THE WORD FINDER

THE

Word Finder

Compiled and edited by J. I. RODALE

With the collaboration of KINGSBURY M. BADGER, M. A.

THEODORE G. EHRSAM, M. A. · MABEL E. MULOCK, B. S.

EDWARD J. FLUCK, Ph. D.

Rodale Press

EMMAUS, PENNSYLVANIA

THE COLLABORATORS

KINGSBURY M. BADGER, M. A.

Professor of English
Boston University

THEODORE G. EHRSAM, M. A.

School of Commerce, Accounts, and Finance
New York University

MABEL E. MULOCK, B. S.

Formerly Head of the English Department
Allentown High School

EDWARD J. FLUCK, Ph. D.

Editor-in-Chief of Rodale Press Publications

PREFACE

To The New Edition

The *WORD-FINDER* is a revised and enlarged edition of three volumes now out-of-print, the *VERB-FINDER,* the *ADJECTIVE-FINDER,* and the *ADVERB-FINDER,* and includes the original Prefaces to those valuable works as well as that to our more recent *THE SUBSTITUTE FOR "VERY."* Thus, the purpose, method, and writing aids of four useful volumes are conveniently embraced in this composite.

What is the *WORD-FINDER?* Is it a new kind of thesaurus? The answer is emphatically "no!" In a thesaurus one looks for substitutes for the word he has in mind. If he wishes to say "large," reference to a thesaurus will supply him with a better word such as "spacious." The *WORD-FINDER,* on the other hand, does not merely yield a substitute word but produces an augmentative word, one to embellish and add to the idea. Thus, in the *WORD-FINDER* by referring to the adjective *large* the user is taught to describe "how large?" by a selected list of words such as *incalculably, incredibly, preposterously, overwhelmingly, prodigiously, inordinately,* etc.

The *WORD-FINDER* has been created to improve a writer's style by adding to the bare-essential words of a sentence. A thesaurus does not do that. It merely assists the user to change such a sentence as "This business had a loss" to some such variant as "This trade suffered a reversal." The *WORD-FINDER,* however, teaches one that "business *droops, expires, falters, founders, simmers,* and *succumbs,"* simply by referring to the noun *business.* And if none of these adjuvant words is precisely what the writer has in mind to describe a languishing trade, the *WORD-FINDER* will tell him, also under the heading *business,* to see *occupation, trade, concern, enterprise, industry, work, commerce,* etc.

Nouns, verbs, and adjectives are listed, alphabetically arranged, and in connection with each such word a list of "augmentatives" is given, that is, words that can be used to condition such a noun, verb, or adjective. In the case of *hill,* for example, the *WORD-FINDER* will furnish either adjectives, such as *gleaming, emerald, moon-swept, verdured, radiant, shadowed, naked, pastoral, defiant,* or verbs, as *hills dot, encroach, flank, greet, interpose,* etc. In the case of the verb *hinder* we are told that a thing can hinder us *unendurably, insurmountably, irritatingly, irksomely* or *burdensomely,* as well as that we should also consult the synonym entries, *retard* and *obstruct.*

It is a simple type of book to use, and immediate results follow in the form of vigorous and deft variety essential to the creation of a literary style. By studying any particular word in the *FINDER* along with its coupling expressions and synonyms the user is enabled to develop a concept and build a thought in such a way that intricate sentences can be evolved from the study of that word. He will find that whatever particular idea he has in mind will rise to fluent proportions under the leavening influence of the *FINDER'S* associated words, that his vocabulary has been increased and his powers of self-expression immeasurably improved.

For example, the sentence, "His cheerful character charmed me very much," contains the adjective *cheerful,* the noun *character,* the verb *charmed,* and the adverbs *very* and *much.* Though it is grammatically correct and genial in thought, it is sadly lacking in specific statement and colorful diction. What exactly are the elements in a *character* that *charm?* And what are the suggestive ingredients of being *cheerful?*

On pages 182-183 of our *WORD-FINDER* the noun *character* has grouped with it a selected list of adjectives that explain and describe it. After studying the columns of epithets descriptive of our word while bearing in mind that this is a *character* that *charms,* we reap a rich harvest of modifers. Depending on the nature of the characteristics that charm us, we can depict our character as *fabulous, munificent, steadfast, liberal, intense, frivolous, gallant, chivalrous, artistic, elusive, exotic, gentle, jovial, airy, gay, sympathetic, magnanimous, many-sided, jaunty, bizarre, racy* and *whimsical,* to cite only a few of the appropriate words that will expand our idea. Thus, if we admire the fay, will-o'-the-wisp facets of a certain personality, we may say, "His elusive character charmed me very much," and we have started on our quest for the specific and the well-delineated. We have, of course, substituted *elusive* for *cheerful,* but *cheerful* and *charmed* are faintly synonymic anyhow, and our purpose is to show what a plenitude of ideas related to our original sentence may be found in the *WORD-FINDER,* rather than merely to adorn the flimsiness of that original sentence.

Since the original modifier of *character* was *cheerful,* what can we learn about ways of modifying that adjective in our book? Words which describe adjectives, verbs, or other adverbs are known as adverbs. On page 189 we find a choice list of such adverbs in association with the word *cheerful*. If we wish to express what we feel about this charmingly elusive character, we can readily avail ourselves of the most pertinent of these modifiers for *cheerful* and transfer it to *elusive*. Thus, we should choose from some such qualifying words as *habitually, blithely, casually, oddly,* or *perplexingly,* if, let us say, we were charmed by the casually elusive character of a Britisher.

The verb of our original thought was *charmed,* and it was described by the barren, inexpressive adverbial phrase *very much.* (Apropos of the feebleness of *very,* be sure to read the Preface from *THE SUB-STITUTE FOR "VERY"* on page XXX of this volume.) On page 185 we find the noun *charm* with its cluster of associated adjectives, among which we note our selection for character, namely *elusive;* this confirms our concept that an elusive character can be charming. On page 186, however, appears the verb *charm,* marked (v) as are all the verbs in this book. Browsing among its adverbs and choosing a few of the most applicable, we find that we can say with import that an elusive character charms *subtly, mysteriously, hauntingly, inexplicably, piquantly,* or *irresistibly.*

As we reflect over all the words associated with *character, cheerful,* and *charm,* which three alone we have studied, we find that from that glittering galaxy of modifiers we can create innumerable combinations relevant to our original thought, but more sumptuously expressed; for an instance, "His piquant charm was of a perplexingly elusive character, haunting, subtle; yet its very intensity was irresistible." From the delicate contours of a silhouette our character has been projected full-featured.

Only words that are evocative, that stimulate and unfurl the wings of the imagination, are of real assistance to the aspiring writer. These are the words that avoid the flat surface of the cliche, that give dimensional depth to the picture we are creating. We believe such words to be found in hitherto unprecedented numbers in this book. They are the ones which, starting from a single unit in combination with another word, will, as they round a phrase, multiply and burgeon into a complete thought, while at the same time often yielding an unlooked-for but brighter image.

The editors sincerely trust that all students of this book will succeed in sending *winged words* on far-flung odysseys to Fame.

EDWARD J. FLUCK, PH. D.

PREFACE

To The Original Adjective-Finder

Adjectives have been excellently defined as "the words of our language that make everything clearer, plainer, more beautiful or more dreadful." Oral or written expression without any adjectives at all would be meager, monotonous, utterly drab and colorless. The word *adjective* comes from the Latin *adjectivus*, meaning "that is added." The only part of English speech to which an adjective may be added is of course a noun. (That is why, in this volume, nouns have been listed alphabetically, with fitting adjectives appended to each noun).

Adjectives are as life blood to the language. William Freeman, in his book *Plain English,* says, "One can't embark upon any type of narrative, from embittered conversation to the conventional post-card, without turning to the adjective for help." For this reason adjectives may be described as the paints with which one brightens and vivifies the scenes and events behind the printed words, and lends fascinating hues to what might otherwise be prosaic and deadly dry.

No matter what writers turn their attention to, they must draw upon the adjective. Of course in certain types of narrative there is less need of the descriptive paint-brush than in others. An interesting study of the actual use of adjectives in various fields of writing has recently been made by Dr. David P. Boder, head of the department of psychology at Lewis Institute. His study—which he has termed the A. V. Q. (Adjective-Verb Quotient)—is a measure of the ratio of adjectives to verbs employed by writers. For example, an A. V. Q. of 20 means that a writer uses 20 adjectives for every 100 verbs he employs. (For a discussion of the verb, see the introduction to THE VERB-FINDER). Dr. Boder has found that of the four principal fields of writing, drama has the fewest adjectives, with an average A. V. Q. of 11. Laws are next, with an A. V. Q. of 20. Fiction has an A. V. Q. of 35; scientific writing, 75. Business letters, according to Dr. Boder's findings, show a relative paucity of adjectives, with only 19 to every 100 verbs. Private letters by inexperienced writers have on an average but 22 adjectives to a hundred verbs. Advertisements, on the other hand, are lavish of adjectives, with an A. V. Q. of 78. Theses written by candidates for the Ph. D. degree are loaded with even more adjectives than are advertisements—88 to 100 verbs! Poetry has what is perhaps a golden mean for proportion of adjectives to verbs—an A. V. Q. of 36. Dr. Boder's studies in this field make it clear that writers use more adjectives than speakers do. The reason for this is not far to seek; writers closeted with their thoughts have unlimited time in which to select appropriate adjectives while those who express themselves orally and extemporaneously do not.

Adjectives suffer, as any part of speech is bound to, if not properly employed. And adjectives, perhaps more than any other part of our language, are subject to wide-spread misuse. The adjective, of all the parts of English speech, is the most recklessly overworked. Both inexperienced and half-educated writers use far too many, and use them far too loosely. The amateur tends to use the first adjective that enters his mind, though that adjective may be shoddy and threadbare from excessive use, or though it may not express exactly what he wishes to say. Wesseen, in his *Dictionary of English Grammar,* calls this *adjectivitis* (a coined word meaning the habit of using many adjectives, especially big ones.)

Poor writers and beginners obscure their meaning by weighting their sentences with too many adjectives. Dr. Boder found in the course of his researches that the fewer the adjectives, the easier any writing is to read. With experience and practice the writer learns to substitute for makeshift, trite adjectives others which express his meaning exactly and vividly. Daniel Webster, as a young man, was bombastic in his speeches, but it did not take him long to discover that the power of a sentence lies chiefly in its meaning, and that forceful writing is that which is most direct. Upon making this discovery Webster became "a great eraser of adjectives," and used only the plainest in his addresses. Yet he won immortality for his eloquence. "You will find," he said, "in my speeches to juries, no hard words, no Latin phrases, no *fieri facias;* and that is the secret of my style, if I have any."

Because the adjective is of all parts of speech the most frequently abused and misused, it has come to be regarded with a suspicious eye by many a worker in words. The late columnist, Arthur Brisbane, termed the adjective the enemy of the noun. Many years before Brisbane's time Voltaire meant exactly the same thing when he said that adjectives are frequently the greatest enemies of the substantives.

"An adjective is, indeed, an addition," wrote William Matthews, in his book, *Words; Their Use and Abuse.* "But, he concludes, "an addition may be an incumbrance, as even a dog finds out when a kettle is tied to his tail. Generally the weakness of a composition is just in proportion to the frequency with which this abused class of words is introduced."

Ernest Weekley, a well-known authority on words, expressed irritation because of the wide-spread tendency to overwork the adjective. For example, some years ago, after an attempt had been made upon the life of Mussolini, the President of the Irish Free State congratulated the Italian dictator upon his "providential escape" from an "odious attack," and sent his "earnest wishes" for a "speedy recovery" from the "infamous attempt" which had caused "utmost indignation."

This sort of thing—with reason—goads Mr. Weekley to exasperation, and in an essay on the adjective he has been led to condemn it as being perhaps our least essential part of speech. But neither Mr. Weekley nor any other worker in words worth his salt scorns the adjective in actual practice. For example, Mr. Weekley, in his book *Cruelty to Words*, speaks of "linguistic absurdities perpetrated by contemporary authors," and "a small leavening of peptonized uplift and dilettante pornography." Here are adjectives a-plenty, and employed by an authority who has declared the adjective the least important part of our language! And though Arthur Brisbane termed the adjective the enemy of the noun, a study of Brisbane's writings reveals that the columnist used approximately 42 adjectives to every 100 verbs he employed.

The adjective has come to have a somewhat unsavory reputation, then, not because there is anything inherently bad about it, but because it is the one part of speech first seized upon and worked to death by novices and inferior writers.

When properly used, however, the adjective is an indispensable tool in the hands of all who would communicate with their fellow men by means of words. Employed with discrimination and restraint it becomes a source of tremendous power. Selection of the exact adjective to convey their meaning has done as much as anything to lend beauty and strength to the writings of men whose names have long since become household words wherever English is spoken. Thomas De Quincy, for example, famed for his style, was a master of the adjective. A single sentence from the pen of the man who wrote *The Confessions of an English Opium Eater* serves to show this:

"His diction blazed up into a sudden explosion of prophetic grandeur."

Had De Quincy used an adjective in connection with the word "diction," this fine sentence would have been spoiled.

Just as an adjective thoughtlessly or carelessly placed can wreck an otherwise excellent sentence, so a fitting adjective inserted at just the proper place can build magic into a sentence. The William

Saroyan play, *Love's Old Sweet Song*, offers an interesting example. Walter Huston, in the role of the leading male character, approaches an ornamental stone lion and in expressing disgust with the situation in which he finds himself, gestures toward the figure, referring to it not as "That lion!" but rather, as "That Abyssinian lion!" The adjective Abyssinian, as the author intended, brings a roar of laughter from the audience.

The danger in using adjectives lies in employing overworked and "tired" adjectives, or adjectives unsuited to the noun with which they are joined. That is the *raison d'etre* for the present volume. In the following pages a host of adjectives, each group appended to the noun modified, offers the user of this book a wide choice in the words so vital to memorable writing.

Very simple adjectives have been avoided except where their use in connection with certain nouns appears to be somewhat unusual. This point is worth a second glance—for quite simple adjectives have frequently aided authors in the moments of their greatest genius. Ernest Hemingway, in describing one of his characters, writes:

"His face was small and white and he had tight lips."

How simple are these adjectives: "small," "white," tight!" And yet they enable one to see that character immediately—and not only to see him, but to be on guard against him.

Indeed, Hemingway is famed for the simplicity of his style. At the other extreme there are writers who do not hesitate to use three words where one would suffice. Rufus Choate, the famous American statesman and orator, was such a man. So prodigal he was of adjectives that it was said that he "drove a substantive-and-six" whenever he spoke. When Chief-Justice Shaw, before whom Choate frequently pleaded, heard that a new edition of *Worcester's Dictionary* was off the press and that it contained 2,500 new words, he cried out, "For heaven's sake, don't let Choate get hold of it!"

Perhaps Choate frightened those who knew him with his verbiage, but he was so skilled in the use of words that he succeeded in spite of an overloaded style. A person of less experience or skill is almost certain to fall disastrously into the octopus arms of elaborate language. And curiously enough, it frequently happens that the amateur writer seeks to express himself in a more or less highly ornamented manner, usually with sad results.

The student, and even the practiced writer, cannot be advised too strongly against the use of long, unusual words. The urge to show off to the reader must be kept down. Not only will the worker in words —if he would possess a clear, vigorous style—guard against employing too many adjectives, but he will avoid the pitfalls and detours and handicaps that are likely to be encountered through the use of excessively elaborate adjectives. The simple adjective is almost always preferable to the unusual adjective.

Of course an adjective not met every day may be employed with profit if it expresses the author's thought better than any other word could, but in general the student—in using the present volume—will find it to his advantage to select such simple and yet vivid adjective-noun combinations as "casual visitor," "speechless agony," "misty diplomacy," "liquid gurgle," "giddy intoxication," and "silvery laughter."

Remember that adjectives—like visitors—become a nuisance only when there are too many of them. The adjective is never the enemy of of the noun until the adjective—like a drowning swimmer—drags down and strangles the noun.

J. I. RODALE.

PREFACE

To The Original Verb-Finder

THE POWER OF VERBS

There is an old saying that "fine words butter no parsnips." But of course they do, and always will—whenever the words have been fine enough. Words act. Think of the information, the insight, the entertainment that words provide through books, plays, radio programs, and sound motion pictures. Words are practical, practical even in the narrowest American sense; that is, they bring in money, support life. Let us be clearer by being more definite.

From the days when Anglo-Saxon and medieval minstrels earned their board by entertainment in mead-hall and castle, to modern times, word-craftsmen have moved and delighted their audiences by telling stories or by expressing thoughts, emotions, and aspirations at once personal and common to all people. In modern times such authors as Kipling, Shaw, Wells, Barrie, Masefield, and Bennett, to mention only a few, have achieved literary eminence by the power of fine words. They, like many other writers, not only have woven bright tapestries in poetry or prose, but also have buttered many a delicious parsnip. Robert Frost found the pen more powerful than the plow—even if he did have to go to England to make sure of it. Edgar Lee Masters wrote himself clear of the stifling influence of the small mid-western town. Edwin Arlington Robinson kept the wolf from his door for years by retelling for the modern world some of the most enchanting of the old romances, as well as by painting satirical portraits of New England townspeople. Arnold Bennett, through a tremendous amount of diligent work—he loved to gloat over the number of words he turned out every day—succeeded in becoming both a first-rate literary "merchant," as he liked to call himself, and one of the best novelists of his time. He lived zestfully by the power of words, and even realized his great desire to own a yacht.

Many other persons, perhaps no more gifted than we, have also succeeded. Although they have not profited greatly in a financial way, or become famous by their ability to write well, they have, nevertheless, shared with the eminent one satisfaction—that of expressing themselves adequately, of communicating their emotions, their thoughts, their opinions, attitudes, and ideals. By the power of well-wrought language they have achieved self-expression and have succeeded in rising from the buried life of a solitary organism to the rich life of communion with their fellows. Such satisfaction, such success is within the reach of all of us.

"But show us the road," people say. "What is the secret? Which way?" There is no one way, of course, for writing is a many-sided, complex art. Nor is there any formula for us to follow, for art is creative and imaginative, by no means a matter of slavish imitation or of scientific procedure. We need not despair, however,—not so long as we have the will to write. A close examination of what good writers produce, cannot fail to reveal to us something about how those works were produced, to give us some hints toward improvement. Arnold Bennett, whose improvement in style was due in large measure to his careful study of other writers, realized that the best novelists were word-conscious, that they sought constantly for strength, for clarity, precision. Incidentally, a good craftsman in writing must always be more than grammatically correct, and he will do well to keep ever in mind those three cardinal principles: strength, clarity, and precision. Bennett, by comparing and examining passages of equal length in the works of a great many novelists, discovered that the better artists—and the better merchants—chose lively adjectives and lively verbs. He discovered, furthermore, that adjectives, unless used charily, overornament; that nouns, unless cut down to a minimum, tend to overweight; but that verbs, if well chosen and skillfully handled, invigorate one's style.

We can see this for ourselves. Every day writers strive vainly to ornament and enrich their expression before they have learned to animate and strengthen it. The result of their striving is too often mere prettiness with no vigor beneath it, writing that is all sweetness and flourishes, a meal of all pastry, a beauty with no grain in it. This is a common fallacy among amateur writers, and even professional writers. They fail to see that ornamental adjectives often blur and obscure their meanings and that too many nouns, especially learned nouns—scientific, psychological, technical terms—bog it down. Expression demands life, not merely the trappings of life; vigor, not merely glitter. The sword must be keen that it may cut and thrust as well as glitter in the sun.

XVI

The true knight fought valiantly in battle; he did not spend most of his time strutting about with his plume, spear-pennant, and lady's scarf rippling in the breeze. The modern athlete, if he would excel on the field of competition, must display strength, agility, and sportsmanship, not merely a good sun-tan, bulging muscles, and his college or club colors. It is not enough that cathedrals be magnificently adorned with tapering spires and beautiful storied windows; they must be firmly braced and buttressed. Likewise, our written or oral expression must be keen-edged, powerful and agile, and well buttressed at the walls. Without a large number of carefully selected verbs, these essentials are impossible; moreover, selection, which is one of the cardinal principles of all art, is far more important than numbers.

Now, after so many generalizations, it is high time we substantiated what we have said about verbs by referring to particular passages in the writing of particular authors, for surely one good illustration is worth at least sixty generalizations.

Perhaps the most obvious use for verbs is to express physical action. In order to illustrate not a mere piling-up but a skillful selection of verbs, let us examine an action-scene from one of John Masefield's poems, *Dauber*. The poet transports his reader immediately to the deck of a clipper. The ship's painter, the "Dauber," and Si, the apprentice, stood by the rail while the swift ship *"tore"* on, *"straining"* her sheets and *"whitening"* her trackway.

> Her **clacking** tackle **tugged** at pins and cleats,
> Her great sails **bellied** stiff, her great masts **leaned:**
> They watched how the seas **struck,** and **burst,** and **greened.** *

On she sailed toward Cape Horn through snow and hail, her spars straining as she was tossed on the toppling billows. Just before she reached the cape, polar snow came *"tumbling"* and *"wavering"* down, *"furring* the ropes with white, *casing* the mast." At the cape all hands were called on deck to combat the storm, and the Dauber was sent aloft to furl one of the sails. As he lay out on the yardarm, *"gripping"* hard and *"clutching"* at the jack, he was sickened by the vast space that yawned just below his feet, where birds were *"mewing"* and *"wheeling."* He felt the wind *"hurl"* the ship on her side, and

> . . . . .darkness **speared**
> At her with wind; she **staggered,** she **careened,**
> Then down she lay. The Dauber felt her go;
> He saw the yard **tilt** downwards. Then the snow
> **Whirled** all about—dense multitudinous, cold—*

It was a terific storm, one that *"whiffled* out men's tears" and put to a severe test their courage and endurance.

---

* Quoted by special permission of the publishers, The Macmillan Company, from *Poems* by John Masefield, 1935. (The boldface and italics are the editor's.)

While we are considering action and the sea, we recall those vigorous lines in Shakespeare's *HENRY V* in which the poet describes the effect of the blast of war on man, ending up with a fine picture of the sea drenching the rocks on the coast.

> Then lend the eye a terrible aspect;
> Let it **pry** through the portage of the head,
> Like the brass cannon; let the brow **o'erwhelm it,**
> As fearfully as doth a **galled** rock
> **O'erhang** and **jutty** his **confounded** base,
> **Swilled** with the wild and wasteful ocean.

Here the imagery of the sea and the coast is employed by the poet, not as the setting of a narrative poem, but to describe the appearance of man when the horrible spirit of war distorts his features. We recall, also, those famous lines from *MACBETH*. Macbeth is hounded by guilt and every noise *"appals"* him. He finds that all Neptune's ocean cannot wash the blood from his hands but that

> "...........this my hand will rather
> The multitudinous seas **incarnadine.**"

Thousands of such powerful lines could be culled from Shakespeare's works. A rereading of some of the famous passages reveals his chary use of lively adjectives, his strong contempt for mere prettiness, for what he called "silken terms" and "taffeta phrases," and his consummate mastery in the use of verbs. Reread, for example, Hamlet's advice to his players, or his soliloquies; Gloucester's speech in the opening scene of *Richard III;* Jacques' description of the seven ages of man, in *As You Like It;* the description of Cleopatra in her barge; Portia's mercy speech; Falstaff's witty lines, especially in *Henry IV* (Part I); or the splendid songs and sonnets. Cull a few phrases such as these:

> **Absent** thee from felicity awhile
> **Godlike** reason **to fust** in us unus'd
> Lilies that **fester**
> **Struts** and **frets** his hour
> Thoughts **people** this little world
> I am **unking'd** by Bolingbroke
> Let the **galled** jade **wince,** our withers are **unwrung.**
> **Screw** your courage to the sticking place
> The cliff that **beetles** o'er his base
> **Paragon** description
> **Beggars** description
> Native resolution **sicklied** o'er with the pale cast of thought
> Daffodils that come before the swallow **dares**

Shakespeare's use of the verb *dares* is an excellent example of the selection of a verb that is neither long nor rare but singularly apt. How better could he have distinguished the daffodil from other flowers or suggested the venturesome nature of the swallow than in these lines?

> "............................ daffodils
> That comes before the swallow **dares**, and take
> The winds of March with beauty................."

Another excellent example of fine selection is to be found in Ophelia's beautiful lament for Hamlet, in which she says,

> "Now see that noble and most sovereign reason,
> Like sweet bells **jangled**, out of tune and harsh."

"Sweet bells jangled." What a perfect phrase to suggest the contrast between noble reason and madness! On one side of the word *bells* we have the adjective *sweet,* and on the other side the verbal adjective, or participle, *jangled.*

So we might continue to quote from Shakespeare and other poets, from Shelly and Byron, Wordsworth and Coleridge, Tennyson and Browning, Keats, and many others. We recall the sound effects in the skating scene in Wordsworth's *Prelude* and in the scene toward the end of Tennyson's *Morte d'Arthur* in which Sir Bedevere carries Excalibur down to the edge of the mere. We remember, also, the remarkable description of storm-clouds in *The Testament of Beauty,* by Robert Bridges. Mention of Keats calls to mind many lines, especially those in his ode *To Autumn* in which he says of the bees, "Summer has *o'er-brimmed* their clammy cells." But since we must stop quoting somewhere, why not with this exceptionally fine example from Keats? Now let us turn to a consideration of the power of verbs in prose. It really makes little difference here whether we speak of poetry or prose, except that poetry is usually more concise and, consequently, more suitable for illustration. Certainly the need and selection of verbs is much the same.

In pure nature description one might not expect to find much action, certainly not so much as in an action-scene such as that quoted from *Dauber* or in any similar action-scene in prose. One might expect to find far fewer verbs than adjectives. Good description of nature, however, is never flat, static, motionless, but always alive. In his story, "The Lagoon," Conrad heightens an effect of stillness and immobility by emphasizing what action there is. Although the lagoon was *"bewitched* into an immobility perfect and final"*, the paddlers found themselves in a world not entirely devoid of motion. "The *churned-up* water *frothed* alongside with a *confused* murmur," the cry of a bird, "discordant and feeble, *skipped* over the smooth water," the voices of the paddlers *"reverberated* between the walls of vegetation," and "darkness *oozed* out from between the trees." In Mary Webb's novel, *Gone To Earth,* we find description that is surpassingly beautiful. Notice how much life she expresses in these two sentences, both of which describe Undern, a farm in Shropshire, England:

> Even in May, when the lilacs **frothed** into purple, **paved** the lawn with shadows, **steeped** the air with scent; when soft leaves **lipped** each other consolingly; when blackbirds sang, **fell** in their effortless way from the green height to the green depth, and sang again—still, something that **haunted** the place set the heart **fluttering.**
>
> In winter the yews and firs were like **waving** funeral plumes and **mantled,** headless goddesses; then the giant beeches would **lash** themselves to frenzy, and, **stooping,** would **scourge** the ice on Undern Pool and the **cracked** walls of the house, like beings **drunken** with the passion of cruelty. *

Here we have description that is alive, alive with suggestive and vigorous words, many of which are verbs.

Poets, novelists, historians; military leaders and peace-makers; statesmen, diplomats, lawyers; journalists, advertisers, and business men—all are men of action, wielders of words, wielders of verbs. Powerful words spurred Napoleon's men to push on over the Alps and down onto the fertile plains of Italy, just as, later, powerful words spurred the Italian army in its conquest of Ethiopia. No little eloquence was required to pass the Great Reform Bill of 1832 in England, or to free negro slaves in America. Salesmen cannot sell, business men cannot transact, diplomats cannot negotiate, lawyers can neither prosecute nor defend without forceful, convincing language. Without words our personalities become feeble and defunct; with words they spring into life. To express ourselves is to live—and where there's a will there's a word.

GUIDE TO THE USE OF VERBS

1. The Contents and Arrangement of the Thesaurus

Every workman requires the special tools, materials, and technique of his particular trade, and it is the function of the VERB-FINDER to provide the word-craftsman with these requisites. We must first go to the lumberyard and mill to see what materials and machinery we have with which to construct the furniture of our thoughts. In addition we must learn the technique of building.

The Arrangement of the Verbs

The Thesaurus consists of verbs, or action-words, listed alphabetically under nouns. These nouns are the subjects of our sentences, and they, together with the verbs listed below them, form the nuclei or cores of the sentences. Immediately below each noun a number of verbs are listed alphabetically with dashes following them, and under this list other verbs are arranged with dashes preceding them. The

---

* Quoted by special permission of the publishers, E. P. Dutton and Company, Inc., from *Gone To Earth,* by Mary Webb. (The boldface is the editor's.)

dashes are used to avoid needless repetition of the nouns. Notice that the verbs in the first list act upon the nouns, and that those in the second list carry out the action of the noun; that is, in the first list the noun is the receiver of the action, usually the object of the verb, and in the second list the doer of the action, or the subject of the verb. For example, under the noun *fire* you will find these two lists and these two relationships between noun and verb.

Fire

feed — (*Fire* is the object and receiver of action)
— crackles (*Fire* is the subject and doer)

Verb Forms

Obviously, not all forms of the verbs can be included in the lists, any more than all sizes and shapes of boards can be piled in the lumberyard. The carpenter must select suitable boards of approximately the right size and then shape them to his needs. Consequently, in the first list under each noun, that in which the verb precedes the dash, you will find the infinitive form of the verb (with the *to* omitted), which is exactly the same form as that of the first person singular of the present indicative. In the second list under each noun, that in which the dash follows the verb, you will find the third person singular or plural form of the present indicative, to agree with the noun preceding. For example:

Fish

prepare — (*Prepare* means *to prepare* or *I prepare*)
— squirms (*Squirms* means *It squirms*)

Brick

build with —s (*Build* means *to build* or *I build*)
—s crumble (*Crumble* means *They crumble*)

No verbals are listed. However, verbals and their value in writing will be discussed in another section of the "Guide."

2. How to Build Sentences

In the Thesaurus you will find thousands of sentences and suggestions for sentences right at hand. Given any thought or feeling that you want to express, all you have to do is to find the one best word to express the action that you want. The sentence is a unit of thought or predication containing a subject and predicate. Given a subject, you can easily find here the other element, the word to set it into motion, to make it alive—the verb.

Selecting the Verb

Let us assume that you hear a bell ringing, and that you wish to communicate to us the sound that you hear and exactly how that sound affects you. It is not enough to say, "I hear a bell ringing." That communicates little, for there are all sorts of bells and all sorts of ringing sounds. *Bell* is your subject, however, and *rings* your action, at least tentatively. Now run your finger down the second column of verbs under *bell* and find a better verb. Perhaps you will choose *chimes, clangs, reverberates, sings,* or *tinkles.* It makes considerable difference. Or suppose you want to describe the way a bird moves through the sky. It is not enough to say "The bird moves," or even "The bird flies." Look down the list under *bird* until you come to a verb that will make the bird *dart, hover, float, wheel,* or what you will. This is the way to find your verb, whether you want a verb that will sell a shirt or one of the latest novels, or a verb that will make a poem magical. The same method enables you to find a verb that acts upon a noun used as its object. To express the idea of disposing of an argument, for example, run your finger down the first column under *argument* until you come to a verb, say *refute.* You now have your sentence: "I will refute the argument."

Cross References

If the procedure described above fails to provide you with the verb you are after, you can search elsewhere. At the foot of the verb lists you will usually find a number of guide words or cross references. "See" leads us, through these words, to other lists of verbs. We refer to these other lists in the following ways: from the generic to the specific word, from the specific to the generic, from synonym to synonym, and from the word listed to a word related but not synonymous. Let us explain.

(a) Generic To Specific

Suppose you have been trying to find a verb to express the sound (song or other sound) that a bird makes. Suppose that *bird,* although it has many such words listed, does not have the right one. Turn, then, to a specific kind of bird, such as *lark, nightingale,* or *grouse.* You will find that different and more specific verbs are listed under these headings to describe the characteristic sounds and actions of these very different birds. A few examples of this generic to specific reference are:

> *poetry*—See *sonnet*
> *profession*—See *teaching, law*
> *gem*—See *diamond, ruby*

(b) Specific To Generic

This is, of course the exact opposite. Some examples are:

diamond—See *gem*
painting—See *art*
bee—See *insect*
musician—See *artist*
law—See *profession*

It is well, if possible, to choose the word you want in the first place; that is, not to be talking vaguely about birds if you mean robins or about art if you mean painting. Nevertheless, you will often find it necessary and profitable to refer from the generic to the specific and from the specific to the generic word.

(c) Synonym To Synonym

Often you will find synonyms among your guide words. You will do well to use them. For example, after looking in vain for a verb to go with *courage,* you can easily and quickly turn to *bravery, fortitude,* or *valor.* Incidentally, in addition to finding the verb you are after, you may decide that *fortitude,* not *courage,* is the noun that you want.

(d) The Related Word

If you refer from *hand* to *claw,* which is not exactly a synonym, you will find good verbs for a claw-like hand. Likewise, if you refer from *anvil* to *bell* or from *art* to *artist* you will find verbs related to your subject. Sometimes you might well refer to a word whose meaning is directly opposite, to an antonym. Many verbs, for example, are used interchangeably with such pairs of words as the following:

Summer and *Winter, comparison* and *contrast, poetry* and *prose.*

3. How to Build Better Sentences

The best way to explain how to build better sentences is to build a few. Below you will find a series of sentences which, although grammatically correct, can stand considerable improvement:

> The red embers sent a strong and ruddy glow from the chimney. Dom Nicholas, the Picardy monk, stood before it. He pulled up his skirts and bared his fat legs to the comfortable warmth. His large shadow appeared in the middle of the room. The firelight shone on either side of his broad person, and in a little pool on either side of his feet, which were spread out. His face had the beery appearance of the continual drinker's, and it was bruised. It was covered with a network of veins, which were purple in ordinary circumstances, but were now violet. He had his back to the fire, but he was cold on the other side.

This is badly written. Why? In the first place, the style is monotonous and choppy because every sentence begins with the subject followed immediately by the verb; secondly, most of the verbs are weak or commonplace; and thirdly, there are too many verbs. If we substitute *diffused* for *"sent"*, *straddled* for *"stood"*, *picked* for *"pulled"*, *escaped* for *"shone"*, and *cut the room in half* for *"appeared in the middle of the room,"* we will sharpen the picture by the use of stronger verbs. If we recast the second sentence by combining it with the third and by beginning it with a prepositional phrase, instead of with the usual subject-verb combination, we will create a much more compact sentence and relieve the paragraph of some of its monotony. We might write it this way:

> Before this straddled Dom Nicholas, the Picardy monk, with his skirts picked up and his fat legs bared to the comfortable warmth.

Thus, in combining the two sentences, we have used two participles instead of the two verbs, *picked* and *bared*. Participles often help us to condense and vary our sentences; moreover they add life to a sentence when used in place of commonplace adjectives. For example, if we place *arched* before *"chimney"* in the first sentence, *dilated* in place of *"large"* in the fourth, and *outspread* before *"feet"* in the fifth, we will greatly enhance the power of the description. Notice the unnecessary clause in the fifth sentence—"which were spread out". By rewriting the sentence with the participle *outspread* before *"feet,"* we eliminate a whole clause, and thus condense the writing without losing any of the meaning. We see now that sentences can be improved in several ways: by substituting strong, precise, colorful, accurate verbs for weak, indefinite, colorless, and inaccurate verbs; by recasting sentences so as to vary, condense, and strengthen their structure by either adding verbals or converting verbs into verbals. Following these principles, we have transformed a crude paragraph into a remarkably fine paragraph. Here it is exactly as R. L. Stevenson wrote it in his story, "A Lodging for the Night:"

> A great pile of **living** embers **diffused** a strong and ruddy glow from the **arched** chimney. Before this **straddled** Dom Nicholas, the Picardy monk, with his skirts **picked** up and his fat legs **bared** to the comfortable warmth. His **dilated** shadow **cut** the room in half; and the firelight only **escaped** on either side of his broad person, and in a little pool between his **outspread** feet. His face had the beery, **bruised** appearance of the continual drinker's; it was covered with a network of **congested** veins, purple in ordinary circumstances, but now pale violet, for even with his back to the fire the cold **pinched** him on the other side. His cowl had half fallen back, and made a strange excrescence on either side of his bull neck. So he **straddled, grumbling,** and **cut** the room in half with the shadow of his portly frame. *

---

* Quoted by special permission of the publishers, Charles Scribner's Sons, from *New Arabian Nights*, by R. L. Stevenson. The editor wrote the first version for the purpose of showing how poor writing can be transformed into good writing. (The boldface is the editor's.)

What a striking portrait this is! Notice the use of the sharp verb *pinched* in place of *was* and of the participles *congested* and *grumbling*.

Since the paragraph above contains no infinitives—it is difficult to find any one selection that will illustrate everything—something remains to be said about the use of this type of verbal. The following words, uttered by Napoleon before his army in Milan, serve as a fine illustration of the effective use of infinitives:

> **To re-establish** the Capitol, **to set up** there the statues of the heroes, **to awaken** the Roman people which for centuries have been paralyzed by servitude—that is the fruit of your victories, that will amaze posterity.

What eloquent words—no matter what our feelings about war and peace—from this man of action! Take out the infinitives and you emasculate the sentence. How comparatively feeble it is when we rewrite it like this:

> The re-establishment of the Capitol, the erection of the statues of the heroes, the awakening of the Roman people which for centuries have been paralyzed by servitude—that is the fruit of your victories, that will amaze posterity.

Observe how heavy and academic this last version is. If you look at these two sentences, one above the other as they stand, you cannot fail to see the power of the infinitive.

4. Diction

A few words should be said about good and bad usage in verbs, for often we find ourselves uncertain as to whether or not a word has been generally accepted as good English. How can we be sure? The VERB-FINDER should help us here. To avoid unnecessary verbiage and confusion, the editors have arranged the verbs in the Thesaurus as simply as possible. You will find only three classifications: slang, colloquialism, and general usage.

Slang

Slang expressions, although sometimes extremely forceful, are often limited in use to a small locality or to a small number of people, to the college campus, to the Southwest, or to baseball, for example. Consequently, outside of its own little sphere it may mean nothing. Moreover slang is often too indefinite, too vague in meaning, to be of much value. For these reasons, when you see a verb listed with quotation marks around it, take care to avoid it in formal writing and to use it informally only where it will be understood. If, however, you feel that the word is sufficiently definite and more vigorous than any other you can think of, use it—but always with quotation marks to indicate that you know exactly what sort of word you are using. Although the

XXV

word may some day be accepted as respectable, at present it must be regarded as questionable.

Colloquialisms

These words, if a bit more respectable than slang, are to be avoided in formal writing, because they are usually peculiar to one section of the country. However, authors often, and rightly, use colloquialisms in dialogue, for which the spoken word rather than the written or literary word is more appropriate.

Good Usage

We are correct when we say that usage determines what is right or wrong in language. Certainly usage is the power behind the dictionary. But we must qualify our statement, for not every word in common usage is the best word or even a good word. The standard for good usage is the standard set by the language customs of the better writers and speakers. In general, the most intelligent, the best educated, the most highly cultured, the most expressive people attain to the most effective and most beautiful expression. On the other hand, in general, persons of lesser intelligence, education, and culture use poorer language; they tend toward the mediocre and the trite, and even fall into barbarisms, improprieties, clumsiness, and confusion. We might make a table like this:

Good Usage (Formal)

Choice Diction (the best)
Good Diction (superior)
Fair Diction (tending toward the mediocre and trite)

Good and Bad Usage (Informal)

Slang
Colloquialisms

Bad Usage (Inexcusable)

Archaisms
Vulgarisms or Barbarisms
Improprieties or Malapropisms
Affection and Pedantry

If we keep in mind some such distinctions in diction we can be liberal and flexible without being uncertain and inconsistent. The VERB-FINDER concerns itself with the first two categories only. The greater part of the Thesaurus is devoted to the first, but the second, because of the good in it, cannot be ignored.

5. The Verb-Finder As a Source of Information

In addition to performing its chief function, that of aiding us in expressing ourselves, The VERB-FINDER also furnishes encyclopedic information. By consulting the verb lists we can obtain valuable information about many subjects and can even construct fairly good dictionary definitions. Certainly a good way to characterize or define a person or thing is to state what that person or thing does, what its actions are. How, for example, can we define a snob, except by stating how a snob acts? What is a snob? The VERB-FINDER tells us that the snob *apes, affects, pretends, cringes, worships, swaggers, overbears,* etc. Do not such verbs characterize this sort of person through his actions? Here is the definition of *snob* given in Funk and Wagnall's unabridged *DICTIONARY*:

> A person who vulgarly **affects** gentility, or **pretends** to a superiority he does not possess; one who **apes** and **cringes** to his superiors and is **overbearing** to those upon whom he looks as beneath him; one who regards wealth or position rather than character. *

In the same way we could find out a great deal about the habits of birds or termites or horses; about the nature and function of literature or sculpture or biology; about the characteristics of salesmen, artists, fools, clowns, sages, philosophers, lovers, or thieves.

KINGSBURY M. BADGER

*The boldface, which does not appear in the dictionary, is the editor's.

PREFACE

To The Original Adverb-Finder

The adverb has been described as "the irresponsible playboy of grammar." According to its name it is simply a word which is "close-to the-verb." *Ad* is a Latin prefix meaning "to," and "adverb" therefore ought to be a word attached only to a verb. But the playboy among words isn't content to unite itself only with verbs. As we all may recall from the days of our schooling, an adverb is a word which may modify not merely a verb, but an adjective, or even another adverb. In the present volume, however, not merely for the sake of simplicity, but because the choicer adverbs are generally found in verb combinations, only adverbs used as modifiers of verbs are treated.

Adverbs—according to what they tell, or according to the questions they answer—are divided into four main groups: 1. time; 2. place; 3. manner; 4. degree. Adverbs which tell "when" are termed adverbs of time: The train will arrive *immediately*. *Immediately* is here an adverb of time.

Adverbs which tell "where" are called adverbs of place: The elderly woman lives *here*. *Here* is an adverb of place.

Adverbs which tell "how" are adverbs of manner: The fellow boasted *preposterously*. *Preposterously* is here an adverb of manner.

Adverbs which tell "how much," "to what extent" or "how many times" are termed adverbs of degree: The crowd applauded *repeatedly*. *Repeatedly* is an adverb of degree.

Adverbs, then, in the writer's kit, are the tools which tell *when, where, how* or *to what degree* about the word which they modify. *When, where, how* and *to what degree* are obviously details which recur time and again in writing of any variety. Obviously, too, vigorous and original words which describe *when, where, how* and *to what degree* are essential to forceful writing of any kind.

The present volume is intended to fill this need—to workers in words an instantly available library of abverbs—adverbs which better-than-average writers have employed in a better-than-average manner.

Within the following pages are innumerable adverb combinations, such as *float nebulously, humble sadistically, impair palpably,* etc. No other text among the thousands of books in the field of word-study can—or even pretends to—offer such aids as are presented by such combinations as these, made ready to the user's fingertips through listing in alphabetical order the verbs modified.

In availing himself of the word aids in this volume, the user should remember that while the adverbs presented herein modify only verbs, and usually end in *ly,* there are certain adverbs which do not have this ending. Examples are *along, ill, beyond, often, why, how, when, upward, afterward, hard, hence, down,* etc.

The user should also keep in mind the fact that though an adverb often ends in *ly* it need not necessarily be so used. If the writer desires either to produce a certain effect, or simply to avoid monotony of expression, he may employ instead a phrase embodying the word he has looked up, minus the *ly* ending. Thus, instead of using *danced zestfully,* he may decide to employ *danced with zest.* Or he may make a phrase suggested by the verb-adverb combination which he has picked upon. For example, instead of saying simply *lash savagely* he may be given the inspiration to write *lash out like a demented man,* or some similar expressive phrase.

The value of THE ADVERB-FINDER will of course be greatly enhanced if the user will encircle those adverbs with whose meanings he is not familiar, and look them up in a good dictionary.

The author wishes to thank Mr. Hayden Norwood and Miss Vernice Reinsmith for their invaluable aid in connection with this book.

J. I. RODALE

PREFACE

To The Substitute For "Very"

The purpose of this book is simple. I could have said *very* simple but if I did, it would hardly be the proper way to start an introduction to a book whose deliberate aim is to campaign for the practical elimination of the word *very*. It is a shot-gun type of word, wandering all over the landscape. It doesn't come to a point. In order to secure a substitute for this word I turn the alphabetically-arranged pages of this book until I come to the word *simple* and search there among the list of adverbs for one which might stand in the place of *very*. The only one that seems to come anywhere near fitting is the word *childishly*. The expression now is *childishly simple* but that doesn't seem to convey the exact nuance of thought that is in my mind.

Below the adverbs under the word *simple* is a group of synonyms, some of which may be found in their alphabetical place in the book with their own little group of satellite adverbs. By searching in one or more such places we may find an adverb that would pair harmoniously with *simple*. The word *plain* seems to be a likely synonym, but its group of adverbs does not yield a satisfactory word. I finally come upon my word—*natural*. Although *natural* is not a close synonym to *simple* many of the adverbs that may be used with it may also be employed with *simple*. In this group I find just the word I am after—*unbelievably*. Now I have it! The purpose of this book is unbelievably simple. Why didn't I think of the word in the first place? *Unbelievably* is not a fancy word, and it should be in every writer's vocabulary. Yet by some freak or perverseness in the workings of our minds these simple expressions elude us. The best writers, therefore, have dictionaries and synonym books at their elbows as they write. We offer this SUBSTITUTE FOR "VERY" book as a form of synonym book.

It is the consensus that the use of the word *very* should be severely rationed. It is too broad. It covers too wide a territory. *Very*, in meaning everything and anything, has come to mean nothing. It is like a writer who refers to brown hair when he might choose one of a half dozen shades of brown. One can say, "Fuel is *very* scarce in this poverty-stricken mountain region," but wouldn't it be closer to the truth and convey a more nearly definite meaning to say, "Fuel is *cruelly* scarce . . . ."? Isn't *magnificently healthy* better than *very healthy?* Isn't *smugly infallible* superior to *very infallible?* Doesn't *hopelessly inadequate* conjure up a more effectual picture than merely *very inadequate?*

I do not know what children would do without the word *very.* In the limited vocabulary of juveniles this word is enthroned in a high place, but we are supposed to grow up. There comes a time when we are expected to do better. We must change our ways.

It seems to me also that the word *very,* in the sense that we treat it in this volume, has a legitimate place in conversation. When you meet a friend you might say, "I am very glad to see that you are well." This is acceptable, perhaps, because our conversation is conducted on a far lower literary level than our writings. In this respect one might say that we are children in conversation. We have not learned to go out into deep water. It would be utterly fantastic if you were to greet an acquaintance with "I am enthusiastically glad to see that you are well." If you accosted him with "I am boundlessly glad to see that you are well," you have only yourself to blame if he crosses you off his social register. Yet, the same words written in the third person do not sound nearly as grotesque.

In speaking we tend to commit grammatical lapses. We split infinitives. We do not complete our sentences. We do other things which would be inexcusable in writing. The uttered word has dissolved into thin air. It does not stand there, black on white, to invite correction. In writing there are some situations that require simple handling and the word *very* may then find chary usage. There are other situations where no other word will do, like "to be in a very fine fix."

There is a special meaning in the usage of the word *very,* in which extreme emphasis is intended. Then, no other word can take its place. Examples are, *this is the very thing you should have done, the very ground trembled, on the very day of his death,* and *caught in the very act.*

In order to avoid a crude parallelism in rhetorical structure, not every adjective in a sentence should be preceded by an adverb. For example, in the simple thought, "He was sorry to see the poor man persecuted," an inexperienced writer might say, "He was genuinely sorry to see the wretchedly poor man so severely persecuted." It would be more effective to say, "He was genuinely sorry to see the poor man persecuted." Choice adverbs used in moderation will lend charm to one's literary style.

There are numerous ways in which the idea of *very* can be varied.

For example, instead of "very generous," say "ultra-generous," instead of "very courteous," "courteous beyond expression." There is another way of introducing variety in connection with the employment of adverbs. Suppose you are seeking for an adverb to place before *haughty* and you decide upon the word *superciliously*: "He was superciliously haughty." In order to get away from the machinelike recurrence of adverb-adjective, adverb-adjective, you may introduce a noun, and say, "He had a superciliously haughty disposition." Again, suppose you have decided on the combination "mercurially fickle." You can improve it markedly by introducing a simile in connection with the adverb. Thus you have "fickle as the mercury in a thermometer." The word *mercurially* suggests a thermometer. Other adverbs will indicate other similes. Try to make a simile out of the expression, *foppishly fashionable*. Study the style of famous writers and notice the tricks and devices they use in order to avoid repetitiousness in the use of adverbs.

There are other words which belong in the same category as *very* and which should be used just as sparingly. They include *greatly, absolutely, really, positively, wonderfully*. This book suggests more suitable words.

J. I. RODALE

A

ABANDON

adjectives
delightful; gleeful; unconscious; passionate; drunken; increasing; intoxicated; idolatrous; hilarious; airy; fanatical; reckless; artistic; dissolute; emotional; melodramatic; universal; insane; humorous; bird-like; wild; childish; desolate; mystic; sensual; cruel; wanton; natural; boyish; typical; joyful; delirious; carefree; ecstatic.

ABANDON (v)

adverbs
shamelessly; ingloriously; regretfully; dramatically; definitely; recklessly; simultaneously; reluctantly; prudently; despairingly; eventually; inhumanly; cravenly; wantonly; childishly; temporarily; pusillanimously; faint-heartedly; pitiably; haplessly; remorsefully; ruefully; sullenly; woefully; wretchedly; contritely; dejectedly; dolefully; mournfully; dispiritedly; mirthlessly; tragically.
(See repudiate, forsake, waive, surrender.)

ABANDONED (a)

adverbs
delightfully; gleefully; hilariously; airily; recklessly; emotionally; insanely; crazily; ridiculously; wantonly; childishly; boyishly; ludicrously; lamentably; pitiably; unblushingly; provokingly; totally; shamefully; widely; maliciously; regretfully.

ABANDONMENT

adjectives
courageous; inhuman; introspective; hasty; moral; spontaneous; shameless; inglorious; melodramatic; notorious; cowardly; reluctant; prudent; despairing; criminal; crazy; odd.

ABASE (v)

adverbs
disgracefully; degradingly; humiliatingly; shamefully; mortifyingly; ruinously; brutally; belittlingly; calumniously; traducingly; mortifyingly; dishonorably; slanderously.
(See humiliate, degrade, disgrace.)

ABASEMENT

adjectives
servile; mortifying; humiliating; cruel; wilful; total; ultimate.

ABBE

adjectives
infidel; pleasure-loving; gay; witty; dissolute; dull; aristocratic.

ABBREVIATION

adjectives
offensive; delicate; apt; cryptic; unintelligible; suggestive; recognizable; remote; felicitous.

ABDICATE (v)

adverbs
altruistically; willingly; voluntarily; dramatically; ignominiously; unaccountably; cravenly; enforcedly; pusillanimously; submissively; shrewdly; pliantly; tractably; passively.
(See abandon, forsake, surrender, repudiate.)

ABDICATION

adjectives
dramatic; ignominious; unaccountable; altruistic; precipitate; unprecedented; reckless; voluntary; enforced.

ABDOMEN

adjectives
ample; protruding; protuberant; pendulous; flaccid; lean; monstrous; sagging.

verbs
develop—; distend—; enlarge—; exercise—; flatten—; knead—; massage—; relax—; rest on—; subject—; support—; thrust forward—; —is bounded by; —is composed of; —is lined; —juts out; —sags.
(See stomach, intestines, paunch, belly.)

ABDOMINAL

misc.
—surgery; —distress; mobilize the—contents.

ABERRATION

adjectives
vulgar; isolated; philosophic; abhorrent; dangerous; spiritual; noteworthy; marked; human; apparent; mental.

ABHOR (v)

adverbs
passionately; unqualifiedly; deeply; uncontrollably; vindictively; undyingly; vigorous-

ly; smoulderingly; malignantly; diabolically; vengefully; inimically; satanically; malevolently; misanthropically; disdainfully.

(See detest, scorn.)

ABHORRENCE

adjectives
unqualified; modern; cold; hard-headed; justified; passionate; rational; uncontrollable; utmost; inexpressive; well-organized; sullen; deadly; respectful; furious; fierce; stealthy; holy; professed; burlesqued.

ABHORRENT

adverbs
excruciatingly; loathsomely; impossibly; utterly; completely; horribly; terribly; abominably; odiously; repulsively; detestably; hatefully; shockingly; unspeakably.

ABIDE (*v*)

adverbs
faithfully; religiously; staunchly; temporarily; permanently; trustworthily; stoutly; steadfastly; diligently; persistently; unabatingly; deathlessly; enduringly; unfalteringly; firmly; constantly; assiduously.

ABILITY

adjectives
unexcelled; superior; transcendent; surpassing; brilliant; eminent; distinguished; commanding; promising; superb; never-failing; proved; rare; unique; marked; conspicuous; discernible; pronounced; obvious; manifest; undeniable; surprising; amazing; astounding; extraordinary; remarkable; phenomenal; superhuman; inherent; innate; intrinsic; natural; vast; immense; limited; mediocre; middle; cold-blooded; uncanny; eerie; latent; administrative; artistic; executive; forensic; histrionic; linguistic; organizing; oratorical; recuperative; selective; storytelling; mature; mystifying; embryonic; intuitive; sensitive; supposed; sheer; versatile; productive; respectable; slender; professional; superlative; dramatic; acquired; individual; strategic; recognized; peculiar; wonted; potential; striking; crafty; constructive; singular; conscienceless; overrated; intellectual; humble; undoubted; uncommon; critical; technical; variant; creative; doubtful; adroit; vocalistic; practical; enhanced; discontented; melodic; universal; conscious; humble.

verbs
analyze—; ascertain—; attribute—; bow to —; bluster about—; confer—; demonstrate

—; destroy—; determine—; develop—; diminish—; display—; distrust—; donate—; endow with—; enhance—; estimate—; evince—; exhibit—; increase—; invest with —; lack—; make use of—; manifest—; mistreat—; outstrip—; outweigh—; pool—; possess—; presume—; prove—; register—; test—; vitiate—; weigh—; —develops; —enables; —enhances; —falls short; —redeems; —undergoes.

(See talent, capability, capacity, faculty, power, skill.)

ABJECT

adverbs
inconceivably; hopelessly; mournfully; pitiably; incurably; basely; incredibly; piteously; horribly; tragically; unbelievably; singularly; miserably; comically; ridiculously; ostensibly; ostentatiously; glumly; dismally; disconsolately; moodily; heavily; ludicrously.

ABLE

adverbs
tremendously; extremely; wonderfully; adequately; marvelously; uncommonly; extraordinarily; astonishingly; brilliantly; superbly; surprisingly; amazingly; remarkably; particularly; consciously.

ABLUTION

adjectives
sacred; ordinary; daily; outward; unwonted; ritualistic.

ABNEGATION

adjectives
manly; unselfish; absolute; subtle; apostolic; heroic; inspired; unsparing.

ABNORMAL

adverbs
grotesquely; distressingly; painfully; pitiably; noticeably; hideously; undoubtedly; positively; emotionally; markedly; patently; harmlessly; mildly; slightly; entirely; admittedly; grievously; repulsively; shockingly.

ABNORMALITY

adjectives
distressing; emotional; allied; fancied; imperceptible; marked; noticeable; hideous; incredible; patent.

ABODE

adjectives
lonely; peaceful; august; blissful; ancient; eternal; Elysian; sheltered; inaccessible;

dolorous; lasting; obscure; desolate; ancestral; claustral; comfortless; indispensable; serene; fit; fixed; permanent; primitive; sequestered; sybaritic; transient; immortal; ramshackle; dreadful; disconcerting; abandoned; secure; blest; troglodytic; unostentatious; luxurious; phantasmal; damp; dreary; perilous; abhorred; melancholy; mean; soft; eremitic; dread.

verbs
choose—; disdain—; make—with; retire to —; seek—; take up—; welcome to—.

ABOLISH (v)
adverbs
ultimately; effectually; virtually; universally; legally; permanently; entirely; dictatorially; tyrannically; destructively; obliteratingly; deleteriously.
(See annul, repeal.)

ABOLITION
adjectives
projected; forcible; universal; virtual; effectual; ultimate; immediate; instantaneous; gradual.

ABOMINABLE
adverbs
incredibly; intolerably; unbelievably; hatefully; utterly; completely; maliciously; oppressively; brutally; flagrantly; detestably; perniciously; viciously; deplorably; diabolically; execrably; noxiously; lamentably; hatefully; villainously; woefully; odiously; abhorrently; repulsively; invidiously; despicably.

ABOMINATION
adjectives
heathenish; hideous; dark; whitewashed; nondescript; loathsome; indescribable; foul; monstrous; gross.

verbs
behold—; cast away—; commit—; delight in—; work—; multiply—; overspread—; perpetrate—; provoke to—; turn away from —.

(See squalor, wickedness, aversion.)

ABORTION
adjectives
cruel; criminal; sterility-inducing; inadvisable; mutilating; illegal; wanton.

verbs
advise an—; anticipate—; avert—; balk at —; bring about—; cause—; contribute to—;

expose to—; frustrate—; have—; impose an—; indicate—; induce—; indulge in—; instruct about—; justify—; lead to—; legalize—; perform—; permit—; precede—; prevent—; procure—; produce—; prove—; provoke into—; resort to—; stop—; submit to—; terminate in—; tolerate—; treat—; undergo—; weaken by—; yield to—; — arises from; —occurs; —results.
(See miscarriage, failure, operation.)

ABOUND (v)
adverbs
plentifully; luxuriantly; astonishingly; endlessly; naturally; primevally; multitudinously; munificently; swarmingly; throngingly; monstrously; boundlessly; excessively; generously.
(See swarm.)

ABRUPT
adverbs
unpardonably; rudely; roughly; instinctively; unconsciously; unfortunately; startlingly; whimsically; intentionally; astonishingly; amusingly; offensively; ridiculously; inexcusably; unforgivably; unexpectedly; unreasonably; momentarily; habitually; unintentionally.

ABRUPTNESS
adjectives
embarrassed; off-hand; startling; uncompromising; whimsical; wolfish; characteristic; brusque; brisk; easy.

ABSCESS
adjectives
hidden; internal; monstrous; fatal; pestilent; cankerous; gnawing; tentacle-like.

verbs
confine—; develop into—; drain—; dress—; evacuate—; exude from—; give rise to—; incise—; inflame—; irritate—; lance—; poultice—; swab out—; —arises; —attains size; —becomes embedded; —bulges; —bursts; —destroys; —develops; —discharges; —forms; —grows; —infiltrates; —inflames; —occurs; —opens; —re-forms; —ruptures; —spreads; —swells.
(See sore, ulcer, tumor, boil.)

ABSCOND (v)
adverbs
villainously; faithlessly; vilely; treacherously; unexpectedly; basely; knavishly; mysteriously; monstrously; nefariously; odiously; lawlessly; mendaciously.
(See flee.)

3

adjectives

utter; cautious; restful; prolonged; total; unaccounted; trying; oppressive; frequent; momentary; undutiful; perilous; considerable; striking; enforced; protracted; continued; pleasing; unauthorized; comparative; apparent; voluntary; everlasting; occasional; intermittent (pl).

verbs

attend—; bear—; berate—; bewail—; deplore—; dote on—; endure—; lament—; mourn—; presuppose—; regret—; support by—; take advantage of—; wail—; grant—; yield to—; —diminishes; —draws; —grows; —increases; —kills; —lessens; —quickens.

ABSENT

(in mind or in person)

adverbs

conspicuously; unfortunately; unaccountably; frequently; irritatingly; apparently; voluntarily; inexcusably; noticeably; purposely; inexplainably; mysteriously; carelessly; usually; provokingly.

ABSOLUTION

adjectives

general; priestly; just; rapturous; timely; insincere; virtual; conscientious; serene; blissful.

ABSOLVE (v)

adverbs

religiously; entirely; wholly; thoroughly; certainly; partly; freely; leniently; placably; sympathetically; forbearingly; compassionately; palliatively.

(See free, pardon, release.)

ABSORB (v)

adverbs

incessantly; wholly; passively; profoundly; partially; racially; nationally; intelligently; intellectually; physically; studiously; hurtfully; mentally; accretively; electively; vocationally; bibulously; crapulently; canniballistically; edaciously; intemperately; ghoulishly.

(See monopolize, engross.)

ABSORBED

adverbs

ridiculously; tragically; utterly; profoundly; shamelessly; mentally; wholly; deeply; completely; rapturously; ecstatically; tensely; eagerly; anxiously; gloomily; ludicrously; foolishly; fatuously; amazingly.

ABSORBENT

adverbs

extraordinarily; scarcely; completely; gradually; quickly; remarkably; marvelously; notably; wonderfully; exceptionally; genuinely; astonishingly; unusually; unfailingly; singularly; particularly; unbelievably; highly.

ABSORPTION

adjectives

bookish; omnivorous; profound; tragic; unflattering; shame-faced; poetic; gradual; mental; tense; detached; droll; indecent; stolid; passive; demoniac; vigorous.

ABSTAIN (v)

adverbs

cautiously; perniciously; carefully; systematically; firmly; voluntarily; austerely; religiously; totally; wilfully; narrowly; wholesomely; cautiously; prudently; discreetly; circumspectly; scrupulously; squeamishly; judiciously; economically; frugally; parsimoniously; sparingly; penuriously; chastely.

(See refrain, withhold.)

ABSTEMIOUS

adverbs

ascetically; piously; wholly; strictly; austerely; rigorously; proudly; awkwardly; fanatically; ridiculously; absurdly; carefully; abominably; cautiously; correctly; habitually; warily; ostentatiously; inconspicuously; glaringly; conspicuously; reluctantly; unctuously; smugly; grimly.

ABSTEMIOUSNESS

adjectives

ascetic; austere; stern; rigorous; calculated; proud.

ABSTINENCE

adjectives

bigoted; excessive; prolonged; total; rash; systematic; forced; holy; marked; firm; strict; self-enforced; austere; cautious; pernicious; absolute; recurrent; partial; half-hearted; protracted; extreme; habitual.

ABSTRACT

adverbs

academically; infinitely; immeasurably; uncomfortably; abstrusely; indefinitely; illusively; remotely; undeniably; obscurely; completely; terribly; entirely; sheerly; thoroughly; immaterially; undefinably; immutably; vaguely; fantastically; chimerically;

extravagantly; eternally; evanescently; transcendentally; unverifiably; preternaturally; spiritually; mystically; conceptually; palpably; patently; speculatively; intuitively; ideologically; empirically; occultly; **visionarily**; doctrinally; hypothetically.

ABSTRACTION

adjectives

mysterious; intense; subtle; hazy; sublime; unquiet; meaningless; thoughtful; dreamy; noble; mythical; shadowy; gloomy; statistical; far-off; eerie; stony; melancholy; moody; tight-lipped; deep; dull; pernicious; wistful; lengthy; grandiose; grave; wonted.

ABSTRUSE

adverbs

disagreeably; unfortunately; vexatiously; remotely; obscurely; profoundly; extremely; unreasonably; unnecessarily; needlessly; foolishly; absurdly; foggily; senselessly; stupidly; inexpediently; enigmatically; annoyingly; heavily; injudiciously; incomprehensibly; highly; unwisely; preposterously; confusingly; bewilderingly; perplexingly; indiscreetly.

ABSURD

adverbs

palpably; perniciously; nakedly; impudently; ludicrously; manifestly; fantastically; quaintly; grotesquely; patently; tragically; comically; perversely; detestably; pathetically; ignominiously; ridiculously; monstrously; grossly; unreasonably.

ABSURDITY

adjectives

palpable; pernicious; unfathomable; essential; naked; impudent; ornithological; ludicrous; moral; manifest; fantastic; quaint; reigning; infantine; grotesque; patent; tragic; perverse; colossal; detestable; inadequate; pathetic; ignominious; cumulative (pl); assorted (pl); ridiculous; monstrous; wholesome; gross; intrinsic; raucous; unreasonable.

verbs

atone for—; behold—; condone—; excuse—; expose—; father—; grieve over—; perpetrate—; smile at—; —destroys; —falls away; —impairs; —saps; —undermines.
(See folly, foolishness, nonsense.)

ABUNDANCE

adjectives

copious; uninterrupted; lavish; unbelievable; natural; flowing; laudable; culinary; theoretical; coveted; peculiar; careless; needless; wasteful; economic; sheer.

verbs

bless with—; conserve—; diminish—; endow with—; groan under—; inherit—; lavish—on; partake of—; pile up—; pour —; sate with—; satiate with—; squander—; surround by—; tap—; weaken by—; — flows; —lies; —melts away.
(See plenty.)

ABUNDANT

adverbs

overwhelmingly; marvelously; happily; fortunately; lavishly; naturally; profusely; uncommonly; unusually; remarkably; ravishingly; staggeringly; surprisingly; unbelievably; incredibly; voluptuously; wonderfully; particularly; amazingly; astonishingly; extraordinarily; fabulously; immeasurably; incalculably; indisputably; inexpressibly; alarmingly.

ABUSE

adjectives

political; unintelligible; intemperate; personal; treasonable; alarming; existing; scurrilous; sore; glaring; triumphant; abundant; filthy; scandalous; pernicious; tyrannical; alleged; disastrous; noisy; humorous; false; indiscriminate; stupid; mighty; virulent; intolerable; horrible; obscene; vicious; violent; flagrant; inhuman; profane; foul; notorious; barefaced; arrogant; shameful.

verbs

brook—; check—; condone—; correct—; cry out at—; curb—; direct—against; drive to —; eliminate—; exchange—; heap—; incur —; pour—; prevent—; reckon up—; remedy —; shovel—on; spare—; spy into—; stumble on—; subject to—; thunder—; tolerate —; wipe out—; —blackens; —damns; — prevails; —s are rife; —s reckon up.
(See perversion, invective.)

ABUSE (v)

adverbs

profanely; notoriously; foully; arrogantly; barefacedly; grossly; scandalously; shamefully; intemperately; treasonably; indiscriminately; alarmingly; scurrilously; perniciously; tyrannically; stupidly; virulently; mightily; obscenely; viciously; violently; inhumanly; flagrantly; heinously; malevolently; malignantly; noxiously; tempestuously; truculently; atrociously; hellishly; roughly.
(See misuse, injure, violate.)

5

adverbs

inexcusably; tragically; absurdly; painfully; scathingly; blisteringly; scandalously; alarmingly; ferociously; noisily; intolerably; pugnaciously; truculently; inhumanly; foully; diabolically; inconceivably; incredibly; obscenely; cruelly; scurrilously; unpardonably; unforgivably; unreasonably; immoderately; virulently; rashly; criminally; preposterously; unbelievably; recklessly; terribly; humiliatingly; profanely; disgracefully; shamefully; insanely; crazily; appallingly; maliciously; lamentably; violently; destructively; rancorously; blasphemously; spitefully; wickedly; revoltingly; illegally; direly; deliriously; horribly.

ABYSS

adjectives

immovable; nethermost; awful; blossoming; unfathomed; threatening; watery; dolorous; howling; moral; infernal; financial; yawning; void; profound; desolate; murky; bottomless; sunless; horrible; widening; black; unavoidable; breath-taking; gaping; immeasurable; hellish; hideous; Stygian.

ACADEMIC

adverbs

incurably; consistently; abstrusely; formally; formidably; illusively; evasively; impracticably; idealistically; impractically; remotely; uselessly; patently; frankly; uncomfortably; completely; dangerously; intrinsically; vaguely; fantastically; unfortunately; dreamily; unserviceably; worthlessly.

ACCEDE (v)

adverbs

heartily; speedily; willingly; unconditionally; amicably; rationally; gladly; genially; grudgingly; boorishly; tacitly; affably; benevolently; courteously; complaisantly; civilly; chivalrously; deferentially.

(See agree, concur, comply.)

ACCELERATE (v)

adverbs

tremendously; expectedly; abruptly; naturally; foolhardily; thoughtlessly; mechanically; intemperately; instantaneously; promptly; hurriedly; startlingly.

(See hasten, quicken.)

ACCELERATION

adjectives

whirling; considerable; impressive; impetu-ous; swift; easy; breath-taking; faulty; smooth; effortless.

ACCENT

adjectives

joyous; respectful; tender; well-bred; practiced; unctuous; affected; ornamental; mincing; vicious; blighting; coarse; peremptory; deliberate; icy; imperative; mocking; taunting; hurried; quivering; thick; clipped; mutilated; lingering; guttural; musical; silvery; mellow; pedantic; bell-like; clarion; insinuating; pleasant; droning; persuasive; melancholy; pitying; agonized; oratorical; professional; plebeian; objectionable; awed; faltering; half-impertinent; dispassionate; searching; trembling; gracious; musing; hushed; sober; measured; warning; meek; bluff; terrible; charming; feeble; soothing; compassionate; audible; smart; distinct; hollow; uncouth; haughty; ringing; honeyed; emphatic; nautical; swaggering; furious; mingled; tearful; crystal; pained; ecclesiastical; hesitant; wistful; authentic; melodious; sonorous; Teutonic; flippant; perceptible; provincial; circumflex; hesitating.

verbs

affect—; betray—; brook—; miss—; muffle—; reiterate in —s; —breaks; —echoes; —weakens.

(See stress, emphasis.)

ACCENT (v)

adverbs

nicely; pedantically; unctuously; joyously; tenderly; affectedly; mincingly; coarsely; deliberately; mockingly; tauntingly; quiveringly; lingeringly; musically; mellowly; insinuatingly; persuasively; falteringly; dispassionately; charmingly; soothingly; uncouthly; haughtily; emphatically; hesitantly; wistfully; melodiously; sonorously; flippantly; haltingly.

(See stress.)

ACCEPT (v)

adverbs

graciously; frankly; unreservedly; grudgingly; lifelessly; courteously; readily; cheerfully; fatalistically; passively; cautiously; phlegmatically; elatedly; enthusiastically; universally; bravely; casually; consciously; eagerly; generally; peacefully; credulously; thankfully; reluctantly; gratefully; reasonably; willingly; unhesitatingly; implicitly; philosophically; good-naturedly; slavishly; glibly; skeptically; impulsively; stoically; magnanimously; complacently.

(See approve.)

ACCEPTABLE

adverbs

unquestionably; charmingly; wholly; delightfully; genuinely; joyously; happily; providentially; luckily; gratifyingly; tragically; comically; vastly; duly; profoundly; admittedly; puzzlingly; infinitely; incalculably; immeasurably; particularly; personally; absolutely; frankly; socially; politically; officially; conventionally; widely; universally; locally.

ACCEPTANCE

adjectives

happy; warm; joyous; incoherent; complacent; wholesale; unanimous; fearless; impulsive; stoical; resigned; public; frank; modified; glib; skeptical; slavish; loathsome; unquestioning; ready; belated; simulated; good-natured; pacific; philosophic; reluctant; social; implicit; relieved; gracious; grudging; fatalistic; passive; phlegmatic; appreciatory; wide; delayed; patient; ironical; cheerful; general; unreserved; universal; credulous; grave; grandiloquent.

verbs

authorize—; coax—; confirm—; elicit—; find—; guarantee—; meet with—; presuppose—; —displays; —precludes.

(See agreement, assent.)

ACCESS

adjectives

impregnable; casual; unrestricted; momentary; exclusive; strange; convenient; direct; expeditious; easy.

verbs

bar—; deny—to; desire—to; disdain—; give—; grant—; seek—; procure—; shut off—; stop up—; survey—; throng—.

(See approach, admittance.)

ACCESSIBLE

adverbs

conveniently; easily; instantly; directly; serviceably; handily; immediately; instantaneously; casually; imperceptibly; inconspicuously; unobtrusively.

ACCESSORY

adjectives

agreeable; scenic; fashionable; cultured; gracious; impressive; colorful; distinctive; exquisite; decorative; tawdry; indispensable; unwilling; criminal.

ACCIDENT

adjectives

unlucky; capricious; untoward; melancholy; singular; unfortunate; comical; happy; felicitous; merest; incalculable; inescapable; preventable; frightful; pure; deplorable; subversive; divine; haphazard; perverse; monstrous; trivial; sheer; malignant; regrettable; vexing; inexplicable; minor; heart-breaking; curious; ghastly; providential; incredible; stupid; dreadful; fatal; predictable.

verbs

answer for—; barring—; breed —s; curb —s; excuse—; fake—; incapacitate by—; subject to—; trace to—; —befalls; —forces; —happens; —occurs; —oppresses; —places.

(See event, mishap.)

ACCIDENTAL

adverbs

scarcely; obviously; presumably; luckily; purposely; wholly; comically; inexplicably; curiously; mysteriously; certainly; undoubtedly; admittedly; undeniably; ludicrously; purportedly; evidently; supposedly; awkwardly; tragically; plainly; rarely.

ACCLAIM

adjectives

critical; tumultuous; public; boisterous; deafening; wide-spread; enthusiastic; spontaneous; immeasurable; resounding; joyous; jubilant; riotous; grandiloquent; noisy; righteous; deserved; universal.

ACCLAIM (v)

adverbs

riotously; grandiloquently; enthusiastically; noisily; tumultuously; boisterously; deafeningly; spontaneously; resoundingly; jubilantly; joyously; obstreperously; thunderously; persistently; turbulently; vociferously; sepulchrally; blatantly; clamorously; flamboyantly.

(See applaud, approve, cheer.)

ACCOMMODATE (v)

adverbs

effectually; appreciatively; easily; nobly; amiably; freely; generously; beneficently; benignly; graciously; impartially; magnanimously; altruistically; benignantly; legally; legitimately.

(See favor, oblige.)

ACCOMMODATING

adverbs

ingratiatingly; amiably; delightfully; obsequiously; ostentatiously; pompously; profusely; helpfully; fawningly; cordially; pretentiously; courteously; habitually; unusually; ominously; grudgingly; willingly; significantly; heartily; civilly; servilely; loftily; exceedingly; gravely; graciously; charmingly; freely; gruffly; politely; bluntly; splendidly; magnificently; surprisingly.

ACCOMMODATIONS
adjectives
luxurious; superior; splendid; modern; complete; princely; excellent; cheery; spacious; genial; straitened; pacific; dismal; comfortable; overnight; transient; capacious; commodious; sorry; mean; ordinary; slender; wretched.

ACCOMPANIMENT
adjectives
regrettable; picturesque; harmonic; supernatural; deprecatory; violent; aesthetic; invariable; undulating; confused; fearful; running; pleasurable; inharmonious; unsuitable; inevitable; throbbing; spirited; vague; faint; discordant; splendid; sinister; satiric; verdant; fiendish; bewitching; fitting; orchestral; indispensable; competent; riotous; listless; unhappy; staccato.

ACCOMPANY (v)
adverbs
listlessly; inevitably; invariably; delightedly; unhappily; fearfully; confusedly; harmoniously; unsuitably; spiritually; intelligently; discordantly; bewitchingly; competently; skillfully; dexterously; gaily; gladly; blissfully; rejoicingly; mirthfully; rapturously; dutifully.
(See escort, follow, attend.)

ACCOMPLICE
adjectives
menial; principal; provocative; vigilant; criminal; unwitting; dastardly; secret; willing; assiduous; inept; perfidious.

ACCOMPLISH (v)
adverbs
effectively; boastfully; deliberately; adequately; culturally; indefatigably; ultimately; substantially; peacefully; divinely; signally; impressively; skillfully; meritoriously; energetically; invincibly; irresistibly.
(See achieve, perform, execute.)

ACCOMPLISHED
adverbs
brilliantly; wonderfully; unusually; marvell-

ously; cleverly; incredibly; undoubtedly; distinctly; expertly; thoroughly; consummately; remarkably; politely; elegantly.

ACCOMPLISHMENT
adjectives
germinant; cultural; mental; limited; fatiguing; glittering; ultimate; substantial; brilliant; peaceful; divine; signal; human; impressive; creative; infinite (pl); successful; superb; scrupulous; notable; worthy; effete; versatile; effective; deliberate; boastful.

verbs
appraise —s; awe by—; credit with—; dwarf—; echo with—; enrich with—; gird oneself for—; hail—; lack—; marvel at—; praise—; strive for—; sum up —s; want (lack)—; —pales; —taunts.
(See achievement, action, deed, feat.)

ACCORD
adjectives
complete; mutual; enthusiastic; technical; sweet; voluntary; sensual; solid; simple; superficial; perfect; generous; hearty; tumultuous; universal; widespread; peaceful; temporary; lasting; harmonious.

ACCORD (v)
adverbs
generously; universally; genially; voluntarily; willingly; grudgingly; superficially; beneficently; gladly; intelligently; benevolently; reasonably; magnanimously; graciously; impartially; altruistically; benignly.
(See agree, conform.)

ACCOST (v)
adverbs
cordially; genially; jovially; graciously; familiarly; rudely; roughly; heartily; acrimoniously; bitterly; bluffly; drunkenly; blithely; gleefully; mirthfully; vivaciously; exultantly; ecstatically; conceitedly; cheerily.
(See greet, address.)

ACCOUNT
adjectives
elaborate; detailed; full; minute; lengthy; analytical; concise; brief; condensed; picturesque; magnificent; beautiful; hackneyed; inspired; felicitous; scanty; fragmentary; sketchy; rambling; inadequate; exact; accurate; veracious; precise; factual; personal; intimate; unaffected; sincere; straightforward; biased; impartial; prejudiced; sober; childish; intelligible; cap-

able; continuous; straight-running; chimerical; absurd; amusing; humorous; whimsical; facetious; thrilling; breath-taking; hair-raising; blood-curdling; lurid; ambiguous; conflicting; contradictory; amazing; disquieting; alarming; ribald; sordid; sprawling; incoherent; statistical; romantic; syllogistic; proselytizing; ironical; informative; lusty; rigorous; indignant; delirious; articulate; uninhibited; charming; fascinating; delightful; absorbing; striking; graphic; vivid; animated; leisurely; belated; garrulous; circumstantial; exhaustive; specific; inferential; synthetic; punctilious; glowing; exaggerated; superficial; singular; unrhetorical; contemporary; profuse; inspired; gloomy; harrowing; technical; wiredrawn; conjectural; malicious; farcical; biographical; voluble; prosaic; racy; awful.

verbs
balance—; boost—; fabricate—; juggle —s; revel in —s; render—; settle—; tally up—; treble the—; attach to your—; call to—; give—of; open—; place to—; take—of; take into—; enliven—; favor with—; furnish—; launch upon—; peruse—; ramble through—; deny—; sum up—; supplement —; thrill to—; —amuses; —bores; —depicts; —differs; —entertains; —maneuvers; —wearies.
(See reckoning, bill, notice, history, report, record, narrative.)

ACCOUNTABLE
adverbs
personally; legally; entirely; wholly; scarcely; officially; morally; partially; solely; admittedly; seriously; terribly; unofficially; really.

ACCRETION
adjectives
scholastic; formalistic; enormous; elaborate; slow-forming; cumulative; natural; hidden; gradual.

ACCUMULATE (v)
adverbs
uselessly; painstakingly; laboriously; toilsomely; eccentrically; penuriously; cautiously; judiciously; prudently; close-fistedly; frugally; parsimoniously; economically; conservatively.
(See collect, gather.)

ACCUMULATION
adjectives
periodic; slow; colossal; perpetual; laborious; appalling; dangerous; insistent; useless; unsmiling; prodigious; ponderous; contorted; massive.

ACCUMULATIVE
adverbs
laboriously; ingeniously; peculiarly; unaccountably; painstakingly; instinctively; irresponsibly; habitually; dangerously; suspiciously; unsmilingly; laughingly; openly; furtively; surreptitiously; cleverly; cunningly; frankly; delightfully; deliriously; whimsically; garrulously; sincerely; unaffectedly; leisurely.

ACCURACY
adjectives
absolute; dependable; historical; businesslike; substantial; precise; unrivaled; scrupulous; tolerable; measurable; predictable; muscular; unfailing; blunt; remarkable; strict; deadly; guaranteed; mechanical; clock-like; excellent; uncanny; timed; impeccable; apparent; unctuous; machine-like; relentless; meticulous; unerring; horrible; photographic; sensitive; nautical; perfect; infinite; rhythmic; diabolical; humdrum; monotonous.

verbs
ascertain—; concede—; depend upon—; reveal—; scout—; test—; vouch for—; —fosters; —sustains
(See precision.)

ACCURATE
adverbs
absolutely; dependably; awfully; terrifyingly; scrupulously; tolerably; unfailingly; remarkably; strictly; uncannily; meticulously; monotonously; veritably; disturbingly; nakedly; essentially; unimpeachably; rigidly; mathematically; scientifically; carefully; particularly; astonishingly; insatiably; avidly; impartially; ostentatiously; punctiliously.

ACCUSATION
adjectives
frivolous; unfounded; monstrous; plaintive; vulgar; horrible; tearful; vague; rash; unanswerable; recurrent; merciless; mock; human; public; groundless; menial; eloquent; positive; keen; railing; sarcastic; indignant; constant; trumped up; nonsensical; sharp; determined; wild; unjust; false; cruel; revolting; wholesale (pl); grave; scurrilous; slanderous; violent; sensational; hasty; playful; vitriolic; villainous.

verbs
balk at—; bring—; clear—; contradict—;

counteract—; defend against—; deny—; disprove—; face—; headline—; heap —s; hurl—; level—at; parry—; refute—; resist —; roar —s; secure against—; set—; splutter—; uncover—; weigh—; withstand—.

(See charge, complaint.)

ACCUSE (v)

adverbs

publicly; consistently; unjustly; deliberately; scurrilously; falsely; sternly; vainly; frivolously; monstrously; plaintively; vulgarly; tearfully; vaguely; rashly; mercilessly; groundlessly; eloquently; indignantly; sarcastically; triumphantly; determinedly; wildly; cruelly; revoltingly; libellously; slanderously; sensationally; ruinously.

(See blame, charge.)

ACHE

adjectives

strange; dull; continual; yearning; maddening; hungry; trifling; brief; cold; numbing; throbbing; muscular; angry; bodily; intolerable; murderous; unbearable; agonizing; intermittent (pl).

verbs

aggravate—; allay—; alleviate—; assuage —; charm—; distress with—; fill with —s; harry by —s; hide—; increase—; mitigate —; mollify—; soothe—; subdue—; tantalize by—; torture by—; —abates; —contracts; —develops; —diminishes.

(See pain, agony, anguish, misery.)

ACHE (v)

adverbs

intolerably; dully; maddeningly; agonizingly; throbbingly; bitterly; sorely; mentally; dismally; tormentingly; torturingly; sharply; interminably; incessantly; monotonously; ceaselessly; periodically.

(See pain, suffer.)

ACHIEVE (v)

adverbs

unbelievably; secretly; laboriously; lastingly; consistently; tirelessly; honorably; gloriously; spiritually; conspicuously; momentously; splendidly; monumentally; superhumanly; signally; creatively; magnificently; spectacularly; breath-takingly; impressively; memorably; heroically; illustriously; valorously; fabulously; significantly.

(See accomplish, gain, acquire.)

ACHIEVEMENT

adjectives

solid; practical; lasting; remarkable; scientific; human; technological; metaphysical; civic; routine; happy; courageous; difficult; universal; authentic; fantastic; consistent; tireless; honorable; laureate; glorious; noble; conspicuous; spiritual; major; momentous; monumental; superhuman; signal; sublime; phenomenal; noteworthy; worthwhile; meritorious; creditable; praiseworthy; creative; constructive; colossal; vast; stupendous; magnificent; artistic; picturesque; rare; unparalleled; unique; spectacular; culminating; breath-taking; stirring; supreme; crowning; Homeric; impressive; memorable; heroic; valorous; illustrious; unfading; poetic; precocious; fabulous; laborious; subtle; immortal; significant; epoch-making; irreproachable.

verbs

belittle—; conceive—; denote—; disparage —; enhance—; facilitate—; hedge about—; laud—; meditate on—; mock at—; plan—; praise—; proclaim—; question—; reaffirm —; rejoice in—; strive toward—; —contributes to; —distinguishes; —goes unrecognized; —mocks.

(See accomplishment, action, deed, feat.)

ACID

adjectives

pungent; aromatic; biting; insidious; corrosive; baneful; mineral; powerful; fatal; astringent; violent; fuming.

verbs

immerse in—; isolate—; neutralize—; treat with—; —bites; —burns; —cauterizes; —corrodes; —dissolves; —eats; —etches; —evaporates; —meets; —penetrates; —scars; —sears; —seeps off.

(See chemical.)

ACID (a)

adverbs

bitterly; maliciously; viciously; purposely; unnecessarily; uncontrollably; hatefully; insidiously; sharply; cynically; spitefully; resentfully; venomously; intentionally; designedly; cunningly; insinuatingly; sarcastically; incisively; shrewdly; antagonistically; needlessly; unwisely.

ACKNOWLEDGE (v)

adverbs

gratefully; appreciatively; tacitly; thankfully; obsequiously; grudgingly; pusillanimously; handsomely; tardily; instinctively; cheerfully; profusely; indulgently; exuberantly; restrainedly; warmly; characteristically; graciously; jocosely; belatedly; glumly; obstreperously; **boisterously**; taciturnly; incoherently.

(See admit, confess.)

ACKNOWLEDGMENT
adjectives
profuse; indulgent; exuberant; restrained; polite; conventional; frank; warm; characteristic; humiliating; enthusiastic; grateful; public; gracious; jocose; courteous; grim; belated; thankful; obsequious; tacit; grudging; handsome; tardy; appreciative.

ACQUAINT (v)
adverbs
intimately; minutely; partially; familiarly; imperfectly; mutely; affectionately; eagerly; reluctantly; entirely; affably; amiably; charitably; amicably; loyally; politely; piously; complacently.

(See tell.)

ACQUAINTANCE
adjectives
vast; mutual; desirable; intimate; eventful; favorable; brilliant; charitable; prosperous; common; conventional; casual; stray; select; congenial; slight; valued; ingenious; inaccurate; preliminary; fair; imperfect; superficial; extensive; critical; tolerable; nodding; astounding; injudicious; chance; passing; temporary; broad; well-born; garrulous; good-humored; varied (pl); amiable; numerous (pl); bowing; renewed; promiscuous; protracted; professional; informal; cursory; first-hand; incomplete.

verbs
bless with—; boast—; crave—; dim—; estrange—; exploit—; greet—; hold—; lend—; pursue—; put away—; renew—; resume—; strangle—; strike up—; urge—; —creeps; —is estranged; —widens.

(See intimacy, friendship, association, friend.)

ACQUAINTED
adverbs
intimately; slightly; favorably; unhappily; fortunately; unluckily; auspiciously; personally; directly; indirectly; well; happily; familiarly; casually; superficially; thoroughly; closely; generally; absolutely; naturally; remotely; barely; insufficiently; hardly; scarcely.

ACQUIESCE (v)
adverbs
grudgingly; silently; reluctantly; feelingly;

pleasantly; cheerfully; tepidly; carelessly; stolidly; sullenly; dignifiedly; cravenly; phlegmatically; grumblingly; tacitly; amiably; passively; candidly; complacently; fatalistically.

(See agree, assent, submit.)

ACQUIESCENCE
adjectives
stolid; tepid; agreeable; sullen; silent; dignified; polite; craven; unanimous; wise; courageous; phlegmatic; grumbling; delighted; tacit; stupid; amiable; passive; desperate; compulsory; candid; reluctant; fatalistic; cheerful; complacent; grudging; grim.

verbs
arrive at—; attain—; draw into—; signify —; soften into—; urge—; wheedle into—.

(See submission, agreement, compliance.)

ACQUIESCENT
adverbs
courteously; willingly; reluctantly; gruffly; grudgingly; graciously; cheerfully; necessarily; unwillingly; happily; pliantly; blithely; devotedly; wholly; glumly; half-heartedly; stolidly; timidly; stupidly; blindly; politely; passively; wisely; tacitly; complaisantly; sullenly; amiably; cunningly; shrewdly; casually; apparently; restrainedly; indifferently.

ACQUIRE (v)
adverbs
righteously; readily; patiently; instinctively; innocently; painfully; unjustly; gloriously; sensibly; ultimately; brutally; systematically; dictatorially; vigorously; ruthlessly; villainously; cruelly; treacherously; barbarously; legally; scientifically.

(See learn, master, attain.)

ACQUIREMENT
adjectives
scientific; glorious; systematic; consequent; linguistic; unrighteous; instinctive; innocent; painful.

ACQUISITION
adjectives
painful; noteworthy; desirable; permanent; eternal; arduous; exciting; superior; territorial; profitless; erudite; patient; mental; valuable; perfunctory; forcible; peaceful; cherished; long-sought.

ACQUISITIVE
adverbs
inordinately; insanely; avidly; eagerly; in-

curably; indiscriminately; universally; peculiarly; incorrigibly; distressingly; gloriously; happily; instinctively; painfully; embarrassingly; systematically; irreclaimably; hopelessly; promiscuously; vexatiously; shamelessly; perpetually; laboriously; insistently; appallingly.

ACQUIT (v)
adverbs
unhesitatingly; legally; unexpectedly; unanimously; generously; triumphantly; entirely; constitutionally; legitimately; tolerantly; graciously; licitly; condescendingly; acquiescently; deferentially.

(See absolve, justify, pardon.)

ACQUITTAL
adjectives
prompt; triumphant; unexpected; honorable; disquieting; undeserved; trumped-up.

verbs
advance toward—; argue for—; ballot for —; beg for—; concede—; decide on—; demand—; deny—; deserve—; direct—; earn —; effect an—; entreat for—; expect—; gain—; hope for—; justify—; merit—; move for—; order—; plead for—; produce —; provoke—; refuse—; request—; secure —; seek—; solicit—; vote on—; win—; —carries; —exonerates; —follows.

(See pardon.)

ACREAGE
adjectives
valuable; vast; fruitful; expansive.

ACRES
adjectives
wooded; impoverished; scant; unworked; well-fenced; paternal; suburban; airy; broad; rolling; broken; untilled; scrubby; verdant; denuded; cultivated; dead; ill-acquired.

ACRIMONIOUS
adverbs
pithily; dryly; sharply; tartly; pungently; wilfully; remorselessly; mercilessly; deliberately; ominously; obnoxiously; malignantly; destructively; roughly; bitterly; pertly; insolently; churlishly; crustily; snarlingly; bitingly; banefully; rancorously; quietly; unsparingly; chronically; unrelentingly; viciously; unnecessarily; hatefully; insidiously; venomously; cunningly; needlessly.

ACROBAT
verbs
—amuses; —arches his back; —awes; —

balances; —clowns; —contorts; —dances; —dazzles; —displays; —dives; —executes; —flexes; —flies; —flips; —folds; —frolics; —gyrates; —hangs; —hurtles; —leaps; —manipulates; —postures; —pyramids; —rebounds; —recovers; —relaxes; —revolves; —rolls; —soars; —somersaults; —spins; —swings; —thrills; —throws himself; —tumbles; —twirls; —twists; —vaults; —waddles; —whirls; applaud—; gape at—; gasp at—; marvel at—.

ACT
adjectives
virtuous; generous; gracious; unspeakable; self-confident; aggressive; dastardly; ruthless; loathsome; detestable; horrific; barbarous; ignominious; brutal; wilful; rash; servile; cowardly; militant; hostile; mutinous; lawless; illicit; churlish; unknown; condescending; reprehensible; compromising; unfortunate; suspicious; ungallant; unwise; impulsive; thoughtless; childish; gauche; dauntless; hardy; hazardous; official; ritualistic; conspicuous; overt; inopportune; voluntary; unremembered; well-planned; expressive; benevolent; needless; oppressive; conscientious; exasperating; arbitrary; sublime; amusing; incongruous; valid; symptomatic; disadvantageous; adumbrative; heroic; authenticated; meritorious; unfeeling; decisive; instinctive; valiant; beneficent; disinterested; crowning; innumerable (pl); offensive; daring; energetic; lugubrious; touching; specific; governmental; noble; salutary; impolitic; disdainful; violent; dishonorable; ferocious; generous; cogitative; unpopular; infamous; creative; atrocious; dreaded; mischievous; imposing; inexpiable; illogical; egotistic; compulsive; overbold; unwarrantable; disgraceful; unauthorized; superfluous; defensible; treasonable; climactic; derisive; craven; irrevocable; impudent.

verbs
achieve—; applaud—; behold—; betray—; bring to pass—; catch in the—; commend—; commit—; condemn—; derive from—; dispense with—; incite—; inspire—; perform —; provoke—; pursue—; smile upon—; take in—; urge in—; view—; visualize—; —abides; —blurs; —commences; —denotes; —overtakes; —unfolds; embody—in; frustrate—; galvanize into—; goad into—; govern—.

ACT
(*statute*)
abolish—; abrogate—; annul—; broaden—; design—; disallow—; invalidate—; invoke

12

—; make void—; outlaw—; proclaim—; put an end to—; repeal—; resurrect—; set aside—; supersede—; suspend—; term—; violate—.

(See bill.)

ACT (v)

adverbs

ignominiously; shamefully; disgracefully; irrationally; impulsively; impetuously; vengefully; abnormally; irregularly; generously; cautiously; coldly; officially; officiously; erratically; superfluously; adversely; involuntarily; admirably; imprudently; ostensibly; mercifully; independently; recklessly; detrimentally; impecuniously; deliberately; frivolously; graciously; viciously; self-confidently; aggressively; unspeakably; ruthlessly; detestably; brutally; wilfully; servilely; mutinously; churlishly; compromisingly; condescendingly; gallantly; impulsively; dauntlessly; disinterestedly; offensively; disdainfully; atrociously; illogically; treasonably.

(See behave, feign.)

ACTING

adjectives

immobile; technical; robust; allegorical; iridescent; extravagant; resolute; creditable; unnatural; effective; apt; adequate; inspired; imitative; wooden; facile; listless; pantomimic; sluggish; unconvincing.

ACTION

adjectives

intelligent; noble; efficient; authoritative; authenticated; sober; riotous; furious; hair-raising; intense; virile; vigorous; muscular; courageous; aggressive; direct; resolute; determined; independent; bold; gallant; heroic; positive; affirmative; decisive; vitalizing; tumultuous; perfidious; impetuous; lively; right; stimulating; frenzied; fervent; glorious; justifiable; regrettable; passionate; unrelated (pl); pointless; spectacular; futile; indiscreet; thoughtless; ill-advised; impulsive; commonplace; immoral; uncontrolled; desperate; contemptible; rash; unhesitating; ruthless; unsocial; negative; destructive; infernal; unconventional; drastic; menial; shameful; distressing; implacable; hysterical; mob; maternal; unprecedented; vivid; pending; coordinated; definite; prompt; preliminary; simultaneous; concerted; collective; selective; absurd; dramatic; restrained; involuntary; organized; unified; isolated; strenuous; mechanical; casual; singular; unguarded; unpremeditated; instinctive; punitive; ad-

mirable; favorable; laudable; unselfish; virtuous; righteous; conscientious; irritant; unscrupulous; individual; cordial; arbitrary; precipitate; abrasive; ill-considered; disinterested; excited; physiological; spirited; sweeping; chivalric; soothing; unopposed; insolent; pantomimic; rebellious; radical; postponed; vicious; incessant; automatic; emotional; enlightened; summary; ceaseless; engrossing; self-contained; lightning; distinguished; feverish; morbid; convulsive; vehement; uncertain; purgative; igneous; reflex; public-spirited; unobstrusive; meritorious; functional; dynamic; clannish; crude; awkward; insane; poisonous; reciprocal; inspired; adventurous; unheralded; unobserved; habitual; significant; deleterious; epic; atrocious; persistent; effectual; perturbative; accelerating; deplorable; trifling; magical; vacillating; prohibited; unholy; unforeseen; spontaneous; sporadic; headlong; logical.

verbs

accelerate—; account for—; advise—; affirm—; atone for—; authenticate—; authorize—; bare—; behold—; burst into—; call into—; chafe for—; classify—; clog—; concentrate—; condemn—; construe—; contemplate—; contrive—; control—; counterfeit—; crystallize—; embark on—; emulate—; enhance—; enter upon—; expedite—; dignify—; diminish—; disguise—; dwarf —; embody—in; frustrate—; galvanize into —; goad into—; govern—; hail—; hamper —; hasten—; hinder—; identify with—; imitate—; impede—; increase—; induce—; influence—; initiate—; intensify—; interpret—; introduce—; justify—; kindle into —; maintain—; motivate—; nullify—; paralyze—; perform—; pledge to—; postpone —; prescribe—; prod into—; produce—; put into—; quicken—; repeat—; repudiate —; restrain—; retard—; revel in—; reverse—; ripen into—; rue—; shame into—; snap into—; spring into—; spur to—; stimulate—; stint—; sum up—; support—; swing into—; threaten—; throw light on—; time—; underprop—; utilize—; weigh—; yield to—; —belittles; —betrays; —blasts; —centers; —confers; —contrives against; —conveys; —divorces from; —predominates; —proceeds from; —rends; —tires; —yields.

(See motion, gesture, act, operation.)

ACTIVE

adverbs

tremendously; keenly; perpetually; enormously; nervously; appallingly; seldom; ter-

13

ribly; amicably; despicably; charitably; helpfully; vitally; dramatically; ostentatiously; shamelessly; absurdly; villainously; ridiculously; admirably; efficiently; pompously; socially; ludicrously; perpetually; politically; singularly; habitually; uncommonly; infernally; vexatiously; suspiciously; subversively; constructively; excitedly; impudently; presumptuously; ardently; rebelliously; obtrusively; insanely; significantly; gravely; persistently; disturbingly; noisily; amazingly; annoyingly; tirelessly; normally; surreptitiously; restlessly; furtively; openly; boldly; incessantly.

ACTIVITY
adjectives
intellectual; bustling; political; characteristic; extra-curricular; charitable; unavailing; elemental; intense; supporting; spasmodic; mischievous; feverish; exaggerated; volitional; sustained; pedagogical; commercial; unrivaled; spontaneous; volcanic; essential; potent; gastric; peculiar; mental; disquieting; productive; suspicious; erotic; cultural; infantile; unfettered; creative; mercantile; hampered; cataclysmic; magnetic; hive-like; fruitful; beneficent; unparalleled; throbbing; fiendish; functional; social; subversive; publicized; philanthropic; outstanding; recreational; buoyant; prodigious; ceaseless; energetic; incessant; tireless; editorial; violent; unedifying; frivolous; manifold; literary; accustomed; stunning; physiologic; purposeless; destructive; influential; malignant; cooperative; inspirational; painful; irresponsible; aesthetic; earthly; kaleidoscopic; zealous; wholesome; morbid; constructive; normal; disciplined; fascinating; dexterous; nefarious; frantic; surreptitious; clandestine; deficient; tortuous; expanding; multiple; conglomerate (pl); diversified; teeming; widespread; innumerable (pl); multifarious; incredible; nervous; passionate; eager; restless; strident; humming; hilarious; fertile; instigated; prosaic; bizarre; vicarious; villainous.

verbs
accompany—; administer—; boil with—; camouflage—; center—; chart—; condemn —; confine—; constitute—; contemplate—; control—; cramp—; cripple—; curb—; dedicate—; deliberate on—; diffuse—; direct —; display—; edge out—; embrace—; engage in—; examine—; focus—; frustrate—; guide—; hamper by—; hum with—; immerse in—; induce—; inhibit—; initiate—; interrupt—; involve—; kindle—; leap into

—; limit—; link—; maintain—; motivate —; nag into—; overshadow—; participate in—; pursue—; regulate—; restrict—; resume—; rouse—; seethe with—; spring into —; spur—; supervise—; undertake—; witness—; —abates; —defeats; —ebbs and flows; —excites; —flares into; —reigns; —stimulates.
(See action.)

ACTOR
adjectives
daring; conspicuous; tragic; eminent; gesticulating; diligent; impulsive; distinguished; celebrated; obscure; godlike; prominent; inimitable; popular; expert; unschooled; recalcitrant; "ham"; strolling; itinerant; persuasive; consummate; competent; forthright; character; skilled.

verbs
applaud—; greet—; key up—; prompt—; —acquits; —administers; —affects; —apes; —blunders through; —burlesques; —conforms to; —appears; —evokes; —executes; —forces; —gesticulates; —impersonates; —interprets; —mimics; —narrates; —parrots; —performs; —personifies; —radiates; —recites; —spouts; —suggests; —wails.
(See player, performer.)

ACTRESS
adjectives
gifted; distinguished; competent; charming; brilliant; subtle; exotic; fascinating; indomitable; obscure; hardened; stately; naturalistic; mediocre; energetic; spirited.

ACUMEN
adjectives
critical; philosophical; rare; financial; intellectual; penetrative; business; distinguished; acute.

ACUTE
adverbs
unwontedly; keenly; actually; remarkably; apparently; astonishingly; unexpectedly; surpassingly; shrewdly; cleverly; uncommonly; fairly; profoundly; thoughtfully; politically; sharply; discriminatingly; naturally; subtly; restlessly; prophetically; reassuringly; penetratingly; craftily.

ACUTENESS
adjectives
consummate; vicious; tense; native; unwonted; proverbial; incredible; godlike; rare; apparent.

ADAGE

adjectives
favorite; familiar; classic; oft-quoted; apt; well-phrased; clumsy; appropriate.

verbs
accept—; call to mind—; conceive—; disprove—; grasp—; interpret—; lean against —; paraphrase—; reiterate—; verify—; — expresses.
(See proverb, maxim, saying.)

ADAMANT

adverbs
wilfully; indomitably; bitterly; unyieldingly; obdurately; pitilessly; unrelentingly; unrepentantly; inexorably; stubbornly; obstinately; mulishly; doggedly; perversely; fanatically; pig-headedly; contumaciously; bigotedly.

ADAPT (v)

adverbs
admirably; skilfully; eminently; artistically; mentally; physically; intellectually; professionally; ingeniously; mechanically; adroitly; dexterously; aesthetically; craftily; competently; consummately; deftly; matchlessly; cleverly; efficaciously; factitiously; gracefully; scientifically; diplomatically; inventively; ingeniously; peerlessly; incomparably.
(See adjust, conform.)

ADAPTABILITY

adjectives
ready; wide-awake; facile; quick.
(See adaptation.)

ADAPTABLE

adverbs
complaisantly; hardly; readily; intelligently; graciously; easily; ingeniously; comfortably; moderately; scarcely; willingly; quickly; dexterously; cleverly; wisely; diplomatically; sagaciously; sympathetically; mercifully; affably; courteously; civilly; companionably; amiably; discreetly; judiciously; wisely.

ADAPTATION

adjectives
judicious; exquisite; conscious; functional; deliberate; scenic; terrestrial; approximate; stereotyped; passive; studious; agile; unfulfilled; inexpensive; ingenious; errant.

ADD (v)

adverbs
fondly; facetiously; significantly; intelligent-ly; wearily; dreamily; sorrowfully; passionately; thoughtfully; mildly; parenthetically; frowningly; hopefully; bluntly; decisively; soothingly; carelessly; regretfully; stridently; hurriedly; unobtrusively; contemptuously; tremulously; doubtfully; self-reproachfully; wistfully; breathlessly; impressively; haughtily; needlessly; falteringly; graciously; tentatively; briskly; generously; coolly; cryptically; slyly; speedily; accurately; erratically; mentally; alternately; materially; freely; jerkily; vertically; diagonally; horizontally.
(See annex, join.)

ADDICT

adjectives
passionate; miserable; confirmed; incurable; depraved; pitiful.

ADDICTED

adverbs
miserably; unfortunately; hopelessly; tragically; incurably; ridiculously; pitifully; irreparably; comically; fatally; incorrigibly; lamentably; unhappily; absurdly; unluckily; distressingly; pathetically; laughably; unreasonably; strangely; curiously.

ADDICTION

adjectives
pedantic; stubborn; tiresome; conspicuous; learned; hopeless; desultory; violent; favorite.

ADDITION

adjectives
incongruous; anachronistic; desirable; simultaneous; pleasing; necessary; costly; significant; worthy; astonishing; dubious; immediate; unprofitable; meager; valuable; substantial; imaginative; gratuitous; indispensable; distinctive; popular.

ADDLED

adverbs
hopelessly; comically; strangely; disastrously; slightly; completely; sweetly; horribly; delightfully; indescribably; visibly; manifestly; uproariously; foggily; vociferously; dazedly; rosily; brokenly; incurably; pathetically; palpably.

ADDRESS

adjectives
impromptu; flattering; impending; emphatic; passionate; pithy; temperate; grave; inaugural; intuitive; masterly; graphic; soldier-like; moving; fervid; insinuating; il-

luminating; commemorative; laudatory; radical; carefully-worded; sensational; postprandial; lengthy; stirring; inspiring; rousing; keynote; eloquent; amatory; ardent; affectionate; lucid; preliminary; charming; naive; stumbling; halting; extempore; incoherent.

ADDRESS

verbs *(speech)*

alter—; charge—with; compose—; concoct —; condense—; curtail—; expand—; grind out—; organize—; pour forth—; reel off—; thunder—.

(See speech, oration, sermon, lecture, discourse.)

ADDRESS (v)

adverbs

informally; cordially; intimately; affectionately; indiscriminately; pretentiously; exclusively; mournfully; passionately; extemporaneously; temperately; fervidly; insinuatingly; stirringly; inspiringly; rousingly; eloquently; ardently; lucidly; intelligently; pugnaciously; pointedly.

(See lecture, discourse.)

ADEPT

adverbs

expertly; scarcely; palpably; undoubtedly; cleverly; ingeniously; incredibly; marvellously; clearly; remarkably; smartly; unimaginably; surprisingly; dangerously; alarmingly; exceptionally; subtly; fearfully; comparatively; confidently.

ADEQUATE

adverbs

completely; excellently; pleasantly; delightfully; remarkably; providentially; sufficiently; scarcely; essentially; suitably; wholly; admirably; quite; satisfactorily; wonderfully; gratifyingly; fortunately; luckily.

ADHERE (v)

adverbs

rigidly; tenaciously; doggedly; staunchly; passionately; strictly; perversely; pertinaciously; scrupulously; unflinchingly; undeviatingly; formally; steadfastly; stubbornly; obstinately; blindly; unalterably; intractably; militantly; contentiously; cantankerously; incorrigibly; immovably; impassively; insistently; bigotedly; sullenly; waywardly, strenuously; religiously; moderately.

(See stick, cling.)

ADHERENCE

adjectives

lingering; firm; strict; scrupulous; unflinch-

ing; passionate; undiscriminating; rigid; undeviating; formal; steadfast; stubborn; obstinate; exact; staunch; apparent; blind; unalterable; inborn; tenacious; dogged; pertinacious; devout; perverse; rash; vigorous; unwise; smug; unswerving; ardent.

ADHERENT

adjectives

staunch; unquestioning; zealous; pious; numbered (pl); faithful; deluded; superstitious; loyal; devout; close; spirited.

ADIEU

adjectives

courtly; final; graceful; gentle; mute; sublime; fearful; silent; grave; painful; brash; condescending; disdainful; despairing; wistful.

ADIPOSE

adverbs

incredibly; irremediably; unfortunately; disagreeably; incurably; unacceptably; distressingly; absurdly; ridiculously; needlessly; ludicrously; damagingly; lamentably; sadly; dangerously; heavily; admittedly; unreasonably.

ADJECTIVE

adjectives

qualifying; explosive; unfactual; decorative; severe; impressive-sounding; apt; augmenting; glowing; sonorous; obsolete; laudatory; rapturous; nauseous; overworked; uncomplimentary; unfavorable; commendatory; descriptive; flattering; inept; obvious; appropriate; exact; distinctive; moving; brilliant; breezy; racy; lurid; lush; picturesque; suggestive; well-chosen; precise.

verbs

accompany by—; adorn with—; allot—; arrange—; attach—; avoid—; bandy—; choose—; classify—; compare—; depend on —; derive—; eliminate—; eschew—; exhaust—; group —s; indulge in —s; juggle —s; lavish —s on; overwork—; pile up —s; reject—; strike out—; stuff with —s; supply with —s; swamp with —s; transpose —s; —answers; —colors; —conveys; —defines; —denotes; —describes; —disappears; —explains; —expresses; —forms; —implies; —interprets; —limits; —modifies; —occurs; —s pad; —points out; —presents; —qualifies; —springs from; —supplies.

(See word.)

ADJUNCT

adjectives

impressive; non-essential; inevitable; external; unusual; absurd; impedimental; artificial.

ADJUST (v)

adverbs

delicately; improperly; satisfactorily; accurately; eventually; fortunately; happily; languidly; harmoniously; nervously; peaceably; enduringly; elaborately; amply; subtly; magnanimously; equitably; mathematically; minutely; precisely; punctiliously; specifically; exactly.

(See settle, fit.)

ADJUSTABLE

adverbs

amicably; easily; instantly; comfortably; necessarily; wisely; conveniently; fortunately; luckily; amazingly; extraordinarily; cunningly; cleverly; naturally; serviceably; handily; peaceably; sensibly.

ADJUSTMENT

adjectives

necessary; temporary; ultimate; long-awaited; peaceful; visual; constant; artistic; enduring; honorable; felicitous; elaborate; studied; rightful; immediate; patriotic; corresponding; ample; scientific; preliminary; harmonious; sensible; subtle; economic; discreet; enforced; poetical; complex; delicate; heart-rending; mental; compensating; calm; prompt; partial; compromised; amicable.

verbs

adopt—; advocate—; challenge—; effect—; honor—; postpone—; recommend—; reject —; stimulate—; submit to—; —obviates; —pleases; —prevents; —satisfies; —settles.

(See regulation, arrangement, settlement.)

ADMINISTER (v)

adverbs

efficiently; steadily; faithfully; methodically; internally; cautiously; economically; corruptly; benignly; wholesomely; incompetently; satisfactorily; formally; ecclesiastically; conventionally; customarily; domestically; wontedly; ethically; vigorously.

(See manage, regulate, settle.)

ADMINISTRATION

adjectives

successful; businesslike; memorable; subservient; corrupt; economical; incapable; filial; benign; stormy; incumbent; spiritual; contemporary; centralized; unified; communal; careful; incoming; civil; eventful; efficient; wholesome; bureaucratic; incompetent; judicial; provincial; internal; stern; progressive; partisan.

verbs

backbite—; consolidate—; dominate—; entrust with—; facilitate—; flout—; hamper —; repudiate—; set up—; —comes into power; —contemplates; —defends; —draws to a close; —justifies; —plows under; —refutes; —relegates to; —vindicates; —wields.

(See government.)

ADMINISTRATIVE

adverbs

capably; stormily; benignly; thoroughly; nonchalantly; conscientiously; patriarchally; paternally; ably; cleverly; sternly; severely; strictly; judiciously; wisely; tolerantly; wholesomely; busily; fussily; majestically; pompously; simply; arrogantly; officiously; laxly; loosely; democratically; dogmatically; tyrannically; sagely; affably; fairly; honestly; incorruptibly.

ADMIRABLE

adverbs

genuinely; virtuously; correctly; laudably; truly; really; unexpectedly; consciously.

ADMIRAL

adjectives

mustachioed; famed; stern; plucky; renowned; redoubtable; capable; undaunted.

ADMIRATION

adjectives

heartfelt; affectionate; ecstatic; whole-hearted; rapturous; unbounded; cordial; genuine; undying; profound; unstinted; grateful; modest; effusive; wistful; unfeigned; passionate; intense; open; frank; enthusiastic; reluctant; waning; grudging; fictitious; perverse; patriotic; youthful; girlish; wondering; amazed; hushed; puzzled; unabashed; sneaking; ardent; mirthful; self-contained; inexpressible; repressed; blind; mute; envious; reiterated; deluded; mutual; unmitigated; critical; loquacious; unrestrained; clamorous; passing; complacent; prolonged; smiling; unwilling; universal; ineffable; impersonal; respectful; astonished; reverent; calculating; noisy; untutored; outspoken; undisguised; unlimited; sympathetic; reciprocal; excessive; maudlin; rapt;

half-envious; magnanimous; indulgent; pitying; healthy; speechless; momentary; enhanced.

verbs
arouse—; challenge—; command—; draw—; elicit—; evoke—; excite—; express—; fill with—; inspire—; lose in—; mirror—; modify—; obtain—; profess—; reap—; reserve—; retain—; season—; strike with—; suppress—; temper—; utter—; win—; — abates; —beams; —buzzes; —cools; — haunts; —moves; —seizes; —wanes; — waxes.
(See amazement, wonder, astonishment, love, respect.)

ADMIRE (*v*)
adverbs
universally; prodigiously; immensely; gushingly; passionately; cordially; legitimately; tremendously; ardently; ecstatically; wholeheartedly; rapturously; effusively; profoundly; wistfully; intensely; mutely; unrestrainedly; loquaciously; complacently; clamorously; ineffably; reverently; outspokenly; frankly; undisguisedly; unboundedly; magnanimously; indulgently; unceasingly; fervently; legitimately; perfunctorily.
(See approve, appreciate.)

ADMIRER
adjectives
idolatrous; credulous; soft; ardent; fervent; enthusiastic; irresponsible; discriminating; solemn; passionate; devoted; staunch; countless (pl); sole; persistent; injudicious; quondam; appreciative; reluctant; blind; over-enthusiastic; fond; rival; well-bred; zealous; hearty.

verbs
abuse—; discourage—; displease—; humor —; indulge—; —acclaims; —adores; — amuses; —applauds; —deifies; —eulogizes; —fawns; —flatters; —glorifies; —gratifies; —idolizes; —lauds; —pays tribute; — pleases; —puffs; —renounces; —reveres; —s throng; —toasts; —worships.
(See favorite, follower, lover.)

ADMISSION
adjectives
grudging; heartfelt; inexorable; damaging; fatal; flattering; virtual; certain; tacit; frank; candid; liberal; naive; irreparable; plain-faced; blunt; obvious; rueful; reluctant; unguarded; brash; arrogant; gracious; ineluctable; quaint; final.

effusively; duly; solemnly; tearfully; parentally; cautiously; gently; paternally; prophetically; frantically; urgently; maternally; stingingly; harshly; bitterly; brutally; sternly; sensibly; ceremoniously; formally; puritanically; scrupulously; rigorously; stringently.
(See reprove, warn.)

ADMONITION
adjectives
soft-voiced; tearful; intensified; plain-spoken; parental; judicious; condescending; moral; cautious; stimulating; gentle; poetical; solemn; prophetic; grave; parting; frantic; urgent; forcible; affectionate; respectful; classical; discouraging; paternal; stinging; whispered; effusive; suave; bold; brazen; prosaic; tedious; beautiful.

verbs
cluck —s; elude—; heed—; merit—; —demoralizes; —distorts; —distracts; —repels; —scorches; —softens.
(See caution, warning, advice.)

ADOLESCENCE
adjectives
uneventful; painful; self-conscious; callow; awkward; gawky; supersensitive; vain; joyous; feverish; shy; coy; brash; brusque; carefree.
verbs
apply for—; authorize—; begrudge—; demand—; insure—; refuse—; win—.
(See entrance.)

ADMIT
adverbs
remorsefully; brashly; candidly; universally; reluctantly; arrogantly; ruefully; grudgingly; privately; semi-officially; willingly; graciously; equably; laughingly; knowingly; tacitly; humbly; formally; dubiously; unreservedly; savagely; unfeelingly; naively; bluntly; unguardedly.
(See acknowledge, confess, concede, grant.)

ADMITTANCE
verbs
buy—; crave—; deny—; desire—; gain—; grant—; request—; seek—.
(See entrance, admission.)

ADMONISH (*v*)
adverbs

ADOLESCENT

adverbs

delightfully; glowingly; dully; painfully; awkwardly; gawkily; sensitively; feverishly; shyly; joyously; obviously; incurably; alluringly; exuberantly; inexpressibly; unbelievably; markedly; radiantly; vividly; excitably.

ADOPT (v)

adverbs

gratefully; dogmatically; advantageously; ostensibly; unanimously; prudently; voluntarily; solemnly; vigorously; obstreperously; judiciously; arbitrarily; ultimately; frankly; deceitfully; apparently; formally; ceremoniously; prudishly; skilfully; tactfully; strategically.

(See espouse, support, maintain.)

ADOPTION

adjectives

solemn; vigorous; obstreperous; timely; judicious; grateful; dogmatic; ostensible; prudent; voluntary; ready.

ADORABLE

adverbs

mysteriously; utterly; altogether; delightfully; confoundedly; bewilderingly; amazingly; wondrously; unexpectedly; unimaginably; miraculously; graciously; coolly; warmly; radiantly; glowingly; joyously; unbelievably; consciously; contentedly.

ADORATION

adjectives

ecstatic; idolatrous; inarticulate; solemn; shy; passionate; young; breathless; unswerving; servile; filial; fervent; boyish; maternal; doglike; restrained; impassioned; cold; soft; silent; rapturous; mad; hushed; quiet; poetic; unlimited; deprecatory.

verbs

bestow—; fall in—; rear in—; repel—; yield to—; —buoys; —captivates; —enslaves.

(See worship, love, prayer, reverence.)

ADORE (v)

adverbs

blindly; angelically; ecstatically; inarticulately; solemnly; shyly; passionately; breathlessly; servilely; filially; fervently; restrainedly; boyishly; worshipfully; impulsively; wantonly; vehemently; warmly; carnally; ruttishly; meretriciously; faithfully; intensely; excessively; fondly; soulfully.

(See worship, reverence.)

ADORN (v)

adverbs

lavishly; sumptuously; elaborately; expensively; attractively; richly; architecturally; ceremonially; lustrously; artistically; triumphally; splendidly; decoratively.

(See decorate, ornament, embellish, gild.)

ADORNMENT

adjectives

lavish; extraneous; expensive; sculptural; architectural; curious; feminine; personal; lustrous; rich; sumptuous; elaborate; garish; gaudy; tasteful.

ADROIT

adverbs

marvellously; cleverly; incredibly; admirably; artfully; remarkably; dangerously; palpably; suspiciously; neatly; matchlessly; craftily; masterfully; wonderfully; uncommonly; consummately; innately; constitutionally; instinctively; inherently.

ADROITNESS

adjectives

masterly; neat; witty; technical; skilled; swift; matchless; wily; manual.

ADULATE (v)

adverbs

extravagantly; prodigally; servilely; vociferously; amorously; abjectly; indiscriminately; fulsomely; humbly; shrewdly; deceitfully.

(See praise, flatter.)

ADULATION

adjectives

tribal; hysterical; prodigal; vociferous; amorous; servile; abject; unnatural; fulsome; indiscriminate.

verbs

bask in—; deluge with—; enjoy—; expose to—; feast upon—; indulge in—; relish—; sicken by—; yield to—; —fatigues.

(See flattery, extravagance, praise, compliment.)

ADULATORY

adverbs

abjectly; fawningly; coquettishly; flatteringly; servilely; tribally; hysterically; politically; sycophantically; unctuously; officiously; ostentatiously; subtly; speciously; openly; disagreeably; disgustingly; blatantly; offensively; fulsomely; lavishly.

ADULT (a)

adverbs

surprisingly; completely; fully; obviously; fairly; precociously; prematurely; undeniably; wisely; mysteriously; emotionally; intellectually; uncommonly; buxomly; indescribably; consciously; appallingly; terribly; suddenly; unquestionably.

ADULTERY

verbs

commit—; condone—; forgive—; indulge in —; justify—; revel in—; take in—.

(See unfaithfulness.)

ADVANCE

adjectives

striking; logical; unflinching; subsequent; economic; orderly; general; sharp; courageous; intellectual; triumphant; successive; perpetual; incessant; definite; studious; haughty; unprecedented; spectacular; prodigious; dizzy; substantial; marked; distinct; material; noteworthy; trifling; modest; tenacious; reconnoitering; arduous; implacable; cautious; glacial; faltering; pugnacious; jaunty; ominous; bold; persistent; menacing; notable.

verbs

characterize—; check—; constitute—; discourage—; facilitate—; fear—; hinder—; mark—; pioneer in —s; reject —s; smile at —; —culminates; —terminates.

(See progress.)

ADVANCE (v)

adverbs

aggressively; cautiously; boldly; jauntily; ominously; menacingly; reluctantly; tremblingly; pugnaciously; progressively; ungracefully; simultaneously; hesitantly; secretly; persistently; hopelessly; inexorably; eagerly; notably; triumphantly; timidly; fearfully; compactly; materially; impulsively; awkwardly; unflinchingly; unprecedentedly; spectacularly; substantially; markedly.

(See progress, promote, enhance.)

ADVANCEMENT

adjectives

revolutionary; material; technical; significant; professional; cultural; economic; scientific; industrial; corresponding; spiritual; signal; long-sought; respective (pl).

verbs

contribute to—; deserve—; desire—; hope

for—; note—; promote—; strike a blow to —; strive for—.

(See promotion, progress.)

ADVANCES

adjectives

tender; lover-like; friendly; surreptitious; tactless; unwelcome; old-fashioned; formal; vigorous; amoristic; bold; boorish; bestial; intimate; circumspect.

ADVANTAGE

adjectives

irretrievable; vile; inevitable; inescapable; obvious; patent; remote; trifling; marked; private; educational; pecuniary; fallacious; immediate; inestimable; enduring; appreciable; unfair; hidden; incidental; underestimated; permanent; contingent; manifold; accidental; worldly; material; human; revolutionary; worth while; practical; unique; physical; substantial; undue; reciprocal; temporary; compensating; theoretical; reasonable; invaluable; surreptitious; matchless; graceless; definite; decisive; adventitious; base; hard-earned; initial; momentary; actual; cultural; exclusive; strategic; shameless; frail; selfish; perishable; unparalleled; mutual; overwhelming; hygienic; unsurpassed; decided; tangible; numerical; signal; partisan; insurmountable; incalculable; ineluctable; irresistible.

verbs

buy with—; cite—; confer—; contemplate —; derive—; discern—; embody—; enjoy —; forbear—; forego—; gain—; hold—; hold forth on the —s of; jeopardize—; lack —; let pass—; offset—; pay back with—; press—; press home—; reap—; sacrifice—; seize upon—; set—against; shear off—; stress—; surrender—; turn to—; use—; vouchsafe—; —accrues; —achieves; —is connected with; —feeds; —slips.

(See profit, victory, benefit.)

ADVANTAGEOUS

adverbs

politically; obviously; essentially; undoubtedly; suspiciously; practically; financially; eventually; immensely; socially; highly; materially; personally.

ADVENT

adjectives

illustrious; early; imposing; spectacular; exciting; miraculous; pretended; anticipated; long-awaited.

adjectives

lunatic; divers (pl); romantic; pioneering; nocturnal; foolish; intriguing; blithe; maritime; amusing; gustatory; prodigious; dramatic; weird; preposterous; boisterous; fascinating; glorious; royal; gallant; flagrant; healthful; spiritual; pleasurable; remarkable; scientific; desperate; petty; vicarious; glamorous; ludicrous; aesthetic; perilous; disgusting; intellectual; wearisome; terrifying; profitless; formidable; calamitous; extraordinary; countless (pl); notorious; stupendous; sensational; fruitful; curious; rambling; peaceful; gay; audacious; epic; colorful; picturesque; sparkling; piquant; joyous; sentimental; diverting; exuberant; chivalrous; colossal; uproarious; unprecedented; hazardous; astounding; extravagant; sordid; banal; indecorous; untoward; foolhardy; promiscuous; trying; unbelievable; singular; fantastic; fearful; incredible; curious; stimulating; stirring; hectic; mad; daring; breath-taking; strenuous; pathetic; amorous; mental; fearsome; quixotic; unique; exotic; stark; erotic; piscatory; disconcerting; picaresque; alcoholic; engrossing; comic; tragic; void; equivocal; agile.

verbs

achieve—; crown with—; dare—; dishonor —; dread—; embark on—; encounter—; expose to—; go in quest of—; hanker after —; hazard—; imperil—; mingle among —s; plunge into—; recount—; ride forth to—; risk—; search for—; seek—; set out upon —; thirst for—; thrill with—; urge to—; weave—; yearn for—; —awakens; —befalls; —diverts; —edges; —enlivens; — grips; —lurks; —sweeps over one; —thrills.
(See quest.)

ADVENTURE (v)

adverbs

amorously; haphazardly; romantically; nocturnally; intriguingly; blithely; prodigiously; dramatically; preposterously; boisterously; gloriously; gallantly; vicariously; glamorously; perilously; breath-takingly; strenuously; fearsomely; quixotically; exotically; erotically.
(See dare, venture, happen.)

ADVENTURER

adjectives

venal; intrepid; astute; adroit; unscrupulous; reckless; ambitious; rapacious; martial; noisy; impudent; colossal; hardy;

dauntless; despondent; amorous; born; charming; calculating; worthless; thieving; hard-bitten; lusty; penniless; unprincipled; sordid.

ADVENTUROUS

adverbs

madly; boldly; avidly; bravely; timidly; rashly; innately; daringly; carefully; crazily; recklessly; gloriously; notoriously; audaciously; romantically; dramatically; vicariously; courageously; foolishly; terribly; eagerly; inherently; joyously; colossally; foolhardily; singularly; breath-takingly; tragically; youthfully; fantastically; madly; boyishly; disconcertingly; incredibly; alarmingly; discreetly; constitutionally; extravagantly; hazardously.

ADVERSARY

adjectives

shallow; maimed; underrated; vanquished; doughty; imaginary; stubborn; stony; formidable; proud; courteous; intangible; hostile; vigorous; resolute; worthy; generous; stout; reluctant; well-matched; stalwart; sinister; deadly; harassed; venomous.

verbs

abash—; avenge one's—; battle with—; challenge—; combat—; conquer—; embrace —; fight against—; frustrate—; harass—; heckle—; mock at—; oppose—; overcome—; overpower—; overrule—; overthrow—; overwhelm—; provoke—; quell—; resist—; shake—; stir up—; summon—; take vengeance on—; terrify—; triumph over—; weed out —s; wrestle with—; —conquers; —defeats; —delivers; —fights; —gives battle; —rages; —strives; —struggles.
(See antagonist, enemy, opponent, foe.)

ADVERSE

adverbs

bitterly; fundamentally; persistently; openly; outspokenly; frankly; traditionally; formidably; irreconcilably; strangely; unaccountably; unfortunately; unhappily; powerfully; unmistakably; unmitigatedly; immoderately; unflaggingly.

ADVERSITY

verbs

acquaint with—; afflict with—; assay one's —ies; bruise with—; cast down by—; cross with—; deliver from—; distress by—; embrace—; endure—; redeem out of—; rejoice in—; smite with—; stand against—;

struggle against—; suffer—; withstand—; wound with—; —crosses; —tests; —threatens; —thwarts; —tries.

(See misfortune, disaster, trouble, affliction, calamity.)

ADVERTISE (v)

adverbs

consistently; effectively; dramatically; blatantly; extensively; intelligently; widely; truthfully; nationally; spectacularly; legally; enormously; limitedly.

(See announce, declare, publish, proclaim.)

ADVERTISEMENT

adjectives

circus; powerful; posthumous; gaudy; effective; urgent; fantastic; modest; glowing; spectacular; fraudulent; deceptive; blatant; shrill; prefatory; alluring; truthful; current; consistent; astute; dubious; adequate; seductive; dignified; exaggerated; misleading; objectionable; competitive; skilful; plaguy; unsharpened; productive.

verbs

accent—; alter—; analyze—; approve—; beautify—; believe—; belittle—; change—; complete—; creep into —s; criticize—; decorate—; discard—; follow through—; form—; heed—; identify—; illustrate—; insert—; issue—; launch—; lay out—; lengthen—; limit—; order—; overestimate —; overlook—; point up—; prepare—; purge—; react to—; recognize—; regulate —; respond to—; run—; scan—; solicit—; spoil—; survey—; turn to —s; underestimate—; weaken—; write—; —admonishes; —announces; —concentrates; —extols; —informs; —infuriates; —misleads; —represents; —warns.

(See announcement, notice, publication.)

ADVERTISING

verbs

abuse—; apply—; believe—; benefit by—; blame—; broaden—; buy—; campaign for —; charge for—; circularize—; clarify—; concentrate—; condemn—; continue—; contract for—; credit—; delineate—; display —; dissect—; disseminate—; eliminate—; emphasize—; employ—; exaggerate—; expend for—; experiment with—; exploit—; flash—; guide—; hail—; immunize to—; insist on—; intensify—; inveigh against—; issue—; judge—; learn—; mail—; minimize—; mislead by—; necessitate—; oppose—; overdo—; pay for—; parallel—;

peruse—; post—; pound away with—; prepare—; praise—; prolong—; promote with —; rate—; require—; resist—; revolutionize—; schedule—; segregate—; sell—; solicit—; specialize in—; spurn—; supplement —; survey—; teach—; time—; uphold—; undertake—; utilize—; value—; wage—; warn by—; welcome—; withhold—; —accomplishes; —advances; —appeals; —attracts; —builds; —colors; —embraces; —familiarizes; —features; —fosters; —increases; —influences; —informs; —infringes upon; —inspires; —invites attention; —markets; —merits; —ministers to; —offends; —organizes; —pays; —persuades; —popularizes; —profits; —promotes; —publicizes; —rewards; —sells; —speeds up; —standardizes; —stimulates; —stirs up; —succeeds; —suggests; —trade-marks; —transcends; —transforms; —urges.

(See announcement, notice, advertisement.)

ADVICE

adjectives

interested; sage; facetious; determinative; wholesome; admirable; rash; hasty; parental; urgent; salutary; serious; dissimilar; competent; authentic; unadulterated; old-fashioned; practical; shrewd; hard-headed; requisite; customary; proffered; medical; appropriate; moderate; supplemental; unprejudiced; concentrated; superfluous; brusque; disconcerting; unselfish; matrimonial; pregnant; brutal; subtle; impartial; conservative; canny; intelligent; expert; explicit; pertinent; dreary; resented; overweening; recurrent; interjected; cautionary; voluntary; unheeded.

verbs

adopt—; bombard with—; burst with—; consider—; consult—; counsel—; deliberate over—; disregard—; drum—into; adopt—; follow—; grind out—; hark to—; heap—; heed—; honor—; ignore—; impart—; judge —; lack—; modify—; ooze—; plan—; ponder—; profit by—; reckon—; regard—; relish—; seek—; shun—; solicit—; subscribe to—; supplant—; swallow up—; volunteer—; weigh—; —aids; —hinders; —leaks out.

(See counsel, instruction, information.)

ADVISABLE

adverbs

undoubtedly; scarcely; financially; discreetly; practically; profoundly; morally; urgently; politically; usually; selfishly; solidly; undeniably; particularly; honestly.

ADVISE (v)

adverbs

earnestly; briefly; urgently; unhesitatingly; fatally; needlessly; rightly; strenuously; coolly; sagely; rashly; shrewdly; moderately; wisely; incompetently; brusquely; disinterestedly; unselfishly; impartially; brutally; solemnly; subtly; explicitly; pertinently; drearily; overweeningly; intelligently; cleverly; cautiously.

(See admonish, counsel, inform.)

ADVISER

adjectives

competent; confidential; ill-humored; technical; conservative; sympathetic; prudent; facetious; spiritual; sagacious; influential; unscrupulous; resourceful; invaluable; altruistic; experienced.

ADVOCATE

adjectives

conspicuous; disinterested; benevolent; keen; stalwart; ardent; earnest; pioneer; militant; unselfish; persistent; distinguished; zealous; uncompromising; prominent; enthusiastic; sincere; warm; strenuous; erudite; adroit; exclusive; ingenious; notorious; active; argumentative; fearless; courageous; competent; aggressive; ironic; staunch; resourceful; idealistic; eloquent; loyal; tactful; obstinate; timorous; vigilant; virile; impassioned; able.

ADVOCATE (v)

adverbs

emphatically; disinterestedly; ostensibly; passionately; absurdly; warmly; fanatically; ardently; characteristically; openly; stalwartly; earnestly; militantly; unselfishly; persistently; zealously; uncompromisingly; eruditely; adroitly; ingeniously; notoriously; fearlessly; competently; idealistically; eloquently; obstinately; timorously; truculently.

(See defend, support.)

AERONAUT

adjectives

adventurous; ardent; intrepid; daring; seasoned; war-worn; accomplished; barnstorming; globe-circling; dashing.

AEROPLANE

verbs

ballast—; bank—; capture—; charter—; christen—; equalize—; experiment with—; explore with—; fabricate—; design—; ground—; herd in—; horse down—; hover

in—; kick—into a spin; kite—; land—; lift —; modify—; navigate—; nose in—; overload—; "pancake"—; pilot—; propel—; revolutionize—; salvage—; shelter—; spiral —; stabilize—; stall—; sustain—; tilt—; underpower—; —alights; —attacks; — banks; —bombs; —cartwheels; —circles; —s compete for; —s convoy; —dashes; — dives; —drones; —flattens out; —folds up; —gleams; —glides away; —gyrates; — hovers; —loops; —manoeuvers; —pierces the sky; —pivots; —propels; —rains gas; —rises; —roars; —rolls; —scoots; —sheds its wings; —skids in; —skims the turf; —slips into the sky; —soars; —swirls; —swoops; —takes off; —taxies out; — throbs; —trundles on the field; —tumbles down; —twirls; —twists; —wings its way; —wings over; —winnows its way; —zooms; —floats down.

(See balloon, plane.)

AFFABILITY

adjectives

gracious; smiling; kindly; offensive; sardonic; rare; dry; dull; heartfelt; cordial; generous; insincere; pleasing; unwonted.

AFFABLE

adverbs

unaffectedly; courteously; comfortably; enthusiastically; pleasantly; placidly; unfailingly; graciously; smilingly; considerately; sincerely; genuinely; cordially; usually; singularly; quietly; remarkably; ostentatiously.

AFFAIR

adjectives

Gargantuan; spiritual; delicate; practical; multifarious; tumultuous; domestic; conventional; financial; droll; disagreeable; pressing; internal; personal; celebrated; complicated; instructive; public; petty; weighty; vast; grave; ecclesiastical; monotonous; corporate; clandestine; passing; quiet; prim; sublunary; uninteresting; intimate; detestable; charitable; masculine; elaborate; dramatic; vigorous; rustic; unsettled; momentous; foolish; flimsy; insignificant; wearisome; troublous; warlike; multitudinous (pl); provocative; secret; temporal; risky; supernatural; deplorable; fatal; community; wretched; barbarous; rollicking; primitive; hasty; reputable; gay; charming; harmless; enchanting; colorful; profitable; resplendent; spectacular; pretentious; colossal; rueful; painful; freakish; sordid; unsavory; tragic; diabolic; disreputable; absurd; distasteful; scandalous; iniquitous; sanguinary; ferocious; blundering; dismal; apathetic; frail-looking; terrestial; academic; amorous; intricate; drawn-out; complex; droll; flippant; bewildering; laborious; different.

verbs
absorb in —s; administer —s; be conversant with—; carry on—s; change—s; characterize—; commit—to; con —s; scan—; conclude—; conduct—; connect—; control —; deal with —s; debate —s; detach from —s; dispute —s; embroil with —s; emerge from—; entangle in —s; expatiate —s; extricate from —s; grapple with —s; grasp —s; guarantee—; guide —s; hinder—; indulge in —s; intrude in —s; jumble up —s; manage —s; meddle in —s; muddle —s; operate —s; order —s; parallel—; persevere in—; pertain to—; picture—; place at the head of —s; pry into —s; shirk —s; snow under with —s; supervene in —s; support—; transact —s; travel from one—to another; undertake—; veil—; weather—; wind up —s; —drags; —intrigues; —prospers; —recurs; —rests; —ripens.
(See business, matter.)

AFFECT (v)
adverbs
gravely; materially; profoundly; visibly; powerfully; indirectly; strongly; detrimentally; vexatiously; adversely; vitally; poignantly; deeply; fundamentally; frequently; primarily; invariably; seriously; painfully; considerably; appreciably; enormously; variously; pleasantly; sensibly; injuriously; intimately; definitely; undoubtedly; differently; unconsciously; peculiarly.
(See touch, melt, incline.)

AFFECTED
adverbs
conceitedly; foppishly; pretentiously; sentimentally; stiltedly; mincingly; simperingly; stagily; abominably; absurdly; ridiculously; ludicrously; disgustingly; pathetically.

AFFECTION
adjectives
true-hearted; dramatic; warm; enthusiastic; filial; reciprocal; hysterical; nervous; natural; tepid; responsive; divine; purest; maternal; tender; intense; spasmodic; inordinate; domestic; dutiful; crushed; subtle; heartwarming; admiring; paternal; overflowing; sympathetic; ludicrous; disappointed; unreciprocated; mutual; demonstrative;

indiscriminating; mature; pious; wifely; unrequited; pastoral; temperate; inflammatory; untried; brotherly; peremptory; tempestuous; rabid; conjugal; well-grounded; doglike; overbrimming; sweet-toned; grateful; impulsive; healthful; involuntary; rational; perishable; playful; forced; respectful; ancient; concrete; trustful; overstrained; passionate; connubial; hollow; vulgar; vile; pretended; boundless; irrepressible; delirious; lasting; tacit; disinterested; sound; profound; nobler; generous; unreasoning; gleeful; coarse; tolerant; doubtful; confessed; foolish; blighted; wavering; long-suffering; stifled; sincere; beautiful; intimate; thoughtful; extreme; sheer; naive; frank; chaste; physical; unbounded; proud; tenacious; priceless; violent; immortal; sworn; zealous; sublime; sweet; sentimental; critical; undying; revived; ephemeral; embedded; calm; chilled; obvious; airy; childish; fastidious; quaint; aristocratic; stiff; awkward; disagreeable; languid; teasing; absurd; spruce; showy; deliberate; injudicious; comical; patent.

verbs
advert to—; alienate—; analyze—; arouse —; attach—to; awaken—; bear—; betoken —; bind by—; bless with—; blind by—; breed—; capture—; chain with—; coerce—; compel—; contain—; crave—; deflect—; demand—; denote—; desire—; detect—; disclose—; display—; earn—; eat up—; elicit —; enforce—; engage—; exempt from—; express—for; feed upon—; force—; gain—; impair—; impress by—; influence—; inspire with—; join in—; kindle—; lend—; manifest—; meet the demands of—; motivate by —; object to—; oppose—; overrule by—; pledge—; pour forth—; preserve—; pretend to—; produce—; promote—; regain—; regard with—; remove—; restrain—; reveal—; scatter—; sense—; shun—; speak—; starve for—; steal—; swear—; temper—; tender—; thwart—; transfer—; transplant —; uproot—; wean from—; weigh—; wrestle with—; —alternates; —bursts out; —ceases; —gets out of bounds; —grows; —links together; —prevails; —spreads; — springs from; —strays; —sways; —thickens; —turns; —warms; —wavers.
(See attachment, love, feeling, emotion.)

AFFECTIONATE
adverbs
enthusiastically; deeply; extremely; dutifully; heart-warmingly; tempestuously; gratifyingly; warmly; sincerely; temperately; im-

24

pulsively; playfully; naturally; paternally; respectfully; innately; essentially; confessedly; beautifully; sweetly; frankly; devotedly; apparently; incongruously; professedly; hypocritically; openly; sentimentally; truly; pretentiously; inherently; intensely; ludicrously; moderately; passionately; consistently; ostentatiously; maternally; spasmodically; obviously; steadily; tacitly; foolishly; intimately; proudly; furtively.

AFFILIATION

adjectives
growing; cosmopolitan; party; cultural; intimate; tender; undesirable.

verbs
arrange—; ascertain—; benefit by—; block —; deny—; destroy—; determine—; establish—; impute—with; maintain—; preclude —; recognize—; sponsor—; suspend—; wangle—; —aims at; —complicates; —engenders.
(See association, connection, relationship.)

AFFINITY

adjectives
peculiar; commercial; elective; natural; uncanny; temperamental; secret.

AFFIRM (v)

adverbs
plausibly; solemnly; plainly; distinctly; facetiously; venomously; categorically; definitely; significantly; constantly; vigorously; smilingly; glaringly; nonchalantly; gravely; splendidly; boldly; brazenly; swiftly; readily.
(See assert, state.)

AFFIRMATION

adjectives
smiling; glaring; nonchalant; grave; splendid; bold; brazen; ready; swift.

AFFLICT (v)

adverbs
distressingly; suddenly; desperately; irremediably; bitterly; poignantly; sharply; undeservedly; recurringly; harshly; fatally; brutally; temporarily.
(See persecute, scourge, harass, trouble.)

AFFLICTED

adverbs
distressingly; direly; tragically; unnecessarily; unfortunately; sadly; miserably; incurably; painfully; agonizingly; wretchedly; grievously.

AFFLICTION

adjectives
respiratory; corporal; irremediable; desperate; bitter; poignant; mute; sharp; undeserved; recurring; rending; harsh; fatal; brutal; palsied; temporary.

verbs
ameliorate—; amend—; bear—; bind in—; break with—; carry—; comfort—; conceal —; deliver—; diagnose—; endure—; grant refuge from—; purify by—; shake off—; visit in—; —bites; —follows; —grows; — persists; —prevents; —refines; —softens; —threatens.
(See trouble, tribulation, distress, grief, misfortune.)

AFFLUENCE

verbs
attain—; bask in—; enjoy—; glitter in—; manifest—; raise to—; reduce from—; revive—; wallow in—.
(See wealth, riches, abundance, plenty.)

AFFLUENT

adverbs
gorgeously; enormously; comfortably; fortunately; pleasantly; agreeably; serenely; snugly; enviably; complacently; sufficiently; smugly; graciously.

AFFORD (v)

adverbs
undoubtedly; scarcely; indiscriminately; abundantly; inadvertently.
(See furnish, yield, produce.)

AFFRAY

adjectives
murderous; nocturnal; head-punching; fierce; bloody; violent.

AFFRONT

adjectives
rude; personal; sacrilegious; deliberate; unmerited; unintentional; intolerable; vile; unnecessary; brutal; boorish; ill-mannered; brazen.

AFFRONT (v)

adverbs
impudently; brazenly; rudely; personally; sacrilegiously; deliberately; unmeritedly; unintentionally; intolerably; vilely; unnecessarily; brutally; boorishly; ill-manneredly.
(See insult, aggravate.)

AFFRONTED

adverbs

easily; definitely; slightly; quickly; increasingly; unreasonably; foolishly; senselessly; absurdly; unjustly; unfairly; deeply.

AFRAID

adverbs

superstitiously; timidly; childishly; queerly; curiously; dreadfully; horribly; perpetually; oddly; strangely; starkly; mysteriously; faint-heartedly; cautiously; timorously; extraordinarily; unquestionably; secretly; terribly; mortally; foolishly; frightfully; constantly; cravenly; temperamentally; distressingly; unwontedly; unusually; incredibly; shudderingly; surprisingly; unutterably; incomprehensibly; obviously; genuinely; suspiciously; idiotically; nervously.

AFTERMATH

adjectives

disastrous; psychological; barren; confused; melancholy; unfortunate; sordid; troublesome; hectic; sorry.

AFTERNOON

adjectives

inspiring; brilliant; dismal; gloomy; ghastly; cheerless; dull; restless; raw; fragrant; serene; wintry; rain-washed; humid; sunless; breezeless; tropical; drowsy; clement; drear; golden; rosy; rain-soaked; darkling; declining; showery; sweltering; formal; glamorous; sultry; miserable; fervid.

verbs

beguile—; devote—; fritter away—; nap away—; pass—; shadow—; tarry till—; while away—; —advances; —pales; —pauses; —pushes forward; —spends itself; —takes wing; —unrolls; —vanishes; —wanes; —wears on.

(See evening.)

AGE

adjectives

pastoral; comfortable; endless; bygone; primitive; seasoned; abominable; imponderable; distant; crabbed; prehistoric; graygrown; infidel; enlightened; feeble; unnumbered (pl); glorious; relative (pl); countless (pl); paleozoic; prolific; venerable; immemorial; aesthetical; barbarous; Pliocene; dim-lit; embittered; susceptible; infinite; green; polished; deathless; heroic; jostling; remote; pre-chromo; realistic; frostless; advancing; ripe; patriarchal; responsive; besotted; waning; historic; prudish; hoary; blissful; geologic; energetic; fabulous; middle; streamlined; advanced; receptive; decrepit; retirement; earnest; unregarded; tender; dingy; glamorous; roistering; marriageable; approaching; homely; renowned; rosy; honored; critical; heartless; prescribed; masquerading; electric; discreet; weak; dull; contented; mature; rotting; ambitious; exorbitant; muddled; revolutionary; live; unresting; premature; credulous; pre-scientific; weary; degenerate; fabled; classical; sententious; hectic; dateless; material; iron-bound; licentious; ruthless; flourishing; indeterminate; haggish; adolescent; sedate; debutante; disillusioned; discretionary; vast; eligible; unhonored; mellowed; inventive; withered; golden; machine; raucous; tabloid; pagan; graceless; robust; sordid; decayed; ripened; unorthodox; practical; vanished; leisurely; stalwart; toddling; primeval; hoary; talking; shallow; successive (pl); sentimental; dangerous; undiscriminating; independent; buried; innumerable (pl).

verbs

advance in—; attain—; clothe—in glory; come of—; decay with—; defy—; denote—; dim with—; enfeeble with—; ensnare with —; exempt from—; honor old—; incapacitate with—; increase with—; judge—; knock at the door of—; limit—; renew—; reveal—; scoff at old—; serve—; stoop with —; succumb to old—; —accounts for; —adorns; —s average; —cracks; —decays; —deposits; —diminishes; —dispels; —enfeebles; —honors; —impairs; —measures; —mellows; —prevails; —privileges; —retards; —shrivels; —steals on; —strikes; —wears; —withers; —wrinkles; —yellows; attribute to—; belong to—; classify —s; corrupt—; denounce—; designate—; divide into—; epitomize—; excel—; fade into —s; gild—; glorify—; mark—; mechanize—; outlive—; pervade—; proclaim—; represent —; symbolize—; terminate—; usher in—; —s behold; —recognizes.

(See maturity, era, epoch, generation.)

AGED

adverbs

prematurely; terribly; tragically; pathetically; patriarchally; dingily; ridiculously; mournfully; uncommonly; desolately; contentedly; rosily; datelessly; lamentably; comfortably; crabbedly; hoarily; feebly; incredibly; wondrously; mellowly; honorably.

adjectives

effective; volcanic; ordained; secret; external; conservative; all-sufficient; subtle; sole; appropriate; divine; supernatural; regulative; luciferal; technical; bureaucratic; bargaining; ubiquitous; organized; conducive; charitable; law-enforcing; mitigating; curative; myriad (pl).

verbs

administer—; assume—; consolidate—; develop—; create—; employ—; exclude from —; license—; obtain—; operate—; register with—; require—; squeeze (colloq.)—; terminate—; weld —s into a unit; —acts for; —advocates; —authorizes; —charges; —commissions; —functions; —handles; —offers; —places; —promotes; —recommends; —stimulates; —surrenders functions.

AGENT

adjectives

dominant; consular; imaginative; enterprising; remedial; unscrupulous; catalytic; cleansing; stimulating; diplomatic; publicity; purchasing; fiscal; coloring; trustworthy; energetic; physical; involuntary; recruiting; confidential; vigilant; corrosive; superfluous; purifying; accredited; cajoling; advance; rapacious.

verbs

appoint—; authorize—; commission—; delegate to—; deliberate—; discredit—; employ —; endow—; evade—; exert—; direct—; frustrate—; hearten—; rely upon—; remunerate—; request—; vest in—; yield to—; —accounts for; —acts for; —agitates; —assists; —bickers; —conducts; —contrives; —deliberates; —distributes; —enforces; —exerts; —implies; —negotiates; —operates; —profits; —represents; —slumbers; —solicits; —stipulates; —transacts; —vanishes.
(See representative, operator, factor.)

AGGRAVATE (v)

adverbs

arrogantly; brutally; continually; obviously; detrimentally; unceasingly; painfully.
(See intensify, irritate, provoke.)

AGGREGATION

adjectives

enormous; notable; glamorous; indefinable; congenial; simple; continuous.

adjectives

wanton; wilful; jealous; conscienceless; fiery; brisk; ruthless; merciless; destructive; ill-timed.

verbs

anger by—; anticipate—; avenge—; bear—; bulwark against—; check—; crush with—; denounce—; dread—; encounter—; oppose —; protest against—; provoke—; renounce —; resent—; resist—; save from—; submit to—; surrender to—; wear out by—; —flourishes; —saps; —staggers; —undermines.
(See assault, attack, intrusion, invasion.)

AGGRESSIVE

adverbs

boldly; offensively; truculently; bluntly; presumptuously; impertinently; unbecomingly; unwarrantedly; daringly; courageously; fearlessly; calmly; steadily; persistently; incurably; gallantly; pluckily; heroically; confidently; doggedly; criminally; savagely; indomitably.

AGGRESSIVENESS

adjectives

male; crocodilian; dynamic; sullen; forced; predatory; war-like; unthinking; brutal.

AGGRESSOR

verbs

agitate against—; badger—; blockade—; curse—; defend against—; denounce—; disconcert—; disorganize—; mobilize against —; punish—; repel—; —assails; —assaults; —depresses; —encroaches; —invades; —provokes; —seizes; —sets upon; —sweeps; —attacks.
(See intruder, trespasser.)

AGGRIEVE (v)

adverbs

mortally; painfully; brutally; bitterly; deeply; heartlessly.

AGHAST

adverbs

utterly; wanly; amazingly; amazedly; astoundingly; wonderingly; blankly; staringly; breathlessly; wordlessly; indescribably; stupidly; tremulously; fearfully.

AGILE

adverbs

nimbly; gracefully; unusually; swiftly; briskly; actively; alertly; surprisingly;

youthfully; slenderly; clumsily; unexpectedly; quickly; dangerously; mentally; physically; smartly; light-footedly; spryly; fleetly; trippingly; lightly.

AGILITY

adjectives
graceful; grotesque; sailor-like; astonishing; spidery; acrobatic; unsurpassed; feline; tigerish; apish; rare; unusual.

AGITATE (v)

adverbs
convulsively; considerably; indescribably; fiercely; greatly; gently; violently; internally; nervously; feverishly; vigorously; incessantly; recurrently; destructively; visibly; intellectually; markedly.
(See disturb.)

AGITATION

adjectives
revolutionary; indescribable; gentle; violent; profane; internal; nervous; legitimate; gloomy; feverish; throbbing; vigorous; indignant; preliminary; incessant; convulsive; recurrent; destructive; inner; student; bewildered; smothered; visible; intellectual; marked; wearying; unflinching; wholesale; righteous; wide-spread.

verbs
accustom to—; admire—; allay—; cease —; discuss—; flutter in—; infect with—; introduce—; keep in—; kindle—; menace by—; express—; produce—; provoke—; resume—; stir—; set up—; understand—; witness—; —arises; —arouses; —disorganizes; —disturbs; —excites; —ignites; — impassions; —moves; —perturbs; —stirs; —terrifies; —unsettles.
(See emotion, commotion, disturbance.)

AGITATOR

adjectives
veteran; headstrong; unscrupulous; earnest; didactic; deft; extreme; sincere; dangerous; willing; adept.

AGONY

adjectives
profound; envenomed; tearless; inglorious; mute; unattended; vulgar; unconquerable; mortal; delirious; fiery; nervous; crowning; supreme; keen; blank; dying; childless; nameless; final; convulsive; hot; thudding; acute; multitudinous (pl); cowardly; utter; rending; loathsome; internal; remittent; prolonged; heartfelt; mental; frightful; exquisite; stern; superstitious; unspeakable; piercing; secret; prophetic; scathing; ill-fated; amorous; helpless; concentrated; cold; excruciating; human; unendurable; spiritual; indescribable; invisible; throbbing; last; speechless; intensified; impotent; bitter; blinding; benumbing; timeless; relentless.

verbs
alleviate—; convulsed in—; distort with—; efface—; endure—; face—; impose—; prolong—; relish—; shriek in—; stir with—; strive in—; struggle in—; wrench in—; writhe in—; —abates; —clutches; —confuses; —despairs; —distresses; —shoots.
(See distress, pain, anguish, torture.)

AGREE (v)

adverbs
pleasantly; universally; tacitly; gravely; solemnly; heartily; voluntarily; magnanimously; cheerfully; listlessly; cordially; completely; meekly; mutually; fervently; blandly; wholly; accordingly; passively; unanimously; comfortably; reluctantly; privately; definitely; amicably; pacifically; tentatively; sensibly; politely; reassuringly; fatuously; verbally; voluntarily; vehemently; emphatically; unhappily; authoritatively; benignly.
(See accord, acquiesce, comply, grant.)

AGREEABLE

adverbs
consistently; obviously; openly; frankly; sweetly; essentially; warmly; gratifyingly; extremely; unaffectedly; courteously; comfortably; pleasantly; placidly; gravely; unfailingly; generously; graciously; smilingly; considerately; sincerely; cordially; quietly; remarkably; ostentatiously; charmingly; singularly; genuinely; happily.

AGREEMENT

adjectives
substantial; stringent; mutual; diplomatic; tacit; loose; amicable; pacific; unanimous; working; preliminary; undisclosed; tentative; moratory; provisional; corrupt; sensible; effective; water-tight; polite; blissful; conscientious; hearty; reassuring; noncommittal; fatuous; despotic; verbal; voluntary; vehement; emphatic; unhappy; compromising; iron-clad; binding; enforced; authoritative.

verbs
accept—; assent to—; avow—; breach of—;

bring to—; cement—; come to—; conform with—; consent to—; consolidate—; construct—; consummate—; declare—; default —; deny—; disregard—; dissent from—; enter into—; execute—; express—; formulate—; fulfill—; illustrate—; imply—; "junk"—; negotiate—; perfect—; prescribe —; reach—; repudiate—; sanction—; scrap —; set forth in—; shape into—; subject to—; tie down with—; violate—; —cements; —consolidates; —expires; —manifests; — reveals; —stands.

(See contract, compact, bargain.)

AGRICULTURAL

adverbs
seriously; playfully; spasmodically; seasonably; showily; enthusiastically; presumptuously; ridiculously; professionally; amateurishly; preachily.

AGRICULTURE

adjectives
scientific; crude; experimental; diversified; mechanical; variegated.

verbs
administrate—; appropriate—; classify—; commercialize—; conduct research in—; control—; cooperate in—; crystallize—; depress —; devastate—; develop—; doom—; educate—; employ in—; encourage—; exploit —; extend—; extend credit to—; feed—; foster—; grant to—; improve—; industrialize—; inflate—; instruct in—; insure—; isolate—; manage—; mechanize—; modernize—; nationalize—; organize—; pertain to —; promote—; protect—; regulate—; replenish—; reshape—; restrict to—; revolutionize—; subsidize—; subsist on—; supervise—; survey—; systematize—; teach—; —benefits from; —domesticates; —economizes; —experiments; —flourishes; —markets; —prospers; —rises; —succumbs to; —suffers; —unfolds; —yields.

(See industry.)

AID

adjectives
material; mutual; quickening; self-denying; welcome; preternatural; vigorous; positive; substantial; prompt; efficient; generous; invaluable; all-important; sovereign; practical; inconspicuous; artificial; fictitious; dubious; healthful; supernatural; gloomy; adventitious; reluctant; priceless; functional; loyal; extraneous; potential; enlightened; specific; vital; essential; sustaining; necessary.

verbs
abolish—; afford—; apply for—; apportion —; assist with—; assure—; avail of—; award—; call upon—; condone—; contribute—; deserve—; dispatch—; distribute—; enlist—; extend—; grant—; howl for—; interpose—; invoke—; lack—; lend—; limit —; march to—; offer—; pledge—; proffer —; prompt—; render—; require—; seek—; speed up—; subsidize—; support with—; swear—; trust in—; volunteer—; withhold —; —arrives; —disappears; —preserves; —redeems; —saves.

(See help, assistance, relief, cooperation, succor, subsidy.)

AID (v)

adverbs
gladly; secretly; modestly; materially; unquestionably; unobtrusively; treacherously; substantially; self-denyingly; vigorously; positively; promptly; efficiently; generously; invaluably; practically; inconspicuously; dubiously; gloomily; reluctantly; loyally; potentially; specifically; essentially; necessarily.

(See help, assist, foster.)

AILMENT

adjectives
neurotic; minor; correctible; physical; incurable; hereditary; emotional; imaginary; pernicious; childish; dreaded; mysterious; vague; mythical; chronic; feminine; nervous; obscure; grave.

verbs
complain of—; cure—; diagnose—; disregard—; ignore—; neglect—; relieve—; rout—; —indisposes; —springs from.

(See malady, illness, sickness, disease.)

AIM

adjectives
instructive; principal; lofty; undeviating; murderous; intelligible; unerring; ultimate; personal; heroic; apparent; conscious; poetic; unselfish; generous; fictitious; ulterior; illusory; deadly; deliberate; laudable; ambitious; elevated; unattainable; logical; altruistic; devotional; basic; sole; cherished; confessed; wild; sordid; infallible; sinister; paltry; futile; frustrated; irrelevant; altered; modest; fundamental; kindred; radical; novel; immediate; primal; vain; impracticable; double; sober; impossible.

verbs
applaud—; attain—; baffle—; cast out—; define—; design—; disguise—; dissipate—;

embrace—; encourage—; endorse—; fulfill
—; picture—; promote—; propose—; realize—; restrict—; sanction—; set forth—;
sum up—; wander from—; —conflicts;
—elevates; —succeeds; —tends; affect—;
avoid—; calculate—; direct—; estimate—;
guide—; hinder—; lead—; level—; mark
—; miss—; point—; take—; train—; —errs.
(See object, end, aspiration, purpose, direction.)

AIM (v)
adverbs
uselessly; deliberately; primarily; instructively; immediately; principally; loftily;
undeviatingly; murderously; unerringly; apparently; heroically; consciously; poetically;
unselfishly; generously; fictitiously; laudably; ambitiously; elevatedly; unattainably;
logically; altruistically; basically; solely;
confessedly; futilely; frustratedly; irrelevantly; modestly; fundamentally; radically;
vainly; soberly; impossibly.

(See aspire, desire.)

AIMLESS
adverbs
lamentably; invariably; unfortunately;
carelessly; happily; blithely; deplorably;
unluckily; unhappily; moodily; gloomily;
deliberately.

AIR
adjectives (*atmosphere*)
crisp; healthful; bracing; balmy; salt;
mountain; vitalizing; tingling; invigorating;
pungent; exhilarating; sparkling; scented;
lofty; comfortable; luminous; polluted;
vapory; unbreathed; troublous; sultry;
jocund; frosty; ambient; stifling; glittering;
precipitant; pernicious; darkened; shadowed; vital; dusky; misty; hushed; viewless; frigid; salubrious; tepid; muffled;
wholesome; vibrant; vacant; raw; impalpable; thin; strangling; nocturnal; atmospheric; rarefied; enervating; delicious;
genial; cleft; unjaded; foggy; fermenting;
heavy; nipping; chilled; vivifying; interlunar; brisk; emerald; buoyant; singing;
deoxidized; dewy; trackless; stinking; fetid;
starry; caressant; scorching; tranquil;
spiced; sharp; soothing; health-giving; circulating; conditioned; compressed; illimitable; translucent; moon-struck; wanton;
sulphurous; pellucid; miasmic; penetrating;
oppressive; desolate; pale; filtered; humidi-
fied; twilight; windless; tempest-charged;
electric; upper; sanctified; cloudless; greedy;
wholesome; dreamy; mineral; limpid;

startled; sun-sweetened; purgatorial; inclement; pestilential; highland; laughing;
murky; soul-sustaining; heaven-high; infected; mellow; free; summering; mouldy;
impregnated; vitiated; toxic; acrid; moon-
tide; dust-scented; crystalline; smoke-sat-
urated; balsam-laden; forest-scented; rain-
swept; clammy; roseate; lifeless; aromatic;
ruffled; buxom; clinging; glimmering;
pleasant; tropic; perfumed; empyreal;
luscious; blue; stagnant; spreading; eddying; transparent; yielding.

verbs
admit—; ascend into—; bask in—; beat—;
blacken—; bore through—; build in—;
change—; charge—; choke—with dust;
compose—; compress—; condition—; consume—; cool—; dance in—; darken—; dart
through—; deprive of—; detect in—; diffuse
—; disappear into thin—; dissipate into—;
distribute—; drink—; embalm—with; embrace—; exhale—; exhaust—; expel—; expose to—; fan—; float through—; flush—;
hallow—; heave into—; hurtle through—;
impregnate—; infect—; inflame—; inhale
—; inject—; liquidize—; load—; lope into
—; melt into thin—; mix with—; mount
into—; navigate—; penetrate—; perfume
—; permeate—; pervade—; pierce—; purge
—; purify—; pursue in—; putrefy—; ravish
—; remove from—; rend—; ride—; ripple
—; rise into—; rule—; sail in—; saturate
—; scent—; seep into—; shelter from—;
smite—; sniff—; split—; stir—; subject to
—; support in—; surge into—; suspend in
—; sweep—; taint—; tinge—; vanish into
—; vitiate—; warm—; —blows; —circles;
—circulates; —consists of; —conveys; —
diffuses; —expands; —fans; —lulls; —murmurs; —palpitates; —reeks; —resounds;
—reverberates; —rings; —ripples; —rushes
by; —scintillates; —seeps in; —sighs; —
singes; —stirs; —surges in; —surrounds;
—swirls; —thickens; —throbs; —trembles;
—whispers; —whistles.

(See atmosphere, wind, breeze, ether.)

AIR
adjectives (*attitude*)
racy; ironical; professional; coquettish;
hesitating; surly; monastic; elegant; proud;
condescending; saucy; insouciant; youthful;
carefree; confident; joyous; buoyant; hospitable; grotesque; perky; deliberate; abstracted; mystic; druid-like; prehistoric;
unctuous; becoming; serious; protecting;
perplexed; ardent; businesslike; inquiring;
passionate; prosperous; dolorous; pathetic;

discomfited; prophetic; judicial; desperate; peculiar; proprietary; confidential; indefinable; plaintive; dejected; distant; self-confident; rustic; cold; patient; fantastical; lackadaisical; pouting; well-bred; encouraging; calm; sweet; polished; devilish; dashing; unaffected; imposing; disappointed; striking; distinguished; excited; tragic; undaunted; artless; pompous; shamed; furtive; playful; genteel; wheedling; pensive; citified; injured; sedate; wanton; roguish; insulted; contrite; womanly; virginal; frivolous; feline; jaunty; meditative; bewitching; sinister; forbidding; portentous; sagacious; riotous; appreciative; courteous; unapologetic; candid; youthful; pitiless; voluptuous; simple; languid; reserved; threatening; imperious; intellectual; reminiscent; glib; deprecating; intolerant; patronizing; passionless; composed; comic; engaging; celestial; virtuous; elegant; exquisite; masterful; aggressive; knowing; shrewd; appraising; sophisticated; elaborate; obedient; tranquil; staid; quizzical; enigmatic; lofty; supercilious; possessive; matter-of-fact; nonchalant; detached; insolent; ominous; dissipated; moody; irrational; belligerent; calculating; obstinate; irritating; scandalized; dogged; harassed; martyred; injured; distraught; shrinking; crestfallen; disconcerted; motherly; suave; exotic; masculine; incorrigible; colloquial; cherubic; critical; indulgent; salubrious; appreciative; deferential; disarming; sly; accommodating; grandiose; spiritual; majestic.

verbs
acquaint with—; address with—; adopt—; affect—; ape—; assume—; bear—of; communicate—; describe—; draw up with—; feign—; give —s to; invest with—; manifest—; treat with—; unfold—; —excites; —pleases.
(See manner, mien, appearance, demeanor, expression.)

AIR
adjectives   *(tune)*
wizard; stirring; martial; light; melancholy; flippant; patriotic; lilting; mournful; plaintive; persistent; haunting; nostalgic; memorable; heartfelt; militant.

verbs
accompany—; arrange—; chorus—; compose—; harmonize—; hum—; play—; recognize—; sing—; spoil—; synchronize—; whistle—; —charms; —cheers; —enchants;

—expresses; —gladdens; —moves; —stirs. (See melody, tune.)

AIRPLANE
adjectives
multi-engined; droning; adventitious; obsolete; commercial; fleet; metal; transcontinental.

AIRY
adverbs
gracefully; exquisitely; boyishly; youthfully; lightly; cheerfully; inexpressibly; racily; blithely; gaily; elegantly; saucily; proudly; carelessly; joyously; confidently; buoyantly; mystically; prophetically; proprietarily; fantastically; devilishly; dashingly; imposingly; artlessly; playfully; wantonly; roguishly; jauntily; bewitchingly; engagingly; elegantly; superciliously; nonchalantly; suavely; smoothly; indulgently; disarmingly; slyly; fashionably; stagily; conceitedly; refreshingly; racially.

AISLE
adjectives
shadowy; cathedral; winding; grassy; gloomy; long-drawn; teeming; pillared; silent; narrow; raucous; leafy; forest; cloistered; slender; gorgeous; moldering.

verbs
amble down—; arch—; block—; bound down—; build—; divide into—; drift down —; extend—; flank—; form—; indicate—; labor up—; negotiate—; obstruct—; open —; pace—; separate by —s; speed down —; tear up—; traverse—; trip down—; walk down—; widen—; —bisects; —divides; —extends; —leads; —runs; —swallows one up.
(See passage.)

ALACRITY
adjectives
marvelous; gladsome; incredible; peculiar; sparkling; unequalled; comical; momentary; light-footed; nimble; feigned; eager; warlike; rhythmic; enthusiastic; headlong; keen; noteworthy; nervous.

ALARM
adjectives
serious; groundless; vague; superstitious; unnecessary; high; nocturnal; perpetual; tremulous; faint; profound; spectral; manifest; shrill; evident; grave; imminent; scandalized; unfounded; painful; imbecile; grim; mute; abrupt; midnight; uneasy; sounding; friendly; grisly; deadly; incessant.

verbs

answer—; bewilder by—; blow—; broadcast—; burden with—; check—; chime—; cry—; discourage undue—; excite—; exclaim in—; give rise to—; incite—; occasion—; peal—; produce—; recoil in—; respond to—; shake with—; shudder in—; signal—; sound—; strike—; suppress—; take—; transmit—; —awakens; —clangs; —demoralizes; —dismays; —disturbs; notifies; —signifies; —spreads; —startles; —steals over one; —subsides; —summons; —surprises; —vanishes; —warns.

(See terror, fright, consternation, apprehension, panic, dismay, fear, dread, warning, signal.)

ALARM (*v*)

adverbs

sincerely; fearfully; seriously; astoundingly; exceedingly; groundlessly; unnecessarily; vaguely; superstitiously; perpetually; faintly; profoundly; manifestly; gravely; painfully; abruptly; incessantly.

(See terrify, frighten, scare.)

ALCOHOL

verbs

abstain from—; apply—; banish—; bloat with—; clean with—; concentrate—; condemn—; consume—; contain—; crave—; denature—; detect—; dilute—; dissolve in —; distill—; dose with—; ferment into—; formulate—; heat with—; indulge in—; injure with—; manufacture—; methylate—; power with—; prod with—; purvey—; redistill—; reduce to—; reek with—; reinforce by—; resist—; respond to—; restrict —; saturate with—; solace with—; stain with—; steep in—; stimulate with—; taint with—; utilize—; vaporize—; —accelerates; —contracts; —deadens; —depresses; —derives from; —dulls; —expands; —flames; —inebriates; —influences; —intoxicates; — menaces; —occurs in; —penetrates; —plays a role; —poisons; —preserves; —ravages; —retards; —soothes; —stimulates.

(See wine, liquor, whiskey, ale, etc.)

ALE

adjectives

nut-brown; home-brewed; spicy; unlimited; earth-cooled; bubbling; foam-flecked; gurgling; spirited; heaven-sent; sparkling; cheery; tempting; joyous.

verbs

appreciate—; brew—; consume—; deal in —; drink—; ferment into—; fill with—; flavor—; gulp down—; guzzle—; hop up —; imbibe—; medicate—; pour—; process —; revel in—; set up to a drink of—; swill—; warm with—; —inebriates; —intoxicates; —matures; —pacifies; —ripens; —sours; —stupefies.

(See beer, liquor.)

ALERT

adverbs

guardedly; extremely; wisely; resolutely; diabolically; eternally; zealously; embarrassingly; cautiously; suspiciously; terribly; comically; capably; amazingly; inordinately; passably; incessantly; mentally; nervously; uncommonly; keenly; coolly; warily; sharply; suavely; briskly; swiftly; signally.

ALERTNESS

adjectives

practical; mental; nervous; paradoxical; keen; fierce; flea-like; scientific; cool; quick; wary; sharp; sly; suave; brisk; swift; signal; undervalued.

ALIBI

adjectives

dubious; unquestioned; plausible; unbreakable; incontestable; air-tight; fantastic; faked; unprovable; admirable.

verbs

allege—; build—; concoct—; dispense with —; establish—; fabricate—; furnish—; introduce—; manufacture—; offer—; perjure —; pose—; prove—; regard—; resort to—; scrutinize—; set up—; snarl—; substantiate —; support—; tender—; verify—; —acquits; —bewilders; —confounds; —disconcerts; —proves.

(See plea, excuse.)

ALIEN

adjectives

unwashed; pseudo-intellectual; criminal; invading; objectionable; well-meaning; spying; unpatriotic; harmless.

verbs

admit—; appoint—; bilk—; comfort—; confuse—; defend—; define—; defraud—; delude—; dominate—; dupe—; exclude—; expel—; exploit—; hinder—; hoodwink—; incite—; legislate against—; naturalize—; outwit—; prejudice against—; restrict—; smuggle—; subsidize—; succor—; tolerate —; —agitates; —consumes; —demolishes; —domiciles; —immigrates; —rends; —resides; —sojourns in; —thwarts.

(See stranger, foreigner.)

adverbs
intrusively; irrelevantly; outlandishly; undeniably; ostentatiously; palpably; essentially; obviously; disagreeably; inimicably; inconceivably; unconcernedly; disinterestedly; relatively; discordantly; impertinently; fantastically; exotically; discordantly; incidentally; multifariously; remotely; strangely; unconformably; extraneously; exceptionally; inadmissably; objectionably; harmlessly; unpatriotically; unquestionably.

ALIENATE (v)
adverbs
irretrievably; completely; irreconcilably; temporarily; permanently; successfully; finally; spitefully.
(See transfer, separate.)

ALIENATION
adjectives
mental; complete; temporary; irreconcilable; permanent.

ALIMONY
verbs
appoint—; approve of—; award—; consent to—; decrease—; entitle to—; fall behind in—; imprison for—; lapse—; reward with—; seek—; settle—on; sue for—; win —; —supports.
(See allowance.)

ALIVE
adverbs
gaily; blithely; barely; resolutely; completely; eagerly; energetically; fortunately; happily; surprisingly; beamingly; briskly; industriously; alertly; animatedly; bustlingly; actively; diligently; friskily; restlessly; strenuously; gloriously; joyously; delightedly; rapturously.

ALLEGATION
adjectives
oft-repeated; prevailing; pointless; irrelevant; unsubstantiated; unsupported; insistent.

verbs
affirm—; blurt out—; declare—; deny—; disprove—; dispute—; disregard—; excuse —; hurl—; justify—; moderate—; overthrow—; persevere in—; plead—; propound —; protest—; prove—; refute—; reprove —; state—; voice—; —condemns; —effects; —supports; —validates; —warrants.

(See assertion, declaration, plea, statement.)

ALLEGE (v)
adverbs
emphatically; repeatedly; pointlessly; irrelevantly; insistently; heatedly.
(See state, maintain.)

ALLEGIANCE
adjectives
ill-defined; supreme; unflinching; unfaltering; passionate; vague; firm; absolute; self-sacrificing; divided; faithful; halfhearted; enthusiastic; constrained.

verbs
abandon—; affirm—; begrudge—; bid for —; cease—to; confer—; declare—; desert —; disavow—; dissolve—; exact—; follow with—; free from—to; gain—; imply—; pledge—; profess—; render—; renounce—; repudiate—; seek—; supplant—; swear—; throw off—; violate—; vow—; withdraw—; —binds; —comforts; —continues; —ties.
(See loyalty, devotion, fidelity, obedience.)

ALLEGORICAL
adverbs
abstrusely; openly; frankly; cleverly; disguisedly; ostensibly; ironically; typically; far-fetchedly; obtusely; complexly; incomprehensibly; palpably; evidently; thinly.

ALLEGORY
adjectives
horrid; tremendous; apt; philosophical; pompous; hidden; inappropriate; far-fetched.

ALLEVIATE (v)
adverbs
cheerily; markedly; tremendously; remarkably; slightly; apparently.
(See relieve, lighten, reduce, lessen.)

ALLEY
adjectives
blind; medieval; inclosing; labyrinthian; squalid; grimy; malodorous; slimy; unpromising; filthy; twisting; green; rat-infested.

verbs
approach—; border—; cower in—; lurk in —; saunter through—; skulk in—; slink through—; strike into—; —crawls with; —reeks; —resembles; —slumbers; —teems with; —turns; —twists; —winds.
(See street, passage, path, walk, way.)

adjectives

suspicious; entangling; defensive; amazing; long-desired; dubious; firm; treacherous; political; unholy; unspeakable; tribal; intimate; loose; epoch-making; bizarre; dissolved; prosperous; unhappy; matrimonial; iniquitous; extraneous; staunch; fitting; corrupt; unsurpassed; nuptial; accursed; formidable.

verbs

achieve—; acquire—; adhere to—; alter—; combine in—; conclude—; connect with—; contract—; contribute to—; defend—; deny —; disapprove of—; dissolve—; enhance —; entangle in —s; form—; found—; knit —; maintain—; preserve—; revise—; revoke—; sanction—; seek—; solidify—; stipulate—; terminate—; unite in—; —augments; —concludes; —crumbles; —discriminates against; —empowers; —enables; — enriches; —entangles; —fortifies; —insures; —knits; —maintains; —preserves; —promises; —reanimates; —reinforces; —rejuvenates; —revives; —solidifies; —stiffens; — stipulates; —sustains.

(See league, union, federation, coalition, relationship.)

ALLIGATOR

verbs

conserve —s; corner—; despatch—; exterminate —s; harpoon—; preserve—; prey upon—; prod—; spy on—; stock with —s; stuff—; —s abound; —attacks; —attains a length; —basks; —bellows; —burrows; — charges; —crawls; —crunches; —crushes; —deposits eggs; —devours; —draws his prey; —emits odors; —flips his tail; — floats; —frequents; —glides; —grunts; — hatches; —hibernates; —inhabits; —lashes; —lies in wait; —makes off with; —matures; —measures; —nips; —retreats; —roars; — slips into the water; —snaps; —splashes; —submerges; —suns; —surges; —swarms; —swings its tail; —tends its young; — thrashes about; —twists; —writhes.

(See reptile, crocodile.)

ALLOT (*v*)

adverbs

fairly; equitably; unjustly; unfairly; satisfactorily; magnanimously; impartially.

(See apportion, distribute, divide.)

ALLOW (*v*)

adverbs

ultimately; generously; grudgingly; graci-

ously; subsequently; tacitly; reluctantly; liberally; handsomely; munificently; reasonably; lavishly; regularly; intermittently; impartially.

(See permit, consent, tolerate.)

ALLOWABLE

adverbs

expressly; always; scarcely; socially; officially; legally; obviously; evidently; patently; unconditionally; reportedly; apparently; unquestionably; indubitably; undoubtedly; manifestly; definitely; explicitly; palpably.

ALLOWANCE

adjectives

liberal; generous; handsome; munificent; reasonable; meager; due; tolerable; lavish; modest; regular; intermittent; niggardly; kingly; stated.

verbs

admit—; allot—; apportion—; award—; concede—; continue—; deduct from—; draw from—; exhaust—; husband—; laud—; limit—; oppose—; pledge—; restrict—; sanction—; spurn—; tolerate—; —astounds; —shrinks; —staggers.

(See salary, wages, amount.)

ALLUDE (*v*)

adverbs

publicly; poetically; indelicately; pointedly; superciliously; jocosely; sarcastically; distinctly; crudely; obscurely; perplexingly; scripturally; casually; playfully; metaphorically; slyly; sneeringly; disdainfully; contemptuously; monotonously; personally; irreverently; subtly; timidly; blasphemously; insultingly; condescendingly; scurrilously; jocularly; abstrusely; respectfully.

(See hint, intimate, refer.)

ALLUREMENT

adjectives

economic; taunting; entrancing; delightful; exquisite; siren; agreeable; overpowering; female.

ALLURING

adverbs

mysteriously; utterly; delightfully; disturbingly; designedly; intentionally; confoundedly; diabolically; bewilderingly; amazingly; unquestionably; wondrously; unexpectedly; surprisingly; coolly; radiantly; joyously; quietly; consciously; unconsciously; tauntingly; tormentingly; overwhelmingly; provokingly.

adjectives

happy; distinct; obscure; incidental; scholarly; crude; contemporary; sarcastic; pointed; topical; perplexing; scriptural; casual; facile; parting; playful; metaphorical; delicate; sly; biverbal; sneering; disdainful; contemptuous; literary; monotonous; personal; indecent; stray; well-timed; irreverent; laudatory; hidden; subtle; mythological; rambling; timid; blasphemous; insulting; condescending; scurrilous; jocular; abstruse; respectful.

verbs

accept—; discern—; endure—; explain—; insert—; sport with—; weave in —s; —s abound; —s clutter; —s crowd; —encumbers; —enriches; —implies; —suggests; —weighs down.

(See reference, hint, suggestion.)

ALLY

adjectives

ancient; formidable; constant; treacherous; invaluable; powerful; brilliant; faithful; indispensable; perfidious; distrustful; illustrious; staunch; natural; sturdy; vigorous; sympathetic; unmanageable; lifelong.

verbs

abuse—; alienate—; combine with—; consult—; defend—; forsake—; outrage—; seek—; take for—; unite with—; welcome —; —collapses; —concurs; —s connive; —contributes; —cools down; —forfeits.

(See colleague, friend, partner.)

ALLY (v)

adverbs

closely; inseparably; exclusively; treacherously; invaluably; faithfully; indispensably; perfidiously; staunchly; naturally; sturdily; sympathetically; vigorously.

(See join, associate.)

ALMS

verbs

allot—; bestow—; contribute—; dole out—; donate—; entreat for—; merit—; ministrate —; pilfer—; provide—; relieve with—; scatter—; scorn—; solicit—; support by—.

(See charity, dole, gift.)

ALOOF

adverbs

coldly; proudly; shyly; timidly; arrogantly; superciliously; intellectually; naturally; dreamily; discourteously; deliberately; resolutely; unsocially; impenetrably; ponderously; inscrutably; mysteriously; maddeningly; becomingly; gruffly; gravely; augustly; imposingly; absurdly; magnificently.

ALOOFNESS

adjectives

natural; sweet; drowsy; dignified; dreamy; dainty; unbending; icy; mystic; abstract; courteous; silent; defensive; impenetrable; absent-minded; Olympian; detached; despairing; pardonable; ponderous; inscrutable; effective; becoming.

verbs

attain—; enshroud in—; maintain—; preserve—; withdraw from—; wrap in—; —dehumanizes; —indicates; —induces; —inhibits; —leads to; —results in; —starves.

(See reserve.)

ALTAR

adjectives

garlandless; dreaded; cold; smokeless; nuptial; honored; glowing; conjugal; auspicious; idolatrous; brazen; impious; favored; lofty; sacrificial; venerable.

verbs

accept on—; adorn—; attend—; bow before —; burn at—; cast down—; consecrate—; dedicate at—; desecrate—; disparage—; elevate—; encrust—; enshrine on—; erect —; hang on—; inscribe on—; lure to—; offer on—; perform at—; raise—; rear—; repose on—; sacrifice at—; stagger to—; swear by—; vow at—; worship before—; —fumes with incense; —graces; —rises; —stands.

(See platform, bier.)

ALTER (v)

adverbs

placidly; ridiculously; radically; appreciably; considerably; materially; profoundly; conspicuously; extremely; subsequently; invariably; frankly; significantly; sensibly; quantitatively; mysteriously; extensively; basically; subtly; markedly; seriously; intangibly; indefinably.

(See vary, change, transform.)

ALTERABLE

adverbs

frankly; conveniently; easily; extensively; fortunately; unfortunately; always; happily.

ALTERATION

adjectives

frank; significant; sensible; trifling; quantitative; mysterious; basic; suggested; extensive; observable; subtle; marked; serious; intangible; indefinable.

verbs
detect—; dispute—; effect—; employ—; indicate—; modify—; ponder—; substitute —; yawn at—; —charms; —displeases; —effects; —enchants; —invalidates; —occurs; —offends; —pleases; —satisfies; — is wrought.
(See modification, change, variation.)

ALTERCATION
adjectives
monstrous; lurid; bitter; gesticulatory; high-pitched; wordy; domestic; deadly; unprovoked; violent; acrimonious.

ALTERNATION
adjectives
mad; periodical; endless; rapid; unconscious; intermittent; infinite.

ALTERNATIVE
adjectives
painful; pleasant; admirable; desperate; intolerable; unthinkable; dire; impossible; practicable; subtle; ghastly; grim; vague; contradictory; undesirable; inescapable; serious.

verbs
arrive at—; bewilder with—; conceive—; confront with—; countenance—; endorse—; explore—; extend—; mystify by—; propose —; reject—; request—; suggest—; —circumscribes; —curbs; —lies open; —limits; —puzzles; —remains.
(See option, preference.)

ALTITUDE
adjectives
bleak; dizzy; infinite; considerable; starlit; moderate; healthful; breezy; breath-taking; excessive; unbelievable; unattainable.

verbs
ascertain—; compute—; elevate—; exceed —; fix—; forfeit—; gain—; gauge—; heighten—; level off at—; maintain—; register—; rise to—; scale—; soar to—; — dazzles; —increases.

ALTRUISM
adjectives
genuine; noble; philanthropic; lofty; feeble; non-existent.

ALTRUISTIC
adverbs
sincerely; fanatically; pompously; vaingloriously; publicly; ostentatiously; extremely; instinctively; characteristically; truly; genuinely; amazingly; essentially; quixotically.

ALUMNUS
adjectives
distinguished; valuable; brother; successful; staunch; dependable; rabid; generous.

verbs
appeal to—; browbeat—; organize—; — associates; —i build; —celebrates; —i constitute; —i convene; —endows; —fosters; —i gather; —i nourish; —pledges; —relives; —i reunite; —revisits; —i stand behind.
(See graduate.)

AMALGAMATION
adjectives
compulsory; racial; ethnic; subtle; industrial; necessary; advantageous; vital.

AMATEUR
adjectives
persistent; enterprising; enthusiastic; complacent; inexperienced; deplorable; superficial; distinguished; literary; gifted.

verbs
bar—; brand as—; close to —s; define—; deride—; distinguish—; encourage—; exempt—; govern—; handicap—; outdistance —; purge —s; repudiate—; restrict —s; rule —s; safeguard—; sanction—; vindicate —; —aspires to; —attains; —barters; — competes; —cultivates; —devotes; —engages in; —participates; —preserves his status; —stresses.
(See novice.)

AMATEURISH
adverbs
hopelessly; youthfully; admittedly; eagerly; fancifully; fantastically; ambitiously; avidly; fervidly; enthusiastically; comically; pathetically; inexpertly; deplorably; unexpectedly.

AMAZE (v)
adverbs
perfectly; absolutely; ludicrously; indignantly; honestly; utterly; unboundedly; mutually; bewilderedly; unutterably; speechlessly; blankly; raptly; helplessly; ineffably; dumbfoundedly; haughtily; unconcealedly; senselessly; horribly.
(See astonish, surprise, astound.)

AMAZEMENT

adjectives

sheer; indignant; fond; honest; stupid; starry-eyed; stupefied; utter; mute; unbounded; rising; mutual; bewildered; half-incredulous; mocking; unutterable; speechless; critical; dawning; blank; rapt; wide-eyed; shocked; helpless; dumbfounded; ineffable; freezing; justifiable; startled; horrified; petrified; haughty; agonized; unconcealed; hurt; smothering; open-mouthed; uneasy; senseless.

verbs

augment—; confound with—; evince—; eye with—; feign—; overwhelm with—; paralyze with—; peer with—; petrify with—; smite with—; stupefy with—; —bewilders; —divulges; —manifests itself; —reveals; —seizes; —stuns.

(See astonishment, confusion, surprise, admiration, awe, bewilderment, perplexity, wonder.)

AMBASSADOR

verbs

accredit—; assign—; authorize—; charge —with; commission—; confer with—; delegate—; dismiss—; dispatch—; empower—; entrust—with; exchange —s; exclude—; exempt—; immunize—; induct—; install—; invest—with; maintain—; nominate—; ordain—; oust—; raise to the rank of—; recall—; retract—; suspend—; turn out—; unfrock—; —abrogates; —arbitrates; —arms with; —carries on; —conveys; —develops; —entreats; —has access to; —intercedes; —mediates; —ministers; —negotiates; —represents; —repudiates; —transmits.

(See agent, minister, official.)

AMBER

adjectives

limpid; pale; rich; clear; electrified; honey-colored; translucent; opaque.

AMBIGUITY

adjectives

unfortunate; verbal; apparent; subtle; disturbing; deliberate; undesirable.

verbs

admit—; brush away—; burden by—; clear away—; cling to—; develop—; disentangle —; dissolve—; distinguish—; express—; obscure with—; oppress with—; reduce—;

remove—; —clouds; —deludes; —occurs; —puzzles; —vanishes.

(See uncertainty, obscurity.)

AMBIGUOUS

adverbs

unfortunately; disturbingly; deliberately; undesirably; evasively; obscurely; distressingly; offensively; suspiciously; undeniably; quibblingly; equivocally; perplexingly; obscurely; mysteriously; vexatiously; seriously; irritatingly; vaguely; disagreeably; insidiously; stupidly; unwisely; objectionably; unacceptably; cunningly.

AMBITION

adjectives

forceful; unbounded; misplaced; personal; warring (pl); criminal; abstracted; reasonable; social; ancestral; uninstructed; worthy; unquenchable; industrial; average; grandiose; sole; thick-sighted; racial; lofty; cherished; lifelong; thwarted; worldly; vaulting; vain; conflicting (pl); daring; unprincipled; insane; intense; unbridled; noisy; darling; foiled; primary; disquieting; peculiar; fierce; humble; honorable; wandering; moderate; sensible; imperial; kingly; persistent; mad; tremendous; sublime; soaring; disappointed; desultory; insatiable; absurd; unreined; corrupt; beastly; misdirected; undying; healthy; satisfied; blind; august; youthful; vulgar; inordinate; life-ruling; troublous; sinister; irreconcilable; political; odious; crushed; tacit; impassioned; private; unscrupulous; persevering; senile; exalted; praiseworthy; modern; resolute; aggressive; consuming; gnawing; spurring; boastful; indiscreet; petty; visionary; conceited; dictatorial; egotistical; dynastic; abjured; hypertrophied; latent; innate; undeviating; tempered; boundless; distempered; focalized.

verbs

achieve—; attain—; badger—; balk—; betoken—; breed—; characterize—; cherish —; chill—; choke with—; commend—; control—; credit—; cultivate—; derive—; devour with—; direct—; display—; dose with —; drop—; dwarf—; endow with—; enslave—; entertain—; exaggerate—; extinguish—; feed with—; fire with—; fling away—; frustrate—; fulfill—; further—; gratify—; hamper—; honor—; humor—; infect with—; inflame with—; inspire—; master—; nurse—; overleap—; placate—; realize—; reawaken—; rein—; relinquish —; restrain—; satisfy—; scoff at—; scotch —; stifle—; stimulate—; subordinate—; temper—; thwart—; whet—; —burns; —s conflict; —emboldens; —lures; —overleaps itself; —pushes; —soars; —suffers; — vaults.

(See aspiration, desire, eagerness.)

AMBITIOUS
adverbs
socially; extremely; unspeakably; inordinately; profoundly; mercilessly; unscrupulously; politically; ruthlessly; odiously; laudably; properly; dangerously; admirably; industriously.

AMBLE (*v*)
adverbs
joyously; industriously; gently; languorously; lazily; impudently; lackadaisically.

(See walk.)

AMBUSH
verbs
assault from—; attack from—; capture by —; conceal in—; draw into—; elude—; employ—; encounter—; hide in—; lay—; lie in—; lurk in—; perish in—; post in—; set up—; station in—; suspect—; tempt into—; walk into—; waylay in—; —arises; —succeeds; —surprises.

(See trap.)

AMEN
adjectives
hearty; hasty; solemn; sincere; throaty; husky; heavenly.

AMENABLE
adverbs
pleasantly; personally; entirely; wholly; scarcely; seriously; terribly; directly; agreeably; accommodatingly; willingly; satisfactorily; sufficiently; fortunately; happily.

AMENDMENT
adjectives
belated; rash; drastic; pending; beneficent; continual.

verbs
abandon—; abrogate—; adopt—; allow—; alter—; complete—; concur with—; deliberate—; disagree with—; discuss—; dismiss —; initiate—; insert—; oppose—; propose —; ratify—; reject—; repeal—; resolve—; subject to—; substitute—; veto—; violate —; —adjusts; —alters; —betters; —compensates; —corrects; —deprives; —expiates; —gives birth to; —modifies; —overthrows; —provides; —reforms; —remedies; —removes; —restricts; —stands.

(See change, improvement, correction.)

AMENITY
adjectives
ancient; social; hard-won; nonsensical; accepted; expected.

AMERICAN
adjectives
dashing; chauvinist; adventurous; eminent; loud; red-blooded; level-headed; intellectual; sensitive; liberal; stout-hearted; rapid-fire; virile; swift-moving; industrial-minded.

adverbs
loyally; thoroughly; completely; independently; dauntlessly; proudly; consciously; resolutely; ostentatiously; ridiculously; adventurously; bravely; essentially; obviously; distinctively; characteristically; insistently; consistently; persistently; dashingly; steadily; coolly; charmingly; informally; violently; volubly; restrainedly; serenely; confidently; unmistakably; undeniably; loudly; quietly; palpably; evidently; level-headedly; stoutly; invincibly.

AMERICANISM
verbs
adhere to—; ally with—; appeal to—; assault—; assert—; assimilate—; awaken—; cherish—; cite—; cultivate—; defend—; develop—; deviate from—; embrace—; endow with—; establish—; explore—; express —; federate—; hearten by—; inculcate—; ingrain—; insure—; interfere with—; laud —; menace—; molest—; motivate by—; pledge to—; proclaim—; promote—; resist—; retain—; retreat to—; ripen—; safeguard—; surround by—; sympathize with—; tamper with—; threaten—; unite in—; uphold—; verse in—; vest in—; —converges with; —embraces; —flounders; —flourishes; —forges through; —fosters; —languishes; —progresses; —promotes; —signifies; —survives.

(See patriotism.)

AMIABILITY
adjectives
impassioned; delightful; sincere; disconcerting; utmost; gushing; easy-going; placid; unwonted; native; condescending; rarefied.

AMIABLE
adverbs
charmingly; unfailingly; always; sincerely; unaffectedly; calmly; serenely; happily; cheerily; naturally; bewitchingly; softly; gently; enchantingly; unwontedly; unusually; habitually; incomparably; modestly;

winningly; ineffably; genuinely; becomingly; refreshingly; wonderfully; sweetly; graciously; frankly.

AMITY

adjectives
godlike; cordial; ghastly; mutual; rough; genial; generous; feigned; jealous.

verbs
abide in—; bind in—; cultivate—; despise —; disrupt—; found upon—; knit in—; link in—; promote—; radiate—; restore—; swear—; unite in—; —conduces; —fosters; —insures.
(See friendship, harmony, good-will, peace.)

AMMUNITION

verbs
assign—; cap—; cast—; consume—; contract for—; discharge—; exhaust—; furnish—; fuse—; guard—; handle—; ignite —; insert—; jacket—; project—; protect—; ration out—; replenish—; safeguard—; secrete—; stack—; store—; transport—; —detonates; —embraces; —saves; —shatters; —undergoes improvement.
(See explosives, shells.)

AMOROUS

adverbs
ardently; erotically; tenderly; lovingly; excessively; ostentatiously; fervidly; adoringly; idolatrously; infatuatedly; passionately; rapturously; yearningly; coquettishly; excitedly; flirtatiously; sweetly; philanderingly; seductively; enchantingly; winningly; wooingly; devotedly.

AMOUNT

adjectives
sufficient; excessive; stipulated; immense; cumulative; dangerous; exhausting; vast; exorbitant; fabulous; incredible; gigantic; indecent; unreasonable; prodigious; unprecedented; fantastic; appalling; colossal; ruinous; incalculable; goodly; sizable; average; traditional; stated; strategic; proportionate; lucrative; harmonious; comfortable; infinite; negligible; inexhaustible; inadequate; moderate; insignificant; undue; maximum; requisite; definite; appreciable; trifling; minimum; perceptible; preponderant; staggering; unheard-of.

verbs
aggregate—; anticipate—; calculate—; compute—; diminish—; discount—; estimate—; expend—; forecast—; gauge—; indicate—;

magnify—; register—; sum up—; total—; view—; withdraw—; —dwindles; —exceeds; —recedes; —reverts; —rises.
(See quantity, total, sum.)

AMOUNT (v)

adverbs
collectively; sufficiently; excessively; immensely; cumulatively; dangerously; exhaustingly; vastly; exorbitantly; fabulously; incredibly; gigantically; indecently; unreasonably; prodigiously; unprecedently; fantastically; appallingly; colossally; ruinously; incalculably; sizably; proportionately; lucratively; harmoniously; infinitely; comfortably; inexhaustibly; moderately; insignificantly; definitely; appreciably; perceptibly; staggeringly.
(See reach, extend.)

AMOUR

adjectives
scandalous; classic; innocent; juvenile; delicate; passionate; fanciful; restless; discreet.

AMPHITHEATER

adjectives
Gargantuan; vast; immense; natural; wooded; colossal; sylvan; shaded; massive; florid; shadowy; splendid.

AMPLE

adverbs
generously; extensively; abundantly; liberally; amazingly; overwhelmingly; gratifyingly; astonishingly; capably; enormously; hugely; voluminously; immeasurably; immensely; magnificently; stupendously; splendidly; wastefully; boundlessly; illimitably; immoderately; incredibly; surprisingly; excessively; preposterously.

AMUSE (v)

adverbs
unconsciously; constantly; superficially; inwardly; genuinely; mightily; whole-heartedly; powerfully; secretly; libidinously; vociferously; considerably; indescribably; falteringly; undisguisedly; obviously; grimly; jovially; highly; impersonally; unspeakably; obscurely; good-humoredly; tolerantly; contemptuously; harmlessly; idly; endlessly; intimately; deliriously; detachedly; cynically; maliciously; puerilely; discreetly; ironically; benevolently; magnificently; haughtily; vaguely; wistfully; unconcealedly; emptily; sophisticatedly; insipidly; sheepishly; meretriciously; irritatingly; wholesomely; child-

39

ishly; intriguingly; fashionably; sparklingly; barbarously.

(See entertain, divert, please.)

AMUSED

adverbs

highly; slightly; definitely; postively; mildly; uproariously; unusually; tremendously; ingeniously; cleverly; constantly; greatly; gaily; indescribably; unspeakably; secretly; tolerably; heartily; idly; grimly; suitably; vaguely; foolishly; oddly; properly; fashionably; conventionally.

AMUSEMENT

adjectives

impersonal; unspeakable; obscure; good-humored; tolerant; worldly; contemptuous; harmless; favorite; abundant; hearty; secret; elegant; solitary; idle; puzzled; after-dark; racy; traditional; endless; intimate; delirious; detached; cynical; malicious; puerile; costly; discreet; innocent; sarcastic; healthy; ironic; benevolent; magnificent; mocking; mild; considerable; grim; undisguised; haughty; round-eyed; vague; wistful; unconcealed; empty; suppressed; sophisticated; scornful; wry; ribald; sly; reminiscent; facile; sheepish; heightened; meretricious; insipid; irritating; wholesome; childish; passing; intriguing; idle; fashionable; time-killing; sparkling; barbarous; evident.

verbs

absorb in—; afford—; attend with—; betray —; contrive—; crave—; cultivate—; dedicate to—; devise—; excite—; fall into—; indulge in—; revel in—; seek—; tickle with—; vary—; —affords; —attracts; —beguiles; —detains; —distracts; —diverts; —engages; —entertains; —grows out of; —invigorates; —relaxes.

(See diversion, entertainment, pastime, sport, pleasure.)

ANACHRONISM

adjectives

ineffective; moral; unconscious; flagrant; painful; bold; impossible.

ANAESTHETIC

verbs

absorb—; administer—; apply—; breathe—; confine—; discover—; dope with—; doze under—; drug with—; employ—; experiment with—; inhale—; inject—; introduce —; localize—; numb with—; relieve with —; sniff—; spray—; undergo—; —allays; —alleviates; —benefits; —benumbs; —comforts; —deadens; —depresses; —dulls; —freezes; —induces; —paralyzes; —relieves; —renders insensible; —restricts.

(See ether, chloroform.)

ANALOGOUS

adverbs

relatively; proportionally; approximately; closely; exactly; nearly; ridiculously; truly; interestingly; strikingly; internationally; remarkably.

ANALOGY

adjectives

striking; ironic; obvious; classic; intellectual; palpable; mysterious; astonishing; exaggerated; secret.

ANALYSIS

adjectives

scientific; flawless; exact; brilliant; learned; careful; thorough; logical; painstaking; vivid; keen-sighted; cautious; sound; cogent; revealing; trenchant; penetrating; rigorous; profound; probing; searching; minute; critical; intensive; microscopic; tortuous; shallow; abstruse; absorbing; unsparing; arbitrary; inadequate; illuminating; erroneous; obscure; involved; ruthless; merciless; complex; devastating; scathing; complete; frank; straightforward; philosophic; metaphysical; auditory; primary; legal; chemical; financial; exhaustive; elaborate; compact; comprehensive; thoroughgoing; grueling; final; interrelated; deliberate; cold; accurate; subtle; pedagogic; lucid; fine-spun; perspicacious; detailed; provocative; dispassionate; uncompromising; acute; ingenious; rational; intensive; tragic; patient; forceful; skilful.

verbs

answer with—; apply—; carry out—; clarify—; defy—; descend to—; display—; elude—; employ—; examine—; exhibit—; explain by—; introduce—; involve—; proceed by—; study—; submit to—; suggest—; summarize—; tabulate—; withstand—; yield to—; —assays; —breaks up; —concludes; —correlates; —cultivates; —decomposes; —defines; —determines; —differentiates; —discovers; —identifies; —precedes; —produces; —reduces; —resolves into; —restricts; —results in; —reveals; —separates; —solves; —teaches; —traces; —uncovers; —unearths.

(See investigation, examination.)

40

adverbs

brilliantly; learnedly; carefully; painstakingly; skilfully; cautiously; trenchantly; rigorously; profoundly; searchingly; minutely; critically; intensively; abstrusely; ruthlessly; mercilessly; scathingly; philosophically; primarily; exhaustively; tiresomely; coldly; offensively; accurately; impersonally; patiently; uncompromisingly.

ANALYZE (v)

adverbs

fully; scarcely; scientifically; adequately; exhaustively; flawlessly; exactly; brilliantly; learnedly; carefully; thoroughly; logically; painstakingly; vividly; skilfully; cautiously; soundly; cogently; penetratingly; rigorously; profoundly; probingly; searchingly; minutely; critically; intensively; microscopically; tortuously; shallowly; abstrusely; unsparingly; inadequately; involvedly; ruthlessly; mercilessly; devastatingly; scathingly; dispassionately; frankly; straightforwardly; philosophically; metaphysically; legally; chemically; financially; exhaustively; elaborately; comprehensively; finally; accurately; subtly; pedagogically; lucidly; perspicaciously; provocatively; dispassionately; uncompromisingly; ingeniously; rationally; patiently; forcefully.

(See discriminate, resolve.)

ANARCHIST

adjectives

moral; intellectual; communistic; theoretical; unthinking; rabid.

verbs

accuse—; apprehend—; combat—; condemn —; denounce—; disperse —s; execute—; expel—; take measures against—; —advocates; —blasts; —conceives; —denies; — disregards; —endeavours; —escapes; —executes; —maintains; —masses; —orates; — plunders; —promotes disorder; —rises; — rules; —scorns; —shatters; —struggles; — theorizes; —violates.

(See communist, terrorist.)

ANARCHISTIC

adverbs

ungovernably; dangerously; alarmingly; naively; youthfully; heedlessly; hatefully; enthusiastically; lamentably; deplorably; openly; actively; defiantly; insurgently; seditiously; restively; insubordinately; mutinously; rebelliously; violently; tumultuously; incorrigibly; persistently; obstinately; treasonably.

adjectives

multitudinous; malignant; emulous; lawless; social; dormant; practical; moral.

verbs

abandon—; bear—; cast into—; conceive—; confuse—; control—; cope with—; crash into—; curse—; degrade by—; drift towards —; exclude—; expel—; fall under—; overthrow—; proclaim—; realize—; revive—; subject to—; suppress—; —abolishes; —advocates; —agitates; —appeals; —conflicts with; —confuses; —connotes; —degrades; —denounces; —destroys; —disorders; — dominates; —emancipates; —frees; —hurls back; —overlaps; —overthrows; —rages; —relates to; —repudiates; —resorts to; — strikes; —threatens; —violates.

(See revolution, confusion, chaos.)

ANATHEMA

adjectives

dire; violent; involuntary; incoherent.

ANATOMY

verbs

advance—; approach—; consult—; develop —; dissect—; practice—; protect—; rely on—; reveal—; segregate—; shrink—; shrivel—; sketch—; wither—; —admits; —analyzes; —applies to; —considers; — deals with; —defines; —denotes; —details; —detects; —develops; —dissects; —investigates; —produces; —rejects; —signifies; — specializes; —teaches; —traces; —treats of.

(See science.)

ANCESTOR

adjectives

rude; far-away; august; pious; dim; divine; symbolical; barbaric; martial; devout; renowned; remote; illustrious; cave-dwelling; heroic; primitive; forgotten; venerable; respected; roistering; adventurous; astute; seafaring; contemporary; solitary-minded; immortal; tainted; prehistoric; talented; frugal; lineal; immigrant; blue-blooded; aristocratic; benighted.

verbs

address—; anger—; bury with—; descend from—; hark back to—; honor—; idealize —; idolize—; inherit from—; invoke—; propitiate—; renounce—; revere—; sleep with—s; swear by—; trace—; venerate—; worship—; —bequeaths; —blesses; —counsels; —fades; —foreruns; —influences; — precedes; —vouchsafes.

(See father.)

adjectives
dubious; pre-human; illustrious; revolutionary; mixed; remote; rustic; insignificant; select; healthy; hard-working; shabby; spiritual; far-renowned.

ANCHOR

verbs
back—; cast—; cat—; come to—; drag—; drop—; fasten—; fish—; forge—; foul—; free from—; grapple with—; ground—; haul up—; heave up—; hoist—; hook—; let fall—; let go—; lie at—; lift—; load—; loose—; moor—to; raise—; rest—; ride at —; shackle—; shoe—; stow—; sweep for —; throw out—; tow—; weigh—; —bites bottom; —branches; —comes home; —drags; —entangles; —fixes itself to; —fouls; —holds; —moors; —resists; —rusts; —secures; —settles; —sinks; —slides down; —stabilizes; —strikes; —takes hold.

ANECDOTAL

adverbs
interestingly; racily; risquily; graphically; sentimentally; boisterously; insipidly; fruitily; drolly; ineptly; dismally; sparklingly; ponderously; edifyingly; endlessly; childishly; pertinently; entertainingly; startlingly; shockingly; amusingly; surprisingly.

ANECDOTE

adjectives
traditional; minute; chatty; amusing; sentimental; familiar; insipid; startling; authentic; childhood; trite; pertinent; fruity; long-buried; small-town; pointed; ponderous; sparkling; endless; harmless; edifying; illustrative; droll; badly-told; touching; gossipy; trifling; dismal; antique; inept; apt; satirical.

verbs
apply—to; avoid —s; collect —s; compile —s; dispel by means of —s; edit —s; elaborate—; enrich with —s; launch into—; manufacture—; narrate—; refer to—; reject—; relate—; retail —s; spice with —s; swell —s; venture—; weaken—; —betrays; —deals with; —entertains; —interests; —treats of.
(See story, narrative, incident.)

ANGEL

adjectives
ministering; painted; household; hovering; expectant; tutelary; accursed; avenging; light-invested; grave; rapturous; cheering; ancient; compassionate; invisible; bewitching; fallen; sensuous; rude; naughty; lugubrious; attendant; sorrowing; accusing; luminous; wrathful; flame-robed; benign; pearl-colored.

verbs
cast out—; conduct—; defy—; degrade—; deify—; etherealize—; exalt—; personify —; pray to—; summon—; transform into—; worship—; —appears; —ascends; —attends; —bears; —blesses; —descends; —exemplifies; —flutters; —guards; —hovers above; —ministers to; —proclaims; —represents; —salutes; —serves; —tends; —watches; —weeps.
(See God, cherub.)

ANGER

adjectives
murderous; sullen; slow; revengeful; momentary; disheartened; fatal; clamorous; fierce; hot; uneasy; headlong; savage; proud; righteous; wholesome; controlled; loyal; strident; terrified; tolerant; inordinate; unjust; unreasoning; merciless; dull; cold; stern; carnal; blistering; ferocious; injurious; mute; violent; implacable; assumed; well-feigned; sham; dumb; speechless; suppressed; smouldering; futile; white; pale; impotent; subdued; kindling; seething; blazing; scorching; consuming; flaring; whirlwind; devouring; passionate; incipient; latent; oblivious; quivering; cooling; frenzied; jealous; parental; black-browed; senseless; restrained; impetuous; uncharitable; genuine; uncontrollable; boisterous; arrogant; icy; savage; contemptuous; insane; confused; concentrated; puzzled; craven.

verbs
analyze—; blind with—; bristle with—; burn with—; cast—upon; cherish—; coddle —; control—; defer—; detour—; disarm—; exhibit—; expostulate in—; flash—; flush with—; incite—; kindle—; manifest—; pacify—; pale in—; project—; provoke—; rage in—; rebuke in—; repent—; revive—; scream in—; slay in—; sting with—; strike in—; swallow—; swell with—; unleash—; upbraid in—; vent—; vex with—; visit—upon; voice—; —abates; —blazes; —boils; —burns; —bursts out; —congeals; —consumes; —dies; —distresses; —exasperates; —falls; —flames; —flares up; —floods; —grieves; —inflames; —melts; —over-excites; —rages; —rises; —ruffles; —simmers; —startles; —subsides; —throbs; —wanes; —waxes.
(See fury, rage, wrath, exasperation, ire,

animosity, resentment, vexation, pique, frenzy.)

ANGER (v)

adverbs

violently; murderously; sullenly; slowly; revengefully; momentarily; fatally; clamorously; fiercely; hotly; savagely; inordinately; righteously; unjustly; unreasoningly; mercilessly; ferociously; injuriously; violently; implacably; speechlessly; futilely; impotently; passionately; frenziedly; jealously; senselessly; genuinely.

(See irritate, displease, offend, provoke.)

ANGLE

adjectives

salient; rakish; technical; astonishing; intricate; remote; projecting; peculiar; social; unfortunate; legal; odd; divergent (pl); elevated; oblique; obtuse; acute; precise; humanitarian.

verbs

bisect—; derive—; draw—; figure—; form —; increase—; inscribe—; maintain—; measure—; proceed from—; produce—; reckon—; trisect—; —adjoins; —corresponds.

ANGLER

adjectives

enthusiastic; insatiable; beginning; ardent; jubilant; expert; practiced; bungling; awkward; skilled; proficient; able.

ANGRY

adverbs

senselessly; sullenly; intolerably; hotly; obviously; righteously; foolishly; ridiculously; dangerously; icily; genuinely; uncontrollably; passionately; violently; sternly; implacably; unjustly; inordinately; insanely; naturally; ludicrously; unnaturally; curiously; strangely.

ANGUISH

adjectives

nameless; unspeakable; excessive; bodily; nauseating; dumb; mental; excruciating; keen; maddening; intolerable; sheer; startled; mortal; hopeless; indescribable; frightful; unbearable; bitter; profound; acute; tearless; soul-piercing; occult; strangling; perpetual; fierce; insufferable; universal; maternal; jealous; subdued; transient; dull; stifling; short-lived; audible; intimate; unuttered; grim; heart-rending; despairing; spiritual; killing; sickening; dark; abrupt;

amazed; insupportable; passionate; sensational.

verbs

burst with—; choke with—; consume with—; cry out in—; endure—; escape—; heal—; hearken to—; heed—; lessen—; overwhelm with—; soothe—; strike with—; suffer—; tremble with—; vent—; wring the mind with—; waste one's soul in—; writhe in—; —oppresses; —rends; —splits; —tears; —wrings.

(See distress, pain, anxiety, agony, misery, torture.)

ANGULAR

adverbs

forbiddingly; unattractively; raw-bonedly; repulsively; stiffly; absurdly; awkwardly; gawkily; pathetically; ludicrously; ridiculously; youthfully; painfully; pitifully; wretchedly; distressingly; crookedly.

ANGULARITY

adjectives

solid; raw-boned; stiff; absurd; awkward.

ANIMAL

adjectives

bold; pugnacious; ferocious; uncongenial; stiff-legged; indigenous; alpine; envenomed; elusive; heroic; familiar; social; patient; malignant; sensual; sentient; domesticated; performing; herbivorous; meek; rational; predatory; carnivorous; outlandish; articulate; restive; balky; well-groomed; ignoble; prowling; hunted; elusive; preternatural; reasoning; hoofed; pampered; white-sterned; emaciated; ruminant; noble; vigorous; throwing; marine; native; diabolical; graminivorous; frugivorous; armorial; agile; grotesque; docile; burly; aquatic; water-loving; amphibious; savage; invertebrate; porcine; devoted; thin-skinned; intelligent; responsive; affectionate; tractable; sagacious; helpless; magnificent; sleek; stunning; reclining; trapped; tethered; wounded; careening; stricken; harassed; fretting; snorting; panic-stricken; squealing; recalcitrant; maddened; infuriated; snarling; blood-thirsty; enraged; depraved; gregarious; prowling; omnivorous; albino; lower; furry; unshod; gaunt; cat-like; thick-skinned; sure-footed; nervous; stray; castrated; cautious; fabulous; marsupial; mangy; pachydermatous; oviparous; refractory.

verbs

breed—s; cage—; classify —s; clutch—;

conserve —s; corral —s; cross —s; decoy
—; derive from—; discover—; distinguish
—; domesticate—; dominate—; educate—;
encounter—; ensnare—; exhaust—; exhibit
—; experiment with—; exploit—; exterminate—; feed—; fondle—; groom—; harness
—; improve—; infuriate—; inspect—; mate
—; pat—; protect—; raise—; reproduce—;
revert to—; search for—; stalk—; suffocate
—; track—; train—; wheel—; —charges;
—s cluster; —curls up; —feeds; —forages;
—gestates; —gnaws; —hibernates; —hunts;
—migrates; —s multiply; —occurs in; —
perishes; —rages; —ranges; —reproduces;
—roars; —scurries; —senses; —sniffs; —
succumbs; —suckles.

(See beast, creature, brute.)

(See also specific animals, such as bear,
cat, lion, etc.)

ANIMATE (v)

adverbs
impiously; fascinatingly; gladly; garrulously; characteristically; vividly; dazzingly;
delightfully; picturesquely; mechanically;
preternaturally.

(See stimulate, rouse.)

ANIMATED

adverbs
delightfully; eagerly; garrulously; excitedly; nervously; happily; rapturously; ecstatically; unusually; hilariously; gleefully;
merrily; lightly; joyously; cheerfully;
blithely; sparklingly; pleasingly; playfully;
racily; energetically; vigorously; restlessly;
resolutely; determinedly.

ANIMATION

adjectives
fascinating; glad; suspended; perspiring;
garrulous; contagious; social; characteristic;
vivid; dazzling; delightful; playful; transient; picturesque; returning; intense; mechanical; preternatural.

verbs
attain—; behold—; bestow—upon; buoy up
with—; breathe out—; burst into—; counterfeit—; enliven with—; evince—; feign—;
fire with—; impart—; incite to—; inject—;
inspire with—; instil—; manifest—; provoke to—; recite with—; restore—; revive
—; sparkle with—; suspend—; vitalize with
—; woo with—; —enlivens; —fatigues;
—flags; —flares up; —jades; —wearies.

(See vivacity, life, gayety.)

ANIMOSITY

adjectives
intensified; personal; sullen; jealous; ecclesiastical; rancorous; deep-seated; vindictive; savage; deadly; implacable; partisan;
smouldering; relentless; emotional; bitter.

verbs
arouse—toward; bear—; break out into—;
effect—; excite—; feed—; feel—; incite—;
incur—; inherit—; manifest—; nurse—; regret—; revive—; stir up—; tend toward
—; unveil—; —alienates; —breaks up; —
damages; —disrupts; —exists between; —
hinders; —wavers.

(See rancor, hatred, enmity.)

ANKLE

adjectives
delicate; generous; fragile; beefy; bony;
wrenched; swollen; immaculate; slender;
aristocratic; well-turned.

ANNALS

adjectives
dramatic; fabulous; mythic; factual; voluminous; priceless; ancestral; contemporary;
tragic; fragmentary; historic; literary;
bloodstained; ancient; gossipy; racy.

ANNEX (v)

adverbs
formally; swiftly; utterly; forcefully; readily; craftily; partially.

(See take.)

ANNIHILATE (v)

adverbs
utterly; surely; swiftly; mercifully; unprecedentedly; craftily.

(See destroy.)

ANNIHILATION

adjectives
utter; sure; swift; terrible; bloody; merciful; beastly; unprecedented; crafty.

ANNIVERSARY

verbs
anticipate—; applaud—; commemorate—;
dramatize—; fete—; institute—; observe—;
disregard—; stamp—; —follows; —is marked by; —recurs.

(See observance, celebration, day, event.)

ANNOUNCE (v)

adverbs
flatly; vociferously; oracularly; mercifully;
sententiously; paternally; clamorously; explicitly; pompously; publicly; simultaneously; reluctantly; solemnly; arrogantly; virtuously; ostentatiously; formally; blandly;

abruptly; jokingly; officially; unreservedly; significantly; jubilantly; gleefully; authoritatively; blithely; flatteringly; finally; mournfully; dramatically; haltingly; brazenly; prematurely; tersely; gayly; briskly.
(See proclaim, advertise, publish.)

ANNOUNCEMENT
adjectives
lurid; flattering; calamitous; conciliatory; final; implicit; successive (pl); encouraging; initial; mournful; drastic; dramatic; droning; halting; formal; brazen; devastating; pending; dire; premature; exclusive; vain-glorious; formidable; post-prandial; terse.

verbs
broadcast—; cheer—; confirm—; declare—; deliver—; dispatch—; disseminate—; misconstrue—; notify by—; reiterate—; rise at—; substantiate—; —astounds; —bursts upon; —gives notice; —proclaims; —publicizes; —overtakes; —takes by surprise.
(See proclamation, advertisement, notice.)

ANNOY (v)
adverbs
blusteringly; obviously; sorely; intensely; greatly; positively; unduly; temporarily; mildly; savagely; markedly; jealously; frivolously; unavoidably; excessively.
(See trouble, aggravate.)

ANNOYANCE
adjectives
petty; unconcealed; prolonged; unique; undue; shocked; temporary; intense; mild; savage; internal; mock; marked; aristocratic; impotent; sharp; repressed; obvious; inhospitable; nervous; dangerous; jealous; frivolous; unavoidable; private.

verbs
avoid—; condemn—; dislike—; flush with —; frown with—; generate—; molest with —; occasion—; plague with—; rumble in —; temper—; tolerate—; vent—; —disgusts; —injures; —persists; —returns; —troubles; —vexes.
(See vexation, irritation.)

ANNOYING
adverbs
mischievously; accidentally; disastrously; devilishly; diabolically; intentionally; outrageously; painfully; teasingly; persistently; unintentionally; purposely; defiantly; revengefully; abominably; exceptionally;

characteristically; wretchedly; tormentingly; maliciously; unbecomingly; increasingly; senselessly; unspeakably; deliberately.

ANNUL (v)
adverbs
virtually; wisely; quickly; unthinkingly; promptly; shrewdly.
(See abolish, reverse.)

ANOINT (v)
adverbs
sacrificially; religiously; perfunctorily; daily; occasionally.
(See smear.)

ANOMALY
adjectives
monstrous; dreadful; curious; noble; racial; peculiar.

ANONYMITY
adjectives
scrupulous; illegitimate; heartless; carefully-preserved; politic; necessary; defensive; desperate; cowardly; enforced.

verbs
bury in—; clothe in—; disguise in—; ensconce in—; hide in—; lend—; maintain —; mystify with—; preserve—; prowl in—; remain in—; resort to—; retire from—; skulk in—; slink in—; steal into—; surround with—; veil in—; write in—; —cloaks; —conceals; —impresses; —masks.
(See secrecy.)

ANONYMOUS
adverbs
mysteriously; naturally; obviously; necessarily; securely; safely; forever; scrupulously; legitimately; politically; defensively; timidly; bashfully; shyly; unaccountably; evasively; hopelessly; irretrievably; astonishingly; vaguely; perplexingly; undecipherably; unfathomably; enigmatically.

ANSWER
adjectives
definite; clinching; efficient; contemptuous; indignant; accurate; concrete; requisite; affirmative; negative; disconsolate; evasive; categorical; magnanimous; flippant; consenting; authoritative; verbal; comprehensive; bewildered; favorable; impatient; economical; unconsidered; worthy; doleful; enigmatical; discouraging; meaningless; deft; admissible; explicit; perfect; memorable; quavering; stubborn; sufficient; ready; boorish; cryptic; measured; boun-

tiful; definitive; vague; vehement; imperious; impertinent; oral; candid; argumentative; haughty; laconic; convincing; soul-sufficing; admirable; casual; amazing; proud; skilful; scorching; rash; incoherent; intelligible; insulting; fit; apt; indulgent; practical; animated; reassuring; respectful; impressive; comforting; satisfactory; courteous; illuminating; logical; conclusive; cool; pertinent; surly; equivocal; irritable; insolent; scathing; lame; harsh; dilatory; unorthodox; uninteresting; relevant; prodigal; disquieting; sardonic; pungent; sharp; exultant; dramatic; breathless; crushing; partial; tentative; cautious; inevitable; instantaneous; simultaneous; ultimate; rueful; unconscious; impromptu; time-honored; prescribed; mechanical; mollified; confident; significant; broken; impetuous; impulsive; fateful; matter-of-fact; irrefutable; agnostic; mild.

verbs
address—; appeal for—; approve—; bark —; bind to—; confine—; constitute—; defend—; deliver—; draw—from; echo—; entreat—; evade—; evolve—; exhort—; express—; extort—; fire back—; fling back —; frame—; fumble—; glean—; hang on —; hit upon—; justify—; marvel at—; merit—; mock—; muffle—; owe—; petition—; protest—; reject—; respond with—; signal—; snap—; stir to—; supply—; sustain—; sweeten—; tabulate —s; tear—from; volunteer—; word—; wrench—from; —accuses; —arises; —charges; —claims; —clamors; —contradicts; —implies; —informs; —invalidates; —pleases; —pledges; —rebuts; —reveals; —satisfies; —solves; —states.
(See reply, retort, response, defense.)

ANSWER (v)
adverbs
gruffly; candidly; haughtily; uncomfortably; energetically; evasively; bluntly; darkly; breathlessly; sulkily; affectionately; sagely; casually; volubly; listlessly; persistently; yawningly; carelessly; pointedly; enigmatically; stubbornly; proudly; definitely; tartly; hysterically; reluctantly; sadly; falteringly; unconcernedly; gravely; doggedly; directly; sententiously; completely; triumphantly; hoarsely; brusquely; laughingly; stolidly; cautiously; curtly; impatiently; nervously; desultorily; affirmatively; visibly; faithfully; bitterly; obstinately; thoughtfully; impetuously; effectually; guardedly; evasively; bravely; readily; distinctly; candidly; respectfully; emphatically; squeamishly; ponderingly; surlily; coherently; challengingly; cynically; bashfully; knowingly; passionately; petulantly; hotly; non-committally; rancorously; instantly; simply; affirmatively; monosyllabically; laconically; directly; excitedly; evasively; indignantly; civilly; mechanically; fantastically; meekly; scoffingly; confusedly; definitely; pathetically; pertinaciously; wistfully; accurately; soothingly; tremulously; peevishly; disconsolately; evasively; categorically; verbally; comprehensively; bewilderedly; economically; worthily; dolefully; enigmatically; deftly; explicitly; perfectly; quaveringly; cryptically; measuredly; vehemently; imperiously; scorchingly; rashly; fitly; aptly; indulgently; animatedly; uninterestingly; relevantly; prodigally; disquietingly; sardonically; partially; tentatively; ruefully; matter-of-factly; mildly.
(See reply, respond, concede.)

ANSWERABLE
adverbs
personally; awfully; painfully; seriously; undoubtedly; terribly; officially; directly.

ANT
adjectives
antenna-manipulating; assiduous; destructive; exemplified; ever-questing; eternally-constructing; encroaching; frugal; formic-producing; garnering; gregarious; greedy; hoarding; harvesting; industrious; persistent; swarming; scurrying; sugar-seeking; store-collecting; troublesome; unpopular; wise.

verbs
burden—; combat —s; consider—; cultivate —s; disturb —s; examine—; exhibit —s; exterminate —s; fall victim to —s; infest with —s; go to —s; observe —s; purge of —s; spray —s; study—; teem with —s; —s abound; —accomplishes; —achieves; —accumulates; —s adapt themselves; —s amass; —ascends; —attacks; —bites; —bores into; —s build; —bustles; —s capture; —s collect; —s colonize; —s consolidate; —s construct; —s contend for; —s converge upon; —crawls; —s crowd; —defends; —s denude the area; —s deposit eggs; —descends; —despoils; —destroys; —s devastate; —devours; —digs; —dissects; —dominates; —dwells; —s eddy from; —emerges; —endures; —s enslave; —entombs; —excavates; —explores; —exudes; —s find their way; —s flit about; —s fly; —forages; —gathers; —gorges; —guards; —harvests; —hastens; —hatches; —heaps; —hibernates; —s hol-

low out; —hustles; —imprisons; —s insinuate themselves; —s invade; —labors; —lays up food; —mates; —s migrate; —s nest; —s nurse their young; —occupies; —s organize; —performs; —s pillage; —s preserve; —s pour in; —races; —s raid; —s ravage; —reconnoiters; —regurgitates; —roams; —roves; —rushes; —scouts; —scurries; —secretes; —seizes; —s share; —shears; —s socialize; —stings; —stores; —stows; —s stream up; —struggles; —s surge out; —survives; —s swarm; —s throng; —transports; —trudges; —utilizes; —vanishes; —wars.
(See insect, termite.)

ANTAGONISM
adjectives
political; bitter; surly; heartfelt; overwhelming; violent; subtle; mutual; professional; recurring; stiffening; fundamental; religious; bristling; deep-seated; social; sectional; persistent; racial; pronounced; ingrained; unrelenting; outspoken; vindictive; implacable; lofty; subdued; traditional; compromising; monosyllabic.

verbs
accentuate—; adjust—; balance—; conquer —; create—; develop—; express—; heighten —; increase—; mark—; oppose—; rack by —; risk—; rouse—; soften—; stimulate—; struggle with—; topple—; weaken—; —thwarts; —weakens.
(See opposition, hostility, resistance.)

ANTAGONIST
adjectives
legitimate; formidable; potential; appointed; contemptible; implacable; dreaded; defeated; crafty; redoubtable; irreconcilable; fallen; wary; agile; relentless; acrid.

verbs
admonish—; belittle—; best—; daunt—; defeat—; fence with—; overcome—; overpower—; overwhelm—; —argues; —assails; —battles; —collapses; —contends; —contests; —counteracts; —disputes; —languishes; —opposes; —relaxes; —slumps; —springs up.
(See opponent, rival, assailant, foe, adversary.)

ANTAGONISTIC
adverbs
violently; bitterly; subtly; fundamentally; persistently; racially; socially; politically; openly; outspokenly; vindictively; traditionally; formidably; unreasonably; irreconcil-

ably; relentlessly; ufterly; strangely; inexplicably; essentially; palpably; undeniably; basically; alarmirgly; unaccountably.

ANTAGONIZE (v)
adverbs
derisively; politically; bitterly; overwhelmingly; violently; professionally; recurringly; fundamentally; religiously; socially; sectionally; persistently; racially; outspokenly; vindictively; implacably.
(See oppose, hinder.)

ANTECEDENT
adjectives
mental; worthy; historic; dwarfish; undeniable; necessary; grammatical.

ANTHEM
adjectives
pealing; eternal; blessed; doleful; joyous; heavenly; resounding.

ANTIC
adjectives
unconscious; infantile; puerile; capricious; ridiculous; glib; sterile; gay; exuberant; mad; absurd; droll; small-boy; mechanical; erratic; drunken; boisterous.

ANTICIPATE (v)
adverbs
curiously; fondly; reasonably; pessimistically; confidently; mentally; ecstatically; gleefully; joyously; originally; pleasurably; eagerly; passionately; blissfully; gloatingly; hungrily; ardently; impatiently; avidly; tremblingly; greedily; reasonably.
(See expect, apprehend.)

ANTICIPATION
adjectives
unhesitating; sensitive; charming; bright; daring; joyful; mysterious; pleasurable; eager; greedy; sanguine; exhilarating; passionate; picturesque; lascivious; tingling; heightened; lively; thrilling; blissful; undefined; morose; gloating; hungry; ferocious; keen; alert; ardent; impatient; avid; trembling; crushing; panic-stricken; reasonable; quivering.

verbs
beam with—; delight in—; look forward with—; pardon—; resist—of; restrain—; revel in—; rob—; toil in—of; tremble in—; —cheers; —enhances; —excites; —gladdens; —incites; —stimulates.
(See expectation, hope.)

ANTICIPATORY

adverbs

joyously; mysteriously; pleasurably; excitedly; hysterically; passionately; thrillingly; hungrily; unreasonably; avidly; impatiently; ardently; keenly; hopefully; eagerly; charmingly; joyfully; mischievously; hastily; incontinently; fervently; anxiously; greedily; impetuously; crazily; madly; feverishly; nervously.

ANTIDOTE

adjectives

specific; effective; cursed; pungent; stupefying; vile.

ANTIPATHY

adjectives

blind; cordial; mortal; unaccountable; mutual; invincible; deep-rooted; natural; rational; bigoted; tacit; peculiar.

verbs

admit—; be born of—; date—; display—; dispose toward—; dwell in—; excite—; hold—; imply—; introduce—; mark—; remove—; rouse—; saturate with—; turn from—; —blazes; —burns; —manifests; —melts; —originates from; —prejudices; —puzzles; —restricts; —takes root.
(See aversion, enmity, dislike.)

ANTIQUARY

adjectives

ardent; musical; distinguished; honorary; eminent; passionate; shallow; classical; hoary; curious.

ANTIQUE

adjectives

charming; spurious; rare; valuable; precious; genuine; colorless; fraudulent.

adverbs

genuinely; expensively; unquestionably; authentically; truly; actually; veritably; really; pricelessly; richly; decoratively; garishly; gorgeously; gaudily; ornamentally; deceptively; fraudulently; cheaply; showily; smartly; trickily; foolishly; flimsily; absurdly; beautifully; unbelievably; spuriously.

ANTIQUITY

adjectives

unknown; remote; honorable; pagan; venerable; traceable; hoar; classical; quaint; dead; historical; respectable; solemn; remote; fabulous; feudal; fascinating; observable.

ANTISEPTIC

adjectives

powerful; intestinal; efficient.

verbs

act as—; advise—; apply—; bathe in—; compare—; develop—; dilute—; discard—; dust with—; embalm in—; employ—; expose to—; glaze with—; immerse in—; impregnate with—; inject—; introduce—; operate with—; paint with—; soak in—; sterilize with—; surround with—; swab with—; wash with—; wrap in—; —acts; —aids; —aims at; —arrests; —burns; —cleans; —combats; —counteracts; —destroys; —exercises; —fulfils; —functions; —influences; —inhibits; —insures; —irritates; —kills; —preserves; —prevents; —protects; —purifies; —reaches; —relieves; —removes; —renders; —replaces; —restrains; —restricts; —retards; —rids of; —serves; —sterilizes; —thwarts.

adverbs

genuinely; effectively; valuably; infallibly; powerfully; extremely; heroically; mildly; perfectly; soothingly; correctively; specifically; simply; safely; beneficially; beneficently; advantageously; commendably; highly; essentially.

ANTITHESIS

adjectives

vile; complacent; inharmonious; striking; complete; false.

ANTLERS

adjectives

budding; branching; cresting; clashing; defiant; deciduous; graceful; gouging; fathom-wide; interlocking; lordly; massive; menacing; pronged; palm-tree (moose); periodically-shed; regal; sail-like (moose); self-entrapping; tined; velvety; vigorously-beating; wicked.

verbs

adorn with—; bear—; brandish—; carry—; decorate with—; form—; gore with—; impale on—; lock—; mount—; ornament with —; renew—; shed—; snag—; solidify—; spear—; spike—; sprout—; stunt—; toss—; weaken—; —branch out; —develop; —fork; —menace; —pierce; —protrude; —rend; —stab; —threaten.
(See horn.)

adjectives
clanging; crude; fiery; harsh; hammer-worn; historic; mighty; massive; steely; spark-emitting; shaping; transforming; traditional; invincible; proving; resistant; unvarying; unyielding; Vulcan-symbolizing.

verbs
balance on—; beat on—; bend on—; clink on—; crack on—; fashion on—; flatten on—; forge on—; hammer on—; harden on —; jangle on—; shape on—; strike—; twist on—; —clashes; —resounds; —rings; —sustains.
(See bell.)

adjectives
touching; breathless; irrepressible; excessive; torturing; slight; supreme; utmost; undue; considerable; deep; vague; absorbing; unsatisfied; paternal; indescribable; fretting; gnawing; indeterminate; haggard; unceasing; infinite; unavoidable; financial; perceptible; predominant; tender; insufferable; connubial; excited; feverish; brooding; trembling; pious; deep-seated; maternal; agonizing; bated; flushed; mortal; worldly; cruel; morbid; devastating; betrayed; hysterical; nerve-racking; frantic; breath-taking; mental; domestic; motherly; painful; intense; unjust; sleepless; poignant; sick; grueling; heart-broken; keen; acute; soul-searing; gratuitous; relieved; drab; unwarranted; common; unspoken; hidden; repressed; troublesome; throbbing; annoying; sudden; subconscious; discernible; undeceived; human; suppressed; wearisome; impatient.

verbs
accompany with—; betray—; burden with —; create—; disturb by—; evince—; free from—; gaze with—; harass with—; increase—; manifest—; overshadow with—; reveal—; seize by—; shake with—; strain with—; trouble with—; wear to shreds with—; —agitates; —clouds; —constricts; —depresses; —disturbs; —etches; —prevails; —seizes; —vexes.
(See solicitude, apprehension, worry, fear, care, misgiving.)

adverbs
over; unnaturally; painfully; laughably; ridiculously; pathetically; lamentably; curiously; eagerly; abnormally; naturally; touchingly; supremely; unduly; deeply; in-describably; perceptibly; tenderly; suspiciously; excitedly; frantically; frenziedly; inexplicably; nervously; timidly; terribly; keenly; pitiably; miserably.

adjectives
luxurious; sumptuous; modern; bachelor; tawdry; gorgeous; immaculate; dignified; old-fashioned; impressive; swanky; spacious; cooped-up; dusty; dingy; squalid; isolated; unpersonalized; ground-floor; terraced; doll-size; private; commodious; magnificent; dirty; immense; whitewashed; dimly-lighted; home-like; shabby; imposing; distinctive; charming; elegant; well-ordered; ill-furnished; communal.

verbs
assign to—s; billet in —s; divide into —s; ensconce in—; fit out—; occupy—; wreck —.
(See room, house.)

adverbs
stupidly; dully; strangely; abnormally; alarmingly; weakly; heavily; stolidly; vacantly; ridiculously; unnaturally; singularly; oddly; curiously; unaccountably; irritatingly; shockingly; callously; coldly; carelessly; hopelessly; unpardonably.

adjectives
selfish; weary; dream-like; despairing; stagnant; incredible; dull; immovable; resigned; settled; curious; growing; strange; enveloping; political; unaffected; accustomed; complete.

verbs
denote—; disturb—; encounter—; engender —; escape—; free from—; forsake—; master—; overcome—; produce—; result in—; rouse from—; signify—; sink into—; suffer —; suppress—; tolerate—; —chills; —paralyzes; —prevails; —signifies.
(See indifference, lethargy.)

adjectives
grotesque; lumbering; chattering; soot-colored; restless; anthropoid; man-like; monstrous.

verbs
descend from—; —chatters; —clambers; —claws; —crouches; —dances; —drops to earth; —gallops off; —imitates; —leaps;

—lodges in; —lumbers; —mimics; —plucks; —resembles; —screams; —springs; —sways; —swings; —yelps.
(See monkey, animal.)

APE (v)
adverbs
comically; sedulously; grotesquely; lumberingly; chatteringly; restlessly; monstrously; shamelessly; ludicrously.
(See imitate, mimic.)

APERTURE
adjectives
narrow; barred; grated; half-moon; yawning; ungarnished; ragged; circular; limiting.

APHORISM
adjectives
favorite; pregnant; cynical; resounding; sparkling; hackneyed; abominable; pithy; selfish.

APOLOGETIC
adverbs
awkwardly; humbly; sincerely; nervously; slavishly; hastily; instantly; preposterously; disgustingly; unnecessarily; skillfully; sufficiently; reluctantly; profoundly; deeply; tearfully; pathetically; incoherently; sheepishly; half-heartedly; confusedly; honestly; openly; generously; embarrassingly; miserably; eagerly.

APOLOGY
adjectives
practical; humble; voluble; metrical; nervous; groveling; abject; handsome; awkward; universal; hasty; muttered; cynical; preposterous; skillful; suitable; sufficient; sincere; rapturous; profound; exaggerated; strongly-worded; pathetic; pitiful; tearful; murmured; mumbled; incoherent; obscure; sheepish; mute; half-hearted; amazed; mental; public; automatic.

verbs
acknowledge—; attack—; attempt—; convey—; elicit—; express—; favor with—; imply—; indulge in—ies; plead for—; refuse—; shame into—; stammer—; tender—; trouble with—; wave aside—; —alters; —atones; —excuses; —vindicates.
(See defense, confession, excuse, plea, alibi.)

APOLOGY (v)
adverbs
meekly; pitifully; gruffly; profusely; humbly; volubly; nervously; abjectly; grovelingly; awkwardly; cynically; exaggeratedly; suitably; skillfully; pathetically; tearfully; incoherently; sheepishly; half-heartedly; automatically.
(See justify, defend, vindicate.)

APOSTLE
adjectives
current; intrepid; inspired; non-ecclesiastical; ordained; recalcitrant; self-appointed; subsequently-commissioned; specifically-chosen; treacherous; virtuous; world-denouncing.

verbs
alienate —s; bar —s; call —s; commission —s; delegate—; elect—; gain —s; gather —s; hail—s; initiate—; lead—s; martyr —s; ordain —s; persecute —s; quote—; regulate —s; select —s; send forth —s; —accompanies; —administers; —advocates; —executes; —leads; —performs miracles; —preaches; —proclaims; —records; —scatters.
(See witness.)

APPALLING
adverbs
grievously; sorely; bitterly; painfully; distressingly; excruciatingly; hauntingly; gruesomely; horridly; piercingly; tormentingly; torturingly; deplorably; disastrously; dreadfully; execrably; fearfully; frightfully; insufferably; insupportably; intolerably; odiously; oppressively; pathetically; ruefully; shockingly; woefully; touchingly; unbearably; terrifically.

APPARATUS
adjectives
dust-collecting; elaborate; abundant; scientific; perceptive; sentient; makeshift; curative; simple; intricate; complicated; ghastly; imperfect; digestive; inefficient; ingenious; culinary; new; ponderous; expensive; thinking; hefting; spectroscopic; murderous; solemn.

verbs
adapt—; adjust—; apply—; demonstrate—; design—; employ—; equip with—; evolve —; experiment with—; gear—; guard—; invent—; manipulate—; modernize—; provide—; put—in motion; set up—; simplify—; tinker with—; toy with—; —facilitates; —functions.
(See device, machine, tool.)

APPAREL

adjectives

glorious; superfluous; trim; homely; fashionable; smart; coarse; becoming; gorgeous; exquisite; ceremonious; luxurious; decorous; flamboyant; plain.

verbs

adorn in—; array in—; attire in—; behold —; change—; clothe in—; deck in—; don —; embroider—; equip with—; fashion—; fit—; furnish—; ornament—; outfit with—; prepare—; provide with—; rig with—; snatch at—; —beautifies; —conceals; —enhances; —proclaims.

(See clothing, dress, raiment.)

APPARENT

adverbs

plainly; conspicuously; downright; undeniably; clearly; definitely; flagrantly; glaringly; notoriously; openly; constantly; easily; strikingly; reasonably; shamefully; outrageously; dangerously; plaguedly; perilously.

APPARITION

adjectives

false; glorious; formidable; celestial; enchanting; distinguished; impatient; frightful; phenomenal; monstrous; intruding; startling; soulless; personal; exquisite; grisly; blushing; unpleasant; bloody; fantastic; overwhelming; ill-omened; black; ghostly; miraculous; horrid; singular; continuous.

verbs

authenticate—; believe in —s; disprove—; divine—; exhibit—; generate—; imagine—; occasion—; perceive—; produce—; shroud —; summon—; —s abound; —appears; —comes forth; —groans; —haunts; —lures; —suspends; —vanishes; —warns.

(See specter, ghost, phantom, illusion.)

APPEAL

adjectives

effective; universal; pathetic; emphatic; overt; contagious; impassioned; dramatic; modern; sorrowful; mute; unwitting; infinite; frail; sudden; potential; lamentable; eternal; frantic; mournful; diversified; rude; artless; inharmonious; constant; visible; urgent; boisterous; manifest; felicitous; irresistible; self-respecting; gastronomic; singular; persistent; troubled; popular; manly; matchless; unconscious; skillful; powerful; agonizing; unanswerable; eloquent; psychological; despairing; qualified; humanitarian; tragic; genuine; lasting; sad; unspoken; pitiable; speechless; crushing; fiery; piteous; tender; shrill; plaintive; hypnotic; sensuous; unavailing; habitual; emotional; enticing; alluring; joyous; visual; wonderful; deafening; logical; lovable; warm; convincing; devout; childish; rare; luxurious; stirring; lusty; courageous; challenging; feminine; public; delicate; artistic; magic; poetic; world-wide; human; timid; hurt; solemn; abject; weak; vague; adventurous; whimsical; strange; sensational; animated; electrifying; magnetic; tremendous; spectacular; imploring; wistful; timely; poignant; demagogical; superficial; panic-stricken; vain; inflammatory; dumb; admirable; olfactory; savory; mysterious; abnormal; sporadic; prophetic; distinct; comprehensive; gripping; unique; strong; intense; spontaneous; overbearing; sympathetic; strident; truculent; blatant; unvoiced.

verbs

abandon—; address—; admit—; afford—; bolster—; broadcast—; claim—; decline—; deny—; desist in—; discourage—; disregard—; enact—; exercise—; file—; give notice of—; grant—; institute—; invoke—; involve—; justify—; lose—; merit—; modify—; nullify—; present—; prevent—; privilege to—; prosecute—; provide—; provide security for—; question—; refuse—; regulate—; rely on—; render—; renew—; resist—; respond to—; review—; rule—; schedule—; stir by—; subject to—; submit to—; succumb to—; support—; voice—; whine—; yield to—; —engrosses; —fails; —reverses.

(See entreaty, petition, application, request, prayer.)

APPEAL (v)

adverbs

strangely; frantically; directly; strongly; confidently; constantly; irresistibly; forcibly; specially; powerfully; perpetually; effectively; dramatically; sorrowfully; mutely; strongly; mournfully; artlessly; rudely; urgently; boisterously; eloquently; tragically; piteously; tenderly; emotionally; shrilly; deafeningly; logically; stirringly; warmly; lustily; courageously; publicly; abjectly; wistfully; stridently; truculently; blatantly; outspokenly; mysteriously; grippingly; uniquely; sympathetically.

(See entreat, invoke.)

APPEAR (v)

adverbs

conspicuously; malignantly; impressively; presently; portentously; perpetually; tardily; distinctly; substantially; simultaneously;

miraculously; hesitatingly; posthumously; anonymously; manifestly; commandingly; mysteriously; astoundingly; exotically; flamboyantly; phlegmatically; demurely; ethereally; slovenly; ferociously; unhealthily; obtrusively; majestically; spectrally; inscrutably.

(See emerge, seem, look, resemble.)

APPEARANCE
adjectives
august; pompous; distinguished; stately; austere; noble; commanding; charming; cordial; worthy; antiquated; venerable; comfortable; immaculate; sleek; well-fed; quaint; luscious; artistic; dainty; lovely; comely; gorgeous; untidy; uncouth; angular; ungainly; forlorn; shabby; genteel; plaintive; somber; mysterious; weird; eerie; astounding; arresting; striking; singular; sprightly; grotesque; rakish; massive; robust; rugged; emaciated; deceitful; cadaverous; unearthly; desolate; quarrelsome; offending; miserable; sullen; disgusting; ungraceful; incongruous; gross; flamboyant; resentful; jaded; phlegmatic; grim; physical; youthful; nautical; grave-like; nun-like; orderly; unkempt; park-like; rabbit-like; clerk-like; mournful; exotic; ethereal; leonine; tolerable; ludicrous; poverty-stricken; fragile; casual; contrite; slovenly; dismaying; unfortunate; disjointed; sunken; bedraggled; animated; faint; diaphanous; picturesque; slothful; worm-eaten; contradictory; stern; benevolent; wretched; vulgar; dilapidated; external; promising; visual; ducal; inviting; ideal; squalid; sedate; outward; greasy; attractive; distinctive; ursine; demure; decorative; satanic; fearful; vacant; independent; portentous; beneficent; dignified; mottled; studious; stupid; timid; opalescent; ferocious; prepossessing; sickly; festive; reconciliatory; tawdry; impoverished; voluntary; scattered; deserted; prosperous; famished; thumbworn; unhealthy; reverential; respectable; swing-like; school-teacherish; unobstrusive; weedy; natty; frank; antediluvian; genuine; brave; flattering; material; palatial; battered; dressy; individual; variegated; watered; majestic; spectral.
verbs
come into—; detect—; disclaim—; discredit —; disfigure—; display—; involve—; greet —; judge by—; observe—; parade—; perceive by —s; present an—; preserve —s; put in—; ruffle—; transfigure—; transform —; —arrests; —belies; —repels.
(See aspect.)

APPEASE (v)
adverbs
inadequately; lightly; painstakingly; fully; completely.
(See pacify, calm, reconcile, propitiate.)

APPELLATION
adjectives
equivocal; false; incongruous; inappropriate; ill-mannered; heathenish; phantom; elegant; jocose; permanent; trite; hated; affectionate.

APPENDIX
verbs (anatomy)
drain—; excise—; freeze—; incise—; inflame—; locate—; perforate—; remove—; —adheres; —bursts; —infects; —poisons; —ravages; —suppurates; —swells.

APPENDIX
adjectives (book)
derogatory; contributory; complementary; concomitant; accessory; essential; explanatory; prolonged; solemn; supernumerary; superfluous; statistical.

verbs
advise by—; affix—; consult—; insert—; refer to—; relate in—; review in—; —concurs; —contributes; —directs; —guides; —introduces.
(See addition.)

APPERTAIN (v)
adverbs
unquestionably; undoubtedly; certainly; solely; exclusively.

APPETITE
adjectives
unmanageable; eager; inordinate; ravenous; cavernous; voracious; squeamish; keen; jaded; gluttonous; rude; depraved; abnormal; unappeased; phenomenal; prodigious; robust; natural; sharpened; vicious; eccentric; enormous; monstrous; gross; gigantic; sensitive; coarse; languid; spongelike; pampered; devouring; herbivorous; rude; husky; boundless; leaden; capricious; perverted; obscene; unashamed; sleepy; sensual; catholic; brutish; perennial; inactive; lusty; insatiate; animal; satisfied; fleshy; overpowering; irrational; beastly; hearty; unreasonable; diseased; postponed; demoniac; surfeited.

verbs
acquire—; allay—; animate—; appeal to—; appease—; bury—; cloy—; comply with—;

52

curb—; delight—; deprave—; depress—; digest with—; express—; gorge—; govern —; gratify—; humor—; impair—; indulge —; obey—; pamper—; pervert—; preserve —; quench—; quicken—; raise—; reduce —; regulate—; relish—; revive—; sate—; satiate—; satisfy—; sharpen—; sicken—; staunch—; stimulate—; stir—; suffice—; suit—; yield to—; whet—; woo—; —anticipates; —diminishes; —drives; —dwindles; —gnaws; —grows; —increases; —languishes; —lessens; —returns; —sleeps.

(See desire, hunger, passion.)

APPLAUD (v)

adverbs

riotously; vociferously; warmly; valiantly; equally; tumultuously; spontaneously; hungrily; thunderously; deafeningly; lavishly; enthusiastically; uproariously; vigorously; wildly; irrepressibly; furiously; vehemently; clamorously; frantically; sycophantically.

(See cheer, laud, praise, admire.)

APPLAUSE

adjectives

spontaneous; thunderous; general; deafening; lavish; boisterous; kindly; willing; tumultuous; enthusiastic; whirlwind; uproarious; widespread; rapturous; intelligent; well-directed; vigorous; wild; hearty; irrepressible; furious; delirious; unqualified; vehement; rolling; sporadic; murmuring; rippling; prolonged; forced; warm; courteous; commendatory; heavy-handed; derisive; unbounded; mocking; frantic; vociferous; wondrous; controlled; inordinate; generous; singular; sycophantic; grateful; sarcastic; hollow; malicious; serious; clamorous; ecstatic; scattered.

verbs

acclaim by—; anticipate—; appreciate—; bask in—; chant—; clap—; commend—; demonstrate—; drink up—; echo—; envy—; express—; gain—; huzza—; laugh out—; long for—; love—; manifest—; merit—; murmur—; pronounce—; raise—; reap—; relish—; rock with—; shake with—; snap —; thunder—; trick into—; voice—; win —; —ascends; —breaks out; —bursts out; —crackles; —delights; —encourages; —gratifies; —interrupts; —lessens; —reverberates; —rings from.

(See cheers.)

adjectives

smooth; polished; firm; cool; full-juiced; red-cheeked.

verbs

blight—; blow down—; bob for —s; bore into—; bruise—; bud —s; chip—; chop—; core—; crate —s; crop —s; crunch—; cultivate—; devour—; dice—; ferment —s; freeze—; gather —s; graft —s; harvest —s; hoard —s; market —s; munch —; palm—; pare—; plant —s; pluck —; preserve —s; press —s; propagate —s; quarter —; redden —s; scrape—; seed—; spray —s; store —s; taste—; vend —s; —s canker; —s ferment; —matures; —rots; —tempts; —s thrive.

(See fruit.)

APPLIANCE

adjectives

approved; base; complicated; suitable; adroit; crude; ingenious; rude; primitive.

APPLICANT

adjectives

gentle; clamorous; qualified; hopeful; admissible; profitable.

verbs

eliminate—; expose—; mortify—; place—; repulse—; —declares; —petitions; —qualifies.

(See candidate.)

APPLICATION

adjectives

diligent; intelligent; conscientious; rigid; assiduous; sedulous; steadfast; utmost; rigorous; concrete; fascinating; platonic; practical; universal; adroit; progressive; broad; specific; thorough; dynamic; degrading; perfunctory; strenuous; steadfast; presumptuous; unflinching; educated; continuing; pertinent; quantitative; undue; formalistic; correct; professional; ceaseless; industrial; systematic; repeated; inviting; ingenious; influential; superior; fruitful; admirable; economic; dexterous; unfriendly; timely.

verbs

attach—; consider—; cure with —s; demand —; detail—; justify—; petition for—; postpone—; present—; reconsider—; reject—; require—; solicit—; —eases; —kills; —modifies; —pends; request—.

(See use, request.)

APPLY (v)

adverbs

assiduously; indiscriminately; skilfully; ten-

53

derly; faithfully; diligently; ingeniously; luxuriously; extensively; incorrectly; dexterously; arbitrarily; consciously; comprehensively; advantageously; artificially; rigorously; directly; usefully; necessarily; promiscuously; adroitly; perfunctorily; professionally; ceaselessly; systematically; admirably; literally; liberally; scientifically; practically; universally.
(See use, utilize, practice, adapt.)

APPOINT (v)
adverbs
providentially; celestially; tentatively; publicly; clandestinely; arbitrarily; voluntarily.
(See establish, ordain, assign, allot.)

APPOINTMENT
adjectives
tentative; lifetime; public; onerous; clandestine; absolute; arbitrary; formal; voluntary.

verbs
assign—; benefit by—; cancel—; confirm—; decline—; decree—; designate—; direct—; dispose of—; engineer—; establish—; fix—; grant—; miss—; order—; perform—; ratify—; shuffle—; stipulate—; thrill by—; wangle—; —confers; —pays; —stands; —vests in one.
(See meeting.)

APPOINTMENTS
adjectives
luxurious; elegant; sumptuous; modernistic; dignified.

APPORTION (v)
adverbs
equitably; equally; fairly; justly; wisely; thoughtfully.
(See allot, distribute, grant, share.)

APPRAISAL
adjectives
silent; objective; luminous; shrewd; searching; rational; cool; desperate; intelligent; nimble; careful; adequate; critical; acute; technical; enlightening; scientific; convincing; prolonged; independent.

APPRAISE (v)
adverbs
critically; covertly; judiciously; conceitedly; knowingly; silently; objectively; shrewdly; rationally; coolly; intelligently; adequately; scientifically; independently.
(See judge, estimate.)

APPRECIATE (v)
adverbs
highly; adequately; justly; deeply; properly; particularly; readily; fully; correctly; sympathetically; mutually; genuinely; heartily; whole-heartedly; passionately; aesthetically; belatedly; artistically; profoundly.
(See esteem, prize.)

APPRECIATION
adjectives
intense; genial; detached; sympathetic; respectful; delicate; impersonal; laughing; bashful; mutual; poetic; innocent; definite; full; critical; hearty; high; true; genuine; discreet; wide; sensitive; wholehearted; clearer; deep; heightened; passionate; stunted; aesthetic; anticipated; patriotic; brilliant; cordial; amazed; generous; affectionate; splendid; reluctant; belated; keen; warmhearted; unsolicited; complete; proper; sensuous; fine; vivid; total; marked; flashing; humorous; expressed; emotional; rarefied; scant; supreme; increased; childish; sincere; oppressive; growing; loyal; hard-driven; rare; radiant; tentative; direct; intellectual; spiritual; alleged; artistic; enthusiastic; profound; youthful.

verbs
differ in—; drink in with—; evoke—; increase—; perceive with—; promote—of; recognize with—; stamp—; —grows; —increases; —rises.
(See esteem.)

APPRECIATIVE
adverbs
genially; sympathetically; laughingly; wholly; definitely; heartily; truly; genuinely; wholeheartedly; deeply; highly; passionately; discriminatingly; cordially; amazingly; pathetically; splendidly; keenly; warmly; completely; properly; childishly; sincerely; increasingly; oppressively; radiantly; delightfully; enthusiastically; gratifyingly; profoundly.

APPREHEND (v)
adverbs
readily; imperfectly; clearly; distinctly; nervously; tremblingly; fearfully; vaguely; acutely; undisguisedly; gnawingly.
(See dread, fear.)

APPREHENSION
adjectives
slumbering; uneasy; maternal; troublesome; nervous; wistful; sickening; sensitive; clammy; hazy; ghostly; trembling; frenzied;

lingering; quivering; fearful; shivering; fickle; rational; feigned; lively; vague; acute; undisguised; suppressed; gnawing; constant; religious; dismal; gloomy; ill-defined; cruel; despondent; remorseful; uncomfortable; foreboding; alarming; abject; distinct; unrelieved; sad; breathless; anguished; piteous; idle; grave; continuous; professed; indignant; daily; delighted; dread; warm; groundless; serious; vain; ever-present; nameless; instant; goading; painful; affected; supreme; right; puerile; terrible; mortal; cowardly; tempered; utmost; murky; miraculous.

verbs
allay—; arouse—; rise above—; becloud —; clear—; crystallize—; deny—; dull—; express—; free of—; ingrain—; look about with—; obtain—; profess—; rejoice in—; remove—; rest on—; sense with—; shake with—; strengthen—; torment by—; warrant—; wear out with—; —assails; — flames; —possesses; —seizes.
(See fear, dread, anxiety, distrust.)

APPREHENSIVE
adverbs
uneasily; nervously; fearfully; vaguely; acutely; constantly; occasionally; dismally; gloomily; cruelly; uncomfortably; alarmingly; distinctly; piteously; idly; gravely; professedly; groundlessly; seriously; namelessly; painfully; supremely; childishly; superstitiously; curiously; strangely; inexplicably; suddenly.

APPRENTICE
adjectives
idle; bright; haughty; hand-picked; drunken; able; practiced; clumsy.

verbs
abuse—; bind—; burden—; chastise—; contact—; dismiss—; employ—; engage—; enroll—; fledge—; instruct—; regulate—; remove—; retain—; school—; serve as—; teach—; —binds himself to; —gathers; — learns; —masters; —practices; —serves; —trains.
(See beginner, novice, student.)

APPRENTICESHIP
adjectives
weary; devious; tedious; long; arduous; strict; sordid; faithful.

APPROACH
adjectives
hackneyed; single; sociological; novel; or-

ganic; traditional; inevitable; oblique; tentative; obvious; impressive; immediate; logical; flanked; insidious; common-sense; majestic; tactful; critical; methodological; natural; simple; wary; galloping; fair; hushed; original; insinuating; wistful; cautious; illuminating; subtle; indirect; shamefaced; stealthy; boisterous; chic; affable; experimental; tolerable; warm; mutual; soft; ample; casual; rapid; cunning; active; timid; gradual; intimate; sympathetic; distant; tumultuous; extraordinary; speedy; hostile; irresolute; ironical.

verbs
bar—; betoken—; construct—; cover—; discover—; discuss—; disguise—; divert—; examine—; foresee—; herald—; hinder—; linger over—; obstruct—; reconstruct—; repel—; restore—; sense—; shun—; watch —; —bodes; —leads.
(See access, way, entrance.)

APPROACH (v)
adverbs
penitently; hilariously; noiselessly; devoutly; remotely; diffidently; cautiously; perilously; sinuously; stealthily; unwarily; dexterously; delicately; humbly; reluctantly; leisurely; suppliantly; obsequiously; blushingly; circumspectly; obliquely; irresolutely; casually; confidentially.
(See advance.)

APPROBATION
adjectives
individual; startled; enthusiastic; unmeasured; modest; full; audible; virtuous; general.

verbs
bestow—; concur in—; declare—; enjoy—; entertain—; express—; mark with—; meet with—; merit—; quote with—; receive—; revoke—; seal in—; voice—.
(See commendation, encouragement, admiration, approval, praise.)

APPROPRIATE (v)
adverbs
selfishly; unceremoniously; thievishly; eagerly; doubtfully; reverently; solely; wastefully; adequately; fraudulently; extravagantly; lavishly.
(See take, assume.)

APPROPRIATION
adjectives
wasteful; blind; adequate; permanent; con-

tinuing; ruthless; fraudulent; extravagant; lavish; excessive; passive; meager.

verbs
assign—; authorize—; bar—; bequeath—; carry on with—; default—; designate—; diminish—; draw—; economize on—; employ—; enact—; exceed—; expend—; finance—; grant—; legislate—; necessitate—; pass—; pinch—; reserve—; restrict—; set apart—; shave—; specify—; transfer—; triple—; —aids; —allows; —enables; — provides; pay—.
(See fund, tax.)

APPROVAL

adjectives
affectionate; highest; delighted; private; priceless; overwhelming; unqualified; monotonous; marked; reiterated; vigorous; patent; warm; unanimous; sage; genuine; condescending; frank; complete; roaring; tacit; maternal; hapless; loud; excited; free; world-wide; unrestrained; languid; partial; social; hearty; widespread; abject; masculine; enthusiastic; grudging; expressed; perfect; denominational; popular; surprised; intense; voiceless; unconscious; distant; reluctant.

verbs
authorize—; bask in—; beam—; clamor—; consent to—; imply—; insure—; intimate —; meet with—; nod—; roar—; sanction—; secure—; stamp with—; trick into—; win —; —encourages; —greets; —heartens.
(See approbation, sanction, commendation, indorsement, ratification.)

APPROVE (v)

adverbs
heartily; warmly; thankfully; strongly; unanimously; instinctively; deliberately; indifferently; condescendingly; cordially; unconditionally; thoughtlessly; entirely; unqualifiedly; rapturously; delightedly; privately; vigorously; sagely; completely; condescendingly; tacitly; partially; enthusiastically; grudgingly; reluctantly; overwhelmingly.
(See commend, sanction, favor.)

APPROXIMATION

adjectives
progressive; well-bred; thematic; urbane; close; clear; definite.

APRON

adjectives
gingham; ridiculous; filthy; frilled; generous; snowy; tiny; flowered; humble; voluminous; diminutive; coarse; greasy; billowy; prophylactic; womanish.

APT

adverbs
adroitly; cleverly; specially; dexterously; felicitously; expertly; intelligently; practically; technically; ably; artistically; capably; cunningly; deftly; handily; ingeniously; proficiently; scientifically; shrewdly; remarkably; unusually.

APTITUDE

adjectives
natural; intellectual; remarkable; judicial; military; special; mechanical; oratorical; hidden; artistic; singular; curious; high; unusual; characteristic; musical; surprising; versatile.

AQUEDUCT

adjectives
subterraneous; ancient; spacious.

ARAB

adjectives
tall; graceful; grave; dressed; big; powerful; surly; harmless; wiry; black-bearded; black-browed; courteous; hawk-faced; fine-looking; excited; fierce-looking; chivalrous; filthy; ragged; imperturbable; amorous.

ARABESQUE

adjectives
elfin; exquisite.

ARBITER

adjectives
unprejudiced; just; trembling; implacable.

ARBITRARY

adverbs
overwhelmingly; extraordinarily; despotically; domineeringly; intolerably; paternally; patriarchally; dictatorially; imperiously; presumptuously; harshly; strictly; severely; tyrannically; oppressively; cruelly; haughtily; obdurately; positively; relentlessly; sternly; neatly; unreasonably; excessively; unbelievably; offensively; dangerously; alarmingly.

ARBITRATION

adjectives
compulsory; bloody; impartial; friendly.

verbs
abide by—; accept—; adopt—; advocate—; ascertain by—; compel—; conduct—; control by—; decide by—; discuss—; employ—;

56

obtain—; put to—; renounce—; respect—; seek—; submit to—; —adjusts; —adverts; —avoids; —awards; —conciliates; —considers; —determines; —judges; —negotiates; —referees; —results in; —settles; —succeeds.
(See decision.)

ARBOR
adjectives
rustic; flowering; sequestered; private; moving; gigantic; latticed; conical; bowery; sultry.

ARC
adjectives
deadly; skyward; graceful; fiery; luminous; friedelite; speed-blurred; controlling; unthinkable; zooming; ethereal; splendid; deficient; recurrent; flaming.

ARCADE
adjectives
blind; massive; sheltered; garish

ARCH
adjectives
dignified; old; majestic; steel-trussed; artistic; echoing; horizontal; darkened; graceful; vast; livid; rustic; crumbling; leafy; peaked; magnificent; triumphal; subtle; elliptical; boundless; crystal; culminant; groined; successive; massive; shadowy; proscenium; titanic; accursed; rainbow; emerald; dazzling; topsy-turvy; inverted; cragged; shallow; stupendous; squashed; overworked; collapsed; glistening; flowery; melancholy; starry; tendriled; brazen; rising; interlacing; dim; somber; fretted.

verbs
adorn—; assemble—; cap—; construct—; crown—; develop—; employ—; erect—; form—; point—; span—; vault—; —carries; —commemorates; —curves; —gives way; —graces; —spans; —spreads; —strides over; —supports.
(See curve.)

ARCH (*v*)
adverbs
servilely; solidly; deeply; majestically; artistically; gracefully; magnificently; triumphally; massively.

ARCHAEOLOGIST
adjectives
distinguished; spectacular; venerable.

ARCHAEOLOGY
verbs
delve into—; derive from—; owe to—; study —; —absorbs; —accomplishes; —attempts; —attracts; —authenticates; —brings to light; —catalogues; —classifies; —collects; —compares; —concerns; —concludes; —conserves; —deals with; —deciphers; —decodes; —designates; —digs; —discovers; —disputes; —excavates; —fills in; —influences; —investigates; —marks; —misleads; —portrays; —preserves; —progresses; —recognizes; —reconstructs; —records; —rejects; —relates; —restores; —reveals; —scratches; —searches; —seeks; —sheds light upon; —surveys; —traces; —uncovers; —unravels.
(See science.)

ARCHAIC
adverbs
hopelessly; entirely; poetically; obviously; admittedly; veritably; venerably; traditionally; respectably; genteelly.

ARCHITECT
adjectives
philandering; eminent; self-constituted; consultant; ingenious; known; cunning; celebrated; fledgling; uninterested; creative; imaginative; successful; general; practical; exuberant; contemporary; admirable; lavish; discreet; romantic; symmetry-loving.

ARCHITECTURAL
adverbs
elaborately; chastely; unmistakably; charmingly; poetically; impressively; elegantly; tastefully; traditionally; nobly; ornately; rustically; historically; ecclesiastically; intricately; fantastically.

ARCHITECTURE
adjectives
primitive; diverse; ornate; semi-classic; elaborate; gilded; garbled; symphonic; charming; curious; rustic; organic; naval; noble; plastic; surrounding; historic; repellent; stodgy; colonial; editorial; ecclesiastical; florid; massive; distinctive; domestic; fantastic; traditional; impressive; intricate; tasteful; incrusted; elegant; incomparable; internal; diverse; rambling; poetic.

verbs
acquaint with—; adorn —; apply—; appreciate—; apprentice to—; build—; characterize—; conceive—; consider—; construct—; create—; crystallize—; decorate—; design

—; desolate—; destroy—; develop—; dress
—; embellish—; embody in—; emphasize
—; encourage—; enrich—; exhibit—; imitate—; immortalize—; practise—; preserve
—; produce—; proportion—; raise—; regard—; regulate—; restore—; resuscitate
—; revivify—; —adorns; —arises; —arranges; —consists; —designs; —details;
—enables; —evolves from; —flourishes; —
implies; —includes; —involves; —ornaments; —requires; —solves; —tends toward;
—trains; —transfigures.
(See building, art.)

ARCHIVES
adjectives
historical; secret; incriminating; inexhaustible; enriched; treasured; indestructible; national; enduring.

verbs
burn—; conserve in—; deposit in—; preserve in—; record in—; register in—; rummage through—; store in—; superintend—;
unlock—; —document; —include; —preserve; —record; —relate.
(See records, documents.)

ARCHWAY
adjectives
grated; sunken; ancient; ponderous; shining.

ARCTIC
adverbs
frigidly; frostily; rigorously; horribly;
shiveringly; bleakly; coldly; freezingly;
glacially; inclemently; piercingly; pinching-
ly; nippingly; rawly; intolerably; killingly;
stiffly; frozenly; unbelievably; unbearably.

ARDENT
adverbs
youthfully; brightly; indiscreetly; amazingly; warmly; tenderly; generously; instinctively; impetuously; furiously; poetically;
passionately; mutually; hastily; impulsively; irrepressibly; ingenuously; irresistibly;
fervently; fervidly; anxiously; avidly; fondly; affectionately; devotedly; hungrily;
yearningly; ambitiously; breathlessly; eagerly; insatiably; wistfully; sincerely; rapturously; ecstatically; racily; glowingly;
feverishly; earnestly; emotionally; acutely;
deeply.

ARDOR
adjectives
clean; bright; open-hearted; indiscreet; fiery;
youthful; beauteous; amazing; cooled; revolutionary; tender; generous; characteristic; instinctive; inexplicable; impetuous;
furious; sacrificial; covert; renewed; dampened; fastidious; poetic; passionate; mutual;
tedious; professional; new-born; obsessing;
war-like; wandering; hasty; impulsive;
ready; redoubled; irrepressible; intrepid;
exaggerating; emulous; heroic; ingenious;
martial; patriotic; lyrical; military; submissive; irresistible; fervent.

verbs
burn with—; confine—; dampen—; effulge
with—; electrify with—; extinguish—; fire
with—; flame with—; heat with—; intensify—; pursue with—; radiate—; spend—;
—abates; —swells; —wanes; —warms; —
waxes.
(See eagerness, zeal, fervor, enthusiasm,
warmth.)

ARDUOUS
adverbs
relatively; tremendously; overwhelmingly;
formidably; unbelievably; supremely; gravely; seriously; administratively; physically;
obviously; naturally; peculiarly; necessarily;
unpleasantly; conspicuously; alarmingly;
dishearteningly; incredibly; intricately; embarrassingly; perplexingly; complexly; desperately; perversely; occasionally.

AREA
adjectives
immense; unexplored; swampy; suburban;
consolidated; misty; outlying; considerable;
combined; vast; interior; populated; arid;
scenic; circumscribed; stagnant; marshy;
interstitial; limited; treeless; straggling;
gale-swept; huge; enormous; bewildering;
prolific; petty; devastated; inconspicuous; decreasing; unobstructed; forest; hazardous;
widening; cultivable; superficial; diminished; liberal; super-productive; pestilential;
varying; cleared; enveloping; trading; unpeopled; restricted; restoration; stone;
faunal.

verbs
apply to—; approach—; bound—; cover—;
cultivate—; define—; denude—; determine
—; distinguish—; encircle—; enclose—;
erect on—; excavate—; fence in—; give
access to—; infest—; level—; limit—; measure—; reclaim—; remove from—; scatter
over—; vacate—.
(See space, tract, portion, ground, yard.)

ARENA
adjectives
fit; conspicuous; commercial; frenzied;
bloody; foggy; diplomatic.

58

verbs
combat in—; conflict in—; contend in—; display in—; emerge from—; enclose in—; flood—; jam—; perform in—; plunge into —; strew—; surround—; throng—.

(See space, field.)

ARGUE (v)
adverbs
persuasively; placatingly; elusively; understandingly; thoughtfully; drawlingly; fallaciously; rationalistically; preposterously; sensibly; captiously; lamely; fairly; roughly; impressively; profoundly; affirmatively; excitedly; hypercritically; vainly; irrationally; indefatigably; wisely; logically; adversely; scientifically; sophistically; deviously; contentiously; cantankerously; discursively; priggishly; clumsily; pettishly; hypothetically; ingeniously; crushingly; exhaustively; lucidly; formidably; tellingly; irrefutably; fruitlessly; acrimoniously; equivocally; irritatingly; stubbornly; superfluously; abusively; circuitously.

(See plead, remonstrate, discuss, dispute.)

ARGUMENT
adjectives
ingenious; powerful; affirmative; reasonable; sound; winning; crowning; notable; crushing; logical; acceptable; exhaustive; irresistible; conclusive; weighty; strong; favorable; effective; broad; doughty; truthful; unanswerable; cogent; forceful; basic; substantial; formidable; lucid; imaginative; eager; precious; matchless; intensive; illuminating; flawless; clear-cut; telling; close-knit; irrefutable; practical; heated; forensic; sonorous; eloquent; vehement; revolutionary; bitter; fiery; sharp; impassioned; ferocious; stale; fallacious; insidious; spurious; old; painful; futile; nervous; confused; specious; needless; feeble; conflicting; fruitless; influential; nation-wide; mild; half-playful; solemn; mathematical; typical; endless; extended; editorial; interminable; constant; protracted; final; prolific; deliberate; persistent; lengthy; wordless; delightful; good-selling; long-standing; widespread; impetuous; inevitable; rapid; brilliant; well-rounded; acrimonious; theistic; undeniable; utilitarian; scientific; moral; inconsiderable; violent; lofty; bloody; dispassionate; solid; grave; vulgar; absent; craven; staple; personal; positive; labored; rational; earnest; commonplace; hair-splitting; ampler; penetrating; embodied; outspoken; equivocal; irritating; convincing; coarse; adverse; timid; stubborn; wearisome; wretched; judicious; superfluous; honest; enticing; slender; abusive; keen; potent; concise; odd; maternal; clear; close.

verbs
admit—; advance—; anticipate—; arm with —; arrange—; attack—; base—; bolster—; bolt—; bring forth—; burnish—; clinch—; color—; combat—; construct—; counter with —; debate—; deduce—; demolish—; derive —from; destroy—; dispense with—; dispute —; dread—; drive home—; employ—; engage in—; enumerate—; explain—; fashion —; force—; found on—; ground upon—; indulge in—; invalidate—; kindle—; maintain—; marshal —s; meet—; open—; oppose—; permit of—; premise—; proffer—; propose—; prove—; provoke—; pursue—; push—; qualify—; question—; rebut—; reduce to—; refute—; reiterate—; remove—; resume—; scorn—; settle—; sift—; steel with—; stir—; substantiate—; support—; weigh—; —appeals; —confounds; —depends on; —drones on; —fades away; — implies; —impresses; —infers; —involves; —rages; —rests on; —s simmer down; —s wax hot.

(See reason, proof, debate, discussion, dispute, controversy.)

ARGUMENTATIVE
adverbs
sagaciously; readily; disagreeably; hotly; sagely; offensively; cleverly; adroitly; ingeniously; reasonably; irresistibly; obstinately; pesteringly; abusively; stubbornly; convincingly; mulishly; irritatingly; dispassionately; earnestly; violently; acrimoniously; brilliantly; impetuously; interminably; endlessly; playfully; solemnly; fruitlessly; mildly; feebly; needlessly; nervously; insidiously; unnecessarily; ferociously; bitterly; significantly; foolishly; intelligently; astutely; shrewdly; vigilantly.

ARID
adverbs
dessicatingly; terribly; rainlessly; horribly; intolerably; unbearably; unproductively; wildly; fruitlessly; treelessly; dustily; insufferably; hopelessly; desperately; bitterly; malignly; pestiferously; agonizingly; heartbreakingly; destructively; murderously; joylessly; desolately; insupportably; dolorously.

ARISE (v)
adverbs
involuntarily; energetically; automatically;

spontaneously; pretentiously; incessantly; majestically; strenuously; readily; imperceptibly; irresistibly; hastily.

(See rise, ascend, mount, proceed.)

ARISTOCRACY

adjectives

odious; genuine; true; privileged; effete; heaven-descended; remarkable; gilded; canine; feudal; landed; moribund; pampered; devout; old; dominant; hereditary; high; admitted; recognized; idle; proud; democratic; industrial; sword-girt; phantasmal; martial.

verbs

attain—; break down—; choose from—; compose—; denote—; distinguish—; imperil —; oppose—; overthrow—; pervert—; privilege—; rank among—; strengthen—; vest in—; weaken—; —abuses; —administrates; —conforms; —degenerates; —develops from; —enlists; —fosters; —governs; —lolls; —predominates; —rules; —wields.

(See nobility, peerage, class, government.)

ARISTOCRAT

adjectives

bloated; proud; ante bellum; wealthy; exiled; hot-tempered; born; disgraced; snobbish; cosmopolitan; country; liberal; embryo; impoverished; stripling; emigrant; soft-voiced.

ARISTOCRATIC

adverbs

proudly; genuinely; truly; admittedly; tenaciously; inherently; innately; fantastically; snobbishly; nobly; actually; elegantly; unaffectedly; avowedly; unquestionably; palpably; essentially; stubbornly; ostentatiously; conspicuously; eminently; grandly; imposingly; magnificently.

ARK

adjectives

doveless; guarded; grounded.

ARM

adjectives

beautiful; tapering; superb; perfect; sculptured; marble-smooth; shaped; spiritual; graceful; delicate; slim; daisy-white; slender; golden; tender; soft; fragile; brawny; muscular; steel; iron; terrifying; strong; powerful; stout; tremendous; muscle-corded; firm; capable; sinewy; enormous; massive; mighty; bony; puny; thin; snaky; frail; lean; plump; thick; rounded; chubby; flab-by; awkward; clumsy; grisly; profaning; threatening; offending; degraded; shattered; wounded; wasted; molded; numb; aching; bruised; limp; drowsy; languid; listless; waving; gesticulating; beckoning; outstretched; clutching; outflung; extended; proffered; hanging; rigid; outspread; wide-open (pl); reaching; classical; uplifted; imploring; dangling; upraised; crossed (pl); wan; throbbing; swaying; swinging; linked; shaking; silken; jeweled; uniformed; khaki-clad; veiled; soapy; bare; powdered; hirsute; overlong; fearful; willing; sheltering; protecting; pacifying; combined (pl); engulfing; encircling; supporting; wandering; longing; waiting; accusing; thankful; reluctant; yearning; affectionate; reassuring; flailing; nerveless; tremulous; developed; incredible; ineffective; enthusiastic; detaining; wriggling; reinforcing; impulsive; derisive; forging; bewildered; rapturous; whirlwind; alabaster; movable; crooked; potent; swirling; remorseless; glittering; generous; unsuspected; mutual; temporal; swordless; disposing; gigantic; resplendent; large; fetching; elephantine; revengeful; pendent; lithe; barren; seraphic; twining; motherly; impatient; fearsome; restful; despised; unwieldy; braving; stiffened; sausage-like; unloaded; gilded; speckled; gnarled; angular; hungry; aching; dingy; cautious; protesting; victorious; desolate; almighty; grotesque; ponderous; rebellious; shaggy; puissant; steadying; poetic; enticing; conjugal; wrathful; sustaining; furbished; oft-bended; pleached; dimpled; grounded; sinuous; shining; dazzling; figured; artificial; feeble; gross; snowy; loving; withered; impeccable; mailed; restful; troublesome; gorgeous; fondling; out-reaching; restraining; springy; naked; lascivious; locked (pl); municipal; amputated; freckled; unreasoning; chapel-like; dusky; official; embracing; unhallowed; burnished; alien; faith-clad; waxen; needful; hairy-fibred; sturdy; akimbo (pl); strangling; glowing; lily; secular; band-aged; steel-strong; dissonant; puffy; boneless; broken; stalwart; whirring; blazoned (pl); branching (pl).

verbs

amputate—; attach—to; bare—; bind—; cast —s around; clasp in —s; cradle in —s; cross —s; dangle on—; develop—; drive-through; embrace in —s; encircle in —s; encumber —s; enfold in —s; entwine in —s; extend —s; extricate —s; flap —s; fling—around; fold —s; gather in —s; hail

with open —s; hang on —s; leap into —s; lend—; lock —s; impair the use of —s; open —s; paralyze —s; proffer—; pluck from —s; recline on—; rotate —s; sling —s; stretch out —s; strip from —s; support in —s; tear from —s; uncover —s; wave —s; wind in —s; wound—; wrap in—; wreathe in —s; —bleeds; —s cling around; — s dandle; —hangs; —projects.
(See limb, wrist.)

ARM (v)

adverbs
imperfectly; impenetrably; superbly; powerfully; mightily; threateningly; incredibly; ineffectively; puissantly; sturdily; stalwartly.

ARMADA

adjectives
air; huge; mighty; ponderous; impressive; death-dealing.

ARMAMENT

adjectives
unchecked; formidable; excessive; national; increased; vaunted; enormous; splendid; considerable.

verbs
appropriate for—; discard—; equip with—; limit—; outlaw—; produce—; rebuild—; reduce—; rehabilitate—; replace—; scale down—; strip of—; —s collapse; —s exceed.
(See force, guns.)

ARM-CHAIR

adjectives
palatial; chintz-covered; cushioned; shabby; restful; spacious; luxurious.

ARMISTICE

adjectives
unspoken; assumed; undeclared; disregarded.

ARMOR

adjectives
adamantine; customary; shining; sunbright; noticeable; virginal; magic; mortal; radiant; incongruous; elaborate; tough; chain; safest; steel-plated; jointless; impenetrable; protective; defensive; invisible; golden; horny; inviolate; spiritual; battered; granite; celestial.

verbs
buckle on—; burden with—; burnish—; clad in—; clothe in—; collect—; cover with

—; defend in—; design—; discard—; employ—; enclose in—; furnish—; harness in —; pad—; pierce—; plate with—; scar—; scour—; sheathe in—; stain—; strip off—; swagger in—; —clashes; —gives way; —hampers; —jingles; —protects; —resists; —shields.
(See steel.)

ARMS
(weapons)

adjectives
purposeful; puny; ruthless; skilfully-handled; unfriendly.

verbs
abate—; abolish—; bear—; burnish—; call to—; chastise with—; defend with—; display—; draw—; engage with—; excel in—; exploit with—; fire—; force with—; furnish —; groove—; invent—; lack—; lay down —; leap to—; march in—; notch—; order —; present—; rally to—; rattle—; repel with—; resist with—; rise in—; shoulder —; smuggle—; surrender—; take by force of—; take up—; throw away—; train in—; wield—; win with—; —clash; —run out.
(See weapons.)

ARMY

adjectives
bristling; cleverly-concealed; cold-staring; death-dealing; destruction-spilling; flashing; sullen; grim-looking; grisly; havoc-playing; malignant; murderous; make-shift; exalted; exultant; invincible; indefatigable; gallant; superb; glorious; determined; splendid; formidable; magnificent; picked; distressed; retreating; doomed; ragged; unpaid; disgruntled; decimated; demoralized; domestic; defeated; pathetic; tarnished; recalcitrant; standing; motor-camping; contending; organized; modern; vast; surging; invading; beleaguering; besieging; heterogeneous; overwhelming; furtive; ravishing; enraged; respective; heathen; cooperating; dwindling; fraternal; opposing; immense; precious; powerful; half-famished; dispersed; concentrated; rude; innumerable (pl); incompetent; victorious; scattered; solid; flying; compact; well-commanded; self-reliant; enthusiastic; principal; desolating; provisional; starry; wrangling; succoring; allied; obstinate; barefoot; omnipotent; shattered; phantom; insurgent; faithful; melancholy; deplorable; routed.

verbs
call out—; clothe—; command—; conscript into—; consolidate—; dash at—; defy—; demobilize—; disband—; discharge—; discipline—; dishearten—; dismiss—; disperse

—; double—; drill—; encompass—; engage—; enlist in—; equip—; evacuate—; furlough—; harry—; hire—; impress into—; improvise—; increase—; join—; mechanize —; mobilize—; motorize—; muster—; organize—; pledge—; provide—; provision —; raise—; recruit—; regiment—; route —; serve in—; supply—; support—; transport—; turn—to flight; —assembles; — blockades; —charges; —converges on; — crusades; —encamps; —intercepts; —mutinies; —pillages; —plunders; —retires; — retreats; —rumbles; —rushes in; —storms; —strikes; —swarms; —wages war.

(See troops, soldiers, forces.)

AROMA
adjectives
fruity; exquisite; peculiar; offensive; fragrant; spicy; pungent; delicious; pleasant; remote; earthly; preprandial; tempting; lingering; sickly; intoxicating; faint; ineffable; questionable; delicate; luscious; quick; penetrating.

verbs
breathe in—; dissipate—; exhale—; imitate —; send forth—; —escapes; —floats; — pervades.

(See perfume, fragrance, odor.)

AROMATIC
adverbs
pleasantly; spicily; fragrantly; redolently; sweetly; pungently; arrestingly; refreshingly; pleasingly; definitely; strongly; delicately; exquisitely; enchantingly; charmingly; drowsily; faintly; overpoweringly; delectably; softly; intoxicatingly; lingeringly; richly; attractively; exotically.

AROUSE (v)
adverbs
thoroughly; seditiously; instantaneously; antagonistically; suddenly.

(See excite, rouse, animate, stimulate.)

ARRAIGNMENT
adjectives
harsh; eloquent; appalling; incredible.

ARRANGE (v)
adverbs
dramatically; delicately; becomingly; temptingly; alphabetically; elaborately; admirably; systematically; beautifully; sensibly; exquisitely; harmoniously; ideally; felicitously; obviously; cleverly; efficiently; hid-

eously; crudely; clumsily; finally; previously; complexly; artistically; mechanically; methodically; ostensibly; confidentially; painfully.

(See classify, dispose, devise, contrive.)

ARRANGEMENT
adjectives
balanced; careful; impeccable; admirable; ideal; pleasant; impromptu; serene; formal; elaborate; desirable; skilful; felicitous; fair; obvious; regular; clever; cordial; efficent; divine; empty; attractive; devious; inequitable; hideous; crude; clumsy; final; judgmatical; fiscal; temporary; previous; spacious; preconcerted; incompatible; defensive; complex; dinette; cunning; provident; inconsistent; due; pleasure-principle; special; dilapidated; artistic; compensatory; mechanical; disconcerting; free-wheeling; line; practical; rectilinear; methodical; curious; graceful; established; fairest; simple; credit; harmonious; picturesque; traditional; fitting; domestic; ostensible; existing; unnatural; systematic; complicated; unsatisfactory; municipal; judicious; ingenious; charming; reciprocal; habitual; old-fashioned; dexterous; cumbrous; confidential; countermanded; painful; spacious.

verbs
adapt—; adjust—; adopt—; cancel—; criticize—; declare—; design—; desire—; determine—; devise—; dispute—; elaborate—; enter into—; furnish—; improvise—; insure—; negotiate—; order—; prepare—; prevent—; reach—; register—; repudiate—; standardize—; style—; welcome—; —conforms to; —disposes of; —prevails.

(See contract, understanding.)

ARRAY
adjectives
formidable; imposing; glorious; impressive; prodigious; rich; colorful; fascinating; enticing; neat; disordered; unsightly; stubborn; bristling; bridal; superb; abounding; motley; glittering; formal; endless; giddy; heterogeneous; bewildering; astonishing; comprehensive; superficial; hostile; confused; gorgeous; meek; gallant; militant; vivid; festival; flimsy; tranquil; immense; bright; terrible; meteor-eclipsing; incomparable; undisciplined; loose; vast; inexhaustible; noble; scattered; threatening; ragged; magnificent; grand; feudal; symmetrical; complete; awful; martial; chaste; white; stern; cold; battle; goodly; wild; flowering.

verbs
attire in—; break—; challenge—; deck in —; display—; draw up—; gaze at—; impose—; loose—; order—; outfit in—; rank in—; renew—; review—; stand in—; — impresses; —stretches.

(See display, exhibition.)

ARRAY (v)
adverbs
tastefully; gloriously; handsomely; formidably; impressively; richly; colorfully; fascinatingly; enticingly; superbly; formally; bewilderingly; superficially; vividly; gorgeously; incomparably; nobly.

(See arrange, marshal.)

ARREST
adjectives
arbitrary; capricious; frequent; summary; indiscriminate; wrongful; friendly; dreamy; injudicious; inspired; resisted; abrupt.

verbs
authorize—; charge with—; compel—; declare—; decree—; defend against—; delay —; demand—; dispense with—; effect—; enforce—; execute—; facilitate—; force to —; immunize against—; interfere with—; obtain—; order—; justify—; place under—; procure—of; release from—; resist—; restrain from—; result in—; secure—of; stop —; subject to—; warrant—; —deters; —s outnumber; —prevents.

(See imprisonment.)

ARREST (v)
adverbs
arbitrarily; unjustly; capriciously; summarily; indiscriminately; wrongfully; abruptly; injudiciously.

(See apprehend, stop, check, restrain.)

ARRIVAL
adjectives
mysterious; initial; late; speedy; unheralded; modest; merry; unconventional; noisy; bustling; timely; impending; abstract; successful; adventitious; seasonable; welcome; opportune; brilliant; unexpected; imminent; dread; anticipated.

ARRIVE (v)
adverbs
jubilantly; ultimately; punctually; incessantly; tardily; mysteriously; unconventionally; bustlingly; adventitiously; seasonably; opportunely; abruptly; expeditiously; slumberously.

(See come.)

ARROGANCE
adjectives
haughty; hard; cool; wounded; odd; splendid; stupid; vulgar; small; aesthetic; hot; unresponsive; tactless; desperate; despotic; supercilious; misstyled; unamiable; masculine; intellectual; tempered; monstrous; cynical; intolerable; meddlesome; ruffling; crested; burgher; blustering; brash; brusque; brisk; bristling; unbridled.

verbs
abandon—; disdain—; endure—; feed—; humble—; loathe—; purge the soul of—; satirize—; —causes; —indicates; —offends; —repels; —vexes.

(See assumption, assurance.)

ARROGANT
adverbs
intolerably; justifiably; noticeably; smugly; insolently; proudly; coolly; offensively; condescendingly; irritatingly; purposely; rudely; unpardonably; incurably; ridiculously; laughably; splendidly; oddly; stupidly; brashly; deplorably; uncivilly.

ARROW
adjectives
poisoned; fiery; answering; strong-shot; vengeful; ultimate; barbed; ineffectual; envenomed; burning; rankling; twanging; buried; eagle-plumed; crafty; featherless; swift; blunt; deadly; death-dealing.

verbs
aim—; barb—; bear—; discharge—; draw —; drop—; feather—; fire—; imbed—; lash—; let fly—; loose—; mark with—; notch—; pierce with—; pinch—; place—; point—; poison—; pour —s; release—; secure—; send—; shape—; shoot—; slay with —; smite with—; string—; throw off—; tip—; wound with—; —carries; —describes an arc; —glances off; —goes to the mark; —leaves; —passes; —penetrates; —pierces; —quivers; —reaches; —rides; —slips; — speeds; —wings.

(See dart, shaft.)

ART
adjectives
elaborate; consummate; undying; pleasurable; delicate; gentle; analogous; remarkable; serious; subtle; new; wonderful; ingenious; experienced; sophisticated; noblest; superb; ripe; gracious; obliging; unsurpassable; fine; tedious; glowing; profound; proficient; great; simple; sincere; glorious; pure; epic; meticulous; surpassing; graphic;

snubbed; aristocratic; modernistic; plastic; decorative; landscape; ancient; rustic; epistolary; contemporary; poetic; constructive; modern; applied; dramatic; elegant; antiquated; pyrotechnic; seeming; inscrutable; suave; finished; vanishing; fine; mystical; living; enviable; esoteric; replaced; cultured; lost; symbolic; fancy; hidden; servile; musical; colorless; blandishing (pl); kindred; perfidious; vital; culinary; fascinating; healing; peaceful; unpremeditated; specious; inventive; cunning; brain-spattering; baneful; fickle; windpipe-slitting; flawless; matchless; structural; virile; indigenous; superhuman; dreadful; tonsorial; imitative; classicizing; black; inharmonious; recreational; canonic; piscatorial; sunny; fertilizing; sublime; instrumental; regal; enrapturing; rational; idealistic; acquired; substantial; representative; lenient; vagrant; agile; equestrian; fearful; grotesque; public; deathless; prosperous; evasive; memorial; coarse; spiritual; abominable; inventive; exalted; mechanical; mortuary; histrionic; indifferent; vicious; living; coactive; quaint; empirical; irregular; incomprehensible; demoniacal; jealous; new-invented; loftier; orthodox: commercial; medical; ceramic; unhallowed: athletic; subservient; florid; classic; exquisite; practical; perishable; spontaneous; immature; elevated; patented; etched; menial; poor; low; voluptuous; illustrative; unlawful; rare; piquant; conspicuous.

verbs
animate—; apply—; appreciate—; attain—; awaken—; become—; breed—; caricaturize —; characterize—; choke—; compose—' comprehend—; conceive—; contrive by—; counterfeit—; cultivate—; dabble in—; deem —; devise—; devote to—; discriminate in —; display—; educate in—; elaborate—; embellish—; encourage—; etch—; evolve—; exaggerate—; execute—; exercise—; facilitate—; further—; glorify—; illustrate— imitate—; inaugurate—; influence—; interpret—; limit—; master—; murder—; originate—; ply—; practise—; preserve—; produce—; purge—; pursue—; refine—; school in—; stifle—; supplement—; sustain —; systematize—; take refuge in—; trace—; verse in—; wed to—; —achieves; —assists; —attains; —builds; —conceals; —depicts; —derives from; —dies away; —disguises; —embodies; —enlightens; —evolves from; —excites; —expresses; —feigns; —flourishes; —functions; —imitates; —lags; —languishes; —ornaments; —portrays; —re-

flects; —remains; —reproduces; —reveals. (See literature, science.)

ARTERY

adjectives
pulsating; hardened; tiny; petty; spiritual; emotional.

verbs
block—; circulate in —s; drain—; expel from—; flow through—; incise—; involve —; ligate—; live in—; lodge in—; nourish —; obstruct—; pump through—; rupture—; sever—; terminate—; —s anastomose; —s ascend; —s branch; —s carry; —s contract; —s deteriorate; —s distribute; —s divide; —s empty; —s function; —s harden; —s join; —s spurt; —s supply; —s thicken; —s throb; —s unite.

ARTFUL

adverbs
instinctively; characteristically; slyly; craftily; subtly; insidiously; stealthily; smoothly; shrewdly; fiendishly; maliciously; astoundingly; astutely; cunningly; insinuatingly; trickily; habitually; adroitly; manifestly; openly; undeniably; knowingly; suavely; ingratiatingly; speciously; expertly; dangerously.

ARTICLE
adjectives   (writing)
respective; undesirable; perfunctory; subsequent; able; valuable; detailed; forceful; inflammatory; unrelated; editorial; antiquarian; foregoing; explanatory; abusive; preliminary; hysterical; noteworthy; famous; fascinating; occasional; thought-provoking; enlightening; hypocritical; exasperating; comprehensive; arresting; lurid; delightful; frivolous; authentic; unusual; informative; striking; disturbing; sane; well-reasoned; sensible; condensed; inspired; vituperative; amusing; recent; fiery; stodgy; leading; stimulating; provocative; well-considered; critical; descriptive; proposed.

verbs
abolish—; administrate—; alter—; amend —; approve—; break—; combine —s; compose—; design—; dismiss—; dispute—; ease out—; emit—; enact—; entreat—; excerpt —; fashion—; form—; found upon—; invoke—; peruse—; point out—; prefix—; promote—; promulgate—; provide—; ratify—; reject—; revise—; rewrite—; sanction—; submit—; summarize—; swerve from—; transgress—; —asserts; —author-

izes; —binds; —compels; —concerns; —denotes; —effects; —exposes; —expostulates; —governs; —guarantees; —impeaches; —indicts; —libels; —regulates; —slanders; —specifies; —stipulates; —treats of.
(See detail, item, clause, editorial, essay.)

ARTICLE
adjectives (an object)
proprietary; admirable; charming; befrilled; practical; previous; metallic; objectionable; bloated; inferior; humblest; aggressive; cardinal; minutest; tempting; conspicuous; distinctive; cumbersome; superior; conceivable; forbidden; ancient; bulky; expensive; flimsy; showy; adulterated; intimate; plated; useful; novel; remarkable; superfluous; indispensable; harsher; inanimate; patented; preceding; fulminated; fugitive; non-durable; particular; obnoxious; important; suitable; necessary; principal; existing; resplendent; forbidden; unmistakable; toilet; serviceable; staple; unsightly; ornamental.

ARTICULATE (a)
adverbs
clearly; particularly; distinctly; emphatically; finely; especially; wonderfully; powerfully; unmistakably; cruelly; meticulously; precisely; exactly; easily.

ARTICULATE (v)
adverbs
precisely; faintly; meticulously; whisperingly; breathlessly; clearly.
(See speak.)

ARTICULATION
adjectives
supple; well-remembered; appreciative; meticulous.

ARTIFICE
adjectives
amazing; shallow; harmless; debasing; delicate; petty; plotted; ingenious; fictional; honest; dazzling; wicked.

ARTIFICER
adjectives
deft; cunning; fierce; sly; suave.

ARTIFICIAL
adverbs
subtly; stiffly; crudely; inelegantly; crassly; grotesquely; gracelessly; ponderously; highly; pretentiously; flashily; floridly; laughably; ridiculously; awkwardly; offensively; outlandishly; affectedly; coquettishly; simperingly; mincingly; stagily; smoothly; slyly; cleverly; adroitly; ingeniously.

ARTILLERY
adjectives
active; coastal; defiance-roaring; doomsounding; death-propelling; deafening; concerted; effective; earth-shaking; enormously-heavy; funeral-voiced; fierce-stabbing; incessant; liberal; offensive; reverberating; silenced; threatening; tumultuous; well-placed.

verbs
assign—; blast with—; capture—; command —; concentrate—; detail—; discharge—; disperse—; elevate—; employ—; encamp—; fear—; forge—; fortify—; improve—; introduce—; mechanize—; mount—; project —; reenforce with—; shelter from—; transport—; —attacks; —batters; —bears; —bombards; —breaks down; —concentrates on; —counters; —demolishes; —deploys; —destroys; —deteriorates; —devastates; —discharges; —fires; —forms; —handles; —harasses; —inflicts; —launches; —manoeuvers; —marches; —masses; —moves up; —occupies; —pounds; —projects; —pushes forward; —ranges; —reassembles; —repulses; —shells; —smashes; —supports; —thunders; —withdraws.
(See cannon, arms.)

ARTISAN
adjectives
tramping; skilled; capable; indolent; impatient; swarthy; humble; subordinate; simple; adroit.

ARTIST
adjectives
capable; excellent; first-rate; gifted; accomplished; competent; versatile; consummate; instinctive; true; creative; unerring; purposive; brilliant; conscientious; authentic; supreme; exquisite; cosmopolitan; keen-eyed; indefatigable; illustrious; great; cynical; world-famous; noted; distinguished; dissipated; weedy; sophisticated; temperamental; dissolute; adverse; melancholy; despairing; sought-after; pandering; unbusiness-like; impecunious; struggling; harassed; ragged; persecuted; misunderstood; detestable; sensitive; human; local; jealous; collaborating; fastidious; contemporary; eminent; eccentric; egotistic; excitable, fashionable; talented; outraged; accomplished; vulgar; scenic; native; mature; skilled;

well-known; inimitable; musical; liberal; unique; successful; sincere; decorative; technical; modern; renowned; interpretative.

verbs
confound—; encourage—; endow—; extol —; imitate—; inspire—; mark—; patronize —; remunerate—; revere—; —accomplishes; —apprehends; —attempts; —conceives; —contributes; —conveys; —creates; —cultivates; —designs; —displays; —elevates; —embodies; —employs; —endeavors; —entertains; —eschews; —executes; —expresses; —forges; —imbibes; —imitates; —opposes; —paints; —patterns; —portrays; —practises; —presents; —pursues; —renders; —reproduces; —reveals; —scorns; — sketches; —struggles with; —typifies; — unearths; —unfolds; —verses himself in.
(See sculptor, painter, musician, writer, poet, creator.)

ARTISTIC
adverbs
superbly; magnificently; delicately; actually; genuinely; indubitably; consummately; vividly; lustily; carefully; deftly; exultantly; studiedly; naturally; colorfully; richly; chastely; virginally; traditionally; radically; nostalgically; instinctively; inherently; innately; learnedly; creatively; unerringly; brilliantly; spontaneously; conscientiously; authentically; exquisitely; keenly; notably; temperamentally; sensitively; fastidiously; eminently; fashionably; inimitably; elegantly; gorgeously; magnificently; splendidly; radiantly; sublimely; bonnily; curiously; dazzlingly; passably; prettily; quaintly; showily; ingeniously; intrinsically; imitatively; academically; readily; correctly; easily; neatly; unaffectedly; crudely; ponderously; adroitly; cleverly; dexterously; intelligently; proficiently; skilfully; deftly; expertly; handily; critically; discriminatingly.

ARTISTRY
adjectives
superb; genuine; consummate; lusty; vivid; infinite; careful; deft; exalted; transcending; sheer; traditional; studied; fanatical.

ARTLESS
adverbs
unaffectedly; delightfully; refreshingly; sincerely; naively; touchingly; wondrously; manifestly; charmingly; ravishingly; exquisitely; deliciously; surprisingly; unbeliev-ably; graciously; ingenuously; alluringly; adorably; innocently.

ASCEND (v)
adverbs
magically; majestically; simultaneously; directly; unwaveringly; lazily; leisurely; personally.
(See mount.)

ASCENDANCY
adjectives
inherent; moral; intellectual; growing; fatal; odious; papal; commercial; personal; complete.

ASCENDANT
adverbs
significantly; prominently; interestingly; materially; substantially; emphatically; chiefly; firmly; cardinally; markedly; primarily; remarkably; signally; vitally; influentially; preponderantly; prevalently; dominantly; authoritatively; absolutely; supremely; blessedly; happily; luckily; unfortunately; adversely; unluckily.

ASCENT
adjectives
marked; breakneck; preliminary; formidable; continual; toilsome; gentle; gradual; measureless; feasible; elevated; winding; tortuous; sheer; interminable; perilous.
verbs
accomplish—; attempt—; fear—; grade—; overcome—; schedule—; top—; —fatigues; —slopes; —tires; —wearies.
(See climb.)

ASCERTAIN (v)
adverbs
accurately; distinctly; dimly; instantaneously; vaguely; unhesitatingly.
(See discover.)

ASCETIC
adverbs
austerely; exceptionally; completely; incomprehensibly; obviously; excessively; terribly; remarkably; innately; naturally; puritanically; rigidly; rigorously; strictly; severely; harshly; arbitrarily; despotically; tyrannically; prudishly; haughtily.

ASCRIBE (v)
adverbs
unanimously; vaguely; openly; modestly; unsparingly; deliberately; unhesitatingly; villainously; frankly.
(See attribute, assign, impute.)

adverbs

pallidly; neutrally; coldly; colorlessly; dingily; dully; faintly; muddily; wanly; pearly.

ASHES

adjectives

quenchless; fallen; gossamer-like; glowing; whitening; lifeless; dreamless; smouldering; sparkless; venerated; charred; damped; cold; livid; vile; volcanic; blackened; dead; humble; feeble.

verbs

collect—; exhaust into—; flick—; gather—; grovel in—; heap—; mix with—; powder —; pulverize—; reduce to—; scorch to—; sift—; sprinkle with—; strew with—; throw out—; —char; —flame; —glow; —pirouette down; —remain; —rest; —settle; —smoulder.

(See cinders, remains, residue.)

ASK (*v*)

adverbs

courteously; equably; genially; discreetly; vaguely; pointedly; cannily; unctuously; spitefully; specifically; evasively; incredulously; querulously; swiftly; bluntly; huskily; contemptuously; relentlessly; persuasively; listlessly; compassionately; placidly; critically; guardedly; grouchily; shrewdly; brusquely; involuntarily; guilelessly; insistently; delicately; piteously; beseechingly; impressively; audaciously; plaintively; ironically; deadly; tremulously; naively; belligerently; provisionally; quizzically; socratically; apprehensively.

(See inquire, question, beg.)

ASPECT

adjectives

interesting; practical; picturesque; attractive; encouraging; smiling; humorous; prepossessing; pleasing; romantic; charming; benevolent; calm; noteworthy; absurd; sinister; ominous; accusing; contradictory (pl); dismal; diabolical; grim; forbidding; jaded; ludicrous; sensual; cynical; unnatural; maddening; gloomy; ridiculous; woebegone; volatile; evanescent; odd; grisly; irrational; controversial; shocking; ethical; ceremonial; physical; legal; psychic; religious; psychological; moral; genetic; scientific; obvious; broad; eternal; suggestive; original; fresh; superficial; ingratiating; beneficent; harsh; astonished; intimate; emotional; national; economic; conventional; unique; grave; formal; ferocious; haggard; drawn; staring; piteous; forsaken; melancholy; wan; miserable; pallid; repulsive; formidable; enticing; cheery; weather-beaten; propitious; feminine; appealing; many-sided; festival; material; transitional; cadaverous; ironic; appalling; dark; interrelated (pl); insinuating; benignant; spiritual; unreal; artificial; unlovely; gloomy; tragic; mournful; neglected; mysterious; reverend; stern; belligerent; bleak; legal; aesthetic; incoherent; deserted; rustic; malign; utilitarian; forlorn; sanguine; primitive; alarming; supernatural; stunned; impressive; imposing; inspiring; weird; rigorous; chilling; intangible; classic; foreign; multiform; cultivated; settled.

verbs

accentuate—; adorn—; afford—; assume—; bear—; behold—; bend—; cloud—; color—; contemplate—; contrast—; dominate—; dramatize—; dwell on—; extol—; gaze at —; intensify—; meet—; muzzle—; regard —; stress—; take on—; turn—; view—; wear—; —speaks.

(See appearance, view, scene, expression, mien, look.)

ASPERSIONS

adjectives

obsolete; hasty; casual; thinly-veiled; bitter; subtle.

verbs

bespatter with—; cast—; let fall—; resort to—; vindicate from—; —besprinkle; —damage; —enrage; —infuriate; —soil; —stain.

(See slander, scandal, calumny.)

ASPIRANT

adjectives

baffled; literary; defeated; penitent; conscientious; judicial.

ASPIRATIONS

adjectives

generous; lofty; noble; national; boundless; passionate; vague; artistic; intellectual; glowing; elegant; pure; awakened; dictatorial; spiritual; unlimited; greedy; earnest; forgotten; exalted; exquisite; long-cherished; fond; sacred; speculative; political; moral; musical; social; scrupulous; secretive; rebuffed; undirected; ladylike; thwarted; professional; humdrum; poetic; determined; enthusiastic.

verbs

cherish—; deride—; dignify—; embody—;

fan with—; further—; give force to—; long with—; nurse—; realize—; restrain—; sigh with—; swamp—; thwart—; —is bounded by; —lifts him; —ripens; —soars.
(See ambition, desire, aim.)

ASPIRE (v)
adverbs
invariably; loftily; nobly; boundlessly; generously; passionately; artistically; intellectually; spiritually; earnestly; socially; professionally; poetically; determinedly; enthusiastically.
(See desire.)

ASS
adjectives
preposterous; incompetent; slow-gaited; conceited; affected; insignificant; arrant; pretentious; patient; gibbering; portentous; egregious; pompous.

verbs
act as—; brand—; breed —es; burden—; call—; corral —es; domesticate —es; employ —; harness—; overtake—; plow with —es; procure—; saddle—; shelter—; stall—; yoke —; —balks; —bears; —brays; —flees; —plods; —roams; —sniffs the wind; —strays; —subsists on.
(See animal.)

ASSAIL (v)
adverbs
abusively; fearlessly; unjustly; vituperatively; untruthfully; vaguely; furiously; keenly; constantly; perpetually; unrelentingly; doughtily; blood-thirstily; rudely; vociferously; audaciously; formidably; boldly.
(See attack.)

ASSAILANT
adjectives
fierce; quick; skillful; deadly; doughty; unrelenting; potent; unwary; blood-thirsty; rude; violent; savage; vociferous; audacious; powerful; bold; formidable; deceased.

ASSASSIN
adjectives
foiled; fiendish; jealous; vile; doomed; cool; professional; cowardly; terrorizing; wolfish; mercenary; well-meaning.

verbs
evade—; execute—; hire—; martyrize—; reward—; subdue—; —attacks; —conspires; —knifes; —lurks; —murders; —slays; —stabs; —terrorizes.
(See murderer.)

ASSASSINATE (v)
adverbs
treacherously; fiendishly; vilely; coolly; tragically.
(See kill.)

ASSASSINATION
adjectives
cold-blooded; murderous; foul; villainous; predatory.

verbs
accomplish—; aim at—; applaud—; attempt —; avert—; execute—; finish—; foment—; loathe—; pay for—; plot—; revenge—; witness—; —kindles.
(See murder, killing.)

ASSAULT
adjectives
intermittent; rude; meditated; critical; damnable; aggravated; gallant; fresh; feeble; furious; formidable; anonymous; salutary; murderous; vigorous; mock; contemplated; desperate; boisterous; drunken; base; vain; magnificent; counter; general; unprovoked; concentrated; criminal; inexplicable; destructive; terrific; simultaneous; felonious; courageous; vicious; serious; determined; savage; wicked; shrewd; frenzied; devastating; thorough-going.

verbs
aggravate—; bear—; carry by—; commit —; constitute—; counter—; defy—; fortify against—; gain by—; incur—; inflict—; intend—; make—upon; overthrow—; parallel—; project—; punish—; renew—; repeat —; repulse—; resist—; rush to—; scorn—; threaten with—; win by—; withstand—; —destroys; —produces; —weakens.
(See attack, charge, invasion, onslaught.)

ASSAULT (v)
adverbs
outrageously; violently; rudely; critically; damnably; gallantly; feebly; murderously; furiously; formidably; vigorously; desperately; boisterously; drunkenly; basely; vainly; magnificently; unprovokedly; criminally; inexplicably; destructively; simultaneously; feloniously; frenziedly; devastatingly.
(See attack, assail.)

ASSEMBLAGE
adjectives
vast; matchless; international; dazzling; brilliant; striking; immense; gracious; ad-

miring; hapless; motley; confused; popular; learned; glittering; melancholy; ludicrous; riotous; dreary; solemn; pitiful; plutocratic; chattering; variegated; august; hushed; listless; inattentive; public.

ASSEMBLE (v)

adverbs

elaborately; festively; tumultuously; confusedly; glitteringly; riotously; drearily; solemnly; pitifully; chatteringly; listlessly; publicly; inattentively.

(See congregate, gather, meet.)

ASSEMBLY

adjectives

fair; stormy; provincial; propitious; august; primary; legislative; glorious; numerous; gay; venerable; representative; illustrious; staid; significant; deliberative; electrified; distinguished; religious; truculent; uncongenial; periodical (pl); artless; orderly; polite.

verbs

address—; appoint to—; call—; compose—; convoke—; dismiss—; gather—; haunt—; lead—; organize—; pervade—; petition—; remodel—; salute—; set—against; unite in —; —abolishes; —adjourns; —annuls; —collects; —communes; —condemns; —congregates; —convenes; —decides; —decrees; —deliberates; —enforces; —excludes; —frames; —invests; —limits; —resolves; —suppresses.

(See meeting, congregation, council, conference.)

ASSENT

adjectives

unqualified; wordless; unanimous; preoccupied; spiritless; reluctant; deep-throated; provisional; silent; rational; requisite; cordial; vague; mournful; universal; callous; intellectual; placid; ready; brief; rapturous; smiling; rough; demure; enthusiastic; perfunctory; deliberate.

verbs

approve—; confess—; declare—; engage—; gain—; gesture—; imply—; mutter—; necessitate—; nod—; obtain—; promise—; purchase—; read—; require—; stir to—; vote—; vow—; win—; withdraw—; withhold—; yield—; —emanates; —signifies.

(See agreement, acquiescence, consent.)

ASSENT (v)

adverbs

grudgingly; appreciatively; graciously; solemnly; benevolently; ironically; indifferently; wordlessly; unanimously; unqualifiedly; spiritlessly; reluctantly; silently; cordially; vaguely; mournfully; callously; demurely; placidly; briefly; rapturously; enthusiastically; perfunctorily; deliberately.

(See concur, acquiesce, yield.)

ASSERT (v)

adverbs

positively; incredibly; blasphemously; unanimously; courageously; peremptorily; persistently; strenuously; dogmatically; emphatically; erroneously; eloquently; lustily; judicially; ignorantly; aggressively; boastfully; truculently; blandly; stalwartly; irresponsibly; autocratically; despotically; arbitrarily; fallaciously; contradictorily; presumptuously; vaingloriously; groundlessly; unequivocally; gratuitously.

(See affirm, state, say, declare.)

ASSERTION

adjectives

ignorant; lofty; vigorous; hare-brained; aggressive; emphatic; blundering; boastful; truculent; reiterated; extravagant; prior; impudent; audacious; wild; bland; complete; incredible; dogmatic; complimentary; intense; loud; incensed; controversial; irresponsible; sweeping; absolute; stalwart; astounding; autocratic; despotic; arbitrary; brutal; blustering; erroneous; pharisaical; fallacious; monstrous; disputable; contradictory; vainglorious; random; groundless; florid; deliberate; colorful; presumptuous; unequivocal; gratuitous.

verbs

affirm—; aver—; conclude—; contest—; contradict—; controvert—; credit—; declare —; defend—; flinch under—; justify—; maintain—; protest—; prove—; qualify—; refute—; sponsor—; support—; —contradicts; —elicits from; —liberates; —persuades; —sets free; —vindicates.

(See statement, declaration.)

ASSERTIVE

adverbs

loftily; aggressively; emphatically; boastfully; truculently; extravagantly; impudently; insolently; audaciously; arrogantly; blandly; confidently; dogmatically; irresponsibly; sweepingly; astoundingly; autocratically; despotically; imperiously; brutally; monstrously; vaingloriously; floridly; presumptuously; preposterously; unequivocally; heedlessly; rashly; brusquely; blatantly.

ASSESS (v)

adverbs
equitably; unjustly; annually; repeatedly.
(See rate.)

ASSET

adjectives
dubious; distinct; domestic; inestimable; stupendous; valuable; perdurable; tangible; priceless; frozen; unassailable; paramount; strategic; scenic; compelling.

verbs
assess—s; bear—; capitalize on—; claim—; collect—s; dissolve—; distribute—s; earn —s; falsify—; fix—; freeze—; include—; inflate—s; inherit—; liquidate—; market—; note—; omit—; possess—; reduce—; represent—; salvage—; take over—; trade—; undervalue—; water—; work—; —s appear; —s increase; —s shrink; convert into —s; deduct from—; defer—.
(See property, resources, effects, possessions.)

ASSEVERATE (v)

adverbs
repeatedly; hotly; continually; sincerely; persistently; whole-heartedly; coldly; pleasantly.
(See declare.)

ASSIDUITY

adjectives
attentive; persevering; unremitting; discriminating; devastating; relentless; parental; bee-like; well-meaning.

ASSIDUOUS

adverbs
conscientiously; painfully; perseveringly; dependably; unremittingly; energetically; industriously; reliably; faithfully; amazingly; unusually; remarkably; loyally; uncomplainingly; unwaveringly; invariably; uniformly; persistently; constantly.

ASSIGN (v)

adverbs
subsequently; precisely; rigorously; pedagogically; frequently; unthinkingly.
(See allot, apportion, appoint.)

ASSIGNMENT

adjectives
elaborate; roving; precise; glamorous; charming; pedagogical; rigorous; impossible; difficult.

verbs
accept—; administer—; advance—; allot—; alter—; appoint to—; apportion—; authorize—; block—; botch—; bungle—; create —; designate—; determine—; dispose of—; earn—; exempt from—; free from—; fulfill—; interest in—; merit—; muff—; nominate for—; pass—; point out—; reject—; relieve of—; set to—; share—; specify—; transfer—; wangle—; —consists of; —denotes; —pays.

ASSIMILATE (v)

adverbs
actively; readily; unhesitatingly; spiritually; painfully; whole-heartedly; easily.
(See absorb.)

ASSIMILATION

adjectives
ready; spiritual; difficult.

ASSIST (v)

adverbs
industriously; chivalrously; materially; cordially; officiously; vigorously; effectively; financially; invaluably; charitably; generously; medically; professionally; scientifically; voluntarily; temporarily; mechanically; indispensably; skillfully; mutually; vicariously.
(See help, aid.)

ASSISTANCE

adjectives
masculine; armed; pecuniary; financial; material; invaluable; ineffectual; extraneous; charitable; generous; medical; scientific; voluntary; professional; temporary; mechanical; outside; indispensable; skilled; additional; tactful; mutual.

verbs
accept—; afford—; contribute—; crave—; disdain—; entreat—; furnish—; further with—; lend—; limit—; present—; procure—; rely upon—; render—; requisition —; solicit—; swear—; win by—; —enables; —encourages.
(See aid, relief, cooperation, help, support.)

ASSISTANT

adjectives
capable; patient; faithful; self-sacrificing; esteemed; untrained; temporary; fledgling; green-eyed; detached; ambidexterous; qualified; voluble; clinical; able; scholarly.

verbs

advance—; appoint—; choose—; dispatch —; —accompanies; —aids; —cooperates; —endeavours; —practices; —stands by.
(See partner.)

ASSOCIATE

adjectives

habitual; blithe; old-time; ill-looking; dignified; daring; vulgar; confidential; barbarian; cherished; hardened; crafty; literary; business; questionable; unsavory; droll; gallant; close; intimate.

verbs

applaud —s; exile —s; idolize —s; prevail upon —s; —s accompany; —s ally with; —s belong; —s cooperate; —s share; —s unite.
(See companion, colleague, partner.)

ASSOCIATE (v)

adverbs

inalienably; intimately; indissolubly; inseparably; profoundly; fraternally; indelibly; habitually; vulgarly; daringly; confidentially; craftily; questionably; drolly; closely.
(See connect.)

ASSOCIATION

adjectives

intimate; gloomy; ancestral; disparate; incidental; promiscuous; philanthropic; mournful; obscure; historical; tenuous; scandalous; polite; charitable; congenial; unpleasant; childish; cherished; tender; undefinable; endearing; memorable; haphazard; obligatory; natural; exclusive; ghastly; imperious; voluntary; indissoluble; subtle; casual; facile; aesthetic; unanalyzed; curious; struggling; unsavory; venerable; daily; picturesque; legendary; democratic; classic.

verbs

admit to—; affiliate with—; awaken—; combine in—; conceive—; confederate into —; conjure up —s; connect with—; deal with—; disband—; disorganize—; disrupt —; distinguish—; endow—; establish—; exclude from—; expel from—; father—; found—; frequent—; immortalize—; incorporate—; laud—; league into—; manage—; nurse—; oppose—; organize—; outlaw—; quarter at—; revive—; support—; terminate—; unite in—; vouch for—; — aims at; —classifies; —s combine; —confers upon; —flourishes; —fosters; —rivals; —sets forth; —springs up.
(See alliance, fellowship, affiliation, connection.)

ASSORTMENT

adjectives

imposing; varied; appealing; hideous; heterogeneous; distinguished; tangled; remarkable; excellent; amazing; complete; exceptional; motley; disintegrated; outstanding; vast; crude; comprehensive; diversified; odd; generous; extensive; incongruous; confused; conglomerated; concentrated; balanced; **weird.**

ASSUME (v)

adverbs

presumptuously; gradually; voluntarily; dogmatically; hypothetically; commonly; vigorously; unconsciously; unlawfully; tacitly; boastfully; superciliously; playfully; theatrically; irritatingly; erroneously; gratuitously; whimsically; groundlessly; complacently; fallaciously; blandly; smugly; ungraciously; baselessly; traditionally; fundamentally; falsely; imperturbably; candidly; placidly; fatuously; humorously; viciously; unpardonably; arrogantly; innocently.
(See undertake, presume, accept, usurp.)

ASSUMPTION

adjectives

tacit; boastful; supercilious; theatrical; sweeping; charitable; playful; irritating; erroneous; verbal; gratuitous; transparent; whimsical; preposterous; groundless; natural; complacent; calm; wearied; unparalleled; fallacious; unwarranted; commonplace; absurd; precarious; mute; hereditary; bland; smug; ungracious; critical; baseless; plausible; traditional; fundamental; reckless; false; imperturbable; candid; gross; placid; random; shallow; unconcealed; fatuous; humorous; vicious; unproved; undue; gentlemanly; unpardonable; arrogant; innocent.

verbs

accept—; adopt—; anticipate—; contest—; grant—; guide by—; lay bare—; limit—; pardon—; predicate upon—; proceed upon —; steer clear of—; sustain—; take up—; throw out—; verify—; warrant—; weigh —; —holds; —implies; —leads.
(See supposition.)

ASSURANCE

adjectives

gracious; positive; easy; lavish; pleasant; solemn; full; happy; sincere; serene; unqualified; mute; respectful; modest; delicate; advance; dispassionate; tender; sufficient; renewed; calm; comforting; blissful; counterfeit; diplomatic; vain; insolent;

convincing; serious; limitless; reciprocal; mutual; characteristic; uncomfortable; ineffable; lukewarm; well-founded; disbelieved; inner; loquacious; inspiriting; exquisite; disheartening; definite; false; absolute; emphatic; melodious; tranquil; dampening; ponderous; smiling; gentle; cool; diminishing; considerable; significant; bland; waning; professional; swaggering; ineradicable; unwavering; infallible; magnificent; smug; defiant; blunt; insensitive; brassy.

verbs
breed—; confirm—; convey—; establish—; flash—; guarantee—; handle with—; inspire—; pledge—; procure—; promise—; renew—; rest in—; secure—; smile—.
(See confidence, conviction, trust.)

ASSURE (v)
adverbs
virtually; solemnly; diligently; indolently; secretly; vaguely; reasonably; positively; lavishly; serenely; unqualifiedly; mutely; respectfully; modestly; tenderly; diplomatically; insolently; convincingly; reciprocally; mutually; characteristically; absolutely; emphatically; tranquilly; blandly; professionally; swaggeringly; unwaveringly; infallibly; defiantly; bluntly.

ASTONISH (v)
adverbs
sublimely; rousingly; amazingly; silently; profoundly; inconceivably; utterly; unboundedly; inexpressibly; blankly; palpably; unmistakably; intensely; unaffectedly; ludicrously; dramatically.
(See amaze, astound, stagger.)

ASTONISHMENT
adjectives
respectful; amused; tempestuous; unrestrained; affronted; silent; rapturous; whimsical; fat; pure; feigned; involuntary; mute; profound; initial; inconceivable; liveliest; unspeakable; utter; unbounded; swift; indignant; delighted; ever-increasing; inexpressible; horrified; dull; dawning; contemptuous; blank; palpable; sardonic; unmistakable; puzzled; intense; fond; breathless; wordless; annoyed; unaffected; acute; uncomfortable; curious; faint; open-mouthed; petrified; bitter; wide-eyed; stupefied; ludicrous; dramatic; sheer; hurt; shocked; bored; bald.

verbs
benumb with—; blink with—; confuse—; elicit—; excite—; express—; feign—; gasp with—; move to—; numb with—; paralyze with—; pretend—; quell—; restrain—; seize with—; stagger with—; stupefy—; supersede—.
(See amazement, surprise, wonder.)

ASTOUND (v)
adverbs
utterly; amazingly; thoroughly; completely; tremendously; dramatically; inexpressibly.
(See astonish, amaze, stagger.)

ASTUTE
adverbs
cleverly; keenly; sagaciously; sagely; wisely; craftily; cunningly; invariably; habitually; unfailingly; adroitly; customarily; discerningly; artfully; manifestly; undeniably; intelligently; shrewdly; deftly; ingeniously; insidiously; judiciously; learnedly.

ASTUTENESS
adjectives
habitual; strategical; devious; native; editorial; customary.

ASYLUM
verbs
abolish—; afford—; attend—; cast into—; claim—; commit to—; deliver up to—; devote to—; escape from—; establish—; flee from—; force into—; found—; guarantee—; grant—; harbor in—; huddle in—; incarcerate in—; invade—; limit—to; maintain—; maltreat in—; preside over—; provide—; refuse—to; remove from—; reside in—; restrict to—; retreat to—; sanctify—; seek—; support in—; torture in—; violate —; —accumulates; —cares for; —deals with; —protects; —shelters.
(See retreat, sanctuary, refuge, institution.)

ATHEISM
adjectives
uncompromising; overt; aggressive; militant; downright; courageous; swaggering.

verbs
cast off—; charge with—; clothe in—; countenance—; despise—; disprove—; destroy—; disapprove—; eradicate—; exhibit —; fall into—; incline toward—; inculcate—; justify—; mourn—; overthrow—; practice—; prate about—; pretend to—; proclaim—; recognize—; reject—; replace —; substitute—; support—; thunder—; unloose—; voice—; —acknowledges; —appears; —captivates; —conceives; —denies;

—disbelieves; —exists; —flounders; —grips; —grows; —lacks; —organizes; —philosophizes; —protests; —quiets down; —startles. (See skepticism, disbelief.)

ATHEIST

adjectives
passionate; impious; positive; extreme; practical.

verbs
convert—; convince—; —arises; —confuses; —defames; —denies; —disbelieves; —discourses; —disregards.
(See skeptic, heretic.)

ATHEISTIC

adverbs
bigotedly; horribly; irreverently; impiously; perversely; fanatically; avowedly; sacrilegiously; profanely; heart-breakingly; grievously; tormentingly; obstinately; stubbornly; unhappily; irrationally; unreasonably; profoundly; irrevocably; immovably; obdurately; openly; essentially.

ATHLETE

adjectives
tall; wiry; well-built; fleet-legged; husky; energetic; lithe; young; scintillant; distinguished; professional; promising; splendid; all-around; barrel-chested.

verbs
address —s; applaud—; coach—; coddle—; condition—; debar—; develop—; commercialize—; exhaust—; experience—; fete—; fit—; govern—; honor—; inspire—; key up —; league —s; match—; oppose—; privilege—; proselyte—; provide for—; solicit—; stimulate—; strain—; subsidize—; time—; —accomplishes; —combats; —competes; —contends; —contests; —endures; —excels; —exhibits; —leaps; —overhauls; —strives; —surpasses; —trains; —vaults; —vies; —wrestles.
(See contestant, player.)

ATHLETIC

adverbs
splendidly; stoutly; noisily; sturdily; healthily; devotedly; robustly; heartily; vigorously; wholesomely; healthfully; magnificently; whole-heartedly; stockily; brawnily; ardently; assiduously; zealously; energetically; gravely; seriously.

ATHLETICS

verbs
bar—; bar from—; coach—; compete in—; create—; develop—; dip into—; dispel—; draft into—; embrace—; encourage—; engage in—; enter into—; establish—; excel in—; favor—; further—; go in for—; improve—; interest in—; pertain to—; practise—; promote—; referee—; score—; skill in—; subordinate—; succeed in—; support —; teach—; train for—; undertake—; utilize—; witness—; —builds; —develops; —occupies; —stirs; —thrills.
(See game, exercise.)

ATMOSPHERE

adjectives
radiant; genial; congenial; rosy; general; ideal; blessed; refreshing; exhilarating; free; invigorating; gentle; homelike; calm; pure; enervating; charming; genteel; mirthful; enchanting; quiet; restful; exquisite; bracing; serene; cordial; genuine; healthful; happy; buoyant; delightful; queenly; hospitable; wholesome; agreeable; jolly; rare; admirable; weird; uncanny; indescribable; electric; amazing; spooky; exciting; creepy; gloomy; stratified; brutal; criminal; dingy; severe; restricted; unhappy; aircooled; sinister; dire; hostile; uneasy; chilling; insidious; polluted; murky; smoky; terrible; fetid; soggy; sour; nauseous; poisonous; dim; small-town; rural; frozen; human; political; learned; adventurous; poetic; slumbrous; fairylike; cosmopolitan; humid; sultry; close; windless; stuffy; living; changed; sheltered; realistic; distinctive; intangible; unfathomable; essential; inimical; apprehensive; thunderous; balmy; swift-moving; colorful; unreal; cool; ethereal; misty; special; enveloping; natural; intoxicating; characteristic; refined; clean; correct; luxurious; pleasant; distinguished; cheerful; ambient; suffocating; limpid; burning; steaming; faint; foul; rayless; grim; tense; vapory; bell-clear; venomous; contagious; quivering; artistic; musical; charged; consistent; intimate; straitened; infective; spiritual; hot; scintillating; transparent; stagnant; ruffling; lucid; rosy; uninteresting; agitated; nervous; romantic; artificial; unearthly; fierce; factitious; sleepy; metropolitan; easy; controlled; surcharged; depressing; lost; medieval; continental; stilted; decorous; respectable; social; intellectual; dewy; drear; summer; frightening; intimate; choked; rich; subtle; unindividual; exciting; clarified; dense; ladylike; dismal; troublous; emotional; roseate; oil-reeking; picturesque; somber; country; sentimental; hallowed; poetic; humid; damp; burdensome; scientific; dust-

less; quivering; reactionary; provincial; pellucid; unconventional; thrilling; livable; indoor; germ-laden; putrid; festive; impersonal; disloyal; elastic; sun-warm; crystal; lifeless; mutual; beamless; evening; tranquil; emerald; precious; furnace-heated; authentic; oppressive; concentrated; uncongenial; wet; commonplace; rarefied; burning; impassive; remote; ever-stormless.

ATMOSPHERE
(air)
verbs
absorb in—; adulterate—; analyze—; combine with—; compose—; constitute—; contaminate—; cool—; befoul—; cleanse—; erupt into—; escape into—; gain access to —; illuminate—; inhale—; invade—; filter —; float in—; mix in—; occupy—; pervade —; pump from—; rarify—; refresh—; release into—; smother in—of; surcharge—; —reeks.
(See air.)

ATMOSPHERE
(element or influence)
verbs
achieve—; break—; breathe—; capture—; charge—; create—; dispel—; dissipate—; distill—; drink in—; electrify—; enhance—; evoke—; indicate—; inform—; leaven—; load—; shatter—; surround—; —hinders; —inspires; —lends; —lures; —mingles; —promotes; —vivifies.
(See influence, environment.)

ATOM
adjectives
primordial; golden; pungent; intrusive; paltry; jarring; meditative; quenchless; homogeneous; gaseous; tormented; intelligent; throbbing; phosphorescent.

ATONE (v)
adverbs
fully; peacefully; heroically; bitterly; finally; vicariously; solemnly; sorrowfully; humbly.
(See pay.)

ATONEMENT
adjectives
heroic; final; least; bitter; vicarious; solemn; innocent.

verbs
emphasize—; make—; modify—; offer—; preach—; punish—; purify by—; refuse—; reject—; repent in—; reward—; sacrifice in—; set at—; —amends; —appeases; —

dawns; —expiates; —reconciles; —redeems; —repairs; —restores; —satisfies; —saves; —vindicates.
(See reparation, satisfaction.)

ATROCIOUS
adverbs
scandalously; outrageously; glaringly; notoriously; horribly; monstrously; inhumanly; harshly; ruthlessly; wickedly; abominably; savagely; barbarously; pitiably; remarkably; incredibly; unbelievably; inexpressibly; inconceivably.

ATROCITY
adjectives
Victorian; lugubrious; unbelievable; monstrous; unprovoked; barbaric; utter; cold-blooded; out-of-the-way.

verbs
attend with—; avenge—; commit—; defend from—; deserve—; expiate—; hide—; inflict—upon; revenge—; subject to—; —horrifies; —shocks; —stupefies.
(See outrage, crime, cruelty, wickedness, blunder.)

ATTACH (v)
adverbs
passionately; unfeignedly; exclusively; violently; devoutly; gratefully; justly; indissolubly; sentimentally; ardently; unashamedly; romantically; hopelessly; insanely; incestuously; uniformly; tenderly; fervidly; emotionally; recklessly; conjugally; avowedly; cynically; excessively; momentarily.
(See annex, fasten.)

ATTACHMENT
adjectives
sentimental; passionate; warped; ardent; violent; deep; affectionate; unashamed; romantic; hopeless; boundless; invisible; insane; warm; incestuous; altruistic; disinterested; uniform; prior; tender; honest; steady; unrequited; fervid; special; emotional; underlying; reckless; filial; conjugal; marked; lasting; growing; lukewarm; serious; avowed; cynical; excessive; momentary.

verbs
absorb by—; affect—; apprehend—; authorize—; cement—; command—; connect—; decree—of; deepen—; deprecate—; devote to—; divide—; enforce—; execute—; fasten —; further—; grant—; process—; recover by—; regulate—; secure—; seize in—; sympathize with—; tack on—; warrant—;

—binds; —perishes; —persists; —survives; —withstands.

(See affection, devotion.)

ATTACK

adjectives

smashing; savage; murderous; fiery; bold; homicidal; ripping; bulldog; tearing; deadly; devastating; ruthless; angry; fierce; brutal; reckless; terrific; treacherous; scathing; hurricane; severe; damaging; formidable; desperate; prolonged; diplomatic; merciless; literary; hand-to-hand; journalistic; verbal; demagogic; vehement; unrestrained; incessant; determined; inexorable; rapid; zestful; impetuous; correct; serious; unexpected; direct; surprise; resounding; logical; vague; mysterious; provocative; sudden; well-organized; sustained; widespread; subtle; persisting; counter; organized; vigorous; withering; open; pulmonary; precipitate; simultaneous; scientific; bitter; damaging; crushing; unprovoked; whirlwind; strategic; oblique; furious; hysterical; peculiar; systematic; secular; outside; ordered; infantry; desultory; threatened; blasphemous; lawless; decisive; barbarous; noisy; seditious; premature; subsequent; convulsive; contemplated; nocturnal; burglarous; unjust; insidious; unfortunate; indiscriminate; ill-natured; abrupt; outrageous; immediate; tumultuous; abortive; violent; ignoble; frontal; satirical; tireless; sagacious; spasmodic; censurable; epileptoid; premeditated; venomous.

verbs

anticipate—; avert—; block—; blunt—; carry—; change—; characterize—; conceive —; concentrate—; consolidate—; counter—; cure of—; defy—; desist from—; direct—; dislodge—; divert—; double—; foresee—; forestall—; guard against—; head off—; immunize against—; induce—; initiate—; intensify—; launch—; mass for—; mount to—; plan—; precipitate—; predispose to —; prepare for—; presage—; pretend—; proceed with—; proclaim—; recover from —; re-enforce—; repel—; repudiate—; repulse—; satirize—; shift—; soften—; subdue—; succeed in—; succumb to—; suppress —; survive—; sustain—; terminate—; throw off—; time—; unite in—; unleash—; usher in—; wind up—; —abates; —arises; —coincides; —defames; —excites; —impends; —injures; —occurs; —overthrows; —recurs; —seizes; —subsides; —succeeds; —sways; —swerves; —swings.

(See invasion, siege, attempt.)

ATTACK (v)

adverbs

ardently; simultaneously; bitterly; scurrilously; fiendishly; virulently; libelously; savagely; anonymously; ridiculously; characteristically; sorely; energetically; vehemently; criminally; unscrupulously; smashingly; murderously; devastatingly; ruthlessly; scathingly; treacherously; verbally; incessantly; determinedly; inexorably; impetuously; venomously; scientifically; unprovokedly; obliquely; blasphemously; decisively; barbarously; prematurely; insidiously; satirically.

(See assail, invade, combat.)

ATTAIN (v)

adverbs

ultimately; cheaply; effectually; artistically; modestly; legally; intellectually; profitably; educationally; singularly; ultimately; scientifically; technically; astronomically; linguistically; incomparably; rarely.

(See achieve, gain, acquire.)

ATTAINMENTS

adjectives

remarkable; artistic; desirable; modest; legal; mental; distinguished; unusual; intellectual; profitable; scholarly; educational; singular; ultimate; ornamental; eminent; scientific; technical; astronomical; linguistic; incomparable; rare.

ATTEMPT

adjectives

sincere; valiant; memorable; sympathetic; serious; honest; admirable; successful; elaborate; ingenious; ambitious; eloquent; careful; kindly; enlightened; reasonable; well-meaning; ill-directed; slow-witted; weak; faltering; feeble; sorry; slightest; bashful; ineffectual; unavailing; half-hearted; laughable; grotesque; hopeless; vain; unfortunate; clumsy; futile; stupid; foolish; fruitless; farcical; mock; foolhardy; despairing; inept; pitiful; nugatory; maladroit; murderous; outrageous; mad; disastrous; dreary; infamous; superhuman; bold; daring; heroic; spectacular; systematic; repeated; definite; organized; long-heralded; vituperative; obvious; belated; freest; picturesque; covert; blind; passionate; abortive; miscarried; unappreciated; curious; numerous; pretentious; early; labored; major; hurried; unsteady; involuntary; extreme; rash; remarkable; creditable; impious; patriotic; rude; youthful; vigorous; embarrassed; misguided; cramplike; isolated; memorable; inconsiderate; arduous; coquettish; ignoble; forcible; deliberate; laudable; forlorn; torturing; charitable; unconstitutional; wicked; complicated; brutal; discouraging; direct; previous; mimic; exorbitant; murderous; strange; unorganized; perpetual; chimerical; excellent; traitorous; premature; uncouth; half-satirical; despicable; inauspicious; villainous; experimental; bare.

verbs
acclaim—; afford—; applaud—; commence —; commit—; complete—; constitute—; defeat—; deter from—; discern—; essay—; evade—; fail in—; fall short in—; foil—; glorify—; honor—; indict for—; interpret —; justify—; oppose—; overcome—; put forth—; recognize—; repel—; repudiate—; restrain—; suffer from—; stimulate—; thwart—; undertake—; warrant—; — blinds; —confounds; —triumphs; —wearies; interrupt—.
(See trial, endeavor, effort, attack.)

ATTEMPT (v)
adverbs
desperately; amateurishly; repeatedly; strenuously; previously; feebly; inadvertently; valiantly; memorably; sincerely; ingeniously; eloquently; reasonably; enlightenedly; falteringly; ineffectually; unavailingly; half-heartedly; grotesquely; futilely; fruitlessly; farcically; ineptly; maladroitly; murderously; outrageously; odiously; hazardously; disastrously; infamously; superhumanly; heroically; spectacularly; daringly; systematically; vituperatively; obviously; picturesquely; covertly; abortively; pretentiously; laboriously; unsteadily; involuntarily; creditably; impiously; patriotically; misguidedly; memorably; arduously; coquettishly; ignobly; forcibly; laudably; forlornly; charitably; unconstitutionally; brutally; exorbitantly; prematurely; uncouthly; half-satirically; despicably; inauspiciously; villainously.
(See endeavor, strive, undertake.)

ATTEND (v)
adverbs
diligently; faithfully; habitually; punctually; consistently; patiently; strictly; frequently; numerously; successively; expertly; rarely; invariably; assiduously; casually; nightly; compulsorily; unavailingly; properly; medically; overflowingly; scantily; profes-

sionally; defectively; suitably; stolidly; unceremoniously; devotedly; cheerfully; intermittently.
(See guard, heed, listen.)

ATTENDANCE
adjectives
assiduous; casual; interminable; nightly; compulsory; constant; unavailing; unrelaxing; agitated; proper; medical; overflowing; increased; scanty; professional; slovenly; defective; suitable; stolid; unceremonious; regular; unasked; devoted; cheerful; surpassed; intermittent.

verbs
advise—; await—; charge for—; command —; compel—; continue—; dance—; delay —; engage—; exact—; expect—; gather in —; increase—; minister in—; order—; resume—; wait in—; win—; —dwindles; — falls off; —grows; —increases; —manifests.
(See audience, congregation.)

ATTENDANT
adjectives
faithful; trained; black-robed; courteous; general; unobtrusive; gaudy; official; mercenary; nervous; chattering; spectacled; skilled; constant; flustered; experienced; obsequious; diligent; brave; dissolute; whispering; excited; inspiring; inseparable; obliging; fez-covered.

ATTENTION
adjectives
gentle; popular; eager; favorable; considerate; respectful; flattering; courteous; charming; gracious; delicate; faithful; thoughtful; keen; interested; undisguised; open-mouthed; undivided; rapt; riveted; absorbed; precise; painstaking; critical; persistent; assiduous; meticulous; scrutinizing; scrupulous; particular; strict; studious; unremitting; unceasing; wide-eyed; skilled; intellectual; pusillanimous; unwavering; obsequious; irritating; odious; casual; unappreciated; scant; trifling; idle; surface; slight; wandering; excessive; concentrated; individual; general; underground; wide; alert; spurious; prompt; special; country-wide; final; increased; considerable; cursory; rival; calm; acute; anxious; unobtrusive; tactful; sharp; serious; deliberate; emphatic; sufficient; abstracted; frowning; ample; enwrapped; unreasoning; ungrudging; momentary; minute; precious; nocturnal; faintest; strained; vague; uninterrupt-

ed; polite; unwonted; willing; careful; admirable; well-meant; irksome; solitary; bland; impersonal; edifying; ill-omened; best; tense; languid; profound; watchful; painful; summary; supreme; deepest; unfatigued; hesitating; manual; undue; reluctant; early; marked; feigned; unwelcome; parental; benumbed; whole-souled; funny; startled; minimum; indifferent; exclusive; breathless; sour; statistical; forced; vital; rational; unflagging; close; listless; animated; universal; insensible; fawning; unmeasured; conscientious; uncaressing; vigilant; affectionate; mournful; cheap; fascinated; earnest; cataleptic; wifely; public.

verbs

absorb—; acquire—of; arouse—; arrest—; bestow—upon; bring to—; call—to; capture —; center—; chide into—; claim—; clamor for—; come to—; command—; compel—; compete for—; concentrate—; confine—; crave—; demand—; desire—; devote—; dictate—; direct—; dispose—; distract—; distribute—; divert—; draw—; enforce—; engage—; engross—; enlist—; escape—; exact—from; excite—; exercise—; exhaust —; exhibit—; fasten—; favor with—; fix —; flash—; focus—; gain—; garner—; hold in—; increase—; influence—; lavish —upon; lend—; load with—; locate—; maintain—; mark with—; merit—; monopolize—; object to—; observe with—; occupy —; pay—; provoke—; reap—; recall—; reduce—; register—; reject—; relax—; require—; resume—; rivet—; secure—; stand at—; stimulate to—; straighten up in—; strike—; strive for—; subject to—; summon—; sustain—; train—upon; turn— toward; warrant—; win—; yield—; —embarrasses; —flags; —lies in; —wanders; —wanes; attract—.

(See gaze.)

ATTENTIVE

adverbs

absorbingly; steadily; intently; alertly; critically; analytically; closely; remarkably; astoundingly; suspiciously; guardedly; mildly; noticeably; intelligently; breathlessly; eagerly; engrossingly; raptly; carefully; considerately; thoughtfully; scrupulously; deferentially; respectfully; obsequiously; decorously; immensely; favorably; courteously; charmingly; graciously; assiduously; unwaveringly; flatteringly; idly; excessively; generally; finally; calmly; anxiously; unobtrusively; tactfully; sharply; politely; earnestly.

ATTEST (v)

adverbs

explicitly; unequivocally; duly; sincerely; authoritatively; freely.

(See confirm, indorse, corroborate.)

ATTIC

adjectives

stuffy; dusty; cobwebby; unused.

verbs

betake oneself to—; climb to—; confine to—; construct—; decorate—; design—; designate to—; enclose—; insulate—; lock in—; lodge in—; modernize—; relegate to—; renovate —; rumble around—; rummage in—; scour —; seclude in—; store in—; utilize—; ventilate—; —contains; —covers; —extends; —holds.

(See garret, room, cellar.)

ATTIRE

adjectives

bedizened; elaborate; motley; disreputable; informal; injudicious; fit; scandalous; crumpled; male; hunting; gala; quaint; drab; fairest; elegant; gay; evening; holiday; unaccustomed; scanty; showy; absurd; feminine; careful; splendid; mourning; unceremonious; picturesque; ornamented; exquisite; tawdry; ostentatious; festal; negligent; substantial; wild; coarse; abbreviated; gaudy.

verbs

acquire—; adorn in—; array in—; checker —; costume in—; deck in—; decorate in—; don—; dress in—; equip with—; flash—; gear in—; outfit in—; pin on—; shroud in—.

(See dress, clothing, apparel, costume.)

ATTIRE (v)

adverbs

somberly; impeccably; fantastically; faultlessly; modishly; scrupulously; superbly; disreputably; informally; fittingly; scandalously; quaintly; drably; elegantly; scantily; unceremoniously; picturesquely; exquisitely; ostentatiously; negligently; coarsely; gaudily.

(See dress.)

ATTITUDE

adjectives

firm; oblivious; listless; denunciatory; truculent; philanthropic; apathetic; scrupulous; unsisterly; composed; studied; absolutory; pathetic; impassive; civilized; rebellious; disconsolate; misanthropic; sensible; figurative; contemptuous; hostile; lukewarm; egotistical; endless; assiduous; subtle; depressive; mental; indolent; contemplative; motionless; orientated; threatening; ridiculous; forlorn; political; basic; insidious; exulting; swaying; slouching; stoical; bellicose; favorable; submissive; positive; procrastinating; fearless; lofty; charming; gallant; gorgeous; piquant; reverent; exalted; resolute; cool; unbending; courageous; affirmative; adamantine; uncompromising; optimistic; light-hearted; complacent; cordial; self-sufficient; devil-may-care; overindulgent; carefree; depressed; serious; morose; sound; healthy; sane; natural; quiet; firm; eager; dignified; obliging; respectful; sympathetic; jubilant; conciliatory; enlightened; cultivated; timid; tolerant; cautious; generous; perfunctory; arrogant; supercilious; self-centered; disdainful; unsympathetic; condescending; patronizing; censorious; lordly; imperious; deprecatory; antagonistic; pugnacious; alien; militant; menacing; detestable; vengeful; devastating; preposterous; catastrophic; treasonable; unfriendly; transient; impolite; resentful; flippant; drooped; unfortunate; irreconcilable; condemnatory; suspicious; callous; pessimistic; dejected; ironical; overconfident; balanced; objective; unconventional; sudden; mature; fluid; familiar; injured; pragmatic; necessary; passive; watchful; worshipful; free; set; easy; quiescent; menial; annoying; defensive; condoning; sentimental; typical; talkative; realistic; various; restrained; destructive; ignorant; moral; ostrich; nonchalant; depreciatory; historical; nervous; benevolent; mutual; constrained; praiseworthy; infantile; graceful; belligerent; consistent; peculiar; suppliant; non-aggressive; defiant; untrammeled; presumptuous; judicial; helpless; negligent; characteristic; unsatisfactory; unpleasant; heroic; charming; strutting; comical; righteous; despondent; wholesome; unjust; hard-boiled; anachronistic; unlike (pl); crouching; fashionable; abnormal; chivalrous; discreet; penitential; peering; hypocritical; business-like; suggestive; forensic; fundamental; rigid; habitual; bipolar; ungraceful; tender; nonsensical; erect; resigned; traditional; warlike; emotional; mute; romantic.

verbs

abandon—; acquire—; adopt—; advocate —; analyze—; assume—; behave in—; breed—; choose—; color—; condemn—; define—; denote—; deplore—; discount—; distort—; dominate—; dramatize—; embrace —; emphasize—; encourage—; exalt—; examine—; exhibit—; explain—; expound—; express—; fall into—; gesture—; give rise to—; hold—; illuminate—; implant—; imply—; inculcate—; indicate—; ingrain—; interpret—; justify—; maintain—; manage —; manifest—; modify—; move to—; obsess with—; overcome—; persist in—; pervert—; portray—; posture—; preserve—; project—; reflect—; regard—; relax—; repose in—of; resent—; revere—; reverse—; sense—; stand in—; study—; —antagonizes; —applies; —implies; —menaces; —prejudices; —prevails; —reveals; —robs; —survives; —warns.

(See position, idea.)

ATTORNEY

adjectives

shyster; sneaking; incompetent; eminent; scurrilous; fashionable; prosecuting; well-tried; wealthy; astonished; illiterate; uneducated; brilliant.

verbs

appoint—; bar—; betray—; bind—; commission—; confer with—; confide in—; consult—; criticize—; delegate—; disbar—; discipline—; dispatch—; employ—; endorse —; engage—; ordain—; procure—; refer to—; reimburse—; retain—; train —s; — acknowledges; —acts; —administers; — advocates; —argues; —assails; —attacks; —bickers; —contracts for; —counsels; — cross-examines; —defames; —defends; — discusses; —examines; —exerts; —exposes; —formulates; —influences; —intercedes; —manages; —objects; —orates; —performs; —pleads; —practices; —prepares; —promotes; —prosecutes; —quibbles; —represents; —solicits; —sues for; —tries; —s wrangle.

(See lawyer.)

ATTRACT (*v*)

adverbs

instinctively; adroitly; romantically; magnetically; commandingly; irresistibly; profoundly; inescapably.

(See draw, engage, induce.)

ATTRACTION

adjectives

supreme; irresistible; queer; sweet; rare; natural; voluptuous; defective; dreadful; morbid; tragic; uncomfortable; fierce; insidious; unrivaled; loudly-heralded; dazzling; outstanding; overwhelming; principal; unusual; foremost; notable; cosmopolitan; physical; manifold; tidal; sexual; pastoral;

scenic; sartorial; historic; instant; growing; current; fleeting; scant; mutual; indefinable; obvious; chief; personal; myriad (pl); time-mellowed; casual; added; unspoken; spiritual; powerful; material; instinctive; clouded; poetical; limitless (pl); specific; resultant; acute; gratuitous; magnetic; electrostatic; hideous; fatal; permanent; feature; secret; coquettish; specious; mysterious; reciprocal; innumerable (pl); intellectual; accelerative; divine; enormous; sylvan; intrinsic; varying; imperious; conjugal; subtle.

verbs
admit—; augment—; cause—; center—; confess to—; exert—; force—; form—; illustrate—; yield to—; —adheres; —allures; —develops; —diminishes; —draws; —enhances; —fades; —lures; —recedes; —unsettles.
(See charm, fascination.)

ATTRACTIVE
adverbs
radiantly; irresistibly; rarely; sweetly; dazzlingly; overwhelmingly; indefinably; divinely; mysteriously; unutterably; powerfully; singularly; charmingly; alluringly; uncommonly; engagingly; undeniably; beautifully; bewitchingly; enchantingly; delightfully; exquisitely; interestingly; daintily; smartly; jauntily; bewilderingly; exotically; tormentingly.

ATTRACTIVENESS
adjectives
varied; bright; inevitable; annoying; physical; unusual; singular.

ATTRIBUTE
adjectives
supernatural; desirable; priceless; fundamental; fantastic; fearful; feminine; senseless; wonderful; detestable; recognizable; splendid; striking; peacock; literary; time-honored; chief; mistaken; characteristic; essential; accessory; homely; moral; intellectual; unalterable; judicial; human; highest; universal; gracious; noble; specific; conventional; sacred; productive; lofty; infinite; known; hereditary; striking; armorial; vacillating; diverse; sovereign; modified.

verbs
ascribe—to; credit with—; determine—; discover—; distinguish—; dramatize—; endow with—; enlarge—; estimate—; eulogize—; honor—; invest with—; limit—; manifest—;
mark—; possess—; recognize—; ridicule—; shed all —s; value—; —enhances.
(See characteristic, symbol, quality, property.)

ATTRIBUTE (v)
adverbs
invariably; solely; entirely; modestly; skilfully; chiefly; basely; falsely; absurdly; innocently; supernaturally; fantastically; senselessly; graciously; nobly; specifically; conventionally.
(See impute, ascribe.)

AUDACIOUS
adverbs
disconcertingly; dauntlessly; rashly; indiscreetly; injudiciously; hot-headedly; foolishly; impudently; incredibly; recklessly; serenely; amazingly; overbearingly; shamelessly; tragically; singularly; strangely; innately; crazily; notoriously; dramatically; terribly; inherently; colossally; foolhardily; breath-takingly; fantastically; alarmingly; offensively; constitutionally; temperamentally.

AUDACITY
adjectives
incredible; utmost; reckless; characteristic; rapid; serene; gay; gorgeous; winning; amazing; sheer; insolent; cynical; cool; unfailing; unparalleled; vigorous; indelicate; heroic; harmless; human; inward; personal; dissolute; splendid; unnecessary; supreme; brilliant; operative; adventurous; unheard-of; aggressive; masculine; magnificent.

verbs
admire—; assume—; cool—; counterfeit—; depart from—; encourage—; exhibit—; relapse from—; reprimand—; shame by—; tame—; thrill at—; venture forth with—; —affronts; —engenders; —perturbs; —shocks; disregard—.
(See recklessness.)

AUDIENCE
adjectives
intelligent; sympathetic; understanding; appreciative; meager; sophisticated; attentive; interested; discerning; approving; imposing; vociferous; distinguished; admiring; enchanted; happy; democratic; meticulous; hilarious; enthusiastic; frenzied; vast; crowded; wide; undetermined; large; huge; fair; capacity; slender; tense; hushed; expectant; whispering; breathless; startled; astonished; mystified; chilled; bewildered; hard-boiled; wayward; cynical; hostile;

critical; ribald; unprecedented; unseen; reading; special; famished; invited; dull; applauding; nightly; respectable; imaginary; apathetic; suspicious; technical; motley; martial; impromptu; select; laughing; legislative; eager; delighted; dead-struck; enormous; gloomy; indiscriminate; polished; tragic; absorbed; satisfied; circular; pitying; listless; reasonable; added; dreary; prospective; elect; stupid; unresponsive; advertent; haughty.

verbs
accustom to—; admit—; appeal to—; assemble—; break up—; command—; convulse—; crave—; delight—; dismiss—; draw—; enslave—; enthuse (colloq.)—; exhort—; grant—; harangue—; hypnotize —; inflame—; lend—; lure—; overwhelm —; panic—; scan—; seek—; survey—; sway —; vouchsafe—; win—; —acclaims; —applauds; —cheers; —claps; —demands; — detects; —gapes; —gasps; —groans; — hisses; —howls; —laughs; —listens; — melts away; —packs; —pays; —responds; —roars; —rustles; —sobs; —stamps; — swells; —thrills; —throngs; —weeps.
(See hearing, interview, conference, gathering.)

AUDITOR
adjectives
skilled; bated; confounded; enchanted.

AUDITORIUM
adjectives
tight-packed; seething; huge; crowded; fire-trap.

verbs
assemble in—; fill—; hire—; jam—; occupy —; receive in—; reverberate through—; throng—; —accommodates; —echoes; — holds; —resounds; —rings with; —seats.
(See building, hall, arena.)

AUGMENT (v)
adverbs
currently; incredibly; scarcely; tremendously; indefinitely; continually.
(See swell, increase.)

AUGURY
adjectives
favorable; evil; happy; reassuring; fearful; grim; heathen; sinister.

AUNT
adjectives
thin; sallow; unflagging; gaunt; sophisticated; worldly; ancient; strait-laced; maiden; pious.

AURA
adjectives
healthful; vague; flashing; evil; invidious; shimmering; tangible; smoky.

AUSPICES
adjectives
authoritative; pleasant; responsible; cordial; favorable; present; flattering; charitable.

AUSPICIOUS
adverbs
highly; opportunely; properly; suitably; happily; fairly; favorably; fortunately; luckily; providentially; remarkably; unusually; duly; consistently; gratifyingly; pleasantly; agreeably; fittingly; delightfully.

AUSTERE
adverbs
gravely; starkly; sombrely; monastically; harshly; puritanically; severely; rigorously; rigidly; uncompromisingly; inflexibly; unsparingly; arbitrarily; tyrannically; sternly; oddly; unfashionably; haughtily; soberly; odiously; unmitigatedly; unbendingly; unrelentingly.

AUSTERITY
adjectives
tempering; neat; wholesome; geometric; beautiful; dark; unrelieved; dignified; seeming; monastic; prayerful; natural; gentle; harsh; unyielding; famous; mild; hoar.

AUTHENTIC
adverbs
undeniably; unquestionably; admittedly; avowedly; unchallengedly; assuredly; professedly; palpably; obviously; evidently; apparently; absolutely; positively; categorically; genuinely; incontestably; indisputably; manifestly; unmistakably.

AUTHENTICITY
adjectives
doubtful; absolute; stylistic; altered; unmistakable; unquestioned; unforgettable.

verbs
accept—; command—; confirm—; dispute—; doubt—; entitle to—; insure—; profess—; prove—; question—; satisfy with—; stamp with—; testify to—; value—; verify—; —holds up; —stands.
(See accuracy.)

adjectives

veteran; competent; wild; versatile; accomplished; important; successful; prolific; eminent; favorite; distinguished; famous; modern; esteemed; engaging; amiable; vivacious; charming; noble; ardent; cheerful; well-meaning; inspiring; sane; disputatious; capricious; irresponsible; untrained; whimsical; perplexed; budding; unknown; putative; sentimental; dogmatic; forgotten; judicious; elusive; nascent; anonymous; irate; gregarious; antique; disillusioned; gifted; recent; alleged; striving; fearless; venerable; aspiring; delightful; remote; contemporary; cunning; neglected; profound; classical; agitated; anxious; vain; juvenile; comic; bigoted; superstitious.

verbs

acclaim—; acquaint with—; animate—; appreciate—; challenge—; criticize—; dishonor—; disturb—; employ—; engage—; enthuse (colloq.)—; exhaust—; frustrate—; honor—; inspire—; laud—; persecute—; plague—; rouse—; slander—; —bewitches; —casts about; —characterizes; —colors; —compels; —compiles; —composes; —creates; —cultivates; —dabbles; —declares; —dedicates; —describes; —devotes; —divines; —dreams; —edits; —exploits; —foreshadows; —gloats; —improvises; —indicates; —instigates; —labors; —languishes; —libels; —moralizes; —motivates; —objects; —originates; —philosophizes; —pirates; —plagiarizes; —produces; —pursues; —retires; —shapes; —soliloquizes; —translates; —voices; discuss—.

(See writer, poet.)

AUTHORITATIVE

adverbs

impressively; eminently; unquestionably; undisputedly; distinctly; reliably; responsibly; dependably; infallibly; highly; supremely; competently; expertly; peerlessly; imposingly; abundantly; respectably; quietly; learnedly; famously; deftly; academically; locally; legally; mildly; magisterially; uncompromisingly; pompously; imperially; condescendingly; truculently; brutally; studiously; specifically; directly; dogmatically; smoothly; suavely; conventionally; solemnly; delicately; finally; venerably; despotically; officially; divinely; habitually; undeniably; proudly; gently; unmistakably; cruelly; ostentatiously.

adjectives

leading; unimpeachable; acknowledged; accredited; recognized; renowned; eminent; unquestioned; well-known; undisputed; distinguished; reliable; responsible; dependable; prominent; infallible; high; foremost; supreme; unchallenged; competent; peerless; imposing; abundant; famous; respectable; quiet; learned; interesting; superior; deft; academic; civil; shocked; local; apostolic; outstanding; parental; legal; mild; arrogated; deputed; magisterial; uncompromising; constituted; imperial; sacred; express; crushing; appointed; condescending; revered; truculent; unique; adequate; humiliating; studious; practical; outraged; shadowy; specific; direct; limited; established; dogmatic; smooth; legitimate; apocryphal; mystic; coordinate; unbounded; sundry; conventional; solemn; centralized; concurrent; sufficient; executive; actual; delicate; minor; harassing; censorial; musical; administrative; standard; venerable; serious; delegated; ecclesiastical; parliamentary; despotic; base; brief; oracular; paramount; spiritual; dissolving; firm; provincial; far-distant; disciplinary; excellent; conferred; all-persuasive; scientific; territorial; governmental; antenatal; coercive; private; discretionary; ministerial; coequal; worn-out; military; provisional; ascertained; mellow; habitual; inspired; sovereign; central; weighty; grammatical; consular; divine; unassailable; sanctified.

verbs

abuse—; accept—; act with—; appeal to—; appoint to—; arm with—; aspire to—; assert—; attain—; boast—; carry—; challenge—; claim—; clothe with—; command —; confer—upon; confirm—; consult—; declare—; decree—; defy—; delegate—; derive—; desire—; discredit—; enforce—; entrust—; establish—; esteem—; execute—; exercise—; extend—; fetter—; flout—; grant —; heighten—; ignore—; inspire—; invest with—; lend—; limit—; mark with—; obey —; possess—; preserve—; pronounce—; question—; quote—; rebel against—; regard with—; register—; reject—; relinquish —; rely upon—; respect—; restrain—; revere—; revolt against—; ridicule—; speak with—; squelch—; submit to—; support—; uphold—; usurp—; weaken—; weigh—; wield—; wink at—; wrest—; yield to—; —s arrest; —s intervene; —s jockey; —melts away; —s speculate.

(See right, jurisdiction, influence, power.)

adverbs

specifically; confidentially; responsibly; infallibly; respectably; locally; magisterially; expressly; practically; specifically; directly; limitedly; legitimately; ecclesiastically; despotically; basely; governmentally; divinely; unassailably; grammatically.

(See confirm, justify.)

AUTOBIOGRAPHICAL

adverbs

honestly; inadvertently; factually; probably; possibly; embarrassingly; amusingly; lightheartedly; blithely; gaily; solemnly; revealingly; lustily; radiantly; indecently; decorously; selectively; happily; lustily; gustily; gloriously; delightfully; unexpectedly; helpfully; analytically; critically; literally.

AUTOBIOGRAPHY

adjectives

factual; honest; intimate; embarrassing; lusty; amusing; accurate; unbelievable.

AUTOCRACY

adjectives

malignant; church; incompetent; pernicious; monstrous.

AUTOCRAT

adjectives

rival; irresponsible; absolute; vigorous; beneficent; ruthless; ancient.

AUTOCRATIC

adverbs

imperiously; tyrannically; unyieldingly; inflexibly; hatefully; meanly; arbitrarily; insolently; arrogantly; overbearingly; openly; brazenly; audaciously; jauntily; teasingly; regally; offensively; obnoxiously; deplorably; intolerably; lamentably; unfortunately.

AUTOGRAPH

adjectives

interesting; stateliest; boldest; facsimile.

AUTOMATIC (n)

adjectives   (gun)

wicked; mean-looking; flashing; blue-nosed; compact; sputtering; deadly.

AUTOMATIC (a)

adverbs

entirely; conveniently; amazingly; optionally; originally; luckily; ingeniously; cleverly; smoothly.

AUTOMOBILE

adjectives

ancient; dusty; long; swerving; lean; unidentified; obsolete; two-seated; rusty; rattlesome; undependable; sleek; streamlined.

verbs

climb into—; construct—; crank—; demolish—; design—; develop—; enclose—; engage—; equip—; improve—; insure—; license—; pilot—; pour out of—; power—; salvage—; —careens; —chugs; —climbs; —crawls; —creaks; —cruises; —descends; —flashes by; —flits by; —hauls; —hurtles; —joggles; —jolts; —lumbers; —moans; —noses; —pants; —pokes; —quivers; —roars; —skids; —slips by; —snarls; —snorts; —spins; —squeaks; —s swarm; —swoops; —transports; —travels; —trundles; —whines; —whirs; —whizzes; —zooms.

(See wagon, train.)

AUTOPSY

adjectives

unfavorable; warmly controverted; ghastly; inevitable; long-drawn-out; purely experimental; gruesome; ensuing; consequent; co-incidental.

verbs

carry on—; complete—; conclude by—; consent to—; consider—; consult—; diagnose by—; dispense with—; evidence by—; examine by—; hold—; inspect—; observe—; order—; perform—; permit—; record—; refuse—; report on—; request—; require —; seek—; subject to—; testify to—; urge —; witness—; —confirms; —determines; —discloses; —discovers; —reveals; —verifies.

(See examination.)

AUTUMN

adjectives

first; radiant; rank; meek; eventful; distributed; colorful; ambient; bounteous; dreary; everlasting; sere; paradisaical; chill.

verbs

enter—; hail—; welcome—; —advances; —basks; —beams; —burnishes; —bursts; —clamors; —colors; —decays; —decks; —declines; —descends; —embellishes; —extends from; —fades; —flames; —flushes; —follows; —garners; —gleams; —harvests; —haunts; —heralds; —lavishes; —matures; —meditates; —merges; —mocks; —paints; —pierces; —pours; —precedes; —presses near; —reaps; —resigns; —ripens; —rushes

in; —rustles; —scatters; —shackles; —
spreads; —sweeps in; —thwarts; —upbraids; —violates; —warns; —wreathes;
—yields.
(See fall.)

AUXILIARY

adjectives
warlike; unexpected; disaffected; thundering.

AUXILIARY (v)

adverbs
patronizingly; officially; officiously; legally; cooperatively; helpfully.

AVAIL (v)

adverbs
freely; promptly; continually; unobtrusively; scarcely; covertly; openly; slyly; villainously; brutally.
(See use.)

AVAILABLE

adverbs
easily; instantly; immediately; presumably;
always; undoubtedly; obviously; evidently;
apparently; unquestionably; scarcely; seldom.

AVALANCHE

adjectives
hoofed; blinding; deep; startling; rocky;
appalling; impending; sun-awakened; stupendous.

verbs
beat—; endure—; evade—; loose—; perish
in—; precipitate—; protect against—; roll
down in—; —crashes; —denudes; —descends; —destroys; —endangers; —gathers
force; —masses; —occurs; —overwhelms;
—plunges; —pours by; —roars; —rushes
by; —suffocates; —swallows; —sweeps
past; —washes along.

AVARICE

adjectives
besetting; anxious; sullen; pecuniary; insatiable; gripping; cruel; greedy.

verbs
decry—; deplore—; detest—; display—;
evince—; gather with—; grovel in—; hoard
in—; staunch—; take up with—; —acquires; —eats; —shrieks.
(See greed.)

AVARICIOUS

adverbs
incurably; avidly; insanely; peculiarly; incorrigibly; distressingly; painfully; embarrassingly; irreclaimably; hopelessly; shamelessly; appallingly; terribly; horribly; churlishly; sordidly; rapaciously.

AVENGE (v)

adverbs
horribly; sufficiently; fiercely; self-appoint-
edly; blood-thirstily; cruelly; finally; primarily; satisfactorily.
(See punish, revenge, vindicate, retaliate.)

AVENGER

adjectives
fierce; blood-stained; unblamed; ordained;
avowed; self-appointed.

AVENUE

adjectives
fine; moonlit; glittering; ignominious; trim;
tidy; intersecting; cobble-stoned; open; fashionable; principal; diagonal; spacious;
densely-shaded; leafy; dwarfish; continuous; noble; tree-lined; gorgeous; melancholy.

verbs
amble down—; approach—; border—; circle—; enter—; gain access to—; light—;
litter—; locate on—; mark—; promenade
—; shade—; shadow—; stroll down—; venture up—; —crosses; —extends; —leads to;
—parallels.
(See road, thoroughfare, way, approach,
street.)

AVERAGE

adjectives
well-gauged; inversely-proportioned; adjusted; stalwart; standardized; skeptical;
unvarying; prevailing; weighted; weighty;
timely.

verbs
adjust—; arrive at—; ascertain—; better
—; compare—; compile—; derive—; determine—; diminish—; distribute over—; divide—; estimate—; evolve—; hit—; lower
—; model on—; obtain—; propose—; reckon
—; record—; refer—; reveal—; strike—;
suggest—; yield—; —amounts to; —compares; —falls; —ranges; —rises; —varies;
—yields.
(See amount.)

AVERSE

adverbs

persistently; unreasonably; ineradicably; unnaturally; innately; openly; avowedly; unrelentingly; tenaciously; immovably; inflexibly; headily; arbitrarily; mulishly; stubbornly; obstinately.

AVERSION

adjectives

persistent; marked; ineradicable; strong; unnatural; staunch; unconquerable; inherent; thorough; instinctive; deep-rooted; instantaneous; utter; hereditary; loathing; inexpressible; proportionate; decided; favorite; extreme; separate; marked; mutual; cold; feminine; undisguised; developed; unreasonable; deadly.

verbs

augment—; cement—; fix—; intimate—; produce—; purge of—; recollect with—; rid of—; side-track—; strengthen—; voice—; —estranges.

(See antipathy, dislike, hatred.)

AVERT (v)

adverbs

cleverly; happily; coldly; swiftly; thoughtfully; dexterously; skilfully; painstakingly; scarcely.

(See prevent.)

AVIATOR

adjectives

daring; illustrious; famous; amateur; imaginative; intrepid; fearless; skilled.

verbs

exhaust—; inform—; license—; overtake—; strain—; test—; —accomplishes; —achieves; —ascends; —attempts; —circles; —controls; —descends; —dips; —endures; —lands; —loops; —manipulates; —navigates; —operates; —perceives; —pilots; —somersaults; —speeds; —takes off; —transports; —views; —zooms.

(See flier, airplane.)

AVID

adverbs

childishly; unnaturally; fatally; obviously; extraordinarily; excessively; anxiously; ardently; breathlessly; hungrily; fantastically; impetuously; zealously; madly; curiously; fervently; queerly; insatiably; sedulously.

AVOCATION

adjectives

ecstatic; pleasant.

AVOID (v)

adverbs

zealously; openly; studiously; industriously; contemptuously; scrupulously; cautiously; purposely; persistently; honorably; sedulously; decorously; involuntarily; totally; vigilantly; absolutely.

(See parry, evade, shun, elude.)

AVOIDANCE

adjectives

total; vigilant; lazy; absolute.

AVOW (v)

adverbs

brutally; simply; enthusiastically; bluntly; plainly; ardently; ostentatiously; boldly; energetically; unequivocally; manfully; gratefully; daringly; commonly; sincerely; savagely; secretly.

(See acknowledge, admit, profess.)

AVOWAL

adjectives

brutal; simple; enthusiastic; blunt; plain; ardent.

AWAIT (v)

adverbs

tensely; anxiously; silently; impatiently; apprehensively; informally; excitedly; tremblingly; breathlessly; courageously.

(See look, wait.)

AWAKE (v)

adverbs

rudely; shudderingly; accidentally; muscularly; singularly; breathlessly; consequently; hauntingly; blissfully; manifestly; spiritually; mechanically.

(See wake.)

AWAKENING

adjectives

rude; first; startled; innocent; new; blissful; moral; consequent; modest; manifest; stormy; spiritual.

AWARD

adjectives

long-coveted; grudging; merited; carefully-computed; just; princely; bounteous; inconsequent.

verbs

adjudicate—; applaud—; arbitrate—; assign—; capture—; consider—; decide—; deliberate—; dispute—; earn—; embody—; examine—; furnish—; grant—; institute—;

judge—; merit—; please with—; praise—; pronounce—; provide—; submit—; win—. (See decision, verdict, judgment.)

AWARE

adverbs

sensitively; painfully; acutely; vividly; sharply; keenly; curiously; psychically; subconsciously; sorely; uncomfortably; wretchedly; pleasingly; happily; rapturously; fully; intensely; suddenly; poignantly; astutely; wholly; neurotically; powerfully; perfectly; desperately; dimly; scarcely; barely; breathlessly.

AWARENESS

adjectives

neurotic; powerful; increased; sensitized.

AWE

adjectives

superstitious; deep; deferential; mysterious; simulated; joyous; strange; cringing; profound; candid; ineffable; vague; devout; tender; respectful; salutary; reverential; meaningful; undefined; fearful; slavish; unwilling; sacred; restraining; inspiring; trembling; adoring; mystic; silent; religious; hideous; inexpressible; supernatural; pious; rapt; ecstatic; dumb.

verbs

approach with—; awake—; bask in—; bind in—; breed—; command—; conduce—; create—; deepen—; develop—of; entertain —of; excite—; eye with—; fill with—; flock round in—; hold in—of; inspire with —; keep in—of; learn with—; mingle with —; oppress with—; overcome with—; remove—; shake with—; stand in—of; strike with—; —afflicts; —arises; —breeds; —overcomes; —shakes; —smites; —stirs; —strikes.

(See amazement, fear, reverence.)

AWKWARD

adverbs

clumsily; ungracefully; bashfully; shyly; gawkily; self-consciously; painfully; embarrassingly; ludicrously; laughably; ridiculously; intentionally; adorably; unconsci-

ously; charmingly; affectedly; momentarily; remarkably; flutteringly; clownishly; amusingly; pathetically; lamentably; unfortunately; helplessly; hopelessly.

AWKWARDNESS

adjectives

adorable; fumbling; mirth-provoking; pleased; unconscious; involuntary; slight; obvious; charming; blundering; affected; bristling; momentary.

verbs

begin in—; bungle with—; disperse—; encounter—; laugh at—; rebuke—; scorn—; —adheres; —embarrasses; —inconveniences. (See clumsiness.)

AWNING

adjectives

luxuriant; striped; woven; rotting; shady; gaudy; ordinary; ready-made; gaily-colored.

AXE

adjectives

keen; lusty; glittering; gallant; rude; sounding; devastating; biting; consecrated.

verbs

apply—; chop with—; clasp—; cleave with —; condemn to—; cool—; execute with—; fashion—; fell with—; forge—; grind—; hack with—; heave—; helve—; hew with —; lay on—; resist—; scar—; shaft—; shape—; sharpen—; slay with—; stroke—; swing—; temper—; turn—; wedge—; whip —; wield—; yield to—; —chips; —cleaves; —decapitates; —falls; —gleams; —glitters; —hacks; —hews; —resounds; —rings; —rusts.

(See hatchet.)

AXIOM

adjectives

simple; religious; moral; accepted; fundamental; irrefutable; educing; settled; divine; intricate; established.

AZURE

adjectives

kindling; greenish; vivid; intense; clear; glowing; cold; cloudless; ambient; smiling; dazzling; beauteous; palpitating.

B

adjectives
charming; ceaseless; drunken; foolish; incoherent; literary; senseless; perpetual; meaningless; idle; excited; irrelevant; soothing; childish; idiotic; pleasant; prattling; confused.

BABBLE (v)

adverbs
drunkenly; grievously; ecstatically; idiotically; weirdly; ingeniously; charmingly; ceaselessly; incoherently; perpetually; meaninglessly; irrelevantly; confusedly.
(See murmur, prattle.)

BABE

adjectives
innocent; unmothered; speechless; maiden; starving; wailing; nursing; testy; naked; unborn.

BABOON

adjectives
malevolent; bouncing; dog-faced; patriarchal; chattering; grotesque; gaping; smirking.

BABY

adjectives
healthy; fat; angelic; grown-up; pallid; sickly-looking; unweaned; peaceful; bewitching; sturdy; squalling; new-born; lonesome; pitiful; wriggling; cunning; squeaking; babbling; sticky; petulant; stronglunged; appealing; featureless; blithesome; staring; mewling; rosy-cheeked; tousled; clamorous; stubborn; disobedient; delicate; inopportune; undisciplined.

verbs
comfort—; cradle—; croon to—; fondle—; indulge—; lull—; mother—; quiet—; rear —; suckle—; swaddle—; tend—; train—; treat as—; wean—; —babbles; —coos; — creeps; —crows; —drools; —moans; — pukes; —plains; —teethes; —toddles; — weeps; —whimpers.
(See infant.)

BABYISH

adverbs
entrancingly; ridiculously; disgustingly; utterly; beamingly; angelically; sturdily; cunningly; appealingly; rosily; delicately; helplessly; clingingly; shyly; absurdly; adorably; completely; artlessly; boisterously; irresistibly; lovably; warmly; lustily; magically; mysteriously; excitedly.

BACHELOR

adjectives
virtuous; level-headed; arrant; vagrant; typical; sexagenary; impeccable; desolate; austere; dashing; predestined; crusty; cynical; solitary; elusive; confirmed; lonely; gruff; perennial; wary; indignant; perpetual.

BACK

adjectives
expressive; prosperous; narrow; wiry; slender; straight; innocent-looking; broad; benevolent; roomy; rigid; brawny; powerful; aching; inexorable; lovely; lithe; obtrusive; bent; naked; cringing; arched; agile; discreet; wrenched; deliberate; lacerated; burly; indiscriminate; stiffening; hairy; ramrod; contemptuous; incurious.

verbs
arch—; bear on—; bow—; buckle on—; clamor at—; huddle on—; hump—; mount —; pluck from—; prick—; recline on—; ride—; set upon—; strip—; sway—; upheave—; —arches; —creaks.

BACK (v)

adverbs
stealthily; consistently; obtrusively; cringingly; agilely; discreetly; deliberately; contemptuously.
(See support, indorse.)

BACKGROUND

adjectives
psychological; Puritan; political; historical; rich; Quakerish; botanical; proletarian; intellectual; educational; cultural; moral; monotheistic; inherited; pictorial; blurred; neutral; changeless; realistic; scenic; unwonted; stereotyped; garish; dense; serrated; meager; complex; star-flecked; shimmering; kaleidoscopic; broad; effective; financial; conspicuous; attractive; authentic; religious; fitting; immaterial; plain; harmonious; rocky; precipitous; theatrical; social; domestic; appropriate; technical; fascinating; vivid; lush; convincing; serene; striking; unforgettable; imaginative; glamorous; enchanting; admirable; impressive; shabby; sinister; cluttered; bizarre; weirdest.

verbs
blend into—; broaden—; enhance—; fade

into—; form—; maintain—; melt into—; paint—; screen—; set into—; weave—; — blends; —brightens; —contrasts; —enhances; —looms; —sets off.
(See setting.)

BACON
adjectives
crisp; tender; tasty; mouldy; crackling; rank; sizzling; tempting.

BACTERIA
adjectives
antagonistic; classified; disease-producing; friendly; gram-positive; harmful; infectious; invading; injurious; lethal; minute; multitudinous; overwhelming; poisonous; secondary; succulent; swarming.

verbs
absorb—; activate—; annihilate—; attack —; class—; combat—; cultivate—; culture —; destroy—; discover—; disperse—; distribute—through; dose with—; examine—; filter—; group—; identify—; immunize against—; inhale—; inoculate with—; investigate—; isolate—; observe—; produce—; propagate—; protect against—; raise—; resist—; separate—; study—; treat —; —behave; —cause; —course through; —disturb; —enter; —form; —increase; — infect; —invade; —irritate; —multiply; —poison; —reproduce; —secrete; —split; —spoil; —survive; —swarm; —dwell.
(See organism, germs.)

BAD
adverbs
flagrantly; destructively; infinitely; harmfully; dangerously; mischievously; violently; vilely; irretrievably; inconceivably; poisonously; abominably; accursedly; perniciously; viciously; basely; deplorably; detestably; diabolically; disastrously; dreadfully; exceptionally; grievously; hatefully; malignantly; obnoxiously; venomously; virulently; manifestly; scandalously; irremediably; irrevocably; immeasurably.

BADGE
adjectives
corrupt; distinctive; decorative; decorous; distinguished; emblematic; glittering; heraldic; identifying; imperial; pompous; pretentious; tarnished; tawdry.

verbs
bear—; blazon with—; flash—; flaunt—; merit—; ornament—; wear—; work—; — betokens; —distinguishes; —heralds; — honors; —indicates; —marks; —signifies.
(See device, emblem.)

BADGER
adjectives
belligerent; biting; aggressive; defensive; fierce; hibernating; ungainly; moody.

verbs
bait—; snare—; trap—; —s abound; — burrows; —charges; —claws; —digs; — dives in; —dwells; —excavates; —flattens out; —growls; —haunts; —hisses; —leaps; —lumbers; —mines; —plunges; —purrs; — retreats; —robs; —rushes; —senses; — seizes; —snarls; —sniffs; —squats.
(See animal.)

BADINAGE
adjectives
lazy; giddy; banal; good-natured; teasing; gay; cheap; frivolous; merciless; untimely.

BAFFLE (v)
adverbs
hopelessly; completely; genuinely; scarcely; continually; shrewdly; slyly; plainly.
(See thwart, frustrate.)

BAFFLING
adverbs
mysteriously; irritatingly; bewilderingly; unaccountably; disturbingly; genuinely; strangely; surprisingly; astonishingly; indescribably; fearfully; disappointingly; utterly; insuperably; dishearteningly; incommodiously; discouragingly; depressingly; terribly; vexatiously; seriously; alarmingly; perfectly; absolutely; incomprehensibly; inconceivably.

BAG
adjectives
sealed; sanitary; shiny; travel-worn; soggy; cloth-covered; bottomless; diminutive; bulky; pendulous.

verbs
bind in—; dip into—; purloin—; rifle—; seal—; secure in—; snatch—; stow—; trap in—; —bulges; —dangles; —emits; — hangs; —sags; —slides; —slips.
(See wallet, satchel.)

BAGGAGE
adjectives
unnecessary; hand; superfluous; mental; multitudinous; clumsy; ponderous; weighty.

verbs
abandon—; attend with—; convey—; dispatch—; encumber with—; lighten—; retrieve—; splotch—; stow—; transport—; tuck—away; —encumbers; —weighs.
(See satchel.)

adjectives

awesome; blood-chilling; dominant; droning; ear-splitting; eerie; fiercely-screaming; lamenting; long-winded; screeching; triumphant; victory-sounding; vengeful.

verbs

adjust—; blow upon—; compress—; elbow —; embrace—; esteem—; finger—; inflate —; introduce—; muffle—; press—; puff up —; regulate—; —bawls; —bellows; —chants; —cries; —drones; —emits; —expands; —groans; —harmonizes; —heaves; —labors; —mourns; —pipes; —proclaims; —rouses; —shrills; —sighs; —stirs; —swells; —wails; —whistles.

BAIL

adjectives

appointed; certified; forfeited; generous; responsible; specified; superficial; trifling; enforced; heavy; necessary; substantial.

verbs

admit to—; allow—; apply for—; assure—; bind with—; collect—; default—; demand —; deny—; designate—; dispense with—; enter—; exempt from—; fix—; forfeit—; furnish—; give—; grant—; gauge—; guarantee—; hold to—; insure by—; justify—; liberate on—; pledge—; post—; procure—; provide—; put up—; raise—; receive—; refund—; release on—; require—; risk—; satisfy with—; set—; set free on—; surrender—; —obligates; —releases.

(See security.)

BAIT

adjectives

tempting; dainty; false; seductive; coveted; treacherous; pernicious; alluring.

verbs

devour—; expose—; feed—; hold out—; proffer—; swallow—; —allures; —ensnares; —entices; —lures; —tempts; —traps.

(See lure, inducement, temptation.)

BALANCE

adjectives

unexpended; fabulous; unnatural; proper; delicate; subtle; artistic; comfortable; unpaid; neutral; sentimental; smooth; floating; adverse; peculiar; precarious; normal; miraculous; economic; trifling; workable; unfavorable; scrupulous; logical; physiological; trembling; accurate.

verbs

achieve—; adjust—; arrange—; attain—; augment—; bear—; bequeath—; control—; deflect—; determine—; disturb—; equalize —; even—; exhaust—; hang in—; hold—; lay in—; maintain—; measure—; reach—; readjust—; recover—; restore—; strike—; supply—; suspend on—; sway—; test—; tip —; totter in—; turn—; upset—; weigh in —; —turns.

(See scales, equilibrium.)

BALANCE (v)

adverbs

precariously; equally; ultimately; harmoniously; unskillfully; exactly; accurately; systematically; uncomfortably; cautiously; dexterously; eventually.

(See poise.)

BALCONY

adjectives

exquisite; overhanging; latticed; moon-drenched; screened; high-perched; vine-clad; narrow; grilled; delicate; frail.

verbs

crowd—; gain—; occupy—; overlook—; peer from—; rail—; salute from—; view from—; —encompasses; —overhangs; —projects; —swarms.

(See gallery.)

BALD

adverbs

shinily; fatly; rosily; hopelessly; nakedly; ruddily; ghastly; ridiculously; laughably; gracelessly; grossly; haggardly; hideously; unashamedly; odiously; shockingly; smilingly.

BALEFUL

adverbs

perniciously; terribly; venomously; malignantly; undeniably; villainously; exceptionally; sadly; grievously; deplorably; lamentably; woefully; shockingly; cruelly; detestably; infernally; irremediably; atrociously; malevolently; incorrigibly; brutally; unpardonably; incredibly; shamefully; iniquitously.

BALK (v)

adverbs

continually; cruelly; particularly; recalcitrantly; exasperatingly; pettishly; provokingly; irritatingly.

(See thwart, frustrate, baffle, disappoint.)

BALKY

adverbs

astonishingly; surprisingly; naturally; incorribibly; wonderfully; unexpectedly; tormentingly; vexatiously; embarrassingly; stubbornly; obstinately; temperamentally; characteristically; abnormally; habitually; usually; uncompromisingly; invariably; consistently; inherently; innately; blithely; unreasonably; provokingly; unaccountably.

BALL
(dance)
adjectives
inauguration; carnival; rustic; impromptu; magnificent; birthday; anniversary; annual; masquerade.

BALL
(object)
adjectives
gilded; glowing; gleaming; bouncing; glittering; devil-guided; luminous; swift; gelatinous; fungous.

BALL
(sport)
adjectives
back-firing; catapulting; foul; fair; ricocheting; trenchant; tangential; sodden; speeding; bombastic; refractory.

verbs
bat—; bobble—; bunt—; chuck—; club—; control—; cover—; drive—; feed —s; fling —; foul—; fumble—; grip—; heave—; hurl —; inflate—; juggle—; lob—; loft—; muff —; pass—; pole—; pop—; project—; pursue—; release—; round into—; smash—; snare—; spear—; strike—; top—; toss—; trap—; waggle at the golf—; whip—; zip —; —bounds; —curves; —hops; —zooms.

BALLAD
adjectives
woeful; doleful; ribald; odious; patriotic; vigorous; dramatic; celebrated; tawdry; rude; merry; scurrilous; tender; lewd; blasphemous; interminable; vulgar; sentimental; brisk; ringing; homely; dolorous; obscene; raucous.

verbs
accompany—; carol—; characterize—; classify—; compose—; measure—; narrate—; print—; revive—; traduce—; translate—; wail—; —celebrates; —deals with; —exploits; —narrates; —relates; —survives; —swells.
(See poem, song.)

BALLET
adjectives
gaudy; glittering; dainty; sumptuous; exquisite; fairylike.

BALLOON
adjectives
gigantic; invisible; floating; lifeless; air-filled; gaseous.

verbs
anchor—; attach to—; ballast—; blow—; burst—; check—; command—; dispatch—; cut away—; deflate—; elevate—; experiment with —s; fire—; guide—; improve—; inflate—; liberate—; lift—; lighten—; man —; navigate—; power—; propel—; steady —; suspend—; swell—; —ascends; —circles; —collapses; —descends; —drifts; —expands; —explodes; —floats; —journeys; —kites; —rises; —sallies; —soars; —spins; —tosses; —wallows.
(See bladder, aeroplane.)

BALLOT
adjectives
approved; adopted; computed; disputed; fatal; political; polled; open; reformed; secret.

verbs
accede by—; acknowledge by—; agree by—; arrange—; assent by—; broadcast—; cast —; circulate —s; choose by—; deposit—; draw up—; employ—; hinge on—; inspect —; introduce—; record—; reform—; reject —; satisfy with—; stuff —s; tabulate —s; tally —s; tamper with —s; —acquits; —affirms; —ascertains; —condemns; —decides; —elects; —eliminates; —installs; —proclaims.
(See vote, ticket.)

BALLROOM
adjectives
huge; improvised; dimly-lit; crowded; decorated.

BALM
adjectives
soothing; fragrant; golden; philosophic; blissful; healing; temperate; assuaging; precious; unguentary; icy.

verbs
anoint with—; exude—; soothe with—; steep in—; yield—; wash off—; —assuages; —charms; —eases; —heals; —mitigates; —soothes; —trickles.
(See ointment, salve.)

BALMY
adverbs
soothingly; refreshingly; softly; comfortingly; curatively; quietly; coolly; gently; mild-

ly; blandly; healingly; gratifyingly; satisfactorily; remarkably; tenderly; mercifully; pleasantly; especially.

BALUSTRADE
adjectives
granite; terrace; sandstone; marble; graceful; wrought-iron; exquisite; carved; shining; quaint; twisting; serpentine; monstrous.

BAMBOO
adjectives
delicate-leaved; pliant; plaited; feathery.

BAN
adjectives
authoritative; blasphemous; cruel; common; harsh; inhibitory; legal; maledictory; proclamatory; senseless; tyrannical; unjust.

verbs
announce—on; command—on; contradict—; curse—; decree—; end—; enforce—; exempt from—; impose—; lift—; proclaim—; publish—; reaffirm—; remove—; renew—; send—; —deprives; —forbids; —offends; —outlaws; —prohibits.

(See notice, taboo, edict, proclamation, excommunication.)

BANAL
adverbs
monotonously; tritely; tiresomely; boringly; disagreeably; drearily; unceasingly; invariably; triflingly; vapidly; inanely; insipidly; intolerably; trivially; unbearably; exhaustingly; wearily; tediously; frivolously; senselessly; vacuously; insufferably; habitually; prosily; uninterestingly.

BANALITY
adjectives
routine; easy; preliminary; gross; unpleasant; boring; dreary; repetitious.

BANANA
adjectives
tempting; sun-hungry; lush; ripened.

BAND
adjectives (company)
aimless; diminished; detached; ferocious; foraging; gladsome; hunted; hapless; march-worn; pillaging; rapine; rollicking; straggling; vandalistic; victorious.

verbs
arm—; associate with—; attach to—; banish from—; bind in a holy—; captain—; collect—; compose—; disperse—; divide into —s; enlist in—; muster—; scatter—; summon—; unite in—; wander in—; —attacks; —invades; —pillages; —plunders; —pursues; —roves; —shrinks.

(See company, group, gang, troop.)

BAND
adjectives (fetter, tie)
ring-stacked; quivered; artful; swaddling; unrelieved; restraining; flexible; iridescent; metallic.

verbs
break asunder the—s; cancel—s; chain in —s; dissolve—; link in —s; release from —s; rend —s; strengthen —s; twist —s; untie —s; untwine —s; weaken—; —s bind; —s encircle; —s fetter; —s shackle.

(See tie, cord, bond, fetter, belt, bandage, chain.)

BAND
adjectives (group)
infuriated; angelic; cycling; alabaster; ruthless; scarlet; riotous; massed; melancholy; marauding; adverse; servile; devoted; encircling; colic; baleful; eager; doomed; notorious; peaceful; full; unbroken; bloody; amiable; swirling; murderous; numberless; resplendent; scattered; reckless; chosen; shadowy; formidable; violent; apathetic; restless; defiant; eternal; itinerant; enthralling; wandering; guerilla; fantastic; sullen; glittering; expectant; valiant; considerable; predatory; snail-like; gallant; mirth-breathing; heroic; enormous; mute; ghastly; scanty; boisterous; prying; mirthful; devoted; adventurous; ambitious; imperious; fairy; social; scattering; brazen; nondescript; partisan; thin; doughty; fierce; worn; insignificant; rival; small; well-armed; thundering; wild; howling; heretical; shabby; unkempt; conspicuous; feeble; mighty; unconquerable; inexhaustible; laborious; invading; brave.

BAND
adjectives (instrumental)
tuneful; stirring; gorgeously-arrayed; regimental; swing; jazz; competent.

verbs
assemble—; compose—; conduct—; engage —; group—; maintain—; organize—; pitch —; strike up—; supervise—; —arouses; —blares; —blasts on; —encourages; —harmonizes; —honors; —marches; —parades;

—performs; —renders; —serenades; —
toots; —troops.
(See orchestra.)

BANDAGE

adjectives
crimsoned; filthy; swathing; emergency;
bloodstained; saving.

verbs
apply—; attach—; border with—; change
—; discard—; fasten—; loose—; replace—;
sew—; sterilize—; stitch—; stripe with —s;
swathe in —s; tighten—.
(See band.)

BANDIT

adjectives
famous; amiable; cold-blooded; ferocious;
ruthless; wily; out-and-out; dark-visaged;
bold; outrageous; notorious; reckless; tantalizing; enraged; burly; restless; lawless.

verbs
defend—; execute—; grant sanctuary to—;
hire—; hunt—; imprison—; infest with —s;
organize—; outlaw—; seclude—; slay—; —
harries; —marauds; —s pillage; —s plunder; —s terrorize.
(See robber, burglar.)

BANDY (v)

adverbs
mercilessly; repeatedly; continuously; freely; haphazardly; thoughtlessly.
(See toss.)

BANG

adjectives
loud; emphatic; thudding; resounding; ear-
splitting.

BANG (v)

adverbs
fitfully; resoundingly; loudly; emphatically; terrifically; crashingly; tremendously;
explosively; thunderously; furiously.
(See thump, resound.)

BANISH (v)

adverbs
utterly; effectually; everlastingly; perpetually; dishonorably; eternally; inescapably;
deservedly; ultimately; reluctantly; cruelly.
(See dismiss, expel.)

BANISHMENT

adjectives
timely; everlasting; perpetual; honorable;
deadly; eternal; inescapable; deserved.

verbs
compel—; consent to—; decree—; doom to
—; order—; repeal—; reside in—; return
from—; suffer—.
(See exile, expulsion.)

BANJO

adjectives
melodious; melancholy; tuneless; twanging;
plunking; soul-fathoming; heart-voicing;
unstrung; voodoo-charming.

verbs
compose for—; employ—; excel at—; finger
—; fret—; harmonize with—; introduce—;
peg—; perform on—; pick—; pluck—; strike
—; string—; strum—; twitch—; —expresses; —lulls; —registers; —serenades; —
sings; —twangs; —vibrates.
(See instrument, music.)

BANK (finance)

adjectives
shiftless; leading; unthrifty; local; financial; depleted; impoverished; badly-man-
aged; safe; insured.

verbs
borrow from—; charter—; conduct—; consult—; deal with—; deposit in—; draw
upon—; equip—; loot—; patronize—; plunder—; run on—; wreck—; —acquires; —
advances; —advises; —amasses; —appropriates; —authorizes; —branches; —cashes;
—charges; —collapses; —consolidates; —
discounts; —dominates; —drafts; —expands; —finances; —flourishes; —guards;
—handles; —incorporates; —insures; —invests; —issues; —loans; —manages; —
mortgages; —negotiates; —operates; —profits; —rates; —regulates; —sanctions; —
serves; —transacts.
(See banker, firm, company, corporation.)

BANK (land)

adjectives
naked; oozy; perpendicular; shagged; grassy; wooded; precipitous; steep; slippery;
tottering; glorious; flowering; rocky; river;
mud; sloping; mossy; willow; sheltering;
forested; shelving; placid; tossing; pine-
clad; green-wooded; rugged; dirt; overhanging; miry; gentle; weedy; curving;
rain-gullied; clay; eroding; tree-lined;
heavily-wooded; glistening; caving; mosquito-infested; rabbit-riddled; willow-tufted;
low-lying; unlimited; enormous; smothering; noisy; frequented; fringed; deep; impassable; unmolested; storm-shaken; weary;
embroidered; permanent; high; bramble-

covered; primrose; chalk; starred; settled; craggy; stifled; ash; wasted; picturesque; marshy; swampy; rugged; herbless; upland; tawny; bounding; beauteous; verdant; calm; rounding; porcelain; encompassing; lonesome; craggy; fraudulent; puddled; never-withering; glittering; blossomladen.

verbs
bask on—; bound by —s; couch on—; fortify —s; overflow —s; scramble up—; shadow—; support—; swell over—; teeter on —; —encircles; —s rise.
(See ridge, pile.)

BANKER
adjectives
conservative; prosperous; resourceful; foremost; international; sophisticated; tall; dignified; mustached; gray-haired; trusted; rich; mean; bearded; cautious; private; leading; upstate; honest; hard-headed; prominent; defaulting; metropolitan; sagacious; astute; expert; established; benevolent; shortsighted; unscrupulous.

verbs
denounce—; envy—; protect—; —absconds; —collects; —contracts; —credits; —deals; —defaults; —embezzles; —executes; —investigates; —proffers; —provides; —refunds; —reimburses; —remits; —safeguards; —secures; —swindles; —traffics in.

BANKRUPT
adverbs
frequently; unfortunately; unhappily; profitably; conveniently; adroitly; inevitably; morally; irretrievably; unaccountably; mysteriously; surprisingly; seriously; temporarily; expediently; smartly; ingeniously; pitiably; dishearteningly; grievously; ruinously; touchingly; hopelessly; heartbreakingly.

BANKRUPTCY
adjectives
inevitable; economic; honest; moral; voluntary; irretrievable.

verbs
adjudge—; administer by—; administrate in —; annul—; arrange for—; arise from—; assent to—; authorize—; avoid—; commit to—; contract—; declare—; decree—; defer —; delay—; discharge from—; drift into—; effect—; embarrass into—; enter—; evade —; examine for—; face—; force into—; head for—; incur—; investigate—; involve

—; liquidate in—; petition for—; record—; reduce to—; relieve by—; save from—; seize in—; settle—; surrender to—; terminate in—; threaten with—; verge on—; —deprives; —divests; —solves; —threatens.
(See failure.)

BANNER
adjectives
bloodless; darkling; tattered; starry; spangled; elastic; prosperous; flaunting; murky; insurgent; bright-colored; gaudy; mimic; emblematical; superb; barbarous; gorgeous; unfurled; horse-tail; hostile; flapping; gay; flamboyant; victorious; appropriate; clustered; sinister; bloodstained; triumphant; rippling; holy; silken; star-faced; faded; historic; impalpable; crimsoned; ragged.

verbs
adopt—; bear—; flaunt—; flout—; gather round—; hail—; hang out—; hoist—; lift —; rally round—; serve—; spread—; stretch out—; unfurl—; unroll—; wave—; —dances; —droops; —flies; —flutters; —inspires; —rises into the air; —streams; —symbolizes; —undulates.
(See flag, standard, ensign.)

BANQUET
adjectives
unpretentious; sumptuous; diplomatic; delicious; fantastical; open-air; luxurious; artistic; unending; exotic; artificial; voluptuous; good-will; Lucullan; elaborate; stately; philanthropic.

BANTER
adjectives
familiar; good-natured; brilliant; delicate; contemptuous; gay; slow; facetious; witty.

verbs
assail with—; chide with—; engage in—; exchange—; indulge in—; pass for—; ridicule with—; turn to—; —entertains; —floats about.
(See ridicule, derision, mockery, repartee.)

BANTER (v)
adverbs
vivaciously; familiarly; brilliantly; delicately; contemptuously; gaily; facetiously; wittily; good-naturedly; slyly; cleverly; satirically.
(See jest, chaff.)

BAR
adjectives
unfeeling; resonant; colossal; extemporized;

statutory; invidious; anticipatory; inexorable; sullen; dissolving; alternating (pl); corporeal; multitudinous (pl); legal; oaken; drink-laden.

BAR
(law)
adjectives
lofty; magisterial; inviolable; relentless; arraigning; ruling; invincible.

verbs
accuse at—; address—; admit to—; appear before—; arraign before—; beseech—; bring to—; cajole—; call to—; defend at —; disagree with—; elect to—; expel from —; influence—; pass—; plead before—; reproach—; resign from—; solicit—; station at—; summon to—; —administers; —advises; —criticizes; —directs; —disciplines; — encourages; —establishes; —exercises; — governs; —grants; —orders; —privileges; —rules.
(See tribunal, law.)

BAR
(obstruction)
adjectives
basic; formidable; frowning; impassable; protective; forbidding; impenetrable; unscalable.

verbs
beat —s; cut —s; escape —s; fence in with —s; strengthen —s; —creates a barrier; — excludes; —hinders; —impedes; —obstructs; —prevents; —prohibits; —restrains.
(See barrier, obstruction, obstacle.)

BAR (v)
adverbs
strongly; unfeelingly; invidiously; inexorably; sullenly; corporeally; legally; determinedly; harshly; ultimately; utterly; unkindly; treacherously.
(See exclude, hinder, obstruct, restrain.)

BARBARIAN
adjectives
ferocious; sanguinary; tumultuous; idolatrous; lusty; obstinate; suspicious; bestial.

verbs
civilize—; conquer—; crush—; culture—; dominate —s; overcome—; quell—; repress —; subdue—; vanquish—; —imitates; —s overthrow; —pillages; —plunders; —subjugates; —sacks.
(See brute, savage, monster.)

BARBARISM
adjectives
medieval; colloquial; unenlightened; dark; heathen; unavoidable.

verbs
brand—; crash into—; degrade to—; descend to—; enslave by—; fall to—; rise from—; stave off—; succeed—.
(See brutality, anarchy.)

BARBARITY
adjectives
execrable; shocking; vulgar; calculated; legal; deliberate; indecent.

BARBAROUS
adverbs
fiercely; savagely; shockingly; deliberately; outlandishly; rudely; inhumanly; brutally; indecently; unforgivably; inherently; instinctively; heathenishly; triumphantly; vauntingly; mercilessly; fiendishly; oddly; uncouthly; bizarrely; grotesquely; cruelly; blatantly; flagrantly; incredibly.

BARD
adjectives
love-stricken; saturnine; high-dreaming; didactic; epic; merry; subtle; pied; mercenary; gifted.

BARE
adverbs
starkly; nakedly; pitiably; shamelessly; distressingly; skimpily; scantily; stingily; pathetically; austerely; painfully; grievously; unfortunately; wretchedly; miserably; cheerlessly; horribly; surprisingly; desolately; dismally; hopelessly; deplorably; utterly; unnecessarily.

BARGAIN
adjectives
mammoth; amazing; selfish; outstanding; remarkable; vaunted; sensational; sharp; fair; sordid; impious.

verbs
agree upon—; bind to—; buy a—; close a —; consider—; contract for—; discuss—; drive a—; enter into—; fulfill—; gobble up —; jump at—; maintain—; propose—; refuse—; release from—; rue—; seal—; search for —s; seize—; settle—; stipulate in—; strike—; strive for—.
(See transaction, contract.)

BARGAIN (v)
adverbs
collectively; indigently; amazingly; selfish·

93

ly; remarkably; sensationally; sharply; fairly; sordidly; impiously; cleverly; shrewdly; stupidly; astutely.
(See agree, contract, stipulate.)

BARGE
adjectives
imperial; ungainly; gorgeous; state; abandoned; sluggish; dingy; gaily-painted; clumsy.

verbs
adorn—; anchor—; board—; christen—; command—; control—; convoy—; cushion —; decorate—; design—; dock—; equip—; escort—; fit out—; land—; lash—; launch —; license—; moor—; navigate—; pilot—; power—; propel—; rig—; shift—; stow—; straddle—; tow—; —coasts; —conveys; — discharges; —drifts; —journeys; —plies; —sails; —slips past; —trades; —transports; —tugs.
(See boat.)

BARK
adjectives (boat)
venturous; perfidious; passing; stranded; swift-winged; lofty; fragile; floating; deep-drawing; foundering; proud; flying; frail; enchanted; storm-tossed.

BARK
adjectives (dog's)
snappish; harsh; fiendish; welcoming; irritated; short; sharp; wild; eager; thundering; swaggering; acute; agonized; imperative; gay; high-pitched; teasing; expressive; ferocious; frenzied; staccato; frantic; furious; deafening; ecstatic; jubilant; ringing; desolate; muffled; defiant; confident; playful.

BARK
adjectives (tree)
sapless; gnarled; rugged; indigenous; silvery; bruised; corrugated; peeling.

BARK (*v*)
adverbs
imperiously; lustily; inopportunely; explosively; joyously; injuriously; snappishly; harshly; fiendishly; welcomingly; irritatedly; sharply; wildly; eagerly; agonizedly; imperatively; teasingly; expressively; ferociously; frenziedly; frantically; deafeningly; jubilantly; desolately; defiantly; confidently; playfully.
(See shout.)

BARN
adjectives
substantial; commodious; solitary; comfortable; cool; tumble-down; ruinous; dilapidated; rickety; rambling; ramshackle; abandoned; neglected; decaying; well-filled; bulging.

verbs
construct—; equip—; erect—; fire—; forage in—; frame—; gather into—; house in—; install in—; remodel—; stable in—; stake out—; store in—; —collapses; —harbors; —shelters.
(See building.)

BAROMETER
adjectives
alternating; disconcerting; steadily-rising; unvarying; vacillating; threatening; faltering.

verbs
adjust—; affect—; compensate—; correct—; depend on—; devise—; employ—; equip with—; experiment with—; expose—; govern—; influence—; learn from—; read—; record—; rely on—; seal—; sheathe—; steady—; test—; throw off—; vouch for—; —assists; —climbs; —demonstrates; —determines; —falls; —fluctuates; —forecasts; —graduates; —indicates; —measures; — oscillates; —predicts; —records; —registers; —represents; —rises; —shows; —sinks; — soars; —threatens; —warns.
(See meter, thermometer.)

BARON
adjectives
medieval; villainous; cattle; feudal; despotic; coal; monocled; proud; impetuous; monstrous.

BARRACKS
adjectives
bleak; disciplinary; grim; cheerless; orderly; solid.

verbs
advance toward—; allot to—; arouse—; arrange for—; assault—; assign to—; censor —; command—; concentrate in—; confine to—; construct—; convert into—; dispatch to—; encamp in—; equip—; extend to—; file into—; fire on—; fortify—; guard—; invade—; protect—; quarter in—; repair to—; report to—; restrict to—; retire to—; sanitize—; station in—; superintend—; survey—; threaten—; —accommodate; —collapse; —house; —lodge; —resound; — spring up.

(See quarters, shelter, building.)

BARRAGE

adjectives
gigantic; advertising; incessant; verbal; rolling; murderous; leaden; shrapnel; deadly; fatal; vicious; violent.

verbs
advance under—; approach—; beat down —; concentrate—; create—; curtain with—; defend against—; defy—; denounce—; disperse—; establish—; extend—; invade—; lay down—; penetrate—; prolong—; reduce —; resist—; restrict—; retreat from—; strengthen—; sweep through—; —cuts off; —holds up; —obstructs; —parries; —protects; —surprises; —threatens.

BARREL

adjectives
dilapidated; hoopless; cobwebbed; mossgrown; sagging; scarred; slimy; stout; warped.

verbs
bung—; measure—; pipe—; pump from—; roll—; store in—; stove in—; tap—; valve —; —bulges; —reeks; —resounds; —thuds; —thunders; —tumbles.

BARREN

adverbs
monotonously; treelessly; desolately; endlessly; infinitely; alarmingly; frightfully; indescribably; immeasurably; comfortlessly; formidably; blankly; inhospitably; illimitably; boundlessly; terrifyingly; perilously.

BARRICADE

adjectives
verdant; feeble; defensive; disputed; stone; bristling; human; effective.

verbs
advance toward—; approach—; assault—; capture—; defend—; denounce—; entrench behind—; erect—; extend—; invade—; pile up—; strengthen—; support—; survey—; sweep through—; threaten—; withdraw—; —annoys; —bars; —blocks; —collapses; —confines; —cuts off; —defends; —fortifies; —parries; —prevents; —protects; —resists; —restricts; —withholds.
(See barrier, obstruction.)

BARRIER

adjectives
golden; external; sufficient; insuperable; material; formidable; subjective; effective;

feeble; obstinate; intervening; screening; conventional; fancied; invisible; insurmountable; stair-like; impassable; airy; serried; moss-draped; dismal; ancient; irregular; surf-beaten; absolute; stout; invincible; powerful; unconquerable; mighty; impenetrable; awesome; lofty; serious; eternal; natural; legal; psychological; economic; cultural; vast; lowered; inadequate; stubborn; artificial; puerile; indefinable; pitiless; traditional; countless (pl); imagined.

verbs
beat—; build—; burst—; confine by—; create—; cross—; erect—; flatten against—; follow—; form—; hurdle—; hurl against—; jump—; rail in with —s; smash—; step over —; strengthen—; surmount—; tear down—; vault—; —bounds; —hinders; —isolates; —limits; —looms; —obstructs; —prevents; —supports; —thwarts.
(See obstruction, barricade.)

BARRISTER

adjectives
conscientious; ambitious; overworked; struggling; smug; briefless; infant; sneering; brilliant; competent.

BASE

adjectives
substantial; solidified; tottering; commodious; crumbling; flattering; immutable; firm; circular.

verbs
advance to—; attach to—; break from—; build on—; challenge—; communicate with —; construct—; create—; decorate—; dump at—; enlarge—; establish—; gather at—; hollow—; issue from—; mould—; protect—; puncture—; rest on—; separate from—; set on—; situate at—; spread on—; store at—; —projects.
(See foundation, basis, bottom.)

BASE (a)

adverbs
intolerably; meanly; ignobly; obscurely; contemptibly; abjectly; unbecomingly; undisguisedly; shamefully; glaringly; flagrantly; unmistakably; palpably; nakedly; brazenly; shamelessly; flauntingly; sorrily; brutishly; rudely; fawningly; obsequiously; cringingly; sneakily; subtly.

BASE (v)

adverbs
primarily; wholly; unsoundly; substantially; totteringly; firmly; immutably.
(See depend.)

verbs
blacken—; condemn—; destroy—; rebuke—; sponsor—; spread—; welcome—; —animates; —breeds; —engenders; —enlivens.
(See game.)

BASEMENT

adjectives
sunless; dark; stone; historical; excavated; dungeon-like; dank; damp; airless; musty; rat-infested.

verbs
climb from—; consist of—; drain—; excavate—; floor—; flood—; form—; relegate to—; rummage in—; well from—.
(See cellar.)

BASENESS

adjectives
inherent; forced; unconfinable; adroit; despicable; apparent; undisguised.

BASHFUL

adverbs
awkwardly; uneasily; boyishly; self-consciously; embarrassingly; uncomfortably; painfully; engagingly; charmingly; peculiarly; strangely; unwontedly; becomingly; naturally; modestly; timidly; fearfully; clumsily; foolishly; distressingly; ridiculously; pitiably; touchingly; adorably; comically; absurdly.

BASHFULNESS

adjectives
uneasy; maiden; engaging; virgin; childish; boyish; graceful; captivating; peculiar; shamefaced.

verbs
feign—; mask in—; shrink in—; —disturbs; —inhibits; —melts; —overcomes; —unfits.
(See modesty, shyness, diffidence.)

BASIC

adverbs
scientifically; fundamentally; essentially; indispensably; admittedly; emphatically; prescriptively; usually; ordinarily; officially; obviously; palpably; conspicuously; explicitly; positively; definitely; unavoidably.

BASIN

adjectives
remarkable; treeless; shallow; vast; starlit; drainage; rock-bottomed; tidal; empty; volcanic; gigantic; pitlike; lacustrine; rustic; beautiful; incrusted; weedy; marshy; na-

tural; fan-shaped; broad; spacious; sumptuous.

BASIS

adjectives
psychological; moral; social; military; commission; logical; scientific; voluntary; geographical; tangible; potential; essential; sustaining; concrete; apperceptive; experimental; daily; hypothetical; structural; universal; simplified; sound; economic; well-established; sensible; rationalized; secure; efficient; profitable; firm; prosperous; indispensable; healthy; solid; equitable; liberal; substantial; broad; possible; false; unsatisfactory; narrow; slippery; temporary; vast; meager; factual; ample; permanent; tenuous; inevitable; reliable; pecuniary; corporative; practical; immovable; flimsy; philosophical; physical; monarchical; creditable; feudal; mechanical; theoretical; dubious; imperishable; fantastic; enduring; lowest.

verbs
build upon—; establish a—; explain on—; form—; found on—; meet on—of; obtain—; place on—; rest on—; rise from—of; shake —; support on—; win a higher—; —consists.
(See foundation, base.)

BASK (*v*)

adverbs
obviously; torpidly; cozily; lazily; drowsily; blissfully; comfortably; sleepily; pleasantly; restfully.
(See luxuriate.)

BASKET

adjectives
enormous; rustic; severe; round; shallow; inexhaustible; wicker; huge; garlanded; split-oak; cup-shaped; upturned; filigree.

verbs
charge—; coil—; convey in—; cram in—; design—; fashion—; lattice into—; load—; measure in—; net—; provision—; stuff—; twine—; weave—.
(See case, chest, box.)

BASKING

adverbs
luxuriously; comfortably; buoyantly; joyously; prosperously; happily; warmly; radiantly.

BASS

adverbs
thunderingly; resonantly; deeply; breezily; boomingly; awfully; mightily; magnificently; toweringly; enormously; stupendously.

BASS
(fish)

adjectives
game; scrappy; small-mouthed; stern; skittish.

BASS
(voice)

adjectives
thunderous; resonant; bawling; masculine; profound; growling; deep; unruly; swelling; mellow; breezy.

BASTION

adjectives
sparkling; absurd; massive; futile; sloping; tower-like; coral.

BAT
(baseball)

adjectives
firm-resounding; decisive; sturdy; uncompromising; stout; spindly; threatening; relentless.

verbs
balance—; choose—; fling—; fondle—; grip —; oil—; paw—; release—; sandpaper—; scrape—; select—; shave—; shorten—; shoulder—; split—; swish—; tape—; weight —; wield—; —cracks; —flies; —slips; —splits.
(See club.)

BAT
(mammal)

adjectives
insectivorous; gloomy; grisly; monstrous.

verbs
attract—; disturb—; ensnare—; entice—; loose—; pursue—; strike—; trap—; —s abound; —clings; —flits; —hibernates; —lurks; —preys upon; —shuns; —sucks; —swoops; —terrorizes; —wheels; —whirls; —whirs; —wings.
(See animal, bird, insect.)

BATH

adjectives
chemical; imperceptible; ice; cold; Diocletian; perfumed; steaming; reducing; discomforting; relaxing; refreshing; portable; warm; soapy; splashing; freezing; medicated; involuntary; tepid; open-air; sun; modern; finely-appointed; immaculate; world-famous; well-equipped; radio-active; mud; matutinal.

verbs
administer—; arrange—; cure by —s; drain —; enter—; immerse in—; lather in—; loll in—; medicate—; perspire in—; rub in—; scald in—; sponge in—; steam in—; treat in

—; vaporize—; —enervates; —exhilarates; —refreshes; —relaxes.
(See water.)

BATHE (*v*)

adverbs
actually; chemically; steamingly; discomfortingly; comfortingly; refreshingly; soapily; splashingly; freezingly; involuntarily; tepidly; immaculately; daily; matutinally; thoroughly.
(See wash.)

BATHER

adjectives
ecstatic; adventurous; timid; floundering; inept; expert.

BATHING

adjectives
unexcelled; luxurious; indiscriminate; clear; clean; surf; safe; ocean.

BATON

adjectives
authoritative; commanding; directing; gilt; guiding; silencing; silver-tipped; suspended.

verbs
carry—; conduct with—; cudgel with—; dash—; direct with—; flourish—; lead—; mark with—; point—; signal with—; strike —; swing—; tap—; wave—; wield—; —guides.
(See wand, sceptre.)

BATTALION

adjectives
repulsed; puny; assaulting; steel-clad; potential; defending; staunch; sturdy; stalwart.

BATTER

adjectives
alert; deftly-moving; eagle-eyed; able-armed; wary; splendid; famous.

verbs
fan—; strike out—; —bats; —bunts; —crashes; —doubles; —drives; —flies; —fouls; —hits; —loops; —pops; —singles; —steals; —triples; —walks.

BATTERY

adjectives
sensitive; galvanic; pointed; discharged; weakened.

BATTLE

adjectives
bitter; hard-fought; furious; terrific; fierce;

raging; frantic; desperate; hot; bloody; savage; gory; gallant; sanguinary; thrilling; glorious; mighty; valiant; decisive; ceaseless; brief; impending; arduous; incessant; strenuous; historic; bloodless; inglorious; exhausting; hopeless; undercover; stiff; ironic; silent; pitched; fateful; phantom; life-long; offensive; parliamentary; dramatic; unrighteous; perpetual; discouraging; hereditary; nameless; memorable; earthly; childish; verbal; crashing; hand-to-hand; immediate; never-ending; weird; raging; naval; puny; intellectual; disastrous; losing.

verbs
arouse a—; clash in—; climax—; conflict in—; contend in—; create—; distinguish in —; doom to—; encounter in—; engage in—; finance—; gain in—; gird for—; give—; honor in—; join—; light the fuse of—; manoeuver—; offer—; overcome in—; pit in—; pitch—; precipitate—; premeditate—; provoke—; pursue—; slay in—; stay—; strive in—; subsist in—; sway—; triumph in—; wage—; —depends on; —ensues; — flashes; —presses; —rages; —rings; — swirls.
(See conflict, encounter, combat, fight, contest.)

BATTLE (v)
adverbs
fiercely; doggedly; invincibly; manfully; heroically; furiously; terrifically; desperately; gallantly; thrillingly; gloriously; valiantly; decisively; ceaselessly; briefly; arduously; incessantly; strenuously; hopelessly; exhaustingly; silently; fatefully; perpetually; childishly; verbally; intellectually; disastrously.
(See fight, encounter, combat.)

BATTLEFIELD
adjectives
immense; immortal; stupendous; rolling; ill-fated; scarred; silent; bloody; bone-strewn; glorious; memorial.

verbs
abandon on—; advance on—; assault on—; campaign on—; clash on—; concede on—; concentrate on—; encounter on—; enmesh on—; exhaust on—; fell on—; mass on—; occupy—; overthrow on—; perish on—; redden—; relinquish—; replace on—; slay on —; suffer on—; surprise on—; surrender on —; test on—; —lies, —reaps a harvest; —reeks; —stretches.
(See field, plain.)

BATTLELINE
adjectives
wavering; bent; far-flung; crushed; crumbling; tottering.

BATTLEMENTS
adjectives
frowning; massive; time-scarred; dim; castellated; crackling; imperial; haunted; escarped; cloud-capped; shining; narrow; gilded; tottered.

BAUBLE
adjectives
ingenious; gilt; worthless; imperial; silken; gorgeous; gleaming; heavy.

BAWD
adjectives
wicked; powdered; notorious; infamous; lewd; libidinous.

BAWL (v)
adverbs
hoarsely; plaintively; pitifully; intermittently; fitfully; loudly; wailingly.
(See cry.)

BAY
adjectives
land-locked; craggy; shallow; native; tranquil; yawning; eddying; noble; silvery; curving; regal; extensive; deep; protective; roaring; billowy; treacherous; glassy; squally; distant; sheltered; whispering; shimmering; murky; shark-infested; broadening; magnificent; protected; misted.

verbs
anchor in—; break on—; dredge—; drop into—; embark at—; enter—; put into—; recede into—; ride—; surround—; —eddies; —extends; —lashes the beach; —narrows; —widens.
(See ocean, river, gulf, harbor.)

BAYONET
adjectives
gleaming; pointless; glistening; fixed; bared; flashing; pitiless; ruthless; slanting; slashing; gory; grisly; merciless; murderous.

verbs
arm with—; attach—; charge with —s; clasp —; clutch—; connect—; defend with—; drive home—; equip with—; fix—; impale on—; insert—; jab with—; juggle—; raise —; repulse with—; rush with—; sheathe—; shield from—; spar with—; stab with—;

struggle with—; thrust—; vanquish with—;
wield—; withdraw—; —catches; —flashes;
—gores; —gouges; —pierces; —sticks.
(See dagger, weapon.)

BAZAAR
adjectives
straggling; languorous; Oriental; romantic;
gay; grubby; modern; noisy.

BEACH
adjectives
artificial; accessible; secluded; clean; sloping; crescent; sandy; curving; private; sunwarmed; beautiful; commodious; gay;
bright; fascinating; golden; rocky; pebbly;
silvery; brilliant; sun-swept; gleaming;
silent; desolate; shelving; surf-smoothed;
windless; mosquito-infested; ancient; calcareous; foamy; private.

verbs
batter—; break on—; dawdle along—; drift
on—; lash against—; pound—; ripple on—;
roam—; run aground on—; settle on—;
sprawl on—; stagger onto—; strand on—;
strew—; throw up on—; —extends; —
gleams; —stretches.
(See shore.)

BEACON
adjectives
eternal; indubitable; towering; revolving;
long-distance; visual; dangerous; spiritual;
gleaming; rebel; warning.

verbs
operate—; provide—; set—; —aids; —blazons; —circles; —directs; —guides; —identifies; —illuminates; —indicates; —leads;
—lights; —marks; —notifies; —rotates; —
shines; —signals; —swings; —warns.
(See fire, light, signal.)

BEADS
adjectives
wired; shining; iridescent; pale; gleaming;
coiled; garish; many-colored; greasy; wood-
en; pea-sized; unstrung; cheap.

verbs
barter with—; color—; count—; crush—;
dye—; facet—; fashion—; grind—; mould
—; mount—; ornament with—; perforate
—; pray with—; shape—; space—; string
—; suspend—; trade—; trim with—; —
glisten; —sparkle.
(See diamond, ornament, drop, jewel.)

BEAK
adjectives
curled; relentless; ravening; golden; brazen;
Wellingtonian; lifelike; twisted; hooked;
powerful; crooked; tuneless.

BEAM
(light)
adjectives
quivering; hazy; dulled; transient; sunny;
noonday; blessed; invisible; silvery; chaste;
stray; steady; unwinking; eternal; creeping; intermittent; half-extinguished; bright;
pallid; guiding; fervid; virgin; naked; feeble; divergent; crimson; intellectual; belated; transverse; kindly; slanting; piercing;
horizontal; penetrating; weird; leaf-en-
tangled; genial; blinding; sunny; burning;
effulgent; gracious; glancing; refracted.

verbs
clothe in —s; emit—; enwreathe with —s;
flash—; fling—; focus—; follow—; furnish
—; gild with —s; isolate—; outshine—;
play—upon; radiate—; shade—; shed—;
shoot—; spot—; throw—; —blazes; —
blinds; —brightens; —creeps up; —dazzles;
—directs; —emanates from; —glitters; —
guides; —penetrates; —pierces; —reflects;
—scorches; —shines; —shoots forth; —
slants; —sweeps.
(See ray, gleam.)

BEAM
(wood)
adjectives
sagging; massive; uncovered; metal-weight-
ed; rough; hand-hewn; exposed; blackened;
tarred.

verbs
arch—; center—; cross —s; fell—; lay—;
saw—; set—; split—; suspend from—; warp
—; —connects; —extends; —projects; —
strengthens; —supports.
(See timber.)

BEAM (v)
adverbs
affably; vaguely; benevolently; radiantly;
hazily; transiently; sunnily; unwinkingly;
chastely; steadily; eternally; intermittently;
pallidly; fervidly; nakedly; intellectually;
feebly; belatedly; slantingly; horizontally;
penetratingly; weirdly; genially; blindingly;
effulgently; graciously.
(See gleam, shine, glitter, glisten.)

BEAMING
adverbs
radiantly; joyously; fairly; delicately; beautifully; becomingly; bonnily; curiously; unconsciously; gorgeously; prettily; rosily;

smilingly; laughingly; ridiculously; foolishly; ruddily; sparklingly; mischievously;
openly; innocently; girlishly; shyly; modestly; frankly; happily; brightly.

BEAR
adjectives
ponderous; huge; crafty; burly; brindled;
fearless; monstrous; murderous; menacing;
untamed; vicious; playful.

verbs
ambush—; bait—; cage—; chain—; confine—; exterminate —s; fatten—; harass—;
madden—; roast—; skin—; stalk—; tame
—; tether—; trap—; —attacks; —burrows;
—charges; —claws; —climbs; —clowns;
—dances; —flourishes; —forages; —gambols; —growls; —grunts; —hibernates; —
hugs; —lumbers; —lurks; —migrates; —
multiplies; —paws; —pounces on; —preys
on; —ravages; —roars; —sheds; —shuffles;
—whelps.
(See animal.)

BEAR (v)
adverbs
patiently; manfully; oppressively; prematurely; extremely; stiffly; valiantly; coldly;
stoically; recklessly; philosophically; heavily; hurriedly.
(See endure, stand, tolerate.)

BEARD
adjectives
sheaved; vigorous; spreading; bushy;
tawny; curly; peaked; dripping; comic; incipient; wiry; rippling; full; tangled;
mangy; grizzled; downy; matted; filthy;
forked; crisp; trim; close-cropped; well-
clipped; Oriental; venerable; unshorn;
hoary; foolish; overgrown; silken; military;
telescopic; verdant; patriarchal; Mephisto-
phelian.

verbs
acquire—; adorn with—; attain—; clip—;
comb—; curl—; dignify with—; disguise
by—; distinguish by—; drag by—; part—;
paw—; pluck off—; pull—; run down—;
scratch—; seize by—; shave—; singe—;
smooth—; stroke—; style—; take by—; trim
—; twitch—; waggle—; weep in—; —
bristles; —blooms; —covers; —glistens.
(See hair, whiskers.)

BEARD (v)
adverbs
boldly; fearlessly; manfully; foolhardily;
playfully; exasperatingly; foolishly; valiantly.
(See defy, oppose, encounter.)

BEARING
adjectives (manner)
modest; timid; manly; noble; courteous;
polished; dignified; tranquil; unpretentious;
unostentatious; imperial; austere; regal;
lofty; haughty; patrician; godlike; majestic; jaunty; lively; gay; contemptuous; disdainful; martial; soldierly; military; clerkly; grave; staid; courteous; queenly; gallant; graceful; intimate; alarming; humble;
courageous; worthy; unbridled; steadfast;
chivalrous; heroic; imperious; rollicking;
straightforward; immitigable.

BEARING
adjectives (meaning)
intimate; immediate; favorable; happy;
vital; frank; tragic; popular; external; direct; mutual.

BEAST
adjectives
skulking; brutish; ingenious; ravenous;
wily; unfriendly; elusive; slippery; wild;
driveling; boisterous; unruly; unsavory;
massive; infuriated; ill-trained; bloody;
savage; grisly; predatory; formidable;
monstrous; maddened; outlandish; venomous; grotesque; fabulous; cross-grained;
beauteous; malicious; cowardly; sanguine;
sulky; unkempt; jaded; voracious; undisciplined; squealing; nocturnal; four-footed;
noble; lordly; cruel; murderous; ferocious;
relentless; marauding; prowling; hostile;
enraged; screaming; snarling; cornered;
charging; frantic; restless; stamping;
crouching; sagacious; cunning; well-bred;
gaunt; hairy; stolid; plodding; shaggy;
rugged; graceless; diminutive; foolish; prehistoric; sleek.

verbs
cage—; chase—; constrain—; depict—; flay
—; hunt—; mount—; pen up—; shelter—;
skin—; slash—; slaughter—; spare—; subdue—; track—; transform into—; —bays;
—cries; —forages; —growls; —grunts; —
prowls; —roams; —subsists; —yelps.
(See brute, monster, animal.)

BEAT
adjectives
receding; impatient; dynamic; incessant;
steady; rhythmic.

BEAT (v)
adverbs
unmercifully; continuously; impatiently; in-

cessantly; rhythmically; languidly; mercilessly; boisterously; joyously; youthfully; manifestly; pleasantly; proportionately; regularly; audibly; unpitifully; unreasonably; horribly; uncontrollably; thoroughly; strenuously; burningly; merrily; lazily; lightly.
(See hammer, smite, strike, chasten.)

BEATIFIC
adverbs
ethereally; mysteriously; divinely; happily; ecstatically; gloriously; rapturously; mystically; devoutly; fervently.

BEATING
adjectives
merciless; tumultuous; fierce; unjust.

verbs
administer—; chastise with—; deserve—; endure—; flatten out with—; punish—; suffer—; throb from—; —intimidates.
(See drubbing, defeat, blows.)

BEATING
adjectives (sound)
loud; insistent; barbaric; tumultuous; staccato.

BEATITUDE
adjectives
infinite; limitless; insouciant.

BEAU
adjectives
ardent; fascinating; devoted; distant; cool.

BEAUTIFUL
adverbs
gloriously; ethereally; dazzlingly; elusively; unearthly; fatally; fleetingly; intangibly; mysteriously; magnificently; fabulously; charmingly; radiantly; exquisitely; matchlessly; fiercely; surprisingly; exotically; sullenly; poignantly; bloomingly; naturally; simply; lustrously; languidly; compellingly; opulently; richly; wondrously; duskily; cruelly; stormily; vitally; singularly; vividly; gracefully; flawlessly; harmoniously; calmly; graciously; serenely; sweetly; childishly; unforgettably; innocently; imposingly; surpassingly; disdainfully; daintily; proudly; wildly; ineffably; triumphantly; ravishingly; weirdly; unconsciously; sternly; devastatingly; darkly; resplendently; robustly; infinitely; pensively; faultlessly; divinely; quietly; vivaciously; glamorously; glitteringly; glowingly; alluringly; unspeakably; adorably; startlingly; chastely; regally; terribly.

BEAUTY
adjectives
glorious; guarded; sable; animal; dazzling; uncultivated; moral; unearthly; distinctive; luscious; inexhaustible; famous; mortal; fleeting; iridescent; passionate; sensuous; gleaming; talented; mysterious; perpetual; mystic; homely; all-pervading; picturesque; infantile; notable; fabulous; radiant; exquisite; unmatched; haughty; reigning; stately; insistent; fierce; surprising; changeful; indescribable; celestial; sullen; naked; blooming; antique; poignant; morose; abstracted; delicate; poetic; unparalleled; mocking; unrivaled; natural; lustrous; wistful; ideal; rare; polished; perennial; languid; indefinable; compelling; opulent; rugged; matronly; rich; wondrous; original; verdant; dusky; cruel; peculiar; marvelous; stormy; despoiled; masculine; singular; indestructible; substantiated; transfigured; intellectual; graceful; harmonious; bedizened; unforgettable; luxurious; surpassing; sacred; evanescent; pictorial; breathless; crystal; excelling; considerable; spiritual; peerless; creative; dainty; speckled; wild; triumphant; weird; celebrated; impersonal; vaunted; plastic; blemished; stern; angelic; dismal; dark; earthly; comprehensible; robust; ripe; melodic; supernal; pensive; tragic; divine; intrinsic; vivacious; glittering; mellow; soul-awakening; tanned; alluring; exclusive; haunting; chaste; bridal; somber; unadorned; fadeless; geometric; impassioned; terrible; regal; majestic; voluptuous; sculptured; artistic; traditional; unexampled; rustic; enhanced; startling; unspeakable; glowing; patrician; pristine; tonic; glamorous; superlative; ornate; quiet; nymph-like; faultless; gnarled; debased; garnished; infinite; midnight; filmy; feathery; refined; gossamer; sheer; resplendent; impalpable; devastating; ravishing; beguiling; unique; lavish; ineffable; intoxicating; commanding; proud; lofty; disdainful; scornful; awesome; imposing; inherent; innocent; restful; unconscious; unspoiled; child-like; lyrical; ethereal; exotic; eerie; serene; calm; colorful; riotous; flawless; nonpareil; vivid; vital; lucid; transcendant; deathless; Grecian; statuesque; rural; odorous; pastoral; colonial; scenic; buxom; pagan; Botticellian; lush; creamy; elusive; fatal; still; sepulchral; guileless; proverbial; unattainable; unveiled; shroud-

ed; stage; intoxicating; sylvan; intangible; consummate.

verbs
achieve—; approve of—; array in—; a-waken—; bathe in—; bless with—; build—; capture—; commend—; deface—; depict—; desire—; desolate the—; drink up—; enamour of—; enhance—; envy—; excel in—; favor with—; gladden by—; glorify—; hanker for—; heighten—; hunger for—; hypnotize by—; impair—; lust for—; maintain—; mar—; outrage—; perfect—; praise—; preserve—; recapture—; rejoice in—; restore—; seek—; smother—; soften—; stain—; surrender—; tinge with—; trample—; unfold—; unmask—; veil—; vouchsafe—; worship—; —abounds; —attracts; —captivates; —charms; —decays; —departs; —enchants; —endures; —enraptures; —entrances; —excites; —fades; —fascinates; —glows; —shines; —stabs; —withers.
(See perfection, charm, loveliness, grace, harmony.)

BECKON (v)
adverbs
significantly; enticingly; captivatingly; smilingly; quaintly; repeatedly; imperceptibly.
(See wave.)

BED
adjectives
soft; snowy; luxurious; comfortable; lovely; quaint; chilly; four-poster; carved; musty; damp; ghoulish; spotless; wretched; pendent; curtained; sagging; painful; rocky; wholesome; cursed; barren; lustful; wormy; pensive; restless; regal; naked; sickly; fruitful; odorous; peaceful; creaking; makeshift; lumpy; hallowed; pebbly; nuptial; feverish; dying; sandy; virgin; sleepless; inviting; aching; pious; tumbled; weary; woeful; spectral; turfy; unhallowed; incestuous.

verbs
canopy—; cast upon—; clamber into—; confine to—; convey to—; couch in—; deck—; decorate—; defile—; enclose—; flop into—; fold—; glide into—; hang from—; heave from—; hurl out of—; kneel beside—; lay out in—; loll on—; lounge on—; mattress—; pillow in—; prop in—; recline in—; repose in—; retire to—; roll in—; rouse from—; sink into—; slumber in—; spring from—; squirm in—; stagger from—; stow in—; strike—; toss in—; toss into—; tuck in—; usurp—; warm—.
(See cot, couch, mattress.)

BED (v)
adverbs
softly; luxuriously; quaintly; comfortably; mustily; damply; nightly.
(See rest.)

BEDECK (v)
adverbs
gaily; gorgeously; fabulously; lavishly; grandly; attractively; picturesquely; gloriously.
(See ornament.)

BEDLAM
adjectives
clamorous; dreadful; foul; frantic; mind-sundering; raging; unsubdued.

verbs
lead into—; subject to—; —abates; —breaks out; —confuses; —deranges; —roars.
(See confusion, noise.)

BEDROOM
adjectives
gaudy; banal; voluptuous; charming; airy; dismal; silent; gloomy; ill-ventilated; dreary; diminutive.

verbs
air—; dash into—; deny—; emerge from—; furnish—; repair to—; retire to—; —contains.
(See room, apartment.)

BEE
adjectives
swarming (pl); laden; anxious; straggling; sucking; noontide; murmuring; stingless; maudlin; industrious; voluptuous; blunt-faced; sexless; restless; marauding; buzzing; bustling; busy.

verbs
handle—; keep —s; —alights on; —breeds; —bristles; —chases; —collects; —colonizes; —darts; —deposits; —dozes; —flits; —forages; —gathers; —gorges; —hibernates; —hums; —impregnates; —s issue; —labors; —mumbles; —murmurs; —nests; —oviposits; —perforates; —plies; —pollinates; —regurgitates; —secretes; —sips; —stings; —stores; —s swarm; —swoops down; —s throng; —tunnels; —wings its way.
(See insect.)

BEECH
adjectives
russet; stalwart; giant; leafy; serpent-rooted.

102

BEER

adjectives

authentic; stout; frothy; pale; foamy; powerful; drowsy.

verbs

abstain from—; addict to—; annihilate—; age—; bottle—; brew—; concoct—; consume—; de-alcoholize—; down—; extract —; gulp—; guzzle—; hop up—; lap up—; manufacture—; market—; process—; quaff —; sample—; sip—; steep in—; stock—; stow away—; strengthen—; swill—; tap —; weaken—; —bubbles; —ferments; — flows; —foams; —froths; —glistens; —intoxicates; —quenches; —thickens; —winks.

(See ale, liquor.)

BEETLE

adjectives

noisome; infuriated; drowsy; iridescent; carnivorous; obscurely-colored; glistening.

verbs

armor—; attack —s; control —s; crush—; exterminate —s; infest with —s; plague with —s; sheathe—; spray—; —bites; — captures; —chews; —destroys; —devastates; —feigns; —forages; —gnaws; —menaces; —s ravage; —scurries along; —tears out; —tumbles along.

(See insect.)

BEFALL (*v*)

adverbs

occasionally; preposterously; happily; unaccountably; auspiciously; inadvertently; inexplicably.

(See happen.)

BEG (*v*)

adverbs

solicitously; ingratiatingly; deprecatingly; appealingly; importunately; urgently; embarrassedly; impudently; clamorously; reproachfully; whiningly; fawningly; grimacingly; piteously; pestiferously; professionally; earnestly.

(See beseech, implore, ask.)

BEGGAR

adjectives

sturdy; amiable; jolly; disciplined; filthy; whining; gloomy; worthless; disgraced; greedy; blind; wandering; monkish; implacable; stalwart; unclean; bareheaded; crippled; loathsome; fawning; grimacing; piteous; penniless; tattered; pestiferous; hideous; impudent; professional; formidable.

verbs

contribute to—; corrupt—; die a—; ease—; feast—; foster—; lodge—; reduce to—; relieve—; repel—; revive—; sink to—; spurn —; —s band together; —complains; —desires; —entreats; —implores; —intrudes; —loafs; —petitions; —pleads; —roams; — shirks; —starves; —struggles; —tramps along.

BEGIN (*v*)

adverbs

jerkily; resentfully; methodically; mechanically; earnestly; hesitatingly; ostensibly; clumsily; euphemistically; sarcastically; argumentatively; oracularly; surreptitiously; savagely; wistfully; eventually; contemporaneously; ecstatically; romantically; insidiously; auspiciously; appealingly; rapturously.

(See commence, originate.)

BEGINNER

adjectives

awkward; anxious; fearful; mere; overconfident; zealous; untried.

verbs

bestow on—; condition—; describe to—; educate—; encourage—; foster—; induce—; pit against—; reveal to—; school—; sponsor—; stimulate—; suggest to—; train—; trouble—; —acquires; —advances; —applies; —contacts; —copes with; —crams; — demands; —embarks on; —emerges; —errs; —experiences; —learns; —plunges into; — questions.

(See novice, apprentice, amateur.)

BEGINNING

adjectives

remote; slow; tentative; crude; auspicious; recorded; amateurish; nebulous; unworkable; humble; long-deferred; promising; simple; tragic; ambitious; mandatory; microscopic; substantial; inconspicuous; modest; casual; sweet; indestructible; unpropitious; unlimited; significant.

verbs

celebrate—; commemorate—; declare—; honor—; initiate—; mark—; proceed from —; read from—; trace—; —introduces; — leads off.

(See origin.)

BEGRUDGE (*v*)

adverbs

habitually; selfishly; unfeelingly; implacably; cruelly; odiously; remorselessly; frowningly.

(See deny.)

BEHAVE (v)

adverbs

unchastely; abhorrently; alluringly; treacherously; erratically; abominably; indifferently; unsociably; diabolically; errantly; debonairly; gawkily; ridiculously; prudently; uncouthly; proverbially; boisterously; obtusely; ludicrously; conclusively; theatrically; drably; courteously; jocularly; artlessly; imposingly; lasciviously; austerely; capriciously; speciously; decorously; callously; irreverently; obstreperously; generously; admirably.

(See act, bear.)

BEHAVIOR

adjectives

artless; imposing; offensive; lascivious; distant; picturesque; humorous; demonstrative; objective; portentous; genetic; outward; baffling; tormenting; prudential; austere; blunt; infantile; rude; stupid; loutish; unfilial; capricious; unparalleled; highhanded; emotional; ungracious; specious; courteous; ingenious; mild; odd; cruel; frantic; despicable; unbecoming; cowardly; disgusting; deferential; creditable; wanton; displeasing; suitable; individualistic; disheartening; noble; unique; odious; decorous; erratic; shameful; senseless; outrageous; shocking; riotous; mysterious; instinctive; decent; manly; intelligent; exceptional; reasonable; circumspect; polite; unmaidenly; childish; detestable; inhuman; callous; irreverent; egocentric; annoying; insulting; abominable; eccentric; obstreperous.

verbs

condone—; dignify—; interpret—; simulate —; soften—; —implies; —improves; —infuriates; —pleases.

(See demeanor, conduct, manner, action.)

BEHEAD (v)

adverbs

publicly; cruelly; wantonly; outrageously; heartlessly; shockingly; abominably; detestably.

(See execute.)

BEHOLD (v)

adverbs

gladsomely; earnestly; unblinkingly; respectfully; rapturously; tremblingly; blankly.

(See contemplate, gaze, look, observe.)

BEING

adjectives

sovereign; invisible; sinful; ungrateful; stormy; neurotic; faulty; inner; loathed; human; transformed; wayward; puny; delusive; reasonable; rare; radiant; rational; uninhibited; amiable; jovial; lively; lovely; sentimental; reasoning; semidivine; supernatural; mythological; legendary; unearthly; exalted; supreme; superior; forceful; intrepid; corporeal; unfortunate; self-conscious; unsheltered; despicable; ominous; intellectual; mysterious; rebellious; subtle; wild; immortal; created; wondrous; incomprehensible; countless; deluded; satanic-looking; helpless; finite; enchanted; malevolent; celestial; terrestrial; infernal; articulate; moral; responsible; spiritual; conscious; unnatural; tame; passionless; progressive; humble; supernal; incarcerated; physical; transcendent.

verbs

corrupt—; eat into—; insinuate into—; oppose—; reject—; subjugate human —s; —s differ.

(See individual.)

BELABOR (v)

adverbs

soundly; cruelly; wantonly; heartlessly; persistently; grossly; unfeelingly; murderously.

(See beat.)

BELCH

adjectives

nauseating; embarrassed; resounding.

BELIEF

adjectives

comforting; sincere; inspiring; venerable; sustaining; profound; cherished; traditional; calm; dispassionate; widespread; ingenuous; indestructible; unshakable; unswerving; staunch; rock-bound; deep-rooted; unwavering; overpowering; long-established; settled; personal; persistent; thoroughgoing; time-honored; inescapable; unquestioning; poetic; fantastic; weird; romantic; quaint; crazy; fanatical; blind; senile; heretical; fatuous; illogical; widely-varying; theosophical; medieval; atheistic; religious; general; common; dogmatic; tottering; badly-shaken; pathetic; childlike; implicit; tacit; supernatural; pragmatical; ancient; serious; exacting; slow; rising;

important; indisputable; eager; unavoidable; prevailing; ineradicable; immemorial; confident; gross; unconscious; contrary; reasonable; theoretic; generous; universal; unassailable; vast; pious; ethical; fundamental; credulous; intellectual; old-fashioned; traditional; discreet; doctrinal; lingering; instinctive; cherished; unflattering; strange; irrational; adorable; spiritualistic; erroneous; grotesque; uncomprehending; popular; stubborn; independent; rote-learned; fatalistic; indomitable; unfounded; growing; stout; superstitious; honest; unstable; rooted; purposive; current; obstinate; divine; peremptory; vague; hoary; dangerous; prevalent; desirable; uncompromising; systematized; battered; consequent; conflicting (pl).

verbs
abandon—; allay—; alter—; annihilate—; apprehend—; arise from—; asphyxiate—; banish—; battle for—; bolster—; blot out—; break down—; cast out—; cherish—; cling to—; comfort in—; confide—; confirm—; conquer—; consider—; contradict—; convict on—; create—; credit—; delude into—; derive—; designate—; destroy—; dispel—; dissipate—; doubt—; draw—; drop—; embody—; embrace—; encourage—; endorse —; entertain—; establish—; evolve—; excite—; expel—; explain—; explode—; expound—; express—; favor—; fetter—; fix —; found upon—; free from—; imply—; incline to—; include—; indoctrinate—; influence—; inherit—; inspire—; justify—; labor under—; lend weight to—; manifest —; master—; nourish—; obliterate—; originate—; outgrow—; perpetuate—; persist in—; persuade in—; present—; profess—; realize—; reject—; relapse into—; relinquish—; repose—in; represent—; repudiate —; rest upon—; retain—; reverse—; rid of —; ripen into—; scotch—; share—; strengthen—; stress—; subdue—; submerge—; support—; surmise—; subscribe to—; trust in —; value—; vindicate—; voice—; waive—; wallow in—; warrant—; witness—; wound —; —s conflict; —decays; —dies; —disappears; —emerges from; —expires; —functions; —intrudes; —melts; —obsesses; — rests on; —springs from; —tempts; —totters; —vanishes; —wanders; —wanes; — waxes low.

(See faith, conviction, persuasion, assurance, doctrine, dogma, creed, opinion, view.)

BELIEVE (v)
adverbs
erroneously; candidly; passionately; frankly; ingenuously; assertively; infallibly; conscientiously; currently; popularly; deliberately; ardently; mournfully; instinctively; dispassionately; unshakably; unswervingly; staunchly; unwaveringly; persistently; unquestioningly; fatuously; illogically; religiously; dogmatically; pathetically; implicitly; tacitly; indisputably; immemorially; reasonably; fundamentally; irrationally; uncomprehendingly; obstinately; unfoundedly; fatalistically; superstitiously; uncompromisingly.

(See suppose.)

BELIEVER
adjectives
devout; ardent; passionate; true; firm; conscientious; tremendous; frantic; lifelong; unquestioning; consummate; fervent; enthusiastic; rapt.

BELITTLE (v)
adverbs
scoffingly; maliciously; subtly; justifiably; surreptitiously; obstreperously; venomously; insidiously; invidiously.
(See· reduce.)

BELITTLEMENT
adjectives
malicious; subtle; justifiable.

BELL
adjectives
peaceful; enchanted; clinking; muffled; tinkling; gentian; chiming; mellow; shimmering; deep; oracular; old; cracked; twilight; clear-toned; insistent; tremulous; sullen; ponderous; clanging; gold-rimmed; discordant; warning; ringing; rankling; sleigh; jingling; pealing; rich-toned; musical; resonant; glittering; dazzling; brass; bronze; doleful; melancholy; drowsy; monotonous; jangling; feeble; faint; rusty; antique; little; clapping; sobbing; vesper; shrilling; sonorous; salvage; sweet; cracked; midnight; mournful; heavy-hanging; tolling.

verbs
adorn—; answer—; bear away—; bless—; cast—; clap—; coat—; consecrate—; crack —; fashion—; flare—; found—; gain—; hallow—; invert—; jangle—; lose—; mould —; muffle—; rattle—; recast—; rivet—; shake —s; shape—; silence—; strike—; swing—; trill—; tune—; —alarms; —assembles; —booms; —calls; —carols; — chimes; —clangs; —clashes; —ding-dongs; —heaves; —honors the dead; —invites; — knells; —marks the hour; —notifies; —

peals; —punctuates; —records; —reverberates; —rolls; —screams; —shrieks; —signals; —sings; —speaks; —strikes; —summons; —taunts; —tinkles; —tolls; —ushers in; —vibrates.
(See instrument, anvil.)

BELLE
adjectives
merciless; waltzing; ballet; faded; traditional; brilliant; raging.

BELLICOSE
adverbs
habitually; constitutionally; inherently; naturally; hopelessly; aggressively; truculently; atrociously; barbarously; brutally; cruelly; fiercely; hatefully; hard-heartedly; maliciously; obdurately; rancourously; resentfully; spitefully; uncharitably; venomously; relentlessly; ruthlessly; outrageously; churlishly; invidiously; fiendishly.

BELLIGERENT
adverbs
naturally; habitually; inherently; incorrigibly; lamentably; incurably; racially; inveterately; intrinsically; fanatically; customarily; admittedly; contentiously; wranglingly; quarrelsomely; malevolently; cruelly; cold-heartedly; irreconcilably; disturbingly; riotously; aggressively; irretrievably; hopelessly.

BELLOW
adjectives
inflated; mysterious; bleating; righteous; forty-acre; overpowering; epochal; hearty; ludicrous; untuneful; cataclysmal; angry; summoning; resonant; stupendous; ear-shattering; huge; tempestuous; inhuman; fantastic; wonder-provoking; throaty; hoarse; terrified; subterranean; hollow.

BELLOW (v)
adverbs
tumultuously; gloomily; piercingly; pleasedly; lustily; bleatingly; heartily; ludicrously; untunefully; resonantly; inhumanly; throatily; subterraneanly; hollowly; barbarously.
(See roar.)

BELLY
adjectives
remorseless; wrinkled; vile.

verbs
band—; belt—; constrict—; fill—; grovel on—; inflate—; stuff—; swell—; thrust into —; —aches; —bulges out; —contains; —hungers; —protrudes; —swells; —vibrates.
(See abdomen, paunch.)

BELONG (v)
adverbs
remotely; infinitely; notoriously; legally; tacitly; anonymously; permanently; patriotically; temporarily; indefinitely; perpetually.

BELONGINGS
adjectives
countless; diminished; age-hoarded; scanty; scattered; pathetic; vestigial.

verbs
carry—; cherish—; endow with—; increase —; injure—; possess—; retrieve—; value —.
(See possessions, property.)

BELT
adjectives
tarnished; studded; endless; embroidered; green-fringed; unbuckled; impenetrable; surrounding; inimitable; controversial; safety; gentian; fertile; swaying; sequoia; flashing.

verbs
adorn with—; apply—; bind with—; carve —; design—; emboss—; flap—; hang at—; inlay—; join —s; load—; loose—; notch—; pattern—; secure with—; strap—; tense—; tighten—; tool—; unclasp—; —borders; —confines; —conveys; —encircles; —girdles; —restrains; —stretches; —supports; —surrounds.
(See band.)

BEMOAN (v)
adverbs
miserably; piteously; sobbingly; gently; chronically; unspokenly; tremulously; wailingly; wretchedly.
(See lament, bewail, deplore.)

BENCH
adjectives   (furniture)
slab; roughly-carved; pew-like; crude; sun-dried; high; dry; disfigured; secluded; notched; Sheraton; offending; judicial; rustic; sympathizing; elevated.

verbs
adorn—; decorate—; design—; display—; indicate—; model—; occupy—; provide—; reserve—; squat on—; tilt—; utilize—; work at—; —affords; —serves; —supports; —topples.
(See seat, table, furniture, chair.)

BENCH

adjectives   **(legal)**

dignified; exalted; honorable; judicial; learned; triumvirate; upper.

verbs

appoint to—; bring before—; elect to—; esteem—; occupy—; preside at—; resign from—; retire from—; return to—; serve at—; vacate—; —accepts; —affects; —approves; —ascertains; —charges; —conducts; —deems; —derives; —exemplifies; —fines; —fixes; —fulfills; —imposes; — judges; —pronounces; —sentences.
(See court.)

BEND

adjectives

distant; graceful; alternate; convex; keen; sharp; magisterial; sudden; tender; tolerant.

BEND (*v*)

adverbs

feebly; impulsively; confidentially; inextricably; mournfully; solicitously; alternately; magisterially; tenderly; tolerantly.
(See turn, curve.)

BENEDICTION

adjectives

low; gentle; healing; apologetic; silver; short; pontifical; perpetual; celestial.

verbs

accompany with—; apply—; attend—; bestow—upon; bless at—; implore—; kneel for—; perform—; pray at—; pronounce—; receive—; seek—; serve at—; shower —s upon; speak—; visit—upon; wreathe in—; —closes; —encourages; —inspires; —opens.
(See prayer, blessing.)

BENEFACTION

adjectives

unknown; gracious; admirable; notorious.

verbs

appeal for—; appreciate—; begrudge—; bestow—upon; cloak—; confer—; contribute —; demand—; expose—; imply—; influence —; judge—; launch—; menace—; offer—; owe to—; publicize—; reduce—; secure—; surprise by—; thwart—; volunteer—; withhold—; —elates; —redeems; —satisfies; — succors.
(See charity.)

BENEFACTOR

adjectives

anonymous; modest; silent; elderly; leading; munificent; life-long; potent.

verbs

appeal to—; betray—; burden—; depend on —; devote to—; distinguish—; employ—; flourish under—; inherit from—; —aids; —bequeaths; —cares for; —comforts; — counsels; —demands; —endows; —establishes; —finances; —fosters; —inquires; —institutes; —lavishes; —patronizes; —profits; —relieves; —retains; —satisfies; —shapes; —succors; —tempts; —volunteers.

BENEFICENCE

adjectives

magical; embodied; leading; heedless; iridescent.

BENEFICENT

adverbs

altruistically; amiably; benignly; charitably; considerately; generously; generally; good-naturedly; kindly; mercifully; sympathetically; tenderly; unselfishly; warmly; bountifully; graciously; indulgently; maternally; paternally; modestly; gently; anonymously; magnificently; simply; unassumingly.

BENEFICIAL

adverbs

permanently; desirably; cumulatively; particularly; reciprocally; mutually; enormously; surprisingly; extraordinarily; satisfactorily; gratifyingly; appreciably; economically; politically; internationally; ultimately; eventually; immensely; essentially; peculiarly; tolerably; generally; universally; absolutely; socially; financially.

BENEFIT

adjectives

permanent; community; important; practical; substantial; lasting; visible; far-reaching; anonymous; persuasive; sweet; merited; accrued; transforming; material; fixed; particular; cumulative; reciprocal; unsurpassed; mutual; enormous; inestimable; overwhelming; extraordinary; incalculable; remarkable; international; economic; educational; tolerable; especial; peculiar; corresponding; patriotic; public; conferred; positive; admitted; innumerable (pl); secluded; essential; immense; desirable; full; doubtful; immediate; surprising; unintended; ultimate; hazardous.

verbs

abolish—; acquire—; attend with—; bequeath —s; bestow—upon; claim—; concede—; confer—upon; defend—; demand—; deprive of—; derive—; disable—; embrace —; enumerate —s; finance—; grant—of; load with —s; mark—; merit—; nullify—; proffer—; reap—; render—; reveal—; secure—; share—; stress—; yield —s; —s accrue; —occurs; —s proceed from.

(See profit, advantage, service, favor.)

BENEFIT (v)
adverbs
questionably; directly; substantially; visibly; anonymously; materially; particularly; cumulatively; reciprocally; unsurpassedly; mutually; inestimably; incalculably; internationally; economically; educationally; peculiarly; correspondingly; admittedly; essentially; unintentionally; ultimately.

(See help, avail.)

BENEVOLENCE
adjectives
unexpected; winged; remarkable; defective; private; expansive; factitious; tolerant; vague; world-wide; significant; muscle-loosening; red-blooded; social; despotic; easy; universal; dominant; sympathetic; amused; innate.

verbs
assist through—; assure one of—; contribute—; depend upon—; disguise—; dispense with—; encourage—; endow with—; exercise—; exploit—; expose—; flourish under —; manifest—; practice—; promote—; reform by—; rejoice in—; rouse—; support with—; surprise by—; withhold—; —aids; —consoles; —delights; —relieves; —shines.

(See bounty, charity, generosity.)

BENIGNANT
adverbs
graciously; invariably; consistently; tenderly; notably; amiably; big-heartedly; mildly; simply; warmly; tolerantly; gently; courteously; smoothly; generously; complacently; genially; thoughtfully; considerately.

BENIGNITY
adjectives
politic; hopeful; inexpressible; suave; soothing; gentle.

BENT
adjectives
artistic; philosophical; natural; immediate; practical.

BEQUEATH (v)
adverbs
mutely; subsequently; generously; acceptably; munificently; extravagantly; liberally; miraculously; unsparingly.

(See transmit.)

BEQUEST
adjectives
subsequent; munificent; acceptable; final; generous; scanty.

BERATE (v)
adverbs
morosely; abusively; furiously; heatedly; indignantly; vociferously; venomously; drunkenly; privately; desperately; deplorably; monstrously.

(See upbraid, reprimand, censure.)

BEREAVEMENT
adjectives
irreparable; personal; domestic; mitigated; intolerable; unforgettable.

BERRIES
adjectives
fresh-picked; luscious; delicious; bunched; packaged; frozen; helpless; scarlet.

verbs
consume—; crate—; crush—; cultivate—; devour—; enjoy—; feast on—; hull—; market—; pluck—; preserve—; relish—; wreathe with—; yield—; —crackle; —flourish; —redden; —ripen; —suspend from; —thrive.

(See fruit, vegetable, flower.)

BESEECH (v)
adverbs
unfeignedly; weepingly; vainly; piteously; charmingly; graciously; guilelessly; exquisitely; sentimentally; fanatically; piously; humbly.

(See beg, entreat, implore.)

BESIEGE (v)
adverbs
ineffectually; resolutely; foolhardily; miraculously; overwhelmingly; vigorously; ragingly; persistently; intermittently; intensively; desultorily.

(See surround, attack.)

BESIEGER
adjectives
arrogant; merciless; infuriated; intrepid; importunate; relentless; tireless; unreasoning; wrathful.

verbs
arm —s; take —s by surprise; taunt —s; —s advance; —s assail; —s assault; —s beleaguer; —s blockade; —s capture; —s hem in.
(See fighter, soldier, troops.)

BESTIAL

adverbs
coarsely; horribly; brutally; fiercely; grossly; indecently; ribaldly; shamelessly; unbelievably; abusively; obscenely; evilly; brutishly; violently; abominably.

BESTOW (*v*)

adverbs
gratuitously; felicitously; improperly; equally; facetiously; unwittingly; philanthropically; munificently; grudgingly.
(See grant.)

BET

adjectives
fatal; reckless; shrewd; timely; underhanded; unfair; unfortunate.

verbs
arouse—; balance—; cancel—; cover—; encourage—; forfeit—; hedge—; instigate—; insure—; lay—; stake—; support—; — stands; —surprises.
(See wager, stake.)

BETRAY (*v*)

adverbs
grossly; deliberately; hideously; vilely; viciously; virtually; infrequently; treacherously; incautiously; bluntly; subtly; heartlessly; venomously; emotionally; mentally.
(See reveal, disclose.)

BETRAYAL

adjectives
gross; deliberate; grave; hideous; vile; vicious.

verbs
avenge—; charge—; commit—; fume at—; lead into—; —divulges; —exposes; —violates.
(See treason, treachery, exposure.)

BETRAYER

adjectives
accidental; circumspect; disloyal; shameless; subtle; treacherous; unwitting.

verbs
accuse—; confront—; denounce—; dishonor —; execute—; vindicate—; —deserts; — discloses; —flees.

BETROTH (*v*)

adverbs
gladsomely; diplomatically; religiously; contemptuously; sordidly; inappropriately; beatifically.
(See give.)

BETROTHAL

adjectives
enforced; happy; opposed; favored; proclaimed; prolonged; signalized; unduly influenced.

verbs
compact—; compound—; consecrate—; consummate—; contract—; dissolve—; fulfill—; honor—; promote—; ritualize—; sanction—; solemnize—; violate—; —affiances; —binds; —couples; —engages; —promises.
(See engagement.)

BETTERMENT

adjectives
permanent; material; economic; moral; human; spiritual; lasting; civic.

BEVERAGE

adjectives
intoxicating; wholesome; fermented; distilled; seductive; beguiling; customary; exhilarating; soothing; mild; constant; limpid; refreshing; invigorating; fragrant; thirst-quenching.

verbs
brew—; carbonate—; consume—; devise—; dispense—; dissolve into—; draw off—; formulate—; infuse—; ladle—; medicate—; quaff—; sip—; tap—; treat—with; weaken —; —cools; —effervesces; —ferments; — foams; —induces; —intoxicates; —percolates; —relieves; —satisfies; —warms.
(See drink, liquor, wine, beer, coffee, etc.)

BEWAIL (*v*)

adverbs
sepulchrally; mournfully; heartbrokenly; blatantly; vigorously; hoarsely; stentoriously; stormily; fearfully; inarticulately; raucously.
(See bemoan.)

BEWILDER (*v*)

adverbs
confusingly; completely; perplexingly; inscrutably; spiritually; pitifully; naively; tragically; childishly.
(See confuse, perplex, mystify.)

BEWILDERED

adverbs

strangely; suddenly; hopelessly; helplessly; mysteriously; alarmingly; gravely; seriously; tragically; disastrously; completely; horribly; terribly; indescribably; obviously; manifestly; dazedly; brokenly; pathetically; laughably; ridiculously; foolishly; undeniably; significantly; painfully; confusedly; embarrassingly; ludicrously; bashfully; modestly; piteously; awkwardly; confoundedly; disturbingly; timidly; vaguely; dangerously; overwhelmingly; unluckily; miserably; wretchedly; indefensibly; ineptly.

BEWILDERMENT

adjectives

blank; growing; vague; dazed; helpless; elated; stunned; weary; hurt; spiritual; disgusted; pitiful; naive; added; incredulous; cross; seeming; sheer; complete; deep; suspicious; dazzling; tragic; childish.

verbs

extricate from—; hide—; lose in—; meet with—; stray in—; tangle in—; wander in —; —confuses; —grows; —perplexes.
(See confusion.)

BEWITCHING

adverbs

dangerously; enchantingly; charmingly; radiantly; indescribably; indefinably; marvelously; startlingly; fatally; ineffably; inexplicably; utterly; delightfully; designedly; diabolically; surprisingly; quietly; consciously; tauntingly; overwhelmingly; provokingly; tormentingly; youthfully; irresistibly; unconsciously.

BIAS

adjectives

distorting; grossest; racial; political; natural; beneficial; theoretic; considerable; economic; favorable; moral; elemental; personal.

verbs

deliver from—; free from—; —clouds; —crops up; —distorts; —inclines one toward; —influences; —leans; —misleads; —prejudices; —rejects; —slopes;. —swerves; —warps.
(See prejudice.)

BIBLE

adjectives

consoling; dignified; family-recording; mutilated; treasured; time-honored; oft-perused; woe-comforting.

verbs

adopt—; advance—; blaspheme—; commend—; conflict with—; dethrone—; embellish—; embrace—; esteem—; execute—; inscribe in—; interpret—; misconceive—; mutilate—; preserve—; reject—; spread—; undermine—; —aims at; —appeals; —authorizes; —condemns; —decrees; —endures; —impresses; —inspires; —presents; —reveals; —sets forth; —stirs; —teaches; —unites; —veils.
(See book, scriptures.)

BIBLIOGRAPHY

adjectives

extensive; sketchy; elaborate; speculative; heavy; selective; analytical; complete; annotated; comprehensive; critical.

BICKER (v)

adverbs

constantly; cantankerously; perpetually; unappetizingly; pettishly; undiplomatically; uncharitably; blatantly; repulsively; incompatibly.
(See dispute.)

BICKERING

adjectives

unseemly; perpetual; unappetizing; petty; diplomatic; international.

adverbs

eternally; spitefully; ill-naturedly; nervously; feverishly; incessantly; tempestuously; fussily; intolerably; quarrelsomely; forever; habitually; ill-temperedly; unnecessarily; shrewishly; continually.

BID

adjectives

subtle; foolhardy; feathery; maddest; miraculous; casual; curt; collusive; contemptuous.

verbs

advance—; dispose of —s; double—; govern—; ignore—; pass—; rattle off —s; redouble—; reject—; retract—; run up—; shout—; submit—; withdraw—; —astounds; —s compete; —s pour in; —suffices.
(See proposal, offer.)

BID (v)

adverbs

mockingly; artfully; graciously; regretfully; shrewdly; imperiously; subtly; foolhardily; madly; casually; curtly; contemptuously.
(See offer, order, direct, ask.)

BIDDABLE

adverbs

graciously; astonishingly; miraculously; devotedly; pliantly; amiably; indifferently; apparently; cunningly; shrewdly; grudgingly; necessarily; glumly; stolidly; stupidly; passively; complacently; wisely; politely; suavely; cheerfully; blindly; blithely; unthinkingly; foolishly.

BIDE (*v*)

adverbs

patiently; habitually; naively; perpetually; ephemerally; transiently; independently; pensively.

(See inhabit, abide, endure.)

BIER

adjectives

watery; beckoning; hasty; hallowed; senseless; wretched; blazing.

verbs

array before—; deck—; decorate—; deposit on—; expose on—; file before—; kneel before—; mourn at—; repose on—; surround —; venerate—; weep at—; worship at—.

(See coffin, frame, grave, altar.)

BIGAMY

adjectives

defiling; forbidden; law-evading; ostracised; perfidious; shameful; titled; wretched.

verbs

charge with—; commit—; condone—; define—; imprison for—; live in—; loathe—; outlaw—; practice—.

(See crime.)

BIGOT

adjectives

fierce; intelligent; splendid; self-satisfied; pernicious; vicious; unsparing.

BIGOTED

adverbs

intolerably; fanatically; narrow-mindedly; obdurately; obstinately; incurably; persistently; hopelessly; offensively; arbitrarily; doggedly; incorrigibly; mulishly; inflexibly; perversely; pig-headedly; stubbornly; intractably; perniciously; wilfully; narrowly; dogmatically; arrogantly; imperiously.

BIGOTRY

adjectives

puritanical; sordid; religious; inveterate; unthinking; patent.

BILE

adjectives

abounding; acrid; complex; reactivated; yellow-green.

verbs

expel—; secrete—; store—; —collects; —converts; —flows; —reacts; —trickles.

(See fluid.)

BILL (invoice)

adjectives

preposterous; inevitable; exorbitant; unexpected; modest; staggering; delusive; long-unpaid.

BILL (law)

adjectives

substitute; pending; mandatory; feasible; amended; revised; comprehensive; militia; drafted; pork-barrel.

BILL (legislation)

adjectives

adopted; accepted; amended; contested; discussed; defeated; dismissed; parliamentary; petitionary; true; revised.

verbs

act on—; advocate—; challenge—; confer on—; confront with—; contest—; deliberate—; draft—; draw—; denounce—; enact —; frame—; hurry—through; incorporate in —; kill—; modify—; originate—; railroad —; reject—; retain—; slap through—; smother—; sponsor—; veto—; urge—; —entails; —looms; —provides; —sets forth; —stipulates.

(See law, legislation.)

BILL (money)

adjectives

limp; dejected; worn; crumpled; charitable; elusive; proud; defaced; carefully-fondled; ragged; crisp; faded; crinkled.

BILL (statement of account)

adjectives

adjusted; dunning; final; lavish; harassing; paltry; peccant; padded; uncollected; overwhelming.

verbs

deduct—; deliver—; discount—; draw up—; enter—; file—; foot—; forward—; pad—; render—; scale—; tuck—away; —itemizes; —overcharges; —s pour in; —s rain in.

adjectives

blatant; blazing; huge; glaring; inappropriate; inartistic.

verbs

censor—; crusade against —s; employ —s; greet with —s; plaster on—; post on—; rebel against —s; —blares; —campaigns; —coaxes; —s dot the highways; —informs; —s line; —s mar; —pictures; —promotes.
(See advertisement.)

BILLOW

verbs

bear on—; beset by—; cleave—; produce—; steer through—; swell into —s; swim through—; —beats; —breaks; —crests; —dances; —endangers; —foams; —overwhelms; —rages; —rears up; —roars; —rolls; —silvers; —surges; .—sweeps on; —swells; —tosses up; —tumbles.
(See wave, breaker.)

BILLOW (v)

adverbs

softly; tumblingly; restlessly; dashingly; furiously; advancingly; foamingly; wrathfully; seethingly; multitudinously; glitteringly; darkly; crestedly.
(See pound.)

BILLOWS

adjectives

inky; heaving; crested; vibrant; slanting; wild-roaring; rocking; undulating; glittering; high; multitudinous; dark; solemn; breaking; proud; unreposing; tawny; ruffian; surging; unblended; foaming; unawakened; rolling; tempestuous; seething; wrathful; dancing; curling; building; ridgy; wafting; advancing; dashing; obedient; sleepless; furious; resistless; cruel; immense; endless; tumbling; glimmering; restless.

BIND (v)

adverbs

indubitably; beautifully; closely; exquisitely; intimately; firmly; conveniently; infinitely; eternally; irrevocably; inextricably.
(See fasten, tie, restrict, restrain.)

BINDING

adjectives

neat; original; practical; imperishable; ornate; exquisite; excellent; worn; mildewed; embossed; leather; drab; linen; luxurious.

BINDING (a)

adverbs

legally; morally; onerously; embarrassing-ly; awkwardly; laboriously; perplexingly; formidably; desperately; dreadfully; outrageously; distressingly; vexatiously; uncomfortably; appallingly; alarmingly; unquestionably; definitely; positively; absolutely; securely; cruelly; truly; inescapably; conclusively; oppressively.

BIOGRAPHER

adjectives

distinguished; veracious; worthy; eulogistic; skilled; faithful; enthusiastic; pedestrian; debunking; ecclesiastical; iconoclastic.

BIOGRAPHICAL

adverbs

palpably; unmistakably; blatantly; evidently; undisguisedly; apparently; openly; flagrantly; accurately; historically; clearly; nakedly; pleasantly; slightly; pseudo-; cruelly; completely; purportedly; intentionally; carelessly.

BIOGRAPHY

adjectives

full-fledged; fascinating; literary; splendid; noble; notable; dignified; readable; compelling; painstaking; vital; rhapsodic; exuberant; fictionalized; authoritative; official; comprehensive; iconoclastic; miniature; definitive; pretentious; sensational; previous; informal; inclusive; reliable; remarkable; famous; picturesque; best-selling; meritorious; colorless; satisfactory; magnified; racy; critical; dull; drab; musty; hero-worshipping.

verbs

acquaint with—; attempt—; cultivate—; illuminate—; interpret—; launch—; live—; record in—; —accounts; —appeals; —attributes; —catalogues; —chronicles; —"debunks"; —defames; —delights; —details; —distorts; —enchants; —eulogizes; —exaggerates; —extols; —fires; —informs; —lauds; —narrates; —pictures; —portrays; —reveals; —sketches; —treats of; —twists; —unfolds.
(See life.)

BIRCHES

adjectives

superb; slim; silver; delicate; colored; snow-hung.

BIRD

adjectives

carrion; landward; flitting; red-breasted; homeward; chattering; fluttering; honey-sucking; soaring; stuffed; widowed; songless; stripe-winged; glowing; ruffled;

choleric; captive; nesting; melodious; succulent; rapacious; flippant; full-throated; chirping; unclean; ominous; insolent; feathered; sober; morbid-looking; migratory; aquatic; timorous; joyful; frightened; grand-limbed; restless; gold-flecked; bewildered; caged; nest-deserted; reckless; human-hearted; singing; fledgling; unhappy; babbling; solemn; cruel; furtive; night; huge; deserted; callow; blind; bright-winged; predatory; cheerful; brooding; herald; unscared; dapple-breasted; silly; ragged; riotous; noxious; pigmy; tropical; sable; striking; raucous; contented; brilliant; ravenous; monstrous; bewildered; imprisoned; mateless; rare; unusual; strange; valuable; roosting; circling; wingless; timid; tenderest; startled.

verbs
breed —s; cage—; capture—; cripple—; dislodge—; encage—; exterminate—; fall prey to —s; flush—; kill off —s; peg—; scatter —s; stuff —s; teem with —s; —s anthem; —ascends; —babbles; —breeds; —broods; —builds; —calls; —carols; — chants; —cheeps; —cheers up; —chirps; —chitters; —s chorus; —s clamor; —s congregate; —croons; —s copulate; —crouches; —cuddles; —darts; —descends; —disgorges; —disports; —drifts; —dwells; —s enliven; —feeds; —fledges; —flits; —floats; —s flock; —flutters; —frequents; —gorges; — gossips; —gushes; —hatches; —haunts; — hovers; —inhabits; —lays; —lights upon; —mates; —migrates; —molts; —mounts; —nests; —s orient themselves; —s pair; —pecks; —perches; —pierces sky; —pipes; —pirouettes; —plaints; —plumes himself; —plunges; —pours out his song; —preens; —preys upon; —probes; —prunes; —s quarrel; —s race; —ranges; —rears; —s roost; —s ruffle their plumage; —s scatter; —s scold; —screams; —scuds; —scurries; — serenades; —shoots; —shuns; —sips; — skips; —soars; —sputters; —s stridulate; —s swarm; —sweeps; —swoops down; — taxies; —traces a circle in the air; —trills; —s troop; —twitters; —unfolds; —vanishes; —wanders; —warbles; —wheels; — whirls about; —whistles; —wings his way; —zooms.
(See animal, fowl.)

BIRTH
adjectives
checkered; illustrious; multiple (pl); doubtful; restless; mystic; abhorred; prodigious; timeless; visible; high; noble; royal; immortal; declining; exotic; heavenly; unnatural; approaching; violent; promiscuous; mortal; majestic; wondrous; adulterated; hallowed; painful; miraculous; princely; portentous; abortive; vernal; unexceptional; worthy; monstrous; ill-starred; fated; celebrated; virgin.

verbs
announce—; assist at—; attend at—; celebrate—; extol—; foretell—; govern—; herald—; honor—; manifest at—; preside over—; record—; register—; rejoice at—; restrict —s; travail in—; —s decline; — occurs.
(See beginning, origin, renaissance.)

BIRTHDAY
adjectives
happy; sad; romantic; memorable; unsung.

verbs
commemorate—; document—; endow on—; fete on—; honor on—; memorialize—; observe—; register—; trace—; —approaches.
(See anniversary.)

BIRTHPLACE
adjectives
forsaken; humble; remembered; sterile.

BIRTHRIGHT
adjectives
unattainable; unbound; bitter; unwhipped; unburned; unchained; separated; precious; inalienable; undeniable.

verbs
claim—; forfeit—; honor—; pawn—; retain—; rob of—; salute—; sell—; sway to —; —entitles; —privileges.
(See privilege, inheritance.)

BISCUITS
adjectives
delicious; crumbly; crisp; brown; golden-topped; delicate.

BISHOP
adjectives
affable; resident; pompous; dignified; massive; dutiful; esoteric; eccentric.

BISON
adjectives
attacked; watered; labored; tamed; horned; roaming; vagrant; herded; captured; slaughtered; conquered; hunted; skinned; galloping; thundered; inhabited; restricted; protected.

verbs
corral—; exterminate—; herd—; shelter—; yoke—; —abound; —bellows; —charges; —grazes; —pastures; —ranges; —roams; —roars; —sheds; —stampedes; —vanishes. (See ox, buffalo, animal.)

BIT
adjectives
needful; tempting; savory; checked; insignificant; fluffy; bright; picturesque; unrelated; choice; fragmentary; imaginary; premature; fantastic; mute; tuneless; disquieting; impossible; brilliant; incredible; dainty; demoralized; charred; flimsy.

BIT
adjectives   (mouthpiece of bridle) double; chain; cruel; champed; curbing; excruciating; maddening; torturous; vexing.

verbs
accustom to—; adjust—; attach to—; callous to—; champ at—; choke on—; control with —; cough out—; fight against—; jerk at—; respond to—; ride—; run away from—; saw at—; shy at—; slaver—; spit out—; stop with—; swallow—; take—between teeth; veer from—; yank at—; —chafes; —clamps tongue; —curbs; —restrains; —slackens; —subdues; —tames; —tortures.

BITE
adjectives
crisp; short; crunching; vicious; murderous; prodigious; good-sized; furious; agonizing; hurried; hasty.

verbs
down—; gulp—; inflict—; —cuts; —heals; —pierces; —wounds.

BITE (v)
adverbs
savagely; impetuously; unmercifully; unexpectedly; annoyingly; passionately; viciously; daintily; crunchingly; murderously; agonizingly; hurriedly; hastily.
(See nibble, chew.)

BITING (a)
adverbs
sarcastically; bitterly; viciously; venomously; insidiously; hatefully; mercilessly; deliberately; churlishly; unsparingly; crustily; insolently; obnoxiously; captiously; censoriously; caustically; acrimoniously; perversely; contumaciously; snappishly; peevishly; uncivilly; ungraciously; abusively.

BITTER
adverbs
maliciously; shrewdly; enviously; viciously; purposely; unnecessarily; uncontrollably; insidiously; invidiously; sharply; cynically; sarcastically; spitefully; jealously; intentionally; cunningly; ironically; insinuatingly; incisively; cruelly; brutally; unwisely; atrociously; malevolently; tauntingly; caustically; diabolically.

BITTERNESS
adjectives
thwarted; rancorous; profound; political; unserviceable; chill; quiet; corrosive; smiling; intense; loathsome; speculative; secret; pent-up; sarcastic; extreme; sectional; unsparing; contradictory; personal; sardonic; unrelenting; acrid; partisan; increased; concealed; concentrated; unspoken; undying; chronic.

verbs
be devoid of—; brush aside—; erase—; evoke—; fan—; intensify—; persecute with —; taste—; temper—; —creeps into; —develops; —flames; —gnaws; —heats; —vexes.
(See malice, rancor.)

BIVOUAC
adjectives
picturesque; solemn; miserable.

BLACK (n)
adjectives
solemn; rusty; pitchy; stark; shining; blistered; exploited; wicked; natural; dense; lustrous; inky; midnight; conservative; rich; dense; impenetrable; oppressive; sable; ominous; heavy; palpable; murky; humid; thick.

BLACK (a)
adverbs
rustily; dingily; deeply; lugubriously; formidably; gloomily; duskily; murkily; pitchily; sombrely; richly; pallidly; dunly; faintly; dully; coldly; unearthly; sepulchrally; mournfully; glossily; glassily; smoothly; astonishingly; incredibly; unspeakably.

BLACKBIRD
adjectives
combative; chuckling; glinting; saucy; scolding; sooty; squabbling; planing; winging; windy; timid.

verbs
—chatters; —chants; —claws; —flaps; —

flutes; —hovers; —migrates; —nests; —plasters; —preys on; —raids; —ravages; —sails off; —warbles.
(See bird.)

BLACKGUARD

adjectives
dissipated; turbulent; foreign; drunken; brutal.

BLACKNESS

adjectives
inky; impenetrable; oppressive; pitchy; soft; sable; ominous; murky; cold; drizzling; unsociable; palpable; heavy; humid; piercing; peculiar; dripping; appalling; corrugated; musty; absolute; quivering; menacing; comforting; Cimmerian; Stygian.

verbs
engulf in—; grope through—; lose in—; peer into—; steer through—; —envelops.
(See darkness.)

BLACKSMITH

adjectives
rural; gnarled; sinewy; mighty; brawny.

BLADDER

verbs
control—; dilate—; distend—; empty—; govern—; inflame—; regulate—; swell—; —bursts.

BLADE
(grass)
adjectives
trembling; springing; wind-rippled; dewy.

BLADE
(man)
adjectives
blushing; foppish; gay; desperate; roistering; brilliant; flashy; overdressed; jolly; generous.

BLADE
(sword)
adjectives
flashing; glittering; whirling; bright; heavy; broad; double-edged; sharp; dull; penetrating; rapier; projecting; fiery; lean; delicate; blameful; bloody; dripping; burnished; avenging; dry; scanty; polished; troublesome; flexible; unwithering; tremulous; freshly-springing; fratricidal; bayleaf-shaped; deadly; reddened; shining; scythe-shaped; trenchant; trusty; unsheathed; well-tempered; worthy.

verbs
carve with—; draw—; drive in—; flash—; forge—; grasp—; heave—; lash with—; redden—; send—home; sheathe—; temper —; withdraw—; —glances off; —lacerates; —pricks.
(See knife.)

BLAMABLE

adverbs
partially; lamentably; unhappily; deplorably; unquestionably; entirely; seriously; directly; indirectly; morally; sinfully; deservedly; completely; personally; atrociously; criminally; enormously; outrageously; censurably; exceptionally; reprehensibly; unbelievably.

BLAME

adjectives
high-repented; worthy; moral; sinful; specific; small; ill-placed; complete; deserved; directed; heavenly.

verbs
absolve of—; account for—; accuse of—; allocate—; attach—to; avoid—; bear—; censure in—; charge with—; conceal—; deflect—; deserve—; devise—; expose to—; free from—; impute—to; incur—; lay—to; merit—; reproach with—; share—; stamp with—; trace—; vindicate one of—.
(See censure, reproach, condemnation.)

BLAME (*v*)

adverbs
unjustly; morally; sinfully; specifically; completely; deservedly; prejudicially; unthinkingly; narrow-mindedly; puritanically.
(See censure, reproach.)

BLAMELESS

adverbs
clearly; innocently; exceptionally; altogether; wholly; consciously; truly; undoubtedly; impeccably; virtually; artlessly; virtuously; happily; essentially; palpably; patently; indisputably; incontestably; indubitably; positively; absolutely; spotlessly; unquestionably.

BLAND

adverbs
inscrutably; gently; politely; mysteriously; amiably; civilly; complacently; courteously; genteelly; good-temperedly; obsequiously; suavely; urbanely; suspiciously; sweetly; affably; cordially; graciously; ingratiatingly; habitually; unfailingly; surprisingly; essentially.

BLANDISHMENT
adjectives
spider-like; sordid; paternal; artless; suave; sneering; oily.

BLANDNESS
adjectives
inscrutable; confidential; amazing; acquired; pretended.

BLANKET
adjectives
dripping; lovely; soaked; gaudy; bright-colored; impenetrable; shaggy; government; smelly; ragged; invisible; undulating; stretched; osier; sulphur; tasseled; warming; comfortable.

verbs
air—; clothe in—; divest of —s; double —s; envelop in —s; fold in—; immerse in—; pattern—; shelter with—; snuggle in—; tuck—in; weave—; wrap in—; —comforts; —consoles; —protects; —shields; —shrouds; —smothers.
(See robe.)

BLANKNESS
adjectives
oblivious; utter; lurid; strange; complete; devastating; overwhelming; inescapable; dire.

BLARE (*v*)
adverbs
steadfastly; vigorously; furiously; shrilly; howlingly; fearfully; cuttingly; startlingly; penetratingly; brassily; warningly; echoingly.
(See bellow.)

BLASPHEME (*v*)
adverbs
scandalously; fearfully; soul-searingly; abominably; raucously; mutteringly; luridly; crudely; shockingly; ominously.
(See swear.)

BLASPHEMOUS
adverbs
scurrilously; luridly; startlingly; horribly; unspeakably; soul-searingly; abominably; hideously; shrilly; raucously; noisily; inarticulately; mutteringly; unutterably; impiously; irreverently; brazenly; openly; wilfully; profanely; perversely; sacrilegiously; fanatically; scoffingly; desecratingly; irreligiously; cynically; intolerably; unbearably; terrifyingly; unregenerately; godlessly; unforgivably; diabolically; ruthlessly; implacably; criminally; indefensibly; inexcusably; unpardonably; flagrantly; iniquitously; scandalously; wickedly; offensively; accursedly; indecorously; infamously; nefariously; obdurately; unconscionably; villainously.

BLASPHEMY
adjectives
loud; lurid; startling; horrible; unspeakable; soul-searing; abominable; willful; hideous; shrill; vast; raucous; intricate; illimitable; half-inarticulate.

BLAST
adjectives
overwhelming; vigorous; short; fierce; furious; golden; hoarse; challenging; unbroken; scorching; stentorian; summoning; shrill; chilling; stinging; icy; polar; startling; passing; careening; suffocating; howling; putrid; eddying; tremulous; stirring; modulated; bitter; spasmodic; heated; bleak; fearful; wintry; pitiless; furnace-like; roaring; infernal; scornful; woeful; cutting; unruly; nightly; parching; wailing; foul; stormy; raging.

verbs
blow—; loose—; prepare for—; set off—; shiver in—; shrink from—; spit out—; time —; unloose—; —bites; —bolts; —decapitates; —displaces; —envelops; —frees; — forces; —raves; —rends; —resounds; — rises; —roars; —rocks; —shakes; —shatters; —shocks; —startles; —unearths; —uproots; —vibrates; —withers.
(See explosion, discharge.)

BLAST (*v*)
adverbs
terrifically; overwhelmingly; vigorously; suffocatingly; thunderously; stunningly; tremendously; dynamically.
(See smite, destroy, frustrate.)

BLATANT
adverbs
clamorously; vociferously; cheeringly; uproariously; screamingly; stentoriously; offensively; unnecessarily; asininely; blunderingly; brainlessly; arrogantly; extravagantly; foolishly; heavily; ineptly; obtusely; senselessly; weakly; awkwardly; boorishly; lustily; indecorously; loudly; ribaldly; obstreperously; tawdrily; coarsely; cheaply; vulgarly; oddly; unwontedly; hoydenishly; monstrously; clownishly; outlandishly.

adjectives
ghastly; solstitial; supersolar; hospitable; fruitful; crimson; mellowed; meridian; fierce; brilliant; torrid; departed; passionate; leaping; flaring; cheery; unclouded; quenchless; final; distant; wondrous; continuous; garish; radiant; far-beaming; careless; sullen; comforting; noontide; bright; splendid; golden; hungry; glowing.

verbs
burst into—; confine—to; diffuse—; extinguish—; feed—; smother—; —beams; — flares up; —illumines; —ravages; —roars; —scorches; —sears; —springs up.
(See flame, fire, light.)

BLAZE (v)
adverbs
magnificently; spectacularly; terrifically; intensely; defiantly; crimsonly; torridly; passionately; flaringly; garishly; radiantly; sullenly; glowingly.
(See flame.)

BLAZONED
adjectives (also emblazoned)
gloriously; goldenly; ceremoniously; glitteringly; grandly; magnificently; pretentiously; colourfully; punctiliously; properly; ritualistically; ceremonially; spectacularly; splendidly; fancifully; fantastically; ostentatiously; flamingly; garishly; gaudily; gaily; majestically; sumptuously; theatrically; noteworthily; deservedly; lustrously; distinctively; honorably; famously; sublimely; immortally; memorably; exaltedly; surpassingly; deathlessly; imperishably; prominently; proudly; imposingly.

BLAZONRY
adjectives
rich; barred; glorious; blood-red; historic; age-old; aristocratic; meaningful.

BLEAT (v)
adverbs
frantically.

BLEATING
adjectives
incessant; piteous; high-pitched; squeaky; helpless; ineffectual.

BLEED (v)
adverbs
internally; sorely; profusely; copiously; continually; excessively; fatally; terrifyingly; unexpectedly; intermittently.
(See exude.)

adjectives
continuous; excessive; fatal; forced; arrested.

verbs
arrest—; benefit from—; check—; coagulate—; combat—; control—; dread—; eliminate—; encourage—; impair by—; induce —; plug—; recover from—; reduce—; result in—; retard—; staunch—; suffer from —; tourniquet—; treat—; witness—; — ceases; —confines; —endangers; —enervates; —impoverishes; —increases; —irrigates; —saps; —shocks; —weakens.
(See hemorrhage.)

BLEMISH
adjectives
superficial; facial; physical; unsightly.

verbs
detect—; discern—; eradicate—; result in —; —blots; —disfigures; —flaws; —impairs; —marks; —mars; —scars; —slurs; —stains.
(See defect, fault, imperfection, flaw.)

BLEND (v)
adverbs
softly; intimately; pleasantly; indistinguishably; cunningly; curiously; skillfully; delicately; inextricably; mildly; expertly; exquisitely; amazingly; incredibly; magically; miraculously; mysteriously.
(See merge, combine, mix, assimilate.)

BLENDING
adjectives
extraordinary; delightful; special; uncopiable; mild; expert; discreet; mellow; master; subtle; delicate; rare; happy; strange; colossal; exquisite.

BLESS (v)
adverbs
sanctimoniously; benignly; spiritually; devoutly; reverently; graciously; silently; eternally; providentially.

BLESSED
adverbs
blissfully; happily; infinitely; richly; unquestionably; gratefully; ecstatically; gloriously; eternally; divinely; magically; mystically; endlessly; tenderly; devoutly; profoundly; fervently; sincerely; devotedly; reverently; immeasurably; warmly; thankfully.

adjectives
unexampled; greatest; inestimable; countless (pl); infinite; fervent; plural (pl); apostolic; unmitigated; needful; earthly; mutual (pl); manifold (pl); priestly; substantial; redeeming; unfelt; silent; certain; rich; supernatural; heavenly; abundant; guttural; over-cordial; unimpaired; unclouded; sundry (pl); unequivocal; endless; providential; choicest; valueless; lasting; lifelong; eternal.

verbs
abound with —s; bestow—upon; cherish—; consecrate with—; crown with —s; inherit —; invoke—; pour —s upon; pronounce—; prove—; realize—; render—; wish—upon; —s attend; —consoles; —descends upon; —s flow from; —hallows; —redeems; —thrills.
(See benediction, favor.)

BLIGHT
adjectives
devastating; mouldy; cruel; venomous; visible; premature; swarming.

BLIND
adverbs
falsely; defiantly; wilfully; mercifully; besottedly; heart-rendingly; wretchedly; pitiably; totally.
(See obscure.)

BLINDNESS
adjectives
obstinate; approaching; helpless; innocent; ultimate; mortal; burning; perspicacious; willful; social; pedantic.

BLINDS
adjectives
copper; painted; window; genteel; dilapidated; secret; shut; much-used.

BLINK (v)
adverbs
solemnly; approvingly; sleepily; drowsily; somnolently; shrewdly; sagaciously; dazedly; incessantly; intermittently.
(See wink, disregard, overlook.)

BLISS
adjectives
truest; rapturous; idiotic; unutterable; hysterical; mortal; conjugal; winged; ecstatic; endless; unforgettable; perennial; purest; youthful; dissolving; ambiguous; matchless; unclouded; virgin; visioned; perfect; con-
nubial; extreme; dreamy; unearthly; ineffable; immortal; highest; domestic; private; perpetual; tranquil; coming; sensual; dead; inward; candid; nameless; eternal; transporting; audacious; mantling; faded; departed; foreshadowed; capricious; passive; paralyzed; everlasting; human; heavenly; imaginary; enormous.

verbs
abide in—; anticipate—; attain—; augment —; dampen—; deluge—; diffuse—; dwell in —; experience—; merit—; reign in—; renounce—; sever from—; share in—; violate —; wither—.
(See rapture, happiness, ecstasy.)

BLISSFUL
adverbs
delightfully; supremely; rapturously; gladly; happily; ravishingly; beatifically; joyously; transportedly; charmingly; joyfully; luxuriously; thrillingly; exquisitely; deliciously; incredibly; fascinatingly; blessedly; truly; idiotically; unforgettably; conjugally; amorously; enormously; eternally; dreamily; ineffably; perfectly; matchlessly; endlessly; youthfully; innocently; ecstatically.

BLISTER
adjectives
benign; dark; burning; malignant; tiny; suppurating; prurient; purulent; unsightly; watery.

verbs
absorb—; acquire—; apply to—; cover with —s; drain—; heal—; infect—; inflame to —; open—; paint—; plague with —s; puff into—; raise—; remove—; rub into—; suffer from—; swell into—; treat—; —annoys; —appears; —burns; —bursts; —inconveniences; —irritates; —pains; —drains.
(See ulcer, sore, boil.)

BLITHE
adverbs
infectiously; charmingly; cheerfully; gaily; healthily; contagiously; habitually; airily; exuberantly; heedlessly; carelessly; nimbly; affectionately; bewitchingly; teasingly; bewilderingly; childishly; girlishly; youthfully; wholeheartedly; enticingly; irresistibly; exhilaratingly; animatedly; gleefully; hilariously; friskily; bonnily; exultingly; happily; jauntily; jovially; joyously; jubilantly; joyfully; laughingly; merrily; mirthfully; playfully; rollickingly; spiritedly; vivaciously; trickily; winsomely.

adjectives

biting; dense; muffled; roaring; driving; raging; terrible; insect; blinding; numbing; howling; merciless; swirling.

verbs

dread—; forecast—; forewarn of—; perish in—; precede—; predict—; shelter from—; —blasts; —blinds; —freezes; —rages; —rattles; —redoubles its force; —rises; —shrieks; —suffocates; —tears; —wheels; —whines; —whirls.

(See wind, disaster, storm.)

BLOCK

adjectives

riveted; clanking; creaking; dedicated; bloody; lifeless; vertical; city.

BLOCKADE

adjectives

never-ending; actual; patriotic; economic; dilatory; menacing; complete; vertical; partial; inescapable; innumerable (pl).

verbs

break—; comply with—; cut off by—; denounce—; detail—; effect—; enforce—; engage in—; foil—; force—; impose—; insure—; maintain—; notify of—; patrol in —; penetrate—; proclaim—; raise—; relieve—; resort to—; retaliate for—; run—; slip out of—; smuggle through—; storm—; subject to—; succumb to—; surrender to—; sustain—; terminate—; undertake—; —binds; —checks; —compels surrender; —confiscates; —denies; —detains; —distresses; —endangers; —interrupts; —isolates; —obtructs; —prohibits; —shuts off; —starves.

(See embargo.)

BLOCKHEAD

adjectives

babbling; inconceivable; prattling; idling; complete; accomplished; practiced; genial; harmless; silly; fond.

BLONDE

adjectives

blithe; fine; sandy; honey-colored; flamboyant; debonair; strident; incurable; brilliant; robust; vivacious; appealing; feather-headed; ravishing; pretty; irresponsible; peroxide; raucous; platinum; stringy; petite; insolent; attractive; natural; bleached; wistful.

adverbs

alluringly; rapturously; heavenly; divinely; seductively; naturally; artificially; goldenly; sandily; ruddily; tawnily; flamboyantly; stridently; brilliantly; vivaciously; bleached-ly; attractively; provocatively; stringily; irresponsibly; prettily; ravishingly; feather-headedly; appealingly; irresistibly; enchantingly; refreshingly; winsomely; fascinatingly; daintily; felicitously; pleasantly; satisfyingly; tormentingly; disturbingly; grievously; inordinately; bewitchingly.

BLOOD

adjectives

distinguished; vigorous; fighting; chivalrous; tainted; foul; fraternal; stale; rank; polluted; dangerous; feverish; tingling; pounding; pulsing; oozing; flowing; mingled; foreign; human; hot; caked; dried; frozen; chilled; sluggish; innocent; spattered; quick; living; turbulent; bereaved; sacred; hostile; young; drowsy; precious; patriot; malapert; rushing; ebbing; jellied; trading; frolicsome; atoning; molten; violent; daring; kindred; nutrient; swift; basic; true; gummy; martyred; heretic; faultless; systolic; wicked; generous; pale; coursing; royal; aspiring; frothy; haughtiest; sanguine; congealed; arrested; excellent; noble; rare; sweet; comfortable; nomadic; corrupt.

verbs

aerate—; baptize in—; bathe in—; besmear with—; blend —s; chill—; cleanse—; congeal—; contaminate—; convey—; cool—; curdle—; defile with—; dilute—; dip in—; draw—; drip—; dye with—; effuse—; enrich—; expel—; fertilize—; flush with—; forfeit—; foul—; freeze—; go down in—; impoverish—; infect—; infiltrate—; infuse —; inhabit—; inoculate—; inure to—; invigorate—; issue from—; let—; oxygenate —; paint with—; poison—; pollute—; purge —; purify—; redden with—; seal with—; secrete—; shed—; soak in—; spill—; splash with—; spout—; stain with—; staunch—; steep in—; stimulate—; stir—; suck—; suffuse with—; swill—; taint—; taste—; thirst for—; transfuse—; wallow in—; win with —; write in—; yield—; —accumulates; —boils; —clots; —coagulates; —courses; —creeps through; —dribbles out; —flows; —gushes; —issues forth; —jets out; —leaps; —oozes; —palpitates; —pours from; —pulsates; —reabsorbs; —rises; —runs; —rushes through; —shoots forth; —spurts; —

stagnates; —streams; —surges; —tinkles; —throbs; —wells up.

adjectives
alarming; apoplectic; choleric; devastating; mounting; tremendous.

verbs
lower— —; normalize— —; relieve high— —; — —descends; — —drops; — —endangers; — —rises; — —startles; — —threatens.
(See barometer.)

BLOODSHED

adjectives
wanton; continued; unspeakable; needless; callous; ruthless.

verbs
attend with—; conquer without—; denounce —; die in—; ease—; end in—; free from—; instigate—; involve—; precipitate—; provoke—; result in—; revel in—; steep in—; suffer—; terminate in—; win through—.
(See massacre, slaughter.)

BLOODTHIRSTINESS

adjectives
bestial; reckless; ghoulish; vampire; leechlike; insatiable.

BLOODTHIRSTY

adverbs
insatiably; recklessly; criminally; bestially; cruelly; abominably; inhumanly; atrociously; brutally; infamously; iniquitously; knavishly; profligately; scandalously; viciously; incorrigibly; lawlessly; nefariously; sinfully; wickedly; horribly; unspeakably; amazingly; systematically; inherently; savagely; ferociously; diabolically; feloniously; fiendishly; flagitiously; foully; vilely; villainously.

BLOOD VESSEL

adjectives
bulging; bursting; flexible; heated; attenuated; overworked; straining; fragile.

verbs
block— —; burst— —; circulate through— —; clog— —; contract— —; course through — —; dilate— —; distend— —; disturb— —; engorge— —; flex— —; harden — —s; infect— —; line— —s; lodge in— —; narrow— —; puncture— —; retract— —; rupture— —; sever— —; staunch— —; tear— —; thin— —; twist— —; conveys — —; — —pulsates; — —shrivels up; — —s spring from; — —throbs; — —yields.
(See artery, vein.)

adjectives
gorgeous; glossy; girlish; delicate; lusty; fragrant; glorious; lingering; artificial; short-lived; semi-tropic; abundant; natural; sweet; faded; bell-like; wonted; youthful; overflowing; renovated; hopeful; welded; roseated; manifold; definite; luxuriant; virgin; citrus; petaled; vivid; vernal; prolific; radiant; amethystine; braided; sensational; plenteous; bunchy; precious; exotic; hidden; perfumed; wholesome; primeval; straying; ethereal.

verbs
blast—; blight—; break into—; exalt—; nip —; smother—; take—off; —colors; —culminates in; —exudes; —floresces; —flourishes; —flushes; —glows; —pales; —promises; —sparkles; —springs from; —tints.
(See blossom, vigor, flower.)

BLOOM (v)

adverbs
unchangingly; abundantly; magnificently; lustily; gorgeously; glossily; youthfully; overflowingly; luxuriantly; prolifically; vernally; exotically; wholesomely; primevally; ethereally.
(See blossom.)

BLOSSOM

adjectives
gorgeous; exquisite; cheerful; bright; fabulous; pure; almond; varicolored; lace-like; fragrant; golden; bursting; myriad; pendulous; showy; petaled; wholesome; marsh; bloodlike; colorful; holy; peach; tender; blazing; curious; living; blighted; pomegranate; sunlit; gaudy; meek; conical; embowering; faded; minute; brimstone; evanescent; odorous; latent; beauteous; topmost; phantom; vernal; winking; barren; mimic; loveliest; storm-beaten; flaming; proud.

verbs
bear—; burst into—; clip—; cover with —s; nip—; press—; produce—; put forth —s; scatter —s; shed —s; shower down —s; trim—; yield—; —buds; —dances; —fades; —flowers; —flutters down; —grows; —opens; —promises; —unfolds; —withers.
(See bloom, flower.)

BLOSSOM (v)

adverbs
magnificently; simultaneously; luxuriantly; fabulously; gorgeously; pendulously; colorfully; curiously; gaudily; conically; eva-

nescently; odorously; vernally; winkingly; flamingly.
(See bloom, flower, prosper, thrive.)

BLOT
adjectives
unsightly; tarnished; shadowy; foul; indelible; wrinkled; messy; adulterate.

BLOT (v)
adverbs
remorselessly; indelibly; blackly; permanently; finally; eventually; carelessly; frequently.
(See spot, efface, obliterate.)

BLOTCH
adjectives
sickly; shadowy; ugly; pale; bloody.

BLOTCHY
adverbs
painfully; disagreeably; incurably; unpleasantly; dingily; obnoxiously; disgustingly; repulsively; distressingly; unbecomingly; hopelessly; embarrassingly; disconcertingly; mortifyingly; alarmingly; fearfully; strangely; oddly.

BLOUSE
adjectives
gaudy; flowered; sheer; soft; warm; padded; diaphanous.

BLOW
adjectives
powerful; hammer-like; heavy; severe; fatal; irresistible; lethal; nasty; cruel; treacherous; descending; resounding; percussive; menaced; serious; decisive; frightful; painful; crushing; aggressive; perennial; threatened; echoless; irreparable; doughty; well-directed; staggering; breathless; final; sharpest; faithless; severe; swashing; annihilating; solid; hollow; drunken; amorous; vicious; impending; dull; dexterous; tetchy; ineradicable; heartless; sacrilegious; accusative; death-wind; implacable; ineffective.

verbs
administer—; aim—; break—; breast—; deal—; encounter—; evade—; exchange —s; execute—; experience—; fall to —s; interchange —s; parry—; rain —s upon; reel under—; strike—; stun with—; survive—; thrust—; trade —s; —descends upon; —resounds; —shatters; —smashes; —stretches one out.
(See stroke.)

BLOW (v)
adverbs
adversely; ceaselessly; placidly; gustily; violently; shrewdly; languorously; keenly; incessantly; spasmodically; irresistibly; resoundingly; lethally; aggressively; annihilatingly; viciously; implacably.
(See howl, sigh, swirl.)

BLOWZY
adverbs
ruddily; healthily; sturdily; rosily; attractively; coarsely; blatantly; noticeably; carelessly; showily; floridly; sunnily; pleasantly; roughly; captivatingly; interestingly; wholesomely.

BLUDGEON
adjectives
crude; effective; honest; critical; rough; swift; devastating.

BLUE
adjectives
heavenly; silent; mermaid; exquisite; canonical; dim; celestial; iceberg; indigo; bright; cadmium; intense; sky; glamorous; turquoise; sapphire; brilliant; ordinary; deep; chalcedony; larkspur; limpid; cobalt; delicate; crystal; anemic; illimitable; somber; opalescent; glossy; boundless; uniform; unbroken; dusty; remotest; wood-smoke; cornflower; purest; periwinkle; light; luminous; royal; aquamarine; aerial; tropic; pallid; sulphurous; frost.

BLUE
adverbs
ineffably; deeply; divinely; heavenly; unspeakably; indescribably; pleasantly; coldly; steely; affectionately; exquisitely; dimly; brightly; intensely; brilliantly; limpidly; delicately; sombrely; boundlessly; dustily; uniformly; remotely; purely; lightly; luminously; royally; frostily.

BLUEBIRD
adjectives
ever-welcome; flitting; glorious; luck-bearing; joyful; memory-haunting; merry-whistling.

verbs
—cheers; —pipes; —speeds; —warbles; —whispers.
(See bird.)

BLUFF
adjectives (cliff)
barren; wind-swept; somber; bare; grass-

grown; bold; low; hazy; fine; sand; scarped; rock-reared.

BLUFF
adjectives (lie)
unadulterated; superb; magnificent; brazen; bold; preposterous.

BLUFF
adjectives (speech or manner)
deceptive; frightening; hearty; imposing; offhanded; pretentious; surly; cruel.

verbs
attempt—; bet against—; boast—; call—; carry out—; get away with—; maintain—; —blinds; —deceives; —deters; —excuses; —frightens; —hoodwinks; —induces; —influences; —serves.
(See lie.)

BLUFF
adverbs
churlishly; rudely; captiously; discourteously; disrespectfully; ill-manneredly; impudently; uncivilly; mischievously; moodily; morosely; perversely; insultingly; impertinently; bitterly; bluntly; boorishly; coolly; grimly; harshly; peevishly; pertly; ruggedly; naturally; characteristically; unpardonably; inexcusably; unpleasantly; playfully; teasingly; tormentingly; nonsensically; disagreeably; unnecessarily; sarcastically; ironically; sourly; unceremoniously; tartly; sullenly; vulgarly; unintentionally; deliberately; indefensibly.

BLUFF (v)
adverbs
unnecessarily; superbly; brazenly; preposterously; boldly; magnificently; characteristically; inevitably; grossly; incredibly; unpardonably; faithlessly.
(See frighten, intimidate.)

BLUFFING
adjectives
brilliant; multifarious; inevitable; characteristic; unexpected.

BLUNDER
adjectives
unhappy; colossal; fateful; irretrievable; astounding; disastrous; egregious; political; awful; brave; absurd; idiotic; tactical; ill-judged; sad; marketing; glorious; gross; serious; irreparable; extravagant; incredible; recent; sorry; idiomatic; curious; unpardonable.

verbs
aggravate—; atone for—; commit—; denounce—; fall into—; redeem —s; repair —s; —confounds; —confuses; —disturbs; —troubles.
(See error, mistake.)

BLUNDER (v)
adverbs
grossly; ludicrously; chimerically; ineptly; awkwardly; colossally; fatefully; irretrievably; disastrously; egregiously; politically; idiotically; irreparably; incredibly; idiomatically; grammatically; unpardonably.
(See bungle.)

BLUNDERER
adjectives
inept; impudent; awkward; supposed; chagrined; finished.

BLUNDERING
adjectives
hopeless; bureaucratic; forward; silly; understandable; impudent.

BLUNT
adverbs
stupidly; boorishly; ignorantly; unintentionally; deliberately; sullenly; unceremoniously; ironically; unnecessarily; disagreeably; unpardonably; inexcusably; insolently; unpleasantly; characteristically; ruggedly; honestly; pertly; peevishly; sternly; severely; harshly; doggedly; rudely; captiously; discourteously; uncivilly; ungraciously; moodily; morosely; perversely; bitterly; coolly; clumsily; ineptly; exasperatingly.

BLUNTNESS
adjectives
occasional; astringent; exasperating; characteristic; righteous; permissible; ugly; accentuated; clumsy; bludgeoning; inept.

BLUR
adjectives
confused; dim; pale; ineffectual; misted; pensive; wavering; shapeless; golden; retreating; vague.

BLUSH
adjectives
soft; crimson; deep; modest; rare; palest; contagious; piteous; guilty; delicate; scarlet; hot; burning; suffusing; lovely; rising; bright; charming; gracious; guileless; west-

ern; innocent; telltale; pure; vivid; quick;
eloquent; mellow; sudden; unseen; fleeting;
short; boyish; puzzled; witching; unbor-
rowed; exquisite.

verbs
color with—es; flash—; hide—; redden with
—es; result in—; suffuse with—; —beautifies; —embarrasses; —glows; —heats; —
inflames; —warms.
(See flush.)

BLUSH (v)
adverbs
furiously; miserably; coyly; elatedly; synthetically; disdainfully; ingenuously; modestly; delicately; eloquently; exquisitely; witch-
ingly; easily.
(See flush, redden.)

BLUSTER (v)
adverbs
furiously; thunderously; fearsomely; tremendously; terrifically; ceaselessly; monotonously; wrathfully; heatedly; vigorously;
vainly.
(See storm, rage, fume.)

BOAR
adjectives
urchin; snouted; angry; chafing; blunt;
bloody; hideous; monstrous.

BOARD (commission)
adjectives
nonpartisan; expert; efficient; glowing;
political; mirthful; superior; ancient.

BOARD (official body)
adjectives
assembled; directing; executive; governing;
advisory; high; honorable; local.

verbs
abolish—; admit to—; bring before—; control—; create—; elect to—; enlarge—; entrust to—; establish—; organize—; provide
—; refer to—; set up—; staff—; —administers; —adopts; —advises; —authorizes;
—agrees; —arbitrates; —condemns; —convenes; —develops; —disposes of; —effects;
—elects; —enacts; —enforces; —exercises;
—investigates; —modifies; —operates; —
outlines; —performs; —promotes; —provides; —reforms; —regulates; —relieves;
—reports; —stimulates; —supports; —
votes.
(See commission, committee.)

BOARD (wood)
adjectives
resplendent; stray; reeking; creaking; uncarpeted; shot-scarred; glistening; cypress;
trophy-laden; decaying; rough-hewn; original; grub; sparing; wine-filled; ugly;
sturdy; flimsy; scanty; groaning; festive;
plenteous.

verbs
adjust—; burnish—; case with —s; cast
upon —s; cover with —s; encase in —s; enclose in —s; finish off—; fit—; frame with
—; hew—; measure—; patter over —s;
plane—; preserve—; reinforce —s; sand—;
scurry over —s; warp—; —bars; —creaks;
—extends; —groans; —rots; —splinters; —
splits; —warps.
(See table, stage.)

BOAST
adjectives
absurd; playful; empty; foolish; truthful;
proudest; ordinary; unique; unadulterated;
vapid; peerless; ignoble; honest; sentimental; fanatic; airy; childish; frantic; prattling; noisy; vain.

BOAST (v)
adverbs
justly; blatantly; unmitigatedly; exuberantly; arrogantly; intoxicatedly; hollowly;
overweeningly; whimsically; vainly; egotistically; vapidly; ignobly; fanatically;
prattlingly.
(See brag, vaunt.)

BOASTFUL
adverbs
extravagantly; absurdly; playfully; foolishly; proudly; vapidly; airily; childishly; boyishly; noisily; blatantly; egotistically; fantastically; grotesquely; palpably; manifestly;
essentially; ludicrously; ridiculously; laughably; offensively; unpleasantly; egregiously;
ignobly; ineffectually; inanely; senselessly;
idiotically; preposterously; dexterously; adroitly; cleverly; indiscreetly; imprudently;
feebly; flimsily; wishfully; stupendously;
magnificently; splendidly; vaingloriously;
blindly; blissfully.

BOASTING
adjectives
egotistical; vain; cursed; extravagant;
blustering; bold; blatant.

verbs
glory in—; indulge in—; make good—; occasion—; speak in—; utter—; —extols; —

menaces; —occasions; —terrifies; —threatens.
(See display.)

BOAT
adjectives
crude; wooden; staunch; frail; uptilted; racing; comfortable; sunken; excursion; distant; tiny; fishing; plying; crowded; plunging; fragile; light; portable; lazy; vile; cheap; whirling; driving; moored; outward-bound; crewless; colossal; iron; vanished; half-beached; clumsy; swift; weather-beaten; well-manned; unanchored; pavilioned; worn-out; illuminated.

verbs
alight from—; anchor—; bail—; becalm—; capsize—; caulk—; detail—; fire up—; fit out—; heave to—; moor—; paddle—; pole —; propel—; punt—; push off—; reserve—; swamp—; —churns; —cleaves the water; —dances; —flops; —flounders; —founders; —glides; —grounds; —nuzzles; —outsails; —pitches; —plies; —ploughs; —sneaks; —swings; —touches at.
(See vessel, ship, canoe, launch, schooner, barge, tugboat.)

BOATMEN
adjectives
wrangling; grizzled; inexperienced; skillful.

BOB
adjectives
ravishing; tawny; smooth; smart; shoulder-length.

BOBOLINK
adjectives
joy-swelling; migratory; coy; rice-seeking; reed-swinging; throaty; questing.

verbs
—boasts; —broods; —chirps; —laughs; —prattles; —rattles.
(See bird.)

BOBWHITE
adjectives
covert; dun-colored; misleading; nature-sheltered; shy; sly; wary.

verbs
—bursts out; —calls; —darts; —displays; —feathers; —feigns; —fights; —flushes; —huddles; —preens; —preys on; —puffs out; —sails; —struts; —swells; —trots; —twitters; —whirrs; —whistles; —wings.
(See quail, partridge, bird.)

BODEMENT
adjectives
tremendous; horrid; accurate; uncanny; precise.

BODICE
adjectives
slim; fitted; jeweled.

BODY   (group)
adjectives
aggregate; august; responsible; disinterested; official; governing; obscure; civil; picturesque; upstanding; formidable; deliberative; eminent; hasty-witted; public; legislative; virtuous; specialized; illustrious; ecclesiastical; unsympathetic; artistocratic; insensate; permanent; obstructive; impartial; intermediary; heterogeneous; pigmy; arbitrating; expansive; elastic; appropriating; unfathomable; long-established; anxious; consulting; sensible; seeming; well-regulated; confirming; alterable; irresistible; distinct; reckless; contemptible; inanimate; numerous.

BODY   (substance)
adjectives
clumsy; angular; boyish; deformed; dangling; hurtling; jerking; squatting; quivering; slouched; struggling; trembling; wan; palpitating; human; paralyzed; mummified; hairy; wrinkled; ruddy; compact; drenched; sodden; bleeding; jarred; relaxed; collapsed; huddled; slumped; sagging; defiant; swaggering; dainty; small-boned; shapely; graceful; delicate; striking; quick; wiry; supple; lithe; sturdy; swift; strong; heavy-muscled; hard; rugged; sinewy; young; vigorous; healthy; sound; vibrant; sensuous; amorous; yielding; passionate; stocky; weightless; stunted; shrunken; emaciated; meager; bronzed; ·slim; stiffened; taut; lethargic; slack; immovable; prone; lifeless; couchant; motionless; prostrate; huge; overgrown; vast; obese; mountainous; lanky; unclean; ragged; neglected; unshaven; detestable; overworked; meek; fear-driven; weary; worn; exhausted; charred; sick; strangled; ailing; ·poverty-weakened; disfigured; bruised; torn; jerking; swooning; soulless; negroid; paralyzed; covered; blanketed; relaxed; frozen; dense; unworthy; well-defended; minute; fever-stricken; anemic; religious; misshapen; pierced; organic; transparent; sovereign; inanimate; subterranean; visible; recumbent; influential; spontaneous; rotund; drowned; tattooed; inert; interlaced; uni-

cellular; statuesque; squirming; convivial; flaccid; defunct; astral; adjacent; contradictory; segregated; idle; capable; cheerful; fluid; qualified; bigoted; unsound; chaste; branching; decent; convulsing; cigar-shaped; erect; twitching; Spagnuoled; decomposed; uncoffined; jovial; exhausted; plump; filiform; weazened; undivided; rubicund.

verbs
adapt—; anoint—; array—; attune—; bare —; batter—; bow—; bury—; cast out—; chill—; cleanse—; cling to—; commit—; consecrate—; consume—; contract—; deck —in; defile—; deplete—; discern—; dismember—; dispose of—; drag—; dwarf—; ease—; edify—; emaciate—; embrace—; endanger—; exhilarate—; expose—; exult in—; fetter—; floor—; gloat over—; govern—; incline—; inflict upon—; inter—; introduce into—; invest—; invigorate—; mangle—; pelt—; pommel—; preserve—; reconstruct—; relieve—; reproduce—; rid —of; saturate—; splatter—; sponge—; stiffen—; sustain—; tenant—; torture—; transmit through—; triumph over—; twist—; vitalize—; waste—; wrap—in; —decomposes; —disintegrates; —festers; —flops; —gleams; —glides; —putrefies; —quivers; —rebels; —reigns; —responds; —slumps; —sprawls; —twitches; —vibrates; —wriggles; —writhes.
(See form, frame, carcass, corpse.)

BOG
adjectives
filthy; logical; sinking; swanky; sphagnous; treacherous; dangerous.

BOG (v)
adverbs
hopelessly; filthily; logically; treacherously; dangerously; fatally; irresistibly; obscurely; unprecedentedly; miserably.
(See fail.)

BOGGY
adverbs
muddily; plashily; squashily; quaggily; swampily; softly; unpleasantly; unhealthfully; unfortunately; pestiferously; undesirably; irrecoverably; irremediably; hopelessly; unluckily; deplorably; disturbingly; plaguedly; impracticably.

BOIL
adjectives (tumor)
erupting; festering; hideous; throbbing; rest-robbing; purplish.

verbs
absorb—; cut—; dissect—; extirpate—; incise—; lance—; paint—; puncture—; — buds; —comes to a head; —disappeared; —forms.
(See abscess.)

BOISTEROUS
adverbs
broadly; intolerably; noisily; clamorously; uproariously; vociferously; turbulently; obstreperously; blatantly; fussily; breezily; convivially; festively; jovially; genially; happily; joyously; joyfully; wildly; madly; crazily; drunkenly; merrily; coarsely; crudely; pugnaciously; discordantly; angrily; excusably; childishly; rudely; Rotarily; uncontrollably; foolishly; fatuously; socially; perpetually; heedlessly; carelessly; thoughtlessly; deliberately; unpardonably; inexcusably; understandably; naturally; affectionately; fraternally.

BOISTEROUSNESS
adjectives
boyish; loud; unrestrained; broad; raucous.

BOLD
adverbs
offensively; audaciously; impudently; rashly; wantonly; indiscreetly; injudiciously; hotheadedly; foolishly; recklessly; presumptuously; amazingly; shamelessly; tragically; singularly; ridiculously; inexplicably; dramatically; inherently; fantastically; alarmingly; temperamentally; dangerously; courageously; adventurously.

BOLDNESS
adjectives
unprecedented; characteristic; decent; self-respecting; uncanny; prodigious; sublime; astonishing; pious; persistent; singular; ill-timed; ridiculous; easy; frank; habitual; felicitous; generous; extreme; foolish.

BOLE
adjectives
twisted; opalescent; resinous; hoary; bossy.

BOLT
adjectives
tremendous; heavy; flimsy; sulphurous; sharp; avenging; death-dealing; heaven-sent.

verbs
adjust—; apply—; clamp on—; connect—; discharge—; drive—; employ—; extract—; fasten—; forge—; heat—; hurl—; manipu-

late—; rivet—; screw—; secure with—; shackle in —s; shoot—; sink—; snap—; strip—; stud—; thread—; tighten—; turn —; undo—; —bars; —expands; —fastens; —locks; —pins; —prevents; —rivets; —safeguards; —seals; —secures; —shrinks; —unties; —withstands.

(See bar.)

BOLT (v)

adverbs
hungrily; avidly; ferociously; grossly; hoggishly; brutishly; barbarously; unrestrainedly; sottishly; permanently.

(See gulp.)

BOMB

adjectives
unsuccessful; exploding; gas; incendiary; volcanic; time.

verbs
bombard with—; clock—; detonate—; direct—; discharge—; drop—; eject—; encase—; examine—; fill—; fire—; fling—; fuse—; hurl—; ignite—; project—; rain —s; release—; set—; shower with —s; time —; toss—; —batters; —bursts; —dynamites; —explodes; —s fly; —hammers; —hums; —plows through; —ruins; —scatters; — shatters; —ticks; —uproots.

(See projectile, shell.)

BOMB (v)

adverbs
cold-bloodedly; unsuccessfully; inhumanly; volcanically; ruthlessly; fiendishly; callously; devilishly; soullessly.

(See attack.)

BOMBARDMENT

adjectives
preliminary; serious; desultory; persistent; intermittent; intensive; aerial; constant; threatened.

verbs
assail with—; command—; concentrate—; conduct—; counter—; defend against—; direct—; flee from—; fortify against—; inflict—; plan—; prepare for—; resort to—; shatter with—; shelter from—; shudder under—; slacken—; unleash—; ward off—; —assails; —attacks; —batters; —damages; —demolishes; —demoralizes; —destroys; —disables; —disheartens; —dispirits; —injures; —reduces; —routs; —rumbles; — scatters; —thunders; —uproots.

(See attack, assault.)

adjectives
oratorical; studied; stilted; rhetorical; empty; loud; pedantic; ranting.

BOMBASTIC

adverbs
magnificently; absurdly; playfully; foolishly; proudly; inanely; vapidly; airily; noisily; childishly; blatantly; fantastically; joyously; ludicrously; ridiculously; laughably; offensively; unpleasantly; ineffectually; senselessly; idiotically; clownishly; preposterously; stupendously; splendidly; blissfully; intolerably; rudely; fatuously; deliberately; crudely; merrily; crazily; convivially; vociferously; uproariously.

BOND

adjectives   (certificate or debenture)
corporation; government; interest-bearing; matured; municipal; negotiable; transferable; utility.

verbs
advise on —s; borrow on —s; cash —s; float —s; inherit —s; investigate —s; issue —s; liquidate—; market —s; number —s; print —s; recommend —s; register —s; repudiate —s; sell —s; serialize —s; transfer —s; —accumulates interest; —matures; — promises.

BOND

adjectives   (investment)
dubious; crinkly; unimpeachable; funding; highly-secured; gilt-edged.

BOND

adjectives   (tie)
textual; unbreakable; inescapable; economic; financial; confidential; cruel; weak; tacit; everlasting; powerful; tenacious; imperishable; invisible; sympathetic; secret; strong; invariable; delusive; indissoluble; indestructible; intellectual; countless (pl); subtle; artistic; single; merry; harmonious; conventional; natural; oppressive; fraternal; eternal; marriage; enduring; close.

verbs
burst —s; contract—; dissolve—; enter—; liberate from—; link with —s; loose —s; maintain—; pledge—; seal—; shatter—; snap —s asunder; tighten—; —cements; — confines; —connects; —constrains; —endures; —enslaves; —fetters; —imprisons; —manacles; —obligates; —restrains; — shackles.

(See band, tie, fetter, obligation, promise.)

BOND (v)

adverbs

indissolubly; unbreakably; inescapably; financially; tenaciously; imperishably; invisibly; conventionally; eternally; oppressively.

BONDAGE

adjectives

infantine; solemn; sweet; petted; deep; hereditary; deadly; commercial; intermittent; mysterious; improvised; voluntary; brittle; tolerable; wholesome; hard; magic; roseate; economical.

verbs

abolish—; bring into—; deliver from—; enforce—; enslave in—; escape from—; free from—; hold in—; impose—; pledge into —; reduce to—; return to—; rid of—; sell into—; serve out—; subject to—; tie in—; —degrades; —warps.

(See slavery, servitude, captivity, subjugation.)

BONE

adjectives

joint; marrow; gaunt; jutting; crumbling; bleached; ravaged-looking; dry; mighty; dismal; poor; tired; aching; trivial; massive; storm-chilled; unsightly; toothsome; aged; blanching; unrememberable; dissevered; aligned; queer-shaped; earthly; chivalric; delicate; distorted; empty; honored; sturdy; white-sown; sound; mastoid; unburied; grilled; uncoffined; shining; petrified; carious; honest; moldering; livid; weary; piteous; cowardly; frontal; pliable; marsupial; steely; brittle; immense; pulsant; femoral; prominent; canonized; spiced; high; saucer-like.

verbs

adhere to—; adjust —s; affect—; assemble —s; bend—; bleach —s; breed in —s; bruise —; cement—; crack—; crush—; cut to—; deform—; dislocate—; distort—; dry—; excavate —s; expose—; fertilize with —s; fracture—; freeze to—; gnaw—; graft—; grind —s; harden —s; heal—; infect—; inflame—; injure—; inter —s; knit—; lengthen—; operate on—; pick—; pierce—; plate —; protect—; rattle —s; realign—; reveal —; scatter —s; set—; shake—; soften—; splinter—; treat—; twist—; unite—; waste —s; wire—; wrap up —s; x-ray—; —s ache; —s creak; —s form; —s frame; — hinges; —s join; —s mature; —s remain; — rots.

BONFIRE

adjectives

solitary; glowing; tremendous; rejoicing.

BONNET

adjectives

dark; coquettish; delicate; starched; battered; flattened; sun; gigantic; hearse-plumed; amazing; poke; durable; dangling; orange-tawny.

BONNY

adverbs

blithely; airily; beautifully; buxomly; rosily; prettily; wholesomely; cheerfully; buoyantly; merrily; jestingly; gaily; lightly; winsomely; joyously; ecstatically; rapturously; simply; dearly; adorably; charmingly; enchantingly; bewitchingly; lovably; irresistibly; tormentingly; teasingly.

BONY

adverbs

awkwardly; fantastically; grotesquely; amusingly; pathetically; complacently; unbelievably; distressingly; angularly; terribly; horridly; oddly; touchingly; grievously; unthinkably; ludicrously; ridiculously; deplorably; lamentably; strangely; queerly; singularly; drolly.

BOOK

adjectives

vade-mecum; reference; glorified; guide; handy; narrow; thin; black; unacademic; unpretentious; amazing; disturbing; terrifying; strange; vital; dynamic; pregnant; monogrammed; original; incisive; passionate; ancient; worn; musty; dusty; littered; moldy; coverless; written; translated; polished; elegant; cynical; illustrated; inferior; painful; heartbreaking; obscure; condemned; ungraceful; dull; tedious; rejected; inadequate; incomplete; fuliginous; obscene; degrading; suggestive; immoral; dreadful; spectacular; shocking; devastating; ill-natured; cursed; blasphemous; seditious; banned; deliberate; quarrelsome; posthumous; sacred; unsigned; anonymous; educative; formidable; scientific; talking; racial; devotional; serious; realistic; truest; provocative; important; notable; warlike; venerable; sophisticated; wise; mature; delicate; learned; informative; readable; clever; agreeable; comprehensive; detailed; popular; best-selling; famous; hilarious; painful; funny; amusing; stimulating; quaint; priceless; rare; difficult; massive; well-made; clear; rich; authentic; factual; authoritative; absorbing; astonishing; accursed; bewitching; clarifying; diverting; enthralling; exhilarating; extraordinary; first; feminine; forthright; glamorous; glorious; heroic; human; hair-raising; irresistible; intimate; magnificent; practical; perfect; remarkable; readable; stirring; superb; scholarly; strangest; sensitive; timely; splendid; unique; vital; witty; grand; ephemeral; melancholy; useful; thought-provoking; valuable; exercise; scrambling; profitable; memorandum; stormy; edifying; musty; indecent; salable; lewd; elementary; illiterate; lucid; enjoyable; commonplace; censored.

verbs
adapt—; admire—; base on—; belittle—; clutch—; con—; cram—; dedicate—; depreciate—; disparage—; distort—; dive into —; edit—; elaborate—; enshrine—; fling —; illustrate—; label—; launch—; mutilate —; permeate—; peruse—; plot—; plunge through—; pour over—; preface—; propagate—; recommend—; resort to—; review —; revise—; ridicule—; satirize—; scan—; search—; slander—; succumb to—; summarize—; thumb—; tilt—; vend—; —abounds in; —breathes; —charms; —defiles; — details; —depresses; —disturbs; —documents; —embodies; —enchants; —enthralls; —inspires; —meanders; —oppresses; —ranks; —shocks; —sparkles; —surges; —transports.
(See volume, novel, fiction, story, biography.)

BOOKCASE
adjectives
bamboo; elegant; built-in; expensive.

BOOKISH
adverbs
hopelessly; learnedly; ostentatiously; arrogantly; proudly; unfortunately; quaintly; amusingly; complacently; colossally; tediously; monotonously; inordinately; obviously; studiously; ardently; unintelligently; vacuously; inanely; showily; blindly; pedantically; superficially; shrewdly; proverbially; profoundly; eruditely; consciously; academically; omnisciently.

BOOKKEEPER
adjectives
provincial; timid; expensive; overworked; lazy; ambitious.

BOOKLET
adjectives
descriptive; illustrated; attractive; authoritative; fascinating; explanatory; valuable; informative; dainty; interesting; constructive; pictorial.

BOOM ·
adjectives (activity or prosperity)
amazing; exciting; fortune-rolling; gigantic; rapidly-subsiding; tidal-wave; overnight.

verbs
accelerate—; advance into—; buoy up by—; burst into—; daze by—; delay—; denote—; follow by—; foretell—; launch—; prepare for—; provoke—; revel in—; revive—; stimulate—; work up—; —advances; — bounds; —cheers; —collapses; —crashes; —encourages; —exhilarates; —fades; —follows; —induces; —prospers; —retards; — roars; —sets in; —swells.
(See prosperity, development.)

BOOM
adjectives (business)
postwar; periodic; unprecedented; glorious; fantastic.

BOOM
adjectives (noise)
dwindling; penetrating; deep; disturbing; muffled; incalculable; subdued.

BOOM (v)
adverbs
hollowly; deafeningly; penetratingly; disturbingly; muffledly; subduedly; sonorously; dully; monotonously; musically; thuddingly; resoundingly; intermittently.
(See roar.)

BOOMING
adjectives
hollow; sonorous; dull; perpetual; deep-toned; monotonous; musical. ·

BOON
adjectives
inestimable; priceless; immortal; unspeakable; delusive; blissful; greater; floral; choicest; smaller.

verbs
accord—; beseech—; bestow—; command —; confer—upon; court—; deny—; entreat —; favor with—; grant—; petition—; pray for—; request—; yield—.
(See blessing, advantage, favor, gift.)

BOOR
adjectives
sottish; churlish; ill-bred; insensible; ignor-

ant; thick-necked; rustic; lascivious; horny-handed; drunken.

BOORISH

adverbs
awkwardly; fantastically; inordinately; offensively; contemptibly; amusingly; unconsciously; unwittingly; artlessly; deliberately; morbidly; prodigiously; colossally; tediously; detestably; bluntly; insufferably; intolerably; unbearably; rudely; abominably; crudely; intentionally; carelessly; shockingly; stupidly; innately; churlishly; ignorantly; drunkenly; impudently; uncivilly; moodily; perversely; insultingly; bitterly; harshly; ruggedly; inexcusably; disagreeably; sourly; unceremoniously; sullenly; indefensibly; outrageously.

BOOTH

adjectives
gaudy; little; secluded; vine-covered; mushroom-topped; rustic; impermanent; miserable; demonstration.

verbs
assemble in—; conduct—; conduct to—; construct—; cover—; erect—; exhibit in—; huddle in—; lead to—; lodge in—; provide —; refresh at—; shelter in—.
(See shelter, stand.)

BOOTS

adjectives
squeaking; shining; swaggering; varnished; spurred; heavy; patched; elaborate; flat-soled; faultless; creaking; lustrous; lacquered; immaculate; fancy; neat; soft; studded; tight; high-heeled; close-fitting; dilapidated; clumsy; shapeless; patent-leather; elastic-sided; cavalier; flappy; muddy.

BOOTY

adjectives
hidden; magnificent; honeyed.

BORDER

adjectives
remote; rickety; dusky; inscribed; gaudy; beauteous; eternal; secluded; variegated; terraced; populous.

verbs
adjust—; broaden—; define—; enlarge—; establish—; extend—; fortify—; illustrate —; mark—; mass at—; menace—; pass through—; patrol—; post at—; ravage—; safeguard—; skirt—; touch—; widen—; — bounds; —limits; —margins; —outlines.
(See edge, limit, boundary, frontier.)

BORE

adjectives
deadly; highest; dreadful; everlasting; colossal; ignorant; ceaseless; veritable; incomparable; intimate; fearful; unmitigated; amiable; horrid; practiced.

BORE (v)

adverbs
faintly; heartily; dreadfully; everlastingly; colossally; ceaselessly; incomparably; unmitigatedly; horridly; agonizingly.
(See annoy, tire, trouble, vex.)

BOREDOM

adjectives
exasperated; intolerable; sinister; petulant; languid; passionless; unbearable; barren; solitary; sheer; genteel; gentlemanly; profound; drowsy; well-bred.

verbs
bear—; chase away—; consign to—; drug into—; endure—; experience—; free from —; pierce—; relieve—; sink into—; succumb to—; threaten with—; —annoys; —gnaws.
(See ennui, annoyance.)

BORESOME

adverbs
intolerably; profoundly; tiresomely; tediously; monotonously; irksomely; uniformly; terribly; inordinately; feebly; exhaustively; dully; mortally; prosily; disgustingly; unbearably; wearily; flatly; stupidly.

BORN (v)

adverbs
royally; posthumously; lowly; painlessly; humbly; legitimately; nobly.

BORROW (v)

adverbs
infrequently; constantly; boldly; shamelessly; persistently; frequently; habitually; cheerfully.
(See obtain, acquire.)

BORROWER

adjectives
solvent; would-be; shameless; infinite; unfortunate.

BOSOM

adjectives
ample; abundant; massive; extensive; capacious; expanded; capital; lovely; warm; flat; weak; aching; bare; maternal; austere; quickened; heaving; corseted; covert; jaded; melancholy; contented; placid; chill-

ed; plenteous; peaceful; brinish; immortal; faithless; complete; genial; tranquil; transparent; virginal; brassy; nectared; sad; blushing; sunburnt; sluggish; inconstant; soft-pleated; undefiled; quivering; virile; bloodless; hard; nursing; murmuring; glassy; palpitating; rock-ribbed; shieldless; agonized; fragrant; chaste; simple; writhing.

verbs
agitate—; assail—; bare—; beat—; chamber in—; cherish in—; clasp to—; cleanse—; embrace—; incense—; live in—; lurk in—; nestle in—; nurse in—; pacify—; pain—; perturb—; plant in—; pluck from—; shelter in—; soothe—; stir—; tear from—; vent—; warm—; wrestle in—; —burns; —heaves; —swells.
(See breast.)

BOSS
adjectives   (colloq.)
political; nervous; high-strung; dominant; invisible; corrupt; arrogant; powerful; level-headed; department; egomaniac; brazen; bilingual; militant; argumentative.

verbs
anger—; esteem—; promote to—; —dictates; —discharges; —employs; —fires; —lashes; —leads; —manages; —masters; —orders.
(See manager, employer, politician.)

BOSS (v)
adverbs
dreadfully; politically; nervously; dominantly; arrogantly; brazenly; argumentatively; dictatorially; highhandedly; imperiously; swaggeringly.
(See direct, dominate.)

BOSSY
adverbs
disagreeably; ludicrously; infinitely; amusingly; officiously; ridiculously; despotically; tyrannically; pompously; characteristically; inherently; arrogantly; superciliously; loftily; clownishly; insistently; persistently; sharply; curtly; efficiently; offensively; detestably; shockingly; naturally; unreasonably; foolishly; excessively.

BOTHERSOME
adverbs
unduly; disagreeably; intolerably; annoyingly; vexatiously; incessantly; persistently; incorrigibly; incurably; offensively; detestably; shockingly; unreasonably; foolishly; noisily; pestiferously; tediously; stupidly; mortally; inordinately; terribly; disgustingly; cantankerously; unmanageably; insufferably; unendurably.

BOTTLE
adjectives
beautiful; shining; labeled; exquisite; spherical; grotesque; unique; ancient; flamboyant; reliable; venerable-looking; narrow-mouthed; half-empty; crown; coveted; unisonant (pl); unfinished.

verbs
brandish—; case —s; charge—; clink—; cluster —s; convey in—; cork—; drain—; drink—; invert—; manipulate—; pour into —; prepare—; produce—; proffer—; quaff from—; smash—; store in—; strain—; transfer to—; transport in—; —carries; —s clink; —contains; —crashes.
(See glass.)

BOTTLE (v)
adverbs
effectively; exquisitely; reliably; permanently; temporarily; securely; skilfully; perpetually.

BOTTOM
adjectives
noble; shallow; luxuriant; sandy; sieve; fertile; blind; leaky; rugged.

verbs
anchor to—; drag—; dredge—; flounder on —; gauge to—; list at—; lower to—; plunge to—; probe to—; recede to—; rest on—; sink to—; transfix to—.
(See base, foundation.)

BOUDOIR
adjectives
scented; perfumed; luxurious; frivolous; beautiful; alluring; enticing; sumptuous; beckoning.

BOUGH
adjectives
pendent; blossoming; projecting; breathless; fruited; pampered; untrimmed; feathery; colored; drooping; stony; topmost; shelving; unpeeled; majestic; prodigal; thick; snow-laden; fluttering; withered; naked; raven; arching; interlaced (pl); long; snow-hung; unwaving; sinewy; barren; fragrant; untrustworthy; clustering (pl); fresh; disenchanted; gnarled; splintered; hanging; billowy (pl); willing; treacherous; reluctant; nodding; denuded; springy;

mossy; stirring; ragged; beechen; innumerable (pl); dripping.

adjectives
fern-covered; huge; scattered; mighty; sunwarmed; tremendous; mossy; sheltering; flat-topped; great; loosened; granite; steel; ancient; glacial.

BOULEVARD
adjectives
spacious; crowded; engirdling; wintry; gay; bright; lighted; festive.

BOUND (v)
adverbs
joyously; gallantly; gracefully; exquisitely; superbly; lithely; sportively; animatedly; freely.
(See leap, spring, dance, frisk.)

BOUNDARY
adjectives
fairy; historical; established; frontier; opposite; outer; definite; geographical; intangible; material; titular; ill-defined; political; utmost.

verbs
break—; dispute—; disregard—; encroach upon—; enlarge—; extend—; fortify—; hang on—; hover over—; indicate—; limit —; line—; mark—; perceive—; reside on —; station at—; transcend —ies; widen—.
(See border, limit, barrier, edge, line.)

BOUNDS
adjectives
abolished; vaulting; narrow; visible; stone-troubled; mad; vulgar; utmost; firm; elastic; graceful; earthly.

verbs
appoint—; break—; confine to—; extend—; hurdle—; infringe on—; leap—; narrow—; overleap all—; prescribe—; set—; transcend —; widen—.
(See boundary.)

BOUNTY
adjectives
beneficent; endless; essential; extravagant; munificent; questionable; reckless.

verbs
bestow—; collect—; deserve—; distribute —; earn—; merit—; pay—; proclaim—; reward with—; scorn—; share—; spread—;

taste—; value—; —encourages; —excels.
(See gift, favor, fee.)

BOUQUET
adjectives
lavish; huge; enormous; absurd; farewell; conventional; nightly; enchanting; exquisite; intriguing; distinctive; superb; animated; sumptuous; tasteful.

verbs
adorn with—; affix—; arrange—; bunch—; clasp—; clip—; cut—; display—; garnish with—; gather—; inhale—; lavish —s upon; pay tribute with—; sniff—; surrounded by —s; tie up—; toss—; wrap—; —cheers; —compliments; —conveys; —enhances.
(See flowers.)

BOURGEOIS
adverbs
obscurely; barbarously; humbly; boorishly; churlishly; roughly; savagely; snobbishly; flauntingly; obviously; manifestly; basely; evidently; indubitably; unquestionably; ignobly; meanly; sorrily; confessedly; admittedly.

BOURGEOISIE
adjectives   (pl)
dispossessed; unconverted; all-pervading; prosperous; ambitious; wealthy; enfranchised; bloated; mercantile.

verbs
address—; besiege by—; class among—; clout (colloq.)—; control—; depend on—; despise—; distinguish—; enslave—; exclude —; familiarize with—; inveigh against—; mingle with—; rank among—; restrain—; tread on—; —arise; —cheer; —congregate; —decay; —gather; —resent; —revolt; —storm; —support; —surround; —triumph.
(See proletariat.)

BOUT
adjectives
match; stiff; humiliating; distressing; winding; dressing; wassail; exciting; boring.

verbs
cancel—; engage in—; indulge in—; stage —; take part in—; time—; witness—; —attracts; —draws; —thrills.
(See contest, conflict, battle.)

BOVINE
adverbs
stolidly; dully; ineptly; absolutely; stupidly; apathetically; calmly; serenely; indifferent-

ly; complaisantly; agreeably; blockishly; doltishly; heavily; idly; obtusely; simply; vacantly; witlessly; prosaically; ridiculously; reposefully; mildly; tranquilly; placidly; tamely; unconcernedly.

BOW

adjectives
noiseless; courteous; flourishing; profound; sweeping; chilly; polite; continuous; Oriental; ceremonious; unbent; mechanical; masculine; formal; conventional; hospitable; drowsy; serious; ironical; garish; humid; humble; grateful; obsequious; sycophantic; inimitable; magnificent; barbaric; sawing; whanging; romantic; historical; burlesque; mischievous; silent; amiable; exaggerated; sardonic; society; manly; valedictory; smashing; frigid; stiff; scarlet; prodigious; liberal; majestic; ethereal; transparent; unctuous.

BOW

adjectives   (archery)
ashen; carefully-adjusted; curiously-fashioned; crude; pliant; servile; trusty; twanging.

verbs
arm with—; bend—; curve—; draw—; employ—; fashion—; form—; joint—; level—; release—; ripple from—; set—; shape—; shoot with—; spring—; string—; tense—; twang—; unleash—; —projects; —quivers; —retracts; —wavers.
(See arrow.)

BOW (v)

adverbs
discriminately; involuntarily; prematurely; languidly; ornately; gallantly; ironically; instinctively; profoundly; gravely; unctuously; passively; distantly; obsequiously; cringingly; formally; mockingly; deferentially; debonairly; submissively; desolately; haughtily; profoundly; dejectedly; Orientally; sweepingly; ceremoniously; drowsily; mechanically; sycophantically; sardonically; majestically.
(See incline, nod, yield, stoop.)

BOWELS

adjectives
lazy; lithe; firm-muscled; engorged; surfeited; stubborn.

verbs
clean out—; clear—; constipate—; dilate—; distend—; ease—; empty—; evacuate—; in-fect—; inflame—; inject into—; insert in—; introduce into—; irritate—; line—; move—; open—; perforate—; purge—; regulate—; relax—; stimulate—; —move; —respond.
(See intestines.)

BOWER

adjectives
complete; myrtle; noontide; bloomless; wavy; heavenly; inmost; comfortless; leafy; over-arching; consecrated; moonlit; sylvan; pleached; native; roseate; apricot-silk; secluded; ravaged; amaranth; pleasant; lyric; noisome; blissful; fragrant; glimmering; newly-woven; close; enchanted; virgin; sequestered.

verbs
canopy with —s; cover—; dwell amid —s; entertain in—; entice into—; hide in—; idealize—; inhabit—; plant with—; shade—; steal into—; —droops; —shades; —thickens.
(See recess, cottage.)

BOWL

adjectives
unmingled; capacious; leathern; meager; ambrosial; flowing; enormous; sealed; pewter; lovely; cloisonne; shallow; flowered; fat; priceless; low; translucid; smooth; shining; adorned; brimming; nut-brown; coarse; coppery; hospitable; friendly.

BOX

adjectives
capacious; dreadful; cumbersome; spacious; stuffed; cozy; convenient; jolly; satin; alabaster; screened; unfurnished; pasteboard; triangular; poetical; wooden; gaudy; proscenium; uncompromising; sunken; hectagonal; oblong; tin; oversize.

verbs
collect in—; encase in—; hide in—; lock—; occupy—; partition—; restore to—; save in —; seal—; search—; shelter in—; —clatters; —contains; —yawns.
(See case, chest, basket.)

BOX (v)

adverbs
firmly; securely; clumsily; cumbersomely; conveniently; hectagonally; tastefully; sumptuously.
(See tie, enclose.)

BOX (v)

adverbs   (prize fight)
invincibly; vigorously; violently; dexterously; nimbly; uncompromisingly; superbly.
(See slap.)

adjectives

stalwart; remarkable; inexperienced; un-equipped; boastful; unruly; dissolute; pre-cocious; clean-cut; nestling; disobedient; thoughtless; reckless; flint-hearted; peevish; starved; shelterless; amorous; military; ir-recoverable; stocky; round-faced; apple-cheeked; rollicking; red-haired; conscripted; sundry; dull; jolly; good-natured; laughing; active; fun-loving; handsome; radiant; live-ly; loving; good-looking; sturdy; absurd; lanky; chubby; honest; mischievous; lubber-ly; aggrieved; vociferous; barefoot; cool; silent; frantic; disappointed; irresponsible; incorrigible; devoted; taciturn; moody; thoroughbred; errant; waggish; flattering; well-grown; pestiferous; ungrateful; beau-tiful; fair; musing; ragged; cocksure; grin-ning; pernicious; lawless; criminal; medal-led; sheepish; bold; sanguine; quick; for-ward; capable; penitent; ruddy; sleeping; rare; rude; sympathetic; leprous; unbridled; unthinking; wayward; budding; white-headed; thin-faced; black-aproned; black-eyed; scornful; lascivious; patient; tender; serviceable; scrubbed; aristocratic; peevish; rascally; vigorous; enamored; swarthy; bril-liant; wild; weedy; daring; tiresome; non-sensical; turbaned; sordid; dreamy; wan-ton; winning; sassy; sportive; insolent; headstrong; ardent; healthy; robust; sedul-ous; aggressive; chivalrous; paltry; insipid; feeble-minded; stolid; clever; pugnacious; problem; gloomy; lonely; fragile; timid; impetuous; boisterous; fiery; heavy-hearted.

BOYCOTT

adjectives

fair; hampering; hostile; personal; private; protective; retaliatory; rigid; unwarranted; universal.

verbs

adopt—; approve—; assail—; coerce by—; counter—; discard—; formulate—; incur—; inflict—; instigate—; institute—; justify—; lift—; organize—; patronize—; prepare for —; proclaim—; punish with—; secure against—; shelter from—; stand firm on—; support—; sweep through—; threaten with —; urge—; warrant—; yield to—; —de-moralizes; —deprives; —incites; —injures; —outrages; —persecutes; —prevents; —pro-tects; —reduces; —starves.
(See embargo.)

BOYISH

adverbs

delightfully; remarkably; sturdily; stoutly; adventurously; daringly; good-naturedly; impetuously; grinningly; happily; joyously; coaxingly; energetically; vigorously; re-freshingly; inextinguishably; vividly; irre-sistibly; robustly; ungovernably; hilarious-ly; facetiously; blithely; cheerfully; buoy-antly; merrily; triumphantly.

BOYLIKE

adverbs

refreshingly; charmingly; irresistibly; utter-ly; inexpressably; ineffably.

BRACE

adjectives

arching; auxiliary; extended; movable; strengthening; sustaining.

verbs

buckle on—; discard—; loosen—; regulate —; strap on—; —clasps; —connects; — holds; —pinches; —presses; —secures; — supports; —suspends; —tightens.
(See support, belt.)

BRACELET

adjectives

flaming; jingling; massive; jeweled; glitter-ing; diamond; flashing; glancing.

BRAG (*v*)

adverbs

immodestly; alcoholically; heartily; swag-geringly; idly; shamelessly; unrestrainedly; bullyingly; insolently; immoderately.
(See boast, vaunt.)

BRAGGADOCIO

adjectives

swaggering; hearty; idle; alcoholic.

BRAGGART

adjectives

strutting; cowardly; insolent; debonair; bullying; unscarred.

BRAID

adjectives   (stripe, ornament)

beaded; encrusting; curiously-patterned; glittering; intricately-woven; silken; em-broidered; tarnished.

verbs

adorn with—; attach—; deck in—; decorate with—; display—; embroider in—; entwine in—; envelop in—; exhibit—; flaunt—; in-terweave —s; knit in—; untwine—; wind

—; —binds; —denotes; —honors; —represents; —slips.

(See ornament.)

BRAID (v)

adverbs

skillfully; dexterously; nimbly; radiantly; verdantly; lustrously; heavily; intricately; curiously.

BRAIDS

adjectives

stubby; heavy; lustrous; jetty; shining; long; twisted; verdant; treble; radiant; glossy.

verbs

confine in—; do up in—; knot—; loose—; plait into—; snip—; tangle—; trim—; twist into—; uncoil—; —fly; —stream from.

(See hair.)

BRAIN

adjectives

editorial; reeling; sobering; inquisitive; clamoring; budding; shrinking; plotting; soothed; human; fevered; maddened; fabulous; boiled; whirling; busy; fertile; comprehensive; excited; dissolving; overseeing; keenest; overheated; immature; distempered; fruitful; logical; teeming; troubled; benumbed; sunburnt; tortured; tired; half-awakened; haunted; seething; rapt; bastard; dying; fatigued; maudlin; loyal; dull; cunning; drunken; scheming; throbbing; bewildered; heavily-taxed; misshapen; feverish; visioning; pure; devious; requisite; burning; addled; callow; young; confused; uncertain; grosser; amiable; brute; disordered; ruthless; maggoty; whisky-addled; flighty; emotive; calculating; celestial; erring; infernal; artless; shrewd; stifled; forging; cool; overtasked; wandering; vacant; sagacious; collective.

verbs

addle—; ballast—; bewilder—; clog—; confuse—; connect with—; craze—; cudgel—; dart through—; dash out—; emanate from —; endow with —s; force—; lash —s; nourish—; overtax—; perplex—; pound through—; prey upon—; rack—; rowel—; sear—; tax—; twist—; weigh upon—; — burns; —conceives; —devises; —fails; — functions; —invents; —lumbers; —races; — weaves; —whirls.

(See mind, intellect.)

BRAINLESS

adverbs

utterly; manifestly; feebly; heavily; blithely; cheerfully; obtusely; fatuously; blatantly; vacuously; incoherently obviously; evidently; oddly; crazily; unfortunately; lamentably; deplorably; admittedly; oafishly; loutishly.

BRAINY

adverbs

acutely; exceptionally; cleverly; astutely; profoundly; solidly; unusually; perspicaciously; reasonably.

BRAKE (n)

adjectives

dusky; shrieking; grinding; tricky; rasping; serviceable; shrill; inadequate; hissing.

verbs

adjust —s; apply—; clamp on—; contact—; depend on—; depress—; devise—; draw—; employ—; exercise—; fit with—; free—; jam on—; operate—; pedal—; press on—; regulate—; release—; tighten—; utilize—; —acts; —arrests; —checks; —controls; — fails; —grips; —locks; —reduces; —safeguards; —screams; —shrieks; —squeals.

BRAMBLES

adjectives

straggling; thorny; neglected.

BRANCH

(division)

adjectives

collateral; subordinate; subsequent; specialized; rudimentary; purifying; despised; architectural; itinerant; local.

verbs

combine —es; consist of —es; corrupt—; diverge into —es; establish—; flourish in all —es; foster—; invest in—; manage—; propose—; separate into —es; spread out into —es; subdivide into —es; subordinate —es; —affiliates with; —booms; —flourishes; — represents; —springs up; —transacts.

(See department, division.)

BRANCH

(tree)

adjectives

waxen; soft; wide; spreading; prominent; overhanging; gigantic; interlaced (pl.); rushing; grown; curving; circumstantial; fragrant; blazing; arching; swaying; murmuring; springy; moss-set; peaceful; long; pendulous; feathery; gnarled; picturesque; independent; coordinate; simpler; towering;

tasseled; gigantic; umbrageous; intruding; flowery; greenwood; nodding; flexible; loaded; heavy; somber; lopped; crackling; beauteous; stirring; thick-leaved; legitimate; plumy; luxurious; virgin; low-bent; delicate; shapely; shattered; phantom; profound; hoary; beauteous; obstructing; isolated; fatal; erect; verdant; flattened; crossing; covered; superfluous; naked; strong; thick; overambitious; luscious; knotted.

verbs
bow—; clip—; crash through—; gnarl—; graft—; hew—; lop off—; perch on—; rock —; trim—; —arches; —s cluster; —decays; —dips; —droops; —drops off; —flowers; —hangs low; —springs out; —supports; — tosses; —withers.
(See twig, limb.)

BRAND
adjectives
competitive; impious; petty; ensanguined; advertised; popular; faithful; largest-selling; reliable; searing; offensive; gloomy; smoldering; casual; blurred; wasted; glimmering; obscure; crooked; standard.

BRAND (*v*)
adverbs
epigrammatically; impiously; pettishly; popularly; offensively; casually; stigmatically; shamefully.
(See mark.)

BRANDISH (*v*)
adverbs
ferociously; victoriously; eloquently; proudly; heroically; gloriously; heatedly; furiously; exuberantly.
(See wave.)

BRANDY
adjectives
powerful; vile; cheap; canteen; aromatic; mulled; life-restoring.

verbs
age—; bottle—; distill—; entertain with—; flavor—; imbibe—; import—; mix with—; regale on—; sip—; tax—; —burns; — flavors; —intoxicates.
(See liquor, whiskey.)

BRASH
adverbs
impulsively; thoughtlessly; indiscreetly; touchily; testily; waspily; peevishly; fretfully; irascibly; rashly; foolhardily; incau-

tiously; carelessly; giddily; wildly; hotheadedly; precipitately; daringly; heedlessly; headily; jauntily.

BRASS
adjectives
unenduring; lusterless; winking; carved; glittering; burnished; time-stained; gorgeous; barbaric; tarnished.

BRASSY
adverbs
arrogantly; audaciously; flippantly; insolently; haughtily; impertinently; impudently; petulantly; saucily; shamelessly; terribly; dictatorily; presumptuously; bumptiously; superciliously; swaggeringly; intolerably; offensively; vexatiously; provokingly; unpleasantly.

BRAT
adjectives
furtive; howling; brawling; ill-mannered; ugly; puny; dirty; unwanted; cheeky; sweet; angelic; unruly; ungrateful; unteachable.

BRAVADO
adjectives
unmanly; soaring; humorous; polished; sheer; pure; pitiable; shallow; ferocious; speechless.

BRAVE (*n*)
adjectives
vanquished; murderous; sensible; aged; venerated; tremulous; reckless; selected; gifted; itinerant.

BRAVE (*a*)
adverbs
physically; indomitably; nobly; conspicuously; inherently; unflinchingly; heroically; magnificently; uncommonly; eminently; gallantly; resolutely; steadily; essentially; confidently; pluckily; valorously; valiantly; remarkably; unbelievably; sublimely; quietly; patiently; exceedingly.

BRAVE (*v*)
adverbs
defiantly; fearlessly; tremulously; recklessly; stalwartly; unselfishly; nobly; passionately; haughtily; staunchly; patriotically.
(See defy, dare.)

BRAVERY
adjectives
personal; shining; physical; insolent; sex-

ual; drunken; indomitable; reckless; flawless; noble; audacious; conspicuous; stupid; witless; inherent; unflinching; heroic; magnificent; outrageous; glittering; uncommon; fearful; unsurpassed.

verbs
act in—; add to—; admire—; display—; exhibit—; marvel at—; put on—; saturate with—; swagger in—; —amazes; —includes; —lies.
(See courage, heroism.)

BRAWL
adjectives
disreputable; drunken; street; friendly; desperate; private; coarsest.

verbs
approach—; batter in—; brook—; cause—; engage in—; force—; incite—; squabble in —; —clamors; —conflicts; —noises; —upsets.
(See quarrel, wrangle, row.)

BRAWNY
adverbs
extremely; indomitably; mightily; overpoweringly; stoutly; sturdily; vigorously; unbelievably; clumsily; awkwardly; admirably; amazingly; exceedingly; incredibly; undeniably; sufficiently.

BRAY (v)
adverbs
hideously; hoarsely; intermittently; solemnly; agonizingly; terrifyingly; idiotically; repeatedly; huskily.
(See howl.)

BRAZEN
adverbs
monstrously; shamelessly; daringly; boldly; presumptuously; unbecomingly; unsuitably; jauntily; airily; arrogantly; impudently; irreverently; disagreeably; ridiculously; offensively; detestably; hatefully; obnoxiously; excessively; foolishly; nauseatingly; indecently; insolently; incredibly; unwarrantably; atrociously; odiously.

BREACH
adjectives
formidable; continual; unpardonable; social; incurable; deplorable; irreconcilable; perceptible; dreadful; momentary; temporary; general; absolute; religious; flagrant; unhealed; monstrous; meditated.

verbs
excuse—; produce—; repair—; smooth over —; suffer—; widen—; —damages; —disrupts; —fractures; —infracts; —infringes upon; —injures; —outlaws; —ruptures; —separates; —violates; —widens.
(See gap, violation, infringement, infraction.)

BREAD
adjectives
warm; stiff; frozen; daily; gnawed; moldy; sacred; rising; substantial; living; rainsoaked; wheaten; insipid; elfin; unleavened; bitter; blessed; broken; sliced.

verbs
apportion—; beg—; blacken—; break—with; brown—; consume—; cram with—; crave—; crumb—; deprive of—; devour—; dispense —; display—; divide—; earn—; knead—; munch—; nibble—; offer—; partake of—; prepare—; process—; provide—; ration—; restrict to—; sell for—; shape—; sustain with—; tax—; vend—; win—; —nourishes; —satiates; —stales; —strengthens.
(See food.)

BREADTH
adjectives
enormous; bare; unmoved; lyrical; viewless; diverse; endless; scant; epical; rippling; glassy; immoderate; spacious; ample; impassable.

BREAK
adjectives
appreciable; notable; numerous (pl.); unhappy; fatal; final; distinct; sharp; complete; agreeable; unhindered.

BREAK (v)
adverbs
eventually; unwarily; theoretically; treacherously; subsequently; deliberately; violently; unreasonably; forcibly; gratuitously; grimly; incoherently; intentionally; threateningly; advisedly; perilously; hilariously; fatally; distinctly; completely.
(See smash, shatter, burst, demolish.)

BREAKDOWN
adjectives
nervous; moral; universal; disastrous; incipient; mental; practical.

BREAKER
adjectives
foaming; ponderous; rising; swelling; ceaseless; never-silent; immense; wicked; enormous; tumbling; reasonless.

land among —s; warn of —s; —booms; —
verbs
crashes; —crushes; —dashes; —destroys;
—flies in; —foams; —lashes; —murmurs;
—passes over; —pounds; —rolls in; —subdues; —swells; —tumbles.
(See wave, billow.)

BREAKFAST
adjectives
sophisticated; substantial; hurried; magnificent; wedding; cheerful; gobbled; belated;
hearty; impromptu; leisurely; gloomy; abstemious; hospitable; pleasant; supplementary; wholesome.

verbs
adjourn to—; announce—; attack—; beckon
to—; bolt—; entertain at—; fast until—;
furnish with—; gobble—; gulp—; miss—;
partake of—; prepare—; provide—; relish
—; rush—; serve—; snatch—; take—; —
appeases; —replenishes; —satiates.
(See meal, dinner, supper, food.)

BREAST
adjectives
defenceless; heaving; secret; cavernous;
beautiful; gloomy; dauntless; billowy;
brooding; snowy; throbbing; dolorous; tortured; rounded; large; tight; swollen; repentant; vast; soothing; barren; sanguine;
suckling; happy; glossy; greasy; watery;
inspired; boiling; bloody; obedient; elongated; half-tamed; calm; martyr; maternal;
well-developed; laboring; hideous; hollow-
swelling; feathered; torpid; shuddering;
fragrant; woolly; sunken; ample; misshap-
en; tumultuous; grief-filled; responsive;
troubled; palpitating; spotted; peaceable;
haughty; silent; careworn; panting; unconscious; pious; guileless; gentle; patriotic;
bare; careless; distended; vice-polluted;
faultless; oppressed; tawny; speckled; stimulated; supporting; snow-cold; tender; infinite; spangled; uplifted; wanton; sagging;
scourged; protruding; mailed; unwary; rugged; stormy; emaciated; full; dulled; immeasurable; harmless; devoted.

verbs
adorn—; bare—; beat—; boil in—; clasp
to—; cling to—; crush to—; distend—; disturb—; dry up—; ease—; exhaust—; expand
—; fold on—; harbor in—; inflame—with;
inflate—; infuse—with; inhabit—; lock in
—; lodge in—; nurse at—; penetrate—;
pillow on—; plant in—; rend—; smite—;
soothe—; strain to—; thunder in—; torment
—; trouble—; warm—; —burns with; —

flutters; —heaves; —secretes; —throbs.
(See bosom, chest, heart.)

BREASTWORK
adjectives
serpentine; substantial; gingerbread; military.

BREATH
adjectives
fiery; venomous; struggling; aimless; bated;
extinguished; unsavory; delighted; sweet-
scented; fragrant; idle; ryhthmic; vulgar;
warbling; unwholesome; morning; fearful;
quivering; foul; blessed; uneasy; snowy;
expiring; lightest; infant; untroubled;
stifled; stertorous; fetid; dumb; transitory;
quick; furtive; tender; ambient; delicate;
meager; surprised; hard; wicked; fluttering; damp; sobbing; quivering; dulcet;
common; harmonious; maiden; tremulous;
full; relieving; divine; clean; soft; rose-
laden; wine-laden; smoking; fugitive; bad;
cosmic; scorching; delicate; invisible; duteous; fleeting; deadly; rude; consuming;
sour; painful; blasting; feverous; spiritual;
tempestuous; undying; vital; icy; frightened; clear; cool; warm; natural; gasping;
miserable; transient; poisonous; cankering;
frosted; panting; rattling; ebbing; infantile;
golden; applausive; difficult; sugary; free;
audible; suspended; transparent; sharp;
worthless; royal; wanting; stinking; fatal;
passionate; hot; balsam; contagious; tobacco; scandalous; blighting; sulphurous; meditative; unanimous; offensive; prophet;
scant; pestilential; holy; failing; vile.

verbs
animate by—; bate—; catch—; discharge—;
draw—; exhale—; exhaust—; frost—; gasp
for—; inhale—; labor for—; lose—; murmur—; pen up—; poison—; puff out—; recover—; regain—; release—; revive—;
sigh—; smother—; stifles—; struggle for—;
suck in—; waste—; —emanates; —reeks.
(See air, respiration, breathing.)

BREATHE (v)
adverbs
stertorously; irregularly; assiduously; audibly; rhythmically; expiringly; uneasily;
untroubledly; transitorily; flutteringly; sobbingly; gaspingly; failingly.
(See inhale, pant, gasp.)

BREATHING
adjectives
cumbered; heavy; light; soft; shallow;
audible; regular; labored; peaceful; fervent;

137

placid; ryhthmical; tender; noisy; fluttered; holy; distressful; steady; abundant; hoarse; hurried; quickened; convulsive; alcoholic; long; quiet.

verbs
arrest—; choke—; correct—; ease—; hamper—; impede—; induce—; interfere with —; labor—; lessen—; obstruct—; restore —; smother—; stimulate—; train—.
(See respiration, breath.)

BREATHLESSNESS
adjectives
induced; parenthetical; distressing.

BREECHES
adjectives
tight; leather; drab; torn; baggy; muddy; tweed; nankeen.

BREED
adjectives
ancient; sporting; selective; unsocial; truer; elastic; pure-blooded; reckless; fabulous; recognized; superior; coarser; irritable; voracious.

verbs
adhere to—; ally—; characterize—; combine—; cross—; defile—; degenerate—; despise—; develop—; display—; distinguish —; domesticate—; examine—; exhaust—; exhibit—; exterminate—; generate—; improve—; mingle—; mix—; originate—; perpetuate—; preserve—; procreate—; propagate—; recognize—; strain—; —competes for; —overruns.
(See race.)

BREED (v)
adverbs
prodigiously; intelligently; luxuriantly; deicately; fabulously; superiorly; selectively.
(See multiply, rear, train.)

BREEDING
adjectives
artificial; exquisite; noble; gentle; courteous; virtuous; soft; tender; essential.

BREEDING
adjectives (animals)
straight-line; selective; fertile; aristocratic.

BREEZE
adjectives
sobbing; varying; desultory; increasing; favorable; roving; blessed; subtle; night;

summer; scented; playful; rising; steadying; native; faint; wayward; rude; slumbering; imperceptible; cooling; voluptuous; sportive; tonic; telltale; dying; sea; balmy; spicy; healthful; blistering; murmuring; chilling; southerly; fresh; blowing; sweeping; unsatisfied; zephyr; sluggish; nimble; ruffling; searching; western; fitful; sacred; wafting; whispering; treacherous; lightest; caressing; languorous; noiseless; lingering; river; lusty; passing; savage; crooning; tantalizing; penetrating; stray; pungent; stinging; vagrant; mild; raw; westerly; hovering; wanton; genial; odorous; vernal; polar; perfumed; salt-laden; lazy; casual; smoky; increasing; swift; uncontrollable; propitious; peaceful; refreshing; ocean; constant; soft; billowing; woodland; stirring; invigorating; tender; sweet; dependable; tantalizing; bracing.

verbs
bask in—; catch—; float in—; head into—; nod in—; rock with—; rustle in—; scent—; tremble in—; wave in—; —billows; —brushes; —caresses; —dies; —fans; —flutters; —freshens; —kisses; —lulls; —pauses; —ruffles; —rumples; —rustles; —scuds by; —sighs; —steals through; —stirs; —sweeps down; —tousles; —wafts; —wanders; —whistles.
(See wind, current.)

BREEZY
adverbs
delightfully; joyously; buoyantly; jovially; irresponsibly; gaily; vivaciously; brightly; wholesomely; heartily; irresistibly; flippantly; merrily; happily; gleefully; laughingly; rapturously; cheerfully; foolishly; childishly; youthfully; pleasantly; charmingly; exquisitely; daintily; agreeably; habitually.

BRETHREN
adjectives
dreamy; venerable; erring; cloudy; luckier; weak; civilized; wicked; twin-souled; speculative; fortunate; renegade; amiable; literary.

BREVITY
adjectives
laconic; pregnant; voluble; algebraic; tabloid; reassuring cynical; businesslike; curt; characteristic; voluminous; fallacious; laudable.

BRIBE
adjectives
base; timely; unworthy; innocent; custom-

ary; efficient; costly; enormous; extravagant; unclenched; septennial.

verbs
administer—; buy with—; condemn—; consent to—; consider—; exact—; extort—; forfeit—; offer—; pay—; pocket—; procure—; refuse—; surrender to—; tender—; yield to —; —abuses; —corrupts; —entraps; —induces; —influences; —offends; —perverts; —purchases; —purloins; —tempts.
(See inducement, graft.)

BRIBERY

adjectives
barefaced; corrupt; covert; daring; flagrant; offensive; open; surreptitious; vile.

verbs
accuse of—; achieve by—; acquit of—; arrest for—; charge with—; conceal—; convict of—; detect—; frustrate—; gain by—; obtain by—; practise—; punish—; purchase by—; remove for—; solicit—; yield to—; —flourishes; —motivates; —procures; —scandalizes; —sways; —tends to.
(See robbery, plunder.)

BRICK

adjectives
mellow; tawny; warm-toned; Georgian; adobe; harsh; sliding; smoke-blackened; enameled; soft; hard; front.

verbs
bake —s; base on —s; build with —s; cart —s; chisel—; construct of—; cut into—; dry —s; face with —s; fireproof —s; front with —s; harden into —s; heave —s; hem in with —s; inlay with —s; inscribe —s; knead into —s; lay —s; measure —s; pave with —s; prepare —s; pyramid —s; reinforce with —s; shape into —s; strain —s; toss —s; trowel —s; wall in with —s; —s collapse; —s crumble; —endures; mold into —.
(See stone.)

BRIDE

adjectives
peerless; prospective; insatiate; passionless; fastidious; virgin; beloved; blooming; perjured; pretty; bonny; first-made; affianced; gallant; truant; contraband; blushing; vivacious; country.

verbs
act as—; announce—; array—; assemble round—; attend—; bestow upon—; capture —; choose—; confuse—; congratulate—; costume—; dress—; drink to—; endow—;
fete—; give away—; greet—; indulge—; kiss—; pledge—; proclaim—; purloin—; serenade—; shower—; toast—; welcome—; win—; yearn for—; —blushes; —pales; —trembles.
(See queen, sweetheart.)

BRIDEGROOM

adjectives
destined; embarrassed; fickle; sturdy; youthful; happy; busy; shy; recreant; bold; brisk.

BRIDGE

adjectives
substantial; indigenous; antiquated; well-constructed; picturesque; rude; covered; mighty; famous; sturdy; swinging; massive; arched; iron; railroad; rustic; medieval; hideous; battered; spiritual; wooden; commodious; fortified; trembling; wide; narrow; rambling; portable; draw; proud; trussed.

verbs
arch—; block—; chain—; construct—; cross —; design—; destroy—; draw—; engineer —; flow under—; fortify—; gird—; imperil —; load—; lower—; overhaul—; patrol—; pattern—; plan—; strain—; suspend from —; sweep away—; —arches; —collapses; —connects; —conveys; —links; —spans; —supports; —surmounts; —totters; —unites.
(See span, support, structure.)

BRIDGE (v)

adverbs
successfully; picturesquely; massively; medievally; spiritually; proudly; tremblingly; diplomatically.
(See connect, link.)

BRIEF

adjectives
apostolic; honest; argumentative.

BRIEF (a)

adverbs
ridiculously; delightfully; agreeably; pitifully; disappointingly; tragically; mercifully; humanely; unreasonably; dramatically; smartly; inexcusably; characteristically; remarkably; satisfactorily; surprisingly; pleasantly; compactly; laconically; conveniently; curtly; commendably; strikingly; sensibly; wisely; prudently; tersely.

BRIEF CASE

adjectives
bulging; dog-eared; important-looking; mys-

terious; over-stuffed; resplendent; secret-
charged; shabby; shiny; streamlined.

verbs
clasp— —; cram into— —; dig into— —;
extract from— —; fasten— —; pack in—
—; strap— —; stuff— —; whip open— —;
— —bulges.
(See bag, satchel.)

BRIGADE
adjectives
advancing; combined; battle-toughened;
favored; heroic; invincible; thundering.

verbs
command—; compose—; divide—; drill—;
enlist in—; enroll—; form—; inspect—; instruct—; make up—; organize—; train—;
transfer to—; transport—; —charges; —
forages; —hunts; —marches.
(See gathering, regiment, troops, army.)

BRIGAND
adjectives
ferocious; ruthless; fugitive; veritable.

BRIGHT
adverbs
indescribably; dazzlingly; miraculously; ingeniously; amazingly; splendidly; magnificently; unbelievably; unusually; wonderfully; marvellously; artificially; scintillatingly; starrily; intolerably; painfully; bewilderingly; blindingly; unwontedly; suspiciously; crystally; luminously; radiantly; splendidly; unbearably; intensely; gaudily.

BRIGHTEN (*v*)
adverbs
intensely; momentarily; perceptibly; vividly; dazzlingly; artificially; bewilderingly;
superficially; blindingly; unnaturally; intellectually; matchlessly.
(See cheer, illuminate.)

BRIGHTNESS
adjectives
tranquil; dazzling; artificial; scintillant;
starry; shifting; shining; superficial; painful; intolerable; transcendent; bewildering;
enlivening; unfathomed; expansive; glowing; gradual; sharp; windy; steely; rising;
cold; blinding; unmoving; burning; unwonted; fiery; suspicious; poisonous; crystal.

BRILLIANCE
adjectives
youthful; mental; stylistic; dazzling; scintillating; roseate; intellectual; utmost; epigrammatic; feverish; crystal; signal; magnificent; polished; matchless; daring; spontaneous; eye-aching; uncanny; solemn; inevitable; lustrous.

verbs
boast—; hide—; impress with—; intensify
—; polish into—; radiate—; shade—; shine
in—; sing of—; sparkle with—; strike with
—; —amazes; —dazzles; —overpowers; —
pervades.
(See splendor.)

BRILLIANCY
adjectives
unnatural; dreamlike; exquisite; sufficient;
solar; heightened; blinding; imposing;
strange; ivory-like; technical; irregular;
sparkling; superhuman.

BRILLIANT
adverbs
scintillatingly; miraculously; cleverly; ingeniously; notably; amazingly; signally; socially; intellectually; dazzlingly; smartly;
inexpressibly; indescribably; surprisingly;
splendidly; undoubtedly; incredibly; unusually; wonderfully; ostentatiously.

BRIM
adjectives
sparkling; medium-sized; huge; picot;
glancing; rolling.

BRINE
adjectives
restless; bitter; mid-sea; rushing; audacious; fragrant; rolling; hoary; fateful; eye-
offending; first-made; desolate; level; glassy; hissing.

BRING (*v*)
adverbs
lightly; finally; rarely; slyly; festinately;
constantly; painfully; accordingly; vividly;
inevitably; continuously; obviously; ultimately; simultaneously; vaguely.
(See carry, conduct, convey.)

BRINK
adjectives
plashy; dim; breezy; chilling; eternal;
shadowy; rushy; precipitous; utmost; abrupt; sandy; giddy.

BRINY

adverbs

bitterly; brackishly; acridly; hotly; pungently; toughly; saltily; spicily; sharply; unsavorily; strongly; disagreeably; unpleasantly; horribly; aromatically; perceptibly; pleasingly; subtly; odoriferously; sufficiently; magnificently; properly.

BRISK

adverbs

tremendously; apallingly; helpfully; efficiently; singularly; habitually; excitedly; noisily; restlessly; nimbly; gracefully; energetically; cheerfully; actively; alertly; vivaciously; surprisingly; youthfully; capably; unexpectedly; quickly; dangerously; smartly; spryly; fleetly; trippingly; lightly; busily.

BRISKNESS

adjectives

keen; flavored; characteristic.

BRISTLE (v)

adverbs

defiantly; horridly; furiously; pugnaciously; militantly; bellicosely; belligerently; vindictively.

(See argue.)

BRITISH

adverbs

incurably; stolidly; loyally; sensibly; respectably; obstinately; stubbornly; proudly; unconditionally; obviously; manifestly; essentially; securely; permanently; urbanely; imperturbably; serenely; soundly; stoutly; devotedly; ardently; staunchly; punctiliously; incorruptibly; correctly; virtuously; shrewdly.

BRITISHER

adjectives

sound; solid; sensible; usual; well-fed; obstinate; muddling.

BRITTLE

adverbs

unfortunately; regrettably; exceedingly; smartly; delicately; crisply; lamentably; deplorably; deceptively; unexpectedly; surprisingly; slightly; highly; overly; extremely; evidently; unprofitably; unserviceably; inconveniently; impracticably.

BROAD

adverbs

splendidly; magnificently; illimitably; extensively; spaciously; liberally; boundlessly; infinitely; immensely; admirably; amply; adequately; grandly; majestically; expansively; inexpressibly; capaciously; roomily; extremely; enormously; endlessly; epically; immoderately; unbelievably.

BROADCAST

adjectives

commercial; unsponsored; regional; nationwide.

BROADCAST (v)

adverbs

grandiloquently; commercially; regionally; universally; temporarily; professionally; annually; popularly.

(See speak.)

BROADCLOTH

adjectives

bullet; lava; popular; shantung.

BROADEN (v)

adverbs

marvelously; appreciably; tremendously; noticeably; immeasurably; imperceptibly; abruptly; gradually.

(See enlarge, expand.)

BROADSIDE

adjectives

genuine; fearful; death-dealing; thundering; tremendous; crashing.

BROCADE

adjectives

jeweled; ancient; gorgeous; stiff; correct; bright; exquisite; historic.

BROCHURE

adjectives

innocent; artistic; modern; intimate; expensive; slender; rare.

BROGUE

adjectives

adorable; quaint; little; soft; clouted; brisk; Irish.

BROIL

adjectives

murderous; internal; prolonged; fierce.

BROKER

adjectives

disreputable; dummy; staid; loose-living; middle-aged.

BRONZE

adjectives

precious; valuable; burnished; enduring; immortal; inimitable; monumental; lined.

BRONZE (a)

adverbs

richly; tawnily; deeply; elaborately; strangely; incongruously; sumptuously; splendidly; magnificently; shimmeringly; ruddily; beautifully; superbly.

BROOD

adjectives

callow; straggling; lowering; hideous; unmanageable; erring; enormous; hapless; late-begotten; human; successive; spurious; shameful; dusky; hateful; writhing; silver; bastard; erratic; gorgeous; infernal; venomous; boreal; heavenly; noisy; viperous.

verbs

bring forth—; cherish—; cultivate—; exhibit—; gather—; give birth to—; hatch—; hover over—; incubate—; mother—; nest —; nourish—; nurse—; nurture—; orphan —; rear—; select—; tend—; tolerate—; warm—; —clucks; —follows; —originates from.

(See offspring, race, flock.)

BROOD (v)

adverbs

solitarily; somberly; vacantly; enviously; mournfully; reverently; haplessly; humanly; bitterly; maternally; superstitiously; fruitlessly; drearily; despondently.

(See ponder, meditate.)

BROODING

adjectives

subsequent; bitter; melancholy; constant; maternal; superstitious; concentrated; fruitless; dreary; despondent.

BROOK

adjectives

sluggish; delectable; south-sloping; unreposing; rapid; boisterous; wandering; brawling; glassy; careless; shallow; hidden; sedgy; rain-full; thirst-inviting; defiled; rippling; weedy; gushing; tumbling; mazy; copious; unsunned; struggling; babbling; gurgling; glittering; limpid; unseen; patient; peaceful; passionless; rushing; shrunken; inland; reedy; swift-running; crisped; hurrying; rushy; pellucid; happy; murmuring; narrow; silver; bisecting; cool; meandering; sweet; perennial; dancing; transparent; rocky; mountain; sparkling; companionable; pebbly; winding; wild; clear; woodland.

verbs

bog in—; bound—; bridge—; cast into—; frequent—; haunt—; pass over—; splash in—; swell—; wade in—; —babbles; —bubbles; —bursts forth; —chatters; —dances; —flows on; —frolics; —groans; —gurgles; —gushes; —murmurs; —races along; —rambles; —ranges; —sings; —swells; —whirls.

(See stream.)

BROOM

adjectives

careless; coarse; ever-questing; immaculate; industrious; lopsided; restless; rude.

verbs

apply—; brandish—; employ—; fill—; peddle —s; tie into—; trim—; twist—; wield —; —brushes; —collects; —delves; —gathers; —raises; —removes; —renews; —routs; —unearths.

(See brush.)

BROTH

adjectives

comforting; stomach-fortifying; satisfying; substantial; tasteless; watery.

verbs

ladle—; sip—; spoon—; strain—; test—; —nourishes; —simmers; —steams; —warms.

(See soup.)

BROTHER

adjectives

kind; indulgent; gentle; arbitrary; fiendish; cruel; illustrious; amorous; truant; healthful; affectionate; poor; unworthy; unemotional; new; distinguished; sworn; loftier; recreant; admirable; manly; ecclesiastical; true; foster; lost; ungrateful; renowned; awe-stricken; heroic; neglected; harrowed; malleable; rebellious; dismal; elder; serious; devoted; erring; unseemly; eligible; aristocratic; obvious; undeniable; slow-witted; indubitable; heavy-going; paretic; blood; model; imperial; puissant.

BROTHERHOOD

adjectives

bristly; critical; human; great; blood; subtle; meritable; idealized; diplomatic; close; cordial; indissoluble; spontaneous; sworn.

verbs

address—; ally with—; associate with—; band into—; cherish—; create—; devote to —; establish—; fraternize with—; fuse in —; head—; join—; league in—; obey—;

organize—; protect—; persecute—; regale —; resign from—; rupture—; salute—; support—; sustain—; tie to—; unite—; —acts; —aids; —arrays against; —convenes; —declines; —equalizes; —flourishes; —instructs.

(See society, fellowship.)

BROTHERLY
adverbs
extremely; heart-warmingly; hardly; affectionately; cordially; intimately; sincerely; sympathetically; amicably; heartily; benevolently; benignly; charitably; considerately; lovingly; unselfishly; tenderly; accommodatingly; good-naturedly; graciously; warm-heartedly; adoringly; devotedly; fondly; adorably; charmingly; admirably; helpfully; companiably; congenially; surprisingly; unexpectedly.

BROUGHAM
adjectives
cozy; little; well-appointed; shiny.

BROW
adjectives
handsome; delicate; beautiful; illumined; bland; amiable; fair; classical; lofty; manly; noble; social; lily; triumphant; low; white; clouded; black; heavy; straight; dark; blonde; rosy; sunburned; freckled; bushy; shaggy; roughened; grizzled; thick; puckered; ruffled; knotted; furrowed; wrinkled; corrugated; contracted; drawn; sad; troubled; overcast; mournful; brooding; swarthy; interrogative; scowling; frowning; stormy; startled; puzzled; plucked; painted; fine; pencilled; arched; whimsical; thin; peaked; curved; meeting (pl.); beetling; well-carved; prominent; level; lifted; placid; tranquil; damp; perspiring; fevered; heaving; crotchety; ironical; pimpled; elderly; austere; intelligent; glistening; deplorable; massive; haughty; dusky; livid; thoughtful; withered; innocent; craggy; calm; angry; weather-beaten; clammy; thorn-pierced; healthful; callow; serene; high; cold; shadowy; intellectual; gloomy; heated; royal; guilt-steeled; scarred; infant; sacred; surly; purpled; upturned; snowy; unaltered; crownless; throbbing; pensive; broiling; olive-tinctured; thunderblasted; burning; imperious; sun-kissed; barbarian; hopeless; relaxed; rugged; imperial; bewitching; pale; amiable; unsullied; bent; immense; blue-veined; threatening; unkind; pain-knotted; laurel-laden; impenetrable; deep-pent; channeled; ingenuous;

contemptuous; stately; conquest-branded; inky; triumphant; wreathed; pedantic; pitying; kindred; profulgent; wizard; animated; stunned; mild; milky; crescent; haggard; earnest; broad; gracious; bared; hooded; bloodless; aching; youthful; dreamy; overhanging; polished; pallid; worn; drooping; godlike; candid; transparent; bald; anxious; smarting; bent; pretty; unsullied; mummied; unwritten; warlike; ensanguined; resigned; sober; compressed; regent; dauntless; overwhelming; spiritual; hazel; burthened; projecting; mobile; airy; averted; peaceful; bronzed; careworn.

verbs
arch—; contract—; crown—; elevate—; flush—; furrow—; gild—; harden—; kiss —; knit—; lift—; mop—; plait—; pluck —s; pucker—; purse—; quirk—; shadow —; singe—; smite—; smooth—; uplift—; wrinkle—; —s bridge; —darkens; —menaces; —s struggle together; —throbs.

(See forehead, eyebrow, countenance.)

BROWBEATEN
adverbs
submissively; shamefully; meekly; disgracefully; humiliatingly; disconsolately; humbly; abjectly; frightfully; horribly; terribly; fearfully; unhappily; incredibly; astoundingly; alarmingly; coweringly; tremulously; dreadfully; nervously; portentously; unforgivably; evidently; visibly; indefensibly.

BROWN
adjectives
lustrous; vehement; russet; unsightly; golden; country; dainty; mellow; shining; turf; ruddy; crisp; curious; grayish; glossy; twilight; yellowish; chestnut; pinkish; autumnal; gleaming; sedate.

BROWN (a)
adverbs
ruddily; lustrously; deeply; richly; gloriously; curiously; crisply; lightly; tawnily; sumptuously; splendidly; superbly; shimmeringly; magnificently.

BROWSE (v)
adverbs
phlegmatically; contentedly; intellectually; placidly; happily; abstractedly; absently.
(See nibble, feed, graze.)

BRUISE
adjectives
livid; marring; hurting; vast; innocent; cruel.

verbs

apply to—; bandage—; heal—; incur—; inflict —s; produce—; receive—; salve—; soothe—; treat—; —dents; —disables; —discolors; —disfigures; —hurts; —infects; —injures; —lacerates; —mangles; —mars; —swells; —weakens.

(See injury, contusion.)

BRUISE (v)

adverbs

ineradicably; severely; agonizingly; disfiguringly; horribly; temporarily; villainously; mercilessly.

(See injure, hurt.)

BRUNETTE

adjectives

small; vivacious; indeterminable.

BRUNETTE (a)

adverbs

wondrously; gloriously; adorably; strikingly; petitely; vivaciously; piquantly; irresistibly; charmingly; saucily; startlingly; captivatingly; fascinatingly; distinctly; radiantly; glowingly; darkly; provocatively; astonishingly; starrily; artificially; naturally; skilfully; enchantingly; bewitchingly.

BRUSH

adjectives

deft; burnishing; illuminating; frugal; obliterating; purging; scavenging; sweeping.

verbs

apply—; attach—; cleanse with—; dust with —; employ—; paint with—; scrub with—; shape—; shine with—; smooth over with—; spread with—; stroke—; sweep with—; wipe with—; —refreshes; —renews; —revives.

(See broom.)

BRUSH

adjectives (artist)

potent; profound; lavish; fragrant; skillful.

BRUSH

adjectives (plant)

leafy; stunted; ragged; meager; aboriginal; sage; alert; tangled; fringing; rabbit; icy; dangerous; flaming; scrawny; crackling.

BRUSH (v)

adverbs

aimlessly; haughtily; hastily; tenderly; effectively; vivaciously; skillfully; interminably; monotonously.

(See wipe.)

BRUSQUE

adverbs

dashingly; fussily; hurriedly; impetuously; hastily; precipitately; urgently; expeditiously; fitfully; boisterously; furiously; outrageously; roughly; uproariously; violently; excitedly; stormily; extravagantly; ostentatiously; hysterically; uncontrollably; irrepressibly; turbulently; wildly; rampageously.

BRUTAL

adverbs

abominably; terribly; unspeakably; villainously; systematically; needlessly; inherently; harshly; sharply; savagely; coarsely; ferociously; nefariously; detestably; indecently; obtrusively; ostentatiously; foully; insolently; caustically; venomously; perversely; incorrigibly; inhumanly; cruelly; atrociously; obdurately; truculently; maliciously; intentionally; treacherously; outrageously; ruthlessly; stonily; barbarously; virulently; diabolically; invidiously; blatantly; flagrantly; openly; resolutely.

BRUTALITY

adjectives

quaint; sacrificed; horrible; primitive; suave; frantic; unspeakable; blind; amazing; unintelligent; villainous; continued; systematic; noisy; downright; needless; inherent; harsh; sharp; ugly; savage; coarse; ferocious; sheer.

verbs

appall by—; breed—; expose—of; imbue with—; inculcate—; indulge in—; refrain from—; subject to—; teach—; treat with—; —cuts; —degrades.

(See cruelty.)

BRUTE

adjectives

shy; perverse; treacherous; conscious; unfeeling; perfect; nasty; polite; ferocious; tawny; horrid; goaded; barbarous; hardy; lustful; grazing; repulsive; drunken; noxious; greedy; innocent; bristling; savage; ponderous; cowardly; self-confessed; surly; dangerous; ruffian; untamed; lowest; husky; sulky; selfish; canny; accursed; exhausted; avenging; cold-blooded; menacing; maddened; bulky; foul; bestial; blundering; evil; designing; ugly; meanest; villainous; merciless; gross; dissipated; burly; callous.

verbs

bring out—; charm—; ensnare—; hypnotize —; polish—; quell—; silence—; slay—;

tame—; worship—; —bolts; —charges; — rends; —survives; —thunders.
(See animal, beast.)

BUBBLE

adjectives

headed; ascending; crystalline; iridescent; innumerable (pl.); lazy; broken; pricked; intoxicating; soothing; pretty; sparkling; flimsy; flattened; beaded; wandering; empty.

verbs

agitate into —s; blow —s; cover with —s; delude with —s; emit —s; produce —s; send forth —s; —amuses; —dances; —dissipates; —drifts; —escapes; —explodes; —fascinates; —floats; —rises; —scintillates; —springs from; —swells.
(See balloon.)

BUBBLE (v)

adverbs

gayly; effervescently; hissingly; foamingly; exhilaratingly; joyously; sputteringly.
(See flow, whirl.)

BUCK (v)

adverbs

spiritedly; suddenly; abruptly; belligerently; spitefully; venomously; wildly.
(See prepare, plan.)

BUD

adjectives

springing; kindling; swaying; bloomless; sluggish; tender; dejected; bursting; fadeless; unexpanded; flower-enfolding; sweetest; masked; dripping; wayside; sulking; terminal; leaf-enfolded; axillary.

verbs

blast—; blight—; clip—; form—; frost—; graft—; kill—; nip—; sprout —s; —s appear; —breaks into bloom; —bursts forth; —s cluster; —s crowd together; —decorates; —develops; —expands; —flowers; —glistens; —matures; —multiplies; —produces; —projects; —promises; —prospers; —reveals; —sprouts; —swells; —unfolds.
(See flower, plant, bulb.)

BUDGET

adjectives

biennial; admirable; bearskin; balanced; moderate; scanty; heart-shaking; ordinary; family; tentative; extraordinary.

verbs

balance—; institute—; jeopardize—; promul-

gate—; prune—; reduce—; shape—; slash —; stagger under —s; swell—; tax—.
(See estimate, plan.)

BUDGET (v)

adverbs

impecuniously; meticulously; biennially; admirably; annually; tentatively; shrewdly; dexterously; wisely; conservatively.

BUFF

adjectives

rich; golden; glowing.

BUFFALO

adjectives

aggressive; belligerent; bellowing; charging; furious; grunting; humping; powerful; possessive; primitive; prairie-lording; stampeding; roaming.

verbs

domesticate—; exterminate—; farm with—; herd—; overrun with—; plough with —s; protect—; pursue—; stampede—; tame—; teem with—; water—; yoke—; —gores; — grazes; —grunts; —lumbers; —ranges; — roams; —wallows in mud.
(See bison, ox, animal.)

BUFFETINGS

adjectives

reminiscent; repeated; merciless; unkind; intermittent.

BUFFOON

adjectives

enormous; gluttonous; ordinary; stammering; pantomime.

BUFFOONERY

adjectives

exhibitionist; engaging; wanton; mad.

BUG

adjectives

annoying; encroaching; gregarious; insidious; invincible; inoffensive; obnoxious; over-companionable; persevering; patrolling; pestiferous; shelter-seeking; shrilly-serenading; undaunted; diminutive; droning; hovering; jeweled; predatory; piping; snug; vagrant; villainous; vigorous; wiggling.

verbs

destroy—; dissect—; exterminate —s; observe—; spray—; swat—; —s blight; —s bore; —s breed; —s lurk; —stings; —sucks.
(See insect.)

145

adjectives

blaring; bold; dominant; duty-calling; invocative; piercing; silence-shattering; rousing; sonorous; lamenting; peace-lulling.

verbs

assemble at—; awaken by—; march to—; overblow—; rally to—; respond to—; retire to—; scale—; sound—; —alarms; —arouses; —blares; —blasts; —calls; —declares; —echoes; —orders; —signals; —summons; —trumpets; —wails; —wakens; —warns.

(See instrument, horn, trumpet.)

adjectives

elephantine; slender; sinewy; enduring; curious; heroic; gigantic; warlike; sturdy; ascetic; proportional.

ostensibly; impregnably; simultaneously; airily; irrevocably; variously; intelligently; synthetically; stoutly; expressly; sturdily; magnificently; substantially; enduringly; proportionally; secularly; incomparably; ecclesiastically; shabbily.

(See erect, construct, raise.)

adjectives

timid; prominent; independent; empire; sturdy; hard-working; ambitious; wonderful; body; pioneer; home; prospective; vigorous; devastating.

verbs

—alters; —bids; —commissions; —constructs; —contracts for; —designs; —determines; —develops; —directs; —draws; —employs; —erects; —establishes; —estimates; —excavates; —fireproofs; —guarantees; —initials; —leases; —operates; —profits; —remodels; —renovates; —specifies; —submits; —undertakes.

(See carpenter.)

adjectives

imposing; magnificent; attractive; palatial; rich; adorned; handsome; spacious; wonderful; beautiful; pretentious; fine; substantial; comfortable; monster; mammoth; giant; towering; commercial; Gargantuan; ancient; antiquated; century-old; grim; obsolescent; vestigial; solid; massive; great; stone; immense; gawky; ramshackle; barnlike; flimsy; rickety; rambling; straggling; squatting; cluttered; dirty-looking; sour; dingy; grimy; false-fronted; smoke-stained; bleak; gloomy; wretched; ugly; forlorn; sinister; peculiar; somber; severe; white-walled; red-roofed; multicolored; gaunt; red-bricked; weathered; ivy-grown; long; flat; low; clustered; silent; gilt-domed; unique; sun-flooded; commodious; consistorial; barrack-like; pagan; secular; combustible; oppressive; aggressive; impertinent; tame; uninteresting; proposed; dismal; conventual; tumble-down; unpretentious; heterogeneous; detached; ill-looking; conservative; irregular; opulent; profane; speculative; old-fashioned; well-constructed; extensive; monumental; decayed; moss-covered; useful; ghostlike; worthy; notable; beggarly; ruinous; eccentric; contemporaneous; flanking; arsenal-like; murky; unoccupied; sleepy; deserted; shabby; admonitory; elegant; dilapidated; ecclesiastical; capacious; incomparable; proud; drab.

verbs

clutter up—; demolish—; design—; dominate—; enlarge—; erect —s; evacuate—; extend—; inhabit—; lodge in—; modernize —; raze—; renovate—; restore—; revolutionize—; segregate into—; separate—; throng through—; —looms; —pierces; —straddles; —towers.

(See edifice, structure, house, barn.)

adjectives

feeble; electric; flickering; unveiled; rarefied; myriad (pl.); inanimate.

adjectives

spring; early-flowering.

verbs

bury—; cultivate—; insert—; market—; raise—; sow—; uproot—; —blossoms; —buds; —bursts; —develops; —dilates; —flowers; —nourishes; —radiates; —sends off roots; —stores; —takes root; —tides over.

(See flower, plant, bud.)

adjectives

inquisitive; disconcerting; noticeable; awkward.

adverbs

roundly; awkwardly; disconcertingly; noticeably; inquisitively; prominently; pro-

trudingly; enormously; horribly; abnormally; grotesquely.
(See swell, protrude.)

BULK
adjectives
grotesque; enormous; huge; tremendous; great; black; haughty; proper; mastodonic; insufficient; surging; tawny; cumbrous; low; broad; shadowy; imposing; shaggy; massive; shattered; considerable; vast; languid; full; voluptuous; overgrown; ugly; wavering; helpless; insufficient; ponderous; credent; colossal; crude; patched; bluff; terrifying; faceless; non-irritating; Amazonian; flying; clean-limbed; portly; physical; crushing; overwhelming; threatening.

BULK (v)
adverbs
enormously; heavily; cumbrously; overwhelmingly; threateningly; ponderously; terrifyingly; portentously.

BULKY
adverbs
enormously; awkwardly; immensely; massively; mightily; monstrously; crudely; inelegantly; lumpishly; stupendously; grotesquely; queerly; strangely; imposingly; overwhelmingly; ponderously; suspiciously; clumsily; unnecessarily; laughably; ridiculously; deceptively; ludicrously; grossly; delusively.

BULL
adjectives
incorrigible; snorting; mad; infuriated; rumbling; fretful; savage; raging; veritable.

verbs
bait—; brand—; breed—; bring—to bay; castrate—; chafe—; combat—; enrage—; exhibit—; infuriate—; jab—; market—; mistreat—; outnumber —s; plague—; rope —; slaughter—; slay—; torment —; —bellows; —butts; —charges; —collapses; —emerges; —gores; —grazes; — leaps; —paws; —perspires; —rages; —retires; —rushes; —snorts; —vaults; —wearies; raise—.
(See animal, cattle.)

BULLDOG
adjectives
hideous; squirming; pedigreed; ferocious.

BULLET
adjectives
moaning; well-directed; paper; answering; shrieking; ricocheted; caroming; whistling; spattering; soft-nose; flattened; harmless; powder; telltale; whining; whizzing; fiery; screaming; thudding; dum-dum; explosive.

verbs
cap—; design—; hail —s; jacket—; mold —s; project—; riddle with —s; shower —s; squirt —s; stream —s; —attains a speed; —s buzz by; —careens; —glances off; — grazes; —s hammer; —s patter; —penetrates; —pierces; —ricochets; —s spatter; —speeds toward; —swerves; —wavers; — whines; —whistles by; —s wing past.
(See shot, projectile.)

BULLETIN
adjectives
confidential; monotonous; public.

BULLY
adjectives
beastly; blustering; loutish; strutting; prostrate.

BULLY (v)
adverbs
mildly; blusteringly; loutishly; struttingly; overbearingly; diplomatically; pertly; flatly; endlessly; securely; firmly.
(See intimidate.)

BULWARK
adjectives
sturdy; mighty; everlasting; broken; seaward; riddled; splintered; heaven-sustaining; granite; eternal; flimsy; invulnerable.

BUMP
adjectives
dull; heavy; inadvertent.

BUMPKIN
adjectives
small-town; awkward; city; country; overgrown.

BUMPTIOUS
adverbs
aggressively; offensively; disagreeably; absurdly; impertinently; ridiculously; egotistically; presumptuously; pretentiously; vainly; boastfully; ostentatiously; priggishly; unblushingly; brazenly; ludicrously; laughably; quaintly; comically; stupidly; boyishly; fantastically; immensely; complacently; foolishly; senselessly; extravagantly.

adjectives
delectable; indigestible; round; flat; plump.

BUNCH

adjectives
scattered; beautiful; horrible.

BUNDLE

adjectives
withered; compact; parti-colored; ribboned; exceptional; fine; emaciated; darkish; unwieldy; swaddled; inert; flat; sodden; queer-shaped; precious; muddy; helpless; numerous (pl.); cached; wrinkled; endless; malevolent.

verbs
bind in—; collect in—; contain in—; disorder—; encumber with —s; fasten in—; gather—; group in —s; load down with —s; shift —s; untie—.
(See parcel, package.)

BUNDLE (*v*)

adverbs
unceremoniously; compactly; inertly; flatly; endlessly; securely; firmly; unceremoniously.
(See bind, tie, roll.)

BUNGALOW

adjectives
rose-clad; richly-furnished; swanky; luxurious; screened; rustic; rambling; dark; unpretentious; beloved; picturesque.

BUNGLE (*v*)

adverbs
tragically; atrociously; characteristically; repeatedly; ineptly; generally; idiotically; diplomatically; strategically.

BUNGLING

adjectives
general; inept; patient; characteristic; repeated.

BUNGLING (*a*)

adverbs
awkwardly; clumsily; boorishly; loutishly; shyly; bashfully; ineptly; inexpertly; unskilfully; self-consciously; incompetently; vexatiously; hopelessly; diffidently; timidly; pitifully; helplessly; pathetically; plaintively; outlandishly; pitiably; miserably; sorrily; sadly; grievously.

adjectives
dancing; heaving; ringing; rocking; warning.

BUOYANCY

adjectives
reckless; supreme; glad; youthful; virile; unutterable; natural; positive.

BUOYANT

adverbs
positively; joyously; affectedly; naturally; supremely; happily; suddenly; excitedly; unexpectedly; blithely; gleefully; rapturously; lightly; airily; gaily; hilariously; jovially; warmly; delightfully; delightedly; briskly; cheerily; jauntily; jubilantly; lightheartedly; disarmingly; merrily; playfully; irrepressibly; laughingly; smilingly; engagingly; irresistibly; confidently; enthusiastically; fervently; hopefully.

BURDEN

adjectives
grievous; financial; intolerable; painful; unwomanly; deadly; increasing; mutual; fragrant; double; various (pl); accumulated; racking; enticing; unnecessary; venerable; drowsy; precious; fatal; sinister; clattering; unescapable; never-lifted; serious; economic; appropriate; perpetual; fiery; passive; insufferable; monstrous; secret; baneful; oppressive; onerous; corresponding; expensive; equivalent; sweet; heavy; clerical; sheer; melancholy; aggravating; grim; common; unequal; unjust; dangerous; inevitable; cold; prodigious; ever-growing; staggering; crushing; unendurable; unbearable; cumbersome; over-heavy; dreadful; terrific; gruesome; undue; unusual; strange; pitiful; manifold (pl).

verbs
absorb—; ameliorate—; assume—; bear—; bend under—; chafe at—; deliver of—; ease—; groan under—; hamper with—; impose—; labor under—; lay on—; lighten —; load with—; overwhelm with—; shift —; shoulder—; stagger under—; suffer under—; support—; sustain—; unload—; —bows one down; —crushes.
(See load, cargo, weight, oppression, encumbrance.)

BURDENSOME

adverbs
grievously; financially; socially; intolerably; painfully; increasingly; unnecessarily; inescapably; seriously; economically; insuffer-

ably; monstrously; really; oppressively; aggravatingly; vexatiously; irritatingly; unequally; unjustly; dangerously; prodigiously; unendurably; dreadfully; terrifically; unduly; unusually; strangely; pitifully; calamitously; disastrously; unfortunately; tragically; gravely; cumbrously; embarrassingly.

BUREAU
adjectives
topographical; time-blackened; well-organized; devoted; legal; complete; self-supporting.

BUREAUCRACY
adjectives
smug; Teutonic; decadent; hardhearted; centralized.

BUREAUCRATIC
adverbs
complexly; unfortunately; portentously; ominously; dangerously; smugly; comfortably; democratically; autocratically; dictatorially; dominantly; imperiously; administratively; absolutely; arbitrarily; undeniably; hopelessly; irresistibly; terribly; unluckily; fairly; justly; unjustly; surprisingly; increasingly; overwhelmingly.

BURGLAR
adjectives
apprehensive; cautious; cunning; conscientious; felonious; stealthy; unscrupulous; chagrined; amateur; bungling; professional.

verbs
absolve—; accuse—; acquit—; apprehend —; condemn—; convict—; denounce—; detect—; imprison—; investigate —s; jail —s; protect against—; shield—; slay—; vindicate—; wound—; —alarms; —arouses; — invades; —plunders; —sacks; —terrorizes.
(See robber, highwayman, bandit.)

BURIAL
adjectives
obscure; golden; forgotten; Christian; interesting; hasty; premature; decent; respectable; proper; reverent; dismal; pagan.

verbs
assist at—; attend—; authorize—; commend to—; conceal by—; consecrate at—; console at—; draw out—; embalm for—; entitle to—; eulogize at—; notify of—; preach at —; preside over—; solemnize—; superintend—; uncover—; —disposes of.
(See death, funeral.)

BURLESQUE
adjectives
credible; polite; modified; exuberant; profane; farcical; vulgar; risque.

BURLESQUE (a)
adverbs
broadly; racily; absurdly; comically; cleverly; ludicrously; bombastically; caustically; sarcastically; ironically; satirically; extravagantly; cuttingly; adroitly; drolly; farcically; politely; profanely; coarsely; laughably; monstrously; ridiculously; refreshingly; delightfully; oddly; bizarrely; preposterously; unpardonably; whimsically; quizzically; uproariously; clownishly; chaffingly; scurrilously; derisively; scoffingly; exquisitely; deftly; expertly.

BURLESQUER
adjectives
hilarious; sheer; apt; clever; practiced.

BURN (v)
adverbs
destructively; smolderingly; luridly; noisily; mortally; inwardly; radiantly; shockingly; ruddily; intensely; steadfastly; dimly; sullenly; fitfully; ardently; distressfully; miraculously; inadvertently; glowingly.
(See scorch, consume.)

BURNING
adjectives
senseless; everlasting; endless.

BURRO
adjectives
dusty; dirty; shaggy; lop-eared; lazy; baldfaced; bobbing; munching.

BURST
adjectives
instant; passionate; indignant; convulsive; periodical; dreadful; sudden; fresh; unexplained; fiery; ungovernable; resplendent; scented; spontaneous.

BURST (v)
adverbs
turbulently; spontaneously; impetuously; appallingly; scornfully; involuntarily; hoarsely; ceaselessly; indignantly; periodically; ungovernably; resplendently.
(See break.)

BURTHEN
adjectives
breathless; delicate; sad; weighty; sorry.

BURY (v)

adverbs

quietly; reverentially; worshipfully; solemnly; splendidly; impecuniously; shabbily; awesomely; spectacularly.

(See hide, conceal.)

BUS

adjectives

shrieking; steady; dependable; rumbling; lantern-hung; lumbering; gaudy; sight-seeing.

verbs

board—; enter—; jam—; route—; station —; —conducts; —crawls along; —disgorges passengers; —flounders; —jolts; —rolls along; —rumbles; —snorts; —traverses.

(See automobile.)

BUSH

adjectives

tough; elder; laurel; sickly; interminable; towering; rose; fiery; projecting; elderberry; pathless; silent; clustering; naked; sheltering; berried; whortleberry; embracing; sparse; spiny; flourishing; jessamine; spreading; secret; scrubby; gnarled; stiff; stunted; woody; flowering; scraggly; unkempt; mesquite; indigo; patient; blooming; broad; pyramidical; gorse; vase-shaped; irregular; curious; round-topped; twiggy; shriveled; stumpy; sodden.

verbs

conceal in—; cultivate—; dwell in—; grow over with—es; hide in—; lie in—; lose in—; nest in—; nestle in—; prune—; pry in—; shroud in—; skirt—; spring from—; take to —; tangle in—; wind in and out among—es; —blooms; —blossoms; —branches; —flourishes; —protects; —screens; —spreads; — tangles; —yields.

(See shrub, thicket.)

BUSINESS

adjectives

queer; fateful; ugly; hypothecary; mercantile; intelligent; stirring; fascinating; centralized; stiff; ungentle; bloody; snug; unpleasant; keyhole; curious; suspended; profitable; complicated; awkward; terrible; remunerative; weary; rationalized; wretched; unreasonable; sordid; ethical; vengeful; phenomenal; tidy; bustling; superfluous; reputable; flourishing; dangerous; serious; reliable; shameful; discouraging; dubious; late-afternoon; ecclesiastical; villainous; dreadful; dreary; executive; temporal; poor; single; roaring; delightful; toilsome;

prosperous; urgent; abstract; illegal; deplorable; unsound; definite; rascally; foul; weighty; stern; solemn; unavoidable; congenial; tedious; momentous; rural; legitimate; extensive; fiery; scratchy; urgent; civil; thriving; swift; blistering; risky; petty; competitive; extended; ordinary; solvent; brisk; lifelong; arduous; tangled; sorry; scurvy; delectable; unscrupulous; dirty; fast-growing; perfunctory; uncrowded; paramount; timely; weighty; subnormal; domestic; miserable; chancy; piratical; prodigious; nefarious; litigated; experimental; well-managed; urgent; hazardous; irrational; creative; exclusive; detailed; ruined; illustrious; muddled; tranquil; reckless; speculative; banking; primary; astounding; fecund; roundabout; essential; menaced; dull; drab; trivial; slack; stupid; pure; unmitigated; heartbreaking; backbreaking; brusque; honest; successful; sound; interesting; lucrative; blessed; rushing; gigantic; immense; tremendous; colossal; modern; increasing; dismal; shady; distasteful; degrading; unsavory; despicable; dark; knavish; damnable; cruel; fearful; ugly; tedious; distressing; nervy; nasty; sad; tiresome; unconstructive; stable; droll; ticklish; queer; silly; increasingly-profitable; substantial; amazing; ever-increasing; secure; ready-made; dependable; troublesome.

verbs

absorb—; accommodate—; adjust—; administer—; badger—; blast—; bolster—; charge with—; confess to—; corrupt—; debate—; democratize—; depress—; derive—; disorganize—; dispose of—; disrupt—; dominate —; drum up—; embark into—; employ in —; endanger—; envelop in—; establish—; evolve—; expedite—; exploit—; foster—; increase—; interfere with—; liquidate—; make inroads into—; meddle in—; mess up —; nurse—; plunge into—; quit—; regulate —; restrict—; resurrect—; revivify—; shift —; slow down—; speed up—; stabilize—; stimulate—; suspend—; swallow up—; symbolize—; tie up—; transact—; undertake—; underwrite—; wrap up in—; —booms; — bounds up; —branches out; —climbs; — droops; —expands; —expires; —falters; — flourishes; —flows; —founders; —lags; — looms; —nets; —simmers; —succumbs.

(See occupation, trade, matter, affair, interest, concern, enterprise, duty, industry, work, commerce.)

BUSINESSLIKE

adverbs

insistently; consistently; briskly; cheerfully;

alertly; keenly; intelligently; curiously; terribly; unreasonably; delightfully; urgently; definitely; positively; absolutely; thriftily; competently; competitively; thoroughly; ordinarily; ardently; scrupulously; astoundingly; essentially; dully; brusquely; honestly; successfully; soundly; immensely; tremendously; tediously; drolly; comically; amazingly; dependably; actively; assiduously; devotedly; eagerly; energetically; industriously; officiously; vigilantly; notably; smartly; zealously; shrewdly; courteously; methodically; craftily; astutely; cleverly; uniformly; capably; ingeniously; felicitously.

BUSINESSMAN
adjectives
average; hard-boiled; shrewd; prudent; substantial.

BUST
adjectives
laurel-crowned; glowing; imperial; negligible; animated; portrait-like; protuberant; resurrected; placid; sculptured.

BUSTLE
adjectives
empty; heroic; sudden; feverish; indescribable; silent; hospitable; intervening; noisy.

BUSTLE (v)
adverbs
valorously; heroically; feverishly; indescribably; hospitably; noisily; officiously; clamorously; indignantly.
(See stir.)

BUSTLING
adverbs
restlessly; fitfully; eagerly; zealously; inefficiently; noisily; happily; affectionately; fondly; vexatiously; everlastingly; ceaselessly; cheerily; moodily; hastily; ardently; actively; energetically; industriously; assiduously; diligently; earnestly; enthusiastically; nervously; excitedly; impetuously.

BUSY (v)
adverbs
hurriedly; interferingly; noisily; officiously; irritatingly; animatedly; industriously; ambitiously; casually; perfunctorily.

BUSY (a)
adverbs
agreeably; delightfully; ceaselessly; charmingly; briskly; cheerfully; intelligently; constantly; curiously; unreasonably; competently; ordinarily; astoundingly; tremendously; comically; amazingly; actively; eagerly; zealously; energetically; smartly; ostentatiously; craftily; cleverly; capably; boyishly; noisily; happily.

BUSYBODY
adjectives
gifted; interfering; old; free lance; gaping; nosy.

BUTCHER
adjectives
benevolent; inexorable; unfeeling; latent; mortal; skilled.

BUTCHER (v)
adverbs
indiscriminately; dexterously; inexorably; unfeelingly; mortally; professionally; methodically; heartlessly; cruelly; wantonly; atrociously.
(See slaughter, kill.)

BUTCHERY
adjectives
horrible; atrocious; deadly; murderous; wartime.

BUTLER
adjectives
impassive; peremptory; perfect; shrinking; hovering; worried; excellent; solemn; diminutive; competent; grizzled.

BUTTER
adjectives
rancid; molten; honeyed.

verbs
adulterate—; cart—; churn into—; color—; crock—; daub with—; deal in—; draw—; exude—; flavor—; grease—; lay on—; market—; melt—; mould—; pot—; ration out—; ripen—; separate—; solidify—; spread—; stir in—; test—; thicken—; work—.

BUTTER (v)
adverbs
sufficiently; goldenly; lavishly; liberally; scantily; meagerly; penuriously; politically.

BUTTERFLY
adjectives
painted; giddy; ingenious; chromatic-winged; bright; honey-sipping; social; gilded; quivering; sipping; marrying; blossom-like; slim; jet; loppy-winged; admired; gaudy; lazy; dainty; fluttering; poising.

verbs

attract—; distinguish—; frame—; hurt—; identify—; preserve—; pursue—; —beautifies; —ies cluster; —flits about; —flutters; —ies gather; —ies hibernate; —lays eggs; —migrates; —mimics; —pollinates; —spins; —sports; —twinkles.

(See moth.)

BUTTON

adjectives

saucer; shining; blue-jerkined; glittering; showy; blazing; fantastic.

verbs

adorn with —s; attach—; card —s; decorate with —s; drill —s; fondle—; grind —s; mold —s; ornament with —s; perforate —s; polish—; press out —s; sew on—; sort —s; stamp out —s; stud with —s; undo—; —affixes; —decorates; —fastens; —signifies.

(See knob, ornament.)

BUXOM

adverbs

agreeably; cheerfully; delightfully; attractively; genially; gaily; hilariously; noisily; lightly; merrily; joyously; charmingly; entrancingly; seductively; captivatingly; fascinatingly; humorously; vivaciously; bonnily; cheerily; gleefully; heartily; jauntily; jovially; jubilantly; playfully; sportively.

BUY

adjectives

exceptional; special; extraordinary.

BUY (*v*)

adverbs

secretly; eagerly; dearly; methodically; recklessly; exceptionally; extraordinarily.

(See purchase.)

BUYER

adjectives

reluctant; unintelligent; reckless; unwilling; avid; adept; ultimate; discriminating; prospective; timorous.

verbs

cater to—; coax—; coddle—; commission—; employ—; forewarn—; petition—; —bargains; —dickers; —obtains; —s pour in; —purchases.

(See customer.)

BUYING

adjectives

hand-to-mouth; cash; unintelligent; abnormal; collective; curtailed.

BUZZ

adjectives

humming; roaring; somnolent; baleful.

BUZZ (*v*)

adverbs

violently; roaringly; somnolently; balefully; monotonously; grindingly; painfully; repeatedly; intermittently; raucously; irritatingly.

(See hum, murmur.)

BUZZARD

adjectives

eternal; circling; watchful; carrion-feeding; waiting; patient.

verbs

—dips; —flaps his wings; —hovers; —soars.

(See bird, fowl.)

BUZZING

adjectives

loud; melancholy; repeated; intermittent; raucous.

BY-PRODUCT

adjectives

dubious; usual; unforeseen.

BYSTANDERS

adjectives

casual; innocent; mere; fascinated; inoffensive-looking; pathetic; sympathetic; superstitious.

verbs

collide with—; entertain—; regale—; strike —; —boo; —cheer; —gather; —hoot; —recognize; —threaten; —witness.

(See spectator, crowd.)

BYWAY

adjectives

deserted; dark; bowered; romantic.

C

CAB

adjectives
dilapidated; high; ridiculous; dejected; creaking; hansom; ramshackle.

CABIN

adjectives
malodorous; ruined; dreary-looking; little; sweet; deserted; primitive; ugly; tumble-down; abandoned; friendly; roomy; windowless; stuffy; spacious; airy; adobe; rustic; frontier; willow; dilapidated; dismal; second-class; unventilated; sanitary; lonely; embowered; remote; populous; tourist.

verbs
allot—; approach—; confine to—; coop in—; crawl into—; dwell in—; huddle in—; inhabit—; lodge in—; occupy—; situate—; thatch—; —flames; —shelters.
(See hut, house, compartment, cottage.)

CABINET

adjectives
quaint; treasure; lacquered; sound-proof; bedstead; canopied; moist; drunken; medicine; reliable; antiquated.

CABINET

adjectives (governmental)
austere; absolute; didactic; dictatorial; disorganized; resolute; united; unsympathetic; vacillating; weak-kneed.

verbs
address—; appoint to—; call—; consult—; convoke—; corrupt—; dismiss—; dissolve—; elect to—; represent in—; summon—; —administers; —advises; —confers; —consists; —convenes.
(See committee, council, ministry.)

CABLE

adjectives
heavy; electric; steel-wire; enormous; light; underground; overhead.

verbs
insulate—; lay—; reclaim—; reenforce—; sheathe—; snap—; solder—; stretch—; —communicates; —connects; —rusts; —transmits.
(See rope, line, chain, conduit, pipe.)

CACKLE

adjectives
sickly; vacant; occasional; sociable; foolish; prodigious.

CACKLE (v)

adverbs
obstreperously; sociably; harshly; prodigiously; raucously; stridently; disagreeably; triumphantly; proudly; jubilantly; exuberantly.
(See laugh, chatter, babble.)

CACTUS

adjectives
spiny; mammoth; massive; hardy; scraggly; fantastic; prickly; succulent; large.

CAD

adjectives
sensual; slimy; rotten; brutal; discreet; elderly; ineffable.

CADAVEROUS

adverbs
horribly; forbiddingly; frightfully; spectrally; foully; grimly; gruesomely; hideously; haggardly; monstrously; odiously; shockingly; stiffly; uncannily; fearfully; alarmingly; incredibly; dreadfully.

CADENCE

adjectives
self-possessed; monotonous; odd; singsong; calm; deep; mimic; best-measured; tinkling; merry; queer; wild; sardonic; nasal; minor; rollicking; weird; hideous; entreating; slightest; slurred; strange; rhythmic; musical; affectionate; lingering; effective; gentle; elegant; exotic; passionate; varied; soul-like; plagal; pathetic; pleading; enchanting; sorrowful.

CAFE

adjectives
innumerable (pl); continental; eccentric; gaudy; dingy; sumptuous; garish; gay; air-conditioned; pleasant; obscure; modest; smart; modern.

CAFFEINE

adjectives
unfriendly; stimulating.

adjectives

subterranean; quarantined; awful; gilded; bamboo; wire; delicate; adjourning; wicker; pretty.

verbs

bar—; beat—; burst—; chain—; confine in —; convey in—; coop in—; escape from—; fetter in—; flit from—; hoist—; house in—; imprison in—; muffle in—; release from—; seal—; thrive in—; transport in—; wire in —.

(See prison.)

CAKE

adjectives

huge; fluffy; stale; abominable; peatlike; fresh; big; luscious; ancestral; oaten; incalculable; sacrificial; decomposed; fatal; successful; election; rich; moist; tender; smooth; white; pound; futile.

verbs

celebrate with—; crust—; decorate—; feast on—; flavor—; frost—; ice—; knead—; mix—; moisten—; mold—; munch on—; ply with—; regale with—; relish—; shape —; share—; spice—; squash—; sweeten—; yearn for—; —appeals; —appeases; —attracts; —crumbles; —falls; —rises; —stales.

(See bread.)

CALAMITY

adjectives

sudden; near; appalling; frightful; dire; staggering; tremendous; universal; public; painful; evident; undeserved; national; family; inevitable; crowning; impending; ominous; dreadful; absurd; mysterious; natural; inexhaustible; grotesque; unspeakable; ultimate; extraordinary; surrounding; bitter; colossal; temporal; undisguised.

verbs

afflict with—; avert—; avoid—; bear—; beset with—ies; drive to—; free from—; inflict with—; investigate—; involve—; laugh at—; mourn—; overcome—; restore from—; rush to—; save from—; survive—; —arises; —confounds; —damages; —descends; —distresses; —foreshadows; —injures; —menaces; —recurs; —smites; —threatens; —troubles.

(See misfortune, disaster, adversity.)

CALCULABLE

adverbs

easily; accurately; obviously; analytically; rationally; fairly; exhaustively; arithmetically; scientifically; precisely; exactly; laboriously; imposingly; impressively.

CALCULATE (*v*)

adverbs

mentally; abstractly; arithmetically; shrewdly; convincingly; precisely; astronomically; mathematically; slavishly; systematically; perpetually; strikingly; nicely; artfully.

(See compute, reckon.)

CALCULATION

adjectives

abstruse; optimistic; hasty; mental; abstract; pragmatic; intricate; colorless; chill; arithmetical; trained; shrewd; barren; imposing; convincing; rough; mental; unsettling; hard; stupendous; easy; moderate; absurd; deliberate; prudent; precise; laborious; memorable; astronomical; elaborate; vain; mathematical; calm; monotonous; craniometrical; cool; systematic; slavish; perpetual; reasonable.

verbs

adjust—; adopt—; arrange—; average—; check—; cite—; compute—; denounce—; err in—; estimate—; facilitate—; frame—; perform—; prove—; reckon—; speed—; tabulate—; think out—; upset—; —deceives; —determines; —fits; —indicates; —results in.

(See computation, reckoning.)

CALDRON

adjectives

seething; spiteful; great; live; bubbling; ancestral; hellish; boiling; monstrous; magic.

verbs

agitate—; cook in—; cool—; fry in—; steep in—; —boils; —bubbles; —overflows; —pours out; —seethes; —simmers; —steams.

(See kettle, pot.)

CALENDAR

adjectives

proposed; universal; unscriptural; modern; present; scientific.

verbs

appear on—; count on—; designate on—; introduce—; judge by—; keep—of; pencil —; readjust—; reckon by—; regulate—; revise—; scratch out of—; —computes; —denotes; —determines; —s differ; —groups; —indicates; —measures; —serves; —signifies.

(See list, schedule.)

CALF

adjectives

capering; soft-eyed.

verbs
beget—; corral—s; fatten—; fetter—; groom—; infect—; lasso—; offer—; pasture—; pet—; rend—; sacrifice—; slaughter—; stable—; —bawls; —browses; — grazes; —kicks; —shies; —suckles; — whines.
(See animal.)

CALF
(leg)
adjectives
well-turned; unwearying; aching; pretty.

CALIBER
adjectives
high; stern; rare; meager; spectacular; mental; various.

CALL
adjectives
urgent; impatient; hurried; frantic; startled; strenuous; amazing; mystic; persistent; insistent; ceaseless; gallant; thrilling; voiceless; feeble; muffled; strong; canny; joyous; ringing; strident; clarion; screeching; staccato; calm; melodious; loud; musical; excited; effectual; pitiful; petulant; stirring; incoming; home-coming; solemn; doleful; providential; skyward; languid; vigorous; cheering; quavering; inconsiderate; bugle; emphatic; clamorous; person-to-person; night; echoing; high-pitched; immediate; impassioned; immortal.

verbs
evade—; ignore—; register—; respond to —; rise at—; trumpet—; whistle—; yield to—; —beckons; —bursts forth; —deludes; —drifts; —gladdens; —saddens.
(See shout, cry, summons, invitation.)

CALL
(visit)
adjectives
deathless; enormous; unending; ceremonious; emergency; neighborly; unexpected; convenient; innumerable (pl); close; honorable; hasty; protracted; reliable; bewildering; personal.

CALL (*v*)
adverbs
insistently; urgently; frantically; persistently; feebly; ringingly; stridently; screechingly; melodiously; musically; pitifully; petulantly; dolefully; languidly; passionately; vigorously; quaveringly; clamorously; emphatically; echoingly; irresistibly; officially; severely; alternately; bluntly; facetiously; despairingly; technically; irreverently;

extemporaneously; plaintively; mysteriously; familiarly; delicately; subsequently; indifferently; timorously; imperiously; cordially; tauntingly; cautiously; virtually; proverbially; unconscionably; sportively; graciously; lustily.
(See summon, bid, invite.)

CALLER
adjectives
white-haired; talkative; bedraggled; irate; bashful; unexpected; disappointed.

CALLING
adjectives
suitable; honorable; money-making; effectual; incessant; primordial; gainful; lawful.

verbs
answer—; awake to—; bend to—; consider —; continue in—; exalt—; exercise—; feel —; follow—; give up to—; heed—; profess to—; succeed in—; surrender to—; —bids; —invites; —invokes; —summons.
(See vocation, occupation, trade, profession.)

CALLOUS (*a*)
adverbs
coldly; unfeelingly; stolidly; senselessly; obtusely; apathetically; strangely; abnormally; weakly; heavily; vacantly; singularly; oddly; curiously; unaccountably; irritatingly; vexatiously; coolly; unpardonably; inexcusably.

CALLOUSNESS
adjectives
extreme; bitter; cruel; harsh; icy; incurred; repellent; brutal; self-imposed; criminal.

verbs
breed—; develop—; display—; expose to—; immunize to—; relapse into—; —blinds; — forms; —grows; —prevents; —ridicules.
(See callous, cruelty.)

CALLOW
adverbs
crudely; intolerably; uncompanionably; insufferably; rawly; youthfully; unintelligently; rudimentally; coarsely; thoughtlessly; heedlessly; vacuously; fatuously; surprisingly; awkwardly.

CALLUS (n)

adjectives

burning; carefully-tended; horny; leathery; reducible; stubborn; thickening; toil-worn; cushiony; cracked; shell-like.

verbs

apply to—; cut—; expose—; form—; pad—; peel—; press on—; rub into—; salve—; scrape—; slice—; soften—; soothe—; treat —es; wear —es; —aches; —burns; —hardens; —indurates; —irritates; —pains; — thickens.

(See callousness.)

CALM

adjectives

imperturbable; equable; deathly; reproachful; ominous; unutterable; desolate; sullen; philosophic; mental; studied; sensual; false; somber; solemn; classic; customary; comparative; jaded; forced; alert; secretive; unnatural; dovelike; delightful; unbroken; untroubled; restful; flawless; concentrated; hallowed; inmost; underlying; Sabbath; delicious; sweet; bitter; disciplined; stately; unalterable; shimmering; breathless; expressionless; succeeding; prosaic; windless; splendid; night; rigid; eternal; perfect; disquieting; outward; threatening; mysterious; legislative; passionless; remote; lucid; constant; serene; professional; melancholy; colossal; awful; inward; solid; habitual; unapologetic; sad; sacred; stolid; maddening; level; shuddering; kindred; dead; planetary; everlasting; propitious; apparent; judicial.

verbs

agitate—; break—; bring—; disturb—; end —; maintain—; preserve—; retain—; shatter—; suspend—; —bewitches; —delays; — detains; —enchants; —endures; —irritates; —rests; —settles on; —soothes.

(See tranquillity, stillness, serenity.)

CALM (a)

adverbs

pleasantly; delightfully; comfortingly; comfortably; habitually; sweetly; imperturbably; serenely; equitably; ominously; unutterably; philosophically; unnaturally; restfully; inwardly; unalterably; splendidly; mysteriously; perfectly; maddeningly; apparently; suddenly; strangely; pathetically; judicially; indulgently; coolly; placidly; gravely; passively; patiently; quietly; soberly; tranquilly; deliberately; silently; amicably; gently; smoothly; mildly; nonchalantly.

CALM (v)

adverbs

ominously; philosophically; falsely; somberly; soberly; mentally; comparatively; unnaturally; expressionlessly; prosaically; outwardly; mysteriously; passionlessly; professionally; serenely; propitiously; judicially; apparently.

(See lull, appease, hush.)

CALMNESS

adjectives

perfect; deathlike; icy; irritating; tense; sleepy; sudden; terrible; deliberate; strange; stony; peculiar; solitary; intrepid; honest; dreadful; collected; pathetic; fierce; unwonted; unmerciful; dreamy; judicial; proud; displeasing; settled; cold; imperturbable.

CALORIES

adjectives

accumulated; actinic; beneficial; burdening; life-sustaining; stored-up.

verbs

burden with—; calculate—; contain—; define—; determine—; express in—; govern —; increase—; lessen—; measure—; obtain —; regulate—; require—; supply—; vary—; —suffice.

(See unit.)

CALUMNIATORY

adverbs

criminally; scandalously; grossly; wilfully; flagitiously; dangerously; substantially; veritably; avowedly; abominably; detestably; extremely; illegally; nefariously; unfortunately; unluckily; openly; deliberately; maliciously; venomously; libelously; scurrilously; foully; slanderously.

CALUMNIOUS

adverbs

deliberately; inherently; naturally; habitually; unfortunately; unpleasantly; disagreeably; detestably; abominably; hatefully; malignantly; maliciously; poisonously; venomously; viciously; insinuatingly; slyly; subtly; scandalously; wilfully; dangerously; extremely; openly; foully; unforgivably.

CALUMNY

adjectives

gross; frequent; willful; barbarous; backwounding; transparent; private; flagitious; hideous; popular; superstitious.

verbs

accuse of—; asperse with—; characterize

by—; charge with—; diffuse—; invent—; propagate—; raise—; repudiate—; subject to—; utter—; —blights; —defames; —detracts; —imputes to; —injures; —libels; —misrepresents; —slanders.

(See slander, aspersion, accusation.)

CALVINISTIC
adverbs
rigidly; soundly; strictly; unyieldingly; inflexibly; faithfully; scrupulously; unbendingly; loyally; puritanically; chastely; punctiliously; literally; precisely; rigorously; unaffectedly; unimpeachably; frankly; openly; avowedly; sincerely; obstinately; stubbornly; obdurately; intolerantly; proudly.

CAMARADERIE
adjectives
careless; spirited; joyous.

CAMEL
adjectives
gloomy-eyed; crouching; fast; cream-colored; browsing; patient; fleet; miserable; baggage; fine-riding; beautiful; prodding; magnificent; kneeling; swift; sure-footed.

verbs
domesticate—; load—; mount—; train—; water—; —bolts; —consumes; —fasts; —gurgles; —jolts; —kneels; —nibbles; —rages; —roars; —shakes; —stores; —sweats; —thrives.

(See animal.)

CAMEO
adjectives
exquisite; precious.

CAMERA
adjectives
television; candid; clicking; heavy; leveled.

verbs
adjust—; arm with—; besiege with —s; conceal—; focus—; insert in—; level—; load—; operate—; pose before—; regulate —; sit before—; utilize—; —aids; —captures; —catches; —copies; —enlarges; —espies; —grinds out; —obtains; —pictures; —records; —registers; —reproduces.

CAMOUFLAGE
adjectives
pleasant; pious; shallow; discreditable; impenetrable; foolish.

CAMP
adjectives
hostile; dismantled; horrible; concentration; deserted; aboriginal; circumvallating; permanent; temporary; picturesque; fortified; turbulent; peaceful; comfortable; armed; spacious; attractive; modest; thriving; selected; opposite; lawless; antagonistic; divided; nightly; luxurious; chaotic.

verbs
arouse—; beleaguer—; besiege—; command —; concentrate—; conduct—; conduct to—; divide into —s; escort to—; pitch—; proclaim—; put out of—; quarter at—; split into —s; strike—; —busies; —buzzes; —hums; —rises; —swarms.

(See barracks.)

CAMP (*v*)
adverbs
ostentatiously; conveniently; permanently; temporarily; turbulently; lawlessly; nightly; luxuriously; strategically.

CAMPAIGN
adjectives
triumphant; ill-fated; successful; whispering; perfunctory; systematic; demographic; vigorous; anti-crime; collective; energetic; fruitless; gubernatorial; brilliant; tremendous; aggressive; virulent; victorious; independent; indiscriminate; plausible; preliminary; piratical; comprehensive; subtle; long; tedious; bloody; doggerel; wearisome; approaching; powerful; persistent; perfidious; journalistic; deliberate; devouring; lulled; preceding; critical; anti-feminist; amatory; mighty; brilliant; thrilling; worldwide; far-flung; intense; thorough; guerrilla; national; educational; money-raising; recruiting; secret; quiet; off-stage; complete; exacting; sanguinary; haphazard; extraordinary.

verbs
broaden—; carry on—; conduct—; embark on—; feature—; focus—; foster—; inaugurate—; initiate—; inspire—; intensify—; launch—; map out—; participate in—; plan —; plot—; promote—; push—; stir—; sway —; swing—; transcend—; wage—.

(See operation, contest, appeal.)

CAMPAIGN (*v*)
adverbs
vigorously; triumphantly; ill-fatedly; vaingloriously; perfunctorily; systematically; energetically; fruitlessly; brilliantly; gubernatorially; aggressively; virulently; independently; indiscriminately; perfidiously; comprehensively; tediously; educationally; extraordinarily; haphazardly.

(See operate.)

adjectives
agitated; ogling; leering; scheming; artful; active; seasoned.

adjectives
scattered (pl); unsuspecting.

adjectives
forsaken; gleaming; rosy; flickering; bright; glowing; tiny; cozy; smoking; central.

adjectives
dignified; attractive.

adjectives
highly-colored; discarded.

verbs
cap—; dent—; deposit in—; dump —s; grade—; heap —s; label—; litter with —s; manufacture—; package —s; penetrate—; put up in—; save in—; seal—; shape—; shelve—; —preserves; —protects; —rusts.
(See cup.)

adverbs
staunchly; stoutly; shrewdly; indomitably; loyally; dauntlessly; stolidly; generously; cannily.

adjectives
shining; picturesque; slender; enchanting; stagnant; inland; crude; sluggish; beautiful; tree-lined; intestinal; vast; network; practicable; intracoastal; alimentary; auditory; winding; lotus-paved; irregular; pestiferous; tortuous; marble-lined; glittering; terrestrial; ribbonlike; semicircular; shadowed; vestigial.

verbs
bank—; block—; border by—; bridge—; circle—; construct—; drain—; dredge—; fortify—; lay out—; line—; lock—; navigate —; obstruct—; project—; tow through—; —communicates; —connects; —conveys; —irrigates; —retains; —shortens; —unites.
(See channel, duct, passage.)

adjectives
base; preposterous.

adjectives
ephemeral; fluffy; fragile; gladsome; green-gold; restless; song-bursting; twittering.

verbs
—carols; —peeps; —trills; —tweets.
(See bird.)

adjectives
malignant; hereditary; inoperable.

verbs
ascribe to—; control—; detect—; diagnose —; discover—; engraft—; examine for—; excise—; indicate—; lecture on—; localize —; recognize—; reveal—; sacrifice to—; suffer from—; suspect—; treat for—; —advances; —appears; —courses through; —develops; —disables; —eats away; —extends; —lodges; —lurks; —results; —spreads.
(See tumor, disease.)

adverbs
hopelessly; lamentably; malignantly; incurably; irremediably; morbidly; painfully; distressingly; inoperably; sorely; agonizingly; grievously; horribly; dolorously; frightfully; pitiably; woefully; tragically.

adjectives
myriad; tall; bronze; brilliant; huge; silver.

adverbs
glowingly; whitely; tropically; lambently; scintillatingly; flamingly; smolderingly; incalescently; intensely; fiercely; sulphurously; overpoweringly; intolerably; unendurably; incredibly.

adverbs
blazingly; dazzlingly; effulgently; brightly; radiantly; intolerably; gloriously; luminously; refulgently; resplendently; splendidly; magnificently; garishly; lustrously; vividly; genially; mildly; exceedingly; surprisingly; gratefully; agreeably; magically.

adverbs
utterly; openly; honestly; innocently; simply; sincerely; artlessly; deliberately; resolutely; roughly; directly; downright; frankly; ingenuously; naively; naturally; plainly; unflatteringly; delicately; nakedly; soberly;

palpably; evidently; manifestly; truthfully; veraciously; bluntly; indulgently; particularly; scrupulously; unaffectedly; unnecessarily; inexcusably; faithfully; unreservedly; respectfully; incorruptibly; crudely; painfully; gaily; unfeelingly; characteristically; habitually; amazingly; humorously; unexpectedly; engagingly; alarmingly; charmingly.

CANDIDACY

adjectives
insurgent; unsuccessful.

verbs
announce—; avow—; back—; boost for—; campaign for—; criticize—; decide—; discuss—; interest in—; offer for—; promote —; propose—; protest—; reject—; rob of—; select for—; support—; work for—.

CANDIDATE

adjectives
potential; gubernatorial; legitimate; senatorial; aspiring; glamorous; receptive; prospective; rejected; unexceptionable; proper; eligible; formidable; leading; opposing; passive; alternative; presidential.

verbs
choose—; doom—; endorse—; favor—; groom—; handicap—; honor—; idealize—; squelch—; uphold—; —aspires to; —offers; —orates; —"slings mud"; —stumps; —thunders; - -triumphs.
(See contestant.)

CANDIED

adverbs
deliciously; delectably; lusciously; richly; densely; thickly; indissolubly; substantially; sweetly; fruitily; generously; agreeably; palatably; deceptively.

CANDLE

adjectives
dumb; newfangled; paraffin; shining; beeswax; flickering; brief; gigantic; guttering; meek; neglected; tall; ghastly; blessed; diminutive; melancholy; flaring; spent; cabbage-headed; half-burned; lighted; sputtering; waning; snuffed; long-wicked.

verbs
dip —s; extinguish—; mould —s; snuff—; —decorates; —drips; —flickers; —gutters; —illuminates; —melts; —shadows; —shines; —shrinks; —sputters; —stains; —tapers.
(See light, lamp.)

CANDLESTICK

adjectives
squat; slender; graceful.

CANDOR

adjectives
crude; unfailing; ingenuous; shameless; maidenly; winning; half-rebellious; friendly; perfect; pervading; utmost; gay; transparent; unwonted; incomparable; painful; dignified; unfeeling; fresh; apparent; characteristic; piercing; brotherly; stainless; endearing; illuminating; violent; good-humored; unashamed; unsuggestive; uncompromising; amazing; wholesome; spiritual; direct; heartfelt; vigorous; humorous; unexpected; courageous; perfect; devastating; engaging; openhearted; rustic; unruly; alarming; comical.

verbs
acclaim—; boast—; discourse with—; dispose toward—; express—; feign—; honor —; judge with—; radiate—; —brightens; —frees; —shines; —shocks; —strains; —surprises.
(See frankness, impartiality, fairness, sincerity.)

CANDY

adjectives
silk; atrocious; hard; lime; delicious; tempting; nutritious.

verbs
bribe with—; congeal into—; consume—; decorate—; feast on—; flavor—; hanker for—; immerse—in; inspissate—; proffer—; regale with—; thicken—; —appeals; —crystallizes; —sickens —stales; —vanishes.
(See cake.)

CANE

adjectives
lithe; long; ebony; ivory-headed; silver-headed; Malacca; gold-headed; slender; impenetrable; light; flexible; leaded; jewelled; silver-topped; beribboned.

verbs
beat with—; brandish—; carve—; enamel —; flex—; flog with—; flourish—; jab with —; joint—; lean on—; notch—; poise—; sheathe—; tap with—; utilize—; —supports.
(See stick, staff, whip.)

CANINE

adjectives
affectionate; luckless.

adjectives
groveling.

CANKER

adjectives
vengeful; gnawing.

verbs
banish—; infect with—; slough—; spray—; —consumes; —corrupts; —decays; —depraves; —destroys; —develops; —devours; —discharges; —diseases; —eats; —envelops; —gnaws; —grows; —indisposes; —poisons; —pollutes; —rusts; —spreads; —tarnishes.
(See cancer, ulcer, sore.)

CANKEROUS

adverbs
increasingly; injuriously; poisonously; corrosively; blightingly; irremediably; incurably; painfully; distressingly; troublesomely; pitiably; unfortunately.

CANNED

adverbs
perfectly; exquisitely; expertly; faultlessly; irreproachably; hygienically; scientifically; soundly; carefully; well; safely; home; prophylactically; guardedly.

CANNIBALS

adjectives
gigantic; raging.

CANNON

adjectives
least-accessible; monstrous; small; academical; clumsy; ugly; yawning; widely-sloping; terraced; prostrate; grumbling; booming; brazen-throated; improvised; boulder-choked; distant; useless; breaching; spiked; roaring; frowning; lateral; brazen; belching; thundering; hostile.

verbs
capture—; charge—; discharge—; level—; load—; man—; mount—; sight—; silence —; train—upon; —batters; —blazes away; —booms; —emits; —explodes; —menaces; —pounds; —recoils; —revolves; —roars; —rolls; —salutes; —throws; —thunders; — vollies.
(See gun, weapon.)

CANNONADE

adjectives
tremendous; sullen.

adverbs
astonishingly; shrewdly; weirdly; uncommonly; infinitely; suavely; smoothly; adroitly; cleverly; diplomatically; artfully; subtly; cunningly; naturally; craftily; guilelessly; astutely; foxily; deeply; knowingly; politically; discreetly; intelligently; sharply; wisely; sagely; sagaciously; alertly; smartly.

CANOE

adjectives
stealthy; canvas-covered; capsized; frail; careening; racing; dug-out; birchen; lonely.

verbs
ballast—; capsize—; cruise in—; fashion—; guide—; handle—; launch—; level—; model —; navigate—; overturn—; propel—; race in—; right—; rig up—; sail—; stabilize—; steer—; trim—; twist—; waterproof—; weight—; —dips; —glides; —outsails; — rocks; —slips.
(See boat.)

CANOEIST

adjectives
seasoned.

CANON

adjectives
hospitable; highest; continent; aesthetic; worthy; obtrusive; waterless; metrical.

CANONICAL

adverbs
strictly; highly; conformably; obtrusively; ecclesiastically; monastically; pontifically; illustriously; conventionally; formally; habitually; ordinarily; regularly; acceptably; rigidly; typically; uncompromisingly; evangelically; sacredly; prophetically; inviolably; expressly.

CAN OPENER

adjectives
maligned.

CANOPY

adjectives
moon-proof; damask; shifting; irremovable; drooping; arched; orb-like; moth-flitted; overhead; luminous; oblique; skyey; silken; flowery; crimson; celestial; velvet; azure; somber; verdant; umbrageous.

verbs
bracket—; couch under—; embroider—; hang out—; spread—; support—; suspend —; —circles; —covers; —decorates; —

hangs over; —hoods; —projects; —protects; —shades; —shelters; —surmounts.
(See pavilion, tent.)

CANT

adjectives
specious; traditional.

CANTER

adjectives
clumsy; brisk; undeniable; preliminary.

CANTER (v)

adverbs
clumsily; briskly; carelessly; steadily; spiritedly; half-heartedly; unevenly; monotonously; jouncingly; pleasurably; lazily.
(See trot.)

CANVAS

adjectives
mute; melancholy; billowing; snowy; smoke-darkened; gigantic; towering; shimmering; famous; important; dark-colored; mighty; somber; rickety; defiled; broad; idly-flapping; mimic; remarkable; inflammable.

verbs
bleach—; daub—; depict on—; display on —; dye—; execute on—; garment in—; line with—; live under—; portray on—; retain on—; spread—; surface—; transfer to—; weave—; —blinds; —filters; —protects; —screens.
(See cloth, sail, tent, picture, painting.)

CANVASS

adjectives
frantic; extensive; national; house-to-house; thorough; misleading; hotly-contested; electoral; industrious; effective.

CANYON

adjectives
deepening; lowland; tributary; carved; narrow; sharp; shallow; dreaded; deserted; winding; mile-deep; color-flaming; hollow; bare; hard; blind; frowning; weird; wind-swept; somber; snow-clad; treeless; mist-filled; nave-like; mystic; rocky-bottomed; grand.

verbs
carve—; collect in—; delve in—; enter—; erode into—; explore—; flow through—; stream through—; traverse—; widen—; — beautifies; —extends; —narrows; —skirts; —traverses; —widens.
(See gorge, valley.)

adjectives
rakish; coon-tail; checked; grimy; shabby; demure; bulging; peaked; close-fitting; visored; tall; shako-like; thin; plumed; gauze; paltry; flaring; jaunty; blue-tasseled; night-spangled; frilled; perforated; traditional; funnel-shaped; lace; muslin.

verbs
adjust—; admire—; appear in—; clap—on; crown with—; don—; fashion—; fling—; hurl—in air; line—; pattern—; peak—; —balloons; —blows off; —covers; —distinguishes; —fits; —perches; —protects; —shades; —shields; —surrounds; —warms.
(See hat, cover.)

CAPABILITIES

adjectives
ultimate; brilliant; admitted; generous; endless.

verbs
admit—; apprehend—; ascertain—; boast of—; confirm—; convince of—; demand—; destroy—; display—; discover—; doubt—; drain—; enlarge—; establish—; evince—; examine—; exhibit—; gift with—; investigate—of; perceive—; possess—; recognize —; reward—; strike one with—; trust in—of.
(See ability, capacity, skill.)

CAPABLE

adverbs
unusually; brilliantly; remarkably; normally; generally; immensely; naturally; highly; notably; efficiently; sufficiently; incredibly; exceptionally; energetically; potentially; influentially; adroitly; cleverly; dexterously; deftly; discreetly; expertly; ingeniously; indefatigably; tirelessly; intelligently; practically; skilfully; proficiently; felicitously; handily; neatly; pleasantly; willingly; thoroughly; technically; shrewdly; entirely; gratifyingly; prepossessingly; agreeably.

CAPACIOUS

adverbs
unusually; incredibly; extensively; extremely; sweepingly; magnificently; broadly; splendidly; grandly; superbly; unbelievably; wonderfully; marvellously; illimitably; infinitely; admirably; majestically; roomily; enormously; remarkably; notably; famously; renownedly; formidably; singularly; uncommonly; particularly.

adjectives

imitative; business; temporal; assimilative; remarkable; absorptive; negative; productive; private; normal; functional; boundless; superior; reserve; carrying; immense; phenomenal; histrionic; unbounded; equestrian; bestowed; fruitful; partisan; sovereign; native; fatal; individual; narrowest; physical; psychological; proper; everlasting; increasing; cubical; wage-earning; reputed; creative; intellectual; interpretative; notable; productive; automatic; honorary; earning; predatory; constitutional; dignified; uncommon; extensive; aggregate; daily; destructive; magical; executive; exceptional; innate; latent; automatic; enlarged; varying; inexhaustible; bear-like; extraordinary; tremendous; ultimate; human; seating; consulting; mental; social; official; business; threefold; spiritual; prehensile; advisory; endless; singular; considerable; utmost; marked; unique; stunted; amazing; unparalleled; infinite; limitless; incredible; strange; cold-blooded; meanest; inherent; natural; fertile; implanted; expert; unsuspected; sufficient; demonstrated; flexible; inborn; benevolent; hidden; varied; contrasted; formidable.

verbs

cultivate—; delineate—; demonstrate—; develop—; endow with—; engender—; enlarge —; exceed—; exert to—; expand—; gauge —; impair—; increase—; limit—; measure —; nourish—; overestimate—; reduce—; sharpen—; —dwindles; —wanes.

(See ability, talent, power, space, position, office.)

CAPE

adjectives (clothing)

dark; all-enveloping; velvet; cloth; dusky; ghostly; chestnut; graceful; small; fluttering.

CAPE

adjectives (land)

stupendous; huge; rocky; famous; grassy.

CAPER

adjectives

wild; queer; prancing; droll; weird; drunken; inexplicable.

verbs

cut —s; dance in—; execute—; frolic in —s; jump in —s; leap in —s; perform—; prance in—; run into—; skip in—; sport in—; twist in—.

(See prank, trick, leap, spring.)

CAPERING

adjectives

gleeful; lamb-like; idle.

CAPITAL

adjectives (city)

seething; delightful; mad; hospitable; national; inland; stricken; remote; proud; brilliant; sophisticated; intellectual; financial; provincial; faraway; critical; highland; ancient; gilded; sculptured; flowery; peerless.

CAPITAL

adjectives (financial)

ample; slender; insufficient; borrowed; local; surplus; invested; ready; maximum; accumulated; potential; enchanting; embellished; tolerable; available; abundant; organized; skittish; enlightened; unproductive.

verbs

accumulate—; amass—; calculate—; contribute—; convert into—; distribute—; employ—; exploit—; favor—; fix—; float—; furnish—; gain—; guarantee—; impair—; increase—; insure—; invest—; organize—; produce—; protect—; subscribe—; withdraw—; —earns; —finances.

(See money, wealth, stock.)

CAPITALISM

adjectives

regenerated; decadent; imperialistic; monopolist.

verbs

abuse—; attack—; base on—; berate—; condemn—; creep upon—; denounce—; deplore—; favor—; oppose—; overthrow—; prejudice against—; rebuild—; reform—; reject—; revive—; support—; vindicate—; —collapses; —concentrates; —evolves from; —exploits; —flourishes; —promotes; — possesses; —retards; —rules; —speeds up; — topples; —tyrannizes.

CAPITALIST

adjectives

foolish; old-style; hard-boiled; new-risen; timid; satanic; retired; world-famed; local; noted; universal; desirable; unregenerate; designing.

CAPITULATION

adjectives

dishonorable; unexpected; so-called; careful; generous.

adjectives
cruel; revolting; monstrous; swift; boyish; accidental; magnificent; slightest; youthful; expensive; sudden; unaccountable; feminine; passing; innocent; common; irresistible.

verbs
act on—; depend on—; humor—; lead by—; leave to—; restrain—; subject to—; —determines; —fancies; —fixes; —forms; —governs; —guides; —turns.
(See whim, fancy, notion.)

CAPRICIOUS

adverbs
waywardly; whimsically; wantonly; playfully; captiously; unreasonably; amusingly; ridiculously; delightfully; irresistibly; strikingly; extravagantly; senselessly; humorously; cruelly; childishly; irresponsibly; unaccountably; girlishly; incorrigibly; intractably; curiously; foolishly; preposterously; nonsensically; drolly; comically.

CAPSULE

adjectives
compact; dehiscent; formidable; gelatine; handy; metallic; portable; soluble; transparent; unappetizing.

verbs
administer—; cover with—; dissolve—; dose with —s; enclose in—; form in—; heat—; medicate—; melt—; perforate—; seal in—; swallow—; —bursts; —contains; —cures; —envelops; —opens; —sheaths; —surrounds.
(See case.)

CAPTAIN

adjectives
turbulent; portly; doughty; gallant; dauntless; resourceful; inspiring; imperturbable; wily; bluff; honest; naval; brutal; steady; reliable; plump; rubicund; grave; calm; wigged; staff; blustering; youthful; sagacious; usurping; triumphant; modish; unwilling; unapproachable; senior; russet-coated; victorious; mutinous; self-sufficient; spectacular; valiant.

verbs
beseech—; betray—; commission—; commune with—; dread—; elect—; elevate to —; entreat—; promote to—; rank as—; raise to—; —assigns; —authorizes; —commands; —heads; —leads; —orders; —roars; —survives; —thunders; —upbraids.
(See leader, commander.)

adverbs
disagreeably; offensively; irritatingly; needlessly; groundlessly; wilfully; unpleasantly; truculently; cantankerously; capriciously; whimsically; irresponsibly; provokingly; fitfully; contrarily; uncomfortably; excitably; petulantly; intolerably; unpardonably; irascibly; irritably; fretfully; inexplicably; fractiously; sarcastically; woefully.

CAPTIVE

adjectives
illustrious; beautiful; sullen-eyed; barbaric; slaughtered; hopeless; hapless; delighted; luckless; trapped; defenseless; willing; unhappy; devoted; cowardly; shamed; spent; princely; august.

verbs
acquit—; bind—; cage—; carry away—; chain—; deliver—; detain—; enslave—; exchange —s; fetter—; free—; humble—; liberate—; mutilate—; restore—; slaughter —s; struggle with—; subdue—; take—; torture—.
(See prisoner.)

CAPTIVITY

adjectives
killing; limitless; perpetual; weakening; prolonged.

verbs
bring into—; cancel—; carry into—; counsel in—; dash into—; deliver from—; desolate in—; detain in—; dwell in—; enforce—; escape from—; feel—; hold in—; incarcerate in—; languish in—; lead into—; pine in—; resign to—; sell into—; shut in—; sink into —; subject to—; submit to—.
(See bondage, slavery.)

CAPTURE

adjectives
final; violent; rich; gallant; important; nefarious; imminent.

CAPTURE (*v*)

adverbs
triumphantly; previously; brilliantly; finally; violently; gallantly; nefariously; shrewdly; skillfully; dexterously; slyly; viciously; cruelly; wantonly.
(See apprehend, arrest, seize.)

CAR

adjectives
spectral; rheumatic; unobtrusive; high-

toned; high-priced; heavenly; short-lived; sumptuous; rushing; antiquated; magnificent; fast; refrigerator; private; outmoded; jangling; streamlined; swift; horse; electric; dull; faded; forward; triumphal; airborne; pellucid; impressive; frivolous; ill-smelling; clanging; luxurious; excellent; appointed; fine-looking; gay; resplendent; ancient; battered; touring; rattling; scraggly; ramshackle; decrepit; small; shabby; disreputable; armored; torpedo-shaped; queer; coffin-shaped; showy; motor; gaudy; rakish; spectral; death; twisted; crippled; expensive; charging; oncoming; hurtling; roaring; pursuing; departing; passing; jolting; bouncing; purring; lurching; brilliant; swinging; mud-splashed; full-length; close-parked; halted; gleaming; massive; roomy.

verbs
check—; convey in—; crowd—; crush beneath—; demolish—; draw—; fuel—; grease —; guide—; jaunt in—; load—; polish—; power—; proceed in—; ride in—; scramble from—; smash—; tow—; transport in—; tumble from—; wheel—; —backfires; —s collide; —s file by; —glides; —glistens; —groans; —hums; —purrs; —rattles; —serves; —skids; —skims; —speeds; —traverses; —whizzes by.
(See automobile.)

CAR
adjectives (railroad)
clanking; gliding; heavily-laden; obdurate; rattling; runaway; swaying; unmanned; unwieldy; weighty; trundling; creaking; brawling.

verbs
attach—; brake—; couple —s; derail—; design—; dispatch—; electrify—; equip—; gear—; haul—; hook on—; light—; load—; model—; number—; refrigerate—; shunt—; signal—; station—; streamline—; switch—; transport in—; —chugs along; —s collide; —rattles by; —rumbles past; —rusts.
(See coach.)

CARAVAN
adjectives
innumerable (pl); floating; assembled; angelic; formidable; long-winding; slow-crawling; trekking; vast; imposing; lonely; patriarchal; stately; sluggish.

verbs
arm—; attack—; burden—; convoy—; encounter—; engage—; equip—; guard—; guide—; halt—; head—; hire—; lead—; route—; set upon—; tour in—; —assembles; —marches; —perishes; —sets forth; —starves; —travels; —traverses; —treks; —troops by; —wanders.
(See company, cart, wagon.)

CARAVANSARY
adjectives
frivolous; huge; pretentious; courtyard.

CARBOHYDRATES
adjectives
essential; tissue-building; fortifying; vital; woody.

verbs
analyze—; burn up—; characterize—; class as—; consist of—; consume—; contain—; depend on—; distribute—; form—; induce —; lack—; —benefit; —energize; —fuel; —occur in; —produce; —reveal; —serve as.
(See compound.)

CARBON
adjectives
amorphous; crystallized; free; elemental; ebon; smudgy; uncombined.

verbs
anaylze—; clean—; combine with—; compound with—; crystallize—; deposit—; filter with—; free—; give off—; illuminate —; produce—; reduce to—; —blackens; —condenses; —decolors; —joins with.
(See element.)

CARCASS
adjectives
bloodstained; bovine; flaccid; gross; swarming; fresh-bitten; floating; putrefying; snake-bitten; swollen; miserable; mutilated; handsome; lifeless; rascally; partly-devoured; warm; bleeding; frozen; corrupt; bloody.

verbs
bury—; cast out—; drape—; drop—; glut —; hide—; mutilate—; prostrate—; rend —; reveal—; scatter —s; suspend—; tear —; tread upon—; —decays; —decomposes; —disintegrates; —putrefies; —rots.
(See body, frame.)

CARD
adjectives (calling)
ill-judged; official; engraved; neatly-typed; attention-compelling.

CARD
adjectives (playing)
best; false; winning; shuffled; precious; worn; greasy; stacked.

verbs

arrange —s; box —s; cheat at —s; draw —; flash—; gather —s; introduce —s; mark —s; pack —s; perforate—; shuffle —s; stack —s; stake —s; stencil —s; throw up —s; trump—; wager on —s; —s allot; —designates; —slides; —slips; —warrants.

CARDINAL
(bird)

adjectives
brilliant-plumaged; crested; flitting; music-flooding; regal; scarlet-flashing; sun-reflecting; pine-homing.

verbs
cage—; tame—; —plumes; —whistles.
(See bird.)

CARE

adjectives
scientific; secret; degrading; unhappy; reverential; dull; business; public; sincere; harassing; artistic; dismal; ill-reputed; wasting; fastidious; considerate; domestic; humbler; stimulating; carping; patient; unquiet; paternal; medical; ministering; nice; meanest; gigantic; thoughtful; bounteous; sharp; fatherly; elaborate; watchful; timely; indefatigable; peculiar; jealous; anxious; cankering; institutional; painstaking; tender; sufficient; chary; honest; reverent; fearful; scrupulous; rankling; loving; never-ceasing; heavy; sleepless; grisly; meticulous; considerable; fostering; wrinkled; persistent; efficient; extreme; municipal; tell-tale; providential; sympathetic; ignoble; wearying; warlike; chief; overpowering; conscientious; earth-born; practical; untuned; unremitting; apparitional; scrutinizing; eating; arduous; fevered; conquered; alliterative; preventive; utmost; prodigious; perpetual; silent; commonplace; judicious; self-intrusted; mortal; same; knowing; vexing; heavy; particular; gnawing; magnificent; altruistic; reverent; pale; touching; loving; consumptive; excellent; shallow; pastoral; intrusive; daintiest; prudent; exaggerated; vigilant; infinite; special; unusual; foreboding; exacting; sinful; late; surgical; maternal; miserable; sheltering; sordid; rigid; pitying; colossal; intensive; queenly; distracting; peremptory; ancient; religious; studious; sedulous; solicitous; protective; hospitable; exquisite; admirable; tender; expert; rooted; squalid; searing; wrinkling; stern; ageless; minute; tireless; human; pressing; deliberate; visible; foolish; constant; inevitable; unctuous; inadequate; masterly; incessant; patriarchal.

verbs
abolish—; banish—; bend with—; bestow —upon; brood with—; charge with—of; choke with—; conduct with—; delegate—of; demand—; deride—; devote—to; discharge —s; disclaim—; drive away—; droop with —; drown—; dull with—; ease—; escape —; exempt from—; exercise—; foster with —; free from—; fret with—; harass with —; heal —s; intrust—of; kill —s; lavish— upon; lay aside—; lift —s; load with—; lose —s; merit—; observe—; oppress with —; overcome with—; perform with—; redouble—; relax—; release from—; rest from —; rout—; shake off—; share —s; soothe —s; sour with—; twist with—; unload —s; wash away—; waste with—; weigh down with—; wrack with—; wring with—; yoke with—; —ceases; —s chafe; —s consume; —s linger; —perplexes; —pursues; furrow with—.
(See concern, anxiety, worry, caution.)

CARE (*v*)

adverbs
particularly; hardly; assiduously; violently; chiefly; scientifically; reverentially; artistically; patiently; paternally; medically; bounteously; indefatigably; jealously; anxiously; painstakingly; tenderly; sufficiently; scrupulously; never-ceasingly; meticulously; efficiently; conscientiously; unremittingly; arduously; magnificently; providently; touchingly; prudently; exaggeratedly; surgically; maternally; religiously; studiously; sedulously; solicitously; hospitably; exquisitely; expertly; patriarchally; domestically.
(See worry.)

CAREER

adjectives
decent; brilliant; military; creative; sterile; medical; hard-working; subsequent; honorable; prosperous; notable; checkered; literary; wasted; remarkable; tremulous; serene; cinematic; philanthropic; ill-starred; unblemished; generous; victorious; adequate; kind; unsentimental; stormy; eventual; buoyant; editorial; distinguished; definite; uninterrupted; artistic; academical; parliamentary; changed; rough; terrible; desperate; horrible; riotous; laboring; dignified; forceful; wandering; martial; theatrical; inglorious; unwearied; conjugal; pale; rollicking; joyous; diplomatic; coarse; low; anti-social; recognized; remorseless; official; political; placid; dazzling; wild; agitated; tragic; unscrupulous; clerical; independent; legal; triumphant; mercantile; honest; pro-

fessional; obscure; shameful; disastrous; unadvanced; unswerving; irresistible; journalistic; heavenly; active; normal; marvelous; termagant; bloody; picturesque; celibate; hapless; saintly; inspiring; fluctuating; celebrated; astonishing; story-book; startling; extraordinary; exceptional; amazing; incredible; meteoric; budding; illustrious; clean; vivid; noted; imposing; sensible; fine; assured; magnificent; promising; serious; versatile; invincible; famous; portentous; spectacular; dramatic; sensational; eventful; colorful; breathless; adventuresome; exciting; arduous; quick; tempestuous; mad; extravagant; challenging; tumultuous; controversial; erratic; servile; turbulent; disturbed; revolutionary; happy; rollicking; blithe; disappointing; lonely; hopeless; lively; active; busy; vicious; infamous; strange; tormented; brutal; enigmatic; seafaring; forensic; golfing; burdened; moneymaking; pleasurable; public; scholastic; college; peripatetic; discomforting; scientific; posthumous; brief; true; indecorous; sufficient; chosen; diverging; material; limited; glittering; fixed; fortuitous; penitential; subsequent; prone.

verbs
achieve—; aspire to—; blast—; carve out —; checker—; close—; commence—; crown —; date—; embark on—; embrace—; endanger—; enter upon—; enthrall by—; further—; jeopardize—; litter—; mar—; mark —; pursue—; renounce—; smash—; stunt —; terminate—; unfold—; wreck—.
(See achievement, course, life, profession.)

CAREFUL
adverbs
prudently; vigilantly; alertly; attentively; meticulously; extremely; particularly; intelligently; scrupulously; conscientiously; decorously; dutifully; obediently; admirably; thoughtfully; deliberately; ridiculously; significantly; comfortingly; considerately; warily; cautiously; absolutely; energetically; definitely; discreetly; wisely; singularly; strangely; sagacously; expertly; nervously; unduly; characteristically; naturally; usually; laughably; uneasily; elaborately; unobtrusively; satisfactorily; exaggeratedly; habitually; fastidiously; solicitously; sedulously; unusually; infinitely; lovingly; prodigiously; indefatigably.

CARELESS
adverbs
inexcusably; nonchalantly; casually; gaily; airily; indecently; recklessly; wantonly; vexatiously; irritatingly; amusingly; laughably; imprudently; indiscreetly; dangerously; perilously; significantly; noticeably; heedlessly; thoughtlessly; deliberately; indifferently; inconsiderately; unwarily; irresponsibly; absolutely; lazily; idly; unaccountably; inexplicably; impossibly; listlessly; languidly; defiantly; rebelliously; ostentatiously; flauntingly; stupidly.

CARELESSNESS
adjectives
aristocratic; criminal; elaborate; assumed; habitual; inveterate; idle; lovable; studied; superb; unpardonable; willful; culpable; deliberate.

verbs
berate—; breed—; condone—; countenance —; decry—; denounce—; inculcate—; inveigh against—; neglect in—; occasion—; punish—; regret—; resent—; utter in—; warn against—; wear an air of—; — disturbs; —worries.
(See neglect.)

CARESS
adjectives
condescending; complacent; fond; final; gentle; hasty; haughty; impulsive; impassioned; perfunctory; sympathetic; mesmeric; bitter-sweet; adolescent; dizzying; monotonous; turbulent; vicarious; exploratory; casual; mellowing; playful; sustained; infinite; indescribable; fierce; pussy-cat; rude; vague.

verbs
bestow —es on; cherish —es; countenance —es; delight in —es; encourage —es; favor with —es; fondle—; hunger for —es; intermix with —es; invite —es; long for —es; overwhelm with —es; ward off —; welcome —; —es allure; —es burn; —es cheer; —es endear; —es offend; —es soothe.
(See embrace, kiss, flattery.)

CARESS (v)
adverbs
endearingly; ecstatically; adoringly; sympathetically; warmly; lovingly; roughly; thrillingly; imploringly; affectionately; blissfully.
(See embrace, kiss, court.)

CAREWORN
adverbs
irritably; distressingly; intolerably; uncomfortably; dejectedly; sadly; anxiously; wretchedly; grievously; miserably; pitiably;

horribly; sorely; sorrily; heartbreakingly; unbearably; piteously; bitterly; dismally; hopelessly; unutterably; tragically; extremely; incredibly; gravely; outrageously; **indescribably.**

adjectives
guarded; guilty; indifferent; precious; smuggled; surreptitious; undeclared; worthless.

verbs
burden with—; dampen—; discharge—; disinfect—; haul—; hoist—; import—; inspect —; insure—; land—; levy on—; load—; salvage—; ship—; tax—; transport—; underwrite—; —ballasts; —weighs.
(See freight, load, burden.)

CARNAL
adverbs
loosely; sensually; intemperately; luxuriously; voluptuously; grossly; shamelessly; wantonly; rakishly; bestially; erotically; indecently; self-indulgently; dissipatedly; intemperately; licentiously; coarsely; unbelievably; obscenely; evilly; sinfully; vilely; detestably; odiously.

CAROL
adjectives
gay; haunting; joyous; lively; merry; rustic; round; ancient; swelling; warbled.

verbs
bellow—; bless in—; burst into—; celebrate with —s; chorus—; compose—; dance to—; exercise—; flute—; hallow—; join in—; listen to —s; practise—; praise—; revive —; scream—; warble—; —cheers; —encourages; —expresses; —rings out; —sounds; —survives; —warms.
(See song, hymn.)

CAROUSE (v)
adverbs
hilariously; drunkenly; sordidly; squalidly; riotously; viciously; rollickingly; tumultuously; turbulently; wildly.
(See drink, celebrate.)

CARPENTER
adjectives
village; rare; retired; veteran.

verbs
employ—; hire—; —bevels; —chisels; —constructs; —designs; —frames; —hammers; —joins; —labors; —levels; —mea-

sures; —molds; —mortises; —notches; —s organize; —pins; —rules; —sands; —saws; —smooths; —tenons; —tails; —wedges.
(See worker, workman.)

CARPET
adjectives
sumptuous; grassy; mossy; wind-woven; flaunty; matted; frayed; brilliant; swampy; varicolored; taupe; worn; dusty; odorous; dirty; heavy; gay; stair; soft; suspended; treacherous; patternless; fiber; deep-pile; thick; handsome; bright; eye-offending.

verbs
dance on—; design—; dust—; fringe—; kneel on—; litter—; market—; match—; patch—; prostrate on—; scour—; shampoo —; shred—; spread on—; strew on—; tack down—; warp—; weave—; —beautifies; —covers; —decorates; —protects; —shields; —slides.
(See fabric, rug.)

CARRIAGE
(manner)
adjectives
military; dashing; haughty; vigorous; graceful; violent; reckless; frank; toiling; unbending; indifferent; picturesque; internal; fierce; unpretentious; gentle; courteous; reverend; elegant; exquisite; superb; certain; sedate; fine; dignified; stately; soldierly; upright; erect; insolent; intelligent; swaggering; unwieldly; faulty; obstinate; headstrong; peculiar; sanctimonious.

CARRIAGE
(vehicle)
adjectives
imperial; rough; decent; elegant; horseless; lumbering; travelling; countless; handsome; heavy; painted; lurching; wooden-wheeled; ramshackle; musty; moldy; rickety.

verbs
bar—; burden—; dispatch—; draw—; fashion—; guard—; guide—; harness—; load—; ornament—; provide—; tow—; wheel out —; —accommodates; —bounces; —conveys; —jolts; —rattles; —rocks; —rolls; —rumbles; —sways; —transports; —winds its way.
(See car, vehicle, coach.)

CARRION
adjectives
foolish; unsavory; putrefied.

CARRY (v)
adverbs
imperfectly; occasionally; triumphantly;

habitually; surreptitiously; imperceptibly; valiantly; ultimately; infallibly; delicately; laboriously; unfalteringly; accommodatingly; unconsciously; jauntily; continuously; unanimously; infallibly; slavishly; penitently; ostentatiously.
(See convey, bear, transport.)

CART

adjectives
creaking; retreating; fatal; ungainly; heavy; laden; shabby; jaunty.

verbs
direct—; draw—; grease—; harness to—; harvest with—; license—; load—; mount —; operate—; peddle on—; pile in—; provide—; team—; traverse by—; wheel—; —clatters; —conveys; —creaks; —jolts; —looms; —pitches; —progresses; —rumbles; —wheels.
(See vehicle, truck.)

CARTOON

adjectives
animated; completed; contemporary; much-remarked.

CARTOON (v)

adverbs
derisively; animatedly; sarcastically; satirically; diplomatically; viciously; humorously; blisteringly.
(See picture, design.)

adjectives • CARTOONIST
ribald; clever.

verbs
—attacks; —caricatures; —characterizes; —colors; —conceives; —contributes; —copies; —crystallizes; —denotes; —designs; —distorts; —draws, —engages in; —exaggerates; —executes; —illustrates; —implies; —indulges in; —irritates; —lampoons; —misrepresents; —mocks; —offends; —prints; —qualifies; —represents; —sets forth; —supplies; —sways; —wields.
(See artist.)

CARTRIDGE

adjectives
blank; buck-shot; cylindrical; deadly; highly-charged; inflammable; trusty; hoarded.

verbs
arm with —s; belt —s; box —s; case —s; distribute —s; fit—; form into—; ignite—; insert—; load with—; provide—; replenish —s; shape—; store—; —bursts; —detonates; —explodes; —penetrates.

CARVE (v)

adverbs
curiously; richly; marvelously; elaborately; skillfully; exquisitely; delicately; ornately; cunningly; ingeniously; fantastically; medievally; wearily.
(See sculpture, engrave, fashion.)

CARVING

adjectives
elaborate; fantastic; relief; grotesque; intricate; salvaged; weatherworn; delicate; splendid; flat; ornamental; hand; exquisite; artistic; ill-favored; medieval.

verbs
adorn with—; auction off—; destroy—; discover—; display—; embellish with—; exhibit—; fret with—; ornament with—; skill in—; unearth—; —hardens; —lasts; —illustrates.
(See sculpture, art.)

CASCADE

adjectives
foaming; perpetual; shimmering; feathery; pearly; motionless; veritable; gushing; showy; dazzling; musical; enthusiastic; blonde; roaring; tossing; magnificent.

verbs
lose in—; surmount—; sweep over—; —churns; —descends; —erodes; —falls; —foams; —pours over; —roars; —rumbles; —thunders.
(See waterfall.)

CASCADE (v)

adverbs
sibilantly; foamingly; perpetually; shimmeringly; gushingly; dazzlingly; roaringly; magnificently; awesomely; spectacularly.

CASE
(box)
adjectives
huge; packing; worn; oblong; odd-shaped; platinum; ponderous; concrete; jeweled; venerable-looking; tarnished.

verbs
buckle on—; ease—; frame in—; loose—; peel off—; strap on—; strip off—; unclasp —; —covers; —protects; —shields.
(See sheath, box, chest.)

CASE
(legal term)
adjectives
arguable; trying; contested; noted; curious; pending; simple; celebrated; criminal; collateral; disputed; brilliant; trivial; hope-

less; analogous; unaccountable; hardened; pathetic; exceptional; idiopathic; inexplicable; celebrated; pressing.

verbs
advise upon—; assign to—; bring—to trial; clinch—; conduct—; confer on—; contend with—; dispose of—; expedite—; fashion—; frame—; handle—; injure—; judge—; peruse—; plead—; prejudice—; present—; prove—; recount—; rest—; reverse—; review—; support—; sway—; testify in—; try —; unravel—; —hangs fire; —proves.

CASE
adjectives (medical term)
virulent; incurable; chronic; grave; critical; abnormal; dangerous; surgical.

verbs
cure—; diagnose—; encounter—; improve —; isolate—; protract—; relieve—; remedy —; succumb to—; treat—; —occurs; —recovers; —yields.
(See disease.)

CASE
adjectives (situation)
flattering; excellent; exceptional; important; striking; clear; conspicuous; rare; factual; difficult; intricate; severe; complicated; overwhelming; diverse; notable; eminent; necessitous; simplified; weird; inevitable; outrageous; analagous; stubborn; notorious; absurd; inevitable; insoluble; unpardonable; convincing; speculative; twisted; discussed; common; definite; desperate; recent; important; laughable; isolated; sole; parlous; pathetic; extreme; unforeseen; aggravated; deceptive; illustrative; lamentable; specific; evident; authentic; perplexing; superfluous; blessed; parallel; handsome; falsified; battle-scarred; imaginary; unrecognized; well-prepared; remarkable; mournful; special; pitiful; innumerable (pl); suppositious; sporadic; selective (pl); extraordinary; meritorious; multifarious (pl).

CASEMENT
adjectives
clasping; ivied; shaded; rattling; glimmering; ill-shut; oriel; wide; magic.

CASH
adjectives
evanescent; ample; pitiless; unquestionable;

predatory; leaking; safe; cold; ambrosial; immediate.
verbs
amass—; appropriate—; check—; convert into—; demand—; discount for—; forward —; guard—; hoard—; involve—; register —; release—; secure—; transact with—; turn into—; —circulates; —flows through; —pours in.
(See coin, currency, money.)

CASKET
adjectives
precious; handsome; bronze; wrought; imposing; leaden; contrary; inlaid; glorious; draped; guiltless; scaly.

verbs
bank—; bless—; cache—; conceal—; decorate—; discover—; encrust—with; enrich—with; entrust—to; file past—; inter in—; lay in—; lower—; mourn at—; penetrate —; rob—; unearth—; unlock—; value—; —reveals.
(See box, chest, coffin.)

CAST
adjectives (drama)
capable; supporting; remarkable; insignificant; mythical; revengeful; fiery; fantastic; medieval; morbid; heterogeneous; desperate; undramatic; frivolous; stony.

verbs
allot to—; annoy—; applaud—; assemble —; assign to—; bestow on—; bring together —; choose—; coach—; congratulate—; direct—; dismiss—; dominate—; introduce—; manipulate—; provide—; recruit—; ruffle —; scan—; select—; train—; try out for—; —bows; —disbands; —impresses; —justifies; —mutilates; —performs; —produces; —rehearses; —renders.
(See actors.)

CAST
adjectives (glance)
pensive; pinkish; determined; wistful; meditative; wonted; somber; pale; mirthful; changeful.

CAST (v)
adverbs
rashly; humbly; weakly; demurely; bluntly; pensively; determinedly; wistfully; meditatively; somberly; mirthfully.
(See hurl, throw, fling.)

CASTANETS
adjectives
clicking; distant; jittering; rhythmic; noisy.

CASTAWAY

adjectives

lonely; assembled (pl); starving; lean; cadaverous; despairing; frantic; gaunt.

CASTE

adjectives

learned; distinct; priestly; inconvenient; sacerdotal; perpetual; ethic; transparent; time-honored.

verbs

ally with—; define—; distinguish—; forfeit —; form—; found—; isolate—; loathe—; organize—; preside over—; privilege—; qualify for—; restrict—; revile—; unite—; weld—; —aggregates; —collects; —confines to; —excludes; —groups; —practices; —inhabits; —resembles; —serves; —succumbs.
(See class, rank.)

CASTIGATION

adjectives

heartening; malicious; soul-deadening; deserved.

CASTLE

adjectives

ruined; haughty; baronial; ancient; Moorish; huge; grim; serviceable; razed; shimmering; inconvenient; ancestral; dream; medieval; moated; fairy; grandiose; princely; formidable; bastioned; ruined; cloud; stuccoed; enchanted; moldering; stupendous.

verbs

abide in—; assail—; bar—; besiege—; dominate—; dwell in—; fly to—; force—; ransack—; sack—; storm—; undermine—; —crumbles; —decays; —quakes; —shadows; —topples; —yields.
(See fortress, stronghold, mansion, building.)

CASTOR OIL

adjectives

disgusting; disguised; healing; malignant; nauseating; stomach-turning; skillfully-administered; repulsive; viscous.

verbs

administer— —; capsule— —; decoct— —; dose with— —; employ— —; express— —; inject— —; — —aggravates; — —cleans; — —induces; — —loosens; — —lubricates; — —nauseates; — —purges; — —relieves.
(See oil.)

CASUAL

adverbs

charmingly; nonchalantly; habitually; coolly; presumably; indeterminately; usually; provokingly; vexatiously; vaguely; perplexingly; unfortunately; undoubtedly; absolutely; positively; heartbreakingly; insufferably; intolerably.

CASUALNESS

adjectives

charming; practiced; hushed; lacerating; easy.

CASUALTY

adjectives

unforeseen; distressing; unlooked-for.

CAT

adjectives

clawing; long; tawny; enigmatic; gaunt; watchful; two-faced; ubiquitous; stray; sleek; despicable; huge; Persian; sinuous; predatory; singed; staid; spitting; plump; slinking; suspicious; cold; slow-witted; round-eyed; mewing; quick; harmless; contented; calculating; tiger; musing; lemon; sheltered; homeless; foiled; prudent.

verbs

pet—; stroke—; —arches; —claws; —climbs; —clutches; —darts; —devours; —laps; —leaps; —licks; —meows; —paws; —purrs; —preys on; —slinks; —sniffs; —sprawls; —springs; —washes.
(See animal, kitten.)

CATACOMB

adjectives

vaulted; literary; secret; large.

CATALOGUE

adjectives

descriptive; endless; illustrated; dry; melancholy; amplest; technical; diabolical; wearying; complete; seasonal; beautiful.

verbs

choose from—; clarify—; compile—; edit—; enter in—; index—; insert in—; issue—; list in—; order from—; prepare—; print —; publish—; set up—; —advertises; —confuses; —describes; —enumerates; —explains; —fascinates; —features; —lists; offers; —pictures; —prices; —registers; —systematizes.
(See list, record.)

CATAPULT

adjectives
deadly; powerful; regulated; vicious; well-aimed.

verbs
discharge—; draw—; fire—; gear—; invent—; lay siege with —s; manipulate—; release—; storm with —s; —batters; —bombards; —damages; —harms; —hurls; —overcomes; —propels; —stones.
(See cannon.)

CATARACT

adjectives
shining; superb; sounding; roaring; earthquaking; fiery; remorseless; smoky; pouring; opaque; tireless; foaming.

verbs
lose in—; spout —s; stem—; view—; —churns; —crashes; —dashes down; —descends; —falls; —flashes; —foams; —leaps; —pours over; —precipitates; —roars; —rumbles; —rushes over; —surges; —sweeps down; —wears away.
(See waterfall, flood, cascade.)

CATASTROPHE

adjectives
tremendous; awful; imminent; historical; welcome; dire; impending; tragic; inevitable; general; calamitous; world-wide; ironical; picturesque; national; unexpected; crowning; unavertable; overwhelming; breath-taking; dreadful; unforeseen.

verbs
avert—; culminate in—; experience—; inflict with—; mourn—; plunge into—; result in—; rush to—; suffer—; survive—; —distresses; —looms; —overwhelms; —shocks; —threatens.
(See disaster, misfortune.)

CATASTROPHIC

adverbs
tragically; unmitigatedly; disastrously; extremely; ruinously; ominously; significantly; appallingly; deplorably; staggeringly; unspeakably; extraordinarily; shockingly; absolutely; unfortunately; unluckily; calamitously; incredibly; gravely; direly.

CATCH

adjectives
meager; passionate; little; obstinate; remarkable; maximum; uncommon; attractive.

CATCH (fishing)

adjectives
boasted; briny; exaggerated; gleaming; meager; modest; silvery; scaly; thrilling; traditional.

verbs
acquire—; bait—; devour—; display—; ensnare—; exhibit—; lure—; market—; net —; prepare—; prize—; relish—; scale—; transport—; value—; —amazes; —disappoints; —impresses; —increases.

CATCH (v)

adverbs
unceremoniously; impulsively; instinctively; convulsively; mechanically; red-handedly; charmingly; inadvertently; essentially; unerringly; passionately; obstinately; remarkably.
(See seize, clasp, clutch.)

CATCHER (baseball)

adjectives
adroit; alert; courageous; clumsy; befuddled; dependable; fumbling; unpredictable.

verbs
—blocks; —covers; —encourages; —fumbles; —misses; —muffs; —recovers; —signals; —steadies; —tags.

CATCHING

adverbs
highly; easily; dangerously; epidemically; pestilentially; unfortunately; acutely; widely; perilously; seriously; extremely; decidedly; unquestionably; astonishingly; frightfully; absolutely; remarkably; alarmingly; curiously; awfully; critically; definitely; fatally; positively.

CATCHY

adverbs
irresistibly; sweetly; indefinably; mysteriously; luckily; unutterably; powerfully; singularly; charmingly; engagingly; undeniably; bewitchingly; enchantingly; delightfully; daintily; smartly; jauntily; youthfully; tormentingly; teasingly; hauntingly; unexpectedly; surprisingly; genuinely; miraculously; luckily; unprecedentedly.

CATEGORICAL

adverbs
positively; undeniably; avowedly; broadly; certainly; emphatically; explicitly; formally; markedly; peremptorily; solemnly; reliably; authentically; axiomatically; evidently; manifestly; undoubtedly; indisputably;

irrefutably; solidly; soundly; unmistakably; uncomfortably; conclusively; gratefully; cheeringly; disturbingly; dogmatically.

CATEGORY

adjectives
amiable; poetic; astonishing; definite; separate; neat; depressing; reasonable; odious; scholastic.

verbs
add to—; bring into—; disagree with—; discard—; exclude from—; express in—; group in—; interest in—; list in—; recognize—; reduce to—; regard—; relegate to —; understand—; upset—; —consists of; — deals with; —derives from; —differs from; —includes; —represents.
(See class, division, condition, predicament.)

CATER (v)

adverbs
exclusively; delectably; democratically; professionally; amiably; commonly; stealthily; unaccountably.
(See provide, supply, furnish.)

CATERPILLAR

adjectives
bristly; evil-horned; fuzzy; harmless; inching; plushy; sojourning; whither-bent.

verbs
combat —s; cultivate —s; examine—; exterminate—; infest with —s; observe—; spray —s; teem with —s; —s abound; —s attack; —s bore into; —s collect; —crawls; —despoils; —devours; —emerges; —s gather; —hibernates; —s invade; —s molt; —s ravage; —secretes; —spins a cocoon.
(See insect.)

CATHEDRAL

adjectives
Gothic; Doric; staid; sleepy; dim; mystic; peaceful; medieval; miniature; quaint; magnificent; majestic; unfinished; elaborate; spacious; Roman.

verbs
approach—; congregate in—; construct—; design—; erect—; explore—; found—; glorv in—; hallow—; install in—; preside over —; pour from—; raise—; revere—; worship at—; —awes; —echoes; —impresses; —induces; —inspires; —looms; —shadows; —towers.
(See church, tabernacle.)

CATHOLIC

adverbs (general sense)
broadly; comprehensively; unusually; prevalently; magnanimously; remarkably; liberally; comfortably; generally; decently; sagaciously; intelligently; admirably; reasonably; generously; dependably; charitably; intellectually; discerningly; perceptively; obviously; manifestly; nobly; unselfishly.

CATTLE

adjectives
blooded; grazing; crazed; unkempt; roving; peaceful; scraggy; weak; driven; fine; drowsy; stolen; bedded; wild; long-horned; bartered; mottled; reclining; tainted; lazy; sweltered; murrained; domesticated; meanest; draught; thin.

verbs
corral—; dehorn—; exchange for—; infect —; market—; raise—; slaughter—; stampede—; tend—; tether—; —bellow; —freeze; —graze; —huddle; —low; —pasture; —plod; —roam; —stagger.
(See animal.)

CAUSATION

adjectives
natural; eternal; inevitable.

CAUSE

adjectives (agent or reason)
abundant; scattered (pl); obnoxious; specific; proximate; predisposing; pressing; apparent; fundamental; hopeless; unavoidable; immediate; prolific; duplicating; rational; dreadful; effective; underlying; mighty; noble; just; sacred; worthy; legitimate; endless; redeeming; supernatural; spectacular; apparent; assignable; faltering; secondary; physical; universal; growing; innocent; predominant; remote; unknown; scandalous; sensational; plausible; permanent; transient; fatal; potential; weighty; assignable; prominent; internal; erroneous; contributory; subjective; temperance; amorous; glorious; breaking; eternal; ultimate; paramount; unconscious; frequent; princely; philosophical; natural; mistaken; malignant; alleged; latent; discreditable; recorded; celebrated; sordid; economic; primeval; mitigating; constitutional; sensible; ennobling; determining; mechanical; infallible; propelling; hated; secondary; obvious; habitual; minute; idiotic; antecedent; justifiable; primal; creative; irritating; efficient; unkind; notable; unwitting; extraneous; lawful; unaccountable; identical; ex-

citing; worthy; immoral; functional; vanquished; multifarious (pl); impious; trivial; sublunary; artificial; ridiculous; everlasting; similar; righteous.

verbs

acquaint with—; advance—; allege—; appraise—; approach—; ascertain—; ascribe —to; assign—; attach—; attribute—to; concern with—; cure—; deal with—; debate—; declare—; define—; demonstrate—; determine—; discover—; display—; dwell upon —; eliminate—; eradicate—; estimate—; explain—; fathom—; inquire into—; judge —; laugh at—; obliterate—; obviate—; overcome—; perceive—; procure—; regard —; relieve—; remand—; remove—; report —; reveal—; reverse—; rue—; seek—; serve as—; state—; strike at—; suggest—; surmise—; suspect—; trace—to; weigh—; —prevails; —resides in.

(See reason, motive, source, origin.)

CAUSE

adjectives   (aim, principle, movement)
adopted; alien; championed; espoused; glorious; lost; noble; sacred; undying.

verbs

adopt—; advocate—; approve—; betray—; bolster—; bow to—; champion—; cleave to —; contribute to—; defame—; desert—; devote to—; die for—; do ill to—; embrace —; encourage—; engage in—; enlist in—; espouse—; favor—; forsake—; further—; guide—; harm—; injure—; interpret—; justify—; labor for—; maintain—; misinterpret—; pay tribute to—; persecute—; plead—; praise—; promote—; rally to—; scorn—; serve—; speak for—; sponsor—; spurn—; struggle for—; suffer for—; sunder—; support—; transgress—; tread—under foot; unbraid—; vindicate—; withdraw from—; —perishes; —prospers; —suffers; —triumphs.

(See aim, principle, movement.)

CAUSE (v)

adverbs

inadvertently; noxiously; specifically; fundamentally; apparently; unavoidably; rationally; legitimately; supernaturally; spectacularly; physically; universally; predominantly; fatally; potentially; subjectively; eternally; ultimately; philosophically; malignantly; allegedly; mechanically; infallibly; unaccountably; artificially; righteously.

(See induce, effect.)

CAUSTIC

adverbs

bitterly; unpardonably; unreasonably; mildly; maliciously; hatefully; sharply; acrimoniously; cruelly; brutally; atrociously; resentfully; venomously; ominously; needlessly; incisively; sarcastically; ironically; cunningly; mercilessly; churlishly; unsparingly; perversely; abusively; uncivilly; intolerably; captiously; obnoxiously; unbearably; tauntingly; unwisely; malevolently; unwontedly; habitually; unwarrantably; disagreeably; unpleasantly.

CAUTION

adjectives

superfluous; common; vast; habitual; infinite; singular; subtle; inborn; abominable; timid; commendable; puerile; conscientious; wonted; just; extraordinary; prudent; preliminary; unholy; philosophic; extreme; losing; intended; vigilant; necessary; worldly; superior; redoubled; stealthy; reverent; niggardly; beneficent; utmost; curious; patriotic; friendless.

verbs

advise—; deaden—; exercise—; heed—; indicate—; inspire—; lessen—; motivate by —; necessitate—; perform with—; proceed with—; sound a note of—; throw—to the winds; —safeguards; —wanes.

(See prudence, care.)

CAUTIOUS

adverbs

discreetly; prudently; wisely; significantly; ludicrously; suspiciously; habitually; singularly; unnecessarily; timidly; extraordinarily; alertly; stealthily; curiously; strangely; oddly; outlandishly; sagaciously; expertly; deftly; foolishly; unwontedly; nervously; excitedly; idiotically; incomprehensibly; queerly; cravenly; faintheartedly; genuinely; unduly; inexplicably; laughably; characteristically; gravely; uneasily; extravagantly; elaborately; quietly; unobtrusively; undoubtedly; inherently.

CAVALCADE

adjectives

straggling; grim; martial; scampering; gorgeous; furbished; infinite; brilliant; large.

CAVALIER

adjectives

attentive; boyish; tall; gallant; bold; comely; free; sprightly; deformed; stout-hearted; effeminate; high-spirited; trusty; plumed; pretentious; victorious; arrogant; broken-down; gay; impecunious.

CAVALRY

adjectives

bedizened; best-mounted; thundering; foaming; dismounted; exploiting; dashing; irregular.

CAVE

adjectives

lonely; lovely; moonlit; dark; damp; stalactite; virtual; glistening; unexplored; enormous; ice; magical; winding; abandoned; unlighted; shore-cliff; fretted; destined; toothless; coral; forlorn; shadowy; unfathomed; tiny; deep; cold; yawning; unimagined; sapphire; vaulted; low-browed; monstrous; dewy; gloomy; spacious; coastal.

verbs

abandon—; bar—; block—; bury in—; crawl into—; creep into—; discover—; dwell in —; grope in—; harbor in—; inhabit—; issue from—; lodge in—; retire to—; roll from—; scoop out—; seal—; shelter in—; —echoes; —resounds.

(See hole, recess.)

CAVERN

adjectives

fairy-like; verdurous; dark; beautiful; marvelous; mysterious; ghostly; enormous; notchy; desolate; crystal; unfathomed; smudged; obscure; glaucous; horrid; smoky; dusky; ominous; spacious; tongueless; rifted; sparry; precipitous; gloomy; gelid; mossy; inaccessible; scorched; murmuring.

CAVERNOUS

adverbs

darkly; dimly; vastly; mysteriously; alluringly; deeply; dangerously; alarmingly; irresistibly; fantastically; gloomily; obscurely; duskily; murkily; sombrely; astonishingly; marvellously; frighteningly; indistinctly; strangely; terribly; hideously; formidably; awfully.

CAVITY

adjectives

dark; dungeon-like; hideous; conical.

verbs

cap—; dilate—; drain—; drill—; empty—; fill—; grind—; irrigate—; line—; obliterate —; tap—; treat—; —contains; —weakens.

(See hole, cave, hollow, excavation.)

CAVORT (v)

adverbs

blithely; friskily; gaily; spiritedly; joyously; sportively; grotesquely; gracefully; idiotically; pleasingly.

CEASE (v)

adverbs

functionally; abruptly; presently; suddenly; definitely; temporarily; prematurely; entirely; eventually.

(See discontinue, stop, refrain.)

CEDAR

adjectives

spicy; stunted; gray-sheathed; pyramiding; tall; slim; fantastic; distorted; stately; lordly; vast; majestic; somnolent; dark; mighty; drooping.

CEDE (v)

adverbs

superfluously; entirely; willingly; temporarily; outwardly; prematurely; partially.

(See surrender, relinquish, grant.)

CEILING

adjectives

beamed; frescoed; gorgeous; lofty; gilded; festooned; clouded; vault-like; fallen; damp; stained; crumbling; grimy; dirty; arched; slanting; sagging; dingy; domelike; moulded; ornamented; pictured; sloped; mirrored; reflecting.

CELEBRATE (v)

adverbs

hilariously; painfully; pompously; traditionally; obstreperously; appropriately; dissolutely; justly; discreetly; jubilantly; enthusiastically; dramatically; elaborately; barbarously; deliberately; raucously; gorgeously; nationally.

(See commemorate, observe.)

CELEBRATED

adverbs

locally; justly; universally; eminently; notably; illustriously; nationally; genuinely; rightfully; appropriately; brilliantly; remarkably; exceptionally; fitly; especially; particularly.

CELEBRATION

adjectives

discreet; jubilant; enthusiastic; centenary; forthcoming; final; dramatic; flourished; bicentenary; misconstrued; elaborate; decennial; gaudy; monster; roaring; barbarous; deliberate; raucous; gory; gorgeous.

verbs
arrange for—; climax—; deserve—; disturb
—; enter—; extol—; fete with—; hold—;
indulge in—; launch—; observe—; plan—;
retain—; —commemorates; —exhausts; —
honors; —overjoys; —surprises.
(See observance.)

CELEBRITY
adjectives
half-forgotten; rare; permanent; cosmopolitan; revered; glittering; dead; contemporary; available; innumerable (pl);
continental; immediate; literary; envious;
frustrated; fastidious; world-wide; posthumous.

CELERITY
adjectives
swift; amazing; deft; surprising; indescribable; dramatic; magical; characteristic;
reckless; miraculous; incredible; rounded;
admirable; ingenious.

CELERY
adjectives
crunchy; crisp; green; curled.

CELL
adjectives
fungal; transition; sylvan; poor; mossy;
dermal; reflective; solitary; overcrowded;
photo-electric; filthy; drafty; narrow; tiny;
whitewashed; dingy; cement-floored; steel;
quiet; dreary; dismal; naked; cloistered;
eremitic; waxen; monastic; longitudinal;
convent; inmost; uncouth; unused; ambrosial; functional; albumenoid; wretched;
semi-transparent; prophetic; gloomy; uncomfortable; wind-rocked; message-sending;
tender; solemn; primordial; dungeon-like.

verbs
bind in—; brood in—; cloister in—; confine
in—; dwell in—; ensconce in—; force—;
gain—; imprison in—; lodge in—; pour
from—; range in—; remand to—; retire to
—; share—; store in—; track to—.
(See room, cavity, chamber.)

CELL
adjectives (biological)
amoebic; detached; enlarged; enemy; floating; gelatinous; malignant; normal; structural.

verbs
build —s; destroy —s; feed —s; motivate
—s; nourish —s; protect —s; regenerate
—s; renew —s; stimulate—; —s adhere to;

—s degenerate; —fulfills; —s increase; —s
multiply; —s perform; —shrivels; —specializes; —s store; —s work.
(See unit, compartment, blood.)

CELLAR
adjectives
dark; reeking; damp; fire-stopped; verminous; spacious; nether; dry; shallow; rat-
infested.

verbs
carpet—; convert—; cool in—; dampen—;
descend to—; drain—; emerge from—; enter by—; flood—; grope in—; inhabit—;
illumine—; lodge in—; stock in—; store in
—; —conceals; —extends.
(See basement, vault, room.)

CELLULOID
adjectives
brittle; explosive; flimsy; highly-inflam-
mable; inexpensive; pretentious; shining;
showy.

verbs
compose of—; derive from—; employ—; encase in—; manufacture—; mould—; polish
—; press—; season—; shape—; stain—;
turn—; utilize—; —covers; —cracks; —
imitates; —protects; —serves as; —shields;
—shrivels.
(See material.)

CEMENT
adjectives
crack-proof; grayish; impenetrable; marble;
plastic; protecting; resisting; tested; unyielding.

verbs
apply—; blast—; bore into—; calcine—;
coat with—; compact—; compound—; crush
—; grind—; lay—; mix—; slake—; surface
with—; —adheres; —binds; —clinkers; —
crumbles; —dehydrates; —glues; —hardens;
—secures; —sets; —solidifies; —walls in.
(See mortar, plaster.)

CEMENT (*v*)
adverbs
firmly; securely; fixedly; perpetually; eternally; enduringly; permanently.
(See join, fasten.)

CEMETERY
adjectives
walled; tiny; bleak; dismal; weed-grown;
desolate; neighboring; pauper.

CENSER

adjectives

floral; coveted; gilded; flame-like; smoking.

CENSOR

adjectives

royal; strict; sternest; formidable; official; prejudiced; incompetent.

verbs

assign to—; elect—; escape —s; moderate for —s; offend —s; submit to —s; —approves; —bans; —bars; —blames; —clamps down; —condemns; —criticizes; —cuts out; —examines; —exercises; —guards; —grants; —inquires; —inspects; —investigates; —judges; —preserves; —prohibits; —reviews; —slashes; —supervises; —torments.

(See critic.)

CENSORIOUS

adverbs

sharply; mercilessly; ominously; destructively; needlessly; venomously; invidiously; viciously; unsparingly; churlishly; snappishly; obnoxiously; unpleasantly; disagreeably; remorselessly; relentlessly; dryly; roughly; rudely; cleverly; spitefully; sarcastically; maliciously; malevolently; bitterly; ruthlessly; uncompromisingly.

CENSORSHIP

adjectives

moralistic; strict; recent; rigid; vague; effective; religious; powerful; insidious; official; actual; iron; voluntary; rigorous.

verbs

announce—; clamp down—; concoct—; enforce—; establish—; exercise—; impose—; indicate—; institute—; pass—; practise—; submit to—; tighten—; —cuts; —militates; —outlaws; —prevails; —slashes; —supervises; —suppresses.

(See superintendence, revision, criticism, censure.)

CENSURABLE

adverbs

seriously; unquestionably; exceptionally; lamentably; deplorably; deservedly; justly; avowedly; properly; strictly; fairly; unfortunately; unhappily; unluckily; obviously; manifestly; plainly; conspicuously; grievously.

CENSURE

adjectives

moral; heavy-handed; violent; declamatory; implicit; critical; reluctant; ecclesiastical; perpetual; just; erroneous; undeserved; awful; lewd; implied.

verbs

avoid—; cringe under—; endure—; escape —; incur—; smart under—; wag one's tongue in—; —abates; —looms; —repels; —threatens.

(See blame, disapproval, criticism, revision, censorship.)

CENSURE (*v*)

adverbs

morally; violently; critically; reluctantly; ecclesiastically; perpetually; undeservedly; impliedly; scornfully; gravely; captiously; freely; scathingly.

(See reprove, rebuke, upbraid.)

CENSUS

adjectives

national; biennial; previous; rough; partial.

CENTER

adjectives

musical; inspiring; nervous; spiritual; cultural; permanent; intellectual; exclusive; allied; important; residential; veritable; principal; information; overpopulated; dead; banking; distributing; key; trading; financial; industrial; bustling; civic; business; urban; railroad; unique; metropolitan; important; steamship; legislative; exact; religious; commercial; smart; creative; harmonious; congested; prosperous; subtle; dazzling; storm; enlightened; fashionable; remote; accessible; strategic; tessellated; eternal; relative.

verbs

balance at—; collect at—; converge toward —; diffuse from—; draw to—; emerge from —; fall toward—; form in—; gravitate toward—; group in—; intersect at—; move toward—; occupy—; proceed from—; radiate from—; revolve around—; root in—; throw off—.

(See middle.)

CENTRAL

adverbs

conveniently; acceptably; appropriately; diplomatically; advantageously; exactly; comfortably; satisfactorily; relatively; approximately; strategically; practically.

CENTRALIZATION

adjectives

elaborate; rigorous; bureaucratic; political; absorbing; hierarchical.

CENTURY

adjectives

populous; modern; countless (pl); tempestuous; romantic; untold; preceding; myriad (pl); glorious; previous; unborn; hoary; present; noiseless; stormy; arduous; brilliant; successive (pl); amusing; senile.

verbs

endure for —ies; fade into —ies; gild—; measure in —ies; span —ies; roll into—; — abounds in; —creeps past; —draws to an end; —elapses; —unwinds.

CEREAL

adjectives

nourishing; tempting; whole-grain; steaming; golden-wheat; farinaceous.

verbs

bleach—; combine—with; consume—; cultivate—; diet on—; exploit—; moisten—; prepare—; produce—; refine—; steam—; sweeten—; —comprises; —flourishes; —furnishes; —nourishes; —provides; —stimulates; —strengthens; —supplies.

(See grain.)

CEREBRUM

adjectives

divided; convalescent; convoluted; boiling; membrane-wrapped; throbbing; overlapping.

verbs

affect—; injure—; penetrate to—; —compacts; —comprises; —consists of; —controls; —files away; —forms; —is divided into; —is enveloped in; —presides over; —occupies; —overlaps; —regulates.

(See brain.)

CEREMONIAL

adjectives

voodoo; elaborate; fitting; impressive; quaint; stately; insignificant; rich; tiresome; pompous; compulsive; enormous; insulting; cumbrous; wailing; magnificent; frivolous; burdensome; overpowering; curious.

CEREMONIOUS

adverbs

admirably; devoutly; elaborately; meticulously; punctiliously; appropriately; highly; decorously; reverently; traditionally; properly; conventionally; magnificently; splendidly; royally; barbarically; impeccably; reverentially; beautifully; irreproachably; majestically; extravagantly; wondrously; superbly.

CEREMONY

adjectives

preparatory; customary; lawful; scant; whimsical; decent; curious; fetish-like; anointing; approaching; diabolical; bloody; dedicatory; solemn; picturesque; ancient; hazardous; occult; impressive; religious; elaborate; tedious; appalling; venerable; appropriate; outrageous; stately; somber; reverent; enforced; time-consecrated; incongruous; peculiar; inauguration; imposing; formal; august; notable; gracious; futile; melancholy; fantastic; colorful; calm; dignified; punctilious; grim; savage; icy; painful; superstitious; primitive; undue; funeral; final; outward; ritualistic; appointed.

verbs

beautify—; bore with—; endure—; enrich —; observe—; officiate at—; preserve—; ritualize—; shorten—; stand on—; wed with —; —commemorates; —drags; —entails; —honors; —ruffles.

(See rite, form, solemnity, formality, sacrament.)

CERTAIN

adverbs

actually; definitely; positively; absolutely; undeniably; assuredly; solidly; substantially; decisively; categorically; incontestably; irrefutably; conclusively; officially; plainly; indisputably; acceptably; unfortunately; unhappily; fortunately; luckily; humiliatingly; terribly; reasonably; comfortably; authoritatively.

CERTAINTY

adjectives

absolute; inevitable; old; humiliating; terrible; established; polite; painful; perfect; ultimate; unbreakable; considerable; simple; comfortable; practical; swift; astounding; reasonable; atrocious; dark; inevitable; instant; instinctive; automatic; positive; boyish; monumental; fierce; unerring; dead; towering.

verbs

accept as—; authenticate—; be born of—; confirm—; demonstrate with—; destroy—; inform of—; neglect—; postulate as—; question—; surrender to—; venture on—; verge on—; —relieves; —satisfies.

(See confidence, assurance, conviction, fact, truth.)

CERTIFICATE
adjectives
gilded; original; engraved; baptismal; round; marriage; laudatory; authenticated; sales.

verbs
attest by—; bear—; collect —s; confirm—; counterfeit—; dispense—s; esteem—; forge —; furnish with—; garner—s; issue—; register—; revoke—; seal—; suspend—; witness—; —assures; —authorizes; —certifies; —guarantees; —licenses; —restricts; — specifies; —testifies.

(See declaration, document, testimony.)

CERTITUDE
adjectives
reasonable; fresh; inward.

CESSATION
adjectives
sudden; entire; instant; negative; good-humored; gradual; complete; premature.

CHAFF
adjectives
mocking; antiquarian; absurd.

verbs
bear up—; beat out—; drive away—; fan—; flay out—; gather—; pick from—; scatter—; separate from—; sift out—; weed out—; winnow—; wipe away—; —flies away.

(See straw.)

CHAFF (v)
adverbs
banteringly; unmercifully; considerably; mockingly; excessively; humiliatingly; boisterously; bitterly; coquettishly; hostilely; enigmatically; frivolously.

(See banter, ridicule, jest.)

CHAGRIN
adjectives
natural; evident; universal; jealous; bitter; secret.

verbs
arouse—; conceal—; devour by—; display —; excite—; feel—; meet with—; observe —; profess—; smile away—; steep in—;

touch with—; —daunts; —fumes away; — suffuses; —waxes.

(See mortification, **vexation**, humiliation, confusion.)

CHAIN
adjectives
linked; secular; leash; endless; indissoluble; unbroken; firm; lengthening; household; ponderous; rattling; long-worn; mesh; nocturnal; clanking; winding; golden; flowery; galling; resplendent; multitudinous (pl); massive; continuous; impressive; feudal; adamantine; ascending; everlasting; dangling; countless (pl); gleaming; indivisible; bolted; door; bloody; glittering; rosy; trembling; human; roaring; shrieking; howling; jingling; hateful; shameful; curious; will-forged; stout; giant; relentless; binding; restraining; damaging; mental; intangible.

verbs
affix—; bind in —s; bolt—; burst—; condemn to —s; dally with—; deliver from —s; drag in —s; draw—; encircle with—; encompass in—; fasten—; file—; hedge —s about; knit—; link in—; loose —s; manacle in —s; pluck off —s; shake off —s; smite at—; strive in —s; tangle—; tighten —; unravel—; untwist—; wreathe in —s; —clanks; —engirdles; —falls off; —fetters; —rattles; —yields.

(See bond, shackle.)

CHAIN (v)
adverbs
ingloriously; secularly; indissolubly; unbrokenly; firmly; ponderously; everlastingly; indivisibly; stoutly; bindingly; relentlessly; restrainingly; intangibly.

(See restrain, fasten.)

CHAIR
adjectives
rocking; lounge; slim; worm-eaten; leather; pillowed; straight; glowing; prominent; swinging; covered; over-stuffed; cane-seated; long-legged; solitary; classic; rickety; capacious; proffered; marble; cushioned; inhospitable; mahogany; rigid; magisterial; split-bottomed; professorial; confessional; narrow; Morris; substantial; dangling; exiguous; ornamental; adjustable; high; triumphal; anatomical; editorial; rustic; fragile; carved; tipped-back; mural; gilt; lower; vacant; cozy; heavy; upholstered; soft; comfortable; club; arm; formidable; easy; roomy; favorite; noble; battered; faded; untrustworthy; worn; invalid; dilapidated; uncertain; overturned; adjoining;

groaning; clattering; reversible; swivel; basket; wing; Windsor; hideous; creaking; wicker; walnut; hickory; iron; horsehair; rattan; curule-back; expectant.

verbs

accept—; advance to—; appropriate—; bound from—; descend from—; drop into—; ensconce in—; hoist from—; jerk out of—; loll back in—; monopolize—; motion to—; occupy—; offer—; perch on—; plump into —; resign—; retire to—; shift in—; shrink back in—; sink in—; slump in—; snuggle in—; splinter—; sprawl all over—; straddle—; throne in—; tip—back; uprear in—.
(See seat, bench.)

CHAIRMAN

adjectives
temporary; anecdotal; prosy.

verbs
—adjourns; —bangs; —conducts; —delegates; —dismisses; —exercises; —occupies; —opens; —performs; —presides; —vetoes.
(See president.)

CHALICE

adjectives
cup-like; poisoned; silver; exuberant; sacred.

CHALLENGE

adjectives
visual; roguish; hoarse; loud; singing; heroic; silent; singular; provocative; sonorous; contemptuous; roistering; gay; feeble; stormy; direct; unsuccessful; peremptory; demoniac; concentrated; insolent; manifest; artistic; chivalrous; pert; mocking; puny; derisive; laughing; flippant; devil-may-care; malicious; sinister; menacing; truculent; fierce; wanton; snarling; angry; sharp; strident; stern; riotous; sweeping; tremendous; formidable; ringing; constant; perpetual; high-pitched; subtle; stimulating; reasonable; vague; unvoiced; startling; blue; definite; objective; hysterical.

verbs
arouse—; blaze—; cringe before—; debate —; defy—; deliver—; fling—; howl—; hurl —; ignore—; meet—; open to—; point—; read—; refuse—; ridicule—; scorn—; take up—; whistle—; —echoes; —rings; —resounds; —withers.
(See defiance, objection, exception, accusation, charge.)

CHALLENGE (v)

adverbs
egotistically; gruffly; justly; promptly; insolently; bravely; provocatively; sonorously; directly; peremptorily; demoniacally; pertly; mockingly; sinisterly; sternly; stridently; formidably; hysterically; definitely; startlingly; fiercely; wantonly; snarlingly.
(See defy, dare, brave.)

CHAMBER

adjectives
conjugal; aspiring; well-guarded; underground; silent; sordid; desolate; bare; nuptial; operating; comfortable; antique; mean; solitary; echoing; sepulchral; voluptuous; subterranean; subaqueous; privy; mystic; chill-looking; glorious; airy; accursed; ducal; treasure; mutilated; respective; chilling; uppermost; gloomy; dismal; unstable; haunted; untenanted; noble; repulsive; empty; crumbling; grimy; dusty; vaultlike; lethal; burial; inner; low-ceilinged; tiny; circular; unexplored; spacious; lofty; gilded; confined; packed.

verbs
abide in—; array in—; attend—; build—; carve—; convey into—; dress up—; empty —; gather in—; hie to—; invite to—; retire to—; seal—; seep into—; withdraw into —; —echoes.
(See room, cell, hall.)

CHAMPAGNE

adjectives
effervescent; brisk; excellent; cool; dashing; sparkling; tingling; convivial; atmospheric; gurgling; winking.

verbs
age—; blend into—; bucket—; cask—; characterize—; christen with—; consume—; cork—; drown in—; flavor—; foul—; ice —; lose in—; mature—; mix—; produce—; proffer—; revel in—; sip—; steep in—; support by—; swill—; tap—; toast with—; uncork—; urge on with—; —arouses; —bubbles; —effervesces; —exhilarates; —ferments; —fizzes; —glitters; —inspires; —intoxicates; —matures; —numbs; —sparkles; —unsteadies.
(See wine, liquor.)

CHAMPION

adjectives
undistinguished; formidable; invincible; undoubted; avowed; opposing; proper; ardent; conspicuous; valiant; illustrious; celebrated; sturdy; solitary; devoted; victori-

ous; doughty; undaunted; energetic; stalwart; lusty; redoubtable; brave; resolute; determined; unswerving; uncompromising; foremost; self-admitted; noble; gaunt; royal; prospective; fanatical; loyal; strange; defeated; fearless; resistless.

verbs
acclaim—; applaud—; challenge—; combat—; condition—; crown—; defeat—; defy—; develop—; disable—; dispute—; fear—; hail—; laud—; overthrow—; present—; proclaim—; protect—; provide—; — appears; —competes; —contends; —defends; —engages; —maintains; —performs; —renders; —represents; —teaches; —trains; —upholds; —vanquishes.
(See defender, winner, hero, conqueror.)

CHAMPIONSHIP
adjectives
intrepid; intemperate; conjugal; hyper-enthusiastic; vigorous; notable.

CHANCE
adjectives
slim; fluctuating; lost; opening; opportune; miraculous; lifetime; calculable; divine; slight; desperate; matrimonial; sporting; robust; limited; faint; ironical; impossible; evil; unforeseen; additional; mere; slender; golden; reasonable; fighting; undue; exceptional; brilliant; precious; main; endless; favorable; fortunate; magnificent; good-sized; fair; happy; unlooked-for; convenient; pure; barest; slightest; remote; small; equal; unfortunate; desperate; fatal; frustrated; awful; unfair; hazardous; repeated; fortuitous; amazing; timely; unlimited; glamorous; impartial; full; incorruptible; individualized; complicated.

verbs
advance—; await—; blast —s; brood over —; dispose of—; forfeit—; grab at—; grasp —; imperil —s; intercept by—; invite—; jump at—; leap at—; lessen —s; mind—; muff—; obviate—; rush for—; scoff at—; seize—; shun—; spy by—; stake on—; subject to—; yield to—; —begets; —controls; —detains; —determines; —dies; —fades; — fails; —governs; —guides; —leads.
(See fortune, luck, possibility, hazard, risk, probability.)

CHANCELLOR
adjectives
great; fallen; iron.

CHANDELIER
adjectives
cut-glass; crystal; interesting; central; dazzling; immense; prism-fringed; brilliant; glistening.

CHANGE
adjectives
singular; momentous; subtle; logical; ministerial; definite; threatened; healthful; indescribable; amazing; innovational; perceptible; incestuous; personal; far-reaching; periodical; remarkable; random; striking; varying; gradual; fluctuant; refreshing; incessant; vindictive; rhythmic; continual; rapid; industrial; tragical; stupendous; extraordinary; infinitesimal; withering; physiological; molecular; fine; hideous; enjoyable; radical; ceaseless; generating; appreciable; agreeable; constant; profound; prelusive; frequent; cunning; coincidental; instantaneous; delicate; fearful; acceptable; painful; pathetic; alarming; implied; essential; numerous (pl); eternal; intermediate; never-ending; distressing; partial; genuine; far-reaching; healing; startling; elaborate; drastic; magical; notable; wholesome; comprehensible; monotonous; revolutionary; unaccountable; permanent; consolidating; accumulated; progressive; astonishing; unimportant; political; social; economic; structural; miraculous; obliterative; corresponding; desirable; succeeding; fundamental; constant; violent; geophysical; asthmatic; marked; sudden; degenerative; inexpedient; miserable; extensive; solar; mortal; impending; metamorphic; observable; electrical; agreeable; flattering; malignant; pathological; valuable; secular; lightning-like; fermentative; welcome; seasonal; noticeable; decided; verbal; pleasing; ceaseless; convulsive; panoramic; periodic; beneficent; numerable (pl); realized; much-needed; alleged; abrupt; necessary; sly; wide; complex; enduring; practical; problematic; undeniable; unvarying; tangible; quiet; kindliest; peaceful; noteworthy; magical; refreshing; propitious; vital; tactful; serious; dramatic; vast; thrilling; epoch-making; cataclysmic; arbitrary; doleful; terrific; saddening; inevitable; visible; kaleidoscopic; psychic; psychological; adolescent; bodily; daily; physical; technical; natural.

verbs
accomplish—; advance—; advise—; advocate—; anticipate—; await—; bemoan—; beset by —s; bless—; compel—; concede—; confirm—; contemplate—; debate—; deplore

—; destine for—; dread—; effect—; execute
—; exhort—; fathom—; frown upon—; hinder—; impart—; inaugurate—; indicate—;
induce—; mourn—; occasion—; oppose—;
perceive—; prescribe—; promise—; pronounce—; prophesy—; propose—; report—;
stir to—; suffer—; undergo—; warrant—;
work—; —accompanies; —arises from; —
equalizes; —modifies; —occurs; —perplexes.
(See variation, alteration, transition.)

CHANGE (v)

adverbs
accordingly; singularly; momentously; logically; definitely; healthfully; indescribably;
amazingly; perceptibly; personally; refreshingly; incessantly; industrially; tragically;
stupendously; infinitesimally; molecularly;
radically; appreciably; profoundly; instantaneously; acceptably; partially; eternally;
genuinely; drastically; momentously; magically; notably; wholesomely; permanently;
progressively; economically; miraculously;
desirably; fundamentally; electrically; pathologically; seasonally; undeniably; noticeably; unvaryingly; tangibly; propitiously;
vitally; arbitrarily; chemically; climatical-
ly; technically.
(See alter, shift, reform.)

CHANGEABLE

adverbs
bewilderingly; vexatiously; curiously; characteristically; constantly; impulsively; provokingly; giddily; fitfully; capriciously; inexcusably; wantonly; recklessly; carelessly;
injudiciously; ridiculously; fantastically;
temperamentally; dramatically; inconsiderately; selfishly; rashly; indiscreetly; unstably; outrageously; unbelievably; tactlessly; unwisely; shiftily; erratically; restlessly;
nervously; weakly; timidly; irresolutely;
irresponsibly; unreliably; unfortunately; deplorably; wilfully.

CHANNEL

adjectives
correct; proper; earthly; turbulent; precipitous; somber; legitimate; inconsequent; subterranean; intricate; dreaming; transparent; colossal; destined; practical; devious;
manifold; diplomatic; regular; sound; conservative; productive; selfish; fortuitous;
tranquil; oozy; funnel-like; free-flowing;
foaming; tortuous; contorted; rock; unmapped; river; slender; deepened; narrow; bur-
rowed; boiling; miniature; uncounted; nois-
ier; personal; ample; powerful; smiling;
artistic; sequestered.

verbs
deepen—; dredge—; explore—; flow into
—; narrow—; obstruct—; pilot through—;
slide into—; sound—; stray into—; swell
—; trench—; turn into—; waft across—;
—extends; —widens.
(See canal, avenue, route, stream.)

CHANNEL (v)

adverbs
deeply; subterraneously; intricately; deviously; diplomatically; contortedly; narrowly; mysteriously.

CHANT

adjectives
intoned; low; deep-toned; barbaric; monotonous; fragmentary; musical; frenzied;
rhythmical; sonorous: rude; solemn; wild;
pathetic; droning; mellow; melancholy; triumphant; virginal; wailing; aspirated; joyful; impassioned; antiphonal; liturgic; Gre-
gorian; weird; doleful; guttural; nasal;
funeral; ominous; intellectual; wordless;
outlandish; obstreperous; pagan; tribal;
lachrymose; eerie.

verbs
accompany—; answer with—; compose—;
intone—; introduce—; mock—; mourn—; recite—; respond with—; sing—; take up—;
throw off—; troll—; uplift—; utter—; warble—; —celebrates; —consists of; —haunts;
—influences; —praises; —resounds.
(See song, melody.)

CHANT (v)

adverbs
angelically; barbarically; musically; monotonously; rhythmically; sonorously; solemnly; pathetically; mellowly; triumphantly;
wailingly; impassionedly; antiphonally; gutturally; ominously; outlandishly; obstreperously; lachrymosely.
(See intone.)

CHAOS

adjectives
stagnant; aboriginal; conquered; formless;
barren; shapeless; revolutionary; dark; living; wonderful; glaring; resulting; fierce;
cluttered; Stygian; boundless; black; idiotic;
financial; human; approaching; turmoiling;
whirring; tumultuous; leaden; primeval;
unintelligible; blank; entertaining; stimulating; appalling; ghastly; stricken; smothering; gloomy; hopeless; pathetic; bewildering; jumbled; indescribable; cultural; social; economic; industrial; political; primordial; age-long; blind; temporary; strident; ancient.

verbs

beset by—; build out of—; free from—; kindle—; plunge into—; produce—; resolve —; restore from—; rise out of—; survey—; swim through—; —arises; —confounds; —distresses; —overwhelms; —reigns; —roars; —rules; —threatens.

(See confusion, disorder.)

CHAOTIC

adverbs

fiercely; lamentably; uproariously; riotously; noisily; wildly; hysterically; tumultuously; turbulently; hopelessly; madly; distressingly; disturbingly; ominously; alarmingly; threateningly; perplexingly; confusedly; confusingly; indescribably; bewilderingly; pathetically; appallingly; idiotically; senselessly; needlessly; deplorably; unreasonably; unjustifiably; inconceivably; absurdly; perversely; unhappily.

CHAP

adjectives

wild; expensive; likable; sturdy; little; queer; good-looking; affable; lovable; facetious; fortunate; engaging; nice; clear-eyed; clever; capable; bully; jolly; handsome; slender; peaceable; decent-looking; shrewd; stout-hearted; sensible; fastidious; plucky; quiet; reserved; harmless; taciturn; undecided; irresolute; steady; unimpressive; callous; burly; massive; disappointed; solemn; roguish; belligerent; stocky; contriving; smirking; seagoing; oldish; well-mannered; polite; charming.

CHAPEL

adjectives

dimly-lighted; wattled; bare; dreary; lofty; exquisite; fragrant; ivied; unimposing; nonconformist; encircling; compulsory; ancient; carved; gilded; brown-tiled; quaint; old-fashioned; lapis lazuli; private; quiet; forgotten, white-spired; shabby.

verbs

consecrate—; dedicate—; enlarge—; establish—; found—; frequent—; gather at—; grant to—; install in—; maintain—; occupy —; perform in—; revere at—; summon to —; worship in—; —accommodates; —awes; —beckons; —enshrines; —serves; —solaces.

(See church.)

CHAPERON

adjectives

seedy; glowering; inadequate.

CHAPERON (v)

adverbs

conscientiously; inadequately; willingly; cheerfully; nominally; perfunctorily.

(See protect.)

CHAPTER

adjectives

tedious; individual; interesting; brilliant; stimulating; thrilling; solemn; miserable; immortal; spacious; singular; striking; morbid; unwritten; subsequent; supplementary; vivid; crisp; pleasant; debonair; racy; vivacious; fascinating; profoundly-illuminating; surprising; flaming; remarkable; crucial; satirical; provocative; circumspect; concluding; gloomiest; analogous; staccato; explanatory; didactic; drifting; detailed; secret.

verbs

arrange in—s; branch into—s; constitute—; contradict—; divide into—s; head—; introduce—; organize—; pen—; record in—; refer to—; section into—s; touch up—; —deals with; —depicts.

(See category, paragraph, story.)

CHARACTER
(quality, personality)

adjectives

vexatious; illustrious; first-rate; exceptional; celebrated; sheer; toothsome; prosy; composite; parasitic; private; fabulous; axiomatic; positive; nefarious; negative; munificent; salient; deleterious; stern; tempting; formal; reflective; sturdy; undecided; durable; substantial; apoplectic; cabalistic; melodramatic; provisional; indifferent; unscrupulous; vindictive; steadfast; estimable; personal; central; religious; fictional; finite; grasping; hollow; peculiar; composite; intrinsic; amiable; honest; uncelebrated; analogous; distinctive; intellectual; roving; liberal; alarming; feeble; notorious; pedestrian; sad; unspotted; moral; high-toned; daring; intense; diverse; frivolous; startling; half-obliterated; august; gallant; chivalrous; amazing; odious; elevated; heterogeneous; unwieldly; ridiculous; artistic; refulgent; elusive; absorbing; wanton; depraved; timid; trembling; unstable; virtuous; unsullied; robust; arduous; singular; dynamic; determinate; contrasting; beautiful; historical; vicious; interesting; inviolate; seductive; romantic; chameleon-like; miscellaneous; eccentric; arbitrary; powerful; clerical; defective;

murderous; unworthy; pristine; anecdotic; ferocious; sterling; spontaneous; ardent; presumptuous; headstrong; appealing; irresolute; lofty; sinister; luminous; feminine; extraordinary; contrary; eminent; acquired; general; goblin; complimentary; cold; passionless; checkered; obliterated; suspicious; unpractical; public; philological; simplest; primitive; prominent; unpleasant; minor; capricious; voluptuous; nobler; double; outward; antiquated; native; patriotic; deadly; improvident; accursed; external; ungainly; admirable; urgent; dubious; gloomy; melancholy; haughty; imperious; odd; domestic; massive; unique; dry; hard; assumed; fraudulent; heart-rending; exotic; self-reliant; bucolic; pacific; tempestuous; rightful; fictitious; random; complete; exhaustive; timely; idealistic; moral; unemotional; vigorous; epigrammatic; joyous; gentle; sacred; dissolute; flawless; reckless; genial; indelible; reigning; seasoned; lovable; indigenous; predominating; subordinate; unsavory; clean; natural; jovial; shallow; uninspiring; blackened; loquacious; homophonic; physiognomic; hermit; sensational; utilitarian; disturbing; hard-bitten; dwarfish; degrading; flabby; authoritative; jellyfish; picturesque; theocratic; tragic; fluctuating; literary; airy; modish; coquettish; desperate; incidental; colorful; irreproachable; vulgar; veritable; rugged; decorative; compendious; undefined; implacable; pontifical; imperfect; articulate; antithetical; legendary; opaque; tranquil; true; arid; mysterious; commanding; historical; surreptitious; observing; current; grandiose; gay; sympathetic; charming; functional; apathetic; vain; lyrical; nondescript; zigzag; explicit; inherited; statuesque; well-established; trivial; national; contemptible; hurried; hostile; material; accidental; vicious; doubtful; motley; congratulatory; enigmatical; prerogatived; external; abandoned; inviolable; vehement; monochromatic; uncommon; poisonous; sensuous; dicrotic; magnanimous; coherent; positive; semidivine; normal-sized; strenuous; affectionate; ethereal; disfiguring; irregular; forceful; idealistic; poetical; constipating; spiritual; grave; biographico-historical; proud; lying; submissive; many-sided; dutiful; upright; worthless; homely; humorous; insignificant; imperishable; gentlemanly; useful; abusive; decorous; indecisive; cosmopolitan; vague; dangerous; treasonable; atrocious; half-paternal; factitious; unsteady; shadowy; rude; wooden; impassioned; villainous; yielding; architectural; gross;

specific; conscientious; firm; hereditary; unimpeachable; sporting; harmonious; strong; contrasting; unnatural; dominant; special; bright; emphatic; desert; clear-cut; defined; handsome; stainless; collective; corporate; speculative; critical; eclectic; savory; loose; resolved; nebulous; advanced; impeccable; authentic; unblemished; rare; chosen; sophisticated; celestial; saint-like; docile; creditable; cute; attractive; virile; adamantine; curious; idiosyncratic; jaunty; bizarre; adventurous; comic; fantastic; silent; methodical; satisfied; staid; solidified; reticent; dull-witted; timorous; infantile; saturnine; soft; phlegmatic; vacillating; planless; traditionless; varied; racy; infamous; base; notorious; vengeful; unscrupulous; mercenary; obstinate; preposterous; racial; Mephistophelean; Puritan; hieroglyphic; seditious; quasi-public; figurative; youthful; semi-private; artificial; grave; cursive; specialized; representative; confidential; voluntary; individual; composite; intimate; interpolated; unequivocal; abnormal; unified; holy; incidental; deepest; ironic; realistic; abstract; contemporary; secondary; well-rounded; famous; well-known; picaresque; functionless; minor; queer; well-conceived; bygone; rough; Brobdingnagian; deliberate; light; splendid; principal; credible; ambitious; memorable; leading; burlesque; whimsical; quaint; flamelike.

verbs

alter—; analyze—; behold—; besmirch—; blacken—; brand—; breathe—; clear—; debase—; defend—; degrade—; denote—; detract from—; disclose—; display—; elevate—; embody—; emulate—; estimate—; express—; mask—; mold—; paint—; purify—; redeem—; reflect—; rehabilitate—; respect—; reveal—; slur—; traduce—; transform—; undermine—; warp—; —achieves; —breaks down.

(See constitution, nature, personality, temperament.)

CHARACTER
(role in drama or literature)

adjectives

biblical; dramatic; heroic; historic; legendary; mythological; fictional; personated; comic; tragic; contemporary.

verbs

assume—; compound—; conceive—; delineate—; depict—; differentiate—s; display—; distort—; draw—; interpret—; introduce—; invent—; juggle—s; merge into—; play—; portray—; produce—; roll into—; unfold—; —impresses; —represents; —symbolizes.

CHARACTERISTIC
adjectives
distinctive; prevalent; hereditary; congenial; essential; distinguishing; dominant; marked; personal; cheering; salient; general; diffusive; artistic; definite; admirable; farseeing; attractive; familiar; striking; swampy; psychical; unfailing; outstanding; individual; unmitigated; rife; recurring; external; commanding; visible; fundamental; praiseworthy; unsuspected; social; unique; national; spiritual; physical; emotional; peculiar; graceful; common; commendable; prudent; conspicuous; habitual; desirable; major; endearing; whimsical; useful; vicious; vulpine; supposed; reprehensible; tiresome; fictitious; radical; fatal; changeable; facial; group; racial; mental; climactic; local; rudimentary; tell-tale; complex; noticeable; great; unavoidable; inclusive; conceivable; differentiated.

verbs
abolish—; conceal—; disclose—; feign—; interpret—; manifest—; normalize—s; — appeals; —condemns; —differs; —distinguishes; —enhances; —heightens; —persists; —resembles.

(See trait, feature, attribute, quality, idiosyncrasy.)

adverbs
distinctly; particularly; superbly; singularly; specifically; specially; racially; inherently; definitely; typically; essentially; genuinely; truly; normally; significantly; notoriously; notably; touchingly; indelibly; intrinsically; substantially; practically; markedly; supposedly; presumably; ordinarily; naturally; fundamentally.

CHARACTERIZATION
adjectives
masterly; subtle; dramatic; first-rate; cursory; striking; curious; essential; accurate; contemptuous; intimate; convincing; appreciative; hopeful; delicate; musical; beneficent; genial; humorous; fine; readable; delightful; amazing; short; pithy; tricky; finely-etched; vivid; naive; exhaustive; spirited; shrewd; vigorous; sympathetic; penetrating; sharp; amusing; superb; hard-boiled.

CHARACTERIZE (*v*)
adverbs
justly; frivolously; positively; nefariously; negatively; substantially; provisionally; indifferently; amiably; honestly; distinctively; feebly; odiously; absorbingly; voluptuously; nobly; fraudulently; exotically; tempestuously; fictitiously; unsparingly; authoritatively; colorfully; irreproachably; vulgarly; sympathetically; charmingly; enigmatically; saturninely; villainously; seditiously; confidentially; intimately; ironically; realistically; credibly; whimsically; abnormally; quaintly; timorously; timidly; dynamically; romantically.

(See distinguish.)

CHARGE
adjectives
false; bayonet; untrue; competent; reiterated; swift; avaricious; substantiated; needy; specific; piebald; unlucky; excessive; gallant; ridiculous; unexpected; baleful; sensational; grievous; galloping; calumnious; tremendous; insulting; bloody; injudicious; precious; ignoble; generous; emotional; nominal; desperate; undiscriminating; exorbitant; modest; moderate; blasphemous; extortionate; spectacular; cruel; swift; impetuous; unburned; roaring; disgraceful; fluctuating; sole; typical; scrupulous; disputed; express; insurance; fair; immediate; humiliating; frivolous; warlike; motherly; boisterous; monstrous; quoted; atrocious; warehousing; bitter; additional; preposterous; ungrateful; unmerited; unnecessary; serious; mighty; cynical; horrible; defamatory; grotesque; homicide; criminal; dissenting; formal; groundless; trivial; indirect; swaggering; startling; accusing.

CHARGE
(*accusation*)
adjectives
absurd; civil; criminal; false; lying; specific; preposterous; unfounded; unjust; unsupported; unwarranted; substantial.

verbs
advance—; answer—; brand with—; brush aside—; conclude—; convey—; couch—; deny—; drone—s; fire—at; frame—against; incur—; justify—; lessen—s; level — at; lodge—s against; motivate—; prefer—s against; protest—; squash—s; refute—; repudiate—; splutter—s; spring—; suppress—; vindicate from—; voice—; — arises from; —rifles; —vexes; —wanes.

(See accusation, complaint.)

CHARGE
(duty, trust)

adjectives

burdensome; entrusted; costly; difficult; doubtful; inevitable; trying.

verbs

assign—; commit to—of; comprehend—; ease—; execute—; fail in—; fulfill—; impose—upon; obey—; perform—; release from—; resign—; shirk—; tend—.

(See duty, trust, custody, care, responsibility, management.)

CHARGE
(rush)

adjectives

driving; furious; concerted; blind; headlong; fruitless; onslaughting.

verbs

ambush—; block—; command—; cut down in—; dodge—; hasten to—; hinder—; lead—; precipitate—; rush to—; succumb to—; —conquers; —overcomes; —overwhelms; —succeeds; —surges; —surprises.

(See attack, assault.)

CHARGE (v)

adverbs

temporarily; strictly; bluntly; excessively; falsely; reiteratedly; specifically; ridiculously; unexpectedly; sensationally; calumniously; injudiciously; ignobly; exorbitantly; spectacularly; unscrupulously; bitterly; humiliatingly; unmeritedly; criminally; accusingly; groundlessly; startlingly; indirectly.

(See effort, impose, assault.)

CHARGEABLE

adverbs

conveniently; easily; indubitably; definitely; morally; officially; unquestionably; positively; absolutely; unfortunately; unluckily; inopportunely; legally; equitably; incontestably; explicitly; certainly; justly; properly; legitimately.

CHARGER

adjectives

foaming; wearied; stamping; restless.

CHARIOT

adjectives

black-lacquered; fiery; colliding; triumphal; colossal; four-horse; glossy; flaming; visionary; sumptuous; fierce.

verbs

arm—; depict—; display—; guide—; mount—; ornament—; rein—; —clanks; —conveys; —mows down; —overturns; —s parade; —rolls by; overthrow—.

(See vehicle, carriage.)

CHARITABLE

adverbs

humanely; amiably; benevolently; considerately; generously; lovingly; philanthropically; sympathetically; tenderly; unselfishly; bounteously; complaisantly; mercifully; blessedly; liberally; graciously; freely; tolerantly; unsparingly; munificently; bountifully; astonishingly; admirably; superbly; dependably; genuinely; sincerely; truly.

CHARITY

adjectives

moral; tender; intellectual; remedial; precarious; sniffing; gracious; truest; indiscriminate; princely; spasmodic; grudging; blessed; uncommanded; impulsive; abused; mutual; easy-going; voluntary; unwise; pious; unpublished; natural; aggressive; casual; deadened; superb; neighborly; learned; false; estimable; impressive; endless; confining; rigid; forbidden; tender.

verbs

administer—; appeal to—; assist through—; beseech—; bind with—; contribute to—; entitle to—; influence—; interest in—; lack —; necessitate—; pour forth—; relieve through—; remove from—; subject to—; subscribe to—; temper with—; —alleviates; —ameliorates; —declines; —enables; —grows; —heals; —revives; —suffers from.

(See love, benevolence, tolerance, alms.)

CHARLATAN

adjectives

preying; industrial; accomplished; ingenious; barred; shameless; ambitious.

CHARM

adjectives

flattering; awakened; glittering; soothing; outward; unusual; rare; quiet; distinct; untitled; healing; substantial; paltry; artless; haunting; subtle; inexplicable; personal; awful; lovely; mysterious; indescribable; celestial; imputed; wintry; forbidden; central; veiling; increasing; unique; insinuating; lyric; melodious; superficial; irresistible; heathenish; zestful; home-like;

traditional; distinguished; peculiar; wonder-working; soul-subduing; terrible; inscrutable; voluptuous; conversational; unspeakable; immortal; fictitious; native; unholy; substantial; compact; nostalgic; understanding; piquant; ineffable; delicious; grave; sensitive; vast; inimitable; compelling; indefinable; feminine; quaint; extraordinary; unmodish; seductive; individual; radiant; unfailing; poetic; flirtatious; fastidious; genuine; literary; changeable; reigning; essential; vocal; chief; haunting; quieting; inherent; serene; external; insouciant; modest; striking; incommunicable; inexhaustible; naturalistic; lasting; singular; stately; appropriate; rugged; intrinsic; crowning; restful; picturesque; decorative; elfin; ripening; definite; ideal; sovereign; softening; alluring; nameless; ethereal; inner; dishevelled; potent; spontaneous; simple; flying; material; exotic; unflagging; bitter-sweet; rose-tinted; fatal; suffocating; wild; astonishing; graphic; piquant; varied; recognized; original; perennial; captivating; superlative; brilliant; peaceful; magic; wistful; shy; magnetic; elusive; merry; fleeting; revealing; compensating; persuasive; devastating; certain; ardent; innate; indigenous; unusual; florid; sedate; mature; ancient; lasting; unhurried; lazy; languorous; unsuspected; vexing; thoughtless; ugly; thwarted; melancholy; flexible; chemical; immortal; historic; gala; dimpling; professional; youthful; topographical; provocative; auroral; scenic; domesticated; infantile; old-fashioned; boyish; naive; languorous.

verbs
apply—; attain—; eclipse—; emanate—; enchant with—; endow with—; enhance—; exercise—; loose—; lend—; radiate—; reflect—; resist—; retain—; savor—; survey—s; underrate—; win with—; —appeals; —conquers; —disarms; —dissolves; —enslaves; —fades; —melts; —pervades; —wanes.
(See fascination, beauty, spell, incantation, attraction.)

CHARM (*v*)
adverbs
delectably; bewitchingly; artlessly; outwardly; angelically; hauntingly; inexplicably; subtly; uniquely; mysteriously; indescribably; celestially; lyrically; melodiously; superficially; irresistibly; peculiarly; conversationally; genuinely; essentially; vocally; inherently; insouciantly; modestly;

strikingly; alluringly; ethereally; spontaneously; exotically; unflaggingly; seraphically; piquantly; perennially; captivatingly; superlatively; magnetically; elusively; devastatingly.
(See fascinate.)

CHARMING
adverbs
indescribably; delightfully; bewilderingly; amazingly; unquestionably; wondrously; surprisingly; radiantly; ineffably; wholly; joyously; blithely; consciously; tormentingly; overwhelmingly; provokingly; unimaginably; mysteriously; graciously; gravely; youthfully; exotically; alluringly; downright; exquisitely; genuinely; ingenuously; incomparably; irresistibly; rapturously.

CHART
adjectives
imperfect; neat; workman-like; cosmographical; authoritative; unusual; tattered; triumphal; fever; mystic; customary.

verbs
ascertain by—; calculate by—; compile—; consult—; depend on—; issue—; publish—; refer to—; scan—; stud—with; survey—; utilize—; —assists; —benefits; —directs; —furnishes; —indicates; —informs; —outlines; —plans; —reveals; —supplements; —sustains.
(See map, charter.)

CHART (*v*)
adverbs
unobtrusively; imperfectly; invisibly; vaguely; neatly; cosmographically; customarily; professionally; expertly; skillfully.

CHARTER
adjectives
accepted; approved; disputed; adopted; granted; grand; rejected; ratified; restored; submitted; revitalized.

verbs
abolish—; grant—; issue—; renew—; revoke—; —allows; —expires; —legalizes; —permits; —privileges.
(See deed, document, lease, agreement, contract, right, immunity.)

CHARY
adverbs
thriftily; stingily; selfishly; closely; parsimoniously; penuriously; frugally; providently; unreasonably; prudently; singularly; superfluously; curiously; needlessly;

unpleasantly; coolly; discreetly; cautiously; guardedly; warily; meanly; sordidly; greedily; cannily.

CHASE
adjectives
spirited; exciting; invisible; emulous; piteous; desultory; vague; dull; panting; delicious; wild-goose; fruitless; protracted; mad; perpetual; hectic; stern; blissful; grim; hard; desperate; cruel; lengthy; weary; heartbreaking; frenzied; thrilling.

verbs
follow—; forsake—; plan—; prolong—; pursue—; refrain from—; swerve from—; undertake—; —ensues; —fatigues.
(See pursuit, hunt.)

CHASE (v)
adverbs
spiritedly; madly; perpetually; excitingly; desperately; cruelly; heartbreakingly; thrillingly; remorselessly; grimly.
(See pursue, track, hunt.)

CHASM
adjectives
bloody; fearful; unfathomable; infinite; azure; brazen; billowy; bottomless; immense; fateful; watery; formidable; chalk; sunlit; unaccountable; Alpine; narrow; roaring; remarkable; wide; rock-walled; wonderful; dizzy; precipitous.

verbs
break into—; bridge—; cross—; disrupt into—; hollow—; open into—; rend—; rut with—s; span—; —breaches; —divides; —extends; —gapes; —interrupts; —resounds; —slants; —yawns.
(See gulf, gap, opening.)

CHASTE
adverbs
delicately; artistically; architecturally; virtuously; incomparably; beautifully; modestly; incorruptibly; unaffectedly; tastefully; classically; supremely; marvellously.

CHASTEN (v)
adverbs
amply; awfully; unnecessarily; physically; publicly; ruthlessly; brutally; fiendishly; triumphantly; soullessly; odiously; lawfully; legally.
(See punish, whip, correct.)

CHASTISEMENT
adjectives
awful; earthly; unnecessary; literary; physical; maternal; public.

CHASTITY
adjectives
sacred; constant; spotless; cold; enforced; fruitless; habitual; pure; stainless; incomparable.

verbs
affect—; blemish—; dedicate to—; despoil—; enforce—; honor—; impose—upon; laud—; mar—; practice—; pretend—; seduce from—; suspect—of; testify to—; violate—; —extends; —prescribes.
(See purity, virtue.)

CHAT (v)
adverbs
vivaciously; confidentially; mirthlessly; desultorily; emptily; pleasantly; informally; comfortably; loquaciously; frivolously; incessantly; jovially; aimlessly; absurdly; nervously; garrulously; carelessly; constantly; superficially; inconsequentially; amiably.
(See talk, gossip.)

CHATEAU
adjectives
imposing; dilapidated; turreted; ruined.

CHATTER
adjectives
rapid; mirthless; empty; convulsive; frothy; furious; confidential; pleasant; informal; short; comfortable; lively; neighborly; slipshod; unexpected; vivacious; social; friendly; loquacious; backstairs; mere; idle; egotistical; gay; joyous; competent; frivolous; merry; subdued; precocious; incessant; jovial; aimless; absurd; nervous; irresponsible; rattle-brained; garrulous; careless; constant; superficial; indignant; inconsequential; unfailing; bootless.

CHATTER (v)
adverbs
exuberantly; incessantly; complacently; volubly; monotonously; blithely; woefully; excitedly; affably; obstreperously; vivaciously; querulously; unrestrainedly; perplexingly.
(See chat, talk, gossip.)

CHATTY
adverbs
interminably; sociably; hospitably; heartily; genially; cordially; intimately; casually;

happily; companionably; affably; cosily; gregariously; fluently; gabbily; garrulously; nonsensically; glibly; harmlessly; revealingly; cheerfully; dangerously; indiscreetly; venomously; maliciously; indiscriminately.

CHAUFFEUR

adjectives
recommended; liveried; fur-clad; peaceful; sleeping; uniformed; wary; practiced; able; expert.

CHAUVINISTIC

adverbs
pretentiously; bombastically; flauntingly; triumphantly; swaggeringly; magniloquently; boastfully; brassily; highly; obviously; absurdly; foolishly; vapidly; noisily; ostentatiously; blatantly; fantastically; ludicrously; ignobly; inanely; stupendously; splendidly; vaingloriously; airily; blithely; manifestly; impudently.

CHEAP

adverbs
absurdly; unreasonably; contemptibly; indifferently; miserably; pitifully; ridiculously; laughably; worthlessly; unspeakably; incredibly; amazingly; attractively; undoubtedly; indubitably; tolerably; passably; really.

CHEAT (v)

adverbs
perpetually; infernally; villainously; flagrantly; scandalously; vilely; cleverly; shrewdly; diplomatically.
(See defraud, trick.)

CHEATING

adjectives
infernal; villainous; tyrannical; risky; disguised; cowardly; flagrant; glorious; freeboot.

verbs
amount to—; associate with—; bar for—; condone—; convict of—; depose for—; dispose toward—; implicate in—; indict for—; obtain by—; practice—; tolerate—; — affects; —besmirches; —blemishes; —dishonors; —lowers; —mars.
(See fraud, deception, imposition, delusion.)

CHECK

adjectives
bank; thief-proof; signed; gigantic; cancelled; reversible; formidable; sublime; indispensable; distinct; invaluable; generous; salutary; health-giving; contrasting; wholesome; constitutional; temporary; perceptible; accurate; worn; pallid; deplorable; effective; absolute.

CHECK (v)

adverbs
cleverly; fortunately; powerfully; abruptly; temporarily; effectively; formidably; systematically; constitutionally; perceptibly; accurately; absolutely.
(See impede, curb, restrain.)

CHEEK

adjectives
apple-red; crimson; cherry-colored; ruddy; ruddled; flushed; burning; fat; flaming; glowing; pretty; scarlet; blushing; fevered; blazing; rosy; incarnadining; pale; tranquil; sallow; livid; pasty; pallid; ashen; death-like; wan; triangular; lean; sunburnt; tanned; mottled; ebony; smudged; singed; painted; downy; smooth; boyish; placid; fresh; cold; sweet; firm; amiable; withered; weather-beaten; wrinkled; leathery; haggard; careworn; wizened; wasted; darkened; hollowed; cavernous; sunken; emaciated; bony; heavy; forged; rough; unshaven; flabby; jelly-like; puffed; comfortable; plump; soft; sleep-flushed; icy; droopy; hard; marble; freckled; pockmarked; scarred; smarting; tremulous; pendent; upturned; unresponsive; wind-freshened; consumptive; sweat-damp; infantile; peachy; delicate-rounded; high; warm; transparent; wide; strong; protruding; mangy; prominent; sinister; bronzed; tender; sinewy; distended; damask; blanched; dimpled; unprofaned; marked; veined; unworthy; straining; melting; pellucid; brown; tear-stained; mantling; placid; waning; quivering; faded; smiling; furrowed; smutted; tear-sodden; pinched; rubicund; glowing; lank; clear; pink; flaccid; swarthy; untasted; shrunken; shaded; blanched; cracking; languid; bloodless; emaciated; waxen; virgin; harlot; kissing; delicate; changing; inflamed; sunny; white; yellow-cowslip; childish; worn; proud; jutting; silver; drawn; amiable; animated; peony-colored; pinched; haggard; unreluctant; blooming; freshening; massive; lifeless; purplish-mottled; carmine-colored.

verbs
blanch —s; brighten —s; color —s; cool —s; corrugate —s; daub —s; dimple —; empurple —s; fan —; flame —s; flush —s;

hollow —; lean on —; moisten —s; paint —s; pat —; puff —s; redden —s; smite —; stain —s; stream down —; swell —s; tint —; varnish —; waste —; wrinkle —; —s blush; —s burn; —s fade; —s glisten; —s glow; —s hang; —s pale.

(See face.)

CHEEKY

adverbs

pertly; brassily; insolently; impertinently; insufferably; offensively; impudently; brazenly; flippantly; shamelessly; unpleasantly; disagreeably; saucily; swaggeringly; arrogantly; audaciously; provokingly; terribly; odiously; ridiculously; presumptuously; daringly; detestably; abominably; unwarrantably; jauntily; unbecomingly.

CHEER
(shout of applause)

adjectives

national; tumultuous; ironical; forced; admiring; hysterical; loud; rousing; shrill; hearty; panting; frenzied; rippling; irrepressible; patient; thunderous; incomparable; immense; blithe; lofty; pathetic; heart-strengthening; daily; mingled; answering; encouraging; sunny; lusty; universal; undaunted; wedding; unanimous; ringing; triumphal; measureless; traditional; good; intimate; massive; whooping; vociferous; solemn; silvery; evil; melancholy; uncertain.

verbs

celebrate with —s; depart with —s; draw —; echo—; grudge—; hail—; incite to —s; judge by —s; kill —; lessen —s; participate in —; raise —; rejoice in —; thunder —; — abates; — ceases; — dies; — fades; — greets; —rouses; — sweeps; — wanes.

(See applause, cheering.)

CHEER (v)

adverbs

raucously; rabidly; lustily; wildly; vociferously; enthusiastically; heartily; jovially; mirthfully; tumultuously; hysterically; rousingly; shrilly; frenziedly; irrepressibly; thunderously; incomparably; encouragingly; undauntedly; unanimously; triumphantly.

(See praise, applaud.)

CHEERFUL

adverbs

habitually; pleasantly; naturally; irrepressibly; immensely; blithely; vociferously; placidly; serenely; vivaciously; charmingly; refreshingly; youthfully; casually; calmly; hilariously; maddeningly; vexatiously; merrily; jauntily; airily; exuberantly; heedlessly; bewilderingly; surprisingly; unexpectedly; strangely; oddly; unwontedly; exhilaratingly; contentedly; lightly; gladly; complacently; tolerably; genially; jovially; jubilantly; briskly; smilingly; winsomely; noticeably; perplexingly; unbelievably; extraordinarily.

CHEERFULNESS

adjectives

unabated; placid; imperturbable; undiminished; sparkling; consistent; weary; hysterical; natural; charming; growing; healthy; infectious; contagious; uncomplaining; pensive; constrained; forced; renewed; spasmodic; affected; perennial; usual; weird; desperate.

verbs

animate with—; conceal—; denote—; diffuse—; dispose toward—; exhibit—; exude—; feign—; fight with—; free with—; inspire—; invade with—; reflect—; regain—; restore—; revive—; season with—; temper with—; welcome—; —comforts; —eases; —encourages; —exhilarates; —pervades; —stimulates.

(See optimism, buoyancy.)

CHEERING

adjectives

earnest; frenzied; fresh; unusual; loud; vociferous.

verbs

accelerate—; conduct—; direct—; drown in—; encounter—; join—; lead—; promote—; repress—; —acclaims; —animates; —compliments; —dies down; —echoes; —encourages; —heartens; —enlivens; —gladdens; —greets; —indicates; —overwhelms; —resounds; —stimulates; —subsides; —swells; —welcomes.

(See applause, ovation, cheer.)

CHEERING

adverbs

reasonably; brightly; definitely; encouragingly; reassuringly; propitiously; comfortingly; helpfully; positively; unusually; finally; tolerably; moderately; fairly; somewhat; downright; wholly.

adverbs

dismally; grievously; unhappily; sorely; sadly; unpleasantly; disturbingly; utterly; horribly; drearily; piteously; woefully; deplorably; pathetically; needlessly; discouragingly; dishearteningly; hopelessly; desolately; oppressively; extremely; undeniably; unutterably; wretchedly; peculiarly; cruelly.

CHEERY

adverbs

sturdily; resolutely; brightly; consistently; charmingly; healthily; infectiously; ;contagiously; professionally; philosophically; spontaneously; loudly; serenely; placidly; courageously; confidently; reassuringly; hearteningly; encouragingly; valiantly; gallantly; refreshingly; pleasantly; cordially; attractively; delightfully; calmly.

CHEESE

adjectives

milk; pyramided; vintage; large; ripe; stale; mouse-eaten; rancid; dry.

verbs

coagulate into—; consume—; enclose—in; grate—; import—; introduce—; loaf—; manufacture—; market—; mix—; pack—; process—; refrigerate—; roll—; slice—; spread—; sprinkle with—; toast—; turn into—; —moulds; —ripens.

adverbs

achieve with—s; analyze—s; apply—s; compose of—; concentrate—; devise—; employ—; 'evaluate—; extract—; force by—s; impregnate with—; involve—; mix—; obtain—; precipitate—; prepare—; produce—; resist—; synthesize—; —accomplishes; —acidizes; —acts; —alkalizes; —alters; —attracts; —catalyzes; —s combine; —converts; —counteracts; —depends on; —neutralizes; —poisons; —preserves; —reacts; —transforms.
(See substance.)

CHEMICALS

adjectives

injurious; common; inexpensive; mixed; synthetic.

CHEMIST

adjectives

renowned; brilliant; ruthless; analytical; alleged.

adjectives

agricultural; pure; applied; industrial; theoretical.

CHERISH (v)

adverbs

secretly; mutually; innocently; piously; tenderly; reverently; fondly; unconsciously; vociferously; tenaciously.
(See protect.)

CHERISHED

adverbs

carefully; affectionately; absurdly; highly; sentimentally; tenderly; reverently; ardently; fondly; ridiculously; stoutly; passionately; truly; sincerely; genuinely; whimsically; lovingly.

CHERRY

adjectives

fermented; fiery; ripened; blushing; pale.

CHEST
(part of body)

adjectives

stalwart; barrel; bulging; professional; corded; massive; out-muscled; superb; self-confident; thick; plump; brawny; skinny; cadaverous; cavernous; puny; meager; bony; unathletic; feeble; narrow; broad; pigeon; deep-sprung; expanded; wizened; sagging; crushed; collapsed; heaving; hollow; battle-scarred; inflated; hairy; soldierly; portentous; chubby; excessive; vainglorious; ample; laboring; decorated; tattooed.

verbs

blow out—; contract—; crush—; deflate—; deform—; develop—; expand—; flatten—; inflate—; lock up in—; loosen—; massage—; pierce—; puff out—; rend—; seal in—; stretch—; thump—.

CHEST
(receptacle)

adjectives

lopsided; crammed; treasure; battered; scarred; wooden; nail-studded; rivet-bound; stout; oaken; ironbound; corded; roped; brass-mounted; refrigerating; musty; capacious; ornate; plenteous; sacred; fireproof; ample.

CHEW (v)

adverbs

viciously; contentedly; placidly; hungrily; vigorously; continuously; tranquilly; normally; restrainedly; noisily; crushingly.
(See nibble, munch, crunch.)

adverbs

distinctly; smartly; fashionably; exceptionally; dramatically; fabulously; demurely; cleverly; artistically; stylishly; slenderly; effectively; correctly; trimly; conservatively; sparklingly; brilliantly; barbarically; expensively; conventionally; habitually; elegantly; quietly; handsomely; becomingly; intriguingly; appropriately.

CHICKADEE
(*titmouse*)

adjectives

black-capped; cheerful; lisping; flocking; lusty; evergreen-loving.

verbs

—carols; —chats; —chirps; —clings; —flits; —frolics; —hops; —preys on; —shrills; —somersaults; —whistles.
(See bird.)

CHICKEN

adjectives

cackling; snowy; browned; fragrant; smoking; drawn; rudimentary.

verbs

behead—; breed—; dine on—; excite—; exhibit—; fatten—; infest—; pen up—; prey on—; relish—; roast—; savor—; spice—; stuff—; —clucks; —flutters about; —gobbles up; —invades; —lays; —molts; —pecks; —perches; —scratches; —scurries; —squawks; —struts.
(See fowl, bird.)

CHICKENHEARTED

adverbs

notably; laughably; ridiculously; ludicrously; constitutionally; unwontedly; timorously; avowedly; shamefully; effeminately; dastardly; basely; solicitously; appallingly; astoundingly; wonderfully; amazingly; surprisingly; inexplicably; shockingly; fearfully; tenderly; obviously; disgracefully; outrageously; infamously; incurably.

CHIDE (*v*)

adverbs

scowlingly; mildly; severely; reprovingly; moderately; kindly; harshly; embarrassingly; vociferously; violently; sharply; shyly; intelligently; churlishly; mercilessly; legitimately; sternly.
(See admonish, censure, scold.)

adjectives

churlish; stormy; gallant; meaningful.

CHIEF

adjectives

indulgent; revered; supreme; prominent; gangster; powerful; local; native; usurping; polygamous; picturesque; murderous; mountain; desert; brigand; hereditary; indignant; deputed; reticent; patriarchal; despotic; venerable; artful; descendant; influential; kind; uncrowned; tribal; dominating; brave-hearted; gentle; generous; formidable; independent; invincible; responsible; crimson-stained.

verbs

advance to—; depose—; execute—; forsake—; guard—; hail—; hang—; idolize—; name—; oppose—; patronize—; rank as—; restore—; serve—; swerve from—; torture—; —commands; —inveighs; —leads; —orders; —rejoices.
(See head, leader, commander, captain.)

CHIEFTAIN

adjectives

feudal; bearded; putative; simple; desert; venerable; bandit; lifeless.

CHIFFON

adjectives

multitone; bright; filmy; sinuous.

CHILD

adjectives

delightful; charming; dutiful; cherubic; enchanting; divine; brilliant; bright; rosy; nice; capable; contented; accomplished; gifted; intelligent; respectable-looking; well-bred; supernatural; fun-loving; eager; exemplary; affectionate; studious; lovable; responsive; winsome; wistful-eyed; misty-eyed; golden-haired; fair-skinned; well-formed; comely; prepossessing; immaculate; prim; unnatural; normal; typical; average; growing; obedient; meek; humble; tactful; old-fashioned; subdued; repentant; contrite; tractable; tranquil; absorbed; silent; reflective; problem; sensitive; bewildered; shy; shrinking; artistic; emotional; unreasonable; nervous; highstrung; neglected; adorable; confused; sickly; delicate; frail; rickety; ragged; spindling; colorless; nondescript; angular; ugly; brutal; beastly; wretched; impertinent; rebellious; spoiled; spiteful; petted; precocious; audacious; impetuous; headstrong; heartbroken; prostrate; unhappy; miserable; forlorn; terrified; adored; admired; afflicted; frightened; greedy; wayward; unruly; exasperating; foolish; grown-up; offensive; refractory; obstreperous; monstrous; stubborn; obdurate; burdensome; unwitting; artless; retarded; stolid; annoying; slow-growing; defective; stupid; sturdy; pot-bellied; lean-faced; leggy; plain; thin; big-eyed; sallow; chubby-faced; regretful; toddling; prattling; wailing; screaming; sobbing; play-loving; beauty-loving; staring; frail; convalescing; engrossed; mere; weeping; casual; innocent; puzzled; venturesome; quizzical; adventurous; riotous; finicky; changeling; romantic; cockney; vaudeville; aristocratic; infant; drowsy; rash; loathed; unflinching; defective; culpable; pouting; petulant; conscientious; minor; wanton; dazed; eloquent; sanguine; forward; reticent; gallant; virtuous; vixenish; beaten; delightful; impious; crippled; exceptional; precious; churlish; talented; robust; engrossed; roguish; heaven-obscuring; loyal; turbulent; houseless; nurtured; tender; unborn; adolescent; simple; sole; heavenborn; cherished; complaining; blind; foolish; vagrant; comparative; scampering; weakest; credulous; guileless; merciless; illegitimate; sacred; fractious; proud; vivacious; burnt; pampered; abused; ambidextrous; healthy; unruly; passionate; undisciplined; self-willed; posthumous; fretful; imitative; melancholy; untutored; docile; migratory; princely; lily-shining; cunning; secretive; unmanageable; victorious; bewitching; sad-looking; riotous; unquenchable; wondrous; slumbering; veritable; eccentric; imaginative; flaxen-haired.

verbs
attend—; awaken—; bear—; befriend—; beget—; bereave—; bring forth—; build-up—; burden—; chastise—; cherish—; circumcise—; comprehend—; conceive—; correct—; debilitate—; deliver—; develop—; discipline—; disinherit—; dispossess ; educate—; emaciate—; embrace—; encourage—; exhort—; expose—; father—; fondle—; forsake—; govern—; harden—; inspire—; lull—; lure—; name—; nourish—; nurse—; oppress—; punish—; rear—; reassure—; remain—; restrain—; revive—; scold—; sire—; spoil—; teach—; tempt—; train—; trust—; understand—; wean—; whip—; —babbles; —clambers; —clamors; —contracts a disease; —dis-

obeys; —heeds; —moans; —pines; —rebels; —skips; —sobs; —strays; —struggles; —thrives; —wails; —weeps.
(See offspring, son, daughter, descendant, boy, girl, infant.)

CHILDHOOD
adjectives
earliest; amazing; seeming; narrow; nightmare-ridden; neglected; sheltered; imaginative; distorted; light-hearted; bleak; lonely; cheerless; spindle-legged; pathetic; precocious; inconsiderate; captious; mysterious; docile; blooming; unappreciative; serene; satisfied; joyous; humble; meditative; healthy; ripe; passive.

verbs
acquire in—; affect—; care for during—; conceive in—; dominate—; form during—; govern—; inculcate in—; learn in—; mould during—; preserve in—; recall—; rejoice in—; reminisce about—; restrict—; revert to—; teach in—; train in—; —contributes; —flees; —lapses; —ripens into; —strays.
(See infancy, youth.)

CHILDISH
adverbs
foolishly; disagreeably; utterly; unpleasantly; unexpectedly; shamefully; dreadfully; inexplicably; deliberately; unreasonably; ill-temperedly; pathetically; unbearably; wretchedly; senselessly; unaccountably; stubbornly; obstinately; horridly; ridiculously; sullenly; flagrantly; awkwardly; gawkily; unhappily; indecorously; outlandishly.

CHILDLIKE
adverbs
innocently; delightfully; simply; artlessly; guilelessly; naively; radiantly; joyously; charmingly; rosily; contentedly; lovably; meekly; adorably; foolishly; chubbily; wonderfully; bewitchingly; irresistibly; appealingly; utterly; touchingly; alluringly; unaffectedly; ingenuously; frankly; sweetly.

CHILDREN
adjectives
passive; fidgety; hostile; supersensitive; refractory; shy; obtrusive; irresponsible; prison; native; illegitimate; semi-hypnotized; bickering; gawky; mercurial; wondering; stoical; egotistical; unimaginative; pampered; promising; bright; worthy; wholesome; angelic; charming; marvel-

lous; carefully-bred; blithe; laughing; rollicking; smiling; audacious; happy; playful; prankish; romping; sturdy; robust; lusty; noisy; clamoring; clattering; frantic; screaming; unkempt; ragged; verminous; unwashed; wide-eyed; stocky; golden-haired; long-legged; quaintly-garbed; chubby; enormous; gayly-dressed; tiny; naked; half-grown; thick-legged; growing; underweight; undernourished; sickly; imperfectly developed; abandoned; heartbroken; frightened; radiant; desolate; trembling; pale; unloved; uncared-for; hungry; homeless; irresponsible; healthy; syphilitic; motherless; restless; squabbling; homespun; true; shivering; bedazed; vagrant; heartless; degenerate; crippled; unruly; earnest-hearted; vexing; starry; promising; natural; unreasonable; unbridled; fiery-blooded; outcrying; myriad; notorious; ill-bred; vulgar; ill-favored; exquisite; fresh; white-faced; silent; insolent; smutty; hovering; pert; dirty; squalling; fretful; sycophantic; mischievous; destitute; glorious-eyed; maddened; strumous; garrulous; hilarious; delinquent; violent; erring; handicapped; unlettered; vociferous; cruel; neglected; veritable; vigorous.

CHILL
adjectives
horrid; penetrating; biting; shrinking; severe; mental; violent; curious; embarrassing; noticeable; hopeless; sharp; congestive; sudden; inexplicable; slight; damp; timid; dry; icy; bone-penetrating; deathly; vault-like; bitter; uncomfortable; balmy; growing; cold; increasing; dreadful; comfortless; shaking.

verbs
blow—; chatter with—s; experience—; expose to—; overcome by—; produce—; prolong—; quiver with—; run—; seize with—; sense—; shake with—; shiver with —; shudder with—; strike with—; survive —; treat for—; —accompanies; —affects; —creeps in; —depresses; —injures; — numbs; —penetrates.
(See sensation, cold.)

CHILL (v)
adverbs
bitingly; severely; violently; hopelessly; noticeably; sharply; suddenly; inexplicably; bitterly; increasingly; dreadfully; mortally; painfully.

CHILLY
adverbs
suddenly; inexplicably; curiously; slightly; uncomfortably; dreadfully; alarmingly; keenly; tremulously; visibly; uncommonly; unendurably; strangely; unaccountably; unpleasantly; dangerously; unusually; unwontedly; inexcusably; indefensibly.

CHIME
adjectives
musical; pathetic; dolorous; silvery; sweet-toned; unhurried; clear; jubilant; silver; soothing; unvaried; religious; faint; heavenly.

CHIME (v)
adverbs
drowsily; harmoniously; mischievously; dolorously; unhurriedly; jubilantly; soothingly; religiously; faintly; heavenly; musically, clearly.
(See ring.)

CHIMERICAL
adverbs
strangely; fantastically; grotesquely; wildly; eccentrically; erratically; quaintly; curiously; baselessly; foolishly; exceptionally; peculiarly; extraordinarily; unaccountably; extravagantly; preposterously; fabulously; dreamily; fancifully.

CHIMNEY
adjectives
rotten; smoking; natural; stubborn; ample; curious; spiraled; defective; tottering; stumpy; low; ungainly; blackened; ghostly; clustering; open-throated; sparkless; disused.

verbs
block—; blow down—; clean—; connect—; construct—; convey through—; dampen—; decorate—; design—; escape through—; extend—; fire—; inspect—; lodge in—; muffle—; obstruct—; pass through—; suck up—; support—; —breathes; —carries off; —diffuses; —discharges; —draws off; —exhales; —fumes; —leaks; —reeks; —smokes; —topples; —tumbles.
(See passage.)

CHIN
adjectives
out-thrust; curious; jutting; determined; provocative; elongated; significant; prominent; dominant; fighting; obstinate; aggressive; protruding; stubborn; molded;

prognathous; rounded; square; retreating; bulldog; cleft; portly; dimpled; daintily; shaped; clean-cut; aristocratic; triangular; pointed; strong; rounded; sensitive; delicate; demure; quivering; protesting; scrubby; stubbled; unshaven; bristly; sunken; curbed; callow; tremulous; weak; girlish; bevelled; unflinching; lowered; firm; heavy; mutinous; marred; bruised; impudent; receding; arrogant; trembling; dumpy; formless; patrician; slack-set; full; granite; gray-bearded; seamy; witching; clean-shaven; sagging; generous.

verbs
box—; caress—; chafe—; dimple—; dip—; double—; furrow—; guard—; hollow—; pillow—on; razor—; roughen—; smooth—; strike on—; stroke—; stubble—; tickle—; —juts out.
(See jaw.)

CHINA
(*country*)
adjectives
ancient; colorful; present-day; famine-cursed; tasteful.

CHINA
(*dish*)
adjectives
atrociously-patterned; colorful; decorated; egg-shell; fragile; glazed; mongrel; ancestral; mended; imported; lustered; lustrous; treasured; superb; rare; delicate; magnificent; glorious; exquisite; dainty.

verbs
bake—; carve—; decorate—; design—; exhibit—; fire—; glaze—; inherit—; lithograph—; manufacture—; model—; mold—; paint—; preserve—; print—; process—; produce—; trace on—; trim—; turn—; vitrify—; —attracts; —sparkles.
(See porcelain.)

CHINAMAN
adjectives
slant-eyed; sinister; innocent; cryptic.

CHIP
(*counter or disk in game*)
adjectives
accumulated; cashed-in; clicking; ivory; ominous; nested; red-and-blue; rattling; plastic; stacked.

verbs
accumulate—s; amass—s; ante—; calculate—; cash—s; mark—s; pile up—s; revalue—; toss in—; wager—; —s rattle; —s represent.

CHIP (*v*)
adverbs
laboriously; unweariedly; characteristically; disfiguringly; hurtfully; disastrously; idiotically; carelessly.

CHIPMUNK
adjectives
burrowing; chipping; conspicuous; beautifully-striped; darting; free-roving; fence-travelling; gleaming; marauding; scampering.

verbs
—chirps; —emerges; —ranges; —scurries; —stores.
(See squirrel, animal.)

CHIPPER
adverbs
blithely; heartily; gaily; cheerily; wholesomely; briskly; actively; ably; laughingly; light-heartedly; sunnily; smartly; alertly; energetically; happily.

CHIPS
(*fragments*)
adjectives
infinitesimal; coarse; falling; scattered; shapeless; raw; valueless.

verbs
break into—; chisel into—; chop into—; cut into—; fly into—; gather—; hack into —; hew into—; piece into—; separate into—; split into—; —accumulate; —clutter up; —fly; —gather; —strike.
(See fragment, piece.)

CHIRP (*v*)
adverbs
shrilly; disdainfully; rapturously; ecstatically; joyously; contentedly; obstreperously; cheerfully; maddeningly; noisily; incessantly; obtrusively; deafeningly; unendingly; subduedly; discordantly.
(See twitter.)

CHIVALRIC
adverbs
patriotically; loyally; fanatically; devotedly; fantastically; bigotedly; faithfully; chauvinistically; unnecessarily; showily; ostentatiously; genuinely; sacrificially; pi-

ously; religiously; ardently; zealously; uncompromisingly; impulsively; sincerely; sublimely; martially; fiercely; incorruptibly; staunchly; inviolably; excessively.

CHIVALROUS
adverbs
delicately; devotedly; politely; generously; magnanimously; innately; inherently; traditionally; racially; suavely; gallantly; civilly; pleasantly; ardently; fervently; courteously; extremely; gently; urbanely; smoothly; obsequiously; amiably; ceremoniously; attentively; blandly; ingratiatingly; pleasingly; tactfully.

CHIVALRY
adjectives
morbid; belated; unsullied; old-fashioned; rekindled; deficient; fantastical; poetic; latent; knightly; gay; misplaced; exaggerated; distant; feudal; religious; delicate; loyal; medieval; undaunted; vaulted; celestial; youthful; generous.

verbs
affect—; attend with—; attribute to—; awaken—; bend toward—; blind by—; celebrate—; charge with—; commend for—; confer on—; dispense with—; educate for —; encounter—; equip for—; institute—; knight for—; reward—; —constitutes; —decays; —dies; —flourishes; —flowers; —prevails; —survives.

(See gallantry, courtesy, bravery.)

CHLOROFORM
adjectives
colorless; ethereal-odored; insidious; penetrating; pungent; sickish-sweet; sleep-producing.

verbs
administer—; anesthetize with—; dissolve in —; dose with —; expose —; gelatinize —; inhale —; melt —; overcome with —; sniff —; solidify —; subject to —; — acts; — boils; — decomposes; — dissolves; — dulls; — eases; — lessens.

(See anaesthetic.)

CHOCK-FULL
adverbs
generously; utterly; satisfactorily; inconveniently; dangerously; sloppily; carefully; calculatedly; accurately; happily; luckily; absolutely; surprisingly; gratifyingly; entirely; brimmingly; nicely.

CHOCOLATE
adjectives
thick; creamy; burning; sugary; tasty; bitter; rancid; delicious.

CHOICE
adjectives
inevitable; sensible; indefensible; ideal; hasty; shrewd; ultimate; emotional; distinguished; alternate; definite; conscious; free; happy; mistaken; unlimited; fortunate; sympathetic; logical; wise; moral; wide; important; half-humorous; unrestricted; endless; arbitrary; uncorrupted; critical; unessential; irrelevant; nonsensical; ideal; solicitous; scrupulous; ghastly; admirable; satisfactory; premium; perfect; sturdy; bitter; loathed; boundless; random; unaccountable; injudicious; intelligent; first; deliberate; perfect; haphazard; excellent; doubtful; mercenary; dazzling; appropriate; resolute; righteous; prudent; haughty.

verbs
abide by —; applaud —; bind to —; commend —; conceal —; contend with —; delight in —; determine —; encourage —; envy —; extend —; favor —; guard —; indicate —; justify —; leave —; overrule —; regulate —; restrict —; widen —; yield to —.

(See alternative, option, preference, election.)

CHOICE
adverbs
unusually; exquisitely; valuably; indubitably; unquestionably; evidently; manifestly; incomparably; inimitably; singularly; particularly; inestimably; invaluably; exceptionally; alluringly; temptingly; exotically; incalculably; immeasurably; imposingly; infinitely; sumptuously; inexpressibly; utterly; absolutely.

CHOIR
adjectives
soothing; plumed; enraptured; chantry; surpliced; cathedral; full-throated; extraordinary; immortal; starry; constellated; matin; white-robed; angelic; sweet-voiced; ritual; dusky; captive; silent; mystic; pausing; shining; winged; invisible.

verbs
accompany —; coach —; compose —; conduct —; direct —; employ —; establish —; garb —; invite —; organize —; pitch —; regulate —; retain —; stimulate —; support

—; train —; — answers; —anthems; — carols; — chants; — croaks; — croons; — devotes; — invokes; — is situated; — performs; — practises; — rehearses; — renders; — resounds.
(See chorus, singers.)

CHOKE (v)
adverbs
horribly; fiendishly; murderously; hellishly; painfully; furiously; fatally; mortally; partially; savagely.
(See strangle, throttle.)

CHOLERA
adjectives
Asiatic; devastating; dread; horrible; life-snuffing; malignant; pestilential; spreading; impartially-dealing; ravaging.

verbs
afflict with —; arrest —; attack with —; cause —; control —; distinguish —; expose to —; inoculate against —; overcome —; prevent —; protect against —; quarantine —; recognize —; recover from —; resemble —; scourge with —; stamp out —; subdue —; subject to —; suffer from —; treat for —; — affects; — infects; — invades; — irritates; — occurs; — prevails; — ravages; — spreads; — subsides; — travels; — visits.
(See disease, epidemic.)

CHOLERIC
adverbs
inveterately; terribly; extremely; excitedly; irascibly; habitually; touchily; cantankerously; exceptionally; intolerably; dangerously; hotly; petulantly; restively; incorrigibly; inherently; incurably; alarmingly; irritatingly; unbearably; unreasonably; senselessly; miserably; unfortunately; ill-temperedly; plaguedly; waspishly; querulously.

CHOOSE (v)
adverbs
promiscuously; precisely; deliberately; unanimously; inevitably; fastidiously; invariably; sedulously; universally; constitutionally; tactfully; tastefully; unselfishly; sensibly; shrewdly; ultimately; emotionally; definitely; mistakenly; sympathetically; logically; morally; unrestrictedly; arbitrarily; critically; irrelevantly; nonsensically; scrupulously; admirably; unaccountably; injudiciously; haphazardly; appropriately; resolutely; righteously; prudently; instinctively; finally; discreetly; speedily.
(See select, prefer.)

CHOP
adjectives
breaded; congealed; dripping; double; evenly-browned; fat; juicy; oozing; bony; shriveled.

verbs
broil —; butter —; devour —; digest —; dine on —; enjoy —; garnish —; grill —; heat —; pepper —; preserve —; relish —; roast —; salt —; savor —; season —; trim —; — burns; —simmers; — sizzles; — steams.
(See meat.)

CHOP (v)
adverbs
savagely; vigorously; ambitiously; hurriedly; leisurely; grimly; regularly; ineffectively; monotonously; continuously.

CHORAL
adverbs
melodiously; harmoniously; lyrically; fundamentally; originally; essentially; tunefully; euphoniously; symphoniously; orchestrally; effectively; splendidly; magnificently; sweetly; primarily; simply; elaborately; complicatedly.

CHORD
adjectives
harmonic; emotional; sympathetic; tender; responsive; peremptory; compassionate; triumphant; thunderous; preliminary; opening; impromptu; maddening; wailing; noisy; closing; sobbing; dreamy; dashing; nerve-racking; rare; vibrant; responsive; strong; broad; determined; familiar; answering; conscious; throbbing; susceptible; airy; sonorous; breaking; plenteous; liquid; sensitive; dominant.

verbs
pluck —; sound —; twang —; — charms; — shivers; — thrills; —trembles.
(See tendon, string.)

CHORE
adjectives
old-fashioned; bitter; small; domestic; weary.

verbs
dispatch —s; do —s; perform —s; plan —;
—s bind; —s devolve on; —s occupy; —s
settle on.
(See job, duty, task.)

CHORISTER
adjectives
impatient; poor; supercilious; monotonous.

CHORUS
adjectives
noisy; welcoming; general; angry; fearful;
jangling; affirmative; derisive; obtrusive;
hallelujah; exhausted; tender; deafening;
hoarse; booming; familiar; whispering;
pessimistic; eerie; intricate; mighty; hair-
raising; shrill; musical-comedy; shrieking;
unending; recurrent; tuneful; abusive; masterly; jubilant; echoing; universal; horrend-
ous; solemn; jolly; deep; screaming; hideous; vernacular; subdued; unprecedented;
dirge-like; clamorous; wild; unfaltering;
multitudinous (pl); seasonable; seditious;
blasphemous; bibulous; mumbling; gleeful;
meaningless; ranting; discordant.

verbs
accompany —; coach —; collect —; conduct —; constitute —; flow from —; join in
on —; laugh in —; manage —; organize
—; pitch—; regulate—; repeat—; take
up —; train —; transpose —; utter —;
whine in —; — breaks out; — chants;
— executes; — harmonizes; — imitates; —
practices; — rehearses; — renders; — reports; — resounds; — revels; — revives;
— shrills; — spreads; — swells.
(See choir, song, refrain.)

CHRIST
adjectives
agonized; crucified; unheralded; infallible;
merciful; glorious; death-triumphant; pur-
ple-robed; sorrowing; thorn-crowned; unconquerable; comforting.

verbs
acknowledge —; apprehend —; beseech —;
bless —; bow before —; conform with —;
consecrate to —; contemplate —; deny —;
discern —; endow with —; esteem —; fight
for —; follow —; forsake —; herald —;
interpret —; preach —; preserve —; protect —; receive —; reject —; unveil —;
uphold —; — ascends; — bears; — heals;
— passes; — prophesies; — redeems; —
represents; — rises; — rules; — suffers;
— teaches; — toils.
(See God, Jesus.)

CHRISTIAN
adjectives
sincere; misguided; professing; preeminent; heartfelt; genuine.

CHRISTIAN
adverbs
devoutly; sincerely; ardently; fervently; devotedly; faithfully; humbly; meekly; piously; religiously; sanctimoniously; beatifically; joyously; blessedly; reverently; solemnly; benignly; honestly; genuinely; benevolently; mercifully; tolerantly; humanely;
charitably; obviously; unmistakably; plainly; evidently; openly; avowedly; professedly.

CHRISTIANITY
adjectives
admirable; dogmatic; muscular; mysterious;
primitive; sustained; sympathetic; profound.

verbs
conceive —; convert to —; cut off from —;
denote —; embrace —; exalt —; extirpate
—; follow —; found —; illustrate —; implant —; inculcate —; live in —; lose faith
in —; manifest —; obscure —; persecute
—; plant —; preach —; profess —; regard
—; reject —; restore —; spread —; support —; teach —; trace —; — concerns; —
embodies; — grows; — progresses; — redeems; — saves; — transcends; — triumphs.
(See religion, faith.)

CHRONIC
adverbs
avowedly; incurably; unfortunately; finally;
obstinately; stubbornly; lingeringly; mildly; firmly; deplorably; grievously; pitiably;
indubitably; manifestly; evidently; palpably; obviously; unquestionably; distinctly;
plainly; incontrovertibly; unmistakably.

CHRONICLE
adjectives
sensuous; pagan; commonplace; objective;
calm; gay; fascinating; detailed; lively;
scandalous; stirring; heroic; racy; salty;
wistful; tender; humorous; courageous;
mocking; faithful; vivid; massive; memorable; poignant; unique; gripping; incomparable; lofty; moving; human; vigorous;
episodic; broad-spoken; tedious; zestful;
medieval; tattered; factual; dusty; fast-
moving; personal; sententious; intimate.

verbs

accumulate in —; arrange —; compare —; compile —; complete —; compose —; devote — to; examine —; forge —; keep —; preserve —; recite —; refer to —; skeletonize —; — consists of; — contains; — contradicts; — conveys; — disposes; — determines; — embraces; — presents; — recollects; — registers; — reveals; — sets down; — treats of.

(See record, account, narrative, diary, history.)

CHRONICLER

adjectives

matter-of-fact; scandal-loving; contemporaneous.

CHRONOLOGICAL

adverbs

accurately; carefully; meticulously; fussily; absolutely; dependably; tolerably; infallibly; scrupulously; strictly; uncannily; unimpeachably; avidly; punctiliously.

CHRONOLOGY

adjectives

dismal; distilled; condensed; meaningful; mouldering; simple; uneventful; unvarnished; verified.

verbs

arrange —; ascertain —; base — on; check —; compare — with; correlate —; develop —; explain —; fix —; interest in —; preserve —; reckon —; settle —; telescope —; verse in —; — classifies; — computes; — depends on; — enumerates; — includes; — indicates; — measures; — provides; — records; — reveals; — survives; — traces.

(See science, time.)

CHRYSANTHEMUM

adjectives

huge; tawny; bronze; brave; pink; golden; great; pale; shaggy; yellow; calm.

CHUBBY

adverbs

adorably; sweetly; cheerily; buxomly; huskily; rosily; pleasantly; happily; cheerfully; sturdily; healthily; stoutly; laughably; ridiculously; lovably; admirably; ludicrously; stupidly; heavily; laughingly; gaily; blithely; bonnily; winsomely; handsomely; terribly.

CHUCKLE

adjectives

appreciative; affectionate; naive; long; delicious; humorous; benevolent; sepulchral; melancholy; mirthless; low; little; slow; deep; noiseless; vicious; gloating; evil; sneering; irreverent; exultant; gratuitous; ghastly; unpleasant; eerie; soft; childish; crazy; husky; shrewd; mild; elfish; asthmatic; inward; dry; communicative; contagious; cruel; palpitating; suppressed; sly; insulting; bitter; inward; prolonged; coarse; fearful; tremulous; joyous; grim.

CHUCKLE (v)

adverbs

inaudibly; casually; maliciously; gruffly; waggishly; inwardly; fearfully; hollowly; appreciatively; affectionately; naively; humorously; benevolently; sepulchrally; mirthlessly; noiselessly; gloatingly; sneeringly; irreverently; exultantly; gratuitously; unpleasantly; huskily; elfishly; contagiously; asthmatically; insultingly; bitterly; tremulously; joyously; grimly.

(See laugh.)

CHUMMY

adverbs

delightfully; helpfully; devotedly; intimately; sympathetically; companionably; affectionately; cordially; warmly; sincerely; heartily; amicably; affably; wonderfully; frankly; graciously; loyally; distinctly; enthusiastically; congenially; marvellously; unselfishly; staunchly; generously; steadfastly; courageously.

CHURCH

adjectives

venerable; impressive; calm; dignified; simple; famous; historical; imposing; ancient; hoary; handsome; exquisite; fashionable; enormous; frescoed; small; gray; loopholed; ivy-clad; colonial; belfry-towered; country; white-washed; fly-bitten; square-towered; parabolic; village; parish; dismal; silent; superfluous; competing; huddling; dedicated; pillaged; dissenting; buttressed; belfried; cathedral; sumptuous; ornate; friendly-looking; tremendous; dominating; ambitious; primitive; prosaic; barnlike; uncouth; spireless; gloomy; established; conservative; olive-green; sandstone; decent; remote; comprehensive; self-denying; laborious; unwearied; ancient.

verbs

assemble in —; baptize in —; christen in —; confirm in —; consecrate —; deface —; drift away from —; enrich —; establish —; esteem —; file into —; forsake —; gather in —; hie to —; interpret —; laud —; liberalize —; neglect —; orient —; present to —; ransack —; respect —; salute —; unite —; wed in —; worship in —; — absolves; — inspires; — molds; — moulders; — wanes.

(See temple, cathedral, chapel, tabernacle, sanctuary, congregation.)

CHURCH-GOERS

adjectives

austere; backbiting; backsliding; devout; earnest; dogmatic; fervent; grave; heaven-aspiring; hypocritical; morose; long-faced; puritanical; salvation-seeking.

verbs

appeal to —; appoint —; join —; patronize —; prevail on —; respect —; witness —; — abandon; — attend; — authorize; — band; — commune; — conform; —congregate; — contribute; — control; — convene; — criticize; — endow; — flow by; — grow; — ignore; — organize; — provide; — rally; — sneer; — stream past; — support. (See congregation.)

CHURCHY

adverbs

devoutly; hypocritically; ostentatiously; sententiously; unctuously; devotedly; fashionably; unwearyingly; pompously; dramatically; dutifully; properly; appropriately; adequately; meticulously; punctiliously; obediently; piously; sentimentally; obsequiously; pharisaically; sanctimoniously; conscientiously; righteously; pretentiously.

CHURL

adjectives

drunken; seditious; sturdy; vulgar; brash; brazen.

CHURLISH

adverbs

inordinately; bluntly; sullenly; stupidly; basely; ruggedly; fantastically; awkwardly; offensively; unconsciously; unwittingly; artlessly; deliberately; colossally; detestably; insufferably; intolerably; unbearably; rudely; crudely; abominably; intentionally; shockingly; innately; boorishly; ignorantly; harshly; disagreeably; outrageously; indefensibly; vulgarly; brazenly; coarsely; brashly; brassily; contemptibly; shamefully.

CHURN (v)

adverbs

irrationally; viciously; vigorously; wildly; impressively; awesomely; grimly; tumultuously; thunderously; deafeningly.

CIDER

adjectives

piercing; tangy; aromatic; acid.

CIGAR

adjectives

smooth; mild; mellow; vile; unlighted; butted; disheveled; half-smoked; aromatic; excellent; villainous; rank; rough; exotic; inevitable; refreshing.

verbs

box —; chew on —; clip —; clutch —; crave —; display —; extinguish —; flick —; grade —; import —; inhale —; insert —; manufacture —; mold —; object to —; pocket —; point —; produce —; proffer —; puff on —; pull at —; roll into —; shape —; smoke —; wave —; wrap —; yearn for —; — appeals; — burns; — glows.

CIGARETTE

adjectives

disconsolate; soggy; indispensable; lightly-fingered; monogrammed; bungled; unlighted; blended; acrid; quashed; dangling; proffered; pasty; formless; customary.

verbs

blend —s; carton —s; choke on —; consume —s; cough on —; discard —s; fumble for —; grade —; inhale —; mentholize —; moisten —; package —; perfume —; proffer —; purvey —; tip —; toast —; turn out —; wave —; — dies; — dries out; — fumes; — glows; — smoulders; — stales.

CIMMERIAN

adverbs

gloomily; darkly; vastily; expansively; extensively; terrifyingly; frightfully; luridly; sunlessly; tenebriously; umbrageously; obscurely; dimly; shadily; murkily; sombrely; stupendously; appallingly; hideously.

CINDERS

adjectives

besieging; blinding; blazing; cruel; drifting; catapulting; dusty; feathery; gritty; inky; murky; smudgy; sooty; sharp; stinging.

verbs

arrest —s; deposit —s; eject —s; form —s; pile —s; quench into —s; rake —s; reduce to —s; sift —s; throw off —s; turn to —; — die; — fly; — glow; — lodge; — pop; — sear; — smoulder.

(See coal, residue, ashes.)

CIPHER

adjectives

valueless; inextricable; constant.

CIRCLE

adjectives

conversational; social; illustrious; exclusive; gilded; artistic; political; aristocratic; literary; fashionable; wealthy; financial; wide; brilliant; well-bred; bigoted; select; limited; cheery; charmed; real; ideal; convivial; erratic; perfect; dim; pale; iron; eddying; disintegrated; blurred; broken; enclosing; great; sweeping; sturdy; charmed; intimate; executive; solemn; predestined; concentric; cosmopolitan; bizarre; widening; charred; ceremonial; ringing; collapsed; ever-enlarging; original; vicious; agricultural; splendid; decorative; leading; influential; distinguished; smartest; elastic; pleasant; closed; petty; educational; esoteric; polished; interior; operatic; ultrafashionable; awkward; extended; deep; ruddy; vast; walled; uninterrupted; conservative; privileged; noisy; wavering; pallid; giddy; curious; deft; professional; diplomatic.

verbs

accomplish —; assemble in —; bar from —; circumscribe —; cleave —; complete —; cut —; disband —; emit from —; form —; flutter in —; guard —; hallow —; inscribe —; insert in —; join —; lead into —; narrow —; pour in —; revolve —; round —; spin in —; swell —; trace —; — disintegrates; — widens.

CIRCLE (v)

adverbs

demurely; erratically; solemnly; wideningly; ceremonially; viciously; awkwardly; noisily; waveringly; curiously; treacherously.

(See surround.)

CIRCLED

adverbs

darkly; ominously; closely; gloriously; radiantly; strangely; completely; hopelessly; fatally; alarmingly; perplexingly; unexpectedly; suddenly; roseately.

CIRCUIT

adjectives

respectful; due; electric; unbroken; annual; elliptical; tedious; irregular; spacious; voltaic; short.

verbs

administer —; appoint to —; attach to —; complete —; discontinue —; divide into —s; enclose within —; form —; plug into —; regulate —; remodel —; retain —; ride —; supervise —; travel —; visit —; — comprises; — consists of; — prevails; — transmits.

(See district, course.)

CIRCUITOUS

adverbs

exasperatingly; terribly; needlessly; tediously; wearisomely; monotonously; vexatiously; undesirably; unsuitably; extremely; hopelessly; endlessly; sadly; tortuously; intricately; crookedly; deviously; disturbingly; distressingly; dangerously; suspiciously; obscurely; alarmingly; astonishingly; bewilderingly; wretchedly; unduly.

CIRCULAR

adjectives

inviting; descriptive; confidential; brief; significant; sluggish.

verbs

announce by —; display —; distribute —; lay out —; request —; shower —s; subscribe to —; summon by —; — advertises; — colors; — describes; — explains; — informs; — proclaims; — propagates.

(See communication, publication, letter.)

adverbs

perfectly; absolutely; symmetrically; artistically; ceremonially; originally; decoratively; significantly; smartly; fashionably; curiously; brokenly; naturally; elliptically; impressively; architecturally; theatrically; harmoniously.

CIRCULATE (v)

adverbs

immediately; greedily; continually; widely; extensively; briskly; industriously; limitedly; considerably; enormously; sluggishly; periodically; selectively; inadequately; effectively; normally.

(See disseminate, diffuse.)

CIRCULATION

abnormal; adequate; aroused; deficient; defective; engorged; impaired; lax; hindered; over-stimulated; rapid; sluggish; simulated; tonic.

verbs
aid —; carry on —; check —; constrict —; depress —; increase —; impair —; impede —; improve —; maintain —; obstruct —; overtax —; promote —; quicken —; quiet —; relieve —; restore —; speed up —; stimulate —; throw into —.

CIRCULATION
(newspaper, magazine, etc.)

adjectives
amazing; limited; considerable; vast; enormous; select; huge; extensive; sluggish; periodical; suspended; defective; repressed; throttled; inadequate; effective; brisk; normal.

verbs
augment —; boost —; build —; double —; fix —; heighten —; increase —; lose —; maintain —; promote —; reduce —; — climbs; — drops; — gains; — jumps; — sags; — spurts; — wanes.
(See distribution, number, quantity.)

CIRCUMFERENCE
adjectives
extensive; vast; extreme; luminous.

CIRCUMJACENT
adverbs
closely; influentially; contributively; advantageously; interestedly; actively; importantly; anxiously; indivisibly; inseparably; consequentially; momentously; potently; authoritatively; closely; cooperatively; helpfully; serviceably; opportunely; concernedly; sympathetically; watchfully; warily; providently; alertly; heedfully.

CIRCUMLOCUTORY
adverbs
tiresomely; tediously; unnecessarily; amateurishly; monotonously; maddeningly; vexatiously; impossibly; undesirably; ineptly; unsuitably; extremely; excessively; incurably; incorrigibly; insistently; pedantically; pedagogically; academically; hopelessly; digressively; ramblingly; sadly; inexcusably; inefficiently.

CIRCUMSCRIBE (*v*)
adverbs
narrowly; severely; precisely; closely; rigorously; definitely; clearly; specifically.
(See confine, defense, limit.)

CIRCUMSPECTION
adjectives
exact; utmost; administrative; continual; pious; sly.

CIRCUMSTANCE
adjectives
dominant; antecedent; analogous; formal; favorable; encouraging; exceptional; fortunate; imagined; extenuating; mitigating; accompanying; hurried; external; altered; similar; actual; existing; ensuing; diverse; subsequent; attendant; concomitant; accessory; contingent; manifold; contributory; leading; collateral; expeditious; unfortunate; equivocal; droll; adventitious; novel; romantic; auspicious; pitiful; fortuitous; identical; peculiar; incredible; unsafe; interesting; faulty; minute; formidable; easy; irritable; providential; ridiculous; encumbered; isolated; painful; affluent; present; disastrous; striking; arduous; discouraging; obsolete; momentary; incidental; dreadful; unforeseen; unpropitious; disquieting; untoward; promiscuous; straitened; forgotten; extraordinary; mysterious; uncontrollable; suggestive; singular; suspicious; sordid; curious; comfortable; accidental; unbelievable; peculiar; unlucky; delicate; unpromising; adverse; differing; historical; accidental; evanescent; inexplicable; potent; varying (pl); ignoble; probable; embarrassing; trying; sordid; intellectual; advantageous; astonishing; iniquitous; distressing; trifling; disheartening; agreeable; brutal; reduced; domestic; precarious; impressive; remarkable; frivolous; perplexing; dramatic; diametric; moderate; prevailing; complicated; sensational.

verbs
ascribe to —; attend with —; depend on —; detail —; engender —; impress with —; meet —; overcome by —; ponder —; recount —; relish —; respond to —; rest on —; shape —; stress —; struggle against —; weigh —; — accompanies; — alarms; — alters; — arises; — determines; — forces; — hampers; — imputes; — prevents; — surrounds; — wavers; — yields.
(See condition, incident, cause, occurrence, situation, feature, environment.)

CIRCUMSTANTIAL

adverbs

sensationally; remarkably; insignificantly; trivially; favorably; temporarily; extenuatingly; aggravatingly; coincidentally; fortuitously; unpropitiously; unfavorably; suspiciously; adversely; adventitiously; critically; incidentally; contradictorily; corroboratively; reasonably; plausibly; speciously; credibly.

CIRCUS

adjectives

Jacksonian; bloody; tented; political; traveling; tinseled; three-ring.

verbs

admit to —; "ballyhoo" —; operate —; perform at —; stage —; yearn for —; — amuses; — blares; — displays; — engages; — enlivens; —entertains; — exhibits; — parades; — roams; — tours; — travels; — troups.
(See show.)

CITADEL

adjectives

celebrated; straw-built; unguarded; ancient; social; aerie; capitulated; impregnable; pensile; undefended.

verbs

attack —; bar from —; command —; construct —; erect —; establish —; evolve —; fortify —; man —; pour from —; retreat to —; scale —; siege —; storm —; — contains; — defends; — defies; — guards; — protects; — rises; — stores; — towers; — withstands.
(See fortress.)

CITATION

adjectives

corroborated; ample; apt; ludicrous; partial.

CITE (*v*)

adverbs

earnestly; partially; amply; aptly; accurately; authoritatively; relevantly; sensationally; fortuitously; strikingly.
(See quote, mention.)

CITIZEN

adjectives

belligerent; busy; esteemed; perspicacious; small-salaried; luckless; prosperous; distinguished; patched; individual; prejudiced; plodding; enlightened; enthusiastic; inde-
finite; unworthy; substantial; intelligent; god-fearing; ordinary; peaceable; law-abiding; unoffending; disillusioned; callous; staid; home-loving; ornamental; defenseless; competent; simple; plain-speaking; public-spirited; conscious; active; conspicuous; callous; vile; half-starved; influential; venerable; indignant; average; private; generous; illustrious; cultivated; grave; respectable; admirable; eminent; cloaked; reputable; representative; loyal; worthy; useful; law-abiding; duteous; bespectacled; patriotic; well-known; honorable; lamented; mutinous; plain; simple; quiet; easygoing; innocent; tight-lipped; august; pugnacious; disgruntled; beleaguered; iron-bellied; wistful; regretful; ordinary; humble; average; mere; prosaic; typical; able-bodied; courageous; husky; young; stalwart; bibulous; sanguine; careless; selfish; blind; serious-minded; straight-thinking; reckless; conscientious; high-minded; foremost; valued; wealthy; prominent; leading; outstanding; revered; self-sacrificing; hard-working; progressive; zealous; loyal; kindly; honest; decent; cultured; altruistic; worthy; well-meaning; stolid; solid; independent; untrammeled; noble; exemplary.

verbs

conscript —s; disfranchise —; entitle as —; harangue —s; interview —; oppress —; privilege —; protect —; regiment —s; register as —; tax —; wheedle —s; —s assemble; —s demand; —s elect; — enjoys; — possesses; — protests; —s rally; —s vote; — vows.
(See individual, inhabitant.)

CITIZENRY

adjectives

outraged; humble; contented; greasy; dignified.

CITIZENSHIP

adjectives

national; commonplace; robust; conscientious.

verbs

accept —; acquire —; admit to —; apply for —; cancel —; confer — upon; declare —; deprive of —; desire —; divest of —; drop —; establish —; forfeit —; obtain —; refuse—; renounce—; revoke—; — confers; — entitles; — privileges; — protects.

adjectives

throbbing; bustling; seething; hustling; thriving; growing; brutal; busiest; wealthiest; progressive; unperturbed; huge; teeming; headlong; glorious; rushing; stirring; energetic; modern; flourishing; busy; enterprising; gay; laughing; lighthearted; sleeping; dead; quiet; wicked; free; sinstained; wilted; worth-while; corrupt; ruined; content; intolerant; fanatical; smoldering; dull; murky; grimy; congested; drab; squalid; ugly; commonplace; worse-lit; widespreading; outermost; rich; influential; prosperous; conservative; trading; selfsame; shimmering; noble; thronged; unruly; cathedraled; melancholy; mighty; breathless; ruinous; humming; resplendent; coastal; swarming; fascinating; inspiring; sunken; deserted; gilded; distinguished; diversified; hopeful; distracted; mirthful; opulent; queer; glittering; long-shaped; peaceful; friendly; shivering; glamorous; lamplit; rock-built; annihilated; joyous; menacing; elegant; youthful; mansion-decked; ambitious; nether; imperial; titanic; restless; enchanted; pagan; pleasure; tropical; typical; slumbering; prospective; maritime; clustering; affrighted; melancholy; earthcommanding; advertised; drowned; wondrous; gorgeous; hard-boiled; powerful; awakened; isolated; industrious; ancient; crooked; tortuous; snakelike; rising; unhappy; undefended; cursed; commercial; voluptuous; plague-stricken; congested; wailing; spacious; vast; helpless; holocaust; pest-ridden; torpid; passive; dejected; garrisoned; well-washed; appreciative; ruined; constricted; thriving; decayed; masterful; wrought; luxurious; well-ordered; spirited; advancing; altar-decked; silenced; crowded; provincial; beleaguered; cordial; death-stricken; verdureless; once-famous; heathen; attractive; jeweled; well-watered; eternal; plague-stricken; negligent; viceladen; spire-adorned; sin-compassed; roguehaunted; monolithic; hapless; besieged; materialistic; nebulous; commercial; sinburdened; austere; sunless; unrivalled; futuristic; enthralling; delightful; majestic; marvelous; fabulous; aspiring; great; lovable; desirable; coveted; fascinating; benignant; scintillating; proud; bright; fairest; naughty; impregnable; beautiful; staid; silent; moonlit; dream; lovely; colorful; gray-blue; snow-white; unique; grand; mysterious; adventurous; glittering; dying; buried; bombarded; monotonous; muffled; agate; polyglot; golden-doomed; appealing; infant; native; cosmopolitan; royal; tourist; shipbuilding; lake-girted; guardian; prehistoric; alabaster-like; holy; flat-roofed; oriental-looking; walled; medieval; legendary; industrial; pontifical; celestial; exotic; homogeneous; lurid; confused; incredible; burning; meticulous; leading; principal; vibrant; far-flung; populous; fortified; conquered; well-kept; ever-growing; sun-baked; parched-brown; gentlemannered.

verbs

abide in —; adjoin —; annihilate —; approach —; assault —; banish from —; besiege —; burn —; congregate in —; corrupt —; crowd —; deface —; defend —; deluge —; depopulate —; desolate —; destroy —; doom —; encompass —; erect —; establish —; flank —; harbor in —; haunt —; huddle in —; impoverish —; inhabit —; inundate —; issue from —; lay siege to —; lay waste to —; march through —; migrate to —; mold —; oppress —; pen up in —; pillage —; pollute —; raze —; rule —; sack —; scatter through —; shake —; stake out —; steal over —; strike —; survey —; swallow up in —; take —; tarry in —; tax —; terrorize —; veer toward —; wall in —; war on —; warn —; — acclaims; — basks; — decays; — expands; — flourishes; — forges ahead; — hums; — reeks; — roars; — simmers; — sprouts; — straggles; — towers.

(See town, community.)

CITYLIKE

adverbs

extraordinarily; significantly; unexpectedly; surprisingly; undeniably; meticulously; deliberately; artificially; naturally; disagreeably; agreeably; discordantly; ostentatiously; inharmonoiusly; superciliously; arrogantly; pathetically; ludicrously; ridiculously; foolishly; awkwardly; busily; enterprisingly; prosperously; proudly; fashionably; grandly; incongruously.

CIVIL

adverbs

smoothly; coolly; correctly; properly; appropriately; scarcely; politely; affably; warmly; graciously; sweetly; fawningly; idly; nonchalantly; unexpectedly; suddenly; carefully; officiously; unctuously; blandly; obligingly; complacently; obsequiously; ingratiatingly; tactfully; diplomatically; sagaciously; wisely; necessarily; condescendingly; urbanely; decorously; fashionably;

punctiliously; meticulously; admirably; conventionally; stiffly; demurely; primly; precisely; cautiously; warily.

CIVILIAN
adjectives
meddlesome; covenanted; humdrum; conceited; wretched.

CIVILITY
adjectives
unforced; sad; cold; sweet; creeping; fawning; base; chill; ancient; restrained; interchanged (pl); impetuous; idle; unmeaning.

verbs
accept with —; act with —; answer with —; breed —; cherish —; conform to —; consider —; employ —; deny —; lack —; oblige with —; observe —; occasion —; preserve —; respect —; teach —; train in —; treat with —; want —; — befits.
(See courtesy, politeness.)

CIVILIZATION
adjectives
brutalized; luminous; distinctive; potential; perished; private; primitive; ancient; increasing; vast; varied; overvaunted; bloated; progressive; sophisticated; troubadour; moral; decadent; earthly; ordered; material; contemporary; turbulent; strange; advancing; complex; indigenous; mechanical; passionate; refined; higher; saturated; enlightened; decent; perilous; sick; alien; technical; crumbling; disintegrating; effete; bygone; older; long-vanished; artistic; archaic; forgotten; unique; extraordinary; so-called; cracked; industrial; megalopolitan; superficial; luxurious; urban; domestic; barbaric; aboriginal; agrarian; national; crude; fastidious; majestic; unrecorded; belligerent; chivalrous; selfish; solid; positive; pernicious; prosy; modern; curious; attendant; perfected.

verbs
blot out—; break down—; contribute to—; court—; cradle—; destroy—; doom—; extol—; flout—; found—; fuse—s; infect—; menace—; promote—; raise—; shame—; standardize—; threaten—; —advances; —asserts itself; —decays; —declines; — enslaves; ;—falls; —inflicts; —mars; —perishes; —progresses; —reverts to type; —sweeps onward; —wanes.
(See enlightenment, progress, refinement, advancement, culture.)

CLAD
adverbs
richly; elaborately; gaudily; wretchedly; fully; scantily; shabbily; raggedly; poorly; luxuriously; carefully; carelessly; recklessly; absurdly; fashionably; ridiculously; ludicrously; grotesquely; honorably; unfashionably; garishly; wantonly; laughably; clownishly; seductively; gaily; gorgeously; glamorously; awkwardly; incongruously; outlandishly; expensively; cheaply; smartly; handsomely; drably; extravagantly; economically; tastefully.

CLAD (v)
adverbs
decorously; symbolically; grossly; imperfectly; fittingly; partially; scantily; scarcely; heavily; warmly; harmoniously.
(See dress.)

CLAIM
adjectives
additional; faint; ardent; extenuating; misleading; exaggerated; extravagant; curative; substantiated; indisputable; enormous; groundless; confidential; bitter; exclusive; plausible; intellectual; unquenchable; notorious; complacent; intolerable; advertising; hereditary; unjustifiable; unprophetic; slender; peculiar; sales; fraudulent; rhetorical; accumulating; valid; remaining; worthless; reproachful; respectable; illegal; embroidered; time-honored; extortionate; suitable; contested; obsolete; conflicting (pl); imperial; inexorable; insistent; professional; modest; abiding; prior; rival; inflated; fanciful; questionable; incredible; preposterous; unsavory; false; pecuniary; parental; royal; special; implacable; imperative; unusual; difficult; depreciating; relative.

verbs
adjust—; annul—; assert—; attest to—; base—on; cede—; combat—; confirm—; consider—; contradict—; debate—; defy—; demolish—; denounce—; deny—; dismiss —; dispose of—; dispute—; doubt—; establish—; exempt from—; expose—; forfeit—; honor—; iron out—s; justify—; lay—to; offset—; press—; protest—; reconcile—; record—; refute—; renounce—; retain—; shatter—; smile at—; stake out—; stultify—; substantiate—; support—; surrender—; verify—; waive—; —s diminish; —s dissolve.
(See pretension, demand. title. right.)

CLAIM (v)

adverbs

persistently; strenuously; confidently; assuredly; adroitly; falsely; boldly; vociferously; exorbitantly; ardently; exaggeratedly; groundlessly; unjustifiably; reproachfully; fraudulently; extortionately; inexorably; professionally; insistently; incredibly; legitimately; validly; fancifully; preposterously; implacably; imperatively.

(See assert, affirm, maintain.)

CLAIRVOYANT

adverbs

remarkably; unmistakably; mysteriously; unquestionably; marvelously; prophetically; mesmerically; hypnotically; naturally; extraordinarily; undeniably; absolutely; indisputably; incontestably; traditionally; inherently; palpably; infallibly; conclusively; phenomenally; triumphantly; evidently; manifestly; obviously; incredibly; astonishingly; astoundingly; startlingly.

CLAMBER (v)

adverbs

aimlessly; bravely; laboriously; ceaselessly; clumsily; unsteadily.

(See climb.)

CLAMMY

adverbs

unpleasantly; disagreeably; horridly; horribly; loathsomely; disgustingly; offensively; repulsively; hatefully; necessarily; distastefully; manageably; stickily; adhesively; cohesively; coldly.

CLAMOR

adjectives

full-voiced; ghastly; noisy; tremendous; hideous; hellish; impatient; violent; nerve-straining; deafening; general; mournful; never-ceasing; heart-warming; popular; raucous; frenzied; turbulent; orchestral; sudden; staccato; venomous; savage; ministerial; excited; wretched; smothered; deplorable; loud; ignorant; exacting; blind; vulgar; universal; confirmatory; persistent; dismal; querulous; fulsome; vague; virile; impertinent; muffled; uncontrollable; petty; frightful; selfish; national; thunderous.

verbs

cease—; ease—; fill with—; harken to—; lose in—; prolong—; raise—; vent—; — abates; —bursts forth; —deafens; —

drowns; —peals; —rings; —rumbles; — thickens; —wanes; —waxes.

(See uproar, tumult, din, racket.)

CLAMOR (v)

adverbs

dissentingly; noisily; vociferously; obstreperously; shrilly; hideously; hellishly; mournfully; raucously; frenziedly; turbulently; venomously; wretchedly; deplorably; persistently; dismally; querulously; fulsomely; impertinently; thunderously; uncontrollably.

(See bawl, roar.)

CLAMOROUS

adverbs

noisily; impatiently; surlily; angrily; happily; eagerly; hungrily; deafeningly; madly; frenziedly; suddenly; excitedly; wretchedly; blindly; persistently; anxiously; querulously; vaguely; uncontrollably; selfishly; restlessly; explosively; alarmingly; menacingly; hysterically; enthusiastically; ungovernably; significantly; fanatically; boisterously; jubilantly; joyously; shrilly; uproariously; ominously; importunately; appallingly; impressively; extraordinarily; unwontedly; urgently.

CLAN

adjectives

critical; prolific; original; feudal; clamorous; sturdy; romping; murderous; visionary; hostile; rival.

verbs

assemble—; associate with—; connect with —; descend from—; dissolve—; father—; found—; grace—; join—; lead—; muster —; organize—; prohibit—; represent—; rule—; trace—; unify—; —gathers; —marauds; —pillages; —plunders; —terrorizes.

(See tribe.)

CLANDESTINE

adverbs

romantically; furtively; sordidly; inviolately; strictly; necessarily; unhappily; guiltily; subtly; curiously; unsavorily; evasively; stealthily; slyly; skulkingly; terribly; miserably.

CLANG

adjectives

imperious; fearful; warning; horrid; windy; glad; melancholy; lingering; hollow; ecstatic; nonchalant; resounding; harsh; discordant; metallic; muffled; funereal; brassy; vibrating.

CLANG (v)
adverbs
discordantly; infernally; resonantly; imperiously; fearfully; horridly; hollowly; ecstatically; vibratingly; metallically; funereally; dismally.

CLANGOR
adjectives
mad; sudden; merry; deafening; reverberative; impatient.

CLANGOROUS
adverbs
madly; terrifyingly; violently; riotously; horribly; jubilantly; cheeringly; mournfully; funereally; sadly; alarmingly; warningly; menacingly; joyously; happily; joyfully; stirringly; thunderously; sweetly; softly; harmoniously; deeply; deafeningly; sonorously; melodiously; mellifluously; heartily; hearteningly.

CLANK
adjectives
steady; metallic; tiny; tinkling.

CLANNISH
adverbs
incurably; delightfully; loyally; incorrigibly; eternally; characteristically; inherently; sturdily; stoutly; noisily; quietly; devotedly; staunchly; dependably; truly; racially; locally; provincially; intrepidly; indomitably; intrinsically; dangerously; alarmingly; actively; definitely; vigorously.

CLANNISHNESS
adjectives
unconquerable; enforced.

CLAP
adjectives
friendly; frightful; genial.

CLAP (v)
adverbs
conclusively; vigorously; dutifully; noiselessly; unobtrusively; frightfully; thunderously; genially; enthusiastically; freely; monotonously; liberally; appreciatively; sympathetically; gratefully; welcomingly; ceaselessly.
(See applaud.)

CLARIFY (v)
adverbs
successfully; intellectually; admirably; miraculously; satisfactorily; completely; partially; painstakingly; generally; notably.
(See illumine, clear.)

CLARITY
adjectives
intellectual; painful; interpretative; unsurpassed; sparkling; aching; diamondlike; enervating; sickening; miraculous; admirable; fragrant; intense; sunlit; irrefutable; quiet; cold; crystal.

CLASH
adjectives
furious; threatened; explosive; angry; contemporaneous; rude; syncopated; sharp; memorable; initial; street; recurrent; joyous; violent; naval; brisk; soundless; bloody; metallic; muffled; inter-racial.

verbs
attack with—; avoid—; collide with—; embroil in—; engage in—; incite—; produce—; recoil from—; recount—; result in—; strike with—; —conflicts with; —echoes; —peals; —resounds; —shocks; —thunders; —warns.
(See crash, collision, opposition, noise.)

CLASH (v)
adverbs
unpleasantly; antagonistically; explosively; rhythmically; furiously; angrily; rudely; sharply; initially; recurrently; violently; muffledly; thunderously; intermittently; instinctively.
(See hurtle, crash, disagree.)

CLASHING
adverbs
unfortunately; unhappily; hostilely; inimically; contradictorily; unpropitiously; constantly; pugnaciously; truculently; ill-naturedly; contentiously; quarrelsomely; unnecessarily; ill-advisedly; hastily; antagonistically; foolishly; irritably; unreasonably; senselessly; miserably; hotly; frightfully; pathetically; vexatiously; bitterly; rudely; violently; frequently; furiously; crudely; sharply.

CLASP
(embrace)
adjectives
conventional; dewy; impulsive; uncoercive; warm; comforting; gentlemanly; gentle; confiding; cruel; lingering; eager; cold; firm; frantic; healthy; strong.

adjectives
gilt; ornate; clicking.

CLASP
(*general*)
verbs
affix—; brace—; buckle—; cleave—; connect—; fit—; fumble with—; furnish with—; gird with—; hook—; join—; strain—; —bars; —embraces; —encircles; —fastens; —grasps; —insures; —interlocks; —overlaps; —secures.
(See hook, embrace, lock.)

CLASP (*v*)
adverbs
convulsively; deliberately; fondly; unprofitably; familiarly; sensually; hungrily; severely; frantically; impulsively; comfortingly; confidingly; cruelly; lingeringly; coldly; firmly; despairingly.
(See grasp, grapple, clutch.)

CLASS
(*school*)
adjectives
academic; attending; assembled; bespectacled; diligent; elementary; fixed; grade; grouped; graduating; freshman; intermediate; lecture; overworked; primer; primary; advanced; subdivided; unlimited.

verbs
address—; admit to—; attend—; change —es; conduct—; divide into—es; examine —; lecture—; limit—; promote—; raise—; rate—; unite—; —answers; —assembles; —choruses; —competes; —graduates; —recites; —reviews; —sings; —studies.

CLASS
(*social*)
adjectives
arrogant; unclaimed; ruthless; vast; emergent; ruling; history-conscious; leisure; spurious; laboring; useful; humble; technical; servile; degraded; generic; social; diversified; privileged; conflicting; piratical; consistent; submerged; collected; represented; traditional; dole-receiving; peaceful; better; vicious; inarticulate; dominant; rapid; various (pl); exclusive; despised; venal; conspicuous; liberated; opulent; irresponsible; possessionless; obnoxious; corresponding; lower; agrarian; distinct; noticeable; exploiting; vulgar; inferior; irreconcilable; wealthy; cultured;

upper; cultivated; best; preferred; conservative; industrial; intellectual; proletarian; illiterate; submerged; artisan; contented; prosperous; working; object; odious; mediocre; truant; rising; central; middle-aged; indivisible; appointive; chivalrous; holy; iron-bound; vigorous; skeptical; unimpassioned; economic.

verbs
arouse—; bow to—; consort with—; do away with—es; educate—; elevate—; enslave—; fix—; free—; level—; liberate—es; lower—es; separate—; stifle—; —es arise; —es gravitate; —idolizes; —predominates; —rebels.
(See caste, rank, order.)

CLASSIC
adjectives
perfumed; bristling; venerable; favorite; beloved; noblest; unforgettable; purest; intellectual; juvenile; immortal; rare.

CLASSICAL
adverbs
superbly; acceptably; admittedly; elegantly; easily; gracefully; readily; academically; artistically; chastely; correctly; felicitously; naturally; unaffectedly; modestly; unpretentiously; undoubtedly; deservedly; avowedly; pleasingly; aptly; appropriately; commendably; deservedly; admirably; laudably; universally; uniformly.

CLASSICISM
adjectives
capricious; cold; ethical.

CLASSICS
verbs
accept—; acquaint with—; assimilate—; associate with—; bar—; criticize—; delve into—; discuss—; edit—; educate in—; familiarize with—; favor—; forsake—; instruct in—; introduce to—; model on—; pertain to—; place among—; prefer—; quote—; regard—; revel in—; tabulate—; verse in—; —exemplify; —guide.
(See literature, history, biography, religion.)

CLASSIFICATION
adjectives
racial; minute; inexact; detailed; price; misleading; occupational; moral; lucid; compendious; social; principal; broad; fixed.

verbs

allocate—; arrange—; assign—; assume—; attempt—; confirm—; correct—; distinguish—; employ—; exclude—; exhaust—; formulate—; head—; lead—; observe—; place in—; question—; recognize—; reduce—; retain—; separate into—; subordinate—; systematize—; —allows; —orders; —permits.

(See arrangement, group.)

CLASSIFY (v)

adverbs

carefully; ignorantly; conveniently; racially; minutely; exactly; misleadingly; lucidly; compendiously; socially; broadly.

(See arrange.)

CLASSMATE

adjectives

erstwhile; condescending; fun-loving; heckling; parasitic; superiority-inflicting; snubbing; snobbish; unapproachable; whilom.

verbs

compete with—s; enroll with—s; hail—s; prompt—s; recognize—s; reunite with—s; tutor—; —advances; —chooses; —s clash; —cribs (colloq.); —disenrolls; —s elect; —fails; —"flunks"; —graduates; —s honor; —recites; —vacations.

(See member, student, companion, friend.)

CLASSROOM

adjectives

grimy; gloomy; stuffy; modern; noisy.

verbs

absent from—; "barge" into—; bustle into —; buzz through—; clutter up—; congregate in—; dismiss from—; disorder—; equip—; illuminate—; preside over—; retain in—; rule—; scurry through—; survey—; —clamors with; —hums.

(See room.)

CLATTER

adjectives

prodigious; city-bred; glib-tongued; authoritative; confused; subsided; metallic; hideous; delectable; rousing; ringing; harsh; sudden; rhythmic; wild; hysterical; swift; reverberating; castanet.

CLATTER (v)

adverbs

recklessly; dissonantly; prodigiously; confusedly; metallically; hideously; ringingly; harshly; wildly; hysterically; furiously; excitingly; rudely.

(See tramp.)

CLAUSE

adjectives

complicated; misleading; expatiatory; particular; introductory; compensatory; sweeping; glacial; insidious; qualifying; solemn; independent; appended; ambiguous; flexible; limiting; adjective; adverbial; noun; appositional; descriptive; secret; hidden.

verbs

actuate—; condemn—; cudgel—; denounce—; evade—; "fake"—; frame—; insert—; insist on—; introduce—; kill—; legalize—; motivate—; occasion—; order—; ponder—; question—; sacrifice—; rule against—; unearth—; violates—; —bars; —cedes; —denotes; —embodies; —governs; —guards against; —joins; —provides; —stipulates; —varies; —wills.

(See provision, article, part.)

CLAW

adjectives

grimy; hooded; bloody; scarifying; holy; ominous; nipping; powerful; burrowing; slimy; acute; prehensile; scaly; sheathed; quivering; dirt-encrusted; feeble; invisible.

verbs

arm with—s; clip—s; clutch in—s; grapple with—s; grasp in—s; grip in—s; hook in —s; lay hold with—s; pare—; seize in—; sharpen—s; snip off—s; strike with—s; try —s on; —s flash by; —s lacerate; —s miss; —s rend; —s rip; —s scrape; —s scratch; —s snatch; —s tear.

(See talon, nail, clutch, hand.)

CLAW (v)

adverbs

wildly; fiercely; bloodily; ominously; feebly; voraciously; hungrily; viciously; hatefully; fiendishly; frantically; frightfully; sadistically.

(See scratch.)

CLAY

adjectives

clammy; cradling; humble; barren; encumbering; painted; sun-baked; impure; rebellious; uncoffined; tenacious; senseless; fruitful; unconsecrated; well-trodden; unconscious; breathless; human; eventful; sodden; reddish; brittle; damp.

verbs

cart—; cast—; chisel—; cleave—; color—; compound—; daub with—; dry—; fashion of—; fire—; form of—; line with—; mix—; moisten—; mould—; paint—; plaster with

—; prepare—; refine—; rise from—; seal with—; shape with—; soil with—; temper —; tread into—; —cements; —hardens; —moulders; —pastes; —resists; —sinks; —succumbs; —wears.

CLEAN

adverbs
hygienically; immaculately; neatly; spotlessly; stainlessly; tidily; trimly; sweetly; refreshingly; satisfactorily; punctiliously; meticulously; fragrantly; wholesomely; healthily; fastidiously; exquisitely; scrupulously; surgically; personally; shiningly; glowingly; delightfully; gratefully; comfortably; perfectly; faultlessly; impeccably; consummately; neatly; sprucely; radiantly; superbly; incredibly; finically; fussily; fanatically; daintily; sturdily; acceptably; passably; indifferently; presumably; appreciably.

CLEAN (v)

adverbs
immaculately; scrupulously; ambitiously; superficially; fussily; diligently; indifferently; ostentatiously; industriously; scientifically; passably; thoroughly; generally; fastidiously; exquisitely; enviably; orally; spotlessly; surgically; aridly.
(See wash.)

CLEANING

adjectives
distinctive; scientific; effective; exclusive; passable; spasmodic; thorough; general.

CLEANLINESS

adjectives
sterile; sweet; life-saving; fastidious; exquisite; notable; enviable; oral; scrupulous; spotless; personal; surgical; nice; general; arid; sinewy.

verbs
advise —; emphasize —; enjoin —; extol —; honor —; lack —; maintain —; necessitate —; preach —; respect —; sacrifice —; teach —.
(See hygiene.)

CLEAR

adverbs
explicitly; intelligibly; definitely; graphically; unmistakably; beautifully; crystally; unsurpassably; remarkably; unequivocally; decisively; startlingly; essentially; terribly; extraordinarily; easily; smoothly; positively; definitely; absolutely; unquestionably; obviously; plainly; categorically; incontestably; happily; comfortingly; satisfactorily.

CLEAR (v)

adverbs
tolerably; auspiciously; systematically; substantially; crystally; dramatically; poetically; unequivocally; limpidly; essentially; admirably; partially; annoyingly.
(See clarify, elucidate, explain.)

CLEAR-HEADED

adverbs
shrewdly; naturally; subtly; extremely; alertly; consciously; intentionally; discreetly; unexpectedly; infallibly; precociously; coldly; penetratingly; singularly; astoundingly; cleverly; astutely; craftily; profoundly; discriminatingly; manifestly; obviously; significantly; dangerously; alarmingly; perspicaciously; unwontedly.

CLEARING

adjectives
eloquent; unproductive.

CLEARNESS

adjectives
unaccustomed; ever-increasing; unsurpassable; agonizing; masterly; noonday; crystal; remarkable; sufficient; dramatic; admirable; diminished; poetic; crystalline; unequivocal; decisive; limpid; startling; essential; burning; horrible; nauseous; eerie; abominable; impulsive; calculating.

CLEATS

adjectives
longitudinal; transverse; rubber; football; leather; damaging; dangerous.

CLEFT

adjectives
unsunned; mossy; deep; gaping; vertical; narrow; steep.

CLEMENCY

adjectives
executive; merciful; benignant; gracious; bountiful; charitable; magnanimous.

verbs
allow —; beg —; display —; dispose toward —; exercise —; exhibit —; forgive in —; grant —; incline toward —; insure —; offer —; oppose —; promise —; recommend —; soften with —; suggest —; temper with —; — adds; — spares.
(See forbearance, mercy.)

CLEMENT

adverbs

mercifully; sympathetically; tolerantly; moderately; mildly; compassionately; humanely; understandingly; unexpectedly; piteously; charitably; ruthfully; sagaciously; wisely; discerningly; generously; benevolently; shrewdly; magnanimously.

CLENCH (v)

adverbs

convulsively; tightly; firmly; unrelentingly; severely; agonizingly; hopelessly; unceasingly; hysterically; tremblingly; abruptly; fearfully; genially; characteristically; appallingly; deftly; painfully.

(See clutch.)

CLERGY

adjectives

modest; fashionable; regional; corrupt; parochial; reverend; fanatical.

verbs

benefit by —; connect with —; distinguish —; divide —; exempt —; oust from —; persecute —; robe —; set apart —; support —; unfrock —; — advocates; — authorizes; — consecrates; — devotes; — embraces; — engineers; — ministers; — preaches; — privileges.

(See clergyman, minister.)

CLERGYMAN

adjectives

worthy; ordained; well-informed; influential; leading; superannuated; fussy; distinguished; eminent; disgraced; spineless; diffident; respected; deserving; unsuccessful; welcome; elderly; purring.

verbs

abide by —; bar —; confess to —; confide in —; delude —; ordain —; persecute —; qualify as —; revere —; — beseeches; — blesses; — delivers; — endeavors; — intones; — orates; — pleads; — preaches; — teaches; — voices; — waxes.

(See minister.)

CLERIC

adjectives

minor; prim; devout; righteous; exhorting; mild; inoffensive; shepherding; soul-directing.

CLERICAL

adverbs

monotonously; fastidiously; punctiliously; tediously; importantly; primarily; modestly; humbly; pompously; primly; precisely; fanatically; comically; unsuitably; slavishly; humbly; elegantly; gently; mildly; unassumingly; unpretentiously; ostentatiously; flauntingly; worthily; influentially; fussily; sedately.

CLERK

adjectives

shabby; confidential; delicate; officious; trustworthy; discreet; minor; embarrassed; assessing; unsympathetic; dispensing; efficient; obsequious; hard-working; quick-witted; gouging; small; studious; wise; lynx-eyed; vigilant; plodding; sneering; genial; generous; courteous; diligent; satisfactory; busy; conscientious; meticulous; orderly; dapper; impecunious.

verbs

advance —; discharge —; ordain —; promote —; retain —; — accounts; — announces; — collects; — corresponds; — documents; — enters; — greets; — rates; — records; — sells.

(See employee.)

CLEVER

adverbs

notably; strikingly; consummately; diabolically; slyly; fiendishly; peculiarly; artfully; marvellously; adroitly; incredibly; admirably; remarkably; dangerously; palpably; obviously; undeniably; suspiciously; neatly; matchlessly; craftily; masterfully; wonderfully; constitutionally; innately; instinctively; inherently; subtly; cunningly; capably; competently; proficiently; deftly; discreetly; handily.

CLEVERNESS

adjectives

notable; insolent; insinuating; satiric; striking; meretricious; considerable; consummate.

verbs

accompany with —; deceive with —; display —; envy —; exhibit —; market —; necessitate —; perform with —; question —; reward —; shed —.

(See skill, ingenuity.)

CLICK

adjectives

faint; whispered; resolute; dry; animated; soulless; jarring; indignant; responsive; metallic; sharp; hollow; emphatic; mysterious; mechanical; significant.

adverbs

teasingly; faintly; animatedly; indignantly; metallically; jauntily; gaily; significantly; spontaneously; mechanically; repeatedly; intermittently.

(See sound.)

CLIENT

adjectives

trembling; desirable; gilded; prospective; fair; courtroom; stolid; indifferent; obstinate; timid; whilom; unfortunate; parasitical; rich; likely; uninvited; much-injured; oppressed; distinguished.

CLIENTELE

adjectives

discriminating; conservative; distinguished; congenial; refined; select; restricted; discerning; diversified; financial; desirable; exacting; influential; fine.

CLIFF

adjectives

smooth; vertical; lofty; abrupt; ebony; frowning; iron-stained; black; distant; ochre; scarped; hoary; jutting; fringing; treacherous; honeycombed; populous; inaccessible; naked; formidable; perpendicular; snowy; desolate; picturesque; precipitous; ragged; rude; radiant; unexpected; perilous; buttressed; stupendous; abrupt; craggy; majestic; impending; fearful; steep; frosty; sheer; rugged; overhanging; reeking; implacable; cloudy; haughty; cloud-encircled; broken; great; colossal; lofty; gigantic; tremendous; high; mighty; towering; giant; barren; bald; bare; wild; tinted; tortuous; weathered; wind-worn; crumbling; jagged; crude; sinister; grotesque; fantastic; limestone; granite; rocky; thorn-clad; narrow; iron-walled; ferny; orchard-crowned; heavily wooded; forest-covered; icebound; broad; bold; receding; sculptured; sloping.

verbs

clamber up —; climb —; fall from —; overhang —; peer from —; reconnoiter —; scale —; skirt —; slither over —; suspend from —; throw from —; tumble from —; — looms up; — rises; — sinks.

(See crag, precipice.)

CLIMATE

adjectives

dry; marvelous; summer; outdoor; world-famous; incomparable; mild; kindly; inviting; pleasant; enervating; rugged; healthful; bracing; life-prolonging; gracious; superb; gentle; beneficent; maligned; semitropical; oppressive; delicious; glowing; balmy; invigorating; divers (pl); burning; listless; villainous; various (pl); boreal; hyperequatorial; bland; trying; exhausting; arctic; dry; sultry; severe; trick; tropical; exhilarating; salubrious; temperate; genial; frowning; delightful; subduing; smiling; perfect; year-round; propitious; equable; fittest; tranquil; ocean; lovely; stern; excellent; unbearable; bitter; forbidding; rigorous; harsh; rotten; poisonous; arid; high; wonderful; winter; southern; atmospheric; variable; capricious; altered; seasonal; coldest; humid; torrid; damp; changing.

verbs

accustom to —; adapt to —; ascribe to —; chart —; malign —; record —; seek —; succumb to —; — affects; — batters; — braces; — depends on; — destroys; —devastates; — discourages; — invigorates; — irritates; — enlivens; — prevails; — ravages; — restores; — revives; — sickens; — stimulates.

(See weather.)

CLIMAX

adjectives

characteristic; appalling; fit; momentous; glorious; culminant; unforgettable; sad; dramatic; exquisite; progressive; prepared; surprising; approaching; autumnal; frolicsome; disgraceful; ingenious; horrifying; grandstand; poignant; emotional; proper; unexpected; thunderous; oratorical; inevitable; marvelous; stupendous; glowing; inescapable; pulsating; deft; unsatisfactory; lightninglike.

verbs

abate at —; ascend to —; culminate in —; deduce —; delay —; delight in —; foreshadow —; hurtle to —; lax after —; postpone —; prelude —; prepare for —; rise to —; — dies; — excites; — interests; — occurs; — surprises.

(See culmination, extreme.)

CLIMAX (v)

adverbs

inevitably; appallingly; momentously; gloriously; unforgettably; dramatically; exquisitely; disgracefully; horrifyingly; poignant-

ly; emotionally; unexpectedly; oratorically; marvelously; stupendously; tragically; comically.
(See finish.)

CLIMB
adjectives
lewd; beastly; upward; breezy; steady; wonderful; sporty; muscle-racking; long; hard; uphill; winding; persistent; plodding; blistering; dizzy.

verbs
accomplish —; ascend —; attain —; boast of —; cease —; enjoy —; gird for —; mount to —; negotiate —; prepare for —; reconnoiter for —; scale —; spur to —; toil up —; — excites; — exhausts; — exhilarates; — fatigues; — thrills; — wearies.
(See ascent.)

CLIMB (v)
adverbs
nimbly; perversely; strenuously; reluctantly; desperately; lamely; steadily; ploddingly; dizzily; dexterously; skillfully; laboriously; unceasingly; determinedly.
(See clamber, scale.)

CLIMBER
adjectives
expert; social; respectable; superior; snobbish; repulsed; wonderful; ambitious; intrepid; mountain; indefatigable; aggressive.

CLIMBING
adjectives
hot; venturous; exhausting; tedious; fruitless; arduous.

CLIME
adjectives
serene; inclement; cloudless; delightful; sunless; inhospitable; blissful; celestial; rougher; torrid; pleasant; eastern; drear; hostile; sunny; glorious; radiant; changeful; distant; genial; unknown; capricious; fair; happy; scenic; southern; rigorous.

CLING (v)
adverbs
adhesively; tenaciously; desperately; blindly; credulously; firmly; faithfully; purposefully; heavily; persistently; timorously; affectionately; endearingly; invariably; exhaustingly.
(See hang.)

CLINIC
adjectives
public; impersonal; domestic; courtesy; private; convenient; indispensable.

verbs
admit to —; attach to —; attend —; conduct —; contribute to —; endow —; establish —; extol —; install —; institute —; maintain —; practise in —; subsidize —; support —; visit —; — adjusts; — administers; — advises; — cures; — diagnoses; — discovers; — investigates; — observes; — records; — specializes; — surveys; — tabulates; — treats.
(See school, instruction, institution.)

CLIP (v)
adverbs
fantastically; closely; raggedly; dexterously; evenly; painfully; skillfully; roughly.
(See trim.)

CLIPPER
adjectives
lofty; heavy; sparred; lean; graceful; swift.

CLIQUE
adjectives
irresponsible; campus; mutinous; ruling; esoteric; secret; nominating.

CLOAK
adjectives
leopard-skin; hooded; constitutional; bad-fitting; ludicrous; tattered; snatched; feathery; dusky; frieze; cardinal; ungathered; shimmering; girlish; sodden; voluminous; long; sweeping; tinseled; mantled; impervious; full.

verbs
bear under—; bury in—; drape—about; draw—; envelop in—; fashion—; fasten—; garment in—; line—; loose—; pluck off—; raise—; spread—; stain—; wrap in—; —conceals; —covers; —disguises; —hides; —hoods; —mantles; —masks; —protects; —secretes; —shelters; —warms.
(See coat, mask, garment, disguise.)

CLOAK (v)
adjectives
constantly; completely; ludicrously; shimmeringly; voluminously; sweepingly; imperviously; snugly; warmly; comfortably; parsimoniously.
(See conceal, mask.)

CLOCK

adjectives

brass-bound; clanging; unvarying; vigilant; ingenious; tall; glowing; synchronous; illuminated; noisy; chiming; solemn; dignified; pine; delirious.

verbs

read—; set—; wind—; —alarms; —chimes; —clangs; —s disagree; —fools; —gains; —heralds; —indicates; —knells; —lies; —misses; —rings; —strikes; —ticks off; —tolls; —trembles; —vibrates; —warns. (See watch.)

CLOD

adjectives

finite; loamy; frozen; wormy; icy; kneaded; sluggish; plow-cloven.

CLOISTER

adjectives

shady; open; solemn; personal; dilapidated; mournful; monkish; restful; beautiful.

CLOISTERED

adjectives

conventionally; monastically; happily; willingly; voluntarily; perpetually; consecratedly; religiously; inviolably; piously; holily; devoutly; reverently; fervidly; eagerly; blessedly; prayerfully; securely; unassailably; safely.

CLOSE

adjectives

summary; speedy; rapid; long-expected; official; bloody; glorious; victorious; tragic; rollicking; undramatic.

CLOSE (v)

adverbs

securely; peremptorily; lazily; reluctantly; abruptly; grimly; instantly; spasmodically; virtually; unexpectedly; wistfully; hermetically; discreetly; summarily; officially; victoriously; tragically.
(See terminate, end.)

CLOSENESS

adjectives

furtive; essential; unwinking.

CLOSET

adjectives

well-filled; portable; glazed; stuffy; cedar; hall; dark; tiny; shallow; obscure.

verbs

air—; conceal in—; creep from—; crowd—; deposit in—; enclose in—; force—; hide in—; imprison in—; invade—; lock in—; occupy—; recess in—; repose in—; retire into—; retreat into—; rummage in—; seclude in—; secrete in—; shut in—; store in—; unlock—; ventilate—.
(See chamber, room, recess.)

CLOSE-TONGUED

adverbs

discreetly; prudently; wisely; judiciously; sagely; quietly; thoughtfully; reflectively; unusually; habitually; philosophically; astutely; cleverly; laconically; reticently; safely; invariably; cautiously; warily; circumspectly; loyally; smartly; consistently; shrewdly.

CLOT

adjectives

convenient; cohesive; fibrous; embolic; gelatinous; hardened; semisolid; stubborn.

verbs

coagulate in—; cohere in—; congeal into—; dissolve—; form—; mass in—; mat with —s; melt—; —cements; —checks; —hardens; —lumps; —stems.

CLOTH

adjectives

worsted; patented; irreproachable; beautiful; nonshrinkable; sturdy; long-fibred; handsome; silver-striped; imported; rugged; soft; subdued; fine-textured; rich; dressy; quality; cool; smart; suave; silky; smooth-textured; wool; long-wearing; summer; unfinished; featherweight; zephyrweight; superlative; firm; striped; two-ply; knife-edge; durable; baize; painted; elegant; hair; spotless; brocaded; coarse; fluttering; thin; cotton; vile; greasy; trailing; polishing; draped; snowy; immaculate.

verbs

adorn—; bias—; cast—over; darn—; emerge from—; finger—; gather—; saturate—; shroud in—; spin—; strain through—; weave—; wrap in—; —adorns; —hangs; —indicates.
(See fabric, wool, silk, cotton, drapery, material.)

CLOTHE (v)

adverbs

comfortably; miserably; profusely; uniformly; irreproachably; beautifully; handsomely; coolly; smartly; suavely; spotless-

ly; coarsely; immaculately; vilely; seductively; temptingly; ravishingly; glamorously; appropriately; faultlessly; inappropriately; incongruously; formally; ordinarily; voluminously; hideously; drably
(See dress, attire.)

CLOTHED
adverbs
richly; elaborately; gaudily; wretchedly; fully; scantily; shabbily; raggedly; luxuriously; carefully; elegantly; carelessly; recklessly; absurdly; fashionably; ridiculously; ludicrously; honorably; unfashionably; garishly; laughably; gaily; seductively; gorgeously; glamorously; rakishly; awkwardly; incongruously; outlandishly; expensively; cheaply; smartly; handsomely; drably; extravagantly; economically.

CLOTHES
adjectives
gay; seductive; feminine; tempting; gorgeous; ravishing; glamorous; bright; fluttering; sensible; fresh; clean; appropriate; harmonized; picture-book; well-cut; ready-made; fashionable; faultless; evening; unkempt; dusty; bedraggled; ragged; patched; town; shiny; stained; dirty; cast-off; inappropriate; lanky; ill-fitting; loose-hanging; awkward; free; incongruous; horrible; dreadful; deplorable; bizarre; rakish; gaudy; nobby; vivid; outlandish; astonishing; everyday; working; riding; queer; country; shabby; summer; immaculate; disordered; ordinary; patriarchal; expensive; swaddling; drenched; bespattered; mud-covered; formal; voluminous; Easter; foolish; smart; dependable; famous; individualized; well-tailored; fine; hand-tailored; comfortable; hideous; baggy; dowdy; string-colored; advertised; pepper-and-salt; drab.

CLOTHING
adjectives
ragged; tailored; travel-stained; indispensable; fastidious; tattered; cast-off; sad; nondescript; complicated; soiled; frayed; legal; dreadful; russet; mortal; small; scant; flashy; drenched; ruined; seedy; personal.

verbs
alter—; array in—; bare of—; cast off—; closet—; design—; discolor—; display—; divest of—; doff—; don—; fashion—; lack—; launder—; model—; outwear—;

penetrate—; purvey—; refurbish—; rend —; renew—; saturate—; store—; strip off—; style—; swaddle in—; tailor—; tatter—; vest in—; —allures; —belies; —chafes; —denotes; —expresses; —flutters; —masquerades.
(See dress, raiment, apparel.)

CLOUD
adjectives
slate-colored; puffy; snow-white; gray-blue; mauve; silver; opaline; dense; glittering; golden; crisp; hazy; bluish; sun-filled; dazzling; thin; misty; drifting; passing; hurrying; scattering; rolling; racing; soaring; flying; scudding; broken; rifted; wild; black; frayed; breaking; gritty; paunchy; blood-colored; bulbous; swollen; cumulus; dark; darkening; endless; sullen; rolling; disastrous; angry; menacing; thunder; lowering; heavy; shapeless; curtain; exemplary; leaking; massed; low-hanging; opaque; distant; tangible; unvarying; tiniest; wind-spun; mysterious; mountain; smoke; desolate; incandescent; moon; crimson; flitting; flaky; eternal; sanguine; wind-driven; mantling; dangerous; glimmering; wrinkled; coifing; airy; veiling; purple; fugitive; pasturing; delicate; radiant; coppery; eddying; foggy; melting; lachrymose; mournful; embattled; scattered; perpetual; thick; sun-rimmed; sacred; chariot; sunset; darksome; rainy; luminous; vast; severing; bursting; downpouring; sullen; brilliant; serrate; smothered; lurid; dull; restless; sundering; envious; massive; gilded; fleecy; flowing; hovering; fat; clammy; perturbed; poisonous; westward-stationed; murmurous; suffocating; interwoven; tear-laden; battlemented; dripping; many-folded; perceptible; pillared; inky; irrevocable; feathery; dusking; orange; infernal; sulphurous; amber; canvas; cinerous; wondrous; rosy; billowy; soft-gray; sable.

verbs
ascend to—s; aspire to—s; bivouac in—; checker with—s; cleave—s; clothe in—; curtain with—s; deck with—; descend from —; fan off—; float in—; gild—; lose in—; penetrate—; pierce—; ride upon—; sail on—; slip into—; vanish into—; withdraw into—; wreathe in—; —billows; —blankets; —blots out; —creeps up; —curls; —darkens; —descends; —dims; —discharges; —disperses; —drenches; —drifts; —flees; —freaks; —gushes; —hides; —hovers; —hurries; —lifts; —melts;

—menaces; —mottles; —mounts; —musters; —obscures; —obstructs; —overcasts; —overshadows; —s part; —s pockmark the sky; —races; —rebuffs; —s scatter; —screens; —scurries; —shrouds; —smoulders; —soars; —s stream by; —sweeps down; —swirls up; —threatens; —vanishes; —veils; —wanders; —weeps; —whitens; —wings by.

CLOUD (v)
adverbs
heavily; densely; hazily; mistily; rollingly; scuddingly; blackly; sullenly; disastrously; mysteriously; foggily; mournfully; sulphurously; luridly.
(See shade.)

CLOUDLESS
adverbs
gloriously; beautifully; brightly; brilliantly; dazzlingly; radiantly; sunnily; garishly; refulgently; pitilessly; mercilessly; hotly; breathlessly; happily; luckily; fortunately; joyously; splendidly; magnificently; enchantingly; pleasantly; delightfully; ravishingly; pleasurably; refreshingly; cheeringly; enjoyably; utterly.

CLOUDY
adverbs
mistily; darkly; rosily; densely; hazily; thinly; thickly; completely; partly; occasionally; wildly; gloomily; sullenly; dismaly; angrily; windily; mysteriously; suddenly; delicately; foggily; perpetually; brokenly; luridly; fleecily; suffocatingly; surprisingly; hopelessly; ominously; menacingly; discouragingly; faintly; muggily; dunly; distressingly; disturbingly.

CLOVER
adjectives
incarnate; scented; sweet-smelling; blooming; nodding; bee-calling.

CLOWN
adjectives
sweet; bungling; loutish; sad; yawning; brokenhearted; roguish; impudent; grimacing; rollicking; whimsical; appreciated.

verbs
play—; —antics; —burlesques; —caricatures; —entertains; —farces; —frolics; —grimaces; —jigs; —mimics; —pantomimes; —portrays; —somersaults; —taunts.
(See fool.)

CLOWN (v)
adverbs
professionally; hilariously; divertingly; sophisticatedly; loutishly; roguishly; impudently; grimacingly; rollickingly; whimsically.
(See jest.)

CLOWNISH
adverbs
roguishly; impudently; whimsically; comically; madly; foolishly; provokingly; everlastingly; incurably; teasingly; irresistibly; boorishly; waggishly; jocosely; roughly; innocently; merrily; blithely; joyously; boyishly; entertainingly; rowdily; indecorously; unbecomingly; extravagantly; horridly; amusingly; unwontedly; hilariously; habitually; delicately; deliberately; unceasingly; incessantly; tiresomely.

CLUB
(*society*)
adjectives
influential; literary; luxurious; attractive; sumptuous; social; enthusiastic; industrial; exclusive; permanent; flourishing; musical.

verbs
affiliate with—; associate with—; bar from—; "blackball" from—; charter—; contribute to—; form—; found—; house—; organize—; pledge to—; preside over—; —assembles; —benefits from; —convenes; —elects; —springs up.
(See organization, association.)

CLUB
(*weapon*)
adjectives
mossy; powerful; formidable; threatening; respect-inspiring; sturdy; purposeful.

verbs
arm with—; bat with—; batter with—; bear—; brandish—; carve—; clutch—; cudgel with—; exercise—; extend—; flog with—; flourish—; hurl—; rule with—; strike with—; subdue with—; submit to—; threaten with—; whirl—; wield—; yield to—.
(See cudgel, bat.)

CLUBFOOTED
adverbs
unfortunately; hopelessly; irremediably; crookedly; monstrously; hideously; slightly; pathetically; unmistakably; noticeably;

grotesquely; fantastically; outlandishly; miserably; wretchedly; helplessly; strangely; pitiably; woefully.
(See crippled.)

CLUCK (v)

adverbs
busily; anxiously; industriously; maternally; absorbedly; endlessly; cheerfully; fondly; pleasantly; unrestrainedly.
(See chatter.)

CLUE

adjectives
inescapable; priceless; vital; suggestive; recondite; fancied; elusive; definite; flawless; tangible; exhausted; magnificent; startling; surprising; bewildering; slender.

verbs
discover—; divulge—; efface—; follow up—; join—s; muddle up—; produce—; recognize—; scatter—s; strike upon—; tackle—; thread—s together; trace—; track down—; uncover—; unearth—; unravel—; yield—; —convicts; —crumbles; —guides; —indicates; —perplexes; —puzzles; — solves; —warns.
(See intimation, hint.)

CLUMP (v)

adverbs
aimlessly; monotonously; painfully; laboriously; tiredly; woefully; miserably; desolately; lachrymosely; loutishly; rudely.
(See thump.)

CLUMSINESS

adjectives
grotesque; intolerable; wasteful; massive; inexcusable; wanton; marked.

verbs
accentuate—; attend with—; decry—; display—; feign—; lack—; perform with—; ridicule—; simulate—; —annoys.
(See awkwardness.)

CLUMSY

adverbs
childishly; awkwardly; gawkily; inexpertly; adorably; provokingly; vexatiously; unconsciously; involuntarily; obviously; charmingly; ludicrously; ridiculously; laughably; cheerfully; momentarily; naturally; objectionably; unnecessarily; foolishly; unluckily; ungraciously; hopelessly; helplessly; bashfully; shyly; painfully.

CLUSTER

adjectives
superb; globular; kindling; luscious; indefatigable; delicate; shining; drowsy; dense; vivid; telltale; peaceful; gleaming; grapelike; many-branched; rich.

verbs
assemble in—; cultivate—; emerge from—; form in—; gather in—; group in—; halve —; join—; pluck—; swarm in—; tear—; unite in—; —collects; —droops.
(See group.)

CLUSTER (v)

adverbs
gayly; abundantly; luxuriously; lusciously; lovingly; globularly; delicately; gleamingly; richly; darksomely.
(See crowd.)

CLUTCH

adjectives
detaining; fibrous; ungainly; evil; frantic.

verbs
avoid—; clasp in—es; draw into—es; escape—; evade—; fasten—es; free from—; grasp in—es; grip in—; lock in—es; seize in—; snatch from—es; strive in—es; struggle in—es; trap in—es; wrench from—es.
(See grasp, grip, hold.)

CLUTCH (v)

adverbs
frantically; conclusively; desperately; instinctively; covetously; rapaciously; nervously; unconsciously; detainingly; vigorously; fiercely; fanatically.
(See grasp, grip.)

COACH

adjectives
ponderous; gilded; lazy; decayed; liveried; rolling; hackney; rumbling; gilt; clumsy; deserted; ancient; motor; imperial; rattling; elaborate; dingy; passenger; lurching.

verbs
alight from—; attend—; carve—; convey in—; draw—; gild—; hire—; jog along in—; journey in—; ornament—; travel in—; upset—; —approaches; —careens; —jolts; —jounces; —rumbles; —speeds on; —traverses.
(See carriage.)

COACHMAN

adjectives

superannuated; ridiculous; stiff; dignified; glossy; supercilious; liveried; crest-emblazoned.

COADJUTANT

adverbs

willingly; profitably; politically; conveniently; favorably; suspiciously; heartily; voluntarily; reluctantly; cheerfully; agreeably; confessedly; admittedly; avowedly; acquiescently; contentedly.

COAL

adjectives

dull; burning; glowing; red; roseate; glimmering; living; dying; soft; purloined; hard.

verbs

bake on—s; char—; devour—; fire—; fuel with—; heave—; ignite—; kindle—; lay on—s; power by—; quench—; rake—; scuttle—; transport—; —darkens; —emits gas; —glows; —soils.
(See carbon, ember.)

COALESCENT

adverbs

actually; easily; monotonously; valuably; scientifically; fortunately; probably; amazingly; surprisingly; indistinguishably; homologously; convertibly.

COAL FIELDS

adjectives

bleak; dreary; grime-shrouded; honeycombed; exhausted; abandoned; producing; pit-fallen; valuable; wealth-yielding; worked-out; anthracite; bituminous; lignite.

verbs

capture— —; cede— —to; conserve— —; control— —; dominate— —; employ in— —; exhaust— —; exploit— —; inherit— —; invade— —; replenish from— —; transport from— —; utilize— —; value— —; work— —; — —boom; — —extend; —range; — —supply.

COALITION

adjectives

favorable; fresh; genuine; lasting; instantaneous; political; superfluous; tardy.

verbs

ally in—; blend in—; federate—; form—; fuse in—; improvise—; support—; unite in—; —aids; —connects; —forces; —insures; —offers.
(See alliance, union.)

COARSE

adverbs

disagreeably; abominably; intolerably; unbearably; basely; bluntly; carelessly; hideously; unutterably; stupidly; pathetically; odiously; blatantly; insufferably; awkwardly; boorishly; intentionally; deliberately; unpardonably; barbarously; indecorously; ribaldly; tawdrily; vulgarly; hoydenishly; rowdily; shockingly; heavily; horridly; monstrously; obtrusively; outlandishly; impossibly.

COARSENESS

adjectives

crass; disgusting; homely; hopeless; innate; gorgeous; humiliating; savage; revolting; provincial; vulgar; unvarying.

verbs

acquire—; alleviate—; display—; exhibit —; modify—; pardon—; polish off—; refine—; retain—; sand away—; smooth—; —embarrasses; —inflames; —irks; —irritates; —rasps; —vexes.
(See rudeness, vulgarity.)

COAST

adjectives

unguarded; rock-bound; frequented; desolate; craggy; foggy; adjacent; perilous; eerie; crystal; lowly; bold; sea; sandy; high; verdant; pathless; imperfect; shining; chalk; viny; inhospitable; picturesque; trimmed; rectangular; fateful; misty; extended; iron-bound; remarkable; rebelling; melancholy; weather-beaten; forlorn; murky; azure; colorful; historic; rough; deserted; irregular; dangerous; harborless; barren; indented; shallow; flat; tranquil; elongated; sun-kissed.

verbs

abide on—; batter—; blockade—; border —; depart from—; enlarge—; expel from —; fortify—; guard—; invade—; land on—; move up—; patrol—; pebble—; scout—; skirt—; spy—; travel along—.
(See shore, beach.)

COAT

adjectives

tattered; greasy; dirty; damaged; dusty; shiny; comfortable; dinner; expensive; heavy; shapeless; buttoned; tawny; rhythmic; striped; outer; flimsy; cloth; pajama; sopping; laced; collarless; soft; fleecy; fresh; clean; distinguished; simple; boxy; tailored; custom-made; threadbare; protective; stunning; immaculate; voluminous; enticing; frogged; magic; russet; fetching; fustian; holiday; shabby; smartest; useful; raglan.

verbs
clothe in—; design—; discolor—; divest of—; dry-clean—; embroider—; encase in—; fray—; gird with—; jacket in—; model—; peel off—; press—; provide—; ruin—; seam—; split—; strip off—; style —; tailor—; tatter—; weave—; —envelops; —glitters; —protects; —warms.
(See garment, overcoat.)

COAT-TAIL

adjectives
dangling; elongated; formal; flippant; funereal; restless; tentaculate; twisting; sweeping.

verbs
alter—; cling to—; embroider—; fray—; hoist—; line—; press—; rend—; shorten—; soil—; suspend from—; tatter—; tread on—; wrinkle—; —covers; —drags; —protects.
(See coat.)

COAX (v)

adverbs
irresistibly; tantalizingly; endearingly; slyly; treacherously; lewdly; sweetly; angelically.
(See persuade.)

COBWEB

adjectives
dusty; patterned; glittering; hanging; iridescent.

verbs
abound with—s; brush away—; capture in—; dart from—; elude—; enmesh in—; ensnare in—; entangle in—; entwine in—; evade—; fringe with—; lace with—; spin—; strain in—; struggle in—; weave —; —s gather; —hangs from; —traps.
(See web, net, snare, network.)

COCK

adjectives
belligerent; bullying; cavalier; calcarate; defiant; domineering; clarion-sounding; game; strutting; spur-brandishing; vainglorious; vanquishing; victorious.

verbs
breed—s; excite—; —announces the morn; —battles; —crows; —heralds the dawn; —pecks; —perches; —rages; —scurries; —struts.
(See fowl, bird, rooster.)

COCKNEY

adverbs
unmistakably; markedly; rowdily; frankly; honestly; loyally; toughly; helpfully; sturdily; stoutly; idly; unaffectedly; heartily; healthily; humbly; chaffingly; churlishly; sorrily; originally; raffishly; menially; clownishly.

COCKROACH

adjectives
defiant; glistening; horned; invading; inexpugnable; scurrying; ubiquitous; crackling; reddish-brown; filthy; vile; obscene; offensive; nasty; foul; abominable; beastly; repulsive; immodest.

verbs
abound with—es; bait—; crush—; detest—; exterminate—; plague with—; poison—; rid of—; spray—; —infests; —multiplies; —scuds; —scurries; —wanders.
(See insect.)

COCK-SURE

adverbs
calmly; confidently; deeply; professedly; unshakably; arrogantly; egotistically; positively; provokingly; determinedly; doggedly; happily; vainly; insolently; loquaciously; tranquilly; blandly; foolishly; swaggeringly; magnificently; smugly; brassily; brazenly; heedlessly; cavalierly; importantly; blusteringly.

COCKTAIL

adjectives
aromatic; relaxing; reassuring; shudder-producing; stimulating; sticky; welcome.

verbs
chill—; concoct—; dispatch—; down—; drain—; flavor—; ice—; join in—; level—; mix—; partake of—; soak up—; tolerate—; vary—; water—; —exhilarates; —intoxicates; —quickens; —stimulates; —warms.
(See drink, liquor, whiskey.)

COCOON

adjectives
dainty; clumsy; fragile; silken; bark-powdered; suspended; swinging; silver-grey; ovate; webby.

verbs
burst from—; emerge from— encase in—; enclose in—; envelop in—; flutter from—; raise from—; spin—; swathe in—; tend—; weave—; —expels; —flowers; —hatches.

(See envelop, case.)

CODE
adjectives
changing; rigid; moral; unwritten; ambitious; voluminous; detailed; accepted; logical; traditional; ruthless; peculiar; lasting; ancient; true; rigorous; artificial; strict; odious; professed; sexual; chivalrous; elaborate; social.

verbs
decipher—; draft—; elaborate—; enforce—; formulate—; guard—; honor—; impose—; intercept—; interpret—; jeopardize—; observe—; preserve—; protect—; relay—; respect—; sanction—; subject to—; translate—; —amends; —restricts; —systematizes.

(See system, law, legislation.)

COEFFICIENT
adverbs
clannishly; collusively; concertedly; unanimously; fraternally; companionably; collectively; jointly; amazingly; surprisingly; remarkably; notoriously; supremely.

COEQUAL
adverbs
evenly; symmetrically; adaptably; broadly; generously; good-humoredly; amiably; cooperatively; affably; placidly; serenely; scrupulously; carefully; contentedly; apparently; notoriously; easily.

COERCION
adjectives
vulgar; parental; ruthless; painstaking; deliberate; wily.

verbs
advocate—; apply—; bar—; control by—; drive to—; employ—; exercise—; gain by—; govern by—; irk by—; oppose—; rebel at—; resist—; resort to—; restrain by—; retain by—; separate by—; submit to—; —antagonizes; —inflames; —intimidates.

(See compulsion, force, restraint, constraint.)

COERCIVE
adverbs
illegally; substantially; disagreeably; officially; brutally; martially; enforceably; necessarily; forcibly; violently; inexorably; irresistibly; peremptorily; ruthlessly; cruelly; intolerably; authoritatively; unjustly; outrageously; unreasonably; unlawfully; unjustifiably; inauspiciously; injudiciously; openly; furtively; slyly; actually.

COFFEE
adjectives
steaming; strong; savory; weak; adulterated; delicious; best; morning; aromatic; muddy-looking; tepid; syrupy; finest; selected; black; rancid.

verbs
brew—; cultivate—; grind—; gulp down—; ice—; imbibe—; market—; percolate—; pound—; roast—; serve—; sniff—; sweeten—; tend—; tin—; wash down with—; yield—; —refreshes; —rouses; —stales; —stimulates; —wakens; —weakens.

(See tea, drink.)

COFFER
adjectives
depleted; hoarded; mouldy; grudging; opulent; overflowing; well-guarded.

verbs
bind—; burden—; burst—; bury in—; deposit in—; enrich—; force—; hoard in—; lay up in—; line—; ornament—; plunder—; preserve in—; ransack—; seal—; secure—; stuff—; suck—dry; swell—; treasure in—; —yields.

(See treasury.)

COFFIN
adjectives
insignificant; sumptuous; unlowered; precious; naked; flaming; rude; hard; misshapen; stately; large.

verbs
attend—; bear—; confine in—; decorate—; disinter—; encase in—; inter in—; mourn at—; remove from—; rest in—; rob—; seal—; sleep in—; stand around—; trail—; transport—; view—; weep at—; —receives; —sinks.

(See casket, case.)

adverbs

gravely; deeply; absorbedly; perplexedly; abstrusely; abstractedly; studiously; frowningly; fixedly.

(See meditate, think.)

COGITATION

adjectives

gloomy; matrimonial; fragmentary; groping; manifold.

COIFFURE

adjectives

rustling; waved; elaborate; charming; conservative; monstrous; ingenious; gleaming; eccentric; affected; severe; elegant; sculptured.

COIL

adjectives

adamantine; tortured; lustrous; ceaseless; flat; irregular; steel; long; snakelike; hideous; opal; cumbrous; temporal; brilliant; mortal; collapsed; limp; shining; twisting.

COIL (v)

adverbs

lavishly; ceaselessly; flatly; irregularly; hideously; cumbrously; limply; twistingly; intricately.

(See twist.)

COIN

adjectives

fair; bogus; deceptive; well-worked; unadulterated; glittering; nimble; ancient; valuable; artificial; rare.

verbs

assort—s; collect—s; convert into—; counterfeit—; deposit—; devaluate—; fashion —; hoard—s; melt—; mold—; mutilate—; pocket—; press—; stamp—; treasure—; uncover—; unearth—; value—; —circulates; —clinks; —depreciates; —represents; —wears thin.

(See cash, money, metal.)

COINCIDE (v)

adverbs

exactly; oddly; strangely; sardonically; singularly; amazingly; romantically; happily; fortunately; curiously; minutely; unexpectedly; tragically; occasionally; extraordinarily; crazily; closely.

(See agree.)

COINCIDENCE

adjective

strange; odd; singular; sardonic; happy; horrible; cruel; amazing; romantic; lucky; mere; crazy; curious; minute; unexpected; accidental; unusual; overdone; tragic; occasional; extraordinary; powerful; unfortunate; uncomfortable; suggestive.

verbs

discern—; discuss—; evidence—; illustrate—; involve—; marvel at—; report—; strike—; witness—; wonder at—; —amazes; —blends; —confounds; —occurs; —startles.

(See correspondence, agreement.)

COLD
(illness)

adjectives

harrassing; head; chest; bronchial; miserable; stubborn.

verbs

dispose toward—; down by—; engender—; expose to—; guard against—s; indispose by—; nurse—; predispose to—; resist—; subject to—; —lowers resistance; —strikes; —subsides; —weakens.

(See sickness.)

COLD
(weather)

adjectives

hostile; icy; intense; biting; deadly; stinging; cruel; casual; arctic; deathlike; encroaching; inescapable; bitter; paralyzing; freezing; wondrous; immense; retreating; purifying; interminable; midnight; piercing; stubborn; extreme; troublesome; ambient; heavy; penetrating; Stygian; monstrous.

verbs

blanket against—; brave—; chatter with—; endure—; expose to—; huddle in—; inure to—; paralyze by—; resist—; stem—; —abates; —bites; —blasts; —creeps in; —freezes; —nips; —persists; —pinches; —refreshes.

(See winter.)

COLD

adverbs

uncomfortably; intolerably; unfortunately; impossibly; frigidly; bitingly; piercingly; icily; wintrily; disagreeably; inconveniently; unpleasantly; uninvitingly; unluckily;

terrifically; dreadfully; frightfully; unnecessarily; dangerously; intensely; cruelly; penetratingly; increasingly; freezingly; nippily; perilously; unbearably.

COLD-HEARTED
adverbs
bitterly; unpleasantly; disturbingly; relentlessly; cruelly; outrageously; inhumanly; unsympathetically; terribly; dreadfully; incurably; habitually; temperamentally; constitutionally; obviously; manifestly; shamefully; unbelievably; astonishingly; actually; selfishly; naturally; inexplicably; fearfully; inexorably; uncharitably; unfortunately.

COLDNESS
adjectives
dewy; incisive; still; sudden; faithless; superficial; wintry; relentless; increasing; contemptuous; supreme; lofty; studied; mortified; intellectual; selfish; fancied; disdainful.

COLLABORATE (v)
adverbs
unreservedly; successfully; harmoniously; artfully; skilfully; imaginatively; superbly; brilliantly; startlingly; enthusiastically.
(See work, cooperate.)

COLLABORATION
adjectives
direct; efficient; permanent; enduring; spiritual.

COLLAPSE
adjectives
moral; constant; painful; cataclysmic; progressive; widespread; nervous; complete; disgraceful; simulated; eventual; imminent; inevitable; pretended; subsequent; tragic; alleged; disastrous.

verbs
fall into—; guard against—; hasten—; insure—; predict—; shrink in—; sink into—; verge on—; —discourages; presage—.
(See exhaustion, failure, ruin.)

COLLAPSE (v)
adverbs
utterly; invariably; tragically; partially; fatally; completely; ruinously; disastrously; fearfully; wretchedly; dramatically.
(See fall.)

COLLAPSIBLE
adverbs
conveniently; laughably; comically; dangerously; perilously; easily; cleverly; cunningly; neatly; handily; ingeniously; tidily; quickly; instantly; disastrously; momentarily; tragically.

COLLAR
adjectives
ermine; greasy; soft; fur; oppressive; enormous; clerical; obdurate; snug; upstanding; celluloid; muzzle; resplendent; faultless; diminutive; onerous.

verbs
crane at—; engrave—; fumble with—; harness in—; insert in—; jewel—; pleat—; ring with—; slip out of—; split—; strain at—; suspend from—; tug at—; —bands; —binds; —chains; —chokes; —encircles; —encompasses; —fetters; —ornaments; —restrains; —shrinks; —wreathes; —yields; —yokes.

COLLEAGUE
adjectives
word-compelling; melancholy; congressional; conscientious; efficient; critical; turbulent; immediate; peripheral; redoubtable; ardent; gifted; pagan; older; experienced; artful; disgruntled; atrabilious; professional; distinguished.

verbs
aid—; ally with—; assemble—s; associate with—; bow to—; cooperate with—; debate with—; emulate—; enjoin—; favor—; inveigle—into; lead—; sever from—.
(See associate, accessory, ally.)

COLLECT (v)
adverbs
painlessly; systematically; haphazardly; eagerly; privately; scientifically; gloriously; remarkably; exclusively; posthumously; dramatically; actively; cantankerously; indiscriminately; laboriously; sedulously; periodically; assiduously.
(See accumulate, group.)

COLLECTION
adjectives
wonderful; arresting; suggestive; pretentious; rare; attractive; ponderous; complete; expensive; priceless; weird; heterogeneous; haphazard; motley; vague; private; interesting; useful; fair; authentic; miscellaneous; entertaining; tolerable; ave-

rage; classified; individual; comprehensive; annotated; voluminous; scientific; varied; hideous; exciting; representative; enticing; adequate; imaginative; brilliant; extensive; world; superb; spring; advanced; copious; incongruous; considerable; notable; vast; glorious; remarkable; exclusive; thrilling; posthumous; original; magnificent; active; dramatic; infinite; zoological; cantankerous; startling.

verbs
accumulate—; amass—; delay—; display—; equal—; examine—; exhibit—; herd—; insure—; join—; lead—; mass—; prize—; raise—; rifle—; speed—; suspend—; treasure—; uncover—; unearth—; value—; yield—; —depicts; —symbolizes.
(See heap, group.)

COLLECTIVE
adverbs
effectively; efficiently; agreeably; typically; officially; undeniably; comprehensively; indivisibly; unanimously; substantially; broadly; indefinitely; locally; significantly; representatively; startlingly; surprisingly.

COLLECTIVE BARGAINING
adjectives
conciliatory; deferred; haggled; generalized; tactless; tolerant; prolonged; summary.

verbs
abolish— —; acclaim— —; achieve through — —; acquire— —; activate— —; base on— —; criticize— —; demand— —; discuss— —; drift into— —; employ— —; enjoy— —; exercise— —; forbid— —; object to— —; oblige by— —; oppose— —; organize— —; prohibit— —; recognize— —; restrict— —; support— —; — —enables; — —functions; — —improves; — —insures; — —involves; — —recognizes; — —secures; — —upholds.
(See negotiation.)

COLLECTOR
adjectives
ardent; modest; assiduous; insatiable; advanced; passionate; entranced; curious; enthusiastic; worthy; unceasing; discriminating; prominent; budding.

verbs
avoid—; evade—; rob—; waylay—; —accumulates; —acquires; —amasses; —assembles; —classifies; —compiles; —dis-

plays; —embezzles; —evades; —exhibits; —prizes; —recovers; —solicits; —sues; —values.

COLLEGE
adjectives
aggressive; liberal; commercial; general; aspiring; rival; venerable; electoral; denominational; junior; endowed.

verbs
administer—; attach to—; bar from—; charter—; enroll at—; establish—; father —; found—; incorporate—; invest—with; pursue in—; register at—; reopen—; respect—; restrict—; staff—; suspend from—; —accommodates; —conducts; —confers; —expels; —honors; —instructs; —lodges; —offers; —prepares.
(See school, university.)

COLLEGIATE
adverbs
ostentatiously; airily; knowingly; smartly; ridiculously; pompously; clannishly; arrogantly; thoroughly; strictly; proudly; determinedly; resolutely; correctly; faintly; laughably; properly; academically; actively; becomingly; unimpeachably; respectably; admirably; satisfactorily; duly; responsibly.

COLLISION
adjectives
fierce; monstrous; inevitable; chance; actual; violent; personal; fatal; frequent; successive; clear; serious; menacing; exciting; amusing; sudden; sharp; fateful; imminent; expensive.

verbs
avoid—; foresee—; insure against—; result in—; swerve from—; warn against—; —batters; —dashes; —destroys; —entangles; —impairs; —necessitates; —rends; —upsets.
(See clash, impact, conflict, encounter, shock.)

COLLOQUIAL
adverbs
informally; easily; admissibly; chattily; provincially; pleasantly; frankly; agreeably; comfortably; familiarly; sociably; ingenuously; childishly; simply; naturally; unceremoniously; unconventionally; recklessly; candidly; artlessly.

adjectives
prolonged; fruitful; serious; peaceful.

COLLUSIVE

adverbs
shrewdly; dangerously; illegally; astutely; fraudulently; surreptitiously; subtly; cleverly; craftily; cunningly; incontrovertibly; undeniably; unluckily; unfortunately; openly; abominably; unwisely; dishonestly; palpably; manifestly; essentially; substantially; deplorably; unhappily; artfully; inauspiciously; openly.

COLON
(part of body)

adjectives
distended; inactive; inflamed; impacted; sluggish; varicose.

verbs
abscess—; accumulate in—; block—; constrict—; distend—; drain—; excise—; flush—; force from—; incise—; inflame—; irrigate—; lubricate—; oil—; purge—; ulcerate—; wash—; irritate—.
(See intestine, bowel.)

COLONEL

adjectives
crusty; old; courtly; benign; gallant; cultured; rum-rotten.

COLONIAL

adverbs
strictly; authentically; architecturally; characteristically; distinctly; respectably; acceptably; accurately; admirably; attractively; boldly; originally; gallantly; charmingly; pleasantly; hospitably; spaciously; formally; beautifully; markedly; significantly; remarkably; conspicuously; faithfully; loyally; generously; broadly.

COLONIST

adjectives
pacific; early; hardy; patriotic; affluent; desperate; original; God-fearing; ever-encroaching.

COLONY

adjectives
abandoned; congenial; agricultural; depressing; independent; outlying; foreign; smart; wealthy; summer; colorful; wrangling; unique; devoted; robust; exempted; hale; dusky; tropical; proprietary; flour-

ishing; inheriting; remote; suburban; wretched; pretty; conquering; segregated; feeble; adjacent; dependent.

verbs
administer—; ban from—; cede to—; defend—; evict from—; free—; govern—; immigrate to—; launch—; maladministrate—; seize—; set up—; transfer to—; —flounders; —founders; —prospers; —rebels; —revolts; —riots; —smoulders; —wars on.
(See settlement.)

COLOR

adjectives
gorgeous; enchanting; rich; shining; clear; dazzling; uniform; subdued; gleaming; unheroic; quiet; faded; reticent; dull; canary; natural; artificial; exuberant; youthful; spirited; vibrant; kaleidoscopic; iridescent; full; lavish; live; vague; harmonious; piebald; sensuous; emotional; crude; raw; delicate; fragile; soft; false; basic; popular; rising; watery; gaudy; daring; welcome; flashy; isolated; normal; clean; complementary; solid; delightful; unwonted; radiant; dulled; hectic; thick; fatty; varied; dark; deep; decorative; brilliant; flying (pl); lustrous; subtle; intermediate; grimy; instrumental; tremendous; local; hideous; detestable; festive; staring; prismatic; heightened; glowing; incredible; warm; flickering; grinding; reassuring; unusual; new; water; factitious; equatorial; autumn; mellow; rapturous; ethereal; tender; faint; sickly; superb; crowded (pl); somber; profuse; motiveless; bright; exuberant; jumbled (pl); sleek; flamboyant; livid; solemn; sad; agreeable; riotous; pastel; summer; prominent; conventional; gay; seasonal; bold; plain; fluctuating; vigorous; orchestral; exquisite; dirty; garish; impregnated.

verbs
abhor—; accentuate—; alter—; array in—; assume—; bathe in—; bedeck with—; blend—; brush on—; burnish—; clothe in—; convey—; dash with—; deck in—; deprive of—; dim—; dip in—; disguise—; enamel with—; exhibit—; flush with—; grade—; indulge in—; invest with—; lend—; lose—; mix—; overcharge with—; paint in—; portray in—; retain—; shade—; sprinkle—; steal—from; subdue—; sully—; tone—; touch with—; vary—; —arrests; —dazzles; —distinguishes; —ebbs; —emanates from; —enhances; —flames; —flow-

ers; —glares; —glows; —harmonizes; —heightens; —mingles; —mounts; —predominates; —runs rampant; —sickens; —soothes; —sparkles; mask—.
(See hue, blush.)

COLOR (v)

adverbs
amusingly; distinctly; faintly; unevenly; angrily; painfully; brilliantly; synthetically; violently; conspicuously; obscurely; exquisitely; highly; gorgeously; enchantingly; uniformly; vibrantly; iridescently; lavishly; emotionally; crudely; fragilely; gaudily; daringly; normally; decoratively; harmoniously; festively; incredibly; factitiously; flamboyantly; conventionally; exquisitely; garishly.
(See tint, tinge.)

COLORFUL

adverbs
gorgeously; strikingly; beautifully; garishly; gaudily; remarkably; famously; bizarrely; barbarically; incredibly; delicately; daintily; pleasantly; agreeably; artistically; splendidly; brilliantly; magnificently; superbly; flashily; gaily; cheerfully; strangely; impressively; extraordinarily; riotously; outlandishly; fantastically; extravagantly.

COLORING

adjectives
illusive; youthful; fanciful; mustard; vivid; admirable; tender; somber; warm; luxurious; genuine; motley; special; clear; mellow; rich; artificial; musical; radiant; gorgeous; deep; lustrous; neutral; delightful; flawless; appropriate.

COLORLESS

adverbs
monotonously; dully; cheerlessly; wanly; pallidly; neutrally; dismally; drearily; discouragingly; grievously; sorely; sadly; utterly; piteously; deplorably; pathetically; cruelly; wretchedly; singularly; oppressively; hopelessly; dishearteningly; needlessly; horribly; unpleasantly.

COLT

adjectives
frolicking; uncomely; dark; unhandled; youthful; awkward; wanton; unbroken; rough; handsome.

verbs
corral—; curb—; groom—; exercise—; loose—; mount—; stable—; —balks; —frisks; —gallops off; —grazes; —hurdles; —neighs; —pastures.
(See animal, horse.)

COLUMN
(architectural, military, etc)

adjectives
twisting; resistless; ascending; noble; tall; solid; marble; sturdy; dusty; massive; huge; vast; soaring; classic; stark; interpretative; warlike; somber; shattered; steel-clad; venerable; marching; flowered; lucrative; attacking; airy; perpendicular; crystal; slender; parallel; surging; monumental; vertebral; isolated; lofty; unending; advancing; ivory-shaped; vaporous; rostral; fragile; majestic; internal; spouting; graceful; gigantic; fantastic; glittering; luminous; rising; fluted; copulated; clustered.

verbs
ambush—; attach to—; construct—; destroy—; encircle—; erect—; file in—; head —; join—; line up in—; reinforce—; rule into—; shake—; shape—; shatter—; shield—; —crumbles; —marks; —supports; —swerves; —tapers; —vibrates; —winds.
(See line, post, shaft.)

COLUMN
(journalistic)

adjectives
mercurial; exciting; fascinating; informative; interpretative; hackneyed; inspiring; authoritative.

verbs
caption—; condense—; dash off—; devour —; edit—; evolve—; excerpt—; feature—; head—; limit to—; print—; publish—; rewrite—; syndicate—; title—; —berates; —conveys; —demeans; —interests; —inveighs against; —libels; —prejudices; —scandalizes.
(See writing, editorial.)

COMA

adjectives
deathlike; glassy-eyed; mild; rigid; trancelike; wide-staring.

verbs
affect with—; arouse from—; awake from—; emerge from—; fail in—; fall

into—; lapse into—; mutter in—; relieve—; sink into—; succumb to—.
(See unconsciousness, lethargy.)

COMB
(animal)

adjectives
cresting; crimson; defiant; flaunting; proudly-borne; imperial; nodding; superbly-curving; waggish.

verbs
adorn with—; curry—; develop—; ruffle—; serrate—; —crests; —matures; —protrudes; —waves.
(See crest.)

COMB (v)

adverbs
sleekly; briskly; dreamily; languidly; dexterously; effectively; left-handedly; gently.
(See brush.)

COMBAT

adjectives
frequent; ensuing; single; fierce; blood-stirring; aerial; chivalric; imaginable; beauteous; armed; hourly; historic; isolated; sportful; savage; noiseless; gladiatorial; primeval; mortal; feminine; caveman; merry; exciting; pitched; mimic; open-air; close; rude.

verbs
challenge in—; clash in—; collapse in—; crave—; dare—; disdain—; engage in—; face—; gird for—; heat—; incite to—; join in—; lay low in—; offer—; pledge to—; prick to—; view—; ward off—; —burns; —devastates; —rages; —seethes.
(See contest, battle, struggle, bout, contention.)

COMBAT (v)

adverbs
continually; effectively; fiercely; aerially; mortally; historically; savagely; gladiatorially; fatally; rudely; overwhelmingly; victoriously; thunderously; surgingly.
(See fight, struggle.)

COMBATANT

adjectives
successful; colossal; effective; unpropitious.

verbs
distinguish—; engage—; face—; fence with—; beat—; irk—; join—; lock with—; oppose—; overwhelm—; surround—; tri-

umph over—; unsnarl—s; —contends; —vanquishes; —wins.
(See contestant, fighter.)

COMBATIVE

adverbs
absurdly; ferociously; foolishly; noisily; unreasonably; immoderately; truculently; pugnaciously; irresponsibly; blatantly; insolently; openly; challengingly; daringly; teasingly; vexatiously; offensively; lamentably; unfortunately; quickly; boyishly; egotistically; vaingloriously; conceitedly; boldly; unpleasantly; disagreeably.

COMBINATION

adjectives
charming; rare; wonderful; striking; perfect; lovely; pretty; extraordinary; amazing; unusual; curious; grotesque; strange; foolish; occasional; lucky; strategic; simplest; unbeatable; agricultural; mental; brilliant; intricate; intellectual; exclusive; special; ecstatic; positive; possible; seasonable; solemn; subtle; gigantic; magnificent; extensive; weird; nutritive; synergistic; inexplicable; incongruous; pleasing; industrial; vigorous; ingenious; color; skillful; equilibrious; pernicious; bright; bold; distasteful; dramatic; compelling; illegal; fortunate; roomy; irresistible; unholy; dextrous.

verbs
achieve—; attain—; balk at—; capture—; conceal—; guard—; hide—; join—; justify—; lock in—; reveal—; seal—; warn against—; weld—; —conflicts; —strengthens; evolve—.
(See union, alliance, league, coalition.)

COMBINE (v)

adverbs
intricately; successfully; euphoniously; felicitously; skillfully; dexterously; chemically; wisely; shrewdly; gorgeously; charmingly; extraordinarily; strategically; grotesquely; agriculturally; mentally; intellectually; subtly; weirdly; inexplicably; incongruously; industrially; ingeniously; perniciously; dramatically; legally; irresistibly; unfortunately.
(See unite, merge.)

COMBUSTIBLE

adverbs
readily; dangerously; unfortunately; perilously; easily; alarmingly; dreadfully; unhappily; conveniently; temptingly; hazard-

ously; appallingly; advantageously; distressingly; unluckily; disastrously; sadly; direly; sorely; deplorably; inauspiciously; spontaneously; instantaneously; explosively.

COMBUSTION

adjectives
fitful; spontaneous; resultant; dire; disastrous; chemical; destructive.

verbs
accompany with—; destroy by—; excite to—; kindle to—; prevent—; produce—; protect against—; reduce by—; resist—; result in—; save from—; support—; throw into—; —consumes; —devours; —eats; —generates; —heats; —rages.
(See outbreak, disturbance.)

COME (v)

adverbs
laboriously; reluctantly; decently; prosaically; richly; undeniably; vividly; argumentatively; inevitably; fitfully; steadily; intermittently; confidently; rarely; voluntarily; briskly; warily; peaceably; archly; spasmodically; vehemently; distinctly; unquestionably; drunkenly; rapidly; silently; hopefully; swiftly; hesitatingly; deliberately; monotonously; sporadically; obliquely; seasonably; drowsily; wondrously; indiscriminately; assiduously; ponderously; slyly; jauntily.
(See arrive, approach.)

COMEDIAN

adjectives
eminent; slapstick; popular; audacious; acrobatic; facile.

COMEDIENNE

adjectives
eccentric; apt; world-renowned; clever; scintillating.

COMEDY

adjectives
brilliant; pleasing; charming; restrained; intelligent; rich; social; suave; earnest; ironic; clever; satirical; light; sardonic; fluffy; riotous; farcical; roaring; buoyant; high; tiresome; wry; ineffective; sickly; alleged; fantastic; absurd; lamentable; tragic; mournful; burlesque; macabre; amateur; romantic; artificial; plain; fancy; veritable; crisp; wary; lascivious; admirable; sentimental; slapstick; optimistic; frivolous; robust; complicated; poetic; eccentric.

verbs
applaud—; conclude—; dramatize—; enact—; indulge in—; perform—; present—; produce—; revel in—; write—; —burlesques; —characterizes; —delights; —depicts; —enlivens; —entertains; —lightens; —relishes; —satirizes.
(See play, drama, representation.)

COMELY

adverbs
altogether; sufficiently; surprisingly; bloomingly; rosily; ruddily; roughly; singularly; vividly; serenely; innocently; proudly; unconsciously; robustly; quietly; unspeakably; admirably; unexpectedly; charmingly; pleasantly; gracefully; jauntily; smartly; tidily; specially; pleasingly; attractively.

COMET

adjectives
splendid; wandering; refulgent; vagrant; thunder-toned.

verbs
analyze—; calculate—s; control—; describe—; discover—; distinguish—; — examine—; expel—; focus on—; identify—; interested in—; observe—; recognize—; regard—; separate from—; study—; witness—; —approaches; —burns; —deviates; —diminishes; —emits; —excites; —flashes; —influences; —speeds; —travels; —wanes.

COMFORT

adjectives
blessed; genial; gentle; thoughtful; priceless; bracing; cold; increased; dubious; poor; scant; miserable; physical; plush; velvety; spiritual; knee-deep; old-fashioned; modern; intellectual; home; comparative; measurable; smug; temporary; ordered; necessary; summer; easy; great; shirtsleeve; refreshing; jaunty; ideal; constant; breezy; smart; luxurious; every; physical; whispering; quiet; superior; social; superb; cheerful; supreme; extra; genuine; continental; casual; suffused; melancholy; rural; restful; urban; heavenly; untold; heating; scantiest; maximum; perpetual; swinish; joyous; fireside; filthy; mysterious; dispensing; material; exclusive; blissful; indisputable; needed.

verbs
afford—; augment—; delight in—of; deprive of—; derive—from; draw—from; fill with—; insure—; maintain in—; mini-

ster to—; rear in—; refuse—; restore—; scorn—; subsist in—; take—from; withhold—.

(See ease, solace, consolation, encouragement.)

COMFORTABLE
adverbs
altogether; pleasantly; utterly; finally; increasingly; physically; comparatively; immeasurably; snugly; happily; easily; refreshingly; luxuriously; quietly; socially; supremely; genuinely; mysteriously; blissfully; serenely; contentedly; unexpectedly; immensely; definitely; deliciously.

COMFORTER
adjectives
effectual; wayside; despairing; gorgeous; sympathetic; placating.

COMICAL
adverbs
absurdly; pleasantly; brilliantly; cleverly; ironically; riotously; uproariously; tiresomely; tediously; highly; effectively; fantastically; complexly; eccentrically; intentionally; deliberately; daintily; dazzlingly; hilariously; mercilessly; bitterly; fatuously.

COMMA
adjectives
checking; favored; interfering; interspersed; omitted; perfunctory; setting-off; indispensable; jutting; obstructing.

verbs
designate by—; dot with—s; invert—; mark with—; pause at—; punctuate with—; —clarifies; —denotes; —indicates; —interrupts; —punctuates; —separates.
(See mark, interval, pause, delay.)

COMMAND
adjectives
brisk; snarled; definite; sharp; stern; brusque; crisp; curt; despotic; peremptory; absolute; authoritative; unconditional; tyrannical; facile; supreme; independent; imperious; iron; deathless; masterly; fluent; unconcerned; stentorian; low-voiced; shouted; spoken; hoarse; shrill; raucous; sole; unified; urgent; last; hurrying; prompt; effective; divine; implied; incisive; suggestive; rudimentary; consequential; shaky; tactful; phenomenal; incomparable; geographical; instant; cold; lawful; unique; disguised; renewed; vigorous; immediate;

irregular; enthusiastic; instinctive; military; snapped; fierce; unlimited; laudable; pernicious; admirable; stifled; long-desired; rapturous; strenuous; intermingling; respective; just.

verbs
assume—; attend—; await—; bear—; boast—; comply with—; condescend to—; constitute—; defy—; execute—; fulfill—; lose—; obey—; release from—; relieve from—; relinquish—; respond to—; send forth—; stand ready at—; sway by—; thunder—; transgress—; understand—; waive—; —confuses; —enrages; —rings; —splits the air; —startles.
(See order, charge, mandate, authority, leadership, control.)

COMMAND (v)
adverbs
imperiously; authoritatively; intellectually; impatiently; laughingly; peremptorily; petulantly; definitely; brusquely; crisply; curtly; despotically; unconditionally; tyrannically; independently; stentorianly; hoarsely; shrilly; raucously; urgently; promptly; effectively; incisively; tactfully; phenomenally; incomparably; vigorously; immediately; enthusiastically; instinctively; fiercely; laudably; perniciously; justly.
(See order, direct.)

COMMANDER
adjectives
trusted; plucky; dashing; able; spectacular; immediate; insulted; victorious; regimental; immovable; illustrious; panic-stricken; fiery; respected; half-clad; venerable; renowned; indomitable.

verbs
appoint to—; exalt—; obey—; raise to—; rank as—; —assigns; —assumes; —authorizes; —campaigns; —controls; —directs; —disposes of; —exercises; —grants;— overrules; —pensions; —plans; —rules.
(See master, officer, captain, leader.)

COMMANDING
adverbs
harshly; fussily; sternly; briskly; definitely; sharply; crisply; curtly; despotically; peremptorily; authoritatively; imperiously; hoarsely; shrilly; raucously; urgently; incisively; tactfully; coldly; vigorously; enthusiastically; insultingly; offensively.

COMMANDMENT

adjectives

harsh; fussy; express; stern; abrupt; strait; unwritten; divine.

verbs

annul—; charge with—; delight in—; deliver—; disregard—; forbid by—; forsake—; fulfill—; hearken to—; neglect—; rebel against—; reject—; send forth—; transgress—; tremble at—; violate—; urge—.

(See command, precept, law, order, warning.)

COMMEMORATE (v)

adverbs

jubilantly; appropriately; fitly; justly; splendidly; gloriously; annually; royally; simply; serenely; privately; publicly; passionately; sincerely.

(See celebrate.)

COMMEMORATIVE

adverbs

tenderly; reverently; publicly; appropriately; affectionately; permanently; nobly; deeply; triumphantly; faithfully; perpetually; graciously; worthily; adequately; suitably; gratefully; humbly; lastingly; enduringly; splendidly; magnificently; fittingly; beautifully; especially; impressively; felicitously.

COMMENCE (v)

adverbs

ceremoniously; busily; prosperously; daily; accustomedly; jocosely; meticulously; amiably; comfortably; conventionally; shrewdly.

(See begin, start.)

COMMENCEMENT

adjectives

elementary; prosperous; propitious; belated; annual; current.

COMMEND (v)

adverbs

grandiloquently; strongly; extravagantly; chiefly; emphatically; warmly; meritedly; flatteringly; heartily; fulsomely; boundlessly; scantily; meagerly.

(See recommend.)

COMMENDABLE

adverbs

altogether; especially; meritoriously; emphatically; particularly; eminently; unusually; unimpeachably; gloriously; admirably; worthily; highly; markedly; uncommonly; definitely.

COMMENDATION

adjectives

sorry; emphatic; extravagant; warm; merited; well-meant; gentle; widespread; worthy; hearty.

verbs

bestow—upon; consider—; convey—; deliver—; deserve—; discharge from—; express—; favor with—; flatter with—; gain—; regard—; respect—; silence—; solicit—; still—; value—; welcome with—; —abates; —ceases; —extols; —graces; —lauds; —praises; —recedes.

(See approbation, approval, praise, recommendation.)

COMMENSURATE

adverbs

exactly; appropriately; approximately; suitably; undeniably; properly; adjustably; tolerably; remarkably; meticulously; essentially; mathematically; scrupulously; carefully.

COMMENT

adjectives

favorable; approving; polite; appreciative; triumphant; grateful; important; significant; interesting; persuasive; sane; civilized; fretful; intelligent; shrewd; laconic; enlightening; cultured; prosaic; inappropriate; characteristic; dry; stumbling; trivial; bewildered; incoherent; wild; trite; open; gloomy; dubious; direct; vigorous; crisp; daring; pungent; scathing; sharp; penetrating; humorous; witty; jesting; facetious; upstart; quick; running; spontaneous; disgruntled; constant; exquisite; philosophic; speculative; editorial; cartoon; pamphleteering; country-wide; local; mental; printed; verbal; moralizing; censorious; detailed; curious; whispered; audible; casual; passing; critical; wistful; rare; contemporary; inane; enthusiastic; playful; cheerful; cynical; caustic; unsympathetic; perverse; churlish; uncomplimentary; endless; sour; abundant; cheering; quaint; considerable; public; analytic; needless; inconsequential; musical; stupid; jocular; introductory; prophetic; skeptical; authoritative; enlivening; lavish; vulgar; resentful; acrimonious.

verbs

analyze—; arouse—; attach—; bear—; betray into—; challenge—; conceal—; cram with—; deride—; elicit—; evince—; evoke—; excite—; issue—; lavish—on; occasion—; provoke—; subject to—; underline—; —criticizes; —disconcerts; —elucidates; —enlightens; —flatters; —illuminates; —illustrates; —interprets; —penetrates; —squelches.

(See remark, observation, explanation.)

COMMENT (v)

adverbs

grumblingly; haughtily; admiringly; dryly; audibly; grimly; favorably; approvingly; politely; appreciatively; gratefully; significantly; interestingly; sanely; fretfully; intelligently; shrewdly; laconically; prosaically; inappropriately; characteristically; tritely; gloomily; dubiously; vigorously; crisply; pungently; scathingly; penetratingly; humorously; facetiously; spontaneously; philosophically; speculatively; editorially; locally; mentally; verbally; inanely; wistfully; playfully; cheeerfully; cynically; caustically; endlessly; sourly; cheeringly; quaintly; publicly; analytically; inconsequentially; stupidly; jocularly; drolly; flatteringly; prophetically; skeptically; authoritatively; lavishly; vulgarly; resentfully; acrimoniously; pityingly.

(See remark, observe.)

COMMENTARY

adjectives

significant; brilliant; sad; ironic; biting; pure; dazzling; binding; striking; authentic; curious; philosophic; keen; critical; rollicking; satiric; stressed; subtle; whimsical; penetrating; ludicrous; panoramic.

COMMENTATOR

adjectives

genial; philosophical; dramatic; unknown; hostile; political; inelegant; unseen.

COMMERCE

adjectives

nascent; enlarged; far-flung; unsullied; peaceful; flourishing; lawless; enhanced; expanding; international; vast; increasing; interstate; long-established; petty.

verbs

blockade—; derange—; develop—; encourage—; engage in—; hinder—; imperil—; insure—; interchange—; invade—; join in—; levy on—; negotiate—; open—; profit by—; protect—; regulate—; restrict—; route—; safeguard—; stimulate—; stint—; subsidize—; traffic in—; —dwindles; —flourishes; —transports; —wanes.

(See trade, business, intercourse, traffic, communication.)

COMMERCIAL

adverbs

sordidly; blatantly; profitably; readily; thrivingly; flourishingly; prosperously; productively; unaccountably; satisfactorily; fairly; openly; frankly; avowedly; uninterestingly; brilliantly; insistently; briskly; cheerfully; keenly; terribly; competently; thoroughly; dully; tediously; comically; actively; successfully; assiduously; energetically; shrewdly; craftily.

COMMERCIALISM

adjectives

blatant; camouflaged; high-powered.

COMMISERATION

adjectives

exaggerated; false; gentle; tender; light; regretful; sincere.

verbs

act in—; assist out of—; attend with—; behold in—; conceal—; defy—; deserve—; disdain—; distress with—; excite—; express—; feign—; lack—; pretend—; succumb to—; tear with—; tender—; wrack with—; wring with—.

(See compassion, pity, sorrow.)

COMMISSION

adjectives

perilous; permanent; promised; glorious; royal; simple; delicate; accredited; illicit; flattering; nonpartisan; legislative; eminent; joint; mixed; innocent; imaginary; unspoken; gabbling; much-desired.

verbs

accept—; appoint to—; assume—; authorize—; buy—; charge with—; confer—upon; delegate to—; deliver—; devise—; discharge—; dispatch—; empower—; entrust with—; execute—; tender—; undertake—; warrant—; —empowers; —instructs; —orders; —ranks; —specifies.

(See mission, delegation, errand, trust.)

adjectives
imperial; mouth-dripping; perfunctory; supercilious; unbending; bribe-swallowing; porcine.

COMMIT (v)
adverbs
consciously; irrevocably; unconsciously; habitually; sinfully; wilfully; rarely; solemnly; vilely; deliberately; unreservedly; fearlessly; criminally; treacherously; shrewdly; mysteriously; antagonistically; swiftly; veritably; vulgarly.
(See assign, entrust.)

COMMITMENT
adjectives
careless; imaginary; solemn; revealed; judicial; official.

COMMITTEE
adjectives
advisory; influential; corresponding; reception; adjuvant; self-constituted; associational; intractable; select; prudential; vigilance; chagrined; strong; supreme; grand; advisory; special; executive; proper; socialistic; pacific; utilization.

verbs
appear before—; appoint to—; arm—; corral—; dominate—; hamstring—; head—; invent—; preside over—; set up—; taunt—; —advises; —bans; —bars; —condones; —denounces; —evinces; —favors; —functions; —proclaims; —retorts.
(See group, board.)

COMMODIOUS
adverbs
sufficiently; adequately; advantageously; expediently; handily; serviceably; valuably; luckily; conveniently; pleasantly; appropriately; fortunately; splendidly; completely; excellently; spaciously; cheerily; comfortably; capaciously; extremely; admirably; roomily; particularly; suitably; uncommonly; exceptionally.

COMMODITY
adjectives
precious; agricultural; respected; unwanted; unctuous; valuable; opposite; essential; leading; vital; industrial; prized; necessary.

adjectives
culinary; evasive; vapid; conventional; tedious.

verbs
beautify—; enrich—; exalt—; express—; sink into—; soar above—; utter—; —bores; —fails to impress; —tires; —wearies.
(See platitude, remark.)

adverbs
undeniably; insignificantly; trivially; indifferently; particularly; ridiculously; negligibly; cheaply; contemptibly; immaterially; miserably; pitifully; shabbily; wretchedly; distinctly; laughably; remarkably; surprisingly; stupidly; monotonously; prosaically.

COMMON-SENSE
adjectives
practical; supreme; salty; shrewd; courageous; hard-headed.

verbs
accept as— —; argue with— —; characterize by— —; demand— —; derive by— —; develop— —; display— —; endow with— —; evince— —; exhibit— —; forsake— —; judge with— —; lack— —; override— —; perceive with— —; require— —; violate— —; — —prevails.
(See judgment, understanding.)

COMMONWEALTH
adjectives
corrupted; co-operative; precarious; ancient; native; advanced; free; industrial; individual.

COMMOTION
adjectives
nervous; subdued; hurried; violent; sudden; faint; diurnal; inner; economic; mysterious; sad; strong; tremendous.

verbs
engage in—; excite—; quell—; quiet—; still—; throw into—; —agitates; —bristles; —confuses; —disorders; —irritates; —perturbs; —rages; —recurs; —rises;—stirs; —subsides; —terrifies.
(See agitation, excitement, tumult, disturbance, turmoil, riot, stir.)

COMMUNE (v)

adverbs

spiritually; intimately; immortally; rapturously; ineffably; wordlessly; mentally; intellectually; constantly; socially; devoutly; worshipfully; divinely.

(See confer, converse.)

COMMUNICABLE

adverbs

highly; easily; perilously; alarmingly; dangerously; scarcely; freely; openly; secretly; rapidly; slyly; electrically; directly; conveniently; instantly; fearfully; frightfully; hardly; mysteriously; quickly; expeditiously; advantageously; expediently.

COMMUNICATE (v)

adverbs

duly; unknowingly; felicitously; thrillingly; formally; efficiently; gracefully; uniquely; swiftly; economically; rapidly; constantly; continuously; belligerently; garrulously; crudely; slyly; telepathically; directly; anonymously; sympathetically; confidentially; treacherously; conveniently; unreservedly; spiritually; clandestinely; telegraphically; precariously; domestically.

(See impart, transmit.)

COMMUNICATION

adjectives

efficient; sincere; graceful; rich; unique; swift; economical; rapid; easy; constant; continuous; belligerent; inarticulate; garrulous; profane; flimsy; crude; covert; sly; underhanded; world; visual; electrical; papal; aerial; interstate; telepathic; unrestricted; telltale; articulated; direct; anonymous; sympathetic; confidential; treacherous; depressing; convenient; unreserved; spiritual; slow-moving; pregnant; clandestine; evil; friendly; mercantile; unlimited; secure; radio; telegraphic; privileged; pretended; domestic; precarious.

verbs

break—with; contrive—; cut off—; deliver—; draw—; establish—with; exchange —s; interfere with—; reestablish—; relay—; scatter—; set up—with; stimulate—; —conveys; —expresses; —imparts; —informs; —proceeds from; —purports to; —requests.

(See intercourse, conference, correspondence, message, letter.)

COMMUNION

adjectives

immortal; rapturous; ineffable; friendly; wordless; mental; intellectual; intimate; untroubled; constant; social.

COMMUNISM

adjectives

lawless; isolated; outright; iconoclastic; jealous; possessive; intolerant.

verbs

advocate—; aspire to—; bow to—; combat—; decry—; denounce—; draw the line against—; embrace—; envision—; eradicate—; espouse—; flirt with—; incite to—; riddle with—; seethe with—; spread—; storm toward—; suppress—; taint with—; war on—; —abolishes; —derives from; —destroys; —equalizes; —menaces; —levels; —reconstructs; —undermines; —idealizes.

(See socialism.)

COMMUNIST

adjectives

subtle; unadulterated; rabid; confirmed; covert; active.

verbs

ban—; bar—; condemn—; denounce—; deport—; evict—; forbid—; harbor—; organize—s; recognize—; regulate—; reproach—; shelter—; style as—; —advocates; —agitates; —antagonizes; —exhorts; —expresses; —dreams; —influences; —opposes; —orates; —practices; —proclaims; —s riot; —struggles; —supports; —undermines; —vows.

(See socialist.)

COMMUNISTIC

adverbs

honestly; dangerously; sincerely; intrepidly; daringly; audaciously; enthusiastically; actively; furtively; slyly; openly; obviously; convincingly; absurdly; alarmingly; recklessly; inherently; appallingly; bitterly; outright; downright; thoroughly; entirely; subtly; deceptively; startlingly; surreptitiously.

COMMUNITY

adjectives

benighted; enlightened; forward; average; model; decent; beautiful; ideal; prideful; ambitious; busiest; enterprising; self-respecting; progressive; aggressive; sturdy; self-sustaining; comfortable; isolated; much-maligned; antagonistic; sprawling; ecclesiastical; overcrowded; treeless; civilized; closely-knit; urban; country; laboring; alien; polyglot; quiet; residential; pioneer; rural; sacred; tropical; industrial; monastic; conservative; organized; homogeneous; composite; enormous; fortress-like; curious; moral; congenial; guileless; self-supporting; hostile; opulent; veritable; seafaring; serene; drainageless; expanding; sober; scattered.

verbs
acquaint with—; beautify—; burden—; confine to—; dominate—; dwell in—; elevate—; establish—; expel from—; filter into—; forsake—; govern—; offend—; organize into—; pervade—; present to—; represent—; rule—; unite in—; —elects; —fosters; —levies; —shares; —supports.
(See city, town, village, public, society, association, people.)

COMPACT
adjectives
convenient; social; indissoluble; comfortable; voluntary; earthly; unwritten; imaginary; binding; favorable.

verbs
admit to—; authorize—; compose—; confirm—; contract—; draw up—; frame—; fulfill—; gather in—; join—; knit in—; plan—; ratify—; seal—; sign—; solemnize—; weld in—; —aids; —allies; —consolidates; —insures; —protects; —strengthens; —supports.
(See covenant, agreement, pact, treaty, contract.)

COMPANION
adjectives
beloved; wonderful; alluring; pleasant; charming; gentle; beautiful; popular; trusted; genial; attractive; true; faithful; devoted; wonted; burly; happy; thoughtful; useful; fit; illustrious; bosom; constant; intimate; inseparable; indefatigable; daily; gayest; jolly; jocose; meticulous; amiable; agreeable; lively; entertaining; droll; emaciated; pale; slim; young; feeble; stocky; lithe; rough; double-crossing; profligate; undesirable; sneering; doubtful; fickle; morose; weak; pitiable; gloomy; craven; irate; dispirited; tense; shrinking; prostrate; intellectual; drinking; mysterious; familiar; unsuspecting; grave; normal; authentic; eager; boon; ardent; engaging; quaking; environed; ghastly; po-

lite; unique; troublesome; disappointing; lifelong; blithe; confederate; friendly (pl); semi-conscious; equivocal; spruce; subsidiary; often-tried.

verbs
associate with—; consort with—; engage—; entertain—; hire—; join—; lack—; lead—; long for—; reproach—; reunite with—; seek—; share with—; sway—; vie with—; —entertains; —escorts.
(See comrade, associate, ally.)

COMPANIONABLE
adverbs
pleasantly; agreeably; always; charmingly; unusually; genially; truly; faithfully; happily; thoughtfully; gaily; amiably; comfortably; entertainingly; curiously; politely; delightfully; inestimably; congenially; distinctly; unobtrusively; quietly; cheerfully; sociably; cosily; chattily.

COMPANIONSHIP
adjectives
genial; noble; voluntary; coarse; revered; endeared; creative; neighborly; thoughtful; indiscriminate; intimate; delightful; human; dull; honorable; dark; inestimable; mutual; helpful; satisfactory; refined; sympathetic; loving; mysterious; loyal; gay; humorous; pleasant; exclusive; friendly.

verbs
avoid—; break—; conceal—; crave—; delight in—; denounce—; desire—; hunger for—; invite—; join in—; lack—; limit—; lose—; maintain—of; object to—; seek—; win—; withdraw from—.
(See association, company, intimacy, fellowship, society.)

COMPANY
(association, companionship)
verbs
crave—; cultivate—; curse—; delight in—of; detest—; forbid—; forsake—; grace with—; miss—; placate—; refrain from—; regain—of; request—; sever from—; thrust into—of; woo—; —amuses; —bores; —departs; —dwindles; —entertains; —straggles in.
(See companionship.)

COMPANY
(corporation)
verbs
absorb—; bankrupt—; buy up—; charter—; consolidate—; defraud—; embezzle from—;

232

found—; incorporate—; manage—; merge
—; reorganize—; ruin—; —branches out;
—recovers; —profits; —survives.
(See corporation, firm.)

COMPANY
(general)
adjectives
subsidiary; lightheaded; respectable; assembled; scanty; ubiquitous; jocund; devout; treasonable; select; panic-stricken;
choice; trading; merry; congenial; licentious; loathsome; saintly; high-born; agreeable; mysterious; villainous; ennobling;
distinguished; defunct; brilliant; pleasant;
enterprising; cosmopolitan; animated; sus-
pecting; enchanting; glamorous; immortal;
great; picturesque; unobtrusive; sympathetic; jovial; buoyant; refined; talented;
detestable; rascally; infernal; wild; chartered; generating; transmission; gigantic;
aggressive; forward-looking; reputable;
commissary; projected.

COMPANY
(military division)
verbs
ambush—; assign to—; command—; desolate—; discontinue—; dispatch to—; divide
into—ies; enlist in—; evolve—; forge—;
head—; manoeuvre—; overtake—; partition—; separate—; spy on—; train—; —retreats; —traverses.
(See army, troops.)

COMPARABLE
adverbs
invidiously; scarcely; highly; easily; definitely; analogously; proportionally; relatively; homogeneously; interestingly; pertinently; distinctly; curiously; significantly;
favorably; deservedly; worthily; excellently; appropriately; suitably; fittingly; properly; decently.

COMPARE (v)
adverbs
invidiously; egotistically; unavoidably;
faithfully; favorably; unintentionally; approvingly; challengingly; odiously; metaphorically; significantly; caustically; classically; drolly; poignantly; dismayingly; conscientiously; directly; accurately; unfavorably; brutally; inevitably; aptly.
(See observe.)

COMPARISON
adjectives
vigorous; productive; challenging; odious;

cost; metaphorical; insignificant; self-in-
vited; curious; outworn; caustic; retrospective; classic; droll; poignant; dismaying; conscientious; direct; accurate; momentary; invidious; hateful; significant;
unfavorable; brutal; strained; inevitable.

verbs
attempt—; bear—; belittle—; consider—;
despair of—; despise—; disdain—; draw—;
fail in—; flaunt—; illustrate—; institute—;
invite—; judge—; lend to—; lose by—;
place beyond—; ridicule—; scoff at—;
stand—; subject to—; suffer by—; —brings
out; —emphasizes; —measures; —parallels;
—suggests.
(See illustration, simile.)

COMPARTMENT
adjectives
separate; concealed; rear; public; water-
tight.

verbs
coil in—; couch in—; decorate—; design—;
distribute in—; divide in—; dwell in—;
lay out—; occupy—; ornament—; panel—;
partition into—s; prepare—; retain—;
seal—; separate into—s; space—s; widen—;
—accommodates; —adjoins; —allows; —
permits.
(See section, chamber, part, division.)

COMPASS
adjectives
narrow; golden.

verbs
attract—; box—; manipulate—; navigate
with—; observe—; plan with—; plot
with—; suspend—; trust—; chart—; —describes; —deviates; —directs; —guides;
—indicates; —informs; —leads; —limits;
—marks; —measures; —pilots; —records;
—routes; —safeguards; —surveys.
(See instrument.)

COMPASSION
adjectives
pitying; proud; deep; sincere; involuntary;
august; womanly; delicate; angelic; bleeding; intolerable; melancholy; infinite;
chivalrous; moving; affectionate; protective; scornful; profound; hurried; infallible; tender; faint; sweet; bored; dying;
divine.

act in—; arouse—; conceal—; consume with—; contain—; display—; excite—; express—; feign—; fill with—; melt in—; minister with—; mourn in—; move to—; plead for—; pretend—; reveal—; stir to—; succor in—; take—upon; touch with—; weep in—; wrack with—; wring with—; —humanizes; —tempers.

(See commiseration, pity, sympathy, mercy.)

COMPASSIONATE
adverbs
keenly; sympathetically; understandingly; charitably; graciously; leniently; humanely; mercifully; pityingly; tenderly; disarmingly; softly; utterly; gently; tolerantly; indulgently; mildly; magnanimously; comfortingly; effectively; deeply; sincerely; delicately; infinitely; chivalrously; affectionately; profoundly; divinely.

COMPATIBLE
adverbs
easily; happily; felicitously; fortunately; unusually; harmoniously; amiably; agreeably; pleasantly; joyously; obviously; essentially; manifestly; supremely; famously; gracefully; opportunely; auspiciously; comfortably; amicably; extremely; unquestionably; unaccountably; surprisingly; fundamentally; notably.

COMPATRIOT
adjectives
assumed; grateful; affected.

COMPEL (v)
adverbs
flatly; ultimately; adroitly; reluctantly; strategically; artfully; slyly; politely; subtly; indirectly; truculently; legally; privately; troublesomely; economically; mysteriously; aggressively.

(See make, force.)

COMPENDIOUS
adverbs
remarkably; surprisingly; pleasingly; compactly; amazingly; laconically; tersely; conveniently; exceedingly; expertly; inexpressibly; faultlessly; commendably; laudably; extraordinarily; strikingly; sensibly; prudently; synoptically; concisely; neatly; cleverly; adroitly; agreeably; usefully; helpfully; advantageously.

COMPENDIUM
adjectives
astonishing; encyclopedic; similar.

COMPENSATE (v)
adverbs
adequately; amply; partially; grudgingly; sufficiently; satisfactorily; financially; tolerably; pecuniarily; ultimately; abundantly; solemnly; fully; barely; genially; nobly; voluntarily; loyally.

(See pay, replace.)

COMPENSATION
adjectives
adjusted; ample; satisfactory; dwindling; eternal; objective; financial; reassuming; tolerable; pecuniary; abundant; fixed; heartless; solemn; reasonable; adequate; dynamic; ultimate.

COMPENSATORY
adverbs
satisfactorily; safely; securely; luckily; happily; allowably; considerately; honorably; calculatingly; accurately; remuneratively; retroactively; highly; cleverly; acceptably; soundly; sensibly; wisely; adjustably; amply; financially; tolerably; generously; reasonably; adequately; ultimately; prudently; sufficiently.

COMPETE (v)
adverbs
hotly; hilariously; unrestrainedly; unrestrictedly; freely; spectacularly; constructively; legitimately; ruinously; destructively; bitterly; actively; intensely; keenly; strenuously; effectively; formidably; unprecedentedly; meaninglessly; individually; internally; domestically; internationally; critically; primarily; unfairly; unequally; aggressively; benevolently; basely; dishonorably; ruthlessly; hopefully; triumphantly.

(See contend, strive.)

COMPETENCE
adjectives
notable; cold; easy technical; hard; unruffled; modest; financial; mental; utmost; professional; decent; occupational; bare; sufficient.

verbs
allot—; amass—; bestow—upon; enlarge—; exhaust—; fritter away—; furnish—; in-

herit—; insure of—; lack—; live off—;
provide—; require—; rob of—; run
through—; secure—; —dwindles; —suffices.
(See wealth.)

COMPETENT
adverbs
thoroughly; remarkably; highly; brilliantly; exceptionally; influentially; deftly; ingeniously; intelligently; proficiently; excellently; capably; discreetly; smartly;
shrewdly; consummately; prepossessingly;
undoubtedly; unquestionably; manifestly;
completely; perfectly; notably; modestly;
sufficiently.

COMPETITION
adjectives
unrestrained; unlimited; unrestricted; utterly unbridled; free; full; spectacular; unregulated; constructive; legitimate; ruinous; destructive; bitter; active; intense;
keen; severe; sharp; heavy; strenuous;
serious; effective; unprecedented; formidable; meaningless; puny; individual;
world; internal; native; water-power; utility; truck; domestic; socialistic; international; critical; interstate; adjudicable;
tangled; unwanted; constant; increased;
enhanced; primary; counter; supplantive;
unfair; unequal; hampering; foreign; savage; eager; formidable; pecuniary; marginal; benevolent; consequent; base; dishonorable; aggressive; harsh; ruthless;
anarchical; hopeful; triumphal.

verbs
cripple—; curb—; discourage—; eliminate—; exclude—; face—; nurture on—;
obliterate—; offer—; overcome—; promote—; reduce—; sharpen—; squelch—;
stamp out—; stimulate—; suppress—; survive—; sustain—; —abates; —eases; —enlivens; —grinds; —steels; —tempers;
—threatens.
(See rivalry, contention, strife.)

COMPETITIVE
adverbs
bitterly; actively; enthusiastically; brutally;
ruinously; intensely; keenly; sharply;
strenuously; formidably; primarily; savagely; appealingly; contentiously; pugnaciously; destructively; stimulatingly; rousingly;
dangerously; cruelly; barbarously; desperately; mischievously; trickily; cunningly;
shrewdly; deceptively; unfairly.

COMPETITOR
adjectives
insurgent; easygoing; formidable; alert;
dangerous; cruel; honest; lame; veteran;
motor; throat-cutting; husky; local; direct;
active.

verbs
bankrupt—; defeat—; dispose of—; eliminate—; engage—; equal—; harass—;
judge—; mass—s; outdistance—; outstrip
—; rival—; suppress—; vanquish—; vie
with—; —contests; —endeavors; —gains;
—objects; —s organize; —retires; —stimulates.
(See contestant, opponent, rival, antagonist.)

COMPILATION
adjectives
intelligent; magnificent; handy; voluminous; exact; wretched; unoriginal; subsequent; important; systematic; hasty; valuable.

COMPLACENCY
adjectives
philosophical; bland; cynical; benign;
pleased; yielding; melancholy; smug; superb; amiable; pleasant; light; foolish;
placid; meek; oily; agreeable; affectionate.

verbs
announce with—; approach with—; breathe
—; breed—; characterize—; display—;
dwell in—; exhibit—; gain—; jolt out of—;
observe with—; puncture—; rebuke—; receive with—; regard with—; resent—;
satirize—; shake—; shock out of—; smile
with—; —reigns.
(See satisfaction, serenity.)

COMPLACENT
adverbs
oddly; serenely; calmly; placidly; maddeningly; smugly; conceitedly; arrogantly; incredibly; imperturbably; vexatiously; pleasantly; comfortably; affably; blandly; gently; graciously; composedly; tranquilly;
sedately; contentedly; cheerfully; entirely;
good-humoredly; curiously; resolutely; admirably; justifiably.

COMPLAIN (*v*)
adverbs
shrewishly; bitterly; sorrowfully; dismally;
audibly; feelingly; grievously; drawlingly; drearily; vehemently; respectfully;

peevishly; humorously; angrily; constantly; unjustly; ignorantly; pathetically; formally; jealously; frivolously; vexatiously; chronically; vigorously; dolefully.
(See grumble, murmur.)

COMPLAINT
adjectives
infantile; troublesome; vehement; loud; private; belated; frequent (pl); timid; alarming; mournful; loathsome; rash; angry; incipient; constant; fatal; unjust; prevalent; ignorant; fond; quavering; pathetic; distressing; formal; jealous; frivolous; dysenteric; pulmonary; vexatious; unintelligible; irritating; wailing; individual; public; chronic; paternal; vigorous; hoarse; well-founded; well-formed; pleasant; bitter; doleful; defensive; frenetic; praiseful; threnodic.

verbs
amend—; burden with—; complicate—; contract—; develop—; dismiss—; ease—; investigate—; issue—; lodge—against; mourn—; murmur—; pour out—; propogate—; renew—; rid oneself of—; set forth—; suffer—; swallow—; terminate—; usher in—; utter—; whisper—; withdraw —; —irritates; —s rain in; —recurs; —saddens; —wanes; —waxes.
(See grievance, lamentation, ailment, accusation, disease.)

COMPLAISANCE
adjectives
ready; affectionate; discreet; supple; sad; veiled.

COMPLAISANT
adverbs
amiably; benignly; kindly; warm-heartedly; indulgently; good-humoredly; benevolently; considerately; tenderly; accommodatingly; obligingly; sweetly; unaffectedly; comfortably; pleasantly; gravely; generously; happily; graciously; quietly; unobtrusively; remarkably; charmingly; gallantly; gently; urbanely; gracefully.

COMPLEMENTARY
adverbs
unusually; fortunately; remarkably; usefully; serviceably; happily; luckily; auspiciously; delightfully; pleasantly; absolutely; completely; entirely; thoroughly; mutually; opportunely; profitably; advantageously; conveniently; astonishingly; ingeniously.

COMPLETE
adverbs
absolutely; finally; happily; fortunately; luckily; satisfactorily; remarkably; unbelievably; magnificently; splendidly; extraordinarily; ideally; actually; delightfully; ceremonially; royally; formally; legally; officially; really.

COMPLETE (v)
adverbs
rapidly; swiftly; partially; gradually; skillfully; conventionally; finally; respectably; absolutely; delightfully; entirely; satisfactorily; casually; determinedly; superbly.
(See finish, perfect.)

COMPLETENESS
adjectives
unapproached; exhaustive; ethical; frightful; conventional; ruthless; respectable; final; round; absolute; firm; delightful.

COMPLETION
adjectives
apparent; advanced; divine; glorious; malevolent; plentiful; prophetic; stony; timely; unexpected; premature.

verbs
accomplish—; achieve—; attain—; await—; celebrate—; commemorate—; consent to—; desire—; expedite—; predict—; speed—; time—; —exhausts; —tires.
(See accomplishment, fulfillment, conclusion, end.)

COMPLEX
adjectives
repressed; haunting; sadistic; exceeding; flourishing; superior; vague; parlor; calamity; familiarity; modern; unreconciled; knitting; permanent; inferiority; narcissistic.

verbs
affect by—; analyze—; attribute to—; banish—; comprehend—; develop—; disentangle—; form—; indicate—; interpret—; involve—; nurture—; psychoanalyze—; relieve—; remove—; subject to—; understand—; unravel—; —chains; —consumes; —fetters; —seeks an outlet; arm with—.
(See complication, fear, influence.)

236

adverbs

bewilderingly; disturbingly; irritatingly; needlessly; seriously; embarrassingly; ambiguously; evasively; strangely; oddly; exceedingly; vaguely; astonishingly; bafflingly; unintelligibly; unnecessarily; tiresomely; painfully; harassingly; impossibly; intricately; perplexingly; confusingly; confoundedly; plaguedly; disconcertingly.

COMPLEXION

adjectives

flawless; clear; transparent; creamy; ivory; putty; sallow; apoplectic; pale; long; faded; unflushed; sanguine; fresh; ruddy; healthy; port-wine; choleric; beery; sunburnt; olive; sandy; swarthy; unnatural; delicate; dazzling; pleasant; muddy; blotchy; pretty; dark; ruined; shadowed; private; country; embrowned; coarse; variable; rubicund; jealous; florid; leaden; tanned; pallid.

verbs

beautify—; blemish—; blot—; change—; clear—; coarsen—; darken—; discolor—; dot—; inflame—; mar—; paint—; praise—; redden—; smirch—; tan—; tinge—; wither —; wrinkle—; —brightens; —freckles; —glows; —shines.

(See character, color, hue.)

COMPLEXITY

adjectives

astonishing; endless; infinite; ever-growing; abstract; ornate; serried; political; extraordinary; exciting; amazing; bewildering; differentiated; cosmic; baffling; increasing; technical.

verbs

attend with—; comprehend—; confine—; delve into—; disintegrate—; dispose of—; dissolve—; embrace—; evolve—; extricate from—; investigate—; involve—; reduce—; regard—; result in—; simplify—; solve—; sweep away—; —amazes; —discourages; —puzzles; —vanishes.

(See intricacy, complication, entanglement.)

COMPLIANCE

adjectives

immediate; faithful; servile; suave; entreating; implicit; infantile; calm; strict.

verbs

balk at—; betoken—; bow in—; coerce into—; demand—; desire—; enforce—; fall into—with; gain—; move to—; necessitate —; press for—; profess—; propose—; refuse—; request—; signify—; utter—; yield—.

(See submission, concession, acquiescence.)

COMPLIANT

adverbs

obligingly; gently; readily; willingly; vexatiously; slavishly; obsequiously; pleasantly; meekly; timidly; obediently; supinely; spinelessly; weakly; devotedly; passively; submissively; deferentially; affectionately; faithfully; loyally; unwillingly; rebelliously; sweetly; gladly; implicitly; childishly; calmly.

COMPLICATED

adverbs

hopelessly; senselessly; foolishly; necessarily; purposely; seriously; dangerously; ominously; sadly; perplexingly; embarrassingly; unavoidably; queerly; strangely; alarmingly; interestingly; disconcertingly; bafflingly; astonishingly; unintelligibly; ridiculously; confusingly; bewilderingly; desperately; painfully; plaguedly.

COMPLICATION

adjectives

serious; unseen; interesting; threatening; sad; annoying; embarrassing; military; endless; ingenious; delicate; everlasting; perplexing; indispensable; annoying; constant; dangerous; simple; psychological; dizzying; fresh; queer; added; social; imaginative; international; unforeseen.

verbs

avoid—; bar—; catch in—; develop—; free from—; guard against—; induce—; involve—; prevent—; result in—; solve—; suffer—; —abates; —arises; —endangers; —occurs.

(See complexity, entanglement, intricacy, confusion.)

COMPLICITY

adjectives

potential; secret; treacherous; eager; energetic; guilty; deceptive.

verbs

accuse of—; act in—with; charge with—; clear of—; convict of—; deal in—; free of—; imprison for—; involve in—; suspect of—; vindicate of—.

(See guilt.)

COMPLIMENT

adjectives

genial; pleasant; admirable; handsome; rare; high; generous; apt; polite; fervid; sincerest; respectful; justified; honest; delicate; smooth-tongued; high-flown; flowery; stilted; grudging; left-handed; fulsome; dubious; youthful; peculiar; unphilosophical; noncommittal; questionable; erudite; abstracted; subtle; appropriate; gentle; awkward; indirect; feminine; gratifying; truculent; stipulated; supreme; piquant; munificent; bombastic; professional; superlative; gallant; ephemeral; deferential; mawkish; double-barreled; formal; undeniable; sugared; two-edged; exaggerated; idle; well-turned; tactful; novel; affectionate; ghastly; hyperbolic.

verbs

accept—; acknowledge—; allow—; bestow—; deliver—; disdain—; expect—; extend—; favor with—; greet with—; imply—; pay—; present—; receive—; return—; turn—; —commends; —flatters; —pleases; —praises; —soothes.

(See greeting, remembrance, congratulation, praise.)

COMPLIMENT (v)

adverbs

warmly; genially; admirably; handsomely; rarely; highly; generously; aptly; fervidly; sincerely; justifiedly; delicately; stiltedly; grudgingly; fulsomely; dubiously; eruditely; subtly; appropriately; awkwardly; indirectly; gratifyingly; bombastically; supremely; piquantly; professionally; superlatively; gallantly; deferentially; mawkishly; formally; undeniably; exaggeratedly; idly; affectionately; hyperbolically.

(See praise.)

COMPLIMENTARY

adverbs

delightfully; flatteringly; gallantly; charmingly; politely; exaggeratedly; absurdly; smilingly; chivalrously; adoringly; pleasingly; highly; sincerely; appropriately; affectionately; truly; honestly; grudgingly; dubiously; questionably; subtly; gently; indulgently; pompously; supremely; deferentially; handsomely; lovingly.

COMPLY (v)

adverbs

promptly; strictly; willingly; gladly; partially; slavishly; humbly; irritably; nonchalantly; bitterly; sourly; grimly; carelessly.

(See agree, consent.)

COMPONENT

adjectives

essential; necessary.

adverbs

fundamentally; essentially; necessarily; indispensably; unavoidably; constitutionally; organically; vitally.

COMPOSE

adverbs

nominally; identically; wholly; partly; artistically; largely; simultaneously; incessantly; luckily; prolifically; abundantly; charmingly; picturesquely; didactically; pretentiously; ludicrously; vilely; monstrously; allegorically; monumentally; orchestrally; historically; fantastically; chorally; crudely; elaborately; vitally; gravely; dramatically; humorously; gracefully; creatively; realistically.

(See lull, calm.)

COMPOSER

adjectives

native; brilliant; voluminous; contemporary; eminent; operatic; productive; talented; anxious; instinctive; ultramodern; bestknown; foremost; outstanding; exuberant; modernist; versatile; pharisaical; famous; hack; master; deft; practiced.

COMPOSITION

adjectives

decorative; didactic; careless; pretentious; ludicrous; tragic; vile; dishonorable; artistic; unwieldy; monstrous; secular; monumental; reposeful; allegorical; touching; fugitive; orchestral; historical; intensive; feminine; studied; capricious; fantastic; motley; choral; essential; elaborate; crude; important; vital; grave; dramatic; humorous; graceful; striking; aesthetic; creative; realistic.

verbs

adjust—; alter—; arrange—; compound—; deliver—; fashion—; form—; frame—; interpret—; order—; polish—; prepare—; print—; release—; reshape—; score—; toss off—; transpose—; versify—; vocalize—; —involves.

(See essay, story.)

COMPOSURE

adjectives
perfect; kind; gentle; magnificent; incomparable; unruffled; flintlike; utmost; splendid; absolute; unimpaired; astonishing; solemn; curious; labored; grave; hard; horrible; contemptuous; reticent; equable; uncanny; airy; mournful; melancholy; marble; seeming; insolent; extraordinary; austere; inflexible; strained; undisturbed; dogged; comparative; amiable; cruel; unshakable; affected.

verbs
blemish—; break—; enjoy—; feign—; handle with—; maintain—; mar—; meet with—; preserve—; recover—; regain—; settle in—; shake—; shock out of—; view with—; —disarms; —follows.
(See equanimity, serenity.)

COMPOUND

adjectives
hypothetical; monstrous; metallic; disastrous; ferrous; utmost; rankest; argenteous; thermoplastic; harmonious; complicated; deliquescent; linguistic; tantalizing; elaborate; ingenious; chemical; incongruous.

verbs
absorb—; analyze—; break down—; characterize—; combine in—; derive—from; devise—; dissolve—; form—; heat—; indicate—; make up—; meet—; mix—; prescribe—; stir—; stimulate—; unite in—.
(See mixture, combination.)

COMPREHEND (v)

adverbs
fully; perfectly; readily; rightly; intelligently; discriminatingly; partially; scientifically; deeply; accurately; generally; dispassionately; tardily; masterfully; instinctively.
(See grasp, understand.)

COMPREHENSION

adjectives
conspicuous; intelligent; calm; infant; social; absent; discriminating; untrained; perfect; martial; vast; human; growing; enlightened; scientific; deeper; accurate; easy; imaginative; adequate; general; faithful; quick; dispassionate; gathering; complete; unparalleled; tardy; masterly; instinctive; dawning.

verbs
achieve—; affect—; attain—; attempt—; benumb—; enlarge—; exhibit—; extend—; feign—; go beyond—; grasp—; include in—; lack—; listen with—; simulate—; stagger—; view with—; warp—; —dawns; —results in.
(See understanding, apprehension, knowledge.)

COMPREHENSIVE

adverbs
wonderfully; broadly; unusually; fortunately; cogently; liberally; tolerantly; tolerably; fairly; extremely; luckily; purposely; explicitly; advantageously; generously; admirably; delightfully; superbly; conspicuously; nobly; strikingly; unquestionably; impressively; astonishingly.

COMPRESS (v)

adverbs
firmly; severely; savagely; bitterly; tightly; angrily; powerfully; dramatically.
(See crowd.)

COMPROMISE

adjectives
expensive; unworthy; lean; sensible; timid; tolerable; workable; proposed; wise; self-sufficient; practical; judicious; tacit; occasional; dignified; negotiated; imaginable; ineffectual; prudent; pitiful; strange; cowardly; ultimate; wretched; curious; scorning.

verbs
accept—; achieve—; agree upon—; announce—; arrange—; arrive at—; attempt —; come to—; conclude—; consent to—; draw up—; effect—; extend—; maintain—; offer—; result in—; risk—; —adjusts; —decides; —recommends; —reconciles; —settles; —soothes.
(See agreement, settlement, promise.)

COMPROMISING

adverbs
unfortunately; possibly; alarmingly; leniently; sensibly; reasonably; opportunely; fearfully; timidly; timorously; bravely; courageously; senselessly; scandalously; recklessly; indiscreetly; curiously; indubitably; injudiciously; awkwardly; unluckily; evasively; unhappily; unwisely; shockingly; appallingly; rashly; appeasingly.

239

COMPULSION

adjectives

silent; irresistible; subtle; fascinated; armed; legal; restraining; unrecognized; physical; sad; temperamental; moral; strong; inescapable.

verbs

accept under—; act in—; appear under—; commit under—; confess under—; develop by—; devise by—; exercise—; involve—; obey under—; rebel at—; resist—; restrain by—; submit under—; wring out by—; —exculpates; —forces.

(See coercion, force, necessity, restraint, obligation.)

COMPULSORY

adverbs

disagreeably; hatefully; substantially; significantly; dangerously; disturbingly; implicitly; strictly; rigidly; hideously; flagrantly; wisely; sensibly; cruelly; detestably; odiously; wickedly; irksomely; arbitrarily; officially; locally; inescapably; fortunately; annoyingly; tediously; prosily; vexatiously; needlessly; ineffectively; irresistibly; silently; subtly; sadly; inexorably; stringently; peremptorily; terrifyingly; actually; authoritatively; absolutely; dominantly; imperiously; originally; sternly; necessarily.

COMPUNCTION

adjectives

slight; severe; grievous; motherly; evident; mathematical; natural; bitter.

COMPUTATION

adjectives

careful; sardonic; arithmetical; subsequent; moderate; impressive; ridiculous.

verbs

calculate—; check—; correct—; corroborate—; employ—; err in—; estimate—; fail in—; fall short of—; find by—; increase—; inspect—; prove—; reach by—; reckon—; scorn—; —accounts for; —differs; —helps; —indicates.

(See calculation, reckoning.)

COMPUTE (*v*)

adverbs

accurately; sketchily; carefully; arithmetically; mathematically; geometrically; impressively; ridiculously; statistically; scientifically.

(See calculate, estimate.)

COMRADE

adjectives

worthy; fastidious; gallant; benevolent; wounded; self-denying; placid; hackneyed; suffocated; inseparable (pl); little; garrulous; abiding; agreeable; wonder-loving; intellectual; exhausted; needy; sensible; merry; conforming; loyal; bickering; gluttonous.

verbs

aid—; applaud—; assist—; associate with —; betray—; forsake—; fraternize with—; gain—; march with—; protect—; share with—; shield—; treasure—.

(See companion, associate, mate.)

COMRADELY

adverbs

loyally; devotedly; sympathetically; cordially; warmly; helpfully; heartily; amicably; affably; frankly; distinctly; congenially; unselfishly; staunchly; generously; courageously; gallantly; agreeably; faithfully; gaily; comfortably; entertainingly; curiously; unobtrusively; quietly; sociably; chattily.

COMRADESHIP

adjectives

happy; warm; flattering; unconditional; spiritual; impossible; ceaseless; genuine; kindly; pleasant; tragic; deep-hearted; constant; simple; rare; international; lifelong; sympathetic; unspeakable.

CONCEAL (*v*)

adverbs

cleverly; effectually; criminally; partially; instinctively; feloniously; dexterously; deliberately; stupidly; ignorantly; guiltily; conscientiously; fearfully; scrupulously.

(See hide, suppress.)

CONCEALMENT

adjectives

expedient; ignorant; stupid; coarse; juggling; ladylike; watery.

verbs

appear from—; attempt—; disclose—; divulge—; effect—; intend—; lay bare—; necessitate—; offer—; place in—; reveal— of; seek refuge in—; suspect—; uncover—; veil in—; wrap in—.

(See secretion, seclusion, privacy.)

CONCEDE (v)

adverbs

deferentially; completely; unexpectedly; apologetically; willingly; generally; tactfully; frankly; generously; tamely; gently; freely; liberally.

(See yield, admit.)

CONCEIT

adjectives

devastating; quaint; mere; whimsical; colossal; comical; solemn; peculiar; lessening; sanguine; keen; erroneous; piteous; stupid; rational; boyish; staple; enigmatic; graceful; profound; doubtful; partial; presumptuous; lively; ingenious; gallant; noble; true; innocent; earthy; gross; fantastic; literary; passing; imperious; self-centered; melancholy; artificial; sickening; modest; fabulous; false; platonic; vain; immense.

verbs

bare—; cloud with—; deplore—; devour with—; display—; fill with—; humor—; puff up with—; rebuke—; shatter—; soak in—; swallow up by—; tickle—; wallow in—; ween—; —disgusts; —exaggerates; —inflames; —overestimates; —overvalues; —prejudices; —robs; —twists.

(See egotism, pride, vanity.)

CONCEITED

adverbs

harmlessly; ludicrously; solemnly; piteously; ridiculously; arrogantly; intolerably; stupidly; gracelessly; presumptuously; innocently; grossly; fantastically; offensively; imperiously; sickeningly; immensely; disgustingly; foolishly; inordinately; contemptibly; amusingly; ingenuously; artlessly; complacently; prodigiously; colossally; unconsciously; unwittingly; awkwardly; foppishly; simperingly; stagily; abominably; laughably; pathetically; noisily; theatrically; transparently; unreasonably; loftily; grandly; undeniably; extremely; palpably; remarkably; incredibly.

CONCEIVABLE

adverbs

scarcely; possibly; readily; easily; fantastically; reasonably; sensibly; hardly; barely; obscurely; oddly; grotesquely; faintly; ridiculously; probably; presumably; romantically; preposterously; theoretically; fancifully; appallingly.

CONCEIVE (v)

adverbs

wondrously; hastily; chastely; humbly; craftily; admirably; distinctly; harshly; instantly; empirically; artistically; ingeniously; effectually; erroneously; majestically; nobly; inspiringly; popularly; narrowly; uniquely; morally; politically; cynically; definitely; puerilely; sentimentally; liberally; nebulously; intellectually; romantically; unchristianly; traditionally; previously; exaltedly; dramatically; subjectively; aesthetically; musically; competitively; peculiarly; erroneously; vitiatedly; incongruously; spontaneously; idealistically; judicially; crudely; grandly; divinely; immaculately; sympathetically.

(See understand, imagine.)

CONCENTRATE (v)

adverbs

swiftly; mentally; logically; intensely; fruitfully; protractedly; deliberately; achingly; devoutly; exhaustively; grimly; intently; desperately; incessantly; persistently; passionlessly; impassionedly; carefully; ambitiously; wholly.

(See focus.)

CONCENTRATION

adjectives

mental; intense; logical; zestful; vague; dreamy; undue; fruitful; physical; protracted; deliberate; agonized; aching; devout; exhausting; grim; perpetual; desperate; implacable; administrative; deadly; intent; desired; completed; incessant; persistent; pronounced; impassioned; careful; gigantic.

verbs

affect—; cultivate—; direct—; gain by—; gather in—; lose in—; necessitate—; produce—; require—; strive for—; —collects; —empowers; —enables; —intensifies; —strengthens; —unifies.

(See condensation, contraction.)

CONCEPT

adjectives

cynical; ethereal; social; major; permanent; simple; beneficent; fundamental; negative; petty; platonic; economic; emotional; rational; mystical; anthropopsychic; consonant; abstract; steady; liberal; heroic; ridiculous; idiotic.

verbs

accept—; build up—; discard—; express—; form—; guard—; hallow—; idealize—; join in—; lose—; master—; produce—; reshape—; reverence—; symbolize—; —develops; —disappears; —fades; —grows.
(See idea, conception, thought, notion.)

CONCEPTION
adjectives

majestic; noble; lofty; proud; inspiring; popular; beautiful; imperial; powerful; daring; profound; accurate; just; coherent; ingenious; undiluted; curious; unique; narrow; haziest; raw; immature; moral; military; brilliant; mental; political; cynical; definite; puerile; sentimental; novel; liberal; fixed; abstract; easy; inward; general; nebulous; artistic; imaginative; intellectual; evolutionary; theologic; ethical; romantic; freer; objective; movie; arabesque; unchristian; utopian; traditional; previous; exalted; true; delicate; grotesque; distinguished; gross; crude; dramatic; sensuous; wildest; essential; subjective; aesthetic; musical; dynamic; faintest; fickle; competitive; physical; adequate; theoretical; ancient; poetic; original; admirable; peculiar; erroneous; vitiated; serviceable; advanced; incongruous; spontaneous; idealistic; hysterical; cherished; judicial; fabulous; dim; vague; crude; gracious; rival; radiant; grand; different; proper; divine; immaculate; sordid; dominant; sympathetic; continental.

CONCEPTION
verbs

accept—; acquire—; attain—; base—; blur—; broaden—; clarify—; classify—; color—; confuse—; derive—; destroy—; disrupt—; divorce from—; embody—; endow—; enlarge—; envisage—; exalt—; expound—; fulfill—; gain—; give—; implant—; inherit—; justify—; perfect—; ponder—; reflect—; rest on—; revise—; school in—; set aside—; translate—; —exists; —denotes; —forms; —prevails.
(See idea, notion, concept, impression, imagination.)

CONCERN
(*business*)
adjectives

pioneer; long-established; competing; successful; dominating; settled; private; commercial; ultra-respectable; prospective; pretentious.

CONCERN
(*feeling*)
adjectives

sweet; kindly; tender; mild; affectionate; anxious; eager; charitable; intense; human; sympathetic; pitying; agonizing; real; honest; deep; serious; grave; consuming; jealous; secondary; irritable; superfluous; dramatic; suprasensual; primary; personal; lifelong; general; vital; ever-pressing; mutual; patent; complex; terrestrial; interior; materialistic; temporal; immediate; flourishing; pressing; extreme; disquieting; ethical; soft; menial; waking; paramount; nonchalant; hypochondriacal.

verbs

cause—; contemplate with—; create—; demonstrate—; detect—; ease—; engage—; excite—; feel—; feign—; frown with—; involve—; lift—; manifest—; neglect—; plead—; pretend—; question—; regard with—; relate with—; share—; throw into—; trouble with—; —vexes.
(See anxiety, care.)

CONCERN (*v*)
adverbs

feverishly; intelligently; intimately; immensely; intensely; principally; solely; tenderly; mildly; affectionately; humanly; anxiously; eagerly; charitably; sympathetically; gravely; consumingly; jealously; dramatically; mutually; patently; materially; disquietingly; ethically; passionately.
(See worry.)

CONCERNED
adverbs

deeply; anxiously; financially; nationally; personally; appallingly; vitally; scandalously; curiously; excitedly; nervously; strangely; unaccountably; justly; responsibly; unfortunately; uneasily; importantly; heavily; solicitously; inseparably; undeniably; painfully; seriously; gravely; primarily; materially; surreptitiously; secretly.

CONCERT
adjectives

classical; orchestral; spiritual; thrilling; indoor; monster; basic; charitable; home; impromptu.

CONCERTED
adverbs

effectively; influentially; efficiently; strongly; irresistibly; favorably; clannishly; irrepressibly; invincibly; alertly; thoughtfully; resolutely; vigilantly; guardedly; securely;

legally; legitimately; warrantably; justifiably; formidably; confidently; ably; authoritatively; adaptably.

CONCESSION

adjectives

radical; scandalous; surprising; trivial; veritable; voluntary; momentary; mutual; temporary; secret; valuable; unconscious; generous; dignified; minor; gracious; reciprocal; commercial; vital; unwise; unlimited; cowardly; benevolent; original; liberal; sufficient; pencil-making; political; unusual; unworthy.

verbs

accept—; allot—; allow—; appreciate—; claim—; demand—; exact—; execute—; exploit—; force into—; grant—; obtain—; receive—; refuse—; scorn—; submit to—; warrant—; yield—; —admits; —ameliorates; —fails; —infers; —mitigates.

(See privilege, right, favor, allowance.)

CONCILIATION

adjectives

harmonious; promoted; predetermined; unattainable; replete; voluntary; amiable; tender; lenient.

verbs

accept—; achieve—; attempt—; bring into—; declare—; dispute—; effect—; hope for—; offer—; open avenues of—; promote—; recommend—; strive for—; tease into—; welcome—; win—; —harmonizes; exhibit—.

(See reconciliation.)

CONCILIATORY

adverbs

hopefully; possibly; presumably; properly; justly; wisely; sagaciously; favorably; sensibly; reasonably; soundly; fairly; profoundly; craftily; subtly; shrewdly; deceptively; fortunately; decently; respectfully; generously; honestly; appropriately; judiciously; impressively; moderately.

CONCISE

adverbs

gratifyingly; remarkably; satisfactorily; surprisingly; pleasingly; pleasantly; briefly; compactly; crisply; laconically; tersely; conventionally; conveniently; exceedingly; curtly; pointedly; inexpressibly; faultlessly; commendably; laudably; extraordinarily; strikingly; necessarily; sensibly; wisely; prudently.

CONCLUDE

adverbs

sorrowfully; erroneously; inevitably; cynically; peremptorily; definitely; abruptly; pessimistically; tartly; amicably; summarily; jocosely; confidently; coolly; officially; triumphantly; contemptuously; reasonably; legitimately; brilliantly; theoretically; logically; humiliatingly; despairingly; irresistibly; obviously; rationally; preposterously; statistically; ultimately; fallaciously; tragically; hypothetically; misleadingly.

(See end, close.)

CONCLUSION

adjectives

official; generalized; conducive; triumphant; intelligible; contemptuous; doubtful; still; strict; legitimate; practical; definite; inevitable; vile; languid; painful; speculative; spiritualistic; solid; meager; practiced; satisfactory; reasonable; brilliant; virtuous; lurid; adventurous; foregone; theoretic; suitable; logical; compulsory; negative; ungracious; erroneous; murdering; palpable; bloody; humiliating; consolatory; dreary; preliminary; impotent; happy; sterile; demonstrated; scientific; auspicious; pregnant; valuable; horrible; devastating; despairing; portentous; irresistible; victorious; trivial; obvious; rational; abrupt; preposterous; statistical; ultimate; farcical; astonishing; surprising; fallacious; lame; subversive; opposite; tragic; hypothetical; critical; spooky; necessary; tricky; misleading.

verbs

accept—; admit—; arrive at—; base—on; bias—; bring to—; build—; carry to—; confirm—; crown—; deduce—; delude—; divine—; draw—; enunciate—; escape—; establish—; formulate—; induce—; influence—; jump to—; lead to—; march to—; perceive—; prejudice—; reach—; refute—; reinforce—; seek—; set down—; shake—; shape—; strengthen—; substantiate—; support—; sustain—; tolerate—; weigh—; win—; —fades; —follows.

(See decision, determination, deduction, completion.)

CONCLUSIVE

adverbs

satisfactorily; officially; doubtfully; legally; definitely; painfully; reasonably; ungraciously; positively; absolutely; decisively; arbitrarily; dogmatically; incontestably;

categorically; tyrannically; unmistakably; brutally; hopelessly; firmly; disagreeably; peremptorily; unconditionally; finally; uncannily; unalterably; happily.

CONCOCTION
adjectives
promoting; bitter; delicious; fatal; philanthropic; potent.

CONCOMITANT
adverbs
usually; habitually; naturally; presumably; probably; inevitably; recurrently; occasionally; reasonably; definitely; ordinarily; assuredly; undoubtedly; apparently; evidently; unavoidably; inescapably; painfully; unfortunately; strangely; miraculously; always; providentially; significantly; luckily; deliberately; designedly.

CONCORD
adjectives
never-ending; everlasting; universal; perfect; gentle; sweeping; jarring.

CONCOURSE
adjectives
fortuitous; . gallant; immense; abusive; vast; numerous (pl); divine; affected; orderly; deep.

CONCRETE
adverbs
convincingly; satisfactorily; actually; explicitly; expressly; objectively; substantially; sensibly; perceptibly; representatively; appreciably; unequivocally; unmistakably; demonstrably; intelligently; decisively; intelligibly; comprehensibly.

CONCUR (v)
adverbs
entirely; amiably; directly; heartily; half-heartedly; diplomatically; affably; casually; tentatively; provisionally; privately; unboundedly; tranquilly.
(See agree.)

CONCUSSION
adjectives
hearty; fearful; tremendous; momentary; enormous.

CONDEMN (v)
adverbs
unjustly; unmercifully; irrevocably; universally; intentionally; mildly; mercilessly; unhesitatingly; petulantly; emphatically;
unanimously; bitterly; publicly; unqualifiedly; unhesitatingly; blindly; severely; drastically; indignantly; barbarously; formally.
(See censure, blame.)

CONDEMNATION
adjectives
bitter; unqualified; sharp; public; critical; sweeping; unhesitating; blind; severest; vigorous; censorious; sorrowful; active; reverberating; drastic; unhesitating; iniquitous; unanimous; cruel; scornful; indignant.

verbs
announce—; deserve—; fall into—; judge —; launch—; merit—; procure—of; pronounce—; repent—; reproach with—; spare—; steep in —; —blames; —censures; —inflames; —libels; —slanders.
(See denunciation.)

CONDENSATION
adjectives
amazing; conjoined; hasty; literal; moderate; sensible; viscous.

verbs
effect—; hasten—; —compresses; —concentrates; —converts; —crowds; —eliminates; —hardens; —intensifies; —purifies; —reduces; —thickens; —vaporizes; —heats.
(See contraction.)

CONDESCEND (v)
adverbs
urbanely; graciously; ostentatiously; hypocritically; patronizingly; haughtily; languidly; stiffly; benignantly; amusingly; gently; amiably; magnanimously.
(See yield.)

CONDESCENSION
adjectives
gradual; ostentatious; hypocritical; patronizing; lofty; haughty; languid; stiff; graceful; benignant; edifying; condoling; infinite; good-natured; familiar; awful; terrifying; presidential; amusing; gentle; utmost; amiable; degrading.

CONDITION
adjectives
excellent; perfect; satisfactory; ideal; pathological; prepossessing; happy; blissful; remarkable; unusual; stringent; robust; righteous; tumbled; primitive; dilapidated; neglected; unsanitary; crowded; miserable; terrible; deplorable; woeful; pitiful; gloomy; below par; demoralized;

alarming; untidy; fatigued; distracted; productive; senile; mental; unsettled; financial; gaseous; ultimate; permanent; natural; relaxed; garrulous; hard; analogous; harsh; proper; normal; correct; genial; glamorous; inspiring; delectable; humane; contemporary; dangerous; chaotic; changing; temporal; local; grim; corrupt; pleasant; evil; unfavorable; quiet; working; early; stipulated; defined; varying; existing; hazardous; severe; embryonic; calamitous; operating; parlous; servile; underlying; rational; peculiar; degraded; wretched; degenerate; interesting; flowing; discouraging; artificial; erotic; fluctuating; adverse; slight; disabled; neglected; ill; molten; outward; altered; poisoned; responsive; ameliorated; inferior; industrial; abject; starving; infamous; foot; expressed; optical; grievous; flourishing; inchoate; ultimate; top-notch; depraved; unsightly; unbailed; distressing; threatening; unsatisfactory; disturbed; semi-barbarous; undated; prolonged; chronic; stagnant; delicate; incompatible; belligerent; vapory; hopeless; molecular; rigid; fluid; atmospheric; frightful; impaired; moribund; aeronautical; helpless; critical; social; intellectual; established; humblest; embarrassed; bruised; political; drooping; prostrate; arid; thriving; ragged; dreadful; introverted; muddy; complicating; traffic; subgrade; unique; cheeky; destitute; nourishing; visceral; taut; contrasting; inflammatory; amorphous; surrounding; climatic; hypnotic; healthy; antecedent; clogged; encumbered; sober; lamentable; crippled; acute; pecuniary; opposing; ignoble; temporary; famishing; incurable; elastic; seraphic; upset; identical; light; irritated; anguished; tubercular; gruelling; convulsive; befuddled; unhygienic; defenseless; spasmodic; morbid; equivalent; special; cold; heterogeneous; disordered; atomic; perilous; habitable; succulent; certain; unbearable; deterrent; cataleptic; humbler; prevailing; linguistic; odd; sophisticated; desolate; quick; ruinous; exhausted; disastrous; bewildering; desiccated; foolish; precise; replenished; humble; itching; depleted; slovenly; idyllic; impassable; negative; perplexed.

verbs
abolish—; accept—; accustom to—; adapt to—; affect—; aggravate—; alter—; ameliorate—; analyze—; appraise—; avoid—; benefit by—; better—; cavil—; check—; comply with—; comprehend—; conquer—;

consider—; contribute to—; convert—; cope with—; create—; depend on—; designate —; diagnose—; discover—; elucidate—; embrace—; encounter—; enter on—; eradicate—; exaggerate—; exemplify—; exempt from—; foresee—; fulfill—; govern—; heal—; ignore—; impose—; improve—; inform of—; investigate—; judge—; manifest—; mark—; neglect—; obviate—; portray—; prophesy—; protest—; recognize—; rectify—; regard—; regulate—; rejuvenate—; relieve—; remedy—; restore—; rule—; scorn—; simulate—; stabilize—; stipulate—; subject to—; submit to—; taint—; thrive on—; treat—; ward off—; welcome—; yield to—; —arises; —attends; —characterizes; —culminates in; —embitters; —ensues; —evolves; —indicates; —permits; —persists; —prevails; —provokes; —recurs; —reflects; —shifts; —spreads; springs from—; —threatens; —vanishes; —warrants; —yields to.
(See state, plight, situation.)

CONDITIONAL
adverbs
wisely; definitely; stringently; deplorably; properly; unfortunately; explicitly; reasonably; ungraciously; tersely; curtly; offensively; repugnantly; humiliatingly; auspiciously; trivially; favorably; rationally; surprisingly; trickily; equivocally; provokingly; treacherously; deviously; perplexingly; unacceptably; fantastically.

CONDONE (*v*)
adverbs
sentimentally; magnanimously; freely; sanctimoniously; unqualifiedly; humanely; broad-mindedly; intelligently; tenderly; affectionately; willingly; absolutely.
(See pardon.)

CONDUCIVE
adverbs
actually; essentially; significantly; distinctly; fundamentally; valuably; originally; splendidly; meritoriously; superbly; indubitably; definitely; expressly; enduringly; surprisingly; virtually; actively; serviceably; indispensably; profitably; indescribably; indisputably.

CONDUCT
adjectives
private; meritorious; exemplary; commendable; efficient; high; sane; civilized; plausible; consistent; circumspect; chivalrous; gallant; lazy; mannerless; unmanly; un-

ruly; annoying; indecorous; flagitious; instinctive; rebellious; licentious; abstemious; intemperate; editorial; criminal; theatrical; active; shameless; cruel; precipitate; fraudulent; inexplicable; barbarous; unyielding; daring; ungenerous; dishonest; peaceful; angelic; perverse; questionable; refractory; intolerable; neutral; patriotic; discreditable; irreproachable; disloyal; flagrant; flighty; analytical; unruly; outrageous; flamboyant; unethical; forward; arbitrary; obstreperous; bearish; boorish; courteous; perceptive; irascible; mad; depraved.

verbs
approve—; better—; correct—; decry—; denounce—; deprecate—; elevate—; emulate—; guide—; improve—; impugn—; influence—; interpret—; loathe—; pursue—; restrain—; shape—; —agitates; —conforms.
(See behavior.)

CONDUCT (*v*)
adverbs
inelegantly; rigidly; honorably; intelligently; prudently; improvidently; solemnly; marvelously; diligently; privately; secretly; commendably; efficiently; circumspectly; indecorously; rebelliously; licentiously; meritoriously; intemperately; editorially; criminally; theatrically; shamelessly; precipitately; fraudulently; barbarously; inexplicably; unyieldingly; daringly; dishonestly; peacefully; perversely; questionably; irreproachably; disloyally; analytically; unethically; arbitrarily; obstreperously; boorishly; courteously.
(See escort, lead.)

CONDUCTOR (*electric*)
adjectives
central; extended; brass; faulty; fixed; insulated; metallic; prime; water-tight.

verbs
ground—; insulate—; pass through—; shield—; tape—; —carries; —conveys; —shocks; —transmits.

CONDUCTOR (*escort or guide*)
adjectives
gifted; orchestral; philharmonic; natural; theatrical; amiable; poor; talented; celebrated.

verbs
tip—; uniform—; —accompanies; —collects; —directs; —escorts; —leads; —lectures; —motions; —signals; —guides.
(See guide, leader, escort.)

CONDUIT
adjectives
earthen; flood; secret; circuitous; transmitting; subterranean; water.

verbs
block—; bury—; clog—; connect—; drain —; force through—; issue from—; obstruct—; paint—; pipe through—; pour from—; pump through—; run through—; spout from—; —channels; —communicates; —conveys; —distributes; —freezes; —irrigates; —leads; —leaks; —protects; —rusts; —spouts; —transmits; —channels.
(See channel, canal, pipe, passage.)

CONE
adjectives
long; slender; truncated; symmetrical; veritable.

CONFECTION
adjectives
tasteless; mystic; sundry; delightful; cooked; appetizing; delicate.

CONFEDERATION
adjectives
absolute; powerful; vigorous; active; loyal.

CONFER (*v*)
adverbs
secretly; ostentatiously; freely; proposedly; hurriedly; briefly; privately; personally; officially; nationally; informally; ominously; endlessly; amicably; annually; softly; treacherously; rebelliously.
(See give, consult.)

CONFERENCE
adjectives
friendly; all-night; midnight; afternoon; dinner; proposed; rapid; hurried; whispered; brief; private; personal; long; wearisome; fateful; remarkable; regional; diplomatic; astronomical; family; official; arms; plenipotentiary; national; sad; radical; recent; emergency; worth-while; informal; preliminary; secret; ominous; homespun; amicable; endless; intended; extraordinary; soft; affable; casual; overheard; annual.

verbs

adjourn—; address—; break off—; bring before—; buckle down to—; close—; demand—with; dissolve—; gather in—; herald—; meet in—; preside over—; represent at—; resume—; sponsor—; urge—; —assembles; —collapses; —convenes; —discusses; —elects; —ensues; —formulates; —governs; —honors; —outlaws; —passes; —resolves; —rules.

(See consultation, assembly, meeting, council.)

CONFESS (v)

adverbs

ruefully; subsequently; truthfully; naively; timorously; hesitatingly; blushingly; penitently; candidly; gaily; blankly; humbly; frankly; affectionately; artlessly; shamefully; indiscreetly; unavailably; tacitly; touchingly; reciprocally; mortifyingly; abjectly; tearfully; belatedly; mysteriously; sincerely.

(See acknowledge, admit.)

CONFESSION

adjectives

tender; precious; eloquent; hopeful; naive; humble; honest; frank; full; complete; difficult; horrifying; shameful; deadly; indiscreet; voluptuous; phlegmatic; unavailing; liberal; honorable; tacit; plenary; revealing; bashful; touching; pitiful; reciprocal; soft; mortifying; abject; sham; constant; ecclesiastical; tearful; cool; belated; unconscious; mysterious; derisive; sincere; youthful; unsworn.

verbs

acknowledge—; beat out—; demand—; deny—; dictate—; drag out—; evidence—; force—; pour out—; record—; render—; repudiate—; rescind—; secure—; sign—; urge—; witness—; —absolves; —alleviates; —amends; —humbles; —humiliates.

(See statement.)

CONFIDANT

adjectives

intimate; faithful; special; ever-receptive; sympathetic.

CONFIDE (v)

adverbs

tearfully; languidly; apologetically; falteringly; timidly; loyally; genially; divinely; joyously; blithely; serenely; placidly; patriotically; arrogantly; spiritually; intellectually; unhesitatingly; profoundly; utterly; tactlessly; implicitly; tranquilly; pathetically; personally; charmingly; unsuspectingly; absolutely; unboundedly; complacently; wistfully.

(See trust. commit.)

CONFIDENCE

adjectives

gentle; sublime; fine; loyal; supreme; soft; wedded; divine; marvelous; ecstatic; gay; genial; joyous; blithe; touching; cheerful; certain; perfect; fullest; resolute; complete; boundless; utmost; limitless; inviolable; serene; calm; placid; sorry; silent; sober; patriotic; popular; renewed; immovable; easy; abiding; stern; arrogant; thrusting; spiritual; intellectual; infinite; presumptuous; invincible; unhesitating; sordid; utmost; assumed; strict; obliging; overweening; profound; veiled; restored; undiminished; buoyant; fullest; sincerest; utter; vanished; inspired; mutual; tactless; quiet; secure; fulsome; sketchy; unusual; industrial; heart-rending; tranquil; prophetic; pathetic; liberal; devilish; strong; superb; robust; shaken; animated; personal; imposing; charming; public; reminiscent; radiant; humble; preternatural; unsuspecting; absolute; unlimited; innocent; celebrated; unbounded; harassed; habitual; complacent; unreasonable; loving; admiring; snaring; heartfelt; unbroken; implicit; tender; childish; exaggerated; curious; sufficient; eager; wistful; vigorous; community; aboriginal.

verbs

beget—; betray—; blend in—; break—; breed—; buttress—; destroy—; dull—; dwell in—; earn—; enjoy—; establish—; evince—; evoke—; exchange—; express—; found in—; gravitate into—; honor with—; inspire—; interchange—; justify—; merit —; misplace—; mistrust—; reek—; regain—; register—; reject—; rejoice in—; renounce—; repose—in; restore—; root—in; shake—; share—; stimulate—; swear—; treat in—; undermine—; violate—; warrant—; weaken—; win—; —prevails; —soars; —wavers.

(See trust, faith, assurance, reliance.)

CONFIDENT

adverbs

absolutely; unreasonably; justifiably; egotistically; blatantly; extravagantly; gravely; seriously; shrewdly; assuredly; assuringly;

comfortably; comfortingly; sublimely; loyally; marvellously; genially; joyously; blithely; cheerfully; completely; calmly; placidly; quietly; serenely; imperturbably; sternly; presumptuously; overly; foolishly; fully; securely; unusually; tranquilly; impressively; charmingly; innocently; radiantly; unsuspectingly; habitually; complacently; curiously; encouragingly; courageously; egregiously; preposterously; rashly; absurdly; unjustifiably; unwarrantably; groundlessly; erroneously; profoundly.

CONFIDENTIAL

adverbs
strictly; necessarily; solemnly; terribly; mysteriously; portentously; ominously; seriously; vitally; stupendously; scrupulously; inviolately; momentously; significantly; essentially; intimately; sacredly; impressively; formidably; extremely; supremely.

CONFIGURATION

adjectives
geographical; tortured; certain; edifying; fundamental; classic.

CONFINE (v)

adverbs
exclusively; undeservedly; prudently; inexorably; mainly; remorselessly; necessarily; sedulously; comparatively; narrowly; continuously; irksomely.
(See restrict, restrain.)

CONFINEMENT

adjectives
solitary; respectful; prolonged; comparative; narrow; continuous; feverish; rigid; instant; irksome.

CONFIRM (v)

adverbs
speedily; stirringly; rapidly; strikingly; miraculously; unanimously; explicitly; concretely; abundantly; singularly; unexpectedly; instantaneously; amply; particularly.
(See affirm.)

CONFIRMATION

adjectives
complete; concrete; documentary; supplemental; splendid; singular; unexpected; instantaneous; unconscious; unexamined; fresh; particular; ample.

verbs
add the weight of—; ascertain—; authenticate—; dread—; establish—; inspect—; investigate—; maintain—; rejoice in—; sanction—; settle—; strengthen—; —assures; —convinces; —corroborates; —encourages; —fortifies; —legalizes; —proves; —ratifies; —removes doubt; —supports; —verifies.
(See ratification, proof.)

CONFLAGRATION

adjectives
frequent; devastating; disastrous; brilliant; nation-wide; mounting; enormous; widespread; delightful; amorous; raging; perpetual.

verbs
battle—; beat down—; contend with—; fight—; fan—; kindle—; prevent—; quell —; smother—; —blazes; —bursts out; —consumes; —deforests; —denudes; —dies; —envelops; —extends to; —menaces; —rages; —razes; —roars; —spreads; —threatens.
(See fire, blaze.)

CONFLICT

adjectives
triumphant; gigantic; stupendous; long; arduous; amorous; constant; eternal; ceaseless; sensational; heroic; dramatic; deliberate; determined; serious; severe; sharp; irrepressible; terrible; bitter; wasteful; violent; fierce; wanton; emotional; moral; general; visible; notorious; open; direct; external; coming; local; unfortunate; inevitable; sanguinary; approaching; irreconcilable; internal; civilized; irritating; unexpected; enormous; hopeless; impending; obstinate; fighting; deadly; desperate; immediate; disastrous; conscientious; earnest; class; bloody; obvious; unrelenting; savage; decisive; fiery; trying; mental; territorial; genial; protracted; brutal; decorous; tragic; linguistic; hopeless; commercial; hideous; armed; tumultuous; selfish; subjective; periodic; uncertain; psychic; intestinal.

verbs
avert—; avoid—; draw into—; elude—; end—; engage in—; experience—; explode in—; foment—; precipitate—; prolong—; provoke—; raise—; run into—; —bobs up; —bursts out; —consumes; —engulfs; —rages; —rends.
(See strife, battle, antagonism.)

CONFLICT (v)

adverbs

amorously; arduously; eternally; ceaselessly; sensationally; heroically; dramatically; deliberately; irresponsibly; violently; terribly; wantonly; emotionally; notoriously; morally; externally; locally; inevitably; irreconcilably; obstinately; desperately; disastrously; conscientiously; unrelentingly; savagely; decisively; mentally; commercially; tumultuously; subjectively.

(See interfere.)

CONFLUENCE

adjectives

riotous; harmonious; thickest; torrential; raging; seething; undistinguishable; peaceful; grateful.

CONFORM (v)

adverbs

tactfully; placidly; pusillanimously; complacently; docilely; strictly; entirely; rigidly; inflexibly; artistically; artificially; legally.

CONFORMATION

adjectives

athletic; peculiar; well-sculptured.

CONFORMITY

adjectives

complacent; pusillanimous; docile; strict; rigid.

CONFOUND (v)

adverbs

eternally; mysteriously; inexplicably; unspeakably; fathomlessly; gropingly; helplessly; inextricably

(See confuse.)

CONFRONT (v)

adverbs

bravely; indignantly; furiously; impudently; boldly; fearlessly; carelessly; brazenly; dramatically; theatrically; vociferously.

(See face, oppose.)

CONFUSE (v)

adverbs

paradoxically; wildly; deliberately; intricately; endlessly; inextricably; disastrously; emotionally; momentarily; infinitely; significantly; chaotically; intellectually; indescribably; feignedly; mentally; feverishly; socially; psychologically; mysteriously; purposely.

(See perplex, embarrass.)

CONFUSED

adverbs

delightfully; mysteriously; vaguely; perplexingly; hopelessly; strangely; comically; disastrously; completely; horribly; indescribably; visibly; manifestly; palpably; uproariously; tipsily; foggily; dazedly; rosily; brokenly; happily; incurably; pathetically; laughably; ridiculously.

CONFUSION

adjectives

joyous; cheerful; honest; orderly; multiple; endless; inextricable; strange; disastrous; hideous; sad; raging; wildest; lusty; deliberate; emotional; slight; flushed; misty; crimson; seeming; impersonal; peaceful; complete; topographical; blissful; momentary; deepening; infinite; picturesque; sweet; chaotic; irretrievable; tense; inextricable; hopeless; perpetual; crystalline; bosky; horrid; general; utter; utmost; ominous; significant; seeming; gibbering; dire; considerable; delightful; pretty; dreadful; studied; intellectual; speculative; indescribable; handsome; indistinct; tremendous; bubbling; multiform; feigned; visible; musical; whirling; mental; metaphysical; apparent; dusty; feverish; social; psychological; mysterious; manifold; crazy; melancholy; uproarious; disturbing; advertized; puzzling; commodious; vociferous; smiling.

verbs

afflict with—; boil with—; cover—; create—; deliver to—; eliminate—; embroil with—; fall into—; fill with—; flounder in—; grapple with—; heap—; lose in—; provoke—; retire in—; subdue—; subject to—; throw into—; weather—; work—; —aggravates; —ensues; —rises; —surrounds.

(See tumult, consternation, disorder, commotion, agitation, distraction.)

CONGEAL (v)

adverbs

instantaneously; readily; perfectly; partially; entirely; ultimately; normally; swiftly; rapidly; completely.

(See freeze.)

CONGENIAL

adverbs

completely; pleasantly; unusually; agreeably; charmingly; entertainingly; jovially; truly; happily; amiably; comfortably; curiously; delightfully; inestimably; distinctly;

unobtrusively; quietly; cheerfully; sociably; cosily; highly; exceedingly; unexpectedly; affably; unpretentiously; unaffectedly; artlessly.

CONGESTED

adverbs

hopelessly; inconveniently; dangerously; inordinately; needlessly; desperately; irremediably; impossibly; horribly; alarmingly; purposely; intentionally; stupidly; foolishly; senselessly; inextricably.

CONGESTION

adjectives

plethoric; cerebral; abnormal; prolonged; urban; slight; permanent.

verbs

accumulate—; clear—; heap in—; increase—; relieve—; —retards; —bars; —blocks; —crowds; —disorders; —hampers; —hinders; —impairs; —masses; —obstructs; —overcomes; —produces; —spreads; —weakens.

(See confusion.)

CONGLOMERATE

adverbs

ingeniously; heterogeneously; democratically; unmistakably; undeniably; utterly; curiously; interestingly; bewilderingly; confusedly; kaleidoscopically; staggeringly; internationally; unintelligibly; confusingly; diffusely; outlandishly; bizarrely; barbarically; inimitably; noisily; astoundingly; extravagantly; oddly; strangely.

CONGLOMERATION

adjectives

kaleidoscopic; multitudinous; staggering; curious; imperial.

CONGRATULATE (*v*)

adverbs

civilly; warmly; cordially; sincerely; dutifully; ceremoniously; facetiously; humbly; genially; volubly; effusively; solemnly; heartily; fulsomely; fiendishly.

(See sympathize.)

CONGRATULATIONS

adjectives

dutiful; abortive; ceremonious; facetious; humble; warmest; genial; voluble; solemn; heartiest.

verbs

acknowledge—; appreciate—; beam—; convey—; deliver—; deserve—; dismiss—; exchange—; express—; extend—; flood with—s; offer—; pay—; rejoice in—; return—; shower—; telegraph—; warrant—; wave away—; —gratify.

(See felicitation, sympathy.)

CONGRATULATORY

adverbs

pleasantly; dutifully; filially; grudgingly; ceremoniously; facetiously; happily; joyously; heartily; warmly; genially; jovially; jocosely; waggishly; proudly; solemnly; blessedly; rapturously; ecstatically; coolly; civilly; courteously; officially; politely; perfunctorily; obsequiously; unctuously; sententiously.

CONGREGATE (*v*)

adverbs

temptingly; silently; conservatively; piously; scantily; annually; triumphantly; sorrowfully; formally; diplomatically; dutifully.

(See gather.)

CONGREGATION

adjectives

motley; cultivated; dissolving; silent; dissenting; pious; foul; dispersing; scanty; sunburned; shaggy; staid; conservative.

verbs

assemble—; bless—; break up—; call—; come into—; cut off from—; distract—; gather—; offer to —; preach to—; rile—; sanctify—; separate from—; —breaks into song; —issues forth; —responds; —worships.

(See assembly, gathering.)

CONGRESS

adjectives

chaotic; international; bicameral; complaisant; musical; unique; legislative; filibustering.

verbs

discipline—; elect to—; empower—; importune—; prevail upon—; prod—; represent in—; seat in—; storm—; sway—; —adjourns; —appropriates; —assembles; —authorizes; —confers on; —confirms; —convenes; —debates; —deliberates; —designates; —dissolves; —frames; —functions; —interviews; —lags; —legislates; —meets; —rebels; —reforms; —regulates; —rejects; —revises; —suspends; —taxes. (See assembly, conference, legislature.)

CONGRESSMAN

adjectives
conspicuous; humorless; accomplished; grandiloquent; rabble-rousing; argumentative; glorified.

verbs
appeal to—; berate—; bribe—; criticize—; elect—; invite—; petition—; rally to—; reserve for—; run for—; select—; support—; —addresses; —men assemble; —men convene; —declines; —deliberates; —discusses; —filibusters; —introduces; —issues; —orates; —proposes; —protests; —questions; —represents; —signs; —withdraws.
(See legislator, senator, member.)

CONGRUITY

adjectives
separate; manifest; apparent; gratifying; practical; theoretical.

CONGRUOUS

adverbs
wholly; wonderfully; appropriately; nicely; exactly; accurately; entirely; aptly; adroitly; studiously; carefully; considerately; thoughtfully; becomingly; pertinently; relatively; agreeably; altogether; duly; happily; felicitously; opportunely; superbly; extraordinarily.

CONJECTURE

adjectives
whispered; frail; simple; stimulating; vague; languid; rational; bewildered; shrewd; right; straining; probable; plausible; sanguine; hurried; vacillating; speculative; half-hinted; serious; wild; cynical; fruitless; premature; alarming; vague.

verbs
absorb in—; base on—; cast—; conclude from—; form—; gather from—; infer from—; inject—; judge on—; offer—; propose—; scoff at—; scorn—; throw—; —guesses; —puzzles; —surmises.
(See guess, hypothesis, surmise, supposition, inference.)

CONJUNCTION

adjectives
successive; particular; clumsy; covert; helpful.

CONJUNCTURE

adjectives
fortunate; frequent; prodigious; delicate; straight; critical.

CONJURATION

adjectives
detestable; measured; spirited; inviolable; occult; mystic.

CONNECT (v)

adverbs
closely; organically; intimately; indissolubly; collaterally; innocently; eminently; honestly; inseparably; originally; exclusively; subtly; physiologically; remotely; unconsciously; persistently; matrimonially; adequately; lucratively; harmoniously; intellectually; surreptitiously; invisibly; uniformly; rigidly; profitably; vitally; perniciously; internationally.
(See join, link.)

CONNECTION

adjectives
reciprocal; physiological; closest; definite; remote; natural; intimate; unfathomable; unconscious; persistent; unbroken; illicit; valuable; influential; apparent; multifarious; judicious; matrimonial; fragmentary; uninterrupted; shameless; casual; obvious; adequate; touching; apparent; numerous; lucrative; remote; inevitable; mercantile; harmonious; manifold; intellectual; surreptitious; invisible; sole; florid; uniform; rigid; profitable; neat; positive; irregular; plausible; vital; pernicious; direct; deepwater; international; brief; genetic.

verbs
block—; break—; contract—with; disclaim —; dissolve—; establish—; fasten—; invalidate—; join in—with; link in—with; maintain—; mark—; mention in—with; prevent —; prohibit—; rend—; repudiate—; run in —with; sever—; snap—; —binds; —ties.
(See union, alliance, relationship, affiliation, association.)

CONNECTIVE

adjectives
social; iconoclastic; ineffectual; sturdy; tried.

CONNIVING

adjectives
petty; treasonable; clever; skillful; foxy; selfish.

251

adjectives
appreciative; true; profound; ogling; dramatic; amateur.

CONNOTATION
adjectives
biological; original; conventional; proper; sentimental; hazy.

CONQUER (*v*)
adverbs
technically; triumphantly; intellectually; eventually; honorably; personally; ultimately; romantically; basely; scientifically; partially; irresistibly.
(See win.)

CONQUEROR
adjectives
ultimate; sottish; roving; indigenous; vulgar; rapacious; satiate; daunted; virile; invisible; illustrious; single-handed; lesser.

verbs
hail—; herald—; honor—; overthrow—; proclaim—; welcome—; —acquires; —attains; —campaigns; —defeats; —enslaves; —gains; —invades; —masters; —overcomes; —pursues; —retreats; —subdues; —subjugates; —vanquishes; —wars.
(See hero, army.)

CONQUEST
adjectives
intellectual; territorial; illusory; unprovoked; honorable; vainglorious; continental; shameful; prophetic; industrial; imperial; personal; doubtful; amatory; remote; ultimate; easy; dazzling; barren; adventurous; romantic; material; barbarian; complete; base; air; unbroken; momentary; perpetual; fresh; hard-won; social; scientific; partial; furtive; rapid; notorious; feminine; irresistible; radical.

verbs
achieve—; acquire by—; crown—; effect—; enjoy the fruits of—; frustrate—; gain by—; herald—; inspire—; plunge into—; reap—; repel—; revel in—; revenge—; spread—; subdue by—; threaten—; win—; —captivates; —falters; —subdues; —subjugates; —succeeds; —stifles.
(See victory, triumph.)

adjectives
smooth; haunting; latent; intellectual; padded; inflexible; insufferable; awakened; strenuous; quickening; guilty; drugged; beaten; stoned; sensitive; reproachful; artistic; obsessed; national; tender; obtuse; uneasy; straightforward; delicate; vast; floating; scientific; sensitive; capricious; filial; indulgent; fastidious; individual; obdurate; seared; well-seasoned; masterful; stricken; resolved; struggling; agonizing; heavy; unsilenced; proscriptive; renewed; peaceful; corrupted; condemning; fierce; judicial; worrying; ethical; aesthetic; perverse; poor; wounded; high; mute; alarmed; keen; free; super-developed; healthy; supreme; determined; clear; untroubled; twinging; aching; writhing; elastic; sluggish; bomb-proof; democratic; prickly; literary; celebrated; puritan; political; approving; private; childish.

verbs
alarm—; appeal to—; arouse—; cauterize —; compromise—; defile—; disburden—; ease—; examine—; fetter—; free—; invoke—; muffle—; offend—; pad—; purge —; quiet—; rectify—; rule by—; salve—; sear—; shake—; sour—; square—; suppress—; torment—; wake—; weaken—; wound—; wring—; —assails; —blames; —condemns; —convicts; —impels; —reproaches; —plagues; —prompts; —reproves; —slumbers; —tortures; —troubles; —twinges; —upbraids; —whispers.
(See judgment.)

CONSCIENTIOUS
adverbs
terribly; puritannically; extremely; rigorously; sternly; austerely; deeply; painfully; rigidly; stiffly; decorously; properly; unimpeachably; irreproachably; becomingly; stringently; dutifully; amenably; respectably; scrupulously; incorruptibly; courageously; lamentably; uncomfortably; ostentatiously; unnecessarily; carefully; foolishly.

CONSCIENTIOUSNESS
adjectives
exemplary; deep; historical; magnificent; stubborn; commendable; heroic.

CONSCIOUS
adverbs
fully; acutely; painfully; vividly; sharply; altogether; keenly; curiously; tinglingly; psychically; sorely; happily; uncomfortably;

wretchedly; pleasantly; rapturously; intensely; suddenly; poignantly; astutely; wholly; partially; slowly; wearily; actually; bitterly.

CONSCIOUSNESS
adjectives
full; private; inner; drowsier; ennobling; waking; joyous; veiled; guilty; perverted; bitter; instinctive; ever-abiding; susceptible; dawning; dim; proud; individual; well-founded; disagreeable; acute; living; unadmitted; amiable; gloomy; pleased; uplifting; mortifying; vivid; present; dreadful; despotic; widened; glad; glowing; impersonal; ineffable; half-bewildered; wordless; religious; glimmering; astonishing; sudden; joyful; intense; demure; collective; profound; transitory; shamefaced; lucid; reviving; inward; shaky; disintegrated; beatific; humble; native; growing; diffused; human; continental; pained; financial; class; political; social.

verbs
bestow—; bring to—; develop—; display—; drag to—; enfold—; indicate—; jar into—; lose—; obscure—; obsess—; percolate—; possess—; precede—; retain—; rub into—; seize with—; thrust into—; vanish from—; waken to—; —brings; —evolves.
(See sensation, feeling, intuition.)

CONSCRIPTION
adjectives
ruthless; established; legislated; mandatory; selective; indiscriminative.

CONSECRATE (*v*)
adverbs
specially; religiously; ceremoniously; hallowedly; reverently; formally; fittingly; impressively.
(See dedicate, hallow.)

CONSECRATED
adverbs
divinely; ecclesiastically; eternally; sacredly; early; devoutly; devotedly; faithfully; humbly; reverently; splendidly; conspicuously; avowedly; deeply; practically; notably; eminently; heroically; illustriously; piously; solemnly; gloriously; signally.

CONSECRATION
adjectives
immortal; pathetic; tragic; perpetual; ecclesiastical.

CONSECUTIVE
adverbs
conveniently; endlessly; monotonously; meticulously; punctiliously; carefully; accurately; impressively; rarely; handily; painstakingly; comfortably; accommodatingly; appropriately; properly; tediously; invariably; methodically; systematically; exactly; significantly; actually.

CONSENT
adjectives
unanimous; magnanimous; particular; ardent; tacit; grudging; reluctant; common; hard; general; cringing; mutual; unwilling; formal; personal; passive; generous; grumbling; effective; mournful; gracious.

verbs
announce—; batter into—; blush—; crave —; deny—; desire—; extend—; nod—; serve with—; suffer—; swear—; win—; wink—; write—; yield—.
(See acquiescence, compliance, approval, agreement.)

CONSENT (*v*)
adverbs
reluctantly; unwittingly; tacitly; handsomely; gloomily; instantly; sulkily; cheerfully; wisely; legally; unanimously; ardently; magnanimously; grudgingly; cringingly; mutually; unwillingly; formally; personally; passively; generously; mournfully; graciously; blandly.
(See agree, concur.)

CONSEQUENCE
adjectives
natural; territorial; eventual; disastrous; cruel; tremendous; necessary; self-evident; dramatic; dire; logical; inevitable; direct; lurking; ambushed; far-reaching; political; educational; perilous; unavoidable; permanent; favorable; momentous; sensational; serious; instantaneous; important; natural; surprising; paramount; probable; horrible; evil; debasing; fruitful; deplorable; certain; fatal; utmost; ethical; awful; unexpected; deepest; unforeseen; equivalent; temporal; invisible; viewless; heavy; mechanical; mischievous; injurious; dreadful; remoter; unshunned; catastrophic; desirable; possible; incalculable; wretched;

disagreeable; appalling; wonderful; beneficent; brilliant; obvious; patent; inescapable; vital; enormous; tragic; devastating; demoralizing; calamitous; unhappy; embarrassing; ultimate; physiological; emotional; social; financial; moral; risky; comical; small; foolish; involved; detailed; legal.

verbs

abide by—; appreciate—; avert—; balk at—; conceal—; dread—; deter by—; escape—; face—; ignore—; portray—; realize—; shun—; suffer—; torment by—; —ensues; —follows; —results in.

(See issue, result, outcome, importance, distinction, consideration.)

CONSEQUENTIAL

adverbs

evidently; ludicrously; ridiculously; arrogantly; pompously; stupidly; gracelessly; presumptuously; impressively; ostentatiously; grossly; fantastically; grotesquely; immensely; inordinately; amusingly; complacently; colossally; awkwardly; stagily; foppishly; laughably; theatrically; loftily; extremely; unbelievably; absurdly.

CONSERVATISM

adjectives

zealous; sprightly; stubborn; passionate; industrious; extreme; moderate; innate; disillusioned; smug; hearty; emotional.

verbs

abolish—; admire—; characterize by—; embody—; engender—; enliven—; epitomize—; hinder by—; practice—; preserve—; prod—; produce—; satisfy—; school in—; shrink from—; swerve from—; swing toward—; —crops up; —fears; —retains; —safeguards.

(See stability, conventionality.)

CONSERVATIVE

adjectives

uncompromising; extreme; staunchest; gruesome; obstinate; grim; sturdy; born; honest; cynical; stuffy; hidebound.

adverbs

incurably; tenaciously; consistently; obstinately; stubbornly; half-heartedly; permanently; solidly; stiffly; unchangeably; fixedly; firmly; immovably; resolutely; irrevoc-

ably; steadfastly; unalterably; inactively; quietly; passively; zealously; passionately; smugly; contentedly; pertinaciously; temperamentally.

CONSIDER (v)

adverbs

intrinsically; impartially; tenderly; duly; carnally; prospectively; lightly; maturely, accordingly; politically; honestly; anxiously; tentatively; dispassionately; seriously; previously; arithmetically; erroneously; respectfully; matrimonially; rationally; theoretically; belatedly; paternally; philosophically; delicately; momentously; sympathetically; unselfishly; posthumously; temporarily; shallowly; economically; sordidly; morally; optionally.

(See ponder, contemplate.)

CONSIDERABLE

adverbs

seriously; worthily; assuredly; notably; prominently; essentially; substantially; critically; imposingly; gravely; materially; remarkably; significantly; signally; vitally; momentously; impressively.

CONSIDERATE

adverbs

courteously; thoughtfully; tenderly; officiously; politely; deferentially; respectfully; appropriately; unusually; obsequiously; deliberately; generally; astutely; keenly; shrewdly; tenderly; mercifully; tolerantly; benevolently; charitably; generously; carefully; prudently; providently; hospitably; alertly; vigilantly; scrupulously.

CONSIDERATION

adjectives

theoretic; paternal; belated; distinguished; favorable; humanitarian; ethical; vital; special; tedious; individual; secondary; close; palpable; philosophic; calm; striking; delicate; tremendous; seeming; abstract; solemn; gracious; serious; momentous; indisputable; respectful; monetary; sympathetic; elusive; salient; important; unselfish; quiet; melancholy; ostensible; due; prime; obvious; mature; practical; minor; limited; partial; long; sedate; candid; fuller; posthumous; unspeakable; distracted; chivalrous; remote; keen; theoretical; various (pl.); confidential; thoughtful; reasoned; dominant; scanty; unhurried; careful; fatherly; triumphant; temporal; elaborate; predominant; common; ultimate;

judicial; weighty; practical; conscientious; difficult; half-hesitating; half-assenting; exclusive; enlarged; grateful; weightier; rational; unpleasing; regrettable; foregoing; strategical; valuable; distinguished; momentary; urgent; scant; earnest; fair; fascinating; finer; grave; profoundest; pragmatic; marked; primary; careful; tender; prudent; dispassionate; cool; logical; intelligent; sordid; false; shallow; selfish; money; economic; material; moral; liberal; collateral; painful; constant; immediate; accumulated; optional; theoretical; rough; personal.

verbs
analyze—; bar—; compel—; dally with—; demand—; extend—; fade from—; gain—; increase—; merit—; quit—; stifle—; view with—; —actuates; —impresses; —sways.
(See thought.)

CONSIGN (v)

adverbs
everlastingly; formally; customarily; tacitly; solemnly; definitely; willingly; commercially.
(See command, commit.)

CONSISTENCY

adjectives
muddy; smoothest; possible; fatal; unwavering; foolish; religious; external; unbroken; theoretical; chewy; conscious.

verbs
boil into—; depart from—; disrupt—; doubt—; establish—; give—to; induce—; practise—; preach—; preserve—; profess—; pursue with—; remain in—; return to—; sacrifice—; stand on—; vary in—; —habituates; —harmonizes.
(See harmony.)

CONSISTENT

adverbs
admirably; dependably; conscientiously; imperturbably; undisturbedly; invariably; equitably; monotonously; conformably; prosaically; agreeably; regularly; habitually; usually; uncompromisingly; queerly; unfailingly; properly; relatively; obstinately; unreasonably; reliably; altogether; courageously; unpleasantly; vapidly; extraordinarily; virtuously.

CONSOLATION

adjectives
bitter; inexpressible; profound; hollow; proudest; infallible; homely; tangible; mean; supreme; perfunctory; divine; substantial; wonderful; ironic; religious; orthodox; clumsy; feeble; abiding; inward; infinitesimal.

verbs
admit of—; convey—; derive—; dismiss—; dispense with—; grant—; impart—; offer —; rejoice in—; seek —; secure—; take— from; —ameliorates; —cheers; —comforts; —encourages; —mitigates; —recompenses; —relieves; —solaces; —soothes.
(See solace, comfort, relief, support.)

CONSOLE (v)

adverbs
profoundly; hollowly; infallibly; perfunctorily; divinely; substantially; ironically; religiously; clumsily; feebly; inwardly; infinitesimally; precipitately.
(See cheer, sympathize.)

CONSONANT

adjectives
concurring; mute; nasal; unaspirated; slurred; elided; rumbling; jarring; harsh; true.

CONSORT

adjectives
ill-fated; gentle; sovereign; hovering; poor; feeble; wasted.

CONSPICUOUS

adverbs
highly; creditably; distinctly; gloriously; intentionally; disagreeably; unpleasantly; vainly; personally; eminently; exaltedly; arrogantly; absurdly; foolishly; unwisely; politically; deliberately; elaborately; fashionably; garishly; gaudily; loudly; noisily; officiously; unfortunately; shamefully; awkwardly.

CONSPIRACY

adjectives
rebel; domestic; tacit; abortive; awkward; finespun; well-contrived; criminal; fraternal; elaborate; organized; ravishing; purported; irresistible; monstrous; political; dark; infamous; grim; pleasing; silent; popular; crackbrained; malevolent; nationwide; alley; fatal.

verbs

block—; charge with—; combine in—; conceal—; contrive—; convict of—; disclose—; discover—; excite—; foil—; hatch—; incite—; indict for—; instigate—; intrigue in—; involve in—; plot—; punish—; strengthen—; uncover—; unearth—; — brews; —damages; —fails; —flourishes; —injures; —ripens; —succeeds.

(See plot, intrigue.)

CONSPIRATOR

adjectives

resident; audacious; crafty; baffled; chief; uneasy.

CONSPIRATORS

adjectives

capricious; criminal; fearful; illegal; implicated; fellow; mercenary; reprehensible; treasonable; plotting; seditious.

verbs

arm—; charge—; convict—; disclose—; execute—; expose—; foil—; hang—; join—; punish—; shield—; —chortle; —combine; —contrive; —devise; —engage; —intrigue; —plan; —plot.

(See plotter.)

CONSTABLE

adjectives

discomfited; discredited; learned; unskilled; blustering; rural; overmaligned.

verbs

appoint—; arm—; authorize—; commit to—; consign to—; deputize—; elect—; empower—; enroll—; escape—; overrule—; rank—; serve as—; uniform—; —administers; —arrests; —enforces; —fines; —imprisons; —quells; —sells.

(See officer, police.)

CONSTANCY

adjectives

infatuated; dangerous; unremitting; inviolable; unchangeable; admirable; true; inflexible; invincible; wonted.

verbs

admire—; amaze at—; attack—; attend with—; bear with—; boast of—; break—; commend—; conduct with—; endure with—; esteem—; exhibit—; inspire—; justify—; laud—; maintain—; occasion—; persist in—; praise—; require—; test—; tolerate with—; value—.

(See faithfulness, stability, fidelity.)

adjectives

golden; arched; bright; brilliant; shimmering.

verbs

appear in—; describe—; distinguish—; dominate—; examine—; form—; name—; obscure—; observe—; steer by—; stud with—; study—; treat of—; —awes; —burns; —embodies; —guides; —illuminates; —mystifies; —portrays; —reveals; —symbolizes.

(See stars.)

adjectives

unseen; general; overwhelming; considerable; mournful; visible; silent; inexpressible; comprehensible; unutterable; momentary; frightened.

verbs

betray—; feign—; fill with—; manifest—; overwhelm with—; prostrate with—; recover from—; shock into—; suppress—; terrify with—; terrorize with—; throw into—; —amazes; —confounds; —dismays; —falls; —incapacitates; —surprises.

(See fear, terror, alarm, panic.)

adjectives

intractable; chronic; stubborn; recurring; harrowing; drug-induced.

verbs

afflict with—; alleviate—; cure of—; doctor for—; dose for—; ease—; flush away—; intensify—; overcome—; produce—; relieve—; remedy—; treat—; warn against —; —hints at; —irks; —necessitates; —obstructs; —sets in.

(See disease.)

adjectives

large; urban; foremost; urgent; enthusiastic.

adjectives

enraptured; characteristic; parsimonious; material; chemical; valuable; necessary; saline; primal; eternal; colored; approved; irreducible; soluble; youthful; enlightened; influential.

verbs
analyze—; assemble—s; authorize by—s; break into—s; determine—s; discern—; distinguish—; gather—; lose—; obey—; represent—s; —s assist; —s complain; —s compose; —s diminish; —elects; —s represent.
(See part, element, ingredient.)

CONSTITUTE (v)
adverbs
singularly; legally; fairly; splendidly; remarkably; amorphously; magnificently; physically; morally; peculiarly; delicately; intellectually; undeniably.
(See compose, establish.)

CONSTITUTION
(general)
adjectives
frail; splendid; diseased; amorphous; healthy; remarkable; strong; loose-jointed; robust; magnificent; physical; moral; iron; peculiar; vigorous; delicate; oligarchical; paper; emotional; consolidated; rugged; well-knit; feeble; glorious; powerful; provisional; permanent; liberal; imperial; intellectual; ancient; sickly.

CONSTITUTION
(governmental)
adjectives
amended; consolidated; hammered-out; botched-up; intrenched; framed; liberal; oligarchical; standardized.

verbs
abandon—; abide by—; abuse—; adopt—; alter—; amend—; clarify—; construe—; defend—; draft—; embody in—; establish—; flaunt—; form—; found—; frame—; improve—; interpret—; modify—; nullify—; ordain—; organize—; preserve—; ratify—; ruin—; stabilize—; tamper with—; twist—; violate—; —abolishes; —decrees; —defines; —grants; —guides; —limits; —prescribes; —prohibits; —provides; —regulates; —sets forth; —totters.

CONSTITUTION
(physical)
adjectives
amorphous; emotional; frail; iron; magnificent; powerful; robust.

verbs
benefit—; brace—; build up—; disturb—; enervate—; exercise—; improve—; inherit—; invigorate—; overtax—; renew—; revitalize—; revivify—; run down—; shatter—; strain—; strengthen—; undermine—; weaken.
(See physique, structure. temperament, character.)

CONSTRAIN (v)
adverbs
unquestionably; unnaturally; artificially; severely; rigidly; commercially; embarrassedly; tyrannically; bitterly; formally;; mercilessly.
(See compel, oblige.)

CONSTRAINT
adjectives
tyrannous; bitter; evident; mute; gloomy; sorrowful; curious; formal; sharp; awkward; merciless; heavy; slight.

verbs
act under—; exercise—; lessen—; manifest—; occasion—; pale under—; prevent—; produce—; resist—; speak with—; subdue—; tug at—; —binds; —checks; —confines; —prohibits; —represses; —tightens; —voices.
(See force, compulsion, pressure, restraint, restriction.)

CONSTRICT (v)
adverbs
rigorously; harmfully; icily; painfully; automatically; physiologically; partially; insufferably; intellectually.
(See compress, contract.)

CONSTRICTION
adjectives
harmful; icy; oppressive; deep; hampering; morbid; marked; express.

CONSTRUCT (v)
adverbs
hastily; diaphanously; patiently; rudely; variously; studiously; ingeniously; dramatically; bizarrely; artistically; ruggedly; flawlessly; primitively; durably; majestically; musically; substantially; solidly; legitimately; technically; scientifically; rudely; crudely; enduringly; flimsily.
(See build, manufacture.)

adjectives

complicated; unsurpassed; improved; patented; rigid; rugged; initial; complex; flawless; exclusive; superb; famous; primitive; ingenious; harmonic; durable; imperfect; majestic; sublime; riveted; mistaken; institutional; pithy; exquisite; immediate; superior; flattering; constitutional; artful; custom-built; excellent; evasive; strained; questionable; peculiar; musical; dependable; substantial; shrewd; sturdy; malicious; dramatic; contemplated; solid; recent; steel-truss; highway; engineering; correct; worst; wrong; strict; illegitimate; charitable; technical; crude.

CONSTRUCTIVE

adverbs

helpfully; critically; definitely; remarkably; valuably; significantly; magnificently; sensibly; fundamentally; essentially; liberally; splendidly; creatively; clearly; saliently; strikingly; explicitly.

CONSTRUE (v)

adverbs

variously; maliciously; confusedly; shrewdly; erroneously; charitably.

(See interpret.)

CONSUL

adjectives

dignified; autocratic; duly-appointed; officiating; protective; prudent; self-important; artful; wily; fastidious.

verbs

appeal to—; appoint—; authorize—; beseech—; charge—with; choose—; elect—; name—; present—; recall—; receive—; retain—; slay—; withdraw—; —advises; —anticipates; —holds office; —promotes; —promulgates; —proposes; —protects; —rejects; —reports; —represents.

(See magistrate, representative, counselor.)

CONSULT (v)

adverbs

selfishly; philosophically; confidentially; timidly; vainly; distressingly; solemnly; informally; anxiously; earnestly; gravely; deliberately; privately; frequently; protractedly.

(See deliberate, discuss.)

adjectives

solemn; whispered; hasty; informal; mature; anxious; actual; serious; religious; rapid; timely; earnest; vociferous; short; grave; deliberate; private; frequent; brief; protracted; muffled.

verbs

advise—; assist at—; call—; confer in—; deliberate in—; demand—; follow—; go into—; meet in—; secure—; seek—; —advises; —concludes; —decides; —ensues; —exposes; —guides; —results in.

(See conference, council.)

CONSUME (v)

adverbs

annually; ravenously; leisurely; utterly; relatively; ultimately; unwarily; industrially; ferociously.

(See burn, destroy.)

CONSUMER

adjectives

desirable; hard-working; mortgaged; ultimate; humble; general; unorganized (pl.); unprotected; unwary; trusting; duped.

CONSUMMATION

adjectives

desirable; relentless; harmonious; supreme; fitting.

CONSUMPTION

adjectives

needful; cold; languorous; melancholy; domestic; laryngeal; pulmonary; equitable; conspicuous; old-fashioned; annual; food; slackening; residential; industrial; diminishing.

verbs

afflict with—; consume with—; contract—; cure—; infect with—; inherit—; predispose to—; smite with—; suffer with—; tend towards—; treat for—; waste away with—; —atrophies; —attacks; —decomposes; —destroys; —invalids; —lingers; —preys on; —rots; —takes a toll; —wreaks.

(See tuberculosis, disease.)

CONTACT

adjectives

friendly; richest; effective; stimulating; intimate; personal; close; casual; fleeting; intermittent; brief; abrupt; superficial; bitter; difficult; banal; brutish; human; nation-wide; diplomatic; domestic; prolonged; mere; necessary; constant; alert; accidental; sonorous; immediate; direct; uninterrupted; unrestricted; terrible; intellectual; social; osculatory; slight; unclean; extensive; miscellaneous; spontaneous; careless; rude; proffered; lawless; responsible.

verbs
abolish—; approve of—; balk at—; bring into—; conceal—; defile by—; enter into—; establish—; favor—; harbor—; join in—; lose—; maintain—; modify—; negotiate—; oppose—; profit by—; reestablish —; renew—; uncover—; vary—.
(See connection.)

CONTAGION
adjectives
rigid; terrible; deadly; delicious; virulent.

verbs
check—; convey by—; engender—; expose to—; guard against—; harbor—; isolate—; propagate by—; quarantine—; restrain—; spread—.
(See pestilence, plague. infection.)

CONTAGIOUS
adverbs
highly; dangerously; pestilentially; unfortunately; acutely; widely; perilously; seriously; extremely; exceedingly; decidedly; unquestionably; frightfully; absolutely; remarkably; alarmingly; curiously; awfully; critically; definitely; fatally; positively; notoriously.

CONTAIN (*v*)
adverbs
virtually; fully; partially; entirely; fittingly; snugly; amazingly; completely; substantially.
(See hold.)

CONTAINER
adjectives
transparent; airtight; offsize; metal; standardized; smart; huge.

CONTEMPLATE (*v*)
adverbs
objectively; actually; soberly; vaguely; philosophically; consciously; listlessly; curiously; absorbedly; dreamily; serenely; profoundly; rapturously; complacently; severely; plaintively.
(See meditate.)

CONTEMPLATION
adjectives
frowning; ravishing; precocious; listless; passing; will-less; curious; celestial; absorbed; deep; hopeless; cold; solitary; mystic; dreamy; serene; wondering; academic; narrow; unfettered; profound; continued; sundry; comprehensive; silent; lofty; spiritual; complacent; zealous; rapturous; lonely; steadfast; habitual; pleasurable; melancholy; selfish; leaden; severe.

verbs
absorb in—; arouse from—; drift in—; engross in—; hold in—; fall into—; lose in—; meditate in—; molest in—; rejoice in—; soar in—; steep in—; swathe in—; wrap in—; —beholds; —colors; —pictures; —reflects; —stirs.
(See reflection, thought, meditation.)

CONTEMPLATIVE
adverbs
deeply; thoughtfully; reminiscently; prophetically; studiously; closely; ponderingly; abstractedly; intelligently; philosophically; sagely; wisely; leisurely; thoroughly; habitually; pensively; anxiously; eagerly; curiously; queerly; oddly; coldly; academically; zealously; loftily; mysteriously; calmly.

CONTEMPORARY
adjectives
admirable; poetic; fiendish; celebrated; unanimous; skeptical; disillusioned; eminent; cheery; erudite; wholesome; northern; smaller; male.

adverbs
conveniently; embarrassingly; undeniably; obviously; certainly; unquestionably; evidently; curiously; admittedly; presumably; probably; possibly; supposedly; oddly; incontrovertibly; authentically; actually; categorically; authoritatively; ironically.

CONTEMPT
adjectives
inexplicable; beautiful; impersonal; concentrated; dignified; undisguised; supercilious; exaggerated; inexpressible; reckless; fierce; lofty; veiled; half-compassionate; uncharitable; faint; deprecating; emphatic; cynical; spendthrift; withering; utmost; considerable; unreasoning; infinite; ineffable;

indiscriminate; bitterest; thorough; profound; uncompromising; notable; alternate; characteristic; deep-rooted; loud; ironical; arrogant; irrepressible; supreme; utter; habitual; geniune; biting; absolute; irrevocable; noisy; blighting; ineffable; unequivocal; notable; paternal; grand; magnificent; eloquent; smiling; good-natured; factitious; unfeigned; ardent; courageous; illimitable; aristrocratic; lofty; cavalier; holy; highbred; cold; stern; skeptical; icy; scornful; gloating; exasperating; shocked; keen; apparent; thundering; hereditary; growing; sudden; shattering; inherited; sweeping; high-nosed; friary.

verbs
admit—; awake—; bear—; breed—; convey—; deserve—; disdain—; entertain—; excite—; fill with—; foster—; gesture—; hurl—; imply—; place in—; pour out—; profess—; provoke—; regard with—; shield from—; sigh with—; smile—; spurn—; tinge with—; treat with—; veil—; wither with—; —arises; —deepens; —dies; —flickers; —infuriates; —terrifies; —shrivels up.
(See disdain, scorn, derision.)

CONTEMPTIBLE
adverbs
abominably; odiously; detestably; hatefully; shockingly; unspeakably; despicably; invidiously; woefully; lamentably; noxiously; execrably; flagrantly; intolerably; incredibly; disgustingly; utterly; outrageously; horribly; inexpressibly; notoriously; infamously; glaringly; monstrously; wickedly; remarkably.

CONTEND (*v*)
adverbs
pedantically; strenuously; incredulously; physically; laboriously; forcefully; narrowly; fiercely; boldly; stoutly; optimistically; senselessly; shrewdly; ridiculously; acrimoniously; ironically; undeviatingly; vigorously.
(See oppose.)

CONTENT
adjectives
sufficient; scholarly; organic; prescribed; sociological; trusting; universal; infinite; spacious; final; anti-religious; deepest; intimate; nestling; incongruous; supreme; wondrous; wise; greedy; drowsy; dreamy; measureless; immortal; blissful; cubical;

infantile; scrutinized; radiant; adequate; muddy; gorgeous; endless; significant; melodic; shrewd; fluid; flinty; fermented; logical; corrupt; imbecile; unaggressive; protein; perfect; physical; sweet; scented; quiet; intellectual.

CONTENTION
adjectives
stout; brave; optimistic; bloody; senseless; ridiculous; fierce; unnatural; ravishing; rival; critical; acrimonious; basic; general; ironical.

verbs
abandon—; cast out—; contest—; dispute—; endorse—; illustrate—; justify—; match—; raise—; refute—; rend with—; support—; —lingers; —upsets.
(See strife, conflict, struggle, dispute, argument, dissension.)

CONTENTIOUS
adverbs
characteristically; incorrigibly; disagreeably; loftily; shrewdly; intelligently; stupidly; doggedly; foolishly; bitterly; unnecessarily; testily; mildly; impetuously; violently; mulishly; stolidly; abusively; unreasonably; habitually; hotly; offensively; absurdly; pretentiously; brazenly.

CONTENTMENT
adjectives
inward; homelike; childish; stolid; rapturous; sweet; complete; thoughtless; perfect; placid; domestic; rare; abiding; happy; odd; new; supreme; drowsy; ineffable; sleepy; sinking.

verbs
achieve—; attain—; bathe in—; desire—; destroy—; feign—; fill with—; pretend—; purr—; realize—; relax in—; resign in—; result in—; seek—; sigh in—; sink into—; smile with—; strive for—; struggle for—; swathe in—; view with—; yearn for—; —evades; —proceeds from.
(See satisfaction, happiness, gratification.)

CONTENTS
adjectives
valuable; varied; lively; treasurable; illuminating; deadly; gruesome; nauseous; horrific; strange; discursive; golden; heterogeneous; problematical; sluggish; terse.

verbs
add to—; assimilate—; dehydrate—; discharge—; eject—; empty—; expel—; gut of—; imbibe—; master—; pound—; rob of—; stir—; —escape.
(See ingredients.)

CONTEST

adjectives
unequal; remarkable; obstinate; decisive; interstate; animated; bloody; deadly; dread; formal; sanguinary; passionate; inevitable; pending; civic; naked; spirited; frightful; ceaseless; violent; diplomatic; jarring; dramatic; tremendous; culminating; emotional; costly; tedious; amicable; bitter; mighty; audacious.

verbs
attend—; "ballyhoo"—; cheer—; debate—; develop into—; dispute—; emerge from—; enter—; invite to—; lose—; prepare for —; relish—; renew—; strive in—; struggle in—; vie in—; win—; witness—; — awards; —excites; —proceeds.
(See tournament, competition, dispute, dissension.)

CONTEST (v)

adverbs
fiercely; energetically; gallantly; bitterly; unequally; remarkably; obstinately; decisively; animatedly; bloodily; passionately; inevitably; ceaselessly; violently; diplomatically; dramatically; amicably; audaciously.
(See oppose, dispute.)

CONTESTANT

adjectives
feeble; leading; vindicated; keen; rival; earnest; obstinate; invincible; indefatigable.

verbs
equip—; reduce—s; —achieves; —applies; —battles; —competes; —contends; —endures; —gains; —overcomes; —races; —rivals; —strains; —strives; —struggles.
(See competitor, rival.)

CONTINENCE

adjectives
absolute; vowed; eternal; inordinate; lofty; ascetic; monastic; impenetrable; inviolable.

CONTINENT

adjectives
rich; new; powerful; remote; sunken; commanding; unexhausted; sunny; undiscovered; virgin; unborn; unmapped; orbed; infinite.

verbs
abound on—; bound—; communicate with —; cover—; discover—; divide—; explore—; exploit—; govern—; inhabit—; populate—; rule—; sail for—; span—; speed across—; study—; tranquilize—; travel—; traverse—; wage on—.
(See land, country.)

CONTINGENCY

adjectives
remote; various (pl); fatal; imaginable; impossible; dangerous; unforeseen; future.

verbs
admit—; conceive—; consider—; contemplate—; exempt from—; expose to—; foresee—; forestall—; fortify against—; free from—; involve—; prepare for—; regard—; subject to—; —befalls; —occurs; —requires.
(See chance, possibility, accident, hazard.)

CONTINGENT

adjectives
various (pl); assorted (pl); fresh; obligatory; unlimited; valuable; denominated; incidental.

adverbs
accidentally; unexpectedly; fortuitously; unfortunately; presumably; casually; unluckily; advantageously; possibly; remotely; imaginably; gravely; distantly; presciently.

CONTINUANCE

adjectives
further; simultaneous; perpetual; dogged; indefinite.

verbs
balk at—; bore by—; detest—; forswear—; hinder—; insure—; lapse—; prohibit—; shrink from—; speed—; stay—; urge—; —adds; —confirms; —engulfs; —improves; —inculcates; —irks; —oppresses; —perfects; —preserves; —renders.

CONTINUATION

adjectives

sketchy; mirthful; interminable; ruthless; casual; fluent; moderate.

CONTINUE (v)

adverbs

presumptuously; relentlessly; calmly; uncomplainingly; dauntlessly; voluntarily; passionately; stealthily; triumphantly; obstinately; jerkily; thoughtfully; facetiously; affably; mercilessly; hopefully; defiantly; imperturbably; treacherously; blandly.

(See persevere.)

CONTINUITY

adjectives

historic; unbroken; inexplicable; long-sighted; strict; general; agreeable; grim.

CONTINUOUS

adverbs

maddeningly; providentially; monotonously; tiresomely; intolerably; incredibly; grimly; dangerously; indescribably; unbearably; alarmingly; frightfully; crazily; insufferably; solemnly; ruthlessly; appallingly; cleverly; dismally; noisily; provokingly; automatically.

CONTORT (v)

adverbs

misshapenly; facilely; inanely; horribly; capriciously; drolly; spasmodically; frantically; sinisterly; agilely; facially; sneeringly.

(See twist, wrench.)

CONTORTION

adjectives

deprecatory; wonderful; frightful; spasmodic; joyful; frantic; sneering; sinister; unsystematic; slight; facial; agile.

CONTOUR

adjectives

delicate; vertical; bodily; inviting; ground; vague; pleasing; facial; rugged; muscular; hard; skeletal; cranial; childish; chubby; snug; effeminate; pronounced; rounded; sharp; youthful; wasted; swinging; voluptuous; pert; harsh; smooth; girlish; sagging; exquisite.

CONTRABAND

adjectives

confiscated; exported; proclaimed; prohibited; seized; smuggled.

verbs

ban as—; carry—; confiscate—; deal in—; declare as—; destroy—; export—; forbid as—; forfeit—; import—; list as—; proclaim as—; prohibit as—; seize as—; smuggle—; supply—; traffic in—.

(See arms, supplies.)

CONTRACT

adjectives

fat; solemn; valid; conjugal; stamped; workable; favorable; vowed; true; signed; nullified; binding; huge; definite; gilt-edged; legal; repudiated; direct; airtight; substantial; advantageous; invariable.

verbs

abandon—; amend—; breach—; cancel—; celebrate—; cleave to—; depart from—; dispense with—; execute—; forfeit—; fulfill—; interpret—; jockey over—; jump—; land—; modify—; rebel at—; revoke—; term—; terminate—; violate—; void—; waive—; win—; —binds; —discloses; —expires; —holds; —implies; —specifies; —stipulates.

(See compact, agreement, arrangement, bargain, promise.)

CONTRACT (v)

adverbs

violently; vigorously; bindingly; definitely; legally; advantageously; substantially; physically; spasmodically; intermittently; solemnly.

(See narrow, shrink.)

CONTRACTION

adjectives

muscular; inevitable; continuous; sharp; deep; nervous; concentric.

verbs

allow for—; produce—; regulate—; tend toward—; —abbreviates; —apostrophizes; —condenses; —confines; —diminishes; —draws; —hampers; —lames; —limits; —narrows; —reduces; —restricts; —shortens; —shrinks.

(See condensation.)

CONTRACTOR

adjectives

certain; labor; alert; scheming; enriched; resourceful; purloining.

CONTRADICT (v)

adverbs

expressly; violently; inexplicably; constantly; embarrassingly; fatuously; flagrantly; mutually; bewilderingly; curiously; logically; extravagantly; vulgarly; boorishly; curtly; ill-manneredly; explicitly; directly. (See say.)

CONTRADICTION

adjectives

violent; inexplicable; constant; embarrassing; slight; irreconcilable; moral; breathtaking; productive; idealistic; disruptive; imaginary; self-corroding; fatuous; accumulated; social; flat; absurd; apparent; flagrant; painful; notable; mutual; bewildering; amazing; curious; logical; affectionate; extravagant.

verbs

affirm—; brook—; claim—; deny—; discern—; encompass with—; endure—; forbid—; indulge in—; involve—; object to—; offset—; press—; profess—; prove—; reconcile—; solve—; sustain—; utter—; —irritates; —perplexes; —proposes; —yawns. (See opposition, paradox, inconsistency.)

CONTRADICTORY

adverbs

strangely; oddly; naively; subtly; blatantly; inexplicably; embarrassingly; irreconcilably; disruptively; absurdly; flagrantly; pugnaciously; truculently; amazingly; curiously; apparently; obviously; palpably; illogically; bewilderingly; flatly; fiercely; directly; fatally; unbecomingly; defiantly.

CONTRAPTION

adjectives

happy; pleasing; refreshing; delicious; charming; excellent; attractive; pleasant; effective; interesting; encouraging; true; striking; vivid; marked; sharp; pronounced; momentous; notable; smashing; amazing; astounding; unbelievable; startling; surprising; puzzling; quaint; odd; curious; cruel; violent; prosaic; dismal; amusing; abrupt; ludicrous; deft; precise; tremendous; instructive; dramatic; intense; singular; gratifying; possible; ghastly; artificial; obvious; favorable; crazy; delightful; subtle; melancholy; piquant; gloomy; contemporaneous.

verbs

contemplate—; contrive—; design—; destroy—; devise—; employ—; extricate from—; immerse in—; interest in—; invent—; mesh in—; plan—; set up—; test—; work out—; —attracts; —envelops; —puzzles. (See device.)

CONTRAST

adjectives

clear; exciting; flattering; bitter; brilliant; remote; poignant; startling; unfavorable.

verbs

accentuate—; cap—; disclose—; emphasize—; mark—; place in—; present—; resent—; revel in—; serve as—; strike—; study—; vow—; —glares; —grows; —interests. (See comparison.)

CONTRAST (v)

adverbs

vividly; sharply; strangely; whimsically; bitterly; strikingly; violently; picturesquely; invidiously. (See compare.)

CONTRIBUTE (v)

adverbs

materially; unceasingly; indirectly; voluntarily; considerably; cheerily; altruisticly; willingly; liberally; simultaneously; singularly; gloomily; voluminously; conspicuously; effectively; powerfully; notably; anonymously; originally; technically; fundamentally; uniquely; meritoriously; formidably; permanently; characteristically. (See give, furnish.)

CONTRIBUTION

adjectives

important; notable; anonymous; epoch-making; significant; distinctive; voluminous; august; practical; passionate; magnificent; literary; original; technical; fundamental; valuable; unique; varying; copious; charming; worthy; liberal; heartfelt; generous; sole; fascinating; splendid; superb; meritorious; formidable; serious; permanent; solid; genuine; enduring; tangible; priceless; cultural; private; statesmanlike; creative; cooperative; definite; negligible; phantom; invigorating; timely; characteristic; startling; immediate.

verbs

begrudge—; collect—; deluge with—s; favor with—; gather—s; offer—; sacrifice—; solicit—; squeeze—out of; —exemplifies; —s pour in.
(See alms.)

CONTRIBUTOR

adjectives

distinguished; prolific; occasional; prospective; sparkling; anonymous; forgotten; flourishing; industrious; scholarly; well-remembered; frequent.

verbs

advertise for—s; appeal to—s; approach —s; back by—s; pay—; promise—; satisfy—; seek—s; serve as—; —aids; —endows; —furnishes; —raises; —rallies; —responds; —supports; —writes.
(See supporter.)

CONTRIBUTORY

adverbs

helpfully; advantageously; liberally; commercially; cooperatively; charitably; economically; encouragingly; generously; harmoniously; jointly; obligingly; originally.

CONTRITION

adjectives

veritable; authentic; apparent; heartfelt; warm; mock; pitiful; sudden; blind.

verbs

afflict with—; arise from—; break with—; bruise with—; display—; dissolve in—; exhibit—; languish in—; melt in—; pray in—; reduce to—; repent in—; sow—; strike with—; suffer—; wear with—; weep in—; —softens.
(See sorrow, remorse.)

CONTRIVANCE

adjectives

clumsy; mechanical; various (pl); discarded; ingenious; kindred; well-fitted; curious; perfect; mysterious; fun-making; excitement-arousing; dumpy; rickety; admirable; mock; peculiar; delightful; tricky; intricate; labor-saving; quaint; malignant.

CONTRIVE (v)

adverbs

ingeniously; cunningly; sedulously; curiously; cleverly; providentially; indirectly; scientifically; mechanically; mysteriously; intricately; malignantly; maliciously; viciously; bitterly; revengefully.
(See scheme, invent.)

CONTROL

adjectives

powerful; menial; supervisory; easy; heroic; thought; political; centralized; mysterious; transcending; absolute; repressive; automatic; effective; determined; collective; benevolent; inadequate; virtual; irremissible; remote; autonomous; inventory; democratic; effortless; rigorous; working; parental; precise; undisputed; production; autocratic; perfect; substantial; self-assumed; immediate; hypnotic; arbitrary; excellent; iron; firm; entire; permanent; complete; full; supreme; exclusive; nominal; limited; partial; hectic; craven; hateful; sinister; degrading; systematic; ordered; social; ancestral; merchandising; unjust; civilian; traffic; nerve; scientific; strong; external; silent; boundless; planned; private; growing; critical; steady.

verbs

acquire—; assume—; attest to—; centralize—; concentrate—; demonstrate—; divorce—; endanger—; entrust with—; establish—; exempt from—; exercise—; exert—; fight—; gain—; grab—; lose—; maintain—; manifest—; release—; respond to—; seek—; seize—; settle in—of; teach—; trick into—of; vest—in; win—; —changes hands; —rests with.
(See regulation, restraint, domination, command.)

CONTROL (v)

adverbs

absolutely; imperiously; arbitrarily; powerfully; heroically; politically; mysteriously; dictatorially; automatically; determinedly; benevolently; adequately; virtually; democratically; effortlessly; rigorously; autocratically; hypnotically; exclusively; nominally; partially; privately; critically; steadily.
(See regulate, restrain.)

CONTROVERSIAL

adverbs

highly; unfortunately; temptingly; inevitably; religiously; violently; tediously; painfully; excitably; vehemently; stupidly; obstinately; endlessly; bitterly; intricately; dangerously; traditionally; diplomatically; perplexingly.

CONTROVERSY

adjectives

perplexing; pending; long-standing; religious; violent; acrimonious; vehement; tedious; frequent; painful; external; important; bitter; political; sectarian; ferocious; exciting; pending; contemptible; heated; long; warm; drawn-out; endless; intricate; arduous; acrid; terrific; lively; scorching; threatening; dangerous; ancient; long-forgotten; legal; economic; international; diplomatic; clerical; parlor; silly; unfortunate; unexpected; waning.

verbs

appraise—; arouse—; avoid—; carry on—; clarify—; cut through—; dismiss—; engage in—; entangle in—; involve in—; judge—; occasion—; perpetuate—; plunge into—; precipitate—; shrink from—; stir up—; suppress—; sway by—; unleash—; view—; wage—; —arises from; —blasts; —convulses; —fizzles; —flares; —rages; —spits.

(See dispute, contention, debate, feud.)

CONTUMACIOUS

adverbs

stubbornly; stiffly; defiantly; hotly; permanentally; habitually; insufferably; intractably; unmanageably; uncontrollably; foolishly; ridiculously; mutinously; violently; restlessly; lawlessly; seditiously; ungovernably; openly; formidably; irreconcilably; alarmingly; dangerously; unaccountably; obstreperously; inveterately; malevolently; distressingly.

CONTUMELIOUS

adverbs

blatantly; absurdly; airily; egotistically; unpardonably; fantastically; insufferably; extremely; audaciously; flippantly; saucily; shamefully; bumptiously; brassily; offensively; provokingly; unpleasantly; disagreeably; intolerably; arrogantly; haughtily; unreasonably; senselessly; idiotically; unwisely; indiscreetly; imprudently.

CONTUSION

adjectives

severe; fatal; painful; serious; violet-hued; predominant.

verbs

acquire by—; anoint—; bandage—; cure—; dress—; infect—; inflame—; irritate—;

produce—; relieve—; suffer—; treat—; —bruises; —crushes; —enervates; —heals; —incapacitates; —injures; —swells.

(See bruise, injury.)

CONUNDRUM

adjectives

stock; baffling; fascinating; improvised; stale; original.

CONVALESCENCE

adjectives

tolerable; hard-won; adequate; drowsy; slow; uncertain; maddening.

verbs

affect—; delay—; doze through—; discharge from—; ease through—; interrupt—; nurse through—; regain during—; revive in—; shorten—; strengthen in—; treat during—; visit during—; while away—; —advances; —cures; —overcomes; —proceeds.

(See recovery, improvement.)

CONVALESCENT

adjectives

petulant; selfish; irritable; impatient; implacable; whining; whimsical.

adverbs

happily; fortunately; securely; finally; contentedly; easily; tolerably; slowly; painfully; actually; pleasantly; luckily; gratefully; thankfully; affably; normally; definitely; apparently; blessedly; cheerfully; charmingly; truly; presumably; undoubtedly; decisively.

CONVENIENCE

adjectives

domestic; timesaving; greater; money-saving; every; ultra-fashionable; incidental; notable; modern; homelike; foresighted; admirable; earliest; consequent; passing; delightful; added; safe; metropolitan; undoubted; tremendous; general.

verbs

adopt—; afford—; allow—; appreciate—; avail oneself of—; await—of; enjoy—; extend—; lack—; marry for—; offer—; pay for—; permit of—; possess—; require—; —comforts; —eases; —saves.

(See comfort, ease, opportunity.)

CONVENIENT

adverbs

particularly; comfortably; highly; properly; acceptably; admirably; marvelously; tremendously; safely; delightfully; exceptionally; perfectly; completely; incredibly; wholly; extraordinarily; singularly; suitably; duly; unusually; ingeniously.

CONVENT

adjectives

suppressed; measureless; once-famous; secluded; peaceful; cloistered.

CONVENTION
(*custom*)

adjectives

timid; operatic; faith-healing; classic; universal; social; civic; restricting; rigid; facile; poetic.

CONVENTION
(*meeting*)

adjectives

radical; national; projected; provincial; famous; cheap; wide-open; labor; advertising.

verbs

appoint to—; assemble in—; boycott—; brand—; cavort at—; control—; denounce—; elect at—; emanate in—; hold—; join—; meet in—; open—; preside at—; represent at—; run away with—; stage—; —abolishes; —adjourns; —alters; —bestows; —considers; —convenes; —nominates; —prepares; —proclaims.

(See meeting, conference, congress, council, assembly.)

CONVENTIONAL

adverbs

properly; formally; strictly; habitually; naturally; normally; ordinarily; positively; usually; uncompromisingly; typically; rigidly; stiffly; consistently; absurdly; needlessly; carefully; arrogantly; affectedly; shyly; bashfully; ostentatiously; pretentiously; pompously; meticulously; insistently.

CONVENTIONALITY

adjectives

pleasant; sterile; frigid; precise; ceremonious; cutting; supreme.

verbs

accept—; adhere to—; base on—; beat down—; blind by—; breach—; break—; break away from—; buttress by—; chal-

lenge—; contradict—; defer—; defy—; discard—; disregard—; drop—; flout—; follow—; hamper—; hate—; heed—; obey—; overthrow—; ridicule—; sacrifice to—; satirize—; shatter—; shelter—; smash—; subject to—; violate—; wall in by—; —allows; —determines; —hampers; —permits; —recognizes; —sanctions; —settles; —supports; —upholds.

(See custom, usage, habit, rule, form, practice.)

CONVERGE (*v*)

adverbs

sharply; suddenly; gradually; obviously; abruptly; unexpectedly; consequently; fatally; tragically; significantly.

(See approach.)

CONVERSANT

adverbs

thoroughly; intimately; slightly; fortunately; luckily; auspiciously; expertly; liberally; deeply; profoundly; shrewdly; reportedly; supposedly; reputably; ingeniously; cleverly; intelligently; capably; advantageously; consummately; perfectly.

CONVERSATION

adjectives

desultory; sedate; forcible; vapid; whispered; exquisite; subsequent; inane; trivial; informal; temporary; difficult; frank; touching; calm; natural; cheerful; animated; private; bristling; preliminary; thoughtful; philosophical; savory; embellished; unspecific; mysterious; idyllic; interminable; earnest; measured; gossip-riddled; filthy; reminiscent; considerable; agreeable; subdued; hurried; distracting; energetic; gentle; frivolous; sparkling; undertoned; low-voiced; real; heavenly; pleasant; enchanting; fascinating; egotistic; previous; appreciative; personal; direct; tumultuous; memorable; vivacious; amiable; improbable; intelligent; offhand; comfortable; inmost; casual; serious; bold; liberal; idle; scattered; curious; apparent; ribald; spicy; extravagant; delightful; interesting; sustained; passing; dramatic; diligent; sublimated; piquant; rational; select; easy; graceful; protracted; intimate; eager; edifying; mercurial; running; sportive; open; sociable; antiquarian; inimitable; brilliant; clear; persuasive; sympathetic; sane; coherent; amicable; enthralling; luminous; famous; witty; aphoristic; hilarious; amusing; bantering; facetious; smiling; light; explosive; spirited; lively;

sprightly; negligible; everyday; ordinary; aimless; drifting; languishing; flickering; scattered; intermittent; halting; jerky; wandering; lagging; jumbled; fitful; indefinite; elusive; spiritless; extended; inconclusive; timorous; wearisome; fatuous; insipid; lazy; lackadaisical; muttered; bold; impractical; pert; leery; hidebound; loud; superfluous; irate; embattled; hideous; concerting; coarse; obscene; illiterate; successful; dinner table; eyebrow; traveled; healthy; emotional; quiet; cultured; confidential; startled; amazing; conspicuous; condensed; brief; rapid; promiscuous; unblushing; spontaneous; sudden; chatty: general; developed; simple; polite; absorbed; imaginary; uninterrupted; harmless; dutiful; plausible.

verbs

address—to; conduct—with; connive at—; direct—; divert—; drag into—; dull—; engage in—; essay—; forego—; guide—; infuse into—; interrupt—; key—; lead into—; narrate—; nurture—; open—; overhear—; plunge into—; prolong—; refrain from—; rush into—; shatter—; shift—; shoulder—; snatch at—; suspend—; swing —back to; transcribe—; —breaks out; —drifts on; —evolves from; —flames; —flows; —languishes; —lapses; —palls; —precedes; —rambles; —ranges; —scintillates; —skips from; —streams away; — stumbles upon.

(See dialogue, intercourse, communication, conference, talk.)

CONVERSATIONAL

adverbs

amiably; stiffly; sociably; affably; pompously; garrulously; provincially; gruffly; laconically; informally; calmly; naturally: cheerfully; jovially; helpfully; unwontedly; agreeably; eagerly; gently; brilliantly; enchantingly; illuminatingly; fascinatingly; vivaciously; intelligently; comfortably; casually; seriously; idly; curiously; spicily; ribaldly; drunkenly; convivially; interestingly; dramatically; gracefully; intimately; graciously; wittily; amusingly; facetiously; happily; luckily; intermittently; abstractedly; fitfully; inconclusively; yawningly; insipidly; lazily; loudly; blatantly; noisily.

CONVERSATIONALIST

adjectives

fluent; elegant; absorbing; gifted; interesting; brilliant.

CONVERSE

adjectives

earnest; eager; grave; sagacious; purposeful; covert.

CONVERSE (v)

adverbs

vivaciously; fluently; freely; interestingly; agreeably; courteously; affably; desultorily; acrimoniously; sedately; inanely; trivially; informally; temporarily; frankly; touchingly; animatedly; privately; brilliantly; philosophically; mysteriously; distractedly; curiously; ribaldly; piquantly; rationally; dramatically; gracefully; mercurially; inimitably; persuasively; sympathetically; coherently; amicably; enthrallingly; hilariously; banteringly; aimlessly; pointlessly; intermittently; jerkily; laggingly; fitfully; indefinitely; fatuously; insipidly; timorously; superfluously; irately; emotionally; confidentially; promiscuously; spontaneously; politely; absorbedly; uninterruptedly; harmlessly; pointedly.

(See talk, chat.)

CONVERSION

adjectives

spiritual; infinite; romantic; tardy; religious; abrupt; imminent; vivid.

CONVERT

adjectives

proposed; immovable; enthusiastic; docile; devout; irrevocable.

verbs

baptize—; direct—; gather—s; guide—; lead—s; make—; preach to—; —accepts; —acknowledges; —changes; —embraces; —falls from grace; —forsakes; —gains; —professes; —rallies; —substitutes; — transfers.

(See disciple, follower.)

CONVERT (v)

adverbs

religiously; frequently; enthusiastically; sincerely; passionately; conscientiously; irresistibly; intellectually; rationally; unalterably; solemnly.

(See apply, use.)

CONVERTIBLE

adverbs

readily; easily; handily; economically; quickly; conveniently; instantly; serviceably; instantaneously; advantageously; ingeniously; deftly; dexterously; fortunately;

luckily; accommodatingly; adaptably; providentially; promptly; profitably; altogether; unquestionably; happily.

CONVEY (v)
adverbs
naturally; forcefully; exquisitely; imperceptibly; delicately; competently; peculiarly; luxuriously; privately; diplomatically; tactfully; ceremoniously.
(See carry, transport.)

CONVEYANCE
adjectives
miserable; competent; shaky; tenantless; impossible; peculiar; ornamental; creditable; luxurious; available; modern; private; usual.

verbs
construct—; convoy—; design—; draw—; drive—; escort—; guide—; lead—; load—; lubricate—; mechanize—; model—; pull—; power—; restrain—; transport in—; trust—; upset—; —rattles; —rumbles; —transmits.
(See carriage, vehicle.)

CONVICT
adjectives
political; pardoned; vital; wily; shivering; rat-faced; horrified; fear-dazed; filthy; degraded; villainous.

verbs
apprehend—; chain—; deliver—; execute —; expose—; free—; pardon—; parole—; punish—; rehabilitate—; reprieve—; sentence—; train—; transfer—; try—; —breaks jail; —confesses; —escapes; —invades; —offends; —prowls; —rebels; —reforms; —serves.
(See criminal, culprit, prisoner.)

CONVICT (v)
adverbs
invariably; circumstantially; insidiously; politically; villainously; sternly; intellectually; positively; unmistakably; deliberately; solemnly; theoretically; swiftly; secretly; overwhelmingly; legally.
(See condemn.)

CONVICTION
adjectives
arresting; passionate; humbling; doubtful; historic; conscientious; true; firm; perverse; random; instantaneous; stern; indefeasible; youthful; profound; rapturous; frail; unsettled; irresistible; unshaken; widespread; deep; popular; honest; intellectual; inbred; esteemed; fixed; religious; coessential; subjective; sincere; rational; unalterable; vivid; calm; reasonable; extravagant; remote; positive; instinctive; unmistakable; steel; thorough; moral; antagonistic; internal; jocular; definite; persistent; deliberate; paternal; tried; innermost; solemn; intimate; unspoken; well-known; theoretic; extreme; socialistic; immediate; unutterable; prophetic; perfect; earnest; sober; clear; accepted; assured; lively; joyous; thrilling; exhilarating; lasting; steadfast; stubborn; ineradicable; unassailable; unsullied; unquestioning; independent; heroic; fierce; strong; intense; absolute; personal; individual; horrible; torturing; unaccountable; disagreeable; wild; grim; unfortunate; weary; pathetic; humanitarian; aesthetic; increasing; growing; light; odd; swift; overwhelming; comfortable; latent; naive; dawning; instinctive; secret.

verbs
accept with—; awaken to—; bring—; carry—; cherish—; develop—; express—; fire—; form—; guide by—; indoctrinate—; ingrain—; justify—; lack—; lay down with—; lead to—; profess—; reiterate—; rouse—; share—; stand by—; —accrues; —burdens; —deserts; —grows; —restrains; —springs; —wavers.
(See faith, belief.)

CONVINCE (v)
adverbs
demonstratively; despairingly; rationally; solemnly; reluctantly; unalterably; profoundly; stubbornly; firmly; thoroughly; passionately; conscientiously; irresistibly; honestly; intellectually; religiously; reasonably; positively; theoretically; overwhelmingly; secretly.
(See satisfy.)

CONVIVIAL
adverbs
warmly; extremely; hospitably; sociably; fraternally; cosily; gregariously; entertainingly; chattingly; hilariously; waggishly; uproariously; pleasantly; merrily; gaily; blithely; affably; highly; agreeably; sportively; facetiously; boisterously; noisily; obstreperously; jovially; lovingly; festively; heartily.

CONVIVIALITY

adjectives
dried; dead; joyous; infectious; communicable; sparkling.

CONVOCATION

adjectives
jocund; ecclesiastical; heterogeneous; noble; clamorous; political; incessant.

CONVOKE (v)

adverbs
legitimately; legally; formally; annually; flagrantly; solemnly; ceremoniously; perfunctorily.
(See call, gather.)

CONVOY

adjectives
lumbering; speeding; rushing; protective; unwelcome; sequestering.

CONVULSION

adjectives
popular; perilous; suicidal; gleaming; rare; burnished; hammered; tarnished; public; hysterical; spasmodic; passionate; sardonic; civic; fearful; ghastly; strong; horrid; freakish; dreadful; moral; amiable; seething; mighty; mad.

verbs
attend with—; pass through—; produce—; quiet—; shake with—; stiffen in—; treat for—; writhe in—; —arises from; —recurs; —seizes.
(See spasm, fit, paroxysm.)

COO (v)

adverbs
plaintively; murmurously; softly; romantically; gently; lovingly; affectionately; delicately.
(See whisper.)

COOING

adjectives
soft; melancholy; subdued; mournful; gentle; lullabied; hushed.

COOK

adjectives
outlandish; splendid; superb; excellent; peerless; lusty; furious; surprised; sleepy-eyed; excited; pious; covetous; studious; cursed.

COOK (v)

adverbs
excellently; arduously; outlandishly; superbly; peerlessly; unsurpassingly; appetizingly; deliciously; exotically; delicately; tastefully; experimentally.
(See prepare.)

COOKERY

adjectives
master; tasty; experimental; unpalatable; hopeless; praiseworthy.

COOKIES

adjectives
delicious; stale; fresh; newly-baked; holiday; refrigerator.

COOKING

adjectives
delicate; unsavory; hygienic; casual; indifferent; superb; incomparable.

verbs
delight in—; plan—; practise—; provide—; relish—; school in—; skill in—; teach—; turn to—; —invites; —tempts.

COOL

adverbs
refreshingly; comfortably; uncomfortably; suddenly; unusually; gratefully; sufficiently; extremely; somewhat; moderately; unexpectedly; surprisingly; luckily; unfortunately; unluckily; terribly; beautifully; delightfully.

COOL (v)

adverbs
rapidly; sufficiently; scientifically; nocturnally; professionally; autumnally; abnormally; mechanically.
(See chill.)

COOL-HEADED

adverbs
quietly; calmly; equably; dispassionately; gravely; imperturbably; moderately; patiently; wisely; serenely; stoically; tolerantly; judiciously; sensibly; habitually; temperamentally; luckily; provokingly; sanely; extremely; superbly; astutely; admirably; amazingly; cautiously; warily; discreetly.

COOLNESS

adjectives
alluring; masterful; grateful; soft; admirable; nocturnal; cynical; obstinate; pro-

fessional; smooth; twinkling; utmost; undisturbed; slumberous; dim; correct; apparent; matchless; welcome; sudden; autumnal; inhuman; sneering; delicious.

COOPERATE (v)

adverbs

alternately; enthusiastically; gladly; consciously; respectably; willingly; harmoniously; courteously; advantageously; wholesomely; benevolently; mechanically; agriculturally; heartily; voluntarily; sympathetically; spontaneously; successfully.

(See help, unite.)

COOPERATION

adjectives

peaceful; matchless; loyal; genuine; courteous; close; harmonious; wise; generous; advantageous; wholesome; benevolent; municipal; unwavering; active; constant; cordial; constructive; munificent; emotional; agricultural; merchandising; public; international; pontifical; hearty; voluntary; stabilizing; spontaneous; sympathetic; immense; universal; conscious; indispensable; successful; powerful.

verbs

act in—with; advocate—; balk at—; court—; develop—; display—; dispose toward—; effect—; enlist—; exhibit—; foster—; lack—; necessitate—; pledge—; practise—; result in—; stress—; teach—; urge—; work in—with; —helps; —overcomes; —produces; —saves.

(See action, participation.)

COOPERATIVE

adverbs

wonderfully; serviceably; ardently; energetically; intelligently; zealously; actively; overwhelmingly; ingeniously; skilfully; willingly; grudgingly; instantly; loyally; genuinely; wisely; generously; advantageously; benevolently; unwaveringly; cordially; munificently; heartily; spontaneously; immensely; indispensably.

COORDINATE (v)

adverbs

logically; rationally; physically; functionally; excellently; delicately; mentally; muscularly; exactly; definitely; skilfully.

COORDINATION

adjectives

rational; physical; functional; excellent; delicate; mental; local; muscular.

verbs

arrange—; display—; hamper—; impair—; improve—; involve—; lose—; obstruct—; perform with—; proceed in—; regulate with—; require—; study—; supervise—;

—effects; —pleases.

(See harmony.)

COP

adjectives

strutting; hidebound; bullying; pompous; brass-buttoned; mace-brandishing; dictatorial; obliging; humanitarian.

COPE (v)

adverbs

successfully; bravely; heroically; continually; prevailingly; stalwartly; fearlessly; surprisingly.

(See strive.)

COPIOUS

adverbs

overwhelmingly; lavishly; naturally; needlessly; amply; luxuriantly; abundantly; aboundingly; exuberantly; affluently; inexhaustibly; overpoweringly; prodigally; handsomely; excessively; wantonly; unreasonably; remarkably; inexpressibly; fabulously; extraordinarily; astonishingly; amazingly; particularly; wonderfully; staggeringly; surprisingly; unbelievably; marvellously; fortunately; profusely.

COPPER

adjectives

shining; old; burnished; simmering; gleaming; hammered; tarnished.

verbs

alloy—; coat with—; dissolve—; grub out—; heat—; line with—; mine—; mold—; oxidize—; process—; produce—; purify—; refine—; sheathe in—; smelt—; work in—; —conducts; —insulates; —occurs; —oxidizes; —resists.

(See metal.)

COPSE

adjectives

woven; thick; rambling; summer; luxuriant.

COPY
(general)

adjectives
spirited; modified; examined; literal; certified; advance; drab; uninteresting; exact; laborious; attested; feeble; unique; mimeographed; photostatic; burlesque; fair; fragmentary; engrossed; virtuous; identical; pale; lame; stray; questionable; fraudulent; plaster; unexpurgated.

COPY
(journalism)

adjectives
badly-typed; blue-penciled; interlined; intelligible; transcribed; thumb-worn; sadly-deleted; smudgy.

verbs
arrange—; butcher—; deride—; damage—; edit—; enliven—; expand—; improve—; lengthen—; outline—; overbalance—; overdo—; point up—; read—; rearrange—; review—; set—; shorten—; simplify—; tone up—; write—.
(See advertisement.)

COPY
(reproduction)

adjectives
authentic; accurate; flattering; pathetic; preposterous; sketchy; veritable.

verbs
alter—; attest—; bequeath—; change—; collect—ies; distribute—ies; embellish—; forward—; garnish—; guard—; mail—; pattern—; refer to—; retain—; rewrite—; sign—; transcribe—; translate—; witness —; —appears; —exemplifies; —imitates; —reproduces.
(See imitation, duplicate, pattern.)

COPY (v)

adverbs
accurately; silently; extensively; uninterestingly; literally; exactly; laboriously; uniquely; photostatically; fairly; fragmentarily; identically; fraudulently; faithfully.
(See reproduce, imitate.)

COPYRIGHT

adjectives
popular; valid; world-wide; ineffective; disregarded.

verbs
apply for—; assign—to; defeat—; grant—; infringe on—; invalidate—; reconvey—; renew—; take out—; violate—; —expires; —protects; —secures.
(See right, patent.)

COQUETRY

adjectives
spasmodic; childish; unconquerable; open; feeble; modest; shy; clumsy; graceful; unconscious; native.

COQUETTE

adjectives
laughing; cold-blooded; superannuated; natural; insolent; typical; attractive; little.

COQUETTE (v)

adverbs
saucily; laughingly; insolently; attractively; modestly; shyly; slyly; gracefully; endearingly; lovingly; temptingly; irresistibly; naturally; precociously; shamelessly.
(See flirt.)

COQUETTISH

adverbs
charmingly; shamelessly; wantonly; enchantingly; irresistibly; unconsciously; deliberately; intentionally; effectively; laughingly; coolly; defiantly; inherently; naturally; awkwardly; shyly; incorrigibly; incurably; gracefully; attractively; typically; provokingly; openly; shamefully; clumsily; exquisitely; consciously; demurely; adorably; captivatingly; bewitchingly; reprehensibly; ardently; zealously.

CORAL

adjectives
pearl-hued; polished; blushing; branching; intricately-structured; imperishable.

verbs
abound in—; bedeck in—; deposit—; distribute—; employ—; fashion of—; fish for—; form—; inlay with—; market—; obtain—; polish—; procure—; secrete—; tint—; touch with—; trade—; trim with—; utilize—; value—; —attaches to; —covers; —crusts; —decorates; —flourishes; —ornaments; —grows; prize—.

adjectives

long; dangling; spinal; tense; frayed; durable; vital; hempen; subtle; sensitive; encircling; creaking; tangled; silver; penny; taut.

verbs

attach by—; bind with—; bite—; break—; cast away—; cut asunder—; draw—; gnaw at—; knit—; lengthen—; loop—; loose—; pull—; sever—; sterilize—; strengthen—; tie—; wind—; —binds; —snaps.
(See string, chain.)

CORDIAL

adjectives

best; exhilarating; warming; stimulating; animating; revivifying.

adverbs

eagerly; spontaneously; graciously; sincerely; warmly; heartily; genially; politely; courteously; unwontedly; ostentatiously; obviously; unusually; pleasantly; agreeably; indulgently; civilly; affectionately; devotedly; intimately; quietly; sympathetically; freely; openly; amicably; frankly; gallantly.

CORDIALITY

adjectives

genial; apparent; unexpected; pleasing; intoxicating; unaffected; great; condescending; businesslike; warm; utmost; loud; unofficial.

verbs

display—; doubt—; exhibit—; fraternize with—; greet with—; hate with—; lack—; resent—; respect—; return—; strive in—; —beckons; —bespeaks of; —cheers; —comforts; —exhilarates; —induces; —warms.
(See sincerity, ardor, affection.)

CORE

adjectives

inmost; putrefied; burning; endearing; festering; hidden; vibrant.

verbs

bore into—; cut from—; destroy—; dig to—; eat at—; extract—; feed upon—; fill to—; imbed at—; loosen—; pare to—; putrefy at—; remove—; rot at—; sheathe —; stab to—; surround—; taste to—; touch to—; wring to—; —contains; —disintegrates; —remains; discard—.
(See heart.)

CORK

adjectives

popping; large; leaking; obstinate; unbudging.

CORN

adjectives

military; starving; unsickled; sprinkled; bounteous; strengthening; bladed; scanty; lusty; golden; bruised; dry; pungent; waving; tall; ripening; thriving; rustling.

verbs

blast—; consume—; feed on—; furrow—; gather—; grind—; harvest—; husk—; market—; parch—; pluck—; prepare—; reap—; sack—; scatter—; shell—; shock—; sift—; sow—; stack—; store—; strip—; thrash—; tread out—; wither—; wreathe in—; —blossoms; —ripens; —rustles; —shoots up; —sustains; —sways; —waves.
(See cereal, grain.)

CORNER

adjectives

favorite; accessible; comfortable; cozy; tranquil; quiet; hintermost; secluded; sheltered; sunny; shaded; obscure; murky; isolated; removed; remote; vine-covered; grassy; theological; neglected; wickedest; overstuffed; coolest; tight; ill-smelling; outward; twisting; propitious; genteel; adjacent; inconspicuous; awkward; unexpected; arbored; hooded; hazardous; farthest; dim; dark; squalid; somber; cooperative; unpretentious; neighboring; idle.

verbs

bevel—; cower in—; crouch in—; droop in—; dwell in—; emerge from—; fall in—; hinge—; move to—; obscure in—; pray in—; round—; sharpen—; sit in—; sulk in—; sweep in—; tuck in—.
(See niche.)

CORNFIELD

adjectives

waving; swaying; sweltering; immense; dense; luxuriant; exuberant; discouraged; struggling.

CORNICE

adjectives

ornamental; hand-wrought; elaborate; topheavy; scrolled; jutting; overhanging.

CORNUCOPIA

adjectives
generous; filled; flowing; bounteous; redolent; replete; plenteous; expansive; well-assorted; full-variety; assuring.

COROLLARY

adjectives
necessary; reasonable; definite; consequent; maintained; sustained; abrupt; inevitable; eventual; invariable.

CORONATION

adjectives
earthly; princely; poetical; seraphic; triumphant; glorious; climacteric.

CORONET

adjectives
vast; jeweled; braided.

CORPORAL

adjectives
insignificant; stately; impressive; awkward; imposing; exacting; domineering.

CORPORATION

adjectives
prosperous; civil; remarkable; bloated; modern; soulless; giant; moneyed; world-renowned; flourishing; dummy; tremendous; prominent; large.

verbs
bankrupt—; build up—; charter—; combine in—; constitute—; control—; dominate—; form—; found—; head—; join in—; outlaw—; preserve—; rule— unite in—; —advertises; —branches out; —develops; —employs; —grows; —undersells.
(See company, firm, association.)

CORPS

adjectives
diplomatic; detached; meager; well-tried; judiciary; terrible; executive; attacking; admirable; celebrated.

verbs
assign to—; captain—; command—; enlist in—; form—; join—; lead—; organize—; quarter—; station—; uniform—; —assembles; —attacks; —charges; —combats; —encamps; —marches; —patrols.
(See army.)

CORPSE

adjectives
poor; little; galvanized; sundried; good-looking; bleeding; dripping; handsome; desiccated; mangled; unrecovered; mutilated; disfigured; peaceful; lovely; charred; shriven; bloated.

verbs
animate—; attend—; bear—; bury—; collect—s; desert—; destroy—; discover—; disinter—; dismember—; dispose of—; drag for—; exhume—; grapple for—; hide—; hunt—; identify—; inter—; lament—; lay out—; mourn—; preserve—; recognize—; regard—; restore—; strew with—s; stumble on—; trip over—; view—; —decays; —decomposes; —disintegrates; —putrefies.
(See remains, carcass.)

CORPULENT

adverbs
unfortunately; incredibly; unhappily; incurably; comfortably; contentedly; distressingly; absurdly; ridiculously; ludicrously; lamentably; sadly; blithely; joyously; dangerously; heavily; gracefully; admittedly; funnily; unreasonably; incorrigibly; irremediably; complacently; mournfully; dramatically; complainingly.

CORPUSCLE

adjectives
bulbous; life-bearing; oxygen-supplying; scavenging; striving; surging; vitally-laden.

verbs.
divide into—s; furnish with—s; increase—s; lower—s; study—; tear down—; —acts; —attacks; —bursts; —destroys; —envelops; —immunizes; —provides; —reproduces; —resists; —splits; —wanders about.

CORRAL

adjectives
rickety; shabby; flaming; palisaded; guarded; over-crowded; incarcerating; confining.

verbs
accept—; acknowledge—; devise—; allow —; authorize—; counteract—; direct—; follow—; fumble for—; invite—; judge—;

modify—; need—; offer—; perform—; print—; refuse—; rejoice in—; resent—; subject to—; substitute—; superintend—; —amends; —improves; —neutralizes; —revises.

(See punishment, discipline.)

CORRECT
adverbs
strictly; formally; fashionably; habitually; ordinarily; positively; uncompromisingly; rigidly; stiffly; insistently; absurdly; carefully; arrogantly; affectedly; ostentatiously; pretentiously; pompously; meticulously; punctiliously; dependably; scrupulously; infallibly; uncannily; disturbingly; unimpeachably; mathematically; insatiably; avidly.

CORRECT (v)
adverbs
painstakingly; constructively; helpfully; sufficiently; harshly; courteously; agreeably; adequately; reasonably; grammatically; infallibly; tactfully; rudely; crudely; curtly; sincerely; obnoxiously.

(See right, reprove.)

CORRECTION
adjectives
courteous; agreeable; autograph; strong; uranographical; adequate.

verbs
accept—; acknowledge—; advise—; allow —; authorize—; counteract—; direct—; follow—; fumble for—; invite—; judge—; modify—; need—; offer—; perform—; print —; refuse—; rejoice in—; resent—; subject to—; substitute—; superintend—; —amends; —improves; —neutralizes; —revises.

(See punishment, discipline.)

CORRECTNESS
adjectives
reasonable; superb; grammatical; irreproachable; lavish; infallible; tactical; rigid.

CORRELATE (v)
adverbs
mutually; definitely; significantly; properly; seriously; exactly; statistically.

(See correspond.)

CORRELATION
adjectives
definite; significant; proper; serious; exact; high; statistical.

CORRESPOND (v)
adverbs
confidentially; exactly; extensively; commonly; spiritually; relatively; curiously; prominently; obviously; superficially.

(See correlate.)

CORRESPONDENCE
adjectives
extensive; poetical; contraband; mutual; clandestine; spurious; noteworthy; seditious; mere; frank; subsequent; spicy; voluminous; lifelong; irresponsible; varied; intimate; diplomatic; heated; imperishable; amatory; objectionable; spiritual; copious; cipher; empirical; commercial; glorious; ungrammatical; vivacious; indiscreet; desultory; relative; curious; sympathetic.

verbs
answer—; conduct—with; enter into—with; establish—with; express—with; file—; influence—; interchange—; invite—; maintain—; manage—; neglect—; open—with; receive—; renew—; return—; safeguard—; treat—; —communicates; —enlightens.

(See communication, intercourse, letter.)

CORRESPONDENT
adjectives
humble; prominent; eavesdropping; sympathetic; flattered; international; energetic; special; active; reliable; diplomatic; warshy; persistent; punctilious.

CORRIDOR
adjectives
vaulted; angling; lengthened; spacious; interminable; golden; gloom-shrouded; dreamland; solitary; labyrinthine; tortuous; majestic; deserted; dusty; footworn; myriad (pl); curtained; endless; sloping; bleak; thronged; polished; resounding; murky; circular; concrete; black; eerie.

verbs
brighten—; clatter in—; cross—; darken—; glimmer through—; guard—; light—; line—; narrow—; pass through—; patrol —; run through—; scrub—; shuffle along—; stroll in—; sweep—; traverse—; watch—; widen—; —connects; —joins; —links; —opens into; —resounds with; —unites.

(See gallery, passage, hall.)

CORRIGIBLE

adverbs

submissively; meekly; humbly; wisely; sensibly; sensitively; fortunately; luckily; happily; easily; willingly; reasonably; intelligently; impressibly; moderately; actually; genuinely; tolerably; surprisingly; unusually; probably; presumably.

CORROBORATE (*v*)

adverbs

substantially; partially; reliably; fully; undeniably; undoubtedly; convincingly; authentically.

(See confirm, support.)

CORROBORATIVE

adverbs

wholly; entirely; partially; satisfactorily; scarcely; collusively; unfortunately; shamefully; unhappily; completely; circumstantially; exactly; generally; authentically; absolutely; warrantably; intrinsically; significantly; impressively; precisely; authoritatively; credibly; inferentially; terribly; fortunately; substantially.

CORRODE (*v*)

adverbs

perniciously; morally; detrimentally; psychically; permanently; fatally; irreparably; irremediably.

(See consume.)

CORROSIVE

adverbs

poisonously; terribly; destructively; irreparably; injuriously; harmfully; wastefully; hopelessly; dangerously; perniciously; rankly; banefully; detrimentally; disastrously; ruinously; irremediably; undoubtedly; seriously; unquestionably; positively.

CORRUGATION

adjectives

delicate; microscopic; faint; threadlike; fluted; transverse; deep; shallow; intense; decided.

CORRUPT

adverbs

incredibly; loathsomely; utterly; infamously; secretly; notoriously; officially; politically; perniciously; basely; generally; grossly; crassly; abominably; shamelessly; openly; admittedly; detestably; odiously; execrably; scandalously; outrageously; darkly; maliciously.

CORRUPT (*v*)

adverbs

flagrantly; undesignedly; dishonorably; profoundly; incredibly; wondrously; loathsomely; utterly; infamously; notoriously; perniciously; basely; generally; systematically; satanically.

(See spoil, debase.)

CORRUPTION

adjectives

chronic; mercenary; medieval; chill; unparalleled; dishonorable; profound; incredible; wondrous; loathsome; utter; infamous; hidden; unhappy; ensuing; glossy; political; foulest; civic; official; business; notorious; pernicious; base; miry; monetary; general.

verbs

attend with—; befoul with—; charge with—; conceive in—; cripple by—; defend from—; deliver from—; denounce—; fall into—; fatten on—; feast on—; infect with—; loathe—; perish in—; practise—; preserve from—; rot with—; sow—; subject to—; taint with—; —blemishes; —breaks up; —contaminates; —decomposes; —depraves; —despoils; —destroys; deteriorates; —disintegrates; —dissolves; —extends to; —perverts; —putrefies; —undermines; —violates.

(See perversion, pollution, demoralization, dishonesty, decay.)

CORSET

adjectives

armor-plated; confining; curve-restricting; corrective; breath-expelling; gusseted; hampering; health-destroying; torturing; iron-clad; stout; tightly-laced.

verbs

discard—; divest of—; encircle in—; fit—; lace—; loose—; pierce—; squeeze into—; tighten—; —binds; —covers; —molds; —narrows; —protects; —shapes; —stiffens; —smooths; —strangles; —straps; —supports.

COST

adjectives

trifling; nominal; moderate; inflated; minimum; enormous; appalling; excessive; prodigious; huge; average; comparative; fearful; spiritual; low; relative; ultimate; superfluous; prevailing; exorbitant; admini-

strative; prime; inevitable; extra; classical; operating; additional; insignificant;
evident; initial; proper; increasing; outrageous; haulage; aggregate.

verbs
absorb—; avoid—; bear—; calculate—;
defray—; forfeit—; heighten—; incur—;
maintain—; omit—; prate about—; rate—;
reckon—; shave—; shoulder—; spare—;
whittle down—; —astounds; —piles up;
—soars; —varies; recoup—.
(See price, expense, loss.)

COSTLY
adverbs
enormously; appallingly; unreasonably;
fearfully; outrageously; unusually; exorbitantly; absurdly; gorgeously; unwarrantably; senselessly; wickedly; elegantly; flagrantly; unbelievably; extremely; inestimably.

COSTUME
adjectives
charming; brilliant; fetching; clever; intriguing; perfect; gorgeous; colorful;
nativity; ornamented; elaborate; unconventional; indelicate; inappropriate; con-
vict-like; native; flamboyant; ballet; bizarre; theatrical; local; allegorical; crepe-
paper; abbreviated; authentic; gala; billowing; stiff; characteristic; gaudy; lavish;
fantastic; lugubrious; variegated; rhetorical; exquisite; daring; singular; mournful;
picturesque; old-fashioned; grotesque; embroidered; quaint; antique; swagger;
flattering; jacketed; capricious.

verbs
array in—; attire in—; change—; deck
in—; design—; devise—; disguise in—;
divest of—; don—; embroider—; fashion—; launder—; mend—; model—; parade
in—; pose in—; recognize—; tailor—;
trim—; —dazzles; —enhances; —interprets; —symbolizes.
(See dress, garment, clothing.)

COSY
adverbs
comfortably; snugly; luxuriously; entertainingly; pleasurably; gratefully; refreshingly; sweetly; hospitably; cheerfully; companionably; heartily; intimately; socially;
easily; confidentially; agreeably; pleasantly; truly; curiously.

COT
(*cottage*)
adjectives
hurdled; weed-inwoven; chimneyed; cozy;
overgrown; rose-thatched; sheltered; unpretentious; picturesque; ivied; tenanted.

COT
(*bed*)
adjectives
iron; lowly; downy; snug; sleep-forbid-
ding; lumpy; miserable; untidy; tumbled.

verbs
erect—; pounce on—; slumber on—; throw
oneself upon—; toss on—; —creaks.
(See bed, couch.)

COTERIE
adjectives
half-serious; playful; philosophical; select;
exclusive; cabal; formidable; numerous;
assembled.

COTTAGE
adjectives
thatched; attendant; prim; peaceful; coquettish; straggling; green-shuttered; nestling; squat; smoke-grimed; vine-clad; secluded; luxurious; abandoned; modest;
dim-lit; enchanted; attractive; cozy; ancient; rustic; authentic; pert; suburban;
eerie; mysterious; gray; small; tidy;
weathered; low; lovable; dream; midget.

verbs
abide in—; adorn—; brighten—; construct—; dot with—s; dwell in—; erect—;
forsake—; furnish—; inhabit—; lease—;
lodge in—; rent—; repair to—; shade—;
shelter—; —cheers; —invites; —s line;
—secludes.
(See house, hut, cabin, lodge.)

COTTON
adjectives
speckled; glorified; striped; absorbent;
excellent; lovely; sheer; snowy; feathery.

verbs
apply—; bale—; clean—; clothe in—; cultivate—; dye—; export—; gin—; market—;
pack with—; pad with—; pick—; prey
on—; print on—; raise—; saturate—;
sterilize—; swab with—; thread—; twist—;
wad—; weave—; wrap in—.
(See cloth, thread.)

adjectives

frosty; hollow; narrow; unruffled; fiery; uncurtained; rushy; slippery; nuptial; tortured; stony; bridal; resplendent; sumptuous; festal; luxurious; be-tumbled; eastern; rude; restless; soft; broad; low; big; grassy.

verbs

clamber on—; defile—; ensconce on—; exalt —; fling upon—; lie on—; recline on—; rest on—; roll off—; sprawl on—; stretch upon—; stuff—; upholster—; —invites; —tempts.

(See bed, sofa.)

COUCH (v)

adverbs

cautiously; gracefully; flatteringly; tactfully; fastidiously; expressively; diplomatically.

(See express.)

COUGH

adjectives

bad; monotonous; persistent; sinister; low; irritable; slight; little; sharp; tremendous; sepulchral; muffled; hectic; distressing; hacking; dubious; apologetic; troublesome; churchyard; shattering; discreet; annoyed; wheezing; timid; dismal; hollow; smothered; premonitory.

verbs

affect with—; afflict with—; bark—; characterize by—; contract—; dose—; ease—; relieve—; stifle—; subdue—; suffer with—; —attacks; —disturbs; —drowns; —expels; —expresses; —indicates; —irritates; —persists; —strangles; —warns; —weakens.

COUGH (v)

adverbs

incessantly; huskily; heavily; significantly; discreetly; agonizingly; apologetically; monotonously; persistently; sinisterly; sepulchrally; muffledly; hectically; hackingly; distressingly; troublesomely; exhaustingly; wheezingly; dismally.

(See sound.)

COUNCIL

adjectives

local; advisory; official; ecclesiastical; church; intermediate; undecided; lawful; executive; general; private; separated; motley; municipal; imposing; irresponsible; elective; legislative; wicked; common; maiden.

verbs

admit to—; appoint—; assemble—; bar from—; call—; command—; dismiss—; dissolve—; frame—; gather—; hear—; herald—; sit in—; summon—; —advocates; —bans; —condemns; —decrees.

(See assembly, cabinet.)

COUNSEL
(advice)

adjectives

profound; wise; simple; humane; sane; sweet; gratuitous; anxious; politic; grave; external; insidious; weighty; sworn; heartsome; friendly; erroneous; paternal; vigorous; stout-hearted; medical; expert; wholesome; diffident; ill; intelligible; divided; prudent; crooked; unanimous; lenient; spiritual; senseless; psychiatric; valorous; sage; distracted; appealing; infernal; misguided; financial.

verbs

accept—; amend—; ask—; bestow—; condemn—; decree—; denounce—; engage—; enter—; examine—; execute—; follow—; hearken unto—; hint—; implore—; lack—; lend—; mislead—; plead—; prize—; propose—; receive—; reject—; seek—; speak—; take—; —displeases; —guides; —prevails; —sways; deliver—; forsake—.

(See advice, admonition, consultation.)

COUNSEL
(attorney)

adjectives

opposing; experienced; prosecuting; leading; clever; learned; adroit; defending; burly.

COUNSEL (v)

adverbs

earnestly; sternly; wisely; simply; humanely; sanely; gratuitously; gravely; insidiously; weightily; erroneously; paternally; medically; expertly; prudently; senselessly; leniently; sagely; misguidedly; financially.

(See advice, admonish.)

COUNSELOR

adjectives

civil; general; prime; private; prophetic; worthy.

verbs

confer with—; confide in—; empower—; entrust with—; heed—; praise—; retain—; —advises; —advocates; —charges; —cross-examines; —deliberates; —demands; —devises; —insinuates; —instructs; —orates; —perjures; —persuades; —pleads; —plots; —practises; —proposes; —recommends; —schemes; —summarizes; —sums up.

(See lawyer, attorney.)

COUNT

adjectives

grieved; amorous; fraudulent; noble; bonafide; unctuous; bogus.

COUNT (v)

adverbs

definitely; clearly; confidently; silently; legally; partially; entirely; trustingly; basically.

(See compute.)

COUNTENANCE

adjectives

pleasing; amiable; romantic; happy; polite; reverent; smiling; reckless; oval; sturdy; ponderous; eager; grotesque; alert; lugubrious; dejected; long; solemn; rueful; pathetic; idiotic; dull; expressionless; vacant; haughty; frank; serious; gracious; open; thin; simpering; bleeding; battered; convulsed; astute; ingenuous; keen; livid; pale; roseate; dark; clouded; impassive; smug; bland; remote; soft; ordinary; homely; harsh; rumpled; haggard; worn; savage; dirty; hated; evil; stern; brazen; truculent; sullen; grim; frowning; fearful; holy; large; patient; mobile; eloquent; moist; heavy; serenest; rubicund; cheerful; blooming; half-startled; vivacious; menacing; sardonic; animated; colorless; tragic; beaming; austere; whimsical; withered; undue; shiny; discontented; speaking; princely; saturnine; meager; changed; wan; melancholy; reserved; humorous; tranquil; placid; commanding; ruddy; striking; interesting; uncomely; troubled; pallid; malignant; incensed; scandalized; shriveled; truthful; overcast; saddened; branded; joyous; swarthy; repulsive; priestly; unveiled; hueless; watchful; elevated; triumphant; graceful; angry; ferocious; meditative; villainous; mottled; scarred; bloated; tragic; independent; apathetic; spirit-sighted; benignest; puzzled; sculptured; resolute; angelic; household; horror-stricken; familiar; belligerent;

blandest; quiet; sleepy; florid; meek; distorted; philosophic; martial; infantile; undenoted; piteous; ashen; marble; courageous; plain; superior; flushed; sallow; rueful.

verbs

agitate—; avert—; behold—; bury—in; change—; darken—; distress—; flush—; lift up—; pale—; sadden—; scan—; study—; unmask—; wrinkle—; —beams; —glares; —glowers; —glows; —rebukes; —resembles; —sharpens; —shines; —wavers.

(See face, appearance.)

COUNTERFEIT

adjectives

gross; specious; notorious; worthless; plausible; ostensible; cheap; clever; apish; vulgar; ingenious; tawdry.

verbs

accept—; beguile with—; circulate—; discover—; expose—; fashion—; forge—; identify—; mark—; pass—; reproduce in—; scout as—; stamp—; transform—; withdraw—; work—; —assumes; —copies; —deceives; —defrauds; —differs; —disguises; —imitates; —pretends; —resembles; —simulates.

(See imitation, copy.)

adverbs

grossly; speciously; notoriously; worthlessly; obviously; cleverly; adroitly; deftly; perfidiously; deceptively; cunningly; craftily; unscrupulously; artfully; skilfully; dexterously; ingeniously.

COUNTERMAND (v)

adverbs

dramatically; severely; unjustly; legally; treacherously; unexpectedly; rebelliously; effectively.

(See contradict, oppose.)

COUNTERPART

adjectives

precise; painful; unworthy; institutional; modern; earthly; exclusive; emotional; feminine; dense; stooped; elaborate; shrunken.

COUNTRY

adjectives

beloved; enchanting; interesting; advanced; aristocratic; conservative; quaint; small; peaceful; diminutive; weak; underdeveloped; backward; crude; great; mesa; plain; broken; art-producing; flourishing; mountainous; picturesque; cultivated; unrevealed; continental; twilight; desolate; extensive; open; nightmare; exotic; surrounding; drowsy; outlying; inefficient; dun; solitary; barren; sterile; inaccessible; agricultural; wasted; undulating; fainting; familiar; roadless; pine; principal; competing; swampy; illustrious; standardized; gracious; adoptive; thinly-settled; mysterious; semi-pastoral; neighboring; ravaged; habitable; promising; useless; indissoluble; watered; wooded; unexplored; rolling; songless; primitive; modern; poor; parsimonious; unhappy; secluded; peaceful; virgin; unspoiled; exquisite; rugged; arid; dry; dead; deserted; prairie; landscape; imperiled; proud; timbered; droll; level; populous; self-lifted; alpine; respective; lonesome; prosperous; fresh; civilized; undiscovered; fragrant; invaded; overcrowded; thankless; farming; ungraded; hard; unoffending.

verbs
assault—; benefit—; bleed—; bombard—; conquer—; depart from—; desolate—; despoil—; devastate—; distress—; dominate—; dumbfound—; exploit—; fortify—; free—; govern—; honor—; invade—; lay waste—; love—; march through—; plunge —into war; ravish—; repair to—; reverence—; return—; rouse—; ruin—; saddle —; salute—; scurry about—; serve—; travel—; unify—; —endures; —protects; —seethes; —tries.
(See territory, region, nation, state, kingdom, republic.)

COUNTRYMAN
adjectives
seditious; unpolished; rapacious; unhappy; erring; well-fed; suffering; petitionary; humble.

verbs
aid—; appeal to—; elevate—; entertain—; greet—; invite—; mold—; repatriate—; school—; subject—; unite—; uplift—; welcome—; —men aid; —men assemble; —men congregate; —men gather; —men rally; — rejoices.
(See citizen, farmer, peasant.)

COUNTRYSIDE
adjectives
remote; lonely; rolling; charming; picturesque; gossiping; peaceful; pleasant; suburban.

verbs
beautify—; defile—; denude—; depict—; describe—; devastate—; dot—; eulogize—; familiarize with—; haunt—; invade—; landscape—; paint—; plague—; preserve—; prowl about—; range—; roam—; scour—; storm—; terrorize—; unite against —; —abounds with; —echoes; —teems with.
(See country, land, farm, region.)

COUPLE
adjectives
sober; strolling; loving; inseparable; devoted; curious; ill-assorted; delectable; stately; venerable; plump; amorous; retiring; worthy; withered; happy; struggling; prudent; moneyless; elderly.

verbs
attach—; betroth—; bless—; conjoin—; connect—; dance in—s; divide—; divorce—; engage—; eye—; fasten—; halve —; join—; knit—; leash—; link—; loose—; pair—s; rend—; sever—; split—; tie—; troop in—s; unite—; yoke—.
(See partners.)

COUPLE (v)
adverbs
inevitably; normally; abnormally; hideously; logically; shrewdly; generally; poetically.
(See connect, joint.)

COUPON
adjectives
detachable; hoarded; interest-bearing; neatly-clipped; prepayment; significant; worthless; separable.

verbs
bear—; cash—; clip—; count—s; date—; detach—; identify—; issue—; present—; rate—; register—; save—; snip—; value—; —certifies; —claims; —promises; —represents.
(See certificate, ticket.)

COURAGE
adjectives
splendid; noble; peerless; sublime; superb; ardent; joyous; proud; frank; quiet; simple; patient; dogged; hot; fiery; fighting; wavering; oozing; rising; swelling; stony; unwonted; creative; philosophic; hereditary; moral; ratlike; steadfast; careless; impetuous; indomitable; shamed; unsurpassed; blended; brute; unflinching;

matchless; rare; moral; desperate; pitiful; undiminished; reawakening; husbanded; conscious; exalted; tremendous; tried; reviving; immortal; reckless; abundant; intelligent; ancient; stubborn; personal; devoted; unshaken; passive; sublime; incredible; admirable; habitual; steady; romantic; undismayed; drooping; magnificent; foolhardy; hopeful; animal; exceptional; imperious; placid; dignified; conspicuous; stand-up; renewed; native; undaunted; obdurate; revolutionary; worn; sober; knightly; unfailing; adamantine; audacious; heroic; passive.

verbs
acclaim—; applaud—; blend with—; boast—; bolster—; cultivate—; daunt—; equip with—; exhibit—; extol—; gain—; imbue with—; instill—; lose—; maintain—; manifest—; muster—; plant—; pluck up—; raise—; reflect—; renew—; require—; reveal—; rouse—; screw up—; shake—; shatter—; stiffen—; stimulate—; stir up—; strain—; strengthen—; strut with—; summon—; take—; temper—; whistle up—; —droops; —endures; —flags; —mounts; —rises; —runs high.

(See bravery, fortitude, heroism, valor.)

COURAGEOUS
adverbs
dangerously; rashly; temperamentally; alarmingly; fantastically; foolhardily; colossally; breath-takingly; terribly; admirably; dramatically; notoriously; crazily; strangely; singularly; amazingly; recklessly; unbelievably; foolishly; romantically; heroically; youthfully; boyishly; disconcertingly; extravagantly; splendidly; nobly; superbly; proudly; quietly; patiently; doggedly; enduringly; morally; steadfastly; impetuously; consciously; stubbornly; devotedly; personally; sublimely; habitually; magnificently; calmly.

COURSE
(*direction*)
adjectives
splendid; admirable; sedate; sagacious; reasonable; sensible; serpentine; winding; sinuous; dizzy; desultory; twisting; circuitous; irregular; roundabout; sanguinary; rich; airy; resistless; dangerous; extreme; disagreeable; meteoric; advisable; straight; secretive; indefensible; devious; speedy; politic; heedless; prudent; fixed; middle; needful; unexplored; comfortable; unenvious; erratic; alternative; traditional; len-

ient; stupid; evil; dreary; fatal; mild; tortuous; endowed; systematic; peevish; indirect; frail; zigzag; feverish; rigorous; magnanimous; decisive; stony; immutable; desperate; exemplary; circular; natural; prescribed; luminous; unsilent; prolonged; headlong; initiatory; arduous; hereditary; extreme; strange; motley; conquering; skyward; unscrupulous; uniform; impetuous; tangential; precarious; profligate; tardy; basalt; tearless; curvilinear; lusty; coercive; orderly; ambiguous; long; shady; rapid; endless; wheeling; intermitting; destined; practical; furious; fair; bloody; normal; excellent; spherical; tranquil; doubtful; victorious; aimless; uneventful; peculiar; respective; contrary; irresistible; economical; diurnal; swift; precipitate; majestic; preparatory.

verbs
advance—; alter—; appoint—; bend—; blow off—; chart—; check— commend—; conceal—; condemn—; continue in—; cut off from—; decide on—; denote—; determine—; dictate—; direct—; disturb—; drift in—; embark on—; fix—; follow—; hinder—; hold—; illumine—; impede—; interrupt—; lead—; leave to—; map—; mark—; modify—; order—; outrun—; persevere in—; pervert—; plot—; praise—; pursue—; rebuke—; resolve on—; return to—; reverse—; run—; set—; settle on—; shape—; shun—; steer—; stem—; stick to—; subdue—; swerve from—; travel—; tread—; turn—; upbraid—; veer from—; wander off—; wing—; —fluctuates; —runs; —shifts; —winds; —zigzags.

(See direction, line, conduct.)

COURSE
(*study*)
adjectives
advanced; logical; pedagogic; technical; rigorous; difficult; condensed.

verbs
abandon—; change—; choose—; complete—; comprise—; conduct—; cut—; deride—; divide into—s; elect—; emphasize—; establish—; evaluate—; finish—; flunk (colloq.)—; follow—; fulfill—; initiate—; model—upon; pursue—; renew—; revise—; set up—; speed up—; —equips; —intends to; —prepares.

COURSE (v)

adverbs
tortuously; swiftly; windingly; circuitously; sinuously; irregularly; deviously; erratically; impetuously; tranquilly; irresistibly; precipitately.
(See travel.)

COURT
(*enclosed yard*)

adjectives
cobbled; gravelly; dusty; muddy; noisy; paved; tiled; rubbish-filled; neglected; sunless; gloomy; discouraging.

verbs
approach—; besiege—; build—; cross—; fill—; guard—; measure—; pace—; retire to—; roof—; shut up in—.

COURT
(*law*)

adjectives
vested; open; stuffy; instituted; hospitable; primitive; voluntary; spiritual; temporal; silent; petrified; superior; imperial; gloomy; papal; punctilious; murky; merciless; respectable; sapient; strict; corrupt; packed; primitive; competent; inferior; international; circuit; criminal.

verbs
adjourn—; adjudicate in—; beseech—; blockade—; call into—; coerce—; defy—; dismiss—; exploit—; hale into—; haul into—; liberalize—; override—; overrule —; pack—; petition in—; preside over—; reform—; rejuvenate—; remake—; resort to—; revamp—; strangle—; submit to—; sway—; tamper with—; vow in—; —awards; —convenes; —fines; —grants; —impounds; —judges; —recognizes; —renders a decision; —restrains; —upholds.
(See tribunal, judge.)

COURT
(*royal*)

adjectives
ceremonious; tavern; ostentatious; revolutionary; dilapidated; ecclesiastical; spacious; cloistered; envious; weedy; pontifical; assiduous; ambitious; magnolia; pompous; gloomy; admirable; sportive; untidy; dripping; bosky.

verbs
break up—; dispatch to—; entertain at—; establish—; fete at—; forsake—; hold—;

honor at—; join—; muster—; open—; present at—; preside at—; station at—; —flourishes; —glories in.

COURT (v)

adverbs
lustfully; assiduously; steadfastly; absurdly; ostentatiously; subtly; romantically; devotedly; shyly; masterfully; wildly; incessantly; languidly; impetuously.
(See attract, woo.)

COURTEOUS

adverbs
exquisitely; deeply; quietly; deferentially; perfunctorily; thoughtfully; extravagantly; tenderly; formally; naturally; dangerously; scarcely; scantily; traditionally; languidly; lazily; grimly; cordially; outwardly; genuinely; provokingly; gracefully; particularly; charmingly; gravely; loftily; meticulously; punctiliously; unfailingly; inherently; reverently; suspiciously; unexpectedly; especially.

COURTESY

adjectives
matchless; perfect; fine; gentle; exquisite; spiritual; deep; quiet; understanding; deferential; insinuating; decent; stately; dignified; perfunctory; thoughtful; extravagant; strained; serious; benevolent; stolid; dissembling; unclean; tender; formal; condescending; studied; national; natural; dangerous; official; gracious; scant; neighborly; poor; traditional; senatorial; caressing; straining; languid; special; grim; pressing; obvious; common; cordial; outward; intolerable; particular; graceful; charming; impersonal; doubtful; princely; international; oily; obliging; grave; last; lofty; wayward; patient; rigid; genuine; meticulous; unfailing; cold; automatic; southern; foreign; mickle; inherent; utmost; unusual; sacred; measured; novel.

verbs
accord—; air—; allow—; deny—; deserve—; disdain—; greet with—; imbue with—; misplace—; offer—; overstrain—; praise—; respect—; return—; scorn—; show—; strain—; stress—; temper with—.
(See politeness.)

COURTIER

adjectives
hovering; splendid; decrepit; senile; veteran; garrulous; subtle; shrewd; wary; pompous; vainglorious; sapient; extrava-

gant; absolute; gallant; dissipated; smirking; expectant; avaricious; eulogizing; gaudiest.

COURTSHIP

adjectives

strange; careful; subtle; devoted; romantic; shy; masterful; wild; long; gradual; unhappy; customary; incessant; orthodox; languid; harassed.

verbs

attend in—; chaperon—; conduct—; delight in—; flatter during—; involve in—; lengthen—; pay—; pledge in—; prolong—; pursue with—; reject—; respond to—; revel in—; rush—; sway by—; verse in—; —ends; —expires; —flags; —softens.

(See friendship.)

COUSIN

adjectives

worthy; philological; valiant; capricious; stalwart; pious; enormous; gentle; favorite; distant; pallid; bloody; aristocratic; impecunious; remote; loutish.

COVE

adjectives

fascinating; shallow; sunlit; quiet; wooded; eddying; drowsy; snug.

COVENANT

adjectives

sacred; solemn; binding; common; perpetual; broad; eternal.

verbs

agree upon—; alter—; annul—; break—; confirm—; declare—; defile—; destroy—; draw up—; ensure—; enter into—; establish—; forsake—; invert—; mind—; obey—; profane—; record—; respect—; sever—; stabilize—; stipulate in—; swear to—; transgress—; void—.

COVER

adjectives

fairest; ephemeral; glazed; dewy; precious; enameled; soiled; coarse; garish; friendly; illuminated; excellent; practical; floor; protective; grassy; underdone; loathsome; reversible; detachable; flimsy; inmost; frail; weedy; sorry; luxuriant; ghostly; variegated; conical.

verbs

attach—; clap on—; form—; improvise—; lift—; ornament—; raise—; remove—; screw on—; slide—on; take to—; wrap in—; —clothes; —conceals; —defends; —encloses; —envelops; —hides; —hinges; —overlays; —overspreads; —projects; —protects; —rests upon; —screens; —shelters; —surfaces.

(See case, lid, canopy, roof, spread, shelter.)

COVER (v)

adverbs

instinctively; adequately; grotesquely; insufficiently; inadequately; exhaustively; partially; garishly; protectively; loathsomely; flimsily; fraily; luxuriantly; conically.

(See conceal, hide.)

COVET (v)

adverbs

burningly; obviously; lustfully; jealously; bloodthirstily; sinfully; viciously; insanely; instinctively; economically; vulgarly; basely; detestably; infamously.

(See crave.)

COVETED

adverbs

eagerly; highly; passionately; enviously; wickedly; earnestly; excitedly; justifiably; sinfully; fondly; impatiently; keenly; hungrily; greedily; desirously; wishfully; wistfully; insatiably; avidly; madly; ambitiously; rabidly; invidiously; jealously; yearningly; ardently; curiously; fervently.

COVETOUSNESS

adjectives

excited; justifiable; bloodthirsty; unholy; inordinate; eager; rapacious.

COW

adjectives

serene; spotted; fat; milch; gentle; gaunt; fractious; ambitious; sad; mooing; contented.

verbs

breed —s; feed —s; herd —s; infect —; inspect —; raise —; slaughter —; test —; —s graze; —s huddle; —s leap; —s lumber; —s pasture; —s plod; —s roam; —s trail.

(See cattle, animal.)

COWARD

adjectives

thrasonical; arrant; vulgar; miserable; hulking; base; egotistic; contemptible; mannish; notable; faithless; detestable; abject; conscienceless; crafty; blaspheming; blatant; devout; infernal; pale; infamous.

verbs
bar —; brand as —; denounce —; designate as —; develop into —; intimidate —; ostracize —; proclaim —; regale —; reproach —; slay —; sneer at —; stigmatize as —; taunt —; — faints; — falters; — fears; — flees; — pales; — pleads; — protects; — shakes; — shies; — slanders; — slinks; — trembles; — whimpers; — yields.

COWARDICE
adjectives
empty; servile; moral; ineffable; vilest; abject; unexpected; palpable; strange.

verbs
banish —; brand with —; breed —; charge with —; conceal —; curb —; denounce —; display —; exhibit —; feign —; flaunt —; flee in —; hide —; loathe —; mark —; overcome —; protest —; rage at —; soil with —; vindicate of —; — defiles; — demoralizes; — shames.

(See timidity.)

COWARDLY
adverbs
abjectly; unexpectedly; vilely; feebly; shamefully; suddenly; basely; miserably; contemptibly; hideously; detestably; abominably; pitiably; notoriously; infamously; secretly; pathologically; helplessly; hopelessly; embarrassingly; pathetically; irremediably; consciously.

COWBELL
adjectives
jangling; battered; brassy; silvery; tinkling; musical; matutinal; vespertine.

verbs
attach—; hang on—; respond to—; tie on—; —clangs; —clanks; —dangles; — directs; —echoes; —greets; —jangles; — suggests; —sways; —swings; —tinkles; —tolls.

(See bell.)

COWBIRD
adjectives
attending; herd-following; hoarsely-commenting; perching.

verbs
—crowds out; —gurgles; —intrudes; — warbles.

(See bird.)

COWBOY
adjectives
elemental; daredevil; equestrian; bright; crooning; weather-beaten; saddle-hardened; hard-riding.

verbs
employ—s; quarter—s; —brands; —breaks horses; —breaks loose; —charges; —corrals; —drives; —herds; —lassoes; — mounts; —punches cattle; —ropes; —rounds up; —rustles; —stampedes; —trails; — whoops; —wrangles.

COWER (*v*)
adverbs
gloomily; weakly; shrinkingly; ignobly; basely; abjectly; servilely; palpably; pusillanimously; spinelessly.

(See crouch, squat.)

COY
adverbs
timidly; diffidently; shyly; modestly; retiringly; bashfully; blushingly; humbly; nervously; demurely; primly; pleasantly; adorably; uneasily; engagingly; gracefully; captivatingly; delightfully; sweetly.

COYOTE
adjectives
gaunt; night-prowling; howling; sneaking; sly; wary; pusillanimous.

verbs
frighten by—s; trap—s; —s abound; —s attack; —s bark; —burrows; —s carry off; —cries; —destroys; —digs; —gallops; — hides; —howls; —infests; —inhabits; — laps; —lurks; —mangles; —prowls; — ranges; —screams; —scurries; —slinks; —sneaks; —s surround; —wails; —yaps; —yips; —yowls.

(See animal.)

CRAB
adjectives
roasted; reluctant; soft-shelled; luscious; invading; semi-transparent; side-walking; scurrying; sodden; swiftly-moving.

verbs
broil—; capture—; catch—; devil—; roast —; steam—; —claws; —crawls; —weighs.

CRABBED
adverbs
bitterly; unnecessarily; unwarrantably; vexatiously; sourly; perplexingly; natural-

ly; innately; horribly; detestably; abominably; persistently; obnoxiously; unpleasantly; constantly; permanently; incurably; unreasonably; intractably; stubbornly; plaguedly; discourteously; rudely; uncivilly; tactlessly; coolly; pertly; obtrusively; snarlingly.

CRACK (blow)

adjectives
sharp; smart; mannish; punitive; admonitory; disciplinary; surreptitious; **vindictive**; solar plexus; resounding.

CRACK (fissure)

adjectives
shallow; minute; widening; seamy; ragged; fearful; devastating.

verbs
close—; fill—; peer through—; seal—; seep through—; shine through—; squeeze into—; stretch out—; trace—; widen—; —breaks; —bursts; —damages; —endangers; —gapes; —opens; —separates; —weakens; —widens; —yawns.
(See chasm, gap, opening.)

CRACKLE

adjectives
snapping; faint; sickening; brittle; cheery; warning; ominous; starchy; silken.

CRACKLE (v)

adverbs
cheerily; fiercely; industriously; faintly; sickeningly; furiously; threateningly.
(See sound.)

CRADLE

adjectives
tiny; earthen; equatorial; leafy; stony; hollow; procreant; clumsy; swaddling; unostentatious; animal-skin; rocking.

verbs
attend—; bar—; carry in—; decorate—; deck—; discard—; dream in—; fall from—; jig—; lull in—; mount—; nurture in—; repose in—; rest in—; rock—; shelter in—; sleep in—; snatch from—; stifle in—; sway—; swing—; unveil—; watch over—.
(See bed.)

CRADLE (v)

adverbs
comfortingly; endearingly; maternally; cozily; domestically.
(See bed.)

CRAFT (boat)

adjectives
stately; leaky; weatherly; ponderous; ghostly; frail-looking; multitudinous (pl); tidy; ill-equipped; clumsy; unseaworthy; aging; tiny; speedy; graceful; small; trim; little; slow; toiling; disabled; staunch; makeshift; slender; strange-looking; waterlogged; ridiculous.

CRAFT (skill)

adjectives
hellish; inexhaustible; vulpine; consummate; purloined; mechanical; extraordinary; manual; devilish; elfin; earthly; astonishing; slippery; subtle; inveterate; intervening; peaceful; ancient; coy; crude; indolent; pleasurable; strange-looking; diabolical; contentious; waterlogged.

verbs
apply—; beguile with—; counterfeit—; devote to—; display—; exhibit—; follow—; learn—; master—; perform with—; pursue—; skill in—; study—; trick with—; verse in—; —deceives; —occupies; —thrives.
(See skill, trade.)

CRAFTINESS

adjectives
uncanny; cold; weird; deft; astounding; practiced.

CRAFTSMAN

adjectives
expert; skilled; master; trained; seasoned; meticulous; experienced; sincere; able; erudite; polished; thoroughgoing; wandering; sedentary.

CRAFTSMANSHIP

adjectives
rare; unusual; exquisite; delicate; centuries-old; superb; authentic; progressive; skilled; custom.

CRAFTY

adverbs
suavely; subtly; urbanely; artfully; designingly; dangerously; commercially; alarmingly; suspiciously; extremely; singularly;

profoundly; unexpectedly; deftly; astutely; inscrutably; habitually; warily; cautiously; wisely; invariably; politically; deliberately; shamefully; fiendishly; expertly; horribly.

CRAG

adjectives
stupendous; bare; massive; far-distant; gray; lofty; inaccessible; steep; tottering; yellow; weathered; sustaining; overhanging; dense-wooded; fantastic; impregnable; rocky; mountain; shaggy; slippery; shrubless; jagged; splintered; accumulated; bald; jutting; morselled; whinstone; descendent; beetling; giant-snouted; lichencovered; dizzy; gaunt; lordly; shredded; precipitous; storm-washed; airy.

verbs
ascend—; batter—; beat—; blow from—; catch on—; clasp—; cling to—; expose—; peer from—; precipitate from—; scale—; scan—; storm—; strand on—; swing from—; topple from—; —hinders; —juts out; —menaces; —slopes; climb—.
(See cliff, rock.)

CRAM (v)

adverbs
completely; reputedly; fully; intellectually; enormously ;swellingly; hoggishly; bestially.
(See crowd, squeeze.)

CRAMP

adjectives
agonizing; distressing; hindering; musclefettering; paralyzing; torturing; violent.

verbs
affect with—; alleviate—; cause—; contract with—; ease—; massage—; predispose to—; produce—; rack with—; seize with—; take with—; —agonizes; —attacks; —benumbs; —constricts; —extends; —incapacitates; —knots; —numbs; —pains; —paralyzes; —pinches; —restrains; —stiffens; —tortures.
(See pain.)

CRANE
(*bird*)

adjectives
eerie-sounding; frog-questing; mournful; shadowy; ungainly; voracious; eternally-wading.

verbs
—alights; —antics; —circles; —clowns; —croaks; —dances; —drifts down; —

evades; —hops; —leaps; —skips; —stalks over; —trumpets; —wades; —whoops.
(See bird.)

CRANK

adjectives
ridiculous; complete; usual; veritable; unenviable; decided.

CRANK (v)

adverbs
laboriously; sweatingly; difficultly; stiffly; energetically; spiritedly.
(See turn.)

CRASH

adjectives
ominous; incessant (pl); reverberating; thunderous; dazzling; successive (pl); hideous; simultaneous (pl); fearful; confused; heavy; blinding; railroad; grinding; tremendous; almighty; tumultuous; occasional; mighty; light; rolling; heart-shaking; impending; vicious; loud; fatal; resounding; dull; heavy; smashing; distant; disastrous; terrific; rending; ear-splitting; dangerous; sudden; hollow; rhythmic; splintering.

verbs
avert—; avoid—; escape—; produce—; witness—; —breaks; —bursts; —crushes; —dashes; —resounds; —ruins; —shatters; —shivers; —shocks; —smashes; —splinters; —thunders.
(See noise, collapse, ruin, failure.)

CRASH (v)

adverbs
sickeningly; haphazardly; ominously; incessantly; reverberatingly; thunderously; simultaneously; heavily; grindingly; tumultuously; rollingly; fatally; resoundingly; disastrously; terrifically; rendingly; earsplittingly; hollowly; splinteringly.
(See collapse, smash.)

CRASSNESS

adjectives
unutterable; despicable; undescribable; hopeless; irritating; inane.

CRATER

adjectives
extinct; ancient; gaping; active; grasscovered; weed-grown; smoking; exhausted; submerged; cindery; cuplike; thundering; roaring; seething.

verbs

fly over—; form—; run from—; —boils; —
bubbles; —discharges; —disgorges; —
ejects; —emits; —erupts; —forms; —furrows; —hardens; —pours out; —roars; —
rumbles; —seethes; —simmers; —smokes;
—spouts; —throws up.

(See volcano.)

CRAVAT

adjectives

unknotted; voluminous; unkempt; nice;
well-chosen; correct; becoming; flowing;
resplendent.

verbs

admire—; color—; display—; knot—; purchase—; purvey—s; spot—; tie—; —
adorns; —blazes; —encircles; —harmonizes; —muffles; —ornaments; —protects;
—shields; —shocks.

(See tie, necktie.)

CRAVE (*v*)

adverbs

irresistibly; humbly; instinctively; insatiably; inordinately; intensely; earnestly;
unappeasingly; incessantly; uncontrollably;
violently; persistently; abnormally; vaguely; maternally; erotically; spiritually; insensately.

(See desire, want.)

CRAVEN

adjectives

stricken; confessed; marked; cowering;
fearful; cringing; crass.

CRAVING

adjectives

intense; earnest; unappeasable; eager; incessant; uncontrollable; violent; persistent;
tenacious; unbeautiful; spasmodic; frivolous; abnormal; maternal; unsatisfied;
mysterious; endless; forbidden; sporadic;
instinctive; premature; erotic; insatiable;
cruel; vague; mastered; spiritual; insensate; intermittent.

verbs

annul—; appease—; conceal—; dispatch—;
ease—; frown on—; harbor—; indulge—;
master—; quell—; repress—; resist—;
satisfy—; still—; stir up—; sublimate—;
—overpowers; —seizes.

(See passion, appetite, hunger, desire,
longing, leaning, entreaty.)

CRAWL (*v*)

adverbs

interminably; sluggishly; softly; wearily;
tortuously; bestially; dejectedly; sorrowfully; toilingly; determinedly.

(See grovel, creep.)

CRAZE

adjectives

fashionable; dull; amusement; midsummer;
newest; freakish; passing; temporary.

verbs

adopt—; denounce—; despise—; develop
into—; fancy—; follow—; ignore—; inaugurate—; overcome—; succumb to—;
—affects; —attracts; —dies; —fades; —
flashes; —seizes; —spreads.

(See mania, caprice.)

CREAK (*v*)

adverbs

stridently; irritatingly; monotonously; continually; disturbingly; intermittently;
rhythmically.

(See sound.)

CREAKING

adjectives

strange; cautious; imperceptible; massive;
ear-teasing; inaudible.

CREAM

adjectives

rich; pure; oily; stainless; intellectual;
vanishing; rejuvenating; penetrating; superb; cosmetic; dulcet; soothing; massage;
unguent.

verbs

add—; anoint with—; apply—; beat—;
churn—; convert—; dilute—; filter—;
form—; gather—; mature—; mix—; moist-
en with—; pasteurize—; purify—; rub
in—; separate—; serve—; skim—; sour—;
spread—; stir—; sweeten—; whip—; —
foams; —froths; —greases; —mantles;
—rises.

CREAMERY

adjectives

spotless; inviting; appetizing; efficient;
germ-proof; hermetic; ship-shape.

CREASE (*v*)

adverbs

deftly; readily; disgustingly; offensively;
intolerably.

(See wrinkle.)

CREATE (v)

adverbs

obviously; artistically; unconsciously; independently; unexpectedly; painstakingly; artificially; fantastically; specially; fancifully; complicatedly; permanently; forcibly; harmoniously; uniquely; individually; abstractly; brilliantly; imaginatively; inferiorly; gigantically; intellectually; sublimely; beneficently; ceaselessly; figuratively; literally.

(See make, produce.)

CREATION

adjectives

huge; fantastic; special; foreordained; artistic; fanciful; witty; reflective; grave; complicated; primal; permanent; sculpturesque; forcible; surrounding; psychological; brute; harmonious; unique; individual; abstract; brilliant; dormant; pedigreed; rhythmical; coordinating; visible; ungainly; imaginary; human; various; wide-reaching; evolutionary; artificial; immediate; divine; patented; rejuvenated; pendulous; previous; inferior; gigantic; poetical; violent; splendid; serio-comic; aboriginal; false; aerial; memorable; intellectual; infinite; approved; bountiful; special; sublime; beneficent; genial; warm; inanimate; travailing; catastrophic.

verbs

abolish—; behold—; condemn—; contradict—; counterfeit—; curse—; grasp—; illustrate—; improve—; inspire—; mar—; understand—; —collapses; —reflects.

(See world, universe.)

CREATOR

adjectives

responsible; unworthy; rival; benevolent; conscious; omnipotent.

verbs

betray—; consecrate to—; eulogize—; honor—; praise—; revere—; spring from—; worship—; —animates; —decrees; —divines; —empowers; —fashions; —grants; —moulds; —ordains; —originates; —produces; —reveals; —rules; —works.

(See God, inventor.)

CREATURE

adjectives

rare; likable; upstanding; honest-looking; lovable; admirable; brilliant; luscious; docile; glorious; winning; fine; great-hearted; fascinating; gentle; amiable; demure; marvelous; shy; thin; shortsighted; anemic; limitary; tiny; spiritless; forlorn; obscure; slipshod; ravishing; frugal; despicable; smitten; archaic; perennial; little; dull; yellowish-white; faithful-looking; foolish; struggling; furry; rational; perfect; smooth; pretty; plausible; absurd; doll-like; finite; delicate; sentimental; divine; web-footed; insensible; industrious; drugging; stricken; nasty; ill-bred; inconsequent; voracious; carnivorous; graceful; effeminate; singular; crawling; eyeless; fictitious; overflowing; threadbare; fantastic; bewildering; amphibious; pusillanimous; sensitive; hideous; perverse; desperate; inquisitive; silly; helpless; dependent; brutal; faithful; charming; loathsome; formidable; clear-eyed; harmless; fiery; frail; overgrown; carnal; phlegmatic; unhappy; purest; plainest; kind-hearted; magnanimous; artless; predatory; ever-interesting; nervous; timorous; blunt; pleasant; clambering; monstrous; indigenous; affectionate; sensible; cordial; loving; sweetest; dearest; stealthy; gregarious; insignificant; decrepit; two-fold; strenuous; easy; anxious; poor; unteachable; writhing; tortured; piteous; strange; romantic; sickly; faded; kindly; stout; untidy-looking; flowery; harlequin-like; ridiculous; glorious; foul; infinitesimal; hapless; reasonable; amendable; worthy; horned; love-maddened; coarse-grained; unwashed; flexible; noxious; hairless; diminutive; beastly; poor-spirited; unpolished; veiled; healthy-looking; governmental; discouraged; mendacious; precious; paltry; good-humored; vile; sagacious; dismal-looking; vagrant; nomadic; ferocious; primest; stupid; exquisite; grotesque; exotic; miserable; intellectual; irascible; insufferable; silk-clothed; obliging; goodly; inarticulate; new-made; natural; crooked; shameless; fawn-eyed; gigantic; bewitching; non-aggressive; fickle; thoughtful; grave; wistful; tolerable; human; fearful; sincere; cherubic; yearling; dainty; tallowy; slight; girlish; dawdling; beautiful; ravenous; injudicious; timid; sinful; driven; sweated; magnificent; doe-eyed; clinging; frenzied; heartless; ferocious-looking; impudent; fairest; mongrel; dying; wasted; vivid; earnest; grasping; sylphlike; fine-looking, gorgeous-looking; pretty; dark-eyed; spirited; handsome; elegant; dazzling; furtive; crafty; scheming; wily; baffling; uncanny; wise; cunning; uncouth; spineless; affrighted; gentle; meek-spirited; weak; weary; luckless; poor; humble; long-legged; gaunt; gangling; angular; ragged; emaciated; loose-jointed; lanky; cadaverous-faced; weird; strange; odd-looking; stodgy; porkish; kind; plump; flabby; huge; muscular; poised; self-confident; vital; energetic; big; forthright; hearty; blithe; buxom; sprightly; flippant; self-assured; capricious; sad; ugly; humdrum; stunted; strong-willed; stubborn; obstinate; queer-looking; humpbacked; passive; senseless; idiotic; silliest-looking; star-eyed; sinuous; beady-eyed; slim; bird-like; yellow-striped; half-wild; shy; feathered; migratory; feline; screeching; aquatic; lone; marsh; biting; crawling; forest; pathological; merry; wild; thankless; winged; troublesome; bloodthirsty; obstinate; mangy-looking; broken; disintegrated; dirty; disheveled; unshorn; emaciated; filthy; ragged; detestable; menacing; primitive; worthless; undesirable; vicious-looking; tarnished; distressing; careless; wretched; half-blind; tottering; imaginary; mythical; fastidious; talkative; plain; huddle; two-legged; newly-evolved; vehement; gaudy; unvapory.

verbs
cage—; curse—; despise—; distress—; eye—; feed—; hunt—; hurt—; kill—; loathe—; oppress—; slay—; tame—; torture—; trap—; —echoes; —senses; —stirs; —walks.
(See being, animal.)

CREDENCE
adjectives
qualified; ready; partial; definite; unwarranted.

CREDENTIALS
adjectives
required; college; personal; time-tested; intellectual; valid; sufficient.

verbs
accept—; arm with—; bear—; check—; display—; doubt—; falsify—; forge—; forward—; honor—; investigate—; lose—; present—; provide with—; sign—; —attest to; —entitle; —reveal.
(See testimonial.)

CREDIBLE
adverbs
deeply; implicitly; actually; presumably; reliably; soberly; conceivably; certainly; assuredly; possibly; positively; impress-

ively; fairly; reasonably; plausibly; probably; speciously; potentially; peradventurously; haply; obviously; unreservedly.

CREDIT
adjectives
unlimited; tentative; threatened; retirement; weakening; unquestioned; everlasting; cooperative; implicit; highest; fullest; personal; moral; comparative; small; unfailing; exhausted; practical; rescinded; domestic; long-term; foreign; extended.

verbs
accept—; accumulate—; ascribe to—; bolster up—; claim—; deserve—; expand—; extend—; favor with—; honor—; obtain —; redound—; rehabilitate—; secure—; share—; strain—; warp—.
(See confidence, trust, faith, prestige, influence.)

CREDIT (v)
adverbs
conveniently; ignorantly; tentatively; everlastingly; implicitly; fully; personally; morally; unfailingly; practically; locally; formally; unhesitatingly.
(See believe.)

CREDITABLE
adverbs
highly; altogether; admirably; becomingly; deservedly; duly; richly; splendidly; notably; eminently; conspicuously; remarkably.

CREDITOR
adjectives
importunate; inexorable; sourest; bloody; persistent; detaining; unfeeling.

verbs
avoid—; cajole—; dismiss—; escape—; evade—; hold off—; pay—; satisfy—; settle with—; —s rise; —assails; —demands; —depends; — descends upon; —s dwindle; —forces; —harasses; —importunes; —menaces; —stands; —sues; — threatens; —trusts.

CREDULITY
adjectives
good-natured; popular; heretical; human; great; unfathomable; reluctant; common; ignorant; curious; scornful; emotional; unshakable; grave; innocent.

verbs

appeal to—; assume—; attack—; bless with—; clothe in—; disguise—; invite—; lose—; preserve—; produce—; register—; remove—; strain—; tax—; transcend—; value—; —accepts; —aids; —astounds; —expires.

(See faith, belief.)

CREDULOUS

adverbs

good-naturedly; reluctantly; instantly; readily; gullibly; foolishly; thoughtlessly; unthinkingly; boyishly; eagerly; enthusiastically; fondly; blindly; innocently; gravely; stupidly; superstitiously; idiotically; laughably; guilelessly; artlessly; ingenuously; childishly; ardently; ignorantly.

CREED

adjectives

everlasting; common; rigid; narrow; respective (pl); noble; vulgar; delicious; confused; fashionable; senseless; rebellious; especial; ancient; healthful; soulless; hopeful; dominant; creative; polemic; cynical; procreative; strange; primeval; adopted; universal; heavenly.

verbs

accept—; adopt—; advance—; alter—; bind to—; displace—; fix—; follow—; formulate—; instill—; institute—; learn—; scoff at—; shake—; support—; subscribe to—; tangle—; teach—; —decays; —summarizes.

(See belief, faith.)

CREEK

adjectives

brawling; briny; winding; log-jammed; silvery; yearning; cheery; echoing; tortuous; emerald; dry; dirty; ice-fringed; dimpled; swollen; fresh-water; unruly; hidden; muddy; scanty; cool; pebbled; tiny; whispering; roaring.

verbs

bridge—; dam—; explore—; fish—; follow —; navigate—; paddle down—; span—; wade in—; —babbles; —bends; —branches off; —dances; —drenches; —gurgles; —harbors; —irrigates; —joins; —overflows; —penetrates; —sings; —twists; —widens; —winds.

(See brook, stream.)

CREEP (v)

adverbs

slyly; mechanically; noiselessly; timidly; cautiously; blindly; stealthily; piteously; meekly; invisibly; mysteriously; ultimately.

(See crawl, grovel.)

CREEPER

adjectives

blooming; luxuriant; spiky; parasitic; interlacing; indigenous; deciduous; poisonous; woody.

CREPE

adjectives

sheer; rayon; tailored; trim; crinkly; clinging; webby.

CRESCENDO

adjectives

rending; sudden; deafening; wild; gradual; muffled.

CRESCENT

adjectives

silvery; paling; sardonic; delicate; sharp; black; stormy.

verbs

adopt—as; attach—; carry—; carve—; decorate with—; design—; employ—; form —; mold—; ornament with—; rest upon—; shape—; trace—; —embellishes; —fades; —glimmers; —signifies; —symbolizes.

CRESS

adjectives

matted; mantling; pungent; tasty; crisp; fresh.

CRESSET

adjectives

blazing; burning; hanging; pendent; swinging; polished; shining; glowing.

CREST

adjectives

ferny; higher; snow-streaked; silver; flamelike; fire-tipped; glittering; ancestral; blazing; upturned; haughty; snowy; kindled; polished; gory; uncontrolled; crimson; golden; bald; towering; glimmering; turret; flaming; stainless; overhanging; compassed; princely; confused; proud; slide-scarred; knife-edged; cloven; tranquil; hissing; lofty; whitening; windy; cockatoo; mountain; jagged; distant.

verbs
affix—; bear—; brighten—; dance on—; elevate to—; erect—; fix—; helmet with—; let fall—; mount to—; plate with—; recognize—; seal with—; strike—; —bristles; —crowns; —droops; —ornaments; —plumes; —signifies; —symbolizes; —undulates; —waves; —wreathes.
(See comb, crown.)

CREVICE
adjectives
barren; rock; narrow; winding; snug; sunken; distant; mysterious.

CREW
adjectives
rollicking; skulking; pestilent; fiendish; motley; vulgar; lachrymose; revolutionary; enthusiastic; marauding; rebellious; persevering; well-organized; worthless; mumbling; rough-and-ready; scribbling; numerous; humorous; back-biting; unhallowed; horrid; dilapidated; whining; besotted; stammering; dispirited; oriental-looking; strange; gaunt; merry; mutinous; gay; adventurous; rugged; coarse-fibred; indigent; stout; burly; handy; unruly; sleepy; ground; marooned; insubordinate; changing; sullen; annihilated; rascal; tiring; nefarious; madcap; banished.

verbs
address—; arouse—; assemble—; augment —; banish—; bestir—; captain—; capture —; command—; consult—; control—; curse—; direct—; dissemble—; engage—; enlarge—; exclude—; gather—; hire—; order—; organize—; oversee—; quarter—; rescue—; rule—; —accomplishes; —boards; —conspires; —embarks; —mans; —mutinies; —rebels; —revels.
(See crowd, company.)

CRIB
adjectives
lace-ruffled; comfortable; safeguarded; padded; wicker; swinging; basket.

CRICKET
adjectives
lusty; creaking; humming; chirping; drumming; incessant.

verbs
plague with—s; —chirps; —fiddles; —rubs; —sings; —shrills.
(See insect.)

CRIME
adjectives
cherished; wretched; horrible; nameless; consummate; atrocious; conspicuous; inhuman; futile; prevailing; heinous; juvenile; unmilitary; sexual; solitary; hideous; unpardonable; darkest; inexplicable; absolute; flagitious; imputed; dreadful; reiterated; malicious; enormous; grave; legalized inexpiable; foul; dastardly; monstrous; locutionary; godless; devastating; cloistered; subsequent; gory; imaginable; heathenish; organized; earthly; unknowing; successful; petty; blackest; heart-crazing; flagrant; diversified; gloomy; aboriginal; perfect; crowning; greedy; calculated; cunning; unnatural; nefarious; infamous; barbarous; abominable; obscene; grisly; violent; gruesome; scandalous; brutal; fiendish; cowardly; ungrateful; hair-raising; unpunished; unsolved; unprevented; serious; professional; modern; vocal; attempted; conceivable; pitiful; incredible.

verbs
abet—; accuse of—; allege—; alleviate—; assail—; atone for—; avenge—; avoid—; betray—; breed—; cancel—; charge with —; check—; cloak—; condone—; contemplate—; contrive—; cover—; detect—; diminish—; divulge—; eradicate—; expiate —; extenuate—; fatten on—; grapple with —; hatch—; impute—to; involve in—; mark with—; perpetuate—; plot—; predispose to—; prosecute—; punish—; reconstruct—; restrain—; sentence for—; smash—; sully with—; suspect of—; taint with—; uncover—; urge—; witness—; —flourishes; —stains; —thrives.
(See offense, misdeed, sin, wrong.)

CRIMINAL
adjectives
irreclaimable; petty; condemned; roving; professional; notorious; dangerous; vicious; utter; conscienceless; piratical; organized (pl); runaway; calculating; confirmed; willful; visible; timorous; skulking; bloody; blackjacked; ruthless; hypothetical; potential; clever; perfect; experienced; frenzied; hardened; desperate; miserable; unfortunate; parricidal; adult; cinematographic; self-confessed; grotesque; incipient; enterprising; habitual; elusive; courageous; fleeing; daring.

verbs

apprehend—; arrest—; charge—; close in on—; coddle—; convict—; detain—; develop into—; harbor—; infest with—s; involve—; lash—; mark—; parole—; penalize—; point out—; pounce upon—; prosecute—; punish—; rehabilitate—; restrain—; retrieve—; round up—; sentence —; shame—; thwart—; —commits; —s congregate; —defies; —habituates; — haunts; —indulges; —plots; —reforms; —repents; —rifles; —schemes; —stalks; —swindles.

(See culprit, prisoner.)

adverbs

shockingly; outrageously; brutally; grossly; basely; iniquitously; despicably; abominably; pestilentially; accursedly; damnably; diabolically; infernally; noxiously; vilely; virulently; preposterously; corruptly; atrociously; viciously; profligately; scurvily; scandalously; heinously; fiendishly; incorrigibly; irreclaimably.

CRIMSON

adjectives

deepest; angry; dull; burning; fever; richest; russet; clear; glowing; spiritual.

CRINGE (v)

adverbs

humbly; servilely; slavishly; menially; brokenly; defeatedly; grotesquely; timorously.

(See cower, fawn.)

CRINKLE

adjectives

crisp; pleasant; laughing; traitorous; effacing; merry; mischievous.

CRIPPLE

adjectives

neglected; wealthy; awful; hopeless; deformed; grotesque; drab; grizzled; rag-wrapped; whining.

CRIPPLED

adverbs

hopelessly; helplessly; pitiably; deplorably; tragically; permanently; temporarily; crookedly; slightly; terribly; fearsomely; incredibly; pathetically; pitifully; cruelly; horribly; brutally; deliberately; curiously; strangely; sadly; painfully; dreadfully; indescribably.

CRISIS

adjectives

mighty; momentous; great; tremendous; supreme; fearful; serious; grave; domestic; legislative; intense; emotional; economic; agricultural; unprecedented; spiritual; psychological; political; industrial; national; moral; recurring; financial; banking; favorable; naive; interminable; contemporary; unquiet; distressing; religious; commercial; deplorable; revolutionary; majestic; peculiar; tragical; approaching; memorable; nervous; over-estimated; exciting; sternest; rapid; diplomatic; noisy; striking; desperate.

verbs

aggravate—; avert—; confront with—; cope with—; face—; handle—; improve—; lead up to—; mark—; precipitate—; provoke—; reach—; suffer—; toil over—; weather—; —besets; —grips; —grows; —indicates; —occurs; —passes; —wears off.

(See emergency, exigency.)

CRISP

adverbs

delicately; crunchily; frailly; deliciously; tastily; neatly; concisely; curtly; pithily; crumbly.

CRISPNESS

adjectives

buttery; crunchy; blanched; pleasant; refreshing; airy; invigorating; icy.

CRITERION

adjectives

economic; post-factum; inadequate; surer; whimsical; corresponding.

verbs

admit as —; allow as —; award on —; base on —; conclude by —; decide by —; distinguish as —; establish —; estimate by —; gauge by —; judge by —; mark —; measure by —; present —; produce —; reach —; represent —; test by —.

(See standard, rule, law, test.)

CRITIC

adjectives

superficial; facetious; astute; dramatic; generous; literary; interpretative; level-headed; penetrating; routine; quibbling; shortsighted; ingenious; unsparing; carping; exacting; fastidious; contemporary; music; unperceived; unknown; crabbed; inimitable; bitter; theatrical; vigorous; judicious; inimical; celebrated; fair-minded; aggressive; arrogant; opinionated; over-subtle; ignorant; self-constituted; amateur; thoughtful; passionate; clumsy; educational; creative; penetrating; textual; profound; robust; vicious; haughty; persistent; radical; alert; fearless; toilsome; impartial; snarling; invidious; discriminating; unfriendly; surly; grave; primitive; captious; malevolent; merciless; conscientious; competent; sincere; pure; serious; sober; sanguine; enthusiastic; tolerant; disinterested; keen; ablest; authoritative; master; indisputable; first-rate; leading; eminent; noted; outstanding; caviling; jaundiced; befuddled; sarcastic; cynical; pious; caustic; hostile; pertinacious; belligerent; gloomy; ill-disposed; lethargic; incipient; typical; exaggerating; blatant; incessant; thoroughgoing.

verbs
confound —s; silence —s; — appraises; — assails; — asserts; — attacks; — belittles; — blames; —s chatter; — disparages; — exalts himself; — gauges; — gloats; — interprets; — inveighs; — lauds; — opposes; — praises; — pronounces; — rails; — shuns; — snipes at; — weighs.
(See judge, censor.)

CRITICAL

adverbs
facetiously; astutely; generously; penetratingly; ingeniously; unsparingly; exactingly; fastidiously; crabbedly; bitterly; vigorously; judiciously; aggressively; ignorantly; thoughtfully; clumsily; gracelessly; creatively; viciously; haughtily; persistently; constructively; alertly; fearlessly; courageously; impartially; gravely; captiously; mercilessly; malevolently; conscientiously; keenly; authoritatively; tolerantly; ably; caustically; disagreeably; obnoxiously; unpleasantly.

CRITICISM

adjectives
adverse; favorable; brief; hostile; inductive; malevolent; shallow; argumentative; satisfactory; eerie; comparative; dramatic; querulous; harsh; exacting; withering; reverential; hazy; reprobative; numberless (pl); carping; sophistical; irritating; mordant; metaphysical; trenchant; depressing; cold; merciless; absurd; captious; comprehensive; loud; eager; detailed; negative; audible; severe; social; benevolent; injurious; rational; gentle; satiric; ungenerous; prejudiced; spasmodic; unintended; vigil-

ant; frank; dispassionate; scathing; watchful; cheery, acute; unsparing; sweeping; philosophical; loving; implicit; impartial; outside; caustic; sustained; literary; praiseless; biting; stimulating; musical; acrimonious; premature; qualifying; energetic; stupid; reflected; skeptical; unkind; affected; epigrammatic; candid; careful; intelligent; lucid; searching; healthy; salutary; expert; constructive; justified; corrective; witty; ironic; acrid; barbed; endless; lengthy; copious; vehement; stormy; murderous; libelous; bitter; faultfinding; peculiar; slurring; boorish; small-minded; sullen; stringent; factional; journalistic; partisan; aesthetic; presumptuous; subjective; implied; snobbish; retrogressive.

verbs
base — on; bow to —; chafe at —; dispense with —; distort —; draw —; elicit —; endure —; evoke —; expose to —; heap —; hurl —; indulge in —; justify —; pour forth —; provoke —; refrain from —; squelch —; stifle —; subject to —; welcome —; — cites; — confounds; — marks; — stirs; — takes root.
(See censure, judgment, examination.)

CRITICIZE (*v*)

adverbs
adversely; editorially; harshly; constructively; scoffingly; constantly; insidiously; fiercely; severely; rationally; malevolently; querulously; witheringly; reprobatively; irritatingly; trenchantly; depressingly; mercilessly; captiously; comprehensively; injuriously; impartially; caustically; acrimoniously; prematurely; energetically; candidly; stupidly; intelligently; searchingly; expertly; correctively; ironically; acridly; copiously; vehemently; libelously; slurringly; boorishly; presumptuously; subjectively; snobbishly.
(See censure, reprove.)

CRITIQUE

adjectives
elaborate; exquisite; instructive; poetical; preliminary; commendatory.

CROAK

adjectives
prophetic; monotonous; booming; empty; bellowing; rusty; harsh; discordant.

CROAK (v)

adverbs

tunelessly; roughly; discordantly; inauspiciously; prophetically; monotonously; sinisterly; nocturnally.

(See sound, complain.)

CROCKERY

adjectives

coarse; crudely-shaped; garishly-decorated; homely; humble; over-glazed; paunchy; porous.

verbs

advertise —; bake —; collect —; crack —; craze —; decorate —; display —; exhibit —; glaze —; mould —; paint —; place —; polish —; rattle —; shelve —; smash —; store in —; unearth —.

(See porcelain, china.)

CROCODILE

adjectives

rabbit-footed; slow-living; armored; slimy; stealthy; tearful; preying; slithering; death-dealing.

verbs

— ambles; — bathes; — cracks; — crunches; — crushes; — dives; — floats; —s herd; — invades; — lashes; — slithers; — snaps; — snorts; — splashes; — suns itself; — swims; — whips its tail.

(See reptile.)

CROCUS

adjectives

fatted; lusty; blooming; gay; adventurous; winter-defying; pioneer; spring-bannered.

CRONE

adjectives

withered; gaunt; old; haggard-visaged; dried-up.

CRONIES

adjectives

familiar; odious; bridge-playing; coarse-mouthed; illiterate; race-track; philandering.

CROOK

adjectives

dirty; filthy; loathsome; ordinary; obsequious; terrible; artificial; international; sneaking; whitecollar; capable.

CROOKED

adverbs

unstably; sinuously; jaggedly; darkly; indirectly; implicitly; covertly; cunningly; craftily; strategically; profoundly; diplomatically; shiftily; bafflingly; bewilderingly; insidiously; unscrupulously; disgracefully; perfidiously; treacherously; infamously; contemptibly; scurvily; disloyally.

CROON

adjectives

cheerful; plaintive; melodic; heart-touching; depth-sounding; hollow-ringing; weird; savage.

CROON (v)

adverbs

soothingly; harmoniously; comfortingly; pleasingly; gently; pathetically; sentimentally; romantically; maternally; cheerfully; plaintively; melodiously; touchingly.

(See sing.)

CROP

adjectives

catch; fateful; encouraging; anticipated; bumper; unmanufactured; ungathered; varied; abundant; sprouting; diminished; mildewed; uncertain; agricultural; plenteous; bountiful; scanty; customary; fast-ripening; phenomenal; profitable; huge; staple; immense; luxuriant; tender; supreme; worthless; superior; lavish; fodder; teeming; unfailing; annual; stunted; newly-planted; increased.

verbs

affect —; blast —; blight —; devastate —; devour —; harvest —; injure —; pluck —; produce —; reap —; salvage —; trample —; yield —; — fails; — flowers; —matures; — rustles; — shrivels; — sprouts; — withers.

(See harvest, fruit.)

CROSS

adjectives

customary; blazoned; glimmering; absolving; shameful; abhorred; momentary; reeking; planted; sunken; pastoral; radiant; scarlet; ebony; patient; cold; marble; enameled.

verbs

award —; bear —; curse —; deliver one to —; deny —; embrace —; endure —; erect —; fight for —; glory in —; hallow —; idolize —; kneel before —; mark with —; nail to —; plant —; sign with —; take up —; trust in —; uphold —; vow by —; wear —; worship at —; — leads; — saves; — signifies; — symbolizes.

adverbs

petulantly; perpetually; unreasonably; habitually; disagreeably; sullenly; morosely; gloomily; unbearably; pathetically; tragically; shockingly; waywardly; restively; glumly; crustily; cantankerously; brutally; sternly; forbiddingly; needlessly; gracelessly; unpardonably.

CROSS (v)

adverbs

freely; laterally; obliquely; boldly; accommodatingly; rapidly; devoutly; diagonally; inevitably; cautiously.

(See pass.)

CROSS-EXAMINATION

adjectives

merciless; extraordinary; lengthy; wearisome; pointless; inquisitive; three-cornered.

CROSSING

adjectives

memorable; deserted; careful; transpolar; smooth.

CROSSNESS

adjectives

accustomed; habitual; infectious; morbid; ascetic; acid; bitter; morose.

CROUCH (v)

adverbs

menacingly; sullenly; squatly; tensely; servilely; odiously; threateningly; alertly; aggressively.

(See squat, cringe.)

CROUPIER

adjectives

impassive; efficient; tight-lipped; spidery; inscrutable; grim.

CROW

adjectives

wandering; feeble; poaching; carrion; saucy; heavy-winged; boisterous; amazing; bold; startled; predatory; noisy; ragged; shrill.

verbs

domesticate —; hood —; snare —; tame —; throttle —; — annoys; — caws; — clamors; — claws; — fights; —s flock; — harms; — imitates; — isolates; — quarrels; —ravages; — robs; — roosts; — scours; — shrieks; —s swarm; — thieves; — uproots; — wrangles.

(See bird.)

CROW (v)

adverbs

triumphantly; derisively; harshly; loudly; feebly; saucily; boisterously; boldly; shrilly; monotonously; repeatedly; discordantly.

(See vaunt, brag.)

CROWD

adjectives

discordant; noisy; sportive; yelling; cosmopolitan; shouting; odd; oppressive; silent; rushing; eager; gaping; interminable; boisterous; passing; thick-pressed; promiscuous; voluble; madding; unreasonable; dark-robed; mercenary; miserable; streaming; heartless; hurrying; trembling; unabashed; mingled; surrounding; luckier; gossipy; village; horrid; gloomy; strangling; sympathetic; whispering; assembled; moving; motley; curious; excited; talented; discharged; enthusiastic; threatening; starry; tremendous; seething; scurrying; supper-hungry; still; gentlemanly; jocund; vulgar; dull-faced; self-controlled; dispersing; distinguished; colorful; indiscreet; serried; unfeeling; anxious; quiet; applauding; swirling; weary; malicious; tumultuous; buffeting; raucous; unnumbered; scattered; unhesitating; thickening; impatient; baser; patriotic; good-sized; advancing; watching; awful; jeering; gesticulating; angry; dense; outraged; idle; giddy; well-bred; debauching; surging; thinned; pitying; excited; laughing; unworthy; worthwhile; picturesque; ignoble; cheering; fickle; gazing; prostrate; reformed; exulting; incoming; thoughtless; visionary; sacrificial; virile; idealistic; helpless; ribald; wild-scrambling; myriad-tongued; thronging; dignified; merry; spiteful; purblind; suffering; brilliant; animated; somber; preoccupied; gay; drunken; handsome; glittering; friendly; well-behaved; orderly; healthy; complacent; awed; admiring; acclaiming; morbid; reverent; interested; sober-faced; tranquil; devout; convivial; attentive; hilarious; half-tipsy; roistering; thirsty; rollicking; mirthful; merry-making; congenial; jubilant; good-natured; vivacious; whimsical; smart; sophisticated; well-dressed; expensive; screaming; obstreperous; hooting; queer; enormous; hushed; tatterdemalion; hard-looking; tough; suspicious; quick-acting; realistic; bargaining; heterogeneous; listening; waiting; strolling; murmuring; chattering; milling; swarming; elbowing; lurching; shoving; swaying; eddying; writhing; turbulent; hustling; indifferent; bustling; hostile; challenging; troublesome; pestering; victorious; restless; blood-mad; quarrelsome; frenzied; frightened; wavering; panicky; bibulous; bourgeois; casual; residential; exultant; modern; ubiquitous; famished; impoverished; gaudy; vigorous; powerful; unreflective; increasing; critical; slow-moving; thawing.

verbs

bewilder —; bore —; cater to —; disassociate from —; disperse —; draw —; excite —; harangue —; key up —; plunge into —; steal among —; tower above —; wait with —; — assembles; — clusters; — collects; — dissolves; — gapes at; — gathers; — groans; — hoots; — jams; — jeers; — jostles; — lionizes; — mills about; — mutters; — packs into; — pours from; — presses; — retreats; — scurries; — seethes; — speculates; — stares; — storms; — surges; — swarms; — swerves; — throngs; — wavers.

(See multitude, throng, mob, horde.)

CROWD (v)

adverbs

uncomfortably; amiably; perplexingly; alertly; warmly; thickly; odiously; abundantly; desperately; discordantly; oppressively; boisterously; promiscuously; maddeningly; volubly; unreasonably; horridly; curiously; enthusiastically; vulgarly; colorfully; indiscreetly; tumultuously; buffetingly; raucously; impatiently; gesticulatingly; giddily; animatedly; somberly; complacently; admiringly; acclaimingly; morbidly; roisteringly; hilariously; rollickingly; mirthfully; congenially; vivaciously; obstreperously; suspiciously; listeningly; murmuringly; chatteringly; turbulently; indifferently; bustlingly; victoriously; exultantly; ubiquitously.

(See swarm.)

CROWN

adjectives

silken; crimson; golden; glittering; olive; thorny; kingly; giddy; accursed; treacherous; fruitless; glorious; admired; tufted; starry; molten; embellished; hemispherical; woven; brilliant; rejected; glistening; fadeless; celestial; hoary; clustering; bloomless; flaming; imperial; dread; piercing; blessed; laurel; tiny; jeweled; caplike; magnificent; discarded; pointed; long-expected; unused.

verbs

anoint —; aspire to —; bear —; bequeath —; blemish —; bless —; cast away —; claim —; conform to —; corrupt —; deliver

up —; deprive — of; deprive of —; disgrace —; disown —; encompass by —; gild —; inherit —; lay aside —; lift off —; merit —; offer —; pawn —; profane —; raise —; ransom —; refuse —; reject —; remove —; renounce —; repossess —; resign —; revere —; sear —; serve —; shave —; spurn —; tear off —; wear —; weave —; wreathe —; yield to —; yield up —; — flourishes; — rules; — shines.

CROWN (v)

adverbs

visibly; fittingly; spiritually; goldenly; glitteringly; gloriously; brilliantly; celestially; imperially; magnificently.

(See complete.)

CROWNING

adjectives

glorious; gorgeous; colorful; victorious; jubilant.

CRUCIFIX

adjectives

great; gaunt; ghastly; little.

CRUCIFY (v)

adverbs

miserably; horribly; barbarically; brutally; fiendishly; morally; literally; figuratively.

(See punish.)

CRUDE

adverbs

crassly; gracelessly; harshly; stiffly; awkwardly; barbarously; offensively; ignorantly; bashfully; intolerably; unluckily; baldly; unfortunately; offensively; coarsely; roughly; shiftlessly; quaintly; unsophisticatedly; ill-manneredly.

CRUDENESS

adjectives

honest; blunt; crass; vulgar; elemental; unsavory; natural; primitive.

verbs

abhor —; affect —; alter —; breed —; characterize by —; convert — into; correct —; cure of —; develop —; display —; exhibit —; loathe —; lose —; produce —; recoil from —; regard —; silence —; temper —; work —; — alarms; — annoys; — detracts; — shocks.

CRUDITY

adjectives

jocular; stylistic; frontier; obvious; careless; obsolete; sincere.

adjectives

blood-smeared; organized; unsparing; abysmal; complacent; fiendish; devouring; inhuman; strange; reckless; super-rogatory; amiable; wanton; lawless; innate; stern; execrable; hellish; ignorant; atrocious; thriving; intolerable; apparent; abominable; hideous; savage; existing; peculiar; dull; unimaginable; indescribable; unnecessary; foul; barbarous; malevolent; official; violent; devastating; seeming; narrow; incestuous; lecherous; unavenged; social; callous; irrational; insensate; instinctive; moody; excessive; insidious; unbridled; merciless; monotonous; shameful; needless; brutal; persistent; increasing; petty; continuous.

verbs

batter with —; boast of —; delight in —; display —; dispose to —; encounter —; exhibit —; govern with —; impose —; inflict —; manifest —; mask —; master with —; mitigate —; perpetuate —; practise —; prompt —; protect from —; provoke —; repent—; repress—; reproach for—; revel in —; revenge —; subject to —; suffer from —; tolerate —; yield to —; — distresses; — oppresses; — pains; —surpasses.

(See brutality, tyranny.)

adjectives

intrepid; involuntary; world; enchanting; southern; successful; rest-giving; romantic; difficult; strenuous; notable; delightful; varied; premier; attractive; wonderful.

verbs

anticipate —; direct —; embark on —; enjoy —; entertain on —; escort —; leave on —; navigate —; observe on —; operate —; organize —; plan —; promote —; relax on —; sail on —; travel on —; — accommodates; — attracts; — consists of; — embraces; — enthralls; — envelops; — furnishes; — includes; — inspires; — invigorates; — provides; — rests; — thrills.

(See voyage, journey, trip.)

adjectives

vigilant; protected; submersible; mighty; sojourning; tourist-laden.

adjectives

occasional; forsaken; paltry; stale; mouldy; hoarded; grudging; life-sustaining.

verbs

accept —; beg —; break into —s; brush away —; catch —; cover with —s; dress with —s; dry —; fall into —s; finger into —s; gather —s; mouth —s; pick up —; prepare with —s; reduce to —s; step on —; sweep away —s; thicken with —s; throw away —s; toss —s to.

adverbs

coarsely; gradually; completely; totally; disastrously; fatally; finely; unexpectedly; thoroughly; partially.

(See decline, decay.)

adjectives

gradual; complete; ear-splitting; total; erosive; timely; pathetic.

adverbs

viciously; rudely; roughly; destructively; pathetically; carelessly; hideously; slatternly.

(See smash.)

adjectives

distinct; audible; sickening; clear; sharp; decisive; monotonous.

adverbs

hungrily; viciously; furiously; bestially; rapaciously; eagerly; greedily; distinctly; audibly; sickeningly; sharply.

(See eat.)

adjectives

perennial; lifesaving; insane; emotional; organized; humanitarian; noble; pathetic; anti-crime.

verbs

assemble—; bless—; champion—; direct—; endorse—; engage in—; expedite—; inspirit—; instigate—; launch—; lead—; oppose—; organize—; plan—; prepare for —; support—; wage—; —advances; —

campaigns; —conquers; —crushes; —defeats; —defends; —endeavors; —realizes; —revives; —succeeds; —undertakes; — wrestles with.

(See enterprise, movement, warfare.)

CRUSADE (v)
adverbs

vaingloriously; actively; religiously; perennially; insanely; emotionally; nobly; pathetically; gallantly; zealously; victoriously; inspiredly.

CRUSADER
adjectives

gallant; overzealous; anti-vice; young; medieval; valiant.

CRUSH (v)
adverbs

perfectly; deliberately; tenderly; softly; completely; painfully; carelessly; nervously; rigorously; spiritually; overwhelmingly; finally.

(See smash.)

CRUST
adjectives

favoring; scanty; stony; overpublicized; upper; fruitful; flaky; external; treacherous; shallow; brittle; well-browned; flimsy; hardened; fluted.

verbs

beg for—; break—; coat with—; compose —; contract into—; cover with—; deposit —; dissolve—; dry into—; feed—; form—; gnaw—; harden into—; hide under—; line with—; mass into—; munch—; penetrate —; puncture—; render—; scrape—; season —; slice—; —crumbles; —forms; —hardens.

(See casing, shell.)

CRUTCHES
adjectives

badly-worn; needed; helpful; tapping; supporting; betraying; stout; taped.

CRY
adjectives

raucous; feeble; painful; melancholy; guttural; heartsick; cornered; shrill; sharp; solitary; importunate; hoarse; choking; satirical; earnest; furious; thrilling; unanimous; pathetic; protesting; strident; peevish; battle; human; broken; triumphant; warning; petulant; wailing; plaintive; bootless; simultaneous; responsive; similar; distinct; suppressed; avenging; defiant; boastful; inspiring; drunken; pitiful; long-drawn; careless; passionate; supreme; piercing; unending; desolate; discordant; vociferous; prayerful; exultant; half-suppressed; half-demoniac; funeral; answering; terrified; inharmonious; impious; aspiring; yapping; plausible; premature; inevitable; harsh; ugly; shivering; stifled; strangled; joyous; wild; unearthly; despairing; clamorous; sharp; hissing; death-dealing; maniacal; piteous; amazed; comfortable; weird; impassioned; startling; rallying; unceasing; solitary; untenable; delirious; admiring; wrathful; everlasting; universal; prevailing; farthest-sounding; shuddering; inarticulate; gurgling; long; half-hysterical; dirgelike; loud; incoherent; perpetual; distressing; wrenching; sobbing; agonizing; brief; happy; smothered; full-mouthed; drawling; peculiar; fearful; fierce; ribald; far-resounding; odious; ineffable; continuous; mocking; supplicating; terrible; patriotic; noisy; dismal; expostulating; welcoming; ghastly; mutual; exulting; jubilant; ecstatic; joyful; delighted; gladdening; naive; inspiriting; wistful; stimulating; high; soft-noted; insistent; clarion; squeaky; rasping; clangorous; heart-chilling; babyish; heartbroken; dismayed; solemn; whimpering; breathless; stricken; important; frenzied; frantic; gulping; muffled; wanton; insulting; contemptuous; groaning; derisive; murder; fiendish; horror-stricken; anguished; spiteful; barbaric; sighing; yearning; low; appealing; hysterical; entreating; ominous; involuntary; frightened; haunting; elfin; sporting; familiar; asinine; wheezy; wordless; destructive; fluttering; incessant; scattered; hurtling; penetrating; vibrating; soul-shaking; dolorous; mournful; provocative; revolutionary; multitudinous (pl).

verbs

echo—; flee at—; force out—; give ear to—; hearken to—; heed—; let slip—; mock—; raise up—; repeat—; roar—; take up—; utter—; voice—; wring—from; —arouses; —awakens; —bursts forth; —disturbs; — fills; —jars; —resounds; —reverberates; —rises; —scares; —shatters; —wanes.

(See outcry, exclamation, scream, shriek, howl, lamentation, wail, plaint, yell.)

CRY (v)
adverbs

discordantly; querulously; reproachfully; jealously; hoarsely; earnestly; inarticulate-

297

ly; heartbrokenly; dishearteningly; flippantly; vehemently; enthusiastically; persistently; piteously; sternly; passionately; jovially; tempestuously; haughtily; indignantly; incoherently; irritably; energetically; contemptuously; exultantly; reprovingly; ringingly; gaily; disconsolately; unrestrainedly; tauntingly; feverishly; peremptorily; tantalizingly; falteringly; mirthfully; spontaneously; sympathetically; stormily; unanimously; petulantly; wailingly; drunkenly; passionately; piercingly; agonizingly; vociferously; jubilantly; ecstatically; inspiritingly; solemnly; spitefully; sighingly; hysterically; involuntarily; ominously; wordlessly; incessantly; dolorously; yearningly; bitterly; inwardly.
(See wail, weep.)

CRYING
adjectives
harsh; endless; irrational; awkward; bitter; remorseful; stormy; furious.

CRYPT
adjectives
mournful; venerable; quiet; mossy; dismal; mouldy; time-honored; ancestral.

CRYPTOGRAM
adjectives
magic; involved; difficult; mysterious; puzzling; baffling; tortuous.

CRYSTAL
adjectives
shimmering; transparent; pellucid; celestial; strange; fluffy; slow-frozen; gleaming; stinging; flashing; ice; diaphanous; needle-like; lambent; glittering; perilous; quartz; tempting; tremulous; fragile; long; jagged; tiny; irregular.

verbs
adorn with—; aggregate into—; clear—; concentrate in—; congeal into—; delve for—; dig out—; discover—; dissolve—; drip—s; freeze into—; gaze into—; mass into—; melt—; quaff—; search—; —adheres to; —beams; —darkens; —shines; —sparkles.
(See glass.)

CUB
adjectives
self-willed; young; modest; helpless; clumsy; awkward; closely-watched.

CUCKOO
adjectives
cowled; domineering; echoic; masterful; unmaternal; melancholy; ravenous; usurping; vehement.

verbs
—calls; —chucks; —deposits; —ejects; —flits; —mocks; —shrills; —shies away; —surveys; —wheels.
(See bird.)

CUDDLE (*v*)
adverbs
cozily; snugly; comfortably; lovingly; fondly; maternally; gently; affectionately; tenderly.
(See nestle.)

CUDGEL
adjectives
short; heavy; thick; bloody; bludgeoning; murderous.

verbs
attack with—; awe with—; beat with—; belabor with—; brandish—; combat with—; cross—s; defend with—; resist—; scar with—; shake—; smite with—; strike with —; swing—; take up—; terrify with—; wave—; wield—; —descends; —fells; —stuns.
(See club.)

CUE
(*billiards*)
adjectives
ash-wood; leather-tipped; nicely-balanced; pliant; well-seasoned; tapering; graceful.

verbs
aim—; bridge—; chalk—; crack—; draw with—; indicate with—; point—at; rest—on; retip—; score with—; skill with—; slide—; tip—; —slides; —bends; —slips; —strikes; —warps.

CUE
(*braid*)
adjectives
carefully-braided; bristling; coiled; limp; genteel; powdered; protruding; scrupulous.

verbs
braid into—; clip—; cut—; exhibit—; fashion—; plait—; powder—; roll—; tie into —; twist into—; —dangles; —grows.

CUE
(signal)

adjectives

cryptic; answering; guiding; secret; suggestive; politic; strategic.

verbs

answer—; begin on—; enter on—; forget —; heed—; hint with—; mind—; miss—; muff—; pronounce—; remember—; speak —; signal with—; wait for—; whisper—; —arrives; —comes; —enables; —warns.
(See hint, suggestion, intimation.)

CUFF
(sleeve)

adjectives

sheer; possible; transparent; organdy; starched; immaculate; chafing; frilled.

CUISINE

adjectives

local; national; appetizing; exceptional; world-famous; perfect; excellent; tempting; distinctive; wholesome; unsurpassed; distinguished; tasty; matchless; splendid; finest; delicious; unrivaled; superlative; renowned.

CULMINATION

adjectives

over-ripe; dizzy; fitting; probable; ultimate; untimely.

verbs

ascend to—; attain—; bask in—; crown—; develop to—; display—; encourage—; establish—; form—; herald—; look forward to—; reach—; rise to—; speed—; take pride in—; urge—; —occurs; —takes place.
(See end.)

CULPRIT

adjectives

wretched; miserable; shameful; apprehended; confessed.

CULT

adjectives

capricious; ridiculed; emotional; diverse; aesthetic; sweet; love; sentimental; idiotic; nudist; moribund; moral; eminent; logical; exclusive; religious; bizarre; unconventional; secret; sinister.

verbs

adopt—; denounce—; despise—; develop—; embrace—; inaugurate—; join—; organize—; perpetuate—; succumb to—; take up—; —affects; —attracts; —believes; — devotes; —fades; —interests; —practices; —spreads; —worships.
(See belief, system, ritual.)

CULTIVATE (v)

adverbs

diligently; extensively; sedulously; passionately; intensively; freely; generously; assiduously; fastidiously; systematically; intellectually; profitably; continuously.
(See work.)

CULTIVATION

adjectives

proper; intensive; fictional; continuous; hot-house; forced.

CULTIVATOR

adjectives

prosperous; sensible; practiced; apt; skilled; trained.

CULTURE

adjectives

snob; diligent; literary; rational; spiritual; high; musical; splendid; unprecarious; profound; virile; brilliant; superior; natural; substantial; polite; simple; harmonious; pronounced; untrammeled; mellow; older; mature; age-old; traditional; borrowed; inherited; acquired; vulgar; inferior; dangerous; national; warmed; raw; wide; universal; abundant; vast; considerable; intellectual; indigenous; cruel; pagan; autonomous; alien; civil; rounded; religious; exhilarating; prescriptorial; petty; nascent; curious; active.

verbs

absorb—; acquire—; assimilate—; attain—; borrow—; disparage—; fetter—; flout—; imbibe—; lack—; perpetuate—; propagate —; relegate—; retard—; shed—; spread —; stifle—; —broadens; —enhances; —enlightens; —improves; —polishes; —raises; —refines.
(See refinement, enlightenment, education.)

CULTURE (v)

adverbs

laboriously; diligently; naturally; abundantly; indigenously; spiritually.

CULTURED

adverbs

elaborately; ostentatiously; laboriously; diligently; painfully; highly; profoundly;

brilliantly; naturally; inherently; innately; widely; curiously; delightfully; consciously; obviously; unquestionably; tastefully; genuinely; unaffectedly; bookishly; aimlessly; methodically; scholastically; generally.

CUMBERSOME

adverbs

bulkily; ponderously; gravely; awkwardly; ungracefully; embarrassingly; unmanageably; vexatiously; impossibly; clumsily; massively; stiffly; grotesquely; fantastically; heavily.

CUNNING

adjectives

giddy; diabolical; cordial; tough; stalwart; gentle; sly; fiendish; premeditated; malicious; devilish; peculiar; infinite; instinctive; unconscious; revengeful; stealthy; artful; swift.

verbs

acquire through—; apply—; beguile with—; calculate with—; cheat with—; check—; cover—; deceive by—; devise by—; display—; dispose to—; employ—; entrap by—; excel in—; exercise—; exhibit—; expose—; frame with—; impart—; puff up with—; school in—; trick by—; work—; —hides; —deceives.
(See craft, deceit, trickery, skill, ingenuity.)

adverbs

diabolically; slyly; fiendishly; maliciously; adroitly; cleverly; adeptly; artfully; subtly; insidiously; dangerously; commercially; extremely; astoundingly; profoundly; deliberately; sagaciously; cautiously; carefully; invariably; habitually; incurably; astutely; customarily; ordinarily.

CUP

adjectives

bitter; enameled; verdant; tulip-tinted; silver; red; lacquer; lordly; gold-encrusted; pink-sprigged; intoxicating; crowning; delicate; inebriating; consecrated; lustrous-petaled; sapphire; thin; large; thimble-like; quivering; graceful; odd; vicious; little; demure; coveted; fragile; impersonal; hygienic; invigorating.

verbs

burnish—; drain—; drink—; fill—; finger —; overflow—; partake of—; pour—; quaff—; sip—; share—; steep in—; swell over—; taste—; wash—; win—; —con-

tains; —flows; —runs over; —sparkles; —steams.

CUPID

adjectives

wrestling; painted; devilish; effective; love-darting.

CUPIDITY

adjectives

native; personal; marked; avaricious; expressive.

CUPOLA

adjectives

gigantic; spherical; delicate; gilded; triumphant; towering; opulent.

CUR

adjectives

mean; mongrel; crooked; ragamuffin; contemptible; treacherous; bedraggled; crouching; worthless; cruel-hearted; impenetrable; mangy; carnal; half-starved; yelping.

CURATE

adjectives

perpetual; narrow; egotistical; impecunious; up-to-date; shuffling; pleasant; genial.

CURATIVE

adverbs

effectively; eventually; soothingly; pleasantly; safely; powerfully; speedily; valuably; mythically; infallibly; originally; rarely; expensively; heroically; strangely; miraculously; mysteriously; permanently; remarkably; fraudulently.

CURB (*v*)

adverbs

intentionally; beneficently; spasmodically; stringently; sternly; harshly; brutally; dictatorially; tyrannically.
(See stop.)

CURE

adjectives

renowned; timely; single; simple; sovereign; contemptuous; radical; drastic; fascinating; little; strange; natural; permanent; jagged; miraculous; efficacious; impersonal; so-called; immediate; alleged; prospective; instant; remarkable; sordid; accurate; elaborate; deepest; fraudulent.

verbs
accelerate—; accomplish—; advocate—; applaud—; apply—; approve—; effect—; hasten—; indicate—; perform—; produce —; proffer—; render—; seek—; trust—; work—; —follows; —results.
(See treatment, remedy.)

CURE (*v*)
adverbs
sufficiently; radically; permanently; miraculously; efficaciously; impersonally; immediately; remarkably; fraudulently; professionally; medically; presumably; partially; temporarily.
(See help.)

CURIOSITY
adjectives
high; sympathetic; logical; healthy; frank; profound; sublime; respectful; natural; reverent; indifferent; lively; breathless; instant; insatiable; passionate; intense; intelligent; vague; sedate; pregnant; half-ironic; mingled; eager; oblique; romantic; ardent; unhealthy; heartless; inflamed; intellectual; jealous; ethnological; indefatigable; laboratory; half-cunning; sheer; calculating; impertinent; kind; latent; amused; overwhelming; excited; persevering; overpowering; vacant; tremulous; typographical; rude; beneficial; blunt; morbid; prying; laudable; irresistible; imperious; unenvious; enlightened; gluttonous; languid; anthropological; idle; discontented; unobtrusive; innocent; frightened; contemptuous; unquenchable; ghoulish; sullen; regretful; literary; kindred; weak; mutual; obtrusive; ill-bred; endless; sharp; delighted; vulgar; childlike; indolent; unsated; gratified; evident; noble; unallayed; baffled; passionate; geographical; prejudiced; piqued; chastened; reluctant; persistent; polite; burning; malicious; cordial; professional; importunate; considerable; great; rampant; immense; inordinate; widespread; untiring; undiminished; penetrating; unappeased; quenchless; devouring; itching; momentary; passing; detached; mild; waning; small; faint; stirring; lazy; undisguised; growing; vast; objective; troubled; worried; timid; nervous; furtive; covetous; indecent; greedy; gruesome; avid; prurient; burdensome; leering; sinister; forbidden; impious; perverse; eclectic; visual; disoriented; titillating; gaping; startled; **sudden; scared.**

verbs
admit—; arouse—; awaken—; blame—; burst with—; cater to—; develop—; devour with—; display—; evince—; excite—; exhibit—; experience—; feed—; gratify —; manifest—; move by—; overcome—; pique—; practice—; prompt by—; repel—; repress—; satisfy—; seize with—; spur on by—; steam with—; —grows; —impels; —motivates; —prevails.
(See interest, thirst.)

CURIOUS
adverbs
incurably; meanly; inquisitively; intellectually; daringly; crassly; offensively; frightfully; gracelessly; grossly; maliciously; malevolently; unbearably; odiously; roughly; childishly; innocently; wonderingly; impertinently; impudently; unpardonably; inexcusably; hatefully; coarsely.

CURL
adjectives
soft; radiant; salt-wet; shining; drenched; sawdust; flat; vine; floating; countless (pl); short; upturned; sweeping; treasured; thick; mustache; twisted; moistened; lustrous; streaming; falling; disordered; luxuriant; clustering; smoky; stray; sunny; mutinous; glossy; careless; burnished; soft; copious (pl); copper-colored; white; blond; fluffy; gold; silky; black; brown; nut-brown; wire-gold; resolute; blue; massive; willful; protruding; tossing; doubtful; tight; glossy; loose; impracticable; tumbled; stubborn; fluttered; strange; powdered; damp; superabundant (pl); straggling; crisp; rolled; knotted; short; flaxen; corkscrew; dark; riotous; raven; unruly; fuzzy; dishevelled; dusty; gleaming; puffy.

verbs
admire—s; adorn with—s; assume—; arrange—s; clip—s; dress in—s; finger—s; fondle—s; form—s; promote—s; ribbon—s; shake—s; sun—s; tangle—s; tie into—s; twist into—s; wind into—s; —s attract; —s run riot; —s stream; —s wave.
(See hair.)

CURL (*v*)
adverbs
deftly; gracefully; riotously; indolently; systematically; scornfully; disdainfully;

charmingly; lustrously; luxuriantly; mutinously; carelessly; copiously; loosely; dishevelledly.
(See twist.)

CURRENCY

adjectives

spurious; immediate; auxiliary; new; crisp; special; separate; weak; universal; valueless; tropical.

verbs

accept—; adopt as—; coin—; counterfeit—; debase—; deflate—; depreciate—; exchange for—; guard—; honor—; inflate—; issue—; legalize—; rate—; recall—; stabilize—; stamp out—; tender—; value—; —changes; —wobbles.
(See money, coin.)

CURRENT

adjectives

friendly; irresistible; dangerous; treacherous; gentle; perilous; tricky; mighty; powerful; terrific; swift; racing; shifting; swirling; churning; weltering; streaming; air; glacial; tidal; descending; broad; undulating; steady; smooth; pulling; noiseless; skeptical; romantic; vital; philosophical; social; subtle; stinging; buoyant; fluvial; crystal; atmospheric; arduous; swollen; silver; favoring; conflicting; eddying; ceaseless; contrary; plunging; gushing; descending; mealy; clean; sweeping; lessening; warm; life; haze-enveloped; brown; greasy; running; rippling; timetossed; smooth; moisture-bringing; genial; wild; dreamy; alternating; unbroken; great; strengthened; brinish; galvanic; nauseous; cool; vicious; mazy; low-voiced; prattling; mysterious; permeating; fruity; twisting; lucent; contagious; intellectual; artistic; unseen; integrated; fatal.

verbs

allay—; attune to—; chart—; dam—; defile—; deviate from—; escape—; impede—; oppose—; retard—; ruffle—; stem—; —absorbs; —drives; —forces; —glides; —jets; —originates at; —pushes; —rolls on; —runs on; —shatters; —shifts; —springs from.
(See stream, movement, course.)

CURRICULUM

adjectives

rational; traditionary; academic; narrow; rigid; daily.

verbs

approve—; arrange—; balance—; complete—; constitute—; consult—; contemplate—; decide on—; detail—; fix—; investigate—; load—; offer—; outline—; pursue—; recommend—; regulate—; reject—; run through—; secure—; select—; supervise—; work out—; —covers; —embraces; —entails; —equips; —instructs in; —prepares for; —requires; —satisfies; —trains; —provides.
(See course, study.)

CURSE

adjectives

sobbing; vile; futile; snarling; unintelligible; fervent; dazzling; exasperated; muttered; bitter; great; hot; muffled; steamy; primal; intolerable; irritable; cunning; deep; valiant; haunting; sterile; well-hurled; dread; inevitable; long-forgotten; unutterable; sardonic; primeval; murmuring; blaspheming; shrieking; canceled; smothered; latent; fiendish; furious; primordial; abiding.

verbs

annul—; bait with—; blast—at; breathe—; bring—upon; cast—; croak—; dread—; endow with—; growl—; heap—s upon; hurl—at; mutter—; pronounce—; redeem from—; remove—; shake off—; smite with —; speak—; stifle—; swear—; taunt with —; voice—; wish—; woo—; —bodes ill for; —falls upon; —s pour out; —prevails; —stings.
(See denunciation, imprecation, oath.)

CURSE (v)

adverbs

endlessly; furiously; wrathfully; persistently; belligerently; bitterly; jovially; vulgarly; coarsely; blasphemously; unintelligibly; fervently; exasperatedly; hotly; intolerably; irritably; fiendishly.
(See swear.)

CURTAIL (v)

adverbs

sharply; considerably; drastically; harmfully; detrimentally; abruptly; unexpectedly; nominally; promptly.
(See reduce.)

CURTAILMENT

adjectives

prompt; drastic; unparalleled; harmful; sharp; detrimental.

CURTAIN

adjectives

falling; flapping; wavering; honey-colored; hotel-red; roseate; dirty; mud-brown; cloudless; azure; sinister; black; accordion-pleated; ruffled; embroidered; jeweled; gingham; crisp; bright; chintz; organdie; cretonne; gaily-colored; heavy; felt; wry; old; rich-toned; cheerful; skimpy; hanging; triangular; strong; final; gray; cloudy; dimity; wadded; clinging; billowy; improvised; sunshiny; undrawn; jonquil; silk; blue; light-pierced; dusky; exasperating; crimson; luminous; dazzling; impalpable; tawdry; convenient; sun-lace; formless; tattered.

verbs

adjust—; close—; draw—; drop—; emerge from—; fade behind—; hide behind—; lift—; lower—; peep through—; spread—; stretch out—; —flutters; —protects; —quivers; —shades; —sways.

(See drapery.)

CURTNESS

adjectives

semi-growling; autocratic; sudden; unfeeling; brusque; harsh; perfunctory.

CURTSY

adjectives

majestic; mock; graceful; delicate; practiced; bobbing; deferential.

CURVE
(*bend as of a highway*)

adjectives

gradually-descending; magnificent; unprotected; precipitous; graceful; sinuous; hairpin; wide-swung; continuous.

verbs

approach—; assume—; bank—; collide on —; crowd at—; dart around—; eliminate —; negotiate—; round—; screech around—; turn over on—; upset on—; warn of—; whiz round—; —confronts; —endangers; —hazards; —menaces; —obscures; —represents; —slants.

CURVE
(*general*)

adjectives

seductive; sensuous; luscious; ardent; entrancing; magnificent; graceful; exquisite; winsome; dizzy; dazzling; sweeping; bold; wide; scraped; scornful; disdainful; fleshy; opulent; slim; dignified; sensitive; close-coiled; easy; concave; sheltering; irregular; flat; hairpin; downward; lax; convex; subtle; symmetrical; gigantic; sheltered; painted; wavering; drooping; phosphate; additional; cuspidated; majestic; continuous; caustic; lineless; living; epicycloidal; precipitous; prudish; luxurious; aquiline; flowing; gracile; ceaseless; rich; tender; sweeping; alluring; yielding; self-sought; exquisite; glimmering.

CURVE
(*line of deviation on a graph*)

adjectives

double; reverse; reciprocal; transcendental; mechanical; radical; radial; peculiar.

verbs

construct—; describe—; generate—; interest in—; intersect—; obtain—; study—; trace—; transform—; —corresponds to; —degenerates; —envelops; —falls; —indicates; —recedes; —represents; —sinks.

(See deviation, line.)

CURVE (*v*)

adverbs

perceptibly; seductively; sensuously; entrancingly; magnificently; exquisitely; winsomely; sweepingly; boldly; abruptly; dangerously; sinuously.

(See bend.)

CUSHION

adjectives

pillow; rustling; elastic; silken; multicolored; bright-hued; thin; downy; soft; velvet; damask; faded; reclining; convertible; form-fitting; slippery; loose-seat; padded; ample; natural.

verbs

conceal with—; cover—; embroider—; fringe—; furnish with—; kneel on—; lay on—; loll on—; offer—; place—under; relax against—; repose on—; rest on—; sit on—; stuff—; —decorates; —eases; —graces.

(See pillow.)

CUSPIDOR

adjectives

stately; ill-placed; fanciful; vulgar; avoided; obstreperous; spattered.

CUSTODIAN

adjectives

possible; official; sole; faithless; temporary; definite.

adjectives
safe; protective; temporary; court; jealous; zealous; watchful.

verbs
accept—of; acknowledge—of; advise—of; authorize—of; commit to—of; confine to—of; direct—of; preserve—of; resent—of; retain—of; subject to—of; —amends; —improves; —neutralizes; —protects; —rectifies; —restrains; —superintends.
(See care, imprisonment.)

CUSTOM

adjectives
august; precious; gracious; venerated; pleasant; sentimental; quaint; bizarre; effete; mutable; ancient; immemorial; time-honored; convenient; prudent; barbaric; pagan; primitive; yearly; native; austere; civilized; tribal; nightly; family; social; old-fashioned; southern; administrative; religious; accepted; wild; gay; universal; innocent; disinterested; reprehensible; contrasting; established; observed; prevailing; casual; frequent; habitual; recognized; classic; homogeneous; antiquated; unwonted; barbarous; charming; burial; pious; genteel; blind; stupid; laudable; national; long-continued; kingly; transient; excellent; preserved; ludicrous; prescribed; early; depraved; usual; infuriating; political; traditional; obsolete; enlightened; invariable; offensive; salutary; idiotic; well-known; uniform; familiar; reverent; exuberant; discrepant; monastic; praiseworthy; queer.

verbs
adhere to—; break—; cherish—; cling to—; conform to—; corrupt—; defend—; defer —; defy—; deprecate—; develop—; discharge—; establish—; esteem—; extenuate —; flout—; honor—; impose—; inaugurate —; maintain—; mar—; mock—; observe—; overlap—; overwhelm by—; respect—; retain—; reverence—; revert to—; revive —; run counter to—; stamp out—; —demands; —dictates; —governs; —intimidates; —narrows; —runs back to; —springs from; —stales; hamper by—.
(See usage, conventionality, practice, habit.)

CUSTOMARY

adverbs
scarcely; quaintly; queerly; graciously; pleasantly; conveniently; charmingly; stu-

pidly; infuriatingly; idiotically; amusingly; locally; racially.

CUSTOMER

adjectives
potential; quondam; gay; prospective; tough; favored; fussy; cautious; flighty; lavish; famous; resident; difficult; hard; hideous; soldier; quick; hungry; capricious; disgruntled; excellent; grumpy; dark; lathered; noble; open-aired; profitable; residential; favored; satisfied; admiring; discriminating; picnic; slippery; famished; potential; passing; steady; destructive.

verbs
approach—; bargain with—; beckon to—; deal with—; encourage—; entice—; furnish —; guarantee to—; mulct—; refund to—; round up—s; satisfy—; seek—; smirk at—; tempt—; urge—; —bickers; —complains; —orders; —purchases; —responds; —selects; —s support; —s troop in.
(See purchaser, buyer.)

CUT

adjectives
sharp; sincere; substantial; long; ragged; vile; inelegant; vertical; tremendous; duck-bellied; delicate; fearful; whimsical.

verbs
bandage —; bathe —; bleed —; cleave —; disinfect —; dress —; incise —; infect —; inflict —; open —; salve —; sew —; stitch —; suffer —; suture —; treat —; wound with —; — divides; — heals; — pains; — penetrates; — removes; — separates; — severs.
(See wound.)

CUT (v)

adverbs
completely; exquisitely; cruelly; violently; deliberately; effectively; diagonally; summarily; snobbishly; obliquely; transversely; keenly; generously; heartlessly.
(See gash.)

CUTLASS

adjectives
gleaming; dripping; naked; sturdy; heavy; serviceable; dangling; undimmed.

verbs
arm with —; brandish —; carve with —; chop with —; dull —; flourish —; furnish with —; hew with —; sever with —;

sharpen —; shield from —; thrust —; wave —; wield —; work —; yield to —; — menaces; — pierces; — slashes; — slays.
(See sword, weapon.)

CUTLERY

adjectives
flashing; steely; keen-edged; ivory-handled; adaptable; concealed; cleverly-applied; sundering.

verbs
clean —; dent —; employ —; glaze —; grind —; harden —; inspect —; manipulate —; manufacture —; monogram —; place —; plate —; polish —; provide with —; require —; scour —; sharpen —; spread —; stain —; temper —; utilize —; — clatters; — glistens; — jingles; — resists.
(See instrument, tool.)

CYCLE

adjectives
irregular; uncharted; business; elemental; repetitious; past; never-failing; comprehensive; pleasant; distinct; imaginary; endless; unvarying; normal.

verbs
approve —; avert —; complete —; compute —; continue in —; end —; form —; move in —; obviate —; pass through —; recognize —; recur during —; regain during —; resume —; revolve in —; span —; study —; — gauges; — indicates; — possesses; — promises; — represents.
(See period.)

CYCLONE

adjectives
human; lurking; impending; destructive; periodic; seasonable; threatening; rumbling; whirling.

CYLINDER

adjectives
metal; stubby; rotary; inscribed; clay; reciprocating; wicker; unsymmetrical.

verbs
bolt —s together; bore —; compress in —; construct —; design —; employ —; grind —; insert in —; operate —; — circles; — contracts; — expands; — lags; — leaks; — revolves; — rolls; — rotates; — turns.

CYMBAL

adjectives
tinkling; brazen; clashing; vibrating; jubilant; sounding; heartful.

CYMBALS

adjectives
bronzed; clashing; tinkling; empty-sounding; gypsy; triumphant; traditional.

verbs
cast —; clash —; crash —; play on —; rub —; sound —; strike —; — clash; — echo; — quiver; — resound; — ring; — tinkle.

CYNIC

adjectives
unfeeling; bitter; cold-blooded; licentious; ferocious; unmoved; wandering; cruel; irreverent; sensual; intolerable; sated; singular; imperturbable; consistent; decided; admirable; cheery; depressed; despairing.

CYNICAL

adverbs
bitterly; harshly; gloomily; contemptuously; derisively; scornfully; sneeringly; disdainfully; morosely; witheringly; superciliously; pitifully; censoriously; abusively; scandalously; outrageously; dryly; cuttingly; disparagingly; insufferably; pompously; arrogantly; bumptiously.

CYNICISM

adjectives
prevalent; abstract; consummate; immeasurable; meretricious; searing; cold-blooded; bitter; new-found; grinning; smooth; ugly; sinister; unbearable; rough; infamous; arid; appalling; polished; selfish; philosophical; repellent; analytical; thin; querulous; apparent; disdainful; genial.

verbs
adopt —; attain —; base on —; clothe in —; condemn —; criticize —; dethrone —; display —; dispose of —; don —; exhibit —; exercise —; fall into —; fetter with —; imply —; indulge in —; ingrain —; mask —; provoke —; regard with —; ridicule —; uphold —; — cloaks; — develops; — emphasizes; — evolves; — flourishes; — outrages; — seeps in.
(See contempt, sarcasm, distrust, pessimism.)

CYPRESS

adjectives
towering; gigantic; bearded; hoary; patriarchal.

adjectives

absolute; perturbed; grieved; obstinate; mighty; omnipotent; craven; ruthless.

adjectives

masterful; frantic; neurotic; vainglorious; pride-eaten; ambitious; power-driven.

D

adjectives
giant; yellow; nodding; flaunting; vernal; coquettish.

DAGGER

adjectives
bloody; bronze; gold-hilted; curved; flint; short; heavy; gleaming; well-sharpened.

verbs
attack with —; blunt —; brandish —; conceal —; draw —; dull —; edge —; flourish —; hack with —; nuzzle —; pare with —; pluck with —; point —; reel under —; run — through; sharpen —; sheathe —; shoot —; speak —s; stab with —; threaten with —; thrust —; wave —; wield —; — inflicts; — nicks; — penetrates; — slays; — wounds.
(See knife, weapon.)

DAILY
adjectives (newspaper)
conservative; provincial; radical; yellow; blatant; local; syndicated.

DAINTINESS

adjectives
exquisite; fastidious; unwonted; inimitable; inborn; personal; superlative; luxurious; preening; faultless.

DAINTY

adjectives
carefully-prepared; prized; coveted; diet-robbing; sugared; tempting; toothsome.

verbs
allure by —; crave —; desire —; feed on —; pamper with —; prepare —; promise —; provide —; relish —; reward with —; share —; spice —; store —; surrender to —; — appeals; — delights; — pleases.
(See food.)

adverbs
fastidiously; exquisitely; subtly; extremely; gracefully; charmingly; girlishly; personally; faultlessly; fashionably; meticulously; primly; demurely; delicately; particularly; scrupulously; pleasingly; immaculately; sweetly; fragrantly.

DAISY

adjectives
white; buttercup-hued; English; innocent; unabashed; golden-hearted; question-eyed; love-telling.

verbs
adorn with —; arrange —ies; bear —ies; chain —ies; cultivate —ies; disclose —ies; gather —ies; grow —ies; pin —ies; pluck —ies; scatter —ies; trim with —ies; — blooms; — blossoms; —ies deck; —ies dot; — flowers; — folds; — lurks; — opens; — sleeps; —ies sprinkle; — winks.
(See flower.)

DALE

adjectives
smiling; piny; flowery; wooded; dark; fragrant; shadow-dappled.

verbs
abandon —; bedeck —; bloom in —; grow in —; haunt —; hide in —; inhabit —; retreat to —; roam in —; scatter through —; situate in —; speed over —; wander in —; — invites; — protects; — shelters; — slopes; — winds.
(See valley, dell, vale.)

DALLIANCE

adjectives
pleasant; silken; delightful; primrose; lunar; playful; gentle.

DALLY (*v*)

adverbs
dangerously; carelessly; playfully; indifferently; procrastinatingly; seductively.
(See delay, trifle.)

DAM

adjectives (water)
gracious; milky; restless; undermined; log; earth-filled; broken; frothy; noisy; gushing; beaver.

verbs
bank —; burst —; construct —; install —; level —; overflow —; pipe from —; reinforce —; sweep away —; — bars; — blocks; — breaks; — bridges; — confines; — controls; — discharges; — halts; — impounds; — irrigates; — leaks; — obstructs; — preserves; — prevents; — protects; — restrains; — supplies.
(See barrier.)

DAMAGE

adjectives

moral; irreparable; considerable; inestimable; permanent; malicious; substantial; sudden; serious; material; pecuniary; noticeable; characteristic; infinite; unspeakable; accidental; consequent; enormous; hidden; resultant; unliquidated; willful; unmistakable; punitive.

verbs

account for —; compute —; counteract —; countervail —; distress by —; forestall —; guard against —; inflict —; measure —; mitigate —; offset —; pay —s; receive —; recoup —; recover —; reveal —; survey —; sustain —; — flows from; — impairs. (See destruction, injury, harm.)

DAMAGE (v)

adverbs

seriously; morally; irreparably; inestimably; permanently; maliciously; substantially; materially; noticeably; characteristically; infinitely; unspeakably; accidentally; consequently; enormously; resultantly; unmistakably; punitively; wilfully; revengefully; woefully; unscrupulously; savagely. (See injure. hurt.)

DAMASK

adjectives

heavy; silk; crimson; mingled; traditional; imported; luxurious; gorgeous.

DAME

adjectives

coquettish; scented; imperious; high-nosed; resolute; fairest; rawboned; admiring; glowing; ruffled; peerless; keen-eyed; beauteous; antiquated; sinful; blooming; handsome; disdainful; solicitous; chaste; tissued; wanton; affrighted.

DAMNABLE

adverbs

utterly; odiously; completely; horribly; shockingly; profoundly; venomously; infernally; consummately; unnaturally.

DAMNATION

adjectives

eternal; relentless; utter; deep; everlasting; irretrievable; consummate.

DAMP

adjectives

murk; occidental; death; soothing; uncheerful; choking; senseless; sickly.

adverbs

slightly; clammily; chillingly; penetratingly; rawly; stuffily; noxiously; foggily; depressingly; inescapably; pestilentially; mistily; mysteriously; coldly; smotheringly; muggily; soggily; soddenly; icily; piercingly; frigidly.

DAMPNESS

adjectives

clammy; chilling; penetrating; stuffy; unctuous; consistent.

DAMSEL

adjectives

pulchritudinous; beauteous; young; calmeyed; dainty; efficient; demure; frank; attractive; shrieking; lovelorn; stout; faery; comely; flounced; frail; frolicsome; officiating; citified; rubicund; haggling; distressed; dashing; misguided; hapless.

verbs

attend—; avow to—; captivate—; cherish —; court—; dishonor—; distress—; misuse—; nurture—; protect—; win—; woo—; —attracts; —blushes; —curtsies; —dreams; —droops; —faints; —frolics; —simpers; —twitters; —yearns. (See woman, girl.)

DANCE

adjectives

rhythmic; divine; ingenious; frantic; wild; passionate; pulse-quickening; queer; eccentric; weird; mazy; absurd; freak; astonishing; grotesque; shambling; classic; old-fashioned; curious; square; folk; ritual; holiday; religious; moonlight; native; exotic; reveling; intricate; pompous; judicious; ballet; risque; characteristic; monopolized; fading; confident; scandalous; Moorish; bewitching; quaint; impish; carnal; exquisite; naked; overture; languid; fairy; mystic; howling; murdering; eternal; evening; amusing; sporadic; erotic; sunset; slow; serene; mirthful; astronomical; revolving; barbaric; spectacular; yearlong.

verbs

accompany—; assemble at—; attend—; blend with—; burst forth in—; contort in—; dress for—; embrace in—; escort to—; grace—; invite to—; join in—; lead off—; leave—; master—; open—; perfect—; perform—; polish—; popularize—; rejoice in—; render—; revel in—; study—; survey—; take part in—; vary—; weary of—;

—breaks; —circles; —enchants; —expresses; —interprets.
(See waltz, minuet.)

DANCE (v)
adverbs
frivolously; bewitchingly; gracefully; divinely; exquisitely; violently; vivaciously;
solemnly; triumphantly; angelically; strenuously; eccentrically; grotesquely; picturesquely; seductively; wantonly; gleefully;
incessantly; rhythmically; ingeniously; religiously; weirdly; shamblingly; ritually;
exotically; quaintly; impishly; carnally; exquisitely; serenely; mirthfully; barbarically;
spectacularly; skillfully; zestfully.

DANCE FLOOR
adjectives
deserted; pretentious; polished; gleaming;
inviting; seductive; mirror-smooth.

DANCE HALL
adjectives
common; tawdry; overcrowded; revolting; frivolous; forcibly-gay.

verbs
assemble at— —; attend — —; congregate
in— —; crowd— —; file into— —; frequent
— —; gather at— —; introduce to— —;
popularize— —; supervise— —; wander
around— —; — —appeals; — —breeds; —
—corrupts; — —offers; — —swarms with;
— —swelters.

DANCER
adjectives
merry; good; superb; delightful; graceful;
light; rhythmic.

verbs
applaud—; fete—; fire—; inspire—; train
—; —awes; —delights; —entertains; —executes; —exercises; —exerts; —expresses;
—interprets; —flies; —flutters; —frisks;
—glides; —s jostle; —leaps; —performs;
—personifies; —pirouettes; —pivots; —
practises; —prances; —s promenade; —
quivers; —registers; —springs; —suggests;
—wheels; —whirls.
(See acrobat.)

DANCING
adjectives
outlandish; outrageous; exquisite; convulsive; titillating; rhythmic; habitual; acrobatic; furious.

DANDELION
adjectives
straggling; common; autumnal; late-blown;
frost-braving; starry; fairy-seeded; omnipresent; humble.

DANDY
adjectives
amiable; professional; hypocritical; dapper;
ingratiating; surreptitious; superficial; perfumed; silk-stockinged.

DANGER
adjectives
ever-impending; imminent; looming; hidden; gathering; unseen; unknown; fancied;
mythical; inevitable; unceasing; vile; imaginary; indefinite; miserable; acute; extreme; august; constant; remote; significant; undiluted; discernible; obvious; immediate; overwhelming; inherent; grave;
pretended; apparent; approaching; potential; future; unavoidable; recurring; spicy;
unexampled; real; countless (pl).

verbs
admit—; avert—; avoid—; beset by—;
blind to—; brave—; confront with—; court
—; create—; demonstrate—; duck—; eliminate—; emphasize—; entail—; exaggerate
—; exempt from—; expose to—; face—;
flee—; foresee—; foretell—; free from—;
guard against—; harbor—; ignore—; increase—; incur—; indicate—; induce—;
involve—; laugh at—; lessen—; lie in—;
minimize—; overcome—; pluck from—;
ponder—; realize—; recognize—; remain
in—; risk—; scoff at—; scorn—; sense—;
shield from—; state—; stem—; taste—;
underestimate—; visualize—; weigh—;
wink at—; woo—; —attends; —impends;
—looms; —lurks; —subsides.
(See peril. hazard, risk.)

DANGEROUS
adverbs
secretly; imminently; mythically; inevitably; miserably; acutely; extremely; remotely; obviously; overwhelmingly; gravely; potentially; unavoidably; critically;
ominously; terribly; incredibly; horribly;
palpably; openly; manifestly; conspicuously.

DANGLE (v)
adverbs
mockingly; loosely; tantalizingly; irritatingly; erotically; teasingly; playfully.
(See hang.)

adverbs

effeminately; sartorially; extremely; elegantly; absurdly; smartly; importantly; expensively; brightly; exquisitely; trimly; sprucely; neatly; nimbly; alertly; gracefully; jauntily; nattily; consciously; swankily; sleekly; becomingly; ornamentally.

DARE (*v*)

adverbs

impiously; virtuously; dauntlessly; boisterously; foolhardily; courageously; impetuously; bravely; unhesitatingly.
(See defy, challenge.)

DAREDEVIL

adjectives

reckless; lovable; hopeful; invincible; adventure-seeking; conquering; amiable.

DARING

adjectives

moon-faced; virtuous; dauntless; remorseless; speculative; boisterous; foolhardy; harmonic.

adverbs

dangerously; rashly; temperamentally; fantastically; alarmingly; foolhardily; breathtakingly; colossally; terribly; dramatically; notoriously; crazily; strangely; singularly; shamefully; amazingly; recklessly; incredibly; unbelievably; foolishly; boldly; avidly; bravely; audaciously; romantically; vicariously; courageously; youthfully; boyishly; disconcertingly; extravagantly.

DARK

adjectives

perilous; fierce; haunted; shuddering; leafy; lugubrious; frosty; shadowed; impenetrable; ambrosial; silent; abysmal; peaceful; fragrant; creeping; intricate; tinkling.

adverbs

mysteriously; impenetrably; perilously; shudderingly; lugubriously; peacefully; abysmally; dismally; fragrantly; suddenly; appreciably; blessedly; fearfully; frightfully; alarmingly; intensely; totally; utterly; pitchy; eerily; unnaturally; bewilderingly; oppressively; increasingly; uneasily; thickly.

adverbs

obscurely; opaquely; murkily; partially; gloomily; unaccountably; perceptibly; inauspiciously; nocturnally; totally; utterly; unnaturally; bewilderingly; increasingly; bafflingly; prematurely; comparatively; mysteriously; generally; devouringly; fatefully; mercifully.
(See shade. obscure.)

DARKENING

adjectives

sudden; gradual; appreciable; perceptible; fathomless; ominous; unprecedented.

DARKNESS

adjectives

blank; blessed; friendly; cozy; deep; hampering; intense; total; opaque; utter; black; somber; pitchy; eerie; unnatural; bewildering; baffling; breathless; preternatural; environing; enveloping; oppressive; choking; stabbing; formless; deepening; increasing; reverberating; howling; Stygian; dense; dripping; silvery; velvety; scented; barbaric; leafy; mental; gross; eternal; uneasy; quiet; serene; abrupt; heavy; muffling; premature; comparative; outer; silent; chilly; blessed; mysterious; general; feudal; blind; lifting; gathering; stormy; horrible; abiding; smooth; fetid; midnight; regnant; fateful; cavernous; dumb; inmost; perennial; wormy; circumambient; thick; devouring; looming; brooding; revolutionary; gay; hot; desert; shadowy; fearful; horrid; merciful; hilltop; windy; marble; healing; unfathomed; priestly; chaotic; abysmal; impending; inwoven; double; lustrous; embarrassing.

verbs

abide in—; accustom to—; beam in—; burnish by—; burrow into—; cast into—; conceal in—; descend to—; disappear into—; discern in—; dispel—; distinguish in—; dread—; dwell in—; encompass by—; encounter—; engulf in—; enlighten—; glow through—; grope in—; haunt—; illumine—; keep in—; lapse into—; laugh at—; lose in—; peer into—; pierce—; plunge into—; prowl in—; pursue in—; remain in—; roam in—; scatter—; shine in—; sink into—; sparkle in—; stumble in—; survey—; toil in—; tread in—; wander in—; wrap in—; yield to—; —approaches; —blinds; —blots out; —broods; —deepens; —depresses; —descends; —devours; —eclipses; —embalms; —embraces; —encompasses; —endures; —enfolds; —ensues; —falls; —flees; —folds over; —gathers; —grows; —hides; —mantles; —melts; —obscures; —prevails; —robes; —shadows; —shrouds; —spreads; —steals upon; —surrounds; —swallows up; —terrifies; —thickens; —veils.

(See gloom, obscurity, shadow.)

DARKY

adjectives

rollicking; superstitious; stalwart; ragged; ingenious; septic-looking; magic-footed; tattered; greasy; cringing; blissful; wool-thatched.

DARLING

adjectives

spunky; plucky; extravagant; spoiled; over-indulged; pampered.

adverbs

utterly; adorably; sweetly; lovably; seductively; charmingly; captivatingly; enchantingly; bewitchingly; tenderly.

DART

adjectives

fiery; false; envenomed; swift; imperceptible; slender; sudden; goading; bullet-like; lightning; dribbling; sickening; spirit-quelling; singing; flaming; shining.

verbs

aim—; blunt—; blow—; brandish—; dash —; defend with—s; envenom—; feather—; flash—; interpose; remove—; poison—; polish—; shake—; shield from—; shoot—; spear—; tip—; thrust—through; —hisses by; —soars; —strikes; —whizzes by; —wounds.

(See missile, spear, shaft, weapon, arrow.)

DASH

adjectives

final; blind; despairing; fiery; flying; headlong; inadvertent; tremendous; meaningful; splendid; giddy; joyous; brilliant; surreptitious; eloquent; refreshing; gallant; rosy.

DASH (v)

adverbs

gently; aimlessly; turbulently; hurriedly; immediately; madly; blindly; inadvertently; despairingly; splendidly; joyously; gallantly; eagerly; anxiously; furiously; victoriously; unrestrainedly; violently.

(See hurl.)

DASHING

adverbs

showily; jauntily; gallantly; pretentiously; proudly; vainly; gorgeously; dramatically; theatrically; spectacularly; sumptuously; boldly; rashly; valiantly; pluckily; stoutly; audaciously; dauntlessly; confidently; fashionably; stylishly.

DATA

adjectives

curious; strange; one-sided; accompanying; available; existing; latest; relative; interesting; relevant; fascinating; convincing; accurate; basic; factual; important; significant; extensive; erroneous; obscure; modern; corrective; research; programmed; official; scientific; technical; merchandising; precise; recorded; necessary; incomplete; impeccable; authentic; intimate; historical; biographic.

verbs

accept—; accumulate—; analyze—; attest by—; authenticate—; catalogue—; collect —; elaborate—; furnish—; gather—; improve—; present—; produce—; study—; survey—; synthesize—; track down—; —indicate; —measure; —prove; —reveal; —show.

(See fact, information.)

DATE

adjectives

ineffective; arbitrary; fixed; exact; recent; ancient; prescribed; decisive; closing; historical; equivalent; significant; future; remote; immediate; memorable; subsequent; calamitous; lasting; endless; tentative; dark; dividing; equinoctial.

verbs

ascribe—to; assign—to; bear—; calculate —; cancel—; confirm—; denote—; determine—; extend—; fix—; forestall—; inscribe—; insert—; jot down—; limit to—; mark with—; reckon—; refer to—; require—; set—; specify—; —denotes; —expires.

(See time, duration.)

DATE (v)

adverbs

variously; significantly; recently; historically; tentatively; unquestionably; subsequently.

(See record.)

311

adjectives
unsightly; wretched; pitiful; artless; spattered; colorful.

DAUB (v)
adverbs
wretchedly; hideously; hatefully; amateurishly; carelessly; halfheartedly.
(See smear, soil.)

DAUGHTER
adjectives
loyal; considerate; true; dutiful; self-sacrificing; stubbornly-devoted; tiny; plump; brisk; pretty; beautiful; hardhearted; militant; rebellious; errant; irreconcilable; sedate; tomboy; virginal; debutante; spoiled; idolized; virtuous; modern; outspoken; tender; chaste; marriageable; repentant; gay; beldam; buxom; blithe; debonair; short; untutored; fragile; mangled; abominable; peerless; loving; expiring; flighty; uncultured.

verbs
adopt—; adore—; bear—; berate—; betroth—; bring forth—; chastise—; cherish —; conceive—; confer on—; delight in—; fondle—; long for—; market—; marry off—; mold—; pamper—; preach to—; present with—; nurse—; rear—; rebuke—; rejoice in—; reprimand—; seduce—; woo —; —elopes; —graces; —inherits; — pleads; —shames; —shocks.
(See child, girl, person, woman.)

DAUNTLESS
adverbs
heroically; courageously; recklessly; rashly; resolutely; splendidly; superbly; joyously; proudly; fiercely; morally; carelessly; impetuously; stubbornly; magnificently; exceptionally.

DAVENPORT
adjectives
sagged; restful; upholstered; comfortable; dumpy; deep.

DAWDLE (v)
adverbs
perversely; idly; languidly; tantalizingly; calmly; everlastingly; lightly; somnolently; lazily; lackadaisically; irritatingly; aimlessly.
(See dally.)

DAWDLING
adjectives
calm; everlasting; lackadaisical; nonchalant; idle; purposeless.

DAWN
adjectives
black; crawling; opalescent; dirty; gray; thick; crimson; golden; pitiless; pearl; cool; false; dismal; cheerless; wet; pale; perfect; premature; faint; hushed; slow; tropical; clear; stormy; countless (pl); roseate; autumnal; northern; waking; hazy; kindling; crude; softly-breaking; radiant; wintry; savage; streaked; low; dappled; amorous; reddest; tender; noonday; bashful; tempestuous; joyful; azure; unmellowed; crepuscular; smothering; melancholy.

verbs
behold—; foretell—; front—; herald—; journey till—; precede—; rise at—; usher in—; wait for—; wake with—; warn of—; —arouses; —ascends; —blazons; —blushes; —breaks; —cheers; —creeps on; —flares; —flees; —flushes; —glimmers; —pierces; —ripens into day; —surges; —surprises; —steals over; —verges with.
(See daylight.)

DAWN (v)
adverbs
finally; abruptly; clearly; brilliantly; incisively; eerie; troubled; gorgeous; antiphonal; hazy; phosphorescent.
(See lighten.)

DAY
adjectives
adventurous; agreeable; arduous; alternate; anxious; auspicious; beautiful; brilliant; buoyant; broiling; blowing; bitter; bloody; blank; bygone; blissful; brave; burning; bright; bustling; boyhood; bountiful; battering; commendable; chaotic; cloudy; cool; crisp; calm; coronation; courageous; clear; checkered; capricious; cheerless; catechizing; corsair (pl); credulous; colorful; crowded; careless; canicular; vivid; carefree; dim; dayless; decisive; declining; dying; dull; disastrous; dismal; dramatic; drab; drizzling; dedicated; diviner; domestic; degenerate; dangerous; decadent; delightful; depression (pl); dark; dragging; dreary; dusty; despairing; distracting; dead; dumb; drowsy; dancing; eventful; empty; epochal; endless; expiring; everlasting; ensuing; eternal; enchant-

ed; enlightened; exciting; evil; exceptional; fateful; first; fatiguing; fatal; funeral; flourishing; former; festal; fragrant; fairy; frosty; foul; gentle; glorious; grinding; gloomy; gushing; garish; gallant; garden; golden; gay; glamorous; gambling; hectic; hot; holy; happy; hopeful; halcyon; honest; historic; humid; homesick; happy-go-lucky; innocent; illustrious; indelible; intercalary; ideal; idle; irretrievable; irreclaimable; interleaving; judgment; jocund; joyous; laborious; late; luckless; long; lively; lazy; limpid; lagging; lifeless; memorable; mysterious; miserable; melancholy; motionless; magnificent; monastic; muted; medieval; momentous; opulent; northern; noisy; newborn; natal; nuptial; neophyte; overbusy; old; opal-colored; proverbial; piercing; peevish; present; prosperous; preceding; proud; perfect; pretty; pleasant; pessimistic; pre-medieval (pl); postwar (pl); planless; phlegmatic; primitive; parsimonious; pilgrim; palmy; quondam; restful; rainy; recurring; reckoning; rosy; romantic; regal; raucous; roisterous; red-letter; ruminant; righteous; splendid; sultry; sunless; silent; soggy; silver; strenuous; summer; somnolent; sorry; smiling; sullen; sinking; sodden; scornful; solitary; serene; superb; solar; sordid; short; simple; somber; sinister; supplementary; sizzling; scorching; tiresome; slumberous; topsy-turvy; tumultuous; toil-stained; triumphal; tedious; temperamental; visionary; torrid; unreal; untroubled; unremembered; vanished; campaigning; victorious; vagabond; vacant.

verbs
appoint—; await—; bemoan—; behold—; bless—; busy—; cap—; cloud—; contemplate—; crown—; curse—; decree—; denounce—; dispose of—; divide—; drag out —s; ease—; enliven—; endure—; grace—; herald—; honor—; keep—; kill—; lament —; lose—; mar—; measure—; name—; observe—; peak—; record—; regret—; rejoice—; reminisce of—s; rest by—; rue—; rule—; save—; solemnize—; waste—; win—; —advances; —affords; —approaches; —breaks; —cheers; —closes; —comforts; —darkens; —dawns; —dazzles; — declines; —decreases; —dies; —drags by; —s elapse; —is born; —lags; —mounts; —oppresses; —peers forth; —races by; —saddens; —s shorten; —unfolds; —vanishes; —wanes; —waxes; —wears off.
(See time. age, generation.)

DAYBREAK

adjectives
glimmering; resplendent; glorious; joyous; gratifying; welcome; salutary; golden.

DAYLIGHT

adjectives
fading; burning; broad; wintry; sick; gray; haggard; dying; garish; partial; glimmering; adequate; diffused; beautiful; blessed; obscure; unnatural; scented; yellow; primrose.

verbs
employ—; keep in—; let in—; surrender to—; —appears; —approaches; —arouses; —breaks; —burns; —dawns; —dazzles; —dies; —diffuses; —discloses; —envelops; —fades; —filters through; —floods; —illumines; —pours in; —promises; —seeps in; —shines; —suffuses; —unfolds; —vanishes; —wanes.
(See day, light. dawn.)

DAZE

adjectives
fatuous; open-mouthed; sodden; staggering; effacing; somnambulistic.

DAZED

adverbs
stupidly; unaccountably; genuinely; disturbingly; strangely; indescribably; fearfully; insuperably; depressingly; terribly; alarmingly; unreasonably; vaguely; uncomfortably; inexplicably; awkwardly;; extremely; helplessly; pitifully; tragically; sadly; hopelessly; dangerously.

DAZZLE (v)

adverbs
suddenly; glamorously; resplendently; purposely; bewilderingly; awesomely; blindingly; fatuously; hopelessly; fatally.
(See blind, bewilder.)

DEACON

adjectives
dutiful; long-faced; solemn; ruling; parsimonious; funereal-looking; sleek-haired; sin-denouncing.

adverbs
appoint—; elect—; ordain—; unfrock—; —administers; —admonishes; —advises; —assists; —attends; —awes; —baptizes; —christens; —collects; —disperses; —dis-

313

tributes; —performs; —prays; —preaches; —provides; —reproves; —serves; —supervises; —visits.
(See minister, elder, officer.)

DEAD

adjectives
stricken; unseen; illustrious; beloved; pitiful; humble; heroic; war; ghastly; gallant; moldering; enduring; sainted; venerable; imponderable; silent; turbaned; decaying; ungathered; coffined; spectral; pestilential; unconscious; restless; mighty; dearest; honorable; untimely; vulgar; faithful; precious; passionless; floating.

verbs
awaken—; bemoan—; blaspheme—; bury —; commemorate—; consort with—; curse —; defile—; disinter—; embalm—; entomb—; honor—; judge—; mourn—; number—; record—; reincarnate—; remember—; revive—; rise from—; rob—; —sleep on; —wither.
(See carcass, corpse.)

DEADLOCK

adjectives
hopeless; partial; growing; convenient; relentless; quarterless; fatal.

DEADLY

adverbs
disastrously; noxiously; virulently; exceptionally; irremediably; woefully; execrably.

DEAF

adverbs
totally; insufferably; irritatingly; vexatiously; annoyingly; pitiably; slightly; utterly; deplorably; lamentably; unfortunately; stubbornly; callously; deliberately; unhappily; pitifully; tragically; forlornly; desperately; moodily; lonesomely.

DEAL

adjectives
neighborly; momentous; shady; dirty; legitimate; ill-savored; unprotected; square; devised; financial; business; backstairs; important; great; vast; infinite; complete; skin; wandering; famished; sensational; new; tremendous; parlor; wonder; made-to-order; timed-to-the-minute; combination; bargain; smashing; pace-setting; thrilling.

verbs
arrange—; bargain—; benefit by—; carry on—; clinch—; close—; concoct—; disclose—; engage in—; engineer—; engross

in—; enter—; involve in—; participate in—; put over—; transact—; unfold—; —fizzles (colloq.); —promises.
(See transaction.)

DEAL (v)

adverbs
ceremoniously; promptly; ruthlessly; bountifully; primarily; heedlessly; discreetly; severely; summarily; zestfully; scientifically; munificently; adequately; rigorously; gratuitously; momentously; legitimately; financially; sensationally; thrillingly; persuasively; exclusively; competently; plainly; brilliantly.
(See negotiate, distribute.)

DEALER

adjectives
opulent; persuasive; ignorant; unscrupulous; keen; double; individual; antique; honest; retail; exclusive; plain; implement; competent.

DEALINGS

adjectives
hard; plain; decent; gracious; unauthorized; shrewd; double; quick; sharp; satisfactory; dishonest; high-minded; generous; rough; hazardous; strenuous; undiplomatic; wanton; unscrupulous; fair; nefarious; punctilious; extensive; business; wise; patient; highhanded; furtive; ruthless.

DEAN

adjectives
callous; pompous; incompetent; meticulous; impeccable; impinging; smug.

DEAR

adverbs
infinitely; adorably; admirably; delightfully; affectionately.

DEARTH

adjectives
barren; deplorable; notable; absolute; sickening; hapless; agreeable.

DEATH

adjectives
brave; beautiful; happy; glorious; heroic; gentle; gallant; calm; romantic; tranquil; painless; swift; reasonable; merciful; natural; appropriate; deliberate; certain; sure; untoward; early; premature; melancholy; tragic; baleful; lamented; instantaneous; quick; sudden; vicious; grappling; grisly; grim; horrible; ghastly; dreadful; beastly;

ignominious; slow; lingering; physical; spiritual; temporal; somatic; cool; enfolding; tearful; sleeping; silent; long; unified; inflexible; ensuing; imbecilic; latent; cruel; intellectual; partial; honorable; immediate; recent; deplored; radiant; shadow-like; diverse(pl); mysterious; uniform; delicious; ugly; moral; fearful; drowning; threatened; awful; gradual; merited; devouring; foreboding; impending; immortal; stalking; unlooked-for; tardy; covetous; bright; unspeaking; heartening; atrocious; disgraceful; adulterate; direful; slaughtering; humane; engrossing; sacrificial; unsubstantial; bloody; maternal; helpless; poetic; violent; affronted; unregretted; flaming; unnoticed; instant; sacred; everlasting; manly; glowing; timeless; malignant; agonizing; eternal; obscure; placid; present; golden; ultimate; approaching; protracted; unrewarded; subsequent; tithed; untimely; distressing; hideous; watery; senseless; dusty; accidental; sequent; tuberculous; occasional (pl); ominous; excruciating; voluptuous; shameful; dramatic; pale; wasted; miserable; princely; paralyzing; drier; opportune; delaying; stony; self-abased; sulphurous; overshadowing; unanticipated; propagating; strong; shrouded; scurvy; treacherous; fierce; unavoidable; unseen; mellow; loathsome; temporal; living.

verbs

administer—; announce—; apprise of—; avert—; bore to—; brood on—; cause—; cheat—; condemn to—; confirm—; contemplate—; dance with—; deliver from—; deserve—; designate—; devise—; dramatize —; endure—; evade—; exact—; experience —; expiate—; face—; feign—; frighten to —; gamble with—; give up to—; guard till; —harass to—; harry to—; hasten—; hunger for—; induce—; join in—; laugh at—; long for—; mete out—; mock—; mourn—; overcome—; persecute unto—; poise at the brink of—; pour—on; predestine to—; prepare for—; preserve from—; quail before—; recoil from—; repose in—; repulse—; rescue from—; result in—; revenge—; scorn—; seal with—; send to—; sentence to—; snatch from—; spare from—; spell—; spurt—; stay—; struggle against —; submit to—; suffer—; symbolize—; threaten with—; triumph over—; usher in—; ward off—; warrant—; welcome—; wreak—; yield to—; —alters; —claims; —clamors; —concludes; —dances; — dawns; —devours; —dogs; —embitters;

—engulfs; —ensues; —follows; —grieves; —grins; —harvests; —humbles; —intervenes; —invades; —lurks; —menaces; — parts; —reveals; —shades; —shadows; —spreads; —stalks among; —stings; — supervenes; —swallows up; —terminates; —triumphs; —vanquishes; —walks; — strikes.

(See extinction, destruction, slaughter, mortality.)

DEBASE (v)

adverbs
obscenely; miserably; shamefully; tragically; ruinously; unavoidably; irrevocably; irreparably; tyrannically.
(See degrade, humiliate.)

DEBASED

adverbs
grossly; abjectly; morally; perfidiously; treacherously; disgracefully; darkly; infamously; arrantly; vilely; contemptibly; shamefully; bestially.

DEBATABLE

adverbs
highly; unquestionably; definitely; obviously; profoundly; endlessly; turbulently; violently; critically; dangerously; excitingly; hotly; amusingly; readily; easily; reasonably; rationally; concretely; equivocally; hypothetically; precariously; speciously; logically.

DEBATE

adjectives
stormy; profound; mental; inward; parliamentary; foul; keen; acrimonious; notable; instructive; picayune; animated; interrupted; open; free; public; obstructive; lively; endless; prolix; fierce; impassioned; mock; lifelong; extemporaneous; considerable; political; epistolary; vigorous; newspaper; turbulent; organized; heated; disorderly; spirited; exciting; familiar; long-winded; noisy; hot; brotherly; amusing; teleological; loud; dialetical.

verbs
admit to—; assemble for—; climax—; contend during—; deliberate on—; draw into —; engage in—; enter into—; indulge in—; involve in—; judge—; practise—; prepare —; resolve into—; settle—; subject to—; welcome—; wrangle during—; —concludes; —discusses; —revolves about.
(See dispute, controversy, combat, contest, discussion.)

DEBATE (v)

adverbs
abundantly; extensively; futilely; inwardly; profoundly; mentally; instructively; animatedly; openly; publicly; endlessly; fiercely; impassionedly; extemporaneously; considerably; politically; vigorously; turbulently; heatedly; spiritedly; noisily; hotly; amusingly; loudly; dialectically; acrimoniously; shrewdly.
(See argue, discuss.)

DEBATER

adjectives
cogent; convincing; tight-lipped; ready; interlocutory.

verbs
coach—; judge—; prepare—; train—; verse—; —argues; —assembles; —asserts; —assures; —cajoles; —concludes; —contends; —convinces; —declares; —discusses; —disputes; —engages; —gestures; —illustrates; —informs; —points out; —refers to; —refutes; —registers; —shouts; — voices.
(See speaker.)

DEBAUCH

adjectives
veritable; riotous; rudimentary; prolonged; unwonted; limitless; grisly; abnormal; drunken; secret; fictional.

DEBAUCHED

adverbs
pitiably; grossly; terribly; horribly; shamelessly; abjectly; lamentably; openly; shamefully; morally; disgracefully; infamously; notoriously; arrantly; vilely; contemptibly; bestially; voluptuously; wildly; dissolutely; brutishly; indecently.

DEBAUCHERY

adjectives
brutal; sensual; profligate; titled; coarse; truant; corrupt; perverse.

DEBILITY

adjectives
languid; attendant; general; extreme; congenital; nervous; spectral; physical.

DEBRIS

adjectives
accumulated; rock; floating; chaotic; fragmentary; sad; littered; hopeless.

verbs
emerge from—; crumble to—; fall amidst —; rise from—; scatter—; search—.
(See ruins, remains, fragments, rubbish.)

DEBT

adjectives
common; enormous; stale; ancestral; crushing; credit; impaired; recoverable; petty; immeasurable; incalculable; heavy; tremendous; huge; lawful; honest; long-standing; mounting; urgent; floating; discharged; everlasting; terrible; dubious; regulating; desperate; profound; gambling; unpayable, joint; countless; paltry.

verbs
abolish—; acknowledge—; amass—; assume —; cancel—; clear—; confront with—; contract—; die in—; discharge—; dissolve —; encumber with—; free from—; harass with—; incur—; overwhelm with—; plunge into—; repay—; repudiate—; scale down—; smart under—; swell—; unload—; wipe away—; —jumps; —rises; —soars.
(See obligation, liability.)

DEBTOR

adjectives
prodigal; luckless; shabby; insolvent; grateful; broken.

verbs
accommodate—; bind—; bond—; demand of—; die—; harass—; harry—; hound—; imprison—; insure—; jail—; limit—; oblige—; press—; release—; subject—; sue —; —abolishes; —appeals to; —borrows; —discharges; —falls delinquent; —promises; —reduces.

DEBUT

adjectives
operatic; successful; daring; startling; notable; eventual.

DEBUTANTE

adjectives
pretty; awkward; career-seeking; altar-bound; dazzling; successfully-launched; expensive; luxury-seeking.

DECADE

adjectives
present; recent; stormy; independent; successive; mauve; ironical; past; coming; prosperous; legendary.

verbs
approach—; celebrate—; include in—; infuse in—; form in—; recall —s; recognize—; survive—; vanish with—s; — advances; —elapses; —ensues; —envelops; —flourishes.
(See period, time.)

DECADENCE
adjectives
pale; sentimental; brilliant; passionate; pathetic; fragrant; vegetating; mouldy.

verbs
abandon to—; arouse from—; awake from —; crumble into—; fall into—; incur—; lapse into—; prevent—; produce—; resist —; result in—; rise out of—; slide into—; steep in—; suffer—; threaten with—; — approaches; —beckons; —girdles; —sleeps in.
(See deterioration, decay.)

DECADENT
adverbs
cankerously; decrepitly; effetely; corrosively; corruptibly; irreparably; incurably; irremediably; lamentably; deplorably; pitifully; viciously; degenerately; corruptly; unbelievably; astoundingly; pitiably; hopelessly.

DECAY
adjectives
inevitable; melancholy; symbolic; premature; elegant; slow; mental; swift; physical; flamboyant; approaching; common; perpetual; integral; picturesque; unperceived; sensible; dry; gradual; inexorable; fatal; lichened.

verbs
accelerate—; arrest—; attack by—; bar—; conceal—; delay—; doom to—; exempt from—; fall into—; presage—; preserve from—; reek of—; resist—; subject to—; suffer—; —bores into; —sets in.
(See deterioration, decomposition, corruption.)

DECAY (v)
adverbs
fearfully; disastrously; inevitably; symbolically; prematurely; mentally; swiftly; physically; picturesquely; sensibly; inexorably; gradually; fatally; obviously; partially; invisibly.
(See rot, disintegrate.)

DECEIT
adjectives
charming; dreamlike; dear; radiant; adored; coquettish; remorseful; blind; beguiling; unprincipled; fatal.

verbs
abhor—; avoid—; breed—; commit—; conceal—; contrive by—; depart from—; dispose to—; dwell in—; indulge in—; intend—; nourish—; quit—; redeem from —; shroud—; suspect—; unearth—; utter —; wallow in—; work—; annoys; — counters; —falsifies; —flourishes; —harms; —irks; —misleads; —pricks; —tricks; reprove—.
(See fraud, deception. trick, stratagem, cheating.)

DECEITFUL
adverbs
inherently; naturally; habitually; characteristically; temperamentally; subtly; shrewdly; astutely; carefully; deliberately; insidiously; smoothly; fiendishly; maliciously; astoundingly; deftly; dangerously; insinuatingly; horribly; abominably; shamefully; daringly; surprisingly; unexpectedly; expertly.

DECEIVE (v)
adverbs
deliberately; grossly; palpably; bitterly; eternally; prodigiously; blackly; mightily; heartlessly; systematically; basely; purposely; vilely; villainously; treacherously.
(See mislead.)

DECEIVER
adjectives
systematic; heartless; gracious; seductive; gay; artful; politic; insidious; crafty.

DECENCY
adjectives
ordinary; sheer; conventional; common; mere; enforced; requisite; wanton; political; true; social; eminent; respectable; temperate; native; disregarded.

verbs
breed in—; conform to—; dress in—; dwell in—; execute with—; expect—; inject into—; insist on—; maintain—; manage with—; observe—; perform with—; practise—; pretend—; violate—; —befits; — flourish; —requires; outrage—.
(See propriety, modesty, decorum.)

DECENT

adverbs

decorously; utterly; entirely; honestly; modestly; admirably; habitually; conventionally; eminently; innately; inherently; notably; chastely; suitably; naturally; appropriately; unobtrusively; superbly; remarkably; essentially; palpably; obviously; extraordinarily; unaffectedly.

DECEPTION

adjectives

palpable; gross; downright; swaggering; detestable; obvious; systematic; pious; venial; innocent; intentional; harmless; inevitable; economic; relative; facial; deliberate; refined; universal.

verbs

apply—; avoid—; commit—; conceal—; devise—; dispose to—; expose—; fall into —; fear—; form—; imagine—; impose— upon; justify—; perform—; produce—; practice—; suspect—; unearth—; unfold—; —harms; —injures.

(See deceit, craft, cunning, trickery, fraud.)

DECEPTIVE

adverbs

palpably; grossly; detestably; obviously; cruelly; systematically; methodically; intentionally; purposely; maliciously; harmlessly; deliberately; childishly; innocently; teasingly; criminally; cleverly; astutely; adroitly; expertly; carefully; meanly; despicably; contemptibly; disgracefully; terribly.

DECIDE (v)

adverbs

adversely; conclusively; discreetly; positively; affirmatively; irrevocably; authentically; impartially; wisely; tentatively; peremptorily; glumly; confusedly; arbitrarily; simultaneously; impulsively; virtually; unanimously; eventually; conspicuously; grudgingly; favorably; magnanimously; sensibly; temperately; resolutely; unalterably; authoritatively; haphazardly; prematurely; precipitately; tactically; emphatically; spectacularly; promptly; theoretically; academically; technically; politically; speedily.

(See determine, resolve.)

DECISION

adjectives

favorable; comforting; sagacious; well-considered; careful; correct; perfect; practical; magnanimous; sensible; unfettered; unbought; accurate; straightforward; just; calm; temperate; final; irreparable; irrevocable; invincible; expectant; inexorable; peremptory; sweeping; important; resolute; unflinching; firm; unmistakable; unalterable; unchanged; authoritative; unbiased; weighty; momentous; august; arbitrary; vacillating; haphazard; premature; abrupt; precipitate; rapid; instant; hasty; intuitive; quick; swift; hair-trigger; dangerous; desperate; ruinous; illegal; adverse; judicial; critical; temporal; ticklish; major; iniquitous; unanimous; last-moment; applauded; perplexing; tactical; controlling; definite; profitless; cryptic; tentative; overt; successive; prompt; emphatic; due; unbalanced; disastrous; solemn; demurred; spectacular; supreme; indolent; instant; practical; ruling; belated; blamable; strict; impartial; theoretical; calculated; epoch-making; heart-searching; resolute; sudden; daring; executive; tremendous; resounding; academic; unwise; crushing; initiatory; technical; adverse; political; rumored; sundry (pl).

verbs

abide by—; accept—; acclaim—; adhere to—; analyze—; circumvent—; confirm—; contest—; dictate—; enforce—; execute—; greet—; hail—; hand down—; influence—; obey—; prejudice—; reach—; render—; reverse—; stiffen—; subject to—; submit to—; swing—; voice—; weigh—; —embroils; —favors; —foreshadows; invalidates; —takes place; —wavers.

(See settlement, conclusion, verdict.)

DECISIVE

adverbs

alarmingly; conclusively; definitely; scarcely; mercifully; fortunately; happily; favorably; comfortingly; practically; justly; irrevocably; inexorably; sweepingly; importantly; firmly; unmistakably; unalterably; authoritatively; authentically; weightily; augustly; intuitively; swiftly; desperately; critically; iniquitously; solemnly; tremendously; politically.

DECK

adjectives

hurricane; forward; promenade; white-scoured; bright; snowy; spotless; glistening; holystoned; sloping; inclining; reeling; pitching; slippery; slimy; unscrubbed; shattered; spacious; blazing; cluster-lighted; splinter-strewn; awninged; watery;

crowded; ghostly; creamy; tapered; windswept; ocean; long; great; open; comfortable; gay; sun; broad; shot-torn; shuddering; wave-set; steamer; stricken; bloody; unobstructed; wreckage-laden.

verbs
batter—; burst—; clear—; cover—; dash on—; glimmer on—; keep above—; lash—; lie on—; pace—; scatter on—; shatter—; splinter—; sprawl on—; stand on—; sun on —; toss on—; tramp—; view from—; wave from—; —extends; —runs.
(See platform. floor.)

DECLAMATION
adjectives
rhetorical; strident; stuttering; insipid; passionate; empty; facetious; sounding.

verbs
alter—; burst into—; compose—; dispute—; influence—; inspire—; publish—; render—; repeat—; set forth—; stir up—; thunder—; utter—; —embodies; —exacerbates; —expresses; —proves; —shocks; —stirs.
(See speech. oration, oratory.)

DECLAMATORY
adverbs
absurdly; effusively; unnecessarily; foolishly; ridiculously; ludicrously; amusingly; bombastically; pompously; arrogantly; pretentiously; stridently; passionately; fervently; emptily; facetiously; sententiously; laughably; piously; grandiloquently; floridly; preachily; pedantically; frothily; flashily; flamboyantly; blatantly.

DECLARATION
adjectives
culminating; remarkable; far-echoing; formal; droll; insulting; emphatic; public; appalling; passionate; blunt; voluntary; candid; downright; bold; determining; significant; official; profound; strong; solemn; superior; positive; vehement; frequent; rigid; important; absolute; distinct; undisguised; open; customary; fierce; friendly; supplementary; bitter; passionate; abasing; unmistakable.

verbs
adopt—; announce—; belie—; constitute—; decry—; dispute—; expound—; immortalize—; inspire—; introduce—; issue—; present—; proclaim—; publish—; set forth—; —contradicts; —embodies; —influences; —pleads; —proves; —shocks.
(See assertion, statement.)

DECLARATORY
adverbs
plainly; comfortingly; reassuringly; explicitly; clearly; analytically; broadly; substantially; literally; honestly; simply; significantly; intelligibly; authoritatively; formally; emphatically; bluntly; officially.

DECLARE (v)
adverbs
vociferously; formally; publicly; emphatically; passionately; bluntly; candidly; boldly; significantly; officially; solemnly; vehemently; absolutely; distinctly; openly; fiercely; bitterly; unmistakably; conceitedly; enthusiastically; pedantically; petulantly; grimly; virtually; impatiently; contemptuously; stoutly; hypocritically; privately; haltingly; inconclusively; antagonistically; formally; shamelessly; speciously; archly; hotly; earnestly; rapturously; severely; wrathfully; repeatedly; unanimously; solemnly.
(See affirm, state.)

DECLINE
adjectives
marked; considerable; general; ultimate; lingering; terrific; unquestionable; alarming; social; drastic; prolonged; accelerated; sad; subsequent; premature; short; dreary; unaccountable; hopeless; marked; incipient; ominous; partial; unprecedented; indubitable.

DECLINE (v)
adverbs
peremptorily; repeatedly; progressively; blandly; spinelessly; respectfully; steadily; gently; invariably; bluntly; querulously; rapidly; gravely; firmly; quietly; majestically; ultimately; alarmingly; socially; acceleratedly; subsequently; prematurely; drearily; unaccountably; hopelessly; ominously; partially; indubitably; unprecedentedly.
(See languish, bend.)

DECLIVITY
adjectives
slight; dread; gentle; abrupt; steep; obstructing.

DECOMPOSITION
adjectives
chemical; spontaneous; painful; tedious; rapid; erosive; timely.

verbs
crumble into—; fall into—; incur—; lapse into—; object to—; prevent—; produce—; resolve into—; result in—; slide into—; suffer—; threaten with—; undergo—; — abates; —continues; —distributes; —separates.
(See disintegration, decay.)

DECORATE (v)
adverbs
elaborately; exquisitely; profusely; picturesquely; garishly; inelegantly; charmingly; lavishly; gaudily; quaintly; splendidly; tastefully; mournfully; superfluously; sumptuously; superbly; festively; gorgeously; pictorially; richly; tastefully; delicately; ornately; ostentatiously; characteristically; formally; realistically; murally; scenically; fantastically; architecturally; grotesquely.
(See adorn, embellish.)

DECORATION
adjectives
coveted; incidental; pictorial; simulated; profuse; mistaken; disturbing; quiet; rich; new; superb; modern; regal; tasteful; delicate; contemporary; delightful; ornate; ostentatious; personal; excessive; last-moment; characteristic; silver; detailed; glaring; formal; realistic; eye-filling; sense-curdling; painted; elaborate; polychrome; mural; casual; sober; religious; lateral; lavish; unobtrusive; sparkling; scenical; stupendous; sculptural; simple; fantastic; costly; lifeless; colorless; architectural; molded; grotesque; subordinated.

DECORATIVE
adverbs
delicately; incidentally; properly; quietly; richly; superbly; regally; tastefully; delightfully; ornately; excessively; formally; elaborately; casually; soberly; lavishly; unobtrusively; pleasantly; agreeably; appropriately; graphically; picturesquely; romantically; unusually; beautifully.

DECORATOR
adjectives
prominent; competent; resourceful; professional; amateur; over-ambitious; aspiring; over-nice; classically-inclined.

DECOROUS
adverbs
becomingly; modestly; essentially; socially; strictly; scrupulously; carefully; invariably; habitually; ordinarily; dependably; politely; fashionably; punctiliously; conventionally; civilly; respectfully; reverentially; deferentially; ceremoniously; decently.

DECORUM
adjectives
external; stately; perfect; naughty; social; artistic; strict; pallid; unyielding; scrupulous; grave; public.

verbs
adhere to—; act with—; behave with—; cling to—; clothe in—; hedge by—; maintain—; mantle in—; nourish—; observe—; preserve—; require—; safeguard—; shed —; shock—; wallow in—; —lapses; —prevails; —restrains.
(See politeness, decency, propriety.)

DECREASE
adjectives
sagging; marked; dripping; noticeable; proportional.

DECREASE (v)
adverbs
imperceptibly; immeasurably; relatively; markedly; proportionally; noticeably; amazingly; astonishingly; tragically; fatally; woefully.
(See diminish, reduce.)

DECREE
adjectives
judgment; repealing; castigatory; omnipotent; law; august; tyrannical; eternal; emergency; royal; unalterable; unfathomable; divine; imperial; established; stern; oppressive; changeless; pitiless; unexecuted; irreversible; obnoxious; generous; paternal; laconic; primeval; absolute; extemporary.

verbs
adjust—; affirm—; alter—; annul—; bow to—; break—; carry out—; condemn—; confirm—; contest—; declare—; delay—; enforce—; favor—; issue—; mold—; obey—; oppose—; overleap—; proclaim—; promulgate—; repeal—; resist—; reverse —; revoke—; shape—; sign—; submit to—; sustain—; trample upon—; —banishes; —bans; —conscripts; —disposes of; —prohibits.
(See law, edict, mandate, ordinance, decision, rule.)

DECREE (v)

adverbs
irrevocably; tyrannically; legislatively; formally.

(See enact.)

DECREPIT

adverbs
helplessly; prematurely; dangerously; pitiably; hopelessly; pathetically; terribly; deplorably; heartbreakingly; hoarily; dodderingly; feebly; totteringly; crazily; incurably; weakly; lamentably; pitifully.

DECREPITUDE

adjectives
premature; dangerous; helpless; hampering; fretful; onrushing; subtle.

DEDICATE (v)

adverbs
pompously; respectfully; tacitly; solemnly; chiefly; wholeheartedly; sincerely; humbly; flatteringly; appreciatively; modestly; arrogantly; worshipfully.

(See consecrate, devote.)

DEDICATION

adjectives
handsome; nauseating; flattering; honorary; memorable; cursory; nominal.

DEDUCE (v)

adverbs
psychologically; rationalistically; unscientifically; logically; immediately; daringly; legitimately; profoundly; modestly; shrewdly.

(See conclude.)

DEDUCTIBLE

adverbs
immediately; legitimately; legally; logically; naturally; liberally; fortunately; ultimately; deceptively; possibly; unquestionably; inferentially; authentically; authoritatively; generously; substantially.

DEDUCTION

adjectives
immense; entomological; immediate; pure; sound; unverified; daring; trifling; logical; legitimate; profound; liberal; analogical; ultimate; false; bibulous; dipsomaniacal; modest; sagest; possible; hazardous; labored; spurious; genuine.

verbs
allow—; arrive at—; bear out—; claim—; confirm—; contemplate—; contradict—; debate—; decide on—; deny—; derive—; draw—; err in—; form—; reach—; reason —; secure—; —confuses; —follows.

(See demonstration, proof, inference.)

DEED
(general)

adjectives
sundry (pl); good; glorious; worthy; wise; brilliant; maniacal; meritorious; glamorous; notable; unforgettable; momentous; brave; courageous; heroic; mighty; doughty; rash; evil; dangerous; terrible; dishonest; desperate; inhuman; dirty; brutal; treacherous; violent; bloodthirsty; unholy; harsh; vainglorious; atrocious; silly; tacit; valiant; contemplated; passionate; unnatural; charitable; shameful; cursed; radiant; rueful; conspicuous; piteous; peaceful; wicked; hideous; masterful; execrable; heinous; bloody; lustful; chivalric; honorable; long; traitorous; virtuous; foulest; selfish; corrupt; unjust; steadfast; tragic; dastardly; magnanimous; historic; pious; truculent; knightly; disgraceful; manful; irrevocable; dragon; untried; lovely; sculptured; fiendish; lawless; persistent; deathless; fell; amazing; kindred; hazardous; darkest; venturous; stern; ill; unostentatious; precious; baleful; title; daring; horrible; barbarous; fearful; evil; remorseless; blazing; kind; sublime; caitiff; generous; wholesome; human; reckless; vile; abhorrent; loyal; pure; kingly; senseless; undying; grander; impeachable; noble; despicable; myriad (pl).

verbs
acclaim—; achieve—; answer for—; applaud—; ascribe to—; attempt—; bear out—; belittle—; blame—; bless—; boast of—; celebrate—; commemorate—; commend—; commit—; consent to—; contrive —; dare—; die in—; dignify—; dispense with—; dread—; emulate—; enshrine—; execrate—; glory in—; govern—; hallow—; honor—; incite to—; judge—; justify—; match—; noise—; perform—; please by—; proclaim—; promote—; recompense—; record—; relate—; resent—; render—; repent—; report—; reprove—; reward—; rue—; serve in—; shudder at—; sing of—s; spur to—; spurn—; void—; vouch for—; —awes; —flames; —indicates; —lives; —shames.

(See act. feat, performance, reality, exploit, achievement.)

adjectives

restless; violet; uncomprehensible; over-brimming; mystic; uncreated; populous; airy; avenging; waveless; unfathomable; glimmering; laughing; lonely; vasty; waiting; blue; windless; lethal; boundless; lower; muffled; sunnier; sacred; regal; quiet; lampless; charmed; wind-obeying; shuddering; dreary; tranquil; unsounded; dangerous; mid-sea; transparent; unclosing; immeasurable; presumptuous; unnatural; tempest-wrinkled; dark-blue; innumerable (pl); murmuring; voiceless; remorseless; finny; unapparent.

verbs

abound in—; ambush from—; cast into—; conceal in—; delve in—; draw into—s; fill—; gaze at—; hide in—; lower to—; pierce—; pursue through—; recede into—; thunder in—; venture from—; —engulfs; —resounds.

adverbs

abysmally; inscrutably; mysteriously; unfathomably; quietly; immeasurably; profoundly; immensely; dangerously; hideously; prodigiously; wondrously; obviously; enormously; astonishingly; marvellously; unutterably; fabulously; curiously; amazingly.

DEEPEN (v)

adverbs

insensibly; sufficiently; unconsciously; unfathomably; boundlessly; shudderingly; immeasurably; unnaturally; remorsefully.

(See intensify.)

DEEP-SEATED

adverbs

intrinsically; inherently; stubbornly; obstinately; incurably; intensely; traditionally; customarily; racially; frequently.

DEER

adjectives

shy; brown; agile; astonished; stricken; shadowy; wounded; tame; antlered; plentiful; exquisite; graceful; sobbing; sleek; truant; fleet; swift.

verbs

chase—; follow—; herd—; lasso—; shelter —; skin—; rouse—; wound—; —bounds; —darts; —frequents; —haunts; —leaps; —roams; —sheds; —shies; —shuns; — treads; —treks.

(See animal.)

adverbs

rustily; unrecognizably; terribly; hopelessly; unpardonably; inexcusably; irreparably; irremediably; frightfully; grimly; horribly; grossly; odiously; shockingly.

DEFAME (v)

adverbs

libelously; viciously; revengefully; wantonly; hatefully; treacherously; illegally; spitefully; ruinously.

(See slander.)

DEFAULT

adjectives

glaring; notorious; serious; infinitesimal; covert; punishable.

verbs

arrest—; commit—; convict of—; expect—; expose—; force—; impose—; mend—; occasion—; pardon—; penalize—; practise—; punish—; record—; urge—; —deprives; —occurs.

(See neglect, omission, failure, deficiency.)

DEFEAT

adjectives

avowed; acknowledged; tremendous; crushing; graceful; overwhelming; shameful; ignoble; humiliating; signal; bitter; gory; ugly; rudest; inevitable; ultimate; impending; intellectual; trivial; unconditional; vain; stinging; unwilling; serious; sheer; later; subsequent; disheartening; crowning; humble; expensive; insignificant; final; inglorious; decisive; utter; undisguised; damned; ignominious; logical; ridiculous; unexpected; smashing; dreadful; heart-broken; averted; telling; encompassed; paralyzing; creditable; pet; disastrous; spiritual; dispirited; irretrievable.

verbs

acknowledge—; administer—; bear—; brand with—; brood over—; contribute to —; court—; destine to—; doom to—; emerge from—; foredoom to—; foresee—; gesture—; go down in—; invite—; involve—; meet—; pave the way for—; suffer —; thrive upon—; visualize—; writhe at—; —encompasses; —shakes.

(See repulse, loss, ruin.)

DEFEAT (v)

adverbs

incessantly; absolutely; successively; decisively; utterly; subsequently; exultantly;

crushingly; overwhelmingly; effectually; gloriously; shamefully; ignobly; humiliatingly; signally; bitterly; inevitably; ultimately; unconditionally; finally; ignominiously; logically; paralyzingly; disastrously; spiritually.
(See whip, thrash.)

DEFECT
adjectives
basic; vital; grave; serious; glaring; important; dominant; simple; secondary; minor; flagrant; fatal; unfortunate; psychic; functional; mental; mechanical; characteristic; uncorrected; possible; qualitative; latent; undeniable; structural; fair; abominable; constitutional; aggravated; concealed; palpable; inconspicuous; unexpected; temporary; manifold; serious; surface; complementary (pl); immense; obvious; capital; woeful; postural; inherent; radical; glaring; poetical; perilous; speculative.

verbs
analyze—; compensate for—; discover—; eliminate—; judge—; indicate—; make up for—; minimize—; produce—; rectify—; remedy—; shackle by—; spot—; stamp—; suffer from—; supply—; —impairs; —taints.
(See imperfection, blemish, fault, foible. flaw, shortcoming.)

DEFECTIVE
adverbs
unacceptably; unfortunately; grossly; carelessly; crudely; objectionably; provokingly; vexatiously; definitely; altogether; shamefully; outrageously; obviously; perceptibly; palpably; indefensibly; inexcusably.

DEFECTION
adjectives
contemplated; temporary; momentary; growing; relative; moral; impulsive.

DEFENDANT
adjectives
heroic; private; scared; frightened; worried; perjured.

verbs
accuse—; acquit—; aid—; attack—; bail—; befuddle—; bind—; challenge—; charge—; cross-examine—; discharge—; enjoin—; guard—; question—; represent—; restrain —; vindicate—; —answers; —attests; —

counters; —declares; —defies; —denies; —maintains; —perjures; —pleads; —resists; —swears; —vouches; —vows.
(See defender, champion, advocate.)

DEFEND (v)
adverbs
elaborately; vigorously; gallantly; warmly; strenuously; stoutly; formidably; spiritedly; desperately; principally; subtly; ardently; philosophically; valorously; sturdily; passively; staunchly; brilliantly; obstinately; eloquently; competently; courageously; vigorously; determinedly; impassionedly; sensationally; unexpectedly; heroically; spiritlessly; aggressively; effectually; mutually; instinctively; unfailingly; injudiciously; unapproachably.
(See guard, protect.)

DEFENDER
adjectives
ardent; lawful; impenitent; philosophical; bold; brave; valorous; uncompromising; stout; sturdy; staunch; unconquerable; clever; gallant; passive; sincere; brilliant; steadfast; obstinate; habitual; eloquent.

verbs
acclaim—; banish—; challenge—; charge —; deploy—s; drive out—; hail—; honor —; reward—; —assails; —averts; —counters; —forsakes; —guards; —protects; —repels; —restrains; —upholds; —wards off.
(See defendant, advocate, champion.)

DEFENSE
adjectives
spirited; competent; noble; brilliant; courageous; strong; formidable; valiant; vigorous; long; determined; unassailable; involuntary; bungling; impassioned; half-hearted; weak; sensational; awkward; compelling; half-amused; adequate; national; manufactured; critical; inartificial; organized; offensive; frenzied; conceivable; unexpected; steadfast; natural; dignified; rare; spiritless; obstinate; pretty; armed; heroic; plausible; aggressive; uncompromising; honest; sorry; effectual; questionable; uncouth; eloquent; moral; capital; elaborate; gallant; adamantine; projected; womanly; leisurely; prompt; powerful; compensatory; mutual; instinctive; self; unfailing; minute; anomalous; injudicious; unapproachable.

verbs

abandon—; achieve—; argue in—; arise in—; batter—; bolster—; build—; bungle —; buttress—; demolish—; employ—; imperil—; map out—; prepare—; propound —; rally—; reenforce—; rehabilitate—; rush to—; sharpen—; smash—; spring to—; stand in—; stiffen under—; survey—; throw up—; vow—; —breaks; —crumbles; —crumples; —interposes.

(See protection, plan.)

DEFENSELESS

adverbs

tragically; unhappily; pathetically; silently; horribly; suddenly; surprisingly; utterly; bitterly; sadly; unexpectedly; scandalously; shockingly; calamitously; fatally; ignominiously; ominously; mysteriously; inexplicably.

DEFENSIVE

adverbs

eagerly; humbly; hastily; skilfully; reluctantly; angrily; confusedly; openly; awkwardly; nervously; instantly; preposterously; unnecessarily; sufficiently; profoundly; tearfully; pathetically; incoherently; sheepishly; embarrassingly; miserably; slavishly; disgustingly; deeply; half-heartedly; honestly.

DEFER (v)

adverbs

suavely; unfeignedly; condescendingly; pleasantly; scrupulously; particularly; servilely; resentfully; punctiliously; ungrudgingly; habitually; admiringly; carelessly; sympathetically.

(See delay.)

DEFERENCE

adjectives

unfeigned; suave; condescending; pleasant; exceeding; scrupulous; blissful; unfailing; chivalrous; particular; bullying; servile; secret; resentful; respectful; awesome; self-restraining; punctilious; exquisite; due; apparent; ungrudging; utmost; habitual; admiring; careless; sympathetic.

verbs

acknowledge—; allow—; bestow—; bow in—; choose out of—; claim—; conduct with—; entitle to—; grant—; nod in—; pay—; proceed with—; render—; respect —; respond to—; tender—; transact with —; treat with—; yield—.

(See respect, regard.)

DEFERENTIAL

adverbs

charmingly; pleasantly; properly; respectfully; scrupulously; exceedingly; unfailingly; chivalrously; punctiliously; exquisitely; duly; apparently; habitually; carefully; courteously; delightfully; devotedly; loyally; modestly; affably; amiably; gallantly; ceremoniously; ingratiatingly; tactfully; dutifully; decorously; sweetly; cordially.

DEFIANCE

adjectives

calm; silent; rare; quiet; fine; daring; resolute; firm; gay; mirthful; drawling; roaring; fierce; raucous; shrill; blatant; willful; ruffian; snarling; monstrous; shamefaced; reckless; desperate; murderous; mock; sneering; indignant; open; curious; passionate; exhilarating; quivering; quotable; shrinking; cringing; thundering; puny; irritating; perceptible; sudden; nomadic; scornful; admirable; maledictory; frank; potential; nonchalant; hurt; robust; half-frightened; schoolgirlish; unrighteous; mute; bristling; mortal; contemptuous; solitary; mutual; bold; actual; successful; patient; implied; indomitable; still; suppressed; savage.

verbs

attempt—; breathe—; fling—at; foster—; glare—; greet with—; hurl—; quell—; scorn—; shout—; snort—; sponsor—; stand firm in—; throw—at; uphold—.

(See challenge, opposition, provocation, contempt, rebellion.)

DEFIANT

adverbs

calmly; rarely; silently; quietly; boldly; resolutely; firmly; blithely; fiercely; blatantly; shrilly; monstrously; desperately; mockingly; indignantly; openly; sullenly; curiously; strangely; irritably; frankly; mutely; moodily; indomitably; stubbornly; obstinately; inexplicably; justly; defensibly.

DEFICIENCY

adjectives

unavoidable; fatal; evident; mental; technical; previous; glaring; psychological; marked; organic; suprarenal; noticeable.

verbs

accentuate—; allow—; balance—; compensate for—; condone—; correct—; counter-

act—; detect—; manifest—; mend—; observe—; presage—; reveal—; supply—; weep for—; —glares; —occurs.
(See defect, imperfection, shortcoming, inadequacy.)

DEFICIENT
adverbs
fatally; evidently; mentally; technically; markedly; glaringly; noticeably; crudely; lamentably; unfortunately; sadly; miserably; pitifully; woefully.

DEFICIT
adjectives
genuine; increasing; successive; alleged; alarming; startling; unaccountable.

verbs
accumulate—; arrest for—; bear—; calculate—; estimate—; expose—; falsify—; finance—; force—; halt—; mend—; pile up—; protect against—; reveal—; stagger through—; suspect—; uncover—; wipe out —; —arises; —deprives; —dwindles; —occurs.
(See deficiency.)

DEFILE
adjectives
dark; tangled; lofty; wild; rugged; rocky; towering; mountain; dangerous.

DEFILEMENT
adjectives
solemn; majestic; zonal; constructive; compact; straggling.

DEFINE (*v*)
adverbs
boldly; closely; sharply; sufficiently; particularly; bluntly; precisely; explicitly; accurately; crudely; arbitrarily; exactly; interestingly; subjectively; objectionably; essentially; technically; vigorously; invidiously; imperfectly; objectively; brilliantly; informally; vaguely; scientifically.
(See interpret, limit.)

DEFINITE
adverbs
crisply; bluntly; accurately; arbitrarily; interestingly; sharply; oddly; objectionably; thoroughly; brilliantly; pleasingly; acceptably; comfortingly; intelligibly; conspicuously; reliably; dogmatically; officially; authoritatively; authentically; vividly; graphically; comprehensibly.)

DEFINITION
adjectives
accurate; crude; representative; arbitrary; abstract; exclusive; exact; precise; interesting; perfervid; subjective; sharp; clearcut; objectionable; famous; preliminary; unchallenged; healthy; thoroughgoing; essential; positive; vigorous; technical; analogous; invidious; objective; brilliant; informal; vague; scientific; elastic; reasonable; serviceable; imperfect.

verbs
apply—; arrive at—; construct—; determine—; establish—; restrict—; search for —; stretch—; supply—; understand—; weaken—; —defines; —describes; —determines; —enlightens; —explains; —expresses; —fixes; —limits; —satisfies; —specifies; —unfolds.
(See explanation, description, comment, exposition, interpretation.)

DEFLATION
adjectives
sweeping; monetary; postwar; credit; vicious; severe; sharp; salient; encroaching.

verbs
guard against—; master—; prepare for—; produce—; prophesy—; protect against—; release—; remedy—; repair—; sink into—; —affects; —injures; —looms; —menaces; —occurs; —produces; —reduces; —remedies; —repairs; —ruins.
(See collapse.)

DEFORMED
adverbs
woefully; physically; hideously; sadly; monstrously; congenitally; pitiably; lamentably; mysteriously; inexpressibly; horribly; deplorably; wretchedly; distressingly; incurably; irremediably; sorrily; crookedly; grossly; gruesomely; repulsively; terribly.

DEFORMITY
adjectives
apoplectic; unexpressed; pockmarked; physical; mocking; hideous; monstrous; foul; passing; hereditary.

verbs
accentuate—; avert—; brace—; correct—; enhance—; fake—; guard against—; iron out—; minimize—; overcome—; prevent—; produce—; result in—; torture into—; twist into—; —disfigures; —distorts; —impairs; —recurs.
(See blemish, abnormality.)

DEFRAUD (v)

adverbs

deliberately; coolly; villainously; cleverly; knavishly; deceitfully; unsuspectingly; deftly; sagaciously; financially.
(See cheat.)

DEFRAY (v)

adverbs

individually; regularly; belatedly; tardily; unhesitatingly; handsomely; regally; completely.
(See pay.)

DEFT

adverbs

unusually; admirably; wondrously; enviably; nimbly; marvellously; amazingly; remarkably; consistently; harmoniously; socially; conversationally; felicitously; appropriately; intelligently; shrewdly.

DEFTNESS

adjectives

marvelous; amazing; remarkable; skillful; marked; noteworthy.

DEFY (v)

adverbs

haughtily; sullenly; recklessly; arrogantly; undauntedly; menacingly; calmly; resolutely; fiercely; raucously; blatantly; snarlingly; desperately; murderously; mockingly; passionately; frankly; nonchalantly; righteously; mutely; bristlingly; mortally; contemptuously; savagely.
(See challenge, dare.)

DEGENERACY

adjectives

deplorable; nervous; physical; dissolute; irreparable; abject.

DEGENERATE

adjectives

unmoral; lazy; pathological; hopeless; irretrievable.

adverbs

grossly; outrageously; poisonously; corruptly; viciously; brutally; shabbily; effetely; decrepitly; dangerously; hopelessly; helplessly; woefully; abjectly; disgracefully; infamously; contemptibly; shamefully.

DEGENERATION

adjectives

infectious; eventual; apparent; inflammatory; progressive.

DEGRADATION

adjectives

moral; physical; unmerited; hideous; absolute; habitual; excessive; concomitant; stunting; deep; present.

DEGRADE (v)

adverbs

hopelessly; materially; ruinously; morally; unmeritedly; hideously; absolutely; deeply; shamefully; disgracefully; humiliatingly.
(See debase, disgrace.)

DEGREE

adjectives

large; high; fullest; surpassing; extreme; maximal; marked; slightest; infinitesimal; limited; imperceptible; tiny; small; astonishing; extraordinary; remarkable; amazing; startling; unusual; singular; diverse; vulgar; moderate; disgraceful; unsatisfactory; disconcerting; appalling; pre-eminent; uncanny; rare; greatest; practicable; fair; irreparable; increasing; sufficient; corresponding; artificial; intolerable; advanced; superlative; requisite; microscopic; moderate; alarming; considerable; high; unprecedented; varying; feverish; lavish; passable; measurable; adroit; incalculable; slow; adequate; improbable; surpassing; admirable; pronounced; fine; incredible; unabated; evergrowing; remote; minute; awe-inspiring; comparative; diminished; unwonted; gentle; significant; valuable; modified; paramount; unparalleled; sublime; imposing; traditional; extravagant; shameless; certain; cunning; excessive; reasonable; notable; unusual; uncommon; successive; illuminating; unsolicited; impudent; ancient; striking; valued; least; coveted; honorary; impressive; academic; doctorate; transcendent; subordinate; multiform.

verbs

ascend by—s; attain by—s; award—; change by—s; coax by—s; confer—; elevate —; exalt—; honor—; improve by—s; intensify—; lead by—s; limit—; mark—s; match—; overrate—; raise—; respect—; sharpen by—s; suffice to—; turn by—s.
See extent, rank, amount, station, position, title.)

DEITY

adjectives

tutelar; heathen; sylvan; ubiquitous; innumerable (pl); patron; anthropomorphic; beneficent; temperamental; pagan; presiding; vestal; glorious; gloomy; tremendous; graceful; accursed; vital; protecting; incarnate; ascended; impotent; inferior; patronymic; numerous (pl); disowned; injured; dangling; benevolent; oracular; contemporary; iron; dishonorable; solemn.

verbs
absorb in—; adore—; appease—; befit—; believe in—; break away from—; complain to—; conceive of—; create—; defy—; deny—; despise—; dethrone—; enthrone—; incense—; offend—; please—; pray to—; renounce—; signify—; worship—; —creates; —interposes.
(See God, divinity.)

DEJECTED
adverbs
inconceivably; hopelessly; mournfully; pitiably; incurably; incredibly; piteously; horribly; tragically; alarmingly; unbelievably; singularly; oddly; strangely; miserably; comically; unreasonably; ridiculously; youthfully; ostensibly; openly; glumly; disconsolately; moodily; heavily; ludicrously.

DEJECTION
adjectives
vague; querulous; profound; complete; utter; intense; bewildered; utmost; deep; miserable; spiritless; passionate; weary.

verbs
bow in—; bury in—; cast into—; forsake —; humiliate into—; imply—; lower into —; manifest—; register—; shroud into—; sink into—; succumb to—; sustain—; throw into—; —deepens; —envelops; —fells; —weakens; —provokes.
(See depression, melancholy, discouragement.)

DELAY
adjectives
considerable; majestic; lingering; enforced; useless; injurious; unaccountable; inexplicable; petty; incomprehensible; anterior; proverbial; infamous; extended; dull; dangerous; corresponding; avoidable; needless; tedious; prolonged; slight; long; hazardous; endless; disappointing; fatal; strange; enforced; irksome; heartbreaking; exasperating; unconscionable; grievous; amorous; vexatious; sweet; parliamentary; characteristic; innumerable (pl).

verbs
advise—; brook—; counsel—; effect—; eliminate—; entail—; importune—; necessitate—; obtain—; occasion—; produce—; promise—; rebel against—; subject to—; trace—; work—; —endangers; —hinders.
(See procrastination, obstruction.)

DELAY (v)
adverbs
immeasurably; unaccountably; injuriously; temporarily; unfortunately; unreasonably; painfully; enforcedly; uselessly; incomprehensibly; infamously; tediously; fatally; disappointingly; irksomely; heartbreakingly; exasperatingly; unconscionably; grievously; vexatiously; characteristically; amorously.
(See dally. postpone.)

DELECTABLE
adverbs
refreshingly; invitingly; appetizingly; delicately; excitingly; charmingly; alluringly; altogether; consistently; irresistibly; unusually; remarkably.

DELEGATE
adjectives
messenger; rural; assembled (pl); interested; legal; ardent; recusant; lone; autochthonous.

verbs
act as—; appoint—; commission—; depute —; employ—; engage—; entrust to—; instruct—; send—; —s assemble; —attends; —s confer; —s convene; —s determine; —exercises; —manages; —performs; —represents; —wearies; —yells.
(See deputy, substitute. representative.)

DELEGATE (v)
adverbs
expressly; successfully; impressively; formally; nominally; authoritatively.
(See order.)

DELEGATION
adjectives
hilarious; impressive; express; representative; pathetic; dependable; authorized; random; select.

verbs
address—; appoint—; assemble—; entrust to—; instruct—; sway—; —attends; —chants; —cheers; —confers; —convenes;

—journeys; —represents; —subscribes to; —supports; —switches to; —votes; —wearies.

(See committee.)

DELETERIOUS
adverbs

malignly; abominably; painfully; grievously; oppressively; noxiously; perniciously; dreadfully; horribly; exceptionably lamentably; woefully; extremely; incredibly.

DELIBERATE
adverbs

evidently; sagaciously; good-humoredly; coolly; duly; sagely; wisely; gravely; ominously; vexatiously; calmly; terribly; impressively; solemnly; consciously; exaggeratedly; cleverly; curiously; pleasantly; prudently; anxiously; courteously; quietly; intently; thoughtfully; particularly; attentively; observantly; carefully; craftily; smartly; skilfully; shrewdly; cautiously; warily; discreetly.

DELIBERATE (v)
adverbs

earnestly; sagaciously; coolly; good-humoredly; sagely; gravely; calmly; solemnly; skillfully; prudently; protractedly; slowly.

(See debate, consider.)

DELIBERATION
adjectives

evident; sagacious; mature; good-humored; cool; sage; equable; grave; terrible; immense; studied; calm; solemn; joint; unexampled; impressive; congressional; knowing; conscious; curious; pleasant; skillful; prudent; public; anxious; due; maddening; courteous; protracted; considerable; massive; cutting; slow; disdainful; anguished.

DELICACY
adjectives

proper; conceivable; lineal; respectable; penetrating; covert; autumnal; fastidious; unexpected; pastel; epicurean; unbounded; ephemeral; substantial; native; exquisite; subtle; spiritual; fine; false; piercing; esteemed; great; extreme; innate; special; instinctive; charming; graceful; imaginable; fine; artistic; manly; morbid; feminine; queenly; dreamlike; complicated; bashful; dangling; exquisite; tempting; infinite; international; raw; pompous; toothsome.

DELICATE
adverbs

exquisitely; incredibly; beautifully; airily; frailly; crisply; freshly; harmoniously; pleasingly; agreeably; sweetly; bewitchingly; daintily; delightfully; ravishingly; gracefully; artistically; richly; properly; fastidiously; ephemerally; subtly.

DELICIOUS
adverbs

altogether; inexpressibly; exquisitely; pleasantly; daintily; felicitiously; palatably; appetizingly; ambrosially; utterly; unexpectedly; pungently; spicily; fragrantly; richly; stimulatingly; lusciously; sweetly.

DELIGHT
adjectives

pure; chastened; true; sincere sacred; home-felt; ecstatic; rapturous; whimsical; jubilant; tittering; utter; sheer; keen; complete; subtle; bizarre; unexpected; unnatural; strange; surprised; awed; supreme; incredulous; wondering; noisy; clamorous; wild; unrestrained; frantic; perfervid; frenzied; ungovernable; unqualified; unending; immeasurable; inexhaustible; tremendous; inexpressible; ineffable; unspeakable; unholy; dumb; fiendish; scornful; malevolent; perverted; painful; fierce; infectious; malicious; vain; frustrated; untrammeled; unalloyed; unfailing; sensuous; passionate; Epicurean; sadistic; childish; gastronomic; boyish; businesslike; chief; generous; intimate; inborn; naive; paroxysmal; extravagant; exalted; rare; drooling; varied; abiding; ardent; insatiate; frank; impossible; anticipatory; redoubled; secret; incommunicable; emulous; riotous; perfumed; idiotic; comforting; flitting; continual; awed; perpetual; sensational; occult; barren; subsequent; deep; dull; mournful; wild; swift; infinite; solicitous; rarefied; siren; lasting; inward; calm; buoyant; sentimental; unfelt; bitter; false; seasonable; hurricane; inexplicable; perpetual; hourly; hysterical; stunned; malignant; surprised; unquiet; trenchant; callous; celestial; rude; intense; ever enduring; laughing; unequalled; gay; unutterable; exquisite; flagging; soft; inebriating; subsiding; delicate; royal; bubbling; vivid; undefined; delicious; taste-tempting; mingled; languorous; unconcealed; nebulous; vigorous; rapturous; wild-beast; fresh; immortal; inestimable; divine; true; savage; anticipatory; astonished; cordial; pretended; rich; impish; tremulous; spiteful; obvious; special; young; unmanaged; vicious; dreamy; innocent; unchecked; preposterous; genuine; rare; giggling; measureless; peculiar; silly; breathless; sweet; placid; unmixed; fair; warm; lingering; singular; musical; mutual; fragmentary; serious; composed; dissembled; temporal; wanton; whimsical; eager; animated; vague; sustained; audible; subdued; capricious; seductive; consummated; manifold (pl).

verbs
afford—; bathe in—; behold with—; derive —; drink in—; enjoy—; exalt—; express—; extol—s of; fall into with—; feed with—; feel—; fill with—; find—in; gaze with—; hail with—; hide—; inspire—; listen with —; mar—; mount in—; offer—; pour—; recall with—; redden in—; shiver with—; smile in—; snuff out—; spread—; submerge in—; taste—; teem with—; turn to—; turn—into; weep with—; win—; yield—; —comes; —flees; —fleets; —pierces; —shines; —tempers.
(See happiness, rapture, joy, entertainment, pleasure, satisfaction.)

DELIGHTFUL
adverbs
charmingly; whimsically; utterly; strangely; unexpectedly; supremely; immeasurably; ineffably; delicately; freshly; cordially; innocently; peculiarly; particularly; youthfully; sweetly; glamorously; enchantingly; pleasantly; gracefully; entertainingly.

DELINEATE (*v*)
adverbs
graphically; minutely; humorously; familiarly; truthfully; recognizably; unsurpassedly; impartially; satirically.
(See depict, describe.)

DELINEATION
adjectives
humorous; familiar; truthful; recognizable; subtle; unsurpassed; impartial.

DELINQUENCY
adjectives
seeming; imaginary; juvenile; egregious; blameworthy.

DELINQUENT
adverbs
criminally; woefully; viciously; indiscreetly; enormously; outrageously; censurably; reprehensibly; objectionably; villainously;

wretchedly; monstrously; loosely; unpardonably; inexcusably; carelessly; deliberately; indifferently; purposely; wantonly; wickedly; accidentally; shamefully; scandalously; disreputably; heedlessly; rashly; foolishly.

DELIRIOUS
adverbs
wildly; woefully; dangerously; alarmingly; crazily; violently; frantically; madly; feverishly; helplessly; critically; terribly; incoherently; oddly; strangely; hysterically; startlingly; uncontrollably; turbulently; distractedly; restlessly.

DELIRIUM
adjectives
mad; tossing; restless; extreme; raving; emotional; critical; blissful; confused; terrible; dreamy; prolonged; fierce; maniacal; insane.

verbs
break out into—; characterize—; dance in —; excite to—; haunt—; indicate—; induce—; murmur in—; produce—; quake with—; rave in—; seize with—; stimulate to—; suffer—; tremble with—; wander in—; —attacks; —exhausts; —impairs; —occurs.
(See insanity, hallucination, excitement, enthusiasm, rapture.)

DELIVER (*v*)
adverbs
simultaneously; conveniently; eloquently; solemnly; habitually; coldly; duly; consequently; sullenly; resolutely; impassionedly; volubly; hazardously; inarticulately; daily; promptly; tardily; reproachfully.
(See give, transfer.)

DELIVERANCE
adjectives
immediate; abrupt; miraculous; timely; tardy; gracious; hazardous.

verbs
achieve—; aid in—; arrange—; commemorate—; complete—; desire—; effect—; hope for—; offer—; order—; pray for—; rejoice in—; seek—; work for—; yearn for—; —liberates; —rescues; —sets free; —yields.
(See rescue, release, salvation.)

DELIVERER

adjectives
would-be; commanding; deliberate; graceful; intrepid; chance.

verbs
acclaim—; hope for—; pray for—; send—; thank—; welcome—; yearn for—; yield to—; —dispatches; —disburdens; —disposes of; —liberates; —orders; —rescues; —rids; —saves; —sets forth; —sets free; —surrenders; —releases.

DELIVERY

adjectives
resolute; voluble; impassioned; happy; complex; hazardous; inarticulate; measured; certified.

DELL

adjectives
bosky; mysterious; darksome; shaded; dreamy; labyrinthine; pathless; pastoral; narrow; hollow; diminutive; desolate; untrodden; resounding; budded; healthy; briery.

verbs
abandon—; bloom in—; frolic in—; grow in—; haunt—; hide in—; inhabit—; leap in—; perform in—; retire to—; retreat into—; ring through—; seek—; shelter in —; wander in—; —invites; —protects; — soothes; —winds.
(See valley, dale.)

DELUGE

adjectives
dawn-tinted; fiery; overflowing; binding; veritable; fearful; eternal; lawless; smothering; silvery; perfect; delectable; swashing; drowning; vapory.

verbs
bury under—; drown in—; escape—; fall before—; perish in—; pour—; release—; shower—; suffer from—; swell into—; vent—; —abates; —breaks loose; —confronts; —demolishes; —descends; —destroys; —floods; —harms; —occurs; —proceeds; —submerges; —sweeps away.
(See flood.)

DELUSION

adjectives
nightmare; cherished; fixed; superstitious; generous; grandiose; ignorant; insane; partial; monstrous; mental; shattered; anthropocentric; hollow; false; phantasmic; treasured; crazy; tenderhearted; unconquerable; pleasant; systematized; salutary; popular; miserable; long-detached; equal; mere; uncomfortable; plausible; stage; optical; pernicious; fond; empty; financial; neat; mocking; tragic; psychotic; somnolent.

verbs
cast out—; cure of—; destroy—; develop—; dismiss—; dissipate—; foster—; give up to—; guard against—; labor under—; share—; slip into—; suffer—; —exists; — misleads; —pursues.
(See illusion, deception, error, fallacy, hallucination.)

DELUSIVE

adverbs
cunningly; smoothly; insidiously; fallaciously; unfairly; starkly; inevitably; slyly; fraudulently; mendaciously; untruthfully; mistily; deceptively; ironically; strategically; incredibly; artfully; erroneously; dishonestly; perfidiously; unsoundly; trickily; treacherously; groundlessly; heretically; disingenuously; evasively; grimly.

DELVING

adjectives
curious; industrious; bibliographical; mental; scientific; relentless.

DEMAGOGUE

adjectives
consummate; selfish; irresponsible; fluent; political; inveterate; notorious; captious.

verbs
abandon to—; become the prey of—s; cultivate—; descend from—; despise—; play—; prove—; rule as—; stoop to—; —agitates; —appeals; —defends; —esponses; —fires; —influences; —leads; —obtains; —opposes; —orates; —panders; —suits; —sways; — undertakes.
(See politician, orator, leader.)

DEMAND

adjectives
ceaseless; incessant; insistent; constant; ever-increasing; rapid; mounting; growing; overwhelming; unabated; uncompromising; intransigent; persistent; obstinate; stern; strong; extreme; shouted; clamorous; roaring; exorbitant; modern; intermittent; inevitable; inescapable; irresistible; general; consistent; fluctuating; exigent; imperious; peremptory; vehement; exacting; outrag-

eous; blustering; unfortunate; unjust; unfair; relentless; surly; impossible; arrogant; abnormal; excessive; enlarged; unlimited; important; normal; human; social; industrial; consumer; decorative; popular; peculiar; multitudinous (pl); ever-changing; diminishing; emotional; unique; concrete; embarrassing; sufficient; immediate; preparatory; half-resentful; half-appealing; urgent; brusque; imaginative; craving; immense; inadmissable; definite; worthy; unprecedented; voiced; authoritative; effectual; fanatical; earnest; unsatisfied; insidious; widespread; essential; renewed; complex; paternal; insulting; nervous; remorseless; uproarious; intense; importunate; voluntary; unreasonable; necessary; explicit; widening; infrequent (pl); temporary; never-ending; feverish; unheeded; logical; sternest; tremendous; live; nationwide; huge; terrific; steady; gigantic; additional; ridiculous; temporal; emphatic; exaggerated; transient; continuing; unconditional; audacious; progressive; monstrous; arbitrary.

verbs
accede to—; accomplish—; acquiesce in—; agree to—; attend—; besiege with—s; browbeat with—s; clarify—; comply with —; confront with—; create—; deny—; divine—; dwarf—; echo—; evoke—; fulfill —; grant—; ignore—; indulge—; meet—; obey—; parry—; press—; reiterate—; reject—; respond to—; satisfy—; stabilize —; supply—; thunder—; unite in—; utter —; voice—; wake to—; yield to—; —astounds; —diminishes; —grows.

(See requirement.)

DEMAND (*v*)
adverbs
vibrantly; savagely; gutturally; greedily; persistently; relentlessly; frantically; unreasonably; brusquely; exorbitantly; rapaciously; sternly; bluntly; ruthlessly; briskly; scornfully; triumphantly; indignantly; truculently; riotously; clamorously; impetuously; obviously; despairingly; exactingly; unanimously; staunchly; imperatively; ultimately; stridently; cruelly; arrogantly; unconscionably; assuredly; gruffly; hungrily; curtly; incessantly; uncompromisingly; definitely; arbitrarily; formally; imperiously; sharply; furiously; virulently.

(See order, request.)

DEMEANOR
adjectives
smiling; calm; dignified; unassuming; staid; modest; composed; sweet; gentlemanly; unruffled; gentle; majestic; lordly; torpid; hangdog; wild; cold; impassive; commonplace; surly; savage; ferocious; fickle; inscrutable; accustomed; somber; unflinching; immoral; peculiar; interested; punctilious; solemn; courtly; popular; menacing; comical; contemptuous; sober; widespread; coy; laughing; obtuse; offensive; quiet; proud; sanctified; subdued; violent; pompous; puritanical; tacit; sage; haughty; meditative; cheerful; courageous; undaunted; resolute; private; unbending; unusual; unostentatious; reserved; stately; confident; cringing; dispassionate; aggressive; turbulent.

verbs
adopt—; alter—; disdain—; disguise—; exhibit—; judge by—; maintain—; mask—; soften—; trust—; —changes; —expresses; —irritates; —registers; —shames; —signifies.

(See behavior, mien.)

DEMENTED
adverbs
idiotically; sadly; inexplicably; foolishly; witlessly; frenziedly; incoherently; oddly; strangely; wildly; distractedly; dangerously; alarmingly; peculiarly; woefully; hopelessly; deplorably; pitiably; startlingly; uncontrollably; ungovernably; pathetically; tragically; unaccountably; mysteriously; stupidly; feebly; confusedly; noticeably; palpably; obviously; unmistakably; perceptibly; plainly.

DEMISE
adjectives
speedy; approaching; early; inevitable; heroic; premature; sad; lamented; long-awaited.

DEMOCRACY
adjectives
forward-looking; sham; industrial; passion-ridden; unlimited; enraged; semieducated; true; shrewd; humorous; multitudinous; kindly; economic; formidable; representative; pure; inclusive; rampant; qualified; experienced; financial; primitive; fierce.

verbs
attack—; betray—; contribute toward—; destroy—; foster—; imperil—; instill—;

jeopardize—; ordain—; preserve—; retain —; satirize—; supplant—; sustain—; threaten—; tread down—; —advances; —degenerates; —elevates; —flourishes; —functions; —levels; —marches ahead; —prevails; —survives; —asserts itself.

(See government, people, republic.)

DEMOCRATIC

adverbs

marvellously; tolerantly; broadly; unusually; magnanimously; foolishly; admirably; remarkably; embarrassingly; rampantly; amusingly; extremely; eminently; notoriously; openly; liberally; impartially; highmindedly; violently; vociferously; unselfishly; charitably.

DEMOLISH (v)

adverbs

utterly; ruinously; brutally; cruelly; savagely; thoughtlessly; bestially; bloodthirstily; uncompromisingly; fiercely.

(See destroy.)

DEMON

adjectives

heroic; insatiable; unabashed; devastating; wrestling; fiery; angry; fragile; screaming; monstrous; cruel; heartless; horrible; demoralizing; protecting; trap-door; satellite; seeming; malignant; treacherous; avenging; restraining.

verbs

attribute to—; call forth—; dismiss—; drive out—; endow with—; exorcise—; introduce—; possess—; rout—; sacrifice to —; worship—; —controls; —destroys; —disturbs; —dominates; —dwells in; —enters; —frightens; —haunts; —infests; —inflicts; —inhabits; —leads; —prevails; —rules; —surrounds; —wails.

(See devil, spirit.)

DEMONIAC

adverbs

screamingly; insatiably; fierily; angrily; cruelly; monstrously; heartlessly; horribly; malignantly; maliciously; treacherously; revengefully; venomously; excitably; feverishly; hysterically; wildly; frantically; frenziedly; sensationally; dramatically; bitterly; invidiously; ruthlessly; brutally; atrociously; infamously; flagrantly; nefariously; viciously; grossly; infernally.

DEMONSTRATE (v)

adverbs

lucidly; tastefully; repeatedly; strictly; abundantly; practically; phenomenally; experimentally; fully; conceitedly; conclusively; convincingly; substantially; triumphantly; abstractedly; forcefully; abstrusely; approximately; ocularly; precisely; visually; cordially.

(See show, indicate.)

DEMONSTRATION

adjectives

patriotic; subtle; triumphant; abstract; abstruse; forceful; approximate; corrupt; dramatized; familiar; ocular; charitable; grandiose; active; enthusiastic; attention-compelling; simple; interesting; convincing; dynamic; startling; spot; irresistible; sales-producing; breath-taking; quick; inspiring; emphatic; salivary; quadrennial; amazing; rigorous; precise; rigid; noisy; striking; visual; grand; superb; flattering; riotous; dramatic; bitter; hostile; unfriendly; armed; elaborate; outward; cordial.

verbs

answer by—; apprehend—; crown—; defy —; establish by—; harangue—; mar—; offer—; stage—; subject to—; support—; thwart—; understand—; —exposes; —proves.

(See celebration.)

DEMONSTRATIVE

adverbs

readily; easily; triumphantly; forcefully; dramatically; spectacularly; actively; enthusiastically; interestingly; convincingly; startlingly; irresistibly; amazingly; noisily; strikingly; flatteringly; elaborately; outwardly; cordially; heartily; offensively; delightfully; charmingly; amiably; vexatiously; provokingly; foolishly; unbecomingly; unnecessarily; frankly; brazenly; boldly; ominously; markedly; conspicuously; disagreeably.

DEMORALIZE (v)

adverbs

profoundly; partially; utterly; speedily; swiftly; incredibly; socially; morally.

(See corrupt.)

DEMORALIZATION

adjectives

incredible; widespread; social; linguistic; nervous.

verbs
aid in—; check—; guard against—; influence—; prevent—; produce—; protect from —; yield to—; —corrupts; —deprives; —destroys; —envelops; —lowers; —reduces; —seeps in; —unnerves; —weakens.
(See corruption.)

DEMURE
adverbs
affectedly; prudishly; coyly; timidly; shyly; delightfully; gravely; quietly; unaffectedly; conspicuously; deliberately; discreetly; tranquilly; placidly; soberly; submissively; harmoniously; meekly; cleverly; purposely; ostentatiously; unnaturally; stiffly; primly; puritanically; priggishly; bashfully; skittishly; admirably; attractively; alluringly; blushingly.

DEMURENESS
adjectives
stately; slumberous; timid; lofty; aloof; deceptive; becoming.

DEN
adjectives
careless; stifling; stuffy; dark; trackless; moldy; unsanitary; loathsome; steamy; horrible; hidden; dreary; turreted; fresh-dug.

verbs
abide in—; cast into—; confine to—; convert into—; crouch in—; drive from—; dwell in—; escape to—; habitate—; hibernate in—; hide in—; immure in—; lodge in—; lurk in—; nestle in—; pace—; retire to—; retreat to—; smoke out of—; stow in—; visit—; stray about—; —conceals; —hides; —reeks.
(See lair, cave, hut, retreat.)

DENIAL
adjectives
incredulous; amused; bold; vehement; armed; cynical; indignant; visual; arrogant; gracious; telegraphic; rigid; furious; steadfast; vigorous; smiling; disarming; chivalrous; utter; peremptory; quibbling; naive; positive; emphatic.

verbs
accept—; brook—; color—; conceal with —; counter—; evoke—; ignore—; lash out—; prepare—; rebut—; request—; resign to—; spurn—; storm—; —contradicts;

—discourages; —irks; —peeves (colloq.); —refuses; —refutes; —repulses; —wearies.
(See contradiction, refusal, restraint.)

DENIZEN
adjectives
long-eared; finny; astute; stately; furred; feathered; forgotten; permanent.

verbs
accept—; acquaint—; admit—; allow—; fill with—s; furnish with—s; grant to—; make—of; offer—; people with—s; populate with—s; privilege—; —dwells; —enjoys; —obtains; —occupies; —prospers; —settles.
(See inhabitant, citizen, native.)

DENOUEMENT
adjectives
curious; interesting; melodramatic; iridescent; tragic; crowning; premature.

DENOUNCE (*v*)
adverbs
vehemently; furiously; sternly; unsparingly; scoffingly; insultingly; bitterly; scathingly; obstreperously; violently; vociferously; witheringly; astoundingly; dramatically; vitriolically; mercilessly; roundly.
(See accuse.)

DENSITY
adjectives
sufficient; mean; different; tangled; repellent; depthless; frightful.

DENT
adjectives
sizable; slightest; permanent; cruel; hideous.

DENTIST
adjectives
ruthless; unfeeling; ultra-schooled; late-edition; glorified; hit-or-miss.

verbs
consult—; visit—; —anaesthetizes; —applies; —assembles; —caps; —closes; —drills; —examines; —extracts; —fastens; —files; —fills; —furnishes; —grinds; —inserts; —operates; —practises; —prepares; —preserves; —restores; —shapes; —treats.

DENUNCIATION
adjectives
withering; mystic; astounding; fiery; glib; unmerited; furious; spiteful; playful;

severest; loud; intemperate; sweeping; grand; impartial; effective; thorough; resounding; impassioned; dramatic; vitriolic; ominous; unsupported; combative; rabid; angry; utter; preliminary; filthy; violent; merciless.

verbs

announce—; authorize—; blast—; characterize by—; defy—; indulge in—; reiterate —; thunder—; tolerate—; —accuses; —affects; —alarms; —condemns; —deluges; —frightens; —humbles; —informs; —inveighs against; —punishes; —ruins; —scathes; —sears; —threatens; —warns; —weakens.

(See condemnation, accusation.)

DENUNCIATORY

adverbs

scarcely; dogmatically; scandalously; needlessly; strongly; bitterly; acrimoniously; jealously; enviously; inexcusably; scurrilously; abusively; profanely; execrably; thunderously; cruelly; caustically; harshly; ungraciously; ferociously; ruthlessly; sarcastically; dryly; severely; unsparingly; exceptionably; indefensibly; viciously; terribly.

DENY (v)

adverbs

hotly; unequivocally; promptly; absolutely; bitterly; indignantly; effectively; peremptorily; stoutly; inhospitably; crossly; cravenly; unselfishly; strenuously; passionately; categorically; justly; vehemently; flatly; shamelessly; arrogantly; disarmingly; positively; naively.

(See contradict, renounce.)

DEPART (v)

adverbs

voluntarily; peacefully; mysteriously; seriously; cheerfully; clandestinely; noiselessly; radically; precipitately; momentously; daringly; agitatedly; unprecedentedly; abruptly.

(See leave, quit.)

DEPARTMENT

adjectives

subsidiary; vast; systematized; countless (pl); elementary; remote; significant; drabbest; immense; irrational; beautiful; capable; experienced; vocational; public; vulgar; administrative; insular.

verbs

allot to—; assign to—; bestow upon—; boss—; branch into—s; break into—; close —; control—; convert—; create—; divide into—s; establish—; organize—; portion into—s; preside over—; regulate—; supervise—; —administers; —caters to; —handles; —practises.

(See part, division, section, branch.)

DEPARTURE

adjectives

clandestine; abrupt; refreshing; noiseless; instant; radical; precipitate; revolutionary; momentous; impending; mysterious; unannounced; impetuous; calm; imminent; immediate; rollicking; sudden; hurried; frank; frequent (pl); speedy; hasty; considerate; approaching; contemplated; daring; dinnerless; agitated; noticeable; exceptionable; controlled; compelled; maiden; expected; awaited.

verbs

arrive at—; assure of—; await—; enjoy—; facilitate—; fear—; laugh at—; notice—; occasion—; plan—; prepare—; regret—; speed—; spur to—; take—; —divides; —frees; —nears; —partitions; —saddens; —separates; —severs; —sunders; prevent—.

(See deviation, withdrawal, separation, death.)

DEPEND (v)

adverbs

utterly; unfailingly; exclusively; materially; completely; mathematically; virtually; ultimately; directly; perpetually; apparently; irksomely; fatuously; absolutely; haplessly.

(See lean, trust.)

DEPENDABILITY

adjectives

superb; absolute; steady; impeccably; invariable; inflexible.

DEPENDENCE

adjectives

utter; lifetime; helpless; indirect; apparent; perpetual; disgraceful; irksome; increasing; sure; fatuous; absolute; harmless; magnified; ultimate; humble.

DEPENDENT

adjectives

servile; wise; beggarly; penniless; mutual; weaker; helpless; hapless.

DEPENDENT

adverbs

pitifully; completely; partially; sadly; helplessly; unhappily; grievously; sullenly; subserviently; servilely; fawningly; obsequiously; hopelessly; desperately; wholly; meekly; touchingly; pathetically.

DEPICT (v)

adverbs

symbolically; aesthetically; dramatically; graphically; powerfully; deftly; starkly; episodically; vividly; mercilessly; shrewdly; realistically; fearlessly.

(See delineate, describe.)

DEPICTION

adjectives

episodic; merciless; stark; shrewd; realistic; fearless; vivid.

DEPLETE (v)

adverbs

entirely; largely; physically; utterly; definitely; swiftly; suddenly; fatally; woefully; financially.

(See exhaust.)

DEPLETION

adjectives

corresponding; physical; excessive; utter; definite; sudden; swift.

DEPLORABLE

adverbs

piteously; unwontedly; terribly; seriously; gravely; direly; especially; signally; distressingly; wretchedly; exceptionably; bitterly; dismally; woefully.

DEPLORE (v)

adverbs

sincerely; satirically; prophetically; loudly; tearfully; pitifully.

(See lament, regret.)

DEPORTMENT

adjectives

habitual; exigent; correct; laudable; exceeding; proper; maidenly; fashionable; graceful; amiable; blameless; fine; unexpected; inexplicable; grave; incredible.

DEPOSIT

(*general*)

adjectives

superficial; alluvial; extensive; stratified; evanescent; coralline; affected; fertile; untouched; inexhaustible; graphite; modest; fossiliferous; sacred; required; fabulous; immense; nominal; sedimentary; buttery; driftwood; precious; phosphate; turquoise; bank; large; unexpected.

DEPOSIT

(*money or property*)

adjectives

nominal; actual; legal; stipulated; optional; binding; good faith.

verbs

accumulate for—; bank—; collect—s; commit—to; deliver—; demand—; entrust with —; guard—; invest—; place—; pledge—; receive—; require—; restore—; return—; squander—; withdraw—; —benefits; —increases; —settles.

DEPOSIT (v)

adverbs

deliberately; daintily; noiselessly; hastily; superficially; extensively; inexhaustibly; evanescently; fabulously; immensely; unexpectedly.

(See place.)

DEPOSITOR

adjectives

luckless; frightened; hypothetical; poor; illiterate; ingenuous; middle class; unlocated; unfortunate; ultimate; robust.

DEPOT

adjectives

cavalry; temporary; commissary; indispensable; prearranged; stationary.

DEPRAVED

adverbs

wickedly; shamelessly; grossly; outrageously; corruptly; brutally; dangerously; awfully; hopelessly; woefully; abjectly; disgracefully; infamously; contemptibly; notoriously; shamefully; arrantly; dissolutely; indecently; perfidiously.

DEPRAVITY

adjectives

precocious; moral; joint; vicarious; total; horrible; rude; contented; professional; humorous.

DEPRECATE (v)

adverbs

forcibly; timidly; periodically; modestly; markedly; increasingly; hurriedly; mildly; vigorously; pleadingly.

(See disapprove.)

DEPRECATION

adjectives
timid; hurt; pleading; periodic; modest; hurried; abysmal.

DEPRECATORY

adverbs
timidly; pleadingly; modestly; elaborately; unnecessarily; urgently; importunately; clamorously; solicitously; compassionately; sympathetically; tenderly; critically; abusively; accusingly; sarcastically; sharply; trenchantly; censoriously.

DEPRECIATION

adjectives
marginal; disastrous; marked; ever-increasing; substantial; radical; elaborate.

DEPRESS (v)

adverbs
particularly; fearfully; dreadfully; vaguely; obviously; acutely; drastically; economically; financially; industrially; spiritually; nationally; mentally; nervously.
(See lower.)

DEPRESSED

adverbs
alarmingly; dangerously; gloomily; incurably; inconceivably; incredibly; horribly; woefully; dismally; gravely; seriously; inconsolably; sadly; unreasonably; desperately; piteously; pitifully; tragically; wanly; unduly; unnecessarily; moodily; lamentably; darkly; wearily.

DEPRESSING

adverbs
sadly; alarmingly; needlessly; terribly; unreasonably; unaccountably; inexplicably; dreadfully; acutely; grimly; painfully; cursedly; grievously; unfortunately; sorely; unluckily; intolerably; tremendously; cruelly.

DEPRESSION
(*business*)

adjectives
prolonged; agricultural; successive (pl); mild; general; current; exaggerated; dreadful; evil; aching; acute; drastic; major; vast; long; business; economic; financial; industrial; national; world; price; severe.

DEPRESSION
(*general*)

adjectives
paralyzing; epidemic; enveloping; growing; inflation.

verbs
aggravate—; alleviate—; banish—; emerge from—; intensify—; mitigate—; offset—; plunge into—; prolong—; relapse into—; survive—; tackle—; thaw out—; weather —; —annihilates; —blights; —grips; —hits; —slashes.
(See dejection, melancholy, discouragement, despondency.)

DEPRESSION
(*spirits*)

adjectives
low; nervous; sundry (pl); sympathetic; frequent; spiritual; constant; mental.

DEPRESSION
(*surface*)

adjectives
sheltered; circumscribed; shallow; cup-like; deep; noticeable; amphitheatrical; saucer-like; extreme.

DEPRIVATION

adjectives
haphazard; stringent; total; ruinous; violent; vicious; indigent.

DEPTH

adjectives
generous; unguessed; shielding; protective; underlying; deceptive.

verbs
advance from—s; attain—; bear through —s; descend to—s; discover in—s; explore —s; foul in—s; gauge—; harbor in—; judge—; launch into—s; measure—; penetrate to—of; pitch to—s; preserve from—s; probe—s; raise from—s; reach—; reflect in—; repose in—; rise from—; scour—; search—; thrust into—; venture beyond—; —closes round; —covers; —embraces; —exceeds.
(See extent, measure.)

DEPTHS

adjectives
dizzy; profound; unfathomable; considerable; perpendicular; homely; crystalline; fertile; remorseless; tremendous; melancholy; nethermost; giddiest; slumberous; remote; hollow; blank; soundless; somber; seeming; distant; inmost; glassy; shadowed; abysmal; lost; awesome; limpid; unknown; cavernous; hideous; liquid; secret; aesthetic; hidden; wondrous; unexplored; lowest; unserviceable; passionless; sleeping; adverse; warm; darkest; pearly; evil;

unimagined; ghostly; annulling; prodigious; shapeless; voiceless; forest; folded; calm; reflective; slimy; cold; frozen; agitated; yawning; luminous; inaccessible; superhuman; insatiable; pathless; dewy; vast; music-haunted; wakening; clear; shameful; gloomy; abhorrent; nightmare; sylvan; subterranean; apparent; Stygian; secure.

DEPUTY
adjectives
dishonest; hateful; gun-toting; indolent; tense; amiable; strict; presumptive; pernicious; corrupt; radiant.

verbs
appoint—; authorize—; bribe—; corrupt —; depose—; elect—; employ as—; evade —; oust—; rebuke—; swear in—; —aids; —arrests; —assists; —enforces; —fines.
(See representative, agent, delegate.)

DERANGE (v)
adverbs
irreparably; seriously; mentally; functionally; extensively; sexually; mechanically.
(See confuse.)

DERANGED
adverbs
eccentrically; incoherently; madly; strangely; unaccountably; inexplicably; queerly; foolishly; dangerously; peculiarly; woefully; hopelessly; helplessly; deplorably; pitiably; lamentably; shockingly; uncontrollably; mysteriously; noticeably; obviously; unmistakably; perceptibly; terribly.

DERANGEMENT
adjectives
mental; extensive; functional; obstinate; obsessional; intermittent.

DERBY
adjectives
battered; cherished; perforated; shabby; broken; battle-scarred; aggressively-tilted; ancient; salvaged.

DERELICT
adjectives
human; moral; physical; sleeping; floating; wretched; barnacle-incrusted.

verbs
abandon—; defend—; desert—; discover —; lift—; observe—; pity—; reduce to—; relinquish—; seize—; —s assemble; —s

congregate; —drifts; —flounders; —s infest; —limps in; —s overrun; —suffers; —s swarm.

DERIDE (v)
adverbs
steadily; correspondingly; opprobriously; sourly; scornfully; lightly; ribaldly; coarsely; brutally; mercilessly; bitterly; loudly; boisterously; unsparingly; contemptuously; sharply; stingingly.
(See ridicule, jeer.)

DERISION
adjectives
mysterious; sour; scornful; light; ribald; unconquerable; coarse; brutal; merciless; filthy; bitterest; loud; boisterous; approving; pressed; uneasy; foul; unsparing.

verbs
bait with—; be in—; cackle in—; call forth —; chuckle in—; expose to—; express—; give vent to—; laugh in—; mock in—; open to—; ridicule in—; scorn—; sting by—.
(See ridicule, mockery, scorn, sarcasm.)

DERISIVE
adverbs
sharply; arrogantly; pompously; mockingly; sarcastically; cynically; offensively; officiously; disagreeably; unbearably; insufferably; mysteriously; sourly; lightly; blithely; airily; ribaldly; disrespectfully; coarsely; grossly; brutally; ignorantly; crudely; mercilessly; clumsily; bitterly; loudly; boisterously; enviously; foully.

DERIVATION
adjectives
remote; theoretical; unanswerable; grotesque; indirect; authentic.

DERIVATIVE
adjectives
direct; traceable; flattering; acknowledged; questionable.

verbs
accept—; confuse—; develop—; discover —; employ—; form—; gain—; generate—; market—; obtain—; process—; produce—; recognize—; reduce—; substitute—; use—; utilize—; —emanates from; —originates; —supplants.
(See product, word.)

337

DERIVE (v)

adverbs

recently; evidently; shamelessly; primarily; corruptly; ultimately; essentially; remotely; theoretically; grotesquely; endlessly.

(See obtain.)

DEROGATORY

adverbs

shamefully; enviously; bitterly; venomously; vengefully; maliciously; scandalously; disagreeably; peevishly; petulantly; falsely; slanderously; abusively; injuriously; shockingly; unreasonably; unwarrantably; indefensibly; vindictively; dreadfully; mercilessly; ruthlessly; openly; shamelessly; deliberately; viciously.

DERVISH

adjectives

demented; dancing; filthy; whirling; frenzied.

DESCEND (v)

adverbs

quickly; unexpectedly; noiselessly; sharply; gradually; hastily; giddily; benignly; impartially; laboriously; gracefully; fearsomely; pompously.

(See fall.)

DESCENDANT

adjectives

lineal; direct; eager; legitimate; homeward-flown; pure-blooded; glorious; degenerate; remote; immediate; impoverished; ill-starred; hybrid; presumed; winsome; indolent; guilty; genuine; unmixed.

verbs

acquire—; advertise for—; characterize—; extract—; leave—; nourish—; transmit to—; —s assemble; —belongs to; —carries; on; —s congregate; —s convene; —s gather; —s honor; —s inherit; —s respect; —s settle; —s spring from; —s wrangle over.

(See posterity, offspring, issue.)

DESCENT

adjectives

rapid; direct; steep; aristocratic; hasty; gradual; rocky; pitiless; precipitous; stately; deep; smooth; laborious; graceful; harsh; unblemished; ladderlike; armed; sheer; illustrious; dateless; artistic; pompous; actual; noble; maternal; barbarous; flashing; uninterrupted; royal; divine; fearsome; slow.

verbs

attempt—; balk at—; ease—; dread—; flow upon—; halt—; hazard—; hinder—; manage—; menace—; observe—; plan—; point for—; prepare—; prevent—; resume —; venture—; —dizzies; —frightens; —sharpens; —slopes.

(See fall, deterioration, slope, attack, raid.)

DESCRIBE (v)

adverbs

ludicrously; graphically; adequately; admiringly; pathetically; trippingly; accurately; derisively; justly; feelingly; expansively; compactly; comprehensively; elegantly; elaborately; felicitously; minutely; traditionally; eloquently; illuminatingly; succinctly; superlatively; subsequently; erroneously; fittingly; imperfectly; contemptuously; facetiously; impressionistically; boisterously; radiantly; glowingly; sentimentally; humorously; animatedly; verbally; uncensoredly; tersely; intimately; satirically; suggestively; enticingly; distortedly; imaginatively; realistically; vaguely; colorfully; briefly; essentially.

(See delineate, depict.)

DESCRIPTION

adjectives

facetious; minute; impressionistic; boisterous; admirable; exquisite; graphic; detailed; contemporary; radiant; entangled; magnificent; luminous; eloquent; adjectival; distinctive; impassioned; felicitous; faithful; elaborate; extended; racy; preceding; picturesque; punctual; lengthy; frivolous; leisurely; sublime; tolerable; restrained; appropriate; enthusiastic; illustrated; ludicrous; harrowing; truthful; accurate; glowing; sentimental; vivid; hopeless; humorous; animated; unpleasant; lucid; primitive; verbal; censored; admirable; unexcelled; pompous; threadbare; negative; terse; rhapsodical; intimate; pathetic; satiric; suggestive; enticing; distorted; savage; imaginative; authoritative; realistic; adequate; abridged; silent; magnificent; robust; vague; damning; flashing; colorful; complicated; recondite; brief; modest.

verbs

amend—; base—; baffle—; beggar—; color—; defy—; detail—; enter into—; fit—; limit—; paragon—; quote—; suit—; verify—; —centers; —clarifies; —colors; —combines; —delineates; —depicts; —

equals; —excels; —explains; —furnishes; —illuminates; —illustrates; —implies; —impresses; —introduces; —motivates; —paints; —pictures; —portrays; —presents; —provides; —suggests; —surpasses; —tires; —vivifies; —wearies.
(See portrayal, representation, definition.)

DESCRIPTIVE
adverbs
graphically; vividly; effectively; unusually; remarkably; facetiously; minutely; admirably; splendidly; magnificently; eloquently; faithfully; elaborately; extensively; racily; tolerably; appropriately; enthusiastically; ludicrously; accurately; humorously; intimately; savagely; authoritatively; adequately; vaguely; briefly; modestly; realistically.

DESECRATION
adjectives
impudent; attempted; wanton; impious; daring; inconoclastic.

verbs
accuse of—; admit—; confess—; criticize for—; enjoy—; ignore—; indulge in—; preserve from—; rear in—; sentence for—; spit—; suffer—; threaten—; —injures; —involves; —pains; —nauseates; —undermines.
(See violation.)

DESERT
adjectives
dreary; irreclaimable; flat; melancholy; rude; mountainous; rocky; burning; lifeless; alkaline; pathless; encompassing; arid; forbidding; reactionary; scorching; unspeakable; mysterious; dreadful; measureless; voiceless; bare; palpable; comfortless; vast; withered; desolated; uninhabitable; barren; waterless; open; grim; dangerous; cactus; sandy; silent; illimitable.

verbs
advance through—; border—; chart—; conceal in—; dwell in—; frequent—; gain—; inhabit—; lead into—; lose in—; patrol—; redeem—; retire to—; retreat to—; roam —; span—; swallow up by—; track—; wander in—; —envelops; —howls; —menaces; —parches; —threatens.
(See merit, reward, solitude, waste.)

DESERT (v)
adverbs
woefully; heartlessly; easily; virtually; basely; cruelly; impulsively; treasonably; wilfully; criminally; wantonly; finally.
(See forsake, abandon.)

DESERTED
adverbs
cruelly; criminally; hastily; shamefully; ingloriously; humiliatingly; mercilessly; ruthlessly; inhumanly; brutally; wickedly; iniquitously; scandalously; ignominiously; wantonly; inconsiderately; groundlessly; wilfully; deliberately; unhappily; ungratefully; wretchedly.

DESERTION
adjectives
contemplated; cruel; impulsive; treasonable; willful; proverbial; wholesale; criminal; wanton.

DESERVE (v)
adverbs
equally; notoriously; perpetually; fittingly; unreservedly; distinctly; eminently; wholeheartedly; undeniably.
(See merit.)

DESIGN
(intention)
adjectives
ultimate; honorable; base; fell; ill-conceived; rash; deadly; deep; evil; deliberate; stern; wicked; ostensible; malicious; oppressive; serious; importunate; hostile; ambitious; joyous; true-meant; immoral; misguided; criminal; evident; vile; matrimonial; disgusting; mischievous; far-reaching; avowed; traitorous; aggressive; lawful; villainous; perfidious; nefarious.

verbs
admit—; adopt—; approve—; arrange—; carry out—; conceive—; concur on—; declare—; discover—; disguise—; execute—; form—; frustrate—; harbor—; plan—; pursue—; relinquish—; settle on—; undertake —; —aims; —fails; —requires.
(See scheme, plan, purpose, project, intention.)

DESIGN
(pattern)
adjectives
authentic; immense; elaborate; inscrutable; constructive; fierce; beautiful; arabesque; border; intricate; sporting; famous; artist-

ic; ethical; fanciful; matchless; polychromatic; structural; well-known; conventional; monstrous; impractical; flowing; simple; graceful; anatomical; chevron; deliberate; heavy-duty; tentative; distinctive; exclusive; transitional; interior; conservative; unfathomable; palpable; engineering; harmonious; attractive; central; classical; crude; quaint; scientific; unintelligent; grotesque; aliform; vast; gorgeous; geometrical; efficacious; secular; smart; original; unusual; nautical; advanced; stitched; modern; staggering; unjust; superior; functional; systematic; wise; dramatic; compass; thoughtful; ingenious; feathery; engraved; mosaic; curious; huge; exotic; general; novel; tangled; cut; dried; gay; rational; brilliant; stunning; annulose.

verbs
arrange—; carve—; conceive—; contrive—; develop—; draw—; elaborate—; embellish; —embroider; —employ—; engrave—; execute—; hammer—; mark—; model—; paint —; plan—; prescribe—; sketch—; strike—; submit—; teach—; trace—; work—; —decorates; —denotes; —depicts; —improves; —ornaments; —represents; —signifies; —stresses.
(See pattern, ornament, sketch, model, representation.)

DESIGN (v)
adverbs
scientifically; properly; solely; exquisitely; seriously; admirably; specially; primarily; harmoniously; expressly; artfully; elaborately; charmingly; masterfully; skillfully; intricately.
(See intend.)

DESIGNATE (v)
adverbs
incriminatingly; innocently; erroneously; euphoniously; strictly; specifically; appropriately; felicitously; aptly; fittingly; properly; correctly.
(See identify.)

DESIGNATION
adjectives
appropriate; playful; substitutive; territorial; felicitous; apt; proudest; patrician; fitting; proper; correct.

verbs
appoint—; arrange—; arrive at—; decide —; denote—; describe—; determine—; indicate—; justify—; name—; point out—;
prepare for—; refuse—; search for—; — appeals; —serves.
(See mark, name, title, epithet, arrangement.)

DESIGNER
adjectives
experienced; noted; scenic; landscape; master; skilled; leading; functional.

DESIRABLE
adverbs
utterly; enchantingly; irresistibly; temptingly; alluringly; seductively; pleasantly; quietly; intensely; vaguely; darkly; acutely; inordinately; infinitely; genuinely; specially; absurdly; practically; conveniently.

DESIRE
adjectives
intense; longing; laudable; childish; sweet; gallant; brutal; extravagant; haughty; unextinct; fair; express; elevated; deferred; sensuous; corrupt; sentimental; customary; ardent; imperious; vague; earnest; devoted; prayerful; crushing; passionate; overpowering; innocent; noble; hearty; morbid; quaint; amiable; imperative; commendable; lifelong; insatiable; irresistible; confused; dark; furious; comfortable; cold; mistaken; automatic; lost; cordial; acute; unjust; scant; feeble; magnanimous; instinctive; slightest; warm; fond; faintest; inordinate; subtle; burning; infinite; sincere; countless (pl); selfish; conscientious; petty; frenzied; anxious; mad; implacable; consuming; inhibited; troublesome; deliberate; illimitable; excessive; benevolent; impatient; keen; pure; gnawing; restless; parching; unsatisfied; prevailing; quick; impetuous; known; longing; genuine; unlawful; subdued; strong; unacknowledged; high; insane; hot; dangerous; dominant; vehement; ungratified; dimmest; vain; proud; fiery; carnal; special; evident; unholy; torturing; inflamed; scattering; anxious; nervous; appeased; individual; egotistical; wolfish; bloody; ravenous; amorous; defrauded; emotional; covetous; honest; untamable; aimless; chaste; practical; feverish; mistaken; dwarfed; perceptible; wild; increasing; repressed; sacred; soft; delicate; wistful; sordid; ungenerous; laudable; lascivious; false; philanthropic; quenchless; unbaffled; phlegmatic; personal; boundless; loving; touching; lurking; popular; absurd; reasonable; senile; universal; apparent.

verbs

accomplish—; aggravate—; appease—; arouse—; attain—; awake—; balk—; beat with—; breed—; burn with—; cater to—; chasten—; cherish—; communicate—; conquer—; curtail—; eat up with—; entertain —; equal—; exercise—; experience—; exploit—; express—; feed—; flash—; gratify —; humble—; humor—; inflame—; inhibit—; instil—; intensify—; kindle—; lack —; languish in—; loose—; master—; melt into—; nourish—; obscure—; obsess with —; overbalance—; prompt—; provoke—; quell—; quench—; quicken—; quiet—; raise—; realize—; refine—; relinquish—; repress—; reward—; satisfy—; seethe with —; seize with—; sharpen—; smother—; subjugate—; sublimate—; submit to—; tangle—s; temper—; throttle—; thwart—; undermine—; yield to—; —consumes; — disquiets; —embodies; —endures; —fires; —hounds; —hungers; —impels; —motivates; —rules; —tortures; —urges on.

(See longing, craving. learning, wish, appetite, passion, impulse, request, aspiration.)

DESIRE (v)

adverbs

passionately; earnestly; ardently; eminently; obviously; insistently; presumably; unquestionably; particularly; intensely; consistently; unanimously; gallantly; extravagantly; brutally; sensually; customarily; imperiously; overpoweringly; nobly; heartily; morbidly; quaintly; insatiably; automatically; cordially; acutely; inordinately; burningly; infinitely; implacably; consumingly; benevolently; impatiently; gnawingly; genuinely; unlawfully; vainly; vehemently; carnally; torturingly; egotistically; ravenously; amorously; emotionally; chastely; delicately; wistfully; sordidly; ungenerously; lasciviously; boundlessly; touchingly; personally; absurdly.

(See want, wish.)

DESIROUS

adverbs

intensely; longingly; childishly; extravagantly; expressly; sentimentally; ardently; imperiously; earnestly; prayerfully; passionately; heartily; morbidly; insatiably; darkly; furiously; inordinately; sincerely; selfishly; madly; consumingly; troublesomely; impetuously; insanely; hotly; vehemently; proudly; anxiously; perceptibly; covetously; enviously; wistfully.

DESIST (v)

adverbs

abruptly; entirely; partially; completely; willingly; mutually; wisely; lazily; temporarily; subsequently; eventually; deliberately; totally.

(See stop, cease.)

DESK

adjectives

broad; secluded; ancient; battered; mahogany; flat; smooth; rickety; large; carved; Renaissance; polished; oak; dull; grimy; matutinal; reading; writing; spindle-legged; ransacked; roll-top.

verbs

anchor to—; beat—; clutter up—; cover—; dust—; dawdle at—; erect—; flank—; litter —; lock—; pad—; plop at—; rummage in—; seal—; smite—; stack on—.

(See table, stand, pulpit.)

DESOLATE

adverbs

grimly; utterly; profoundly; desperately; dreadfully; indescribably; singularly; supremely; bleakly; unutterably; tragically; bitterly; unbearably; intolerably; oppressively; appallingly; drearily; emptily; dismally; wildly; fearfully; perceptibly.

DESOLATION

adjectives

blazing; harsh; lifeless; utmost; dusty; grim; willful; utter; profound; dreadful; whispering; universal; wintry; careless; degraded; rightful; indescribable; chaotic; haunted; blank; unrevenged; fancied; barren; rapid; fresh; burlesque; weird; withered; mighty; icy; rocky; striking; heartsick; singular; immense; rugged; bleak.

verbs

behold—; blast—; bury in—; clothe with—; curse with—; decry—; doom to—; dwell in—; emerge from—; face—; fade into—; fall to—; inhabit—; lift from—; mourn—; repair—; —encroaches; —entombs; —overcomes; —overwhelms; —sets in.

(See loneliness, waste, region.)

DESPAIR

adjectives

absolute; pessimistic; calm; tragic; mute; mild; stolid; endless; unending; savage; dim; sick; grim; appalling; sudden; dismal; irremediable; human; dumb; crushed; whimsical; comfortless; comical; sham;

smothered; secure; beautiful; reluctant; inward; rash; deep; perplexed; spiritual; cold; keen; suppressed; rigid; abysmal; proud; solitary; rayless; sad; abhorred; sheer; errorless; black; reckless; pleased; utmost; mad; wild; lonely; scientific; blank; patient; speechless; passionate; pitiful; comfortless.

verbs

comfort in—; crush with—; doom to—; drive to—; end in—; engender—; fan into —; gasp with—; lift from—; lighten—; listen to—; plague with—; rack with—; rescue from—; save from—; seize with—; shake with—; sink in—; slump into—; spring from—; sweep away—; swoon in—; turn to—; unveil—; wring with—; yield to—; —chills; —grips; —grows; —hovers over; —poisons; —sets in; —settles in; —wells up; —withers; —wracks.

(See hopelessness, discouragement, despondency.)

DESPERADO
adjectives
slinking; sleepless; unarmed; bloodthirsty; ferocious; brutal; murderous; bestial.

DESPERATE
adverbs
tragically; wildly; mutely; savagely; helplessly; grimly; appallingly; suddenly; dismally; dumbly; comically; inwardly; proudly; madly; pitifully; fatally; frantically; cruelly; curiously; awfully; miserably; shockingly; fearfully; obstreperously; ungovernably; excitedly; hysterically; rashly; recklessly.

DESPERATION
adjectives
sheer; blind; melancholy; suicidal; frantic; sullen; utter; ruthless; momentary; stubborn; light-hearted.

DESPICABLE
adverbs
utterly; contemptibly; inexpressibly; shamefully; basely; terribly; outrageously; scandalously; notoriously; meanly; generally; incredibly.

DESPOND (v)
adverbs
daily; morbidly; deeply; profoundly; suicidally; utterly; sullenly; mournfully; tearfully; abnormally; unduly; unreasonably.
(See worry.)

DESPONDENCY
adjectives
temporary; morbid; deep; dire; frank; profound; suicidal; despairing; utter; pronounced; stifling; sullen; mournful.

verbs
beset with—; burden with—; chase—; create—; encourage—; envelop in—; express—; forbid—; indulge in—; labor under —; lament—; sink in—; throw into—; wallow in—; —darkens; —deforms; —depresses; —drowns; —envelops; —oppresses; —overcomes; —seeps in; —torments; —triumphs.
(See despair, depression, dejection.)

DESPONDENT
adverbs
temporarily; morbidly; deeply; direly; ominously; significantly; frankly; openly; admittedly; incurably; profoundly; suicidally; dangerously; alarmingly; desperately; sullenly; inexplicably; palpably; mournfully; habitually; ordinarily; inordinately; irremediably; pathologically; temperamentally.

DESPOT
adjectives
merciful; outraged; insulted; fierce; angered; petty; absolute; egotistic; monstrous; municipal; dangerous; predatory; benevolent; arrogant; small-souled; stern; hot-tempered; cruel; rank; vicious; iron-willed.

DESPOTIC
adverbs
relentlessly; ruthlessly; overbearingly; overwhelmingly; intolerably; imperiously; presumptuously; harshly; severely; oppressively; cruelly; obdurately; haughtily; insufferably; unreasonably; terribly; fearfully; dreadfully; incredibly; unwarrantably; dangerously; foolishly; barbarously; heartlessly; recklessly; outrageously; monstrously; viciously; benignly.

DESPOTISM
adjectives
unlimited; mild; barbarous; native; military; benign; agelong; ceremonious; astonished; combined (pl); absolute; irresistible; insupportable; irresponsible; capitalistic; reckless; heartless; rapacious; subsequent; iron.

verbs
adopt—; allay—; apply—; crush under—; establish—; exercise—; expose to—; form

—; free from—; guard against—; launch
—; organize—; preserve from—; protect
from—; relax—; submit to—; support—;
surrender to—; throw off—; tolerate—;
—compels; —controls; —enslaves; —governs; —limits; —restrains; —survives; —
wills.
(See tyranny.)

DESSERT
adjectives
abbreviated; frugal; colorful; frozen;
tempting; cold; delicious; nourishing; gay-
looking; tiny.

DESTINATION
adjectives
mutual; secret; final; natural; appointed;
moral; different; inevitable; deeper; suitable; proposed; outlandish; religious.

DESTINY
adjectives
false; manifest; impossible; loftiest; wondrous; unaccomplished; unhappy; auspicious;
blighted; terrible; myriad (pl); precarious;
transcendent; magnificent; deathless; resolute; outwitting; uncertain; circumvolving;
inevitable; natural; moral; human; changing; common; momentous; eternal; desolate; future; sunless; noble; solemn;
bright; inexorable; tragic; divine; high;
evil; inherited; strange; evident; kindest;
ultimate; proud; ill-starred.

verbs
abide by—; accept—; bless—; carve—;
chart—; command—; condemn by—; evade
—; expand—; fight out—; fulfill—; guide
—; master—; mold—; pursue—; seal—;
shape—; solve—; steer—; struggle with—;
succumb to—; supervise—; ward off—;
waylay—; work out—; —appoints; —
awaits; —beats; —bewails; —carries out;
—conspires; —decrees; —dogs; —dooms.
(See fortune, doom, fate, lot.)

DESTITUTE
adverbs
absolutely; sadly; utterly; helplessly; hopelessly; pennilessly; unquestionably; miserably; wretchedly; appallingly; comparatively; abjectly; astonishingly; peculiarly;
distressingly; embarrassingly; horribly.

DESTITUTION
adjectives
absolute; utter; penniless; hopeless; abandoned; indigent.

verbs
abandon to—; avoid—; engulf by—; escape
—; forsake to—; imply—; lift from—;
leave in—; reduce to—; throw into—;
verge on—; —approaches; —deprives; --
increases; —menaces; —stalks.
(See poverty, want.)

DESTROY (*v*)
adverbs
deliberately; wantonly; ruthlessly; partially; foolishly; irreparably; frequently; simultaneously; eternally; ultimately; unwittingly; rigorously; utterly; effectually;
thoughtlessly; universally; mutually; eventually; indiscriminately; consequently; lawlessly; practically; remorselessly; deliberately; inevitably; mercilessly; incalculably.
(See ruin, demolish.)

DESTROYER
adjectives
fierce; parasitic; brutal; plowing; ruthless; courteous; soulless.

DESTRUCTION
adjectives
sudden; instant; universal; wanton; daily;
self; total; wild; brilliant; mutual; eventual; willful; indiscriminate; probable; consequent; miserable; practical; comprehensive; threatening; remorseless; deliberate;
useless; apparent; utter; flashing; inconceivable; inevitable; ominous; merciless;
incalculable; ultimate; sheer; wasting; lawless; necessary; subsequent.

verbs
attempt—; await—; behold—; bring on—;
contemplate—; crumble into—; dash to—;
deliver from—; ensure—; foredoom to—;
incline to—; invite—; involve in—; lead
to—; leap to—; lure to—; redeem—; rejoice in—; rescue from—; revel in—;
revenge—; rush to—; seek—; send to—;
shower—; smite with—; sweep with—;
suffer—; thirst for—; woo—; work—.
(See ruin.)

DESTRUCTIVE
adverbs
appallingly; unnecessarily; drunkenly; hysterically; angrily; riotously; deliberately;
designedly; wantonly; universally; widely;
horribly; unbelievably; lethally; instantly;
eventually; indiscriminately; probably; infallibly; remorselessly; inconceivably; ominously; mercilessly; incalculably; ultimately;
wastefully; carelessly; thoughtlessly; needlessly; meanly; hatefully; systematically.

adverbs

merely; irregularly; disconnectedly; lazily; quaintly; exasperatingly; fatally; carelessly; unsystematically; heedlessly; negligently; nonchalantly; indifferently; blithely; smilingly; wantonly; intolerably; imperturbably; vexatiously; unluckily; placidly; serenely; plaguedly.

DETACHMENT

adjectives

alert; hard; fierce; philosophic; lofty; cool; aloof; displayed; detailed; reserved; various (pl); ever-proceeding; beautiful; hastily-gathered; successive; indolent; numerous (pl).

DETAIL

adjectives

rich; decorative; sickening; harmonious; intimate; perturbing; enduring; incredible; visual; elaborate; irrelevant; minute; ornate; amusing; personal; trivial; luscious; troublesome; unpoetical; fictitious; superficial; architectural; repugnant; alarming; impeccable; sensuous; outstanding; conventional; authentic; characteristic; confusing; ingenious; harrowing; technical; tedious; cumbersome; painful; disgusting; exquisite; complete; distinctive; profound; vivid; profuse; charming; unimportant; commonplace; agonizing; remaining; ornamental; profligate; petty; admirable; picturesque; remarkable; significant; sharp; graphic; fervid; reliable; voluminous; appropriate; devastating; realistic; revolting; hateful; trifling; little; worrisome; vexatious; delicate; subtle; gossiping; brief; merest; dull; complicated; tiniest; circumstantial; grim; sordid; collateral; sufficient; loveliest; essential; unusual; perplexing; mean; unrevealed; cleverest; homely; domestic; biographical; scenic; endless; methodical; exact; statistical; clear; restless; hampering; subordinate; heterogeneous; vulgar; needless; topographical; pedantic; faultless; historical; meager; concise; irksome; dreary; myriad (pl).

verbs

array—s; authenticate—s; avoid—; chronicle—s; contribute to—; correlate—s; describe—s; dig out—s; dispense with—; divulge—; dwell upon—; enumerate in—; furnish with—s; grapple with—; grasp—; intersperse—s; marshal—s; master—s; memorize—s; note—s; observe—s; offer in—; parade —s; rehearse—s; relate—s; repeat—s; reveal—s; set forth—s; spare—s; study—s; suppress—s; thrash out—s; treat in—; underestimate—; unearth—; waive —; wrestle with —s; —s bewilder; —s bore; —s elude; —s enrich; —s leak out; —s weary.

(See particular, item, part.)

DETAIL (*v*)

adverbs

minutely; intimately; visually; elaborately; irrelevantly; amusingly; trivially; lusciously; poetically; superficially; significantly; conventionally; authentically; characteristically; tediously; completely; profusely; vividly; picturesquely; fervidly; voluminously; realistically; vexatiously; briefly; sordidly; endlessly; exactly; methodically; statistically; vulgarly; meagerly; irksomely; drearily.

(See narrate.)

DETAILED

adverbs

accurately; explicitly; clearly; meticulously; punctiliously; richly; horribly; intimately; incredibly; elaborately; minutely; amusingly; alarmingly; ingeniously; tediously; painfully; disgustingly; exquisitely; completely; vividly; graphically; admirably; remarkably; sharply; reliably; appropriately; realistically; hatefully; delicately; briefly; circumstantially; sordidly; unusually; cleverly; statistically; endlessly; exactly; clearly; needlessly; faultlessly; drearily; irksomely.

DETAIN (*v*)

adverbs

forcibly; unavoidably; successfully; honorably; ingloriously; vexatiously; outrageously; accidentally; unhappily.

(See keep, arrest.)

DETECT (*v*)

adverbs

easily; cleverly; shrewdly; casually; astutely; logically; artfully; slyly; brilliantly; scientifically; accidentally.

(See discover, uncover.)

DETECTION

adjectives

casual; successful; skillful; logical; artful.

verbs

avoid—; baffle—; elude—; escape—; evade —; fear—; flee—; frustrate—; hide from

—; stumble upon—; suffer—; —alarms; —discloses; —exposes; —informs; —reveals.
(See discovery, disclosure.)

DETECTIVE
adjectives
private; geological; dental; shrewd; competent; hard; luckless; district; burly; typical; tireless; great; heroic; unsympathetic.

verbs
baffle—; commission—; dispatch—; elude —; employ—; escape—; evade—; hire—; inform—; reward—; —accuses; —corners; —discloses; —discovers; —disguises; — dogs; —executes; —exposes; —guards; — hounds; —hunts; —inquires; —inspects; —investigates; —masks; —nabs; —observes; —protects; —pursues; —raids; — reveals; —runs down; —searches; —spies; —studies; —suspects; —tracks; —tracks down; —trails; —uncovers; —unearths; —watches.
(See officer, police.)

DETENTION
adjectives
prolonged; honorable; inglorious; compulsory; vexatious; outrageous; accidental; unhappy.

DETERIORATE (*v*)
adverbs
sadly; horribly; physically; mentally; morally; bodily; inevitably; steadily; intellectually; lamentably; seriously; markedly.
(See impair.)

DETERIORATION
adjectives
physical; bodily; inevitable; mental; nervous; steady; intellectual; lamentable; serious; marked.

verbs
defend from—; detect—; employ in—; exaggerate—; preserve from—; pretend—; produce—; save from—; undergo—; — abates; —arises; —continues; —degenerates; —depresses; —destroys; —impairs; —injures; —seeps in.
(See corruption.)

DETERMINATION
adjectives
obvious; inflexible; intrinsic; great; zealous; steadfast; tireless; grim; deathly;
feverish; personal; supernatural; insistent; passionate; sudden; abrupt; settled; bounding; equal; fixed; prescient; mighty; harsh; forceful; intelligent; calm; accurate; cool; early; tangible; selfish; chronological; unwilling; stubborn; dogged; warm; uniform; indefatigable; judicial; desperate; controlling; unanimous; persistent; obstinate; invincible; unflinching; resolute; cold; immutable; precise; whole-souled; ruthless; iron; inexorable; pudgy; manifest; drunken; earnest; indomitable.

verbs
change—; equip with—; flash—; forge—; inspire—; hail—; obsess with—; plod along in—; quench—; reiterate—; reward—; sharpen—; strengthen—; struggle in—; —achieves; —triumphs; —wanes.
(See decision, resolution.)

DETERMINE (*v*)
adverbs
absolutely; happily; objectively; unanimously; shrewdly; passionately; accurately; precisely; resolutely; sternly; conclusively; immediately; unceremoniously; inflexibly; zealously; grimly; stubbornly; doggedly; invincibly; unflinchingly; ruthlessly; inexorably; manifestly; indomitably; largely.
(See decide.)

DETERMINED
adverbs
firmly; inordinately; immovably; irrationally; illogically; childishly; irrevocably; stubbornly; officially; mightily; finally; courageously; quietly; inexorably; harshly; feverishly; passionately; intelligently; calmly; coolly; selfishly; desperately; ruthlessly; drunkenly; crazily; earnestly; curiously; fatally.

DETEST (*v*)
adverbs
fundamentally; thoroughly; positively; unreasonably; infinitely; exaggeratedly; definitely; markedly; obviously; noticeably; unhallowedly; violently.
(See hate.)

DETESTABLE
adverbs
utterly; incredibly; unbelievably; hatefully; abominably; completely; flagrantly; viciously; deplorably; lamentably; diabolically; noxiously; terribly; generally; woefully; odiously; repulsively; despicably; intolerably; insufferably; horridly.

adjectives
infinite; prolonged; exaggerated; definite; marked; noticeable.

DETHRONE (v)
adverbs
ignominiously; completely; shamefully; dishonorably; pusillanimously; courageously; cowardly; brutally; violently; forcefully.
(See usurp.)

DETONATION
adjectives
remote; mystic; continuous (pl); muffled; tremendous; furious; sharp; spasmodic.

verbs
accompany by—; attribute—to; enkindle—; fire—; muffle—; produce—; result in—; —echoes; —erupts; —expels; —occurs; —reports; —rips; —shocks; —stuns; —thunders; —uproots; —violates.
(See explosion.)

DETOUR
adjectives
weary; lightning; quick; disconcerting; unexpected; wrong; bumpy; long; roundabout; wretched.

DETRACTION
adjectives
timid; rude; subtle; uninitiated; aggravated.

DETRIMENT
adjectives
clogging; acute; raw; unbiased; grave; serious.

verbs
accept—; acquire—; admit—; burden with —; cause—; free from—; harbor—; incur —; load with—; repair—; replace—; suffer —; sustain—; —accrues; —affects; —harms; —impairs; —injures; —weakens.
(See injury, loss, damage, harm.)

DETRIMENTAL
adverbs
undeniably; economically; financially; physically; terribly; unluckily; intentionally; maliciously; designedly; substantially; enormously; incalculably; irreparably; irremediably; seriously; personally; disgracefully; unintentionally; incidentally; palpably; essentially; disastrously; woefully.

DEVASTATE (v)
adverbs
virtually; generally; appallingly; spiritually; systematically; aimlessly; heartlessly; fiendishly; tyrannically; viciously; ferociously; brutally.
(See ruin.)

DEVASTATING
adverbs
unimaginably; horribly; incredibly; ruinously; inhumanly; savagely; vastly; universally; viciously; sinfully; iniquitously; extensively; irremediably; irrevocably; irrecoverably; heinously; dismally; calamitously.

DEVASTATION
adjectives
cyclonic; general; appalling; forest; spiritual; systematic; aimless.

DEVELOP (v)
adverbs
precociously; enormously; advantageously; harmoniously; indirectly; majestically; copiously; riotously; subsequently; perfectly; logically; habitually; unexpectedly; definitely; independently; inordinately; exclusively; rationally; invariably; extraordinarily; tediously; arduously; irrationally; intricately; belatedly; artistically; culturally; muscularly; socially; economically; mentally; physically; deftly; imposingly; continuously; poetically; subsequently; coherently; vindictively; scientifically; progressively; morally; spectacularly; aesthetically; uniquely; deviously; legitimately.
(See complete, unfold.)

DEVELOPMENT
adjectives
extraordinary; astonishing; startling; amazing; rapid; meteoric; long; tedious; arduous; extravagant; irrational; intricate; vast; extensive; slow; evolutionary; gradual; belated; deliberate; hirsute; artistic; cultural; muscular; social; economic; modern; mental; physical; noble; high; deft; majestic; effective; logical; imposing; egregious; intellectual; secluded; surface; inferred; diversified; further; general; continuous; eventual; recent; poetic; subsequent; surprising; coherent; architectural; vindictive; enriching; compensatory; scientific; progressive; basic; disproportionate; laudable; harmonic; individual; impartial; strained; wholesome; previous; promising; technical; organic; moral; multifarious;

psychosexual; magnificent; glorious; institutional; consequent; thematic; peculiar; spectacular; recent; liturgical; safety; empiric; aesthetic; intensive; industrial; defective; external; remoter; unique; devious; expansive; legitimate; profligate; multiple (pl); arrested.

verbs
arrest—; attain—; await—; check—; contribute to—; encourage—; enfeeble—; evaluate—; foresee—; forestall—; foster—; hail—; hamper—; hasten—; hinder—; impair—; keep abreast of—; paralyze—; retard—; review—; revolutionize—; rush—; speed—; spur—; stimulate—; stunt—; trace—; undergo—; visualize—; witness—; —germinates from; —proceeds; —surges forward.
(See evolution, growth, expansion, enlargement.)

DEVIATE (v)
adverbs
unconventionally; grossly; materially; peculiarly; slightly; frequently; momentarily; anomalously; occasionally; abnormally; unaccountably; oddly; exceptionally; strangely; weirdly.
(See stray, wander.)

DEVIATION
adjectives
peculiar; slight; gross; material; frequent (pl); anomalous; momentary; occasional.

verbs
accept—; allow—; ascertain—; cause—; determine—; doubt—; eliminate—; govern —; measure—; observe—; recognize—; render—; suspect—; tend toward—; —destroys; —shocks; —strays; —varies.
(See variation, divergence, error.)

DEVICE
adjectives
ingenious; grotesque; elaborate; great; fertile; clockwork; amazing; safety; unworkable; wicked; stale; petty; crude; devious; clumsy; happy; shallow; rhetorical; patriotic; labor-saving; convenient; frugal; improved; successful; hard; simple; shrewd; cunning; artful; clever; magical; sundry (pl); sufficient; heraldic; alignment; desperate; quaint; local; singular; comfortable; playful; artificial; supreme; effective; ancient; symbolic; noble; ceremonial; makeshift; curious; economic; excellent;

scholastic; rotary; timesaving; automatic; protective; hazardous; discredited; suitable; chosen; favorite; optical; childish; treacherous.

verbs
abandon—; adopt—; affect—; contrive—; employ—; equip with—; finance—; hit upon —; invent—; launch—; manufacture—; patent—; resort to—; scorn—; utilize.
(See invention, scheme, strategem, symbol.)

DEVIL
adjectives
excellent; incarnate; unsympathetic; deceitful; poor; red; charming; imaginary; flaming; fever-scourged; cruel; stubborn; attractive; little; frisky; obstinate; greedy; latent; merry; destroying; exorcised; surly; eternal; good-looking; chained-up; burning; interior; tempting; mocking; malicious; foreign; raging; daring; conjuring.

verbs
bargain with—; cast out—; conquer—; conspire with—; contend with—; curb—; defy—; deny—; destroy—; drive out—; emancipate from—; exorcise—; expel—; flee from—; follow—; grapple with—; league with—; offend—; personify—; possess by—; preserve from—; "raise"—; rebuke—; resist—; sacrifice to—; scorn—; steer toward—; subject to—; take up with —; worship—; —betrays; —conjures; —deceives; —deludes; —ensnares; —enters; —entices; —harries; —mocks; —oppresses; —rules; —spurs; —tempts.
(See demon, spirit, evil.)

DEVILISH
adverbs
hatefully; inconceivably; iniquitously; irretrievably; incredibly; incorrigibly; atrociously; infernally; shockingly; manifestly; openly; exceptionably; horribly; outrageously; incurably; obdurately; stubbornly; nefariously.

DEVILTRY
adjectives
good-humored; inexhaustible; stock; petty; ineradicable.

DEVIOUS
adverbs
obscurely; circumbendibusly; sinuously; unfortunately; astutely; adroitly; unnecessarily; strangely; oddly; ominously; cur-

iously; provokingly; vexatiously; suspiciously; cleverly; cruelly; intricately; amazingly; confusingly; deliberately; craftily; sharply; fatally; obviously; inscrutably; perplexingly.

DEVISE (v)

adverbs

ingeniously; carefully; cunningly; peculiarly; subtly; specially; grotesquely; elaborately; crudely; deviously; clumsily; conveniently; frugally; ˙ shrewdly; sufficiently; comfortably; artificially; effectively; symbolically; economically; curiously; automatically; scholastically; hazardously; suitably; amazingly.

(See contrive, invent.)

DEVOLVE (v)

adverbs

wholly; unexpectedly; absurdly; startlingly; weightily; heavily; normally; politically; traditionally.

(See transmit.)

DEVOTE (v)

adverbs

exclusively; properly; faithfully; unstintingly; passionately; intensely; unreservedly; exclusively; civilly; fearlessly; zealously; earnestly; tenderly; uniquely; expressly; profoundly; religiously; patriotically; personally; mutually; humbly; doggedly; dumbly; blindly; obviously; absurdly; heroically; submissively; unselfishly; sentimentally; conscientiously; unswervingly; untiringly; recklessly; fervidly; deathlessly; assiduously; conjugally; unimpeachably; unobtrusively; agelessly; sublimely; patiently.

(See dedicate, consecrate.)

DEVOTED

adverbs

piously; profoundly; childishly; earnestly; personally; ardently; completely; humbly; mutually; doggedly; blindly; foolishly; queerly; absurdly; heroically; deeply; extremely; submissively; unselfishly; tenderly; sentimentally; exclusively; dangerously; conscientiously; genuinely; passionately; unswervingly; exquisitely; ostentatiously; conspicuously; reverently; staunchly; assiduously; fondly; unobtrusively; sublimely; patiently; openly.

DEVOTEE

adjectives

impious; reverent; average; enthusiastic; ardent; fresh; rabid; distinguished; meek; worshiping; religious; theosophic; highminded; indigent; true; congenial; servile.

verbs

attract—; gain—; interest—; victimize—; —s assemble; —clamors; —s congregate; —consecrates; —s convene; —dedicates; —denounces; —disparages; —esteems; —exhibits; —indulges in; —introduces; —offers; —practices; —pursues; —worships.

(See follower.)

DEVOTION

adjectives

profound; wearied; religious; patriotic; infantile; earnest; lifetime; studied; personal; detached; complete; humble; mutual; dogged; real; dumb; blind; open; queer; absurd; increased; heroic; wholehearted; obvious; deep; impious; discouraged; endless; extreme; continued; distant; submissive; unselfish; outdated; painful; tender; sentimental; spiritless; exclusive; dangerous; unceasing; conscientious; genuine; passionate; pure; unparalleled; unswerving; evening; exuberant; capable; angry; faithful; untiring; constant; unconditional; exquisite; ardent; disinterested; unostentatious; conspicuous; undiminished; reverent; speculative; reckless; consecrated; fervid; wifely; deathless; absolute; doglike; unfaltering; respectful; mystic; desperate; obsequious; chivalric; staunch; inextinguishable; cheerful; manly; bigoted; costliest; austere; solitary; unalterable; ceremonious; idyllic; efficient; assiduous; extemporary; conjugal; outstanding; abiding; unimpeachable; incessant; fondest; invisible; protective; unobtrusive; passing; nunlike; reunited; ageless; sublime; patient.

verbs

accept—; bestow—; cease—; command—; excite—; exploit—; extend—; favor with —; glorify—; interrupt—; lavish—upon; pay—; show—; tender—; —abates; —wanes; —warms.

(See zeal, allegiance, attachment, love, worship, adoration, fidelity, religion.)

DEVOUR (v)

adverbs

ravenously; omnivorously; voraciously; greedily; rapidly; utterly; brutally; fiendishly; hoggishly; bestially; rudely.

(See eat, consume.)

DEVOUT

adverbs

profoundly; earnestly; completely; humbly; queerly; whole-heartedly; piously; submissively; unselfishly; unceasingly; reverently; conscientiously; faithfully; ardently; loyally; assiduously; unobtrusively; admirably; sincerely; solemnly; fervently; meekly.

DEW

adjectives

drenching; fragrant; cleansing; damp; dripping; murky; lethal; sparkling; heavy; melodious; filmy; glittering; glistening; warm; moonlit; starry; starlight; hoary; scented; gracious; moistening; quivering; spangled; prodigal; fiery; melancholy; ambrosial; new-dropped; fattening; ghastly; pestilent; gleaming; undried; cold; blinding; richer; unconcealing; sunlit; gathering; bitter; innocent; softest; melting; nocturnal; lingering; mellifluous; healing; falling; sickly; silvery.

verbs

bathe in—; bedabble with—; brush away—; deck with—; dip in—; dissolve in—; distill—; flower in—; sip—; spray with—; steep in—; sweep away—; wash with—; wet with—; —chills; —dabbles; —drenches; —drops; —falls; —freshens; —glistens; —moistens; —pearls; —refreshes; —revives; —spangles; —strengthens; —thickens; —twinkles.

(See moisture, tears, drop.)

DEXTERITY

adjectives

reasonable; digital; polite; amazing; bland; graceful; manual; unusual; marvelous; incredible; rapid; superior; wonderful; admirable; cool; indescribable; automatic; fatal.

DEXTEROUS

adverbs

reasonably; unusually; politically; blandly; amazingly; wonderfully; admirably; automatically; incredibly; dangerously; skilfully; particularly; consciously; proudly; ostentatiously; dramatically; expertly; felicitiously; discreetly; advantageously; acutely; shrewdly; scientifically; quickly; consummately; spectacularly; opportunely; astutely.

DIABOLIC

adverbs

inconceivably; iniquitously; incredibly; incorrigibly; atrociously; infernally; shock-ingly; manifestly; openly; flagrantly; exceptionably; horribly; outrageously; incurably; obdurately; stubbornly; nefariously; villainously; execrably; accursedly; inhumanly; ruthlessly.

DIABOLISM

adjectives

everlasting; widespread; apparent; marked; noticeable; flagrant.

DIADEM

adjectives

priceless; imperial; starry; kingless; stellated; royal; regal; ducal.

DIAGNOSE (v)

adverbs

precisely; accurately; exactly; correctly; medically; solemnly; bacteriologically; logically; scientifically; casually; conscientiously; astutely.

(See study.)

DIAGNOSIS

adjectives

exact; definite; bitter; unpromising; correct; medical; solemn; bacteriological.

verbs

conduct—; confirm—; embrace in—; form —; reach—; record—; study—; value—; weigh—; —assures; —determines; —discovers; —distinguishes; —errs; —identifies; —reveals; —warrants.

(See conclusion, judgment.)

DIAGRAM

adjectives

legible; clear; confused; graphic; explanatory; key; brief.

verbs

compose—; constitute—; draw—; examine —; exhibit—; experiment with—; improve —; mark—; measure—; outline—; produce —; —charts; —demonstrates; —directs; —illustrates; —points out; —represents; —symbolizes.

(See plan, outline, map, drawing, illustration.)

DIAL

adjectives

wavering; luminous; recessed; spacious; graduated; moss-grown; sun.

verbs

adjust—; affect—; center—; check—; discover by—; employ—; furnish with—; provide—; refer to—; set—; spin—; watch—; —aids; —counts; —describes; —directs; —indicates; —measures; —points to; —regulates; —revolves; —substantiates; —times.

(See compass, watch.)

DIALECT

adjectives
drawling; guttural; hinterland; crude; broad; garrulous; vulgar; handed-down; ancestral; forcible; unintelligible; strange; multiplying (pl); unpleasant; peculiar; nasal; native; authentic; queer; rural; overaccented; delicious; amorous; gibbering; purest; expressive; barbarous; quaint; untutored; hissing; unmusical.

verbs
adopt—; affect—; converse in—; drop—; influence—; interpret—; lay aside—; missound—; modify—; overcome—; recognize —; study—; understand—; —amuses; —confuses; —corrupts; —missounds; —retains; —vanishes.

(See language, speech.)

DIALOGUE

adjectives
fabulous; witty; short; solemn; natural; spontaneous; earnest; happy; hurried; vivid; delightful; tender; adequate; poetic; urbane; sparkling; final; mysterious; amusing; fast-paced; wooden; frothy; delicious; rapier-like; brilliant; imaginary; merry; wasted; feeble; dramatic; realistic; sustained.

verbs
carry on—; compile—; compose—; confine —to; contrive—; enter into—; entertain with—; inject into—; introduce in—; involve in—; launch into—; transcribe—; —animates; —concerns; —engrosses; —enlivens; —passes; —praises; —vivifies; interests in—.

(See conversation, talk.)

DIAMOND

adjectives
paste; oblong; spurious; illicit; sparkling; enormous; square-cut; pendent; blazing; icy; fair-sized; uncut; monstrous; starry; flashing; unlimited (pl); countless (pl); elemental; flaming; smuggled.

verbs
admire—; adorn with—; deck with—s; imbed—; mine—s; polish—; prize—; quarry

—s; set—; win—; yield—s; —crowns; —flames; —flashes; —gleams; —glimmers; —glistens; —glitters; —glows; —reflects; —scintillates; —sparkles.

(See gem, stone, jewel.)

DIAPHRAGM

adjectives
crude; concave; heaving; parchment; tough; bisecting.

DIARY

adjectives
careful; meteorological; intimate; manuscript; joyous; cryptic; copious; vigorous; authoritative; conscientious; well-kept; informal; informative; gossipy; risque; bold; revealing.

verbs
cherish—; enter in—; expose—; hide—; inscribe in—; jot in—; peep into—; prepare—; publish—; recollect by—; record in—; refer to—; repose in—; scan—; —collects; —contains; —covers; —notes; —observes; —relates; —reveals.

(See record, account, book, literature.)

DIATRIBE

adjectives
notorious; violent; revengeful; brutal; incessant.

verbs
break out in—; conclude—; direct—; erupt —; fire—; fulminate—; indulge in—; regret—; set off—; thunder—; utter—; vent —; —abuses; —arouses; —contributes; —exaggerates; —offends; —provokes; —shocks.

(See invective, tirade, discourse, discussion.)

DICE

adjectives
lucky; loaded; rattling; false; unfailing; irresistible; seductive.

verbs
bet on—; box—; cast—; cheat at—; gamble with—; jostle—; load—; lose by—; play with—; scatter—; shake—; shoot—; throw —; toss—; win at—; —clack; —clink; —decide; —fall; —rattle; —reveal; —settle; —topple; —turn.

DICTATE

adjectives
definite; unheeded; vicious; infernal; soundest; passionate; fascist.

DICTATE (v)

adverbs
amiably; simultaneously; personally; definitely; viciously; infernally; passionately; bestially; heartlessly; fiendishly; reasonably.
(See command.)

DICTATION

adjectives
aimless; laborious; imperious; rapid; accurate; careless.

DICTATOR

adjectives
military; musical; cruel; unseen; benevolent; philosophic; willful; occult; imperious; ranking; domestic.

verbs
appeal to—; develop into—; entrust—with; fall before—; follow—; name—; prate about—s; serve under—; succumb to—; —authorizes; —bans; —checks; —coerces; —crushes; —decrees; —exercises; —forbids; —forces; —fulminates; —governs; —orders; —prescribes; —rules; —tyrannizes; —violates; —wields.
(See tyrant, monarch, ruler.)

DICTATORIAL

adverbs
absolutely; politically; offensively; unashamedly; officiously; ostentatiously; imperially; regally; imperiously; cruelly; unwarrantably; disagreeably; needlessly; arrogantly; haughtily; superciliously; hatefully; carefully; obstinately; dogmatically; fanatically; fantastically; deliberately; insolently; saucily; impertinently; bumptiously; brazenly; shamelessly; presumptuously.

DICTATORSHIP

adjectives
absolute; military; political; proletarian; economic; stultifying; unashamed; irregular; temporary; household; bloody; mighty; inefficient; imperial; popular; literary; fruitless.

verbs
accept—; assume—; attempt—; create—; cultivate—; curtail—; elect to—; entrust—to; establish—; exercise—; install—; lust for—; repulse—; revolt against—; set up

—; serve under—; shake—; succumb to—; yield to—; —coerces; —compels; —crushes; —holds sway.
(See despotism, control, rule.)

DICTION

adjectives
stilted; meticulous; parietal; exquisite; tragic; dignified; metaphorical; illogical; artless; terse; elaborate; glowing; extravagant; loitering; poetic; racy; fashionable; classical; unadorned; overwhelming; peculiar; crabbed; bold.

DICTIONARY

adjectives
comprehensive; dusty; voluminous; exhaustive; unabridged; unusable; historical; universal; excellent; rhyming; biographical; scholarly; pronouncing; scriptural; phonetic; synonymic; grammatical; weighty; authoritative.

verbs
abridge—; compile—; consult—; edit—; enlarge—; have recourse to—; provide—; publish—; resort to—; revise—; —aids; —arranges; —classifies; —confirms; —contains; —decides; —defines; —determines; —informs; —interprets; —pictures; —verifies.
(See book.)

DICTUM

adjectives
energetic; famous; harsh; bold; brisk; final.

DIDACTIC

adverbs
tiresomely; tediously; wearisomely; monotonously; conceitedly; learnedly; instructively; endlessly; absurdly; egotistically; indefatigably; disagreeably; unpleasantly; ostentatiously; diffusely; preachily; sharply; academically; eruditely; expertly; bumptiously.

DIDACTICISM

adjectives
solemn; sugar-coated; obvious; patent; marked; unintelligent.

DIE (v)

adverbs
ultimately; unaccountably; wholly; utterly; valiantly; peacefully; sullenly; violently; gloriously; proudly; recently; providentially; stoically; pennilessly; invariably; hap-

lessly; blissfully; huskily; respectively; honorably; mysteriously; quiveringly; holily; abruptly; shamefully; accidentally; religiously; rebelliously; precipitately.
(See perish.)

DIET
adjectives
abstemious; starvation; daily; piscatory; ample; proper; modern; scant; mixed; varied; balanced; ordinary; exclusive; monotonous; nut; fastidious; invented; staple; nourishing; enriched; astringent; vitaminized; spurious; vegetarian; optimum; adequate; coniferous; correct; predominant; meat; peculiar; skimpy; rigid; sensible; intellectual; carnivorous; dangerous; strict; liquid; heavy.

verbs
adhere to—; adopt—; alter—; change—; commend—; complete—; compound—; discuss—; employ—; exclude from—; increase —; mix—; modify—; place on—; prescribe—; recover on—of; reduce—; regulate—; restrict—; spare in—; subsist on—; supplement—; vary—; yield to—; —cures; —influences; —nourishes; —reduces; —
(See fare, victuals. ration, food.)
stimulates; —supplies; —sustains.

DIETETICS
adjectives
compulsory; insipid; accessory; elementary; fundamental.

verbs
engross in—; instruct in—; interest in—; study—; —adapts; —cautions; —comprises; —cures; —defines; —extends to; —inquires; —observes; —prevents; —reforms; —regulates; —solves; —systematizes; — aids.
(See hygiene.)

DIFFER (v)
adverbs
radically; racially; decidedly; essentially; widely; profoundly; chemically; entirely; acutely; sharply; markedly; noticeably; perceptibly; infinitesimally; psychologically; mentally; religiously; gravely; appreciably; strikingly; palpably; vitally; significantly; fundamentally; philosophically; prodigiously; intrinsically; structurally.
(See disagree.)

DIFFERENCE
adjectives
sharp; marked; acute; honest; conscientious; noticeable; perceptible; decided; evident; inconsequent; infinitesimal; scant; slight; petty; racial; psychological; mental; religious; matrimonial; grave; insuperable; subtle; bitter; radical; simulated; conceded; actual; essential; utmost; striking; outstanding; profound; vast; appreciable; noteworthy; tremendous; palpable; calm; assignable; important; fresh; material; vital; sad; qualitative; pathetic; supreme; happy; minute; amazing; factional; original; significant; indefinable; supposed; superficial; magical; tribal; fundamental; irrepressible; deep-seated; philosophical; irreconcilable; prodigious; intrinsic; temporary; structural.

verbs
acquaint with—; appreciate—; bury—s; cancel—; compensate for—; correlate with —s; debate—; define—; determine—; discern—; discuss—; dread—; expose—; illustrate—; master—; notice—; obliterate—; observe—; reconcile—s; rest—s; settle—; smooth out—; —appears; —s arise; —s estrange; —s flare up; —prevents.
(See disagreement, discrimination, variation, inequality.)

DIFFERENT
adverbs
multifariously; incidentally; impertinently; harmlessly; objectionably; inadmissibly; unconformably; strangely; remotely; outlandishly; undeniably; palpably; essentially; grotesquely; disagreeably; pleasantly; obviously; inconceivably; discordantly; fantastically; exotically.

DIFFERENTIATE (v)
adverbs
legitimately; generously; elaborately; acutely; bluntly; properly; distinctly.
(See distinguish.)

DIFFERENTIATION
adjectives
subtle; elaborate; proper; acute; blunt.

DIFFICULT
adverbs
relatively; tremendously; overwhelmingly; formidably; unbelievably; supremely; seriously; administratively; physically; obviously; naturally; peculiarly; particularly;

strangely; curiously; conspicuously; alarmingly; patently; evidently; dishearteningly; impossibly; intricately; perplexingly; desperately.

DIFFICULTY
adjectives

immense; great; huge; tremendous; enormous; overwhelming; formidable; redoubtable; unbelievable; amazing; supreme; innumerable (pl); grave; serious; agrarian; domestic; emotional; administrative; technical; diplomatic; physical; economic; religious; appalling; financial; fiscal; evident; obvious; inherent; identical; underlying; insurmountable; vital; peculiar; practical; necessary; problematic; familiar; initial; insuperable; unpleasant; lamentable; invincible; conspicuous; unforeseen; functional; alarming; recurrent; endless; disheartening; relative; principal; censorship; bargaining; visual; baffling; impending; incredible; considerable; unprecedented.

verbs

adjust—; attend with—; belittle—; beset by—; breathe with—; clear up—; comprehend—; conclude—; confront with—; conquer—; contend with—; demonstrate—; double—; eliminate—; encounter—; escape —; estimate—; evade—; experience—; go to the root of—; grapple with—; grasp—; impose—; impress with—; iron out—; labor in—; minimize—; obliterate—; obviate—; pass—; perceive—; raise—; remedy—; rouse with—; shirk—; smooth away—; stir up—; strew with—; surmount—; weigh —; wrestle with; —ies accumulate; —ies arise; —grows out of; —intervenes; —looms; —persists.

(See obstacle, hindrance, quarrel, trouble.)

DIFFIDENCE
adjectives

delicate; rustic; becoming; excessive; amused; half-boyish; proper.

verbs

attack—; disperse—; enter into with—; indulge in—; lay aside—; manifest—; practise—; proceed from—; speak with—; teach —; —afflicts; —assails; —creeps over; —prevents; —shames; —submits to; —terrifies; —wounds.

(See bashfulness.)

DIFFIDENT
adverbs

delicately; provincially; becomingly; excessively; amusingly; laughably; ridiculously; needlessly; properly; nervously; anxiously; dreadfully; painfully; bashfully; blushingly; demurely; quietly; shyly.

DIFFUSE
adverbs

tiresomely; tediously; monotonously; vexatiously; endlessly; verbosely; copiously; circuitously; disagreeably; provokingly; pedantically; stupidly; dully; indirectly; interminably; prosily; maddeningly; notoriously.

DIFFUSE (v)
adverbs

naturally; delicately; excessively; wastefully; widely; copiously; freely; liberally; perplexingly.

(See scatter, disseminate.)

DIFFUSENESS
adjectives

rhythmical; excessive; expansive; limited; unshadowed; beaming; theoretical.

DIFFUSION
adjectives

wide; cultural; original; soft; vast; inexpressible; universal.

DIG
adjectives

sly; intentional; vicious; sarcastic; witty; humorous; retaliative.

DIG (v)
adverbs

laboriously; perseveringly; viciously; intentionally; purposively; industriously; indefatigably.

(See work, labor.)

DIGEST
adjectives

interesting; careful; considered; chronological; fact.

DIGEST (v)
adverbs

complacently; rapidly; internally; interestingly; carefully; chronologically; intelligently; mentally; cleverly; briefly.

(See absorb, classify.)

DIGESTION

adjectives
torpid; agreeable; disturbed; superb; sound; pure.

verbs
activate—; affect—; allay—; disturb—; govern—; impair—; improve—; interrupt —; promote—; regulate—; reinvigorate—; retard—; sour—; stimulate—; upset—.
(See health.)

DIGIT

adjectives
lone; disassociated; menacing; insignificant; discounted.

verbs
calculate—; count—; dismember—; divide into—s; decorate—; employ—; exercise—; express in—s; flex—; indicate—; memorize—; number—; ornament—; run into—s; sever—; spoil—s.
(See toe, finger, figure, number.)

DIGNIFIED

adverbs
properly; proudly; informally; graciously; simply; pleasantly; nobly; serenely; calmly; quietly; gravely; faultlessly; elaborately; coldly; indescribably; ridiculously; superbly; naturally; magisterially; matchlessly; sternly; impressively; incongruously; austerely; professionally; pompously; senselessly; gently; disagreeably; repellently; notoriously; augustly; fashionably; solemnly.

DIGNITARY

adjectives
honorable; famous; professional; local; robot; titular; learned.

DIGNITY

adjectives
proper; proud; upright; informal; happy; delicate; external; lofty; lauded; gracious; supreme; simple; majestic; pleasant; complacent; noble; robust; brave; serene; calm; quiet; grave; unwinking; studied; measured; faultless; immaculate; elaborate; sure; stilted; cold; severe; savage; impaired; faded; obedient; mysterious; social; impassive; indescribable; forensic; dashing; waddling; ridiculous; outraged; poised; trembling; spacious; potential; outward; stoical; superb; forced; unbroken; ageless; natural; silent; sententious; sad;

irresistible; magisterial; distant; matchless, undeserved; ill-timed; spiritual; patriarchal; wonted; smug; scholastic; gruesome; military; threatened; short-lived; stern; pious; panoplied; leisure-class; frowning; impressive; spectral; incongruous; white; celestial; mutilated; austere; professional; youthful; additional; senseless; mournful; sedate; pompous; mock; epic; inherent; insulted; gentle; careless; unprecedented; Wagnerian.

verbs
achieve—; cast off—; detract from—; develop—; discard—; dispose of—; enhance —; grope for—; halo in—; inject—; impair—; impart—; invest with—; lend—; maintain—; outrage—; preserve—; retain —; rob of—; shed—; shrug aside—; stress —; surpass—; sustain—; treat with—; vindicate—; win—.
(See eminence, honor, distinction.)

DIGRESS (v)

adverbs
irrelevantly; deviously; slightly; politically; fascinatingly; descriptively; boringly; dryly; interminably; illogically.
(See wander, deviate.)

DIGRESSION

adjectives
pleasing; slight; bitter; political; fascinating; irrelevant; unintegrated; wise; agreeable; descriptive; periodic (pl).

DIGRESSIVE

adverbs
vexatiously; endlessly; wordily; verbosely; diffusely; copiously; circuitously; disagreeably; provokingly; tiresomely; unintelligibly; pedantically; vaguely; stupidly; dully; ramblingly; indirectly; interminably.

DILAPIDATED

adverbs
terribly; wretchedly; miserably; sorely; pathetically; dreadfully; ruinously; hideously; outrageously; fantastically; shabbily; shockingly; inconceivably; greatly; inexpressibly; worthlessly.

DILAPIDATION

adjectives
general; wholesale; pathetic; ragged; tumble-down; remnantal.

DILATE (v)

adverbs
endlessly; visibly; abnormally; intolerably; unprecedentedly; continuously; unreasonably.
(See swell.)

DILATORY

adverbs
injuriously; uselessly; needlessly; vexatiously; irritatingly; senselessly; unaccountably; obstinately; stubbornly; dangerously; exasperatingly; unconscionably; characteristically; habitually; gravely; terribly; impertinently; indolently; stupidly; languidly; listlessly; inertly; slothfully; drowsily; dreamily; inexcusably; unpleasantly; gallingly.

DILEMMA

adjectives
economic; awkward; annoying; ancient; veritable; insoluble; cruel; moral; pitiful; agonizing; dire; frightful; doubtful; sentimental; unpleasant; terrible; desperate; inescapable; hopeless.

verbs
balk at—; drift into—; elude—; escape from—; extricate from—; face—; founder on—; grasp—; rescue from—; seize—; solve—; take—by the horns; —baffles; —confronts.
(See choice, predicament.)

DILIGENCE

adjectives
characteristic; sullen; unwearied; savage; conscientious; guilty; true; extraordinary; exceeding; utmost; duteous; scrupulous; tenderest; dire; indefatigable; persevering; dusty; yellow; unsparing; tireless; unwonted.

verbs
admire—; apply—; dispatch with—; display—; exercise—; exert—; note—; nourish —; repay—; report—; require—; reward —; rule with—; show—; summon—; —accomplishes; —persists; —pleases.
(See industry, care, application.)

DILIGENT

adverbs
extraordinarily; carefully; innately; studiously; assiduously; industriously; busily; constantly; doggedly; faithfully; loyally; indefatigably; conscientiously; exceedingly; duteously; scrupulously; tirelessly; habitual-ly; trustworthily; energetically; pleasantly; surprisingly; zealously; devotedly; officiously; briskly; ostentatiously; conspicuously; diplomatically; astutely; shrewdly.

DIM

adverbs
mysteriously; obscurely; strangely; curiously; oddly; nebulously; dully; faintly; cloudily; confusingly; perplexingly; disturbingly; wretchedly; miserably; pallidly; imperceptibly; unaccountably; plaguedly; infernally; dreadfully.

DIM (v)

adverbs
perceptibly; scarcely; mystically; prematurely; dramatically; awesomely; effectively; abruptly; perceptibly.
(See darken, obscure.)

DIMENSION

adjectives
important; narrow; reduced; dominating; prodigious; mere; colossal; ideal; mathematical; basic; toylike; supernatural; hugest; portentous; relative; corporal; gigantic; stupendous; miniature; scanty; horizontal; volcanic; enormous; manageable; palatial; moderate; ambitious; noble; desired; imperial; spacious; confined; incompatible.

verbs
compute—; describe—; discover—; draw—; expand—; explore—; find—; furnish—; measure—; mistake—; reach—; reduce—; require—; speculate on—; supply—; take —; —bounds; —confuses; —exceeds; —represents; —shrinks.
(See magnitude, size, extent.)

DIMINISH (v)

adverbs
perceptibly; partially; proportionally; steadily; materially; insignificantly; sensibly; seriously; vastly; appreciably; intolerably; sensibly; continuously.
(See reduce, lessen.)

DIMINUTION

adjectives
appreciable; sensible; continuous; perceptible; subtle; covert; gradual.

DIMNESS

adjectives

mystic; lovely; gracious; unreal; chequered; shadowy; dreamlike; holy; religious; premature; vast; lonely; cobwebby; misty.

DIMPLE

adjectives

reluctant; fugitive; elusive; tantalizing; fleeting; impertinent; wanton; roguish; neighboring.

verbs

bait with—; break into—; depress into—; expose—; flash—; form—; hollow into—; laugh—; mark with—; part in—; practise —; repay in—; reveal—; smile—; —captivates; —dances; —delights; —lures; —smiles; —twinkles.

DIN

adjectives

terrible; infernal; sudden; outrageous; jocund; clanging; alarming; competing; wheezing; awful; chaotic; terrific; rude; discordant; horrible; chattering; general; ominous; exclamatory; ear-splitting; merry; lively; plaintive; deafening; ever-waxing; furious; vexatious; wild; humming; resounding; reverberating; echoing; shattering; intermittent; frightful.

verbs

diminish—; drown—; endure—; muffle—; penetrate—; raise—; silence—; tremble at —; —awakens; —blasts; —breaks; —dies away; —ensues; —fades; —hisses; —reverberates; —roars; —streams forth; —waxes louder.

(See noise, clamor, uproar, rattle.)

DINE (v)

adverbs

prodigally; sumptuously; ostentatiously; regally; piggishly; opulently; delectably; luxuriously; gaily; talkatively; impressively; miserably; simply; abundantly; belatedly; modestly; ceremoniously; diplomatically; formally.

DINER

adjectives

agitated; gay; talkative; Epicurean; gluttonous.

verbs

cook for—; entertain—; greet—; satiate—; suit—; welcome—; —indulges; —overeats; —relishes; —samples; —stuffs; —tastes; —tips.

DINGY

adverbs

bleakly; terribly; obscurely; gloomily; faintly; disagreeably; repulsively; hatefully; disgustingly; unpleasantly; monotonously; incredibly; pitiably; surprisingly; unexpectedly; discouragingly; hopelessly; inexcusably; dishearteningly; depressingly.

DINING-ROOM

adjectives

oak-paneled; charming; huge; typical; sweltering; cheerless; tapestried; dim; quiet; empty; resplendent.

DINNER

adjectives

impressive; princely; charming; old-fashioned; pleasant; elaborate; sumptuous; delicious; gala; respectable; cheerful; good; decent; tolerable; stupid; miserable; oppressive; masculine; state; simple; abundant; belated; expensive; modest; incredible; endless; savory; magnificent; wretched; melancholy; solitary; periodical; ceremonious; diplomatic; woman-cooked; desolate; doubtful; formal; midnight.

verbs

accompany at—; address at—; attend—; dance at—; dispatch—; drop in for—; enliven—; hobnob at—; invite to—; prepare—; relish—; revel at—; ring for—; sample—; savor—; serve—; spread for—; tear at—; —cools; —nourishes; —satisfies; —steams.

(See meal.)

DIP

adjectives

invigorating; exhilarating; morning; tallow; convulsive; curious.

DIP (v)

adverbs

heavily; abnormally; invigoratingly; exhilaratingly; convulsively; curiously; continuously.

(See lower.)

DIPHTHERIA

adjectives

malignant; mild; tentative; membranous; controlled; dread.

verbs

afflict with—; carry—; contract—; describe —; diagnose as—; doctor for—; immunize to—; infect with—; inoculate against—; isolate—; quarantine for—; recognize—; seize with—; succumb to—; suffer from—; treat for—; —attacks; —inflames; —rages; —ravages; —takes its toll.

(See disease.)

DIPLOMACY

adjectives

tortuous; wasted; secret; minute; private; unskilled; shrewd; consummate; formal; proper; misty; tricky.

verbs

acquire—; adjust with—; adopt—; boast —; conduct with—; control by—; cultivate —; destroy—; detect—; dole out—; employ—; encourage—; exert—; favor—; fit for—; found in—; gain by—; infiltrate—; instruct in—; introduce—; manage with—; necessitate—; negotiate—; propose—; school in—; suggest—; —achieves; —attains; —conceals; —reconciles; —smooths out; — wins.

(See tact, shrewdness, craft.)

DIPLOMAT

adjectives

clever; astute; seasoned; distinguished; veteran; wary; consummate; Oriental; skillful; traditional; old-style; career; formal; suave; scholarly; incredulous; eminent; deft; accomplished; practiced.

verbs

appoint—; employ—; entrust to—; introduce—; invest—with; privilege—; prove —; receive—; select—; —arranges; — conciliates; —conducts; —humors; — "joshes"; —manages; —proposes; — smooths; —suggests; —tricks.

(See ambassador.)

DIPLOMATIC

adverbs

subtly; cunningly; shrewdly; artfully; gravely; wisely; craftily; smoothly; suavely; cleverly; astutely; instinctively; habitually; skilfully; formally; deftly; adroitly; tactfully; profoundly; courteously; cannily; discerningly; nimbly; sagaciously; sagely; blandly; wisely; affably; calculatingly; strategically.

DIPLOMATIST

adjectives

career; cunning; unscrupulous; acute; supple; wary; tenacious; dexterous; decorated.

DIRECT

adverbs

delightfully; pleasantly; helpfully; comfortingly; charmingly; gratifyingly; satisfactorily; pleasingly; ingenuously; frankly; candidly; honestly; courageously; boldly; unequivocally; agreeably; surprisingly; conveniently; childishly; bluntly; sincerely; unaffectedly; unflatteringly; crudely; curiously; strangely.

DIRECT (*v*)

adverbs

vaguely; intelligently; generally; competently; practically; brilliantly; magnificently; disastrously; dangerously; legislatively; habitually; relentlessly; ultimately; academically; arbitrarily; ignobly; intellectually; intricately; eccentrically; hurriedly; curtly; calmly; frivolously; vigorously; automatically; vainly; verbally; uniformly; perseveringly; astutely; dramatically; independently; victoriously.

(See control, guide.)

DIRECTION

adjectives

unlooked-for; vague; intelligent; competent; general; steady; practical; brilliant; magnificent; indicated; careful; unified; cohesive; disastrous; dangerous; legislative; opposite; forbidden; habitual; desirable; inhibited; oblique; relentless; distinguished; succinct; ultimate; academic; retrograde; homeward; arbitrary; ignoble; businesslike; complicated; intellectual; intricate; low-toned; eccentric; crisp; voluble; concise; hurried; curt; calm; explicit (pl); contradictory; transversal; dazzling; frivolous; minute.

verbs

comply with—; determine—; divert from —: drift in—; err in—; face in—of; gaze in—; give—to; heed—; incline—; lack—;

observe—s; respond to—; reverse—; tend in—of; train in—; transmit—s; turn in—; —swerves; —wavers.
(See instruction, course. position.)

DIRECTNESS

adjectives
commendable; uncanny; bull-headed; downright; pleasing; brisk; characteristic; engaging; arrowlike; uncompromising; simple; unstudied; brutal; revealing; clipped; unabashed; manly; military; impulsive; naive; brusque.

DIRECTOR

adjectives
capable; painstaking; regional; financial; shadowy; honorable.

DIRGE

adjectives
mournful; wailing; beautiful; prophetic; wrathful; death; funeral; undifferentiated; weird.

verbs
chant—; compose—; intone—; introduce—; moan—; occasion—; perform—; renew—; sing—; soothe with—; sound—; utter—; wail—; —commemorates; —laments; — mourns; —saddens.
(See song, poem, music.)

DIRT

adjectives
stubborn; encrusted; soft; excess; sweaty; grayish; imbedded; accumulated; unspeakable.

verbs
acquaint with—; breed in—; cast out—; defile with—; fleck with—; fling to—; frolic in—; grind into—; ingrain with—; originate from—; plant in—; pluck from—; pollute with—; scrape away—; search in—; throw—; tread in—; wade in—; wallow in—; wash away—; —accumulates; —adheres; —befouls; —clings; —soils.
(See earth, soil, filth, squalor.)

DISABILITY

adjectives
total; grim; physical; permanent; financial; partial; inescapable.

verbs
attend with—; bring on—; complain of—; cope with—; create—; cripple by—; emancipate from—; gloat over—; increase—; labor under—; lessen—; remove—; stress —; —paralyzes; —prevents; —restricts; —tortures.
(See inability, incompetence, impotence, weakness.)

DISABLE (v)

adverbs
totally; physically; permanently; financially; partially; inescapably; tragically; woefully; completely; entirely.
(See handicap.)

DISABLED

adverbs
tragically; oddly; sadly; utterly; strangely; dangerously; grimly; totally; partially; physically; mentally; irremediably; irrecoverably; lamentably; pitiably; deplorably; pitifully; unnecessarily; helplessly; hopelessly; recently.

DISADVANTAGE

adjectives
distinct; physical; immense; tactical; serious; obvious; ungenerous; initial; economic; particular; individual; undue; painful; tremendous.

verbs
balance—; conceal—; confront with—; deprecate—; endure—; fight at—; hurdle—; labor under—; place at—; overcome—; regret—; sell at—; surmount—; tug at—; uproot—; weight with—; —hinders; — injures; —obstructs.
(See injury, loss, inconvenience, detriment, drawback, hindrance.)

DISADVANTAGEOUS

adverbs
financially; socially; decidedly; distinctly; physically; immensely; strategically; seriously; obviously; manifestly; unfortunately; economically; particularly; unduly; painfully; tremendously; perniciously; disastrously; horribly; exceptionally; infernally; irremediably.

DISAGREE (v)

adverbs
spiritedly; violently; emphatically; excessively; unwittingly; vehemently; internally; utterly; bitterly; acridly; reasonably; emotionally; rationally; spitefully; venomously.
(See differ, contradict.)

DISAGREEABLE

adverbs

pathetically; utterly; atrociously; outrageously; obviously; senselessly; unreasonably; unnecessarily; horribly; disgustingly; bitterly; deliberately; unintentionally; habitually; gravely; rankly; indecently; disrespectfully; odiously; painfully; unfortunately; unbearably; plaguedly; obnoxiously; dismally; shockingly; harshly; cruelly.

DISAGREEMENT

adjectives

vehement; internal; utter; bitter; acrid.

verbs

abandon—; attribute—to; avoid—; cancel —; cause—; engross in—; evade—; expose to—; feign—; indulge in—; live in—; overcome—; pacify—; remove—; settle—; — disgusts; —displeases; —offends; —vexes.
(See difference, contention, quarrel, dispute.)

DISAPPEAR (v)

adverbs

mysteriously; unaccountably; abruptly; miraculously; evanescently; unquestionably; gradually; totally; effectually; unexpectedly; irretrievably; virtually.
(See vanish, recede.)

DISAPPEARANCE

adjectives

unexpected; unexplained; irretrievable; inexplicable; sudden; gradual; virtual.

verbs

achieve—; credit—to; discover—; effect—; fear—; feign—; investigate—; solve—; witness—; —astounds; —baffles; —mystifies.
(See escape.)

DISAPPOINT (v)

adverbs

acutely; obviously; grievously; wretchedly; woefully; bitterly; continually; visibly; childishly; distinctly; overwhelmingly; inevitably; vaguely; deeply; poignantly; remorsefully; horridly; mutually; perpetually; cruelly; repeatedly.
(See frustrate, baffle.)

DISAPPOINTED

adverbs

sadly; hopelessly; bitterly; heartbreakingly; irrecoverably; obscurely; grievously; distinctly; overwhelmingly; obviously; manifestly; inexpressibly; vaguely; definitely; deeply; poignantly; horribly; woefully; repeatedly; disconcertingly; tragically; bleakly; senselessly; foolishly; pitiably; terribly; inconsolably; forlornly; miserably; wrtechedly; cruelly.

DISAPPOINTING

adverbs

cruelly; bitterly; harshly; sharply; overwhelmingly; unbearably; sadly; grievously; distinctly; inexpressibly; vaguely; woefully; searingly; pitiably; wretchedly; terribly; tragically; fearfully; definitely; deeply.

DISAPPOINTMENT

adjectives

minor; obscure; scathing; bitter; grievous; distinct; overwhelming; obvious; hurt; expressive; inevitable; resultant; burning; vague; outward; unhappy; deep; poignant; remorseful; unrepressed; horrid; woeful; classic; mutual; perpetual; cruel; melancholy; repeated; callous; demoniac.

verbs

adjust—; conceal—; deserve—; dole out—; entail—; feign—; oppress with—; preclude —; pretend—; produce—; shoulder—; sob —; soothe—; suppress—; taste—; —dampens; —ensues; —irks; —rankles; —saddens; —teaches; —wounds.
(See frustration, dissatisfaction, chagrin, misfortune, defeat.)

DISAPPROBATION

adjectives

express; strong; bitter; haughty; hesitant; ready; spontaneous.

DISAPPROVAL

adjectives

envious; ponderous; unmistakable; cold; emphatic; mounting; marked; absent-minded; prim; shocked; icy; unanimous; stern; distinct; tragic; wordless; consistent; harsh; lofty; undisguised; united; violent; ungracious; frigid.

verbs

anticipate—; earn—; indicate—; mask—; prompt—; quench with—; register—; relax —; signify—; snort—; storm—; vent—; —abates; —dampens; —descends; —oppresses; —silences; —vexes.
(See condemnation, censure.)

DISAPPROVE (v)

adverbs

distinctly; heartily; obviously; strongly; unmistakably; coldly; emphatically; primly; icily; unanimously; consistently; sternly; wordlessly; harshly; violently; ungraciously; frigidly.

(See criticize, grumble.)

DISARMAMENT

adjectives

effective; universal; unilateral; worldwide; wide-spread.

verbs

affect—; agree to—; approve of—; confer on—; demand—; disagree upon—; introduce—; join in—; propose—; secure—; urge—; —deprives; —divests; —promises; —reduces; —secures; —strips; —terrifies; —weakens.

DISASTER

adjectives

black; dreadful; messy; hideous; terrible; unmitigated; unbearable; cataclysmic; overwhelming; serious; stupendous; titanic; ultimate; irreparable; irretrievable; marital; economic; melodramatic; planetary; cosmic; social; family; metaphysical; political; commercial; matrimonial; personal; unforeseen; unaccountable; unprecedented; indefinable; dim; imaginary; merited; dire; instant; sheer; sad; fresh; grievous; increasing; appalling; sweet; financial; subsequent; irremediable; awful; ominous; ignominious; illimitable; apparent; widespread; impending; unmerciful.

verbs

circumvent—; court—; force into—; foredoom to—; head for—; investigate—; invite—; meet with—; obviate—; presage—; prophesy—; provoke—; rush into—; salvage from—; shield from—; sow the seeds of—; spell—; suffer—; threaten—; —befalls; —dogs; —impends; —jars; —overtakes; —overwhelms; —sweeps.

(See calamity, catastrophe, mishap, misfortune, accident.)

DISASTROUS

adverbs

overwhelmingly; wholly; irremediably; inexpressibly; horribly; politically; strategically; ruinously; dreadfully; hideously; cataclysmically; seriously; stupendously; ultimately; irreparably; economically; soc-

ially; unaccountably; direly; appallingly; financially; apparently; unmercifully; exceptionally; shockingly.

DISAVOW (v)

adverbs

explicitly; deservedly; modestly; completely; distinctly; partially; honestly; earnestly; heatedly; excitedly; repeatedly.

(See disclaim.)

DISAVOWAL

adjectives

distinct; modest; complete; craven; rash; deliberate.

DISBELIEF

adjectives

scornful; cynical; heartsick; raucous; stuttering; total.

verbs

acquire—; adjust—; alter—; assert—; attack—; conceal—; drift into—; express—; form—; hint—; mantle—; pretend—; strip of—; —angers; —annoys; —persists; —refuses; —vexes; —rejects.

(See doubt, distrust, incredulity, skepticism.)

DISC

(See disk)

adjectives

flat; brilliant; polished; keen; turned; crude.

DISCARD (v)

adverbs

ruthlessly; consequently; permanently; gradually; partially; entirely; carelessly; uncaringly; selfishly; obliviously; cruelly.

(See throw, reject.)

DISCERN (v)

adverbs

dimly; faintly; clearly; scornfully; acutely; truthfully; shrewdly; enlightenedly; keenly; jealously; raptly; suspiciously.

(See distinguish, see.)

DISCERNIBLE

adverbs

easily; scarcely; quickly; obscurely; dimly; clearly; plainly; eventually; humanly; amazingly; startlingly; fatally; distinctly; intuitively; dangerously; definitely; positively; momentarily; hardly.

DISCERNING

adverbs

notoriously; profoundly; deeply; sagaciously; judicially; philosophically; expertly; adroitly; cleverly; keenly; astutely; shrewdly; solidly; quickly; brilliantly; acutely; intelligently; ingeniously; discriminatingly; wisely.

DISCERNMENT

adjectives

shrewd; human; enlightened; acute; rapt; keen; jealous.

DISCHARGE

adjectives

watchful; judicious; successful; assiduous; instant; thunderous; conscientious; ignominious; offensive; immediate; luminous; electrical; profuse; vigilant; faithful; occasional; copious.

verbs

absorb—; arrest—; check—; emit—; mop out—; purify—; stop—; suck out—; —burns; —drips; —gushes; —inflames; —irritates; —itches; —renews; —varies; —wanes.

(See firing, blast.)

DISCHARGE (v)

adverbs

instantaneously; intelligently; conscientiously; ingeniously; adequately; capably; briskly; faithfully; fully; punctually; judiciously; watchfully; assiduously; ignominiously; offensively; vigilantly.

(See remove, stop.)

DISCIPLE

adjectives

ardent; doubting; youthful; ignorant; inquiring; leading; prolific; uncritical; blunt; renowned; wholehearted; faithful; fervent; humble; patient; temporary; tractable; immediate; civil; primitive; hopeful; trusted.

verbs

accept—; address—; baptize—; cast out—; choose—; command—; distinguish—; instruct—; lead—; rebuke—; teach—; win—; —advances; —apprehends; —believes; —deserts; —establishes; —expounds; —fasts; —follows; —forsakes; —ministers; —prays; —propagates; —records; —understands.

(See convert, follower.)

DISCIPLINARIAN

adjectives

harsh; ferocious; stern; incompetent; ineffectual; strong-minded.

DISCIPLINE

adjectives

mental; hard; strict; unsympathizing; monastic; religious; stern; patient; firm; virtuous; gentle; effective; military; grim; iron; inflexible; rigorous; compulsory; irksome; inexorable; cellular; unfeeling; imaginative; infracted; systematic; painful; affectionate; heroic; moral; speculative; conventual; unrelenting; secret; peculiar; spasmodic; needful; unflagging; questioned; sound; absolute; perfect; modern; prudent; monastic; iron.

verbs

abate—; chafe under—; dread—; enforce —; fuse with—; impose—; maintain—; neglect—; preserve—; relax—; subject to —; wreck—; —deteriorates; —exacts; —falters; —loosens; —wavers; —weakens.

(See training, subjection, punishment, correction.)

DISCIPLINE (v)

adverbs

conscientiously; admirably; ardently; faithfully; patiently; strictly; morally; physically; rigorously; daily; harshly; severely; mentally; unsympathizingly; monastically; religiously; virtuously; gently; effectively; grimly; inflexibly; irksomely; inexorably; unfeelingly; conventionally; unflaggingly; soundly; prudently.

(See train, correct, punish.)

DISCLAIM (v)

adverbs

privately; modestly; excitedly; vehemently; repeatedly; violently; noisily; vigorously; grumblingly; eloquently; fluently; loudly; definitely; weakly; spiritedly; competently; aggressively; promptly; compellingly.

(See deny, renounce.)

DISCLOSE (v)

adverbs

immodestly; irreverently; recently; immediately; fully; shamelessly; modestly; staggeringly; gradually; startlingly; sensationally; diplomatically; dramatically; formally; monstrously; unflatteringly; ruthlessly.

(See reveal, expose.)

DISCLOSURE

adjectives

important; staggering; startling; gradual; cumulating; sensational; diplomatic; dramatic; undeniable; flattering; wide; formal; monstrous.

verbs

anticipate—; guard against—; prepare for —; prevent—; publish—; view—; —accuses; —liberates; —menaces; —precipitates; —reveals; —shocks; —threatens; —unfolds; —yields; —shames.

(See revelation, exhibition, display, discovery.)

DISCOLORATION

adjectives

repulsive; mottled; superficial; unsightly; dark; obtrusive.

DISCOMFIT (v)

adverbs

completely; embarrassingly; humiliatingly; momentarily; comically; immediately; spitefully; playfully; calculatedly.

(See humiliate, defeat.)

DISCOMFITURE

adjectives

momentary; comical; old-fashioned; humiliating; nettled; barbed.

DISCOMFORT

adjectives

conscious; visible; emotional; acute; general; agitated; human; prudent; personal; slight; apparent; uncommon; steaming; petty; postprandial; myriad (pl); picturesque; indefinite; sordid; eerie; social; mental; heavy; unendurable; heated; hospitable.

verbs

allay—; alleviate—; chafe in—; chuckle at—; endure—; inflict—; remove—; return with—; share—; suffer—; —disheartens; —dismays; —forces; —grows; —leads; —pains.

(See uneasiness, distress, pain.)

DISCONCERTED

adverbs

embarrassingly; awkwardly; deeply; profoundly; visibly; obviously; painfully; amazingly; terribly; significantly; palpably; vaguely; momentarily; considerably; violently; unmistakably; inexplicably; inadvertently; hopelessly; desperately; irreparably; vexatiously; grievously; glumly; strangely; slightly; mysteriously; oddly.

DISCONSOLATE

adverbs

visibly; apparently; sadly; heavily; pathetically; pitiably; unreasonably; irrationally; appallingly; drearily; grimly; sullenly; resentfully; oddly; ostentatiously; gloomily; biliously; pitifully; profoundly; hopelessly; wearily; desperately; unbearably; unutterably; bitterly; touchingly; genuinely; pensively; mopishly; moodily; dully.

DISCONTENT

adjectives

heavy; economic; real; inevitable; chronic; moderate; prevalent; dreadful; weary; divine; habitual; sullen; desperate; patent; renewed; thoughtful; querulous; perpetual; brawling; thralled; epidemic; popular; vain; moody; gloomy; unruly; smoldering; muttered; latent; futile; growing; impious; sublime; audible; ancient; widespread; aggravating.

verbs

articulate—; awake—; calm—; curse in—; excite—; foment—; murmur—; mutter—; revolt in—; rumble—; seethe with—; sow —; spread—; —afflicts; —flames; —flares; —gathers; —impairs; —sours.

(See dissatisfaction, uneasiness.)

DISCONTINUE (v)

adverbs

peremptorily; permanently; temporarily; abruptly; gradually; suddenly; surprisingly; spectacularly.

(See cease, stop.)

DISCORD

adjectives

exquisite; gay; jarring; hidden; ludicrous; mournful; factional; international; jangling; grating; quavering; unmusical; melodious; bitter; unappeasable; striking; distressing; intestinal; inevitable; civic; fluctuant; causeless; lingering; fearful; multitoned.

verbs

accept—; breed—; clash in—; conquer—; correct—; fall to—; ferment—; foment—; hush—; intensify—; master—; overcome—; produce—; silence—; sow—; subject to—;

suffer—; swallow up in—; terminate in—; wipe out—; yield to—; —confounds; —destroys; —follows; —jars; —reigns; —strains.

(See dissension, disagreement, contention, strife, antagonism.)

DISCORDANCE
adjectives
bewildering; complicated; noisy; deafening; incipient; harsh; covert.

DISCORDANT
adverbs
bewilderingly; surprisingly; unexpectedly; unendurably; roughly; harshly; disagreeably; impossibly; intolerably; ludicrously; bitterly; ridiculously; oddly; strangely; exceptionally; shockingly; queerly; strikingly; distressingly; inevitably; racially; essentially; fundamentally; ideologically; unreasonably; distinctly; incongruously; incompatibly; terribly; irreconcilably.

DISCOURAGE (v)
adverbs
sepulchrally; entirely; distinctly; churlishly; wisely; heartbreakingly; pathetically; habitually; profoundly; deeply; unreasonably; ruthlessly; permanently.

(See depress, dishearten.)

DISCOURAGEMENT
adjectives
combined; heartbreaking; pathetic; habitual; profound; countless (pl).

verbs
conceal—; mask—; pretend—; produce—; register—; succumb to—; turn in—; yield to—; —abates; —chills, —dampens; —ensues; —hinders; —obstructs; —oppresses; —suppresses; —depresses.

(See despair, depression, dejection, obstacle.)

DISCOURSE
adjectives
admirable; amiable; gay; pleasant; amusing; instructive; didactic; short; humorous; ingenuous; stirring; amazing; connected; rambling; flagging; rhymed; romantic; eloquent; serious; excellent; pointed; identical; separate; vehement; fallible; intended; doctrinal; harmonic; correct; sweet; voluble; sharp; remarkable; fair; bold; moral; witty; common; erratic; profound; unsympathizing; venial.

verbs
admit in—; change—; comprehend—; control—; delight in—; deliver—; devour—; draw out—; enter into—; fill with—; interchange—; invite—; leave off—; open—; peruse—; publish—; render—; spice—; venture on—; waste—; —differs; —enchants; —ensues; —matures.

(See address, speech, dissertation, oration, conversation.)

DISCOURSE (v)
adverbs
pleasantly; accurately; prophetically; eloquently; abstrusely; incredibly; delightfully; confusingly; impressively; admirably; amiably; gaily; authoritatively; amusingly; instructively; didactically; ingenuously; humorously; stirringly; romantically; ramblingly; volubly; morally; unsympathetically.

(See speak, converse, lecture.)

DISCOURTEOUS
adverbs
churlishly; sullenly; bluntly; snarlingly; angrily; deliberately; offensively; truculently; hotly; ignorantly; intentionally; unwittingly; brutally; harshly; captiously; sulkily; pertly; saucily; repulsively; venomously; perversely; contemptibly; purposely; impudently; shamefully; crudely; roughly; impertinently; disgracefully; inherently; grossly; tactlessly; morosely; arrogantly; boldly; insolently; trenchantly; maliciously; contemptuously.

DISCOURTESY
adjectives
seeming; gross; prevalent; personal; rough; contemptuous.

DISCOVER (v)
adverbs
finally; subsequently; readily; traitorously; astoundingly; amazingly; spectacularly; startlingly; thrillingly; remarkably; stupendously; trivially; miraculously; scientifically; painfully; revolutionizingly; astonishingly; momentously.

(See disclose, ascertain.)

DISCOVERY
adjectives
cheery; delightful; heartening; pleasant; beautiful; astounding; amazing; startling; spectacular; interesting; thrilling; far-reaching; marvelous; remarkable; important; stupendous; paleontological; radical; grievous; awkward; trivial; disconnected; public; godlike; decorative; miraculous;

scientific; striking; painful; epoch-making; bold; notable; pristine; archaeological; grand; useful; initiatory; pictorial; revolutionary; glorious; mineral; laboratory; outward; astonishing; momentous; fatal; salutary; uncomfortable.

verbs
announce—; anticipate—; bring forth—; communicate—; conjure up—; corroborate —; culminate in—; discredit—; examine —; finance—; follow up—; hail—; honor —; lead to—; obtain—; pursue—; report —; stumble on—; verify—; —benefits; —discloses; —reflects; —sheds light on; —underlies.
(See detection, disclosure, revelation, exposure.)

DISCREDITABLE
adverbs
hideously; secretly; subtly; palpably; manifestly; evidently; sadly; terribly; calamitously; foully; abjectly; basely; shamefully; disgracefully; notoriously; scandalously; opprobriously; outrageously; shockingly; appallingly; pitifully.

DISCREET
adverbs
astutely; reasonably; habitually; safely; loyally; admirably; cautiously; warily; wisely; sagaciously; carefully; tremendously; invariably; rarely; absolutely; dependably; naturally; thoughtfully; considerately; oddly; superbly; shrewdly; craftily; marvelously; unerringly; consummately; prudently; vigilantly; cannily; scrupulously; sharply.

DISCREPANCY
adjectives
ironical; peculiar; irreconcilable; slight; curious; minute; embarrassing; minor; frightful; strange.

verbs
admit—; attribute—to; avoid—; clarify—; conceal—; detect—; exhibit—; expose—; harass by—; observe—; overlook—; produce—; remove—; reveal—; search for—; —displeases; —offends; —surprises; —worries.
(See variation, difference, disagreement.)

DISCRETION
adjectives
over-wide; limited; safe; heroic; admirable; tremendous; official; sufficient; arbitrary; peaceable; victorious; unshaken; expert; invariable; rare; absolute; wiser; unrestrained; undefined.

verbs
act with—; answer with—; defer in—; doubt—; employ—; exercise—; guide with —; lack—; leave to—; necessitate—; practise—; preserve with—; school in—; yield to—; —befits; —distinguishes; —separates.
(See prudence, wisdom, judgment.)

DISCRIMINATE (v)
adverbs
sharply; nicely; emotionally; mentally; infallibly; racially; carefully; rationally; fastidiously; intelligently; scrupulously; aesthetically; artistically; dramatically; unjustly; sagaciously.
(See distinguish, contrast.)

DISCRIMINATING
adverbs
keenly; carefully; cautiously; expertly; unusually; oddly; shrewdly; nicely; fastidiously; scrupulously; naturally; infallibly; habitually; critically; duly; wisely; sagaciously; impeccably; deeply; sharply; cleverly; thoughtfully; prudently; meticulously; delicately.

DISCRIMINATION
adjectives
nice; emotional; mental; infallible; racial; preconceived; careful; rational; fastidious; intelligent; scrupulous; due; innate; geographical; open; aesthetic; ineffable; unfair; impeccable; artistic; dramatic; unjust; laborious; sensory; sagacious; rare.

verbs
apply—; approve—; attempt—; avoid—; credit—; develop—; employ—; exercise—; imply—; lack—; note—; nourish—; pretend—; tolerate—; touch with—; —bites; —earns; —rewards; —separates; —succeeds; —vexes.
(See difference, distinction.)

DISCURSIVE
adverbs
tediously; garrulously; ramblingly; fascinatingly; interestingly; tiresomely; vexatiously; provokingly; illogically; irrelevantly; disputatiously; prosily; maunderingly; verbosely; digressively; effusively; frothily; palaveringly; chattily; tattlingly; senselessly; loquaciously; pratingly; preachily.

DISCUSS (v)

adverbs
animatedly; calmly; intellectually; glibly; heatedly; unreservedly; widely; exhaustively; seriously; despondently; enigmatically; gravely; academically; audibly; robustly; noisily; eagerly; languidly; critically; lucidly; penetratingly; brilliantly; masterfully; amiably; passionately; argumentatively; violently; vitriolically; challengingly; acutely; ethically; fruitfully; colorfully; extensively; elegantly; frankly; inconclusively; philosophically; protractedly; trivially; pertinently; acridly; reasonably; sympathetically; satisfyingly.

(See argue, debate.)

DISCUSSION

adjectives
lucid; penetrating; brilliant; popular; masterful; amiable; lively; doubtful; friendly; agreeable; noisy; heated; passionate; animated; spirited; brisk; keen; argumentative; violent; vitriolic; challenging; enthusiastic; acute; radical; voluble; calm; dignified; intelligent; serious; thoughtful; embittered; acrimonious; academic; nationwide; unofficial; earnest; curtailed; spicy; lusty; ethical; fruitful; cultural; colorful; intensive; critical; concise; detailed; prearranged; extensive; fiery; unexpected; current; everlasting; elegant; miserable; frank; preliminary; fair; complicated; inconclusive; philosophic; protracted; intolerable; scientific; squalid; productive; unprofitable; perpetual; trivial; free; speculative; excited; political; domestic; salutory; group; metaphysical; stormy; pertinent; theological; wearisome; idle; grave; acrid.

verbs
advocate—; avoid—; balk at—of; block—; break into—; center—upon; characterize —; cut short—; deserve—; dominate—; drag into—; enter—; evoke—; exclude from—; influence—; launch into—; merit—; open—; plunge into—; promote—; provoke —; refrain from—; sidetrack—; —enlightens; —informs; —follows; —opens up; —takes place.

(See debate, argument.)

DISDAIN

adjectives
condescending; supercilious; pardonable; chill; withering; pathetic; haughty; hightoned; quick; icy; cynical; aggressive; bitter; well-bred; invincible; lofty; aristocrat-

ic; ineffable; proud; profound; incredulous; unutterable; constructive; uncharitable; scornful; vile; utmost; listless; cold; monotonous; immovable; unquenchable; contemptuous.

verbs
call in—; conceive—; confer—upon; convert to—; cool—; deserve—; disregard—; entertain—for; jeer in—; regard with—; reject with—; reply in—; reproach with—; retire in—; scan with—; sting with—; suffer —; taunt in—; treat with—; turn up one's nose in—; upbraid with—; view with—; wrinkle one's nose in—; —displeases; — embitters; —grows; —infuriates; —melts; —offends; —pierces; —swells; —vexes.

(See contempt, scorn, arrogance.)

DISDAIN (v)

adverbs
sneeringly; churlishly; superciliously; condescendingly; witheringly; icily; haughtily; cynically; bitterly; aristocratically; proudly; uncharitably; scornfully; coldly; contemptuously.

(See shame, scorn.)

DISDAINFUL

adverbs
arrogantly; foolishly; senselessly; fantastically; scornfully; youthfully; superciliously; pathetically; absurdly; ridiculously; ludicrously; laughably; haughtily; icily; loftily; aristocratically; proudly; profoundly; unutterably; uncharitably; humiliatingly; nonchalantly; coolly; bumptiously; blusteringly; brazenly; imperiously; insolently; flippantly; boldly.

DISEASE

adjectives
mental; malignant; lurking; prevalent; hideous; pestilential; casual; vague; infectious; incurable; mystifying; loathsome; obscure; virulent; contagious; incipient; insidious; organic; curious; communicable; subtle; fatal; childish; indigenous; inherent; devastating; corrupting; frightful; tropical; inexorable; dread; devilish; pulmonary; inveterate; epidemic; tumorous; lingering; unconquerable; chronic; bewildering; horrible; secondary; intercurrent; febrile; fungus; advanced; inflammatory; foul; sporadic; moral; constitutional; wasting; unique; well-feigned; long-extinct; progressive; unripe; nutritional; resultant; purulent.

verbs

accelerate—; afflict with—; aggravate—; alleviate—; arrest—; attribute—to; awaken —; battle—; beget—; bow down with—; breed—; carry—; characterize—; check—; combat—; communicate—; complicate—; contract—; control—; convey—; deal with —; detect—; diagnose—; disseminate—; efface—; eliminate—; engender—; eradicate —; exempt from—; expose to—; exterminate—; forestall—; fortify against—; foster —; harden to—; heal—; immunize against —; implant—; import—; induce—; infest with—; inherit—; intensify—; introduce—; isolate—; languish with—; master—; overcome—; predispose to—; recognize—; recover from—; rekindle—; relieve—; resist —; smite with—; stamp out—; succumb to—; suffer from—; transmit—; usher in —; ward off—; wrestle with—; —advances; —breaks out; —consumes; —declines; —destroys; —emaciates; —fastens itself upon; —flourishes; —gains a foothold; —hangs on; —lingers; —lurks; —manifests itself; —menaces; —plagues; —prevails; —progresses; —rages; —ravages; —runs rampant; —spreads; —springs up; —stalks; —strikes; —subsides; —threatens.

(See ailment, disorder, malady, pestilence, plague, epidemic.)

DISEASED

adverbs

horribly; unfortunately; appallingly; pitiably; cankerously; pitifully; pathetically; awfully; disgustingly; alarmingly; dangerously; mentally; hideously; incurably; irremediably; irrecoverably; infectiously; virulently; insidiously; organically; curiously; fatally; inherently; congenitally; frightfully; chronically; morally.

DISFAVOR

adjectives

absolute; mingled; high; stern; increasing; lasting; bitter.

verbs

bring into—; deserve—; dispense—; draw —of; earn—; experience—; fall into—; familiarize with—; incur—; mar with—; pour—; pretend; regard with—; roar—; shower—; spread—; taste—; —affects; — attends; —handicaps; —hinders.

(See disapproval, dislike.)

DISFIGURED

adverbs

grotesquely; queerly; crookedly; horribly; strangely; fantastically; grossly; grimly;

hopelessly; terribly; shamefully; tragically; slightly; odiously; repulsively; pitifully; pathetically; comically; bitterly; deliberately.

DISGRACE

adjectives

hideous; concealed; unmitigable; bewailed; final; crying; sad; eternal; calamitous; nominal; intolerable; foul; invisible; pardonless; indelible; manifold; infinite; glorified; personal; continual; inescapable.

verbs

acknowledge—; augment—; betray—; bewail—; derive—; dishonor with—; dread —; experience—; fall into—; heap—upon; incur—; join in—; lay—upon; lie in—; reflect—; revenge—; rise from—; shrink from—; subject to—; suffer—; sustain—; —blemishes; —deprives; —mars; —shames; —undoes.

(See reproach, infamy, ignominy, disrepute, dishonor.)

DISGRACE (v)

adverbs

publicly; wrongfully; hideously; finally; eternally; calamitously; intolerably; infinitely; personally; wantonly; spitefully; intentionally; revengefully.

(See humiliate, shame.)

DISGRACED

adverbs

permanently; shamefully; terribly; odiously; horribly; sadly; calamitously; disastrously; eternally; momentarily; inexplicably; inescapably; palpably; personally; deeply; darkly; disreputably; notoriously; publicly; outrageously; pathetically; deservedly.

DISGRACEFUL

adverbs

outrageously; wickedly; infamously; scandalously; brutally; flagrantly; atrociously; criminally; dissolutely; foully; hideously; unmitigably; intolerably; indelibly; unforgettably; grossly; shamelessly; patently; palpably; unmistakably; utterly; inexpressibly.

DISGRUNTLED

adverbs

obscurely; bitterly; distinctly; obviously; visibly; openly; inevitably; vaguely; naturally; understandably; sorely; frankly; seriously; fiercely; silently; evidently; sullenly; quietly; wretchedly; miserably; fretfully; peevishly.

DISGUISE

adjectives
neutral; clever; absurd; thin; mystical; inanimate; terror-striking; strange; modest; filthy; effective; reverend; deceptive; extraordinary; impenetrable; customary; smiling; logical; credulous; troublesome; opaque; desperate.

verbs
assume—; attempt—; cloak with—; contrive—; counterfeit by—; deck in—; detect —; don—; invent—; lurk beneath—; penetrate—; pierce—; recognize—; see through —; strip off—; take refuge in—; throw off—; —alters; —conceals; —deceives; —disfigures; —masks; —misleads; —succeeds; —transforms.
(See pretense, mask, cloak, dress, costume.)

DISGUISE (v)

adverbs
perfectly; handsomely; cleverly; absurdly; thinly; mystically; strangely; effectively; deceptively; extraordinarily; slyly; logically; subtly.
(See mask, cloak.)

DISGUISED

adverbs
cleverly; absurdly; thinly; strangely; modestly; effectively; deceptively; extraordinarily; impenetrably; mysteriously; exactly; ridiculously; cryptically; furtively; stealthily; darkly; inviolately; secretly; palpably; harmlessly; falsely; fraudulently; unfairly; maliciously; artfully; perfidiously; mischievously; skilfully; comically; trickily; successfully; completely.

DISGUST

adjectives
implacable; sharp; vast; exasperated; angry; outraged; inherent; profound; creeping; shuddering; secret; icy; silent; honest; personal; evident; furious; intense; sheer; indignant; intolerable; weary; mingled; infinite; considerable; mutual; supreme; deep; sullen; philosophical; sickened; cruel; loathing; bewildered; excessive; previous; violent.

verbs
arouse—; assert—; attend with—; awake —; conquer—; control—; depict—; drown —; excite—; raise—; retreat in—; sicken in—; shun in—; shrug—; —deters; —dissuades; —nauseates; —offends; —wounds.
(See aversion, abhorrence, repugnance, distaste.)

DISGUST (v)

adverbs
presumably; thoroughly; implacably; profoundly; secretly; personally; evidently; intensely; intolerably; considerably; mutually; supremely; cruelly; loathingly; excessively; violently.
(See revolt, offend.)

DISGUSTED

adverbs
immeasurably; terribly; utterly; bitterly; painfully; intolerably; dreadfully; tremendously; exceedingly; morally; heartily; secretly; obviously; openly; sharply; profoundly; intensely; deeply; violently.

DISH

adjectives
humble; distinguished; glorious; different; tempting; delicious; time-honored; warmed-over; exotic; appetizing; delicate; fattening; sumptuous; velvet; lordly; rattling; tempting; priceless; savory; attractive; fascinating; toothsome; succulent; elaborate; unwholesome; economical; earthen; kingly; chafing; tasty; pewter; substantial; rich; sparkling; unornamental; fatal; fragile; glittering; nutritious; strange; clean; dirty; anomalous; conventional.

verbs
cover—; devour—; dip into—; eschew—; garnish—; hurl—; pile—; relish—; sauce —; scour—; serve—; smash—; sprinkle—; wipe—; —clatters; —nourishes; —rattles.
(See plate, platter, cup, food.)

DISHEARTEN (v)

adverbs
dismally; inwardly; decidedly; partially; purposely; unintentionally; completely; tragically; finally.
(See discourage, depress.)

DISHEARTENED

adverbs
profoundly; exceedingly; pathetically; deeply; remarkably; extremely; mysteriously; significantly; vaguely; completely; intense-

ly; utterly; miserably; wretchedly; wearily; finally; increasingly; signally; inexplicably; unaccountably; strangely; oddly; queerly.

DISHEVELED

adverbs
carelessly; negligently; wildly; merrily; laughably; shamefully; thoughtlessly; terribly; exceedingly; blithely; indifferently; untidily; recklessly; lazily; rudely; heedlessly; lumpishly.

DISHONEST

adverbs
instinctively; inherently; innately; naturally; characteristically; traditionally; slyly; racially; insidiously; invidiously; shrewdly; fiendishly; maliciously; astoundingly; trickily; surreptitiously; habitually; speciously; manifestly; essentially; abominably; detestably.

DISHONESTY

adjectives
rank; mercantile; unself-conscious; childlike; acquired.

verbs
accuse of—; conceal—; convict of—; cover —; deny—; dispose to—; expose—; renounce—; reveal—; tempt to—; uncover —; —colors; —defiles; —disgraces; — scars; —shames; —stains; —violates; — wanes.
(See fraud, cheating.)

DISHONOR

adjectives
whispered; partial; foul; ultimate; deathless; base.

verbs
bear—; bring into—; clothe in—; defile with—; die in—; meet with—; plague by—; pronounce—; root in—; sow—; stain with —; suffer—; tempt with—; tread down in—; undergo—; —blemishes; —blurs; — hounds; —lies.
(See insult, reproach, disgrace, disrepute.)

DISHONORED

adverbs
scandalously; distinctly; notoriously; infamously; publicly; permanently; unutterably; indelibly; irremediably; unforgettably; desperately; ignominiously; basely;

shamefully; unjustly; unfairly; opprobriously; foully; reportedly; allegedly; immeasurably; immensely.

DISILLUSION

adjectives
stupendous; postwar; chill; bitter; heartbreaking.

DISILLUSION (v)

adverbs
precipitately; cruelly; completely; politely; immodestly; frankly; unthinkingly; abruptly; fiendishly; shrewdly; wisely; foolishly.
(See free, liberate.)

DISILLUSIONED

adverbs
pitiably; miserably; wretchedly; sadly; suddenly; early; unhappily; unexpectedly; cruelly; bitterly; dismally; grimly; appallingly; tremendously; inconsolably; despairingly; hopelessly; heartbreakingly.

DISILLUSIONMENT

adjectives
cruel; unembittered; complete; furious; devastating; haughty; polite.

verbs
increase—; incur—; move to—; protect against—; reject—; suffer—; —ages; — banishes; —begets; —depresses; —descends; —disappoints; —displaces; —frees from; —rocks; —sets in; —settles over; —shatters; revenge—; —arouses.

DISINCLINATION

adjectives
intolerable; deep-rooted; definite; stubborn; unreasoning.

DISINFECTANT

adverbs
effectively; infallibly; powerfully; extremely; heroically; mildly; perfectly; soothingly; correctively; specifically; simply; safely; beneficially; advantageously; commendably; highly; essentially; intrinsically.

DISINFECTION

adjectives
efficient; rigorous; unstinted; disciplinary; punitive.

verbs
practise—; subject to—; —destroys; — guards against; —nauseates; —offends; —ousts; —overcomes; —prevents; —purifies; —rejects; —routs; —safeguards.

DISINHERITED

adverbs

unfairly; unfortunately; properly; unjustly; deservedly; unluckily; miserably; wretchedly; crushingly; summarily; audaciously; cruelly; deliberately; curtly; wrongfully; unwarrantably; inexcusably; unreasonably; inauspiciously; logically.

DISINTEGRATE (v)

adverbs

deliberately; steadily; relentlessly; rapidly; financially; slowly; hopelessly; mentally; socially; progressively; internally; abruptly; completely; locally.

(See crumble, decay.)

DISINTEGRATION

adjectives

rapid; financial; slow; relentless; hopeless; mental; social.

verbs

blast into—; break into—; control—; demand—; detach by—; effect—; expose to—; hasten—; influence—; produce—; tend toward—; undergo—; —blurs; —destroys; —modifies; —multiplies; —proceeds from; —reduces; —separates; —sets in.

(See decay, decomposition.)

DISINTERESTED

adverbs

personally; truly; neutrally; sufficiently; obviously; manifestly; satisfactorily; demonstrably; sternly; judiciously; honestly; undeniably; avowedly; acceptably.

DISK
(see disc)

adjectives

scintillating; whirling; rotating; advancing; menacing.

verbs

affix—; emerge from—; grind—; hollow—; hurl—; mount—; roll—; send—; shape—; shoot—; strike—; whirl—; —careens; —loops; —protects; —revolves; — rises; —rotates.

(See plate.)

DISLIKE

adjectives

profound; inordinate; violent; instinctive; active; malicious; deep; intense; maddening; involuntary; abnormal; innate; virulent; entire; fundamental; colonial; mu-

tual; haughty; peculiar; ardent; reasoned; expressed; incurable; foolish; irrational; everlasting; contemptuous; personal.

verbs

betray—; conceal—; consider with—; feed —; feign—; fume—; grow into—; harbor —for; impel by—; incur—; kindle—; mask —; regard with—; shudder with—; subject to—; warrant—.

(See distaste, repugnance, aversion, antipathy, hatred.)

DISLIKE (v)

adverbs

strongly; inherently; notoriously; heartily; profoundly; inordinately; violently; instinctively; maliciously; deeply; intensely; maddeningly; involuntarily; virulently; fundamentally; mutually; incurably; irrationally; personally; contemptuously; cordially.

(See disapprove, hate.)

DISLOCATE (v)

adverbs

dreadfully; fatally; tragically; calamitously; critically; severely; cruelly; devastatingly.

(See separate, dislodge.)

DISLOCATION

adjectives

serious; complex; cursory; temporary; tentative; remediable.

verbs

adjust—; bind—; cure—; exercise—; force —; impede—; involve—; place in—; prevent—; produce—; suffer—; submit to—; treat for—; —alarms; —pains; —swells.

(See displacement, disorder.)

DISLODGE (v)

adverbs

successfully; viciously; brutally; triumphantly; vigorously; severely; expeditiously; resolutely.

(See remove, eject.)

DISLOYAL

adverbs

shamefully; treacherously; perfidiously; disgracefully; extremely; secretly; publicly; boldly; cruelly; basely; subtly; bitterly; openly; unpardonably; incredibly; surprisingly; unexpectedly; eventually; shabbily;

tremendously; abjectly; unutterably; unscrupulously; **infamously**; contemptibly; ingloriously.

DISMAL

adverbs
drearily; drably; lonesomely; abjectly; disconsolately; irremediably; soddenly; sadly; wretchedly; excessively; irrecoverably; deeply; horribly; profoundly; incorrigibly; incurably; darkly; solemnly; anxiously; sombrely; despondently; fixedly; sullenly; heavily; dangerously; ominously; cheerlessly; intensely; terribly.

DISMAY

adjectives
incredulous; unutterable; direct; pale; goggle-eyed; stark; nameless; evident; vague; abject; dumb; genuine; dawning; dark; terrified; alarmed; extreme; mad; immeasurable; utter; indescribable; ineffable; panic-stricken.

verbs
contemplate—; cope with—; discover—; heap—; mitigate—; paralyze with—; read —; recoil in—; rout—; shake with—; spread—; swoon with—; view with—; —daunts; —defeats; —discourages; —engulfs; —threatens.
(See consternation, terror, alarm, fear.)

DISMAY (v)

adverbs
thoroughly; abjectly; dumbly; genuinely; extremely; immeasurably; utterly; indescribably; bullyingly.
(See alarm, frighten.)

DISMAYED

adverbs
unaccountably; deeply; profoundly; unreasonably; illogically; dreadfully; alarmingly; fearfully; incredibly; starkly; evidently; vaguely; abjectly; genuinely; terribly; extremely; immeasurably; significantly; utterly; indescribably; remarkably; notably; visibly; wildly; bewilderingly.

DISMISS (v)

adverbs
reluctantly; summarily; finally; courteously; instantly; contemptuously; flatly; lightly; curtly; abruptly; harshly; ignominiously; impudently; brusquely; uncouthly.
(See discharge, banish.)

DISMISSAL

adjectives
contemptuous; harsh; ignominious; brusque; impudent; abrupt; summary; instant; immediate.

verbs
annul—; bow—; counsel—; demand—; denounce—; indicate—; justify—; order—; punish by—; request—; seek—; suffer—; threaten with—; urge—; wave—; —discourages; —liberates; —rectifies; —releases; —sets free.
(See discharge, removal.)

DISOBEDIENCE

adjectives
continued; alleged; filial; repeated; defiant; wilful; persistent.

verbs
construe as—; correct—; express—; fall into—; foster—; instigate—; nourish—; punish for—; reprimand for—; revenge—; rue—; subscribe to—; —annoys; —begets; —develops; —erupts; —irks.
(See defiance.)

DISOBEDIENT

adverbs
stubbornly; obstinately; impudently; impertinently; insolently; arrogantly; constantly; continually; haughtily; obdurately; peevishly; boldly; openly; flagrantly; invidiously; sullenly; morosely; carelessly; wildly; inexcusably; unduly; deliberately; consciously; flauntingly; laughingly; brazenly; allegedly; provokingly; extremely; dreadfully; rebelliously; resentfully; defiantly; restively; impatiently; resolutely.

DISORDER

adjectives
allergic; emotional; turbulent; careless; forlorn; homelike; miry; tousled; musty; unparalleled; wild; lawless; riotous; diffuse; frightful; inconsistent; tumultuous; frenzied; virulent; violent; considerable; moving; curing; gay; infectious; mental; prevailing; direst; accumulated; seeming; spasmodic; strange; degenerate; nutritional; infantile; grave; spiritual; underlying; momentary; current; shameful; neurotic; statistic; extreme; deep-seated; admired; contagious; curious; chaotic; physical; picturesque; complete; pleasant; inconceivable; ensuing; chronic; half-mended; infernal; indescribable; harlequinesque; nervous; radical; immaculate; moral.

verbs
accompany—; ascribe to—; benefit—; caution against—; fall into—; foment—; indicate—; introduce—; plague with—; produce —; relieve—; remedy—; remove—; rout—; spring from—; succumb to—; vanquish—; —surges ahead; —threatens.
(See confusion, chaos, disturbance.)

DISORDERLY
adverbs
remarkably; notoriously; turbulently; truculently; outrageously; noisily; flagrantly; violently; wildly; riotously; lawlessly; frightfully; gayly; uproariously; convivially; genially; laughingly; daringly; inconsiderately; indescribably; inconceivably; ungovernably; uncontrollably; curiously; contagiously; momentarily; mutinously; gravely; alarmingly; ominously; significantly; terrifyingly; tumultuously; tempestuously; viciously; extravagantly; excitedly.

DISPARAGEMENT
adjectives
caustic; cynical; systematic; ruthless; unsparing; merciless.

verbs
bring into—; commit—; deserve—; express —; hurl—; impose—; intend—; involve in—; justify—; lose by—; reproach for—; speak—; vilify with—; —annoys; —belittles; —degrades; —disgraces.

DISPASSIONATE
adverbs
imperturbably; provokingly; vexatiously; serenely; calmly; deeply; immovably; apparently; dreadfully; coldly; completely; carelessly; nonchalantly; discouragingly; utterly; singularly; stolidly; stonily; coolly; soberly; judicially; sagely; wisely; securely; tranquilly; placidly; philosophically; tolerantly.

DISPATCH
adjectives
calamitous; hostile; amazing; quick; marvelous; summary; rapid; convenient; diplomatic; hourly; insolent; elaborate; amended; swift; equal; vivid; detailed; telegraphic; simultaneous; importunate; important; explanatory; outspoken; uncensored; satisfactory; frequent (pl).

verbs
announce—; arrive with—; attend to—; cable—; carry—; convey—; deliver—; depart with—; hasten—; leave on—; obey—; order—; receive—; relay—; report—; rush —; seal—; send—; smuggle in—; speed—; transfer.
(See message, telegram.)

DISPATCH (v)
adverbs
mercifully; secretly; summarily; rapidly; diplomatically; insolently; telegraphically; swiftly; simultaneously; satisfactorily; frequently; conveniently; hastily.
(See send, forward.)

DISPEL (v)
adverbs
effectually; instantly; immediately; entirely; frankly; innocently; humanely; charmingly; testily.
(See withdraw, dissipate.)

DISPENSATION
adjectives
benign; critical; merciful; mysterious; special; divine; providential; heavenly; frugal; afflicting; artistic; favorable.

verbs
administer—; allow—; arrange—; claim—; conduct—; deliver—; deserve—; grant—; manage—; obtain—; order—; provide—; receive—; require—; reward with—; seek —; sue for—; undertake—; urge—; warrant—; —distributes; —pardons; —releases.
(See distribution, pardon, exemption.)

DISPENSE (v)
adverbs
vicariously; bountifully; gracefully; liberally; naturally; mercifully; divinely; providentially; frugally.
(See distribute, administer.)

DISPLACEMENT
adjectives
sympathetic; successive (pl); unmerited; slight; hazardous; careless; capacious.

verbs
indicate—; occasion—; order—; request—; seek—; set—; threaten with—; —disposes of; —embarrasses; —liberates; —occurs; —rectifies; —releases; —remedies; —shifts.
(See removal, discharge, dismissal.)

DISPLAY
adjectives
alluring; ceremonial; enviable; ostentatious; tawdry; unrivaled; garish; blatant;

enchanting; gorgeous; grisly; creditable; pitiful; emotional; lurid; audacious; glaring; splendid; obtrusive; amazing; magnificent; appropriate; lavish; legitimate; ludicrous; frequent (pl); color; thaumaturgic; remarkable; aggravating; autumnal; fabulous; breath-taking; triumphant; fanatical; heroic; pedantic; attractive; modern; gaudy; mass; beautiful; official; merciless; singular; wild; arresting; material; prominent; extraordinary; romantic; single-handed; elaborate; vast; brilliant; haunting; many-colored; prodigal; boasted; vulgar; maladroit; provocative; vivid; mere; admirable; barbarous; temporary; tasteful; profuse; superfluous; quixotic; childish; unfortunate; dazzling; fan-shaped.

verbs
abhor—; adorn—; arrange—; feed on—; furnish—; gape at—; nose among—s; prepare—; unfurl—; view—; wonder at—; —advertises; —appeals; —attracts; —describes; —exhibits; —explains; —expresses; —glitters; —represents; —unfolds.
(See exhibition, show.)

DISPLAY (v)
adverbs
pompously; flamboyantly; tastefully; magnificently; realistically; conspicuously; charmingly; habitually; refreshingly; equally; palpably; ostentatiously; vaingloriously; smartly; temptingly; vulgarly; eminently; lavishly; dazzlingly; entrancingly; alluringly; ceremonially; garishly; blatantly; pitifully; audaciously; legitimately; mercilessly; ludicrously; singularly; prodigally; temporarily; superfluously.
(See exhibit, expose.)

DISPLEASE (v)
adverbs
stupidly; purposely; markedly; unsophisticatedly; rudely; frankly; seriously; pettishly; ungenerously; lastingly; coldly; boorishly; carelessly; inadvertently.
(See anger, offend.)

DISPLEASED
adverbs
remarkably; extravagantly; extremely; uneasily; wearily; anxiously; miserably; unreasonably; unaccountably; sorely; heavily; horribly; vexedly; painfully; grievously; bitterly; cheerlessly; fiercely; savagely; markedly; visibly; openly; frankly; seriously; permanently; implacably; coldly;

alarmingly; dangerously; unspeakably; profoundly; deeply; inordinately; justly; rightly.

DISPLEASURE
adjectives
smothered; surprised; fierce; marked; sore; sovereign; unsophisticated; frank; everlasting; serious; noble; petty; ungenerous; lasting; cold; divine.

verbs
avoid—; conceal—; display—; dread—; heighten—; incur—; indicate—; languish in—; meet with—; occasion—; provoke—; risk—; shoulder—; signify—; snort—; —annoys; —irks; —mounts; —overwhelms.
(See dissatisfaction, vexation, dislike, resentment, disapproval.)

DISPOSE (v)
adverbs
carelessly; antagonistically; religiously; briefly; favorably; symmetrically; ornamentally; effectually; graciously; immediately; variously; gracefully; peaceably; coolly; effectively.
(See settle, adjust.)

DISPOSITION
adjectives
pacific; amenable; amiable; covetous; docile; morose; winsome; credulous; mercurial; bromidic; penurious; depraved; petulant; avaricious; peevish; jovial; bad; sweet; equable; contentious; balky; impetuous; fiery; angelic; vivacious; unyielding; confiding; cheery; vacillating; sunny; sullen; bitter; eager; cordial; raving; delicate; characteristic; generous; noble; litigious; rough; envious; well-oiled; jealous; vicious; masterful; dreamy; increasing; testamentary; passionate; princely; violent; chilly; humane; puerile; stubborn; contemplative; unconquerable; melancholy; inquisitive; affectionate; bloodthirsty; resolute; tractable; pious; dogged; ungodly; virtuous; commiserating; natural; excellent; romantic; kind; similar; charming; pliant; stupid; tame; grateful; tranquil; speculative; favorable; skillful; alert; neurotic; suitable; innate; ingenuous; friendly; adventurous; traitorous; faithful; indolent; eager; shirking; sociable; prevailing; incomprehensible; unpredictable; classic; combative; tunable; phlegmatic; peremptory; dangerous; buoyant; secret; magnificent; thoughtful; brooding; aesthetic; primitive; humane; amicable; irregular;

submissive; methodical; venomous; fantastical; timid; hereditary; restless; roving; retiring; imperious; absolute; noxious; further; hysterical.

verbs
abuse—; admire—; alter—; change—; complete—; consider—; contrive—; derange—; disguise—; evince—; excuse—; indulge—; inherit—; judge—; punish—; soften—; sour—; specify—; submit to—; touch—; view—; —comprehends; —inclines; —precipitates; —restores; —secures.
(See mood, will, propensity, inclination, tendency, temperament.)

DISPOSSESS (v)
adverbs
forcibly; legally; harshly; irregularly; doggedly; calmly; cruelly; selfishly.
(See eject, remove.)

DISPUTANT
adjectives
scientific; forensic; obstinate; moral; voiceless; excited.

DISPUTATION
adjectives
public; scholastic; private; learned; religious; doubtful; prodigious; wrangling.

DISPUTATIOUS
adverbs
troublesomely; immensely; tremendously; egregiously; elaborately; intricately; eccentrically; egotistically; loftily; superciliously; tyrannically; dogmatically; extremely; learnedly; academically; provokingly; disagreeably; unpleasantly; obtrusively; officiously; conceitedly; astutely; pugnaciously; hotly; captiously; churlishly; remarkably; marvellously.

DISPUTE
adjectives
doctrinal; theological; inevitable; learned; angry; bitter; dull; vain; laughing; demoralizing; serious; uncontrollable; pending; cold; international; academic; free; conceivable; long-standing; violent; notable; fierce; perpetual; territorial; fruitless; factional; leisurely.

verbs
adjudicate—; adjust—; arbitrate—; beguile into—; conciliate—; meditate—; quash—; quell—; solve—; suppress—; take part in—;

—arises; —bubbles; —evaporates; —flares up; —foreshadows; —overshadows; —rages.
(See discussion, contest, controversy, quarrel.)

DISPUTE (v)
adverbs
skillfully; acrimoniously; consciously; angrily; subsequently; inhumanly; successfully; publicly; privately; religiously; prodigiously; fiercely.
(See argue, wrangle.)

DISQUIET
adjectives
vague; emotional; constant; restless; growing.

DISQUIET (v)
adverbs
chiefly; solely; thoroughly; abruptly; subtly.
(See alarm, disturb.)

DISQUIETUDE
adjectives
serious; vague; mental; extreme.

verbs
arouse—; fear—; fill with—; infest with—; occasion—; pass with—; relay—; sow—; subject to—; trouble with—; view with—; wait with—; —alarms; —disturbs; —envelops; —spreads.
(See alarm, anxiety, fear, agitation.)

DISQUISITION
adjectives
political; clever; popular; lengthy; wordy; learned.

DISREGARD
adjectives
insane; cynical; reckless; defiant; persistent; total; unabashed; bland; pagan; brutal; generous; utter; blithe; calm; benevolent; selfish; cruel; jaunty; entire; drunken; astonishing; habitual; strange; superb; apparent; contemptuous; sublime; peremptory.

DISREGARD (v)
adverbs
incessantly; chronically; totally; utterly; contemptuously; insanely; cynically; recklessly; defiantly; persistently; totally; unabashedly; blandly; brutally; generously;

utterly; blithely; calmly; benevolently; recklessly; entirely; habitually; sublimely; peremptorily; selfishly.

(See ignore, overlook.)

DISREPUTABLE

adverbs

notoriously; infamously; exceedingly; generally; utterly; scandalously; opprobriously; fearfully; dissolutely; admittedly; villainously; grossly; drunkenly; coarsely; shamefully; horribly; remarkably; incredibly; unbelievably; abjectly; pitifully; ingloriously; shockingly; atrociously; viciously.

DISREPUTE

adjectives

(See disgrace.)

verbs

beget—; bring into—; clothe in—; cure of —; depart in—; disguise—; fall into—; ignore—; incur—; indicate—; instigate—; leave in—; return in—; vow—; —dampens; —excludes; —showers; —underlies.

(See disgrace, dishonor.)

DISRESPECT

adjectives

(See rudeness.)

verbs

augment—; bear—; disguise—; display—; free from—; manifest—; mention with—; nourish—; proceed from—; reprimand for —; smother—; stoop to—; suffer—; tolerate—; —indicates; —profanes; —troubles.

(See dishonor, rudeness.)

DISRESPECTFUL

adverbs

irreverently; boundlessly; utterly; blandly; recklessly; persistently; defiantly; totally; brutally; cruelly; entirely; impiously; jauntily; rashly; boldly; astonishingly; elaborately; ostentatiously; openly; habitually; chronically; strangely; particularly; peculiarly; contemptuously; disparagingly; derisively; ironically; rudely; bumptiously.

DISSATISFACTION

adjectives

unending; personal; prevailing; universal; seeming; increasing; evident; undifferentiated; rebellious; widespread.

verbs

anticipate—; be subject to—; beget—; conduct with—; confine—; exhibit—; experience—; express—; occasion—; overcome —; pretend—; smother—; veil—; —disquiets; —irks; —perplexes.

(See discontent, disapproval, displeasure.)

DISSATISFIED

adverbs

slightly; vaguely; wholly; strangely; entirely; increasingly; palpably; evidently; visibly; openly; sullenly; morosely; secretly; obviously; deeply; desperately; horribly; querulously; glumly; gloomily; austerely; sternly; implacably; crabbedly; perversely; continually.

DISSECT (v)

adverbs

mercilessly; tranquilly; scientifically; studiously; thoroughly; painstakingly; absorbedly.

(See cut, criticize.)

DISSEMBLE (v)

adverbs

politely; slyly; deeply; artfully; skillfully; ingeniously.

(See hide, conceal.)

DISSEMINATE (v)

adverbs

widely; unsparingly; insidiously; nationally; universally.

(See spread, circulate.)

DISSENSION

adjectives

considerable; frightful; irreconcilable; humiliating; internal; bitter; sharp; disastrous; factional; growing; intestinal; grave; turbulent; angry; perpetual.

verbs

brew—; crush—; excite—; halt—; incite —; instigate—; investigate—; review—; stir with—; —arises; —breaks out; —flares; —grows; —menaces; —tears; —threatens.

(See discord, strife, quarrel, contention, feud.)

DISSENT

adjectives

metaphysical; profound; internal; grave; effective; ignorant; ill-natured.

verbs

accept—; apprehend—; arouse—; constitute—; enter—; explain—; free of—; ignore—; interpose—; overlook—; question —; tolerate—; trace—; voice—; —prevails; —sunders.

(See disagreement, difference.)

DISSERTATION

adjectives

moral; illuminating; exhaustive; stilted; learned; rhapsodic; elaborate; pedantic; physiological; scholarly.

verbs

absorb in—; censor—; compose—; criticize—; dedicate—to; engage in—; launch upon—; level—at; pause in—; prepare—; study—; —carries; —concerns; —discusses; —treats.

(See discourse, speech, lecture.)

DISSIMULATION

adjectives

polite; deft; practiced; splendid; skilled.

DISSIPATE (*v*)

adverbs

abruptly; partially; voluptuously; senselessly; reprehensibly; carelessly; excessively; incessantly; disgustingly; jovially; recklessly; fashionably; tragically; thoughtlessly.

(See dispel.)

DISSIPATION

adjectives

voluptuous; senseless; reprehensible; careless; excessive; mild; incessant; besetting; solitary; minor; disgusting; jovial; reckless; polished; recreative; fashionable.

verbs

consume by—; defy—; denounce—; engage in—; imbibe in—; investigate—; lose in—; practise—; relinquish—; squander in—; warn against—; —corrupts; —endangers; —enslaves; —grinds; —penalizes; —wears.

(See diversion, crime.)

DISSOLUTE

adverbs

frightfully; utterly; irretrievably; gracelessly; irremediably; boundlessly; wantonly; recklessly; grossly; wildly; shamelessly; outrageously; perversely; irreclaimably; senselessly; remarkably; grotesquely; manifestly; abysmally; lawlessly; disgracefully; criminally; obdurately; heinously; gravely; sensually; intemperately; rakishly.

DISSOLUTENESS

adjectives

frightful; reckless; ferocious.

DISSOLUTION

adjectives

impending; natural; continual; ultimate.

DISSOLVE (*v*)

adverbs

partly; mutually; mysteriously; harmlessly; entirely; thoroughly; perfectly; experimentally.

(See melt.)

DISSONANCE

adjectives

excruciating; wild; unpleasant; barbarous; weird; raucous; harsh.

DISTANCE

adjectives

hazy; mean; weary; legendary; celestial; deepest; drowsy; magnificent; shooting; dusty; tantalizing; spacious; untold; extreme; impossible; obscure; safe; unattainable; perihelion; zenith; infinite; considerable; entire; visible; cautious; respectful; widening; exquisite; excessive; proportionate; inaccessible; twinkling; vast; unvarying; surlier; inscrutable; musket-shot; hailing; limited; unknown; inadequate; supporting; remote; short; surprising; observing; terrible; uncertain; linear; measured; delicate; mellow; dimmer; indefinite; required; insurmountable; discreet; sufficient; pathless; beautiful; unapproachable; everincreasing; misty; retrospective; walking; previous; assaulting; unbridgeable; riding; running; dangerous; mean; enormous; indeterminate; broadening.

verbs

annihilate—; estimate—; fade in—; fall at—; indicate—; mark—; measure—; proportion—; rise in—; span—; stand in—; traverse—; —alienates; —enchants; — lends; hold at—.

(See space.)

DISTASTE

adjectives

profound; sordid; intellectual; furious; extreme; scornful; cynical; patient; passionate; startling; evident.

verbs
banish—; bring into—; conceive—for; cultivate—for; develop—; dismiss—; excite—; express—; heal—; imply—; inherit—; nourish—; pamper—; possess—for; produce—; regard with—; relinquish—; rescue from —; view with—; —develops; —implies; —menaces.

(See aversion, dislike, antipathy.)

DISTASTEFUL
adverbs
horribly; deeply; profoundly; sordidly; intellectually; furiously; extremely; exaggeratedly; startlingly; shockingly; inordinately; extraordinarily; remarkably; immensely; dreadfully; evidently; manifestly; palpably; fundamentally; essentially; sickeningly; nauseatingly; sorrily; plaguedly; bitterly; grimly; frightfully.

DISTENSION
adjectives
pale; chronic; acute; pestilential; fatal; feminine.

DISTENTION
verbs
attend with—; blow into—; conceal—; fill to—; force into—; guard against—; imbibe to—; inflate to—; labor under—; prevent—; produce—; protect from—; —follows; —harms; —injures; —pains; —sunders.

(See expansion, inflation.)

DISTILL (*v*)
adverbs
imperceptibly; specially; powerfully; elaborately; delicately; experimentally; expertly; painstakingly.

DISTILLATION
adjectives
elaborate; strong; renewed; delicate; powerful.

DISTINCT
adverbs
particularly; cruelly; meticulously; precisely; exactly; easily; accurately; wonderfully; especially; clearly; emphatically; separately; effectively; powerfully.

DISTINCTION
adjectives
striking; pedantic; arresting; moral; sweeping; manifest; artificial; crude; material; considerable; supreme; theoretical; grave; philosophic; fundamental; military; superfluous; arbitrary; ethical; social; exclusive; unreal; cruel; topographical; solid; trade; unusual; ancient; perceptible; unhappy; obvious; immediate; dubious; essential; man-made; additional; unique; sage; minor; threefold; nervous; racial; deep; literary; ephemeral; financial; singular; subtle; natural; sole; invidious; repugnant; family; color; worldly; coveted; grand; preeminent; unenviable; individual; popular; groundless; slender; fleeting; fanciful; frivolous; honorable; constitutional; sensible; moral; race; artistic; broad; innate; particular; careless; visible; inglorious.

verbs
achieve—; attain—; blur—; carry—; convey—; discern—; draw—; earn—; enhance —; grant—; hunger for—; level—; maintain—; obliterate—; obtain—; perceive—; perpetuate—; recognize—; reduce—; sense —; serve with—; trace—; uphold—; warrant—; yearn for—; yield—.

(See eminence, prominence, renown.)

DISTINCTNESS
adjectives
surprising; exquisite; sufficient; arbitrary; tragic; unmistakable; vivid; considerable; growing; luminous.

DISTINGUISH (*v*)
adverbs
curiously; logically; justly; pedantically; crudely; theoretically; philosophically; fundamentally; arbitrarily; obviously; uniquely; sagely; singularly; subtly; invidiously; unenviably; groundlessly; fancifully; frivolously; sensibly; morally; artistically; broadly; scientifically.

(See discriminate, discern.)

DISTINGUISHABLE
adverbs
easily; readily; generally; entirely; particularly; diversely; divergently; differentially; broadly; carefully; instantly; conveniently; immediately; altogether; separately; unmistakably; plainly; decidedly; satisfactorily; positively; definitely; absolutely; clearly.

DISTINGUISHED
adverbs
brilliantly; extraordinarily; internationally; academically; illustriously; notably; remarkably; admirably; matchlessly; profes-

sionally; prominently; nationally; supremely; impressively; splendidly; augustly; imperishably; ecclesiastically; heroically; immortally; honorably; enviably; eminently; strikingly; manifestly; singularly.

DISTORT (v)
adverbs
momentarily; painfully; fatally; obviously; ludicrously; hideously; fantastically; insanely; madly; jokingly; fiendishly
(See twist, misrepresent.)

DISTORTED
adverbs
wilfully; perniciously; purposely; deliberately; deceptively; visibly; obviously; clearly; palpably; frightfully; excessively; dreadfully; intentionally; falsely; adroitly; craftily; wickedly; academically; disputatiously; remarkably; fatally; elaborately; completely; partially; loosely; fantastically; grotesquely; grossly; harmfully; utterly; maliciously; astutely; cleverly.

DISTORTION
adjectives
pale; fatal; obvious; imbedded; elaborated; ludicrous; intentional; fantastic.

DISTRACTION
adjectives
infinite; compelling; manifold; powerful; sweet; skillful; extreme; artificial; material; innocent; bewildered; beneficial; endless; blind; great; cautious.

verbs
attend with—; avoid—; blind to—; condemn—; drive to—; fear—; justify—; labor under—; lock out—; occasion—; result in—; shut out—; view with—; —arises; —confuses; —diverts; —intercepts; —interrupts; —perturbs.
(See confusion, disorder.)

DISTRESS
adjectives
simulated; palpable; widespread; pecuniary; horrible; mental; mortal; violent; keenest; intellectual; obvious; sore; obstinate; poignant; genuine; fearful; hideous; fancied; sentimental; dark; blind; generalized; terrified; needless; supreme; spiritual; bitter; fatherless; sensitive; financial; painted; severe; extreme; pathetic; heart-

searching; recurrent; sharp; sublime; deep; chronic; painful; insupportable; bare; wide-eyed; cowering; dire; evident; unrelieved; supposed; public.

verbs
afflict with—; aggravate—; answer—; bawl —; behold in—; consume with—; counsel in—; deliver from—; embolden by—; expose to—; give rise to—; pity—; relieve—; soothe—; submit in—; suffer—; wait in—; wring with—; —afflicts; —crazes; —gnaws.
(See suffering, pain, misery, agony.)

DISTRESS (v)
adverbs
deeply; shockingly; mentally; triumphantly; dreadfully; palpably; pecuniarily; horribly; mortally; violently; obviously; sorely; poignantly; genuinely; fearfully; hideously; sentimentally; needlessly; recurrently; supremely; spiritually; chronically; painfully; insupportably; direly; publicly.
(See grieve, wound.)

DISTRESSING
adverbs
extremely; remarkably; awfully; painfully; sorely; profoundly; deeply; appallingly; horribly; gravely; shockingly; incredibly; unspeakably; unmentionably; mentally; violently; keenly; poignantly; genuinely; hideously; supremely; bitterly; insupportably; evidently; unutterably; intensely; seriously; starkly; uncommonly; acutely; fundamentally; unduly; immoderately; unusually.

DISTRIBUTE (v)
adverbs
genially; exclusively; uniformly; indecisively; judiciously; equally; geographically; geometrically; irregularly; indefinitely; equitably; plentifully; scientifically; socially; ultimately; unlimitedly; symmetrically; lavishly; visibly; wastefully.
(See allot, apportion.)

DISTRIBUTION
adjectives
wide; general; equitable; liberal; wasteful; scientific; social; impracticable; ultimate; uniform; respective; symmetrical; rude; democratic; extensive; unlimited; lavish; indiscriminate; geographical; high; low; visible.

verbs
arrange—; bless with—; comprehend—; control—; effect—; enjoy—; increase—;

377

influence—; mention—; prepare for—; prevent—; reject—; sanction—; urge—; — abates; —aids; —disposes; —enriches; — involves; —reduces.

(See arrangement, disposition.)

DISTRICT

adjectives
outlying; thinly-populated; fashionable; simple; rural; residential; industrial; swankiest; congested; pastoral; remote; congressional; newly-gained; urban; scenic; sanitary; fertile; squalid; arid; extensive; coterminous; financial; genial-hearted; native; affected; accessible; dispatching; productive; adjacent; tenement; various (pl); charming; malodorous; populous.

verbs
appoint to—; assign to—; comprise—; constitute—; control—; divide into—s; dwell in—; elect to—; hedge in—; inhabit—; manage—; occupy—; separate into—s; supervise—; vest in—; —affords; —embraces; —envelops; —includes; —takes in; —thrives.

(See region, tract, locality, territory, circuit.)

DISTRUST

adjectives
cynical; grim; profound; paternal; morbid; reserved; instinctive; lurking; painful; lessening; vigilant; vulgar; palpable; mutual; abiding; inward; deep; prejudicial; unreasonable; vague; dawning; marked; foul.

verbs
accuse of—; acquire—; approach with—; augment—; awaken—; breed—; earn—; entertain—; eye with—; foster—; incur—; intensify—; mark with—; regard with—; silence—; view with—; warrant—; — appears; —enters; —grows; —sprouts.

(See doubt, suspicion.)

DISTRUST (v)

adverbs
instinctively; heartily; constantly; unavoidably; cynically; profoundly; morbidly; painfully; vigilantly; palpably; mutually; abidingly; deeply; unreasonably; vaguely; markedly.

(See suspect, doubt.)

DISTRUSTFUL

adverbs
gravely; alertly; watchfully; constantly; grimly; altogether; positively; profoundly; chronically; habitually; temperamentally; morbidly; painfully; instinctively; intuitively; inwardly; secretly; openly; unreasonably; vaguely; suspiciously; obnoxiously; disagreeably; wisely; warily; quietly; prudently; faintly; uneasily; seriously; momentarily; anxiously; sagaciously; nervously; timidly; horridly; skeptically.

DISTURB (v)

adverbs
inwardly; particularly; wantonly; perceptibly; profoundly; permanently; materially; deeply; grievously; emotionally; functionally; mentally; mutually; exceptionally; powerfully; pathologically; intellectually; violently; electrically; psychically; internally; glandularly; rudely; unnecessarily; unpleasantly.

(See annoy, perturb.)

DISTURBANCE

adjectives
civil; spasmodic; organic; emotional; terrific; mutual; atmospheric; insurrectionary; functional; mental; exceptional; powerful; gastric; strange; pathological; magnetic; widespread; intellectual; violent; electrical; psychic; visual; emotional; internal; agitated; glandular; serious; rude; unnecessary.

verbs
accompany by—; aggravate—; allay—; attend with—; continue—; engender—; foment—; free from—; generate—; relieve —; suffer from—; —arises; —fizzles out (colloq.); —subsides.

(See tumult, confusion, commotion, uproar, clamor.)

DISTURBING

adverbs
faintly; vaguely; definitely; seriously; gravely; alarmingly; significantly; evidently; manifestly; irrationally; palpably; visibly; noticeably; unreasonably; needlessly; maliciously; meddlesomely; shockingly; turbulently; fussily; restlessly; excitably; hysterically; tantalizingly; bitterly; miserably; intolerably; horribly; unpleasantly; disagreeably; obnoxiously; exceptionally

adjectives

(See neglect.)

verbs

cast into—; come into—; drop into—; excuse—; fall into—; lapse into—; lose by—; overcome—; parch by—; proceed from—; regret—; rot away in—; rouse out of—; rust from—; stifle by—; weaken by—; —affects; —deteriorates; —prevents; grows into—.

(See neglect.)

adjectives

briny; oozy; impassable; rain-soaked; muddy; filthy; deep.

verbs

bog in—; fall into—; level—; mire in—; plunge in—; turn in—; —ensnares; —forms; —furnishes; —serves.

(See trench, channel.)

adjectives

sea-going; hiccup; time-honored; popular; strident; amorous; doleful; woeful; sentimental; irrelevant.

verbs

carol—; compose—; dash off—; entertain with—; hum—; mourn—; mute—; pipe—; warble—; welcome with—; —amuses; —celebrates; —cheers; —flows; —lulls; —praises; —resounds.

(See air, poem, song, tune.)

adjectives

perfumed; pillowed; rickety; commodious; luxurious; resplendent; inviting; comfortable.

adverbs

spectacularly; gracefully; unerringly; precipitately; abruptly; harrowingly; thrillingly; bravely; courageously.

(See plunge, drop.)

adjectives

(See deviation.)

verbs

allow for—; bridge—; check—; correct—; flow in—; follow—; generate—; illustrate —; increase—; intersect—; occasion—; produce—; question—; relate with—; test —; —affects; —arises; —diminishes; —occurs; —proceeds from; —separates; —widens.

(See deviation, disagreement, difference.)

adverbs

extraordinarily; resolutely; definitely; sharply; interestingly; disputatiously; positively; harshly; discordantly; disagreeably; uncongenially; incompatibly; inaptly; terribly; endlessly; pitiably; painfully; exceptionally; deliberately.

adverbs

utterly; harmlessly; momentarily; intellectually; economically; mysteriously; inexplicably; sharply; markedly; remarkably; notably; acutely; perceptibly; gravely; insuperably; racially; subtly; essentially; strikingly; fundamentally; radically; appreciably; materially; amazingly; significantly; superficially; extremely; irreconcilably; prodigiously; temperamentally; intrinsically; completely.

adjectives

social; congenial; harmless; pleasurable; staple; childish; constant; unending; favorite; momentary; contemporary; popular; infantile; intellectual; sturdy; innocent; outdoor; decorous; unique; languid; incidental; seasonable; healthful; economical; agreeable; mysterious; attacking; exquisite; exhilarating.

verbs

advocate—; allow—; amuse with—; conceive—; consider—; contrive—; employ—; engage in—; forget in—; invent—; look for—; need—; occupy with—; search for—; sprout—; suggest—; —attracts; —benefits; —entertains; —excites; —fatigues; —gratifies; —withholds.

(See amusement, recreation, entertainment, sport, relaxation, pastime.)

adjectives

delightful; continental; extraordinary; infinite; outward; merry; magnificent; grave; picturesque.

adverbs

frequently; immensely; delightfully; extraordinarily; infinitely; outwardly; merrily; magnificently; pleasurably; childishly; constantly; intellectually; uniquely; healthfully; economically; agreeably; exquisitely; exhilaratingly.

(See turn, withdraw.)

DIVERTING

adverbs

deviously; erratically; circuitously; endlessly; delusively; sharply; cleverly; artfully; adroitly; skilfully; mysteriously; cunningly; deceptively; insidiously; trickily; meretriciously; wickedly; amusingly; entertainingly; playfully; sportively; clumsily; merrily; joyously; wittily; pleasantly; cheerily; roguishly.

DIVIDE (v)

adverbs

customarily; transversely; horizontally; conveniently; finely; subtly; wisely; evenly; longitudinally; miraculously; hopelessly; equally; formally; critically; scientifically; fatally; geographically; appropriately; arbitrarily; factionally; racially; unexpectedly; originally.

(See separate, sever.)

DIVIDEND

adjectives

illegitimate; substantial; reasonable; regular; generous.

verbs

advise of—; allot—; announce—; bear—; declare—; distribute—; draw—; invest—; mail—; obtain—; pay—; present—; promise—; report—; yield—; —s accrue; —s suffice; —s support; share in—.

(See portion, amount, money.)

DIVINITY

adjectives

anthropomorphic; ancient; omnipresent; scholastic; sylvan; jealous; false; actual; utter; strange; winged; favorite; sarcastic; dying; tutelar; polemical.

verbs

attain—; claim—; conceive—; concern—; embrace—; encounter—; express—; invoke —; manifest—; preach—; reflect—; reject —; unite in—; verse in—; —governs; — inspires; —rules; —stirs.

(See deity, God.)

adjectives

venereal; contending; formal; minutest; critical; various (pl); proposed; scientific; astonishing; equitable; isolated; distinct; fatal; assaulting; heroic; antecedent; primary; geographical; arbitrary; appropriate; factional; racial; unexpected; original.

verbs

arrange in—s; attempt—; avoid—; cement —; control—; distinguish—; draw from—; enforce—; establish—; form—; include in —; lead—; mark—; note—; number—; observe—; place in—; separate into—s; struggle for—; supervise—; zone—; — comprises; —consists of; —distributes; —widens.

(See distribution, part, section.)

DIVORCE

adjectives

salubrious; irregular; hateful; unwholesome; deadly; collusive; welcome; longsought; publicized; worth-while; surprise; framed.

verbs

abuse—; agree to—; apply for—; approve of—; consent to—; contemplate—; declaim against—; favor—; grant—; involve in—; lament—; pronounce—; recognize—; resort to—; sanction—; stay—; sue for—; terminate in—; warrant—; —cleaves; — corrupts; —dissolves; —frees; —privileges; —separates; authorize—; prevent—; tolerate—.

(See separation, marriage.)

DIVORCED

adverbs

irrevocably; unhappily; unfortunately; frequently; regularly; unjustly; unluckily; grievously; rightfully; properly; legally; loosely; distinctly; justifiably; judicially; profitably; recently; correctly; felicitously; irreconcilably.

DIZZINESS

adjectives

swift; paralyzing.

verbs

attend with—; diagnose—; feign—; induce —; occasion—; overcome—; produce—; strike with—; sway in—; take with—; treat for—; —diminishes; —ensues; — envelops; —forewarns; —perplexes; —relaxes; —suggests.

(See giddiness, confusion.)

adverbs

hopelessly; suddenly; helplessly; dangerously; alarmingly; slightly; completely; blindly; dimly; confusedly; mistily; obscurely; glaringly; sickeningly; frightfully; fearfully; inadvertently; muzzily; abnormally; deliriously; incoherently; crazily; light-headedly; uncontrollably; oddly; curiously; strangely; queerly.

DOCILITY

adjectives

noiseless; submissive.

DOCK

adjectives

shipping; humming; dingy; ancient; wet; neat.

DOCKET

adjectives

(See calendar.)

verbs

appear on—; arrange—; cancel—; file—; inclose in—; mention in—; prepare—; produce—; rearrange—; run through—; seal —; search—; strike—; survey—; —authorizes; —contains; —dispenses with; —indicates; —revolves; preserve—.

(See calendar, list.)

DOCTOR

adjectives

young; learned; vivacious; resourceful; inscrutable; lauded; illustrious; indefatigable; old-fashioned; provincial; would-be; mellifluous; tall; capable; country; handpicked; easy-going; fashionable; distracted; badgered; reverend; worthy; murderous; talented; mystic; eminent; discreet; budding; regimental.

verbs

(See physician.)

DOCTRINAL

adverbs

rigidly; austerely; augustly; sternly; undeviatingly; absurdly; devoutly; strictly; tenaciously; persistently; insistently; consistently; wholly; conscientiously; meticulously; punctiliously; ceremoniously; ritualistically; dogmatically; obstinately; stubbornly; stiffly; dismally; fundamentally; zealously; abstractly; comfortably; placidly; primarily; horribly.

adjectives

dismal; dangerous; fundamental; heretical; pernicious; incestuous; outworn; decided; zealous; positive; blessed; conflicting; revolutionary; mystical; audacious; subversive; traditional; exoteric; recondite; cold; abstract; sound; pleasant; sensational; elevated; valid; accursed; denominational; living; recurring; enlarging; rigid; evil; deliberate; vulgar; licentious; nefarious; blighting; barbarous; opposite; cherished; characteristic; unflinching; republican; unedifying; undefiled; devilish; dubious; hermeneutical; time-honored; orthodox; comfortable; vague; pregnant; imported; erroneous; traditive; evolutionary; heterodox; wildest; primary; essential; tantalizing; evangelical; shallow; bold; religious; horrible; sentimental; deistical; contrary; practical.

verbs

accept—; adhere to—; adopt—; advocate —; apply—; attack—; believe—; blaspheme—; bolster—; challenge—; commit to—; concur in—; define—; demolish—; derive—from; echo—; enunciate—; epitomize—; espouse—; expound—; illustrate—; immerse in—; impart—; inculcate—; invoke —; nullify—; obey—; pledge to—; practise—; preach—; promulgate—; propound —; put forth—; refer to—; reject—; sin against—; spread—; teach—; understand —; unite in—; —astounds; —confounds; —embraces; —governs.

(See teaching, belief, dogma, principle, precept.)

DOCUMENT

adjectives

genuine; routine; epic; intimate; tremendous; human; effective; dull; trustworthy; ethnological; authoritative; vivid; revealing; precious; obnoxious; colorless; official; controversial; immortal; fundamental; notable; living; ecclesiastical; diplomatic; temperate; extraordinary; unique; amazing; public; formidable; illuminating; brief; decorous; forceful; momentous; dangerous; pathetic; significant; rambling; equivocal; flimsy; finicky; noteworthy; singular; irreproachable; trenchant; unpublished; fatal; different-looking; authentic; ponderous; uncommon; insidious; iconographic; respective (pl); edifying.

verbs

arrange—; crowd with—s; cull from—;

draw up—; entrust with—; explore through —s; file—; inscribe in—; preserve—; produce—; refer to—; release—; scan—; seal —; search—; sign—; survey—; term—; value—; witness—; —asserts; —authorizes; —enlightens; —entitles; —informs; —points out; —proves; —records; —serves; — verifies.

(See paper, evidence, proof, record.)

DOCUMENTARY
adverbs
inescapably; genuinely; trustworthily; ecclesiastically; legally; amazingly; formidably; briefly; momentously; dangerously; significantly; irreproachably; fatally; ponderously; trenchantly; uncommonly; unexpectedly; surprisingly.

DODDERING
adverbs
tremulously; quaveringly; helplessly; feebly; pleasantly; uncertainly; hopelessly; desperately; decrepitly; wanderingly; erratically; confusedly; bewilderedly; pathetically; bravely; prematurely; nervously; besottedly; drunkenly; slowly; wearily.

DOG
adjectives
wistful; spineless; mauled; loutish; shambling; squat; well-shaped; mongrel; tubby; stray; wolf-like; well-bred; barking; marauding; placid; slinking; whipped; cringing; huge; lion-like; cross-grained; savage; vicious; sedate; beaten; avid; yelping; raging; inestimable; alien; clean; rabid; murderous; angry; hungry; handsome; stately; jubilant; worthless; gigantic; lean; gallant; happy; famished; miserable; reliable; frail; little; woolly; deep-chested; disgraceful-looking; couchant; myopic; demented; tawny; treacherous; panting; half-wolf; stripe-tailed; surly; brutal; stranger; accursed; unconscionable; patient; fierce; snapping; chivalrous; jovial; vagrant; atheistical; thievish-looking; voiceless; lame; sneaking; sad; craven; traitorous; thirsty; bipedal; gentlemanly; elderly; mangy; hellish; lounging.

verbs
cast to—s; coax—; crop—; cudgel—; lash —; soothe—; stone—; unleash—; whip—; —barks; —bays; —clambers; —crouches; —darts by; —dashes by; —depredates; — frisks; —gnaws; —growls; —herds; — howls; —invades; —laps; —licks; —limps; —lurks; —menaces; —performs; —points; —preys; —pursues; —retrieves; —skulks;

—slinks off; —snaps; —snarls; —strays; —tears; —trots away; —whimpers; — whines; —wrangles; —yelps; —yowls.

(See animal, puppy.)

DOGGED
adverbs
stubbornly; obstinately; boundlessly; excessively; resolutely; sullenly; morosely; pertinaciously; glumly; silently; irresistibly; obdurately; implacably; inveterately; bravely; heroically; endlessly; surprisingly; unexpectedly; mulishly; perversely; blindly; intractably; fanatically; wilfully; intrepidly; enterprisingly; fiercely; churlishly; grouchily; moodily; crustily; grumpishly.

DOGMA
adjectives
wide-rooted; delicate; dangerous; religious; deflating; dour; theological; pungent; narrow; entrenched; intolerant; pure; sheer; rash; inscrutable; fundamental; negative; sweeping.

verbs
abandon—; assert—; defend—; expound—; follow—; formulate—; impose—; inherit—; justify—; preach—; proclaim—; propound —; put forward—; question—; sanction—; save—; state—; teach—; —convinces; — denounces; —flourishes; —satisfies; — vanishes.

(See doctrine, principle.)

DOGMATIC
adverbs
unwarrantably; disagreeably; confidently; marvelously; unaccountably; egotistically; cruelly; harshly; severely; conceitedly; bumptiously; ecclesiastically; tyrannically; officially; inexorably; stiffly; dangerously; dourly; narrowly; fundamentally; purely; utterly; singularly; austerely; arrogantly; proudly; unyieldingly; solidly; absolutely; definitely; positively; fanatically; superficially; intolerantly; provincially; remarkably; fussily; peremptorily; emphatically; solemnly.

DOINGS
adjectives
hot-headed; habitual; subsequent; infinite; valiant; ill; sinister; factual.

DOLE
verbs
apply for—; apportion—; approve of—; deprive of—; dispense—; distribute—; di-

vide—; drop from—; entitle to—; impart —; issue—; reduce to—; reward—; relinquish—; subsist on—; —eases; —supports. (See alms, charity.)

DOLEFUL

adverbs

habitually; temperamentally; utterly; ceaselessly; deeply; darkly; foolishly; unreasonably; vexatiously; needlessly; remarkably; singularly; oddly; oppressively; inarticulately; silently; immoderately; unutterably; fundamentally; extravagantly; dismally; abjectly; glumly; gloomily; lugubriously; dreadfully; biliously; horribly.

DOLL

adjectives

mature; gorgeous; absurd; rag; exquisite; mutilated; adorable; cherished; brainless; dancing; dressed-up; dilapidated; moon-faced; battered.

verbs

collect—s; display—; dress—; entertain with—; name—; present with—; repair—; sleep with—; tire of—; wind—; yearn for —; —attracts; —cheers; —dangles; —pleases; —satisfies; —simpers; —sleeps; —surprises; —walks. (See toy.)

DOLLAR

adjectives

precious; shrunken; tangible; advertising; paltry; appreciating; solitary; minted; countless (pl); depreciating; inflated; purchasing.

verbs

adopt—; beg—; coin—s; count—s; counterfeit—; deflate—; devaluate—; earn—; fill with—; flash—; furnish with—; inflate—; issue—; lose—; mint—s; present with—; print—s; proffer—; rate—; reduce to—; reject—; relinquish—; soil—; tear—; value —; worship—; —s accrue; —adorns; —attracts. (See money, coin.)

DOLTISH

adverbs

unutterably; strangely; dully; apathetically; singularly; oddly; curiously; unaccountably; inscrutably; abysmally; grotesquely; palpably; essentially; incurably; irremediably; callously; shockingly; soddenly; sullenly; vacuously; ridiculously; lumpishly; grossly; coarsely; direly; blandly; stupidly; stolidly.

DOMAIN

adjectives

temporal; spiritual; allied (pl); speckless; ancestral; rough-hewn; extended; unexploited; bleak; ecclesiastical; obscure; shifting; elastic; scanty; shattered; melancholy; eminent; imperial; unassailable; forbidden; flourishing; impenetrable; outlying; all-pervading; vast.

DOME

adjectives

golden; majestic; great; granite; shallow; saucer-like; gilded; blue-tiled; truncated; bell-shaped; silent; glorious; velvety; vaulted; star-fretted; tremulous; inevitable; isolated; monastic; gaping; observatory; firmamental; clustered; shadowy; ribbed; Moorish; towering; heaven-pointing; illuminated; porphyroid.

verbs

adorn—; ascend to—; cradle in—; decorate —; dwell in—; enlarge—; gild—; illuminate—; poise on—; round off in—; stud—; survey—; swell—; —arches; —attracts; —resounds; —revolves; —shields; —sparkles; —spreads; —totters. (See roof, building.)

DOMESTIC

adverbs

incurably; delightfully; cozily; comfortably; exaggeratedly; elaborately; ostentatiously; blatantly; offensively; conspicuously; hopelessly; charmingly; narrowly; insistently; flamboyantly; proudly; absurdly; impressively; vexatiously; boundlessly; entirely; pretentiously.

DOMESTICITY

adjectives

smug; safe; dull; suburban; hard-won.

verbs

acquaint with—; avoid—; balk at—; dabble in—; eliminate—; escape—; feign—; glance into—; incur—; indulge in—; pretend—; school in—; swallow by—; trap by—; wallow in—; weary of—; wrap in—; —annoys; —appeals; —bores; —involves; —restrains; —shelters. (See affair.)

DOMICILE

adjectives

luxurious; semi-detached; sumptuous; self-contained; sanctified; historic; commodious; tempting.

DOMINANT

adverbs

disturbingly; arrogantly; prominently; interestingly; strangely; substantially; emphatically; markedly; primarily; remarkably; vitally; virtually; dangerously; luckily; alarmingly; fortunately; unluckily; strongly; invincibly; inescapably; supremely; disagreeably; unpleasantly; officiously; selfishly; ruthlessly; inconsiderately; politically; unfortunately; insistently; manifestly; obviously; terribly; loftily; sternly; extraordinarily.

DOMINATE (*v*)

adverbs

atavistically; powerfully; effectively; tyrannically; overwhelmingly; sternly; inevitably; insistently; solely; persistently.

(See govern, control.)

DOMINATION

adjectives

lofty; overwhelming; hard; stern; cortical; banded; extraordinary; inevitable; insistent; sole; extended.

verbs

break away from—; condemn—; curse by —; dwell in—; enlarge—; enrich—; establish—; foster—; join—; subject to—; submit to—; suffer under—; trace—to; —compels; —inflicts; —reaps; —rules; —thrives.

(See control, dominion, rule, government, tyranny.)

DOMINEERING

adverbs

disagreeably; ridiculously; amusingly; tyrannically; unreasonably; characteristically; arrogantly; clownishly; persistently; airily; shockingly; politely; officiously; ludicrously; despotically; pompously; inherently; superciliously; loftily; insistently; sharply; detestably; offensively; naturally.

DOMINION

adjectives

sole; hereditary; dim; voracious; hard; unlimited; uncurbed; supreme; gross; drear.

verbs

control—; exercise—over; explore—; form —; gain—; grant to—; grasp—; inhabit—; integrate—s; procure—over; recognize—; rule—; rule with—; sever—from; sway—; yield to—; —comprises; —extends to; —obeys; —serves; govern—.

(See sovereignty, authority, nation, empire, kingdom.)

DONATE (*v*)

adverbs

munificently; generously; charitably; anonymously; amply; lavishly; splendidly; meagerly; grudgingly; complainingly.

(See give, contribute.)

DONATION

adjectives

generous; ample; munificent.

DONKEY

adjectives

laden; tiny; gray; straggling; diminutive; plodding; modest; gentle; omnipresent; neat-stepping; patient.

verbs

burden—; fetter—; lash—; lasso—; pasture —; tether—; water—; —ambles; —balks; —draws; —grazes; —hauls; —kicks; —pulls; —shies; —snorts.

(See animal, ass.)

DOOM

adjectives

impending; ultimate; irrevocable; ignominious; inescapable; dreadful; tragic; distant; thankful; inevitable; eternal; mysterious; dark; self-wrought; everlasting; inscrutable; stormy; graceless; fatal; approaching; imminent; perpetual; dubious; ultimate.

verbs

announce—; assign—; avoid—; bear—; bide—; consign to—; curse—; draw to—; dread—; fix—; fly to—; foresee—; foreshadow—; foretell—; hasten to—; move to—; near—; precipitate—; pronounce—; read—; revoke—; seal—; sound—; spell —; threaten—; —closes in; —impends.

(See judgment, fate, destiny.)

DOOM (*v*)

adverbs

irrecoverably; irrevocably; apparently; everlastingly; prophetically; ultimately; ig-

nominiously; inescapably; dreadfully; tragically; inevitably; eternally; mysteriously; inscrutably; fatally; cruelly.
(See condemn, ruin.)

DOOMED
adverbs
irretrievably; finally; mortally; endlessly; terribly; ultimately; irrevocably; ignominiously; inescapably; dreadfully; tragically; inevitably; eternally; mysteriously; darkly; everlastingly; inscrutably; perpetually; unhappily; utterly; evidently; manifestly; fatefully.

DOOR
adjectives
massive; battered; paneled; reluctant; clamped; iron-bound; barricaded; heavy; monumental; lovely; sun-blistered; baffling; carved; solid; grilled; unyielding; bolted; humble; weather-beaten; cathedral; unlatched; ponderous; stout; studded; opening; squeaking; communicating; yawning; cringing; ancient; worm-eaten; hacked; clanging; front; fateful; mystic; perpetual; unfrequented; love-crowned; substantial; impervious; moldering; revolving; portcullis; lodge; postern; sloping; sliding; hospitable; intermediate; veiled; padded; unguarded; infernal; impalpable; paternal; mossy; adamantine; unhinged; arched; mountain; shattered; curtained; guilty; shrunken; dilapidated; feeble.

verbs
appear at—; arch—; attain—; bar—; barricade—; batter down—; beat down—; bolt—; clamor at—; command—; commune at—; darken—; defend—; encamp at—; escort to—; exclude from—; fling open—; force—; gather at—; glimmer through—; guard—; guide to—; hammer on—; hinge —; hover about—; jam—; peep through—; pry at—; repulse from—; slam—; steal through—; stream through—; tap on—; tarry at—; tend—; venture through—; — admits; —creaks; —groans; —squeaks; — yawns.
(See entrance, portal, gate, opening, doorway.)

DOOR-BELL
adjectives
(See bell.)

verbs
adjust—; answer—; attach—; connect—; hang—; press—; quiet—; ring—; sound—;

—announces; —chimes; —disturbs; —interjects; —interrupts; —jingles; —pierces; — warns.
(See bell.)

DOOR-KNOB
adjectives
(See knob.)

verbs
adjust—; attach—; fasten to—; force—; grasp—; handle—; hug—; jiggle—; manipulate—; mark—; move—; ornament—; palm—; release—; toy with—; try—; tug at—; turn—; soil—; —gives way; —turns.
(See handle, knob.)

DOOR-MAN
adjectives
hulking; hard-faced; resplendent; staring; ruthless; gigantic.

DOORWAY
adjectives
sheltered; stately; doorless; curtained; unpretentious; pilastered; time-stained; flamboyant; enticing; impressive; unsavory; sculptured.

verbs
admit through—; adorn—; darken—; embellish—; enter—; file through—; flutter past—; huddle in—; jostle into—; loom in—; observe from—; occupy—; open into —; ornament—; pursue through—; scamper through—; shadow—; —beckons; —divides; —exhibits; —invites; —separates.
(See door.)

DORMANT
adverbs
temporarily; transiently; healthily; momentarily; latently; passively; inertly; heavily; lethargically; inactively; mysteriously; importantly; smoulderingly; symbolically; impenetrably; inferentially; fortunately; naturally; quiescently.

DOSE
adjectives
minimum; enormous; nauseous; attenuated; curative; large; graduated (pl); tremendous; unpalatable; minute; occasional; nontoxic; potable; protective; moderate; monstrous; therapeutic; homeopathic.

verbs
adjust—; administer—; advocate—; apply —; calm with—; concoct—; decrease—;

increase—; inject—; ladle out—; measure —; portion out—; prepare—; prescribe—; reduce—; refuse—; regulate—; repeat—; suggest—; swallow—; —alleviates; —relieves; —suffices.

(See portion, draught, amount, medicine.)

DOTING

adverbs
foolishly; absurdly; inordinately; childishly; tenderly; ludicrously; tempestuously; frankly; proudly; significantly; ridiculously; openly; ostentatiously; fatuously; fervently; idolatrously; ardently; inarticulately; inexpressibly; madly; fervidly.

DOUBLE-FACED

adverbs
subtly; cunningly; insidiously; notoriously; infamously; surreptitiously; artfully; craftily; deceitfully; remarkably; dangerously; cleverly; alarmingly; distressingly; maneuveringly; plaguedly; adroitly; successfully; underhandedly; shrewdly; proverbially; manifestly; suavely; sanctimoniously.

DOUBT

adjectives
premonitory; wondering; casual; growing; reasonable; prudent; impending; recurring; faint; presumptuous; insinuating; audacious; uneasy; horrid; black; wistful; serious; disturbing; grisly; consuming; bitter; sickening; momentary; angry; torturing; cynical; passionate; formless; unmerited; nagging; insidious; mean; conflicting; anxious; painful; pecuniary; timid; sarcastic; considerable; solitary; lingering; inseparable; floating; paralyzing; melancholy; remorseful; hideous; sorrowing; thronging; rational; hopeless; jealous; tragic; unwelcome; injurious; dark; coquettish; blasphemous; unclaimed; childish; oft-repeated; religious; unanswerable; good-humored; constitutional; grave; fiendish; sagacious; cloudy; broken; desperate; earthly.

verbs
assail with—; attend with—; banish—; breed—; brush away—; burden with—; cast into—; chill with—; circulate—; clear up—; cloud with—; conceive—; convey—; crush—; defy—; dissipate—; dissolve—; eliminate—; entertain—; erase—; express —; falter in—; fight—; interpose—; occasion—; oppress with—; raise—; remove—; rend with—; resolve—; strike with—; sustain—; sweep away—; torture with—; trouble by—; voice—; wrap in—; wring

with—; —creeps in; —encompasses; —incenses; —lingers; —lurks; —overshadows; —prevails; —pursues; —springs up; —stabs; —taints.

(See uncertainty, distrust, disbelief, incredulity, skepticism.)

DOUBT (v)

adverbs
casually; growingly; reasonably; recurringly; seriously; disturbingly; consumingly; sickeningly; momentarily; formlessly; painfully; jealously; childishly; gravely; sagaciously; paralyzingly.

(See distrust, suspect.)

DOUBTER

adjectives
fastidious; sneering; puny.

DOUBTFUL

adverbs
altogether; reasonably; seriously; gravely; vexatiously; still; wholly; timidly; vaguely; hazily; bewilderingly; mysteriously; enigmatically; ignorantly; distractedly; nervously; uncertainly; embarrassingly; elusively; remarkably; singularly; inexplicably; oddly.

DOUGH

adjectives
tasteless; crisp.

verbs
cake—; knead—; leaven—; mix—; mould —; moisten—; prepare—; punch—; set—; shape—; sprinkle—; sweeten—; transform —into; work—; —ferments; —puffs; —rises.

(See mass.)

DOUGHNUT

adjectives
lunch-counter; sugary; forbidden.

DOVE

adjectives
crooning; staid; strengthless; mellow-mourning; lonely; sucking; milk-white; cooing; brooding; silver; snowy.

verbs
tame—; toy with—; —bills; —broods; —coos; —crouches; —grieves; —haunts; —moans; —mourns; —murmurs; —plains; —sails; —trembles; —trumpets; —tumbles; —walks.

(See bird.)

DOWAGER

adjectives
ugly; old; **decorous**; ill-tempered; amiable.

DOWDY

adverbs
indescribably; dismally; untidily; vaguely; shamefully; embarrassingly; pitiably; incredibly; unfashionably; inexcusably; indifferently; nonchalantly; blithely; carelessly; gloriously; laughingly; placidly; **self-consciously**; unconscionably; inordinately; unpardonably; vexatiously; downright; smudgily; grimily; lazily; **obstinately**; slouchily; gaily; negligently.

DOWER

adjectives
unconscious; fragrant; generous; sufficient; convenient.

DOWN

adjectives
solitary; dewy-glooming; callow; loaning; soft; undulating (pl); hushless (pl); beautiful; swelling (pl).

DOWNCAST

adverbs
terribly; unreasonably; needlessly; gloomily; glumly; inordinately; emphatically; dourly; sorely; irrationally; inexplicably; moodily; alarmingly; dangerously; incurably; inconceivably; incredibly; horribly; woefully; gravely; seriously; inconsolably; desperately; tragically; unduly; wearily.

DOWNFALL

verbs
anticipate—; approach—; bring about—; drag into—; escape—; expect—; experience—; fear—; guard against—; heed—; **meet**—; pitch to—; promise—; protect from —; recover from—; tumble to—; warn **of**—; —destroys; —engulfs; —teaches.
(See disgrace, ruin, destruction.)

DOWNPOUR

adjectives
torrential; thinning; increasing; steady; drenching; tropical.

DOWRY

adjectives
(See gift.)

verbs
agree upon—; amass—; assign—; assure **of**—; bestow—; demand—; endue with—;

furnish—; grant—; guarantee—; increase —; marry for—; pay—; present with—; provide—; return—; seek—; —compensates; —impoverishes; —satisfies; —shrinks.
(See endowment, **gift**, property, portion, reward.)

DOZE

adjectives
noontide; surreptitious; sudden; heavy; fitful; nightmare-ridden; comfortable; wakeful; uncomfortable.

DOZE (*v*)

adverbs
peacefully; slumberously; surreptitiously; fitfully; comfortably; wakefully; interminably; lazily.
(See sleep, drowse.)

DRABNESS

adjectives
colorless; external; bleak; blank.

verbs
clothe in—; compensate for—; conceal—; envelop by—; expel—; exude—; observe—; relieve—; shroud in—; throw off—; —depresses; —displeases; —drowns; —offends; —oppresses; —overwhelms; —seeps in; —suits.
(See dullness, monotony.)

DRAFT
(*air*)

adjectives
icy; adventurous; sparkling; severe; swift.

verbs
admit—; avoid—; breathe—; create—; draw—; expose to—; force—; guard against—; inhale—; place in—; prevent—; produce—; protect against—; shiver in—; sit in—; —effects; —enters; —escapes; —harms; —passes through.
(See current, air, breeze.)

DRAFT
(*money*)

verbs
address—; approve—; cash—; date—; defer—; draw—; honor—; pay with—; produce—; send—; tender—; wire—; write—; —enables; —orders; —suffices.
(See money.)

DRAG (*v*)

adverbs
painfully; listlessly; dejectedly; bodily;

heavily; tenderly; stubbornly; forcibly; despondently; unwillingly; sternly.
(See haul, trail, pull.)

DRAGON

adjectives
undulant; cave-hid; gilded; fabulous; swift; full-gorged; transfixed; ugly; hideous; murderous; Hydra-headed; green; monstrous; bloodthirsty.

verbs
beset by—; cast out—; confront by—; crush—; pacify—; prevail against—; rout —; slay—; strike at—; vanquish—; — claws; —destroys; —fumes; —guards; — hisses; —licks; —menaces; —ravages; — snorts; —spouts forth; —swallows up; — symbolizes; —tramples; —vanishes; — wails; —writhes.
(See monster, serpent.)

DRAIN

adjectives
(See ditch, pipe, trench.)

verbs
clog—; connect to—; consign to—; dig—; discharge in—; drop into—; employ—; enter—; flush—; furnish—; insert—; pour down—; —carries off; —clears; —preserves; —prevents; —serves; washdown—.
(See gutter, channel. trench, ditch, pipe.)

DRAIN (v)

adverbs
steadily; thoroughly; partially; unscrupulously; unsparingly; entirely; completely; painfully.
(See empty, exhaust, deplete.)

DRAMA

adjectives
spiritual; modern; languid; excessive; loquacious; moving; honest; courageous; stirring; sturdy; classic; dazzling; intense; irrepressible; successful; trivial; stark; high; spectacular; unpretentious; lyric; terrific; painful; crucial; ineffective; unsettled; sensational; hidden; sinister; comic; touching; grim; vivid; gloomy; tragic; dynamic; many-sided; homely; homespun; heartrending; agonizing; absorbing; daily; rousing; weird; romantic; enthralling; raw; elemental; episodic; moon-lit; grisly; moribund; terrestrial; breathless; turgid; far-flung; unrelenting; throbbing; intensified; psychological; adulterous; quiet; piquant; stupendous; thrilling; philosophical;

judicial; realistic; naturalistic; poetic; merciless; pitiless; constructive; decadent; fierce; historical; mimic; powerful; religious; impending; oft-rehearsed; voiceless; equestrian; potential; tragic; social; great; well-ordered; transpired; blustering; nefarious; well-arranged; celebrated; revolutionary; sublime; epic; passionate; vast; heroic; propaganda; depressing; exhilarating.

verbs
cast—; enact—; fashion—; foreshadow—; ground in—; intensify—; pervade—; portray—; recreate—; reform—; revive—; sense—; sketch—; spell—; take part in—; temper—; unfold—; —depicts; —electrifies; —stirs; —teeters; —unrolls.
(See play, composition, performance, tragedy, literature.)

DRAMATIC

adverbs
spectacularly; absurdly; impressively; extravagantly; emphatically; foolishly; ridiculously; laughably; profitably; undoubtedly; evidently; palpably; grotesquely; fantastically; unusually; admittedly; excessively; movingly; highly; lyrically; sensationally; weirdly; romantically; breathlessly; enthrallingly; quietly; psychologically; stupendously; marvellously; abundantly; thrillingly; mercilessly; historically; undeniably; powerfully; potentially; sublimely; epically; vastly; heroically; passionately; exhilaratingly; touchingly; immensely; intensely; boundlessly.

DRAMATIST

adjectives
celebrated; contemporary; deft; practiced; renowned; distinguished.

verbs
acclaim—; applaud—; condemn—; criticize—; inspire—; praise—; reward—; support—; sympathize with—; —composes; — conceives;— concocts; —entertains; —excels; —foreshadows; —implies; —motivates; —moves; —plans; —presents; — prevails; —relates; —stirs; —yields.
(See writer, playwright, author.)

DRAPE

adjectives
extreme; modified; easy; natural; smart; athletic; careless; fashionable; poised; proper; graceful.

DRAPE (v)

adverbs

artistically; sparingly; carelessly; archly; smartly; fashionably; properly; gracefully; gloomily; vividly; voluminously; richly; flutteringly; monotonously; fantastically; gorgeously; judiciously; dustily.

(See hang, adorn, cover.)

DRAPERY

adjectives

sweeping; gloomy; gleaming; damask; smoke-grey; vivid; chiffon; voluminous; sad; silvery; rich; orchid; taffeta; window; glistening; festooned; stifling; floating; filmy; sable; well-managed; snowy; fluttering; verdant; monotonous; undulant; translucent; sonorous; graceful; gorgeous; golden; diaphonous; flying; silken; judicious; soft; streaming; sooty; gauzy; fantastic; witching; ambulant; chintz; voile; dusty.

verbs

admire—; arrange—; clothe in—; cover with—; decorate with—; dress in—; festoon in—; fold—; furnish with—; hang—; model—; place—; select—; strip of—; suspend—; weave—; —adds —dresses; —enhances; —graces; —offsets; —ies part.

(See curtain, cloth, material.)

DRASTIC

adverbs

cruelly; intensely; inhumanly; emphatically; unscrupulously; pitifully; powerfully; intensely; virulently; poignantly; harshly; resolutely; immensely; strenuously; incisively; violently; desperately; brutally; trenchantly; strikingly.

DRAUGHT

adjectives

copious; literary; roaring; shallow; mellow; crystal; daring; refreshing; beneficial; delirious; frequent (pl); nectared; unpalatable; portentous; long; hearty; ample; fresh; considerable; acid; grateful; magic; liquorish; fiery; nut-brown; immortal; mingled (pl); fatal; assisted.

verbs

concoct—; down—; drain—; draw off—; empty—; finish in one—; imbibe—; mix—; order—; partake of—; rejoice in—; tap—; —effervesces; —foams; —quenches; —revives; —sates; —soothes; —suffices.

(See drink.)

DRAW (v)

adverbs

fiercely; reluctantly; passionately; mournfully; caressingly; silently; swiftly; contentedly; lazily; demurely; passively; haughtily; apprehensively; irresistibly; reproachfully; inevitably; hastily; affectionately; tenderly; symbolically; exquisitely; sophisticatedly; sketchily; grotesquely; impeccably; hideously; apologetically.

(See depict, sketch, pull.)

DRAWBACK

adjectives

tremendous; undeniable; numerous (pl); practical; definite.

verbs

accept—; anticipate—; control—; expect—; involve—; lack—; necessitate—; overcome —; produce—; pronounce—; refuse—; relax—; reveal—; weigh—; —diminishes; —hinders.

(See disadvantage, hindrance, defect.)

DRAWER

adjectives

secret; gilt-labelled; locked; hidden; stuffed; filled.

verbs

arrange in—; conceal in—; decorate—; discover in—; draw out—; examine—; explore —; fit in—; lock—; muss—; obtain from—; ornament—; rummage in—; search in—; wade through—s; —contains; —exposes; —reveals; —sticks; —swallows.

(See case, box.)

DRAWING

adjectives

water-color; modernistic; free-hand; magnificent; clever; amazing; delectable; symbolical; beautiful; holy; exquisite; sophisticated; sketchy; charcoal; crude; sturdy; grotesque; impeccable; bewildering; distinguished; detailed; icicle-like; naturalistic; hideous.

verbs

collect—s; embellish—; exhibit—; interest in—; model for—; pen—; pencil—; pose for—; praise—; produce—; scratch out—; sit for—; sketch—; study—; translate—; —attracts; —depicts; —imparts; —represents; —reveals; —symbolizes.

(See sketch, picture.)

adjectives
frescoed; honest; staid; spacious; marble-floored.

DRAWL

adjectives
tantalizing; unexcited; calm; level; lazy; musical; indistinct; mountain; innocent; maddening; affected; enchanting; slow; steady; masculine; comforting; pleasant; ingenious; listless; haughty; sardonic; husky; amusing; amiable; quiet; soft; confidential; high; emphatic.

verbs
acquire—; adopt—; affect—; catch—; copy—; correct—; employ—; inject—; mimic—; mumble—; recognize—; retain—; translate —; understand—; utter—; —fascinates; —intrigues; —irritates; —loiters; —pleases.
(See speech, utterance, accent.)

DRAWL (v)

adverbs
slowly; wearily; tantalizingly; lazily; musically; indistinctly; maddeningly; affectedly; enchantingly; steadily; comfortingly; pleasantly; listlessly; sardonically; huskily; amusingly; amiably; softly; calmly.
(See speak, sound.)

DRAWLING

adverbs
lazily; sleepily; indifferently; carelessly; drowsily; yawningly; insolently; arrogantly; stupidly; impudently; slowly; indistinctly; affectedly; listlessly; languidly; huskily; interminably; endlessly; tiresomely; slackly; slouchily; leisurely; deliberately; apathetically; dully; maunderingly; inarticulately; singularly; faintly; idly; inertly; dreamily; inexcusably.

DREAD

adjectives
despising; wondrous; superstitious; half-conscious; silent; mysterious; contagious; ignorant; sickening; apprehensive; maddening; unreasonable; secret; speechless; mysterious; lurking; shrinking; shadowy; slavish; inexplicable; haunting; unimaginable; nameless; inexpressible; morbid; somber; fresh; blank; irrational; racking; stark; mutual; constant; unnamed; obscene; unnatural; foolish; abnormal; salutary; oppressive; decorous; ill-defined; vague; shuddering; subconscious; feminine; incomprehensible; grinding; popular; nervous;

pious; unformulated; poignant; supernatural; recurrent; indefinable; unfathomable; overwhelming; inspiring.

verbs
attend with—; awaken—; cause—; cure of—; diagnose—; disguise—; dwell in—; hide in—of; induce—; nourish—; obsess with—; oppress by—; overcome—; produce —; provoke—; put away—; regard with—; relinquish—; ripen into—; shake with—; wrap in—; —causes; —dogs; —inspires; —overcomes.
(See fright, horror, terror, awe.)

DREAD (v)

adverbs
righteously; vaguely; habitually; superstitiously; ignorantly; apprehensively; unreasonably; secretly; speechlessly; shrinkingly; inexplicably; hauntingly; unimaginably; inexpressibly; morbidly; somberly; irrationally; starkly; mutually; constantly; unnaturally; foolishly; oppressively; vaguely; nervously; piously; poignantly; supernaturally; recurrently; indefinably; unfathomably; overwhelmingly.
(See fear, anticipate.)

DREADFUL

adverbs
unutterably; unspeakably; horridly; abominably; tragically; gloomily; incredibly; indescribably; absolutely; starkly; uncommonly; amazingly; astonishingly; cruelly; shockingly; startlingly; perniciously; damnably; disastrously; ruinously; arrantly; reprehensibly; execrably; irremediably; insupportably; appallingly; repulsively; abhorrently; sickeningly; calamitously; cataclysmally.

DREAM

adjectives
aerial; aching; amazing; ambitious; amusing; amethystine; angelic; antenatal; appalling; astonishing; attenuated; bad; baleful; balmy; beastly; beatific; beauteous; besetting; bewildering; bitter; blessed; blighting; blissful; botched; boyish; bucolic; captured; changing; chaste; cherished; childhood; clear; clouded; colored; confused; consecrating; constant; conversational; daring; crazy; dark; day-appearing; dazzling; dead; dearest; deep; delicate; delicious; delirious; delusive; depressed; disconnected; discordant; disjointed; disordered; distorted; distressing; disturbed; divine; dotard; doubtful; dreadful; ecstat-

ic; drowsy; embodied; empty; enthralled; external; evil; exacerbated; exquisite; extraordinary; extravagant; exuberant; fabulous; faded; fairy tale; false; fanatical; fanciful; fancy; fantastic; favorite; fearful; feverish; fitful; flashing; flattering; fleeting; floating; fond; foolish; fragile; friendly; frightful; futile; ghastly; girlish; glorious; gloomy; golden; gorgeous; grandiose; grotesque; half-forgotten; half-remembered; hashish; hateful; haunting; hazy; hideous; horrible; horrid; horrifying; hovering; idle; idyllic; illusory; immortal; impossible; impressive; incommunicable; industrial; ineffaceable; ingenuous; insistent; inspiring; interlunar; interminable; intransitive; invisible; iridescent; jeweled; jostling; journeying; jocund; languorous; lasting; lethargic; liquored; lifelong; liberal-minded; living; loftiest; lotuseating; lowly; luxurious; mad; maddening; magical; magnificent; melancholy; materialized; millennial; misty; mournful; mooning; morbid; nightly; nightmare; obliging; particular; pensive; perfectible; perishing; odorous; oppressive; ominous; painful; perpetual; persistent; picturesque; pipe; poetic; pompous; poor; preposterous; prophetic; quarrelsome; protracted; pure; quaint; quaking; qualm-filled; quarrelsome; quavering; queenly; quenchable; quick; quieting; querimonious; querulous; questionable; quirky; quizzical; remarkable; restless; resurrected; ridiculous; rockingchair; romantic; rosy; senseless; sensual; significant; shameful; shattered; shivering; short-lived; sin-chastising; sprinkling; singular; sleepless; slow; smiling; solid; stern; strange; summer; sweet; symbolic; telepathic; tender; terrific; terrifying; thoughtless; topsy-turvy; torturing; transitory; trivial; troubled; tumultuous; unborn; uneasy; unmeaning; unpleasant; unquiet; unremembered; unshakable; unsubstantial; untold; vague; veritable; vernal; vicious; visionary; vivid; waking; wandering; waning; wavering; whirling; whiskey; whispered; wicked; winged; wildering; wildest; wistful; wretched; youthful; zestful.

verbs
awake from—; babble in—; blend in—; break—; calm—s; cast into—; conceive in—; create in—; delight in—; destroy—; dissipate—; exist in—; explain—; fade to —; fly away in—; foresee in—; forget—; fulfill—; glimpse in—; haunt—; hearken to—; indulge in—; interpret—; lose in—; nurse—; pass from—; perpetuate in—;

produce—; realize—; rule—s; shake off—; shatter—; sink into—; slumber in—; spin —; suffer in—; transform—; understand—; wander in—; —betokens; —crumbles; —disturbs; —flees; —flowers; —foretells; —haunts; —overpowers; —overshadows; —presages; —prophesies; —puzzles; —reveals; —signifies; —startles; —terrifies; —torments; —troubles; —warns.

(See illusion, reverie, fancy, fantasy, hallucination, vision.)

DREAM (v)
adverbs
unchastely; delectably; romantically; splendidly; confusedly; fondly; contentedly; ambitiously; amusingly; astonishingly; blissfully; dazzlingly; deliciously; deliriously; disconnectedly; drowsily; distressingly; dreadfully; ecstatically; emptily; evilly; exquisitely; extravagantly; exuberantly; fabulously; fanatically; fancifully; fleetingly; gloomily; gorgeously; grotesquely; horribly; inspiringly; interminably; maddeningly; magnificently; oppressively; pensively; perpetually; persistently; picturesquely; poetically; prophetically; ridiculously; romantically; senselessly; sensually; significantly; vividly; waveringly; zestfully; deliriously.

(See fancy, imagine.)

DREAMER
adjectives
egotistic; inefficient; preposterous; imaginative; languishing; impractical; hair-splitting; drowsy; pathetic; soppy; deep; blissful; solitary; delirious; superstitious; utopian; stony.

DREAMY
adverbs
languidly; somnolently; lazily; delightfully; terribly; wonderfully; slightly; deliciously; comfortably; cosily; amazingly; amusingly; inattentively; carelessly; abstractedly; beatifically; boyishly; constantly; irritatingly; naturally; habitually; inherently; provokingly; wistfully; wickedly; vaguely; yearningly; longingly; sweetly; strangely; tenderly; uneasily; thoughtlessly; sleepily; quaintly; remarkably; restlessly; perpetually; crazily; deeply; divinely; ecstatically; extraordinarily; fancifully; fantastically; foolishly; girlishly; gloriously; hatefully; idly; interminably; pensively.

adjectives
mute; funereal; cacophonous; soporific; appalling; blank.

DREGS

adjectives
wretched; bitterest; painful; basest; final; bottom; last.

DRENCH (v)

adverbs
instantaneously; entirely; thoroughly; fully; fatally; refreshingly; repeatedly.
(See flood, overflow.)

DRESS

adjectives
fetching; charming; daring; motley; gay; luxurious; trim; exquisite; gorgeous; delicious; evening; sky-blue; conventional; simple; starched; stiff; immaculate; adorable; homely; conspicuous; sophisticated; gauzy; filmy; gleaming; dishevelled; faded; dirty; frumpy; torn; crumpled; rumpled; flecked; queer; shabby; tattered; muslin; voile; serge; bridal; ostentatious; proper; irreproachable; azure; alpaca; holiday; low-necked; traveling; brocade; silk; hand-embroidered; ceremonial; wedding; picturesque; metal; native; turquoise; satin; fringed; beaded; buckskin; fluttering; flowing; insufficient; favorite; voluminous; old-style; detailed; antediluvian; unpretending; flaunting; shaggy; scant; plain; sumptuous; tight-fitting; sober; decorous; splendid; fantastical; ecclesiastical; airy; clean; yellow; fresh; somber; different; good-looking; extraordinary; school-girlish; flowered; varicolored; trailing; made-over; soft; sheer; identical; suitable; frivolous; flame; nondescript; gaudy; dazzling; cute; vivid; wearable; outlandish; martial; orchestral; distinctive; well-made; exceptional; fashionable; tinted; gala; lively; rich; basic; bloody; negligent; obsolete; impeccable; tailored; elegant; romantic; loose; glittering; quaint; rainy day; ragged; olive-green; outdoor; red; tulle; ballerina; becoming; masculine; fitted; boyish; convenient; hideous; fleshly; enchanting; rustic; indecent; shiny; wretched; flattering; versatile; foppish; manly; similar; alluring; gingham; incomparable.

verbs
adorn—; ban—; complete—; delight in—; don—; fancy—; fray—; gather—es; hem—; iron—; long for—; pleat—; shorten—;

stitch—; straighten—; —befits; —clings; —rustles.
(See apparel, attire, gown, frock, clothing.)

DRESS (v)

adverbs
sparsely; impecuniously; exquisitely; ravishingly; punctiliously; fastidiously; extravagantly; flamboyantly; garishly; gaudily; flashily; uninvitingly; smartly; opulently; alluringly; superfluously; tastefully; picturesquely; gorgeously; expensively; impeccably; conservatively; fashionably; resplendently; somberly; foppishly; fantastically; drably; identically; ostentatiously; modestly; primitively; brilliantly; scrupulously; fetchingly; daringly; trimly; immaculately; dishevelledly; ceremonially; ecclesiastically; nondescriptly; distinctively; martially; obsoletely; negligently; rustically; shabbily; gallantly.
(See garb, attire, array.)

DRESSER

adjectives
consummate; flashy; top-notch.

DRESSING

adjectives
elaborate; court; surgical; decongestive; somber; passionate; undisciplined; artificial.

verbs
admire—; apply—; bedeck in—; change—; compliment—; complete—; concoct—; eat with—; occupy with—; prepare—; scrutinize—; serve with—; signal for—; soak through—; soil—; tear off—; wear—; —appeals; —eases; —preserves.

DRESSMAKER

adjectives
domestic; fashionable.

DRIFT

adjectives
pearly; scudding; glacial; pallid; irresistible; wind-swept; fallacious; wordy; imaginative; social; passing; intended; amoral; steaming; feathery; powdery; blinding; treacherous.

DRIFT (v)

adverbs
delightfully; quietly; naturally; casually; waywardly; lazily; smoothly; unconscious-

ly; hopelessly; tranquilly; alternately; irresistibly; indecisively; purposelessly; scuddingly; glacially; fallaciously; blindly.
(See wander, deviate.)

DRIFTER

adjectives
shiftless; disgruntled; utter.

DRIFTWOOD

adjectives
dancing; scattered.

DRILL

adjectives
arduous; painful; sword; emergency; stiff; dusty; grammatical.

DRILL
(*instrument*)

verbs
attach—; man—; power—; sharpen—; sink —; yield to—; —beats out; —bores; —forces; —grinds; —plunges into; —strikes; —uncovers.
(See tool, machine.)

DRINK

adjectives
refreshing; useful; stimulating; seductive; sleepy; sparkling; zestful; hearty; robust; mellow; keen-tasting; acidulous; exhilarating; cooling; thirst-quenching; superb; delicate; delicious; appetizing; nutritious; soothing; innocuous; long-deferred; effervescent; frosty; fermented; hot; heady; tinkling; fiery; stiff; repulsive; steaming; choice; soft; wholesome; excellent; restorative; limpid.

verbs
abandon—; adulterate—; cool—; derive—from; err through—; ferment—; gulp—; ice—; indulge in—; offer—; rage with—; reek of—; regale with—; serve—; sour—; stagger with—; swallow—; thirst for—; —affects; —appeals; —assuages; —debauches; —depraves; —enslaves; —exhilarates; —intoxicates; —nourishes; —quenches; —refreshes; —satiates; —stimulates; —transforms; reel with—.
(See liquid, beverage, liquor, draught.)

DRINK (*v*)

adverbs
abstemiously; excessively; ravenously; plentifully; vilely; greedily; intemperately; copiously; thirstily; systematically; deeply; convivially; bestially; insatiably; inconsolably; loyally; deliberately; injudiciously.
(See sip, imbibe.)

DRINKER

adjectives
lusty; confirmed; chronic; mean; deadly; fat; unforgivable; suspicious; intemperate; unhealthy; inured; obstinate; problem.

DRINKING

adjectives
conspicuous; hard; excessive; copious; free; easy; constant; injudicious.

DRIP (*v*)

adverbs
monotonously; drearily; steadily; ceaselessly; intermittently; maddeningly; torturingly.
(See drop, fall.)

DRIVE
(*campaign*)

adjectives
(See campaign.)

verbs
abandon—; abate—; captain—; conduct—; deadlock—; forsake—; hail—; inaugurate —; join—; lash into—; launch—; map out —; organize—; stage—; wage.
(See campaign, effort.)

DRIVE
(*general*)

adjectives
fashionable; beautiful; urban; weed-grown; gravel; jolting; scenic; cliff-skirting; magnificent; wood; curving; public; leaf-strewn; coquina; steep; winding; fatal; monster; determined; concentrated; concerted; organizational; solitary; conclusive; oppressive; phenomenal.

DRIVE
(*road*)

adjectives
(See road.)

verbs
amble along—; approach—; bar—; choke —; circle—; clear—; conceal—; crowd—; direct to—; emerge from—; enter—; follow —; gallop along—; hedge—; meet in—; park in—; patrol—; ramble along—; roll

along—; shout from—; skirt—; widen—; zoom into—; —beckons; —circles; —flanks; —winds; —zigzags.
(See road, avenue.)

DRIVE (v)
adverbs
ridiculously; irresponsibly; oppressively; tirelessly; tensely; erratically; heedlessly; blithely; electrically; masterfully; involuntarily; cautiously; leisurely; steadily; briskly; simultaneously; helplessly; tumultuously; precipitately; grimly; drunkenly; ineptly; furiously; irresistibly; contemptuously.
(See impel, propel.)

DRIVEL
adjectives
maudlin; meaningless; puerile; sentimental.

DRIVER
adjectives
addlebrained; grim; recumbent; cruel-visaged; skilled; trusted; insolent; sweating; wretched; reckless; superb; acrobatic; benumbed; drunken; inept; unlicensed.

verbs
apprehend—; blame—; convict—; direct—; employ—; fine—; hire—; jail—; license—; pay—; request—; summon—; tip—; trust —; —charges; —compels; —complies; — hails; —halts; —signals; —urges; arrest—.
(See engineer, operator.)

DRIZZLE
adverbs
driving; steaming; slow; spiritless; early-morning; fine; thick; cold; chill; falling.

DROLL
adverbs
entertainingly; laughably; naturally; racially; endlessly; remarkably; quaintly; oddly; deliciously; marvellously; piquantly; robustly; whimsically; fancifully; fantastically; grotesquely; genially; jeeringly; good-naturedly; spontaneously; chattily; sardonically; delightfully; coarsely; quietly; irrepressibly; irresistibly; playfully; unaccountably; inexhaustibly; effervescently; waggishly; facetiously; outlandishly.

DROLLERY
adjectives
broad; absurd.

DROMEDARY
adjectives
helmless; patient.

DRONE
adjectives
sonorous; teasing; supine; liturgic; stingless; luxurious.

DRONE (v)
adverbs
mechanically; somnolently; sonorously; monotonously; teasingly; maddeningly; dully; stupidly.
(See sound, idle.)

DRONING
adverbs
wearily; endlessly; prosaically; academically; pretentiously; incessantly; languidly; indifferently; leisurely; tiresomely; monotonously; intolerably; insufferably; unbearably; maddeningly; eternally.

DROOP
adjectives
discouraged; affectionate; pensive; pathetic; childish; weary; dissatisfied.

DROOP (v)
adverbs
gloomily; mournfully; cheerlessly; pathetically; languidly; dejectedly; alarmingly; tenderly; visibly; sleepily; pensively; wearily; tremulously.
(See fade, faint.)

DROP
(fall)
adjectives
sickening; sheer.

DROP
(liquid)
adjectives
minute; needle-like; pearly; crystal; myriad (pl); ambrosial; beady; glittering; blistering; infinitesimal; foolish; fresh; morning; congealed; twinkling; priceless; falling; tearful; insolent; bitterest; contiguous; bitter; ruddy; mournful; burning.

verbs
absorb—; add—; administer—; dispense —s; distil in—s; draw off—; drink—; dry —s; exude—; fall in—s; form—; give off —s; instill—s; mix with—s; moisten with —s; prepare—; save—; shed—; shower—; spill—; squeeze—; sweat—; wipe away—s;

—s appear; —s dampen; —s descend; — evaporates; —glitters; —issues from; —s stream from; —wets.
(See moisture.)

DROP (v)
adverbs
miraculously; swiftly; quietly; carelessly; listlessly; gently; significantly; tearfully; alarmingly; methodically; mournfully; lazily; heavily.
(See fall.)

DROPSY
adjectives
(See disease.)

verbs
affect with—; afflict with—; aggravate—; cure—; fall into—; incur—; relieve—; suffer from—; swell with—; treat for—; —appears; —arises; —destroys; —enlarges; —inflates; —overcharges; —pains.
(See disease.)

DROSS
adjectives
(See scum.)

verbs
allow for—; bloat with—; convert from—; dissolve into—; give off—; heap—; leave —; mass—; mix with—; mound—; purge of—; refine—; separate—; scum—; skim off—; —detracts; —floats; —remains.
(See impurity, waste, scum.)

DROUGHT
adjectives
devilish; burning; severe; prolonged; unparalleled; unprecedented; insatiate; scorching; extensive; continued; stagnant; extreme.

verbs
endure—; expose to—; flee—; prepare for —; prevent—; relieve—; subject to—; succumb to—; suffer from—; —burns; —continues; —descends; —destroys; —dries; — grips; —parches; —ravages; —ruins; — scorches; —sears.
(See heat.)

DROVE
adjectives
immense; countless.

DROWNING
verbs
avoid—; bewail—; escape—; guard against —; mark—; rescue from—; —bereaves; —takes its toll.

DROWSE (v)
adverbs
sorrowfully; deliciously; lazily; wearily; carelessly; comfortably; continually.
(See sleep.)

DROWSINESS
adjectives
overwhelming; overpowering; delicious; petulant; slight; bored; morbid.

DROWSY
adverbs
irresistibly; pleasantly; dully; deliciously; overwhelmingly; heavily; comfortably; cosily; warmly; fortunately; suddenly; fitfully; uncomfortably; inconveniently; overpoweringly; fatally; quietly; tranquilly; quietly; restfully; peacefully; drunkenly; pleasingly; mysteriously; startlingly; alarmingly; feverishly; hypnotically; dangerously; constantly; languorously; gradually; imperceptibly; idly; inertly; torpidly; lumpishly; dreamily; wearily.

DRUBBING
adjectives
(See beating.)

verbs
administer—; deserve—; earn—; expect—; impose—; inflict—; merit—; protect from—; punish with—; render—; scream under—; suffer—; threaten with—; undergo—; yield to—; —benefits; —cures.
(See beating.)

DRUDGE
adjectives
weary; household; casual; incessant; faithful; cautious; miserable; sickly; ordinary; domestic.

DRUDGE (v)
adverbs
monotonously; wearily; casually; incessantly; faithfully; miserably; domestically; deadeningly; depressingly; ceaselessly; degradingly; tediously; mechanically; unremittingly; grievously; unendingly; commercially.
(See work, labor.)

adjectives

tiresome; deadening; depressing; ceaseless; degrading; low; tedious; mechanical; grievous; unremitting; severest; formal; old-time; unending; initial; youthful; mercenary; pretty.

verbs

charge—to; condemn—; decline—; detail to—; earn by—; employ for—; expose to—; fade under—; fall into—; flee—; heap—upon; impose—upon; perform—; punish with—; put to—; release from—; relieve —; require—; subject to—; toil in—; —chokes; —wearies; —wears.

(See toil, work, labor.)

DRUG

adjectives

opiate; antisyphilitic; spicy; ancient; various (pl); somniferous; impotent; fatal; injurious; valuable; convenient; officinal; nerve-exciting; deleterious; evil-smelling; subtle; incompatible; nauseous; diluted; oonoxious; illicit; habit-forming; powerful; futile; sleep-inducing; insidious; pernicious; deadly.

verbs

addict to—; administer—; apply—; diminish—; distribute—; employ—; inhale—; label—; peddle—; prescribe—; purvey—; recommend—; rely on—; saturate with—; smuggle in—; swallow—; traffic in—; treat with—; turn to—; —affects; —aids; —allays; —alleviates; —antidotes; —controls; —heals; —induces; —poisons; —purges; —scours; inject—.

(See narcotic, poison, potion.)

DRUGGED

adverbs

disgustingly; hopelessly; pleasantly; overwhelmingly; heavily; comfortably; overpoweringly; fatally; mysteriously; startlingly; shockingly; alarmingly; dangerously; languorously; gradually; imperceptibly; inertly; dreamily; injuriously; subtly; insidiously; wickedly; inhumanly; habitually; incidentally; accidentally; deliberately; cruelly.

DRUM

adjectives

deafening; rolling; cask-like; sullen; insistent; furious; sardonic; deep-throated; bellowing; exploding; jarring; perpetual; droning; boisterous; revolving; muffled; recruiting; thumping; unbraced; churlish; distant; weird; rattling; repeating; monotonous.

verbs

belabor—; hearken to—; muffle—; rattle—; sound—; strike up—; thump—; —beats; —booms; —murmurs; —rolls; —stirs; —thunders; —warns; —welcomes.

DRUM (v)

adverbs

fretfully; vigorously; deafeningly; sullenly; insistently; furiously; jarringly; perpetually; droningly; muffledly; thumpingly; weirdly; monotonously.

(See beat, pound.)

DRUMBEAT

adjectives

furious; rapid; swift; staccato; far-off.

DRUMSTICK

verbs

accept—; approve of—; beat with—; bless with—; covet—; dress—; examine—; eye —; favor—; pick at—; regard—; reject—; relish—; request—; select—; squabble for —; —appeals; —appeases; —attracts.

(See meat, food.)

DRUNK

adverbs

comically; gloriously; jovially; convivially; pleasantly; beastly; soddenly; happily; deliciously; unconsciously; heartily; vacuously; fatuously; ribaldly; funnily; smartly; deeply; sleepily; drowsily; tragically; helplessly; hopelessly; terribly; utterly; desperately; dangerously; fantastically; grotesquely; palpably; morosely; glumly; woefully; mournfully; lovingly; ridiculously; ludicrously; lamentably; deplorably; pitifully; truculently; quarrelsomely; amiably; magnificently; obnoxiously; furiously; boisterously; outrageously; noisily; chattily; dizily.

DRUNKARD

adjectives

heavy; cursing; quarrelsome; hopeless; confirmed; amiable; uncouth; magnificent; congenital; half-stupefied; reformed; infatuated; habitual; unproductive; swinish; incorrigible; abandoned.

verbs

abhor—; apprehend—; commit—to; confine—; cure—; direct—; humor—; incense

—; lock up—; perplex—; punish—; steady —; stupefy—; treat—; —assails; —disturbs; —partakes; —raves; —reels; —revels; —shocks; —staggers; —teeters; —totters; —wavers.

DRUNKENNESS
adjectives
habitual; seasonal; babbling; intemperate; usual; perpetual; rash.

verbs
abuse in—; addict to—; chain in—; cure—; denounce—; extirpate—; feign—; frown on—; imbibe to—; overcome by—; prevent —; saturate into—; seize by—; simulate—; soak into—; treat for—; yield to—; —appalls; —destroys; —envelops; —harms.

DRY
adverbs
terribly; painfully; horribly; intolerably; unbearably; unprofitably; unproductively; treelessly; dustily; torridly; hopelessly; desperately; heartbreakingly; destructively; insupportably; feverishly; parchedly.

DRYNESS
adjectives
unhealthful; satirical; extreme; intolerable.

DUALITY
adjectives
antagonistic; apparent; incredulous; baffling; unbelievable; inescapable.

DUBIOUS
adverbs
momentarily; strangely; horribly; anxiously; painfully; oddly; ominously; curiously; embarrassingly; remarkably; terribly; openly; dreadfully; frightfully; vaguely; frankly; obscurely.

DUCK
adjectives
iridescent; gabbling.

verbs
—beats water; —dives; —quacks; —rests on the water; —wings; —whirls past; —whirs.
(See fowl, bird.)

DUCT
adjectives
non-functional; necessary; essential; much-used.

verbs
discover—; draw through—; follow—; form—; introduce—; mark—; meet—; observe—; pass through—; perfect—; retreat through—; tap—; —communicates; —contains; —conveys; —directs; —dispatches; —guides; —runs; —secretes; —transmits; —turns.
(See passage, canal, conduit, pipe, channel.)

DUE
adverbs
legally; officially; naturally; recently; inescapably; conveniently; properly; justly; fairly; rightfully; reasonably; warrantably; legitimately; indefeasibly; allowably; equitably; substantially; imperatively; morally; immediately; opportunely; unexpectedly.

DUEL
adjectives
single-handed; mortal; formidable; celebrated; straight-out; valiant; political; judicial; desperate; inevitable; fatal; violent; informal; impromptu; bloody; spectacular; protracted; farcical; grudging; grim; solemn; honor-prompted.

verbs
arrange—; challenge to—; demand—; enter —; excuse from—; fight—; practise for—; stab in—; succumb in—; vanquish in—; witness—; —acquits; —decides; —discharges; —ensues; —entrances; —scars; —settles; —tests.
(See combat, encounter.)

DUES
adjectives
ecclesiastical; ample; usual.

DUET
adjectives
lively; little; long; thrilling; sentimental.

DUGOUT
adjectives
primitive; shallow; damp; foul-smelling; wartime; protective.

DUKE
adjectives
gracious; mighty; renowned; comical; fierce; noble; worthless; compassionate; virtuous; fantastical; banished; necessitous; covetous.

adverbs

abysmally; indifferently; insensitively; stupidly; strangely; stolidly; apathetically; vacantly; vacuously; ridiculously; unnaturally; singularly; oddly; peculiarly; curiously; unaccountably; inscrutably; irritatingly; vexatiously; shockingly; callously; coldly; carelessly; hopelessly; unpardonably; inexplicably; intolerably; heavily.

DULLNESS

adjectives

mysterious; pardonable; intolerable; tired; heavy; lonely; narrow; legitimate; ungenial; unbelievable; desperate; utter; everyday; kindly; incipient; vacant.

verbs

bar—; consign to—; contemplate—; correct —; curse—; dread—; mark by—; possess —; ridicule—; shroud in—; stagnate in—; tolerate—; —bores; —castigates; —distresses; —endangers; —irks; —maddens; — overwhelms; —pervades; —provokes; — surrounds.

(See apathy.)

DUMB

adverbs

pathetically; tragically; completely; suddenly; abysmally; wondrously; amazingly; stupidly; breathlessly; surprisingly; mysteriously; unutterably; wordlessly; silently; reticently; inarticulately; voicelessly; inexplicably.

DUMPY

adverbs

ridiculously; sturdily; robustly; clumsily; ludicrously; grotesquely; strangely; oddly; peculiarly; dwarfishly; elfishly; compactly; stubbily; stockily; outlandishly; comically; tragically; curiously; unfortunately; brawnily; stalwartly; stoutly.

DUNES

adjectives

darkened; shifting; lonely; sea-cast; high; tufted; transverse; desolate; shadowy; sandy; blistering; roasting; waterless; uninhabitable.

DUNGEON

adjectives

airless; subterranean; underground; miserable; bleak; awful; villainous; pagan; priestly; gloomy.

verbs

air—; bind in—; burst—; cast into—; clap into—; commit to—; conceal in—; confine to—; doom to—; dwell in—; escape from —; fling to—; gather in—; guard—; hide in—; imprison in—; incarcerate in—; lock in—; mold in—; rescue from—; rot in—; solace in—; storm—; —harbors; —incarcerates; —reeks.

(See cell, prison, hole.)

DUPE

adjectives

confiding; fair; penitent; innocent; credulous; intended; egregious.

DUPLICATE

adjectives

original; reversed.

verbs

appear in—; deliver—; encounter—; enter —; file—; furnish—; grant—; order—; part with—; provide—; purchase—; reserve—; retain—; save—; send—; sign—; supply—; take in—; transfer—; transmit—; void—; —copies; —repeats.

(See copy, replica.)

DUPLICITY

adjectives

infinite; twofold; unconscious; unworthy; patent; obvious.

DURABILITY

adjectives

utmost; increasing.

DURATION

adjectives

blooming; indefinite; customary; variable; perpetual; uncertain; momentary; endless; irregular; probable; limitless; comprehensible.

verbs

allow for—; calculate—; depend on—; fade in—; forbid—; grant—; limit—; mark—; pass—; portion—; prepare for—; propose —; time—; —continues; —lasts; —restricts; —suffices; —terminates.

(See period, time, era.)

DUSK

adjectives

growing; premature; eternal; grateful; gathering; friendly; mournful; dolorous; rainy; wet; winter; moonlit; thickening; deepening; early; glittering; clear; whispering; soft; sweet; mellow; warm; humid; cool; softening; glimmering; green; deep; blue; moon-silvered; breathing.

verbs
diminish in—; dip in—; grope through—; haunt—; retire at—; wait for—; —clouds; —descends; —drifts in; —dulls; —gives away; —harbors; —hovers; —obscures; — reveals; —shades; —shadows; —swallows; —thickens; —treads.
(See twilight, evening, darkness.)

DUSKY
adverbs
prematurely; eternally; mournfully; thickly; softly; sweetly; deeply; dimly; inkily; sombrely; dingily; murkily; obscurely; nebulously; gloomily; glimmeringly; fragrantly; weirdly; fearfully; frightfully; pleasantly; restfully; peacefully; shadily; coolly; drearily; forlornly; desolately.

DUST
adjectives
cosmic; yellow; shining; fainting; dying; trifling; impalpable; valiant; undisturbed; shapeless; dreadful; sodden; titillating; red; desert; thick; blue; gray; heavy; blinding; oppressive; choking; stagnant; siliceous; shameful; trodden; dedicated; honored; long-committed; animate; fine; staining; unlovely; lonely; garnered; historical; rolling; scentless; murderous; material; injurious; sleeping; brown-colored; leveled; sunny; sunlit; suffering; kindred; burning; dim; scanty; feathery; illumined; senseless; slumbering; delicate; sacred; tawny; crumbling; vile; powdered; invisible; atomic; whirling; torturing; atmospheric; spiraling; hatred; stirred; gritty; smelly; filthy; parched; wayside; pervading; dissipating; mounting; precious; learned; flaming; uncontrolled; floating; undivided.

verbs
beat—; cake with—; carpet with—; clot with—; clothe in—; crumble to—; decompose into—; drag down to—; fall into—; filter—; form into—; go down in—; grovel in—; impregnate with—; issue from—; kick up—; lift from—; mar with—; mix with—; moulder in—; parch with—; reduce to—; remand to—; repose in—; return to—; roll in—; scatter—; scrape off—; scuff through—; shake off—; shower—; smite—; soil with—; spring from—; stamp

—; stir up—; trail in—; tread in—; turn to—; write in—; —beclouds; —chokes; — clings to; —creeps in; —gathers; —permeates; —settles; —shrouds; —thickens.
(See ashes, powder, rubbish, earth.)

DUST (*v*)
adverbs
furiously; animatedly; industriously; vigorously; listlessly.
(See clean, polish.)

DUSTY
adverbs
disagreeably; intolerably; parchedly; painfully; uncomfortably; impalpably; dreadfully; terribly; abominably; unbearably; heavily; blindingly; oppressively; chokingly; shamefully; vilely; grittily; hatefully; filthily; pervasively; untidily; grossly; carelessly.

DUTIFUL
adverbs
carefully; beautifully; painfully; meticulously; punctiliously; assiduously; ostentatiously; passionately; pretentiously; obviously; scrupulously; devotedly; affectionately; primly; precisely; constantly; marvellously; sternly; officiously; efficiently; terribly; actively; energetically; publicly; submissively; competently; anxiously; solicitously; respectfully; politely; courteously; austerely; diplomatically; mechanically; grimly; piously; dully; rigorously; odiously; fondly; constantly; unfailingly.

DUTY
adjectives
irksome; self-assumed; unpleasant; imperative; simple; stern; domestic; humanest; arduous; boring; differential; obnoxious; official; expedient; obvious; religious; paternal; stooping; manifold (pl); bounden; inescapable; unending; inefficient; inviolable; particular; useful; terrible; serious; wide-reaching; unloved; indispensable; colorless; ever-esteemed; active; humbler; costuming; civic; social; pedagogic; creative; vexatious; nerve-racking; constitutional; public; appropriate; disagreeable; sad; monotonous; weary; dangerous; exhausting; exacting; uncongenial; painful; respective; definite; foolish; routine; submissive; competent; obstructionary; forcible; hardest; responsible; laborious; barbarous; conjugal; onerous; anxious; sickening; perilous; special; competent; childlike;

charitable;additional; ministerial; necessary; paramount; rental; far-off; pleasurable; professorial; momentous; military;
eternal; vile; devotional; peremptory; respectful; easy; polite; generous; melan
choly; intimate; principal; filial; unforgot-
ten; imperious; eventual; matutinal; major;
discriminating; blockading; wifely; incumbent; austere; consular; immediate;
habitual; noble; irresistible; sworn; diplomatic; protective; distasteful; lowliest;
fearful; unfamiliar; mechanical; tyrannous; slothful; solemn; earthly; grim;
cursed; dull; high; pious; repugnant;
homely; harsh; unhappy; rigorous; derelict;
multifarious (pl); stern-voiced; nebulous;
odious; manifest; tripartite.

verbs

assign—; assume—; attend to—; charge
with—; comply with—; consign—to; define
—; discharge—; disengage from—; encroach on—; engross in—; fail in—; fulfill—; impose—on; inculcate—; infringe
on—; lessen—; meet—; neglect—; obey—;
perform—; perish in—; pledge to—; pursue—; relieve of—; repudiate—; restrain
by—; scrap—; shirk—; shoulder—; slacken
in—; stand firm on—; stress—; surrender
—; swerve from—; teach—; transgress—;
—allows; —binds; —embraces; —enjoins;
—impels; —inspires; —permits; —presses;
—pricks on; —slackens; —weighs.

(See responsibility, business, work, obligation. function.)

DWARF

adjectives
deformed; rickety; stirring.

verbs
employ—; engage—; harbor—; gift—with;
jeer at—; ridicule—; —antics; —busies;
—carries off; —chuckles; —climbs; —
covers; —dances; —hobbles; —hops; —
mimics; —performs; —prances; —struts.

(See animal, manikin, clown.)

DWARFED

adverbs
hopelessly; mysteriously; grotesquely; fantastically; irremediably; unhappily; unfortunately; unluckily; singularly; oddly;
strangely; queerly; sturdily; clumsily; elfishly; compactly; stockily; outlandishly;
tragically; curiously; stalwartly; stoutly;
pathetically; pitifully.

DWELL (v)

adverbs
luxuriously; languidly; pleasurably; laughingly; principally; impatiently; spaciously;
lingeringly; occasionally; affectionately;
impecuniously; inharmoniously; eternally;
gloomily; artfully; gratefully; royally; unostentatiously; sedately; uncouthly; dismally; humbly; indefinitely.

(See live, abide.)

DWELLER

adjectives
dullest; admirable; planned; distinguished.

DWELLING

adjectives
planned; steadfast; isolated; ancestral;
royal; prolonged; primitive; pretentious;
ancient; snow-enveloped; forgetful; undisturbed; clustered; rustic; unostentatious;
habitable; rapturous; odorous; sedate; time-
stained; ambitious; tranquil; dismantled;
rambling; uncouth; dismal; neglected;
blank; underground; graceful; comfortable;
humblest; stately; lovely; impressive; obscure; fabulous; patriarchal; communal;
quaint; red-tiled; lacustrine; frail; abandoned.

verbs
assign to—; choose—; confine to—; decorate—; destroy—; enter—; erect—; fire—;
flood—; grace—; lay waste—; move into—;
occupy—; preserve—; purchase—; raze—;
renovate—; restore—; retire to—; return
to—; surround—; ventilate—; —appeals;
—crumbles; —harbors; —invites; —shelters.

(See house, residence, abode.)

DWINDLE (v)

adverbs
amazingly; alarmingly; partially; insensibly; rapidly; markedly; obviously; scarcely; abruptly; logically; tragically; fatally.

(See decrease, diminish.)

DYE

adjectives
angry; synthetic; crimson; vegetable; progressive; autumnal.

DYNAMIC

adverbs
admirably; energetically; responsibly; socially; fortunately; acceptably; helpfully;
usefully; stimulatingly; interestingly; actively; progressively; commercially; powerfully; effectively; efficiently; mightily.

DYNAMITE

adjectives
potential; **swift**; powerful.

verbs
arm with—; attack with—; blast with—; charge with—; contain—; convert into—; employ—; experiment with—; fire—; ignite —; mine with—; prepare—; shell—; test —; touch off—; —blasts; —blows up; — damages; —destroys; —disrupts; —explodes; —rends; —shakes; —shatters; — threatens; —uproots; —wrecks.

(See explosive, powder.)

DYNAMO

adjectives
(See motor.)

verbs
acquaint with—; employ—; examine—; exhibit—; operate—; provide—; ruin—;

study—; —aids; —converts; —deposits; —excites; —generates; —induces; —purrs; —revolves; —rotates; —supplies; —transforms.

(See machine, generator, motor.)

DYNASTY

adjectives
reigning; unoffending; remote; trembling; continuous; unbroken; imperial; semifeudal.

verbs
begin—; carry on—; cut short—; denounce —; found—; inaugurate—; maintain—; overthrow—; perpetuate—; rear—; —declines; —rules; —stems.

(See race, government, sovereignty.)

E

EAGER

adverbs

extremely; youthfully; girlishly; boyishly; childishly; unspeakably; inordinately; suspiciously; significantly; admirably; wonderfully; industriously; energetically; actively; alarmingly; adorably; ardently; fervidly.

EAGERNESS

adjectives

apologetic; utmost; excessive; passionate; extraordinary; manifest; restrained; childish; youthful; intelligent; dashing; sheer; liberal; hasty; hawk-eyed; feverish; fatal; diffident; fresh.

verbs

burn with—; conceal—; cure of—; display —; impart—; incite—; instil—; intensify —; moderate—; possess—; pursue with—; resist—; satiate—; stimulate—; temper—; —irritates; —devours; —exasperates; —maddens; —vexes.

(See impatience, fervor, intensity, zeal, ardor, impetuosity.)

EAGLE

adjectives

ravening; screaming; conquering; stuffed; rampant; princely; soaring; immense; gilded; empty; famished; symbolical; home-building.

verbs

cage—; exalt—; shelter—; —attacks; —braves; —captures; —circles; —clasps; —cleaves sky; —climbs; —destroys; —drives home; —drops; —eyes; —falls; —floats; —hawks; —hooks; —inspires; —moults; —preys on; —robs; —sails; —screams; —sights; —signifies; —soars; —surveys; —sweeps; —swoops; —symbolizes; —terrorizes; —thieves; —watches; —wheels; —zooms.

(See bird.)

EAR

adjectives

sensual; perked; dull; deaf; dozing; treacherous; attentive; unconscious; reasonable; good; licentious; thrifty; unheeding; helpless; eager; attending; sickly; pregnant; vouchsafed; kindest; external; deafened; listless; acute; greedy; reluctant; quick; sympathetic; large; cultivated; sensitive; passionate; gentler; foreboding; practiced; tesselated; apprehensive; furry; blushing; thievish; instinctive; loathing; listening; flapping; velvet; pleased; willing; public; sweet; enthusiastic; charmed; pendulous; living; dreaming; gorgeous; lobe-shaped; bewitched; trembling; ravished; waiting; dying; married; sickly; savage; aged; favorable; idle; insensible; untutored; modest; patient; inner; general; outwearied; kissed; fortified; fancy; inquisitive; royal; expectant; shuddering; reeling; mortal; unaccustomed; thoughtful; startled; proper; uninitiated; astonished; raptured; erect; impaired; innumerable (pl); flat; ill-developed; silken; uncultivated; ample; honest; grateful; aching; middle; cupped; drooping; constant; wakeful; sealed; vexed; burning; haughty; world; unwearied; uneducated; pointed; fainting; lewd; startled; straining; close-lying; public; couchant; senseless; inaudible; sylvan; favorable; leaning; hooded; untaught; silky; delicate; close-set; dainty; fine; gracious; velvety; well-set; quick; exact; sharp; critical; appreciative; alert; keen; cocked; intent; vigilant; cabbage; flabby; cauliflower; prominent; angular; preposterous; bruised; ungladdened; thick; long-lobed; enormous; stiff; droll; outstanding; uncomprehending; unattuned; unresponsive; cynical; inhospitable; unfailing; musical; irritated; entranced; thrilled; welcoming; delighted; shell-like; modern; royal; jeweled; ringing; jaunty; aloof; gullible; frisky; unjaded; well-trained; wiggly; tweaked; pert; questioning; hopeful.

verbs

abuse—; attune—to; beat against—; bend —; block—; box—; charm—; cleanse—; cock—; crop off—; deceive—; delight—; depend on—; din into—; drain—; dull—; gain—; impart to—; incline—; insert in—; irrigate—; lend—; lodge in—; meet—; muffle—; mutilate—; prick—forward; rend —; resound in—; strike—; twitch—; weary —; whisper in—; wiggle—; —s betray; —s buzz; —s devour; —discharges; —rings; —throbs; —tingles; stuff—.

(See head, ear-drum.)

verbs

affect—; attack—; burst—; fall upon—; incise—; infect—; inflame—; injure—; meet—; perforate—; pierce—; rupture—; shatter—; split—; strike—; stun—; treat—; wound—; —admits; —pains; —protects; —vibrates.

(See membrane, ear.)

EARLY

adverbs

unusually; exceptionally; conveniently; amply; unnecessarily; remarkably; uncomfortably; unpleasantly; gloriously; appropriately; sufficiently; ridiculously; needlessly; opportunely; comfortably.

EARN (v)

adverbs

professionally; determinedly; lawfully; honestly; criminally; astoundingly; rapidly; drudgingly.

(See gain, procure.)

EARNEST

adverbs

enthusiastically; seriously; unusually; truly; zealously; fervently; ridiculously; habitually; eagerly; graciously; cordially; resolutely; desperately; tenaciously; inflexibly; unusually; extremely; gravely; solemnly; remarkably; indubitably; incredibly; emphatically; heartily; passionately; deeply.

EARNESTNESS

adjectives

simple; fixed; grave; intense; eager; conscientious; impressive; tragic; passionate; beseeching; aggressive; perpetual; burning; profound; characteristic; devout; somber; cold; honest; forgetful; dogged; taciturn; habitual; mighty; sanctified; mournful; solemn; downright; visible.

verbs

adopt—; allege—; begin with—; conduct with—; declare in—; endeavor with—; enter in—; express—; feign—; inculcate—; indicate—; instil—; pledge—; supplicate with—; touch by—; watch with—; —recommends; —secures.

(See ardor, sincerity, seriousness.)

EARNINGS

adjectives

scanty; exiguous; individual; fabulous; present; undistributed; sky-rocketed; hard-won; slender; stabilized.

verbs

attach—; bag—; bank—; collect—; curtail —; demand—; distribute—; enhance—; increase—; invest—; merit—; mortgage—; pledge—; save—; withdraw—; withhold—; —accrue; —decline; —recompense; —top.

(See wage, salary, pay.)

EAR-PHONE

verbs

adjust—; clamp on—; display—; furnish —; mislay—; pick up with—; require—; seek—; speak into—; —aids; —amplifies; —assists; —benefits; —clarifies; —communicates; —relieves; —rescues.

EARTH

adjectives

social; fructifying; plashy; stony; melancholy; calcareous; sunburned; verdant; daedal; thirsty; kindly; unviolated; groaning; fragrant; porous; frozen; transformed; sullen; gloomy; arching; molten; voluble; gaping; laboring; green-girt; hostile; distraught; disembowelled; chapped; unconsidered; spherical; moist; gaunt; wounded; awakening; bare; native; spongy; gladdened; powdered; delightful; frostbound; renovated; shocked; shackled; perennial; messy; reconciling; nursing; synthetic; dull; prosaic; barren; despised; hungry; sanguine; encumbering; clodded; faithless; unawakened; arid; pendulous; easeful; wearied; sun-spangled; unyielding; virgin; mangled; filial; consecrated; turfless; frost-crisped; horrible; ancient; parched; sordid; absorbent; unmoistened; alluvial; stagnant; troubled; patient; various-mingled (pl); sinful; profiting; beleaguered; teeming; life-giving; habitable; darkened; spacious; healthy; odorous; unsinning; narrowing; menaced; lawful; burying; beauteous; faded; deep; peopled; trembling; desolate; indubitable; sleepy; bright; red; ashy; black; devastated; ordinary; shaken; fresh-turned; primeval; tenacious; widened; savage; fainting; fresh-plowed; chafed; harsh; central; pleasant; reluctant; silvery; waiting; finished; substantial; ridgy; imminent.

verbs

beautify—; blast—; bless—; bore into—; cling to—; command—; crawl upon—; create—; creep upon—; deface—; depart from —; explore—; fertilize—; gain—; grovel on—; inhabit—; inherit—; landscape—; mantle—; paw—; perish from—; plant—; plow—; pluck from—; rake—; reign on—;

replenish—; return to—; scatter over—; scorch—; scour—; sink into—; swoop to—; till—; tramp over—; trample—; veil—; wrestle with—; —abounds with; —blooms; —flowers; —heaves; —moulders; —nourishes; —quakes; —revolves; —sustains; — swallows up; —teems; —throbs; —trembles; —whirls; —renews.

(See world, globe, ground, soil, land.)

EARTHLY

adverbs
sordidly; selfishly; meanly; mercenarily; ungenerously; temperamentally; habitually; gracelessly; incredibly; basely; grossly; inconceivably.

EARTHQUAKE

adjectives
unusual; slumbering; murderous; all-devouring; disastrous; tremendous; submarine.

verbs
behold—; flee from—; record—; warn of—; —blights; —blots out; —crumbles; —destroys; —devastates; —jars; —razes; — reduces; —rends; —ruins; —rumbles; — shakes; —shatters; —subsides; —takes toll; —thunders; —topples; —wrecks.

(See tremor, shock, vibration.)

EASE

adjectives
amateur; blessed; ignoble; rakish; natural; light-hearted; tolerable; considerable; somnolent; charming; comparative; consequent; luxurious; extraordinary; miraculous; frivolous; insidious; rhythmic; dreamy; muscular; dignified; stately; material; solid; democratic; loose; astonishing; affluent; slothful; masterly; bloodless; constant; reckless; beauteous; cross-legged; disastrous; inglorious; cool; chivalric; deceptive; apparent; corrective; extreme; graceful; tranquil.

verbs
couch at—; court—; dwell in—; enhance—; enjoy—; envy—; interpose—; lack—; leap with—; live at—; loll in—; perform with—; procure with—; recline in—; rest at—; sacrifice—; seek—; spend in—; vault with—.

(See comfort, luxury.)

EASE (v)

adverbs
appreciably; greatly; partially; materially; markedly; miraculously; apparently; ostensibly; gracefully.

(See alleviate, soothe.)

EAST

adjectives
blustering; incandescent; lucid; purpling; blushing; blank; mummied; eyeless; fervid; mournful; bloodless.

EASY

adverbs
unusually; incredibly; remarkably; ridiculously; perfectly; comfortably; fairly; distinctly; definitely; naturally; conveniently; absolutely; suspiciously; unquestionably.

EAT (v)

adverbs
inordinately; leisurely; fastidiously; barbarously; enormously; bestially; heartily; regularly; hurriedly; swiftly; wolfishly; insufficiently; ravenously; incontinently; excessively; sparingly; plentifully; noisily; irrevocably; surreptitiously; swinishly; gluttonously.

(See consume, devour.)

EATABLE

adverbs
safely; deliciously; lusciously; definitely; perfectly; conveniently; unquestionably; wholesomely; avowedly; warrantably; assuredly; properly.

EATING

adjectives
mass; impudent.

verbs
abstain from—; coax into—; consider—; consume in—; exhaust by—; forbid—; reduce—; refrain from—; stimulate—; —appeases; —benefits; —bolsters; —encourages; —exhilarates; —fattens; —nourishes; —produces; —reassures; —revives; —satiates.

(See food, feeding.)

EAVES

adjectives
overhanging; lofty; dripping; gargoyled; sheltering.

adjectives
reduced; constant; alternate.

adverbs
constantly; alternately; markedly; noticeably; scarcely; partially; wholly; entirely; slowly; tragically; fatally; rapidly.
(See flow, 'move.)

adjectives
grizzled; flowing.

adverbs
effervescently; gushingly; violently; hysterically; outrageously; turbulently; riotously; obstreperously; naturally; excitedly; stormily; ungovernably; uncontrollably; terribly; highly.

adjectives
youthful; sulphurous; trifling; present.

adjectives
genial; amazing.

adverbs
highly; outlandishly; ostentatiously; fantastically; oddly; offensively; incurably; proudly; flagrantly; peculiarly; inexplicably; inscrutably; temperamentally; egotistically; exasperatingly; comically; pitiably; unfortunately; abnormally; wantonly; singularly; unaccountably; extravagantly; insanely; capriciously; whimsically; uncomfortably; unusually.

adjectives
gentle; hopeless; individual; amiable; violent; drunken; troublesome; benevolent; ghastly; moderate; asinine.

verbs
acquire—; adopt—; affect—; allow—; attribute to—; betray—; blame on—; condemn—; develop—; feign—; govern—; laugh at—; mimic—; overlook—; palliate —; pardon—; produce—; ridicule—; sense —; stray into—; tolerate—; —amuses; —offends; —perplexes.
(See oddity, idiosyncrasy.)

adverbs
highly; completely; sacredly; judicially; lawfully; legally; reverently; strictly; soundly; literally; evangelically; faithfully; positively; infallibly; irrefutably; dogmatically; authoritatively; doctrinally; authentically; officiously; reverently; fanatically; deeply; devoutly.

adjectives
death-groan; congenial; sonorous; eternal; faint; stunning; distorted; awaking; heartbreaking; softened; jovial; dreary; drumming; startling; sullen; melodious; unimpressive; woodland; respectable; evasive; sparse; prophetic; sharp; metallic; trashy; reverberating; resonant; hovering; wearisome; laughing; ringing; deep-resounding; high; multiplied; somnolent; battling; vibrant; obedient; mad; bellowing; wheezing; wild; tragic; mocking; haunting; silvery; reminiscent; trembling; slumbering.

verbs
evoke—; listen for—; prolong—; silence—; stir—; voice—; —answers; —breaks; — dies away; —fades; —hurls back; —repeats; —resounds; —returns; —reverberates; —rings; —roars; —shrills; —sings out.
(See sound, voice.)

adverbs
buoyantly; contemptuously; piously; responsively; cheerily; ominously; dubiously; joyously; anxiously; heartily; falteringly; stupidly; congenially; sonorously; faintly; heartbreakingly; jovially; drearily; sullenly; melodiously; evasively; prophetically; metallically; reverberatingly; wearisomely; ringingly; vibrantly; obediently; hauntingly; mockingly; reminiscently; tremblingly.
(See reverberate, resound.)

adjectives
mysterious; swift; dismal; temporary; absolute; ominous.

verbs
identify—; observe—; predict—; record—; study—; suffer—; throw into—; —blinds; —cloaks; —clouds; —darkens; —deprives; —dims; —extinguishes; —hides; —intercepts; —intervenes; —obscures; —occurs; —overcasts; —screens; —shadows.
(See darkness.)

ECLIPSE (v)

adverbs

exultantly; mysteriously; swiftly; dismally; temporarily; absolutely; ominously; skillfully; treacherously; eventually; partially; entirely; scarcely; finally; triumphantly.

(See surpass, excel.)

ECONOMICAL

adverbs

properly; methodically; systematically; carefully; frugally; stingingly; successfully; highly; overly; habitually; admirably; utterly; wonderfully; remarkably; pitifully; practically; shrewdly; thriftily; parsimoniously; selfishly; unnecessarily; shabbily; ungenerously; sordidly; miserably; necessarily; wisely; cheerfully; churlishly.

ECONOMICS

verbs

affect—; alter—; apply—; attack—; control—; deal with—; determine—; devote to—; employ—; experiment with—; govern —; improve—; manage by—; observe—; regulate—; school in—; specialize in—; understand—; —assumes; —discerns; —flourishes; —regards; —serves.

(See science.)

ECONOMIST

adjectives

professional; orthodox; political; academic.

ECONOMY

adjectives

vulnerable; rugged; centralized; reasonable; regimental; actual; domestic; scrupulous; excessive; benign; solitary; desperate; smooth-running; careful; ultimate; numerous (pl); political; drastic; niggardly; expensive; operating; utmost; satisfying; random; ready; careful; capitalistic; animal; internal; democratic; rigid; spiritual; unequalled; household; strictest; outstanding; supernatural; gasoline; false; agricultural; physical.

verbs

betray—; decree—; denounce—; disparage —; effect—; encourage—; favor—; hail—; ignore—; instil—; maintain—; necessitate —; observe—; plan—; practise—; promote—; require—; sacrifice—; systemize—; tighten—; undertake—s; —assures; —preserves; —saves.

(See management, frugality, thrift.)

ECSTASY

adjectives

sheer; delicate; mounting; artistic; tingling; silent; trembling; insane; voluble; bedazzled; boundless; untaught; brainless; anguished; mingled; delicious; spiritual; quiet; simulated; inexpressible; wonderful; unquestioned; consuming; momentary; wonderful; gentle; heaven-breathed; stolen; spontaneous; restless; modern; awed; undivided.

verbs

blast—; blunt—; burst into—; emerge from —; enthrall in—; experience—; flow in—; flutter in—; glow with—; increase—; indulge in—; inspire—; quiver with—; recall in—; respond to—; swoon in—; throw into —; tingle in—; transport into—; tremble with—; wake to—; —dissolves; —excites; —flushes; —pervades; —pulsates; —rules; —stirs.

(See bliss, happiness, delight, rapture, joy, enthusiasm.)

ECSTATIC

adverbs

rapturously; happily; unrestrainedly; blissfully; youthfully; blessedly; delightfully; extravagantly; preposterously; romantically; enthusiastically; fervently; eagerly; passionately; deeply; thrillingly; breathlessly; glowingly; hysterically; significantly; obviously; charmingly; ravishingly.

ECZEMA

verbs

exude from—; pick at—; rub—; salve—; suffer from—; treat—; x-ray—; —burns; —cracks; —discharges; —excretes; —inflames; —irritates; —itches; —pains; —smarts; —spreads; —stings; —tingles; —torments.

(See disease.)

EDDY

adjectives

whirling; murmuring; brilliant; wild; twisting; nervous; blue; boiling; curled; dimpling.

EDDY (v)

adverbs

irresistibly; whirlingly; murmuringly; wildly; twistingly; boilingly; dimplingly; ceaselessly; monotonously; dangerously; rapidly; sickeningly.

(See whirl, swirl.)

adjectives

shadowed; sharpened; upturned; natural; outermost; foaming; thin; extremest; trembling; distinctive; cord; jutting; keen; cruel; marshy; raveled; cutting; frayed; frowsy; smooth-quarried; relentless; perilous.

verbs

bevel—; blunt—; crimp—; double—; drive to—; dull—; escape—; file—; flounder on—; heave over—; round—; set on—; sharpen—; slip from—; smite with—; smooth—.

(See border, verge, boundary.)

EDIBLE

adverbs

safely; undeniably; deliciously; lusciously; wholesomely; healthfully; delightfully; warrantably; refreshingly; daintily; agreeably; palatably; pleasantly; acceptably; appetizingly; definitely; highly.

EDICT

adjectives

late; strict; fearful; imperial; royal.

verbs

decry—; denounce—; enforce—; frame—; fulfill—; impose—; infringe on—; introduce —; invalidate—; issue—; legalize—; nullify—; proclaim—; revoke—; spurn—; support—; —bans; —corrects; —declares; —reforms; —stands; —subjugates.

(See decree, mandate, proclamation, ordinance.)

EDIFICATION

verbs

break down—; contribute to—; contrive—; demolish—; destroy—; dismantle—; dispense—; inspire—; justify—; profane—; promote—; prompt—; provide—; ravage—; ruin—; scoff at—; deserve—.

(See enlightenment, education, instruction, improvement.)

EDIFICE

adjectives

gaunt; holy; ramshackle; massive; timeworn; solid; sumptuous; humble; sacred; ghostly; enchanted; shattered; spiritual; historic; august; vast; splendid; stately; public; imposing; spacious; social; heathen; elaborate; ecclesiastical.

verbs

convert—; demolish—; destroy—; dismantle —; erect—; modernize—; profane—; raise —; ravage—; raze—; renovate—; ruin—; —collapses; —crumbles; —moulders; —topples.

(See building, structure, house.)

EDIT (v)

adverbs

skillfully; artfully; exquisitely; originally; hastily; voluminously; sympathetically; crudely.

(See prepare, check.)

EDITION

adjectives

revised; voluminous; choice; camouflaged; pirated; limited; reprint; enormous; successive (pl); telescoped; exquisite; lavish; rare; illustrated; muggier; original; ornamented; annotated; abridged; cherished; privately-printed.

verbs

amend—; annotate—; arrange into—; change—; collect—s; conceive—; copyright —; correct—; criticize—; examine—; exhaust—; favor—; furnish—; illustrate—; issue—; mend—; order—; prepare—; print —; publish—; quote from—; revise—; —abounds with; —corrects; —informs; —surpasses.

(See issue, work, book, publication, copy.)

EDITOR

adjectives

vituperative; country; important; cable-desk; guileless; pugnacious.

verbs

consult—; employ—; —arranges; —conceives; —condemns; —conducts; —criticizes; —describes; —details; —exposes; —expunges; —inserts; —manages; —pens; —plans; —prepares; —publishes; —refuses; —relates; —revises; —scorns; —selects; —suggests; —supervises.

(See journalist, publisher.)

EDITORIAL

adjectives

conspicuous; calumnious; rousing; occasional; learned; rattling; fearless.

verbs

censor—; commend—; compose—; contribute—; criticize—; grind out—; popularize —; prepare—; revise—; set up—; venture

—; word—; —embarrasses; —exonerates; —exposes; —insinuates; —intimates; —recounts; —relates; —shocks; —suggests; —unloads.

(See article, writing.)

adverbs

reliably; officially; responsibly; ridiculously; sagely; egotistically; unquestionably; notoriously; flatteringly; astutely; adroitly; obviously.

EDITORIALIZE (v)

adverbs

?latedly; pompously; calumniously; learnedly; fearlessly; ponderously; fanatically; oracularly; languidly; pathetically.

(See write, talk.)

EDUCATE (v)

adverbs

simultaneously; properly; insensibly; imperfectly; adequately; superficially; genteelly; rigorously; bookishly; progressively; classically; technically; intensively; practically; liberally; musically; undisciplinedly; systematically; formally; artistically; legitimately; aesthetically; religiously; snobbishly; methodically; scholastically; primitively; physically; idealistically; vocationally; competently.

(See instruct, teach.)

EDUCATION

adjectives

bookish; purposive; self-acquired; intellectual; progressive; priggish; aimless; technical; elementary; spiritual; mass; classical; advanced; intensive; practical; inevitable; meager; imperfect; precarious; previous; liberal; musical; systematic; military; evolutionary; formal; invigorating; confused; undisciplined; barren; wasteful; superficial; artistic; legitimate; adequate; aesthetic; wider; practicable; far-reaching; preparatory; humane; specific; religious; methodical; labored; compulsory; scholastic; primitive; interior; physical; positive; idealistic; vocational; regular; rudimentary; competent.

verbs

achieve—; broaden—; deny—; dominate—; enforce—; foster—; furnish—; glean—; influence—; laud—; liberalize—; neglect —; promote—; retard—; —biases; —broadens; —cultivates; —develops; —enlightens; —forms; —spreads.

(See culture, enlightenment, development, training.)

EDUCATIONAL

adverbs

highly; unusually; inconceivably; uncommonly; delightfully; alarmingly; formidably; distressingly; monotonously; agreeably; helpfully; tiresomely; necessarily; advantageously; acceptably; slightly.

EERIE

adverbs

uncommonly; uncannily; supernaturally; dreadfully; terribly; unusually; singularly; oddly; curiously; queerly; unnaturally; inexplicably; remarkably; frightfully; appallingly; gruesomely; grotesquely; undeniably.

EFFACE (v)

adverbs

rapidly; gradually; partially; entirely; totally.

(See obliterate, cancel.)

EFFECT

adjectives

similar; profound; influential; immediate; harmonious; beneficent; picturesque; pernicious; reactionary; ventriloquial; verbal; visible; fleeting; nutritive; continuous; external; displeasing; fearful; biologic; adverse; soothing; equal; singular; enormous; contractile; tragic; radiant; emotional; designed; salutary; useful; sinking; palpable; excellent; demoralizing; perceptible; social; festive; elegant; stimulating; smooth; modern; ultimate; tonic; fatal; harmful; cumulative; spacious; stunning; disastrous; probable; deterrent; dying-duck; powerful; atmospheric; characteristic; putrefactive; indirect; heavenly; grotto; depressing; electrical; sustained; pronounced; hypnotic; particular; recreational; prejudicial; recurrent; stabbing; continuous; important; enervating; naturalistic; exhilarating; varied; striking; outdoor; lamplight; remote; psychological; honest; combined; dreadful; decisive; charming; fair; gabardine; rejuvenating; theatrical; plaster; gravitating; dramatic; wondrous; devastating; incredible; summary; injurious; impressive; permanent; secondary; enchanting; artistic; malevolent; pathetic; accumulating; sedative; rare; extrinsic; detrimental; contrary; harmonic; metrical; rhythmical; astringent; prismatic; incomparable; startling; hardening; deleterious; decorative; supreme; paralyzing; bewildering; debasing; tranquillizing; luminous; strange; uncanny; stiffening; mechanical; striped; harsh; moral; architectural; broadening;

finished; unfailing; entrancing; orchestral; inspired; instantaneous; vivid; stormy; considerable; alkalizing; deteriorating; similar; preternatural; appreciable; marvellous; outrageous; racial; metrical; subversive; chromatic; maleficent; invigorating; ordinary; pyramidical; noble; depressing; thrilling; noticeable; rude; sinister; intended; massed; bracing; detectable; geophysical; brilliant; persuasive; enduring; distinguished; terrestrial; healthful; reciprocal; dampening; unfortunate; oratorical; regulating; tremendous; solemn; awful; polyphonic; unreal; unifying; distinctive; exotic; practical; flowered; composite; desired; invigorating; lasting; pompous; preservative; curative; magical; peculiar; unusual; textural; gratifying; subsequent; smartest; manifested; propitious; astounding; touching; suave; inevitable; twilight; dynamical; preponderant; secular; baneful; momentary; prized; destructive; dignified; perishing; thermometric; tragic; marked; binding; bizarre; half-veiled; required; scanty; baleful; exquisite; minute; kaleidoscopic; resultant; disintegrating; powerful; rhetorical; possible; absurd; mere; healing; imposing; tingling; fructifying; crushing; organ; luxurious; correspondent; errant; surprising; subtle; delicate; legitimate; acoustical; ill; variegated (pl); narcotic; nugatory; elevating; comic; deadly; sculptural; outward; happy; calamitous.

verbs

accentuate—; achieve—; analyze—; attain —; banish—; comprehend—; conceive—; counteract—; curse—; demonstrate—; destroy—; disturb—; elicit—; escape—; evaluate—; exercise—; exert—; gauge—; heighten—; ignore—; lessen—; mar—; mark—; match—; minimize—; mitigate—; neutralize—; notice—; observe—; obviate —; occasion—; offset—; predict—; prevent—; recapture—; record—; rehearse—; remove—; rob of—; speculate on—; strive for—; suffer from—; time—; trace—; visualize—; weaken—; witness—; —endures; —persists; —wears off.

(See result, realization, end, aim.)

EFFECT (v)

adverbs

speedily; insidiously; skillfully; advantageously; simultaneously; satisfactorily; unconsciously; tremendously; promptly; periodically; profoundly; perniciously; beneficently; externally; fearfully; adversely; soothingly; singularly; emotionally; percep-

tibly; demoralizingly; ultimately; fatally; harmfully; powerfully; characteristically; recurrently; continuously; remotely; decisively; theatrically; devastatingly; incredibly; injuriously; permanently; malevolently; pathetically; supremely; bewilderingly; debasingly; mechanically; unfailingly; racially; depressingly; curatively; gratifyingly; propitiously; dynamically; subtly; comically; calamitously.

(See accomplish, achieve.)

EFFECTIVE

adverbs

satisfactorily; highly; pleasantly; undeniably; profoundly; remarkably; sufficiently; powerfully; extremely; adequately; serviceably; practically; unusually; tremendously; admittedly.

EFFECTIVENESS

adjectives

theatric; amazing; histrionic; architectural; outstanding; dramatic; general; pictorial; decorative; haphazard; marvelous; maximum.

verbs

attain—; attend with—; augment—; direct with—; dispose with—; employ—; execute with—; follow with—; function with—; impair—; increase—; mar—; operate with —; prevent—; produce—; pursue with—; treat with—; weaken—; —accomplishes; — comforts; —decides; —produces; —rectifies; —renders.

(See efficiency, power.)

EFFECTUAL

adverbs

thoroughly; consummately; elaborately; perfectly; finally; immediately; felicitously; fortunately; highly; completely; absolutely; altogether; utterly; surprisingly.

EFFEMINATE

adverbs

disgustingly; unfortunately; unpleasantly; disagreeably; pitiably; fearfully; weakly; nervously; softly; languidly; horribly; extremely; timidly; infirmly; remarkably; vexatiously.

EFFERVESCENT

adverbs

highly; unusually; delightfully; amusingly; sparklingly; frothily; ebulliently; energetically; enthusiastically; excitedly; irrepressibly; restlessly; violently; mercurially; tempestuously; impulsively; curiously; remarkably; excessively; foolishly.

EFFETE

adverbs
horribly; lamentably; pitiably; tragically; unfortunately; deplorably; undeniably; remarkably; significantly; unsubstantially; uselessly; emptily; hopelessly; obviously.

EFFICACIOUS

adverbs
(See efficient.)

EFFICACY

adjectives
untamable; proved; constitutional; feeble.

EFFICIENCY

adjectives
calm; bustling; normal; productive; awkward; chaotic; devastating; vaunted; pedagogical; modest; maximum; extreme; technical; superior; industrial; impaired; top; outstanding; administrative; dreadful; physical; individual; creative; working; up-to-date; antiseptic; defensive; stolid; executive; incredible; added; increased; slender; swift; cleansing; expanding.

verbs
achieve—; admit—; assimilate—; demand —; destroy—; discharge with—; display—; effect—; enforce—; exhibit—; impair—; increase—; lack—; prove—; rate—; weaken—; —produces; —promotes; —saves.
(See ability, power.)

EFFICIENT

adverbs
remarkably; unusually; obviously; busily; incredibly; completely; sensibly; wisely; officiously; pleasantly; gracefully; politely; irritatingly; ostentatiously; horribly; satisfactorily; skilfully; expertly; cleverly; adroitly; ingeniously; shrewdly; ably; invaluably; surprisingly; unbelievably; uncommonly.

EFFIGY

adjectives
silent; grotesque; gilded; insensible; clumsy; crowned; sceptered; pompous; full-length; sad; recumbent; ghastly; transfixed; rueful; granite.

verbs
bear—; burn—; carry—; damn in—; display—; draw in—; dress up—; execute in—; hang in—; mount—; prepare—; —copies; —depicts; —destroys; —dramatizes; —illustrates; —portrays; —represents; —ridicules.
(See image, figure.)

EFFORT

adjectives
sheer; obvious; ceaseless; insane; sporadic; powerful; convulsive; belated; manful; stringent; fanatical; bitter; renewed; daring; conciliatory; overt; pitiful; thwarted; ponderous; childish; rash; humble; feeble; emotional; culminating; futile; creditable; clumsy; persistent; crowning; strained; zealous; individual; abortive; desperate; unscrupulous; constrained; infantile; frantic; untiring; slightest; reasonable; laborious; fragmentary; prolonged; wasted; proud; unsuccessful; painful; indomitable; stupendous; superior; strenuous; sustained; conscious; concentrated; active; stern; Herculean; visible; pictorial; vigorous; charitable; automatic; dynamic; heroic; mightiest; literary; concerted; willful; strong; intermittent; bounding; mental; feverish; immense; utmost; tentative; paramount; extra; oracular; extant; superhuman; conversational; languid; consecutive; tireless; unionized; wearisome; insufferable; historical; fruitless; human; best; spasmodic; persevering; editorial; effectual; baffled; irrelevant; determined; vague; misdirected; rash; sincere; spontaneous; notable; crude; violent; vain; inadequate; collective; immense; energetic; perilous; organized; powerful; undue; conceivable; formidable; periodic; praiseworthy; pioneering; never-ceasing; continued; self-denying; willing; exhausting; arduous; constructive; moral; fitful; creative; initial; expiratory; bizarre; rain-making; remedial; serious; apparent; sober; sympathetic; painstaking; offensive; special; colloquial; ridiculous; everlasting; sedulous; anxious; united; patient; plastic; maiden; pathetic; dutiful; generous; repetitive; financial; belated; poetic; obstinate; volunteer; co-operative; communal; religious; appropriate; published; unremitting; diligent; supreme; avowed; expired; earnest; enforcement; passionate; future; pretentious; evident; bluffing; murderous; barren; sublimest; kindly; sincere; vexed; ambitious; operatic; courageous; unwise; individual; unflinching; restraining.

verbs

belittle—; bend—; berate—; cheer—; compensate for—; concentrate—; coordinate —s; counter—; crown—; decry—; dwarf—; endorse—; enlist—s; entail—; exert—; expend—; fail in—; focus—s on; galvanize—; garble—; glorify—; hamper—; impede—; intensify—; justify—; key up for—; lend—; mock—; nullify—; quicken—; redouble—; repay—; repel—; reward—; scotch—; spare—; squander—; slacken—; stir to—; succumb to—; suppress—; suspend—; thwart—; —attains; —bears fruit; —exhausts.

(See attempt, endeavor, exertion.)

EFFRONTERY
adjectives
calculated; humorous; brazen; incredible; unabashed; hardy; vulgar; matchless.

EFFULGENT
adverbs
radiantly; glaringly; sparklingly; scintillantly; shimmeringly; dazzlingly; luminously; lustrously; unbelievably; remarkably; brilliantly; garishly; splendidly; brightly; incredibly; unexpectedly; showily; gaudily; flashily; tremendously.

EFFUSION
adjectives
amatory; tender; pathetic; vocal; gymnastic; osculatory; lyrical; rich; boisterous; copious; labored; characteristic; reducing; irrepressible; unnecessary; vaporing; hypocritical; merry; hypercritical.

EFFUSIVE
adverbs
garrulously; lavishly; chattily; enthusiastically; explosively; excessively; needlessly; ridiculously; foolishly; inappropriately; unpleasantly; comically; endlessly; noticeably; amusingly; overly; absurdly.

EGG
adjectives
pendent; ostrich; whipped; fried; poached; scrambled; hot.

verbs
addle—; beat—; burst from—; coddle—; crate—s; deposit—; emerge from—; gather —s; germinate in—; guard—s; hatch from —; hunt—; impregnate—; incubate—; market—; nest—; originate in—; poach—; puncture—; scramble—; sit on—; snatch—; spring from—; start from—; whip—; — brings forth; —curdles; —produces.

EGO
adjectives
exaggerated; inflated; restless; exalted; hard; poised; fretted; bubbling; monarchical; suppressed; assertive.

verbs
bolster up—; commiserate—; excite—; express—; foster—; gratify—; inflate—; pervert—; reflect—; satiate—; satisfy—; soothe —; submerge—; understand—.

(See personality, individuality.)

EGOISM
adjectives
sullen; puppyish; dramatic; tyrannical; justifiable; elemental; narrowing; unlimited; psychopathic; holy; sublime; sentimental; comfortable; collective; passionate; colossal; animal; narcissistic.

EGOTISM
adjectives
outrageous; instinctive; explicable; monstrous; intense; superb; stultifying; passionate; blustering; savage; solid; immense; baseless; absurd; ruthless; unselfish; indecent; vivacious; supreme; undisguised; magnanimous; friendly; dreary; compound; naive; absolute; slightest; importunate; young; cultivated; placid.

verbs
allow—; annihilate—; apologize for—; avoid—; banish—; brand—; criticize—; excuse—; justify—; pardon—; pierce—; produce—; recommend—; resist—; —absorbs; —bores; —dominates; —irks; — occupies; —offends.

(See conceit, vanity, self-esteem.)

EGOTIST
adjectives
diseased; sentimental; offensive; supreme; turbulent; hateful; fantastic; sheer; unmalleable; harmless; power-hungry.

EGOTISTICAL
verbs
shamefully; arrogantly; absurdly; outlandishly; palpably; obviously; highly; profoundly; inexcusably; ponderously; blatantly; boastfully; vaingloriously; ridiculously;

noisily; curiously; unashamedly; disagreeably; offensively; foolishly; extremely; habitually; incredibly; blindly.

EJACULATE (v)
adverbs
sarcastically; faintly; incredulously; blankly; feelingly; sententiously; forcefully; vigorously; caustically; admiringly; joyfully; fiercely; piously; angrily; indelicately; hollowly; muffledly.
(See exclaim, call.)

EJACULATION
adjectives
customary; heartfelt; fervent; profane; pious; startled; angry; indelicate; religious; barbarous; hushed; hollow; muffled.

EJACULATORY
adverbs
violently; ridiculously; needlessly; noisily; importantly; egregiously; highly; arrogantly; blatantly; suddenly; startlingly; shockingly; ludicrously; stertorously; vociferously; monstrously; immensely; outlandishly.

EJECT (v)
adverbs
forcibly; copiously; abruptly; vigorously; determinedly; suddenly.
(See discharge, expel.)

ELABORATE (v)
adverbs
minutely; successfully; eloquently; ingeniously; ridiculously; pompously; ramblingly; fully.
(See develop, perfect.)

ELABORATE
adverbs
extremely; excessively; unnecessarily; arduously; egregiously; incredibly; ostentatiously; ingeniously; skilfully; intolerably; preposterously; fearfully; unduly; inappropriately; suitably; ceremoniously; oddly; singularly; significantly; pompously; laboriously; marvellously; beautifully.

ELABORATION
adjectives
ingenious; quaintest; ridiculous; polychronic; productive.

ELASTIC
adverbs
conveniently; expediently; comfortably; immensely; extremely; marvelously; resiliently; sturdily; wonderfully; powerfully; effectively; adequately; diplomatically; buoyantly; springily; notably.

ELASTICITY
adjectives
molecular; virtual; joyous; dangerous.

verbs
acquire—; calculate—; depend on—; deprive of—; lessen—; limit—; lose—; recover—; remove—; require—; return by—; strain—; stress—; test—; —overcomes; —resists; —restores; —varies.

ELATED
adverbs
unduly; hysterically; strangely; oddly; curiously; highly; naturally; ecstatically; rapturously; proudly; quietly; properly; unusually; brightly; enthusiastically; triumphantly; merrily; exultantly; confidently; pertly; priggishly; smugly; dramatically; boastfully; indescribably; irrepressibly.

ELATION
adjectives
short-lived; undue; cruel; hysterical; strange.

ELBOW
adjectives
bony; touching; angular; fat; massive; crooked; dimpled; immaculate; hard; inert.

verbs
brace—; cap—; extend—; fit on—; fracture—; jab with—; join—; jostle with—; move—; nudge with—; pad—; prop on—; raise—; rest on—; skin—; strain—.
(See joint, arm.)

ELDER
adjectives
disillusioned; itinerant; unsuspecting; ruling; grumpy.

verbs
appeal to—; assemble—s; burlesque—; consult—; entreat—; exhort—; gather—s; grieve—; heed—; honor—; ordain—; persuade—; respect—; revere—; succeed—; worry—; —advises; —counsels; —decrees; —heads; —interposes; —judges; —officiates; —pardons; —presides over; —punishes; —rebukes; —warns.
(See deacon, minister, ruler.)

adverbs

respectably; unquestionably; soberly; reliably; safely; pleasantly; comfortably; graciously; sourly; augustly; gravely; admittedly; frightfully; depressingly; incurably.

ELECT (v)
adverbs

unanimously; tacitly; spontaneously; subsequently; optionally; popularly; municipally; decisively; willingly; virtually.
(See choose, select.)

ELECTION

adjectives

farcical; obligatory; ensuing; local; optional; subsequent; degrading; frank; popular; financial; municipal.

verbs

announce—; campaign for—; climax—; conduct—; doom—; gain—; inveigh against—; merit—; nullify—; officiate at—; postpone—; propose—; revoke—; riot at—; stay—; swing—; —installs; —results in.
(See vote.)

ELECTIONEER (v)
adverbs

blatantly; flatteringly; obviously; humorously; pompously; volubly; wheedlingly; politically; masterfully; passionately; journalistically.
(See plan, campaign.)

ELECTIVE
adverbs

freely; unconditionally; fortunately; highly; frankly; wisely; generously; broadly; extensively; liberally; tolerantly; widely.

ELECTRICITY
adjectives

dynamical; spiritual; galvanic; wondrous; helpful; servant-like; static.

verbs

activate—; apply—; charge with—; communicate by—; conduct—; connect—; conserve—; consume—; develop—; direct—; discharge—; employ—; generate—; harness —; induce—; measure—; resist—; supply —; transmit—; utilize—; wire for—; — circulates; —emanates from; —flows; — magnetizes; —radiates from; —shocks; — vitalizes.

adjectives

tasteful; sartorial; unusual; impaired; gracious; extreme; solid; stately; sculptured; cheerless; superficial; concise; unfailing; luxurious; voluptuous; sovereign; chill; refining; quiet; palatial; simple; futile; dainty; urban; indescribable; modish; restrained; decorous; envied; dark; classic; restless; certain; bright; supercilious; inborn; airy; rustic; rich; cautious; inherent; chaste; subdued; austere; correct; lazy; shabby; social; verbal; defiant; peculiar; pristine.

verbs

abandon—; arrange with—; behave with —; breed in—; demonstrate—; destroy—; detest—; display—; dress with—; effect—; indulge in—; instruct in—; polish with—; surrender to—; treasure—; tutor in—; yield to—; —charms; —graces; —impresses; — prevails; —wins.
(See refinement.)

ELEGANT
adverbs

tastefully; graciously; quietly; indescribably; modishly; richly; chastely; naturally; unerringly; exquisitely; quaintly; discriminatingly; correctly; superbly.

ELEGY
adjectives

Sapphic; biblical; funeral; lamenting; somber; pastoral.

ELEMENT
adjectives

instinctive; structural; romantic; automatic; subtle; personal; opposing; radical; mutable; flavoring; incongruous; rare; hereditary; picturesque; lawless; thinkable; lymphatic; volitional; aesthetic; disproportionate; jarring; conservative; fragmentary; chemical; undefined; necessary; nationalistic; ominous; simple; discordant; valuable; discrepant; professional; poetic; complex; unalloyed; salient; airy; fighting; unlikely; limpid; primal; negligible; essential; various (pl); devouring; lurking; perverse; dramatic; exhilarated; commonest; dissolving; dreadful; unchained; recessive; liberal; unimaginative; diviner; mercantile; physic; criminalistic; regressive; nutritional; denominative; ambient; basic; ancient; uncanny; lesser; heterogeneous; individual; maltreated; unobstructed; conflicting; sensual; insignificant; cultivated;

honest; inflammable; primordial; cheerful; chalky; fantastic; simplest; positive; dominant; pitiless; divergent; pagan; lawless; inextinguishable; repeated; elliptic; seasonal; melancholy; ungenial; desirable; erotic; distinct; furious; vitamin; mineral; dissatisfied; prim; grim; sufficient; sensitive; minority; moral; decisive; sedate; opaque; disturbing; contradictory; connate; supernatural; determining; sound; hostile; visible; ultimate; fundamental; irreconcilable; bodily; contending; ideal; artistic; divers (pl); permanent; diversifying; natural; serenest; primary; untamed; eternal; incompatible; principal; unloosed; glorious; subtle; insane; comic; burning; lazy; humorous; slow; speculative; vital; harmless; food; important; valuable; mysterious; emotional; backsliding; infelicitous; restful; venal; subjective; neutralizing; metaphysical; dimorphous; cultured; celestial; alien.

verbs
coalesce—s; constitute—; disintegrate—; fathom—; inject—; introduce—; master—; mix—; nourish—; play to—; rouse—; stress—; submerge—; surrender—; symbolize—; unearth—; unite—s; —disturbs; —pervades; —predominates.
(See ingredient, constituent.)

ELEMENTAL
adverbs
distinctly; obviously; simply; powerfully; irresistibly; purely; absolutely; solely; manifestly.

ELEMENTARY
adverbs
clearly; purely; sheerly; singularly; simply; exclusively; woefully; amazingly; lamentably; unfortunately; significantly; gravely; momentously; seriously.

ELEMENTS
(*weather*)
verbs
bar—; barricade against—; combat—; conquer—; contend with—; struggle with—; yield to—; —destroy; —deteriorate; —determine; —disintegrate; —flash; —fret; —govern; —rust; —wreck.
(See earth, air, fire, water.)

ELEPHANT
verbs
anger—; arouse—; climb on—; domesticate —; mount—; spear—; train—; travel upon —; —bathes; —batters; —charges; —

draws; —flings; —hisses; —lumbers; —performs; —rages; —rams; —remembers; —roars; —runs amuck; —spears; —tosses; —trumpets.
(See animal.)

ELEVATE (*v*)
adverbs
morally; perceptibly; proudly; correspondingly; scarcely; partially.
(See raise, lift.)

ELAVATED
adverbs
reputably; highly; estimably; honorably; majestically; eminently; unusually; consciously; nobly; gloriously; immensely; remarkably; uncommonly; notably; famously; conspicuously; illustriously; splendidly; brilliantly; prominently; sacredly.

ELEVATION
adjectives
corresponding; proud; displeased; moral.

ELEVATOR
adjectives
special; arch; fast; slow; decorated; express.

verbs
accelerate—; block—; burden—; control—; crowd—; disable—; employ—; enter—; file out of—; install—; jam—; jostle in—; level—; man—; manipulate—; operate—; overload—; pour from—; retard—; ring for—; signal—; station at—; stream from —; —ascends; —descends; —drops; —facilitates; —hoists; —hums upward; —plunges; —transfers; —zooms.
(See platform, aeroplane.)

ELF
adjectives
happy; semi-respectable; sportive; cunning; troublesome; perverse; bad; imperturbable; vagrant; scribbling.

ELFISH
adverbs
delicately; mischievously; sportively; cunningly; perversely; vagrantly; uncannily; weirdly; impishly; undeniably; laughably; amusingly; naturally.

ELIGIBLE
adverbs
legally; capably; competently; wholly; unusually; highly; undeniably; exceptionally;

socially; becomingly; conveniently; obviously; evidently; admirably; financially.

ELIMINATE (v)
adverbs
completely; utterly; entirely; abruptly; virtually; outrageously; tyrannically; courageously; completely.
(See separate, remove.)

ELIXIR
adjectives
wondrous; imperious; youth-giving; immortal; nectarous; divine.

ELLIPSE
verbs
bound by—; circle in—; course—; cut into —; define; —describe—; disfigure—; draw —; execute—; fashion—; form—; shape into—; sketch—; wheel in—; —belts; — entertains; —frames.
(See circle.)

ELM
adjectives
hedgerow; overshadowing; lofty; spindling; immemorial; vaulted; ancient; graceful; sighing.

verbs
entwine—; rock—; trim—; —branches; — flowers; —groans; —nods; —protects; — quivers; —shades; —sheds; —shelters; — stirs; —tapers; —towers; —waves.
(See tree.)

ELOPE (v)
adverbs
blithely; lovingly; spiritedly; clandestinely; surreptitiously; furtively; secretly; slyly; stealthily; impetuously.
(See run, flee.)

ELOQUENCE
adjectives
manly; grand; bold; persuasive; gloomy; transcending; bitter; melodic; florid; voluble; wheedling; candid; political; impressive; native; seductive; caustic; hardy; stately; indignant; impersonal; sonorous; patriotic; solemn; resistless; cold; clear; pathetic; silent; denunciative; masterful; masculine; insidious; solid; flatulent; astonishing; awful; touching; imperishable; impetuous; religious; native; saucy; audacious; attractive; brilliant; passionate; luminous; clarion-like; convincing; additional; parliamentary; journalistic; fiery;

rich; insinuating; supreme; consummate; rude; unstudied; lofty; picturesque; simple; fervent; abusive; prompt; gorgeous; sublime; worthy; copious; popular; ecclesiastical.

verbs
breathe out—; burst out in—; disregard—; drown in—; endow with—; prompt—; resist—; utter—; woo with—; —acquits; — colors; —flowers; —flows from—; —glitters; —induces; —moves; —pierces; — strikes; —sways.
(See speech, fluency, elegance, utterance.)

ELOQUENT
adverbs
powerfully; marvelously; incisively; impressively; dramatically; vigorously; sensationally; brilliantly; pleadingly; pithily; loftily; sublimely; touchingly; vehemently; passionately; exceptionally; astonishingly; attractively; highly; uncommonly; simply; consummately; irresistibly; persuasively.

ELUCIDATE (v)
adverbs
graphically; clearly; extensively; thoroughly; patiently.
(See describe, explain.)

ELUDE (v)
adverbs
exasperatingly; continually; slyly; ingeniously; cleverly; repeatedly; irritatingly.
(See evade, avoid.)

ELUSIVE
adverbs
cunningly; deceptively; insidiously; trickily; meretriciously; fraudulently; cleverly; artfully; abominably; evasively; adroitly; subtly; treacherously; archly; unbelievably; highly; alarmingly; singularly; terribly.

ELYSIAN
adverbs
delectably; beatifically; ecstatically; divinely; rapturously; ravishingly; seraphically; sweetly; celestially.

EMACIATED
adverbs
pitiably; outrageously; scandalously; miserably; shakily; wirily; sparely; gauntly; haggardly; tenuously; shockingly; terribly; unusually; wretchedly; unwarrantably; shamefully.

EMANATION

adjectives
divine; miasmal; primitive.

EMANCIPATION

adjectives
bourgeois; unconditional; prospective.

EMBALM (v)

adverbs
carefully; elaborately; skillfully; marvelously; artfully; professionally.
(See preserve.)

EMBALMING

adjectives
elaborate; marvelous; skilled.

EMBARGO

adjectives
silly; alternative; virtual.

verbs
adopt—; apply—; assail—; authorize—; clap on—; condemn—; counter—; declare —; effect—; employ—; enforce—; impose —; instigate—; justify—; lift—; patronize —; proclaim—; propose—; support—; threaten—; urge—; —checks; —hinders; —restrains; —starves.
(See hindrance, impediment, injunction, restraint.)

EMBARK (v)

adverbs
gleefully; sadly; joyfully; formally; unmolestedly; freely; tardily; eventually; hastily.
(See begin, venture.)

EMBARKATION

adjectives
businesslike; unmolested.

EMBARRASS (v)

adverbs
disconcertingly; satirically; startlingly; perceptibly; sadly; slyly; perplexingly; visibly; painfully; pecuniarily; secretly; acutely; considerably; strangely.
(See harass, shame.)

EMBARRASSED

adverbs
singularly; curiously; oddly; strangely; profoundly; awkwardly; deeply; shamefully; shyly; financially; socially; distressingly; painfully; publicly; secretly; timidly; occasionally; vaguely; slightly; greatly; horribly; visibly; angrily; acutely; considerably; helplessly; hotly.

EMBARRASSMENT

adjectives
visible; flattering; painful; evident; pecuniary; nervous; tingling; angry; secret; acute; considerable; strange.

verbs
betray—; blush in—; conceal—; contribute to—; ease—; flush in—; guard against—; lead to—; manifest—; pardon—; relieve—; —hinders; —prevents; —silences.
(See chagrin, perplexity.)

EMBASSY

adjectives
overburdened; heaven-like; loving.

EMBELLISH (v)

adverbs
peculiarly; handsomely; profusely; tastefully; poetically; artistically; architecturally; rhetorically; flamboyantly; gaudily; beautifully; lavishly.
(See adorn, ornament.)

EMBELLISHED

adverbs
ornately; tastefully; gaudily; crudely; garishly; beautifully; artistically; gorgeously; smartly; showily; unnecessarily; highly; extravagantly; excessively; richly; gayly; daintily; elegantly; chastely; simply.

EMBELLISHMENT

adjectives
poetical; artistic; architectural; rhetorical.

EMBER

verbs
blanket—s; conceal beneath—; fan—; feed —s; heap on—s; heat on—s; poke—s; quench—s; rake—s; roast in—s; stir—s; strew over—s; toast on—s; —blazes; —burns; —s comfort; —dies; —expires; —flames; —glows; —heats; —s sleep; —smoulders; —s warm; —chars.
(See coal, ashes, cinders.)

EMBERS

adjectives
rose-red; burnt-out; glowing; smoldering; latent; dying; dangerous; pale; dim; fading; glimmering; throbbing; slumbering; raked; inextinguishable; feeble; ruddy; ashen-gray; blue; crumbling; smoky.

adverbs
deeply; permanently; irremediably; unfortunately; justifiably; hopelessly; irrecoverably; secretly; profoundly; morbidly; sullenly; unhappily; strangely; naturally; pathetically; violently; savagely; dejectedly; desperately.

EMBLAZON (v)
adverbs
vividly; richly; weirdly; brilliantly; astonishingly; colorfully.
(See adorn, shine.)

EMBLAZONED
adverbs
gorgeously; colorfully; artistically; brilliantly; wonderfully; marvelously; ceremonially; magnificently; splendidly; sumptuously; dramatically; richly; glitteringly; brightly; highly.

EMBLAZONING
adjectives
dim; fiery; weird; astonishing.

EMBLEM
adjectives
talismanic; portentous; ecclesiastical; gorgeous; hieroglyphical; conventional; mortuary; graven-lined; masonic; sepulchered.

verbs
bear—; bedeck with—s; distinguish with —s; engrave—; enrich with—s; insert—; reward with—; select—; scrutinize—; vie for—; —attests; —denotes; —expresses; —flutters; —indicates; —represents; —suggests; —symbolizes; —testifies.
(See representation, symbol, sign, badge.)

EMBLEMATIC
adverbs
characteristically; truly; ecclesiastically; gorgeously; splendidly; highly; remarkably; particularly; obscurely; appropriately; suitably; graphically; felicitously; extraordinarily; uncommonly; manifestly.

EMBODIMENT
adjectives
stirring; organic; adequate; striking; rough.

EMBODY (v)
adverbs
satisfactorily; stirringly; organically; strikingly; adequately; roughly; successfully; convincingly.
(See combine, form.)

EMBRACE
adjectives
clinging; maddening; bearlike; straining; wordless; rapturous; mute; passionate; quiet; transparent; pure; warm; turbulent; meek; fervid; hard; stimulating; emotional; sorrowing; soothing; fierce; strict; firm; chill; rugged; silent; romantic; locked; welcoming; timid; tight; tepid; kind; lank; stormy; stiff; clumsy.

verbs
avert—; avoid—; blush at—; break—; check—; clasp in—; delight in—; enclose in—; force—; gather in—; lock in—; resist—; seek—; shelter in—.
(See clasp.)

EMBRACE (v)
adverbs
tenderly; blithely; lasciviously; licentiously; cheerfully; responsively; affectionately; warmly; fitfully; passionately; voluntarily; devoutly; boldly; clingingly; maddeningly; wordlessly; rapturously; emotionally; mutely; turbulently; sorrowfully; soothingly; fiercely; firmly; ruggedly; romantically; timidly; tepidly; clumsily; stormily.
(See caress, clasp.)

EMBRASURE
adjectives
gloomy; mighty.

EMBROIDER (v)
adverbs
dexterously; delicately; ecclesiastically; strangely; brilliantly; artfully; skillfully; fantastically.
(See sew, ornament.)

EMBROIDERY
adjectives
brilliant; sad; glittering; ecclesiastical; fancy; eyelet; cross-stitch; lace; delicate.

EMBROILMENT
adjectives
bloody; wearisome; needless; furious.

verbs

abort—; disengage—; enclose—; examine
—; form—; hatch—; kill—; nourish—;
shape—; stifle—; stimulate—; surround—;
—develops; —dwells in; —enfolds; —impresses; —matures; —occupies; —originates; —ripens.

(See germ, beginning.)

EMERALD

adjectives

living; veined; encrusted; sparkling; striking; great; square; exquisite.

verbs

adorn with—; cover with—s; delight in—;
favor—; guard—; lure with—; purchase
—; secrete—; value—; —crowns; —dazzles;
—gleams; —glimmers; —glitters; —scintillates; —shines.

(See jewel, gem, diamond.)

EMERGE (v)

adverbs

dramatically; noiselessly; coolly; gradually;
luminously; transcendingly; reluctantly;
mystically; shyly; abruptly; unmistakably.

(See rise, come.)

EMERGENCY

adjectives

fearful; prolonged; sudden; fiscal; threatening; temporal; frequent; peculiar; unexpected; popular; pressing; unusual; serious;
desperate; international.

verbs

anticipate—; bow to—; challenge—; confront with—; cope with—; ease—; face—;
guard against—; handle—; iron out—;
lessen—; meet—; resign to—; rise to—;
—arises; —exists.

(See crisis, exigency, necessity.)

EMETIC

verbs

act as—; administer—; does with—; employ
—; prescribe—; suggest—; swallow—; —
aids; —corrects; —counteracts; —cures; —
empties; —excites; —induces; —produces;
—prostrates; —remedies; —stimulates.

(See medicine, laxative, enema.)

EMIGRANT

adjectives

unfortunate; greenhorn; bewildered; aggressive.

verbs

admit—; advocate—; assist—; campaign
for—; dodge—; embark on—; halt—; occasion—; prevent—; record—; shift—; stir
—; undertake—; —drifts; —flows; —
lapses; —relieves; —streams; —trickles.

(See exodus, departure, immigration.)

EMINENCE

adjectives

lofty; intellectual; grassy; bright; conspicuous; crested; humble; narrowed; specific;
abrupt; sudden; immediate; gentle; incontestable; commanding; inland; archaeological; practicable; affected; sacred; cliffy;
deserted; professional; unblemished; gigantic; noble.

verbs

ascend to—; assume—; attain—; command
—; deserve—; elevate to—; enjoy—; enthrone in—; hope for—; merit—; perch
in—; rise to—; shoot to—; surpass in—;
tower in—; worship—.

(See distinction, fame.)

EMINENT

adverbs

notably; internationally; ecclesiastically;
politically; socially; distinctly; illustriously;
splendidly; proudly; conspicuously; honorably; deservedly; brilliantly; famously.

EMISSARY

adjectives

paid; secret; trustworthy; discreet.

verbs

assign—to; dispatch—; employ—; entrust
with—; interview—; send—; —announces;
—carries; —communicates; —conveys; —
corresponds; —furnishes; —imparts; —implies; —informs; —performs; —pries; —
promotes; —relays; —reports; —represents;
—scouts; —spies.

(See agent, messenger, ambassador.)

EMISSION

adjectives

non-luminous; watery.

EMOLUMENT

adjectives

stipendiary; unearned; colossal; untaxable.

verbs

calculate—; consider—; deny—; deprive
of—; derive—; earn—; enjoy—; forfeit—;

obtain—; pocket—; produce—; reap—; receive—; return—; seek—; —amends; —atones for; —comforts; —compensates; —improves; —rewards; —satisfies.

(See advantage, gain, profit.)

EMOTION

adjectives

poignant; intellectual; enthusiastic; touched; pent-up; gentle; repressed; inscrutable; barbaric; profound; blushing; conflicting; fierce; dark; complex; vague; vindictive; turbulent; painful; dominant; disturbing; desirable; private; desperate; kindled; human; extraordinary; petty; ardent; suitable; exulting; tremulous; generous; primitive; perfect; sudden; passionate; unquiet; joyful; parental; unmaidenly; chivalric; opposite; irrevocable; decadent; violent; indescribable; timid; charitable; passive; transient; repentant; trembling; contending; diverse; tumultuous; untried; sensitive; irrepressible; scornful; rapid; lively; mingled; suppressed; distinct; contradictory; intricate; dead; keen; sincere; adult; unstable; overwhelming; evident; patriotic; quivering; natural; intense; irreproachable; educated; anguished; elusive; corresponding; religious; tender; similar; singular; gushing; innocent; inner; spontaneous; aesthetic; genuine; hot-headed; silent; excited; immature; shallow; cheap; neat; compelling; inelastic; visible; awe-inspiring; incomprehensible; strong; sham; momentary; adulterated; sociable; inward; intimate; surcharged; acute; sustained; sympathetic; wandering; rebellious; compassionate; catholic; outward; tragic; burning; awakened; volcanic; uncontrollable; ineffable; synthetic; perverted; antagonistic; distressful; frozen; deepest; inmost; swelling; ill-concealed; pleasing; vehement; undisciplined; unfathomable; dumb; subdued; passion-hued; haggard; inexpressible; encompassing; unrestrained; facile; full-fledged; causeless; primal; deadened; inwrought; honest; confused; incomparable; personable; incongruous; incredible; indefinable; devastating; vivid; depressive; overpowering; simultaneous; old-fashioned; mysterious; unearthly; ultimate.

verbs

appeal to—; arouse—; awaken—; batter down—; betray—; blunt—; cherish—; choke—; conquer—; control—; cover—; curb—; disentangle—s; experience—; express—; falsify—; feign—; hide—; kindle —; lavish—on; move with—; overflow with

—; palpitate with—; play with—; prompt by—; pulsate with—; quake with—; quiver with—; register—; respond to—; restrain —; still—; suppress—; sway with—; toy with—s; tremble with—; vanquish—; vent —; whip up—; wrench by—; wring with—; —s clash; —s conflict; —governs; —recurs; —s riot; —seizes; —surges; —vacillates.

(See feeling, sensation, passion, perturbation, agitation.)

EMOTIONAL

adverbs

peculiarly; deeply; ardently; unstably; eagerly; warmly; quickly; strongly; obviously; fervently; uncontrollably; ungovernably; impetuously; impulsively; hysterically; unsteadily; remarkably; inherently; naturally; expressively; violently; highly; unusually.

EMOTIONALISM

adjectives

crude; seething; accursed; florid.

EMPEROR

adjectives

illustrious; reigning; ambitious; ardent; haughty; tyrannical.

verbs

admire—; assassinate—; attend—; bow to —; cringe before—; crown—; fete—; guard —; hail—; huzza—; pledge to—; present to—; succeed—; wait upon—; —addresses; —conquers; —decrees; —dismisses; —pardons; —receives; —rules; —subdues.

(See king, monarch.)

EMPHASIS

adjectives

lingering; menacing; stubborn; marked; terrific; daring; allowable; improper; extravagant; dreadful; indignant; prodigious; fretful; passionate; prevailing; serious; trivial; joyous; sufficient; ethical; victorious; appealing; artistic; attenuated; sarcastic; flattering; languid; tantalizing.

verbs

bear—; convey—; express with—; focus upon—; lay—upon; lose—; mark—; note—; observe—; require—; shift—; voice—; —accentuates; —affirms; —delivers; —forces; —imbeds; —implies; —impresses; —inculcates; —insists; —instils; —points; —sharpens; —stresses.

(See stress, force.)

adverbs

significantly; repeatedly; effectively; victoriously; graciously; boastfully; adequately; menacingly; stubbornly; markedly; daringly; improperly; extravagantly; indignantly; fretfully; passionately; seriously; trivially; sufficiently; appealingly; artistically; tantalizingly.

(See stress, impress.)

EMPHATIC

adverbs

stubbornly; terribly; fretfully; joyously; aggressively; boldly; loftily; truculently; extravagantly; impudently; insolently; audaciously; arrogantly; blandly; confidently; sweepingly; dogmatically; astoundingly; autocratically; despotically; imperiously; monstrously; presumptuously; preposterously; rashly; blatantly; sarcastically.

EMPIRE

adjectives

calm; powerful; mighty; disintegrating; formidable; distracted; extensive; audacious; vain; populous; consolidated; celestial; peerless; permanent; veritable; effeminate; far-reaching; full-fledged; supernatural; gentle; colonial; barbaric; mercantile; spiritual.

verbs

bind—; bound—; build—; carve—; cement —; command—; conquer—; consolidate—; create—; destroy—; dictate—; disentangle —; divide—; forsake—; found—; govern —; invade—; overthrow—; police—; rock —; rule—; seek—; shake—; spread through —; unite—; wreck—; yoke—; —dwindles; —extends; —falls; —perishes; —ranges; —sickens; —staggers.

(See state, nation, dominion, sovereignty, kingdom.)

EMPLOY (v)

adverbs

habitually; conspicuously; vigilantly; anxiously; faithfully; uselessly; frequently; thriftily; steadily; methodically; profitably; gainfully; vigorously; skillfully; magically; unceasingly; temporarily; advantageously; peacefully; sparingly; incessantly; hazardously; individually; occasionally; domestically; legitimately; remuneratively; suitably; figuratively; ingloriously; systematically; actively.

(See use, work.)

EMPLOYEE

adjectives

conscientious; rank-and-file; valued; prudent; salaried; unionized.

verbs

agitate—s; assign—to; coerce—; command —; discard—; dismiss—; dock—; engage —; engross—; enroll—; intimidate—; manage—s; misuse—; regulate—s; supervise —s; —s demand; —exerts; —obeys; —s organize; —s recess; —s strike.

(See worker, workman, laborer, clerk.)

EMPLOYER

adjectives

philosophic; recusant; apprehensive; prospective; banded (pl).

verbs

demand of—; persuade—; picket—; plead with—; seek—; —acquires; —advertises; — assigns; —controls; —disposes; —economizes; —engages; —fires; —hires; —locks out; —pities; —procures; —provides; — refuses; —regulates; —supervises; —sympathizes; —tyrannizes; —understands.

(See master, owner, manager.)

EMPLOYMENT

adjectives

unconscious; hazardous; individual; occasional; domestic; legitimate; remunerative; regressive; useful; suitable; skillful; congenial; responsible; continuous; money-making; figurative; seasonable; inglorious; obvious; temporary; lucrative; profitable; regular; diverse; military; justifiable; creative; systematic; gainful; mercantile; initial.

verbs

acquire—; apply for—; assign—; avoid—; carry on—; devote to—; evade—; fit for—; insure—; necessitate—; offer—; procure—; pursue—; receive—; regulate—; reject—; seek—; stabilize—; stimulate—; throw out of—; —fluctuates; —maintains; —occupies; —preserves; —satisfies.

(See occupation, vocation, calling, business, profession, trade, job.)

EMPRESS

adjectives

chimerical; power-drunk; haughty.

EMPTINESS

adjectives

divine; ultimate; horrid; echoing; civilized; gnawing; spiritual; wide; desolate; bleak; blank; black; void; gaping; yawning.

EMPTY (v)

adverbs

surreptitiously; completely; partially; automatically.

(See deplete, exhaust.)

EMPTY

adverbs

hopelessly; deplorably; lamentably; desperately; completely; almost; obviously; visibly; dreadfully; desolately; bleakly; startlingly; awfully; dismally; unbelievably; palpably; contemptibly; unhappily; unfortunately; wretchedly.

EMULATION

adjectives

literary; perpetual; generous; envious.

EMULSION

adjectives

light; sensitive; suspended; cloudy.

ENACT (v)

adverbs

comparatively; gravely; legally; prohibitively; legislatively; socially; illegitimately; dictatorially; forcefully; dogmatically.

(See perform, accomplish.)

ENACTMENT

adjectives

statutory; prohibitive; legislative; social; revolutionary; legal.

ENAMEL

adjectives

tinted; lucid; brittle; brilliant.

ENAMOURED

adverbs

crazily; besottedly; wholly; rapturously; blindly; immensely; ecstatically; ardently; passionately; idolatrously; fervidly; deeply; inordinately; absorbingly; perilously; dangerously; absurdly; hopelessly; helplessly.

ENCHANT (v)

adverbs

magically; ravishingly; sweetly; uniquely; mysteriously; powerfully; fantastically; mystically; passionately.

(See charm, fascinate.)

ENCHANTED

adverbs

utterly; delightfully; marvellously; oddly; perfectly; curiously; unquestionably; irresistibly; openly; avowedly; completely.

ENCHANTING

adverbs

delightfully; charmingly; seductively; bewitchingly; girlishly; youthfully; marvellously; radiantly; daintily; exquisitely; courteously; divinely; gracefully; brightly; chivalrously; politely; attentively; urbanely; ingratiatingly; genially; extremely; curiously; oddly; uncommonly.

ENCHANTMENT

adjectives

grave; sweet; rapt; unique; age-old; powerful; mysterious; perpetual; varied; divine; social; heightened; drear; cool; true; aristocratic; gloomy; mystic.

verbs

brew—; cast—; drink in—; endow with—; exercise—; gaze with—; invest with—; lend—; respond to—; steep in—; succumb to—; touch with—; view with—; —allures; —assails; —beguiles; —bewitches; —captivates; —charms; —cloaks; —delights; —enraptures; —enslaves; —expires; —fascinates; —fetters; —influences; —overpowers; employ—.

(See charm, fascination.)

ENCOMIUM

adjectives

unjust; warm; eulogistic; heaped-up (pl).

ENCOUNTER

adjectives

loose; strange; accidental; constant; fierce; ordinary; bloody; murderous; romantic; amiable; strong; awkward; fatal; vile; pugilistic; sharp; chivalrous; previous; bitter.

verbs

anticipate—; avoid—; calculate—; clash in—; confess to—; contemplate—; dare—; engage in—; experience—; expose to—; fear —; flush from—; intend—; join—; launch —; match in—; plan—; relate—; risk—; shrink from—; shun—; venture—; welcome—; —follows; —unsteadies.

(See meeting, collision, contest, conflict, battle.)

ENCOUNTER (v)
adverbs

repeatedly; proudly; frequently; occasionally; obliquely; cheerfully; unexpectedly; fearlessly; accidentally; murderously; romantically; amiably; awkwardly; fatally; chivalrously; bitterly.

(See meet, confront.)

ENCOURAGE (v)
adverbs

smoothly; openly; jovially; tremendously; sympathetically; willingly; specially; genially; unduly; adroitly; enormously; affectionately; consistently; wordlessly; unceasingly; remotely; cordially; professionally.

(See aid, assist.)

ENCOURAGEMENT
adjectives

enormous; lifelong; affectionate; consistent; wordless; unceasing; remote; slender; managerial; cheerful; cordial; melancholy; fresh; misplaced.

verbs

afford—; impart—; lend—; rally to—; thrive on—; —animates; —cheers; —comforts; —enlivens; —exhilarates; —heartens; —impels; —incites; —induces; —inspires; —kindles; —promotes; —prompts; —reassures; —restores; —stimulates.

(See help.)

ENCOURAGING
adverbs

cheerily; genially; gravely; enormously; affectionately; immensely; highly; silently; cordially; sincerely; resolutely; decisively; impulsively; discreetly; deliberately; helpfully; amicably; confidently; enthusiastically; reassuringly; sympathetically; actively; genuinely; exceptionally; prudently; thoughtfully; reliably.

ENCROACH (v)
adverbs

steadily; progressively; unconsciously; brazenly; perpetually; aggressively; belligerently; martially; pugnaciously.

(See trespass, intrude.)

ENCROACHMENT
adjectives

noteworthy; perpetual.

verbs

justify—; observe—; prevent—; rant against—; recognize—; resent—; resist—; revenge—; seize by—; tolerate—; wrest by—; —arouses; —deprives; —disables; —irritates; —offends; —outrages; —perils; —robs; —violates.

(See intrusion, invasion.)

ENCUMBER (v)
adverbs

perilously; hopelessly; monstrously; tragically; fatally; tyrannically; viciously; pathologically.

(See hinder, impede.)

ENCUMBRANCE
adjectives

vast; hopeless; monstrous.

verbs

accept—; attach—; discharge—; dispel—; divest of—; free from—; load with—; master—; struggle with—; suffer—; —annoys; —burdens; —clogs; —complicates; —embarrasses; —hampers; —harasses; —hinders; —impedes; —obstructs; —oppresses; —presses; —restrains.

(See load, burden, hindrance, impediment.)

ENCYCLOPEDIA
adjectives

skeptical; exhaustive; character; walking; biographical; all-inclusive.

verbs

appear in—; compile—; comprehend—; consult—; discover in—; edit—; employ—; refer to—; require—; scan—; —comprises; —educates; —enlightens; —explains; —illustrates; —informs; —instructs; —specifies; —teaches.

(See book.)

END
adjectives

dreary; practical; extreme; definite; private; lofty; selfish; ambitious; sordid; common; remote; swanlike; unsavory; equivocal; inexorable; surprising; personal; muchcoveted; teleological; adequate; ornamental; technical; ulterior; contingent; unpitied; desirable; special; worthier; appointed; hideous; latter; petty; sad; professed; untimely; abhorred; economical; wretched; radiant; conscious; tapering; immortal; futile; spiritual; individual; chief; shameful; ephemeral; extravagant; lifeless; blunt; preconceived; ultimate; gracious; disastrous.

verbs
accomplish—; achieve—; attain—; bend to —; catch—; constitute—; continue until—; contrive—; discern—; draw to—; endure to—; fear—; fulfill—; further—; hasten—; indicate—; justify—; maintain till—; obtain—; pause at—; pray for—; progress toward—; pursue—; push to—; put to—; scorn—; serve—; sever—; sleep till—; stave off—; subserve—; waste—; welcome —; work out—.
(See purpose, intention, aim, object, goal.)

END (v)
adverbs
invariably; eloquently; feebly; amicably; mournfully; abruptly; fatally; badly; tragically; comically; sorrowfully; dramatically; coldly; virtually; intelligibly; disastrously; breathlessly; inevitably; miserably; ultimately; insignificantly; ominously; appropriately; abruptly; gradually; poetically; swiftly.
(See finish, stop.)

ENDANGER (v)
adverbs
seriously; frequently; foolishly; absurdly; carelessly; jauntily; bravely; ridiculously.
(See imperil, risk.)

ENDEARMENT
verbs
address—to; cajole with—s; caress in—; coax with—s; court with—s; exhibit—; feast on—; flatter with—s; fondle in—; pat with —; refrain from—s; secure—of; serenade with—s; utter—; wheedle with—s; whisper —s; woo with—s; —annoys; —s charm; —flatters; —pleases.
(See caress, affection, love.)

ENDEAVOR
adjectives
enthusiastic; painstaking; deformed; vain; apparent; infinite; earnest; tenacious; mournful; incessant; rash; awful; patient; desperate; passionate; humane; utmost; high; speedy; organized; fruitless; fair; stern; honest, unsuccessful; ceaseless; beneficent; personal; therapeutic; urgent; self-protective; strenuous; fierce; psychoanalytic; sanctified; junior; charitable; dead; suicidal; dull; strong; philanthropic; continuous; decorative; intellectual; foolish.

verbs
bless—; conceal—; direct—; dwarf—; emulate—; encourage—; exert in—; extend—;
forestall—; forsake—; frustrate—; inspire —; lessen—; oppose—; plan—; put forth—; renew—; smile on—; struggle in—; —contributes; —ennobles; —helps; —sweeps away.
(See attempt, effort, struggle.)

ENDEAVOR (v)
adverbs
scrupulously; vainly; forcefully; energetically; constantly; primarily; inadequately; feebly; conscientiously; fruitlessly; unconsciously; gravely; heroically; ineffectually; eternally; enthusiastically; painstakingly; apparently; earnestly; tenaciously; mournfully; incessantly; patiently; desperately; passionately; humanely; strenuously; charitably; intellectually; foolishly.
(See try, strive.)

ENDING
adjectives
insignificant; ominous; tragic; gigantic; physical; abrupt; fittest; appropriate; gradual; beautiful; soft; poetic; swift.

ENDLESS
adverbs
horribly; apparently; almost; irritatingly; hopelessly; vexatiously; terrifyingly; incalculably; maddeningly; fabulously; unendurably; fearfully; frightfully.

ENDORSE (v)
adverbs
enthusiastically; tentatively; legally; legitimately; criminally; dishonestly; optimistically.
(See approve, agree.)

ENDORSEMENT
adjectives
enthusiastic; tentative.

verbs
(See indorsement.)

ENDOW (v)
adverbs
richly; invariably; exceptionally; wisely; lavishly; liberally; speedily; suitably; splendidly; mentally; spiritually; hypocritically; naturally; intellectually; physically; rarely; uncommonly.
(See give, donate.)

adjectives

mental; spiritual; intrinsic; hypothetical; natural; decorative; intellectual; physical; rare; literary; uncommon.

verbs

assure of—; bequeath—to; bestow—upon; confer—upon; deserve—; furnish—; grant —; inherit—; lavish—on; leave—to; obtain —; present—; provide—; secure—; settle —on; solicit—; stipulate—; vest—; wheedle —; will—; —eases; —enriches; —provides for; —rescues; —supports.

(See bounty, gift, money.)

ENDURABLE

adverbs

scarcely; grimly; barely; hardly; philosophically; stoically; tolerably; heroically; reasonably.

ENDURANCE

adjectives

dignified; calm; physical; marvelous; pained; resolute; unparalleled; silent; heroic; unlimited; patient; passive; superhuman; moral; stout; brave.

verbs

attain—; bear with—; discipline to—; enhance—; harden—; impose on—; limit—; prolong beyond—; replenish—; tax—; torment beyond—; —conquers; —ebbs; —fades; —fails; —surpasses; —sustains; —terminates; —wanes.

(See persistence, fortitude, patience, forbearance.)

ENDURE (v)

adverbs

placidly; firmly; coldly; irksomely; everlastingly; impatiently; consciously; simply; daily; permanently; dignifiedly; heroically; naturally; intellectually; physically; passively; morally; stoutly; bravely.

(See suffer, bear.)

ENEMA

verbs

employ—; endure—; inject—; introduce—; order—; prepare—; prescribe—; recommend—; resort to—; urge—; —aggravates; —aids; —appeases; —comforts; —eases; —enervates; —exasperates; —infuriates; —purges; —quickens; —relieves; —soothes; —weakens.

(See medicine, laxative, emetic.)

adjectives

approaching; spiteful; transalpine; routed; hereditary; partisan; scrupulous; fearful; generous; retreating; domestic; vanquished; damaging; embittered; pernicious; confiding; political; patient; sagacious; faithful; malarial; sworn; potential; stern; cruel; legendary; mysterious; invisible; avowed; discomfited; malicious; vigilant; treacherous; intrenched; formidable; destructive; prejudiced; pleasant; bigoted; subtle; legionary; inveterate; aggressive; contemptuous; external; visionary; fanatical; unfair; bitter; self-reliant; resolute; common; skulking; service; ferocious; pregnant; imaginary; alien; courageous; loathed; penniless; rival; devouring; butchering; lurking; malignant; exposed; deadly; cunning; unrelenting; panic-stricken; implacable; erstwhile; exasperated; indefatigable; insidious; ruthless; vehement; vindictive.

verbs

acquiesce to—; ambush—; annihilate—; approach—; baffle—; beleaguer—; betray to —; charge—; chase—; confront—; crush—; cultivate—; curse—; deliver—; demoralize—; destroy—; disarm—; eliminate—; elude—; engage—; enslave—; entrap—; erase—; excoriate—; exterminate—; face—; fall into the hands of—; foil—; forgive—; harass—; hold—at bay; hurl back—; intercept—; inveigh against—; judge—; massacre—; mislead—; mollify—; negotiate with—; outstrip—; overpower—; overwhelm—; prey upon—; provoke—; persecute—; pursue—; rage at—; reproach—; reveal—; rid of—; scatter—; slay—; smite —; subdue—; survey—; trap—; vanquish —; yield to—; —clamors; —conspires; —falls; —invades; —launches; —lures; —lurks; —plots; —retires; —retreats; —slanders; —withdraws; overthrow—.

(See adversary, antagonist, foe, opponent, rival, competitor.)

ENERGETIC

adverbs

spasmodically; courageously; consistently; actually; indefatigably; gloriously; conspicuously; monumentally; phenomenally; creatively; colossally; stupendously; patiently; strikingly; laboriously; magnificently; spectacularly; breath-takingly; supremely; impressively; valorously; indomitably; nervously; joyously; formidably; prodigiously;

fitfully; restlessly; tremendously; appallingly; suspiciously; excitedly; disturbingly; normally; abnormally.

ENERGETICS
adjectives
metaphysical; speculative; philosophic.

ENERGY
adjectives
active; indomitable; wonted; untiring; feverish; progressive; torrential; resistless; undiminished; imperfect; newborn; constructive; cheering; felicitous; nervous; twofold; contortionary; difficult; joyous; murderous; characteristic; wondrous; abundant; lagging; formidable; surpassing; stern; resolute; boundless; uncommon; impressive; superhuman; vigorous; untamable; repressed; cumulative; imparted; latent; prevailing; overmastering; enormous; sustained; rebellious; dynamic; mysterious; creative; deceptive; tireless; youthful; fervid; patient; inexhaustible; biological; triumphant; collective; relentless; inherent; passionate; vital; vehement; available; unfaltering; invincible; exhaustless; multiform; tameless; undivided; flagging; due; never-ceasing; dampened; stormy; hopeful; tidal; liquid; administrative; striking; unabated; incalculable; intellectual; volcanic; intrepid; convulsive; destructive; sleepless; tremendous; expansive; prodigious; long-discordant; presidential; unmeasured; enlightened; hollow; despairing; impetuous; spiritual; terrible; native; productive; indefatigable; mastering; excited; reposing; diligent; discursive; overflowing; manly; radiant; well-directed; unparalleled; potential; pathetic; mechanical; unaided; concentrated; rapid; fitful; industrious; subtle; compulsive; throbbing; unwearying; distorting; hypothetical; dulled; intensive; dauntless; dashing; hopeful; ridiculous; biting; fiery; reckless; grim; capacious; rank; incomparable; magnetic; useful; unimpeded; subatomic; desperate; ruthless; vivid; searching; reserve; marked; superfluous; wasteful; dogged; restless; impartial; restricted; ultimate; scientific; electric; kinetic; mental; singular; superabundant; structural; moral.

verbs
absorb—; bend—toward; build up—; center —; conserve—; consume—; control—; convert into—; dedicate—to; demand—; derive —from; develop—; devote—to; discharge —; dissipate—; display—; drain—; endow with—; exhibit—; expend—; fill with—;

flood with—; focus—upon; fritter away—; gather—; increase—; liberate—; organize —; provide—; relax—; renew—; release —; resuscitate—; retard—; reward—; smother—; spend—; squander—; store up —; tax—; transform—; transmit—; unleash—; unlock—; utilize—; waste—; — deteriorates; —flags.
(See force, power, vigor, strength, zeal.)

ENERVATING
adverbs
undeniably; terribly; unfortunately; dangerously; unbelievably; alarmingly; deplorably; definitely; horribly; strangely; oddly; visibly; hopelessly; deeply.

ENFEEBLED
adverbs
pitiably; miserably; wretchedly; hopelessly; irremediably; visibly; apparently; manifestly; outrageously; cruelly; extraordinarily; curiously; nervously; languidly; unquestionably; ominously; mysteriously; horribly; inexplicably.

ENFEEBLEMENT
verbs
brace—; fortify—; give way to—; guard against—; incur—; invigorate—; languish in—; produce—; relax in—; resist—; sustain—; totter in—; —cramps; —deprives; —drains; —impoverishes; —prevents; — reduces; —saps; —unhinges.

ENFORCE (v)
adverbs
rigorously; arrogantly; rigidly; stringently; steadily; strictly; promptly; obstinately; sufficiently; aggressively; roughly; nominally; doggedly; painstakingly.
(See force, compel.)

ENFORCEMENT
adjectives
vigorous; sufficient; rough; rigid; aggressive.

ENGAGE (v)
adverbs
professionally; professedly; obviously; industrially; industriously; controversially; earnestly; actively; pitifully; extensively; variously; picturesquely; successfully; continuously; seriously; actively; willingly; exclusively; amicably; hotly; demurely;

jointly; bindingly; allegedly; partially; obstinately; bloodily; pecuniarily; indecisively; intensively.

(See pledge, indulge.)

ENGAGEMENT

adjectives
binding; alleged; partial; bloody; obstinate; quasi-voluntary; pecuniary; long-standing; memorable; indecisive; pressing; wordy; professional.

verbs
agree upon—; announce—; anticipate—; arrange for—; attend—; break—; cancel—; celebrate—; contract—; defer—; desire—; enroll—; free from—; fulfill—; liberate from—; obtain—; prolong—; release from —; terminate—; —affiances; —betroths; —binds; —pairs; —pledges; —surprises.

(See betrothal, promise.)

ENGAGING

adverbs
irresistibly; charmingly; captivatingly; youthfully; delightfully; pleasantly; adorably; sweetly; gracefully; winningly; interestingly; fascinatingly; amiably; quietly; modestly; pertly; saucily; lovingly; attractively; enchantingly; unusually; artlessly; innocently; indefinably; extraordinarily; singularly.

ENGINE

adjectives
locomotive; palpitating; lifeless; mutilated; cruel; deadlier; mysterious; inanimate; atmospheric; fettered; awesome; devilish; asthmatic; rotary; monstrous; phenomenal; ubiquitous.

verbs
coal—; cool—; develop—; devise—; fuel—; lubricate—; muffle—; oil—; pilot—; repair—; —backfires; —batters; —buzzes; —chugs; —clatters; —coughs; —dies; —drives; —drones; —racks; —recoils; —roars; —snarls; —sputters; —throbs; —transforms; —utilizes; —wavers.

(See machine, mechanism.)

ENGINEER

adjectives
painstaking; consulting; self-styled; distinguished; research; topographical.

verbs
consult—; employ—; require—; —alters; —arranges; —bridges; —computes; —constructs; —contrives; —designs; —devises; —invents; —manages; —measures; —plans; —performs; —schemes; —suggests; —supervises; —undertakes.

(See driver, operator, manager.)

ENGINEERING

adjectives
automotive; unrivaled; chemical; civil; electrical; mechanical.

ENGLAND

verbs
ally with—; defame—; defend—; govern —; honor—; integrate—; invade—; journey to—; maim—; reign over—; represent—; revere—; rule—; —acclaims; —bleeds; —endures; —honors; —laments; —triumphs; —vanquishes.

(See country, democracy, republic, monarchy.)

ENGLISH

adjectives
clipped; civilized; thoughtful; simple; fatuous; rhythmic; plain; rough.

verbs
accent—; analyze—; comprehend—; converse in—; correct—; corrupt—; criticize—; falter in—; improve—; interpret—; polish —; purify—; render in—; rhyme—; speak —; study—; translate—; —changes; —derives from; —develops; —evolves.

(See language, literature.)

ENGRAVE (v)

adverbs
delicately; handsomely; daintily; indelibly; exquisite; curious; extraordinary; reproduced; vivid; delicate; deft; skillful.

(See carve, imprint.)

ENGRAVING

adjectives
exquisite; curious; extraordinary; reproduced; vivid; delicate; deft; skillful.

ENGROSS (v)

adverbs
constantly; deeply; chiefly; earnestly; wholly; entirely; sympathetically; entirely; passionately; successfully.

(See absorb, occupy.)

ENHANCE (v)

adverbs

enormously; vastly; radically; inexpressibly; fascinatingly; consequently; attractively.

(See increase, magnify.)

ENIGMA

adjectives

inexplicable; incomprehensible.

verbs

deal in—s; disclose—; dissect—; dissolve—; explain—; express in—; investigate—; question—; ransack—; screen in—; scrutinize—; shroud in—; solve—; —baffles; —conceals; —mystifies; —perplexes; —puzzles; —seals.

(See riddle, mystery, puzzle.)

ENIGMATIC

adverbs

bewilderingly; vexatiously; obscurely; inscrutably; oddly; curiously; peculiarly; singularly; precariously; bafflingly; unaccountably; infernally; unreasonably; inexplicably; unnecessarily.

ENJOIN (v)

adverbs

peremptorily; rudely; dictatorially; harshly; sternly; firmly; casually.

(See command, forbid.)

ENJOY (v)

adverbs

intensely; habitually; unconsciously; sagaciously; contemplatively; languidly; poignantly; acutely; hugely; profoundly; keenly; wholesomely; amazingly; vastly; tranquilly; tremendously; passively; evanescently; maliciously; mentally; meditatively; feverishly; indolently; mischievously; voluptuously; trivially; domestically; serenely; aesthetically; innocently; personally; wholeheartedly; imaginatively; idly; unpretentiously; heartily; reasonably; consciously; contemplatively.

(See gratify, like.)

ENJOYABLE

adverbs

thoroughly; utterly; occasionally; always; keenly; profoundly; heartily; immensely; altogether; delightfully; luxuriously.

ENJOYMENT

adjectives

republican; evanescent; passive; malicious; mental; meditative; different; full; feverish; stately; immediate; indolent; rapt; healthy; affected; frequent; novel; separate; mischievous; voluptuous; perfect; unwonted; trivial; unmolested; prosperous; domestic; serene; sublunary; aesthetic; surfeited; lazy; suppressed; joint; innocent; personal; whole-hearted; imaginative; idle; aimless; gluttonous; amused; refined; open; mystical; tranquil; solid; solitary; statutory; unpretentious; keen; hearty; animal; civil; wholesome; evident; reasonable; frank; conscious; exclusive; contemplative.

verbs

afford—; bless with—; charge with—; covet—; crave—; derive—; desire—; detract from—; forestall—; grasp—; indulge in—; interrupt—; lead to—; limit—; manifest—; prove—; pursue—; quench—; savor with—; scatter—; seize—; share—; spoil —; subdue—; temper—; —engrosses; —monopolizes; —occupies; —palls; —refreshes.

(See pleasure, entertainment, delight, satisfaction, happiness.)

ENLARGE (v)

adverbs

unboundedly; quickly; dangerously; abnormally; unduly; gradually; continuously; threateningly.

(See expand, broaden.)

ENLARGEMENT

adjectives

remarkable; gradual; ignorant; undue; continuous.

verbs

advocate—; attempt—; check—; curb—; curtail—; demand—; influence—; justify—; limit—; necessitate—; plan—; prepare—; prevent—; procure—; promote—; regulate —; require—; restrain—; restrict—; strangle—; strive for—; survey—; warrant —; —absorbs; —enhances; —exalts; —improves.

(See increase, extension, development, expansion, growth.)

ENLIGHTENMENT

verbs

communicate—; direct—; express—; furnish —; impart—; need—; occasion—; plan—; plead for—; present—; prompt—; seek—; shed—; signify—; strive for—; supply—; support—; suppress—; taste—; —acquaints;

—assists; —awakens; —edifies; —exhilarates; —progresses; —revives.
(See wisdom, advancement.)

ENMITY

adjectives
secret; everlasting; oblivious; lifelong; passionate; irreconcilable; unwarrantable; stolid; intense; dark.

verbs
abolish—; allay—; disarm—; drown—; earn—; enact through—; express—; frown upon—; ground on—; harbor—; incite—; incur—; nurse—; overcome—; perceive—; place—between; ponder—; set—between; sow—; vanquish—; —abates; —breaks; —separates; —severs; —splits.
(See hostility, ill-will, opposition, antagonism, hatred, animosity.)

ENNUI

adjectives
listless; eternal; mortal.

verbs
affect with—; bore with—; curse with—; die of—; divert—; feel—; overcome—; produce—; resent—; save from—; signify—; subdue—; suffer from—; taste—; weary with—; wrap in—; —abates; —attacks; —bereaves; —despairs; —dethrones; —grows; —is born; —palls; —vexes; —victimizes; —weights.
(See weariness, languor.)

ENORMOUS

adverbs
incredibly; preposterously; inordinately; tremendously; fabulously; astonishingly; absolutely; extraordinarily; indescribably; positively; frightfully; alarmingly.

ENQUIRE (v)

adverbs
innocently; hopefully; continually; persistently; annoyingly; repeatedly; fervently.
(See ask, question.)

ENRAPTURED

adverbs
obviously; utterly; inordinately; particularly; strangely; surprisingly; completely; deeply; indubitably; wonderfully; mysteriously; highly; avowedly.

ENRICH (v)

adverbs
prodigiously; delectably; abundantly; magnificently; elaborately; immensely; ultimately; considerably; ornately.
(See adorn, embellish.)

ENRICHMENT

adjectives
resultant; minor; ornate.

ENROLLMENT

verbs
check—; dismiss from—; enter in—; erase from—; inscribe in—; list—; mark—; merit —; place on—; qualify for—; record in—; refer to—; register in—; seek—; view—; —acknowledges; —approximates; —certifies; —embodies; —increases; —notes.
(See record.)

ENSCONCE (v)

adverbs
snugly; firmly; comfortably; safely; cozily; warmly; domestically.
(See sit, repose.)

ENSEMBLE

adjectives
impressive; rustic; harmonious; neighborhood.

ENSIGN

adjectives
national; armorial; fluttering.

verbs
cheer—; guard—; humble—; lift up—; march under—; plant—; protect—; raise—; rally round—; salute—; scatter—; shred—; spread—; tatter—; unfurl—; —advances; —blazes; —flutters; —signifies; —symbolizes; hang up—.
(See standard, flag.)

ENSLAVEMENT

verbs
cast into—; decry—; deliver from—; denounce—; drive into—; free from—; hamper by—; liberate from—; prevent—; quit —; reduce to—; release from—; repel—; return to—; submit to—; throw into—; —deprives; —disgusts; —hinders; —restrains; —stifles; —subjugates.
(See bondage, subjugation, subjection, slavery.)

428

ENTANGLE (v)

adverbs

inextricably; equally; unnecessarily; thoroughly; fatally; tragically; unfortunately; matrimonially; domestically; ceaselessly; rashly.

(See tangle, involve.)

ENTANGLEMENT

adjectives

inextricable; unnecessary.

verbs

avoid—; charm into—; extricate from—; inveigh into—; knit—; lure into—; prevent —; remove—; risk—; snare in—; unfold—; unravel—; trap in—; weave—; —complicates; —confuses; —distresses; —embarrasses; —embraces; —impedes; —implicates; —involves; —pains; —perplexes; escape—.

(See intricacy, complication, tangle.)

ENTER (v)

adverbs

gradually; inconspicuously; presumptuously; peremptorily; calmly; belligerently; triumphantly; obtrusively; intimately; minutely; hurriedly; intelligently; gratefully; optimistically; promptly; controversially; casually; ceremoniously; boldly; unlawfully; pompously; abruptly; simultaneously.

(See penetrate, insert.)

ENTERPRISE

adjectives

profitable; amazing; legitimate; individual; heterogeneous; successful; commercial; regional; dignified; lofty; voluntary; economic; vulgar; protracted; inadequate; stupid; philanthropic; characteristic; romantic; fresh; monumental; desperate; year-round; unscrupulous; blameless; ill-starred; magnanimous; daring; equal; vivid; manly; costly; co-operative; active; chimerical; honorable; venturesome; formidable; uncertain; serviceable; perilous; glorious; prodigious; productive; fabulous; nautical; mundane; infernal; gigantic; prominent; dangerous; hazardous; brilliant; illegal; crusading; charitable; appalling; audacious; inviting; indomitable; laudable; imaginative; delicate.

verbs

abandon—; arm for—; consider—; display —; embark on—; endanger—; enlist in—; enroll in—; exploit—; finance—; hazard—; imperil—; initiate—; manage—; partake in—; persist in—; risk—; stimulate—; struggle in—; swear to—; undertake—; venture on—; —fails; —flourishes; —prospers; —requires; —succeeds; —thrives.

(See project, task, work, undertaking.)

ENTERPRISING

adverbs

unusually; amazingly; daringly; laudably; brilliantly; prodigiously; cleverly; skilfully; alertly; smartly; energetically; marvelously; wonderfully; astutely; zealously; strenuously; earnestly; oddly; briskly; vigorously; indefatigably; industriously; diligently; intrepidly; confidently; uncommonly; competently.

ENTERTAIN (v)

adverbs

momentarily; seriously; pretentiously; fabulously; jovially; charmingly; extensively; lavishly; sumptuously; gravely; royally; tolerably; gaily; steadily; hospitably; vaguely; ponderously; uniformly; erroneously; rudely; incessantly; boisterously; casually; cleverly; musically; laboriously; incidentally; sparklingly; fitfully.

(See amuse, divert.)

ENTERTAINER

adjectives

talented; professional; terrified; master.

verbs

acclaim—; announce—; applaud—; boo—; deride—; encore—; encourage—; engage—; heckle—; hire—; hiss—; order—s; produce —; provide—; seek—s; supply—s; — amuses; —bores; —delights; —diverts; — enlivens; —exhibits; —performs; —pleases; —practises; —wearies.

(See hostess, actor.)

ENTERTAINING

adverbs

brilliantly; pleasantly; highly; agreeably; racily; undoubtedly; unusually; charmingly; elaborately; distinctly; delightfully; cleverly; gallantly; amusingly; wittily; sportively; hilariously; roguishly; noisily; admirably; impressively; merrily; comically; ridiculously.

ENTERTAINMENT

adjectives

charming; rude; hospitable; society; elaborate; endless; incessant; boisterous; casual; youthful; distinguished; amateur; critical; mutual; princely; diversified;

clever; friendly; dramatic; musical; honorable; momentary; laborious; sumptuous; guest; evening; varied; sparkling; incidental.

verbs
accord—; afford—; announce—; applaud—; approve of—; buy—; desire—; furnish—; guarantee—; lack—; perceive with—; prepare—; produce—; provide—; seek—; stage —; supply—; surprise with—; —annoys; —bores; —delights; —diverts; —enlivens; —interests; —pleases; —tires; —wearies.
(See performance, amusement, delight, diversion, enjoyment, recreation, hospitality.)

ENTHRALLED
adverbs
irresistibly; utterly; completely; wondrously; mysteriously; rapidly; rapturously; ecstatically; blissfully; strangely; deeply.

ENTHRONE (v)
adverbs
solemnly; grandly; ceremoniously; magnificently; pompously; regally; spectacularly.
(See raise, elevate.)

ENTHUSIASM
adjectives
rash; increasing; unbounded; fanatical; heartiest; warm; passionate; noisy; generous; ill-judged; romantic; voluble; girlish; glowing; exaggerated; weakening; boundless; fervent; ubiquitous; academic; rapt; unrestrained; passing; patriotic; polemical; rousing; gushing; uncontrolled; uncommon; positive; lyric; religious; intense; irrepressible; beautiful; delirious; vapid; proud; popular; impetuous; smoldering; healthy; altruistic; fierce; contagious; usual; greedy; human; available; misguided; rapturous; solemn; latent; unreflecting; honest; dwindled; instant; wild; frantic; temporary; buoyant; fervid; virginal; virtuous; genuine; inexhaustible; boyish; sweet; joyous; earnest; hearty; lofty; flamboyant; divine; common; contagious; actual; infectious.

verbs
admire—; arouse—; awaken—; beam with —; beget—; chill—; dampen—; dim—; display—; evoke—; express—; feed—; fire with—; halt—; imbue with—; impart—; inspire with—; muster—; pour forth—; rationalize—; respond to—; rouse—; share —; spend—; suppress—; sustain—; tolerate

—; vibrate with—; —blazes; —blinds; — bubbles; —flags; —flows; —melts away; — pales; —penetrates; —perishes; —rises; —spreads; —subsides; —wanes; —waxes.
(See zeal, ecstasy, eagerness, earnestness, ardor, fervor, passion.)

ENTHUSIAST
adjectives
prominent; dreaming; zealous; culpable; martial; religious; inconsiderate; baffled; harebrained; romantic.

ENTHUSIASTIC
adverbs
unusually; sincerely; delightfully; keenly; profoundly; actively; immediately; zealously; glowingly; passionately; fanatically; warmly; generously; girlishly; fervently; childishly; loudly; boundlessly; raptly; intensely; irrepressibly; beautifully; impulsively; impetuously; fiercely; instantly; wildly; sweetly; joyously; infectiously; extravagantly; strikingly; ardently; exceptionally.

ENTITLE (v)
adverbs
unquestionably; incorrectly; legally; fully; completely; thoroughly; clearly.
(See justify.)

ENTITY
adjectives
abstract; operative; self-acting.

ENTRAILS
adjectives
massy; palpitating; intolerable.

ENTRANCE
adjectives
clairvoyant; auspicious; reputed; complicated; triumphant; unperturbed; hospitable; bricked-up; ceremonious; stormy; sudden; ragged; dirty; fitting; changeful; bursting; unobserved; sheltered; adjacent; brilliant; noisy; swaggering.

verbs
bar—; block—; camouflage—; circle—; clog —; command—; conceal—; convey to—; direct to—; disdain—; effect—; fight for—; flank—; forbid—; forsake—; gain—; guard —; lead to—; obtain—; penetrate—; procure—; reject—; win—; force—.
(See access, door, entry, gate, introduction, opening.)

ENTRANCED

adverbs

perfectly; enthusiastically; utterly; irresistibly; naturally; obviously; noticeably; visibly; delightfully; ecstatically; happily; rapturously; wholly; irrecoverably.

ENTRANT

verbs

admit—; assign—; award to—; file—; herd —s; insert—; introduce—; judge—; limit —s; privilege—; receive—; register—; require—; reward—; select—; welcome—; —s compete; —s flow past; —influences; — participates; —subscribes to.

(See beginner, applicant, competitor.)

ENTREAT (v)

adverbs

civilly; brokenly; pathetically; frankly; patronizingly; earnestly; tenderly; sighingly; fondly; urgently; reproachfully; persistently; humbly; noisily.

(See plead, urge.)

ENTREATY

adjectives

earnest; fond; urgent; boisterous; reproachful; persistent; hospitable; humble; previous; repeated (pl).

verbs

allow—; answer—; comply with—; consent to—; grant—; harass with—ies; hawk—ies; heed—; protest—; rebuff—; recite—; repulse—; resist—; tender—; tolerate—; vex with—; yield to—; —irritates; —persuades; —requests.

(See request, petition, appeal.)

ENTREE

verbs

anticipate—; arrive at—; await—; ban—; choose—; demand—; give—to; gulp—; limit—; prepare—; prevent—; procure—; provide—; refuse—; relish—; select—; serve—; value—; —tempts.

(See dish, food.)

ENTRENCH (v)

adverbs

firmly; safely; protectively; defensively; deeply; securely.

(See intensify, fortify.)

ENTRY

adjectives

forcible; partial; abrupt; official; illegal; discursive; triumphant; burglarious; grandiloquent; mere; magnificent.

verbs

cancel—; certify—; duplicate—; file—; inscribe—; insert—; jot down—; limit—s; note—; post—; record—; register—; reject—; solicit—ies; strike out—; tabulate ies—; welcome—; wipe out—; —s flood.

(See entrance, access, hall.)

ENVELOP (v)

adverbs

thickly; gaseously; materially; impenetrably; nebulously; obscurely.

(See surround, inclose.)

ENVELOPE

adjectives

gaseous; rigid; material; impenetrable.

verbs

address—; assign to—; enclose in—; fold —; gum—; knife—; pen—; seal—; stamp —; tear—; wrap in—; —bears; —confines; —contains; —covers; —encases; —protects; —surrounds.

(See wrapper, case, sheath.)

ENVELOPMENT

adjectives

nebulous; curious; obscure; ungrateful.

ENVIABLE

adverbs

utterly; eminently; vaguely; intensely; apparently; obviously; highly; undeniably; uncommonly; invidiously.

ENVIRONMENT

adjectives

unnatural; accidental; fictitious; cultural; gay; friendly; refined; smart; spiritual; stately; refreshing; restricted; unambitious; ideal; hostile; economic; early; playhouse; suitable; specific; luxurious; pseudo-social; moral; fitting; cooling; healthful; unsuited; niggardly; native; unfavorable; frontier; unusual; human; felicitous; musical; nationalistic; physical; fertile; limited.

verbs

adjust to—; alter—; control—; create—; dominate—; endure—; escape from—; fit—; harmonize with—; lift from—; modify—; shape—; share—; —corrupts; —exerts; —influences; —moulds; —shapes; — strengthens; —weakens.

(See surroundings, circumstances, conditions.)

adjectives

immediate; sheltered; picturesque; straggling.

ENVY

adjectives

petty; daggered; jealous; vile; powerless; ghoulish; malignant; poignant; pardonable; bitter; secret; gnawing; public; private; strenuous; illiberal; mixed; unnatural; sharp; sick-bed.

verbs

arouse—; awaken—; conceal—; discipline —; evoke—; excite—; exempt from—; express—; fill with—; incite—; incur—of; infect with—; move by—; murmur—; occasion—; provoke—; raise—; regard with—; sicken with—; stab with—; —blazes up; — convulses; —envelops; —inflames; —narrows; —prejudices; —swells; —threatens.
(See malice, desire, jealousy.)

ENVY (v)

adverbs

secretly; sincerely; pettishly; jealously; vilely; powerlessly; ghoulishly; malignantly; bitterly; gnawingly; privately; unnaturally; painfully.
(See suspect, desire.)

EPHEMERAL

adverbs

fleetingly; wondrously; transiently; shiftily; sadly; precariously; tantalizingly; vexatiously; transitorily; evanescently; mortally; perishably; briefly; heartbreakingly.

EPIC

adjectives

peopled; magnificent; grand; unscrupulous; extant; future; literary; counterfeiting; ponderous; medieval; pietistic; eternal; heroic; familiar; lengthy.

adverbs

traditionally; fabulously; nationally; racially; universally; nobly; significantly; majestically; splendidly; dramatically; tragically; brilliantly; deathlessly; imperishably; timelessly; sweepingly; consummately; amazingly; highly; magnificently; staggeringly; incomparably; grandly.

EPICURE

adjectives

jovial; classical; facetious; cultured; suave; fastidious; precise.

adverbs

fastidiously; delicately; luxuriously; sensuously; indulgently; daintily; discriminatingly; greedily; highly; openly; manifestly; intemperately; voluptuously; rakishly; wildly; inordinately; lamentably; extremely; deliberately; avowedly.

EPIDEMIC

adjectives

veritable; dangerous; disastrous; prevailing; periodical; acute; terrible; infectious.

verbs

approach—; constitute—; curtail—; eradicate—; fend against—; inoculate against—; succumb to—; —appears; —breaks out; — consumes; —devastates; —lingers; —prostrates; —rages; —ravages; —sweeps; — swells; —wanes.
(See disease, plague, cholera, smallpox.)

adverbs

locally; universally; currently; recently; sweepingly; commonly; prevalently; generally; infectiously; contagiously; noxiously; pestilentially; virulently; unfortunately; diffusively; dangerously; disastrously; periodically; acutely; terribly; curiously; obscurely; inexplicably; mysteriously.

EPIDERMIS

verbs

affect—; apply to—; blemish—; dab—; damage—; daub—; flay—; form—; impair —; infect—; injure—; mar—; repair—; restore—; salve—; scratch—; shed—; smear on—; —coats; —covers; —defends; —encases; —peels; —tans; —regenerates.
(See skin.)

EPIGRAM

adjectives

sparkling; feeble; biting.

verbs

abound in—s; compose—; enjoy—; indulge in—; inscribe—; master—; recite—; resent —; translate—; vent—; —charms; —condenses; —debases; —expresses; —irks; — points out; —provokes; —puzzles; —revenges; —satirizes; —stings; —consists of.
(See saying, poem, writing.)

EPIGRAMMATIC

adverbs

facetiously; waggishly; sententiously; laconically; crisply; curtly; neatly; quaintly;

pithily; concisely; summarily; wittily; cruelly; harshly; sarcastically; clownishly; drolly; jocosely; playfully; smartly; consciously; vexatiously; endlessly.

EPISODE

adjectives
impressive; dramatic; colorful; ludicrous; tragical; unsavory; extraordinary; pungent; exciting; wearing; pathetic; undignified; magnificent; ugly; continental; momentous; stirring; detached; mystical; peaceful; quixotic; picturesque; unforeseen; human; moving; trivial; soul-stirring; unfinished.

verbs
arrange—s; brood upon—; continue—; dramatize—; finish—; interject—; interpose—; introduce—; involve in—; number —s; recount—; refer to—; relate—; repeat —; resume—; —climaxes; —concerns; — crops up; —embraces; —entertains; —implicates; —intervenes.
(See incident, event, occurrence, action, story.)

EPISTLE

adjectives
famous; closely-written; absurd; tearful; heartfelt; imperial; business; monotonous; gracious; elegant; maternal; perplexing.

verbs
address—; compose—; delay—; deliver—; dispatch—; inspire—; laud—; pen—; prepare—; seal—; —aims at; —communicates; —consoles; —conveys; —declares; —explains; —indites; —instructs; —links; — relates; —reunites; —reveals; —strays; — wanders; —waxes.
(See letter, communication, writing.)

EPITAPH

adjectives
lying; mournful; pompous; uxorious; chiseled; inordinate; pitiable; simple; celebrated; original; dusty; sly; faithful; ancestral; wise; fitting; appropriate; irreverent.

verbs
bestow—on; compose—; conceive—; define —; deliver—; deserve—; hang—on; incorporate in—; inscribe—; interpret—; judge —; merit—; render in—; —adorns; —de-

scribes; —familiarizes; —glitters; —glorifies; —honors; —records; —reflects; — slanders; —vulgarizes.
(See inscription.)

EPITHET

adjectives
deranged; obnoxious; profane; insulting; deprecatory; opprobrious; polite; repeated; contumelious; endearing; courteous; balanced; fatal; significant.

verbs
answer—; apply—; bandy—s; bestow— upon; christen with—; comprehend—; convey—; design—; employ—; fix—; glory in—; indulge in—; justify—; originate—; pelt with—s; rain—s; represent with—; scatter—s; stuff with—s; —belongs; —designates; —disgraces; —justifies; —qualifies; —signifies; —terms.
(See phrase, expression, adjective, designation.)

EPITOMIZE (*v*)

adverbs
successfully; wittily; artfully; completely; shrewdly.
(See summarize, discuss.)

EPOCH

adjectives
geological; brilliant; colonial; misguided; glacial; legendary; memorable; impersonal; agitated; eventful; warfaring; climacteric; barbarous; revolutionary; haunted; chronological; antique; pagan.

verbs
begin—; commemorate—; create—; divide into—s; enhance—; form—; indicate—; inherit from—; mark—; open—; outlive—; refer to—; remember—; venerate—; — declines; —embraces; —glides on; —impresses; —produces; —provides; —survives.
(See period, era, time.)

EPOCHAL

adverbs
distinctly; significantly; markedly; notably; unforgettably; shamefully; brilliantly; memorably; legendarily; fabulously; imperishably; matchlessly; startlingly; stupendously; incalculably.

EQUABLE

adverbs
comfortably; pleasantly; dependably; naturally; happily; habitually; inherently; se-

renely; faultlessly; monotonously; reliably; drearily; methodically; agreeably; fairly; vexatiously; always; enviably.

EQUAL

adverbs
fairly; satisfactorily; agreeably; monotonously; symmetrically; broadly; practically; reasonably; legitimately; lawfully; admittedly; avowedly; synonymously; sufficiently; apparently; obviously; manifestly; evidently; incontestably.

EQUALITY

adjectives
rude; cozy; perfect; social; moral; legitimate; large; unrestricted; eternal; condescending.

verbs
abuse—; acquire—; admit—; approach—; assert—; assume—; attain—; demand—; denounce—; deny—; destroy—; disturb—; endow with—; maintain—; plead—; practice—; prate about—; prevent—; proclaim —; refuse—; require—; —breeds.
(See equilibrium, right, fairness, justice.)

EQUANIMITY

adjectives
astonishing; cool; unruffled; suave.

verbs
admire—; accept with—; approve—; bear with—; command—; concede with—; demonstrate—; digest with—; disregard with —; dwell in—; endure with—; justify—; keep in—; maintain—; possess—; recommend—; recover—; require—; restore—; suffer with—; swallow with—; wonder at —; —continues; —impresses; —persists; —surprises.
(See composure, serenity.)

EQUATION

adjectives
quadratic; personal; explanatory.

EQUILIBRIUM

adjectives
natural; balanced; unstable; happy; atmospheric.

verbs
attain—; check—; correct—; display—; exhibit—; gain—; guard—; illustrate—; maintain—; preserve—; restore—; threaten—.
(See balance, proportion.)

EQUIPAGE

adjectives
lumbering; huge; gilded; sumptuous; sufficient; somber.

EQUIPMENT

adjectives
technical; complete; optional; brilliant; recreational; obsolete; extensive; standard; defective; scanty; scientific; physical; inadequate; vocal; motorized; primitive; superior; ample; necessary; mental; intellectual.

verbs
acquire—; allot—to; complete—; contrive —; devise—; guard—; install—; modernize—; provide—; repair—; shield—; transport—; utilize—.
(See outfit, apparatus.)

EQUIPOISE

adjectives
boasted; unusual; vaunted.

EQUITABLE

adverbs
wisely; reasonably; duly; plainly; profoundly; prudently; rationally; sensibly; providently; expediently; justly; impartially; honorably; fairly; squarely; lawfully; legally; allowably; absolutely; legitimately; properly; scrupulously; punctiliously.

EQUIVALENT

adjectives
thermal; fair; modern; universal; financial; precise.

adverbs
meticulously; convertibly; tantamountly; avowedly; broadly; currently; customarily; regularly; naturally; wontedly; mathematically; genuinely; officially; strictly; basically; precisely; materially.

EQUIVOCAL

adverbs
vexatiously; irritatingly; purposely; intentionally; ambiguously; craftily; subtly; adroitly; cleverly; dubiously; debatably; insecurely; vaguely; mysteriously; ticklishly; obscurely; untrustworthily; unreliably; provokingly; cunningly; unfairly; artfully; fraudulently; perfidiously; insincerely; highly.

ERA

adjectives

crude; garish; showy; industrial; uninspired; commercialized; brief; comparative; colonial; illuminated; vamp; cultural.

verbs

acclaim—; announce—; enhance—; gild—; glorify—; hallow—; mark—; open—; symbolize—; typify—; usher in—; vulgarize—; —advances; —dawns; —emerges; —passes.

(See period, epoch, time.)

ERASURE

adjectives

lineal; untidy; unsightly; careless; blotchy; neat; nearly-invisible.

ERECT

adverbs

sturdily; staunchly; bravely; gallantly; loftily; firmly; grandly; rigidly; boldly; admirably; conspicuously; consciously; stiffly; proudly; imperiously; arrogantly.

ERECT (v)

adverbs

loftily; firmly; grandly; staunchly; toweringly; eloquently; triumphantly.

(See build, raise.)

ERECTNESS

adjectives

firm; conscious; natural; easy; military.

EROSION

verbs

activate—; check—; occasion—; overcome —; prevent—; produce—; protect from—; risk—; subject to—; —damages; —disintegrates; —endangers; —occurs; —strains; —weakens.

(See destruction, decay, acid.)

EROSIVE

adverbs

dangerously; wastefully; distressingly; disturbingly; unprofitably; harmfully; disastrously; detrimentally; deplorably; irremediably; inexpediently; increasingly; unfortunately; unnecessarily; grossly; outrageously; appallingly.

EROTIC

adverbs

amorously; tenderly; seductively; ardently; captivatingly; unduly; notably; particularly; interestingly; rapturously.

ERRAND

adjectives

mysterious; arrogant; uncouth; discouraging; slightest; reluctant; urgent; mournful; stumbling; futile; various (pl); wondrous.

verbs

accept—; administer—; bear—; commission for—; consent to—; discharge—; dispatch on—; execute—; fail in—; fake— (colloq); feign—; journey on—; send on—; speed on—.

(See mission, commission, communication.)

ERRANT

adverbs

incurably; nonchalantly; carelessly; incorrigibly; irresponsibly; gaily; happily; rapturously.

ERRATIC

adverbs

irregularly; habitually; characteristically; provokingly; unreliably; strangely; curiously; inscrutably; irresponsibly; inconsiderately; naturally; restlessly; mercurially; vagrantly; incurably; inveterately; fitfully; whimsically; capriciously; contrarily; uncomfortably; foolishly; inconsistently; marvelously; terribly.

ERRONEOUS

adverbs

tragically; purposely; carelessly; fallaciously; materially; foolishly; illogically; deceptively; intentionally; blunderingly; misleadingly; slightly; altogether; dreadfully; unpardonably.

ERROR

adjectives

manifest; inextricable; fatal; capital; successful; intellectual; deep-seated; common; vulgar; sweet; silly; trivial; apparent; gross; earthly; popular; strange; destructive; outstanding; biting; feeble; shallow; weak; mountainous; egregious; universal; ignoble; bare; venial; tactical; childish; unavoidable; curious; annoying; unguessed; statistical; innumerable (pl); scientific; serviceable; crumbling; pernicious; wild; warm; fantastic; glaring; opposite; chronic; dietetic; pleasing; previous; petty; profound; matrimonial; irretrievable; infinite; fundamental; unwelcome; counter; haughty; serious; damned; tempest-winged; typographical; monstrous; unfortunate; irremediable.

abound in—s; acknowledge—; adhere to—; aggravate—; atone for—; befog—; betray into—; build on—; cast out—; chafe at—; claim—; combat—; conquer—; correct—; counteract—; debate—; detect—; dispel—; escape—; expiate—; expose—; fall into—; forsake—; involve in—; lead into—; learn from—; lift above—; minimize—; neutralize—; overrule—; produce—; rebuke—; rectify—; reduce—; regret—; reject—; relinquish—; remove—; retrieve—; root in—; rue—; sense—; uncover—; unveil—; utter —; vanquish—; war against—; ward off—; wrestle with—; —contaminates; —deludes; —destroys; —impedes; —misleads.
(See fault, blunder, mistake, inaccuracy.)

ERUDITION
adjectives
mock; scholarly; extraordinary; specious.

verbs
abuse—; admire—; demand—; demonstrate —; denote—; digest—; employ—; exhibit —; feign—; freight with—; indicate—; judge—; justify—; oppress—; regard—; represent—; require—; —gratifies; —impresses.
(See knowledge, learning, wisdom.)

ERUPT (v)
adverbs
prematurely; terrifically; violently; prodigiously; volcanically; thunderously; crashingly; blindingly.
(See burst, explode.)

ERUPTION
adjectives
ruddy; cutaneous; memorable; terrific; copious; violent; prodigious; simultaneous; volcanic.

verbs
break forth in—; fear—; force—; hinder—; occasion—; prevent—; subject to—; —appears; —bursts; —discharges; —ejects; — emits; —harms; —issues forth; —occurs; —overwhelms; —shatters; —showers; — spreads.
(See outbreak, outburst.)

ESCAPADE
adjectives
suspicious; political; rash; youthful; drunken.

ESCAPE
adjectives
miraculous; precious; destitute; momentary; trivial; ignoble; impossible; marvelous; perilous; ultimate; hairbreadth; extraordinary; hair-raising; strong.

verbs
aid—; allow—; assist in—; attribute—to; conceal—; conspire—; cut off—; desire—; despair of—; effect—; enable—; guard against—; hinder—; insure—; investigate —; permit—; prevent—; scorn—; shun—.
(See flight, excuse, evasion.)

ESCAPE (v)
adverbs
exultantly; miraculously; temporarily; narrowly; easily; resolutely; audaciously; incessantly; barely; momentarily; ignobly; marvelously; perilously; ultimately; extraordinarily; hair-raisingly.
(See flee, elude.)

ESCORT
adjectives
military; proper; honorary; lounging; insufficient; barbaric.

verbs
accept—; attend in—; choose—; command —; desire—; employ—; form—; invite—; require—; serve as—; —abandons; —accommodates; —accompanies; —conducts; —conveys; —deserts; —guides; —lectures; —manages; —nurses; —protects; —serves; —supervises.
(See guard.)

ESCORT (v)
adverbs
tumultuously; barbarically; formally; ceremoniously; grandly; magnificently; regally; royally; gaily.
(See attend, follow.)

ESPIONAGE
adjectives
ostentatious; stealthy; cleverly-concealed; sympathetic.

ESPOUSE (v)
adverbs
obstinately; warmly; passionately; rabidly; ardently; rashly; impatiently; sincerely; treacherously.
(See undertake, assume.)

adjectives
ardent; rabid; rash; impatient.

ESSAY

adjectives
satirical; controversial; historical; critical; introductory; moral; discursive; provocative; delightful; notable; apathetical; celebrated; detached; literary; elaborated; sublime; fragmentary; informative; admirable; kindred; penetrating; classical; enlightening; presumptuous; remarkable.

verbs
abandon—; accept—; agree with—; attack —; caption—; compose—; criticize—; discuss—; elaborate—; judge—; laud—; offer —; praise—; prepare—; preserve—; propound—; —attempts; —encourages; —expresses; —implies; —meditates on.
(See composition, endeavor, attempt, effort, exposition.)

ESSAYIST

adjectives
critical; classical; aggressive.

ESSENCE

adjectives
seductive; intentional; tenfold; concrete; lasting; solitary; everlasting; spiritual; subtle; carnal; divine; congenial; electric; enduring; singular; ethereal; poetic; meager; heavenly; invisible; articulate; omnipresent; distinct; penetrative; volatile; rubylike; thin; fiery; winged; glassy; sensuous; impalatable; immutable.

verbs
apply—; convey—; counterfeit—; cover with—; distil—; exhale—; extract—; flavor with—; instil—; perfume with—; prepare —; preserve—; procure—; resign—; rub in—; sprinkle—; steep in—; —nauseates; —penetrates; —pervades; —refreshes; — sickens; —sinks in.
(See substance, perfume, odor, scent.)

ESSENTIAL

adjectives
salient; **vital; food;** absolute; minimum; basic.

verbs
ascertain—; cloud—; constitute—; deprive of—; destroy—; discern—; dispense with —; establish—; lack—; master—; obstruct —; **overlook—;** prove—; require—; restore

—; strain—; suppress—; understand—; withhold—; —necessitates; —represents; — vanishes.
(See element, principle, quality.)

ESSENTIAL

adverbs
highly; absolutely; cardinally; emphatically; gravely; momentously; vitally; fundamentally; primarily; signally; significantly; urgently; extraordinarily; inordinately; seriously; utterly; peculiarly; unusually.

ESTABLISH (v)

adverbs
infallibly; conclusively; firmly; pompously; ultimately; solidly; definitely; indispensably; officially; permanently; triumphantly; incontestably; sufficiently; extensively; formally; rudely; splendidly; ancestrally; palatially; administratively.
(See show, prove.)

ESTABLISHED

adverbs
permanently; enduringly; stably; inviolately; thoroughly; immemorially; traditionally; generally; commonly; familiarly; conventionally; socially; regularly; officially; long; recently; firmly; easily; legally; emphatically; inescapably.

ESTABLISHMENT

adjectives
monastic; modest-looking; productive; immense; rude; conventional; splendid; primitive; odorous; penal; permanent; consular; separate; extensive; palatial; domestic; immediate; select; ancestral; manufacturing; ultimate; princely; meat-curing; administrative; costly; respectable-looking.

verbs
attack—; bar from—; conduct—; dictate —; enlarge—; evict from—; found—; guard—; hallow—; join—; legalize—; maintain—; nurture—; offend—; patronize—; set up—; superintend—; underwrite —; —crumbles; —fails; —flourishes; — prospers.
(See organization, institution.)

ESTATE

adjectives
manorial; residuary; **intestate;** unencumbered; landed; ancestral; precarious; competent; distressed; dark; scanty; fabulous;

feudal; impoverished; ecclesiastical; paltry; low; poor; outlying; hushed; sublunary; pretentious; unspeakable; meager; strange; uncorrupted; seignorial.

verbs
administer—; auction off—; charge to—; confiscate—; disable—; dissipate—; doom —; fall from—; fritter away—; lease—; maintain—; mortgage—; reapportion—; rent—; scorn—; settle—; shift—; tax—; —declines; —prospers; —shrinks.
(See property, possessions.)

ESTEEM
adjectives
great; rising; profound; exalted; proudest; racial; envious; impious; general; bright; favorable; sincerest.

verbs
command—; conceal—; deserve—; drop from—; enjoy—; entertain—; forfeit—; gain—; grow in—; hide—; hold in—; increase—; lose—; regard with—; value—; win—; —cools; —fades; —grows.
(See regard, respect, honor, favor, worth, opinion, value.)

ESTEEM (*v*)
adverbs
particularly; profoundly; racially; generally; sincerely; logically; enviously.
(See respect, honor.)

ESTIMABLE
adverbs
entirely; generally; highly; profoundly; undeniably; creditably; unimpeachably; obviously; worthily; dreadfully; respectably; dully; extremely; priggishly.

ESTIMATE
adjectives
impartial; production; exact; sanguine; contemptuous; accurate; accepted; modest; conservative; rough; truer; provisional; respectful; private; critical; utmost; exaggerated; judicious; reasonable; professional; slighting; undue; exaggerated; fallacious; moderate; current; contradictory; erroneous; inadequate; fantastic; theoretical; lightning.

verbs
accept—; arrive at—; attempt—; beggar—; calculate—; compute—; correct—; denounce —; entertain—; exaggerate—; extend—;

forward—; govern—; harbor—; offer—; reach—; reel off—s; sway—s; —agrees; —coincides; —differs; —errs; —falls short; —indicates.
(See computation, calculation, value.)

ESTIMATE (*v*)
adverbs
conservatively; variously; accurately; critically; approximately; authoritatively; unhesitatingly; wildly; unerringly; calculatingly; fallaciously; erroneously; inadequately; fantastically; theoretically; professionally; provisionally; worthily.
(See value, appraise.)

ESTIMATION
adjectives
worthy; reverend; excessive; ludicrous; ungalled; avowed; exalted; aristocratic.

ESTRANGED
adverbs
pitiably; altogether; tragically; pathetically; curiously; inexplicably; mysteriously; oddly; silently; obviously; evidently; coldly; hatefully; temporarily; deeply; permanently; stubbornly; relentlessly; visibly; idiotically; astonishingly; lamentably.

ESTRANGEMENT
adjectives
transient; political.

verbs
bear—; brood over—; complete—; incur—; mourn—; pine in—; prevent—; rebel against—; sink in—; submit to—; suffer—; —agonizes; —burns; —dejects; —depresses; —desolates; —disheartens; —isolates; —oppresses; —pains; —wearies.

ETCH (*v*)
adverbs
vividly; powerfully; movingly; delicately; skillfully; artfully; dexterously; strikingly.
(See draw, sketch.)

ETCHING
adjectives
powerful; delicate; moving.

ETERNITY
adjectives
self-enshrined; dead; endless; shoreless; present; measureless; indivisible; dreadful; tiny.

438

accept—; believe in—; dwell in—; endure for—; foretaste—; glimpse—; leave to—; pass through—; probe—; prolong to—; reach—; reveal—; seems—; sing of—; spend in—; wander through—; —effaces; —exists.
(See immortality.)

ETHER
adjectives
luminiferous; finer; limpid; luminous; elastic; celestial; boundless; subtle.

verbs
administer—; apply—; float in—; put under —; sleep under—; spray—; —anaesthetizes; —affects; —deadens; —diminishes; —dims; —dissolves; —drowns; —dulls; —moderates; —numbs; —palls; —reduces; —stupefies.
(See anaesthetic.)

ETHEREAL
adverbs
daintily; airily; insubstantially; lightly; buoyantly; incredibly; delicately; vivaciously; whimsically; blithely; gracefully; sportively; inexpressibly.

ETHICAL
adverbs
punctiliously; meticulously; highly; systematically; unfailingly; ostentatiously; laboriously; carefully; naturally; habitually; professionally; strictly; rigidly; happily; gracefully; politely; diplomatically; marvellously; conscientiously; dutifully; amenably; absolutely.

ETHICS
adjectives
professional; inflexible; strict; dreary; government; ministerial; legal; cheerless; bad; heightened.

verbs
adopt—; consider—; control by—; digest—; discourse on—; embrace—; exhort—; impose by—; improve—; instruct in—; involve—; judge—; live up to—; obligate by—; observe—; rebel against—; rely on—; test—; versed in—; —directs; —guides; —provides; —raises.
(See science, rules, philosophy.)

ETIQUETTE
adjectives
fixed; punctilious; stiff; established; courtly; exclusive; rigid.

verbs
apply—; conduct with—; educate in—; impose by—; inform on—; judge by—; loosen —; observe—; polish—; practise—; prescribe—; require—; study—; transact with —; transgress—; —bans; —demands; —forbids; —improves; —obliges; —prohibits; —tames; —ties.
(See code, rules, decorum.)

EULOGISTIC
adverbs
sententiously; sincerely; properly; suitably; regularly; duly; smugly; sanctimoniously; hypocritically; highly; impressively; dramatically; immeasurably; unnecessarily; sonorously; artfully; brilliantly; magnificently; admirably; splendidly; unctuously; sycophantically; speciously; fulsomely.

EULOGIZE (*v*)
adverbs
unctuously; flamboyantly; effusively; lavishly; flatteringly; deceptively; slyly; treacherously; deceivingly.
(See laud, praise.)

EULOGY
adjectives
barren; unmeasured; artful; embarrassed; swallowing; lengthened; brilliant; indiscriminating; sorry; glowing; sounding.

EUPHEMISTIC
adverbs
cleverly; artfully; adroitly; ironically; sarcastically; wittily; smoothly; humorously; plausibly; pompously; rhetorically; merrily; teasingly; neatly; felicitously; pleasantly; inoffensively.

EUPHONY
adjectives
gushing; sheer.

EUROPE
verbs
communicate with—; denounce—; embattle —; embroil—; introduce in—; invade—; ring through—; rock—; rule—; sail for—; seize—; shock—; tour—; unite—; —allies with; —arms; —copies; —envies; —ex-

ports; —imitates; —imports; —quakes; —repudiates; —seethes; —simmers; —stands; —voices; —wars.
(See continent.)

EVACUATION
adjectives
copious; sanguinolent; alvine.

verbs
advocate—; authorize—; command—; compel—; deplore—; direct—; facilitate—; force—; impose—; insist on—; prepare—; prescribe—; promote—; resist—; submit to —; suggest—; withdraw in—; —relinquishes; order—.
(See withdrawal, discharge.)

EVADE (*v*)
adverbs
gracefully; studiously; partially; slyly; treacherously; cleverly; dexterously.
(See avoid, shun.)

EVALUATION
adjectives
clinical; clear.

EVANESCENT
adverbs
flittingly; impermanently; briefly; ephemerally; precariously; transiently; transitorily; perishably; mortally; sadly.

EVANGELISTIC
adverbs
ardently; zealously; sincerely; earnestly; successfully; eagerly; persistently; fervently; devotedly; fervidly; passionately; assiduously; solemnly; happily; joyously; enthusiastically; rapturously; superbly; intensely; unwearyingly; devoutly.

EVASION
adjectives
elaborate; endless; dexterous; pitiful; terror-stricken; treasonable; sly .

verbs
addict to—; criticize—; decry—; detect—; employ—; endure—; forbid—; force—; frustrate—; practice—; require—; shift in —; shuffle in—; stammer in—; suspect—; trouble with—; wrap in—; —assists; —shelters.
(See subterfuge.)

EVASIVE
adverbs
unfortunately; disturbingly; deliberately; undesirably; ambiguously; equivocally; distressingly; offensively; insultingly; suspiciously; undeniably; quibblingly; perplexingly; bewilderingly; obscurely; mysteriously; seriously; irritatingly; stolidly; vaguely; disagreeably; insidiously; significantly; stupidly; unwisely; objectionably; cunningly; cleverly; adroitly.

EVE
adjectives
autumn; dew-glistening; sealing; keener; momentous; thoughtful; dewy; ghostly; deepening.

EVENING
adjectives
lingering; tranquil; happy; occasional; curious; long; fatal; autumnal; cold; frosty; red; triumphant; sad-colored; ravishing; chilly; awkward; bacchanal; bridal; calm; swift-falling; unfortunate; deepening; sorrowful; unillumined; bronzed; sleepy; balmy; eventful; golden; peaceful; imperial; ensuing; purple; gusty; premature; sober; dewy; ghostlike; dull; shadowy; memorable; grateful; languorous; bygone; dusky; hectic; delirious; warm; muggy; uncomfortable; cheerful; amazing; preceding; quiet; starry; harmonic; roseate.

verbs
approach—; await—; chill—; cloud—; crown——; draw toward—; gild—; hush—; last till—; occupy—; overcast—; ramble through—; return at—; rift—; rise at—; solemnize—; still—; sup at—; toil till—; usher in—; —approaches; —closes; —cools; —declines; —dies; —dims; —fades; —falls; —flies; —reposes; —shades; —sobers; —steals on.
(See twilight, dusk.)

EVENNESS
adjectives
velvet; insipid; boring; smooth; pleasant.

EVENT
adjectives
solemn; unbeatable; important; comprehensive; festival; outward; outstanding; sensational; trivial; huge; memorable; extraordinary; tragic; thrilling; embarrassing; disgusting; headline; contemporary; gigantic; strange; sweet; perturbing; crowning; subsequent; tremendous; strik-

ing; confused; fortunate; true; fierce; natural; unlooked-for; obscene; preposterous; dignified; sublime; momentous; inescapable; ultimate; startling; dramatic; pivotal; exciting; deplorable; celestial; mysterious; fateful; propitious; supreme; remarkable; future; sinful; minutest; detectable; stormy; dark; hurried; bizarre; unforeseen; stirring; fortuitous; unexpected; tempestuous; miraculous; boding; melancholy; overshadowing; succeeding; naked; recurrent; domestic; insignificant; humiliating; hastened; intermediate; calamitous; historical; previous; disastrous; happy; current; impolite; pin-point; dire; dreadful; preventable; antecedent.

verbs
acclaim—; applaud—; ascribe—to; attend —; beget—; commend—; detail—; dramatize—; explain—; fashion—; forecast—; ·foresee—; govern—; interpret—; mark—; narrate—; ponder—; predict—; presage—; rehash—; resume—; rue—; scan—; seize upon—; shape—; stamp—; view—; witness —; —commemorates; —confuses; —evolves; —portends; —represents; —results in; —underlies.
(See occurrence, incident, episode, consequence, issue, fortune.)

EVICT (*v*)
adverbs
raucously; sternly; heartlessly; coldly; cruelly; dictatorially; vigorously; harshly; peremptorily; abruptly; legally; forcefully; formally.
(See expel, dispossess.)

EVICTION
adjectives
harrowing; tragic; pitiful; heartless.

EVIDENCE
adjectives
silent; fearful; happiest; overwhelming; corroborative; further; official; tangible; repeated; spectroscopic; additional; damnatory; damaging; multiplied; irrefutable; confirmatory; circumstantial; diagnostic; documentary; substantial; signal; stronger; moral; noisy; convincing; incontrovertible; concrete; inadmissible; marked; apocryphal; explicit; abundant; bibliographical; contemporaneous; irrelevant; customary; secondhand; definite; palpable; visual; unmistakable; ·authentic; touching; effectual; white-spotted; legendary; sufficient; internal; contemporary; speechless; striking; ex-traordinary; certain; conspicuous; gratifying; remarkable; scientific; faintest; absolute; unassailable; revealing; external; pragmatic; ungarbled; trustworthy; material; corrected; hearsay; impressive; factual; ample; cumulative; manifest; undoubted; lawful; modest; conclusive; positive; indubitable; unanswerable; unexceptionable; incontestable; breathing; experimental; reasonable; truthful; overt; concentrated; supporting; decisive; hopeful; notable; unconscious; considerable; undeniable; direct; usual; unerring; outward; archaeological; satisfactory; unequivocal; presumptive.

verbs
accept—; accumulate—; adduce—; alter—; amass—; base on—; confirm—; confront with—; contradict—; corroborate—; credit —; deduce—; deny—; destroy—; digest—; emphasize—; examine—; falsify—; ferret out—; gaze on—; interpret—; invoke—; offer—; overrate—; overrule—; parade—; perjure—; produce—; proffer—; recite—; regard—; reject—; review—; ruin—; search for—; seek—; sift—; submit—; substantiate—; sum up—; team with—; transcend—; unearth—; verify—; weigh—; yield to—; —collates; —damns; —discloses; —piles up; —supports; —sustains; —warrants.
(See fact, testimony, proof, demonstration.)

EVIDENT
adverbs
fearfully; overwhelmingly; irrefutably; convincingly; substantially; explicitly; unmistakably; sufficiently; strikingly; materially; conclusively; undeniably; flagrantly; easily; plainly; clearly; glaringly; reasonably; shamefully; outrageously; pitifully; dangerously; plaguedly; perilously; fortunately.

EVIL
adjectives
once-abounding; attendant; besetting; multiplied (pl); alleged; cave-keeping; substantial; dreadful; terrible; secret; manifest; necessary; infinite; inevitable; heaviest; familiar; scandalous; restless; trifling; unseen; remediable; impending; incalculable; desperate; unsubduable; imminent; weakheaded; manifold (pl); partial; temporary;

crying; accursed; ominous; future; thirsty; iniquitous; imaginary; approaching; unavoidable; abstract; moral; fixed; ruthless; necessary; human; accumulated; insidious; immeasurable.

verbs
abhor—; abolish—; abstain from—; aggravate—; alleviate—; ameliorate—; atone for—; avoid—; banish—; beset by—; besmirch with—; blind to—; breed—; cast out —; combat—; compensate for—; cope with —; counteract—; counterbalance—; cure—; deliver from—; denounce—; deplore—; dispose to—; dwell in—; effect—; eradicate—; evince—; exempt from—; fortify against —; imply—; insinuate—; intend—; intensify—; lapse into—; loathe—; master—; mitigate—; overcome—; persist in—; personify—; promote—; punish—; repent—; stir up—; strike at—; submit to—; suffer—; symbolize—; tackle—; tempt with—; uncover—; unite against—; uproot—; —befalls; —degrades; —menaces; expose to—; resist—.

(See wickedness, sin, iniquity, disaster, misfortune, reverse, injustice, wrong, affliction.)

adverbs
cruelly; flagrantly; hatefully; dangerously; mischievously; violently; irretrievably; inconceivably; poisonously; viciously; iniquitously; shamefully; incredibly; brutally; incorrigibly; atrociously; infernally; shockingly; woefully; sadly; villainously; irremediably; scandalously; manifestly; openly; avowedly; exceptionally; obnoxiously; disastrously; detestably; diabolically; perniciously; basely; irrevocably; horribly.

EVINCE (*v*)
adverbs
noticeably; markedly; unmistakably; obviously; sickeningly; partially; undoubtedly.
(See show, indicate.)

EVOLUTION
adjectives
regressive; rapid; uninterrupted; accelerated; lingual; mental; inevitable; intricate; uncertain; social; orderly; pious; masterly; creative; deliberate; mystic; eternal; cosmic; daring; terrestrial.

verbs
climb in—; complete—; confirm—; effect—; examine—; influence—; manifest—; observe—; produce by—; represent—; resolve by—; roll in—; speed up—; support —; verify—; —lifts; —progresses; —ripens; —spreads; —transmits; —unfolds.
(See development, growth.)

EVOLVE (*v*)
adverbs
scientifically; illogically; rapidly; perpetually; acceleratedly; mentally; intricately; uncertainly; splendidly; creatively; mystically; socially; daringly.
(See develop, complete.)

EWE
adjectives
mild-faced; fulsome.

EXACT
adverbs
infallibly; unimpeachably; strictly; literally; rigorously; scrupulously; painstakingly; punctiliously; mathematically; scientifically; unerringly; meticulously; authentically; absolutely; dependably; terrifyingly; uncannily; monotonously; essentiallly; astonishingly; impartially; ostentatiously; manifestly; graphically; astonishingly.

EXACT (*v*)
adverbs
rigidly; inexorably; harshly; cruelly; legally; painfully; strictly; formally.
(See demand, extort.)

EXACTION
adjectives
dictatorial; tyrannous.

EXACTITUDE
adjectives
graphic; conscientious; mathematical; clear-cut; scrupulous.

EXACTNESS
adjectives
scrupulous; close; ironical; crystalline; literal; elaborate; legal; unfailing; painful; technical; historical; mathematical.

EXAGGERATE (*v*)
adverbs
monstrously; sensationally; absurdly; vaingloriously; recklessly; grossly; amusingly;

crudely; grotesquely; rhetorically; journalistically; palpably; virulently; turbulently.
(See lie, magnify.)

EXAGGERATION

adjectives
sensational; cruel; striking; reckless; pardonable; gross; reactionary; amusing; crude; grotesque; rhetorical; passionate; journalistic; delicious; intense; palpable; rowdy; virulent; turbulent.

verbs
addict to—; anticipate—; blame—; confess —; decry—; guard against—; mark by—; reduce—; relate with—; represent—; ridicule—; sneer at—; tolerate—; warn of—; —adds; —amuses; —entertains; —harms; —misleads; —offends; —overwhelms.
(See overstatement.)

EXALT (v)

adverbs
boundlessly; loftily; indefinitely; religiously; mystically; sentimentally; blissfully; joyfully; spiritually; vividly; feverishly; impassionedly; hysterically.
(See magnify, elevate.)

EXALTATION

adjectives
religious; mystic; essential; sentimental; blissful; joyful; spiritual; high; nervous; vivid; dreamy; curious; feverish; impassioned; personal; unimaginable; mesmeric; perfect; harmonic.

EXALTED

adverbs
eminently; highly; conspicuously; notably; distinctly; gloriously; illustriously; splendidly; proudly; honorably; imposingly; majestically; wonderfully; remarkably.

EXAMINATION

adjectives
blind; impromptu; oral; minute; dispassionate; separate; unprejudiced; astute; unimpassioned; thoughtful; perfunctory; microscopic; critical; accurate; detailed; severe; competitive; censorial; elaborate; premarital; unsparing; stiff; fruitless; preventative; periodic; careful; searching; verbal; expert; posthumous; simultaneous; hasty; anatomical; exacting; unbiased; cooler; tedious; cursory; hostile; placid; frequent (pl); monotonous; brusque; caustic; judicial; meticulous; subsequent; systematic.

verbs
compete in—; conduct—; cram for—; crib in—; fail in—; flunk—; merit—; pass—; perform—; prepare for—; resort to—; select by—; subject to—; submit to—; summon for—; tackle—; undergo—; urge—; waive—; —discloses; —proves; —reveals.
(See scrutiny, investigation, search, review, autopsy, inquiry, test.)

EXAMINE (v)

adverbs
minutely; curiously; critically; superficially; studiously; gravely; closely; attentively; expertly; subsequently; ostensibly; hastily; rigorously; briefly; blindly; dispassionately; separately; astutely; perfunctorily; thoughtfully; microscopically; severely; competitively; premaritally; unsparingly; fruitlessly; preventatively; periodically; verbally; expertly; posthumously; simultaneously; anatomically; unbiasedly; tediously; cursorily; hostilely; placidly; monotonously; brusquely; caustically; judicially; meticulously; systematically; subsequently.
(See scrutinize, inspect.)

EXAMPLE

adjectives
pernicious; glaring; magnificent; picturesque; genuine; colorful; notorious; admirable; subsequent; fond; familiar; notable; remote; fatal; stirring; savage; disastrous; illustrious; shining; encouraging; extreme; servile; debasing; effective; melancholy; comparative; innumerable (pl); legible; elaborate; excellent; cruelest; supreme; imitated; striking; foremost; tardy; ultimate; enlightening; noble; unique; analogous; uncommon; impressive; attainable; painful; recorded; vicious; vindictive; concrete; classic; splendid; pathetic; judicious; morbid; eloquent; conspicuous; astounding; contagious; flagrant; haphazard; executive; pregnant; high-poised; rare; instructive; formidable; heroic; valuable; patriotic.

verbs
afford—; cite—; cull—; display as—; emulate—; encourage—; enumerate—s; exhibit —; follow—; glorify—; imitate—; interpret—; make—of; pattern on—; unearth—; view—; —defiles; —illustrates; —incites; —proves; —verifies.
(See instance, sample, specimen, model, illustration, precedent.)

EXASPERATING

adverbs
dreadfully; unbearably; intolerably; oddly; vexatiously; intentionally; unwittingly; innocently; terribly; tormentingly; naughtily; raspingly; bitterly; savagely; relentlessly; ungovernably; unusually; occasionally.

EXASPERATION

adjectives
religious; renewed; increased; inner; sardonic; frequent; intense; sudden; continual; increasing; incessant.

verbs
account for—; bear—; dispose to—; enrage with—; forbear—; incense with—; increase —; incur—; inflict—; irritate to—; load with—; occasion—; plot to—; remedy—; shiver with—; subject to—; torment to—; vent—; —disposes; —explodes; —harms; —wells up.
(See anger, irritation, provocation.)

EXCAVATION

adjectives
abandoned; lone; gaping; desolate.

verbs
direct—; discover during—; employ in—; engage in—; examine—; forbid—; place—; plan—; prevent—; require—; tunnel—; unearth in—; watch—; —divulges; —exposes; —impairs; —lays bare; —progresses; —reveals; —ruins.
(See cavity, hole.)

EXCEED (v)

adverbs
frequently; illegally; surprisingly; splendidly; astonishingly; notably; memorably; wildly.
(See transcend, surpass.)

EXCEL (v)

adverbs
unexpectedly; conspicuously; immeasurably; peculiarly; intrinsically; individually; comparatively; marvelously; surpassingly; materially; unusually; trivially; matchlessly; supremely; dramatically; genuinely; consistently; exceedingly.
(See surpass, transcend.)

EXCELLENCE

adjectives
highest; intrinsic; exceeding; compensatory; artistic; rare; individual; comparative; marvelous; unobtrusive; eternal; surpassing; minor; architectural; material; unapproached; unusual; trivial; matchless; supreme; dramatic; acoustic; professional; peerless; genuine; unrivaled; unvarying; known; consistent; unsurpassed; dateless; superior; self-made; brand-new.

EXCELLENCY

adjectives
reverend; moral.

EXCELLENT

adverbs
dependably; consistently; consciously; reliably; obviously; evidently; palpably; incomparably; matchlessly; surprisingly; brilliantly; artistically; genuinely.

EXCEPTION

adjectives
notable; memorable; violent; trifling; marked; conspicuous; solitary; occasional; delightful; important; innumerable (pl); rare; possible; inexcusable; honorable.

verbs
answer—; appeal for—; ban—; bar—; declare—; defend—; demand—; examine —; expose to—; justify—; lodge—; produce—; protect—; provide—; rule—; state —; take—to; —appears.
(See objection, omission.)

EXCEPTIONAL

adverbs
undoubtedly; highly; indubitably; conspicuously; delightfully; notably; famously; memorably; inimitably; peculiarly; eccentrically; fantastically; exotically; outlandishly; grotesquely; unconventionally.

EXCESS

verbs
accumulate—of; addict to—; burn—; eliminate—; gather—; protest—; rebuke—; refrain from—; remove—; reject—; regret —; reprove—; scatter—; spread—; waste —; —disgraces; —intoxicates.
(See extravagance, surplus, residue, intemperance.)

EXCESSES

adjectives
poor; mad; factional; deplorable; utmost; sanguinary; hideous; extravagant; intolerable; morbid; dangerous; clumsy; mischievous; wildest; witty; persistent; loathsome; personal; dreadful; careless; strained.

EXCHANGE

adjectives

typical; significant; inevitable; dexterous; mute; mutual; unauthorized; solemn; sympathetic; friendly; intimate; immediate; whispered.

verbs

agree on—; allow—; authorize—; counteract—; demand—; dote on—; give in—; grant—; lose through—; operate—; permit —; plan—; procure—; profit by—; promote —; reject—; return in—; solicit—; win—.
(See trade, traffic.)

EXCHANGE (v)

adverbs

mutely; significantly; dexterously; solemnly; sympathetically; intimately; immediately.
(See accept.)

EXCHANGEABLE

adverbs

readily; easily; conveniently; equitably; allowably; obviously; scarcely; legally; hardly; adaptably; commercially; negotiably; reciprocally; properly; warrantably; necessarily; assuredly.

EXCITABILITY

adjectives

morbid; rabid; easy; choleric.

EXCITABLE

adverbs

terribly; abnormally; easily; highly; uncommonly; unusually; temperamentally; naturally; habitually; unfortunately; absurdly; childishly; ridiculously; oddly; curiously; strangely; mysteriously; slightly; disturbingly; painfully; dangerously; significantly; extremely; excessively; outlandishly; uncontrollably; ungovernably; wildly; fussily; inexplicably; deplorably.

EXCITATION

adjectives

unnatural; noticeable; spiritual; frenzied; marked.

EXCITE (v)

adverbs

strongly; mutinously; painfully; sedulously; intensely; fiercely; supernaturally; wildly; vivaciously; pleasurably; contagiously; artificially; tremulously; exhaustingly; bound-lessly; terrifically; preternaturally; sensuously; coarsely; riotously; scandalously; hilariously; hectically; intellectually.
(See arouse, stimulate.)

EXCITEMENT

adjectives

intense; fierce; vast; fascinated; fevered; constant; glowing; supernatural; wild; vivacious; pleasurable; abated; contagious; considerable; gradual; turbulent; aggressive; remorseful; stirring; flushed; perpetual; overpowering; artificial; tremulous; insolent; solemn; strong; hasty; feeble; exhausting; innocent; bubbling; dangerous; pale; adventurous; subdued; joyous; composed; avid; pleasant; tense; probable; peculiar; delicious; momentary; nervous; deep; delirious; emotional; gross; diseased; uncontrollable; sheer; cerebral; contemporary; unprovoked; healthful; frantic; involuntary; frenzied; boundless; high; extraordinary; smothered; terrific; preternatural; sensuous; coarse; perpetual; inconceivable; drawled; riotous; scandalous; hilarious; correspondent; suppressed; mental; hectic; painful; veritable; previous; neutral; intellectual; revolutionary.

verbs

arouse—; avoid—; buzz with—; calm—; conceal—; contain—; crave—; eliminate—; flash—; flush with—; guard against—; induce—; respond to—; rock with—; seethe with—; sense—; stir to—; suppress—; thirst for—; thrive on—; wheeze with—; —blazes; —dies away; —fades; —leaps high; —shines in one's eyes; —smolders; —subsides; —surges.
(See perturbation, commotion, agitation, stimulation.)

EXCLAIM (v)

adverbs

wildly; curiously; breathlessly; softly; thoughtfully; boisterously; fiercely; delightfully; acidly; admiringly; jovially; facetiously; angrily; incredulously; distressfully; bitterly; enthusiastically; solemnly; blankly; saucily; triumphantly; impulsively; testily; gleefully; savagely; boastfully; regretfully; profanely; tragically; piteously; sharply; reproachfully; anxiously; ostentatiously; disappointedly; unadvisedly; fervently; joyously; rapturously; faintly; audibly; stifledly; abruptly; ardently; helplessly; enthusiastically; frantically; shockedly; gutturally.
(See ejaculate, shout.)

EXCLAMATION

adjectives

joyous; rapturous; passionate; angry; fiery; furious; half-suppressed; faint; nervous; incoherent; mourning; audible; half-articulated; impatient; stifled; abrupt; homely; ardent; helpless; enthusiastic; sharp; frantic; indistinct; vivid; pleased; assenting; guttural; shocked.

verbs

burst out in—; drown—; elicit—; emit—; heed—; mark with—; mouth—; pour forth —; pronounce—; protest with—; startle by—; suppress—; utter—; —delights; — expresses; —pains; —resounds; —surprises.

(See outcry, utterance, cry.)

EXCLAMATORY

adverbs

dramatically; absurdly; ludicrously; needlessly; unnecessarily; noisily; violently; offensively; vexatiously; loudly; cholerically; angrily; enthusiastically; blatantly; conspicuously; boldly; urgently; impressively; ridiculously; gustily; coarsely; grossly; sympathetically; terribly; frightfully.

EXCLUDE (*v*)

adverbs

strictly; vigorously; expressly; deliberately; entirely; cautiously; jealously; utterly; rigorously; persistently.

(See omit, prevent.)

EXCLUSION

adjectives

stereotyped; utter; impolitic; studied; strictest; rigorous; perpetual; persistent.

EXCLUSIVE

adverbs

socially; discriminatingly; absurdly; wisely; necessarily; snobbishly; proudly; haughtily; carefully; significantly; purposely; designedly; unreasonably; offensively; formally; officially; safely; rigidly; ridiculously.

EXCLUSIVENESS

adjectives

scornful; fastidious.

EXCOMMUNICATION

verbs

banish to—; brood over—; delay—; demand—; denounce—; deplore—; deserve—; fulminate—; incur—; prevent—; prohibit —; pronounce—; rebel against—; repent—;

restrain—; sentence to—; submit to—; suffer—; threaten with—; —ejects; —excludes; —exiles; —expels; —interdicts; — separates; —shuts out.

(See separation, expulsion.)

EXCRESCENCE

adjectives

preternatural; hideous; annoying; ugly.

EXCRETION

adjectives

wasteful; useless; diminished.

verbs

encourage—; expel during—; facilitate—; halt—; necessitate—; observe—; occasion —; prevent—; produce—; promote—; provoke—; reduce—; require—; stimulate—; suppress—; throw out in—; —cleanses; — exhausts; —occurs; —pains; —purges.

(See discharge.)

EXCRUCIATING

adverbs

terribly; unbearably; visibly; obviously; piteously; unnecessarily; inexpressibly; dreadfully; appallingly; insufferably; insupportably.

EXCURSION

adjectives

amatory; vague; opportune; equestrian; pedestrian; novel; episodical; periodical; rural; provincial; preliminary; piratical; involuntary; compulsory; sporting; restless; predatory; hunting; sketching; torch-light.

verbs

anticipate—; arrange—; delight in—; depart on—; embark on—; escape on—; join —; organize—; plan—; prevent—; start on —; take—; undertake—; venture on—; enjoy—.

(See journey, trip, expedition.)

EXCUSABLE

adverbs

easily; readily; scarcely; hardly; apparently; plausibly; fairly; barely; legitimately; defensibly; reasonably.

EXCUSE

adjectives

apparent; plausible; sheepish; sufficient; audible; penitent; ominous; coy; lawful; puerile; crazy; fair; generous; bare; specious; voluble; cleanly-coined; deft; bashful;

dingy; unblushing; flimsy; useful; reasonable; truthful; ready; legitimate; good; slightest; time-honored; inept; fabricated; unspeakable.

verbs
accept—; beg for—; condone—; defend with—; demand—; denounce—; furnish—; hatch—; invent—; judge—; offer—; plead —; pray for—; present—; produce—; propose as—; request—; require—; seek—; seize on—; shape—; —absolves; —acquits; —amends; —exonerates; —explains; —infuriates; —justifies; —patches up; —releases; —suffices; —vindicates.
(See plea, reason, apology.)

EXCUSE (*v*)
adverbs
ostensibly; pleasantly; apparently; plausibly; sheepishly; audibly; penitently; ominously; coyly; speciously; volubly; deftly; reasonably; ineptly.
(See forgive, pardon.)

EXECRATION
adjectives
terrible; half-smothered; frantic.

EXECUTE (*v*)
adverbs
imperfectly; faithfully; unquestionably; intensively; beautifully; simultaneously; brilliantly; stoutly; momentously; bureaucratically; thoroughly; successfully; duly; splendidly; unremittingly; vigorously; summarily; gracefully; practically; skillfully; admirably; knowingly; linguistically; economically; rudely; justifiably; secretly; intrepidly; imposingly; crudely; magnificently.
(See administer, perform.)

EXECUTION
adjectives
linguistic; efficient; imperfect; economic; justifiable; rude; supreme; secret; immediate; intrepid; unrivaled; imposing; brilliant; hopeful; bloody; crude; magnificent; vigorous; facile.

verbs
await—; cite—; condemn to—; delay—; deliver over to—; demand—; enforce—; entrust—to; escape—; obstruct—; postpone —; reprieve from—; risk—; stay—; warrant—; witness—; —expiates.
(See performance, accomplishment, death.)

EXECUTIVE
adjectives
able; industrial; admirable; signal; energetic; insignificant; high-powered; tyrannical; overbearing; pompous.

adverbs
responsibly; highly; legally; carefully; cautiously; supremely; imperiously; authoritatively; royally; municipally; arbitrarily; masterfully; imposingly; efficiently; brilliantly; magnificently; splendidly; vigorously; intrepidly; unquestionably; proudly; effectively.

EXECUTOR
adjectives
literary; financial; grasping; efficient.

EXEMPLARY
adverbs
admirably; famously; notably; conspicuously; illustriously; effectively; elaborately; supremely; strikingly; nobly; impressively; uncommonly; uniquely; splendidly; eloquently; heroically; valuably; dramatically.

EXEMPLIFICATION
adjectives
historic; unostentatious; significant.

EXEMPLIFY (*v*)
adverbs
richly; strikingly; effectively; vaingloriously; histo ically; significantly; unostentatiously; per ectly.
(See illustrate, prove.)

EXEMPT
adverbs
legally; officially; notably; explicitly; expressly; wisely; craftily; fortunately; adroitly; cleverly; politically; absolutely; automatically; unaccountably; mysteriously; happily; luckily; inexplicably; radiantly.

EXEMPTION
verbs
acquire—; beg—; command—; demand—; enjoy—; grant—; merit—; plead—; procure—; protest—; purchase—; renounce—; select for—; —debars; —excludes; —frees; —removes; —unburdens.
(See immunity. freedom, privilege.)

adjectives

unwearied; bodily; vigorous; appropriate; pedestrian; social; sinister; manly; vacation; habitual; arbitrary; daily; princely; exhilarating; useless; ruthless; mechanical; conscientious; active; simple; unlawful; righteous; well-planned; equitable; monotonous; generous; virtuous; intelligent; fatiguing; effortless; unbiased; perpetual; delectable; injudicious; joyous; constant; conscious; graceful; unwonted; painful; divine; continued; utmost; preposterous; efficient; courtly; mental; gymnastic; unremitting; insufficient; unquestionable; enlightened; nocturnal; ecstatic; memorial; devilish; gentle; graduated; strenuous; mere; internal; plentiful; violent; muscular; recreative; intellectual; anteprandial.

verbs

adapt—to; apply—; assign—to; carry out —; delight in—; deprive of—; diminish—; forego—; graduate—; indulge in—; neglect —; perform—; practise—; recommend—; refrain from—; repeat—; restrict—; resume; —develops; —enlivens; —exhilarates; —tires.

(See act, action, activity, exertion, practise, drill, use.)

EXERCISE (v)

adverbs

diversely; exclusively; violently; ruthlessly; bodily; unweariedly; vigorously; appropriately; socially; habitually; uselessly; mechanically; delectably; joyously; painfully; gymnastically; unremittingly; insufficiently; mentally; nocturnally; muscularly; strenuously; recreatively.

(See exert, apply.)

EXERT (v)

adverbs

strenuously; vocally; undoubtedly; vigorously; unscrupulously; prodigiously; assiduously; incredibly; desperately; extraordinarily; laudably; incessantly; courageously; productively; vainly; unusually; seriously.

(See exercise, apply.)

EXERTION

adjectives

unaccustomed; equivalent; utmost; strenuous; prodigious; assiduous; redoubled; incredible; vigorous; individual; useless; unremitted; desperate; extraordinary; vio-

lent; fresh; intrepid; laudable; incessant; supernatural; polite; diurnal; courageous; fortunate; physical; mental; ceaseless; laborious; unusual; productive; ungracious; vain; joint.

verbs

abhor—; break under—; carry—of; delay —; hinder—; increase—; kindle—; manifest—; produce by—; render—; resist—; reveal—; rouse to—; stimulate to—; waste —; —agitates; —aggravates; —fags; —fatigues; —restores; —taxes.

(See effort, struggle, endeavor.)

EXHALATION

adjectives

ammoniacal; mephitic; ceaseless; foggy; loathsome; unwholesome; noxious.

EXHAUST (v)

adverbs

stertorously; utterly; finally; financially; totally; seemingly; mutually; racially; ruthlessly; practically; physically; spiritually.

(See deplete, prostrate.)

EXHAUSTED

adverbs

utterly; well-nigh; pitiably; shockingly; alarmingly; pathetically; portentously; ludicrously; laughingly; feebly; wheezily; grievously; faintly; perceptibly; visibly; unusually; naturally; obviously.

EXHAUSTION

adjectives

worn; mutual; racial; nervous; sheer; ruthless; practical; physical; spiritual.

verbs

approach—; carry on to—; collapse in—; cure—; diminish—; discuss to—; drain to—; drop in—; induce—; occasion—; produce—; reach—; recuperate from—; reduce to—; succumb to—; tax to—; —destroys; —enervates; —ensues; —incapacitates; —perils; —prostrates.

(See fatigue, weariness.)

EXHIBIT

adjectives

studious; mercantile; bulky; archaeological; educational; pitiable; admirable; startling; doleful; representative.

EXHIBIT (v)

adverbs

immodestly; markedly; unexpectedly; pretentiously; shamelessly; obscenely; gratuitously; glaringly; curiously; muscularly; conspicuously; educationally; persuasively; studiously; representatively.
(See show, display.)

EXHIBITION

adjectives

retrospective; permanent; positive; invidious; wholesale; detailed; spectacular; amazing; spontaneous; portentous; barefaced; frequent (pl); incomparable; theatrical; fanciful; competitive; foremost; remarkable; pitiable; noticeable; notable; comic; degrading; disgusting; enormous; colonial; spirited; creditable; outstanding; florid; symbolical.

verbs

acclaim—; applaud—; appreciate—; bill—; boycott—; display—; inspect—; participate in—; sponsor—; throng—; witness—; —amazes; —amuses; —astounds; —commemorates; —draws; —entertains; —fascinates; —instructs; —opens; —profits.
(See display, spectacle, show.)

EXHILARATE (v)

adverbs

vivaciously; briskly; momentarily; strangely; voluptuously; joyously.
(See excite, cheer.)

EXHILARATING

adverbs

tremendously; immensely; vigorously; wonderfully; boundlessly; highly; buoyantly; briskly; hilariously; vivaciously; sparklingly; radiantly; splendidly; superbly; surprisingly; astoundingly.

EXHILARATION

adjectives

brisk; inexplicable; momentary; elated; strange; voluptuous; joyous.

verbs

burst into—; dampen—; defer—; discourage—; enliven by—; flush in—; impart—; inspire—; kindle—; leap in—; move to—; produce—; refrain from—; repress—; skip in—; stimulate—; subdue—; suppress—; —animates; —frisks; —rollicks; —sparkles.
(See stimulation, gladness, cheer.)

EXIGENCY

adjectives

unexpected; various (pl); present.

verbs

adapt to—; contribute to—; create—; ease —; escape—; judge—; labor under—; meet —; relieve—; rise to—; satisfy—; stress—; subject to—; tolerate—; —claims; —demands; —necessitates; —pinches; —presses; —requires; —threatens.
(See necessity, demand, need, emergency.)

EXILE

adjectives

needy; administrative; imperious; melancholy; lifelong; scarred; cynical; penniless; wandering; impudent; multitudinous (pl); outlandish; prejudiced; lasting; pensive; political; communal; venturous; vagabond; involuntary; indiscriminate.

verbs

abandon to—; authorize—; banish into—; cast into—; condemn to—; die in—; doom to—; dwell in—; endure—; enter—; escape —; flee from—; follow into—; force into—; imprison in—; languish in—; liberate from —; recall from—; release from—; relegate to—; retire to—; shut in—; waste in—; —depresses; —saddens; —veils.
(See banishment, expulsion.)

EXILED

adverbs

miserably; pitiably; wretchedly; desolately; unjustifiably; deservedly; homelessly; forlornly; ignominiously; shamefully; savagely; lamentably; unhappily; shockingly; mercilessly; permanently.

EXIST (v)

adverbs

beggarly; parasitically; uninterruptedly; contemporaneously; naturally; impecuniously; cheerlessly; amicably; smoothly; gracefully; individually; primitively; socially; bodily; irregularly; animally; grossly; amiably; miserably; thoughtlessly; meagerly; spiritually; imperiously; carelessly; contemplatively; exaltedly; desolately; torpidly; lifelessly; narrowly; rudely; tranquilly; virtuously; drably; romantically; separately.
(See live, continue.)

adjectives
smooth; carefree; graceful; refined; individual; primitive; savage; reasoned; ordered; social; bodily; irregular; well-regulated; illusive; animal; dreamlike; feeble; gross; amiable; theoretical; political; obscure; intrinsic; objective; miserable; universal; thoughtless; meager; spiritual; waking; eternal; harmonious; future; contained; independent; imperious; dominating; substantial; fractional; careless; contemplative; complicated; sad; precarious; imaginary; distracted; poetical; whole; peaceful; horrible; tangible; exalted; desolate; schizophrenic; divided; wretched; spectral; general; common; artistic; warped; torpid; lifeless; unostentatious; destructive; ephemeral; secluded; charmed; congenial; tormented; dissipated; petty; restless; humdrum; semi-monastic; infantile; determined; untarnished; secular; actual; intra-uterine; mere; restrained; narrow; genuine; inevitable; stormy; moribund; inscrutable; superficial; dubious; perennial; rude; adolescent; unreal; unending; wasted; self-fixed; country; tranquil; bright; virtuous; pampered; unsympathizing; vulgar; drab; long-forgotten; material; beneficent; treacherous; triumphant; undisciplined; tropical; pleasurable; honorable; romantic; unnecessary; indolent; diversified; untroubled; separate; beauteous.

verbs
admit—of; animate—; annihilate—; contemplate—; dedicate—to; demonstrate—of; deny—of; determine—; disbelieve—; dispute—; drag out—; eke out—; grant—; guide—; heighten—; ignore—; imperil—; invigorate—; justify—; loathe—; obliterate—; pop into—; preserve—; recognize—; rule—; shape—; shatter—; struggle for—; suspect—of; sustain—; threaten—; uproot —; verify—; —bores; —continues; —wearies.
(See reality, fact, life.)

EXIT

adjectives
eccentric; clear; funnel-shaped; joyful; mysterious; hurried.

verbs
bar—; barricade—; burst from—; chain —; dramatize—; emanate from—; excrete through—; file from—; give—; issue from —; padlock—; perceive—; scorn—; search for—; sigh for—; trickle through—; witness —; —discharges; —effuses; —ejects; — erupts; —expels.
(See passage, doorway.)

EXODUS

adjectives
dramatic; wholesale; gradual.

verbs
consent to—; encounter—; force—; plan—; overtake—; speed—; start—; trace—; — abates; —attains; —commences.
(See departure, emigration.)

EXONERATE (*v*)

adverbs
completely; partially; fully; satisfactorily; entirely; unconditionally; impartially.
(See pardon, acquit.)

EXONERATED

adverbs
completely; honorably; recently; wholly; justly; happily; luckily; fortunately; easily; glibly; smoothly; craftily; publicly; properly; rightfully; legally; entirely; unquestionably; unconditionally.

EXORBITANT

adverbs
insanely; intolerably; terribly; extremely; frightfully; criminally; illegally; preposterously; inordinately; egregiously; fantastically; outrageously; outlandishly; crazily; flagrantly; grossly; incredibly; enormously; prodigiously; amazingly; glaringly; appallingly.

EXOTIC

adjectives
illustrious; tiny; rare.

EXPAND (*v*)

adverbs
progressively; rapidly; limitlessly; sufficiently; continually; sanely; monstrously; ingeniously; lustily; adroitly; tremendously; marvelously; subsequently; intellectually; ephemerally; explosively; economically; industrially; muscularly; noisily; inevitably; imperially; poisonously; chaotically.
(See dilate, enlarge.)

EXPANSE

adjectives
treeless; sealike; dreary; tranquil; sunny; shadowless; still; boundless; undulating; great; prodigious; shining; broad; vast;

trackless; bare; uncharted; endless; prairie-like; glassy; barren; pale; serene; berg-filled; measureless; limitless; windless.

EXPANSION

adjectives

transcendent; fanlike; marvelous; tremendous; subsequent; intellectual; cruel; ephemeral; vital; free; explosive; economic; prodigious; temperamental; industrial; reflex; muscular; important; noisy; amazing; ill-directed; inevitable; major; rapid; imperial; conceivable; healthful; chaotic; enormous.

verbs

advocate—; check—; confine—to; cover—; curtail—; demand—; evince—; force—; influence—; justify—; limit—; nip—; plan —; prevent—; regulate—; speed up—; strangle—; suppress—; terminate—; —continues; —ends; —follows.
(See enlargement, increase, extension, development.)

EXPANSIVE

adverbs

conveniently; adaptably; broadly; signally; remarkably; wonderfully; incredibly; exceptionally; naturally; amply; roomily; spaciously; capaciously; comfortably; amazingly.

EXPATRIATION

adjectives

instant; delayed; enforced; prolonged.

EXPECT (v)

adverbs

confidently; unreasonably; half-heartedly; gloomily; romantically; anxiously; vaguely; plainly; apparently; breathlessly; presumptuously; blissfully; sanguinely; ardently; benevolently; vainly; mystically; fondly; rationally; erroneously; impossibly; evidently; extravagantly; tremulously; hourly.
(See anticipate, hope.)

EXPECTANCY

adjectives

reasonable; shuddering; dread; eager; lounging; tranquil; wistful; vigilant; anxious; homeless.

EXPECTANT

adverbs

happily; joyously; mysteriously; excitedly; hysterically; passionately; thrillingly; unreasonably; impatiently; ardently; keenly;
eagerly; charmingly; joyfully; fervently; anxiously; crazily; madly; nervously; confidently; vainly; hopefully.

EXPECTATION

adjectives

blissful; confident; sanguine; harrowing; exorbitant; pecuniary; ardent; benevolent; florid; vain; reasonable; appreciative; mystic; fondest; remote; rational; continual; erroneous; future; protracted; exaggerated; impossible; evident; sure; tremulous; delightful; brilliant; ulterior; anxious; hopeful; hourly; indefinite; visionary; commensurate; extravagant; distant.

verbs

await with—; blast—; confirm—; darken —; encourage—; excite—s; fall short of—; fulfill—; gamble in—; glow with—; prolong —; quiver with—; shine in—; thwart—; torment with—; warrant—; whirl in—; —becomes; —fails; —grows; —perishes; —shrinks.
(See anticipation, prospect, hope.)

EXPECTORATE (v)

adverbs

nauseously; excessively; disgustingly; continually; foully; filthily.
(See spit, expel.)

EXPECTORATION

adjectives

excessive; sustained.

verbs

diminish—; discharge in—; effect—; eject in—; eliminate in—; emit in—; encourage —; evict in—; excrete in—; expel in—; forbid—; hack with—; increase—; interrupt—; promote—; retch in—; warn against—; —clears; —disgorges; —dislodges.
(See sputum, spit, saliva.)

EXPEDIENCE

verbs

balance—; base on—; befit—; charge with —; conform to—; consider—; consult—; doubt—; employ—; necessitate—; require —; resort to—; sacrifice to—; suit—; —controls; —embarrasses; —guides; —perplexes; —rules; —silences; —violates.
(See utility, propriety.)

adjectives

seducing; astute; unlawful; financial; dangerous; temporary; favorite; happy; simple; unworthy; desperate; fertile; splendid; shifty; sensible; customary; physical; various (pl); effective; readiest.

adverbs

politically; immediately; wisely; necessarily; strategically; properly; undoubtedly; opportunely; luckily; eminently; ingeniously; indisputably; astutely; dangerously; temporarily; boldly; roughly; cleverly; subserviently; usefully; adaptably.

EXPEDITION

adjectives

implemented; conquering; disastrous; maritime; elaborate; dangerous; Odyssean; hostile; filibustering; nervous; suicidal; successful; predatory; brazen; particular; nefarious; exploring; favorite; notable; rescue; zoological; costly; memorable; punitive; much-vaunted; perilous; sanguine; swiftest; abortive.

verbs

command—; defer—; endanger—; fit out—; guard—; hasten on—; head—; organize—; overwhelm—; prepare—; set forth on—; sponsor—; spur—; support—; undertake—; venture on—; —claims; —cruises; —discloses; —discovers; —sights; —uncovers; —winters.

(See journey, excursion, enterprise.)

EXPEDITIOUS

adverbs

earnestly; smartly; briskly; alertly; eagerly; intently; resolutely; vigorously; actively; energetically; uncommonly; highly; miraculously.

EXPEL (*v*)

adverbs

brutally; unceremoniously; painfully; peremptorily; summarily; abruptly; heartlessly; formally.

(See banish, eject.)

EXPEND (*v*)

adverbs

usefully; lavishly; prodigally; unwisely; honestly; modestly; extravagantly; frugally; annually; prudently; unreasonably; unfortunately; judiciously.

(See employ, consume.)

adjectives

increasing; modest; lavish; unstinted; extravagant; frugal; loose; annual; prudent; unreasonable; prodigal; corresponding; large; undue; unfortunate; speediest; nervous; judicious; equivalent.

verbs

afford—; approve—; check—; deplore—; furnish—; grudge—; incur—; invest in—; involve—; pare down—; provide for—; purvey—; recruit—; require—; restrict—; return—; —acquires; —amounts; —crushes; —drains; —exhausts; —impoverishes; —purchases.

(See outlay, expense, payment.)

EXPENSE

adjectives

useless; prodigal; major; extreme; ruinous; extraordinary; minimum; profitless; miscellaneous; crushing; enormous; improper; maintenance; inescapable; considerable; financial; operating; imperial; advertising; personal; monstrous; trifling.

verbs

advance—; appropriate for—; defray—; dread—; entail—; increase—; incur—; involve—; necessitate—; pay—; pool—; rate —; save—; slice—; spare—; survey—; trim—; —arises; —galls; —increases; —rises; —weighs.

(See cost, expenditure, outlay.)

EXPENSIVE

adverbs

tremendously; absurdly; unreasonably; ridiculously; excessively; dreadfully; cruelly; inordinately; extremely; enormously; inevitably; inconceivably; naturally; inexpressibly; impossibly; uselessly; ruinously; foolishly; exorbitantly; extortionately; illegally; criminally; extravagantly; wastefully; abominably; amazingly; immoderately; outrageously.

EXPERIENCE

adjectives

early; expensive; novel; dreamy; profound; tragic; deadly; purifying; diversified; trying; literate; mystical; unpleasant; salient; glorious; colorful; jarring; transitory; throbbing; absolute; tedious; major; bitter; inductive; unique; considerable; personal; vigilant; spiritual; preparatory; ripe; universal; uniform; various (pl); unguessable; deplorable; practical; exceptional;

accumulated; anticipatory; horrid; disgraceful; blind; dangerous; invariable; salutary; deep-reaching; thrilling; unfavorable; memorable; financial; satisfying; professional; manifest; initial; exhaustive; confident; vulgar; perplexing; architectural; distressing; worldly; gradual; vast; crushing; fatal; intellectual; enormous; deceptive; sensory; funny; ludicrous; private; evolutionary; rich; unfortunate; sacred; extensive; infallible; disillusioning; unalterable; costly; waking; deep; versatile; amorous; augmented; collegiate; exhilarating; bitter; reportorial; traumatic; unmatched; fascinating; pioneering; imperfect; agonizing; preliminary; aesthetic; direful; dismal; analytic; hereditary; veridical; fateful; rough; pathogenic; droll; public; bitter-sweet.

verbs
accumulate—; achieve—; analyze—; attain —; cite—; continue—; deduce from—; derive—; discolor—; diversify—; enjoy—; exaggerate—; furnish—; gain—; grow out of—; marshal—; narrate—; prepare—; reject—; relate—; relive—; review—; seek —; survive—; tax—; understand—; undertake—; unfold—s; unify—s; utilize—; — delights; —discloses; —embitters; —enriches; —fathers; —guides; —harrows; — teaches; —unnerves; —verifies; —warns.
(See experiment, proof, practice, knowledge.)

EXPERIENCE (v)
adverbs
alternately; tediously; profoundly; tragically; mystically; gloriously; colorfully; uniquely; spiritually; variously; uniformly; practically; deplorably; horridly; financially; professionally; manifestly; fatally; intellectually; ludicrously; privately; unalterably; exhilaratingly; dismally; fatefully; drolly; accidentally.
(See endure, suffer.)

EXPERIENCED
adverbs
amazingly; smartly; cunningly; adeptly; adroitly; carefully; skilfully; unusually; competently; proficiently; ingeniously; masterfully; eminently; impressively; scarcely; broadly; profoundly.

EXPERIMENT
adjectives
lengthy; innumerable (pl); vagrant; happily-conceived; foregoing; weak; partial; cheap-money; exploded; extensive; hypnotic; ethical; unpleasant; rigid; awkward; transoceanic; trifling; memorable; vulgar; instructive; promising; crude; telepathic; gainful; unsought; hazardous; opposite; rash; inductive; vaunted; soon-abandoned; leading; momentous; complicated; supplementary; socialistic; definite; social; important; dangerous; innocent; philosophical; graceful; good-natured; analytical; disastrous; ingenious; interesting; costly; trustworthy; exhaustive; agricultural; continuous; lateral; doubtful; unfailing; amusing; preliminary; practical; revolutionary; wild; pedagogical; endless; tremendous; colossal; meticulous; interminable; absurd; mad; conclusive; cautious; daring; radical; crucial; ignoble; tentative; atrocious; laboratory; epochal; gigantic; novel; singular; misguided; deplorable; ignorant; clumsy; ill-advised.

verbs
benefit by—; conduct—; contrive—; design —; doom—; embark on—; engage in—; indulge in—; interpret—; perform—; prove by—; submit to—; tolerate—; —fails; — fares; —saddens; —suggests; —yields.
(See trial, attempt, test.)

EXPERIMENT (v)
adverbs
indefatigably; extensively; hypnotically; awkwardly; memorably; vulgarly; instructively; crudely; gainfully; hazardously; rashly; inductively; complicatedly; definitely; dangerously; philosophically; exhaustively; agriculturally; continuously; amusingly; practically; interminably; absurdly; cautiously; daringly; radically; crucially; ignobly; tentatively; ignorantly; ill-advisedly; clumsily.
(See try, test.)

EXPERIMENTAL
adverbs
definitely; avowedly; fantastically; openly; extensively; crudely; boldly; dangerously; exhaustively; wildly; amusingly; absurdly; madly; cautiously; clumsily; awkwardly; courageously; adventurously; expensively; heroically; tentatively.

EXPERIMENTATION
adjectives
zealous; clinical; persistent; rigid; controlled.

adjectives
distinguished; eminent; authentic; technical; nautical; transplanted; moral; monetary; illumination; industrious; irrigation; undisputed; tight-mouthed; acknowledged; accomplished; high-salaried; acoustical; competent; independent; manufacturing; efficiency; decoding; practical; able; two-fisted; qualified; outstanding; self-appointed.

verbs
acclaim as—; affront—; applaud—; cope with—; demand—; develop into—; employ —; flatter—; judge by—; nominate—; regard as—; require—; trust—; try—; —conquers; —criticizes; —excels in; —judges; —manages; —masters; —practises; —scowls.
(See specialist, master.)

adverbs
skilfully; obviously; reasonably; unusually; ably; adroitly; capably; competently; technically; mechanically; deftly; efficiently; handily; ingeniously; inventively; smartly; masterfully; proficiently; readily; oddly; curiously; professionally; admirably; prodigiously; uncommonly; miraculously; surprisingly.

EXPIATION
adjectives
tragic; particular; penitential; complete.

EXPLAIN (v)
adverbs
proudly; patiently; quaintly; amply; candidly; plausibly; speciously; prefatorily; redundantly; superfluously; passionately; comprehensively; adequately; essentially; partially; definitely; solemnly; carefully; sulkily; presently; sufficiently; hesitatingly; casually; paradoxically; tenderly; technically; voluntarily; minutely; undauntedly; elaborately; effectively; inaudibly; lengthily; immaterially; confusedly; ingeniously; laboredly; immediately; incongruously; philosophically; sympathetically; volubly; competently; psychologically; invaluably; tardily; apologetically; illogically; concisely; facetiously; fundamentally; comically; prosaically; disarmingly; lamely; casually; haltingly.
(See interrupt, elucidate.)

EXPLANATION
adjectives
plausible; inaudible; immaterial; lucid; hesitating; dreaded; comprehensive; confused; ingenious; satisfactory; labored; immediate; mechanistic; unreserved; fantastic; dynamic; vivid; philosophical; disjointed; incongruous; sympathetic; voluble; abbreviated; competent; adequate; scientific; rational; palliative; indiscreet; pathological; glib; specious; consequent; blind; various (pl); psychological; paralyzing; muddled; invaluable; tardy; groundless; half-true; apologetic; supreme; parenthetical; useless; attempted; flimsy; illogical; overwhelming; blithe; clarifying; concise; simplifying; aesthetic; petulant; facetious; fundamental; reasonable; common-sense; comic; struggling; tedious; elaborate; prosaic; matter-of-fact; air-tight; fictional; disarming; diluted; casual; lame; halting.

verbs
amplify—; bear—; clarify—; clear—; comprehend—; condemn—; confirm—; defy—; devise—; drown out—; elaborate—; emerge with—; frame—; fumble for—; grasp—; muddle—; offer—; stammer—; swallow—; tender—; wind up—; yield—; —clarifies; —involves; —rests on; —simplifies.
(See exposition, solution, interpretation, key.)

EXPLANATORY
adverbs
satisfactorily; aptly; effectively; sufficiently; definitely; clearly; lucidly; acceptably; liberally; roughly; carefully; crudely; artfully; skilfully; adroitly; sagely; wisely; craftily; sincerely; genuinely; plausibly; ingeniously; vividly; graphically; competently; glibly; discreetly; tardily; flimsily; fundamentally; intelligently; elaborately; casually; lamely.

EXPLETIVE
adjectives
muttered; raucous; exasperated; choice; foul-mouthed; energetic; unmeaning.

EXPLICIT
adverbs
elaborately; clearly; fully; succinctly; tersely; curtly; definitely; undeniably; unusually; highly; oddly; unnecessarily; needlessly; carefully; meticulously; strangely; curiously; noticeably; graphically; broadly; dogmatically; officially; imperiously; decisively; formally; solemnly; ominously.

EXPLODE (v)

adverbs

indignantly; successfully; prematurely; squarely; sharply; terrifically; volcanically; frightfully; violently; tremendously; initially; deafeningly; horribly; titanically; dreadfully; disastrously; catastrophically.
(See burst, erupt.)

EXPLOIT

adjectives

boldest; illustrious; quick-witted; antique; ludicrous; memorable; heroic; jocular; gigantic; engineering; dread; phenomenal; daring; dashing; transcendent; brilliant; decisive; hazardous; exuberant; unmatched; imagined; valorous; news; psychic; hair-raising; atrocious; spectacular.

verbs

achieve—; boast of—; close—; conceive —; design—; dream of—; perform—; plot —; recount—; resent—; set forth—s of; share in—; succeed in—; witness—; view —; —reverberates.
(See deed, act, feat, achievement.)

EXPLOIT (v)

adverbs

unethically; arrogantly; fully; indefensibly; ruthlessly; profitably; assiduously; cleverly; industrially; competitively; agriculturally; capitalistically; unreasonably; hideously; nationally; unscrupulously.
(See persecute, oppress.)

EXPLOITATION

adjectives

competitive; pagan; agricultural; middleman; capitalistic; reasonable; hideous; coastwise; national.

verbs

accomplish by—; achieve through—; carry on—; conduct—; consider—; curtail—; decry—; denounce—; delve into—; expose to —; frown on—; instigate—; investigate—; prohibit—; prosper through—; renounce—; resist—; reveal—; view—; —agitates; — enriches; —impoverishes; —ransacks; — reigns.
(See employment, utility, profit.)

EXPLORATION

adjectives

titanic; celebrated; linguistic; nocturnal; unproductive; extensive; arctic; authentic; geographical; daring; world-girdling; fervid; perilous; exhaustive; exotic.

verbs

absorb in—; conduct—; deserve—; discover by—; discuss—; frustrate—; instigate—; plan—; prepare for—; relate—; resume—; subscribe to—; tire of—; undertake—; — ascertains; —determines; —discloses; —inquires; —investigates; —proves; —reveals.
(See search, examination, investigation.)

EXPLORE (v)

adverbs

intelligently; carefully; completely; morbidly; zealously; undauntedly; adventurously; intrepidly; untiringly; scientifically; methodically.
(See examine, search.)

EXPLORER

adjectives

enterprising; zealous; undaunted; adventurous; literary; fortunate; intrepid; untiring; hardy; scientific.

EXPLOSION

adjectives

premature; sharp; terrific; volcanic; frightful; violent; intermittent; numbing; tremendous; deplorable; initial; deafening; magnificent; strange; horrible; dreadful; rending; staccato; titanic; disastrous; gigantic; soul-shattering; catastrophic.

verbs

augment—; forestall—; investigate—; produce—; threaten—; —alarms; —casts out; —damages; —discharges; —drives out; — ejects; —emits; —erupts; —jars; —reports; —rocks; —scars; —shatters; —shocks; — showers; —sunders; —thunders; —violates.
(See outburst, discharge, detonation.)

EXPLOSIVE

verbs

employ—; play with—; toy with—; threaten with—; touch off—; warn of—; —alarms; —blows off; —bursts; —damages; —detonates; —discharges; —drives out; —ejects; —erupts; —jars; —rocks; —shatters; — shocks; —showers; —thunders; —violates.
(See gunpowder, dynamite.)

adverbs

dangerously; reportedly; ominously; alarmingly; highly; unusually; allegedly; undeniably; notoriously; abominably; hazardously; perilously; precariously; ticklishly; terrifically; frightfully; tremendously; horribly; disastrously; easily; readily.

EXPLOSIVENESS

adjectives
volatile; choleric; ready.

EXPONENT

adjectives
able; distinguished; outstanding; scholarly; preeminent; quasi-authoritative; skilled; sole; impressive; faithful; philosophical.

EXPORT

verbs
allow—s; ban—; boycott—s; confiscate—s; deal in—s; demand—s; dispose of—s; dump—s; exchange—s; halt—s; levy against—s; license—s; minimize—s; permit—s; produce for—; reduce—s; restrain—; ship—s; speculate in—s; stimulate—; suspend—; tax—s; underwrite—s; value—s; —s decline; —s rise.

EXPORTER

verbs
bargain with—; communicate with—; consult—; exchange with—; impose on—; license—; order from—; purchase from—; remit to—; restrain—; subsidize—; tax—; —deals in; —demands; —disposes of; —dumps; —invests; —produces; —speculates; —values.

EXPOSE (*v*)

adverbs
shamelessly; unequivocally; unblushingly; reputedly; blasphemously; fearlessly; dangerously; conspicuously; piteously; improperly; sufficiently; ultimately; virtually; subsequently; unwisely; shrewdly; partially; lucidly; subtly; thrillingly; incautiously; graphically; relentlessly; ruthlessly; definitely; imprudently; inevitably.
(See denounce, accuse.)

EXPOSITION

adjectives
comprehensive; simply written; progressive; ever-varying; precise; lucid; striking; suitable; masterly; contemporaneous; courteous; erroneous; chronological; classic; sound; scientific; clear; serious; accurate; amusing; brilliant; pretentious; concise; skillful; enthusiastic; daring; illuminating; consummate; distinguished; subtle; straightforward; ethnographical; thrilling; well-reasoned; graphic; sane; forcible; passionate; lucid; fresh.

verbs
arrange—; attend—; conduct—; display at —; enter into—; finance—; hearken to—; interpret—; launch into—; present at—; prohibit—; publish—; recount—; render—; report—; show at—; view—; —advocates; —awes; —confuses; —explains; —expounds; —interests.
(See display, exhibition, essay, composition, explanation.)

EXPOSITORY

adverbs
clearly; drearily; dully; endlessly; dismally; wearily; droningly; lucidly; intelligibly; unusually; definitely; admirably; agreeably; needfully; suitably; skilfully; soundly; accurately; acceptably; artlessly; realistically; critically; wonderfully.

EXPOSTULATE (*v*)

adverbs
softly; fiercely; petulantly; madly; mildly; wrathfully; amicably; frantically; frankly.
(See protest, remonstrate.)

EXPOSTULATION

adjectives
mad; mild; wrathful; lingering; amicable; frantic; frank.

EXPOSURE

adjectives
horrible; projected; undue; serviceable; fatal; bleak; inevitable; imprudent; fearless; initial; earnest; intelligent; courageous; sociological; wanton; definite; ominous; startling; sensational; ruthless; unremitted; incautious; cruel; relentless; blatant.

verbs
anticipate—; deserve—; entail—; escape—; guard from—; lay open to—; prohibit—; protect from—; sentence to—; subject to—; suffer from—; view—; —deprives; —discloses; —displays; —divulges; —endangers; —expels; —reveals; —shames.
(See disclosure, revelation.)

EXPOUND (*v*)

adverbs
repeatedly; grimly; clearly; gravely; quaintly; mystifyingly; incomprehensibly; patiently.
(See explain.)

EXPRESS

adjectives
roaring; aerial; limited; endless.

adverbs

audibly; cordially; admirably; resignedly; lightly; precisely; visually; optimistically; poetically; pointedly; metaphorically; significantly; inelegantly; openly; peevishly; wittily; independently; frivolously; accurately; obviously; submissively; vaguely; delicately; urgently; exquisitely; eloquently; privately; succinctly; indignantly; mildly; figuratively; adequately; bluntly; repeatedly; inadequately; gratefully; forcibly; voluntarily; lucidly; ingenuously; courteously; pithily; whimsically; graphically; stupidly; placidly; felicitously; affably; affectedly; angelically; animatedly; arrogantly; appropriately; arbitrarily; benevolently; blandly; buoyantly; capriciously; caressingly; characteristically; calculatingly; contemptuously; creatively; deceptively; delicately; demurely; diabolically; dubiously; ecstatically; equivocally; ferociously; formidably; genially; grammatically; gravely; grimly; grotesquely; humorously; forbiddingly; impassionedly; indescribably; indignantly; instinctively; introspectively; journalistically; jovially; knowingly; legitimately; loftily; lugubriously; luminously; majestically; martially; meekly; melodiously; memorably; metaphysically; charmingly; mirthlessly; mutinously; momentarily; nobly; nonsensically; nostalgically; owlishly; patriotically; peculiarly; pedantically; pensively; pessimistically; petulantly; pitifully; plaintively; portentiously; radiantly; recklessly; sardonically; saturninely; savagely; secretively; sheepishly; shrewdly; sinisterly; smugly; solemnly; soothingly; sourly; superbly; spiritedly; spontaneously; sternly; strainedly; submissively; sullenly; synonymously; technically; transparently; treasonably; tritely; truculently; ultimately; uniformly; vicariously; viciously; vindictively; vivaciously; vividly; volubly; warily; wistfully; wryly; yearningly.

(See say, utter.)

EXPRESSION

adjectives

adequate; affable; affected; agonized; airy; alchemistical; all-conquering; altered; amazed; ambiguous; angelic; animated; anxious; apologetic; appalled; appealing; appraising; appropriate; arbitrary; arrogant; artistic; assertive; astonished; austere; banal; beatific; belligerent; benevolent; bewildered; bitter; blameless; bland; bleak; broken; brutish; buoyant; cabalistical; calm; capricious; careless; caressing; ceremonious; characteristic; charming; chastened; chivalric; calculating; comical; commanding; conciliatory; confidential; consecrated; conspicuous; consummate; contemplative; contemptuous; contended; contrite; countless (pl); courteous; creative; criminal; crystalline; cunning; curious; dazed; deceptive; deliberate; delicate; demoniac; demonstrative; demure; depressed; despairing; diabolic; disagreeable; disdainful; distasteful; dolorous; dithyrambic; dogged; dominant; dramatic; dreamy; dubious; dumb; ear-pleasing; eager; earnest; ecstatic; elegant; embossed; emotionless; emphatic; encouraging; equivocal; etherealized; exalted; evanescent; expectant; exterior; facial; faintest; fanglike; faraway; far-off; felicitous; feline; ferocious; fervent; fiendish; fierce; figurative; fine; fixed; fleeting; forbidding; forced; forlorn; formidable; freezing; frequent; frightened; frowning; frustrated; fundamental; furtive; genial; gentle; gladsome; glazed; gloomy; glorified; graceful; grammatical; grave; grim; habitual; grotesque; grouchy; haggard; half-absorbed; half-articulate; half-humorous; half-downright; half-pathetic; half-hearted; half-indulgent; half-suspicious; hangdog; happy; hard; hard-set; haunting; heart-broken; hearty; hereditary; homely; honest; hopeless; horrible; horrid; hospitable; humorous; ideal; idiotic; idyllic; ill-natured; imaginative; imbecilic; immobile; impassioned; imploring; implied; impressive; incidental; incredulous; indescribable; indignant; indirect; infinite; injured; inquiring; inscrutable; instinctive; intense; intent; introspective; jolly; journalistic; jovial; joyous; kindly; knowing; lackluster; legitimate; listening; listless; literary; lofty; lovable; lucid; lugubrious; luminous; majestic; malign; martial; martyrlike; maudlin; meaningful; meek; melancholy; melodious; memorable; menacing; merry; metaphysical; mirthless; moody; momentary; moral; mutinous; mysterious; mystic; noble; noncommittal; nonsensical; nostalgic; noteworthy; odd; ominous; open; outward; owlish; plain; pleasing; pantomimic; particular; passionate; patriotic; peculiar; pedantic; peevish; pensive; perfect; periphrastic; perplexed; pessimistic; petulant; physiognomic; pithy; pitiful; placid; plaintive; plastic; pleasant; poetic; poignant; popular; portentous; predatory; preoccupied; prim; professional; proper; provoking; prose; puzzled; quaint; quarrelsome; queer; questioning; quiet; quizzical; radiant; rapt; rare; rebuked; reckless; relaxed; remarkable; repelling; resentful; resolute; respective; rueful; sagacious; sad; sarcastic; sardonic; saturnine; saucy; savage; secretive; self-concentrated; seraphic; serio-comic; serious; set; severe; sharp; sheepish; shocked; shrewd; sicklied; significant; sincere; singular; sinister; slight; slow; sly; smileless; smug; soft; softened; solemn; soothing; sorrowful; sour; spacious; superb; spirited; spontaneous; sprightliest; stealthy; stern; stony; strained; structural; submissive; subtle; sulky; sullen; surprised; sweet; synonymous; taut; technical; tender; tense; theoretical; thoughtful; thought-saving; thwarted; tragic; transparent; treasonable; trite; triumphal; triumphant; troubled; truculent; ultimate; unanimous; unbelieving; unbounded; uncompromising; unelaborated; unconscious; uneasy; unfit; unforgettable; unguarded; uniform; unmoved; unstudied; unusual; upright; vacant; vague; various (pl); vehement; venomous; vibratory; vicarious; vicious; victorious; vindictive; violent; virtuous; visual; vivacious; vivid; voluble; warlike; warm; wary; wavering; **well-bred; whimsical;** wild; wily; wistful; **woebegone;** wondering; wordless; worn; worried; wry; yearning.

verbs
achieve —; assume —; crave —; cry out **for** —; cultivate —; distort —; divest of —; efface —; fathom —; fix —; limit —; recollect —; stifle —; strive toward —; struggle for —; translate —; understand —; wear —; — congeals; — plays; — settles.
(See utterance, statement, assertion.)

EXPRESSIVE
adverbs
clearly; particularly; distinctly; emphatically; beautifully; especially; wonderfully; accurately; powerfully; effectively; cruelly; remarkably; sympathetically.

EXPRESSIVENESS
adjectives
mobile; pregnant.

EXPULSION
adjectives
pathetic; forcible; virtual.

verbs
accept—; anticipate—; criticize—; demand —; employ —; face —; favor —; inflict —; influence —; order —; promote —; punish with —; resign to —; secure —; suffer —; threaten with —; welcome —; — benefits; — corrects; — shames.
(See discharge, dismissal.)

EXPURGATED
adverbs
mercilessly; unnecessarily; relentlessly; priggishly; carefully; zealously; absurdly; needlessly; hopelessly; inanely; ridiculously; primly; spinsterishly; puritanically; mawkishly; properly.

EXQUISITE
adverbs
daintily; charmingly; enchantingly; delicately; matchlessly; remarkably; beautifully; utterly; delicately; airily; incredibly; wonderfully; gracefully; harmoniously; richly; melodiously.

EXTEMPORANEOUS
adverbs
genuinely; sincerely; honestly; obviously; rigidly; strictly; avowedly; artlessly; spontaneously; crudely; thoughtlessly; carelessly; delightfully; impulsively; manifestly.

EXTEMPORIZE (*v*)
adverbs
jocosely; freely; humorously; artfully; skillfully; clumsily; cleverly; shrewdly.
(See improvise.)

EXTEND (*v*)
adverbs
spaciously; understandingly; beseechingly; widely; liberally; skillfully; infinitely; beneficently; enormously; generously; gradually; laterally; additionally; internationally; invitingly.
(See lengthen, project.)

EXTENSION
adjectives
infinite; enormous; generous; ideal; dangerous; gradual; further; lateral; additional; international; widest.

verbs
advocate —; check —; confine —; curtail —; grant —; justify —; influence —; limit

—; nip —; open —; permit —; plan —; plead for —; prevent —; regulate —; strangle —; terminate —; — accommodates; — eases.

(See increase, addition, expansion, enlargement.)

EXTENT

adjectives
dangerous; uncivil; unjust; perceptible; amazing; probable; unprecedented; monstrous; considerable; far-reaching; reasonable; enormous; vast; unusual; boundless; solemn; important; limitless; sufficient; immense; greater; fearful; astonishing; satisfying; bewildering; disproportionate.

verbs
ascertain —; carry to —; consider —; define —; estimate —; exercise to —; limit —; occupy to —; reach —; recognize —; rule — of; serve —; understand —; — alarms; — allures; — consists; — forces; — reduces.

(See amount, size, magnitude, degree.)

EXTERIOR

adjectives
impenetrable; rustic; indifferent; fearless; attractive; commonplace; grave; showy; valorous; calm; amphibious; passive; listless; visible; expansive; impassible; quiet; soft; cold; stolid.

EXTERMINATE (v)

adverbs
ruthlessly; gradually; certainly; speedily; inevitably; totally; subsequently; entirely; cruelly; blindly; finally.

(See destroy, remove.)

EXTERMINATION

verbs
attempt —; banish to —; demand —; drive into —; end in —; engage in —; guard against —; plan —; prevent —; prophesy —; protect against —; pursue to —; repel —; war on —; warn against —; — destroys; — drives out; — eliminates; — extirpates; — forces out; — reduces; — rids.

EXTINCTION

adjectives
final; certain; hurried; speedy; inevitable; total; subsequent.

verbs
blot into —; decay into —; demand — of; deplore —; doom to —; flicker into —; guard against —; meet —; mourn —; plan —; prevent —; suffocate into —; surrender to —; threaten with —; warn against —; witness —; yield to —.

(See destruction, extermination.)

EXTINGUISH (v)

adverbs
instantly; temporarily; instantaneously; abruptly; promptly; rudely; hastily; swiftly.

(See destroy, remove.)

EXTOL (v)

adverbs
frequently; highly; loudly; continually; flatteringly; lavishly; shrewdly; purposely; ostensibly; sincerely.

(See exalt, praise.)

EXTORT (v)

adverbs
soullessly; miserly; graspingly; meanly; exorbitantly; usuriously; heartlessly.

(See wring, force.)

EXTORTION

adjectives
oppressive; multiplied (pl); baffled; criminal.

EXTORTIONATE

adverbs
criminally; highly; illegally; terribly; absolutely; positively; unbelievably; cruelly; harshly; tyrannically; greedily; rapaciously; sordidly; meanly; ravenously; insatiably.

EXTRACT

adjectives
liquid; liberal; embryonic; subsequent; garbled; glandular; misquoted.

verbs
administer —; copy —; deduce —; derive —; discharge —; distil —; draw forth —; elicit —; employ —; evolve —; issue —; obtain —; prepare —; quote —; view —; — finishes; — flavors; — represents.

(See essence, selection.)

EXTRACT (v)

adverbs
freshly; imperfectly; wilfully; liberally; subsequently; glandularly; erroneously; illegally.

(See draw, select.)

EXTRACTION

adjectives

oral; foreign; noble.

EXTRANEOUS

adverbs

unessentially; relatively; definitely; obviously; naturally; discordantly; exotically; curiously; strangely; mysteriously.

EXTRAVAGANCE

adjectives

fine; reckless; ostentatious; unusual; tasteless; absurd; oratorical; rough; gorgeous; favorite; complete; unwarrantable; incipient; lavish; wasteful; senseless; frightful; old-time; wicked; imaginable; utmost; elegant; profligate; forensic; bromidic; unjustified; flagrant.

verbs

check —; cloak in —; consort with —; court —; criticize —; guard against —; indulge in —; involve in —; regret —; rue —; sacrifice to —; smack of —; stimulate —; supply —; warn against —; — corrupts; — destroys; — drains; — fetters; — impoverishes; — inflames; — reigns; — shocks.

(See waste, excess.)

EXTRAVAGANT

adverbs

wantonly; foolishly; madly; rapturously; lavishly; happily; drunkenly; wildly; blithely; wickedly; improvidently; fantastically; outrageously; vulgarly; proudly; ostentatiously; extremely; absurdly; ridiculously; pompously; outrageously; gayly; inordinately; exceedingly; incredibly; magnificently; splendidly; gorgeously; recklessly; fully; senselessly; flagrantly; immensely.

EXTREME

adjectives

absurd; delirious; fantastic; spiritualistic; unhealthy; uttermost; strenuous; blunt; precise; calculable; dangerous; glorious; exhaustive.

verbs

avoid—; delight in—; dress in—; drive to —; employ—; endure—; leap to—; moderate—; proceed to—; reach—; run to—; shun —; temper—; twist to—; warn against—; —begets; —blinds; —confuses; —destroys; —disturbs; —endangers; —maddens.

(See excess.)

EXTREMITY

adjectives

dire; sensuous; dread; ultimate; desperate; furthest; remotest.

EXUBERANCE

adjectives

glorious; effervescent; fantastic; brash; floral; prodigal; fitful; incondite; brisk.

verbs

attest by—; avoid—; burst into—; correct —; drain of—; exhaust—; hide—; indulge in—; inject—; lessen—; play with—; repress—; spoil—; steep in—; suppress—; teem with—; —astonishes; —overflows.

(See abundance, luxuriance, excess.)

EXUBERANT

adverbs

gloriously; fantastically; profusely; prodigally; excessively; inordinately; uncommonly; oddly; immensely.

EXUDE (v)

adverbs

aromatically; disgustingly; vilely; sickeningly; freely; abnormally gradually.

(See discharge, flow.)

EXULT (v)

adverbs

vauntingly; openly; enthusiastically; triumphantly; boastfully; happily; gloatingly; drunkenly.

(See rejoice, triumph.)

EXULTANT

adverbs

loudly; noisily; proudly; pompously; splendidly; magnificently; quietly; deeply; childishly; triumphantly; happily; incredulously; boastfully; humbly; rapturously; ecstatically; incoherently; profoundly; joyously; jubilantly; elatedly; delightedly; immensely; exceedingly; remarkably.

EXULTATION

adjectives

vaporous; justifiable; fierce; savage; childish; honest; incoherent; facetious; wonted; sublimest; raptured; menacing; splendid.

verbs

affix to—; avert—; bat—; bathe—; blear—; blink—; cast —s upon; catch—; cloud—; cock—; darken—; dazzle—; delude—; di-

late—; dim—; divert—; examine—; extract from—; feast —s upon; glue —s upon; goggle—s; inflame—; intrigue—; irrigate —; irritate—; moisten—; narrow—s; offend —; paste—s on; pin—s on; pucker up—s; rivet—s on; roll—s; screw up—s; shadow —s; shield—s; snag—; soften—s; soothe—s; stagger—; strain—s; suffuse—; tear—s away; test—; tire—s; veil—s; —s acquiesce; —s beam; —s blaze; —s brood; —s bulge; —s challenge; —s climb; —s dance; —s devour; —discerns; —s drift; —s drink in; —embraces; —s fall; —s flash; —s flicker; —s flinch; —s glare; —s gleam; —s glint; —s glitter; —s glow; —s kindle; — penetrates; —s plead; —probes; —s protrude; —s redden; —rests upon; —roams; —roves; —scans; —scorns; —scrutinizes; —shines; —smarts; —s smoulder; —s snap; —s sparkle; —s squint; —s study; —s swell; —s swim; —s twinkle; —s twitch; —s water; —s waver; —s widen; —s beseech.
(See sight.)

EYE (v)
adverbs
wistfully; piercingly; candidly; keenly; curiously; suspiciously; boldly; challengingly; squarely; critically; sternly; pathetically; attentively; thoughtfully; timidly; painfully; hungrily; contemptuously; unwaveringly; inquisitively; significantly; frigidly; derisively; moodily; covetously; soulfully; bleakly; dispassionately; fastidiously; stonily; sullenly; darkly; insatiably; beseechingly; alertly; mischievously; inquiringly; absently; abstractedly; amazedly; ardently; arrogantly; benignly; bestially; bewilderedly; bewitchingly; earnestly; enviously; intently; lovingly; piteously; intelligently; pleadingly; heavily; humorously; formidably; gaily; glassily; glintingly; glitteringly; maudlinly; joyously; mysteriously; professionally; raptly; sheepishly; steadfastly; studiously; superficially; uncritically; vacantly; watchfully; wisely; wolfishly; wonderingly; wordlessly; venomously.
(See watch, observe.)

EYEBALLS
adjectives
fierce; searing; burning; gorgeous; dead; bugle; rolling; protruding; swimming; staring; dilated; half-eaten.

EYEBROW
verbs
arch—s; cock—; corrugate—s; darken—s; jet—s; knit—s; pluck—s; quirk—; raise—; slant—s; thin out—s; tidy up—s; —s beetle; —s curve; —s shag.

EYEBROWS
adjectives
bushy; shaggy; fierce-looking; supercilious; calm; haughty; broad-arched; peaked; high; pencil-line; sandy; mastic-darkened; solemn; prominent; raised; tangled; thick; curved; heavy; bristly; stiff; silky; delicate; wispy; perfect; bent; drawn; uneven; surprised; sardonic; elevated; uplifted; bold; gloomy; mismated; boyish; languid; ginger; thin; proud; twitching; pepper-and-salt; disapproving.

EYELASHES
adjectives
sooty; dusky; mascaraed; artificial; tear-drenched; dense; dark-fringed; thick; long; sopping; dark; uplifted; beaded; blinking; sandy; absurd; beautiful; long-lashed; heavily-fringed.

verbs
bat—; clip—; lift—; —brush; —droop; —flash; —flatter; —flicker; —flutter; —fringe; —glisten; —guard; —quiver; —repose; —shade; —shimmer; —sleep; —sweep; —veil.

EYELIDS
adjectives
quivering; quiet; swollen; shaken; withered; heavy; drooping; long-fringed; broad; worn-off; fluttering; wrinkled; straight-cut; languid; trembling; waxen; bronze; bluish; opaque; leaden; tired; limp; hanging; half-closed; narrowed; closed; shriveled; lazy; tremulous; thin; pain-wrenched.

verbs
drop—; fringe—; kiss—; lift—; raise—; squeeze—; wag—; weigh—down; —ache; —droop; —fall; —flutter; —quiver: —sleep; —slumber; —twitch.

EYES
adjectives
able; abnormal; absent; accusing; abstracted; aching; actual; admirable; adorable; adoring; adulterated; adventure-seeking; aesthetic; affrighted; affronted; agate; age-dimmed; agonized; age-blue; alien; all-seeing; alluring; almond; altered; amazed; amber-colored; ambitious; amiable; amorous; amused; angered; anguished; ani-

mated; anxious; apathetic; appealing; appraising; appreciative; apprehending; approving; archeological; ardent; arrogant; ash-rimmed; assailing; assenting; astonished; astounded; attentive; attractive; august; austere; authoritative; autumn-leaf; avaricious; averted; avid; awakened; awe-inspiring; azure-tinted; baby-blue; bad; baffling; bagged; baleful; bashful; battered; battle-aged; battle-lighted; beadlike; beady; beady-bright; beaming; beautiful; beauty-loving; beetling; bemused; benignant; bent; beseeching; bestial; bewildered; bewitching; bilberry; big; bilious; bland; blazing; blue; bleak; bleared; blissful; blood-injected; bloodshot; bodeful; bold; bonny; boring; boundless; bovine; bright; brightened; brimming; brooding; brown; bruised; brown-flecked; bulbous; bulging; burrowing; bursting; button; calculating; calm; candid; canny; capricious; careless; cat-like; cautious; cavernous; celestial; challenging; chance-met; changeable; charmed; chaste; chastening; childish; cheerful; chilly; chocolate-brown; civic; clear; clever; clinging; close-set; closing; clouded; coal-black; cold; colorless; color-loving; commanding; commemorative; commiserating; compassionate; compelling; concealed; concerned; condemnatory; confused; congested; contemplative; contemptuous; contracted; contumelious; conventional; convivial; convulsed; cool; countless; courageous; covert; covetous; craving; created; critical; crumpling; crystal-clear; cunning; curious; cynical; dancing; dangerous; dark-fringed; dark-lashed; death-darting; darkness-dazed; darting; dazzled; deadly; deceiving; decorous; deep; deep-circled; deep-curtained; deep-set; deep-socketed; deep-sunk; defenseless; defiant; dejected; deliberating; delighted; delightful; demanding; demon; demure; deprecating; derisive; descriptive; desolate; despair-glazed; despairing; devastating; devilish; devouring; dewy; dilated; directing; discerning; discolored; discomfited; discontented; discovering; disdainful; disillusioned; dispassionate; dissatisfied; displeased; disquieting; dissecting; dissipated; distasteful; distempered; distended; distracting; distressed; disturbed; divining; dizzy; dog-true; doubtful; dovelike; downcast; dramatic; downdropped; dreadful; dream-shrouded; dream-swept; dreamy; dreary; drink-filmed; drooping; drowsy; dry; dull; dusky; dying; eager; eagle; eagle-gray; eagle-

keen; earnest; educated; effective; effeminate; eloquent; eluded; embittered; emerald-green; empty; enameled; enamored; enchanted; energetic; enigmatic; enlarged; enlivening; enormous; enthralled; entranced; envious; epiphyseal; evasive; ever-lusterless; ever-moving; ever-questing; evil; examining; excited; expanding; expectant; expiring; expert; expressionable; expressive; extraordinary; exulting; faded; failing; fainting; fairer; faithful; falcon; familiar; far-gazing; far-off; farseeing; farsighted; fascinated; fastened; fastidious; fatal; fatherly; fathomless; fatigue-dimmed; favoring; fear-filled; feminine; fear-glazed; fear-laden; fearful; fearless; feeble; ferocious; ferret; feverish; fidgety; fierce; fiery; filmed; finding; fine-wrought; fishlike; fishy; fixed; flashing; flat-blue; fleshy-looking; flickering; flinty; flowerlike; flustered; fluttering; foolish; forbidden; foreboding; foreign; forgiving; formidable; formless; foul; frank; freezing; fresh; fretful; fright-filled; frightened; frosty; frowning; frozen; furious; furtive; galled; gamesome; gay; gazelle; gemlike; gentle; ghastly; gifted; gimlet; gin-cleared; girlish; glad; glaring; glassy; gleaming; glimmering; glinting; glittering; gloating; globular; glorious; glossy; glowering; glowing; glutton; goggling; golden; golden-brown; good; grave; gray; gray-steel; great; greedy; gross; grotesque; groveling; guarded; guiding; guileless; guilty; gypsy; habituated; haggard; hale; half-closed; half-defiant; half-repentant; half-shut; half-veiled; happy; harassed; hardened; haughty; haunting; hawk-brown; hazel; healthy; heart-broken; heart-reaching; heartless; heart-sick; heated; heavenly; heavy; heavy-lidded; heedless; hollow; honest; hooded; horny; horrified; hostile; housewifely; hovering; human; humble; humid; humorous; hyacinth-blue; hungry; hunted; hurt; hypnotic; hypnotized; ice-blue; icy; idealistic; ill-omened; immobile; immortal; impartial; imperious; implacable; imploring; impudent; incandescent; incredulous; incensed; incurious; indifferent; indignant; indolent; indomitable; indulgent; inebriate; inexorable; inexperienced; inferior; inflamed; innocent; innumerable; insolent; inquiring; inquisitive; insane; inscrutable; insipid; insistent; intelligent; intent; interrogating; intricate; intriguing; introspective; intrusive; intuitional; inventive; inward; inward-turning; iris-blue; jade; jaded; irradiant;

462

jaundiced; jewel; jolly; joy-filled; joyous; joy-pronouncing; keen; keen-puckered; kind; kindled; knowing; kohl-rimmed; laboring; lackluster; lackadaisical; lambent; landlubber; languid; languorous; large; lascivious; lashless; laughing; leaden; lecherous; leering; lenient; level; lidless; life-darting; lifted; light; limpid; lingering; liquid; listless; livid; living; loathing; lodestar; lofty; longing; lovable; love-deep; love-laden; love-lit; love-weary; loving; lucent; lurid; lumpy; lurking; lusterless; lustrous; lynx; madonna; magisterial; magnificent; mahogany; malevolent; malicious; malignant; mangling; martial; masculine; maternal; mature; maudlin; mean; medicinable; meditating; melancholy; melting; memory-ridden; menacing; microscopic; merciless; merry; meteor; mild; military; milky; miraculous; miscast; mischievous; miserable; mismatched; mistaking; misty; mocking; modest; moist; moistened; Mongolian; monstrous; moody; mortal; mortified; motionless; mottled; mournful; murderous; muddy-brown; musing; musty; mutinous; myopic; myriad; mysterious; mystical; mystifying; naked-bladed; narrow; national; neighboring; normal; observant; observing; obsidian; offering; ogling; onyx; opal; opaque; opening; oriental; outraged; outstanding; outward; overflowing; overhanging; overstrained; oxlike; owlish; pain-dimmed; pain-filled; pain-lashed; painful; pale; pale-blue; pallid; pansy-blue; pansy-dark; passing; passionate; paternal; patient; peacock; peeping; peering; peevish; pellucid; penetrating; pensive; perceiving; peremptory; perspicuous; persuasive; perverse; philosophical; phoenix; piercing; piglike; pious; piteous; pitying; placid; plaintive; pleading; pleasant; poetic; polished-looking; pondering; preoccupied; ponderous; popping; porcine; possessive; pouchy; powerful; practiced; pragmatic; predatory; probing; prodigious; profane; professional; prominent; prompting; prophetic; protecting; protuberant; proud; provocative; public; puffed; punished; purblind; pure; purged; purple; prying; puzzled; querulous; questioning; quick; quick-lifted; quick-shifting; quiet; quizzical; radiant; raccoonlike; raging; random; rapt; ratlike; ratty; ravenous; ravished; realmless; rebel; rebelling; rebuking; red-rimmed; reddened; reflecting; reflective; reluctant; remarkable; remote; reproachful; resplendent; retrospective; re-

verent; reverted; revengeful; rheumy; richest; rival; riveting; roaming; roguish; rolling; romantic; rose-colored; round; roving; ruddy; ruddy-brown; rueful; rust-colored; sad; saddened; sagacious; sanguine; sarcastic; sardonic; satiated; saturnine; saucy; savage; scandalized; skeptic; scornful; scowling; screwed-up; scrutinizing; sea-blue; sea-gray; sea-green; sea-spent; searching; searchlight; seductive; seeing; selfsame; sensible; seraphic; sere; serene; serious; serpent; shaded; shadow-nurtured; shadowed; shadowy; shifting; sharp; sheepish; shifty; shimmering; shining; shrewd; shrinking; shrouded; shy; sibylline; sidelong; sightless; silent; silly; single; sinister; skeptical; sky-blue; skyey; slant; slate-colored; slaty; sleep-sodden; sleepless; sleepy; slight; slitty; sly; small; smart; smarting; smiling; smoke-blue; smoldering; snake; snapping; sober; sodden; soft-winged; solemn; solicitous; solitary; sorrowing; soul-telling; soulful; soulless; sour; sparkling; speaking; spectacular; speculating; speculative; spell-set; spirit-beaming; sphered; splendid; sprightly; sprouting; stainless; starlike; staring; spirit-thrilling; stark; starry; starting; steady; steadfast; stealthy; steaming; steel; steel-bright; steel-cold; stinging; steely; stern; stony; stormy; strained; strange; straying; streaming; striking; strong; studious; stupefied; subtle; subdued; sud-filled; suffering; suffused; sullen; sulky; sulphurous; sultry; sunken; sun-clear; sun-dazzled; sunshiny; superb; superficial; surprised; surveying; suspicious; sweeping; swimming; swollen; sympathetic; Tarquin; taunting; tawny; tear-blurred; tearful; tear-marred; tear-ridden; tear-wet; telescopic; telltale; tempestuous; tender; terrible; terrifying; terror-glazed; threatening; terrorized; terror-stricken; thankful; tiger; thirsty; thoughtful; tigerish; time-dimmed; timorous; tiny; tip-tilted; tired; tired out; tolerant; tormented; tormenting; tortured; topaz; touching; town-bred; trained; traitorous; tranquil; tremendous; transcendent; transparent; zinc-colored; tremulous; triumphal; triumphant; trouble-strained; truant; truculent; true; trustful; trustless; twinkling; unabashed; unaccountable; unaccustomed; unaided; unaltering; unbelieving; unannointed; unavoided; unblended; unblinded; unblinking; uncanny; uncaptious; uncertain; unclouded; uncomprehending; unconscious; uncritical; uncultivated; uncurious; undaunted; uneasy; unencumbered; unemotional; unenlightened; unenvious; unfathomable; unflickering; unflinching; unfriendly; uninitiate; unkind; unlearned; unnatural; unoperated; unpitying; unpredictable; unpleasant; unpracticed; unprejudiced; unprepossessing; unpresumptuous; unresponsive; unrevealing; unrewarded; unscrupulous; unseeing; unshackled; unshaded; unsmiling; unsophisticated; unspeakable; unsullied; unsuspecting; untamed; unterrified; untrained; untutored; untroubled; unusual; unwearied; unworldly; upbraiding; upraised; upturned; ugly; urgent; vacant; vacuous; velvet-soft; vague; veering; veiled; veilless; veiny; velvety; vengeful; venomous; vigilant; violet-blue; virgin; visionary; visionless; vivid; vulgar; wailing; waiting; wandering; wanton; war-wearied; waxen; warning; wary; washed; wasted; watchful; watery; weak; weary; weasel; weather; weeping; welkin; whimsical; well-known; well-spaced; wicked; wide; wide-open; wild; willful; wincing; winking; wintry; wise; wistful; wolfish; wonderful; wondering; wondrous; wood-nymph; wordless; worldly-wise; worn; worried; worshipped; wrathful; wretched; yellow; yielding; youthful; zestful.

EYESIGHT

adjectives

partial; unsealed; failing; precious; weakening; impaired; inefficient; palsied; neglected.

F

FABLES

adjectives

comic; antique; contextual; wretched; trivial; impious; vivid; gorgeous; romantic; traditional; prehistoric; fantastic.

FABRIC

adjectives

political; attractive; sturdy; fine-wearing; ultra-smart; notable; practical; choicest; worsted; ideal; pure; wool; superb; tropical; rich; wearable; soft; exclusive; easy-draping; hard-finished; select; popular; excellent; mellowed; non-shrinkable; favored; summer; luxurious; wonderful; wear-packed; good-looking; sparkling; cool; expensive; original; sensational; iridescent; shivered; delicate; tinted; lustrous; gaudy; spangled; colorful; lightweight; soft-textured; quality; comfortable; easy-fitting; long-living; neutral color; rugged; famous; firm; extraordinary; lovely; apparent; hairy-surfaced; casual; unsubstantial; imported; cobweb; resilient; massive; durable; stately; identical; novelty; sheer; gossamer; distinctive; social; impregnated; misty; symmetrical; textile; clinging; accentuated; husky; brawnier; loomed; patterned.

verbs

construct—; fashion—; frame—; plan—; rebuild—; renovate—; spin—; supply—; threaten—; weave—; —awes; —endures; —inspires; —tatters.

(See cloth.)

FABRICATE (v)

adverbs

ingeniously; cleverly; hypocritically; plausibly; affectedly; falsely; maliciously; slyly; traitorously; convincingly.

(See devise, construct.)

FABRICATION

adjectives

wholesale; feeble; delicious; clumsy.

FABULOUS

adverbs

foolishly; extravagantly; egregiously; terribly; abominably; absurdly; laughably; outlandishly; whimsically; maliciously; fantastically; outrageously; mythically; ironically; perversely; romantically; utterly; manifestly; openly.

FACADE

adjectives

exquisite; unlovely; venerable; florid.

FACE

adjectives

absorbed; accusing; aggrieved; adored; aged; aghast; aging; agitated; agonized; alert; alluring; amazed; amiable; amused; flabby; angelical; angry; anguished; angular; animated; anxious; apathetic; apprehensive; approving; arresting; aquiline; arch-female; aristocratic; arrogant; artificial; ascending; ascetic; ashen; assiduous; astonished; astounding; attentive; attractive; audacious; auroral; austere; automaton; averted; awe-swept; awful; babyish; begrimed; baleful; barren; battered; beaming; beardless; beauteous; beefy; beloved; benevolent; benign; benignant; beseeching; besmeared; bestial; bewildered; bewitching; biddable; big; big-boned; big-featured; black; blackened; black-eyed; blanching; bland; blank; blear-eyed; blind; blissful; blistered; blithe; bloated; blood-faint; bloodless; bloodstained; bloodthirsty; bloody; blossomy; blubbering; blue-white; blurred; blushing; bold; bony; boulder-colored; boyish; bright; broad; broad-cheeked; brooding; brown; bruised; brutal; brutish; bucolic; burning; businesslike; cadaverous; calloused; calm; cameo; candid; capable; carbonadoed; careless; cavernous; careworn; carved-bone; cast-iron; celestial; chagrined; chalklike; changing; charitable; charming; charred; chastened; cheated; cheerful; cherubic; childlike; choleric; chubby; clammy; clawed; clean-cut; clean-shaven; clear-cut; clever; close; clouded; coarse; cold; cold-creamed; collapsed; colorless; combative; comely; comfortable; comical; commanding; complaining; complicated; composed; condemning; confident; congealed; congested; consumptive; contorted; contracted; convulsed; copper-bronzed; coppery; cordial; corpselike; corrugated; country-looking; cowardly; crafty; craggy; creamy-white; crude; cruel; crystal; cunning; curious; cynical; cynically-lined; dainty; daring; dark; darkened; dark-huddled; dazed; deadly; deadly-white; dead-white; death-like; deathly-pale; death-marked; debauched; deceptive; deep-lined; deeply-marred; dejected; delicate; delicately-formed; delicately-modeled; delighted; demure; delightful; denunciatory; despairing; despotic; determined; devilish; dewy; diffident; dignified; dimpled; dirty; disagreeable; disapproving; discolored; discontented; disdainful; disfigured; disillusioned; dismal; disordered; dissipated; distinct; distinguished; distorted; distracted; disturbed; doleful; dour; downcast; dowdy; drained; dreadful; dreary; dripping; droll; drooped; drowsy; dryad; dubious; dull; dusky; dust-colored; eager; earnest; easy-mannered; effeminate; elfin; eloquent; elusive; emaciated; embarrassed; eminent; enchanting; encrimsoned; energetic; enigmatic; enormous; enraptured; erstwhile; ethereal; ever-changing; everlasting; ever-welcome; evil; exceeding; expectant; exposed; expressionless; expressive; exquisite; eyeless; familiar; faded; fainting; fair; faithful; fallen; famine-stricken; famous; fanatical; fascinating; fat; fatigued; fatuous; fawning; fear-contorted; fearless; ferret-like; fervent; fiery; fighting; filled; fine; fixed; flabby; flamboyant; flat; flattened; flattered; fleshless; fleshy; flinty; flowerlike; flower-tinted; fond; foolish; forbidding; forced; foreign; formed; forsaken; forward; frail; frank; fraternal; freckled; fresh; friendly; frightened; frightful; froglike; frosted; furious; frosty; frozen; full; full-charged; furrowed; furtive; fuzzy; gamin; gaping; gaunt; gay; genial; ghastly; ghastly-pale; gigantic; girlish; gleaming; glistening; glittering; gloating; glory-beaming; glowing; glum; gnarled; gnomish; godlike; golden; good-humored; grotesque; good-natured; grained; granite; granite-gaunt; granite-hewn; grateful; grave; great; greenish-hued; grim; grinning; groping; gross-bloated; gruesome; guileless; gypsy; haggard; hair-fringed; hairless; half-averted; half-shrinking; half-haunted; handsome; hapless; happy; harassed; hard; hard-boiled; hard-muscled; harsh-featured; haughty; hate-clouded; hawklike; hearty; healthy-looking; heart-shaped; heated; heavenly; heat-flushed; heavy; helpless; heroic; hideous; hideously-scarred; well-bred; high-cheekboned; high-spirited; hirsute; hollow; holy; home-ly; honest; horrible; horror-stricken; hostile; huddled; humble; humorous; hungered; hungry; hunted; husklike; hypocritic; icy; idiotic; ignominious; illuminated; immemorial; immortal; immovable; impassive; imperial; imperious; imperturbable; impish; implacable; imploring; impudent; incredulous; indifferent; indignant; indomitable; ineffable; ineffectual; inelegant; inexorable; inexpressible; inexpressive; infant; infantine; inflamed; infuriated; ingenious; innocent; innumerable (pl); inoffensive; inscrutable; intellectual; intelligent; interesting; intrepid; irregular; irritable; isolated; ivory; jolly; jovial; keen-featured; kill-joy; kind; kindling; kindly; lampblack; large; lantern-jawed; laughing; lean-cheeked; leathery; leering; lemon-yellow; lifeless; little; lined; lineless; line-old; listening; listless; lively; livid; loathsome; locked; long; long-chinned; lordly; lovable; lovely; loving; gay; lowering; luminous; lustrous; majestic; malarial; malicious; malignant; maniacal; manly; mantling; marble; marred; martial; martyr; masklike; masked; massive; meager; meek; melancholy; memorable; merciless; merrier; mild; mirth-lit; miserable; mistrustful; mobile; mocking; modeled; motionless; monstrous; moon-colored; moonlike; moon-shaped; motherly; mottled; mottled-red; mournful; mud-besmeared; much-desired; muddy; mummied; murderous; muscular; mutilated; mutinous; mysterious; naked; nervous; neurotic; noble; noncommittal; noseless; objective; nutcracked; observant; obtuse; oil-smeared; oil-streaked; oily; olive; ominous; open; oval; overcast; pain-chiseled; pain-distorted; painted; pale; pansy-shaped; pallid; parchment; passionate; passionless; pasty; pasty-white; patient; patrician; peaceful; peaked; peerless; peaked; pearly; peasant; peevish; pensive; perfect; perfectly-formed; perished; perpendicular; perspiring; pert; pictured; phantom-like; piggish; pimply; pinched; piquant; piteous; pitiable; pitying; pitted; placid; plain; plaintive; pleasant; pleasing; plump; pock-marked; poetic; pointed; poker; porcelain-tinted; potent; powdered; powerful; precipitous; predestinate; premature; prematurely-aged; prevaricating; pretty; prison-pale; proud; puckered; pudding; pudgy; puffed; puffy; pugnacious; puny; purple-colored; putty-colored; puzzled; quaint; queenly; quiet; quivering; rabbity; radiant; rage-torn;

466

rage-twisted; rain-drenched; rapt; ratlike; ravaged; rebellious; reckless; red; refined; reflective; relentless; reproachful; resigned; resolute; respectable; responsive; restless; reticent; retributive; retrospective; reverent; reversed; ridged; rigid; roguish; rosepetal; rose-tinted; rosebud; rosy; roughly-hewn; round; rubicund; ruddier; rueful; rustic; ruthful; sad; sagacious; saintly; sallow; salt-stung; sanguine; sardonic; satanic; saturnine; saucy; scandalized; scapegrace; scared; scarlet; scarred; scheming; scholarly; scornful; scowling; scraggly; scratched; scrawny; screech-owl; seamed; scrutinizing; searching; seared; sedate; self-assured; selfless; sensitive; sensual; sentimental; serene; serious; serpent; serpentine; set; shaded; shamed; shameful; sharp-featured; sharply-angled; shaven; shining; shocked; shockingly disfigured; shrewd; shrouded; sick-looking; sickly; sightless; silent; silly; simpering; simple; sin-scarred; sinister; slant-eyed; sleek; sly; small; smashed; smiling; smile-lit; smirking; smoke-begrimed; smooth; smooth-coated; smooth-pale; smudged; smutted; snarling; sneering; sober; soft; soldierly; sorrow; somber; sorrowful; sorrowing; sorry; spare; sparkling; speaking; spectral; spirited; spiritual; splotched; staring; spongy; square; stark; square-jawed; square-jowled; startled; startling; steadfast; steady; steaming; stern; still; stolid; stone; stony; storm-beaten; stout; straight; straight-featured; strenuous; straightforward; strained; stubbly; streaming; stricken; striking; subdued; strong; strong-featured; stupid; sublime; sulky; sullen; sun-bitten; sun-browned; sunburned; sun-darkened; sun-scorched; sunken; sunny; surly; suspicious; swarthy; sweat-marked; sweat-streaked; sweating; sweet; tabid; tallow; swollen; tanned; tawny; tear-dabbled; tearful; tear-stained; tear-streaked; tear-wet; teary; tender; tense; terrible; thin; thoughtful; threatening; tight; tightening; tight-lipped; tight-skinned; tilted; time-stained; time-worn; timid; tired; toothless; tortured; tough; towering; tragic; tranquil; transfigured; transformed; transparent; triumphant; treacherous; troubled; trunkless; twisted; twittering; ugly; unabashed; unbelieving; unconscious; uncouth; uncovered; underhung; uneasy; unforgetful; unfriendly; unhealthy; unintellectual; unkempt; unlighted; unlined; unmoved; unpenciled; unreadable; unrejoicing; unremembering; un-

shaven; unscathed; unsmiling; unspoiled; unsunny; unsympathetic; untroubled; unwashed; unwithered; unworldly; unworried; unwrinkled; uplifted; uptilted; upturned; upward; vacant; vacuous; varnished; vanished; vapid; varying; veiled; vellum-colored; vicious; villainous; vindictive; virginal; vivacious; vulturish; waning; wan; washed; wayward; waxen; weak; weather-beaten; weather-stained; weather-worn; wedge-shaped; wee; weird; well-cut; well-featured; well-groomed; well-known; well-remembered; whimsical; whiskered; white; wicked; whitewashed; wide-eyed; wine-flushed; winsome; winter-blighted; wiry; wistful; withered; wizened; woebegone; woeful; wolfish; womanly; wonder; wrinkled; wooden; working; worn; worried; wrathful; wry; yearning; young; youthful; yeoman-built; arch; delicately-cut; frolic; lean; sleeping; slender.

verbs

animate—; blanch—; contort—; distort—; draw—; flush—; furrow—; illumine—; mop —; obscure—; pinch—; pucker up—; puff up—; read in—; scrutinize—; stamp—with; submerge—; suffuse—with; tense—; wrinkle—; —beams;— bleaches; —blooms; —brightens; —charms; —clouds; —creases; —darkens; —fascinates; —flames; — gleams; —glows; —lights up; —pales; — purples; —relaxes; —resembles; —smarts; —whitens.

(See countenance, features.)

FACE (*v*)

adverbs

haughtily; resolutely; squarely; undauntedly; challengingly; listlessly; courageously; indomitably; unflinchingly; immovably; accusingly; agitatedly; alluringly; animatedly; amiably; apathetically; apprehensively; arrogantly; ashenly; audaciously; bewitchingly; austerely; callously; chastenedly; cherubically; comically; composedly; cordially; cynically; despotically; determinedly; diffidently; disdainfully; disillusionedly; distractedly; dolefully; dourly; drearily; dubiously; eloquently; energetically; enigmatically; fanatically; fatuously; fawningly; guilelessly; humbly; hypocritically; idiotically; impassively; imperiously; imperturbably; impishly; implacably; imploringly; incredulously; indifferently; intrepidly; majestically; maniacally; martially; meekly; miserably; mutinously; neurotically; obtusely; ominously; passionately; passionlessly; pertly; priggishly; piquantly; piteously; potently; precipitously; prematurely; radiantly; rebelliously; raptly; recklessly; relentlessly; reticently; reverently; roguishly; ruefully; schemingly; selflessly; sensually; sentimentally; serenely; smirkingly; sneeringly; stubbornly; tenderly; tensely; tragically; treacherously; uncouthly; unintellectually; unsmilingly; unsympathetically; wistfully; woefully; wrathfully.

(See meet, confront.)

FACETIOUS

adverbs
comically; waggishly; entertainingly; inappropriately; unseasonably; happily; merrily; youthfully; smartly; unfortunately; fantastically; quick-wittedly; nimbly; clownishly; jovially; convivially; whimsically; amusingly; pleasantly; foolishly; banteringly; teasingly; drolly; fatuously; remarkably.

FACETIOUSNESS

adjectives
grave; sparkling; cheery; dull; unwitty.

FACETS

adjectives
sparkling; gleaming; well-cut.

FACIAL

adjectives
refreshing; hasty; stimulating; cleansing.

FACILE

adverbs
skilfully; dexterously; extremely; unusually; cleverly; adroitly; artfully; neatly; ingeniously; felicitously; deftly; smartly; expertly; capably; competently; intelligently; enthusiastically; eagerly; earnestly; amenably; heartily; glibly; conveniently; pliantly; smoothly.

FACILITATE (v)

adverbs
readily; necessarily; skillfully; automatically; unsurpassingly; commercially; mechanically; briskly; unfailingly; completely.

(See advance, hasten.)

FACILITIES

adjectives
housekeeping; intermediate; clinical; educational; characteristic; technical; limitless; equal; extra; modern; recreational; convenient; marvelous; unmatched; complete; astonishing; culinary; superior; abundant; inadequate; merger; available; unsurpassed; banking; admirable; improved; mechanical; surprising; fatal; elaborate; telegraphic; musical; subsequent; terminal; rapid-transit; existing; sanitary; commercial.

FACILITY

verbs
abuse —; accomplish with —; afford —; break down —; compose with —; contribute to —; hinder —; impede —; increase —; learn with —; manage with —; perform with —; permit of —; prove —; provide —; utilize —; wipe out —; — accelerates; — lightens; — lubricates.

(See ease.)

FACSIMILE

adjectives
diminished; alleged.

FACT

adjectives
mere; ugly; unassorted (pl); stark; unvarnished; statistical; unpalatable; vital; ultimate; iron; serious; gratifying; timely; curious; salient; undoubted; indisputable; astonishing; surprising; marvelous; miraculous; magnificent; confounding; unheard-of; singular; extraordinary; incredible; unforeseen; rarest; private; enviable; subtle; outstanding; isolated; well-established; simple; unfortunate; significant; smallest; natural; cosmic; accomplished; psychological; grim; historic; lamentable; practical; dominant; sordid; illuminating; governing; eternal; insuppressible; inexplicable; remarkable; systematizing; ineluctable; conceded; multifarious (pl); straight-from-the-shoulder; scientific; interesting; striking; noteworthy; accepted; inexorable; cruel; prosaic; hard; sprightly; inescapable; persistent; settled; essential; contradictory; embellished; deniable; stubborn; fundamental; revolting; unanswerable; disgraceful; unrelated; concomitant; intriguing; optical; naked; undeviating; instructive; damaging; changing; fluid; amazing; full; free; cold; startling; elemental; important; demonstrated; unconventional; permanent; visible; notorious; well-ascertained; brutal; preliminary; relevant; bitter; admitted; melancholy; deplorable; embodying; memorable; bare; palpable; unquestionable; authenticated; cardi-

nal; incontrovertible; worthy; final; ultimate; absolute; graphical; quiet; special; patent; unsuspected; unguessed; reasonable; architectural; dark; mysterious; concrete; palpitating; delightful; irresistible; delicious; unimpugnable; analogous; sinful; well-known; conspicuous; clear; distinct; firm; passionless; impartial; noticed; meticulous; illuminating; scanty; inert; vivid; tremendous; previous; exact; formidable; unconnected; first; empirical; acoustical; external; perpetual; bald; encouraging; physical; plain; ascertained; convincing; horrific; central; negative; basic; tangible; indubitable; geological; suggestive; trivial; rudimentary; clenching; acquired; outward; adduced; inconvenient; major; self-evident; commonplace; verifiable; supreme; actual; positive; sheer; apparent; acknowledged; ethical; diverting; sober; unpleasant; disturbing; unpoetic; tragic; queer; fantastic; colorful; fabulous; notable; stirring; buried; laborious; discovered; overwhelming; exhaustive; multitudinous (pl); detailed; hazy; confusing; experimental; paradoxical; observed; challenging; superficial; im-
material

verbs

accept —; account for —; accumulate —s; allude to —; amplify —; apprise of —; array —s; ascertain —; ascribe — to; assail —; assemble —s; attest to —; awake to —; bear out by —; belittle —; bemoan —; blind to —; blur —; bring — to light; bring home —; certify —; cite —; collate —; color —; confirm —; conform to —; confront with —; construe —; cram with —s; credit —; debate —; deduce —; demonstrate —; deny —; deplore —; digest —; disclose —; disentangle —s; disguise —; distort —; divulge —; dodge —; embrace —; emphasize —; establish —; evidence by —; exhaust —s; exploit —; expound —; face —; found on —; garble —s; generalize —s; glean —s; grant —; grapple with —; grasp —; harp on —; ignore —; impress with —; interpret —; juggle —s; master —; misconstrue —; misrepresent —; mull over —s; obscure —; oppose —; outweigh —; overlook —; override —; ponder —; question —; recapitulate —s; reconcile —s; refute —; regale with —s; rehash —s; represent as —; rest upon —; run counter to —; sift —s; stress —; stud with —s substantiate —; suppress —; trace — to; transform —s; unearth —; verify —; weigh —; wrestle with —; —s co-

here; — dawns; — depresses; — disquiets; — illustrates; — looms; — sinks in; —startles; — supports; — verifies.

(See truth, act, incident, statement.)

FACTION

verbs

attach to —; avoid —; combine —s; criticize —; defend —; disturb —; divide into —s; extinguish —; join —; maintain —; rend into —s; run into —s; sort into —s; split in —s; spread —; support —; suppress —; unite —s; — abandons; — declines; — dictates; — disperses; — springs from.

(See party, opposition.)

FACTIONS

adjectives

fluctuating; petty; discordant; embittered; wretched; defeated; turbulent; atrocious; execrable; fierce; mischievous; warring; hostile; rival; musical; exasperated; oligarchical; various; aristocratic; contending; internal; respective; opposing; imprisoned; reconciling.

FACTOR

adjectives

selective; dietary; prominent; etiological; potent; growth; various (pl); significant; vital; psychological; unfortunate; inestimable; additional; causative; determining; indispensable; compensating; prime; intellectual; dependable; encouraging; underlying; distinct; astounding; contributory; fundamental; outside; limiting; legendary; inherited; unquestioned; environmental; important; practical; dominant; industrial; external; material; essential; responsible; decisive; narcissistic; ecclesiastical; obvious; negligible; despised; dangerous; racial; geographical; constitutional; constant; motivating; all-pervasive; avoidable; incalculable.

verbs

belittle —; consider —; coordinate —s; embrace —; establish —; influence by —; limit —s; ponder —; reckon —; reveal —; unravel —; weigh —; —s converge; — determines; — emerges; —looms; —s militate against; — predisposes; — dominates.

(See element, constituent, influence, cause.)

FACTORY

adjectives

besieged; enormous; noisy; irrepressible.

verbs

boycott —; conduct —; control —; convert —; destroy —; dispose of —; equip —; erect —; establish —; examine —; improve —; inspect —; maintain —; man —; manage —; observe —; picket —; promote from —; strip —; supervise —; — employs; — idles; — produces; — specializes in.

(See plant, mill, shop, building.)

FACULTY

adjectives

contemplative; divine; unworn; ruling; bounded; healthful; bigoted; domestic; artful; visualizing; ready; rational; corporeal; biased; imaginative; perceptive; distinct; trained; reasoning; intellectual; remarkable; scientific; benumbed; integral; honorable; unimpaired; sterner; reciprocal; courageous; practised; departmentalized; balancing; glorious; winged; natural; rare; unique; primary; worldly; efficient; sublimest; wondrous; higher; dormant; aesthetic; elaborative; human; visual; imitative; cardinal; potential; awakened; penetrating; governing; administrative; spiritual; critical; cogitative; analytical; abnormal; treacherous; moral; finite; antipodal; comparative; common; creative; inventive; uncanny; obstinate; acute.

verbs

arouse —; assist —; collect —s; concentrate —ies; cultivate —ies; dazzle —; develop —ies; dull —ies; endow with —; exercise —; exhibit —; hamper —; impair —; manifest —; rally —ies; reclaim —; recruit —ies; retain —; strain —; strengthen —; stupefy —; waste—ies; — decays; — enables.

(See power, capacity, ability, skill, talent.)

FAD

adjectives

commendable; expensive; dietary; crazy; innocent; passing.

verbs

addict to —; adopt —; advocate —; annihilate —; attribute — to; conceive —; condemn —; criticize —; cultivate —; deter —; dispose to —; frown on —; gibe at —; indulge in —; nourish —; produce —; pursue —; ridicule —; start —; warn against —; — exaggerates; — passes; — seizes; — spreads; — sprouts.

(See fancy, fashion, hobby, whim.)

FADE (v)

adverbs

partially; gracefully; strangely; autumnally; hauntingly; dismally; inevitably; corporeally; depressingly; tragically; lingeringly.

(See droop, decay.)

FAGGED

(fagged-out)

adverbs

utterly; inexpressibly; dangerously; alarmingly; haggardly; gauntly; hopelessly; irrecoverably; lamentably; pitiably; wretchedly; miserably.

FAGGOT

adjectives

wintry; blazing; ashy; glazing.

FAIL (v)

adverbs

miserably; tragically; unquestionably; ridiculously; deplorably; essentially; deservedly; constantly; conspicuously; unwittingly; signally; lamentably; ignominiously; eventually; despicably; grievously; partially; scholastically; abjectly; habitually; inexplicably; indefensibly.

(See decline, deteriorate.)

FAILING

verbs

aggravate —; alter —; anticipate —; apprehend —; breed —; brood over —; compensate for —; deserve —; detect —; discover —; establish —; excuse —; exploit —; forgive —; incur —; mention —; pardon —; produce —; promote —; supply —; — enfeebles; — overtakes.

(See fault, foible, shortcoming, failure, deficiency, infirmity, defect.)

adverbs

indubitably; visibly; hopelessly; shockingly; feebly; weakly; languidly; decrepitly; desolately; shakily; perceptibly; manifestly; patently; conspicuously; noticeably; rapidly; inevitably; finally; slowly; obviously; avowedly; brokenly; wretchedly; pitifully; undoubtedly; languishingly; hopelessly; fatally; incurably; infirmly; strangely.

FAILINGS

adjectives

radical; common; inherited; proudest.

adjectives
impending; eventual; despicable; grievous; pathetic; distressed; architectural; expensive; wasteful; baking; partial; corresponding; miserable; irritating; repeated; dismal; celebrated; melancholy; appalling; foredoomed; regretted; vacillatory; consecutive (pl); preliminary; scholastic; abject; pitiable; sensible; ignominious; hideous; frantic; predestined; lamentable; mental; conspicuous; habitual; heroic; inexplicable; unhappy; indefensible; depressing; sudden; gigantic; pioneering.

verbs
ameliorate —; avert —; brood over —; court —; face —; foredoom to —; foretell —; grapple with —; indemnify against —; insure against —; offset —; overcome —; precipitate —; predict —; punish —; view as —; — disheartens; — dismays; — impends; — invalidates; — looms.
(See bankruptcy, neglect, short-coming, failing.)

FAINT

verbs
anticipate —; avert —; fall into a —; feign —; fight off —; produce —; recover from —; revive from —; rouse from —; simulate —; sink in —; stay —; treat for —; — confuses; — depresses; — enfeebles; — ensues; — weakens.
(See fit, paroxysm, convulsion.)

adverbs
woefully; terribly; incredibly; illegibly; powerlessly; visibly; noticeably; conspicuously; obviously; wretchedly; helplessly; dangerously; alarmingly; dreadfully; mysteriously; strangely; oddly; curiously; wearily; breathlessly; drowsily.

FAINT (v)

adverbs
ostensibly; charmingly; abruptly; unexpectedly; calculatingly; intermittently; designingly.
(See despond, fade.)

FAINTNESS

adjectives
present; humiliating.

adjectives
fashionable; cruel; slumbering.

adverbs
invariably; honestly; beautifully; equitably; always; indubitably; incontestably; legally; scrupulously; meticulously; carefully; dutifully; cautiously; discreetly; reasonably; surprisingly; astutely; logically; sensibly; expediently; providently; admirably; pleasantly; grudgingly; primarily; tolerably; exceptionally; satisfactorily; remarkably; generously; strictly; rigidly; impartially.

FAIR-GROUNDS

adjectives
populous; spacious; frequented.

FAIRNESS

adjectives
supposed; scrupulous; pretended.

verbs
assail —; bestow with —; dispute —; doubt —; exhibit —; judge —; necessitate —; repay —; reward —; seek —; violate —; yield to —; — pleases.
(See justice, impartiality, honesty.)

FAIRY

adjectives
adventurous; pitiless; rough; omnipotent; venturous; good; fiendish.

verbs
transform into —; —ies array; — assumes; — charms; — circles; — dances; — darts; — enchants; — flits; — frisks; — frolics; — gambols; — hies away; — inhabits; — leaps; — meddles; —revels; — scampers; — sings; — tricks; — trips; — warbles.
(See angel, spirit.)

FAIRYLAND

adjectives
vague; misty.

FAITH

adjectives
abiding; indestructible; consolatory; sublime; gladder; scrupulous; passionate; mutual; ripening; childlike; obliterated; obliged; nobler; inflexible; implicit; efficient; pure-eyed; grim; unbounded; whimsical; plighted; sturdy; radiant; joyful; religious; rising; unbroken; rational; potential; blind;

unquestioning; manly; lesser; unfeigned; humble; trusting; unfailing; utter; undying; secure; absolute; conflicting (pl); fervid; melancholy; sincere; optimistic; earnest; all-absorbing; heartier; devouring; habitual; immaculate; lofty; unwavering; sacramental; supreme; dumb; helpless; good; willing; generous; unalterable; unshaken; true; fugitive; orthodox; public; exulting; purblind; quickened; implied; heart-enrooted; inviolate; stalwart; tardy; obedient; blighting; impious; feeble; down-sunken; deathless; customary; active; shattered; sinless; material; profound; infirm; honorable; transcendent; barren; simple; steadfast; plural (pl).

verbs
apostatize from —; break — with; cling to —; confirm —; dampen —; endure with —; exhibit —; found upon —; forsake —; fortify —; inculcate —; inspire —; invalidate —; justify —; maintain —; manifest —; mould —; persecute for —; pervert —; pin — in; preach —; proclaim —; profess —; purge —; reawaken —; reiterate —; retain —; rivet — in; shake —; share —; sway by —; voice —; — melts away; — perishes; — quickens; — stands; — survives; — wavers.
(See assurance, belief, conviction, confidence, trust.)

FAITHFUL
adverbs
affectionately; loyally; duly; honorably; scrupulously; rigidly; deeply; grimly; resolutely; sturdily; undeviatingly; joyously; blindly; humbly; utterly; absolutely; optimistically; earnestly; heartily; unwaveringly; unalterably; inviolately; steadfastly; actively; flatteringly; abjectly; punctiliously; meticulously; actively; simply; unaffectedly; candidly; openly; incorruptibly; uncommonly.

FAITHFULNESS
adjectives
utter; assertive.

verbs
believe in —; build —; cherish —; create —; demand —; display —; encourage —; justify —; necessitate —; overshadow —; praise —; prove —; rely on —; require —;

reward —; suspect —; try —; — falls; — shines; — supports; — trusts.
(See loyalty, fidelity, constancy, allegiance, devotion.)

FAITHLESS
adverbs
shamelessly; terribly; abominably; timorously; basely; faint-heartedly; brazenly; coolly; openly; obdurately; detestably; execrably; audaciously; perversely; hypocritically; evasively; artfully; perfidiously; cunningly; insidiously; surreptitiously; dreadfully; unbelievably; unexpectedly; direly; disastrously; shamefully.

FAKE
verbs
conceive—; contrive—; denounce—; detect —; divine—; expose—; father—; inspire—; invent—; palm off—; perform—; plan—; plunder with—; practice—; regard as—; reveal—; shape—; taboo—; uncover—; work—; —deceives; —entrances; —fascinates; —fools; —perturbs.
(See swindle, sham, deceit.)

FALL
adjectives
tremendous; jade-green; weary; graceful; repeated (pl); preceding; virtuous; sloping; gleaming; deadliest; intertangled; bubbly; clattering; answering; melodious; dying; instantaneous; uncropt; thundering.

verbs
(See autumn.)

FALL (v)
adverbs
ultimately; noiselessly; subsequently; perpendicularly; insensibly; involuntarily; supinely; disdainfully; melodiously; resistlessly; unceasingly; inertly; precisely; incoherently; unwittingly; leisurely; dreamily; violently; intermittently; disconcertingly; fitfully; ponderously; thunderingly.
(See drop, descend.)

FALLACIOUS
adverbs
deeply; grossly; utterly; obviously; sorrily; patently; manifestly; wretchedly; clumsily; grotesquely; fantastically; absurdly; oddly; scientifically; deliberately; speciously;

egregiously; horribly; laughably; flimsily; nonsensically; evasively; blunderingly; deceptively; intentionally; perversely; shamefully.

FALLACY

adjectives
glittering; discarded; deepest; gross; sophistical; pathetic; discovered.

verbs
accept—; admit—; challenge—; correct—; demonstrate—; denounce—; discover—; disperse—ies; disprove—; explode—; rationalize—; reveal—; ridicule—.
(See delusion, error, deception, misconception.)

FALLIBILITY

adjectives
extreme; obvious; apparent.

FALLIBLE

adverbs
precariously; embarrassingly; obscurely; timidly; indecisively; vaguely; occasionally; foolishly; weakly; inconclusively; deceptively; speciously; carelessly; casually; remarkably; frequently; bewilderingly; blithely; thoughtlessly; inconsequentially; impulsively; untenably.

FALLING

adjectives
unconscious; swift; desperate.

FALLOW

adverbs
aridly; unfruitfully; unprofitably; naturally; carelessly; shiftlessly; passively; inactively; unproductively; purposely; improvidently; rudimentally; roughly; calmly; tentatively; temporarily; deliberately; advisedly; provisionally; wisely.

FALSE

adverbs
subtly; stiffly; crudely; inelegantly; crassly; grotesquely; laughably; ridiculously; awkwardly; outlandishly; stagily; cleverly; ingeniously; obviously.

FALSEHOOD

adjectives
practised; flattering; incredible; base; clumsy; downright; palpable; grotesque; blushing; deliberate; infamous; pardonable; ingenious; cheerful; illusive; hidden; hypocritical; conventional; fawning; tortured; twisted.

verbs
accept—; admit—; avoid—; challenge—; confess—; demonstrate—; denounce—; disprove—; explode—; refrain from—; utter —; —dishonors; —pervades; —reeks; —sours; —taints.
(See lie, counterfeit, mistake, error.)

FALSENESS

adjectives
glittering.

FALSETTO

adjectives
tender; querulous; mincing; anxious; senile.

FALSIFIER

adjectives
wretched; conscienceless; insidious; adept.

FALSIFY (v)

adverbs
mystifyingly; abundantly; basely; prodigiously; incredibly; clumsily; palpably; grotesquely; deliberately; infamously; ingeniously; hypocritically; fawningly.
(See misrepresent, distort.)

FALTER (v)

adverbs
technically; abruptly; quaveringly; meekly; habitually; agedly; feebly; unattractively; repeatedly; recurrently; absurdly; ridiculously.
(See tremble, hesitate, waver.)

FAME

adjectives
fabulous; dying; boundless; imperishable; philosophic; volatile; hallowed; bastard; genuine; partial; lawful; glorious; prophetic; academic; inferior; abstract; soaring; shouting; patrimonial; monumental; artistic; tremendous; spotless; matchless; immense; unqualified; illustrious; extensive; prodigious; horrible; imaginary; eternal; posthumous; spurious; stainless; spreading; vague; inordinate; legal; faultless; immortal; nascent; worthy; untainted; sinister; international; equal; envious; additional; dead; serial; unpolluted; lifelong; enduring; deadly-purchased; dingy; long.

verbs

achieve—; acquire—; amass—; covet—; dazzle with—; destine to—; establish—; exalt to—; recapture—; renounce—; secure —; snatch at—; vault to—; —expands; —glows; —reaches; —rests on; —waxes.

(See renown, reputation, eminence, glory, notoriety.)

FAMILIAR
adverbs

thoroughly; intimately; wholly; cordially; affably; unceremoniously; informally; heartily; conversantly; entirely; highly; accessibly; courteously; perfectly; completely; habitually; wontedly; long; companionably; chattily; sociably; suavely; blandly; graciously; tactfully; genially; openly; publicly; avowedly; remarkably; undoubtedly; somewhat.

FAMILIARITY
adjectives

growing; sentimental; impertinent; legitimate; insolent; becoming; affectionate; misdirected; easy; sheer; hourly; dear; curious; intimate; democratic; personal; sweet; profane.

FAMILY
adjectives

sorrowing; aristocratic; human; peaceable; imperial; citrus; helpless; defenseless; hereditary; unnurtured; well-governed; ancient; illustrious; immediate; distinguished; ever-growing; affluent; respectable; numerous; aristocratic; discriminating; exaggerating; impecunious; influential; well-ordered; harmonious; attractive; pious; august; aghast; impoverished; meritorious; indigent; regal; talented; jarring; proud; national; wrangling; mignonette; well-regulated; homeless; powerful; intimate; decayed; short-lived; close-mouthed; stiff-necked; divided; frugal; brawny; destitute; increasing; lively; handsome; chivalrous; patrician.

verbs

contribute to—; dominate—; evict—; head —; hold—together; inspire—; join—; maintain—; respect—; reunite—; rule—; stir—; warp—; —flourishes; —overflows; —quarrels; —unites; —wrangles.

(See clan, tribe.)

FAMINE
adjectives

impending; desperate; pining; consuming; fearful; feverish.

verbs

bring—; die in—; expose to—; incur—; keep—at bay; lament—; perish in—; recover from—; suffer—; threaten with—; —attacks; —besieges; —blights; —clings; —devastates; —distresses; —ensues; —frustrates; —punishes; —prevails; —ravages; —reduces; —subdues.

(See destitution.)

FAMISHED
adverbs

incredibly; dreadfully; shamefully; abominably; unbelievably; utterly; starvingly; actually; haggardly; gauntly; horribly; shockingly; startlingly; heartbreakingly; emaciatedly; hungrily; insatiably; breathlessly; pitiably; awfully; murderously; terribly.

FAMOUS
adverbs

illustriously; brilliantly; notoriously; terribly; internationally; prodigiously; tremendously; distinctly; gloriously; honorably; deservedly; ingloriously; ignobly; horribly; imperishably; splendidly; politically; proudly; nobly; undeniably; remarkably; reputably; signally; amazingly.

"FAN"
(devotee)
verbs

breed—s; collect—s; produce—s; supply—s; —acclaims; —applauds; —attends; —cheers; —s congregate; —s flock to; —indulges in; —is addicted to; —praises; —pursues; —s rally; —responds; —"roots" for; —s turn out.

(See fanatic, devotee.)

FAN
(implement)
adjectives

cooling; breezy; whirling; flirting; feather; winnowing.

verbs

employ—; install—; regulate—; —agitates; —airs; —blasts; —blows; —buzzes; —cools; —churns; —creates a draft; —drives; —eases; —refreshes; —relieves; —revol-

ves; —rotates; —supplies; —urges; —ventilates; —whizzes.
(See propeller.)

FAN (v)

adverbs
coolingly; breezily; whirlingly; refreshingly; pleasingly; irritatingly; maddeningly;
furiously; feverishly.
(See cool, ventilate, rouse.)

FANATIC

adjectives
revolutionary; religious; unflinching; murderous; vegetarian; sour; crazed; recognized; unbalanced; miserable; vicious; passionate.

verbs
combat—; control—; enlist—; inflame—; intoxicate—; oppose—; ridicule—; scorn—;
transform into—; —accomplishes; —s band;
—charms; —explodes; —fevers; —imagines; —infects; —inveighs against; —kindles; —prates; —prattles; —rants; —stirs;
—undermines; —uproots.

FANATICAL

adverbs
intolerantly; illiberally; narrowly; provincially; wildly; madly; insanely; terribly; unfortunately; fantastically; outrageously; outlandishly; unreasonably; stupidly; crazily;
ribaldly; eccentrically; sharply; deeply; earnestly; fervently; fervidly; zealously; feverishly; hysterically; ungovernably; excitably; deliriously; moodily; dangerously;
dreadfully.

FANATICISM

adjectives
ignorant; remorseless; arrogant; insupportable; growing; unbridled; harsh; contemptible; lamented; religious.

verbs
control—; delude by—; display—; evince—;
express—; fire with—; heat with—; incline to—; incur—; inflame with—; manifest—; overwhelm by—; persecute for—;
plant the seed of—; tolerate—; —disqualifies; —drains; —exaggerates; —ferments;
—governs; —impresses; —inhibits; —intoxicates; —overdoes; —prejudices; —prohibits; —rends; —stimulates; —sunders; —
terrifies.
(See intolerance, superstition.)

FANCIER

adjectives
sensitive, professional.

FANCIFUL

adverbs
gloriously; illusively; abstractly; fantastically; notionally; delusively; chimerically;
phantasmagorically; romantically; fugitively; whimsically; momentarily; imperishably; extravagantly; deceptively; insubstantially; fabulously; inventively; voluptuously; comfortingly; ecstatically; ardently;
playfully; wildly; grotesquely; absurdly;
ludicrously; laughably; ridiculously; beautifully.

FANCY

adjectives
passing; distorted; subjective; sportive;
delicate; religious; bubbling; enthusiastic;
deluding; school-girl; ingenious; boundless;
superstitious; starry; virgin; quainter; tenderer; changeful; fond; disturbed; poetical;
stray; youthful; difficult; ungrateful; irritable; popular; flesh-imprisoned; wild; prodigal; subtle; shadowy; groundless; ridiculous; childish; morbid; curious; vagrant;
wayward; thick-coming (pl); fluttering;
riotous; trustworthy; fermenting; exquisite;
languid; incipient; airiest; feeble; preposterous; lingering; sudden; busy; extravagant; fickle; romantic; correlated; luxuriant; restless; quaint; hopeless; hypochondriacal; cruel; angry; later; odd; gushing;
fecund; timorous; sweet; strange; voluptuous; gentle; mystical; insistent; long-
faded; quick-springing; torpid; ardent;
credulous; rambling; captious; wheeling;
playful; giddy; unfirm; crude; disordered;
unreciprocated; fastidious; irregular; excited; distempered; ever-veering; pardonable; unearthly; waking; fragrant; flying;
footless; viewless; fugitive; worthless; delicious; violent; gloomy; wild-looking;
mere; weak-hinged; scheming; frivolous;
hideous; thoughtful; unsettled; whimsical;
diseased; quavering; extraordinary; idolatrous.

verbs
breed—; build with—; catch—; chime with
—; cure of—; crystallize—; dally with in
—ies; draw upon—; excite—; fit—; free
from—; indulge in—; lead by—; press upon
—; reject—; restrain—; —conceives; —

flees; —flickers; —ies gather; —pursues; —
—reigns; —roams; —rushes; —travels; —
—wakes; —wanders.

(See fantasy, conceit, whim, caprice.)

FANCY (v)

adverbs

chimerically; erroneously; subjectively; enthusiastically; boundlessly; superstitiously;
tenderly; poetically; ridiculously; childishly;
morbidly; waywardly; romantically; voluptuously; frivolously; whimsically; idolatrously.

See imagine, dream.)

FANDANGO

adjectives

shuffling; mad; whirling; wild.

FANFARE

adjectives

dying; sounding; glorious; wild; raucous.

FANGS

adjectives

sharpened; bloody; poisoned; harpy; particular; mimic; dripping; unseen; enormous; knotted; viewless.

verbs

bury—in; display—; escape—; expose—;
imbed—; insert—; shed—; strike with—; —
drive at; —fold back; —gnaw; —pass into;
—penetrate; —perforate; —pierce; —poison; —puncture; —spike.

(See claw, talon, nail.)

FANTASTIC

adverbs

illusively; deliciously; wildly; queerly; sadly; vainly; strangely; oddly; curiously;
mysteriously; romantically; whimsically;
extravagantly; fabulously; divertingly;
playfully; grotesquely; absurdly; ludicrously; laughably; horribly; ridiculously; unreasonably; irrationally.

FANTASY

adjectives

satirical; utopian; errant; delirious; babbling; wild; causeless; bewildering; vivid;
sinful; incestuous; conjectural; winged;
shadowy; scant; hideous; blasphemous;
guiltless; sinuous; shaping; aboriginal;
gracious; hateful; cherished; ingenious;
cosmic; unconscious.

verbs

delight in—; devise—; express in—; frame
in—; flutter in—; imagine in—; live in—;
project—; retreat into—; scatter—; soar in
—; stray in—; travel in—; view—; wander
in—; —attracts; —beckons; —gallops; —
hovers; —melts away; —roams; indulge
in—.

(See image, illusion, fancy, dream, phan-
tasy, caprice.)

FAR

adverbs

incredibly; fabulously; outlandishly; outrageously; remotely; inaccessibly; impossibly;
immeasurably; fantastically; wearily; extremely; surprisingly; dangerously; disturbingly; discouragingly; heartbreakingly;
terribly; lamentably; pitifully; incalculably.

FARCE

adjectives

coarse; physical; ghastly; gayest; moral;
boisterous; solemn; gigantic; social; bawdy;
glorious; brisk.

FARCICAL

adverbs

comically; laughably; ridiculously; ludicrously; fantastically; outlandishly; noisily;
boisterously; uproariously; racily; ribaldly;
coarsely; satirically; genially; socially;
brilliantly; crudely; gayly; solemnly; gloriously; hilariously; spectacularly; luminously; nonsensically; extravagantly; preposterously; senselessly; ironically; cleverly;
waggishly; facetiously; merrily; jocosely;
whimsically; drolly; bombastically; irresistibly; tremendously.

FARE

adjectives

monotonous; dainty; palatable; delicious;
sumptuous; heavenly; primitive; meager;
frugal; unwholesome; humble; ambrosial;
acceptable; penitential; bounteous; monastic; substantial.

FARE
(passage money)

verbs

calculate—; call for—; demand—; deposit
—; extend—; forfeit—; furnish—; mislay
—; necessitate—; produce—; reduce—;
reject—; remit—; request—; require—; supply—; take up—.

(See money, amount, price.)

476

FARE (v)

adverbs

sumptuously; disastrously; monotonously; deliciously; primitively; penitently; bounteously; substantially; monastically.

(See live, suffer.)

FAREWELL

adjectives

stern; ceremonious; affectionate; cheerful; fervent; edifying; wifely; remaining; inimitable; sublime; reluctant; mock; secret; fantastical; dilated; hasty; tender; thundering; summary; courteous; sobbing; heart-breathed; horrible; silent; mute; long; touching; mechanical.

verbs

anticipate—; bid—; bless at—; deter—; express—; mourn—; pour out—; prolong—; regret—; remember—; shorten—; take—; wave—; weep—; —depresses; —distresses; —ensues; —pains; —saddens; —terminates.

FAR-FETCHED

adverbs

laboriously; ridiculously; ineptly; irrelevantly; absurdly; ludicrously; unfortunately; clumsily; outlandishly; discordantly; inappropriately; pointlessly; senselessly; foolishly; studiously; sedulously; speciously; vapidly; inanely; stupidly; doltishly; remarkably; vacuously; childishly.

FARM

adjectives

stud; hospitable; deserted; scattered; exhausted; allodial; collective; extensive; productive; diversified; isolated; fruitful; well-cultivated.

verbs

abandon—; cultivate—; dwell on—; equip —; establish—; forsake—; grow on—; inhabit—; labor on—; leave—; maintain—; overrun—; raise on—; settle on—; till—; transform—; vacation on—; —deteriorates; —employs; —furnishes; —nestles; —produces; —provides; —supplies.

(See land, tract, district.)

FARMER

adjectives

incautious; florid; peasant-like; hard-handed; embattled; prosperous; stricken; indifferent; sheep; border-line; enlightened; sinewy; gentleman; close-fisted; liberal-hearted; disingenuous; venturesome; stout; industrious; plodding.

verbs

grubstake—; subsidize—; tax—; —cultivates; —fertilizes; —flourishes; —furrows; —garners; —gathers; —harvests; —hoes; —labors; —markets; —ploughs; —prunes; —reaps; —slaves; —sows; —spades; — thrives; —tills; —plucks.

(See countryman, peasant.)

FARM-HOUSE

adjectives

pleasant; smiling; comfortable-looking; stout.

verbs

abandon—; care for—; conceal—; describe —; dwell in—; erect—; gather in—; locate —; long for—; renovate—; restore—; search for—; surround—; threaten—; welcome—; yearn for—; —deteriorates; —nestles; —stands; retire to—.

(See dwelling, building, house.)

FARMING

adjectives

speculative; diversified; intensive; fertile; scientific.

FASCINATE (v)

adverbs

bewitchingly; enchantingly; inexplicably; infinitely; absurdly; irresistibly; singularly; carnally; voluptuously; dangerously.

(See charm, enchant.)

FASCINATED

adverbs

inexpressibly; inordinately; incomprehensibly; radiantly; innocently; incredibly; marvellously; artlessly; unconsciously; utterly; thoroughly; completely.

FASCINATING

adverbs

adorably; attractively; bewitchingly; charmingly; inexpressibly; dazzlingly; radiantly; innocently; designedly; intentionally; cleverly; incredibly; undeniably; marvellously; inordinately; dangerously; winningly; artlessly; unconsciously; utterly; highly; thoroughly; teasingly; smartly; consciously; craftily; seductively; completely.

adjectives

painful; potent; enchanting; dread; charming; horrible; occult; absorbing; inexplicable; perilous; acute; infinite; tremulous; inexhaustible; ominous; youthful; absurd; irresistible; singular; divine; wild; carnal; indefinable; wonderful; dangerous; shuddery; personal.

verbs

apply—; cast—; employ—; lie under—; overcome—; prevent—; resist—; succumb to—; surrender to—; sweep on by—; tantalize with—; withstand—; yield to—; —attracts; —binds; —compels; —draws; —freezes; —haunts; —impels; —masters; —overpowers; —perils; —prevails.

(See enchantment, charm, influence, attraction.)

FASCISM

adjectives

distinct; aggressive; insidious; power-drunk; efficient; masterful; stultifying.

verbs

admit to—; establish—; infect with—; inspire—; join—; oppose—; smack of—; succumb to—; support—; yield to—; —advocates; —aims at; —attacks; —campaigns; —controls; —crushes; —deprives; —embodies; —enforces; —girds its loins; —organizes; —ousts; —prohibits; —regulates; —revolts; —riots; —violates; —welds.

(See movement.)

FASHION

adjectives

convincing; casual; improving; scimitar; belated; futile; paternal; masterly; promising; authentic; sumptuous; peculiar; sinister; bourgeois; summery; changing; refreshing; military; charming; comical; vigorous; cold-blooded; casual; coat; outstanding; debonair; dress; sensational; gay; important; hurried; righteous; tawdry; wicked; pernicious; bygone; graceful; latest; effeminate; aesthetic; school-boy; regal; exclusive; foolish; beastly; fickle; mythical; tragic; fine; quaint; excellent; picturesque; debased; florid; symbolic; polluted; seemly; obedient; faultless; orderly; jovial; delicate; hearty; squalid; metropolitan; expensive; liberal; excited; impulsive; infantine; unstudied; unostentatious; accepted; surly; taciturn; shifting; smart; early; appealing; distinctive; formless; hellish; malignant; piquant; self-respecting; desultory; unbecoming; perfect; coordinating; candid; straightforward; corduroy; fantastic; rare; oriental; prevailing; serious; high-and-mighty; outlandish; simple; superficial; identical; classic; perpendicular; intrusive; orthodox; rude; bungling; haphazard; obvious; offensive; primitive; phlegmatic; soldierly; dramatic; feminine; fanciful; diverting; characteristic; feeble; brilliant; stimulating; fastidious; clownish; enervating; window-shutter; democratic; brutal; halting; obsolete; fugitive; literary; noble; obstinate; materialistic; unceremonious; ornate; reckless; romantic; humblest; patriarchal; gossipy; chatty; forced; upstart; plain; childish; united; inconvenient; awkward; listless; vague; antique; bovine; lavish; merciless; beneficent; contradictory; womanly.

verbs

accommodate—; anticipate—; appraise by —; attune to—; balk at—; create—; decree —; follow—; influence—; purvey—; rule—; set—; style—; —derives from; —dies out; —endures; —fades; —flickers out; —prevails; —roots in.

(See mode, method, usage, style.)

FASHION (v)

adverbs

primitively; crudely; superbly; flawlessly; deftly; tenderly; meticulously; delicately; comically; sensationally; gaily; perniciously; aesthetically; quaintly; picturesquely; symbolically; unostentatiously; fantastically; rudely; haphazardly; offensively; dramatically; characteristically; fastidiously; democratically; ornately; awkwardly.

(See style, make.)

FASHIONABLE

adverbs

completely; occasionally; enthusiastically; seriously; carefully; entirely; thoroughly; uncommonly; extraordinarily; habitually; conventionally; decorously; highly; modishly; socially; conformably; stylishly; jauntily; conspicuously; resolutely; determinedly; exquisitely; foppishly; flirtatiously; pretentiously; famously; notoriously; splendidly; reputably; eminently; imposingly; impressively; inveterately.

FAST

adverbs

incredibly; expeditiously; smartly; actively; mercurially; nimbly; remarkably; amazingly; marvellously; miraculously; unaccountably; intolerably; breathlessly; dangerously; alarmingly; hazardously; bewilderingly; terrifically; insanely; inordinately; immoderately; immeasurably; incalculably.

FAST (v)

adverbs

stubbornly; continually; frequently; tediously; determinedly; fatally; fanatically; rigorously; monastically; severely.

(See starve, abstain.)

FASTEN (v)

adverbs

securely; attractively; firmly; gaily; fastidiously; competently; snugly; closely; permanently; temporarily.

(See fix, secure.)

FASTIDIOUS

adverbs

inordinately; extravagantly; daintily; precisely; primly; exquisitely; neatly; habitually; punctiliously; rigidly; strictly; rigorously; arbitrarily; admirably; marvellously; meticulously; priggishly; delicately; captiously; censoriously; scrupulously.

FASTIDIOUSNESS

adjectives

aristocratic; complete; extreme; studied.

FASTNESS

adjectives

forest; wild; remote; unillumined; mountain; inaccessible; rugged; desolate; solitary.

FASTS

adjectives

frequent; bitter; tedious; hunger-strike.

FAT

adjectives

twofold; juicy; rancid; waxy; resinous; insoluble; additional; indigestible.

verbs

accrue—; accumulate—; acquire—; compose of—; devour—; digest—; emulsify—; fight against—; grow—; guard against—; live on—of; overcharge with—; prevent—; produce—; provide—; provoke—; put on —; reduce—; ridicule—; store up—; supply —; —blossoms; —forms; —nourishes; —sizzles.

(See flesh.)

adverbs

inexpressibly; unhappily; incredibly; incurably; laughably; lamentably; comfortably; contentedly; distressingly; absurdly; ridiculously; ludicrously; sadly; joyously; dangerously; heavily; gracefully; admittedly; funnily; unreasonably; incorrigibly; complacently; complainingly; mournfully; dramatically; pathetically; gracelessly; shapelessly; waddlingly.

FATAL

adverbs

unhappily; unfortunately; lamentably; deplorably; grievously; inevitably; presumably; usually; heartbreakingly; obscurely; darkly; strangely; oddly; curiously; mysteriously; unaccountably; irresistibly; inexorably; violently; mercifully; inescapably.

FATALISM

adjectives

vulgar; stubborn; reckless; hysterical; inevitable.

FATALISTIC

adverbs

inveterately; unshakably; implicitly; soberly; staunchly; confidently; incorrigibly; positively; gloomily; delusively; dispassionately; stubbornly; fantastically; calmly; unreasonably; irrationally; unfathomably; vaguely; actually; absurdly; destructively; insanely; credulously; securely; doctrinally.

FATALITY

adjectives

irresistible; all-powerful; inexorable; stark; strange; ironical.

FATE

adjectives

indulgent; tempted; solemn; inexorable; ultimate; special; pure; untoward; unchallenged; relentless; kindly; subsequent; uncommon; cruel; bitter; ignominious; blind; baffling; cramping; tragic; hostile; fixed; adverse; obedient; precious; unenviable; inevitable; awful; varied (pl); incumbent; obdurate; dismal; probable; narrower; tear-compelling; fairest; obliging; uncertain; evil; chequered; vanquished; whimsical; dedicated; happy; pursuing; favoring; deplorable; melancholy; endangered; ungentle; oracular; fabled; vulgar; worldly; harsh; indifferent; ruthless; unconscious; impending; proper; insensate; hapless; thwarting; sundering; monarchial; horrible; undoubted; ample; leafless; ungracious.

verbs
accept—; challenge—; cloud—; confront by —; dodge—; fulfill—; hinge on—; impose by—; mould—; outwit—; preside over—; prophesy—; resign to—; scoff at—; seal—; share—; work out—; —crushes; —deals; — destines; —engulfs; —fashions; —hangs; — moulds; —orders; —pushes; —singles out; —tortures.
(See destiny, necessity, doom, death.)

FATED
adverbs
blindly; adversely; inexorably; inevitably; imperiously; relentlessly; inauspiciously; ominously; portentously; luckily; auspiciously; resistlessly; direly; blessedly; obscurely; propitiously; unluckily; unpropitiously.

FATHER
adjectives
doting; implacable; prosaic; crusading; reverend; illustrious; active; improvident; bustling; electioneering; mitered; groveling; virtuous; joyful; ill-tempered; fond; dreadful; peevish; noble; ghostly; banished; honored; earthly; obdurate; hilarious; strenuous; formidable; vain; hollow; heartless; persecuted; imperial; uncowled; stricken; avaricious; spendthrift; unsuspecting; benignant; narrow-praying; blustering; indulgent; worthy; irate; grimy; jaunty; tender; scholarly; venerable; adoptive; remorseful; impecunious; avaricious; dissolute; judicious; temporal; deceiving; autocratic.

verbs
adopt —; adore —; ape —; idolize —; obtain —; owe to —; respect —; revere —; — advises; — aids; — allows; — assents; — corrects; — declares; — guards; — guides; — maintains; — moulds; — neglects; — nourishes; — pampers; — permits; — pets; — presents; — prevents; — pro-

tects; — punishes; — restrains; — scolds; — spoils; — supports; — thrashes.
(See parent, ancestor, author, mother.)

FATHERLAND
adjectives
icebound; heavenly; pleasant; memorable.

FATHERLESS
adverbs
unhappily; forlornly; unluckily; unfortunately; helplessly; drearily; desolately; miserably; wretchedly; pitiably; disconsolately; haplessly; deplorably; cheerlessly; dismally; obviously.

FATHERLY
adverbs
dutifully; indulgently; severely; gently; unnecessarily; quietly; wisely; proudly; providently; lovingly; generously; warmly; humanely; benevolently; sympathetically; comfortingly; amiably; lovingly; graciously; complaisantly; bounteously; benignly; mercifully; magnanimously; tenderly; warmly; softly; accommodatingly; usefully; considerately.

FATHOMLESS
adverbs
abysmally; profoundly; mysteriously; vastly; quietly; shudderingly; drearily; tranquilly; dangerously; immeasurably; incalculably; voicelessly; terrifyingly; inscrutably.

FATIGUE
adjectives
industrial; wild; insidious; extreme; expressed; decreased; unexplainable; excessive; pure; dangerous; painful; mental; undue; alcoholic; sheer; deep; unparalleled; harsh; dreamy; curing; resultant; intolerable; unwonted.

verbs
allay —; alleviate —; avoid —; correct —; dispel —; droop in —; eliminate —; endure —; induce —; inure to —; lessen —; measure —; produce —; recover from —; recuperate from —; — daunts; — dulls; — ensues.
(See exhaustion, weariness.)

FATIGUED

adverbs

inexpressibly; alarmingly; desperately; extremely; excessively; immeasurably; remarkably; inexplicably; painfully; mentally; physically; inordinately; deeply; intolerably; utterly; terribly; seriously; haggardly; gauntly; frightfully; mysteriously; unreasonably; quickly.

FATUITY

adjectives

parental; unspeakable; apparent.

FATUOUS

adverbs

unspeakably; tiresomely; foolishly; vacuously; inanely; idiotically; senselessly; absurdly; waggishly; terribly; preposterously; egregiously; intolerably; emptily; nonsensically; bombastically; pompously; absurdly; vaguely; insignificantly; ordinarily; habitually; frivolously; inconsequentially; endlessly; wearily; plaguedly.

FAUCET

adjectives

defective; rushing; singing; whistling; mixing; shining; dripping.

FAULT

adjectives

inherited; earthly; unforgivable; social; existing; distinctive; unbelievable; beastly; serious; cold; rankest; vile; outfacing; innumerable (pl); grave; glaring; inherent; headstrong; potent; grossest; unpardonable; undeserved; evident; grievous; universal; punishable; irremediable; apparent; brilliant; contrasted; unexpiable; venial; gracious; unwilling; prime; rash; technical; shunning; pernicious; excusable; tragic; ill-favored.

verbs

accept —; atone for —; beset by —; burden with —; compensate for —; confess —; conquer —; denounce —; disclose —; evince —; excuse —; find —; flay —; guard against —; iron out —s; lapse into —; lay — on; overlook —; spare —; subdue —; — blemishes; — glares; — mars.

(See error, mistake, offense.)

FAULTLESS

adverbs

perfectly; incredibly; utterly; marvellously; inexpressibly; obviously; manifestly; immac-

ulately; superbly; splendidly; absolutely; fashionably; rarely; technically; ineffably; remarkably; completely; theoretically; comparatively; exquisitely; overwhelmingly; matchlessly; morally; mechanically; artistically; unapproachably; unbelievably.

FAULTY

adverbs

technically; mechanically; obviously; provokingly; undeniably; intentionally; designedly; purposely; unfortunately; reprehensibly; grievously; inexcusably; unpardonably; irremediably; curiously; strangely; grossly; frightfully; slightly; unfortunately; strategically; absurdly; stupidly; cruelly; ludicrously; horribly.

FAVOR

adjectives

distinguished; heavenly; fairy; generous; sweet; fashionable; unmistakable; dissembled; supreme; gracious; royal; political; special; childish; imperial; ephemeral; trifling; scientific; singular; flattering; divine; equivalent; princely; preferential; ecclesiastical; gastronomical; private.

verbs

bask in —; bestow —; beg —; bid —; compete for —; confer — on; court —; curry — with; deny —; design —; dispense —s; efface —s; entertain — of; fall out of —; flow in — of; meet with —; seek —; win —; yield —s; — fattens.

(See kindness, benefit, advantage.)

FAVOR (v)

adverbs

patently; particularly; manifestly; fruitlessly; universally; unduly; corruptly; incidentally; uncannily; generously; sweetly; politically; childishly; ephemerally; scientifically; singularly; gastronomically; ecclesiastically; privately.

(See support, encourage.)

FAVORABLE

adverbs

highly; profoundly; obviously; certainly; sweetly; cordially; sincerely; undoubtedly; unqualifiedly; unconditionally; heartily; enthusiastically; immediately; graciously; singularly; flatteringly; publicly; unmistakably; considerately; openly; remarkably; marvelously; auspiciously; zealously; actively; altogether.

adjectives

universal; overwhelming; particular; exclusive; profligate; prime; especial; eternal; general; reigning; indulged; current; perennial; summer; envious; unquestioned.

verbs

acclaim—; admire—; bestow on—; cheer—; choose—; cultivate—; deny—; grant—; gratify—; mark as—; receive—; regard as —; respect—; reveal—; shine on—; —effaces; —requests; —tumbles; —wins.

(See companion, associate, friend, etc.)

adverbs

undeniably; obviously; universally; currently; apparently; enviably; curiously; strangely; unreasonably; openly; offensively; flauntingly; pleasantly; attractively; socially; companionably.

FAVORITISM

adjectives

personal; opposing; apparent; political; annoying.

FAWN

adjectives

sportive; tender; new-roused; nursling; startled; leaping; gamboling; gentle.

FAWN (v)

adverbs

obsequiously; servilely; tenderly; sportively; gently; calculatingly; schemingly; slyly; traitorously; impiously.

(See flatter, cringe.)

FAWNING

adverbs

unctuously; fulsomely; servilely; humbly; slavishly; flatteringly; cringingly; abjectly; basely; meanly; obsequiously; pliantly; subtly; sycophantically; shamelessly; artfully; craftily; shrewdly; pretentiously; knavishly; deceitfully; unscrupulously; openly; unashamedly; deferentially; submissively.

FEALTY

adjectives

unswerving; lifelong; forsworn.

adjectives

jealous; stark; harrowing; palpitating; phantasmal; mutual; sneaking; conjectural; prodigious; womanly; unaccustomed; indefinable; hideous; chilling; mingled; wonted; ghoulish; political; sweeping; degrading; irrational; surging; sharp; chasmed; mortal; deadly; supernatural; troubling; unnerving; predominant; anguished; superstitious; unspoken; ghastly; servile; abysmal; lingering; clutching; lurking; fretful; foolish; bashful; childlike; oppressive; nagging; maiden; rising; exaggerated; pet; selfish; trembling; horrible; incredible; reverential; unreasonable; haunting; depressive; pathological; scrupulous; spiritual; morbid; ghostly; prudent; dreadful; lessening; natural; vague; numbing; perpetual; general; feminine; hurtful; impatient; premonitory; growing; momentary; various (pl); nameless; slight; pious; never-buried; secret; recanting; specific; universal; strange; excessive; holy; bloodless; slavish; inextinguishable; age-old; terrible; physical; conflicting; faint-footed; prophetic; grim; pale-hearted; pleasing; devouring; tormenting; pitiable; distressing; tender; gloomy; distracted; idiotic; incomprehensible; continual; groundless; petrified; nervous; helpless; anxious; savage; primitive; uneasy; unutterable; remorseless; unaccountable; respectful; inexpressible; unnamed; shuddering; startling; trivial; shivering; yearning; dark; paltry; mysterious; dominant; crushing; scarce-hidden.

verbs

allay—; banish—; beset by—; bespeak—; brush aside—; counteract—; curtail—; dismiss—; dispel—; dissipate—; drown—; eliminate—; entertain—; eradicate—; evoke —; express—; foster—; ground—upon; harbor—; harness—; impregnate—; ingrain—; inspire—; intensify—; justify—; modify—; nourish—; obliterate—; petrify with—; play on—; quake with—; quell—; quiet—; rule by—; rout—; scoff at—; share—; shiver with—; soothe—; subdue—; surmount—; vanquish—; —blights; —chills; —clutches; —coerces; —dominates; —drives; —evaporates; —fetters; —hounds; —insinuates itself; —lurks; —materializes; —melts; —motivates; —numbs; —obsesses; —overshadows; —prevails; —preys upon; —racks; —subsides; —takes possession.

(See dread, terror, apprehension, dismay, consternation, fright, anxiety.)

FEAR (v)

adverbs

unjustifiably; instinctively; inexpressibly; grossly; unreasoningly; jealously; harrowingly; irrationally; superstitiously; abysmally; oppressively; exaggeratedly; unreasonably; hauntingly; pathologically; morbidly; momentarily; secretly; excessively; pitiably; distressingly; incomprehensibly; groundlessly; inexpressibly; mysteriously.

(See dread, apprehend.)

FEARFUL

adverbs

indefinably; childishly; unusually; unwontedly; nervously; superstitiously; fretfully; foolishly; bashfully; incredibly; unreasonably; morbidly; prudently; dreadfully; naturally; vaguely; perpetually; momentarily; constantly; namelessly; secretly; slightly; excessively; strangely; terribly; prophetically; grimly; tormentingly; pitiably; distressingly; tenderly; gloomily; idiotically; incomprehensibly; groundlessly; helplessly; anxiously; uneasily; unutterably; unaccountably; inexpressibly; shudderingly; shiveringly; darkly; coldly; mysteriously; timidly; queerly; curiously; starkly; timorously; genuinely; suspiciously; significantly.

FEARLESS

adverbs

unquestionably; utterly; curiously; oddly; unnaturally; habitually; temperamentally; always; bombastically; boastfully; pretentiously; ostentatiously; apparently; avowedly; allegedly; amazingly; incredibly; confidently; boldly; valiantly; intrepidly; calmly; serenely; quietly; courageously; firmly; doggedly; resolutely; determinedly.

FEASIBLE

adverbs

easily; smoothly; clearly; undeniably; practically; apparently; oddly; entirely; completely; unbelievably; patently; palpably; manifestly; possibly; scarcely; hardly; conceivably; perhaps; uncertainly; doubtfully.

FEAST

adjectives

solemn; artistic; annual; sinful; memorable; sumptuous; continuous; constant; horrible; royal; ample; joyful; Lucullan; endless; sacrificial; accustomed; pagan; popish; marshaled; rural; movable; fashion-able; bountiful; convent; princely; wondrous; funeral; impious; nobler; inimitable; superfluous; triumphal; Saturnalian; sun-born; purveying; vernal; reasonable.

verbs

anticipate—; bless—; cater at—; celebrate with—; crown—with; destine for—; enjoy —; enter—; entertain at—; gather for—; gorge at—; hold—; honor at—; invite to—; join in—; partake of—; plan—; prepare—; rejoice at—; —cheers; —commemorates; —gratifies; —refreshes.

(See entertainment, repast, anniversary.)

FEAST (v)

adverbs

convivially; recklessly; annually; triumphantly; bountifully; gluttonously; unstintedly; sumptuously; memorably; idolatrously; lavishly.

(See dine, eat, gratify.)

FEASTING

adjectives

mutual; swinish.

FEAT

adjectives

notable; merchandising; piteous; prodigious; additional; superhuman; inconsiderable; extraordinary; curious; noble; herculean; elaborate; pugilistic; haughty; brilliant; spectacular; dashing; marvelous; warlike; magic; miraculous; incomparable.

verbs

acclaim—; accomplish—; advertise—; applaud—; duplicate—; emulate—; enact—; enjoy—; equal—; exploit—; gasp at—; perfect—; perform—; practise—; praise—; recount—; regale with—; watch—; work—; —awes; —dazzles; —delights; —displays; —enthralls; —pleases; —punctures.

(See act, performance, deed, exploit, achievement.)

FEATHER

adjectives

flying; rumpled; motionless; courteous; superincumbent; molted; decorative; draggled; animated; varicolored (pl); lofty; silky; mottled; drooping; variegated (pl).

verbs

adorn with—; attach—; bristle with—s; clothe with—s; cover with—s; crop—s; decorate with—s; deck with—s; display—s; exhibit—s; fledge with—s; furnish—s; molt —s; ornament with—s; pick—s; pluck—; plume with—s; preen—s; provide—s; ruffle —s; rumple—s; rustle—s; shake—s; smooth —s; strip of—s; wave—; wear—s; —floats; —tickles.

(See ornaments.)

FEATURE
(of the face)

verbs

age—s; blur—s; characterize—s; cheat of —; cloak—s; cloud—s; contort—s; define —s; discern—s; distinguish—s; inherit—; mark—; obliterate—s; scar—; sketch—; weary—; —s beam; —s express; —s glare; —s glisten; —s gloom; —indicates; —s pucker up; —s shine.

(See shape, form, face.)

FEATURE
(part)

verbs

acclaim—; applaud—; appraise—; bar—; conceal—; detect—; eliminate—; embody—; evince—; execute—; incorporate—; negate —; plan—; present—; preserve—; recognize—; schedule—; strike at—.

(See item, characteristic, point.)

FEATURE (v)

adverbs

exclusively; faultlessly; consistently; animatedly; monotonously; characteristically; classically; conspicuously; disastrously; decorously; distinctively; distortedly; dominatingly; eloquently; graphically; harmoniously; irrationally; legitimately; offensively; picturesquely; piquantly; perennially; specifically; dominantly.

(See portray, delineate.)

FEATURES

adjectives

active; added; additional; advanced; agitated; agreeable; air-cooling; alabaster; altered; amazing; angular; angelic; animated; anxious; aristocratic; aquiline; arrogant; ascetic; attractive; astonishing; automatic; awkward; battered; bearded; bearish; bold; beauteous; benevolent; benignant; bewitching; bizarre; bloated; brightest; blurred; bronzed; Caesarean; calm; characteristic; charming; chiseled; clean-cut; classical; clear-cut; clearly-chiseled; coarse; comely; comfortable; commonplace;

composed; concealed; conforming; conspicuous; constructive; contorted; convenient; convulsed; corpselike; correct; craggy; crowning; daring; dark; decorated; decorous; delicate; delightful; desirable; desperate; determined; detestable; difficult; disastrous; distinctive; distinguishing; distorted; distressing; divers; diversified; dominant; dripping; dominating; dusky; eager; ebon; eloquent; effective; elongated; embarrassing; embrowned; engrossing; entrancing; essential; epic; evil; exasperating; exceptional; exclusive; expansive; exploitational; expressive; exquisite; extraneous; extraordinary; fabric; fair; familiar; fascinating; ferocious; fervent; fierce; fine; finely-cut; firm; flawless; flexible; flowerlike; forbidding; fundamental; gaunt; gay; genial; gentle; geologic; glorious; graphic; grave; haggard; handsome; hand-tailored; harmonious; hawk-like; haughty; healthful; heavy; high; high-priced; homely; hueless; humorous; immovable; important; impassive; impressive; indelible; indistinguishable; ineffable; inherited; innocent; insensible; insipid; intellectual; interesting; iron; intriguing; irrational; kindly; lamentable; large; leading; lean; legitimate; light; long; lovely; majestic; malignant; marked; massive; medieval; melancholy; mild; minor; mobile; mocking; modern; molded; monstrous; natural; neat; new; noble; notable; noteworthy; noticeable; objectionable; offensive; operating; occult; oppressive; original; ornamental; outstanding; paindrawn; pain-seamed; pallid; passionless; particular; passionate; patented; patrician; peaked; perplexing; peculiar; perennial; persisting; personal; physical; picturesque; piquant; pivot-turning; placid; plastic; positive; pock-marked; poignant; practical; predominant; prevailing; prominent; protective; proscriptive; quality; questionable; quivering; quizzical; rare; recognized; recreational; recurring; redeeming; refined; regular; remarkable; restful; revolting; rigid; rough; rugged; sad; safety; saggy; salient; saturnine; scapegrace; scenic; scowling; sculptured; sensational; Semitic; semi-constructional; sensitive; serious; severe; shrunken; significant; sharp; singular; sinister; slumbering; small; smiling; socialistic; softened; sophisticated; sordid; sorry; sport; special; specific; splendid; square; stain-preventing; stellar; sterile; stern; striking; strategic; strong; structural; style; suffering; sunken; superior; swarthy;

swollen; symmetrical; tanned; thoughtful; tightly-drawn; ugly; unaffected; uncertain; ineloquent; unique; unmistakable; unrevealed; unshaven; unsightly; unusual; upraised; useful; valuable; visible; varied; vital; vivid; wasted; weazened; welcome; well-balanced; well-cared-for; well-cut; well-marked; well-proportioned; worn-out.

FECUNDITY

adjectives
incredible; mental; artificial.

FEDERAL

adverbs
impressively; inescapably; finally; predominantly; imperiously; authoritatively; officially; imperatively; compulsively; autocratically; decisively; conclusively; grandly.

FEDERATION

adjectives
loose; irksome; compact.

verbs
accomplish—; ally with—; condense into—; contract—; dismember—; establish—; form —; join—; organize—; propose—; readjust —; unite—; —advocates; —authorizes; — campaigns; —controls; —delegates; —despairs; —develops; —manages; —performs; —supports.

(See league, alliance, association, union.)

FEE

adjectives
ceremonious; unpredictable; hateful; wandering; prodigious; undeserved.

verbs
accept—; augment—; beg for—; bill—; calculate—; command—; demand—; entitle to —; execute—; expect—; fatten on—; fix—; grant—; hold in—; incur—; limit—; merit —; perform for—; procure—; promise—; refuse—; require—; rob of—.

(See payment, reward, wage.)

FEEBLE

adverbs
pitiably; lamely; hunchedly; forlornly; lugubriously; pleasantly; comfortably; placidly; admittedly; distressingly; passively; plaintively; touchingly; helplessly; utterly; frequently.

FEEBLENESS

adjectives
infantine; boyish; inherent; gathering; negligent; accustomed.

verbs
commit to—; conceal—; convince of—; cure —; degenerate into—; delight in—; fall in —; feign—; guard against—; imply—; indicate—; inflict—; loathe—; minimize—; mourn—; pity—; produce—; resist—; ridicule—; —afflicts; —deters; —prevents.

(See debility, weakness, infirmity.)

FEED (v)

adverbs
serenely; omnivorously; sumptuously; gluttonously; continually; artfully; carefully; delicately; dietetically; scientifically; consistently; regularly; beneficially; sparingly.

(See nourish, subsist.)

FEEDING

adjectives
careful; destructive; faithful; delicate; worthy; fast.

verbs
abstain from—; administer—; anticipate—; attempt—; call for—; crown—with; encourage—; force—; gorge in—; invite to—; join in—; manage—; partake of—; plan—; prepare—; provide—; regulate—; rely upon —; serve—; surfeit—; supervise—; — chokes; —nourishes; —refreshes; —satiates; govern—.

(See food, eating.)

FEEL (v)

adverbs
instinctively; genuinely; sweetly; exquisitely; amiably; turbulently; reverently; maternally; triumphantly; graciously; exuberantly; vindictively; poetically; spontaneously; tyrannically; morbidly; mutually; congenially; compassionately; philanthropically; vehemently; profoundly; spiritually.

(See touch, grope, handle.)

FEELING

adjectives
grateful; peculiar; deep-souled; instinctive; undiminished; sensitive; partisan; genuine; suppressed; subdued; pragmatic; sweet; exaggerated; repressed; empty; artistic; exquisite; amiable; ardent; selfish; con-

gealed; sad; vague; solemn; painful; exasperated; intuitive; strange; sickening; horrible; ineffable; bitter; ancient; feudal; passionate; regenerated; turbulent; dreadful;
reciprocal; lofty; high-wrought; bewildered; unmistakable; soapy; reverent; excited;
cognate; sacred; anti-clerical; preponderant; triumphant; imaginative; sublime; gracious; expansive; tender; profound; humble; vindictive; apparent; inward; unshared; poetic; spontaneous; remorseful;
strangled; exuberant; tight; revolted; morbid; hostile; tyrannical; pent-up; shamed;
kindly; grosser; evident; aesthetic; enthusiastic; unfounded; overcharged; mutual;
subconscious; rancorous; remorseful; diminished; absurd; universal; annoying; intense; haughty; strange; telltale; fantastic;
congenial; burning; dim; compassionate;
appreciative; philanthropic; suspicious;
ruffled; discordant; queer; ripened; awesome; uneasy; sick; half-ironical; half-
superstitious; affectionate; dysphoric; nervous; innermost; mingled; maternal; erroneous; poignant; acute; stilted; upleasant;
differentiated; unfilial; immoral; rarest;
uncanny; overburdened; potent; unworthy;
felicitous; vehement; complicated; dormant;
fortified; taut; strained; dissimilar; mercenary; jealous; devotional; democratic; unhappy; wounded; pious; fancied; resultant;
superior; uncomfortable; profound; mightiest; domestic; warm; hangdog; worn-out;
ill; benevolent; indescribable; restless; blissful; liberal; selfish; holiest; lingering; contrary; half-defined; resentful; noble; national; subtler; ungovernable; amicable;
subordinate; individual; refreshing; genial;
embarrassed; lethargic; unspeakable; sincere; kindred; tight-throated; breathless;
repressed; energetic; martial; honest; playing; heady; oldish; forlorn; uncertain;
spiritual.

verbs

abate—; analyze—; awaken—; capture—;
cherish—; deaden—; disturb—; divulge—;
engender—; evince—; evoke—; excite—;
experience—; express—; foster—; gratify
—; guard—; harbor—; impart—;
inflame—; inhibit—; injure—; instill—;
manifest—; mask—; modify—; outrage—;
pen up—; petrify—; probe—; provoke—;
quicken—; regard with—; reveal—; rouse
—; soothe—; stir up—; strain—; strengthen
—; subdue—; suffuse with—; tamper with
—; tinge—; vent—; voice—; wound—; —

blossoms; —dominates; —envelops; —explodes; —impends; —impresses; —overpowers; —overwhelms; —persists; —pervades; —pours from; —rests upon; —runs
high; —subsides.

(See sensation, emotion, sentiment, consciousness, conviction.)

FEET

adjectives

tender; multitudinous; dancing; delicate;
pattering; marshy; scuffing; indolent; industrious; accursed; reluctant; whispering; un-
delaying; dainty; wicked; wanton; unwearied; aimless; overlarge; charming; rugged;
untrammelled; twinkling; trampling; faltering; restless; uncertain; racing; dimpled; fear-sped; clammy; golden; errant;
daring; blistered; webbed; tripping; willing; strolling; straddling; small; silvery;
marshalled; angel; dangling; swift; flying;
aristocratic; slender; tortured; erring; distorted; impious; unshod; wary; bare; romping; glorious; shuffling; noiseless; stumbling; wandering; shod; trembling; claw;
moccasined; scurrying; cautious; hurried;
shoe-encased; churlished; infinitesimal; desultory; approaching; substantial; windy;
hastening; airy; grappling; morning-wing-
ed; mournful; running; consecrated; stag-
dering; myriad; veined; spreading; peace-
abiding; wayward; bleeding; rushing;
careless; adroit; feathery; bruised; radiant; big; muddy; charging; dirty; countless; silent; aching; echoing; shrivelled;
calloused; sagging; desperate; lagging;
leaden; wild; timorous; ivory-channeled;
skipping; eager; jumping; cursed; stealthy;
faultless; tiny; swirling; swift; frenzied;
nimble; ample; heroic; huge; tottering;
none-too-steady; unsure; immovable; obstinate; halting; dragging; indifferent; sweaty;
ragged; graceless; slipshod; deformed;
crippled; swollen; faltering; arched; slim;
elongated; narrow; cloven; squared; padded; innumerable; slippered; heavily-shod;
sandaled; velvet; clay; piggish; clattering;
thudding; hobbled; stockinged; satined; rub-
bered; thumping; pounding; wandering;
scampering; stamping; marching; little;
shuffling; naked; parched; outraged; uncivilized; trusting; tireless; wary; bound;
tangled; unseen; departing; protruding; unguided; educated; prodding; frantic; creeping; booted; thick; mad; clawing; immortal; fetter-incumbered; plundering.

FEIGN (v)

adverbs

calculatingly; slyly; cleverly; expressly; treacherously; artfully; skillfully; deftly; fawningly; dissolutely; roguishly; knavishly.

(See pretend, simulate, assume.)

FEINT

adjectives

preliminary; solitary; diplomatic.

FELICITATION

verbs

accept—; acknowledge—; anticipate—; bestow—; compliment with—; delight in—; enjoy—; exchange—; express—; extend—; greet with—; incur—; inspire—; offer—; present—; produce—; promote—; pronounce—; receive—; return—; thank for—; —pleases.

(See congratulation.)

FELICITOUS

adverbs

auspiciously; opportunely; happily; supremely; superbly; grandly; splendidly; inexpressibly; undeniably; altogether; consummately; utterly; singularly; unexpectedly; harmoniously; delightfully; rapturously; extremely; unusually; uncommonly.

FELICITY

adjectives

earthly; engaging; exalted; supreme; expressional; uninterrupted; singular; eternal; true; pastoral; curious; domestic; Arcadian.

FELLOW

adjectives

chuckle-headed; absurd; lovable; tainted; jolly; sturdy; brash; lusty; amiable; scurvy; woodland; underbred; fine-spoken; clever; clean-living; intelligent; tractable; generous; light-hearted; industrious; bustling; common-looking; gaunt; ill-visaged; jovial-looking; loathsome; riotous; unrefined; honorary; guileless; robustious; muffled; massive; great-shouldered; muscled; lewd; merry; manly; sharp; amiable-looking; impudent; feeble; noble; pestilent; funniest; good-natured; hearty; broad-faced; dapper; fierce; valiant; cunning; admirable; wiry; sallow; enviable; heartless; worthless; indignant; craggy-faced; gnomish; odd; unaccountable; fluctuating; irresolute; voluble; slender; prattling; hilding; captious; hale; hard-bitten; big; handsome; back-slapping; rollicking; villainous; good-hearted; easy-going; devil-may-care; kindly; lawless; open-hearted; brilliant; gentle-mannered; plausible; unthoughtful; innocent; sneaking; talkative; enthusiastic; unstudious; vulgar-looking; officious; engaging; swarthy; smock-faced; coal-blackened; florid; prettier; magnificent-looking; gallant; hulking; meager; verdant; stale; licentious; white-bearded; hatchet-faced; sheepish; awkward; respected; desperate; foppish; bluff; blunt; indiscreet; self-assured; conceited; celestial; melancholy; abominable; beetle-browed; powerful; marvelous; witty; eloquent; prodigious; fine; staring; inexorable; ghostly; disgruntled; capricious; insignificant; simpering; intelligent; courageous; good-humored; roguish; ignorant; noisy; unweighing; notable; good; dull; vicious; dissolute.

FELLOWSHIP

adjectives

sweet; pleasant; superficial; close-linked; accursed; generous.

verbs

admit—; build up—; enjoy—; enter into—; entitle to—; honor—; instil—; obtain—; necessitate—; participate in—; receive in—; refuse—; reject—; renounce—; separate from—; share in—; shatter—; unite in—; —honors; —predominates.

(See companionship, association.)

FELON

adjectives

acquitted; larcenous

FELONIOUS

adverbs

dastardly; outrageously; contemptibly; obviously; openly; heinously; infamously; basely; grossly; shamelessly; scandalously; brutally; atrociously; scurvily; diabolically; terribly; frightfully; horridly; insanely; venomously; fiendishly.

FELT

adjectives

faded; clean.

FEMALE

adjectives

buxom; irresponsible; elderly; frivolous; elegant; delicate; sour-faced; anemic; hysteric; shivering; tattered; bewildered; unimpeachable; upholstered; parthenogenetic; large; desirable; muscular; unattached; angular; firm-faced; formidable; grim.

FEMININE
adverbs
daintily; sweetly; delightfully; ravishingly; ineffably; seductively; bewitchingly; charmingly; lovably; utterly; provokingly; wantonly; weakly; dependently; irritatingly; clingingly; comfortingly; gracefully; graciously; altogether.

FEMININITY
adjectives
stigmatized; collective; rampant; disquieting; flagrant; desirable.

FENCE
adjectives
woven-wire; straggling; distorted; elaborate; bushy; pitiless; verbal; locust; split-rail; hurdle; whitewashed; spiritual; weather-beaten.

verbs
break through—; construct—; erect—; fortify with—; hurdle—; jump—; leap—; level —; provide—; repair—; skirt—; straddle —; surround with—; —bars; —defends; — deters; —encloses; —guards; —hinders; — limits; —partitions; —protects; —repels; — restricts; —screens; —shields; —wards off; —yields.
(See defence, wall.)

FENCE (v)
adverbs
deftly; skillfully; artfully; vigorously; expertly; professionally; fascinatingly; mentally; courageously; intelligently; arrogantly.
(See evade, shift.)

FENDER
verbs
attach—; bump—; clod—; crack—; damage —; dent—; run into—; rust—; secure—; splash—; split—; spray—; streamline—; strike—; —s collide; —guards; —prevents; —protects; —rattles; —shimmies; — squeaks; —vibrates.

FERMENT
adjectives
putrid; foreign; alcoholic; microscopic; anarchistic; violent; subtle; tumultuous; active; political; irresistible.

FERMENT (v)
adverbs
putridly; alcoholically; microscopically; violently; subtly; tumultuously; politically; irresistibly; actively.
(See decay, excite.)

FERMENTATION
adjectives
vinous; offensive; natural.

verbs
agitate to —; control —; employ —; excite to —; give rise to —; hinder —; incur —; occasion —; produce —; subject to —; suffer —; undergo —; work —; — aids; — results; — sours; — subsides.
(See decomposition, transformation.)

FERN
adjectives
discolored; luxuriant; water-loving; minute; exquisite; metallic; lacelike; sprouting.

FEROCIOUS
adverbs
savagely; inexpressibly; cruelly; diabolically; unspeakably; atrociously; brutally; pretentiously; comically; dutifully; unduly; mercilessly; ruthlessly; inhumanly; malevolently; coldly; unnaturally; unbelievably; stonily; barbarously; heinously; utterly; uncommonly; unutterably.

FEROCITY
adjectives
gloomy; deft; reckless; uncommon; brutal; diabolic; dull; pitiless; cruel; vigilant; admirable; frightful; unmitigated; martial; senseless; terrific; moist; clammy; mad; hair-raising; ill-concealed; blazing; incredible; unlimited; ungovernable; lurid; smoldering.

verbs
abate —; display —; escape —; fire with —; generate —; incur —; inflame to —; occasion —; ponder —; provoke to —; recover from —; salve —; shake with —; subdue —; — alarms; — blights; — destroys; — frightens; — overwhelms; — terrifies.
(See cruelty, fury.)

adjectives
improvised; antiquated; electric.

FERTILE
adverbs
creatively; productively; luxuriantly; abundantly; fruitfully; teemingly; richly; plenteously; inexhaustibly; incredibly; remarkably; superbly; amazingly; incomparably; matchlessly; satisfactorily; surprisingly; naturally; highly; completely.

FERTILITY
adjectives
triumphant; personal; exuberant; teeming; superior; incredible; inexhaustible; dauntless; absolute; amazing; singular; improved; intellectual; unrivaled; incomparable.

FERTILIZER
verbs
advocate —; apply —; broadcast —; employ —; enrich with —; gorge with —; introduce —; purchase —; stock with —; supply —; — enhances; — enriches; — generates; — replenishes.

FERVENT
adverbs
warmly; sincerely; ardently; zealously; eagerly; significantly; earnestly; actively; utterly; heartily; fanatically; uncommonly; remarkably; contagiously; piously; magnetically; eloquently; feverishly; passionately; youthfully; dynamically; intensely; tremendously; solemnly; amazingly.

FERVID
adverbs
intensely; emotionally; contagiously; infectiously; feverishly; nervously; peculiarly; oddly; curiously; abnormally; strangely; glowingly; hotly; impressively; rapturously; breathlessly; zealously; absorbingly; fanatically; impetuously; magnificently.

FERVOR
adjectives
contagious; inward; renewed; religious; superficial; unprecedented; magnetic; disinterested; eloquent; undiminished; poetic; feverish; lurid; intolerable; passionate; revolutionary; equinoctial; meridian; devotional; exalted; involuntary; racy; youthful; vain; primitive; nationalistic; dynamic; patriotic; blazing; fascinating; emotional; intense; defensive; animated; tremendous; artificial; lyric; solemn; romantic; prophetic; loving; simple; noontide.

verbs
arouse —; bridle —; cool —; execute with —; fill with —; flush with —; inflame with —; instil —; join with —; pitch to —; quench —; replace —; shape with —; starve —; sweat with —; waste —; — animates; — boils; — blazes; — glows; — rages; — torments.

(See ardor, intensity, zeal, enthusiasm.)

FESTAL
adverbs
delightfully; joyously; charmingly; companiably; chattily; convivially; noisily; happily; jovially; gregariously; magnificently; splendidly; brilliantly; sparklingly; sumptuously; highly; elaborately; extravagantly; uproariously; unexpectedly; ineffably; tumultuously; excitedly; inexpressibly; innocently; spontaneously; exultantly; radiantly; supremely; highly.

FESTER (v)
adverbs
malignantly; hideously; horridly; disgustingly; fatally; repeatedly; continually; agonizingly; hatefully; devastatingly.

(See pain, suffer.)

FESTIVAL
adjectives
solemn; religious; torchlight; domestic; magnificent; sumptuous; nocturnal; carousing; democratic; annual; circling; memorial; high; brilliant; recurring; community; notorious; extravagant; licentious; elaborate; holiday; clamoring; grandiose.

FESTIVE
adverbs
hilariously; boisterously; uproariously; informally; happily; gaily; gloriously; utterly; absurdly; ineffably; blithely; irrepressibly; merrily; unaccountably; unexpectedly; noisily; magnificently; intimately; spontaneously; radiantly; tumultuously; inexpressibly.

FESTIVITY
adjectives
brilliant; boisterous; final; compelled; holiday; maudlin.

FESTOONS

adjectives
scalloped; looping; flung; graceful; ethereal.

FETE (v)

adverbs
ceremonially; blithesomely; handsomely; joyfully; magnificently; sumptuously; annually; memorially; brilliantly; notoriously; extravagantly; elaborately; grandiosely.

(See celebrate, feast.)

FETID

adverbs
offensively; rankly; horridly; unbearably; mustily; suffocatingly; impossibly; unspeakably; abominably; noisomely; terribly; disagreeably; frightfully; malodorously; foully; strongly; grossly; pestilentially; unwholesomely; perniciously; poisonously; extremely; inconceivably.

FETISH

adjectives
popular; patriotic; exploded; carved; wooden; much-loved.

FETTER

verbs
chain with —s; clap into —s; commit to —s; escape —s; fasten —s; free from —s; hobble in —s; impose —s; load with —s; loose —s; release from —s; relieve of —s; relinquish —s; secure —s; shackle with —s; shake off —s; — binds; — checks; — confines; — constrains; — guards; — hinders; — prevents; — restrains; — restricts; — tortures; — vexes.

(See bond, shackle, chain.)

FETTERS

adjectives
gratuitous; triple; brazen; rose-blossom; adamantine; galling; unmeasured; creed-imposed; riven; fleshly.

FEUD

adjectives
fatal; fresh; bitter; fruitful; private; lasting; internal; dismal; revamped; primeval; mutual; tribal; relentless; grim; long-standing; age-long; nasty; murderous; deadly; domestic; personal; ancient; futile; hereditary.

verbs
activate —; arouse —; beget —; carry on —; clash in —; convert into —; declare —; enjoy —; entangle in —; inflame into —; instigate —; interrupt —; justify —; prevent —; rankle into —; renew —; root out —; — agitates; —continues; — disturbs; — flares up; — originates; compete in —.

(See strife, hostility, enmity, animosity, bitterness, quarrel.)

FEUDALISM

verbs
abhor —; bring under —; check —; convert into —; incline to —; influence —; overthrow —; practise —; recognize —; reject —; subject to —; support —; — bridles; — clutches; — deprives; — originates; — persists; — reduces; — stultifies; — survives; — treads on; — tyrannizes.

(See system.)

FEUDATORY

adjectives
mutinous; disaffected; tyrannical.

FEVER

adjectives
contagious; eruptive; ravenous; rheumatic; cruel; irregular; low; violent; fitful; prevalent; swamp; intermittent; bilious; high; malignant; unhallowed; infectious; splenic; rapid; raging; morbid; gnawing; malarial; typhus; envious; puerperal; riotous; obvious; tortured; lurking; deadly; perpetual; acute; childbed; hunting; burning; inflammatory; slow.

verbs
accompany by —; allay —; attend with —; characterize by —; come down with —; contract —; control —; develop —; heighten —; induce —; predispose to —; reduce —; retard —; transmit —; — burns; — consumes; — continues; — devours; — grips; — heats; — infects; — persists; — rages; — smoulders; — subdues.

(See excitement, disease.)

FEVERISH

adverbs
cruelly; violently; terribly; highly; extremely; obviously; dangerously; alarmingly; uncomfortably; fearfully; deliriously; acutely; dreadfully; hysterically; deplorably; burningly; restlessly; wildly; unusually; uncommonly; curiously; peculiarly.

FEW

adjectives

unscornful; far-visioned; desperate; favored; comparative; privileged; hateful; chosen.

FEW

adverbs

remarkably; extremely; strangely; lamentably; significantly; deplorably; miserably; wretchedly; fortunately; happily; curiously; mercifully; presumably.

FIASCO

adjectives

mountainous; official.

FIBER

adjectives

fleecy; pusillanimous; secret; ancestral; civic; resonant; ligneous; crude; tough; tenacious; delicate; flaccid; genuine; spiritual; moral; quivering; unexperienced; twisting; intellectual; sensitive; coarser; maguey.

FIBRE

verbs

bind with —; compose of —; connect —s; consist of —; develop —; draw into —; exhibit —; furnish with —; join —; knot —; produce —; rig with —; shred —; stretch —; swathe in —; twist —; weave —; — connects; — girdles; — hangs; — links.

FIBRIN

adjectives

coagulated; increased; exudative.

FICKLE

adverbs

disgustingly; uncertainly; unstably; mercurially; changeably; irresolutely; capriciously; whimsically; unfortunately; remarkably; exceedingly; sensationally; undependably; unhappily; deplorably; habitually; temperamentally; irresolutely; erratically; waywardly; terribly.

FICTION

adjectives

luxuriant; native; sensational; convenient; evasive; romantic; serious; bold; mythological; improbable; extravagant; picturesque; conventional; monstrous; short-lived; distinguished; unmitigated; frothy; introspective; current; sentimental; contemporary.

verbs

cast away —; compose —; condemn —; consume —; criticize —; desire —; devise —; distinguish from —; embroider —; prefer —; produce —; reject —; relate —; select —; steep in —; turn into —; — charms; — confuses; — copies; —delights; — diverts; — enchants; — informs; — influences; — instructs; — interests; — pleases; — poisons; — transports; — unwinds.

(See story, novel, narrative, myth.)

FICTITIOUS

adverbs

harmlessly; allegedly; avowedly; undoubtedly; whimsically; nonsensically; suppositiously; extravagantly; probably; grotesquely; fantastically; ironically; obviously; manifestly; ingeniously; romantically; preposterously; utterly; surprisingly; completely; hypothetically; dreamily; innocently; wildly.

FIDDLE

adjectives

nocturnal; uncivilized.

FIDDLER

adjectives

diligent; rascal; rollicking; peripatetic.

FIDELITY

adjectives

conjugal; eye-taking; doglike; unswerving; undying; utmost; undeviating; eternal; scrupulous; minute; marvelous; assured; realistic; rigid; inviolable; subtle; flawless; dull; unwavering; long-tried; intense; reverent; sober; unblemished; sorrowful; lifelike; profound; historic; pastoral; diving; true-hearted; noteworthy; everlasting.

verbs

abuse —; appreciate —; arouse —; bestow —; buy —; depend on —; endow with —; entwine with —; exact —; incur —; instil —; nourish —; rivet —; shake —; strengthen —; support with —; swear —; threaten —; violate —; — endears; — endures; — palls; — perishes.

(See faithfulness, loyalty.)

FIDGET (*v*)

adverbs

uneasily; unceasingly; impatiently; painfully; embarrassedly; unpleasantly; secretly; fruitlessly; suppressedly.

(See move, stir, jump.)

FIDGETY

adverbs

suspiciously; terribly; unnecessarily; annoyingly; vexatiously; uneasily; uncomfortably; fussily; officiously; clamorously; excitably; hysterically; foolishly; impatiently; irrepressibly; curiously; peculiarly; oddly; odiously; strangely; significantly; atrociously: unpleasantly; extremely; needlessly.

FIELD

verbs

capture —; clothe —; crop —; deplete —; dominate —; double —; encumber —; entrench —; fence —; invade —; litter —; lord over —; pioneer —; plod across —; preempt —; replenish —; sow —; tap —; tramp across —; usurp —; wall —; — extends; — lies; — slumbers; — stretches.

(See meadow, land.)

FIELDER
(baseball or cricket)

verbs

contract for —; fire —; hire —; release —; trade —; — catches; — chases; — covers; — drops; — fields; — holds out; — juggles; — misjudges; — muffs; — races; — runs; — slides; — slips; — snares; — spears; — sprints; — steals; — stops; — returns; — traps; — whips.

(See player, athlete.)

FIELDS

adjectives

gray-green; emerald; frost-bitten; whitened; glistening; ripened; sun-parched; windswept; sparse; billowing; fertile; soft; wet; untrodden; picturesque; stubble; rolling; tremendous; uncrowded; virgin; untouched; fruitless; crimsoned; bloody; drowned; molding; barren; swamped; useful; conquered; disturbed; tented; grazing; plowed; fragrant; archaeological; fenceless; weedy; spring; amaranth; aesthetic; desolate; rain-gullied; swelling; smoky; blossoming; wanton; hunting; encompassing; uncarved; well-dressed; twilight; fallow; unchartered; productive; silken; wintry; remnant; subterranean; feathered; extensive; beautiful; economic; poisonous; illimitable; tobacco-jetted; hard-fought; coal; industrial; deserted; joyless; sedgy; abandoned; untried; magnetic; interpretative; somber; azure; languishing; stricken; teeming; sequestered; electrostatic.

FIEND

adjectives

despiteful; foul; stout; incarnate; shivering; father; consummate; possessing; kindred; infernal; abandoned; impetuous; cursed; lubber; human; delicate; malignant; viewless; glaring; sneering.

FIENDISH

adverbs

unspeakably; inexpressibly; uncommonly; brutally; incomprehensibly; unthinkably; odiously; atrociously; heinously; flagrantly; outrageously; outlandishly; grotesquely; inscrutably; barbarously; coldly; stonily; diabolically; inhumanly; unnaturally; defiantly; ominously; ungovernably; uncontrollably; insatiably.

FIERCE

adverbs

implacably; incredibly; intentionally; barbarously; cruelly; ungovernably; impetuously; vehemently; uproariously; brutally; outrageously; fantastically; abruptly; uncontrollably; savagely; irrepressibly; sarcastically; dreadfully; bitterly; explosively; irately; blusteringly; relentlessly; pitilessly; remarkably; amazingly.

FIERCENESS

adjectives

unscrupulous; brutal; suppressed; dramatic; intense.

FIG

adjectives

luscious; large; tasty; over-ripe.

FIGHT

adjectives

inextricable; unflinching; miscellaneous (pl); portentous; isolated; murderous; desultory; bloody; furious; sublimated; ensuing; serious; trench; unavailing; arduous; heavy; futile; ever-losing; factional; running; desperate; winning; memorable; successful; strenuous; tumultuous; showdown; sea-convulsing; manful; vulturous; incessant; dreadful; unequal; dubious; mortal; bitter.

verbs

accept —; augur —; conduct —; evade —; gird for —; lack —; participate in —; reopen —; rouse to —; schedule —; show —;

stage —; wage —; witness —; —embitters; — grows; — rages; — wanes; — waxes; pledge to —; precipitate —.

(See strife, struggle, battle, conflict, combat.)

FIGHT (v)

adverbs

murderously; desultorily; furiously; unavailingly; memorably; strenuously; manfully; dubiously; mortally; viciously; vaingloriously; stolidly; simultaneously; rebelliously; gallantly; doggedly; magnificently; sanguinarily; ostentatiously; vindictively.

(See combat, battle, struggle.)

FIGHTER

adjectives

infuriated; stubborn; considerable; effective; unimaginable; undisciplined; malicious; fearless; reputed; aggressive; ruthless.

verbs

cheer —; condition —; cow —; cuff —; goad —; hack —; incite —; sponge —; spur —; urge —; — bangs; — beats; — bruises; — clinches; — cuts; — dances; — dodges; — drops; — ducks; — feints; — flinches; — jumps; — practises; — punches; — reels; — retreats; — sags; — skips; — slams; — slips; — tallies; — taps; — whacks; — winces.

FIGMENT

adjectives

seductive; idle; imaginative.

FIGURE

verbs

accept —s; bandy —s; cite —s; compile —s; delineate —s; deluge with —s; juggle —s; publish —s; quote —s; scribble —s; splotch —s; —s claim; —s pour in; — soars.

(See digit, number, amount.)

FIGURE
(general)

adjectives

able; absurd; advancing; allegorical; aged; alluring; ample; appealing; ardent; arrestive; athletic; august; battered; belligerent; beloved; benignant; bent; bestial; blue-clad; blurred; bony; bouncing; bulky; buoyant; buxom; cherubic; clever; cloyed; colorful; colossal; comfortable; comical; comparative; compelling; conspicuous; contorted; cool; cosmopolitan; courtly; cowering; crabbed; credible; crouched; crumpled; curious; dainty; dark; dashing; defenseless; defiant; dejected; demure; departing; desolate; dignified; dim; diminutive; discreet; dismal; distinguished; distorted; dominant; domineering; dramatic; draped; drawn; dressed; dwarfed; eager; elegant; emaciated; emblematical; enameled; enchanting; energetic; enigmatic; enormous; epauletted; erect; eternal; excited; exquisite; exuberant; famous; fatigued; fashionable; fawning; flat; flexible; foregoing; forlorn; formless; frail; fragmentary; full-grown; furtive; gagged; gallant; gaunt; geometric; ghastly; girlish; glowing; gorilla-like; grandiose; grappling; grave; grotesque; heroic; growing; haloed; heavy; horrid; huddled; hurrying; ideal; imperious; incalculable; independent; indifferent; indistinguishable; inert; influential; innocent; inscrutable; insignificant; interesting; international; irridescent; irrelevant; jaunty; kneeling; lagging; lawless; lax; leading; lean; legendary; limping; literary; lithe; little; lost; lumbering; lurid; lurking; magnetic; majestic; marvelous; masculine; massive; mean; melancholy; memorable; menacing; minor; mocking; miserable; misshapen; monosyllabic; motionless; mountainous; mournful; muffled; mummy-like; mythic; naive; national; nautical; neglected; negligible; nervous; noble; notable; nude; odious; ominous; ornamental; osseous; outlandish; outstanding; pale; panting; pathetic; perfect; petite; pinched; picturesque; pitiful; plastic; pliant; podgy; poetic; poignant; portentous; powerful; preserved; principal; prominent; prone; prostrate; puny; quadrilateral; quaint; quivering; quixotic; rapid; rare; reclining; recumbent; reeling; related; respected; resplendent; retreating; ridiculous; rigid; romantic; rounded; rustic; salient; sardonic; sauntering; semi-legendary; shaking; shameless; shapeless; shrewd; silent; shrinking; shriveled; shuddering; shrouded; silhouetted; sinister; sluggish; skinny; sleek; smart; sob-shaken; solitary; somber; spiritless; sprawled; spry; stalwart; stiff; stocky; stolid; stooping; straight; stricken; strong; stunted; stupendous; sunburned; superb; supple; svelte; swaying; sylphlike; symbolical; tabulated (pl); talented; tatterdemalion; tense; thick-set; tottering; unattractive; tragic; tremendous; trim; truculent; turbulent; typical; uncouth; uniformed; unique; unkempt; unobtrusive; veiled; venerable; vigorous;

vestlike; wasted; weak; well-loved; well-molded; whirling; white-clad; wild; winsome; wiry; wizened; wooden; worthy; tall; wretched; writhing; young; radiant; quaking; queenly; quiet.

FIGURE
(*physique*)

verbs

blur—; conceal—; corset—; develop—; enhance—; forge—; guard—; illuminate—; jeopardize—; nurture—; silhouette—; uncoil—; visualize—; —looms; —s mill; —symbolizes; —writhes.

(See shape, form.)

FIGURE (*v*)

adverbs

conspicuously; deliberately; absurdly; prominently; allegorically; appealingly; belligerently; benignantly; colorfully; comically; domineeringly; dramatically; irrelevantly; fashionably; grandiosely; lawlessly; luridly; mythically; negligibly; picturesquely; portentously; ornamentally; saliently; typically; unobtrusively.

(See calculate, contrive.)

FILE
(*catalogue or cabinet*)

verbs

arrange in—; assemble in—; catalogue—; clean—; destroy—; dig into—; feed—; go through—; lodge in—; prepare—; preserve in—; pull from—; rank in—; refer to—; search—; store in—; wade through—; —aids; —arranges; —facilitates; —separates.

(See list, catalogue, collection, cabinet.)

FILE
(*general*)

adjectives

endless; extensive; newspaper; glittering; moldering; lengthening; four-ranked; successive (pl); straggling; droning.

FILE
(*tool*)

verbs

employ—; slide—; yield to—; —abrades; —evens; —finishes; —glazes; —gnaws; —grates; —grinds; —nicks; —polishes; —reduces; —removes; —restores; —scratches; —sharpens; —smooths; —wears down.

FILE (*v*)

adverbs

sedately; painstakingly; noiselessly; endlessly; monotonously; stragglingly; patiently; ceaselessly; solemnly; incessantly.

(See smooth, cut, walk.)

FILIBUSTER (*v*)

adverbs

bombastically; wordily; vigorously; exasperatingly; venomously; repeatedly; uncontrollably.

(See hinder, prevent, argue.)

FILL (*v*)

adverbs

adequately; creditably; efficiently; generously; amply; faultlessly; cleverly; partially; greedily; graciously; constantly; skillfully; exclusively; scantily; systematically.

(See satisfy, occupy.)

FILLING

adjectives

continuous; systematic; adequate.

FILM
(*camera*)

adjectives

color; sooty; celluloid; supersensitive; exposed; iridescent.

FILM
(*covering*)

adjectives

transitory; glossy; sanguine; adherent; shadowy; permanent; half-drawn; base; clogging.

verbs

break—; cover with—; emerge from—; penetrate—; remove—; —dims; —envelops; —floats; —forms; —grows; —hides; —hinders; —obscures; —prevents.

(See membrane, cover.)

FILM
(*picture*)

verbs

acclaim—; applaud—; ban—; bar—; censor—; criticize—; cut—; develop—; enjoy —; expose—; feature—; guard—; legalize —; manipulate—; preview—; rave about—; —burlesques; —satirizes; —portrays.

adjectives
squalid; undiluted.

verbs
abhor—; collect—; detest—; drag through
—; expose—; fling—; forbid—; gather—;
live in—; loathe—; purge of—; reek with
—; remove—; revolt at—; shun—; suffer
—; swarm with—; wallow in—.
(See dirt.)

FILTHY
adverbs
grossly; coarsely; unspeakably; incredibly;
grotesquely; horribly; abominably; grimily;
foully; beastly; offensively; slovenly; squalidly; unpardonably; inexcusably; unreasonably; needlessly; hideously; unwarrantably;
piteously; pitiably; deplorably; outlandishly; wretchedly; singularly; exceptionally;
extraordinarily.

FIN
verbs
cut off—s; course with—s; cruise with—s;
employ—s; injure—; insert—s; paddle with
—s; support with—s; swim with—s; —s
flap; —s flip; —s lash; —s navigate; —s
project; —s propel; —s steer.

FINAL
adverbs
tragically; conclusively; heartbreakingly;
egotistically; pompously; acrimoniously; officially; irrevocably; ultimately; catastrophically; elaborately; hopelessly; decisively; absolutely; definitely; unmistakably; inevitably; unchangeably; unimpeachably; dogmatically; authoritatively; authentically;
clearly.

FINALE
adjectives
ludicrous; wonderful.

verbs
approach—; compose—; encore—; enjoy—;
perfect—; play—; rehearse—; render—; —
completes; —concludes; —delights; —disposes of; —ends; —pleases; —terminates;
—winds up.
(See end, conclusion.)

FINALITY
adjectives
unmistakable; consecrated; unshakable;
helpless; brutal.

FINANCE (v)
adverbs
niggardly; soundly; scientifically; ceremoniously; pragmatically; ingenuously; professionally; unscrupulously; unethically; ingeniously.
(See provide, manage.)

FINANCES
adjectives
declining; pitiful; low; unsound; prospective.

verbs
accumulate—; amass—; clear up—; conceal—; deplete—; destroy—; drain—; imperil—; manipulate—; patch up—; pervert
—; provide—; rally—; shake—; strain—;
—accrue; —accumulate; —dwindle.
(See income, revenue, funds.)

FINANCIAL
adverbs
inescapably; naturally.

FINANCIER
adjectives
unscrupulous; accurate.

verbs
beseech—; curb—; employ—; provide—;
ruin—; —accomodates; —accumulates; —
amasses; —collects; —conducts; —controls;
—demands; —deposits; —invests; —judges;
—levies; —manages; —operates; —persuades; —recruits; —secures; —supports;
—swindles.
(See manager.)

FIND
adjectives
consequent; definite; important; right;
ghastly.

FIND (v)
adverbs
inevitably; eventually; invariably; conclusively; ultimately; locally; intuitively; distinctly; frequently; officially; promptly; con-
sequer y; definitely.
(Se acquire, attain, discover.)

adjectives

malicious; specific; pertinent; scientific.

verbs

chance on—; consider—; determine—; elucidate—; endorse—; examine—; expose—;
furnish—; inquire about—; inspect—; labor
for—; observe—; owe—to; pay for—; pick
up—; preserve—; procure—; produce—;
provide—; reveal—; supply—; view—; —
aids; —clarifies; —reveals.

(See discovery.)

FINE

verbs

anticipate—; agree upon—; condemn to—;
evade—; exact—; execute—; exempt from
—; impose—; incur—; lament—; levy—;
obtain—; pass—on; pronounce—; remit—;
settle—; subject to—; suffer—; —compensates; —punishes; —reduces; —releases; —
restrains.

(See penalty, money, sum, payment.)

FINE (v)

adverbs

heavily; unscrupulously; punitively; legally;
unethically; maliciously; cruelly; sternly.

(See dispossess, punish, attack.)

FINERY

adjectives

metropolitan; priceless; grotesque; worthless; gaudy; tawdry; verdant; shimmering;
bright; thin; elaborate; ruinous; scarlet;
barbaric; natural.

verbs

addict to—; adorn in—; appreciate—; bedeck in—; clothe in—; crave—; deck in—;
decorate in—; degenerate into—; display—;
dress in—; envy—; exhibit—; indulge in—;
observe—; prefer—; sport (colloq.)—; view
—; —amazes; —attracts; —impresses; —
consoles.

(See ornament, splendor.)

FINES

adjectives

enormous; aggregate; unfair; wholesale.

FINGER

verbs

beckon with—; bend—; cramp—; cut—;
distend—; drum with—; extend—; level—

at; prick—; snap—s; —s clutch;—s fly; —s
fumble with; —s hover near; —s twist; —s
twitch.

(See digit, thumb, hand.)

FINGER (v)

adverbs

significantly; nervously; delicately; tremulously; feverishly; tremblingly; intimately;
lingeringly; caressingly; fumblingly; rheumatically; lustfully; authoritatively; cannily; agilely.

(See handle, touch.)

FINGERNAIL

verbs

bite—; break—; chew—; claw with—; clean
—; clip—; cream—; dig with—; employ—;
excavate with—; file—; jag—; manicure—;
polish—; round—; shape—; split—; trim—;
—s attract; —s scratch; —s shine.

FINGERNAILS

adjectives

rose-tinted; pointed; unimpeachable; untidy; long; sharp; shiny-rouged; talon-like;
crooked; yellow; polished.

FINGERS

adjectives

guiding; tapering; prisoned; tremulous; uncut; slim; deft; searching; exquisite; listless; merciless; dimpled; slender; artistic;
patient; careless; knotted; dewy; numbed;
icy; outstretched; fevered; imitative; sharp;
clumsy; nimble; skilled; ferocious; plastic;
hushing; bloody; trembling; unresisting;
needle-marked; guiding; interlacing; chubby; jeweled; pointed; weary; marble; radiant; horny; gloved; ineffectual; groping;
invisible; ghostly; pensive; accusing; sensitive; solicitous; shaking; reverent; lily;
grubby; bruised; flitting; dextrous; lingering; fairy; waxen; talented; intimate;
tense; rosy; unseen; cruel; pale; bony;
moistened; lean; nervous; quick; grimy;
courageous; forced; benumbed; dirty; benign; rapid; transparent; shriveled; brown;
coral-tipped; rosy-nailed; soft; rose-tinted;
vigorous; premonitory; amethyst; skeleton;
effacing; pinching; clutching; tenacious; solemn; iron; glowing; choppy; mortal; beckoning; swathed; royal; pilfering; sudden;
microscopic; wasted; barky; unraised; nico-
tine-stained; false; hungry; catechising;
heavily-ringed; uncontrolled; gentle; caressing; limp; lax; hesitating; idle; pitying;

beguiling; chilled; awkward; ready; cautious; scorched; imperative; feeble; fluttering; disengaged; itching; indignant; warning; denunciatory; admonitory; busy; exploring; cold; prying; covetous; searching; blundering; greedy; mischievous; playful; meddling; offensive; slight; thieving; usurious; exploratory; tapping; snatching; gripping; fumbling; grasping; emphasizing; stiff; rheumatic; tendril-like; skinny; fleshy; blunt-tipped; thick; ruthless; plump; lustful; felonious; deadly; predatory; sinewy; powerful; rough; agile; smudgy; soiled; dingy; square; flat; stubby; freckled; curled; strong; spatulate; arched; huge; crooked; firm; authoritative; steady; experienced; well-groomed; manicured; quick; canny; excited.

FINGER-TIPS
adjectives
reverent; slim; caressing; calloused; semiconscious; warm; sensitive; chill; gentle.

FINICKY
adverbs
frivolously; idly; inanely; uncommonly; absurdly; unreasonably; ludicrously; primly; priggishly; vexatiously; bumptiously; loudly; unnecessarily; intolerably; tiresomely; inordinately; extravagantly; elaborately; pitifully; ridiculously; shabbily; amazingly.

FINISH
adjectives
elaborate; high; literary; permanent; pictorial; sleek; glace; gleaming; harmonious; artistic; lustrous; meticulous; smooth; ill-conceived; warm; mellow; oratorical; scholarly; surface; admirable; exquisite; attractive; interior; rare; delicate; subtle.

verbs
acquire—; adorn with—; anticipate—; await—; design—; destroy—; exhibit—; lay —; mar—; obtain—; plan—; polish to—; prepare—; produce—; provide—; restore —; select—; —perfects.
(See perfection.)

FINISH (v)
adverbs
uniformly; leisurely; deliberately; neatly; minutely; solemnly; abstractedly; hurriedly; elaborately; lustrously; meticulously; exquisitely; delicately; subtly.
(See complete, end.)

FINISHED
adverbs
perfectly; unquestionably; irrevocably; recently; satisfactorily; smoothly; politely; irremediably; finally; consummately; highly; definitely; unfortunately; beautifully; fundamentally; exquisitely; wonderfully; amazingly; faultlessly; cleverly; ingeniously; expertly; artistically; elaborately; splendidly.

FINITE
adverbs
materially; inevitably; essentially; mortally; lamentably; fitly; tragically; appropriately; evanescently; merely; transitorily; passingly; humanly.

FIRE
adjectives
scattering; withering; blasting; raging; scorching; penal; scared; continuous; purging; oracular; crimson; cheerful; incessant; smoldering; suicidal; contagious; dormant; enfilading; unquenchable; horrid; eternal; dullest; answering; celestial; heavenly; constant; heavy; ethereal; gnawing; latent; cozy; untoward; baleful; closest; starry; aromatic; blinding; plumed; combined (pl); elemental; fearful; liquid; inextinguishable; rolling; long-suffering; barbed; singular; permeating; blinking; fruitless; accustomed; lambent; all-consuming; volcanic; ardent; innumerable (pl); central; lively; unfathomed; insatiate; mirrored; living; destructive; well-directed; unwonted; pulsating; cordial; sweet; slumbering; murderous; impetuous; undermining; swift; mystic; golden; unapparent; unavailing; mocking; molten; soul-scorching; subtile; ruddy; capricious; cleansing; solar; blazing; terrific; plucky; feeble; strange; electric; corrosive; tempestuous; powerless; conflicting; thrifty; deadly; flaming; beamless; dusky; twilight; overwhelming; tremulous; soft; unspotted; grim; roaring; intolerable; lurid; well-directed; effective; flickering; baser; raking; devastating; tempering; azure; deep; spiritual; restless; steady; opalescent; remorseless; avenging; divine; nightly; slow; pale; fresh-lit; instantaneous; animating; vestal; monumental; branding; hallowed; turf; boisterous; pernicious; ancestral; incipient; unhallowed; galling; solitary; musketry; unhealthful; ravenous; wild; disastrous; immortal; wandering; smokeless; ceaseless; considerable; impassioned; appalling; magic; incense; illumin-

ating; sea-coal; immeasurable; unearthly; velvet; dead; drowsy; desultory; extraordinary; insignificant; languid; freezing; diverging; chaster; commingling; subterranean; parental; mortal; specifical; waning; unslackened; merry; fanatical; respective; elfin; spiral; conquering; theologic; everlasting; fluttering; hoarded; dreadful; open; hot-burning; council; actual; covered; hectic; kindly; combined; prophetic; shafted; impatient; inward; sleeping; mad; suppressed; bright; flashing; purifying; undivided; amber; sheathing; lightless; fierce; sprightly; vaporous; telling; crackling.

verbs
assail with—; concentrate—; douse (colloq.) —; extinguish—; feed—; intensify—; lower—; quench—; rake—; replenish—; revive—; smother—; stoke—; torture with—; vent—; witness—; yield to—; —breaks out; —consumes; —crackles; —devastates; —devours; —flashes; —gnaws; —leaps; —menaces; —rages; —ravages; —razes; —reaches out; —roars; —scorches; —shrivels; —slakes down; —smolders; —snaps; —sputters; —whips through.
(See blaze, flame, conflagration.)

FIRE (v)
adverbs
electrically; witheringly; blastingly; scorchingly; incessantly; fearfully; destructively; lethally; murderously; perniciously; mortally; fiercely; shatteringly; devastatingly.
(See explode, burn, blaze.)

FIREFLY
verbs
capture—; welcome—; —blinks; —cheers; —emits; —flames; —flashes; —flickers; —glimmers; —glitters; —glows; —illuminates; —lights; —scintillates; —shimmers; —spangles; —sparkles; —twinkles; —winks.
(See insect.)

FIRELIGHT
adjectives
flickering; wan; lifeless; bright; glaring; warm; drab; dull.

verbs
behold—; emit—; neglect—; observe—; provide—; quench—; —blinks; —casts; —cheers; —flames; —flashes; —flickers; —

gleams; —glimmers; —glows; —illuminates; —rages; —sparkles; —transmits; —twinkles; —warms; —warns.
(See light.)

FIREPLACE
adjectives
rustic; capacious; radiant; immense; stone; clean-swept; spacious; desolate; high; cheery; white-tiled.

verbs
congregate around—; crackle in—; delight in—; gather 'round—; lounge around—; nestle near—; pave—; provide—; rejoice 'round—; toast at—; —blinks; —cheers; —furnishes; —glimmers; —heats; —illuminates; —welcomes.

FIREWORKS
verbs
arrange—; attack with—; cast—; celebrate with—; charge with—; dedicate with—; design—; display—; execute—; exhibit—; honor with—; prepare—; present—; start —; —appear; —burn; —conclude; —cover; —disturb; —excite; —explode; —harm; —represent; —spark; —splutter.

FIRING
verbs
attend to—; commence—; halt—; inspire—; instigate—; lead to—; minimize—; perceive —; prepare for—; prevent—; prohibit—; require—; restrain—; slacken—; start—; subject to—; warn against—; —ceases; —destroys; —ruins; —wanes.
(See attack.)

FIRM
adjectives
salvaging; futile; magnanimous; munificent; enterprising; business; successful; mercantile; bankrupt.

verbs
alter—; associate with—; bankrupt—; designate—; establish—; head—; indict—; join —; manage—; supervise—; —advises; —agrees; —delivers; —dissolves; —engages; —perishes; —promotes; —sells; —solicits; —trades; —transacts.
(See partnership, corporation, company.)

adverbs
stably; dependably; securely; safely; sufficiently; satisfactorily; immovably; obdu-

rately; stubbornly; severely; wisely; care
fully; affectionately; paternally; desperate·
ly; sullenly; relentlessly; pitilessly; curious·
ly; remorselessly; primly; priggishly; officially; professionally; vexatiously; unnecessarily; resolutely; decisively; emphatically; remarkably; singularly; particularly;
uncommonly.

FIRMAMENT
adjectives
beautiful; boundless; darkling; airy; star-
spangled; full-arched; starry; azure; cloudless; aerial; spacious; frosty; all-encircling;
unquestionable; rolling; economic; overcast;
pellucid; twinkling; terrestrial; expectant.

FIRMNESS
adjectives
desperate; gloomy; relentless; curious; remorseless; fatal; necessary; exemplary;
practical; miscalled; fresh; equal; temperate; unexampled; futile.

FISH
adjectives
fin-twinkling; fiery; armored; magnificent;
surface; fatted; voracious; darting; glistening; golden; artificially-grown; live; game;
broiled; diminutive; silly; slim; silvery;
tawny; iridescent; sodden; much-comforted;
playful; meddlesome; mystical; speckled;
bony; lacelike; cartilaginous; salmonoid;
shining; putrid; floating; edible; brain-
giving.

verbs
abound in—; catch—; cure—; drag for—;
feed—; harbor—; limit—; plant—; prepare
—; raise—; shred—; steam—; yield—; —
darts off; —deposits eggs; —flashes past; —
flops about; —hovers near; —inhabits; —
schools; —spawns; —squirms; —swoops
past.

FISH (v)
adverbs
intently; contentedly; placidly; somnolently;
abstractedly; ruminatively; enthusiastically;
skillfully; professionally; devotedly.
(See search, seek.)

FISHERMAN
verbs
ban—; enthrall—; license—; permit—; tantalize—; tempt—; —anchors; —angles; —
attempts; —baits; —casts; —catches; —
collects; —courts; —displays; —disturbs;

—elicits; —enthuses (colloq.); —hauls in;
—hooks; —nets; —occupies; —pulls; —
snaps; —strives; —struggles with; —supplies; —trawls.

FISHERMEN
adjectives
energetic; skillful; stalwart; unsuccessful;
professional; lowly; ideal; shabby; devoted;
rude.

FISHING
verbs
acclaim—; ban—; bar—; contemplate—;
control—; employ in—; offer—; permit—;
popularize—; prevent—; rely on—; supervise—; thrive on—; tutor in—; —bores; —
disturbs; —diverts; —entertains; —lags; —
pleases; —supplies; —supports; —tests; —
tires; —yields.
(See sport.)

FIST
adjectives
clenched; rocklike; parental; fat; helping;
husky; tense; skillful; clumsy; practised;
dimpled; huge; solid; hamlike; giant;
heavy; ample; pudgy; iron; hard-knuckled;
useful-looking; great; raw; calloused;
knotted; gnarled; vengeful; angry; furious;
shaking; defiant; rage-driven; smashing;
whirling; swinging; pounding; thudding;
closed; hairy; doubled; impotent; knuckle-
torn; rock-laden; mailed; choking; eager;
oxlike.

verbs
bandage—; box with—; clasp in—; clench
—; close into—; conceal in—; dodge—;
double into—; drive with—; feint with—;
fight with—; flourish—; fold into—; grasp
with—; injure—; lay on with—; shake—;
strike with—; swing—; wield—; —clutches;
—crushes; —descends; —grips; —shoots
out; —staggers.
(See hand (colloq. for fist.)

FISTICUFFS
adjectives
childish; brutal; scientific.

FIT
adjectives
fainting; plethoric; smooth; trim; excellent;
slenderizing; violent; immoderate; jealous;
snug; periodical; poetic; painful; dreadful;
melancholy; sullen; apoplectic; hysterical;

natural; morose; economical; perfect; permanent; wild; suave; comfortable; superior; proper; lasting; soft; custom; superb; correct; assured.

verbs
ail with—; anticipate—; attack with—; burst into—; check—; convulse in—; cure of—; fall into—; fear—; master—; scream in—; seize with—; shake with—; sweat in —; take with—; throw into—; treat for—; —exhausts; —possesses; —seizes; —wracks.
(See spasm, convulsion, paroxysm.)

adverbs
remarkably; splendidly; magnificently; capably; competently; expertly; skillfully; amazingly; opportunely; conveniently; appropriately; brilliantly; robustly; sturdily; gratifyingly; pleasantly; unusually; marvelously.

FIT (v)
adverbs
snugly; exquisitely; adorably; peculiarly; permanently; specifically; curiously; delicately; smoothly; periodically; economically; superbly.
(See adorn, wear.)

FITFUL
adverbs
erratically; irregularly; capriciously; vexatiously; undependably; unsystematically; haltingly; changeably; inconstantly; terribly; oddly; restlessly; waywardly; fantastically; whimsically; captiously; inconsistently; surprisingly; unpleasantly; disturbingly.

FITNESS
adjectives
practical; vital; exquisite; highest; personal; harmonious; absolute; visible.

FIX
adjectives
awkward; monetary; erroneous; frightful; dreadful.

FIX (v)
adverbs
hypnotically; firmly; arbitrarily; unalterably; inherently; accurately; steadily; steadfastly; ingeniously; rigidly; awkwardly; momentarily.
(See fasten, secure, arrange.)

FIXED
adverbs
irrevocably; firmly; irresistibly; finally; resolutely; permanently; unalterably; inevitably; immovably; persistently; immutably; steadfastly; obstinately; ineradicably; irretrievably; indelibly; traditionally; officially; absolutely; inviolately.

FLABBERGASTED
adverbs
wondrously; breathlessly; mysteriously; unutterably; unspeakably; utterly; completely; helplessly; confusingly; confoundedly; obviously; embarrassingly; peculiarly; entirely; ludicrously; comically; pitiably.

FLABBY
adverbs
uselessly; pliably; flexibly; limply; malleably; inadequately; slackly; helplessly; hopelessly; wretchedly; miserably; terribly; disgustingly; vexatiously; dreadfully.

FLAG
adjectives
rippling; hoisted; wind-swayed; tattered; crimson; insulted; back-blown; radiant; saucy; faltering; drooping; enchanted; movable; fluttering; enormous; quadrangular; constabulary; tricolored; shameful; lozenge-shaped; scoured; ominous; hearth; withered; common; many-colored; gaudy; simplest; easiest; veranda; garish; unfurled; hostile; invincible; draped; precious; historic.

verbs
accept—of; bear—; crowd 'round—; display—; elevate—; extend—; flaunt—; guard—; half-mast—; haul down—; hoist —; jeopardize—; level—; moor—; nail—; pay homage to—; rally 'round—; unfurl—; wave—; —ascends; —cheers; —descends; —flutters; —symbolizes; —unfurls; —whips in the breeze.
(See banner, ensign.)

FLAGRANT
adverbs
arrantly; notoriously; patently; strikingly; incredibly; unconcealably; scandalously; publicly; grossly; atrociously; indecorously; indiscreetly; iniquitously; nefariously; reprehensibly; shamelessly; unconscionably; exceptionally; emphatically; indefensibly; wickedly.

adjectives
vicious; promotional; remarkable; definite;
noticeable.

FLAKES
adjectives
lazy; starry; quivering; fervent; wandering; hoariest; ash; thick-descending; jetty;
crackling; crunchy; flavor-packed; discolored; sun-ripened; delicately-browned; whole-
wheat; tender; luscious; flying; snow; wavering; radiant; whirling; white; mated;
blinding; elfish.

verbs
blow—; break into—; chip off—; cover
with—; cut into—; dress in—; fall in—;
peel in—; powder with—; scale—; scrape
into—; separate into—; silver with—;
spread with—; strip into—; —descend; —
fly; —pave.
(See fragment, chip.)

FLAMBOYANT
adverbs
conspicuously; openly; ostentatiously; brazenly; daringly; audaciously; floridly; sonorously; pompously; egotistically; rhetorically;
bombastically; flashily; noisily; terribly;
marvelously; uproariously.

FLAME
adjectives
vivid; dancing; flapping; unshapely; lean;
bursting; unresting; pitiless; candle; hungry; fever; solar; sunny; fragrant; cheerful; inward; pointed; dying; lambent; livelier; spiritual; devouring; sacrificial; quickening; unconsuming; conscious; immediate;
celestial; dull; low-lit; pure; changeless;
ruddy; sulphurous; polluted; generous; inferior; floating; rival; innocent; sacred;
showering; mutual; enormous; heavenly;
self-divided; restless; pale; earnest; pallid;
elusive; ethereal; many-colored; irregular;
guiding; quick; darting; stiller; variegated;
white; ardent; tired; leaping; noiseless;
flickering; lawless; wasting; writhing; hurrying; subtle; penetrating; torturing; amorous; evangelic; lurid; vital; feeble; blue;
scarlet; greenish; luminous; dreadful; incandescent; vengeful; empyreal; midnight;
heavenward; sudden; irregular; joyful; inexorable; springing; clearest; delusive; intermittent; chastening; accustomed; outrageous; withering; purer; livid; authentic;

spiral; cold; radiant; captive; flashing;
baleful; inextinguishable; mumuring; rapid; quenchable; serpent; seraphic; furious; ill-dissembled; all-absorbing; sullen;
wrathful; prismatic; loyal; purple; liquid;
bickering; deep-red; mounting; embracing;
peaceful; creeping; unshelterable; blessed;
vestal; transported; avenging; breathing;
oxyhydrogen; tossing; productive; lustral;
coral; powerful; imagined; internal; ceaseless; roaring; unchanging; unimprisoned;
silver; gigantic; lustrous.

verbs
burst into—; deliver up to—; dim—; extinguish—; feed—; kindle—; spout—; spray
with—; —blisters; —breathes; —chars; —
consumes; —crackles; —curls; —devours;
—flickers; —hovers over; —leaps; —licks;
—overcomes; —plays; —rages; —ravages;
—roars; —spreads; —spurts; —subdues; —
subsides; —trembles; —wanes; —wavers.
(See fire, blaze.)

FLAME (v)
adverbs
gorgeously; vividly; lambently; spiritually;
sacrificially; ruddily; dartingly; writhingly;
amorously; inextinguishably; unquenchably;
sullenly; wrathfully; furiously; mountingly;
ceaselessly; lustrously.
(See blaze, burn.)

FLANK
adjectives
bleeding; belathered; vertical; universal;
monstrous; cavernous; bulging; heaving;
towered.

FLANNEL
adjectives
spotless; tawdry; immaculate; easily-clean-
ed; rough.

FLAP (v)
adverbs
aimlessly; incessantly; irritatingly; monotonously; lustily; carelessly; impotently;
characteristically.
(See beat, flutter, quiver.)

FLARE (v)
adverbs
vividly; repeatedly; luminously; torridly;
heatedly; destructively; celestially; ethereally; balefully; blindingly; luridly.
(See flicker, dazzle, blaze.)

FLASH

adjectives
incessant; vicious; simultaneous (pl); continual (pl); temporary; vivid; rapid; illuminating; serpentine; forked; lurid; brilliant; sardonic; momentary; fiery; intellectual; blinding; deafening; free; intolerable; luminous; long-lingering; quick; eager; impetuous; sulphurous; flambeaux; electric; astonishing; meteoric; rhythmic; quivering; kaleidoscopic; sublime; downward; opalescent; white; clean-cut; fitful.

verbs
create—; criticize—; develop into—; disclose—; display—; fire—; produce—; rebound in—; repeat—; ridicule—; shoot—; strike with—; wait for—; —appears; —arouses; —astounds; —attracts; —blazes; —bursts; —directs; —displays; —disturbs; —exposes; —flares; —flaunts; —flouts; —gleams; —ignites; —illumines; —indicates; —occurs; —passes over; —relinquishes; —reveals; —signals; —spurts; —vanishes; —violates.
(See blaze, gleam.)

FLASH (v)

adverbs
briefly; brilliantly; gloriously; vindictively; instantaneously; irresistibly; fiercely; restlessly; intermittently; radiantly; lambently; simultaneously; serpentinely; luridly; electrically; meteorically; kaleidoscopically; opalescently; fitfully.
(See sparkle, gleam.)

FLASH-LIGHT

verbs
douse (colloq.)—; employ—; necessitate—; replenish—; resort to—; supply—; —beams; —blinks; —brightens; —dazzles; —exposes; —flickers; —floods; —glares; —glimmers; —guides; —illuminates; —reflects; —reveals; —shines; —spots; —uncovers.
(See light.)

FLASH-LIGHT
(photography)

verbs
anticipate—; ban—s; bar—s; blink at—; conceal—; employ—; guard against—; jump at—; permit—; pose for—; protect from—; refuse—; —enrages; —explodes; —illumines; —interrupts; —irritates; —pops; —reveals; —scares; —startles; —surprises.
(See flash.)

FLASHY

adverbs
pretentiously; gaudily; garishly; flauntingly; daringly; highly; wonderfully; cheaply; grossly; coarsely; attractively; ornately; smartly; pompously; gorgeously; indecorously; unbecomingly; rudely; provincially; outlandishly; fantastically; grotesquely; dreadfully; horribly.

FLASK

adjectives
supernal; primitive; tapering; liquor; pocket-size.

FLAT

adverbs
monotonously; tiresomely; vapidly; disagreeably; invariably; intolerably; uninterestingly; wearily; tediously; endlessly.

FLATS

adjectives
dangerous; vile; sumptuous; inhospitable; cluttered; crowded; sewage-polluted; fertile; streaming; occidental; windowed; various; tenement; lurid.

FLATTER (v)

adverbs
obsequiously; fondly; grossly; hugely; slavishly; unduly; artfully; immeasurably; prettily; cunningly; adeptly; adroitly; deftly; coyly; treacherously; deceptively; coarsely; egregiously; sleekly; fatuously; expertly.
(See compliment, praise.)

FLATTERED

adverbs
happily; blushingly; pleasantly; rosily; smilingly; highly; pleasingly; delightfully; convivially; excitedly; jubilantly; artlessly; inordinately; uncommonly.

FLATTERER

adjectives
impudent; cunning; defective; adept; adroit.

FLATTERY

adjectives
coarse; temporizing; sordid; graceful; innumerable (pl); gross; egregious; judicious; servile; friendly; unconscious; grateful; sleek; supple; dulcet; cautious; fatal; infinite; verbal; blazoned; expert; delicate; commonplace.

verbs
abhor—; accept—; addict to—; conceal with —; court—; detest—; endure—; expand under—; fall for—; feed with—; fool by—; savor of—; steel to—; succumb to—; thicken with—; withstand—; yield to—; —deceives; —soothes; —tricks.
(See adulation.)

FLAUNT (v)
adverbs
arrogantly; insultingly; saucily; pertly; exasperatingly; tantalizingly; maliciously; subtly; coyly; mortifyingly.
(See parade, show.)

FLAVOR
verbs
acclaim—; adulterate—; affect—; create—; detect—; dislike—; extract—; marvel at—; mask—; protect—; retain—; scent—; smell —; —appetizes; —burns out; —delights; —dies; —rivals; —stales.
(See taste, savor.)

FLAVOR (v)
adverbs
delectably; delicately; exotically; appetizingly; pungently; inimitably; matchlessly; characteristically; originally; temptingly; palatably; exhilaratingly; toothsomely; incomparably.
(See season, taste.)

FLAVORING
verbs
add—; dislike—; employ—; impart—; inject—; lack—; mix with—; necessitate—; savor—; season with—; select—; spice with —; taste—; try—; —enhances; —flatters; —pleases; —stings; —teases.
(See extract, spice, etc.)

FLAVORS
adjectives
marvelous; exotic; luscious; appetizing; oleaginous; pleasant; juicy; spirited; unapproachable; delicate; aristocratic; pungent; inimitable; distinctive; exclusive; minty; matchless; characteristic; delicious; intellectual; imaginative; full-bodied; treacherous; international; original; satisfying; grand; extra-fresh; odorous; acrid; individual; abominable; faint; infused; sublime; palatable; tender; supreme; exhilarating; delicious; native; tempting; subtle; apparent; mellow; reminiscent; unique; mild; tangy;
toothsome; peculiar; balanced; smoky; dry; hearty; popular; unusual; fine; criminal; appetizing; old-time; incomparable; clinging.

FLAW
adjectives
foul; inherent; blemishing; inscrutable; apparent; age-old; inherited.

verbs
accept—; conceal—; consider—; constitute —; detect—; develop—; discern—; discover —; eradicate—; exempt from—; free from —; guard against—; hide—; jade with—s; overcome—; —blemishes; —mars; irons out —.
(See defect, blemish, imperfection, fault, crack.)

FLAWLESS
adverbs
perfectly; incredibly; marvelously; utterly; unbelievably; delicately; simply; tastefully; chastely; obviously; superbly; splendidly; absolutely; technically; ineffably; completely; comparatively; exquisitely; matchlessly; artistically.

FLEE (v)
adverbs
incontinently; instinctively; peremptorily; precipitately; timorously; tremulously; impetuously.
(See run, abandon.)

FLEECE
adjectives
delicate; silky; plenteous; warm.

FLEECY
adverbs
warmly; softly; comfortingly; comfortably; incredibly; genuinely; agreeably; pleasantly; tenderly; sleekly; smoothly; shaggily; delightfully; snugly; delicately.

FLEET
verbs
antiquate—; assemble—; assign to—; command—; dispatch—; expand—; increase—; mobilize—; observe—; order—; recondition —; —anchors; —blockades; —celebrates; —cruises; —exhibits; —files in; —journeys;

—migrates; —navigates; —passes; —performs; —plies; —sails; —shifts; —ships; —speeds; —travels.
(See squadron, navy.)

adverbs
incredibly; nimbly; gracefully; marvelously; splendidly; remarkably; expeditiously; smartly; actively; lightly; mercurially; inordinately; unwontedly; naturally; unusually; surprisingly; amazingly; trippingly.

FLEETING
adverbs
impermanently; evanescently; mortally; transiently; transitorily; perishably; quickly; temporally; illusively; elusively; sadly; unhappily; ephemerally; pitifully; terribly.

FLEETNESS
adjectives
sleek; eager; easy; unapproachable; swift.

FLEETS
adjectives
allied; provisional; myriad; trade; mimic; royal; confederate; formidable; cumbrous; grim; multitudinous; death-dealing.

FLESH
adjectives
mortifying; famished; fever-stricken; palatable; cumbrous; festering; quivering; lank; unsavory; overroasted; flower-tinted; soft; pink; sun-bronzed; ivory; pale; waxen; bruised; shuddering; swollen; dusty; exhausted; putrefying; carrion; miserable; half-cooked; pierced; mad; attractive; common; living; sweet; tender; transfigured; dead; redundant; yielding; warm; lumpy; scalded; mangled; tainted; wrinkled; ample; muscular; decrepit; quaky; firm; human; crawling; swooping; swelling; slippery; sensitive; blooming; decaying; rebellious; seraphic; gangrenous; overwearied; quick; aching; adhering; mutinous; torn; elaborate; dressed; sinful; avaricious.

verbs
accumulate—; chafe—; char—; crucify—; denounce—; derive from—; flavor—; gain —; gather—; grind—; inject into—; market —; mutilate—; produce—; reduce—; waste —.
(See meat, fat.)

FLESHY
adverbs
mortifyingly; cumbrously; comfortably; burdensomely; embarrassingly; dreadfully; inordinately; dangerously; amiably; miserably; wretchedly; clumsily; awkwardly; strangely; warmly; stockily; alarmingly; heavily; hideously; shockingly; wholesomely; merrily; nonchalantly; cheerfully.

FLEXIBLE
adverbs
conveniently; adaptably; suitably; appropriately; diplomatically; agreeably; pliantly; tractably; complaisantly; affably; pleasantly; indulgently; easily; manageably; smoothly; fortunately; properly.

FLICKER
adjectives
curious; small; tiny; rapid; abrupt; unseen.

verbs
emit—; observe—; reduce to—; repeat—; shake with—; vibrate in—; —annoys; — dies out; —disturbs; —flames; —mottles; — remains; —warms; —warns; —wavers.
(See light.)

FLICKER (*v*)
adverbs
inscrutably; involuntarily; fitfully; rapidly; incessantly; repeatedly; mysteriously; interminably.
(See flutter, waver.)

FLIER
verbs
employ—; examine—; exhaust—; inform—; license—; overtake—; strain—; test—; — achieves; —accomplishes; —ascends; —attempts; —charts; —circles; —controls; — descends; —dips; —endures; —lands; — loops; —manipulates; —navigates; —operates; —perceives; —pilots; —somersaults; —speeds; —takes off; —transports; — zooms.
(See aviator, aeroplane.)

FLIES
adjectives
lazy; insolent; gilded; unfortunate; shrivelled; swarming; glittering; incautious; stinging; vicious; bothersome.

504

FLIGHT

adjectives

pattering; comely; droning; fagging; impetuous; wheeling; gay; labored-looking; ceaseless; joyous; temporary; cankerous; vehement; tireless; unreturning; bold; poetic; rhythmic; self-same; erratic; hysterical; epochal; prolonged; intertwined; nuptial; mocking; impeded; principal; common; angry; unjust; disguising; pretended; ignominious; airy; troublesome; perceptible; humanitarian; risky; mediocre; freshening; industrious; frolic; promiscuous; illuminated; tremendous; precipitate; untried; aery; lagging; filmy; fleeting; rapturous; fearful; perilous; howling; ambitious; imperial; interminable; ponderous; winding; higher; unwearied; intrepid; hurried; undulating; unbounded; upward-hovering; never-ending; impudent; swift; rickety; tremulous; transitory; wide; worn; persistent; cloistered; cowardly; voluptuous; orderly; annual; unsustained; measureless; distant.

verbs

accomplish—; accustom to—; attempt—; depart in—; drop in—; hasten in—; impede —; lose in—; mount in—; move to—; observe—; plan—; pursue in—; record—; resume—; retreat in—; sally forth in—; scatter—; soar in—; witness—; —exhausts; —fails.

(See journey, trip.)

FLIGHTY

adverbs

comically; wantonly; cheerfully; happily; merrily; charmingly; vexatiously; curiously; deliriously; strangely; oddly; queerly; alarmingly; dangerously; insanely; whimsically; wildly; capriciously; fantastically; lightly; drunkenly; heedlessly; thoughtlessly; carelessly; inadvertently; remarkably; utterly.

FLIMSY

adverbs

absurdly; airily; vaguely; tenuously; unreasonably; nonsensically; foolishly; slightly; ridiculously; miserably; wretchedly; contemptibly; pitifully; unmanageably; unserviceably; objectionably.

FLING

adjectives

overhand; disdainful; senseless; disjointed; surreptitious; ill-natured.

FLING (*v*)

adverbs

mechanically; dramatically; fiercely; jauntily; simultaneously; impetuously; violently; harshly; carelessly; savagely; tauntingly; disdainfully; ill-naturedly; contemptuously; extravagantly.

(See hurl, cast.)

FLINTS

adjectives

stubborn; clattering; brittle; steely.

FLIPPANCY

adjectives

extravagant; friendly; verbal; studied; marked; open; definite; disgusting.

FLIPPANT

adverbs

impertinently; carelessly; insouciantly; audaciously; daringly; brazenly; charmingly; attractively; giddily; heedlessly; jauntily; saucily; unblushingly; shamelessly; wantonly; unduly; disrespectfully; comically; inappropriately; unbecomingly; inopportunely; youthfully; glibly; smartly; inconsiderately; sacrilegiously; terribly.

FLIRT

adjectives

saucy; harmless; wild.

FLIRT (*v*)

adverbs

blatantly; shamelessly; saucily; wildly; outrageously; unconscionably; boldly; coyly; shyly; immodestly; voluptuously; arduously; impassionedly; trivially; desultorily.

(See coquette, love.)

FLIRTATION

adjectives

sly; anonymous; literary; unworthy; miserable; pleasant; hit-and-run; trivial; desultory; detached; discreet; swift; arduous; meaningful; mere; summer; unimpassioned.

verbs

arouse—; arrest—; cease—; coach—; commit—; continue—; delight in—; express in —; interrupt—; overlook—; recount—; regard as—; renew—; school in—; tease in —; —deceives; —excites; —grows; —inspires; —invites; —involves; —stimulates.

adverbs

innocently; harmlessly; amusingly; designedly; resolutely; definitely; systematically; assiduously; sedulously; charmingly; noticeably; curiously; oddly; habitually; seductively; irresistibly; coquettishly; philanderingly; merrily; openly; obviously; palpably; whimsically; engagingly.

FLIT (*v*)

adverbs

errantly; feverishly; vaguely; joyously; tantalizingly; momentarily; casually; ephemerally; temporarily.
(See flutter, fly.)

FLOAT (*v*)

adverbs

nebulously; airily; buoyantly; lazily; gracefully; listlessly; majestically; drowsily; delicately; miraculously; gorgeously; lumberingly; glitteringly.
(See move, billow, creep, drift, hover.)

FLOATS

adjectives

gossamer; lumbering; horse-drawn; glittering; beautiful; papier-mache; river; gorgeous; glorious.

FLOCK

adjectives

close-pinned; golden; crowding; divided; trembling; scattered; endless; fleecy; blood-bought; patriarchal; afflicted; nibbling; snowy; browsing; timorous; homeward; clustering; healthful; pictorial; benighted.

verbs

appeal to—; call on—; care for—; guide—; journey in—; manage—; muster—; preach to—; supervise—; travel in—; —assembles; —congregates; —flees; —gathers; —journeys; —occupies; —supports; —swarms.
(See pack, group, herd, congregation.)

FLOCK (*v*)

adverbs

protectively; reposefully; timorously; clusteringly; pictorially; benightedly; habitually; characteristically; seasonally.
(See assemble, crowd.)

adjectives

intoxicating; impetuous; sluggish; vitreous; soaking; mighty; torrential; creeping; short-lived; devastating; human; babbling; untamable; spring; savory; copious; shoreless; seething; passing; brackish; fearful; crystal; maddened; foaming; phenomenal; raging; steaming; shining; redundant; weltering; unfathomable; shaded; disastrous; shallow; uncurling; surging; horned; isle-fretted; moon-lit; breaking; all-destroying; advancing; overflowing; post-glacial; drenching; shedding; glowing; turbid; sparkling; storied; wondrous; full; eternal; main; wasteful; lashing; fiery; glassy; urgent; tranquil; azure; furious; unbroken; frigid; ice-imprisoned; tropical; roaring; all-engulfing; gathering; clearest; fretful; unwelcome; poured-out; eddying; vaporous; theoretic; wandering; widespread.

verbs

abate—; ameliorate—; check—; dam—; guard against—s; halt—; mitigate—; recoil from—; stem—; swirl with—; unloose—; —cripples; —devastates; —inundates; —overwhelms; —recedes; —submerges; —sweeps away.
(See deluge.)

FLOOD (*v*)

adverbs

fatally; partially; impetuously; torrentially; devastatingly; untamably; copiously; seethingly; foamingly; phenomenally; ragingly; disastrously; drenchingly; sparklingly; furiously; roaringly; eddyingly.
(See overflow, submerge, drench.)

FLOOR

adjectives

watery; dark-stained; polished; topmost; unpretentious; sanded; desolate; glassy; olive; opalescent; light; stained; glittering; gleaming; seedy; oaken; translucent; sinking; mosaic; drafty; musty; gritted; amethystine; spotless; desert-yellow; charred; cloudy; slimy; draughty; well-swept; untrodden; mirrored; clammy; brazen; tremulous; expansive; diamond-paved; planet-powered; dilapidated; brick; herbless; carpetless; conscious; vaster; threshing; blazing; shining; scholastic; marble; iron-bound; tessellated; tiled.

verbs
board—; cement—; crowd—; inlay—; joist —; lay—; litter—; nail to—; polish—; rest on—; root to—; scrape—; shellac—; slip on—; splinter—; strew—; swab—; tread on —; varnish—; warp—; wax—; —collapses; —creaks; —rots; —sags; —supports.
(See surface, platform.)

FLORID
adverbs
ruddily; uncommonly; dangerously; alarmingly; healthily; intensely; freshly; blowzily; warmly; wholesomely; unusually; remarkably; oddly; habitually; unwontedly; naturally.

FLOUNDER (v)
adverbs
bewilderingly; haphazardly; awkwardly; comically; clumsily; helplessly; wretchedly.
(See stumble, struggle.)

FLOUNDERING
adjectives
haphazard; ignoble; awkward; laughable.

FLOUR
adjectives
ill-mixed; unadulterated; unbolted; bleached.

verbs
bag—; barrel—; bin—; bleach—; brush off —; cover with—; employ—; grade—; grind into—; manufacture—; mill—; mix with—; obtain—; pulverize into—; reduce to—; select—; sift—; sprinkle—; triturate into—; —dusts; —whitens.
(See cereal, powder.)

FLOURISH
adjectives
ornamental; periodic; sudden; joyous; eloquent; graceful; festive; indignant; brazen.

FLOURISH (v)
adverbs
chiefly; luxuriously; gloriously; vigorously; periodically; gracefully; festively; brazenly; heartily; boisterously.
(See thrive.)

FLOURISHING
adverbs
highly; uncommonly; remarkably; prosperously; successfully; sturdily; steadily; indubitably; certainly; materially; apparently; evidently; manifestly; splendidly; magnificently; obviously; fortunately; luckily; deservedly; extremely.

FLOUT
adjectives
wounding; brash; resounding.

FLOW
adjectives
inward; sonorous; cheerful; increasing; intermitting; eternal; long-accustomed; dual; lurid; spontaneous; irrepressible; beneficent; sluggish; restless; maladjusted; seething; social; dolorous; endless; lateral; never-ending; excessive; constant; boisterous; agreeable; continuous; metrical; wavy; taintless; melodious; uneventful; quiescent; exuberant; imaginative; babbling; enclasping; incessant; gracious; balanced; rhetorical; unceasing; rippling; perpetual; lyrical; literary; everlasting.

verbs
accelerate—; bar—; check—; control—; dam—; diminish—; direct—; increase—; induce—; lessen—; prevent—; produce—; re-establish—; reiterate—; restrain—; still —; stimulate—; —advances; —ceases; —progresses.
(See stream, current, outpouring, fluency, abundance.)

FLOW (v)
adverbs
diffusely; noiselessly; divergently; tortuously; incessantly; lazily; mutely; sluggishly; inevitably; serenely; spontaneously; vehemently; placidly; seethingly; melodiously; quiescently; babblingly; rhetorically; perpetually; lyrically.
(See move, pass, float.)

FLOWER
verbs
arrange—s; array—s; awaken—s; bear—s; blanket with—s; crush—; cultivate—s; cull —s; fertilize—s; gather—s; landscape with —s; pluck—; press—; putter among—s; strew with—s; surround with—s; trample —; —s beckon; —s bob; —s cascade; —s cluster; —droops; —s drink in; —emerges; —fades; —nods; —ravishes; —shrivels; —springs up; —sways in the breeze; —unfolds; —withers; —waves.
(See blossom, plant, rose, lily, etc.)

FLOWER (v)

adverbs
adverbs
resplendently; fragrantly; consummately; opulently; transiently; garishly; pendulously; wantonly; fugitively; vernally; deathlessly; luxuriantly; autumnally; vernally.
(See blossom, bloom.)

FLOWERS

adjectives
fragrant; spicy; graven; inwrought; constellated; starry; drooping; withering; consummate; tender; venturesome; wasted; amassing; wave-reflected; hybrid; thirsting; flamelike; wilting; carven; modest; spangled; variable; tissued; varicolored; opulent; delicate; pearling; transient; venomous; exotic; shy; climbing; homely; balmy; bewailing; garish; budding; laughing; uncropped; prim; thriving; fresh; expanded; dewy; perishable; sculptured; sweet; maiden; transitory; unfolding; unpretentious; satisfactory; pendulous; mystic-passion; wanton; fugitive; brilliant; rootless; storm-marred; busy; wilted; unthroned; immeasurable; infinite; scattering; manifold; sweet-tipped; festal; precious; thorny; summer-swelling; gazing; fair-named; visionary; indomitable; sanguine; waxen; multicolored; richly-colored; brightly-hued; frost-white; gorgeous; faded; fragile; printless; clustering; choicest; curious; crocus; wayside; artificial; unfolded; beauteous; tinted; tributary; achromatous; welcome; air-sown; mysterious; glowing; helpless; sweet-smelling; vernal; fullest; big; gallant; splashy; shaded; deathless; moisture-loving; classic; new-bloomed; unblown; heaven-plated; soft-breathing; incense-mingling; snow-white; changing; scented; meanest; fairest; pressed; foolproof; heartier; hand-planted; unperishing; promiscuous; luxuriant; earthly; autumnal; votive; ligulate; new-sprung; fantastic; torn; dissimilar; saffron; silvery; languishing; thread-hung; barren; uncourted; flourishing; enameled; discriminating; cleftborn; belated; sculptured; innocent; unconscious; prolific; resting; crimson-petalled; woodland; departed; chief; goodly; angel-missioned; breathing; stately; golden-hearted; overflowing; wordlike.

FLOWERY

adverbs
absurdly; ridiculously; bombastically; pompously; egotistically; importantly; blatantly; ornately; elaborately; ludicrously; bumptiously; sonorously; sententiously; egregiously; outlandishly; fantastically; inordinately; senselessly; preposterously; extravagantly.

FLUCTUATE (v)

adverbs
feverishly; violently; transiently; perceptibly; normally; cyclically; seasonally; economically.
(See waver, vary.)

FLUCTUATION

adjectives
violent; silken; alternate; transient; considerable.

FLUENCY

adjectives
extreme; rare; deplorable; inexhaustible; sweet; inimitable; impressive; illimitable.

verbs
acquire—; administer with—; declaim with —; deliver with—; discharge with—; dispatch with—; emit—; exhibit—; express with—; flow with—; increase—; orate with —; pen with—; proceed with—; promote—; recite with—.
(See ease.)

FLUENT

adverbs
amazingly; surprisingly; admirably; consistently; enviably; gracefully; readily; naturally; habitually; easily; felicitously; rhythmically; delightfully; wonderfully; strikingly; splendidly; eloquently; impressively.

FLUFFY

adverbs
delightfully; delicately; deliciously; warmly; softly; smoothly; remarkably; surprisingly; correctly; comfortably; comfortingly; deeply; amazingly; genuinely; uncommonly; extremely; distinctly; completely; lightly.

FLUID

adjectives
innumerable (pl); life-giving; gummy; intoxicating; subtle; vapid; sizy; scarce; lacteal; germinating; dark-hued; amber-colored; opaque; overabundant; turbid; electric; illusive; bleaching; unwholesome; precious; drinkable; vital; inky; incompressible; ethereal.

verbs

absorb—; consume—; discharge—; drain—; draw off—; effuse—; employ—; expel—; exude—; generate—; inject—; introduce—; secrete—; spill—; tap—; —circulates; —stains.

(See liquid, liquor, gas.)

FLUIDITY

adjectives

noticeable; linguistic; remarkable.

FLURRY

adjectives

undeniable; smiling; spiteful; abortive; pinwheel; angry.

FLUSH

adjectives

hectic; bloomy; unwonted; happy; momentary; blackish; brick-red; dull-red; fiery; gentle; helpless; fading; rosy; mahogany; perceptible; embarrassed; uneasy; novel; irritated; delicate; angry.

verbs

arouse—; cover with—; emit—; glow with —; overcome—; produce—; provoke—; redden into—; robe with—; subdue—; suffuse with—; —allures; —animates; —ebbs; —exasperates; —mantles; —overspreads; —throbs; —veils.

(See glow, blush, excitement, bloom.)

FLUSH (v)

adverbs

painfully; faintly; violently; delicately; miserably; singularly; passionately; transparently; hectically; unwontedly; rosily; perceptibly; embarrassingly; angrily.

(See blush, glow, thrill.)

FLUSHED

adverbs

extremely; drunkenly; feverishly; excitedly; apoplectically; alarmingly; dangerously; significantly; shyly; embarrassingly; ruddily; rosily; violently; angrily; furiously; madly; insanely; terribly; dreadfully; inordinately; frightfully; unnaturally; unusually.

FLUSTERED

adverbs

nervously; awkwardly; clumsily; significantly; helplessly; pitifully; weakly; terribly; agitatedly; hopelessly; ineptly; dis-

tractedly; distressingly; comically; absurdly; unreasonably; distinctly; undoubtedly; unwontedly; merrily; gloriously; drunkenly; tipsily.

FLUTE

adjectives

meditative; pastoral; oaten; perpendicular; enchanted; breathing.

verbs

dance to—; employ—; finger—; ornament —; pipe—; pitch—; practise on—; render on—; scale—; sound—; tootle on—; transpose on—; —blends; —cheers; —complains; —enraptures; —harmonizes; —shrills; —utters; —whines; —whistles.

FLUTTER

adjectives

unconscious; faint; indescribable; continual; perpetual; gay; sleek.

FLUTTER (v)

adverbs

recurrently; lightly; tremulously; gently; wantonly; ominously; convulsively; persistently; gaily; indescribably .

(See tremble, fluctuate.)

FLY

adjectives

aggressive; officious; untrapped; pestering; stuttering; intolerable.

verbs

abandon to—ies; bar—ies; guard from—ies; harbor—ies; protect from—ies; screen off —ies; torture with—ies; —ies breed; —buzzes; —ies crawl; —drones; —glitters; —ies infest; —lays eggs; —lights on; —plagues; —settles; —torments; —ies swarm.

(See insect.)

FLY (v)

adverbs

professionally; gracefully; undauntedly; breath-takingly; basely; fantastically; cheerily; intrepidly; instinctively; precipitately; characteristically; swiftly; unerringly.

(See soar, flee.)

FLYER

adjectives

feathered; unsuccessful; dare-devil; intrepid; courageous; fearless; inimitable; daring; great; world-wide; seasoned; professional; careful; negligent; lawless; nerveless.

FOAM

adjectives

tainted; snow-soft; circumambient; ocean; fantastic; dashing; driven; creamy; panting; loose; wasteful; pale; fleet; lacteal; rainbow-colored; sea; rolling; fragile; salt; sweet; flamelike; delicious; wind-tossed; yeasty; fleecy; border; crested; carded; moonlit; seething; springtide; surging; uneasy; luminous; enchanted; twinkling; cruel; crawling; constellated; barren; sparkling; wild.

verbs

aggregate—; beat to—; boil to—; break into —; cover with—; crest with—; emit—; ferment—; fill with—; fleck with—; toss off—; —bubbles; —drips off; —effervesces; —floats; —froths; —gurgles; —issues from; —reams; —scuds; —smothers; —streaks; —washes.

(See froth.)

FOCUS

adjectives

constant; sharp; blurred; careful; precise; accurate.

FOCUS (v)

adverbs

sharply; precisely; accurately; deftly; skillfully; blurredly; scientifically; exactly.

(See concentrate, adjust.)

FOE

adjectives

prostrate; headless; murderous; mortal; prejudiced; vanquished; imaginary; spectral; intestinal; foreign; malicious; private; prevailing; ruthless; fierce; inveterate; exhausted; ghastly; remorseless; embodied; overweening; fallen; formidable; mailed; bigoted; blushing; contemptible; sensuous; inferior; daring; wily; ribald; wicked; sternest; unseen; countless (pl); implacable; victorious; ferocious; bitter; monstrous; invading; immortal; inexorable; mental; invisible; effective; heartless; treacherous; insolent; despicable; ubiquitous; stubborn; blaspheming; deadliest; cunning; contending; faint; blood-seeking; hereditary; lurking; bitterest; over-confident; one-time; hellish; persistent; dark; encircled; external; mocking; unexpected; savage; alert; hostile; ironclad; captured; defeated; cowering; principal; dastardly.

verbs

curse—; defy—; denounce—; disarm—; discover—; dislodge—; embolden—; grapple with—; halt—; inflame—; inflict on—; inveigh against—; overwhelm—; persecute—; puzzle—; reconcile—; subdue—; vanquish —; —advances; —approaches; —assaults; —attacks; —falls; —looms up; —strikes.

(See enemy, adversary, opponent, antagonist.)

FOG

adjectives

transparent; antarctic; autumnal; dank; treacherous; opalescent; thick; black; rolling; gray; heavy; white; pea-soup; dense; chill; contagious; low-lying; relentless; increasing; germ-laden; midsummer; silent; drooping; blinding; impenetrable; miasmal; curling; dismal; decided; wall-like; opaque; blanketing; heartless.

verbs

cut—; dispel—; disperse—; dissipate—; emerge from—; fathom—; grope in—; penetrate—; —abates; —blankets; —clears; —creeps up; —devours; —fades; —lifts; —settles on; —swallows up; —wraps around.

(See mist, haze, darkness.)

FOGGY

adverbs

mysteriously; unluckily; unfortunately; thickly; slightly; lightly; strangely; alarmingly; fearfully; dangerously; frightfully; impossibly; darkly; impenetrably; muddily; hazily; vaporously; wetly; mistily; nebulously; murkily; uncommonly; opaquely.

FOIBLE

adjectives

harmless; amiable; pitiable; laughable; pleasant; cheery; understandable.

verbs

acknowledge—; correct—; cure of—; detect —; disclose—; discover—; entail—; expose—; inherit—; observe—; overcome—; perceive—; produce—; resent—; reveal—; ridicule—; screen—; tempt—; —appears; —arises; —hinders; —irritates; —results.

(See fault, failing, weakness, defect, frailty.)

FOIL

adjectives

glistening; glittering; gleaming; sharp; glinting; swift.

adjectives

enchanting; mazy; misty; snapping; secret; drowsy; brazen; caressing; snowy; floating; dimpled; thick; amorous; effeminate; ample; vaporous; voluminous; wind-flowing; loosened; deep-shadowed; clammy; becoming; sweeping; glistening; filmy; radiant; horizontal; fatal; strangling; gold-fringed; overhanging; graceful; meaningless; pinching; shivering; unapproachable.

FOLD (v)

adverbs

tensely; neatly; unconsciously; ostentatiously; quaintly; placidly; threateningly; wearily; voluminously; tenderly.

(See embrace, clasp.)

FOLDER

adjectives

descriptive; illustrated; well-printed; lucid; advertising.

verbs

arrange in—; assemble in—; attach to—; collect in—; destroy—; distribute—s; go through—; lodge in—; pass out—s; place in—; pore over—; prepare—; preserve in —; pull from—; refer to—; search in—; store in—; —advertises; —contains; —discloses.

(See catalogue, record.)

FOLIAGE

adjectives

cloudy; profuse; scattering; sapless; admirable; gracious; feathered; fresh; brilliant; luxuriant; delicate; evanescent; tropical; polished; gorgeous; golden; bright; tinted; silvery; bluish-gray; tender; scarlet; autumnal; shining; clustering; wasted; observable; sunny; dense; colored; fiery; blunt; curly; knotted; entangled; massive; dropping; ruddy; fresh; rustling; scant; softened; umbrageous; dying; intervening; voluminous; graceful; ornamental; protecting; overhanging; disease-resistant; impenetrable; screening; glossy.

verbs

admire—; bear—; behold—; decorate with —; don—; drench—; refresh—; shed—; shower—; sprout—; welcome—; yield—; — abounds; —adorns; —appears; —bathes; —blooms; —dies; —rustles; —shadows; — surrounds; —trembles.

(See leaves.)

adjectives

illuminated; ponderous; rare; inestimable; unhandy.

FOLK

adjectives

quick-witted; trivial; cross-tempered; quarrelsome; finical; guileful; guarded; suspicious; anxious; furtive; purposeful; true-hearted; famished; complacent; eavesdropping; ordinary; old-fashioned; showy; shadowy; placid; unexcitable; wee; shepherd; pert; novelty-loving; scribbling; fashionable; timorous; humble; hard-working; religious; peaceful; indigenous; unwieldy; slow; heavy; pale; prosperous; happy; furtive; cunning; hysterical; well-mannered; reaping; invincible; marooned; congenial; worthy; bourgeois; plain.

FOLKS

verbs

amuse—; enjoy—; please—; study—; visit —; —abide by; —adhere to; —admit; — cherish; —cleave to; —cling to; —congregate; —flourish; —follow; —frolic; —gambol; —gather; —inherit; —instil; —persevere; —resent; —revel.

(See people, nation, family, relatives.)

FOLLOW (v)

adverbs

instinctively; abjectly; trustfully; inevitably; irresistibly; reverently; wistfully; obsequiously; relentlessly; heedlessly; slavishly; reluctantly; unswervingly; gallantly; mechanically; traditionally; dutifully; dumbly; placidly; mutely; logically; religiously; grudgingly; undeviatingly; automatically; implicitly; doggedly; devoutly; diligently; sedulously.

(See chase, pursue.)

FOLLOWER

verbs

attract—s; beget—s; beguile—; conduct—; dictate to—; direct—; exhort—; fascinate —; gather—s; goad—; instruct—; retain—; secure—s; spurn—s; woo—s; —accepts; — accompanies; —admires; —assists; —imitates; —obeys; —practises; —s preserve; — serves.

(See disciple.)

adjectives

heterogeneous; heretical; despairing; immediate; unruly; conservative; obsequious; faithful; diffident; egregious; wayworn; insuperable; sincerest; discontented; favorite; influential; scattered; stout-hearted; deluded.

FOLLOWING

adjectives

prodigious; tremendous; overbearing; unnatural; popular; huge; national; inspired.

verbs

guide—; instruct—; retain—; secure—; spurn—; whip up—; —adheres; —attends; —disbands; —pursues.

(See follower.)

FOLLY

adjectives

sheer; ludicrous; violent; prostrate; wilful; gratuitous; vain; shouting; stupendous; industrious; crowning; derogatory; egregious; serious; rash; present; deplorable; superfluous; sordid; idiotical; capricious; incurable; human; sentimental; disastrous; daring; amiable; pernicious; extreme; enormous; impious; obvious; ingrained; youthful (pl); amorous; harmless; pretty; wild; glaring; covert; pretentious; incredible; ridiculous; countless (pl); flagrant; repudiated; irritating; repented; repeated; absurd; intermittent (pl).

verbs

accuse of—; balk at—of; commit to—; decry—; deplore—; discern—; emancipate from—; fall into—; flatter into—; guard against—; lure into—; mitigate—; regret —; ridicule—; rue—; run after—ies; scorn —; uncover—; vex with—; work—.

(See foolishness, indiscretion, absurdity, infatuation.)

FOMENTATIONS

adjectives

copious; generous; applied; restful; unexpected.

FOND

adverbs

foolishly; unutterably; inordinately; infatuatedly; undyingly; obsequiously; genuinely; unwontedly; particularly; remarkably; childishly; extremely; tenderly; mawkishly; warmly; filially; dutifully; enthusiastically; intensely; spasmodically; ludicrously; demonstratively; temperately; tempestuously; gratefully; impulsively; respectfully; passionately; sincerely; beautifully; frankly; proudly; violently; sentimentally; deeply; heart-warmingly; gratifyingly; temperately; innately; essentially; confessedly; ridiculously; ostentatiously; understandably; justly; devotedly; incongruously; professedly; obviously; palpably.

FONDNESS

adjectives

thoughtful; foolish; maternal; exaggerated; inordinate; unutterable; inbred; infatuated; undying; obsequious; undiscriminating; genuine; unwonted; particular; remarkable; regal; evident; childish; solicitous; usual; extreme; gruesome; hoarded; faithful; unusual; tender; mawkish; precocious.

FOOD

adjectives

unwholesome; essential; wholesome; synthetic; spiritual; health; celestial; unsating; best; marvelous; intellectual; digestible; exceptional; repulsive; abundant; nutritious; natural; precious; unscrupulous; untasted; leathery; toothsome; heedful; unusual; attractive; delicious; inferior; unsavory; highly-spiced; concentrated; smoking; inedible; nectar; canned; adulterated; medicinal; palatable; enjoyable; protective; satisfying; superb; substantial; desirable; piscatorial; frosted; frozen; tonic; out-of-season; obnoxious; packaged; non-fattening; tempting; accustomed; rejuvenating; cheapest; sharp-tasting; execrable; inadequate; concentrated; well-cooked; raw; fundamental; automatic; elaborate; ambrosial; plenteous; delectable; scanty; superb; assimilated; vitalizing; luscious; world-famous; choice; dainty; tasty; good; fine; appetizing; excellent; splendid; inspired; insufficient.

verbs

absorb—; accumulate—; anoint—; assimilate—; bolt—; brown—; consume—; contaminate—; convey—; crave—; deprive of —; devitalize—; dilute—; dispense—; dole out—; expel—; flavor—; forage for—; freight—; masticate—; munch—; order—; partake of—; peptonize—; predigest—; prescribe—; puke—; purvey—; ration—; refine—; requisition—; restrict—; season—; shovel down—; snatch at—; sniff—; subsist on—; vomit—; withdraw—; wolf—; —agrees with; —decreases; —ferments; —irritates; —putrefies; —sustains; —upsets.

(See nourishment, nutriment, meat, bread, rations, victuals, viands, refreshments.)

FOOL

verbs

appear like—; play the—; prove oneself a —; put the—upon; remain—; ridicule—; suspect oneself—; think one a—; turn—; —apes; —beckons; —capers; —complains; —counterfeits; —disregards; *—diverts; —dotes; —gambols; —ignores; —jests; —lets slip; —mistakes; —possesses; —prates; —preaches; —sidles; —mocks.

(See idiot, clown.)

FOOL (v)

adverbs

amiably; ignorantly; wantonly; pitifully; blindly; hatefully; vulgarly; tediously; clumsily; unfeelingly; ungratefully; venomously; deliberately; sportively; shallowly.

(See deceive, trick.)

FOOLERIES

adjectives

bygone; humorous; insouciant.

FOOLHARDY

adverbs

ignorantly; youthfully; boldly; ridiculously; absurdly; sadly; recklessly; fecklessly; carelessly; daringly; desperately; rashly; idiotically; preposterously; indiscreetly; extravagantly; imprudently; childishly; dangerously; terribly; senselessly.

FOOLING

adjectives

gracious; admirable; airy; flippant.

FOOLISH

adverbs

ridiculously; absurdly; ludicrously; unreasonably; insanely; extravagantly; idiotically; ineptly; inanely; irrationally; childishly; stupidly; blatantly; brainlessly; fatuously; injudiciously; rashly; simply; weakly; altogether; supremely; senselessly; fantastically; manifestly; grossly; pathetically.

FOOLISHNESS

adjectives

potent; drunken; colossal; unspeakable.

verbs

awaken—; cast aside—; confess—; convert into—; criticize—; forsake—; govern by—; grieve over—; ignore—; indicate—; persuade to—; practise—; pretend—; provide —; reprimand—; resent—; ridicule—; rue —; shape—; sneer at—; suffer for—; — amuses; —befits; —persists; —smarts; — tempts; prevent—.

(See folly, absurdity; imprudence, indiscretion.)

FOOLS

adjectives

calf-like; luckless; flatulent; simple-minded; amiable; bleating; superstitious; superannuated; ignorant; weak-minded; poor; dappled; wanton; blind; pitiful; blasted; badgering; family; dull; impractical; incapable; honest; besotted; blundering; hateful; crack-brained; veritable; tuneful; precious; misguided; puling; pale; scrawny; wretched; vulgar; allowed; frantic; proud; tedious; witty; clumsy; gullible; strait-laced; soft; dull-eyed; shallow; learned; sweeter; unfeeling; inconstant; damnable; ungrateful; hairy; accursed; motley; officious; positive; brazen; venomous; yawning; consummate; obstinate; conspicuous; fond; deliberate; contemplative; rash; patient; scoundrelly.

FOOT

adjectives

wandering; blistered; emphatic; itching; fiery; stealthy; mutilated; inaudible; noiseless; crushing; punctilious; spurning; feathered; ponderous; restless; fearful; godlike; diminutive; forgetful; cautious; unresisting; swelled; slight; slender; bounding; maladjusted; individual; tentative; struggling; cloven; careless; investigating; nimble; fairy; exquisite; shapely; tiniest; beautiful; small; bare; dangling; naked; extended; sensitive; sandaled; exploring; large-booted; gout-ridden.

verbs

ail—; bandage—; bare—; brace—; chafe —; control—; drum—; elevate—; expose—; injure—; journey on—; lame—; lay—on; massage—; plant—; plunk (colloq.)—; scramble to feet; shod—; shuffle feet; spring to feet; stagger to feet; stamp—; trample under—; wander on—; —aches; —drags;

—pounds; —presses; feet scurry; —sinks in; —soils; feet slacken their pace; —treads on; —trips; —lags; —marks; feet patter.

FOOTFALL

adjectives
lightest; stealthy; pattering (pl).

FOOT-HILLS

adjectives
desolate; barren; uninhabitable.

FOOTHOLD

adjectives
meager; scant; precarious; tentative.

verbs
acquire—; apply—; climb by—; contrive—; devise—; effect—; employ—; gain—; grab —; lose—; manage—; necessitate—; recover—; relax—; release—; warrant—; —agonizes; —enables; —saves.
(See support, hold.)

FOOTING

adjectives
insecure; surer; friendly; uncertain; indispensable; equal; solid; unsteadfast; treacherous; unsteady.

FOOTLIGHTS

verbs
crave—; diminish—; employ—; hover at —; reach—; require—; —attract; —color; —deceive; —divert; —emblazon; —enhance; —flash; —flatter; —flood; —glare; —illumine; —shine; —soften; —suffuse.
(See light, stage, theater.)

FOOTMAN

adjectives
servile; stiff-necked; powder-headed; select.

FOOT-NOTE

adjectives
humble; elusive; helpful; necessary.

FOOTPRINTS

adjectives
fading; fiery; veritable; dim; blurred; blood-stained; halting.

FOOTSTEP

verbs
anticipate—; characterize—; dim—; identify—; listen for—; muffle—; obliterate—;

pad—; recognize—; trace—; tread in—; —destroys; —exposes; —lags; —mars; —marks; —patters; —presses; —resounds; —reveals; —sinks in; —soils; —surprises; —warns; anticipate—.
(See step.)

FOOTSTEPS

adjectives
ringing; impartial; martial; harmless; pattering; plainer; faltering; retreating; ethereal; cautious; shuffling; early; tranquil; hastening; hurried; tottering; hallowed; errant; unwary; coming; paternal; trembling; visiting; rapid; parting; softened; rustling; foul; light; bounding.

FOOTSTOOL

adjectives
radiant; battered; comfortable.

FOOTWAY

adjectives
grass-grown; discernible; winding.

FOOTWEAR

adjectives
superior; expensive; exclusive; comfortable.

FOP

adjectives
priggish; suave; conceited; bold; overdressed; rash; silk-stockinged.

FOPPERIES

adjectives
exaggerated; indescribable; undesirable; unthinkable.

FOPPISH

adverbs
effeminately; fashionably; gallantly; preposterously; foolishly; ludicrously; absurdly; senselessly; conceitedly; ostentatiously; showily; flauntingly; jauntily; blithely; habitually; outlandishly; outrageously; disgustingly; pretentiously; proudly; pridefully; detestably; offensively; abominably.

FORAGING

adjectives
criminal; adept; clumsy; exploratory.

FORAYS

adjectives
occasional; frequent; sudden; ill-starred; remorseless; endless.

FORBEARANCE

adjectives

friendly; generous; unusual; wonderful; abounding; systematic; passive; unexpected; affectionate; good-natured; gentle.

verbs

admire—; commend—; conduct with—; end—; endure with—; excel in—; extort—; feign—; indulge in—; justify—; laud—; learn—; occasion—; practise—; praise—; pretend—; submit with—; suffer—; treat with—; —surprises.

(See patience, mercy, indulgence, tolerance.)

FORBID *(v)*

adverbs

specifically; ostentatiously; positively; dogmatically; rudely; pugnaciously; reluctantly; vehemently.

(See restrain, hinder, prevent.)

FORBIDDING

adverbs

sternly; disagreeably; unreasonably; unpleasantly; wryly; frightfully; gracelessly; grossly; grimly; shockingly; roughly; repulsively; monstrously; horridly; haggardly; dreadfully; odiously; appallingly.

FORCE

adjectives

tangential; orthogonal; material; automatic; selling; striving; provisional; elastic; diminished; perturbative; brainless; all-compelling; intensified; organizing; victorious; quickening; despoiling; radial; disturbing; insurgent; expeditionary; ethical; considerable; available; dramatic; hoplite; campaigning; resistless; influential; chemical; odious; cumulative; inadequate; powerful; imperious; sufficient; tremendous; superior; crushing; irresistible; apogee; vital; antagonistic; extraordinary; deadly; imperial; sullen; enduring; overwhelming; thwarting; civilizing; working; financial; deterring; conflicting; enormous; deterrent; molecular; static; latent; incomprehensible; invading; opposing; mechanical; insuperable; inorganic; vast; mental; formidable; unvarying; headlong; superior; intense; artistic; demoralized; meditative; self-formed; scattered; unguided; blind; striking; social; constant; besieging; threatening; protective; centrifugal; centripetal; objective; spiritual; ignoble; unwieldy; retarding; natural; frictional; universal; concentrated; entire; spontaneous; operant; devitalizing; permanent; virile; efficient; blasphemous; exuberant; attacking; unrestrained; creative; excessive; electro-motive; well-disciplined; human; reverberating; impelling; synthetic; injurious; swelling; explosive; negative; indivisible; malevolent; instrumental; reactionary; fivefold; overpowering; subterranean; repellent; auxiliary; comparative; insignificant; genuine; meager; potent; fearful; harnessed; terrible; unknown; frontier; outnumbered; selective; cohesive; divided; frightful; calculable; fluid; disturbing; controlling; muscular; superhuman; physical; ameliorative; unaided; brute; tragic; moral; missionary; numerical; defending; living; nervous; passionate; innovating; armed; all-pervading; compulsory; disheartened; elemental; original; lacking; famished; available; hostile; demoniac; peculiar; bodily; uncommon; magnetic; mere; undiminished; pneumatic; lifting; terrifying; supplementary; persuasive; domestic; ascensional; revolting; overmastering; equivalent; driving; deep; remedial; vegetative; sheer; dubious; competent; incisive; generative; unrelenting; sacred; quiet; unmerciful; educational; dynamic; almighty; omnipresent; effectual; wavering; plastic; dumb-gazing; supernatural; unrestricted; destructive; reliable; tractive; emotional; multiple; caressing; illustrative; ethereal; subversive; masterful; philosophical; colonial; unseen; international; furious; economic; wave-whirled; gravitating; sustaining; mercenary; much-needed; propulsive; undeniable; motley; subtle; ceaseless; bull-like; sales; uniformed; unpitying; elevatory; inherent; royal; obstructive; dominant; great; contending; innate; imperious; constructive; psychological; exigent; exhausted; prevalent; warring; primal.

verbs

absorb—; accelerate—; acquire—; assail by —; combat—; concentrate—s; defy—; diminish—; discipline—s; dislodge by—; divert —; employ—; focus—upon; join—s; gather —s; generate—; hamper—; harmonize—s; harness—; impede—; intensify—; let loose —s; marshal—s; mass—s; muster—s; neutralize—; nullify—; rally—s; react upon with—; recruit—s; resist—; resort to—; stymie—; suspend—; suppress by—; transmit—; triumph over—; utilize—; weaken—; —s battle; —s engulf; —impels; —s motivate; —subdues; —subsides; —s underlie; —s war.

(See energy, power, strength.)

FORCE (v)

adverbs

deliberately; instinctively; ruthlessly; offensively; gradually; automatically; dramatically; antagonistically; financially; ignobly; spontaneously; blasphemously; malevolently; potently; demoniacally; incisively; dynamically; psychologically; odiously.

(See oblige, compel.)

FORCEFUL

adverbs

impressively; immensely; unwontedly; admirably; intensely; ably; dynamically; potentially; persuasively; vigorously; invincibly; sublimely; eloquently; influentially; strikingly; effectively; effectually; energetically; intentionally; deliberately; trenchantly; vehemently; violently; sensationally; boldly; passionately; vividly.

FORD

adjectives

practicable; convenient.

FOREARMS

adjectives

wiry; sinewy; hairy.

FOREBEARS

verbs

admire—; claim—; commemorate—; extol —; honor—; inherit from—; invent—; judge—; receive from—; uphold—; venerate—; wean away from—; —achieve; —accomplish; —found; —inspire; —instil; —lead; —migrate; —produce; —settle; —suffer.

(See ancestors.)

FOREBODING

verbs

arouse—; assail by—; cast aside—; disperse—; fly from—; heed—; realize—; relate—; ridicule—; —advises; —betokens; —divines; —foretells; —oppresses; —overhangs; —prophesies; —signifies; —warns.

(See apprehension, anticipation, prognostication.)

FOREBODINGS

adjectives

vague; gloomy; dismal; unfavorable; cynical; sorrowful; dim; retroactive; chilling; undefinable; wretched; sinister; grim; inexplicable; incorrect.

FORECAST

adjectives

judicious; vivid; conservative; surprising; accurate; exultant; enlightened; broad; prophetic; provident.

verbs

abide by—; arise from—; believe—; commend—; flout—; heed—; inquire of—; provide—; read—; rectify—; ridicule—; study —; trust—; —advises; —anticipates; —dejects; —indicates; —predicts; —promises; —warns.

(See prophecy, estimate.)

FOREFATHERS

adjectives

crusading; physical; pioneering.

FOREFINGER

adjectives

absolute; gnarled; coercive; swarthy; grimy; argumentative; slim; beckoning; pointed; long; flapping; thick; blunt; admonitory; crooked; mocking.

FOREHEAD

adjectives

flaming; tattooed; unfretful; expanded; marble; smooth; swarthy; luminous; tanned; pale; pallid; mantling; frowning; mountainous; square; fretted; bulging; lofty; spacious; jutting; powerful; branded; fabled; dusky; livid; ample; dirty; well-developed; unsustained; knobby; somber; tranquil; exquisite; disfigured; shaped; wide; massive; cloudless; wrinkled; deep-grooved; damp; moist; perspiring; mean; calm; burning; towering; bold; throbbing; princely; well-shaped; fine; narrow; aristocratic; intelligent; brainy; anxious; receding; unbashful.

verbs

cloud—; distinguish by—; furrow—; knot —; mop—; raise—; scar—; —wrinkles; —puckers; —pulsates; —throbs.

(See face, head.)

adverbs

harmlessly; objectionably; inadmissably; unconformably; strangely; remotely; irrelevantly; outlandishly; undeniably; ostentatiously; palpably; essentially; obviously; disagreeably; inconceivably; relatively; discordantly; impertinently; fantastically; exotically; intrusively; inimically; disinterestedly; extraneously.

FOREIGNER

adjectives

high-born; cursed; invading; enlightened; hated; distinguished.

verbs

accept—; admit—; allow—; Americanize—; beguile—; deport—; enhance—; entertain —; examine—; limit—s; lodge—; naturalize—; reject—; school—in; smuggle in—s; welcome—; —s colonize; —s crowd; —s intrude; —s settle in.

(See alien.)

FORERUNNER

adjectives

elegant; early; indigenous.

FORESEE (*v*)

adverbs

dimly; timorously; morbidly; clairvoyantly; vividly; mysteriously; supernaturally; unerringly.

(See anticipate, prepare, foretell.)

FORESIGHT

adjectives

shrinking; patriotic; economic; fiery; sagacious; divine; prudent; keen.

FOREST

adjectives

dull; motionless; intricate; illimitable; isolated; teak; aboriginal; virgin; lonely; primeval; ilex; adjacent; unawakened; green-haired; trackless; preservable; cathedral-vaulted; thick-studded; favoring; natural; solemn; tropical; impenetrable; solitary; mildew; uncleared; enchanted; rank; moon-illumined; great; silent; desolate; interminable; incense-bearing; magnificent; fragrant; murmuring; umbrageous; blackened; sun-filled; flaming; black; golden; tinted; unspoiled; moaning; boundless; thicketed; still; thick; rude; untrodden; dripping; shadowed; unwilling; melancholy; somber; tangled; pine-carpeted; infinite; tantalizing; hazy; unbroken; coniferous; panther-peopled; odorous; stretching; hoary; intervening; matted; immense; majestic; fast-darkening; surrounding; dreary; leafless; silver-powdered; limitless; disenchanted; unsurveyed; thrifty; unwholesome; girdling; trackless; frowning; consuming; scathed; ancient; encircling; mighty; massy; monotonous; luxuriant; sleeping; uncouth; miniature; black-bearded; encroaching; slumberous.

verbs

conserve—s; denude—s; deplete—; dot with —s; entangle in—; fell—; guard—; harbor in—; infest—; invade—; jeopardize—s; level—; patrol—; poach in—; preserve—; raze—; skirt—; thin out—; wipe out—; —abounds in; —encircles; —extends; —flourishes; —ranges; —whispers.

(See jungle.)

FORETELL (*v*)

adverbs

portentously; sensationally; uncannily; clairvoyantly; accurately; unerringly.

(See predict, portend, foresee.)

FORETHOUGHT

adjectives

divine; anxious; endless; deliberate.

verbs

commend—; decide with—; discipline to—; employ—; exercise—; exhibit—; indulge in —; mark by—; necessitate—; note for—; praise—; provide—; save by—; submit to —; urge—; —assures; —determines; —enables; —impedes; —influences; —obviates; —overcomes; —prepares; —reaps.

(See consideration, prudence, precaution.)

FORFEIT

adjectives

unredeemable; profitless; vain.

verbs

call—; demand—; exact—; impose—; incur—; lose—; offer—; pay—; penalize with —; punish with—; redeem—; remit—; subject to—; take—; —clears; —deprives; —redeems; —releases; —ruins.

(See fine, penalty.)

FORFEIT (v)

adverbs
automatically; legally; irrevocably; inevitably; provisionally; nominally.
(See fine, pay.)

FORGE

adjectives
gleaming; sounding; flashing.

FORGE (v)

adverbs
laboriously; dexterously; artfully; audaciously; deliberately; daringly; subtly.
(See force, push.)

FORGERY

adjectives
literary; flimsy; deliberate; audacious.

FORGET (v)

adverbs
mercifully; promptly; speedily; momentarily; eternally; wantonly; deliberately; conveniently; prudently; flagrantly.
(See ignore, neglect, overlook.)

FORGETFUL

adverbs
lamentably; carelessly; idly; inattentively; senilely; agedly; hopelessly; deplorably; unfortunately; conveniently; tactfully; forgivingly; gracefully; irritatingly; provokingly; vexatiously; incurably; helplessly; nervously; weakly; treacherously; sadly; terribly; inexcusably; criminally; tragically.

FORGETFULNESS

adjectives
conceivable; dull; momentary; frank; heavenly; atrocious; slumberous; unkind; eternal.

FORGIVE (v)

adverbs
graciously; magnanimously; indulgently; meekly; heartily; mutually; patiently; solemnly; cordially; spiritually.
(See excuse, acquit.)

FORGIVENESS

adjectives
infinite; mutual; implored.

FORGIVING

adverbs
gracefully; indulgently; wisely; discreetly; wholly; tolerantly; tactfully; generously; graciously; infinitely; nobly; magnanimously; charitably; benignly; unexpectedly; surprisingly; chivalrously; gallantly; affably; extremely.

FORGOTTEN

adverbs
sadly; altogether; unhappily; conveniently; cold-heartedly; unfeelingly; wretchedly; unpardonably; inexcusably; carelessly; brutally; thoughtlessly; mercilessly; selfishly; ungratefully; thanklessly; friendlessly; desolately; forlornly; miserably; disconsolately; appallingly; shockingly.

FORK

adjectives
gesticulating; triple; excoriated; soft; tender; furrowy; vibrating; tuning.

verbs
barb with—; brandish—; cast with—; convey on—; draw with—; hook with—; impale on—; jab with—; lift—; pursue with —; stab with—; —pierces; —prongs; —spears; —transfers.
(See knife.)

FORLORN

adverbs
lonesomely; terribly; pitiably; pathetically; uncommonly; utterly; listlessly; silently; glumly; resignedly; profoundly; weirdly; singularly; immensely; blankly; unutterably.

FORM

adjectives
absurd; active; acute; admirable; adorable; aesthetic; aggravated; airy; ample; analogic; angular; antique; apparent; archaic; archangelic; architectural; artistic; athletic; attenuated; barbarous; barest; beastlike; beautiful; bent; bestial; bewildering; bewitching; birdlike; blanketed; blasting; bleeding; bliss-inspiring; bloated; bounding; boyish; briefest; brigand-like; broken; buckskin-clad; burly; changing; charming; chaste; childish; chronic; circular; clamorous; classic; clothed; codified (pl); collectible; colloidal; comely; commanding; compact; complicated; concentrated; conciliatory; concrete; condensed; constitutional; contrary; convenient; conventional; corrupt-

518

ed; countless (pl); creeping; crowded; crumpled; cultivated; cumulative; curvilinear; debasing; cylindrical; dainty; decrepit; desired; definite; democratic; detailed; determinate; diabolic; diluted; disguised; disrobed; dissolving; distressing; distribution; durable; earliest; ecstatic; elastic; elegant; elliptic; emasculated; erect; ephemeral; epistolary; equitable; established; erroneous; eventual; exaggerated; express; expurgated; exquisite; faded; fair; faltering; famished; fan-shaped; fantasmalike; fantastic; faultless; feigned; feminine; fiery; flawless; flitting; floral; fluid; fragile; fruitful; gallant; fundamental; garbled; gaseous; gigantic; gasping; gaunt; geometrical; ghostly; glancing; gleaming; gloomy; glorious; glowing; gnarled; graceful; goodly; graceless; grandiose; granular; graphic; greyhound-like; groaning; guileless; handsome; harmless; harmonic; heavenly; herculean; heroic; historic; horrible; huddled; hulking; human; hungry; hurrying; ill-clad; imposing; improvisational; incoherent; inconvenient; indirect; individual; indurate; inert; inexorable; infantile; ingenious; intimate; instrumental; intricate; irritated; jovial; jostling; kicking; languid; lanky; lifeless; long; low; magnified; majestic; malignant; mainfold; manly; mantled; maritime; metrical; microscopic; milder; mitigated; moderate; modified; moldering; monophonic; monumental; motionless; motley (pl); moving; mundane; myriad; mythologic; native; never-shifting; needle-shaped; obese; offensive; oligarchic; operatic; organic; outward; palpable; palatable; particular; pathetic; permanent; plastic; pliant; poetic; pompous; portly; prescribed; pretentious; printed; pristine; prone; proper; prostrate; protesting; proverbial; provincial; puerile; puerperal; pure; quantitative; quivering; rebellious; recitative; recumbent; regular; related; reluctant; repugnant; respectful; retiring; rhythmic; robust; rigid; sardonic; scholastic; semicircular; semi-elliptical; senseless; serpentine; shadowy; shaky; shapely; simple; shivering; shriveled; shrouded; sinking; shrunken; singular; skeleton; slender; slim; smug; slouching; slumping; spare; spectral; spheroidal; spiritualized; squalid; staggering; standard; startling; stately; stiff; strange; strong; structural; struggling; stunted; subsumed; suffering; suitable; superb; swallow-tailed; symmetrical; tall; tapering; technical; tedious; theistic; thickening; thin;

tiny; titanic; tortuous; tottering; towering; traditional; transient; typical; unadulterated; unblemished; undulating; undying; unhealthy; unimaginable; unintelligible; united; unmatched; unnatural; unphonetic; unremembered; unsubstantial; unusual; vacant; valuable; vaporous; varied; vast; veiled; venerable; vicarious; villanelle; virulent; visible; visionary; warlike; wasted; wedge-shaped; weird; well-balanced; willowy; feeble; coherent; wolflike; wooden; writhing; conversational; peculiar; pedagogic; peerless; phantom.

verbs
accept—; adhere to—; assume—; conventionalize—; develop—; distort—; enhance —; evince—; gain—; insist on—; jeopardize—; lend—to; model on—; pattern—; retain—; scoff at—; standardize—; —embraces; —sways.
(See method, ritual, style, model.)

FORM (*v*)
adverbs
voluntarily; theoretically; successively; gracefully; dexterously; expeditiously; inadvertently; prematurely; originally; insensibly; ultimately; delicately; collectively; ingeniously; durably; aesthetically; constitutionally; cumulatively; democratically; diabolically; ephemerally; erroneously; fantastically; geometrically; grandiosely; majestically; organically; symmetrically; tortuously.
(See shape, mould.)

FORMAL
adverbs
extremely; unusually; officially; strictly; conventionally; dogmatically; ritualistically; legally; ecclesiastically; absolutely; undeviatingly; explicitly; solemnly; ceremoniously; curiously; gracefully; splendidly; brilliantly; terribly; awesomely; punctiliously; meticulously; particularly; needlessly; coldly; unnecessarily; foolishly.

FORMALITY
adjectives
concluding; statuesque; affected; stiff; precise; professional; imposing; architectural; stately; icy; tired; tiring; degrading; rigid; joyless.

verbs
adopt—; break—; conduct with—; conform to—; discard—; dress in—; don—; ease—;

519

encase in—; end—ies; endure—; engage in —; execute with—; exercise—; insist on—; observe—ies; perform—ies; peach—ies; preserve—ies; relax—; require—; school in —; shed—; shun—; —corsets; —exasperates; —retards; —stifles; —preserves.
(See conventionality, ceremony.)

FORMATION

adjectives
geological; humanistic; proper; peculiar; meteoric; tertiary; harmonic; crude; various (pl); fantastic; shaft-like; remarkable; delusional; delicate; inanimate; slow.

verbs
abet —; aid —; bar —; check —; conceal — of; discover —; divest of —; emerge from —; precede —; prevent —; shake —; sponsor —; suppress —; whip into —; — breaks; — divides; — splits; — takes place.
(See arrangement, development.)

FORMULA

adjectives
mathematical; moral; abstract; original; magical; aphoristic; invariable; devotional; bristling; perfected; barren; creative; dead; noble; majestic; definite.

verbs
accept—; apply—; apprise of—; bungle—; change—; coin—; compound—; compute—; devise—; employ—; evolve—; express in—; falsify—; fetter by—; fulfill—; reduce to—; simplify—; utilize—; work from—; —clarifies; —curbs; —states.
(See rule, form, prescription, principle, ritual.)

FORMULATE (v)

adverbs
peculiarly; scientifically; enterprisingly; academically; skillfully; dexterously; crudely; professionally.
(See plan, prepare.)

FORMULATION

adjectives
academic; scientific; definite; crude.

FORSAKE (v)

adverbs
reluctantly; unnaturally; disastrously; faithlessly; shamefully; churlishly; unfeelingly.
(See abandon, quit, leave.)

FORSAKEN

adverbs
desolately; lamentably; desperately; helplessly; shockingly; utterly; unhappily; coldheartedly; unfeelingly; wretchedly; miserably; appallingly; friendlessly; mercilessly; unpardonably; thoughtlessly; cruelly; brutally; disconsolately; dreadfully; pitifully.

FORT

adjectives
outlying; improvised; grim; silent; impregnable; well-garrisoned; deserted; strategic; hidden; camouflaged.

FORTIFICATION

adjectives
wasted; noble; remarkable; permanent; extensive; grim; stupendous; medieval; tremendous; useless; antiquated.

verbs
arm —; assail —; charge —; erect —; fire on —; maintain —; march to —; necessitate —; plan —; provide —; require —; shatter —; — defends; — guards; — overlooks; — preserves; — protects; — repels; — shields; — surrounds; — yields.
(See castle, stronghold.)

FORTIFY (v)

adverbs
unwaveringly; speedily; stalwartly; mysteriously; testily; crudely; powerfully; permanently; grimly; medievally; antiquatedly; extensively.
(See defend, guard, protect, resist.)

FORTITUDE

adjectives
Christian; matchless; admirable; uncomplaining; unpretentious; placid; remarkable; surprising; stoic; unshakable; intestinal; sustained; physical; iron; enduring; calm; extraordinary; sufficient; stolid.

verbs
admire —; arm with —; bear with —; commend —; conduct with —; consider —; endure with —; excel in —; exhibit —; laud —; mark by —; occasion —; practice —; praise —; require —; summon —; tolerate with —; treat with —; — amazes; — surprises.
(See courage, endurance, strength.)

520

FORTRESS

adjectives

level; mighty; permanent; improvised; baronial; gloomy; island; feminine; garrisoned; inaccessible; dismantled; frowning; seductive; insulated; frost-locked; grim; walled; magnificent; medieval; ragged; beleaguered; rock-bound; impregnable; isolated.

FORTUITOUS

adverbs

curiously; obviously; luckily; presumably; casually; wholly; comically; inexplicably; mysteriously; admittedly; ludicrously; certainly; providentially; frequently; purportedly; evidently; luckily; awkwardly; pleasantly; tragically; undependably; uneasily; uncertainly; opportunely; ironically; favorably; conveniently.

FORTUNATE

adverbs

blessedly; splendidly; politically; incidentally; moderately; luckily; unwontedly; propitiously; systematically; regularly; uniformly; brilliantly; inherently; triumphantly; inexpressibly; inscrutably; signally; notoriously; unaccountably; unwarrantably; significantly; mysteriously; immensely; marvellously; ultimately; enviably; conveniently; ingeniously; accidentally; reasonably; highly; extremely; happily; fairly; auspiciously; luckily; providentially; remarkably; unusually; consistently; gratifyingly; pleasantly; agreeably; fittingly; delightfully; appropriately.

FORTUNE

adjectives

fairer; munificent; fallen; rude; adverse; cursed; blessed; varying; colossal; competent; considerate; gracious; splendid; political; forlorn; individual; shattered; ample; stupendous; unparalleled; equal; favorable; blind; moderate; stormy; good; fitful; frowning; drooping; public; invulnerable; tottering; wretched; rare; fluctuating; enormous; crooked; humbled; squandered; dire; subsequent; brilliant; indulgent; inconstant; princely; changing; gloomy; wild; patrimonial; narrow; fierce; keen; adventurous; sunny; superior; promising; dissipated; extraordinary; desperate; fouler; spiritual; broken; prodigious; relenting; signal; hostile; unconfirmed; fretted; sure; disastrous; dependent; ultimate; doubtful; waning.

verbs

accumulate —; amass —; bemoan —; bewail —; dissipate —; establish —; fall into —; garner —; hazard —; mend —; net —; prophesy —; reap —; recoup —; replenish —; restore —; retrieve —; stake — on; struggle for —; tempt —; wipe away —; wreck —; —s ascend; —s crash; — ebbs; — fails; — favors; — flows; — melts away.

(See chance, fate, destiny, estate, possessions, success, wealth.)

FORWARD (v)

adverbs

conscientiously; progressively; unselfishly; magnanimously; munificently; disastrously; ultimately.

(See advance, send.)

FORWARDNESS

adjectives

intrusive; brusque; brash.

FOSSIL

adjectives

Paleozoic; contained; stone-pervaded; mammalian; minute; significant.

FOSTER (v)

adverbs

cunningly; gradually; effectually; deliberately; diligently; cordially; subtly; diabolically; treacherously; philosophically.

(See support, promote.)

FOULNESS

adjectives

horrid; Stygian; dank; miasmic.

FOUNDATION

adjectives

massive; explanatory; moral; splendid; well-laid; unorthodox; rational; permanent; slender; substantial; antiquated; shifting; virtual; respectable; monstrous; dangerous; durable; treacherous; solid; floating; everlasting; enviable; philosophic; sufficient; economical; lasting; broad; crumbling; reciprocal; thrilling; slenderizing.

verbs

build —; correct —; deprive of —; dig at —; erect —; founder at —; ground on —; jeopardize —; lay —; protect —; ruffle —; sap —; shake —; strike at —; undermine —; — crumbles; — remains; — shudders; — stands; — supports.

(See base, basis, principles.)

FOUNDER

adjectives
traditional; energetic; patient; spiritual.

FOUNDLING

adjectives
helpless; undernourished; scantily-clad.

FOUNT

adjectives
sapphire; never-failing; continual; perennial; babbling; sacred; consecrated; youth-giving.

FOUNTAIN

adjectives
paved; wide-spreading; inexhaustible; burning; searchless; trickling; foul; ancient; perennial; bitter; many-voiced; spouting; celestial; ever-filling; welling; untainted; fresh; life-sealed; gurgling; weedy; pleasant; fire-laden; reedy; living; perpetual; hillside; fiery; soulless; bubbling; distant; sporting; earthly; fresh; ceaseless; gushing; unlocked; unfailing; lightning; cool; ablutionary; flashing; geyserlike.

verbs
admire —; choke —; illuminate —; — bubbles; — dances; — flings; — floods; — gleams; — gurgles; — gushes; — plays; — sallies; — scintillates; — sings; — sparkles; — splashes; — spouts; — sprinkles; — spurts; — twinkles; — weeps.
(See spring, brook, spray.)

FOUNTAIN-PEN

verbs
feed —; fill —; illustrate with —; pocket —; press on —; regulate —; reserve in —; store in —; transcribe with —; uncap —; — blotches; — drips; — leaks; — scratches; — spills; — stains.
(See pen.)

FOWL

adjectives
domestic; plump; glossy; long-billed; gluttonous; winged; screaming; sea; poor; miserable; ravenous; fearful; wild; skinny; sapless; lagging; ungainly; succulent; lean.

verbs
behead —; boil —; breed —s; call —; catch —; devour —; feed —s; house —s; roast —; serve —; shoo —; snare —; steal —; — cackles; — crows; —s flock; —s gather; — pecks; — scratches.
(See hen, rooster, bird, chicken, turkey, duck, etc.)

FOX

adjectives
stealthy; caverned; cunning; loping; sly; sleek; slinking.

verbs
chase —; ensnare —; farm —; pursue —; raise —es; skin —; trap —; — burrows; — claws; — darts; — digs; — displays; — excavates; — fools; — leaps; — outwits; — preys on; — roams; — tricks.
(See animal.)

FOXY

adverbs
naturally; cautiously; shrewdly; artfully; abominably; treacherously; trickily; subtly; sharply; evasively; skilfully; adroitly; astutely; deceptively; cunningly; unexpectedly; profoundly; unusually; diplomatically; insidiously; deplorably; unfortunately; strategically; commercially; financially; cannily.

FOYER

adjectives
bare; grotesque; sumptuous.

FRACAS

verbs
bridle —; curb —; describe —; enjoy —; enter —; indulge in —; inflame to —; inquire into —; instigate —; interrupt —; invite —; involve in —; occasion —; prevent —; produce —; quell —; raise —; referee —; — annoys; — irritates; — subsides; — unnerves.
(See fight, brawl, uproar, disturbance.)

FRACTION

adjectives
insignificant; minute; undue; slender; mixed.

verbs
break into —s; denote —; diminish to —; dispense with —; dispute —; divide into —s; dwindle to —; express —; include —;

indicate —; instruct in —s; measure by —; observe —; piece into —s; reduce to —; — irks; — puzzles.

(See fragment.)

FRACTIOUS

adverbs

unmanageably; irritatingly; distressingly; undeniably; notoriously; uncontrollably; ungovernably; abominably; detestably; petulantly; highly; utterly; terribly; peculiarly; singularly; oddly; queerly; churlishly; excitably; snappily; captiously; cantankerously; restively; intolerably; utterly.

FRACTURE

verbs

cast —; compound —; depress —; examine —; expose —; fasten —; incur —; inflict —; prevent —; produce —; recognize —; reconcile —; reduce —; splice —; splint —; support —; x-ray —; — divides; — heals; — mends; — shocks; — splits; — splinters; — unites.

(See rupture, breach.)

FRAGILE

adverbs

delicately; infirmly; weakly; languidly; increasingly; terribly; totteringly; tremulously; decrepitly; defensely; flimsily; nervously; frightfully; shakily; hopelessly; irremediably; uncommonly.

FRAGMENT

adjectives

unrelated; expurgated; enormous; intelligible; welcome; warlike; sparkling; numberless (pl); cumbrous; colossal; tattered; insignificant; scattered (pl); hissing; weary; whirling; clattering; chaotic; shattered; quarried; incoherent; isolated; misty; artless; halting; detached; ill-smelling; connected; cometary; heterogeneous; massive; indubitable; massy; rough; curious; countless (pl); weary; fancy; important; disjointed; grand; beauteous; sculptured; pitiful; brilliant; restless; exquisite.

verbs

break into—s; cast into—s; cherish—s; conceal—s; discard—s; excise—s; extract—s; gather up—s; hack into—s; preserve—s; reduce to—s; retain—s; rip into—s; scatter —s; splinter into—s; strew—s; tear into—s; —embarrasses; —s fill; —projects; —s scatter.

(See part, portion, piece, remnant, chip.)

FRAGRANCE

adjectives

fruity; heady; worldly; delicious; favorite; faint; clinging; delightful; ardor-awakening; sweet; visible; strong; tea; delicate; full-blown; nocturnal; powerful; cloverlike; midsummer; ambrosial; breathing; wholesome; odorous; salty; diffusing; fog; subtle; autumnal; exotic; worldly; unmatched; feverish; ineffable; homelike; dewy; aromatic; spicy; manifold; healthful; nutlike; honied; evanescent; blended; provocative; woody; sense-dissolving; embodied; balmy.

verbs

admire—; anoint with—; delight in—; diffuse—; emit—; exude—; fill with—; gather —; inhale—; savor—; share—; veil in—; yield—; —assaults; —clouds; —edifies; — floats; —outlasts; —permeates; —pleases; —scents; —stirs.

(See sweetness, odor, perfume, scent, smell.)

FRAGRANT

adverbs

pleasantly; spicily; redolently; sweetly; pungently; arrestingly; refreshingly; seductively; pleasingly; alluringly; strongly; delicately; faintly; exquisitely; enchantingly; charmingly; overpoweringly; overwhelmingly; delectably; intoxicatingly; lingeringly; exotically; romantically; evanescently.

FRAIL

adverbs

terribly; pitifully; unusually; increasingly; nervously; feebly; decrepitly; languidly; defenselessly; helplessly; hopelessly; appallingly; shockingly; miserably; wretchedly.

FRAILTY

adjectives

human; decorous; female; universal; patent; obvious; apparent; inexcusable.

verbs

admit—; condemn—; confess—; crush—; cure—; disguise—; draw—; fall into—; hide—; inherit—; overcome—; play on—; remove—; reveal—; seek—; surrender to —; tempt—; tolerate—; treat—; —s cheat; —shames.

(See weakness.)

FRAME

adjectives
consistent; wasted; mortal; lordly; narrow; thrilling; graceful; universal; spreading; comfortable; lean; becoming; ebonite; tottering; decrepit; unhelpful; nerveless; ponderous; imposing; corporal; unbreathing; stalwart; elastic; weary; lank; long-limbed; grateful; smitten; impassioned; growing; iron; sinful; kindred; anxious; well-knit; wretched; ultimate; chilled; feeble; inexplicable; racked; bent; gilded; blanket-covered; spiritless; huge; husky; faltering; tortured; powerful; pain-worn; portly; delightful; luminous; gaunt; slender; fine; massive; reluctant; dying; arabesque; unlovely; large; meager; hardy; well-proportioned; trembling; oddest; tuneful; irksome; emaciated; attentuated; vigorous; buxom; vital; mystic; uneasy; moldering; unpleasant; perforated; unresisting; shriveled; goodly; measured; spare; matchless; hardy; ethereal; unearthly; daring; vandal; delicate; physical; shrunken; magnificent; seductive; vast; rugged; muscular; vigorous; sky-scraper; flexible; gigantic; stocky; osseous; thick-set; hard; light; wiry; loose; stolid; weak.

verbs
adjust—; brace—; construct—; dissolve—; enclose in—; enter into—; fashion—; fence with—; fix to—; lodge in—; move—; overthrow—; place in—; regulate—; set in—; set up—; shape on—; weave on—; —arises; —collapses; —s differ; —shuts out; —stretches.
(See structure, case.)

FRAME (v)

adverbs
brilliantly; picturesquely; substantially; inexplicably; vaguely; gracefully; imposingly; luminously; seductively.
(See devise, contrive, plan.)

FRAMEWORK

adjectives
rigid; skeletal; essential.

FRANCHISE

adjectives
elective; tangible; legal; limited.

verbs
acquire—; admit to—; advocate—; bequeath —to; deprive of—; enjoy—; establish—; exercise—; forbid—; grant—; invest with —; limit—; possess—; purchase—; renew —; restore—; seek—; sell—; violate—; —benefits; —empowers; —exempts; —privileges; —protects.
(See right, exemption, freedom.)

FRANK

adverbs
delightfully; charmingly; bitterly; cruelly; attractively; distressingly; unusually; characteristically; sarcastically; crudely; appallingly; refreshingly; inordinately; artlessly; innocently; ingenuously; plainly; guilelessly; unaffectedly; apparently; strikingly; naively.

FRANKNESS

adjectives
manly; irrevocable; perfect; natural; cordial; timid; placid; virtuous; medical; absolute; inestimable; unsophisticated; superfluous; careless; unprepossessing; engaging; simple; uncomplimentary; brotherly; military; hearty; beautiful; intimate; indolent; imperious; brisk; medieval; sardonic; straightforward; youthful; uninhibited; repellent; naive; savage; genial; painful.

verbs
admit—; confess with—; declare with—; experience—; inflict—; meet with—; occasion—; permeate with—; relish—; require —; return—; reveal—; —annoys; —cuts; —disquiets; —hurts; —mortifies; —nettles; —offends; —pains; —pricks; —ruffles; —stings; —wounds.
(See candor, fairness, liberalism.)

FRANTIC

adverbs
irritably; passionately; distractedly; feverishly; hysterically; nervously; wildly; eccentrically; crazily; fanatically; incoherently; insensately; rabidly; starkly; acutely; desperately; uncontrollably; irrepressibly; unappeasably; ungovernably; terribly; pitifully; frightfully.

FRATERNAL

adverbs
genially; convivially; generously; warmly; indulgently; closely; remotely; intimately; congenially; harmoniously; tranquilly; dependably; quietly; remarkably; securely; comfortably.

adjectives

unremitting; shameful; presumable; wretched; economic; mercenary; pious; gigantic; petty; manifest; glaring; meditated; flagrant; barefaced.

verbs

beguile with—; commit—; cover—; declaim against—; design—; detect—; discern—; draw into—; engage in—; execute—; impose—upon; indulge in—; glory in—; lament—; perceive—; perpetrate—; practise —; prevent—; punish—; rectify—; reveal —; suspect—; taint with—; uncover—; unearth—; —amuses; —deceives; —dejects; —enables; —provokes; —ruins; —succeeds. (See deception, deceit, trick, dishonesty, cheat, swindle.)

FRAUDULENT

adverbs

criminally; obviously; manifestly; apparently; openly; flagrantly; subtly; artfully; shrewdly; cleverly; adroitly; sharply; smartly; miserably; indefensibly; basely; grossly; knavishly; villainously; disgracefully; ignominiously; meanly; shabbily; unscrupulously; extremely; infamously; notoriously; surreptitiously.

FRAY

adjectives

deadly; fair; bloody; lawless; late; obstinate; youthful; horrid; clamorous; devilish; holy; mimic; thundering; insidious; nefarious.

verbs

charge into—; clash in—; commence—; crush in—; curb—; describe—; indulge in —; inquire into—; instigate—; interrupt—; involve in—; occasion—; plunge into—; raise—; referee—; —boils; —disperses; — frightens; —irritates; —unnerves; —disturbs.
(See fracas, combat, fight, commotion.)

FREAK

adjectives

grotesque; sudden; disgraceful; wanton; fashionable; unaccountable; fierce; impossible; peculiar.

FREAKISH

adverbs

outlandishly; ostentatiously; manifestly; absurdly; shamelessly; intentionally; disgustingly; inexcusably; laughably; idiotically; teasingly; tormentingly; erratically; eccentrically; fantastically; whimsically; particularly; wantonly; waywardly; uncomfortably; frivolously; terribly; unexpectedly.

FRECKLES

verbs

bleach—; conceal—; discern—; encourage —; mark with—; produce—; remove—; spangle with—; sprinkle with—; —cover; —dapple; —discolor; —dot; —embarrass; —mar; —spot; —stain; —variegate.

FREE

adverbs

gloriously; joyously; happily; independently; finally; utterly; completely; absolutely; unconditionally; irrepressibly; irresponsibly; gaily; blithely; merrily; unaccountably; gladly; jubilantly; incredibly; fortunately; luckily; unbelievably; unexpectedly.

FREE (v)

adverbs

ultimately; eventually; legally; economically; filially; unrestrainedly; magnanimously; unquestionably.
(See liberate, release.)

FREEDOM

adjectives

incomparable; bold; unbounded; perfect; unquestioned; unnoticed; personal; newly-regained; unchecked; untrammeled; licentious; perpetual; untamed; unbridled; annihilating; determined; brave; practical; deserving; airy; courtly; subjective; reverent; half-bashful; half-saucy; hopeless; complete; comparative; dignified; economic; accustomed; refined; filial; spotless; exceptional; intellectual; unbroken; unrestrained; priceless; dearly-bought; bloody; unwonted.

verbs

achieve—; advocate—; alienate—; announce—; assert—; break for—; confer—on; curb—; curtail—; deprive of—; encroach on—; expand with—; exult in—; flutter to—; guarantee—; hamper—; heighten—; impair—; imperil—; infringe on—;

menace—; relinquish—; resign—; retain—; strive for—; suppress—; surrender—; thrill in—; trample—; wed to—.

(See liberty, independence, ease, frankness.)

FREEZE (v)

adverbs

nightly; seasonally; spectrally; glacially; dangerously; tragically; formidably; permanently.

(See congeal, chill.)

FREEZING

adjectives

unexpected; bulk; seasonal; costly; artificial.

FREIGHT

adjectives

human; perishable; superannuated; additional; weary; animate; precious.

verbs

bear—; charge for—; convey by—; deduct for—; deposit—; despatch by—; export—; handle—; hold up—; load—; pay—; protect —; store—; transport by—; —s collide; —costs; —weighs.

(See cargo, load, transportation.)

FRENZIED

adverbs

deliriously; joyously; madly; wildly; excitedly; feverishly; insanely; fanatically; violently; completely; pathetically; jealously; inexpressibly; appallingly; alarmingly; dangerously; abnormally; incurably; deplorably.

FRENZY

adjectives

astonishing; fanatical; violent; selfish; poetic; complete; pathetic; maddening; full; jealous; dread; untimely; dreadful; inexpressible.

verbs

anticipate—; attack in—; dart with—; drive to—; fall into—; fight with—; imbue with —; incur—of; indulge in—; inflame to—; infuriate to—; inspire—; lash into—; plunge into—; provoke—; roll in—; salve —; seize with—; shake with—; shriek in—; strike with—; subject to—; throw into—; unloose—; —alarms; —descends; —disturbs; —seizes.

(See agitation, fury, madness, enthusiasm, fanaticism.)

FREQUENCY

adjectives

determinate; disheartening; distasteful; persistent; increasing; nervous.

verbs

commit with—; condemn—; diminish—; displease with—; encourage—; endure—; enjoy—; impose with—; increase—; justify—; occur with—; necessitate—; reduce—; relax—; repeat with—; return with—; vary—.

(See speed.)

FREQUENT

adverbs

annoyingly; disturbingly; unnecessarily; unusually; recurrently; monotonously; tiresomely.

FREQUENT (v)

adverbs

intermittently; habitually; persistently; carelessly; rashly; daringly; unconventionally; customarily.

(See visit.)

FRESH

adverbs

delightfully; unquestionably; genuinely; lusciously; deliciously; lately; exquisitely; excellently; capitally; superlatively; inimitably; admirably; pleasantly; agreeably; wonderfully; marvelously; emphatically; perfectly.

FRESHNESS

adjectives

original; enviable; dewy; lyrical; immortal; permeating; morning; faded; dreadful; youthful; infinite; cool; guaranteed; astonishing; clean; abounding; genial; delicate; sweet; unsunned; soothing; bracing; glorious; frosty; gay; perennial; breezy; elastic; vernal; odorous; wholesome.

FRET (v)

adverbs

pettishly; childishly; morbidly; irritatingly; unreasoningly; unintelligently; abnormally; pathologically.

(See vex, irritate, tease, annoy.)

FRETFUL

adverbs

whiningly; peevishly; complainingly; nervously; spitefully; feverishly; pathetically; unfortunately; unbearably; intolerably; sullenly; restlessly; capriciously; jealously; appallingly; shockingly; surprisingly; unreasonably; foolishly; needlessly; groundlessly; sadly; unwisely; shrewishly; querulously; cantankerously; restively; perversely; terribly; captiously.

FRIABLE

adverbs
desirably; admirably; sufficiently; satisfactorily; duly; frangibly; impalpably; wonderfully; astonishingly; surprisingly; superbly; splendidly; adequately; amply.

FRIAR

adjectives
coarse; unreverend; unhallowed; bungling; mendicant; saucy; true; meddling; frantic; humble; pious.

FRICTION

adjectives
constant; incessant; insufficient; sectional; cheerful; spiritual; unnecessary; destructive; laborious; tidal; continual; unpleasant.

verbs
expose to—; ignite by—; prophesy—; suffer —; sustain—; transmit—; undergo—; — agitates; —blisters; —chafes; —corrodes; —develops; —endangers; —grates; —polishes; —resists; —rubs; —scrubs; — smooths; —stings; —tingles; —torments; — wears away.
(See resistance.)

FRIEND

adjectives
indefatigable; well-meaning; circumspect; valued; discriminating; influential; wonderful; feathered; familiar; perfidious; neglecting; faithless; thankless; all-seeing; political; social; frank; loyal; impressionable; impetuous; fiery; sworn; intimate; gracious; genial; impartial; democratic; discouraging; unprofitable; disinguished; disinterested; ardent; benignant; charitable; obliging; light-hearted; disapproving; enthusiastic; serviceable; congenial; dexterous; hollow; affectionate; distressful; devoted; indiscreet; candid; bubbling; esteemed; immediate; marvelous; illustrious; indisposed; courtly; unfortunate; lasting; solid; lifelong; profligate; distant; utmost; roistering; tyrannous; ancient; medieval; timid; loving; acquainted; unflinching; high-toned; imaginary; lawless; ecclesiastical; sable; caressing; inconstant; confidential; honorable; quondam; bleating; censorious; de-

parted; much-lamented; scrutinizing; numerous (pl); timorous; magnanimous; mute; amiable; philanthropic; treacherous; absent; traitorous; consumptive; blushing; hospitable; lazy; valuable; firm; velvet; festive; veteran; sweet; judicious; coolest; biteless; inebriated; unselfish; inestimable; gentle; spirited; puissant; officious; powerful; epicurean; banished; bosom; inseparable; obliging; staunch; long-sustaining; beloved; worthy; trusty; conservative; liberal; secret; nameless; common; late-embarked; warmest; true; literary; importunate; merry; dissipated; vindictive; benevolent; strong; creditable; rival; family; steadfast; unswerving; unrepentant; provoking; pock-marked; middle-aged; satirical; reasonable; particular; virtuous; modest; long-tried; long-known; gossiping; courageous; unwavering; sympathizing; questioning; suspicious; unconditional; choice; well-tried; false; sad; well-advised; irritable; gifted; prying.

verbs
accept as—; accost—; affront—; alienate —; berate—; betray—; cast away—; concede to—; exasperate—; exempt—s; favor —; forsake—; harbor—; idolize—; join—; lack—; let down—; muster—s; part with—; protect—; sacrifice—; succor—; sustain—; take leave of—s; value—; vex—s; wish—; yield to—; —consoles; —s drift away; — lends a hand; —prevails; —stands by; — supports.
(See associate, ally, companion, favorite.)

FRIENDLINESS

adjectives
patronizing; beaming; familiar; ignoble; truest; genuine; curious; paternal; effusive; heavenly.

FRIENDLY

adverbs
disarmingly; consistently; unquestionably; essentially; extremely; gratifyingly; courteously; placidly; gravely; smilingly; cordially; helpfully; quietly; remarkably; palpably; ostentatiously; condescendingly; singularly; charmingly; genuinely; sincerely; unaffectedly; naturally; delightfully; politely; openly; heartily; scrupulously; loyally; enchantingly; engagingly; altogether.

FRIENDSHIP

adjectives

platonic; distinguished; diplomatic; remarkable; acknowledged; disinterested; traditional; proffered; supercilious; partisan; equal; hereditary; warmest; informal; subsidiary; steadfast; deathless; ardent; resistless; lasting; ancient; problematical; practical; confidential; ill-assorted; heaping; tranquil; precious; intimate; true; poetic; intellectual; pure; lifelong; three-cornered; expedient; serviceable; loyal; commercial; estranged; deep; benevolent; unreturned; familiar; generous; dignified; cordial; warm; patronizing; profound; casual; adoring; unusual; strict; fragile; ominous; well-known; inseparable; unquenchable; passionate; restful; sober; youthful; energetic; bosom; offered; exquisite; literary; ancient; protracted; expansive.

verbs

accept—of; attain—of; bask in—; cultivate —; destroy—; disrupt—; encourage—; endanger—; enhance—; foster—; gain—of; hold out the hand of—; jeopardize—; kill—; manifest—; taint—; voice—; —blossoms; —cools; —fades; —flowers; —ripens.

(See affection, attachment, amity, intimacy, devotion.)

FRIEZE

adjectives

professional; magnificent; dignified.

FRIGHT

adjectives

perfect; whispered; sudden; supernatural; helpless; violent; overwhelming; quivering; collective; intolerable; morbid.

verbs

blanch with—; conceal—; convulse in—; cower in—; crouch in—; die of—; exhaust with—; harrow with—; hesitate in—; impel by—; quake with—; quiver with—; recoil in—; shake with—; start in—; subject to—; sweat with—; take—; thrill with —; throw into—; tremble with—; —abates; —freezes; —paralyzes; —petrifies; —slackens; —shocks; shiver with—.

(See alarm, fear, dismay, terror, consternation.)

FRIGHTEN (v)

adverbs

genuinely; horribly; supernaturally; violently; morbidly; collectively; intolerably; overwhelmingly; instinctively; devilishly; nefariously; insidiously.

(See alarm, terrify.)

FRIGHTFUL

adverbs

hideously; awfully; shockingly; appallingly; grimly; unspeakably; inexpressibly; incalculably; indescribably; peculiarly; particularly; utterly; insupportably; cruelly; brutally; grimly; uncommonly.

FRIGID

adverbs

obnoxiously; calmly; arrogantly; bitterly; languidly; impassively; phlegmatically; unemotionally; indifferently; callously; imperturbably; unconcernedly; maddeningly; discourteously; abominably; insufferably.

FRINGE

verbs

adorn with—; bear—; border with—; deck with—; drape—; edge with—; finish with —; hang by—; knot—; ravel—; rip—; suspend—; swing—; toy with—; —beautifies; —dances; —dangles; —fascinates; —quivers.

(See border.)

FRINGES

adjectives

fleecy; raveling; icy; angry-looking; luxuriant; amber; penumbral; straggling; outermost; solid; mysterious; cotton; ball; scalloped; hand-knotted; luminous; sleek; tattered; tasseled; delicate.

FRIPPERY

adjectives

feminine; tawdry; meretricious.

FRISK (v)

adverbs

joyously; gaily; laughably; unconventionally; youthfully; wantonly; scandalously; thoughtlessly; dissipatedly.

(See leap, skip, frolic.)

FRISKING

adjectives

joyous; carefree; unconventional; animal.

FRISKY

adverbs

youthfully; childishly; vivaciously; nimbly; happily; blithely; smartly; eagerly; delightfully; charmingly; interestingly; buoyantly;

jauntily; airily; lightsomely; brightly; joyously; sportively; gleefully; trickily; jocosely; exultantly; jubilantly; irrepressibly; exhilaratingly; indescribably; playfully.

FRIVOLITY
adjectives
scholastic; Gallic; irresponsible; scandalous.

verbs
attack—; beckon in—; celebrate with—; condemn—; denounce—; discard—; display —; exhibit—; pretend—; prevent—; repudiate—; ridicule—; —amuses; —attracts; —excites; —flourishes; —irks; —vexes.
(See frolic, fun.)

FRIVOLOUS
adverbs
wildly; foolishly; entertainingly; absurdly; gaily; blithely; idly; childishly; utterly; senselessly; lightly; ridiculously; ludicrously; capriciously; fantastically; giddily; wantonly; freakishly; blatantly; extravagantly; nonsensically; vacantly; hilariously.

FROCK
adjectives
smartest; charming; sheerer; gleaming; silver; filmy; close-fitting; icy; twice-turned; chic; dowdy; spangled; gayest; refreshing; fashionable.

verbs
adore—; alter—; arrange—; compliment on —; design—; discard—; dislike—; display —; don—; envy—; fit—; injure—; purchase—; renovate—; select—; slip into—; yearn for—; —attracts; —becomes; —befits; —exposes; —flatters; —reveals; —slenderizes.
(See garment, gown, dress, robe.)

FROG
verbs
can—s; farm—s; persecute—s; —blinks; —burrows; —croaks; —damages; —dips; —s disperse; —dives; —evolves; —excavates; —jumps; —leaps; —snatches; —swims; —trills.
(See animal.)

FROGS
adjectives
croaking; reasonable; vulgar.

FROLIC
adjectives
carnal; lively; midnight.

verbs
bridle—; curb—; enter into—; gambol at —; gather for—; indulge in—; interrupt—; invite to—; observe—; provide—; reprimand—; revel at—; savor—; subdue—; suffer for—; —amuses; —delights; —tempts.
(See merriment, sport, prank, fun.)

FROLIC (*v*)
adverbs
boyishly; gleefully; jocundly; winsomely; exuberantly; sportively; blithesomely; drunkenly.
(See leap, skip, play.)

FROLICSOME
adverbs
genially; gaily; gleefully; vivaciously; irrepressibly; mirthfully; hilariously; noisily; boisterously; laughingly; merrily; jovially; joyously; brightly; lightly; delightedly; happily; jauntily; immensely; immeasurably; infectiously; pleasantly; playfully; waggishly; amazingly.

FRONDS
adjectives
dark; sempiternal; pinnate; magnificent; beauteous; waving; hoving.

FRONT
adjectives
formidable; starry; atheist; willing; bastionlike; undaunted; proud; defying; bold; blazoned; blushless; time-stained; ivory; immediate; pompous; ardent; honorable; confident; veneered; gallant.

verbs
bound—; direct to—; display—; edge—; erect—; enter—; face—; forge to—; form at—; furnish—; limit—; move to—; pertain to—; place at—; provide—; scale—; situate at—; skirmish on—; station at—; unite—; —crumbles; —extends; —shields.
(See rear.)

FRONTIER
verbs
charge—; command—; defend—; dispatch to—; extend—; guard—; inhabit—; invade —; repel at—; scale—; settle on—; shun—; situate on—; station at—; thrust to—; unite

—; —advances; —bounds; —limits; —
presses forward; —recedes; —resists; —
shifts; —surrounds.
(See border, boundary.)

FRONTIERS
adjectives
narrow; indefensible; remotest; flexible;
dangerous; maritime; rude; guarded; expanding; constraining.

FROST
adjectives
flowery; white; radiant; pondering; wondrous; make-believe; ceaseless; wintry; dazzling; crackling; sharp; keen; relentless;
singeing; killing; envious; autumn; audacious; piercing; blighting; withering; fet-
tering; bitter; heavy; gray; iridescent;
chilly; hard; snapping; untimely; hoar.

verbs
form—; hang with—; lace with—; trace
with—; —bites; —chills; —covers; —damages; —decorates; —descends; —designs;
—draws; —etches; —falls; —glimmers; —
glistens; —glorifies; —injures; —lingers;
—nips; —projects; —settles on; —sharpens; —silvers; —sprays; —transforms.
(See snow.)

FROSTY
adverbs
sharply; refreshingly; bitterly; appetizingly; freshly; bleakly; bitingly; nippingly;
terribly; cruelly; destructively; slightly; invigoratingly; delightfully.

FROTH
adjectives
sudden; flowery; flying; idlest.

verbs
agitate to—; beat to—; boil to—; break
into—; churn up—; cover with—; crest
with—; emit—; ferment to—; fleck with—;
shake into—; toss off—; —bubbles; —
creams; —effervesces; —floats; —foams; —
gurgles; —issues from; —reams.
(See foam.)

FROTHY
adverbs
lightly; airily; volatilely; thickly; effervescently; sparklingly; lusciously; fizzily; deliciously; genuinely; attractively; invitingly.

FROWN
adjectives
ominous; ireful; discontented; blackening;
mournful; rumorous; bitter; puzzled; chilling; feudal; gloomy; sternest; habitual;
steady; churlish; crusty; fastidious; gathering; old-fashioned; restrained; drunken;
petulant; searching; angry; pedantic; unfeeling; charming; fleeting; deep-furrowed.

verbs
assume—; blemish with—; contract in—;
cringe before—; disclose—; display—; form
—; incur—; observe—; overcome—; perceive—; rebuke with—; relax—; suppress
—; wrinkle into—; —belies; —commands;
—corrugates; —creases; —deters; —expresses; —intimidates; —punishes; —reprimands; —terrorizes.
(See scowl.)

FROWN (v)
adverbs
sullenly; belligerently; blackly; wrathfully;
inauspiciously; reprovingly; dismally; majestically; ferociously; austerely; ominously; mournfully; bitterly; sternly; habitually;
churlishly; petulantly; uncongenially.
(See scowl.)

FROWZY
adverbs
carelessly; roughly; inexcusably; neglectfully; dreadfully; miserably; nonchalantly;
wretchedly; merrily; cheerfully; indifferently; unconcernedly; inordinately; terribly;
excitedly.

FRUGAL
adverbs
carefully; necessarily; thriftily; cautiously;
warily; watchfully; ostentatiously; habitually; naturally; amazingly; cooperatively; inherently; meanly; sensibly; providently;
moderately; parsimoniously; admirably; intelligently; judiciously.

FRUGALITY
adjectives
ostentatious; necessary; apologetic; helpful;
customary; habitual; native.

verbs
bare—; commend—; conceal—; conduct
with—; display—; endure—; expose to—;
found—; justify—; mark—; occasion—;

practise—; praise—; reduce to—; relieve—; require—; resent—; resign to—; reveal—. (See economy, thrift.)

FRUIT

adjectives

forbidden; copious; unavailing; immediate; fairy; delicious; grateful; acid; just; divine; mellow; pulpy; ambrosial; monthly; teeming; autumnal; fuller; beatific; wholesome; fragrant; delightful; deciduous; luscious; bitter; discordant; blessed; apparent; bleeding; sacred; proper; gushing; clustering; golden; compensating; disastrous; ruddy; detested; glorious; exotic; immortal; alluring; natural; noble; fresh; cordial; panting; wandering; fairest; legitimate; sunripened; vigorous; personal; pouting; celestial; cherished; ripe; fallacious; unknown; blushing; sole; mellow; seasonal; proper; wind-tossed; choicest; dazzling; tolerable; ornamental; sprouting; ripe-cheeked; remarkable; nectarine; oversized; divinest; flesh-colored; rotten; wormy.

verbs

attack—; bear —; blight—; blossom into—; consume—; damage—; develop into—; diet on—; gather—; load with—; partake of—; produce—; reap—; relish—; replenish with —; savor—; serve—; spray—; store—; yield—; —abounds; —delights; —rots; — satiates.
(See crop, harvest.)

FRUITFUL

adverbs

profitably; satisfactorily; unusually; prolifically; luxuriantly; admirably; genuinely; copiously; abundantly; teemingly; sparsely; apparently; ordinarily; remarkably; sufficiently; surprisingly; plentifully; richly; uberously.

FRUITFULNESS

adjectives
mellow; uncommon; tropical.

FRUITION

adjectives
instant; tantalizing; unalloyed; ceaseless.

FRUITLESS

adverbs

grievously; disappointingly; inconsequentially; terribly; disconcertingly; ruinously; unfortunately; unluckily; wretchedly; miserably; pitiably; pathetically; naturally; inevitably; irremediably; sadly; dreadfully.

FRUMPISH

adverbs

crabbedly; morosely; perversely; moodily; sulkily; intolerably; utterly; doggedly; grumpily; peevishly; crustily; inscrutably; vaguely; sourly; unreasonably; habitually; usually; disagreeably.

FRUSTRATE (v)

adverbs

effectually; treacherously; legitimately; vindictively; jealously; subtly; basely; temporarily.
(See prevent, defeat, disappoint.)

FRUSTRATION

verbs

avoid—; balk at—; condemn—; curb—; denounce—; endure—; hurdle—; overcome—; resent—; subdue—; suffer—; —baffles; — circumvents; —defeats; —deters; —harms; —hinders; —injures; —interrupts.
(See failure, defeat, disappointment.)

FRYING-PAN

verbs

adhere to—; blacken—; brandish—; cleanse —; dent—; employ—; escape—; grease—; mix in—; necessitate—; place in—; polish —; scour—; —clatters; —jangles; —rattles; —shines; —sizzles.
(See pan.)

FUEL

adjectives

premium; inflammable; volatile; self-sustaining; exhausted; available; solid; fresh.

verbs

acquire—; burn—; employ as—; fill with—; furnish—; ignite—; necessitate—; obtain—; produce—; replenish—; require—; select—; supply—; —explodes; —flames; —heats; — illumines; —inflames; —sustains.
(See wood, coal, etc.)

FUGITIVE

adjectives

gallant; young; suppliant; mangled; royal; solitary; panting; sole; wretched; stricken; returning; frenzied.

verbs

conceal—; deter—; endanger—; espy—; harbor—; nab—; prevent—; protect—; pur-

sue—; search for—; shelter—; track down
—; —absconds; —deserts; —escapes; —
flees; —hides; —journeys; —wanders.
(See prisoner.)

adverbs
elusively; shyly; evasively; remotely; evanescently; transiently; ephemerally; etheral-
ly; nebulously; perishably; mortally; temporally; transitorily; unhappily; sadly; unfortunately; tormentingly.

FULFILL (v)
adverbs
magnificently; admirably; conscientiously;
abundantly; moderately; approximately;
swiftly; blindly; ultimately; immutably;
adequately; partially.
(See accomplish, complete.)

FULFILLMENT
adjectives
adequate; abundant; mere; rigid; speedy;
partial.

verbs
accomplish—; allow—; anticipate—; attain
—; attempt—; concede—; defeat—; effect
—; execute—; express—; grant—; perform
—; pray for—; predict—; promote—; reach
—; supply to—; yearn for—; —completes;
—disappoints; —satiates; —satisfies.
(See accomplishment, realization.)

FULL
adverbs
moderately; satisfactorily; sufficiently; completely; fortunately; gloriously; abundantly; measurably; adequately; liberally; generously; pleasantly; agreeably.

FULLNESS
adjectives
quiet; flaring; swelling; grim; apparent;
arduous; generous; lavish; flaccid; abounding; messy; eloquent; all-excluding; immeasurable; molded.

FUMBLE (v)
adverbs
casually; nervously; drunkenly; clumsily;
fruitlessly; tremulously; ineffectually; absurdly; pedantically.
(See blunder, flounder, miss, stumble.)

FUME (v)
adverbs
indignantly; sulphurously; poisonously; unendurably; odoriferously; exasperatedly; angrily; wrathfully; blatantly; prodigiously.
(See rage, bluster.)

FUMES
adjectives
noxious; greasy; odoriferous; resinous; unendurable; earthly; unkindly; poisonous;
fishy; devilish; disagreeable; sulphurous.

verbs
bear—; blow—; disperse—; discharge—;
emit—; exhale—; fill with—; flood with—;
give off—; inhale—; scent—; send forth—;
spray with—; —creep out of; —mantle; —
overcome; —pass off; —perfume; —please;
—preserve; —rise; —smother; —stifle; —
vanish.
(See vapor, smoke.)

FUN
adjectives
spirited; capital; innocent; fairy; hilarious;
practical; legitimate; gentle; monstrous;
genuine; nonsensical; boisterous; monotonous; tremendous; bitter; nasty; ill-timed;
painful.

verbs
carouse in—; create—; drown—; entertain
with—; exclude—; indulge in—; play for—;
poke—at; pretend in—; spare—; —amuses;
—ceases; —cheers; —diverts; —enlivens;
—grows; —relaxes; —wearies.
(See frolic, joke, mirth, gayety, merriment, amusement.)

FUNCTION
adjectives
ministerial; vital; legitimate; valuable; useful; manifold (pl); ritualistic; perverted;
nerve; judicial; impaired; aesthetic; beneficent; natural; economic; animal; normal;
consular; religious; executive; cherished; intellectual; pitiable; hospitable; cognitive;
imitative; precise; sacerdotal; essential; basest; appropriate; principal; civilian; impaired; numerous (pl); social; obsolete; inescapable; diminished; proper; primary; indispensable; frightful; spiritual; gracious;
ecclesiastical; sociological; diversified (pl);
imperfect; varied (pl); episcopal.

verbs

abuse—; arrest—; associate with—; block —; centralize—; check—; delegate—to; discharge—; embarrass—; energize—; exercise —; fulfill—; impair—; improve—; invest with—; magnify—; perform—; preserve—; promote—; regulate—; resume—; restore—; subserve—; vest—in; —s overlap one another.

(See duty.)

FUNCTION (v)

adverbs

automatically; efficiently; biologically; splendidly; sluggishly; elaborately; ministerially; beneficently; economically; indispensably; spiritually.

(See perform, discharge.)

FUND

verbs

abscond with —s; abuse—; administer—; advance —s; allocate —s; allot —s; appropriate —s; audit—; bolster—; campaign for —s; deplete—; divert from—; draw from —; embezzle —s; endow with—; juggle —s; misappropriate —s; muster —s; pool —s; seek —s; solicit —s; stretch —s; struggle for —s; supplant—; swell—; utilize—; —benefits; —dwindles; —increases; —s roll in.

(See money, capital.)

FUNDAMENTAL

adverbs

definitely; indispensably; radically; significantly; essentially; ineradicably; inherently; intrinsically; virtually; substantially; absolutely; fairly; basically; undeniably.

FUNDAMENTALS

verbs

cleave to—; cling to—; deviate from—; doubt—; exhaust—; implant—; inculcate—; inform in—; instruct in—; interfere with—; involve—; necessitate—; preserve—; recognize—; regard—; reiterate—; rely on—; require—; revere—; subject to—; submit to—; sway from—.

(See essential, rule, principle, law.)

FUNDS

adjectives

stabilization; exhaustless; contingent; accumulated; unlimited; reserve; insurance; pegging; special; slush; inexhaustible; char-

itable; needed; unlimited; unequalled; tremendous; misused; supplemented; baffling; available; endowment; meager; misappropriated.

FUNERAL

adjectives

leafy; lugubrious; genteel.

verbs

announce—; arrange—; ease—; eulogize at —; expend on—; follow—; reign at—; mourn at—; observe—; officiate at—; preside at—; proceed at—; toll at—.

(See death.)

FUNEREAL

adverbs

solemnly; lugubriously; quietly; reverently; murmurously; depressingly; gloomily; disconsolately; dismally; gravely; heavily; horribly; oppressively; sadly; dully; mournfully; cheerlessly; frightfully; lamentably; dolefully; incredibly; unnecessarily; absurdly; extremely; inordinately.

FUNGUS

adjectives

decayed, dismal.

verbs

cover with—; divest of—; neglect—; nourish—; —chokes; —corrupts; —damages; — encrusts; —enervates; —flourishes; —gathers; —harms; —injures; —invades; —kills; —overruns; —penetrates; —poisons; —ripens; —spreads; —rots.

(See plant.)

FUNNY

adverbs

hilariously; laughably; excruciatingly; uproariously; comically; wholesomely; divertingly; delightfully; drolly; drily; quaintly; entertainingly; merrily; facetiously; smartly; extravagantly; ridiculously; fantastically; whimsically; outlandishly; extremely; exceedingly.

FUR

adjectives

shimmering; sleek; rich; warm; glossy; jet; ruffled; luxurious; silk-soft; semiprecious; camouflaged; prickly; ice-covered; tawny; sumptuous; imitation; expensive; woolly; fuzzy.

verbs

adjust—; clothe in—; deck with—; display —; dress in—; encase in—; face with—; fluff—; hunt for —s; line with—; muffle in —; ornament with—; sheathe in—; strip of —; stroke—; trade in —s; trim with—; value—; wrap in—; —encircles; —envelopes; —flies; —protects.

(See coat, skin, hair.)

FURIOUS

adverbs

senselessly; sullenly; suddenly; intolerably; hotly; justly; obviously; foolishly; ridiculously; dangerously; alarmingly; terribly; dreadfully; coldly; genuinely; uncontrollably; passionately; violently; sternly; implacably; unjustly; inordinately; insanely; naturally; ludicrously; unnaturally; curiously; oddly; strangely; unappeasably; recklessly; inconsiderately; blindly; savagely; jealously; indescribably; tragically; absurdly; hysterically; inanely; idiotically; groundlessly; boisterously; desperately; murderously; fearfully; frightfully; fiercely; truculently; diabolically; brutally; needlessly; horribly.

FURLOUGH

adjectives

delightful; precious; desired; short; happy.

verbs

absent on—; authorize—; beg—; concede—; defer—; demand—; earn—; favor with—; forbid—; grant—; leave on—; license—; obtain—; order—; overstay—; permit—; refuse—; request—; restrict—; return from —; take—; warrant—.

(See vacation.)

FURNACE

adjectives

fiery; sacred; untiring; molten; smelting.

verbs

bake in—; cast into—; dry in—; feed—; fire —; fuel—; install—; issue from—; operate —; rake—; start—; supply—; tap—; tend —; —burns; —converts; —emits; —exhales; —heats; —sighs.

(See stove.)

FURNISH (v)

adverbs

abundantly; defectively; meanly; gaudily; bizarrely; adequately; scantily; sumptuously; tastefully; exquisitely; luxuriously; rudely; drably; modernistically.

(See provide, supply.)

FURNITURE

adjectives

scanty; enduring; somber; haircloth; simple; meager; hand-made; custom-made; time-worn; elegant; unfriendly; commodious; ecclesiastical-looking; space-saving; antique; luxurious; rude; best-styled; massive; costly; dim; drab; incidental; hideous; rickety; bulky; modernistic; streamlined.

verbs

appoint—; arrange—; clutter with—; cover —; damage—; decorate—; design—; equip with—; fill with—; inherit—; nick—; outfit with—; overcrowd with—; place—; polish —; possess—; scratch—; select—; stock with —; store—; van—; —fits; —harmonizes; —matches; —suffices.

(See equipment, outfit, chair, table, etc.)

FUROR

adjectives

bacchic; devilish; raucous; riotous; frenzied.

FURROW

adjectives

sounding; foul; fat; unmeaning; roaring; mucky; silvery; sonorous; fruitless; shining; rectangular; dry-drawn; unthrifty; vertical.

FURTIVE

adverbs

craftily; adroitly; cleverly; uncommonly; habitually; suspiciously; strangely; oddly; curiously; warily; evasively; mysteriously; cryptically; whisperingly; needlessly; significantly; unduly; cautiously; extremely; remarkably; particularly.

FURY

adjectives

domestic; utmost; irresistible; civil; unappeasable; suppressed; violent; tempestuous; warlike; unabated; reckless; undiminished; exasperated; empty; whirling; drink-engendered; satiate; direful; fierce; concentrated; snake-locked; everlasting; fighting; manifest; indiscriminate; inconsiderate; uncontrolled; steelhearted; perfect; hellish; exterminating; blistering; blindfold; mineral; revolutionary; mad; governable; bestial; increasing; unreasoning; sparkling; unbridled; coming; sudden; implacable; chaotic; overpowering; disappointed; savage; unchained; vindictive; obvious; concentrated; pretty; jealous; unrelenting; indescribable; blind; incarnate; tragic.

verbs
blast with—; conceal—; dignify—; drive to —; encounter—; engender—; fan—; fly into —; gaze in — at; mutter in—; rage in—; roar in—; seethe with—; simmer with—; vent—; whip into—; work into—; —abates; —increases; —lets down; —subsides.
(See anger, rage, passion, frenzy, excitement.)

FUSE
adjectives
unreliable; burning; hissing; short; time.

FUSILLADE
adjectives
murderous; fierce; random; furious; brutal; bloody; merciless.

verbs
discharge—; emit—; keep up—; pour—; protect from—; rain—; run from—; shower —; spout—; swear—; warn of—; withstand —; —assaults; —butchers; —ceases; —executes; —levels; —massacres; —mows down; —shatters; —terrorizes.
(See volley, barrage.)

FUSION
adjectives
fiery; graceful; necessary; remarkable.

FUSS
adjectives
indignant; noisy; quarrelsome; sudden; nasty; unspeakable.

FUSSY
adverbs
needlessly; tiresomely; irritatingly; restlessly; excitedly; foolishly; ineptly; unduly; eternally; noisily; annoyingly; feverishly; briskly; officiously; uneasily; twitteringly; naggingly; abominably; detestably; unbearably; remarkably; intolerably; hatefully.

FUTILE
adverbs
lamentably; invariably; unfortunately; deplorably; helplessly; unluckily; unhappily; feebly; weakly.

FUTILITY
adjectives
clumsy; apparent; sweet; fantastic; magnificent; obvious; patent; accepted.

verbs
battle with—; bemoan — of; break in—; contend with—; curse—; dispose of—; evade—; fritter into—; lapse into—; lose in —; manifest—; object to—; recognize—; reduce to—; result in—; screen—; strike at —; while away in—; —appears; —confronts; —conquers; —dies.
(See uselessness, worthlessness.)

FUTURE
adjectives
ever-better; magnetic; blest; naturalistic; impending; imminent; immediate; luminous; physical; immortal; distant; impossible; eternal; financial; promising; boundless; uncertain; commercial; brilliant; infinite; interesting; cruel; ruthless; secure; dubious; dim; black; significant; controlling; happy; measureless; hopeless; cheerful; supramundane; heterogeneous; somber; altered; terrestrial; fantastic; invisible; far-stretching; friendless; permanent; real; gloomy; glorious; unlimited; profitable; assured; lurid; long-time; cosmopolitan.

verbs
anticipate—; blast—; chart—; cloud—; despair of—; endanger—; entrust to—; explore —; fear for—; figure out—; forecast—; foretell—; gamble away—; gaze into—; glance into—; guide—; hope for—; jeopardize—; lay — open; menace—; mortgage —; overshadow—; peer into—; project into —; prophesy—; read—; risk—; save for—; secure—; stake — on; view—.
(See outlook.)

G

adjectives
sculptured; towering; fantastic; peaked.

GADGET

adjectives
life-saving; lethal; noise-making; educational.

GAIETY

adjectives
fictitious; unfeigned; served; wild; airy; fortunate; exuberant; uncanny; bounding; fatigued; inward; forced; brilliant; charming; facile; heedless; social; jaded; seeming; careless; prevalent; nimble; leaden; affectionate; bewitching; sparkling; teasing; surface; delirious; animating; exhausting; false; spurious; customary; ironical; childlike; mock; embarrassed; tempered; alternate; enticing; unearthly; wholehearted.

verbs
(See gayety.)

GAIN

adjectives
glorious; immense; sure; intellectual; eternal; substantial; capital; selfish; adequate; personal; speculative; happy; immediate; indubitable; obvious; fruitful; fallacious; indicated; unhallowed; qualitative; scanty; treacherous; pecuniary; proper; equivalent; territorial; untold; mystic; appreciable; unjust; corporate; hopeless.

verbs
accomplish—; acquire—; begrudge—; claim —; content with—; count—; derive—; dissipate —s; forego—; promise—; register—; seek—; serve for—; spurn—; struggle for —; yield—; —astonishes; —benefits; —decreases; —increases; —mounts; —outweighs.
(See profit, advantage.)

GAIN (v)

adverbs
vastly; legally; lawfully; ethically; deservedly; definitely; unquestionably; incredibly; consistently; incessantly; singularly; substantially; gloriously; immensely; speculatively; indubitably; unhallowedly; pecuniarily; territorially; subtly.
(See profit, win.)

GAINFUL

adverbs
amazingly; securely; certainly; magically; mysteriously; unexpectedly; productively; surprisingly; admirably; luckily; fortunately; happily; providentially; adequately; curiously; valuably; oddly; legally; definitely; unquestionably; incredibly; gloriously; immensely; subtly; pecuniarily; financially; singularly.

GAIT

adjectives
staid; swinging; rolling; stooping; shuffling; awkward; majestical; unremitted; aerie; true; haggard; lofty; shambling; weary; gentle; traveling; unnatural; pacing; common; ponderous; rapid; stately; princely; habitual; heavy; feeble; swaggering; musing; measured; lumbering.

verbs
change—; fix—; go at—; hobble in—; limp in—; lumber in—; mimic—; mock—; practise—; quicken—; recognize—; settle down to—; shift—; slacken—; slow up—; solemnize—; stagger in—; steady—; stumble in—.
(See walk, step.)

GALAXY

adjectives
splendid; cooperative; successive (pl).

GALE

adjectives
treacherous; spicy; approaching; lurid; angry; shrieking; tearing; frantic; passing; sunrise; dreadful; furious; boisterous; merry; heavy; southern; viewless; favoring; odor-scented; cold; wet; carping; keel-compelling; sinking; coming; mocking; pleasant; heroic; terrific; strenuous; destroying; freshening; gracious; shadowy; rising; balmy; sighing; reveling.

verbs
buck—; combat—; encounter—; —abates; —accelerates; —arises; —blusters; —carries away; —damages; —disperses; —fans; —fumes; —lashes; —rages; —rampages; —

riots; —screams; —shrieks; —stiffens; — sweeps away; —violates; —whips up; — wreaks.

(See breeze, current, wind, tempest.)

GALL

adjectives
burning; soul-tormenting; hypercritical.

GALLANT

adjectives
open-handed; trim; gay; pleasant-spoken; boisterous; high-spirited; faultless; chivalric.

adverbs
splendidly; valorously; heroically; courteously; unwontedly; unusually; consistently; habitually; inherently; intrepidly; fearlessly; boldly; courageously; resolutely; adventurously; bravely; audaciously; firmly; confidently; daringly; dangerously; pluckily; fiercely; doughtily; urbanely; suavely; dutifully; blandly; graciously; obsequiously; ingratiatingly; immeasurably.

GALLANTRY

adjectives
generous; uncouth; delicate; desperate; sheepish; wonted; conspicuous; boyish; distinguished; rare; calm; consistent; premature; excessive; imputed; timeless; self-conscious; overdone; elaborate; natural; practical; noticeable.

verbs
accost with—; applaud—; attend with—; bear with—; behave with—; breathe—; conduct with—; court with—; deck in—; defend with—; display—; escort with—; exaggerate—; exchange —s; exhibit—; lay aside—; mock—; premeditate—; rejoice in —; —captures; —steals away; —wins.

(See bravery, courage, heroism, chivalry, prowess.)

GALLERY

adjectives
elliptical; gilded; elaborate; dirty; immense; encircling; frequented; extensive; whispering; formal; gracious; classical; ignorant; subterranean; loaded; starlit; vaulted.

verbs
assemble in—; exhibit in—; guide through —; hang in—; lounge in—; occupy—; par-

ade through—; play to—; proclaim from—; rail—; set up in—; speak from—; subdue —; support—; visit—; —edifies; —heckles; —hushes; —surrounds.

(See corridor, balcony, audience.)

GALLOP

adjectives
thunderous; false; perilous; rapid; soundless; clattering; morning; daily; historic; breathless.

GALLOP (v)

adverbs
furiously; picturesquely; gallantly; stiffly; thunderously; swiftly; perilously; clatteringly; breathlessly.

(See run, trot.)

GALLOWS

verbs
bring to—; cheat—; condemn to—; conduct to—; correct on—; deliver from—; deserve —; erect—; escape—; execute on—; hang on —; inflict—; punish on—; reprieve from—; save from—; sentence to—; threaten with —; —cures; —tames; —terrifies; —terrorizes.

(See gibbet.)

GAMBLE (v)

adverbs
habitually; inveterately; suavely; besottedly; professionally; foolhardily; passionately; improvidently.

(See risk.)

GAMBLER

adjectives
passionate; ready; riverboat; incarnate; prodigious; professed; besotted; adept; inveterate; skilled; sleek; suave.

GAMBLING

verbs
abhor—; bewail—; campaign against—; cheat at—; defraud at—; degenerate into—; denounce—; hedge in—; play at—; rail at —; resist—; resort to—; risk in—; shackle to—; share in—; speculate in—; stake for —; thrive on—; trap in—; wager on—; —destroys; —disgraces; —dismembers; — harms; —preys on; —relaxes; —ruins; — wrecks.

(See game.)

adjectives

wanton; noisy; joyous; insufferable; dainty; uncouth; frolicsome; pleasant; childish.

adjectives

mocking; dangerous; toilsome; impious; heroic; risky; thrilling; open; intricate; formidable; tedious; shut; attractive; daily; mimic; impassioned; unmeaning; poetic; lawful; Olympic; card; disappearing; contested; skillful; endless; arrayed; highpowered; intellectual; bickering; strenuous; political; national; cordial; nobler; entrancing; tight; overtime; professional; heated.

verbs

announce—; cheat in—; dabble at—; emerge from—; enjoy—; enliven—; enthuse (colloq.) over—; feature—; follow—; improve —; indulge in—; invent—; join in—; judge —; master—; practise—; referee—; quarrel at—; score—; share—; strive in—; view—; witness—; —amuses; —contents; —cripples; —delights; —diverts; —entertains; —enthralls; —excites; —stales; —tires; — wanes; —wearies.

(See contest, recreation, sport.)

(*animals*)

verbs

bag—; cherish—; destroy—; ensnare—; enthrall by—; exterminate—; follow—; preserve—; prey upon—; relish—; rouse—; search for—; stalk—; trap—; view—; — abounds; —flees; —flourishes; —thrives; pursue—.

(See animal.)

adverbs

amusingly; enliveningly; briskly; smartly; energetically; divertingly; happily; entertainingly; unusually; marvellously; enthusiastically; airily; blithely; buoyantly; exhilaratingly; hilariously; delightfully; jauntily; jovially; merrily; playfully; rollickingly; roisteringly; waggishly.

adjectives

vehement; embryo; experienced; common; desperate; lukewarm.

verbs

associate with—; attract—; break up—; control—; disperse—; form—; head—; hire —; join—; lead—; manage—; regulate—; reprimand—; supervise—; —dissipates; — gathers; —meets; —operates; —separates; —troops in.

(See group, band, company, crew, crowd, squad.)

verbs

(See gangway.)

verbs

affect with—; cure—; decompose with—; defile with—; heal—; infect with—; lop off —; occasion—; result in—; seize with—; treat for—; —begins; —corrupts; —endangers; —pains; —oozes; —sets in; —spreads.

verbs

accuses—; apprehend—; battle—; consort with—; employ—; round up—; rub out—; track down—; —bribes; —foments; —"hides out"; —intimidates; —maltreats; —murders; —s operate; —s organize; —revenges; —smuggles; —snuffs out; —terrifies; —terrorizes; —wounds.

(See thief.)

verbs

ascend—; assemble at—; climb—; confine to—; crowd—; enter by—; file down—; hoist—; leave by—; lower—; pass down—; raise—; rush up—; stream down—; stride up—; take up—; —accommodates; —extends; —bridges.

(See platform.)

adjectives

wide; appalling; unbridgeable; tremendous; invisible; innumerable (pl); perceptible; ghastly; apparent; long; conversational; glaring.

verbs

break into—; bridge—; cut—; discover—; enter—; escape through—; form—; mend —; notch into—; open into—; pass through

538

—; patch—; span—; stop—; wear into—; —diminishes; —heals; —interrupts; —separates; —unites; —widens.

(See passage, breach.)

GARAGE

verbs

direct to—; equip—; grease at—; inspect at—; maintain—; operate—; paint at—; polish—; repair in—; stock—; store in—; wash at—; —distributes; —furnishes; —harbors; —itemizes; —services; —supplies; manage—; weld at—.

GARB

adjectives

fantastic; offensive; splendid; angelic; penitential; puritanical; sacred; dazzling; holiday; traditional; eccentric; shaggy; fleshy; severe; brighter; half-clerical; ecclesiastical; curious; symbolic; rustic; pompous; mourning; disordered; humble; shapeless; picturesque; antique; chronic; somber.

GARB (*v*)

adverbs

immaculately; spectacularly; fantastically; puritanically; eccentrically; ecclesiastically; symbolically; rustically; drably; somberly; modestly.

(See clothe, array, dress.)

GARBAGE

verbs

accumulate—; complain of—; destroy—; discard as—; disintegrate—; dispose of—; dump—; heap—; incinerate—; litter with —; object to—; separate—; sterilize—; strew with—; utilize—; —contaminates; —decomposes; —fertilizes; —menaces.

(See waste.)

GARBLED

adverbs

hopelessly; senselessly; sadly; ridiculously; vexatiously; incoherently; wildly; deliberately; carelessly; ignorantly; disastrously; indescribably; intentionally; maliciously; dishonestly; unfairly; cunningly; adroitly; mischievously; terribly; inexcusably; indefensibly; horribly.

GARDEN

adjectives

colonization; mellowing; exotic; luxuriant; bowery; celebrated; fateful; private; curious; aquatic; countless (pl); tranquil; radiant; delicious; odorous; fabled; spacious; desolate; ample; rustic; walled; extensive; seedy; orchard; ravaged; shady; tiny; broken; terraced; revived; alluring; vigorous; suburban; enchanted; sequestered; neglected; stately; weedless; beautiful; untidy; hanging; sunny; formal; productive; magnificent; illuminated; rock; delightful; dainty.

verbs

cultivate—; delve in—; fence—; fringe—; girdle—; hedge in—; plan—; plot—; preserve—; putter in—; rejoice in—; sow—; sprinkle—; stroll through—; till—; tour—; transplant to—; wall in—; water—; —delights; —flourishes; —thrives.

(See yard.)

GARGLE

verbs

advise—; advocate—; apply—; bathe with —; dilute—; employ—; prepare—; require —; treat with—; wash with—; —cools; —eases; —heals; —relieves.

(See liquid, preparation.)

GARISH

adverbs

cheaply; glitteringly; unpleasantly; surprisingly; unexpectedly; intensely; crudely; discordantly; inharmoniously; rudely; monstrously; obtrusively; pretentiously; pompously; spectacularly; dramatically; unbecomingly; ridiculously; intensely; preposterously.

GARLAND

adjectives

funereal; live; jeweled; lovely; immortal; leafy; beauteous; victorious.

verbs

bear—; compete for—; crown with—; deck with—; display—; festoon with—s; lay—; mantle with—; reward with—; set—upon; swathe in—; wind—; —adorns; —decorates.

GARMENT

adjectives

drenched; banqueting; tattered; ordinary; sacerdotal; wretched; voluminous; trailing; coarse; operating; dignified; delicate; fragile; sober; mortal; perennial; discarded; stage; bridal; transparent; necessary; glittering; rustic; vaporous; shabby; shapeless; magic; exquisite; clean; flimsy; seductive; upper; radiant; charity; appropriate; superb; snowy; sweeping; fluttering; flattering; luxurious; handsome; custom; cool; elegant; exclusive; poisoned; untimely; imperial; dusty; modest; everlasting.

verbs

admire—; damage—; design—; dishevel—; display—; dye—; envy—; exhibit—; fashion—; fumigate—; injure—; model—; repair—; sew—; shroud in—; strip off—; sweat in—; weave—; yearn for—; —attracts; —befits; —clings to; —flatters; —reveals.

(See dress, coat, gown.)

GARNISHED

adverbs

tastefully; beautifully; generously; gayly; colorfully; invitingly; attractively; pleasingly; decoratively; becomingly; gorgeously; showily; simply; lusciously; deliciously; elaborately; cleverly; laboriously; ingeniously; unbelievably.

GARRET

verbs

accumulate in—; ascend to—; betake to—; conceal in—; deposit in—; evict from—; furnish—; heap in—; hoard in—; inhabit —; lodge in—; mount to—; preserve in—; remove to—; renovate—; reserve in—; search in—; stock in—; store in—; stow away in—; —garners; —projects; —totters.

(See attic, room.)

GARRISON

adjectives

intrusive; ample; large; floating; stalwart; retreating; slender; beleaguered; sturdy; strong; well-manned.

verbs

assault—; beset—; besiege—; bombard—; build—; charge—; erect—; fire upon—; invade—; maintain—; march upon—; quarter in—; reinforce—; station at—; threaten—; —defends; —guards; —shields; —surrenders; —withdraws.

(See fortification.)

GARRISON (v)

adverbs

sturdily; feebly; inadequately; stalwartly; smartly; prodigiously; effectually; adeptly.

(See supply, furnish.)

GARRULITY

adjectives

senile; unflagging; increased; nauseous; feminine; usual; boring; customary.

GARRULOUS

adverbs

endlessly; tediously; happily; chattily; genially; illuminatingly; knowledgeably; tiresomely; toothlessly; cacklingly; ribaldly; merrily; nauseatingly; unusually; habitually; highly; inescapably; incorrigibly; ponderously; monotonously; feverishly; excitedly; mumblingly.

GAS

adjectives

illuminating; foul; lethal; vivifying; incandescent; subtle; insidious; continuous; nebulous; congealed; fermenting; beneficent; transmuted; superseded; liquefied; mystery; deadly; noxious; injurious; rarefied; offensive; healthful.

verbs

accumulate—; battle—; bottle—; burn—; develop—; exhale—; guard against—; inhale—; isolate—; overcome by—; saturate with—; —asphyxiates; —emerges; —escapes; —expands; —flows; —fouls; —lifts; —poisons; —rises; —seeps in; —fuels.

(See oxygen.)

GASH

adjectives

deep; ghastly; fearful; fatal; abominable; hideous; deadly; murderous; bloody.

GASH (v)

adverbs

mortally; deeply; fatally; abominably; hideously; murderously; fearfully; savagely; fiendishly; diabolically.

(See slash, cut, tear.)

GASP

adjectives

convulsive; painful; long; grieving; struggling; broken; terrific; fitful; gurgling; last.

GASP (v)

adverbs

incredulously; breathlessly; unintelligibly; audibly; convulsively; fitfully; dramatically; brokenly; startlingly.

(See pant, breathe.)

adjectives

rusty; unclosed; churlish; inexorable; curtained; yawning; swinging; wooden; steel; decorated; awful; moon-lit; spectral; monumental; thronged; fast-locked; characteristic; facile; infernal; adamantine; massive; mosque; million-dollar; forbidden; figured; eastern; widest; celestial; huge; planched; applauding; painted; hospitable; silent; folding; sculptured; gorgeous; occidental; shadowy; postern; seaward; enchanted; grim; guarded; wicket; latched.

verbs

admit at—; bar—; beat against—; besiege —; fling open—; furnish—; guard—; knock on—; latch—; mend—; pass through —; repair—; storm—; swing on—; —bars; —hangs; —prevents.

(See opening, entrance, door.)

GATEWAY

adjectives

dilapidated; massive; secluded; crumbling; decorated; illumined.

GATHER (v)

adverbs

methodically; unpretentiously; seditiously; amiably; posthumously; tenderly; laboriously; noiselessly; cautiously; comprehensively; assiduously; formally; gaily; annually; riotously; raucously; exclusively.

(See assemble, congregate, accumulate.)

GATHERING

adjectives

informal; gay; insufficient; considerable; quiet; blind; assiduous; fashionable; indignant; annual; uncultured; democratic; eclectic; prompt; distinguished; noisy; unruly; riotous; unusual; raucous; notable; select; exclusive.

verbs

address—; arrange—; call—; collect into—; compose—; disperse—; dissipate—; enrage —; govern—; guide—; lead—; prevent—; provoke—; pull—; sway—; swell—; threaten—; —buzzes; —clamors; —contributes; —crowds; —impresses; —murmurs; — packs; —proposes; —views.

(See assembly, crowd.)

GAUDY

adverbs

unusually; unutterably; terribly; shockingly; extravagantly; oddly; gracelessly; unexpectedly; ridiculously; childishly; preposterously; horribly; offensively; disgustingly; unpleasantly.

GAUGE

verbs

adjust—; affect—; apply—; attach—; devise—; employ—; examine—; refer to—; test—; —advances; —ascertains; —determines; —fluctuates; —limits; —marks; — measures; —mounts; —notes; —records; — registers; —safeguards; —warns.

(See measure, standard.)

GAUGE (v)

adverbs

accurately; scientifically; correctly; skillfully; professionally; logically; mentally.

(See measure, estimate.)

GAUNT

adverbs

forbiddingly; haggardly; crookedly; unbelievably; terribly; awfully; unpleasantly; disagreeably; touchingly; miserably; portentously; wretchedly; ominously; alarmingly; horribly; uncommonly; meagerly; wanly; pallidly.

GAUZE

adjectives

theatrical; motionless; artful; vague; dappled; filmy.

verbs

apply—; bandage with—; brace with—; clean—; disinfect—; guard with—; join with—; sterilize—; strain through—; support with—.

(See fabric, silk.)

GAVEL

verbs

administer—; bang—; beat with—; drum —; employ—; hammer with—; heave—; inflict with—; knock—; rap with—; sound —; strike with—; —entreats; —hushes; — interferes; —interrupts.

(See hammer.)

GAWKY

adverbs

incredibly; pitiably; ludicrously; absurdly; inexcusably; sadly; utterly; remarkably;

clownishly; deliberately; pretentiously; comically; grotesquely; outlandishly; sensationally; theatrically; stupidly; heavily; youthfully.

GAY

adverbs
gracefully; boyishly; lightly; cheerfully; inexpressibly; racily; blithely; airily; saucily; proudly; carelessly; joyously; confidently; buoyantly; mystically; fantastically; devilishly; dashingly; artlessly; disarmingly; refreshingly; fashionably; racially; playfully; wantonly; roguishly; bewitchingly; engagingly; radiantly.

GAYETY

verbs
beget—; blush with—; commend—; displace—; eclipse—; feign—; flush in—; imbue with—; indulge in—; release—; revive —; rollick in—; thirst for—; unloose—; wreathe in—; yield to—; —blazes; —bubbles up; —cheers; —refreshes; —reigns; —ripples; —wearies.
(See merriment, fun, frolic, sport, liveliness, vivacity.)

GAZE

adjectives
uncertain; tributary; penetrating; mute; orphaned; relentless; quiet; kindred; probing; inquiring; abstracted; presumptuous; loving; searching; uncomplaining; earnest; averted; steady; enraptured; somber; maternal; inspiring; animated; shrewd; level; answering; admiring; bright; intent; compelling; concentrated; modest; steadfast; unwinking; calm; large; curious; living; dark; keen; vulgar; shrinking; piercing; hostile; disembodied; fervid; trained; appalling; complacent; unrestricted; astonished; lecherous; universal; dimmed; commanding; patient; long; prying; magic; painful; strained; imploring; ardent; melancholy; motionless; malevolent; questioning; different; tender; impartial; rapt; sullen; passionate; disdainful; reverent; magisterial; drowsy; mild; fixed; undeviating; yearning; enamored; ferret-like.

verbs
avoid—of; fix—on; quail beneath—; screen from—; shun—; stand at—; strain—toward; turn—upon; wilt beneath—; wince

beneath—; writhe under—; —chills; —falls; —falters; —pierces; —searches; —wanders.
(See look, stare, glare.)

GAZE (v)

adverbs
vacantly; indifferently; inquiringly; deliberately; mournfully; impassionedly; trustfully; steadfastly; searchingly; furtively; blankly; defiantly; wistfully; dreamily; intently; sympathetically; impertinently; apprehensively; menacingly; disconsolately; reflectively; piercingly; keenly; obtrusively; insinuatingly; mockingly; beseechingly; profanely; piteously; perplexedly; meditatingly; yearningly; shrewdly; lecherously; ardently; malevolently.
(See look, stare.)

GEAR

adjectives
new-fashioned; dainty; dangerous; diminishing; adamantine; shapeless; bloody; military.

verbs
change—; connect—s; damage—s; drive in —; equip with—; fit with—; grease—; lock—; provide—; put into—; repair—; reverse—; rip—; strip—s; throw into—; —grinds; —s mesh.
(See equipment, mechanism.)

GEAR (v)

adverbs
adequately; delicately; mechanically; intricately; complicatedly; highly; scientifically.
(See prepare.)

GELATINE

verbs
abhor—; box—; coat with—; contain—; convert into—; contaminate—; dissolve—; garnish—; mold—; prepare—; relish—; serve—; shape—; utilize—; —preserves; —shakes; —shimmies; —trembles; —wobbles.

GEM

verbs
adorn with—s; collect—s; cut—; discover —; display—; engrave—; fashion—; girdle with—s; mine for—s; polish—; prize—; unearth—; value—; weigh—; —delights; —glistens; —glitters; —illuminates; —scintillates; —spangles.
(See stone, jewel, emerald, diamond, ruby, etc.)

GEMS

adjectives

sparkling; infusorial; twinkling; expensive; superb; flashing; shining; glittering; oracular; priceless; dainty; sunborn; reflecting; radiant; costly; animated; burnished; brilliant; carven.

GENEALOGY

verbs

admit—; commend—; dig up—; insert in—; interest in—; investigate—; mark—; note in—; praise—; reckon—; record—; register—; trace—; view—; —enumerates; —exhibits; —proves; —verifies.

(See record.)

GENERAL

adverbs

admittedly; broadly; surprisingly; necessarily; astonishingly; mysteriously; inexplicably; naturally; unaccountably; unwarrantably; fortunately; illimitably; sweepingly; inclusively; significantly; evidently; amazingly; dreadfully.

GENERAL (*army*)

adjectives

politic; intrepid; merciful; permanent; commanding; grim; skilled; knowing; trained; clever; bungling; immortal; cruel; brash; stubborn; brutish; worsted; incipient; respective (pl); sagacious; shelved.

verbs

commission as—; decorate—; promote to—; respect—; salute—; —accuses; —administrates; —authorizes; —castigates; —commands; —conducts; —controls; —disposes of; —entrusts; —exercises; —leads; —maltreats; —orders; —plans; —posts; —quarters; —supervises; —terrorizes.

(See officer, commander, leader, chief.)

GENERALITIES

adjectives

polite; vague; inane; solemn; inept; illogical; meaningless.

GENERALITY

verbs

agree on—; arrive at—; avoid—; comment on—; comprehend—; confine to—s; deal in —s; descend from—s; evade—; guide—s; judge—; limit to—s; propound—; question —s; relegate to—s; resort to—s; restrain —s; skip—s; sound—s; stress—s; test—.

(See statement.)

GENERALIZATION

adjectives

easy; mystic; embracing; fantastical; scientific; hazardous; metaphysical; unsupported.

GENERATE (*v*)

adverbs

spontaneously; swiftly; sturdily; corruptly; endlessly; ceaselessly; intemperately; prolifically.

(See produce, reproduce, propagate.)

GENERATION

verbs

activate—; beget—; compute—; expose to —; glorify—; introduce—; laud—; praise —; reckon—s; remove from—; urge—; —arises; —s cherish; —s gather; —s heap; —s inherit; —involves; —s issue from.

(See period, time, age.)

GENERATIONS

adjectives

modest; innumerable; spontaneous; remote; sturdy; pompous; extremest; corrupt; countless; endless; coming; rising; future; spirited; existing; depraved; succeeding; frustrated; spurious; perished; analytical; tongueless; false; illiterate; whole; experimental; aesthetic; ceaseless; previous; intemperate; traveling.

GENERATOR

verbs

drive—; employ—; operate—; simplify—; —alternates; —converts; —draws; —heats up; —produces; —revolves; —rotates; —whines; —whirs; —winds.

(See machine, apparatus, dynamo.)

GENEROSITY

adjectives

impetuous; impulsive; unwonted; eager; judicious; amazing; consummate; pious; trustful; unparalleled; scornful; fond; divine; hearty; bitter; lavish; hospitable; celestial; careless; unquestioning; understandable; widespread; designing; dastardly.

verbs

admit—; bestow with—; commend—; credit —; distrust—; endow with—; exceed in—; expose—; flatter—; indulge—; owe to—; practise—; praise—; reveal—; rival—; shower with—; subscribe with—; temper with—; —bribes; —delights; —deprives; —drains.

(See benevolence.)

GENEROUS

adverbs

sincerely; quixotically; fantastically; ostentatiously; publicly; extremely; altruistically; charitably; benevolently; instinctively; distinctly; spontaneously; lavishly; extravagantly; habitually; truly; genuinely; amazingly; notably; essentially; magnificently; splendidly; essentially; unselfishly.

GENIAL

adverbs

pleasantly; courteously; affably; amiably; heartily; merrily; jovially; altogether; consistently; resolutely; fraternally; comfortingly; charmingly; cordially; delightfully; engagingly; marvelously; extraordinarily; unusually; habitually; conspicuously.

GENIALITY

adjectives

frank; shrewd; artificial; suave; hearty; boyish; artistic; feigned; real; soothing; effervescent; everlasting; annoying.

verbs

accustom to—; bask in—; diffuse—; flush with—; light up with—; practise—; receive with—; smile with—; welcome with —; —animates; —cheers; —delights; —endears; —exhilarates; —inspires; —warms.

(See cordiality, cheerfulness, warmth.)

GENIUS

adjectives

consummate; presiding; intellectual; inherent; interpretative; evil; unique; sublimest; engineering; sheer; ardent; sceptered; acute; fanciful; eloquent; bounding; sartorial; extraordinary; executive; untutored; unfettered; renovated; amiable; universal; persistent; various (pl); rare; decorative; sardonic; prodigious; military; solemn; solitary; gloomy; dramatic; inventive; erratic; hereditary; singular; fresh; organizing; malignant; incredible; financial; disciplined; obscure; recessive; rich; evident; peculiar; diabolical; culinary; assured; stupendous; poetical; veritable; commanding; mathematical; autocratic; superior; musical; misdirected; unclarified; intrepid; dormant; harsher; precocious; strange; brightest; gigantic; statesmanlike; vigorous; feminine; inventive; meditative; political; desultory; unique; pining; irritated; artificial; middling; majestic; maiden; innate; contriving; sullen; capricious; saturnine; fertile; legislative; bountiful; puissant; tutel-

ary; individual; creative; special; ethnic; massive; fiery; lofty; true; masterly; evil; mature; adroit; tragic; predominant; mundane; characterized.

verbs

acclaim—; attain—; befriend—; endow with—; exhibit—; inspire—; marvel at—; nourish—; nurture—; produce—; recognize —; starve—; tincture—with; trifle with—; waste—; worship—; —aspires to; —creates; —enlightens; —produces; —fructifies; —glows; —ripens; —triumphs.

(See talent, power, creator, artist.)

GENTEEL

adverbs

proudly; nobly; aristocratically; inherently; genuinely; truly; admittedly; tenaciously; handsomely; elegantly; impressively.

GENTILITY

adjectives

brave; stripped; plated; faded; shabby; penniless; sham; decayed; decadent; worn; worked; noticeable .

verbs

bear with—; borrow—; claim—; confute—; convey—; counterfeit—; cultivate—; degrade from—; diffuse—; exhibit—; expel—; patronize—; pursue—; recognize—; reveal —; stand on—; vanquish—; —decays; —enhances; —fades; —graces.

(See dignity, politeness, elegance, refinement.)

GENTLE

adverbs

considerately; sympathetically; indulgently; remarkably; particularly; affably; curiously; compassionately; mercifully; understandingly; softly; tolerantly; calmly; forbearingly; patiently; gravely; quietly; serenely; complaisantly; politely; ingratiatingly; amazingly.

GENTLEMAN

adjectives

worthy; dignified; conservative; old-fashioned; prosy; antique; majestic; country; whiskered; eligible; aristocratic; credulous; digressive; gallant; decorous; opulent; polished; decrepit; unusual; chivalrous; superannuated; curious; studious; lovely; legal-looking; vacuous-looking; benevolent; eccentric; elderly; ceremonious; fastidious;

venerable; scholarly; valiant; flippant; loyal; downright; reverend; inane; decayed; clerical; suave; heedless; sober; fat; landed; frayed; frail; silk-stockinged.

verbs
admire—; bear like—; be born—; behave like—; conduct like—; define—; denote—; disguise as—; educate as—; grace—; mellow into—; pass for a—; perfect—; produce—; respect—; transform into—; welcome—; —considers; —forbears; —honors; —reproaches; —respects; —submits; —sympathizes; —understands.

GENTLENESS
adjectives
stately; infinite; intelligent; supreme; caressing; surface; unassuming; deprecating; wonted; unbelievable; tender; heartfelt.

GENTLEWOMAN
adjectives
shrewd; virtuous; fresher; dainty; elegant.

GENTRY
adjectives
landed; minor; cocked-hat; light-fingered.

GENUINE
adverbs
unquestionably; veritably; obviously; manifestly; unimpeachably; indubitably; essentially; authentically; incontestably; substantially; inimitably; invaluably.

GEOGRAPHY
verbs
add to—; confuse—; familiarize with—; perfect—; refer to—; resort to—; subdue—; verse in—; —defines; —describes; —explains; —informs; —reveals; —treats of.
(See science.)

GERM
verbs
check—s; combat—; crawl with—s; destroy —; detect—; disseminate—s; eliminate—s; fall prey to—; filter—s; harbor—; identify —; infect with—; infest with—; isolate—; resist—; sow—s; track down—; transmit—; —inhabits; —invades; —lodges in; —migrates; —multiplies; —strikes; —thrives.
(See disease.)

GERMICIDE
verbs
advocate—; disinfect with—; employ—; flush with—; fumigate with—; wash with —; —allays; —arrests; —cleans; —cures; —destroys; —evaporates; —exterminates; —heals; —overpowers; —prevents; —purifies; —rids; —routs; —sterilizes.
(See disinfection.)

GERMS
adjectives
natural; fruitful; virulent; organic; pernicious; fundamental; floating; delicate; vegetable; infant; marauding; infectious; prolific; insidious.

GESTICULATE (v)
adverbs
violently; ludicrously; dramatically; expressively; suavely; gleefully; impatiently; sweepingly; airily; affectedly; ecstatically; significantly; authoritatively.
(See gesture.)

GESTURE
adjectives
wild; authoritative; mental; ponderous; conciliatory; magnificent; ungoverned; convulsive; dreadful; despairing; angry; spontaneous; imploring; eloquent; generous; affectionate; threatening; pitying; ferocious; airy; truculent; dignified; dramatic; expressive; vulgar; romping; abrupt; symbolic; fine; impetuous; helpless; parting; joyous; excited; gentle; sweeping; negative; impatient; uncouth; insolent; respectful; tentative; violent; spasmodic; careless; grateful; absurd; polite; gleeful; animated; significant; vehement; arbitrary; regal; emphatic; heroic; deprecatory; faint; pretty; chivalrous; spectacular; interrogatory; emotional; superstitious; childish; renunciatory; magnanimous; effective; imperceptible; furious; inexplicable; disparaging; frivolous; courtly; menacing; frail; analyzing; pioneering; possessive; benignant; scarce; wide; graceful; invincible; masterful; quick; noble; imperious.

verbs
accompany with—s; ape—; emphasize with —; employ—; execute—; express by—; indulge in—; imitate—; mix with—; moderate —s; motion with—; note—; perform—; record—; refuse—; restrict—s; ridicule—; speak with—s; signify by—; —s express; —s harmonize.
(See motion, posture.)

GESTURE (v)

adverbs

wildly; ponderously; magnificently; convulsively; despairingly; spontaneously; generously; ferociously; truculently; vulgarly; symbolically; uncouthly; animatedly; vehemently; regally; emphatically; spectacularly; menacingly; benignantly; imperiously; masterfully.

(See gesticulate.)

GEYSER

verbs

—blows off; —boils; —bubbles; —darts; —ejects; —emits; —erupts; —explodes; —gurgles; —gushes; —jets; —plays; —pours; —relaxes; —ruins; —shoots; —snorts; —spouts; —spurts; —swells; —throws off.

(See spring, fountain.)

GHASTLY

adverbs

incredibly; unbelievably; inexpressibly; horribly; awfully; fearfully; shockingly; portentously; appallingly; monstrously; formidably; weirdly; terribly; utterly.

GHOST

adjectives

sheeted; gigantic; livid; lofty; gliding; glowing; drab; pale; frighted; silvery; collaborating; sweet; songless; pathetic; slender; reflected; mad; aimless; restless; peaceful; infernal; beckoning; disturbed; pensive; pious; haunting; handsome; graphical; headless; shrouded; honest.

verbs

give up—; harbor—; perceive—; raise—; shape—; speak to—; —beckons; —cries; —flits; —follows; —glares; —haunts; —howls; —points; —prowls; —pursues; —returns; —scares; —shadows; —stalks; —torments; —vanishes; —visits.

(See apparition, phantom, spirit, shade, soul.)

GHOSTLY

adverbs

weirdly; alarmingly; immaterially; spectrally; uncannily; appallingly; mysteriously; inscrutably; horribly; terribly; inexplicably; comically; strangely; curiously; oddly; unbelievably; remarkably; singularly.

GIANT

adjectives

mental; financial; rich; juicy; shock-headed; glorious; massy; mysterious; petrified; supernormal; stupendous; genial; peaceable; useless; pastoral; deformed; hideous; monstrous.

verbs

conquer—; crush—; dread—; flee from—; grapple with—; mount—; overthrow—; quell—; wrestle with—; —heaves; —inhabits; —menaces; —overpowers; —overwhelms; —roars; —shoulders; —terrifies; —threatens; —tramples.

(See monster.)

GIBBER (v)

adverbs

ghoulishly; drunkenly; disgustingly; idiotically; aimlessly; inanely; unintelligibly; insanely.

(See chatter, jabber.)

GIBBET

adjectives

shameful; gloomy; intellectual; menacing; ancient; unused; life-snatching.

verbs

chain to—; condemn to—; conduct to—; deserve—; erect—; escape—; execute on—; gaze at—; punish on—; save from—; send to—; sentence to—; suffer—; tie to—; —frightens; —glooms.

(See gallows.)

GIBE

adjectives

rude; insolent; stinging; jocose; exultant; nasty; bitter; raucous; friendly.

GIDDINESS

verbs

anticipate—; bring on—; condemn—; cure —; delight in—; faint with—; fall in—; incur—; occasion—; repent—; stagger with —; swim with—; tolerate—; whirl with—; —bewilders; —confuses; —creeps over; —envelops; —infuriates; —maddens; —ruins; —vexes.

(See dizziness.)

GIDDY

adverbs

wildly; heedlessly; distractedly; carelessly; dreamily; happily; rapturously; blithely;

capriciously; wantonly; deliriously; incoherently; foolishly; irresolutely; irresponsibly; amazingly; reprehensibly; erratically; fitfully; fantastically; unstably; freakishly; waywardly; captiously; frivolously.

GIFT

adjectives
charming; lasting; valuable; expensive; mental; worthless; poetic; lovely; heavenly; worth-while; exceptional; inalienable; practical; satirical; equal; especial; divine; conversational; ample; promised; fragile; higher; festive; peaceful; myriad (pl); fair; genuine; lyrical; hospitable; innate; pious; glozing; distinctive; versatile; gracious; sacramental; brilliant; healing; compensating; acceptable; wonderful; appropriate; sweet; random; suitable; melancholy; unavailing; entrusted; transcendent; golden; youthful; fecund; rare; graceful; clever; placating; superlative; godlike; lyrical; trifling; sponsorial; unique; prophetic; precious; pure; cankering; free; mysterious; ineffable; cherished; imitative; peerless; wondrous; oratorical; clever; dangerous; matchless; propitiatory; social; costly; formidable; different; spicy.

verbs
apologize with—; bestow — upon; cherish—; cultivate—; endow with—; enhance —; exercise—; favor with—; grant—; honor with—; lavish —s upon; offer—; proffer—; scorn—; surprise with—; value—; —delights; —elates; —enriches; —impresses; — obligates; —persuades; —s pour in.
(See present, endowment, talent, benefaction, contribution.)

GIFTED

adverbs
brilliantly; unusually; wonderfully; magnificently; notably; consummately; peculiarly; expertly; intellectually; eminently; admirably; illustriously; aptly; conspicuously; extraordinarily; supremely; uncommonly; highly.

GIGANTIC

adverbs
incredibly; stupendously; tremendously; unbelievably; inexpressibly; colossally; prodigiously; overwhelmingly; terrifyingly; appallingly; marvellously; terribly; astonishingly; astoundingly.

GIGGLE

adjectives
rich; girlish; antiquated; sudden; nervous; loud.

verbs
burst into—; convulse in —s; cure of —s; degenerate into —s; laugh in —s; set into —s; suppress—; throw into —s; utter—; — annoys; —bores; —disgusts; —disturbs; — interrupts; —sickens; —sparkles; —tickles; —wearies.
(See laugh.)

GIGGLE (*v*)

adverbs
nervously; hysterically; self-consciously; intermittently; abruptly; explosively; coquettishly; alluringly.
(See snicker, titter.)

GILD (*v*)

adverbs
radiantly; lavishly; artfully; tastefully; professionally; superfluously; richly; ornamentally.
(See cover, color.)

GILL

verbs
breathe with—; close—; cuff—; draw into —; expand—; furnish with—; stroke—; inhale through—; strain—; —absorbs; — admits; —flaps; —inhales; —quivers; —receives; —sucks; —swells.

GIN

adjectives (liquor)
meditative; sullen; accursed.

verbs
abstain from—; denature—; distill—; imbibe—; legalize—; loathe—; reek of—; resist—; —destroys; —dulls; —grogs; —inebriates; —influences; —intoxicates; —overcomes; —regales; —seduces.
(See liquor.)

GIRAFFE

verbs
anger—; arouse—; cage—; exhibit—; lasso —; pet—; train—; —ambles; —batters; — browses; —forages; —gallops; —s herd; — kicks; —plucks; —roams; —straddles.
(See animal.)

547

adjectives

sylvan; docile; unaffected; much-courted; cuddlesome; dear; delightful; stricken; robust; athletic; country; serving; frowzy; wishy-washy; tawdry; expensive; clumsy; urgent; watchful; passionate; anserine; adolescent; elegant; slim; confiding; artful; sensible; true; scrawny; giddy; sweet; gentle; beautiful; ornamental; casual; suitable; frail; sympathetic; light; colored; timbrel; ambitious; radiant; exotic; truthful; semi-wild; utilitarian; blushing; alluring; unregulated; debilitated; loitering; singsong; impecunious; trembling; dependent; sullen; charming; pluckiest; dainty; sober; uneducated; freckle-faced; worthless; industrious; ridiculous; swarthy; sophisticated; vigorous; decent; virtuous; enthusiastic; patrician; perverse; unruly; willful; flippant; comely; awkward; sad; shiftless; peevish; commonplace; emotional; suicidal; coquettish.

verbs

betroth—; bud into—; consort with —s; —beguiles; —blushes; —charms; —dances; —giggles; —loves; —lures; —mystifies; —pouts; —prates; —smiles; —sulks.

(See infant, child, youth, damsel.)

GIRTH
adjectives

generous; broad; immense; cumbersome; muscular; spanless; bountiful.

GIST
verbs

convey—; define—; deviate from—; explain —; follow—; glimpse—; overlook—; phrase —; sum up—; translate—; understand—; wade through—; —deals with; —denotes; —lies in; —necessitates.

(See substance, core, essence.)

GIVE (v)
adverbs

exclusively; grudgingly; charitably; benevolently; abundantly; grumblingly; discriminately; spontaneously; magnificently; methodically; unsparingly; discreetly; conscientiously; periodically; impartially; infallibly; subsequently; wantonly; invariably; ultimately; intentionally; substantially; prodigally; legitimately.

(See bestow, accord, grant.)

adjectives

undiscerning; venerable; judicious; Indian.

GLACIER
adjectives

grinding; upended; extinct; immense; unnamed; glistening.

verbs

climb—; consolidate into—; cross—; form —; melt—; press into—; slide into—; warn of—; —chokes; —confronts; —creeps; —derives from; —drifts; —glistens; —glitters; —glows; —lodges; —sparkles.

(See stream, ice, snow.)

GLAD
adverbs

genially; laughingly; wholly; definitely; heartily; truly; genuinely; wholeheartedly; amazingly; pathetically; childishly; sincerely; radiantly; delightedly; enthusiastically; profoundly; quietly; visibly; boundlessly; solemnly; exceedingly; gloriously; rapturously; hysterically; excitedly; serenely.

GLADE
adjectives

rustling; steep; hopeful; enchanted; shaded; woodland; mossy; purple; shadowy; umbrageous; sheltered; tropic.

GLADNESS
adjectives

tender; whimsical; quiet; visionary; subdued; visible; sunny; hidden; bursting; boundless; solemn; ignorant; maniacal; exceeding; glorious; unfeigned; abrupt; tranquil; immortal; effervescent; sober; ebullient.

verbs

bring on—; cloak in—; comprehend—; couch in—; crush—; derive — from; deserve—; dispense—; emit—; enliven with —; exude—; flush with—; occasion—; overwhelm—; quell—; radiate—; send out—; trample—; —confuses; —enhances; —speaks.

(See delight, exhilaration, joy, pleasure.)

GLAMOROUS
adverbs

seductively; delightfully; undeniably; beautifully; gloriously; irresistibly; peculiarly; utterly; adorably; charmingly; exotically;

wantonly; girlishly; deliberately; carefully; calculatingly; immeasurably; inconceivably; incomparably; naturally; purposely; cleverly; bewitchingly; unconsciously; darkly; brilliantly; **entrancingly.**

GLAMOUR

adjectives

harmless; **romantic;** laughing; longing; sophisticated; midnight; theatrical; lingering; pictorial; extraneous; fortuitous.

verbs

capture—; create—; deck in—; dim—; invest with—; recapture—; sacrifice—; savor —; surround with—; win with—; yield to —; —allures; —attracts; —awes; —bewitches; —charms; —dazzles; —deceives; —deludes; —enchants; —entrances; —fades; —fascinates; —magnetizes; —stirs; —wears off.

(See charm, enchantment, fascination, glory, spell.)

GLANCE

adjectives

tender; sidelong; mirthful; dreamy; wistful; mechanical; furtive; fierce; maternal; reproachful; hasty; keen; languid; quick; pitying; uneasy; mingled; oblique; timid; mischievous; departed; pure; half-inviting; flaming; penetrating; vindictive; imploring; comprehensive; passing; interrogatory; approving; satisfying; chastened; sinister; deep; hostile; malevolent; tranquil; curious; apologetic; crawling; mortal; wild; expressive; mournful; fantastical; unseeing; fiery; covert; careless; bridling; suspicious; clear; significant; inquiring; admiring; rapid; errant; frightened; unintercepted; single; heartfelt; nervous; wandering; absorbing; baleful; annihilating; superficial; farewell; dull; bird; momentary; vertical; frank; casual; contemptuous; supplicating; conciliatory; fleeting; expectant; indolent; genuine; sudden; sharp; malign; critical; heavy; meteor; furious; meaning; steady; hurried; meager; backward; irresistible; exquisite; surprised; evil; dubious; compassionate; venomous; irresolute; proud; soulful; swift; pleading; expiring; confused; cold; mild; satanical; luminous; ripened; abstracted; frowning; murderous; incidental; saucy; **ominous;** wondering; beseeching; appealing.

verbs

bestow — upon; cast — upon; detect at a—; flash—; intercept—; quail beneath—; rivet —upon; shift—; shoot — at; steal — at; survey at—; —chills; —falters; —pricks; — rests on; —strays.

(See look, gleam, glimpse, flash.)

GLANCE (v)

adverbs

curiously; complacently; suspiciously; furtively; rebelliously; piercingly; cursorily; indifferently; disconsolately; disdainfully; involuntarily; contemptuously; critically; reproachfully; apprehensively; surreptitiously; wistfully; inquisitively; significantly; tenderly; malignantly; covertly; casually; instinctively; passionately; imperiously; intuitively; dubiously; deferentially; maliciously.

(See beam, gleam, glitter.)

GLAND

adjectives

lymphatic; dormant; secretive; master; lively; sex; ineffective; swollen; abnormal.

verbs

affect—; block—; graft—; inflame—; reduce—; reinvigorate—; transplant—; —controls; —enlarges; —functions; —indurates; —opens into; —pours forth; —produces; —responds; —secretes; —suppurates; —swells.

(See organ.)

GLARE

adjectives

savage; bright; burning; furious; warning; ghastly; gaudy; blinding; blistering; sun; dull; interested; meteoric; dancing; kingly; fearful; fiery; pale; lurid; ruddy; rifted; wild; frozen; desert; awful; brazen; blank; merciless; yellow; chill.

verbs

bask in—; bate—; cast—; destroy with—; fix—; incur—; ignore—; mark—; observe —; relieve—; remove—; shade—; shine with—; —angers; —blinds; —dazzles; — exposes; —lights; —reveals.

(See light, look, gaze, splendor.)

GLARE (v)

adverbs

ferociously; **comically;** fiercely; scowlingly; balefully; resentfully; vindictively; hostilely; stonily; remorselessly; oddly; blazingly.

(See frown, stare.)

adjectives

undersized; sapphire; frosted; gleaming; spilled; parenthetical; arid; iridescent; bifocal; misted; delicate; preparatory; smoky; sumptuous; watery; tarnished; steaming; shattered; spattering; neglected; molten; poor; distorted; stained; cobwebbed; superstitious; irregular; untasted; social; translucent; medieval; brimming; swirled; rimmed; uncolored; inverted; dimpling; opaque.

verbs

brandish—; blow—; cast—; chip—; clink —s; color—; cover with—; crack—; drain —; engrave—; etch on—; file—; fondle—; frame with—; glaze with—; grind—; mold —; nick—; pulverize—; shape—; shatter—; split—; stain—; —s clash; —s clatter; —s clink.

(See crystal, mirror.)

GLAZE

adjectives

dreamy; monotonous; sincere; defiant; granite; iridescent; thin; death.

GLEAM

adjectives

rare; momentary; occasional; varied (pl); silvery; dazzling; diabolic; sorrowful; cool; phosphorescent; portentous; troubled; lurid; livid; fiery; brilliant; distant; convex; dull; new; hateful; crafty; starry; subdued; unpleasant; sulphurous; metallic; stray; elusive; polar; waning; pallid; summer; flickering; bountiful; bright; ruddy; spasmodic; pale; alluring; determined; ineffectual; faint; vagrant; tearlike; broken; wilder; solitary; opaline; visionary; formless; evanescent; greasy; angry; illusive; moon-lit; splendid.

verbs

behold—; cast—; diffuse—; emit—; flare into—; flash—; light up with—; obscure—; reflect—; send—; shoot—; spread—; — blazes; —dazes; —dazzles; —flickers; — glitters; —illuminates; —pales; —shimmers; —shudders; —sparkles; —twinkles.

(See light, flash, beam, ray.)

GLEAM (v)

adverbs

weirdly; unnaturally; ominously; tigerishly; obscurely; fitfully; dangerously; momentarily; dazzlingly; diabolically; phosphorescent-

ly; portentously; sulphurously; pallidly; spasmodically; flickeringly; evanescently; illusively.

(See shine, glow.)

GLEE

adjectives

rapturous; malicious; unconscious; strange; noisy; defying; childish; uncouth; unbidden; counterfeited; fiendish; sparkling; tumultuous; pelting; innocent; laughing; intemperate; venturous; chortling.

verbs

advance with—; bubble with—; condemn—; dance in—; display—; exhibit—; exude—; feign—; flaunt—; grin with—; increase—; jump in—; laugh with—; leap in—; occasion—; plunge into with—; rub the hands in—; sport with—; titter in—; turn into—; —envelops; —infects; —spreads.

(See mirth, gayety, merriment, joy.)

GLEEFUL

adverbs

blithely; enthusiastically; infectiously; innocently; happily; irresistibly; completely; naturally; elatedly; triumphantly; joyously; light-heartedly; merrily; hilariously; sportively; utterly; openly; laughingly; noisily; effervescently; ecstatically; wholesomely; habitually.

GLEN

adjectives

peaceful; shadowy; shrubby; narrow; unfrequented; mountain; leafy; woody; silent; obscurest; darkened; solitary; shaded; sunless.

GLIB

adverbs

blandly; smoothly; cleverly; adroitly; deceptively; astutely; suspiciously; blatantly; suavely; socially; professionally; unctuously; fluently; nimbly; easily; felicitously; dexterously; affably; complaisantly; urbanely; civilly; politely; ingratiatingly; entertainingly; persuasively; resourcefully; amazingly; extraordinarily; strikingly.

GLIBNESS

verbs

admire—; beget—; criticize with—; deliver with—; impede—; judge by—; mistrust—; perform with—; practise—; praise—; proceed with—; speak with—; unfold with—;

utter with—; —charms; —deceives; —delights; —impresses; —misleads; —oils.
(See fluency.)

GLIDE (v)
adverbs
smoothly; gracefully; unobtrusively; serenely; majestically; sinuously; noiselessly; dreamily.
(See slide, slip.)

GLIMMER
adjectives
misty; fading; uncertain; ghostly; pale; gleaming; dying; quivering; ignorant; confused; faint; quiet; pallid.

GLIMMER (v)
adverbs
dimly; phosphorescently; spasmodically; intermittently; evanescently; uncertainly; pallidly; gaily; mistily.
(See gleam, shine.)

GLIMPSE
adjectives
intriguing; touching; vivid; interesting; incidental; electric; vague; marvelous; amusing; faint; transient; picturesque; tempting; comforting; occasional; tantalizing; leafy; fleeting; delicious; shadowy; shimmering; cautious; prophetic; furtive; chilly; flashing; unveiled; mysterious; passing; murky; desired.

verbs
afford—; catch—; deny—; detect at—; drink in—; flash—; hope for—; obtain—; prevent—; procure—; win—; yearn for—; yield—; —dazzles; —delights; —glimmers; —glitters; —perforates; —reveals; —shimmers; —shines.
(See flash, glance.)

GLINT
adjectives
moiled; rigid; ravishing; fiery; murderous; nasty; wicked.

GLINT (v)
adverbs
suspiciously; antagonistically; brutally; angrily; murderously; wickedly; fiendishly; viciously; vindictively.
(See gleam, flash, glitter.)

GLISTER
adjectives
faint; ruddy; scornful; spotless.

GLITTER
adjectives
prismatic; gilded; steely; intense; jeweled; scaly; fiery; mercurial; dangerous; sinister; streaked; sarcastic; dull; wandering; pristine; weary; effeminate; blinding; ghastly; opulent; gaudy.

GLITTER (v)
adverbs
lustrously; prismatically; intensely; mercurially; sinisterly; coldly; devilishly; blindingly; opulently; gaudily.
(See sparkle, gleam, flash.)

GLOAT (v)
adverbs
spitefully; hilariously; selfishly; pettishly; triumphantly; hatefully; jealously; vindictively; morbidly; victoriously.
(See covet, lust, ogle.)

GLOBE
adjectives
terrestrial; habitable; ponderous; gorgeous; spotty; gluey; heavenly; stupendous; terraqueous; bewildering; celestial; native; many-mortaled; whirling; spinning; careening.

verbs
circle—; circumnavigate—; consult—; discern on—; employ—; fill—; form into—; girdle—; perfect—; refer to—; revolve—; rotate—; suspend—; —defines; —describes; —explains; —points; —represents; —rolls; —rotates; —spins; —whirls.
(See ball, sphere, earth, world.)

GLOBULAR
adverbs
amazingly; overwhelmingly; stupendously; astonishingly; astoundingly; totally; inconceivably; boundlessly; extraordinarily; unprecedentedly; strangely; unwontedly; surprisingly; singularly.

GLOBULES
adjectives
teeming; swarming; insignificant; minute; porous.

adjectives

congregated; dark; ascetic; deepening; shady; solemn; hopeless; malodorous; partial; anxious; lingering; additional; thick; funereal; desponding; murkier; dishwater; moving; gathering; chilly; fixed; slumbrous; melancholy; impenetrable; somber; sacred; grateful; ceaseless; minister; surrounding; forest; eternal; atmospheric; unromantic; perpetual; sepulchral; profound; pregnant; damp; warm; divine; convent; azure; woven; settled; sullen; dungeon; foreboding; sympathetic; twilight; wintry; intensified; lurid; coiled; starving; unavailing; heavy; persistent; dreary; pervasive; darkling; glowing; unobtrusive; dangerous; conventional; glorious; coppery; verdurous; gorgeous; adamantine; arched; natal; cheerless; silent; sable; oppressive; dank; languid; prairie; utter; ethereal; delicate; sheer; blighting; roseate; abnormal; rich; curtained; sibylline; haunting; stained; shadowed; Stygian.

verbs

assimilate—; cast upon—; detach from—; dispel—; envelop in—; exude—; harbor—; overcome—; overhang with—; overwhelm with—; pierce—; wrap in—; —assails; —deepens; —dwells on; —oppresses; —pervades; —settles on; —thickens.

(See darkness, obscurity, melancholy, sorrow, misfortune, despondency, dejection.)

GLOOMY

adverbs

abjectly; helplessly; depressingly; incurably; inconceivably; hopelessly; incredibly; piteously; horribly; tragically; unbelievably; singularly; unreasonably; miserably; needlessly; comically; ridiculously; ostensibly; obviously; desperately; heavily; sadly; mournfully; moodily; pensively; sulkily; inconsolably; desolately; disconsolately; dismally; gravely; woefully; glumly; wanly; unnecessarily; irritatingly.

GLORIFY (v)

adverbs

insanely; enthusiastically; boisterously; lovingly; martially; sumptuously; posthumously; eternally; physically; radiantly; ancestrally; feudally; imperially; romantically; regally; matchlessly; barbarically.

(See praise, adore.)

adverbs

effulgently; brilliantly; splendidly; superbly; unexpectedly; martially; inestimably; radiantly; proudly; regally; ecstatically; peculiarly; matchlessly; supremely; barbarically; distinctly; solemnly; sublimely; remarkably; eminently; imperishably; transcendently.

GLORY

adjectives

ghastly; martial; gaping; reflected; sumptuary; posthumous; fainter; semblance; coeternal; inevitable; liquid; elemental; sudden; butchered; native; physical; inner; athletic; shining; paternal; short-lived; earthly; radiant; proud; ancestral; gentle; false; golden; pristine; endless; evolving; hirsute; mild; celestial; eclipsed; incipient; abandoned; lustrous; living; feudal; spectacular; insubstantial; universal; passive; imperial; romantic; artistic; transient; setting; crimson; western; lineal; lasting; regal; undulating; naked; meridian; peerless; ebbed; imperishable; meteoric; shadowy; flaming; ecstatic; boasted; crowning; supernal; floral; lambent; heroic; scenic; promised; unclouded; unknown; peculiar; unclasped; matchless; lesser; barbaric; original; untasted; quiet; everlasting; pinnacled; bloody; departing; concentrated; sole; inestimable; imaginary.

verbs

accentuate—; bask in—; blaze in—; blind to—; crown with—; debilitate—; dissipate —; elect to—; encircle with—; elevate to —; extol—; flaunt—; mark for—; participate in—; reflect—; revel in—; reward with—; raise to—; shed—; —passes; —shines; —suffuses; revivify—.

(See honor, fame, renown, pomp, splendor, grandeur, praise.)

GLOSS

adjectives

opaque; ultimate; faultless; brilliant; shining; raven; stimulating; firm.

GLOVE

adjectives

frosted; leathern; long; slim; cloth; fringed; greasy; primrose; easy; cheveril; snug-fitting; warm; worn.

GLOW

adjectives

lurid; phosphorescent; rainbow; pallid; vinous; rich; fitful; silvery; ruby; vague; starry; full; strong; suffusing; warm; chastened; dim; joyous; transparent; luminous; dreamy; brilliant; soft; scorching; fiery; mystical; pectoral; molten; original; reflected; white; youthful; inward; comfortable; feverish; unaccustomed; sunset; faint; summer; somber; evening; latent; wavering; conscious; clustering; earthly; fearful; hectic; tropic; genial; emotional; refracted; refulgent; ethereal; blessed; hideous; sorrowing; tremulous; seraphic.

verbs

agitate to—; burn to—; clothe in—; emit—; feel—; heat to—; kindle—; pale—; quench —; quicken to—; shade—; suffuse with—; —brightens; —captivates; —cheers; —declines; —deepens; —flushes; —guides; —illuminates; —irradiates; —lights up; —radiates; —scorches; —shines; —subsides; —warms.

(See flush, animation, ardor, warmth.)

GLOW (v)

adverbs

morosely; intensely; luminously; nebulously; sardonically; auspiciously; mellowly; perceptibly; luridly; phosphorescently; mystically; vaguely; ruddily; feverishly; genially; hectically; ethereally; tremulously; seraphically.

(See shine, beam.)

GLOWING

adverbs

radiantly; softly; dimly; perceptibly; brilliantly; splendidly; gorgeously; endlessly; magnificently; sumptuously; constantly; ineffably; lustrously; phosphorescently; vividly; brightly; intensely; resplendently; marvellously; luridly; richly; fitfully; joyously; transparently; whitely; faintly.

GLUM

adverbs

dismally; incurably; stupidly; cheerlessly; immovably; terribly; hopelessly; lugubriously; darkly; anxiously; despondently; curiously; profoundly; heavily; drearily; dangerously; dreadfully; abnormally; significantly; silently; unreasonably; sulkily; mopishly; strangely; disconsolately; exasperatingly.

GLUT (v)

adverbs

swinishly; brutishly; disgustingly; inordinately; madly; unrestrainedly; ravenously.

(See gorge, eat.)

GLUTTONOUS

adverbs

unbelievably; insanely; disgustingly; repulsively; strangely; crudely; grossly; hungrily; greedily; voraciously; extremely; excessively; wolfishly; inordinately; recklessly; dangerously; extravagantly; horribly; horridly; ravenously; insatiably; offensively; revoltingly; abominably; incredibly.

GNARLED

adverbs

roughly; ruggedly; scraggily; crookedly; sturdily; agedly; stumpily; robustly; massively; tenuously; thickly; rheumatically; gauntly; wirily.

GNASH (v)

adverbs

incessantly; frenziedly; horribly; furiously; fiercely; hungrily; fiendishly; dreadfully; insanely.

(See rage, fume, storm.)

GNAW (v)

adverbs

hungrily; ravenously; furiously; madly; brutishly; bestially; vigorously; ferociously; famishedly.

(See chew, bite.)

GOAD

adjectives

insistent; galling; sharp; inexorable.

GOAL

adjectives

veiled; ultimate; luminous; common; glittering; incentive; stimulating; selfsame; receding; unreachable; refined; successive (pl); utmost; mortal; illusory; desired; tertiary; inevitable; traditional; amaranthine; mysterious; hard-gained; fictitious.

verbs

achieve—; attain—; bar—; cherish—; defeat—; effect—; forge forward—; gain—; guard—; hamper—; move toward—; propel toward—; realize—; strive for—; surmount to—; sway from—; swerve from—; swing from—; touch—; push toward—.

(See end, aim, destiny, mark.)

adjectives
romantic; silky; browsing; sure-footed; metamorphosed; mutinous; sacrificial.

verbs
domesticate—; clip—; exercise—; fleece—; herd—s; pasture—; shear—; stall—; tether —; —attacks; —butts; —forages; —grazes; —leaps; —pastures; —supplies; —yields.
(See animal.)

GOBLET

adjectives
knobbed; embossed; smoke-colored.

GOD
(*divine being*)

adjectives
faultless; unalterable; sacred; immortal; stern; everlasting; deathless; compassionate; ever-living; serene; inspiring.

god
(*idol*)

adjectives
monstrous; extemporal; bestial; goat-nursed; stalwart; unappeasable; bleating; victim-nourished; appeasable; defiant; contending; drunken; fire-robed; distant; tinseled; winged; capricious; exasperated; petty; crumbled; artificial; blinded; associate; banished; inexorable; unsolicited; false; materialized; frivolous; deposed; auxiliary.

verbs
banish—; beseech—; blaspheme—; defy—; deify—; discover—; exalt—; herald—; implore—; invoke—; placate—; propitiate—; recognize—; reveal—; revere—; revile—; vow before—; worship—; wrestle with—; —commands; —grants; —guides; —illumines; —judges; —ordains; —prevails.
(See deity, divinity, idol, ruler, creator, Jesus Chirst.)

GODDESS

adjectives
libidinous; voluptuous; impending; fickle; glorious; loving; beauteous.

GODLESS

adverbs
horribly; impiously; perversely; fanatically; recklessly; avowedly; sacrilegiously; blasphemously; profanely; heartbreakingly; graciously; obstinately; obdurately; unhappily; irrationally; unreasonably; immovably; openly; skeptically; materially; agnostically; faithlessly; indifferently.

GODLIKE

adverbs
wondrously; peerlessly; angelically; seraphically; undeniably; charitably; sweetly; piously; virtuously; humbly; beatifically; consecratedly; spiritually; reverently; purely; incredibly; utterly.

GODLY

adverbs
beautifully; devotedly; humbly; piously; reverently; consistently; devoutly; actively; justly; remarkably; eminently; notably; transcendently; earnestly; zealously; illustriously; wondrously; consecratedly; faithfully.

GOLD

adjectives
fraud-accumulated; burnished; sculptured; transparent; crystal; molten; wrought; mealy; fretted; refined; virgin; bright; hard-earned; rusted; intense; gleaming; mossy; dominant; vaporous; tested; gravel; supple; gaudy; damning; barbaric; powdered; sterilized; coronation; beaten; clearest; drowned; countless; vile; richest; hoarded; stamped; fluid; fairy; blowing; musty; shimmering; iridescent; cloudy; streaked; shining; fragrant; faint; floral; glittering; ruined; banked; clean; coarse; ruddy.

verbs
alloy—; amass—; beat out—; bless with—; bribe with—; delve for—; desire—; dig for —; discover—; emboss with—; hammer—; harden—; heap—; hide—; hoard—; load with—; melt—; mine—; pan—; plot for—; roll—; salvage—; search for—; separate—; spurn—; squander—; thirst for—; treasure —; —blinds; —chains; —charms; —clinks; —corrupts; —curses; —degenerates; —glitters; —glistens; —occurs; —sparkles.
(See metal, element, treasure.)

GOLF

verbs
compete in—; concentrate on—; contend at —; enjoy—; gamble at—; improve—; pair off in—; practise—; tie in—; score in—;

—beguiles; —diverts; —engrosses; —entertains; —excites; —exerts; —interests; — wearies.
(See sport, game.)

GOLF COURSE
verbs
compete on—; construct—; cover—; design —; develop—; extend—; form—; idle on —; open—; operate—; visit—; wander over —; —attracts; —beckons; —stretches.

GONG
adjectives
clangorous; dreadful; sounded; resonant; echoing.

verbs
clash—; drum on—; hammer—; hearken to —; strike—; —alarms; —assembles; — calls; —clanks; —clatters; —deafens; —resounds; —reverberates; —signals; — sounds; —summons; —surprises; —thunders; —vibrates.
(See bell.)

GOOD
adjectives
indifferent; supreme; possible; garnered; public; tender; unimagined; infinite; irreconcilable; celestial; chief; ultimate; timely; final; permanent; common; spiritual; sovereign; unmitigated; worldly; satiating; everlasting; unchanging; weak; universal.

verbs
accept—; admire—; approve of—; ascertain—; augur—; commend—; devote to—; distinguish by—; endorse—; expound—; favor—; invite—; laud—; nullify—; offer —; relish—; repay—; reward—; welcome —; —benefits; —merits; —pleases; —profits; —prospers.
(See advantage, benefit, virtue, welfare.)

adverbs
exceptionally; wonderfully; incontrovertibly; undeniably; absolutely; faultlessly; commercially; spiritually; materially; supremely; innately; naturally; inherently; essentially; unusually; uncommonly; consistently; fairly; completely; unquestionably; intrinsically; genuinely; pricelessly; unutterably.

GOOD-HUMORED
adverbs
delightfully; pleasantly; genially; merrily; jovially; immensely; unfailingly; invariably; wholesomely; amazingly; marvelously; patiently; visibly; notably; remarkably; indulgently; considerately; graciously; generously.

GOODNESS
adjectives
mantled; wholesome; innate; inherent; natural; hearty; infinite; adorable; undeserved; essential; true; full; awful; delicious; breathing; invisible; unusual; universal; tasty; obedient; hypocritical.

GOODS
adjectives
glittering; worldly; perishable; unwanted; transitory; worthless; non-durable; treasured.

GOOD-WILL
verbs
abuse—; cultivate—; dispense—; earn—; enjoy—; evoke—; favor with—; foster—; further—; gain—; grant—; inculcate—; inherit—; merit—; obtain—; pay with—; permit—; procure—; promote—; regard with —; seek—; sell—; solicit—; speak with—; spread—; win—; work for—; —privileges; —wanes.
(See reputation, favor.)

GOOSE
verbs
—attacks; —braves; —cackles; —captures; —circles; —clasps; —cleaves sky; —climbs; —destroys; —dives; —drives; —drops; — eyes; —floats through; —hawks; —hooks; —moults; —perches; —preys on; —robs; —sails; —screams; geese sever themselves; —sights; —soars; —sweeps.
(See bird.)

GOPHER
verbs
—burrows; —devastates; —digs; —honeycombs; —scuds.
(See animal.)

GORE
adjectives
stiffened; gladiatorial; sacred; dusky; quivering; unheeded; stagnant; hideous.

GORGE

verbs

cut—; descend into—; dig—; enter—; furrow—; hollow—; scoop out—; scour—; skirt—; traverse—; wear—; —bends; —confronts; —deepens; —extends; —frightens; —slopes.

(See canyon.)

GORGE (*v*)

adverbs

unrestrainedly; hungrily; ravenously; brutishly; swinishly; nauseously; habitually; insatiably; immoderately.

(See glut, eat.)

GORGEOUS

adverbs

brilliantly; splendidly; magnificently; uncommonly; unusually; dazzlingly; resplendently; superbly; supremely; glitteringly; vividly; richly; harmoniously; imposingly; impressively; extravagantly; inordinately; strikingly.

GORGES

adjectives

twisting; shadowy; picturesque; sunlit; wondrous; narrow; deep; unscaled; roaring; windy; desolated; immediate; mountainous; intricate; melting; protected; tremendous; rock-fanged.

GORILLA

verbs

—challenges; —chews; —cries; —crushes; —drums; —entertains; —nurses; —rages; —raids; —roars; —rushes; —shies; —tears; —terrifies; —wanders.

(See animal.)

GORY

adverbs

unspeakably; horribly; murderously; distressingly; wretchedly; hideously; abominably; beastly; grossly; awfully.

GOSPEL

adjectives

political; radiant; fiery; bitter; gradual; everlasting; healing; long-repeated; timeworn; helpful.

verbs

carry—; crusade—; decry—; denounce—; explode—; herald—; narrate—; preach—; propagate—; propound—; spread—; transmit—.

(See truth, story, narrative, tale, teachings, Bible, Scriptures.)

GOSSIP

adjectives

habitual; savory; baseless; interested; slanderous; mighty; idle; laggard; good-natured; dashing; careless; ubiquitous; censorious; drowsy; cheerful; impertinent; agreeable; withering; contemporaneous; neighborhood; useful; whispered; undercover; vulgar; insignificant; malicious; scandalous; social; ugly.

verbs

cackle—; center—on; circulate—; deal out —; exchange—; feed on—; indulge in—; interchange—; interest in—; ladle out—; savor—; sputter—; whisper—; —buzzes; —floats about; —libels; —maligns; —slanders.

(See rumor.)

GOSSIP (*v*)

adverbs

gregariously; inanely; incautiously; inimically; indiscreetly; loquaciously; baselessly; habitually; slanderously; censoriously; impertinently; witheringly; vulgarly; maliciously; jealously; enviously; treacherously.

(See talk, rumor, tattle.)

GOVERN (*v*)

adverbs

inharmoniously; dictatorially; paternally; intricately; nobly; tyrannically; bureaucratically; autocratically; democratically; plutocratically; ruthlessly; despotically; aristocratically; ephemerally; legitimately; perfidiously; constitutionally; prudently.

(See rule, control.)

GOVERNMENT

adjectives

hard up; executive; tyrannical; municipal; patriarchal; long-lived; authoritarian; radical; shameful; jealous; odious; provincial; paternal; stable; supernatural; ruthless; despotic; representative; aristocratic; free; unprosperous; ephemeral; puppet; vacillating; irresponsible; legitimate; mushroom; acknowledged; ill; deceased; consular; perfidious; industrious; consolidated; constitutional; orderly; imperial; dangerous; respective; monarchial; central; moral; provisional; prudent; autonomistic; conservative; totalitarian; bankrupt.

verbs

abuse—; balance—; castigate—; centralize —; control—; corrupt—; criticize—; defraud—; hoodwink—; jeopardize—; lose faith in—; maintain—; obliterate—; plot against—; preserve—; reverence—; revolt against—; surrender—to; undermine—; upbraid—; usurp—; —capitulates; —cooperates with; —crumbles; —functions; —launches; —regulates; —subsidizes; —succors; —teeters; —thrives.

(See administration, authority, management.)

GOVERNOR

adjectives

sturdy; testy; saûcy; assiduous; unerring.

verbs

appoint—; criticize—; draft for—; honor—; impeach—; nettle—; nominate for—; override—; remove—; welcome—; —abuses; —administers; —admonishes; —allows; —authorizes; —s confer; —consents; —controls; —s convene; —executes; —heads; —oppresses; —pilots; —represents; —reprieves; —resides at; —rules; —steers; —vetoes; —visits.

(See master, ruler, guardian.)

GOWN

adjectives

fragile; star-sprinkled; long; flowing; tattered; curtailed; goodly; fluttering; sleeveless; sophisticated; rusty; glamorous; enticing; dull; flapping; saffron; flounced; ruffed; rustling; conventional; silk; close-fitting; sacred; furred; soiled; waxen; low-cut.

verbs

admire—; damage—; design—; don—; exhibit—; fashion—; fit—; model—; repair—; sew—; shed—; tread on—; yearn for—; —becomes; —exposes; —flatters; —flows; —flutters; —reveals; —ripples; —s vary.

(See dress, robe, garment.)

GOWN (v)

adverbs

exquisitely; tastefully; dully; ecclesiastically; spectacularly; gaily; strikingly; vividly; richly; ornately.

(See dress, garb.)

GRAB (v)

adverbs

ruthlessly; despotically; fanatically; autocratically; selfishly; brutishly; vulgarly; nefariously; offensively.

(See seize, clutch, grasp.)

GRACE

adjectives

exquisite; petitionary; tempting; homicidal; impartial; luxuriant; aerial; fruitless; reviving; crowning; singular; refined; supple; literary; lasting; gleaming; natural; apt; gloomy; nameless; strengthening; ineffable; quiet; soft; fluent; tranquil; tolerable; precise; wild; resolute; majestic; lazy; vigorous; inward; flexuous; nobler; sovereign; supreme; jocund; infant; caressing; redeeming; animating; gentle; negligent; perceptible; restoring; extreme; fugitive; melancholy; manly; extenuating; demure; bewildering; boundless; matchless; youthful; inexplicable; happy; evolvent; lingering; saving; ideal; summer; irresistible; extraordinary; antique; old-fashioned; loathsome; condescending; insinuating; chivalrous; swaying; sufficient; outward; pardoning; habitual; infinite; feminine; musical; living; rude; lascivious; languished; fugitive; jaunty; superb; careless; celestial; needful; easy; sinuous; divine; touching; subtle; good; peculiar; maiden; classical; awkward; virginlike; golden; regal; languid; invigorating; charming; courtly; ravishing; unconscious; casual; heavenly; winsome; winning; poetic; tactful; fraternal; sweetest; mundane; tragic; abounding; fastidious; heroic; hopeless; girlish; perfect; cordial; righteous; pastoral; serious; calm; stately; lordly; truer; lurid; celestial; slow; modern; airy; eloquent; simple; sportive; hidden; stupendous; breezy; beauteous; social; pitying; fleeting; coy; capricious; inimitable; facile; undulating; human; inferior.

verbs

admire—; approach—; attain—; commend —; conduct with—; divest of—; endow with —; exhibit—; express with—; form with—; imitate—; invoke—; lend—; move with—; possess—; serve with—; —attracts; —distinguishes; —charms.

(See favor, kindness, mercy, prayer, beauty, love.)

557

GRACEFUL

adverbs

amiably; pleasantly; unusually; definitely; slenderly; skillfully; wonderfully; delightfully; uncommonly; naturally; habitually; instinctively; exquisitely; singularly; aptly; ineffably; quietly; softly; lazily; supremely; extremely; superbly; matchlessly; youthfully; irresistibly; extraordinarily; ineffably; carelessly; charmingly; unconsciously; felicitously; unaffectedly; attractively; quaintly.

GRACELESS

adverbs

harshly; stiffly; awkwardly; crudely; offensively; grotesquely; bluntly; carelessly; appallingly; rudely; clumsily; shockingly; inexcusably; viciously; lawlessly; indecorously; incorrigibly; indiscreetly; obdurately; stubbornly; indefensibly; shamefully; obstinately; frightfully; terribly.

GRACIOUS

adverbs

charmingly; delightfully; indulgently; cordially; courteously; unusually; consistently; habitually; exceedingly; sincerely; warmly; hospitably; eagerly; amenably; heartily; suavely; ceremoniously; obsequiously; deferentially; attentively; unctuously; ingratiatingly; benevolently; kindly; considerately; unusually.

GRADATION

adjectives

subtle; organic; beautiful; cold; fractional; manifest; intermediate; ravishing; insensible; rapid; minute; infinitesimal.

GRADE

adjectives

laborious; convenient; intermediate; successive (pl); correct; seasonal; lower.

verbs

approve—; branch into —s; classify —s; compare —s; criticize—; delineate —s; enter—; examine—; organize—; promote—; recognize—; skip—; withdraw—; —guarantees; —indicates; —promises; —satisfies.
(See degree, step, rank, division.)

GRADE (v)

adverbs

legitimately; fairly; delicately; skillfully; laboriously; scholastically; provisionally; academically; nominally.
(See calculate, estimate.)

GRADUAL

adverbs

progressively; comparatively; intentionally; purposely; significantly; wisely; designedly; necessarily; inevitably; imperceptibly; slowly; inexpressibly; extremely; sensibly; intelligently; subtly; insidiously; cleverly; deliberately; shrewdly.

GRADUATE

verbs

assemble —s; confer on—; congratulate —s; employ—; enlist—; examine—; fete—; gift —; honor—; laud—; pose as—; praise—; present to—; privilege—; train—; —completes; —excels in; —harks back; —qualifies; —understands.
(See student.)

GRADUATE (v)

adverbs

creditably; subsequently; formally; ultimately; eventually; respectfully.
(See win, finish.)

GRAFT

adjectives

foreign; niggling; vigorous; huge; amazing; regular; stupendous; successful.

verbs

devise—; employ—; induce—; introduce—; support—; yield to—; —accomplishes; —attracts; —begets; —flourishes; —instils; —interests; —intrigues.
(See fraud.)

GRAIN

adjectives

burdening; natural; waving; distinct; fine; springing; gathered; sprouting; garnered; hardy; scanty; coarse; vintage; pungent; generous; well-ripened; rustling; indigenous.

verbs

bag—; cast — to; char—; collect—; distill from—; feed on—; ferment—; gather—; glean—; harvest—; injure—; plant—; prepare—; prize—; reap—; sow—; stack—; yield—; —fattens; —flourishes; —invites; —nourishes; —ripens.
(See seed, crop.)

GRAMMAR

verbs

abide by—; abuse—; conform to—; criticize —; disregard—; fumble with—; heed—; judge—; master—; obey—; observe—; relish—; violate—; —concerns; —confuses; —demands; —explains; —informs; —ordains; —rules.

(See rhetoric.)

GRAND

adverbs
impressively; imposingly; magnificently; infinitely; sublimely; majestically; augustly; eminently; superbly; illustriously; ineffably; essentially; fundamentally; resplendently; remarkably; transcendently.

GRANDEUR

adjectives
wild; political; religious; weird; imposing; solemn; primitive; tantalizing; gloomy; inherent; contemplative; tumultuous; superior; ancient; superlative; labored; monotonous; human; venerable; sustained; shadowy; rough; solitary; husbanded; superficial; desolate; poetic; magnificent; severe; false; massive; hideous; infinite; melodious; pristine; architectural; sarcastic; deceitful; dilapidated; original; savage; civic; sublime; dreary.

verbs
abate—; acquaint with—; borrow — from; contemplate—; debase—; discipline—; emulate—; equal—; exhibit—; intimate—; love —; parade—; perceive—; reduce—; ridicule—; rise in—; sacrifice—; stagger by—; touch with—; witness—; —diminishes; —expands; —impresses; —impels; —soars.

(See display, splendor, elegance.)

GRANITE

adjectives
unhewn; barren; straited; enduring; everlasting; defiant; cumbersome.

verbs
build on—; carve from—; chip—; crack—; demolish—; hammer—; hew from—; lay—; mix—; pave with—; pierce—; quarry—; shatter—; smooth—; spike—; split—.

(See rock, stone.)

GRANT

adjectives
authentic; fairest; legislative; definite.

GRANT (v)

adverbs
liberally; tacitly; exclusively; subsequently; courteously; grudgingly; graciously; originally; readily; fairly; legislatively; definitely.

(See allow, permit.)

GRAPE

adjectives
shrivelled; luscious; choicest; ripened; celestial; rare; intoxicating; blossoming; autumn; noble; sweet; rich; sour.

GRAPES

verbs
abound with—; bag—; bear—; crate—; gather—; glean—; harvest—; mash—; seed —; skin—; squash—; suck—; —hang; —ripen; —ferment.

(See fruit.)

GRAPPLE

adjectives
iron; death; watchful; painful; damaging; bruising.

GRAPPLE (v)

adverbs
frantically; painfully; bruisingly; fiercely; vigorously; methodically; firmly.

(See clutch, seize.)

GRASP

adjectives
relaxing; iron; monstrous; bitter; prosperous; slender; weak; oblique; unrelaxing; stiffening; consumptive; immature; godlike; unaccommodating; intuitive; conscious; fearful; warm; tenacious; hot; masculine; cordial; prophetic; mental; timorous; vigorous; incisive; childish; octopus-like; passionate; dying; despotic; encyclic; double; fevered.

verbs
beguile into—; carry off in—; crush in—; elude—; entice into—; evade—; gain—; loosen—; relax—; release—; shake from—; wrest from—; yank (colloq.) from—; —bruises; —pains.

(See grip, embrace.)

GRASP (v)

adverbs
frantically; avariciously; selfishly; rudely; firmly; convulsively; cordially; impetuously; tightly; loosely; greedily; unrelaxingly; tenaciously; passionately; despotically.

(See seize, clutch.)

adjectives

tangling; waving; succulent; full-grown; pure; lush; new; long; gentle; fruitful; comfortable; pleasant; dull; starved; trampled; straggling; luxuriant; cut; dry; reedy; dripping; wiry; gaunt; shaven; parched; associated; pinched; nutritious; tedded; flowering; scented; aromatic; delicate; wilted; mossy; rank; russet; aquatic; ornamental; bladed; inland; silent; tumbled; hindering; peopled.

verbs

clip—; crop—; fence off—; mow—; pasture on—; plow through—; sow—; sprinkle—; tread on—; —beautifies; —blankets; —carpets; —cloaks; —covers; —creeps up; —dots; —flows; —pushes up; —spreads; —springs up; —trembles.

(See herb, plant, hay, pasture.)

GRASSHOPPER

verbs

exterminate—; plague with—s; swarm with —s; —alights; —chews; —chirrups; —s damage; —leaps; —limps; —races; —reposes on; —secretes; —sings; —sips; —skips; —s strip; —vaults; —wings.

(See insect.)

GRATE

adjectives

gaping; glowing; abhorred; ponderous; old-fashioned.

GRATE (v)

adverbs

harshly; unendurably; roughly; irritatingly; exasperatingly; monotonously; continually; ceaselessly; repeatedly.

(See rub, irritate.)

GRATEFUL

adverbs

utterly; heartily; thankfully; sincerely; pathetically; significantly; inexpressibly; curiously; oddly; volubly; openly; obviously; extremely; inordinately; delightedly; embarrassingly; overwhelmingly; speechlessly; extravagantly; genuinely.

GRATIFICATION

adjectives

refined; instant; external; personal; aesthetic; innocent; pretty; natural; sensual; speechless; solitary; idle; perfect; vilest; profound; correspondent; intellectual; emotional.

verbs

afford—; anticipate—; bestow—; consider with—; crave—; derive—; experience—; express—; incur—; indulge in—; observe with—; obtain—; offer—; receive—; — attends; —recompenses; —satisfies.

(See satisfaction, pleasure, reward.)

GRATIFIED

adverbs

extremely; highly; uncommonly; happily; proudly; pleasantly; inordinately; ineffably; visibly; noticeably; naturally; marvellously; wonderfully; overwhelmingly; volubly; shyly; utterly; inexpressibly.

GRATIFY (v)

adverbs

lustfully; sexually; aesthetically; profoundly; adequately; personally; sensually; intellectually; emotionally; innocently.

(See please, indulge.)

GRATITUDE

adjectives

admiring; endless; intense; natural; virtuous; innocent; deep; passionate; permanent; respectful; noble; erring; bewildered; elementary; pathetic; tender; meek; universal; heartfelt; devout; profound; earnest; fervent; reverent; patriotic; humble; genuine; characteristic; everlasting; sincere; simple.

verbs

acknowledge with—; earn—of; exact—; expect—; express—; feel—; reject—; return in—; reward with—; thrive on—; touch with—; —embarrasses; —humiliates; —justifies; —overflows; —pains.

(See appreciation, adoration, affection.)

GRATUITOUS

adverbs

unexpectedly; surprisingly; acceptably; generously; pleasantly; unnecessarily; cordially; genially; graciously; tactfully; helpfully; impulsively; incredibly.

GRAVE

adjectives

prehistoric; volcanic; nameless; humble; grassy; putrid; innocent; artless; shallow;

desolate; nobler; trodden; sullen; yawning; unmarked; liquid; triumphant; ecstatic; dishonored; burning; solitary; watery; tenantless; sacred; ocean; unblessed; pauper; heaving; insatiate; curtained; scented; bloody; untimely; populous; dusky; mimic; new-made; gloomy; hastily-dug; forgotten; gaping; unmade; dismal; destitute; obscure; dreary; mattress; close-set; stone; inglorious.

verbs
bequeath to—; confine to—; couch in—; hound to—; lie in—; loot—; lower into—; mourn over—; pillage—; pray at—; rest in—; shudder in—; sleep in—; slumber in—; snatch from—; tear open—; turn in —; unearth—; weep at—; wrest from—; —reconciliates; —silences; —snatches; —swallows.
(See tomb, death.)

adverbs
habitually; critically; alarmingly; preternaturally; profoundly; intensely; extremely; frightfully; indescribably; essentially; incalculably; downright; emphatically; cruelly; shockingly; inconceivably; momentously; signally; eventfully; pregnantly; impressively; urgently; solemnly; saliently; portentously; grievously; deplorably; insupportably; disastrously; exceptionably.

GRAVEYARD
adjectives
various (pl); silent; ancestral; country; populous.

GRAVITATE (v)
adverbs
naturally; habitually; paradoxically; customarily; ominously; affectionately; supernaturally; awfully; specifically.
(See attract, sink.)

GRAVITATION
adjectives
irresistible; mutual; pervading; touching; constant.

GRAVITY
adjectives
mock; fantastic; portentous; comic; habitual; sustained; becoming; superb; accustomed; unusual; ominous; dreamless; amused; paradoxical; affectionate; sudden;

heavy; elaborate; melancholy; supernatural; dark; colder; awful; attentive; abundant; specific; technical; pompous; frowning; affected.

verbs
challenge—; mitigate—; preserve—; recover—; repel—; robe in—; —alters; —attracts; —directs; —draws; —exercises; —forces; —increases; —influences; —produces; —restricts; —tends.
(See seriousness, solemnity, importance.)

GRAY
adjectives
smiling; salt; mottled; austere; soft; ashen; joyless; fallow; bluish; uncertain; subtle; dark; pearly; dappled; warm; smart; dim; gleaming.

GRAYNESS
adjectives
spring; arrested; dense; spectral; grim; premature; recurring; whitish.

GRAZE (v)
adverbs
peacefully; contentedly; ruminatively; habitually; ceaselessly; monotonously; beneficially.
(See feed.)

GREAT
adverbs
supposedly; naturally; unaffectedly; apparently; fairly; substantially; essentially; fundamentally; downright; immeasurably; incalculably; pleasantly; surprisingly; incredibly; marvellously; wonderfully; amazingly; unusually; singularly; admittedly; undeniably; distinctly; illustriously; reputably; conspicuously; eminently; brilliantly; famously; locally; nationally; internationally; splendidly; sublimely; deservedly; transcendently; memorably; remarkably; unassumingly.

GREATNESS
adjectives
false; intellectual; enduring; moral; natural; ingenuous; true; simple; affected; immeasurable; veiled; esteemed; imperial; patent; corresponding; undiminishable; deserved; apparent; recognized.

verbs

achieve—; advertise—; attain—; bestow—upon; contemplate—of; envy—; expatiate on—; gain—; inspire—; perceive—; pursue—; reach—; seize—; sweep into—; thrust—upon; —affects; —appeals; —elevates; —fetters; —serves; —torments.

(See magnitude, eminence, distinction, importance, seriousness.)

GREED

adjectives

pulpit; inordinate; disappointed; reckless; instinctive; intrenched; insatiable; rapturous; internecine; misapplied; misdirected; methodical; physical; miserly.

verbs

clog with—; curse with—; devour with—; indulge—; loathe—; occasion—; overcome with—; prey upon—of; quench—; resent—; satiate—; torment with—; vanquish—; —annoys; —chokes; —deforms; —drags; —drains; —repels; —shames; —sickens; —stints; —tempts.

(See avarice.)

GREEDY

adverbs

inordinately; covetously; avidly; ravenously; insatiably; voraciously; incurably; incorrigibly; strangely; instinctively; painfully; embarrassingly; irreclaimably; hopelessly; shamelessly; perpetually; appallingly; shamefully; scandalously; indecently; brazenly; palpably; unmistakably; obviously; openly; manifestly.

GREEK

verbs

accent—; decipher—; interpret—; laud—; smatter—; translate—; utter—.

(See language, literature.)

GREEN

adjectives

shimmering; woodsy; opaque; dense; diversified; aqueous; resonant; luxuriant; dull; quiet; waving; pale; varied; feathery; delicate; wanton; pistache; exquisite; emerald; dim; faint; mossy; luminous; malachite; leaping; neutral; festive; luscious; slimy; lesser; consecutive; tender; tainted; translucent; glossy; arbute; rusty; delicious; willow; fresher; serpent; turquoise.

GREENERY

adjectives

tangled; moist; varying; well-kept.

GREET (*v*)

adverbs

affably; jovially; charmingly; affectionately; cordially; effusively; ardently; sympathetically; benignly; blandly; genially; brusquely; civilly; fraternally; perfunctorily; hilariously; boisterously.

(See hail, accost, address.)

GREETING

verbs

accost with—; address—to; approach with —; embrace in—; evoke—; exchange—s; express—; ignore—; meet with—; nod—; return—; salute with—; shun—; —arouses; —surprises; —welcomes.

(See salutation, salute, welcome, compliment.)

GREETINGS

adjectives

cordial; civil; playful; absent; kindly; usual; respectful; undemonstrative; paschal; fraternal; joyous; spasmodic; innumerable; sad; perfunctory; affable; effusive; hospitable; hilarious; daily; neighborly; flustered; boisterous; inaudible; affectionate; holiday; warm; mutual; unspoken.

GREGARIOUS

adverbs

jovially; socially; politically; companionably; incurably; heartily; naturally; instinctively; inherently; pleasantly; hospitably; freely; sociably; healthily; wholesomely; briskly; unusually; normally.

GRENADE

verbs

charge with—; catapult—; employ—; fire —; flee from—; fling—; hurl—; roll—; —assaults; —bursts; —dispenses; —explodes; —s harass; —injures; —maims; —levels; —s terrorize; —wounds.

(See bomb, shell.)

GRENADIER

adjectives

gallant; grim; warlike; various (pl); pleasant; gaudy; eye-pleasing.

GRIDIRON
(colloq. for football field)

verbs

battle on—; clash on—; compete on—; condition—; construct—; cover—; design—; excel on—; injure on—; meet on—; pack —; subsidize—; swarm—; witness on—; — attracts; —extends; —beckons; —lies.

(See field, battlefield.)

GRIEF

adjectives

reproachful; national; silent; burning; irremediable; hysterical; immoderate; hopeless; purposeless; needless; passionate; private; strong; sincere; idle; truer; beauteous; half-smothered; poignant; chastening; successive (pl); domestic; lasting; overwhelming; elegiac; endless; casual; unutterable; remorseful; hateful; proud; sudden; mortal; inconsolable; innocent; conjectured; barren; sacred; sentimental; angry; deeper; selfish; lighter; paroxysmal; unmanly; stark; arbitrary; single; withered; fettered; ancient; vanished; callous; uncontrollable; compensated; inward; perished; cloudy; unavailing; fundamental; relentless; utmost; forecasted; wayward; bitter; eternal; touching; present; household; greatest; genuine; pure; young; excessive; second; extravagant.

verbs

assail with—; assuage—; bring to—; confide—in; disguise—; drown—; emerge from —; fight—; overcome by—; overwhelm with —; rush into—; smite with—; stifle—; submerge—; —abates; —lessens; —overwhelms; —spends itself.

(See sorrow, sadness, anguish, distress, tears.)

GRIEVANCE

adjectives

intense; industrial; undoubted; lofty; maritime; maudlin; intolerable; eternal; permanent; serious; heartfelt; deep; deadly.

verbs

adjust—; air—; allege—; arbitrate—; bound with—; conceal—; detail—; exploit —; iron out—; outline—s; recount—; voice —; yield to—; —justifies; —warrants.

(See wrong, injustice, resentment, complaint.)

GRIEVE (v)

adverbs

perpetually; obstinately; silently; unfeignedly; hysterically; immoderately; hopelessly; passionately; poignantly; endlessly; remorsefully; uncontrollably; bitterly; touchingly; genuinely; excessively; extravagantly.

(See lament, mourn.)

GRIEVOUS

adverbs

deplorably; lamentably; sadly; piteously; distressingly; intolerably; appallingly; horribly; unaccountably; unwarrantably; irremediably; unutterably; uncontrollably; bitterly; touchingly; genuinely; grimly; sorely; cruelly; inexpressibly; inordinately; terribly.

GRILLING

verbs

conduct—; cringe from—; criticize—; denounce—; dread—; escape—; overdo—; resent—; suffer—; tense for—; withstand—; wrestle with—; yield to—; —exposes; — irritates; —reveals; —threatens.

(See questioning, examination, inquiry, inquisition.)

GRIM

adverbs

horribly; terribly; cruelly; bitterly; unutterably; unaccountably; unwarrantably; acutely; austerely; brutally; cynically; morosely; perversely; discourteously; sullenly; unceremoniously; impolitely; horridly; sternly; severely; depressingly; oppressively; heavily; forlornly; frightfully; irredeemably.

GRIMACE

adjectives

admiring; mocking; mental; fantastic; convulsive; furious; comical; passing; sour; droll; cold; dissatisfied; idiotic; wry; harrowing.

GRIMACE (v)

adverbs

facetiously; fiercely; humorously; dourly; mockingly; fantastically; convulsively; furiously; drolly; idiotically; wryly.

(See leer, sneer, smirk, scowl.)

adverbs

inexcusably; unspeakably; merrily; laughably; nonchalantly; carelessly; offensively; hopelessly; inevitably; momentarily; repulsively; irretrievably; laughingly; smudgily; dustily; darkly; grotesquely; fantastically; outlandishly; shamelessly; unconcernedly; coolly; indifferently; unashamedly.

GRIN

adjectives

tigerish; noble; wooden; homely; amused; cast-iron; broad; triumphant; insolent; sardonic; lewd; specious; jubilant; ingenuous; incredible; mocking; leering; sympathetic; understanding; unmitigated; lopsided; sheepish; saucy; fiendish; doubtful; relieved; affable; sly; horrible; courageous; infectious; whimsical; saturnine.

verbs

attempt—; break into—; broaden into—; conceal under—; expand in—; force—; manage—; master—; muster—; provoke—; restrain—; salute with—; smother—; stab with—; wear—; wrinkle into—; —creases; —delights; —embarrasses; —fades; —lurks; —recurs; —widens; —wreathes.
(See smile, smirk.)

GRIN (*v*)

adverbs

genially; wistfully; bashfully; flatteringly; sheepishly; affably; stupidly; skeptically; amiably; sympathetically; complacently; impudently; derisively; ironically; toothlessly; ruefully; fulsomely; tantalizingly; wryly; broadly; engagingly; craftily; lewdly; jubilantly; ingenuously; saturninely.
(See smirk, laugh, smile.)

GRIND
(*colloq. for drudgery*)

verbs

abhor—; avoid—; coach—; detest—; enforce—; labor on—; necessitate—; perform at—; plod at—; reduce to—; toil away at —; —crushes; —exacts; —harasses; —prepares; —oppresses; —sharpens; —torments; —wearies; —wears down.
(See drudgery, labor, work.)

GRINNING

adverbs

foolishly; facetiously; fatuously; vacuously; vacantly; cheerfully; happily; mischievous-

ly; teasingly; pertly; tormentingly; suavely; blandly; indulgently; slyly; broadly; triumphantly; jubilantly; sheepishly; joyously; sympathetically; mockingly; elaborately; openly.

GRIP
(*grasp*)

adjectives

tight; paralyzing; momentary; firm; muscular; nervous; burning; remorseless; herculean; frantic; throttling; fiendish; intellectual.

verbs

loosen—; relax—; release—; —pains; —reassures; —slips; —strains; —wearies.
(See clutch, grasp.)

GRIP
(*colloq. for valise*)

verbs

clasp—; clutch—; fit into—; grab—; insure —; load in—; seize—; stow—; —wearies.
(See satchel, bag.)

GRIP (*v*)

adverbs

fervently; licentiously; momentarily; nervously; remorselessly; frantically; fiendishly; vigorously; selfishly; figuratively.
(See seize, grasp.)

GRIPE

adjectives

convulsive; mincing; communicated.

GRIT
(*sand*)

adjectives

blinding; parching; grinding; unpleasant; rough.

verbs

brush away—; conceal—; dissolve—; fill with—; free of—; gather—; scour with—; sieve—; sift—; slip on—; sprinkle with—; strain off—; sweep away—; wash away—; —chokes; —impairs; —injures; —irritates; —scratches.
(See sand.)

GRITTY
(*plucky*)

adverbs

pluckily; sturdily; stoutly; resolutely; indomitably; firmly; courageously; spunkily.

GRITTY
(sandy)

adverbs

roughly; harshly; coarsely; crudely; grossly; impossibly; uselessly; desirably; friably; suitably; properly; unduly; terribly; remarkably; extremely; uncommonly; excessively.

GRIZZLED

adverbs

wintrily; crabbedly; hoarily; dingily; sadly; gently; gloriously; patriarchally; fabulously; honorably; proudly; mellowly; vainly.

GROAN

adjectives

rheumatic; tortured; deep; indignant; expiring; solemn; ghastly; frequent (pl); fierce; thrilling; smothered; unutterable; subdued; loud; bubbling; agonizing; dying; heartrending; deadly; dismal; passionate; unsolaced; convulsive; self-accusing; mirthful; gurgling; heavy; mortifying; unwilling; bitter; penitential.

verbs

blanket—; convulse with—; drown—; emit —; murmur—; restrain—; stifle—; utter—; —distresses; —disturbs; —haunts; —rends; —resounds; —subsides.
(See moan, sigh, sound.)

GROAN (v)

adverbs

audibly; painfully; agonizingly; dreadfully; inwardly; bitterly; involuntarily; unutterably; heartrendingly.
(See moan, complain, scream.)

GROOM

adjectives

diminutive; natty; surly; envious; unpolished; sturdy; surfeited; industrious; bashful; nervous; worried.

GROOM (v)

adverbs

foppishly; tastefully; immaculately; nattily; handsomely; fittingly; appropriately; decoratively; impressively.
(See dress, brush.)

GROOMED

adverbs

perfectly; carefully; immaculately; recently; lately; meticulously; punctiliously; primly; starchily; fastidiously; fashionably; especially; obviously; manifestly; freshly; radiantly; sophisticatedly; remarkably; elaborately.

GROOVE

adjectives

habitual; prosaic; uncongenial.

verbs

excavate—; fall into—; flow in—; force along—; furrow—; hollow out—; lapse into —; lie in—; mark with—; obstruct—; provide—; rust in—; sink into—; slide in—; throw out of—; travel in—.
(See channel, rut, routine, course.)

GROPE (v)

adverbs

futilely; blindly; vaguely; wildly; ineffectually; dazedly; mentally; uncertainly.
(See feel, search.)

GROSSNESS

adjectives

intermingled; material; mortal; swinelike.

GROTESQUE

adverbs

outlandishly; fantastically; clownishly; elaborately; ornately; abnormally; eccentrically; monstrously; singularly; oddly; curiously; exceptionally; egregiously; unusually; extraordinarily; queerly; unconscionably; capriciously; whimsically; extravagantly; barbarically; horribly; uncommonly; immeasurably; unnaturally; absurdly; ridiculously; ludicrously; highly.

GROTTO

verbs

adorn—; construct—; excavate—; exhibit—; ornament—; nestle in—; retreat to—; — beautifies; —delights; —displays; —echoes; —pleases; —shades; —solaces.
(See cave, recess, cavity.)

GROUCH

verbs

irritate—; nurse—; serve—; tolerate—; — complains; —deplores; —frets; —frowns;

565

—growls; —grumbles; —laments; —moans; —roars; —scowls; —wails; —whines.
(See anger, bitterness, ferocity.)

GROUND
(earth)
adjectives
analogical; habitual; ticklish; enchanted; avowed; crinkled; soggy; slightest; shaky; tedious; rugged; fragrant; difficult; sanctified; vantage; unexpressed; sterile; dry; azure; emotional; vulgar; tainted; solid; interesting; attractive; plausible; pastel; teeming; scientific; spacious; moaning; moral; delicate; callous; bordering; hallowed; innate; wounded; cultivated; fissured; commanding; incontrovertible; common; terraced; happy; conceded; illogical; dangerous; practical; rough; insufficient; good; bloody; reasonable; haunted; holy; treacherous; proper; thirsting; technical; theological; sluttish; slippery; burning; vivid; eudaemonistic; trampled; adequate; sanctified; superior; extensive; shuddering; filthy; familiar; untouched; unmarked; spawning; various (pl); debatable; heartless; quaking; reigning; cleared; obscure; ridgy; aesthetic; desolate; plain; ornamented; intuitive; neutral; remoter; grassy; subjective; dwelling; dewy; irregular; consecrated; excellent; tenable; dubious; sole; base; sectional; tufty; objective; highest; waste; alien; precise; casting.

verbs
assign—to; carpet—s; cast to—; congest—s; cultivate—; encamp on—s; gain—; parch —; plod over—; plow—; shift—; spade—; stand—; strew—; trample—; tread—; work —; writhe on—.
(See earth, soil, land, clay, dirt.)

GROUNDLESS
adverbs
nonsensically; flimsily; foolishly; absurdly; undeniably; palpably; obviously; patently; manifestly; maliciously; inconclusively; inconsistently; irrationally; unreasonably; inexcusably; unscientifically; unwarrantably; delusively; fallaciously; illogically; untrustworthily; unsubstantially; intentionally; deliberately; deceitfully; malignly; perversely; disastrously; ruinously; ridiculously.

GROUNDS
(reasons)
verbs
afford—for; attack on—; maintain—; object on—.
(See reason, consideration, premise, motive, inducement.)

GROUNDWORK
verbs
accomplish—; add to—; depend on—; enhance—; exhibit—; expand—; finish—; form—; hurry—; lay—; manage—; perform —; plan—; spurn—; supervise—; undermine—; —benefits; —precedes.
(See basis, foundation.)

GROUP
adjectives
ancillary; afflicted; exclusive; oncoming; limited; select; co-ordinated; ethnic; personified; heterogeneous; non-listening; cultural; pedimental; garrulous; chattery; valid; specialized; waning; geographical; parental; enthusiastic; civic; statuesque; spurious; flitting; sparse; straggling; considerable; loitering; vocational; remarkable; federated; unscrupulous; racial; efficient; distinct; sympathetic; lethargic; careless; weird; complete; dominant; diversified; overlapping; huddled; gesticulating; noisiest; lazy; divers (pl); representative; congenial; curious; listless; clustering; odious; humiliated; stalwart; grotesque; irregular; silent; lounging; intramural; brilliant; singular; denominational; allegorical; fearful; impressive; loquacious; detached; emblematic; spectacular; hedgehog; jovial; executive; jeering; sullen; craning; militant; prolific; controlling; anarchical; indispensable; producing; tractable; mournful; isolated; sobbing; pressure; elaborate; hostile; molecular; negligible; decorative.

verbs
assemble in—; belong to—; break with—; cluster in—; collect in—; compose—; divide into—s; disperse—; draft—; form—; gather —; huddle in—; lead—; scatter in—; segregate—s; split into—s; stand in—; work in —; —congregates; —co-operates; —gathers; —roves; —s spring up; —survives; — thins; —visions; —wanes; —yields.
(See crowd.)

566

GROUP (v)

adverbs

systematically; logically; categorically; picturesquely; vocationally; carelessly; representatively; congenially; elaborately; decoratively.

(See cluster, crowd.)

GROUPINGS

adjectives

picturesque; molecular; effective; attractive; fundamental; confused; huddled; fragmentary; photographic.

GROUSE

verbs

bag—; pelt—; retrieve—; roast—; —alights; —bellows; —booms; —cackles; —clucks; —dodges; —drums; —flutters; —glides; —grumbles; —haunts; —hides; —hoots; —roves; —ruffles; —rustles; —scratches; —scurries; —squats; —struts; —thumps; —thunders.

(See bird.)

GROVE

adjectives

shadowy; inviolate; sacred; melancholy; Elysian; lofty; haunted; celestial; primeval; pathless; fringed; boundless; musical; hoary; warbling; thriving.

GROVEL (v)

adverbs

obsequiously; humbly; servilely; slavishly; flatteringly; abjectly; debasingly; shamelessly.

(See cringe, fawn.)

GROW (v)

adverbs

tremendously; luxuriously; abundantly; proportionately; sensibly; vigorously; culturally; inevitably; formidably; abnormally; densely; miraculously; infinitely; ulcerously; wantonly; pendulously; phenomenally; intellectually; malignantly; tropically; vernally; spiritually.

(See increase, develop.)

GROWL

adjectives

meaning; significant; warning; low; audible; indignant; guttural; angry; friendly; fierce.

GROWL (v)

verbs

break into—; charge with—; emit—; enrage to—; incur—; mutter—; reiterate—; restrain—; stifle—; utter—; —arouses; —s drown; —eclipses; —reverberates; —rises from; —terrifies; —terrorizes; —thunders; —vibrates.

(See rumble, complaint, roar, grunt.)

GROWL (v)

adverbs

ominously; pugnaciously; disapprovingly; menacingly; furiously; warningly; audibly; ferociously; formidably; irascibly; surlily; gutturally.

(See grumble, snarl.)

GROWTH

adjectives

coarse; sturdy; vigorous; rock-loving; spontaneous; miraculous; arborescent; continuous; ulcerous; wanton; rooted; pendulous; phenomenal; inoperable; luxuriant; ghostly; stunted; monstrous; perpetual; stupendous; morbid; cancerous; unpleasant; intellectual; remarkable; tropical; unconscious; parasitic; healthy; native; scanty; incessant; record; evolutionary; puny; unexampled; developmental; unequal; hasty; mushroom; successive (pl); intervening; unbroken; astounding; endless; vital; rapid; sterile; outward; nutritious; proper; innate; funguslike; differenial; continuous; enormous; plant; malignant; sudden; psychic; unabated; contorted; wayside; vernal; marked; knotty; tremendous; arrested; constant; fateful; lush; spiritual; secular; unkept; strong; millennial; bushy; dense.

verbs

augment—; check—; control—; foster—; govern—; hinder—; induce—; promote—; stunt—; suppress—; thwart—; retard—; strengthen—; witness—; —commences; —develops; —swallows up.

(See development, increase, extension, enlargement.)

GRUDGE

adjectives

private; personal; economic; ancient; bitter.

verbs

annul—; avenge—; bear—; brush aside—; bury—; cherish—; engender—; harbor—;

incur—; lay aside—; nurse—; owe—; pursue—; relinquish—; resent—; warrant—; —troubles; —vexes.

(See malice, hatred, antipathy, rancor, enmity, resentment.)

GRUESOME

adverbs

horribly; cadaverously; horridly; unbearably; forbiddingly; squalidly; frightfully; grimly; grossly; monstrously; odiously; repulsively; shockingly; appallingly; intolerably; dreadfully; impossibly; inconceivably; unspeakably; inexpressibly; indescribably; preposterously; exceedingly.

GRUFF

adverbs

unnecessarily; intolerably; uncivilly; discourteously; needlessly; naturally; habitually; unfortunately; deliberately; unconsciously; rudely; grossly; sullenly; churlishly; intentionally; discouragingly; reluctantly; professionally; bluntly; curtly; captiously; moodily; abusively; boorishly; sarcastically; crudely; clumsily; snarlingly; venomously; significantly; surprisingly; particularly; remarkably.

GRUMBLE (v)

adverbs

captiously; discontentedly; pessimistically; forebodingly; cantankerously; vindictively; monotonously; gloomily.

(See growl, snarl.)

GRUNT

adjectives

complacent; mingling (pl); peculiar; roaring; occasional; satisfied; whining; disdainful; rebellious; startled; long; swinish.

verbs

acquiesce with—; answer with—; concede with—; manage—; resent—; snort—; suffer—; understand—; tolerate—; —annoys; —disturbs; —irritates; —s subside.

(See growl.)

GRUNT (v)

adverbs

audibly; complacently; peevishly; contemptuously; swinishly; disdainfully; rebelliously; appreciatively; approvingly.

(See croak, mumble, bray, stammer.)

GUARANTEE

adjectives

sufficient; money-back; sensational; satisfaction; iron-clad; official; further; serious; perpetual; limited; broken; vague; unfulfilled.

verbs

accompany with—; afford—; apply for—; base—on; break—; chain to—; consider—; demand—; enforce—; enter into—; forfeit —; fulfill—; propose—; test—; utilize—; witness—; —assures; —secures; —suffices.

(See security, reparation, insurance, protection, safeguard, safety.)

GUARANTEE (v)

adverbs

solemnly; unconditionally; unethically; unequivocally; scrupulously; fully; reliably.

(See promise, pledge.)

GUARD

verbs

arouse—; assign—to; bait—; conceal—; decoy—; deride—; double—; eject—; escape —; evade—; flank with—s; hail—; limit —; mount to—; muster—; post—; rile—; stand on—; station—; —manhandles; — patrols; —seizes; —s swarm; —s swarm round.

(See sentry, patrol.)

GUARD (v)

adverbs

closely; jealously; adequately; warily; zealously; rigidly; exclusively; circumspectly; sedulously; dependably.

(See defend, watch.)

GUARDED

adverbs

cautiously; carefully; watchfully; constantly; warily; discreetly; prudently; vigilantly; respectfully; affectionately; tenderly; devotedly; reverently; piously; punitively; sternly; skillfully; successfully; effectively; adroitly; cleverly; subtly; heavily; inefficiently; carelessly; insufficiently; perfectly; scrupulously; pitilessly; faithfully; temporarily; currently; elaborately; invincibly.

GUARDIAN

adjectives

ghostlike; gloomy-winged; particular; faithful; wary; fearless; dissembling; glistering; zealous; legal; appointed; temporary; greedy.

verbs

appoint—; **choose**—; **commit to**—; **employ**
—; entrust—; necessitate—; respect—; —
administers; —defends; —executes; —governs; —guides; —manages; —performs; —
preserves; —protects; —supervises; —
watches.

(See guard, defender, keeper.)

GUARDS

adjectives

pitiless; **dependable**; **provost**; vigilant;
dust-choked; abdominal; imperturbable;
scrupulous; inexorable; affrighted; angelic;
advanced; obsequious; fearful.

GUESS

adjectives

admirable; happy; accepted; shrewd; instinctive; various (pl); ridiculous; **worst**;
elaborate; wild.

verbs

attempt—; base—on; calculate—; chance—;
estimate—; form—; hazard—; measure—;
necessitate—; vary—; venture—; weigh—;
withdraw—; —amazes; —coincides; —deceives; —rescues.

(See conjecture, surmise, supposition, speculation.)

GUESS (*v*)

adverbs

shrewdly; **instinctively**; profoundly; cleverly; skillfully; miraculously; intuitively;
luckily; unerringly.

(See imagine, suppose.)

GUEST

adjectives

illustrious; forward; flirting; solitary; plebeian; gathering (pl); sparing; ungreeted;
adoring; applauding; agreeable; telltale;
long-awaited; welcome; neglected; lovelorn; parting; delightful; fastidious; distinguished; elegant; congenial; kingly; tedious; unexpected; taciturn; believing; late;
surreptitious; terrible; unloved; continual;
invited; straggling; boisterous; sour; involuntary; princely; glorious; entranced;
sundry (pl); favorite; dreaded; ship-
wrecked; tolerated; frivolous; sybaritic;
celestial; crowding; transient; honored;
monster; mortal.

verbs

arrange—s; **circulate among**—s; **delight**—s;
escort—; fete—; honor—; lodge—; prepare
for—; regale—; speed—; —s assemble; —
departs; —s mill about; —returns; present
—.

(See visitor, friend.)

GUFFAW (*v*)

adverbs

coarsely; **boisterously**; **crudely**; obstreperously; sardonically; ribaldly; vulgarly;
rudely; unrestrainedly; frivolously; drunkenly.

(See laugh.)

GUIDANCE

adjectives

tactful; energetic; vocational; celestial;
continuous; psychiatric; genial; economic;
perverse; fresh; cheering; altruistic.

verbs

bring under—of; commit to—; direct—of;
entrust to—of; manage—; necessitate—; observe—; operate under—; relinquish—; remove—; resist—; respect—; supervise—;
teach by—; —controls; —influences; —preserves; —protects; —trains.

(See protection, patronage, direction.)

GUIDE

verbs

commit to—; employ—; exhort—; provide
—; —climbs; —conducts; —controls; —
courses; —directs; —explains; —indicates;
—influences; —leads; —lectures; —manages; —pilots; —plans; —points out; —
rambles; —supervises; —tests; —trains.

(See conductor, pilot.)

GUIDE (*v*)

adverbs

fearlessly; **intelligently**; **insensibly**; tactfully; genially; altruistically; competently; intrepidly.

(See steer, conduct.)

GUIDES

adjectives

magnetic; careless; portly; trustworthy;
baldpated; impassive; unerring; competent;
powerful; greasy; spiritual; trusty; loving;
infallible; intrepid; mysterious; sun-swart;
foolhardy.

verbs
admit to—; elect to—; impede—; organize
—; regulate—; supervise—; support—; —
aids; —benefits; —controls; —dispenses; —
educates; —exhibits; —honors; —offers; —
pursues.
(See association, fraternity, society,
corporation, brotherhood.)

GUILE

adjectives
political; baleful; false; innocent; spiritual;
fatal; venerable; smooth; sweet.

GUILELESS

adverbs
unaffectedly; apparently; delightfully; incredibly; refreshingly; touchingly; childishly; wonderfully; manifestly; charmingly;
ravishingly; surprisingly; unbelievably; ingenuously; youthfully; unquestionably; candidly.

GUILT

adjectives
mutual; accessorial; exultant; hideous; apparent; open; inexpiable; stubborn; frustrate; tyrannic; supposed; bounteous; admitted; dread; enormous; ineffable; occulted; imputed; traitorous; murderous; uneasy; multiplied; heinous; miserable.

verbs
accept—; adduce—; ascertain—; betray—;
blush with—; conceal—; exhibit—; experience a sense of—; expose—; hide—; incur
—; induce—; measure—; prove—; repudiate—; reveal—; shoulder—; take—; uncover—; —attends; —dishonors; —shames.
(See sin, offense, wrong, crime.)

GUINEA-PIG

verbs
breed —s; dissect—; experiment with—; inject into —s; propagate —s; test —s.
(See animal.)

GUISE

adjectives
altered; secret; abstracted; fitting; festal;
mortal; novel; startling; attractive; celestial; compellent; lowly; truthful; human;
opalescent; reputable; gentler; murky; artful; silken; modern; winning.

adjectives
accustomed; tinkling; roaring; vigilant;
humming; strumming; vibrant.

verbs
accompany with—; brush—; employ—; finger—; feet—; handle—; peck—; pick on—;
pluck—; provide—; serenade with—; string
—; strum—; tune—; twang—; —delights;
—harmonizes; —moans; —throbs; —tinkles.
(See banjo.)

GULF

adjectives
voracious; winding; foaming; starlit; yawning; impassable; remoter; deep; tragic; unfathomable; roaring; pebbly; fiery; envious;
breaking; starry; mystic; mediate; azure.

verbs
bridge—; deepen into—; dip into—; span—;
—absorbs; —confronts; —hides; —opens;
—roars; —separates; —sweeps.
(See chasm, separation, whirlpool,
bay, vortex.)

GULL

adjectives
curving; circle; flannel; flapping; laughing;
fading; strenuous; notorious; gleaming.

verbs
—barks; —bullies, —chatters; —s colonize;
—darts; —fishes; —floats; —s flock; —s
fraternize; —s prey on; —rends the air; —
robs; —roves; —sails; —screams; —shrills;
—skims; —soars; —squalls; —swoops; —
wails; —wheels; —wings out to sea.
(See bird.)

GULLIBLE

adverbs
credulously; foolishly; weak-mindedly; dully; inanely; weakly; thoughtlessly; blindly;
unthinkingly; easily; disastrously; unfortunately; fatuously; vacuously; childishly; superstitiously; confidently; exceptionally; obviously; manifestly; absurdly; ridiculously;
idiotically; imprudently; indiscreetly; witlessly; brainlessly; amazingly; unexpectedly.

verbs

excavate—; force along—; form—; furrow —; hollow into—; rise from—; scramble up —; straddle—; —deepens; —extends; —graduates; —opens.

(See gorge, channel, hollow, gutter, ditch, gulf.)

GULP (v)
adverbs

noisily; disgustingly; hungrily; vulgarly; eagerly; nauseously; rapaciously; ravenously.

(See swallow, eat.)

GUM
verbs

barrel—; consume—; dissolve—; glue with —; harden into—; secrete—; spread—; utilize—; twist—; yield—; —issues from; —preserves; —prevents; —stiffens.

GUMS
adjectives

enormous; toothless; odorous; lucid; precious; aromatic.

GUN
adjectives

honeycombed; squirrel; strong; pneumatic; murdering; resounding; hungry; rapid-fire; threatening; crackling; truculent; booming; resonant.

verbs

brave —s; cover with—; deflect—; jab—at; level—at; loose—at; man —s; mount—; muster —s; notch—; sheathe—; sight—; train—on; whip out—; —barks; —belches fire; —blazes away; —bombards; —booms; —s clatter; —demolishes; —enfilades; —glints; —grumbles; —jams; —pours; —roars; —rumbles; —spits; —spurts; —thunders; —volleys; —whines.

(See rifle, cannon, musket, pistol.)

GUN-FIRE
verbs

attack with—; break into—; charge with—; dodge—; flee from—; order—; rake with —; retreat from—; spatter with—; —assaults; —breaks loose; —crackles; —damages; —destroys; —disperses; —explodes; —reverberates; —tears up; —terrorizes.

(See firing, bombardment, fusillade, shots, volley.)

verbs

agitate—; blast with—; charge with—; compound—; discharge—; inflame—; kindle—; reek with—; store—; —detonates; —explodes; —flashes; —smokes.

(See ammunition, dynamite, explosive.)

GURGLE
adjectives

slobbery; liquid; rich; childish; thick; horrible; oozing.

GURGLE (v)
adverbs

drearily; monotonously; pleasantly; musically; melodiously; ceaselessly; perpetually; spasmodically.

(See hiss, ripple, whisper.)

GUSH (v)
adverbs

copiously; spontaneously; terrifically; roaringly; richly; impetuously; foamingly; unrestrainedly; loquaciously.

(See rush, flow.)

GUSHING
adverbs

elaborately; volubly; fluently; foolishly; effusively; sentimentally; ecstatically; rapturously; joyously; inanely; absurdly; ridiculously; inconsequently; excitedly; nervously; warmly; racily; breathlessly; hysterically; impressively; pretentiously; ostentatiously; showily; unpleasantly; offensively; uncommonly; habitually; constantly; impetuously; vivaciously; tiresomely; endlessly; interminably.

GUST
adjectives

chill; fitful; hot; unusual; violent; fierce; stormy; buffeting; extreme; passionate; sudden; scented; eddying; angry.

GUSTO
adjectives

culinary; geyserish; racy; joyous; wholesome; great; inartistic; rare; sardonic; hearty; solemn.

verbs

discharge in—; drag in—; drift down—; furrow—; jostle into—; lodge in—; recline in—; slope to—; stream down—; sweep into —; wear away—; —carries away; —irrigates; —drains;.

(See channel, ditch, groove.)

adverbs

deeply; brokenly; inarticulately; pleasantly; heavily; outlandishly; exotically; grotesquely; absurdly; mockingly; thickly; hesistantly; distinctly; extremely; undisguisedly; surprisingly.

H

HABIT

adjectives

moral; ferocious; mental; celestial; tranquil; quasi-religious; barbarian; sedentary; unclean; desultory; unrestrained; invariable; systematic; social; separate; idle; economical; sober; contrary; old-fashioned; disconcerting; lifelong; healthful; steady; taciturn; lifetime; precious; established; estranged; unsettled; long-existing; philosophical; popular; spendthrift; cleanly; incurable; religious; offensive; courteous; innate; sidewalk; ill; parti-colored; vulgar; devilish; aquatic; fixed; personal; priceless; dissolute; important; peculiar; cherished; sociable; outdoor; baneful; migratory; industrious; indelicate; retrospective; steady; gregarious; exasperating; tutored; psychological; fastidious; immoral; virtuous; asthmatic; intense; wandering; acquired; uncanny; vicious; comparative; harmless; injurious; prevalent; confirmed; spending; abominable; feminine; deadly; expensive; drinking; mating; unsightly; bloodcurdling; unhygienic; pernicious; voracious; proper; degrading; unproductive; intemperate; honorable; natural; unfortunate; orderly; watchful; flabby; dainty; epicurean; cherished; virile; judicious; ineradicable; purgative; disputatious; busy; convivial; frugal; industrious; temperate; ascetic; studious; nascent; leisurely; hurtful; depraved; mean; intoxicating; careless; fatal; constant; inexcusable; incompatible; physical; silly; dreadful; disgusting; beguiling; autocratic; sluggish; roving; debauched; evil; remorseless; ingrained; domestic; active; awkward; licentious; luxurious; extravagant; artificial; dishonest; mourning; filthy; untoward; piscatory; unmanageable; corrupt; slovenly; indolent; humble; simple; unfixed; dietetic; stylish; unassuming; sordid; demure; synthetic; deliberate; daring; terrible; worse; improvident; intellectual; watchful; unconscious; detestable; dangerous.

verbs

acquire—; adopt—; assume—; break up—; breed—; check—; contract—; cultivate—; deplore—; develop—; discard—; dissolve —; diverge from—; eradicate—; establish —; fall into—; gain—; inculcate—; induce —; indulge in—; instill—; protest against —; pursue—; regulate—; relinquish—; re-

nounce—; set up—; teach—; unlearn—; upset—; —accustoms; —binds; —compels; —loses its hold; —persists; —roots; —takes possession.

(See custom, practice, inclination.)

HABITATION

adjectives

devoted; personal; moving; crude; squalid; humble; peaceful; dismal; commodious; isolated.

HABITUAL

adverbs

idly; disconcertingly; incurably; deliberately; carefully; peculiarly; traditionally; inherently; harmlessly; unfortunately; automatically; ineradicably; studiously; dreadfully; awkwardly; dangerously; methodically; prosaically; conveniently; unconsciously.

HACKNEYED

adverbs

tiresomely; boresomely; ineffectively; tritely; prosaically; typically; bookishly; learnedly; academically; pedantically; professionally; banally; conventionally; pedagogically; unctuously; sententiously; wearisomely; stupidly; monotonously; flatly; terribly; dully.

HAEMOGLOBIN

verbs

break down—; combine with—; count—; destroy—; enrich—; gain in—; lessen—; measure—; study—; —circulates; —conveys; —crystallizes; —dispenses; —oxidizes; —provides.

HAG

adjectives

unseemly; edentate; withered; repulsive; blear-eyed; hideous; ferocious; wretched; wicked; secret; black; midnight.

HAGGARD

adverbs

terribly; alarmingly; surprisingly; pitiably; pathetically; fearfully; unwontedly; extremely; frightfully; mysteriously; significantly; distressingly; disturbingly; gauntly; shockingly; appallingly; wearily; uncommonly; singularly; strangely; cruelly.

adjectives
continuous; lashing; sonorous; pearly; sulphurous; incessant; cursing; dreadful.

verbs
deluge with—; escape—; pour—; send down —; shower with—; volley—; —assails; — chills; —descends; —desolates; —falls; — pierces; —ravages; —shatters; —spatters; —stones; —tattoos; —whistles round.
(See rain, snow.)

HAIL (*v*)

adverbs
exultingly; rapturously; imperatively; enthusiastically; resoundingly; boisterously; thunderously; obstreperously; vigorously.
(See salute, accost.)

HAIR

adjectives
abnormal; abominable; abounding; abundant; agglutinated; alluring; amber; amorous; ash-blonde; ash-colored; asthetic; auburn; back-blown; backward-streaming; bad; battling; beautiful; bleached; blowing; blond; blue-black; bobbed; boyish; braided; brick-colored; bright; bristling; brittle; bronzed; brunette; brushed; bushy; carefully-brushed; careless; carroty; chestnut; close-curling; close-cut; close-trimmed; clustering; coal-black; coiled; colored; copious; coppery; corn-colored; correct; cottony; crinkly; crisp; crownless; cumbersome; curled; dabbled; dark; dazzling; dewy; disarranged; dirty; discolored; disheveled; disordered; drab; dressed; dripping; drowning; dull; dusky; dusty; dyed; ebon; effulgent; elaborately-dressed; electrified; erect; entangled; excessive; faded; fair; falling; fiery; filthy; fine; finespun; flamelike; flattened; flaxen; flecked; floating; flowing; fluffy; fluttering; flying; forlorn; frizzed; frowzy; fussy; fuzzy; garlanded; glamorous; gleaming; glinting; glittering; glorious; glossy; golden; gorgeous; gray; graying; greasy; grimy; grizzled; haggard; hard; harsh; hay-colored; hazel; heavy; helmeted; hempy; henna; hoary; honey-colored; horrent; horrible; horrid; impeccable; impetuous; incredible; iron-gray; jet; jet-black; jeweled; kinky; knotted; lambent; lank; lifeless; light; limp; long; loosening; loosewaved; lovely; luminous; lustrous; luxuriant; mahogany; marcelled; marvelous; massive; matted; metallic; mis-dressed; misty;

mortal; mouse-colored; muddy; mussed; mustard-colored; neat; neglected; nut-brown; objectionable; oily; odorous; over-bleached; overgrown; overlong; pale; palled; pallid; palsied; parted; pendulous; perfumed; plaited; plentiful; plastered; pomaded; poppied; portentous; powdered; precious; prematurely-gray; prim; princely; problematical; prodigious; profuse; puffed; queenly; quiet; radiant; ragged; raven; ravishing; rebellious; reddish; reddled; refractory; reverend; ribboned; rich; riotous; rippling; romantic; rough; ruffled; rumpled; russet; rusty; sandy; satiny; scant; scattered; scented; scorched; scraggly; sculptured; shadowy; shaggy; sheeny; shining; shingled; short; short-cropped; silken; silver-gilt; silvery; sleek; slender; slicked; sluttish; smoky; smoothed; smothering; snowy; soft; soggy; spiky; spilling; sprouting; starchy; steel-gray; stiff; stiff-looking; straggly; straight; straw-colored; streaked; subtle; streaming; strength-giving; stringy; strong; stubbly; stubby; sun-blanched; sunny; sun-bleached; sustaining; swart; sylvan; swarthy; sweaty; taffy; tangled; tawny; thick; tidy; time-hallowed; tiny; tousled; tow-colored; tumbled; turbulent; twining; twisted; two-toned; unbound; uncompromising; unconquered; uncurled; undone; undulating; unhealthy; unkempt; unkinked; unmanageable; unruly; untidy; unwashed; usurping; vegetable; velvety; venerable; vibrant; vivid; voluminous; waved; wavy; waxed; well-brushed; well-known; weltering; wet; wild; wind-blown; wind-rumpled; wind-whipped; wiry; wondrous; wreathless; youthful; zephyr-blown; burnished.

verbs
arrange—; beribbon—; braid—; curl—; deck—; discipline—; dishevel—; fluff out—; glue down—; groom—; ruffle—; rumple—; train—; whisk back—; —bristles; — frames; —gleams; —glistens; —glows; — luxuriates; —projects; —ripples; —shimmers; —shines; —straggles; —waves.
(See beard, whiskers, curls.)

HALCYON

adverbs
gently; calmly; peacefully; gratefully; delightfully; gloriously; enviably; agreeably; providentially; happily; sunnily; smoothly; charmingly; blissfully; comfortably; beatifically; cloudlessly; unbelievably; refreshingly; felicitously; miraculously; incomparably.

HALE

adverbs

delightfully; sturdily; stoutly; vigorously; vivaciously; cheerily; healthily; soundly; hardily; robustly; ordinarily; vibrantly; exuberantly; remarkably; incredibly; exceptionally; unwontedly; enthusiastically; unbelievably; cheerfully.

HALF-HEARTED

adverbs

obviously; unconcealedly; openly; frankly; manifestly; curiously; indifferently; timidly; indecisively; lazily; indolently; insolently; capriciously; indeterminately; irresolutely; phlegmatically; languidly; nonchalantly; carelessly; inattentively; imperturbably; extraordinarily; inexplicably; unaccountably; irresponsibly; insouciantly; vexatiously; lackadaisically; noticeably; conspicuously.

HALL

adjectives

moody; boundless; cerulean; pillared; gilded; naked; windy; dimly-lighted; spacious; brilliant; low-browed; gaslit; upper; festal; voiceless; lofty; hospitable; marble-paved; ancestral; ancient; unillumined; dusky; enormous; capacious; shallow; subterranean; barrel-vaulted; main; oak-lined; paternal; palatial; roofless; lonely; ample; gloomy; ethereal.

verbs

appropriate—for; assemble in—; convert—into; gather in—; grace—; jam—; loiter in —; occupy—; receive in—; transact in—; preside over—.

(See building, room, auditorium, passage, entry.)

HALLOW (*v*)

adverbs

traditionally; solemnly; formally; religiously; pompously; perfunctorily.

(See reverence, bless.)

HALLUCINATION

adjectives

visionary; engendering.

verbs

abolish—; dispose to—s; entertain—s; expel—; molest with—; produce—; suffer—s; wander into—; welter in—; wrap in—; —

annoys; —arises; —envisions; —harasses; —hounds; —preys upon; —suggests; —sweeps away; —worries.

(See delusion, illusion.)

HALLWAY

adjectives

frigid; austere; narrow.

HALO

adjectives

majestic; radiant; glistening; hollow.

verbs

award—; crown with—; display—; fashion —; form—; garland with—; invest with—; spread—around; suspend—; weave—; — appears; —blinks; —encircles; —encompasses; —girdles; —glorifies; —hovers over; —radiates; —surrounds; —wreathes.

(See glory, circle, light.)

HALT

adjectives

panting; dead.

verbs

bring to—; call—; come to—; command—; earn—; fall to—; induce—; merit—; necessitate—; plead for—; sound—; stumble to —; urge—; —refreshes; strengthens; — vivifies.

(See truce.)

HALT (*v*)

adverbs

abruptly; irresolutely; awkwardly; instantaneously; jarringly; completely; permanently.

(See stop, cease.)

HAMLET

adjectives

scattered (pl); rude; nameless; obscure; favored; humble; huddled; disheveled; insignificant.

HAMMER

adjectives

ponderous; polished; deafening.

verbs

beat with—; clasp—; crush with—; drive with—; employ—; flourish—; guide—;

labor with—; rap with—; shape with—; smite with—; strike with—; swing—; tap with—; wield—; —injures; —menaces; —suffices.

(See gavel, club, hatchet.)

HAMMER (v)

adverbs

untiringly; repetitiously; energetically; deafeningly; maddeningly; industriously; monotonously; vigorously; thunderously.

(See beat, pound.)

HAMMOCK

adjectives

concealing; leafy; creaking.

verbs

bear in—; cradle in—; ensconce in—; hang in—; hide in—; loll in—; nest in—; relax in—; rest in—; shroud in—; sling—across; slip into—; suspend—; turn into—; —holds; —swings; —upsets.

(See bed, couch.)

HAMPER (v)

adverbs

disastrously; tragically; purposely; fatefully; seriously; painfully; cruelly; superfluously.

(See impede, restrain.)

HAND

verbs

aspire to—of; beckon with—; callous—; clap—s; clasp in—; clench—; denote with —; employ—; extend—; flex—; flick—; flourish—; gain—of; indicate with—; join —s; paralyze—; proffer—; pump—; spread —; splint—; tender—; wring—; —quivers; —trembles; —twitches.

(See palm, claw, fingers, marriage.)

HANDCLASP

adjectives

latticed; fluid; fervent.

HANDFUL

adjectives

paltry; unshackled; comparative; thorny; scanty; scattered; promiscuous.

HANDICAP

adjectives

difficult; generous; cruel; troublesome; personal.

verbs

burden with—; compensate for—; gain—; impose—; insist on—; load with—; offset—; overcome—; require—; resent—; suffer under—; survive—; —alters; —equalizes; —evens; —hampers; —penalizes; —reduces.

(See disadvantage.)

HANDICAP (v)

adverbs

hopelessly; heavily; physically; psychically; spiritually; economically; maritally.

(See hinder.)

HANDKERCHIEF

adjectives

glaring; necktie; napkin; shabby; scandalous; unclean; tear-stained; immaculate; wadded.

verbs

adorn—; border—; display—; embroider—; expose—; fringe—; monogram—; perfume —; pocket—.

(See cloth, silk, linen.)

HANDLE

adjectives

knob; lever; hollow; detachable; composition; substantial.

verbs

clasp—; clutch—; deprive of—; fly off—; grab—; grasp—; grip—; hold by—; manage—; manipulate—; nab—; operate—; snatch—; twist—; —controls; —protrudes; —regulates.

(See knob.)

HANDLE (v)

adverbs

effectively; dexterously; summarily; severely; rudely; technically; awkwardly; individually; arbitrarily; competently; urgently; suavely; adroitly; skillfully.

(See manipulate, touch.)

HANDLING

adjectives

masterly; ill; indecisive; adroit; clever; rough; technical; dexterous; unexceptionable; guileful; skillful.

HANDS

adjectives

able; accursed; accomplished; achieving; active; admonishing; aged; affectionate; agile; agitated; aggressive; airy; almighty; ambitious; angelic; applauding; aristocratic; armed; arresting; artistic; atrocious; audacious; automatic; avaricious; awkward; balmy; barbarous; bare; beautiful; beckoning; begrimed; bejeweled; beneficent; benumbed; beseeching; bewildered; black; branded; black-gloved; blanched; bleeding; blistered; blithe; bloodless; bloody; blundering; bony; botanic; bounteous; bountiful; brawny; broad; bronzed; brown; bruised; brutal; bungling; burning; callous; capable; careless; caressing; casual; cautious; cemented; chafed; chamois-gloved; chapped; charitable; cheap; cheery; chill; chilly; childish; chopped; chubby; clammy; clapping; clasping; clawing; clawlike; clean; clenched; clever; cold; clinched; clumsy; clutching; coarse; comforting; colossal; confident; conscious; considerate; consoling; cordial; craven; cringing; crooked; cunning; curative; cushionlike; dainty; damaging; darting; deadly; deeply-tanned; defiling; deft; deformed; delegated; delicate; deprecating; despairing; despoiling; detaining; dexterous; diamond-ringed; disguised; dirty; dimpled; discolored; disdainful; disengaged; disrobing; divine; dogmatic; dolllike; dominating; dreadful; drooping; drink-shaken; dubious; dying; eager; eclipsing; eloquent; emaciated; emphatic; enameled; enchanting; energetic; envious; erudite; ever-open; ever-awakening; excellent; execrable; expensive; experienced; expert; explanatory; exploring; exquisite; extended; eye-instructed; fair; facile; failing; fairy; faithful; false; faltering; fanless; fastidious; fatigued; favoring; fearless; feeble; ferocious; fevered; fidgety; fiery; filthy; fine; firm; flabby; flaccid; flattering; flawless; fleshless; fleshy; flexible; floury; fluttering; foam-white; folded; foraged; frank; frantic; fratricidal; freckled; free; frenzied; friendly; fumbling; furtive; fussy; gaunt; gauntleted; generous; gentle; gesticulating; girlish; gloating; glorified; gloved; glowing; gnarled; gorilla; gracious; grasping; graspless; greasy; green; grimy; groomed; groping; grubby; guiding; hairy; hallowed; hamlike; hammerhard; handsome; hanging; hard; hard-palmed; hasty; hateful; healthful; hearty; heavy; heavy-veined; heedless; helpful;

helping; high; hollowed; holy; honest; honored; horny; hospitable; hovering; huge; human; humble; hurried; icy; idle; ignoble; immaculate; immediate; immense; immortal; impatient; imperious; impious; imploring; impulsive; incarnadined; inconsequent; indignant; indiscriminate; indolent; indomitable; ineffective; inexperienced; infant; innocent; innocuous; inquisitive; insistent; instinctive; instrumental; intelligent; interpretative; intractable; intruding; invisible; iron; irresolute; irresponsible; irreverent; ivory; jerking; jeweled; kindly; knotted; knuckled; labor-calloused; lacerated; lacerating; lame; languid; lavish; lax; lean; leathery; legible; lemon-scented; lenient; dishpan; wise; liberal; limp; listless; lithe; little; locked; lone; long; long-fingered; long-stretched; long-taloned; loose-hanging; lordly; loving; lustful; mailed; magnetic; malicious; malignant; manacled; manicured; manipulating; martial; massive; masterly; maternal; meager; menacing; merciful; mere; mighty; ministering; miscalculating; mittened; moist; molded; motionless; mottled; mournful; much-ringed; murderous; munificent; nameless; narrow; neighborly; nerveless; nervous; nestling; niggardly; nimble; noiseless; numbed; offending; old-looking; olive; outdoor; outflung; outstretched; pale; pallid; palsied; pampering; parched; parricidal; passive; patrician; peaceful; persistent; persuasive; pierced; pious; pitiless; placid; plastic; plenty-dropping; plump; poised; portraying; powder-blackened; powerful; practiced; pragmatic; praying; presumptuous; priestly; prim; primitive; prodigal; profane; proffered; prompt; proper; protective; providential; providing; pudgy; puffy; pulpy; pure; quavering; quizzical; rash; rapacious; raw; reassuring; reaching; reckless; relaxed; remorseless; relentless; reluctant; resolute; respectful; responsive; restless; restraining; reverent; rheumatic; rigid; rigorous; ringed; ringless; robust; rose-leaf; rose-petal; rosy; rough; royal; rude; ruinous; ruthless; sacred; sacrilegious; sallow; satiny; saving; sceptered; scheming; scholarly; scornful; sculptured; searching; seared; severe; sinless; shadowy; shaking; shapely; shattered; shiny; shriveled; shuddering; signaling; sin-avenging; sinew-swelled; sinewy; skeleton; skillful; slack; slender; slim; slimy; slippery; slow; sly; small; smooth; smudgy; snowy; soaked; soft; soiled; solid; soot-grimed;

577

staying; steady; stealthy; stiffened; stodgy; stout; straggling; straining; strange; strengthening; strong; stubby; subtle; sudden; suing; sunburned; supine; supple; supplicating; supporting; sure; surreptitious; sustaining; swarthy; swollen; sympathetic; tactful; tainted; tampering; tanned; tapering; tear-dampened; tempestuous; tender; thick; thievish; thin; threatening; throttling; tied; tight-clasped; timid; tiny; tiring; titanic; toil-hardened; toilworn; toiling; torn; trained; translucent; transparent; treacherous; trembling; tremendous; tremulous; trusting; tugging; twitching; tyrannous; unaided; uncertain; unclasped; unconscious; uncovered; unequal; unerring; unfamiliar; unfettered; ungainly; ungloved; ungrudging; uninhibited; unlineal; unresisting; unresponsive; unseen; unskilled; unsparing; unsteady; unswerving; untrained; untrembling; unvenerable; unwilling; uplifted; upstretched; useful; useless-looking; usurious; valorous; victorious; viewless; vigorous; violent; vital; vulgar; wan; wandering; wanton; warm; warning; warring; wasted; water-shriveled; wavering; waxlike; weather-browned; welcoming; well-bred; well-cared-for; well-formed; well-shaped; willing; withered; work-hardened; lifeless; working; work-marked; wounded; work-soiled; wrapped; wrinkled; wretched; clear; soothing; upraised; spider; sprawling; sprightly; vandalous; vast; veined; venerated.

HANDSOME
adverbs
dazzlingly; gloriously; intangibly; matchlessly; fiercely; surprisingly; sullenly; compellingly; richly; darkly; duskily; cruelly; stormily; vitally; singularly; imposingly; impressively; proudly; sternly; triumphantly; resplendently; glowingly; startlingly; regally; glamorously.

HANDWORK
adjectives
painstaking; plodding; patient; deft.

HANDWRITING
adjectives
sprawling; attested; unmistakable; feeble; quavering; distinctive; intelligent; inelegant; bold; clear; poor; scrawly; uncultivated; crabbed.

verbs
admire—; alter—; counterfeit—; decipher —; develop—; forge—; judge—; recognize —; —fascinates; —flourishes; —reveals; — wavers.
(See writing.)

HANDY
adverbs
extremely; providently; conveniently; exceptionally; remarkably; carefully; delightfully; cleverly; unusually; perfectly; uncommonly; thoughtfully; noticeably; incomparably; serviceably; advantageously; practically; appropriately; readily; ingeniously; miraculously.

HANG (v)
adverbs
fatefully; debatably; imminently; dolefully; fondly; precariously; waveringly; indecisively; tenderly; listlessly; stubbornly; conspicuously; breathlessly; lankly; disconsolately; doggedly; flaccidly.
(See lynch, execute.)

HANGINGS
adjectives
leafy; wholesale; sumptuous; inflammable.

HAPHAZARD
adverbs
casually; carelessly; indolently; informally; adventitiously; incidentally; nonchalantly; indifferently; fortuitously; delightfully; abominably; terribly; atrociously; reprehensibly; joyously; merrily; irresponsibly; gloriously; dreadfully; inconveniently.

HAPPEN (v)
adverbs
opportunely; propitiously; auspiciously; allegedly; subsequently; historically; spontaneously; mysteriously; logically; promptly.
(See occur, befall.)

HAPPENINGS
adjectives
alleged; accidental; subsequent; historical; ordinary; spontaneous; vital; invented; unbelievable; strenuous; mysterious.

HAPPINESS
adjectives
boundless; excited; fireside; tranquil; resultant; connubial; crowning; legitimate; incomparable; wild; overwhelming; keen;

grave; peaceful; celestial; passive; humble; supreme; human; cheap; vulgar; true; romantic; buoyant; puerile; subsequent; unproductive; unclouded; scant; pure; golden; glowing; earthly; mutual; secret; rapturous; eternal; visionary; unexpected; highest; solid; unexcelled; redundant; unutterable; radiant; sublunary; sublime; unappreciated; dizzy; surface; delusive; temporal; exquisite; soft; personal; dear; strange; domestic; virulent; poor; neighborly; pastoral; exalted; joyous; healthy; close-woven; superhuman.

verbs
achieve—; assail—of; bar from—; betoken —; breathe—; conceal—; convert to—; derive—from; destroy—; extract—from; hamper—; inhale—; jeopardize—; overrate—; predestine to—; promote—; recapture—; rescue—; salvage—; shut out—; stake everything on—; strive for—; struggle for —; tend toward—; voice—; void—; yield —; —endures; —evades; —fades; —lingers; —reposes in; —touches; —visits; —wanes.

(See prosperity, gladness, delight, pleasure, bliss, joy, comfort, enjoyment, satisfaction.)

HAPPY
adverbs
radiantly; beamingly; beautifully; bonnily; curiously; rosily; smilingly; ridiculously; openly; innocently; childishly; shyly; modestly; frankly; brightly; rapturously; excitedly; tranquilly; quietly; incomparably; wildly; keenly; overwhelmingly; supremely; secretly; unutterably; joyously; ecstatically; ineffably; profoundly; tenderly; deliriously; breathlessly.

HARANGUE
adjectives
mere; soporific; seditious; inflammatory; tempestuous; conciliatory; soldierly; unintelligible; coherent; explanatory; fiery; belligerent.

HARANGUE (v)
adverbs
bombastically; vehemently; seditiously; tempestuously; unintelligibly; coherently; fiercely; belligerently; vigorously.

(See orate, address.)

HARASS (v)
adverbs
consistently; grievously; ceaselessly; perpetually; maddeningly; irksomely; irritatingly; exasperatingly; incessantly.

(See distress, persecute, trouble.)

HARASSMENT
adjectives
ceaseless; perpetual.

HARBOR
adjectives
immense; sun-splashed; sunlit; little; green-bordered; earthly; exposed; secret; miniature; landlocked; fortified; blue; restless; mountain-bound; all-creating; bustling; glassy; neutral; matchless; noble; placid; sheltered; fair; unrivaled.

verbs
admit to—; afford—; anchor in—; assign to—; blockade—; drift to—; lie in—; lodge at—; obtain—; put into—; seek—; set out of—; slip into—; —accommodates; —conceals; —protects; —quarters; —shelters.

(See refuge, haven, shelter, retreat.)

HARD
adverbs
stonily; wilfully; unyieldingly; pitilessly; obdurately; unrelentingly; unrepentantly; inexorably; stubbornly; obstinately; mulishly; doggedly; perversely; fanatically; resolutely; determinedly; unmercifully; cruelly; maliciously; vengefully; implacably; bitterly; sternly; unreasonably; manifestly; palpably; undeniably.

HARDEN (v)
adverbs
glacially; excessively; immoderately; perpetually; scientifically; methodically; mechanically.

(See season, invigorate.)

HARDIHOOD
adjectives
slipshod; reckless; barbaric; desperate.

HARDNESS
adjectives
iron; steely.

verbs
allay—; arm with—; crust with—; deliver from—; dissemble—; inure to—; incur—;

loathe—; overcome—; penetrate—; produce
—; rub off—; shed—; suffer—; —defends;
—endures; —protects; —resists.

(See difficulty, harshness, cruelty, severity.)

HARDSHIP
adjectives
continued; increasing; inevitable; nameless;
physical; appreciable; incredible; tremendous; unnecessary; unexpected; early; unre-
pining.

verbs
allay—; alleviate—; ameliorate—; bear—;
bow under—; condemn to—; ease—; endure
—; entail—; evade—; groan under—; impose—; inflict—; learn through—; oppress
with—; share—; suffer—; taste—; tolerate
—; torment with—; —anguishes; —destroys; —discourages; —presses.

(See privation, injury, affliction, adversity, trouble, pain.)

HARDY
adverbs
resolutely; intrepidly; courageously; stoutly; sturdily; robustly; boldly; fortunately;
indubitably; obviously; indefatigably; dependably; strongly; staunchly; vigorously;
stalwartly; inexhaustibly; courageously;
audaciously; pluckily; wonderfully; irresistibly; astonishingly; prodigiously.

HARE
adjectives
purblind; timorous; fluffy; flying.

HARLEQUIN
adverbs
erratically; capriciously; changeably; mercurially; kaleidoscopically; vagrantly; waywardly; fleetingly; nimbly; swiftly; fleetly;
trippingly; stagily; dramatically; spectacularly; comically; trickily; lightly; clownishly; jocosely; waggishly; fabulously; entertainingly; laughingly; mockingly.

HARM
adjectives
sullen; bodily; enormous; substantial; tremendous; imminent; delicious; irreparable;
incalculable; chief; outward; serious; personal.

verbs
anticipate—; avert—; commit—; correct—;
counterbalance—; forgive—; heed—; inflict
—; lament—; offset—; prevent—; protect
against—; rectify—; remedy—; render—;
resent—; ruminate upon—; save from—;
suffer—; sustain—; weigh—; —afflicts; —
angers; —distresses; —pains; —threatens.

(See injury, damage, evil, wrong.)

HARMFUL
adverbs
terribly; immediately; ultimately; distinctly;
admittedly; obviously; maliciously; venomously; deliberately; innocently; unconsciously; ignorantly; intentionally; purposely; irrevocably; irremediably; calamitously; disastrously; dreadfully; outrageously; atrociously; perniciously; exceptionably; deplorably; uncommonly; frightfully; immeasurably; incalculably.

HARMLESS
adverbs
innocently; distinctly; assuredly; avowedly;
obviously; manifestly; definitely; altogether;
utterly; comparatively; allegedly; perfectly; impeccably; virtually; substantially;
practically; negligibly; essentially; presumably; reasonably; assuredly.

HARMONIOUS
adverbs
agreeably; fortunately; sweetly; luckily; unquestionably; happily; felicitously; unbelievably; unexpectedly; sociably; ineffably; cordially; heartily; obviously; manifestly; sincerely; highly; entirely; uncommonly; remarkably; particularly; delightfully; serenely; exquisitely; seraphically; gloriously; inexpressibly.

HARMONY
adjectives
ingenious; distinguished; plaintive; serene;
subtle; thrilling; ringing; sublime; unutterable; amiable; developed; divine; ravishing; inner; absolute; complete; whirlwind;
primal; undisturbed; entire; methodical;
perfect; ethereal; general; incomparable;
celestial; angelic; pre-established; exquisite; multitudinous (pl); many-sounding;
unbroken; heavenly; household; deceiving;
liquid; delightful; peculiar; inarticulate;
eternal; discordant; canarylike; complicated; blatant; enchanting; weird; insured;
glorious; limitless; soft; subdued; inexpress-

ible; aerial; unconjectured; color; intoxicating; far-linked; elemental; impromptu; autumnal; wonderful; rugged; lugubrious; consonant; palatable; chiseled.

verbs
admire—; beget—; bind into—; cement—; compose into—; destroy—; dispose toward —; insure—; maintain—; melt into—; stress —; strike—; weave in—; work in—; —charms; —delights; —emanates from; —enchants; —grows; —pervades; —prevails; —smooths.
(See friendship, agreement, peace, consistency.)

HARP
adjectives
murmuring; piano; neglected; cunning; mysterious; sullen; reproofless; impaled; aeolian; smitten; solemn; sounding; sweet; tuneful.

verbs
flow from—; marry to—; pitch—; string—; strum—; touch—; tune—; waken—; welcome—; —chimes; —disarms; —enervates; —entrances; —pleases; —reverberates; —rings out; —sings; —sleeps; —soothes; —thrills; —trembles; —whispers.
(See guitar, banjo.)

HARP (*v*)
adverbs
exclusively; repetitiously; irksomely; naggingly; inexorably; bitterly; moodily; venomously; groundlessly; sullenly.
(See persist, repeat.)

HARPING
adjectives
constant; mysterious; celestial.

HARROW (*v*)
adverbs
mercilessly; cruelly; superfluously; gratuitously; sadistically; grimly.
(See wound, distress, torture.)

HARSH
adverbs
dreadfully; needlessly; unnecessarily; bitterly; inexplicably; austerely; irritably; discourteously; forbiddingly; irritatingly; inexcusably; deliberately; maliciously; incredibly; unreasonably; vengefully; disconcertingly; tyrannically; despotically; dogmatic-

ally; imperiously; authoritatively; terribly; uncompromisingly; stubbornly; cruelly; unmitigatedly; mercilessly.

HARSHNESS
adjectives
terrible; stubborn; momentary; sinister; mellowed.

verbs
apply—; assail with—; avoid—; clash with —; correct—; creak with—; pardon—; resent—; resist—; rub with—; shed—; subdue—; taste—; temper—; thunder—; —arises from; —displeases; —grates; —sours.
(See severity, cruelty, hardness.)

HARVEST
adjectives
terrible; reaped; pecuniary; costly; easy; sorrowful; rich; bounteous; promising; uncertain; preposterous; golden; ripened; abundant; heavenly; full; fair; millennial; hidden; glorious; unshared; full-sheaved.

verbs
bear—; celebrate—; enrich—; gather—; glean—; heap—; house—; invite to—; mar —; promise—; reap—; rear—; ruin—; sickle—; toil in—; treasure—; —cheers; —contents; —glows; —graces; —repays; —rewards; —satisfies; —wearies.
(See crop, yield, product, reward, fruit, proceeds, result, return.)

HASTE
adjectives
heedless; breathless; duteous; delirious; phantom; disciplined; desperate; unseemly; wrathful; fiery; undue; hot; wild; indecent; purblind; unscrupulous; lamentable; eager; irreverent; barbarous; clumsy; nervous; noiseless; mad; frantic; reckless; uncivil; feverish; deadly; frenzied; disgraceful; rash; ruthless; moderate; dread; incredible; unusual; straining; over-credulous; tremulous; generous; noticeable.

HASTEN (*v*)
adverbs
instinctively; obsequiously; anxiously; vastly; materially; dutifully; nervously; unscrupulously; irreverently; frantically; uncivilly; feverishly; incredibly; tremulously.
(See urge, hurry.)

HASTY

adverbs
disgracefully; inexcusably; rudely; unforgivably; shamefully; hysterically; impetuously; impulsively; ridiculously; unnecessarily; unfortunately; madly; insanely.

HAT

adjectives
drab; shiny; tomato-colored; glazed; straw; rusty; soiled; silk; glossy; discolored; sleek; napless; chocolate; absurd; shabby; ordinary; archaic; hereditary; beaver; crownless; conical; jaunty; battered; distinguished; befeathered; beribboned; broad-brimmed; sugar-loaf; hard; high; cocked; cavernous; flattish; stunning; featherweight; felt; rush; high-crowned; flopping; dilapidated; fantastic; misshapen; much-worn; coquettish; beguiling; casual; slouched; formless; distinctive; fashionable; devastating; smart; shovel; horrible; becoming; plumed; infinitesimal; shapeless; dun-colored; soft; fetching; flowered; slouch; dishpan-shaped; delicate; battered; cunning.

verbs
clap on—; cock—; deck—; design—; discard—; display—; doff—; don—; fancy—; fashion—; plume—; scorn—; shed—; sport (colloq)—; tide—; tip—; trim—; wave—; —awes; —flatters; —s fly; —perches; —protects; —reposes on; —shocks; —teeters.
(See cap, helmet.)

HATCHET

verbs
brandish—; crush with—; drive—into; employ—; flourish—; hew with—; knock down with—; sharpen—; smite with—; split with —; strip with—; strike with—; threaten with—; wield—; yield to—; —cuts; —destroys; —lacerates; —menaces; —severs; —splits; —subdues; —wounds.
(See axe, hammer, club, bat, gavel.)

HATE

adjectives
high-strung; prejudiced; vigorous; counterfeiting; morbid; malevolent; racking; vanquished; constant; hideous; sectional; murderous; savage; steadfast; individual; groveling; immortal; deadly; inflexible; unfilial; grudging; envious; despotic; lodged; impious; heavy; ancestral; sullen; ill-dissembled; consuming; unrelenting; strong; bitter; mutual; irrevocable; quenchless; shameful; successful; unspoken; misbegotten; unmistakable; supernatural; vehement.

HATE (v)

adverbs
perniciously; implacably; cordially; insatiably; invariably; vindictively; jealously; instinctively; mutually; passionately; inflammably; politically; irrepressibly; unconquerably; groundlessly.
(See detest, dislike.)

HATED

adverbs
utterly; abominably; repugnantly; mortally; intolerably; impossibly; incredibly; completely; shockingly; detestably; disgustingly; insufferably; horribly; terribly; odiously.

HATEFUL

adverbs
bitterly; utterly; unspeakably; odiously; offensively; completely; abominably; disgustingly; insufferably; intolerably; horribly; terribly; shockingly; profoundly; uncommonly; intensely; unnaturally; curiously; passionately; venomously; infernally; furiously; consummately.

HATER

adjectives
reputed; persistent.

HATRED

adjectives
native; innate; instinctive; internal; caustic; patient; deadly; profound; intense; bitter; rancorous; mutual; unaffected; unnatural; unsleeping; hidden; curious; lifelong; strong; ineradicable; passionate; moody; fierce; obscure; inextinguishable; revolutionary; inflammable; virtuous; vigorous; apparent; venomous; smiling; inexorable; immodest; antique; ancient; fanatical; unleavened; hearty; national; raw; implacable; political; irrepressible; partisan; nauseous; jealous; racial; infernal; base; active; indurated; color; perfidious; relentless; furious; vindictive; violent; unconquerable; baffled; undying; consuming; groundless.

verbs
allay—; appease—; breed—; cherish—; conceal—; deepen—; depict—; deplore—; endure—; excite—; focus—upon; incite to —; justify—; kindle—; manifest—; nour-

ish—; nurse—; placate—; regard with—; quicken—; scatter—; shower with—; stir up—; summon—; sustain—; turn to—; voice—; —blazes; —bubbles; —convulses; —embitters; —festers; —impels; —lingers; —maligns; —stings; —subsides; —ravages; —rends; —sunders; —wanes; —waxes.

(See abomination, animosity, antagonism, contempt, enmity, hostility, indignation, jealousy.)

HAUGHTINESS
adjectives
staring; unconscious; self-approving.

HAUGHTY
adverbs
arrogantly; deliberately; pompously; absurdly; unreasonably; unnecessarily; offensively; ridiculously; egotistically; insolently; bumptiously; imperiously; superciliously; impertinently; shamefully; laughably; swaggeringly; presumptuously; contemptuously; contemptibly; justifiably; atrociously; extremely; unusually.

HAUL (v)
adverbs
economically; daily; professionally; customarily; speedily; laboriously; vigorously; painfully; lumberingly.

(See pull, draw, drag.)

HAUNCHES
adjectives
powerful; cold.

HAUNT
adjectives
genteel; childhood; authenticated; private; familiar; hideous; reptile; undergraduate; classical; cheerful; frequent; gay; frightful; native; brightened; strange; indigenous; delightful; swampy; deserted; weary; unaccustomed; popular; picturesque; mysterious; public; garden; melodious; shaded; inaccessible.

HAUNT (v)
adverbs
bewitchingly; lecherously; dejectedly; privately; hideously; frightfully; indigenously; mysteriously; bewilderingly.

(See persecute.)

HAVEN
adjectives
windless; beauteous; spacious; commodious; sheltered; wished.

verbs
admit to—; afford—; bar from—; conceal in—; enter—; establish—; flee to—; lodge —; retreat to—; seek—; —accommodates; —consoles; —protects; —quarters; —shelters; —solaces; —supports; —welcomes.

(See harbor, shelter, refuge, retreat, asylum.)

HAVOC
verbs
anticipate—; come to—; create—; cry—; decry—; fortify against—; pass into—; play —; practise—; repair—; resist—; survey—; witness—; work—; wreak—; —confounds; —distresses.

(See destruction, waste, ruin.)

HAWK
verbs
—alights; —attacks; —dashes; —destroys; —dodges; —floats; —glides; —gyrates; — pounces on; —preys on; —prowls about; — sails; —scans; —screams; —screeches; — seizes; —severs; —skims; —soars; —somersaults; —squeals; —sweeps down; —twists; —swerves; —swoops; —wheels around; — whistles.

(See bird.)

HAWKER
verbs
license—; patronize—; —advertises; —attracts; —babbles; —barks; —barters; — bears; —bellows; —carries; —disposes of; —cries; —expatiates on; —jabbers; —plies; —prates about; —rants about; —rattles off; —spiels; —travels; —vends; —wanders.

(See merchant, salesman.)

HAY
adjectives
nutritious; crisping; new-mown; fragrant; sun-scorched; fresh; half-tanned.

verbs
basket—; bundle—; cart—; cock—; conceal —; consume—; fork—; hook—; load—; market—; mow—; pitch—; preserve—; rake —; press—; spade—; stack—; store—; toss —.

(See grass.)

adjectives
high-shouldered; proverbial.

HAZARD

adjectives
structural; lessened; unreasonable; reduced; glorious; industrial; temporary; human; intrinsic; specified; extreme; blind; skidding; physical; tremendous; awful; extraordinary; perilous; dust.

verbs
avoid—; dally with—; dare—; doubt—; eliminate—; expose to—; face—; incur—; obviate—; overcome—; preserve from—; risk—; run—; stand—; stake on—; venture —; view—; —allures; —endangers; —obstructs; —perils; —threatens.

(See chance, risk, danger, peril, stake.)

HAZARDOUS

adverbs
extremely; recklessly; perilously; presumably; obviously; manifestly; unreasonably; gloriously; tremendously; awfully; extraordinarily; mysteriously; ominously; alarmingly; terribly; attractively; alluringly; notoriously; undeniably; adventurously; exceedingly; strangely.

HAZE

adjectives
blossomy; luminous; suspended; soft; emotional; hueless; silver; blue; purple; smoke; gauzy; transparent; waterish; golden; mellowing; murky; burning; yellow; soft; faint; autumnal; amber; glittering; diaphanous; fictitious; Indian Summer; nebulous; iridescent; mournful; dim; gray; damp; misty; penumbral; somnolent; fluid; shimmering; reddish; sumptuous; moonlit; drowsy; vanishing; undefinable; deepening; shining; tremulous; glimmering; noontide; languorous.

verbs
clear—; disappear in—; falter in—; grope in—; lose in—; mingle with—; penetrate—; —develops; —dims; —encompasses; —lifts; —frosts; —hangs; —hovers over; —melts; —mists; —obscures; —rests on.

(See vapor, smoke, mist, fog, obscurity, clouds.)

adverbs
dangerously; obscurely; dimly; incredibly; curiously; oddly; strangely; queerly; peculiarly; particularly; unpleasantly; unintelligibly; incomprehensibly; intentionally; deliberately; perilously; vexatiously; darkly; nebulously; uncertainly; foggily.

HEAD

adjectives
abominable; aching; acknowledged; addled; administrative; aggressive; ambitious; ample; antique; apprehensive; ashen; aspiring; asymmetrical; attentive; auburn; auspicious; averted; bald; bandaged; banished; battered; bedraggled; beautiful; beloved; bent; bewildering; blameless; blighted; blunt; bobbed; bowed; boyish; braided; brainless; bright; bristling; bruised; bullet; burnished; bursting; bushy; cavernous; classic; clean; clean-swept; clear; close-clipped; clumsy; coiffed; collective; comely; common; confused; copper; country; cowering; craven; cropped; crowned; crumpled; crushed; curious; curling; cursed; dark; dastardly; deathless; defending; deathlike; defenseless; defiant; delicate; delightful; desperate; devoted; diminished; disordered; dispirited; distant; dizzy; doll-like; downcast; downy; drooping; drowsy; drunken; dusky; early-silvering; elegant; elegantly-wigged; elfin; elongated; enticing; erect; executive; extravagant; fanciful; fascinating; fast-whitening; feathered; feeble; fine; finely-molded; firm; flame-red; flattened; flaunted; flaxen; fleshy; flowerless; forked; forlorn; frizzled; frowzy; gasping; ghastly; gleaming; glossy; golden; golden-mouthed; good-natured; gossipy; graceful; graduated; grizzled; grotesque; hairless; hairy; handsome; happy; haughty; heaven-saluting; heavy; heavy-jawed; heavy-jeweled; helmeted; helpless; henna; hideous; high-held; hoary; hooded; hopeless; horny; horrible; horrid; huge; hunted; ignorant; immortal; impassioned; imperial; imperious; impotent; impressive; impudent; impulsive; inclined; incongruous; inert; inexperienced; inquisitive; intellectual; intelligent; intermediate; intervening; iron-gray; irregular; irrevocable; joyful; keen; kingly; kinky; knavish; languid; large; learned; leonine; limp; lingering; little; living; logical; lofty; lolling; long; long-haired; lowered; low-lying; magnificent; mangled; massive; meek; melancholy; menacing; mighty; military; mob-

capped; molded; mossy; mottled; mountainous; muddy; mummylike; nightcapped; nodding; obsequious; obtuse; old; oval; ovate; overhanging; overheated; packed; palsied; pantomime; patchily-bald; patchy; patriarchal; patrician; pendent; pensive; periwigged; pictured; picturesque; plebeian; plumy; poetic; powdered; practical; presumptive; pretty; prostrate; proud; remarkable; queenly; racking; regal; responsible; restless; retracted; reverend; ridiculous; rolling; romantic; round; rude; saintly; satiny; saucy; sculptured; seemingly-devoted; sensible; shaggy; shaken; shamed; shapely; shameless; shaven; shiny; shrunken; sickly; silken; simple; sleek; sleeping; sleepless; slender; slightly-bald; small; smooth; snowy; sorrow-bowed; sovereign; spaniel; specular; spiritual; splendid; sprouting; square; stained; stately; steady; steaming; steel-hard; stupid; sturdy; suave; subtle; sufficient; sumptuous; sun-baked; sun-bleached; sunburned; tangled; thorny; thick-curled; thorn-crowned; throbbing; tilted; titled; titular; tombless; tonsured; tormenting; tossing; tousled; tremendous; troublesome; turbaned; twisted; ugly; uncovered; uncrowned; undishonored; unhonored; unkempt; unmellowed; unprotected; unshaven; unsuspecting; upheld; uptilted; upturned; veiled; venerated; virile; virtual; vivacious; vulgar; wabbling; wagging; weak; weary; weird; well-balanced; well-bleached; well-constructed; well-formed; well-poised; well-proportioned; well-shaped; whimsical; white-wigged; wigged; wobbly; woolly; yoke-encumbered; youthful.

verbs
adorn—; balance on—; bare—; bob—; bow —; cock—; crown—; erect—; hang—; incline—; involve—; pillow—; pound—; raise —; split—; surge to—; tilt—; wag—; waggle—; —buzzes; —protrudes; —reels; — sings; —spins; —swims; —throbs.
(See skull, mind, crown.)

HEADACHE
adjectives
frightful; agonizing; excruciating; satisfactory; attendant; racking; incessant; violent; splitting; insidious.

verbs
aggravate—; allay—; alleviate—; assail with—; attack with—; banish—; confine with—; cure—; dispose of—; ease—; groan with—; incur—; mitigate—; relieve—; remedy—; soothe—; subdue—; subject to—; temper—; throb with—; treat for—; —ensues; —indisposes; —prostrates; —returns; —weakens; —yields to.
(See pain.)

HEADDRESS
adjectives
gleaming; horned; immense.

HEADING
adjectives
cabalistic; comprehensive; general; definite.

HEADLAND
adjectives
graceful; misty; picturesque.

HEADLIGHT
adjectives
dazzling; blinding; blinking.

verbs
adjust—; dim—; extinguish—; focus—; regulate—; shun—; turn on—; —beams; —blinds; —dazzles; —flares; —flickers; —glares; —gleams; —illuminates; —penetrates; —reflects; —reveals; —shimmers; —shines.
(See light.)

HEADLINE
verbs
consult—; garner —s; hush down —s; pop into —s; scan —s; —alarms; —amazes; —announces; —asserts; —attracts; —awakens; —blares; —blazes; —blazons forth; —discloses; —disquiets; —hints; —misleads; —proclaims; —reports; —s protest; —suggests; —screams (colloq.); —shrieks; (colloq.).

(See title, advertisement, announcement, proclamation.)

HEADQUARTERS
adjectives
harried; military; ecclesiastical.

verbs
assume — at; convey to—; direct from—; dispatch to—; inhabit—; move into—; operate from—; order from—; repair to—; report to—; respect—; transact at—; —an-

nounces; —bars; —conceals; —decrees; —harbors; —issues; —reinstates; —shelters.

(See quarters, center, residence, house.)

HEADSTRONG
adverbs
stubbornly; wilfully; indomitably; doggedly; obdurately; obstinately; absurdly; ridiculously; unreasonably; violently; untractably; cantankerously; unmanageably; ungovernably; uncontrollably; persistently; inveterately; habitually; dreadfully; frightfully; inherently; incorrigibly; hopelessly; invincibly; sturdily; extremely.

HEAL (v)
adverbs
marvelously; miraculously; permanently; temporarily; superficially; medically; scientifically.

(See cure, repair.)

HEALING
adjectives
divine; sovereign; transient; miraculous.

HEALTH
adjectives
accustomed; decayed; comely; hardy; declining; failing; rude; tolerable; inexhaustible; robust; rustic; shattered; delicate; fundamental; glowing; particular; ever-uncertain; buxom; departing; saving; comparative; sweet; virile; ruddy; rose-tinted; vibrant; summer; absolute; universal; buoyant; positive; vigorous; precarious; glorious; moral; trying; blasted; flagrant; lonely; redundant; informing; frail; invigorating; dynamic; impaired; feeble; infirm; inexhaustible; exuberant; reacquired; required; physical; drunken; mental.

verbs
bankrupt—; battle for—; brace—; bubble with—; confer — upon; cultivate—; deprive of—; deteriorate in—; drain upon—; drink —; enjoy—; entrust—; foster—; hazard—; impair—; imperil—; improve—; influence —; injure—; insure—; lower—; maintain —; promote—; preoccupy with—; recapture —; restore to—; sacrifice—; sap—; shatter —; strive for—; sustain—; undermine—; —breaks; —continues; —fails; —improves; —suffers.

(See welfare, prosperity, strength.)

HEALTHFUL
adverbs
presumably; allegedly; bracingly; invigoratingly; restoratively; curatively; notoriously; reputably; famously; distinctly; remarkably; wonderfully; demonstrably; manifestly; evidently; undeniably; marvellously; unquestionably; extremely.

HEALTHY
adverbs
robustly; normally; unusually; admirably; wonderfully; fortunately; tolerably; fundamentally; comparatively; altogether; completely; buoyantly; vigorously; radiantly; gloriously; exuberantly; sturdily; happily; constitutionally; remarkably; excellently; magnificently; splendidly.

HEAP
adjectives
moldering; promiscuous; mountainous; tumbled; contorted; dismaying; enormous; undistinguishable; solemn; compost; wretched; writhing; convulsed; bony; wind-driven; sprawled; silvery; shapeless; lifeless; apparent; hoarded; inextricable; despicable.

verbs
accumulate into—; amass—; cast into—; collect in—; cone—; form—; gather into—; level—; lie in—; load into—; pile up—; relegate to—; rise in—; stand in—; store up—; throw into—; —grows; —overwhelms; —rises.

(See pile, mass.)

HEAP (v)
adverbs
massively; promiscuously; impartially; confusedly; profusely; indiscriminately; contortedly; convulsively; shapelessly; inextricably.

(See pile, accumulate.)

HEAR (v)
adverbs
accidentally; distinctly; occasionally; keenly; inevitably; audibly; dumbly; unconsciously; subconsciously; perpetually.

(See listen, perceive.)

HEARER
adjectives
eloquent; complacent; indefatigable; critical; attentive.

verbs

attract—s; bore —s; convince —s; crave—;
enchant—; impress—; inflame—; inform—;
instruct—; interest—; move—; obtain—;
preach to—; tire—; weary—; —assents; —
complies; —heeds; —judges; —learns; —
listens; —perceives.

(See audience, listener, spectator.)

HEARING

adjectives

respectful; impaired; defective; harsh; distinct; impartial; favorable; younger.

verbs

accede to—; bar from—; block—; crave—;
defer—; dull—; favor with—; grant—;
judge—; prejudice—; preside at—; question
—; rant at—; sustain—; weaken—.

(See meeting, investigation.)

HEARKEN (*v*)

adverbs

wistfully; respectfully; expectantly; eagerly;
nervously; excitedly; cautiously; instinctively.

(See hear, perceive, listen.)

HEART

adjectives

abysmal; aching; adulterate; affectionate;
affection-starved; agitated; alien; alienated;
anguished; animated; anxious; ardent;
arid; attentive; barren; bursting; base;
beating; beauty-broken; beauty-loving; beclouded; beefy; befuddled; besotted; bewildering; black; bland; blank; blazoned;
bleeding; blighted; boding; bounding;
brave; breaking; breathless; broken; brute;
bucklered; burdened; burning; bursting;
busy; callous; careless; cheerful; cheering;
cheery; childlike; clamorous; cold; compassionate; conscious; conservative; constant; constricted; contented; contrite; coreless; corrupted; courtly; covetous; cowardly; critical; crushed; dark; darkened;
dauntless; dazzling; dead; deceitful; dedicated; defying; delicate; delighted; desolate; despairing; disappointed; discontented; diseased; divided; dormant; double;
doubting; drained; dreary; drowsy; dull;
duteous; eager; echoing; ecstatic; editorial;
effeminate; emptied; enchanted; encouraged; energetic; entranced; erring; ever-beating; everlasting; exacting; excited;

fainting; faithful; false; famished; **fam**ous; farseeing; fascinated; faultless; **fear**ful; fecund; feeble; feminine; fevered;
fiendish; fierce; fiery; firm; fleshy; flinty;
wrung; fluttering; foolish; forestalled; forever-shattered; fragrance-laden; frail;
frank; freer; fretted; frightened; frostbound; frosted; frowning; frozen; gallant;
general; generous; gentle; genuine; girlish;
gleeful; graceless; grateful; gravel; grieved; guileless; half-snared; hammering; happy; haughty; heavenly; heavy; heedless;
hereditary; heroic; hidden; humanitarian;
humble; hungering; hurrying; hushed; idolatrous; impassioned; impious; impressionable; improvident; impulsive; inconstant;
indecent; individual; indolent; indurated;
inmost; inner; innocent; intense; irritable;
joyous; kind; kindling; kindred; laboring;
lacerated; laggard; languid; laughing; lavish; leaden; life-giving; light; lively; living; lofty; lonely; long; long-enduring;
long-pent; long-wandering; longing; loudly-beating; love-pampered; loving; low; low-hushed; maddening; manful; manly;
marble; mean; meditative; merry; mighty;
moist; mourning; mountain; moved; mysterious; mystic; naked; noble; obdurate; open;
oppressed; orphaned; outraged; overburdened; overflowing; overfull; overladen;
overworked; pained; palpitating; passionate; paternal; pearly; penitent; pent; perfect; perplexed; perturbed; perverse; pinched; pious; pitiless; pitying; plighted; poisoned; poor; popish; popular; poverty-stricken; private; profane; profound; propelled; prophetic; proud; pulsating; puny;
pure; pusillanimous; quaking; queenly;
queer; quenched; quick-beating; quick-breathed; quickened; rapt; rapture-filled;
ravaged; rebellious; reckless; relenting; repressed; responsive; restless; returning;
reverent; riotous; rising; rocky; rough;
royal; rude; rugged; rusting; saddened;
satisfied; scented; scheming; scorching;
seated; self-accusing; sensitive; shadowy;
shallow; sheer; shuddering; sickly; sincere; sinewy; singing; single; sinking;
slight; slow; smitten; smothered; softened;
solitary; somber; sore; sorrowful; spotless; stagnant; stainless; stalwart; starry;
steadfast; sterner; still-renewed; stirring;
stony; stout; straitened; stricken; strong;
struggling; stubborn; sturdy; suffocating;
sullen; sunny; superstitious; susceptible;
swelling; sweltering; sympathetic; tavern-like; tempest-tossed; **tender**; terrified;

thankful; thoughtless; thought-propelled; throbbing; thumping; tortured; tossed; towering; trembling; tremulous; troubled; trusting; tumultuous; turbulent; tyrannous; unassisted; uncaged; unconjectured; undivided; uneasy; unfettered; unfortified; unfrozen; unguarded; universal; unmoved; unpurchasable; unquickened; unquiet; unselfish; unsophisticated; unsuspecting; untutored; unwavering; unworn; unyielding; upright; vacant; veritable; virgin; wakening; wandering; warm; wasting; waxing; wayward; weak; weary; well-contented; well-disposed; wicked; widowed; wild; wintry; withering; womanly; wooing; wordless; worldly; worried; worshipping; wounded; wretched; yearning; zealous.

verbs
appeal to—; beguile—; chill—; depress—; dilate—; ease—; engage—; enshrine in—; furrow—; gather—; gladden—; harden—; hug to—; lay open—; melt—; mend—; pluck at—; pour out—; smite—; stab to—; stimulate—; take to—; warm—; wring—; —awakens; —betrays; —bleeds; —blinds; —contracts; —craves; —expands; —fails; —hungers; —jumps; —misgives; —overflows; —palpitates; —pines; —pounds; —prompts; —quakes; —races; —responds; —sinks; —softens; —swells; —throbs; —ticks; —yearns.
(See essence, core, pulse, organ, affection, passion, courage, strength.)

HEARTBEAT
adjectives
tumultuous; vexing.

HEARTBREAK
adjectives
terrible; human.

HEART DISEASE
verbs
convalesce from— —; correct— —; cure of — —; examine for— —; incur— —; indicate— —; recover from— —; resist— —; suffer from— —; treat— —; — —degenerates; — —dilates; — —menaces; — —pains; — —ravages; — —subsides.
(See disease, sickness, malady.)

HEARTH
adjectives
blazing; domestic; lonely; imperial; glittering; familiar; heavenly; glowing; inmost; desolated; tiled; hospitable; altar; ancestral; dreary; lowly; sordid.

HEARTLESSNESS
adjectives
cruel; perfect; undisguised; criminal.

verbs
bare—; brook—; conceal—; deny—; excuse —; steep in—; wither into—; —bites; —contrives; —crushes; —dejects; —despairs; —embitters; —lurks; —murders; —pains; —strikes; —wounds.
(See cruelty.)

HEARTY
adverbs
sincerely; enthusiastically; graciously; spontaneously; warily; impressively; rapturously; eagerly; cordially; impetuously; impulsively; openly; splendidly; sympathetically; devotedly; cheerily; jovially; entirely; exceptionably; extremely; unusually; noticeably; conspicuously; especially.

HEAT
adjectives
primitive; intense; intercepted; parching; hardening; dulling; destructive; resisting; sulphurous; automatic; self-regulating; unifying; genial; ordinary; subterranean; excessive; steaming; shimmering; white; fervent; gray; heartburning; yellow; incandescent; dancing; breathless; blood-red; imminent; midday; prickly; internal; sweltering; fierce; subtle; central; controlled; oppressive; tempered; incarnate; scalding; blistering; ferocious; feverish; heroic; fortunate; visceral; vague; withering; imperial; scorching; restless; blinding; tremulous; torturous; masculine; radiant; deadly; incremental; defying; infernal; furious; palpable; saturating; wet; devoted; overpowering; polished; rash; false; aching; clean; efficient; dependable; effortless; healthful; boisterous; instant; steady; terrestrial; boiling; unspeakable; tropical; love-devouring; uniform; intolerable; bristling; generous; luminous; beneficial; glowing; perpendicular; savage; unendurable; suffocating; kindly; animal; brooding; fantastic; sickening; fierce; quivering; stifling; freezing; stimulating; intolerable; exceptional; fluent; temperate; extreme; concentrated; continuous; expensively-produced; transmuted; burning.

apply—; bask in—; control—; foment—; generate—; maintain—; measure—; raise —; regulate—; relieve—; sustain—; swelter in—; swoon from—; transform into—; treat with—; utilize—; —blights; —blisters; —encompasses; —escapes; —evolves; —parches; —scorches; —stifles; —subsides.
(See fire, flame.)

HEAT (v)

adverbs
fiercely; intensely; destructively; sulphurously; automatically; excessively; subtly; oppressively; · witheringly; scorchingly; palpably; blisteringly; tropically; intolerably; beneficially; suffocatingly; concentratedly.
(See warm.)

HEATH

adjectives
flowery; vast; uncultivated; blasted; magnificent; pastoral; bleak; tottering; menacing; stultifying; ugly; murky; dismal.

verbs
clip—; crop—; cut—; grow—; plant—; roof with—; tend—; thatch with—; utilize —; —abounds; —banks; —blazes; —flourishes; —flowers; —perfumes; —stretches.
(See land, area, plant, flower.)

HEATHEN

adjectives
benighted; tiresome.

HEATHENISH

adverbs
shamelessly; cruelly; deliberately; grossly; ignorantly; savagely; brutally; barbarously; unconscionably; inordinately; terribly; dreadfully; unbelievably; inexpressibly; atrociously; shamefully; brazenly; ostentatiously; openly; crudely; blindly; darkly; coarsely; rudely; brutishly; shockingly; appallingly.

HEAVE (v)

adverbs
bodily; fulsomely; breathlessly; spasmodically; tumultuously; intermittently; laboriously; oppressively.
(See throw, lift.)

HEAVEN

adjectives
frosty; righteous; luminous; cloudless; precipitating; overhanging; bounteous; transfigured; untrod; starry; sublunar; clear; subjugated; high; bending; miniature; smiling; avenging; tranquil; angry; broad; firmamental; unfolding; swelling; bending; unrelenting; gladsome; spangled; insulted; unpavilioned; troubled; merciful; unimagined; clear-eyed; naked; unclouded; pitying; crystal; hollow; influent; frowning; slumberless; impenetrable; jealous; deepening; unimaginable; sweet; vaulty; cloudless; piteous; encompassing; unpitying; remote; glorious; star-deserted; crystalline; unobstructed; immeasurable; middle; material; warm-colored; pinky-purple; bland; placid; stainless; sick; scoffing; propitious; flaming; deaf.

verbs
abide in—; ascend to—; bless in—; conduct to—; contemplate—; deny—; depart for—; depict—; descend from—; dwell .in—; enthrone in—; gain—; long for—; look up to —; offend—; prepare for—; prevail in—; rail at—; reign in—; reside in—; rest in—; rise to—; seek—; steal into—; transport to—; trust in—; visit in—; win—; —s dazzle; —s look down; —s open; —promises; —radiates.

(See paradise, sky, Providence, God.)

HEAVENLY

adverbs
delectably; ecstatically; divinely; utterly; altogether; consummately; ineffably.

HEAVINESS

adjectives
unaccustomed; palpable; dreamy; lifeless; curious; embraced; languid; singular; deceptive; moody.

verbs
augment—; burden with—; cast—over; counterbalance—; discard—; drowse under —; dump—; enter with a sense of—; lament —; seize with—; shed—; —angers; —dejects; —displeases; —enrages; —manifests; —oppresses; —saddens; counterpoise—.

(See weight, gravity, sadness, despondency, dejection.)

HEAVINGS

adjectives

tumultuous; needless; intermittent.

HEAVY

adverbs

grievously; financially; painfully; economically; unwarrantably; dreadfully; pitifully; gravely; unendurably; increasingly; unnecessarily; inescapably; seriously; insufferably; dangerously; unusually; strangely; unfortunately; cumbrously; monstrously; oppressively; aggravatingly; vexatiously; unjustly; tragically; embarrassingly.

HECKLER

verbs

"bounce" out—; court—; encounter—; oust —; remove—; subdue—; —annoys; —bests; —bothers; —catechizes; —chastises; —contends; —derides; —examines; —irks; —irritates; —plagues; —questions; —scolds; —teases; —wrangles.

(See pest, audience.)

HECTIC

adverbs

feverishly; terribly; tensely; excitably; emotionally; crucially; breathlessly; hysterically; impetuously; poignantly; thrillingly; violently; hotly; angrily; decidedly; bitterly; intensely; peculiarly; curiously; strangely; queerly; extremely; inexplicably; unaccountably; unwarrantably; unusually.

HEDGE

adjectives

lofty; wayside; impenetrable; rustic; decorative; thorny; prickly; flowery.

HEED

adjectives

prudent; accurate; immediate; absent.

HEED (v)

adverbs

carefully; scrupulously; painstakingly; anxiously; prudently; cautiously; instinctively; characteristically; habitually.

(See attend, notice, regard.)

HEEDLESS

adverbs

provokingly; intolerably; inherently; habitually; thoughtlessly; incorrigibly; stupidly; nonchalantly; indifferently; wilfully; obstinately; stubbornly; sadly; grievously; cruelly; pathetically; unwisely; foolishly; frivolously; inexcusably; recklessly; rashly; dangerously; deplorably; lamentably; incurably; shockingly; frightfully.

HEEL

adjectives

hindermost; unmesmerized; official; wavering; hoofed; despotic; miry; flying; cloven; heavy.

verbs

blister—; click—s; clutch at—s; cool—s; crush with—; drive—into; hang up by—s; squat on—s; trample beneath—; —s clatter; —s kick up dust.

(See foot, end, bottom.)

HEIFER

adjectives

illustrious; languid; breathing.

HEIGHT

adjectives

level; pinnacle; considerable; winged; excessive; unsuspected; glimmering; definite; prayerful; azure; wooded; extreme; odorous; pernicious; opposite; embattled; sequestered; serene; gigantic; hoary; mountain; empty; dizzy; commanding; tiptoeing; entrenched; glittering; extravagant; windworn; crystal; preposterous; towering; dark; craggy; moon-bewildering; garden; considerable; grand; sunlit; yonder; stream-riven; fixed; heavenly; immortal; fantastic; mounting; reachless; impressive; matchless; panoramic; helpless; immeasurable; divine; daring; obvious; empyreal; utmost; heroic; lofty; bristling; perilous; superb; dusky; eloquent; slippery; desolate; gleaming; barren; sovereign; immense; barometric; melancholy; distant; emerald; rocky; stately; adverse; unscalable; noble; massy; sunscorched; bleak; appointed; waxen; grassy; historic; fortified; starry-headed; inordinate; difficult; full; gray; grave; rugged; precipitous; supernal; financial.

verbs

ascend to—; attain—; attempt—; average —; depend on—; descend—; discover—; fall from—; gain—; mount—s; raise to—; reach—s; rise to—; scale—; set on—; situate on—; soar to—; view from—; —amazes; —slopes down.

(See altitude, stature, eminence, zenith, summit.)

adverbs

atrociously; abominably; diabolically; criminally; brutally; shamefully; basely; feloniously; flagitiously; flagrantly; deliberately; foully; villainously; viciously; wickedly; incalculably; iniquitously; immeasurably; inexpressibly; grossly; shamelessly; indecently.

adjectives

spiritual; immediate; unexpected; lineal; natural; indolent; unwitting; blissful; legitimate; recognized; lavish; contentious; beauteous; joyous; adopted; prodigal; illustrious; peasant-born; true; spendthrift; gilded; impatient.

verbs

apportion to—s; bear—; bequeath to—; curse—; endow—; enrich—; extort from—; guard—; impose on—; nominate—; present with—; prey on—s; tax—s; will to—; yearn for—; —acquires; —is entitled to; —overjoys; —succeeds.

(See offspring, child.)

adjectives

pitiless; multitudinous; impious; dismal; high-vaulted; yawning; gratuitous; incipient; tangible; monster-teeming; ever-burning; social; inevitable; fabled; jealous; fearsome; inextricable; earth-consuming.

verbs

boil in—; burn in—; chain in—; condemn to—; damn to—; deliver from—; descend to—; doom to—; dwell in—; embark for—; escape—; lead to—; parch in—; plunge into—; punish in—; purify in—; sink in—; torment in—; torture in—; —breaks loose; —devours; —flames; —gapes; —scorches; —shadows; —threatens.

(See torment, torture, flame.)

adverbs

barbarously; fiendishly; inhumanly; inexpressibly; unutterably; indecently; abysmally; accursedly; basely; flagitiously; nefariously; enormously; monstrously; outrageously; obscenely.

adjectives

thronging; prosperous; passive; obedient.

verbs

abandon—; control—; course—; ease—; govern—; handle—; lash to—; menace—; manipulate—; meddle with—; mind—; operate—; order to—; post at—; slander—; steer at—; wrestle with—; —cares; —directs; —guides.

(See wheel, guidance, helmet, pilot, guide, command; control, administration.)

adjectives

pith; vicious-looking; fire; leather; superb; spiked; conical; flat-topped; glittering.

verbs

arm with—; attire in—; balance—; bear—; break through—; furnish—; open—; pad—; penetrate—; pierce—; polish—; provide—; supply—; top with—; —clanks; —crowns; —defends; —prevents; —protects; —reflects; —resists; —rests on.

(See hat.)

adjectives

indispensable; senseless; agreeable; distinct; explanatory; simple; invaluable; adventitious; slender; ever-present; effective; sympathetic; availing; unbiased; beneficial; relative; mutual; timely; injurious.

verbs

afford—; clamor for—; consent to—; furnish—; invoke—; obtain—; present—; procure—; profit by—; promise—; provide—; purchase—; refuse—; render—; seek—; —ameliorates; —amends; —augments; —benefits; —delivers; —extricates; —relieves; —remedies.

(See aid, assistance, remedy, relief, succor, co-operation, support.)

adverbs

chivalrously; effectually; materially; cheerfully; perversely; personally; generously; precipitately; leisurely; adventitiously; sympathetically; beneficially; mutually.

(See aid, assist, alleviate.)

HELPFUL

adverbs

ingratiatingly; amiably; delightfully; obsequiously; ostentatiously; pompously; unspeakably; amazingly; providentially; accommodatingly; cordially; willingly; eagerly; courteously; habitually; unusually; significantly; heartily; resolutely; dutifully; civilly; servilely; loftily; exceedingly; extremely; gravely; graciously; charmingly; freely; gruffly; roughly; awkwardly; childishly; lovingly; affectionately; skillfully; politely; bluntly; generously; splendidly; surprisingly.

HELPFULNESS

adjectives

patient; cordial; mutual; unassuming.

HELPLESS

adverbs

pitiably; weakly; incurably; intentionally; gloomily; abjectly; depressingly; desolately; inconceivably; ludicrously; comically; horribly; woefully; dismally; gravely; seriously; inconsolably; sadly; desperately; obviously; unreasonably; piteously; tragically; actually; absolutely.

HELPLESSNESS

adjectives

silent; ignominious; sudden; revealed; unconscious; utter; galling; bitter.

verbs

accuse of—; alleviate—; attack—; conceal —; degenerate into—; discover—; grieve over—; increase—; lament—; relieve—; remedy—; retire into—; ridicule—; scorn —; sink into—; —amazes; —angers; — crushes; —despairs; —distresses; —oppresses.

(See weakness.)

HELPMATE

adjectives

devoted; feeble; imperious.

HELTER-SKELTER

adverbs

horribly; laughingly; hilariously; precipitately; confusedly; boisterously; joyously; triumphantly; hastily; breathlessly; impetuously; riotously; tumultuously; uproariously; madly; wildly; inordinately; extraordinarily; tempestuously; happily.

HEMISPHERIC

adverbs

broadly; surprisingly; expansively; extensively; liberally; hospitably; comprehensively; increasingly; generously; magnanimously; necessarily; commonly; strangely; designedly; intentionally; significantly; preferably.

HEMORRHAGE

verbs

arrest—; check—; control—; delay—; diminish—; excite—; induce—; prevent—; produce—; repress—; risk—; stem—; succumb to—; suffer—; treat—; —ceases; —diminishes; —endangers; —ensues; —gushes; — pours; —recurs; —spouts.

(See discharge, bleeding, blood.)

HEN

adjectives

scrawny; rained-on; cackling; maternal; speckled; teeming (pl); unsung; matronly-minded.

verbs

(See chicken, bird.)

HERALD

adjectives

pale; perfect; tempestuous; flame-tongued; sad-faced.

HERB

adjectives

winged; aromatic; tender; fragrant; artificial; vivid; bespangling; poisonous; tufted; enchanted; beneficial; culinary; trodden; baneful; pungent; grassy.

verbs

administer—; collect—s; crop—s; cultivate —s; devour—; feast on—s; feed on—s; flavor with—s; garnish with—s; gather—s; market—s; overgrow with—s; prescribe—s; yield to—; —abounds; —cures; —flowers; —stimulates; —withers.

(See plant, grass.)

HERBAGE

adjectives

sprouting; autumnal.

HERCULEAN

adverbs

distressingly; arduously; obscurely; obviously; evidently; notably; desperately; formidably; toilsomely; laboriously; operosely; stoutly; gigantically; hardily; overwhelmingly; robustly; irresistibly; inexhaustibly; wirily; unconquerably; invincibly; astonishingly; remarkably; inexpressibly; admirably; wondrously; enormously; onerously; extraordinarily; tremendously.

HERD

adjectives
bellowing; stolid; fear-crazed; vulgar; weanling; scaly; meager; wild; wanton; maddening; weaponless; turbulent; servile; careless; drooping; wandering; innumerable (pl); untamable; countless (pl); incomparable; quiet; gentle; sarcastic; nightmare; diminishing; woolly; profane; galloping; tempting.

verbs
abandon—; assemble in—; associate with—; break—; breed in—; cluster in—; congregate in—; control—; destroy—; drive—; gather in—; guard—; join—; lead—; mingle among—; prey on—; rule—; single out of—; slaughter—; stall—; stampede—; —lows; —grazes; —perishes; —ranges; —treks.
(See rabble, crowd, flock.)

HEREDITARY

adverbs
supposedly; probably; definitely; questionably; sadly; unfortunately; allegedly; highly; occasionally; decidedly; basically; intrinsically; invariably; naturally; ineradicably; lamentably; possibly; undoubtedly.

HEREDITY

adjectives
contaminated; established; epileptic; definite; patent.

verbs
boast of—; claim—; degenerate from—; disparage—; doubt—; envy—; interest in —; praise—; renounce—; revere—; revile —; scorn—; stain—; trace—; transmit by —; —burdens; —constrains; —decays; — governs; —heightens; —influences; —instills; —polishes; —weakens.
(See ancestors, birth, father.)

HERESY

adjectives
literary; passing; downright.

verbs
abhor—; accuse of—; confess—; create—; curb—; dare—; defeat—; denounce—; destroy—; excommunicate for—; incur—; interpret as—; protest—; renounce—; revenge —; ridicule—; scan—; shake off—; work—; —denies; —enrages; —mocks; —offends; —scoffs; —taints; —tolerates.

HERETIC

verbs
approve—; burn—; consider—; curb—; denounce—; deprive—; disapprove of—; disperse—s; ignore—; lament—; punish—; regard—; reject—; ridicule—; scoff at—; tolerate—; weed out—s; —denies; —disbelieves; —disobeys; —disregards; —enrages; —mocks; —offends; —preaches; —professes.

HERETICS

adjectives
obstinate; upstart; vile; gruff; brash.

HERITAGE

adjectives
national; rich; common; splendid; precious; deathless; destined; princely; classic; inalienable; unexpected; useless; noble; sempiternal; dramatic.

verbs
acquire—; administer—; allot—; bequeath —; bestow—; bless—; cherish—; claim—; curse—; devolve—; endow—; entitle to—; envy—; execute—; extort—; govern—; present—; preserve—; provide—; reserve—; shear of—; stipulate—; transmit—; —devolves; —overjoys; —provides.
(See inheritance, birthright, estate.)

HERMIT

adjectives
stalwart; genial; lesser; lone; withered; solitary.

HERO

adjectives
unambitious; grotesque; noble; ghostly; beauteous; self-made; admirable; laureled; wonder-working; overbearing; martyred; spiritual; chivalrous; scatterbrained; ornithological; fettered; picturesque; classic; omnipresent; unassuming; stalwart; fabulous; incompetent; energetic; honored; renowned; contemporary; mythic; legendary; vulgar; gentle; immaculate; doughty; stout;

worthy; transcendental; portentous; immortal; barbarous; discomfited; erring; illustrious; incomparable; splendid.

verbs
acclaim—; admire—; cheer—; decorate—; distinguish—; emulate—; enhance—; esteem —; glorify—; hail as—; honor—; identify oneself with—; indebt to—; pity—; respect —; reverence—; shoulder—; supplant—; sympathize with—; venerate—; worship—; —achieves; —braves; —conquers; —courts; —deserves; —excels in; —fades; —regales; —rescues; —rises; —suffers; —withers.
(See champion, character, actor, God.)

HEROIN
verbs
addict to—; analyze—; confiscate—; crave —; derive—from; dissolve—; dose with—; drug with—; forbid—; import—; ingest—; inject—; insufflate—; smuggle—; subject to —; —allays; —anaesthetizes; —depresses; —enslaves; —numbs; —relieves; —victimizes.
(See narcotic, drug.)

HEROINE
adjectives
persecuted; peerless; sentimental; fallen; durable; revengeful.

verbs
acclaim—; identify oneself with—; worship —; —beguiles; —bewitches; —blushes; — captivates; —charms; —enchants; —enraptures; —entrances; —fascinates; —gladdens; —ravishes; —shrinks; —suffers; — transports; —wins.
(See character, hero.)

HEROISM
adjectives
volcanic; unmatched; reckless; romantic; foredoomed; cowering; potential; fierce; intolerant; dauntless; latent; melodramatic; ostentatious; vulgar; showy.

verbs
abate—; aim at—; commend—; conduct with—; contemplate—; crown with—; display—; emulate—; extol—; frown upon—; illustrate—; imitate—; laud—; perform—; reflect—; reward—; sacrifice to—; —dazzles; —glorifies; —merits; —sparkles.
(See valor, courage, bravery, fortitude.)

HERON
verbs
—calls; —circles; —colonizes; —croaks; — fishes; —flaps; —gossips; —impales; — roosts; —shies away; —snaps up; —soars; —squawks; —wades; —wings.
(See bird.)

HERONS
adjectives
long-necked; crested; great; night; long-beaked; stately; graceful.

HESITANCY
adjectives
strange; grave; characteristic; reserved; courteous; apparent; awkward; blushing.

HESITANT
adverbs
capriciously; captiously; uncertainly; reluctantly; doubtfully; stammeringly; changeably; indecisively; timidly; weakly; irresolutely; deliberately; falteringly; waveringly; feebly; tormentingly; infirmly; unsteadily; tremulously; significantly; fearfully.

HESITATE (v)
adverbs
fatally; ominously; dubiously; thoughtfully; inexplicably; imperceptibly; timorously; characteristically; coquettishly; momentarily.
(See vacillate, falter.)

HESITATION
adjectives
sensitive; obvious; imitative; painful; surprised; charming; inexplicable; imperceptible; timorous; controlled; characteristic; awkward; coquettish; momentary; ineloquent.

verbs
banish—; conceal—; decry—; deny—; grieve over—; lament—; pretend—; reproach—; shrink in—; stagger in—; stammer in—; tear with—; —confounds; —endangers; —frustrates; —haunts; —loses; — perplexes; —prevents; —shames; —tortures; —embarrasses.
(See doubt, uncertainty.)

HEW (v)
adverbs
roughly; bravely; ambitiously; vigorously; industriously; stalwartly; robustly; untiringly.
(See cut, sever.)

HIDE

adjectives

tawny; spotted; shaggy; strange-colored; swarthy; horny; silken; callous; precious; crafty; withered; tanned.

HIDE (v)

adverbs

effectually; obscurely; modestly; instinctively; completely; craftily; skillfully; subtly; avariciously.

(See conceal, mask, cloak.)

HIDEBOUND

adverbs

inordinately; deplorably; unfortunately; stubbornly; obstinately; oddly; curiously; provincially; narrowly; dogmatically; intolerantly; fanatically; immovably; inflexibly; perversely; tenaciously; doggedly; mulishly; ungenerously; terribly; notably; notoriously.

HIDEOUS

adverbs

outrageously; inordinately; extraordinarily; unbearably; grossly; terribly; indescribably; starkly; grotesquely; immoderately; monstrously; piteously; cruelly; shockingly; dreadfully; pathetically; horribly; repulsively; inexpressibly; appallingly.

HIDEOUSNESS

adjectives

naked; unshaped; outward; grim; gross.

HIDING-PLACE

adjectives

primeval; undisturbed; criminal; undiscovered; discreet.

HIERARCHY

adjectives

lofty; definite; centralized; disciplined; administrative; apostolical.

HIGH

adverbs

eminently; prominently; gigantically; monstrously; terrifyingly; incredibly; inordinately; supremely; toweringly; enormously; immensely; infinitely; astonishingly; essentially; extraordinarily; fabulously; preposterously; prodigiously; unsuitably; impossibly; confoundedly; frightfully; horribly; immeasurably; incalculably; delightfully; gloriously; marvellously; particularly; pecu-

liarly; dangerously; perilously; hazardously; singularly; strikingly; woefully; cruelly; awfully; wonderfully; miraculously.

HIGHBORN

adverbs

aristocratically; nobly; notably; gently; undeniably; obviously; evidently; unmistakably; unquestionably; proudly; consciously; illustriously; eminently; admittedly; palpably; undeniably; avowedly; allegedly; probably.

HIGHNESS

adjectives

imperial; incredible; unspeakable; breathless.

HIGH-SPIRITED

adverbs

unusually; delightfully; infectiously; ineffably; happily; radiantly; irrepressibly; hilariously; boisterously; blithely; merrily; mirthfully; teasingly; mockingly; contagiously; charmingly; immeasurably; ardently.

HIGHWAY

adjectives

crooked; invisible; leaf-hung; imperial; dusty; dubious; traffic-crowded; smooth; sleek; arterial; tree-lined; panoramic.

verbs

block—; cruise on—; drive along—; follow —; frequent—; keep to—; laud—; motor along—; patrol—; perceive—; protect—; roll along—; stream down—; traverse—; tread—; —connects; —divides; —endures; —gleams; —leads to; —winds.

(See road, thoroughfare, way.)

HIGHWAYMAN

verbs

apprehend—; defend against—; execute—; hang—; overtake—; protect from—; pursue—; resist—; —appropriates; —deprives of; —escapes; —frequents; —frightens; —gorges on; —plagues; —preys upon; —terrorizes; —victimizes.

(See robber, thief.)

HILARIOUS

adverbs

uproariously; merrily; heartily; noisily; infectiously; contagiously; enthusiastically; effervescently; audaciously; mischievously; intensely; uncommonly; deliriously; unbecomingly; convulsively; irrepressibly; unmanageably; irresponsibly; joyously; blithely; enviably; delightfully; sociably; foolishly; nonsensically; senselessly; consummately; utterly; unrestrainedly; uncontrollably; youthfully; magnificently; jubilantly; inexplicably; warrantably; gleefully.

HILARITY

adjectives
audacious; mischievous; intense; reckless; increasing; delirious; unbecoming; misdirected.

verbs
attempt—; conceal—; conduce to—; enliven to—; excite to—; feign—; flush with—; inspire—; overcome with—; provoke—; reduce—; season with—; spend in—; temper —; —brightens; —diverts; —fades; —flows; —palls; —pours from; —seizes; —solaces; —tires; —wanes; —wearies.
(See mirth, glee, gayety, jollity.)

HILL

adjectives
gleaming; moon-tortured; green-clad; emerald; autumn-tinted; moon-swept; dense; verdured; moonlit; silver; verdant; radiant; silent; shimmering; bright; stony; tawny; soft; rolling; gentle; peak; shadowed; scarred; rock-ribbed; primeval; neighboring; dripping; innocent; reverberating; ferny; naked; forest-cinctured; long-contested; alluring; picturesque; arid; delicious; slanting; soilless; heathery; dry; parched; savage; desolate; ghastly; treeless; volcanic; lower; square-topped; uprooted; eternal; full-grassed; lavish; granite; terraced; breezy; heaped; ever-changing; windy; environing; many-faced; vine-covered; overhanging; massive; bare; steep; incomparable; squalid; encompassing; disturbed; sequestered; pastoral; haughty; bald; bleak; commanding; breezy; ancient; folded; pulpy; conical; cup-shaped; quaking; parched; steadfast; skirting; everlasting; undulating; opprobrious; huge; inferior; barren; disconsolate; invisible; chalk; low-lying; alluvial; rolling; smooth; dawning; wooded; remote; defiant; eternal; silent; dominating; romantic; pestilent; rhododendron; distant; thicketed; sunny; dusty; windy; colored; precipitous; echo-giving; sun-baked; classical; retiring; cindery; pine-clad; spotless; milken; swelling; carven; monumental; forked; savage; timbered; rocky; rock-ribbed; answering; ice-clad; templed; leaping; heathery; pastoral; reeking; distorted; detached; high; utmost; flowery; populous; bustling; fertile; bedimmed; dreary; dark; cloud-capped; sun-kissed; umbrageous; misty; lowering; superb; billowy; consecrated; sterile; craglike; dewy; trembling.

verbs
ascend—; cap—; clear away—; coast down —; crown—; descend—; dwell in —s; heap into —s; observe from—; peep over—; retreat to —s; scale—; settle in —s; stray to —s; survey from—; toil up—; tumble down —; —arises; —charms; —s dot; —s encroach; —s entrance; —flanks; —s greet; —interposes; —shades; —shadows; mount —.
(See heap, mountain.)

HILLOCK

adjectives
scattered (pl); mortal; isolated; palmy; snowy.

HILLSIDE

adjectives
exposed; rounded; blackened; placid; flower-starred; pine-plumed; swelling; sunburned; slippery; sloping; stony; rocky; steep.

verbs
belt—; conceal in—; conduct to—; devastate —; frequent—; inhabit—; mount—; outline —; ravage—; roam—; rove—; settle on—; stream down—; survey—; —blooms; —charms; —flowers; —slopes.
(See hill, bank.)

HILLTOP

adjectives
arduous; breezy; grassy; sun-begoldened.

HIND

adjectives
loitering; heartless.

HINDER (*v*)

adverbs
unendurably; insurmountably; irritatingly; tremendously; irksomely; painfully; burdensomely.
(See retard, obstruct.)

HINDRANCE

adjectives
outward; tremendous; insurmountable.

verbs
condemn—; contribute—; decry—; endure
—; erect—; grieve over—; lament—; object
to—; overcome—; present—; provide—; remove—; —embarrasses; —frustrates; —objects; —perplexes; —perturbs; —prevents;
—threatens.
(See obstruction, obstacle, interruption, delay, restraint, disadvantage.)

HINGE
verbs
attach with—; bind with—; hang on—; join
with—; lift off—; lubricate—; manipulate
on—; nail—; pin—; pivot on—; prop on—;
rest on—; revolve on—; swing on—; turn
on—; —groans; —supports; —unites; —
yields.
(See joint.)

HINGES
adjectives
rusty; rusted; pregnant; musical.

HINT
adjectives
significant; practical; private; curious; advantageous; prompt; dark; rude; lavish;
sundry (pl); ineffectual; equivocal; grotesque; doubtful; oblique; vague; suggestive; friendly; occult; elusive; unintelligible; insinuated; intimated.

verbs
afford—; catch—; comprehend—; contemplate—; convey—; derive — from; heed—;
ignore—; infer—; interpret—; perceive—;
proffer—; provide—; respond to—; seek—;
seize on—; suggest—; weigh—; —distresses; —implies; —indicates; —insinuates; —
promises.
(See intimation, insinuation, suggestion.)

HINT (v)
adverbs
barely; delicately; obscurely; wickedly; privately; bashfully; significantly; curiously;
vaguely; suggestively; unintelligibly.
(See intimate, imply.)

HIPPOPOTAMUS
verbs
—ambles; —bathes; —charges; —crushes;
—damages; —dives; —floats; —s herd;
—puffs; —scoops; —sinks; —snorts; —submerges; —splashes; —swims; —tramples.
(See animal.)

HIPS
adjectives
supple; spacious; smooth; rounded; flabby;
powerful; streamlined; swaying; bolstered;
slim; sinewy; snake-like.

HIRELING
adjectives
sanguinary; base.

HISS
verbs
deride with—; disapprove with —s; dread
—; drive away with —s; emit—; express in
—; greet with—; ignore—; inject—; overhear—; revile with—; scorn with—; utter
—; voice in—; whisper—; —drowns; —
disparages; —disturbs; —heckles.
(See sound, noise.)

HISS (v)
adverbs
menacingly; vehemently; venomously; sibilantly; spitefully; viciously.
(See whisper, sound, sing.)

HISTORIAN
adjectives
eloquent; contemporary; romancing; hostile;
elegant; fact-grubbing; ecclesiastical; celebrated; apt.

HISTORIC
adverbs
minutely; authoritatively; authentically; accurately; specifically; allegedly; avowedly;
evidently; obviously; verifiably; graphically; scarcely; valuably; splendidly; eminently; significantly; serviceably; admirably; indubitably; undeniably.

HISTORICAL
adverbs
slightly; suggestively; traditionally; pleasantly; entertainingly; reminiscently; extravagantly; crudely; accurately; extraordinarily; dully; monotonously; tiresomely; artistically; thrillingly; graphically; entirely;
instructively; nostalgically; broadly; generally; altogether; closely.

HISTORY
adjectives
administrative; thrilling; painful; fashion;
family; significant; ecclesiastical; contemporary; much-revised; educational; diplo-

matic; stormy; dazzling; tragic; informal; revolutionary; fateful; detailed; typographical; limited; subsequent; pertinent; simple; painstaking; scathing; episodical; future; institutional; human; lamentable; uneventful; monumental; inglorious; noble; pathetic; spiritual; artistic; chronological; natural; eminent; curious; remote; consecutive; authentic; sacred; profane; feigned; forgotten; informative; terrible; impartial; tumultuous; confused; picturesque; incontrovertible; financial; commercial; secret; ancestral; copious; accurate; narrative; inductive; impartial; venerable; social; governmental; international; aesthetic; piteous; wondrous; separate; tender; eventful; glorious; wretched; wisdom-woven; tribal; invaluable; naval; religious; prejudiced; conjectural; school; unrecorded; benevolent; problematical; winged; eventful; gradual; fragrant; subsequent; early; economic; anecdote; magnificent; musical; political; dignified; literary; exhaustive; fantastic; subsequent; authoritative.

verbs
burrow into—; "debunk"—; delve into—; derive from—; dig through—; exhibit in—; expatiate on—; falsify—; garnish—; glean from—; informalize—; modify—; record—; recount—; review — of; shape—; suppress —of; telescope—; trace—; unfold—of; — dates back to; —enchants; —enshrines; — extends to; —recurs; —reflects; —throws light upon.
(See narrative, tale, story, book, account.)

HISTRIONIC
adverbs
attractively; technically; alluringly; seductively; extravagantly; spectacularly; ludicrously; dramatically; absurdly; brilliantly; splendidly; inexpressibly; unexpectedly; illustriously; magnificently; competently; melodramatically; ably; tragically; operatically; stagily; stupendously; sensationally; incurably; immensely; pleasantly;' exaggeratedly; uncommonly; remarkably; fantastically.

HIT
verbs
acclaim as—; anticipate—; applaud—; chance—; effect—; gain—; obtain—; pray

for—; pronounce—; provide—; score—; strike—; —astonishes; —delights; —enriches; —reveals; —surprises.
(See blow, success, stroke, victory, triumph.)

HIT (v)
adverbs
severely; viciously; repeatedly; injuriously; cruelly; brutally; vigorously.
(See strike, beat, pound.)

HITCH (v)
adverbs
unconsciously; impatiently; unexpectedly; clumsily; mechanically; automatically.
(See fasten, attach.)

"HITCH-HIKER"
verbs
accommodate—; arrest—; bar —s; convey —; dispose of—; forbid—; maroon—; outlaw—; pick up—; prohibit—; —attacks; —begs; —"bums"; —bunks (colloq.); —"chisels"; —clambers aboard; —dodges; —s dot; —freights; —legs; —signals; —tramps; —thumbs.

HIVE
adjectives
scandalous; prolific; considerable; overloaded; nest.
verbs
board in—; crowd—; destroy—; forsake—; gather in—; inhabit—; issue from—; locate in—; lodge in—; occupy—; store in—; swarm to—; watch over—; —busies; —buzzes; —houses; —shelters; —teems; —worships.
(See swarm, crowd, bees, box, home.)

HOARD (v)
adverbs
avariciously; jealously; niggardly; meanly; fanatically; selfishly; desperately.
(See store, accumulate.)

HOARSE
adverbs
curiously; strangely; alarmingly; dangerously; fearfully; inexplicably; speechlessly; stridently; harshly; coarsely; raucously; unpleasantly; gruffly; angrily; sepulchrally; deeply; gratingly; terrifyingly; suddenly; uncommonly; extraordinarily; remarkably; discordantly; terribly; horribly; excruciatingly.

HOARY

adverbs
venerably; patriarchally; ripely; perfectly; snowily; gracefully; distinctly; majestically; gloriously; honorably; splendidly; conspicuously; grandly; nobly.

HOAX

verbs
accept—; conceive—; contrive—; denounce —; espy—; frame—; impose — upon; manufacture—; perpetrate—; plan—; practise —; reveal—; spring—; vend—; —amuses; —deceives; —mystifies; —ridicules; —succeeds; —scares; —victimizes.
(See deception, joke, trick.)

HOBBLE (*v*)

adverbs
painfully; feebly; laboriously; miserably; slowly; waveringly; falteringly.
(See limp, falter, walk.)

HOBBLING

adverbs
ineffectually; lamely; quietly; forlornly; wretchedly; limply; stumblingly; brokenly; distressingly; grievously; woefully; slowly; painfully; awkwardly; cumbrously; dreadfully; pathetically; sadly; uncomfortably; sturdily; crookedly; gayly; mournfully.

HOBBY

adjectives
dominant; fascinating.

verbs
advocate—; allow—; dabble in—; devote to —; excel at—; favor—; indulge in—; permit—; pursue—; ride—; school in—; suggest—; sympathize with—; tinker with—; trifle with—; —amuses; —delights; —diverts; —enthralls; —occupies; —relieves.
(See occupation, interest, vocation, topic, plan, pursuit.)

HOBNOB (*v*)

adverbs
jovially; fraternally; loquaciously; extravagantly; boisterously; democratically.
(See associate, mingle.)

HOG

adjectives
goaded; ill-bred.

verbs
auction —s; breed —s; exhibit—; fatten—; market—; pen—; roast—; slaughter—; stable—; stick—; —devours; —farrows; —grunts; —hobbles; —snorts; —squeaks; —squeals; —wallows; —yields.
(See animal, pig.)

HOLD (*grip*)

adjectives
spiritual; demoniac; tenacious; vise-like; passionate; careless; fragile; imploring; pocket.

verbs
bar—; break—; catch—; correct—; divert —; emerge from—; escape—; evade—; force—; gain — on; knit—; loose—; maintain—; mend—; obtain—; seize—; take—; —slips; —supports; —yields.
(See grasp, grip, authority, power, stronghold, refuge.)

HOLD (*ship*)

verbs
assemble in—; ballast—; cache in—; chain in—; conceal in—; condemn to—; confine to —; couch in—; hide in—; lock in—; provide—; replenish—; stock in—; store in—; stow in—; stuff—.
(See interior, prison.)

HOLD (*v*)

adverbs
stubbornly; desperately; proudly; tenaciously; securely; frenziedly; obstinately; inviolably; jealously; staunchly; tenderly; tremulously; deferentially; permanently; stoutly; hungrily; tentatively; gingerly; dexterously; automatically; diplomatically.
(See grasp, clutch.)

HOLDING

adjectives
large; theoretical; allotted.

"HOLDUP"

verbs
abet—; appropriate in—; curb—; deprive in —; escape—; execute—; frustrate—; plague with —s; protect from—; reduce —s; resist —; surprise in—; —appalls; —terrorizes.
(See assault, robbery.)

HOLE

adjectives
huge; nest; shallow; halfway; effective; deep; ragged; obvious; death-spitting; oc-

casional; furtive; treacherous; dull; ghastly; obscure; ominous; vast; circular; expansive; inmost; gaping.

verbs
bore—; burrow—; conceal—; drill—; drive
—; escape—; excavate—; hollow—; lurk in
—; perforate—; pick —s; pierce—; plant in
—; plug—; rot in—; sink into—; smother in
—; thrust into—.
(See opening, cavity, pit, flaw, defect, hollow.)

HOLIDAY
adjectives
enforced; universal; conventional; invigorating; golden; pastoral; piecemeal; summer; sunshine; sparkling.

HOLINESS
adjectives
pharisaical; penitential; assumed; outward.

verbs
brighten with—; cherish in—; commend—; dedicate to—; diffuse—; dispose to—; dwell in—; glow with—; manifest—; possess—; seek—; share—; shroud in—; touch with—; violate—; —beautifies; —charms; —glorifies; —inspires; —purifies.
(See sanctity, piety, sacredness, purity.)

HOLLOW
verbs
bellow through—; blow through—; bore—; depress—; enclose—; excavate—; fashion—; occupy—; rest in—; shape—; shelter in—; sink into—; thrust into—; —interposes.
(See cavity, depression, channel, basin, valley, hole.)

HOLLOWNESS
adjectives
dreadful; echoing.

HOLLOWS
adjectives
fleshless; intricate; unsuspected; desolate; windless; curving; curdled; starved; fearful; marshy; dreadful; dampish; arid; delicate; wide; cloudy; gaping; grassy.

HOLY
adverbs
reverently; sacredly; divinely; altogether; consummately; perfectly; utterly; eternally; gloriously; infinitely; celestially; spiritually; ineffably; majestically; triumphantly; solemnly; consecratedly.

HOMAGE
adjectives
poor; devoted; disinterested; glorious; reluctant; decorous; regal; unpurchasable; lowly; dreadful; wild; respectful; spontaneous; corporate; due; assiduous; grateful; humble; instinctive; loyal.

verbs
acknowledge—; bow in—; demand—; do—; kneel in—; offer—; owe—; present—; profess—; render—; renounce—; submit to—; swear—; yield — to.
(See respect, deference, obeisance, loyalty.)

HOME
adjectives
kitchen; inn; lodge; nest; suitable; well-ordered; contemporary; devout; rustic; frugal; veritable; industrial; blazing; discriminating; earthly; deep-thatched; undiscovered; devastated; deep-sea; kindred; humble; hereditary; antiquated; exclusive; delegated; desolate; charming; handsome; eternal; secluded; cheerful; terrestrial; stately; gay; cool; inviting; vast; ancestral; unfathomable; peaceful; tainted; remote; simple; material; fond; sheaf-gathered; commodious; sumptuous; unpretentious; reeking; love-guarded; sordid; trim-built; stainless; convenient; historic; palatial; sullen; cloudy; sylvan; silent; distinguished; year-round; fine; perfect; holiday; ideal; primeval; airy; wanton; antenatal; sheltered; chaotic; glory; flooded; peasant; spacious; uninhabitable; artistic; eternal; comfortable; resplendent; imperiled; tiny; congenial; dismantled; annihilated; defenseless; orthodox; dainty.

verbs
abide at—; admire—; banish from—; bless
—; cleave to—; cut loose from—; dream of
—; escort—; evict from—; flee from—; frequent — of; install in—; lodge at—; long for—; lounge at—; master—; nurse in—; prefer—; preserve—; prize—; provide—; repair to—; sequester in—; survey—; tie to
—; troop—; uproot from—; wander from
—; welcome—; —beckons; —charms; —cheers; —comforts; —delights; —eases; —protects; —shelters.
(See abode, house, residence, dwelling.)

HOMELESS

adverbs

miserably; wretchedly; desolately; pitiably; cruelly; bitterly; unhappily; incredibly; unfortunately; unluckily; forlornly; pitifully; deservedly; naturally; oddly; curiously; particularly; outrageously; desperately; dreadfully; hopelessly; helplessly; lonesomely; friendlessly; inconceivably; unbelievably; definitely; ironically; disconsolately; dismally; drearily.

HOMELY

adverbs

forbiddingly; awkwardly; clumsily; frightfully; gracelessly; gauntly; haggardly; horribly; monstrously; shockingly; undeniably; simply; plainly; manifestly; curiously; unaffectedly; strangely; dully; avowedly; undisguisedly; outlandishly; indifferently; uncommonly; oddly; cheerfully; sturdily; imperturbably; wholesomely; pleasantly; unconcernedly.

HOMESICK

adverbs

actually; seriously; evidently; manifestly; signally; dangerously; alarmingly; fearfully; frightfully; truly; irrecoverably; desperately; extraordinarily; naturally; slightly; extremely; comprehensibly; bitterly; ruefully; sorely; insatiably; woefully; miserably; sadly; wretchedly; appallingly; shockingly; critically; unaffectedly; irremediably; unaccountably; terribly.

HOMESICKNESS

adjectives

drear; desperate; dread; supportable; nostalgic; prolonged; pronounced.

verbs

affect with—; conceal—; control—; doom to —; intensify—; moan in—; waste in—; yield to—; —afflicts; —arises; —depresses; —eats; —fatigues; —mars; —recurs; —saddens; —steals over; —troubles; —wracks.

(See nostalgia, sadness.)

HOMILY

verbs

address—; ascribe — to; attribute—; compose—; cultivate—; deliver—; excel in—; issue—; preach—; pronounce—; —awes; —bores; —edifies; —explains; —impresses; —moralizes; —pursues; —tires; —wearies.

(See sermon, discourse.)

HONEST

adverbs

absolutely; naturally; sincerely; honorably; morally; downright; altogether; completely; ingenuously; innately; inherently; unreservedly; habitually; constitutionally; virtuously; courageously; bravely; fearlessly; candidly; impartially; fairly; faithfully; sometimes; usually; spasmodically; incorruptibly; loyally; punctiliously; meticulously; respectably; reputably; scrupulously; trustworthily; conscientiously; frankly; inviolably; stainlessly; staunchly; uprightly; utterly; strictly; basically; unimpeachably; fundamentally; essentially; unshakably; apparently.

HONESTY

adjectives

basic; unimpeachable; unquestioned; belated; savage; strict; intrinsic; childlike; shakable; tribal; crystal; rigid; sham; confirmed; intellectual; surface; apparent.

verbs

approve—; assert—; boast of—; conduct with—; consider—; corrupt—; depend on—; desire—; inspect—; instill—; praise—; proclaim—; require—; respect—; test—; trust —; try—; undermine—; violate—; —repays; —rewards; —shines.

(See integrity, sincerity, fairness.)

HONEY

adjectives

pure; limpid; thick; flavored; fine; fermented; amber; sweet; nectareous.

HONEYSUCKLE

verbs

attire in—; bear—; cultivate—; naturalize —; ripen—; shower—; suck—; —attracts; —beautifies; —blooms; —clings; —clutches; —crawls; —creeps; —entwines; —exudes; —flowers; —garlands; —glorifies; —scents; —wreathes.

(See flower, plant, shrub, vine.)

HONOR

adjectives

dropsied; chivalrous; grave; cleansed; distinguished; well-earned; disinterested; enduring; foolish; royal; material; artistic; literary; scientific; sensitive; unprecedented; worldly; assaulted; blushing; academic; unviolated; unending; proffered; divine; proclaiming; professional; questionable; murdered; high; hereditary; especial; bridal; double; unsullied; primitive; imposing; petty; immortal; moral; worthy; blushing; liberal; empty; posthumous; fading; false; unblemished; sunny; perpetual; troublesome; maiden; special; unwonted; proud; dangerous; unsolicited; unexpected; longtransmitted; diplomatic; low-declined; conspicuous; haughty; civic; reverent; jealous; innumerable (pl); scrupulous; dangerous; platonic; strict; dimmed; unpretending; doubtful; sacred; slight; actual; mother-city.

verbs
accord—; assail—; attest to—; avenge—; bestow—; clothe with—; confer—upon; covet—; heap—; invoke—; lavish—; outrage —; pay—; preserve—; reflect upon—; sacrifice—; satisfy—; sell—; solicit—; stain—; steal—; sully—; vie for—; walk away with —; —overjoys.
(See esteem, respect, chastity, virtue, glory, reverence, reputation, dignity.)

HONOR (*v*)
adverbs
chastely; scrupulously; undeviatingly; academically; uniquely; faithfully; royally; materially; artistically; scientifically; scholastically; professionally; perpetually; posthumously; diplomatically; formally.
(See revere, esteem, respect.)

HONORABLE
adverbs
reputably; supposedly; allegedly; unshakably; irreproachably; sincerely; strictly; fundamentally; naturally; basically; dependably; reliably; altogether; innately; virtuously; fearlessly; intrepidly; courageously; impartially; incorruptibly; loyally; carefully; apparently; utterly; staunchly; scrupulously; meticulously; remarkably; notably; notoriously; illustriously; eminently; utterly.

HOOD
adjectives
riven; purpled; drooping.

HOODLUM
(*colloq.*)
breed—s; chastise—; denounce—; disperse —s; punish—; shelter—; warn—; —annoys; —absconds; —baffles; —damages; —drifts; —dodges; —escapes; —evades; —s gang; —s gather; —harms; —snatches; —threatens.
(See gangster, robber, thief, criminal.)

HOOF
verbs
caulk—s; file—s; muffle—s; paw with—s; protect—s; shoe—s; stamp—s; trim—s; —s clang; —s clank; —s clatter; —s clink; —s drum; —s furrow the ground; —s pound; —s roar; —strikes; —thuds.
(See foot.)

HOOFS
adjectives
stamping; cloven; devilish; edged; delicate; ironshod; flying; plunging; unshod; clattering; clumsy; galloping; clanging; rattling; death-dealing; heavy; awkward.

HOOK
adjectives
nail; peg; rusty; anchoring.

verbs
arm with—; angle with—; bait with—; bend with—; capture with—; cast—; drag with—s; draw—; grapple with—; grasp with—; hang on—; raise with—s; seize with—; snare with—; suspend from—; —catches; —cuts; —links; —penetrates; —secures; —snags.
(See clasp, snare, trap, pin.)

HOOT
adjectives
terrified; clanging.

HOOT (*v*)
adverbs
disconsolately; dismally; dolefully; scoffingly; monotonously; eerily; mockingly; jeeringly.
(See deride, denounce, shout.)

HOP (*v*)
adverbs
nimbly; agilely; gaily; swiftly; lightly; sportively; merrily.
(See jump, frisk, bound.)

HOPE
adjectives
ardent; debarred; lingering; honest; deathless; best; sustaining; tremendous; awakened; buried; presumptuous; unearthly; fond;

sole; latent; fiery; buoyant; visionary; absurd; unacknowledged; dead; darkened; false; trusting; unbounded; flowering; roseate; strained; sanguine; groveling; unraveled; indefatigable; twin-born; beautiful; inexperienced; baffled; extravagant; winged; frustrated; high-hearted; generous; departing; dauntless; quenchless; ripening; pale-cheeked; blighted; reverent; perfect; deceptive; patient; half-revealed; smallest; wildest; renewed; gray-haired; inspiriting; troublous; faltering; bursting; dazzling; holy; glorious; wandering; reactionary; lingering; flickering; dying; ardent; heartfelt; improbable; ruined; faded; freshening; blasted; fair; reasonable; trembling; increasing; slender; toppling; absolute; indefinite; dull; atrocious; vague; half-rallied; fruitless; parched; fervent; unchristian; untransmitted; histrionic; definite; decaying; broken; submissive; withered; forlorn; confident; earthly; full; fluttering; savage; pure; budding; tranquil; ultimate; shattered; vague; dreamy; inhaling; celestial; boundless; barren; thrilling; stubborn; ambitious; tortured; dear; flattering; sweet; delusive; feeble; troubled; hovering; unworthy; impossible; natural; blessed; disappointed; prophetic; bright; raised; vain; realized; fallacious; dawning; gaudy; vulgar; future; delicious; exultant; brilliant; odious; perpetuating; latent; polite; desperate; famished; appointed; rekindled; reckless; improbable; countless (pl); yearning; feverish; joyous; sleeping; pathetic; obedient; spacious; intenser; perpetual; confiding; remote; innocent; grim; philosophic; cheerful; unheeded; supreme; trusting; undying; abandoned; inconsistent; earnest; greedy; blossoming.

verbs
afford—; attain—; base—on; blast—; blight —; center—s in; cherish—; cling to—; console with—; crush—s; culminate in—; dash —s; defer—; delude with—; discourage—; divest of—; entertain—; exaggerate—; fall from—; falsify—; flush with—; frustrate—; fulfill—; hatch—; hold out—; impart—; infuse—; inspire—; justify—; kindle—; pin —s on; prompt—; relinquish—; restore—; rouse—; splinter—; stimulate—; substantiate—; undermine—; voice—; —blossoms; —collapses; —deserts; —exalts; —flickers; —glimmers; —is born; —leaps high; — lingers; —looms; —mounts; —perks up; —

sinks; —springs; —stirs; —vanishes; — wanes; realize—.
(See trust, reliance, expectation, optimism, anticipation.)

HOPE (v)
adverbs
vainly; fervidly; philosophically; optimistically; piously; fondly; desperately; fervently; devoutly; irresistibly; ardently; deathlessly; presumptuously; reverently; fallaciously; fruitlessly.
(See pray, desire, wish.)

HOPEFUL
adverbs
joyously; mysteriously; unaccountably; pleasurably; excitedly; hysterically; passionately; thrillingly; unreasonably; impatiently; ardently; keenly; eagerly; charmingly; joyfully; fervently; patiently; gloriously; fairly; increasingly; stubbornly; naturally; exultantly; pathetically; philosophically; earnestly; crazily; presumptuously; fondly; absurdly; reverently; extraordinarily.)

HOPEFULNESS
adjectives
desperate; perennial; gentle; indulgent.

HOPELESS
adverbs
probably; apparently; unfortunately; pitiably; wretchedly; miserably; forlornly; utterly; desperately; disconcertingly; insuperably; absolutely; calmly; tragically; bitterly; stolidly; grimly; appallingly; secretly; blankly; speechlessly; frantically; utterly; extremely; undeniably; obviously; manifestly; finally; frightfully.

HOPELESSNESS
adjectives
utter; cruel; black; dark; despairing.

verbs
bow down by—; complain of—; confront with—; doom to—; fret over—; groan with —; incline to—; lose in—; overcome—; paralyze with—; recognize—; reflect—; shroud in—; weight with—; —afflicts; —agonizes; —anguishes; —burdens; —clouds; —deadens; —desolates; —deters; —discourages; —saddens; —submerges; —weakens.
(See despair, despondency, pessimism, sadness.)

adjectives

miserable; motley; implacable; maddened; antlike; gray; conquering; impious; existing; vandal; rabble; elfish; veteran; rebellious; bleeding; barbarian; retreating; moving; turbulent; infuriated; undisciplined; roving.

verbs

accumulate—; congregate—; gather in—; spring from—; —bands; —concentrates; —congests; —crowds; —crushes; —disbands; —disperses; —dwells; —flocks; —floods; —howls; —migrates; —mills about; —packs; —roams; —scatters; —stampedes; —strays; —swarms; —throngs; —thunders; —wanders.

(See crowd, swarm, pack, throng, multitude.)

adjectives

heavy; landscape; flushed; solar; soft; endless; ruddy; glowing; magnificent; dim; open; historical; sunny; misty; tinted; dull; dusky; hazy; mother-of-pearl; contracted; lost; dreadful; vaporous; moral; circling; wide; intellectual; mental; imperial; boundless; ever-receding; expanding; far-off.

verbs

blacken—; broaden—; emerge from—; enlarge—; expand—; hesitate on—; loom on —; obscure—; open—; survey—; widen—; —beckons; —broadens; —embraces; —lightens; —recedes.

(See line, range, border, boundary.)

adjectives

toppling; dolorous; signaling; heavenly; masked; crescent; pellucid; sultry; impatient; lusty; sullen; formidable; barbarous; monstrous; cruel; long; twanging; curving; gilded; distinct; insistent; audacious; clangorous.

verbs

bear—; defend with—; develop—; drive—s into; impale on—s; loose—s; pierce with—; pinion down with—; —butts; —drills; —s endanger; —s frighten; —s gore; —s lance; —s prick; —s punch; —s puncture; —s rip; —s spike; —s threaten; —s wound.

(See antler, pin, point.)

verbs

arouse—s; provoke—s; —attacks; —basks in; —bites; —hums; —s infest; —inflicts; —s nest; —perforates; —pierces; —pricks; —regurgitates; —riots; —s swarm.

(See wasp, bee, insect.)

adverbs

grimly; unexpectedly; surprisingly; naturally; inevitably; dismally; alarmingly; awfully; frightfully; tremendously; unforgettably; unspeakably; inexpressibly; abhorrently; sickeningly; nauseatingly; unbearably; intolerably; incredibly; wildly; gruesomely; dreadfully.

adverbs

disgustingly; repulsively; shockingly; appallingly; offensively; abominably; atrociously; intolerably; unbearably; hideously; frightfully; unbelievably; incredibly; peculiarly; outrageously; unaccountably; positively; unendurably; insufferably; uncommonly; unduly.

adverbs

utterly; amazingly; dreadfully; astoundingly; blankly; startlingly; breathlessly; wordlessly; appallingly; indescribably; fearfully; inexpressibly.

adjectives

profound; damp; amused; attendant; alien; gentle; bragging; ignorant; scaly; untold; speechless; weary; blank; cloudy; congenial; superstitious; instinctive; unmitigated; invariable; distant; pious; ridiculous; accumulated; gloomy; hovering; incredulous; indescribable; quaint; formless; dismal; pursuing; sleepy; blank; misbegotten; fantastic; grisly; inseparable; supernumerary; unspeakable; stunned; anxious; nameless; ghastly; large-eyed; inconvenient; silent; inconceivable; insuperable; peculiar; infinite; tragic; cold; pungent; unimaginable; affected; incredible; dreary; unaccountable; shadowy; grim; journalistic; stunned; burlesque; incumbent; inactive; uncouth; utter; imaginary; positive; irrational; piercing; unfeigned; frightful; inexorable; intolerable; bloody; distant; mingled (pl); pale; unburied; childlike.

verbs

banish—; chill with—; conceal—; depict—; enhance—; expose—; freeze with—; ponder over—; recoil in—; reconstruct—; rise to the height of—; strike—; survey—; transfix with—; view with—; witness—; — grows; —strikes.

(See fear, dread, consternation.)

HORSE

adjectives

mustang; livestock; startled; dozing; hot; unbroken; riderless; steaming; petrified; winged; prancing; enchanted; massive; heavy; plodding; unwilling; spurred; vicious; docile; broken-down; unweaned; ghostly; pack; chubby; unmanageable; mettlesome; reluctant; well-broken; spirited; redoubtable; outspent; sorry; maniacal; generous; light-limbed; restive; bang-tailed; great-limbed; true; beautiful; foam-flecked; mottled; moth-eaten; dilapidated; straining; stalking; solemn; ramping; slender; rawboned; sweating; plow; blazed-faced; well-breathed; arrogant; unafraid; fiery; exhausted; weary; bony; dispirited; disemboweled; jibbing; drooping; jaded; foam-lipped; indifferent; admirable; harrowed; blooded; plunging; corn-stuffed.

verbs

bed down—; corral—; breed—s; currycomb —; guide—; harbor—; hobble—; jockey—; lash—; leap from—; mount—; pace—; rein in—; round up—s; saddle—; spur—; stable —; straddle—; tether—; tumble off—; — balks at; —bolts; —bucks; —canters; — capers; —caracoles; —champs at the bit; —dances; —falls to feeding; —founders; — hurdles; —neighs; —paws; —plods; — prances; —quivers; —races; —rears; — shies; —shivers; —snorts; —tramples; — trots; —vaults; —veers; —wheels; — whickers; —whinnies.

(See colt, animal, mare.)

HORSEBACK

verbs

canter on—; charge on—; convey by—; excel on—; exhibit on—; gallop in on—; journey on—; joust on—; mount—; race on—; sport on—; traverse on—; trot on—; vault on—.

(See horse.)

HORSEMAN

adjectives

brave; coated; mystic; unwary; gallant; solitary; admirable; steel-clad; headless; unhorsed.

verbs

—men assemble; —bestrides; —breeds; — charges; —coaches; —controls; —exhibits; —fancies; —flogs; —halts; —lashes; —manages; —mounts; —performs; —pets; — plods; —rears; —reins in; —spurs; — strokes.

(See rider, cowboy, soldier.)

HORSEMANSHIP

adjectives

consummate; daring; showy; superb.

HOSE

adjectives

stout; dusty; russet; silken; gossamer; diaphanous; cotton; worsted; shrunken.

HOSE
(conduit)

verbs

burst—; couple—; drench with—; pump through—; sprinkle with—; water with—; —bursts; —conducts; —conveys; —showers.

(See pipe.)

HOSIERY

adjectives

unsatisfactory; beautiful; sheer; cobwebby.

verbs

don—; draw on—; mend—; rip—; roll—; shed—; snag—; snap—; —fades; —glistens; —runs.

HOSPITABLE

adverbs

graciously; warmly; delightfully; cordially; generously; bounteously; liberally; munificently; splendidly; magnificently; freely; handsomely; pleasantly; sociably; happily; merrily; heartily; jovially; genially; urbanely; companionably; informally; gregariously; remarkably; immensely; courteously; enthusiastically; exuberantly; inordinately; good-naturedly; unobtrusively; lavishly; quietly; genuinely; charmingly; wholeheartedly.

HOSPITAL

adjectives

contemporary; improvised; convalescent; dingy; special; cheerless; contagious.

adjectives

courteous; sailorlike; effusive; uncommon; exuberant; mellowed; proverbial; rival; discreet; lasting; stinted; princely; elegant; undiscriminate; thankful; rural; good-natured; dignified; generous; professional; profuse; reluctant; wonted; hearty; cordial; unobtrusive; cheerful; genial; unwearying; lavish; quiet; warm; surpassing; genuine; old-time; luxurious; hearty; charming; homelike; famous; unique; cordial; warm-hearted; incredible; gracious; reluctant; extempore; southern; wholehearted.

verbs

dispense—; enjoy—; maintain—; offer—; practise—; provide—; repay—; reward—; ruffle—; share—; warm with—; —blossoms; —charms; —cheers; —dwindles; —eases; —flourishes; —flows; —relieves.

(See entertainment, generosity, friendship.)

adjectives

dejected; ungracious; disagreeable; heavenly; secondary; routed; subtle; benignant; tragic; starry; affable; reluctant; straggling; new-found; genial; angelic; crusading; illimitable; shadowy; numerous; overweening; inseparable; chafing; kind; legionary; indignant; embattled; celestial; spangled; assaulting; heathen; conquering; amiable; heavenly; pensive; battle-broken; visionary; countless; smiling; ranting; ill-fated; motley; square; swarthy; ethereal; tombless; venerable; frugal; innumerable; hurrying; mustering; frank; miserable; prospective; glorified; radiant; niggardly; weary; generous; bewildered.

verbs

besiege—; honor—; praise—; —amuses; —appears; —approves; —befriends; —bids; —charms; —comforts; —delights; —enlivens; —flatters; —greets; —plans; —presides; —provides; —relieves; —welcomes.

(See entertainer, actor, friend.)

adjectives

temporary; noble; popular; impromptu; attentive; exuberant; lavish; ambitious; small; fat; good-natured; fair; charming; gracious; air; amiable; tidy; buxom.

adverbs

coldly; politely; secretly; surreptitiously; inscrutably; openly; candidly; absurdly; hatefully; malevolently; venomously; maliciously; viciously; ominously; portentously; villainously; inscrutably; inexplicably; irreconcilably; antagonistically; dangerously; alarmingly; curiously; strangely; oddly; queerly; unreasonably; irrationally; exceptionally; tragically; inconveniently; irrevocably; horribly.

adjectives

determined; quiet; small; quenched; implacable; slumbering; languid; perpetual; unexpressed; sudden; smiling; unnecessary; undiluted; expensive; alert; expectant; uncompromising; indecent; provoking; bitter; unintermitting; implacable; innate; jealous; frequent (pl); wily; deadly; concealed; smoldering; methodical; intuitive; evident; legislative; defensive; interfering; neighborly; unprofitable; fanatical.

verbs

arouse—; break—s; cease—; encourage—; engage in—s; enter—s; evince—; excite—; fan—; incur—of; loose—s; renew—s; suspend—s; temper—; view with—; —frightens; —grows.

(See enmity, animosity, opposition, warfare, anger.)

adverbs

devilishly; horribly; unbearably; unusually; remarkably; abnormally; feverishly; unnaturally; angrily; dangerously; apparently; unseasonably; strangely; intolerably; sufficiently; scarcely; inordinately; queerly; peculiarly; curiously; unfortunately; oppressively; swelteringly; stiflingly; bakingly; blazingly; suffocatingly; intensely.

adjectives

superb; smart; first-class; fine; famous; quiet; dignified; luxurious; distinguished; friendly; notable; favored; complete; beachfront; residential; delightful; attractive; skyscraper; seaside; centrally-located; modern; perfect; cheerful; warm; inviting; traditional; unique; outstanding; swanky; distinguished; exclusive; apartment; ambitious; wooden; cozy; commercial; resort;

small; provincial; rambling; frame; vermin-infested; temperance; convenient; grand; comfortable; charming; nice; hospitable; cosmopolitan; well-kept; well-organized; innumerable (pl); glamorous.

verbs
convene at—; dwell at—; inhabit—; loll in—; patronize—; retain at—; stow away in—; —accommodates; —caters to; —comforts; —delights; —employs; —flourishes; —offers; —provides; —serves; —welcomes; —furnishes.

(See inn, house, building, tavern.)

HOUND
adjectives
overrash; cadaverous; lean; ugly; couchant; degenerate; long-eared; deepmouthed; patient; fox; aged; hot; scent-snuffing; baffled; phenomenal; howling; licking; fawn-colored; thirsty-looking; cunning; toothless; graceful.

verbs
pat—; quiet—; unleash—; whip—; —bays; —dashes by; —growls; —s harry; —howls; —points; —pursues; —snarls; —tears; —whines; —yelps; —yips.

(See dog, animal.)

HOUR
adjectives
accustomed; additional; agonizing; all-glorious; amazing; appointed; arid; atoning; awful; baleful; bitter; black; bleak; blessed; blighted; blue-eyed; bounteous; brawling; breakfast; breathless; brief; bright; calm; captive; careful; cheerless; closing; cloudless; comfortless; coming; conditioned; confident; consecrated; countless (pl); cramped; critical; crucial; customary; darkened; darkling; dawning; definite; delicious; designated; desirable; disastrous; discouraged; dolorous; dread; dreadful; dream-haunted; dreaming; dreary; drinking; dull; dusky; early; eerie; elected; ensuing; enthusiastic; eventful; evil; exciting; fair; famished; fatiguing; favored; fearful; fervent; feverous; flaming; forbidden; forgetful; forlorn; forsaken; fragrant; fruitful; generous; gentle; giddy; gleeful; gloom-clad; glutted; gory; gradual; hallowed; happy; hateful; hazy; heavenly; heavy; heinous; heterogeneous; hushed; hustling; hypnotic; idle; illuminating; imperious; impossible; impressionable; impressive; inaus-

picious; incessant; industrious; inevitable; instant; interminable; jocund; jovial; joyful; jubilant; laborious; languorous; lasting; lazy; leisure; lingering; lonely; long; luckless; lyric; meet; melancholy; memorable; merciless; meridian; merry; midnight; moonlit; mortal; mourning; murderous; natal; new-fledged; niggard; noteless; nuptial; old; optional; pallid; particular; parting; passing; peaceful; perilous; placid; pleasant; precious; precise; prefixed; prescribed; promised; rare; regretful; regulated; retributive; rosy-fingered; sacred; sauntering; secret; serene; serious; shadowed; shiny; short; sleepless; slow-paced; social; soft; solemn; somber; sorrowful; spent; splenetic; starless; stormy; strange; suffering; sunny; sunset; superincumbent; supreme; surviving; swift; tedious; thorny; thoughtful; thrilling; torturing; tranquil; transient; treacherous; trembling; tremulous; troublous; trysting; twilight; unbearable; unborn; unconscionable; unfortunate; unlucky; unnatural; unreturning; unseasonable; unsuspecting; untroubled; usual; valuable; vast; vehement; vesper; voluptuous; wakeful; wasted; weary; wedlock; weird; weeping; white-robed; wholesome; wild; wonted; working; wretched.

verbs
appoint—; budget—s; consume—s; count —s; crowd—; devote—s to; employ—; fix —; fritter away—s; kill—s; laze away—s; note—; postpone—; read—of day; reckon —; regulate—s; set—; —approaches; —s crawl by; —s drag; —elapses; —s fly; —s lag; —s ripen; —strikes; —s wear on.

(See time, occasion.)

HOUSE
adjectives
mansion; miserable; enchanting; cat-encumbered; solitary; scattered (pl); gloomy; dilapidated; true; pretentious; archetypal; echoing; painted; battlemented; imperial; ambitious; dignified; quaint; religious; gaunt; comfortable; straggling; disreputable; showy; imaginative; practical; reminiscent; adjacent; shiftless; austere; aristocratic; poultry; gliding; modest; tile-roofed; haunted; burnished; conspicuous; illustrious; farm; gnarled; jolly; deserted; squatty; lonely; first-run; widespreading; rayless; darksome; crafty; magnificent; ancestral; lofty; supply; substantial; idyllic; shamble; economical; town; continental;

shell-pitted; giddy; shabby; pillaged; lady-like; shameful; dower; blithe; ugly; hallowed; powerful; low-browed; inviting; tenement; triangular; terraced; humble; wretched; wattled; dull; lucrative; untenantable; paltry; inconvenient; dreamy; ruined; ducal; ill; country; dismantled; useless; gay; gambling; naughty; celestial; neat; treasure; festive; warm; jovial; sunny; luxurious; embellished; pharmaceutical; comfortable-looking; log; dwelling; tremendous; unpeeled; well-insulated; mobile; trembling; gay-roofed; little; popular; swarming; stuccoed; irregularly-scattered (pl); handsome; respectable; bleak; hospitable; ill-furnished; filthy; dirty; isolated; thatch-roofed; cane; respected; faltering; unobtrusive; ancient; narrow; flimsy; reigning; royal; desolate; fair; vast; treasure; identical; tumble-down; boxlike; unquiet; crowded; parental; eery; model; lodging; commodious; stately; unreal; excellent; pretentious; swell-front; shutterless; old-fashioned; once-fashionable; clattering; adobe; ranch; sheltering.

verbs
adorn—; bedizen—; billet in—; demolish—; design—; ensconce in—; inhabit—; model —; pattern—; refurbish—; renovate—; sanctify—; shatter—; tenant—; undermine —; waddle into—; —hushes; —looms; —nestles; —springs up.
(See building, abode, home.)

HOUSE (v)
adverbs
luxuriously; warmly; faithfully; imperially; quaintly; disreputably; practically; shiftlessly; austerely; aristocratically; hospitably; magnificently; economically; shabbily; commodiously; pretentiously.
(See shelter, protect.)

HOUSEHOLD
adjectives
ducal; decorous; quiet; turbulent; tyrannical; literary; minute.

HOUSEKEEPER
adjectives
active; manifest; procrastinating.

HOUSEKEEPING
adjectives
modern; efficient.

HOUSEWIFE
adjectives
fastidious; primitive; chaste; querulous; busy; lazy.

HOUSING
adjectives
better; overcrowded; low-cost; planned; government-supported.

HOVEL
adjectives
poverty-stricken; ruinous; lowly; wretched

HOVER (v)
adverbs
perpetually; perilously; caressingly; ceaselessly; expectantly; eagerly; protectingly; lovingly.
(See flutter, linger.)

HOWL
adjectives
long; loud; piteous; increasing; reverberate; unearthly; occasional; barbaric; tumultuous; deep; wild; ghastly; triumphant; angry; prolonged; fearful; dismal; lugubrious.

verbs
break into—; muffle—; prolong—; subdue —; unleash—; utter—; —arises; —astonishes; —breaks out; —distresses; —frightens; —penetrates; —pierces; —rends; —rips through; —terrifies; —confuses.
(See cry, wail, noise.)

HOWL (v)
adverbs
dismally; incessantly; bleakly; victoriously; gruesomely; sickeningly; heart-rendingly; ironically; blatantly; eerily.
(See roar, wail.)

HOWLING
adjectives
melancholy; weird; ear-rending.

HOYDENISH
adverbs
gaudily; boisterously; coarsely; noisily; conspicuously; flauntingly; blatantly; publicly; shamelessly; barbarously; boorishly; remarkably; lamentably; extravagantly; queerly; unfortunately; horribly; indecorously; monstrously; indecently; terribly; outlandishly; outrageously; wantonly; ri-

baldly; particularly; shabbily; provincially; shockingly; uncivilly; extremely; horribly; inexcusably.

HUBBUB
adjectives
chaotic; universal; confused; inarticulate.

HUDDLE
adjectives
low; confused.

verbs
band in—; concentrate in—; congregate in —; crowd in—; crush in—; emerge from—; flock in—; gather in—; lie in—; mingle in —; move in—; throng in—; tumble into—; spring from—; swarm in—; —confuses; —disperses; —writhes.
(See group, crowd.)

HUDDLE (v)
adverbs
pathetically; sluggishly; comfortably; protectingly; snugly; patiently; instinctively; dolorously.
(See crouch, pack, crowd.)

HUE
adjectives
intense; stone; tender; undecided; vivid; varied (pl); native; prismatic; exuberant; deathly; roseate; unalterable; ashy; glorious; brimstone; golden; somber; autumn; ghastly; celestial; pallid; pronounced; rainbow; healthy; firm; unshimmering; kindred; slaughterous; predominating; faint; myriad (pl); intense; unwithering; sad; blended; heavenly; tawny; universal; melodious; tempting; chameleon; damask; sulphurous; manifold (pl); livid; pallid; pure; lovely; somber; curious (pl); virgin; sublimer; azure; florid; ghastly; voluptuous; enchanting; homely; lurid; brassy; sightly; rich; fair; unwashed; fading; sunburned; evanescent; normal; unnatural; brilliant; predominant; wild; unpropitious; delicate; unfading; charming; different; changing; sanguine; decided; dazzling; doubtful; generous; washed-out; nondescript; aerial; shifting; burnished; iridescent; gorgeous; undying; kaleidoscopic; twilight; various (pl).

verbs
blend—s; dab—; daub with—; dim—; dip into—; enhance—; flush—; mix—; paint—;

smear—; stroke—; teem with—; —brightens; —delights; —enchants; —fades; —glows; —melts; —merges.
(See color, shade.)

HUG
adjectives
affectionate; exemplary; ecstatic.

HUG (v)
adverbs
brazenly; amorously; affectionately; ecstatically; lustily; brutishly; stalwartly; tenderly; voluptuously; lasciviously.
(See clasp, grip, embrace.)

HUGE
adverbs
remarkably; bulkily; monstrously; awkwardly; stupendously; grossly; grotesquely; queerly; impossibly; overwhelmingly; ponderously; prodigiously; sensationally; unusually; formidably; unduly.

HULK
adjectives
lumbering; shallow; unprizable; lifeless.

HULL
adjectives
polished; rough; swift; graceful.

verbs
confine to—; discard—; divest of—; enrobe in—; equip with—; fashion—; shed—; shell —; swathe in—; wrap in—; —armors; —covers; —encases; —encompasses; —encrusts; —envelops; —hides; —protects; —reverberates.
(See frame, blanket.)

HUM
adjectives
busy; murmurous; beelike; soft; bubbling; hideous; endless; peaceful; lily-muffled; dolorous; distant; discordant; hoarse; pleasant; sonorous; faint; musical; drowsy.

verbs
endure—; heed—; ignore—; join in—; muffle—; perceive—; raise—; subdue—; —attracts; —bothers; —charms; —delights; —disturbs; —plagues; —waxes.
(See murmur.)

HUM (v)

adverbs
tremulously; blithely; discordantly; hoarsely; sonorously; drowsily; musically; melodiously; monotonously.
(See drone, buzz, croon.)

HUMAN

adjectives
frail; feeble; fallible.

adverbs
charitably; generously; sympathetically; compassionately; kindly; tenderly; lovingly; mercifully; graciously; understandingly; intelligently; gently; uncommonly; remarkably.

HUMANE

adverbs
benevolently; tenderly; intelligently; consistently; dependably; charitably; comfortingly; considerately; graciously; warmly; mercifully; philanthropically; altruistically; patriotically; generously; leniently; admirably; wonderfully; actively; naturally; habitually.

HUMANITARIAN

adverbs
constructively; altruistically; benevolently; beneficently; public-spiritedly; generously; sincerely; actively; compassionately; effectively; admirably; superbly; magnificently; nobly; worthily; eminently; immensely; intensely; definitely; broadly.

HUMANITY

adjectives
enslaved; misshapen; outraged; frail; struggling; downtrodden; common; kindred; communal; exalted; suffering; unexpected; active; frank; sturdy; armed; heated; rugged; semi-tropical; multiform; profound; natural; polluted; redeemed; despairing; glorious; rekindled; warm; adorned; consistent; chained.

verbs
claim for—; contemplate—; contribute to—; educate—; enrich—; exhibit—; found on —; imitate—; regard—; observe—; pity—; portray—; prompt by—; relieve—; rely on —; rule—; stir—; uplift—; —inclines; —mitigates; —restrains.
(See mankind, human nature, compassion, tenderness, kindness, benevolence, civilization, world.)

HUMAN NATURE

verbs
appeal to—; attribute to—; benefit—; bewail—; characterize—; contemplate—; lament—; observe—; regard—; rely on—; scrutinize—; subjugate—; —balks at; —behaves; —evolves; —pursues; —responds; —revolves.
(See character, disposition, temperament, constitution, mankind, humanity.)

HUMBLE

adverbs
quietly; unusually; sincerely; modestly; shyly; timidly; obsequiously; submissively; abjectly; astoundingly; timorously; unassumingly; guiltily; demurely; devoutly; reverently; solemnly; gravely; consecratedly; penitently; contritely; sadly; unexpectedly; unnecessarily; extremely.

HUMBLE (v)

adverbs
abjectly; painfully; utterly; profoundly; unmeritedly; shamefully; sadistically; vindictively.
(See debase, humiliate.)

HUMBLENESS

adjectives
whispering; profound.

HUMBUG

adjectives
solemn; intolerable; sleek; hypocritical; dishonest.

HUMDRUM

adverbs
flatly; dully; stupidly; uninterestingly; monotonously; intolerably; usually; habitually; conspicuously; laboriously; tediously; prosily; dismally; wearisomely; tiresomely; prosaically; endlessly; interminably; baldly; disgustingly; ponderously; heavily; impossibly; curiously; unbearably.

HUMID

adverbs
suffocatingly; sultrily; horribly; dreadfully; frightfully; unusually; uncommonly; highly; extremely; excessively; damply; muddily; soggily; reekingly; drippingly; oppressively; uncomfortably; relatively; remarkably; surprisingly.

adjectives
oppressive; rotten; dense; unusual; relative; extreme; unwholesome; uncomfortable.

HUMILIATE (v)
adverbs
bitterly; horribly; ineffably; profoundly; spitefully; hatefully; jealously; * enviously; treacherously.
(See humble, debase, shame.)

HUMILIATED
adverbs
extremely; deeply; profoundly; intolerably; shamefully; unnecessarily; needlessly; intentionally; deliberately; cruelly; bitterly; painfully; brutally; publicly; utterly; direly; sorely; deplorably; scandalously; outrageously; inexcusably; unforgivably; criminally; shockingly; basely; terribly; dreadfully.

HUMILIATION
adjectives
painful; jovial; utter; imagined; frequent; just; ineffable; anticipated; profound; deep; unmerited; subsequent.

verbs
bow in—; break in—; deserve—; end in—; expose to—; incur—; inure to—; invite—; go down in—; kneel in—; overcome with—; pretend—; purchase by—; resign to—; sink in—; submit to—; suffer—; walk in—; — humbles; —shames; —tortures.
(See mortification, dishonor, ignominy.)

HUMILITY
adjectives
proud; abrupt; deep; profound; singular; matchless; laughable; egotistic; mock; vast; mild; utmost; true; provoking; apparent; shamed; cringing; honest; servile; false; respectable; marked; passionate.

verbs
accept with—; affect—; breathe—; commend —; feign—; fill with—; gown in—; practice—; relish—; submit with—; walk with —; —contents; —satisfies; —tempers.
(See modesty, humiliation.)

HUMMING
adjectives
gentle; intermittent; audible; drowsy.

verbs
—beaks; —chirps; —flits; —hops; —hums; —skims about.
(See bird.)

HUMOR
adjectives
gay; ironic; wonted; savage; drawling; malicious; lively; cantankerous; dismal; sportive; piquant; homely; arrogant; mingled; delighted; good; robust; devastating; oppressive; mixed; clumsy; puppy; whimsical; tender; resistless; genial; boisterous; bubbling; caustic; pestilent; parched; jeering; grave; playful; unhappy; gentle; satirical; headstrong; frank; companionable; unaccountable; secondhand; good-natured; capricious; obliging; black; little; melancholy; arresting; pleasant; ponderous; audacious; grim; true; spleeny; splenetic; cynical; acrid; biting; fertile; irresistible; lordly; proper; sarcastic; racy; inexhaustible; overwhelming; excellent; charming; fiery; delightful; vile; morbid; insolent; grotesque; fantastical; broad; quizzical; seditious; grave; holiday; unruffled; sly; subtle; bawdy; effervescent; ironic; fickle; reigning; buoyant; ebullient; ill-concealed; quaint; impatient; serious; flattering; irrepressible; admirable; sneering; ready; quiet; wholesome; fireside; mocking; reckless; testy; bitter; coarse; choice; sectional; ill; unconfined; sanguine; unfailing; trading; gossiplike; querulous; careless; salty; unquarrelsome; sardonic; irregular; universal; exquisite; farcical; Rabelaisian; aqueous; comparative; limited; pitiless; painful; acute; sullen; toplofty; spontaneous; sulphurous; meditative; burlesque; irreverent; unhappy; bizarre; corresponding.

verbs
appreciate—; attempt—; bar—; color with —; conceive—; delight in—; disdain—; execute—; indulge in—; milk dry of—; regale with—; sense—in; subdue—; subtilize—; tame—; —abates; —bores; —eases; —effervesces; —enlivens; —flashes; —flows; —palls; —pales; —penetrates; —ruffles; — scintillates; —shines through; —wanes; — wears thin.

(See disposition, mood, caprice, whim, fancy, fun, mirth, merriment, play.)

HUMOR (v)
adverbs

patronizingly; slyly; indulgently; consciously; ironically; maliciously; whimsically; grotesquely; fantastically; subtly; mockingly; coarsely; sardonically; irreverently.
(See laugh, giggle.)

HUMOROUS
adverbs

smartly; sharply; habitually; temperamentally; wittily; unusually; uncommonly; delightfully; pleasantly; keenly; charmingly; entertainingly; divertingly; waggishly; robustly; lustily; gustily; noisily; boisterously; outrageously; irrepressibly; spontaneously; naturally; broadly; cleverly; brilliantly; whimsically; merrily; comically; wonderfully; endlessly; uncommonly; highly; amazingly; unfailingly.

HUNCH
verbs

believe in—; consider—; contemplate—; deal in —s; follow—; heed—; indulge in—; inspire with—; mark—; observe—; pursue —; stake on—; submit to—; trust—; —implies; —hints; —proves; —suggests.
(See impression, belief.)

HUNCHBACKED
adverbs

unfortunately; pitiably; incurably; slightly; crookedly; grotesquely; terribly; dreadfully; nonchalantly; gallantly; bravely; extremely; possibly.

HUNGER
adjectives

coarse; alleviated; gaunt; gluttonous; deep; ravening; healthful; vulturous.

verbs

abate—; abolish—; appease—; excite—; expire from—; faint in—; press by—; quiet—; risk—; satiate—; satisfy—; spur on by—; stave off—; suffer—; weaken by—; —irritates; —predisposes; —threatens; —vexes.
(See craving, desire, appetite, famine.)

HUNGRY
adverbs

insatiably; terribly; slightly; greedily; pitiably; incessantly; habitually; extremely; unspeakably; alarmingly; ravenously; eagerly; seriously; gauntly; cadaverously; glut-

tonously; healthily; wolfishly; impatiently; avidly; wistfully; curiously; strangely; irritably; awfully; restlessly; fretfully.

HUNK
adjectives

substantial; seditious; luscious; juicy; flavorful.

HUNT
adjectives

fruitless; scavenger; vengeful; man.

HUNT (v)
adverbs

mercilessly; patiently; anxiously; fruitlessly; enthusiastically; intrepidly; passionately; wantonly; humanely; daringly.
(See seek, search, pursue.)

HUNTER
adjectives

venerable; winged; passionate; unsuccessful; novice; persistent; pugnacious; gold; lifelong; unthinking; wanton; humanity; outstanding; fair-weather; daring; intrepid.

HUNTING
adjectives

purposed; realistic.

HURDLE
verbs

balk at—; brace—; break—; construct—; erect—; fence with—; fly over—; fortify with—; gain—; jump—; leap over—; spring over—; stride—; take—; vault—; —bars; —encloses; —obstructs; —topples.
(See barrier, frame, fence.)

HURL (v)
adverbs

viciously; heedlessly; relentlessly; vigorously; boisterously; stalwartly; prodigiously; thunderously; flagrantly; tempestuously.
(See fling, cast.)

HURRICANE
adjectives

untamed; furious; aimless; tempestuous; lightning.

verbs

cast away by—; dread—; encounter—; perish in—; report—; wallow in—; —bedevils; —breaks; —bursts; —ceases; —confuses; —destroys; —devastates; —falls upon; —

overthrows; —persecutes; —rages; —ravages; —rends; —riots; —shrieks; —sweeps; —takes toll; —violates; —whirls.

(See storm, tempest, typhoon, snow, blizzard.)

HURRIED
adverbs
unfortunately; carelessly; inefficiently; urgently; nervously; harassingly; terribly; intensely; monstrously; foolishly; ineptly; excitedly; feverishly; hysterically; restlessly; violently; wildly; irrepressibly; impolitely; uncivilly; discourteously; boorishly; ungraciously; furiously; breathlessly; desperately; unduly; indecently; unscrupulously; clumsily; madly; noticeably; visibly; obviously.

HURRY
adjectives
monstrous; national; raging; frivolous; hot.

HURRY (v)
adverbs
nervously; merrily; conservatively; gallantly; furtively; tremulously; precipitately; anxiously; madly; feverishly; mechanically; blindly; confusedly.

(See hasten, dispatch.)

HURT
adjectives
unbandaged; real; painful; dull; deep; permanent; growing; bodily; mortal; nagging; aroused.

HURT (v)
adverbs
grievously; hideously; deeply; permanently; acutely; bodily; fatally; superficially; incurably.

(See injure, damage, wound.)

HURTFUL
adverbs
mischievously; intentionally; deliberately; innocently; unconsciously; dreadfully; perniciously; maliciously; obnoxiously; legally; disastrously; venomously; villainously; exceptionably; deplorably; pitiably; lamentably; wretchedly; sadly; reprehensibly; confoundedly; hopelessly; purposely; irremediably; dangerously; alarmingly; seriously; hopelessly; desperately; unusually; incredibly.

HURTLE (v)
adverbs
recklessly; swiftly; spectacularly; gloriously; furiously; blazingly; daringly; fiercely.

(See throw, hurl.)

HUSBAND
adjectives
frigid; itinerant; shiftless; distraught; loveselfish; unworthy; allowing; truant; worthless; war-blinded; unfaithful; affianced; attached; exacting; impecunious; obstinate; unhopeful; disgruntled; cynical; captive; coarse; instructive; ill; indolent; divorced; heavy; uxorious; precise; devoted; appreciative; scandalous; imaginary; bereaved; cruel; cantankerous; wild; noble; generous; dissipated; irascible; maddening; distracted; ingenious; indignant; fiery; stolid; jealous.

verbs
abide with—; attend—; chide—; divorce—; nag—; obtain—; rebuke—; respect—; serve —; submit to—; —abandons; —chastises; — defends; —deserts; —domineers; —heads; —lords over; —philanders; —rebukes; — represses; —reprimands; —reproves; — rules; —supports.

(See master.)

HUSBANDRY
adjectives
prolific; animal; skilled; economical.

HUSH
adjectives
sudden; expectant; breathless; dread; timeless; primeval; windless; unbreathing; evening; instinctive; religious; all-pervasive; awed; deadly; starlight; deep; peculiar; grim; instant.

verbs
command—; demand—; enforce—; expect —; impose—; pierce—; procure—; reduce to—; restore—; seek—; split—; spread—; welcome—; —calms; —charms; —deepens; —delights; —disturbs; —ensues; —hangs heavy; —invades; —pervades; —rules.

(See stillness, silence, quiet.)

HUSH (v)
adverbs
significantly; breathlessly; instinctively; peculiarly; cautiously; temporarily; abruptly.

(See silence, repress, suppress.)

HUSHED

adverbs

solemnly; reverently; quietly; quickly; unusually; wonderfully; swiftly; inordinately; uncommonly; gloomily; irritably; suddenly; breathlessly; instinctively; deeply; profoundly; grimly; instantly; particularly; peculiarly; curiously; queerly; horribly; oddly; infinitely; strangely; temporarily; momentarily; eternally.

HUSK

adjectives

scholastic; fruitless; bearded; wrinkled.

HUSKY
(strong)

adverbs

vigorously; robustly; mightily; powerfully; sturdily; stoutly; irresistibly; incontestably; inexhaustibly; stubbornly; soundly; magnificently; splendidly; remarkably; brutally; immensely; prodigiously; evidently; incredibly; obviously; manifestly; palpably; surprisingly; matchlessly.

HUSKY
(voice)

adverbs

faintly; deeply; murmurously; languorously; hoarsely; softly; audibly; throatily; seductively; seriously; dreadfully; terribly; deliberately; stagily; whisperingly; melodiously; musically; raucously; brutally; sepulchrally; hollowly; permanently; temporarily; purposely; alarmingly; amazingly; fearfully; slightly.

HUSSY

adjectives

cantankerous; brazen; brash; loud-mouthed.

HUSTLE (v)

adverbs

unceremoniously; precipitately; abruptly; undignifiedly; characteristically; breathlessly; enthusiastically.

(See hurry, hasten.)

HUSTLING

adverbs

restlessly; constantly; fitfully; zealously; noisily; happily; everlastingly; ceaselessly; cheerily; actively; energetically; assiduously; diligently; earnestly; eagerly; excitedly.

HUT

adjectives

unaired; mud-walled; abandoned.

HYBRID

adverbs

undeniably; obviously; cheaply; miserably; indiscriminately; palpably; manifestly; peculiarly; singularly; unaccountably; noteworthily; fantastically; unfashionably; professedly; quaintly; promiscuously; heterogeneously; openly.

HYDROGEN

adjectives

nascent; carbureted.

HYENA

verbs

—attacks; —battles; —barks; —carries away; —crushes; —devours; —feeds on; —inhabits; —laughs; —overpowers; —preys on; —scavenges; —stalks.

(See animal.)

HYGIENE

verbs

deride—; heed—; improve—; instruct in—; obey—; practise—; preach—; prescribe—; promote—; scorn—; verse in—; violate—; —defends; —extends to; —guards against; —preserves; —prevents; —resists; —sustains.

(See science, health, cleanliness.)

HYGIENIC

adverbs

wonderfully; satisfactorily; unusually; unquestionably; commendably; appreciably; safely; warrantably; authoritatively; properly; duly; appropriately; securely; perfectly; completely; agreeably; prophylactically; sanitatively; sanitarily; usefully; remarkably; wholesomely; avowedly; allegedly; matchlessly; superbly; supremely; acceptably; splendidly.

HYMN

adjectives

celestial; anguished; tuneful; joyful; measured; ceaseless; wrathful; pious; solemn; undying; ancient; impassioned; nuptial; appropriate; choral; swelling; pretty; dreadful; metaphorical; edifying; impious; vernal; sentimental; angelic; warbled; exulting.

614

verbs
adore with—; arrange—; carol—; chant—; compose—; express in—; honor with—; hum —; quote—; rehearse—; whistle—; worship with—; —bursts forth; —delights; —extols; —glorifies; —honors; —praises; —resounds; —thanks.

(See song, composition, poem, music.)

HYPERBOLE
adjectives
eloquent; extravagant; original.

HYPNOTIC
adverbs
mysteriously; scientifically; strangely; professionally; amateurishly; allegedly; curiously; oddly; inscrutably; questionably; incredibly; supposedly; probably; possibly; slightly; incontrovertibly; dreadfully; fearfully; alarmingly; frightfully; highly; uncommonly; curatively; helpfully; experimentally; dangerously; terrifyingly; marvellously; ominously.

HYPNOTISM
verbs
advocate—; approve of—; consent to—; deride—; induce—; inject—; interest in—; fall into—; place under—; practise—; resist —; submit to—; succumb to—; treat by—; utilize—; witness—; —amends; —cures; —influences; —intrigues; —relieves.

(See sleep, spell.)

HYPOCHONDRIAC
adverbs
gloomily; dismally; incurably; unfortunately; miserably; sadly; distressingly; alarmingly; disturbingly; fanatically; insensately; unreasonably; irrationally; pitiably; blankly; abjectly; despondently; heavily; biliously; dreadfully; grimly; lamentably; lugubriously; inordinately; senselessly; helplessly; hopelessly; desperately; surprisingly.

HYPOCRISY
adjectives
smooth; habitual; adjusted; smug; unsleeping; transparent; coarse; blustering.

verbs
accuse of—; befog with—; blanket in—; clothe in—; couch in—; denounce—; despise —; detest—; discern—; explode—; feed—; oil with—; protest—; prove—; purge of—;

repent—; steep in—; trick by—; —beguiles; —deceives; —disgusts; —frames; —veils.

(See insincerity, pretence, sham, affectation, trickery.)

HYPOCRITE
adjectives
honest; mealy-mouthed; vamped-up; cruising; canting; consummate; sharp; pompous; oily; lowborn.

verbs
denounce—; despise—; detect—; detest—; discern—; expose—; purge—; —affects; —beguiles; —binds; —blinds; —deceives; —disgusts; —feeds; —feigns; —oils; —poisons; —pretends; —tricks; —veils.

(See liar, snob.)

HYPOCRITICAL
adverbs
shamefully; obviously; palpably; evidently; scandalously; notoriously; infamously; outrageously; atrociously; undependably; faithlessly; disloyally; sanctimoniously; openly; falsely; contemptibly; atrociously; abominably; detestably; flagrantly; artfully; insincerely; evasively; flatteringly; ingeniously; perfidiously; craftily; shrewdly; basely; dangerously; terribly.

HYPOTHESIS
adjectives
problematical; unreal; rationalistic; unverified; monstrous; creative; metaphysical; untenable; tentative; scientific; cherished; inaccurate; superficial; unlikely.

verbs
accept—; advance—; apply—; argue on—; build up—; condemn—; consider—; deduce —; demonstrate—; depend on—; deride—; dispute—; draw—; evolve—; frame—; put forth—; reason by—; rest on—; state—; work on—; wreck—; —assumes; —embraces.

(See theory, supposition, assumption, information, fact.)

HYPOTHETICAL
adverbs
thinly; disguisedly; obviously; manifestly; usually; cleverly; shyly; serviceably; usefully; dubiously; vaguely; obscurely; precariously; supposably; academically; presumptively; stimulatingly; probably.

adjectives

military; imminent; continual; giggling.

verbs

augment—; blaze into—; convulse with—; excite to—; goad to—; indicate—; indulge in—; laugh in—; overcome—; prevent—; produce—; remedy—; restrain—; soothe—; struggle in—; subject to—; —attacks; —bubbles; —disturbs; —hovers near; —occurs; —presses; —wrecks.

(See nervousness, excitement, anger.)

adverbs

wildly; foolishly; remarkably; unreasonably; rabidly; loudly; nervously; intentionally; habitually; conveniently; profitably; contemptibly; provokingly; pitiably; unduly; insufferably; deliberately; miserably; helplessly; incoherently; capriciously; erratically; uncontrollably; ungovernably; incurably; incorrigibly; disconcertingly; distressingly; dreadfully; deliriously; furiously; passionately; angrily; fanatically; violently; uncommonly; highly.

I

ICE

adjectives

enchanted; tinkling; never-melting; thick-ribbed; confounded; congealed; treacherous; translucent; cerulean; gathered; perennial; anchor; polished; liquefied; crevassed; cushioned; crashing; everlasting; grinding; blue-white; glittering; phosphorescent; pellucid; transparent; overwhelming; drifted.

verbs

chip—; congeal to—; crush—; engulf in—; scar—; scrape—; shave—; sheet with—; smooth—; thaw—; tong—; —barricades; —blocks; —clinks; —drifts; —gleams; —glistens; —jams; —shimmers; —shines.
(See diamond, light, snow.)

ICEBERG

adjectives

glittering; sharp; jagged; ghostly; colossal; murderous; silent; ominous.

ICE-BOAT

adjectives

dainty; swift; wind-swept; dashing; gliding.

ICE-DRIFT

adjectives

heavy; ruinous.

ICICLE

adjectives

pendent; petrified; callous; living.

verbs

chip—; flow from—; —crashes; —s decorate; —drips; —endangers; —gleams; —glistens; —glitters; —shimmers; —shines; —suspends from; —thaws; —s weight.

ICINESS

adjectives

calm; bitter; calculated.

ICING

adjectives

rich; creamy; sparkling; sugar.

ICONOCLASTIC

adverbs

terribly; habitually; temperamentally; brutally; critically; harshly; inconsiderately; impiously; evilly; cruelly; dreadfully; unreasonably; wantonly; deliberately; irreverently; atheistically; disrespectfully; blasphemously; profanely; idiotically; egotistically; unintelligently; pretentiously.

ICY

adverbs

terribly; unbearably; significantly; horribly; unexpectedly; perilously; dangerously; hazardously; fearfully; impossibly; remarkably; peculiarly; curiously; hideously.

IDEA

adjectives

abiding; absorbing; abstract; adequate; admirable; aggressive; amazing; antiquated; approximated; artistic; ascetic; associated; attractive; bare; baseless; basic; beautiful; blasphemous; bold; brilliant; casual; charming; clashing; cherished; chimerical; classical; clear; cognate; cold; commanding; complete; confused; concrete; confined; conflicting; concluding; congealed; contemporary; contemptible; contrasting; conventional; crafty; critical; crude; cryptic; delicious; delirious; democratic; despicable; destructive; determinate; devouring; dim; disastrous; distinct; divergent; divine; dominant; dynamic; economical; educational; elementary; elevating; embryo; empty; endearing; entangled; entire; erroneous; essential; evolutionary; exaggerated; excellent; explicit; explosive; extraordinary; faintest; false; fantastic; fashionable; fastidious; fixed; flattering; fleeting; forward-moving; fundamental; funny; geographical; graceful; grandiose; grotesque; habitual; hazy; heathen; heroic; immature; impalpable; impolitic; impure; inane; inconceivable; inconvenient; industrial; ingenious; innate; insane; irruptive; jolly; literary; lofty; ludicrous; malicious; manifest; meditative; melodic; miscalled; mistaken; momentary; monarchic; musical; moral; money-making; nascent; nebulous; new; noble; notorious; novel; obvious; oft-repeated; opulent; original; pastoral; patentable; perfect; philosophical; picturesque; platitudinous; plebeian; poetical; ponderous; popular; preconceived; preposterous; prevailing; previous; primitivistic; private; profit-making; progressive; puzzling; quaint; radical; rational; realized; remote; repressed; retrogressive;

revolutionary; romantic; selling; sensational; sentimental; singular; sketchy; slightest; snob; sound; speculative; spiritual; spontaneous; spurious; stable; startling; sterling; stern; stimulating; striking; structural; sufficient; suggested; synthetic; systematic; tasteful; tempting; terrible; theologic; theoretical; traditional; tranquilizing; tutelary; twisted; ugly; unhappy; underlying; undesired; unexpected; unfulfilled; uninteresting; universal; unjust; unsound; vagrant; vague; vaporous; varied (pl); vile; well-grounded; whimsical; widespread; womanish; wonderful.

verbs

absorb—; amplify—; apprehend—; assemble—s; assimilate—s; balk at—; boil down —; brood upon—; cherish—; clarify—; color—; communicate—to; conceive—; concentrate on—; conform to—; contribute—; convey—; crystallize—; cultivate—; curb —; deride—; devote to—; disclose—; discredit—; dispel—; dissociate—from; divest of—; divulge—; elaborate on—; embed—in; endorse—; entertain—; entrench—; envisage—; evolve—; explode—; exploit—; expound—; favor—; fertilize—; formulate —; foster—; grasp—; grope for—; guard —; hail—; harbor—; hatch—; hit upon—; illuminate—; illustrate—; imbue with—; implant—; impose—; impregnate with—; incubate—; inculcate—; inspire—; interchange—s; invest with—; jot down—; launch—; modify—; mold—; mull over—; nourish—; obliterate—; obsess with—; overflow with—; patent—; pervert—; pioneer with—; play with—; ponder—; pounce upon —; promote—; promulgate—; pursue—; rally to—; recoil from—; refute—; reject —; relish—; repudiate—; retain—; reverse —; revive—; root—in; scoff at—; scorn—; set forth—; spike—; sprout—; stifle—; sum up—; superimpose—; suppress—; surrender to—; sustain—; symbolize—; toy with—; unfold—; visualize—; —clings; —s crowd; —dominates; —emanates from; —emerges; —endures; —flashes upon; —germinates; —haunts; —incorporates; —is born; —lurks; —matures; —permeates; —persists; —pops up; —predominates; —prevails; —progresses; —seeps in; —springs from; —takes shape; —wells up; embody in—; instil—; master—.

(See thought, opinion, design, plan, project, conception, impression, apprehension, ideal, belief, theory.)

verbs

assimilate—; betray—; cherish—; cling to —; consecrate to—; cultivate—; defend—; depart from—; elevate—s; embody—; exemplify—; extol—; forsake—; foster—; further—; imbue with—; inculcate—; ingrain—; inspire—; instill—; maintain—; mutilate—; nourish—; nurse—; owe to—; personify—; play havoc with—; preserve—; sacrifice to—; satisfy—; shatter—; shape—; symbolize—; weld to—; worship—; —aims at; —binds; —inspires; —permeates; — rests upon; realize—.

(See model, pattern, standard.)

adverbs

chimerically; dreamily; fantastically; perfectly; impossibly; extravagantly; romantically; preposterously; notionally; unsubstantially; whimsically; vaporously; entertainingly; emphatically; beautifully; charmingly; emptily; nebulously; speculatively; ridiculously; vaguely.

IDEALISM

adjectives

crystallized; poetical; romantic; moral; altruistic; impulsive; abstract; soaring; poignant.

verbs

breathe—; clothe in—; decry—; dwell in—; encourage—; found on—; inculcate—; marvel at—; nurse—; prate about—; sacrifice to—; temper with—; value—; voice—; tinge with—; —affirms; —compensates; —denies; —hampers; —melts; —reigns; —teaches; —transcends.

(See honesty, confidence, faith, trust.)

IDEALIST

adjectives

unconscious; rash; fatuous.

verbs

chain—; criticize—; delude—; disenchant —; disillusion—; enthrall—; frustrate—; hamper—; —cherishes; —contemplates; —despises; —dreams; —envisions; —regards; —sacrifices; —speculates on; —values.

(See poet, writer, philosopher, artist, author.)

IDEALITY

adjectives

refined; poetic; muzzy; confused; muddled.

IDEALS

adjectives
chivalrous; romantic; fatal; perfect; undigested; adequate; false; poetic; elevating; sublime; temperate; vague; educational; cherishing; retrograde; fanciful; picturesque; exalted; abstract; empty; ultimate; spiritual; collective; theoretical; factitious; racial; intangible; entrancing; complete; visionary; industrial; literary; ascetic; divine; unfulfilled; tutelary; cherished; degrading; distant; bric-a-brac; noble; affecting; unavowed; unclean; ethical; secret; antiquated; stern; unattainable.

IDENTIFICATION

adjectives
imputed; obliterated; spurious.

IDENTIFY (*v*)

adverbs
unconsciously; mystically; irrevocably; peculiarly; mechanically; ecclesiastically; prominently; nominally.
(See recognize, ascertain.)

IDENTITY

adjectives
concealed; conscious; obliterated; substantial; separate; sweet; veritable; undiscovered; revealed; fictitious.

verbs
assure of—; conceal—; convince of—; demand—; determine—; discourage—; doubt —; establish—; forfeit—; grope for—; lose —; merge—with; preserve—; recognize—; reveal—; seek—; substantiate—; suggest—; suspect—; —leaks out; —perplexes; prove—.
(See similarity, individuality, accuracy.)

IDIOCY

adjectives
sublimest; teeth-chattering; morbid; impertinent.

IDIOM

adjectives
delicate; racial; succinct; racy; vulgar; national; quaint; absurd.

verbs
approve of—; cherish—; excel in—s; express in—; familiarize with—; interpret—; maintain—; repeat—; speak in—; translate —; transmit in—s; —amuses; —confuses; —differs; —glows; —perplexes.
(See expression, phrase, speech, dialect, jargon, word, thought.)

.DIOSYNCRASY

adjectives
personal; morbid; sickly; separate.

verbs
ban—; dispense with—; foster—; humor—; imitate—; indulge in—; inherit—; parade —s; permit—; protest—; question—; restrain—; ridicule—; tolerate—; transmit—; understand—; warrant—; wonder at—; — embarrasses; —perplexes; —puzzles.
(See eccentricity, characteristic, habit.)

IDIOT

adjectives
mad; contemplative; congenial; insolent; blinking; sloppy; sentimental; monumental; stargazing; optimistic; notorious.

verbs
bar—; behave like—; conceal—; content—; control—; guard—; incarcerate—; lament —; manage—; mistrust—; play—; please —; shelter—; tolerate—; treat—; witness —; —amuses; —blinks; —dotes on; —giggles; —mistakes; —misunderstands; — ogles; —stares.
(See fool, imbecile, dunce, lunatic.)

IDIOTIC

adverbs
pathetically; hopelessly; incurably; congenitally; insolently; monumentally; crazily; purposely; maddeningly; utterly; foolishly; infatuatedly; rashly; recklessly; simply; childishly; nonsensically; blatantly; dully; extravagantly; grossly; idly; inappropriately; injudiciously; obtusely; ridiculously; senselessly; unwisely; stolidly; stupidly; spoonily.

IDLE

adverbs
vexatiously; languidly; lazily; slothfully; constitutionally; preferably; naturally; habitually; obesely; contemptibly; selfishly; sleepily; delightfully; continually; obstinately; stupidly; deliberately; torpidly; stubbornly; irresponsibly; reprehensibly; inexcusably; unduly; remarkably; strangely; unusually; dreadfully.

IDLE (v)

adverbs
frivolously; disreputably; intellectually; listlessly; aimlessly; wantonly; blissfully; degenerately; disgracefully; talkatively.
(See trifle, loaf.)

IDLENESS

adjectives
disgraceful; good-night; busy; unwilling; chatty; disreputable; intellectual; enforced; compulsory; conscientious; ancient; shapeless; elegant; rapturous; summer; absent; fatal; listless; sheer; aimless; settled; inert.

verbs
avoid—; banish—; denounce—; dread—; excuse—; hatch in—; maintain in—; pillow in—; repose in—; reproach—; revel in—; shake off—; stagnate in—; thrive in—; wallow in—; waste in—; —beguiles; —breeds; —demoralizes; —destroys; —harms; —poisons; —rusts; —shames; —tempts; —wearies.
(See indolence, futility.)

IDLER

adjectives
luxurious; busy; dependent; shiftless; studied; practiced.

IDOL

adjectives
burning; particular; subterraneous; lifeless; baser; grim; brass; vile; well-painted; matinee; youthful; gross; shapeless; gilded; bewitching; celebrated.

verbs
bless—; bow before—; cast down—; chant to—; clasp—; found—; mock—; offer to—; profane—; prostrate before—; renounce—; sacrifice to—; serve—; worship—; —embodies; —represents.
(See image, representation, effigy, notion, fallacy, hero, altar.)

IDOLATROUS

adverbs
fanatically; foolishly; infatuatedly; fatuously; inordinately; fantastically; extravagantly; irrationally; fervently; ridiculously; absurdly; oddly; passionately; superstitiously; credulously; bigotedly; wildly; enthusiastically; rabidly; grossly; inconceivably; blindly.

IDOLATRY

adjectives
social; long-upheld; popular; passionate; bloody; religious; foolish; enthusiastic.

IDOLIZE (v)

adverbs
inordinately; foolishly; lovingly; adoringly; passionately; madly; religiously; fervently; faithfully; fanatically.
(See adore, worship.)

IDYLLIC

adverbs
blissfully; romantically; sentimentally; rapturously; ecstatically; fancifully; extravagantly; inexpressibly; indescribably; beautifully; marvelously; utterly.

IGNITE (v)

adverbs
spontaneously; abruptly; dangerously; spectacularly; swiftly; furiously; startlingly; brilliantly; mechanically.
(See kindle, excite, rouse, burn.)

IGNOBLE

adverbs
basely; undeniably; surprisingly; despicably; unbelievably; horribly; contemptibly; grossly; consciously; deliberately; innately; naturally; inexpressibly; hopelessly; notoriously.

IGNOMINIOUS

adverbs
shamefully; contemptibly; ingloriously; scandalously; abjectly; arrantly; shockingly; dreadfully; terribly; unmentionably; outrageously; obscurely; inexpressibly; unbelievably; humbly; vaguely.

IGNOMINY

adjectives
imputed; complete; undesired.

verbs
arise from—; base on—; bear—; bow in—; confess to—; cover with—; crumble into—; endure—; eradicate—; fall into—; hide in —; reveal—; rise above—; spring from—; subject to—; suffer—; veil—; —chains; —degrades; —dishonors; —pursues.
(See disgrace, dishonor, infamy, defeat.)

IGNORAMUS
adjectives
splendid; hopeless; obvious; posturing.

IGNORANCE
adjectives
presumptuous; simple; personal; intelligent; self-loved; brutal; complete; deplorable; widespread; absolute; prevailing; singular; guilty; primitive; genteel; amazing; gross; fatuous; pure; universal; mingled; sheer; miraculous; timid; sanctified; blissful; faithless; desperate; profound; admirable; modest; entire; woeful; unpained; learned; crass; barbaric; swirling; helpless; disconcerting; honest; deep; extreme; violent; popular; general; culpable; intense; daring; dense; blind; humble; spotless; impertinent; naked; glooming; united; intellectual; polished; manifold; feigned; maidenly; perpetual; childish.

verbs
alienate through—; bare—; betray—; brand —; breed—; conceal—; condemn—; confess —of; deplore—; emancipate from—; expose —; forgive—; foster—; lapse into—; mock —; nurture—; remain in—; remedy—; scoff at—; shroud in—; tolerate—; yield to—; —blinds; —darkens; —deforms; —prejudices; —shames.
(See stupidity, foolishness, illiteracy.)

IGNORANT
adverbs
hopelessly; blissfully; dully; abjectly; absurdly; shamefully; utterly; merrily; stupidly; crassly; stolidly; contentedly; obviously; terribly; criminally; inexcusably; unfortunately; deplorably; curiously; strangely; grossly; woefully; painfully; helplessly; deeply; culpably; amazingly; uncommonly.

IGNORE (v)
adverbs
snobbishly; blandly; blatantly; antagonistically; scornfully; contemptuously; sneeringly; uncivilly; impudently.
(See snub, disregard.)

ILL
adjectives
oppressive; infinite; unmitigated; cruel; invisible; obscure; vindictive; false; malign; financial; cureless; sundry (pl); swooning; foulest; specific; dreadful; violent; approaching; virulent; knowing; earthly; willing; matchless; economic; hastening; invented.

verbs
banish—; better—; correct—; decry—; defend from—; destroy—; endure—; expatiate on—; feign—s; foreshadow—s; grieve over —; incur—; number—s; occasion—; remedy —; suffer—; unravel—; work—s; —s befall; —s beset; —s confront; —s disappear; —s distress; —s imperil; —shadows.
(See evil, misfortune, disease, pain.)

ILL
adverbs
seriously; desperately; slightly; temporarily; violently; honestly; strangely; fatally; mortally; naturally; extremely; cruelly; incurably; terribly; irrecoverably; unhappily; unfortunately; woefully; recently.

ILL-BRED
adverbs
boorishly; crassly; grossly; downright; unbelievably; notoriously; shamelessly; terribly; unbearably; offensively; barbarously; cruelly; intolerably; shamefully; deplorably; lamentably; woefully; obnoxiously; extremely; dreadfully; curiously; obviously.

ILLEGAL
adverbs
notoriously; admittedly; obviously; dangerously; trickily; shamelessly; vaguely; obscurely; flagrantly; perilously; riskily; openly; daringly; audaciously; villainously; viciously; flagitiously; shamefully.

ILLEGALITY
adjectives
obvious; apparent; declared; widespread.

verbs
censor—; charge—; conceal—; condemn—; criticize—; cure of—; deal with—; espy—; foster—; oppose—; permit—; protest—; punish—; rectify—; taint with—; tolerate —; war on—.
(See crime, dishonesty.)

ILLEGIBLE
adverbs
utterly; quasi; entirely; hopelessly; shamefully; vexatiously; carelessly; childishly; purposely; intentionally; deliberately; aged-

ly; scrawlingly; indecipherably; pompously; unfortunately; unluckily; crampedly; deplorably; woefully; strangely; unusually; habitually; uncommonly; feebly.

ILLEGITIMATE
adverbs
nefariously; criminally; obviously; admittedly; horribly; cruelly; woefully; deliberately; dangerously; riskily; hazardously; audaciously; daringly; heinously; extremely; curiously; flauntingly; flagrantly; shamelessly; hopelessly; notoriously.

ILLIBERAL
adverbs
fanatically; narrowly; bigotedly; stingily; meanly; basely; selfishly; cruelly; parsimoniously; sordidly; uncharitably; necessarily; temperamentally; innately; naturally; habitually; prejudicially; provincially; dogmatically; stupidly; unreasonably; penuriously; shabbily; exceedingly; remarkably; notoriously.

ILLICIT
adverbs
criminally; obviously; shamefully; furtively; stealthily; perilously; ignominiously; strangely; desperately; contemptibly; horribly; cruelly; dangerously; fearfully; unaccountably; terribly.

ILLITERACY
adjectives
pitiful; undesirable; brutish; inert.

verbs
campaign against—; conceal—; condemn—; curse with—; excuse—; hide—; induce—; judge—; nourish—; plead—; rectify—; reform—; remedy—; ridicule—; shroud in—; test—; tolerate—.
(See ignorance, blunder, error, stupidity.)

ILLITERATE
adverbs
boorishly; shamefully; provincially; hopelessly; helplessly; innocently; unduly; lazily; slothfully; shamelessly; surprisingly; unexpectedly; woefully; deplorably; amazingly; utterly; remarkably; unreasonably; inexplicably; pitiably; sadly; completely; barbarously; terribly.

ILL-MANNERED
adverbs
unpardonably; unforgivably; crudely; sensationally; boorishly; exceptionally; woefully; pitifully; ignorantly; hopelessly; offensively; curiously; strangely; inexplicably; oddly; surprisingly; terribly; amazingly; inordinately; inexcusably; utterly; positively; unbearably; unendurably; ungraciously; flagrantly; boisterously.

ILL-NATURED
adverbs
peevishly; fretfully; meanly; unbearably; innately; naturally; constitutionally; curiously; strangely; inexplicably; oddly; querulously; viciously; brutally; maliciously; slanderously; obviously; dreadfully; implacably; harshly; sternly; unutterably; completely; irremediably.

ILLNESS
adjectives
deadly; wearisome; passing; desperate; pernicious; chronic; prolonged; unsuspected; fatal; exhausting; disabling; frequent (pl); trifling; acute; separate; particular; severe; protracted; slow; gradual; wearing; dangerous; absolute; serious; violent; hopeless; lingering.

verbs
attend with—; combat—; contract—; convalesce from—; cure—; diagnose—; exempt from—; guard against—; hinder by—; induce—; recuperate from—; report—; succumb to—; suffer—; —abates; —debilitates; —enfeebles; —prostrates; —seizes; —weakens.
(See disease, malady, sickness, ailment, complaint, indisposition.)

ILLOGICAL
adverbs
strangely; absurdly; vexatiously; alarmingly; dangerously; ridiculously; ominously; perilously; irrationally; terribly; deliberately; ignorantly; shortsightedly; unstably; trickily; speciously; inordinately; irritatingly; wildly; viciously; particularly; dreadfully; uncommonly; impulsively; evasively; foolishly.

ILLUMINATE (v)
adverbs
singularly; brilliantly; gloriously; vividly; feebly; sparklingly; indirectly; partially.
(See brighten, adorn.)

ILLUMINATION

adjectives

full; softened; glorious; public; burning; phosphoric; faintest; brilliant; secondary; partial; competent; rude; veritable; indirect.

ILLUMINE (v)

adverbs

clearly; vividly; brilliantly; fully; faintly; publicly.

(See adorn, brighten.)

ILLUSION

adjectives

self-imposed; transparent; phantasmagorical; egregious; optical; innocent; grave; desired; ambrosial; childlike; brief; gorgeous; fantastic; strange; dramatic; auditory; kindred (pl); terrifying; momentary; sacred; brilliant; vague; exquisite; romantic; beloved; concrete; shattered; spectral; charming; dazzling; sweet; pleasing; multiplied (pl).

verbs

awaken from—; beguile with—; cherish—; complete—; create—; cultivate—; destroy —; dispel—; dispose of—; dissolve—; entertain—; extirpate—; harbor—; illustrate —; maintain—; mask—; prolong—; shatter—; strip of—; suffer—; sweep away—; triumph over—; uncover—; wander in—; —blinds; —crumbles; —haunts; —lulls; —persists; —prevails; —robs; —stupefies.

(See misconception, delusion, hallucination, idea, fallacy.)

ILLUSIVE

adverbs

fancifully; imaginarily; romantically; ideally; whimsically; extravagantly; fabulously; notionally; insubstantially; visionarily; fantastically; phantasmally; spectrally; imaginatively; chimerically; wildly; singularly; preposterously; absurdly; unreasonably; ridiculously; irrationally.

ILLUSTRATE (v)

adverbs

profusely; copiously; adequately; abundantly; humorously; liberally; vividly; lavishly; dramatically; admirably; splendidly; graphically; superbly; instructively; vivaciously; curiously; decoratively.

(See draw, engrave, describe.)

ILLUSTRATION

adjectives

supposititious; striking; sublime; graphic; prophetic; amusing; practical; accompanying; superb; helpful; gorgeous; excellent; plentiful; delightful; crude; sufficient; fearful; extreme; lithographic; sketchy; notable; instructive; apt; vivacious; curious; profuse; inimitable; elaborate; occasional; decorative; interesting; irrelevant; concrete; dreamy; brilliant; cogent; vivid; dramatic; fair; typical; forcible; modest; touching; well-known; supreme; elusive; descriptive; pleasant; puerile; exotic; magnificent.

verbs

afford—; commend—; criticize—; design—; display—; draw—; embellish—; exhibit—; lend to—; popularize—; pour forth—s; — adorns; —attracts; —caricatures; —depicts; —emphasizes; —exemplifies; —explains; — glorifies; —indicates; —interests; —proves.

(See comparison, example, picture, sketch, photograph.)

ILLUSTRIOUS

adverbs

splendidly; brilliantly; distinctly; broadly; orably; famously; proudly; unimpeachably; generally; conspicuously; imperishably; hondeservedly; enviably; nobly.

ILL-WILL

verbs

bear—; derive—; display—; haunt by—; incite—; incur—; infect with—; level—at; mock with—; moderate—; nourish—; poison with—; regard with—; repent—; resent—; scorn—; —barks; —bites; —blinds; — chills; —curdles; —disturbs; —lashes.

(See malice, hatred, antipathy, resentment, rancor, grudge.)

IMAGE

adjectives

dead; latest; fixed; dull; mimic; remembered; faint; delusive; watery; sacred; mental; faithful; concise; imperial; wavering; colossal; familiar; pathetic; discreet; wandering; visionary; helpless; fallen; blurred; falsest; contrasted; imperfect; radiant; licentious; agreeable; vague; tissued; thronging (pl); sweetest; tremulous; reduced; indistinct; sainted; idolatrous; teasing; rude; carved; graven; serene; sublime; heavenly; impassive; bronze; waxen;

scattered (pl); flying; livid; exact; unsculptured; spitting; distorted; monstrous; confused; hampered; lovely; mysterious; visible; newborn; ludicrous; perceptible; royal; peace-bearing; magnified; graceful; wonder-working; wrinkled; heroic; constant; effective; fallen; luminous; palpitating; deathlike; fantastic; delicate; pleasant; vivid; poetical; horrible; foul; votive; reflex; compendious; dreamlike; artificial; subordinate; molten.

verbs
bow before—; call up—; carve—; confront with—; conjure up—; convey—; distort—; efface—; etch—; evoke—; evolve—; exalt —; focus—; perpetuate—; picture—; preserve—; project—; reflect—; reject—; retain—; scorn—; stamp—; summon—; transform—; transmit—; —blooms; —gleams; —glimmers; —represents; —terrifies.

(See imitation, representation, conception, idea, figure, statue, hallucination, picture.)

IMAGERY

adjectives
mental; external; woven; obscene; metaphorical; definite; amorphous; oriental; passionate; childish; vivid; pensive; carven; sculptured; learned; wondrous; colorful; glowing; inapplicable.

IMAGINABLE

adverbs
scarcely; easily; readily; horribly; illusively; barely; possibly; hardly; dimly; vaguely.

IMAGINARY

adverbs
undoubtedly; probably; highly; possibly; unquestionably; assuredly; vexatiously; pitiably; hypothetically; supposedly; illusively; definitely.

IMAGINATION

adjectives
luxuriant; emotional; proud; copious; splendid; morbid; ardent; vivid; exacting; realizing; kindling; atavistic; inquisitive; teeming; creative; youthful; pure; retired; somber; poetic; sympathetic; rustic; capricious; irreverent; kindly; lively; indolent; veracious; astounding; exuberant; glorious; fertile; constructive; powerful; sanest; diseased; dim; contemporaneous; heated; restless; headlong; respective; fond; sluggish; cultivated; warm; historic; disorderly; ardent; ribald; popular; foul; cumulative; daring; tensest; fruitful; disordered; morbid; pure; solitary; retired; limitless; salty; fever-driven; agile; plastic; epic; hyperbolical; inventive; apt; quick; gifted; robust; defective; delicate; irrepressible; unconfinable; dire; dark; mortal; heated; distempered; boyish; idealizing; burning; jaded; penetrating; scientific; riotous; melancholic.

verbs
ballast—; capture—; check—; confine—; confound—; curb—; develop—; distort—; drift in—; dull—; enslave—; exercise—; fire—; flow from—; inflame—; infuse into —; kindle—; nurture—; parade before—; pursue in—; revel in—; seize—; spur—; stagger—; stain—; stimulate—; stretch—; tax—; transcend—; breaks loose—; —elucidates; —envisages; —pictures; —recoils; —runs away; —soars; —vaults.

(See conception, image, fancy, fantasy, vision, mind, brain, power.)

IMAGINATIVE

adverbs
highly; wildly; violently; unstably; obviously; creatively; inventively; usefully; inconsistently; untrustworthily; romantically; admirably; wonderfully; remarkably; brilliantly; artistically; extremely; deeply; beautifully; inordinately; fearfully; dangerously.

IMAGINE (v)

adverbs
optimistically; poetically; nobly; vainly; fondly; swiftly; vividly; vaguely; naively; emotionally; morbidly; ardently; capriciously; irreverently; indolently; exuberantly; heatedly; sluggishly; daringly; irrepressibly; scientifically; riotously.

(See dream, suppose, fancy.)

IMAGININGS

adjectives
vain; bilious; untutored; profound; fervid; horrible; chimerical; fertile; mystic; audacious.

IMBECILE

adjectives
financial; inept; vacuous; egregious.

adjectives
vehement; congenital; wonted; cheerful; incurable.

verbs
confirm—; contemplate—; contend against —; cure—; curse with—; foster—; lament —; punish—; reduce to—; shelter—; sustain—; verge on—; —confounds; —damages; —endangers; —irks; —itches; —maddens; —provokes.
(See foolishness, feebleness, stupidity.)

IMBED (v)
adverbs
deeply; firmly; permanently; snugly; concretely; securely.
(See bury.)

IMBIBE (v)
adverbs
copiously; sympathetically; insensibly; generously; freely; liberally; unstintingly.
(See drink, absorb, assimilate.)

IMBIBING
adjectives
generous; profuse; ravenous insatiate.

IMBUE (v)
adverbs
thoroughly; deeply; wholesomely; morally; naturally; insidiously; tacitly; psychologically.
(See impress, tinge.)

IMITATE (v)
adverbs
ludicrously; successfully; fearlessly; superfluously; inimitably; consciously; effectively; exquisitely; preposterously; authentically; creditably; slavishly; palpably; obviously.
(See impersonate, simulate, copy.)

IMITATION
adjectives
literal; unintentional; corrupt; preposterous; considerable; cunning; sorry; dead; wretched; lifeless; authentic; cheap; mortifying; makeshift; exaggerated; showy; flattering; excellent; creditable; sickly; curious; slavish; miserable; laughable; clumsy; accurate; effective; vociferous; direct; narrative; palpable; elaborate; obvious; apish.

verbs
alter—; condemn—; disguise—; praise—; recognize—; reduce to—; savor of—; — borrows; —defaces; —falters; —feeds on; —injures; —mimics; —models; —ransacks; —resembles; —steals.
(See copy, counterfeit, parody.)

IMITATIVE
adverbs
cleverly; skillfully; brilliantly; adroitly; expertly; unconsciously; deliberately; preposterously; fantastically; cheaply; admiringly; derisively; laughably; accurately; effectively; devotedly; affectionately; extraordinarily; perfectly; apishly; absurdly.

IMITATIVENESS
adjectives
selective; sycophantic; vigilant; wary.

IMITATOR
adjectives
literal; servile; accidental; circumspect.

IMMACULATE
adverbs
usually; perfectly; extraordinarily; completely; admirably; wonderfully; amazingly; utterly; faultlessly; consummately; sprucely; neatly; tidily; daintily; delicately; nattily; beautifully; pleasantly; attractively; wondrously; indescribably; entrancingly.

IMMATERIAL
adverbs
vaguely; definitely; admittedly; palpably; ephemerally; transiently; momentarily; temporarily; wholly.

IMMATURE
adverbs
ridiculously; disgustingly; rosily; appealingly; helplessly; delicately; shyly; absurdly; hopelessly; sweetly; wretchedly; crudely; surprisingly; coarsely; roughly; thoughtlessly; shiftlessly; terribly; unsuitably; unfortunately; preposterously; unbelievably; miserably; painfully; awkwardly; adorably; gawkily; feverishly; obviously; noisily; blithely; inexpressibly; markedly; dully; ingeniously; garrulously; incredibly.

IMMENSITY
adjectives
vast; involved; sublime; actual; unfriendly; unknowable; roofless; increate.

IMMERGE (v)

adverbs

partially; abruptly; wholly; suffocatingly; fatally; protectively; instinctively.

(See plunge, dip.)

IMMERSION

adjectives

continuous; partial; total.

IMMIGRANT

verbs

assimilate—s; awe—; bar—s; check—s; confuse—; distress—; finance—s; limit—s; perplex—; puzzle—; reduce—s; refuse—; shelter—; succor—; —Americanizes; —s crowd to; —lands; —settles.

(See alien, foreigner, stranger.)

adverbs

indiscriminately; transiently; recently; outlandishly; awkwardly; bewilderingly; conspicuously.

IMMIGRATION

adjectives

indiscriminate; limited.

verbs

assimilate—; ban—; check—; control—; curtail—; discourage—; finance—; govern —; harbor—; influence—; limit—; permit —; reduce—; restrict—; stimulate—; —distresses; —fluctuates; —shifts; —slackens.

(See invasion, penetration.)

IMMINENT

adverbs

immediately; terribly; ominously; perilously; dangerously; significantly; portentously; dreadfully; woefully; alarmingly; suddenly; fatally; gloomily; dismally; actually; inevitably; inescapably.

IMMOBILE

adverbs

stiffly; rigidly; curiously; absolutely; oddly; strangely; inexplicably; sternly; severely; altogether; stolidly; implacably; inimically; harshly; stubbornly; stupidly; phlegmatically; skeptically; uncomprehendingly; silently; statically.

IMMOBILITY

adjectives

intelligent; skeptical; perfect; awe-inspiring; deathly; masklike.

IMMODERATE

adverbs

foolishly; fantastically; palpably; wildly; inexcusably; hysterically; woefully; notoriously; inanely; distressingly; grievously; miserably; grossly; astoundingly; singularly; outlandishly; glaringly; fundamentally; naturally; innately; habitually; unfortunately.

IMMODEST

adverbs

dreadfully; inordinately; reprehensibly; wantonly; seductively; alluringly; shamefully; terribly; inexcusably; unpardonably; naturally; always; spitefully; unconsciously; deliberately; thoughtlessly; alarmingly; coarsely; grossly; crassly; brazenly; flagrantly; notoriously; offensively; horribly.

IMMODESTY

verbs

accuse of—; array in—; chasten—; decry—; denounce—.

(See coarseness, obscenity.)

IMMOLATE (v)

adverbs

religiously; selflessly; traditionally; customarily; perfunctorily; cruelly; barbarically.

(See sacrifice.)

IMMOLATION

adjectives

determined; enforced.

IMMORAL

adverbs

grossly; openly; audaciously; daringly; obstinately; insufferably; crassly; flagrantly; heinously; terribly; obviously; extraordinarily; blithely; carelessly; incurably; unwarrantably; iniquitously; criminally; viciously; brazenly; scandalously; infamously; notoriously; sadly; atrociously; brutally; despicably; incorrigibly; malevolently; obdurately.

IMMORALITY

adjectives

coarse; cruel; wanton; flagrant; ugly; blatant; obvious; evident; daring; reprehensible; impenitent; hardened; hopeless; notorious; gross; boundless.

IMMORTAL

adverbs
divinely; gloriously; ineffably; immemorially; sublimely; sacredly; illustriously.

IMMORTALITY

verbs
achieve—; admit—; allege—; assure of—; commune with—; crown with—; deny—; destine to—; dwell in—; earn—; escape to —; flourish in—; rejoice in—; seek—; win —; —degrades; —endures; —exempts.
(See infinity, permanence, stability, sanctity, holiness.)

IMMOVABLE

adverbs
obstinately; stubbornly; altogether; completely; stiffly; firmly; stably; permanently; fixedly; inveterately; indestructibly; quietly; tenaciously; mulishly; inexorably; doggedly; wilfully; inertly; dogmatically; horribly; sternly; harshly; obdurately.

IMMUNE

adverbs
naturally; happily; fortunately; luckily; freely; properly; warrantably; authoritatively; legally; exceptionably; constitutionally; presumptively; duly; legitimately.

IMMUNITY

adjectives
national; glorious; happy; tolerable; various (pl); just; precarious; comparative.

verbs
acquire—; break—; confer—upon; enjoy—; favor with—; grant—; guarantee—; hope for—; induce—; observe—; preserve—; prove—; purchase—; test—; —exempts; —frees; —lasts.
(See exemption, freedom.)

IMMUTABLE

adverbs
divinely; sacredly; naturally; celestially; spiritually; permanently; securely; timelessly; marvelously.

IMP

adjectives
impudent; squabbling; mercurial; sturdy; unmerciful.

IMPACT

adjectives
modulated; joyous; sharp; abrupt; physical.

verbs
calculate—; prepare for—; prevent—; resist —; —communicates; —destroys; —drives; —impresses; —jams; —pinions; —presses; —rends; —resounds; —shatters; —splits; —stamps; —vibrates; —violates; —wedges.
(See collision, force, contact, blow.)

IMPAIR (v)

adverbs
palpably; seriously; disastrously; permanently; superficially; fatally; dangerously; cruelly.
(See ruin, injure, weaken.)

IMPALPABLE

adverbs
evanescently; transitorily; ephemerally; vaporously; nebulously; vexatiously; tormentingly; evasively; intangibly; teasingly; curiously; oddly; alluringly; altogether.

IMPART (v)

adverbs
concisely; confidentially; abundantly; secretly; trustingly; tacitly; freely; uninhibitedly.
(See communicate, give, grant, disclose.)

IMPARTIAL

adverbs
thoroughly; carefully; judicially; meticulously; particularly; admirably; properly; scarcely; cautiously; punctiliously; affectionately; paternally; grudgingly; cleverly; astutely; craftily; sagaciously; wisely; reasonably; prudently; keenly; sharply; shrewdly; perfectly; discreetly; considerately; politically; moderately; faithfully; scrupulously; conscientiously.

IMPARTIALITY

adjectives
editorial; historic; deliberate; absolute; pretended; imperial; known; magnanimous; perfect.

verbs
approve of—; commend—; conduct with—; depart from—; encourage—; favor with—; feign—; judge with—; maintain—; observe —; perform with—; practice—; praise—;

prescribe—; preserve—; profess—; seek—; stamp with—; submit to—; veer from—; witness with—; —assures.

(See fairness, justice, equity.)

IMPASSABLE
adverbs
utterly; completely; undeniably; obviously; clearly; obstinately; desperately; hopelessly; incontrovertibly; admittedly; evidently; manifestly.

IMPASSIONED
adverbs
rapturously; ecstatically; ardently; fervently; feverishly; utterly; sublimely; eloquently; fervidly; amorously; gloriously; vehemently; wildly; fiercely; enthusiastically; fanatically; eagerly; impulsively; impetuously; irrepressibly; excitedly; utterly; violently; foolishly; vainly.

IMPASSIVE
adverbs
stoutly; phlegmatically; stupidly; dully; stolidly; apathetically; neutrally; quietly; serenely; provokingly; resolutely; deliberately; frightfully; alarmingly; dreadfully; ominously; portentously; deafly; blindly; obtusely; obdurately; languidly; indifferently; uncommonly; deeply; carelessly; callously; imperturbably; maddeningly.

IMPATIENCE
adjectives
intolerable; nervous; polyglot; vehement; thwarted; balked; obvious; angry; insolent; feverish; languishing; demonstrative; rash; surprised; ungovernable; helpless; ill-concealed; unreasonable; singular; restless; filial; enraged; domineering; passionate; ferocious; repressed; uncalculating; rude; burning; subdued; bored; irritating; fidgety.

verbs
betray—; burn with—; calm—; chastise—; crack with—; detect—; dispose toward—; enrage with—; fever with—; prance with —; rage in—; remedy—; sheathe—; spur on by—; struggle with—; warn against—; —amazes; —angers; —grasps; —irritates; —stings; control—.

(See restiveness, restlessness, uneasiness, nervousness.)

IMPATIENT
adverbs
peevishly; fretfully; wildly; violently; vehemently; nervously; unduly; peckishly; vexatiously; surprisingly; inexcusably; incorrigibly; irritatingly; provokingly; feverishly; habitually; always; unpardonably; eagerly; happily; rapturously; childishly; inordinately; extremely; oddly; curiously; strangely; remarkably; unaccountably; inexplicably; unreasonably; disagreeably; unnecessarily.

IMPEACHMENT
adjectives
unfair; soft; withering; amusing.

verbs
acquit of—; anticipate—; carry—; clamor for—; conduct—; demand—; expose to—; justify—; lament—; prevent—; proceed to —; remove by—; suggest—; —disqualifies; —shames; —suspends.

(See accusation, arraignment, trial, arrest.)

IMPECCABLE
adverbs
admittedly; wholly; notoriously; altogether; clearly; exceptionally; consciously; unquestionably; utterly; notoriously; virtuously; incomparably.

IMPECUNIOUS
adverbs
wretchedly; pitiably; admittedly; obviously; terribly; woefully; uneasily; desperately; evidently; manifestly; strangely; curiously; destitutely; distressingly; embarrassingly; alarmingly; hopelessly.

IMPEDE (v)
adverbs
unaccountably; tragically; purposely; premeditatedly; totally; partially; mechanically.
(See hinder, obstruct.)

IMPEDIMENT
adjectives
sundry (pl); formidable; sluggish; occasional; visible; unaccountable.

verbs
admit—; bear—; breed —s; brush aside—; correct—; cure—; curse—; hurl aside—; pass—; remove—; resist—; —chains; —con-

628

strains; —delays; —disconcerts; —hinders; —irritates; —obstructs; —petrifies; —restrains; —restricts; —strangles; —vexes.

(See obstruction, hindrance, obstacle, difficulty, bar, barrier, encumbrance.)

IMPEL (v)

adverbs
blindly; steadily; simultaneously; instinctively; naturally; normally; sexually; emotionally; subconsciously.

(See drive, urge, incite.)

IMPENETRABLE

adverbs
dimly; darkly; densely; thickly; massively; absolutely; utterly; strangely; mysteriously; altogether; terribly; fearfully; blindly; unaccountably; solidly; pathlessly; inscrutably; hopelessly; defiantly; stubbornly; definitely; manifestly.

IMPERATIVE

adverbs
vitally; essentially; fundamentally; urgently; pressingly; harshly; severely; austerely; arbitrarily; absolutely; legally; tyrannically; strictly; rigidly; uncompromisingly; inexorably; dreadfully; highly.

IMPERCEPTIBLE

adverbs
altogether; definitely; materially; infinitesimally; miserably; comparatively; almost; unaccountably; impalpably; evanescently; nebulously; vaporously; obscurely; fuzzily; curiously; symbolically; inferentially; covertly.

IMPERFECT

adverbs
crassly; grossly; carelessly; obviously; manifestly; inexplicably; disastrously; wretchedly; unsatisfactorily; defectively; sketchily; crudely; disgustingly; annoyingly; inexcusably; hopelessly; unbelievably.

IMPERFECTION

adjectives
hateful; technical; degrading; moral.

verbs
alter—; complain of—; conceal—; criticize —; detect—; expose—; gloat over—; mani-

fest—; note—; observe—; perceive—; remove—; reveal—; view—; x-ray for —s; —blemishes; —mars.

(See deficiency, fault, blemish, defect, flaw, shortcoming.)

IMPERIAL

adverbs
arrogantly; dogmatically; haughtily; regally; magisterially; domineeringly; royally; grandly; splendidly; pompously; proudly; beneficently; dictatorially; generously; cruelly; authoritatively; tyrannically; bossily; fussily; absolutely; supremely; magnificently; boldly.

IMPERIL (v)

adverbs
outrageously; recklessly; foolhardily; gallantly; thoughtlessly; intrepidly; daringly.

(See endanger, risk.)

IMPERIOUS

adverbs
disagreeably; regally; ridiculously; amusingly; tyrannically; arbitrarily; unreasonably; arrogantly; clownishly; airily; shockingly; unwarrantedly; officiously; ludicrously; despotically; hatefully; pompously; inherently; superciliously; loftily; haughtily; proudly; sharply; offensively; naturally; rudely; grossly.

IMPERIOUSNESS

adjectives
mighty; apparent.

IMPERISHABLE

adverbs
gloriously; lustrously; solemnly; splendidly; sublimely; eminently; magnificently; memorably; brilliantly; immutably; unchangeably; forever; grandly; astonishingly; incomparably.

IMPERSONAL

adverbs
coldly; vaguely; ineptly; indifferently; politely; disagreeably; evasively; nonchalantly; casually; frigidly; disinterestedly; vexatiously; unpardonably; horribly; detestably; broadly; sweepingly; generally; arrogantly.

IMPERSONATE (v)
adverbs

inimitably; jocosely; vulgarly; lewdly; dexterously; shrewdly; artfully; histrionically; adequately; fancifully; phlegmatically.

(See represent, assume.)

IMPERSONATION
adjectives

heroic; scattered (pl); inadequate; succeeding; fanciful; phlegmatic.

IMPERTINENCE
adjectives

light; stunning; intrusive; damned; chirping; superb; delicate; female; fond; idiotic; preposterous.

IMPERTINENT
adverbs

grossly; ignorantly; foolishly; senselessly; inanely; unreasonably; disrespectfully; deliberately; crudely; purposely; intentionally; subtly; furtively; openly; flagrantly; defiantly; stupidly; unfortunately; idiotically; preposterously; astoundingly; blithely; outlandishly; crassly; brazenly; blatantly; ostentatiously; rudely; superciliously; saucily; pertly; bumptiously; shamelessly; boisterously; swaggeringly; terribly.

IMPERVIOUS
adverbs

tightly; snugly; callously; securely; satisfactorily; scientifically; hermetically; hopelessly; entirely; utterly; manifestly; reportedly; allegedly; actually; genuinely.

IMPETUOSITY
adjectives

characteristic; jocose; vehement; sinewy; flamboyant; irresistible.

verbs

attack with—; bear—; bridle—; check—; curb—; flame with—; mistrust—; obey—; overcome—; reply with—; repress—; rush into with—; subdue—; suppress—; —blunders; —endangers; —forces; —spurs; —tempts.

(See eagerness, passion, enthusiasm, exuberance, violence.)

IMPETUOUS
adverbs

foolishly; wildly; childishly; rashly; recklessly; thoughtlessly; inconsiderately; uncontrollably; violently; blithely; merrily; happily; precipitately; dangerously; generously; delightfully; enchantingly; engagingly; astonishingly; uncommonly; highly; roughly; boisterously; explosively; stormily; noisily; vivaciously; restlessly; indiscreetly; wantonly; adventurously; dreadfully.

IMPETUS
adjectives

accumulated; momentous; logical; considerable; enormous; great; fresh; intellectual; moral; united; desired.

verbs

acquire—; add—; bridle—; curb—; gather —; mistrust—; receive—; repress—; rush with—; struggle for—; —carries; —destroys; —directs; —forces; —overcomes.

(See momentum, impulse, incentive, stimulus.)

IMPIETY
adjectives

pure; natural; heinous; filial; negative; sacrilegious.

IMPIOUS
adverbs

dreadfully; disrespectfully; reprehensibly; irreverently; scornfully; terribly; scoffingly; deliberately; purposely; insultingly; inordinately; extraordinarily; ostentatiously; unforgivably; offensively; audaciously; frowardly; waywardly; blasphemously; profanely; unspeakably; infamously; astoundingly.

IMPLACABLE
adverbs

hopelessly; terribly; appallingly; shockingly; horribly; inexorably; harshly; sternly; severely; amazingly; suddenly; temperamentally; pitilessly; remorselessly; ruthlessly; cruelly; stolidly; immovably; uncommonly; remarkably; notoriously.

IMPLANT (v)
adverbs

deeply; vigorously; insidiously; skillfully; artfully; scientifically; artificially; subconsciously.

(See instill, plant.)

IMPLEMENTS
adjectives

martial; agricultural; trashy; crude; homemade; medicinal; fantastic; facile; ungainly; gainly.

IMPLICATE (v)

adverbs

rashly; vaguely; tacitly; socially; treacherously; shamefully; premeditatively; thoughtlessly; spitefully.

(See involve, entangle.)

IMPLICATION

adjectives

materialistic; covert; historical; moral; practical; far-reaching; small; tacit; social.

verbs

convey—; deny—; detect—; detest—; dodge —; fathom—; involve—; judge—; justify —; lament—; leave to—; pale at—; prove —; —confuses; —disturbs; —entangles; — entwines; —hints; —infers; —irritates; — shocks.

(See suggestion, entanglement, deduction, inference.)

IMPLICIT

adverbs

allusively; inferentially; expressly; subtly; secretly; doctrinally; indirectly; covertly; understandably; carefully; profoundly; cunningly; diplomatically; artfully.

IMPLORE (v)

adverbs

piteously; heartrendingly; beseechingly; plaintively; fruitlessly; ceaselessly; noisily; blatantly; repetitiously.

(See beg, entreat.)

IMPLY (v)

adverbs

obviously; virtually; suggestively; meaningfully; vaguely; slanderously; slyly.

(See signify, infer.)

IMPOLITE

adverbs

unbelievably; subtly; deliberately; ignorantly; crudely; awkwardly; unintentionally; purposely; inexcusably; habitually; always; cruelly; appallingly; shockingly; uncivilly; imprudently; indiscreetly; unfortunately; offensively; distastefully; openly; intentionally; superciliously; arrogantly; boisterously; roughly; noisily; grossly; brazenly; flagrantly.

IMPORT
(meaning)

adjectives

sinister; serious; mystic; peaceful; physiological; enormous; direful; violent; spiritual; immediate; ominous; mysterious; weighty; reliable; hideous.

verbs

bear—; contemplate—; convey—; discern—; doubt—; overlook—; question—; value—; weigh—; —amazes; —baffles; —betokens; —disconcerts; —implies; —indicates; —interests; —involves; —perplexes; —states.

(See meaning, purport, signification, importance, significance.)

IMPORT
(trade)

adjectives

vast; domestic; agricultural; mineral; excisable; dutiable.

IMPORT (v)

adverbs

exclusively; professionally; domestically; agriculturally; annually; legally.

IMPORTANCE

adjectives

paramount; distressing; incalculable; portentous; relative; pressing; subordinate; considerable; direct; practical; outstanding; primary; unworthy; vital; supreme; unspeakable; signal; slight; moral; overwhelming; valetudinarian; genuine; artistic; fictitious; decisive; intrinsic; comparable; rising; overstrained; anticipatory; preeminent; consequent; infinite; tremendous; historic; utmost; overshadowing; trifling; negligible; lingering; transcendent; commercial; strategic; proportionate; significant; requisite; enormous; commanding; vast; honorable; commercial; secondary; endless; profound; glowing; fundamental; grave; vanishing; conspicuous; apparent; absolute; mighty; plenary; immense; major; increasing; exaggerated; sufficient; exceptional; constitutional; far-reaching; perpetual; startling; cultural; infinitesimal; true; evident; ultimate; radical.

verbs

accentuate—; amplify—; assume—; attach —to; belittle—; bolster up—; convey—; detract from—; diminish—; dwarf—; enhance —; exaggerate—; feign—; imbue with—;

manifest—; minimize—; overemphasize—; overestimate—; overrate—; overwhelm with —; puff out with—; rob of—; signify—; stress—; swell with—; underestimate—; underrate—; weigh—of.

(See value, consequence, worth.)

IMPORTANT
adverbs
highly; urgently; gravely; seriously; materially; scarcely; terribly; extraordinarily; mysteriously; secretly; implicitly; unusually; personally; internationally; immeasurably; incalculably; ominously; vitally; genuinely; infinitely; tremendously; historically; commercially; exceptionally; peculiarly; particularly; oddly; astonishingly; profoundly.   :

IMPORTS
(merchandise)
verbs
blockade—; curtail—; affect—; gain in—; increase—; levy on—; restrict—; stimulate —; tax—; —dwindle; —recede; —wane.

(See merchandise, wares.)

IMPORTUNATE
adverbs
persistently; endlessly; teasingly; provokingly; annoyingly; vexatiously; harrassingly; bothersomely; indiscreetly; incredibly; inappropriately; inconsiderately; inveterately; clamorously; unpleasantly; disagreeably; obnoxiously; piteously; pathetically; dreadfully; uncommonly; highly.

IMPORTUNE (v)
adverbs
shamelessly; rapturously; irritatingly; persistently; pressingly; incessantly; ceaselessly.

(See implore, beg.)

IMPORTUNITIES
adjectives
precluded; trivial; renewed.

IMPORTUNITY
verbs
ease—; endure—; experience—; indulge in —; labor under—; relax—; restrain—; sacrifice to—; satisfy—; suffer—; yield to—; —annoys; —chafes; —clamors; —goads; — irks; —irritates; —pains; —torments; — troubles.

(See insistence, urge, demand.)

IMPOSE (v)
adverbs
inordinately; wilfully; deliberately; tyrannically; disgracefully; legally; tactlessly; selfishly; thoughtlessly.

(See command, enjoin.)

IMPOSING
adverbs
splendidly; brilliantly; tremendously; magnificently; sublimely; incomparably; undeniably; satisfactorily; carefully; sensationally; dramatically; solemnly; remarkably; grandly; nobly; significantly; eminently; signally; immensely; enormously.

IMPOSITION
adjectives
tyrannical; disgraceful; illegal; tearful.

verbs
agree to—; avert—; avoid—; bar—; burden with—; enforce—; escape—; inflict—; levy—; necessitate—; overcome—; pay—; punish with—; refuse—; subject to—; suffer—; suspect—; —irks; —irritates.

(See abuse, tax, oppression, burden.)

IMPOSSIBILITIES
adjectives
wild; apparent; utter; undesired.

IMPOSSIBILITY
verbs
accomplish—; achieve—; admit—; argue—; attempt—; consider—; contemplate—; fret over—; hurdle—; lessen—; master—; overcome with—; remove—; render—; stress—; strip of—; wander in—; —chafes; —torments.

IMPOSSIBLE
adverbs
highly; probably; practically; altogether; presumably; allegedly; obviously; manifestly; evidently; naturally; hopelessly; desperately; wildly; utterly; absurdly.

IMPOSTOR
adjectives
privileged; crafty; latent; artistic; ignorant; vile; wretched.

IMPOTENCE
adjectives
peevish; terrorized; pitiful; glaring; languishing; unstable.

632

verbs
afflict with—; betray—; bewail—; denounce
—; expose—; feel—; feign—; grieve over
—; incur—; jibe at—; reduce to—; —agonizes; —displeases; —limits; —provokes; —
restrains; —shames; —torments.
(See weakness, deficiency, fatigue, inefficiency.)

IMPOVERISHED

adverbs
somewhat; pitiably; ruinously; slightly; altogether; utterly; considerably; hopelessly;
helplessly; incredibly; grievously; embarrassingly; distressingly; indigently; terribly;
wretchedly; unfortunately; unbelievably;
immeasurably.

IMPOVERISHMENT

verbs
conceal—; descend to—; discover—; dread
—; endure—; further—; grind to—; inflict
—; reduce to—; relieve—; steep in—; suffer
—; tax to—; wallow in—; —attends; —
distresses; —embitters; —scorches.
(See poverty, distress, need, privation.)

IMPRACTICABLE

adverbs
absurdly; terribly; notionally; absolutely;
utterly; foolishly; manifestly; obviously;
desperately; hopelessly; formidably; awkwardly; perplexingly; completely.

IMPRECATION

adjectives
dreadful; articulated; profane; elaborate;
good-natured; loud; tumultuous; petulant;
solemn; unprecedented.

verbs
abuse with—s; blacken with—; blast with
—; crush with—; curse with—; fling—at;
hurl—at; lash out—; mutter—; perish under
—; pour out—; scorn—; shower—; whip
with—; wilt under—; —frightens; —outrages; —pains; —stings.
(See oath, curse, denunciation.)

IMPREGNABILITY

verbs
attack—; beat at—; condemn—; defy—;
deny—; derive—from; lessen—; overcome
—; prove—; threaten—; —assures; —coun-

teracts; —deteriorates; —discourages; —
obstructs; —perishes; —represses; —repulses; —resists; —withstands.
(See strength, toughness, tenacity, security.)

IMPRESS (v)

adverbs
deeply; immensely; tremendously; vividly;
profoundly; indelibly; forcibly; pitilessly;
unduly; disagreeably; strikingly; palpably;
vehemently; painfully; emotionally; humorously; solemnly; mysteriously; charmingly;
austerely; superficially; fraudulently; spiritually; permanently.
(See affect.)

IMPRESSION

adjectives
vivid; mysterious; external; erroneous;
weak; correct; tremendous; optimistic; ex-
changed (pl); charming; curious; chilling;
half-preternatural; hoarse; dual; instantaneous; ineffaceable; misleading; ludicrous; sprawling; artistic; pleasant; immediate; violent; indelible; favorable; austere;
cultural; false; lasting; explicable; earliest;
subtle; majestic; feeble; deep; imperfect;
unanalyzed; current; superficial; dissimilar;
severest; half-farcical; painful; ungainly;
prominent; suitable; profound; undiscernible; confused; intelligible; surface; repellent; powerful; momentary; unwelcome;
mistaken; uneasy; desolate; penetrating;
firm; childhood; sensual; journalistic; consequent; perceptible; private; acoustic; lively; dominant; outward; nameless; needful;
orderly; illusory; delightful; divine; vague;
amusing; ill-founded; fraudulent; faint;
obscure; distinct; sincere; irresistible; all-
pervading; antecedent; awful; reverent;
indefinable; absolute; personal; grotesque;
unmistakable; dangerous; maximum; chief;
cheerful; undiscernible; spiritual; superstitious; comparative; prevalent; permanent;
credulous; scarlike.

verbs
absorb—; analyze—; communicate—; confirm—; convey—; correct—; create—; crystallize—; deepen—; discount—; dissipate—;
dull—; efface—; evoke—; formulate—;
gain—; give rise to—s; interpret—; jumble
—; justify—; record—; reproduce—; sharp-
en—; soften—; stamp—; strengthen—; sum-

marize—s; sum up—; sustain—; translate
—; verify—; weaken—; —fades; —flickers
out; —persists; —prevails; —seeps in.
(See effect, result, picture, action, achievement.)

IMPRESSIVE
adverbs
tremendously; splendidly; touchingly; deeply; uncommonly; oddly; incredibly; surprisingly; majestically; royally; powerfully; profoundly; unmistakably; sincerely; affectingly; overwhelmingly; mysteriously; inexplicably; strangely; subtly; vaguely; immensely.

IMPRINT (v)
adverbs
deeply; indelibly; permanently; artistically; strongly; professionally; skillfully.
(See print, stamp, mark.)

IMPRISON (v)
adverbs
temporarily; unjustly; legally; permanently; tyrannically; harshly; perpetually.
(See confine, restrain.)

IMPRISONMENT
adjectives
ignorant; severe; subsequent; prolonged; dreary; unjust; tyrannical; perpetual.

verbs
cast into—; condemn to—; confine to—; doom to—; frown upon—; inflict—; justify —; lament—; release from—; resort to—; sentence to—; suffer—; —bridles; —deprives; —deters; —divests; —gags; —scandalizes.
(See restriction, prison.)

IMPROBABLE
adverbs
altogether; entirely; curiously; palpably; highly; wholly; naturally; presumptively.

IMPROMPTU
adverbs
awkwardly; obviously; delightfully; enchantingly; diffidently; undisguisedly; spontaneously; gracefully; altogether; evidently; warmly; cordially; sincerely; wholly; charmingly.

IMPROPER
adverbs
shockingly; altogether; terribly; wantonly; carelessly; insolently; impudently; highly; inappropriately; offensively; flagrantly; defiantly; obstinately; ignorantly; bumptiously; recklessly; rashly; indiscreetly; imprudently; vexatiously; disagreeably; unpleasantly; wildly; incorrigibly; dreadfully; subtly; vaguely.

IMPROVE (v)
adverbs
markedly; rapidly; tremendously; suitably; infinitely; unquestionably; artificially; verbally; gradually; admirably; progressively; intellectually; definitely.
(See enhance, gain.)

IMPROVEMENT
adjectives
artificial; needed; pronounced; astonishing; invariable; substantial; admirable; ecclesiastical; religious; theoretical; decorative; laudable; salutary; effective; urban; progressive; noteworthy; sensible; revolutionary; eternal; intellectual; sensational; definite; industrious; profitable; corresponding; outstanding; internal; general; countless; continual; objective; perceptible; beneficial; concrete; perpetual; proposed; acoustic; mutual.

verbs
acclaim—; adopt—; applaud—; campaign for—; depart for—; evince—; experience—; institute—; manifest—; mark—; note—; observe—; pioneer—; promote—; push—; register—; restrict—; retard—; subject to —; undertake—; venture—; win—; yield—.
(See reform, recovery.)

IMPROVIDENT
adverbs
lamentably; unfortunately; culpably; hopelessly; incorrigibly; vexatiously; tragically; unbearably; impossibly; heedlessly; recklessly; rashly; thoughtlessly; inattentively; negligently; arrantly; flagrantly; cruelly; brutally; shiftlessly; injudiciously; wildly; impulsively; senselessly; culpably.

IMPROVISE (v)
adverbs
freely; dexterously; artistically; roughly; crudely; professionally; brilliantly.
(See extemporize, perform.)

IMPROVISED

adverbs

hastily; visibly; obviously; cleverly; skillfully; experimentally; oddly; instantly; adroitly; comically; adequately; successfully; impulsively; brilliantly; splendidly; marvellously; crudely; dexterously.

IMPRUDENT

adverbs

incorrigibly; hopelessly; altogether; carelessly; heedlessly; wantonly; strangely; wastefully; defiantly; disagreeably; rashly; recklessly; desperately; wildly; flagrantly; curiously; obstinately; utterly; precariously; indiscreetly; adventurously; dreadfully; astonishingly; uncommonly; highly.

IMPUDENCE

adjectives

overbearing; shameless; brazen; amazing; useless; passable; increasing; unbounded; bland; stupefying; happy; uncommon; magniloquent; interrupting.

IMPUDENT

adverbs

disgustingly; obstinately; stubbornly; stolidly; incurably; incorrigibly; oddly; strangely; curiously; noticeably; visibly; openly; flagrantly; noisily; boisterously; ostentatiously; recklessly; rashly; insolently; snobbishly; arrogantly; hopelessly; offensively; disagreeably; insufferably; heedlessly; wantonly; ignorantly; deliberately; purposely; terribly; astoundingly; surprisingly; habitually; occasionally; always.

IMPULSE

adjectives

peculiar; sudden; abrupt; unconscious; bibulous; burning; mad; perverse; speculative; visionary; violent; admirable; kindly; generous; irresistible; poetical; unintelligent; mutual; wandering; malignant; choice; successive (pl); lively; kinesthetic; changing; mighty; repressed; spontaneous; august; inward; dreadful; confiding; grateful; rash; strong; suspended; dramatic; subtle; pleasurable; lyrical; natural; deepest; simpler; animating; maddening; national; mysterious; creative; popular; simultaneous; senseless; unanimous; intensified; headlong; sonorous; inexplicable; selfsame; involuntary; overmastering; fierce; missionary; repressed; deep-reaching; celestial; morbid; immortal; disturbing; frustrated; blind; vital;

governing; patriotic; analytic; upward; primary; chivalrous; wondrous; initial; common; romantic; instinctive; primitive; powerful; lightning; consecutive; intensifying; restless; motivating; piquant; unreasoning; singular; cordial; original; separate; drunken; obscure; latent; aristocratic; unguarded; indescribable; isochronous; unequaled; unprecedented; boisterous; warm; regular; excitable; westward; varying (pl); recurrent; uncontrollable; mastering; transcendent; catlike; electric; artistic; praiseworthy.

verbs

arouse—; block—; blunt—; choke—; control —; cultivate—; curb—; deaden—; destroy —; direct—; eradicate—; exercise—; exhaust—; follow—; impart—; manifest—; obey—; perform on—; respond to—; restrain—; sense—; sidetrack (colloq.)—; stifle—; subordinate—; suppress—; yield to—; —departs; —overwhelms; —persists; —rends; —sweeps over; —travels.

(See motive, incentive, impetus, ambition, desire.)

IMPULSIVE

adverbs

charmingly; utterly; habitually; temperamentally; innately; obviously; incorrigibly; wildly; enchantingly; alarmingly; extraordinarily; unstably; undependably; unreliably; indescribably; interestingly; dangerously; flightily; lamentably; deplorably; terribly; incredibly; imprudently; indiscreetly; bewitchingly; enthusiastically; irresistibly; heedlessly; adventurously; fanatically.

IMPURE

adverbs

definitely; positively; terribly; unfortunately; lewdly; indelicately; grossly; crassly; brazenly; indecently; foully; immodestly; obscenely; coarsely; lamentably; deplorably; meretriciously.

IMPURITY

verbs

cleanse of—; contaminate with—; defile by —; expel—; fling forth—; free from—; guard against—; inhale—; pollute with—; prevent—; purge of—; rid of—; swarm with—; tempt to—; —corrupts; —s deluge; —detracts from; —enters; —offends; — spreads.

(See dirt, filth, pollution, infection, squalor.)

adjectives
unworthy; injurious; scandalous.

IMPUTE (*v*)

adverbs
generally; erroneously; fallaciously; lavishly; speciously; injuriously; scandalously; unworthily; slanderously; viciously; vindictively.
(See charge, attribute.)

INABILITY

adjectives
sheer; restless; obvious; consequent; patent.

verbs
accept—; afflict with—; certify as to—; conceal—; dwell on—; judge—; observe—; overcome—; recognize—; regard—; remove—; respect—; —disqualifies; —distresses; —disturbs; —limits; —pains; —restrains; —restricts; —shames.
(See inefficiency, incompetence, helplessness, weakness, impotence, stupidity.)

INACCESSIBLE

adverbs
hopelessly; almost; desperately; altogether; presumably; allegedly; reportedly; remotely; utterly; incredibly; maddeningly; lamentably; preposterously; deplorably; positively; definitely; terribly; incredibly; tragically.

INACCURACY

adjectives
demoniac; unintentional; slight; gross.

verbs
calculate—; conceal—; condemn—; contain—s; correct—; couch in—; criticize—; curse—; deal in—; detect—; observe—; overlook—; plague with—s; prove—; rectify—; suffer—; —astonishes; —overwhelms.
(See error, blunder, mistake, misconception.)

INACCURATE

adverbs
lamentably; unacceptably; definitely; scientifically; mathematically; hopelessly; culpably; criminally; deliberately; slyly; utterly; slightly; fallaciously; mendaciously; purposely; carelessly; incautiously; calculably; positively; craftily; subtly; vaguely; bewil-

deringly; unbelievably; erroneously; accidentally; blunderingly; deceitfully; illusively; nefariously; egregiously.

INACTION

adjectives
unaccustomed; dreadful; silent; fruitless; enforced; inevitable; prolonged.

INACTIVE

adverbs
necessarily; helplessly; tragically; unfortunately; preferably; habitually; naturally; temperamentally; lamentably; unhealthfully; unluckily; lazily; languidly; torpidly; idly; indolently; sleepily; indifferently; lumpishly; passively; unintelligently; terribly; incredibly; hopelessly; undependably; unreliably; unhelpfully; sluggishly; vexatiously; disagreeably; cruelly; selfishly.

INACTIVITY

adjectives
sluggish; hopeless; enforced; protracted.

INADEQUACY

verbs
compensate for—; cure—; curse—; demonstrate—; denounce—; inveigh against—; observe—; overcome—; refer to—; regard—s; suffer from—; —chafes; —distresses; —hampers; —hinders; —limits; —overwhelms; —pains; —plagues; —restrains; —restricts; —tortures; —undermines; —vexes.
(See lack, deficiency, need, deficit.)

INADEQUATE

adverbs
hopelessly; entirely; lamentably; deplorably; miserably; wretchedly; cruelly; bitterly; wholly; utterly; disproportionately; deliberately; incredibly; stingily; criminally; iniquitously; mercilessly; ruthlessly; grievously; pitifully; altogether.

INADMISSABLE

adverbs
legally; socially; conventionally; altogether; definitely; positively; usually; highly; objectionably; inconveniently; unfortunately; unluckily; exceptionally.

INADVERTENT

adverbs
unfortunately; negligently; forgetfully; carelessly; inexcusably; unintentionally; la-

mentably; gracelessly; dreamily; reprehensibly; thoughtlessly; absently; disconcertingly; altogether.

INADVISABLE
adverbs
highly; altogether; utterly; wholly; completely; prudently; commercially; financially; personally; socially; locally; expediently; positively.

INANE
adverbs
fatuously; foolishly; witlessly; utterly; unconscionably; senselessly; hopelessly; vexatiously; curiously; irritatingly; disagreeably; impossibly; tenuously; vaguely; vacuously; thoughtlessly; absently; irrationally; flimsily; contemptibly; uselessly; futilely; oppressively; ridiculously.

INANITY
adjectives
oppressive; mythological; expressional.

INAPPLICABLE
adverbs
hopelessly; entirely; unserviceably; distressingly; ridiculously; wretchedly; outlandishly; discordantly; incongruously; inappropriately; unseasonably; definitely; utterly; disappointingly; vexatiously; ineptly; unfortunately; unluckily.

INAPPROPRIATE
adverbs
distinctly; deplorably; unfortunately; reprehensibly; subtly; dimly; sadly; definitely; indecorously; irreverently; wantonly; terribly; deliberately; unconsciously; tragically; comically; unbecomingly; inaptly; offensively; vexatiously; awkwardly; embarrassingly; highly; exceptionably; objectionably; inconveniently; immeasurably; remarkably; flagrantly; absurdly; ridiculously; wildly; altogether; senselessly; ludicrously; entirely; completely; discordantly; oddly; curiously; hilariously; incongruously; exceptionally; extremely; distressingly; dreadfully.

INARTICULATE
adverbs
unfortunately; diffidently; shyly; awkwardly; timidly; gruffly; ridiculously; ludicrously; extremely; taciturnly; heavily; stammeringly; tremulously; stiffly; gawkishly; silently; laconically; curtly; reticently; reservedly; gravely; bewilderingly; strangely; unwisely.

INARTISTIC
adverbs
grossly; crudely; childishly; amazingly; remarkably; strangely; unbelievably; painfully; cruelly; loudly; garishly; tawdrily; cheaply; blatantly; forbiddingly; shapelessly; crookedly; gracelessly; stiffly; awkwardly; clumsily; hideously; frightfully; horribly; shockingly; gaudily.

INATTENTION
adjectives
sheer; consequent; impolite; trivial.

INATTENTIVE
adverbs
rudely; disagreeably; visibly; obviously; significantly; dreamily; drowsily; remarkably; heedlessly; mindlessly; impolitely; insolently; arrogantly; superciliously; scornfully; learnedly; impertinently; openly; distractedly; vacantly; absently; vacuously; negligently; vexatiously; defiantly; provokingly; extremely.

INAUDIBLE
adverbs
almost; unfortunately; miraculously; pleasantly; intentionally; deliberately; painfully; distressingly; irritatingly; provokingly; disappointingly; unnecessarily; carelessly, mumblingly; confusedly; faintly.

INAUGURATE (v)
adverbs
ceremoniously; jubilantly; ostentatiously; enthusiastically; triumphantly; festively.
  (See install, begin.)

INAUSPICIOUS
adverbs
deplorably; direly; dreadfully; grievously; ominously; portentously; lamentably; pitifully; signally; woefully; wretchedly; miserably; oppressively; sadly; curiously; definitely; desperately; extremely.

INCANTATION
verbs
bewitch with—; chant—; charm with—; defy—; moan—; mouth—; mutter—; mumble—; pour forth—; practise—; ridicule—;

whisper—; —amuses; —beseeches; —cures; —enchants; —exorcises; —summons; recite —. ·

(See song, magic, sound, melody, tune, air, harmony, ballad, poem.)

INCAPABLE

adverbs

helplessly; desperately; pitiably; languidly; ineptly; stupidly; grossly; arrantly; carelessly; terribly; provokingly; woefully; utterly; extremely; obviously; embarrassingly; miserably; wretchedly; unserviceably; hopelessly; clumsily; doltishly; vapidly; obtusely; deliberately; feignedly; undisguisedly; frankly.

INCAPACITY

adjectives

permanent; social; innate; ruinous; witless; confessed.

INCARNATION

adjectives

blameless; critical; astonishing; previous; distributive.

INCAUTIOUS

adverbs

definitely; undoubtedly; wildly; vexatiously; alarmingly; perilously; tragically; dangerously; terribly; recklessly; rashly; absurdly; unreasoningly; irresponsibly; unwittingly; doltishly; stupidly; foolishly; senselessly; amazingly; witlessly; youthfully; unpardonably.

INCENSE

adjectives

grateful; lavish; mystic; rare; impatient; delicate; hoarded; perpetual; dreadful; hallowed; stale.

verbs

bear—; breathe—; offer—; pray with—; scatter—; scent with—; suffuse with—; —ascends; —clouds; —curbs; —fumigates; —mists; —perfumes; —permeates; —pervades; —rises; —rolls; —smokes; —sweetens.

(See perfume, breath, fragrance, odor, aroma, spice, flowers.)

INCENTIVE

adjectives

noblest; renewed; conceivable; external; powerful; perpetual; high; especial.

verbs

arouse—; crush—; design as—; restore—; smother—; —beckons; —encourages; —excites; —induces; —inflames; —influences; —inspires; —prevails; —provokes; —springs from; —spurs; —stirs; —sways.

(See ambition, motive, inducement, provocation, influence, inspiration.)

INCESSANT

adverbs

intolerably; unbearably; mysteriously; garrulously; needlessly; maddeningly; vexatiously; curiously; oddly; incredibly; torturously; tormentingly; painfully; agonizingly; plaguedly; infernally; peculiarly; crazily.

INCH

adjectives

furthest; shuddering; single; available; proverbial; last.

INCIDENT

adjectives

tragic; astonishing; romantic; fictitious; cheery; comic; marvelous; simultaneous; moving; thrilling; well-connected; pleasing; dramatic; principal; ludicrous; trifling; amusing; terrifying; noteworthy; curious; related; significant; humorous; minutest; absurd; disturbing; long-forgotten; developing; ignoble; cruel; well-invented; chief; burlesque; dreadful; historic; picturesque; maddening; outstanding; shameful; illustrative; fruitful; illuminating; creditable; affecting; noticeable; distorted; unimportant; stirring; weird; dramatic; unrelated; spectacular; poetic; expected; traumatic; petty; noble; innocent; nonsensical; absurd; frightful; monotonous.

verbs

ascribe—to; climax—; compile—s; devise—; found on—; illustrate—; lead up to—; misinterpret—; narrate—; record—; relate—; shudder at—; vivify—; —demonstrates; —exasperates; —exposes; —occurs; —reveals.

(See event, circumstance, occurrence, episode.)

INCIPIENT

adverbs

mildly; indeterminately; fortunately; apparently; obviously; definitely; luckily; manifestly.

adjectives
deep; unauthorized; curving; external.

INCISIVE

adverbs
clearly; sharply; acrimoniously; maliciously; sarcastically; cruelly; bitterly; scornfully; inquisitively; strangely; remarkably; quickly; painfully; terribly; needlessly; harshly; severely; sternly; questioningly; gruffly; intensely; acutely; caustically; vigorously; impressively; autocratically; magisterially; piercingly; poignantly; fanatically.

INCITE (v)

adverbs
deliberately; treacherously; spitefully; vindictively; artfully; slyly; dangerously; perversely; intentionally; maddeningly; passionately; violently; overwhelmingly; excessively.
(See stimulate, arouse.)

INCLEMENT

adverbs
stormily; disastrously; severely; harshly; roughly; forbiddingly; incredibly; remarkably; surprisingly; unexpectedly; unnecessarily; unreasonably; injudiciously; needlessly; frigidly; bitterly; keenly; coldly; austerely; relentlessly; arbitrarily; tyrannically; cruelly; mercilessly.

INCLINATION

adjectives
undue; irresistible; religious; conspicuous; matrimonial; sensual; jaunty; treacherous; particular; respectful; haughty; profound; courteous; natural; mutual.

verbs
acquire—; beget—; endow with—; evince —; follow—; gratify—; obviate—; oppose —; repress—; restrain—; sharpen—; smother—; stifle—; stimulate—; suppress—.
(See desire, tendency, propensity, aim.)

INCLINE

adjectives
wicked; slow; stony; flinty.

INCLINE (v)

adverbs
significantly; beneficently; unconsciously; tolerantly; favorably; seriously; piously; respectfully; benevolently; philosophically; naturally; diversely; subconsciously; affectionately; viciously; peaceably; wickedly.
(See slope, lean.)

INCLOSE (v)

adverbs
completely; darkly; securely; snugly; safely; oppressively; mechanically; thoroughly; lovingly.
(See surround, circumscribe.)

INCLOSURE

adjectives
delicious; little; dark; circular; large; grassy; mosque; square; walled; utilitarian.

INCLUDE (v)

adverbs
ultimately; parenthetically; implicitly; fundamentally; specifically.
(See comprehend, inclose.)

INCLUSIVE

adverbs
broadly; generally; promiscuously; indiscriminately; democratically; comprehensively; pleasantly; agreeably; satisfactorily; sufficiently; astonishingly; diplomatically; courteously.

INCOHERENCE

adjectives
colossal; maddening; affectionate; intentional.

INCOHERENT

adverbs
stammeringly; inarticulately; timidly; nervously; hysterically; wildly; feverishly; tragically; chokingly; sobbingly; sorrowfully; sadly; eagerly; enthusiastically; excitedly; frantically; frenziedly; fanatically; insanely; screamingly; bewilderingly; hopelessly; perplexingly; extremely; helplessly; strangely.

INCOME

adjectives
slender; living; taxable; ample; modest; lowered; comfortable; net; retirement; moderate; steady; gratifying; definite; diminished; precarious; subsequent; substantial; national; slim; meager; inadequate; unimpaired; dependable; prosperity; nice; splendid; profitable; cash; good; daily.

verbs
aid—; augment—; budget—; control—; curb—; curtail—; derive — from; devastate—; diminish—; divert from—; expand —; fritter away—; glean—; invest—; reduce—; stabilize—; tax—; —fluctuates; — oscillates; —rises; —wanes.
(See profits, revenue, proceeds, salary, wages.)

INCOMPATIBLE
adverbs
frankly; hopelessly; admittedly; evidently; manifestly; innately; temperamentally; unusually; admittedly; unfortunately; unluckily; violently; sadly; bitterly; acutely; stupidly; signally; remarkably; irreconcilably; openly; strangely; dreadfully; irremediably; highly.

INCOMPETENCE
verbs
cure—; decry—; denounce—; diminish—; display—; eliminate—; exclude—; maim with—; object to—; overcome—; remedy—; remove—; —arises; —corrupts; —cramps; —cripples; —hampers; —hinders; —prevails; —unnerves; —weakens.
(See inefficiency, inability, stupidity, dullness, carelessness.)

INCOMPETENT
adverbs
incredibly; hopelessly; irremediably; idly; lazily; stupidly; doltishly; immeasurably; unfortunately; ignorantly; frankly; surprisingly; unexpectedly; unmitigably; maddeningly; provokingly; presumably; allegedly; possibly; utterly; amazingly; terribly; uncommonly.

INCOMPREHENSIBLE
adverbs
incoherently; unreasonably; unnecessarily; unusually; highly; evasively; delusively; deliberately; utterly; vexatiously; perplexingly; inscrutably; mysteriously; symbolically; provokingly; unaccountably; curiously; uncomfortably; cryptically; embarrassingly.

INCONGRUITIES
adjectives
careless; apparent; pitiful; inexplicable; curious.

verbs
abolish—; commit—; detect—; perceive—; rectify—; sense—; smile at—; utter—; — arises; —denotes; —fouls; —glares; —inconveniences; —interferes; —intrudes.
(See discord, sin, wrong, discrepancy, error, mistake.)

INCONGRUOUS
adverbs
ridiculously; fantastically; utterly; grotesquely; painfully; awkwardly; embarrassingly; completely; strangely; oddly; curiously; crudely; pitifully; inexplicably; mysteriously; unpleasantly; unhappily; unreasonably; flimsily; discordantly; inharmoniously; inartistically; noticeably; terribly; highly.

INCONSEQUENTIAL
adverbs
foolishly; utterly; senselessly; inanely; manifestly; legally; quite; evasively; trivially; absurdly; ridiculously; wretchedly; quibblingly; illusively; speciously; inordinately; unusually; obviously.

INCONSIDERABLE
adverbs
altogether; modestly; miserably; comparatively; practically; pitiably.

INCONSIDERATE
adverbs
thoughtlessly; selfishly; cruelly; crassly; constantly; harshly; surprisingly; terribly; pitiably; wretchedly; miserably; ignorantly; carelessly; hideously; bitterly; inexcusably; unpardonably; grossly; flagrantly; noticeably; notoriously; naturally; characteristically; utterly; uncharitably; inadvertently; heedlessly; rashly; recklessly; ruthlessly; impulsively; impetuously.

INCONSISTENCY
adjectives
curious; astounding; allowable; charming; political; apparent; innocent; uncommon; feminine.

verbs
accuse of—; argue—; charge—; despise—; display—; exhibit—; frown on—; imply—; observe—; practise—; prove—; unfold—; wonder at—; —confounds; —contradicts; — distresses; —irks; —perplexes; —vexes.
(See discord, stupidity.)

INCONSISTENT

adverbs

unfortunately; manifestly; carelessly; heedlessly; illogically; indiscreetly; dangerously; embarrassingly; politically; expediently; habitually; strangely; ridiculously; annoyingly; provokingly; perilously; horribly; fantastically; utterly; highly; uncommonly; provokingly; unreliably; unstably; impulsively; vaguely; preposterously; egregiously; stupidly; blatantly; injudiciously; astoundingly.

INCONSOLABLE

adverbs

bitterly; miserably; utterly; sadly; mournfully; desolately; uncommonly; manifestly; evidently; unhappily; hopelessly; dismally; lamentably; dreadfully; drearily; ruefully; disconsolately; forlornly; desperately; pitiably; pathetically; hysterically; tragically.

INCONSPICUOUS

adverbs

timidly; diffidently; shyly; busily; usually; habitually; preferably; naturally; deliberately; vaguely; quietly; obscurely; discreetly; wisely; modestly; unassumingly; unaffectedly; meekly; sweetly; gracefully; serenely; contentedly.

INCONSTANT

adverbs

notoriously; flagrantly; blithely; recklessly; ruthlessly; pitilessly; carelessly; reprehensibly; obviously; curiously; habitually; temperamentally; highly; egregiously; inordinately; unfortunately; unstably; unreliably; dreadfully; gaily; restlessly; erratically; capriciously; waywardly; incorrigibly.

INCONVENIENCE

adjectives

least; possible; accidental; immediate; unnecessary; mutual; supposed.

verbs

abuse with—; avert—; bemoan—; hurdle—; ignore—; lead to—; observe—; rectify—; remedy—; spare—; submit to—; suffer—; —arises; —interferes; —torments.

(See disadvantage, drawback, handicap, trouble, misfortune.)

INCONVENIENT

adverbs

highly; seriously; embarrassingly; provokingly; irritatingly; utterly; troublesomely; awkwardly; unseasonably; financially; expensively; inconsiderately; extremely; unmanageably; terribly; curiously; hideously.

INCORRECT

adverbs

shamefully; carelessly; unfortunately; incautiously; idly; viciously; deliberately; intentionally; evasively; mendaciously; criminally; unaccountably; inexcusably; foolishly; inconsistently; speciously; troublesomely; hopelessly; wretchedly; intentionally; erroneously; fallaciously; obviously; manifestly; deceitfully; infamously; cruelly; indefensibly.

INCORRIGIBLE

adverbs

presumably; altogether; utterly; deplorably; manifestly; evidently; allegedly; notoriously; tragically; wretchedly; stubbornly; obdurately; mulishly; perversely; waywardly; obstinately; hopelessly; terribly; viciously; impenitently; gracelessly; heartbreakingly; unspeakably; portentously.

INCREASE

adjectives

corresponding; apparent; abnormal; ultimate; prodigious; anticipated; rational; periodical; sporadic; inevitable; goodly; relative; imperceptible; unprecedented; unexampled; happy; subsequent; sharp; considerable; marked; progressive; definite; commensurate; concomitant; enormous.

verbs

anticipate—; calculate—; check—; cite—; compute—; decree—; derive — from; entitle to—; estimate—; occasion—; order—; promote—; rejoice in—; reward with—; stimulate—; urge—; welcome—; yield—; —cheers; —enthuses (colloq.).

(See addition, expansion, growth, reward.)

INCREASE (v)

adverbs

materially; alarmingly; acutely; enormously; perseveringly; notably; perceptibly; grotesquely; grossly; enormously; noticeably; infinitely; relentlessly; boundlessly; perpetually; proportionably; stupendously; manifestly; abnormally; rationally; sporadically; commensurately; concomitantly.

(See multiply, enlarge, extend.)

INCREDULITY

adjectives

concealed; total; impertinent; angry; pathetic; complete; petulant; polite.

verbs

arouse—; convert to—; display—; dispose to —; expose to—; ignore—; incur —; indicate —; prompt—; receive with—; remove—; study with—; —distresses; —irks; —robs; —vexes.

(See amazement, disbelief, distrust, confusion, surprise, perplexity, wonder.)

INCREDULOUS

adverbs

blindly; youthfully; suspiciously; openly; distrustfully; skeptically; doubtfully; frankly; laughingly; amusedly; teasingly; blasphemously; scoffingly; gracelessly; impolitely; rudely; ignorantly; totally; impertinently; angrily; pathetically; comically; politely; petulantly.

INCREMENT

adjectives

unearned; substantial; annual.

INCRIMINATING

adverbs

definitely; positively; manifestly; unquestionably; incontrovertibly; unfortunately; unexpectedly; unanswerably; tragically; implicitly; gravely; seriously; dangerously; alarmingly; ominously; dreadfully; inescapably; profoundly; momentously.

INCULCATE (v)

adverbs

weightily; firmly; vigorously; forcefully; unforgettably; vividly; skilfully; academically.

(See implant, impress.)

INCUR (v)

adverbs

legitimately; thoughtlessly; indulgently; lamentably; excessively; superfluously.

(See assume, accept.)

INCURABLE

adverbs

definitely; positively; grievously; altogether; presumably; supposedly; allegedly; hitherto; lamentably; deplorably; tragically; pur-

portedly; wretchedly; unhappily; unfortunately; hopelessly; essentially; normally; usually; fundamentally; unluckily.

INCURSIONS

adjectives

dangerous; nocturnal; savage; hostile.

INDEBTED

adverbs

deeply; insolvently; embarrassingly; seriously; hopelessly; helplessly; gravely; heavily; slightly; pleasantly; increasingly; everlastingly; enormously; tremendously; unbelievably; gratefully; thankfully; personally; profoundly; inextricably.

INDECENT

adverbs

horribly; slightly; tremendously; altogether; somewhat; utterly; flagrantly; boisterously; carelessly; recklessly; viciously; offensively; shamelessly; broadly; grossly; publicly; unbelievably; inexcusably; inexpressibly; culpably; vilely; villainously; grossly; outrageously; basely; insufferably; criminally; perniciously; nefariously; heinously.

INDECIPHERABLE

adverbs

strangely; exotically; mysteriously; altogether; almost; evidently; deliberately; purposely; unfortunately; horribly; oddly; outlandishly; hopelessly; dimly; faintly; presumably; supposedly; sadly; provokingly; bewilderingly; perplexingly; disconcertingly; maddeningly; vexatiously; disappointingly; unaccountably; inscrutably; enigmatically; fantastically.

INDECISION

adjectives

ludicrous; chronic; momentary; fatal; gentlemanlike; habitual; costly; temporary; customary.

INDECISIVE

adverbs

evasively; waveringly; hesitantly; timorously; feebly; weakly; timidly; provokingly; maddeningly; abjectly; habitually; always; uncertainly; perplexingly; bewilderedly; irresolutely; variably; capriciously; unstably; mercurially; fitfully; unreliably; strangely; curiously; unaccountably; inexplicably; unpleasantly; disagreeably; indolently.

INDECOROUS

adverbs

unintentionally; flagrantly; rashly; impudently; irreverently; outlandishly; outrageously; deliberately; fantastically; disagreeably; unpleasantly; unacceptably; boorishly; crassly; grossly; rudely; stupidly; coarsely; impolitely; discourteously; habitually; intentionally; gracelessly; awkwardly; terribly; oddly; strangely.

INDEFATIGABLE

adverbs

sturdily; stoutly; robustly; apparently; evidently; manifestly; inordinately; surprisingly; astoundingly; astonishingly; unexpectedly; marvellously; almost; pluckily; indomitably; manfully; actively; zealously; nimbly; strenuously; resolutely; busily; restlessly; amazingly; marvellously; miraculously; unbelievably.

INDEFINITE

adverbs

exasperatingly; politically; sagaciously; evasively; delusively; craftily; maddeningly; bewilderingly; perplexingly; preposterously; crudely; cruelly; bitterly; weakly; timorously; viciously; vaguely; deliberately; vexatiously; embarrassingly; foggily; casually; mysteriously; obscurely; enigmatically; distressingly; inordinately; inscrutably; terribly; highly.

INDELICATE

adverbs

conspicuously; gracelessly; shamefully; immodestly; grossly; rudely; wantonly; improperly; openly; defiantly; boorishly; intrusively; coarsely; indecorously; unsympathetically; obtusely; impertinently; unbecomingly; loudly; boisterously; obscenely; foully; viciously; villainously; flauntingly; flagrantly; terribly; inexcusably; incorrigibly; unbelievably.

INDEPENDENCE

adjectives

sturdy; industrial; patrimonial; constitutional; proud; aggressive; inexorable; supreme; cherished; characteristic; fearless; modest; virtual; personal; mental; extraordinary; immediate; daring; lofty; rough; uncouth; insolent; wrathful; virtual; unsurpassed; leisurely; saucy; harmonic; masterful; inflexible.

verbs

afford—; assert—; assume—; boast—; breed—; cherish—; defend—; encroach on —; enjoy—; favor—; inspire—; maintain —; preserve—; prize—; quell—; relish—; respect—; restore—; revel in—; safeguard —; share—; strive for—; suppress—; taste —; undermine—; —increases; —irritates.

(See strength, freedom, liberty, privilege, power, security, individuality.)

INDEPENDENT

adverbs

immeasurably; delightfully; selfishly; resolutely; manfully; openly; arrogantly; rightfully; freely; happily; boldly; courageously; tenaciously; fortunately; luckily; nationally; fearlessly; intrepidly; extraordinarily; inordinately; miraculously; unbelievably; marvellously; affluently; comfortably; absolutely; entirely.

INDEX

adjectives

refractive; flattering; classified; elaborate; cephalic; prosaic; analytical; unusable; helpful.

INDIAN

adjectives

bronze-skinned; wily; athletic; dark-looking; garrulous; stealthy; keen-sighted; cigar-store.

verbs

govern —s; overcome —s; tutor —s; — dances; —fishes; —s flourish; —hunts; —s maraud; —s pillage; —s plunder; —s roam; —scalps; —shrieks; —slays; —squats; — trails; —vanishes; —s war; —whoops.

(See savage, native, barbarian.)

INDICATE (v)

adverbs

fairly; specifically; definitely; broadly; irresistibly; unmistakably; forcibly; conclusively; accurately; vaguely; tersely; vividly.

(See designate, signify.)

INDICATION

adjectives

suspicious; surface; perceptible; powerful; vouchsafed; definite; convincing; genuine; obvious; smiling; picturesque; cold; peculiar; sufficient; unmistakable; syntactic; conjectural.

verbs
afford—; await—; derive — from; exaggerate—; follow—; forsake—; heed—; measure —; neglect—; note—; observe—; reduce—; respect—; —denotes; —enlightens; —hints; —implies; —misleads; —promises; —signifies.
(See evidence, symptom, sign, manifestation.)

INDICTMENT
adjectives
extraordinary; blistering; quashed.

verbs
advocate—; demand—; dismiss—; draw up —; endorse—; ignore—; justify—; launch into—; oppose—; plead—; present—; propose—; protest—; quash—; suffer—; suspend—; upset—; witness—; —engrosses; — shames.
(See accusation, charge.)

INDIFFERENCE
adjectives
polished; apparent; entire; lordly; chilling; nodding; forced; Olympian; dreadful; blind-walled; perfect; suicidal; semi-barbarized; luxurious; exquisite; moral; complete; purposeless; immense; lofty; offhand; careless; calm; public; artless; gallant; simulated; nonchalant; discouraging; utter; singular; profound; stolid; drunken; lethargic; negligent; gloomy; cold-blooded; passive; hardened; stony; supreme; evident; listless; curious; delightful; disdainful; callous; unteachable; reckless; criminal; affected; studied; proud; political; wandering; cynical; mere; uncomfortable; affable; heartbreaking.

verbs
attain—; bare to—; buttress with—; **case in** —; commend—; cultivate—; cure of—; ice with—; feign—; lure by—; maintain—; mourn—; profess—; regard with—; shed—; signify—; slight by—; —chills; —depresses; —dulls; —torments.
(See apathy, carelessness, impartiality.)

INDIFFERENT
adverbs
dully; stupidly; strangely; stolidly; apathetically; vacantly; ridiculously; singularly; oddly; peculiarly; curiously; unaccountably; irritatingly; vexatiously; shockingly; callously; coldly; carelessly; hopelessly; unpardonably; inexplicably.

INDIGENT
adverbs
pitiably; constantly; seriously; tragically; pathetically; needlessly; shiftlessly; lazily; idly; impecuniously; miserably; wretchedly; helplessly; hopelessly; strangely; mysteriously; unaccountably; unwarrantably; incomprehensibly.

INDIGESTION
verbs
anticipate—; develop—; dose for—; fume with—; induce—; palliate—; reap—; seize with—; sow—; suffer from—; —agonizes; —attacks; —crucifies; —indisposes; —tortures; —vanishes; —wracks.
(See sickness, disease, pain.)

INDIGNANT
adverbs
horribly; wildly; violently; mildly; justly; righteously; deeply; loudly; boisterously; drunkenly; foolishly; profoundly; justifiably; dangerously; properly; silently; a-larmingly; furiously; resentfully; inordinately; absurdly; foolishly; needlessly; unaccountably; unusually; unwarrantably; unappeasably; implacably; sternly; harshly; stonily; irrecoverably; vengefully; bitterly; sorely; sadly; grievously.

INDIGNATION
adjectives
virtuous; unrelaxed; unmitigable; righteous; mollified; noble; repressed; rising; natural; speechless; furious; pent-up; tempered; sincere; loyal; moral; capacious; overwhelming; expressive; popular; utmost; hearty; tumultuous; superb; becoming; impotent; uncommon; foaming; dignified; satirical; passionate; warm; astonished; violent; cruel; fiery.

verbs
blow up in—; burn with—; curb—; dread —; embitter by—; experience—; heap— upon; incense with—; move to—; mantle—; overflow with—; pour out—; quench—; restrain—; rock with—; rouse—; scorn—;

shock into—; shriek—; snort with—; swell with—; vent—; —blinds; —effervesces; —glows; —mounts; —waxes.

(See anger, violence, contempt, fury, rage, wrath, resentment, passion.)

INDIGNITY

adjectives

excessive; various (pl); supposed; glaring; sensible; amusing; intolerable; harsh; fresh; egregious.

verbs

ignore—; nurse—; persecute with—s; prompt—; punish—; restrain—; revenge—; subject to—; submit to—; suffer—; —aggravates; —heats; —inflames; —kindles; —riles (colloq.); —stings; —vexes; —nettles.

(See insult, injury, offense, outrage, contempt.)

INDIRECT

adverbs

perplexingly; disturbingly; distressingly; intricately; needlessly; absurdly; circumbendibusly; deliberately; evasively; irritatingly; atrociously; maliciously; unhappily; unnecessarily; circuitously; craftily; nefariously; artfully; adroitly; astutely; outrageously; outlandishly; insidiously; shiftily; ingeniously.

INDISCREET

adverbs

amazingly; gravely; dreadfully; dangerously; compromisingly; thoughtlessly; heedlessly; carelessly; youthfully; awkwardly; unsophisticatedly; unconsciously; rashly; recklessly; imprudently; innocently; harmlessly; impulsively; stupidly; incomprehensibly; surprisingly; egregiously; idiotically; senselessly; ridiculously; madly; unbelievably; strangely; curiously; inexpressibly.

INDISCRETION

adjectives

manifest; culpable; racy; childish; abominable; lamentable.

verbs

abandon—; absolve from—; assail—; commit—; conceal—; conduct with—; curb—; curtail—; mar by—; mute—; rationalize—;

repent—; soil with—; suffer for—; —reflects; —scandalizes; —shames; —tempts.

(See error, mistake, recklessness, foolishness, act.)

INDISPENSABLE

adverbs

vitally; fundamentally; essentially; presumably; supposedly; allegedly; purportedly; curiously; oddly; strangely; utterly; emphatically; imperatively; unquestionably; absolutely.

INDISPOSITION

adjectives

casual; slight; physical.

verbs

aggravate—; correct—; detain by—; evince —; increase—; induce—; irritate—; recover from—; rectify—; sweeten—; —confines; —deters; —hampers; —hinders; —interrupts; —repels; —restricts; —tantalizes; —vexes.

(See reluctance, unwillingness, aversion, illness.)

INDISPUTABLE

adverbs

curiously; altogether; legally; officially; authoritatively; evidently; palpably; manifestly; oddly; mysteriously; professedly; scientifically; mathematically; technically; strangely; incomprehensibly; positively; absolutely; truly.

INDISTINCT

adverbs

curiously; unfortunately; deliberately; intentionally; inaudibly; purposely; bewilderingly; confusedly; chaotically; dimly; faintly; remotely; vexatiously; unsatisfactorily; unacceptably; fantastically; miserably; wretchedly; lamentably; grievously; deplorably; disagreeably; unexpectedly; mysteriously; carelessly; obscurely; vaguely; sadly.

INDIVIDUAL

adjectives

happy-looking; erratic; numerable; jocular; distinguished; determinate; obscure; coatless; dismal; intelligent; unchanged; transfigured; progressive; independent; self-centered; disciplined; tattered; troublesome; reasonable; bellicose; enfeebled; conservative; irresponsible; thinking; noxious; adventurous; acquisitive; privileged; enthusiastic; laborious; intoxicated; gifted; uncommon; dignified; arrogant; vanishing; unworthy; ill-conducted; beef-faced; unlucky; scant-haired; hardy; amoral; fearless; quiet-spoken; remarkable; enterprising; under-slung; myriad (pl); peculiar; famed; delightful; relaxed, maladjusted; hesitant; harmonious; unprepared; unhappy; perverse.

verbs
bequeath to—; characterize—; depend on—; direct to—; dwarf—; ignore—; incense—; insulate—; intrude on—; isolate—; mold—; shape—; support—; —achieves; —strives.
(See person, being.)

INDIVIDUALISM
adjectives
rugged; blind; intense; excessive; pioneering; exaggerated; ruinous; obtrusive.

INDIVIDUALITY
adjectives
separate; abstract; persistent; piquant; genuine; characteristic; pronounced; intense; well-equipped; powerful; indolent; decided; magnetic; distinct.

verbs
assert—; cherish—; contrive—; crush—; desert—; distinguish by—; divest of—; efface—; enlarge—; impart—; inspire—; justify—; lose—; maintain—; mold—; preserve—; reflect—; respect—; retain—; sacrifice—; season with—; shield—; submerge —; sustain—; throttle—.
(See personality, independence, strength, freedom, liberty, power, security.)

INDOLENCE
adjectives
lifeless; alternate; listless; habitual; regal; dreamy; inert; bland; easy; lackadaisical.

verbs
avoid—; banish—; bask in—; breed—; deplore—; dispose to—; overcome—; pillow in —; reproach—; revel in—; shake off—; stagnate in—; stretch in—; strangle by—; wallow in—; waste in—; —demoralizes; — destroys; —ensnares; —rusts.
(See idleness, apathy, lethargy, procrastination.)

INDOLENT
adverbs
lackadaisically; delightfully; abominably; atrociously; comfortably; drowsily; lazily; deplorably; meretriciously; inexcusably; inherently; constitutionally; obstinately; gaily; blithely; contentedly; immovably; slothfully; feebly; wisely; vexatiously; maddeningly; restfully; peaceably; peevishly; quietly; serenely; brilliantly; mentally; unpardonably; unforgivably; selfishly; heavily; torpidly; stubbornly; inconsiderately; amazingly; thoughtlessly.

INDOMITABLE
adverbs
sturdily; resolutely; determinedly; surprisingly; unexpectedly; marvelously; invincibly; vigorously; staunchly; stubbornly; heroically; gallantly; bravely; boldly; courageously; habitually; hardily; irresistibly.

INDORSE (v)
adverbs
enthusiastically; unwittingly; unsuspectingly; legitimately; laconically.
(See attest, approve, confirm.)

INDORSEMENT
adjectives
peremptory; terse; enthusiastic; ill-natured; laconic; premature.

verbs
authorize—; carry—; examine—; necessitate—; note—; pen—; question--; refuse—; require—; respect—; seek—; sign—; transfer by—; witness—; —confirms; —sanctions.
(See approval, sanction, ratification.)

INDUCE (v)
adverbs
automatically; involuntarily; effectively; strongly; fawningly; cleverly; slyly; immorally; patiently.
(See influence, persuade, urge.)

INDUCEMENTS
adjectives
soul-sustaining; flattering; principal.

adverbs
coin—; contrive—; decline—; frame—; hold out—; ignore—; offer—; repeat—; —

646

determines; —influences; —motivates; —
persuades; —procures; —sways; —urges.
(See incentive, motive, stimulus, provocation.)

INDUCTIONS

adjectives
absolute; reflective; subsequent; logical;
dangerous.

INDULGE (v)

adverbs
excessively; fallaciously: incontinently; unscrupulously; moderately; incessantly; passionately; heartily; luxuriantly; habitually;
viciously; sensually; immorally.
(See gratify, satisfy, allow.)

INDULGENCE

adjectives
idle; habitual; passing; social; partial; expensive; pampered; rare; caustic; plenary;
legal; vicious; indeterminable; unseasonable; vile; unrestrained; sensual; excessive;
prolonged; maternal; classic; immoral; pitying; polite; complaint; further; unaesthetic.

verbs
abstain from—; beg—; check—; curb—;
curse—; feast on—; grant—; humor with—;
live in—; permit—; practise—; reproach
for—; share in—; temper—; tempt to—;
treat with—; wallow in—; yield to—; —
fattens; —gratifies; —shackles; —weakens.
(See gratification, luxury, sin, crime,
wickedness, violence.)

INDULGENT

adverbs
unfortunately; over; unhappily; lazily;
carelessly; spasmodically; intermittently;
tenderly; lovingly; unwisely; sympathetically; sadly; idly; thoughtlessly; unluckily;
short-sightedly; foolishly; vacuously; affectionately; graciously; complacently; serenely; good-naturedly; tolerantly; torpidly;
benevolently; warmly; humanely; ridiculously; excessively; uncommonly.

INDUSTRIALIST

verbs
enrich—; organize—; protect—; rouse—;
satisfy—; spur—; support—; urge—; —achieves; —derives; —directs; —governs; —
labors; —plies; —plods; —pushes; —submerges; —supplies; —yields to.
(See boss, executive, banker, farmer, manager.)

INDUSTRIOUS

adverbs
painfully; perseveringly; dependably; unremittingly; energetically; actively; carefully;
constantly; temperamentally; characteristically; busily; reliably; amazingly; unusually;
uncomplainingly; happily; cheerfully; unwaveringly; invariably; uniformly; persistently; insistently.

INDUSTRY

adjectives
domestic; ignorant; large; indefatigable;
honest; urban; diversified; pious; prodigious; persistent; purposeless; scheduled;
languid; necessitous; productive; peaceable;
incomparable; much-vexed; myriad-shaped;
indigenous; extraordinary; untiring; vast;
growing; refining; charming; laudable;
seasonal; unwearied; promising; middling;
patient; technical; all-absorbing; mingled;
damnable; unflagging; depression-born; unfaltering; modest; native; skilful; adoring;
subsidized; persistent; unaided; predominating; dark-armed.

verbs
blossom into—; bulwark—; chastise—; cow
—; cripple—; dislocate—; dominate—;
evolve into—; father—; fortify—; foster—;
gag—; merge—s; modernize—; organize—;
paralyze—; prod—; reconstruct—; regulate
—; rejuvenate—; resurrect—; retard—; revitalize—; revive—; sovietize—; speed up
—; stimulate—; subsidize—; threaten—;
tie up—; —booms; —buzzes; —collapses;
—flourishes; —languishes; —perks up; —
rallies; —squirms.
(See business, company, manufacture,
trade, profession, enterprise, pursuit, vocation.)

INEFFECTIVE

adverbs
tragically; pitifully; surprisingly; disappointingly; utterly; wholly; strangely; suddenly; finally; painfully; curiously; singularly; unluckily; occasionally; feebly; weakly; tiresomely; languidly; stodgily; pitiably.

INEFFICIENCY

verbs
affirm—; characterize by—; condemn—;
couch in—; degenerate to—; execute with—;
observe—; plague with—; rectify—; relapse

into—; remove—; suffer from—; —accounts for; —bankrupts; —impoverishes; —scandalizes; —ruins; overlook—.

(See carelessness, stupidity, indifference.)

INEFFICIENT

adverbs

tragically; hopelessly; pitiably; miserably; wretchedly; helplessly; feebly; provincially; ignorantly; ineptly; clumsily; awkwardly; nervously; bashfully; shyly; self-consciously; inexpertly; crudely; grossly; flagrantly; crassly; surprisingly; harmlessly; dreadfully.

INELEGANT

adverbs

crudely; slightly; uncommonly; highly; gracelessly; awkwardly; boorishly; garishly; stiffly; rudely; inartistically; roughly; gaudily; grotesquely; artificially; vulgarly; coarsely; remarkably; unbelievably; incredibly.

INEPT

adverbs

stupidly; frightfully; foolishly; vacuously; terribly; comically; unfortunately; incompetently; miserably; wretchedly; senselessly; painfully; embarrassingly; unserviceably; lamentably; deplorably; pitiably; dreadfully.

INEQUALITIES

adjectives

inevitable; seeming; shameless; mountainous; irritating; supplementary; patent; sensible; glaring; gross; parallactic; slight; planetary.

INEQUALITY

verbs

complain of—; conduce to—; consider—; detect—; dispute—; frown on—; grieve over—; lament—; observe—; occasion—; owe to—; reconcile—; rectify—; treat with —; —glares; —shocks· —unbalances.

(See injustice, inferiority.)

INERT

adverbs

passively; dully; drowsily; heavily; indolently; lethargically; noddingly; quietly; sluggishly; stupidly; torpidly; dreamily; idly; lazily; lumpishly; sleepily; motionlessly; somnolently; apathetically; callously; habitually; unusually; uncommonly; phlegmatically; unconcernedly; imperturbably.

INERTIA

adjectives

gross; somber; amiable; ordinary; insurmountable.

verbs

display—; fall into—; force—; lull into—; overcome—; reform—; shed—; stimulate—; subject to—; suspend—; weary of—; while away in—; —consumes; —dulls; —prevents; —resists; —weakens.

(See indolence, idleness.)

INEVITABLE

verbs

accept—; bow to—; buck—; condone—; defer—; foresee—; foretell—; ignore—; predict—; prophesy—; resign to—; resist—; submit to—; yield to—.

(See fate.)

adverbs

tragically; embarrassingly; naturally; terribly; certainly; fatally; lamentably; fortunately; happily; awfully.

INEXCUSABLE

adverbs

wholly; altogether; entirely; manifestly; naturally; shamefully; hopelessly; flagrantly; scandalously; unfortunately; unluckily; irremediably; absolutely; admittedly; gravely; seriously.

INEXHAUSTIBLE

adverbs

boundlessly; generously; abundantly; luxuriantly; gorgeously; happily; naturally; apparently; miraculously; fortunately; surprisingly; evidently; marvelously; inexplicably; mysteriously; curiously; oddly; utterly; strangely; copiously; exuberantly; lavishly; gratefully; pleasantly.

INEXORABLE

adverbs

terribly; unfeelingly; unsympathetically; brutally; stiffly; severely; hard-heartedly; stonily; coldly; utterly; unreasonably; unaccountably; inexplicably; pitilessly; merci-

648

lessly; scornfully; pitiably; miserably; craftily; rigidly; uncompromisingly; austerely; haughtily; cruelly; tyrannically; imperiously; unsparingly; puritanically; authoritatively.

INEXPEDIENT
adverbs
palpably; obviously; awkwardly; inconveniently; embarrassingly; perplexingly; intricately; vexatiously; disconcertingly; bewilderingly; obstructively; objectionably; viciously; manifestly; utterly; clearly; painfully; glaringly; grossly; senselessly; terribly; grotesquely.

INEXPENSIVE
adverbs
surprisingly; amazingly; curiously; naturally; gratifyingly; delightfully; fortunately; conveniently; attractively; prudently; unexpectedly; cleverly; luckily; agreeably; pleasingly; remarkably; quite; comparatively.

INEXPLICABLE
adverbs
altogether; fantastically; utterly; strangely; inscrutably; mysteriously; peculiarly; mystifyingly; obscurely; darkly; capriciously; captiously; wantonly; impulsively; curiously.

INFALLIBILITY
verbs
acquire—; admit—; assure of—; boast of—; confirm—; confute—; deride—; doubt—; judge—; overrate—; praise—; promise—; prove—; puff up with—; reveal—; strain —; tempt—; test—; witness—.
(See skill, judgment, ability, ingenuity.)

INFALLIBLE
adverbs
unctuously; smugly; pompously; arrogantly; sapiently; sagaciously; practically; usually; consciously; reputably; notoriously; admittedly; apparently; supposedly; avowedly; bumptiously; maddeningly; gallingly; offensively; ostentatiously; proudly; blusteringly; swaggeringly; curiously.

INFAMOUS
adverbs
scandalously; vilely; notoriously; unjustly; unutterably; inexpressibly; grossly; crassly; brazenly; wickedly; odiously; atrociously; unbelievably; incredibly; ingloriously; un-

mentionably; shamefully; arrantly; shockingly; outrageously; pitifully; atrociously; shabbily; fantastically; uncommonly; deplorably.

INFAMY
adjectives
unutterable; callous; clumsy; vilest; perpetual; crushing; immortal.

verbs
bear—; blot out—; brand—; challenge—; consign to—; deface with—; denounce—; doom to—; endure—; hold up to—; incur—; infer—; inflict—; mire with—; scar with —; suffer—; work—; —disgraces; —pains; —shames; stain with—.
(See disgrace, dishonor, shame, scandal.)

INFANCY
adjectives
smiling; philologic; unlearned; fretting; cherub; innocent; dauntless; endless; careless; slumbering; unpracticed; mewling.

verbs
cloud—; develop in—; emerge from—; extend—; form in—; foster from—; guide through—; impress in—; mould in—; nourish in—; nurse in—; plead—; regress to—; soothe in—; terrorize in—; train in—; utter in—; —precedes; —unfolds.
(See childhood.)

INFANT
adjectives
well-educated; squalling; bewildered; undipped; unvaccinated; sucking; clay-faced; blue-lipped; baptized; conventional; miraculous; swaddling; ragged; hungry; mute; speechless; suffering; sentient; premature; trustful; vigorous.

verbs
christen—; cradle—; cuddle—; govern—; guard—; guide—; pamper—; quell—; soothe—; suckle—; swaddle—; swathe—; wean—; —bawls; —chatters; —howls; — mewls; —prattles; —pukes; —scampers about; —squalls.
(See child, baby.)

INFANTRY
adjectives
redoubtable; intrenched; disciplined; unsupported; trampling; well-armed; spiritless.

verbs
collect—; distress—; snipe at—; —advances; —assails; —besieges; —charges; —defends; —guards; —harries; —invades; —maneuvers; —marches; —mops up; —parries; —peppers; —presses; —reconnoiters; —retreats; —shields; —storms; —strikes; —wars on.
(See army, regiment, soldier.)

INFATUATION
adjectives
judicial; sad; incomprehensible; girlish.

verbs
besot with—; blame—; blind with—; deride —; fire by—; free from—; infect with—; overcome by—; provoke—; resist—; suffer —; stun by—; —dazzles; —dopes; —overwhelms; —perturbs; —ruffles; —ruins; —sharpens; —thrills.
(See love, charm, passion, tenderness.)

INFECTION
adjectives
diphtheritic; acute; common; respiratory; wide-spread; bacterial; innocent; recurrent; severe.

verbs
breathe—; combat—; cope with—; contract —; convey—; diagnose—; eradicate—; escape—; expose to—; exterminate—; immunize against—; incise—; introduce—; localize —; predispose to—; purge of—; risk—; scatter—; transmit—; —derives from; —enters; —lingers; —ravages; —spreads.
(See disease, malady, plague.)

INFECTIOUS
adverbs
highly; dangerously; easily; alarmingly; uncommonly; definitely; positively; portentously; slightly; supposedly; allegedly; probably; surprisingly; remarkably; particularly; acutely; seriously; gravely; fearfully.

INFER (*v*)
adverbs
hastily; carelessly; vaguely; unfoundedly; unreasonably; absurdly; rationally; irresistibly; confidently.
(See imply, gather, deduce.)

INFERENCE
adjectives
decisive; ruinous; vague; astounding; pathological; unfounded; unreasonable; bare; typographical; absurd; rational; charitable; irresistible; justifiable; sharp.

verbs
accept—; argue—; condemn—; conclude—; consider—; deduce—; derive—from; dispute—; draw—from; indulge in—s; justify —; pour out—s; resent—; respect—; scoff at—; scorn—; —implies; —indicates; —insinuates; —troubles.
(See opinion, thought, conclusion, consequence.)

INFERENTIAL
adverbs
probably; carelessly; naturally; logically; ruinously; vaguely; obscurely; incontrovertibly; soundly; unreasonably; absurdly; fallaciously; shrewdly; undeniably; covertly; obviously.

INFERIOR
adverbs
hopelessly; comparatively; pitifully; manifestly; palpably; shockingly; appallingly; terribly; unmistakably; oddly; curiously; patently; apparently; greatly; dreadfully; mentally; physically; essentially; materially; utterly; inexplicably; unaccountably; unacceptably.

INFERIORITY
adjectives
decent; mental; intellectual; alleged; admitted.

verbs
burden with—; conceal—; consider—; curse —; detect—; experience—; fret over—; lament—; prove—; overcome—; suffer—; —anguishes; —cramps; —gnaws; —shames; —stings; —vexes.
(See complex, inequality, injustice, mediocrity.)

INFERNO
adjectives
gasoline; raging; lurid; hot; white.

INFEST (*v*)
adverbs
horribly; pestiferously; peculiarly; grossly; luxuriantly; unpleasantly; extraordinarily; perniciously; fatally.
(See overrun, haunt, annoy.)

adjectives
perilous; professed; stalwart.

adjectives
foolish; matrimonial; religious.

verbs
admit—; blot with—; commit—; confess—; flaunt—; inspire—; motivate—; repent—; reproach for—; sully with—; —dejects; —desolates; —destroys; —disgraces; —dishonors; —poisons; —stains; —taints; —threatens.
(See unfaithfulness, treachery, sin.)

verbs
advocate—; consider—; curb—; fill by—; halt—; introduce by—; lead to—; observe —; permeate through—; receive—; travel by—; —alarms; —breeds; —endangers; —preserves.
(See penetration.)

adverbs
gloriously; spiritually; divinely; ineffably; vastly; mysteriously; impenetrably; boundlessly; immensely; incomprehensibly; fearfully; occultly; unknowably; inexpressibly; incalculably; unapproachably; unfathomably; immeasurably.

verbs
ascend into—; dwell in—; infringe on—; lead to—; measure—; pattern—; range in —; represent—; understand—; yield to—.
(See eternity.)

adverbs
decrepitly; weakly; languidly; brokenly; defenselessly; helplessly; pitiably; unbelievably; horribly; lamentably; pathetically; nervously; powerlessly; shakily.

adjectives
physical; hideous; besetting; divine; mortal; unique; growing; venial; deplorable; quotidian; speedy.

verbs
bare—; bear—; brace—; discover—; escape —; lament—; linger in—; master—; pretend—; relieve—; suffer—; trample on—; —blights; —constrains; —desolates; —despairs; —enfeebles; —gnaws; —relents; —restrains.
(See weakness, feebleness, illness, disease.)

adverbs
superficially; fatally; excessively; chronically; temporarily; painfully; treasonably.
(See provoke, excite.)

adverbs
highly; criminally; uncommonly; easily; dangerously; seriously; illegally; hazardously; perilously; probably; indubitably; instantly; terribly; extremely.

adjectives
excessive; fatal; chronic.

verbs
allay—; avert—; check—; clear up—; confine—; diminish—; excite—; indicate—; palliate—; reduce—; relieve—; subdue—; undergo—; —abates; —accompanies; —extends to; —proceeds; —ravages; —sustains.
(See infection, sore, ulcer, pain.)

verbs
advocate—; authorize—; block—; border on —; condemn—; criticize—; distrust—; head for—; predict—; propose—; puff by—; resort to—; spike—; suffer—; threaten—; veer from—; —benefits; —devaluates; —dilates; —distends; —enhances; —swells.
(See expansion, prosperity, depression, success.)

adverbs
rigidly; obdurately; stiffly; arrogantly; austerely; autocratically; brutally; strictly; imperiously; domineeringly; tyrannically; sharply; rigorously; hardly; haughtily; inexorably; peremptorily; severely; uncompromisingly; unsparingly; sternly; hatefully; notoriously; intolerably; heartbreakingly; obstinately; tenaciously; resolutely; de-

terminedly; stubbornly; unreasonably; consistently; immovably; indomitably; unflinchingly.

INFLICT (v)

adverbs

thoughtlessly; painfully; cruelly; heavily; superfluously; unpleasantly; perniciously.

(See impose, strike.)

INFLUENCE

adjectives

prevailing; inspirational; disintegrating; brutalizing; powerful; benignant; incalculable; tidal; starry; tyrannical; fructifying; sinister; corrosive; parental; controlling; good; withering; gentler; similar; malevolent; baneful; potent; intimate; political; soft; corrupt; personal; iron; sullen; defiant; hypnotic; restless; formative; considerable; disorganizing; maleficent; variable; appealing; cogent; malign; permanent; mephitic; evil; favorable; insidious; pathetic; depressing; scathing; consequent; important; solemn; educational; disastrous; restraining; controlling; enormous; gentle; diminishing; inhibiting; compelling; helpful; mesmeric; mysterious; deadly; healing; persuasive; warping; demoniac; sober; useful; fair; stabilizing; decisive; overgrown; beauteous; internal; unquestioned; uncanny; court; mellow; moonlight; human; morbid; fierce; undue; wide; partisan; precious; magical; reviving; environmental; divine; hypnotic; genial; disciplinary; evangelical; adverse; favorable; prodigious; conservative; calamitous; censorial; baleful; demoralizing; ultimate; subtle; revolutionary; wholesome; destined; dispiriting; sobering; extensive; marked; destructive; foreign; soothing; vague; reassuring; mitigated; pernicious; gracious; jangling; exhilarating; sympathetic; refining; prenatal; stupefying; quickening; heinous; softening; enlightening; literary; guiding; imponderable; predisposing; invigorating; moral; repressing; ethnographical; incalculable; territorial; desolating; broadening; omnipotent; overgrown; weakening; irritating; lasting; liberal; credible; spreading; tremendous; single; sinister; poetical; disquieting; profound; invariable; witching; dominating; unconscious; balmiest; hasty; compensating; ultimate; environing; secret; disturbing; proportional; steadying; damping; unperceived; dwarfing; ennobling; corrupting; subtle; secondary; political; immense;

beneficent; various (pl); salutary; vast; transcendent; despotic; commanding; trivial; sovereign; civilizing; protective; nerve-depleting; subjective; potential; blighting; wide-spread; many-mingled; reflex; problematical; sacred; sweet; transitory; misleading; ethical; marvelous; awful; antecedent; beneficial; unmindful; pernicious; jealous; vivifying; magical; subsequent; unexampled; infinite; invasive; emotional; soothing; tranquilizing; blasting; benumbing; propitious; aesthetic; toughening; gladdening; immediate; suggestive; carnicular; lost; predominating; underhand; materializing; mollifying; all-embracing; unconditional; mitigating; restraining; icy; moderating; celestial; superlative; narrowing; inaugurating; perceptible.

verbs

arrest—; bow to—; broaden—; come under —of; cramp—; curb—; diffuse—; exercise —; exert—; fall under—; impose—; infuse —; labor under—; lend—; manifest—over; measure—; multiply—; paralyze—; preserve from—; press—; promote—; reflect—; resist—; spread—; stem—; subject to—; survive—; wield—; yield to—; —bends; — corrupts; —declines; —extends to; —prevails; —reigns; —sways; —undermines; — wanes.

(See control, sway, prestige, persuasion, authority, strength, power.)

INFLUENCE (v)

adverbs

profoundly; powerfully; significantly; phenomenally; subsequently; adversely; unduly; vitally; strikingly; insensibly; unwillingly; remotely; benignantly; brutalizingly; parentally; malevolently; banefully; hypnotically; depressingly; exhilaratingly; despotically; jealously; morbidly; restrainingly.

(See induce, compel.)

INFLUENTIAL

adverbs

highly; remarkably; mysteriously; darkly; extremely; generally; peculiarly; politically; financially; notoriously; ominously; dangerously; alarmingly; helpfully; socially; nationally; sagaciously; powerfully; disastrously; enormously; quietly; calmly; tremendously; profoundly; artfully; immensely; persuasively; craftily; openly; obviously; palpably; manifestly; inexplicably; unaccountably; marvelously; wisely; secretly.

adjectives
vast; miraculous; steady.

INFORM (*v*)
adverbs
tremulously; blandly; personally; authoritatively; gruffly; unequivocally; officially; credibly; curtly; superficially; confidentially; comprehensively; fallaciously; dogmatically.
(See instruct, notify.)

INFORMAL
adverbs
graciously; intimately; delightfully; carelessly; charmingly; elaborately; deliberately; artfully; intentionally; happily; sweetly; pleasantly; amiably; agreeably; enchantingly; surprisingly; naively; remarkably; attractively; naturally; oddly; unexpectedly; heartily; cordially; diplomatically; exceedingly; habitually.

INFORMALITY
adjectives
pleasant; admirable; well-bred; delightful; charming.

INFORMATION
adjectives
instructional; imparted; common; broiling; miscellaneous; superficial; authentic; precise; vague; coordinating; scanty; solid; criminal; practical; household; substantial; summarized; trustworthy; factual; accurate; elusive; genuine; scientific; encouraging; inviting; astounding; exact; useful; further; detailed; comprehensive; false; up-to-the-minute; startling; practical; reliable; usable; behind-the-scenes; understandable; fallacious; gloomy; invaluable; superfluous; curious; anterior; accumulated; tabulated; profit-building; current; comparative; restricted; dogmatic; fascinating; unpleasant.

verbs
abound in—; absorb—; accumulate—; acquire—; authenticize—; bear—; buttress—; clamor for—; compile—; contribute—; convey—; coordinate—; correlate—; derive—; dig out—; digest—; dispense—; disseminate—; distort—; divulge—; elicit—; falsify—; garner—; glean—; impart—; misinterpret—; plead for—; prod for—; pump for —; relay—; rely on—; retail—; solicit—;

summon—; suppress—; tabulate—; thirst for—; unburden oneself of—; utilize—; verify—; volunteer—; vouchsafe—; wheedle—; withhold—; worm—; yield—; —embodies; —leaks out.
(See knowledge, intelligence, data, facts, understanding, wisdom, science, statistics.)

INFRACTION
verbs
accuse of—; chastise for—; condemn—; detect—; fine—; harass by—; lament—; overlook—; penalize—; plague with—s; suffer —.
(See breach, error, violation, infringement.)

INFREQUENT
adverbs
painfully; frigidly; usually; remarkably; vexatiously; probably; luckily; fortunately; gratifyingly; uncertainly; erratically; undeniably; mysteriously; inscrutably; happily; negligibly.

INFRINGEMENT
verbs
abet—; allege—; curb—; enjoin—; observe —; protest—; punish—; resent—; restrain —; rue—.
(See violation, breach, infraction.)

INFUSION
adjectives
organic; putrescible; imperceptible; sterilized; steeped; imaginable; dormant.

INGENIOUS
adverbs
cleverly; artfully; skilfully; unusually; notably; famously; remarkably; adroitly; particularly; artistically; diplomatically; admirably; amazingly; marvelously; helpfully; extremely; capably; intelligently; unbelievably; exceedingly; dexterously; expertly; deftly; resourcefully; smartly; shrewdly; incredibly.

INGENUE
adjectives
raw; artless; guileless.

INGENUITY
adjectives
considerable; mechanical; inventive; misguided; speculative; wonderful; naive;

fiendish; subtle; puerile; interwoven; productive; devilish; unbetrayed; calumnious; extraordinary; conjectural.

verbs
acknowledge—; conceive by—; defy—; demand—; display—; employ—; excel in—; encourage—; endow with—; exercise—; feign—; invent by—; observe—; profit by —; strain—; swathe in—; tax—; witness—; —conquers; —triumphs.
(See infallibility, skill, ability, genius.)

INGENUOUS

adverbs
youthfully; openly; childishly; pleasantly; unsuspectingly; candidly; naturally; sincerely; innocently; honestly; frankly; bluntly; marvellously; unusually; unexpectedly; utterly; exceedingly; extraordinarily; surprisingly; amazingly; strikingly; astonishingly; miraculously; unaffectedly.

INGRATIATING

adverbs
deliberately; skilfully; artfully; politically; purposely; pleasantly; craftily; disgustingly; abjectly; insidiously; invidiously; diplomatically; amiably; curiously; elaborately; obsequiously; ceremoniously; suavely; gently; courteously; urbanely; gallantly; unctuously; blandly; cordially; affably; civilly; extremely.

INGRATITUDE

adjectives
occasional; habitual; horrible; foul; base.

verbs
brood over—; complain of—; denounce—; expose to—; suffer—; taint with—; treat with—; wipe out—; —barbs; —bites; —bruises; —oppresses; —pains; —pierces; —provokes; —shames; —thrives; —undermines.
(See oppression, infidelity, treachery, selfishness.)

INGREDIENTS

adjectives
healing; costly; dry; delicious; sifted; accidental; sweetening; unintelligible; prominent; basic; malicious; principal; choicest; modern; balanced; seething; pernicious; commonplace; poisonous; necessary; muddy; nutritive; nourishing.

verbs
adjust—; analyze—; calculate—; concoct of —; denounce—; discover—; gather—; measure—; memorize—; mix—; note—; prepare —; produce—; reduce—; separate—; skimp on—; test—.
(See parts, elements, materials.)

INHABIT (v)

adverbs
thinly; comfortably; successively; wretchedly; swarmingly; solely; misguidedly; placidly; domestically; humbly.
(See abide, dwell, live.)

INHABITANTS

adjectives
strange; glorious; unmolested; unobtrusive; aboriginal; intimate; permanent; larger; wretched; respective; awe-struck; diverse; fortunate; cordial; respectable; unambitious; rustic; brawny; feathered; defenceless; plague-stricken; tender; placid; amazed; pious; ancient; wretched; swarming.

verbs
confer on—; consider—; entitle — to; grant to—; privilege—; regulate—; rule—; urge —; —attend; —benefit; —complain; —congregate; —dwell; —enjoy; —frequent; —organize; —rejoice; —revolt; —rise; —tenant; —welcome.
(See individual, native.)

INHALE (v)

adverbs
audibly; deeply; luxuriously; spasmodically; gaspingly; sharply; agonizingly; laboriously.
(See breathe.)

INHARMONIOUS

adverbs
unpleasantly; inexplicably; annoyingly; disastrously; inexcusably; unreasonably; utterly; frequently; mysteriously; obscurely; unnecessarily; strangely; disgustingly; fearfully; ominously; significantly; unbelievably; oddly; curiously; extremely.

INHERENT

adverbs
disturbingly; ineradicably; indubitably; obviously; manifestly; fortunately; happily; palpably; deeply; essentially; fundamentally.

INHERIT (v)
adverbs

legally; unexpectedly; spectacularly; dramatically; nominally; traditionally; customarily; fortunately.

(See receive, possess, derive.)

INHERITANCE
adjectives

dismal; fairest; fallen; ill-starred; astounding; storied; entailed; occasional; moderate; racial.

verbs

administer—; bequeath—; bless with—; come into—; confirm—; derive—from; divide—; enjoy—; entitle to—; forfeit—; forsake—; grant—; lay claim to—; portion—; preserve—; profit by—; relinquish—; restore to—; scatter—; squander—; succeed to —; tax—; —enriches; —falls to.

(See legacy, estate, money, property, profits.)

INHIBITION
verbs

detect—; express—; harass by—; incur—; persecute with—; proceed from—; remove —; suffer—; sympathize with—; veil—; vent—; —arrests; —disappears; —haunts; —plagues; —restrains; —restricts; —torments; —tortures.

(See restraint, fear, complex, restriction.)

INHOSPITABLE
adverbs

strangely; rudely; uncivilly; inexcusably; curiously; coldly; unpardonably; deliberately; openly; ostentatiously; purposely; discourteously; oddly; inexplicably; unaccountably; miserably; wretchedly; terribly; gruffly; brusquely; roughly; distinctly; unsociably; churlishly; ungraciously; forbiddingly; extremely; unforgettably; peculiarly; remarkably; significantly.

INHUMAN
adverbs

brutally; brutishly; curiously; incredibly; savagely; unbelievably; strangely; deliberately; barbarously; cruelly; ferociously; atrociously; ruthlessly; relentlessly; fiendishly; fantastically; viciously; diabolically.

INIMICAL
adverbs

essentially; radically; fundamentally; altogether; naturally; antagonistically; malevolently; maliciously; secretly; mysteriously; inexplicably; unaccountably; strangely; unreasonably; obviously; oddly; unexpectedly; palpably; manifestly; significantly; sadly; violently; spitefully; constitutionally; ominously; dangerously.

INIMITABLE
adverbs

altogether; remarkably; utterly; incomparably; peerlessly; brilliantly; perfectly; artistically; preciously; peculiarly; delightfully; faultlessly; avowedly; reputedly; presumably.

INIQUITIES
adjectives

conjugal; juvenile; aged; crowning; manifest.

INIQUITOUS
adverbs

atrociously; unbelievably; inexpressibly; unspeakably; obscenely; heinously; invidiously; egregiously; inordinately; exceptionally; unmentionably; diabolically; grievously; irremediably; banefully; criminally; unwarrantably; immorally; unimaginably; viciously; nefariously; malevolently; impiously; unconscionably; basely; vilely; savagely.

INIQUITY
verbs

acquit of—; bring forth—; cleanse of—; cling to—; conceive of—; confess—; defile with—; delight in—; disclose—; drown in —; forgive—; foul with—; perish in—; punish for—; purge of—; rebuke—; redeem from—; reveal—; steep in—; taint with—; turn from—; work—; —flourishes.

(See sin, wickedness, abomination, crime.)

INITIATE (v)
adverbs

festively; ceremoniously; dramatically; annually; imaginatively; originally; forcefully; beneficently.

(See begin, instruct, introduce.)

INITIATION
adjectives

practical; exceptional; unwilling; elementary; baptismal.

adjectives

unusual; private; unfettered; individual; untrammeled; unparalleled; aggressive; independent; popular.

verbs

cripple—; crush—; curb—; demonstrate—; develop—; display—; encourage—; exhibit —; imbue with—; kill—; manifest—; observe—; praise—; provoke—; reward—; —activates; —yields.

(See originality, ability, skill, genius, proficiency.)

INJECT (v)

adverbs

hypodermically; intravenously; insidiously; spitefully; slyly; salaciously; maliciously; medically; scientifically; methodically.

(See put, introduce, insert, interject.)

INJUDICIOUS

adverbs

thoughtlessly; senselessly; foolishly; indiscreetly; imprudently; childishly; heedlessly; vengefully; ignorantly; unintentionally; unfortunately; sadly; disastrously; blindly; rashly; impulsively; impetuously; adventurously; heedlessly; inexpediently; recklessly; wantonly; stupidly; ridiculously; absurdly.

INJUNCTION

adjectives

solemn; serious; conflicting; sternest; strict; vehement; permanent; pretty; curt; tacit; restraining; temporary.

verbs

apply for—; consecrate—; deny—; enforce —; grant—; hand down—; justify—; obey —; refuse—; suspend—; sustain—; —bans; —bars; —blocks; —restrains; —restricts; —ties up.

(See action, order, instructions, command, requirement.)

INJURE (v)

adverbs

severely; dangerously; wilfully; critically; incurably; shockingly; permanently; unwittingly; atrociously; wantonly; gravely; internally; materially; irreparably.

(See damage, hurt, wound.)

adjectives

atrocious; potent; wanton; conscious; protracted; sinister; dreaded; serious; widespread; multiplied; repeated; grave; previous; internal; incredible; permanent; material; mental; disabling; irreparable; incalculable.

INJURIOUS

adverbs

distinctly; presumably; definitely; positively; irremediably; slightly; surprisingly; distressingly; unintentionally; indiscreetly; mysteriously; maliciously; deliberately; desperately; highly; perniciously; seriously; destructively; tragically; outrageously.

INJURY

verbs

avenge—; bewail—; compensate for—; entail—; expose to—; inflict — upon; insure against—; occasion—; preserve from—; proclaim—; receive—; recover from—; recuperate from—; resist—; suffer—; sustain—; work—; —cripples; —outrages; —restricts; —unnerves.

(See wound, damage, wrong, outrage, mischief, pain, injustice.)

INJUSTICE

adjectives

murderous; temporary; wanton; cruel; tyrannic; abominable; cruelest; flagrant; social; crowning; peculiar; horrible; artistic; shocking; unspoken; treacherous; inherent; unintentional; immemorial; atrocious; gross.

verbs

accept—; attack—; belabor—; bewail—; brood over—; cite—; crush with—; decry —; denounce—; detect—; eliminate—; extirpate—; impose—; inflict—; lament—; inveigh against—; persist in—; reek of—; remedy—; sense—; shrink from—; swallow —; wallow in—; work—.

(See inequality, injury, unfairness, grievance, wrong.)

INK

adjectives

corroding; potent; sympathetic; invisible.

verbs

battle with—; blacken with—; blot with—; cloud with—; color with—; dilute—; dip into—; drip—; eject—; expel—; reservoir

—; smear—; smirch with—; —blurs; —spatters; —spots; —stains.
(See paint.)

INMATES
adjectives
temporary; cowering; exasperating; feeble-minded; querulous; miserable-looking; destitute; licentious; unhappy; mad.

INN
adverbs
dwell in—; establish—; frequent—; keep—; lodge in—; maintain—; put up at—; repair to—; reside in—; sojourn at—; stop at—; —accommodates; —houses; —invites; —provides; —quarters; —warms; —welcomes.
(See hotel, home, apartment, tavern.)

INNOCENCE
adjectives
harmless; loveliest; virgin; extreme; spotless; intrinsic; recognized; inviolable; unsuspecting; helpless; strange; fulsome; unabashed; childish; deliberate; despairing; injured; elaborate; pretended; starry; lofty; conscious; departed; primitive; heavenly; gentle; hapless.

verbs
assert—; betray—; commend—; despoil—; feign—; guard—; hallow—; immortalize—; jeopardize—; maintain—; plead—; prey on —; protest—; prove—; seduce—; smile in - -; vindicate—.
(See purity, simplicity, sincerity.)

INNOCENT
adverbs
delightfully; childishly; naturally; legally; sweetly; presumably; girlishly; charmingly; playfully; beautifully; helplessly; apparently; manifestly; palpably; irresistibly; gently; essentially; virtuously; positively; artlessly; sincerely; unaffectedly; ingenuously; frankly; admirably; unbelievably; happily; refreshingly; naively; touchingly; wonderfully; alluringly; graciously; ravishingly; exquisitely; alluringly; adorably.

INNOCUOUS
adverbs
utterly; advantageously; valuably; unobjectionably; vacuously; inoffensively; negligibly; presumably; probably; wholesomely; safely; undoubtedly; definitely.

INNOVATION
adjectives
striking; political; unquiet; distasteful; ghastly; outward; unauthorized; startling; tyrannical; interesting; radical; endless; inexpedient; recent; countless (pl).

verbs
champion—; clamor for—; curb—; demand —; disapprove of—; discourage—; favor—; plan—; protest against—; resist—; sprout —; stay—; suspect—; welcome—; —attracts; —improves; —revolutionizes; encourage—.
(See change, improvement, style, fashion, movement.)

INNUENDO
adjectives
unspoken; malicious; biting; salacious.

verbs
convey by—; employ—; indulge in—; insinuate by—; interpret—; utter—; —annoys; —hints; —implies; —intimates; —libels; —peeves (colloq.); —puzzles; —slanders; —suggests.
(See insinuation, suggestion.)

INOCULATE (*v*)
adverbs
successfully; scientifically; experimentally; automatically; prudentially.
(See protect, insert, introduce, inject.)

INOFFENSIVE
adverbs
utterly; safely; negligibly; warrantably; assuredly; surely; completely; wholly; avowedly; indubitably; satisfactorily; fairly; probably; quietly; amiably; diplomatically; wisely; sagaciously; discreetly.

INOPERATIVE
adverbs
provokingly; vapidly; vexatiously; hopelessly; idly; lately; legally; harmlessly; untenably; wholly; utterly.

INOPPORTUNE
adverbs
awkwardly; embarrassingly; vexatiously; wholly; singularly; peculiarly; financially; politically; commercially; disastrously; unfortunately; presumably; socially; signally;

seriously; unfortunately; unluckily; inexpediently; inaptly; clumsily; stupidly; foolishly; terribly; sadly; miserably; wretchedly.

INQUIRE (v)

adverbs
solicitously; perfunctorily; boldly; mischievously; curiously; sarcastically; diligently; concernedly; incredulously; laconically; superficially; placidly; ominously; bluntly; officially; passionately; skeptically; apprehensively; dolorously; innocently; curtly.

(See ask, seek, question.)

INQUIRER

adjectives
individual; diligent; curious; historical; philosophical; profane.

INQUIRY

adjectives
investigational; liberal; audacious; vindictive; studious; calm; dispassionate; laconic; rigorous; extensive; horrified; breathless; minute; confidential; particular; skeptical; recent; diligent; patient; successful; urgent; sarcastic; apprehensive; exacting; troubled; cold; sanctioned; sleepy; dolorous; fruitless; competent; respectful; troublesome; subsequent; eager; physical; point-blank; thorough; sincere; innocent; direct; discreet; pertinent; scientific; suave; vain; solid; indefinite; tentative; strict; sad; accurate; unthinking; suspicious; sarcastic; mild; hospitable; formal; curt; brisk; brash.

verbs
bombard with—s; conduct—; deter—; institute—; meet—; occasion—; overwhelm with —s; press—; provoke—; pursue—; push—; renew—; repeat—; reply to—; resume—; subject to—; waive—; —discloses.

(See question, investigation, research, examination.)

INQUISITION

adjectives
tyrannous; ceaseless; imperious; bootless; comfortable; solemn; merciless; cruel.

verbs
demand—; escape—; fall foul of—; justify —; launch—; occasion—; propose—; search by—; suggest—; sweep by—; —explores; —irks; —proves; —reviews; —trespasses.

(See investigation, inquiry, research.)

INQUISITIVE

adverbs
inordinately; offensively; curiously; oddly; persistently; maliciously; meddlesomely; tiresomely; offensively; venomously; innocently; harmlessly; miserably; distressingly; unpardonably; inexcusably; discourteously; unforgivably; dangerously; significantly; alarmingly; intellectually; scientifically; intrusively; pryingly; mysteriously; egregiously; openly; expertly; officiously; relentlessly; impolitely; boundlessly; insatiably.

INQUISITORS

adjectives
delegated; persecuting; mealy-mouthed; death-dealing.

INROADS

adjectives
destructive; perpetual; frequent; constant; serious; casual; blighting.

INSANE

adjectives
wildly; slightly; probably; mildly; presumably; avowedly; violently; slightly; permanently; periodically; pathetically; tragically; recently; allegedly; notoriously; dangerously; pitiably; miserably; hopelessly; irremediably; irrecoverably; dreadfully; incurably; utterly; deliriously; fanatically; eccentrically; hysterically; incoherently; distressingly.

INSANITY

adjectives
true; warlike; intellectual; temporary; dire; pious; incipient; incurable; speculative; hysterical; harmless; systematic; delusional; hereditary.

verbs
anticipate—; banish—; border on—; condemn to—; correct—; detect—; discern—; drive to—; hush—; lament—; lead to—; observe—; plead—; produce—; sense—; simulate—; subdue—; suffer—; thrust into —; treat—; —desolates; —imprisons; — seizes; overcome—.

(See mania, madness, frenzy, delirium.)

INSATIABLE

adverbs
greedily; voraciously; miserably; shamelessly; hungrily; terribly; pitiably; rapacious-

ly; unbelievably; curiously; strangely; grossly; avidly; covetously; cravingly; sordidly; openly; manifestly.

INSCRIBE (v)
adverbs
lightly; erroneously; appropriately; decoratively; legibly; hieroglyphically; tenderly; officially; historically.
(See imprint, write.)

INSCRIPTION
adjectives
analogous; trilingual; sham; inappropriate; monumental; absorbing; cuneiform; simple; lofty; horizontal; decorative; legible; duplicate; flattering; mural; libelous; hieroglyphical; ominous; effaced.

verbs
bear—; carve—; chisel—; decipher—; engrave—; furnish—; mark—; pen—; place —; study—; survey—; trace—; word—; — adorns; —commemorates; —dedicates; — denotes; —heads; —indicates; —records; — reminds.
(See record, handwriting, monument, document.)

INSCRUTABLE
adverbs
mysteriously; oddly; hopelessly; curiously; impenetrably; altogether; strangely; utterly; unaccountably; wholly.

INSECT
adjectives
individual; venomous; luminous; aculeate; industrious; blundering; coral; silken-winged; bloated; noisome; dormant; swarming; glittering; populous; all-devouring; melodious; gorgeous; countless (pl); injurious; ubiquitous; energetic; acquisitive; sweet; throbbing; mottled; destructive; painless; annoying; voracious; multitudinous (pl).

INSECTS
verbs
allure—; breed—; combat—; exterminate—; feed on—; hunt—; lure—; net—; overrun with—; trap—; —annoy; —buzz; —demolish; —devour; —dismantle; —distress; — fertilize; —hum; —nest; —pest; —plague; —pupate; —ravage; —sap; —settle on; — swarm; —swirl; —undergo a metamorphosis; —creeps.
(See individual insects.)

INSECURE
adverbs
pitiably; alarmingly; distressingly; fearfully; hopelessly; flimsily; embarrassingly; awkwardly; vaguely; bewilderingly; precariously; dangerously; carelessly; inexcusably; critically; ominously; perilously; curiously; dreadfully; horribly; undeniably; fatally; continuallly; wearily; professionally; pathetically; apprehensively; uncomfortably; anxiously; tormentingly; grievously; financially.

INSENSIBLE
adverbs
curiously; stolidly; dully; apathetically; sluggishly; languidly; torpidly; utterly; callously; indifferently; phlegmatically; drowsily; somnolently; sleepily; stupidly; dazedly; obtusely; lethargically; imperturbably; inattentively; unconcernedly; unbelievably; incredibly.

INSEPARABLE
adverbs
affectionately; insistently; physically; scientifically; technically; financially; politically; logically; commercially; naturally; cohesively; firmly; solidly; tenaciously; securely; legally; authoritatively; officially; warrantably.

INSERT (v)
adverbs
parenthetically; expressly; daily; meticulously; formally; officially; logically; derogatorily.
(See inject, interject.)

INSIDIOUS
adverbs
peculiarly; subtly; dangerously; alarmingly; appallingly; cunningly; shrewdly; terrifyingly; particularly; shockingly; ominously; uncomfortably; deceptively; surreptitiously; elusively; fraudulently; slyly; profoundly; cleverly; artfully; astutely; shabbily; wickedly; perfidiously; shamefully; trickily.

INSIGHT
adjectives
clearer; intuitive; vivid; profound; spiritual; rare; true; mythic; penetrating; partial; uncanny; sympathetic; psychological;

pathetic; keen; intellectual; comprehensive; steady; sagacious; curious; imaginative; prophetic; dramatic; clearest; scientific; objective; valid; mature; mystic.

verbs

acquire—; endow with—; flash—; follow with—; furnish with—; gain—; give—; lack—; obtain—; possess—; ripen into—; understand through—; —comprehends; —discerns; —fathoms; —penetrates; —perceives; —rewards; —searches.

(See understanding, wisdom.)

INSIGNIA

adjectives

distinguishing; military; graceful.

INSIGNIFICANCE

adjectives

paltry; essential; sallow; miserable; puny.

verbs

bury in—; crouch in—; dwindle into—; fade into—; pale into—; plunge into—; reduce to—; ridicule—; scorn—; sink into—; spring from—; suffer—; —engulfs; —prostrates; —swallows.

(See obscurity, seclusion, trifle, oblivion.)

INSIGNIFICANT

adverbs

altogether; negligibly; admittedly; avowedly; inconsequentially; weakly; pitifully; contemptibly; ridiculously; vaguely; absurdly; fatuously; inanely; pathetically; terribly; ultimately.

INSINCERE

adverbs

woefully; curiously; obviously; strangely; indubitably; palpably; hopelessly; arrantly; evidently; shamefully; transparently; absurdly; slyly; evasively; pretentiously; flatteringly; cruelly; insidiously; bitterly; clearly; unmistakably; grossly; dreadfully.

INSINCERITY

verbs

abhor—; charge with—; clog with—; condemn—; detect—; embroider with—; engage in—; falsify with—; incline toward—; witness—; —adulterates; —deceives; —disgraces; —disguises; —distorts; —forfeits; —shames.

(See unfaithfulness, treachery, deception, hypocrisy.)

INSINUATE (v)

adverbs

brazenly; slanderously; coyly; pointedly; delicately; calumniously; offensively; adroitly; covertly; reticently; outrageously.

(See imply, hint, suggest.)

INSINUATION

adjectives

calumnious; conscientious; adroit; slanderous; covert; nasty; reticent; evil; unguarded; offensive; outrageous; terrible; unfortunate; slow.

verbs

contemplate—; dare—; defeat—; deliver—; dispose of—; omit—; perceive—; weigh—; wince at—; —alludes; —creeps in; —hints; —implies; —informs; —instills; —shocks; —suggests.

(See accusation, innuendo, intimation, suggestion, hint.)

INSIPID

adverbs

stupidly; feebly; unusually; habitually; naturally; hopelessly; tiresomely; vacuously; fatuously; colorlessly; vexatiously; tediously; prosaically; dully; doltishly; inertly; passively; phlegmatically; listlessly; lackadaisically; recklessly; uninterestingly; monotonously; depressingly; unbearably.

INSIPIDITY

adjectives

conventional; slumbrous; stereotyped.

INSIST (v)

adverbs

hotly; glowingly; indignantly; belligerently; stolidly; perversely; deliberately; pedantically; resolutely; pointedly; pertinaciously; disobligingly; uniformly; emphatically; vehemently; strenuously; obstinately; blandly; sternly; eloquently.

(See urge, persist, press.)

INSISTENCE

adjectives

stern; steadfast; deliberate; important; melancholy; eloquent; perpetual; pathetic; stereotyped.

verbs

assert with—; increase—; relax—; require —; silence—; steel against—; stick with—;

—annoys; —conquers; —determines; —irks; —relents.

(See persistence, determination, intensity, perseverance.)

INSISTENT

adverbs

vexatiously; tiresomely; intolerably; annoyingly; captiously; peevishly; cruelly; tyrannically; discourteously; violently; disagreeably; unpleasantly; hospitably; generously; aggressively; inescapably; urgently; embarrassingly; pestiferously; cantankerously; distressingly; dictatorially; resolutely; firmly; tenaciously; obstinately.

INSOLENCE

adjectives

haughty; increasing; disobedient; smiling; beefy; studied; ferocious; displeasing; gigantic; personal; insane; wanton; flat-faced; mutinous; puffed.

INSOLENT

adverbs

unbearably; atrociously; arrogantly; proudly; haughtily; arrantly; inordinately; egregiously; intolerably; ridiculously; unpardonably; disrespectfully; terribly; flippantly; pertly; saucily; crudely; grossly; abusively; outrageously; outlandishly; scandalously; loudly; brazenly; crassly; bumptiously; imperiously; highly; audaciously; inexcusably.

INSOLVENT

adverbs

pitiably; suddenly; finally; pathetically; unfortunately; admittedly; hopelessly; sorrowfully; desperately; deeply; unluckily; unhappily; impecuniously; embarrassingly; ruinously; unaccountably; inexplicably; mysteriously; curiously; incredibly; needlessly.

INSOMNIA

verbs

afflict with—; conquer—; correct—; ease—; grapple with—; labor under—; release—; subject to—; suffer—; —hinders; —interferes; —provokes; —stupefies; —unnerves; —weakens.

(See disease, pain.)

INSOUCIANT

adverbs

inconsiderately; blithely; giddily; dizzily; heedlessly; dreamily; gaily; cheerily; carelessly; unconcernedly; imperturbably; recklessly; rashly; serenely; calmly; heartily.

INSPECT (v)

adverbs

intently; circumspectly; fastidiously; judiciously; rigidly; periodically; personally; cursorily; cautiously; painstakingly.

(See examine, investigate.)

INSPECTION

adjectives

immediate; rigid; bare; painstaking; periodic; cursory; cautious; personal.

INSPIRATION

adjectives

passionate; fatal; unmistakable; fresh; happy; healthier; subtle; verbal; sudden; heroic; divine; adequate; overpowering; mystic; elevated; dramatic; inward; maternal; incarnate; mighty; unbiased; natural; irrepressible; sustaining; struggling; feeblest; laborious; ennobling.

verbs

conflict with—; derive—from; exhaust—; foster—; gain—; kill—; presage—; pray for—; preserve—; restore—; suppress—; whisper—; —cheers; —flags; —rallies; —seizes; —visits; —wells from.

(See enthusiasm, fervor, influence, genius.)

INSPIRE (v)

adverbs

religiously; divinely; nocturnally; unceasingly; invariably; passionately; fatally; happily; subtly; verbally; heroically; mystically; dramatically; maternally; irrepressibly; feebly; laboriously; tenderly.

(See kindle, arouse, rouse, animate.)

INSTABILITY

adjectives

emotional; molecular; psychic; permanent; mental.

verbs

aggravate—; betray—; buttress—; condemn—; convey—; deplore—; detect—; judge—; lament—; lead to—; observe—; reflect on—; reform—; support—; survey —; —irks; —threatens.

(See weakness, impotence.)

INSTALL (*v*)

adverbs

magnificently; ceremoniously; regularly; comfortably; formally; scientifically; modernistically; charitably; governmentally; legislatively; dictatorially.

(See establish, place.)

INSTALLMENT

verbs

administer—; commend—; consent to—; direct—; glorify—; herald—; honor by—; influence—; inspire—; invite to—; observe—; occasion—; perform—; plan—; preside at —; seek—; view—; —climaxes; witness—.

(See payment.)

INSTANCE

adjectives

contradictory; isolated; individual; noteworthy; wonderful; abundant; well-authenticated; striking; inconsiderable; parallel; continued; dramatic; precise; memorable; far-famed; admirable; melancholy; conspicuous; arresting; notable; forcible; unfortunate; characteristic; splendid; abortive; comparable; notorious; tragic; recorded; solitary; unrelated; typical; worthy; particular; extreme; delightful; present; illustrious; rare; undeniable; remarkable.

verbs

afford—; cite—; contradict—; demand—; dispute—; experience—; furnish—; multiply —s; offer—; point out—; provide—; quote —; ridicule—; solicit—; study—; —exemplifies; —illustrates; —indicates; —proves; —reminds.

(See example, illustration, precedent.)

INSTANT

adjectives

unseasonable; luminous; approaching; flashing; terrible; fleeting; single; breathless; fatal; swift.

verbs

accomplish in an—; convey in—; depart for —; emerge in—; flicker out in—; pause for —; separate for—; —passes; —presses.

(See moment, hour, time.)

INSTIL (*v*)

adverbs

ridiculously; subtly; insidiously; cleverly; slyly; perfidiously; covertly; mystically; paternally; scholastically.

(See introduce, impress, implant.)

INSTINCT

adjectives

poetic; indefinable; impulsive; hereditary; faithful; natural; holy; warm; brutal; prophetic; profoundest; subtle; dramatic; vague; combative; protective; military; proper; religious; beneficent; noble; aesthetic; conservative; inherited; artistic; self-preserving; denied; invisible; maternal; unerring; refined; gentle; deepest; semi-barbaric; perverted; animal; sterile; amorphous; conservative; universal; deep-rooted; formal; ennobled; delicate; driving; human; heroic; grosser; native; transcendental; tameless; sympathetic; long-dormant; disorderly; journalistic; monastic; social; irresistible; fine; quality; predominating; **provident**; spiritual; tender; wonderful; mechanical; prudential; fiery; grateful; innate; sudden; scientific; imperative; sure; trained; superhuman; speculative; irrrelevant; snob; groping; gregarious; terrible; herd; independent; fortunate; selective; kindly; unconscious; purest; common; iconoclastic; logical; racial; brutal; derogatory.

verbs

cloud—; control—; curb—; develop—; endow with—; follow—; gratify—; numb—; obey—; offend—; pander to—; rely on—; repress—; rouse—; stir—; succumb to—; suppress—; thwart—; violate—; —deceives; —guides; —impels; —motivates; —persists; —s war within.

(See impulse, desire, skill, nature.)

INSTITUTION

adjectives

frail; cherished; extraordinary; charitable; religious; popular; temporary; essential; instrumental; professional; venerable; august; notable; existing; ecclesiastical; sacerdotal; preparatory; necessary; time-honored; infant; remarkable; major; peculiar; sundry (pl); aristocratic; feudal; fiduciary; diverse (pl); flourishing; ancient; dignified; free; popular; bestial; inevitable; liberal; respective; lauded; social; distinctive; dominant; economic; benevolent; perfidious; bureaucratic; long-established; various (pl); abhorrent; moneyed; powerful; notorious; parochial; superb; monstrous.

verbs

abolish—; acclaim—; bar from—; charter —; commit to—; confirm—; discard—; endow—; grant to—; herd in—s; lampoon—;

maintain—; patronize—; support—; undermine—; —crumbles; —flourishes.

(See establishment, club, society, school.)

INSTRUCT (v)

adverbs

peremptorily; urgently; artistically; solemnly; forcefully; adequately; laconically; ethically; clinically; parochially; tediously; theoretically; intellectually; facetiously; vaguely; academically; formally; inspirationally; diligently.

(See teach, command, direct.)

INSTRUCTION

adjectives

adequate; hurried; scattered; bloody; laconic; inevitable; careful; explicit; brave; ethical; botanical; clinical; stimulative; parochial; official; minute; thoughtful; elementary; theoretical; intellectual; facetious; pleasurable; cabled; hazy; vague; religious; tedious; classroom; parliamentary.

verbs

abide by—; attend to—; authorize—; comply with—; conform to—; contravene—; counsel—; deluge with—; desire—; disqualify for—; follow—; hearken to—; impart—; lack—; overwhelm with—s; prescribe—; profit by—; radio—; refuse—; —corrects; —guides.

(See teaching, information, education.)

INSTRUCTOR

adjectives

clerical; capable; competent; sober; sordid; reticent.

INSTRUMENT

adjectives

physical; master; keyboard; gracious; godlike; negotiable; outstanding; dictating; grand; musical; ingenious; expensive; unfit; precision; potent; rude; glorious; philosophical; penitent; facile; perfect; rough; extraordinary; noble; exceptional; component; heavenly; murderous; incomprehensible; spellbound; blunt; passive; unconscious; compact; scorned; supple; astronomical; serviceable; quaking; dental; cunning; greedy; sacred; tolerable; immediate; graceful.

verbs

contaminate—; contrive—; devise—; employ—; encase—; fashion—; forge—; guard —; hamper—; hinder—; introduce—; lubricate—; manipulate—; obstruct—; perform with—; project—; resist—; utilize—; yield to—.

(See tool, utensil, method, document, machine.)

INSTRUMENTAL

adverbs

definitely; helpfully; necessarily; admittedly; covertly; secretly; furtively; openly; proudly; ostentatiously; usefully; diabolically; benevolently; obscurely; inscrutably; valuably; serviceably; fortunately; capably; competently.

INSUBORDINATE

adverbs

insufferably; unbearably; intolerably; recklessly; rashly; brazenly; sullenly; subtly; openly; unaccountably; deliberately; arrantly; accidentally; purposely; unconsciously; unpardonably; hopelessly; grossly; crassly; flagrantly; slyly; audaciously; mutinously; seditiously; treacherously; incredibly; restively; impatiently; egregiously; amazingly; dangerously; childishly; senselessly.

INSUBORDINATION

adjectives

sharp; colonial; criminal; flagrant; rank.

INSUBSTANTIAL

adverbs

terribly; hopelessly; tragically; nebulously; imaginatively; dreamily; pitifully; wretchedly; airily; tenuously; vaguely; dimly; altogether; blankly; obviously; utterly.

INSUFFERABLE

adverbs

utterly; disagreeably; incredibly; altogether; haughtily; boisterously; rudely; arrantly; grossly; crassly; crudely; boorishly; arrogantly; swaggeringly; scornfully; loudly; maliciously; slanderously; invidiously; importunately; abhorrently; odiously; generally.

INSUFFICIENT

adverbs

pitiably; tragically; wretchedly; altogether; stingily; parsimoniously; unbelievably; evidently; palpably; ungenerously; thoughtlessly; piteously; miserably; criminally; incredibly; shockingly; appallingly; awfully.

adverb

incredibly; happily; safely; securely; narrowly; narrow-mindedly; bigotedly; fanatically; contentedly; smugly; dogmatically; stupidly; surprisingly; naturally; peacefully; complacently; inordinately; rustically; provincially.

INSULT

adjectives

harsh; unfeeling; endurable; rash; crowning; biting; personal; cruel; grossest; veiled; monstrous; fresh; mortal; stinging; deadly; persistent; dire; supposed; petty.

verbs

avenge—; barb with—; bawl—; brook—; condone—; decry—; endure—; exchange —s; fling—at; hurl—at; ignore—; shout—; suffer—; take affront at—; —grieves; — infuriates; —libels; —rebuffs; —slanders; pardon—.

(See outrage, offense, wrong.)

INSULT (v)

adverbs

scurrilously; desperately; vilely; impudently; grossly; brazenly; outrageously; sullenly; wantonly; unendurably; monstrously.

(See affront, abuse, offend.)

INSULTING

adverbs

horribly; unpardonably; intolerably; unbearably; insufferably; boorishly; cruelly; subtly; covertly; sneeringly; cynically; ironically; openly; deliberately; intentionally; inexcusably; coarsely; grossly; publicly; superciliously; impudently; flagrantly.

INSUPPORTABLE

adverbs

altogether; evidently; manifestly; fantastically; obviously; heavily; tragically; pitiably; wretchedly; lamentably; indubitably; visibly; shockingly; pitifully; physically; painfully; grievously; finally; oppressively; tormentingly.

INSURANCE

verbs

collect—; consider—; examine for—; obtain —; pay—; prefer—; refuse—; regulate—; transfer—; value—; undertake—; under-

write—; —guarantees; —indemnifies; —invests; —lapses; —provides; —reassures; —safeguards.

(See security, guarantee.)

INSURE (v)

adverbs

prudentially; customarily; rashly; paradoxically; conventionally; conservatively; liberally.

(See protect, assure.)

INSURGENTS

verbs

accede to—; beat down—; check—; disperse —; inflame—; kindle—; quell—; repel—; repulse—; rout—; stir—; subdue—; — arise; —conspire; —demand; —dictate; intrigue; —occupy; —oppose; —overthrow; —plot; —revolt; —spring up; —tyrannize.

(See enemy, rebel, foe, rival, competitor.)

INSURMOUNTABLE

adverbs

heavily; oppressively; appallingly; manifestly; admittedly; apparently; perplexingly; bafflingly; absurdly; desperately; seriously; gravely; unfortunately; curiously; altogether; legally; disconcertingly; embarrassingly; awkwardly; cruelly.

INSURRECTION

adjectives

muting; wide-spread; hopeless; subsequent; servile; absurd; serious; laughable; domestic.

verbs

check—; conspire—; crush—; encourage—; engage in—; excite—; finance—; foment—; head—; inflame—; instigate—; kindle—; plot—; quell—; resist—; restrain—; support—; suppress—; —alarms; —breaks out; —bursts forth; —dismays; —endangers; — menaces; —sweeps away; —threatens.

(See revolution, rebellion, fight.)

INTACT

adverbs

blessedly; luckily; fortunately; incredibly; happily; visibly; safely; securely.

INTANGIBLE

adverbs

evanescently; undeniably; practically; dimly; vaguely; obscurely; fleetingly; provokingly; legally; foggily; indeterminately; temporally; darkly; unintelligibly; naturally; mysteriously; faintly.

INTEGRITY

adjectives

territorial; constitutional; innate; unimpeachable; sturdy; delicate; unassailable; sterling; unbending; unquestioned; determined; administrative; incorruptible; moral; transparent; intellectual; perfect; stubborn; stern; indisputable.

verbs

blemish—; breed—; commend—; doubt—; esteem—; impair—; laud—; maintain—; note—; preserve—; question—; require—; reserve—; retain—; reward—; root in—; taint—; test—; trust—; sacrifice—; vow—.
(See honesty, virtue, truth, sincerity.)

INTELLECT

adjectives

cultured; keen; expanded; happy; considerable; godlike; high; stern; jaded; powerful; sluggard; prostrated; ruthless; unclouded; benighted; noble; restless; unguided; comprehending; austere; elevated; sluggish; brilliant; ordinary; lofty; inferior; articulate; frightened; active; provincial; haggard; fertile; ripening; profound; undying; imperial; superior; aroused; cultivated; crudest; discerning; prepared; meddling; humble; cold; resourceful; human; shadowy; penetrating; colossal; wavering; uninformed; grasping; singular; mightiest; reasoning; many-sided; stagnant; refined; stirring; seraphic; all-subtilizing; amazing; constructive; massive; eternal.

verbs

balance—; cobweb—; cultivate—; destroy—; dissipate—; distort—; educate—; enlarge—; enthrone—; excel in—; expand—; impair—; judge—; perfect—; reflect—; shake—; sharpen—; stunt—; train—; weigh —; —comprehends; —deteriorates; —discerns; —enslaves; —revolts; —speculates.
(See brain, mind, understanding, intelligence.)

INTELLECTUAL

adverbs

proudly; blatantly; swaggeringly; consciously; brilliantly; immensely; keenly; sharp-

ly; shrewdly; astutely; highly; profoundly; seriously; soberly; cleverly; solidly; alarmingly; incredibly; gravely; heavily.

INTELLIGENCE

adjectives

earliest; remorseless; keen; patient; banded; reassuring; native; alarming; sluggish; subtlest; extreme; swift; alert; shrewd; melancholy; luminous; elusive; mysterious; afflicting; morbid; restless; human; vulgar; musing; diagnostic; presiding; matrimonial; conscious; coherent; welcome; obvious; informed; supreme; unwonted; infinite; unexpected; hideous; magnified; detached; unfailing; lofty; meanest; mediocre; wide; untutored; vivid; concentrated; prophetic; polished; quick; weakened; precocious; unclouded; creative; clear; rapid; rarefied; omniscient; cheering; passive; divine; sympathetic; disagreeable; crushing; cold; hard; penetrating; astounding; musical; sharp; sad; singular; diseased; supreme; bizarre; energetic; pure; sagacious.

verbs

approach with—; assert—; bow to—; brim with—; dim—; dull—; endow with—; exercise—; gamble on—; impart—; mock—; radiate—; register—; reveal—; sharpen—; subjugate—; —controls; —dominates; —governs.
(See ability, intellect, insight, mind, wisdom, talent.)

INTELLIGENT

adverbs

unwontedly; keenly; patiently; naturally; alarmingly; subtly; extremely; swiftly; alertly; shrewdly; mysteriously; vigilantly; restlessly; consciously; obviously; supremely; unexpectedly; unfailingly; infinitely; broadly; loftily; vividly; prophetically; creatively; precociously; clearly; omnisciently; cheeringly; sympathetically; divinely; disagreeably; coldly; penetratingly; warmly; astoundingly; singularly; sagaciously; apparently; cleverly; profoundly; fairly; thoughtfully; politically; discriminatingly; manifestly; exceedingly; significantly.

INTELLIGIBLE

adverbs

wholly; fairly; hardly; easily; surprisingly; scarcely; explicitly; instantly; graphically; unmistakably; strikingly; barely; clearly.

verbs

abstain from—; addict to—; atone for—; avoid—; betray—; burst with—; cure—; drown in—; err through—; fall into—; forego—; indulge in—; outlaw—; rack by —; sink into—; slide into—; —burns; —clouds; —defaces; —degenerates; —dissipates; —reigns; —sickens.

(See drunkenness, excess, debauchery, wickedness.)

INTEMPERATE

adverbs

foolishly; fatally; recklessly; dangerously; rashly.; unaccountably; senselessly; extravagantly; voluptuously; luxuriously; wildly; rakishly; drunkenly; dreadfully; occasionally; habitually; notoriously; absurdly; preposterously; dissolutely; indiscreetly.

INTEND (*v*)

adverbs

characteristically; primarily; virtually; incalculably; originally; complimentarily; ostensibly; wantonly; subtly; unquestionably; maliciously; tyrannically; amiably; cruelly; dictatorially; loyally; jocularly; irreverently.

(See design, propose.)

INTENSIFY (*v*)

adverbs

vividly; inordinately; furiously; dramatically; emotionally; subjectively; morbidly; infinitely; fiercely; tragically; gloriously.

(See aggravate, emphasize, magnify.)

INTENSITY

adjectives

intermediate; decreasing; dreadful; lyrical; savage; scorching; barbarous; varying; unsurpassable; dramatic; clear; severe; low; unequal; mystical; emotional; subjective; white-faced; waning; morbid; infinite; desired; fierce; bare; dramatized; tragic; peculiar; heightened; glorified.

verbs

denote—; exhibit—; glow with—; increase —; live with—; measure—; note—; observe —; register—; relax—; revive—; slacken —; —grows; —overcomes; —strains; —taxes; —tires; —trebles; —wanes.

(See energy, force, strength, power, zeal.)

adjectives

deliberate; wicked; mad; late; charitable; swift; amorous; bad; fierce; conscious; absurd; unlawful; evil; original; sublime; obvious; malicious.

adverbs

curiously; strangely; absently; wholly; abstractedly; oddly; deeply; eagerly; deliberately; carefully; wisely; impressively; earnestly; seriously; closely; resolutely; diplomatically; considerately; thoughtfully; critically; studiously; markedly; vigilantly; flatteringly; raptly; breathlessly; zealously; uncommonly.

INTENTION

adjectives

serious; deliberate; immoral; especial; tyrannous; docile; murderous; honorable; ulterior; honest; supposable; amiable; emotional; benignant; cordial; cruel; benevolent; wicked; wise; avowed; hospitable; definite; travelling; alleged; evil; dictatorial; loyal; earthly; original; industrial; festive; greedy; hostile; fixed; charitable; unconscious; evident; speculative; objective; cold; calculated; liberal; apparent; pacific; testamentary; treacherous; profound; matrimonial; suicidal; warlike; irreverant; jocular; private.

verbs

burst with—; cancel—; communicate—; conceal—; declare—; deny—; disavow—; disclaim—; err in—; impede—; miscarry—; misconstrue—; mistake—; proclaim—; purify—; reaffirm—; reiterate—; relinquish—; stick to—.

(See plan, aim, desire, purpose.)

INTERACTION

adjectives

ethical; unsuspected; incessant; harmonious.

INTERCEPT (*v*)

adverbs

subtly; dexterously; slyly; treacherously; inimically; jealously; hatefully; selfishly; zealously; perfidiously.

(See seize, take, prevent.)

INTERCHANGE

adjectives

healthful; interesting; provident; sweet; social; savage; constant; wearisome; pleasant; mutual; rapid; unfettered.

INTERCOURSE

adjectives

sexual; amicable; continual; free; frigid; convivial; pleasant; innocent; mutual; beautiful; intimate; unrestrained; sweet; genial; delightful; formal; beneficial; unhappy; courteous; social; personal; vile; intimate; habitual; commercial; unreserved; constant; diplomatic; friendly; frequent; intellectual.

verbs

abstain from—; avoid—; bind by—; carry on—; discontinue—; employ—; encourage —; engage in—; limit—; open—; overindulge in—; prevent—; prohibit—; refrain from—; relax—; stimulate—; survey—; — balances; —debilitates; —declines; —increases.

(See communication, commerce, conversation, traffic, transaction.)

INTERDICT (v)

adverbs

solemnly; formally; legally; tyrannically; dictatorially; officially; religiously.

(See restrain, repress.)

INTEREST

verbs (attention or concern)

absorb—of; accentuate—; alienate—; attach — to; awaken—; betoken—; catch—; cultivate—; dim—; display—; distract—; eclipse —; elicit—; engage—; enlist—; evoke—; excite—; exude—; feed—; feign—; focus—; inspire—; intensify—; kill—; kindle—; lend —; manifest—; muster—; note with—; pique—; quicken—; recapture—; regain—; revive—; rivet — upon; share—; smother—; stimulate—; sustain—; switch—; whip up —; —abates; —s bind; —centers on; — deepens; —ebbs; —endures; —fades; — flags; —mounts; —palls; —picks up; — wanes; engross—.

(See concentration, attention, vigilance.)

INTEREST

adjectives (general)

far-flung; special; national; religious; commercial; personal; passing; indulgent; individual; detached; momentous; property; selfish; minority; friendly; complicated; irresistible; affected; benevolent; primary; historic; philanthropic; superstitious; restrained; exorbitant; busy; final; jarring;

well-meant; equal; presbyterian; literary; pecuniary; mercantile; great; attentive; missionary; extreme; evident; general; popular; genuine; lively; mournful; careful; bosom; paradoxical; private; growing; central; probable; pathetic; worldly; fraternal; universal; renewed; confessed; touching; paramount; amused; sudden; indifferent; satirical; feverish; certain; philosophic; intelligent; lasting; considerable; painful; respective; appalling; intense; thoughtful; overrated; immense; absorbing; surpassing; ultimate; connected; warm; widespread; national; stealthy; furtive; insistent; proprietary; vital; languid; energetic; diverse; bibliographical; thrilling; ennobling; peculiar; intellectual; overmastering; economic; vital; theoretical; active; gloomy; bankrupt; principal; endless; suave; urgent; sustained; human; racial; keenest; direct; jealous; discriminating; tepid; shadowy; languid; overmastering; contemporaneous; extraordinary; exclusive; philosophical; characteristic; surpassing; aesthetic; childish; anthropological; particular; enduring; extraneous; antiquarian; truant; exaggerated; crowning; inimical; lofty; revived; enormous; satisfying; undisturbed; parochial; medieval; ancient; awesome; never-ceasing; student; sectional; humanitarian; public-spirited; diminished; real; sincere; insatiable; courteous; pathological; unutterable; coincidental; deepest; involved; expressional; inexhaustible; controlling; active; exceptional; long-nursed; wistful; faintest; unconquered; vaguest; passionate; grim; chauvinistic; lukewarm; vested; ethical; interwoven; compounded; dark; conflicting; perfunctory; elusive; persistent; particular; academic; world-wide; critical; heightened; potential; imperialist; affectionate; ignorant; domestic; alarmed; burning; solicitous; stirring; sordid; discriminating; perplexing; antipodal; lingering; dissimilar (pl).

INTEREST
(*financial*)

verbs

affect—; amass—; cater to—; cherish—; control—; defend—; enlarge—; enumerate —; fortify—; foster—; merge—; promote —; regulate—; represent—; safeguard—; strengthen—; subverse—; unite—s of; weld —s of; —s flourish; —s overlap; —s prosper.

(See business, advantage, good, benefit.)

667

INTEREST
(*money*)

verbs

bear—; borrow on—; calculate—; charge —; claim—; compound—; entitle to—; fix —; figure—; forfeit—; obtain—; reckon—; request—; return—; subtract—; —accrues; —compensates; —taxes.

(See amount, sum, money, profit.)

INTEREST (*v*)

adverbs

proportionately; consistently; particularly; profoundly; excessively; keenly; genuinely; ingeniously; intensely; moderately; religiously; commercially; selfishly; affectionately; benevolently; philanthropically; paradoxically; jealously; philosophically; passionately; perfunctorily; academically; potentially; solicitously.

(See concern, excite.)

INTERESTING

adverbs

thrillingly; absorbingly; breathlessly; specially; historically; extremely; generally; genuinely; intensely; vitally; economically; extraordinarily; particularly; pathologically; vaguely; curiously; keenly; charmingly; strangely; attractively; pleasantly; engrossingly; marvelously; especially.

INTERFERE (*v*)

adverbs

boisterously; materially; consciously; energetically; unreasonably; irrationally; officiously; arrogantly; providentially; destructively; judicially; jealously; enviously; vindictively.

(See conflict, intermeddle, intervene.)

INTERFERENCE

adjectives

slightest; untimely; impertinent; feeble; ill-judged; arrogant; avoidable; unwarranted; providential; destructive; judicial; intolerant; mutual; optical; hostile; unexpected; unauthorized; supernatural; jealous; imperative; humane; watchful; hot; outside; needless; powerful.

verbs

brook—; counteract—; encounter—; inveigh against—; justify—; oppose—; overcome—; provoke—; refrain from—; resent—; restrict—; tolerate—; withdraw—; —agitates;

—blocks; —chokes; —clogs; —disheartens; —distresses; —hinders; —impedes; —meddles; —retards.

(See opposition, collision, intervention, resistance, hostility, obstacle.)

INTERIOR

adjectives

distinctive; ambitious; distinguished; sumptuous; superb; opaque; domestic; webby; capacious; unmodified; colonial; costly; austere; musty; dusty; wretched; pierced.

verbs

acquaint with—; advance into—; creep into —; display—; enter—; harmonize—; invade —; line—; lose in—; penetrate—; press into —; pry into—; push into—; situate in—; withdraw into—; worm into—; —awes; —impresses; —unfolds.

(See jungle, recess, middle, center.)

INTERJECT (*v*)

adverbs

bitingly; devoutly; unexpectedly; harshly; abruptly; piercingly; rudely; coarsely; fiercely; wittily; indignantly; unreasonably; nervously; ferociously; instructively; irritatingly.

(See inject, insert.)

INTERLINE (*v*)

adverbs

warmly; richly; comfortably; luxuriously; expensively; matchlessly; ornamentally.

INTERLOCUTOR

verbs

employ—; —acquaints; —amuses; —announces; —asserts; —communicates; —corrects; —explains; —expresses; —informs; —instructs; —interferes; —interposes; —introduces; —intrudes; —leads; —prompts; —opens; —outlines.

(See speaker, debater, actor, clown.)

INTERLUDE

adjectives

strange; musical; brief; charming; circling; underworld; calm.

INTERMENT

adjectives

pious; showy; honorable.

INTERMINGLE (v)

adverbs

gregariously; grotesquely; democratically; unrestrictedly; swarmingly; offensively; perpetually; extraordinarily.

(See mingle, mix.)

INTERMISSION

adjectives

seasonable; lucid; irregular (pl); much-needed.

INTERMIXTURE

adjectives

occasional; subtle; helpful.

INTERPOSE (v)

adverbs

unwillingly; deftly; providentially; mercifully; mysteriously; deliberately; fortunately; designedly; vainly; aggressively; zealously; blankly.

(See intervene, interrupt.)

INTERPOSITION

adjectives

deft; timely; providential; renewed; merciful; divine.

INTERPRET (v)

adverbs

literally; objectively; narrowly; allegorically; sympathetically; intelligently; boldly; unfavorably; adequately; superficially; metaphysically; speculatively; offensively; poetically; charitably; mythologically.

(See translate, construe, render.)

INTERPRETATION

adjectives

superficial; corresponding; metaphysical; polyphonic; diverse (pl); legal; rabbinical; speculative; conflicting; mental; probable; ingenious; thoughtful; offensive; fascinating; authoritative; understandable; subtle; mystic; poetic; mythological; imperfect; lyric; base; musical; scriptural; allegorical; inexperienced; uncharitable.

verbs

abuse—; accept—; advance—; broaden—; contemplate—; correct—; deduce—; evolve —; hand down—; infer—; lend—; misconstrue—; misquote—; offer—; reiterate—; reject—; question—; scorn—; —mutilates; —signifies.

(See conception, explanation, idea.)

INTERPRETER

adjectives

urbane; euphuistical; noble; zealous; penetrating; coarse; apt; false; picturesque.

INTERROGATE (v)

adverbs

sumptuously; rudely; impudently; roughly; impishly; boldly; formally; characteristically; frankly; pompously; fraternally; authoritatively.

(See question, examine.)

INTERROGATION

adjectives

incredible; fresh; impish; wondering.

INTERRUPT (v)

adverbs

rudely; joyously; hastily; frequently; blatantly; judiciously; indignantly; earnestly; conveniently; peremptorily; momentarily; irrelevantly; abruptly; vaguely; temporarily; prematurely; spasmodically; repetitiously.

(See interpose, obstruct, retard.)

INTERRUPTION

adjectives

frequent; serious; spasmodic; jarring; abrupt; stern; absolute; continual; palpable; reasonable; momentary; temporary; unseemly; extraordinary; external.

verbs

attempt—; beg—; forgive—; hinder with —; tolerate—; welcome—; wince at—; witness—; —angers; —disturbs; —infringes; —provokes; —severs; —thwarts.

(See pause, rudeness, impudence, delay.)

INTERSPERSE (v)

adverbs

widely; thoroughly; comfortably; regularly; conveniently; occasionally; methodically.

(See mix, scatter, distribute.)

INTERTWINE (v)

adverbs

inextricably; elaborately; amorously; delicately; endlessly; complexly; haphazardly; artfully; skilfully; curiously.

(See entangle, twine, wind.)

INTERVAL

adjectives

slender; irregular; fitting; considerable;

feeding; torpid; measured; painful; equidistant; suitable; stated; frequent (pl); wide; fathomless; varying (pl); tranquil; rapid; indeterminate; endless; rare; twilight; reasonable; precious; dreadful; starless; recurring; lucid; mystical; harmonic; immeasurable; brief; stipulated; enormous; ensuing; conceivable; stolen; lesser; unflattering; spasmodic; long.

verbs
administer at—s; bridge—; consider in—; designate at—s; doze at—s; fill—; fritter away—; grant—; increase—s; pause for—; regulate—s; review—; sleep at—s; span—; —annoys; —delays; —separates; —vanishes.

(See space, pause, distance.)

INTERVENE (v)
adverbs
actively; impetuously; diabolically; miraculously; demoniacally; indiscreetly; venomously; slyly; paternally; hatefully; habitually; jealously.

(See interpose, interrupt.)

INTERVENTION
adjectives
armed; miraculous; indiscreet; diabolical; perpetual; untoward; demoniacal.

verbs
appeal for—; approve of—; consider—; decry—; denounce—; deplore—; employ—; exercise—; frame—; grant—; necessitate—; plead for—; seek—; terminate—; —aids; —annoys; —impedes; —interrupts; —irks; —relieves; —wanes.

(See opposition, interference, resistance.)

INTERVIEW
adjectives
satisfactory; valuable; confiding; affecting; complicated; unauthorized; interesting; clandestine; frequent; stormy; remarkable; painful; expressive; tussling; unchaperoned; vesper; transient; short-sighted; frank; preliminary; childish; protracted; brief; unexpected; psychoanalytic; parting; unsatisfactory; disastrous.

verbs
allow—; chronicle—; conclude—; confine—to; demand—; draw into—; elicit in—; endure—; evade—; grant—; obtain—; promise—; publish—; report—; request—; seek

—; shirk—; terminate—; transpire at—; —degrades; —reveals; —tires; —wearies.

(See discussion, talk, conversation, conference.)

INTERVIEW (v)
adverbs
genially; professionally; confidentially; journalistically; daily; secretly; clandestinely; politically.

(See question.)

INTERWEAVE (v)
adverbs
artfully; intimately; mysteriously; dexterously; laboredly; elaborately; delicately; ornamentally; richly; intricately.

(See weave, intermingle.)

INTERWEAVING
adjectives
labored; dexterous; endless; elaborate; delicate.

INTESTINE
verbs
afflict—; attach to—; attack—; block—; clog—; constrict—; distend—; ferment in—; penetrate—; poison—; puncture—; obstruct —; putrefy in—; strangle—; twist—; —absorbs; —adheres; —coils; —discharges; —functions; —kinks; —mats; —provides.

INTIMACY
adjectives
annoying; agreeable; increasing; pleasant; peculiar; apparent; unfriendly; amorous; unseemly; lifelong; affectionate; curious; surprised; seeming; daily; closest; sudden; true; delicious; clandestine; immemorial; homely; rare; patronizing; embarrassed; mutual.

verbs
attempt—; brook—; court—; crush—; desire —; display—; draw back from—; enjoy—; enter with—; establish—; forbid—; question—; poison—; press into—; relax—; resist—; ripen into—; solicit—; strike up—; —arises; —mitigates; —reveals; —springs up.

(See friendship, fellowship, companionship, love, tenderness.)

adverbs

exceptionally; reprehensibly; curiously; inordinately; strangely; charmingly; closely; unusually; uncommonly; pleasantly; affectionately; embarrassingly; oddly; sweetly; confidentially; particularly; peculiarly; singularly; artlessly; cordially; devotedly; companionably; agreeably; gently; graciously; unbecomingly.

INTIMATE (*v*)

adverbs

bitterly; silently; darkly; distinctly; simultaneously; tacitly; mystically; officially; unpleasantly; slyly; diabolically; delicately; plausibly.

(See hint, indicate.)

INTIMATION

adjectives

slightest; evident; injurious; mystical; official; silent; scattered; delicate; subjective; free; previous; unpleasant.

verbs

acknowledge—; advance—; contemplate—; dare—; furnish—; heed—; perceive—; ridicule—; seek—; weigh—; —creeps in; —denotes; —hints; —indicates; —informs; —interests; —leaks out; —notifies; —suggests.

(See accusation, innuendo, hint, suggestion, implication.)

INTIMIDATE (*v*)

adverbs

illegally; jealously; forcefully; unfairly; fiercely; ferociously; ruthlessly; formidably; economically; physically; deliberately; rudely.

(See frighten, scare, threaten.)

INTIMIDATED

adverbs

brutally; constantly; illegally; criminally; unquestionably; evidently; horribly; cruelly; tyrannically; daily; perceptibly; ignorantly; ridiculously; spinelessly; terribly.

INTOLERABLE

adverbs

absolutely; painfully; finally; naturally; odiously; grievously; oppressively; grimly; abhorrently.

adjectives

fierce; unchecked; ecclesiastical; fiery; narrow; marked; wicked.

verbs

accuse of—; attend with—; campaign against—; deplore—; indicate—; observe—; overcome—; provoke to—; show—; suffer from—; —scorns; —shames; —treads on; —vitiates.

(See fanaticism, wickedness.)

INTOLERANT

adverbs

harshly; sternly; austerely; fretfully; rigidly; dogmatically; professionally; narrowly; ignorantly; generally; inexcusably; unduly; unpleasantly; disagreeably; terribly; inconsistently; strangely; extremely; conspicuously; arrogantly; superciliously; emphatically; stubbornly; obdurately; unyieldingly; cruelly; bitterly; provincially; fanatically; doctrinally; mulishly; doggedly; impatiently; fiercely; officially.

INTONATION

adjectives

pitying; different; soft; searching; ascending; calm; genuine; limpid; liquid; sweet; steadfast; wilful; contemptuous; languorous; asthmatic; nasal; characteristic; bellowing; lazy; nervous; guttural; perceptible; muffled.

INTONE (*v*)

adverbs

sanctimoniously; languorously; sepulchrally; melodiously; sweetly; gutturally; monotonously; characteristically.

(See speak, recite, sing.)

INTOXICATION

adjectives

subduing; complete; serene; habitual; partial; sweet; giddy; prolonged; utter; helpless.

INTRACTABLE

adverbs

perversely; incorrigibly; provokingly; vexatiously; unbearably; intolerably; stubbornly; wilfully; offensively; defiantly; utterly; doggedly; stolidly; wildly; capriciously; uncontrollably; cantankerously; mulishly; pitifully; violently; obstinately; scandalously;

sullenly; waywardly; formidably; hopelessly; restively; peevishly; churlishly; inveterately; narrow-mindedly.

INTRENCH (v)
adverbs
strongly; safely; securely; inviolably; firmly; strategically; protectively.
(See encroach, invade, entrench.)

INTREPID
adverbs
valorously; gallantly; chivalrously; boldly; feignedly; conversationally; swaggeringly; boastfully; audaciously; spunkily; resolutely; determinedly; heroically; valiantly; pluckily; marvellously; remarkably; uncommonly; adventurously; firmly; apparently; stoutly.

INTRICACY
verbs
comprehend—s; conceal in—s; conduct through—s; cut off—s; ease—; enmesh in —s; entangle in—s; involve—s; lessen—; map out—s; overcome—; probe—s; understand—; unravel—s; —bewilders; —complicates; —perplexes; —puzzles.
(See complication, complexity, tangle, confusion, obstruction.)

INTRICATE
adverbs
perplexingly; obscurely; obstructively; hopelessly; strangely; unduly; embarrassingly; objectionably; needlessly; terribly; deliberately; tortuously; subtly; awkwardly; formidably; provokingly; unnecessarily; clumsily.

INTRIGUE
adjectives
romantic; genuine; peaceful; violent; perpetual; criminal; sinuous; revolutionary; paltry; scandalous; sordid; ambitious; political; continental; double; indefatigable; dynastic; sacrilegious; abortive; tortuous; poor; clever; private.

verbs
bristle with—; conspire—; detect—; enjoy —; expose—; fall into—; infuse—; involve in—; meddle with—; plot—; plunge into—; share in—; stimulate—; uncover—; unearth —; —accomplishes; —deceives; —embarrasses; —mystifies.
(See adventure, plot, scheme, mystery.)

INTRODUCE (v)
adverbs
deliberately; simultaneously; ceremoniously; advantageously; casually; decorously; mischievously; commercially; conventionally; perfunctorily; unblushingly; orchestrally; formally.
(See present, insert, commence.)

INTRODUCTION
adjectives
preliminary; basic; promiscuous; impressive; appreciative; conventional; appropriate; perfunctory; coveted; improbable; wearisome; illicit; unblushing; depressing; orchestral; embarrassing; formal; labored.

verbs
contribute to—; crave—; demand—; manoeuvre—; plan—; prefix—; refuse—; survey—; wangle—; —agitates; —comments on; —communicates; —delights; —eulogizes; —explains; —makes known; —prepares; —presents.

INTRODUCTORY
adverbs
pleasantly; favorably; agreeably; courteously; smoothly; graciously; cordially; eulogistically; approvingly.

INTROSPECTION
adjectives
cold; morbid; pitiless.

INTROSPECTIVE
adverbs
curiously; unwontedly; unfortunately; unduly; overly; oddly; habitually; naturally; highly; sorrily; ominously; dangerously; morbidly; sensitively; pitifully; moodily; incurably; deplorably; lamentably; absurdly; miserably; incorrigibly; inveterately.

INTRUDE (v)
adverbs
presumptuously; bumptiously; rashly; irksomely; startlingly; irritatingly; exasperatingly; selfishly; jealously; obnoxiously; perpetually; pompously; impertinently; forcibly; abruptly; unwontedly.
(See obtrude, invade, encroach, intrench.)

INTRUDER

adjectives

base; peaceful; queenly; friendly; troublesome; miserable; solitary; murderous; burglarous.

verbs

dislodge—; dispose of—; eject—; evict—; ignore—; object to—; punish—; warn—; —disrupts; —encroaches; —forces; —infringes; —invades; —oversteps; —transgresses; —trespasses; —usurps.

(See robber, thief, villain, intrusion, invader, enemy.)

INTRUSION

adjectives

pompous; foul; resented; impertinent; forcible; involuntary; pale; swift; abrupt; noisy; hated; unwonted; rude.

verbs

deplore—; embitter by—; enter by—; excuse —; inform of—; loathe—; observe—; prevent—; protect from—; refuse—; threaten —; —disturbs; —pains; —violates; resent—.

(See intruder.)

INTRUSIVE

adverbs

obnoxiously; provokingly; annoyingly; uncommonly; meddlesomely; inexcusably; discourteously; inquisitively; amazingly; pertly; insolently; rudely; miserably; insidiously; abominably; maliciously; crudely; ignorantly; disgustingly; tiresomely; terribly; grossly; brazenly; persistently; unpardonably; troublesomely.

INTRUST (v)

adverbs

particularly; subsequently; willingly; tacitly; faithfully; confidently; authoritatively; cautiously; legislatively; medically; economically; pecuniarily; financially.

(See confide, commit.)

INTUITION

adjectives

divinest; deepest; pure; unerring; special; sensible; extraordinary; mysterious; half-desolate; womanly; instinctive; judicious.

INTUITIVE

adverbs

amazingly; marvellously; miraculously; naturally; uncommonly; highly; unusually; impulsively; vaguely; unscientifically; absurdly; inconsequently; notoriously; psychically; distinctly; infallibly; strangely; oddly; curiously; fantastically; unbelievably; astonishingly; incredibly; inconsequentially.

INVADE (v)

adverbs

ruthlessly; perilously; outrageously; ferociously; heartlessly; monstrously; totally; unnaturally; belligerently; bellicosely; illegally.

(See encroach, intrench, trespass.)

INVADER

adjectives

ruthless; ferocious; upstart; heathen; petty; expelled; filthy; ragged.

verbs

battle—; beat back—; drive off—; expose to —; harass—; repel—; resist—; vanquish—; withstand—; —assaults; —eludes; —encroaches; —entrenches; —infringes; —intrudes; —penetrates; —ravages; —violates.

(See enemy, intruder, army, troops, soldiers, multitude, robber.)

INVALID

adjectives

habitual; brave; gallant; bedridden; incurable; reeling; bawling; hopeless; feverish; nervous; marked; secluded; chronic; weak; despairing; comfortable; eager.

verbs

comfort—; delight—; discharge—; encourage—; entertain—; exhaust—; pension—; raise—; render—; report—; shelter—; treat —; visit—; —despairs; —recovers; —struggles.

adverbs

untenably; undeniably; groundlessly; absurdly; fallaciously; evasively; deceptively; cunningly; deplorably; legally; unluckily; unfortunately; inoperatively; spuriously; meretriciously.

INVALIDISM

adjectives

temporary; cruel; continual; increasing; nervous; chronic.

INVALIDITY

adjectives

established; judicial; utter; obvious.

INVALUABLE

adverbs

inestimably; extremely; marvellously; pricelessly; unusually; incredibly; astoundingly; wonderfully; indubitably; notoriously; distinctly; manifestly; prodigiously; extraordinarily; inexpressibly; unconscionably; unbelievably.

INVARIABLE

adverbs

incredibly; wonderfully; surprisingly; comfortingly; steadily; consistently; amazingly; warrantably; essentially; fundamentally; intrinsically; monotonously; habitually; drearily; tiresomely; hatefully; conventionally; agreeably; prosaically; typically; doctrinally; deliberately; wisely; purposely; designedly.

INVASION

adjectives

meditated; atrocious; premature; rebel; fratricidal; pioneer; advancing; contaminating; unauthorized; hostile; apparent; lawless; threatened; long-continued; air.

verbs

avert—; curb—; defend against—; deplore —; fight—; inform of—; plan—; persist in —; protect from—; repel—; resist—; stage —; stem—; suffer—; threaten—; yield to—; —destroys; —embitters; —succeeds.

(See raid, aggression, infringement, encroachment, violation.)

INVECTIVE

adjectives

indignant; opprobrious; unreasonable; furious; insulting; bitter; indiscriminate; coarsest; classical; fierce; witty; heated.

verbs

burst into—; deluge with—s; discharge—; drench with—; express in—; flay with—; fling—at; hurl—at; pour forth—; provoke —; rail—; rain—s; roar—; shoot at—; suffer—; shower—s; volley—s at; —angers; —denounces; —embitters.

(See sarcasm, abuse, oath.)

INVEIGH (v)

adverbs

censoriously; violently; bitterly; spitefully; vindictively; cantankerously; treacherously; acrimoniously; acidly; blasphemously; insidiously; sternly; roughly; ruthlessly; ferociously.

(See censure, reproach, rail.)

INVENT (v)

adverbs

deftly; creatively; infernally; matchlessly; diabolically; inexhaustibly; sensationally; dangerously; maliciously; technically; fantastically; poetically; prodigally; marvelously; spectacularly; singularly.

(See devise, contrive, discover, originate.)

INVENTION

adjectives

matchless; sad; infernal; stupendous; neoteric; diabolical; dangerous; exorbitant; gymnastic; multitudinous (pl); fervid; inexhaustible; florid; sensational; proposed; dangerous; numerous (pl); distributive; sheer; malicious; divine; technical; melodic; considerable; labor-saving; arbitrary; modern; fantastic; admirable; plausive; poetic; harassing; breath-taking; greatest; perfected; prodigal; modistic; topical; feeble; honest; marvelous; remarkable; sensational; patented; amazing.

verbs

accelerate—; beget—; commemorate—; contrive—; devise—; exploit—; introduce—; laud—; paralyze—; perfect—; seek—; stumble on—; submit—; suppress—; —eases; —enlightens; —improves.

(See discovery, patent, device, stratagem, improvement.)

INVENTIVE

adverbs

cleverly; amazingly; ingeniously; skilfully; wonderfully; expertly; surprisingly; profitably; scientifically; extraordinarily; conveniently; handily; crudely; curiously; shrewdly; broadly; expediently; fortunately; necessarily; unusually; uncommonly; highly; resourcefully; magnificently; dexterously; unbelievably; deftly; competently; capably; delightfully; fortunately; luckily; inexhaustibly; admirably.

INVERSION

adjectives

unnatural; monstrous; total.

INVERT (v)

adverbs

confusingly; perplexingly; complicatedly; abnormally; eccentrically; characteristically; humorously; habitually.

(See reverse, turn, overthrow.)

INVEST (v)

adverbs

fraudulently; annually; temporarily; forcibly; financially; shrewdly; austerely; astutely; strategically; judiciously; modestly; initially.

(See clothe, dress, surround.)

INVESTIGATE (v)

adverbs

promptly; personally; intensively; duly; vigorously; anatomically; tediously; assiduously; tranquilly; legislatively; analytically; diligently; intellectually; comprehensively; judicially; conclusively; abstractly; inquisitively; physiologically; methodically; aimlessly.

(See examine, inquire, probe.)

INVESTIGATION

adjectives

vast; anatomical; tedious; empiric; unprejudiced; eager; assiduous; futile; patient; tranquil; personal; cautious; legislative; analytical; literary; diligent; shouldered; racial; intellectual; careful; clinical; elaborate; journalistic; contemporary; comprehensive; judicial; hostile; rigorous; subsequent; conclusive; minuter; abstract; introspective; inquisitive; empirical; embarrassing; physiological; methodical; aimless.

verbs

carry on—; conduct—; contribute to—; dismiss—; exhaust—; facilitate—; institute—; ponder—; promise—; submit to—; summarize—; throttle—; yield to—; —brings to light; —concentrates; —convinces; —discloses; —drags; —indicates; —reveals; —wearies.

(See inquiry, examination, research, inquisition.)

INVESTMENT

adjectives

sound; gilt-edged; attractive; healthy; strategic; permanent; lifetime; elaborate; comparative; conservative; judicious; defence-less; economical; individual; modest; initial; desirable; careful; extraordinary; substantial; definite.

verbs

convert—; derive from—; discourage—; gain by—; impair—; necessitate—; preserve —; profit by—; pyramid—; represent—; sacrifice—; safeguard—; sell out—; subscribe to—; —accumulates; —crashes; —diminishes; —skyrockets (colloq.).

(See stocks, shares, bonds, property, interest, money.)

INVESTORS

adjectives

institutional; individual; hypothetical; multitudinous; thoughtful; painstaking.

INVIGORATE (v)

adverbs

artificially; scientifically; medically; alcoholically; mentally; physically; emotionally; beneficially; hurtfully; detrimentally.

(See animate, encourage.)

INVIGORATING

adverbs

pleasantly; highly; refreshingly; definitely; notoriously; conspicuously; unquestionably; wholesomely; fortunately; infallibly; gratefully; unexpectedly; surprisingly; strangely; marvellously; curiously; wonderfully; permanently; gloriously; progressively; restoratively; incredibly; miraculously; splendidly; remarkably; magnificently.

INVINCIBLE

adverbs

sturdily; stoutly; amazingly; unexpectedly; proudly; notoriously; conspicuously; surprisingly; preposterously; incredibly; genuinely; apparently; evidently; manifestly; curiously; strangely; oddly; fantastically; indomitably; insuperably; doggedly; stubbornly; obstinately; mightily; powerfully; splendidly; magnificently; irresistibly; mysteriously; unbelievably.

INVISIBLE

adverbs

mysteriously; curiously; strangely; incredibly; oddly; fantastically; designedly; provokingly; disappointingly; vexatiously; minutely; mistily; foggily; mystically; significantly.

INVITATION

adjectives

colorful; specific; long-standing; cordial; smart; flattering; outright; friendly; cheerful; implied; indefinite; actual; unanswered; clamorous; open; unexpected; sinister; original; unauthorized; pressing; liberal; hearty; perpetual; vague; inescapable.

verbs

answer—; besiege by —s; decline—; dine by —; draft—; ignore—; issue—; limit—; long for—; prepare—s; present—; prize—; procure—; —allures; —amuses; —delights; —flatters; —gladdens.

(See summons, call, question.)

INVITE (v)

adverbs

cordially; formally; frequently; graciously; peculiarly; forcibly; daintily; vociferously; specifically; flatteringly; originally; nominally; suavely; fatally; ostensibly.

(See ask, induce, summon, call.)

INVITING

adverbs

charmingly; delightfully; pleasantly; coolly; refreshingly; warmly; cordially; hospitably; marvellously; unexpectedly; attractively; bewitchingly; cordially; cheerfully; heartily; politely; comfortably; lusciously; delectably; alluringly; temptingly; irresistibly; wonderfully; surprisingly.

INVOCATION

adjectives

brief; unknown; sweet; solemn.

INVOKE (v)

adverbs

eloquently; ardently; solemnly; incessantly; reverently; briefly; earnestly; verbally; monotonously.

(See pray, beseech, beg.)

INVOLVE (v)

adverbs

markedly; shockingly; tragically; unfathomably; inextricably; hopelessly; abstrusely; problematically; ultimately; tremendously; scandalously.

(See implicate, include, entangle, embarrass.)

INVULNERABILITY

verbs

acclaim—; appreciate—; boast—; charge—; demand—; doubt—; estimate—; mistrust—; relax—; respect—; shake—; strain—; test —; threaten—; —defends; —sustains; — irks.

(See strength.)

INVULNERABLE

adverbs

proudly; ominously; happily; fortunately; consciously; remarkably; strongly; obviously; manifestly; completely; supposedly; presumably; apparently; allegedly; securely; safely; tenably; snugly; confidently.

IODINE

verbs

apply—; antidote—; disinfect with—; inject —; impregnate with—; paint with—; smear —; tint with—; treat with—; —poisons; —relieves; —safeguards; —sterilizes.

(See chemical, antiseptic, medicine.)

IRASCIBLE

adverbs

insufferably; highly; hotly; moodily; cholerically; capriciously; inexplicably; temperamentally; habitually; naturally; inexcusably; unreasonably; illogically; snappishly; querulously; contentiously; excitably; restively; uncommonly; rudely; captiously.

IRATE

adverbs

dangerously; alarmingly; highly; unusually; terribly; inexplicably; extremely; fearfully; sullenly; silently; noisily; tempestuously; unreasonably; savagely; senselessly; moodily.

IRE

adjectives

political; vengeful; patriot; noble; raging; avenging.

verbs

appease—; arouse—; assuage—; avert—; awake—; draw—of; dread—; ferment—; flush with—; fume with—; glow with—; moderate—; pale with—; provoke to—; shake with—; sharpen—; shelter from—; slake—; subdue—; —effervesces; —erupts; —riots.

(See anger, rage, wrath, passion, vexation, temper.)

IRIDESCENT

adverbs

shimmeringly; beautifully; amazingly; uncommonly; gloriously; splendidly; magnificently; delicately; daintily; flashily; curiously; oddly; marvellously; inexplicably; unexpectedly; attractively; highly; uncommonly.

IRKSOME

adverbs

tediously; wearily; heavily; distastefully; monotonously; dully; stupidly; vaguely; unpleasantly; dismally; drearily; oppressively; onerously; laboriously; vexatiously; provokingly; formidably; grievously; bitterly.

IRON

adjectives

adamantine; crushing; hot; assimilated; magnetized; tempered; redcoated; stubborn; rusted.

verbs

alloy with—; cast—; employ—; forge—; gird with—; hammer—; lathe—; magnetize —; mold—; plate with—; polish—; puddle —; roll—; shackle in—; shod with—; smelt —; utilize—; weld—; —clangs; —corrodes; —grates; —masters; —rusts.
(See metal, steel.)

IRONICAL

adverbs

bitterly; suddenly; justifiably; calmly; sarcastically; shrewdly; terribly; insolently; acidly; keenly; scoffingly; sneeringly; mockingly; tauntingly; teasingly; cleverly; perspicaciously; astutely; inscrutably; unduly; rudely; disagreeably; offensively; openly.

IRONY

adjectives

discordant; malignant; secret; terrible; masterly; characteristic; calm; strange; fearless; melancholy; subtle; laughing; delicate; enchanting; quaint; unconscious; wanton; unpleasing; fine; gentle; trivial; dramatic; civilized; somber; delicious; amiable; tragic.

verbs

afford—; aim at—; convey—; exhibit—; imply—; pierce with—; prick with—; recognize—; relish—; stress—; suggest—; suspect

—; tinge with—; wince at—; —amuses; — barbs; —cuts; —nips; —penetrates; —rebukes.

(See sarcasm, satire, ridicule, mockery.)

IRRADIATION

adjectives

intense; imponderable; hidden; compulsory.

IRRATIONAL

adverbs

pathetically; portentously; absurdly; ridiculously; senselessly; stupidly; irascibly; fallaciously; crazily; preposterously; extravagantly; alarmingly; strangely; oddly; unwontedly; impulsively; evasively; nonsensically; obstinately; foolishly; incredibly.

IRRECLAIMABLE

adverbs

hopelessly; tragically; legally; virtually; lamentably; deplorably; altogether; presumably; allegedly; shamefully; viciously; impenitently; defiantly; recklessly; unfortunately; unluckily; lucklessly; wickedly; unconscionably; conclusively; apparently; manifestly.

IRRECOVERABLE

adverbs

desperately; hopelessly; lamentably; unfortunately; sadly; unhappily; utterly; presumably; probably; allegedly.

IRREDEEMABLE

adverbs

hopelessly; strangely; cruelly; officially; unluckily; legally; authoritatively; curiously; mysteriously; probably; definitely; unquestionably; incontrovertibly; absolutely.

IRREGULAR

adverbs

shamefully; disgracefully; furtively; openly; strangely; deplorably; cruelly; dangerously; secretly; unfortunately; terribly; slightly; gravely; seriously; suspiciously; egregiously; highly; utterly; wildly; lamentably; unpardonably; inexcusably; unsatisfactorily; unacceptably; disagreeably; disgustingly; indiscreetly; imprudently; unhappily.

IRREGULARITIES

adjectives

technical; faint; odd; quaint; exasperating; clumsy; rugged; fatal; ruddy.

IRREGULARITY

verbs

acknowledge—; adjust—; admit—; commit —; condone—; detect—; disperse—; file down—; generalize—s; lament—; magnify —; note—; penalize—; perform—; relent—; rue—; —debars; —disqualifies; —impedes. (See abnormality, error, mistake, wrong, oversight.)

IRRELEVANCE

adjectives

boring; inextricable; apparent; complete; established.

IRRELEVANT

adverbs

disturbingly; vexatiously; insolently; suddenly; shrewdly; sadly; purposely; deliberately; hopelessly; uselessly; unserviceably; impracticably; impertinently; nonchalantly; casually; coolly; outlandishly; inappropriately; incongruously; exceptionally; oddly; unreasonably; foolishly; inanely; ridiculously; absurdly; unbelievably.

IRRELIGIOUS

adverbs

outlandishly; irreverently; curiously; terribly; unpardonably; conspicuously; flagrantly; inconceivably; sadly; flauntingly; inveterately; offensively; quietly; stolidly; stubbornly; immovably; impiously; grievously; irremediably; atheistically; indifferently; ostentatiously; dreadfully; strangely.

IRREMEDIABLE

adverbs

evidently; unluckily; grievously; sadly; unfortunately; presumably; possibly; apparently; hopelessly; forlornly; curiously; singularly; extraordinarily; peculiarly; particularly; avowedly; significantly; heartbreakingly; queerly; incomprehensibly.

IRREPARABLE

adverbs

curiously; hopelessly; oddly; strangely; unfortunately; unluckily; bitterly; cruelly; dismally; absolutely; apparently; obviously; manifestly; indubitably; palpably; haplessly; unhappily; distressingly; disturbingly; grievously.

IRREPRESSIBLE

adverbs

obstreperously; riotously; uproariously; cur-iously; vexatiously; alarmingly; obviously; wantonly; mischievously; garrulously; independently; absolutely; offensively; restlessly; boisterously; noisily; feverishly; hysterically; violently; hot-headedly; fanatically; impulsively; disagreeably; unbecomingly; strangely; blatantly.

IRREPROACHABLE

adverbs

notoriously; consistently; conspicuously; generally; altogether; unquestionably; wholly; presumably; emphatically; positively; incontrovertibly; ineffably; assuredly; warrantably; securely; acceptably; implicitly; impressively; probably.

IRRESISTIBLE

adverbs

charmingly; delightfully; utterly; absolutely; wholly; fascinatingly; inexhaustibly; altogether; persuasively; indomitably; argumentatively; logically; consciously; personally; oddly; singularly; powerfully; attractively; strangely; evidently.

IRRESOLUTE

adverbs

feebly; timidly; indecisively; weakly; singularly; senselessly; strangely; particularly; incredibly; foolishly; pliantly; hesitantly; infirmly; capriciously; whimsically; lamentably; oddly; captiously; nervously; restively; stupidly; unwisely; noticeably; dreadfully; timorously; tremulously; warily.

IRRESPONSIBLE

adverbs

gaily; blithely; insouciantly; nonchalantly; wantonly; hopelessly; singularly; deplorably; curiously; outlandishly; fantastically; oddly; strangely; vexatiously; unpleasantly; maddeningly; wildly; heedlessly; utterly; painfully; incorrigibly; alarmingly; dangerously; intolerably; palpably; sadly; incredibly; inveterately; temperamentally; incurably; obviously.

IRREVERENT

adverbs

impiously; flagrantly; offensively; unforgivably; rudely; grossly; crudely; thoughtlessly; unbecomingly; painfully; unutterably; unspeakably; arrantly; invidiously; insolently; terribly; crassly; brazenly; senselessly; utterly; blasphemously; sacrilegiously; deliberately; singularly; peculiarly; carelessly;

unpardonably; ignorantly; boorishly; insultingly; outrageously; scandalously; shamefully; egregiously; irremediably.

IRREVOCABLE
adverbs
lamentably; terribly; disastrously; ruinously; calamitously; hopelessly; desperately; sadly; lamentably; horribly; tragically; seriously; gravely; legally; pitiably; validly; indelibly; unintentionally; patently; inexorably; fortunately; happily.

IRRIGATION
adjectives
minute; plenteous; land-saving; colonic.

IRRITABILITY
verbs
control—; exaggerate—; fan—; lament—; manifest—; observe—; plague to—; rouse to —; salve—; stimulate—; —annoys; —lessens; —pains; —vexes.
(See irritation.)

IRRITABLE
adverbs
silently; resentfully; extremely; evidently; horridly; fiercely; violently; bitterly; absurdly; senselessly; foolishly; unreasonably; increasingly; slightly; definitely; hotly; furiously; mightily; unbearably; intolerably; grievously; sorely; ludicrously; plaguedly; annoyingly; wretchedly; miserably; distinctly; unfairly; deeply; easily; unhappily; comically; unjustly; ill-temperedly.

IRRITATE (v)
adverbs
unduly; nervously; perpetually; exasperatingly; sharply; temporarily; psychologically; physically; childishly; needlessly; excessively; superfluously.
(See provoke, vex, annoy, offend.)

IRRITATION
adjectives
stifled; puerile; deep-seated; concealed; nervous; perpetual; passing; burning; infinite; teasing; increasing; private; lulling; sharp; temporary; psychological; childish; consequent; needless; excessive.

verbs
allay—; alleviate—; arouse—; augment—; bear—; check—; convey—; endure—; excite —; expose to—; express—; fume with—;

master—; relieve—; respond to—; seethe with—; stimulate—; stir up—; subject to—; thunder—; —bursts forth; —ferments; —lashes; —subsides.
(See pain, anger, impatience, vexation, temper, irritability.)

ISLAND
adjectives
extensive; weedy; barren; fragrant; glacier-polished; sea-girt; adjacent; desolate; smiling; marshy; imaginary; rugged; low; swampy; ill-fated; oozy; barricaded; secluded; moraine; river-girt; bare; cozy; floating; uninhabited; beautiful; verdant; glittering; serene; wretched; industrial; volcanic; antique; irregular; classical; sterile; rocky; roaming; substantial; dismal; sun-drenched; southern; romantic; veritable; uttermost; jeweled; remote; late-sacked.

verbs
banish to—; batter—; bombard—; desolate —; encompass—; infest—; isolate—; maroon on—; overrun—; populate—; plunder —; rule—; settle on—; sight—; strand on —; strew with —s; stud with —s; surround —; survey—; take root on—; winter on—; —blooms; —chains; —s dot; —enchants; —flowers; —overlooks; —shelters; —swarms with; —veers off; —yields.
(See land, shore.)

ISLE
adjectives
oozy; lofty; desolate; peaceful; flat; bloomy; mystic; shady; weeping; volcanic; low; wooded; hateful; pumice; bee-pasturing; tributary; foamless; outlying; execrable; high-favored; storm-encompassed.

ISOLATE (v)
adverbs
pathetically; voluntarily; effectively; dismally; advisedly; temporarily; virtually; morally; politically; physically; formidably; geographically; financially; economically; legally.
(See segregate, separate.)

ISOLATED
adverbs
somewhat; lamentably; fortunately; happily; necessarily; cruelly; bitterly; preferably; remotely; terribly; relatively; comparatively; desolately; drearily; singularly;

oddly; curiously; particularly; strangely; deliberately; unwillingly; inconveniently; inhospitably; snugly; safely; securely; unsociably.

ISOLATION
adjectives

moral; lonely; luxurious; infinite; blank; self-centered; studied; prompt; sectional; moribund; lofty; exposed; sheltered; physical; stupendous; selfish; desolate; deliberate; absolute; anguished; formidable; self-perceived; geographical; awful; magnificent; economic; financial; terrible.

verbs

advocate—; bear—; condemn to—; contemplate in—; delight in—; dread—; dwell in —; expel into—; meditate in—; penetrate —; procure—; punish by—; resign to—; retire into—; risk—; shake from—; suffer —; wrap in—.

(See privacy, solitude, loneliness, seclusion, retirement.)

ISSUE (v)
adverbs

spuriously; portentously; anonymously; particularly; publicly; officially; politically; controversially; triumphantly; victoriously; colorfully; significantly.

(See result, terminate, proceed.)

ISSUE
adjectives

sequent; political; momentous; controversial; great; fruitful; genuine; fundamental; ethical; indirect; unlimited; clear; dearest; profuse; precarious; degenerate; precise; vital; moral; abundant; tragic; confused; doubtful; remarkable; fascinating; colorful; basic; supreme; stupendous; irrelevant; insignificant; luckier; proposed; proud; concrete; adverse; felicitous; unlucky; immeasurable; tremendous; happy; disinherited; discussable; uncertain; dreadful; coming; involved; wartime; particular; recent; national; unforeseen.

verbs

analyze—; ban—; clarify—; confuse—; crystallize—; debate—; decline—; determine —; dismiss—; dodge—; dramatize—; duck —; dwarf—; elaborate on—; entangle—; evade—; force—; forego—; gloss over—; inject—; judge—; obliterate—; outlaw—; prejudice—; scrutinize—; set forth—;

sharpen—; side-step—; speed—; split on—; state—; subordinate—; swamp—; tackle—; terminate—; —burns; —s conflict; — emerges; —involves.

(See outcome, result, consequence, question, point.)

ITCHING
adjectives

considerable; intense; profuse; excessive; unbearable.

verbs

affect with—; aggravate—; allay—; cure —; ease—; increase—; relieve—; remedy —; renew—; soothe—; wash—; —annoys; —attends; —indicates; —maddens; — tickles; —torments; —vexes.

(See disease, pain, torment, torture.)

ITEM
adjectives

important; inconspicuous; imperative; various (pl); replacement; indispensable; popular; rarest; fascinating; seasonable; considerable; middling; crucial; drab; related; restricted; associated; central; profit; essential; outstanding; lively; unpretentious; derogatory.

verbs

calculate—s; charge—; check—; classify—; compute—s; enter—; enumerate—s; exempt —; muster—s; note—; plow through—s; register—; specify—; total—s; —tempts.

(See amount, details.)

ITERATION
adjectives

monotonous; caressing; deliberate.

ITINERANT
adverbs

irresponsibly; necessarily; compulsively; happily; willingly; recklessly; pleasantly; profitably; adventurously; extravagantly; vagrantly; politically; lazily; vapidly; inanely; foolishly; vigilantly; nomadically; erratically; restlessly; vexatiously; peculiarly; outlandishly; whimsically; expensively; grievously; piteously; interestingly; fascinatingly; thrillingly; attractively; amazingly; unaccountably; idly.

verbs

approve—; arrange—; contemplate—; describe—; draw up—; follow—; measure—; plan—; prepare—; refer to—; study—; —delights; —informs; —mentions; —proposes.

(See program, plan, project, scheme.)

adjectives

waxen; tinted; delicate; rose-ensanguined; carved.

adjectives

clinging; poison; variegated; linked; wandering; climbing; embowering.

verbs

crown with—; direct—; train—; —bowers; —canopies; —clasps; —climbs; —clings; —creeps; —curls; —decorates; —feeds on; —hangs; —hides; —jackets; —leaps; —nods; —twines; —twists; —wanders; —wreathes.

(See plant, flower, vine.)

J

JAB (v)

adverbs
viciously; repeatedly; verbally; savagely; bitterly; ferociously; brutally; vindictively; malignantly.
(See thrust, poke, dig.)

JABBER (v

adverbs
bestially; perpetually; enthusiastically; excitedly; cheerfully; effusively; idiotically; loquaciously.
(See talk, babble, chatter.)

JACKDAW

verbs
tame—; —babbles; —cackles; —caws; — chatters; —clacks; —flits; —frequents; — gabbles; —gossips; —hops; —imitates; — jabbers; —steals; —thieves.
(See bird.)

JACKET

adjectives
undress; soft; bright; embroidered; wadded; silk; familiar; long; reversible; ill-fitted; clumsy.

verbs
adorn—; box in—; conceal under—; divest of—; don—; emerge from—; fortify with —; fray—; stain—; tatter—; utilize—; — preserves; —protects.
(See coat, overcoat, cloak.)

JADE

adjectives
veriest; outworn; brazen-faced; veined; unruly; tired.

JADED

adverbs
wearily; exhaustedly; gaspingly; tiredly; haggardly; uncommonly; gauntly; entirely; finally.

JAGGED

adverbs
angularly; dangerously; roughly; ruggedly; sharply; crookedly; obliquely; curiously; fearfully; perilously; strangely; hazardously; terribly; ominously; frightfully; unpleasantly; painfully; disagreeably; horridly; hideously; distressingly.

JAIL

adjectives
fantastic; infernal; distasteful; pleasant; comfortable.

verbs
break—; clamp in—; clap into—; commit to—; confine to—; deliver from—; deposit in—; detain in—; dwell in—; free from—; guard—; imprison in—; incarcerate in—; languish in—; parole from—; patrol—; release from—; secure in—; slap into—; — confines; —corrects; —penalizes; —rehabilitates.
(See prison.)

JAM

adjectives
absolute; fearful; traffic; inextricable.

JANGLE (v)

adverbs
crudely; dissonantly; inharmoniously; irritatingly; blatantly; exasperatingly; ceaselessly; hideously.
(See clang, clash.)

JAR

adjectives
dripping; giddy; subsequent; intestinal; mortal; endless; importunate; tempestuous; family-sized; inharmonious; treble.

JAR (v)

adverbs
rudely; terrifically; tempestuously; roughly; disastrously; mysteriously; awkwardly; economically.
(See jolt, shock, grate.)

JARGON

adjectives
wretched; broken; unscientific; courtly; meaningless; commonplace; unintelligible; barbarous; infernal; pitiful; busy.

verbs
babble—; chatter—; despise—; interpret—; master—; prate—; ring with—; translate

—; —confounds; —confuses; —delights; —grates; —perplexes; —prevails.

(See language, dialect, slang, speech.)

JAUNDICE

verbs
afflict with—; induce—; occasion—; tincture with—; treat for—; —appears; —deranges; —discolors; —disquiets; —distresses; —torments; —worries; —attacks.

(See disease.)

JAUNDICED

adverbs
biliously; querulously; regrettably; unhappily; incurably; slightly; jealously; evidently; visibly; clearly; unmistakably; highly; fulvously; inferentially; prejudicially; blindly; provincially; narrowly; fanatically; dogmatically; stupidly; illiberally; terribly.

JAUNT

adjectives
pleasure; summer; daring; mental.

JAUNTY

adverbs
blithely; carelessly; buoyantly; fashionably; delightfully; smilingly; nonchalantly; wholesomely; charmingly; lightly; brightly; insouciantly; laughingly; swaggeringly; heedlessly; wantonly; happily; rollickingly; saucily; comically; ludicrously; whimsically; cheerfully; gaily; gleefully; airily; heartily; joyously; playfully; sportively; marvelously; effervescently; jubilantly; remarkably.

JAW

adjectives
set; prominent; stern-set; grinning; outstanding; poisonous; delicate; mastic; bloody; protruding; resolute; aristocratic; firm; square-cut; pugilistic; marble; powerful; massive; protuberant; horrible; ponderous; unshaven; hollow; underhanging; infernal; poor; weasel; monstrous; champing; brutal; malevolent; grim; ravening; snarling; mighty; square-set; strong; clamped; industrious; determined; dogged; hard; iron; formidable; heavy; immense; bulging; clean-cut; elastic; inflexible; locked; lean; recessive; foaming; loose; distended; uplifted; pikelike; scarred; flaring; gaping; yawning; snapping; triangular; pier-like; haggard; beefy; flabby; jutting; projecting; lower; prognathous; combative; fighting; sagged; drooping; hanging; fallen; sharp; tense.

verbs
brace—; click—s; crack—; fracture—; tear with—s; wire—s; work—s; —s clasp; —s close; —s crunch; —s crush; —drops; —s embrace; —s foam; —gapes; —juts out; —sags; —s snap; —s tighten.

(See teeth.)

JAY

verbs
—destroys; —hops; —mimics; —s mob; —pipes; —preys on; —scolds; —screams; —shies; —tears; —teases.

(See bird.)

JAZZ

verbs
beat out—; blare—; bridle—; entertain with—; inspire—; mute—; record—; repress—; revolt against—; seethe with—; sprinkle with—; trumpet—; welcome—; —agitates; —arouses; —batters; —cradles; —evolves from; —predominates; —reigns; —rushes.

(See music, melody, song, noise.)

JEALOUS

adverbs
inordinately; insanely; madly; wildly; furiously; violently; slightly; somewhat; justly; reasonably; naturally; intensely; venomously; pitiably; pathetically; unutterably; vengefully; supposedly; allegedly; probably; suspiciously; miserably; wretchedly; groundlessly; unbearably; insufferably; wonderfully; basely; disgracefully; contemptibly; foolishly; dangerously; deplorably; unbearably.

JEALOUSY

adjectives
insensate; fond; green-eyed; intense; self-harming; dangerous; popular; continual; savage; lively; maternal; mutual; inventive; instinctive; furious; narrow; mad; excessive; exaggerated; needless; lurking; smoldering; petty; miserable; frantic; unreasonable; improvident; habitual; acute; sensitive; active; selfish; fiercest; exalted; self-betraying; watchful; rare; retrospective; sentimental; malignant; factional; alternating; blinding; naive; overwrought; commercial; rancorous; undefined.

verbs
abhor—; arouse—; beget—; conceal—; cure
—; curse with—; dread—; extinguish—;
fire—; incur—; nourish—; occasion—;
overcome—; squirm in—; strangle—; —
blasts; —corrodes; —dictates; —disturbs;
—frustrates; —grips; —harms; —magnifies; —pains; —perverts; —poisons; —subsides; —torments; —tortures; —wanes.
(See suspicion, distrust, curiosity, selfishness.)

JEER
verbs
cripple with—; deride with—; flog with—;
flout with—; incur—s of; inflict—; heat
with—s; pelt with—s; punish with—s; scorn
—s; silence—s; stone with—s; —bruises; —
disconcerts; —mocks; —perturbs; —taunts;
—unnerves; —upsets.
(See taunt, ridicule, derision, sneer, laughter.)

JEER (v)
adverbs
scornfully; sardonically; vindictively; sarcastically; enviously; bitterly; spitefully;
acrimoniously; acidulously.
(See mock, ridicule.)

JEERING
adverbs
scornfully; irreverently; disrespectfully;
contemptuously; derisively; cruelly; bitterly; savagely; mockingly; insultingly; outrageously; superciliously; sarcastically;
basely; tauntingly; dreadfully; tormentingly.

JEOPARDIZE (v)
adverbs
recklessly; rashly; foolhardily; absurdly;
superfluously; idiotically; madly; passionately; deliriously.
(See risk, imperil, endanger.)

JERK (v)
adverbs
spitefully; instinctively; desperately; ludicrously; furiously; intermittently; ignominiously; frantically; mechanically; repetitiously; violently.
(See twitch, snatch.)

JERKY
adverbs
unnaturally; abnormally; lamentably; miserably; deplorably; pitiably; incurably; reg-

ularly; strangely; spasmodically; convulsively; suddenly; inexplicably; curiously;
fitfully; recurrently; restlessly; singularly;
peculiarly; surprisingly; woefully; frightfully.

JEST
verbs
beware of—s; enjoy—; fashion—; flash—s;
glean—s; harass with—; interpret—s; refine—; repeat—; season with—; share—;
speak in—; suppress—; time—; —affronts;
—amuses; —cures; —delights; —pains; —
ridicules; —slings; —taunts.
(See joke, witticism, parody, satire.)

JEST (v)
adverbs
indelicately; indecently; subtly; amiably;
recklessly; satirically; slanderously; scurrilously; wittily; boisterously; unrestrainedly; foolishly.
(See joke, clown, fool.)

JESTER
verbs
appreciate—; encourage—; humor—; maintain—; retain—; —aims; —attempts; —
directs; —diverts; —entertains; —excites;
—indulges; —jokes; —makes game of; —
makes merry; —makes sport of; —provokes;
—treats.
(See clown, actor.)

JESTING
adverbs
roguishly; mischievously; broadly; teasingly; tormentingly; merrily; banteringly;
waggishly; facetiously; playfully; comically;
frivolously; whimsically; airily; idly.

JESUS
verbs
accept—; behold—; betray—; blaspheme—;
crown—; crucify—; follow—; forsake—;
glorify—; hallow—; invest—with; proclaim
—; reject—; —bleeds; —comforts; —cures;
—forgives; —heals; —reigns; —rises; —
saves; —suffers; —weeps.
(See Christ, God.)

JETS
adjectives
silvery; sparkling; glittering; branching;
augmenting.

adjectives
dull; cloudy; glistening; glittering; sparkling; sullied; dumb; barbaric; treasured; molten; rich; costly; heavenly; gleaming; glowing; burnished; eternal; graceful; propitious; best; fluid.

verbs
begem with—; box—; collect—s; display—; exhibit—; insure—; mount—; offer—; pawn —; retrieve—; set with—s; stud with—s; swathe in—s; value—; —adorns; —awes; —s bedeck; —dazzles; —flashes; —gleams; —glistens; —glitters; —ornaments; —sparkles.
(See gem, diamond, gold, pearl, ruby.)

JEWELER
verbs
—adorns; —deals in; —decorates; —determines; —estimates; —furnishes; —imports; —inscribes; —mounts; —prices; —prizes; —purveys; —sets; —values; —vouches for; —insures.
(See merchant.)

JEWELRY
adjectives
abundant; delicate; ponderous; glimmering; subtlest; starry; resplendent.

JILT (*v*)
adverbs
senselessly; brazenly; cruelly; heartlessly; capriciously; frivolously; selfishly; disgracefully.
(See flirt, coquette.)

JINGLE
adjectives
petulant; spasmodic; clear; discordant; pleasant; foolish.

JINGLE (*v*)
adverbs
melodiously; musically; petulantly; spasmodically; discordantly; gaily; genially; pleasantly; propitiously.
(See ring, resound.)

JOB
adjectives
rapid; life-toning; craftsmanlike; daily; tedious; practical; identical (pl); thankless; nefarious; constricting; definitive; dirty; difficult; bungling; advertising; hack-writing; unpleasant; needless; remodeling; political; surrealistic; executive; assured; thorough; faultless; royal.

verbs
abandon—; abolish—; apply for—; attack —; buckle down to—; bungle—; chuck—; contemplate—; cut out for—; decry—; despatch to—; equip for—; fumble at—; harness to—; jeopardize—; land (colloq.)—; nail—; quail at—; register for—; swing into—; tackle—; threaten—; undertake—; usurp—; wangle—; —fazes (colloq.); —materializes.
(See position, work, situation, employment, engagement.)

JOCOSE
adverbs
facetiously; waggishly; convivially; playfully; whimsically; foolishly; fatuously; pleasantly; drolly; clownishly; banteringly; quick-wittedly; humorously; fantastically; teasingly; whimsically; quibblingly; entertainingly; happily; naturally; cheeringly.

JOCULAR
adverbs
immensely; always; habitually; entertainingly; genially; amiably; charmingly; divertingly; dependably; heartily; wholesomely; good-naturedly; characteristically; amusingly; agreeably; waggishly; broadly; banteringly; comically; drolly; dryly; whimsically; facetiously; merrily; pleasantly.

JOCULARITY
adjectives
nervous; perplexed; forced; mock.

JOCUND
adverbs
pleasantly; wittily; archly; cheerfully; amusingly; heartily; irrepressibly; blithely; admirably; imperturbably; consistently; naturally; charmingly; lustily; noisily; boisterously; incomparably.

JOG (*v*)
adverbs
monotonously; ceaselessly; cheerfully; automatically; conventionally; dismally; uneventfully; tediously; arduously; toilsomely.
(See shake, push, jar, jolt.)

685

adverbs
enthusiastically; obsequiously; slavishly; matrimonially; lustily; indissolubly; devoutly; mechanically; temporarily; snugly.

(See add, annex, knit.)

JOINT

adjectives
diminishing; stiffened; distorted; affected; enlarged; stubborn; firm-knit.

verbs
bandage—; cement—; connect at—; dislocate—; displace—; fit—; form—; hinge—; lay—; limber up—; lubricate—; mend—; nodulate—; shake out of—; strengthen—; support—; sustain—; turn on—; —creaks; —squeaks.

(See bone.)

JOKE

adjectives
rude; matter-of-fact; practical; outrageous; affectionate; oft-repeated; grave; crowning; pathetic; sly; obscene; indelicate; cynical; mocking; foolish; fermented; repressed; bibliomaniacal; deplorable; mutual; uncountable (pl); endless; inopportune; wonderful; delicious; off-color; miserable; particular; impish; questionable; horrible; priceless.

verbs
censor—; exchange—s; flash—; guffaw at —; interpret—; laugh at—; perpetrate—; refine—; report—; retail—s; season with —; share—; swap (colloq.)—s; time—; understand—; —affronts; —amuses; —caps; —climaxes; —delights; —offends; —pains; —stings; —wears thin.

(See jest, witticism, parody, satire.)

JOKER

adjectives
absolute; loud-tongued; misused.

JOLLITY

adjectives
innocent; unrestrained; frenzied; youthful.

verbs
arrest—; dampen—; dip in—; enjoy—; feed —; immerse in—; occasion—; overcome with—; prolong—; relent—; repent—; share

—; split in—; steep in—; yield to—; —exhausts; —inebriates; —palls; —prevails; —wanes.

(See fun, mirth, merriment, relaxation, recreation, laughter.)

JOLLY

adverbs
immensely; invariably; consistently; heartily; wholesomely; delightfully; tremendously; inveterately; indomitably; constitutionally; naturally; habitually; unusually; uncommonly; extravagantly; exceedingly; unsuitably; blithely; merrily; sportively; teasingly; tormentingly; mockingly; inopportunely; roguishly; unquenchably; whimsically; exuberantly; mischievously; impishly; marvelously.

JOLT

adjectives
staggering; nasty; gigantic; painful.

JOLT (v)

adverbs
heavily; crunchingly; staggeringly; terrifically; thunderously; rudely; destructively; disastrously.

(See shock, grate, jar.)

JOLTING

adjectives
unendurable; incessant.

JOURNAL

adjectives
musical; vivacious; naked; satirical; enterprising; independent; distinguished; inflated; pompous; veracious.

JOURNALIST

adjectives
well-informed; eminent; cultured; conscientious; flamboyant; inspired; death-defying; disreputable; able; irresponsible; brilliant; prolific.

verbs
bribe—; condemn—; congratulate—; criticize—; fear—; hire—; —awes; —composes; —corrupts; —describes; —edits; —expounds; —humanizes; —itemizes; —publishes; —reports; —serves; —sums; —vulgarizes.

(See writer, reporter, publisher, editor.)

JOURNEY

adjectives

frightful; tedious; dreaded; proposed; fruitless; interesting; expeditious; fatiguing; fatal; costly; weary; innumerable (pl); arduous; self-appointed; unspeakable; dismal; unsteady; stately; longing; measureless; long; foggy; subsequent; daily; harrowing; troubled; wearisome; leisurely; evangelizing; extended; unexpected; uneventful; triumphant; adventurous; shorter; rumored; aimless; perilous; sentimental; celebrated; plodding; memorable; romantic; toilsome; infinite; mysterious; accursed; triumphal; pleasant; homeward.

verbs

accompany on—; break—; contemplate—; embark on—; enjoy—; plan—; proceed on —; quicken—; set out on—; shape—; undertake—; —benefits; —fatigues; —interests; —pleases; —tires; —wearies.

(See trip, tour, voyage.)

JOURNEY (v)

adverbs

tediously; fruitlessly; fatiguingly; fatally; arduously; dismally; daily; harrowingly; leisurely; uneventfully; triumphantly; aimlessly; perilously; memorably; romantically; triumphally.

(See travel, tour.)

JOURNEYINGS

adjectives

tiresome; constant; endless; costly.

JOVIAL

adverbs

immensely; extremely; heartily; wholesomely; amusingly; cordially; warmly; teasingly; companionably; sociably; convivially; happily; pleasantly; comfortably; familiarly; amiably; freely.

JOY

adjectives

earth-born; malignant; fiendish; serene; spirit-piercing; unreasoning; intense; sounding; ineffable; tumultuous; material; inexpressible; deceitful; exultant; domestic; vernal; secret; insecure; temporary; concentrated; inward; unbelieving; early; awkward; cradle; pretty; profound; unchecked; immortal; innumerable (pl); hearty; guilty; furious; deluding; fierce; thankful; transient; palpable; rapturous; strange; frank; unsubstantial; unbidden; grateful; youthful; deep; innocent; parental; deluding; lasting; spontaneous; superabundant; benevolent; eloquent; insidious; savage; unsuppressed; strained; increasing; mutual; triumphant; corroding; shivering; brief; embodied; overborne; sheer; wonderful; passionate; voluptuous; chastised; sober; unchecked; passionless; indistinct; heavenly; reviving; lively; presented; common; unappreciated; gentle; truant; boisterous; exulting; wild; celestial; overwhelming; plenteous; aching; general; quiet; unimaginable; ghastly; restrained; expectant; lustful; holy; exquisite; submissive; monumental; lovely; worldly; universal; passing; attainable; petty; dangerous; doubtful; unprecedented; incommunicable; tender; true; withered; acute; fleeting; artistic; beguiled; sharp; natural; wretched; thronged; unutterable; solemn; diversified; infant; curious; unmingled; abiding; murmuring; inconceivable; unmitigated; gushing; homely; unbodied; tranquil; flawless; majestic; equable; sedate; taintless; blustering; boundless; Lethean; amazed; delirious; incredulous; life-giving; purest; wordless; ill-natured; costlier; bridal; keen-witted; mild; suffused; refined; barbaric; human; overmastering; deepest; religious; radiant; breathless; narrow; thrilling; mixed; constant; vivid; explosive; animal; comforting; never-fading; lofty; stolen; unmingled; heartfelt; supreme; palpitating; eager; disguised; unbounded; hideous; abstract; perennial; eternal; prolonged; beatific; social; hackneyed; intoxicating; equal; filial; stern; fretful.

verbs

anticipate—; awaken—; blight—; conceal —; dampen—; derive—; experience—; extinguish—; forego—; impart—; intoxicate with—; leap for—; revel in—; snatch—; swoon with—; throw into a paroxysm of—; veil—; —floods the soul; —mounts; —riots in his eyes; —rises.

(See fun, mirth, merriment, happiness, pleasure, rapture.)

JOYFUL

adverbs

triumphantly; victoriously; magnificently; splendidly; brilliantly; naturally; exceedingly; marvelously; wonderfully; elatedly; exuberantly; overwhelmingly; quietly; secretly; proudly; humbly; gratefully; thankfully; utterly; speechlessly; unspeakably; inexpressibly; ineffably; rapturously; ecstatically; obviously; visibly; openly; professedly; apparently; downright; decidedly; infinitely; immeasurably; properly.

tutionally; disinterestedly; impartially; inflexibly; objectively; adversely; shallowly.

(See decide, discern, discriminate, consider.)

JOYOUSNESS

adjectives
symbolic; trustful; subdued.

JUBILANT

adverbs
naturally; marvellously; duly; triumphantly; happily; unspeakably; loudly; deeply; noisily; exultantly; boisterously; clamorously; immoderately; hilariously; vivaciously; spiritedly; tremendously; emphatically; riotously; turbulently; tumultuously; appropriately; hearteningly; utterly; unusually; noticeably; visibly; unconcealedly; secretly.

JUBILEE

adjectives
fierce; careless; wildly-celebrated.

JUDGE

adjectives
existing; rash; self-appointed; sagacious; equitable; discriminating; sympathetic; competent; imaginary; sole; honorable; terrible; ruthless; fitting; elective; dyspeptic; supreme; eminent; worthy; rightful; ecclesiastical; upright; learned; fastidious; capable; brutal; wicked; finicky; frowning; dispassionate; wanton; constitutional; capital; shrewd; disinterested; favorable.

verbs
appeal to—; appear before—; appoint—; elect—; impeach—; oust—; —administers; —admonishes; —assigns; —authorizes; —awards; —condemns; —deliberates; —determines; —grants; —hears; —holds; —investigates; —outlaws; —pardons; —penalizes; —presides; —pronounces; —sentences; —weighs.

(See president, umpire, congressman, senator.)

JUDGE (v)

adverbs
summarily; harshly; rigidly; rashly; righteously; wrathfully; hastily; cursorily; superficially; sentimentally; sagaciously; discriminatingly; equitably; competently; ruthlessly; ecclesiastically; learnedly; fastidiously; brutally; wickedly; wantonly; consti-

JUDGMENT

adjectives
solid; impartial; casual; profound; unerring; veritable; astonishing; declamatory; primitive; clearest; unfavorable; unimpeachable; scornful; verdant; aesthetic; historical; stern; intellectual; inappropriate; solemn; melodious; capricious; moral; subtle; snap; considered; artistic; sound; healthy; noble; fundamental; manifest; perverted; educated; critical; righteous; biased; discriminating; unflattering; jealous; ripe; tolerant; affectionate; cold; inflexible; popular; calm; awful; invaluable; depraved; unbiased; sober; silent; ready-made; disciplined; erroneous; imitative; military; discretionary; irritating; full-grown; burning; superior; qualitative; withering; adverse; objective; masculine; exulting; poetic; shallow; strict; true; interested; brawling; temperate; kindly; false; settled; unstable; dispassionate; rash; presentative; tautological; individual; unmerciful; reformed; lame; tried; admirable; enlightened; harsh; synthetic; advanced; maturer; ablest; retributive; cooler; strong; simple.

verbs
confirm—; derange—; distort—; endorse—; enfeeble—; exercise—; formulate—; impair—; impose—; impugn—; influence—; interfere with—; modify—; obtain—against; pass—; pervert—; pronounce—; render—; reverse—; ripen—; stimulate—; suspend—; temper—; venture—; voice—; waive—; warp—; withhold—; —affirms; —coerces; —impels.

(See decision, decree, sentence, verdict, opinion.)

JUDICIAL

adverbs
gravely; seriously; discreetly; officially; scarcely; pompously; magisterially; sagaciously; competently; capably; honorably; equitably; calmly; ruthlessly; cruelly; serenely; discriminatingly; supremely; eminently; fastidiously; coldly; deliberately; brutally; dispassionately; shrewdly; disinterestedly; impartially; splendidly; wonderfully.

adjectives
elective; appointive; corrupt; effective; independent.

JUDICIOUS
adverbs
remarkably; admirably; unusually; surprisingly; carefully; thoughtfully; soberly; sensibly; discreetly; keenly; acutely; astutely; discerningly; profoundly; considerately; uncommonly; wisely; habitually; temperamentally; dependably; reliably; comfortingly.

JUG
verbs
crack—; drain—; mold—; replenish—; seal —; shape—; shatter—; sterilize—; stew in —; store in—; —preserves; —protects; —tapers.
(See glass.)

JUGGLE (*v*)
adverbs
dexterously; skillfully; marvelously; professionally; verbally; grotesquely; spectacularly.
(See manipulate, handle.)

JUGGLING
adjectives
grotesque; verbal; remarkable.

JUICE
adjectives
concocted; helleboric; resinous; vegetable; rich; natural; savory; precious; rare-flavored; cooling; sweetened; vilesome; gastric; autumnal; acrid; necessary; fermented; joyful; bilious; ruddier; inspissated; gelatinuous; pungent; viscous; aerial; nectarian.

verbs
derive—from; dilute—; draw off—; drink —; express—; extract—; flavor with—; moisten with—; relish—; save—; secrete—; squeeze out—; strain—; suck—; suffuse—; tap—; wring out—; —dries; —drips—; exudes; —flows; —intoxicates; —oozes.
(See liquid, water, fluid, solution.)

JUICY
adverbs
lusciously; deliciously; palatably; sufficiently; scarcely; slightly; satisfactorily; sufficiently; delightfully; wonderfully; remark-ably; surprisingly; unexpectedly; drippingly; soppingly; terribly; delectably; extremely.

JUMBLE
adjectives
absurd; sad; wearisome; confused; incoherent.

JUMBLED
adverbs
hopelessly; terribly; intricately; miscellaneously; heterogeneously; miserably; unsystematically; promiscuously; chaotically; carelessly; confusedly; inexcusably; indefensibly; hastily; perplexingly; distressingly; disconcertingly; indiscriminately; indistinguishably; erratically; wantonly; dreadfully; impossibly; unimaginably; desperately; inextricably; frightfully; messily.

JUMP
adjectives
daring; awkward; high; corkscrew; vehement.

JUMP (*v*)
adverbs
nimbly; lightly; lumberingly; daringly; threateningly; smartly; gingerly; awkwardly; precipitately; rashly; gallantly; gracefully; thoughtlessly; agilely.
(See hop, spring, bound.)

JUMPY
adverbs
strangely; curiously; nervously; hysterically; foolishly; inanely; ostentatiously; painfully; shockingly; incurably; appallingly; helplessly; hopelessly; desperately; pitifully; stupidly; childishly; fearfully; unreasoningly; irremediably; pathetically; tragically.

JUNCTURE
adjectives
present; alarming; dangerous.

JUNGLE
adjectives
encroaching; hobo; steaming; unhealthy; uninhabited; vibrant; familiar; artificial; impenetrable; misty.

verbs
abandon in—; beat—; clear—; conceal in—; creep through—; cultivate—; desert—; explore—; guide through—; hack through—;

infest—; inhabit—; invade—; lose in—; overhang with—; penetrate—; tangle in—; thread through—; trudge through—; —enmeshes; —hems in; —looms; —swamps; —terrifies.

(See woods, thicket, forest.)

JUNK

adjectives
toy; majestic; gaudy; bright.

verbs
cart—; collect—; consume—; convert—; deal in—; discard—; dispose of—; eject—; employ—; enlist—; exhume—; fill with—; peddle—; refuse—; sack—; salvage—; sweep away—; utilize—.

(See rubbish, mess, sewage, waste.)

JURISDICTION

adjectives
reciprocal; exclusive; consular; provisional; military; constitutional; doubtful; competent; ecclesiastical; conflicting (pl).

verbs
abolish—; arrive within—; assume—; demand—; exempt from—; exercise—; extend —; free from—; include in—; infringe on —; invade—; limit—; relax—; resent—; subject to—; submit to—; vest—in; —embodies; —empowers; —extends.

(See authority, power.)

JURIST

adjectives
ermined; impartial; eminent; able; robed.

JURY

adjectives
absurd; impartial; swayed; emotional; prejudiced.

verbs
address—; appoint—; bribe—; challenge—; charge—; intimidate—; lay before—; panel —; plead with—; submit to—; summon—; swear in—; —acquits; —ballots; —conducts; —considers; —decides; —deliberates; —discharges; —haggles; —indicts; —meditates; —judges; —recommends; —retires; —takes oath; —withdraws.

(See tribunal, committee, hearers, court, judge.)

JUST

adverbs
undeniably; absolutely; impartially; admittedly; admirably; profoundly; unerringly; veritably; astonishingly; clearly; unimpeachably; uncommonly; unusually; appropriately; sternly; solemnly; soundly; nobly; fundamentally; righteously; coldly; tolerantly; strictly; temperately; dispassionately; entirely; manifestly; substantially; roughly; terribly; frightfully; remarkably.

JUSTICE

adjectives
distributive; poetical; passionless; ridiculous; temperate; biased; manifest; remarkable; substantial; inordinate; exemplary; swordless; armed; dreadful; summary; strictest; reasoned; eternal; stern; ultimate; resolute; unfailing; knavish; irascible; poetic; distorted; impartial; criminal; universal; rough-handed; wild; even-handed; scanty; presiding; sparing; perfect; divine; social; retributive; conservative; inflexible; vindictive; moral; common; private; ample; striking; strict; tardy; conceded; recompensive; bare; drowsy; immovable; equal; exact; slow; cruel; tied-up.

verbs
achieve—; administer—; advance—; defeat —; deny—; despair of—; dispense—; do — to; elude—; execute—; hamper—; imperil —; insure—; mete out—; obstruct—; paralyze—; preserve—; render—; taint—; thirst for—; trample—; —evolves; —grows; —hinges on; —rests.

(See righteousness, right, virtue, purity, truth.)

JUSTIFIABLE

adverbs
eminently; splendidly; scarcely; expediently; entirely; legally; morally; unquestionably; substantially; fundamentally; essentially; possibly; supposedly; presumably; apparently; sufficiently; reasonably; plausibly; barely; advantageously.

JUSTIFICATION

adjectives
substantial; abundant; gradual; creative; theoretical.

adverbs

completely; amply; definitely; sufficiently; reasonably; righteously; unmistakably; manifestly; undoubtedly; substantially; abundantly; theoretically.

(See excuse, absolve, warrant.)

adverbs

prodigiously; precipitately; sharply; abnormally; prominently; frightfully; dangerously.

(See protect, protrude.)

K

KALEIDOSCOPIC

adverbs

variably; restlessly; changefully; colorfully; shiftily; perilously; unstably; waveringly; interestingly; dizzily; artfully; terribly; surprisingly; amazingly; incredibly; perplexingly; mysteriously; queerly; inconveniently; oddly; dreadfully; uncertainly.

KANGAROO

verbs

—balances; —carries; —expels; —fights; —gnashes; —hops; —jumps; —pouches; —races; —nibbles.

(See animal.)

KEEN

adverbs

intelligently; unwontedly; sharply; acutely; naturally; subtly; extremely; shrewdly; sensibly; mysteriously; obviously; supremely; unfailingly; infallibly; prophetically; precociously; penetratingly; astoundingly; singularly; uncannily; sagaciously; wisely; apparently; obviously; profoundly; thoughtfully; exceedingly.

KEENNESS

adjectives

hereditary; uncanny; catlike.

KEEP (v)

adverbs

perniciously; charitably; surreptitiously; deliberately; shamelessly; tenderly; sedulously; discreetly; stubbornly; courteously; religiously; undeviatingly; ceaselessly; perpetually; inevitably; ostentatiously; jealously.

(See preserve, celebrate, observe, maintain.)

KEEPER

adjectives

pernicious; charitable; inquisitive.

verbs

appoint—; dodge—; elude—; escape—; install—; evade—; —abandons; —administers; —attends; —chastises; —controls; —governs; —guards; —inspects; —preserves; —prosecutes; —pursues; —retains; —scans; —snatches.

(See manager, guardian.)

KEEPING

adjectives

watchful; devoted; perfect.

KEN

adjectives

inscrutable; human; widest.

KENNEL

adjectives

loathsome; dubious; extensive; ghostly.

KERCHIEF

adjectives

bleached; pale; square-drooping.

KETTLE

adjectives

prophetic; simmering; melting; steaming.

verbs

beat—; brew in—; brush—; drain—; polish —; replenish—; scour—; scrub—; stew in —; strike—; strum on—; —chirps; —gleams; —hisses; —hums; —simmers; —sings; —trills; —whistles.

(See caldron, pot, tub, vat.)

KEY

adjectives

crystal; romantic; feeble; excellent; foreboding; tentative; strategic; interrogative; ponderous; unwieldy; tingling; massy.

verbs

belt —s; fit—; force—; fumble with—; inject—; grope for—; insert—; jangle—; mislay—; pocket—; ram — into; respond to—; —s clank; —s jingle; —s rattle.

KEY

(music)

adjectives

rigid; plaintive; tender; sad; minor; cracking.

KEYBOARD

adjectives

console-like; magic; complicated; master.

verbs

belabor—; caress—; dance on—; finger—; journey over—; perform on—; pounce upon

—; recite on—; render on—; run along—; skip over—; trip along—; work—; — gleams.

(See instrument, banjo, piano.)

KEYNOTE
verbs
elaborate on—; fire—; hit—; introduce—; reach—; recognize—; reveal—; seek—; sound—; strike—; touch—; —arouses; —attracts; —excites; —impresses; —interests; —stirs.

(See point, policy, idea.)

KEYSTONE
adjectives
indispensable; all-supporting.

KICK
adjectives
mighty; harmless; ceremonious.

KICK (v)
adverbs
affectionately; profanely; unmercifully; brutally; furiously; spasmodically; carelessly; frantically; simultaneously; unceremoniously; savagely; clumsily; murderously; madly; viciously; vindictively; ferociously.

(See oppose, resist, recoil.)

KID
adjectives
healthy; irresponsible; squalling.

KIDNAPPER
verbs
apprehend—; contact—; negotiate with—; prosecute—; pursue—; —abducts; —decoys; —delivers; —demands; —directs; —entices; —frightens; —lures; —operates; —snatches; —spirits away; —surveys; —threatens.

(See thief, robber, murderer.)

KIDNEY
adjectives
hard-worked; distressing; paining.

verbs
belt—; block—; congest—; dilate—; engorge —; impair—; inflame—; obstruct—; pad—; support—; —enlarges; —excretes; —filters; —floats; —fuses; —moves; —swells.

(See bladder, liver, organ, intestines.)

KILL (v)
adverbs
incessantly; simultaneously; accidentally; designedly; uselessly; intentionally; instantly; wantonly; ferociously; brutally; pitilessly; insanely; savagely; basely; sportively.

(See murder, slay, assassinate.)

KILLER
adjectives
tyrannical; pitiless; brutal; mad.

KILLING
adjectives
merciless; unrestricted; unsolved.

verbs
atone for—; avenge—; conceal—; confess —; contrive—; indulge in an orgy of—s; lament—; observe—; perform—; plan—; resent—; revenge—; stifle—; uncover—; unearth—; warrant—; witness—; —awes; —incenses; —infuriates; —offends; —puzzles; —shocks.

(See murder, slaughter, massacre, assassination.)

KIN
adjectives
blood; nearest; surviving.

KIND
adjectives
refractory; voracious; abstracted; unexpected; corresponding; literal; positive; unworthy; fraternal; direst; various (pl); wondrous; honey-gathering; tingling; haphazard; curious; mortal; fascinating; heavier; weakest; baser; unlike; particular; noblest; sprightliest; restless; elaborate; expensive; barbarous; branching; peculiar; indifferent; unsatisfied; awful; lonesome; effectual; defensive; increasing; adventurous; equivocal.

adverbs
graciously; generously; hospitably; helpfully; unexpectedly; extremely; exceedingly; habitually; naturally; indulgently; gently; mistakenly; thoughtfully; lovingly; unaffectedly; effusively; officiously; sincerely; cordially; unspeakably; unusually; uncommonly; openly; apparently; noticeably; unselfishly; sympathetically; amiably; affably; unwontedly; considerately; humanely; complaisantly.

KINDLE (v)

adverbs

patiently; skillfully; daily; purposely; premeditatively; punctually; swiftly; spectacularly; vividly.

(See ignite, burn, inflame, rouse.)

KINDLINESS

adjectives

tranquil; clear; close-fisted; proverbial; eager; unaffected; sincere; comfortable.

KINDNESS

adjectives

gracious; ostentatious; undiminished; manifest; systematic; sickening; honey; paternal; sneaking; fraternal; mysterious; selfsame; indulgent; mistaken; loving; thoughtful; false; mellow; anxious; maddening; touching; like; present; patient; generous; fair; subtle; covetous; usurious; impersonal; marked; quizzical; proffered; grave; considerable; lukewarm; cruel; extreme; homely; exceeding; benevolent; natural; indolent; remorseful; hospitable; commended; native; cordial; unbought; forbearing; apparent; untaught.

verbs

bestow—upon; bless with—; confer—; enslave by—; extend—; overflow with—; render—; scatter—; trust—; —charms; —comforts; —conquers; —converts; —enriches; —gladdens; —melts; —shines; —soothes.

(See tenderness, tolerance, charity.)

KING

adjectives

maleficent; deposed; uncrowned; shameful; tributary; wily; grisly; besieging; cautious; guarded; crafty; lofty; apostate; bereaved; loving; nominal; bonanza; well-intentioned; penitent; harlot; veritable; anointed; uxorious; lawful; captive; prostrate; rightful; boastful; mythological; guileless; pious; colorless; blameless; lottery; faithless; untamed; sanguine; unwholesome; resplendent; fangless; landless; provincial; incredulous; fratricidal; licentious; dissimulating.

verbs

acknowledge—; anoint—; consort with—s; crown—; dethrone—; exile—; forsake—; guard—; honor—; praise—; respect—; serve—; —abdicates; —administers; —awes; —commands; —governs; —reigns; —rules; —surveys.

(See monarch, queen, god, ruler.)

KINGDOM

adjectives

infernal; peasant; teeming; animal; mineral; island; watery; moss-hung; hereditary; unconquerable; petty; stout; little; enchanting; enduring; dull; vassal.

verbs

banish from—; conquer—; divide—; forsake—; govern—; grant—; infect—; inhabit—; invade—; overthrow—; partition—; reign over—; renounce—; resign—; rule—; serve—; skirt—; split—; subdue—; —embraces; —extends; —ranges.

(See kingship, realm, monarchy, jurisdiction, dominion, empire.)

KINGLY

adverbs

undeniably; admittedly; consciously; notably; admirably; strikingly; astonishingly; superbly; estimably; magnificently; splendidly; consummately; expertly; aristocratically; nobly; unimpeachably; judiciously; benevolently; resplendently; absolutely; authoritatively; influentially; supremely; autocratically.

KINGSHIP

verbs

abdicate—; abolish—; accept—; bestow—upon; forsake—; honor—; invest—with; ordain to—; propose—; respect—; survey—.

(See kingdom.)

KINSHIP

adjectives

emotional; spiritual.

KINSMEN

adjectives

distinguished; lamented; honorable; moldering.

KISS

adjectives

salt; sterile; spiritlike; melancholy; squandered; multiplied (pl); successive (pl); bought; barren; piteous; breathless; rapturous; wafted; indulgent; passionate; energetic; perfunctory; burning; glowing; inplacable; ungiven; farewell; hot; silent;

fleeting; mute; deep-drawn; fruitful; horizontal; cancerous; treacherous; lovely; sisterhood; famished; tempting; punctuating; loving; holy; sovereign; furious; honeyed; guileless; humbled; fervent; furtive; impassioned; ardent; rarely-tempered; admiring; compassionate; serio-comic; reverent; vigorous; abstracted; random; sincere; airy; moist; reassuring; iron; eager; hasty; laughing; latter; timorous; broken; delicious.

verbs
bestow—upon; blow—; blush at—; brush—; cement with—; cling in—; dab—; dot with —; pluck—; press—; print—upon; promise with—; resist—; sever—; smother with—s; snatch—; steal—; taste—; tempt with—; wed in—; yield—; —disturbs; —enraptures; —entrances; —pecks; —quenches; —subdues; —thrills.
(See caress, embrace.)

KISS (v)
adverbs
passionately; resoundingly; reverently; clumsily; violently; tenderly; airily; ravenously; earnestly; brazenly; soberly; intimately; exultantly; crudely; tantalizingly; fondly; perfunctorily; devoutly; dutifully; vivaciously; mutely; timorously.
(See caress, salute, embrace.)

KISSING
adjectives
voluptuous; continual; heated; promiscuous; ignominious; passioned.

KITCHEN
adjectives
commodious; fragrant; detached; reeking; itinerant; greasy; pretty; well-designed.

verbs
avoid—; consign to—; convey from—; drudge in—; equip—; inspect—; loiter in —; preside over—; retire to—; rule—; scrub—; slave in—; survey—; sweat in—; toil in—; work in—; —enslaves; —gleams; —shines; —smells of.
(See home, room, shop, factory, laboratory.)

KITES
adjectives
carrion; marauding; ravenous.

KITTEN
adjectives
imaginary; striped; playful; impish.

verbs
pet—; stroke—; —amuses; —antics; — basks; —capers; —diverts; —frisks; — frolics; —gambols; —laps; —meows; — plays; —romps; —toys with.
(See cat, puppy, lamb, baby, calf.)

KNACK
adjectives
mechanical; instinctive.

KNAVE
adjectives
cowardly; luckless; unthrifty; lunatic; base; poor; gallant; false; arrant; jealous; decayed; shrewd; ingenious; foolish; rascally; whoreson; beetle-headed; flap-ear; misshapen; pestilent; foul-mouthed; calumnious; scurvy; railing; wrangling; thin-faced; fantastical; doting; sooty; veritable; sinful.

KNAVERY
verbs
brew—; check—; condemn—; confess—; curb—; despise—; escape—; frustrate—; observe—; resist—; shun—; suffer—; suspect—; unfold—; witness—; yield to—; — jars; —shocks; —tempts.
(See wickedness, villainy, vice, crime.)

KNAVISH
adverbs
arrantly; downright; notoriously; grossly; consummately; egregiously; abominably; atrociously; villainously; viciously; infamously; daringly; wickedly; brazenly; extraordinarily; outrageously; monstrously; unbelievably; sinfully; terribly; insufferably; unscrupulously; insidiously; ingloriously; lawlessly; disreputably; scandalously; incorrigibly; shamelessly; astoundingly .

KNEAD (v)
adverbs
savagely; industriously; vigorously; laboriously; mechanically; experimentally; patiently; wholesomely; furiously.
(See fashion, massage, mould, mix.)

KNEE
adjectives
guiding; shaking; shaken; bended; knotted; twinging; naked; rocky; suppliant; feeble;

mailed; pliant; trembling; faltering; up-gathered; relentless; silken; immaculate; sagged; well-molded; sagging; bony; flaccid; tottering; wobbly; weak; exposed; bare; numb; stalwart; buckling; jutting; drawn-up; clasped; scratched; dimpled; enticing.

verbs
bend—; beseech on—s; bow—; brace—; bruise—; climb on—; drop on—; entreat on —s; fall upon—; flex—; implore on—; sink to—; smite—; supplicate on—; —s buckle; —s fold; —s sag; —s weaken.

KNEEL ·(v)

adverbs
heavily; laboriously; devoutly; submissively; reverently; blindly; prayerfully; imploringly; meekly; religiously; adoringly .
(See surrender, bend.)

KNELL

adjectives
doleful; perpetual; inevitable.

KNIFE

adjectives
ill-directed; harmful; murderous; crooked; keen; burning; long; two-edged; broad; sharp-pointed; naked; big; tempered; curved; brass-handled; blunt; hatchetlike; pointless; whetted; blood-stained.

verbs
brandish—; carve with—; clasp with—; fling—; flourish—; hack with—; heave—; hone—; hurl—; pare with—; pocket—; sheathe—; slash with—; slay with—; stab with—; thrust—; whirl—about.
(See sword, stiletto.)

KNIGHT

adjectives
moralizing; valiant; dauntless; adventurous; tender-smelling; solitary; gallant; cheerful; virgin; sinful; dissembling; blended; belted; irreverent; greasy; assailing; tight-lipped; stalwart; particular; fabled; dubbed; brave.

KNIGHTLY

adverbs
dauntlessly; intrepidly; courteously; gallantly; invariably; habitually; splendidly; superbly; magnificently; generously; chivalrously; distinctly; eminently; nobly; bene-

volently; delightfully; charmingly; pleasantly; affably; uncommonly; unusually; exceptionally.

KNIT (v)

adverbs
indefatigably; industriously; vigorously; busily; exquisitely; laboriously; patiently; domestically; artistically; beneficially; healthfully; swiftly; monotonously.
(See tie, unite, join, weave.)

KNITTING

verbs
abandon—; admire—; busy with—; commend—; concentrate on—; display—; enjoy —; exhibit—; instruct in—; interrupt—; observe—; occupy with—; survey—; teach —; unravel—; —annoys; —bores; —contents; —delights; —fascinates; —satisfies; —takes form.
(See work.)

KNOB

adjectives
battered; rusty; bent; twisted; turning.

verbs
adjust—; affix—; force—; furnish—; grasp —; grope for—; handle—; jiggle—; locate —; manipulate—; move—; raise—; shake —; turn—; —juts out; —opens; —resists; —submits.
(See handle.)

KNOCK

adjectives
welcome; jarring; thundering; timid; hesitating; parlous; cheerful; imperative; timorous; hard; unwonted; resounding.

KNOCK (v)

adverbs
sharply; clamorously; deliberately; accidentally; respectfully; irritably; resoundingly; unwontedly; thunderously; echoingly; startlingly.
(See rap, clash, beat, strike.)

KNOLL

adjectives
neighboring; sandy; moon-lit; wooded; treeless; timber-covered; rising; verdant.

KNOT

adjectives
inextricable; mystic; intricate; unsuccess-

ful; curious; murderous; true-love; shaggy; salient; writhing; snaky; sagest; feathered.

verbs
curl into—; disentangle—; do up in—; draw into—; form—; knit into—; loop into—; loose—; secure with—; unravel—; untwine —; weave into—; —assures; —mystifies; — perplexes; —puzzles.

KNOTTED

adverbs
dreadfully; tightly; nervously; angrily; inextricably; roughly; strangely; queerly; loosely; carelessly; deliberately; unevenly; jaggedly; hopelessly; terribly; untidily; indiscriminately; mischievously; maliciously; incurably; irreparably; perniciously; vexatiously; inexcusably.

KNOW (v)

adverbs
precisely; intimately; distinctly; intuitively; authoritatively; affectionately; grimly; casually; graciously; jocularly; abstractly; instantaneously; superficially; alliteratively; imperfectly; officially; familiarly; presumably; academically; traditionally; personally; fallaciously.

(See apprehend, realize, understand, ascertain, recognize.)

KNOWLEDGE

adjectives
technical; subtle; painful; pleasurable; experimental; distinct; tinctured; hearsay; extensive; intuitive; slight; detailed; repugnant; profound; dark; uncanny; sudden; acquired; human; systematic; psycho-analytic; copious; elementary; unique; well-known; definite; fuller; academic; intimate; precise; rudimentary; prodigious; barren; bookish; extemporary; unimparted; uncertain; critical; boundless; accurate; specialized; exhilarating; unwelcome; superior; guilty; dangerous; swift; unrelated; superficial; miraculous; worldly; unutterable; imperfect; substantial; immense; preliminary;

fluent; growing; untimely; proficient; inestimable; complete; improved; practical; symbolic; consummate; masterful; extraordinary; previous; satisfying; medieval; organized; theoretical; advanced; wearisome; crafty; instinctive; varied; seeming; increased; thorough; lawful; inexhaustible; phenomenal; accumulated; comprehensive; preternatural; gradual; learned; unerring; scientific; definite; clearer; objective; special; lesser; naturalistic; adequate; hard-won; competent; masculine; shrewd; natural; deeper; desecrated; inherited; cynical; rapidly-acquired; delivering; deep-fetched; limited; dread; defective; positive; indisputable; fallacious; educational; gossipy; colloquial; all-embracing; traditional; questionable; acquired; laborious; working; premature; verified; superfluous; meager; personal; astronomic; contemptuous; inward; actual; earthly; secure; rooted; fiendish; fascinating; up-to-the-minute; priceless; happiest; nobler; inferior; well-founded; momentary; unrivaled.

verbs
absorb—; accumulate—; acquire—; apply —; arm with—; assimilate—; attain—; augment—; broadcast—; confront with—; contribute to—; convey—; cultivate—; derive —; digest—; disavow—; disseminate—; draw upon—; employ—; enlarge—; enrich with—; equip with—; evince—; evolve—; exhibit—; expand—; extend—; feed with—; flash—; flaunt—; grope for—; illuminate with—; impart—; imply—; obscure—; pool —; prize—; promulgate—; purchase—; record—; retain—; retard—; safeguard—; soak up—; spread—; thirst for—; treasure —; utilize—; yearn for—; —enlightens; — boils down to.

(See learning, facts, information, understanding, wisdom.)

KNUCKLE

adjectives
bleeding; white; pudgy; bruised; skinned; swarthy; abraded; brass.

L

adjectives
progressive; registered; bothersome.

verbs
affix—; destroy—; investigate—; note—; require—; scan—; seal with—; slap on—; stamp—; —attests; —clings; —describes; —designates; —indicates; —represents.
(See mark, stamp, notice, badge, trademark.)

LABEL (v)

adverbs
legally; sarcastically; laconically; carelessly; perfunctorily; cursorily; painstakingly; methodically; decoratively; attractively; concisely; symbolically; fantastically; characteristically.
(See classify, mark.)

LABOR

adjectives
enormous; arduous; sedentary; colossal; persevering; unskilled; lofty; conscientious; praiseworthy; enlightened; earnest; patient; painful; fastidious; graver; uplifting; exhausting; toilsome; unceasing; intellectual; self-imposed; initiatory; faithful; incredible; useless; indefatigable; ceaseless; reproachful; assiduous; unsparing; manual; wonderful; immense; manifold; ill-paid; unimaginable; attendant; unremitting; nocturnal; incessant; endless; grievous; journalistic; intermittent; wearisome; strenuous; unrequited; exploited; loving; sleepless; sweated; diligent; untiring; confining; unceasing; steadfast; imperative; degraded; superfluous; insurgent; inconceivable; fantastic; bucolic; herculean; honorable; skilled; mighty; guiltless; daring; infinite; moderate; effective; congenial; smoke-grimed; gratuitous; united; earnest; unbroken; painstaking; influential; powerful; culinary; unselfish; historical; interrupted; successive (pl); backbreaking; previous; subordinate; organized; active; unwearying; vilified; productive; tremendous; exacting; harsh; aspiring; patient; painful; tedious; ideal; untasked; convict; dreadful; rural; additional; sylvan; pleasant; astrological;

oppressed; wonted; tutorial; symbolical; evasive; menial; ever-successful; short-lived; literary; coarse; ferocious; professional; ministerial; heartbreaking.

verbs
absorb in—; bleed (colloq.)—; discipline—; enslave—; free from—; mar—; necessitate —; organize—; placate—; prohibit—; recompense—; recuperate from—; regulate—; reward—; stimulate—; supplement—; surmount—; thrive upon—; undertake—; — profits; —reaps; —supports; —sustains.
(See work, workers, task, industry, toil, production.)

LABOR (v)

adverbs
systematically; incessantly; indefatigably; assiduously; unmercifully; industriously; vigorously; tirelessly; prodigiously; diligently; tumultuously; arduously; fastidiously; unsparingly; gratuitously; congenially; productively; exactingly; unwontedly; tutorially; symbolically; menially; ferociously; professionally.
(See work, toil, drudge.)

LABORATORY

adjectives
destructive; stupendous; metallurgical.

verbs
dissect in—; emit from—; employ in—; establish—; experiment in—; inspect—; investigate in—; lecture in—; manufacture in—; prepare in—; rig out—; stock—; test in—; tinker in—; turn out of—; verify in —; work in—; —discloses; —nauseates; — reeks of; —discovers.
(See kitchen, shop, factory.)

LABORER

adjectives
diverting; solitary; bucolic; devoted; potential; agricultural; diligent; luckless.

LABORIOUS

adverbs
extremely; oppressively; intricately; objectionably; unexpectedly; surprisingly; unremittingly; sedulously; overwhelmingly; enormously; immensely; painfully; incred-

ibly; grievously; strenuously; fantastically; moderately; dreadfully; pleasantly; wholesomely; backbreakingly; elaborately; wearisomely; terribly; undeniably; unbelievably.

LABYRINTH
adjectives
slimy; close; mighty; vast; trackless; burning; weary; watery; aboreal; inextricable.

LABYRINTHINE
adverbs
intricately; hopelessly; perplexingly; curiously; queerly; alarmingly; amazingly; dreadfully; surprisingly; mysteriously; dangerously; perilously; complexly; sinuously; tortuously; troublesomely; circuitously; vexatiously; terrifyingly; ominously.

LACE
adjectives
tawdry; exquisite; cream; supernumerary (pl); billowing; meandering; delicate; passementerie; erring; fluttering; elaborate; tarnished; creamy; tinted.

LACE (v)
adverbs
tightly; suffocatingly; fashionably; injuriously; oppressively.
(See fasten, tie, bind.)

LACERATION
verbs
incur—; inflict—; occasion—; soothe—; sterilize—; stitch—; suture—; tourniquet—; —appals; —bares the bone; —distresses; —heals; —horrifies; —inflames; —pains; —scars; —shocks; —throbs; —tortures.
(See wound, injury, pain, cut.)

LACK
adjectives
pretended; noticeable; all-round; deplorable; disorderly; overwhelming; impressive; plentiful; definite; obvious.

verbs
atone for—; bare—; bemoan—; compensate for—; confess—; decry—; disclose—; imply —; perceive—; recognize—; recompense for —; remedy—; sense—; suffer—; supply—; suspect—; —crushes; —disgraces; —handicaps; —humbles; —irks; —offends; —ostracizes; —saddens.
(See inadequacy, need, want.)

LACK (v)
adverbs
lamentably; puzzlingly; vainly; essentially; wretchedly; sorely; utterly; sadly; deplorably; definitely; obviously; tragically; dramatically.
(See need, want.)

LACKADAISICAL
adverbs
nonchalantly; ostentatiously; obviously; foolishly; sentimentally; romantically; languidly; dreamily; inanely; provokingly; drunkenly; stupidly; crazily; pretentiously; foppishly; vainly; unnaturally; artificially; languishingly; heavily; terribly; gravely; thoughtfully.

LACKEY
adjectives
saucy; liveried; silk-stockinged.

LACONIC
adverbs
meagerly; unsatisfactorily; emphatically; disappointingly; vexatiously; habitually; tersely; drily; drolly; crisply; curtly; comprehensively; summarily; trenchantly; curiously; oddly; officially; arrogantly; cynically; laudably; neatly; compactly; sententiously; professionally; provokingly; remarkably; wonderfully; notably; famously; uncommonly; highly; amazingly; incredibly; effectively.

LACONISM
adjectives
formal; concise; annoying; notable.

LACQUERS
adjectives
decorative; shiny; protective; gaudy; bright.

LAD
adjectives
malicious; lethargic; raw; daring; sober; gallant; joyous; vigorous; singular; loutish; fine; gentlemanly; valiant; painstaking; capable; ambitious; blithe; sensitive; sweet; rosy; mad; delirious; promising; struggling.

LADDER
adjectives
petal-woven; corded; rude; commodious; symbolical; palpable; golden; heavenly.

verbs

ascend—; clamber up—; drop from—; employ—; extend—; hoist—; leap up—; mount —; rung—; scale—; scramble up—; shake —; shift—; support—; teeter on—; —aids; —bridges; —conveys; —dizzies; —totters; travel up—.

(See steps, stairs.)

LADY

adjectives

demure; spare; grave; worthy; estimable; double-dealing; venerable; generous; gallant; out-sized; perennial; gracious; blushing; haughty; pitiful; excellent; accomplished; wretched; audacious; quick-fingered; quick-witted; quick-eyed; sacred; horny-handed; virtuous; sweet; innocent; good-natured; courageous; beauteous; incredulous; celestial; disloyal; hopeful; miserable; conventional; decorous; well-mannered; dejected; soft-spoken; square-faced; starched; profound; interested; autocratic; languid; well-brought-up; masterful; delicate; highbred; pink-cheeked; reverend; vixenish; colossal; dignified; elderly; flustered; skeptical; diminutive; blameless; giddy; charming; gentle; fortunate; little; chubby; prudent; pleasant-spoken; exotic; sentimental; thricefair; pleasant-spirited; desolate; poor; wrong; chic; acidulated; chaste; agreeable; prepossessing; illustrious; elegant; glittering; ingenuous; favorite; metallic; solicitous; pearly-robed.

LADYLIKE

adverbs

oppressively; exquisitely; absurdly; delightfully; overwhelmingly; fastidiously; foolishly; agreeably; pleasantly; graciously; comically; modestly; demurely; coyly; decorously; genteelly; formally; properly; fashionably; appropriately; conventionally; aristocratically; politely; courteously; ostentatiously; stylishly; elegantly; ceremoniously; stiffly; awkwardly; pretentiously; affably; complaisantly; charmingly; enchantingly.

LAG

adjectives

cultural; common; noticeable.

LAGOON

verbs

approach—; cover—; cross—; describe—; enclose—; enter—; form—; observe—; open into—; row in—; sail in—; separate—; skirt—; swim in—; —appears; —beckons; —extends; —invites.

(See lake, bay, pond.)

LAIR

adjectives

frigid; equatorial; shaggy; rosy; dreadful; jungle; deathless.

verbs

conceal in—; corner in—; discover—; dwell in—; ensconce in—; enter—; expose—; harbor in—; lodge in—; nestle in—; recline in—; repose in—; retreat to—; reveal—; track to—; uncover—; venture upon—; —comforts; —reeks; —shelters.

(See den, refuge, retreat.)

LAKE

adjectives

shimmering; tranquil; climbing; lily-mantled; darkling; grassy; azure; misty; stagnant; placid; bitter; weedy; far-reaching; encircling; shattered; picturesque; forest-bosomed; crystal; encompassing; starry; lovely; seething; translucent; calm-flowing; rumored; universal; parent; sleeping; lucid; contrasted; burning; smiling; argent; glittering; airy; lonely; ruffled; liquid; mirrored; fringed; dazzling; noble; dusky.

verbs

angle in—; cast into—; encompass—; fish in—; navigate—; ramble by—; row on—; sail—; shade—; sight—; skim over—; skirt —; slip into—; surround—; waft across—; —affords; —dazzles; —gleams; —glimmers; —laps; —mirrors; —reflects; —ripples; —shimmers; —spangles; —winks; —yawns.

(See lagoon, river, stream, bay, pond, sea.)

LAMB

adjectives

bleating; parti-colored; sinful; sacrificial; silly; twinned; heaven-sent.

verbs

brand—s; cuddle—; fatten—s; market—; roast—; sacrifice—; slaughter—; —baas; —bleats; —capers; —frisks; —frolics; —gambols; —grazes; —nuzzles; —prances; —symbolizes.

(See kitten, calf, sheep, animal, baby, puppy, cat.)

LAMBENT

adverbs

delicately; gently; flickeringly; effulgently; flashingly; gloriously; steadily; luminously; phosphorescently; shimmeringly; softly; recurrently; lustrously; scintillatingly; unusually; peculiarly; strangely.

LAMENT

adjectives

constant; loud; inevitable; lugubrious; passionate.

LAMENT (v)

adverbs

dolorously; pitifully; pathetically; eternally; morbidly; passionately; lugubriously; quaveringly; tearfully; abnormally; hysterically; affectionately.

(See weep, wail, grieve.)

LAMENTABLE

adverbs

altogether; downright; pitiably; bitterly; sorely; direly; utterly; exceptionally; shockingly; appallingly; horribly; unusually; extremely; fearfully; frightfully; tragically; wretchedly; indescribably; sadly; absolutely; unspeakably; inexpressibly; singularly.

LAMENTATION

adjectives

piteous; moderate; importunate; frantic; grand; purposeless; loud; diabolical; silent; sublime; quavering; burlesque.

verbs

censure—; deplore—; fill with—; forego—; forestall—; regret—; restrain—; staunch—; stifle—; utter—; wail in—; —arises; —ceases; —encompasses; —haunts; —increases; —rends the air; —resounds; —weakens.

(See tears, sadness, grief, sorrow.)

LAMP

adjectives

flickering; wharf; quenchless; fragrant; incandescent; glimmering; respectable; acetyline; blear; trembling; mirrored; tawdry; frail; light-giving; intoxicating; ill-trimmed; wasting; pendulous; failing; rain-splashed; glow-worm; festooned; slow-sliding; meteoric; impudent; innumerable (pl); classic; sleepy; street; eternal; oil-dried; fluorescent; midnight; smoky; outburnt; shaded; reading; bronze; copper; shining; winking; flashing; soft; colored; tiny; sputtering; gas; oil; luminous; twinkling; vital; studious; flaring; kindled; dewy.

verbs

blast—; deck with—s; extinguish—; grope for—; quench—; restore—; strangle—; suspend—; switch on—; —beautifies; —blinds; —brightens; —cheers; —comforts; —directs; —enhances; —fails; —flickers; —glimmers; —glows; —mellows; —reveals; —shines; —silhouettes.

(See light, candle, flame, fireworks, match, sunshine, twilight, spark.)

LANCE

adjectives

ill-headed; gleaming; thirsty; leafy; quivering; strong; shivered; rusted; splintered; unused.

verbs

cast—; charge with—s; harpoon with—; shatter—; slay with—; spear with—; splinter—; stab with—; thrust—; wield—; —cripples; —defends; —disfigures; —injures; —maims; —pierces; —scratches; —shivers; —splinters; —splits; —threatens; —wounds.

(See spear, sword, stiletto.)

LAND

adjectives

brawny-breasted; weather-beaten; tempting; wide; uninhabited; fruitful; radiant; rolling; toiling; devastated; depreciated; desolate; swampy; bleeding; cultivated; uncharted; intolerant; sylvan; eloquent; unshorn; exhausted; delightful; twilight; favored; death-polluted; dying; delectable; woeful; venerable; alluvial; granitic; barren; arable; heavenly; sickly; dewy; contiguous; pastoral; sun-soaked; virgin; enchanted; ceded; broad; monotonous; flat; factious; romantic; quaggy; guilty; boggy; habitable; sterile; forbidden; allodial; lifeless; gasping; sheltering; delicious; forsaken; debatable; enlightened; guileless; dirty; mortgaged; dawning; smiling; genial; sullen; scorched; superior; unhappy; untraveled; chivalric; gracious; inspirational; wretched; time-stricken; foreign; extreme; sprightly; listening; neighboring; untilled; goodly-growing; fertile; fallen; long-promised; hostile; springtime; sinless; disburdened; dipping; defenceless; unappropriated; wilderness; unoccupied; well-contented; watered; dependent; curtained; ruined; gentler;

sorrow-stricken; shadowy; hazy; ice-prisoned; white; useless; beautiful; vacation; placid; tight; upheaved; sculptured; aesthetic; undulous; dim; vast; tranquil; irrigable; rich; blatant; fabled; misty; scrubby; furrowed; shadowless; antique; divers (pl); unseated; high-cost; touch-and-go; sluggish; marshy; fettered; hollow; bustling; native; derelict; waste; heath; many-tinted; boundless; prosperous; bountiful; invisible; timeless; sodden; unexplored; unconcerned; financial; fairy; luxuriant; exhaustless; desirable; agricultural; surrounding; night-enfolded; spiritual; unknown; gullied; middling; hereditary; distant; alien; dismembered; stubble; blossoming.

verbs

apportion—; bargain for—; cede—; claim —; cleanse—; corrupt—; cultivate—; darken—; defile—; denude—; despoil—; dower —; engulf—; enrich—; exploit—; fertilize —; inhabit—; inherit—; lease—; link—; nurse—; plow—; portion—; purge—; rule —; scour—; sow—; squat on—; sweep—; till—; vest—s in; —abuts; —adjoins; — yields.

(See earth, soil, ground, farm.)

LANDHOLDER
adjectives
wealthy; pampered; heavily-taxed; frugal.

LANDING
adjectives
rude; haphazard; prosaic; steamboat; three-point; perfect; fatal; forced.

verbs
anticipate—; bar—; contemplate—; effect—; forestall—; hinder—; hope for—; impede —; limit—; meet at—; prepare for—; prohibit—; salute—; superintend—; survey—; swoop to—; view—.
(See platform, finish.)

LANDLADY
adjectives
callous; slipshod; overpositive; shrieking; untrained; half-distracted; miserly.

LANDLORD
adjectives
absentee; lonely; liberal; grasping.

LANDMARK
adjectives
ghostly; tall; treasured; celebrated; obliterated; ancient; historical; well-kept; awe-inspiring.

LANDSCAPE
adjectives
ideal; imaginative; volcanic; broad; wet; dreary; reposeful; shadowy; manifold (pl); glorious; delicate; gliding; desolate; dismal; rolling; inspiring; autumnal; harmonious; limited; extravagant; bewildered; poetical; suggestive; naked; receding; twilight; motionless; mystic; glimmering; colored; austere; stupendous; delicious; ungenial; ravaged; forbidding; bitter; peaceful; perfect; winter; untrodden; melancholy; impressive; serious; shivering; imposing; large; dreamy; terrestrial; hoary; lunar; hazy; sunlit; glowing; variegated; pastoral; scarred; vernal; withered; dim; embrowned; distant.

verbs
clutter—; contemplate—; denude—; desecrate—; design—; dot—; enhance—; exhibit—; gaze on—; gild—; glorify—; integrate—; intersperse—; perfect—; photograph—; regard—; scrutinize—; shade—; tinge—; view—; —charms; —delights; — educates; —gratifies; —spreads; —stretches.
(See country, countryside, view, scene, picture, scenery.)

LAND-SLIDE
adjectives
fashion; fatal; crushing; spectacular.

LANE
adjectives
dark; solitary; hedgerowed; grassy; seaward; rambling; turfy; cattle-haunted; leafy; pleached; neighboring; winding; miry; isolated; infrequent; sandy; rectory; bowery; dirty; rutty; hollow; shaded; forest; high-walled; quiet; deep-shaded.

verbs
adhere to—; bolt down—; clear—; follow —; labor up—; lurk in—; mantle—; pause in—; rest in—; scamper down—; shade—; shadow—; shun—; skirt—; tarry in—; veer from—; —diverges; —flanks; —meanders; —spirals; —swerves; —twists; —wanders; —winds.
(See road, alley, passage, path, street, thoroughfare, walk.)

LANGUAGE

adjectives

various (pl); symbolical; evasive; abusive; well-known; clear; understandable; simple; clarified; easy; peculiar; profane; psychoanalytic; lovely; figurative; neighboring; luminous; ungracious; graceless; energetic; ominous; satirical; adopted; subservient; impassioned; rhythmical; strenuous; lucid; emphatic; precise; noble; judicious; conversational; similar; amicable; forcible; violent; unseemly; flexible; musical; refined; primitive; wide-spread; copious; metrical; native; expressive; unmistakable; worthy; passionate; maternal; extinct; warming; dead; universal; reviling; elegant; opprobrious; inoffensive; biblical; scrupulous; classical; provincial; concise; sublime; appropriate; nervous; unintelligible; official; elaborate; stilted; bombastic; temperate; winning; cordial; sensible; semibarbarous; mystic; glowing; tart; strong; persuasive; inadequate; provocative; hearty; lustful; animated; rude; decorous; uncensored; remarkable; felicitous; colloquial; declarative; emotional; melodious; informal; striking; paradoxical; imaginative; contemptuous; coarse; embellished; pleasurable; impossible; vehement; rugged; vigorous; idiomatic; austere; traditional; high-flown; hidden; spiritual; characteristic; artificial; lifeless; sacred; colorless; symbolic; euphonious; literary; immoderate; festive; impious.

verbs

abuse—; bolt—; broaden—; clothe in—; command—; corrupt—; decipher—; decode —; defile—; interpret—; manipulate—; master—; mold—; mutilate—; purify—; restrict—; revive—; strangle—; vitalize—; vulgarize—; —abounds in; —bears witness; —bristles with; —flows; —lilts; —survives.
(See speech, dialect, slang, jargon.)

LANGUID

adverbs

listlessly; dreamily; lazily; idly; deliberately; deliciously; softly; blissfully; unwontedly; delightfully; pensively; thoughtfully; wearily; mildly; strangely; unusually; peculiarly; alarmingly; ominously; oddly; dispiritedly; dejectedly; indifferently; indolently; inertly; uncommonly; woefully; significantly; particularly; constitutionally; objectionably; exasperatingly; provokingly; inveterately.

LANGUISH (v)

adverbs

piteously; idly; gradually; pathetically; sickly; wanly; pensively; wearily; dreamily; amorously; listlessly; unwontedly; blissfully; lazily; agonizingly; passionately; ceaselessly; lovingly.
(See pine, droop, faint, weaken.)

LANGUOR

adjectives

increasing; ladylike; apparent; wearisome; delicious; gentle; delightful; pensive; passionless; restive; melancholy; sensuous; dreamy; amorous; unwonted; listless; gracious; soft; blissful; divine; mortal; exceeding; lazy.

verbs

complain of—; depress into—; diffuse—; droop in—; exhibit—; exude—; fall into—; perceive—; relieve—; shake off—; sink into —; sway with—; —arrests; —floats over; —oppresses; —pervades; —spreads.
(See lassitude, exhaustion, weariness.)

LANKY

adverbs

unbelievably; comically; ludicrously; increasingly; awkwardly; clumsily; bashfully; haggardly; hungrily; terribly; pathetically; woefully; weedily; gauntly; slenderly; extremely; preposterously; fantastically; impressively; dreadfully; inexpressibly; curiously; laughably; particularly; peculiarly; strangely.

LANTERN

adjectives

port-colored; multicolored; treacherous; exquisite; smoky; ill-smelling.

LAP

adjectives

flowery; mossy; verdant; commodious; soft; inviting.

LAP (v)

adverbs

greedily; thirstily; affectionately; hungrily; fawningly; cringingly; ingratiatingly.
(See lick, eat.)

LAPSE

adjectives

careless; temporary; momentary; single; liquid; deplorable; smooth; strong; venial;

703

occasional; incredible; atrocious; enormous; soothing; sad; moral; melancholy; abrupt.

verbs
attribute—to; dispel—; emerge from—; expose to—; fall into—; glide into—; recover from—; sink in—; slip into—; spend—; suffer—; vacate—; —avails; —decays; flow into—.
(See mistake, error, indiscretion.)

LAPWING
adjectives
wanton; swift.

LARCENY
adjectives
petit; grand; mammoth.

LARDER
verbs
deposit in—; drain—; exhaust—; hang in —; invade—; load—; purge—; raid—; replenish—; resort to—; sack—; stock—; store in—; tap—; —abounds in; —conserves; —gratifies; —overflows; —preserves.
(See stock, supply, store.)

LARGE
adverbs
extremely; incalculably; incredibly; immeasurably; preposterously; exceedingly; particularly; overwhelmingly; infinitely; enormously; monstrously; prodigiously; astoundingly; marvelously; remarkably; notoriously; uncommonly; immoderately; inordinately; signally; strikingly; amazingly; tremendously; immensely; comparatively; incomparably; imposingly; formidably; sensationally; unusually; amply; satisfactorily; sufficiently.

LARK
adjectives
veritable; merry; late; full-throated; mounting; morning; winging.

verbs
—carols; —chants; —chimes; —chirrups; —circles; —composes; —s congregate; —s flock; —heralds the dawn; —improvises; —instills; —molts; —ravishes; —sharps; —showers melody; —shrills; —slurs; —sprinkles notes; —squats; —startles; —strains; —trills; —whistles.
(See bird.)

LASH
adjectives
drooping; burning; sweeping; sooty; dark; arrowy; invisible; sleepy; scattered (pl); fluttering; glistening; torturing; flickering; stinging; inky; silky; languid; bristly; downcast; molten; delicate; pale; long; flaxen; biting; verbal.

LASH (v)
adverbs
viciously; furiously; frenziedly; maniacally; vilely; brutally; sadistically; murderously; madly.
(See whip, scold, beat, punish.)

LASHING
adjectives
ominous; merciless; cruel; interrupted; crippling; bloody; bitter; mad; furious; fierce; frenzied; maniacal.

verbs
bemoan—; bestow—upon; cringe under—; crucify with—; denounce—; experience—; gloat over—; inflict—; suffer—; wince at —; writhe under—; yield to—; —angers; —convulses; —cows; —infuriates; —maddens; —subdues; —tortures.
(See scolding, punishment, beating.)

LASS
adjectives
prettiest; lowborn; morbid; enticing; dark-eyed; bouncing; tidy-looking; flat-faced; modest; buxom; bewitching; pleasant; vivacious; smiling.

LASSITUDE
adjectives
despairing; general; poppied; speechless; languorous; drowsy; dreamy; hopeless.

verbs
combat—; depress into—; diffuse—; droop into—; exhibit—; induce—; perceive—; remedy—; shake off—; sink into—; tie with —; yield to—; —arrests; —envelops; —floats over; —flows over; —oppresses; —pervades; —spreads; —takes hold.
(See languor, exhaustion, weariness, fatigue.)

LAST (v)
adverbs
interminably; unendurably; unreasonably; briefly; unconsciously.
(See endure, continue, remain.)

704

LATCH

adjectives
clinking; welcoming.

LATE

adverbs
extremely; horribly; preposterously; hideously; terrifyingly; alarmingly; significantly; dreadfully; intentionally; deliberately; carelessly; unfortunately; disastrously; calamitously; nonchalantly; lazily; inconsiderately; strangely; curiously; understandably; habitually; inexcusably; unpardonably; inexplicably; ungraciously; excusably; justifiably; unavoidably; apologetically; incredibly; vexatiously; unluckily; inordinately; terribly; uncommonly.

LATENESS

adjectives
preposterous; repeated; excusable.

LATENT

adverbs
imperceptibly; mysteriously; inferentially; implicitly; unsuspectedly; darkly; confusingly; mistily; indistinguishably; astoundingly; unhappily; impenetrably; unfortunately.

LATHER

adjectives
sudsy; brushless; shaving; foamy; plentiful; softening.

verbs
agitate to—; beat up—; burst into—; confect—; enjoy—; exercise into—; form—; give—; mix into—; sponge with—; swathe in—; thrash up—; wash in—; whip into—; work up—; —agrees with; —bubbles; —cleanses; —foams; —fortifies; —froths; —gushes; —overflows; —penetrates; —purifies; —refreshes; —sinks deep; —sputters; —stimulates; —tingles.
(See cream, soap, foam, froth.)

LATIN

verbs
acquaint with—; deliver in—; discourse in —; express in—; honor—; interpret—; mumble—; recite—; spout—; translate—; vent—; —bewilders; —confuses; —conveys; —dismays; —distracts; —flourishes; —revives; —stumps (colloq.).
(See dialect, language, literature.)

LATITUDES

adjectives
utmost; boundless; beloved; heliographical; medieval.

LATTICES

adjectives
stormy; antique; caged.

LATTICEWORK

adjectives
quaint; artistic; delicate.

LAUD (v)

adverbs
flatteringly; fawningly; foolishly; extravagantly; sincerely; fervently; enthusiastically; passionately; exaggeratedly.
(See sing, praise, celebrate.)

LAUDATORY

adverbs
fawningly; flatteringly; admiringly; politically; unctuously; officially; ostentatiously; fulsomely; subtly; appreciatively; blatantly; lavishly; sincerely; moderately; humbly; unnecessarily; reluctantly; eloquently; heartily; solemnly; warmly; profusely; effusively; highly; excessively.

LAUGH

adjectives
scornful; cackling; incredulous; wild; abrupt; gruesome; childish; simple; gay; subdued; hoarse; low; relieved; inaudible; approving; forced; rippling; mild; familiar; horrid; distracted; funny; hard; little; tremulous; unpleasant; wheezy; triumphant; irritating; crackling; gentle; noisy; spiteful; uneasy; jeering; sarcastic; mocking; eerie; sinister; terrible; unmelodious; hearty; arch; frightful; constrained; blunt; malicious; sweet; vain; ringing; young; enchanting; trifling; suppressed; loud; evil; coarse; chuckling; fierce; jovial; silent; slight; cheery; rapturous; polite; merry; choked; melodious; careless; clumsy; gibing; cold; gurgling; startling; humorous; tinkling; boisterous; wild; impish; fearsome; bitter; drunken; sweet; mirthless; meaningful; fiendish; bubbling; wicked; harsh; ironical; taunting; tuneful; carnivorous; hysterical; delicious; silver; horse; self-conscious; childlike; joyous; grating; gasping; throaty; deep; hearty; good-humored; half-desperate; discordant; brit-

tle; characteristic; woeful; roguish; irritable; rattling; complacent; derisive; convulsive; hospitable; mingled (pl); sardonic; sonorous; supercilious; astonished; penitent; rueful; angry; sobbing; weak; musical; tittering; bursting; ghostly.

LAUGH (v)

adverbs

incredulously; gruesomely; tremulously; triumphantly; irritatingly; spitefully; jeeringly; sarcastically; triflingly; jovially; boisterously; humorously; impishly; drunkenly; mirthlessly; fiendishly; gratingly; discordantly; complacently; convulsively; sardonically; sonorously; superciliously; musically; croakingly; gleefully; mordantly; uproariously; jauntily; ruefully; derisively; significantly; ironically; constrainedly; sheepishly; unquenchably; grimly; idiotically; dramatically; jubilantly; exultantly; reassuringly; gustily; insolently; immoderately.

(See roar, giggle, snicker, titter.)

LAUGHABLE

adverbs

ludicrously; comically; monstrously; ironically; absurdly; quaintly; delightfully; uncommonly; moderately; scarcely; heartily; frankly; amusingly; prankishly; pleasantly; rousingly; stimulatingly; cleverly; admissibly; outlandishly.

LAUGHTER

adjectives

silent; delighted; thistle-down; immoderate; boisterous; mingled; shrill; subdued; uncontrolled; resonant; restrained; refreshing; rude; discordant; ill-natured; smothered; derisive; inward; mocking; deluded; resolute; hearty; artificial; soft; wild; hysteric; cackling; lifeless; zealous; delicious; high-pitched; murmurous; joyous; careless; frank; wholesome; meaningless; lovely; honest; unbelted; babbling; intellectual; faltering; Homeric; irreverent; rapid; irresistible; internal; confident; everlasting; hysterical; rippling; childish; unholy; sincerest; rollicking; bitter; mortal; intermingling; wilder; beery; innocent; immortal; foolish; free; bubbling; silvery; sudden; scary; throaty; excessive; gushing; hoarser; treble; shallow; fairy; savage; riotous; inheld.

verbs

break into—; burst into—; check—; constrain—; convulse in—; dimple in—; draw —; elicit—; enjoy—; evoke—; excite—; explode in—; flood with—; forgive—; join in —; occasion—; provoke—; raise—; reel in—; refrain from—; repress—; roar with —; rock with—; roll in—; scorn—; split with—; stifle—; stab with—; suppress—; swallow—; tumble into—; turn to—; wrinkle into—; —dances; —delights; —distorts; —ebbs; —explodes; —fizzles out (colloq.); —flows; —jars; —jets; —punctures; —quivers; —resounds; —rings out; —spills from; —warms; —wins.

(See mirth, grin, smile, merriment, snicker.)

LAUNCH

verbs

anchor—; appoint—; buffet—; endanger—; navigate—; propel—; repair—; slap—; view from—; —capsizes; —chugs; — circles; —courses; —cruises; —dances in; —drifts; —glides; —noses past; —ploughs; —rocks; —steams; —transports.

(See boat, tugboat, motor-boat, ship, steamer, schooner, yacht, vessel.)

LAUNCH (v)

adverbs

simultaneously; ceremoniously; auspiciously; vigorously; politically; enthusiastically; formally; diplomatically.

(See start, begin.)

LAURELS

adjectives

congregated; unsunned; untwined; bright; barren; fadeless; windless; unplucked; mingling.

verbs

acquire—; bestow—; blast—; crown with —; display—; envy—; garnish with—; look to—; merit—; reap—; regain—; repose on —; rest on—; retire on—; reward with—; seek—; snatch—; —delight; —enhance.

(See medal, prize, reward, trophy, crown.)

LAVA

adjectives

disintegrated; fluid; naked; incandescent; basaltic; massed; molten; smoking.

verbs
discharge—; disgorge—; drool—; emit—; pour—; puke—; spew—; —boils; —bubbles; —bursts; —courses down; —crushes; —deluges; —devastates; —envelops; —erupts; —expands; —flows; —gurgles; —inundates; —issues from; —oozes; —overflows; —percolates; —ravishes; —solidifies; —streams from; —swoops down.

(See water, mortar, liquid, plaster, bullet.)

LAVISH

adverbs
astoundingly; extravagantly; exceedingly; overwhelmingly; regally; royally; ridiculously; exorbitantly; profusely; disgustingly; inordinately; needlessly; unnecessarily; ostentatiously; proudly; pompously; wastefully; improvidently; thriftlessly; foolishly; inanely; witlessly; idiotically; generously; charitably; benevolently; benignly; amiably; graciously.

LAVISH (v)

adverbs
impulsively; vainly; extravagantly; regally; royally; affectionately; tenderly; passionately; adoringly; liberally; immoderately; recklessly.

(See spend, bestow.)

LAVISHNESS

adjective
glittering; sparse; regal.

LAW

adjectives
immutable; sacred; penal; violated; stringent; fundamental; impartial; salutary; comprehensive; valid; international; eternal; sumptuary; important; traditional; inexorable; remedial; flagitious; changeless; singular; angry; constricting; physical; standing; secular; unwritten; common; mild; conciliatory; criminal; invariable; certain; efficacious; unfailing; adequate; inoperative; severest; bloody; existing; conscription; never-to-be-formulated; geometric; organic; unspectacular; non-corporation; bogus; supreme; primitive; scientific; radiant; antiquated; prohibitory; uniform; rigorous; hideous; undiscriminating; drastic; continuous; all-building; recorded; subjective; severe; inescapable; biting; benignant; unconstitutional; sharp; evident; economic; oppressive; empirical; righteous; anatomic; deathless; conservation; mun-

dane; beneficent; harsh; sumptuary; ceremonial; querulous; sanguine; chancery; rigid; outraged; unequal; civil; social; hidden; substantive; obnoxious; mortal; stern; slavery-fashioned; ungracious; admirable; dramatic; academic; irreversible; active; indwelling; immovable; murderous; primal; unwieldy; tyrannical; blind; furious; unreasoning; crude; complex; clumsy; fiery; brutal; underlying; strictest; sordid; indiscreet; fantastical; expiring; ridiculous; restraining; proposed; express; protective; ultimate; martial; fallible; human; intolerant; preadjusted; physiological; clocklike.

verbs
amend—; administer—; apply—; array against—; bow to—; challenge—; circumvent—; clarify—; codify—; comply with—; comprehend—; conform to—; defy—; denounce—; dispute—; disregard—; dodge—; draft—; elude—; enact—; enforce—; expound—; flout—; forge—; forsake—; frame —; grind out—s; heed—; impose by—; infringe—; instigate—; interpret—; invoke—; mock—; modify—; nullify—; promulgate—; rail against—; ratify—; repeal—; repudiate —; resist—; run afoul of—; stiffen—; subject to—; supersede—; supplant—; suspend —; sustain—; systematize—; tamper with —; tighten—; transgress—; uphold—; — broadens; —clamps down; —curbs; —decrees; —defines; —differentiates; —empowers; —isolates; —prescribes; —relaxes; —restricts; —sanctions; —stipulates.

(See bill, statute, ordinance, regulation, edict, decree, mandate, rule, legislation.)

LAW-ABIDING

adverbs
carefully; duly; cautiously; respectfully; reputably; generally; habitually; usually; remarkably; always; scarcely; voluntarily; conscientiously; ordinarily; publicly; obviously; uniformly; invariably; obediently; willingly; passively; actively; faithfully; loyally; devotedly; superbly; consistently; customarily; exceptionally; notably.

LAWFUL

adverbs
definitely; expressly; explicitly; officially; ordinarily; prescriptively; properly; duly; acceptably; admissibly; equitably; constitutionally; downright; completely; funda-

mentally; authentically; singularly; emphatically; unquestionably; unimpeachably; currently; altogether.

LAWLESS
adverbs
dangerously; alarmingly; youthfully; heedlessly; daringly; audaciously; lamentably; deplorably; openly; actively; defiantly; insurgently; seditiously; restively; insubordinately; mutinously; rebelliously; tumultuously; treasonably; incorrigibly; persistently; obstinately; incredibly.

LAWLESSNESS
adjectives
rash; irresponsible.

verbs
assail—; condemn—; condone—; countenance—; crush—; decry—; denounce—; infest with—; reform—; suffer—; survive—; subscribe to—; yield to—; —breaks out; —fascinates; —grinds; —offends; —oppresses; —reigns; —spreads; —sullies.
(See crime, vice, anarchy, communism, wickedness, sin.)

LAWN
adjectives
dewy; grassy; upland; smooth; squared; summery; sunny; carpetlike; sun-baked; unkempt; dew-besprinkled; russet; spacious; sleek; sun-bathed; well-kept; flowered; shadow-chequered; wintry; sun-soaked; moon-lit; thick; velvety.

verbs
adorn—with; besprinkle—; border—; design —; fence in—; gird—; hedge in—; injure —; mow—; pluck from—; romp on—; shadow—; sprinkle—; tread—; —beautifies; —carpets; —clothes; —creeps; —extends; —flowers; —slopes.
(See grass, field, garden.)

LAWSUIT
adjectives
vexatious; improper; ugly; ruinous; prolonged; endless; trumped-up; expensive.

verbs
avoid—; bear—; condemn—; contest—; drop—; elude—; encounter—; incur—; institute—; judge—; propose—; saddle with —; subpoena for—; support—; wrangle

over—; —confounds; —drags; —harasses; —perplexes; —tires; —wearies.
(See litigation, suit, case, prosecution.)

LAWYER
adjectives
crooked; gray-haired; briefless; solemnfaced; shyster; contemporary; constitutional; struggling; well-trained; prominent; competent; sharp; cunning; tricky; conceited; supercilious; dignified; profound; learned; callow; bullying; quick-witted; capable; unconventional; eccentric; eminent; good; skinflint; rascally; kindly.

verbs
employ—; retain—; —addresses; —advocates; —appeals; —battles; —blusters; — cavils; —charges; —confounds; —cross-examines; —defends; —expounds; —interprets; —litigates; —objects; —outwits; — pleads; —pounds; —practises; —queries; —questions; —quibbles; —shifts; —solicits; —strives; —wrangles.
(See orator, congressman, senator, attorney.)

LAX
adverbs
surprisingly; inscrutably; mysteriously; deliberately; criminally; negligently; leniently; indulgently; lamentably; incomprehensibly; regrettably; terribly; disastrously; calamitously; scandalously; outrageously; atrociously; dangerously; ominously; carelessly; languidly; lazily; indifferently; unusually; unwontedly; habitually; inexcusably; noticeably; obviously; apparently; dreadfully.

LAXATIVE
verbs
addict to—s; advocate—; dose with—; employ—; necessitate—; order—; require—; resist—; resort to—; suggest—; —abuses; —cleanses; —cures; —dispels; —eases; — loosens; —purges; —relieves; —unloads.
(See medicine, enema, remedy.)

LAXITY
adjectives
social; moral; parental.

LAYERS
adjectives
peripheral; thin; successive; innumerable;

reflecting; stratified; conglomerate; favorable; superficial; aerial; saline; serrated.

LAYMEN
adjectives
impertinent; unhallowed; incompetent; unpracticed.

LAYS
adjectives
embroidered; melodious; deathless; mirthful; mystic.

LAZINESS
adjectives
intense; mental; incorrigible; lifelong; noticeable.

LAZY
adverbs
unbelievably; deliciously; delightfully; utterly; incurably; inexcusably; openly; flauntingly; nonchalantly; blithely; carelessly; admittedly; vauntingly; intensely; mentally; incorrigibly; horribly; selfishly; inconsiderately; ungraciously; curiously; unpardonably; impudently; blatantly; flagrantly; insufferably; unbearably; lethargically; languidly; heavily; lumpishly; inertly; dreamily; sleepily; drowsily; terribly; provokingly.

LEA
adjectives
windy; russet; flowery; darkening; emerald; shadowed; rich; calm.

LEAD
adjectives
hissing; murderous; dull; unencumbered; smoke-blackened; merciless; proper.

verbs
cast—; expose—; fuse—; melt—; mine—; refine—; sheet—; smelt—; solder—; treat with—; unearth—; weight with—; —corrodes; —poisons; —softens; —tarnishes.
(See metal, iron, steel.)

LEAD (v)
adverbs
deceitfully; gallantly; boldly; intrepidly; triumphantly; victoriously; mercilessly; ceremonially; dexterously; ultimately; fatefully; enterprisingly; illustriously; imagin-

atively; reluctantly; gallantly; despotically; fanatically; energetically; intelligently; unscrupulously; nominally; ecclesiastically; incomparably; supremely.
(See command, direct, guide.)

LEADER
adjectives
enterprising; illustrious; reluctant; doubtful; foremost; cavalry; political-minded; creative; imaginative; naive; eminent; come-by-chance; spiritual; fanatical; party; befeathered; distinguished; despotic; conspicuous; prudent; prominent; submissive; insurgent; acknowledged; subjugated; ascetic; inspiring; quality; moderate; unquestioned; energetic; intelligent; self-constituted; unscrupulous; popular; typical; halting; patriot; nominal; revolutionary; adored; ecclesiastical; incomparable; brilliant; knightly; liberal; natural; recognized; crestfallen; typical; supreme.

verbs
adhere to—; distinguish—; emulate—; engage—; flock to—; gather 'round—; pattern on—; rally 'round—; support—; trust—; —arises; —commands; —conducts; —controls; —directs; —fires; —guides; —harangues; —influences; —marshals; —pilots; —presides; —unites; —voices.
(See minister, clergyman, boss, manager, official.)

LEADERSHIP
adjectives
lamentable; vital; accepted; inspired; vigorous; skillful; unchallenged; fashion; undisputed; intelligent; consummate; compensating; careful; aggressive; heroic; daring; recognized; judicious; palsied.

verbs
anticipate—; assume—; commend—; compete for—; crave—; favor—of; follow—; flourish under—; grant—to; offer—; overthrow—; prosper under—of; recognize—; rely on—; require—; settle—; stress—; strive for—; succeed to—; sustain—; trust to—; yield to—.
(See command, direction, guidance, protection, patronage.)

LEAF
adjectives
dancing; folded; garrulous; delicate; weary; laurel; latest; rueful; retuse;

voluminous; withered; minutest; rustling; medicinal; sleeping; braided; tender; plaited; glossy; primordial; peopled; drifted; vibrant; blushing; flattering; needlelike; drooping; notched; lanceolate; stirring; succulent; heedless.

LEAFAGE
adjectives
rustling; spreading; luxuriant.

LEAGUE
adjectives
united; endless; weary; hostile; moribund; nuptial; immeasurable; remarkable; unconscious; stormy.

verbs
ally with—; appeal to—; associate with—; band into—; crack—; criticize—; enter—; excite—; join—; renounce—; resuscitate—; —assists; —confers on; —defends; —safeguards; —sanctions; —shelters; —threatens; —unites.
(See society, club, organization, union, association.)

LEAGUE (v)
adverbs
inseparably; nuptially; protectively; firmly; perpetually.
(See combine, unite, associate.)

LEAK
verbs
block—; bare—; choke—; dam—; detect—; drill—; indicate—; master—; plug—; repair—; riddle with—s; seal—; spring—; —drains; —frightens, —gapes; —sinks; —weakens; —yawns.
(See hole, gap, flow.)

LEAKY
adverbs
dangerously; intentionally; slightly; unconscionably; uselessly; inconsequentially; suspiciously; mysteriously; ominously; treacherously; apparently; wastefully; terribly; unfortunately; miserably; extremely; fearfully; increasingly; wretchedly.

LEAN (v)
adverbs
slumberously; placidly; mechanically; gracefully; slantingly; wearily; impulsively; perilously; listlessly; indolently; dizzily; confidentially.
(See incline, recline, slope, tend, depend.)

LEAP
adjectives
imperious; breezy; astonishing; demoniacal; sudden; flying; rash; concealed; vigorous; mortal; quick; tremendous; horrid; queer; bold; gathered.

verbs
admire—; attempt—; calculate—; complete —; dare—; endeavor—; observe—; perfect —; practice—; rebound from—; record—; venture—; —amazes; —awes; —impresses.
(See feat.)

LEAP (v)
adverbs
lissomely; simultaneously; blithely; surefootedly; frolicsomely; nimbly; spryly; boisterously; perilously; demoniacally; boldly; vigorously; swiftly; agilely.
(See jump, spring, bound.)

LEARN (v)
adverbs
aptly; brilliantly; instinctively; normally; precociously; scientifically; pedagogically.
(See acquire, attain, master, obtain.)

LEARNER
adjectives
incipient; reputed; polite; awkward; brilliant.

LEARNING
adjectives
typical; harsh; crabbed; abstruse; unorganized; worldly; barren; superficial; serviceable; detrimental; optimistic; polite; philosophic; higher; extensive; carnal; varied; introvertive; inconsiderable; subtle; radiant; classical; supposed.

verbs
consume—; digest—; drink in—; feed on—; foster—; impart—; lack—; overestimate—; revive—; shun—; stamp out—; swallow—; test—; underestimate—; value—; wonder at—; —crowns; —discerns; —enlightens; —flourishes; —intoxicates; —penetrates; —polishes; —serves; —shines; —sobers; —speeds; —upbraids.
(See knowledge, wisdom, facts, information, understanding.)

LEASE
verbs
approve—; cancel—; comply with—; de-

mand—; enjoy—; gain—; grant—; ignore —; nullify—; obtain—; renew—; study—; terminate—; violate—; —expires; —guarantees; —protects; —runs out; —satisfies; extend—.

(See contract, pact, treaty, promise, agreement.)

LEASH

verbs
attach—; drag on—; exert—; hunt on—; lug on—; ply—; pull at—; secure with—; slip—; strain—; tow on—; tug at—; —confines; —controls; —restrains; —restricts; —yields; draw in—.

(See chain, strap, cord, string.)

LEATHER

adjectives
superlative; bronzed; well-oiled; sumptuous; dusty.

verbs
bind in—; bleach—; buff—; coat—; convert into—; damage—; dip—; drum—; paddle —; pickle—; roll—; shave—; soak—; spray —; stretch—; tan—; treat—; trim—; —creaks; —discolors; —preserves.

(See cotton, cloth, wool.)

LEATHERY

adverbs
darkly; stubbily; sturdily; sallowly; grubbily; robustly; pleasantly; vigorously; unbelievably; dilapidatedly; increasingly; oddly; quaintly; fantastically; grotesquely; uncommonly; remarkably; noticeably; conspicuously.

LEAVE

adjectives
tedious; gracious; affectionate; ceremonious; sick; instant.

LEAVE (v)

adverbs
unceremoniously; inadvertently; incautiously; judiciously; unwittingly; politely; diplomatically; reluctantly; prudently; voluntarily; affectionately; ultimately; irrevocably.

(See depart, retire, start.)

LEAVES

adjectives
tender; dank; trembling; unstirring; murmuring; myriad; aromatic; cordial; soggy; shifting; shivering; shimmering; frosted; glittering; withered; dewy; arching; glossy; listening; rustling; crumpled; brilliant; interlaced; ripened; dentated; glistering; crystal; frost-crisped; close-shut; pounded; suspended; motionless; pendant; lusty; sere; implicated; delicate; clustering; scented; amorous; soft; silken; summer; verdant; healing; fading; painted; falling; crowded; velvet; rejected; sweet; barren; yellowing; crimson; brazen; lapping; shining; russet; serrated; fingery; languid; twinkling; silent; retuse; dying; drifted; mantling; blanched; steaming; sweeping; wind-tossed; flaming; tiny; soiled; age-worn; vellum; tremulous; hardy; gay; autumn; burning; polished; dark; copious; mottled; sweet-fern; wintry; fanlike; agitated; coarse; grasslike; lucent; twining; fair; false; bruised; remembered; swarth; sodden; porcelain; unwritten; many-tinted; beauteous; drooping; wild; somber; parti-colored; joyous.

verbs
bedew—; decorate with—; flush—; gather —; scatter—; shed—; sprout—; thatch with —; tinge—; —blazon; —blend; —drift down; —droop; —float down; —flutter; —mat; —overspread; —quiver; —redden; —rustle; —shade; —shower down; —swirl; —tremble; —unfold; —wave; —whisper; —wilt; —wither.

(See foliage, plant.)

LECTURE

adjectives
edifying; inaugural; compulsory; scientific; interminable; wide-spread; celebrated; didactic; boring; ill-attended.

verbs
assimilate—; attend—; concoct—; deliver —; instruct by—; preach—; profit by—; temper—; —admonishes; —asserts; —assists; —attracts; —confounds; —interests; —perplexes; —rebukes; —reprimands; —reproaches; —stirs; —uplifts.

(See lesson, speech, address, narration, narrative; oration.)

LECTURE (v)

adverbs
tediously; graphically; eruditely; vividly; edifyingly; scientifically; interminably; didactically; boringly; inspiringly; inspirationally; eloquently.

(See address, discourse, speak.)

adjectives
shaven; dangerous-looking; slippery; narrow; pine-clad; overhanging; rocky; dirty-backed; solid; basalt; shaded; craggy; projecting; bare; inaccessible; shelving.

verbs
clamber up—; cleave to—; cling from—; hover on—; hug—; lean from—; peer over —; pitch from—; scale—; teeter on—; totter on—; tumble from—; —gives way; — juts; —projects; —protrudes.
(See edge, ridge, shelf, reef.)

LEECH

verbs
apply—; breed—es; employ—; fatten—; — absorbs; —adheres; —bleeds; —clings; — cures; —draws; —evacuates; —extracts; —heals; —relieves; —remedies; —sticks; — sucks.
(See parasite, physician, doctor.)

LEER

adjectives
impudent; jealous; complacent; silly; half-triumphant; roguish; fawning; malignant.

LEER (v)

adverbs
obscenely; idiotically; spitefully; impudently; murderously; despicably; sardonically; jealously; complacently; malignantly; fawningly; roguishly.
(See look, sneer, glance, stare.)

LEERY

adverbs
slightly; altogether; artfully; cunningly; trickily; warily; guardedly; cleverly; suspiciously; diplomatically; strategically; cautiously; prudently; deliberately; discreetly; coolly; habitually; cannily; charily; politically; vigilantly; dependably; uncommonly; carefully.

LEG

adjectives
excellent; bowed; rickety; timber; gouty; graceful; sturdy; bandy; lower; convulsed; stockinged; shapely; long; fluted; sinewy; brawny; spindle; incased; thin; shivering; toothsome; amputated; thread-like; leaden; muscular; bony; pitiful; tiny; slender; knotted; hacked; jagged; hairy; gaitered; lovely; graceful; bulging; slim.

verbs
admire—; bow—s; brace—; condition—s; elevate—; expose—; fetter—s; fracture—; massage—; peer at—s; reel on—s; reveal —; straddle with—s; strengthen—; trust —s; —s entwine; —s fly; —protrudes; —s sag; —supports; —s taper; —s twitch; —s weary.
(See foot, knee.)

LEGACY

adjectives
supplemented; limited; personal; precious; unexpected; hereditary.

verbs
administer—; allocate—; anticipate—; bequeath—; contemplate—; court—; deprive of—; direct—; envy—; fritter away—; grant—; inherit—; parcel—; partition—; provide—; reckon—; —dwindles; —enriches.
(See estate, property, money, wealth, inheritance, resources.)

LEGAL

adverbs
entirely; incontrovertibly; admittedly; unquestionably; allowably; authoritatively; duly; prescriptively; warrantably; presumptively; absolutely; unimpeachably; equitably; constitutionally; properly; securely.

LEGEND

adjectives
fearful; golden; traditionary; fanciful; facile; splenetic; heroic; marvelous; primeval; shadowy; serviceable; diffused; epic; fading; picturesque; contemporary; medieval; confusing; profane; puissant; fictitious; interminable; conventional.

verbs
blast—; carry on—; confute—; demolish—; destroy—; detach from—; discard—; dispel —; dispose of—; embroider—; emerge from —; exploit—; extenuate—; interpolate—; lampoon—; perpetuate—; peruse—; —attests to; —grows from; —persists; —portrays.
(See story, tale, myth, lie, narrative.)

LEGENDARY

adverbs
wholly; vestigially; acceptably; admittedly; daringly; inventively; romantically; fanci-

fully; ingeniously; purportedly; theoretically; notionally; fairly; authentically; presumably; doubtfully; probably; highly; vaporously; heroically; picturesquely; pleasantly.

LEGIBILITY
verbs
admire—; appreciate—; approve—; commend—; demand—; desire—; emblazon—; esteem—; extol—; heighten—; increase—; praise—; prize—; regard—; recommend—; value—.

LEGIBLE
adverbs
clearly; perfectly; gratifyingly; pleasantly; crudely; altogether; neatly; plainly; easily; distinctly; definitely; precisely; graphically; unmistakenly; scrawlingly; hieroglyphically; eventually; pleasingly; extremely; immediately; satisfactorily.

LEGION
adjectives
gallant; ragged; puissant; well-disciplined; iron-breasted; scouring; locust; swarthy; victorious; invincible.

verbs
array in—; assemble—; decimate—; direct —; fill with—s; follow—; gather—; overthrow—; secure—; sustain—; unite in—; —congregates; —defends; —drifts; —engages; —flocks; —participates; —serves; —strives.
(See army, crowd, association, enemy.)

LEGISLATE (v)
adverbs
precipitately; shrewdly; beneficently; malignantly; oppressively; economically; socially; constitutionally; perniciously; ecclesiastically; appropriately; arbitrarily; unscrupulously.
(See effect, enact.)

LEGISLATION
adjectives
oppressive; economic; sumptuary; social; preferential; intemperate; critical; unconstitutional; pernicious; injurious; ecclesiastical; educational; dangerous; absolute; remedial; appropriate; defunct; amendatory; arbitrary; refined; adverse; unscrupulous; undesirable; vindictive; class.

verbs
acclaim—; admire—; broaden—; enact—; enforce—; influence—; invalidate—; jam—through; lobby for—; motion for—; pile up —; propose—; sanction—; schedule—; sponsor—; stifle—; strangle—; sustain—; urge —; veto—.
(See law, bill, statute, ordinance, regulation.)

LEGISLATIVE
adverbs
augustly; imposingly; strictly; exclusively; oppressively; coolly; impersonally; absolutely; scrupulously; impartially; finally; irrevocably; wisely; providentially.

LEGISLATOR
verbs
criticize—; elect—; invest—with; nominate —; —attempts; —authorizes; —s convene; —deliberates; —devises; —interprets; —judges; —moves; —proposes; —propounds; —serves.
(See congressman, senator, politician, statesman.)

LEGISLATURE
verbs
appoint to—; nominate for—; recommend to—; —affirms; —appropriates; —confirms; —defeats; —deliberates; —dismisses; —enacts; —frames; —overrules; —passes; —propounds; —reveals; —revokes; —suspends; —congregates; —convenes.
(See congress, parliament, legislator, government.)

LEGITIMATE
adverbs
wholly; unquestionably; substantially; plainly; unqualifiedly; unimpeachably; authoritatively; authentically; genuinely; verily; allowably; unconditionally; justly; absolutely; duly; properly; completely; rightly.

LEISURE
adjectives
scant; elegant; extreme; endowed; practicable; sour; patient; graceful; multitudinous; everlasting; abundant; fallow; infinite; precious; tranquil; unbroken; spiritual; ample; dignified; literary; sufficient; unholy; superfluous; holiday; dilettante; calm; machine-created; wasted.

verbs
bankrupt of—; beautify—; burden with—; court—; devote—to; discipline—; dispense with—; employ—; enjoy—; fill—; indulge at —; occupy—; pursue at—; rejoice in—; retire into—; revel in—; reward with—; steal —; wallow in—; weary of—; —civilizes; —delights; —enriches; —entombs; —polishes.
(See time.)

LEMON

verbs
bear—s; box—s; crate—s; cultivate—; express from—; extract from—; flavor with —; gather—s; harvest—s; pack—s; peel—; pickle in—; pierce—; scent with—; ship—s; sort—s; squeeze—; wrap—; —clings; —puckers; —ripens.
(See fruit.)

LEND (*v*)

adverbs
grudgingly; conveniently; conditionally; gracefully; innocently; legitimately; unscrupulously; willingly; gratuitously.
(See accommodate, assist, furnish.)

LENDER

adjectives
legitimate; money; licensed; unscrupulous.

LENGTH

adjectives
learned; barbarous; apparent; extortionate; manlier; abbreviated; intolerable; variable; irregular; average; ludicrous; unaltered; extreme; considerable; unconscionable; enormous; interminable; majestic; pellucid; lamentable; shameful; immoderate; standard; ancient; unwieldy; startling; weary; apportioned; slender; infinite; wondrous; measured; treacherous; vine-clad.

LENGTHEN (*v*)

adverbs
indefinitely; ludicrously; unconscionably; interminably; immoderately; infinitely; disproportionately.
(See extend, stretch.)

LENGTHY

adverbs
interminably; intolerably; tiresomely; monotonously; unbelievably; endlessly; ramblingly; reminiscently; diffusely; effusively; wretchedly; miserably; wearisomely; unconscionably; ludicrously; sadly; terribly; shamefully; incredibly; inexcusably.

LENIENT

adverbs
habitually; conveniently; indulgently; affectionately; spasmodically; considerately; mercifully; courteously; hospitably; graciously; weakly; supinely; deliberately; gently; calmly; absent-mindedly; nervously; pacifically; reasonably; blandly; purposely; lamentably; unduly; wisely; helpfully; disgustingly; feebly; temperately; tolerantly; complaisantly; compassionately; humanely; exceedingly.

LENITY

adjectives
half-contemptuous; half-calculated; sufficient; vaunted; customary; assumed; apparent.

LENS

adjectives
immense; photographic; concave; shadowy; convex; powerful.

LEOPARD

verbs
bag—; creep up on—; ensnare—; infest with—s; skin—; trap—; —attacks; —barks; —charges; —claws; —climbs; —depredates; —devours; —drags off; —lies in ambush; —pounces; —preys on; —pulls down; —rages; —roars; —screams; —seizes; —slaughters; —slinks; —springs; —stalks; —steals upon; —wails; —infests.
(See animal, lion, tiger.)

LEPER

verbs
ban—; bar—; cleanse—; cure—; heal—; incarcerate—; isolate—; purge—; quarantine—; restore—; segregate—; shelter—; —befouls; —begs; —contaminates; —defiles; —infects; —stigmatizes; —suffers; —taints,
(See beggar, invalid, parasite.)

LEPROUS

adverbs
fatally; tragically; horribly; unfortunately; miserably; wretchedly; infirmly; incurably; pitiably; morally; mortally; indubitably; dreadfully.

adjectives

local; organic; mechanical; healed.

LESSEN (v)

adverbs

abnormally; scientifically; beneficially; mechanically; gradually; agreeably; appreciably.

(See diminish, reduce, decrease.)

LESSON

adjectives

crowning; salutary; rude; strategical; humiliating; valuable; distasteful; sacred; deathless; wholesome; exemplary; object; copious; pioneer; curious; striking; stern; impressive; instructive; ethical; important; nobler; outstanding; painful; baneful; tremendous; fruitful; needful; hard; silent.

verbs

assign—; deliver—; experience—; expound —; imply—; inculcate—; instill—; memorize—; preach—; project—; rebel at—; recite—; spice—; yield—; —penetrates; —rebukes; —reprimands; —sinks in.

(See lecture, talk, speech, moral.)

LETHARGY

adjectives

intellectual; torpid; icy; blind; pleasant; patriarchal; complete; apparent; inglorious; passive; utter.

verbs

arouse from—; breed—; descend into—; fade into—; fall into—; fix in—; lie in—; lift from—; mumble in—; overcome—; — attacks; —blinds; —chokes; —envelops; — hinders; —paralyzes; —restrains; —seduces; —seizes; —stupefies.

(See languor, weariness, fatigue, exhaustion, lassitude.)

LETTER

adjectives

rare; deprecatory; terrible; much-discussed; anonymous; unfeeling; complimentary; entertaining; amusing; exhaustive; innumerable; confidential; charming; loathsome; vitriolic; insolent; threatening; overbearing; pensive; seditious; amiable; commendatory; pitiful; subjoined; promised; obliging; impassioned; strange; incoherent; obscure; incomprehensible; bulky; pattern; civil; simple-minded; subsequent; obnoxious; elementary; discursive; nonsensical; dead; unfriendly; repentant; passionate; adulatory; indiscreet; ill-spelled; runic; affectionate; shameful; orderly; menacing; luminous; feigned; curt; immediate; interminable; pithy; gilt; full; convincing; esteemed; accusing; interesting; specific; deep-cut; reprehensive; pastoral; brief; terse; condensed; emphatic; exculpatory; beautiful; eloquent; touching; conspicuous; good; unjust; delicious; sweet; patient; wise; tender; painful; abusive; round-robin; often-recurring; chance-preserved; introductory; burning; generous; handsome; mystical; explanatory; racy; exquisite; slanderous; ill-written; libelous; crafty; brusque; unsound; stilted; pleading; naive; denunciatory; easy-flowing; inevitable; long; reproachful; sparkling; enigmatical; depressing; assisting; condemnatory; faded; fatal; clandestine; ridiculous; agreeable; hasty; impudent; enthusiastic; unauthenticated; taunting; dedicatory; chatty; kind-hearted; cheery; journalistic; happy; timely; conclusive; effective; admonitory; indignant; spiteful; pathetic; dainty; memorable; sad; begging; witty; misguiding; resounding; fascinating; inquisitive; occasional; compromising; laconic; needless; unfinished; genuine; obedient.

verbs

append to—; bear—; besiege with—s; bombard with—s; censor—; communicate by—; convey—; deluge with—s; devise—; devour —; dictate—; frame—; peruse—; post—; scribble—; seal—; skim through—; speed—; suppress—; welcome—; —acquaints; —assures; —breathes; —cheers; —commends; —commissions; —consoles; —conveys; — expatiates; —gushes; —imparts; —links; —s pour in; —reveals; —unites.

(See communication, note, correspondence, message, telegram.)

LEVEL

adjectives

portentous; maintenance; conversational; unlovely; vulgar; conciliating; preeminent; remunerative; childish; artistic; unending; windy; desirable; reflecting; usual; varying; harmless; unmeaning; humdrum; common; ordinary.

verbs

attain—; defile—; degrade to—; destroy—; discover—; drain—; elevate to—; find—;

gain—; hold—; jump to—; lie within—; maintain—; mark—; preserve—; raise above—; reduce to—; regress to—; sink to —.

(See height, depth, altitude, summit, mark.)

adverbs
meticulously; exactly; monotonously; conveniently; smoothly; endlessly; uniformly; tiresomely; changelessly; drearily; continuously; symmetrically; roughly; unevenly; ruggedly; fairly.

LEVER

verbs
adjust—; apply—; brace—; heave out with —; jack with—; manipulate—; yank (colloq.)—; —disembowels; —dislodges; —elevates; —expels; —lifts; —overthrows; —pries open; —raises.

(See handle, bar.)

LEVITY

adjectives
incorrigible; enervate; uncanonical; responsive; unpardonable; superficial; dreadful; careless; shameful; bitter; exquisite; undesirable; foolish; unnecessary; unbecoming; surface.

LEVY

adjectives
forced; undisciplined; successive (pl).

LEWD

adverbs
ribaldly; boisterously; inexcusably; gustily; evilly; immodestly; shamelessly; wantonly; habitually; inexplicably; unaccountably; unwarrantably; hilariously; terribly; ostentatiously; unscrupulously; crudely.

LIABILITY

verbs
account for—; admit—; burden with—; clog with—; confess—; display—; exempt from —; free from—; impose—; limit—; load with—; meet—; relieve of—; saddle with —; shoulder—s; —cramps; —deters; —disheartens; —hampers; —impedes; —imposes; —obligates; —oppresses; —shackles; —weighs.

(See trouble, responsibility, misfortune, reverse, debt, obligation.)

LIABLE

adverbs
criminally; undeniably; unfortunately; financially; morally; legally; unhappily; fatally; inescapably; inevitably; embarrassingly; deeply; inconveniently; properly; ethically; prescriptively.

LIAR

adjectives
congenial; false-hearted; designing; monstrous; virtuous; probable; political; prophesying; beneficent; notorious; endless; generous.

verbs
accuse—; avoid—; condemn—; criticize—; despise—; judge—; punish—; reprimand—; reproach—; shame—; spurn—; support—; —beguiles; —blinds; —contrives; —convinces; —deceives; —devises; —forges; —fumbles; —invents; —libels; —raves; —relates; —slanders; —stabs; —violates.

(See criminal, robber, thief, hypocrite, quack.)

LIBATION

adjectives
wonted; copious; devout.

LIBEL

adjectives
infamous; poisonous; criminal; seditious; scandalous; outrageous; intentional; anonymous; atrocious.

verbs
accuse of—; contradict—; convict of—; denounce—; disprove—; forge—; incur—; institute—; introduce—; oppose—; publish—; rebut—; serve—; sue for—; —accuses; —alleges; —assails; —charges; —declares; —defames; —discredits; —implies; —slanders.

(See slander, rumor.)

LIBERAL

adverbs
naturally; habitually; generally; always; extremely; charitably; considerately; lavishly; thoughtfully; ostentatiously; grudgingly; calculatingly; carelessly; unwarrantably; improvidently; moderately; bountifully; generously; munificently; handsomely; unwisely; unselfishly; thoroughly; unfailingly; dependably.

LIBERALISM

adjectives

militant; enlightened; extreme; journalistic.

verbs

absorb—; adopt—; advocate—; convert to —; criticize—; crusade for—; cultivate—; endanger—; exercise—; inculcate—; interpret—; plant—; plead for—; restrain—; scorn—; stifle—; stimulate—; unite in—; weaken—; —affords; —aims at; —emerges from; —involves; —prevails; —thrives.

(See democracy, freedom, socialism, communism, movement.)

LIBERALITY

adjectives

unstinted; decent; unbounded; mutual; enlarged; patriotic.

LIBERATE (v)

adverbs

promptly; magnanimously; industrially; philosophically; politically; temporarily; economically; nobly; rationally; partially; subversively.

(See free, release, deliver.)

LIBERTY

adjectives

elemental; unwarrantable; glorious; philosophical; wild; popular; hard; political; natural; temporary; unrestrained; sanctioned; economic; industrial; religious; ignoble; pagan; secure; atheistic; unequalled; unbridled; headstrong; false; stormy; intermittent; universal; rational; partial; subversive; adored; masculine; excessive; perfect; lyric; dearly-bought.

verbs

abdicate—; champion—; concede—; confiscate—; conspire against—; defend—; deprive of—; encroach upon—; enjoy—; forsake—; grant—; imperil—; infringe upon —; invade—; jeopardize—; maintain—; prate of—; purchase—; sacrifice—; scorn —; sequester—; shackle—; spurn—; suppress—; suspend—: taint—; threaten—; violate—; —crumbles; —perishes; —vanishes.

(See rights, freedom, privilege, independence.)

LIBRARY

adjectives

provincial; extensive; circulating; immense;

somber; reference; astronomical; valuable; comprehensive; well-balanced; technical.

verbs

bequeath to—; browse in—; bury in—; cherish—; confine to—; drink from—; endow—; enrich—; establish—; labor in—; refer to—; repose in—; resort to—; revel in—; shelve in—; subscribe to—; —circulates; —collects; —entombs; —feeds; — fines; —lends; —nourishes; —preserves; — records; —safeguards; —stores.

(See book, literature.)

LIBRETTOS

adjectives

innocuous; unappealing; poetical; complete.

LICENSE

adjectives

passionate; poetic; uncontrolled; mocking; wanton; warrantable; unpunished; unchecked; transport; boldest; amplest; unbridled; graceful; roving; ignoble; extraordinary; democratic; driving; vending.

verbs

abuse—; acknowledge—; concede—; deny —; display—; draw—; enjoy—; forge—; grant—; inspect—; obtain—; observe—; practise under—; require—; revoke—; withdraw—; —authorizes; —permits; —protects; —vouches.

(See right, privilege.)

LICENSE (v)

adverbs

legally; medically; authoritatively; officially; nominally; wantonly; properly.

(See permit, authorize.)

LICENTIOUS

adverbs

unwarrantably; riotously; ungovernably; dissolutely; wickedly; despicably; contemptibly; terribly; disgustingly; viciously; unimaginably; dreadfully; unexpectedly; villainously; wildly; rakishly; deplorably; lamentably; unforgivably.

LICENTIOUSNESS

adjectives

unbridled; evil; uncurbed; repeated.

verbs

campaign against—; check—; curb—; defend—; denounce—; explode—; harbor—;

impute to—; inflict—upon; regret—; taste
—; tolerate—; tumble into—; witness—;
—irks; —occurs; —offends; —prevails; —
reigns; —vexes.

(See wickedness, vice, sin.)

LID

adjectives
just-raised; placid; translucent; drooping;
long; sly; flaming; veinous; opaque; blue-
veined; drowsy; flower-soft; fringed; unsullied; squinted; lower; eternal; coarse;
triangular-shaped; low; wrinkled; conscious; timorous; heavy.

verbs
clamp—on; clap—on; fit—; force—; overlay—; plant—on; pry—off; seal—; tap—;
tighten—; —conceals; —preserves; —prevents; —protects; —resists; —restrains; —
screens; —yields to.

(See cover, canopy.)

LIE

adjectives
glittering; vicious; monkey-faced; vivid;
spectral; glib; painted; plausible; sin-born;
wanton; endless; improbable; consoling; intolerable; libelous; deadliest; drowsing;
diplomatic; ungentlemanly; organized; conventional; filthy; original; convincing; blaspheming; preposterous; gracious; sustained; surpliced; costly; pious; calm; quaint;
shameless; damnable; dumb; helpless; glorious; puny; rotten; absurd; magnificent;
unnumbered; iniquitous; measured; poisonous; deliberate; purchased.

verbs
acknowledge—; censure—; condemn—; condone—; confess to—; decry—; detect—;
evolve—; promulgate—; propagate—; reject—; rend—; reveal—; spill—s; uncover
—; utter—; —blackens; —cheats; —cloaks;
—defrauds; —dishonors; —falsifies; —fetters; —frees; —perplexes; —swindles.

(See crime, statement, falsehood, misre-
presentation.)

LIE (v)

adverbs
nervelessly; slothfully; smoothly; perversely; atrociously; malignly; glibly; supinely;
profusely; portentously; outrageously; mutely; composedly; plausibly; wantonly; libelously; preposterously; shamelessly; iniquitously.

(See fabricate, misrepresent.)

LIEUTENANT

adjectives
lion-hearted; self-important; selected.

LIFE

adjectives
abhorred; abject; abnormal; abstract; aboriginal; abundant; academic; active; act-
ion-craving; affluent; agonized; agreeable;
agricultural; all-embracing; altruistic;
amazing; ambrosial; angelic; antecedent;
antenatal; artificial; ascetic; astonished;
austere; bad; beneficent; benevolent; blameless; blithe; blooming; boulevard; bountiful; bright-eyed; broad; broken; brute;
bubbling; buoyant; busy; bygone; bird-
cage; cankerous; carefree; careful; changing; charmed; civic; civilized; cloistral;
cold-blooded; collective; college; colorful;
commercial; commonplace; communal; concentrated; consistent; constant; contemplative; contemporary; contemptuous; convenient; convulsive; cordial; corporate; cosmic;
country; crescent; cruel; crystal; cultivated;
cultured; darkened; darkling; darting;
deadening; decorous; deep-bosomed; defaced; delightful; democratic; demonstrable; deplorable; desultory; devouring;
diffusive; diminished; diplomatic; disastrous; discontented; disfigured; dishonored;
disjointed; disposed; dissipated; dissolute;
distasteful; distracted; dividing; double; domestic; doubtful; dull; dusky; dutiful; easy-
going; eccentric; economic; effete; effective;
effeminate; elemental; emancipated; embittered; emotional; enlarging; ennobling;
ephemeral; equal; erotic; equivocal; essential; eternal; eventful; existing; exotic; expanding; external; extinguished; exuberant;
exultant; factitious; familiar; farcical;
farmyard; fascinating; fashionable; fast-
fleeing; fast-withering; fettered; feudal;
feverish; fictionized; flabby; flickering;
floating; flourishing; foreign; fragrant;
free; friendless; frisking; frivolous; frugal;
fruitful; fugitive; fullest; genuine; gushing;
grimy; groovelike; gypsy; half-revealed;
hapless; hard-working; harmless; healthful;
helpful; hideous; hoary; high-pressure;
homely; honest; human; humdrum; hygienic; ideal; idyllic; imagined; imaginative;
immortal; impatient; impeccable; imper-

fect; imperiled; imperishable; impish; incarnate; increasing; independent; individual; indulgent; industrious; infantile; informal; inglorious; inherent; inner; innermost; insect; unsociable; integrated; intellectual; intense; interior; intimate; irresponsible; irregular; joyless; kindly; knowable; laborious; large; licentious; lifeless; liquid; listless; literary; livable; loathed; long; low; lush; lusterless; luxurious; magnanimous; many-sided; married; material; maximum; meditative; melancholy; mental; meteoric; middle-married; milder; millennial; mingled; mirthful; miserable; modest; monastic; monotonous; moral; mortal; moving; multitudinous (pl); mythological; namby-pamby; nervous; nobler; nomadic; objectless; obscure; old-maidish; ordinary; orgiastic; outer; out-of-town; outside; paltry; palpitating; pampered; parasitic; parental; peaceful; perilous; permeating; perverted; phenomenal; pioneer; plausible; pleasant; plenteous; practical; precarious; prevailing; priceless; private; progressive; prosperous; prosaic; provincial; prudent; pseudo-social; psychical; public; pulsating; pulseless; pure; quickening; radical; rampant; realistic; redundant; regular; rejuvenated; reproductive; renovated; restive; restless; retired; revolutionary; rhythmical; rollicking; rough; roving; ruddy; rural; sacred; sacrificial; scandalous; scanty; secluded; secret; secular; sedentary; sensuous; sequestered; serene; sheltered; shifting; shudderable; simpering; simple; singing; single; skilful; sky-wedded; sleeping; slow-moving; sluggish; smiling; smug; snug; sobered; social; solitary; sophisticated; spiritual; spontaneous; sportive; starved; steady; sterile; stimulating; straggling; strenuous; studious; subsequent; sunless; sunlit; supersensual; sustaining; sweet; swinish; tangled; temperate; tempestuous; tender; terrestrial; thin-spun; thoughtless; thwarted; toilsome; torpid; tortured; tragic; tramping; tree; trite; troubled; tumultuous; turbulent; tyrant; unambitious; unassuming; unbearable; unceasing; unchanging; unconventional; uncircumscribed; undeniable; unendurable; undistinguished; uneventful; unjaded; unprofitable; unprosperous; unrealized; unresisting; unsatisfactory; unseen; unseparable; unsettled; unsightly; unsophisticated; unstable; upright; useful; urban; various (pl); vagrant; vicious; veritable; vigorous; vile; virtuous; wagering; wandering;

warm; wasted; wayside; wayward; well-lost; wholesome; wild; winged; wistful; womanly; wonted; workless; worldly; worthless; worthy; wretched; youthful; action-filled; adequate; adventurous.

verbs

abbreviate—; alter—; bare—of; beautify —; blight—; blot out—; burst into—; carve —; challenge—; cling to—; commence—; comprehend—; conceive—; consecrate—to; cope with—; dedicate—to; degrade—; delve into—; depict—; deplete—; detach from—; devote—to; devour—; disorganize—; dissipate—; diversify—; drag out—; drain of—; embitter—; endanger—; endow with —; enhance—; ennoble—; equip for—; erase—; exemplify—; face—; flash into—; flinch from—; foreshorten—; foster—; fritter—away; galvanize into—; gamble—on; immerse in—; insulate against—; intercede for—; interpret—; intrude upon—; invade—; isolate—; jeopardize—; maim—; maintain—; manifest—; mar—; mend—; mock—; mold—; muddle through—; nourish—; oppress by—; pay with—; permeate —; plunge into—; portray—; probe—; prolong—; race through—; radiate—; rebuild —; reconstruct—; rekindle—; resuscitate —; retire from—; revel in—; routinize—; shock into—; skim through—; snuff out—; squander—; stake—on; submerge—; sum up —; sustain—; taste—; terminate—; thirst for—; tranquilize—; trifle away—; uplift —; vitiate—; warp—; weigh—; —blossoms; —buzzes by; —disintegrates; —ebbs; —evolves; —flowers; —flows; —hangs; — —s intertwine; —persists; —pulsates; — quickens; —rallies; —surges; —trudges on; —unfolds; —withers.

(See career, existence.)

LIFELESS

adverbs

dully; inactively; languidly; inertly; lazily; idly; torpidly; quiescently; silently; actually; heavily; passively; sluggishly; unusually.

LIFETIME

verbs

concentrate in—; curtain—; devote—to; endure—; fill—; guide through—; pledge—; pour into—; record—; seek—; spend—; spin —; strive—; stumble through—; terminate —; withstand—; wrap in—; —grinds; — slides by; —wearies.

(See time, age, century.)

LIFT (v)

adverbs

momentarily; stalwartly; vigorously; feebly; reverently; instinctively; responsively; daintily; involuntarily; alertly; simultaneously; perceptibly; stealthily.

(See elevate, raise, support.)

LIGAMENT

verbs

rupture—; sever—; strain—; strengthen—; stretch—; suture—; tear—; tie—; treat—; —attaches; —binds; —connects; —couples; —extends; —fastens; —joins; —reinforces; —supports; —unites.

(See muscle, cord, tie, bond.)

LIGATURE

verbs

apply—; —arrests; —binds; —checks; —clamps; —collapses; —compresses; —constricts; —contracts; —curbs; —heals; —remedies; —restrains; —squeezes; —stems; —strangulates.

(See bandage, tape.)

LIGHT

adjectives

accusing; adequate; advancing; all-beholden; all-surprising; altering; amber; ample; amusing; angelic; angry; approaching; arrowy; artificial; ashy; attractive; auroral; austral; available; baleful; beacon; becoming; bewildering; blinding; blinking; blissful; blithe; burning; borrowed; bright; broken; brutal; calm; celestial; center; chalky; changeless; chastening; chatoyant; cheering; clear; cloudless; collateral; comforting; confused; congealed; contrasting; cool; coppery; coruscating; crystal; curious; dancing; danger-dissipating; dark; dawning; dazzling; day; deadly; deceitful; deceptive; deep; defiant; delusive; departing; despairing; despondent; dewy; dim; diaphanous; diffused; dirty; discernible; disheveled; distant; distressing; divine; doubtful; dreadful; dreamy; dry; dusky; dying; earliest; effulgent; elfin; enlivening; enkindling; emerging; emitting; erroneous; emotional; eternal; evening; everlasting; evermoving; factitious; fading; faint; fair; falling; fanning; feeble; featureless; filtered; fitful; flaming; flaring; flash; flashing; flighty; fluctuating; fluttering; fuller; garish; gas; gentle; ghastlier; ghostly; gladsome; glancing; glaring; glazed; gleaming; gleamy; glimmering; glorious; glowing; gradual; hallowed; hard; harnessed; harsh; hateful; hazy; heavenly; holy; hovering; illimitable; immortal; imperfect; inaudible; incandescent; indefinite; indistinct; ineffable; inexorable; influential; inner; innumerable (pl); inquisitive; insolent; intellectual; interfused; internal; intrinsic; inward; irreligious; joyous; laborious; leaning; legendary; lessening; lesser; liquid; literary; livid; lofty; lonelier; lovely; luminous; lunar; lurid; malicious; marquee; melancholy; mellow; melting; meridian; meteor; midday; mingling; ministering; minute; mobile; momentary; morning; mourning; murderous; murky; myriad (pl); mysterious; naked; native; nebulous; nocturnal; northern; obscured; odor-giving; opalescent; opposing; patient; pecuniary; peerless; perpetual; petulant; phantasmal; phantom; phosphorescent; piercing; pitiless; planetary; poisoned; political; primogenital; prismatic; propitious; pure; purging; quivering; rackless; rational; ravishing; reflected; remoter; restored; returning; revealing; rising; roseate; rough; ruddy; rush; rushing; sanctioned; sanguine; satisfactory; sacred; scattered (pl); serious; sectarian; serene; sevenfold; shaping; shadowing; shifting; shimmering; shining; shrouded; sickly; slanting; smoky; smothered; soft; solar; solitary; sparkling; stagnant; starry; steady; steely; straggling; streaming; strengthened; subtle; sudden; suffering; sullen; sulphurous; summer; sunset; swimming; tempered; tender; terrific; time-wasting; timid; transmitted; transparent; tremulous; trembling; uncanny; unaccustomed; unapproached; twinkling; uncertain; unclouded; uncreated; undivided; undoubted; undulating; undying; unenvied; unfading; unfavorable; unnatural; unpitying; unsettled; unshadowed; unshaken; unsifted; unspeakable; untainted; unwavering; unwelcome; unwilling; upspringing; vacillating; valiant; varied; vehement; victorious; wandering; waning; warming; wave-divided; wavering; weak; weeping; weird; welcoming; well-diffused; well-loved; wishing; wistful; wondrous; worldly; zigzag.

verbs

adjust—; bathe in—; blot out—; centralize —; douse (colloq.)—; extinguish—; flood with—; focus—upon; glory in—; grope for —; kindle—; muffle—; obscure—; radiate —; refract—; rejoice in—; shed—upon; shield from—; soften—; wreathe in—; —

720

blazes; —blinds; —blinks; —creeps in; —dances; —dazzles; —diffuses; —dwindles; —exposes; —fades; —filters in; —flares; —flickers; —gleams; —glitters; —glows; —illumines; —penetrates; —pierces; —seeps in; —stabs; —streams in; —streaks; —twinkles; —wanes; —wavers; —wells from; —winks.

(See lamp, candle, flame, fireworks, match, sunshine, spark.)

adverbs
insignificantly; extremely; exceedingly; unusually; uncommonly; unbelievably; airily; buoyantly; brilliantly; garishly; pallidly; faintly; indifferently; passably; tolerably; ordinarily; scarcely; manageably; conveniently; happily; jauntily; briskly; brightly; cheerfully; surprisingly; bewilderingly; comfortably; gloriously; mysteriously; unaccountably.

LIGHT (v)
adverbs
brilliantly; spectacularly; visibly; adequately; scantily; partially; gracefully; blindingly; cheerfully; exquisitely; vividly.
(See illumine, illuminate, ignite.)

LIGHTEN (v)
adverbs
blazingly; blindingly; dreadfully; terrifyingly; vividly; explosively; spectacularly.
(See flash, illuminate.)

LIGHT-HEARTED
adverbs
cheerfully; exhilaratingly; genially; good-humoredly; naturally; temperamentally; laughingly; optimistically; roguishly; briskly; blithely; brightly; buoyantly; bonnily; hilariously; youthfully; hopefully; jauntily; jubilantly; winsomely.

LIGHTNESS
adjectives
imaginative; graceful; innumerable (pl); dry; extreme; cheerful; exquisite; boyish; sheer; buoyant; inexpressible.

LIGHTNING
adjectives
blind; parching; internal; wicked; uncommunicated; consuming; volcanic; unleashed; lovelier; poisonous; irreversible; silent; mercy-winged; congregated; artificial; naked; sheet; baleful; arrowy; reverberating; restless; glaring; keener; livid; harmless; nimble; diffused; yoked; indirect; vivid; deadly.

verbs
—bolts; —chars; —cleaves; —dances; —darts; —demolishes; —destroys; —flames; —flashes; —flickers; —glows; —ignites; —illumines; —illuminates; —plays; —rends; —reveals; —streaks; —terrifies; —wreaks; —zigzags.

(See light, lamp, storm, thunder, spark, tornado, typhoon, wind, hurricane.)

LIKE (v)
adverbs
scarcely; extremely; metaphorically; universally; faithfully; persistently; constantly; mutually; momentarily; superficially.
(See fancy, approve, choose.)

LIKELY
adverbs
fairly; somewhat; plausibly; reasonably; speciously; hardly; perhaps; questionably; undoubtedly; dependably; positively.

LIKENESS
adjectives
striking; unaltered; unsubstantial; intrinsic; rude; tangible; graphic; distorted; hideous; speaking; inaccurate; mysterious; generic; grotesque; immortal; mutual; faithful; famous; executed; momentary; consistent; family; rudimental; mute; persistent; phantasmal.

LILIES
adjectives
lazy; sculptured; unsullied; lolling; slumbrous; gleaming; water; waxen; vast; ineffable; fair; pure; languid; pale; sere; mystic; robust; careworn; wind-sown.

LILY
verbs
attire in—; bear—; blight—; crown with —ies; cultivate—ies; stain—; sully—; tint —; —blushes; —ies clothe; —droops; —fades; —ies fester; —flourishes; —glistens; —heaves; —nods; —symbolizes; —unfolds; —withers.
(See flower, plant.)

LIMB
adjectives
vast; swollen; rigid; unshapely; weary;

wan; trembling; unnatural; withered; unbroken; willing; fervid; coarse-featured; uncouth; unfettered; mangled; gouty; childish; sturdy; knotted; writhing; arching; leafless; half-frozen; scabby; severe;. tossing; leprous; shivering; pulsed; oily; corded; stiffened; languid; immovable; unhewn; shrunken; painful; degraded; gangling; puny; little; putrefying; chafed; feeble; naked; denuded; burning; helpless; drooping; sinewy; long-laboring; jaded; massive; thin; weather-beaten; charred; loving; queenly; bare; crippled; paralytic; distorted; wreathing; gentle; tawny; tender; wondrous; supplemental; mutilated; delicate; bending; shuddering; exquisite; lithe; agile; artificial; palsied; aged.

verbs
amputate—; bare—; brace—; char—; cramp—; deform—; develop—; drag—; employ—; exercise—; fracture—; inject into —; paralyze—; strain—; torture—; —shrinks; —supports; —withers.
(See leg, foot, body, elbow.)

LIME-LIGHT
verbs
avoid—; bask in—; crave—; earn—; emerge from—; extinguish—; fade from—; gain—; glory in—; quench—; seek—; steal —; throw into—; —dazzles; —glows; —notorizes; —publicizes; —smoulders; —wanes.
(See fame, publicity, notoriety, renown, reputation.)

LIMES
adjectives
arching; quiet-leaved; bitter; ripened.

LIMIT
adjectives
narrow; rigid; geographic; predetermined; municipal; severe; definite; maximum; uttermost; extended; lazy; ultimate; treaty; broad; hallowed; corporate; judicious; narrowest; practicable; confined; ancient; utmost; wiser; extreme; true; insurmountable; fenceless; transcending; glimmering; constitutional; remotest; legitimate; sanctified; certain; whimsical; original; modest; sensible; reasonable; appointed.

LIMIT (v)
adverbs
grammatically; rigidly; definitely; constitutionally; narrowly; infinitely; scientifically; inescapably; practically; mathematically; morally; fastidiously.
(See confine, restrict, circumscribe.)

LIMITATIONS
adjectives
spheric; rigid; constitutional; reasonable; proper; narrow; hereditary; infinite; inner; scientific; inevitable; immediate; self-imposed; mortal; finite; inescapable; practical.

verbs
abandon—; acknowledge—; amend—; circumscribe—; circumvent—; discern—; dispel—; dispute—; enforce—; escape—; establish—; extricate from—; impose—; prescribe—; subject to—; transcend—; —bar; —bridle; —check; —confine; —constrain; —curb; —expire; —fetter; —incarcerate; —repress; —restrain; —restrict; —yoke.
(See restriction, restraint, limit.)

LIMITED
adverbs
indescribably; legally; unfortunately; strictly; viciously; exclusively; unchangeably; necessarily; conveniently; rigidly; ridiculously; wickedly; inexcusably; traditionally; conventionally; legislatively; excessively; absurdly; wisely; imperiously; irrevocably.

LIMITLESS
adverbs
incredibly; expansively; awesomely; terribly; broadly; generously; inexpressibly; unutterably; incomprehensibly; fearfully.

LIMITS
verbs
act with—; authorize—; bind by—; compress—; define—; exceed—; extend—; fall within—; indicate—; lift—; measure —; narrow—; order—; overstep—; sanctify—; slip over—; sound—; transgress—; urge to—; —bar; —constrain.
(See bounds, restraint, restriction, scope, limitations.)

LIMP
adverbs
languidly; wearily; lankly; soggily; wetly; sadly; hopelessly; helplessly; absurdly;

laughably; feebly; powerlessly; flabbily; pliantly; flimsily; ludicrously; drunkenly; breathlessly; utterly; ridiculously.

LIMP (v)

adverbs
laboriously; painfully; sorely; hideously; piteously; pathetically; feebly; jadedly; wanly; uncouthly; repulsively.
(See hobble, walk, falter.)

LIMPID

adverbs
beautifully; transparently; coolly; serenely; clearly; pellucidly; innocently; trustingly (eyes); ripplingly; translucently.

LINE

adjectives
fine; skirmish; untutored; soft; flowing; harmonious; never-ceasing; demolished; graceful; melodic; undulating; depending; transparent; rippling; continuous; scientific; collateral; advancing; extended; capricious; oblique; sounding; intertwisted; impromptu; important; imaginary; beautiful; impregnable; policy; gleaming; opposing; exiled; converging; occasional; legitimate; feeling; half-illegible; pencil-traced; tighter; sensuous; emphatic; inspiring; minute; fleeting; never-varying; fringing; sharpened; youthful; subtle; insuperable; agitated; endless; divergent; special; curving; dainty; never-relaxing; flexible; roaring; sensitive; equinoctial; curling; flimsy; absolute; straight; feudal; suave; dignified; body-traced; crisp; wide; well-proportioned; smart; smart-draping; distinguished; tapering; easy; exclusive; distinctive; vulnerable; ravaged; sonorous; unbroken; monastery; bread; uneven; ragged; cramped; parallel (pl); eccentric; sleepless; irregular; pathetic; wabbling; quivering; ensuing; paternal; wavering; decided; eastward; fringing; fortified; etched; shapely; style; constricting; exterior; remotest; rent; successive (pl); slim; stirring; insolent; decisive; mystic; long; urbane; broad; tedious; swagger; classic; apostolic; complete; swinging; transcontinental; surging; stunning; weight-bearing; traditional; characteristic; honied; poetic; circumvallating; radial; moral; interconnecting; natural; jeweled; slender; wanton; rambling; trim; immortal; smart-tailored; ever-lengthening; stubborn; sleek; sun-tempting; back; dauntless; luxuriant; unreturning; fantastic; momentous; placid; solemn; noiseless; intertangled; infinitesimal; oblique; shoddy; eloquent; narrative; witty; preparatory; hypothetical; impassioned; unpunctuated; inimitable; telegraphic; harsh; effective; circling; competing; bristling; faint; intrenched; brilliant; vanquished; horizontal; cabalistic; sinuous; preconcerted; completed; well-defined; stateliest; unfading; glittering; never-ending; allied; quaint; experimental; nodal; prosaic; radiating (pl); trimmer; industrial; intellectual; heroic; improvised; illustrious; admirable; hard; grim; humble; imitative; ghostly; foul; swelling; touching; foolish; connecting; imperiled; unpolished; bobbing; unrelated; brief; plumb; slimmer; compact; simple; unconquered; vocal; holy; therapeutic; theoretic; charging; ferocious; thought-tracked; genealogical; sublime; fleshly; surging; dividing.

verbs
alternate—s; blur—; delineate—; derive—from; eradicate—; extend—; foul—; fracture—; intersect—; overrun—; scale—; thread—; trace—; warp—; wipe out—s; —bounds; —s coincide; —deviates; —digresses; —dips; —grades; —graduates; —limits; —parallels; —progresses; —s radiate from; —refracts; —represents; —straggles; —swerves; —veers; —verges; —wobbles.
(See mark, boundary, outline, route, road.)

LINEAGE

adjectives
ancient; imperial; injured; honorable.

LINEAMENTS

adjectives
haughtiest; stricken; pallid; striking; noble; dead; hideous; mental; exaggerated; warworn; strong; sculptured; impertinent; personal; shifting.

LINED
(*wrinkled*)

adverbs
deeply; humorously; scowlingly; ripely; puckeringly; agedly; patriarchally; terribly; significantly.

LINEN

adjectives
blood-clotted; snowy; dubious; age-yellowed; spotless; filthy; foul; stout; dainty; immaculate; embroidered; outward-surging; convent.

verbs
array in—; attire in—; bleach—; brocade
—; carbonize—; card—; comb—; disentangle—; drape—; dress—; embroider—;
fringe with—; garb in—; gird in—; grade
—; hackle—; hank—; ret—; soak—; spin
—; vest in—; warp—.
(See cloth, silk, velvet.)

LINGER (*v*)
adverbs
tenderly; affectionately; vaguely; monotonously; boringly; obtrusively; wearily; confusedly; regretfully; perilously; idly; irresolutely; indecisively.
(See loiter, saunter.)

LINGUIST
adjectives
skilled; ready; manifold; comparative; accomplished; brilliant; celebrated.

LINIMENT
verbs
administer—; apply—; drench with—; yield
to—; —cools; —limbers; —mollifies; —palliates; —relaxes; —relieves; —restores; —
soothes.
(See medicine, iodine, tonic, remedy, ointment, salve.)

LINING
verbs
strip of—; stud with—; —chafes; —coats;
—crusts; —inflames; —jackets; —pads; —
preserves; —sheathes; —wads.
(See cloth, silk, velvet, wrapper.)

LINK
verbs
cement—; dissolve—; fuse—; partition into
—s; pivot on—; rend—; sever—; solder—;
sunder—; terminate—; —affiliates; —allies;
—bridges; —cleaves; —coincides; —communicates; —correlates; —facilitates; —fetters; —hinges; —leagues; —shackles; —
spans; —unites; —leashes.
(See chain, bond, tie, ring, union, part,
ligament, ligature.)

LINK (*v*)
adverbs
indissolubly; inextricably; rhythmically; inevitably; inseparably; perpetually; incessantly; slanderously; humorously; incongruously; incompatibly.
(See join, connect, unite.)

adjectives
intervening; thought; special; connecting;
accustomed; mystic; clay-cold; adamantine;
successive; breezy.

LINNET
verbs
—collects; —s flock; —mimics; —pipes; —
warbles.
(See bird.)

LINOTYPE
verbs
dump—; ink—; melt—; print from—; set—;
trim—; —assembles; —casts; —clanks; —
composes; —distributes; —facilitates; —
stereotypes; —transcribes.
(See type, metal.)

LION
adjectives
tameless; tawny-bearded; prisoned; rampant; jagged-jawed; wondrous.

verbs
encounter—; rouse—; slay—; —attacks; —
carries off; —claws; —creeps upon; —devours; —drags off; —forages; —glares;
—growls; —menaces; —paws; —preys on;
—purrs; —rages; —rampages; —roams; —
roars; —rolls over; —slaughters; —springs;
—stalks; —stretches; —tears; —yawns.
(See animal, tiger, leopard.)

LIONIZE (*v*)
adverbs
bizarrely; enthusiastically; customarily; fraternally; hospitably; jovially; congenially;
sportively; agreeably.
(See glorify, adore, exhibit, display.)

LIPS
adjectives
kissing; bridled; bearded; ripe; marble;
burning; dimpled; fervent; rosy; trembling;
quivering; seldom-parted; seductive; pendulous; curdled; ruddy; seeking; tender; sensitive; clear-cut; blistering; coward; car-
mine; glowing; loving; gaping; languid;
wet; rosy; pallid; sinful; placid; down-
drawn; brazen; dewy; blanched; swollen;
bold; parching; flaccid; pursed; tightened;
generous; thin; gummed-up; villainous;
straight; pale; discolored; unpainted;
roughed; pinched; dry; rosebud; ruby;
whitening; crystal; shiny; coral; wide;

over-red; livid; bloodless; velvet; blanched; cerise; lead-colored; flower-petal; sardonic; projecting; compressed; unbreathing; protruding; heavy; half-open; full; purpled; flower-soft; traitorous; dainty; milk-fed; loose; eloquent; scornful; curse-laden; icy; mute; opened; stern; set; fevered; fettered; fleshless; babbling; mortal; ample; living; warm; sealed; eased; tired; willing; gifted; insatiable; sinuous; unseen; mobile; contorted; angel; squandering; innocent; imperial; firm; uncaressing; love-enkindled; luscious; appreciative; hueless; perjured; voluptuous; lifeless; dying; republican; wax-red; grim; nectared; bristled; mocking; unfettered; gnarled; miserable; careless; winning; girlish; sallow; frothing; lax; slight; haughty; proud; retracted; sad; voiceless; severed; curled-up; flashing; skinny; full; incense-breathing; sensuous; intertwisted; carved; calm; pure; thirsty; grosser; guarded; writhing; drooping; obsequious; shrunken; puckered; slanderous; relaxing; half-pouting; crooked; pendulous; mellow; prehensile; meager; tortured; honeyed; unclosed; averted; starved; covetous; convivial; unclean; well-cut; ineffectual; scorched; passionate; leopard; lily; stammering; infant; panting; cracked; stifling; rapid; chiseled; milkless; wrinkled; long-silent; devout.

verbs
compress—; depress—; excoriate—; glue—; gnaw—; lock—; parch—; pucker—; purse —; seal—; smack—; sully—; thin—; tumble from—; wring from—; —beguile; —curl; —falter; —pout; —proclaim; —profane; —protrude; —quiver; —scorn; —snarl; —stir; —thin; —tremble; —writhe; —yield.
(See mouth.)

LIQUID
adjectives
malodorous; viscous; foul; limpid; combustible; sparkling; denser; anesthetizing; lifeless; ecstatic; rosy; plain; noxious; queer-looking; seminal; unliquidating; colorless; swarming; consecrated; putrid; opaque.

verbs
charge—; chill—; dabble in—; deluge with —; dilute—; discharge—; drain—; draw off —; exude—; gargle—; gulp—; imbibe—; immerse in—; infiltrate—; inject—; precip-

itate—; spout—; squirt—; steep in—; strain —; submerge—; tap—; —babbles; —gurgles; —ripples; —saturates.
(See water, fluid, liquor, beverage, drink.)

LIQUOR
adjectives
amber; muddy; intoxicating; crimson; fuming; pleasant; drowsy; rebellious; sparkling; grand; spiritual; hateful; nectarial; exquisite; stimulating.

verbs
abstain from—; age—; carouse with—; compound —; dilute—; distill—; ferment—; grade—; imbibe—; overindulge in—; perfume—; reek of—; reel with—; restrict—; stamp—; sublimate—; sweeten—; tax—; traffic in—; —inebriates; —stupefies.
(See whiskey, brandy, beer, ale, wine.)

LISP (*v*)
adverbs
affectedly; mincingly; insipidly; captivatingly; emulously; irritatingly; annoyingly; sibilantly.
(See utter, talk, speak.)

LISSOME
adverbs
slenderly; daintily; youthfully; girlishly; beautifully; attractively; unusually; uncommonly; delightfully; softly; yieldingly; tenderly; gracefully; charmingly.

LIST
adjectives
inexhaustible; extensive; provisional; authoritative; stupendous; representative; eligible; pompous; voting; growing; metrical; interminable; fatal; appalling; shining; gratifying; alarming; casualty; diversified; abbreviated; annotated; prescribed; protesting; mere; certain; inexorable; illegitimate.

verbs
approve—; audit—; check—; circularize—; compile—; delete—; enroll in—; extend—; investigate—; muster—; rattle off—; recapitulate—; review—; supplement—; swell—; —accounts; —calendars; —catalogues; —computes; —declines; —dwindles; —enumerates; —indexes; —measures; —polls; —recedes; —registers; —schedules; —scores; —sums up; —wanes.
(See schedule, sum, amount, account, record, statistics, statement, program.)

LISTEN (v)

adverbs

apprehensively; indulgently; intently; attentively; dreamily; compassionately; piously; obediently; intelligently; impassively; reflectively; languidly; aimlessly; sympathetically; interminably; gratifyingly; raptly.

(See attend, heed, hearken, obey.)

LISTENER

adjectives

attentive; sympathetic; untutored; intelligent; chance; anxious; uninitiated; puzzled; radiant; discriminating; unprejudiced; admiring; individual; laconic; impassive; wondering; mute; rapt; unobtrusive; defiant; close; trembling.

verbs

admonish—; bar—; bore—; enchant—; entrance—; inform—; reproach—; rouse—; spellbind—; —absorbs; —bends an ear; —s chorus; —considers; —eavesdrops; —grasps; —hearkens; —heeds; —pricks up his ears; —regards; —senses; —wearies.

(See audience, congregation, hearer, visitor, guest, crowd.)

LISTLESS

adverbs

provokingly; languidly; inertly; lazily; dully; carelessly; heedlessly; indifferently; irritatingly; vexatiously; arrogantly; obviously; visibly; unaccountably; inexplicably; insufferably; impolitely; discourteously; insolently; inconsiderately; helplessly; drowsily; distractedly; dreamily; terribly; amazingly; surprisingly; dreadfully.

LITERAL

adverbs

painfully; punctiliously; insufferably; legally; meticulously; intolerably; ostentatiously; professionally; officiously; unctuously; learnedly; academically; boresomely; unduly; unnecessarily; mercilessly; ruthlessly; unimaginatively; prosaically; mathematically; correctly; severely; uncompromisingly; curiously; exaggeratedly; awfully; uncommonly.

LITERATURE

adjectives

vigorous; national; contemporary; classical; related; city-bred; romantic; descriptive; illustrated; tinted; creative; imperishable; vernacular; inventive; satirical; critical; superficial; current; periodical; obscene; extensive; mainstream; complete; forensic; personal; ancient; primitive; social; significant; majestic; disciplined; prolific; imaginative; vitalized.

verbs

acclaim—; appreciate—; assail—; bar—; censor—; create—; criticize—; dabble in—; delve into—; evaluate—; execute—; foster —; haunt—; interpret—; nurse—; patronize —; relish—; revaluate—; sanctify—; stabilize—; unify—; —charms; —communicates; —conveys; —enlightens; —delights; —enraptures; —eternizes; —expresses; —immortalizes; —incites; —informs; —inspires; —portrays; —provides; —redeems; —reveals; —stimulates; —transfuses; —transports.

(See art, story, biography, newspaper, press, essay, fiction, poetry, writing, book, magazine.)

LITIGATION

adjectives

expensive; sufficient; recent; weary; furious; prolonged; bitter.

verbs

appeal—; clinch—; discharge—; dispose of —; dispute—; evidence—; execute—; judge —; speed—; support—; —apprehends; —arraigns; —clashes; —distrains; —drags; —embroils; —impeaches; —indicts; —jars; —prosecutes; —squabbles.

(See lawsuit, case, suit (law), argument, verdict, results, decision, settlement.)

LITTER

adjectives

sable; terrible; intellectual; huge.

LITTER (v)

adverbs

confusedly; untidily; sloppily; haphazardly; disheveledly; obtrusively.

(See scatter, separate, intersperse.)

LITTLE

adverbs

precious; confoundedly; pitiably; inconsequentially; remarkably; miserably; cruelly; incredibly; inadequately; infinitesimally; wretchedly; blessedly.

LIVE
(alive)

adverbs

actively; mentally; amazingly; animatedly; perilously; briskly; eagerly; mysteriously; sensitively; energetically; spiritually; fiercely; unmistakably; joyously; secretly; keenly; spiritedly; emotionally; intellectually; persistently; tragically; enterprisingly; exuberantly; vigorously; undeniably; restlessly; substantially; strongly; warmly; wretchedly; vivaciously; vitally; acutely; flourishingly; impatiently; tenaciously; exultantly; resolutely; happily.

LIVE (v)

adverbs

lavishly; dangerously; originally; expansively; improvidently; actively; profligately; opulently; ostentatiously; excessively; inconsequentially; affluently; gloriously; immortally; significantly; luxuriously; fantastically; penuriously; pretentiously; sumptuously; dissolutely; harmoniously; religiously; precariously; blithely; exclusively; spiritually; economically; abstemiously; scandalously; barbarously; monotonously; strenuously.

(See exist, abide, dwell.)

LIVELIHOOD

adjectives

meager; humble; bare; reputable; honest.

verbs

acquire—; afford—; bereave of—; command —; derive—from; draw—from; earn—; furnish—; gain—; grub—; insure—; maintain—; offer—; procure—; reap—; scrape together—; strip of—; yield—.

(See living, support, sustenance, income, wages, salary.)

LIVELINESS

verbs

animate with—; frolic in—; manifest—; radiate—; sparkle in—; stimulate—; — cheers; —effervesces; —elates; —enlivens; —exhilarates; —gladdens; —inspirits; — perks up.

(See animation, action, activity, vivacity, life.)

LIVELY

adverbs

immensely; joyously; noisily; naturally; unwontedly; unbelievably; briskly; gloriously; conspicuously; strikingly; fitfully; abnormally; dramatically; ostentatiously; ridiculously; singularly; habitually; disturbingly; pleasantly; refreshingly; enchantingly.

LIVER

adjectives

unchaste; torpid; spotted.

verbs

afflict—; attack—; congest—; damage—; derange—; disorganize—; impair—; infect —; —deteriorates; —discharges; —ejects; —excretes; —expels; —functions; —lodges; —purifies; —secretes; —shrivels.

(See bladder, organs, heart, kidney.)

LIVERY

adjectives

silver; reclusive; religious; gorgeous; cunning; destined; sober; bare; showy; beauteous; humble; drab-colored; gilded; royal; special.

LIVES

adjectives

best-regulated; scandalous; infinite; sedentary; weary; frivolous; deplorable; millennial; constricted; barbarous; valueless; luxurious; fateful; uncultivated; eventful; precious; regimented; craven; misplaced; strenuous; acceptable; fashionable; worthy; stunted; solitary; unnumbered; pale; virgin; disordered; imaginative; carnivorous; intermittent; lawless; divided; brutish; monotonous.

LIVESTOCK

verbs

auction off—; brand—; confine—; corral—; deal in—; free—; insure—; obliterate—; pasture—; shelter—; stable—; tend—; tether—; water—; —grazes; —sickens; — stampedes; —tramples; —wanders.

(See cow, horse, cattle, oxen, mule, sheep, lamb.)

LIVID

adverbs

terribly; hideously; terrifyingly; painfully; awfully; gruesomely; darkly; dreadfully; ashenly; coldly.

LIVING

adjectives

riotous; monotonous; concentrated; fruitful; flourishing; luxurious; scandalous; enjoyable; precarious; lucrative; gracious; contemporary; successful; happy; reckless; useful; dissipated; sufficient; vicarious; fat; independent; complicated; healthier; clean; ascetic; cheap; moderate; contented; strenuous; satisfactory; pleasurable; honorable; generous; primitive; scanty; quiet; fine; inexpensive; congenial; restful; wasteful.

verbs
acquire—; afford—; derive—from; earn—; eke—; fend for—; furnish—; gain—; garner—; glean—; offer—; simplify—; wrest —from.
(See livelihood, support, sustenance, income, wages, salary.)

LIZARD
verbs
—burrows; —claws; —crawls; —dives; — erects; —flies; —frequents; —invades; — paddles; —poisons; —preys upon; —reproduces; —sheds; —slithers; —suns itself; — swims.; —whips its tail; —wounds; — wriggles.
(See reptile, animal, snake.)

LOAD
adjectives
bounteous; dark; weary; precious; concentrated; work; moaning; dead-weight; groaning; grievous; cumbrous; harsh; life-compelling; monstrous; tremendous.

verbs
ameliorate—; augment—; bear—; bend under—; bow by—; collect—; discharge—; droop under—; strap—on; support—; weigh —; —burdens; —clogs; —encumbers; — hampers; —impedes; —oppresses; —overwhelms; —restrains; —weakens.
(See burden, weight, pressure.)

LOAF (v)
adverbs
contentedly; idly; improvidently; dreamily; disgracefully; drunkenly; corruptly; enjoyably; congenially; wastefully.
(See dawdle, lounge, loiter, loll.)

LOAM
adjectives
fresh; woodland; tenacious; yielding; smeared.

LOAN
adjectives
brief; willing; stagnant; inadequate; exorbitant.

verbs
acknowledge—; advance—; amortize—; confer—upon; contract—; contribute—; extend—; facilitate—; float—; force—; grant —; inveigle—; launch—; obtain—; pledge —; press—; procure—; raise—; solicit—; subscribe—; —gratifies; —indebts.
(See debt, money, funds, payment.)

LOATHSOME
adverbs
unspeakably; abominably; disgustingly; mortally; sickeningly; insufferably; intolerably; uncommonly; impossibly; utterly; completely; horribly; repulsively; detestably; shockingly; hatefully.

LOATHING
adjectives
indignant; deepest; instinctive; enormous.

LOBBY
adjectives
commodious; magnificent; new; busy; quiet; economical; impressive; appointed; cheerful; furnished; luxurious.

verbs
appropriate—; decorate—; frequent—; lounge in—; pace—; page in—; retire to —; retreat to—; throng—; wait in—; — connects; —echoes with; —resounds; — swarms.
(See hall, corridor, passage, room.)

LOCAL
adverbs
apparently; allegedly; merely; luckily; strongly; unquestionably; evidently; emphatically.

LOCALITY
adjectives
affected; attractive; residential; memorable; isolated; miserable.

verbs
acclimate to—; annihilate—; assign to—; canvass—; examine—; explore—; fix—; in-

habit—; investigate—; mold to—; scan—; scour—; search—; seek—; select—; sever from—; shift—; view—; —militates.

(See territory, region, neighborhood, vicinity, district.)

LOCATE (v)
adverbs

systematically; centrally; conveniently; precisely; picturesquely; distinctly; matchlessly; conveniently; strategically; geographically.

(See place, establish.)

LOCATION
adjectives

pleasant; choice; favored; unexcelled; preferred; ideal; unique; matchless; convenient; superb; beautiful; quiet; splendid; particular; strategic; changing; available; interesting; hazardous; advantageous; geographical; outstanding; efficient; mythical; industrial; peculiar; unrivaled.

LOCK
(hair)
adjectives

unkempt; curling; raven; clustering; flowing; luxuriant; thin; dangling; straggling; whitened; crisped; snaky; golden; recalcitrant; massy; obstinate; bushy; truant; glossy; sunny; intertwining; straying; shining; tumbled; dense; shaggy; well-groomed; shorn; stiff; flat; dripping; hoary; clustering; sparse; unruly; fearful; floating; silken; careless; scanty; disheveled; plaited.

LOCK
(mechanical)
adjectives

shattering; languid; crude; mitered; profuse; keyhole; intricate; burglar-proof.

verbs

adjust—; design—; force—; jimmy—; pick —; set—; tamper with—; test—; unbar—; withdraw—; —clasps; —clicks; —embraces; —repulses; —resists; —responds; —seals; —secures.

(See bolt, bar.)

LOCK (v)
adverbs

discreetly; cautiously; prudently; mechanically; automatically; modestly; suspiciously; covetously; staunchly.

(See fasten, fix, secure.)

LOCOMOTIVE
verbs

board—; derail—; dismount from—; fuel —; propel—; —chugs; —halts; —hammers; —overtakes; —pants; —puffs; —screeches; —shrieks; —shuffles; —speeds; —sputters; —stammers; —steams;. —traverses; — wails; —wheezes; —whizzes.

(See train, engine.)

LOCUST
verbs

crush—; exterminate—s; —bores; —burrows; —s cloud; —cymbals; —destroys; — drones; —drums; —s migrate; —molts; —s plague; —rasps; —rattles; —sings; —sucks; —s swarm; —s symphonize; —undergoes; —s descend.

(See insect, grasshopper.)

LODGE
adjectives

ivy-covered; rude; supreme; nightly; country; hunting.

verbs

abandon—; charter—; confine to—; enjoy —; invite to—; luxuriate in—; occupy—; organize—; repose in—; reside at—; retire to—; retreat to—; vacate—; —accommodates; —comforts; —harbors; —shelters; — solaces.

(See club, home, residence, society, room.)

LODGE (v)
adverbs

snugly; firmly; fatally; temporarily; miserably; congenially; uniquely; conveniently; strategically; advantageously; industrially; permanently.

(See stay, remain, abide.)

LODGING
adjectives

inferior; hard; primitive; comfortable; barren.

verbs

afford—; assure of—; demand—; engage—; enjoy—; find—; furnish—; grant—; guarantee—; inquire into—; lease—; offer—; procure—; scorn—; secure—; seek—; warrant—; —delights; —refreshes; —shames.

(See shelter, refuge, room, rest, repose, sanctuary.)

LOFTY

adverbs

arrogantly; notoriously; incalculably; ridiculously; eminently; majestically; exaltedly; impressively; imposingly; proudly; toweringly; incredibly; tremendously; imperiously; strangely; ludicrously.

LOG

adjectives

smoldering; inanimate; unhewn; hollowed; flaming; back; blazing; hickory; yule; drunken; senseless; floating; ostensible; patent; moldered.

verbs

batter with—; bear—; char—; fire—; hew —; ignite—; kindle—; poke—; stir—; toast over—; vault—; —chills; —flames; —fuels; —glows; —seethes; —smokes; —smoulders.

(See club, wood, flame, fire, board, timber.)

LOGIC

adjectives

unerring; remorseless; persistent; energetic; soundest; dangerous; delightful; rigorous; symbolic; feminine; erstwhile; convincing; uncharitable; unanswerable; aesthetic; dispassionate; vast; cruel; hasty; imperfect; triumphant; inexorable; simple; compelling; pitiless; easy; strict; subtle; inevitable; unyielding; blundering; naked; suicidal.

verbs

condemn—; defy—; demonstrate—; endorse —; govern by—; indicate—; judge—; lame —; practise—; question—; reduce to—; refute—; require—; review—; warp—; ween from—; —analyzes; —annihilates; —convinces; —deduces; —determines; —dictates; —evolves; —prevails; —solves; —speculates.

(See reason, theory, accuracy.)

LOGICAL

adverbs

entirely; historically; skilfully; unfailingly; admirably; justly; remarkably; inevitably; . unerringly; alarmingly; inexorably; fearfully; inescapably; undeniably; amazingly; uncommonly; wholly.

LOINS

adjectives

unknown; frozen; supple; girt; proper.

LOITER (v)

adverbs

undecidedly; jauntily; lackadaisically; tantalizingly; idly; luxuriously; persistently; excessively.

(See loaf, dawdle, lounge, loll.)

LOLL (v)

adverbs

luxuriantly; idly; listlessly; carelessly; wearily; impassively; frivolously; wantonly.

(See lounge, loaf, dawdle.)

LONE

adverbs

desolately; noticeably; distinctly; prominently; tragically; cheerlessly; remotely; intensely; solitarily; terribly; remarkably; uniquely; dreadfully.

LONELINESS

adjectives

supreme; visionary; abstracted; infinite; mossy; tragic; bowery; unutterable; oppressive; indescribable; multitudinous; infinitesimal; appalling; palatial; dreary; empty; bitter; unbearable; intolerable.

verbs

abate—; assuage—; conceal—; decry—; dissipate—; drive away—; evince—; fear—; guard against—; heighten—; overcome—; ravage by—; shroud in—; stress—; succumb to—; —accompanies; —assails; —engulfs; —envelops; —penetrates.

(See seclusion, solitude, isolation, dullness.)

LONELY

adverbs

strangely; unbelievably; unaccountably; naturally; oddly; forlornly; unbearably; unendurably; unnecessarily; distressingly; portentously; infinitely; tragically; unutterably; bitterly; intolerably; drearily; appallingly; indescribably; inexpressibly; pitiably; irremediably; pathetically; cruelly.

LONESOME

adverbs

dismally; reminiscently; gloomily; serenely; lazily; jealously; unhappily; terribly; intensely; peevishly; fretfully; drearily; supremely; absurdly; inexpressibly; grievously; hopelessly; pathetically; deservedly; unexpectedly; remarkably; curiously; dimly; vaguely; startlingly; extremely.

LONG

adverbs

extraordinarily; endlessly; interminably; monotonously; unbearably; ridiculously; excessively; remarkably; singularly; extremely; unbelievably; unnecessarily; sufficiently; tediously; inexcusably; unserviceably; unconscionably; incredibly; diffusely; tiresomely; wearily; terribly; curiously; unaccountably; unwarrantably.

LONG (v)

adverbs

nostalgically; impassionedly; wildly; sentimentally; fondly; inexplicably; fruitlessly; morbidly; restlessly; irresistibly; insatiably; singularly; inexpressibly; lingeringly; buoyantly; irrationally.

(See yearn, crave.)

LONGEVITY

verbs

contribute to—; derive—; endure—; enjoy —; entail—; evoke—; forestall—; hinder—; increase—; induce—; invest with—; procure—; produce—; provoke—; secure—; shatter—; —enfeebles; —results.

(See health.)

LONGING

adjectives

wild; nostalgic; vain; impassioned; sympathetic; premature; indefinite; wholesome; satisfied; strange; unpenetrated; mad; hopeless; immortal; musical; fond; earnest; unconscious; unchaste; new-born; inexplicable; vague; anxious; unceasing; indefinable; passionate; animal; earliest; patent; potent; half-deadly; half-voluptuous; persistent; bitter; fruitless; diseased; morbid; innermost; undefined; restless; ungratified; irresistible; painful; cruel; insatiate; ceaseless; upward; uncontrollable; faded; singular; doglike.

verbs

abate—; conceive—; devour by—; fulfill—; gratify—; hatch—; live in—; quench—; respect—; sate—; satisfy—; suffer—; uproot—; —burns; —destroys; —gnaws; — palls; —tantalizes; —tears at.

(See desire, yearning, craving, nostalgia.)

LOOK

adjectives

absent; agonized; alabaster; appealing; alert; amorous; animated; approving; arch; ardent; artless; attenuated; backward; bantering; beaming; beguiling; beseeching; bewildered; bitter; black; brazen; bleached; brown; bullying; burning; careworn; colorless; comic; compassionate; complacent; comprehensive; conjunctive; contemptuous; contented; counterfeit; critical; cross; crystal; cunning; curious; cursory; damp; dazed; deadly; deep; defiant; dejected; delicate; delirious; demure; deserted; despairing; desperate; despondent; dim; discontented; disdainful; dismal; dissipated; dissembling; distasteful; disturbed; doubting; downcast; drawn; dreamy; droopy; dubious; dying; elusive; enthralling; envious; expectant; exultant; fair; faraway; far-off; fearful; fear-stunned; flashing; frequent (pl); frightened; furtive; gentle; gloomy; glowering; glum; good; gracious; grateful; grave; grieved; guileless; haggard; half-laughing; hanging; haunting; heartbroken; helpless; honest; hopeless; hostile; hunted; hurried; hurt; icy; impertinent; imploring; indignant; innocent; inquiring; inscrutable; intelligent; intent; intimidating; irreverent; jaunty; keen; kind; knowing; languid; latent; lean; lingering; loftiest; longing; lowering; luminous; melancholy; melodramatic; merry; mild; mischievous; momentary; moody; mute; mysterious; naughty; obdurate; oblique; occasional; ogling; ominous; open; outdoor; pale; pathetic; penetrating; perplexed; phantasmal; piercing; pitiful; plaintive; pleading; predatory; preoccupied; prepossessing; prolonged; provocative; puzzled; queenly; queer; questioning; quick; quizzical; rakish; reluctant; resigned; reverend; riveted; robust; rueful; roguish; rowdy; rugged; sad; saucy; scared; scornful; scowling; searching; seeking; seraphic; serene; serious; shy; shamed; sidelong; significant; silky; silly; smart; soft; somnambulistic; sorrowful; sour; spectral; speculative; speechless; spiteful; sprightly; startled; steady; staunch; stealthy; stereotyped; stiff-necked; strained; stricken; stunned; sulky; sullen; surprised; suspicious; swift; swarthy; sweetest; tearful; thick; timely; threatening; timid; tired; tranquil; truculent; unfathomable; unflinching; ungentle; unguarded; united; unrestful; unseeing; unusual; vacant; valiant; vexed; vindictive; vivid; waiting; wan; weak; weather-beaten; welcoming; wild; whimsical; wistful; wise; withering; woebegone; wonderful; wondering; worn; worshipful; yearning.

acclaim with—; belie—; conceal—; confuse —; evade—; flash—; manufacture—; quail before—; shoot—; snatch—; sneak—; sour —; —challenges; —cows; —probes; —rebukes; —scorches; —shines; —wanes; —wavers; —withers.

(See glance, gaze, scrutiny, glimpse.)

LOOK (v)

adverbs

amorously; beseechingly; cursorily; compassionately; demurely; disdainfully; impertinently; dubiously; haggardly; reverently; ominously; pathetically; provocatively; intimidatingly; roguishly; seraphically; speculatively; vacantly; vindictively; witheringly; uncomprehendingly; covertly; sagaciously; stonily; meditatively; disconsolately; ferociously; ponderingly; wistfully; raptly; keenly; frivolously; mockingly; sheepishly; woefully; querulously; significantly; incredulously.

(See gaze, glance, stare.)

LOOM

adjectives

rustling; webless; creaking; interwoven; ages-old; wooden; handicraft; triumphant; primitive; magic; precious.

LOOM (v)

adverbs

ominously; thunderously; portentously; threateningly; impressively; belligerently; direly; stupendously; awesomely.

(See shine, rise, appear.)

LOOSE

adverbs

dangerously; fearfully; oddly; inexplicably; perilously; hazardously; distinctly; insecurely; inexcusably; terribly; accidentally; mysteriously; undeniably; unstably; carelessly; incautiously.

LOOSEN (v)

adverbs

radically; sufficiently; comfortably; medically; beneficially; healthfully; scientifically; partially.

(See free, separate, unfasten.)

LOOT

verbs

appropriate—; bag—; bicker over—; conceal—; divide—; embrace—; feed on—;

forage for—; gather—; nab—; parcel—; plunder for—; pocket—; ransack for—; sack for—; scramble for—; smuggle—; snap up —; snatch—; strip of—; suckle on—; vie for—; wean on—.

(See spoils, plunder, graft.)

LOQUACIOUS

adverbs

interminably; wildly; garrulously; chattily; maliciously; undeniably; highly; endlessly; inanely; glibly; clackily; flippantly; tiresomely; insufferably; amusingly; vexatiously; incredibly; hysterically; verbosely; repetitiously; dreadfully; amazingly; strangely; nonsensically.

LOQUACITY

adjectives

irrepressible; nervous; unlimited; noticeable.

LORD
(gentleman)

adjectives

stalwart; pampered; truant; absolute; predestined; rapacious; dread; native; gracious; illustrious; dethroned; worthy; courteous; brindled; merry; distressed; mocking; sovereign; faithless; new-trothed; filthy; scurvy; unworthy; unnatural; self-complacent; honored.

LORD
(divine being)

verbs

accept—; beseech—; bow to—; cherish—; exalt—; invoke—; offer unto—; praise—; pray to—; supplicate—; worship—; —anoints; —bestows; —controls; —heals; —judges; —masters.

(See God, Christ, Jesus.)

LORDLY

adverbs

arrogantly; insufferably; naturally; imposingly; impressively; absurdly; ridiculously; ludicrously; magnificently; splendidly; magnanimously; majestically; distinctly; notoriously; eminently; conspicuously; superciliously; imperiously; incredibly; proudly; laughably; curiously.

LORE

adjectives

slothful; poetic; listless; childlike; astrologic; legendary; idle; mythical; sublimest; exhaustless; technical; nauseous; immortal;

deceptive; inmost; shining; civilizing; gentlest; lascivious; mystic; legal; golden; preternatural; eternal; divinest.

verbs
acquire—; arm with—; banish—; comprehend—; delve into—; exaggerate—; gather —; ignore—; initiate into—; instruct in—; master—; perpetuate—; preserve—; steep in—; strip of—; substantiate—; unearth—; —deludes; —impresses; —misleads; —survives.
(See legend, tale, story, wisdom, learning.)

LOSER
verbs
condole—; declare—; deprive—; deride—; dispossess—; draw—; jeer—; renounce—; ridicule—; spot—; sympathize with—; — beseeches; —blunders; —complains; —deplores; —discards; —fails; —falls; — grumbles; —laments; —pledges; —prates; —protests; —sacrifices.
(See failure.)

LOSS
adjectives
consequent; wasteful; proportional; total; threatened; mournful; irreparable; considerable; excessive; disastrous; serious; unendurable; continual; awakened; prospective; infinite; intolerable; vague; frightful; heavy; trifling; financial; tragic; fearful; trivial; melancholy; sickening; crushing; shocking; inconsiderable; dear; moisture; perceptible; slight; petty; gainful; immeasurable; ultimate; imminent; undetectable; aggregate; lamentable; moneyed; irretrievable; tremendous; frightful; complete; appalling; preventable; numerical; maiden; partial; positive; anticipated; grievous.

verbs
absorb—; attribute—to; bemoan—; brood over—; cloak—; compensate for—; concede —; counterbalance—; curtail—; deplore—; grieve over—; incur—; lament—; lighten—; mourn—; occasion—; offset—; outweigh—; recoup—s; redress—; regard—; reimburse —; repent—; report—; retrieve—; smart under—; suffer—; sustain—; swallow—; — anguishes; —maddens; —s mount; — shames; —s soar.
(See bankruptcy, defeat, failure, misfortune.)

LOST
adverbs
irrecoverably; irretrievably; recently; altogether; forever; temporarily; lamentably; deplorably; utterly; strangely; curiously; terribly; unfortunately; incredibly; miserably.

LOT
adjectives
adjacent; adventurous; vacant; disreputable; enviable; dreary; toilsome; cheerless; loose-living; human; picturesque; unfortunate; homely; future; worthless; scrubby; uncomfortable; cloudless.

verbs
administer—; apportion—; assign—; bequeath—to; cast—s; deplore—; detail—; dispense—; distribute—s; draw—s; elect by —; embrace—; parcel—; partition—; remedy—; sacrifice—; share—; throw—in with.

LOTION
adjectives
creamy; soothing; cool; pleasant; unguent.

verbs
bathe with—; dilute—; dissolve in—; gargle —; immerse in—; saturate with—; steep in —; vend—; —beautifies; —heals; —perfumes; —purges; —purifies; —refreshes; — repairs; —repels; —soothes.
(See ointment, salve, soap.)

LOUD
adverbs
boisterously; terribly; crashingly; fearfully; impressively; unbelievably; clamorously; deafeningly; tumultuously; infernally; uncommonly; strangely; unnecessarily; unduly; appallingly; shockingly; thunderously; tempestuously; shrilly; objectionably; explosively; unmistakably; insufferably; unbearably.

LOUD-SPEAKER
verbs
boom through—; muffle—; suppress—; thunder through—; —amplifies; —bellows; —blares; —blasts; —deafens; —discharges; —grates; —produces; —shrieks; —startles; muzzle—.
(See bugle, bagpipe, trumpet.)

LOUNGE

verbs

assemble in—; dawdle in—; decorate—; dillydally in—; gather in—; idle in—; loaf in—; loiter in—; loll in—; relax in—; retire to—; saunter into—; skulk in—; slouch in—; —soothes; —swarms.

(See bedroom, room, chair, apartment.)

LOUNGE (v)

adverbs

idly; disconsolately; unambitiously; lasciviously; slothfully; trivially; comfortably; shamelessly; sensually.

(See recline, rest.)

LOUNGERS

adjectives

cultivated; suave; beach; dingy-looking.

LOUT

adjectives

foolish; gross; clumsy; lazy.

LOVABLE

adverbs

entirely; charmingly; delightfully; bewilderingly; bewitchingly; fascinatingly; indescribably; inexpressibly; unusually; uncommonly; tenderly; graciously; sweetly; attractively; engagingly; amiably; enchantingly; captivatingly; irresistibly; genially; heartily; ingratiatingly; adorably.

LOVE

adjectives

abiding; absorbing; abstract; adulterous; all-absorbing; all-discerning; ambitious; animal; animated; approving; ardent; arduous; artless; baffled; barbaric; barefaced; beholding; betrayed; bleeding; blissful; boundless; bounteous; brave; brittle; brotherly; burning; calculating; casual; celestial; changeful; changeless; changing; chasing; childlike; chastising; chivalrous; clandestine; condemned; coerced; comely; common; comprehensive; condescending; confessed; confiding; connubial; consanguine; consenting; consoling; condemned; conventional; corrupt; costly; courtly; cunning; cutting; dear; deathless; debasing; debatable; deep-buried; deepening; deep-rooted; deep-seeing; depraved; descending; despised; despiteful; dire; disgusting; distilling; divine; domestic; duteous; earnest; earthly; eloquent, embittered; emblematic; endearing; enduring; enlightened; ennobl-

ing; enthusiastic; equal; entrancing; erring; everlasting; exacting; exceeding; faddist; faithful; faithless; false; fantastical; fastidious; fathomless; faultless; feigning; fervent; festering; filial; florid; flustered; foolish; forgiving; forgotten; fostering; fraternal; frustrated; genuine; glorified; great; hapless; hard-believing; heavenly; heavy; hereditary; holy; highest; hoarded; hollow; heroic; honest; honor-loving; hopeless; humble; humiliated; hungry; illicit; imagined; immoderate; immortal; immune; impetuous; inborn; inbred; incalculable; inestimable; inexpressible; inextinguishable; inextricable; infinite; instinctive; intense; intellectual; intimate; invincible; irradiating; jealous; languid; lavish; lessening; lifelong; lively; light; limitless; living; long-suffering; lordliest; loveless; loveliest; luminous; manly; masterful; matchless; maternal; meek; melancholy; meritorious; militant; misguided; mother; mutual; mystical; nameless; nascent; newborn; never-wearying; new-found; noble; noiseless; obdurate; obscure; obsequious; one-sided; overmastering; painful; palsied; paltry; pardonable; parental; passionate; pathetic; perennial; persistent; philosophic; physical; pigeon; platonic; potential; pounding; predominating; proffered; primal; profound; prosperous; protecting; provident; public; puerile; pure; purifying; rational; real; reasonable; reassuring; recovering; redeeming; redoubtable; relenting; remorseful; rending; renouncing; repentant; repudiated; responsive; resurgent; reunited; reverent; romantic; sacrificial; satiated; selfish; self-renouncing; sensual; sensuous; sentimental; sham; shamed; shameless; shining; shy; silent; sin-destroying; sinful; sleepless; spiritual; spontaneous; steadfast; stilled; stimulated; stirring; strong; stupendous; sustaining; sweet; sweet-suggesting; tamed; tender; thankful; thoughtful; thwarted; tragic; tranquil; transient; transparent; true; true-confirmed; trusting; truthful; unalterable; unavailing; unbecoming; unbounded; unchanging; unconquerable; undying; unconscious; unexaggerated; unfashionable; unfathomable; unfocused; unfortunate; universal; unlawful; unmanly; unpropitious; unqualified; unquestioned; unreasonable; unregarded; unrelenting; unrequited; unrestful; unreturned; unruly; unsatisfactory; unselfish; unspoken; untaught; unutterable; unvowed; unwed; valiant; vigorous; violent; virtue; virtuous; visionary;

734

vivacious; vivid; wandering; wanton; warped; wasted; wasteful; weakening; welcoming; well-deserved; well-earned; well-known; well-quitted; willing; wilting; wonder-filling; wondrous; wonted; worst; worthiest; wrenching; wronged; yearning; youthful; zealous.

verbs
abide in—; arm with—; awaken—; cultivate—; enthrone in—; excite—; feign—; fire with—; forsake—; fulfill—; idealize—; inculcate—; instill—; insure—; lavish—upon; overflow with—; overshadow—; pine for—; proffer—; profess—; recapture—; reject—; revive—; ripen into—; scorn—; shatter—; smite with—; strangle—; sublimate—; —anguishes; —burns; —chastens; —dawns upon; —enchains; —endures; —ennobles; —illumines; —inspires; —reigns; —seizes; —smites; —tortures; —vanishes; —wells up; —wounds.
(See passion, tenderness, friendship, affection, devotion, infatuation.)

LOVE (v)

adverbs
irretrievably; immortally; fondly; passionately; instinctively; engrossingly; disinterestedly; possessively; ardently; inordinately; uniquely; jealously; profoundly; devotedly; virtuously; violently; exquisitely; heroically; exclusively; utterly; unrequitedly; illicitly; carnally; steadfastly; mawkishly; abstractly; adulterously; arduously; artlessly; boundlessly; blissfully; celestially; casually; clandestinely; connubially; corruptly; deathlessly; debasingly; fantastically; fastidiously; fathomlessly; feigningly; fervently; festeringly; inexpressibly; languidly; masterfully; parentally; philosophically; physically; zealously; platonically; rationally; romantically; sensually; sensuously; spiritually; spontaneously; sustainingly; transiently; unfathomably; vigilantly.
(See like, admire, adore.)

LOVELINESS

adjectives
solitary; perennial; attractive; boasted; female; soft; budding; informing; surpassing; vernal; uncommon; evanescent; shamed; enchanting; exquisite; ineffable; radiant; virgin; pensive; fragile; lustrous; unnoticed; luminous; chaste; uncultivated; exceeding; passing; twofold; sheer; pristine; inner; genuine; ethereal; breath-taking;

moral; unaccountable; unthrifty; winning; supernal; superb; imperious; sensuous; placid; scattered; petite; tempestuous; modest; incomparable; stately; mild; exalted; opulent; conventional.

verbs
admire—; adorn with—; appreciate—; bloom in—; cultivate—; deface—; devour —; flaunt—; garment in—; glow with—; mar—; praise—; preserve—; sully—; taint —; —charms; —dazzles; —enchants; —endures; —glitters; —haunts; —hypnotizes; —shines; —surpasses.
(See beauty, grace, charm, splendor.)

LOVELY

adverbs
charmingly; adorably; indescribably; utterly; delicately; gracefully; delightfully; absorbingly; artlessly; exquisitely; gently; softly; ineffably; enchantingly; radiantly; breath-takingly; unutterably; sweetly; genuinely; superbly; incomparably; incredibly; completely.

LOVER

adjectives
tender; considerate; laggard; betrothed; melancholy; disconsolate; romantic; passionate; despairing; hot; beseeching; universal; entwined (pl); advanced; weary; ardent; triumphant; meek; changing; newly-plighted; lifelong; patriarchal; listening; whispering; greatest; fond; ethereal; accepted; estranged; impassioned; tragic; redeeming; remorseful; starved; hesitating; loathsome; lowly; memorable; enthusiastic; forsaken; notable; subtle; clinging; faithful; monastic; unhappy; distracted; true; flaming-breasted; truant; sleepless; sempiternal; pattern; fearful; credulous; youthful.

verbs
anger—; deceive—; exact from—; excite—; inflame—; renounce—; reward—; ridicule —; sting—; —beams; —blesses; —capers; —caresses; —desires; —devotes; —dotes upon; —dreams; —frets; —muses; —reflects upon; —repents; —reveres; —s rift; — sacrifices; —sighs; —thirsts; —treasures; —woos; —yearns; —yields.
(See suitor, sweetheart, admirer, friend.)

LOVING

adverbs
ardently; tenderly; exceedingly; excessive-

ly; ostentatiously; proudly; fervently; adoringly; idolatrously; infatuatedly; passionately; rapturously; yearningly; wistfully; coquettishly; flirtatiously; excitedly; sweetly; seductively; devotedly.

LOW
adverbs
inconceivably; extremely; abysmally; exceedingly; uncomfortably; peculiarly; mysteriously; alarmingly; curiously; inconveniently; unnecessarily; unduly; impossibly; terribly; disagreeably; unpleasantly.

LOWER (v)
adverbs
mechanically; cautiously; appreciably; materially; economically; charmingly; coyly; tremulously; bestially.
(See reduce, drop, depress, diminish, fall.)

LOWLY
adverbs
childishly; inconceivably; sweetly; humbly; surprisingly; modestly; plainly; humbly; unpretentiously; unaffectedly; marvellously; admirably; wondrously.

LOYAL
adverbs
unaffectedly; genuinely; unquestionably; unimpeachably; sincerely; utterly; undeviatingly; sturdily; stoutly; faithfully; constantly; devotedly; unswervingly; negatively; positively; incredibly; reliably; dependably; steadily; militantly; patriotically; obediently; eagerly; ardently; meticulously; tremendously; utterly; uncommonly; steadfastly.

LOYALTY
adjectives
unswerving; instinctive; recovered; fastidious; stanch; inflexible; unconditional; fresh; religious; willing; unflinching; enthusiastic; savage; indestructible; mistaken; human; habitual; obstinate; fervent; filial; tenacious; intense; racial; quixotic; passionate; clan; true; ardent; alternate; unwavering; devoted; unchanging; affectionate; vaunted; basic; stubborn.

verbs
acknowledge—; attend with—; awaken—; chain by—; command—; discharge with—; exact—; fix—; follow with—; inspire—; overcome—; owe—; pledge—; profess—; protest—; prove—; retain—; reward—;

shift—; stress—; submit with—; sustain—; —ennobles; —flames; —prevails.
(See faithfulness, devotion, love, faith, zeal.)

LUBBERLY
adverbs
heavily; awkwardly; ridiculously; laughably; absurdly; good-naturedly; unmanageably; inconveniently; unfortunately; terribly; lazily; massively; lumpishly.

LUBRICANT
verbs
enlist—; feed—; inject—; react to—; —benefits; —clears; —eases; —facilitates; —frees; —lightens; —nourishes; —promotes; —quickens; —relieves; —smooths; —speeds; —unclogs; —waxes.
(See oil, soap, lather.)

LUBRICATE (v)
adverbs
thoroughly; seasonally; periodically; mechanically; systematically; annually.
(See facilitate.)

LUCID
adverbs
unusually; beautifully; satisfactorily; transparently; clearly; vividly; brilliantly; splendidly; especially; peculiarly; oddly; brightly; curiously; particularly; distinctly; luminously; delightfully; amazingly; astonishingly.

LUCK
adjectives
imaginable; ragged; blundering; unmerited; hard; monumental; good; ill; incredible; unearned; foolish.

verbs
ascribe to—; bemoan—; beset by—; bewail —; deplore—; earn—; encounter—; face —; fall into—; stake on—; trust to—; —attends; —befalls; —chases; —deals; —deserts; —disheartens; —ebbs; —favors; —mocks; —pursues; —singles out; —soars.
(See chance, fortune, risk, misfortune, reverse.)

LUCKLESS
adverbs
wretchedly; miserably; always; consistently; unfortunately; habitually; markedly; notoriously; distinctly; positively; unhap-

pily; conspicuously; disastrously; calamitously; deplorably; lamentably; constantly; altogether; pitiably; dreadfully; uncommonly.

LUCKY
adverbs
always; inexplicably; auspiciously; fortunately; inherently; blessedly; shrewdly; deservedly; adroitly; triumphantly; advantageously; inexpressibly; deucedly; remarkably; surprisingly; inscrutably; notoriously; unaccountably; unwarrantably; mysteriously; strangely; oddly; curiously; immensely; cleverly; admirably; wonderfully; miraculously; marvellously; ingeniously; conveniently; boastfully; surpassingly; accidentally; reasonably; assuredly; casually; incidentally; unexpectedly; blessedly.

LUCRATIVE
adverbs
commendably; admirably; enviably; commercially; happily; duly; naturally; distinctly; definitely; astonishingly; surprisingly; mysteriously; measurably; incalculably; moderately; immensely; tremendously; exceedingly; pleasantly; immoderately; unexpectedly; satisfactorily; profitably; advantageously; curiously; unbelievably.

LUDICROUS
adverbs
immoderately; grotesquely; fantastically; curiously; uproariously; extravagantly; monstrously; whimsically; quaintly; outlandishly; eccentrically; preposterously; drolly; contemptibly; decisively; strangely; irresistibly; inconceivably; amazingly; intensely; unexpectedly; marvellously; inordinately.

LUGUBRIOUS
adverbs
miserably; wretchedly; inconsolably; determinedly; ostentatiously; funereally; gloomily; ridiculously; inordinately; uncommonly; terribly; unbearably; absurdly; unreasonably; pompously; showily; dreadfully; solemnly; demurely; grimly; disconsolately.

LULL (*v*)
adverbs
deliciously; magically; miraculously; momentarily; intermittently; sweetly; melodiously; maternally; affectionately.
(See hush, subside.)

LULLS
adjectives
reverberate; hopeless; magic; intermittent.

LUMBER (*v*)
adverbs
ponderously; heavily; monotonously; peacefully; stupidly; phlegmatically; lifelessly; solidly; soddenly; stolidly; passionlessly.
(See move, walk, stagger.)

LUMINARY
adjectives
legal; heavenly; glorious; kindliest.

LUMINOUS
adverbs
brilliantly; gloriously; effulgently; radiantly; splendidly; magnificently; phosphorescently; resplendently; scintillantly; shimmeringly; intermittently; steadily; beautifully; remarkably; intensely; extremely; unusually.

LUMPISH
adverbs
stupidly; dully; awkwardly; stolidly; boorishly; ignorantly; incredibly; remarkably; fantastically; terribly; inertly; drowsily; heavily; listlessly; languidly; lazily.

LUMPS
adjectives
rude; painful; lifeless; restive; solid; phlegmatic; deformed; soft; persistent; translucent; sympathetic; painless; obstinate; helpless; sodden; monstrous.

LUNATIC
adjectives
criminal; privileged; harmless; wild; rough.

adverbs
wildly; unmanageably; ungovernably; violently; absurdly; uproariously; ravingly; frenziedly; drunkenly; deliriously; daftly; fanatically; fantastically; strangely; curiously; unaccountably; irresponsibly; suddenly; frantically; dreadfully.

LUNCH
adjectives
well-balanced; belated; frugal; costly; convivial; substantial; suitable; abundant; half-wrapped; cold.

LUNCH (v)

adverbs
frugally; convivially; substantially; abundantly; swiftly; fraternally; hospitably; gaily; appetizingly; insatiably.
(See eat, dine.)

LUNCHEON

adjectives
grim; enormous; hilarious; sacrilegious; scant; well-attended.

verbs
conclude—; cram in—; design—; digest—; honor at—; indulge in—; savor—; scorn—; tender—; welcome to—; —appeals; —beguiles; —cheers; —contents; —inaugurates; —lubricates; —nourishes; —satisfies; —tempts.
(See supper, dinner, breakfast, meal, food, repast.)

LUNG

adjectives
prodigious; spongy; bursting; choked; skeleton; delicate; iron.

verbs
collapse—; compress—; congest—; deflate —; enter—; envelop—; examine—; infect —; inflate—; perforate—; scar—; solidify —; spot—; traverse—; waste—; —decays; —expands; —heaves; —labors; —retracts; —rots; —shrivels.
(See balloon, chest.)

LURCH (v)

adverbs
drunkenly; crazily; perilously; dizzily; rashly; abruptly; sensually; fatally; comically.
(See stagger, sway, roll.)

LURE

adjectives
constant; obvious; velvet.

verbs
bait—; betray into—; expose to—; follow —; inveigle into—; manoeuvre—; risk—; spread—; succumb to—s; swindle by—; — attracts; —beguiles; —deceives; —deludes; —enchants; —ensnares; —entices; —tempts; —tricks; —victimizes.
(See bait, temptation.)

LURE (v)

adverbs
delusively; obscenely; lustfully; coyly; lasciviously; sexually; sensually; joyously; suavely; wantonly.
(See tempt, attract.)

LURID

adverbs
sensationally; disgracefully; terribly; remarkably; reprehensibly; inordinately; comically; ridiculously; gloomily; dismally; awfully; repulsively; obscurely; deeply; dingily; faintly; ruddily; oddly; strangely; peculiarly.

LURK (v)

adverbs
slyly; obscurely; insidiously; deceptively; treacherously; diabolically; instinctively; viciously; grimly.
(See prowl, steal, stalk.)

LUSCIOUS

adverbs
remarkably; admirably; particularly; delectably; deliciously; pleasantly; attractively; invitingly; agreeably; acceptably; gratefully; daintily; delicately; appetizingly; sweetly; richly; peculiarly; uncommonly; unusually.

LUSH

adverbs
abundantly; luxuriantly; amazingly; unusually; particularly; freshly; refreshingly; remarkably; juicily; marvellously; admirably; attractively.

LUST

adjectives
short-sighted; careless; burning; monstrous; ruffian; healthy; mad; hurtful; amber-scented; mute; melancholy; sordid; ignoble; worldly; hellish; alien; decrepit; devilish; unnatural; exceeding; inbred; vile; ever-craving; coarse; concupiscible; greedy; fleshy; intemperate; tyrannous; ominous; drunken.

verbs
abhor—; cater to—; cool—; conquer—; couch in—; extinguish—; intoxicate with—; loathe—; melt in—; quench—; resist—; satiate—; sink in—, —blemishes; —burns; —

738

consumes; —corrupts; —decays; —defiles; —frenzies; —maddens; —massacres; —overthrows; —ruins; —scandalizes.
(See wickedness, sin, abomination, **iniquity**.)

LUST (v)

adverbs
obscenely; insatiably; devilishly; ceaselessly; monstrously; madly; mutely; sordidly; ignobly; unnaturally; vilely; pervertedly; concupiscibly; intemperately; intoxicatedly; ominously.
(See desire, long.)

LUSTER

adjectives
joyless; exceeding; collective; dazzling; sparkling; added; undiminished; feeble; refreshing; smooth; vitreous; glossy; dull; intolerable; classic; freshening; full; subdued; feverish; transient; ethereal; brilliant; iridescent; penetrating; timid; ancient; soft; purer; growing; spectral; hoary; starry; nebulous; pearly; antique; welcome; sulphurous; natural; hungry; original.

LUSTY

adverbs
remarkably; robustly; vigorously; unusually; enviably; sturdily; exceptionally; extraordinarily; amazingly; notoriously; dependably; luckily; fortunately; incredibly; surprisingly.

LUTE

adjectives
short-stringed; warbling; enfeebling; fragile; long-neglected; ravishing.

LUXURIANCE

adjectives
tropical; unchanged; prodigal; rank; wild.

verbs
abate—; attire in—; burst forth in—; cushion in—; display in—; feed on—; indulge in—; prune—; ransack—; soak in—; surrender to—; taste—; wallow in—; —diffuses; —enslaves; —entices; —flourishes; —inebriates; —overwhelms.
(See wealth, luxury.)

LUXURIANT

adverbs
abundantly; unusually: tropically; amazing-

ly; uncommonly; exceptionally; unbelievably; naturally; surprisingly; profitably; amply; satisfactorily; richly; incalculably; advantageously; opportunely.

LUXURIATE (v)

adverbs
blissfully; joyously; exaggeratedly; carnally; sentimentally; drunkenly; wantonly; profanely; riotously; boastfully.
(See lavish, bestow.)

LUXURIOUS

adverbs
delightfully; pleasantly; agreeably; actually; unexpectedly; amazingly; indescribably; unconsciously; inordinately; extravagantly; gratifyingly; comfortably; refreshingly; enjoyably; enchantingly; cheerfully; blissfully; extraordinarily; incredibly; elaborately; expensively; gorgeously; happily.

LUXURY

adjectives
refined; lapping; useless; unfailing; sublime; elaborate; costly; leafy; swinish; expensive; voluptuous; hateful; sordid; manly; easy; light; innocent; prejudicial; incommunicable; colossal; subtle; multiform; unusual; gorgeous; invalid; higher-priced; rare; harmless; accustomed; profuse; wanton; superfluous; unequaled; almost-forgotten; cramping; attendant; sleek; pagan; indecent; unnecessary; sensual; idle; unobtrusive; quiet; secluded; modern.

verbs
afford—; bless with—; contemplate—; couch in—; crave—; diffuse—; dispense with—; intoxicate with—; lack—; loll in—; nurse in —; pamper with—; revel in—; steal—; swathe in—; thirst for—; —cushions; —hinders.
(See luxuriance, wealth.)

LYMPH

adjectives
pellucid; transparent; lava.

verbs
absorb by—; discharge—; dissolve in—; extract—; exude—; inject in—; secrete—; —

assimilates; —attenuates; —coagulates; —deteriorates; —dilutes; —escapes; —flows; —percolates; —streams.

LYNCH (*v*)

adverbs
madly; ferociously; bestially; insanely; swiftly; horrifyingly; sadistically; heartlessly; cruelly; tigerishly.
(See kill, murder, hang, punish.)

LYRE

adjectives
slumberous; sparkling; sweet-toned; tuneful; darling; lascivious.

LYRICAL

adverbs
sweetly; smoothly; tunefully; fluently; unusually; completely; utterly; curiously; softly; gently; clearly; enchantingly; fascinatingly; euphoniously; pleasantly; agreeably; roughly; perfectly; crudely; correctly; harmoniously; remarkably; magnificently; splendidly.

LYRICS

adjectives
poignant; rural; conventional; occasional; studied; dramatic; satirical; infrequent; sentimental.

M

MACHIAVELLIAN

adverbs

shrewdly; craftily; unbelievably; astutely; wickedly; colossally; designingly; subtly; arrantly; dreadfully; archly; crookedly; evasively; viciously; dangerously; alarmingly; curiously; fearfully; insidiously; nefariously; invidiously; profoundly; cleverly; notoriously; deceptively; heinously.

MACHINATE (v)

adverbs

diabolically; politically; unscrupulously; subtly; insidiously; perfidiously; treacherously; ambitiously.

(See plot, scheme.)

MACHINATIONS

adjectives

sublime; subtlest; insidious; political; perfidious.

MACHINE

adjectives

unmoral; cosmic; efficient; propaganda; specialized; vending; merciless; infernal; admirable; memorial; vast; fantastic; protected; ponderous; domestic; cranky; undependable; ill-omened; senseless; electrical; slow; expensive; leased; extraordinary; radical; omnipresent; colossal.

verbs

abolish—; clog—; construct—; control—; demonstrate—; exalt—; fuel—; humanize —; install—; lubricate—; master—; meter —; putter with—; sublimate—; subordinate —; tamper with—; tinker with—; transmute —; worship—; —accommodates; —clicks; —enslaves; —functions; —roars; —rumbles; —stamps.

(See engine, apparatus, instrument, drill, elevator, generator, dynamo, mechanism.)

MACHINE-GUN

verbs

nest—; place—; set up—; —bellows; — blasts; —chatters; —deafens; —drums; — fulminates; —mows down; —mutters; — rakes; —raps; —rat-tat-tats; —rends; — retaliates; —reverberates; —rolls; —spatters; —tattoos; —yammers (colloq.); — crackles.

(See gun, **cannon**, pistol, revolver, rifle.)

MACHINERY

adjectives

physical; warlike; experimental; elaborate; agricultural; complicated; economical; tireless; arbitration; internal; domestic; suspended; educational; cumbrous; subtle; stupendous; disinterested; specialized; budgetary; commonplace; dread; multiplied; comprehensive; **unified**; **irrigating**; newfangled.

MAD

adverbs

incoherently; fanatically; hopelessly; incurably; pathetically; violently; distractedly; bewilderedly; frantically; insanely; suddenly; periodically; hysterically; wildly; tragically; irrecoverably; irremediably.

MADMAN

verbs

arouse—; chain—; coddle—; **confine**—; cudgel—; enchain—; enkindle—; fetter—; harness—; immure—; imprison—; incarcerate —; infuriate—; isolate—; liberate—; manacle—; overpower—; perturb—; pinion—; pique—; restrain—; shackle—; subdue—; yoke—; —dotes; —drivels; —flames; — foams; —fumes; —gibbers; —leers; — rages; —rambles; —raves; —scowls.

(See fool, idiot.)

MADNESS

adjectives

feigned; apparent; inexplicable; amorous; sweet; mingled; incipient; mysterious; strange; mob; tender; autumnal; supernatural; solemn; studied; sacred; solitary; cruel; voluntary; midsummer; centrifugal; harmonious; moody; utter; suicidal; decided; sad; merry; **drunken**.

verbs

cloud with—; feign—; ramble in—; rave in —; —aberrates; —afflicts; —deranges; — diseases; —disorders; —embroils; —infects;

—invalidates; —possesses; —ravages; —seizes; —shatters; —taints; —unbalances; —undermines; —warps.

(See frenzy, insanity, stupidity, delirium, hysteria, mania.)

MAELSTROM

verbs

circumvent—; sweep into—; —agitates; —boils; —buffets —churns; —circulates; —drenches; —flings; —foams; —gyrates; —jets; —revolves; —rolls; —spouts; —threatens; —trundles; —whirls.

(See whirlpool, rain, river, turmoil, torrent, waves.)

MAGAZINE

adjectives

short-lived; humorous; independent; reputable; liberal; entertaining; lively; all-around; popular; foremost; smart; fast-growing; up-to-date; progressive; incipient; sectarian; well-storied; short-story.

verbs

censor—; contribute to—; dip into—; disseminate—s; extol—; glean from—; hawk —s; launch—; linotype—; peruse—; rack —s; sanction—; scan—; set up—; —accounts; —blazes; —chronicles; —circulates; —condenses; —delineates; —depicts; —digests; —polls; —promulgates; —records; —reports; —reviews; —summarizes; —supports.

(See literature, newspaper, press, publication, book, story, volume.)

MAGIC

adjectives

supernatural; practised; foul; peculiar; curative; traditional; subtle; powerful; sheer; wild; all-subduing; aimless; lush.

verbs

conjure up by—; contrive—; exercise—; influence by—; practise—; reek of—; skill in —; —bedevils; —bewitches; —casts spells; —divines; —enchants; —exorcises; —fascinates; —forecasts; —foretells.

(See incantation, trick, miracle, manipulation.)

MAGIC

adverbs

bewilderingly; occultly; cleverly; subtly; amazingly; undeniably; wondrously; miraculously; curiously; strangely; unbelievably; wickedly; ascendanty; weirdly; cabalistically; mystically; mysteriously; slyly; obviously; presumably.

MAGISTERIAL

adverbs

officiously; ostentatiously; authoritatively; arrogantly; superciliously; offensively; vexatiously; sternly; severely; harshly; cruelly; tyrannically; rigidly; unnecessarily; ridiculously; absurdly; gravely; solemnly; droningly; coldly; strictly; intolerably; overbearingly; imperiously; pretentiously; stiffly; magnificently; ceremoniously; arbitrarily.

MAGISTRATE

adjectives

unmeriting; proud; violent; teasing; lawful; principal; inferior; directing; venal; elective; civil; presiding; stipendiary.

verbs

commit to—; impeach—; plead with—; vest in—; —acquits; —administers; —arbitrates; —arraigns; —assigns; —authorizes; —commands; —concedes; —deprives; —determines; —dispenses; —empowers; —exempts; —exonerates; —grants; —judges; —pronounces; —prosecutes; —restrains; —reviews; —sanctions; —sentences; —summons.

(See judge, consul, legislator, governor, president.)

MAGNANIMITY

adjectives

delicate; unbounded; peaceable; critical; rough; splendid; unlimited.

MAGNANIMOUS

adverbs

unusually; dependably; conspicuously; wonderfully; remarkably; unexpectedly; surprisingly; delightfully; beneficently; magnificently; utterly; habitually; unwontedly; unselfishly; generally; loftily; chivalrously; admirably; generously.

MAGNETIC

adverbs

highly; strongly; amazingly; surprisingly; delightfully; attractively; charmingly; unusually; powerfully; potently; preponderantly; influentially; persuasively; temptingly; irresistibly; unaccountably; immensely; extremely; remarkably.

MAGNETISM

adjectives
permanent; terrestrial; animal; proudest; universal.

MAGNIFICENCE

adjectives
mournful; profuse; calculated; theatrical; oriental; solid; fancied; barbaric; gorgeous; stern; multiplied; tawdry; ephemeral; pristine; unquestionable; snowy; lavish; incredible; wide-spread; somber.

MAGNIFICENT

adverbs
splendidly; gorgeously; grandly; sumptuously; brilliantly; gaudily; regally; extraordinarily; remarkably; marvelously; ceremonially; majestically; pompously; formally; highly; unspeakably; beautifully; elegantly; overwhelmingly; stupendously; colossally; resplendently; richly; imposingly; sublimely; matchlessly; impressively.

MAGNIFY (v)

adverbs
stereoptically; enormously; stupendously; gloriously; theatrically; barbarically; audaciously; scientifically; mechanically; prodigiously.
(See enlarge, exaggerate, augment.)

MAGNITUDE

adjectives
enhanced; prodigious; audacious; infinite; imposing; sensible; intermediate; considerable; swelling.

verbs
amplify—; comprehend—; extend—; heighten—; limit—; reduce—; restrict—; swell to —; —abates; —diminishes; —soars.
(See dimension, extent, greatness, measurements.)

MAGPIE

verbs
molest—; persecute—; tame—; —amuses; —chatters; —cheeps; —scolds; —shies; — steals; —talks; —thieves.
(See bird.)

MAHOGANY

adjectives
massive; rich; heavy; clumsy.

MAID

adjectives
unwilling; thoughtless; imprudent; poor; lowly; sentimental; lovelorn; wronged; meek; graceful; chariest; expiring; cleaner; sun-swart; deflowered; wretched; deceitful; sprightly, dark-tressed; loud-screaming; ungrateful; uncommon; guileless; kind; virtuous; fasting; blooming; lurking; milking; volatile; butterfly; kittenish; old; heavenly; stainless; recreant; pretty; chaste; simple; buskined; confiding; serving; stately; pale; impassioned; virginal; orphaned; fair; cruel; careless.

MAIDEN

adjectives
modest; guileless; simple; barefoot; dimpled; timid; white-veiled; sainted; home-keeping; cherry-cheeked; rosy-lipped; burlesque; gleeful; toddling; pastoral; dejected; snow; movie-mad; timid; willful; loose-girdled; affectionate; hapless; orbed; pale; avaricious; virtuous; rigid; decked; broad-backed; unfortunate; bright-eyed; enamored.

MAIDENHOOD

adjectives
delectable; stainless; frank; lean; profaned; blooming.

MAIDENLY

adverbs
demurely; coyly; sedately; shyly; decorously; becomingly; modestly; blushingly; rosily; suitably; properly; sweetly; graciously; conventionally; attractively; quietly; serenely; bashfully; appropriately.

MAIL

adjectives
glittering; ubiquitous; outgoing; departed; brisk.

verbs
assemble—; bag—; bear—; certify—; classify—; collect—; communicate by—; consign to—; convey—; defraud by—; distribute—; flood—; fly—; insure—; loot—; plunder—; register—; rifle—; transmit by—.
(See message.)

743

MAIN

adjectives

troubled; unfathomable; whitening; infinite; boundless; molten; azure; pulseless; tideless; billowed; murmuring; immeasurable; moaning.

MAINTAIN (v)

adverbs

stubbornly; willfully; inexorably; unreservedly; automatically; gallantly; scrupulously; peremptorily; diabolically; resolutely; unblushingly; stoutly; intensely; ignorantly; vigorously; inflexibly; normally; agreeably; perpetually; progressively; jealously; adequately.

(See claim, sustain, support, affirm.)

MAINTENANCE

adjectives

continued; scanty; perpetual; fitting; progressive; standing; adequate; jealous.

MAIZE

adjectives

tall; spiky; twinkling; sun-loving; ripening; towering; tasseled.

MAJESTIC

adverbs

splendidly; gloriously; brilliantly; imposingly; solemnly; ceremonially; augustly; sublimely; impressively; grandly; formally; pompously; superbly; imperially; loftily; sumptuously; gorgeously.

MAJESTY

adjectives

essential; ghostlike; wonted; collective; impressive; angered; sluggard; unfamiliar; sheer; serene; characteristic; conscious; outraged; awful; singular; tranquil; dreadful; comparable; gentle; vigorous; tropical; sweet; rare; commanding; overshadowing; apparent; unspeakable; glittering; unascended; inaccessible; colossal; shadowy; mutilated; certain; dispelled; clouded; unshakable; rayless; ineffable; grotesque; ethereal; swarthy; dramatic; imperious; pastoral; sublime; somber.

MAJORITY

adjectives

overwhelming; popular; hostile; legislative; phenomenal; vast; handsome; compact; emphatic; bare; preponderant; ignorant; enlarged.

verbs

attain—; bow to—; endow with—; gain—; increase—; pile up—; poll—; purchase—; reach—; render—; sway—; swell—; —balances; —carries; —determines; —exceeds; —overtops; —overwhelms; —predominates, —prevails; —surpasses.

(See generality, age, minority, multitude, throng, crowd.)

MAKE (v)

adverbs

powerfully; eventually; inevitably; ultimately; unquestionably; crudely; obviously; inadvertently; advisedly; persistently; unwittingly; unhesitatingly; temporarily; subsequently; superbly; indiscriminately; laboriously; lawfully; delicately; scientifically.

(See create, compose, invent, manufacture.)

MAKESHIFT

adverbs

cleverly; ingeniously; obviously; carelessly; shiftlessly; adroitly; permanently; clumsily; awkwardly; evidently; dexterously; smartly; handily; pitifully; crudely; presumably; miserably; wretchedly; comically; suitably.

MAKE-UP

verbs

apply—; blanch under—; disguise with—; renew—; represent by—; strip of—; —ages; —alters; —clogs; —colors; —embellishes; —ornaments; —smudges; —tones.

(See paint, color, disguise, mask, pose, pretense, sham.)

MALADIES

adjectives

putrid; incurable; terrible; relievable; organic; infinite; still-clinging; kindred; mortal; deadly; grievous; past-cure; corporeal; painful; expensive; pestiferous; reparable.

MALADJUSTMENT

adjectives

serious; temperamental; deep-seated.

MALADROIT

adverbs

absurdly; unexpectedly; ridiculously; laughably; comically; ludicrously; surprisingly; inexpertly; clumsily; awkwardly; shyly; bashfully; deliberately; purposely; intentionally; helplessly; pitiably; miserably; wretchedly; hopelessly; oddly; stupidly; obtusely; gawkily; embarrassingly; shockingly; uselessly.

MALADY
verbs
afflict with—; aggravate—; allay—; arrest —; communicate—; contract—; control—; diagnose—; eradicate—; expose to—; immunize against—; infest with—; inherit—; isolate—; recognize—; succumb to—; withstand—; —consumes; —lingers; —menaces; —prostrates; —reasserts itself.
(See ailment, disease, infection, illness, sickness.)

MALE
adjectives
monstrous; inexhaustible; art-shy; dominant; rival; smug.

verbs
attract—; lure—; —begets; —fertilizes; — fructifies; —fuses; —generates; —husbands; —implants; —impregnates; —incorporates; —infuses; —preserves; —procreates; — propagates; —sires; —unifies.
(See parent, father.)

MALEDICTION
adjectives
profane; parting; bitter; hearty; muffled.

verbs
address with—s; bluster—; call down—; fulminate—; invoke—; thunder—; utter—; —abuses; —anathematizes; —clamors; — curses; —denounces; —execrates; —scolds; —threatens.
(See curse, slander, denunciation.)

MALEVOLENT
adverbs
viciously; vengefully; savagely; terribly; brutally; sternly; harshly; incredibly; mercilessly; relentlessly; ruthlessly; unspeakably; desperately; villainously; alarmingly; dangerously; notoriously; infamously; criminally; actively; nefariously; inordinately; utterly; incurably; inescapably; heinously; dreadfully; rancorously; spitefully; barbarously; bitterly.

MALICE
adjectives
burning; insane; fairy; devilish; venomous;

ancient; fiendish; sportful; serpent; deepest; diabolical; ingenious; crafty; partisan; womanly; warm; dancing; genial; cold-blooded; ferocious.

verbs
bear—; betray—; breed—; excite—; express —; harbor—; impel to—; impute to—; incite—; intend—; provoke—; recoil from—; regard with—; rile to—; sense—; shudder at—; sow—; tinge with—; view with—; wreak—upon; —embitters; —harasses; — hardens; —harries; —molests; —ripens.
(See bitterness, grudge, ill will, envy, anger, rage, violence, wrath.)

MALICIOUS
adverbs
flagrantly; dangerously; violently; irretrievably; inconceivably; poisonously; abominably; accursedly; perniciously; viciously; basely; deplorably; diabolically; disastrously; dreadfully; exceptionally; grievously; hatefully; venomously; violently; manifestly; subtly; irremediably; irrevocably; immeasurably; villainously; sadly; woefully; shockingly; cruelly; infernally; atrociously; incredibly; shamefully; iniquitously.

MALIGN
adverbs
ominously; portentously; dangerously; undeniably; disastrously; calamitously; ruinously; venomously; poisonously; treacherously; ruthlessly; relentlessly; slanderously; incredibly.

MALIGNANT
adverbs
openly; deliberately; studiously; hatefully; curiously; incorrigibly; evilly; desperately; outrageously; cruelly; bitterly; harshly; venomously; truculently; atrociously; dangerously; poisonously; abominably; perniciously; disastrously; exceptionally; grievously; subtly; sadly; woefully; shockingly; infernally.

MALIGNITY
adjectives
impure; incredible; factious; fiendish; drunken; elaborate; devilish.

MAMMALS
adjectives
branch-building; aquatic; ungulate.

adverbs

colossally; gigantically; incredibly; unbelievably; inconceivably; immeasurably; monstrously; incalculably; mythically; stupendously; toweringly; overwhelmingly.

MAN

adjectives

able; acclaimed; alert; ambitious; amiable; anile; arbitrary; armed; austere; available; avaricious; bad; bald; bearded; beetle-browed; bemused; benevolent; benighted; bibulous; big-waisted; bizarre; blind; bloody; boastful; bony; boorish; boyish-looking; brawny; brilliant; broken; broken-hearted; burly; business; cadaverous; cannon-voiced; carefree; careful; carnal; celebrated; charming; chipper; coming; commercial; compassionate; completed; condemned; conscientious; contemplative; corpulent; corruptible; cultivated; cumbersome; cunning; cynical; dapper; dauntless; deathless; decorous; defeated; deep-dimpled; difficult; dilatory; disappointed; disengaged; disinterested; dissipated; double-chinned; dull; dumb; dusky; dynamic; easy-going; eccentric; effeminate; egotistic; elemental; eloquent; emancipated; embarrassed; energetic; enterprising; entertaining; envious; envisaging; estimable; exact; excellent; exceptional; exemplary; experienced; fair-haired; family; famous; fat; fierce; fine-looking; fine-shaped; firm; fit; flaunting; florid; formidable; fractious; frail; frivolous; frustrated; full; full-rigged; function-free; fussy; gallant; general; genial; godless; gossiping; graceless; great-hearted; gregarious; half-naked; handicraft; hard-fisted; hard-working; hawk-headed; headless; heavy-built; heroic; highbred; hoary; homely; honest; hooked-nose; hospitable; hot-tempered; huge; human; humorous; hungry; husky; idle; ill-instructed; ill-natured; illustrious; imperious; impertinent; impious; incomparable; incredible; incurious; indefatigable; indispensable; industrious; influential; informed; ingrateful; inner; inscrutable; intemperate; intrepid; irate; isolated; jolly; jovial; key; kind; knowing; lank; large; lawless; lean; lettered; literary; little; lonely; lovable; magnificent; magnified; married; masterless; mediocre; meditative; meek; merciful; merry; middle-aged; mild-appearing; mild-mannered; mincing; moaning; modest; much-experienced; mustached; myopic; myriad-

wrinkled; mysterious; narrow-minded; new-married; niggardly; noble; obstinate; olive-skinned; omnivorous; overconfident; over-sexed; pallid; pampered; patriarchal; petrified; phenomenal; plain-spoken; phlegmatic; plighted; politic; poorly-dressed; pragmatical; premature; primitive; prominent; proper; propertied; prospering; prudent; pushing; puzzled; quiet; rapid-fire; rational; ready; red-eyed; reflective; repentant; reticent; rich; riddled; rising; rough-looking; round; ruthless; sad; sane; saturnine; savage; seafaring; selfish; self-helping; self-isolated; self-made; self-poised; sensitive; sensual; sharp-eyed; sharp-witted; shock-headed; silent; silly; simple-minded; sinful; sleek; sleight-of-hand; smoking; sober; society; soft-voiced; sound; spoiled; spotted; square-set; squat-figured; staunch; steel-sinewed; stocky; strange; strange-voiced; stray; studious; successful; sullen; sunburned; superior; supple; sure-poised; sweaty; taciturn; talented; tempestuous; tender-hearted; toothless; tormented; ugly; unabashed; unabsolved; unadaptable; unbookish; unbreakable; unburied; uncompanionable; unfortunate; ungrateful; universal; unlettered; unquestioning; unrepentant; unrevolving; untidy; untutored; upright; useless; wayfaring; well-conditioned; wealthy; well-informed; well-proportioned; whimsical; witless; wind-swept; wiry; wise; worthy; vague; wretched; vain; vigorous; virtuous; yellow-visaged; voluptuous; youthful.

MANACLE

adjectives

mortal; menacing; hampering.

verbs

bind with—; clamp on—; don—; fetter with —; forge—; —bridles; —checks; —confines; —constrains; —controls; —curbs; —handcuffs; —prohibits; —restrains; —restricts; —secures; —shackles; —tethers.

(See fetter, restraint.)

MANAGE (*v*)

adverbs

economically; dexterously; effectively; humanely; judiciously; exclusively; bunglingly; artistically; ingeniously; peremptorily; governmentally; politically; systematically; conservatively; prudently; profitably; incompetently; adroitly; admirably.

(See conduct, supervise, administer, handle.)

adverbs
easily; smoothly; carefully; thriftily; commercially; financially; scarcely; altogether; strategically; subtly; strangely; readily; diplomatically; unexpectedly; quietly; tractably; tactfully.

MANAGEMENT
adjectives
municipal; marvelous; topsy-turvy; duped; frightened; conservative; generous; consolidated; wise; dietary; bungling; systematic; operative; prudent; profitable; admirable; good; adroit; clumsy; wasteful; incompetent; group; capable; vigorous.

verbs
acquire—; administer—; charge with—; conduct—; contrive—; control—; decry—; demean—; denounce—; direct—; enact—; guide—; manipulate—; master—; qualify for—; shift—; skill in—; superintend—; —negotiates; —transacts.
(See direction, government, economy, conduct, charge, legislature, owner, manager.)

MANAGER
adjectives
dexterous; peremptory; unyielding; operatic.

verbs
install—; —directs; —governs; —heads; —helms; —inspects; —orders; —oversees; —pilots; —regulates; —steers; —superintends; —supervises; —surveys; —threatens.
(See boss, industrialist, employer, superintendent, leader, management, owner.)

MANDATE
adjectives
constitutional; official; illegal; tragic; scholastic; royal; titular.

verbs
cite—; comply with—; enact—; issue—; lay down—; prescribe—; remand—; seal—; yield to—; —appoints; —bids; —commands; —controls; —decrees; —deposes; —directs; —dictates; —enjoins; —imposes; —ordains; —proclaims; —summons; —orders.
(See law, measure, decree, edict, command, warrant, regulation, ordinance, order, summons.)

adjectives
flowing; tossing; dripping; luxuriant; braided; hanging; illimitable; plaited; leonine; sudden; flaring.

verbs
brush—; corrugate—; crumple—; gnarl—; knot—; roughen—; ruffle—; rumple—; seize by—; stroke—; toss back—; —adorns; —crests; —droops; —erects; —flows; —fringes; —ripples; —shags.
(See hair, mustache, whiskers, plumage, beard.)

MANEUVER
adjectives
adroit; loving; little; ingenious; thrilling; sordid; political; important; inexplicable; pernicious; odious; shabby; perfunctory; legal; sensational; innocent; dishonest; decisive; skillful; polished; ticklish; ladylike; bold; engineering; intricate.

verbs
achieve—; circumvent—; commit—; contrive—; design—; detail—; enact—; evolve—; execute—; expedite—; organize—; outline—; participate in—; perform—; perpetrate—; practise—; project—; propose—; sanction—; systematize—; transact—; —conceals; —juggles; —temporizes.
(See method, strategy, tactics, subterfuge, trick, move.)

MANEUVER (v)
adverbs
skillfully; adroitly; ingeniously; thrillingly; dexterously; perfunctorily; legally; sensationally; decisively; diplomatically; boldly; rashly; daringly; intricately.
(See plan, scheme.)

MANFUL
adverbs
boldly; bravely; confidently; courageously; firmly; gallantly; hardily; intrepidly; sturdily; pluckily; resolutely; spunkily; valorously; nobly; honorably; virtuously; dauntlessly; splendidly; indomitably; stoutly; venturesomely; venturously; admirably.

MANGLE (v)
adverbs
hideously; shamefully; murderously; ruth-

lessly; savagely; bestially; brutishly; insanely; stupidly; outrageously; sordidly; perniciously.

(See torture, tear.)

MANHOOD

adjectives
generous; neglected; ripe; moral; sober; prosperous; blasted; pitiless; riper; stormy; toilworn; debonair; relentless; martial; remorseless; civilized; sturdy; vigorous; returning.

MANIA

adjectives
sad; dreadful; melancholy; fantastic; undoubted; infernal.

verbs
amount to—; control—; obsess with—; —abates; —attacks; —crazes; —deludes; —deranges; —enthuses (colloq.); —excites; —fades; —impassions; —rages; —wanes.

(See madness, insanity, frenzy, hysteria, delirium.)

MANIAC

adjectives
religious; raving; fettered; gesticulating; fugitive.

verbs
arouse—; chain—; confine—; enchain—; fetter—; harness—; imprison—; incarcerate—; isolate—; liberate—; overpower—; restrain—; shackle—; subdue—; —flames; —foams; —fumes; —howls; —leers; —rages; —rambles; —raves; —scowls.

(See madman.)

MANIFEST

adverbs
unwisely; conspicuously; demonstrably; distinctly; explicitly; boldly; strikingly; publicly; fortunately; unluckily; brazenly; shamefully; pitifully; alarmingly; fearfully; clearly; glaringly; plainly.

MANIFEST (v)

adverbs
obscurely; plainly; vividly; predominantly; broadly; speciously; exclusively; strenuously; universally; frankly; ingenuously; externally; exaggeratedly; conspicuously; whimsically; outwardly; directly; morbidly; physically.

(See reveal, show.)

MANIFESTATION

adjectives
incipient; exaggerated; contemporaneous; external; remarkable; terrestrial; temporary; visible; startling; conspicuous; moderate; astounding; fiery; impolitic; practical; imperial; special; whimsical; extraordinary; outward; historical; tawdry; distinct; decrepit; amplified; direct; recorded; morbid; external; troublesome; extravagant; physical.

verbs
discourage—; overshadow—; ponder—; render—; suppress—; —alludes to; —attests; —bears out; —conveys; —discloses; —evidences; —expresses; —implies; —indicates; —proves; —purports; —reveals; —signifies; —suggests; —symbolizes.

(See indication, evidence, display, disclosure, demonstration.)

MANIKIN

verbs
drape on—; photograph—; view—; —demonstrates; —depicts; —displays; —exhibits; —illustrates; —imitates; —impersonates; —mimics; —models; —parades; —personifies; —projects; —represents.

(Seee model.)

MANIPULATE (v)

adverbs
delicately; deceptively; dexterously; mysteriously; tactfully; secretly; adroitly; technically; surgically; automatically; mechanically; conservatively; deftly.

(See operate, handle.)

MANIPULATION

adjectives
secret; delicate; adroit; technical; surgical; mechanical; automatic; localized; conservative; deft.

verbs
absorb in—; admire—; circumvent—; contrive—; disparage—; employ—; execute—; necessitate—; observe—; practise—; refrain from—; resort to—; skill in—; transact—; —exercises; —stimulates.

(See magic, strategy, trick, mischief, management, treatment.)

MANKIND

adjectives
menaced; married; miserable; unregenerate; redeemed; beauteous.

verbs
admonish—; apprize—; beguile—; benefit —; confer on—; edify—; enlighten—; humanize—; immortalize—; judge—; liberate —; present to—; raise—; trace—; —achieves; —deifies; —evolves; —progresses; — wars on; —worships.
(See civilization, world, family, population, race, society.)

MANLINESS

adjectives
ancient; rugged; ripening; native; barbarous.

MANLY

adverbs
boldly; sturdily; admirably; wonderfully; stoutly; robustly; courageously; valiantly; gallantly; pluckily; resolutely; confidently; adventurously; heroically; fiercely; staunchly; candidly; splendidly.

MANNA

adjectives
animal; celestial; hidden; unexpected; heavenly.

MANNER

adjectives
absorbing; abstracted; acceptable; accessible; accustomed; acquiesced; affable; affectionate; aggressive; agitated; aimless; alarming; altered; ambiguous; amicable; amplest; apologetic; appropriate; approved; argumentative; aristocratic; arrogant; artificial; artist-like; assuming; astonishing; attitudinizing; authoritative; awkward; bantering; barbarous; base; bizarre; blackguardly; bland; bookish; boyish; brotherly; brusque; brutal; buoyant; burlesque; businesslike; calm; candid; casual; caustic; cautious; charming; chatty; cheap; chilling; circuitous; classical; clerkly; cogitating; collected; commodious; compendious; complacent; comprehended; confidential; connected; consummate; continuous; conventional; coquettish; cordial; corporate; correct; correctional; courteous; courtly; cowardly; creditable; crushing; cunning; customary; dainty; dazzling; debonair; deceptive; deferential; defying; delicate; de-

lightful; depraved; deranged; derisive; derivative; despiteful; desultory; detached; dictatorial; different; diffident; dignified; discovered; discreditable; disdainful; disillusioned; disagreeable; derogatory; disquieting; distinctive; distressful; dreadful; earnest; elegant; embarrassed; enchained; enchanted; endearing; engaging; engrossed; entertaining; enviable; erratic; exasperating; exceptional; exhaustive; expressive; extraordinary; fantastic; fawning; festive; filial; finished; formal; forthright; frank; friendly; frugal; gallant; gentle; glaring; gleeful; greedy; guilty; guileless; gross; haphazard; harmonious; haughty; hearty; heavy; heedless; heroic; hideous; hospitable; hurried; identical; illiberal; imitating; immortal; impatient; impeccable; imperfect; imperturbable; imploring; incomparable; incomprehensive; incongruous; independent; indescribable; indispensable; indolent; inexplicable; ingenious; ingratiating; inimitable; insinuating; insolent; insulting; interesting; intimate; intolerant; intricate; invidious; invincible; irreproachable; irreverent; irritated; joyless; kind; kingly; lamblike; languid; laughing; lawabiding; legitimate; lethargic; lifelike; loathed; longing; ludicrous; maidenly; majestic; manufactured; masonic; masterful; meek; meditative; metaphorical; methodic; modern; modest; monotonous; muffled; musing; native; negligent; obsessive; obstinate; odd; offensive; orderly; ordinary; orthodox; outrageous; particular; overbearing; patronizing; peerless; peculiar; perfunctory; persuasive; pert; pettish; picaresque; piquant; piteous; plausible; poetic; polished; polite; pompous; positive; pragmatic; precise; premature; prepossessing; priestlike; profitless; promiscuous; proper; propitiatory; prosy; protesting; provoking; punctilious; quiet; rational; rattling; realistic; reasonable; reckless; refreshing; reluctant; repulsive; respectable; rough; roundabout; rustic; ruthless; satisfactory; saucy; savage; self-reliant; selfsame; sensational; sententious; sentimental; serene; shoddy; signal; silken; similar; simplified; simulated; sketchy; soft; slovenly; social; solemn; spectacular; spurious; stainless; suave; sublime; substantial; suitable; summary; sumptuous; supercilious; superficial; superlative; systematic; tactful; tender; terrifying; theoretical; thoughtful; touching; two-fold; triumphant; tumultuous; typical; unaccountable; unaffected; unassuming; uncompromising; undemonstrative; undiscriminating; un-disguised; unemotional; unenthusiastic; un-even; uneventful; unforgettable; ungrac-ious; unique; unmistakable; unobtrusive; unofficial; unostentatious; unprecedented; unpremeditated; unprincipled; unprofitable; unreserved; unsightly; unswerving; un-usual; unwavering; uproarious; urbane; warning; warring; wholesome; winning; vivacious; youthful; laughable.

verbs
affect—; acquire—; adopt—; ape—; corrupt —s; embolden—; evolve—; flaunt—s; in-culcate—s; modify—; recover—; revitalize —; revolt against—s; tolerate—; transform —; —bullies; —cools; —enrages; —s root in; —shocks; adapt—.

(See behavior, air, method, style, manner-ism, vogue, mode, mien, means.)

MANNERISM
adjectives
inscrutable; developing; humiliating; mus-ical; romantic; severe; compulsive; obstrep-erous.

verbs
abandon—; accentuate—; addict to—; affect —; caricaturize—; conventionalize—; en-dow with—; fall into—; inherit—; jeer at —; mimic—; mock—; ridicule—; satirize —; sustain—; —dandifies; —exemplifies; —individualizes; —simpers.

(See manner, eccentricity, style, method.)

MANNERLY
adverbs
inherently; naturally; carefully; beautifully; pleasantly; agreeably; studiously; unaffect-ed|y; ostentatiously; always; scarcely; bare-ly; urbanely; suavely; smoothly; affably; gallantly; chivalrously; obsequiously; re-spectfully; humbly; unctuously; blandly; gracious|y; genially; heartily; modestly; quietly; unfailingly; ceremoniously.

MANNIKIN
adjectives
flesh-hinged; mortal; god-driven; mechanic.

MANSION
adjectives
cheerless; mossy; determinate; ostentatious; commodious; moldered; noble; desolate; ex-ecutive; hospitable; dim; fatigued; reticent; old; feudal; happy; elegant; studious; soli-tary; heavenly; blissful; rich-chambered; eterna|; sun-mellowed; stout; substantial; white-pillared; gloomy; dolorous; marble; noisy; aristocratic; baronial; shut-up; palat-ial; intricate; stately; extensive; stormy; steady; temple like; beautiful; decorated; colonnaded; antiquated; fragile.

verbs
convert—; dwell in—; haunt—; inhabit—; modernize—; occupy—; permeate—; redec-orate—; remodel—; renovate—; reside in —; restore—; —awes; —houses; —inspires; —quarters.

(See castle, structure, palace, residence, house, apartment.)

MANTLE
adjectives
judicial; imperial; furred; motley; verdant; somber; russet; silver; curious; sable; in-visible; ermine; many-colored; grassy; flowery; stained; autumn.

MANUAL
adjectives
comprehensive; illustrated; constructive; in-formative; training; exquisite; helpful; complete.

MANUFACTURE (v)
adverbs
exclusively; prosperously; rudely; synthetic-ally; coarsely; reputably; legally; success-fully; preeminently.

(See make, create, invent, compose.)

MANUFACTURER
adjectives
coarsest; recalcitrant; obdurate; prominent; exclusive; reputable; preeminent; alert; successful.

MANUSCRIPT
adjectives
maltreated; moldered; crabbed; blazoned; lost; delusive; illuminated; scrawly; cunei-form; origina|; religious; written; quaint; typed; rare; valuable; long-penned.

verbs
acknowledge—; approve—; attest—; com-pile—; cull—; decipher—; decline—; edit —; engross in—; polish—; publish—; re-ject—; rewrite—; scratch out—; scrawl—; scribble—; transcribe—; witness—.

(See story, novel, message, romance, theme, thesis, volume.)

adjectives
density; topographical; previous; rude; accurate; road; aerial; changing.

verbs
design—; draft—; scale—; sketch—; —acquaints; —apprizes; —charts; —communicates; —conveys; —delineates; —describes; —details; —directs; —enlightens; —estimates; —guides; —imparts; —informs; —pilots; —portrays; —represents; —specifies.
(See chart, diagram, outline, plan.)

MARAUDER

adjectives
sanguine; terrible; ferocious; licentious; burglarious; deadly; stealthy.

MARBLE

adjectives
mottled; blended; breathing; variegated; wrought; remarkable; chill; polished; synthetic; lusterless; ponderous; snowy; chiseled; cold; imitation.

MARCH

adjectives
torturing; severe; fruitless; tedious; silent; famous; dreary; rapid; forced; cautious; circuitous; toilsome; dreadful; disorderly; victorious; bloody; irresistible; hobbling; retrograde; triumphant; arduous; dramatic; confused; slow; glorious; stealthy; measureless; marvelous; magnificent; unprecedented; stately; prolonged; endless; ordered; steady; stormy; victorious; general; monotonous.

verbs
command—; direct—; extend—; force—; renew—; resort to—; retard—; review—; steal—on; —advances; —circuits; —deviates; —parades; —precedes; —rambles; —shuffles; —straggles; —veers; —wends; —zigzags.
(See charge, advance, action, move, attack.)

MARCH (*v*)

adverbs
pompously; triumphantly; steadily; tirelessly; leisurely; endlessly; menacingly; circuitously; stalwartly; uninterruptedly; briskly; morosely; intrepidly; aimlessly; ignominiously; fruitlessly; cautiously; irresistibly; arduously; dramatically; magnificently; monotonously.
(See advance, walk.)

MARCHER

verbs
—advances; —jogs; —journeys; —normalizes; —patrols; —plods; —proceeds; —promenades; —rambles; —roves; —salutes; —saunters; —shuffles on; —strolls; —struts; —threads his way; —tramps; —treads; —trudges.
(See traveler, tourist, passenger.)

MARE

adjectives
striking-looking; nervous; high; infuriated; whinnying; placid; brood; riderless; sleek; calico; thoroughbred.

verbs
break—; bridle—; check—; curb—; curry—; groom—; mount—; rein in—; —bares; —balks; —canters; —conveys; —foals; —gallops; —hurdles; —neighs; —prances; —shies; —trots; —whinnies.
(See horse, colt, mule, donkey. ass, pony.)

MARGIN

adjectives
invisible; flowery; satisfactory; embarrassing; narrowing; refreshing; substantial; distinct; sedgy; slight; regular.

MARGINAL

adverbs
broadly; safely; dangerously; insecurely; permissibly; perilously; riskily; hazardously.

MARINER

adjectives
shipwrecked; ancient; sunswart; chartless; faint-hearted; cowering; cautious; ingenious; homesick; deft; seaworthy.

MARK

adjectives
destructive; decisive; gracious; distinguished; well-founded; separate; dreadful; wedge-shaped; venerable; evident; conspicuous; special; privy; unobtrusive; peculiar; visible; imperceptible; external; transient; deepened; brilliant; delicate; guiding; aimless; unchanging; indelible; tiny.

verbs
bear—; better—; detect—; hold—; over-
shoot—; recognize—; regard—; scale—;
scrutinize—; surpass—; toe—; —attests to;
—betokens; —brands; —characterizes; —
denotes; —directs; —guides; —identifies;
—indicates; —periods; —ranks; —relates
to; —signalizes; —signifies; —symbolizes;
—symptomizes.
(See goal.)

MARK (*v*)
adverbs
distinctly; gratefully; delicately; unalterably; conspicuously; dismally; boldly; indelibly; obviously; destructively; venerably;
privately; peculiarly; imperceptibly; externally; aimlessly; brilliantly.
(See brand, stamp, indicate.)

MARKET
adjectives
immediate; limited; glutted; rising; alternative; volume; extensive; matrimonial;
prominent; inchoate; essential; public; prosperous; domestic; non-competitive; bristle;
eager; growing; wide; open; huge; blooming.

verbs
barter in—; bear—; bottle up—; bull—;
congest—; deflate—; dominate—; dump on
—; flood—; glut—; invest in—; job in—;
kill—; negotiate in—; overload—; procure
—for; purvey at—; quote—; ravage—;
speculate in—; stabilize—; survey—; swamp
—; tax—; trade in—; traffic in—; transact
at—; underbid—; vend in—; —booms; —
fluctuates; —oscillates; —sags; —slumps.
(See exchange, trade, business, speculation, store, merchandise.)

MARKETABLE
adverbs
permanently; highly; seasonably; readily;
easily; scarcely; always; occasionally; fad-
dishly; uncertainly; remarkably; positively;
currently; advantageously; profitably; opportunely; extremely; unusually; stably;
durably; steadily; invariably; conveniently;
fortunately.

MARRIAGE
adjectives
mercenary; reckless; indissoluble; heterodox; cradle; wealthy; international; immediate; advantageous; previous; unhappy;
crude; dubious; ungentle; placid; conjectural; unworthy; bogged; subsequent; ill-
starred; spiteful; wondrous; fat; ceremonious; intelligent; dubious; possible; ideal;
continual; intended; somber; imprudent;
hasty; impending; private; ensuing; repented; plural; honorable; brilliant; acceptable;
sudden; monstrous; morganatic; uncertain;
consanguineous; impecunious; impromptu;
loveless; convenient; derogatory; ill-match-
ed; idiotic; imprudent; impetuous; necessary.

verbs
absolve—; annul—; attend—; bless—; cement—; consummate—; contract—; dissolve
—; ensure—; give in—; indicate—; precipitate—; romanticize—; sancitfy—; sanction
—; terminate—; undermine—; —materializes; —sanctifies; —unites; plunge into—.
(See hand, wedding, nuptial, union, matrimony.)

MARROW
verbs
chill to—; convey through—; freeze—; inculcate in—; infect—; ingrain in—; moisten
with—; suppurate—.
(See blood, being, bone, soul.)

MARRY (*v*)
adverbs
inadvertently; subsequently; advantageously; eventually; hastily; shamefully; recklessly; indissolubly; dubiously; congenially;
spitefully; ceremoniously; imprudently; honorably; morganatically; lovelessly; impecuniously; conveniently; imprudently; impetuously.
(See espouse, wed.)

MARSH
verbs
bog down in—; drain—; dwell in—; flourish
in—; infest—; inhabit—; mire in—; rehabilitate—; sink in—; slough in—; thrive in
—; —breeds; —contaminates; —inundates;
—menaces; —reeks; —stagnates; —submerges.
(See island, peninsula, swamp, valley,
jungle, forest.)

MARSHAL
adjectives
provost; undaunted; fiery; daunted.

MARSHAL (v)

adverbs
sternly; vigorously; militaristically; undauntedly; patriotically; dutifully; gallantly.
(See arrange, adjust, settle.)

MARSHES

adjectives
malarial; pestiferous; inhospitable; dreary; fever-haunted; deadly; venomous; unmarshlike; treacherous; desolate; steaming.

MART

adjectives
humming; considerable; desperate; imperceptible; prosperous.

MARTIAL

adverbs
splendidly; brilliantly; gorgeously; portentously; ominously; dominantly; belligerently; contentiously; predominantly; magnificently; noisily; grimly; subtly; ostentatiously; deliberately; offensively; fearfully; daringly.

MARTIN

verbs
—aids; —arrays; —attacks; —banks; —s colonize; —s journey; —migrates; —pierces; —preys on; —rounds; —scratches; —skims; —smooths; —spreads.
(See bird, swallow.)

MARTYR

adjectives
ancient; unheralded; exulting; patient; resolute; selfish; grave; unpractical; fiery; sainted; magnanimous; crucified.

MARTYRDOM

adjectives
heroic; disdainful; uplifting; voluntary; long-sought.

MARVEL

adjectives
admiring; fantastic; infinite; accomplished; dreamlike.

verbs
accomplish—; admire—; behold—; gape at —; paint—; stand aghast at—; —amazes; —astonishes; —astounds; —awes; —baffles; —bewilders; —dazes; —dazzles; —dumb-founds; —electrifies; —fascinates; —flabbergasts (colloq); —overwhelms; —strikes dumb; —stuns; —stupefies; —staggers.
(See wonder, beauty, radiance, splendor, mystery, success.)

MARVEL (v)

adverbs
secretly; fantastically; infinitely; mutely; impassively; joyously; candidly.
(See wonder, amaze.)

MASK

adjectives
servile crescentlike; grisly; laughing; smiling; newest; impenetrable; lifeless; impassive; theatrical; acquired; hideous; wanton; deceitful; well-trained; sun-expelling; dainty; waxen; placid; tragic; changing; child-faced; stately.

verbs
adjust—; cloak with—; doff—; emerge from —; fashion—; —beguiles; —blinds; —conceals; —deceives; —deludes; —depicts; —disguises; —eclipses; —lures; —portrays; —veils; don—.
(See cloak, disguise, make-up, masquerade.)

MASK (v)

adverbs
partially; cunningly; demurely; servilely; impassively; wantonly; deceitfully; daintily; tragically; deceptively; treacherously; hideously; ironically; slyly.
(See disguise, hide, veil, masquerade.)

MASON

verbs
employ—; hire—; —achieves; —blocks; —carves; —chips; —chisels; —constructs; —drills; —erects; —fabricates; —forges; —frames; —heaves; —hews; —lugs; —models; —molds; —rears; —shoulders; —sunders.
(See worker, workman.)

MASONRY

adjectives
roofless; arched; delicate; beautiful.

MASQUERADE

adjectives
brilliant; glittering; ghastly; savage; phantom; speaking; ironic; ghostly.

verbs

attend—; organize—; plan—; reveal—; — bamboozles (colloq.); —beguiles; —blinds; —cloaks; —conceals; —counterfeits; —curtains; —decoys; —deludes; —diverts; — eclipses; —enlivens; —hoodwinks; —lures; —masks; —muffles; —mystifies; —relaxes; —screens; —secretes; —shades; —shrouds; —stifles; —suppresses; —veils.

(See mask, disguise, misrepresentaion, dance, sham.)

MASQUERADE (v)

adverbs

bizarrely; brilliantly; savagely; ironically; enthusiastically; spectacularly; joyously; ceremonially; formally; perfunctorily.

(See mask, hide, veil, disguise.)

MASS
(general)

adjectives

heterogeneous; midnight; bucking; regimented; gloomy; immense; agitated; promiscuous; frowning; withered; helpless; physical; mighty; confused; prosaic; frantic; vulgar; ever-moving; phalanxed; unmanaged; specious; aggregate; straggling; celebrated; clinking; homogeneous; inert; buttressed; tangled; wrestling; ungrateful; disloyal; neutral; spheroidal; somber; animated; woolly; ponderous; oscillating; floating; bloated; crashing; continuous; seething; chaotic; heaving; solid; desiccated; melancholy; pulplike; discouraging; whirling; remarkable; gigantic; fermenting; tumultuous; imposing; gummy; ill-defined; nebulous; rushing; roaring; irresistible; flickering; whale-like; luminous; continuous; immeasurable; indiscriminate; glowing; gross; steely; leaping; sinking; cutting; amorphous; bristling; repugnant; insensible; dark; impending; unbroken; burnished; entangled; pinnacled; conglomerate; gigantic; agitated; restless; incoherent; inarticulate; quivering; resplendent; rough; packed; incandescent; unyielding; accumulating; inanimate; successive (pl); tough; leathery; somber; indistinct; charred; gelatine.

MASS
(lump, assemblage, heap, etc.)

verbs

accumulate—; aggregate—; bulk—; cement in—; cluster in—; compile—; constitute—; crush—; disintegrate—; dissolve—; embody —; focus in—; heap in—; integrate—; lump in—; measure—; muster—; scrape—; verge in—; —expands; —ferments; —rises; — soars; —swells; —thickens; —towers; — transcends.

(See dough, generality, crowd, amount, heap.)

MASS
(religion)

verbs

administer—; anthem—; attend—; bow at —; chant—; chorus—; devote to—; give praise at—; kneel at—; mumble—; perform —; worship at—; —glorifies; —invokes; — offers; —salvages; —uplifts.

(See church, rite, ceremony, sacrament.)

MASSACRE

adjectives

atrocious; brutal; indiscriminate; cruel; fierce; horrid; dreadful; treacherous; wholesale; judicial; bloody .

verbs

decry—; denounce—; execute—; expire in —; frown on—; lust for—; perpetrate—; plot—; rebuke for—; reproach for—; resign to—; succumb in—; yield to—; —despatches; —enrages; —ensanguines; —incenses; —rages; —scandalizes; —scars; —stains; —threatens.

(See bloodshed, killing, murder, assassination, slaughter, violence.)

MASSAGE

adjectives

invigorating; stimulating; scientific; frictional; healing.

verbs

—enlivens; —exhilarates; —invigorates; — limbers; —quickens; —refreshes; —regenerates; —relaxes; —relieves; —soothes; —smooths; —ungnarls.

(See remedy, medicine, liniment, masseur.)

MASSAGE (v)

adverbs

industriously; actively; invigoratingly; stimulatingly; scientifically; healingly; beneficially.

(See rub, knead.)

adjectives

singular; vapory; quadrangular; comet-shaped; thunderous; dusky; cosmic; exultant; dense; congested; multitudinous; surging; accumulated; struggling; huddled; flame-shaped; crushing; impenetrable; enormous; enthusiastic; metallic; hurrying; disorderly; grateful; cross; incensed; vast; bold; fleeing; irregular; illiterate; listening; glittering; shadowy; dusky; dull; huge; menacing; obedient; luminous.

MASSES
(*people*)

verbs

benefit—; cajole—; deride—; educate—; enkindle—; enslave—; exhort—; exploit—; ferment—; inflame—; indoctrinate—; lift —; move—; rally—round; subjugate—; submerge—; sway—; tread on—; weld—; —erupt; —revolt; —seethe.

(See public, population, multitude, mob, society, throng, crowd.)

MASSEUR

verbs

train—; —comforts; —eases; —kneads; — manipulates; —massages; —pats; —pounds; —quiets; —rectifies; —rubs; —spanks.

(See massage.)

MASSIVE

adverbs

enormously; awkwardly; stupendously; impossibly; overwhelmingly; grotesquely; strangely; ponderously; grossly; monstrously.

MAST

adjectives

staggering; derrick-like; ripened; tapering; straining; naked; raking; towering; broken; snapped.

verbs

clamber up—; erect—; lash to—; lower—; nail to—; raise—; rig—; sail before—; spring—; step—; strain—; —creaks; —extends; —rises; —splinters; —supports; — sustains; —sways.

(See post, beam.)

MASTER

adjectives

imperious; profound; lurid; disloyal; captious; contemporary; testy; intriguing; sweet; urban; provincial; absolute; clouted; majestic; unrighteous; supreme; former; money; dish-faced; prayer; inglorious; independent; exasperating; unsuccessful; tyrannical; foremost; inward; school; mystic; industrial; noble; undisputed; accepted; perturbed; indignant; formidable; marvelous; proficient; blithe; shrewd; unworthy; injudicious; intractable; manful; jovial.

verbs

acknowledge—; appeal to—; attend—; betray—; bow to—; conspire against—; emulate—; enjoin—; follow—; salute—; serve —; supersede—; —authorizes; —censures; —controls; —directs; —disciplines; —enslaves; —governs; —guides; —judges; — lashes; —oversees; —rewards; —rules; — supervises.

(See expert, husband, commander, employer.)

MASTER (*v*)

adverbs

skillfully; imperiously; profoundly; absolutely; majestically; tyrannically; undisputedly; formidably; marvelously; proficiently; shrewdly; jovially; injudiciously; dictatorially.

(See handle, rule, command.)

MASTERPIECE

adjectives

ambitious; fair; exquisite; crisp; vivid; brief; restrained; unequaled; unsurpassed; literary; involuntary; eminent; symphonic; heroic.

verbs

acclaim—; accomplish—; achieve—; applaud—; appreciate—; cast—; chance upon —; contemplate—; emulate—; esteem—; examine—; extol—; hail as—; interpret—; laud—; match—; pay tribute to—; praise —; reproduce—; rival—; study—; transcribe—; value—; work—; —excels; —depicts; —portrays; —reposes in; —surpasses; —survives; —transcends.

(See picture, photograph, portrait, painting, model, plan, statue.)

adjectives
unrivaled; intelligent; barbarous; seductive; technical: imperfect; physical; complete.

verbs
aim at—; assay—; assert—; assume—; attain—; command—of; crown with—; dispute—; distinguish by—; exercise—; gain —; maintain—; match—; perform with—; prove—; regain—; relinquish—; spur to—; strive for—; struggle for—; surpass—; wield—; —awes; —dominates; —prevails; —sways.
(See perfection, proficiency, skill.)

MATCH
(*fire*)

verbs
apply—; dip—; extinguish—; ignite—; impregnate—; quench—; scratch—; smother —; tip—; touch off—; —chars; —devours; —dies; —enkindles; —flickers; —fuses; — glows; —incinerates; —simmers; —singes; —smoulders; —sputters.
(See lamp, light, flame, fire.)

MATCH
(*general*)

adjectives
brilliant; unwise; brief; ordinary; shameful; suitable; mad; rich; honorable; championship; unholy; inappropriate; love.

MATCH
(*parallel, mate, boot, etc.*)

verbs
arrange—; challenge to—; compete i -; contest—; enter—; judge—; negotiate—; officiate at—; promote—; prove—for; regulate—; scorn—; spurn—; view—; witness —; —corresponds; —duplicates; —mirrors; —parallels; —pairs; —resembles.
(See bout, fight, race (sport), contest.)

MATCH (*v*)

adverbs
equally; boldly; madly; rashly; foolhardily; brilliantly; unwisely; honorably; shamefully; improvidently.
(See oppose, challenge, defy, dare.)

MATE

adjectives
trembling; truant; incongruous; all-beautiful; nested; afflicted; vile; sincere; sweet; shivering; unloved; lovely; unkind; brooding; equal; imprudent; inharmonious; beauteous.

verbs
abandon—; choose—; compete for—; desert —; discard—; divorce—; espouse—; estrange from—; forsake—; guard—; join —; protect—; quit—; relinquish—; renounce —; vie for—; —matches; —parallels; —resembles.
(See comrade, husband, wife, friend.)

MATERIAL
(*general*)

adjectives
biographical; suggestive; front-page; illustrative; corrosive; supplementary; ennobling; inexhaustible; complex; delicate; gauzy; acoustical; intellectual; suitable; biblical; health; preserved; objectionable; documentary; infinite; mournful; hilarious; extensive; tangible; concentrated; factual; authoritative; vast; repressed; anthropological; exquisite; impressionable; ample; outside; moraine; underworld; heterogeneous; mailable; muscle-building; copious; rustable; combustible; superfine; prepared; quality; misleading; rubberlike; tenacious; unpromising; noble; rugged; infantile; washable; special; volatile; polished; positive; elastic; unformed; nutritive; discordant; packaging; cool; raw; molten; protective; illustrative; septic; superlative; conglomerating; basic; rude; superfluous; durable; versatile; abrasive; miraculous; abundant; unimpeachable; picturesque; inorganic; fragmentary; coarse; scanty; shining; intractable; disjointed; choicest; insulating; mulch; thematic.

MATERIAL
(*information*)

verbs
absorb—; accumulate—; amass—; arrange —; array—; assemble—; assort—; catallogue—; collect—; compile—; concentrate on —; delve into—; digest—; disseminate—; gather—; glean—; group—; jot down—; marshal—; muster—; rake up—; reduce—; sift—; simplify—; treat—; unify—.
(See knowledge, facts, science, copy, information, wisdom.)

MATERIAL
(matter)

verbs
allot—; amass—; apportion—; assemble—; consume—; derive—from; drain—; exhaust —; expend—; garner—; heap—; lay in—; load—; manipulate—; measure—; order—; reserve—; sift—; squander—; stock with—; store—; waste—; —fritters away.

(See cloth, drapery, ingredients, supply, food, merchandise.)

adverbs
grossly; flagrantly; selfishly; highly; essentially; vitally; fundamentally; gravely; eminently; indispensably; crassly; seriously; urgently.

MATERIALISM

adjectives
ruthless; dialectical; advanced; practical; lifeless; brutal; unreligious; coarse; scientific; crass.

verbs
absorb by—; accentuate—; cloak—; degenerate into—; disparage—; infest with—; lapse into—; shrink from—; sink into—; tend to—; transmute—; —blasphemes; —desecrates; —doubts; —hardens; —perverts; —profanes; —questions; —scorns; —wanes.

(See modernism, paganism, atheism, realism.)

MATERNAL

adverbs
fondly; fiercely; tenderly; solicitously; possessively; obsessively; jealously; proudly; comfortingly; unduly; naturally; habitually; admirably; charmingly; sweetly; placidly; serenely; imperturbably; dominantly; indulgently; good-humoredly; warmly; softly; bounteously; generously; providently; curiously; thoughtfully.

MATERNITY

verbs
anticipate—; arouse—; balk at—; delight in —; endear to—; exalt—; guard—; impair —; overwhelm by—; prepare for—; prevent —; pride in—; recognize—; train for—; —bores; —nauseates; —secures.

MATHEMATICS

verbs
advance by—; apply—; base on—; compile by—; demonstrate—; depend on—; dispute —; fathom by—; ferret out by—; formulate —; introduce—; —computes; —disciplines; —educes; —enthralls; —sharpens; —solves; —systematizes; —trains; —verifies; —weighs.

(See science, logic, solution, problem.)

MATING

adjectives
auspicious; seasonal; beneficial; integral.

MATRIARCHAL

adverbs
venerably; insistently; tyrannically; gently; tenaciously; uncommonly; highly; imperiously; oddly; naturally; unyieldingly; obviously; irrevocably; proudly; haughtily.

MATRIMONY

verbs
abhor—; blast—; cloud—; commit to—; consent to—; dissolve—; embark on—; entice into—; evade—; reconcile to—; sacrifice to —; scorn—; spurn—; surrender to—; —circles; —exacts; —knits; —mars; —preserves; —shackles; —survives; —torments; —unites.

(See marriage, wedding, nuptials, union.)

MATRON

adjectives
substantial; sober; ancient; stately; ailing; bulky; sharp-faced; fluttering; dignified; sober-suited; modest; pedantic; gracious; haughty.

verbs
appoint—; tip—; train—; vest in—; —administers; —assists; —cradles; —furnishes; —inspects; —manages; —obliges; —presides —reinforces; —resides; —serves; —superintends; —supervises; —supplies.

(See servant, housekeeper, wife.)

MATRONLY

adverbs
pleasantly; proudly; unexpectedly; charmingly; admirably; sedately; demurely; comfortably; serenely; imperturbably; undeniably; sweetly; graciously; happily; gently; tranquilly; placidly; remarkably.

MATTER

adjectives
subject; specific; triturated; perfunctory; doleful; heterogeneous; inconsequential; unimportant; spiritual; combustible; urgent; prudential; luminous; worldly; esoteric; indigent; trivial; imminent; spiritual; superficial; heavy; calcareous; internal; fixed; fluid; humid; dry; unctuous; crude; hard; soft; simple; veiny; compound; similar; organical; imponderable; extraneous; controversial; inevitable; critical; unpalatable; speculative; jesting; granular; erupted; exterior; analogous; ample; essential; brute; country; mineral; weighty; pertinent; waste; baser; suspended; countless (pl); theoretical; pecuniary; impending; critical; putrid; encrusted; tarry; bare; nitrogenous; stony; regrettable; indolent; protuberant; empty; forgotten; ecclesiastical; inert; testamentary; suspended; mighty; graver; inexhaustible; commonplace; relevant; remote; subtle; indifferent; inflammable; financial; earnest; hideous; abstruse; fascinating; temporal; coloring; worthy; woody; perishable; money; unattainable; carbonaceous; artistic; grave; morbid; cognate.

verbs
adjust—; aggravate—; brood over—; clinch —; deal with—; debate—; deliberate—; discuss—; dispute—; elucidate—; expedite—; forsake—; go to the root of—; inquire into —; judge—; mince—s; ponder—; press—; report—; shape—; simplify—; smooth—; visualize—; weigh—; —drifts; —engages; —engrosses; —|ingers; —pertains to.
(See business, affair, event, question, problem.)

MATTRESS

verbs
construct—; fluff—; handle—; hollow—; hump—; launder—; lug—; pad—; quilt—; stitch—; strain—; stuff—; tuck under—; tuft—; —comforts; —cushions; —eases; — molds; —pits; —refreshes; —supports.
(See bed, pillow.)

MATURE

adverbs
suddenly; undeniably; admirably; sensibly; sagaciously; sturdily; responsibly; unexpectedly; remarkably; curiously; strangely; surprisingly; reasonably; sufficiently; presumably; scarcely; thoroughly; progressively; strikingly; completely; fully; obviously; fairly; terribly; precociously; indescribably; gratifyingly; wisely; emotionally; physically; appallingly; supposedly; intellectually; unquestionably.

MATURITY

adjectives
fairest; complete; precocious; ripened; mysterious; surprising; hypothetical; indescribable; emotional; warm; rapid; cold; respectable; serene; luxuriant; sumptuous; buxom.

verbs
abide till—; approach—; attain—; grow in —; impede—; merge into—; settle into—; tarry—; undergo—; —charms; —limits; — mellows; —ripens; —subdues; —sweetens; —teaches; —transforms.
(See development.)

MAUDLIN

adverbs
drunkenly; foolishly; senselessly; incoherently; intoxicatedly; joyously; merrily; crazily; utterly; stupidly; oddly; disgustingly; hopelessly; helplessly; egregiously; heavily; tipsily; gloriously; comically; shamefully; happily; irresponsibly; excitedly; hysterically.

MAUVE

adjectives
soft; pale; brilliant.

MAXIM

adjectives
horrible; favorite; terse; common; sublime; wholesome; elevated; political; shrewd; sagacious; execrable; salutary; ethical; moral; polite; profane; semibarbarous.

verbs
apply—; coin—; comprehend—; condense into—; consider—; defend—; draw from—; interpret—; invoke—; mold—; observe—; propose—; retain—; speculate on—; weigh —; —concludes; —directs; —embodies; — guides; —philosophizes; —relates to.
(See adage, proverb.)

MAXIMUM

verbs
assign—; attain—; calculate—; conduct to —; distend to—; establish—; reach—; record—; test—; strain—; strike—; weigh—; —bears; —corresponds; —limits.
(See amount, average, degree, position, status, limit.)

adjectives

quaint; murmuring; surging; tangled; institutional; flitting; uncouth; moon-loved; flowery; backward; vague; hopeless; musky-circled; mirthful; tortuous; statistical; mystic; intriguing; shadowy; winding; insane; bewitching; laborious; shifting; curious; intoxicating.

verbs

crack—; dissolve—; entangle in—; extricate from—; grope through—; guide through—; immure in—; retrace—; struggle through —; submerge in—; wander in—; weave—; —bewilders; —confounds; —confuses; — entwines; —perplexes; —puzzles; —twists; —winds; —wreathes.

(See mystery, perplexity, problem.)

MEADOW

adjectives

romantic; grassy; intervening; frost-flowered; luxuriant; bloody; fruitful; slushy; starry; outlying; tender; enameled; smooth; saturated; dewy; serene; mountain; sheltered; bright; undulating; extensive; quaint; parched; dim-seen; damp; open; homely; scorching; laughing; swelling; rolling; billowy; unmown; emerald.

verbs

amble through—; crop—; cultivate—; drench—; dress—; luxuriate in—; mow—; paint—; parch—; pasture in—; plough—; prance in—; romp in—; stain—; —blooms; —extends; —invites; —scents; —slopes.

(See field, grass, flowers, plant, country, lawn.)

MEAGRE

adverbs

pitifully; scantily; miserably; wretchedly; pitiably; deplorably; lamentably; pathetically; unnecessarily; unaccountably; unreasonably; criminally; stingily; meanly; cruelly; bitterly; hopelessly; desperately; incredibly; unbelievably; meretriciously; skimpily; contemptibly.

MEAL

adjectives

supplementary; sunset; ominous; scanty; small; floating; satisfying; well-balanced; belated; abominable; miserable; vegetable; frugal; hearty; hasty; elaborate; slender; indigested; sumptuous; savory; lavish; hot; jovial; quick; homelike; sailor-cooked; quiet; infantile; dismal; miraculous; assured; plenteous; solitary; luxurious; economical; accustomed; superb; delectable; tempting; perfect; appetizing; famous; marvelous; generous; tasty; home-cooked; thrilling; abundant.

verbs

beg—; consume—; despatch—; dispose of —; enhance—; lubricate—; relish—; savor —; snatch—; terminate—; —nourishes; — proceeds; —sustains; —tempts.

(See dinner, luncheon, food, breakfast, supper.)

MEALY-MOUTHED

adverbs

insufferably; perversely; pretentiously; humbly; deceitfully; mendaciously; perfidiously; hypocritically; cunningly; insidiously; treacherously; invidiously; trickily; meretriciously; atrociously; abominably; satirically; inconceivably.

MEAN

adverbs

abominably; terribly; stingily; viciously; maliciously; horribly; incredibly; inordinately; unbelievably; brutally; cruelly; bitterly; greedily; shamefully; despicably; outrageously; disgracefully; treacherously; selfishly; jealously; enviously.

MEANING

adjectives

mysterious; common; inexpressible; pathetic; doubtful; mythical; majestic; secondary; imploring; earnest; ominous; ambiguous; solemn; veiled; gentle; odious; candid; double; true; remote; ultimate; uncertain; specific; significant; obvious; generous; wicked; eucharistic; fearful; undecipherable; patriotic; platonic; heavenly; universal; philosophical; shrunken; painful; lawful; mean; historic; symbolic; irresolute; serious; deadly; unmistakable; plain; dark; intelligible; cloudy; abstruse; legitimate; moral; profound; folded; hideous; concrete; precise; borrowed; infinite; intellectual; spiritual; unaffected; unattractive; huge; hybrid; cryptic; secular; sexual; incredible; second; elusive; considerable; instant; involved; vague; express; accumulated; vital.

verbs

absorb—; adulterate—; apprehend—; ascribe—to; bestow—upon; clarify—; comprehend—; discover—; elaborate on—; elucidate—; embody—; extricate—from; grasp —; illustrate—; imply—; impregnate with —; pervert—; ponder—; reflect upon—; seek—; sum up—; translate—; weigh with —; wresle with—; attach—to.

(See reason, significance.)

MEANS

adjectives

iniquitous; effective; downright; legitimate; solid; extraordinary; vociferous; plunging; continuous; ample; systematic; peaceful; prying; drastic; efficient; radical; clumsy; hygienic; scantiest; slender; superficial; rapid; showy; artificial; honorable; comfortable; undue; subtle; unlawful; effectual; vast; superior; remote; mysterious; unexplained; considerable; subservient; further; highhanded; useful; indispensable; occult; earthly; inarticulate; mechanical; pecuniary; approved; devious; gigantic; accidental; instrumental; faint; conflicting; realistic; blessed; inadequate; extremest; practicable; readiest; apparent; double; abundant; unrestrained; speediest; lavish; quick; individual; moderate; miraculous; flagitious; potent; valuable; creditable; instinctive.

verbs

adopt—; attain—; contrive—; desire—; devise—; employ—; find—; invent—; meditate on—; outline—; resort to—; secure—; supplant—; suggest—.

(See agency, method, way, manner, policy.)

MEASLES

verbs

afflict with—; attack with—; convey—; develop—; dispose to—; immunize to—; isolate—; stud with—; usher in—; —abates; —blotches; —endangers; —erupts; —fades; —infects; —invades; —patches; —spreads; —stains; —weakens.

(See sickness, malady, disease, smallpox.)

MEASURE
(general)

adjectives

effectual; dictatorial; decisive; mystic; unconstitutional; delightful; harsher; faltering; aesthetic; star; buskined; domestic; extreme; classical; diminished; good; considerate; large; hostile; rustic; merriest; precautionary; equal; discriminatory; infinite; quaint; drastic; pending; intemperate; judicious; repressive; defiant; puretoned; irregular; solemn; unattainable; compulsory; undeserved; hygienic; conservative; corrective; preventive; radical; contemptuous; potent; energetic; conciliatory; violent; pernicious; tempestuous; sinister; undaunted; scant; retaliatory; large; fluctuating; rhythmical; brimming; galloping; tuneful; vigorous; airy; stringent; generous; just; final; unexpected; accurate; weightiest; flowing; unrhymed; stately; financial; sweeping; inevitable; hostile; ample; aggressive; individual; tyrannical; dusty; highhanded; swelling; smallest; compromise; dulcet; preliminary; prompt; satisfactory; boundless; sterilizing; sufficient; proposed; doubtful; desperate; tedious; irregular; considerate; quantitative; rude; severe; vulgar; hasty; lavish; strained; pacific; debated; stark; concentrated; burning; central; centuried; organic; diverse (pl); eugenic; suitable; disciplinary; ruinous; emergency; corresponding; undreamed; contestable; gracious; bold; oppressive.

MEASURE
(legislation, course.)

verbs

adopt—; advance—; advocate—; block—; combat—; defy—; effect—; enact—; enforce—; execute—; exert—s; force—through; install—; institute—; introduce—; outlaw—; pilot—; promote—; promulgate —; reject—; repass—; resort to—; subscribe to—; suggest—; threaten with—s; — affords relief; —clamps down on; —corrects; —embodies; —embraces; —evolves from.

(See bill, law, rule, ordinance, statute, mandate.)

MEASURE (v)

adverbs

scientifically; mechanically; accurately; consciously; effectually; constitutionally; aesthetically; mystically; classically; equally; intemperately; judiciously; financially; individually; tediously; quantitatively; lavishly; radically.

(See gauge, rule, estimate.)

MEASUREMENTS

adjectives
micrometrical; accurate; geodetic; refined.

verbs
adopt—; appraise for—; ascertain—; calculate—; cling to—; collect—; confirm—; deduce—; derive—; determine—; estimate —; probe—; reckon—; report—; review—; sound—; stipulate—; —allow; —coincide with.

(See magnitude, size, dimension.)

MEAT

adjectives
lean; sizzling; homely; substantial; immortal; choleric; wretched; corrupted; unctuous; miserable; wholesome; manufactured; perishable; fatty; generous; preserved; tainted.

verbs
abstain from—; broil—; brown—; carve—; consume—; crave—; dispatch—; dive into —; dress—; dry—; extract from—; grill—; grind—; inspect—; market—; parch—; pickle—; prepare—; refrigerate—; roll—; salt—; savor—; shred—; store—; tenderize —; tub—; weigh—; —ages; —deteriorates; —putrefies.

(See flesh, game, food, stew.)

MECHANIC

adjectives
shrewd; roused; expert; trained; competent; skilled.

MECHANICAL

adverbs
cleverly; ingeniously; dexterously; marvelously; dully; automatically; altogether; accurately; conveniently; advantageously; profitably; precisely; unerringly.

MECHANISM

adjectives
literal; extremely delicate; intricate; lifeless; wondrous; dexterous; primary; gorgeous; elaborate; inanimate; greasy; interior; insensate; unconscious; instrumental.

verbs
acquaint with—; analyze—; approve—; construct—; design—; develop—; explain—; improve—; inspect—; install—; invent—;

operate—; substitute—; tamper with—; tinker with—; understand—; —eases; — performs; —specializes; —speeds.

(See gear, engine, machine, dynamo, apparatus.)

MEDAL

verbs
accord—; award—; bestow—; cast—; confer—; decorate with—; engrave—; favor with—; grant—; honor with—; inscribe on—; jingle—s; mold—; present with—; prize—; strike—; —commemorates; —distinguishes; —encourages; —records; —represents; —signifies; —symbolizes.

(See laurels, trophy, badge, memorial, reward.)

MEDDLESOME

adverbs
vexatiously; irritatingly; maliciously; incredibly; unaccountably; maddeningly; incurably; offensively; unpleasantly; disagreeably; unbelievably; busily; officiously; unpardonably; intrusively; invidiously; atrociously; inexcusably; curiously; inquisitively; inveterately; unscrupulously; incorrigibly; grievously.

MEDIA

adjectives
sympathetic; turbid; diffracting; fluctuating.

MEDICATION

adjectives
pre-anesthetic; proper; penetrating; soothing.

MEDICINAL

adverbs
warrantably; highly; splendidly; advantageously; incidentally; profitably; strangely; oddly; beneficially; opportunely; properly; admirably; wonderfully; extraordinarily; amazingly; surprisingly; unaccountably; extremely; acceptably; uncommonly; usefully.

MEDICINE

adjectives
loathed; cooling; sudorific; preventive; multiplying; domestic; reform; heavenly; native; proprietary; astringent.

verbs
administer—; anoint with—; dispense—; endorse—; gulp down—; instil—; measure—; overdose with—; prescribe—; reject—;

specialize in—; swallow—; verse in—; — allays; —alleviates; —palliates; —purges.

(See iodine, emetic, enema, laxative, liniment.)

MEDIOCRE
adverbs

hopelessly; indefensibly; undeniably; stupidly; dully; stodgily; uninterestingly; boresomely; tediously; monotonously; crudely; crassly; inexcusably; unaccountably; surprisingly; amazingly; terribly; unexpectedly; unwarrantably; awkwardly; provincially; tiresomely; dreadfully; pitiably; miserably; wretchedly.

MEDIOCRITY
adjectives

solemn; witless; practiced; superlative.

verbs

allow—; approve—; attain—; avoid—; condemn—; cringe in—; criticize—; disparage —; lift from—; respect—; —begets; —endures; —eclipses; —perseveres; —starves; —subjugates; —succeeds.

(See inferiority.)

MEDITATE (v)
adverbs

pensively; gloomily; seriously; morbidly; sedately; dispassionately; bitterly; wilfully; restlessly; whimsically; religiously; serenely; monotonously; characteristically; habitually.

(See muse, ponder, reflect, think.)

MEDITATION
adjectives

profound; portentous; heavenly; important; threadbare; silent; devout; thoughtless; restless; solemn; pensive; starred; whimsical; crude; fearful; plotting; holy; rapid; sullen; lofty; numerous (pl); serene; reconstructive; continual.

verbs

abide in—; absorb in—; bathe in—; build in—; discern through—; draw from—; fall into—; fix in—; immerse in—; neglect—; recall in—; recess in—; recline in—; shroud in—; spend in—; steep in—; wander in—; weave in—; wrap in—; —ensures; —nurses; —solaces; —strengthens.

(See contemplation, thought, philosophy, reflection, reverie.)

MEDITATIVE
adverbs

gravely; quietly; habitually; temperamentally; strangely; naturally; seriously; soberly; deeply; profoundly; studiously; reminiscently; remarkably; unduly; thoughtfully; inscrutably; solemnly; earnestly; dangerously; pensively; wistfully; philosophically; pointedly.

MEDIUM
adjectives

congenial; diaphanous; sympathetic; fleeting; meteoric; tangible; appropriate; accurate; ethereal; desirable; suitable; pictorial; cooling; proselytizing; surrounding; reliable; graphic; inaccurate; just; ridiculous; interpreting; ambient; pulsing; circulating; supporting; favored; laborious.

MEEK
adverbs

gently; quietly; submissively; modestly; humbly; supplicatingly; serenely; disgustingly; obsequiously; unnecessarily; provokingly; stupidly; miserably; wretchedly; tragically; passively; tranquilly; patiently; placidly; philosophically; gracefully; sedately; demurely; contentedly.

MEEKNESS
adjectives

proud; subdued; female; reverent; swaggering.

MEET (v)
adverbs

coincidentally; accidentally; nocturnally; surreptitiously; forcibly; casually; unwaveringly; tacitly; traditionally; solemnly; memorably; convivially; temperately; fraternally.

(See confront, encounter.)

MEETING
adjectives

turbulent; commonplace; accidental; pleasant; pietistic; traditional; conducive; friendly; solemn; merry; accidental; fortunate; momentous; revival; immediate; memorable; fictitious; soul-trying; convivial; midweek; agitated; temperance; memorial; factious; revolutionary.

verbs

address—; anticipate—; arrange—; ban—; convoke—; devise—; dwell on—; enjoy—; forecast—; foster—; plan—; plot—; promote—; shun—; —brightens; —charms; —delights; —excites; —pains; —quickens; —rekindles; —revives; —sharpens; —thrills; —unites.

(See convention, conference, hearing, assembly, appointment, encounter.)

MELANCHOLY

adjectives

gentle; tranquil; appropriate; natural; funereal; vague; delicious; dull-eyed; hungry; deep; tired; congenital; silent; soft; waning; quiet; gloomy; faithful; inviting; mild-eyed; sweetest; moral; vague; forbidding; bovine; resolute; rude; touching; moody; lovely; customary; profound; savage; constitutional; young; sentimental; somber; depressing.

verbs

charge with—; chase away—; conceal—; discern—; dissipate—; merge into—; sink into—; succumb to—; suffer—; —oppresses; —perks up; —shadows; —touches.

(See gloom, depression, dejection, mood, sadness.)

adverbs

alarmingly; unduly; incurably; stupidly; moodily; churlishly; sullenly; strangely; naturally; inherently; temperamentally; dangerously; doggedly; extraordinarily; inordinately; gloomily; heavily; cheerlessly; unhappily; lugubriously; mournfully; solemnly; dismally; lamentably; glumly; pensively; grimly; desolately.

MELLOW

adverbs

lusciously; delectably; pleasantly; agreeably; softly; richly; naturally; ripely; charmingly; benevolently; harmoniously; melodiously; sweetly; gorgeously; delicately; progressively; groggily; perfectly; adequately; sufficiently; amazingly; surprisingly; astonishingly; unexpectedly.

MELODIOUS

adverbs

delicately; exquisitely; triumphantly; enchantingly; thrillingly; convivially; boomingly; companionably; agreeably; plaintively; ecstatically; sweetly; liltingly; gracefully; meltingly; unutterably; strangely; soothingly; blissfully; lightly; lingeringly; saucily; hauntingly; catchingly; rollickingly; romantically; softly.

MELODRAMA

adjectives

virtuous; cheap; sentimental; exciting; underdone; celebrated; morbid; bloodcurdling.

verbs

applaud—; climax—; compose—; descend to—; dress in—; engage in—; formulize—; hiss—; impassion—; introduce—; lean toward—; overrate—; pattern—on; rehearse —; revive—; ridicule—; sink into—; —appeals; —bores; —exaggerates; —inspires; —intrigues; —lags; —thrives; —thrills; —touches.

(See play, opera, magic, pantomine, performance, tragedy, trick, act, comedy.)

MELODY

adjectives

celestial; untutored; strenuous; cloying; minstrel; delightsome; uplifted; faint-toned; venomed; wild; joyous; wondrous; beguiling; triumphant; exquisite; delicate; ravishing; stirring; vagrant; organic; harmonic; enchanting; sweetest; heavenly; thrilling; booming; siren; high; sky-born; congenial; conjuring; ancient; plaintive; unfailing; untaught; agreeable; liquid; chastened; efflorescent; breaking; consoling; unintelligible; symmetrical; ecstatic; oblivious; unearthly; hireling; nerve-dissolving; elegant; fresh; enchanted; delicious; pathetic; characteristic; rhythmic; facile; inspired; sustained; superabundant; acquired; original; sweet; lilting; exalted; stately; terrible; distinct; enervating; immortal.

verbs

air—; chant—; chorus—; compose—; drench in—; drown—; hum—; imprison—; improvise—; join in—; lilt to—; modulate —; wheedle—out of; —gratifies; —haunts; —heralds; —lingers; —rings out; —soars; —wanes.

(See chant, air, jazz, incantation, song, refrain.)

MELT (v)

adverbs

indistinctly; indefinably; silently; exquisite-

ly; scientifically; methodically; deliciously;
sweetly; appetizingly.
(See dissolve.)

MEMBER

verbs
admit—; coerce—; collaborate with—s; defend—; elect—; entertain—; honor—; invite
—; limit—s; register—; —attends; —s
band; —benefits; —charters; —contributes;
—s convene; —heeds; —s incorporate; —
organizes; —s rally; —undertakes; —votes.
(See faculty, classmate, congressman.)

MEMBERS

adjectives
prominent; mutinous; respectable; superfluous; consistent; confidential; eligible;
eminent; numerous; obscure; vivacious; distinguished; myriad; mateless; influential;
sundry; impecunious; self-respecting; illustrious; discordant; efficient; able; honorable; daring; exemplary; acceptable; conspicuous; representative; worthy; significant; right-thinking; learned; excitable;
geometric; noxious; surviving; discredited;
objectionable; disjointed; privileged; fat;
sturdy; self-respecting; honest; erratic; devout; subsidiary; law-abiding; amiable;
nicely educated; infatuated; disaffected; insubordinate; sundry (pl); corporeal; oracular; useless; unruly; violent; arbitrary;
pronounced; cherished.

MEMBERSHIP

adjectives
distinguished; enormous; compulsory; unstable.

verbs
admit to—; desire—; discontinue—; elect
to—; forfeit—; increase—; invite to—; limit
—; register—; renew—; seek—; tabulate
—; usher in—; vote on—; —concentrates;
—expires; —includes; —requires; —terminates.

MEMBRANE

adjectives
previous; feather-covered; thin; gauzelike.

verbs
affect—; incise—; irritate—; perforate—;
puncture—; shed—; soothe—; stretch—;
swell—; thicken—; ulcerate—; —atrophies;
—bulges; —erodes; —lines; —ruptures; —
vibrates; —wastes.
(See film, eardrum.)

MEMENTO

adjectives
painful; ever-changing; grave; appropriate;
melancholy; lovely; sacred.

MEMORIAL

adjectives
cypress; suitable; tender; dubious; frail;
worthy; peevish; poetic; sculptured; faded;
dogmatic; energetic; living.

verbs
address—; bestow in—; carve—; contribute
to—; dedicate—; draw up—; endow—; engrave—; erect—; inscribe—; merit—; petition for—; raise—; —commemorates; —
credits; —describes; —glorifies; —honors;
—perpetuates; —portrays; —preserves; —
recounts.
(See medal, trophy, monument.)

MEMORIES

adjectives
comfortless; tragic; ungracious; hurting;
multicolored; muscular; grateful; faithful;
hateful; pious; projected; rustling; suggestive; prompt; retentive; feeble; thronging;
lamentable; long-to-be-cherished; conscious;
color; unshaken; magnificent; unwelcome;
artificial; white-lipped; sightless; puissant;
vivid; surprising; ineffable; distinct; jarring; royal; incomparable; healthiest; disastrous; seductive; encyclopedia; disordered; glistening; usurious; aching; retributive; vindictive; solemn; ludicrous; blessed;
confused; melodious; agreeable; natural;
delightful; uncanny; bellicose; dark; animated; passionate; primeval; delicious; immortal; gay; infamous; ballad; dear; capacious; personal; living; impressive; vital;
sacred; withered; sorrowful; pleasant; trifling; haunting; drowsy; fragrant; cherished; gossipy; atrocious; submerged; vapid;
remorseful; tenacious; prodigious; amused;
lingering; bright; stirred; sluggish; human;
personified; resplendent; biographical;
vague; fleeting; half-forgotten; endearing;
dusty; eventful; fragmentary; weary; exhausted; deadly; deficient; precious; unbreathed; overwhelming; ghostlike; distorted; honored; detailed; time-fraught;
everlasting; mutual; unfading; hereditary;
intimate; lofty; public; blurred; rueful;
embarrassed; unaccountable; imperfect;

bitter; accurate; emergent; grisly; musical; phenomenal; inevitable; priceless; unconscious; amazing; lurid; dormant; warming; enticing.

MEMORY
(faculty of remembering)
verbs
blur—; bury in—; cloud—; commit to—; drug—; dull—; engrave upon—; escape—; explore—; impair—; imprint on—; quote from—; strike—; coruscates; —paints; —pictures; —retains; —wanders.

(See mind, brain, consciousness, intellect.)

MEMORY
(reminiscence)
verbs
awaken—ies; blot out—; brood over—ies; cherish—; cling to—; dim—; dispel—; elucidate—; erase—; evoke—ies; freshen—; hallow—; honor—; haunt—; live in—; nurse—; nurture—; obliterate—; refresh—; revive—; shun—; suppress—; swap—ies; toy with—; treasure—; venerate—; —fades; —gnaws; —lingers; —pains; —surges; —survives.

(See remembrance, recollection.)

MEN
adjectives
vainglorious; succeeding; smooth-shaven; trampled; deft; glowing-eyed; up-and-doing; fashion-minded; fallible; able-bodied; orthodox; cringing; soft-conscienced; clear-witted; pusillanimous; decayed; banished; laconic; traitorous; hackneyed; sated; childless; huge-limbed; best-informed; best-tempered; insensate; ruling.

MENACE
adjectives
triple; significant; constant; mingled; dismal; ever-fearful; ominous; positive; deadly; feeble; dangerous; international; wrathful; crushing; serious; perpetual; fierce; terrible; transparent; owl-eyed; enticing; subdued; black.

verbs
avert—; banish—; conceal—; constitute—; denounce—; eradicate—; fear—; guard against—; harbor—; inveigh against—; invoke—; level—; share—; stamp out—; uncover—; ward off—; —endangers; —jeopardizes.

(See threat, peril, danger.'

MENACE (v)
adverbs
seriously; portentously; ominously; dismally; dangerously; perpetually; fiercely; blackly; morally; seductively.

(See threaten, portend.)

MENAGE
verbs
adopt—; attach to—; bully—; conduct—; govern—; head—; install in—; involve—; join—; manage—; occupy—; recommend—; regulate—; superintend—; supervise—; support—; visit—; —bickers; —delights; —disperses.

(See home.)

MEND (v)
adverbs
appreciably; exquisitely; deftly; dexterously; cleverly; artfully; radically; expertly; artistically.

(See repair, patch, improve.)

MENDACIOUS
adverbs
wickedly; venomously; spitefully; vengefully; maliciously; hatefully; viciously; notoriously; infamously; openly; shamelessly; treacherously; dangerously; trickily; craftily; arrantly; undeniably; brazenly; slyly; surreptitiously; atrociously; deplorably; lamentably; oddly; unaccountably; terribly; deliberately; shrewdly; meretriciously.

MENDACITY
adjectives
conscienceless; bugbear; deliberate; habitual; disreputable.

MENIAL
adverbs
odiously; basely; meanly; humbly; obsequiously; cringingly; pliantly; terribly; unaccountably; obediently; subserviently; obscurely; boorishly; pitiably; miserably; wretchedly; churlishly; incredibly.

MENSTRUATION
verbs
arrest—; delay—; disorder—; endure—; establish—; force—; induce—; perform—; retard—; stimulate—; suffer during—; suppress—; —ceases; —commences; —distresses; —exhausts; —fatigues; —impoverishes; —pains; —pauses; —strains.

adjectives

subconscious; practical; assumed; criminal; twisted; careless; subnormal; unbalanced.

verbs

burden—; check—; clog—; contemplate—; contribute to—; develop—; endow with—; exhaust—; furnish with—; impede—; limit —; nourish—; perfect—; relax—; repair—; strain—; tax—; tug at—; undermine—; — evolves from; —flags; —slackens.

(See brain, faculty, cleverness, brilliance, talent.)

MENTION

adjectives

special; passing; honorable; casual; fleeting; complimentary; occasional; copious; nonchalant.

verbs

deserve—; earn—; forbid—; merit—; peeve at (colloq.)—; report—; —alludes to; — describes; —disgusts; —excites; —inflames; —offends.

(See repetition, notice, remark, statement, utterance.)

MENTION (v)

adverbs

secretly; umbrageously; incidentally; mincingly; modestly; casually; nonchalantly; ominously; slanderously; slyly; inadvertently.

(See tell, reveal, relate, advise, expose.)

MENU

adjectives

proper; prescribed; balanced; convalescent; varied; nourishing.

verbs

alter—; approve—; arrange—; check—; compose—; consult—; dispatch—; glean from—; plan—; relish—; serve—; vary—; —appeals; —catalogues; —details; —lists; —nourishes; —offers; —prices; —suggests; —sustains; —tempts.

(See program, list.)

MERCANTILE

adverbs

highly; profitably; successfully; propitiously; negotiably; speculatively; stably; regularly; admirably; advantageously; prosperously; usefully; preeminently; obviously.

MERCENARY

adverbs

stingily; sordidly; basely; penuriously; greedily; deliberately; openly; obviously; manifestly; amazingly; surprisingly; selfishly; shamelessly; avowedly; miserably; wretchedly; blandly; frankly; ungenerously; rapaciously; avariciously; palpably; outrageously; inconsiderately; harshly; extortionately; churlishly; unbelievably; uncommonly.

MERCHANDISE

adjectives

timely; fashionable; quality; heterogeneous; exclusive; styled-right; jointed; seasonable.

verbs

assess—; bargain for—; catalogue—; claim —; close out—; convey—; dispense—; endow with—; evaluate—; hawk—; invest in —; liquidate—; overstock with—; peddle —; purchase—; purvey—; retail—; sacrifice—; salvage—; surrender—; turn over —; underwrite—; wholesale—.

(See imports, material, supply.)

MERCHANT

adjectives

respected; shaggy; successful; affluent; prudent; timorous; independent; prominent; sagacious; enterprising; prosperous; staid; sensible; clear-eyed; retired.

verbs

bargain with—; patronize—; —auctions; — deals in; —dispenses; —disposes of; — hawks; —jobs; —markets; —negotiates; — profits; —purveys; —puts under the hammer; —realizes a profit; —retails; —speculates; —traffics in; —transacts; —vends; —wholesales; —undersells.

(See hawker, jeweler, banker.)

MERCIFUL

adverbs

abundantly; benevolently; benignly; suddenly; habitually; kindly; generously; surprisingly; unaccountably; gravely; happily; fortunately; moderately; remarkably; exceedingly; compassionately; wondrously; uncommonly; infinitely; tenderly.

MERCILESS

adverbs

cruelly; bitterly; terribly; ruthlessly; pitilessly; relentlessly; stonily; sanctimoniously; rigidly; unfeelingly; hard-heartedly; maliciously; basely; incredibly; immovably; unspeakably; coldly; vengefully; unsparingly; tyrannically; sternly; abominably; barbarously; brutally; savagely; uncommonly; habitually.

MERCURIAL
adverbs
blithely; capriciously; delightfully; captivatingly; nimbly; actively; captiously; wantonly; cheerfully; changefully; inconstantly; craftily; unpredictably; problematically; perplexingly; irrationally; unreasonably; vivaciously; fascinatingly; temperamentally; unstably; merrily; erratically; waywardly; vagrantly; restlessly; nomadically; lightly; interestingly; casually.

MERCURY
verbs
administer—; anoint with—; drain—; inject —; scale—; —ascends; —contracts; —corrodes; —descends; —estimates; —expands; —gauges; —graduates; —impends; —measures; —poisons; —sublimates; —threatens; —warns.
(See chemical, medicine, thermometer, barometer.)

MERCY
adjectives
intellectual; wondrous; holy; tender; weakeyed; ill-judged; noble; infinite; crowning; marvelous; common; eternal; devilish; saving; scant; lawful; hopeless; imperial; wonted; mutual; single; pardoning; gentle.

verbs
beg—; crown with—; dispose toward—; excite—; exercise—; extend—; favor with —; forbear out of—; grace with—; grant —; howl for—; implore—; invoke—; judge with—; lack—; lend—; plead for—; recommend—; rejoice in—; soften in—; sue for —; supplicate—; temper with—; tender—; throw upon—of; vouchsafe—; win—; — relents; —restrains; —spares; —thaws; — yields.
(See forbearance, grace, clemency, compassion, pity.)

MERETRICIOUS
adverbs
abominably; atrociously; unmentionably; dreadfully; unspeakably; pretentiously; shamelessly; bawdily; spuriously; indecor-

ously; coarsely; grossly; barbarously; outlandishly; monstrously; horridly; painfully; shockingly; particularly.

MERGE (v)
aaverbs
gradually; perpetually; conveniently; artfully; artistically; unconsciously; completely; superficially.
(See absorb, swallow.)

MERIT
adjectives
unusual; intrinsic; eminent; neglected; spectacular; unpopular; respective; artistic; patient; peculiar; multifarious; remarkable; comparative; indignant; solid; bashful; starving; toilworn; injured; mute; relative; ostensible; supereminent; accumulated; palpable; scientific; telling; strongest; transcendent; distinctive; technical; allsufficient; literary; aesthetic; striking; humbled; uneven; prime; essential; rare; tangible; productive; singular; doubtful; weaker; lap-dog; cardinal; noticeable; satisfying; conspicuous.

verbs
attain—; authorize—; award—; claim—; command—; confer—upon; detract from—; discuss—s; disclaim—; disclose—; dispute —; emulate—; entitle to—; esteem—; exhibit—; impute—to; judge—s; mark with —; overrate—s; rate—; reward with—; rival—; sanction—; test—; value—; vie for—; vindicate—; warrant—.
(See reward, advantage.)

MERIT (v)
adverbs
modestly; genuinely; justly; unquestionably; substantially; incalculably; ostensibly; justifiably; intrinsically; eminently; aesthetically; essentially; conspicuously.
(See deserve, earn.)

MERITORIOUS
adverbs
highly; uncommonly; manifestly; admirably; marvelously; unusually; laudably; exceptionally; splendidly; magnificently; indubitably; satisfactorily; estimably; appreciably; commendably; extremely.

adjectives

spasmodic; boisterous; continual; misplaced; hollow; apparent; considerable; tricksy; inward; thoughtless; sympathetic; ill-timed; quavering; rustic; mocking; chilling; joyous; merciless; excited; openhearted; adventurous; disproportional; infinite.

verbs

contribute to—; disport with—; feign—; frolic in—; frown on—; occasion—; regale with—; rejoice in—; reproach for—; revel in—; romp in—; —amuses; —brightens; — cheers; —convulses; —dies; —drives away care; —eases; —enlivens; —entertains; — flows; —palls; —perks up; —relaxes; — solaces; —titillates.

(See frolic, humor, glee, gayety, laughter, jollity, joy, fun.)

MERRY

adverbs

blithely; happily; mischievously; childishly; excitedly; madly; bewitchingly; ecstatically; joyously; naturally; habitually; inherently; mysteriously; noisily; boisterously; apparently; infinitely; hilariously; facetiously; jovially; genially; convivially; sportively; extremely; delightfully; fascinatingly; comically; drolly; briskly; exceedingly.

MESH

adjectives

mysterious; golden; tangled; guilty; glittering; shattered; legal; airy.

verbs

avert—; construct—; dangle in—; drain through—; elude—; entangle in—; extricate from—; interlace—; thread through—; weave—; —cages; —deceives; —ensnares; —fences off; —nets; —nonpluses; —perplexes; —puzzles; —sifts; —traps.

(See chain, complication.)

MESS

adjectives

nasty; dreadful; horrible; entire; filthy; viscid; savory; unholy; utmost; jovial; hoggish.

verbs

adulterate—; blend—; brew—; concoct—; entangle in—; ferment—; hash—; jumble into—; knead—; pound to—; reduce to—; shuffle into—; unravel—; —complicates; —

confuses; —disarrays; —disorders; —embarrasses; —litters; —muddles; —perplexes; —ruffles; —rumples.

(See junk, rubbish, waste.)

MESSAGE

adjectives

effective; divine; heartfelt; urgent; eternal; lucid; affectionate; turbulent; diabolical; true; expressive; unheeded; heated; spurred; dusty; private; precious; loving; telegraphic; sociological; farewell; verbal; pertinent; leaden; conciliatory; unanswered; assuring; rebukeful; laconic; distinct; luminous; terse; cryptic; hurried; alarming; instant; pitying; mysterious; speechless; heavenly; jubilee; anticipated; thrilling; crumpled; civil; rock-hewn; flattering; peevish; horrid; universal; vaunting; insurgent; faltering; ringing.

verbs

authenticate—; bear—; cable—; charge with—; communicate—; confirm—; convey —; decipher—; despatch—; dictate—; entrust—to; flash—; impart—; interpret—; issue—; narrate—; relay—; report—; signal—; telegraph—; transmit—; —informs; —rings; —stirs; deliver—.

(See errand, dispatch, letter, mail, manuscript.)

MESSENGER

adjectives

celestial; gracious; convenient; pure; winged; mindful; bonded; dusky; mourning; surly; arbitrating; angelic; trustworthy; distempered; shining; impatient; giddy; mystical; special; courageous; strong; churlish; guiltless; awe-stricken; wing-footed; breathless; welcome; better.

verbs

appoint—; assign—; consign to—; delegate —; dispatch—; —apprizes of; —bears; — communicates with; —confirms; —conveys; —declares; —delivers; —embarks; —forwards; —heralds; —imparts; —informs; — races; —reports; —reveals; —speeds; — transfers; —wings.

(See apostle, angel, emissary, delegate.)

MESSY

adverbs

abominably; dreadfully; hopelessly; unnecessarily; unduly; needlessly; confusedly; chaotically; intricately; confoundedly; untidily; shapelessly; irreducibly; inexcusably; unpardonably; unusually; inexplicably; unwarrantably; unspeakably; carelessly; filthily; crazily; surprisingly; extremely; indescribably.

METAL

adjectives

barren; engraving; sonorous; basic; combustible; glittering; mystical; precious; serviceable; non-tarnishable; best-tempered; burnished; invaluable; well-wrought; twisted; gleaming.

verbs

alloy—; assay—; cast—; congeal—; decarbonize—; engrave—; excavate—; hammer out—; model in—; mold—; prospect for—; refine—; render—; sheathe in—; smelt—; stamp—; strike—; value—; weld—; —corrodes; —expands; —oxidizes; —preserves.

(See lead, copper, coin, gold, iron, mineral.)

METAPHOR

adjectives

far-fetched; abundant; developed; suggestive; consistent; bucolic; striking.

verbs

abound with—s; apply—; employ—; —allegorizes; —alludes to; —collates; —colors; —compares; —contrasts; —depicts; —identifies; —illuminates; —illustrates; —likens; —parallels; —personifies; —portrays.

(See figure, word, phrase, paragraph, simile.)

METEOR

adjectives

disastrous; new-forged; unexpected; lurid; ominous; alarming; sudden; wandering; large; mighty; scarlet; cloud-encircled; descending; unctuous; deceitful.

METEORIC

adverbs

luridly; alarmingly; startlingly; swiftly; gloriously; incredibly; glowingly; splendidly; brilliantly; unbelievably; inconceivably; curiously; abruptly; miraculously; strangely; amazingly; astonishingly.

METER
(*instrument*)

adjectives

mystic; unconventional; inaccurate; dainty.

verbs

check—; feed—; flood—; —allots; —appoints; —apportions; —appraises; —assesses; —assizes; —compounds; —dispenses; —estimates; —graduates; —measures; —portions; —plumbs; —probes; —proportions; —records; —scales; —values.

(See barometer, thermometer, mercury.)

METHOD

adjectives

opposite; economical; selfsame; ingenious; inductive; haphazard; peaceful; laborious; scrupulous; numberless; hustling; indirect; exalting; novel; honorable; elaborate; summary; unostentatious; artistic; deductive; radio; unnatural; advantageous; clumsy; gruesome; commercialized; painless; convenient; statistical; authoritarian; getting; instinctive; conservative; picturesque; substantial; unique; dangerous; antiseptic; photographic; modern; up-to-the-minute; unsurpassed; therapeutic; orthodox; old-fashioned; lucid; prudent; time-honored; patented; scientific; sweet; objective; tentative; wholesome; plating; monstrous; philosophical; primitive; factory; despotic; imperturbable; feasible; transient; advertising; suitable; vociferous; unceremonious; naturalistic; lawful; evasive; subjective; preposterous; superstitious; accepted; surreptitious; particular; thoughtful; subversive; dilatory; peculiar; realistic; comely; inferior; outworn; analytic; amazing; humane; unpretending; histrionic; mystical; foolish; political; exclusive; dogmatic; equitable; ever-changing; descriptive; revolting; slack; peaceable; costly; doctrinal; appropriate; shrewd; false; ideal; autographic; financing; simplified; parliamentary; reproductive; pedantic; dictatorial; administrative; mild; barbarous; ignominious; collaborative; time-tried; indistinguishable; desultory; efficacious; inconsequent; injudicious; obsolescent; intuitive; glamorous; subtle; prosodic; avowed; current; fixation; enlarged; straightforward.

verbs

abandon—; abuse—; adopt—; advocate—; antedate—; ape—; apply—; conceive—; condemn—; design—; develop—; devise—; discard—; discover—; employ—; evolve—; exploit—; formulate—; introduce—; justify —; modify—; probe—; propose—; pursue

769

—; reform—; repudiate—; resort to—; revolutionize—; supplant—; supplement—.
(See procedure, process, fashion, manner.)

METHODICAL
adverbs
carefully; habitually; inherently; dependably; reliably; warrantably; overly; punctiliously; meticulously; outlandishly; comically; absurdly; rigidly; painfully; vexatiously; admirably; laudably; naturally; systematically; pleasantly; disagreeably; incredibly; unduly; uncomfortably; terribly.

METICULOUS
adverbs
carefully; painfully; disagreeably; uncomfortably; unduly; curiously; extremely; admirably; laudably; unfailingly; systematically; outlandishly.

METRICAL
adverbs
cleverly; pleasantly; melodiously; carefully; smartly; cunningly; ingeniously; delightfully; tunefully; skillfully; harmoniously; enchantingly; mellifluously; artfully.

METROPOLIS
adjectives
exciting; throbbing; expectant; dazzling; holiday; commercial; perfume; mystical; huge; monstrous.

METTLE
adjectives
invincible; unimproved; scientific.

METTLESOME
adverbs
highly; vivaciously; animatedly; boldly; undauntedly; dauntlessly; cheerfully; sturdily; actively; pluckily; courageously; spiritedly; gayly; uncommonly; remarkably; notoriously; commendably; obviously; unusually; energetically; strenuously; vigorously; intensely; restlessly; ungovernably; uncontrollably; audaciously; valiantly; adventurously.

MEW (v)
adverbs
plaintively; sympathetically; maternally; shrilly; vociferously.
(See cry, wail.)

MICROPHONE
verbs
adjust—; announce through—; broadcast through—; confront—; perform before—; —amplifies; —clarifies; —communicates with; —conveys; —enables; —intensifies; —magnifies; —transmits.
(See loudspeaker.)

MICROSCOPE
verbs
adjust—; contemplate through—; discern through—; employ—; examine under—; focus—; glance into—; incline—; observe under—; peep through—; peer into—; rivet upon—; scrutinize through—; squint through —; view through—; —augments; —detects; —distinguishes; —enables; —enlarges; —exaggerates; —magnifies; —reveals.
(See telescope.)

MICROSCOPIC
adverbs
minutely; infinitesimally; incredibly; curiously; ingeniously; unbelievably; amazingly; imperceptibly.

MIDDLE
verbs
ascertain—; assemble in—; balance in—; cast in—; cleave in—; cling to—; concentrate in—; contract in—; converge on—; designate—; focus on—; intersect in—; narrow toward—; proceed from—; situate in —; split in—; taper toward—; —averages; —centralizes; veer toward—.
(See interior, surface, center, bottom.)

MIDDLE-AGED
adverbs
hopelessly; permanently; persistently; miserably; wretchedly; doggedly; pertinaciously; arthritically; rheumatically; pleasantly; hoarily; venerably; patriarchally; wirily; delightfully; obviously; youthfully.

MIDNIGHT
adjectives
impenetrable; fierce; profoundest; sedentary; sleek; beautiful; drear; blackest.

MIDSHIPMAN
verbs
amuse—; appoint—; consign—to; convey—; delegate—; furlough—; promote—; school

—; train—; —crams; —embarks; —hoists; —marches; —plies; —promenades; — rooms; —sails; —tours.
(See sailor, officer, soldier.)

MIEN
adjectives
stately; gallant; placid; sullen; distant; spirited; haughty; conciliating; graceful; awe-inspiring; impressive; dejected; warlike; thoughtful; majestic; haggard; awkward; portentous; joyless; free; daring; noble; solemn; lofty; bold; withering; somber; undaunted; royal.

verbs
alter—; amend—; assume—; **contemplate** —; convert—; devise—; disguise—; eye—; influence—; modify—; present—; repose—; —awes; —conveys; —distresses; —disturbs; —enhances; —glares; —glows; —inspires; —menaces; —sours; —threatens.
(See demeanor, air, aspect, manner.)

MIGHT
adjectives
eternal; transparent; royal; truehearted; imposing; congregated; individual; withered; conquering; irresistible; apparent; fancied; divine; austere; intimate; unimaginable; ravenous; spacious; towering; resistless; delicious; outworn; borrowed; restless; wholesome; human; overmastering; brutal.

MIGRATION
adjectives
voluntary; forcible; autumnal; barbaric; instinctive.

MILD
adverbs
harmlessly; pleasantly; serenely; compassionately; reasonably; urbanely; blandly; suavely; affably; genially; tolerantly; complaisantly; leniently; judiciously; discreetly; diplomatically; carefully; placidly; imperturbably; philosophically; sedately; demurely; patiently; unctuously; graciously; ingratiatingly; winningly; tactfully.

MILDNESS
adjectives
resigned; mellow; incomparable; delicate.

MILE
verbs
advance—; clear—; detour—; estimate—; extend—; lag—; march—; progress—; pursue—; race—; recede—; total—s; trail for —s; trek—; withdraw—; —s drag; —s separate; —s weary.
(See distance.)

MILEAGE
adjectives
railroad; tire; maximum; gasoline; trip.

MILES
adjectives
dusky; tortuous; uncheered; weary; glistening; merry; laborious; geographical; delectable; glittering; appalling; snow-covered.

MILITARIST
adjectives
battering; greedy; professional; grasping; bloodthirsty; heartless.

MILITIA
adjectives
uniformed; hurrying; insubordinate.

verbs
arm—; arouse—; call out—; drill—; encounter—; enlist in—; discipline—; maintain—; muster—; qualify for—; recall—; regulate—; round up—; train—; —combats; —defends; —guards; —interferes; — mobilizes; —patrols; —pickets; —repels.
(See army, navy, regiment, soldier, troops.)

MILK
adjectives
tepid; acidophilus; skimmed; innocent; pulpy; metabolized; putrid; sour.

verbs
absorb—; administer—; churn—; concentrate—; condense—; contaminate—; curdle —; deprive of—; dilute—; draw—; extract from—; flavor—; pasteurize—; predigest—; rear on—; sip—; skim—; sour—; subsist on—; substitute—; taint—; thicken—; wean on—; —nourishes; —sustains.
(See food, cream.)

adjectives
neighboring; clanking; slander; mortgaged; social; busy; penetrating; muffled.

verbs
design—; establish—; guard—; manage—; operate—; picket—; report to—; set up—; speed up—; stock—; supervise—; —composes; —constructs; —frames; —manufactures; —organizes; —produces; —shuts down; —unionizes.
(See factory, shop, business, company, laboratory.)

MILL (*v*)

adverbs
eddyingly; riotously; alarmingly; tumultuously; disorderly; boisterously; actively.
(See reduce, crush.)

MILLION

adjectives
hardy; countless; shatterproof; mildewed; dark.

MILLIONAIRE

adjectives
senatorial; practical; decrepit; radical; amiable; myopic; eccentric; dirty-handed.

MIME

adjectives
mechanic; deft.

MIMIC (*v*)

adverbs
skillfully; audaciously; sardonically; sedulously; aptly; deftly; professionally; irritatingly; exasperatingly; roguishly.
(See mock, imitate.)

MINARETS

adjectives
slender; delicate; candle-extinguisher.

MINCE (*v*)

adverbs
primly; exaggeratedly; fastidiously; fashionably; wantonly; affectedly; delicately.
(See walk, step.)

MIND

adjectives
agitated; iron; conclusive; grosser; trained; thrifty; astute; observing; unbalanced; liberal; logical; far-seeing; poetic; subtle; self-assured; conniving; contented; invisible; taintless; zealous; capricious; towering; feminine; swift; virtuous; shallow; untutored; courageous; languid; downcast; discriminating; controlling; well-trained; creative; philosophical; illustrious; pulverized; wavering; versatile; earthly; uncomplex; illuminated; earnest; weak; effeminate; careless; mortal; anxious; troubled; unthinking; terrestrial; dispassionate; exalted; elegant; reluctant; sympathetic; backward-looking; vigorous; romancing; ingenuous; tranquil; thoughtful; vulgar; twisted; imaginative; expanding; longing; pensive; unclean; virgin; sublimest; youthful; unconventional; flexible; restless; lethargic; conservative; apprehensive; erring; educated; enlightened; impressible; golden; distracted; lofty; inventive; disordered; undebauched; meditative; invoking; irritated; silly; fractional; preoccupied; giant; pure; soaring; gifted; exploring; ill-trained; independent; active; disburdened; ingenious; colossal; turbulent; callous; affrighted; cultivated; inattentive; exasperated; infinite; writhing; queasy; well-purged; honest; charming; quivering; unconquerable; wooing; ennobling; supersensitive; glowing; speculative; disciplined; scientific; slick; freckled; unfolding; infected; patriarchal; resourceful; unfettered; uninitiated; rude; mute; healthy; determined; mighty; realistic; abject; selfish; learned; far-reaching; devious; discriminating; plastic; brilliant; medieval; flurried; upright; respective; managerial; critical; priggish; sanguine; deferential; mercantile; superstitious; gullible; twofold; finite; percipient; grasping; mournful; wayless; reproductive; docile; theorizing; deliberating; unregenerate; reverential; unhinged; wounded; drunken; unaffected; fatuous; retentive; savage; inhospitable; self-formed; unrebellious; desecrated; diseased; sensitized; keen; serious; frivolous; infinite; robust; dissipated; intuitive; medical; canny; narrow; tabloid; deft; solitary; ductile; undergraduate; scholarly; unclouded; cheerful; nature-loving; idle; devotional; prying; high-sailing; immortal; eternal; petulant.

verbs
addle—; agitate—; assail—; attune—to; baffle—; banish—; bend—; bewilder—; broaden—; burden—; condition—; corrode—; corrupt—; convey to—; cultivate—; debauch—; delude—; depress—; detach—; de-

throne—; disabuse—; disorient—; dispel from—; distort—; divert—; drug—; ease —; emancipate—; enfeeble—; engrave on —; enslave—; explore—; fertilize—; fetter —; filter into—; focus—on; harass—; haunt —; inflame—; impress on—; lodge in—; muddle—; plant in—; penetrate—; permeate —; pervade—; pop into—; rankle in—; reproach—; seep into—; shackle—; sharpen —; stamp on—; steel—; stimulate—; torture —; unbalance—; unbare—; unburden—; unhinge—; unsettle—; warp—; weigh in—; wrench—; —conceives; —dallies; —darts back; —deteriorates; —dictates; —disturbs; —dwells upon; —dwindles; —evolves; —envisages; —masters; —pictures; —probes; —reels; —roams; —seethes; —succumbs; —wanders; —wars.

(See consciousness, brain, imagination, head, intellect, memory.)

MINDFUL

adverbs

considerately; graciously; observantly; attentively; thoughtfully; affectionately; solicitously; tenderly; compassionately; carefully; discreetly; warily; prudently; providently; courteously; admirably; remarkably; sweetly; delightfully.

MINE

adjectives

gnomed; torched; fathomless; well-developed; abandoned; vast; rich; enwombed; exhaustless; hydraulic; inexhaustible.

verbs

abandon—; bore into—; burrow into—; cede —s to; confine in—; descend into—; emerge from—; excavate—; exhaust—; extract from —; gouge—; lower into—; operate—; ravage—; scoop from—; seal—; spring—; survey—; tunnel—; work—; —extends; —yields.

(See vein, earth, ground.)

MINER

verbs

asphyxiate—; confine—; disinter—; lower —; trap—; —bores; —burrows; —descends; —digs; —emerges; —excavates; —extracts; —gropes; —saps; —scoops; —shafts; —strikes; —tunnels; —uncovers; —unearths.

(See mole.)

MINERAL

adjectives

mortal; rare; vitreous; insignificant; tooth-building; essential.

verbs

abound in—s; alloy—; assay—; drill for —s; examine—; excavate—; extract—; prospect for —s; refine—; reveal—; scoop out —; uncover—; unearth—; utilize—; value —; —nourishes.

(See lead, metal, copper, gold, iron.)

MINGLE (*v*)

adverbs

democratically; promiscuously; inextricably; discreetly; affectionately; conspicuously; bizarrely; ostensibly; curiously; blasphemously; curiously; heterogeneously; profanely.

(See associate, mix.)

MINGLING

adjectives

rough; melancholy; charming; strange; promiscuous.

MINIATURE

adverbs

delicately; curiously; fragilely; incredibly; valuably; exceptionally; uncommonly; exotically; quaintly; fantastically; fashionably; modishly; pricelessly; expensively; exquisitely; matchlessly; incomparably.

MINIMUM

adjectives

irreducible; unimportant; smallest.

MINION

adjectives

pliant; sleek; dainty; luxurious; saucy; mindless.

MINISTER

adjectives

weak; debile; empyreal; nonconformist; accredited; formidable; efficient; gracious; sullen; shortsighted; puppet; irritated; gentle; misty; mournful; thoughtful; merciful; respective; refractory; shifty; retired; influential; unprincipled; powerful; grave; obstinate; right-hand.

verbs

appoint—; charge—with; invest—with; ordain—; —chastens; —cheers; —conducts; —converts; —consoles; —corrects; —dissents;

—executes; —imparts; —influences; —meditates; —offers; —officiates; —prays; —performs; —preaches; —rebukes; —reflects; —serves; —tames; —worships.

(See elder, deacon, leader, clergy, rabbi.)

MINISTERIAL
adverbs
gravely; authoritatively; officially; urbanely; suavely; blandly; unctuously; officiously; judicially; solemnly; pompously; professionally; considerately; subserviently; affably; genially; sympathetically; formidably; graciously; gently; influentially; courteously; ostentatiously; pleasantly; agreeably; sternly; cautiously; warily; wisely; admirably; wonderfully; acceptably; curiously.

MINISTRATION
adjectives
unfaltering; kindly; feminine; servile; pulpit; sleuthing; merciful.

MINISTRY
adjectives
maternal; pestilential; virgin; corrupt; tyrannical; radiant; hopeless; arduous; gracious; angelic; stated; bright-winged; incompetent; dictatorial.

verbs
acquaint with—; appoint to—; execute—; forsake—; fulfill—; invest—; obey—; ordain by—; plunge into—; retire from—; suspend from—; train for—; —assents; —chastens; —corrects; —meditates; —officiates; —performs; —rebukes.

(See cabinet, congress, management, government, church, legislature.)

MINK
verbs
dress in—; exhibit—; farm—; market—; prize—; skin—; value—; —burrows; —digs; —dives; —excavates; —inhabits; —shies; —swims.

(See animal, fur.)

MINOR
verbs
advise—; counsel—; cradle—; dictate to—; direct—; govern—; guard—; guide—; instruct—; manage—; model—; mold—; nourish—; prompt—; shape—; sustain—; —anticipates; —assumes; —attains; —matures; —ripens into.

(See child, boy, girl, youth.)

MINORITY
adjectives
enlightened; considerable; miserable; optimistic; aggressive; loud; troublesome; excitable; strong; substantial; intelligent; zealous; fanatic; hopeless; sulky; cultured.

verbs
bind—; defeat—; deprive—; dispense with —; eliminate—; emerge from—; oppress—; organize—; overrun—; overthrow—; tyrannize—; weed out—; —bows to; —engages; —fights; —opposes; —sacrifices; —struggles; —suffers; —thins.

(See childhood, majority, alien, foreigner.)

MINSTRELSY
adjectives
college; crude; barbaric.

MINUET
verbs
compose—; create—; excel at—; fancy—; form—; hum—; lead—; popularize—; step —; walk—; —amuses; —bewitches; —charms; —delights; —dignifies; —fascinates; —flourishes; —graces.

(See dance, waltz.)

MINUTE
verbs
(See moment.)

MINUTE
adverbs
infinitesimally; incredibly; embryonically; microscopically; unbelievably; imperceptibly; extremely; invisibly; undiscoverably; unimaginably; immeasurably; incalculably; inconceivably.

MINUTES
adjectives
joy-absorbing; leaden; immortal; thievish; exquisite; marvelous; soft; miserable; hopeless; breathless; tumultuous; golden; long-cold; precious; weary; interminable; searching; copious; unoccupied; fleeting.

MINUTES
verbs (notes)
depict in—; elaborate on—; enter into—; examine—; extract from—; jot down—; present—; record—; refer to—; report—;

submit—; —describe; —enlighten; —preserve; —recall; —refresh; —retain; —retrace; —specify; —sum up.

(See entry, notes, description, record, item.)

MIRACLE

adjectives

culinary; celestial; numerous (pl); unfathomable; perpetual; incomprehensible; financial; inscrutable; established; blessed; midnight; infinite; recorded; tenderest; gracious; medieval; year-born.

verbs

accept—; accomplish—; achieve—; ascribe —to; behold—; confirm—; contradict—; credit—; deny—; display—; divine—; foretell—; gape at—; hail as—; marvel at—; prophesy—; render—; work—; —astounds; —baffles; —bewilders; —convinces; —inspires; —mystifies; —dumbfounds; —unfolds; —violates.

(See magic, wonder, surprise, mystery.)

MIRACULOUS

adverbs

unbelievably; incredibly; remarkably; wonderfully; solemnly; breath-takingly; divinely; indubitably; warrantably; manifestly; assuredly; unfathomably; inscrutably; extraordinarily; strangely; marvelously; mysteriously; ineffably; stupendously; astoundingly; unquestionably.

MIRAGE

adjectives

holy; distorted; sound; floating; vapory; exquisite.

verbs

blink at—; chase—; contemplate—; paint—; reveal—; speculate on—; view—; —confuses; —dazzles; —deludes; —disperses; —dissolves; —fades; —flickers; —hoodwinks; —lifts; —looms; —melts away; —resembles; —shifts; —tantalizes; —vanishes.

(See maze, sight, view, vision, ghost.)

MIRE

adjectives

tenacious; puddled; lamp-reflecting; sensual; foul; sucking.

verbs

cast into—; drag through—; plunge in—; sink in—; spatter in—; splash in—; stumble in—; struggle through—; trample in—; tread in—; wallow in—; —absorbs; —contaminates; —engulfs; —reeks; —sullies; —swallows.

(See mud, swamp, marsh, dirt.)

MIRROR

adjectives

lie-consuming; spacious; distorting; wavering; retroscope; disposed; silver; gleaming; magic; crystal; glorious; tarnished; liquid; blurred; level; innumerable (pl); convex; concave; enchanted; fleckless; frameless; unflattering; detachable.

verbs

address—; behold in—; consult—; discern in —; espy in—; flash in—; inspect in—; observe in—; panel—; polish—; peep in—; perceive in—; spangle with —s; stare in—; view in—; —exposes; —flickers; —glimmers; —magnifies; —reflects; —reveals; —shimmers.

(See glass, reflection, water.)

MIRROR (v)

adverbs

skillfully; distortedly; waveringly; magically; liquidly; flatteringly; realistically; unfalteringly.

(See reflect, revert.)

MIRTH

adjectives

heart-easing; profane; painful; affected; musing; careless; prolific; uproarious; sunburnt; roguish; petulant; buck-shrieked; innocent; sacred; simple; festal; unquenchable; saturnine; sympathetic; immeasurable; violent; tragical; resounding; boisterous; heathenish; uncouth; harmless; whimsical; fictitious; twinkling; Olympian; pagan; melodious; guiltless; desperate; undissembled; hollow; ill-timed; suppressed; Philistinic; dynamic; quaint; impish; ungrateful; cryptic; exuberant; frolic; rural; hysterical; meditative; unconfined; dignified; pretended; marvelous.

verbs

bar—; bathe in—; choke with—; convulse with—; disguise in—; elicit—; feign—; flood with—; glide into—; light up with—; provoke—; repent—; repress—; reprove—; shake with—; sparkle with—; wreathe in —; —bubbles; —eases; —ripples; —solaces; —swells; —trespasses; —vexes.

(See joy, glee, fun, laughter, hilarity, humor.)

MIRTHFUL

adverbs
irrepressibly; hilariously; boisterously; noisily; scintillatingly; entertainingly; uproariously; blithely; gaily; merrily; playfully; comically; mischievously; roguishly; effervescently; indescribably; youthfully; happily; significantly.

MISANTHROPIC

adverbs
dreadfully; hatefully; cynically; unhappily; miserably; wretchedly; strangely; unaccountably; painfully; stupidly; obdurately; obstinately; fanatically; bitterly; morosely; moodily; cruelly; unreasonably; queerly; incorrigibly; vexatiously; lugubriously; curiously; oddly; anti-socially; unbearably; insufferably; intolerably; unfortunately.

MISAPPREHENSION

verbs
flounder in—; incur—; labor under—; lament—; sense—; —addles; —agitates; bewilders; —confounds; —confuses; —deludes; —distorts; —embarrasses; —muddles; —perplexes; —tortures; —twists.
(See misunderstanding, uncertainty, shame, suspense, misconception.)

MISBEHAVE (*v*)

adverbs
notoriously; ceaselessly; profanely; impishly; unregenerately; drunkenly; fatuously; intolerably; maliciously; wantonly; mortifyingly; wilfully.
(See act, conduct.)

MISCARRIAGE

verbs
agitate to—; avert—; brood over—; convalesce from—; deplore—; incite—; provoke —; succumb to—; ward off—; —bereaves; —disappoints; —disconcerts; —disheartens; —frustrates; —robs; —undermines; —weakens.
(See abortion, failure, mistake, indiscretion, blunder, unhappiness.)

MISCELLANEOUS

adverbs
discouragingly; confusingly; perplexingly; promiscuously; carelessly; hopelessly; delightfully; strangely; unsystematically; un-methodically; curiously; oddly; deliberately; untidily; indiscriminately; typically; characteristically.

MISCHIEF

adjectives
desperate; secret; direst; enormous; desultory; intolerable; tormenting; malicious; wanton; mortifying; anticipated; supernatural; irreparable; impish; private; willful; stomachic.

verbs
actuate—; conceive—; confess—; contrive —; devise—; dog with—; instigate—; molest with—; plague with—; rectify—; share in—; work—; —agitates; —befalls; —besets; —disorganizes; —distresses; —enrages; —grates; —harasses; —hatches; — incenses; —piques; —provokes; —rankles; —ruffles; —torments; —trails.
(See injury, harm, damage, offense, oppression, trouble.)

MISCHIEVOUS

adverbs
incorrigibly; innocently; delightfully; teasingly; harmlessly; viciously; deliberately; childishly; merrily; thoughtlessly; maliciously; vengefully; terribly; intolerably; vexatiously; maddeningly; deliberately; studiously; craftily; shamefully; desperately; secretly; furtively; wantonly; irreparably; impishly; elfishly; purposely; wilfully; openly; defiantly; obstinately; persistently; perniciously; noxiously; naughtily; unbearably; poisonously.

MISCONCEPTION

adjectives
dangerous; huge; unworthy; singular; complete; dreadful; harmful; definite; deliberate; studied.

verbs
dissipate—; expose to—; flounder in—; scent —; twist in—; —addles; —agitates; —bewilders; —confounds; —confuses; —deludes; —distorts; —embarrasses; —endangers; —muddles; —perplexes; —torments; —tortures.
(See error, inaccuracy, fallacy, illusion, misapprehension.)

adjectives
intentional; prankish; private; flagrant; alleged; violent; open.

MISCONSTRUE (*v*)
adverbs
persistently; chronically; inevitably; recurringly; intentionally; profoundly; wilfully; tragically; cavalierly.
(See distort, twist, change.)

MISCREANT
adjectives
loathsome; meaner; apprehended; vile.

MISDEED
verbs
actuate—; boast—; confess—; confine—to; harass with —s; hatch—; lament—; molest with —s; repent—; rue—; share in—; —annoys; —distresses; —dogs; —enrages; —grates; —incenses; —piques; —rankles; —ruffles.
(See crime, deed, offense, conduct.)

MISDEMEANOR
adjectives
trifling; unlawful; ingenious.

MISER
verbs
abhor—; detest—; hiss—; scoff at—; scorn —; torment—; —accumulates; —acquires; —begrudges; —broods; —covets; —endures; —fears; —grasps; —hoards; —pinches; —sacrifices; —scants; —skins; —starves; —stints; —wrests.

MISERABLE
adverbs
wretchedly; unutterably; poignantly; visibly; helplessly; desolately; uncommonly; dismally; lonesomely; heavily; gloomily; drearily; hopelessly; disconsolately; forlornly; abjectly; dejectedly; downright; singularly; peculiarly; bitterly; cruelly; unwontedly; fretfully; sorely; oddly; incurably; intensely.

MISERLY
adverbs
inherently; incurably; basely; selfishly; crazily; stupidly; horribly; avariciously; penuriously; unaccountably; perniciously; mendaciously; sordidly; unspeakably; churlishly; greedily; rapaciously.

adjectives
untried; unrelieved; sticky; disintegrating; life-deserting; unutterable; gnawing; shadow-vested; motionless; . piercing; dim; beauteous; poignant; past; selfish; eternal; uncounted; quiet; consequent; human; tyrannical; vicious; frightful; splendid; lonely; far-off; helpless; slow; unspeakable; seething; extremest; intolerable; parasitical; petty; fictitious; attendant; remediless; lessening; dumb; appalling; deserved.

verbs
allay—; alleviate—; assuage—; augment—; deplore—; escape—; heighten—; lighten—; moan in—; moderate—; mollify—; reduce —; relieve—; repent in—; rid of—; shelter —; spare—; steep in—; waste away in—; —diminishes; —disheartens; —eases.
(See anguish, distress, ache, pain.)

MISFORTUNE
adjectives
unwonted; impending; domestic; terrible; irreparable; vital; serious; human; constant; private; possible; grave; crushing; prevailing; dire; especial; cursed; signal; admitted; unparalleled; lone.

verbs
bear—; beset by—; bow beneath—; endure —; lament—; plunge into—; remedy—; rise above—; shake off—; sob—; suffer—; triumph over—; —afflicts; —assails; —befalls; —blasts; —burdens; —distresses; —gnaws; —harrows; —heckles; —nips; —outstrips; —overtakes; —sleeps; —sours.
(See ill, evil, loss, disappointment, calamity, catastrophe, adversity, affliction, disaster.)

MISGIVINGS
adjectives
serious; shamed; dim; conscientious; restless; nervous; grave; strange; profound; sceptical; ominous.

verbs
admit—; entertain—; excite—; fence with —; flinch beneath—; harbor—; hesitate from—; inspire—; overwhelm by—; shrink in—; wrap in—; wince beneath—; —alarm; —awe; —cloud; —creep over; —disquiet; —haunt; —overwhelm; —prey on; —strike; —torment; —weigh.
(See anxiety, solicitude, worry, apprehension.)

MISGUIDED

adverbs

utterly; unfortunately; wilfully; deliberately; perniciously; unutterably; unhappily; perversely; inconsiderately; foolishly; tragically; lamentably; deplorably; woefully; sadly.

MISHAP

adjectives

untoward; dire; industrial; unavoidable; preventable; serious.

verbs

allay—; avert—; avoid—; bridge—; culminate in—; curtail —s; dodge—; guard from—; labor under—; minimize —s; mourn —; secure from—; share—; succumb to—; —botches; —swallows; —swamps.

(See disaster, accident, misfortune, catastrophe, adversity.)

MISINFORMED

adverbs

lamentably; perfidiously; sadly; bitterly; cruelly; wilfully; deliberately; treacherously; unhappily; unfortunately; maliciously; purposely; peculiarly; unwittingly; erroneously; blindly; stupidly; unwittingly; deceitfully; craftily.

MISJUDGE (*v*)

adverbs

utterly; artlessly; pathetically; perniciously; grossly; deplorably; irritatingly; ludicrously; awkwardly.

(See decide, judge.)

MISLAY (*v*)

adverbs

inadvertently; accidentally; artlessly; senselessly; singularly; absently; disastrously; deliberately; carelessly; obtusely.

(See misplace.)

MISLEAD (*v*)

adverbs

deliberately; treacherously; intentionally; evilly; murderously; unwontedly; perniciously; cruelly; irrationally.

(See decline, cheat.)

MISPLACE (*v*)

adverbs

thoughtlessly; carelessly; absently; casually; unconsciously; unfortunately.

(See mislay.)

MISREPRESENT (*v*)

adverbs

grossly; vindictively; unjustly; scandalously; intentionally; artfully; hatefully; villainously; falsely; hypocritically.

(See distort, falsify.)

MISREPRESENTATION

adjectives

gross; willful; flagrant; specious; singular; monstrous; calculated.

verbs

deceive with—; decry—; denounce—; detect—; disclose—; fall victim to—; fathom —; interpret—; refute—; sense—; suffer from—; —aggravates; —amplifies; —deludes; —distorts; —dupes; —exaggerates; —falsifies; —magnifies.

(See lie, fallacy, deception.)

MISS (*v*)

adverbs

accidentally; coincidentally; seriously; narrowly; dreadfully; tragically; unavoidably; preventably.

(See omit, overlook.)

MISSHAPEN

adverbs

cruelly; bitterly; miserably; pitiably; horribly; unspeakably; pitifully; lamentably; woefully; pathetically; accidentally; congenitally; permanently; unfortunately; unluckily; awkwardly; clumsily; helplessly; hopelessly; irremediably; grotesquely; fantastically; outlandishly; peculiarly; sadly; tragically; crookedly; gauntly; forbiddingly; grossly; frightfully.

MISSILE

adjectives

divine; deadly; terrifying; ineffectual; innocent; squashy; living; unremitting; rebounding; speedy; well-directed.

verbs

arm with—s; assail with—s; direct—; discharge—; fire—; fling—; hurl—; pelt with —s; scatter—s; shoot—s; —shakes; —stabs; —stings; —stuns; —s torment.

(See dart, weapon, arrow, bullet, stone, shot, spear.)

MISSING

adverbs

tragically; hopelessly; irrecoverably; sadly;

blankly; starkly; undeniably; presumably; supposedly; avowedly; unmistakably; mysteriously; strangely; suspiciously; curiously; altogether; allegedly; shockingly; startlingly; disconcertingly; perplexingly.

MISSION
adjectives
intuitive; blushing; world-wide; fruitless; terrestrial; proposed; divine; unearthly; honorable; great; arduous; delicate; merciful; avowed; vicarious; perilous; momentous; indefinite; sublime; apostolic; secret; diplomatic; peaceful; dubious; memorable; celestial; loftiest; subsequent; novel; cultural; consequential; hardy; noble.

verbs
accept—; authorize—; charge with—; confide—to; deter—; entrust with—; equip for —; fulfill—; gain—; hamper—; hasten—; hinder—; impose—upon; journey on—; perform—; proceed on—; reveal—; select for —; speed—; undertake—.
(See errand, commission, purpose, object, view, trust.)

MISSIONARY
adjectives
itinerant; devoted; intelligent; adroit; shabby; gentle; eloquent; conscientious.

MISSPELL (*v*)
adverbs
habitually; intentionally; grossly; carelessly; absently; humorously; stupidly; inanely.
(See spell.)

MISSTATE (*v*)
adverbs
unblushingly; ungenerously; intentionally; artfully; shrewdly; legally; solemnly; cynically; characteristically; humorously; monstrously; eccentrically.
(See distort, falsify, misrepresent.)

MISSTATEMENT
adjectives
willful; unconsidered; ungenerous; planned; leading.

MIST
adjectives
azure; horrid; genial; shimmering; jealous; thin; fragrant; friendly; shrouding; sulphurous; sickening; contaminating; matutinal; morning; undistinguishable; sea-green; starry; dark; whirling; damp; parting; chronic; impenetrable; chilly; indistinct; blinding; luminous; feudal; jeweled; coral; semilucent; opaline; silvery; golden; happy; drenching; rolling; tenuous; square; unwholesome; gleamy; amber; malarial; driving; winged; amorous; earth-born; overhanging; radiant; flaky; descending; opal; heavy; glamorous; impalpable; drifting; odorous; murky; lowering; shifting; stultifying; hoary; rising; northern; ghastly; tremulous; midnight; visionary; feeble.

verbs
emerge from—; falter in—; flounder in—; swathe in—; —befogs; —blinds; —blurs; —clears; —clings about; —darkens; —deepens; —disperses; —encircles; —enfolds; —enshrouds; —envelops; —hangs over; —hides; —lifts; —obscures; —rises; —surrounds; —veils; —wraps.
(See fog, haze, clouds, smoke, spray, steam, vapor.)

MISTAKE
adjectives
grievous; pernicious; curious; strange; dreadful; frightful; pitiful; gross; slight; desperate; fatal; unfortunate; administrative; doltish; tactical; cardinal; traffic; capital; absurd; stupid; deplorable; irritating; felicitous; unavoidable; ludicrous; contradictory; horrible; awkward; petty; tragic; initial; natural; miraculous; cruel; pathetic; military.

verbs
account for—; avoid—; bare—; blush at—; commit—; convince of—; eradicate—; minimize—s; obscure—; observe—; obviate—; overlook—; pardon—; plunge into—; rectify —; regard—.
(See lapse, inaccuracy, fault, falsehood, error, incongruity, indiscretion, blunder.)

MISTAKE (*v*)
adverbs
grievously; grossly; perniciously; curiously; desperately; doltishly; absurdly; felicitously; ludicrously; tragically; pathetically.
(See misunderstand.)

MISTAKEN
adverbs
grossly; curiously; stupidly; senselessly; perversely; stubbornly; awfully; frightfully; blindly; tragically; emphatically; griev-

ously; pitiably; desperately; absurdly; ridiculously; pathetically; horribly; outrageously; manifestly; doggedly; preposterously.

MISTREAT (v)
adverbs
brutally; cruelly; sadistically; evilly; heartlessly; callously; pervertedly.
(See abuse, misuse.)

MISTREATMENT
verbs
bear—; beset by—; bow beneath—; bridle —; brood on—; burden by—; confess to—; endure—; fear—; harass with—; harrow by—; heap—upon; lament—; resent—; revenge—; subdue by—; subject to—; suffer —; —distresses; —embitters; —enrages; —frustrates; —incenses; —numbs; —wrecks.
(See abuse, pain, torture.)

MISTRESS
adjectives
gentle; mature; worthless; doting; fair; merry; accomplished; rare; gracious; white-handed; fine; queenly; slowly-fading; exacting; sovereign; indulgent; flaming; deserted; dread; petty; proud; dainty; virtuous; mischievous; brilliant; coquettish.

verbs
attend—; chain to—; desert—; devote to—; discard—; escort—; harbor—; maintain—; restrain—; serve—; squire—; stray to—; support—; —enslaves; —escapes; —submits.
(See lover, sweetheart, master, matron, friend.)

MISTRUSTFUL
adverbs
prudently; discreetly; habitually; temperamentally; chronically; insolently; anxiously; cautiously; intolerantly; insufferably; uncomfortably; darkly; subtly; sharply; absurdly; jealously; apprehensively; nastily; instinctively; suddenly; vaguely; inwardly.

MISTY
adverbs
strangely; terribly; obscurely; dimly; nebulously; cloudily; smokily; oddly; curiously; extremely; mysteriously; deliberately; dangerously; surprisingly; astonishingly;

perplexingly; frightfully; ominously; intensely; alarmingly; abominably; fragrantly; impenetrably; heavily; gloomily; dismally; drearily; vaporously; frostily; foggily.

MISUNDERSTAND (v)
adverbs
deliberately; obtusely; idiotically; illogically; doltishly; pathetically; characteristically; normally.
(See mistake, disagree.)

MISUNDERSTANDING
adjectives
mutual; future; ever-recurring; chronic; inevitable; costly.

verbs
apologize for—; avert—; avoid—; bridge —; conquer—; cope with—; decry—; eradicate—; expose to—; fear—; grapple with —; guard from—; iron out—; risk—; smooth over—; —alarms; —endangers; —excites; —incites.
(See misapprehension, misconception, controversy, disagreement.)

MISUSE (v)
adverbs
brutally; crudely; ruinously; ungenerously; pitilessly; insensately; irrationally; grievously.
(See mistreat, abuse.)

MITE
adjectives
wee; musical; round-bellied; microscopic.

MIX (v)
adverbs
experimentally; inextricably; confusingly; intimately; determinedly; marvelously; discreetly; curiously; ludicrously.
(See associate, mingle.)

MIXED
adverbs
hopelessly; indiscriminately; perplexingly; delightfully; frightfully; incongruously; artfully; cleverly; beautifully; unbelievably; exasperatingly; vexatiously; curiously; mysteriously; grotesquely; disastrously; advantageously.

MIXTURE

adjectives

singular; strange-looking; flecked; hybrid; curious; whimsical; miscellaneous; bright; prodigious; ineffable; fascinating; effervescent; elemental; incongruous; racemic; unbalanced; incoherent; aromatic; piquant; heavy; paradoxical; greasy; sticky; complicated; engaging; fiery; impotent; confused; irrational; ragged; conglomerate; messy.

verbs

administer—; apply—; boil—; compound—; dilute—; drain—; emerge from—; garnish —; saturate—; stir—; swallow—; —coagulates; —hardens; —simmers; —thickens.

(See compound, medicine, chemical, solution.)

MOAN

adjectives

tender; sullen; insidious; enchanted; solemn; untimely; dying; peevish; stifled; weird; faint; alternate; pathetic; broken; everlasting; repentant; languid; lovely; wailing; low; perpetual; sobbing; desolate; shivering; harmonious; angry; doleful; occasional; harsh; short; mortal.

verbs

emit—; endure—s; muffle—; silence—s; stifle—; swell—s; throttle—; tolerate—; — chills; —disquiets; —escapes the lips; — gnaws; —pierces; —rends; —stirs; — weighs; —wrenches.

(See groan, sigh, whine, sob, cry.)

MOAN (v)

adverbs

dolefully; spasmodically; lugubriously; disconsolately; heartrendingly; fitfully; tremulously; grievously; pathetically; tragically; agonizingly; appallingly; distractedly; desolately; weirdly; inarticulately.

(See groan, mourn, lament, complain.)

MOANING

adjectives

dismal; thunderous; weird; desolate; inarticulate; faint.

MOB

adjectives

pitiless; patriotic; reactionary; lawless; furious; heartless; hostile; bewildering; bawling; swaying; union; emotion-charged; insensate; grinning; unruly; irrationalized;

numerous; surging; distracted; great; mere; clumsy; hot-headed; fickle; ignorant; sadistic; immense; savage; supreme; angry; disorganized; noisy; mingled; infuriated; inflammable; riotous.

verbs

attract—; confront—; frustrate—; harangue —; inflame—; restrain—; sway—; —clamors; —disperses; —heckles; —huzzas; — jeers; —lynches; —pelts; —riots; — swarms; —storms; —withdraws.

(See crowd, masses, multitude, public, throng.)

MOBILE

adverbs

advantageously; curiously; skilfully; ingeniously; suddenly; sadly; variably; inconstantly; curiously; beautifully; handily; splendidly; conveniently; unstably; capriciously; erratically; unsteadily; waywardly; actively; vagrantly; captiously; nomadically.

MOCK (v)

adverbs

sneeringly; heartlessly; derisively; vindictively; sardonically; blandly; hollowly; jeeringly; cynically; impotently; despicably; maliciously.

(See mimic, imitate.)

MOCKERY

adjectives

hollow; unreal; solemn; unsubstantial; empty; cynical; standing; ghastly; forced; impotent; hideous; sardonic; bland.

verbs

bear—; endure—; expose to—; ignore—; persecute with—; provoke—; regret—; roast in—; —agonizes; —discomposes; —disconcerts; —disheartens; —humiliates; —mortifies; —rankles; —ruffles; —saddens; — wearies; —weighs upon; —wounds.

(See irony, derision, banter, sarcasm, ridicule.)

MOCKING

adverbs

hideously; hatefully; laughingly; teasingly; disrespectfully; tauntingly; sarcastically; skilfully; artfully; dramatically; scornfully; entertainingly; rudely; ironically; chaffingly; derisively; insufferably; vexatiously; unbearably; intolerably; disagreeably; unpleasantly; offensively; contemptuously; cruelly; unpardonably; sardonically.

MOCKINGBIRD
verbs
admire—; prize—; —copies; —grieves; —defends; —cackles; —imitates; —jests; —jibes; —mews; —mimics; —pours forth; —scoffs; —shakes music; —shrieks; —utters; —wails; —whistles.
(See bird.)

MODE
adjectives
compact; varying; simpler; desultory; perfected; sagacious; happy-go-lucky; sentimental; singular; adequate; proscribed; equivocal; subconscious; prevailing; pompous; uncivilized; feudal; indispensable; scenical; disagreeable; equitable; progressive; frizzling; questionable; hospitable; artless; peculiar; fleeting; ostentatious; ruinous; expeditious; mercenary; hygienic; languid; cheap; irregular; capricious; enjoyable; ultra-modern; ingenuous; ingenious.

verbs
accept—; approve—; burlesque—; conform to—; consent to—; deride—; endorse—; fix—; govern by—; observe—; overdo—; pattern—; prefer—; protest—; revive—; subscribe to—; —disfigures; —enslaves; —succumbs.
(See fashion, manner, mannerism, vogue, standard, trend.)

MODEL
adjectives
exclusive; stunning; venerable; hallucinatory; dressy; hanging; rustic; unique; classical; mechanical; mangled; conservative; casual; inspired; swagger; straight-line; jigger; uniform; unthrifty; worldly; fancy; lacy; stylish; slim.

verbs
borrow from—; construct—; copy—; depart from—; design—; devise—; draw up—; erect—; emulate—; evolve—; explain from —; follow—; imitate—; improve—; mould —; pattern on—; perfect—; refer to—; reproduce—; serve as—; shape—; —embodies; —represents.
(See example, ideal, design, classics, manikin, masterpiece.)

MODEL (v)
adverbs
deliberately; artistically; sedulously; mechanically; imitatively; conservatively; uniformly; uniquely; fashionably.
(See mould, fashion, shape.)

MODERATE
adverbs
sensibly; admirably; judiciously; sagaciously; wisely; acceptably; reasonably; altogether; frugally; prudently; discreetly; thriftily; modestly; singularly; astonishingly; cautiously; notoriously.

MODERATION
adjectives
false; illogical; genial; equal; due; classical; sworn; practiced; remarkable; notable.

verbs
advise—; caution—; confine to—; counsel —; cultivate—; inure by—; prefer—; prescribe—; prize—; recline in—; seat in—; taper to—; treasure—; treat in—; —calms; —combats; —contents; —sobers; —subdues; —suffices; —tempers.
(See conservatism, caution, temperance, restraint.)

MODERN
adverbs
fashionably; stylishly; acceptably; satisfactorily; sufficiently; delightfully; progressively; refreshingly; presumably; warrantably; conveniently; screamingly; attractively; noticeably; incongruously.

MODERNISM
verbs
accent—; bind in—; cater to—; challenge —; combat—; define—; defy—; diffuse—; dispense with—; evolve—; fashion in—; favor—; immerse in—; temper—; touch with—; welcome—; resist—; —amazes; —attracts; —enhances; —excites; —impresses; —prevails; —refreshes; —transforms.
(See materialism, religion, philosophy, socialism.)

MODEST
adverbs
extremely; girlishly; engagingly: charmingly; peculiarly; becomingly; naturally; fool-

ishly; ridiculously; touchingly; adorably; absurdly; comically; demurely; delicately; decently; decorously; admirably; attractively; pleasingly.

MODESTY

adjectives

shaking; womanly; delicate; singular; maidenly; pleasing; extreme; daring; beauteous; virgin; innate; incredible; hypocritical; unassuming; characteristic; austere; bashful; becoming; habitual; marital; ill-placed; boastful; cold; false; indignant; artful.

verbs

bait with—; counterfeit—; deport with—; discern—; extinguish—; feign—; inculcate —; personify—; recommend—; respect—; veil in—; violate—; wrap in—; —charms; —compels; —enjoins; —guards; —heightens; —hides; —padlocks; —restrains; —shuns; —survives.

(See decency, constraint, bashfulness, humility, purity, reserve.)

MODIFICATION

adjectives

slow; serious; substantive; profound; tiny; prescribed.

verbs

publish with—s; require—s; smooth into—; sober into—; undergo—; vary by—; —appeases; —deviates; —diverges; —hushes; —mollifies; —satisfies; —smothers; —softens; —subdues; —tempers; —tones down.

(See alteration, change, transition, variation.)

MODIFY (*v*)

adverbs

deferentially; partially; essentially; substantially; subsequently; drastically; profoundly; intrinsically; dogmatically.

(See adjust, limit.)

MODISH

adverbs

fashionably; extremely; remarkably; amazingly; oddly; delightfully; attractively; alluringly; temptingly; expensively; extravagantly; absurdly; unexpectedly; stylishly; unusually; uncommonly; astoundingly; daintily; tastefully; elegantly; conventionally; presentably; punctiliously; meticulously; showily; gaudily; quietly; acceptably.

MODULATE (*v*)

adverbs

exquisitely; mellifluously; coherently; harmoniously; musically;

(See adapt, adjust.)

MODULATION

adjectives

indiscriminate; learned; incoherent; inharmonic; mellifluous; surprising.

verbs

accord—; effect—; introduce—; perceive—; resign to—; value—; —delights; —enchants; —finishes; —flatters; —harmonizes; —pleases; —represses; —shades; —soothes; —subdues.

(See accent, adjustment, music, quiet.)

MOILS

adjectives

dynastic; imperial; far-flung; terrestrial.

MOIST

adverbs

excessively; extremely; unpleasantly; disagreeably; dangerously; unfortunately; satisfactorily; sufficiently; disastrously; continually; humidly; oppressively; soggily; swampily; conveniently; productively.

MOISTURE

adjectives

perpetual; heavenly; oppressive; suspicious; refreshing; needed; precipitated; genial; bounteous; dark; filthy; fated; destructive; pleasant; over-much; scant.

verbs

absorb—; boil away—; charge with—; condense into—; dabble in—; deprive of—; diffuse—; dim with—; emit—; exude—; inject —; precipitate—; restrain—; saturate with —; sponge with—; sprinkle with—; suck—; vaporize—; wring from—; —dampens; —irrigates; —refreshes; —seeps in.

(See dew, liquid, water, spray, vapor.)

MOLASSES

adjectives

dark; sorghum; fermented; tasty; rubber-like.

MOLD

adjectives

inflexible; heroic; delicate; vulgar; primitive; ethereal; determined; giant; virtuous;

rude; splendid; human; precision; wintry; gentle; beauteous; hollowed; arbitrary; muscular; different; dark; fresh; mossy; earthly; decaying; mortal; massive.

verbs
(See mould.)

MOLE

verbs
run down—; skin—; —burrows; —devastates; —destroys; —digs; —emerges; —excavates; —menaces; —preys on; —scoops; —shovels; —tunnels; —vacates.
(See animal, miner.)

MOLECULE

adjectives
blundering; organic; asymmetric; infinitesimal.

verbs
blast—; break down—; detect—; dissociate into—s; ionize—s; split—; store in—; weigh —; —attracts; —bombards; —charges; —clings; —collides; —composes; —fascinates; —s group; —s pair off; —puzzles; —retains; —s unite.
(See corpuscle, element.)

MOLLIFIED

adverbs
considerably; mercifully; reasonably; quietly; finally; ultimately; gradually; wholly; gently; visibly; eventually; happily; luckily; fortunately; presumably; somewhat; slowly; greatly; perceptibly; admittedly.

MOMENT

adjectives
decisive; spiteful; uncertain; voluptuous; critical; silent; lyrical; ludicrous; tragic; disagreeable; pictorial; appalling; musing; inspired; leisure; awful; microscopical; infinite; extraordinary; propitious; enlightened; proud; willful; little; heavier; immortal; delightful; high-tide; opportune; prolonged; gravest; radiant; usurped; bitter; highest; prearranged; charming; sulky; brisk; solemn; intuitive; giddy; whirling; supreme; omnipotent; inauspicious; unguarded; precise; culminating; single; blemished; gayest; rare; cantabile; shining; psychological; undecided; spellbound; earliest; vital; dreamy; affected; briefest; dramatic; heartrending; occasional; embittering; cooler; appointed; pleasant; illuminated; wak-

ing; breathless; hungry; ardent; lessened; important; flashing; crucial; theoretical; fading; poignant; fleeting; fateful; exalted; miraculous; pregnant; hostile; erotic; affectionate; necessary; sunny; impressive; reconciling; precise; tense; leisure; staggering; lofty; intimate; startled; inspirational; futile; practical; careless; sardonic; skinned; intent; delightful; lonely; golden; memoried; particular; few (pl); confused; swift; bold; brief; natal; troubled; deplorable; awful; sickening; inexpressible; tingling; cheerless; unnecessary; sunny.

verbs
acclaim—; anticipate—; consume in—; endure—; pause for—; relish—; seize—; snatch—; squeeze—dry; —flits by; —thrills; —troubles.
(See flash, instant, time.)

MOMENTOUS

adverbs
gravely; seriously; importantly; signally; unutterably; immensely; relatively; overwhelmingly; singularly; peculiarly; particularly; impressively; imposingly; strangely; mysteriously; secretly; inscrutably; exceptionally; infinitely; decisively; historically; tremendously; transcendently; insuperably; incomparably.

MOMENTUM

verbs
accumulate—; acquire—; defy—; gain—; lend—to; repel—; resist—; submit to—; withstand—; —batters; —butts; —drives; —impels; —increases; —prods; —shoves; —thrusts.
(See impetus, speed, force, velocity.)

MONARCH

adjectives
constitutional; magnanimous; affable; determined; degenerate; incompetent; conquering; pretentious; maddening; riotous; insolent; absolute; presumptuous; generous; rash; romantic; throned; deposed; new-crowned; ambitious; irrepsonsible; disheveled; unwilling; potent; forest; progressive; luxurious; unengaging; crumpled; affable; sensual; effeminate; puissant; opulent; sagacious; ill-starred; mighty; legendary; capricious; barbarous; factious; turbulent.

verbs

ape—; attack—; attend—; behead—; crown —; depose—; enthrone—; laud—; overthrow—; rebel against—; rule—; submit to—; —abdicates; —compels; —domineers; —imposes; —liberates; —misrules; —oppresses; —ordains; —reigns; —succeeds to; —surveys; —tramples; —yields.

(See emperor, dictator, king, monarchy, nobility, royalty.)

MONARCHY

adjectives

limited; restored; feudal; hereditary; absolute; constitutional; restricted; centralizing; flourishing; undisputed; despotic; serviceable; liberal; free; kingless.

verbs

attack—; destroy—; discontinue—; dispute —; establish—; head—; overthrow—; restore—; revive—; revolt against—; rout—; submit to—; survey—; tolerate—; —compels; —crumbles; —crushes; —falls; —imposes; —oppresses; —taxes; —treads on; —tyrannizes.

(See kingdom, monarch.)

MONASTERY

adjectives

vast; deserted, ruinous; secluded; flourishing.

verbs

cloister in—; conceal in—; desert—; enter —; exile in—; explore in—; foster in—; ramble through—; resort to—; retire to—; retreat to—; seclude in—; sequester in—; shut up in—; supervise—; —charms; —cowls; —disciplines; —embraces; —grants sanctuary; —harbors; —shelters; —soothes; —taboos.

(See prison, seclusion, religion.)

MONEY

adjectives

funded; depreciated; considerable; precious; reluctant; scattering; hoarded; dirty; cheaper; irredeemable; fraudulent; limp; grimy; paper; pin; parental; cold; hard; well-meant; flat; speculator; embezzled; continental; forfeited; worthless; counterfeit; inflated.

verbs

amass—; apportion—; bestow—upon; bilk of—; cling to—; coin—; counterfeit—; covet —; devalue—; divert—from; divest of—; exact—; expend—; extort—; fritter away —; hoard—; importune for—; lavish—upon; mulct of—; pile up—; pilfer—; plunk down—; pocket—; raise—; rake in—; restore—; revaluate—; risk—; salt away (colloq.)—; scrape together—; squander—; utilize—; wheedle—from; wring—from; —dribbles away; —dwindles; —flows in; —melts away.

(See investment, currency, fund, dollar, legacy, coin, cash, capital, inheritance.)

MONGREL

adverbs

despicably; basely; indubitably; indiscriminately; confoundedly; nondescriptly; peculiarly; anomalously; funnily; quaintly; fantastically; undeniably; contemptibly; ridiculously; remarkably.

MONGRELS

adjectives

sycophantic; engaging; brindled; dirty; swinelike.

MONK

adjectives

fanatical; ascetic; tonsured; preaching; cloistered; patient; persecuting; indifferent; excommunicated; abominable; lecherous.

MONKEY

adjectives

horrible-looking; meddling; misanthropic; withered-up; howling; cautious; monocled; grinning; manlike.

verbs

—antics; —s band together; —bounds; —capers; —climbs; —clings; —collects; —cuffs; —entertains; —fascinates; —fights; —frets; —grieves; —grimaces; —grins; —hangs; —howls; —imitates; —laughs; —leaps; —quarrels; —resembles; —scratches; —screams; —squeals; —swings; —tears; —warns; —wheels; —whines.

(See animal, ape.)

MONOCLE

verbs

adjust—; affix—; blink through—; discern through—; dislodge—; employ—; examine through—; fasten—; finger—; flip—; lurk behind—; peer through—; squint through—; tack—to; —dangles; —falls; —hangs from; —magnifies; —screws into.

(See spectacles, telescope, microscope.)

MONOLOGUE

adjectives
indignant; drowsy; inimitable.

MONOPOLIZE (v)

adverbs
selfishly; greedily; pretentiously; dictatorially; craftily; vigorously; legally.

MONOPOLY

adjectives
unlimited; sectional; unified; virtual; national; natural; insidious; wicked; wasteful; wretched; proposed.

verbs
bag—; break down—; confer—upon; denounce—; enjoy—; foster—; free from—; infringe on—; possess—; promote—; protest—; resent—; secure—; —controls; —enriches; —fetters; —gags; —masters; —prices; —reaps; —smothers.
(See power, authority.)

MONOTONE

adjectives
solemn; enchanting; dolorous; maddening; chanting; soothing; weirdly-spoken; mumbling; eternal; indistinguishable.

MONOTONOUS

adverbs
drearily; tediously; dreadfully; boresomely; endlessly; dismally; cheerfully; dully; intolerably; wearily; unbearably; unendurably; garrulously; ponderously; uninterestingly; repetitiously; unvaryingly; vapidly; irksomely; flatly; drowsily; droningly; prosily.

MONOTONY

adjectives
apparent; routine; unused; extreme; inescapable; desolate; endless; gray; maddening; studious; unvarying; fatiguing; deadening; dull; machine-like; unnatural; exasperating; inevitable; tedious; slumberous; loathsome; lazy; painful; hideous; dreary; dreadful; tiresome; wearisome; smooth; objectless.

verbs
allay—; beguile—; bewail—; curse—; deplore—; distract—; emerge from—; endure —; extinguish—; inflict with—; intensify—; object to—; overcome with—; relieve—; repose in—; sink into—; usher in—; while

away—; yawn through—; —abates; —bores; —depresses; —drags; —threatens; —tires; —wearies.
(See drabness, oppression, pain, tedium, boredom.)

MONSTER

adjectives
patient; carniverous; insatiable; sprawling; strong-limbed; grim; hardhearted; unfeeling; cruel; devouring; insatiate; uncouth; slimy; fabled; wallowing; colossal; steaming; papyral; formidable; Briarean; slumbering; vile; modern; entangled; furry; hydra-headed; diabolical; pestilent; grotesque; accursed; eerie; quaint; pediculous.

verbs
abound with—s; beget—; condemn to—; dread—; fear—; overcome—; quell—; satiate—; subdue—; tame—; —coils; —devours; —frightens; —horrifies; —howls; —looms; —offends; —roams; —spouts; —terrifies; —terrorizes.
(See giant, beast, dragon, barbarian, animal; savage; villain; brute.)

MONTH

adjectives
healing; memorable; sweet; dreary; anxious; withered; story-book; ensuing; tedious; corresponding; brief; silent; wintry; tempestuous; treacherous; stretched; gentle; much-abused; crabbed; meager.

verbs
attain in—; endure—; enjoy—; estimate —s; extend—; finish—; indicate—; mark—; pass—; remain—; spend—; survive—; tide over—; waste—; —elapses; —fades; —separates.
(See time, week, year.)

MONUMENT

adjectives
imperishable; wondrous; vast; sarcophagus-like; wasting; lasting; worthy; enduring; extant; venerable; deathless; tawny; stately; strange; gigantic; divine; living; everlasting; endless; colossal; marble; notorious; mysterious; charred; sepulchral; immemorial; pompous; majestic; equestrian; mighty; impressive; lofty; surviving; splendid; kindred; obvious; conspicuous; public.

verbs
boast—; dedicate—; deface—; earn—; elevate—; engrave—; erect—; gild—; inscribe on—; restore—; —adorns; —commemorates; —endures; —glorifies; —immortalizes; —perpetuates; —preserves; —records; —represents; —signifies; —symbolizes; —towers.

(See inscription, trophy, memorial, statue, tomb.)

MONUMENTAL
adverbs
overwhelmingly; stupendously; massively; unbelievably; colossally; gigantically; incomparably; vastly; matchlessly; prodigiously; tremendously; inexpressibly.

MOOD
adjectives
similar; changing; characteristic; grateful; unwavering; rarest; ungentle; furtive; discontented; beguiling; half-dreaming; selfless; mysterious; exquisite; guileful; musing; uncertain; affectionable; wrathful; fantastic; willful; dominant; intemperate; adventurous; morbid; exuberant; genial; articulate; irregular; parleying; silent; ironic; lifelong; rebellious; imperious; bewildered; genial; chaffing; comfortable; freakish; reminiscent; impassioned; subjective; absonant; pensive; unimagined; enchanted; sprightly; sullen; impetuous; rebel; extinguished; mirthful; penitential; disagreeable; wrought-up; thoughtful; receptive; habitual; depressed; philosophic; merry; sentimental; misprized; fear-stricken; romantic; sanguine; pliant; dreamy; exacting; concurrent; raging; beneficial; rapid; garrulous; favorable; variable; placid; wayward; respectful; contemplative; stern; sarcastic; working; expectant; flippant; steadfast; affable; mournful; despondent; indifferent; submissive; idea-less; senseless; frantic; shallow; evanescent; presageful; central; morbid; gruesome; demagogic; indispensable; humane; hysterical; inquisitorial; capricious; alien; jealous; melancholy; habitual; impious; reflective; facetious; chastened; philosophic; anti-radical; religious; docile; hasty; loitering; artificial; successive (pl); dreaded; ascetic; intense; uneven; kindly; changeful; icy; mandatory; shuddering; springtime; berserk; conciliatory; permissive; shifting; minor; angelic; unfavorable.

verbs
combat—; communicate—; crystallize—; defer to—; depict—; dispel—; fathom—; fix —; govern by—; induce—; interpret—; jolt out of—; kindle—; lighten—; overstrain—; rage in—; recall—; reflect—; shock out of —; soothe—; submit to—; succumb to—; sustain—; temper—; voice—; wrap in—; yield to—; —presages; —prevails; —strikes; —vanishes.

(See disposition, melancholy, feeling, emotion.)

MOODY
adverbs
captiously; ominously; sullenly; bitterly; cynically; alarmingly; seriously; unaccountably; occasionally; unreasonably; perplexingly; morbidly; fearfully; portentously; significantly; dangerously; unusually; capriciously; irascibly; fretfully; perversely; glumly; grimly; frequently; rarely; seldom; doggedly; intractably; intolerably; insufferably; unendurably.

MOON
adjectives
envious; filmy; brilliant; full-orbed; Orient; airless; queenly; angry; infantine; misty; fleeting; morning; gibbous; sphered; wintry; melancholy; inconstant; smiling; carven; curved; semi-tropic; lifeless; crescent; triumphant; flying; tranquil; stormy; softer; waxing; prying; dying; mourning; bloody; setting; languorous; red; distorted; pale; cold; waning; mellow; sleepless; listening; harvest; laboring; dying; solitary; shining; hollowed; blazing; marvelous; climbing; broad; sickle; gracious; jealous; watery; fruitless; coined; fair; overcast; wandering; shrouded; slow; haunting; desolate; naked; belated; lingering; sacred; horned; large-lighted; tranquil; smiling; withered; changeless; overwhelming; beauty-seeking; temperamental; winter; unassuming; peeping; summer; round; intense; luminous; full; cruel; yellow; green; harvest; marigold; honey-colored; arctic; hazy; lucent; slow; silvery; frosted; apple-shaped; purple; sad; climbing.

verbs
behold—; encircle—; fringe—; gaze at—; obscure—; veil—; view—; —barges (colloq.); —beams; —blushes; —brightens; —climbs; —dances; —dies; —dips into; —drifts beyond; —emerges; —enamors; —en-

chants; —gleams; —glimmers; —glows; —
impassions; —mellows; —peeps out; —
reigns; —sails over; —scowls; —shimmers;
—silvers; —sinks; —voyages; —wanes; —
waxes.
(See sun, stars, clouds, sky.)

MOONBEAM

adjectives
opalescent; dim; blended; sluiced; cold;
quivering; misty; mellow.

verbs
shed—; wash by—; —brightens; —dances;
—dazzles; —drips; —enchants; —floods; —
glimmers; —hallows; —kisses; —illumines;
—mantles; —shrouds; —silvers; —sparkles;
—sweeps; —swells; —trembles; —whitens.
(See ray, light, radiance, spark, sunshine,
sunlight, twilight, moonlight.)

MOONLIGHT

adjectives
glinting; gentle; sickly; bleached; mellow;
liquid; rich; down-slanting; mystical; cold;
dewy; molten; golden; pleasant; pale; bubbling; magnificent; generous; weird; streaming; faint; white; muffled; fitful; ribboned;
sacred; harvest; painted; vivid; glistening;
tropic; autumn; sallow; milky; tremulous;
slanting.

verbs
bathe in—; drip—; shroud in—; wash by—;
—casts spell; —checkers; —enchants; —illuminates; —kindles; —streaks; —streams
in; —swathes; —sweeps; —unveils; —
wanes.
(See moonbeam.)

MOONSHINE

adjectives
white; sweet; silvery.

MOONSTRUCK

adverbs
crazily; outlandishly; queerly; fantastically;
giddily; foolishly; bewilderingly; ridiculously; undoubtedly; hazily; foggily; daftly; incoherently; deliriously; unstably; heedlessly;
witlessly.

MOOR (*v*)

adverbs
primitively; safely; permanently; seasonally; cautiously; habitually; prudently.
(See fasten, fix.)

MOORING

adjectives
sheltered; primitive; diplomatic.

verbs
anchor to—; attach to—; break—; cable to
—; command—; direct—; drag from—;
drive from—; drop from—; hinder—; quit
—; secure—; shackle to—; slacken—; slip
—; swing at—; wreck in—.
(See post.)

MOOSE

verbs
bait—; breed—; exhibit—; experiment with
—; lure—; pet—; plague with—; stalk—;
stuff—; trap—; —climbs; —frightens; —
haunts; —hurries; —infects; —infest; —
munches; —nibbles; —runs; —scurries; —
shies; —squeals; —shuns; —digs.
(See animal, deer.)

MOPE (*v*)

adverbs
glumly; dismally; gloomily; morbidly; despondently; romantically; drearily; pallidly;
sadly; abnormally.
(See sulk, brood.)

MORAL

adjectives
fearful; strictest; obtrusive; intellectual;
pretty; austerest; admirable; latent; righteous; public; fallible; obvious; creditable;
immovable; political; abstract; philosophical.

adverbs
chastely; sternly; strictly; rigidly; uncompromisingly; intolerantly; righteously; self-
consciously; proudly; apparently; self-righteously; preachily; ostentatiously; blatantly;
presumably; avowedly; virtuously; remarkably; astonishingly; tiresomely; unbelievably; sanctimoniously; unctuously; blandly.

MORALE

verbs
acclaim—; assail—; break down—; destroy
—; fortify—; impair—; instill—; lower—;
shatter—; stimulate—; strengthen—; —ascends; —descends; —sinks; —wanes.
(See nerve, courage, strength, valor, spirit,
virtue.)

MORALIST

adjectives
rigid; fashionable; futile; shallow; pretending; dissembling; confirmed.

MORALITY

adjectives
provincial; austere; puritanical; strait; trite; wholesome; creditable; restrictive; hereditary; flabby; intolerant; rigorous; fastidious; semi-religious; predominant; collar-and-wrist-band; Christian; political; true; scrupulous; marital; speculative.

verbs
abandon—; cant—; contemplate—; develop —; discard—; elevate—; guard—; inspire —; instruct—; observe—; regulate—; revive —; stimulate—; sustain—; uphold—; whitewash (colloq.) —; —crumbles; —decays; — elevates; —enlightens; —improves; —protects; —raises.
(See virtue, purity, integrity, righteousness, honor, truth.)

MORALIZE (*v*)

adverbs
jocosely; piously; monotonously; religiously; paternally; irritatingly; indefatigably.
(See preach, teach.)

MORALS

verbs
annihilate—; communicate—to; compromise —; corrupt—; destroy—; disapprove of—; disregard—; draw—from; emancipate—; improve—; influence—; outrage—; point to —; —degenerate; —deteriorate.
(See lesson, ethics, habit, ideals.)

MORASS

adjectives
drear; dismal; frightful.

verbs
deluge—; dip in—; drain—; emerge from —; immerse in—; penetrate—; plunge into —; soak in—; steep in—; swamp in—; swash through—; wallow in—; wander into —; —bogs; —engulfs; —mires.
(See mire. swamp, marsh.)

MORBID

adverbs
profoundly; abnormally; distressingly; forlornly; dangerously; inordinately; preposterously; crankily; incurably; miserably; pa-

thetically; pitiably; vexatiously; unreasonably; outlandishly; outrageously; disagreeably; intolerably; terribly; irrationally; ominously; horribly.

MORN

adjectives
cloudy; radiant; rosy; returning; balmy; fateful; lily-wristed; incense-breathing; hallowed; double-pillowed; unsullied; gaudy; summer; delusive; valorous; propitious; immortal; breaking; weeping; spring; lagging; misty; struggling; smiling; dismal; endless; gusty; silent; vernal; new-made; awful; refluent; radiant; silver-flecked; blooming; apocalyptic.

MORNING

adjectives
cold; sunless; identical; dreary; propitious; yellow-robed; amber; splendid; dazzling; breezeless; vapory; absorbing; historic; invigorating; precious; faultless; memorable; uneventful; cruel; glorious; listless; duncolored; bridal; dull; delicious; quiet; sullen; dreadful; raw; lurid; misty; clear; shining; perpetual; fresh; auspicious; soft; sharp; frosty; hoary; merry; pallid; portentous; drear; foggy.

verbs
herald—; usher in—; wash—; —ascends; — awakens; —beckons; —blooms; —breaks through; —checkers; —crowns; —dawns; —drones along; —glimmers; —is born; — rises; —shrouds; —smiles; —tints; —uncurtains; —unfolds.
(See dawn, day, afternoon, evening, time.)

MOROSE

adverbs
dismally; incorrigibly; unreasonably; unaccountably; pathetically; unbearably; horribly; crabbedly; cantankerously; churlishly; boorishly; ominously; inordinately; uncommonly; outrageously; inexcusably; rudely; uncivilly; impolitely; ungraciously; inexplicably; inscrutably; silently; suddenly; irascibly; perversely; restively; intractably; implacably; sourly; immovably.

MORPHEUS

verbs
court—; invoke—; resist—; yield to—; — approaches; —caresses; —conquers; — cradles; —delights; —deludes; —enfolds;

—develops; —harasses; —lulls; —purifies; —rejuvenates; —shades; —smooths; — soothes; —strokes; —treads; —weaves.
(See sleep, rest, slumber, lethargy.)

MORSELS
adjectives
tantalizing; epicurean; picturesque; luscious; piquant; nauseous; locutionary; exquisite; petty; piteous; succulent; lawn-wrapped; hungry; delicious; tempting; inviting-looking.

MORTAL
adjectives
contemporary; melancholy; great; rough; rapid; reason-boasting; wretched; sacred; scarcest; meekest; ordinary; venturesome; wee; worn.

MORTALITY
adjectives
indued; miserable; international; enormous; human; waning; dull; recreant; allotted; normal; sad; massed (pl); heaven-oppressed.

verbs
abate—; account for—; constitute—; control —; lower—; rate—; —alarms; —ascends; —decimates; —descends; —effaces; —increases; —piles up; —staggers; —varies; — wanes.
(See death, murder, plague, slaughter, suicide.)

MORTAR
verbs (vessel)
abrade—; beat in—; comminute in—; crumble in—; crunch in—; crush in—; granulate in—; grind in—; pound in—; powder in—; pulverize in—; rasp in—; reduce in—; stamp in—; triturate in—.

MORTGAGE
verbs
assign—; borrow on—; cancel—; confirm—; contract—; convey—; discharge—; foreclose —; fulfill—; grant—; lift—; melt into—; pay off—; undertake—; —assures; —burdens; —devours; —guarantees; —insures; —saps; —warrants.
(See loan, payment, bond, obligation, debt.)

MORTGAGE (v)
adverbs
hopelessly; rashly; improvidently; optimistically; lucklessly.
(See loan.)

MORTIFICATION
verbs
bear—; blush in—; cast into—; color in—; flush in—; hang in—; spare—; stoop in—; submit to—; swallow—; —confuses; —destroys; —crushes; —frustrates; —pains; — sobers; —treads on; —vexes.
(See chagrin, shame.)

MORTIFIED
adverbs
needlessly; horribly; shamefully; cruelly; unreasonably; extremely; humiliatingly; pitifully; naturally; exceedingly; terribly; unnecessarily; unaccountably; inexplicably; modestly; searingly; shockingly; bitterly; sorely.

MOSAICS
adjectives
golden; elaborate; curious; rare; radiant; glorious.

MOSQUITOES
verbs
devour by—; exterminate—; infest with—; spray—; —annoy; —buzz; —disquiet; — draw; —extract; —feast on; —infest; — pester; —plague; —poison; —puncture; — serenade; —suck; —swarm.
(See insects, fly.)

MOSS
adjectives
downy; fragrant; bright; idle; quaggy; silvered; creeping; branched; tender; sea-colored; hanging; velvetlike; bannered; spongy; furred; moldering.

MOTH
adjectives
soft; startled; resurrected; damage-wreaking.

verbs
singe—; snatch at—; —blights; —contaminates; —destroys; —deteriorates; —devours; —flutters; —gnaws; —harasses; —hovers about; —impairs; —s infest; —injures; —s plague; —preys on; —ravages.
(See insects, butterfly.)

adjectives

provident; prudent; glorious; peasant; impatient; frail; beautiful; admirable; pious; doting; mahogany-colored; tedious-working; bereaved; commonplace; potential; infuriated; jealous; indulgent; frowzy; venerable; melancholy; famishing; earthly; vigorous; aggressive; elemental; insatiate; spirited; celestial; prolific; strong-armed; authentic; incestuous; delicate; bountiful; over-fatigued; querulous; imaginary; virgin; green-girdled; sorrowing; devoted; foolish; widowed; subtle; deft; spiteful; adopting; altruistic; unnatural.

verbs

anchor—; cherish—; cling to—; deliver of —; devote to—; hound—; obey—; —bears; —cradles; —conceives; —embraces; —fondles; —forsakes; —nourishes; —nurses; — protects; —punishes; —rears; —rocks; — sacrifices; —suckles; —weans.

(See father, nurse, parent, woman.)

MOTHERLY

adverbs

affectionately; graciously; affably; comfortably; indulgently; gently; sympathetically; understandingly; intelligently; charmingly; unfailingly; tenderly; lovingly; wisely; altogether; admirably; wondrously; marvellously; incomparably; eagerly; happily; joyously; pleasantly; agreeably; good-naturedly; tolerantly; warmly; amiably; complacently; imperturbably; serenely; calmly; quietly; wholesomely.

MOTION

adjectives

ceaseless; visible; measured; dignified; airy; quivering; legal; alternative; perpetual; hesitating; subtle; delighted; stable; inconstant; measureless; appealing; chopping; lulling; spiral; captivating; slow; irregular; sickening; uncertain; nautical; natural; wavy; rapid; mighty; apparent; musical; mincing; proximate; dreamlike; hingelike; graceful; flickering; undulous; mechanic; arresting; awkward; lifelike; ceaseless; obvious; orbital; well-ordered; elliptic; parabolic; intended; revolving; sensible; relative; gyratory; convulsive; gentle; vibratory; dreary; slow; lateral; giddy; planetary; faltering; diurnal; reciprocating; retrograde; scythelike; liquid; horizontal; parallactic; warm; constant; gliding; light-

ning; heavy; rhythmic; astonished; comparative; metallic; erratic; primitive; increasing; habitual; rapturous; universal; admired; inward; feeble; delicious; extravagant; insectlike; unnumbered (pl); tiring; abrupt; veritable; molecular; atomic; nimble; many-valued.

verbs

arrest—; constrain—; express—; ferment into—; guide—; impel—; lose—; practise —; quell—; regulate—; restrain from—; restrict—; retard—; set into—; slide into—; sustain—; whirl into—; —agitates; —expresses; —saps.

(See gesture, flicker, action, movement.)

MOTIONLESS

adverbs

suddenly; silently; warily; breathlessly; strangely; curiously; oddly; watchfully; noiselessly; frightfully; incredibly; absolutely; utterly; statuesquely; unbelievably; miraculously; stealthily; scrupulously; cautiously; prudently; discreetly; secretly.

MOTION PICTURE

verbs

(See "movie.")

MOTIVE

adjectives

chivalrous; tragic; corrupt; predominant; incidental; ambitious; attributed; selfish; altruistic; kind; underlying; commercial; corrupt; worthy; interested; ignoble; greedy; intrusive; conscientious; plausible; priceless; principal; lofty; invented; ostensible; colonial; unmixed; misleading; professional; perplexing; secondary; high; generous; explanatory; interesting; complicated; auxiliary; disinterested; evil; urgent; improper; hedonistic; differing; compelling; imputed; ulterior; patriotic; melodic; inferior; mercenary; fatal; upright; pure; commanding; sufficient; keen; guiding; impugning; impelling; dominant; identical; basilar; ruling; potent; laudable; understandable; cryptic; bread-and-butter; segmented; sculptured; hidden; scarce-known.

verbs

abolish—; acknowledge—; appreciate—; assign—for; attribute—to; destroy—; impute —to; mock—; obscure—; ponder—; probe into—; recognize—; review —s; reward—;

weigh—; —actuates; —governs; —impels; —induces; —inspires; —prompts; —stimulates; —sways.

(See cause, grounds, incentive, impulse, inducement.)

MOTOR

adjectives
creaking; coughing; inactive; compression; oil-driven; whirring; undependable; wheezing.

verbs
accelerate—; choke—; fuel—; recondition —; stall—; —balks; —coughs; —drones; — fails; —fouls; —gasps; —hums; —purrs; —roars; —rasps; —rattles; —splutters; — steams; —whines.

(See generator, machine, engine, propeller.)

MOTORBOAT

verbs
anchor—; buffet—; moor—; test—; throttle —; —bobs; —capsizes; —chugs; —churns; —coughs; —drifts; —heads; —noses for; —splutters; —spurts; —sputters; —whisks; —whizzes; —zooms.

(See launch, ship, tugboat, yacht, vessel, steamer.)

MOTORCYCLE

verbs
straddle—; throttle—; —blasts; —breezes by; —chokes; —chugs; —coughs; —leans; —roars; —shoots by; —splutters; —sputters; —whisks away; —whizzes by; —wriggles; —zigzags.

(See automobile, taxi, motor.)

MOTTO

verbs
adopt—; apply—; coin—; condense into—; design—; devise—; digest—; heed—; inscribe—; misstate—; phrase—; quote—; recite—; recognize—; relish—; sing forth—; —emphasizes; —exalts; —glorifies; —provides; —signifies; —stresses; —symbolizes.

(See poetry, epigram, proverb, parable, saying.)

MOULD

verbs
adjust—; bake in—; cast—; cleave to—; conform to—; design—; drain into—; oil—;

pattern—; pour into—; press—; set in—; shape—; —cools; —fashions; —frames; — hardens; —imitates.

(See form.)

MOULD (*v*)

adverbs
exquisitely; trimly; faultlessly; subtly; realistically; professionally; deftly; skillfully; artistically; symmetrically; sensuously; voluptuously; meretriciously.

(See model, fashion, shape.)

MOULDY

adverbs
dangerously; deeply; poisonously; infectiously; rottenly; putridly; rankly; rancidly; offensively; grossly; noxiously; injuriously; terribly; riskily; presumably; apparently; extremely; obviously; manifestly.

MOUND

adjectives
pious; countless; rural; hideous; grass-grown; craggy; conical; sorrow-laden; shapeless; pyramidal; solitary; moldering.

MOUNT

adjectives
lofty; sloping; tireless; mimic; apocalyptic; flame-fringed; spectacular.

MOUNT (*v*)

adverbs
reluctantly; magnificently; awkwardly; perpetually; gradually; rigidly; reluctantly; mechanically; reticently; stealthily; spectacularly.

(See ascend, rise.)

MOUNTAIN

adjectives
shimmering; bare; cold; eroded; rugged; dizzy; faraway; wintry; forested; beacon-lighted; multitudinous; glacier-laden; pine-encircled; adamantine; dominating; spirit-haunted; cultivated; plain; melancholy; moonlit; steep; uncouthly-cut; beholding; inaccessible; lifeless; precipitous; gloomy; lifeless; variegated; flaring; relentless; soft-looking; enchanted; heaven-reaching; timberless; worshipful; huge; new; craggy; misty; fractured; snowy; moody; severed; tremendous; intervening; prickly; glittering; ruddy; delectable; remote; offensive; jagged; rude; slumbering; overhanging; pensive; eagle-baffling; ice-crowned; terraced;

round-topped; sharp-peaked; redoubtable; messy-looking; environing; tumbling; scarlet; morning; disintegrated; barren; symmetrical; volcanic; vast; everlasting; verdant; fabled; naked; sentinel; scarped; unscaled; windless; towering; colorless; ancient; timbered; gloomy; ponderous; prodigious; unique; weltering; steepy; circumjacent.

verbs
abandon—; ascend—; carve—; circumvent —; fortify—; furrow—; level—; plow through—; reconnoitre—; scale—; straddle —; trudge up—; —awes; —hinders; — looms up; —obscures; —obstructs; —overawes; —shadows; —stands sentinel; — towers.
(See hill, bank, peak, precipice, tower.)

MOUNTAINEERS
adjectives
mythic; benighted; hardy; intractable; redoubtable; wary.

MOUNTAINOUS
adverbs
gloriously; hazardously; terribly; magnificently; splendidly; gorgeously; gloomily; disastrously; impenetrably; densely; impassably; scenically; steeply; bleakly; tremendously; perilously; dangerously; attractively; invitingly; alluringly; adventurously; notoriously; presumably.

MOURN (v)
adverbs
pathetically; sincerely; touchingly; nationally; primitively; tragically; barbarically; oppressively; jealously; querulously; unnaturally; piously.
(See grieve, regret, lament.)

MOURNER
adjectives
flap-mouthed; pensive; desolate; sorrowful; heartbroken.

condole—; console—; sympathize with—; —s attend; —despairs; —s file out; —laments; —grieves; —rends; —s respect; — screams; —sheds; —sobs; —suffers; — wails; —weeps; —groans.

MOURNFUL
adverbs
desolately; forlornly; dismally; drearily; hopelessly; helplessly; bitterly; sadly; tragically; pitiably; unutterably; unspeakably; unbearably; grievously; profoundly; irremediably; disagreeably; uncomfortably; shockingly; cruelly; gloomily; grimly; disconsolately; inconsolably; plaintively; querulously; resentfully; rebelliously.

MOUSE
adjectives
smallest; monstrous; realistic; scampering.

verbs
attract—; bait—; corner—; panic—; pursue —; snare—; stir—; trap—; —burrows; — —cowers; —disturbs; —dodges; —gnaws; —nibbles; —ransacks; —rifles; —rummages; —scampers; —scurries; —scuttles; —whisks.
(See animal.)

MOUSTACHE
verbs
adorn with—; coil—; cultivate—; curl—; dye—; finger—; nourish—; pluck at—; roll —; ruffle—; smooth—; stroke—; trim—; twirl—; twist—; wax—; wipe—; —bristles; —charms; —curls; —droops; —gleams; — trembles; —wilts.
(See mane, beard, whiskers, curls.)

MOUTH
adjectives
smiling; deep; innocent; loud-ringing; mobile; enraged; foamy; sweet; rosy; impressive; good-humored; loving; alkaline; irritable; deathful-grinning; funnel-shaped; compressed; fine; sensuous; musty; winsome; cooing; dimpled; tender; relaxed; generous; unpampered; prudent; extraordinary; wide; wry; foul; brazen; cavernous; resolute; lascivious; delicate; frothy; churning; handsome; full; firm; querulous; ascetic; yawning; coral; ravishing; facile; perilous; puckered; toothless; rabbit; baby; branching; sulky; acid; gaping; arch; eloquent; unmelodious; bloodless; voluble; glad; expressive; economical; breathless; slobbering; serious; savage; insistent; sardonic; purposeful; shapeless; hungry; furnace; munching; painted; heavy; vermilion; distended; luscious; wrinkled; cruel; modeled.

verbs
convey to—; froth at—; honey—; introduce into—; irritate—; padlock—; paint—; pout

793

—; proceed from—; pucker up—; seal—; screw up—; sponge—; smite on—; swab—; —droops; —hardens; —lures; —quirks; — quivers; —relaxes; —tightens; —twitches; —utters.

(See lips, face, opening.)

MOVABLE

adverbs

conveniently; easily; handily; adjustably; cleverly; comfortably; appropriately; serviceably; usefully; freely; readily; lightly; adaptably; conformably; curiously.

MOVE

adjectives

ill-planned; latest; strategic; opening; vulnerable; subordinate; rusty; eccentric; hostile; brilliant; ambitious; fancy; stultifying.

verbs

abet—; alternate —s; attempt—; calculate —; concede—; determine—; devise—; encourage—; guard—; limit —s; speculate on —; study—; undertake—; —captures; —deceives; —misleads; —tricks.

(See march, maneuver, movement.)

MOVE (v)

adverbs

gracefully; automatically; perceptibly; sinuously; precariously; simultaneously; involuntarily; caressingly; violently; rashly; spasmodically; cautiously; deftly; impatiently; rhythmically; profoundly; visibly; sedately; invisibly; fearsomely; serenely; unintelligibly; blithesomely; drearily; stealthily; dubiously; erratically; sluggishly; obliviously; agilely; phelgmatically; passively; invincibly; warily; strategically; abortively; brusquely; tremulously; timorously; martially.

(See step, walk.)

MOVEMENT
(*action, change of position, etc.*)

verbs

accentuate—; accomplish—; attempt—; avoid—; cease—; control—; diminish—; effect—; enliven—; facilitate—; hamper—; impede—; induce—; minimize—; necessitate—; practise—; repeat—; restrain from —; restrict—; reverse—; —agonizes.

(See current, motion, move.)

MOVEMENT
(campaign)

verbs

actuate—; annihilate—; applaud—; ban—; block—; combat—; cripple—; criticize—; defeat—; dominate—; endorse—; engage in —; engineer—; facilitate—; father—; fling into—; found—; frustrate—; govern—; inaugurate—; initiate—; involve in—; launch —; mask—; promote—; quell—; rally to—; sponsor—; support—; —coagulates; —collapses; —commences; —culminates in; — dies; —flourishes; —originates in; —penetrates to; —springs from; —suffers; —symbolizes; —wanes.

(See crusade, fascism, innovation, cause.)

MOVEMENT
(*general*)

adjectives

anxious; contemplated; spasmodic; commendable; romantic; recent; involuntary; strategical; deliberate; planetary; wild; busy; complicated; passionate; graceful; revolutionary; impulsive; metallic; rude; unobtrusive; important; erratic; impatient; abortive; alternative; careless; rhythmic; bustling; wandering; uncapturable; delicate; pending; retrograde; offensive; flank; convulsive; scooping; life-sustaining; contemplated; self possessed; messianic; living; hostile; rebellious; particular; painful; cooperative; bridling; incessant; aesthetic; willowy; celestial; intentional; philanthropic; turbulent; fitting; silent; wasteful; insurrectionary; muscular; imperceptible; dexterous; soothing; foregoing; extensive; composite; clicking; nautical; masterly; terrorist; kneading; responsive; flexible; religious; insensible; tremulous; brusque; grandiose; silly; subsequent; slinking; crushing; fantastic; unconvulsive; guillotine-like; discerning; serpentine; energetic; circumspect; vigorous; recreation; zigzag; interdependent; lyrical; supple; agonized; timorous; hazardous; calm; cabalistic; springy; free; desultory; syncopated; enveloping; unanticipated; blithe; glacial; martial; present; cyclic; toss-over.

MOVER

adjectives
prime; mortal; fairest; unseen.

"MOVIE"

verbs
censor—; construct—; cram—with; direct —; film—; howl at—; inspire—; prevent—;

produce—; repress—; review—; romp through—; —amuses; —appeals; —attracts; —conveys; —depicts; —entertains; —excites; —refreshes; —surges; —thrills.

(See film, play, story.)

MUCOUS

verbs

cast out—; discharge—; eject—; emit—; excrete—; expel—; exude—; secrete—; —drains from; —emanates from; —issues; —lubricates; —moistens; —oozes.

(See secretion, discharge.)

MUD

adjectives

gurgling; oozing; sticky; flung; black; tenacious; dragging; poisonous; treacherous; viscous; sluggish; slimy; clinging; great; ancient; sloshing; hopeless; frozen; fertilizing; dense; respectable; spattered; caked; dried; jellylike.

verbs

bake—; bathe in—; bespatter with—; bog in—; cake—; dabble in—; daub with—; emerge from—; flounder in—; lodge in—; mire in—; plod through—; roll in—; sling —; spatter with—; steep in—; swash through—; wade through—; wallow in—; —cakes; —gurgles; —spatters; —sucks.

(See mire, dirt, filth, swamp, marsh.)

MUDDLE

adjectives

appalling; miserable; vicious; intricate; indescribable.

MUDDLED

adverbs

hopelessly; strangely; unfortunately; helplessly; mysteriously; vaguely; comically; tragically; disastrously; completely; horribly; indescribably; obviously; unmistakably; visibly; manifestly; dazedly; brokenly; pathetically; inexpertly; laughably; foolishly; greatly.

MUDDY

adverbs

untidily; deeply; impassably; horribly; distressingly; grimily; thickly; turbidly; foully; disagreeably; unpleasantly; inconceivably; unexpectedly; astonishingly; impossibly; dangerously; obstructively; swampily; quaggily.

MUFFLED

adverbs

dimly; obscurely; deliberately; unpleasantly; closely; furtively; stealthily; carefully; warily; softly; inaudibly; sepulchrally; confidentially; evasively; tremulously; curiously; peculiarly; faintly; cautiously.

MUGGY

adverbs

unpleasantly; disagreeably; humidly; damply; soggily; suffocatingly; smotheringly; breathlessly; unhealthily; duskily; dimly; obscurely; strangely; remarkably; extremely; peculiarly; confusingly; foggily; mistily; warmly; intolerably; distressingly.

MULE

adjectives

burdened; unshod; bare-backed; toil-enduring; snail-paced; flea-bitten; fruit-laden; sure-footed; lagging; jaded; opinionative; jingling; patient.

verbs

burden—; fetter—; guide—; manage—; rein—; tether—; water—; —balks; —s caracole; —carries; —endures; —groans; —hauls; —haunches; —kicks; —pulls; —shies; —snorts; —strains; —wearies.

(See mare, livestock, animal, donkey.)

MULISH

adverbs

doggedly; intractably; intolerably; disagreeably; unpleasantly; obstinately; sullenly; stubbornly; defiantly; dogmatically; immovably; inflexibly; obdurately; perversely; sulkily; stiffly; tenaciously; waywardly; wilfully; determinedly; obstreperously; remarkably; notoriously; inveterately; confoundedly; terribly.

MULLIONED

adverbs

artistically; elegantly; richly; elaborately; gorgeously; splendidly; magnificently; beautifully.

MULTIPLY (*v*)

adverbs

ceaselessly; prodigiously; exceedingly; miraculously; alarmingly; lustily; mathematically; beneficially; wantonly; deliberately; disconcertingly.

(See increase, enlarge.)

adjectives
vast; breathless; productive; feathered; rude; assembled; furious; buzzing; pleased; barbarous; flocking; lessening; tawny; infuriated; anarchic; immense; applauding; dripping; straggling; carven; hushed; pestilence-stricken; considerable; interminable; prostrate; polluting; thronging; picturesque; kindred; shadowy; overawed; blissful; soaring; promiscuous; babbling; dauntless; heavenly; superfluous; inextinguishable; captive; blind; panting; white-robed; distracted; unthoughtful; dizzy; potent; joyous; clamorous; trampled; groaning; adoring.

verbs
assail—; condemn—; convert—; convey to —; despise—; enthrall—; govern—; harangue—; inspire—; move—; rouse—; rule —; scorn—; —blasphemes; —congregates; —flees; —gathers; —masses; —swarms; —throngs; —worships.
(See crowd, invader, horde, legion, masses, mob.)

MUM

adverbs
discreetly; prudently; wisely; carefully; decently; reliably; securely; sagely; sagaciously; taciturnly; laconically; reticently; quietly; calmly; resolutely; determinedly; uncommunicatively; cautiously; warily; loyally; judiciously; considerately; courteously; shrewdly; judiciously; sensibly; discerningly; remarkably; deliberately; significantly.

MUMBLE (v)

adverbs
inarticulately; vaguely; bashfully; gruffly; querulously; idiotically; roughly; monotonously; irreverently; formidably; outlandishly; grotesquely; gruesomely.
(See mutter, utter.)

MUMMERY

adjectives
ghostly; profane; present; unmeaning.

MUNCH (v)

adverbs
placidly; cozily; contentedly; dreamily; greedily; famishedly; toothlessly; insatiably.
(See chew, nibble, eat.)

MUNICIPALITY

adjectives
obsequious; sham; ring-ridden; patriotic.

MUNIFICENT

adverbs
lavishly; surprisingly; astonishingly; bountifully; extravagantly; incredibly; wastefully; abundantly; bounteously; unimaginably; excessively; preposterously; ostentatiously; exorbitantly; inordinately; magnificently; philanthropically; pompously; notably; charitably.

MURDER

adjectives
cold-blooded; wanton; complicated; anarchic; mightiest; mortal; contested; high-handed; potential; unparalleled; unprovoked; foul; direful; nihilistic; sacrilegious; treacherous; willful; judicial; deliberate; various (pl); ruthless; gruesome.

verbs
atone for—; avenge—; contrive—; cover—; exalt—; execute—; expiate—; perform—; perpetrate—; plan—; plot—; punish—; redeem—; relish—; repent—; reveal—; revenge—; —awes; —confuses; —scandalizes; —terrifies.
(See killing, assassination, massacre, mortality.)

MURDER (v)

adverbs
pitilessly; deliberately; foully; treacherously; inhumanly; wantonly; unprovokedly; direfully; sacrilegiously; gruesomely; ruthlessly; irrationally; sadistically.
(See kill, butcher.)

MURDERER

adjectives
cowardly; viperous; notorious; guilty; cursed; egregious; bloody.

verbs
apprehend—; curse—; execute—; glorify—; hunt—; incarcerate—; inspire—; net—; overtake—; overwhelm—; pardon—; penalize—; reproach—; reveal—; sate—; sentence—; spot—; stain—; terrify—; —contrives; —flees; —stifles.
(See assassin, kidnapper, robber, thief.)

MURDEROUS

adverbs

savagely; cruelly; vengefully; brutally; insanely; fiercely; strangely; alarmingly; dangerously; ominously; dreadfully; portentously; unmistakably; presumably; stealthily; fearfully; enormously; undeniably; incontestably.

MURKY

adverbs

strangely; unaccountably; curiously; dimly; smokily; faintly; obscurely; darkly; duskily; thickly; dangerously; alarmingly; ominously; frighteningly; unseasonably; gloomily; dismally; drearily; dankly; somberly; mistily; muggily; dingily; awfully.

MURMUR

adjectives

awed; sad; long-pent; softer; prolonged; exacting; rapid; prophetic; perpetual; crunching; splashing; faint; applauding; tender; portentous; thrilling; pervading; mimic; sullen; startling; depreciating; powerless; homely; monotonous; rustic; singing; inarticulate; gurgling; hasty; pleasing; shallow; wailing; drowsy; self-contemptuous; hurtful; satisfying; ominous; inarticulate; deepening; mournful; foreboding; whispering; lulling; popular; confused; gentle; kindling; querulous; broken; hushed; perturbed; irrepressible; plaintive; dissentient; cheerful; reverent; hollow; melodious; sympathetic; elusive; low; formidable.

verbs

break—; breathe—; buzz with—s; emit—; melt into—; restrain—; smother—; soften into—; stifle—; still—; subdue—; —floats; —flows; —perturbs; —pervades; —ripples in; —trickles through.

(See hum, sigh, sob.)

MURMUR (v)

adverbs

demurely; complacently; involuntarily; dreamily; drowsily; ceaselessly; whimsically; despondently; moodily; plaintively; apologetically; ruefully; ecstatically; dolefully; hoarsely; deprecatingly; languorously.

(See whisper, mutter.)

MUSCLES

adjectives

well-strung; saddle; noble; flaccid; facial; intestinal; sagging; important; massive; fatigued; aching; expressive; quivering; strengthened; painful; wild; bulging; sturdy; smashing; sledge-hammer; important; strained; swelling; gnarled; swollen; weary; prominent.

verbs

bring—into play; contract—; control—; distort—; embed in—; employ—; enlarge—; exercise—; exert—; expand—; flex—; govern—; incise—; inflame—; invigorate—; limber—; lodge in—; massage—; reeducate —; rejuvenate—; relax—; stiffen—; swell —; tense—; tone up—; weaken—; — atrophy; —bulge; —degenerate; —knot; — quiver; —ripple; —support; —twitch.

(See ligament, body, tendon.)

MUSCULAR

adverbs

amazingly; incredibly; robustly; sturdily; brawnily; athletically; wonderfully; unusually; uncommonly; remarkably; vigorously; powerfully; wirily; admirably; wondrously; soundly; tremendously; invincibly; unbelievably; unconquerably.

MUSE (v)

adverbs

pensively; dolefully; romantically; affectionately; nostalgically; irrelevantly; disconsolately; regretfully.

(See meditate, ponder, reflect.)

MUSES

adjectives

mournful; worst-humored; inspiring; gentle; dreamy; dauntless; humanizing.

MUSEUM

adjectives

local; desolate; veritable; admirable; provincial; miniature.

verbs

assemble in—; bequeath to—; congregate in —; dedicate—to; donate—; endow—; exhibit in—; flock to—; guide through—; muster in—; pack—; ransack—; refer to—; store in—; stream through—; —accumulates; —aggregates; —amasses; —collects; —compiles; —displays; —inspires; —preserves; —sponsors.

MUSIC

adjectives

unregarded; undying; orchestral; barbaric;

instrumental; contemporary; pianoforte; virginal; classical; charming; polyphonic; effective; sparkling; picturesque; elegiac; tragic; sonorous; higher; symphonic; concerted; random; intellectual; homophonic; starry; potential; excellent; secular; voluptuous; low; molten; bold; incidental; mechanized; martial; negroid; jocund; sweet; sinewy; brilliant; torrential; melancholy; mournful; heady; graceful; exquisite; grotesque; vocal; echoing; surging; nationalistic; dumb; ethereal; prismatic; deep-sweet; transporting; melting; evening; tinkling; shrill; steady; enchanted; worthy; unearthly; lively; reeling; dancing; ecclesiastical; liturgical; discordant; seraphic; sensuous; sacred; repining; contrapuntal; roaring; unutterable; half-delirious; pensive; chamber; gay; lilting; mere; persuasive; complex; outlandish; glad; contemporary; preluding; tawdry; delicious; hushed; sparkling; tantalizing; deathless; cadent; sobbing; measureless; brassy; meretricious; triumphant; soul-awakening; grinding; mewling.

verbs
mingle with—; ring with—; set to—; silence —; soften—; strum out—; sway to—; — awakens; —beats; —blares; —charms; — clashes; —electrifies; —elevates; —ensnares; —enthralls; —fascinates; —floats from; —humanizes; —kindles; —lessens; — moans; —mourns; —pauses; —rolls; — sobs; —soothes; —subsides; —swells; — throbs; —tingles; adapt—; drink in—.
(See hymn, modulation, jazz, song, melody.)

MUSICIAN
adjectives
erudite; excellent; graceful; temperamental; foreign-bred; self-taught; skilled; indignant; impertinent; capable; endowed; contemporary; airy; authoritative; eminent; talented; influential.

verbs
acclaim—; accord—; applaud—; encourage —; entreat—; inspire—; welcome—; — bows; —charms; —delights; —dreams; — enchants; —expresses; —interprets; —loosens; —moves; —pours; —renders; — soothes; —speaks; —strays; —thrills.
(See artist.)

MUSKET
adjectives
old-fashioned; smoky; percussion; ancient; unused.

verbs
arm with—; bear—; combat with—; discharge—; employ—; enlist—; force from—; provide—; repel with—; retaliate with—; salute with—; shoulder—; storm with—; wield—; —crackles; —flashes; —glitters; — rattles.
(See gun, pistol, machine gun, rifle.)

MUSLIN
adjectives
saffron; superior; unbleached; spotless; cream-tinted.

MUSSY
adverbs
inexcusably; unpleasantly; untidily; inexplicably; unnecessarily; unaccountably; senselessly; carelessly; shiftlessly; confusedly; chaotically; troublesomely; vexatiously; irritatingly; intolerably; disagreeably; inchoately; incidentally; casually; improvidently; wastefully; inconsiderately.

MUSTACHE
adjectives
cream-colored; tobacco-stained; thick; immature; stiff; iron-gray; jaunty; white; budding; sprouting; sandy; swooping; dashing; curling; tawny; twirled; waxed; indomitable; walrus; sleek; slight; silken; well-trimmed; disdainful; grizzled; blond; silver-streaked; fierce; pepper-and-salt; weedy.

MUSTANG
verbs
retreat before—; break—; breed—s; bridle —; captivate—; check—; confine—to; consign—to; corral—; domesticate—; entrap —; restrain—; round up—s; spur—; stable —; tame—; tether—; —roves; —shies; — wanders.
(See horse.)

MUSTARD
verbs
anoint with—; cultivate—; flavor with—; grind—; mix—; plaster—on; prepare—; relish—; savor—; season with—; smear—;

spice with—; spoon—; spread—; —bites; —flatters; —heightens; —sharpens; —stings. (See salt, spice.)

MUTES

adjectives
obedient; congenital; deaf; wistful.

MUTILATION

verbs
conceal—; fear—; lament—; mend—; punish by—; recover from—; resort to—; sentence to—; suffer—; —attends; —blemishes; —blights; —defaces; —deforms; —deprives; —disfigures; —disables; —handicaps; —pains; —shocks; subject to—.
(See laceration, sabotage, injury, violence.)

MUTINOUS

adverbs
uncontrollably; ungovernably; tumultuously; rebelliously; turbulently; uproariously; unmanageably; riotously; chaotically; dangerously; ominously; portentously; intensely; terribly; alarmingly; doggedly; sullenly; brutally; sternly; murderously; seditiously; truculently; wildly; restlessly; disturbingly; oddly; uneasily; secretly.

MUTINY

adjectives
abortive; famous; practical; incited; exciting; long-planned.

verbs
attempt—; commit—; conspire—; draw into —; encounter—; inspire—; instigate—; invite—; overcome—; quash—; quell—; quench—; rise in—; rouse to—; seethe with —; snuff out—; suppress—; —roars; —smashes; —strikes; —threatens; —unfolds.
(See revolution, rebellion, insurrection.)

MUTTER

adjectives
incessant; drowsy; articulate; growling; low.

MUTTER (v)

adverbs
threateningly; despairingly; incoherently; mournfully; huskily; inaudibly; fitfully; defiantly; savagely; grimly; indistinctly; incessantly; drunkenly; thickly; bestially.
(See murmur, utter.)

MUTTERING

adjectives
internal; magic; bewildered; instant; habitual; unpleasant; inane; drear; visceral.

MUZZLE

adjectives
outstretched; creamy; glittering; shiny; gleaming.

verbs
burst—; clap on—; disengage—; emerge from—; impose—; jam on—; link—; require—; secure—; —checks; —controls; —curbs; —gags; —masks; —prevents; —represses; —restrains; —restricts.
(See brake, collar.)

MYRIADS

adjectives
phantom; propagated; humbler; countless; breathing; swarming; misty.

MYSTERIOUS

adverbs
altogether; strangely; perplexingly; uncomfortably; distressingly; unutterably; occultly; inscrutably; mystically; preposterously; pretentiously; unreasonably; foolishly; unnecessarily; vaguely; cryptically; inordinately; unfathomably; impenetrably; indefinitely; darkly; inviolately; evasively; queerly.

MYSTERY

adjectives
sweet; solemn; unsolved; bewildering; mighty; durable; inscrutable; profound; dread; artistic; baffling; overpowering; woodland; unaccountable; venerable; incarnate; hateful; fashionable; ridiculous; inevitable; unfolded; delicate; gray; unanswerable; ecstatic; unborn; worshipful; embarrassing; unexplored; mild; bearded; abstruse; labyrinthine; sacred; solemn; prime; sublime; peculiar; subtle; unfathomable; hungering; occult; sensational; painful; brooding; wingy; domestic; indescribable; deluding; juggling; physical; shrouding; selfsame.

verbs
absorb in—; cloak in—; comprehend—; concoct—; confront with—; deepen—; delve into—; dispel—; dissipate—; elucidate—; encompass by—; envelop in—; explore—ies of; fathom—; ferret out—; heighten—; init-

iate into—; penetrate—; plumb—; ponder —; reveal—; shroud in—; solve—; unlock —; unravel—; unveil—; wrap in—; — baffles; —prevails; —surrounds.

(See marvel, miracle, enigma, secret, maze.)

MYSTIC

adverbs
casually; vaguely; mysteriously; obscurely; precariously; unintelligibly; unfathomably; inscrutably; curiously; strangely; oddly; queerly; nebulously; symbolically; darkly; inferentially; impenetrably; covertly; magically; incomprehensibly.

MYSTICISM

adjectives
mellow; spiritual; sensuous; dramatic; philosophical.

verbs
achieve—; capitulate to—; chatter—; cloud by—; contemplate—; dabble in—; derive— from; devour—; entertain with—; immerse in—; involve—; poison by—; rationalize—;

ridicule—; speculate on—; steep in—; wallow in—; —deludes; —pervades; —perverts; —poses as.

(See magic, doctrine, belief.)

MYTH

adjectives
nature; heroic; solar; ancient; aboriginal; domestic.

verbs
blast—; conceive—; dispel—; dissipate—; eradicate—; explode—; give rise to—; narrate—; preserve—; shatter—; strangle—; trace—; —antedates; —deals with; —develops; —evolves from; —explains; —grows; —portrays; —reflects; —relates; —reverberates; —survives; —wanes.

(See legend, fiction, story.)

MYTHOLOGICAL

adverbs
fabulously; fantastically; fancifully; presumably; probably; supposedly; speculatively; presumptively; preposterously; presumably; remotely; fantastically; groundlessly; purely; authentically; authoritatively; altogether; wholly.

800

N

adverbs

shrewishly; maddeningly; unceasingly; monotonously; repetitiously; bitterly; acrimoniously; offensively; vehemently; viciously; diabolically.

(See tease, torment.)

NAIL

adjectives

tapering; cruel; brass-headed; sulphurous; diamond; slim; sturdy; bent; rusty.

verbs

cast—; clip off—; drive—; fabricate—s; fasten with—; hammer—; impale on—; mend with—; pound in—; secure with—; strike—; stud with—s; suspend from—; thump—; whack—; —impinges; —pierces; —rivets; —splinters.

(See fang, claw, pin, rivet, point, hook.)

NAIVE

adverbs

charmingly; unexpectedly; ingenuously; quaintly; childishly; incredibly; pitifully; pathetically; absurdly; ridiculously; laughably; ludicrously; unaccountably; inexplicably; surprisingly; sweetly; obviously; overwhelmingly; plainly; disarmingly; delightfully; refreshingly; cheerfully; unsuspiciously; utterly.

NAKED

adverbs

shamelessly; distressingly; pitiably; pathetically; grievously; scandalously; miserably; utterly; painfully; shockingly; horribly; wretchedly; deplorably.

NAKEDNESS

adjectives

primitive; sad; uncomely; cherubic; utter.

NAMBY-PAMBY

adverbs

hopelessly; feebly; pathetically; vexatiously; irritatingly; absurdly; unutterably; disgustingly; reprehensibly; ridiculously; deplorably; incurably; naturally; inherently; detestably; nervously; incomprehensibly; surprisingly; spinelessly; submissively; pliantly.

adjectives

republican; specious; altered; immortal; ambitious; fictitious; high-sounding; low; humble; feigned; aristocratic; charming; potent; endearing; opprobrious; musical; spotless; sacred; unworthy; blighted; generic; prosaic; gentle; uncommon; lasting; mystic; glorious; uncomfortable; interchangeable (pl); fashionable; bucolic; revolting; disreputable; creditable; naked; baptismal; beloved; honored; untarnished; hapless; worthless; ill; fair; mellifluous; doubtful; sonorous; imperial; servant; ancient; deathless; charitable; all-adored; stainless; ragged; abominable; deferential; saucy; everlasting; meaningless; ungentlemanly; hateful; illustrious; dreadful; flattering; inappropriate; grotesque; sheltering; hieroglyphic; long-living; distinguished; imposing; significant; unforgettable; deep-cut; humorous; childish; almighty; noble; unpronounceable; imperishable; respected; contemptuous; complaining; beauteous; musical; impious; wonted; graceless; inconspicuous; revered; phantom; soft; foremost; idolized; lustrous; poisonous; unblemished; influential; important; excellent; famous; good; euphonious; exact; renowned; night-begotten; authoritative; lofty; florid; vaunting; cherished; latinized; assumed; characteristic; family; poetic; suggestive; incongruous; wounded; borrowed; unsoiled; botanical; eminent; alluring; international; classical; inviolable; inoffensive; impressed; heroic; patrician; objectionable; half-mocking; haughtier; shining; fashionable.

verbs

adopt—; append—to; apply—to; assume—; attach interest to—; bear—; besmirch—; bestow—upon; blaspheme—; brand—; coin —; conjure with—; couple—s of; deprecate —; dignify—; dismiss—; divulge—; glorify —; identify with—; inscribe—; link—with; perpetuate—; preserve—; reveal—; scrawl —; stain—; thunder—; usurp—; venerate —; —blazes; —bobs up; —conveys; —derives; —embodies; —implies; —recurs; — shines; —strikes terror; —suggests.

(See title, character, reputation.)

adverbs

speciously; ambitiously; fictitiously; humbly; aristocratically; musically; generically; prosaically; mystically; mellifluously; sonorously; deferentially; significantly; contemptuously; characteristically; offensively; heroically; haughtily; originally; appropriately; promptly.

(See entitle, designate.)

NAMELESS

adverbs

obscurely; curiously; remotely; ingloriously; unhappily; humbly; meekly; strangely; unfortunately; ignominiously; purposely; sadly; significantly; necessarily; abjectly; opprobriously; pathetically; diplomatically; strategically.

NAPKIN

verbs

edge—; fold—; fringe—; gather—; hold —; monogram—; mop with—; ring—; soil —; sponge with—; tuck—; utilize—; whip open—; wrinkle—; —assures; —catches; —protects; —safeguards.

(See handkerchief, cloth, towel.)

NARCOTICS

verbs

abstain from—; addict to—; control—; distribute—; drowse under—; inhale—; inject —; load with—; peddle—; purvey—; smuggle—; specialize in—; swallow—; trade in —; traffic in—; warn against—; —corrupt; —defile; —degenerate; —deteriorate; — ease; —induce; —menace; —poison; —ravage; —stultify; —wreck.

(See drug, heroin, medicine.)

NARRATE (v)

adverbs

bizarrely; absorbingly; vividly; romantically; grippingly; dramatically; movingly; deftly; tensely; vigorously; artfully; prosaically.

(See tell, recite, relate.)

NARRATION

adjectives

dramatic; bare; vivid; gripping; moving; swift; sure; deft; skilled; breathless.

verbs

blend into—; color—; commend—; discuss —; embellish—; enter into—; introduce into

—; publish—; recite—; recount—; rehearse —; resume—; set forth in—; state in—; — delights; —depicts; —enchants; —enthralls; —portrays; —reveals; —unfolds.

(See lecture, story, tale.)

NARRATIVE

adjectives

dry; boasting; comprehensive; epical; enticing; shocking; contemporary; lugubrious; disjointed; digested; romantic; autobiographical; superficial; sober; poetical; imaginative; touching; dramatic; tragic; vivid; melodramatic; sacred; graphic; connected; superb; splendid; fictitious; thrilling; faithful; concise; mirthful; chequered; trustworthy; serious; earnest; authentic; metrical; truthful; personal; descriptive; persuasive; fantastic; voluminous; incredible; celebrated; present; masterly; supernatural; painful; pathetic.

verbs

acclaim—; blend into—; commend—; complicate—; condense—; embellish—; enliven —; impair—; interlard—; introduce in—; peruse—; recount—; set forth in—; spice —; strew throughout—; sum up—; —delights; —enchants; —flows; —portrays; — strikes; —unfolds.

(See fiction, lecture, legend, anecdote, story, tale.)

NARROW (v)

adverbs

appreciably; markedly; abruptly; perilously; impracticably; strikingly.

(See reduce, contract.)

NARROW

adverbs

impossibly; terribly; unbelievably; remarkably; painfully; inconveniently; inexplicably; outlandishly; stingily; frugally; parsimoniously; absurdly; ridiculously; perilously; hazardously; dangerously; inexcusably; outrageously; shockingly; terrifyingly; uselessly; unserviceably; curiously; undesirably; vexatiously; perplexingly; uncommonly.

NARROW-MINDED

adverbs

stubbornly; intolerably; intractably; obdurately; wilfully; incurably; incorrigibly; persistently; fanatically; perniciously; obstinately; hopelessly; mulishly; incomprehensibly; inveterately.

adjectives
ignoble; puritanic; **old-fashioned**; mental; moral; unexpected.

NASTY

adverbs
squalidly; obscenely; **indelicately**; disgustingly; offensively; repulsively; odiously; disagreeably; unnecessarily; unpardonably; indecently; loathsomely; nauseatingly; diabolically; terribly; sickeningly; unhealthfully; pestilentially; dangerously; unsanitarily.

NATION

adjectives
powerful; puissant; guarded; shopkeeping; delivered; advanced; expectant; friendly; regenerated; dusky; surrounding (pl); liberated; disenchanted; grateful; altruistic; respective; warring; neighboring; restless; energetic; impressionable; civilized; happy; peaceable; wretched; impoverished; delusive; motley; swarming; greedy; aggressive; magnificent; resolute; impudent; unpolished; conquered; diverse; unsubdued; maritime; capitalist; woeful; eminent; scientific; long-suffering; declining; raw; mercantile; gentle; moral; uncivilized; stunned; helpless; leaderless; loyal; barbarous; brave; vigorous; ignorant; incredulous; benighted; sacred; homogeneous; burdened; stricken; unfriended; ambitious; progressive; wild; corrupted; exceptional; callous; courageous; brave; enslaved; eager; fickle; ill-assorted; ancient.

verbs
awaken—; blanket—; compensate—; convulse—; envelop—; filch from—; further—; incite—; inflame—; jolt—; liberate—; menace—; realign—; seduce—; terrorize—; trample—; —decays; —embarks on; —quakes; —retaliates; —rises; —s vie for.
(See folk, country, empire, public.)

NATIONAL

adverbs
strongly; ardently; narrowly; broadly; strictly; eagerly; fervently; intensely; devotedly; fiercely; zealously; indifferently; enthusiastically; sharply; selfishly; actively; admirably.

adjectives
intense; spiritual; ardent; growing; evident; forced; powerful.

verbs
advocate—; base on—; breed—; cultivate —; defend—; encourage—; favor—; foster —; institute—; justify—; maintain—; prate of—; prescribe—; respect—; seethe with—; steep in—; threaten—; value—; —characterizes; —comforts; —shields; —smooths.
(See democracy, atheism, socialism, independence.)

NATIONALITIES

adjectives
dominant; jarring; divers; healthy; autonomous.

NATIONALITY

verbs
annihilate—; cast off—; characterize—; color—; denote—; deny—; describe—; distinguish—; efface—; extinguish—; ferret out—; protest—; renounce—; threaten—; —pains; —vanishes.
(See heritage, nation.)

NATIVE

adverbs
unquestionably; genuinely; happily; indigenously; unaffectedly; frankly; plainly; obviously; advantageously; contentedly; indubitably; conveniently; warrantably.

NATIVES

adjectives
frightened; superstitious; credulous; bedizened; grinning; influential; energetic; polygamous; well-connected; indifferent; effeminate; nondescript; bronzed; free-born; wretched; exiled; unprejudiced; guileless; predatory; genuine; belated.

verbs
astonish—; commend—; dispute with—; encounter—; fraternize with—; interrogate—; scuffle with—; —adhere; —adopt; —fashion; —inhabit; —merit; —populate; —praise; —rear.
(See inhabitant, Indian, negro, peasant.)

NATURAL

adverbs
essentially; inherently; artlessly; honestly; ingenuously; openly; unaffectedly; spontane-

ously; simply; frankly; naively; cordially; delightfully; suddenly; altogether; refreshingly; touchingly; wondrously; charmingly; ravishingly; unbelievably; graciously; innocently; alluringly; childishly; guilelessly; youthfully; pleasantly.

NATURALIST
adjectives
well-known; inoffensive; abstracted; wise.

verbs
appeal to—; unfold to—; —breeds; —classifies; —collects; —conserves; —examines; —exhausts; —fathoms; —gazes on; —invades; —investigates; —marvels at; —observes; —preserves; —reflects; —studies; —tabulates; —treasures; —treks; —verifies; —worships.

(See scientist, philosopher.)

NATURALIZATION
verbs
approve—; await—; consider—; deny—; desire—; dispute—; encourage—; gain—; merit—; prepare for—; protest—; qualify for—; question—; seek—; undergo—; —commends; —ensues; —insures; —privileges.

(See citizenship.)

NATURE
verbs
attune to—; conform to—; defy—; endow by —; master—; mirror—; observe—; portray —; reflect—; rely on—; return to—; struggle with—; subdue—; supplant—; take refuge in—; wring from—; —allures; —arrays; —bestows; —decrees; —exacts; —imposes; —molds; —paints; —plays; —rejoices; —sanctions; —shapes; —stages; —thwarts; —unfolds; supplement—.

(See instinct, God, life, convention, conventionality.)

NATURE
adjectives   (*character*)
abject; able; adventurous; affectionate; agitating; angelic; animate; arduous; arrogant; artistic; awakening; awed; belated; beneficent; binding; boisterous; blind; blithesome; bloody; blunt; brooding; brute; bubbling; buoyant; calculating; calm; cantankerous; cautious; capricious; celestial; chivalrous; clinging; cold; combative; communicable; complicated; composite; conceited; concentrated; confiding; conscientious; conservative; contracted; contradictory; contrary; controversial; corporeal; craven; creating; cruel; crumbling; cursed; cynical; daring; darkening; dazzled; definite; delicate; delightful; desperate; determined; diabolical; dictatorial; difficult; diligent, dismal; disordered; distasteful; diversified; domineering; dual; dynamic; easygoing; ecclesiastical; elemental; elevated; emotional; enduring; encouraging; engrossing; erratic; essential; everlasting; evil; exacting; exaggerating; exclusive; exhilarating; expansive; exquisite; external; extraordinary; false; fastidious; fearless; fiendish; fiery; finite; forbearing; forbidding; formidable; frank; friable; frivolous; functional; generous; gloomy; gracious; half-savage; great; gross; hardy; harmonious; harsh; hateful; haughty; hazardous; heaven-born; hereditary; heretical; hidden; hideous; highstrung; honest; honorable; horrible; hostile; human; illustrious; hysterical; immaterial; immutable; imperfect; imperious; impetuous; imperturbable; impracticable; inanimate; incomprehensible; incongruous; indigenous; infectious; infinite; inherent; inmost; inorganic; inscrutable; inspired; intellectual; intense; internal; interpretative; intimate; intrinsic; introspective; intuitive; invertebrate; kind; irritable; latent; lavish; leonine; light; living; lofty; lovable; luxuriant; maimed; magnetic; marked; martial; mean; material; mechanical; melancholy; mid-summer; mercurial; merry; mild; mischievous; miraculous; mismade; moral; murky; mute; mysterious; neutral; niggard; noble; obscure; observant; omnipotent; onerous; operative; opposed; opulent; oracular; ostentatious; outward; painful; paradoxical; parallel; parsimonious; passionate; patriotic; peculiar; pecuniary; personal; phantasmagorical; planetary; playful; pliant; poetic; polished; popular; populous; precise; praiseworthy; prime; primitive; private; probable; prodigal; profaning; prophetic; protracted; proud; quarrelsome; quick; radiant; rash; rational; reasonable; recalcitrant; receptive; recondite; religious; reluctant; restless; retiring; revengeful; rude; sanguine; sardonic; savage; seasonal; self-effacing; self-sacrificing; sensitive; sensuous; sentient; sentimental; severe; shallow; shrinking; silent; sluggish; social; sordid; soldierly; sorry; sound; specific; spiritual; spiteful; spoiled; spontaneous; sterling; stifled; strong; struggling; subordinate; sturdy; subtle; sunny; sympathizing;

swampy; tangible; teaching; temperate; tenacious; thoroughgoing; timid; transitional; transitory; trite; trivial; truthful; ultimate; unadvanced; unblemished; uncompromising; uncultivated; undisciplined; unending; unfatherly; ungentlemanly; ungracious; unique; universal; unoffending; unpoetic; unpredictable; unprofessional; unrepentant; unselfish; unsociable; unstable; untaught; untractable; untrained; upright; vacant; vague, vain; vehement; vengeful; virile; vital; vivacious; voiceless; volatile; volcanic; voluntary; voracious; vulgar; wary; weak; weighty; well-derived; wild; willful; winged; wiry; wistful.

verbs
alter—; ascertain—; bewail—; crush—; determine—; disfigure—; dwarf—; elevate—; flaunt—; indicate—; manifest—; mold—; offend—; recognize—; sate—; temper—; — prompts.
(See character, quality.)

NAUGHTY
adverbs
roguishly; mischievously; childishly; disagreeably; thoughtlessly; embarrassingly; slyly; furtively; innocently; unbearably; maliciously; surprisingly; unwontedly; unusually; vexatiously; remarkably; perversely; incorrigibly; curiously; uncommonly; extremely; scampishly; prankishly; gracelessly.

NAUSEA
verbs
escape—; excite—; induce—; loathe—; relieve—; overcome with—; remedy—; sate to —; seize with—; shock into—; stifle—; suffer—; —agonizes; —disgusts; —dispirits; —grieves; —wearies.
(See vomiting, disgust, resentment, hatred.)

NAUSEOUS
adverbs
terribly; uncommonly; disagreeably; offensively; unnecessarily; unpardonably; unbearably; grievously; painfully; bitterly; obnoxiously; mortifyingly; intolerably; appallingly; hatefully; hideously; insufferably.

NAUTICAL
adverbs
correctly; properly; appropriately; unquestionably; completely; admirably; wildly; charmingly; brightly; nattily.

NAVAL
adverbs
strictly; gloriously; strongly; invincibly.

NAVIGATE (v)
adverbs
precariously; professionally; deftly; skillfully; seasonally; intrepidly; daringly; fearlessly; disastrously.
(See sail, guide, steer.)

NAVIGATION
adjectives
celestial; uninterrupted; protracted; widespread; ocean.

NAVY
adjectives
auxiliary; unexploring; dauntless; protective; strong; fearless; well-manned; undersized; great.

verbs
enlist in—; equip—; maintain—; modernize —; volunteer for—; —defends; —manoeuvres; —patrols; —practises; —recruits; — safeguards; —schools; —trains; —transports; —yields.
(See militia, fleet, army.)

NEAR
adverbs
intimately; advantageously; conveniently; pleasantly; agreeably; handily; surprisingly; remarkably; unexpectedly; ominously; unfortunately; happily; luckily; opportunely; profitably.

NEARNESS
adjectives
immediate; familiar; unknown; breathless.

NEAT
adverbs
painfully; pleasantly; incorrigibly; particularly; remarkably; incomparably; curiously; intolerably; placidly; extremely; admirably; perfectly; habitually; incurably; uniformly; immaculately; daintily; exquisitely; jauntily; attractively; spotlessly; miraculously.

NEATNESS
adjectives
expectant; chilly; unusual; indescribable; extreme; miraculous; meticulous; incomparable.

verbs

cluster into—; cover with—; —beautify; —charm; —decorate; —embellish; —enchant; —enhance; —fascinate; —illuminate; —mantle; —mass; —mist; —patch; —powder; —thicken; —whirl.

(See stars, clouds.)

NEBULOUS

adverbs

vaguely; dimly; obscurely; umbrageously; foggily; mistily; faintly; confusingly; bewilderingly; vaporously; unfathomably; dangerously; hazardously; alarmingly; perplexingly; unpleasantly; extremely.

NECESSARY

adverbs

strictly; hardly; scarcely; entirely; absolutely; completely; undeniably; obviously; definitely; manifestly; unquestionably; financially; economically; apparently; cruelly; unfortunately; unluckily; bitterly; imperatively; unavoidably; tragically; embarrassingly; terribly.

NECESSITY

adjectives

prime; humiliating; absolute; economic; empowered; stern; imperative; sheer; pecuniary; obvious; irresistible; physical; crying; urgent; relative; material; highborn; deplored; indispensable; mathemetical; righteous; pressing; time-honored; everyday; unalterable; inexorable; immutable; dire; expressive; practical; military; objective; cruel; dread; inevitable; invincible; belittling; strict; immediate; vicious; temporary; factitious; mortifying; fatal; unavoidable; logical; desperate; burning; fancied; superfluous; metaphysical; domestic; implacable; unyielding; marvelous; physiological; hypothetical; tragic; bitter; apparent; startling; household; amazing; fast-selling; feminine; clever; business; daily; money-saving.

verbs

argue—; feel—; fortify by—; illustrate—; impel by—; inspire by—; minister to—; obviate—; ponder—; preclude—; relieve of—; skimp on —s; urge—; yield to—; —abates; —arises; —cements; —compels; —forces; —pinches; —s pop up; —presses.

(See fate, emergency, exigency, compulsion, requirement, want, need.)

adjectives

beguiling; withered; distended; ivory; stiffening; corrigible; mottled; humbled; misshapen; glossy; feminine-looking; naked; graceful; gaunt; sinewy; glowing; gleaming; chic; square; distressful; shimmering; stately; snowy; athletic; scalloped; dry-skinned; nervous; wrinkled; thin; flattered; arching; queenly; silly; well-turned; sleek; jeweled; enameled.

verbs

adorn—; arch—; bow—; button at—; clutch by—; crane—; decorate—; dislocate—; exercise—; furbish—; jerk—; massage—; powder—; sever at—; wreathe—; yoke by—.

NECKTIE

verbs

adjust—; criticize—; examine—; knit—; knot—; loosen—; pattern—; print—; spot —; stripe—; weave—; yank (colloq.)—; —blazes; —exaggerates; —flames; —impresses; —infuriates; —matches; —overwhelms; —shocks.

(See cravat, handkerchief.)

NECTAR

verbs

bathe in—; draw — from; drown in—; nourish with—; relish—; secrete—; seek—; sink in—; spout—; suck—; tongue—; —cools; —delights; —intoxicates; —oozes; —gratifies; —steams.

(See sweetness, liquid, beverage, drink.)

NEED

adjectives

individual; imperative; critical; profound; fundamental; airy; spiritual; specialized; self-existing; genuine; unnumbered (pl); warranted; changing; pressing; burning; dubious; desperate; emergency; tragic; primitive; dreadful; urgent; future; spiritual; action-shaping; absolute; obvious; perpetual; definite; private; increasing; artless; shameful; dearest; psychic; extravagant; sorest; inexorable; diverse; economic; home; preliminary; intellectual; emotional; distinct; supreme; pervading; particular; deepest; practical; cruel; bitter; degrading; corporate; quiet.

verbs
anticipate—; ascertain—; awaken to—; beget—; bend to—; conceal—; define—; eliminate—; enunciate—; evince—; emphasize —; express—; meet—; minimize—; minister to—; portray—; reveal—; satisfy—; serve —; smother—; study—; supplant—; supply —; suppress—; survey—; torture by—; voice—; —arises; —dictates; —presses.
(See lack, impoverishment, inadequacy, exigency, necessity, want, poverty.)

NEED (v)
adverbs
direly; imperatively; horribly; desperately; sorely; urgently; critically; fundamentally; spiritually; genuinely; tragically; inexorably; economically; degradingly.
(See lack, require, want.)

NEEDLE
adjectives
magnetic; shining; cambric; trembling; glancing.

verbs
case—; direct—; dodge—; draw—through; grope for—; magnetize—; mend with—; ply —; polish—; prick with—; stick with—; thread—; tug at—; work with—; —designs; —flies; —penetrates; —perforates; —punctures.
(See pin, point.)

NEEDLESS
adverbs
utterly; apparently; altogether; absurdly; obviously; wholly; ridiculously; manifestly; inconsequentially.

NEEDY
adverbs
desperately; undoubtedly; warrantably; tragically; pitiably; pathetically; pitifully; hopelessly; helplessly; surprisingly; avowedly; lamentably; extremely; distressingly; unfortunately; sadly; strangely; unaccountably; obscurely; unquestionably; wretchedly; miserably; inexpressibly.

NEFARIOUS
adverbs
incomparably; abominably; diabolically; extremely; incredibly; unfathomably; wildly; deplorably; dangerously; unconscion-

ably; grossly; scandalously; malevolently; reprehensibly; gracelessly; shamelessly; monstrously.

NEGATIVE
adjectives
strange; audacious; emphatic; startled; definite; clear.

adverbs
feebly; hopelessly; fortunately; luckily; unquestionably; emphatically; flatly; peremptorily; blankly; virtually; completely; incontrovertibly; discouragingly; distressingly; unhappily; unexpectedly; avowedly; allegedly; presumably; probably.

NEGLECT
adjectives
habitual; ostentatious; unintentional; willful; deplorable; hideous; high-spirited; comparative; loving; disdainful; intended; culpable; apathetic; predestined; monstrous; infamous; total.

verbs
atone for—; breed—; charge with—; complain of—; convict of—; die of—; goad by —; pardon—; rescue from—; suffer—; throw into—; wither in—; —corrodes; —damages; —endangers; —harms; —injures; —insults; —rusts; —saps.
(See failure, default, carelessness.)

NEGLECT (v)
adverbs
habitually; ostentatiously; deplorably; hideously; wilfully; disdainfully; apathetically; monstrously; infamously; totally; shamefully; slovenly; impudently; improvidently.
(See ignore, disregard.)

NEGLIGENCE
adjectives
studied; sluggard; tonsorial; official; unwonted; thoughtless; military; criminal; occasional; gross; repeated; lazy; intermittent.

NEGLIGIBLE
adverbs
comparably; comparatively; altogether; somewhat; scarcely; shamefully; ignominiously; infamously; insignificantly; ridiculously; contemptibly; politically; socially; financially.

NEGOTIATE (v)

adverbs
craftily; astutely; ingeniously; zealously; diplomatically; solemnly; tactfully; separately; commercially; internationally.
(See treat.)

NEGOTIATIONS

adjectives
premature; pending; platonic; commercial; proposed; concurrent; abortive; temporal; complex; long-drawn-out; matrimonial; solemn; friendly; mercantile; secret; peace.

verbs
advocate—; assemble for—; bolt—; carry on—; commence—; depart from—; enter into—; favor—; open—; reopen—; renew —; suspend—; terminate—; —bore; —fail; —falter; —flounder; —succeed; —tire; —weary.
(See collective bargaining, meeting, conference.)

NEGRO

adjectives
tattered; superb; shiftless; accused; harassed; free; diligent; music-loving; melodious.

verbs
auction—es; deal in—es; educate—; emancipate—; lynch—; sympathize with—; tolerate—; understand—; uplift—; whip—; —chants; —coaxes; —es congregate; —contorts; —stomps; —"trucks"; —worships.
(See native, denizen, inhabitant.)

NEIGHBOR

adjectives
uncharitable; formidable; reticent; congenial; toxophilitic; pretentious; anarchist; near; marvelous; influential; good; over-bearing; backbiting; stout-shouldered; barbarian; amiable; peaceable; civilized; weaker; territorial; inquisitive; frivolous; infidel; gaping; charitable; calculating; dangerous; wingless; good-natured; barbarous; parallel; singular; perfidious; miserly; pleasant; companionable; afflicted; gossipy; enisled.

verbs
acknowledge—; associate with—; bicker with—; consort with—s; denounce—; drive out—; hedge—; respect—; rouse—s; sanctify—; scandalize—s; wrangle with—; —s

band; —befriends; —complains; —contends; —gossips; —imposes; —quarrels; —rivals; —visits.
(See friend, woman, enemy.)

NEIGHBORHOOD

adjectives
audacious; fashionable; moneyed; residential; frequented; immediate; disreputable; malodorous; adjoining; noisome; deteriorating; gruff.

verbs
arouse—; attract to—; avoid—; crowd—; denounce—; drive from—; explore—; huddle in—; inflame—; master—; preserve—; rule—; scandalize—; shun—; visit—; —appeals to; —bands together; —befriends; —congregates; —petitions.
(See locality, section, city, village, town, district.)

NEIGHBORLY

adverbs
actively; heartily; generously; wonderfully; agreeably; delightfully; helpfully; sincerely; sociably; extremely; unwontedly; incredibly; amicably; chattily; hospitably; gregariously; companionably; remarkably; heart-warmingly.

NEPHEW

adjectives
warming; prodigal; chubby; scapegrace; celebrated; spurious; disinherited.

NERVE

adjectives
firm; strained; tingling; marble; gustatory; languid; irritable; underlying; shaky; delicate; tremulous; sensitive; ragged; gentle; taut; excellent; iron; curious; auditory; miraculous; invisible; sciatic; wailing; harassed; shattered; vibrating; overstrained; optic; inconceivable; adamantine; shrinking; uncertain; tender; overstrung; revolutionary; high-strung; pneumogastric; exhausted; jangled; shuddering; silent; excitable; sympathetic; physical; oversusceptible; overwrought.

NERVELESS

adverbs
pitiably; helplessly; ineffectually; incompetently; curiously; pathetically; distressingly; miserably; wretchedly; ineptly; pitifully; limply; strangely.

verbs

addle—; calm—; constrict—; deaden—; desensitize—; dilate—; disturb—; drag at—; exhaust—; fray—; impinge upon—; irritate —; involve—; jangle—; jolt—; jar—; numb —; pad—; relax—; sever—; shatter—; shock—; soothe—; steady—; stimulate—; strain—; tranquilize—; unstring—; — bristle; —jump; —respond; —snap.

NERVOUS

adverbs

highly; uncommonly; extremely; significantly; pitifully; hysterically; feverishly; unnecessarily; strangely; absurdly; ridiculously; guiltily; curiously; physically; secretly; apparently; timidly; bashfully; childishly; exceedingly; pitiably; pathetically; ludicrously; sadly; touchingly; laughably; miserably; alarmingly; ominously; unfortunately.

NERVOUSNESS

adjectives

concealed; excessive; mere; feverish; subtle.

verbs

allay—; decline into—; enhance—; manifest —; overcome—; overpower—; remedy—; scoff at—; spring from—; suffer from—; — confuses; —debilitates; —deprives; —distresses; —disturbs; —enervates; —enfeebles; —shakes; —strains; —weakens.
(See hysteria, impatience, sickness.)

NERVOUS SYSTEM

verbs

derange— —; ease— —; excite— —; flow through— —; govern— —; guard— — from; impair— —; nourish— —; overwork — —; stimulate— —; strain— —; support — —; tax— —; — —collapses; — — cramps; — —links; — —recovers; — —responds.

NEST

adjectives

drowsy; clamorous; broodless; deserted; eternal; central; quiet; mossy; watery; northern; unmaternal; hungry; enlightened; pensile; well-built; shattered; windless; distant; balmy; spicy; sheltered; warm; cozy.

verbs

camouflage—; construct—; deposit in—; discover—; disturb—; expose—; hollow out —; huddle in—; incubate in—; isolate—; lodge in—; perch in—; pillage—; protect —; pry into—; quit—; retire to—; rob—; scoop out—; swing—; tree—; —comforts; —cradles; —shelters.
(See home, shelter, hole, hive. lair, refuge.)

NESTLE (v)

adverbs

snugly; cozily; domestically; tenderly; drowsily; warmly; affectionately.
(See cuddle.)

NET

adjectives

fishing; anchored; elastic; weblike; impassable; inescapable; closely-woven.

verbs

bag with—; capture in—; cast—; confine in—; construct—; dip—; dredge with—; dry—; fish with—; knit—; lower—; pay out —; repair—; secure with—; slip through— • spin—; spread—; stretch—; sweep into—; swim into—; trap in—; trawl with—; — drifts; —ensnares; —entangles.
(See trap, snare, mesh, network.)

NETTLE (v)

adverbs

intolerably; exasperatingly; maddeningly; spitefully; vengefully; cruelly; formidably; bitterly.
(See provoke, irritate.)

NETWORK

adjectives

gigantic; ramified; endless; ingenious; complicated; broadcasting; national; social.

verbs

bind into—; chain into—; construct—; control—; convey over—; extend—; hook up on —; incorporate—; interfere with—; join—; localize—; present over—; tie up with—; unravel—; weave—.
(See system, net.)

NEUROSIS

verbs

accentuate—; classify—; despise—; dispel —; explain—; group—es; ignore—; pronounce—; resist—; shake—; stem—; suffer from—; usher in—; —attacks; —cripples; —exists; —irritates; —nags; —obsesses; — persists; —upsets.
(See complex, disease, sickness.)

adjectives
advanced; compulsive; unfortunate; life-long; hapless.

adverbs
undeniably; vexatiously; hopelessly; pathetically; absurdly; helplessly; incurably; intolerably; miserably; wretchedly; lamentably; needlessly; unfortunately; exceedingly; curiously; deplorably; incomparably; cursedly; deucedly; conveniently; disgustingly.

NEUTRAL

adverbs
resolutely; dependably; altogether; strictly; rigidly; infallibly; sagaciously; wisely; carefully; cautiously; unimpeachably; sincerely; honorably; respectfully; deliberately; determinedly; indifferently; alertly; judiciously; intelligently; interestedly; evasively; necessarily; pluckily; stoutly; conveniently; steadily; unwaveringly; irreproachably.

NEUTRALITY

adjectives
stern; hostile; selfish; benevolent; malevolent; political; blameless; precarious; armed; maintained; difficult.

verbs
advocate—; break—; commend—; disrupt —; enjoy—; express—; favor—; foreswear —; infract—; maintain—; observe—; pledge—; preserve—; profess—; propose—; renounce—; respect—; uphold—; violate—; —balances; —continues; —endangers; —gratifies.

(See attitude, position.)

NEWCOMERS

verbs
befriend—; criticize—; denounce—; fend off —; judge—; limit—; mold—; pity—; quarrel with—; repel—; snub—; suspect—; train —; wrangle with—; —band; —impress; —invade; hedge—.

(See foreigner, alien, stranger.)

NEWLYWEDS
(*colloq.*)

verbs
davise—; bless—; caution—; endow—; fete —; fetter—; mock—; serenade—; sever—; —beam; —blush; —cherish; —clasp; —coo; —dream; —flush; —honeymoon (colloq.); —nest; —rejoice; —repent.

(See lover, sweetheart, husband, wife, suitor.)

NEWS

adjectives
lamentable; alarming; distasteful; inevitable; ill; current; pleasant; inestimable; cheerful; especial; unwelcome; electrifying; disastrous; positive; serious; fresh; irrelevant; dire; long-expected; glorious; interpretative; astonishing; dreadful; vengeful; amazing; definite; startling; fashionable; comparative; distressing; encouraging; exciting; reassuring; deplorable; stupefying; blackest; domestic; panic; inside; sharp; ominous; hopeful; unacceptable; uncertain; unsatisfactory; major; vital; ghastly; significant; condensed; below-the-surface; latest; accurate; fevered; world; heartbreaking.

verbs
bear—; bound into—; broadcast—; bruit about—; comb for—; crop into—; disseminate—; dominate—; edit—; falsify—; flash into—; glean—; greet—; hail—; impart—; overshadow—; purvey—; relay—; scan—; scream—; sift—; spot—; suppress—; verify —; —blazes; —breaks; —fades; —filters through; —stuns; —trickles in.

(See report, word, rumor, message, telegram.)

NEWSPAPER

adjectives
enterprising; disloyal; daily; influential; sensational; leading; matrimonial; conservative; weekly; contemporaneous.

verbs
blazon on—; clip from—; comb—; creep into—; crumple—; deliver—; hawk—s; peddle—s; peruse—; pore over—; purvey—s; scan—; scoop—; skim through—; supplement—; syndicate—; —campaigns; —circulates; —devotes to; —functions; —suppresses.

(See literature, magazine, periodical, publication, press.)

NEWSPAPERMAN

adjectives
astute; hateful; well-respected; enterprising; bold.

verbs

crowd— —; dash to— —; drift to— —; enjoy— —; mill through— —; pack— —; plunge into— —; stream through— —; taxi 'round— —; tour— —; — —astonishes; — —bewilders; — —clutches; — —enchants; — —excels; — —excites; — —irritates; — —pains; — —sparkles; — —thrills; — —towers; — —unfurls.

(See city.)

NIBBLE (v)

adverbs

tantalizingly; daintily; teasingly; cautiously; intermittently; shyly; coyly.

(See munch, bite.)

NICE

adverbs

extraordinarily; particularly; wonderfully; scrupulously; punctiliously; meticulously; invariably; incomparably; unsurpassably; unquestionably; apparently; obviously; manifestly; admirably; unusually; inherently; exquisitely; marvellously; altogether; remarkably.

NICETY

adjectives

peculiar; critical; professional; scrupulous; utmost; painful.

verbs

accomplish with—; acknowledge—ies; appreciate—; delight in—ies; demonstrate —ies; educate in—ies; express with—; frame in—; manage with—; question—; require—; stand upon—; verse in—ies; — prevails; —ies serve for; offend—ies; operate with—.

(See precision, efficiency, skill, tact.)

NICHE

adjectives

comfortable; murky; opposite; appropriate; temporary.

verbs

assign—; attain—; carve out—; claim—; contrive—; crack—; decorate—; dig—; examine—; fill—; find—; gain—; hew—; hollow out—; molest—; occupy—; place in—; select—; sink into—; —protects.

(See corner, place.)

NICKNAME

verbs

adopt—; assume—; bear—; bedevil with—; bestow—upon; brand with—; coin—; contrive—; define—; dub with—; earn—; incur—; —adheres; —annoys; —clings; —labels; —mocks; —sticks; —survives; —vexes.

(See name, title.)

NICKNAME (v)

adverbs

aptly; sneeringly; vindictively; viciously; scoffingly; slurringly; hatefully; fraternally; jovially; humiliatingly; facetiously.

(See entitle, designate.)

NIGGARDLY

adverbs

grossly; unreasonably; meanly; basely; unutterably; inconsiderately; greedily; unnecessarily; disgustingly; penuriously; sordidly; crassly; unbelievably; terribly; shabbily; despicably; contemptibly; wretchedly; overwhelmingly; unutterably; absurdly.

NIGHT

adjectives

mantling; naked; hopeless; perpetual; long; tedious; dull; brooding; frosty; waxing; restless; feverish; deepening; cloudless; moonlight; stark; unspeakable; cloud-hung; sleepless; hideous; sweating; dim; darksome; sultry; fatal; unfathomable; eternal; earth-shaking; wretched; lyric; carved; impelling; precarious; bespangled; congenial; weary; anxious; noiseless; cheerless; tempestuous; brilliant; magic; tortuous; fearsome; gusty; wakeful; wassail; tolerable; large-eyed; silvery; desolate; romantic; watchful; deep-winding; utter; stifling; memorable; broad-winged; difficult; previous; star-studded; lingering; bridal; stagnant; extended; revolving; abysmal; peerless; summer; capped; subtle; serene; somber; cooling lustrous; light; bottomless; fragrant; dewy; profound; departing; shining; dreamless; drizzly; unalienable; heaviest; glimmering; soft; agate; tourmaline; glass-clear; overcast; milky; ghastly; black; impenetrable; perfumed; smiling; pale; live; black-frost; sable; lurid; moonless; slowly-gathering; eyeless; raving; blessed; eventful; prolonged; irksome; unlanterned; unsocial; stormy; gradual; unseeing; ugly; laboring; fashionable; clear; pallid; bright; golden; sweet-smelling; obscure; dumb;

lingering; limitless; inky; star-silent; earthly; moon-mad; hushed; crimeful; enchanting; divine; shadowy; moonshiny; comfortless; merciless; feeding; pitchy; vaporous; interlunar; supperless; identical; ecstatic; fateful; careful; dreaming; dreary; ill-starred; sweltering; gathering; festival; breathless; humorous; black-faced; azure; auspicious; polar; grim; notable; voluptuous; sightless; lonely.

verbs
contemplate—; fritter away—; lapse into—; lurk in—; pierce—; repose at—; sink into —; —blankets; —calms; —clouds over; — creeps up; —curtains; —depresses; —descends; —drags; —engulfs; —enshrouds; — envelops; —inspires; —mantles; —oppresses; —reigns; —robs; —shades; —tiptoes; — veils; —wanes; —waxes; —yawns.
(See evening, twilight, darkness, dusk.)

NIGHTINGALE
adjectives
wakeful; unenvying; tempestuous; triumphant; full-throated; voluptuous; importunate; undying; beauteous.

verbs
—anthems; —bewails; —bursts out; — chants; —charms; —cheers; —complains; —courts; —crowds; —delights; —enchants; —hurries; —lullabies; —mourns; —pierces; —precipitates notes; —pours forth; —ravishes; —shies; —sings out woe; —sobers; — thrills; —transports; —trills; —utters; — vocalizes; —wails; —warbles.
(See bird.)

NIGHTMARE
adjectives
horrifying; preposterous; fiendish; racking; catapulting; portentous; indistinguishable; intolerable; weird; half-vanishing; hideous; weary; eyeless; horrible; financial; veritable.

verbs
beset with—; conceive in—; convulse in—; fancy in—; free from—; imagine in—; picture in—; plunge into—; sink into—; toss in —; unloose—; —alarms; —chokes; —distresses; —settles on; —strains; —strangles; —suffocates; —terrifies; —tortures; — weighs.
(See menace, dream, vision, delusion.)

NIMBLE
adverbs
actively; alertly; unbelievably; surprisingly; remarkably; miraculously; noticeably; obviously; amazingly; unusually; lightly; deftly; adroitly; cleverly; smartly; expertly; peculiarly; incredibly; dexterously; wondrously; briskly; vigilantly.

NIPS
adjectives
fatal; surreptitious; powerful; piercing.

NITROGEN
verbs
combine with—; derive—from; expel—; extract—; furnish with—; manufacture—; market—; mix with—; obtain—; reveal—; store—; temper with—; unite—with; —dilutes; —evaporates; —extinguishes.
(See chemical, acid, mixture, solution.)

NOBLE
adverbs
naturally; quietly; innately; aristocratically; genuinely; truly; admittedly; tenaciously; inherently; actually; elegantly; splendidly; unaffectedly; avowedly; unquestionably; essentially; eminently; grandly; imposingly.

NOBILITY
adjectives
rapacious; transcendent; conspicuous; dubious; mental; latent; impoverished; inherent; austere; powerless; factious; outraged; certain; pervading.

verbs
acknowledge—; attract—; conceal—; crown with—; display—; enhance—; forfeit—; glory in—; honor—; meet—; rouse—; seat among—; smack of—; steep in—; —characterizes; —distinguishes; —enriches; — graces; —outlives; —pedigrees; —shines.
(See aristocracy, gallantry, monarch, splendor, supremacy.)

NOBLEMAN
adjectives
needy; veritable; self-respecting; impoverished; fiery; dissolute; sporting; eminent.

NOBLENESS
adjectives
natural; native; quiet; free; inborn; innate.

adjectives
violent; hereditary; thoughtful; dissolute; dense; emigrant; malevolent; indolent; faithful; prudent; high-taught; philosophic; dastard; rapacious; cushioned; factious; arrogant; haughty; speculative.

NOD

adjectives
jolly; little; swaggering; impertinent; approving; placid; gracious; wrenlike; imperceptible; insinuating; impatient; laconic; emphatic.

NOD (v)

adverbs
sagely; comprehendingly; vehemently; incisively; crisply; dreamily; benignly; solemnly; drowsily; assuringly; significantly; pensively; urbanely; affably; energetically; complacently; sagaciously; affirmatively; rhythmically; positively; assentingly; jovially; philosophically; speculatively.
(See bow, bend.)

NOISE

verbs
ban—; contribute to—; eliminate—; emit—; endure—; exclude—; guard against—; intensify—; reproduce—; resound with—of; saturate with—; simulate—s of; suppress —; —abates; —s blend; —confuses; — hampers; —hinders; —shuffles; —stuns; — subsides.
(See crash, howl, hiss, din, clash, roar.)

NOISELESS

adverbs
completely; warrantably; avowedly; allegedly; reasonably; absolutely; reputably; incredibly; remarkably; mysteriously; magically; unbelievably; peculiarly; furtively; stealthily; solemnly; awfully; alarmingly.

NOISES

adjectives
sharp; pattering; unfamiliar; rustling; shuffling; sniffling; appalling; sundry; booming; audible; ejaculatory; creaking; thunderous; cowing; ruder; sympathetic; tempestuous; rattling; increasing; frightful; pitiful; snivelling; humming; sinister; melancholy; shattering; prodigious; discordant; stringed; croaking; meaningless; buzzing; roaring; barbarous; sullen; sufficient; continuous; humming; guttural; distant;

singular; dangling; whirring; clumping; ripping; rumbling; loud; damnable; whining; impetuous; swishing; confused; unique; unexplained; confounded; midnight; murmuring; shrill; distinct; sudden; subtler; unexpected; startling; unbelievable; objectionable; doubtful; rushing; softest; ill-resounding; slightest; diabolical; unmeaning; vulgar; outside; explosive; deafening; violent; grating; cool; chirping; jocund; fiendish; spiteful; terrifying; dull; unseemly; vague; harsh; unearthly; everlasting; ceaseless.

NOISY

adverbs
clamorously; vociferously; restlessly; uproariously; happily; childishly; screamingly; thunderously; stentoriously; lustily; ribaldly; naturally; boisterously; oddly; unwontedly; curiously; hoydenishly; audaciously; excitedly; hysterically; wildly; intolerably; provokingly; habitually; uncontrollably; ungovernably.

NOMADIC

adverbs
naturally; inherently; nonchalantly; happily; blithely; habitually; voluntarily; periodically; erratically; aimlessly; restlessly; adventurously; profitably; stubbornly; incurably; incorrigibly; remarkably; curiously; strangely; elusively; extraordinarily; recklessly; indefatigably; merrily.

NOMINAL

adverbs
considerately; altogether; merely; absurdly; obviously; curiously; usually; conventionally; conveniently; generously; deliberately; purposely; prudently; intentionally; deceptively; circumspectly; discreetly; simply.

NOMINATE (v)

adverbs
unanimously; jubilantly; independently; modestly; spontaneously; aptly; democratically; thunderously.
(See name, designate.)

NOMINATION

adjectives
spontaneous; caucus; predetermined; independent; unanimous.

verbs

acquiesce in—; aim at—; arrange—; authorize—; confer—upon; control—; court—; decline—; favor—; limit—s; offer for—; propose—; refuse—; reject—; rejoice in—; second—; seek—; —gratifies; —honors.

(See vote, selection, suggestion.)

NONCHALANCE

adjectives

trenchant; enticing; exasperating; debonair; knavish; affected; exquisite; suave; easy; practiced; deft.

verbs

affect—; assume an air of—; feign—; harden into—; listen with—; penetrate—; prefer—; pretend—; prick—; subdue—; tire of—; —crusts; —impresses; —interests; —irks; —nauseates; —pervades; —provokes; —tantalizes.

(See indifference, carelessness, silence.)

NONCHALANT

adverbs

habitually; blithely; indifferently; arrogantly; superciliously; inherently; naturally; usually; remarkably; studiously; deliberately; ominously; cleverly; intentionally; resolutely; charmingly; attractively; apparently; apathetically; coolly; disinterestedly; carelessly; significantly; decidedly; peculiarly; strangely; wonderfully; uncommonly; unwontedly.

NONDESCRIPT

adverbs

inexplicably; noticeably; conspicuously; curiously; strangely; oddly; hopelessly; unaccountably; unutterably; carelessly; defiantly; needlessly; fantastically; grotesquely; eccentrically; exceptionally; monstrously; singularly; peculiarly.

NONSENSE

adjectives

unmitigated; victorious; fatuous; continued; puerile; idiotic; nimble; incomprehensible; tawdry; driveling; nostalgic; undiluted; inexcusable; intelligible; licentious; good-natured; delicious; unadulterated; abject; frothy; palpable; amusing; blasted; airy; ridiculous; pleasant; absolute; blatant; extravagant; aristocratic.

verbs

dare—; denounce—; disapprove of—; disfavor—; emit—; frown on—; quibble in—; relish—; reproach for—; scoff at—; spare —; swallow—; tolerate—; wrap in—; —clouds; —confuses; —eases; —perplexes; —prevails; —revolts; —romps; —shames; —stigmatizes.

(See absurdity, folly, stupidity.)

NONSENSICAL

adverbs

fantastically; whimsically; utterly; delightfully; completely; charmingly; pleasantly; freakishly; fancifully; quaintly; oddly; wildly; drolly; frivolously; foolishly; absurdly; preposterously; inordinately; wholly.

NOOK

adjectives

sunny; lovely; shadow-haunted; sunnier; shady; obscurest; sequestered; narrow; fleshly; winding; advantageous; cobwebby; sheltered; trysting; secluded; unfrequented; leafy; studious.

NOON

adjectives

drowsy; stainless; calm; summer; joyous; burning; breezy; celestial; ardent; melting; languid; shadeless; sultry; glorious; blue-skied; liquid; sweet; clean; fiery.

NORMAL

adverbs

fairly; wholly; scarcely; altogether; comfortably; admirably; wholesomely; comfortingly; practically; finally; happily; fortunately; luckily; allegedly; avowedly; delightfully; apparently; manifestly.

NOSE

adjectives

aquiline; simple; aggressive; inquisitive; waggling; genial; flexible; innocent; arrogant; astute; weird; rueful; ferret; unerring; pudgy; rubicund; pink; blushing; cherry; streaming; crimson; sunburned; reddened; lavendar-tinted; handsome; diabolic; pug; microscopic; Grecian; fiat; saddle; endless; protruding; intrepid; hooked; well-cut; pointed; arched; showy; little; sensitive; depressed; impertinent; thin; delicate; sharp; meager; twitching; peeled; ruby; exceptional; scornful; typical; flabby; pendulous; enormous.

verbs

cock up—; crinkle—; flatten—; impact in—; sniff up—; spray—; squinch—; thumb—; tweak—; wrinkle—; —bleeds; —curls; —quivers; —streams; —twitches.

(See nostrils, nozzle.)

NOSEY

adverbs

intolerably; despicably; obnoxiously; incurably; incorrigibly; inquisitively; childishly; harmlessly; maliciously; unbearably; dangerously; ominously; alarmingly; odiously; hatefully; poisonously; invidiously; insatiably; intrusively; inordinately; mischievously; impertinently; rudely; officially; singularly; unbelievably; unwarrantably; horribly; inescapably.

NOSTALGIA

verbs

aggravate—; bewail—; crush—; cure of—; deplore—; dread—; ease—; endure—; expect—; foster—; hamper by—; induce—; infect with—; lament—; satisfy—; suffer from —; —discontents; —harrows; —impels; —preys upon; —weighs.

(See homesickness, loneliness, seclusion, sadness.)

NOSTRILS

adjectives

overdelicate; slight; distended; dilated; quivering; tremulous; dullest; creased; straining; sensitive; wide; huge.

verbs

affront—; assail—; clog—; dilate—; discharge from—; irrigate—; lift—; obstruct —; paint—; protect—; spray—; titillate—; —quiver; —tremble.

(See nose.)

NOTABLE

adverbs

universally; nationally; internationally; splendidly; extraordinarily; distinctly; conspicuously; unusually; extremely; illustriously.

NOTE
(*music*)

adjectives

low; full-chested; cool; musical; gracious; flutelike; recognizable; hopeful; pensive; imitative; piping; hoarser; varied (pl); discordant; penetrative; cultural; eternal; mocking; tender; accenting; plaintive; triumphant; vibrant; resounding; rambling; piercing; profound; deepest; sentimental; brooding; mingled (pl); rich; husky; shrill; screech-owl; tingling; simpering; soft; shaken; complaining; dominant; long-drawn; wretched; whimpering; sweeter; prelusive; grieving; mournful; pleasing; soaring; tuneful; teasing; despairing; cocked-hat; golden; tinkling; tentative; air-feeding; fundamental; voluminous; confused; rapturous; wondrous; echoing; pealing; gentle; blending; herald; dirgelike; grandest; warbling; wailing; full; liquid; subduing; resulting; momentary; rasping; trembling; rising; sustained; melodious; untunable; drowsy; rare; faltering; metallic.

verbs

chant—; emit—; hit—; inject—; peal—; pitch—; scale—s; soften—; sound—; stress —; strike—; thump—; utter—; wail—; warble—; —dies away; —reverberates; —shrills; —trembles; —weakens.

(See tone.)

NOTE
(*writing*)

adjectives

fundamental; melting; kindly; mirthful; occasional; ironical; dangerous; congratulatory; courteous; cordial; little; ardent; personal; copious (pl); piercing; crisp; crackling; joyous; subdued; pathetic; loud; tragic; triumphant; brief; hasty; quaint; wild; livelier; sweet; authoritative; changed; satirical; despairing; menacing; endless; pervading; disjointed; expiring; impulsive; warning; insistent; vexed; additional; indefinable; lesser; curious; unexpressive; noble; contemporary; special; optimistic; jubilant; blithest; spry; rebellious; improvised; erudite; admirable; incontrovertible; curt; potent; definite; pleasing; precious; sweet; agreeable; nimble; mental; queer; tense; confidential; illegible; wild; proper; mighty; jeering; choked; depreciated; animated; timid; funeral; authentic; illustrative; tonic; national; short; perfunctory; hieroglyphic; tender; scholarly; warning; flourishing; elaborate; significant; alternate; purer; premonitory; dissentient; impulsive; unmeasured; ironical; bubbling; exquisite; neat; culminating; voluble; flattering; merry; heedful; perjured; marginal; wary; centrifugal; wandering; liked; recurrent; penciled; promissory; inspiring; soiled; descriptive; disconnected; exultant; greatest; impassioned; salutary; prefatory; desultory; fragmentary; hurried; jocund; coaxing; brief; official; kindly; confusing; infallible; unsealed; prophetic; consecutive (pl); simultaneous; dominant; brisk; monotonous; twisted; cursory.

verbs
append—; attest to—; blunt—; deliver—; direct—; dispatch—; interpret—; peruse—; point—at; scrawl—; tender—; veil—in; —elucidates; —engrosses; —explains.
(See message, letter, comment, explanation.)

NOTE (v)
adverbs
consciously; faithfully; vaguely; mirthfully; personally; triumphantly; authoritatively; satirically; curiously; eruditely; perfunctorily; impulsively; ironically; marginally; impassionedly; fragmentarily; officially; prophetically; simultaneously.
(See record, comment.)

NOTED
adverbs
nationally; unusually; brilliantly; splendidly; conspicuously; universally; nationally; locally; happily; curiously; remarkably; famously; singularly; prominently; eminently; fabulously; tremendously; reputably.

NOTEWORTHY
adverbs
distinctly; remarkably; illustriously; undoubtedly; singularly; extremely; unusually; gratifyingly; conspicuously; altogether; admittedly; emphatically; predictably.

NOTHINGS
adjectives
pronounced; airy; empty; pointless; merciful; seeming; sublime; invulnerable; poetical.

NOTICE
adjectives
hypercritical; appreciative; timely; repeated; forbidding; incidental; threatening; attentive; sympathetic; numerous (pl); disparaging; palpable; advance; favorable; sweet; obituary; previous; smiling; appropriate; perceptible; casual; parting; scanty; scrawled; commonplace; hasty.

verbs
bill—; court—; draw—; escape—; observe —; peer at—; review—; scrutinize—; —advises; —attracts; —beckons; —discloses; —enlightens; —imparts; —informs; —instructs; —interests; —intimates; —mentions; —points out; —prescribes; —specifies; —warns.
(See mention, announcement, advertisement, label.)

NOTICE (v)
adverbs
curiously; pityingly; dispassionately; pathetically; graphically; emphatically.
(See observe, see, recognize.)

NOTICEABLE
adverbs
glaringly; shamefully; brazenly; decidedly; singularly; curiously; uncommonly; strikingly; surprisingly; painfully; miserably; shockingly; pitiably; blatantly; distressingly; eminently; prominently; inescapably.

NOTIFY (v)
adverbs
portentously; officially; formally; nominally; sympathetically; appropriately; customarily.
(See tell, inform.)

NOTION
verbs
adopt—; cling to—; convey—; disprove—; distort—; embrace—; entertain—; entrench —; explode—; express—; gather —s; inculcate—; inherit—; justify—; retain—; ridicule—; scoff at—; tolerate—; —misleads; —persists.
(See caprice, conception, idea, opinion, view.)

NOTIONAL
adverbs
strangely; eccentrically; quaintly; fantastically; oddly; grotesquely; capriciously; captiously; remarkably; vexatiously; intolerably; unpredictably; undependably; unreliably; erratically; freakishly; egregiously; inordinately; provokingly; painfully; restlessly; nervously; feverishly; fussily; troublesomely; extremely.

NOTIONS
adjectives
moral; preposterous; inadequate; craziest;

pretty; settled; current; disparaging; odious; patriotic; tolerable; vaguest; baby; sudden; dangerous; modern; eerie; fictitious; illusory; elaborate; predestinarian; vergent; contradictory; diametric; opposed; basic; sensual; distinct; nonsensical; amiable; hateful; obscure; silly; chivalrous; inapplicable; fallacious; mistaken; blind; fabulous; confused; cheerful; half-blown; superstitious; rationalistic; idolatrous; glimmering; exaggerated; rudimentary; faint; vehement; pious; preconceived; feeble; pregnant; previous; monstrous; persistent; economical; dreamy; elementary; idealistic; false; excusable; frugal; civilized; ridiculous; cranky; definite; eccentric; strange; fantastic; crude; conceivable; erroneous; imperfect; ghoulish; half-assimilated; strained; conventional; imbecile; dictator; vitiated; childish; unformed.

NOTORIETY
adjectives
newspaper; despised; unpleasant; criminal; unenviable; public; scandalous; romantic; infamous; melancholy.

verbs
achieve—; acquire—; avoid—; burden with —; delight in—; devote to—; exult in—; flaunt—; heap—on; hunt—; labor under—; outshine—; raise to—; seek—; wallow in—; —attracts; —bridles; —decomposes; —enthrones; —glorifies; —overshadows; —palls; —shames.
(See limelight, fame, publicity, renown, reputation.)

NOTORIOUS
adverbs
nationally; generally; locally; unhappily; illustriously; shamefully; brilliantly; eminently; disgracefully; egregiously; splendidly; magnificently; universally; politically; infamously.

NOURISH (v)
adverbs
beneficially; healthfully; maternally; affectionately; sympathetically; substantially; spiritually.
(See nurture, feed, foster.)

NOURISHING
adverbs
incredibly; notably; admittedly; curiously; altogether; wholesomely; pleasantly; invig-

oratingly; healthfully; highly; uncommonly; exceptionally; extremely; strangely; admirably; notably; noticeably; strikingly; remarkably; substantially.

NOURISHMENT
adjectives
delicious; tasty; concentrated; virtual; sympathetic; necessary; proper; spiritual; healthy; substantial; daily.

verbs
administer—; beg—; decline—; deny—; deprive of—; draw—from; furnish—; gulp down—; impart—; inject—; lack—; offer —; provide—; refuse—; request—; resist—; supply—; volunteer—; —builds up; —comforts; —restores; —satiates.
(See food, nutrition, meal.)

NOVEL
adjectives
powerful; cherished; gifted; historical; pretty; lurid; liberal; daring; surging; trifling; psychological; well-contrived; mysterious; admirable; humorous; meritorious; successful; crude; indecent; imitative; masterly; engrossing; melancholy; improbable; sensational; popular; ambitious; episode; brilliant; ingenious; well-made; subtle; profound; contemporary; fast-moving; dramatic; frank; sympathetic; conventional; distinguished; social; florid; sentimental; slipshod; inflated; proletarian; romantic; biographical; jejune; fine; light; sexfree; sentimental; absorbing; exotic; diverting; comprehensive; vivid; accurate; late; experimental; original; convincing; readable; excellent; magnificent; moving; interesting; pleasant; glowing; enjoyable; grand; fascinating; early; stirring; famous.

verbs
acclaim—; applaud—; clamor for—; climax —; construct—; contemplate—; copyright—; create—; denounce—; devour—; embark on —; engross in—; interpret—; introduce—; peruse—; plan—; portray in—; scribble—; weave into—; —appears; —centers about; —deals with; —depicts; —enthralls; — evolves; —portrays; —reveals; —treats of; —unfolds.
(See fiction, book, manuscript, story, tale.)

NOVELIST
verbs
applaud—; berate—; criticize—; laud—; —

alters; —characterizes; —compares; —composes; —complains of; —copies; —creates; —dedicates; —depicts; —describes; —details; —dictates; —imagines; —indites; — insinuates; —narrates; —pens; —portrays; —rearranges; —relates; —retires; —rewrites; —satirizes; —scribbles; —sets forth; —unfolds.

(See poet, author, journalist, writer, artist.)

NOVELTY

adjectives
solemn; realistic; perfect; myriad (pl); startling; latest; dazzling; ever-changing; puzzling; divine; semi-tropical; constant.

verbs
clamor for—; create—; discard—; exhaust —; indulge in—; invent—; laud—; marvel at—; praise—; quicken with—; seek—; spur on by—; wonder at—; —amuses; —captures; —charms; —dazzles; —delights; — disquiets; —diverts; —entrances; —impresses; —palls.

(See change, innovation, originality, oddity.)

NOVICE

adjectives
anxious; musing; humble; beautiful; bashful.

verbs
advise—; befriend—; discipline—; discourage—; enlighten—; impress—; improve—; instruct—; order—; prime—; train—; — botches; —bungles; —conquers; —drills; — familiarizes; —fumbles; —imitates; —labors; —masters; —practises; —profits; — qualifies.

(See beginner, amateur, apprentice.)

NOXIOUS

adverbs
disastrously; calamitously; terribly; shockingly; appallingly; admittedly; notoriously; irremediably; pestillentially; virulently; inevitably; notably.

NOZZLE

verbs
adjust—; affix—; block—; clog—; dam—; direct—; flow from—; grease—; insert—; introduce—; manipulate—; obstruct—; ooze from—; regulate—; screw on—; service—; —emits; —projects; —protrudes; —spouts; —spurts.

(See nose, pipe, tube.)

NUCLEUS

adjectives
unyielding; convenient; unrivaled; solid.

NUDE

verbs
admire—; adorn—; dismiss—; divest to—; enfold—in; examine in—; expose—; glance at—; model in—; parade in—; pose in—; sanction—; scorn—; strip to—; study—; survey—; undrape to—; —astonishes; —defames; —disgusts; —horrifies; —revolts; — shocks.

(See body, figure, painting, sculpture, statue, drawing.)

adverbs
chastely; innocently; artistically; embarrassingly; shamelessly; distressingly; pitiably; pathetically; grievously; scandalously; sadly; miserably; utterly; painfully; completely; shockingly; wretchedly; horribly; seductively; alluringly; unconsciously; beautifully; deplorably; entirely.

NUISANCE

adjectives
prodigious; insufferable; unmitigated; civic; intolerable; rejected; everlasting; universal.

verbs
abate—; bear—; beset by —s; eliminate—; endure—; exterminate—; harass with —s; harrow with —s; inflict with —s; inveigh against—; overcome—; rectify—; upbraid —; —chafes; —distresses; —encumbers; — irks; —irritates; —offends; —pains; — plagues; —smarts; —weighs on.

(See annoyance, pest, plague, condition.)

NULL

adverbs
abeyantly; absently; baselessly; fabulously; unreally; unsubstantially; inanely; groundlessly; ethereally; airily; visionarily; actually; ridiculously.

NUMB

adverbs
alarmingly; completely; fortunately; blessedly; mercifully; unaccountably; suddenly; occasionally; apathetically; appallingly; sur-

prisingly; pathetically; pitiably; strangely; curiously; oddly; remarkably; inertly; unconcernedly; callously; portentously; ominously; heartlessly.

NUMBER

verbs
affix — to; allot—; ascertain—; check—; conjecture—; decimate —s; demonstrate with —s; deplete —s; dwarf in—; inscribe with —; limit—; memorize—; recall—; recite —s; repeat—; run over —s; select—; — dwindles; —shrivels; —wanes.
(See figure, quantity, amount.)

NUMBER (v)

adverbs
correspondingly; overwhelmingly; countlessly; adequately; prodigiously; extravagantly; increasingly; definitely; interminably; mystically; proportionally; lavishly.
(See count, figure.)

NUMBERS

adjectives
countless; reasonable; considerable; sufficient; requisite; undiminished; fluctuating; unmitigated; incalculable; overwhelming; adequate; infinite; unequal; quantum; subsequent; superior; indeterminate; prodigious; extravagant; stipulated; certain; gentle; qualified; useless; singular; overpowering; gratifying; depleted; unwieldy; immense; actual; unknown; incredible; increasing; harmonious; laggard; jocund; definite; preponderating; fuller; respectable; rhythmic; untold; lofty; superfluous; goodly; augmented; possible; greatest; previous; uncountable; conceivable; scanty; unending; interminable; unvanquishable; diminutive; mystic; comparative; small; mournful; unavoidable; substantial; unrecorded; fiery; choral; fearful; proportional; lavish (pl).

NUMBNESS

adjectives
mental; fortunate; complete; vibrant; deadly; stealthy.

verbs
affect with—; create—; incur—; massage—; overcome with—; receive—; remedy—; — creeps over; —deadens; —dulls; —enfeebles; —hardens; —hibernates; —impairs; — ossifies; —paralyzes; —stupefies.
(See paralysis.)

NUNS

adjectives
undedicate; uncloistered; self-loving; chanting; holy; sincere.

NUPTIALS

verbs
assemble for—; attend—; bless—; celebrate —; consummate—; defer—; discharge—; gather for—; mar—; officiate at—; perform —; plan—; rehearse—; simplify—; solemnize—; —climax; —impress; —join; —symbolize; —unite.
(See marriage, matrimony, wedding.)

NURSE

adjectives
devoted; sedulous; mercenary; sole; hireling; avid; sapient; foul; exemplary; heroic; smart; bustling.

verbs
employ—; notify—; recruit —s; register—; train—; —administers; —allays; —alleviates; —assuages; —attends; —bathes; — cajoles; —cheers; —comforts; —consoles; —dresses; —eases; —massages; —refreshes; —reports; —salves; —smooths; — soothes.
(See mother, doctor, physician.)

NURSE (v)

adverbs
assiduously; devotedly; sedulously; avidly; heroically; maternally; gratuitously; affectionately; sympathetically.
(See attend, tend.)

NURSERY

adjectives
potent; airy; exquisite; huge; profitable.

NURTURE (v)

adverbs
delicately; exquisitely; tenderly; solicitously; appropriately; intellectually; spiritually; lovingly; selflessly.
(See nourish, foster, feed.)

NUTRIMENT

adjectives
appropriate; slight; elemental; intellectual.

verbs
administer—; advise—; digest—; double—; furnish—; infuse with—; lack—; necessitate—; offer—; order—; refuse—; resist—;

rob of—; savor—; spurn—; —aids; —amends; —appeals; —brightens; —improves; —promotes; —refreshes; —renews.

(See nourishment, nutrition.)

NUTRITION

verbs

deprive of—; draw—from; furnish—; improve—; lack—; limit—; maintain—; necessitate—; obtain—; offer—; pervert—; promote—; provide—; refuse—; regulate—; retard—; scorn—; spurn—; supply—; —absorbs; —comforts; —utilizes.

(See nourishment, food, nutriment.)

NUTRITIOUS

adverbs

unusually; wonderfully; remarkably; exceptionally; pleasantly; agreeably; singularly; curiously; scientifically; admittedly; warrantably; delightfully; usefully; extraordinarily; properly; substantially; usefully; valuably; inexpensively; wholesomely; healthfully; conveniently; extremely.

NYMPH

adjectives

slim; skilful; inebriated; ambrosial; attending; woodland; gaudy; jeweled.

verbs

—s array; —awes; —cheers; —charms; —dances; —delights; —frolics; —gambols; —gladdens; —graces; —inspires; —meanders; —rejoices; —roams.

(See fairy, angel, saint.)

O

adjectives

stunted; branched; gnarled; ancestral; enormous; hoary; gouty; rugged; knotted; heaven-delighting; deciduous; mossy; well-worn; monumental; perforated; stern; leafless; doting; twisted; sturdiest; massive; polychromed; stiff.

verbs

beam with—; cleave to—; fell—; moss—; timber with—; —braves; —commands; — crowns; —defies; —droops; —endures; — flourishes; —outlasts; —protects; —reigns; —roofs; —rules; —spreads; —stretches; — towers.

(See tree.)

OAR

adjectives

gliding; cautious; skimming; stalwart; busy; groaning; flashing; ponderous; muffled; paddling; suspended; lingering; laborious; golden; dipping; lazy; languid; rhythmic.

verbs

arm with—; drag—; heave—; manipulate —; paddle with—; ply with—; propel with —; splinter—; steer with—; stroke—; tug on—; —brushes; —cuts; —dips; —furrows; —impels; —splashes; —stirs; —sweeps.

(See paddle.)

OASIS

verbs

come upon—; dwell on—; encounter—; guide to—; refresh at—; seek—; sight—; welcome—; —attracts; —cheers; —delights; —invigorates; —nourishes; —relieves; — renews; —restores; —soothes; —strengthens.

(See fountain, safety, security.)

OATH

adjectives

grating; simultaneous; strange; furious; blood-curdling; infringed; binding; imperial; solemn; dreadful; round; sacred; pretty; horrible; slippery; sailor; continental; protesting; frantic; furious; new-found; consecrating; mouth-filling; royal; fearsome; rude; knightly; deadly; dismal; blistering; raucous; bold-beating; favorite; meaningless; soul-confirming; tremendous; angry; ingenious; inviolable; bombastic; ancient; solemn; confounding; unfeigned; innocent; brave; deep; little; bellowing; muttered; iron-clad; sacramental.

verbs

administer—; break—; cast—; flay with—; hiss—; launch—at; hurl—; repudiate—; spit out—; subscribe to—; utter—; —breaks from; —consummates; —solemnizes; —s stream from; —symbolizes; —vows; falsify under—.

(See curse, invective, ban, imprecation.)

OBDURATE

adverbs

sternly; stubbornly; incorrigibly; implacably; terribly; harshly; roughly; callously; mulishly; cantankerously; grossly; tenaciously; sullenly; perversely; dreadfully; shockingly; dogmatically; austerely; stiffly; uncompromisingly; tyrannically; puritanically; cruelly; bitterly; unaccountably; unbearably; intolerably.

OBEDIENCE

adjectives

military; implicit; hallowed; mechanical; true; fractional; infallible; divine; prompt; strict; characteristic; punctilious; scrupulous; instinctive; faithful; universal; rigid; unquestioning; weary; filial; instant; compliant; blind; passive; voluntary; plausible; slavish; transitory; hideous; docile; reverential.

verbs

abjure—; approve—; coerce into—; demand —; dispute—; enforce—; enslave by—; exact—; feign—; owe—to; profess—; reduce to—; submit in—; suffer—; train to—; yield —; —binds.

(See submission, obeisance.)

OBEDIENT

adverbs

highly; altogether; unfailingly; meekly; submissively; devotedly; affectionately; absurdly; promptly; always; scarcely; deferentially; respectfully; reverently; piously; ridiculously; readily; compliantly; obsequiously;

unctuously; ostentatiously; diplomatically; obviously; stupidly; doltishly; grudgingly; implicitly; meticulously; surprisingly; painstakingly; strictly; passively; grudgingly.

OBEISANCE

adjectives
graceful; surly; humble; profound; ironical; flattering.

verbs
approve—; bow in—; feign—; owe—; pay —; sacrifice to—.
(See homage, obedience, reverence, allegiance, devotion.)

OBESE

adverbs
alarmingly; uncomfortably; comically; tragically; unnecessarily; ridiculously; indescribably; clumsily; dangerously; ominously; significantly; grossly; awkwardly; embarrassingly; lumpishly; unhappily; unfortunately; unbelievably; peculiarly; strangely; dropsically; unaccountably; inherently.

OBESITY

verbs
brood **over**—; dread—; eat into—; fear—; lament—; overcome—; reduce—; remedy—; repress—; resist—; threaten with—; —alarms; —astounds; —dejects; —depresses; —encumbers; —endangers; —hinders; — irks; —restrains; —restricts.
(See stoutness.)

OBEY (*v*)

adverbs
dully; unquestioningly; hypnotically; reluctantly; mechanically; implicitly; systematically; involuntarily; infallibly; filially; punctiliously; scrupulously; rigidly; passively; voluntarily; slavishly; docilely; reverentially.
(See comply, heed.)

OBJECT

adjectives
salient; varied (pl); beloved; conspicuous; well-defined; practicable; spiritual; compassionable; irrelevant; tender; unworthy; contrary; opaque; warlike; foreign; venerable; slipping; benevolent; charitable; repressed; commanding; dark; uncouth; pear-shaped; dreadful; immediate; humanitarian; isolated; chimerical; hideous; accidental; ulterior; characteristic; manifest; fruitful;

darling; concealed; staple; primary; animated; imperfect; half-seen; principal; determinate; sensuous; loathsome; nobler; far-distant; beneficent; desired; frequent (pl); inanimate; forlorn; ornamental; definite; closest; supernatural; impersonal; gruesome; express; homely; prominent; unoffending; acceptable; exclusive; specific; interesting; commonplace; innumerable (pl); solitary; innocent; cardinal; celestial; terrific; natural; secondary; enigmatical; unappetizing; sausage-like; engrossing; incompatible; shining; rugged; sensible; objectionable; visible; baser; sufficient; noteworthy; ostensible; memorable; avowed; sublime; absorbing; pure; visual; alluring; baleful; infamous; remarkable; transparent; repulsive; dusky; legitimate; tangible; dispassionate; praiseworthy; respective; incommunicable; worthy; sole; indifferent; outward; distinct; obtrusive; demagogical; personified; requisite; laudable; engaging; supreme; important; honorable; distinguishing; death-dealing; central; vital; striking; shapeless; petty; sparse; impressive; unreasoning; particular; ludicrous; external; conceivable.

verbs
achieve—; acquaint with—; **aim at**—; attain —; consecrate to—; contemplate—; embrace —; endorse—; expose—; frustrate—; glorify—; labor for—; oppose—; perceive—; pursue—; represent—; reveal—; serve—; —hinders; —interposes; —interrupts; —obstructs.
(See aim, end, view, goal, objective, mission, purpose.)

OBJECT (*v*)

adverbs
strenuously; gruffly; pointedly; perversely; incompatibly; legitimately; passionately; dogmatically; unreasonably; graciously; ludicrously; fruitlessly; snobbishly; ultimately; sturdily; singularly.
(See oppose, disapprove.)

OBJECTION

adjectives
fatal; forcible; futile; insuperable; overt; plausible; critical; insurmountable; principal; gracious; embarrassing; feeble; strenuous; snobbish; ultimate; trivial; various (pl); rooted; violent; further; sturdy; depressing; ingenious; incompetent; singular.

verbs
anticipate—; brush aside—; cease—; disparage—; entertain—; justify—; meet—; outbalance—; overcome—; provoke—; put forward—; reply to—; surmount—; temper —; voice—; —arises; —enlarges; —impedes; —wilts.
(See challenge, exception, opposition, interference.)

OBJECTIONABLE
adverbs
positively; highly; uncommonly; remarkably; unutterably; altogether; definitely; violently; singularly; particularly; personally; professionally; exceptionally; socially.

OBJECTIVE
adjectives
definite; ostensible; constructive; vicious; avowed; economic; clear; precise.

verbs
acclaim—; achieve—; advance upon—; applaud—; back—; complete—; conceal—; deny—; honor—; menace—; surrender—; threaten—; conquer—.
(See object, purpose, goal, mission.)

OBLIGATION
adjectives
financial; solemn; filial; reciprocal; cruel; divine; irksome; contractual; sacred; eternal; inexpressible; mystic; mutual; superadded; maturing; unlucky; pecuniary; deep; universal; external; tacit; parental; religious; corresponding; solemn; effectual.

verbs
accept—; acknowledge—; balk at—; bind by—s; discharge—; disregard—; evade—s; free from—s; fulfill—; impose—; incur—; perform—; place under—; release from—; repudiate—; satisfy—; shirk—; stud with —s; transfer—.
(See bond, debt, mortgage, payment, loan.)

OBLIGATORY
adverbs
dreadfully; rigorously; inescapably; legally; morally; financially; sadly; stringently; rigidly; unfortunately; sternly; inflexibly; appallingly; strictly.

OBLIGE (v)
adverbs
flatteringly; gushingly; reluctantly; infinitely; financially; mutually; morally.
(See please, accommodate.)

OBLIGING
adverbs
pleasantly; amiably; generously; graciously; infallibly; unfailingly; willingly; immediately; gladly; helpfully; expertly; considerately; politely; courteously; tactfully; cordially; heartily; genially; cheerfully; happily; instantly.

OBLITERATE (v)
adverbs
instantaneously; completely; abruptly; wholly; cruelly; dictatorially.
(See efface, blot, remove.)

OBLIVION
adjectives
dusty; complete; mute; utter; dark; sweet; keen; blank.

verbs
accept—; bask in—; bury in—; cast into—; consign to—; doom to—; drag from—; emerge from—; fade into—; flounder in—; gain—; join in—; merit—; overtake—; seek —; sink into—; speed to—; threaten with—; yield to—.
(See insignificance, failure, obscurity.)

OBLIVIOUS
adverbs
vexatiously; carelessly; indifferently; ungratefully; thanklessly; abstractedly; dreamily; drowsily; selfishly; inconsiderately; egotistically; stupidly; apathetically; completely; unfeelingly; utterly; inexcusably; unpardonably; grossly; heartlessly; blindly; cooly; curiously; rudely.

OBNOXIOUS
adverbs
entirely; highly; uncommonly; extremely; deeply; odiously; reprehensibly; unnecessarily; manifestly; curiously; disastrously; exceptionably; detestably; abominably; deliberately; bitterly; shockingly; appallingly; frightfully; unbearably.

OBOE
verbs
finger—; pitch—; render on—; scale—; solo

on—; sound—; tune—; —beseeches; —buzzes; —chants; —confounds; —hums; —mourns; —penetrates; —pleads; —wails; —whispers.
(See bagpipe.)

OBSCENE

adverbs
frightfully; illegally; unimaginably; filthily; terribly; ribaldly; grossly; coarsely; offensively; disgustingly; hatefully; shamefully; lewdly; suggestively; intolerably; broadly; wantonly; meretriciously; abominably; particularly; unexpectedly; unwarrantably.

OBSCENITY

verbs
besmirch by—; censure—; decry—; denounce—; deplore—; devour—; disapprove of—; escape—; foul by—; gorge on—; indulge in—; loathe—; pardon—; repent—; revel in—; wallow in—; —defiles; —nauseates; —offends; —perishes; —revolts; —shocks; —stains; —violates.
(See immodesty, sin, perversion, abomination, corruption.)

OBSCURE

adverbs
lamentably; altogether; curiously; inconveniently; darkly; murkily; cloudily; foggily; mistily; dimly; confusingly; bewilderingly; unintelligibly; unfortunately; unluckily; unaccountably; unnecessarily; unsatisfactorily; vaguely; mysteriously; remarkably; vexatiously; disappointingly.

OBSCURE (v)

adverbs
mysteriously; gloomily; puzzlingly; artfully; purposely; cunningly; hopelessly; patently; diplomatically; politically.
(See darken, eclipse.)

OBSCURITY

adjectives
patient; habitual; deep; obscene; comparative; elusive; humble; ever-deepening; impenetrable; dark; polite; hopeless; smooth; dense; unmerited.

verbs
bury in—; doom to—; drag from—; drive into—; drown in—; exile to—; face—; fade into—; languish in—; perplex with—; plunge into—; retire into—; return to—; sink into—; slip into—; —shields; —veils.
(See darkness, gloom, insignificance, oblivion.)

OBSEQUIOUS

adverbs
blandly; suavely; unctuously; professionally; exceptionally; deferentially; humbly; ingratiatingly; submissively; cringingly; tactfully; curiously; oddly; strangely; unaccountably; slavishly; servilely; abjectly; significantly; mysteriously; pliantly; inexplicably; pitiably; lamentably; sadly; eagerly; reverentially; ceremoniously; unnecessarily.

OBSERVANCE

adjectives
sacred; rigorous; over-curious; strict; puritanical; ceremonious; mute; ritual; superstitious; cordial; religious; cheerful; meticulous; faithful; devout.

verbs
advise—of; advocate—of; celebrate in—; comply with—; demand—; direct—; exact —; extend—; fulfill—; inspire—; join in—; necessitate—; preclude—; relish—; sponsor —; —aids; —obligates; —satisfies.
(See celebration, anniversary, fulfillment)

OBSERVANT

adverbs
keenly; aptly; expertly; skilfully; intelligently; acutely; sharply; critically; terribly; dreadfully; alarmingly; officiously; impertinently; impudently; offensively; vexatiously; carefully; watchfully; cautiously; attentively; remarkably; noticeably; alertly; prudently; thoughtfully; meticulously; amusingly; unusually; punctiliously.

OBSERVATION

adjectives
necessary; specific; dispassionate; punctilious; silent; unaided; personal; quiet; continued; searching; accurate; direct; common; shrewd; watchful; pertinent; judicious; questioning; satirical; surface; natural; homely; penetrating; insignificant; detached; outward; celestial; phrenological; objective; tentative; cursory; august; trifling; encouraging; friendly; consistent; curious; delicate; loving; sufficient; extensive; facetious; astronomical; glib; unlimited; minute; childish; conflicting (pl); discrim-

inating; detailed; mere; abstract; meridional; restless; wondrous; quiet; sundry (pl); original; loose; vague; keen; assiduous; controlled; humorous; insufficient; subsequent; faulty; practiced; meteorological; disconcerted.

verbs

bias—; bolster—; confirm—; elude—; enlarge—s; escape—; exchange—s; guide—s; offer—; record—s; report—; resume—; shun—; voice—; —authenticates; —confirms; —discloses; —reveals; —shocks; —stuns.

(See view, remark, conversation, opinion.)

OBSERVE (v)

adverbs

alertly; philosophically; astutely; slyly; profoundly; significantly; oracularly; sagaciously; parenthetically; studiously; complacently; autobiographically; wistfully; bluntly; impartially; religiously; skeptically; scrupulously; cordially; composedly; spontaneously; infallibly; sentimentally; primly; systematically; punctiliously; shrewdly; pertinently; judiciously; tentatively; facetiously; meteorologically.

(See notice, see.)

OBSERVER

adjectives

stupefied; hasty; wise; phlegmatic; casual; expert; superficial; extraterrestrial; philosophic; silent; attentive; vigilant; practiced; sympathetic; distinguished; rocking-chair; dispassionate; devoted; unprejudiced; uninitiated; scientific; inattentive; careful; careless; numerous; keen-eyed; sagacious; disinterested; unconscious; constant; slight; ignorant; sharp; experienced; political; deliberate; energetic; sarcastic; inexpert; impartial; hasty; indignant.

verbs

admit—s; allow—s; attract—s; confine—s to; deceive—; delude—; limit—s; mislead —; permit—s; present to—s; surprise—s; —beholds; —comprehends; —concentrates; —concludes; —contemplates; —s crowd; —detects; —meddles; —notes; —relishes; —surveys; —views; —witnesses.

(See witness, individual, public.)

OBSESSION

verbs

actuate—; assail by—; beset by—; fret over—; molest with—; plague by—; —annoys; —bedevils; —discomposes; —disquiets; —distresses; —disturbs; —grasps; —grates; —haunts; —hovers over; —inhabits; —inspires; —persecutes; —plagues; —ruffles; —seizes; —tortures; —vexes; —weighs.

(See prejudice, delusion, daydream, idea, hallucination, illusion, nightmare.)

OBSTACLE

adjectives

insuperable; unforeseen; hideous; apparent; tremendous; insurmountable; appalling; usual; effectual; recognized; hopeless; formidable; technical; trifling; prodigious; imaginary; unseen; serious; fatal; stubborn; frightful; infrequent (pl); specific; unexpected; artificial; successful; puny; impending; considerable; practical; impassable; solid-looking; stupendous; petty.

verbs

anticipate—; brush aside—; circumvent—; cut through—; encounter—; gauge—; interpose—; level—; meet with—; overcome—; remove—; surmount—; vanquish—; —arises; —hinders; —restrains; —restricts; —thwarts.

(See bar, impediment, hindrance, difficulty, interference, trouble.)

OBSTINACY

adjectives

senile; dogged; brutal; sheer; wrong-headed; inveterate; hellish; lawless; sufficient; desperate; gentle; suicidal; natural; surprising; misdirected; inflexible; unyielding; invincible; somber.

verbs

adhere with—; attack by—; break—; fatigue—; fight with—; harden into—; induce —; maintain—; narrow into—; rebuke—; relent—; repent—; steel with—; stiffen in —; —conquers; —disconcerts; —endures; —inflames; —perseveres; —persists; —petrifies; —resists; —smothers; —sulks.

(See stubbornness, opposition, antagonism, hostility.)

OBSTINATE

adverbs

doggedly; wilfully; inflexibly; stubbornly; astonishingly; disagreeably; dangerously; incorrigibly; surprisingly; naturally; wonderfully; unexpectedly; implacably; sternly; brutally; inveterately; desperately; habitually; obnoxiously; obdurately; viciously; dreadfully.

OBSTREPEROUS
adverbs
unmanageably; ungovernably; uncontrollably vexatiously; intolerably; habitually; always; altogether; annoyingly; shamefully; mischievously; roguishly; teasingly; tormentingly; violently; wildly; boisterously; viciously; desperately; outrageously; stormily; strangely; unaccountably; unwarrantably; unbelievably; indescribably.

OBSTRUCT (v)
adverbs
deliberately; premeditatedly; doggedly; desperately; unyieldingly; pettishly; formidably; stupidly; forcibly; strenuously; economically; viciously.
(See oppose, retard.)

OBSTRUCTION
adjectives
artificial; mere; insurmountable; blank; formidable; cold; frequent; acute.

verbs
accumulate into—; attempt—; clear away —; complain of—; devise—; localize—; mourn—; offer—; pierce—; purge of—; suffer—; treat—; —arrests; —bars; —clogs; —hinders; —interposes; —resists; —restrains; —shuts out; —stems; —thaws; —delays.
(See impediment, bar, barrier, hazard, hindrance.)

OBTAIN (v)
adverbs
legally; effectually; unethically; surreptitiously; rapaciously; honorably; selfishly; uncharitably; legitimately; singularly; disgracefully; unceremoniously.
(See gain, procure.)

OBTAINABLE
adverbs
recently; currently; conveniently; easily; readily; inexpensively; probably; certainly; assuredly; warrantably; possibly; scarcely; hardly; barely; measurably; later.

OBTRUDE (v)
adverbs
inconsiderately; impudently; irrelevantly,

voluntarily; forcefully; vigorously; selfishly; bluntly; formidably.
(See intrude, encroach.)

OBTRUSIVE
adverbs
inconveniently; irritatingly; pestiferously; inquisitively; impertinently; rudely; inexcusably; boorishly; innocently; mischievously; constantly; miserably; vexatiously; unpardonably; bluntly; meddlingly; meddlesomely; grossly; indecorously; unbecomingly; shockingly; surprisingly; oddly; impolitely; pertly; rudely; inconsiderately; ignorantly; discourteously.

OBTUSE
adverbs
pitiably; terribly; unbelievably; unimaginably; incurably; boorishly; rudely; incomprehensibly; inordinately; shockingly; inexpressibly; callously; stupidly; heavily; stolidly; doltishly; dully; unusually; uncommonly.

OBTUSENESS
adjectives
mental; moral; monumental; colossal; apparent.

OCCASION
adjectives
innocent; ceremonial; last-mentioned; rare; various (pl); utmost; ample; dire; approaching; long-expected; abundant; subsequent; memorable; numerous (pl); lugubrious; insignificant; gala; separate; auspicious; festal; appropriate; trivial; extraordinary; momentous; impressive; everyday; obvious; picturesque; solemn; worldfamous; little-known; grand; festival; ordinary; virtuous; sacred; proudest; notable; exceptional; peculiar; unprecedented; joyful; speedy; multiple; fateful; celebrated; infrequent; mellow; critical.

verbs
afford—; commemorate—; contrive—; feast on—; hunger for—; observe—; offer—; present—; rise to—; seduce by—; seek—; seize —; snatch—; spurn—; —demands; —merits; —prompts; —slips by; —warrants.
(See hour, opportunity, occurrence.)

adverbs

mysteriously; annoyingly; confusingly; bewilderingly; unmistakably; marvellously; undeniably; indubitably; abstrusely; darkly; impenetrably; incomprehensibly; inscrutably; obscurely; vaguely; unfathomably; perplexingly; puzzlingly; disturbingly; peculiarly; strangely.

OCCUPANT

adjectives

voiceless; sheeted; tossing; imaginary; solitary; primitive; sparse.

verbs

confine—; cradle—; discharge—; eject—; evict—; expel—; intrude on—; oust—; remove—; retain—; —s abandon; —admits; —appropriates; —departs; —establishes; —s gather; —nestles; —s pack; —roosts; —s stream from; —tenants; —withdraws.

(See inhabitant.)

OCCUPATION

adjectives

final; praiseworthy; trivial; illegal; congenial; intellectual; agreeable; youthful; earnest; disastrous; hellish; intense; unquiet; beloved; indispensable; triumphant; enviable; sedentary; remunerative; arduous; hazardous; breadwinning; productive; monotonous; strenuous; absorbing; profitable; dignified; various; useful; restful; savory; untidy; joint; undesirable; favorite; degrading; menial; brutalizing; solitary; prosaic; doubtful; unimportant; nightly; chief; ignoble.

verbs

absorb in—; chain to—; cherish—; choose —; comprehend—; despise—; employ in—; engage in—; escape—; follow—; lack—; postpone—; practise—; profit by—; pursue —; qualify for—; seek—; shun—; train for —; —contents; —enthralls; —interests; — rusts; —wearies.

(See business, calling, course, hobby, employment, work.)

OCCUPY (v)

adverbs

extensively; variously; solely; incessantly; densely; assiduously; intermittently; profoundly; temporarily; arduously; triumph-

antly; congenially; intellectually; hazardously; monotonously; strenuously; profitably; menially; prosaically; ignobly.

(See keep, hold, possess.)

OCCUR (v)

adverbs

perpetually; sporadically; coincidentally; propitiously; phenomenally; historically; contemporaneously; miraculously; incredibly; circumstantially; preternaturally; distressingly; fortuitously; deplorably; marvelously.

(See happen, befall.)

OCCURRENCE

adjectives

striking; unusual; shadowy; historical; contemporaneous; miraculous; incredible; biennial; similar; inexplicable; menstrual; determined; alleged; trifling; circumstantial; preternatural; untoward; distressing; supernatural; disgraceful; fortuitous; frequent; shocking; deplorable; unnoticed; joyful; marvelous; unforeseen.

verbs

advertise—; anticipate—; compile—s; count —s; edit—; endure—; experience—; impute —to; meet with—; narrate—; note—; record—; report—; —brings to light; —interrupts; —supervenes; —surprises.

(See course, affair, event, episode, adventure, incident.)

OCEAN

adjectives

treacherous; salt-waved; wild; wreckstrewn; gushing; measureless; distant; dancing; purpling; leaden; madfoam; mighty; voluminous; darkling; momentary; moaning; sanguine; neglected; freshening; circumfluous; turbulent; wasteful; blue; winter; hungry; gleaming; tempestuous; shoreless; wine-dark; surging; charmed; lifeless; bursting; unresting; tossing; illimitable; tumultuous; homeless; boundless; unconfined; ethereal; wasteful; unruffled; infinite; close-lying; yearning; cheerless; boiling; chafed; small-sized; bottomless; mimic; glaucous; vast; calm; unfruitful; resistless.

verbs

brave—; cradle in—; girdle—; harness—; launch on—; —booms; —bubbles; —buffets; —flashes; —foams; —grumbles; —hammers at; —heaves; —lashes; —leaps; —lulls; —

moans; —murmurs; —pitches; —plays; —
ravages; —resounds; —rolls; —shoulders;
—sighs; —smiles; —spumes; —surges; —
swells; —tosses; —washes; —whispers.
(See sea, waves, breakers.)

ODD

adverbs
decidedly; inexplicably; grotesquely; fantastically; unfortunately; positively; extraordinarily; uncommonly; disagreeably; offensively; unpleasantly; awkwardly; comically; boorishly; outlandishly; barbarously;
shamefully.

ODDITY

adjectives
individual; numerous (pl); definite.

verbs
appreciate—; deride—; display—; exhibit
—; marvel at—; reveal—; ridicule—; scoff
at—; scorn—; stare at—; tolerate—; value
for—; —amuses; —astounds; —awes; —
bewilders; —decorates; —dumbfounds; —
flabbergasts (colloq.); —startles; —strikes.
(See eccentricity, novelty.)

ODDS

adjectives
overwhelming; rushing; confounding; fearful; moderate; tremendous; worthless; conceivable; formidable; reckless; highest.

verbs
acquire—; approve—; calculate—; demand
—; discourage—; enjoy—; justify—; play
—; reckon—; reduce—; refuse—; request
—; submit to—; —despair; —increase; —
prevail; —protect.
(See disadvantage, advantage.)

ODE

adjectives
imperishable; turgid; lofty; mortal; patriotic; celebrated.

ODIOUS

adverbs
extremely; uncommonly; extraordinarily;
detestably; abominably; atrociously; unusually; flagrantly; egregiously; intolerably;
incredibly; shockingly; disgustingly; particularly; singularly; peculiarly; monstrously.

ODOR

adjectives
sickening; objectionable; universal; savory;
mingled; musty; offensive; reconciling;
mysterious; undefinable; charnel; thick;
mephitic; delicious; exquisite; peculiar; indescribable; characteristic; prison; vague;
influent; delicate; undesirable; dreamy;
sweet-scented; succulent; fragrant; keen-
edged; greasy; sweetish; spicy; strange;
pervading; fugitive; single-flower; dry; arrowy; autumn; champac; rich; vigorous;
nightly; butyric; body; mystical; dewy;
faint; cloying; perspiration; sweaty; sulphurous; suffocating; poisonous; disagreeable; unsanitary; national; underarm;
subtlest; sour; soft; pungent; balsam;
charming; dainty; languishing; heavy;
grateful; soul-dissolving; aromatic; fecund;
breezy; chafed; durable; evil; intoxicating;
ambrosial; insufferable; subtle; noxious;
distinctive; embarrassing; pleasant.

verbs
combat—; detect—; diffuse—; efface—; emit
—; exhale—; impregnate with—; inhale—;
retain—; snuff up—; waft in—; —assails;
—s commingle; —emanates; —floats from;
—greets; —invigorates; —mingles; —pervades; —sickens.
(See aroma, incense, essence, fragrance,
smell, stench.)

OFFEND (v)

adverbs
mortally; inevitably; desperately; deeply;
morally; spiritually; socially; personally.
(See wound, affront, hurt.)

OFFENDED

adverbs
mortally; heinously; grievously; continually;
slightly; deeply; irreparably; gravely; definitely; unreasonably; senselessly; bitterly;
sorely; grievously; frightfully; distressingly; mightily; dangerously; hotly; obviously;
openly; ludicrously; extremely; absurdly;
foolishly; unfortunately; throughout.

OFFENDER

adjectives
inveterate; hardened; banished; desperate;
misguided; repeating.

verbs
apprehend—; chastise—; detain—; fine—;
forgive—; pardon—; penalize—; punish—;

reform—; resent—; restrict—; reveal—; subject—to; try—; —commits; —displeases; —infringes; —transgresses.

(See loser, criminal, thief, robber.)

OFFENSE

adjectives
criminal; indecent; mortal; dire; flagrant; heinous; aggravated; imputed; trivial; penitentiary; deliberate; actual; supreme; vile; grievous; giddy; voluntary; heavy; continual; superficial; dismissed; similar; odious; impeachable; primitive; slightest; unpardonable; vicious; enormous; grave; excruciating; rank.

verbs
bewail—; commit—; condone—; countenance—; decry—; denounce—; excuse—; fear —; indict for—; lash for—; palliate—; penalize—; punish—; rue—; uncover—; —besmirches; —debases; —defaces; —disgraces; —involves; —libels; —slanders.

(See crime, insult, guilt, misdeed.)

OFFENSIVE

verbs
act on—; assume—; choose—; detail—; dispose to—; launch—; occupy—; plan—; rely on—; take up—; —aggravates; —batters; —drives; —grapples; —harries; — instigates; —invades; —presses; —storms; —strikes.

(See aggression.)

adverbs
distinctly; strikingly; conspicuously; highly; terribly; unexpectedly; boorishly; impertinently; cruelly; bitterly; amazingly; monstrously; daringly; deliberately; purposely; intentionally; unpardonably; inexcusably; execrably; abominably; disagreeably; unnecessarily; unwarrantably; disgracefully; shamefully; aggressively.

OFFER

adjectives
repeated; palliative;. munificent; magnificent; friendly; coherent; intelligent; special; introductory; liberal; amazing; low-priced; unusual; dubious; engaging; particular; disinterested; magnanimous; outstanding; singular; remarkable; unique; combination; inexpensive; generous; hospitable; private; testimonial; unprecedented; polite; irresponsible; spectacular; ridiculous; positive; greatest; free; no-risk; demonstrator; smashing; money-making; quick-starting; astounding; trial; startling; genuine.

verbs
accept—; advance—; avail oneself of—; bombard with—s; consider—; decline—; disdain—; entertain—; hawk about for—s; invite—s; jump at—; present—; press—; propose—; propound—; refuse—; reject—; renew—; resent—; solicit—s; spurn—; tender—; waive—; withhold—; —entices; — satisfies.

(See bid, bribe, gift, opportunity, proposition.)

OFFER (*v*)

adverbs
generously; exclusively; zealously; gratuitously; voluntarily; tentatively; stolidly; temptingly; facetiously; magnanimously; obtrusively; munificently; liberally; dubiously; disinterestedly; uniquely; unprecedentedly; demonstratively; genuinely.

(See bid, propose.)

OFFERING

adjectives
bounteous; princely; freewill; mortuary; exceptional; votive; propitiatory; imposing; annual; rustic; odious; magnificent; appropriate; polluted; sensational; great; strange; intelligent; purest; definite; acceptable; feeble; faithful; worthy; never-fading; extraordinary; remarkable.

OFFICE
(*general*)

adjectives
imperial; holy; ill; drafty; administrative; magnificent; paneled; imposing; nobler; elective; unpretentious; kind; breviary; basest; oldest; established; beneficent; executive; menial; subordinate; domestic; melancholy; appointed; choked; modest; distinct; turbaned; charitable; required; lofty; invidious; courteous; truer; permanent; pious; sceptered.

OFFICE
(*place of business*)

verbs
abandon—; assign to—; clerk in—; collect at—; conduct at—; establish—; glower around—; head—; inquire at—; lodge in—; pour into—; supervise—; transact at—;

transfer—to; usher into—; —buzzes; —dispenses; —drones; —employs; —functions; —hums; —operates.

(See room, building, place.)

OFFICE
(position, duty, etc.)

verbs

abolish—; abuse—; assume—; catapult into —; chain to—; dawdle in—; elevate to—; entitle to—; fill—; hoist into—; hound out of—; induct into—; oust from—; perform —; qualify for—; railroad out of (colloq.) —; resign—; retire from—; slide into—; soar to—; undertake—.

(See capacity, position, job, duty, service.)

OFFICER

adjectives

estimable; rebellious; ranking; administrative; courageous; handsome; gallant; high-minded; energetic; health; faithful; adroit; unscrupulous; sagacious; ragged; efficient; straggling; presiding; preventive; regimental; prefectual; cautious; conservative; consular; arrogant; slothful; executive; subordinate; treacherous; astute; sensitive; embarrassing; resisting; staff; audacious; senior; liberal; peevish; pelting; petty; accomplished; downhearted; hard-working; harassed; mortal; vigilant; competent; superior; liaison; newly-fledged; glaring; unblushing; confidential; native; eminent; forceful; high-spirited; subaltern; disobedient.

verbs

appoint—; consult—; court-martial—; elect —; empower—; refer to—; resist—; —administers; —admonishes; —assembles; —attends; —authorizes; —chastises; —commands; —conducts; —directs; —disbands; —inspects; —records; —serves.

(See constable, deacon, midshipman, detective, commander, general.)

OFFICIAL

adjectives

cruel; incompetent; distinguished; bureaucratic; incorruptible; fearless; intelligent; mere; salaried; corrupt; negligent; faithless; amiable; dignified; foreign; blustering; unappreciative; overdriven; energetic; aesthetic; suspicious; obstinate.

verbs

appoint—; consult—; direct—; elect—; huddle with—s; invest—with; rebuke—; refer to—; serve as—; staff with—s; —administers; —advocates; —s assemble; —attends; —authorizes; —blusters; —chastises; —conducts; —directs; —inspects; —judges; —orders; —presides; —summons.

(See leader, ambassador, legislator, congressman, governor, magistrate, president.)

adverbs

undeniably; admittedly; avowedly; assuredly; obviously; evidently; manifestly; authentically; authoritatively; absolutely; reliably; dependably; solemnly; actually; indubitably; unmistakably; odiously; irresistibly; cruelly; sternly; responsibly; imposingly; shockingly; studiously; weightily.

OFFICIOUS

adverbs

pompously; disagreeably; offensively; foolishly; absurdly; ridiculously; unwarrantably; unnecessarily; proudly; meddlesomely; impertinently; unbecomingly; ceremoniously; ingratiatingly; magisterially; unpleasantly; strangely; egotistically; busily; actively; zealously; smartly; expertly; persistently; ardently; restlessly; alertly.

OFFSPRING

adjectives

precocious; illegitimate; turbulent; new-fledged; frightened; hideous; speckled; spotted; numerous; unfilial; valiant; inferior; diminutive; sole; resulting; fatherless; groveling; motherless.

verbs

bestow—upon; bless with—; enjoy—; idolize—; issue—; mother—; present with—; produce—; promise—; rear—; transmit to —; yearn for—; —blossom; —burden; —comfort; —delight; —gather; —inherit; —torment.

(See fruit, child, heir, brood, generation, descendant.)

OGLE (v)

adverbs

flirtatiously; affectedly; amorously; lasciviously; voluptuously; lustfully; unblushingly; immodestly; brazenly; coyly.

(See look, stare.)

OIL

adjectives

volatile; subtle; raw; golden; unbleached; soothing; midnight; rich; rugged; chemic.

verbs

adulterate—; anoint with—; disseminate—; distil—; distribute—; drill for—; drive by —; extract—; feed—; force—; flush—; fuel with—; lubricate with—; market—; power with—; press—from; prospect for—; pump —; refine—; saturate with—; spout—; — accumulates; —drips; —flows; —seeps through; —smooths.

(See lubricant, fuel.)

OILY

adverbs

unpleasantly; dangerously; surprisingly; admirably; satisfactorily; sufficiently; extremely; uncommonly; significantly; wonderfully; unfortunately; treacherously; hazardously; evenly; mildly; pleasantly; soothingly.

OINTMENT

verbs

absorb—; advocate—; apply—; assimilate —; dose with—; dress with—; plaster—on; prepare—; smear—on; —assuages; — cleanses; —corrects; —draws; —eases; — palliates; —relieves; —remedies; —restores; —salves; —soothes.

(See balm, liniment, lotion, salve.)

OLD

adverbs

genuinely; unquestionably; decrepitly; incredibly; truly; apparently; evidently; obviously; deceptively; smartly; graciously; genteelly; absurdly; beautifully; proudly; valuably; unbelievably.

OLD-FASHIONED

adverbs

ridiculously; charmingly; sedately; sweetly; laughably; eccentrically; obstinately; consistently; serenely; placidly; hopelessly; carelessly; indifferently; pricelessly; whimsically; fantastically; grotesquely; shabbily; innocently; deliberately; intentionally; absurdly; barbarously; unpleasantly; embarrassingly; unconcernedly; nonchalantly; unashamedly; pleasantly; unpretentiously.

OMEN

adjectives

ill; auspicious; prophetic; fearful; unfavorable; parlous; favorable; happy; pleasant; cheery.

OMINOUS

adverbs

unmistakably; significantly; disturbingly; distressingly; sadly; prophetically; alarmingly; unpleasantly; dismally; markedly; noticeably; drearily; fearfully; terribly; heartbreakingly.

OMISSION

adjectives

voluntary; merciful; insidious.

verbs

check—; frown on—; discover—; incur—; lament—; object to—; observe—; overcome —; protest—; rectify—; scoff at—; supply —; —detracts; —irks; —magnifies; —resounds; —scandalizes; —shocks.

(See default, error, mistake.)

OMIT (*v*)

adverbs

premeditatedly; accidentally; tragically; pointedly; voluntarily; mercifully; insidiously; hazardously; rashly; cavalierly.

(See ignore, disregard.)

ONE

adjectives

unsubstantial; eclectic; lisping; heterogeneous; irresistible; delicate; reluctant; silent; memorable; uncivil; awe-inspiring.

ONEROUS

adverbs

unusually; remarkably; uncommonly; formidably; embarrassingly; objectionably; tremendously; grievously; cruelly; unexpectedly; perplexingly; bewilderingly; desperately; irksomely; unaccountably; surprisingly; singularly.

ONLOOKERS

adjectives

uncomprehending; unsophisticated; silent; innocent; conspiring.

ONRUSH

verbs

check—; elude—; instigate—; master—; stem—; —breaks; —deluges; —issues from;

—stampedes; —swamps; —sweeps by; —tramples.
(See onslaught.)

ONSET
adjectives
spiteful; insidious; thunderous; brilliant; impetuous; unyielding; intellectual.

ONSLAUGHT
adjectives
ubiquitous; furious; unscrupulous; merciless; ludicrous; savage; direct; hasty; rapid; murderous.

verbs
anticipate—; check—; curb—; dread—; escape—; fear—; flee from—; fortify against —; prompt—; stem—; subdue—; succumb to—; surrender to—; weather—; witness—; —destroys; —horrifies; —overpowers; —terrorizes.
(See assault, attack, onrush.)

OPALESCENT
adverbs
brilliantly; wonderfully; unusually; colorfully; marvelously; beautifully; uncommonly; splendidly; magnificently; barbarically; remarkably; singularly; peculiarly; particularly; oddly; attractively; gorgeously; wondrously; amazingly.

OPAQUE
adverbs
inconveniently; absolutely; satisfactorily; necessarily; completely; hazily; muddily; cloudily; vaporously; mysteriously; strangely; admirably; disappointingly; smokily; bafflingly; perplexingly; bewilderingly.

OPEN
adverbs
invitingly; mysteriously; conveniently; comfortably; advantageously; yawningly; widely; constantly; continually; evidently; palpably; apparently; indulgently; allowably; legally; officially; hospitably; unconditionally; currently; generously; broadly; liberally; helpfully.

OPEN (v)
adverbs
rarely; partially; tempestuously; listlessly; conveniently; drowsily; automatically; haphazardly; incautiously; beneficently; cautiously; unwarily; modestly; invitingly; portentously; prematurely; symmetrically.
(See reveal, unfold.)

OPEN-HANDED
adverbs
lavishly; extravagantly; liberally; indulgently; foolishly; senselessly; considerately; graciously; benevolently; wastefully; munificently; thoughtfully; freely; hospitably; incomparably; particularly; generously; indiscriminately; diplomatically; strategically; kindly; amazingly; affluently; eminently.

OPEN-HEARTED
adverbs
generously; liberally; charitably; magnanimously; always; dependably; reliably; consistently; indulgently; cordially; candidly; sincerely; frankly; artlessly; unaffectedly; notably; conspicuously; remarkably; splendidly; magnificently; lavishly.

OPENING
adjectives
portentous; moderate; auspicious; friendly; arched; chiseled; ambitious; proffered; numerous (pl); advantageous; premature; crescent; smaller; high-placed; symmetrical.

verbs
await—; desire—; enter—; intersperse with —s; miss—; neglect—; observe—; present —; scuttle through—; seize—; seek—; spurn —; widen into—; —affords; —discloses; —narrows; —offers; —promises; —reveals.
(See chasm, gate, door, opportunity, chance.)

OPERA
verbs
applaud—; aspire to—; attend—; compose —; conceive—; enjoy—; fancy—; patronize —; perform—; produce—; subscribe to—; —allures; —attracts; —captivates; —delights; —diverts; —enamors; —enchants; —enraptures; —enthralls; —fascinates; —flourishes; —thrills.
(See melodrama, theatre, play, music, drama.)

OPERATE (v)
adverbs
onerously; insidiously; mechanically; scientifically; injuriously; skillfully; deftly; effectually; primarily; economically; mystically;

legitimately; viciously; defensively; legally; rhythmically; laboriously; logically; mentally; physiologically; physically; psychologically; disastrously; maligantly; surgically; hygienically.

(See manipulate, manage, handle.)

OPERATION
(general)

adjectives

gradual; primary; difficult; economical; subsequent; celestial; offensive; excessive; gas-wasting; low-gear; efficient; costly; wasteful; expensive; powerful; military; mythic; decisive; ultimate; justifiable; hazardous; expeditious; elaborate; legitimate; vicious; fiscal; industrial; diversified; important; active; gigantic; divine; successful; ceaseless; defensive; relentless; fiery; smooth; business; authentic; undisturbed; unlimited; hygienic; rhythmic; immediate; distinct; vandalic; intermediate; sequential; imperceptible; proposed; tremendous; preliminary; laborious; logical; mental; mining; primitive; brilliant; unprecedented; disastrous; delicate; malignant; surgical; exploratory.

verbs

absorb in—; assimilate in—; coordinate—s; curtail—; demonstrate—; employ—; execute —; expand—; expedite—; facilitate—; frustrate—; mask—; paralyze—; promote —; repeat—; subject to—; suspend—; transact—; —renews.

(See action, activity, process.)

OPERATION
(surgical)

verbs

advocate—; contraindicate—; convalesce from—; entail—; perform—; recover from —; recuperate from—; repeat—; submit to —; undergo—; witness—; —allays; —alleviates; —restores; —revitalizes; —scars. •

(See abortion, procedure, surgery.)

OPERATIVE

adverbs

skilfully; profitably; actively; serviceably; wonderfully; successfully; eminently; conspicuously; amazingly; expertly; deftly; smoothly; dexterously; adroitly; cleverly; usefully; advantageously; currently; locally; incessantly; apparently; evidently.

OPERATOR

verbs

hinder—; recommend—; —controls; —despatches; —effects; —engages in; —executes; —handles; —investigates; —manipulates; —observes; —performs; —plies; —undertakes; —wields.

(See agent, engineer.)

OPIATE

verbs

addict to—s; administer—; inject—; —allays; —alleviates; —anaesthetizes; —balms; —eases; —lulls; —narcotizes; —numbs; —paralyzes; —restrains; —soothes; —tranquillizes.

(See narcotic, drug.)

OPINION

adjectives

conflicting; erroneous; well-founded; preconceived; weightier; fallacious; dispassionate; vulgar; triumphant; optimistic; imperfect; admitted; inconsistent; weening; lagging; mistaken; unequivocal; dissenting; unanimous; immediate; liberal; hard; essential; vain; decorous; ill; misguided; diverse (pl); presumed; clashing; effeminate; half-fabulous; intolerant; hideous; confirmed; candid; desponding; contrary; universal; progressive; plausible; singular; golden; hasty; conciliating; humble; discretional; true; temperate; speculative; undisguised; transient; present-day; contradictory; avowed; realistic; political; extravagant; dwarfed; emancipated; conservative; non-evolutionary; valueless; damning; exaggerated; expert; imperious; religious; public; unbiased; high; antagonistic; unsought; prevailing; adverse; atheistical; critical; reprehensible; authoritative; sincere; unasked; well-informed; monstrous; forceful; swollen; individual; inmost; revolutionary; false; editorial; dissenting; confidential; exalted; adulterated; awed; eccentric; contemptuous; mighty; expressed; implied; prevalent; rash; established; light.

verbs

abandon—; adhere to—; air—; alter—; assert—; base—on; bow to—of; cling to—; coincide with—; concur in—; condemn—; confirm—; controvert—; convert from—; convey—; crystallize—; defend—; dispute —; echo—; embody—; enforce—; formulate —; further—; justify—; modify—; muzzle —; offer—; moderate—; modify—; prepare

—; proclaim—; qualify—; reconcile —s; reflect—; rescind—; reserve—; retain—; shade—; shape—; submit—; subscribe to—; utter—; venture—; voice—; —carries weight; —s clash; —s conflict; —crystallizes; —s differ; —s diverge; —fluctuates; — hinges upon; —prevails.

(See idea, belief, inference, judgment.)

OPINIONATED

adverbs

insufferably; conceitedly; selfishly; egotistically; pompously; arrogantly; domineeringly; dogmatically; bigotedly; narrowly; ridiculously; senselessly; absurdly; foolishly; stubbornly; doggedly; doltishly; intolerably; decidedly; unbearably; unreasonably; offensively; blatantly; brazenly; rudely; grossly; crassly.

OPIUM

verbs

drowse under—; smoke—; smuggle—in; steep in—; trade in—; traffic in—; —allays; —assuages; —benumbs; —blunts; —deadens; —dulls; —enslaves; —mitigates; —palliates; —poisons; —stimulates; —stuns; — stupefies; —subdues.

(See opiate, narcotic, drug.)

OPOSSUM

verbs

—adheres to; —anchors to; —claws; — clings; —feigns; —grips; —licks; —mounts; —pouches; —preys on; —rolls; —seizes.

(See animal.)

OPPONENT

adjectives

formidable; political; honorable; strenuous; extreme; partizan; imaginary; worthy; determined; agile; masterful; malignant; foremost; fervent; energetic; prominent; unsympathetic.

verbs

capitulate to—; conquer—; discredit—; elude—; oust—; overwhelm—; rebuff—; — antagonizes; —condemns; —contends; — contests; —defends; —disputes; —maintains; —objects; —proposes; —resists; —struggles; —yields to.

(See foe, enemy, competitor, antagonist, adversary.)

OPPORTUNE

adverbs

delightfully; seasonably; fortunately; luckily; happily; conveniently; surprisingly; unexpectedly; felicitously; amazingly; particularly; providentially; extraordinarily; splendidly; unusually.

OPPORTUNITY

adjectives

plausible; perennial; exhaustible; golden; favorable; meager; extraordinary; superior; rare; magnificent; abundant; scanty; splendid; spacious; speedy; momentary; favorable; precarious; innumerable (pl); awaited; vast; long-coveted; ample; wasted; tempting; social; characteristic; natural; pleasing; crude; infinite; unusual; propitious; selling; notable; trial; sensational; golden; astounding; money-making; amazing; wonderful; big; superlative; masculine; heaven-sent; ill-annexed; limitless; glorious; boundless; final; well-used; early; convenient; adequate; enervating; indulgent; unequalled; decisive; generous; sorrowful; promising; indefinite; admirable; shrewd; unscrupulous; neglected; educational; irresistible; unsurpassed; growing; attractive; favorable; genuine; lifetime; astonishing; unparalleled; matchless; extra-money; new; profit; surprising; enviable; business; exceptional; non-competitive; grand; greatest.

verbs

afford—; anticipate—; avail oneself of—; awake to—; curtail—for; drain of —s; enlarge —s for; extend—; grasp—; heed—; ignore—; impoverish—for; jump at—; offer —; respond to—; seize—; sense—; snatch —; —beckons; —blooms; —fades; —flees; —knocks; —presents itself; —recurs.

(See occasion, opening, chance, possibility.)

OPPOSE (*v*)

adverbs

conscientiously; violently; stubbornly; diametrically; stoutly; virulently; fiercely; gallantly; obstinately; vigorously; ardently; clamorously; persistently; militantly; zealously; strenuously; cantankerously; radically; determinedly; avowedly; prematurely; fatally; maliciously; seditiously; redoubtably; vainly.

(See resist, combat.)

adverbs
violently; bitterly; subtly; fundamentally; persistently; racially; openly; politically; outspokenly; frankly; candidly; vindictively; fanatically; traditionally; formidably; irreconcilably; relentlessly; utterly; strangely; oddly; ironically; inexplicably; patently; palpably; significantly; basically; alarmingly; unaccountably; unwarrantably; immoderately; unflaggingly; powerfully; unmistakably.

OPPOSITE

adverbs
diametrically; directly; almost; exactly; incompatibly; antagonistically; hostilely; inimically; strangely; mysteriously; contrastingly; oddly; emphatically; curiously.

OPPOSITION

adjectives
cantankerous; uncompromising; radical; persistent; violent; reasonable; serious; determined; slow; powerful; considerable; downright; vigorous; astounding; avowed; rousing; direct; positive; liberal; open; strenuous; peevish; fictitious; bitter; stiffer; virulent; diametric; premature; filibustering; striking; skillful; bloody; fatal; malicious; ticklish; seditious; scholarly; vindictive; parliamentary; frightful; continual; redoubtable; brawling; vain; fierce.

verbs
align with—; antagonize—; anticipate—; batter down—; brook—; browbeat—; confront—; deter—; dispel—; encounter—; incite to—; manifest—; mow down—; mystify—; overcome—; persevere against—; provoke to—; pummel—; raise—; revive—; stimulate—; stir—; vanquish—; —clamors; —melts away; —stiffens.
(See objection, hostility, antagonism, defiance, interference.)

OPPRESS (v)

adverbs
sorely; sternly; vigorously; viciously; ruthlessly; odiously; dictatorially; unremittingly; cruelly; spiritually; rigidly; hideously.
(See persecute, aggrieve.)

OPPRESSION

adjectives
military; ruthless; discomfited; proud; ungrateful; ungracious; needless; odious; iron; long; indefinable; dismal; heavy; unbounded; subordinate; systematic; unremitting; super-inhuman.

verbs
bear—; chain to—; crumble under—; decry —; resist—; sacrifice to—; shake off—; slay by—; struggle with—; tyrannize wtih—; —chafes; —controls; —crushes; —destroys; —frustrates; —hushes; —masters; —ravages; —reigns; —silences.
(See burden, cruelty, tyranny, depression, imposition.)

OPPRESSIVE

adverbs
heavily; unbearably; intolerably; insufferably; dismally; cruelly; barbarously; bitterly; tyrannically; heartbreakingly; gallingly; domineeringly; savagely; brutally; inhumanly; drearily; ruthlessly; needlessly; systematically; incredibly; incomparably; grievously; obnoxiously; shockingly; appallingly; frightfully; odiously; tragically.

OPPRESSOR

verbs
boycott—; chastise—; crumble under—; defy —; denounce—; despise—; fear—; inveigh against—; loathe—; master—; resist—; —chains; —confiscates; —crushes; —despoils; —destroys; —dominates; —enforces; —enslaves; —exterminates; —fetters; —gags; —horrifies; —hushes; —inflicts; —intimidates; —misrules; —oppresses; —outrages; —persecutes; —reigns; —restricts; —rules; —silences; —spies; —suppresses; —terrorizes; —tramples; —tyrannizes; —victimizes.
(See tyrant, dictator.)

OPTIMISM

adjectives
slothful; radiant; placid; sober; incurable; misguided; bourgeois; innate; superb; baseless; unfailing; shallow; feeble; horrible; extravagant; militant; strident; undue; hollow; pretended.

verbs
bolster by—; crown with—; dispel—; feign —; pretend—; voice—; yield to—; —blinds; —cheers; —comforts; —cools; —encourages; —glows; —impresses; —penetrates; —pierces; —prevails; —stimulates; —warms.
(See hope, cheerfulness.)

OPTIMISTIC

adverbs

joyously; mysteriously; unaccountably; unreasonably; pleasurably; thrillingly; impatiently; ardently; charmingly; crazily; radiantly; superbly; unduly.

OPTION

verbs

abandon—; acquire—; assign—to; execute —; exercise—; purchase—; reject—; share —; specify in—; utilize—; vote on—; —expires; —guarantees; —insures; —provides; —relinquishes; —reserves; —seduces; —tempts.

(See choice, alternative, preference.)

OPULENCE

adjectives

lazy; undemocratic; approaching; unearned; sinful.

OPULENT

adverbs

amazingly; incredibly; fantastically; fabulously; magnificently; splendidly; monstrously; unbelievably; superbly; unsurpassably; incomparably; marvellously; miraculously; curiously; inexplicably; enviably; admirably; gloriously; contentedly; complacently.

ORACLE

adjectives

godlike; riddling; received; heathen; sublime; prescient; stalking; ambiguous; literary; ancient; mendacious; burning; commanding.

ORACULAR

adverbs

shrewdly; sapiently; wisely; alarmingly; frequently; confidently; dogmatically; blusteringly; solemnly; piously; mystically; seriously; gravely; soberly; reverentially; portentously; suddenly; remarkably; reputably; allegedly; avowedly.

ORATE (*v*)

adverbs

vaingloriously; verbosely; melodramatically; sonorously; pontifically; seditiously; facetiously; traitorously; thunderously; inspiringly; monotonously; ornately.

(See speak, talk.)

ORATION

adjectives

powerful; sham; eloquent; passionate; infantile; panegyrical.

verbs

blurt out—; comprehend—; criticize—; deliver—; dispute—; frame—; garnish—with; plan—; pour forth—; recite—; render—; spout—; —declaims; —decries; —exhorts; —expounds; —harangues; —incites; —inflames; —informs; —impassions; —sways.

(See declamation, address, discourse, lecture, speech, sermon.)

ORATOR

adjectives

natural; sand-lot; soapbox; idiosyncratic; stay-at-home; brilliant; political; revolutionary; loud-voiced; distinguished; classical; impassioned; effective; discerning; patriotic; genuine.

verbs

distinguish—; introduce—; —addresses; —arouses; —berates; —bombards; —charms; —declaims; —defends; —delivers; —disquiets; —enchants; —enthralls; —fulminates; —gesticulates; —hurls; —incites; —inflames; —mouths; —pleads; —rants; —raves; —spellbinds; —wields.

(See lawyer, demagogue, attorney, congressman, legislator, minister.)

ORATORICAL

adverbs

splendidly; magnificently; emphatically; eloquently; pompously; bombastically; dramatically; comically; absurdly; vainly; egotistically; ridiculously; unctuously; laughably; needlessly; unreasonably; ludicrously; effectively; impressively; imposingly; brilliantly; ardently; passionately; patriotically; grandiloquently.

ORATORY

verbs

amplify—; burst into—; delight in—; excel in—; judge—; pour—; thunder—; —burns; —enchants; —flows from; —floods; —glitters; —glorifies; —hypnotizes; —impassions; —impresses; —persuades; —streams from; —sways; —thaws; —touches.

(See declamation, orator, talk, speech.)

adjectives

huge; brilliant; radiant; glaring; shining; freezing; cold; lifeless; sightless; multitudinous (pl); ruined; piercing; prominent; numerous (pl); intelligent; sickly; serene; mounting; fatal; flaming; parent; unfathomable; wan; planetary; mysterious; small; arch; restless; ruddy; whirling.

ORBIT

adjectives

implicated; moral; common; planetary; definite; independent; lurid; respective; mathematical; elliptic.

ORCHARD

adjectives

abounding; blooming; sappy; starry; fantastic; ravaged; new-planted; wind-swept; dripping; festive; beauteous; aromatic.

verbs

blight—; cultivate—; enclose—; fertilize—; frost—; harvest—; irrigate—; plan—; protect—; prune—; rob—; stock from—; tour —; —blooms; —blossoms; —supplies; — yields.

(See crops, farm, tree, fruit.)

ORCHESTRA

adjectives

errant; magnificent; revamped; mammoth; itinerant; nationally-known; broadcasting; favorite; popular; unrivaled; recording.

verbs

direct—; follow—; guide—; lead—; strike up—; uniform—; —accompanies; —attunes to; —beats time; —blares; —charms; —delights; —enchants; —expresses; —greets; — improvises; —pipes; —performs; —sweeps a chord; —tweedles.

(See band, music, musician.)

ORCHESTRAL

adverbs

splendidly; magnificently; tunefully; harmoniously; delightfully; gorgeously; impressively; sonorously; resoundingly; grandly; superbly; brilliantly; dazzlingly; richly; triumphantly.

adjectives

painful; dreadful; crucial; tremendous; numbing; perilous; premature; coming; fiery.

verbs

bear—; doom to—; endure—; flinch from —; fortify for—; resign to—; submit to—; suffer—; tolerate—; undergo—; wince at—; —agitates; —chastens; —ensues; —proves; —shatters; —sobers; —tests; —verifies.

(See suffering, pain, torture.)

ORDER
(command)

adjectives

peremptory; positive; executive; advance; admirable; divers (pl); liberal; rigid; rarest; extortionate; patriarchal; frantic; vast; abstract; existing; suspicious; preliminary; hostile; spiritual; convulsive; promised; imperative; social; secondary; inferior; sweeping; subsequent; additional; imminent; allied; urgent; superior; makeshift; established; showy; actual; thundering; relenting; conflicting; visible; alphabetical; preposterous; determinate; successive (pl); obstructing; provident; retaliatory; metropolitan; explicit; sinister; treasonable; logical; half-conscious; handsome; privileged; elegant; restricted; marching; spacious; chronological; switchback; notorious; noiseless; unfilled; agrarian; positive; retrograde; tessellated; fraternal; strategic; ill-conceived; sealed; beneficent; contrary; preconcerted; opposite; pretty; gallant; supplementary; internal; welcome; probable; injunction; excellent; shocking; meek; florid; melting; previous; intellectual; gracious; malignant; complacent; lucid; auspicious.

verbs

accept—; comply with—; disregard—; establish—; execute—; flash—; issue—; maintain—; modify—; obey—; preserve—; receive—; record—; rescind—; restore—; violate—; whip into—; —bans; —bars; —compels; —decrees; —hampers; —manifests itself; —reigns.

(See command, commandment, injunction, mandate, discipline.)

ORDER
(organization, system, arrangement)

adjectives

requisite; subsequent; existing; cloistered; festive; favored; valiant; venerable; celestial; vexatious; congenial; imperative; eternal; slender; ethereal; chronological; outward; symmetrical; mystic; eerie; rude; admirable; lower; reiterated; petty; social; solemn; beneficial; dubious; private; revised; economic; different; financial; lofty; honorable; privileged; patrician.

verbs
adhere to—; annihilate—; ape—; bury—; challenge—; establish—; fit into—; institute —; perpetuate—; rage against—; undermine —; —passes; —pervades.
(See arrangement, class, system, government.)

ORDER (*sales*)
verbs
book —s; boost (colloq.)—; confirm—; consign—to; fill—; lose—; overwhelm with —s; procure—; realize—; reject—; ship—; solicit—s; swamp with—s; —s filter in; — grosses; —s mount; —nets; —s pour in; —s slacken.
(See purchase, sales.)

ORDER (*v*)
adverbs
peremptorily; explicitly; indiscriminately; treacherously; bluffly; reluctantly; insolently; sternly; quaintly; imperiously; congenially; pettishly; dubiously; economically; malignantly.
(See command, dictate.)

ORDERLY
adverbs
satisfactorily; unusually; wonderfully; remarkably; particularly; always; altogether; admirably; regularly; uniformly; scrupulously; meticulously; habitually; unwontedly; uncommonly.

ORDINANCE
adjectives
oppressive; divine; surrendered; solemn; secession; ill-starred; detested.

verbs
administer—; cite—; codify—; confirm—; enact—; enforce—; formulate—; frame—; promulgate—; remand—; transgress—; violate—; —commands; —decrees; —directs; —enjoins; —imposes; —legalizes; —ordains; —prescribes.
(See edict, decree, law, legislation, mandate.)

adjectives
useful; good-looking; metallic; massy; pavonine; vermilion-colored; rich; precious; manganese; iridescent; rough.

ORGAN (*general*)
adjectives
full-toned; deep-throated; vital; bodily; singular; discordant; lovely; mysterious; visual; sensual; improper; charming; delicate; deep-laboring; digestive; unique; damaged; sentient; rudimentary; reproductive; respiratory: administrative; generative; ardent; delegated; virile; olfactory.

ORGAN (*of the body*)
verbs
affect—; attack—; cleanse—; congest—; derange—; enliven—; impair—; inflame—; invade—; irrigate—; irritate—; nourish—; tone up—; tune—to; vitalize—; —atrophies; —decays; —functions; —recuperates.
(See heart, kidney, etc.)

ORGANISM
adjectives
finished; vital; political; alert; courageous; aggressive; social; diverse (pl); vegetable; precious; terrific; mysterious; living; active; sensuous; enfeebled; specific; composite; elaborate; molded; unicellular.

verbs
constitute—; culture—; examine—; stain—; study—; —attacks; —excretes; —flourishes; —functions; —invades; —poisons; —reproduces.
(See bacteria, embryo, germ.)

ORGANIZATION
adjectives
inadequate; active; magnificent; complete; accurate; hierarchical; ecclesiastical; farflung; rudimentary; resounding; various (pl); producing; worthy; efficient; sweetly-functioning; secret; farsighted; vital; underlying; scientific; unified; matchless; constitutional; laborious; elaborate; competitive; well-drilled; distributing; independent; eleemosynary; internal; quasi-benevolent; quasi-military; odious; gigantic; monolithic; associational; nervous; abstinence; chartered; well-formed; stupendous; marvelous; militant; mammoth.

verbs
disband—; dominate—; effect—; encourage
—; endow—; envision—; evolve—; foster
—; initiate—; penetrate—; perfect—; preside over—; revive—; sponsor—; subsidize
—; suppress—; weaken—; —expands; —
functions; —s merge.
(See club, league, establishment.)

ORGANIZE (v)
adverbs
admirably; politically; seditiously; treacherously; radically; delicately; efficiently; constitutionally; independently; militantly.
(See arrange, form.)

ORGANIZED
adverbs
highly; carefully; secretly; skilfully; recently; elaborately; simply; surreptitiously; admirably; independently; complexly; regularly; methodically; systematically; strategically; cleverly; intelligently; masterfully; fully; efficiently; marvellously; incomparably.

ORGY
adjectives
bloodiest; speculative; disgusting; emotional; verbal; loathed; sex; lustful; pagan;
midnight; disgraceful; nocturnal; drunken;
sinful; degrading.

verbs
carouse in—; feast in—; indulge in—;
plunge into—; recoil from—; revel in—;
submerge in—; wallow in—; welter in—;
—debauches; —gratifies; —intoxicates; —
nauseates; —palls; —revolts; —wearies.
(See merriment, sin, drunkenness.)

ORIGIN
adjectives
volcanic; unpolished; humble; supernatural;
psychogenic; variant; remote; doubtful;
genial; miraculous; accidental; bourgeois;
genetic; overseas; subjective; celestial;
moral; racial; contractual; recent; classical;
obscure; communal; antique; ultimate; legendary; fiery; modern; ignoble; common;
recent; soulless; synthetic; childish; germinal; historical; illegitimate; plebeian; proximate; abnormal; evolutionary; medieval.

verbs
ascribe—to; derive—from; mist—; outline
—; owe—to; question—; reveal—; shroud—

in; trace—; uncover—; —explains; —revolves about.
(See birth, beginning, cause, source.)

ORIGINAL
adjectives
select; authenticated; uncertain; vivid.

verbs
alter—; conceive—; copy—; counterfeit—;
create—; design—; deviate from—; diverge
from—; duplicate—; exhibit—; fabricate—;
imitate—; modify—; outdo—; overshadow
—; parallel—; prize—; reproduce—; treasure—.
(See model, duplicate, copy.)

ORIGINALITY
adjectives
everyday; characteristic; fixed; refreshing;
unconscious; ignorant; reckless; intellectual;
prophetic; notable; illiterate; absolute; con-
tra-distinguished; transcendent; inspired.

verbs
dispense with—; encourage—; exercise—;
foster—; gain—; induce—; inspire—; lack
—; require—; reward—; stifle—; stimulate
—; stress—; urge—; value—; want—; —attracts; —flourishes; —merits.
(See initiative, novelty, ability, talent.)

ORIGINATE (v)
adverbs
artificially; primevally; mysteriously; exclusively; authenticatedly; germinally; volcanically; celestially; legitimately; normally;
mythically.
(See begin, start.)

ORNAMENT
adjectives
foliated; literary; lovely; sweet; insipid;
conspicuous; enviable; heraldic; wealthy;
feather-inlaid; glittering; distinguished; appropriate; elaborate; characteristic; beseem-
ing; wonted; vacant; simple; trifling; sculptured; complicated; meretricious; showy;
fatal; bedecking; gold-embossed; historic;
desirable; delightful; barbaric.

verbs
convert into—; discard—; fashion—; flourish—; strip off —s; —beautifies; —s bedeck;
—bedizens; —decorates; —embellishes; —

839

emblazons; —enriches; —furbishes; —garnishes; —gilds; —glitters; —spangles; —trims.

(See finery, feather, design, button, bead, braid.)

ORNAMENT (v)
adverbs
grotesquely; gaudily; tastefully; decoratively; profusely; insipidly; conspicuously; appropriately; elaborately; simply; meretriciously; barbarically.

(See decorate, embellish.)

ORNAMENTAL
adverbs
gracefully; pleasantly; delightfully; artistically; unusually; highly; remarkably; tastefully; unbelievably; delicately; structurally; gaudily; floridly; cheaply; richly; scarcely; beautifully; clumsily; daintily; conspicuously; appropriately; barbarically; exotically; impressively; smartly; gorgeously; particularly; noticeably; expensively.

ORNAMENTATION
adjectives
whimsical; graceful; bristling; riotous; hideous; rich; floral.

ORNATE
adverbs
absurdly; unusually; surprisingly; remarkably; highly; uncommonly; peculiarly; curiously; unexpectedly; unwontedly; gaudily; smartly; flashily; richly; gorgeously; splendidly; colorfully; magnificently; brilliantly; architecturally; conspicuously; strangely; attractively; gracefully.

ORPHAN
adjectives
frail; exotic; white-faced; helpless; lonely; homeless.

ORTHODOX
adverbs
regularly; highly; unusually; rigidly; strictly; sternly; severely; uncompromisingly; intolerantly; dogmatically; bigotedly; narrowly; admirably; reverently; consistently; conventionally; conformably; invariably; conspicuously; unyieldingly; soundly; faithfully; truly.

OSCILLATION
adjectives
electric; gorgeous; vibrating; rushing.

OSTENTATION
adjectives
inelegant; mourning; isolated; minor; vain; ironical; brusque.

OSTENTATIOUS
adverbs
deliberately; significantly; purposely; sagaciously; impressively; absurdly; foolishly; egotistically; pompously; blatantly; noisily; arrogantly; dramatically; spectacularly; ridiculously; showily; ludicrously; cheaply; disgustingly; habitually.

OSTRACISM
verbs
deserve—; endure—; live down—; merit—; result in—; —banishes; —castigates; —crushes; —deprecates; —disparages; —excludes; —estranges; —exiles; —outlaws; —reprimands; —secludes; —sequesters; —shuts out.

(See banishment, obscurity.)

OUTBREAK
adjectives
incipient; sporadic; curious; periodical; rebellious; dusky; unexpected; vehement; audible; occasional.

verbs
aggravate—; alleviate—; down—; excite—; foment—; fulminate in—; incite—; instigate —; irritate to—; launch—; mitigate—; provoke—; quell—; quench—; suppress—; —disunites; —embroils; —foams; —fumes; —gushes; —razes; —scorches; —shocks; —thunders; —vents.

(See rebellion, revolution, eruption.)

OUTBURST
adjectives
sudden; restrained; warrantable; wild; spontaneous; mutinous; emotional; overwhelming; eloquent; rash; sacred; passionate; jolly; lyrical; unprecedented; thunderous; tempestuous; national; petulant; swift; sincere; hysterical; thoughtless.

verbs
excite—; plague to—; quell—; quiet—; staunch—; —boils; —discharges; —drains; —distracts; —effervesces; —emanates; —

evacuates; —fevers; —flushes; —gushes; —
heats; —issues; —oozes; —perturbs; —
rages; —storms; —strains; —wears away.
(See explosion, eruption, attack, onslaught.)

OUTCAST

adjectives
nameless; wretched; houseless; miserable;
scathed; diseased; destitute; blighted; reprobated; shamefaced; wronged; ragged.

OUTCAST

adverbs
pitiably; reprehensibly; deservedly; viciously; wretchedly; miserably; wrongfully;
pathetically; pitifully; shamefully; disgracefully; ingloriously; disreputably; scandalously; unfortunately; forlornly; desolately;
obscurely; humiliatingly; cruelly.

OUTCOME

adjectives
eventual; useless; sublime; strangest; felicitous; unlucky; fatal.

verbs
announce—; anticipate—; blight—; contemplate—; declare—; determine—; doom—;
effect—; endanger—; foresee—; predestine
—; predict—; preordain—; prophesy—;
temporize—; threaten—; —disappoints; —
hinges on; —staggers; forestall—.
(See issue, consequence, result, effect.)

OUTCRY

adjectives
passionate; hysterical; absurd; violent; indignant; pitiful; diabolical.

verbs
bawl—; bellow—; mingle with—ies; minimize—; muffle—; restrain—; squeal—; still
—; suppress—; whoop—; —bewails; —
bursts forth; —clamors; —deafens; —deplores; —dies; —fades; —laments; —
scandalizes; —wrings at; raise—; stifle—.
(See cry, exclamation, howl, noise)

OUTFIT

adjectives
colorful; spring; luxurious; pert; demure;
effective; queer.

verbs
accoutre in—; array in—; attire in—; divest
of—; don—; drape—; equip with—; gear

in—; invest in—; prepare—; refurbish—;
renew—; rig in—; slip on—; strip off—;
trap in—; —enrobes; —envelops; —mantles.
(See coat, overcoat, jacket.)

OUTFLOW

verbs
breast—; check—; contend with—; control
—; cope with—; curb—; dam—; filter—;
gauge—; oppose—; resist—; restrain—; restrict—; stem—; —drains; —effuses; —endangers; —exudes; —gushes; —spouts; —
sweeps away.
(See flow, outpouring.)

OUTGROW (v)

adverbs
manifestly; prolifically; unrestrictedly; prodigiously; abundantly; abnormally.
(See surpass, grow.)

OUTLANDISH

adverbs
extraordinarily; surprisingly; strikingly;
ridiculously; boorishly; doltishly; heathenishly; meretriciously; oddly; monstrously;
indecorously; particularly; shockingly; uncivilly; absurdly; egregiously; unaccountably; singularly; unpleasantly.

OUTLAW

adjectives
excommunicated; renegade; tattered; dauntless.

OUTLAW (v)

adverbs
legitimately; legally; socially; morally; spiritually; economically; timorously; passionately; traditionally.
(See interdict, renounce.)

OUTLAY

verbs
absorb—; account for—; allow for—; appropriate for—; atone for—; audit—; exhaust—; expend—; fleece of—; garble—;
invest—; recoup—; recover—; redeem—;
rehabilitate for—; reimburse for—; remit—;
restore—; retain—; reward—; subsidize—;
—bleeds (colloq.); —drains; —indebts.
(See expenditure, expense, money, payment, profit.)

adjectives
manipulative; convenient; retail; common; satisfactory; obscure; constructive; agreeable; sufficient; emotional; noblest; stupendous.

verbs
bore—; bare—; clog—; crave—; drain—; drill—; effuse from—; emanate from—; exude from—; furnish—; gain—; leak from —; perforate—; plug—; provide—; puncture—; seek—; stem—; strive for—; —gapes; —yawns.
(See hole, chasm, opening.)

OUTLINE

adjectives
vague; sublime; cathedral-like; stubbly; shadowy; rude; circular; precise; fine; picturesque; distinct; rolling; faint; graceful; flowing; delicate; charming; crude; undefined; rugged; misty; harsh; unmistakable; broad; melodic; geographical; analytical; tentative; ghastly; soft; rounded; noble; majestic; irregular; angular; spirited; intellectual; arrowlike; imperfect; depressed; monotonous; lambent.

verbs
analyze—; blot out—; conceive—; diagram —; discern—; draft—; draw—; fashion—; launch into—; organize—; plan—; prepare —; scrutinize—; sketch—; stencil in—; trace —; —abstracts; —abbreviates; —condenses; —contracts; —digests; —guides; —represents; —reviews; —shortens; —skims over; —summarizes.
(See figure, line, map, diagram, sketch.)

OUTLINE (v)
adverbs
scholarly; studiously; purposefully; precisely; vaguely; delicately; rudely; crudely; unmistakably; geographically; intellectually; monotonously.
(See sketch, draw.)

OUTLOOK
adjectives
cosmopolitan; confident; savage; philosophic; passionate; desolate; tolerant; humorous; sectional; unwarped; disheartening; superb; model; fundamental.

verbs
alter—; blacken—; broaden—; convert—; darken—; dim—; foster—; modify—; narrow—; overcast—; reverse—; shade—; transform—; widen—; —brightens; —cheers; —disheartens.
(See future, hope.)

OUTPOURING
adjectives
unstudied; passionate; spontaneous; fervent; morbid; unsearchable.

verbs
erupt in—; escape—; evade—; quell—; restrain—; restrict—; stem—; —cools; —diminishes; —eases; —endangers; —immerses; —quenches; —ravages; —relieves; —roars; —swells; —weakens.
(See flow, outflow.)

OUTPUT
adjectives
prolific; excessive; profitable; mechanical; steady.

verbs
amplify—; augment—; decrease—; develop —; diminish—; dwarf—; enlarge—; expand —; govern—; halt—; market—; restrict—; stem—; treble—; utilize—; —climbs; —declines; —depreciates; —dwindles; —ebbs; —overloads; —shrinks; —subsides; —wanes; swell—.
(See production, crops, proceeds, product.)

OUTRAGE
adjectives
intolerant; unparalleled; dreadful; treacherous; uncivil; flagrant; atrocious; hideous; living; frantic; vile; miserable; brutal; cowardly; highhanded; ungentlemanly; rancorous; incredible.

verbs
absolve of—; acquit of—; avenge—; brand as—; commit—; condone—; countenance—; decry—; denounce—; disparage—; fulminate against—; incite—; inflict—; perpetrate —; punish—; —aggrieves; —blights; —debases; —despoils; —fans; —infuriates; —perverts; —stigmatizes.
(See injury, indignity, insult, atrocity.)

OUTRAGE (v)
adverbs
grossly; foully; treacherously; flagrantly;

atrociously; hideously; brutally; sexually; rancorously; incredibly.

(See offend, encroach.)

OUTRAGEOUS

adverbs

barbarously; despicably; incredibly; atrociously; intolerably; insufferably; appallingly; shockingly; execrably; dreadfully; unimaginably.

OUTSKIRTS

verbs

avoid—; circumvent—; direct to—; flank—; fortify—; hover on—; stretch to—; swerve to—; —border; —edge; —encompass; —extend; —parallel; —range; —surround.

(See boundary, border, barrier, edge, line.)

OUTSPOKEN

adverbs

unfortunately; unhappily; unwisely; foolishly; unpleasantly; displeasingly; absurdly; injudiciously; impolitically; indiscreetly; recklessly; pertly; impertinently; disrespectfully; rudely; boorishly; uncivilly; ignorantly; carelessly; brusquely; bluntly; disagreeably; roughly.

OUTSTRIP (v)

adverbs

masterfully; physically; mentally; economically; legally; vigorously; swiftly; overwhelmingly.

(See surpass, outgrow.)

OUTWEIGH (v)

adverbs

enormously; tremendously; markedly; indubitably; characteristically; personally.

(See exceed, surpass.)

OUTWIT (v)

adverbs

cunningly; subtly; deftly; slyly; dexterously; treacherously; nimbly.

(See defeat, surpass, cheat.)

OVARY

verbs

dislocate—; displace—; fertilize—; fructify —; impregnate—; inflame—; operate on—; remove—; sterilize—; —atrophies; —dis-

charges; —distends; —enlarges; —functions; —generates; —germinates; —reproduces; —secretes; —shrivels; —swells.

(See organ.)

OVATION

adjectives

perfect; tremendous; significant; thunderous; enthusiastic.

verbs

rejoice in—; render—; shout—; tender—; voice—; —acclaims; —cheers; —clamors; —gratifies; —honors; —rewards; —rings; —thunders.

(See cheering, celebration, triumph.)

OVERBEARING

adverbs

insufferably; pompously; arrogantly; egotistically; selfishly; tyrannically; importantly; domineeringly; intolerably; disagreeably; imperiously; superciliously; shockingly; appallingly; despicably; contemptibly; impertinently; extremely; presumptuously; terribly.

OVERCOAT

adjectives

heavy; worn; woolly.

verbs

array in—; divest of—; don—; fray—; huddle in—; model—; patch—; peel off—; penetrate—; shed—; tailor—; —assures; —fends off; —guarantees; —insulates; —insures against; —protects; —shelters; —wards off.

(See coat, jacket, outfit, clothing.)

OVERCOME (v)

adverbs

physically; militantly; vigorously; passionately; stoutly; defiantly; mentally; legally; energetically.

(See conquer, master.)

OVERFLOW

adjectives

natural; periodic; kind; spontaneous; simple.

OVERFLOW (v)

adverbs

naturally; prodigiously; periodically; seasonally; spontaneously.

(See flood, fill, pervade.)

OVERGROWN

adverbs

hopelessly; sadly; luxuriantly; weedily; irremediably; irrecoverably; shiftlessly; carelessly; neglectfully; terribly; desperately; irreparably; curiously; inexplicably; unfortunately; unrecognizably.

OVERHEAD

verbs

augment—; charge to—; cover—; cut—; lighten—; meet—; —ascends; —descends; —mounts; —staggers; —swamps.

(See expense, sum, amount, profits.)

OVERHEAR (v)

adverbs

inadvertently; innocently; accidentally; coincidentally; unflatteringly; tragically; fatally; thoughtlessly

(See hear.)

OVERLAP (v)

adverbs

richly; amply; largely; statistically; unavoidably; repeatedly; harmoniously.

(See encroach.)

OVERLOADED

adverbs

tremendously; shamefully; terribly; pathetically; pitiably; dangerously; alarmingly; disastrously; ruinously; dreadfully; unwisely; foolishly; absurdly; wretchedly; unfortunately; imprudently; awfully; bitterly; intolerably; unbearably; cruelly.

OVERLOOK (v)

adverbs

obligingly; tacitly; magnanimously; sullenly; naturally; selfishly; unfeelingly; delicately.

(See neglect, disregard, ignore.)

OVERPOWER (v)

adverbs

vigorously; physically; brutally; lustfully; cruelly; dictatorially; bestially.

(See conquer, overcome.)

OVERRATE (v)

adverbs

grossly; carelessly; confidently; egoistically; mistakenly; fatally; intellectually; morbidly.

(See exaggerate.)

OVERRUN (v)

adverbs

destructively; overwhelmingly; prodigiously; atrociously; brutally; victoriously; pugnaciously; seasonally; periodically.

(See invade, trespass.)

OVERSIGHT

adjectives

unparalleled; unwary; imprudent.

OVERSTATEMENT

verbs

avoid—; concoct—; foist—upon; purvey—; resort to—; —amplifies; —beguiles; —cheats; —colors; —decoys; —deludes; —embroiders; —exaggerates; —heightens; —libels; —lures; —magnifies; —meshes; —misleads; —strains; —stretches; —swindles.

(See exaggeration.)

OVERTHROW (v)

adverbs

decisively; victoriously; illegally; brutally; vindictively; petulantly; mutinously; unrestrainedly; tempestuously; seditiously; passionately; diabolically.

(See overpower, defeat.)

OVERTONE

adjectives

attendant; objectionable; pathetic; brisk.

OVERTURE

adjectives

diplomatic; unfeeling; ineffectual; delicate; joint; friendly.

OVUM

verbs

develop—; discharge—; exude—; fertilize —; impregnate—; secrete—; —enlarges; —generates; —germinates; —reproduces; —unites with; —yields.

(See egg, cell.)

OWE (v)

adverbs

fatally; hopelessly; tragically; fatefully; morally; spiritually; stupendously.

(See obligate.)

OWL

adjectives

moping; staring; melodious; vile; great; horned; nocturnal; clamorous; uncouth.

verbs
—attacks; —bodes; —bolts; —circles; — clamors; —claws; —devours; —flutters; — glides off; —grasps; —hisses; —hoots; — mocks; —perches; —pounces on; —protests; —prowls; —reigns; —sails; —sallies forth; —scans; —screams; —screeches; —shrieks; —skims along; —stares; —wails; — whistles; —explores.
(See bird.)

OWN (v)

adverbs
privately; rightfully; legally; legitimately; originally; enthusiastically; gratefully; luxuriously; selfishly.
(See have.)

OWNER

adjectives
rightful; truculent; same; enthusiastic; untutored; original; favored; dishonest; unfortunate; legitimate.

verbs
divulge—; fine—; indemnify—; levy against —; tax—; —assents; —auctions; —bans; — bars; —disputes; —enlarges; —evicts; — leases; —lodges; —mortgages; —occupies; —prohibits; —renovates; —rents.
(See manager, management, employer.)

OWNERSHIP

adjectives
enthusiastic; beneficial; undisputed; municipal; implied; multiple.

OX

adjectives
stately; primitive; well-fed; fattened.

verbs
burden—; employ—; fetter—; harness—; load—; tether—; water—; yoke—; —balks; —carries; —charges; —gores; —halts; — hauls; —pulls; —rages.
(See buffalo, livestock, animal, bull, cow.)

OXEN

adjectives
patient; meek-eyed; broad-foreheaded; long-suffering.

OXYGEN

verbs
absorb—; administer—; combine with—; curtail—; dissolve—; employ—; extract— from; lack—; liberate—; prepare—; require —; supply—; unite with—; —invigorates; —restores; —resuscitates; —saves; —sustains; —sterilizes.
(See gas, chemical, medicine, tonic.)

OYSTERS

verbs
can—; consume—; crush—; cull—; cultivate—; dislodge—; dry—; farm—; fatten —; grade—; harvest—; irritate—; market —; prey upon—; rake for—; replant—; scallop—; scrape for—; shuck—; stew—; transplant—; —anchor to; —bob around; —imbed; —spawn.

P

adjectives

tranquil;* unperturbed; swift; stealthy;
measured; rapid; restless; incredible; stately; heedless; moderate; breakneck; jaunty;
sluggish; hopping; sauntering; furious; precipitate; brisk; dashing; lively; deliberate;
even; slow; sentry-like; inoffensive; ragged; eager; divers (pl); tremendous;
quick; petty; trembling; evenly-geared; jubilant; killing; portly; quickened; moderate;
feverish; terrific.

verbs

allay—; ease—; hold—; maintain—; quick-
en—; regulate—; set—; slacken—; smooth
—; sustain—; —devours; —tires; —wearies.

(See step, gait, speed, stride.)

PACE (v)

adverbs

stormily; excitedly; moodily; meditatively;
restlessly; furiously; tranquilly; heedlessly;
sluggishly; deliberately; jubilantly; feverishly.

(See walk, amble, step.)

PACIFIC

adverbs

resolutely; calmly; serenely; assiduously;
consistently; diplomatically; earnestly; definitely; urgently; quietly; inherently; naturally; insistently; harmoniously; amicably;
reassuringly; marvellously

PACIFIST

verbs

defend—; denounce—; oppress—; persecute—; support—; —abstains; —advocates;
—arbitrates; —argues; —decries; —hinders; —minimizes; —preserves; —proclaims; —refuses; —resists; —shrinks from.

(See coward.)

PACIFY (v)

adverbs

seductively; profoundly; artfully; domestically; prudently; diplomatically; politically;
nationally.

(See calm, appease.)

adjectives

restless; mechanic; captive; nervous.

PACK

adjectives

damned; crumpled; lathered; baying; clamorous; weighty.

verbs

hunt with—; loose—; muster—; whistle for
—; —attacks; —congregates; —defends; —
deluges; —disbands; —disburses; —flocks;
—gathers; —pursues; —roams; —rushes;
—scatters; —storms; —strays; —surges; —
throngs; —troops; —unites; —wanders.

(See crowd, flock, herd, hive, horde.)

PACK (v)

adverbs

suffoeatingly; densely; scientifically; compactly; tastefully; professionally; deftly;
artfully; medically.

(See bundle, wrap.)

PACKAGE

adjectives

convenient; cumbersome; deceptive; enormous; economical; nifty; seductive; bridal;
sundry; airtight.

verbs

bear—; bow under—; burden with—; cart
—; clutch—; dispatch—; haul—; heap—s
on; load with—s; lug—; relieve of—; stoop
under—; —weighs; —weights.

(See bundle, parcel.)

PACT

adjectives

futile; defensive; warning; unenforceable;
joint; worthless.

verbs

abide by—; acclaim—; bind by—; challenge
—; conclude—; confine—to; disregard—;
fear—; guard—; implement—; inveigh
against—; join—; negotiate—; regard—;
scrap—; sustain—; violate—; —allies; —
insures; —strengthens; —unites; —weakens.

(See treaty, accord, agreement, bargain,
compact, covenant, lease.)

adjectives
shielding; smooth; thick; soothing.

PADDLE

verbs
chastise with—; dip—; drag—; guide with —; ply—; propel—; strain at—; thwack with—; whack with—; —brushes; —dabbles; —flays; —ploughs; —slides; —smacks; —spanks; —steers; —strikes; —sweeps.
(See oar.)

PADDLE (v)

adverbs
noiselessly; desperately; skillfully; deftly; indefatigably; arduously; unerringly; intrepidly.
(See row, propel.)

PADLOCK

adjectives
stout; jingling; burglar-proof; trusty.

PAGANISM

adjectives
aesthetic; poetic; devoted; honest; extreme.

verbs
convert from—; degenerate to—; denounce —; exterminate—; meddle in—; oppose—; practise—; relinquish—; revert to—; sink to—; succumb to—; —blends; —blinds; —destroys; —fancies; —fetters; —outrages; —sacrifices; —worships.
(See atheism, materialism.)

PAGE

adjectives
barren; blistered; storied; long-faded; rattling; historic; fervid; idle; dog-eared; glorious; written; interesting; voluminous; intricate; pregnant; sparkling; colorful; fascinating; provocative; illuminated; labored; naughty; saucy; discolored; classic; poetic; stone; vivacious; succeeding; remote; various (pl); precise; glowing; loitering; impish; vivid; blank; sleepy; luminous; scornful; pretty; knavish; ingenious; unopened; title; lying; wondrous; barekneed; boy scout; well-reputed; wormy; crumbling; long; emblazoned; ample; penciled; large-margined.

verbs
bind—s; charge—with; flick—; flip—; fray —; peruse—s; ponder—; reel off—s; skim over—s; sprinkle—s with; stream across—s; —cumbers; —sparkles; splash across—s.
(See sheet, paper, book, copy, advertisement, picture, text.)

PAGEANT

adjectives
idle; dismal; unsubstantial; extensive; imposing; woeful; inspiring; melodious; martial; ostentatious; magnificent; doleful; colorful; insubstantial; crumbling; fond; warlike; motley; gleamy; proud.

verbs
acclaim—; applaud—; solemnize—; stage —; view—; witness—; —colors; —commemorates; —delineates; —depicts; —glitters; —impresses; —portrays; —predicts; —signifies; —symbolizes; —traces; —wends.
(See celebration, demonstration, parade, spectacle.)

PAGEANTRY

adjectives
adventurous; colorful; antique; ostentatious.

PAGODAS

adjectives
delicate; gilded; slender.

PAIL

adjectives
clicking; brimming; immense.

PAIN

adjectives
racking; sharp; gnawing; tolerable; sympathetic; straining; sleepless; hard-featured; rankling; long-stifled; terrible; labor; passing; dull; keen; lonely; stinging; sacrificial; momentary; unbearable; excruciating; impotent; subtle; passionate; scrupulous; yearning; convulsive; intense; severe; lifelong; wise; palpitating; accusing; secret; willing; ceaseless; ecstatic; unrepentant; divine; sublime; wriggling; fearful; utmost; molten; mortal; pure, exquisite; poisonous; poignant; aromatic; vile; violent; pleasurable; hopeless; soothing; extraordinary; infinite; unendurable; burning; rheumatic; helpless; perpetual; quivering; full-blown; unmitigated; mutual; interrupting; incestuous; fierce; numbing; doggish; peculiar; gratuitous; distorted; mingled (pl); penitential; morbid; licensed; tingling; throbbing; unlanguaged; deteriorated; enduring; cancerous; jealous; ex-

treme; long-drawn; travail; immediate; sweet; aching; transforming; courteous; accepted; recreant; acute; soul-racking; perceivable; hidden; needless; conquering; retributive; anticipated; bodily; afflicting; frightful; remorseful; tender; despairing; positive; stabbing; uncommon; voluntary; eternal; agonizing; heartfelt; longing; unsuccessful; grammatical; stifled; vague; cruel; melancholy; tortuous; frenzied.

verbs

accompany by—; aggravate—; allay—; alleviate—; assuage—; attend by—; combat —; deaden—; deprave with—; experience —; give rise to—; inflict—; intensify—; mark by—; mitigate—; occasion—; pant from—; relieve—; report—; seize with—; soothe—; stifle—; still—; subdue—; throb with—; writhe in—; —abates; —agonizes; —departs; —distracts; —extends to; — flashes up; —gnaws; —gripes; —hammers; —lancinates; —persists; —racks; —radiates from; —shoots; —stabs; —subsides.

(See headache, ill, ache, agony, injury, torture, pang, irritation.)

PAIN (v)

adverbs

acutely; intolerably; excruciatingly; poignantly; unendurably; gratuitously; stabbingly; cruelly; agonizingly.

(See hurt, torture.)

PAINFUL

adverbs

distressingly; terribly; intolerably; slightly; dreadfully; noticeably; apparently; excruciatingly; pitiably; unexpectedly; rackingly; intensely; acutely; extraordinarily; extremely; inordinately; unavoidably; moderately; bitterly; grievously; uncomfortably; unaccountably; pathetically; tremendously; deucedly.

PAINLESS

adverbs

happily; marvellously; miraculously; ostensibly; avowedly; allegedly; unbelievably; blessedly; comfortably; wonderfully; amazingly; incredibly; veritably; unaccountably; gratifyingly.

PAINSTAKING

adverbs

carefully; cautiously; meticulously; strikingly; surprisingly; unexpectedly; deftly; expertly; unusually; habitually; inordinately; unnecessarily; patiently; conscientiously; diligently; remarkably; admirably; consistently; unfailingly; courteously.

PAINT

adjective.

plastic; formidable; war; congealed; melodious; filmy; gaudy; lasting.

verbs

blend—; daub—on; scrape—; smear—; —brightens; —covers; —crusts; —emblazons; —enamels; —enriches; —faces; —fades; —gilds; —glosses; —peels; —preserves; —protects; —sheathes; —sheens; —smudges; —tinges; —tints; —veneers; —waterproofs.

(See complexion, hue, shade, color, ink, make-up.)

PAINT (v)

adverbs

gaudily; sensuously; exquisitely; realistically; artistically; consummately; garishly; formidably; atrociously; professionally; eminently; decoratively.

(See sketch, picture.)

PAINTER

adjectives

impressionist; squalid; supreme; ragged; decorative; itinerant; celebrated; eminent; perpetual; methodical; inexhaustible; extreme; distinguished; peripatetic; atheist; embattled; contemporary; continuous; sanguinary; experienced.

verbs

acclaim—; honor—; model for—; —blocks in; —caricaturizes; —chalks out; —dashes off; —delineates; —depicts; —designs; —enamels; —illustrates; —portrays; —scratches out; —shades; —silhouettes; —sketches; —squares out; —symbolizes; —traces.

(See sculptor, poet, artist, writer, painting.)

PAINTING

adjectives

gracious; barbaric; portrait; ornamental; gaudy; noteworthy; contemporary; immortal; elaborate; effective; labial; delicate; graceful; freakish; unpurchasable; priceless.

verbs
acclaim—; applaud—; authenticate—; copy —; dash off—; embellish—; exhibit—; illuminate—; illustrate—; prize—; value—; —depicts; —personifies; —portrays; —represents; —symbolizes.
(See picture, pattern, sketch, photograph, masterpiece, canvas.)

PAIR
adjectives
pensive; incestuous; assorted; canniest; trusting; happy; inseparable; immense; innocent; elegant; gorgeous; excitable; newly-married; epic; spindle; bereaved; newly-hatched; illustrious; imprudent; wedded; paltry; particular; ill-sorted; lively.

PALACE
adjectives
bridal; magnificent; enchanted; primeval; high-roofed; rural; floating; pleasure; gorgeous; spacious; fantastic; crystal; celestial; colonnaded; sumptuous; ducal; proud; shingle; pretentious; medieval; diminutive; golden-bright; imperial; domed; ethereal.

verbs
assemble in—; barricade—; besiege—; fortify—; guard—; inhabit—; lease—; lodge in—; loot—; plunder—; quarter in—; ransack—; renovate—; retreat to—; sojourn at —; tenant—; —dazzles; —looms; —towers; —yields.
(See house, castle, abode, dwelling, home, mansion.)

PALATABLE
adverbs
extremely; unusually; unexpectedly; delightfully; delectably; lusciously; surprisingly; remarkably; altogether; deliciously; daintily; tastily; toothsomely; pleasantly; definitely.

PALATE
adjectives
effeminate; unperverted; vitiated; crude; gratified; spoiled; censorious.

verbs
cleave to—; harden—; jade—; malform—;

reeducate—; refine—; soften—; tempt—; tickle—; —acclaims; —revolts; —savors; —tempts.
(See taste, appetite.)

PALATIAL
adverbs
gorgeously; splendidly; surprisingly; dazzlingly; brilliantly; luxuriously; overwhelmingly; impressively; imposingly; proudly; magnificently; richly; sumptuously; extraordinarily; magically; superbly; pretentiously; unexpectedly.

PALAVER
adjectives
shameless; windy.

PALE
adverbs
ghastly; horribly; inexplicably; ominously; distressingly; alarmingly; significantly; dangerously; suddenly; strangely; curiously; oddly; sadly; disturbingly; naturally; unnaturally; significantly; unaccountably; noticeably; timidly; nervously; fearfully; apprehensively; remarkably; uncommonly.

PALENESS
adjectives
marble; pastry; deadly; natural; livid; pained; unnatural; grisly.

PALETTE
adjectives
crowded; radiant; glowing.

PALFREY
adjectives
superb; good; small; dainty.

PALISADE
adjectives
gothic; nature-hewn; impregnable.

PALL
adjectives
leaden; fearful; lurid; fleecy; universal; velvet; dark; motionless.

verbs
cast—over; —cloaks; —descends; —disgusts; —enshrouds; —mantles; —nauseates; —subdues; —veils.
(See gloom, darkness, dusk, haze, night.)

PALLET

adjectives
curtainless; wretched; hard.

PALLOR

adjectives
lovely; pasty; chalky; bloodless; petal; luminous; deepening; wan; translucent; ashen; shadowy; ivory; dusky; swarthy; ghastly; moon-lighted; deadly; first-communion.

PALM

adjectives
sweating; ennobling; blistered; labor-hardened; calloused; sentry-like; occasional; branded; virginal; delicate; satin; sudden-moistured; sheltering; upreared; sympathetic; grimy; horny; feathery; white-gloved; slanted; scooped; paddling; moon-lit; verdant; solitary; ashen-colored; graceful; itching; lifeless; gorgeous; supplicating; thrilling; gauntleted; extended; meaningful; open.

verbs
clench—; clinch in—; clutch in—; cover—; cross—with; cup—; grasp in—; read—; retain in—; transfer to—; —itches; —unfolds.
(See hand.)

PALMY

adverbs
altogether; wondrously; happily; desirably; marvellously; miraculously; affluently; luckily; prosperously; agreeably; buoyantly; providentially; unexpectedly; strikingly; unbelievably; exhilaratingly; hopefully.

PALPITATION

adjectives
violent; horrible; blissful; skyey.

PALSIED

adverbs
tragically; venerably; hopelessly; miserably; pitiably; obviously; manifestly; irremediably; shakily; wretchedly; crookedly; infirmly; ingloriously; resentfully; helplessly; pathetically; completely.

PAMPHLET

adjectives
successive; controversial; truth-telling; ironical; little; allegorical; belligerent; scurrilous; libellous; seditious; descriptive.

verbs
circulate—; comment on—; criticize—; digest—; disseminate—s; edit—; issue—; peruse—; publish—; scatter—s; spread—s; —advertises; —discusses; —proclaims.
(See book, catalogue, magazine, publication, periodical.)

PAN

adjectives
greased; brimming; heated.

verbs
blacken—; brandish—; churn in—; grease —; liquefy in—; melt in—; rinse—; roast in—; scar—; scour—; scrape—; —seethes; —simmers; —steams; —whistles.
(See dish, kettle, pot, frying-pan.)

PANACEA

verbs
ascribe to—; brand as—; denounce—; deprecate—; disparage—; introduce—; offer —; proffer—; propose—; scoff at—; scorn —; seek—; sneer at—; spring—; suggest—; —corrects; —cures; —heals.
(See plan, remedy.)

PANE

adjectives
dingy; rain-streaked; twinkling; small; sparkling; quaint; clouded; dim-streaming; greenish; half-translucent; unbreakable.

PANEL

adjectives
worm-fence; complete; horizontal; brick-like.

PANG

adjectives
sweet; jealous; brutal; death; irresistible; abiding; bitter; maddening; acute; morbid; unceasing; still-varying; sharp; fierce; personal; short; impossible; throbbing; deep; joyful; vivid; intolerable; faint; vacant; wasting; icy.

verbs
endure—; —convulses; —cramps; —cuts; —deceives; —deludes; —excruciates; —misleads; —pierces; —shoots through; —tortures; —twinges.
(See pain, ache, affliction, agony, anguish, torture.)

adjectives
terror-stricken; evident; commercial; guilty; precocious; long-feared; uncontrollable; intense; motionless; bewildered; sudden; memorable; subterranean; prevailing; widespread; needless.

verbs
fall into—; flinch in—; flutter in—; halt—; hesitate in—; overcome with—; overwhelm by—; provoke—; quiver in—; result in—; shudder in—; sink into—; stampede in—; survive—; throb in—; throw into—; tremble in—; —deepens; —descends upon; —ensues; —hangs over; —overpowers; —seizes; —spreads.
(See alarm, fright, terror, fear, horror, consternation.)

PANICKY
adverbs
extremely; intensely; absurdly; reasonably; naturally; significantly; astonishingly; suddenly; terribly; nervously; timidly; bashfully; shyly; unaccountably; inexplicably; amazingly; strangely; curiously; unreasoningly; unnecessarily; unfortunately; avowedly; ominously; unluckily.

PANIC-STRICKEN
adverbs
unfortunately; nervously; groundlessly; hysterically; needlessly; terribly; helplessly; utterly; suddenly; horribly; disastrously; appallingly; unaccountably.

PANORAMA
adjectives
surprising; miserable; long-anticipated; characteristic; misty; brilliant; magnificent; limitless; beautiful; moving; specious; glamorous; colorful.

verbs
luxuriate in—; mar—; perceive—; revel in —; shade—; survey—; view—; —awes; —bewitches; —blends; —delights; —enchants; —flows; —gratifies; —impresses; —spreads; —unfolds; —unrolls.
(See landscape, view, picture.)

PANT (v)
adverbs
breathlessly; voluptuously; hoarsely; excitedly; eagerly; exhaustedly; prodigiously.
(See gasp, puff.)

PANTHER
verbs
lasso—; trap—; —attacks; —charges; —claws; —dodges; —glides; —hisses; —leaps; —paws; —rolls over; —scratches; —skulks; —slinks; —snarls; —springs; —tears; —yowls.
(See leopard, animal.)

PANTING
adjectives
voluptuous; hoarse; grievous.

PANTOMIME
adjectives
tongueless; ambiguous; careless; indifferent; shadowy; expressive.

verbs
convey in—; dash off—; denote by—; emphasize—; entertain with—; excel at—; exhibit—; represent in—; signify by—; —amuses; —diverts; —dramatizes; —expresses; —mimics; —outrages; —suggests.
(See drama, magic, comedy, opera, actions, melodrama.)

PANTOMIME (v)
adverbs
animatedly; vigorously; expressively; artistically; suggestively; professionally; obscenely.
(See gesture, gesticulate.)

PANTS
(colloq.)
adjectives
striped; invisible; distinct; tight-fitting.

verbs
alter—; cuff—; divest of—; don—; drape —; hitch up—; patch—; refurbish—; repair—; tailor—; —bag; —flare; —fray; —shriek; —tatter.
(See trousers, coat, suit.)

PAPER
adjectives
pulpy; fluttering; patient; infamous; sensitized; provincial; evening; coppery; impecunious; scented; note; diplomatic; several (pl); fragile; influential; country; old-fashioned; fancy; state; special; descriptive; dreadful; illustrated; inconvertible; white; conventional; respectable; moist; marginal; fly-specked; critical; captured; astounding; humorous; thick; ministerial; mammoth;

precious; chancery; incriminating; exclusive; crumpled; unauthenticated; suspicious; anti-regicide; lithographic; admirable; melancholy; short-lived; neatly-folded; scribbled; motley; snowy; stained; discolored; metropolitan; rag; nice; charred; sundry (pl); notable; transmitted; unsafe; precarious; lined; obnoxious; printed; velvet; brittle; clean; dusty; depreciated; mold-rotten; bond.

verbs
crumple—; deliver—; fiddle with—; glance at—; glaze—; pelt with—; plunge into—; rustle—; score—; search through—; strew with—; —bristles; —circulates; —editorializes; —flutters.
(See sheet, newspaper, article, book.)

PARABLE
verbs
construct—; couch in—; familiarize with—; inculcate by—; interpret—; narrate—; recite—; sum up—; unfold—; value—; —convinces; —describes; —edifies; —moralizes; —teaches.
(See proverb, adage, story, saying, moral, motto.)

PARACHUTE
verbs
bale out with—; dangle on—; float on—; fold—; foul—; inspect—; knot—; leap with —; pack—; patch—; provide with—; repair —; rig—; tug at—; twist—; —checks; —entwines; —expands; —protects; —resists; —safeguards; —settles; —tangles; —unfolds.

PARADE
adjectives
empty; imposing; dusty; unlicensed; halted; spectacular; bizarre; noisy; drunken. '

verbs
climax—; display in—; exhibit in—; flock to—; inspect—; marshal—; muster—; organize—; prink for—; review—; stage—; witness—; —blazes; —files; —glitters; — protests; —surges; —winds.
(See celebration, pageant, demonstration, spectacle.)

PARADE (v)
adverbs
spectacularly; ostentatiously; rebelliously;

aimlessly; imposingly; drunkenly; obstreperously; clamorously; militantly; imposingly.
(See display, show, flaunt.)

PARADISE
adjectives
flower-enameled; painted; pagan; undefiled; terrestrial; youthful; undreamed-of; lively.

verbs
anticipate—; bask in—; breathe—; deny—; deprive of—; drive from—; envision—; glory in—; loll in—; promise—; relish—; surpass—; taste—; transform into—; wallow in—; —enchants; —enraptures; —enthralls; —harbors.
(See heaven, utopia.)

PARADOX
adjectives
cruel; painful; dampening; apparent; permissible; curious; audacious; perpetual; distressing; frivolous; subtle; hideous.

verbs
admit—; afford—; conceive—; confront with —; contemplate—; induce—; involve—; maintain—; propound—; prove—; savor of —; scorn—; skirt—; speculate on—; utter —; —conflicts; —contradicts; —mystifies; —perplexes; —puzzles.
(See statement, lie, truth, contradiction.)

PARADOXICAL
adverbs
strangely; inexplicably; obscurely; ironically; slightly; curiously; particularly; uncommonly; perplexingly; problematically; inscrutably; oddly; preposterously; fantastically; enigmatically; extremely.

PARAGON
adjectives
seeming; earthly; vertical; princely.

PARAGRAPH
adjectives
scandalous; scurrilous; inky; injurious; editorial; priceless; linking; pregnant; pathetic; illuminating; offensive; striking; long; trenchant; involved; complicated; overlong; transitional; brisk.

verbs
aggregate —s; amass —s; arrange in —; confine to—; connect—s; constitute—; couch

in—; divide into —s; indent—; partition into —s; phrase—; quote—; recast—; recount—; stumble upon—; —communicates; —deals with; —embodies; —expresses.
(See sentence, words, thought, statement.)

PARALLEL
adjectives
fitting; astonishing; close; fanciful; fortunate; striking.

verbs
approximate—; attempt—; collate—; contribute—; destroy—; draw—; extend in—; fix —; furnish—; identify—; model—; observe —; render—; tilt—; —balances; —conspires; —copies; —emulates; —reflects.
(See line, comparison.)

PARALLEL (v)
adverbs
precisely; strikingly; coincidentally; astonishingly; fancifully.
(See compare.)

PARALYSIS
adjectives
hysterical; creeping; intellectual; definite; magical; virtual; infantile; numbing.

verbs
affect with—; detect—; feign—; labor under —; languish in—; stun into—; suffer—; — benumbs; —blunts; —creeps upon; —cripples; —deadens; —deprives; —disables; — disqualifies; —halts; —incapacitates; — palls; —sears; —shatters; —silences.
(See disease, lethargy, laziness, stagnation, numbness.)

PARALYZE (v)
adverbs
intellectually; momentarily; permanently; magically; hypnotically.
(See stun, shock.)

PARALYZED
adverbs
completely; partially; unhappily; pitiably; hopelessly; lamentably; curiously; strangely; unaccountably; tragically; helplessly; decrepitly; incurably; irremediably; irrecoverably; pathetically; miserably; wretchedly; apparently; obviously.

PARAPET
adjectives
substantial; rugged; gilded; glistening; silvery; military; gun-studded; ominous; warlike; bloody.

PARAPHRASE
adjectives
harmonic; unique; ingenious; stilted; silly; worthless.

PARAPHRASE (v)
adverbs
skillfully; satirically; ingeniously; uniquely; harmoniously; smoothly; studiously.
(See quote, say.)

PARASITE
adjectives
harmless; business; tiny; formidable; smiling; smooth; detested; destructive; plant; social.

verbs
breed—; detest—; infest with —s; maintain —; nourish—; plague by —s; serve—; tend —; —absorbs; —attaches; —burrows into; —draws; —exacts; —fattens on; --flatters; —frequents; —lodges in; —penetrates; — robs; —sucks; —depends on.
(See cockroach, fly, mosquito, tramp, bugs, leper, leech.)

PARASITIC
adverbs
miserably; submissively; slavishly; helplessly; sycophantically; dependably; subserviently; obsequiously; inexplicably; obscurely; inscrutably; strangely; pitiably; contemptibly; amazingly; singularly; needlessly; pusillanimously; feebly; disgustingly; distressingly; hatefully; odiously; incomprehensibly.

PARASOL
verbs
extend—; hide behind—; poke—; spread—; tilt—; twirl—; —bobs; —caps; —conceals; —defends; —guards; —protects; —screens; —shades; —shields; —shelters; —veils.
(See umbrella, shade, cane.)

PARCEL
adjectives
youthful; bulky; untied; mysterious; clumsy; heavy.

accumulate —s; agglomerate —s; assort —s; deal out—s; deliver—; dispense—s; distribute—s; dole out—s; fumble—; group—s; heap—s; jumble—s; mislay—; mete out—s; rake up—s; share—s; —s litter; —s scatter; —tumbles.

(See bundle, package.)

PARCHED

adverbs
miserably; hopelessly; pitifully; cruelly; unprofitably; wretchedly; feverishly; bitterly; aridly; hotly; terribly; strangely; dreadfully; uncommonly; dangerously; alarmingly; distressingly; ruinously; disastrously; awfully.

PARCHMENT

adjectives
worthy; yellowed; valuable.

PARDON

adjectives
remorseful; free; present; unconditional; long-sought; welcome; humble.

verbs
accept—; beg—; buy—; crave—; expect—; grant—; implore—; invoke—; purchase—; refuse—; seek—; —absolves; —conciliates; —condones; —heals; —placates; —propitiates; —purges; —ransoms; —repairs; — reprieves; —whitewashes (colloq.).

(See forgiveness, mercy, relief, dispensation.)

PARDON (v)

adverbs
magnanimously; benignly; unconditionally; freely; indulgently; leniently.

(See acquit, forgive, excuse.)

PARDONABLE

adverbs
reasonably; justly; expediently; fairly; altogether; innocently; scarcely; wholly; understandably; somewhat; hardly; obviously; palpably; clearly; undoubtedly; undeniably; definitely.

PARENTAGE

adjectives
illegitimate; worshipful; angelic; obscure; unknown; verified.

adverbs
significantly; curiously; importantly; carelessly; noticeably; insignificantly; strangely; inexplicably; unaccountably; deliberately; intentionally; cleverly; deftly; informatively; illuminatingly; casually; pointedly; contemptuously; markedly.

PARENTS

adjectives
unnoticed; natural; evolutionary; dissenting; heroic; stubborn; obdurate; conscientious; frantic; imaginary; stern; careworn; reluctant; distressed; doting; honored; forward; narrow-minded; divine; harsh; vaporing; royal; jolly; lovable; perfect; splendid; health-minded; astonished; indignant; unloving; unscrupulous; grasping; ignorant.

verbs
forsake—; honor—; obey—; reassure—; respect—; revere—; revolt against—; —advise; —bless; —comfort; —discipline; —enlighten; —instruct; —judge; —provide; — punish; —restrain; —train; —tutor; —warn.

(See father, mother, husband, wife.)

PARISH

adjectives
humble; quiet; tiny; beautiful.

PARK

adjectives
permanent; pavilion; urban; extensive; spacious; odious; well-kept; dismantled; wooded; adjacent; artificial; moon-lit; umbrageous; city; cool.

verbs
caper in—; carouse in—; dally in—; disport in—; enclose—; frequent—; frisk in—; frolic in—; gambol in—; holiday in—; inhabit —; rake—; romp in—; tend—; weed—; — amuses; —beguiles; —bores; —diverts; — tires; —wearies.

(See country, field, grass, lawn, garden, meadow.)

PARLANCE

adjectives
theatrical; dramatic.

PARLIAMENT

adjectives
insular; empiric.

verbs
attend—; call—; conduct—; consult—; dissolve—; invest in—; petition—; represent in —; request—; summon—; sway—; —advises; —appropriates; —assembles; —convenes; —debates; —discusses; —frames; —imposes; —levies.
(See congress, senate, meeting, board, legislature, commission.)

PARLIAMENTARY

adverbs
highly; strictly; rigidly; regularly; curiously; pointedly; uncommonly; noticeably; rigorously; formally; unquestionably; impressively; overwhelmingly; magnificently; undeviatingly; splendidly; ceremoniously; gorgeously; scrupulously; meticulously; carefully.

PARLOR

adjectives
wainscoted; fire-lit; ample; long; darkened.

verbs
arrange—; chat in—; confer in—; convene in—; converse in—; deck—; entertain in—; frame—; furnish—; invade—; prepare—; receive in—; retire to—; shoo from—; squire into—; stuff—.
(See room, apartment.)

PARODY

adjectives
mocking; excellent; clever; discerning.

verbs
comment on—; decipher—; elucidate—; lend to—; snigger at—; translate—; —amuses; —caricatures; —distorts; —enrages; —exposes; —mimics; —mocks; —perverts; —ridicules; —roasts; —scoffs; —strains; —twits.
(See ridicule, writing, comedy, joke, jest.)

PAROLE

verbs
acquire—; advise—; advocate—; authorize —; dismiss on—; earn—; forfeit—; foster —; frame—; free on—; grant—; liberate on—; petition for—; plead for—; request—; sanction—; seek—; violate—.
(See pledge, promise, vow, agreement.)

PAROXYSM

verbs
cast into—; choke back—; curb—; discharge in—; fear—; kindle—; mitigate—; provoke to—; quiver with —s; restrain—; suffer—; throw into—; vent in—; —bursts; —disturbs; —explodes; —flares; —frightens; —froths; —incapacitates; —recurs; —rushes; —weakens.
(See convulsion, explosion, recklessness, violence.)

PARROT

adjectives
intrepid; spoiled; well-trained; confounded; petted; loud; mocking.

verbs
cage—; capture—; pamper—; pelt—; teach —; train—; —amuses; —attacks; —claws; —copies; —entertains; —imitates; —mimics; —mocks; —pecks; —perches; —senses; —squawks; —strokes; —whistles.
(See bird.)

PARRY (v)

adverbs
adroitly; deftly; skillfully; professionally; agilely; lithely; invincibly.
(See avert, evade, prevent.)

PARSLEY

verbs
chop—; cultivate—; deck with—; dot with —; dry—; grind—; sprig with—; sprinkle with—; —adorns; —crowns; —decorates; —dresses; —flavors; —garnishes; —seasons; —tones; —tops.
(See vegetable, herb, plant.)

PARSON

adjectives
bibulous; licentious; sociable; agreeable; careless; half-starved; unlucky; serious; sedate; lovable; diligent.

PARSONAGE

adjectives
country; unconventional; pure; generous; commodious; comfortable.

PART

adjectives
tragic; constituent; pompous; closely-fitted; moving; disconsolate; balancing; affected; integral; drossy; prime; splendid; significant; remote; authoritative; confused; convivial; eastern; pendulous; dissimilar; initial; sensitive; intimate; symbolical; animate; imaginative; tender; essential; dis-

tinguished; energetic; conspicuous; swaggering; moneyed; plump; outer; considerable; leading; prominent; decisive; manful; susceptible; formative; timely; striking; negative; tropical; immense; stubborn; uncourteous; oratorical; sequestered; active; subordinate; barbarous; relevant; invaluable; coloristic; abiding; incalculable; prudent; injurious; airy; speculative; theoretical; arid; generous; working; corresponding; aspiring; appropriate; reflex; innermost; understandable; related; declining; conventional; substantial; cumbrous; active; respectable; uttermost; metaphysical; slavish; various (pl); prefatory; effective; creditable; corresponding; over-stately; brilliant; evanescent; hindmost; worshipful; legitimate; retrenched; low; discreet; comedy; wondrous; fundamental; subsequent; external; virtuous; inherent; precipitous; inseparable; singular; choice; dominating; arduous; painful; brute; honorable; amiable; generous; sovereign; obnoxious; worthy; component; outward; membranous; mirthful; serious; vulgar; contiguous; incombustible; unsettled; vulnerable; pleasant; unprofitable; important; pathetic; virtuous; analogous; impertinent; midland; outlying; dissipated; vital; structural; treacherous; adjacent; retired; uninteresting; personal; formal; shady; loud-sounding; individual; restricted; inglorious; ghostly; romantic; impressive; desolate; sudden; prodigious; disjointed; inaccessible; disheartening; intrepid; lamentable.

verbs
accept—; acclaim—; balk at—; convey—; enact—; exaggerate—; live—; master—; perform—; render—; reproduce—; scorn—; sink into—; slip into—; treat—; wangle—; —affords; —allows.
(See lines, detail, character, scene.)

PART (v)
adverbs
despairingly; amicably; haughtily; meekly; convivially; pathetically; formally; romantically; lamentably.
(See divide, separate.)

PARTAKE (v)
adverbs
enthusiastically; joyously; convivially; cheerfully; gratefully; hungrily; ceremoniously; festively; fraternally.
(See share, participate.)

PARTIAL
adverbs
disgracefully; shamefully; illegally; unconstitutionally; openly; palpably; unfortunately; cruelly; bitterly; inexplicably; unjustifiably; unaccountably; miserably; wretchedly; prejudicially; unfairly; unjustly; obviously; openly; defiantly; perversely; curiously; strangely; amazingly.

PARTIALITY
adjectives
parental; sectarian; excessive; overweening; laudable; patent; noticeable.

verbs
avoid—; criticize—; entertain—; gain—; investigate—; lavish—; repel—; report—; shrink from—; —alienates; —distorts; —dotes; —forejudges; —incenses; —irritates; —provokes; —riles (colloq.); —shocks; —warps; —woos.
(See conviction, bias, prejudice.)

PARTICIPANTS
adjectives
interesting; prime; actual; leading.

verbs
cheer—; desire—; goad—; identify—; limit —; reckon as—; register—; seek—; test—; —assemble; —contest; —demonstrate; —enter; —labor; —share; —train; —vie for.
(See contestant, athlete.)

PARTICIPATE (v)
adverbs
willingly; jovially; energetically; heartily; enthusiastically; prominently; futilely; vigorously.
(See share, partake.)

PARTICIPATION
adjectives
undivided; active; human; futile; amateur.

verbs
anticipate—; incapacitate for—; join in—; prepare for—; revel in—; share in—; train for—; vie for—in; welcome—.
(See indulgence, enjoyment, association.)

PARTICLES
adjectives
granulated; seething; invisible; divine; irritating; scattering; constituent; colliding;

shining; impalpable; ultimate; invading; material; distinguishing; great; fruitful; harmful; discoloring; ignoble; gelatine.

PARTICULAR
adverbs
painfully; terribly; absurdly; meticulously; ridiculously; gruffly; scrupulously; conscientiously; extremely; considerately; dependably; reliably; vigilantly; unimpeachably; rigorously; scientifically; curiously; punctiliously; fastidiously; exactingly; inordinately; vexatiously; assiduously; unpleasantly; disagreeably; dreadfully; curiously; unnecessarily; distressingly; nervously; fussily; obnoxiously.

PARTICULARITY
adjectives
circumstantial; undue; over-luxurious.

PARTICULARS
adjectives
unexperienced; remarkable; multiplex; obvious; unnoticed.

verbs
adhere to—; afford—; contemplate—; disregard—; embody—; ignore—; inspect—; omit —; overlook—; mark—; record—; revise—; scan—; slight—; skim—; skip over—; slur —; —absorb; —explain.
(See details, information, facts.)

PARTING
adjectives
gracious; various (pl); undemonstrative; dreadful; present; frivolous; solemn; sweet; sorrowful.

PARTISAN
adjectives
zealous; extreme; undue; conscientious; conspicuous; immovable; long-dreaded; hated; factious.

adverbs
absurdly; rigidly; bigotedly; narrow-mindedly; dogmatically; oddly; strenuously; industriously; actively; thoughtlessly; witlessly; senselessly; unwaveringly; strongly; steadily; stubbornly; obstinately; zealously; confidently; inflexibly; mulishly; resolutely; incomparably.

PARTISANSHIP
adjectives
virulent; verified; insincere; fervid; honest; preposterous.

PARTITION
adjectives
saucer-shaped; unwarranted.

PARTNER
adjectives
semirecumbent; full; dignified; equal; junior; thick-skinned; rock-ribbed; dreadless; erudite; criminal; desperate.

verbs
admit—; couple with—; desire—; forsake —; heed—; require—; silence—; trust—; —agrees; —consults; —contemplates; —debates; —dissolves; —divides; —haggles; — joins in; —profits; —severs; —shares; — squabbles; —s unite.
(See ally, associate, brother, colleague, companion.)

PARTNERSHIP
adjectives
everlasting; effective; lifelong; endless.

verbs
annul—; cement—; combine in—; compose —; dissolve—; inaugurate—; pry apart—; seek—; sever—; undo—; —concurs; —conduces to; —confederates; —cooperates; — conspires; —requires; —seconds; —unites; —withstands.
(See friendship, alliance, company, corporation, society, firm.)

PARTRIDGE
verbs
domesticate—; flush—; startle—; —airs; — amuses; —beats; —bellows; —bills; —captivates; —challenges; —darts; —explores; — feigns; —s flush; —flutters; —glides; — jerks; —nods; —ranges; —roves; —rumbles; —scratches; —squeals; —steals.
(See grouse, bird, bob-white.)

PARTY
(general)
adjectives
assorted; hostile; revolutionary; serenading; tomahawk; staged; raiding; scalping; jovial; retiring; ill-starred; surprise; house; united; scattered; corrupt; fanatical; sectional; wild; antagonistic; dominant; quilting; lively; merry; traveling; singular;

constituted; detached; visionary; invisible; unbiased; exclusive; pleasure; desperate; contracting; foraging; conversation; lawless; luckless; straggling; skulking; disaffected; obtruding; reconnoitering; augmenting; rustic; storming; contending; shipwrecked; skirmishing; covering; excursion; dominant; fatigue; contending; misguided; marching; victorious; select; harmonious; ecclesiastical; scouting; reactionary; inimitable; litigating; all-day; paralyzing; imperial; informal; assaulting; fashionable; defenseless; radiant; bounding; invincible; discontented; amused; aggrieved; torchlight; zealous; ridiculous; joyous; especial; tramping.

PARTY
verbs *(political)*
appraise—; bolt—; cleave to—; consolidate —; dominate—; override—; purge—; rejuvenate—; scatter—; serve—; split—; supplant—; support—; wreck—; —advocates; —cleans house; —collapses; —declines; — flounders.

(See group, gang, following, faction.)

PARTY
verbs *(social)*
attend—; augment—; enliven—; fancy—; flock to—; invite to—; regale—; —amuses; —beguiles; —bores; —cheers; —disgusts; —diverts; —entertains; —palls; —solaces; —wearies.

(See meeting, theatre, ball, entertainment.)

PASS
adjectives
dolorous; desolate; silly; inaccessible; mountain; ragged; permissive; stupendous; perpendicular; gleaming.

PASS (v)
adverbs
translucently; invariably; harmoniously; deliberately; meekly; obliquely; placatingly; economically; wistfully; triumphantly; consciously; tediously; successively; victoriously; irresolutely; sedately; serenely; jauntily; leisurely; dolorously.

(See move, advance.)

PASSAGE
adjectives *(general)*
easy; pathetic; painful; palatial; sparred; tortuous; favorable; rickety; half-remembered; dimly-lighted; hazardous; objectionable; latticed; random; secret; perilous; octave; well-concealed; impassable; wading; sloping; striking; arched; dark; particular; prosperous; speedy; matted; neglected; furious; poetical; disputed; exquisite; descriptive; remarkable; sensational; slippery; precarious; vaulted; circuitous; unedifying; abrupt; narrow-paneled; tedious; practicable; romantic; vivid; characteristic; sumptuous; ill-quoted; brilliant; gloomy; subterranean; stormy; despised; hackneyed; purple; redundant; rhetorical; brief; narrow; thorough; roomy; stirring; significant; secret; political; swift; honey; winding; awful; laudatory; adulatory; untrammeled; disjointed; perihelion; certain; frequent; glowing; oratorical; walled-up; impossible; scorching; alternate; lyric; musical; amorphous; melodious; rumbling; dramatic; instantaneous; treacherous; imaginative; arduous; elevated; lofty; impressive; sublime.

PASSAGE
(literary)
verbs
acclaim—; applaud—; analyze—; blend —s; cite—; delete—; erase—; interpret—; paraphrase—; quote—; —castigates; —expunges; —glows; —reveals; —stings.

(See paragraph, thought, sentence, portion, section, quotation, selection.)

PASSAGE
verbs *(way, avenue)*
accomplish—; bar—; block—; clog—; constrict—; emerge from—; fence in—; gain—; guard—; impede—; jeopardize—; offer—; protect—; quicken—; restrict—; safeguard —.

(See way, access, approach, lobby, exit, corridor, hall.)

PASSENGERS
adjectives
hurrying; unhappy; protesting; hooded; unsuspecting; stealthy; horror-struck; bustling; belated; frivolous; churlish; distinguished; fastidious; half-rate.

verbs
accommodate—; amuse—; assign—to; assure—; bore—; comfort—; enchant—; entertain—; enthrall—; escort—; excite—; guide—; reassure—; reveal to—; tire—; transport—; —fret; —fume; —idle; —tour; —thread; —weary.

(See marcher, audience, gathering.)

PASSION

adjectives

absorbing; acrimonious; afflicting; aimless; angry; ardent; autobiographical; awakened; black; blazing; bestial; base; bad; bitter; bittersweet; blended; boisterous; bottomless; boyish; brutal; burning; bursting; busy; capital; certain; chivalrous; choleric; coarse; comfortable; concentrated; conflicting; contending; contrary; corrosive; damnable; dark; deadly; deathly; deceased; deep; deforming; degrading; delicious; deluding; democratic; departed; determinate; devastating; diabolical; dimmed; distempered; disturbing; divine; earthly; electric; elemental; enduring; energetic; engendered; engrossing; enthusiastic; envied; errant; erratic; eternal; everlasting; evil; exacerbated; exceeding; exciting; exquisite; extraordinary; exultant; fantastical; favorite; fervent; fierce; fitful; flaming; foaming; foul; frantic; frivolous; frozen; frustrated; fugitive; fundamental; futile; gambling; generous; gnawing; gross; guilty; half-accomplished; headlong; hidden; heavenly; high; hurtful; hopeless; human; humble; honest; idealistic; idealized; idiotic; ignoble; illicit; imprudent; inborn; incestuous; indignant; infernal; inflammable; insatiable; instinctive; intellectual; intense; intermediate; invisible; involuntary; ireful; irregular; irrepressible; irresistible; jealous; kindred; lasting; lawless; licentious; loving; lurid; lustful; master; masterful; merry; mischievous; morbid; mortal; mutinous; mutual; newfound; noble; obtuse; original; outrageous; overmastering; overt; overwhelming; palemouthed; pallid; partisan; patriotic; pentup; personate; petty; philanthropic; pitying; preceding; present; prevailing; primal; primitive; private; prosperous; pseudo; radical; raging; rare; rash; religious; repressed; requisite; romantic; rude; ruling; selfish; secondary; silent; sophisticated; sordid; sore; sorry; southern; spectral; speechless; stifled; stirred; stormy; strange; subdued; strong; struggling; sudden; superior; suppressed; swelling; swift; tender; tempestuous; towering; thoughtful; thronging (pl); thwarted; torrid; tragic; tranquil; transient; transitory; triumphant; troubling; true; turbid; tyrannous; unaccustomed; unbridled; unchecked; undying; ungovernable; unhallowed; universal; unnoted; unprofitable; unregulated; unrequited; unsoothed; unsuspected; untainted; untamed; untrained; untried; unwise; unwomanly; unworthy; variable; vehement; vengeful; veritable; vindictive; violent; virile; wanton; warning; wayward; wild; worried; worst; youthful; zealous; exaggerated.

verbs

animate with—; arouse—; boil with—; bridle—; cherish—; declare—; distort with—; enchain by—; evoke—; extinguish—; fly into—; gratify—; impel by—; intensify—; nourish—; pledge to—; quicken with—; reciprocate—; redden with—; respond to—; restrain—; revive—; share—; unleash—; vanquish—; vent—; —consumes; —cools; —inflames; —rules; —seethes; —simmers; —tortures.

(See impetuosity, craving, appetite, ire, enthusiasm, emotion, infatuation, love, indignation.)

PASSIONATE

adverbs

amorously; angrily; cholerically; lovingly; uncontrollably; ungovernably; inordinately; uncommonly; innately; inherently; naturally; notoriously; warmly; ardently; enthusiastically; zealously; earnestly; violently; excitably; captiously; querulously; moodily; mercurially; violently; furiously; impulsively; irrepressibly; strangely.

PASSIVE

adverbs

strangely; apathetically; curiously; disgustingly; provokingly; incomprehensibly; dully; inertly; sluggishly; bluntly; inertly; doltishly; lazily; vexatiously; indolently; obediently; subserviently; hopelessly; servilely; submissively; pliantly; imperturbably; stoically; placidly; meekly; stupidly; stolidly; carelessly.

PASSIVITY

adjectives

despondent; disposed; dejected; dreamy; lazy; inert; stolid; unwavering; slumbrous; dull; dead.

PAST

adjectives

romantic; sorrowful; vanished; voiceless; foolish; monstrous; accumulated; remote; wintry; complacent; immemorial; stormy; immeasurable; gracious; artificial; dim; scarred; remorseless; dark; sinful; mischievous; precious; turbulent; receding; spectral; mysterious; irrevocable; blighted;

ducal; unfathomed; inexorable; changeless; bitter; rough; emotional; ungentle; ambiguous; unrelenting; long-distant; disputable; restored; embalmed; irreproachable; hideous; well-filled; boundless; unrelenting; unhallowed; glorious; ungracious; pathetic; picturesque; melancholy.

verbs

clarify—; decipher—; dip into—; discern—; enrich—; evoke—; grope in—; penetrate—; plumb—; recapture—; recreate—; reflect on —; regret—; relive—; resurrect—; shake off —; —fades; —haunts; —survives; —vanishes.

(See memories, future, life.)

PASTE

adjectives

milk-white; slippery-looking; lackluster; sticky; gelatinous.

PASTEL

adjectives

luscious; summer; gleaming; white.

PASTIME

adjectives

favorite; youthful; kindred; risky; innumerable (pl); gentlemanlike; delightful; brawling; gracious; light; refreshing; uncanonical.

verbs

absorb in—; advocate—; enjoy—; indulge in—; lack—; seek—; —amuses; —cheers; —diverts; —eases; —enlivens; —entertains; —recreates; —solaces; —soothes.

(See game, amusement, diversion.)

PASTOR

adjectives

ungracious; scholarly; zealously; flabby.

verbs

appoint—; ordain—; serve as—; submit to —; venerate—; —administers; —attends to; —consoles; —converts; —guides; —ministers; —negotiates; —pleads; —prays; —preaches; —protects; —rebukes; —reconciles; —rules; —sways; —sympathizes with; —teaches; —visits.

(See minister.)

PASTORAL

adverbs

sweetly; pleasantly; refreshingly; admirably; gently; firmly; mildly; agreeably; pleasingly; acceptably; comfortingly; helpfully; delightfully.

PASTRY

verbs

bolt—; crunch—; despatch—; do honor to —; feast on—; garnish—; gormandize—; knead—; leaven—; munch—; nibble—; roll —; top off with—; —appeals; —attracts; —fattens.

(See food, etc.)

PASTURE

adjectives

recumbent; poisonous; perpetual; sodden; naked; bleak; browsed; boulder-strewn; flowery; pleasant; neighboring; undulous; reeky; stony; verdant; coarse; scant; silver-shrouded.

verbs

abound in—; browse in—; conserve—; devour—; feast on—; feed on—; gnaw—; graze on—; patch—with; plow—; roam—; scrape—; survey—; wander on—; —extends; —fattens; —spreads.

(See grass, field, meadow.)

PAT (v)

adverbs

reassuringly; benignly; affectionately; comfortingly; approvingly; awkwardly; mechanically; caressingly; paternally.

(See tap, caress.)

PATCH

adjectives

vivid; broken; ugly; thrifty; phosphorescent; superficial; numerous (pl); insignificant; single.

PATCH (v)

adverbs

laboriously; awkwardly; deftly; eccentrically; thriftily; superficially; geometrically; pathetically.

(See repair, mend.)

PATE

adjectives

lean; understanding; ponderous; learned; bald; shiny.

adjectives
valuable; formal; longed-for; secret.

verbs
grant—; infringe—; limit—; permit—; request—; restrict—; secure—; seek—; — authorizes; —blocks; —clinches; —empowers; —excludes; —expires; —favors; — guards; —pends; —protects; —seals; — vouchsafes.
(See invention, license, right, privilege.)

adverbs
glaringly; openly; plainly; unmistakably; conspicuously; undisguisedly; lawfully; notoriously; freely; safely; securely.

adverbs
kindly; generously; indulgently; fondly; graciously; proudly; awkwardly; considerately; liberally; clumsily; benevolently; amiably; genially; complacently; complaisantly; tenderly; humanely; benignantly; admonishingly; warningly; pompously; noisily; actively; virtuously; hilariously; autocratically; domineeringly; absurdly; amusingly; happily.

adjectives
beneficient; beauteous; true.

verbs
advocate—; assume—; attempt—; contemplate—; induce—; propose—; wield—; — administers; —cements; —dominates; — governs; —preserves; —protects; —regulates; —reigns; —supplies.
(See power, action, care, control, government.)

verbs
anticipate—; consider—; doubt—of; establish—of; forfeit—; hail—; impose—; respect—; revere—; spare—; venerate—; welcome—; —awes; —burdens; —comforts; —honors; —inspires; —salutes.
(See right, descent.)

adjectives
hollow-worn; pragmatic; steep; hillocky; obliterated; slippery; murmuring; gleaming; damp; luring; zigzag; fringed; twilight; winding; bushy; slender; straitened; adventuresome; hidden; trodden; dissimilar (pl); pleasant; unknown; upward; tempting; circumterrestrial; wild; lone; joyous; numerous (pl); rustling; sinuous; mountain; impracticable; bridle; predetermined; readier; pebbly; tortuous; desolated; endless; outgoing; dusk-shrouded; perilous; silvery; sacred; golden; green-bordered; hazardous; thorny; rough; pleasant; destructive; intricate; unstable; primrose; haughty; delicate; fairylike; factious; grave; beaten; fatal; enticing; pretty; gloomy; overgrown; dreary; chequered; dubious; flashing; conventional; inaccessible; solitary; untried; arduous; blustering; eccentric; homeward; radiating; frequented; lowly; shadowy; perpendicular; stone-flagged; artistic; tiny; intersecting; graveled; destined; somber; labyrinthine; acclivous; giddy; narrow; paved; devious; peaceful; lonesome; pilgrim; darkling; firm; desolate; downward; gravel; doctrinaire; difficult; insecure; shelving; intermediate; climbing; uncharted; converging; unconscious; enchanted; weary; precarious; shady; thankless; triumphal; right; dark; curved; comfortless; coincident; parabolic.

verbs
bury—; choose—; cut—; deck—; depart from—; discern—; establish—; inveigle into —; map out—; reflect—; smooth—; strew —; —allures; —beckons; —diverges; — entices; —invites; —swerves; —veers; — winds.
(See lane, road.)

adverbs
touchingly; unusually; uncommonly; pitiably; infinitely; altogether; poignantly; deeply; grievously; appallingly; shockingly; oddly; immeasurably; heartbreakingly; extraordinarily; dreadfully.

adverbs
terrifyingly; alarmingly; appallingly; shockingly; perplexingly; bewilderingly; confusingly; dangerously; perilously; hazardously; unaccountably; hopelessly; boundlessly; distressingly; calamitously; disastrously; formidably; forbiddingly; ruggedly; impassably; impermeably; impenetrably.

PATHOS

adjectives
infinite; poignant; anxious; half-baked; puerile; sharp; exquisite; melodious; thin; instant; ever-present; intense; sobbing; despairing; expressible; grim; deep; extraordinary; celestial; stern; unfathomable.

verbs
bear—; catch—; endure—; experience—; harbor—; taste—; —affects; —agitates; —dwells; —impresses; —infects; —mantles; —moves; —palpitates; —pierces; —produces; —responds; —shakes; —warms.

(See sadness, unhappiness, suffering, affliction, sorrow, pity, sympathy, passion.)

PATHWAY

adjectives
murmurous; flinty; aerial; swaying; perilous; persistent; segmental; historic; radiant; shadowy; lightning; immemorial; predestined; rocky; lush; overhung; blind; corkscrew; crooked.

PATIENCE

adjectives
human; placid; simple; courteous; uncomplaining; untiring; gracious; pathetic; musing; chaotic; mild; commendable; inexhaustible; heavenly; self-restrained; melancholy; characteristic; strict; infinite; well-established; boundless; admirable; resigned; creditable; unwearying; haggard; struggling; unconscious; genial; elastic; deliberate; long-suffering; tender; saintly; helpless; mock; dogged; counseled; unwearied; bitter; cruel; unexampled; sad; heroic; serene; gentle; endless; trustful; precious; laboring.

verbs
cultivate—; employ—; entail—; exercise—; exhaust—; manifest—; necessitate—; require—; strain—; try—; —dwindles; —fails; —trays; —wears thin.

(See forbearance, perseverance, endurance, fortitude.)

PATIENT

adjectives
bedridden; unruly; noble; satisfied; reluctant; lucrative; passionate; individual; indignant; docile; fever; diabetic; ill; psychopathic; rheumatic; recalcitrant; susceptible; paranoiac; resolved.

verbs
caution—; discharge—; examine—; exhaust —; guard—; hospitalize—; incapacitate—; inspire—; irritate—; nauseate—; refresh—; relieve—; restore—; resurrect—; sponge—; tide—over; —expectorates; —rallies; —recovers; —relapses; —responds to.

adverbs
unbelievably; incredibly; sweetly; gently; imperturbably; uncomplainingly; quietly; serenely; wisely; sagaciously; indulgently; genially; tenderly; affectionately; expertly; persistently; indefatigably; placidly; courteously; charmingly; habitually; infinitely; unwearyingly; doggedly; resolutely; amazingly; uncommonly.

PATRIARCH

adjectives
hoary; dusky; aged; seafaring; aboriginal; venerable.

PATRIARCHAL

adverbs
properly; appropriately; proudly; arrogantly; domineeringly; imperiously; undeniably; uncommonly; incurably; haughtily; tyrannically; immensely; delightfully; amiably; indulgently; unforgettably; venerably; unyieldingly; obviously; obstinately; tenaciously; insistently; jealously; stubbornly.

PATRICIAN

adverbs
undeniably; innately; inherently; naturally; unmistakably; truly; genuinely; dominantly; proudly; palpably; obviously; evidently; manifestly; undeniably; nobly; conspicuously; eminently; exaltedly; renownedly; splendidly.

PATRIOT

adjectives
ardent; virtuous; sterling; devoted; zealous; epistolary; venerable; misguided; sturdy; prejudiced; worthy.

PATRIOTIC

adverbs
splendidly; curiously; ostentatiously; undeniably; nobly; unselfishly; genuinely; magnificently; grandly; unusually; inherently; truly; unquestionably; quietly; naturally; devotedly; conventionally; ardently; actively; assiduously; intelligibly; thoughtful-

ly; discriminatingly; wisely; sagaciously; alertly; vigilantly; altruistically; uncommonly; highly; extraordinarily.

PATRIOTISM
adjectives
fainting; flamboyant; haughty; devoted; pious; religious; uncompromising; engendering; impulsive; vigorous; irrepressible; serious; ardent; epidemic; sincere; jealous; disinterested; fearless; heroic; individual; fervent; sublime.

verbs
acclaim—; advocate—; applaud—; breed—; burst with—; choke—; develop—; exploit —; extinguish—; feign—; guard with—; harbor out of—; inflame with—; inspire—; justify—; kindle—; lampoon—; tear between—.
(See Americanism, love, devotion, loyalty.)

PATROL
verbs
elude—; evade—; maintain—; push through —; —guarantees; —guards; —insures; — paces; —protects; —safeguards; —scours; —traverses.
(See guard, sentry.)

PATROL (v)
adverbs
systematically; vigilantly; ceaselessly; cautiously; periodically; hourly; perpetually.
(See watch, march, protect.)

PATRON
adjectives
gentle; influential; munificent; august; fostering; unbidden; imperial; contemptuous; mighty; passing; perpetual.

PATRONAGE
adjectives
condescending; titled; continued; liberal; constant; increasing; political; admiring; generous; extensive; lucrative; obsequious; advised; loyal; proprietary; aldermanic.

verbs
cherish—; dispense—; enjoy—; extend—; foster—; gain—; seek—; solicit—; swell—; withdraw—; —abets; —advances; —aids;

—benefits; —bolsters; —cheers; —feeds; —influences; —nourishes; —overrides; — succors.
(See guidance, support, encouragement, aid, leadership, protection.)

PATRONIZE (v)
adverbs
deferentially; liberally; advisedly; lucratively; loyally; extensively; habitually.
(See encourage, favor, promote.)

PATRONIZING
adverbs
arrogantly; unduly; insufferably; intolerably; unbearably; intolerantly; pompously; haughtily; overbearingly; absurdly; comically; ludicrously; laughably; foolishly; ridiculously; inanely; terribly; fatuously; loudly; noisily; objectionably; provokingly; disagreeably; unpleasantly; obnoxiously; unreasonably; strangely; incredibly.

PATTERN
adjectives
curious; significant; exclusive; intricate; delicate; existing; original; distinctive; ornamental; complex; decorative; pronounced; wondrous; ageless; accurate; complicated; tasteful; metrical; tremulous; frigid; animal; primitive; blotchy; mental; shadow; effective; whimsical; comprehensive; unknown; arbitrary; geometrical; experimental; mosaic; balanced; agricultural; unpretentious; running; ever-present; schizoid; wanted; rich; vivid; starched; perfect; unconventional; operatic; rudimentary; tawdry; aesthetic; ideal; inconspicuous; characterful; scroll; serene; architectural; everlasting; colorful; new; striped; neat; smart; diversified; selective; beautiful; unususal; quiet; spring; stimulating; popular; plaid; plumage; subdued; dark; striking; artificial; attractive; exclusive; fabric; sprightly; authentic; young-blooded; lacy.

verbs
cling to—; comply with—; conform to—; copy—; devise—; follow—; improve upon —; infringe on—; knit—; mark—; observe —; surpass—; trace—; transcend—; violate —; weave—; —baffles; —exemplifies; — guides; —illustrates; —indicates; —regulates; —represents; —simplifies.
(See copy, ideal, design.)

PATTERN (v)

adverbs
exquisitely; exclusively; intricately; delicately; accurately; whimsically; geometrically; vividly; unconventionally; authentically.
(See copy, model, imitate.)

PATTY

adjectives
solid-looking; overdone; tiny.

PAUNCH

verbs
cram—; develop—; distend—; fill—; gorge —; heave—; load—; pamper—; reduce—; simulate—; stuff—; wad—; —craves; —encumbers; —expands; —gnaws; —protrudes.
(See belly, abdomen, stomach, intestines.)

PAUSE

adjectives
slow; awkward; haunting; appreciable; unconscious; normal; week-end; effect-collecting; thoughtful; cogitative; awful; terrible; pensive; ominous; brief; perceptible; discontented; reminiscent; deep; melancholy; decided; musing; appalling; stifling; suitable; inexplicable; humming; solemn; reticent; doubtful; grateful; considerable; frequent (pl); rapturous; transitory; uncomfortable; eternal; determined; respectful; transient; convenient; ensuing; natural; thrilling; present; discreet; wild-swan; habitual; rhetorical; painful; eloquent.

verbs
abstain from—s; destroy—; incur—; observe—; supply—; waste in—; —arrests; —emphasizes; —ensues; —falls; —halts; —hovers; —hushes; —impresses; —interposes; —interrupts; —intervenes; —persists; —suspends.
(See interruption, interval, lapse.)

PAUSE (v)

adverbs
reflectively; dramatically; reminiscently; instinctively; irresolutely; briefly; delicately; meaningfully; diffidently; lingeringly; ominously; deliberately; pensively; solemnly; discreetly.
(See waver, stop.)

PAVEMENT

adjectives
solitary; unsafe; brick; untrodden; rag-strewn; billowy; shady; deserted; dappled; grass-grown; firmamental; circular; insufficient; damp; marble; noiseless; dimly-lighted.

PAVILION

adjectives
vast; silk; glimmering; sumptuous; luminous; arabesque; gay.

verbs
decorate—; flock to—; garnish—; gather in—; ornament—; throng—; —accommodates; —encloses; —harbors; —protects; —rings; —rises; —shades; —shelters; —spreads; —swarms; —swelters.
(See canopy, tent, building.)

PAW

adjectives
tremendous; searching; tactile; bony; moist; unhallowed; horny; bloody.

PAW (v)

adverbs
fitfully; ineptly; vaguely; savagely; brutishly; clumsily; roughly; searchingly; lustfully.
(See stroke, strike.)

PAY

adjectives
sour; retirement; exorbitant; retroactive; scanty; meager; back; advance.

verbs
acquire—; attach—; claim—; crave—; cut —; derive—; deserve—; draw—; entitle to—; exact—; insist on—; merit—; raise—; restore—; solicit—; yield—; —accrues; —compensates; —defrays; —rewards; —squares (colloq.).
(See earnings, payment, profits, wages, money.)

PAY (v)

adverbs
moderately; handsomely; grudgingly; bounteously; heavily; cheerfully; annually; punctually; roundly; scantily; meagerly; exorbitantly.
(See compensate, reward.)

PAYMENT

adjectives
iniquitous; vicarious; substantial; conven-

ient; easy; permanent; equivalent; coming; political; stipulated; benefit; preliminary; monthly; annual.

verbs
acknowledge—; afford—; await—; cease—; collect—; default—; deserve—; disburse—; evade—; reap—; recover—; refund—; resume—; suspend—; —discharges; —effaces; —pains.
(See pay, profits, wages.)

PAYROLL

verbs
add to—; anticipate—; calculate—; disburse—; distribute—; draw—; guard—; hold up (colloq.)—; insure—; pare down—; prepare—; protect—; reduce—; rob—; survey—; trim—; —increases; —mounts; —surpasses.
(See funds, profits, earnings.)

PEACE

adjectives
intellectual; bitter; profound; durable; dishonorable; unbroken; joyous; healthy; tolerable; enduring; industrial; internal; lovely; lasting; honorable; long-lost; heavenly; mellow-eyed; ineffable; dictated; passionate; meek-eyed; unresting; domestic; rapturous; neighborhood; absolute; unaccustomed; ignominious; settled; endless; everlasting; fruitful; speedy; temporary; ripening; universal; permanent; humiliating; eternal; deep; constant; indescribable; taunting; supplicated; unruffled; uneven; unsuspecting; treacherous; sweet; pale; ultimate; sinless; patched-up; barbaric; prudent; shameful; blissful; perpetual; honeyed; unbroken; inner; wealthy; silken; advantageous; luxurious; infinite; unspeakable; happy; ancient; sacred; poetic; unfluctuating; especial; external; repugnant; intimated; serene; balmy; profound; technical; ignoble; endurable; spiritual; windless; exquisite; riteless; incomparable; shining; fraternal; utter; immemorial; well-earned; pastoral.

verbs
achieve—; agitate for—; assure of—; botch —; breed—; compel—; crusade for—; destroy—; disrupt—; endanger—; enthrone —; further—; herald—; impose—; maintain—; menace—; negotiate—; prate about —; promote—; restore—; risk—; serve—; spurn—; sue for—; symbolize—; threaten

—; unsettle—; upset—; vouchsafe—; —pervades; —prevails; —reigns.
(See harmony, amity, friendship, quiet, tranquillity.)

PEACEABLE

adverbs
inherently; naturally; continuously; resolutely; placidly; mildly; tranquilly; habitually; determinedly; inoffensively; serenely; calmly; imperturbably; unimaginably; curiously; racially; soberly; blandly; unbelievably; uncommonly; reasonably.

PEACEFUL

adverbs
beatifically; serenely; happily; blessedly; rapturously; amiably; pleasantly; contentedly; unbelievably; delightfully; entrancingly; remarkably; gloriously; perfectly.

PEACOCK

verbs
—preens; —prides himself; —stalks; —strides; —strolls; —struts.
(See bird.)

PEAK

adjectives
pinnacled; singular; volcanic; dazzling; furrowed; rounded; perilous; lambent; herbless; snowy; rugged; airy; fierce; savage; glistening; bristling; glittering; isolated; barren; angular; mountain; celestial; gigantic; lofty; successive (pl); precipitous; single; steeple-like; sunlighted; abrupt; ermine-clad; pathless; frowning; craggy; unique; brumal; jagged; environing (pl); rock; multitudinous (pl); scalped; snow-patched; fantastic; snow-covered; solstitial.

verbs
ascend—; cap—; climb—; cuff—; culminate in—; push to—; rise to—; scale—; sharpen—; —commands; —crowns; —heightens; —hovers; —juts; —points; —projects; —rears· —soars; —tapers; —tops; —towers.
(See mountain, tower, hill, top, point, summit.)

PEAL

adjectives
silvery; yawning; merry; angry; repeated; strange; fearful; terrific; dismal; tuneful;

full-hearted; paschal; joyous; hideous; solemn; spasmodic; tremendous; thrilling; dreadful.

PEAL (v)

adverbs

melodiously; softly; gently; gaily; joyously; festively; merrily; angrily; terrifically; solemnly; spasmodically.

(See echo, resound, reverberate.)

PEANUTS

verbs

blanch—; chop—; clean—; consume—; crush—; cultivate—; dig up—; dry—; express from—; extract from—; hawk—; hurl —at; munch—; package—; ripen—; roast —; salt—; shell—; steam—.

PEAR

adjectives

yellow; waxen; withered; mellowing; hoary; blushing; frozen.

PEARLS

adjectives

oriental; ungathered; lustral; barbaric; shimmering; pink; glistening; creamy; iridescent; liquid; imitation; intermingled; sleepy; enormous; carven; inlaid; snowy; pellucid; perfect; melting; glittering.

verbs

collect—; covet—; cultivate—; deposit—in; dissolve—; dive for—; drill—; embellish with—; fish for—; imitate—; polish—; prize —; string—; value—; yield—; —adorn; — decorate; —enhance; —glitter; —ornament.

(See jewel, gem, diamond.)

PEARLY

adverbs

iridescently; beautifully; incredibly; exquisitely; sumptuously; opalescently; frostily; intensely; richly; gorgeously; sweetly; delicately; daintily; incredibly; marvelously; miraculously; creamily; consummately; indescribably; ineffably.

PEARS

verbs

bear—; blight—; box—; bruise—; can—; cook—; crate—; gather—; grade—; infect —; market—; pare—; pluck—; preserve—;

select—; serve—; spray—; stew—; wrap—; —cluster; —decay; —exude; —ripen; — rot; —thrive.

(See fruit, apple.)

PEAS

adjectives

dwarf; delicate; wild.

verbs

box—; can—; crate—; cultivate—; gather —; grade—; harvest—; injure—; plant—; process—; refrigerate—; row—; scoop up —; separate—; shell—; ship—; wash—; — germinate; —mature.

(See vegetables.)

PEASANTS

adjectives

unspoiled; passionate; raw; rude; jubilant; squalid; white-bearded; wretched; shelter-seeking; hopeless; gentle; naked; vindictive; insurgent; healthy-looking; well-dressed; trilingual; downtrodden; distrustful; hard-faced; unforgiving; self-assertive; universal; swarthy; enterprising; bewildered; unlettered; grimy; prating; honest-hearted; ruddy-cheeked; uncultivated.

verbs

agitate—; aid—; appease—; banish—; dominate—; enslave—; exile—; tyrannize over—; —assemble; —clamor; —herd; — economize; —immigrate; —rebel; —revolt; —toil; —uprise; —weary.

(See natives, countryman, farmer, worker, alien, foreigner.)

PEBBLES

adjectives

dewy; rounded; polished; sun-kissed; hard-flung; clean; colored.

PECCABLE

adverbs

unfortunately; unhappily; admittedly; unwontedly; naturally; unquestionably; pitifully; helplessly; probably; alarmingly; outrageously; undeniably; exceptionally; miserably; wretchedly; recklessly; irremediably.

PECULIAR

adverbs

racially; highly; distinctly; definitely; quaintly; strikingly; remarkably; curiously; oddly; highly; outlandishly; exotically; unaccountably.

adjectives

petty; salient; social; seasonal; manifold; awful; definite; well-known; humorous; quaint; minute; arbitrary; marked; intellectual; striking; mental; sectional.

PECUNIARY

adverbs

distinctly; exclusively; wholly; avariciously; fortunately; undeniably; definitely; conveniently; opportunely; luckily.

PEDAGOGICAL

adverbs

unmitigatedly; absolutely; definitely; pedantically; wholeheartedly; monotonously; tediously; loudly; blatantly; opinionatedly; patiently; studiously; meticulously; wisely; tiresomely; intelligently; boresomely; mildly; resolutely; ostentatiously; vainly; egotistically; priggishly; pompously; humbly; modestly; pretentiously; self-consciously; self-righteously; emphatically; insistently; dogmatically; proudly; impossibly.

PEDAGOGUE

adjectives

groveling; admirable; gross; stupid; harassed.

PEDANT

adjectives

sand-blind; miserable; fiery; academic; forward; wrangling.

PEDANTIC

adverbs

unmistakably; unshakably; tiresomely; insufferably; proudly; intolerably; ostentatiously; self-righteously; insistently; vexatiously; primly; assertively; confidently; solemnly; sharply; monotonously; incurably; absurdly; unwarrantably; scrupulously; consciously; punctiliously; unbearably; meticulously.

PEDANTRY

adjectives

display—; encrust with—; engender—; ridicule—; savor of—; scorn—; shake off—; —affects; —concludes; —disgusts; —dogmatizes; —obtrudes; —overestimates; —overacts; —poses; —prejudices; —presumes; —proceeds from; —repels.

(See learning, vanity.)

adjectives

itinerant; flesh; pavement; unscrupulous; stentorian.

PEDESTAL

adjectives

elevated; formal; equal.

verbs

adorn—; bestride—; construct—; erect upon —; mount on—; ornament—; prop on—; repose on—; rest on—; topple from—; totter on—; —affords; —bases; —bolsters; —maintains; —supports; —sustains.

(See base, support, foundation.)

PEDESTRIAN

adjectives

belated; faulty; dust-covered; tall; muscular; travel-stained; raw-boned; successful; ardent; jay-walking.

verbs

accord to—; assist—; block off—s; educate —; endanger—; hamper—; injure—; signal —; warn—; —co-operates; —crosses; —disobeys; —dodges; —evades; —observes; —tires; —tours; —travels; —wearies.

PEDIGREE

adjectives

unbroken; feudal; proud.

PEEP

adjectives

fair; momentary; hasty.

PEEP (*v*)

adverbs

shyly; slyly; shrinkingly; daringly; audaciously; modestly; coyly; flirtatiously.

(See peer, look.)

PEER

adjectives

painstaking; puissant; contemporary; penniless; wrong-incensed; gentle; lustrous; witty; notorious; impecunious; favorite.

PEER (*v*)

adverbs

earnestly; intently; timidly; curiously; cautiously; anxiously; fearfully; furtively; surreptitiously; slyly.

(See peep, look.)

PEERAGE

verbs

bestow—upon; congratulate—; convoke—; create—; entitle—to; forfeit—; influence—; limit—; privilege—; represent—; —adheres; —controls; —convenes; —honors; —serves.

(See aristocracy, nobility.)

PEEVISH

adverbs

unspeakably; unreasonably; unwarrantably; terribly; disagreeably; unfortunately; unpleasantly; horribly; uncommonly; habitually; naturally; querulously; feverishly; childishly; fretfully; captiously; obstinately; incurably; acrimoniously; vexatiously; intolerably; insufferably; unaccountably; inexplicably; curiously; strangely; oddly; significantly; brusquely; snappishly; embarrassingly; humiliatingly.

PEG

adjectives

rustic; wooden; unfitted.

verbs

bind to—; dangle from—; drive—; hammer —; hang on—; hitch to—; insert—; pin with—; pound—; repose on—; tie to—; whittle—; —catches; —fastens; —holds; —projects; —protrudes; —supports; —sustains.

(See nail, hook.)

PELICAN

adjectives

rangy; large-billed; awkward.

verbs

—fishes; —gorges; —plunges; —secretes; —seizes.

(See bird.)

PELLUCID

adverbs

beautifully; admirably; unusually; wonderfully; marvellously; delightfully; incomparably; unsurpassably; limpidly; surprisingly; pricelessly; extraordinarily; inimitably; exquisitely; incomparably; peculiarly.

PEN

adjectives

educated; guided; gifted; severe; unbiased; inexhaustible; spiteful; brilliant; shy; inexpressive; horrible; abler; plaguy; ill-natured; ready; fascinating; vile; enigmatic; substantial; facile; untrained; sprightly; blithesome; humorous; truant; burning; barbarous; dreadful; lucid; inadequate; young; passion-guided; trenchant.

verbs

dip—; exercise—; grasp—; poise—; pour from—; probe—into; scrawl with—; whisk —across; wield—; —assails; —comes to life; —exposes; —falters; —libels; —sears; —unfolds; —voices.

(See fountain-pen, writer, author, pencil.)

PEN (v)

adverbs

obscurely; trenchantly; spitefully; inexhaustibly; brilliantly; expressively; fascinatingly; enigmatically; facilely; passionately.

(See record, compose, write.)

PENAL

adverbs

unnecessarily; cruelly; bitterly; justly; correctively; exceptionally; acidulously; inordinately; egregiously; excessively; mildly; ineffectively; formally; terribly.

PENALIZE (v)

adverbs

ironically; severely; rigorously; painfully; barbarously; harshly; stringently.

(See punish, discipline.)

PENALTY

adjectives

tremendous; painful; mad; inescapable; grievous; similar; severe; proportionate; efficient; enrolled; suitable; spiritual; barbarous; fearful; easy.

verbs

accept—; assert—; assess—; balk at—; condemn to—; decry—; escape—; entail—; evade—; exact—; impose—; inflict—; levy —; pay—; —atones; —recompenses; —rehabilitates.

(See forfeit, fine, punishment, indictment.)

PENANCE

adjectives

fearful; secret; atrocious; purgatorial; easy; spiritual; barbarous; suitable; amorous; cruel; harsh; solemn; hearty; superstitious; severe; lingering; true-hearted; honest.

PENCHANT

verbs

admit—; avoid—; cling to—; eschew—; excite—; exhibit—; incur—; indulge—; —burns; —devours; —disgusts; —irritates; —horrifies; —lusts; —riles (colloq.).

(See desire, inclination, attraction.)

PENCIL

adjectives

stubby; artistic; energetic; mechanical; unsharpened; blunt; coarse.

verbs

clasp—; depict with—; draw with—; drum with—; poise—; scribble with—; sharpen —; tip—; —copies; —dashes off; —delineates; —inscribes; —jots; —marks; —outlines; —scrawls; —scurries; —sketches; —tattoos; —tints.

(See pen.)

PENDANT

adjectives

quaint; inflamed; haughty.

verbs

display—; fashion—; flourish—; hook—; strip off—s; suspend—; —attracts; —bobs; —dazzles; —dangles; —decks; —enhances; —flaps; —fringes; —hangs; —impresses; —ornaments; —swings; —weights.

(See drop, jewel, gem.)

PENDENT

adverbs

terribly; perilously; hazardously; dangerously; decoratively; attractively; delicately; daintily; lustrously; dazzlingly; brilliantly; curiously; strangely; grotesquely; fantastically; quaintly; strikingly.

PENDULOUS

adverbs

heavily; clumsily; awkwardly; corpulently; uncertainly; flabbily; dangerously; indeterminately; wabblingly; loosely; unbecomingly; curiously; strangely.

PENDULUM

adjectives

ponderous; large; rhythmic.

verbs

adjust—; hook—; —controls; —dances; —maintains; —oscillates; —pulsates; —regulates; —rocks; —suspends; —swaggers; —

swings; —tick-tocks; —vibrates; —wags; —waves.

PENETRATE (*v*)

adverbs

accurately; accidentally; decisively; freely; scientifically; discerningly; gradually.

(See pierce, bore, affect.)

PENETRATING

adverbs

curiously; deeply; warrantably; peculiarly; particularly; remedially; soothingly; alleviatingly; surprisingly; remarkably; strikingly; incredibly; unusually; uncommonly; acutely; shrewdly; intelligently; keenly; sharply; discerningly; cleverly; sagaciously; profoundly; incisively; impressively; unfailingly; highly.

PENETRATION

adjectives

profound; calm; accurate; usual; subtle; intuitive; bland; noiseless; perfect; uncanny; characteristic; instinctive; partial; infallible; tender; masterly; sympathetic.

verbs

attempt—; block—; escape—; evade—; force—; induce—; pretend—; resist—; unite by—; wonder at—; —awes; —discerns; —discriminates; —gores; —shoots; —uncovers; —yawns.

(See infiltration.)

PENINSULA

verbs

approach—; fortify—; guard—; inhabit—; near—; overrun—; surround—; view—; watch—; —adjoins; —beckons; —extends; —lengthens; —projects; —protrudes; —reaches; —ranges; —stretches.

(See marsh, island, land.)

PENITENCE

adjectives

haggard; pale; celestial; pathetic; anxious; prescribed.

PENITENT

adverbs

deeply; sincerely; sorrowfully; painfully; naturally; contritely; meekly; humbly; embarrassingly; truly; unduly; ruefully; obviously; evidently; manifestly; pitiably; confessedly; terribly.

PENNILESS

adverbs

pitiably; undeniably; finally; terribly; sadly; frightfully; dreadfully; ruefully; laughably; merrily; blithely; carelessly; nonchalantly; miserably; wretchedly; helplessly; hopelessly; vexatiously; embarrassingly; obviously; humiliatingly; manifestly; actually; evidently; strangely; inexplicably; unaccountably; purposely; intentionally; adroitly; cleverly; resolutely.

PENNY-WISE

adverbs

cleverly; carefully; penuriously; thriftily; cannily; shrewdly; capriciously; extravagantly; wastefully; absurdly; unreasonably; ridiculously; improvidently; lavishly; inconsistently; recklessly; ludicrously; incongruously.

PENSION

adjectives

contributory; liberal; retiring; literary; subsidiary; old-age.

verbs

assign—; authorize—; bestow—upon; derive —from; establish—; exact—; fix—; forfeit —; grant—; merit—; proffer—; provide—; request—; reserve for—; retire on—; welcome—; yield—; —assists; —enables; —encourages; —supports; —sustains.

(See pay, payment, allowance, subsidy.)

PENSIVE

adverbs

abstractedly; incongruously; strangely; silently; absent-mindedly; sweetly; quietly; soberly; anxiously; remotely; dreamily; ruefully; mournfully; dully; deeply; gravely; solemnly; happily; contentedly.

PENTHOUSE

verbs

decorate—; enjoy—; establish in—; furnish —; inhabit—; occupy—; offer—; philander on—; provide—; renovate—; view from—; —allures; —appeals; —attracts; —caps; — crowns; —delights; —enchants; —overlooks; —tops.

(See tower, apartment, roof.)

PENURIOUS

adverbs

intolerably; terribly; necessarily; pitiably; meanly; basely; incomprehensibly; inexplic-

ably; unreasonably; unpardonably; suspiciously; suddenly; inherently; naturally; inconveniently; conspicuously; strangely; incorrigibly; greedily; irremediably; unreasonably; disagreeably; unnecessarily; needlessly; unaccountably; niggardly; miserly; inexcusably; stingily; crustily; gruffly; wretchedly; avariciously; uncommonly; extremely; absurdly; miserably; sordidly.

PENURY

adjectives

cold; hard; frosty; tedious; unvanquishable; sordid; forgetful; utter; gripping; miserable.

verbs

burden by—; conceal—; fear—; feign—; reduce to—; resist—; survive—; —afflicts; — aggrieves; —deprives; —distresses; —embarrasses; —harasses; —irks; —narrows; —necessitates; —pains; —weighs upon.

(See poverty, want, destitution.)

PEOPLE

adjectives

aboriginal; abused; accursed; adventurous; affectionate; agile; alert; amiable; amused; aristocratic; aspiring; astounding; austere; aware; barbaric; benevolent; benighted; bent; border; brave; brusque; bustling; celebrated; charitable; chivalrous; civilized; cold; common; commonplace; communicative; congenial; congregated; conquering; constructive; contemplative; conventional; credulous; cruel; cultivated; debonair; decadent; decent; defenseless; degraded; deluded; democratic; desperate; devoted; diminutive; discontented; distinguished; discriminating; dissipated; distinct; doglike; distressed; egotistical; elbowing; eminent; energetic; enervated; enslaved; enfranchised; engrossing; enlightened; enterprising; erect; estimable; excited; everlasting; expatriated; extravagant; factious; fanciful; fashionable; fertile; fastidious; fickle; filthy; frenzied; fun-loving; friendless; friendly; frivolous; gaily-dressed; gay; generous; gloomy; grateful; great; growing; highminded; homogeneous; humble; humdrum; hurrying; idolatrous; illiterate; impoverished; impulsive; inarticulate; indestructible; indignant; industrious; infatuated; inflamed; infuriated; insane; intense; kind-hearted; interesting; jealous; law-loving; kindly-faced; laboring; learned; liberty-loving; light; lighter; litigious; lively; malicious;

martial; materialistic; mediocre; merry; milling; miserable; modest; missionary-minded; money-making; nice; much-praying; mysterious; neighboring; niggardly; noble; nomadic; notable; noteworthy; obscure; oppressed; outrageous; overfed; packed; panic-stricken; peace-loving; panting; paradoxical; pastoral; peculiar; pediatric; perfect; persistent; persuadable; pessimistic; picturesque; pious; polished; polite; poor; poorly-dressed; practical; precise; prehistoric; preposterous; primitive; progressive; prominent; proud; provoking; quarrelsome; refined; reflective; restless; rich; rigid; rude; rugged; rushing; sagacious; sanguine; seafaring; selfish; sensible; self-seeking; semi-literate; sensitive; sentimental; servile; shabby; shade-loving; sightless; sleek; snobbish; smart; sober; social-minded; solitary; sore; sovereign; special; started; startled; stiff; strange; strong; stupid; sturdy; stylish; supine; substantial; suffering; sufficient; superior; superstitious; swollen; terror-stricken; thoughtful; tempted; thinking; tiresome; thoughtless; timid; tranquil; turbulent; ulcerous; unambitious; unclassical; uncouth; uncultivated; uncultured; unfortunate; unnatural; unobtrusive; unpoetic; unpolished; unreasonable; unreasoning; verbose; vigilant; vigorous; virile; virtuous; visiting; volatile; weak; well-dressed; well-informed; wholesale; wise; wonderful; wondering; worthless; young.

verbs

chide—; color—; conciliate—; corral—; denounce to—; depict—; fraternize with—; instigate—; jolt—; liberate—; outsmart (colloq.)—; portray—; regiment—; tyrannize over—; —arise; —flock to; —gather 'round; —rally to; —revolt; —sanction.

(See English, folk, race, tribe, nation, persons, community.)

"PEP"

verbs

gain—; inject—; lack—; —gains; —brightens; —buoys; —cheers; —emboldens; —endures; —enthuses (colloq.); —glows; —fosters; —impresses; —infects; —inspires; —palls; —reassures; —tingles; —wanes; —warms.

(See energy, power, zeal, vigor.)

PERAMBULATION

adjectives

glad; stealthy.

PERCEIVABLE

adverbs

easily; readily; completely; manifestly; instantly; openly; immediately; perfectly; remarkably; strikingly.

PERCEIVE (v)

adverbs

vividly; tangibly; dimly; sagely; tremulously; instinctively; vaguely; distinctly; superficially.

(See discern, observe.)

PERCENTAGE

adjectives

unknown; doubtful; high.

verbs

calculate—; check—; compute—; cut—; deduct—; demand—; derive—; draw—; exact —; extract—; fix—; reduce—; stabilize—; yield—; —abates; —ascends; —exceeds; —mounts; —staggers.

(See amount, sum, proportion, part, rate, quantity.)

PERCEPTIBLE

adverbs

dimly; readily; scarcely; easily; cruelly; bitterly; instantly; immediately; finally; distinctly; conspicuously; plainly; clearly; mistily; hardly.

PERCEPTION

adjectives

triumphant; keen; dimmest; acute; quick; startling; single; ominous; honest; innate; intuitive; vivid; sharp; intellectual; mental; artistic; sudden; passive; dreamlike; accurate; exquisite; prodigious; vague; confused; sentimental; simultaneous; mystic; infallible; subtle; extra-sensory; spiritual; cloud; sure; steadfast; moral; awful; luminous; interior; penetrating; practical; human.

verbs

attain—; blind—; blunt—; clarify—; display—; dull—; heighten—; stimulate—; warp—; —adjusts; —aids; —appreciates; —apprehends; —fathoms; —matures; —scans; —warns.

(See eye, feeling, sensation.)

PERCH

adjectives

convenient; incongruous; precarious; lofty.

PERCH (v)

adverbs
conveniently; precariously; loftily; importantly; securely; gracefully; daringly.
(See sit, place.)

PERDITION

adjectives
everlasting; bottomless; eternal.

verbs
condemn to—; consume to—; —annuls; —batters; —blasts; —blots out; —confounds; —crashes; —crumbles; —demolishes; —desolates; —devastates; —devours; —engulfs; —eradicates; —overwhelms; —perplexes; —prostrates; —swamps.
(See hell, ruin, destruction.)

PEREMPTORY

adverbs
disagreeably; proudly; dictatorially; extremely; unnecessarily; arrogantly; emphatically; bumptiously; incisively; cuttingly; unwarrantedly; officially; formally; coldly; sharply; sternly; severely; trenchantly; unfortunately; offensively; unwisely; deliberately; habitually; unconsciously.

PERENNIAL

adverbs
conveniently; dependably; delightfully; satisfactorily; reliably; imperishably; comfortably; durably; happily; fortunately.

PERFECTION

adjectives
absolute; delicate; abnormal; classic; spontaneous; aesthetic; time-softened; infinite; divine; optical; fashionable; rare; strained; technical; ineffable; trim; studied; flattering; pure; balanced; complete; supreme; ravishing; final; theoretical; comparative; prosperous; exquisite; unlimited; overwhelming; matchless; constant; minute; moral; true; mechanical; imaginable; artistic; pure; tailored; unapproachable.

verbs
achieve—; acquire—; admire—; approximate—; attain—; disclaim—; emulate—; gain—; invest with—; lack—; mature to—; realize—; ripen to—; sacrifice—to; seek—; strive for—; transcend—; vie for—; —clinches; —crowns; —eludes; —saturates; —seals.
(See beauty, mastery, precision, accuracy.)

PERFIDIOUS

adverbs
dreadfully; treacherously; habitually; racially; inherently; terribly; seditiously; personally; highly; uncommonly; unforgivably; manifestly; cruelly; barbarously; savagely; dangerously; sadly; undeniably; disloyally; untrustworthily; dastardly; basically; horribly; wickedly; deliberately.

PERFIDY

adjectives
armed; household; unspeakable; calculated.

PERFORM (v)

adverbs
unwittingly; gallantly; energetically; creditably; pleasantly; dramatically; conscientiously; theatrically; gratuitously; brilliantly; capably; faithfully; methodically; scrupulously; publicly; effectively; zealously; punctually; rigorously; harmoniously; superlatively; exceptionally; consummately.
(See accomplish, execute, play, act.)

PERFORMANCE

adjectives
relative; theoretical; undignified; smooth; eager; zealous; arduous; singular; dependable; punctual; proved; pirated; exhibition; indubitable; silent; rigorous; maximum; choice; splendid; shoddy; slipshod; pantomimed; effective; harmonious; superficial; sensational; spectacular; laudable; charity; magnanimous; humdrum; incisive; top; charitable; superlative; decennial; periodic; scrupulous; sparkling; exceptional; ill-considered; splendid; faithful; vigorous; painstaking; proper; careless; innocuous; astonishing; fearless; brazen; discreditable; irresponsible; graceful; improper; superb; middling; subsequent; persuasive; impressive; remarkable; brilliant; magnificent; consummate.

verbs
acclaim—; affect—of; applaud—; broadcast —; direct—; engage in—; infuse into—; inject into—; key—; laud—; render—; reward for—; sponsor—; stage—; suspend—; witness—; —involves; —thrills.
(See feat, deed, entertainment, melodrama, play.)

PERFORMER

adjectives
accomplished; creditable; gratuitous; exact.

adjectives

delicate; sweet; enchanted; native; well-remembered; swooning; drowsy; overpowering; excellent; faint; melodic; exquisite; powerful; delectable; floating; rhetorical; soft; pungent; intoxicating; haunting; filthy; lingering; rich; poisoned; attractive; dead; exotic.

verbs

anoint with—; dab—; distill—; douse with —; drench with—; emit—; exude—; haunt by—; inhale—; recognize—; reek with—; saturate in—; spray with—; steep in—; waft—; —clings; —delights; —exudes; — floods; —nauseates; —offends; —oppresses; —overcomes; —overwhelms; —pervades; — pleases; —scents; —tints.

(See aroma, essence, incense, fragrance.)

PERFUME (v)

adverbs

exquisitely; exotically; sweetly; delectably; intoxicatingly; hauntingly; richly; lingeringly; voluptuously.

(See scent.)

PERFUNCTORY

adverbs

arrogantly; smugly; carelessly; disagreeably; unpleasantly; unpardonably; indifferently; apathetically; heedlessly; incautiously; mechanically; thoughtlessly; coolly; unconcernedly; coldly; hastily; inexcusably; inexplicably; unaccountably; horribly; cruelly; unfeelingly.

PERIL

adjectives

approaching; utmost; manifold; sundry (pl); imminent; extreme; extraordinary; real; vague; instant; personal;. probable; attendant; vegetable; serious; formidable; growing; imaginary; nimble; incredible; besetting; innumerable (pl); unavoidable; deadly; slight; weird; ever-recurring; encompassing; great; unexpected.

verbs

anticipate—; brave—; chance—; dare—; defy—; encounter—; expose to—; face—; hazard—; incur—; rescue from—; risk—; steel against—; survive—; terrify by—; venture—; warn of—; —endangers; —jeopardizes; —menaces; —oppresses; —threatens.

(See hazard, danger, menace, risk.)

adverbs

notoriously; notably; undeniably; obviously; terribly; ghastly; miserably; peculiarly; infernally; undisguisedly; unutterably; mortally; bitterly; dreadfully; extremely; inordinately; ominously; mercilessly; prodigiously.

PERIOD
(time)

adjectives

secluded; adequate; successive (pl); tortured; immediate; postwar; remote; unlimited; towering; prehistoric; immature; dismal; prolonged; engine-creating; brief; chronological; pivotal; corresponding; severe; dangerous; characteristic; distinct; critical; definite; mental; extended; smiling; frivolous; traditional; respective; well-defined; pretentious; momentous; dark; potential; bubble; rude; vigorous; stirring; long; glamorous; creative; controversial; dead; spiritual; modern; specified; variable; brilliant; devastating; limited; fruitful; disturbed; predetermined; unquiet; unmoral; corrupt; medieval; immense; pagan; formative; melancholy; calamity; measurable; pretty; reasonable; considerable; conversational; sidereal; productive; eventful; glorious; previous; lurid; palmy; contagious; glacial; noteworthy; tickling; indefinite; nebulous; typical; anomalistic; sluggish; provincial; impressionable; chaotic; comfortable; proscribed; transition; flourishing; definite; pioneering; congested; amusing; long-forgotten; genial; happy; tranquil; expired; stated; moot; shameful; fecund; wondrous; discreditable; creative; probationary; trying.

verbs

characterize—; conclude—; inaugurate—; launch—; perpetuate—; personify—; plunge into—; shorten—; usher in—; —achieves; —advances; —consumes; —dawns; —dies; —elapses; —embarks; —embraces; —expires; —flows; —glides; —intervenes; — terminates.

(See era, epoch, age, cycle, decade, generation.)

PERIODIC

adverbs

regularly; fortunately; reliably; dependably; wisely; ordinarily; invariably; infallibly; officially; necessarily; duly.

adjectives
fledgling; exoteric; esoteric; short-lived; spectacular; fireside; sarcastic; unread.

verbs
dispense—; disseminate—; distribute—; edit —; found—; hawk—; heap —s; hoard —s; launch—; publish—; preserve—; refer to—; scan—; subscribe to—; treasure—; —advertises; —amuses; —delights; —diverts; —illustrates; —informs.

(See newspaper, magazine, publication.)

PERISH (v)
adverbs
desolately; miserably; simultaneously; ignominiously; inevitably; agonizingly.

(See die, decay.)

PERISHABLE
adverbs
highly; uncommonly; unfortunately; remarkably; unluckily; extravagantly; unhappily; particularly; peculiarly; terribly; dreadfully; wastefully; undesirably; inordinately.

PERJURY
adjectives
false; flat; atrocious; cunning; extraordinary.

PERKY
adverbs
roguishly; smartly; saucily; stylishly; fashionably; irresistibly; tomboyishly; quaintly; fascinatingly; interestingly; piquantly; pleasantly; modishly; charmingly; ingeniously.

PERMANENCE
adjectives
historic; unnatural.

verbs
ascertain—; confirm—; establish—; guarantee—; intensify—; retain—of; sense—; threaten—; —drags; —endures; —evaporates; —fades; —flickers; —perseveres; —persists; —protracts; —totters; —weathers.

(See immortality, stability.)

PERMANENT
adverbs
comfortably; securely; admirably; assuredly; warrantably; unquestionably; fortunately; safely; reasonably; steadfastly; unchangeably; durably; inescapably; legally.

adverbs
expressly; generously; always; scarcely; socially; officially; intimately; obviously; evidently; patently; unconditionally; reportedly; reputedly; apparently; unquestionably; manifestly; definitely; explicitly; palpably; luckily; fortunately.

PERMISSION
adjectives
abstracted; unsolicited; verbal; express; requisite; reluctant; willing.

PERMIT (v)
adverbs
unsolicitedly; verbally; expressly; reluctantly; graciously; lazily; incidentally; promiscuously; readily; gratuitously; stolidly; magnanimously.

(See allow, consent.)

PERORATION
adjectives
justly-admired; noble; sprawling.

PERPETRATE (v)
adverbs
cruelly; fiendishly; illegally; vilely; wickedly; lustfully; crudely; murderously.

(See commit, accomplish.)

PERPLEX (v)
adverbs
facetiously; amazingly; sorely; painfully; cunningly; slyly; verbally; mentally.

(See bewilder, confuse.)

PERPLEXING
adverbs
unaccountably; disturbingly; genuinely; indescribably; strangely; fearfully; insuperably; dishearteningly; depressingly; terribly; vexatiously; alarmingly; unreasonably; uncomfortably; vaguely; subtly; awkwardly; stubbornly; extremely; secretly; annoyingly; exasperatingly; inexplicably.

PERPLEXITY
adjectives
inevitable; great; dim; insoluble; unexplained; sad; natural; painful; unrighteous; mingled; hopeless; dangerous; broken-hearted.

verbs
conceal—; flounder in—; grapple with—;

grope in—; hesitate in—; relieve—; tremble in—; unravel—; view with—; —bewilders; —bothers; —burdens; —confuses; —darkens; —embarrasses; —enmeshes; —entangles; —hounds; —muddles; —nets; —overwhelms; —weaves.

(See amazement, incredulity, bewilderment, uncertainty, complication.)

PERSECUTE (v)
adverbs
mercilessly; relentlessly; odiously; pettishly; determinedly; whimsically; remorselessly; senselessly; bitterly; unjustly; repeatedly; unflaggingly; doggedly; incredibly; unfalteringly.

(See oppress, torment.)

PERSECUTION
verbs
bewail—; criticize—; fear—; inflict—; intensify—; intimidate by—; resist—; single out for—; subject to—; suffer—; temper—; —aggrieves; —dispirits; —grinds; —harasses; —haunts; —pains; —offends; —oppresses; —outrages; —tramples; —weighs.

(See oppression, tyranny.)

PERSECUTOR
adjectives
odious; petty; subtle; religious; domestic; determined; unjust; whimsical; cold-hearted; systematic; unmerited; remorseless; senseless; merciless; relentless; languid; fiery; bitter; imperial; miserable; actual; repeated.

PERSEVERANCE
adjectives
unflagging; relentless; tugging; resolute; dogged; steady; indefinite; incredible; majestic; patient; indomitable; scheming; unfaltering; mechanical.

verbs
acclaim—; acquire by—; instil—; reward —; tax—; wed to—; yield to—; —buckles down; —clings; —devotes; —drives; —falters; —fights; —persists; —plods; —plunges.

(See insistence, patience, persistence.)

PERSEVERE (v)
adverbs
steadily; pluckily; characteristically; unflaggingly; relentlessly; resolutely; doggedly;

incredibly; indomitably; unfalteringly; mechanically.

(See continue, persist.)

PERSEVERING
adverbs
resolutely; tenaciously; stubbornly; patiently; gently; mildly; irritatingly; vexatiously; tiresomely; monotonously; wildly; obstinately; mulishly; endlessly; unremittingly; singularly; oddly; peculiarly; awfully; commendably; admirably; terribly; conspicuously; doggedly.

PERSIFLAGE
adjectives
insolent; witty; swift; bantering.

PERSIST (v)
adverbs
archly; insubordinately; doggedly; undauntedly; audaciously; vigorously; stubbornly; enthusiastically; logically; relentlessly; ardently; faithfully; inextinguishably; triumphantly; morbidly; unreasonably.

(See persevere, continue.)

PERSISTENCE
adjectives
marked; ardent; unabated; culpable; faithful; indomitable; cruel; inextinguishable; wonderful; tiresome; patient; triumphant; appalling; morbid; further; uncomplaining; wearisome; adequate; unreasonable.

verbs
dog with—; instil—; tax—; —achieves; —attacks; —continues; —drags; —endures; —fades; —gains; —palls; —survives; —wanes.

(See application, insistence, perseverance.)

PERSISTENT
adverbs
vexatiously; disagreeably; inescapably; unpleasantly; obnoxiously; admirably; remarkably; uncommonly; highly; tiresomely; ardently; passionately; amazingly; incredibly; unreasonably; doggedly; determinedly; obstinately; stubbornly; maddeningly; insufferably; terribly.

PERSON
adjectives
acidulated; acrid; affected; apprehensive; arbitrary; argumentative; arrogant; attrac-

tive; bald-headed; bandy-legged; benevolent; blind; blunt; bold; brazen; brokenhearted; captious; capricious; captivating; charming; chivalrous; clear-headed; comely; commanding; compassionate; conceivable; consoling; consumptive; contemplative; conventional; corpulent; courteous; critical; crotchety; cunning; cute; deformed; delicate; democratic; designing; devout; diabolic; diminutive; disagreeable; discontented; discriminating; domestic; distinguished; divine; double; dubious; easygoing; effeminate; eloquent; erect; eminent; entertaining; estimable; firm; excessive; exotic; fastidious; florid; flourishing; fortunate; frecklefaced; frivolous; garrulous; gentle; ghastly; ghostly; gracious; great; grotesque; grizzily; handicapped; hearty; hard-looking; heavenly; heavy; hook-nosed; humorous; hump-shouldered; ignoble; ignominious; illustrious; imaginary; immense; impeccable; impertinent; impious; inconsiderate; indecorous; indolent; industrious; inelegant; influential; informed; ingenious; inimitable; inquisitive; insignificant; insolvent; just; instructed; intelligent; joking; little; knowledged; laughing; legendary; loquacious; malevolent; malicious; massive; masterly; matching; matter-of-fact; meaner; meek; menacing; mild; milk-livered; mocking; modern; moody; morbid; morose; mortified; namby-pamby; nervous; neurotic; never-smiling; nondescript; normal; obedient; obnoxious; obstinate; obstreperous; obvious; occult; odious; officious; ogreish; ordinary; original; outlandish; outrageous; outwitted; zeal-filled; overbearing; overmastering; overt; overweening; pale; pampered; passable; perfect; perfidious; perjured; persevering; phantasmal; phenomenal; phlegmatic; prejudiced; presumptuous; private; prime; profane; proper; prosperous; pugnacious; punctilious; reckless; reflecting; regular; reputable; respectable; reticent; rude; sacred; scientific; sedate; self-effacing; self-indulging; selfish; selfless; sensitive; sentimental; skilled; slim; slippery; small; smiling; solid; sophisticated; stricken; striking; stuffy; stupid; sublime; substantial; superior; susceptible; talkative; sympathetic; thinking; tiresome; traitorous; unaccountable; unapproachable; unauthorized; uncongenial; uncouth; undesirable; unenterprising; unobtrusive; unpeaceable; unruly; useless; unskilled; unvalued; unwieldy; vindictive; unworthy; venerable; veracious; versatile; virtuous; volatile;

wall-eyed; well-disposed; well-dressed; well-informed; well-intentioned; willful; wild; wily; witty; wordy; worldly; worthy; outstanding; young; assertive; fictitious.

PERSONABLE

adverbs
altogether; charmingly; unusually; uncommonly; highly; remarkably; obviously; undeniably; delightfully; pleasantly; definitely; emphatically; fortunately; admirably; irresistibly; singularly; particularly; completely.

PERSONAGE

adjectives
trusty; eminent; silent; respectable; shabby; grimy; despondent; bitter; pallid; muselike; prominent; venerable; radiant; expansive; leading; all-compelling; allegorical; luminous; historical; leathery; filmy; showy; complex; singular; tutelary; fictitious; arrogant; noble; pompous; exalted; illustrious; subsidiary; favorite; powerful; gnarled; cynical; romantic; miraculous; tragic; nude; stalwart; whimsical; honorable; formidable; poetical; important; tremendous; fine; comely; worthy; ruddy; royal; unimportant; distinguished; sordid; strange-looking; shadowy; august; sympathetic.

verbs
conceal—; esteem—; honor—; introduce—; uncover—; —attracts; —awes; —enhances; —fosters; —graces; —impresses; —inspires; —overwhelms; —thrills.
(See individual, person, character.)

PERSONAL

adverbs
intimately; pleasantly; graciously; undeniably; particularly; unusually; remarkably; highly; uncommonly; specifically; significantly; unpleasantly; definitely; emphatically; obviously; curiously; manifestly; evidently; cruelly; flatteringly; bitterly.

PERSONALITY

adjectives
vivid; perfect; tenuous; fascinating; self-determining; judicial; calumnious; melancholy; unreasonable; erratic; projected; winning; fictitious; operatic; strong; abounding; poetic; vital; charming; intuitive; forceful; robust; integrated; recognizable; eminent; endowed; imaginative; meditative; potent; intense; aggressive; unimpaired;

distinct; agreeable; austere; vigorous; delightful; sinister; conscious; dignified; courteous; general; amiable; unfettered; exciting; dual; sure-fire; predominating; dramatic; arresting; exquisite; variegated; inward; unlicensed; curious; intense; embarrassed; aloof; conspicuous; dominant; big; vibrant; dynamic; powerful; attractive; winning; glowing; composite; serene; underlying; ostensible; unique; thorough; childlike; miserable; wholesome; firm; definite; recurrent.

verbs
absorb in—; build—; destroy—; develop—; disintegrate—; distort—; divest of—; electrify—; enhance—; enrich—; evolve—; lack —; radiate—; relapse into—; shed—; stamp —; stimulate—; submerge—; veil—; vitalize—; warp—; —matures; —s merge; — splits.
(See character, individuality, ego.)

PERSONIFICATION
adjectives
restful; dumpy; shadowy; tremendous.

PERSONNEL
verbs
alter—; charge—with; criticize—; enhance —; increase—; limit—; reduce—; retain—; superintend—; supervise—; train—; —assists; —inspects; —manages; —merits; — strikes; —votes.
(See staff, employees.)

PERSPECTIVE
adjectives
theatrical; artificial; monotonous; accurate; wide; historical; brilliant; scornful; infinite; dim; calm; true; enchanting; celestial; vast; soft; permanent; clear; interminable; deep; remarkable; boundless; artistic.

verbs
adjust—; broaden—; check—; clarify—; contemplate—; depend on—; develop—; gain—; influence—; lack—; maintain—; narrow—; reduce—; —assumes; —astonishes; —clears; —differs; —matures; —warps.
(See outlook, view, position.)

PERSPICACIOUS
adverbs
unusually; keenly; shrewdly; uncommonly; highly; brilliantly; astutely; penetratingly; subtly; craftily; warily; cleverly; undeni-

ably; uncommonly; sharply; sagaciously; wisely; quietly; observantly; gravely; signally; amazingly; marvellously.

PERSPIRATION
adjectives
violent; perpetual; clammy; profuse; excessive; flabby; cold; healthy; copious; odorous.

verbs
bathe in—; check—; drench with—; effuse —; excrete—; exude—; induce—; promote —; —annoys; —beads; —breaks from; — dampens; —drains; —escapes; —filters; — flows; —glistens; —gushes; —oozes; — purges; —reeks; —saturates; —streams from; —trickles.
(See sweat.)

PERSPIRE (v)
adverbs
profusely; perpetually; clammily; excessively; copiously; odorously; disgustingly; nauseatingly.
(See sweat, discharge.)

PERSUADE (v)
adverbs
readily; ultimately; tactfully; forcibly; vigorously; firmly; unobstructively; eloquently; argumentatively; soothingly.
(See convince, induce, urge.)

PERSUASION
adjectives
different; forcible; vigorous; firm; fanciful; deep; kind; parental; instinctive; womanly; melancholy; powerful; unobstructive; eloquent; persistent; argumentative; intimate; undoubting; kindly; soothing; demagogic.

verbs
advocate—; exercise—; possess—; rely upon —; resort to—; yield to—; —baits; —bewitches; —convinces; —entices; —forces; — impresses; —influences; —overcomes; — overwhelms; —seduces; —tames; strive for —.
(See belief, influence.

PERSUASIVE
adverbs
smoothly; irresistibly; graciously; cordially; sternly; suavely; politely; overpoweringly; passionately; enthusiastically; ardently;

overwhelmingly; subtly; insinuatingly; ingratiatingly; imperceptibly; forcibly; violently; loudly; crassly; disagreeably; pleasantly; completely.

PERT

adverbs
saucily; prettily; roguishly; mischievously; brazenly; impudently; insufferably; suddenly; trickily; archly; wantonly; insolently; rudely; flippantly; frivolously; idly; boldly; amazingly; daringly; naughtily; glibly; smartly.

PERTINACITY

adjectives
savage; playful; relentless; unprecedented; unwavering.

PERTINENT

adverbs
opportunely; advantageously; gravely; curiously; significantly; admirably; commendably; undeniably; profitably; happily; remarkably; unexpectedly; strikingly; helpfully; serviceably; usefully; fortunately; harmoniously; critically.

PERTURB (v)

adverbs
irritably; mentally; habitually; mutually; emotionally; superficially; impatiently; pathetically.
(See excite, disturb, agitate.)

PERTURBATION

adjectives
irritable; curious; mental; observed; habitual; internal; planetary; mutual; past; lunar; evident.

verbs
bear—; cool—; endure—; experience—; ferment—; inflict—; provoke—; shake with —; smart under—; wince in—; writhe in —; —chafes; —chokes; —enrages; —infects; —inflames; —jolts; —shakes.
(See excitement, emotion, disturbance.)

PERTURBED

adverbs
naturally; slightly; deeply; inwardly; secretly; obviously; visibly; incomprehensibly; shockingly; inordinately; extremely; curiously; strangely; painfully; pathetically; gravely; seriously; helplessly; subtly; absurdly; momentarily; terribly.

PERUSAL

adjectives
candid; careful; calm; submissive; cool; studied.

PERUSE (v)

adverbs
studiously; exhaustively; intensely; candidly; calmly; coolly; professionally; determinedly; imaginatively; sympathetically.
(See read, scan.)

PERVADE (v)

adverbs
intimately; intensely; foully; insidiously; curiously; morbidly.
(See penetrate, pierce, affect.)

PERVASIVE

adverbs
strangely; utterly; offensively; unpleasantly; disagreeably; delightfully; agreeably; fragrantly; pleasantly; pungently; aromatically; alarmingly; dangerously; deliberately; ominously; suddenly; terribly; sweetly; nauseatingly; acridly.

PERVERSE

adverbs
obstinately; wilfully; stubbornly; intractably; ungovernably; sadly; dreadfully; doggedly; waywardly; wantonly; purposely; deliberately; captiously; capriciously; inexplicably; inscrutably; unexpectedly; uncommonly; malignantly; hatefully; spitefully; fearfully; irritatingly; vexatiously; viciously; mischievously; incorrigibly.

PERVERSION

adjectives
horrible; abominable; monstrous; palpable; sexual; wilful.

verbs
practise—; resort to—; uncover—; unravel —; —abuses; —blemishes; —corrupts; —decimates; —defiles; —distorts; —impairs; —infects; —misdirects; —misleads; —poisons; —warps; —weakens; —misinterprets.
(See abuse, obscenity, corruption.)

adjectives

elaborate; hidden; curious.

verbs

brave—; condemn—; endure—; inflict—
upon; temper—; treat with—; yield to—;
—aggrieves; —angers; —astonishes; —
chafes; —checks; —inflames; —insults;
irks; —jars; —provokes; —resists.
(See obstinacy, stubbornness.)

PERVERT (*v*)

adverbs

odiously; horribly; abominably; monstrously; palpably; wilfully; sexually.
(See debase, falsify.)

PESSIMISM

adjectives

sour; melancholy; polite; morbid; counter-
balancing.

verbs

balance—; droop in—; infuse—; propagate
—; remedy—; ridicule—; shake off—; warrant—; wilt under—; yield to—; —crushes;
—dampens; —dashes; —dejects; —depresses; —despairs; —disconcerts; —disheartens; —preys upon; —prostrates; —reigns;
—represses; —saddens; —shadows; —
shrouds; —weighs upon; —withers.
(See hopelessness, cynicism.)

PESSIMIST

adjectives

confirmed; polite; genial; deliberate.

verbs

desolate—; doom—; paralyze—; —clouds;
—doubts; —complains; —condemns; —
cowers; —disconcerts; —disheartens; —
flinches; —funks; —grumbles; —laments;
—poisons; —quails; —shies; —suspects.

PESSIMISTIC

adverbs

incorrigibly; incurably; deliberately; apparently; stubbornly; obstinately; horribly; unaccountably; gloomily; moodily; mournfully; miserably; wretchedly; intolerably; disgustingly; woefully; pitiably; unreasonably;
morbidly; superstitiously; absurdly; foolishly; ridiculously.

adjectives

domestic; vicious; uninvited; injurious; destructive; lifelong.

verbs

chastise—; eradicate—; extirpate—; —annoys; —inflicts; —molests; —nettles; —
offends; —piques; —plagues; —preys upon;
—racks; —rankles; —riles (colloq.); —
ruffles; —scourges; —torments; —tries; —
vexes.
(See nuisance, disease, plague, insect,
parasite.)

PESTIFEROUS

adverbs

intentionally; purposely; cantankerously; deliberately; wantonly; persistently; continually; unbearably; meanly; maliciously;
venomously; woefully; wretchedly; miserably; curiously; strangely; intolerably; disgustingly; capriciously; naggingly; mischievously; trickily; annoyingly; oddly;
wilfully.

PESTILENCE

adjectives

buoyant; great; hateful; occasional; infidel;
life-poisoning; spreading; instinctive; infectious; tropical; air-borne.

verbs

breed—; confine—to; ease—; free from—;
remedy—; succumb to—; suffer—; survive
—; —abuses; —affects; —aggrieves; —
breaks out; —devastates; —endures; —oppresses; —outrages; —pains; —prostrates;
rages; —ravages; —swamps; —tramples;
—victimizes.
(See contagion, disease, plague.)

PET

verbs

caress—; cater to—; cherish—; court—;
cradle—; cuddle—; embrace—; favor—;
fondle—; hug—; indulge—; maul—; pamper—; patronize—; praise—; serve—; spoil
—.

(See child, baby, kitten, puppy.)

PETALS

adjectives

beauteous; flaming; plumy; richly-tinted;
smoldering; faded; rich; plucked-out;
dusky; yielding; nipped; rained; gauzy;
scriptured; drenched; drifting.

verbs

bag—; dry—; gather—; lacerate—; pluck —; press—; tear—; tint—; —adorn; — blanket; —cup; —drop; —open; —shower; —spread; —strew; —unfold; —wilt.

(See flower, plant, leaf.)

PETITION

adjectives

suitable; begging; respectful; vain; bare; urgent; signed; lengthy; eloquent; specific; unanswered; discarded.

verbs

address—; deny—; enter—; evoke—; file —; press—; repeat—; resort to—; seek in —; solicit—; —appeals to; —s beset; — demands; —pleads; —protests; —suppli- cates.

(See appeal, application, entreaty.)

PETITION (v)

adverbs

fruitlessly; legally; urgently; lengthily; elo- quently; specifically; vainly; slavishly; humbly.

(See entreat, pray.)

PETTICOAT

adjectives

balloon; kilted; elegant; lace-trimmed; braided; ankle-length; old-fashioned; bil- lowy.

PETTINESS

adjectives

ironical; quaint; usual; needless.

PETTISH

adverbs

fretfully; peevishly; annoyingly; nervously; feverishly; childishly; jealously; impossibly; unbearably; intolerably; persistently; miser- ably; curiously; unwontedly; uncommonly; extremely; dreadfully; absurdly; impishly; wretchedly; forlornly.

PETTY

adverbs

frivolously; meanly; insignificantly; ridicul- ously; contemptibly; miserably; absurdly; childishly; pitiably; curiously; singularly; particularly; extraordinarily; extremely; terribly.

,PETULANCE

adjectives

charming; impatient; cowardly; pathetic; habitual; lasting; proud; angry; pouting; becoming.

PETULANT

adverbs

unusually; abnormally; feverishly; nervous- ly; hysterically; fretfully; wantonly; mis- chievously; crossly; captiously; habitually; naturally; strangely; oddly; intolerably; in- excusably; curiously; incorrigibly; disagree- ably; unpleasantly; obnoxiously; hatefully; wistfully; whiningly.

PEW

adjectives

high-backed; respectable; dusty; uncomfort- able; crowded; unused.

verbs

allocate—s; array in—s; commit to—; cram —; cushion—; direct to—; enter—; fill—; kneel in—; occupy—; perch in—; rent—; reserve—; scan from—.

(See place, seat, bench, compartment.)

PHALANX

adjectives

martial; invincible; cunning.

PHANTASIES

adjectives

guilty; childish; unconscious; elaborate; horrid; weird; distempered.

PHANTASY

verbs

coin—; concede—; conjure up—; devise—; dream—; efface—; excogitate—; fabricate —; improvise—; invent—; picture—; strike —; suggest—; —crumbles; —delights; — deludes; —dissolves; —fades; —floats; — passes.

(See picture, vision, image, illusion, de- lusion.)

PHANTOM

adjectives

sceptered; lurid; ghostly; formless; dismal; ugly; transparent; horrible; ignoble; glor- ious; charming; terrible; impudent; holy; melancholy; faithless; summer; granite;

pale; fair; cloudy; colossal; secular; recurring; august; prodigious; pleasurable; deceitful; monstrous; solemn; benignant; dark; simulated; majestic; midnight.

verbs
banish—; devise—; ogle at—; observe—; picture—; spy—; stare at—; —appears; —departs; —dissolves; —evaporates; —fades; —glares; —leers; —looms; —melts away; —passes; —retires; —vanishes.
(See apparition, ghost, vision.)

PHASE
adjectives
various (pl); intimate; personal; extreme; pioneering; ethical; sectional; curious; transitional; manifold (pl); subtle; intermediate; dramatic; conciliating; increasing; unavoidable; varying; unknown; disinterested; ever-changing; important; precise; enthusiastic; nascent; indispensable; interesting; vehement; exceptional; strenuous; submerged; characteristic; delicate; dreadful; periodic; gibbous; special; renewed; pathetic; romantic; significant; peculiar; diversified (pl).

verbs
alter—; assume—; discover—; enjoy—; explore—; exhibit—; form—; interpret—; investigate—; labor through—; master—; pry into—; recognize—; restore—; shape—; undo—; view—; —determines; —melts; —passes; —shifts.
(See condition, state, aspect.)

PHEASANT
verbs
domesticate—; flush—; hunt—; —beats; —bellows; —bills; —challenges; —crows; —feigns; —flutters; —glides; —haunts; —jerks; —pants; —roves; —rumbles; —rustles; —scratches; —steals; —struts; —thumps; —thunders; —whirs.
(See fowl, bird.)

PHENOMENA
adjectives
singular; neutral; visible; manifold; historical; sensible; mental; moral; capricious; multitudinous; brilliant; hypnotic; naked; ordinary; sundry; chromatic; scientific; degrading; spiritualistic; subjective; perplexing; interesting; bowling; entrancing; phonetic; characteristic; absurd; hopeful; remote; impressive; extraordinary; sublime;

universal; curious; ambiguous; social; linguistic; transitory; remarkable; unprecedented; striking; continuing; nervous; natural; capital; disturbing; electrical; kindred; unrelated; sporadic; physical; rare; volcanic; analogous; ingenious; mysterious; poetical; psychic; ghastly; monstrous; psychasthenic; expressional.

PHENOMENAL
adverbs
amazingly; incredibly; strangely; oddly; unbelievably; curiously; particularly; extremely; extraordinarily; abnormally; inexplicably; surprisingly; indubitably; matchlessly; superhumanly; superbly; extravagantly; fantastically; grotesquely; magnificently; splendidly; brilliantly; unutterably; indescribably; mysteriously; strikingly.

PHENOMENON
verbs
account for—; adduce—; aggravate—; belittle—; clarify—; elucidate—; exhibit—; explain—; exploit—; marvel at—; observe —; study—; stumble upon—; uncover—; view—; witness—; —amazes; —deludes; —excites; —indicates; —interests; —proves.
(See sight, miracle, fact, event.)

PHILANTHROPIC
adverbs
nobly; ostentatiously; sincerely; generously; admirably; commendably; unusually; notably; admittedly; consistently; dependably; lavishly; cordially; graciously; benignantly; magnanimously; broadmindedly; charitably; amiably; considerately; bounteously; altruistically; naturally; genuinely.

PHILANTHROPIST
adjectives
pretended; distinguished; irresponsible; long-headed; misguided; sundry (pl); disinterested; paralytic; generous; sanguine; supposed.

PHILOSOPHER
adjectives
pragmatic; classical; political; contemporary; quietistic; talkative; pompous; mystic; awe-stricken; physical; amiable; sour-grape; constitutional; disputative; logical; advanced; grave; weary; deistic; famous; dramatic.

verbs
comprehend—; dispute—; —applies; —asserts; —assists; —concludes; —contemplates; —dreams; —guides; —idealizes; — instructs; —observes; —perceives; —perfects; —proves; —records; —regulates; — restores; —searches; —speculates; —studies; —transcends.

(See idealist, naturalist, scientist.)

PHILOSOPHICAL
adverbs
distinctly; notably; comfortably; consistently; brilliantly; wisely; soundly; serenely; imperturbably; calmly; quietly; sagaciously; comfortingly; gravely; temperately; coolly; thoughtfully; placidly; composedly; tranquilly; deeply; profoundly; intelligently; conspicuously; extraordinarily; consummately.

PHILOSOPHIZE (v)
adverbs
sardonically; eloquently; sagely; politically; pompously; mystically; amiably; logically; gravely; ironically; fatalistically.

(See reason, predict.)

PHILOSOPHY
adjectives
inadequate; high; unruffled; healthful; stoical; occult; organized; clammy; comfortable; false; satisfactory; prudential; flippant; half-sportive; shameless; characteristic; educational; primitive; economic; synthetic; seductive; active; natural; fashionable; mental; terrible; positive; classical; calm; fruitful; natural; unoriginal; eclectic; speculative; fatalistic; cruel; worldly; mature; rude; democratic; sustaining; close-webbed; subtle; unprincipled; ruthless; flexible; pessimistic; reminiscent; archaic; seeming; mystical; stern; cynical; droll; lenient; enlightened; ancient; ultra-radical; social; growing; scholastic; coherent; ethnic; haughty; specious; obtrusive; self-centered; intellectual; authentic.

verbs
air—; bespeak—; condemn—; cultivate—; dismiss—; dispense—; dress out—; elaborate—; embody—; emit—; enshrine—; epitomize—; evolve—; execute—; exemplify—; expound—; formulate—; frame—; imbue with—; indulge in—; oppose—; outline—;

postulate—; quote—; rear on—; set forth—; shape—; share—; sift—; sum up—; voice —; —consoles; —edifies; —pervades.

(See ethics, modernism, psychology, knowledge, wisdom, thought.)

PHLEGMATIC
adverbs
apathetically; dully; temperamentally; naturally; habitually; constantly; irritatingly; impossibly; vexatiously; incredibly; strangely; curiously; racially; maddeningly; oddly; imperturbably; indifferently; stoically; impassively; heavily; coldly; callously; hopelessly; incurably; dreadfully; inexplicably; stolidly; stupidly.

PHOSPHORESCENT
adverbs
mysteriously; brilliantly; strangely; curiously; frightfully; unexpectedly; terrifyingly; iridescently; magically; conveniently; advantageously; alarmingly; weirdly; fantastically; grotesquely; evanescently; serviceably; magnificently; splendidly; luridly; glowingly; amazingly.

PHOTOGRAPH
adjectives
existing; cherished; superb; appropriate; candid; telescopic; luxurious; insouciant; instantaneous; mammoth; irrelevant; dramatic; large; clear; intimate; vivid; gripping; rare; distinctive; beautiful; portrait; brilliant; enlarged.

verbs
blur—; enlarge—; exhibit—; expose—; frame—; illustrate with—; pose for—; request—; shade—; shadow—; snap—; superimpose on—; tint—; —adorns; —catches; —depicts; —fades; —flatters; —lies; — pleases; —reflects.

(See illustration, masterpiece, picture, sketch, portrait.)

PHOTOGRAPHER
adjectives
straggling; traveling; famous.

verbs
patronize—; shield from—; train—; —arranges; —s cluster about; —decorates; — drapes; —endeavors; —exposes; —focuses; —operates; —practises; —rejects; —selects; —shades; —shadows; —snaps; —solicits; — tints; —views.

(See artist.)

PHOTOGRAPHY

adjectives

professional; instantaneous; distinguished.

verbs

apply—; dabble in—; practise—; study—; utilize in—; —advances; —aids; —attracts; —awes; —captures; —impresses; —improves; —prints; —progresses.

(See science, art.)

PHOTOPLAY

adjectives

swift-moving; hilarious; serious.

PHRASE

adjectives

witty; explicit; ill; fantastic; tragic; poisonous; pompous; exclamatory; characteristic; vivid; musical; impressive; commanding; scriptural; glib; expressive; striking; occult; holiday; pedantic; appropriate; subtle; historic; cold; ringing; invariable; redoubled; banal; polished; recondite; learned; idiomatic; canting; studied; varying (pl); euphemistic; penetrative; useful; circuitous; handled; labored; judicial; modern; specific; introductory; depressed; hackneyed; catchy; authority-bearing; indispensable; superfluous; euphonious; overworked; courtly; sharp; isolated; sonorous; ingenious; allusive; convenient; homely; stereotyped; adulating; incoherent; perfect; sarcastic; technical; detached; silvery; obnoxious; ecstatic; metaphysical; vivid; familiar; poetic; poignant; grandiloquent; rabbinical; audacious; honeyed; theological; trivial; celebrated; sacred; pensive; plaintive; prolegomenous; empty; well-worn; suspicious; fanciful; eloquent; vibrant; comfortable; pungent; parliamentary; painful; vague; choice; polite; editorial; vile; swinish; ejaculatory; charming; dark; terrible; painted; inapplicable; high-sounding.

verbs

cling to—; create—; cull—; echo—; employ —; enunciate—; mouth—; omit—; pelt with —s; quibble over—; stumble over—; toss —s at; —enchants; —escapes; —falls upon; —haunts; —intrigues; —illustrates; —originates in; —scalds; —signifies; —springs from.

(See epithet, idiom, metaphor, idea, thought.)

PHRASE (v)

adverbs

subtly; concretely; colloquially; tersely; poetically; redundantly; explicitly; fantastically; vividly; scripturally; glibly; appropriately; euphemistically; ingeniously; obnoxiously; technically; fancifully; pungently; editorially.

(See style, express.)

PHRASEOLOGY

adjectives

accustomed; unhappy; diabolical; realistic; ordinary; commonplace.

PHRASING

adjectives

odd; Ciceronian; intelligent.

PHYSICIAN

adjectives

reluctant; renowned; departing; conscientious; competent; helpful; sagacious; incredulous; understanding; distinguished; eminent; respectable; tolerable; observant; overzealous; consecrated; conservative.

verbs

assist—; communicate with—; confer with —; confound—; consult—; inform—; —administers; —counsels; —decrees; —devotes to; —diagnoses; —examines; —guards; —prescribes; —pronounces; —recommends; —rules; —serves; —warns.

(See teacher, nurse, doctor.)

PHYSIOGNOMY

adjectives

unequivocal; faded; capacious.

PHYSIQUE

adjectives

infinitesimal; ungraceful; delicate; insignificant.

verbs

admire—; approve—; cramp—; endanger —; enfeeble—; esteem—; harden—; improve—; mold—; praise—; reduce—; strain —; strengthen—; vivify—; —deteriorates; —sustains; —toughens.

(See constitution, body.)

PIANIST

adjectives

phenomenal; admirable; fascinating; sleepy.

adjectives

grimy; little; tinkling; mechanical; grand; untuned; hideous.

verbs

attune to—; bang on—; beat—; caress—; finger—; instruct on—; perform on—; pound—; practice on—; scale—; strike—; strum on—; —deafens; —distracts; —enchants; —expresses; —peals; —rends; —resounds; —tinkles

(See keyboard, harp, music, banjo.)

verbs

commit to—; enjoy—; festoon—; meet on —; overhang—; paint—; repose on—; rest on—; retire to—; screen—; shade—; —attracts; —cools; —delights; —refreshes; —spreads.

(See pavilion, porch, courtyard.)

verbs

brandish—; drive—; dull—; implant—; inject—; plunge—; ram in—; twist—; wield —; —chips; —chops; —cleaves; —cracks; —disperses; —eliminates; —gashes; — hacks; —loosens; —minces; —pierces; — rips; —severs; —shatters; —splinters; — slits; —strikes; —sunders; —uproots; — wrenches.

(See hatchet, axe, knife, tool.)

adverbs

hastily; painfully; captiously; contentiously; aimlessly; obediently; precariously; laboriously; cautiously; mercifully; argumentatively; democratically; shrewdly.

(See select, choose.)

adjectives

perpetual; prolonged; never-ending; impromptu.

adverbs

conveniently; serviceably; highly; beautifully; advantageously; profitably; usefully; altogether; intelligibly; graphically; effectively; entertainingly; amusingly; accurately; appropriately; suitably.

adjectives

naturalistic; consistent; coordinated; exaggerated; kaleidoscopic; flaming; ineloquent; amorous; portrait; furry; spectacular; muscular; alert; surreptitious; delicate; dazzling; smiling; luminescent; casual; gay; authentic; elucidating; heavenly; amusing; handsome; paltry; striking; charming; improbable; tender; colored; ineffectual; vivid; conventional; scandalous; arresting; constant; wide; unchanged; forbidding; fascinating; living; veracious; touching; poetic; idyllic; affecting; ensemble; monotonous; pathetic; sacred; classical; religious; unrelated; tragic; philanthropic; dramatic; imaginary; lifeless; vitalized; tone; farspreading; intimate; varied; dreary; unattractive; entrancing; ludicrous; truthful; well-painted; jumbled; provocative; lurid; moderate; radiant; dumb; black; horrible; finished; idealized; breathing; accurate; lively; grim; etched; mental; deplorable; incomparable; fresh; gilt; moving; notable; comprehensive; imposing; ghastly; emblematic; melancholy; crimson; degrading; allegorical; verbal; coherent; lovely; worldfamous; unusual; illuminating; creamy; colorful; outstanding; nature; marvelous; remarkable; alluring; suggestive; candid; contemporaneous; immortal; gloomy; delightful; fleeting; cloud; inimitable; priceless; resplendent; bright; stark; impressive; retinal; choice; instantaneous; incredible; unique; interesting; distinct; decorative; imaginary; blurred; depressing; rhetorical; crude; symmetrical; bewitching; hideous; commercial; glowing; realistic; ghostly; unforgettable; fantastic; penitentiary; composite; dreamy.

verbs

animate—; ban—; blur—; cherish—; clarify —; complicate—; conjure up—; convey—to; delineate—; digest—; distort—; dominate —; embellish—; evoke—; execute—; exhibit—; fade from—; fashion—; harmonize with—; intersperse with—s; mar—; obliterate—; relish—; reproduce—; shade—; shadow—; transmute—; —contrasts with; —depicts; —materializes; —reveals; —revolves around; —unfolds; focus upon—.

(See image, impression, film, canvas, illustration, masterpiece, drawing.)

PICTURE (v)

adverbs

vividly; authentically; artistically; brilliantly; faithfully; eloquently; effectually; scandalously; speculatively; fatalistically; ruthlessly; mystically; cynically; speciously; intellectually.

(See draw, sketch.)

PICTURESQUE

adverbs

highly; uncommonly; magnificently; splendidly; undeniably; wildly; unusually; brilliantly; delightfully; grotesquely; fancifully; fantastically; stupendously; immensely; graphically; singularly; uniquely; oddly; gorgeously; superbly; imposingly; resplendently; sublimely; incomparably; unsurpassably; indescribably; unutterably.

PICTURESQUENESS

adjectives

elaborate; undeniable; vivid; superficial; startling; professional; sublime.

PICTURING

adjectives

dreamy; historical; sumptuous.

PIDDLING

adverbs

absurdly; trivially; vexatiously; idly; foolishly; insignificantly; inconsequentially; horribly; senselessly; stupidly; childishly; preposterously; nonsensically; wastefully; inexcusably; witlessly; ineptly.

PIE

adjectives

silken; leathery-looking; delicious; half-demolished; chattering; browned; fresh; tasty; luscious; steaming.

PIECES

adjectives

inanimate; charming; accessory; exhibitionistic; historical; isolated; perilous; truncated; distinctive; lush; suitable; fugitive; exquisite; impressive; singular; eloquent; dangerous; pendent; crooked; inferior; nimble; complicated; bizarre; honest; vivid; unexpected; ponderous; majestic; solemn; sordid; three-piled; imposing; curious; scientific; adventurous; shaped; bold; atrocious; complex; florid; pathetic; obvious; priceless; detached; merited; miscellaneous; miscreant; neglected; striking; conspicuous;

abject; ignoble; deplorable; dilated; volatile; visionary; popular; choral; fruitful; prodigious; gorgeous; wanton; instrumental; floral; character; infernal; sour; heavy-looking; grease-enveloped; first-rate; mere; abominable; delicate; dominating.

verbs

aggregate—; amass—; batter to—; cement —; clutch—; crack into—; crumble into—; crush to—; disintegrate into—; gather—; integrate—; mold—; portion—; smash to—; split into—; unite—; —constitute; —crash; —scatter.

(See chip, fragment.)

PIER

adjectives

elaborate; compound; tropical; much-used.

verbs

anchor at—; buffet—; construct at—; dock at—; destroy—; enclose—; land at—; lash to—; miss—; moor to—; nuzzle into—; offer —; pound—; reserve—; spray—; wash away—; —extends; —projects; —protects; —stretches.

(See landing.)

PIERCE (v)

adverbs

effectually; fatally; mortally; accurately; deeply; ruthlessly; ferociously.

(See stab, bore.)

PIERCING

adverbs

sharply; keenly; acutely; discerningly; accusingly; unpleasantly; disagreeably; unwontedly; incomparably; significantly; suddenly; painfully; uncomfortably; deliberately; astutely; craftily; cunningly; sagaciously; subtly; inescapably.

PIETY

adjectives

deadened; intense; ingrained; filial; quaint; strait; fervent; practical; scrupulous; unaffected; idiotic; humble; punctual; consistent; tempered; intentional; parenthetical; systematic; individual; infant; celestial; instructed.

verbs

commend—; display—; exhibit—; favor—; feign—; influence—; instil—; laud—; practise—; prefer—; pretend—; protest—; re-

semble—; respect—; revere—; —cheers; —converts; —excels; —inspires; —shields.
(See holiness, patriotism, sanctity, kindness, virtue.)

PIG

adjectives
gaping; fastidious; enormous; impious; cadaverous; good-natured; kicking.

verbs
auction—; exhibit—; fatten—; graze—; market—; pen—; slaughter—; stable—; tend—; trough—; —gobbles up; —grunts; —hobbles out; —snorts; —squeals; —stumbles; —swarms; —wallows.
(See hog, cattle, cow, ox.)

PIGEON

adjectives
nimble; plumaged; monogamous; carrier; useful; homing; well-trained.

verbs
drive—s; capture—; market—s; net—s; tame—s; —broods; —consumes; —coos; —s darken; —darts; —s flock; —flushes; —flutters; —gluts; —incubates; —nestles; —strays.
(See bird.)

PIGGISH

adverbs
horribly; brazenly; crassly; grossly; openly; sadly; unashamedly; greedily; rapaciously; voraciously; noisily; terribly; unbelievably; boldly; hoydenishly; brutally; gluttonously; insatiably; selfishly; naturally; inherently; incorrigibly; inexpressibly; definitely.

PIG-HEADED

adverbs
immovably; stupidly; resolutely; implacably; obdurately; stolidly; incurably; inherently; naturally; temperamentally; obstinately; steadily; inexorably; senselessly; unreasonably; distinctly; unmistakably; cruelly; foolishly; absurdly; inanely; pertinaciously; contumaciously; truculently; offensively.

PIGMENT

adjectives
brilliant; bright; waterproof.

verbs
apply—; approve—; combine—; deposit—; employ—; infuse—; insert—; mix—with; secrete—; —blends; —colors; —constitutes; —enhances; —harmonizes; —imbues; —tinges; —tints.
(See paint, color.)

PILE

adjectives
smoldering; vast; honest; unaffected; scholarly; dignified; heterogeneous; monumental; towering; amorphous; sumptuous; colossal; rambling; immense; enormous; unintelligent; gigantic; blazing; aspiring; proud; gothic; voluptuous; chaotic; sunny; frothy; venerable; gloomy; wretched.

verbs
accumulate—; amass—; disperse—; erect—; heap—; knock down—; level—; mow down —; squash—; rummage through—; scatter —; spread—; strew—; upset—; —topples; —totters; —towers; —tumbles; —wanes.
(See heap, fortune, money.)

PILE (v)

adverbs
methodically; indiscriminately; commercially; toweringly; heterogeneously; monumentally.
(See heap, accumulate.)

PILGRIM

adjectives
travel-weary; true-devoted; humble; adoring; devout; earnest; forlorn; fanatical; passionate; disconsolate; white-robed; ambulant.

PILGRIMAGE

adjectives
perilous; nightly; sentimental; mocking; annual; holy; poetical; earthly; reverential; earned; pious; connubial; stormy; unwilling; long-promised; useless; macabre; angry; weary; zealous; previous; peaceful; inspiring; maiden; amorous; enforced.

PILL

adjectives
gilded; bitter; curative; magic.

PILLAR

adjectives
lasting; well-deserving; fiery; shrinking; fluted; rocky; cloudy; towering; immovable;

886

crossed; crowded; decapitated; beauteous; fantastic; shining; vine-clad; unconscious; tottering; petrified; glistening; massive; lone; huge; gigantic; lofty.

PILLORY

verbs
condemn—; deserve—; expose on—; sentence to—; undergo—; whip on—; writhe on—; —agonizes; —disciplines; —enrages; —frightens; —inflicts; —pains; —rebukes; —threatens; —tortures.
(See punishment, torture.)

PILLOW

adjectives
pretty; fringed; skimpy; seaweed; hard; deaf; feverous; unsolaced; dream-haunted; coal; nut-brown; sleepless; downy; humble; tossed; lacy; comforting; nightmared.

verbs
bury in—; grovel in—; heave—; knead—; mash—; prop up with—s; raise on—s; rearrange—; recline on—; relax on—; repose on—; sink into—; support on—; tarry on—; —comforts; —embeds; —envelops; —hushes; —lulls; —supports; —yields.
(See mattress, bed, cushion.)

PILOT

adjectives
desperate; sagacious; visiting; sublime; competent; wartime; licensed; lightning; skilled.

verbs
—communicates with; —conducts; —governs; —guides; —manages; —navigates; —occupies; —prescribes; —regulates; —sounds; —steers; —weathers.
(See guide, helm.)

PILOT (v)

adverbs
daringly; courageously; intrepidly; gallantly; desperately; sagaciously; competently.
(See direct, guide, steer.)

PIMPLES

verbs
break into—; dot with—; eradicate—; pinch —; salve—; squeeze—; treat—; —blotch; —bunch; —deface; —disfigure; —embarrass; —emboss; —mar; —speckle; —spread; —sprout; —swell; —undermine.
(See blemish.)

PIN

verbs
affix with—; attach with—; bristle with—s; jab with—; join with—; load with—s; locate—; mark with—; plant—; secure with —; tuck in with—; —barbs; —connects; —encloses; —fastens; —lodges; —penetrates; —pricks; —scratches; —stabs; —unites.
(See bolt, hook, horn, needle, nail.)

PIN (v)

adverbs
securely; tidily; firmly; mercilessly; relentlessly.
(See fasten, fix.)

PINCH

adjectives
emphatic; warning; relishing; gentlemanly; record; consecutive (pl); imperial; hurting.

PINCH (v)

adverbs
approvingly; emphatically; warningly; playfully; facetiously; cruelly; spitefully; coyly.
(See squeeze, oppress.)

PINCHED

adverbs
miserably; wretchedly; shamefully; woefully; pitiably; pitifully; sadly; haggardly; gauntly; embarrassingly; terribly; helplessly; unusually; unbelievably.

PINE

adjectives
tossing; pillared; mountain; unpolished; longing; runty; serried; lofty; scrubby; gnarled; wind-swept; odorous; immortal; venerable; swaying; gloomy; scattered; palpitating; vocal; dark; unwavering; parasol; scathed; legendary; rocking; storm-battered; pitchy; quick-growing; fragrant; passionless; blackening; glimmering; glutinous.

verbs
hew—; house under—s; —arches; —exudes; —fans; —graces; —moans; —overspreads; —purrs; —rises; —shadows; —shelters; —sighs; —sings; —tips; —tosses; —towers; —waves; —nods.
(See tree.)

PINE (v)

adverbs
miserably; secretly; homelessly; incessantly;

ceaselessly; tragically; woefully; morbidly. (See long, yearn.)

PINING
adjectives
endless; homeless; heartfelt; secret; lonely.

PINION
adjectives
regal; outworn; borrowed; stooping; joyful; daring; downy; soft-tinted; lightning-braided; fearless; delighted; dusky; trembling; celestial; unimpeded; swanlike; silver; timorous; exultant.

PINK
adjectives
pearl; silver; sparkling; shell; salmon; rose; orchid; delicate; frothy; arresting; translucent; soft; raspberry; light; chalk; lavender; childish; gaudy; pathetic.

PINNACLE
adjectives
far-shadowing; massive; queer; eccentric; silent; lofty; lonely; snow-girt; mountainous; skyey.

verbs
achieve—; adorn—; ascend to—; attain—; descend from—; reach—; set on—; —caps; —crowns; —culminates; —juts; —ornaments; —projects; —rises; —supports; —terminates; —tops; —towers
(See tower, height, zenith, summit, peak, spire.)

PIONEER
adjectives
laboring; primal; rugged; celebrated; veritable; hardy; courageous; daring; undaunted; adventurous; venturous.

verbs
accoutre—; arm—; hark back to—; immortalize—; inure—; ridicule—; —blazes; —braves; —confronts; —conquers; —dares; —endures; —envisions; —equips; —faces; —foresees; —plods; —primes; —rigs.
(See colonist, explorer.)

PIONEER (v)
adverbs
daringly; loyally; laboriously; courageous-

ly; undauntedly; intrepidly; vainly; ruggedly; boisterously.
(See brave, defy, dare.)

PIOUS
adverbs
painfully; primly; sedately; priggishly; disgustingly; hypocritically; sincerely; truly; reverently; pharisaically; self-righteously; ostentatiously; suddenly; conveniently; judiciously; astutely; honestly; pretentiously; apparently; manifestly; evidently; strangely; unwontedly; habitually; temperamentally; keenly; remarkably; notably; distinctly; meekly; ardently; fervently; humbly; intensely.

PIPE
(conduit, etc.)
verbs
attach—; block—; clog—; couple—; explore—; flow through—; insert—; join—; lay—; pass through—; pour into—; stream through—; weld—; —bursts; —carries off; —connects; —conveys; —discharges; —emits; —expands; —freezes.
(See hose, conduit, nozzle, duct, drain.)

PIPE
(general)
adjectives
light; short-stemmed; precious; fragrant; rustic; peace; malodorous; masculine-looking; amber; mellow; rich; ripe; giant; fluted; accursed; golden; affluent; seductive; earthen; pastoral; generous; lascivious; faithful; gleeful; smoke-blackened; organ; wide-stopped; foul.

PIPE
(smoking)
verbs
addicted to—; clean—; crust—; draw on—; enjoy—; mislay—; mouth—; pack—; pocket —; scrape—; stuff—; suck on—; —cakes; —cheers; —eases; —fumes; —glows; —mellows; —solaces; —soothes.
(See tobacco, cigar, cigarette.)

PIPING
adjectives
mellow; sad; loud; mild; harmonious; sweet.

888

adjectives

peculiar; quaint; subtle; original; charming; becoming.

PIQUANT

adverbs

saucily; tartly; racily; gaily; charmingly; delightfully; amazingly; highly; entertainingly; interestingly; sharply; pointedly; amusingly; uncommonly; fascinatingly; vigorously; incisively; impressively; pithily; curiously; smartly; distinctly; arrestingly; catchily.

PIQUE

adjectives

momentary; private; definite; petty; pouting.

verbs

—abashes; —aggravates; —crushes; —disgraces; —enrages; —humbles; —humiliates; —irks; —irritates; —mortifies; —provokes; —rankles; —riles(colloq.); —ruffles; —stirs; —strikes; —treads; —vexes; —wounds.
(See anger.)

PIRACY

adjectives

governmental; undiscovered; intellectual; organized.

PIRATE (*v*)

adverbs

ruthlessly; mercilessly; ferociously; dangerously; notoriously; openly.
(See rob, steal, plunder.)

PIRATES

adjectives

ruthless; smiling; merciless; benevolent; ferocious; uncouth; notable; sanctimonious; wrangling; gallant; notorious; bloody; modern.

verbs

execute—; punish—; resist—; —capture; —chase; —conceal; —confiscate; —cruise; —dare; —despoil; —hang; —murder; —pillage; —ply; —plunder; —rove; —scour; —scuttle; —smuggle; —torture; —venture; —violate.
(See robber, criminal, highwayman.)

verbs

arm with—; brandish—; click—; fear—; flourish—; impound—; load—; snatch—; —cracks; —discharges; —frightens; —kills; —pops; —reports; —rings out; —scares; —sounds; —spits fire; —threatens; —volleys; —wounds.
(See gun, machine-gun, musket.)

PIT

adjectives

fiery; bottomless; infernal; ghastly; fathomless; charnel; abysmal; enchanting; round; stupendous; blazing; murky; sepulchral.

verbs

bore—; burrow—; delve into—; drill—; excavate—; explore—; hollow out—; mine from—; pitch into—; plug—; plunge into—; scoop—; seal—; sound—; —gapes; —traps; —undermines; —yields.
(See hole, opening.)

PITCH

adjectives

extreme; creative; alarming; sharp; overstrained; heightened; uncommon; dolorous; breezy; seething; extraordinary; ruinous; varied; nervous.

PITCH (*v*)

adverbs

drunkenly; plaintively; alarmingly; seethingly; nervously; craftily; professionally; unruffledly; prodigiously; rashly.
(See hurl, toss, throw.)

PITCHER
(*baseball*)

adjectives

all-time; great; clever; smooth; easy-working; jerky; wary; unruffled; valuable; undependable; wild; nerveless; crafty.

verbs

bench—; relieve—; —balks; —blazes; —hurls; —nips; —retires; —strikes; —tightens; —toes the slab; —whips; —winds up; —zips; —burns; —controls; —delivers; —fans.
(See player, athlete, fielder.)

PITCHER
(*crockery*)

adjectives

emptied; handleless; capacious.

adverbs

unhappily; distressingly; woefully; grievously; remarkably; uncommonly; disturbingly; undeniably; unusually; indescribably; singularly; extraordinarily; exceedingly.

PITFALL

verbs

avoid—; beset with—; chase into—; conceal—; encounter—; inveigle into—; lure into—; perceive—; perish in—; rescue from—; save from—; suspect—; tumble into—; warn of—; —captures; —ensnares; —overpowers; —surprises; —traps; cover —.

(See ambush, trap, pit.)

PITHY

adverbs

pungently; drily; drolly; remarkably; smartly; absurdly; amusingly; cleverly; wonderfully; amusingly; trenchantly; paradoxically; scintillatingly; brilliantly; wittily; facetiously; curtly; quaintly; humorously; expressively; inimitably; incomparably; succintly.

PITIABLE

adverbs

shockingly; terribly; definitely; deplorably; grievously; miserably; deservingly; truly; intensely; unspeakably; immeasurably; singularly; especially; particularly; peculiarly; unusually.

PITIFUL

adverbs

gently; comfortingly; mildly; wisely; intelligently; sympathetically; helpfully; compassionately; sweetly; indulgently; tolerantly; mercifully; leniently; immensely; unusually; humanely.

PITILESS

adverbs

coldly; cruelly; sternly; implacably; unappeasably; stoically; bitterly; immovably; terribly; horribly; unbelievably; callously; stubbornly; apathetically; mercilessly; inexorably; woefully; ruthlessly; inexcusably; incalculably; incredibly; inexplicably; unaccountably; dreadfully.

adjectives

slender; remaining; contemptible; meager; trifling; bare; worthless; welcome.

verbs

acquire—; allot—; allow—; beg—; derive—; dole out—; donate—; drain—; draw—; exist on—; live on—; provide—; solicit—; yield—; —contents; —suffices.

(See wages, earnings, money, dole.)

PITY

adjectives

anxious; wondering; contemptuous; melancholy; inexpressible; faded; divine; fluttering; sacred; supplicating; confident; thrilling; scornful; indulgent; misapplied; self-forgiving; infant; ineffable; inner; painful; grave; double; treble; strenuous; unsuspected; tender; infinite; shocked; subtle; languid; affectionate; unutterable; pathetic; immense; foolish; solemn; unfortunate; respectful; anguished; unspeakable; reverent; vanquished; little; careless; continued; skinless; natural; human; divine; profound; angelic; malignant; amazed; indignant; spurious; unrighteous.

verbs

betray—; claim—; eye with—; feign—; implore—of; persecute without—; regard with —; shadow with—; stir to—; submerge in —; waste—on; wrap in—; yield to—; —dries up; —expires; —grips; —moves; —smites; —touches; —tortures.

(See compassion, mercy.)

PLACABLE

adverbs

genially; politely; urbanely; genteely; unexpectedly; impressively; fortunately; luckily; pleasantly; surprisingly; tolerantly; mercifully; blandly; indulgently; reasonably; moderately; thoughtfully.

PLACARD

adjectives

vile; scurrilous; screaming.

verbs

affix—; circulate —s; diffuse —s; disperse —s; display on—; disseminate —s; emblazon with—s; post—; publish—s; set up—; —advertises; —announces; —attracts; —broaches; —heralds; —propagates; —screams; —tempts.

(See announcement, advertisement, notice.)

PLACE

adjectives
friendly; delightful; homelike; ideal; comfortable; mournful; war-torn; shrineless; prosperous; logical; halting; unsanctified; tenable; rough; important; joyous; pathless; contrary; prominent; incompatible; rival; lonely; bearable; distinctive; important; dormant; well-chosen; unwholesome; strange; lofty; perilous; objectionable; vulnerable; conspicuous; exalted; native; dwelling; outraged; burial; odd; gloomy; strategic; alleged; ruinous; nestling; shocking; enviable; supreme; sheltered; estimable; noisome; jubilant; wonted; blithe; permanent; wonderful; armed; mossy; foremost; straggling; appointed; seething; knotty; extensive; ancestral; ultimate; floral; popular; accustomed; nocturnal; resting; glorious; unexpected; breeding; venerable; ill-ventilated; foul-smelling; principal; flame-lit; despicable; craggy; prominent; amusing; waste; monastic; undisputed; unbelieving; desert; cozy; distinguished; suitable; subordinate; ill-omened; desolate; legitimate; unsearchable; important; dilapidated; beautiful; historic; pleasant; precarious; ineffable; slippery; well-ordered; tender; garish; big; ghostly; horrible; authentic; undisturbed; colonized; assigned; appropriate; unexpected; forsaken; special; free; easy; ostentatious; genial; fascinating; necessary; distinct; secondary; private; desecrated; hideous; flowery; cherished; noble; holy; definite; rightful; shallow; honorable; inaccessible; hackneyed; provisioned; customary; cheerless; dainty; humble; respective; sacred; shady; sequestered; wretched; parasitic; urbanized; calculated; prominent; languorous; tenement; wondrous; commodious; enormous; typical; predicted; gorgeous; exclusive; considerable; leafy; dreadful; separated; churlish; melancholy; ticklish; impudent; worthy; doleful; far-off; possible; impassible; evident; fearsome; especial; accessible; depressing; horrid; out-of-the-way; green-watered; abiding; enchanted; well-assured; cheerless; retired; window-barred; unique; rude; benighted; equal; convenient; homely; adequate; sacred; remote; proper; tumbledown; miserable; strange; beautiful; subordinate; desired; envied; decided.

verbs
depart from—; disclose—; dislodge from—; empty—; enjoy—in; fall into—; hold—; occupy—; relegate to—of; retain—; seek—; situate in—; snoop about—; transfer from —; usurp—; vacate—.

(See spot, room, locality, space, position, building, town, city.)

PLACE (v)

adverbs
voluntarily; precisely; unwittingly; obligingly; publicly; unreservedly; poetically; honorably; superficially; temporarily; conspicuously; recklessly; judiciously; impulsively; impersonally; tenderly; logically; objectionably; vulnerably; exaltedly; depressingly; accessibly; uniquely; rudely; subordinately.

(See establish, locate.)

PLACID

adverbs
immovably; sweetly; generously; vexatiously; serenely; terribly; imperturbably; fortunately; singularly; particularly; habitually; temperamentally; coolly; resolutely; stoically; philosophically; demurely; submissively; sedately; icily; patiently; remarkably; unexpectedly; surprisingly.

PLACIDITY

adjectives
spiritual; austere; frozen; eternal.

PLAGIARISM

adjectives
phenomenal; criminal; audacious; discovered; unintentional; obvious; deliberate; barefaced; bald.

verbs
accuse of—; resort to—; —apes; —borrows; —emulates; —mirrors; —models; —parallels; —patterns; —poaches; —purloins; —simulates; —sponges; —steals.

(See theft, dishonesty.)

PLAGUE

adjectives
destroying; wasting; ordaining; abhorrent; prevalent; devastating; immedicable; grasshopper; noxious; virulent; noisome; vile; deadly; dreaded; remorseless; incurable.

verbs
conquer—; control—; disperse—; guard against—; inoculate against—; —breaks out; —creeps through; —decimates; —descends

upon; —rages; —ravages; —slays; —swoops upon; —traverses; —wanes.
(See curse, contagion, disease, infection.)

PLAIN

adjectives
alluvial; dewy; pool-studded; olive-plumed; alluring; torrid; fluctuating; capacious; friendless; brown; sunburnt; smiling; vast; barren; central; abounding; twilight; pensive; mournful; sterile; murderous; ravaged; sunny; harvest-shining; upland; high; delightful; skirting; rugged; rocky; celestial; sandy; trackless; melancholy; comforting; circumfluous; featureless; wan; infernal; illimitable; stubborn; ravished; wide-stretching; idol-burdened; rainy; billowy; fertile; cultivated; extensive; terraced; pastoral; variegated; desolate; prostrate; half-dreary; semibarren; extensive; ethereal; tilted; elevated; semibarbaric; sun-dried; dusky; grassy; placid; cactus; happy; watered; ivory; verdurous; unsheltered; empty; tawny; shimmering; ringing; joyous; delicious; immitigable; flower-paved; smiling; sultry; horrible; boundless; grassless; treeless; long; deep; sandy; wide; deluged; native; chequered; somber; iridescent; sun-blistered; moonlit; pensive; windswept; dazzling; fruitful; burning; ringing (pl); shadowed; immortal; horizon-bounded; stubble; dustbeclouded; undulating; extensive; cattle; classic; redolent; broad; dreary; narrow; soaring; temperate.

verbs
cultivate—; dwell in—; follow—; frequent —; inhabit—; level into—; overlook—; people—; roam—; scan—; till—; travel—; wander over—; —extends; —rolls; —stretches; —unfolds; —unrolls.
(See battlefield, valley, country, land, prairie.)

PLAIN

adverbs (*unadorned*)
emphatically; undeniably; pleasantly; hopelessly; significantly; severely; inartistically; monotonously; invariably; chastely; rigorously; unaffectedly; gracelessly; awkwardly; unfortunately; frightfully; hideously; curiously; singularly; horribly; forbiddingly.

PLAIN

adverbs (*clear*)
delightfully; distinctly; graphically; singularly; curiously; brilliantly; obviously; admirably; conveniently; vividly; unmistakably; extraordinarily; commendably; unusually; extremely; ingeniously.

PLAINNESS

adjectives
rigorous; emphatic; dignified; studious; elaborate; becoming; neat.

PLAIN-SPOKEN

adverbs
fearlessly; bluntly; gruffly; courageously; embarrassingly; irritatingly; dangerously; unwisely; foolishly; senselessly; imprudently; indiscreetly; impoliticly; injudiciously; inexpediently; harshly; offensively; absurdly; ineptly; exasperatingly; awkwardly; harshly; ungraciously; extremely; uncommonly; amazingly; outrageously.

PLAINT

adjectives
pathetic; doleful; somber; noisy.

verbs
breathe—; cease—; detect—; endure—; heave—; reiterate—; renew—; sob—; suppress—; throat—; utter—; whine—; —bursts; —distresses; —fades; —greets; —melts; —moves; —wearies.
(See cry, complaint.)

PLAINTIFF

verbs
allot—; award to—; vest in—; —accuses; —alleges; —appeals; —asserts; —blames; —brands; —challenges; —charges; —contends; —claims; —demands; —denounces; —exacts; —implicates; —imputes; —lodges; —prevails; —reproaches; —waives.
(See defendant, lawyer.)

PLAINTIVE

adverbs
deeply; querulously; tearfully; whiningly; mutteringly; sorrowfully; exasperatingly; sadly; pitifully; endlessly; exceedingly; lamentably; superfluously; unduly; monotonously; obscurely.

PLAN

adjectives
architectural; hazy; delectable; comprehensive; ill-contrived; parricidal; revolution-

ary; extempore; logical; homely; deferred; startling; intricate; makeshift; deliberate; concerted; showy; ambitious; feasible; cherished; immediate; tentative; denominational; trivial; careful; elaborate; insecure; sundry (pl); inscrutable; execrable; frugal; mercenary; eternal; complicated; primitive; frantic; oft-advanced; definite; extended; weird; detailed; welfare; harmonious; enthusiastic; proved; insurrectionary; simple; daring; grandiose; unproductive; long-concealed; tyrannical; far-trumpeted; solid; subtle; clean-cut; different; merchandising; unbelievable; profit-sharing; odd; cooperative; sensational; thrilling; guaranteed; confidential; startling; unusual; powerful; business; stimulating; certified; mail-order; exclusive; helpful; money-making; sales; new; easy; amazing; premium; business-building; selling; unique; coupon; original; complete; astounding; trade; starting; consistent; uttered; foolish; futile; extensive; complex; ultra-modern; vacation; treacherous; rational; intimate; exclusive; pensive; equitable; sagacious; low; time; payment; quixotic; indivisible; cohesive; philanthropic; meritorious; respective; apparent; eternal; widespread; treadmill; miscarried; nefarious; strict; consecutive; first-mentioned; coercive; expensive; melodramatic; best-laid; far-seeing; earnest; educational; strategic; standard; maternal; passioned.

verbs
abandon—; adopt—; advance—; analyze—; bolster—; broach—; buttress—; clarify—; concoct—; contemplate—; crystallize—; defeat—; design—; detail—; devise—; discard —; disclose—; divulge—; draft—; embark upon—; enact—; endorse—; engross in—; evolve—; expound—; foil—; formulate—; frame—; hatch out—; improvise—; inaugurate—; junk—; launch—; map out—; mull over—; obstruct—; pattern—on; promulgate —; propound—; ratify—; revamp—; reveal —; revise—; rout—; sidetrack—; snag—; sponsor—; submit—; terminate—; thwart —; upset—; veto—; withdraw—; —advocates; —s coincide; —crumbles; —embraces; —fizzles; —matures.
(See idea, itinerary, intention.)

PLAN (v)
adverbs
fantastically; subtly; magnificently; purposefully; zealously; methodically; tentatively; divinely; deliberately; meticulously; competently; cunningly; daintily; systematically; gloriously; architecturally; comprehensively; intricately; primitively; harmoniously; tyrannically; sensationally; confidentially; sagaciously; philanthropically; meritoriously; nefariously; strategically.
(See scheme, contrive.)

PLANE
adjectives
realistic; conversational; convex; experimental; inclined; reconnoitering; fast; luxurious; powerful; ascending; vertical; emerald; transport; swift; passenger; streamlined; metal; mail; tri-motored.

verbs
bail out of—; bank—; contact—; fuel—; hop (colloq.)—; license—; maroon—; navigate —; pilot—; throttle—; —bores up; —drones; —flashes over; —gleams; —gyrates; —swoops; —takes off; —taxies out; —twists; —whirs; —wings; —zooms.
(See aeroplane.)

PLANET
adjectives
leaden; populous; wheeling; sin-ridden; vexatious; bawdy; glorious; household; ill; sleepy; turbulent; beautious; virginal; glittering; bruised; influential; perturbed; riming; dead; many-mortalled; spinning; sunless; careering.

PLANK
adjectives
grimy; raw; rotting; sturdy; proposed; political; fastened.

PLANNING
adjectives
adroit; unassuming; constructive; thoughtful; tedious; haphazard.

PLANT
adjectives
experimental; sapient; showy; microscopic; companionless; indigenous; remote; thorny; umbelliferous; greedy; naturalized; obstinate; efficient; marsh; vigorous; leguminous; set; aquatic; insectivorous; luxuriant; aromatic; hardy; celebrated; frost-nipped; reduction; wrinkled; branched; parasitic; intruding; stemless; yielding; ill-assorted (pl); infusorial; characteristic; ornamental; enchanting; liliaceous; baccate; happy; esculent; fragrant; nutritious; ignoble; in-

harmonious; succulent; rank; potted; sun-scorched; dwarf; gaudy; umbrageous; established; trailing; rubbed; redolent; long; water; drooping; wind-fertilized; herbaceous; exotic; native; neglected; curious; conventionalized; ballast; submerged; flowering; unsuccessful; ramshackle; precious.

verbs

cultivate—; develop—; hedge—; nurse—; perpetuate—; pollenize—; propagate—; prune—; scatter —s; strangle—; tend—; trim—; uproot—; vitalize—; —bears; —branches; —droops; —emerges; —flourishes; —flowers; —goes dormant; —puts forth; —roots in; —shoots up; —sprouts; —thrives.

(See bulb, herb, ivy, flower, bud, vine, grass.)

PLANT (*v*)

adverbs

triumphantly; solidly; immovably; advantageously; indigenously; vigorously; aquatically; luxuriantly; characteristically; ornamentally; nutritiously; succulently; conventionally.

(See establish, set.)

PLANTATION

adjectives

flourishing; tidewater; well-managed; substantial-looking; communal; artistic; superabundant; rich.

PLANTER

adjectives

eccentric; remote; poverty-stricken; brusque; affluent; large-scale.

PLANTING

adjectives

permanent; spring; high-growing; experimental.

PLAQUE

verbs

border—; decorate—; exhibit—; figure—; hang—; inscribe on—; insert—; polish—; preserve—; reburnish—; reveal—; study—; unveil—; —acclaims; —commemorates; —honors; —inspires; —ornaments; —shines.

(See metal, ornament.)

PLASH

adjectives

appalling; muffled; startled; noisy.

PLASTER

adjectives

pale-hued; sovereign; peeling; moldering.

verbs

apply—; bedaub with—; cast—; dab—; daub—; mix—; repair—; smear—; spread —; stir—; surface—; —adheres; —cements; —cracks; —crumbles; —crusts; —cures; —encases; —faces; —hardens; —overlays; —surfaces; —survives.

(See paste, paint, cement.)

PLATE

adjectives

special; deep; piping-hot; untouched; burdensome; leaden; circular; photographic; burnished; rimless; elastic; lustrous.

verbs

arrange —s; chip—; cram—; lick—; load —; mar—; retrieve—; scour—; shatter—; stack —s; —crashes; —gleams; —s harmonize; —rotates; —shatters; —shines.

(See dish, disk, platter.)

PLATEAU

adjectives

inhospitable; remote; rock-strewn; undulating; extensive; endless; bare; high.

verbs

ascend to—; cover—; culminate in—; form —; traverse—; view from—; —awes; —extends; —fascinates; —inspires; —rises; —skirts; —stretches.

(See mountain, land, plain.)

PLATFORM

adjectives

movable; desolate; aggressive; rampart; terraced; portico; splintered; mosque; skeletonized; party.

verbs

ascend to—; construct—; crowd—; declaim from—; design—; entertain from—; erect —; flit across—; gather 'round—; jam—; help up—; leap upon—; pace—; perform on —; reveal—; squat on—; straggle over—; —extends; —harbors; —projects; —protects; —rises; —shelters.

(See deck, stage, floor.)

PLATITUDE

adjectives
pompous; sugared; old; theoretic; stale; worthless.

verbs
avoid —s; condemn—; excuse—; fall into —; hide under—; indulge in—; prate —s; take refuge in—; twaddle in—; —bores; — depresses; —dulls; —exasperates; —irks; — lulls; —tires; —vexes; —wearies.
(See proverb, maxim.)

PLATONIC

adverbs
coolly; strictly; altogether; supposedly; perhaps; utterly; amiably; studiously; sedately; thoughtfully; contemplatively; philosophically; calmly; tranquilly; stoically; soberly; demurely; presumably; dispassionately; disinterestedly; decorously; decently; honestly; virtuously; ridiculously; chastely.

PLATONISM

adjectives
delicate; refined; desirable; unsatisfactory.

PLATTER

adjectives
hideous; huge; well-filled; curious.

verbs
arrange —s; garnish—; glean from—; load —; replenish—; stack —s; support—; — crashes; —gleams; —shatters; —sizzles.
(See dish, plate.)

PLAUDITS

adjectives
anticipated; derogatory; noisy; sincere; deserved.

PLAUSIBILITY

adjectives
solemn; delusive; remote; scant; minute.

verbs
admit—; allow—; bear out—; commend—; convince of—; demonstrate—; doubt—; gloss over—; harbor—; lend—; maintain—; mince—; overestimate—; plead—; warrant —; —defends; —enables; —reconciles.
(See sincerity, integrity.)

PLAUSIBLE

adverbs
scarcely; altogether; extremely; manifestly;

reasonably; highly; glibly; apparently; craftily; adroitly; pretentiously; remotely; deceptively; evasively; subtly; cleverly; remarkably; indisputably.

PLAY (*general*)

adjectives
amorous; much-performed; immortal; informal; infant; unfair; melodramatic; morality; careless; idle; fitful; miracle; steady; dignified; devilish; painful; boisterous; prismatic; swift; touching; tempestuous; superficial; fantastic; foul; hampered; harmless; firing; delightful; blithe; imaginative; heedless; stately; heroic; illimitable; desperate; unmatched; prophetic; varying; vivid; frivolous; stodgy; unusual; freak; ceaseless; deft; interminable; tragic; somber; witless; ambitious; wretched; immoral; mutual; brawling; rousing; petty; thin; diplomatic; meaningless; jocund; contemporary; clever; dubious; radical; cut-and-thrust; clumsy; uncontrollable; well-arranged; rapid; supernatural.

PLAY (*theatrical*)

verbs
acclaim—; attend—; commend—; criticize —; revive—; sponsor—; stage—; —bores; —charms; —diverts; —endears; —grips; — holds forth at; —impresses; —intrigues.
(See comedy, humor, opera, movie, melodrama, performance, game, sport, recreation, exercise, fun, amusement.)

PLAY (*v*)

adverbs
fervidly; cleverly; amorously; informally; boisterously; tempestuously; witlessly; blithely; frivolously; immorally; idly; brawlingly; jocundly; clumsily; angelically; capriciously; fantastically; seductively; incomparably; demurely; caressingly; adroitly; recklessly; melodiously; diligently; exquisitely.
(See frolic, romp.)

PLAYED-OUT

adverbs
altogether; finally; pitiably; entirely; miserably; helplessly; pathetically; needlessly; strangely; curiously; wretchedly; alarmingly; completely; undoubtedly; sincerely; utterly.

PLAYER

adjectives
sturdy; accurate; wandering; steely-finger-

ed; ardent; comprising; incompetent; impecunious; phenomenal; orchestral; strolling; professional; inspired; skilled; shrewd; nonchalant.

verbs
cast —s; cheer —s; encore—; "razz"—; recruit —s; spur —s on; star—; subsidize —s; —amuses; —charms; —delights; —dramatizes; —emotes; —enacts; —endears; —entertains; —impresses; —magnetizes; —overacts; —portrays; —redeems; —rehearses; —supports.
(See athlete, actor, musician, etc.)

PLAYFUL
adverbs
rapturously; delightfully; teasingly; ecstatically; happily; amiably; annoyingly; sportively; friskily; amusingly; brightly; vivaciously; archly; coltishly; childishly; amazingly; frolicsomely; merrily.

PLAYFULNESS
adjectives
dignified; reverent; impetuous; elephantine; overburdened; half-serious; quizzical; ferocious; satirical; buoyant; effervescent.

PLAYGROUND
adjectives
endless; city; needed; crowded; well-equipped.

PLAYING
adjectives
unwitting; coloratura; brilliant; ingenious.

PLAYMATE
adjectives
sweet; desirable; agreeable; well-matched (pl); boisterous.

PLAYTHING
adjectives
broken; coarse; colored.

PLAYWRIGHT
verbs
acclaim—; award to—; criticize—; honor —; laud—; recognize—; —caters to; —composes; —contributes; —creates; —designs; —dramatizes; —impresses; —formulates; —offers; —thrives.
(See dramatist, artist, writer, author.)

PLEA
adjectives
suggestive; eloquent; dastard; masterly; eternal; half-stifled; unmoral; impassioned; specious; irrational; pettifogging; ingenious; common; special; confederate.

verbs
address—; anticipate—; endorse—; file—; heed—; impair—; justify—; necessitate—; oppose—; press—; protest—; put aside—; respond to—; satisfy—; support—; witness —; —penetrates; —softens; —touches; —urges.
(See apology, allegation, excuse, prayer.)

PLEAD (*v*)
adverbs
eloquently; persuasively; convincingly; vehemently; indignantly; ostensibly; earnestly; brokenly; meekly; despairingly; touchingly.
(See beg, entreat.)

PLEADING
adjectives
patient; fervent; humble; vain; disinterested; impassioned; guilty; incessant.

PLEASANT
adverbs
consistently; extremely; essentially; sweetly; gratifyingly; courteously; placidly; gravely; unfailingly; graciously; smilingly; cordially; quietly; remarkably; ostentatiously; singularly; charmingly; genuinely; sincerely; unaffectedly; jocosely; whimsically; playfully; facetiously; delightfully; maturely; politely; waggishly; openly; heartily; humorously; scrupulously; enchantingly; engagingly; altogether; urbanely; obligingly; good-humoredly; fearlessly; furtively.

PLEASANTRIES
verbs
banter—; dally with—; enjoy—; exchange —; feast on—; perpetuate—; school in—; sport—; —cheer; —delight; —divert; —ease; —engage; —entertain; —impart; —solace; —titillate.
(See banter, jest.)

PLEASANTRY
adjectives
indigestible; familiar; humoristic; formal; uncouth; ill-timed; fluent; bland; coarse; colloquial.

PLEASE (v)

adverbs

graciously; exceedingly; bewitchingly; inwardly; graciously; instinctively; aesthetically; fleetingly; sensuously; momentarily; blithely; grossly; legitimately; voluptuously; frankly; thrillingly; salaciously.

(See cheer, satisfy.)

PLEASED

adverbs

highly; graciously; exceedingly; momentarily; inordinately; frankly; openly; obviously; extremely; uncommonly; happily; proudly; ineffably; naturally; visibly; noticeably; marvellously; overwhelmingly; utterly; inexpressibly.

PLEASURABLE

adverbs

entirely; delightfully; hilariously; refreshingly; utterly; extremely; surprisingly; unexpectedly; strikingly; acceptably; measurably; moderately; actually; charmingly; splendidly; distinctly.

PLEASURE

adjectives

childish; fleeting; wanton; fearful; personal; supreme; playful; sensual; distinct; extraordinary; faithless; uninterrupted; gross; noisy; birdlike; frank; exalted; sweet; uninstructive; cordial; wild; pensive; agonizing; domestic; private; glorious; cruel; profligate; darling; innocent; unnecessary; tranquillizing; worthy; quiet; infinite; dizzy; sportsmanlike; fantastic; firm; rife; stern; fashionable; youthful; illicit; deceiving; tasteless; sheer; wingless; palling; malicious; guilty; multitudinous (pl); forbidden; grievous; untold; earth-born; selfish; peculiar; girlish; dangerous; melancholy; divine; delicate; ferocious; malignant; headlong; unrevealed; solid; unspeakable; tickling; strange; inoffensive; sensible; quickening; prodigious; infantile; warm; refined; gentle; glittering; curious; sweet; wincing; honest; personal; toiling; unmixed; eternal; giddy; voluptuous; indescribable; puerile; gracious; sensitive; unalloyed; unfeigned; mean; proud; exquisite; idle; profound; monotonous; joint; visible; vivid; scanty; unglorious; sincere; smoking; legitimate; pulsing; mischievous; frank; unabating; questionable; thrilling; frequent (pl); inexpressible; false; compensating; tenfold; primary; royal; grim; mysterious; proper;

simple; hollow; luxurious; profound; petty; monotonous; growing; delicious; dreadful; heartfelt; wholesome; unmeasured; persisting; perishing; agitating; secret; alluring; attendant; calm; celestial; varied; blithe; queer; perpetual; singular; base; harmless; avid; unearned; unreproved; infinite; intellectual; sunny; momentary; solemn; fiendish; mournful; unblinking; costless; kind; evident; prickling; bygone; faint; positive; piquant; sensuous; secondary; melancholy; ecstatic; vicious; malicious; macabre; unremembered; perverse; pure; alien; mere; silent; admirable; unadulterated; fermenting; unsubstantial; dissolute; intense; undisguised; natural.

verbs

addicted to—; afford—; bask in—; dampen —; derive—from; deprive of—; drink up—; enhance—; experience—; forego—; heighten —; indulge in—; partake of—; prolong—; pursue—; rejoice in—; relish—; resign—; sacrifice—; smile in—; squirm in—; taste —; weary of—.

(See gratification, happiness, gladness, delight, enjoyment.)

PLEBEIAN

adverbs

altogether; distinctly; unexpectedly; surprisingly; naturally; inevitably; terribly; pathetically; loudly; roughly; meanly; vexatiously; indecorously; unendurably; singularly; strangely; oddly; overwhelmingly; hopelessly.

PLEDGE

adjectives

sacred; temperance; tender; written; decided; solemn; terse; uncompromising; positive; eternal; uttered; indefinite; uncertain; reliable; unredeemed; noble.

verbs

accept—; administer—; contract—; enter into—; exact—; forfeit—; honor—; offer—; pawn—; redeem—; repudiate—; respect—; subscribe to—; undertake—; violate—; — assures; —binds; —commits; —guarantees; —secures; —ties; —warrants.

(See covenant, agreement, promise.)

PLEDGE (v)

adverbs

solemnly; mutually; enthusiastically; sacredly; tenderly; uncompromisingly; eternally;

definitely; reliably; nobly; nominally; gallantly.

(See promise, assure.)

PLENTIFUL

adverbs

reasonably; unexpectedly; presumably; luxuriantly; scarcely; lavishly; abundantly; adequately; exuberantly; profusely; sufficiently; immeasurably; incalculably; providentially; mercifully; fortunately; luckily; opportunely; auspiciously; happily.

PLENTY

adjectives

admired; wanton; boarded; wasted; unused.

verbs

bless with—; bristle with—; desire—; obtain —; produce—; reign in—; scatter—; shower —; swim in—; wallow in—; wish for—; —abounds; —flows; —teems.

(See abundance, affluence.)

PLIABLE

adverbs

conveniently; opportunely; reasonably; extremely; scarcely; fortunately; luckily; hardly; somewhat; adaptably; suitably; easily; advantageously; comfortably; readily; usefully; measurably; moderately; adequately; remarkably; marvellously; uncommonly.

PLIGHT

adjectives

lamentable; forsaken; sorry; ill; admirable; evil; pathetic; patient; chronic; grievous; shameful; pitiable; dolorous; sad; doleful; sorrowful; unfortunate.

verbs

betray—; exploit—; favor—; foster—; muse on—; reduce to—; swear to—; vow to—; — alarms; —assures; —binds; —contracts; —depresses; —guarantees; —puzzles; — secures; —shocks.

(See condition, predicament, state.)

PLOD

adjectives

painful; prosaic; barefoot.

PLOD (v)

adverbs

contentedly; monotonously; wearily; tire-

lessly; mechanically; ceaselessly; prosaically; steadily; dejectedly; stupidly.

(See tramp, trudge.)

PLODDING

adverbs

patiently; insistently; steadily; doggedly; stubbornly; stolidly; uncomplainingly; laboriously; resolutely; determinedly; admirably; commendably; hopefully; resignedly; firmly; staunchly; unwaveringly; tenaciously; perseveringly; undauntedly; unswervingly; courageously.

PLOT

adjectives

exaggerated; formidable; comprehensive; dramatic; sandy; insidious; tyrannical; thin; thickening; naughty; grassy; murderous; lurid; audacious; inhuman; marshy; detestable; ill-omened; unfrequented; complicated; daisied; infernal; precious; horrible; pretty; fertile; neglected.

verbs

abet—; concoct—; construct—; cook up (colloq.)—; crush—; disclose—; entangle—; fancy—; found—on; frill—; garnish—; get wind of—; harmonize—; hatch—; implicate —; invent—; nip—; plunge into—; resolve —; spring—; summarize—; unmask—; weave—; —derives from; —generates; — smacks of.

(See argument, intrigue, conspiracy.)

PLOT (v)

adverbs

devilishly; maliciously; grimly; infernally; diabolically; formidably; insidiously; tyrannically; audaciously; inhumanly; detestably; perniciously; traitorously; seditiously.

(See scheme, machinate.)

PLOTTER

verbs

exile—; uncover—; —circumvents; —concocts; —contrives; —designs; —devises; — frames; —hatches; —intrigues; —manoeuvres; —overreaches; —schemes; —stoops; — undermines; —snatches

(See conspirator.)

PLOUGH (v)

adverbs

extensively; seasonally; laboriously; deeply; annually.

(See dig, labor.)

PLOVER

adjectives
graceful; scudding; snowy-winged.

PLOW

adjectives
flying; sulky; useful; ancient; improved.

verbs
employ—; equip with—; —bites; —breaks; —cuts; —delves; —digs; —furrows; —grooves; —intrudes; —loosens; —prepares; —uncovers; —wedges; —weeds.

PLUCK

adjectives
invincible; gallant; amazing; redoubtable; unusual; gigantic; great; noticeable.

PLUCK (v)

adverbs
petulantly; surreptitiously; courageously; agitatedly; idiotically; industriously; thievishly; haphazardly.
(See pick, pull.)

PLUCKY

adverbs
unbelievably; unusually; resolutely; naturally; inherently; habitually; remarkably; marvellously; uncommonly; amazingly; courageously; recklessly; determinedly; gallantly; valiantly; intrepidly; undauntedly; stoutly; manfully; tenaciously; indomitably.

PLUG

verbs
cram—into; drive—into; insert—; remove —; tap—; —bars; —blocks; —chokes; —dams; —obstructs; —prevents; —resists; —seals; —stuffs; —traps.
(See stopper.)

PLUG (v)

adverbs
tightly; effectually; firmly; completely; wholly; satisfactorily; efficiently.
(See plod, work.)

PLUMAGE

adjectives
splendid; fantastic; rich-colored; peculiar; rustling; lacy; glossy; entrancing; iridescent; black; glistening; glittering; ribboned; rosy; light; fluttersome; brilliant; demure; unmatchable.

verbs
adjust—; admire—; bear—; bunch—; display—; preen—; prime—; ruffle—; rumple —; smooth—; —adorns; —bedecks; —decorates; —embellishes; —glitters; —nods; —ornaments; —tufts.
(See mane, feather.)

PLUMBING

verbs
approve—; condemn—; criticize—; demolish—; display—; examine—; improve—; install—; lack—; modernize—; renovate—; repair—; sanction—; tear—down; wrench —apart; —sanitizes.
(See pipe.)

PLUME

adjectives
idle; stooping; dancing; waving; funeral; fantastic; sunny; bronze; striped; straining; advanced; rustling; sable; fancy; shining; magnificent; gay; dripping; resinous; fiery; snowy; graceful; shaken; tossing.

PLUMP

adverbs
delightfully; desirably; commendably; terribly; pleasantly; admirably; childishly; overly; unhappily; chubbily; stalwartly; strappingly; thumpingly; extraordinarily; remarkably; charmingly; daintily; rosily; exquisitely; pleasingly.

PLUMPNESS

adjectives
appreciable; unwanted; stodgy; awkward; pleasant.

PLUNDER

adjectives
nefarious; hideous; indiscriminate; winged; licentious; accumulated; plentiful; barbarous; piratical.

verbs
abstain from—; abhor—; acquire—; bag—; commit—; conceal—; convey—; locate—; seize—; share—; smuggle—; submit to—; transfer—; uncover—; —despoils; —ravages; —strips.
(See bribery, loot.)

PLUNDER (v)

adverbs
rapaciously; flagrantly; nefariously; hide-

ously; indiscriminately; barbarously; piratically; lustfully; dictatorially.
(See rob, steal.)

PLUNGE
adjectives
occasional; desperate; constant (pl); useless; despised; sounding.

PLUNGE (v)
adverbs
rashly; daringly; heavily; wildly; impetuously; determinedly; fiercely; violently; desperately.
(See dive, fall, drop.)

PLURALIST
adjectives
splendid; blatant; unblushing.

PLURALITY
verbs
abandon—; amass—; attract—; attribute— to; elect by—; pile up—; question—; require —; secure—; seek—; solicit—; stem—; — chooses; —decides; —determines; —expresses; —follows; —judges; —patronizes.
(See vote, majority, multitude.)

PLUSH
adjectives
moth-eaten; restful.

PLY (v)
adverbs
industriously; constantly; intermittently; diligently; vigorously; ambitiously; unweariedly; indefatigably.
(See work, apply.)

POCKET
adjectives
greedy; sagging; redundant; ragged; attenuated; hidebound; closed; warm; well-filled.

verbs
accumulate in—; button—; charge—with; conceal in—; deposit in—; dig in—; dislodge from—; draw from—; extract from —; fumble in—; grope in—; joggle in—; line—s; quarter in—; tuck in—; —bulges; —jingles; —swells.
(See basket, reservoir, hold.)

POD
verbs
bruise—; crack—; empty—; split—; — binds; —conceals; —defends; —discloses; —encases; —encloses; —enfolds; —faces; —guards; —preserves; —protects.
(See cover.)

POEM
adjectives
poisonous; excellent; patriotic; fantastic; tiny; ancient; typical; conventional; dramatic; simple; mystical; admirable; sentimental; immortal; negligible; genealogical; centenary; lyrical; remarkable; non-dramatic; epic; licentious; heroic; narrative; noble; painful; artificial; humorous; divine; devotional; unified; pastoral; deeply-felt; rare; imperishable; elegiac; Homeric; abiding; commemorative; mere; quizzical; contemplative; puerile; didactic; striking; elegant; personal; impressive; brief; historical; unequal; elevated; preposterous; faulty; primitive; laudatory; symphonic; curious; insipid; amatory; soulless; philosophical; dainty; unpopular; psychological.

verbs
acclaim—; appreciate—; chorus—; create —; evolve—; peruse—; rewrite—; work into—; —amuses; —appeals; —commemorates; —conveys; —depicts; —diverts; — echoes; —expresses; —flows; —inspires; — invokes; —rings; —romances; —sings; — transfuses; —voices.
(See poetry, hymn, ballad, incantation, ditty, epigram, romance, sonnet, dirge, ballad.)

POESY
adjectives
perennial; heaven-bred; inspired.

POET
verbs
acclaim—; appreciate—; award to—; chide —; criticize—; immortalize—; interpret—; laud—; quote—; recognize—; —beautifies; —builds; —chants; —commemorates; — composes; —contributes; —designs; —eternizes; —experiences; —expresses; —impresses; —laments; —offers; —redeems; — rimes; —scans; —sings; —teaches; — thrives; —versifies.
(See author, artist, creator, idealist, novelist.)

POETIC

adverbs

distinctly; delightfully; musically; rhythmically; deeply; melodiously; abstrusely; notably; sublimely; pleasantly; exquisitely; ingeniously; unexpectedly; truly; eloquently; vigorously; passionately; glowingly; impressively; fancifully.

POETRY

adjectives

pastoral; clear; academic; allegorical; visionary; smooth; respectable; lyrical; essential; faulty; satirical; joyful; dramatic; descriptive; subservient; romantic; charlatan; tragic; epic; devotional; delicate; meditative; riotous; spiritual; imaginative; impassioned; bewildering; elder; tender; high-mannered; dreamy; austere; barbarous; glorious; mournful; vague; original.

verbs

conceive—; cultivate—; deliver—; like—; interpret—; mold—; resort to—; toy with —; —charms; —conveys; —delights; — eases; —elevates; —enchants; —endures; —flourishes; —humanizes; —inspires; — narrates; —reflects; —reveals; —softens; — soothes; —springs from.

(See literature, poem, story, sonnet, etc.)

POETS

adjectives

derivative; lofty; erotic; impecunious; contemporary; Ionian; notable; capricious; romantic; quick-conceiving; prominent; sublime; spontaneous; true; subtle; worthy; distinguished; satirical; celebrated; philosophical; tragic; well-known; spasmodic; scurrilous; ecclesiastical; saturnine; laureled; descriptive; sensitive; earnest; prattling; exquisite; synthetic; budding; specific; denominated; authentic; secular; pining; humorous; amorous; lyrical; peasant; ingenious; heathen; isolated; playful; religious; illustrious; mature; esteemed; vernacular; psychic; classical.

POIGNANT

adverbs

intensely; sharply; singularly; curiously; strangely; inscrutably; unexpectedly; apparently; manifestly; painfully; smartly; remarkably; strikingly; unbearably; trenchantly; vividly; suddenly.

POINT
(feature, issue, question, etc.)

verbs

admit—; allow—; attend to—; carry—; concede—; debate—; dispose of—; dodge—; drive home—; dwell on—; emphasize—; grant—; illustrate—; interrogate—; labor —; miss—; pursue—; reinforce—; rule on —; settle—; stress—; sympathize on—; — illustrates; —s interlock.

(See angle, feature, issue.)

POINT
(general)

adjectives

standard; essential; peevish; standing; transitional; original; sore; favorable; vulnerable; geographical; objective; delicate; varying; vindictive; fundamental; advantageous; knotty; statistical; luminous; trivial; weighty; crucial; rallying; superficial; physical; culminating; controverted; dazzling; desired; fiery; inconsiderable; sentimental; thorny; unsavory; noteworthy; narrow; mooted; burning; converging; unguarded; significant; well-selected; worldly; practical; inhuman; chivalric; principal; systematic; pivotal; assailable; prominent; equinoctial; strategic; contrary; suggestive; radiant; favorable; slippery; salient; aesthetic; artistic; remote; material; corrective; designated; matrimonial; elevated; indecomposable; critical; exposed; statistical; disputed; changeless; home-coming; pathetic; conceded; preconceived; minute; projecting; crowning; bitter; unimportant; knotty; decisive; sandy; epigrammatic; rallying; preliminary; characteristic; supreme; saturation; absurd; terminal; contentious; dubious; heterodox; unendurable; stagnant; impressive; dangerous; intangible; inappreciable; restricted; cardinal; determinable; ludicrous; speculative; ample; technical; yawning.

POINT (v)

adverbs

triumphantly; mysteriously; significantly; timidly; conclusively; mournfully; excitedly; scornfully; directly; peevishly; ludicrously.

(See indicate, designate.)

POINTED

adverbs

cruelly; barbarously; hatefully; bitterly; caustically; sarcastically; unmistakably; personally; meanly; maliciously; venomously;

901

impolitely; viciously; intentionally; deliberately; rudely; roughly; ungraciously; bluntly; brusquely; dogmatically; significantly; curtly; crisply; sententiously; bitingly; incisively; impressively.

POINTLESS
adverbs
pitifully; feebly; inanely; fatuously; inconsequentially; insignificantly; monotonously; ponderously; banally; trivially; vaguely; flatly; insipidly; endlessly; foolishly; vacuously; ridiculously; intolerably; tiresomely; absurdly.

POISE
adjectives
calm; serene; contemplative; aristocratic; swerveless; exquisite; intellectual; aloof; physical; domineering; admirable; culminating; coquettish; calculating; mental; dangerous; sturdy; equal.

verbs
acquire—; admire—; affect—; attain—; envy—; exhibit—; lack—; maintain—; practise—; recover—; regard with—; restore—; school in—; shatter—; value—; —assures; —conquers; —controls; —impresses; —polishes; —tones
(See equilibrium, ease, balance, stability.)

POISE (v)
adverbs
serenely; delicately; calmly; daringly; exquisitely; coquettishly; rashly; courageously; undauntedly.
(See balance, pose.)

POISON
adjectives
bottom; virulent; simmering; consuming; offensive; infusing; unseasonable; vanquished; occidental; insidious; intoxicating; infidel; rank; putrefactive; deadly; corrosive; inorganic; delicious; innocuous; slow-working.

verbs
absorb—; antidote—; assimilate—; control—; counteract—; distil—; eliminate—; excrete—; exude—; impregnate with—; infect with—; inject—; neutralize—; reek with—; —accumulates; —circulates; —ravages.
(See germicide, venom, drug.)

POISON (v)
adverbs
insidiously; murderously; premeditatively; maliciously; organically; corrosively; intoxicatingly; basely; diabolically.
(See kill, murder.)

POISONOUS
adverbs
mildly; slightly; fatally; dangerously; mortally; alarmingly; seriously; dreadfully; noxiously; maliciously; venomously; viciously; pestilentially; curiously; unexpectedly; singularly; miserably; manifestly; obviously; invariably.

POKE (v)
adverbs
coyly; tantalizingly; brutally; warningly; cautiously; teasingly; facetiously; delicately; humorously; amorously.
(See thrust, excite.)

POLE
adjectives
boreal; slender; curtained; terrestrial; resonant; telephone; splintered; austral.

POLEMIC
adjectives
staunch; commonplace; bitter; ruthless.

POLICE
adjectives
adequate; lynx-eyed; executive; ubiquitous; ornamental; interested; ineffective; rustic; ingenious; indignant.

verbs
commend—; detail—to; evade—; tangle with—; —accost; —apprehend; —clash; —corner; —escort; —espy; —intimidate; —patrol; —protect; —raid; —regulate; —scout; —trace; —track down; —trail; —trap; —warn.
(See detective, constable.)

POLICY
adjectives
obvious; parsimonious; aggressive; tyrannous; questionable; conservative; enlightened; peace; paltry; time-honored; ecclesiastical; dilatory; prudent; insidious; comprehensive; inconsistent; foreign; cherished; let-alone; well-defined; vacillating; broad; immediate; reasonable; ruinous; cruel; attractive; shameful; honorable; intricate;

liberal; magnanimous; intriguing; devious; public; vicious; dissimulating; beneficent; straightforward; emancipation; subsequent; hostile; medium; prevailing; handsome; odious; maritime; ostensible; shortsighted; Fabian; relentless; habitual; abhorrent; all-important; oppressive; unsound; studied; sound; earnest; logical; determined; rigid; dominant; alternate; consistent; strategic; uniform; alterant; unwavering; reactionary; evasive; effective; crafty; exclusive; kindred; taxing; fiscal; unadulterated; national; increasing; effective; committal; economic; constant.

verbs

abandon—; adhere to—; adjust—; adopt—; advance—; alter—; amend—; chart—; cling to—; defend—; define—; denounce—; dictate—; dominate—; draft—; effectuate—; embark on—; endorse—; enforce—; excoriate—; execute—; expound—; fashion—; forge—; formulate—; frame—; frown upon —; inaugurate—; initiate—; institute—; justify—; modify—; orient—; overhaul —ies; propound—; pursue—; reflect—; resolve—; reverse—; shape—; sponsor—; — embitters; —hinges on; —prevails; —wobbles.

(See principle, theory, course, prudence, procedure.)

POLISH

adjectives
patrician; massive; gleaming; sleek; high.

POLISH (v)

adverbs
painstakingly; superficially; vigorously; industriously; gleamingly; glitteringly; highly; splendidly.
(See rub, smooth.)

POLISHED

adverbs
fashionably; smoothly; suavely; urbanely; socially; smugly; aristocratically; expertly; adroitly; graciously; extraordinarily; admirably; remarkably; incomparably; unsurpassably; matchlessly; splendidly; gorgeously; magnificently; brilliantly; conspicuously; arrogantly; delightfully; charmingly; commendably; elegantly; unctuously; blandly; gravely; affably; gallantly; ingratiatingly.

POLITE

adverbs
dutifully; punctiliously; meticulously; particularly; excessively; deliberately; resolutely; determinedly; naturally; graciously; amiably; delightfully; properly; carefully; cautiously; nervously; awkwardly; clumsily; reluctantly; chivalrously; gallantly; ingratiatingly; suavely; smoothly; urbanely; unctuously; adroitly; formidably; scrupulously; ridiculously; absurdly; remarkably; courteously; obsequiously; affably.

POLITENESS

adjectives
exaggerated; veneered; formidable; pretty; unwavering; hollow; unwearying; determined; freezing; cold; ironical; oriental; indefatigable; grave; affected; insolent; oily; strained; scrupulous; refined; icy.

verbs
applaud—; breach—; conform to—; commend—; enjoy—; exhibit—; laud—; practise—; praise—; struggle with—; —appeals; —conciliates; —pleases; —polishes; —refines.

(See civility, courtesy, gallantry.)

POLITICAL

adverbs
artfully; shrewdly; strategically; craftily; subtly; obviously; manifestly; naturally; keenly; cleverly; necessarily; cunningly; deeply; profoundly; intriguingly; slyly; insidiously; astutely; adroitly; sensibly; judiciously; prudently; soberly; warily; watchfully; expediently; inveterately; wisely; cannily.

POLITICIAN

adjectives
practical; artful; budding; shrewd; designing; unguided; unfledged; malevolent; noisy; timorous; kid-gloved; cunning; ordinary; mechanical; vulgar; hoary; practical; cynical; peanut; conservative; corrupt; cheap; astute; impecunious; unprincipled; redoubtable; superficial; radical.

verbs
corrupt—; oust—; pay tribute to—; support —; —addresses; —administers; —conducts; —contrives; —controls; —directs; —governs; —manages; —orates; —orders; —panders to; —presides; —solicits; —steers.
(See boss, demagogue, legislator.)

POLITICS

adjectives
contemporary; inculcating; domestic; fundamental; partisan; sentimental; crooked; fading; corrupt; practical; economic; financial; moral; befuddled; stormy; puzzled.

verbs
bury in—; dabble in—; delve in—; immerse in—; inveigh against—; meddle with—; muddle in—; participate in—; plunge into —; prostitute—; retire from—; shun—; steer clear of—; tangle with—; verse in—.
(See government, management, affairs, business.)

POLITY

adjectives
primitive; well-ordered.

POLL

adjectives
taxable; voting; straw; nation-wide.

POLLEN

adjectives
wind-blown; insect-borne; widespread.

verbs
carry—; diffuse—; disperse—; disseminate —; dust with—; gather—; issue—; sensitize to—; shed—; sprinkle—; strew—; —drifts; —fertilizes; —germinates; —scatters; —seeds; —sows.

POLLS

verbs
bribe at—; crowd—; entice to—; flock to—; guard—; herd to—; preside at—; rally to —; regulate—; station at—; swamp—; visit —; —protect; —register.

POLLUTED

adverbs
foully; utterly; slightly; poisonously; unnecessarily; infamously; noticeably; visibly; obviously; manifestly; evidently; mysteriously; criminally; dangerously; alarmingly; seriously; pestilentially; odiously; distressingly; illegally; horribly; abominably.

POLLUTION

adjectives
horrible; fat; moral; abhorrent; waterside.

verbs
befoul with—; complain of—; expose to—; labor under—; reproach for—; —brands: —corrupts; —defaces; —defiles; —degrades; —disgraces; —harms; —impairs; —infects; —mars; —offends; —overshadows; —pillages; —saps; —scathes; —shames; —stains; —sullies; —taints.
(See impurity, corruption.)

POLYGAMY

adjectives
praiseworthy; desirable; indiscriminate; outlawed.

POMP

adjectives
painted; regal; mournful; cumbrous; long; worthless; warlike; stately; disposed; solitary; disproportionate; unprecedented; episcopal; vain; bloody; apparent; vulgar; embarrassing; infinite; dazzling; decorative; moving; papistical; liturgical; inimitable; long-drawn; despotic; bloodless; visionary; wonted; wind-blown; solemn; superfluous; contented.

verbs
affect—; display—; exhibit—; relax—; relish—; sacrifice to—; —attracts; —awes; —blazons; —dazzles; —flaunts; —glitters; —sparkles; —splashes; —wearies.
(See display, splendor, magnificence.)

POMPOSITY

adjectives
affable; rollicking; attenuated; affected; bloated; unspeakable.

POMPOUS

adverbs
insufferably; ludicrously; self-righteously; absurdly; gorgeously; officiously; ridiculously; noisily; swaggeringly; affectedly; ostentatiously; blatantly; grandiloquently; splendidly; boastfully; showily; superbly; pettily; dramatically; spectacularly; remarkably; amazingly; drolly; comically; preposterously; crassly.

POND

adjectives
steel-bright; misty; mill; midsummer; fowl; clear; circular; tranquil; darksome; shining; bottomless.

verbs
dabble in—; deposit in—; dive in—; fish in —; immerse in—; merge into—; plunge into—; wade in—; —accumulates; —beautifies; —graces; —laps; —ripples; — sparkles; —washes.

(See lake, water, lagoon.)

PONDER (v)
adverbs
silently; meditatively; sagely; monotonously; seriously; patiently; perplexedly; morbidly; moodily; closely; reverently; meekly; darkly; philosophically.

(See think, reflect, muse.)

PONDEROUS
adverbs
seriously; weightily; gravely; momentously; heavily; mightily; clumsily; awkwardly; impressively; crudely; formally; stiffly; stupidly; dully; flatly; tiresomely; monotonously; prosaically; intolerably; strangely; insipidly; pointlessly; singularly; incomparably; inexpressibly.

PONTOON
verbs
attach—; employ—; equip with—; lower —; moor to—; travel on—; —buoys; —carries; —enables; —floats; —guards against; —holds; —indicates; —insures; —saves; — supports; —sustains.

(See bridge, boat.)

PONY
adjectives
restless; thin; woebegone.

verbs
breed—ies; corral—ies; curry—; guide—; lash—; mount—; saddle—; tether—; tumble off—; —balks; —bolts; —canters; —capers; —paws; —prances; —shies; —trots; — whinnies.

(See horse, colt, mare.)

POODLE
adjectives
wretched; shaved; frolicsome.

POOL
adjectives
rank; glistening; gloomy; palm-edged; stagnant; seething; sullen; slumbrous; slimy; motionless; mirrorlike; broad; willowy; glassy; tepid; rippling; little; whirling; pebbled; dreaming; malarial; shadowed; mottled; shining; iridescent; scintillating; deep; amber; limpid; quiet; flowing; silent; brimming; oblivious; placid; swirling; loathsome; polished; spacious; outdoor; wholesome; dimpled; indicated; narrow; foaming; transparent; reedy; fish; frog; frozen; smooth.

verbs
chlorinate—; construct—; crowd—; dip into —; drain—; house—; plunge into—; splash in—; wade in—; —delights; —glistens; — invites; —laps; —ripples; —shimmers; — simmers; —sparkles; —tempts; dive into—.

(See river, lake, pond.)

POOR
adjectives
fancy; solitary; wily; nameless; neighboring; grateful; undeserving; unattended; shamefaced; neglected; sickly.

adverbs
miserably; wretchedly; deplorably; lamentably; pitiably; pitifully; helplessly; hopelessly; strangely; amazingly; remarkably; terribly; incredibly; unfortunately; unhappily; uncommonly; unusually; embarrassingly; uncomfortably; horribly; desperately; awfully.

POPE
verbs
bow before—; consult—; defy—; support—; visit—; —addresses; —administers; —appeals to; —beads; —blesses; —controls; — governs; —interviews; —officiates; — orates; —prays; —reprimands; —sanctions; —secludes; —supplicates.

(See minister, king.)

POPLAR
adjectives
attendant; showery; huge; shuddering; feathery; towering.

POPPY
adjectives
foolish; scarlet; bloody; flaming; crumpled; memorial.

POPULACE
adjectives
murmurous; giddy; barbarous; infuriated; squalid; malcontent; insolent; virtuous; excited; noisy; irritable.

POPULAR

adverbs

amazingly; incredibly; deservedly; surprisingly; strikingly; particularly; incomparably; unexpectedly; undeniably; manifestly; obviously; definitely; distinctly; evidently; widely; personally; politically; professionally; unmistakably; uncommonly; highly; socially; locally.

POPULARITY

adjectives

contemporary; formidable; respectful; facile; ageless; world-wide; unbounded; amazing; tremendous; zooming; prewar; illogical; apparent; corresponding; increasing; glaring; undeniable; universal; widespread; fickle; assured; fading; undetermined.

verbs

achieve—; attain—; begrudge—; bolster—; hinder—; jeopardize—; reduce—; reinstate —; ride to—; risk—; soar to—; spring into—; suffer—; sweep into—; —declines; —recedes; —tumbles; —wanes.

(See fame, glory, greatness.)

POPULATE (v)

adverbs

thickly; densely; teemingly; sparsely; turbulently; squalidly; swarmingly; homogeneously; animatedly; urbanly.

(See inhabit.)

POPULATION

adjectives

scattered; floating; indolent; communicative; teeming; wage-earning; bucolic; industrious; curious; inflammable; resident; indigenous; migratory; proper; crowded; ancient; coming; stunted; haggard; lifeless; varied; predatory; sparse; strenuous; adventurous; squalid; turbulent; rebellious; surplus; predominant; intractable; hostile; miserable; swarming; aboriginal; motley; much-slaughtered; abstemious; shifting; enormous; nomadic; supplicating; homogeneous; submissive; sufficient; voting; dense; warlike; sluggish; energetic; active; workless; rustic; animated; agricultural; urban.

verbs

control—; decimate—; harbor—; immunize —to; increase—; oppress—; scourge—; teem with—; —ascends; —decreases; —dwindles; —expands; —mounts.

(See masses, mankind.)

POPULOUS

adverbs

uncommonly; definitely; distinctly; overly; congestedly; thickly; problematically; inconveniently; perplexingly; particularly; unpleasantly; unmanageably.

PORCELAIN

adjectives

unglazed; transparent; rare; imported.

verbs

bake—; cast—; decorate—; dip—; finish—; form—; glaze—; mold—; paint—; polish—; prize—; scour—; shape—; shatter—; smooth—; value—; —gleams; —graces; —shines.

(See china, crockery.)

PORCH

adjectives

vine-clad; spacious; sculptured; flowery; dripping; dingy; shrouded; glass-enclosed; jutting; rude; classic; shaded.

PORCUPINE

verbs

anger—; frighten—; —arches; —baffles; —bristles; —climbs; —clings; —defends; —erects; —inflicts; —preys on; —rattles; —rolls into a ball; —rushes; —scares off; —sticks; —wounds.

(See animal.)

PORE (v)

adverbs

painfully; industriously; studiously; bookishly; academically; scholastically; ambitiously.

(See study, ponder.)

PORES

adjectives

subtile; serried; drained-out; minute; clotted; stopped; non-functioning; enlarged; ugly; fine.

verbs

block—; choke—; cleanse—; clog—; contract—; enlarge—; escape from—; filter through—; flow from—; issue from—; obstruct—; penetrate—; plug—; purge—; —discharge; —effuse; —exude; —ooze; —open.

(See skin, hole, opening.)

verbs
barbecue—; condemn—; cure—; devour—; dine on—; examine—; freeze—; garnish—; gobble up—; gnaw—; infect—; inspect—; nibble—; prepare—; putrefy—; relish—; roast—; salt—; sandwich—; serve—.
(See meat.)

POROUS
adverbs
unfortunately; unsalably; inconveniently; unluckily; objectionably; unserviceably; advantageously; intentionally; purposely; curiously; singularly; manifestly; minutely; scientifically; plainly.

PORT
adjectives
alluring; tropical; princely; delectable; centuried; heavenly; intervening; broad-brimmed; broad-armed; tranquil; convenient; favorite; neighboring; unfrequented; swaggering; blockaded; difficult; hostile; much-used.

PORTABLE
adverbs
easily; readily; luckily; conveniently; completely; inexpensively; compactly; invisibly; inconspicuously; particularly; comfortably; lightly; handily; appropriately; serviceably; suitably; instantly.

PORTALS
adjectives
flashing; forbidden; frowning; mysterious; ancient; time-beaten; ruby-colored; massy; gorgeous; somber; subterranean; welcoming; subtle; outer-most; sparkling; gloomy; shadowy; oaken; statue-crowned; ogival; wrought; open; swinging; creaking.

verbs
block—; choke—; crash—; cross—; crowd —; enter—; file from—; filter through—; gain—; invite through—; issue from—; obstruct—; secure—; swarm about—; throw open—; —gape; —welcome; —yawn.
(See door, entrance.)

PORTEND (*v*)
adverbs
gloomily; darkly; unfavorably; banefully; dolefully; evilly; stormily; symbolically; ominously; prophetically; direly.
(See foretell, predict.)

PORTENT
adjectives
unmistakable; vast; fiery; baneful; worse; doleful; evil.

verbs
disregard—; fear—; realize—; recognize—; —depresses; —disconcerts; —disturbs; —frightens; —indicates; —looms; —-oppresses; —promises; —perplexes; —puzzles; —shadows; —shrouds; —warns.
(See warning, meaning.)

PORTENTOUS
adverbs
heavily; grievously; sadly; ominously; gravely; seriously; critically; imminently; unmistakably; direly; solemnly; oddly; significantly; particularly; oddly; dangerously; immensely; sorely; manifestly; frightfully; tremendously; alarmingly; dreadfully; momentously; deeply; profoundly; calamitously.

PORTER
adjectives
suppliant; dark; drowsing; fat; oily; station; slovenly; obsequious; neat; industrious; heavily-laden.

PORTICO
adjectives
antique; classic; gaunt; unfinished; huge.

PORTION
adjectives
dense; important; ascending; priceless; descending; prodigal; hearty; healthful; considerable; flourishing; prescribed; plenteous; energetic; edible; introductory; cascading; dim; minute; mobile; speculative; residual; petty; various (pl); regenerative; generous; chasm-like; valuable; untouched; inviting; vast; integral; tolerable; lofty; broad; compensated; dangerous; uncovered; equitable; unexplored; submerged; astonishing; large; continued; remote; silvery; disinterested; alloted; soluble; superficial; protruding; substantial; picturesque; fleshy.

verbs
allot—to; allow—; break into—s; carve into—s; deal—s; distribute—s; divide

into—s; dole out—s; integrate—s; mete out—s; sample—; share—; stint—; —appeases; —protrudes; —satiates.

(See share, inheritance, quota.)

PORTION (v)

adverbs

fairly; equitably; substantially; prodigally; magnanimously; arbitrarily.

(See share, divide.)

PORTLY

adverbs

inexpressibly; unhappily; incredibly; incurably; laughably; lamentably; comfortably; contentedly; distressingly; absurdly; ridiculously; ludicrously; sadly; joyously; dangerously; heavily; funnily; complacently; complainingly; mournfully; dramatically; pathetically; shapelessly; waddlingly.

PORTRAIT

adjectives

undisputed; ancestral; unfavorable; satirical; penned; unequaled; poetical; gallery; posthumous; deathlike; faded; dark; coarse; staring; notable; vivid; authentic; mezzotint; sharp; vulgar; inimitable; somber-toned; characteristic; spirited; initial; pathetic; unlifelike; gloomy; brilliant; vigorous; distinct; demure; alluring; late; realistic; whole-length; somber; painstaking; delectable; carnationed; rubicund; hard-favored; accurate; sympathetic; untouched.

verbs

admire—; adumbrate—; delineate—; detail—; display—; dress up—; embellish—; hang—; obscure—; pose for—; prepare—; shade—; shadow—; sit for—; sketch—; unveil—; —adheres to; —copies; —depicts; illustrates.

(See masterpiece, painting, picture.)

PORTRAITURE

adjectives

idealized; truthful; moral; rigid.

PORTRAY (v)

adverbs

magnificently; graphically; vigorously; ironically; accurately; vividly; objectively; nebulously; sharply; pathetically; alluringly; realistically; somberly; sympathetically; poetically.

(See picture, paint.)

PORTRAYAL

adjectives

truthful; sympathetic; single-scene; heart-warming; objective; realistic; ethical; ever-fresh.

verbs

achieve—; applaud—; commend—; criticize—; detail—; draw—; enjoy—; practise—; rehearse—; render—; review—; —characterizes; —delights; —depicts; —describes; —relates; —recounts; —unfolds.

(See description, portrait.)

POSE

adjectives

quiet; easy; dignified; habitual; theatrical; traditional; professional; unmistakable; ridiculous; deliberate; conventional; individual; classic; charming; hieratic; autocratic; swan-like; lordly; stiff; heroic; ultimate; hereditary; effective; obsequious; countless (pl).

verbs

affect—; animate—; assume—; carve—; cast—; fashion—; hold—; imitate—; maintain—; overdo—; regard—; ridicule—; shape—; strike—; —appeals; —attitudinizes; —caricaturizes; —characterizes; —copies; —impresses.

(See attitude, posture.)

POSE (v)

adverbs

professionally; importantly; strikingly; statuesquely; dignifiedly; ridiculously; deliberately; classically; autocratically; heroically; obsequiously.

(See balance, poise.)

POSITION

adjectives

absurd; admirable; advantageous; alphabetical; altered; ambiguous; amiable; angular; anomalous; arduous; anonymous; argumentative; artistic; aristocratic; asinine; attributive; awkward; belligerent; brilliant; broad; choice; commanding; compensating; conducive; competitive; conspicuous; consular; contrasting; coveted; creditable; defensive; cramped; crouching; dangerous; definite; degraded; delicate; deplorable; dependent; desirable; desperate; despondent; desultory; detestable; dignified; different; disagreeable; dreadful; dominant; ecclesiastical; elevated; embarrassing; eminent; enviable; envious; erroneous; essential; exalted; exasperating; executive; exposed; extraordinary; fatiguing; fiscal; formidable; fortified; genial; geographical; grand; gratifying; grotesque; handy; hardy; hated; homeless; honorable; idiotic; ignominious; illustrious; imperial; important; impoverished; impregnable; inartistic; insignificant; indefensible; insular; intact; intellectual; interesting; intermediate; irksome; irretrievable; isolated; legal; lucrative; literary; lofty; long-continued; lower; luxurious; masked; mercurial; military; modest; natural-minded; obscure; oceanic; odious; official; opposite; painful; peculiar; perilous; permanent; perplexing; picturesque; pivotal; poised; precarious; precise; premier; prominent; reclining; recognized; reconnoitered; recumbent; relative; relaxed; remarkable; resolute; respectable; responsible; risky; retired; secluded; semi-reclining; serious; shifting; social; solid; stationary; sophisticated; static; strained; strong; strategic; subordinate; subservient; substantial; superfluous; supreme; tedious; technical; tenable; theological; theoretical; thoughtful; threatening; transitional; unambitious; unassailable; uncivil; uncomfortable; unconscious; unendurable; undistinguishable; unequivocal; unfashionable; unfavorable; unique; unlovely; unquestioned; unrivaled; unsupported; unstable; untenable; unworthy; virulent; weak; wicked; worldly; worth-while; wretched.

verbs
acquire—; alter—; aspire to—; challenge—; check—; clarify—; complicate—; compromise—; consolidate—; damage—; defend—; demote—; dignify—; elevate to—; indicate—; jeopardize—; jockey for—; justify—; maintain—; maneuvre for—; regain —; reiterate—; restore—; resume—; retain—; shift—; solidify—; struggle for—; surrender—; survey—; usurp—; wrest — from; —attracts; —reimburses
(See job, situation, rank, status.)

POSITIVE
adverbs
disagreeably; aggressively; boldly; emphatically; truculently; extravagantly; insolently; audaciously; arrogantly; offensively; blandly; calmly; confidently; astoundingly; monstrously; preposterously; rashly; blatantly.

POSSESS (v)
adverbs
legally; intellectually; incontestably; legitimately; intrinsically; originally; potentially; proudly; territorially; undisputedly; conclusively; hereditarily; tranquilly; hazardously; uniquely; enduringly; formally; nominally.
(See own, occupy.)

POSSESSIONS
adjectives
forcible; territorial; illegal; undisturbed; valuable; new; substantial; colonial; uncontrolled; priceless; exclusive; peaceful; dear; steady; imperishable; complete; undisputed; insolent; miserable; calm; vast; limited; overbearing; humble; prized; conclusive; hereditary; earthly; distant; cool; unassisted; narrow; tranquil; cherished; profitable; unquestioned; rightful; kindred; hazardous; naive; small; unique; scenic; remarkable; defiling; precious; enduring; formal; comparative; demoniacal; masterly; favored.

verbs
accrue—; auction off—; command—; cull—; enjoy—; entangle—; estimate—; expand—; forfeit—; gain—; gather—; harbor—; inherit—; liquidate—; mislay—; procure—; reap—; recover—; redeem—; restore—; savor—; value—.
(See estate, assets, fortune, property.)

POSSESSIVE
adverbs
rapturously; ardently; devoutly; jealously; selfishly; fanatically; abnormally; strangely; curiously; maternally; uncommonly; peculiarly; singularly; incorrigibly; foolishly; senselessly; unfortunately; overly; desperately; ridiculously; comically; unpleasantly; embarrassingly; highly; devotedly.

POSSESSOR
adjectives
original; potential; successive (pl); privileged; peaceful; boastful; proud.

POSSIBILITY
adjectives
limping; limitless; remote; easy; dramatic; profit; abstract; contingent; dismal; money-saving; opulent; honest; transcendent; tremendous; horrid; far-reaching; awful; flexible; domestic-social; undiminished;

mental; generous; evolutional; fearful; charming; plausible; iridescent; future; subsequent; divine; envisioned; improbable; extravagant; rhythmic; unfathomable; serene.

verbs
afford—; appreciate—; bolster—; broach—; comprehend—; deny—; determine—; diminish—; disclose—; dissipate—; embroider—; entertain—; envisage—; exhaust—; exploit —; explore—; face—; jump at—; open—; preclude—; raise—; realize—; reject—; ridicule—; rule out—; —appeals to; —dawns upon; —looms; —lurks in; —pales.
(See chance, contingency, potentiality.)

POST
adjectives (*place*)
strategic; arduous; worthless; perilous; impregnable; respective; important; significant; established; permanent; fortified; newly-created; farthest; diplomatic; faint; unbodied; lucrative; sedulous.

verbs
abandon—; assign to—; banish to—; confine to—; establish—; join—; locate—; occupy —; relinquish—; settle at—; station at—; strengthen—; vacate—; —discharges; —lodges; —mobilizes; —quarters.
(See position, situation, job, place, support.)

POST (*v*)
adverbs
ostentatiously; publicly; secretly; strategically; perilously; intermittently; permanently; periodically; diplomatically.
(See mail, send.)

POSTER
adjectives
frigid; salacious; safety.

verbs
circulate —s; diffuse —s; disseminate —s; plaster with —s; publish —s; —advertises; —advocates; —announces; —blazons; —broaches; —flourishes; —hawks; —heralds; —noises about; —proclaims; —promulgates; —trumpets.
(See placard, advertisement, announcement, notice.)

POSTERITY
adjectives
grateful; unloving; forgetful; unworried.

verbs
bequeath to—; hand down to—; record for —; —commemorates; —condemns; —defaces; —disgraces; —emulates; —exhumes; —glorifies; —honors; —inherits; —outshines; —pales; —perpetuates; —reflects; —reproaches; —reveres; —shames; —sullies; —surpasses; —traces.
(See descendants, family, offspring.)

POSTHUMOUS
adverbs
ironically; unfortunately; tardily.

POSTPONE (*v*)
adverbs
indefinitely; vaguely; arbitrarily; discreetly; regularly; permanently; temporarily; ultimately; disappointingly; formally.
(See delay, defer.)

POSTPONEMENT
adjectives
indefinite; unwelcome; regular; long-awaited.

POSTSCRIPT
adjectives
lengthy; apologetic.

POSTURE
adjectives
lifeless; bending; studious; stooping; unusual; healthful; spiritual; reclining; graceful; squatting; thoughtful; ungainly; abject; limp; suggestive; impressive; absurd; inelegant; sitting; unmalicious; faulty; easy; painful; incorrect; recumbent; unmanly; supplicating; favorable; poor.

verbs
acquire—; affect—; alter—; assume—; correct—; derange—; fix—; improve—; maintain—; remedy—; ridicule—; shift—; study —; —apes; —characterizes; —impresses; —mars; —tires.
(See gesture, attitude, pose.)

POSTURING
adjectives
dramatic; virile.

adjectives
fragrant; pretty.

POT

adjectives
earthenware; tea; unusual; molded; glazed; oddly-shaped.

verbs
blacken—; hook—; immerse in—; label—; load—; preserve in—; replenish—; scour—; scrape—; scrub—; —adorns; —boils; —dangles; —glistens; —seethes; —simmers.
(See caldron, kettle.)

POTATION

adjectives
sparkling; nightly; plentiful; spirituous; bubbling; joyous.

POTATO

adjectives
underdone; mashed; baked; frozen; scalloped; sweet; fried; eyeless.

POTENCY

adjectives
tragic; changeful; extraordinary; supernatural; changeful; outstanding; intense; remarkable; long-lived.

POTENT

adverbs
unexpectedly; surprisingly; fatally; peculiarly; singularly; incredibly; amazingly; moderately; scarcely; unusually; commendably; influentially; politically; personally; admittedly; officially; effectively; sufficiently; uncommonly; adequately; overwhelmingly; satisfactorily.

POTENTATE

adjectives
prodigal; rebel; pitiless; powerful; crowned; wealthy; temporal; illustrious; peerless; dread; prudent; wicked.

POTENTIALITY

adjectives
scattered (pl); lasting; remarkable; latent.

verbs
choke—; confer—; cripple—; develop—; discover—; double—; exhaust—; exploit—;

force—; lame—; maim—; muzzle—; realize —; recognize—; shatter—; silence—; strangle—; strengthen—; suppress—; utilize—; weaken—.
(See power, possibility.)

POTION

adjectives
bittersweet; direful; deadly; narcotic; soporific.

verbs
concoct—; dose with—; drain—; gulp down —; lap up—; mix—; quaff—; sip—; swallow—; swig—; swill—; toss off—; wash down—; —nauseates; —palliates; —relieves; —remedies; —restores.
(See dose, medicine, poison, liquid.)

POTTERY

adjectives
shattered; valuable; unusual; native; handmade.

POUCH

adjectives
capacious; gorgeous; bulging.

POULTICE

verbs
apply—; pat on—; smear—; surround with —s; treat with—; —allays; —alleviates; —balms; —comforts; —cures; —eases; —foments; —mitigates; —palliates; —refreshes; —relieves; —remedies; —soaks; —soothes.
(See salve, ointment.)

POUNCE (v)

adverbs
viciously; vindictively; furiously; instantaneously; murderously; diabolically; formidably; belligerently.
(See jump, dash.)

POUND

adjectives
scant; full; generous.

POUND (v)

adverbs
obstreperously; tirelessly; vigorously; lustily; bestially; vociferously; thunderously.
(See beat, strike.)

POUR (v)

adverbs
unceasingly; incessantly; liberally; hospit-

911

ably; effusively; unstintingly; hysterically; liquidly; melodiously; insatiably.

(See flow, stream.)

POUT (v)
adverbs

pettishly; sulkily; prettily; coyly; petulantly; tearfully; despondently.

(See sulk, scowl.)

POVERTY
adjectives

pinching; appalling; relative; hated; imaginary; benumbing; absolute; comparative; inevitable; abject; astonishing; squalid; wretched; genteel; peculiar; hard-working; deepening; irremediable; everlasting; low; continual; lifelong; haughty; distressful; speedy; extreme; general; worthless; utter; honorable; contorted; consequent; disgraceful.

verbs

abhor—; abolish—; accept—; banish—; boast of—; drive off—; outwit—; plead—; prolong—; suffer—; —callouses; —degrades; —dogs; —fetters; —oppresses; —overtakes; —pursues; —ravages; —stalks; —stigmatizes.

(See destitution, impoverishment, need, penury.)

POWDER
(general)
adjectives

smokeless; bronze; ordered; resultant; odorless; moistened; deadly; notorious; fetid; capsulated; dictatorial; heavy; inferior; murderous.

verbs

apply—; dab in—; dip in—; dust with—; prink with—; reduce to—; smear—; spread —; touch up with—; —beautifies; —conceals; —embellishes; —glorifies; —harmonizes; —improves; —mellows; —perfects; —pretties; —primes; —soothes; —tricks; —whitens.

(See make-up, dust, gunpowder.)

POWDER (v)
adverbs

fashionably; flirtatiously; glamorously; exaggeratedly; fascinatingly; bewitchingly; enchantingly.

(See perfume, scent.)

POWER
adjectives

abiding; abrogating; abrupt; absent; absolute; absorbing; abundant; active; advancing; adverse; afflicted; all-consuming; allegorizing; all-embracing; allied; all-inhering; amazing; ample; alternative; amorous; analytic; ancestral; ancient; antipathetic; apostolic; appalling; appointing; arbitrary; arch-angelic; architectural; argumentative; assertive; assumed; autocratic; belligerent; autonomous; balanced; beneficent; bestial; blessed; blighted; boasted; braking; boundless; brilliant; budding; buying; capricious; catapulting; celestial; centralizing; chameleon-like; coercive; chemic; civil; clairvoyant; cloven; coming; clerical; colossal; colonizing; comic; commanding; communicative; complete; compelling; composing; compulsive; concentrated; concocted; confederated; confident; confirming; conscious; considerable; consequent; consistent; constitutional; constructive; contending; contingent; contracting; corporate; cosmic; conversational; cosmetic; creative; critical; crowned; curative; curious; deepening; dangerous; defensive; delegated; deliberative; delicate; delightful; denuding; departed; desolate; despotic; destructive; developed; dictatorial; discretional; discerning; disorderly; disturbing; divine; dominant; dormant; driving; dramatic; dulled; dynamic; earning; earth-prisoned; ecclesiastical; educational; effulgent; elastic; elemental; emotional; enchanted; enhanced; energizing; enlarged; enormous; exceeding; erosive; ever-dreaded; evident; exalted; exceptional; excessive; exchangeable; executive; exhaustive; existing; expansive; exorbitant; explosive; extemporaneous; extraordinary; facile; fangless; fatal; far-reaching; fatherly; feeble; feudal; fertilizing; fierce; filial; financial; first-rate; flawless; flexible; formative; full; formidable; fraudulent; frightful; fundamental; generative; generous; genial; genuine; gigantic; godlike; heartfelt; granted; graphic; grasping; growing; guiding; hateful; healing; heavy; high; heavenly; heroic; hidden; hypnotic; imaginative; immature; immeasurable; immediate; immense; immortal; imperial; impossible; imperialist; implied; inborn; incomprehensible; indefinite; individual; indomitable; industrial; inexplicable; inevitable; infective; infernal; infinite; influential; ingrained; inherent; insensate; inimitable; inner; insensible; insubordinate; intellectual; intelligent; intermittent; interposing; intoxicating; intrinsic; intuitive; inutile; invalid; inventive; inveterate; invincible; invisible; irresistible; irresponsible; jealous; judicial; just; keen; kindly; kingly; lasting; latent; lawless; learning; legal; legislative; lifting; limited; linguistic; living; lordly; lubricating; luminous; luxurious; magical; magnetic; magnifying; maiming; malevolent; malign; marvelous; massive; mastering; mature; mental; mesmeric; microscopic; mighty; miraculous; monarchical; moneyed; moral; motive; mortal; murderous; muscular; narcotic; musical; myriad (pl); mysterious; necessary; necromantic; nefarious; obnoxious; nominal; nutritive; objurgatory; occult; omnipotent; omnipresent; ominous; omniscient; oratorical; oracular; organizing; original; overmastering; oxidizing; overwhelming; paramount; parliamentary; particular; passive; patient; patriarchal; peaceable; peculiar; penetrating; perceptive; pernicious; personal; perilous; periodical; persuasive; plastic; poetic; poisonous; political; potential; practical; preponderant; prevailing; primal; primordial; productive; profit; projectile; prolific; proper; prophetic; protecting; psychologic; public; purchasing; purging; quickening; rare; rational; reasoning; reckless; recumbent; recognized; recuperative; regal; relentless; remarkable; remorseless; renewed; reparative; reportorial; reserve; repulsive; requisite; resisting; restless; restrained; resultant; ripening; rival; revolutionary; rounded; royal; ruling; ruthless; sardonic; satanic; scant; secular; scathing; secret; seductive; seer-like; seething; self-dependent; selfish; self-realizing; self-restraining; sinister; selfsame; self-succeeding; silky; singular; sinless; siren; slow-moving; sole; speculative; sophisticated; spiritual; spontaneous; sprightly; springing; stagnant; startling; stimulating; sufficient; subtle; substantial; sullen; superior; superhuman; supernal; supernatural; supreme; surcharged; surging; surpassing; surprising; sustained; sweet; technical; temporal; terrible; thunderous; tranquil; transcendental; transforming; transporting; tremendous; tumultuous; twofold; tyrannous; ultimate; unappealable; unappeased; unborn; unbounded; uncanny; unconscious; undoubted; unexpected; unearthly; unequaled; unfettered; unfamiliar; unhallowed; uninviting; united; universal; unjust; unlimited; unmeasured; unprecedented; unrivaled; un-

qualified; unrestricted; unseen; unsightly; unspent; unsuspected; untried; unusual; unwearied; unwomanly; uplifting; urgent; utmost; vague; versatile; various (pl); vested; vibrant; victorious; violent; vital; vitalizing; waning; warlike; wearied; wondrous; worsted; worn; smooth; sufficient; self-sustaining.

verbs

abuse—; achieve—; animate with—; ascertain—; bask in—; bid for—; bolster—; bulwark by—; centralize—; check—; climb to —; clip—; clothe in—; confer—upon; consolidate—; crave—; curb—; curtail—; delegate—to; deprive of—; derive—from; dilute —; diminish—; disseminate—; dissipate—; dwarf—; elect to—; endow with—; enhance —; entrust with—; evince—; exercise—; exhaust—; fathom—; fatten on—; forfeit —; generate—; grant—; harness—; impair —; impart—to; impute—to; intensify—; intoxicate with—; lodge—in; lust for—; manifest—; nullify—; offset—; paralyze—; radiate—; regain—; resent—; restrict—; sap —; seize—; sense—; shake—; shear of—; stem—; strip of—; strive for—; surrender —; thirst for—; transmit—; unleash—; undermine—; usurp—; vest—in; vote into —; wield—; worship—; —decays; —declines; —resides in; —wanes; —waxes; —withers.

(See authority, influence, predominance, faculty, force, energy.)

POWERFUL

adverbs

inscrutably; amazingly; omnisciently; dangerously; dreadfully; unbelievably; vigorously; spiritually; influentially; irresistibly; indomitably; intensely; resolutely; acutely; cruelly; brutally; trenchantly; materially; commercially; socially; politically; universally; incredibly; terribly.

POWERLESS

adverbs

pitiably; desperately; hopelessly; inefficiently; altogether; remarkably; deplorably; unhappily; ineptly; awkwardly; clumsily; timorously; terribly; lamentably; miserably; wretchedly; incredibly; curiously; oddly; singularly; pathetically; stupidly; astoundingly; utterly.

PRACTICABILITY

adjectives

concrete; definite; inherent.

PRACTICABLE

adverbs

immediately; usefully; serviceably; opportunely; overwhelmingly; completely; happily; fortunately; conveniently; scientifically; easily; definitely; distinctly; particularly; unexpectedly; strikingly; remarkably; amazingly; luckily; sensibly; profitably; valuably; absolutely; reliably; dependably; positively.

PRACTICAL

adverbs

thoroughly; sensibly; wisely; usefully; commendably; particularly; admirably; fortunately; altogether; sagaciously; splendidly; happily.

PRACTICE

adjectives

ascetic; bayonet; cynical; lucrative; objectionable; lewd; diversified; tedious; competitive; time-honored; arduous; adulterous; traditional; wanton; long; vile; base; private; constant; nefarious; enthusiastic; ancient; shameless; magical; pernicious; assiduous; pagan; treasonable; normal; engineering; recognized; cunning; dangerous; corrupt; horrible; forensic; prevalent; monopolistic; augmented; ungentleman-like; consulting; unvarying; sedulous; ruined; extensive; actual; unique; psychoanalytic; questionable; contrary; licentious; deliberating; consequent; insidious; eminent; degrading; active; flourishing; present; superstitious; robust; irregular; choir; hateful; religious; fascinating; attendant; idolatrous; polygamous; unnatural; universal; prejudiced; comprehensive; revolutionized.

verbs

abandon—; acquire by—; addict to—; adhere to—; adopt—; neglect—; observe—; oppose—; perpetuate—; repress—; resort to—; restrict—; revive—; sanction—; — involves; —survives.

(See habit, conventionality, custom, exercise, performance.)

PRACTICE (v)

adverbs

spontaneously; discordantly; surreptitiously; diligently; vigorously; ambitiously; industriously; assiduously; professionally; sedulously; competitively; privately; forensically; periodically.

(See exercise, train, apply.)

PRACTITIONER

adjectives

successful; unqualified; ardent; ignorant; medical; mercenary.

PRAIRIE

adjectives

bleak; naked; blessed; spacious; teeming; carpeted; flowery; unbroken; corn-bladed; stubble-lined; wild; beautiful; short-turfed; great; undulating; sun-browned; verdant; rolling; broken; shaking.

verbs

course—; dwell on—; inhabit—; retire to—; ride—; roam—; traverse—; trek across—; view—; wander over—; wend across—; — blazes; —bores; —confronts; —extends.

(See plain, valley.)

PRAISE

adjectives

voluble; artless; sincere; partial; vain; moderate; humble; lavish; benignant; ignoble; love-pervaded; perfect; unstinted; aggressive; thriftless; expiatory; copious; unnecessary; untimely; reluctant; cynical; muted; awful; unmerited; unspoken; lofty; eloquent; elicited; unstinted; dolesome; passive; hearty; ill-considered; unworthy; unacceptable; deserved; solemn; ceaseless; partial; enthusiastic; unsought; warm; profane; silent; everlasting; unceasing; flattering; grudging; immortal; endless; virtuous; mingled; profuse; judicious; hollow; unqualified; melodious; implied; veiled; eternal; effusive; great; absent; fair; unbroken; lavish; excessive; exaggerated; intemperate; high; undeserving; compulsory.

verbs

administer—; apportion—; aspire to—; bestow—upon; bloom under—; capture—; deny—; desist from—; earn—; entitle to—; excite—; exhaust—; heap—upon; inspire—; justify—; pour out—; proclaim—; shower —upon; sing—; sum up—; swamp with—; —diminishes; —warms.

(See glory, approbation, compliment, adulation, commendation, applause.)

PRAISE (v)

adverbs

extravagantly; effusively; voluntarily; universally; judiciously; fulsomely; sincerely; flatteringly; rhapsodically; volubly; goldenly; immoderately; lavishly; benignantly; unstintedly; copiously; eloquently; intemperately.

(See extol, laud.)

PRAISEWORTHY

adverbs

deservedly; meritoriously; unusually; admirably; admittedly; conspicuously; modestly; highly; uncommonly; remarkably; exceptionally; undoubtedly; genuinely; highly; singularly; immensely; extremely; impressively; signally; unimpeachably; matchlessly; incomparably.

PRANCE (v)

adverbs

spiritedly; mincingly; vigorously; picturesquely; madly; freakishly; sportively.

(See cavort, spring.)

PRANK

adjectives

hoyden; mad; fruitless; common; wily; extravagant; gamesome; humorous; idle; freakish; youthful.

verbs

anticipate—; beguile with—s; concoct—; dodge—; indulge in—; relish—; smother—; —amuses; —disgusts; —diverts; —irks; —seduces; —tires; —traps; —tricks; —vexes.

(See frolic, joke, jest.)

PRANKISH

adverbs

mischievously; roguishly; teasingly; persistently; unexpectedly; incorrigibly; playfully; innocently; foolishly; absurdly; merrily; persistently; ludicrously; idly; frivolously; remarkably; cleverly; ingeniously.

PRANKSTER

verbs

chastize—; dodge—; evade—; forestall—; rebuke—; reprimand—; reproach—; —beguiles; —concocts; —contrives; —disports; —entertains; —wearies.

(See clown, fool, jester.)

PRATE (v)

adverbs

idiotically; foolishly; maliciously; vindictively; spitefully; boastfully; sacreligiously.

(See talk, chatter.)

PRATING

adjectives

solemn; continuous; noisy; bothersome.

PRATTLE

adjectives

winsome; foolish; intermittent.

PRATTLE (v)

adverbs

vapidly; artlessly; childishly; inanely; coyly; winsomely; foolishly; jejunely; insipidly.

(See talk, chatter, babble.)

PRAY (v)

adverbs

fervently; earnestly; distractedly; conspicuously; solemnly; humbly; devoutly; audibly; passionately; effusively; dumbly; supplicatingly; tremulously; blasphemously; inarticulately; wordlessly; virtuously; fruitlessly; sepulchrally.

(See entreat, beg.)

PRAYER

adjectives

idle; fervent; audible; professional; passionate; effectual; effusive; little; soft; prattled; sobbing; boding; priestly; dumb; nightly; chanted; humble; unuttered; dying; melting; weak; pious; supplicating; creditable; stated; conscious; bootless; earnest; perpetual; weekly; specious; poor; hearty; masticated; wistful; sublime; tremulous; common; granted; sunrise; contemptible; insane; trembling; blasphemous; pattered; morning; awed; inarticulate; wordless; fair; consecrating; virtuous; sepulchral; long-groaned; puling; reluctant; grateful; voluble; thankful; vociferated; wrestling; high-blooded; unlawful; true; pagan; fruitless; pleading; hallowing.

verbs

address—; avert by—; attend—; blend in —; bless in—; bow in—; chant—; console by—; fall down in—; fulfill—; grant—; intone—; kneel in—; offer up—; rattle off —s; unite in—; utter—; —beseeches; —

deifies; —entreats; —glorifies; —importunes; —petitions; —reconciles; —supplicates.

(See benediction, mass, entreaty, confession.)

PREACH (v)

adverbs

unctuously; eloquently; rabidly; narrowly; militantly; independently; sonorously; sanctimoniously; sublimely; vociferously; tiresomely; zealously; austerely; itinerantly.

(See speak, advise, teach.)

PREACHER

adjectives

dissenting; eloquent; judicious; tiresome; poor; dark-lantern; moonlight; fiery; zealous; austere; ordinary; misguided; eminent; opposition; devoted; itinerant; traveling; understanding.

PRECARIOUS

adverbs

obviously; naturally; unduly; admittedly; necessarily; terribly; painfully; gravely; awfully; fearfully; alarmingly; grievously; frequently; peculiarly.

PRECAUTION

adjectives

commendable; polite; absolute; sure; obvious; ordinary; oratorical; futile; former; due; extraordinary; well-known; sensible; businesslike; lifesaving; vigilant; utmost; absurd; remarkably; sanitary; superfluous; vital; undue; attentive.

verbs

advocate—; disregard—; employ—; enforce —; exercise—; heed—; necessitate—; neglect—; observe—; omit—; shelve—; suggest —; urge—; view with—; —assures; — arms; —guards; —preestablishes.

(See caution, care.)

PRECAUTIONARY

adverbs

carefully; punctiliously; meticulously; laudably; strangely; unfailingly; vigilantly; warily; significantly; oddly; ominously; portentously; momentously; unusually; surreptitiously; secretly; furtively; quietly; thoroughly; strikingly.

PRECEDENT

adjectives

laudable; rigorous; historical; auspicious; social; romantic; inappropriate; mighty; semi-barbaric.

verbs

afford—; bolster by—; break—; concede to —; defeat—; establish—; follow—; govern by—; invoke—; quote—; refer to—; shatter —; shun—; suffer from—; —controls; — determines; —enslaves; —justifies; —regulates; —rules.

(See custom, authority.)

PRECEPT

adjectives

repeated; benevolent; mild; excellent; civil; sage; strange; abstruse; divine; averaged; dull; moral; traditional; innumerable (pl); sublime.

verbs

advocate—; authorize—; compile—s; disobey—; dispense—; entrust—; formulate—; fulfill—; issue—; promulgate—; sanction—; submit to—; violate—; —decrees; —dictates; —forbids; —imposes; —instructs; — limits; —ordains; —orders; —prohibits; — requests; —requires; —restrains; —restricts.

(See order, principle, teaching, commandment, instruction.)

PRECINCT

adjectives

attractive; holy; warm; hallowed; consecrated; awful; sordid; local.

PRECIOUS

adverbs

unusually; adorably; remarkably; pricelessly; unreasonably; incredibly; singularly; curiously; altogether; unbelievably; understandably; uncommonly; amazingly; fantastically; immensely; immeasurably; incalculably.

PRECIPICE

adjectives

frowning; dizzy; granite; vertical; dread; superb; hanging; wooded; tremendous; beetling; cloven; rimmed; slippery; ivy-covered; stupendous.

verbs

careen down—; clamber up—; cling to—; hang on—; hazard—; risk—; scan—; slide

down—; survey—; teeter on—; venture on
—; —blocks; —cuts off; —endangers; —engulfs; —jeopardizes; —imperils; —swallows.
(See cliff, mountain.)

PRECIPITATION
adjectives
complete; extraordinary; daily.

PRECIPITOUS
adverbs
steeply; impossibly; dangerously; riskily;
alarmingly; terribly; terrifyingly; incredibly; unreasonably; unspeakably; deucedly;
murderously; roughly; icily; tremendously;
impressively; imposingly; magnificently; superbly; splendidly; grandly; incalculably;
immeasurably; dizzily; stupendously.

PRECISE
adverbs
overwhelmingly; absolutely; dependably;
scrupulously; ridiculously; infallibly; remarkably; uncannily; meticulously; mechanically; monotonously; invariably; deliberately; unimpeachably; rigidly; mathematically;
scientifically; carefully; particularly; painstakingly; rigorously; insatiably; avidly;
necessarily; punctiliously; compellingly; impartially; uniformly.

PRECISION
adjectives
academic; calm; classical; scientific; unerring; rigorous; exquisite; passionate; inflexible; finical; rapid; utmost; careless; nauseating; antique; mechanical; geometrical;
marvelous; rhythmic; remarkable; military;
delighted; mathematical; melancholy; masterly; convincing; grammatical; admirable;
meticulous; faithful; deadly; tolerable; delicate; sufficient; faultless; austere; overwhelming.

verbs
achieve—; applaud—; commend—; demonstrate—; denote—; disclose—; display—;
evince—; exhibit—; lack—; manifest—; reveal—; urge—; —assures; —clarifies.
(See accuracy.)

PRECOCIOUS
adverbs
amazingly; remarkably; smartly; keenly;
unusually; unpleasantly; disagreeably; impertinently; imprudently; knowingly; pertly; offensively; saucily; boldly; flippantly;
bumptiously; obtrusively; oddly; incredibly;
uncommonly; surprisingly.

PRECONCEPTION
adjectives
profound; definite; sentimental; unusual.

PREDATORY
adverbs
cruelly; rapaciously; voraciously; uncommonly; naturally; savagely; maliciously;
wantonly; ravenously; barbarously; incorrigibly; piratically; cleverly; ungovernably;
reprehensibly.

PREDECESSORS
adjectives
resourceful; superstitious; illustrious; ghostly.

verbs
commemorate—; emulate—; excel—; inherit
from—; outshine—; succeed—; surpass—;
trace—; —advise; —bequeath; —construct;
—design; —floor; —found; —frame; —record; —will to.
(See ancestor.)

PREDICAMENT
adjectives
distressing; piteous; unhappy; mechanical;
desperate; awkward; terrible.

verbs
alleviate—; avoid—; disentangle—; enjoy
—; evade—; labor through—; manage—;
risk—; sentimentalize—; shroud—; tackle
—; unravel—; view—; —confronts; —distresses; —embarrasses; —flusters; —restrains; —shames.
(See dilemma, embarrassment, position,
problem, situation.)

PREDICT (v)
adverbs
prophetically; confidently; correctly; lugubriously; mournfully; dismally; darkly; complacently; boldly; astrologically; miraculously.
(See foretell, portend.)

PREDICTION
adjectives
sure-fire; warlike; aristocratic; past; off-

917

hand; dominant; scientific; dismal; astrological; thunderous; poetical; overconfident; remarkable.

verbs
base—on; cast—; challenge—; divine—; justify—; upset—; venture—; verify—; — augurs; —betokens; —bids; —bodes; — excites; —foreshadows; —foretells; —forewarns; —heralds; —indicates; —portends; —precurses; —presages; —prognosticates; —promises; —prophesies.
(See prognostication, prophesy.)

PREDILECTION
adjectives
perverse; striking; traditional; broadheaded; ancient; well-understood.

PREDISPOSITION
adjectives
eternal; obvious; hereditary.

PREDOMINANCE
adjectives
oppressive; hoar; acknowledged; humorous; imperious; definite.

verbs
acquire—; assert—over; attain—; challenge —; gain—; garner—; spread—; —assures; —influences; —leads; —overbears; —overpowers; —overrides; —outweighs; —pervades; —prevails; —rages; —roots in; — succeeds.
(See power.)

PREDOMINANT
adverbs
rightfully; authoritatively; eminently; officially; regularly; imperiously; proudly; offensively; regally; electively; admittedly.

PREEMINENCE
adjectives
distinguished; dignified; established; unquestionable; intellectual.

verbs
acquire—; attain—; crave—; crown with—; culminate in—; demand—; reach—; shadow —; —eclipses; —glorifies; —inflates; —outbalances; —outstrips; —outweighs; —precedes; —prevails; —transcends; —whips.
(See fame, prominence, eminence, excellence.)

PREFACE
adjectives
hilarious; forcible; well-composed; epigrammatic.

PREFER (*v*)
adverbs
vastly; personally; infinitely; particularly; politically; individually; overwhelmingly; unaccountably; emotionally.
(See choose, pick.)

PREFERABLE
adverbs
decidedly; altogether; slightly; definitely; unquestionably; commercially; sensibly; practically; artistically; indubitably; genuinely; popularly; politically.

PREFERENCE
adjectives
personal; particular; exaggerated; political; individual; calculated; affectional; premature; overwhelming; unaccountable; definite.

verbs
acquire—; allow—; determine—; express—; exercise—; fix—; harbor—; indulge in—; list—; mark—; muse over—; offer—; permit—; poll—; select—; shout—; single out —; —culls; —decides; —elects; —espouses; —fancies.
(See choice, alternative.)

PREGNANCY
verbs
detect—; determine—; evade—; examine for—; fear—; generate in—; incur—; induce—; prevent—; procreate in—; produce —; suggest—; yield in—; —alters; —ensues; —increases; —irritates; —multiplies; —nauseates.

PREJUDICE
adjectives
antique; arrogant; feudal; vile; personal; violent; popular; abandoned; tender; ingrained; sectional; unworthy; virulent; vulgar; unflinching; established; unreflective; aristocratical; tainted; logical; conservative; superficial; pious; unconscious; tribal; present; frivolous; patrician; ignorant; senile; unreasonable; miserable; political; tenacious; sexual; bitter; undue; absorbing; intense; inveterate; imperial; unfounded; entrenched; fierce; social; furious; insular; religious; economic; invincible; superstitious.

verbs
arouse—; awaken—; beget—; beset with—; break down—; combat—; defy—; dictate by—; emancipate from—; erase—; exploit —; lampoon—; nourish—; oust—; pander to—; preach—; purge of—; shed—; subserve—; survive—; —distorts; —flourishes; —influences; —persists; —poisons; — shades; —vanishes; —undermines; —weakens.

(See bias, obsession, hate, judgment, opinion.)

PREJUDICE (v)
adverbs
hopelessly; personally; violently; sectionally; vulgarly; aristocratically; logically; unconsciously; ignorantly; irrationally; sexually; socially; inveterately; religiously; economically; superstitiously; politically.

(See injure, hurt.)

PREJUDICED
adverbs
unreasonably; unfavorably; affectionately; indulgently; viciously; maliciously; unfortunately; happily; absurdly; jealously; enviously; unfairly; narrowly; senselessly; terribly; doctrinally; politically; mischievously; indelibly; wrongfully; provincially; fanatically; outrageously; dreadfully; hopelessly.

PREJUDICIAL
adverbs
strongly; unfavorably; criminally; highly; incontrovertibly; definitely; fanatically; outrageously; scandalously; obviously; manifestly; evidently; wrongly; secretly; perniciously; disastrously; exceptionably; grievously; horribly; reprehensibly; inadvisably; unpardonably.

PRELATE
adjectives
haughty; fatuous; foreign; pampered; reverend; gallant; distinguished; princely; shrewd.

PRELIMINARY
adjectives
mysterious; invariable; essential; valuable; inevitable; indispensable.

verbs
anticipate—; arrange—; engage in—; miss —; observe—; settle—; stage—; view—;

—allays; —appeals; —entertains; —heads; —introduces; —leads; —precedes; —prefixes; —ushers in; —bridges; —prepares.

(See introduction, opening, ceremony, preface, prelude.)

PRELUDE
adjectives
fatal; mellow; formal; unpretentious; necessary.

PREMATURE
adverbs
unfortunately; unwisely; thoughtlessly; senselessly; recklessly; ineptly; clumsily; maladroitly; unskilfully; foolishly; imprudently; indiscreetly; disastrously; undiplomatically; inexpediently; calamitously; ill-advisedly; treacherously; sadly.

PREMEDITATED
adverbs
criminally; admittedly; wickedly; brutally; savagely; mischievously; outrageously; scandalously; maliciously; carefully; furtively; conclusively; unanswerably; inferentially; manifestly; cruelly; obviously; nefariously.

PREMISE
adjectives
false; petty; inconceivable; assumed; fundamental; unsound; unexamined; insufficient; academic; specific; cardinal.

verbs
assume—; bank on—; contradict—; depend on—; discuss—; endorse—; establish—; examine—; follow—; guard—; impair—; oppose—; question—; ratify—; rebut—; rely on—; stand upon—; support—; uphold —; verify—.

(See proposition, assumption, supposition, hypothesis.)

PREMONITORY
adverbs
distinctly; formidably; terribly; inferentially; fearfully; thoughtfully; surreptitiously; obviously; manifestly; unmistakably; woefully; horribly; coldly; cruelly; fortunately; subtly; significantly; gravely; deliberately; generously; fraternally; helpfully; suggestively; threateningly.

PREOCCUPATION

adjectives

smiling; intellectual; harassed; religious.

verbs

arouse from—; bury in—; cloud in—; distract from—; erase—; examine in—; immerse in—; interrupt—; necessitate—; notice—; observe—; scan in—; seal in—; view with—; —entertains; —reflects; —revises; —shrouds.

(See reverie, lethargy.)

PREOCCUPY (v)

adverbs

incessantly; intellectually; religiously; studiously; ambitiously; vigorously; clerically; mentally.

(See absorb, occupy.)

PREPARATION

adjectives

ineffectual; anatomical; excellent; nervous; proprietary; essential; initial; frantic; skillful; painstaking; elaborate; manifold; active; warlike; energetic; constant; secret; formidable; impartial; adequate; virtuous; mercurial; vigorous; imperfect; extensive; pain-killing; mighty; scientific; healthful; food; scant; minute; needful; intellectual; effectual; incessant.

verbs

advocate—; demand—; drill in—; justify—; lack—; plunge into—s; —aids; —arms; —arrays; —edifies; —enlightens; —expounds; —familiarizes; —grounds; —implants; —introduces; —organizes; —tunes.

(See qualification, training.)

PREPARATORY

adverbs

gravely; soberly; sadly; woefully; horribly; carefully; cautiously; completely; happily; rapturously; ecstatically; excitedly; frenziedly; heartbrokenly; hastily; deliberately; unwillingly; reluctantly; wildly; eagerly; anxiously; surreptitiously; resolutely; gallantly; thoughtfully; quietly; noisily; serenely; calmly; generously; ardently; piously; reverently; prayerfully.

PREPARE (v)

adverbs

amicably; gallantly; delectably; professionally; tastefully; manifestly; gravely; gratuitously; previously; independently; vigorously; sedulously; duly; amply; privately; cautiously; ceremoniously; wilfully; effectually; elaborately; energetically; formidably; minutely.

(See fit, provide, adapt.)

PREPARED

adverbs

well; badly; completely; scarcely; hardly; wonderfully; remarkably; eminently; fully; admirably; competently; fairly; barely; fortunately; skilfully; carefully; generously; altogether; unusually.

PREPONDERANCE

adjectives

undue; tremendous; noticeable; unquestioned.

PREPONDERANT

adverbs

heavily; unfairly; beneficially; influentially; dangerously; increasingly; politically; socially; dreadfully; unfortunately; imperiously; currently; tellingly; authoritatively; curiously; outrageously; naturally.

PREPOSSESSION

adjectives

personal; sudden; unfortunate; religious; unfavorable.

PREROGATIVE

adjectives

entrenched; personal; enviable.

verbs

allow—; assert—; authorize—; challenge—; demand—; disqualify—; entitle to—; exact—; extend—; grant—; insist on—; merit —; relax—; usurp—; violate—; wield—; —arrogates; —encroaches; —infringes.

(See privilege, right.)

PRESCIENCE

adjectives

slumberous; indistinct; passionate; hollow; unresisted; mystic.

PRESCRIBE (v)

adverbs

punctiliously; wisely; sagely; variously; preposterously; exclusively; legally; specifically; medically; medicinally; methodically.

(See order, advise.)

PRESCRIPTION

adjectives
favorite; exclusive; specific; deep-rooted; legal; unfailing; definite; mystic; age-old.

verbs
acquire—; addict to—; adhere to—; concoct —; dispense—s; fill—; follow—; formulate —; issue—; mix—; order—; recommend—; require—; write—; —alleviates; —eases; —instructs; —palliates; —relieves; —remedies; —soothes.
(See formula, medicine, direction.)

PRESENCE

adjectives
portly; reassuring; immediate; comely; inconspicuous; instant; palpitating; hateful; pale; glorious; visible; posthumous; gracious; protecting; unfamiliar; distinct; august; imposing; resplendent; singular; semiluminous; important; haunting; noiseless; royal; wondrous; palpable; ruddy; tranquil; effulgent; eternal; masked; universal; intolerant; abhorred; grim; imperial; impressive; ignoble; threatened; culprit; enchanting; maternal; detected; solemn; chastening; visionary; transforming; protecting; admirable; close; tender; celestial; gaunt; ramshackle; habitual; blighted; stately; passionate; continual; dreadful; perpetual; animate; pervading; abrupt; excellent; unrecognized; mortal; declared; commanding; dignified; unauthorized; unwelcome; striking; majestic; private; blessed; divine; invisible; engaging; stately; handsome; shadowy; cheering; unconjectured; gentle; combined.

verbs
acknowledge—; advertise—; announce—; ascertain—; conduct into—; detect—; enjoy—; mark—; reveal—; tolerate—; usher into—; —disturbs; —evokes; —impresses; —irritates.

PRESENT

adjectives
immediate; solid; magnificent; spontaneous; elegant; appropriate; ever-fleeting; eternal; realistic; substantial; grief-shadowed; reluctant; alien; visionary; stormy; placid.

verbs
accept—; acknowledge—; bedeck—; beribbon—s; bestow—s upon; conceal—; decline —; guard—s; lavish with—s; offer—; present with—; solicit—; tender—; view—s; —dazzles; —excites; —flatters; —pleases; reconciles; —s shower upon; —stems; dispense—s.
(See gift.)

adverbs
inappropriately; unsuitably; inconveniently; fortunately; happily; conveniently; opportunely; always; seldom; occasionally; objectionably; embarrassingly; unwarrantably; unfortunately; ever; constantly; unexpectedly; auspiciously; generously; considerately; graciously.

PRESENT (v)

adverbs
modestly; formally; humbly; appropriately; reluctantly; satirically; adequately; realistically; brazenly; providentially; ethically; imploringly; casually; repeatedly; materially.
(See give, offer, introduce.)

PRESENTATION

adjectives
technical; diligent; elaborate; artistic; condensed; demon; superb; graphic; ruddy; attractive; dispassionate; illustrative; terse; farewell.

verbs
acknowledge—; administer—; anticipate—; beg for—; favor with—; ignore—; postpone —; propose—; refuse—; reject—; seek—; welcome—; withhold—; —accords; —bestows; —conciliates; —introduces; —reveals.
(See introduction.)

PRESENTIMENT

adjectives
fearful; cold; apt; uneasy; vague; unquiet; undefinable; decisive; guilty.

verbs
argue—; harbor—; heed—; laugh down—; ridicule—; —aggravates; —augurs; —betokens; —bids; —bodes; —disturbs; —excites; —foreshadows; —foretells; —forewarns; —grows; —precurses; —troubles; —visits; —presages.
(See anticipation, apprehension, fear.)

PRESENTMENT

adjectives
counterfeit; vague; forceful; definite.

PRESERVATION

adjectives

perfect; inflexible; miraculous; exquisite; unbelievable.

PRESERVE (v)

adverbs

miraculously; mercifully; unbelievably; marvelously; sagaciously; permanently; painfully; laboriously; durably; prudently; immortally; perpetually.

(See keep, save.)

PRESERVED

adverbs

carefully; reverently; thriftily; skilfully; duly; richly; fortunately; luckily; meticulously; punctiliously; cautiously; perfectly; miraculously; exquisitely; incredibly; well; permanently; inviolately; safely; secretly; doggedly; sacredly; divinely; mysteriously; inexplicably; magnificently; splendidly.

PRESIDENT

adjectives

honorable; unqualified; wearied.

verbs

consult—; impeach—; inaugurate—; induct as—; —addresses; —adjourns; —administers; —advises; —appoints ; —berates; —conducts; —controls; —directs; —drives; —governs; —orates; —orders; —pilots; —presides; —rules; —sanctions.

(See official, chairman, judge, magistrate, executive, legislator.)

PRESS

adjectives

fluctuating; sensational; hostile; radical; daily; periodical; increasing; indefatigable; groaning; gagged; obnoxious; printing; vigilant; militant; bourgeois; respective; converted; brick; clashing; illustrated.

verbs

affiliate with—; divulge to—; gag—; meddle in—; regale—; ruffle—; tumble from—; —alludes to; —argues; —denounces; —discusses; —howls; —screams; —shouts; —spits out; —whirls.

(See literature, magazine, newspaper.)

PRESS (v)

adjectives

sorely; tenderly; vigorously; convulsively;

affectionately; emotionally; hotly; forcibly; desperately; courteously; cautiously; vigilantly; militantly.

(See compress, crowd.)

PRESSING

adverbs

strangely; curiously; immediately; insistently; persistently; inconveniently; instantly; inescapably; direly; embarrassingly; unduly; imperatively; absorbingly; desperately; gravely; critically; significantly; inordinately; portentously; momentously; ominously; peculiarly.

PRESSURE

adjectives

systolic; lingering; diplomatic; lateral; injurious; fierce; unreasoning; excessive; fluid; common; great; stupendous; aggressive; warm; angry; burning; teasing; atmospheric; irresistible; inevitable; convulsive; mechanical; extreme; sympathetic; cordial; normal; persistent; social; tremendous; superincumbent; opposing; diminished; insupportable; delicate; immense; inconstant; uniform; organized; undue; pecuniary; artificial.

verbs

alleviate—; apply—; counteract—; ease off—; employ—; exert—; expose to—; halt—; obliterate—; submit to—; succumb to—; subject to—; wobble under—; work under—; yield to—; —diminishes; —increases; —welds.

(See load, stress, force, power.)

PRESTIGE

adjectives

mysterious; personal; intellectual; frantic; national; original; unprecedented; considerable; glorious; battered; military; relative; enormous; extended; weighty; external.

verbs

acquire—; aspire to—; augment—; capitalize—; crack—; enhance—; enjoy—; extend —to; gain—; guarantee—; impair—; lessen —; lower—; preserve—; revive—; rival—; solidify—; threaten—; weaken—; —declines; —jumps.

(See influence.)

PRESUMABLE

adverbs

readily; reasonably; altogether; sensibly;

credibly; scarcely; hardly; barely; naturally; legally; easily; appropriately; particularly; circumstantially; wholly.

PRESUME (v)
adverbs
unblushingly; boldly; conceitedly; petulantly; insolently; arrogantly; insistently; pettishly.
(See assume, dare.)

PRESUMPTION
adjectives
subsequent; general; arrogant; insistent; petulant; insolent; fundamental; unwarranted; scientific.

PRESUMPTUOUS
adverbs
impertinently; ungraciously; offensively; conspicuously; boldly; audaciously; self-importantly; inexcusably; boorishly; uncivilly; disrespectfully; irreverently; brazenly; ignorantly; flippantly; obnoxiously; atrociously; unpardonably; egregiously; surprisingly; crassly; strikingly; arrogantly; recklessly; indiscreetly; imprudently; unbelievably; daringly; youthfully; obstinately; challengingly; obstreperously; foolishly; senselessly.

PRESUPPOSE (v)
adverbs
arrogantly; confidently; selfishly; carelessly; egotistically; independently.
(See assume, presume.)

PRETEND (v)
adverbs
satirically; childishly; deliberately; extravagantly; chimerically; groundlessly; idiotically; irrationally; sportively.
(See simulate, feign.)

PRETENDER
adjectives
sole; cowled; contemptible; royal.

PRETENSE
adjectives
specious; elaborate; cunning; slight; vile; selfish; theatrical; plausible; vain; boyish; transparent; empty; offensive; innocent; weary; unfounded; scorned; boastful; mere; false; insincere; melancholy; listless; emotional.

verbs
abandon—; accuse of—; afford—; assume —; avoid—; breed—; concoct—; criticize —; don—; eradicate—; fabricate—; garb in—; inveigh against—; justify—; offer—; penetrate—; pierce—; possess—; relax—; ridicule—; simulate—; strip of—; wallow in—; —awes; —deceives; —disguises;—distorts; —encroaches; —masks; —minces; —misbecomes; —misrepresents; —ornaments; —overacts; —overcharges; —perverts; —poses; —strains; —transgresses.
(See disguise, hypocrisy, sham, affectation, subterfuge, deception.)

PRETENSION
adjectives
groundless; ladylike; extravagant; capital; chimerical; present; unreasonable; aesthetic; arrogant; modish; aristocratic; lofty; faint; supernatural; obnoxious; serious; military; specific; rational; foolish; intellectual; genealogical; medieval; additional.

verbs
(See pretense.)

PRETENTIOUS
adverbs
foppishly; stiltedly; mincingly; simperingly; stagily; abominably; absurdly; ridiculously; ludicrously; laughably; disgustingly; pathetically; pompously; arrogantly; noisily; elaborately; cunningly; cleverly; theatrically; transparently; offensively; boastfully; harmlessly; unreasonably; loftily; unnecessarily; fantastically; artlessly; amusingly; prodigiously; colossally; tediously; stiffly.

PRETEXT
adjectives
specious; trifling; vulgar; plausible; worthy; reasonable; friendly; convenient; insignificant.

PRETTINESS
adjectives
bewildering; unearthly; verbal; slim; youthful; stiff; fantastic; painted.

PRETTY
adverbs
innocently; delightfully; rosily; childishly; seductively; alluringly; unbelievably; charmingly; undeniably; naturally; artlessly; unaffectedly; sweetly; unusually; bewitchingly; altogether; remarkably; strik-

ingly; unexpectedly; fascinatingly; wholesomely; radiantly; glowingly; unconsciously; pertly; smartly; artfully; particularly; uncommonly; matchlessly.

PREVAIL (v)
adverbs
ultimately; universally; unanimously; dominantly; uniformly; normally; imperiously; appallingly; annoyingly; turbulently.
(See rule, dominate.)

PREVALENCE
adjectives
marked; imperious; overwhelming; appalling; strong; everlasting; annoying.

PREVALENT
adverbs
widely; generally; currently; recently; naturally; disastrously; unfortunately; inexplicably; significantly; unhappily; unaccountably; ideologically; deucedly; blightingly; destructively; oddly; fashionably; transiently; momentarily; temporarily; insignificantly; briefly; formidably.

PREVENT (v)
adverbs
permanently; effectually; effectively; forcibly; admirably; cautiously; methodically; automatically; mechanically; scientifically; medically.
(See avert, hinder, thwart.)

PREVENTION
verbs
effect—; employ—; investigate—; —averts; —baffles; —blankets; —chokes; —cramps; —disconcerts; —disheartens; —dooms; —encounters; —hampers; —impedes; —nips; —stifles; —thwarts.
(See obstruction, hindrance, impediment.)

PREVENTIVE
adjectives
continual; effectual; admirable; extraordinary.

adverbs
highly; successfully; presumably; helpfully; usefully; actively; moderately; prudently; remarkably; uncommonly; usually; supposedly; credibly; possibly; unquestionably; sometimes.

PREY
adjectives
miserable; finny; helpless; predestined; unexhausted; lawful; accustomed; fair; universal; shattered; specious; legitimate; unambitious; stern; silent; yielding; righteous; reluctant.

verbs
attack—; corner—; descend on—; ensnare—; evade—; fall—to; grasp—; lurk for—; mangle—; pursue—; reconnoiter—; strike—; wrestle with—.
(See victim.)

PRICE
adjectives
unbelievable; prohibitive; exorbitant; heavy; minute; prevailing; comparative; minimum; sacrifice; advancing; rising; prehistoric; dirt-cheap; bottom; wholesale; sensational; competitive; amazing; fabric; specific; cash; low; proportionate; remarkable; sale; moderate; original; ridiculous; extreme; countless (pl); fractional; irresistible; bewildering; unheard-of; insufficient; trivial; possible; popular; basic; fantastic; reasonable; modest; imposing; absurd; attractive; bargain; reduced; exceptional; stiff; outrageous; unjustifiable; frightful; diurnal; internal; history-making; reserve; proportionate; remunerative; fabulous; interesting; impressive; modest; astonishing; anniversary; advertised; democratic; thrifty; wholesale; onerous; money-saving; pleasant; consistent; unusual; national; phenomenal; singular; characteristic; factory-to-you; impressive; astounding; concrete; idle; introductory; retail; disproportionate; losing.

verbs
bolster—; command—; demur at—; depress—; enhance—; fix—; haggle over—; hoist—; inflate—; reduce—; slash—; threaten—; —falls; —fluctuates; —flurries; —shoots up; —soars; —tumbles.
(See cost, amount, fee, tax, expense, value, charge, worth.)

PRICE (v)
adverbs
sensationally; attractively; reasonably; exorbitantly; modestly; economically; prohibitively; ridiculously; outrageously; fabulously; competitively; sensationally; disproportionately.
(See value.)

924

PRICELESS

adverbs
curiously; absolutely; sacredly; definitely; presumably; almost; altogether; sensationally; fantastically; immeasurably; incalculably; naturally; inimitably; superbly; magnificently; indescribably.

PRIDE

adjectives
absurd; adoring; amorous; arrogant; angry; aristocratic; barbarous; bounded; boyish; bubbling; calm; careful; bulldog; carnal; childish; civic; coeval; cold; commendable; competitive; conscious; considerable; contiguous; considerate; contemptible; craggy; daring; counterfeit; dark; defiant; delicious; demon; despairing; determined; disappointed; dormant; drooping; emulated; evident; excessive; exultant; fair; false; fantastical; fatuous; fiendish; fiery; firm; flattered; flowery; foamy; foolish; full-blown; garish; gay; generous; gentle; golden; gracious; grim; guiltless; hasty; haughty; heroic; hidden; high-blown; high-bred; holy; honest; housewifely; hurt; hypocritic; ignorant; imperial; inconsistent; indescribable; indomitable; inordinate; insolent; intellectual; interminable; intolerable; laudable; just; justifiable; legitimate; lingering; local; lofty; lovely; loyal; maiden; martial; masculine; matchless; maternal; melancholy; mingled; moderate; modest; monarchal; moral; morning; mortal; mortified; motley; much-vaunted; narrow; national; noble; obdurate; obstinate; offended; overweening; overwhelming; pardonable; particular; patrician; patriotic; personal; pertinacious; philosophic; piqued; piscatorial; pleasing; plunging; positive; pouting; prim; provincial; proper; purple; rapturous; reassuring; reflected; regal; ruthless; restless; reprehensible; retrospective; sad; sanctimonious; satisfactory; saucy; serpent; school-taught; secret; self-torturing; self-complacent; self-conscious; sensitive; shallow; sheltered; short-lived; signal; silent; single; snobbish; sober; special; spirited; splendid; spotless; stoic; stainless; stranded; stubborn; subdued; stupid; subtle; summer; sweet; tampering; tender; thankless; theatric; touchy; tyrannic; unendurable; ungenerous; unmixed; unsuspected; unvanquished; unwonted; vainglorious; vicarious; voluptuous; welling; wicked; worldly; womanly; wounded; wretched.

verbs
awaken—; beam with—; bloat with—; conceal—; flush with—; fortify—; glow with —; gratify—; humble—; injure—; lacerate —; pocket—; preserve—; reflect—; repress —; restrain—; rouse—; ruffle—; salve—; sting—; stir—; swallow—; swell with—; — animates; —armors; —bloats; —revolts; — supports.
(See conceit, vanity, arrogance, self-esteem.)

PRIEST

adjectives
solemn; white-robed; ministering; venerable; full; dull; frocked; persecuting; attendant; ash-smeared; long-haired; eagle-taloned; half-mad; wandering; native; pretended; sandaled; renegade; officiating; treacherous; unyielding; shameful; stout; rustic; rich; homey; luxurious; solitary; adorned; incensed; idolatrous; little; high; chanting; smooth-tongued; easy-living.

verbs
cloister—; confess to—; ordain—; —admonishes; —addresses; —attends; —baptizes; — blesses; —chants; —confirms; —consecrates; —converts; —fines; —genuflects; —hallows; —imposes; —instructs; —intercedes; —ministers to; —orders; —sanctifies; — serves; —supplicates.
(See minister, clergyman, clergy.)

PRIESTHOOD

adjectives
royal; idolatrous; self-constituted.

PRIESTLY

adverbs
reverently; devoutly; gently; sternly; helpfully; carefully; tolerantly; dutifully; fervently; admirably; estimably; zealously; ardently; diligently; earnestly; unfailingly; consistently; irreproachably.

PRIG

adjectives
sapless; offensive; hopeless; unsocial; obnoxious; well-meaning.

PRIGGISH

adverbs
intolerably; disagreeably; self-righteously; ostentatiously; uncomfortably; deucedly; unbearably; hatefully; immeasurably; unbelievably; miserably; unpleasantly; atrocious-

ly; inflexibly; pretentiously; awfully; suddenly; inveterately; incurably; offensively.

PRIM
adverbs
demurely; sedately; coyly; naturally; disagreeably; incurably; shyly; unsophisticatedly; pleasantly; uncomfortably; innocently; attractively; suddenly; unexpectedly; unaccountably; singularly; remarkably; amazingly; inscrutably; distinctly; self-consciously; bashfully; unnecessarily; needlessly; unfortunately; crudely; virtuously; prettily.

PRIMACY
adjectives
hierarchal; archangelic; established.

PRIME
adjectives
dancing; dominant; golden; autumnal; refulgent; blooming; young; luxuriant; lusty; early; unvalued.

PRIMITIVE
adverbs
unexpectedly; impossibly; intolerably; beautifully; unfashionably; stylishly; restfully; strikingly; pathetically; incredibly; curiously; grotesquely; fantastically; dramatically; spectacularly; uncomfortably; entertainingly; interestingly; singularly; hopelessly; undesirably; quaintly; sweetly; fearfully; miserably; comfortably; happily.

PRIMROSE
adjectives
full-faced; colored; fragrant; meaningful.

PRINCE
adjectives
sovereign; ambitious; praiseworthy; covetous; sagacious; pious; illustrious; merciful; faithful; humane; religious; upright; worthy; trained; petty; imperious; ecclesiastical; independent; chivalrous; tyrannical; scrupulous; economical; democratic; dethroned; barbarian; reigning; renowned; pusillanimous; arbitrary; sweet; auspicious; confiscating.

PRINCELY
adverbs
gorgeously; magnificently; lavishly; splendidly; brilliantly; regally; superbly; nobly; incredibly; indescribably; unutterably; unimaginably; immeasurably; imperiously; absolutely; graciously; gallantly; distinctly; imposingly; impressively; genuinely.

PRINCESS
adjectives
sanctimonious; enchanted; long-despoiled; extravagant; disinherited; meddlesome; overfrivolous.

PRINCIPAL
adjectives
skilled; deft; practiced; renowned; respected.

PRINCIPALITY
adjectives
ecclesiastical; autonomous; tributary; scanty.

PRINCIPLE
adjectives
political; fundamental; moral; poetical; infallible; unsuspected; applicable; acknowledged; essential; immortal; revolutionary; rigid; guiding; ultimate; wholesome; just; competitive; cantilever; inductive; mistaken; common; immutable; particular; thoughtful; sexual; strict; eternal; underlying; false; animating; incorporating; vital; involved; party; maleficent; despotic; sacred; religious; uniform; methodological; architectural; patriotic; latent; antagonistic; vigorous; virtuous; odious; death-bringing; pervading; evolutionary; anti-centralizing; active; chemical; unimpeachable; humanitarian; first; vicious; internal; untrue; inductive; mischievous; settled; rational; human; leading; exhausted; distorted; one-term; critical; intuitive; basic; ruling; durable; adverse; honorable; beautifying; abandoned; intelligible; simple; commonsense; fixed; cooperative; rudimental; scientific; irreconcilable; immaterial; preposterous; philosophical; artistic; cardinal; warlike; favorite; sound; unquestionable; established; high; proper; enlightened; better; novel; demonstrative; sound; self-exploding; moving; dynamic; ethical; phonetic; elementary; unjust; spirited; uniform; dazzling; racial; germinal.

verbs
abhor—; accept—; adhere to—; apply—; base on—; commit to—; comprehend—; compromise—; concur on—; contravene—; deduce—; dispute—; dissect—; embody; —embrace—; endorse—; enunciate—; espouse —; establish—; exemplify—; expound—;

extend—; formulate—; grasp—; illustrate —;inculcate—; infract—; infuse—; instill —; invest with—; invoke—; obscure—; oppose—; pledge to—; proclaim—; promulgate —; refute—; reiterate—; safeguard—; steep in—; trample—; unfold—; utilize—; vaunt —; vindicate—; violate—; —decays; —justifies; —triumphs; —underlies.

(See dogma, doctrine, fundamental, formula, essential, law, rule, policy.)

PRINT

adjectives *(ink)*
vivid; monotone; riotous; conspicuous; well-penetrated; impartial.

PRINT

verbs *(news)*
break into—; compose—; creep into—; dash off—; decipher—; draw up—; impress—; scan—; summarize—; type—; —arouses; —blazons; —broaches; —circulates; —diffuses; —engrosses; —enlightens; —exposes; —heralds; —proclaims; —reports; —reveals; —rumors.

(See press, newspaper, news.)

PRINT

adjectives *(picture)*
unframed; bright; false; colored; sticking; beauteous.

verbs
appreciate—; auction —s; brighten—; collect —s; color—; design—; frame—; imitate —; prize—; select—; study—; value—; —adorns; —attracts; —depicts; —embellishes; —harmonizes; —portrays; —suspends.

(See photograph, picture, painting.)

PRINT (v)

adverbs
slanderously; anonymously; indelibly; elegantly; professionally; impartially; irritatingly; sensationally; boldly; seditiously; scandalously; flatteringly.

(See publish.)

PRINTER

adjectives
enterprising; active; energetic; skilled; deft.

verbs
engage—; prepare for—; —arranges; —bundles; —composes; —copies; —effaces; —

errs; —inscribes; —issues; —measures; —presses; —publishes; —rushes; —sets up; —stains; —transcribes; —types.

(See publisher.)

PRISM

adjectives
refracting; colorful; revolving; perfect.

PRISMATIC

adverbs
gorgeously; iridescently; colorfully; beautifully; magnificently; magically; mysteriously; unbelievably; splendidly; phenomenally; gloriously; awesomely; unexpectedly; strikingly; matchlessly; brilliantly; dazzlingly; bewilderingly; fascinatingly; stunningly; astoundingly.

PRISON

adjectives
expensive; nonsensical; windowless; verbal; polluted; model; various (pl); wiry; medieval; repulsive; gloomy; twilight; squalid; voluntary; glittering; millennial; gilded; unsanitary.

verbs
cast into—; commit to—; languish in—; pine in—; rot in—; scuttle into—; throw into—; —bars; —cloisters; —confines; —encages; —gags; —harbors; —immures; —incarcerates; —paroles; —rehabilitates; —releases; —restrains; —yokes.

(See jail, dungeon, imprisonment, monastery, pillory.)

PRISONER

adjectives
panting; pardoned; life; sullen; self-made; incestuous; affable; emaciated; affable; defiant; careless; high-hearted; unfortunate; well-dressed; distinguished; disheartened; virtual; unprincipled; pale; wounded; linked; sorrowful; feathered; miserable; desperate.

verbs
arraign—; brand—; charge with—; denounce—; exonerate—; guard—; herd —s; incriminate—; indict—; liberate—; lodge—; prosecute—; release—; reproach—; restrain —; saddle—; slur—; stigmatize—; taunt—; twit—; vindicate—; —confesses; —implicates.

(See convict, captive, criminal.)

PRIVACY

adjectives

modified; necessary; outraged; perfect; absolute; tumultuous; defended; domestic; actual; comparative; boudoir; long-enjoyed; pleasing; desirable.

verbs

bottle up in—; couch in—; creep into—; demand—; deny—; destroy—; draw into—; embrace—; enjoy—; ensconce in—; infringe on—; impinge upon—; retire to—; rob of—; ruffle—; seclude in—; sink into—; yearn for —; —buries; —curtains; —fences; —mystifies; —puzzles; —repels; —shrouds.

(See concealment, isolation, seclusion, secrecy.)

PRIVATE

adverbs

strictly; necessarily; diplomatically; securely; safely; supposedly; sacredly; presumably; delightfully; furtively; secretly; particularly; confidentially; officially; intimately; appropriately; mysteriously; inviolably; surreptitiously; reticently; stealthily; pleasantly; happily; fortunately.

PRIVATION

adjectives

rigorous; material; signal; melancholy; revolting; ascetic; inevitable; personal; utmost; bitter; cruel; severe.

verbs

bear—; beget—; conceal—; endure—; experience—; expose to—; incur—; inflict—; meet with—; steel against—; suffer—; undergo—; —agitates; —agonizes; —chafes; —gnaws; —grates; —hinders; —pinches; —purifies; —racks; —smothers; —tortures.

(See hardship, impoverishment, poverty.)

PRIVILEGE

adjectives

royal; peculiar; ancient; valuable; additional; sublime; honorable; desolating; unrestricted; glorious; inestimable; immemorial; treasured; admirable; feudal; obsolete; cut-and-dried; antique; abused; fleeting; exclusive; exceptional; distinguishing; retirement; further; social; franking; chartered; undoubted; ancient; sovereign; accepted; cherished; irresistible.

verbs

abuse—; accord—to; assert—; bestow-upon; claim—; confer—upon; deprive of—; destroy—; encroach on—; extend—to; forego—; grant—; jeopardize—; overstep—; seek—; share—; strip of—; surrender—; wangle—; —enables; —expires.

(See independence, exemption, liberty, right.)

PRIVILEGED

adverbs

highly; especially; unfairly; fortunately; unaccountably; mysteriously; peculiarly; particularly; uniquely; inexplicably; financially; curiously; politically; socially; unusually; deservedly; indulgently; graciously; affectionately; freely; aristocratically; unconditionally; legally; duly; constitutionally; prescriptively; absolutely; properly.

PRIZE

adjectives

priceless; glittering; scarlet-bound; choice; coveted; easy; useless; savory; hard-earned.

verbs

acquire—; award—to; bestow—upon; capture—; collect —s; derive—; draw—; earn —; forfeit—; gain—; glean —s; merit—; obtain—; offer—; reap —s; reward with—; value—; win—; —allures; —enriches; —tempts.

(See laurels, medal.)

adverbs

inordinately; exceptionally; morbidly; casually; affectionately; ardently; exaggeratedly; memorably.

(See value, esteem.)

PRIZE-FIGHTER

verbs

—blocks; —bounds; —clinches; —counters; —dances; —ducks; —feints; —fouls; —groans; —hooks; —jabs; —launches; —levels; —pile-drives; —puffs; —skips; —smashes; —spars; —stabs; —stalls; —shadow-boxes; —trains; —unleashes; —uppercuts; —weakens; —whirls; —winds.

(See fighter, boxer.)

PROBABILITY

adjectives

inconceivable; golden; human; inherent; precarious; imminent.

consider—; contemplate—; erase—; evaluate
—; ground on—; ignore—; invest with—;
point to—; seek—; snort at—; speculate on
—; study—; trace—; —diminishes; —implies; —fathers; —justifies; —tempts.

(See chance, opportunity, possibility.)

PROBABLE

adverbs

highly; circumstantially; scarcely; hardly;
barely; naturally; extremely; confidently;
apparently; reasonably.

PROBATION

adjectives

healthful; troubled; temporary.

PROBATIONARY

adverbs

wisely; prescriptively; experimentally; naturally; sensibly; venturesomely; fortunately; virtually; luckily; distinctly; undoubtedly.

PROBE (*v*)

adverbs

secretly; deeply; curiously; morbidly; surgically; deftly; searchingly.

(See examine, investigate.)

PROBLEM

adjectives

sufficient; invincible; insolvable; residue;
important; age-old; perplexing; harassing;
abstruse; complicated; puzzling; criminal;
psychological; lifelong; farming; everyday;
pretty; metaphysical; decorative; vital; serious; ultimate; speculative; surgical; menacing; technical; arduous; executive; ethical;
comparative; easy; confusing; vast; terrifying; moral; unsolved; dramatic; tremendous; duplex; profound; acute; specific;
changing; individual; challenging; intricate; mathematical; deep; basic; striking;
personal; contemporary; social; workable;
troublesome; transportation; intellectual;
urgent; practical; vexatious; conflicting;
integral; defined; passionless; terrible;
graphic; discouraging; weighty; insoluble;
delicate; great; rising-hour; unanswerable;
rapid; accumulating; mooted; childish; evolutionary; economic; doleful; original; stupendous; pressing; uncontrollable; abstract;
orientation; individual; connected; vexing;
philosophic; veiled; shopping.

verbs

absorb in—; aggravate—; analyze—; approach—; attack—; boil down—; circumvent—; come to grips with—; complicate—;
confront with—; constitute—; contemplate
—; cope with—; deal with—; detour—; dismiss—; dispose of—; dissect—; dodge—;
engross in—; envisage—; expound—; face
with—; focus on—; formulate—; grapple
with—; high-light—; illuminate—; labor
over—; master—; meditate on—; misconceive—; outline—; ponder—; pose—; precipitate—; propound—; restate—; shed light
on—; smooth out—; solve—; struggle with
—; survey—; tackle—; wrestle with—; —s
baffle; —bedevils; —s beset; —embraces;
—looms; —narrows down to; —plagues; —
ruffles; —vexes.

(See riddle, matter, mathematics, predicament.)

PROBLEMATICAL

adverbs

ticklishly; delicately; altogether; precariously; distinctly; fearfully; critically; definitely; painfully; disturbingly; unusually; nicely; obscurely; intricately; perplexingly; curiously; singularly; disconcertingly; vexatiously; plaguedly; extremely.

PROCEDURE

adjectives

characteristic; momentous; amiable; peaceful; unprovoking; abstract; simple; obstinate; intellectual; mystical; well-established;
critical; specific; analytic; scandalous; energetic; wonted; tiresome; practical; routine;
educational; emergency; complicated.

verbs

adopt—; alter—; bear—; condemn—; conduct—; devise—; discharge—; disrupt—;
enact—; execute—; handle—; justify—;
manage—; open—; participate in—; practise—; shape—; study—; suggest—; terminate—; transact—; wind up—; —awes; —
bores; —"clicks".

(See transaction, process, routine, usage.)

PROCEED (*v*)

adverbs

softly; moderately; nonchalantly; systematically; circuitously; divergently; solemnly;
resolutely; vigorously; majestically; awk-

wardly; monotonously; cautiously; methodically; inquisitorially; suspiciously; summarily; critically; amiably; characteristically.

(See advance, progress.)

PROCEEDING

adjectives

rash; solemn; revolutionary; factious; ominous; hot; comely; furious; cumbrous; inquisitorial; cautious; ungrateful; odious; perfect; characteristic; momentous; customary; tumultuous; suspicious; mean; false; summary; manifest; violent; mere; negligent; offensive.

PROCEEDINGS

verbs

annul—; avoid—; conclude—; conduct—; denounce—; disturb—; institute—; legalize —; threaten—; —betray; —bore; —commence; —drag; —tire; —undo; —weary.

(See investigation, action.)

PROCEEDS

adjectives

pecuniary; astounding; unexpected; small.

verbs

deliver—; derive—; devote—to; draw—; inherit—; net—; pay—; procure—; raise—; realize—; reap—; secure—; swell—; treasure—; yield—; —accrue; —accumulate; produce—.

(See income, profit.)

PROCESS

adjectives

administrative; beautifying; combustion; tedious; abrasion; continuing; lucrative; doubtful; elaborate; same; dreary; exclusive; refining; expert; improved; unequivocal; cognitive; delicate; wrapping; ingenious; carving; artificial; evident; fundamental; cultural; glaucomatous; quick-freezing; digestive; tentative; clarifying; fertilizing; subjective; summary; manufacturing; simple; unconscious; intertwined; elementary; pleasant; logical; inductive; volitive; culinary; exacting; continuous; just; cream-choking; regular; inflammatory; obscure; complicated; mental; ricocheting; wasteful; technical; careful; expressive; circumrotary; punitive; reproductive; pressure; patented; sluggish; merciless; inflationary; remedial; primitive; monotypic; dynamic; fascinating; predictable; complex; artful; essential; physical; aquatint; haphazard; phy-

siological; secret; scientific; expensive; oriental; concentrated; painful; embarrassing; minor; bleaching; ordinary; coercive; democratic; purifying; informal; improved; incubating; involuntary; curbing; evolutionary; learning; laborious; uncertain; orderly; rational; inevitable; chemical; diabetic; synthetic; unique; extensive; blood-atonement; new-discovered; searching; creative; psychological; cyanide; deleterious; beneficient; educational; actual; organic; ineradicable; stultifying; variegated; miraculous; deliberate; artistic; torturing; gradual-reduction; persuasive; developed; exasperating; needless; natural; familiar; enlightened; subsequent; chastening; enormous; suitable; morbid.

verbs

accelerate—; advocate—; clarify—; develop —; disclose—; engross in—; facilitate—; hinder—; perfect—; prolong—; push—; regulate—; reject—; retard—; revamp—; reverse—; simplify—; subject to—; terminate—; undergo—; —evolves through; —fabricates; —refines.

(See operation, method, procedure.)

PROCESSION

adjectives

melancholy; pompous; bright; proud; solemn; dim; spangle-clad; funeral; timely; triumphal; torch-light; dull; spontaneous; gaudy; unnoticed; monkish; phantom; festal; unending; ant-like; stately; impressive; historic; parading; demure; triumphant; endless; dripping; religious; sacrificial; white-robed; imposing; mournful; motley; pensive; uniformed; sad; priestly; continuous; rustling; pale; picturesque; straggling; slow; lamentable; penitential; votive.

verbs

arrange—; disconcert—; interpose—; interrupt—; review—; —ambles; —attracts; —blazons; —bowls along; —courses; —displays; —files by; —glides by; —jogs; —paces; —plods; —shuffles; —struts; —trots; —wends.

(See parade, expedition, excursion, marchers, pageant.)

PROCESSIONAL

adverbs

gorgeously; ceremoniously; ceremonially; reverently; harmoniously; magnificently; splendidly; brilliantly; pretentiously; decoratively; decorously; joyously; triumphantly; conventionally; patriotically; mournfully; quietly; majestically; gravely; properly; appropriately.

PROCLAIM (v)
adverbs
formally; proudly; publicly; triumphantly; ostentatiously; loquaciously; boisterously; exuberantly; boldly; enthusiastically; seditiously; exultantly; solemnly.
(See announce, publish.)

PROCLAMATION
adjectives
celebrated; artful; supplementary; seditious; atrocious; insidious; magniloquent; flowery; preliminary; stirring; exultant; solemn; defiant; brilliant; plain-speaking; feeble.

verbs
authorize—; emit—; issue—; post—; prepare—; promulgate—; publish—; recite—; —announces; —blazons; —broaches; —circulates; —diffuses; —disseminates; —heralds; —spreads; —surprises.
(See ban, edict, headline, announcement, notice.)

PROCLIVITY
adjectives
hopeless; sentimental; dangerous; insidious.

verbs
denounce—; endow with—; limit—; promote—; redound to—; temper—; warp—; —affects; —bends; —bids; —conduces; —disposes; —enables; —gravitates; —inclines; —predisposes; —tends; —verges.
(See tendency, inclination, propensity.)

PROCRASTINATION
verbs
addict to—; remedy—; —cools; —defers; —delays; —endangers; —irks; —irritates; —postpones; —prorogues; —protracts; —retards; —stalls; —staves off; —suspends; —waives; —wearies.
(See delay, indolence.)

PROCURE (v)
adverbs
legally; lustfully; lasciviously; salaciously; seasonally; carnally; periodically; sentimentally.
(See acquire, obtain, achieve.)

PRODIGAL
adjectives
good-natured; niggardly; rehabilitated; unconscionable; returning; prodigious; guilty; sinful; wicked; selfish.

adverbs
wastefully; reprehensibly; foolishly; wantonly; dissolutely; sadly; unthriftily; blithely; recklessly; rashly; lavishly; senselessly; thoughtlessly; selfishly; extravagantly; needlessly; immensely; witlessly; absurdly; ridiculously; wickedly; inordinately; unhappily.

PRODIGALITY
adjectives
boundless; reckless.

PRODIGIOUS
adverbs
incredibly; inordinately; amazingly; unbelievably; unaccountably; immeasurably; incalculably; strikingly; miraculously; uncommonly.

PRODIGY
adjectives
flashing; unique; infant; valorous; accompanying; juvenile; extraordinary; necromantic.

PRODUCE
adjectives
scanty; rude; dark; peaceful.

PRODUCE (v)
adverbs
prolifically; lavishly; magically; legitimately; enthusiastically; artificially; characteristically; infallibly; generously; systematically; wantonly; dramatically; luxuriantly; agriculturally; indigenously.
(See generate, yield.)

PRODUCER
adjectives
potential; multitudinous (pl); independent; rich.

PRODUCT
adjectives
national; advertised; fundamental; better; uncrystallizable; commercial; vegetable; salable; sole; glandular; seasonable; staple; meager; pharmaceutic; morphine; accepted; appetizing; attractive; abundant; delicious; wholesome; poisonous; natural; lusty; re-

sultant; non-perishable; noble; choice; dubious; abundant (pl); pristine; spontaneous; admired; extant; filthy; humble; phantastic; extraordinary; good; sensational; amazing; fast-selling; quality; rare; useful; guaranteed; liked; wanted; diversified (pl); allied (pl); abrasive; amphibious; definite; superstandard; multiform (pl); delectable; menacing; insidious; basic; efficient; amalgamated; recent; superior; barbarous; unforced; representative; marvelous; luxurious; dutiable; unpalatable; uniform; miraculous.

verbs
acclaim—; clamor for—; consume—; contribute to—; convert—; degrade—; deposit —; evolve—; finish—; handle—; market—; purvey—; retail—; transform—; transport —; utilize—; waste—.
(See fruit, crop, harvest, output.)

PRODUCTION
adjectives
attractive; quantity; continuous; figure; indigenous; abortive; rhythmical; luxuriant; deep; earned; increased; labored; earnest; aggregate; mechanical; dramatic; chief; finished; varied; conventional; prolific; industrial; assembly-line; plastic; digestible; commercial; poetical; intensive; economic; spontaneous; carnal; appropriate; estimated; curtailed; dramatic; celebrated; aboriginal; vegetable; interrupted; momentary; capacity; crude; intelligent; monstrous; multifarious; maximum; agricultural; dewless; artificial; elaborate; faultless; isolated; immortal; composite; stimulated.

verbs
absorb—; accelerate—; ascribe—to; augment—; bolster—; boom—; cancel—; control—; curtail—; delay—; determine—; disrupt—; doom—; expand—; guide—; hamper—; measure—; quadruple—; rehearse —; scuttle—; simplify—; sponsor—; stimulate—; suspend—.
(See output, product.)

PRODUCTIVE
adverbs
unusually; amazingly; strikingly; miraculously; conveniently; opportunely; profitably; commercially; surprisingly; sensationally; spectacularly; satisfactorily; adequately;

highly; fortunately; experimentally; scientifically; naturally; famously; eminently; remarkably; uncommonly.

PROFANATION
adjectives
proposed; foul; ruinous; picturesque; menaced; lingering; definite; calculated; monstrous.

PROFANE
adverbs
irreverently; brazenly; openly; blasphemously; perversely; sacrilegiously; scoffingly; intolerably; terribly; godlessly; indefensibly; inexcusably; scandalously; wickedly; offensively; indecorously; scurrilously; luridly; startlingly; horribly; unspeakably; abominably; hideously; unbecomingly; shrilly; noisily; mutteringly; unutterably; impossibly; impiously; shamelessly.

PROFANE (v)
adverbs
obscenely; blasphemously; raucously; vulgarly; uncouthly; villainously; barbarously; diabolically.
(See violate, debase.)

PROFANITY
adjectives
inarticulate; smothered; delicate; picturesque; time-honored; extraordinary; unbelievable; purposeless; shocking; disgusting; unmanly; stubborn; raucous; unnecessary; deliberate.

PROFESS (v)
adverbs
ignorantly; ostentatiously; impulsively; boldly; gaily; carelessly; obstreperously; vainly; vigorously; shamelessly; enthusiastically.
(See admit, claim, avow.)

PROFESSION
adjectives
peaceful; rich; dissimilar (pl); dramatic; sacred; lettered; universal; knavish; solemn; kind; respectable; lucrative; clerical; shining; hard-working; shady; pacific; stupid; grave; educated; destined; medical; fraternal; chivalrous; preserved; inherited; honorable; paternal; private; noble; remunerative; knowing; earnest; obvious; elaborate.

verbs
commit to—; contract—; devote oneself to —; engage in—; enter—; fill—; follow—; honor—; overcrowd—; ply—; practise—; prosecute—; prosper in—; pursue—; struggle in—; undertake—; —adjures; —binds; —employs; —engages; —exacts; —obligates; —occupies.

(See calling, employment, industry, law, teaching.)

PROFESSIONAL

adverbs
strictly; scarcely; hardly; highly; expertly; self-consciously; ridiculously; absurdly; suddenly; incredibly; pretentiously; obscurely; insistently; consistently; supposedly; emphatically; assertively; dogmatically; formally; solemnly; conspicuously; unmistakably; prodigiously; ostentatiously.

PROFESSIONALISM

verbs
acquire—; commit to—; denounce—; discontinue—; display—; don—; drop—; exhibit —; practise—; shroud in—; study—; —annoys; —attends; —exacts; —irks; —irritates; —proselytes; —ties; —wearies.

PROFESSOR

adjectives
renowned; theorizing; mournful; dogmatizing; world-famed; controlling; volunteer; unsympathetic; eminent; assiduous; miserable; braintrust; unemployed; unlearned; grave; wizened; wise; absent-minded; kindly; knowing; eccentric; research; modest; masterful.

PROFICIENCY

adjectives
speedy; practical; established; technical; similar; obvious; palpable; notable; demonstrated.

verbs
acquire—; commend—; demand—; gain—; maintain—; misapply—; perceive—; possess —; praise—; profess—; realize—; recognize—; —accomplishes; —conquers; —defeats; —lags; —masters; —outflanks; —overcomes; —prevails; —succeeds; —triumphs; —weathers.

(See mastery, skill, ability, power.)

PROFICIENT

adverbs
obviously; unmistakably; marvelously; amazingly; emphatically; unfailingly; miraculously; singularly; curiously; indubitably; skilfully; expertly; remarkably; unsurpassably; matchlessly; profoundly; dexterously; deftly; felicitously; confidently; cunningly; admirably; commendably; consummately.

PROFILE

adjectives
sloping; inquisitive; clean-cut; architectural; Roman; sable; coin-clear; melancholy; aquiline; energetic; bold; flawless; regular; delicate; fine; vapid; athletic; Grecian; Nordic; gaunt; grisly; smooth; fetching; sagging; gripping; romantic; grim; noble; criminal.

PROFIT

adjectives
generous; quick; sensational; large; cash; clear; general; liberal; tremendous; amazing; steady; spot-cash; repeated; enormous; real; old-fashioned; staggering; unlimited; startling; additional; volume; big; daily; handsome; easy; distributed; potential; competitive; personal; substantial; immense; mutual; divided; moderate; reinvested; small; healthy; material; extortionate; sharp; singular; prospective; present; estimated; inconceivable; colossal; immediate; slender; honest; regular; individual; speculative; utmost; increasing; absolute; illicit; pecuniary; monetary; usurious; abnormal.

verbs
account for—; amass—; ascertain—; assure of—; consume—; create—; derive—from; eat—; educe—; eliminate—; evolve—; net —; pocket—; preclude—; reap—; retain—; spell—; squeeze—; swell—; —accrues; —booms; —evaporates; —lures; —materializes; —piles up; —s rise; —shoots from.

(See income, gain, emolument, pay, money.)

PROFIT (v)

adverbs
sensationally; liberally; enormously; potentially; competitively; personally; moderately; materially; colossally; pecuniarily; usuriously; abnormally.

(See gain, benefit.)

933

PROFITABLE

adverbs

highly; unusually; commercially; financially; professionally; remarkably; surprisingly; amazingly; inordinately; extraordinarily; extremely; unexpectedly; scarcely; hardly; altogether; socially; secretly; mysteriously; shadily; peculiarly; strangely.

PROFLIGATE

adjectives

despairing; lecherous; hopeless; debauched; drunken; unsocial.

verbs

admonish—; chastise—; condemn—; convert from—; punish—; rebuke—; reform—; reproach—; scald—; —brutalizes; —corrupts; —demoralizes; —deviates; —errs; —lapses; —offends; —sins; —slips; —strays; —transgresses; —trespasses; —sinks.

(See scoundrel, villain, criminal.)

PROFOUND

adverbs

mystically; abstrusely; obscurely; pedantically; eruditely; theologically; provokingly; prosaically; gravely; admittedly; politically; sagaciously; distinctly; shrewdly; keenly; astutely; rationally; impartially; thoughtfully; perspicaciously; oracularly; impressively; amazingly; inscrutably; doctrinally.

PROFUSE

adverbs

wonderfully; uncommonly; delightfully; unexpectedly; surprisingly; amazingly; curiously; strangely; exuberantly; luxuriantly; profitably; overly; wastefully; extravagantly; foolishly; senselessly; abundantly; amply; unsparingly; wickedly.

PROFUSION

adjectives

utmost; sheer; lavish; tempting; sumptuous; vernal; incalculable; happy; thick; ostentatious; glossy; luxuriant; extraordinary; disorderly; gothic.

PROGENY

adjectives

little; ungracious; twin-born; vigorous; numerous; enslaved; multiplied.

PROGNOSTICATION

adjectives

gloomy; financial; anguished; supernatural.

verbs

cast—; contemplate—; ignore—; justify—; —augurs; —betokens; —bids; —calculates; —discerns; —excites; —foreshadows; —foretells; —forewarns; —heralds; —points to; —precurses; —predicts; —presages; —promises; —senses; —signifies; —worries.

(See foreboding, prediction, forecast, prophecy.)

PROGRAM

adjectives

rigorous; coherent; laborious; inviting; commercial; aggressive; sponsored; balanced; serious; comprehensive; reading; great; fiction; economical; diagnosed; voluntary; relief; constructive; abstergent; seductive; varied; modernization; entertaining; aesthetic; exhaustive; ultra-professional; systematic; selfsame; sustaining; peace; nationwide; educational; social.

verbs

adhere to—; adopt—; attack—; bowl over —; carry out—; defer—; design—; devote to—; elaborate on—; embark on—; endorse —; evaluate—; evolve—; expand—; familiarize with—; formulate—; initiate—; institute—; integrate—; launch—; map out—; modify—; oppose—; outline—; participate in—; pound away at—; sketch—; submit—; supervise—; swamp—; thread through—; vary—; view—; —embraces; —languishes.

(See itinerary, list, menu.)

PROGRESS

adjectives

educational; marvelous; amazing; unbroken; moral; physical; successful; beneficent; actual; material; phenomenal; torturing; excellent; painful; joyous; eventful; social; obvious; mechanical; sufficient; luxurious; artistic; enormous.

verbs

abate—; achieve—; arrest—; blight—; block—; check—; control—; curb—; curtail —; expedite—; extend—; facilitate—; halt —; herald—; hinder—; impede—; imperil —; indicate—; insure—; keep abreast of—; mark by—; measure—; promote—; record —; retard—; survey—; trace—; yield to—.

(See advance, advancement, civilization, development, growth.)

adverbs

exultantly; boldly; methodically; spectacularly; enormously; swiftly; tardily; phenomenally; socially; mechanically; artistically; markedly.

(See advance, proceed.)

PROGRESSION

adjectives

audacious; endless; constant; harmonic; chromatic; upward.

PROGRESSIVE

adverbs

naturally; unusually; exceptionally; satisfactorily; ambitiously; pseudously; slowly; dependably; reliably; steadily; amazingly; happily; remarkably; startlingly; incredibly; unbelievably; unexpectedly; highly; gratifyingly; solidly; substantially; brilliantly; undeniably.

PROHIBITION

adjectives

virtual; positive; perpetual; reiterated.

verbs

annul—; defy—; denounce—; deplore—; dispute—; enforce—; ignore—; laud—; support—; undermine—; uphold—; urge—; — debars; —forbids; —restrains; —restricts; —revokes; —smothers; —suppresses; —taboos.

(See taboo, embargo, ban, edict.)

PROHIBITIVE

adverbs

meanly; unhappily; unwisely; sordidly; racially; inordinately; senselessly; foolishly; viciously; strictly; sternly; legally; officially; authoritatively; narrowly; dogmatically; imperiously; unwarrantably; unfairly; narrow-mindedly; ineptly; antagonistically; disagreeably; unconscionably; unnecessarily; groundlessly; wisely; necessarily; warily; vigilantly; shrewdly; carefully; financially; prescriptively.

PROJECT

adjectives

ambitious; titanic; resettlement; juvenile; cherished; philosophical; cunning; sublime; modified; unrealized; reclamation; cumbersome; wild; murderous; audacious; brilliant; stupendous; immense; rehabilitation; relief; works; national.

verbs

abandon—; broach—; dedicate—; develop —; discard—; discourage—; expand—; formulate—; horn in on—; incubate—; launch —; lose in—; plan—; quash—; turn down —; —centers upon; —collapses; —goes awry; —marches to completion; —takes shape.

(See idea, design, enterprise.)

PROJECT (v)

adverbs

stereoscopically; distinctly; obtrusively; naively; infinitesimally; sharply; fantastically; ruggedly.

(See extend, jut, protrude.)

PROJECTILE

verbs

bolt—; cast—; discharge—; drive—; emit —; expel—; fire—; heave—; hurl—; pitch —; propel—; shoot—; sling—; toss—; — darts; —forces; —impels; —screams by; —whistles.

(See bomb, bullet.)

PROJECTION

adjectives

rugged; blunted; infinitesimal; gnomonic; jutting; far-reaching; sharp.

PROLETARIAT

verbs

assail—; debar—; denounce—; grind—; incite—; restrain—; restrict—; smother—; stir—; support—; suppress—; trammel—; tyrannize over—; —defies; —degrades; — inflames; —labors; —rises; —revolts; — strikes.

(See bourgeoisie, foreigner, alien, peasant, worker, employer.)

PROLIFIC

adverbs

unusually; highly; distinctly; healthily; sadly; happily; fortunately; amazingly; normally; uncommonly; surprisingly; remarkably; undeniably.

PROLOGUE

adjectives

symphonic; learned; explanatory; necessary; useless; space-filling.

PROLONG (v)

adverbs

indefinitely; unduly; agonizingly; perpetually; embarrassingly; tantalizingly; excessively.

(See lengthen, extend.)

PROMENADE

adjectives
mental; solitary; public; sociable; daily; amorous; fashionable.

PROMINENCE

adjectives
political; literary; excessive; high; rocky; dominating; naked; especial; extraordinary; historical; disturbing; modest.

verbs
attain—; bounce into—; burst into—; deplore—; drag up to—; elevate to—; expose to—; hoist to—; jump into—; lift to—; merit—; mount to—; soar to—; —awes; —commands; —crowns; —exalts; —heightens; —mantles; —perches; —weighs.

(See distinction, fame, eminence.)

PROMINENT

adverbs
unusually; questionably; brilliantly; impressively; wickedly; boldly; audaciously; officially; officiously; curiously; strangely; inexplicably; noticeably; conspicuously; brazenly; eminently; gorgeously; gloriously; radiantly; rightfully; majestically; splendidly; memorably; illustriously.

PROMISCUITY

verbs
condemn—; denounce—; drift into—; refrain from—; shrink from—; suffer—; —agitates; —brews; —corrupts; —deranges; —diffuses; —disorders; —entangles; —reduces; —ruffles; —rumples.

(See indifference, mixture.)

PROMISCUOUS

adverbs
strangely; inexplicably; unaccountably; naturally; inevitably; democratically; significantly; necessarily; shamefully; reprehensibly; embarrassingly; unmanageably; unexpectedly; obviously; complexly; indiscriminately; casually; fortuitously; accidentally.

PROMISE

adjectives
optimistic; heartfelt; significant; solemn; dormant; fertile; considerable; whispered; liberal; maudlin; tremendous; firm; indefin-

ite; conservative; drunken; rash; cheerful; exceptional; remorseful; valiant; unbreakable; vernal; flattering; cheering; gracious; false; definite; scant; pathetic; tacit; doubtful; unredeemed; brilliant; deceiving; high; express; faithful; unfulfilled; light; haughty; scorching; stout-limbed; implied; nugatory; imperial.

verbs
avail oneself of—; carry out—; clutch—; dangle—; dispense—s; elicit—; enforce—; extort—; extract—; fulfill—; gain—; ignore—; issue—; nullify—; puncture—; redeem—; violate—; void—; —binds; —s clash; —electrifies; —implies; —materializes; —pledges; —sanctifies.

(See bond, contract, covenant, compromise, pledge.)

PROMISE (v)

adverbs
blithely; solemnly; vehemently; punctually; devoutly; cheerfully; blandly; speciously; optimistically; liberally; maudlinly; graciously; flatteringly; tacitly; lightly.

(See pledge, assure.)

PROMISING

adverbs
brilliantly; altogether; hopefully; unquestionably; remarkably; uncommonly; highly; splendidly; indubitably; auspiciously; distinctly; definitely.

PROMONTORY

adjectives
beaked; eminent; sea-beaten; keen-faced; salubrious; hoary; rock-girt; remote; mountainous; rugged; wooded; high; moon-bathed; venerable.

PROMOTE (v)

adverbs
infrequently; essentially; subsequently; wisely; swiftly; promptly; tardily; gratuitously; insidiously; seditiously; skillfully; ambitiously.

(See advance, encourage.)

PROMOTER

adjectives
zealous; doughty; enterprising; high-pressure; genial; sports; deft; skilled.

adjectives

picturesque; swift; deserved; lineal; gratuitous; prompt.

verbs

award—; deserve—; favor—; foster—; gain—; merit—; reward by—; secure—; seek—; —ameliorates; —betters; —bolsters; —brightens; —cheers; —elevates; —encourages; —enhances; —enriches; —invigorates; —smooths.

(See progress, advancement.)

PROMPT

adverbs

dependably; reliably; punctiliously; surprisingly; meticulously; carefully; always; curiously; significantly; suspiciously; courteously; considerately; graciously; cheerfully; politely; ingratiatingly; wisely; usually; unfailingly; pleasantly; gratifyingly.

PROMPTING

adjectives

imperious; deep-seated; inner; physiological; base; quiet; serious; definite.

PROMPTNESS

adjectives

absolute; self-satisfied; incredible; well-meant; characteristic; soldierly; utmost; unexampled; noncommittal; deliberate; practiced; remarkable.

PRONOUNCE (*v*)

adverbs

whimsically; unanimously; syllabically; solemnly; unhesitatingly; emphatically; impressively; weightily; definitely; academically.

(See speak, utter.)

PRONOUNCEMENT

adjectives

weighty; impressive; scientific; definite; startling.

verbs

authorize—; await—; circulate—; issue—; post—; prepare—; promulgate—; publish —; relay—; spread—; —blazons; —broaches; —diffuses; —disseminates; —heralds; —proclaims; —rings out.

(See proclamation, announcement.)

adjectives

careful; defective; smooth; facile; slipshod; hasty; inaccurate; local; improper; incorrect; antiquated; slovenly; lip-lazy; faulty; outlandish; uncouth; arbitrary; accepted.

verbs

accentuate—; alter—; aspirate—; bark—; clarify—; correct—; criticize—; detect—; drawl—; drown—; improve—; lament—; mangle—; mutter—; practise—; ridicule—; swallow—; —confuses; —perplexes.

(See accent, utterance.)

PROOF

adjectives

absolute; remarkable; experimental; confirming; ample; undeniable; refined; positive; indisputable; incontestable; irrefragable; actual; traditional; palpable; vulgar; abundant; similar; conclusive; distinct; documentary; lucid; secondary; innate; strenuous; tangible; irresistible; gratifying; strict; historical; convincing; incompatable; forcible; presumptive; convenient; melancholy; corroborative; perpetual; decisive; indubitable; gallery; ocular; bedrock; added; definite; practical; sufficient; triumphant; divine; dingy; authentic; shadowy; exemplary; formal; continuing; quick; legal; hourly; insidious; cruel; doubtful; dramatic; concrete; phenomenal; childhood.

verbs

advance—; cite—; demand—; demonstrate —; devise—; dig—; digest—; draw—; establish—; evince—; prepare—; question—; reflect upon—; seek—; strike at—; —checks; —leaks; —s multiply; —settles; —substantiates; —verifies.

(See argument, evidence, confirmation.)

PROPAGANDA

adjectives

sedulous; sentimental; insidious; insistent; commercial; primitive; blatant; suicidal; incessant; educational; systematic; subversive; sinister; treacherous; political.

verbs

assail—; bedevil with—; denounce—; deny —; direct—at; dispute—; disseminate—; distrust—; doubt—; found on—; grind out —; impregnate with—; ignore—; mask—; pump—into; question—; release—; swallow —; weave—; —bewilders; —convinces; —

deceives; —edifies; —enlightens; —exploits; —familiarizes; —ignites; —implants; —impresses; —inculcates; —inflames; —misinforms; —misrepresents; —pervades; —perverts; —staggers; —startles; —threatens; —undermines.

(See message, doctrine, lie.)

PROPAGATE (v)
adverbs
peacefully; seditiously; agriculturally; radically; cunningly; audaciously; seasonally.

(See increase, reproduce.)

PROPEL (v)
adverbs
vigorously; swiftly; deftly; skillfully; leisurely; brilliantly; valiantly; daringly; rashly.

(See drive, force, impel.)

PROPELLOR
verbs
jerk—; rake—; start—; tug—; yank (colloq.)—; —arouses; —actuates; —calms; —drives; —forces; —halts; —hushes; —impels; —lashes; —revolves; —rotates; —spins; —urges; —whirs; —whizzes; —wrenches.

(See motor, fan.)

PROPENSITY
adjectives
martial; bad; edifying; cruel; feline; gregarious; bucaneering; degraded; mischievous; piscatorial; unsuspected; social; vulgar; erratic; indignant; unconscious; amorous; remarkable; noteworthy; unusual.

verbs
denounce—; gratify—; promote—; temper —; tempt—; —affects; —bends; —bids; —conduces; —disposes; —fancies; —gravitates; —inclines; —tends; —thirsts; —verges.

(See inclination, disposition, proclivity.)

PROPER
adverbs
conventionally; socially; altogether; acceptably; legally; punctiliously; carefully; cautiously; anxiously; graciously; courteously; politely; deferentially; respectfully; reverently; quietly; serenely; laboriously; easily; becomingly; demurely; correctly; unfailingly.

PROPERTY
adjectives
toxic; consular; medicinal; sonorous; outcropped; curative; beneficial; stimulating; private; extensive; desired; elaborate; inalienable; injurious; historical; magnetic; virgin; intellectual; inherent; structural; mechanical; business; essential; surplus; immense; profitable; defunct; physical; admirable; tonic; virtuous; airy; violent; ultimate; poisonous; permanent; living; distinctive; landed; deliquescent; exclusive; health-giving; contested; luminous; papal; adjacent; unpredictable; ice-melting; acid-resisting; agreeable; specific; absolute; phonetic; substantial; acoustic; immutable; unentailed; nutritious; clinging; ancestral; existing; emollient.

verbs
acquire—; allocate—; assess—; confiscate—; deplete—; deprive of—; destine to—; destroy—; exalt—; expropriate—; fence—; guard—; inherit—; insure—; levy on—; liquidate—; retain—; saddle—; squander—; transfer—; —abuts; —includes.

(See estate, legacy, asset, inheritance, possessions.)

PROPHECY
adjectives
unpleasing; vaunting; bitter; humbler; gloomy; drunken; backward-glancing; optimistic; retrospective; impassionate; mad; imposing; painful; fanciful; ominous; dogmatic; numerous (pl); enkindling; maiden; pessimistic; apocalyptic; omnipresent; sanguine; fulfilled; inspired; prospective.

verbs
divine—; fulfill—; ignore—; mock—; scoff at—; sustain—; —augurs; —betokens; —bodes; —excites; —forecasts; —foreshadows; —foretells; —heralds; —points to; —precurses; —predicts; —presages; —promises; —warns.

(See forecast, prediction, foreboding, prognostication.)

PROPHET
adjectives
maddening; dumb; twice-tongued; fiery; courageous; master; disbelieved.

PROPHETIC
adverbs
wildly; hysterically; gravely; seriously;

oracularly; crazily; soberly; gloomily; cynically; sagely; reflectively; thoughtfully; alarmingly; ominously; gloriously; optimistically; groundlessly; profoundly; deeply; boldly; reasonably; sanely; sadly; pessimistically; wishfully; hopefully; sagaciously; intelligently; far-seeingly; perspicaciously; curiously; strangely; startlingly; highly; audaciously.

PROPITIATE (v)
adverbs
flatteringly; servilely; artfully; fawningly; cunningly; shrewdly; timidly; earnestly; studiously.

(See pacify, calm, soothe.)

PROPITIOUS
adverbs
pleasantly; agreeably; seriously; altogether; happily; delightfully; fortunately; opportunely; appropriately; graciously; pleasingly; advantageously; unusually; uncommonly; providentially; entirely; encouragingly; supposedly; singularly; particularly; especially.

PROPORTION
adjectives
cyclonic; impressive; modelled; splendid; respectable; portentous; heavy; exact; cavernous; tremendous; symmetrical; incredible; extensive; luxurious; heroic; sublime; ignoble; overwhelming; exaggerating; classic; inverse; geometrical; colossal; impudent; sizable; gigantic; enormous; proper; monstrous; rotund; sturdy; massive; divine; direct; balanced; faultless; increasing; staggering; unbelievable; inconsiderable; excessive; diminishing; relative; regal; varying; huge; ethical; progressive; majestic; large; meager; just; prodigious; consistent; constituent; pyramid; distinct; major; aldermanic; artistic; slender; clumsy; rude; due; far-reaching; equal; robust; national; vibrating; horrible.

verbs
allot—; allow—; amass—; assign—; assume—s; attain—s; consign—s; contort—; deal —s; deform—s; dispense—s; divide into—s; dole out—s; evaluate—s; indicate—s; misshape—s; preserve—s; retain—s; twist—s; warp—.

(See equilibrium, percentage, size, extent, degree, dimensions, share.)

PROPORTION (v)
adverbs
delicately; exquisitely; admirably; femininely; correctly; superbly; symmetrically; luxuriously; geometrically; massively; regally; meagerly; clumsily; rudely; equally; prodigiously.

(See divide, adjust, apportion.)

PROPORTIONATE
adverbs
fairly; justly; carefully; correspondingly; diplomatically; agreeably; satisfactorily; respectively; congruously; consistently; admissibly; felicitously; acceptably; quantatively; relatively; distinctly; impartially; equitably; laudably; legally; regularly.

PROPOSAL
adjectives
friendly; romantic; infamous; unique; alternative; oral; impracticable; ridiculous; lame; flattering; foolhardy; audacious; ambitious; crackpot; definite.

verbs
accept—; adopt—; argue—; back—; block —; carry out—; commend—; condemn—; denounce—; deride—; dismiss—; entertain —; explode—; heed—; inspire—; oppose—; pooh-pooh—; raise—; reject—; sanction—; submit—; support—; turn down—; vitiate —; withdraw—; —emanates from; —excites; —falls through.

(See bid, proposition, offer, deal, transaction, plan, suggestion, scheme.)

PROPOSE (v)
adverbs
spontaneously; seriously; dogmatically; originally; deliberately; impiously; insidiously; theoretically; philosophically; untenably; ominously; flatteringly; conditionally; passionately.

(See offer, discourse.)

PROPOSITION
adjectives
equitable; due; plausible; theoretical; unintelligible; tough; preposterous; brutal; solemn; definite; businesslike; philosophical; attractive; abstract; meaningless; untenable; ominous; mannerly; distasteful; marvelous; undeniable; dynamical; moneymaking; fundamental; flattering; conditional; general; novel; true; palpitating; astounding.

verbs

acclaim—; applaud—; balk at—; convey—; dedicate—; deliver—; demonstrate—; engage in—; entertain—; fancy—; immerse in—; jeopardize—; lay down—; misconstrue—; reject—; relate—; support—; —allures; —invites; —tempts.

(See offer, proposal, bid, deal.)

PROPOUND (v)

adverbs

academically; philosophically; theoretically; argumentatively; dispassionately; conditionally.

(See offer, propose.)

PROPRIETARY

adverbs

proudly; legitimately; comically; possessively; justly; graciously; absurdly; properly; pompously; ostentatiously; conspicuously; blatantly; ridiculously; modestly; anxiously; watchfully; responsibly; vigilantly; disagreeably; unctuously; suavely; smoothly; blandly; rapturously.

PROPRIETOR

adjectives

affluent; genial; antiquarian; ecclesiastic.

PROPRIETY

adjectives

unconscious; editorial; peculiar; established; equal; perfect; complacent; eminent; dramatic; rigid; obvious; sacred; dreamy.

verbs

adhere to—; admire—; befit—s; conform to—; contravene—s; fulfill—s; impose—; incur—; justify—s; observe—; respect—; satisfy—; suit—; undermine—; —becomes; —binds; —exacts; —obliges; —prescribes; —requires; —saddles.

(See decorum, convenience, decency.)

PROSAIC

adverbs

hopelessly; consciously; dully; flatly; tediously; unimaginatively; monotonously; stupidly; tiresomely; endlessly; unconsciously; pretentiously; pitiably; miserably; vacuously; inanely; diffusely; heavily; drearily; impossibly; terribly.

PROSE

adjectives

rhythmical; impassioned; polyphonic; news-paper; idealistic; strenuous; poetical; rhyming; lucid; glittering; immortal; artistic; famous; dull; heroic; harmonious; sinewy; uncerebral; hard-hitting; straight-from-the-shoulder; extensive; physical; humorous; conventional; flashing; elaborate; measured; conversational; dreamy; grand; mingled; salable; vigorous; poetic; puissant; supple; mellifluous; swift; masculine.

verbs

acclaim—; analyze—; compose—; contemplate—; dwell on—; enjoy—; —abounds in; —amplifies; —bores; —describes; —dilates; —discusses; —protracts; —rambles; —repeats; —swells; —thrills; —wearies.

(See poetry, writing, story, style.)

PROSECUTE (v)

adverbs

actively; recklessly; fearlessly; relentlessly; vindictively; diabolically; legally; spitefully; energetically; impassionedly; repulsively.

(See sue.)

PROSECUTION

adjectives

vigorous; persistent; inevitable; victorious; unceasing.

verbs

avert—; avoid—; demand—; endure—; escape—; evade—; file—; lodge—; order —; prefer—; risk—; suffer—; —brands; —implicates; —saddles; —slanders; —slurs; —stigmatizes; —weighs against.

(See lawsuit, suit (legal), arrest.)

PROSPECT

adjectives

dusky; melancholy; near; gloomy; smiling; brilliant; immediate; favorable; calm; peaceful; hideous; extreme; prosperous; tempting; flattering; consolatory; dazzling; brightening; adjacent; flaming; delightful; honorable; turbulent; bare; feeble; glorious; coveted; varying; bright; scanty; better; dismal; inexpressible; unobstructed; dim; gleaming; domestic; shadowy; repulsive; tempting; spacious; ineffable; glittering; blighted; bleak; dreary; embarrassing; glorious; cheering; depressing; grim; substantial; gay; happy; pleasing.

verbs

bait—; blanch at—; cripple—; dash—;

deter by—; eliminate—; entertain—; gaze at—; guard—; harbor—; insure—s; jeopardize—; open—; relinquish—; relish—; sustain—; tremble at—; —lures; —ponders; —speculates; —tempts; —s wane; —yields.
See future, expectation, view, outlook, chance.)

PROSPER (v)
adverbs
materially; privately; personally; abundantly; excessively; illusively; financially; economically; miraculously; spectacularly.
(See thrive, gain, benefit.)

PROSPERITY
adjectives
material; public; infectious; rapid; nourishing; crass; common; supposititious; deserved; private; ever-increasing; riotous; exemplified; apparent; unexampled; abundant; excessive; fair illusive; sensual; worldly.

verbs
annihilate—; attain—; attribute—to; boom into—; boost—; build—; climb to—; contribute to—; enhance—; enjoy—; experience —; foster—; guarantee—; hamper—; induce—; promote—; re-establish—; retard —; revive—; share in—; —continues; —intoxicates; —permeates; —stems from; —vanishes.
(See boom, happiness, health, inflation.)

PROSPEROUS
adverbs
happily; comfortably; fortunately; extremely; pleasantly; gratifyingly; agreeably; surprisingly; serenely; enviably; snugly; sufficiently; fabulously; independently; tremendously; conspicuously.

PROSTITUTION
verbs
attack—; censor—; drift into—; eradicate —; extirpate—; lapse into—; suffer—; suppress—; wipe out—; —contaminates; —corrupts; —debauches; —defiles; —degrades; —depraves; —discolors; —embitters; —impairs; —mangles; —pollutes; —vitiates; —warps.
(See crime, sin, corruption.)

PROSTRATE (v)
adverbs
reverently; humbly; weakly; fawningly; cringingly; servilely; nervously; speechlessly; utterly.
(See overthrow, overpower, defeat.)

PROSTRATION
adjectives
nervous; servile; indolent; extreme; inanimate; utter.

PROTECT (v)
adverbs
adequately; legally; permanently; chivalrously; amply; unequivocally; honorably; sedulously; sacredly; nominally; automatically; scientifically; parentally; financially; dubiously.
(See defend, guard.)

PROTECTED
adverbs
tenderly; completely; unusually; remarkably; warmly; heavily; affectionately; ardently; carefully; cautiously; vigilantly; constantly; officially; unnecessarily; distinctly; deliberately; strangely; covertly; secretly; openly; successfully; always; legally.

PROTECTION
adjectives
positive; permanent; extra; especial; effectual; benign; immediate; invaluable; inadequate; satisfactory; maximum; parental; sublime; atrocious; mutual; lubricant; efficient; all-around; adequate; momentary; blow-out; generous; fancied; financial; sadvisaged; scanty; extended; gracious; indifferent; humiliating; warm; dubious; inexpensive; weatherproof.

verbs
afford—; bestow—upon; deny—; furnish—; gain—; grant—; insure—; legalize—; maintain—; seek—; sustain—; —assures; —eases; —preserves; —safeguards.
(See guidance, leadership, patronage.)

PROTECTOR
adjectives
guilty; desirable; sole; staunch; potent; courageous.

PROTEIN

adjectives

concentrated; coagulating; necessary.

verbs

absorb—; advocate—; assimilate—; burn—; class as—; consume—; digest—; disintegrate—; inject—; lack—; necessitate—; utilize—; —builds; —corrects; —regulates; —strengthens.

(See food, carbohydrates, starch, sugar, calorie.)

PROTEST

adjectives

indignant; feeble; ineffective; vigorous; humble; passionate; persistent; comic; vociferous; courageous; somber; ancient; incautious; startled; religious; earnest; emphatic; living; masculine; voluble; vehement; inarticulate; shouted; shocked; hurt; stubborn; half-scornful; howled; feigned; energetic; unavailing; timid; manly; undersigned; respectful; harassing; passionate; fiery; undignified; noisy; unwelcome.

verbs

anticipate—; arouse—; awaken—; brush aside—; dismiss—; echo—; elicit—; explode in—; file—; give rise to—; growl in—; grumble—; howl in—; ignore—; issue—; laugh away—; lodge—; maintain—; override—; provoke—; register—; rise in—; scowl—; storm in—; summarize—s; voice —; waive—; —emanates from; —infuriates; —s pour in; —flames forth.

(See complaint, grievance, objection, answer.)

PROTEST (v)

adverbs

drawlingly; vehemently; rebelliously; solemnly; sullenly; violently; keenly; earnestly; lustily; fiercely; indignantly; suavely; energetically; passionately; feebly; extravagantly; ungraciously; formally; persistently.

(See remonstrate, expostulate.)

PROTESTANT

verbs

oppress—; persecute—; —accedes; —acknowledges; —approves; —attends; —contradicts; —criticizes; —demurs; —flays; —opposes; —persecutes; —practices;

—preaches; —protests; —questions; repudiates; —worships; —endorses.

(See church-goers.)

PROTESTANTISM

verbs

approve—; confirm—; convert to—; endorse —; practice—; preach—; promise—; —accedes to; —acknowledges; —contradicts; —demurs; —denies; —differs; —envelops; —flays; —involves; —protests; —questions; —repudiates.

(See religion, Christianity, protest.)

PROTESTATION

adjectives

passionate; jittery; grateful; shrieking; roaring; injurious; characteristic; solemn; extravagant; earnest; amorous.

PROTESTING

adjectives

pure; earnest; vigorous.

PROTRACTED

adverbs

unendurably; endlessly; foolishly; tragically; unhappily; purposely; wickedly; painfully; tiresomely; drearily; unbearably; miserably; wearily; hopelessly; inexplicably; unaccountably; deliberately; purposely; intentionally; distressingly; viciously; lengthily; interminably; unendurably.

PROTRUDE (v)

adverbs

puffily; abnormally; flabbily; unusually; hideously; disgustingly; prominently; exaggeratedly.

(See jut, project, extend.)

PROTUBERANCE

adjectives

horny; auricular; bulging; dimpled; elliptical; flabby; unusual; unsightly.

PROTUBERANT

adverbs

extremely; crookedly; pitiably; seriously; gravely; noticeably; conspicuously; prominently; bulbously; tumorously; alarmingly; dreadfully.

PROUD

adverbs

absurdly; arrogantly; boyishly; coldly; contemptibly; defiantly; excessively; fatuously;

foolishly; haughtily; honestly; rightfully; indescribably; inordinately; justly; moderately; pardonably; rapturously; regally; saucily; secretly; snobbishly; splendidly; stubbornly; stupidly; subtly; tenderly; unendurably; ungovernably; wretchedly; essentially.

PROVE (v)
adverbs
lucidly; axiomatically; irrefutably; conclusively; incontrovertibly; incontestably; ultimately; indubitably; abundantly; substantially; experimentally; undeniably.
(See verify, corroborate.)

PROVERB
adjectives
enigmatical; prudential; silly; ungracious; bold; quaint; untruthful; well-worn. notable.

verbs
apply—; comprehend—; condense into—; contract into—; formulate—; frame—; jewel with—s; memorize—; recall—; refute—; value—; —directs; —embodies; —impresses; —instructs; —moralizes; —prescribes; —sparkles; —teaches; —warns.
(See adage, maxim, motto, epigram.)

PROVIDE (v)
adverbs
graciously; hospitably; duly; suitably; abundantly; sparely; properly; liberally; adequately; specifically; copiously; expressly; indulgently.
(See furnish, supply.)

PROVIDENCE
adjectives
beneficent; special; divine; shocking; indulgent; inscrutable; innocent; adverse; overruling.

verbs
beseech—; depend on—; meditate on—; ponder—; rely on—; —blesses; —creates; —decrees; —elects; —glorifies; —governs; —interposes; —intervenes; —justifies; —ordains; —predestines; —sanctifies; —smiles upon; —upholds.
(See Heaven, God.)

PROVIDENT
adverbs
carefully; cautiously; habitually; generously; thriftily; cannily; scarcely; adequately; satisfactorily; lavishly; extravagantly; proudly; ostentatiously; noticeably; famously; notoriously; wisely; sagaciously; intelligently; admirably; commendably; unfailingly; prudently; considerately; thoughtfully; sensibly; elaborately.

PROVIDENTIAL
adverbs
divinely; fortunately; blessedly; highly; undoubtedly; unmistakably; curiously; mysteriously; strangely; happily; opportunely; auspiciously; gloriously; beneficently.

PROVINCE
adjectives
neighboring; fruitful; extensive; specific; outcrying; petitioning; ostensible; archiepiscopal; opulent; diverse; singular; discordant; subjugated; baffling; petty; dreaded; remote; invaded; turbulent; outlying; detailed; slender; idle; nugatory; qualificatory; stupendous; contradictory; tinned; illiberal; constitutional; suitable; severe; manipulated; complex; uncertain; antimanipulation; miraculous; adequate; obnoxious; ample; sweeping; stringent; institutionalized; standard; highly-important; scanty; illogical.

verbs
banish to—; border—; divide into—; dwell in—; edge—; encroach on—; extend—; inhabit—; lay waste—; occupy—; retire to—; rule—; settle in—; skirt—; tax—; tyrannize over—; visit—; —extends; —harbors; —trades.
(See jurisdiction, kingdom, territory.)

PROVINCIAL
adjectives
uncouth; remote; daring; simple; single-minded; hopeless; ignorant; narrow.

adverbs
narrowly; utterly; hopelessly; boorishly; coarsely; bluntly; brusquely; remarkably; naturally; undisguisedly; illiberally; stupidly; credulously; awkwardly; outlandishly; bashfully; self-consciously; strikingly; noticeably; unexpectedly; obviously; markedly.

PROVISION

verbs

adhere to—s of; annul—; balk at—; contemplate—; decry—; disregard—; enforce —; evade—; exempt from—; heed—; ignore—; incorporate—; infract—; insert—; inveigh against—; nullify—; sanction—; violate—; —amends; —augments; —compels; —eases; —elaborates on; —embodies; —wobbles.

(See clause, amendment, preparation, law.)

PROVOCATION

adjectives

abundant; severe; inscriptional; random; slight; mild.

verbs

agitate—; arouse to—; avoid—; electrify—; enkindle—; evoke—; fan—; foment—; impassion—; inflame—; irritate—; sharpen—; —boils; —disturbs; —fumes; —rages; —seethes; —simmers.

(See defiance, exasperation, hatred, stimulus, incitement.)

PROVOKE (*v*)

adverbs

wrathfully; unwittingly; deliberately; libelously; despicably; needlessly; unduly; abundantly; calculatingly; tremendously; maddeningly; irritatingly.

(See displease, incite, offend.)

PROVOKING

adverbs

particularly; intolerably; naughtily; mischievously; intentionally; deliberately; teasingly; disagreeably; foolishly; seriously; constantly; unbearably; uncommonly.

PROW

adjectives

beaked; glistening; pitch-black; pushing; unremembering; steadfast; reinforced; sharp; shining; gleaming.

PROWESS

adjectives

confirmed; mortal; martial; exploitative; memorable; amatory; mental; bodily; spiritual.

verbs

admire—; diminish—; display—; expose—; necessitate—; obscure—; reveal—; "tout"—;

—beards; —braves; —dares; —defies; —emboldens; —encourages; —defies; — overcomes; —overwhelms; —reassures; —shocks; —ventures.

(See gallantry, power, strength, bravery, valor.)

PROWL (*v*)

adverbs

nefariously; nocturnally; satanically; thievishly; viciously; slyly; characteristically; hellishly; perniciously; rapaciously; fiendishly; mutely.

(See wander, search, sneak.)

PROWLER

adjectives

vicious; thieving.

PROXIMITY

adjectives

welcome; perilous; tantalizing; suspicious.

PRUDE

adjectives

grave; waning; strict.

verbs

avoid—; condemn—; deride—; detest—; ostracize—; ridicule—; scandalize—; — affects; —attitudinizes; —bores; —irritates; —overacts; —patronizes; —poses; —simpers; —sneers; —vexes.

PRUDENCE

adjectives

habitual; rational; tottering; honorable; premeditated; calm; worldly; diplomatic; wise; uniform; traditional; mutual; slow.

verbs

acclaim—; applaud—; bolster with—; cherish—; employ—; endorse—; exercise—; extol—; ignore—; practise—; preach—; violate—; —assures; —cautions; —dictates; — forestalls; —gains; —guards; —prepares; —warns.

(See caution, forethought, consideration.)

PRUDISH

adverbs

ridiculously; comically; awkwardly; provincially; inherently; narrowly; fanatically; provokingly; vexatiously; annoyingly; affectedly; senselessly; ostentatiously; formally; stiffly; obdurately; puritanically; absurdly; ludicrously.

PSYCHOLOGY

verbs

apply—; approve—; delve into—; digest—; dominate—of; employ—; endorse—; illustrate—; involve—; lack—; practise—; —aids; —appreciates; —comprehends; —conceives; —copes with; —evolves; —fathoms; —meditates; —realizes; —studies; —understands.

(See philosophy, science.)

PUBERTY

verbs

anticipate—; attain—; confirm—; digest—; embrace—; reach—; recognize—; reveal—; —arms; —creeps upon; —despairs; —encourages; —envelops; —generates.

(See age, maturity, period.)

PUBLIC

adjectives

receptive; intellectual; alienated; fun-loving; disinterested; aroused; palpitating; surfeited; reverent; morbid; sentimental; trusting; enlightened; gullible; motoring; enduring; theatergoing; authentic; multifarious; indignant; mad; fighting; promiscuous; unorganized; indifferent; jaded; yearning; heartless; blameless; ungrateful; cynical; avid; acquiring; enlightened; attentive; fickle; exacting; ignorant; modern; credulous; importunate; consuming; investing; uneducated.

verbs

appeal to—; beguile—; captivate—; cater to —; deceive—; defraud—; divert—; enlighten—; foist on—; impress—; incite—; scan —; shrink from—; shun—; slip over on—; snare—; swindle—; —applauds; —flocks to; mystify—; present to—.

(See individual, community, masses, mob, nation, observer.)

PUBLICATION

adjectives

illegitimate; ultimate; laborious; conspicuous; wretched; facile; disreputable; posthumous; popular; unrivaled; vigorous; art; fastest-growing; unusual; interesting; outstanding; illustrated.

verbs

achieve—; advertise—; censor—; edit—; emit—; forge—; hatch—; prepare for—;

reach—; restrain—; sanction—; suspend—; translate—; —blazons; —broaches; —circulates; —edifies; —relates.

(See edition, magazine, newspaper, periodical.)

PUBLICITY

adjectives

unwanted; unfavorable; undesirable; immediate; wholesome; unsparing; unpleasant; humiliating; vague; unsavory; national; wide-spread; long-sought.

verbs

achieve—; attain—; avoid—; balk at—; court—; decry—; elude—; favor with—; gain—; leash—; maneuver for—; release—; screen from—; shower with—; shrink from —; shun—; submit to—; suffer—; sustain—; yearn for—; —celebrates; —engulfs; —fames; —glares.

(See limelight, notoriety, fame.)

PUBLIC OPINION

verbs

arouse—; consolidate—; count on—; crystallize—; excite—; formulate—; inspire—; mobilize—; muster—; prize—; rely on—; seek —; suppress—; sway—; value—; —alters; —approves; —condemns; —decides; —denounces; —sanctions; —scorns; —selects; —speculates; —tempers; —vetoes.

(See opinion, belief, sentiment.)

PUBLISH (v)

adverbs

posthumously; exclusively; surreptitiously; libelously; fraudulently; extensively; anonymously; boldly; advantageously; voluminously; compulsorily; seditiously.

(See print, announce, circulate.)

PUBLISHER

adjectives

unscrupulous; ungenerous; august; influential; heroic.

verbs

consult—; entreat—; —advertises; —edits; —emits; —heralds; —proclaims; —rejects; —rushes; —sanctions; —weans.

(See journalist, editor, printer.)

PUCKER (v)

adverbs
resentfully; coyly; teasingly; attractively; quaintly; sweetly; amorously.
(See crease, purse, wrinkle.)

PUDDING

verbs
bake—; cool—; dish—; flavor—; garnish —; mix—; mold—; relish—; serve—; spoon —; steam—; stir—; sweeten—; —curdles; —delights; —graces; —hardens; —tempts; —thickens.
(See cake, food, dessert.)

PUDDLE

adjectives
dirtiest; muddy; slopping; ugly.

PUERILE

adverbs
pitiably; inexplicably; frivolously; ridiculously; unfortunately; fatuously; inanely; trivially; surprisingly; hopelessly; vacuously; ineptly.

PUFF (v)

adverbs
prodigiously; violently; meditatively; reminiscently; pensively; breathlessly; laboredly.
(See blow, pant.)

PUGILISTIC

adverbs
skilfully; notoriously; famously; truculently; quarrelsomely; insistently; contentiously; argumentatively; expertly; eagerly; enthusiastically; zealously; unwarrantably; sturdily; stoutly.

PULL

adjectives
dreadful; energetic; vigorous; hearty; vicious; necessary.

PULL (v)

adverbs
rapidly; laboriously; vigorously; violently; unconscionably; irresistibly; energetically; frantically; tremulously; viciously; forcibly; heartily.
(See draw, haul.)

PULP

verbs
assay—; beat to—; compose of—; convert —; crush to—; derive from—; obtain—;
pound to—; reduce to—; strain through—; test—; tread to—; —adheres; —fattens; —fills; —lines; —stuffs.
(See powder, mass.)

PULPIT

verbs
adorn—; ascend to—; climb to—; encrust—with; erect—; face—; orate from—; preach from—; support—; thunder from—; —attracts; —condemns; —decries; —denounces.
(See desk, platform, rostrum.)

PULSATE (v)

adverbs
rhythmically; markedly; regularly; periodically; throbbingly; violently; flutteringly; feverishly; turbulently; passionately; tremulously; hectically.
(See beat, throb.)

PULSE

adjectives
choral; throbbing; violent; new; bounding; fluttering; burning; ineradicable; languid; feverish; accelerated; rapid; quickened; chaster; pounding; arrested; fleshy; heightened; possible; turbulent; passionate; purple; haggard; energetic; hurried; leaping; firm; wearied; generous; tremulous; immortal; dormant; thrilling; hectic; emotional; inward; audible.

verbs
accelerate—; flag—; quicken—; record—; slow—; stir—; whip up—; —beats; —bounds; —drums; —flows; —flutters; —leaps; —responds; —slackens; —surges; —throbs.
(See stream, flow, vibration.)

PUMP

verbs
elevate—; handle—; labor with—; man—; manipulate—; operate—; require—; work —; —compels; —draws; —eases; —empowers; —enables; —fathoms; —forces; —presses; —pulls; —raises; —rectifies; —squirts; —sucks.

PUN

adjectives
arrant; copious; irresistible; unnecessary; stringing; weak; stupid; childish.

adjectives   **PUNCH**
                          (blow)
essential; crisp; sinewy.

                      PUNCH
verbs   *(drink)*
drain—; flavor—; ladle—; relish—; replenish—; savor—; serve—; sip—; soak in—; spike—; steep in—; swill—; thirst for—; —befuddles; —flows; —inebriates; —lushes; —quenches; —refreshes.
(See liquor, beverage, wine.)

               PUNCTILIOUS
adverbs
overly; carefully; deferentially; ceremoniously; formally; conventionally; officially; meticulously; especially; peculiarly; infallibly; unbendingly; remarkably; particularly; uncommonly; highly; terribly.

                PUNCTUAL
adverbs
usually; seldom; scarcely; infallibly; unfailingly; resolutely; painfully; ostentatiously; disagreeably; satisfactorily; notoriously; noticeably; quietly; serenely; pleasantly; unusually; coolly; habitually; pompously; deferentially; ceremoniously; respectfully; ingratiatingly; singularly.

                PUNGENT
adverbs
spicily; pleasantly; arrestingly; refreshingly; strongly; faintly; overpoweringly; richly; attractively; aromatically; sharply; penetratingly; bitterly; hotly.

                PUNISH *(v)*
adverbs
indiscriminately; summarily; barbarously; cruelly; justly; nominally; sparingly; vindictively; officially; exemplarily; ignominiously; ingeniously; atrociously.
(See discipline, penalize.)

              PUNISHMENT
adjectives
dreadful; supplementary; inhuman; penitentiary; helpless; corporal; vindictive; servile; severe; direful; ignorant; eternal; adequate; express; impending; barbarous; everlasting; official; fitting; permanent; frightful; exemplary; summary; ignominious; brave; insufferable; ingenious; pleasing; dreadful.

verbs
administer—; condemn to—; enforce—; evade—; inflict—upon; mete out—; prohibit —; rain—upon; rebel against—; reserve—for; risk—; subject to—; suffer—; undergo —; —abates; —atones; —frightens.
(See lashing, discipline, torture, torment, penalty.)

                PUNY
adverbs
feebly; miserably; whiningly; undoubtedly; obviously; manifestly; evidently; admittedly; unfortunately; wretchedly; pitifully; deplorably; incomparably; lamentably; shamefully; incurably; incredibly; strangely; unaccountably; hopelessly; discouragingly.

                PUPIL
verbs   *(eye)*
damage—; enlarge—; examine—; exercise —; expose—; film—; harm—; impair—; injure—; mar—; mist—; pierce—; strain—; —contracts; —dilates; —responds.
(See eye.)

                PUPIL
adjectives   *(general)*
apt; docile; individual; dilated; illustrious; ill-omened; interesting; ungifted; alert; unpromising; expressionless; unwilling; incapable; progressive; precocious; impressionable; desired; bewildered; diligent; apathetic; steely.

                PUPIL
verbs   *(student)*
chastise—; encourage—; entertain —s; examine —s; grade —s; graduate—; impart to—; inculcate in—; instil in—; instruct—; limit —s; prepare—; question—; reprimand —; —competes; —comprehends; —crams (colloq.); —demonstrates; —flunks (colloq); —grasps; —passes; —responds; —surpasses; —understands.
(See student.)

                PUPPET
adjectives
gyrating; mere; painted; exceeding; skilled; gesticulating.

verbs
carve—; dress up—; employ—; enjoy—; manipulate—; represent by—; —amuses; —

capers; —delights; —depicts; —diverts; —
enacts; —entertains; —frisks; —impersonates; —mimics; —mocks.
(See clown, doll.)

PUPPY

adjectives
contumacious; playful; hydrophobic; pleasant; tiny; helpless.

verbs
abandon —s; coax—; cuddle—; cudgel—; drown—; leash—; lose—; pet—; play with —; soothe—; train—; whelp —s; whip—; —annoys; —barks; —capers; —darts by; — frolics; —licks; —performs; —pursues; — whimpers; —whines; —yelps.
(See dog, animal, pet.)

PURCHASE

adjectives
remarkable; ill-considered; enforced; judicious; special; important; systematic; infinitesimal; fortunate; careless; opportune.

verbs
cart —s; charge—; check —s; collect —s; deliver—; dispose of—; gather —s; glean —s; inveigle into—; limit —s; mislay—; pile up —s; procure—; redeem—; ship—; weigh—; —s accrue; —loads.
(See merchandise, bundle, parcel, package.)

PURCHASE (v)

adverbs
substantially; advantageously; hypothetically; unwittingly; judiciously; systematically; shrewdly; astutely.
(See buy, acquire, secure.)

PURCHASER

adjectives
careless; persistent; potential.

verbs
advertise for—; allure —s; assure—; deceive—; net—; please—; satisfy—; tempt —; —charges; —complains; —demands; — dispenses; —markets; —patronizes; —procures; —selects; —shops.
(See buyer, customer.)

PURE

adverbs
perfectly; 100%; 99%; chastely; incredibly; warrantably; singularly; incredibly; unsur-

passably; incomparably; consummately; immaculately; spotlessly; absolutely; unadulteratedly; innocently; childishly; devoutly; virtuously; artlessly; genuinely; utterly.

PURGATIVE

adjectives
powerful; stimulating; violent; bitter.

verbs
addict to—s; avoid—s; employ—; —clarifies; —defecates; —expurgates; —filters; — flushes; —frees; —purges; —purifies; — racks; —refines; —removes; —scours; — sifts; —strains; —washes; —weeds.
(See sedative, medicine, remedy, enema.)

PURGATIVE

adverbs
thoroughly; warrantably; successfully; safely; remedially; necessarily; scientifically; naturally; unfailingly; genuinely; receptably.

PURITANICAL

adverbs
painfully; primly; sternly; unyieldingly; inflexibly; unbendingly; rigidly; priggishly; sedately; quietly; stoically; gravely; severely; strictly; austerely; obviously; silently; rigorously; harshly; seriously; learnedly; justly; fairly; ascetically; precisely; forbiddingly; dourly; inexorably; uncompromisingly; stiffly; dreadfully.

PURITANISM

verbs
advocate—; crusade against—; enshrine in —; inflict—; inspire—; practise—; suffer—; tolerate—; —condemns; —consecrates; — narrows; —oppresses; —reveres; —rules; —sanctifies; —simplifies; —smiles; —stints; —tramples.
(See protestantism, christianity.)

PURITY

adjectives
ethical; intellectual; womanly; classical; spotless; rare; pristine; absolute; racial; inexpressible; moral; unconscious; seraphic; touching; delicate; original; infinite; exalted; crystal; coldest; celestial; quiet; immaculate; perfect; impious; comparative; scholastic; sinless; earnest; extreme; displayed; conscious; personal; cherished; political; naked; sufficient; singular; snow-white.

948

verbs
achieve—; admire—; advocate—; attain—; defile—of; incur—; procure—; recommend —; revere—; select—; stain—; taint—; violate—; —awes; —eliminates; —pervades; —satisfies.

(See justice, holiness, innocence, chastity, modesty, morality.)

PURPLE
adjectives
imperial; intense; darkling; dun; regal; pansy; visual; tenderest; livid; rich; ruddy; soft; pale.

PURPORT
adjectives
dramatic; mystical; true; dim.

PURPOSE
adjectives
hellish; undefined; cosmic; syndicating; ambitious; fell; sinister; experimental; better; dire; sworn; pious; excellent; sacramental; critical; reference; avowed; moral; studied; persistent; communal; speculative; lofty; dramatic; practical; underlying; beneficent; voiceless; contrary; serious; artistic; specific; resolute; definite; high; honorable; constant; malignant; reasoned; deliberate; sufficient; laudable; primary; productive; exalted; menial; avowed; large; grim; unchanging; resurging; unswerving; ungenerous; broken; multitudinous (pl); keener; sternest; breeding; sugar-coated; ephemeral; rational; boundless; unaccomplished; restrained; unfathomed; dark; consuming; patient; altruistic; decorative; finite; defensive; distinct; hostile; aggressive; genuine; benevolent; energetic; earnest; common; essential; disinterested; ultimate; sole; poetical; finical; forlorn; flighty; infallible; willful; orbed; insurrectionary; notable; rugged; robust; tragic; humane; philosophical; unheeded; didactic; patriotic; double; extraneous; aesthetic; unchaste; intramural; visual; tolerable; ruthless; noble; corrupt; ulterior; salutary; public; histrionic; educational; patent; malicious; life; manifest; introductory; express; pernicious; heroic; inhospitable; visible; awkward; deadly; theoretical; unvarying; weighty; fraudulent; prudent; propagandist; temporary; deceptive; immediate; precautionary; domestic; abandoned; unsettled; luxurious; salubrious; iron; negative; unlawful; proper; fixed; diabolical; eternal; obstinate; pure;

commercial; industrial; therapeutic; pacific; enduring; divine; microscopic; apposite; doubtful; especial; colloquial; admirable; dumb; insuperable; ineradicable; ostensible; selfsame; infirm; half-formed; prime; economic.

verbs
achieve—; adhere to—; attain—; contrive for—; convey—; crystallize—; defeat—; disclose—; divert from—; divine—; extract —from; fulfill—; galvanize into—; inspire by—; intend for—; interpret—; overcloud —; pursue—; serve—; stiffen—; subserve —; swerve from—; thwart—.

(See end, aim, effect, intention, mission, object, objective.)

PURR (*v*)
adverbs
amiably; demurely; cozily; domestically; comfortably; contentedly; drowsily.

(See murmur, whisper.)

PURSE
adjectives
well-filled; borrowed; evading; slow; slender; humble; yawning; long; cunning; shut; over-gorged; privy.

verbs
clasp—; cling to—; conceal—; consign to —; decorate—; dent—; draw from—; fatten —; fumble in—; lose—; mislay—; pocket—; relinquish—; replenish—; snap—; snatch—; stuff—; suit—; swell—; —accrues; —amasses; —bulges; —flashes.

(See wallet, bag, pocket.)

PURSE (*v*)
adverbs
coyly; squeamishly; fastidiously; cunningly; aristocratically.

(See pucker, wrinkle, crease.)

PURSUE (*v*)
adverbs
adventurously; remorselessly; indefatigably; warily; energetically; lustfully; relentlessly; lasciviously; invariably; resolutely; diligently; doggedly; ardently; stolidly; blandly; sedulously; mechanically; strenuously; zealously; imprudently.

(See chase, follow, seek.)

adjectives

peaceful; immediate; hot; relentless; systematic; agricultural; innocent; intellectual; vigorous; dissipated; artistic; serious; exciting; studious; active; business; industrial; intimate; profitable; unjust; scuffling; professional; energetic; strenuous; relentless; sedentary; brilliant; weird; furious; peaceful; laboratory; vulgar; cultural; dangerous; unique; zealous; eager; imprudent; mercantile; athletic; worthy; hardy; wearisome; military; sluggish; sordid; sylvan; amphibious; lawful; honorable; compulsory; happy; invigorating; dogged; humble; lucrative; ardent; serious; irreparable; useless; rabid; favorite; scientific; ultimate; unavailing; instant; severer; evident; swift; illegitimate; blind; delusive; scholarly; idealistic; sedulous; disordered; engrossing; elevating; uninterrupted; vile; prompt; fascinating; passionate.

verbs

abandon—; avert—; avoid—; contemplate —; devote to—; distract from—; dog in—; engage in—; engross in—; enter—; follow in—; hinder—; hound in—; obstruct—; press—; prevent—; rush in—; spurn—; — annoys; —irks; —threatens.

(See hobby, industry, profession, quest, occupation, business, chase.)

PUS

verbs

cough up—; discharge—; drain—; eject—; emit—; expel—; fester—; localize—; produce—; —befouls; —contaminates; —defiles; —escapes; —exudes from; —fills; — forms; —offends; —oozes from; —pollutes; —reeks; —smears; —spatters; —sullies.

(See saliva.)

PUSH

adjectives

warning; vigorous; desperate; significant; determined; zealous.

verbs

climax—; necessitate—; require—; resist—; —boots (colloq.); —casts; —discharges; — drives; —expels; —favors; —forces; — heaves; —hurls; —impels; —jerks; — launches; —pitches; —startles.

(See charge, attack.)

PUSH (v)

adverbs

cautiously; sententiously; uncompromisingly; unceremoniously; adroitly; instinctively; vigorously; presumptuously; superciliously; unfalteringly; rudely; laboriously; mechanically.

(See shove, impel.)

PUSILLANIMOUS

adverbs

pitiably; insufferably; unhappily; miserably; wretchedly; shamefully; timorously; pitifully; contemptibly; atrociously; meanly; inexplicably; strangely; remarkably; disgracefully; basely; incredibly; hopelessly; disgustingly; pathetically.

PUTTY

verbs

apply—; case with—; coat with—; dab on —; lay—; mold—; plaster—; press—; reduce to—; smear—; spread—; squeeze—; —cements; —conceals; —covers; —faces; — holds; —pastes; —sticks.

(See mortar, plaster, cement.)

PUZZLE

adjectives

inexplicable; provocative; insolvable; fascinating; frightening; baffling.

verbs

disclose—; disentangle—; dissolve—; explain—; extricate—; popularize—; present —; reveal—; scramble—; solve—; study—; unfold—; unravel—; untie—; —baffles; — entertains; —involves; —irks; —irritates; —mystifies; —perplexes.

(See trick, riddle, problem, perplexity.)

PUZZLED

adverbs

strangely; terribly; bewilderingly; bafflingly; bitterly; cruelly; utterly; embarrassingly; painfully; obscurely; profoundly; seriously; completely; admittedly; confusingly.

PUZZLING

adverbs

sadly; naturally; hopelessly; dangerously; seriously; unreasonably; alarmingly; depressingly; unaccountably; disturbingly; genuinely; strangely; indescribably; fearfully; dishearteningly; maddeningly; unusually; terribly; vexatiously; vaguely; definitely; uncomfortably; subtly; awkwardly; extremely; annoyingly; exasperatingly; inexplicably.

Q

QUACK
verbs

betray—; detect—; father—; patronize—; warn of—; —bamboozles (colloq.); —bilks; —cajoles; —deceives; —dupes; —ensnares; —fakes (colloq.); —gammons; —gulls; —hoaxes; —lures; —outwits; —traps.

(See liar, hypocrite, quackery.)

QUACKERY
verbs

denounce—; expose—; practice—; prevent —; support—; worship—; —cheats; —circumvents; —contaminates; —corrupts; —debases; —deludes; —pretends; —swindles; —tricks.

(See quack.)

QUAFF (v)
adverbs

deeply; unhesitatingly; thirstily; eagerly; fraternally; jubilantly.

(See drink, sip.)

QUAGGY
adverbs

hopelessly; impassably; undesirably; soggily; dangerously; uselessly; abominably; strangely; irremediably; unsalably; unfortunately; squashily; swampily; occasionally; seasonally.

QUAIL
verbs

domesticate—; flush—; —barks; —bills; —cruises; —feigns; —flushes; —flutters; —glides; —haunts; —jerks; —nods; —roves; —rumbles; —rustles; —scratches; —squeals; —struts; —tattoos; —trills; —thumps; —thunders; —yelps.

(See bird, bob-white, partridge.)

QUAINT
adverbs

delightfully; demurely; altogether; deliciously; exceptionally; extraordinarily; uncommonly; exotically; unfashionably; enchantingly; attractively; whimsically; bewitchingly; charmingly; pleasantly; alluringly; unusually.

QUAINTNESS
verbs

cultivate—; enjoy—; instil—; notice—; overdo—; practise—; reveal—; ridicule—; —appeals; —attracts; —becomes; —blooms; —deceives; —delights; —intrigues.

(See strangeness, beauty.)

QUALIFICATION
adjectives

inner; original; sterilizing; eminent; remotest; conventional; special; indispensable; scientific.

verbs

arm with—; contemplate—; disclaim—; discount—; dispute—; endow with—; ignore —; impugn—; increase—; seek—; tax—; vouch for—; weigh—; —adapts; —empowers; —enables; —fits; —strengthens; —warrants.

(See power, endowment, essential.)

QUALIFIED
adverbs

competently; capably; entirely; unusually; exceptionally; singularly; well; wonderfully; acceptably; suitably; especially; particularly; incomparably; proficiently; technically; felicitously; obviously; evidently; manifestly; peculiarly; marvelously.

QUALIFY (v)
adverbs

patently; eminently; severely; admirably; splendidly; nominally; scientifically; medically; conventionally.

(See limit, modify, restrict.)

QUALITY
adjectives

absorptive; abstract; adaptive; academic; acoustical; adhering; administrative; aesthetic; affectionate; affrontive; allotted; analytical; anecdotal; antipyretic; appealing; ardent; aristocratic; artistic; atmospheric; authoritative; available; average; blended; blooming; blossom-like; brilliant; cardinal; characteristic; charming; childlike; companionable; chivalric; considerable; contradictory; cooking; correspondent; dependable; daredevil; decorative; deepreaching; deep-rooted; demonstrable; desirable; despised; determining; developmental; diagnostic; disciplinary; disinfectant; distinctive; divine; dogged; distinguished; dramatic; driving; dubious; educational; effective; electric; elusive; embracing; emollient; emotional; empty; enduring; energetic; entrancing; essential; ethical; evident; exasperating; exceptional; fabric; faithless; famous; fertilizing; fatal; feminine; filtering; fine; first; flawless; fleshy; floating; flowery; food; free-lathering; friendly; generous; genial; gentlemanly; genuine; good; gracious; guaranteed; handmade; haunting; health-giving; high; honest; imaginary; imperturbable; indubitable; inefficient; inestimable; infectious; inferior; inherent; inherited; innate; inoperative; insulative; intellectual; integral; intrinsic; introspective; invigorating; lasting; laughable; literary; luxurious; lyrical; machine-like; magnificent; masculine; maternal; maximum; mellow; melodic; mental; militant; minimum; mixing; moral; mordant; musty; mysterious; narcotic; national; nightmare; noble; noticeable; nutritious; objectionable; occult; opiate; outstanding; outward; overlooked; pagan; passive; pedigreed; peculiar; personal; pervasive; physical; pictorial; picturesque; practical; predominant; preeminent; preternatural; prime; primest; profuse; protective; provocative; pulsating; pregnant; pungent; real; realistic; redeeming; relaxing; reliable; remarkable; representative; restraining; robust; romantic; saccharine; ruder; rugged; sachet; sensational; sedative; serious; shameless; sheer; shimmering; showy; singular; slurred; smooth; social; spiritual; sterling; statuesque; sterner; steely; subtle; strengthening; studious; stylistic; subordinate; superior; superlative; syllogistic; tangible; temperamental; tempered; top; toxic; unbeatable; uncertain; unexpected; unfailing; unfitting; unfostered; uniform; united; universal; unreasoning; unquestioned; unsatisfactory; unsought; unsuitable; unsurpassed; untiring; unusual; varied (pl); venomous; vibrating; vital; warlike; wearing; whimsical; windy; womanly; wondrous; zestful; workmanlike; worthy; wretched.

verbs
appraise—; appreciate—; ascribe—to; define—; determine—; discern—; display—; divest of—; endow with—; evaluate—; extol—; impair—; impart—; improve—; inherit—; intensify—; maintain—; recognize

—; refine—; revere—; sacrifice—; share—; temper—; underrate—; —eludes; —predominates.
(See essence, attribute, characteristic, nature.)

QUALM
adjectives
conscience; sudden; bitter; unwonted.

verbs
arouse—; challenge—; incur—; justify—; raise—; register—; satisfy—; suffer—; —abashes; —alarms; —deprives; —frightens; —harrows; —hinders; —impedes; —lingers; —obstructs; —swerves; —unnerves.
(See scruple, fear, misgiving.)

QUANTITY
adjectives
exhaustless; immense; insufficient; unprecedented; unknown; indefinite; changeable; limited; astonishing; enormous; normal; unlimited; illustrative; dumb; untold; abstract; excessive; staggering; substantial; greater; surface; commercial; vast; goodly; monstrous; arbitrary; sufficient; minus; measurable; negligible; distorted; useless; unmanageable; surprising; considerable; incredible; generous; equivalant; adequate.

verbs
accumulate—; amass—; ascertain—; collect —; distribute—; estimate—; gather—; issue —; lessen—; limit—; measure—; muster— of; rake up—; reduce—; regulate—; —dwindles; —masses; —mounts; —soars; —transcends.
(See dose, amount, total, sum.)

QUARANTINE
verbs
demand—; enforce—; escape——; necessitate—; require—; repulse—; resist—; warrant—; —assures; —elapses; —excludes; —fences; —forbids; —houses; —isolates; —protects; —restrains; —restricts.
(See isolation, taboo, ban, boycott.)

QUARREL
adjectives
frequent (pl); monkish; unjust; petty; equivalent; theological; incipient; warranted; dignified; violent; private; intestine;

jealous; holy; comic; ancient; sudden; sharp; false; splendid; empty; continual; wretched; pretty; ecclesiastical; inconsequential; wrongful.

verbs
arouse—; deplore—; evoke—; lament—; patch up—; pick—; provoke—; regret—; repent—; sow—; stir up—; —breaches; —disconcerts; —embitters; —ensues; —gratifies; —rages; —sours.
(See brawl, dissension, disagreement, dispute.)

QUARREL (v)

adverbs
shamelessly; heatedly; pettishly; impertinently; theologically; jealously; acrimoniously; bitterly; squalidly; hatefully; vindictively.
(See dispute, disagree, wrangle.)

QUARRELSOME

adverbs
disagreeably; hotly; offensively; obstinately; abusively; stubbornly; irritatingly; violently; needlessly; nervously; excitably; unnecessarily; bitterly; foolishly; truculently; brutally; intolerably; unsufferably; disputatiously.

QUARRY

verbs
bait—; beguile—; contemplate—; corner—; draw—; gain on—; hole up—; investigate —; offer—; play for—; pursue—; risk—; speculate on—; tree—; vie for—; —delights; —lures; —tempts.
(See prey, victim.)

QUARTERS

adjectives
commodious; limited; exalted; charming; squalid; pleasant; deficient; distant; unsavory; fair; dingy; desolate; fashionable; moderate; heated; precise; comfortable; light-housekeeping; desponding; authoritative; ruined; cramped; ransacked; sumptuous; immigrant; bourgeois; treacherous; humble; unknown; cheerless.

verbs
assign to—; defile—; establish—; invade—; investigate—; locate—; lodge in—; picket —; pitch—; plant—; post—; remove—; report to—; retire to—; set up—; situate—; station at—; take up—; vacate.
(See barracks, place, position, headquarters.)

QUAVER (v)

adverbs
tremulously; weakly; sickeningly; peculiarly; characteristically.
(See shake, tremble, quiver.)

QUAVERING

adverbs
anxiously; diffidently; despairingly; apprehensively; despondently; dismally; dreadfully; nervously; restlessly; solicitously; terribly; tremulously; agedly; eagerly; stammeringly; wearily; abjectly; timidly.

QUEEN

adjectives
refulgent; haughty; fairy; pale; papist; fiend-like; gracious; love-sick; mob-led; stately; legitimate; buxom; helmeted; amorous; crownless; well-intentioned; dark; peerless; uncrowned; crafty; potent.

verbs
attend—; crown—; escort—; guard—; honor—; pamper—; revere—; salaam before —; serve—; squire—; —abdicates; —appeals to; —ascends; —assigns; —commends; —dazzles; —orders; —punishes; —reigns; —rewards; —rules; —symbolizes.
(See king, monarch, ruler.)

QUEER

adverbs
outlandishly; terribly; exotically; egregiously; alarmingly; singularly; abominably; mysteriously; unaccountably; suddenly; dreadfully; ominously; fantastically; uncommonly; extraordinarily; comically; grotesquely; exceptionally; unwontedly; hopelessly; incurably; incorrigibly.

QUEERNESS

verbs
deride—; develop—; incur—; overlook—; permit—; pose—; relieve—; remedy—; ridicule—; study—; tolerate—; —baffles; —creeps into; —infringes; —perplexes; —surprises; —violates.
(See oddity.)

QUELL (v)

adverbs

effectually; forcefully; momentarily; outwardly; effectively; vigorously; legitimately; officiously; legally; demonstrably; brutally.

(See suppress, subdue, crush.)

QUERIES

adjectives

valued; amusing; superstitious; unfortunate; idiotic; sceptical; excellent; everlasting; clattering; desperate; fantastic.

QUERULOUS

adverbs

hatefully; uneasily; restlessly; exceptionally; habitually; extremely; insufferably; disagreeably; pitiably; pitifully; endlessly; crabbedly; morosely; moodily; lonesomely; unhappily; perversely; crossly; sulkily; understandably; helplessly.

QUERY (v)

adverbs

sharply; deprecatingly; deliberately; romantically; significantly; stubbornly; breathlessly; anxiously; curtly; scornfully; perplexedly.

(See question, ask, inquire.)

QUEST

adjectives

chivalrous; eternal; unsuccessful; lawful; terrible; hopeless; contrarious; eager; uncertain; original; evangelical; adventurous; furious; vain; winged; doubtful; childish; selfsame.

verbs

abandon—; aim—at; engage in—; follow—; join in—; justify—; tire of—; value—; —allures; —beguiles; —demands; —eludes;. —escapes; —evades; —leads; —requires; —tempts; —wearies.

(See pursuit, journey, trip, adventure.)

QUESTION

adjectives

compound; innocent; prying; rhetorical; debatable; embarrassing; unvoiced; historic; ultimate; comprehensive; unthinkable; controversial; probing; tentative; pointblank; covert; perfidious; insidious; awkward; searching; identification; artless; incisive; unconscious; sad; vermicular; brute; philosophical; theological; touching; vexed; burning; tabooed; academic; angry; contemptuous; essential; clamorous; suspicious; physical; irrational; prompt; diverse; fundamental; trying; improper; gloomy; immodest; muttered; delicate; difficult; mooted; incessant; pertinent; hideous; intelligent; abstract; stale; celebrated; troublesome; long-pending; dreadful; social: unsettled; idle; constant; bald; agonized; piercing; present; impertinent; deciding; prominent; insolent; disputed; pressing; affable; ambiguous; germane; stern; unanswerable; dormant; sensible; sorrowful; inconvenient; serious; brusque; vital; disencumbered; horrible; frenzied; large; unsuitable; transit; profound; intricate; irritating; imminent; teasing; explosive; argumentative; innumerable (pl); reasonable; concrete; cheerless; ill-bred; cogent; momentous; political; financial; humanitarian; national; absurd; relevant; foregoing; technical; barbed; perennial; multiplying; combustive; tantalizing; beggarly; tremendous; peculiar; perfect; natural; broader; ironical; much-discussed; steep; pending; motherly; untiring; numberless (pl); pregnant; eternal; banal; lustier; dynastic; constitutional; abstruse; unsettled; ever-burning; confidential; ethical; austere; vexatious; economic; insolvable; rude; insatiate; complex; perplexing; basic; uneasy; frivolous; speculative; customary; blunt; trick; similar; exhaustive; civil; religious.

verbs

adjudicate—; bar—; bear upon—; bombard with—s; brood over—; complicate—; comprehend—; confront with—; constitute—; cope with—; darken—; debate—; deluge with—s; dispute—; elucidate—; evade—; face—; fire—at; fling—at; focus on—; formulate—; frame—; go to the heart of—; grapple with—; hammer with—s; hurl—at; open to—; parry—; ply with—s; ponder —; propound—; raise—; revive—; shelve —; shy away from—; solve—; split on—; submit—to; throw light upon—; touch upon—; voice—; wrestle with—; —agitates; —arises; —elicits; —embarrasses; —hangs fire; —involves; —looms; —obtrudes upon; —plagues; —pops up; —poses itself; —relates to; —revolves itself; —rings out; — simmers; —vexes.

(See issue, matter, problem, inquiry, questioning.)

adverbs

importunately; cryptically; audaciously; curiously; vaguely; incredulously; blankly; ruefully; sarcastically; sophistically; prefatorily; minutely; impudently; reluctantly; tactfully; innocently; clamorously; delicately; improperly; sternly; brusquely; momentously; technically; ironically; banally; abstrusely; confidentially; speculatively; bluntly; exhaustively.

(See query, inquire.)

QUESTIONABLE

adverbs

highly; morally; controversially; argumentatively; distinctly; darkly; uncomfortably; naturally; particularly; legally; ticklishly; undeniably; mysteriously; inferentially; conventionally.

QUESTIONAIRE

verbs

circulate—; compile—; conduct—; contemplate—; distribute—; grapple with—; induce from—; infer from—; issue—; mark —; propound—; reply to—; return—; score —; —aids; —decides; —enables; —forecasts; —inquires; —interrogates; —investigates; —irks; —puzzles; —requests; —reveals; —settles.

(See application, petition, appeal.)

QUESTIONING

adjectives

continual; suicidal; interminable; inward; prudent; over-curious.

verbs

avert—; arraign for—; conduct—; dodge —; investigate—; pursue—; refuse—; review—; —agitates; —analyzes; —canvasses; —delves into; —demands; —elicits; —ferrets out; —overhauls; —probes; — pumps; —ransacks.

(See grilling.)

QUEUE

verbs

arrange—; braid—; clip—; dress—; tug at—; twist—; weave—; wind—; wrap—; —attracts; —hangs; —jiggles; —trails; —suspends; —sways; —swings.

(See braid, hair, tail.)

QUIBBLING

verbs

avoid—; brush aside—; check—; detest—; endure—; ignore—; incur—; suffer—; —annoys; —betrays; —deceives; —eludes; —evades; —glosses over; —hampers; — hinders; —irks; —provokes; —shuffles; —taxes; —vexes.

(See evasion, excuse.)

QUICK

adverbs

devilishly; surprisingly; alarmingly; incredibly; wonderfully; efficiently; normally; abnormally; extremely; cruelly; mentally; maliciously; diabolically; remarkably; duteously; feverishly; ordinarily; expertly; impulsively; mercifully; comically; uncomfortably; breathlessly; perilously; marvelously; unaccountably; luckily; astonishingly; dangerously; unbelievably.

QUICKNESS

adjectives

surprising; dizzy; devilish; irresolute.

QUICK-WITTED

adverbs

remarkably; astonishingly; nimbly; commercially; socially; disturbingly; incredibly; simply; admirably; sparklingly; scintillatingly; wonderfully; enviably; scintillantly; naturally; habitually; unsurpassably.

QUIESCENCE

verbs

arouse from—; endure—; lull to—; maintain—; quell to—; snub into—; —abides; —charms; —envelops; —flows; —hushes; —persists; —pleases; —stagnates.

(See lethargy, quiet, repose.)

QUIESCENT

adverbs

temporarily; luckily; fortunately; significantly; customarily; peculiarly; seasonally; remarkably; ominously; naturally; silently; immovably; usually.

QUIET

adjectives

dimmed; remarkable; restful; absolute; undisturbed; restoring; rural; subduing; penitential; endless; dull; luxurious; reverent; lifeless; ominous; domestic; graceful; aimless; formidable; passive; idealic; pastoral; peaceful; enforced.

verbs

brook—; envelop in—; insure—; reduce to —; stir from—; wrap in—; —allays; —appeals; —appeases; —calms; —cools; —governs; —lulls; —maddens; —pervades; —quells; —reigns; —smooths; —soothes.

(See hush, silence, rest, repose, quiescence, peace.)

adverbs

utterly; particularly; carefully; absurdly; cautiously; furtively; stealthily; considerately; attentively; courteously; graciously; pensively; anxiously; deliberately; dreamily; satisfactorily; temporarily; significantly; miraculously; calmly; astonishingly; sullenly; moodily; gloomily; awesomely; terrifyingly; alarmingly; suspiciously; significantly; mysteriously; appallingly; uncommonly.

QUIETNESS

adjectives

inviolable; unobtrusive; external; extreme; pensive; subdued.

QUIETUDE

adjectives

surprising; comforting; unusual; extraordinary; sartorial.

QUILL

adjectives

tuneful; enchanted; porcupine; many-colored; tinkling; venal.

QUIT (v)

adverbs

reluctantly; sadly; dejectedly; eventually; hastily; abruptly; impetuously; significantly; gloomily; mysteriously; consequently.

(See cease, stop.)

QUIVER

adjectives

solemn; convulsive; subtle.

QUIVER (v)

adverbs

nervously; exasperatedly; wantonly; abnormally; violently; sluggishly; markedly; excitedly; passionately.

(See shake, tremble, quaver.)

QUIVERING

adjectives

mysterious; gentle; anxious.

adverbs

nervously; tremulously; helplessly; feverishly; pathetically; pitiably; miserably; visibly; angrily; grievously; timidly; affrightedly; curiously.

QUIZ (v)

adverbs

narrowly; closely; methodically; thoroughly; perfunctorily austerely; vexatiously; rudely; speculatively; civilly; sternly; abstrusely.

(See question, banter.)

QUOTA

adjectives

assigned; respective; insignificant.

verbs

acquire—; allot—; apportion—; attain—; cede—; deal—; derive—; divide—; endow —; fulfill—; furnish—; impose—; pledge —; portion out—; present—; raise—; receive—; subscribe—; supply—; yield—.

(See portion, share, part.)

QUOTATION

verbs

apply—to; bejewel with—s; comprehend—; condense into—; contract into—; eschew—; fling—at; frame—; memorize—; ooze—s; pepper with—s; recall—; refer to—; value —; —directs; —embodies; —exemplifies; —illustrates; —impresses; —instructs; —prescribes; —sparkles; —teaches; —warns.

(See saying, maxim, proverb, passage.)

....QUOTATIONS

adjectives

biblical; poetical; irreverent; copious; innumerable; modest; half-remembered; seasonable; habitual; felicitious; capital; garbled; illustrative; multifarious.

QUOTE (v)

adverbs

copiously; philosophically; widely; extensively; oracularly; preeminently; plaintively; magnanimously; ardently; biblically; poetically; habitually; felicitously; illustratively; multifariously; aptly; erroneously.

(See repeat, extract.)

R

RABBI

verbs
induct—; ordain—; —authorizes; —blesses; —communes; —confirms; —consecrates; —officiates; —performs; —preaches;—ritualizes.

(See minister, priest, teacher.)

RABBIT

adjectives
juicy; misplaced; tasty.

verbs
domesticate—; dress—; experiment with —s; fence out—; pen—; pet—; shoot—; skin—; —bounds off; —burrows; — crouches; —devastates; —digs; —flashes by; —hops; —jumps; —leaps; —nibbles; —plagues; —scampers away; —scurries; —subsists on.

(See animal, pet.)

RABBLE

verbs
arouse—; class with—; concentrate—; court—; dispel—; disperse—; exclude—; harangue—; mingle with—; pander to—; restrain—; rout—; silence—; sway—; —assembles; —congregates; —masses; —mobs; —rules; —rushes; —storms; — surges; —throngs.

(See mob, crowd, proletarian.)

RABID

adverbs
insensately; wildly; unaccountably; dangerously; appallingly; fanatically; eccentrically; terribly; hysterically; downright; curiously; insatiably; violently; bitterly; absurdly; crazily; relentlessly; unbelievably; appallingly; shockingly; incredibly.

RACE
(competition)

verbs
accelerate—; approve—; clinch—; compete in—; contend in—; enter—; judge—; observe—; oppose in—; outdistance in—; postpone—; promote—; protest—; wager on—; —enlivens; —enraptures; —excites; —fascinates; —petrifies; —revives; — thrills.

(See match, game, contest.)

RACE
(general)

adjectives
severed; vengeful; sacerdotal; antipathetic; bloody-minded; fading; earth-born; alien; idle; girdled; amphibious; literary; infinite; indestructible; civilized; chequered; wasted; kindred; blissful; canine; impromptu; solid; tenacious; energetic; fecund; teeming; hectic; fallen; separate; radiant; golden; high-born; beauteous; touchy; savage; warlike; blind; blundering; knightly; proverbial; brave; despicable; barbarous; desperate; well-marked; swarming; obstinate; lascivious; titanic; lawless; hardy; thrifty; ethereal; jocund; elimination; inscrutable; uncultivated; wild; human; contemptible; singing; indigenous; glorious; sturdy; godly; best; fierce; studious; invincible; ill-fated; breathless; oppressed; melodious; long-lived; valiant; sullen; ancient; reprobated; intractable; dominant; unfortunate; subjugated; dwarfish; noble; incapable; aggressive; miserable; bounding; degraded; volatile; well-known; perished; magnificent; frolicsome; dusky; inveterate; unreturning; interesting; ghostly; short-distance; primitive; purblind; domestic; polished; courageous; stoical; decorative; semi-civilized; headlong; gentle; aboriginal; high-hearted; timid; proud; shining; inoffensive; illustrious; pitiless; invalid; unconverted; cultural; hostile; fickle; ruling; backward; impious; antediluvian; rudest; obstacle; delicate; nurtured; greedy; contested; untrustworthy; hard; beastly; vagrant; malignant; feverish; wise; shadowy; interloping; buxom; cognate; active; consequent; awkward; depraved; self-opinionated.

RACE
(nationality)

verbs
characterize—; conquer—; detest—; distinguish—; exterminate—; limit—; mark—; perpetuate—; purify—; sow—; strengthen —; study—; uplift—; —ebbs; —evolves; —perishes; —prospers; —subsists; —vanishes; —wanes.

(See breed, mankind, strain, nationality.)

RACE (v)

tirelessly; vengefully; lawlessly; awkwardly; gloriously; invincibly; boundingly; frolicsomely; courageously; greedily; feverishly; spectacularly.

(See run, scamper, flee.)

RACIAL

adverbs

inherently; strongly; naturally; inseparably; peculiarly; inescapably; indestructibly; tenaciously; proverbially; gloriously; distinctly; significantly; fiercely; dominantly; proudly.

RACK

adjectives

fierce; low-trailing; cruel; commercialized; money-lending; corporeal.

RACKET

adjectives

noisy; gloomy; theatrical; vicious; favorite; flourishing; terrible; resounding.

verbs

—breaks; —clacks; —clashes; —crashes; —deafens; —dins; —drowns; —drums; —penetrates; —pierces; —resounds; —roars; —rumbles; —shakes; —snaps; —splits; —stuns; —thunders.

(See clamor, noise.)

RACY

adverbs

breezily; pungently; pithily; smartly; curiously; brilliantly; pleasantly; boldly; eloquently; piquantly; trenchantly; vigorously; unusually; amazingly; interestingly; arrestingly.

RADIANCE

adjectives

serene; glaring; rapturous; full; ruddy; variegated; clear; reflected; pale; milder; celestial; fathomless; indistinct; farewell; calm; soft; uniform; transitory; subdued; blinding; seraphic; secret; growing; orange; indescribable; mailed; tenderest; warm; flooding; sickly; prismatic; marvelous; bewildering; downcast; fantastic.

verbs

beam with—; blemish—; cloud—; dim—; dull—; eclipse—; extinguish—; glow with —; obscure—; overshadow—; shed—; —blazes; —enchants; —enhances; —flames; —gilds; —gleams; —glistens; —graces; —illuminates; —overspreads; —sparkles; —sublimates; —surrounds; —enlightens.

(See moonbeam, happiness, brilliance.)

RADIANT

adverbs

gloriously; splendidly; conspicuously; noticeably; visibly; happily; joyously; triumphantly; rapturously; ecstatically; jubilantly; exultantly; blissfully; contentedly; serenely.

RADIATOR

verbs

adjust—; bask near—; polish—; throttle—; —affords; —assures; —comforts; —diffuses; —glows; —parches; —scorches; —singes; —simmers; —warms.

RADICAL

adjectives

avowed; univalent; unreasonable; ill-balanced.

verbs

—contaminates; —corrupts; —demoralizes; —disparages; —fulminates; —harangues; —heckles; —ignites; —impairs; —pillories; —poisons; —pollutes; —raves; —taints; —undermines; —vituperates; —anathematizes; —cankers; —condemns.

(See anarchist, socialist, communist.)

adverbs

boldly; daringly; definitely; distinctly; deeply; thoroughly; uncompromisingly; sweepingly; appallingly; necessarily; downright.

RADIO

verbs

broadcast over—; communicate by—; filter into—; toy with—; tune down—; —amplifies; —bears; —blares forth; —bleats; —booms; —clarifies; —contacts; —conveys; —deafens; —disconcerts; —facilitates; —hums; —proclaims; —receives; —transmits; —unites.

(See loud-speaker.)

RAFT

adjectives

well-banded; fatal; formidable; ruined; prodigious; timber.

verbs

climb to—; crowd—; hoist on—; lap—; lash to—; punt—; rig—; slap—; smack—; support on—; sway—; threaten—; —bobs; —dips; —floats; —guides; —rocks; —transports; —troughs.

(See boat.)

adjectives

smoke-stained; gloomy; slender; resonant; skeleton.

verbs

bear on—; bestride—; hang from—; recline on—; repose on—; rest on—; straddle—; —abuts; —affords; —aids; —bolsters; —maintains; —s ring; —snaps; —supports; —sustains; —underprops; —upholds.

(See beam, timber, board.)

adjectives

withering; impetuous; towering; foaming; tacit; guilty; fresh; grievous; righteous; inarticulate; impotent; extreme; cold; merciless; appeasing; disappointed; breathless; gloomy; punic; outflung; murderous; sudden; affectionate; haughty; divine; fierce; animal-like; mightier; furious; resolute; violent; pernicious; appertaining; indescribable; white-hot; unwonted; quick; hostile; unmitigated; sparkling; baffled; generous; unintelligible; silken; tremendous; ceaseless; prophetic; elemental; kindling; stormy; relentless; recurrent; concentrated; mental; pitiful; explosive; instantaneous; trembling; hard-favored; heathen; noble; female; overmastering.

verbs

blind with—; bluster in—; enkindle—; explode in—; fan—; fire with—; flush with—; fly into—; foment—; fume with—; glower with—; inflame with—; justify—; lash into—; pour out—; quiver with—; rouse—; shriek in—; snort with—; sputter with—; storm in—; thunder in—; tremble with—; vent—; work into—; —boils over; —effervesces; —ferments; —seethes; —smolders; —spends itself; —surges; —transports; —vanishes.

(See fury, indignation, anger, impatience, ire.)

adverbs

inwardly; magnificently; incessantly; momentarily; tremendously; fearfully; furiously; dangerously; fiercely; impetuously; foamingly; inarticulately; impotently; murderously; perniciously; unintelligibly; elementally; explosively; mentally.

(See storm, fume.)

adverbs

terribly; carelessly; pitiably; negligently; pathetically; impossibly; irregularly; disgracefully; contemptibly; shabbily; appallingly; shamefully; shockingly; unnecessarily; heedlessly; blithely; gleefully; hoydenishly; tomboyishly; nonchalantly; pitifully; deliberately; mischievously.

adverbs

furiously; violently; tempestuously; angrily; resentfully; virulently; helplessly; stormily; hysterically; needlessly; deliriously; fanatically; feverishly; brutally; fiercely; tyrannically; madly; uncontrollably; bitterly; savagely; rabidly; uselessly; terribly; shockingly.

adjectives

smelly; picturesque; grotesque; flattened; clean; slanting; riddled.

verbs

apparel in—; array in—; deck in—; discard —; divest of—; don—; envelop in—; sheathe in—; shun—; swaddle in—; swathe in—; vest in—; —humble; —humiliate.

(See clothing, raiment, apparel.)

adjectives

intrepid; mutual; memorable; bridge-burning; cavalry; unjustifiable; dreadful; marauding; foraging; rebel; murderous; copious (pl); conducted; similar; swift.

verbs

anticipate—; check—; engineer—; launch—; parry—; plan—; repel—; repulse—; resist —; retaliate for—; shield from—; stem—; —aims at; —assails; —attacks; —beleaguers; —besieges; —harries; —provokes; —saps; —storms; —thrusts at; —violates; —whips.

(See invasion, attack.)

adverbs

lawlessly; intrepidly; memorably; unjustifiably; maraudingly; treacherously; rebelliously; murderously; cunningly; devastatingly; swiftly; belligerently.

(See attack, seize.)

RAIL

adjectives

shattered; sanded; twisted; continuous; purgatorial.

verbs

erect—; grasp—; —barricades; —bars; —checks; —circumscribes; —confines; —encloses; —fences; —fringes; —girdles; — protects; —restrains; —safeguards; — skirts; —terminates; —withstands; —restricts.

(See fence, barrier, barricade.)

RAIL (v)

adverbs

fretfully; bitterly; acrimoniously; acidly; sarcastically; devastatingly; witheringly; relentlessly; pitifully; plaintively; monotonously; copiously.

(See censure, reproach, upbraid.)

RAILROAD

adjectives

infant; pioneered; subtransatlantic; state-owned; opulent; efficient; necessary; well-run.

verbs

plan—; route—; sanction—; tear up—; utilize—; —advertizes; —covers; —enables; —extends; —facilitates; —guarantees; —insures; —invades; —opens; —prospers; — solicits.

RAIMENT

adjectives

snowy; gallant; gay; flying; shining; sumptuous; predestined; scanty.

verbs

admire—; cast off—; divest of—; don—; perk—; remove—; strip of—; swaddle in—; —clothes; —covers; —drapes; —enrobes; —flatters; —laps; —mantles; —muffles; —sheathes.

(See apparel, clothing.)

RAIN

adjectives

drizzling; drenching; summer; impalpable; fiery; mizzling; misty; melting; crushing; silent; blistering; inconceivable; frozen; lukewarm; quiet; dismal; frequent (pl); generous; gusty; recent; fertilizing; sudden; prodigious; hearty; long; continued; cold; abundant; driving; rapid; soft; violent; vernal; invisible; falling; pattering; roaring; passionate; autumn; pouring; swirling; incessant; heavy; pelting; pitiless; quickening; singing; sterile; substantial; windy; mellowing; plenteous; thick; sooty; gusty; healing; love-cast; irised; refreshing; unabated; sheeted; continual; dim; lashing; undecided; sweetest; snow-soft; emerald; chilling; immortal; biting; silver; frozen; constant; superannuated; reluctant; veritable; unprecedented; fitful; uninterrupted; dreary; heaven-sent; swishing.

verbs

brave—; dodge—; —blights; —crescendos; —dashes against; —deluges; —drenches; —drums; —gurgles; —gushes; —inundates; —jets; —lashes; —moistens; —patters; —pelts; —rattles; —relents; —roars; — slithers off; —spatters; —spurts; —teems; —threatens; —thuds; —wanes; —ripples; —trickles.

(See hail, shower, sleet, storm.)

RAIN (v)

adverbs

dismally; heavily; monotonously; desultorily; drizzlingly; prodigiously; abundantly; violently; vernally; patteringly; roaringly; pitilessly; unabatedly; fitfully; unprecedentedly.

(See shower, pour.)

RAINBOW

adjectives

momentary; live; wonderful; myriad (pl); glorified; ephemeral; wondrous; emerald.

RAINY

adverbs

unusually; uncommonly; extraordinarily; terribly; torrentially; softly; dreamily; drowsily; thunderously; drizzlingly; windily; gustily; unfortunately; unluckily; disappointingly; opportunely; seasonally; fortunately; providentially; strangely; gloomily; dismally; drearily; pleasantly; agreeably; lightly; suddenly.

RAISE (v)

adverbs

corruptly; insolently; deferentially; instinctively; eloquently; unscrupulously; defiantly; delicately; significantly; impressively; mechanically; expressively; daintily; warningly; majestically; deliberately; quizzically.

(See lift, elevate.)

RAKE

verbs

drag—; draw—; employ—; tug at—; —dredges; —eliminates; —extricates; —gathers; —grubs; —refines; —scratches; —smoothes; —unearths; —uproots.

RAKE (v)

adverbs

thoroughly; searchingly; painstakingly; questioningly; inquiringly.

(See gather, search.)

RAKISH

adverbs

wildly; recklessly; dissolutely; madly: blithely; gaily; hilariously; idly; merrily; boisterously.

RALLY (v)

adverbs

faithfully; gallantly; ardently; instinctively; fiercely; courageously; heartily.

(See collect, recover.)

RAMBLE (v)

adverbs

garrulously; blindly; monotonously; ceaselessly; maddeningly; purposelessly; pointlessly.

(See stroll, stray.)

RAMBLING

adverbs

pleasantly; quaintly; comfortably; leisurely; irregularly; idly; wantonly; happily; freely; interestingly; endlessly; aimlessly; capriciously; erratically; casually; artlessly; quietly; effortlessly; errantly; desultorily; vagrantly; blissfully.

RAMPANT

adverbs

roughly; obstreperously; uncontrollably; ungovernably; predominantly; buoyantly; noticeably; expansively; singularly; remarkably; naturally; spontaneously; insuppressibly; unmanageably; merrily.

RAMPART

verbs

array on—; batter—; communicate with—; erect—; fret—; pass along—; patrol—; penetrate—; storm—; strengthen—; surmount—; —bulwarks; —defends; —protects; —resists; —surrounds; —unites.

(See defense, fortification, barricade.)

RAMSHACKLE

adverbs

deplorably; hopelessly; discouragingly; challengingly; dingily; dismally; interestingly; inexpensively; terribly; comically; brightly; charmingly; fascinatingly; merrily; curiously; scandalously; completely; rattily; incredibly; manifestly.

RANCID

adverbs

sourly; bitterly; acridly; odoriferously; obviously; outrageously; impossibly; disgustingly; hopelessly; shamefully; mustily; nauseatingly; uselessly; terribly; disagreeably; noticeably; evidently; vexatiously; miserably; undisguisably; visibly.

RANCOR

adjectives

unmitigated; violent; unrelenting; smothered.

verbs

arouse—; betray—; burst with—; defy—; harbor—; inflict—; protest—; repress—; unloose—; wreak—upon; —abuses; —blasts; —embitters; —irritates; —pierces; —shakes; —snarls; —sours; —stabs.

(See grudge, animosity, ill-will, bitterness.)

RANCOROUS

adverbs

unreasonably; senselessly; maliciously; venomously; relentlessly; incorrigibly; outrageously; shamefully; atrociously; dangerously; naturally; alarmingly; fearfully; singularly; insufferably; extraordinarily; violently; fanatically; uncontrollably.

RANGE

adjectives

considerable; extensive; narrow; point-blank; cruising; indicated; effective; enormous; massy; limited; encyclopedic; far-stretching; irregular; cloud-capped; snowy; interminable; billowy; unbounded; easy; flanking; infinite; widened; teeming; formidable; fluid; inexhaustible; vaster; ancient; longitudinal; wonted; unactive; colossal; icy.

verbs
amplify—; ascertain—; broaden—; encompass—; enlarge—; expand—; extend—; localize—; magnify—; narrow—; restrict—; scan—; spread—; sweep—; widen—; —fluctuates; —oscillates; —soars; develop—.
(See horizon.)

RANK
adjectives
high; foremost; crowding; honorable; illustrious; scholarly; serried (pl); unbroken; dense; poetical; bending; unwearied (pl); superior; wasting; preeminent; hostile (pl); distinguished; swaying (pl); teeming (pl); glittering (pl); myriad (pl); titled; depleted (pl); innumerable (pl); obscurest; riddled (pl); stalwart (pl); regular; inferior; extinguished; culinary; extrinsic; intermediate; exhausted (pl); shattered (pl); disordered (pl); relative; jeweled; stately; immortal; intellectual; melancholy; interminable; mournful; rightful; respective; enveloping (pl); princely; gathering (pl); delicate; swelling (pl); fastfalling (pl); equal; riven (pl); reeling (pl).

verbs
accredit—; achieve—; acquire—; ascend to —; aspire to—; assign to—; break—s; denote—; desert—s; divest of—; earn—; eject from—s; elevate to—; forfeit—; honor—; praise—s; promote to—; reduce to—s; respect—; scatter—; shatter—s; signal—s; solidify—s; split—s; swell—s; win—; —dignifies; —eclipses; —glorifies; —outshines; —surpasses; —transcends.
(See degree, grade, caste, class, position.)

RANK (v)
adverbs
deservedly; poetically; obscurely; relatively; intellectually; rightfully; aristocratically; humbly.
(See classify, group.)

RAP (v)
adverbs
smartly; vigorously; authoritatively; viva-

ciously; persistently; furiously; tempestuously.
(See knock, thump.)

RAPACIOUS
adverbs
furtively; terribly; wickedly; scandalously; outrageously; shamefully; greedily; ravenously; insatiably; rabidly; ungovernably; uncontrollably; madly; monstrously; abominably; detestably; peculiarly; astonishingly; unbelievably; uncommonly.

RAPID
adverbs
unbelievably; effortlessly; invisibly; increasingly; mercifully; crazily; expertly; distressingly; painfully; breathlessly; impetuously; perilously; unaccountably; surprisingly; astonishingly; moderately; dangerously; lightly.

RAPIDITY
adjectives
incredible; fair; sufficient; inconceivable; fearful; marvelous; feverish; facial; dexterous; appalling; lightning; extraordinary; extreme; disconcerting; amazing; racial.

RAPIER
verbs
brandish—; evade—; fence with—s; flourish—; parry—; sheathe—; thrust with—; wield—; —lacerates; —penetrates; —pierces; —sheds.
(See sword, lance.)

RAPTURE
adjectives
ultimate; transient; holy; lasting; random; wounding; blissful; pure; speechless; dizzy; boundless; exquisite; heartfelt; divine; mute; radiant; heavenly; guilty; honest; fervid; careless; secret; rhetorical; mysterious; imaginative; maniacal; enveloping; unreasoning; serene; romantic; fading; suppressed; ecstatic; tumultuous.

verbs
breathe in—; cherish—; dilate with—; evoke—; exalt in—; excite—; exclaim in—; express—; feast on—; move to—; muse in —; regard with—; smite with—; speak in —; touch with—; tremble in—; —bewitches; —entrances.
(See ecstasy, delight, delirium, bliss, joy.)

adverbs

supremely; blessedly; truly; idiotically; ineffably; charmingly; unforgettably; enormously; dreamily; innocently; mysteriously; ecstatically; tumultuously; curiously; openly; childishly; rosily; ridiculously; shyly; frankly; excitedly; tranquilly; wildly; unutterably; joyously; tenderly; deliriously.

RARE

adverbs

unusually; valuably; singularly; inimitably; remarkably; pricelessly; incalculably; immeasurably; fantastically; amazingly; unbelievably; momentously; signally; marvelously; incredibly.

RASCAL

adjectives

merry; glaring; bald-pated; meddlesome; lying; barren; mean; consummate; muddy-mettled; mercenary; stretch-mouthed; designing; tawny; lovable; scheming; vile; unmitigated; dishonest; cony-catching; villainous; worthless.

RASCALLY

adverbs

mischievously; outrageously; outlandishly; incorrigibly; unmanageably; fearfully; maliciously; boyishly; trickily; craftily; shamefully; smoothly; atrociously; detestably; insidiously; contemptibly; singularly; appallingly; reprehensibly; treacherously; dishonestly; unregenerately; inveterately; bitterly; hatefully.

RASH

verbs

afflict with—; attribute—to; break into—; daub on—; produce—; solve—; swab—; treat—; —confines; —disappears; —effloresces; —erupts; —fades; —indicates; —irritates; —patches; —plagues; —speckles; —spreads; —subsides.

(See sore, boil.)

adverbs

adventurously; indiscreetly; imprudently; audaciously; unfortunately; wilfully; inconsiderately; foolishly; thoughtlessly; inadvertently; ignorantly; heedlessly; intrepidly; wantonly; desperately; misguidedly; flippantly; absurdly; preposterously; alarmingly; unaccountably; fearlessly.

adjectives

noble; unguided; weakest; stretched; general.

verbs

prevent—; protest—; repent—; rue—; warn against—; —breaks; —chances; —destroys; —endangers; —ignores; —irks; —provokes; —risks; —suffers; —ventures; —vexes; —wrecks.

(See recklessness, audacity.)

RASP (v)

adverbs

harshly; unmelodiously; atrociously; discordantly; gratingly; exasperatingly.

(See grate, file, offend.)

RAT

verbs

experiment on—s; exterminate—s; infest with—s; plague with—s; poison—s; rid of —s; trap—; —burrows; —digs; —excavates; —s frequent; —gnaws; —haunts; —infects; —nibbles; —penetrates; —pillages; —preys on; —ravages; —roves; —scampers; —scurries; —thrives.

(See animal.)

RATE

adjectives

prevailing; reasonable; high; proud; annual; special; low; surprising; respectable; comparable; amazing; expense; balancing; unusual; moderate; stipulated; incredible; differential; fluctuating; minimum; unconscionable; interest; usurious; legal; astounding; tremendous; alarming; reckless; standard; present; noble; rapid; overwhelming; attractive; fearful; death; furious; marvelous; trifling; enormous; modest; prodigious; nominal; unvarying; right; sensible; economical; remarkable; daily; weekly; monthly; thrifty; considerate; extreme; agreeable.

verbs

apply—; assess—; assign—; calculate—; command—; compute—; demand—; deprecate—; determine—; estimate—; fix—; impose—; proportion—; reduce—; slash—; stabilize—; standardize—; subject to—; tax —; —appraises; —corresponds to; —evaluates; —fluctuates; —prevails; —skyrockets; —varies.

(See tax, amount.)

RATE (v)

adverbs
soundly; harshly; disagreeably; furiously; wrathfully; discordantly; scorchingly.
(See appraise, estimate, value.)

RATIFICATION

verbs
fight for—; hinder—; submit for—; —admits; —alters; —attests; —authenticates; —certifies; —concerns; —corroborates; —endorses; —evinces; —indicates; —involves; —recognizes; —seals; —subverts; —upholds; —verifies.
(See approval, confirmation, indorsement.)

RATIFY (v)

adverbs
wisely; amicably; agreeably; ostentatiously; solemnly; internationally.
(See confirm, sanction.)

RATIONAL

adverbs
intelligently; philosophically; soundly; academically; intuitively; sensibly; perfectly; psychologically; coldly; irresistibly; fairly; cosmically; inferentially; elementally; profoundly; fundamentally; presumptively; penetratingly; discernibly; contemplatively; doctrinally; spiritually; innately; ideologically; speculatively; consciously; soberly; speciously; logically; persuasively; convincingly; conclusively.

RATIONS

adjectives
insufficient; deficient; regulation; delicious; balanced; emergency; abundant; scant; half; magic; particular; starvation; wartime.

verbs
allot—; carve—; cast—; consume—; crave —; cut—; deal—; distribute—; divide—; mete out—; parcel—; portion out—; reduce —; replenish—; share—; supply—; —appease; —relieve; —sate; —satisfy; —strengthen.
(See food, diet, supplies.)

RATTLE
(*general*)

adjectives
remote; sudden; tempestuous; globular; unheeded; peremptory; pulsing.

RATTLE
(*toy*)

verbs
chew—; employ—; —amuses; —appeases; —attracts; —clashes; —crashes; —delights; —diverts; —entertains; —fascinates; —interests; —pleases; —subsides; —tinkles.
(See toy, noise, racket.)

RATTLE (v)

adverbs
cacophonously; crisply; peremptorily; tempestuously; rudely; abruptly; irritatingly.
(See clatter, prattle.)

RAUCOUS

adverbs
noisily; curiously; hoarsely; blatantly; boisterously; disagreeably; uncommonly; unusually; unpleasantly; sepulchrally; rudely; raspingly; stertoriously; distinctly; horribly; obnoxiously; unnaturally; offensively; piercingly; peculiarly; curiously; strangely; intolerably; indescribably.

RAVAGES

adjectives
fearful; excessive; increased.

verbs
curb—; preserve from—; stay—; succumb to—; suffer—; —blemish; —blight; —cripple; —damage; —debase; —decimate; —deface; —defile; —desecrate; —disfigure; —embitter; —mutilate; —overwhelm; —prostrate; —ruin; —swamp.
(See damage, injury.)

RAVE (v)

adverbs
senselessly; rapturously; idiotically; drunkenly; fearfully; ominously; furiously; insanely; feverishly; pathetically; passionately; romantically; ecstatically; tumultuously.
(See rage, storm.)

RAVEN

adjectives
presaging; colored; somber; croaking; ominous.

verbs
—attacks; —beaks; —bellows; —bodes; —carries off; —croaks; —destroys; —flits; —kills; —pesters; —plagues; —prates; —preys on; —thieves.
(See bird, crow.)

adjectives
sandy; wooded; picturesque; stained; impenetrable; gaunt; difficult; luminous; inaccessible; bushy; rough; burning; steep; rocky; numerous (pl); precipitous.

RAVISH (*v*)

adverbs
violently; brutally; lustfully; lasciviously; fearfully; viciously; criminally; grossly; sordidly; passionately; bestially; sickeningly.
(See enchant, transport.)

RAVISHING

adverbs
incomparably; delectably; enchantingly; unbelievably; happily; inexpressibly; transportingly; rapturously; ecstatically; divinely; matchlessly; radiantly.

RAW

adverbs
awkwardly; grotesquely; repulsively; unbelievably; angularly; oddly; ludicrously; deplorably; strangely; fantastically; amusingly; pathetically; distressingly; terribly; horribly; grievously; ridiculously; singularly; queerly; drolly; curiously; painfully; crudely; coarsely; thoughtlessly; ignorantly.

RAY

adjectives
solar; deathless; fresh; glaring; dewy; ripening; cheering; evening; gilded; funeral; cosmic; oblique; pounding; visual; scattered (pl); darting; medullary; primary; blushing; early; unrefracted; discomforting; potent; castrated; glowing; lingering; celestial; penetrating; redoubled; luminous; mystic; changing; level; converging; chance; fiery; actinic; tender; unclouded; purest; lurid; overflowing; dimmer; sunny; reviving; dull; fervent; blood-red; transverse; propitious; genial; occasional; beauteous; rising; gladdening; enlivening; killing; hospitable; eternal; controlled; dauntless; diverging; slanting; everlasting; angry; piercing; sportive; parent; heavenly; splendid; dismembered; bewildering; indifferent; curative; reflected; glimmering; dissolving; vertical; illusive; liquid; angelic; streaming; orient; misty; silver; frozen; pensive; radiating; derived; sickly; unwelcome; jubilant; rapid; scorching; dim.

verbs
bend—; diffuse—; dim—; emit—; expose to—; focus—upon; obscure—; shed—; shield from—; shoot—; throw—; —dances; —dazzles; —s diverge; —illuminates; —penetrates; —pierces; —plays upon; —reveals; —shimmers; —streams from.
(See beam, gleam, moonbeam, light.)

RAZOR

verbs
blunt—; brandish—; dull—; employ—; grind—; hone—; nick—; sheathe—; stroke —; strop—; whet—; wield—; —denudes; —incises; —smooths.
(See knife, blade.)

REACH

adjectives
desolating; endless; sighing; automatic; utmost; extended; boundless; upper; illimitable; giddiest; naughty; sandy; vast; arid; easy; keen; timid; wistful; trackless.

REACH (*v*)

adverbs
promptly; simultaneously; automatically; impulsively; conveniently; timidly; ultimately; rapturously; greedily; vainly; wistfully.
(See touch, strike.)

REACT (*v*)

adverbs
discreditably; instantaneously; adversely; strangely; abnormally; divergently; feverishly; violently; passionately; intuitively; romantically; physically; logically; blindly.
(See resist, recoil, oppose.)

REACTION

adjectives
energetic; painful; emotional; necessary; feverish; varied; premature; strong; disastrous; consumer; unequivocal; fatigued; violent; protective; inevitable; deep-seated; vigorous; unexpected; natural; photochemical; uncomfortable; passionate; intuitive; impulsive; instantaneous; chemical; antagonistic; romantic; infantile; chronic; physical; barbarous; pleasant; artificial; individual; astounding; logical; sympathetic; dramatic; blind; unromantic; sanguinary.

verbs
awaken—; control—; defeat—; determine —; emphasize—; evaluate—; excite—; experience—; foresee—; forestall—; induce—;

observe—; produce—; promote—; provoke —; repute—; reverse—; study—; suffer—; test—; —astounds; —ensues; —sets in; — warns.

(See answer, reply, response.)

REACTIONARY

adverbs

commendably; dangerously; manifestly; defiantly; openly; curiously; inexplicably; unaccountably; unreasonably; lamentably; stimulatingly; progressively; energetically; ominously; favorably; admirably; politically; irresolutely; unreliably; antagonistically; painfully; astonishingly; reprehensibly; undependably.

READ (v)

adverbs

omnivorously; perpetually; insipidly; profoundly; nonchalantly; listlessly; attentively; extensively; drowsily; assiduously; advisedly; monotonously; genially; voraciously; habitually; casually; industriously; stimulatingly; desultorily; promiscuously; surreptitiously; haltingly; sporadically; judiciously.

(See peruse, scan, study.)

READABLE

adverbs

instantly; easily; readily; pleasantly; fascinatingly; entertainingly; delightfully; interestingly; scarcely; barely; instructively; highly; uncommonly; remarkably; singularly; definitely; distinctly; plainly; unusually.

READER

adjectives

eager; intelligent; constant; everyday; enthusiastic; serious; gentle; phenomenal; browsing; sagacious; assiduous; casual; insatiable; captious; extensive; persistent; dilettante; confused; unsuspecting; continental; absorbed; negligent; omnivorous; copy; discriminating; stumbling; uncomprehending; fastidious; indefatigable; industrious; prudish; voracious; ponderous; innocent; voluminous; ardent; attentive; arid; rapid; faulty; lifelong.

verbs

absorb—; acquaint—; amuse—; divert—; edify—; enlighten—; entertain—; guide—; inform—; instruct—; lay before—; outrage —; persuade—; tickle—; train—; —appreciates; —browses; —comprehends; —cons;

—consumes; —criticizes; —delights; — delves into; —dips into; —discerns; —enjoys; —gleans; —imbibes; —masters; — peruses; —plunges into; —pores over; — refers to; —scans; —thumbs; —wades through; —apprehends.

(See student, scholar, pupil.)

READINESS

adjectives

dreary; extreme; stubborn; belligerent; astonishing; sulky; useful; disconcerting.

READING

adjectives

essential; constructive; fascinating; stimulating; available; up-to-date; quick; intelligent; delightful; laborious; choral; extensive; assiduous; coarse; prodigious; random; absorbing; hurried; entertaining; tedious; monotonous; desultory; required; attentive; surreptitious; promiscuous; flighty; diverting; irregular; dreary; dull; omnivorous.

verbs

assign—; coach in—; comment on—; define —; enjoy—; expound—; improve—; interpret—; recite—; render—; study—; translate—; unfold—; unravel—; wade through —; —acquaints; —delights; —edifies; —entertains; —serves; —yields.

(See story, lesson, interpretation, book.)

READJUSTMENT

adjectives

heroic; fundamental; sharp; comprehensive; difficult.

verbs

advocate—; demand—; effect—; intensify —; measure—; necessitate—; undergo—; —accommodates; —adapts; —balances; — copes with; —countervails; —equalizes; — evens; —levels; —matches; —poises; —restores; —satisfies; —trims.

(See change, adjustment.)

READY

adverbs

resolutely; instantly; finally; recently; altogether; promptly; eagerly; intrepidly; warily; vigilantly; alertly; evidently; providently; prudently; painfully; carefully; scrupulously; always; unfailingly; heroically; gallantly; formidably; fortunately; luckily; opportunely; reasonably; sensibly; practically; almost.

REAL

adverbs

intensely; fantastically; oppressively; tangibly; vividly; mercilessly; horribly; dangerously; vitally; painfully; starkly; solidly; hideously; grossly; crudely; temporally; mundanely; appallingly; hauntingly; monotonously; ponderously; eternally; sordidly; inexorably; basically; sternly; terribly; gloriously; glamorously; crassly; crudely; humanly; demonstrably; substantially; graphically; stubbornly.

REALISM

adjectives

wounding; decadent; gripping; graphic; unflinching; pure; gross; unshrinking; unpitying; surprising; lifelike; nauseating; inartistic; crude; bare.

verbs

advocate—; compromise—; conform to—; delve into—; dip into—; establish—; examine—; imbibe—; practise—; touch—; transcend—; composes—; —divests; —enthrones itself; —portrays.

(See science, philosophy, psychology, reality, art.)

REALIST

adjectives

destitute; uncompromising; sumptuous; selective; skilled.

REALISTIC

adverbs

dramatically; spectacularly; utterly; unusually; undeniably; distinctly; admirably; notoriously; commendably; surprisingly; unexpectedly; astonishingly; intensely; vividly; mysteriously; incredibly; mercilessly; dangerously; beautifully; delightfully; happily; entertainingly; interestingly; unsurpassably; incomparably; faithfully; startlingly; appallingly.

REALITY

adjectives

grim; sordid; intense; fantastic; naked; oppressive; tangible; passionate; beneficient; clamant; vivid; living; ideal; typical; blunt; mysterious; infinite; waking; existing; sober; practical; elusive; commonplace;
accidental; fearful; unfathomable; clear; conceived; spiritual; concrete; exacting; vulgar; fictitious; specific; merciless; peremptory; subtle; nautical; glassy; horrid; stern; dangerous; vital; painful; stark; solid; gloomy; beneficent.

verbs

bear—; convey—; deal with—; descend to —; divorce from—; endure—; enslave to —; escape—; evade—; face—; flee from—; gain—; gloss over—; grasp for—; ground on—; obscure—; pursue—; question—; return to—; spare—; varnish—; wrap in—.

(See realism.)

REALIZATION

adjectives

hideous; evident; uninterrupted; vivid; devotional; bitter; dawning; living; piteous; stabbing; poseful; shocking; exact; eternal; dark.

verbs

achieve—; anticipate—; attain—; demand —; effect—; fancy—; jar into—; jolt into —; labor under—; register—; strive for—; struggle for—; —completes; —crowns; —dawns; —dazes; —discharges; —fulfills; —grows upon; —perfects; —strikes; —stuns.

(See effect, fulfillment.)

REALIZE (v)

adverbs

sickeningly; nervously; instinctively; emphatically; dimly; speedily; vividly; vaguely; faintly; gloriously; partially; feebly; happily; piteously; stabbingly; shockingly.

(See achieve, complete.)

REALM

adjectives

sterile; populous; empty; untrodden; mysterious; free; rival; sleepy; blissful; boundless; wealthy; sunnier; historic; airy; glorious; unsubstantial; masculine; interminable; intellectual; famous; impenetrable; ancient; loftier; starry; flowery; shuddering; conquered; unproductive; capricious; captivating.

verbs

conquer—; command—; control—; dominate —; dwell in—; explore—; govern—; inhabit

—; invade—; locate—; master—; misrule —; occupy—; overrun—; preside over—; seize—; sway—; visit—.

(See kingdom, region, province.)

REAP (v)

adverbs

meritoriously; vigorously; seasonally; happily; gratefully; handsomely; rightfully.

(See gather, collect.)

REAR

verbs

bring up—; construct—; dog—; guard—; join—; lay—; —closes; —concludes; —determines; —ends; —finishes; —follows; —lags; —nullifies; —shadows; —skirts; —terminates; —trails; —treads.

(See front, back.)

REAR (v)

adverbs

viciously; dangerously; skittishly; wildly; blindly; capriciously; materially; domestically; shelteredly; innocently.

(See raise, elevate.)

REARMAMENT

verbs

advocate—; condemn—; demand—; forbid —; hinder—; limit—; permit—; plan—; question—; reduce—; refuse—; repress—; request—; restrain—; restrict—; sanction —; —abuses; —agitates; —brews; —despairs; —endangers; —incenses; —protects.

(See armament.)

REASON
(general)

adjectives

sensible; valid; potent; indignant; individual; sufficient; sentimental; unshackled; imperceptible; legal; intelligent; physical; holy; sound; artistic; abundant; mere; naked; alleged; supposed; cogent; religious; punitive; exquisite; abstract; shattered; intangible; weighty; passive; mournful; root; indisputable; ostensible; aesthetic; public; human; satirical; unknown; contradicting; inclusive; cold; improbable; crying; philosophic; prosaic; irresistible; calm; special; prudential; earthly; sovereign; obscure; honest; sharp; convincing; sententious; fundamental; liberal; impossible; precise; obvious; justifying; mysterious; firm; foremost; dawning; immense; powerful; natural; plain; unconscious; manly; hamper-

ing; insufficient; overwhelming; carnal; indefinable; inexplicable; righteous; cool; immortal; definite; odious; respectable; trivial; weightiest; evident; hollow; inscrutable; sober; apparent; occult; willful; eternal; bright; pure; practical; benevolent; painful; plausible; logical; absurd; conceivable; organic; pompous; ethnological; inexperienced; unselfish; patent; specious; ultimate; pressing; simple; palpable.

REASON
(grounds, argument, etc.)

verbs

adduce—; advance—; analyze—; assign—for; bolster—; cite—s; conceal—; convey—; cook up—; debate—; discern—; draw—from; elicit—; evidence—; feign—; omit—; outline—s; overstep—; summarize—; —explains; —looms; —motivates; —underlies.

(See excuse, grounds, cause.)

REASON
(intellectual, faculty, common-sense, logic)

verbs

appeal to—; base on—; derange—; employ —; evince—; impregnate with—; invoke—; supplant—; —crumbles; —determines; —dictates; —impels; —ordains; —prevails; —totters; —wanders; —yields to.

(See logic, intellect, sense, sanity.)

REASON (v)

adverbs

coherently; inconsistently; persuasively; solemnly; dialectically; deductively; logically; ridiculously; deviously; ineffectually; intelligently; circuitously; validly; sentimentally; cogently; prosaically; sententiously; plausibly; speciously.

(See argue, debate.)

REASONABLE

adverbs

intelligently; philosophically; soundly; academically; intuitively; sensibly; perfectly; psychologically; coldly; fairly; cosmically; inferentially; elementally; essentially; profoundly; fundamentally; presumptively; penetratingly; discernibly; contemplatively; doctrinally; spiritually; theologically; ideologically; speculatively; consciously; soberly; spaciously; logically; persuasively; convincingly; conclusively.

adjectives
accurate; habitual; profound; lawless; admirable; acute; careful; painstaking; deft; clever.

REASONING

adjectives
seductive; sober; secular; immethodized; speculative; unstable; judicial; vicious; hypothetical; inductive; erroneous; stern; calm; infantile; physiological; precocious; scientific; deliberate; sustained; fallacious; syllogistic; abstract; explicit; conclusive; logical.

REASSURANCE

adjectives
peaceful; hopeful; tremendous; slender.

REASSURING

adverbs
completely; comfortingly; genially; judicially; gravely; amiably; wisely; pleasantly; indulgently; graciously; smpathetically; understandingly; encouragingly; helpfully; hopefully; optimistically; considerately; affectionately; warmly; hospitably; pleasantly; mildly; earnestly; enthusiastically; confidently; definitely; distinctly.

REBEL (*v*)

adverbs
vindictively; heartily; hatefully; intellectually; patriotically; desperately; blindly; abortively; mutely; hopelessly; technically.
(See revolt, defy, resist.)

REBELLION

adjectives
technical; appeasing; incipient; perpetual; gigantic; extensive; righteous; seething; violent; open; unqualified; hurt; blind; abortive; memorable; vain; mute; persistent; universal; manifest; hopeless; futile.

verbs
abet—; confine—; finance—; fire—; foment —; incite to—; intensify—; liquidate—; plan—; plot—; plunge into—; quash—; quell—; repress—; restrain—; set down—; threaten with—; uncover—; verge on—; — breaks out; —perishes; —seethes; —stirs; —undermines.
(See insurrection, mutiny, revolution.)

adverbs
sullenly; doggedly; drearily; unhappily; bitterly; incorrigibly; incurably; unmanageably; sadly; justly; rightfully; intelligently; sensibly; wildly; cruelly; insensately; furiously; violently; uncontrollably; cantankerously; atrociously; detestably; unreasonably; justifiably; naturally; woefully; stubbornly; obstinately; desperately; dangerously; ominously; unfortunately; unluckily; unwisely; finally; instantly; resentfully; angrily; secretly; quietly.

REBELS

adjectives
intellectual; patriotic; incorrigible; vile; contending; repentant; desperate.

verbs
exile—; punish—; restrict—; silence—; — arise; —arm; —betray; —conspire; —corrupt; —defy; —infringe upon; —intrigue; —mutiny; —plot; —resist; —strike; —violate; —withdraw.
(See insurgents, opponent.)

REBUFF

adjectives
unforeseen; stupid; rude; unsympathetic; studied; complete; deserved.

verbs
cower before—; impel—; incur—; render —; resist—; sense—; smart under—; undergo—; withhold—; —chills; —crushes; — cuts; —insults; —jostles; —raps; —reviles; —revolts; —scandalizes; —shocks; —slaps; —smarts; —snubs.
(See insult, defeat, rebuke, refusal.)

REBUFF (*v*)

adverbs
superciliously; sneeringly; rudely; aristocratically; impertinently; proudly; vindictively.
(See resist, repulse, repel.)

REBUFFED

adverbs
definitely; unreasonably; distinctly; neatly; saucily; arrogantly; needlessly; unwarrantably; insolently; impudently; impertinently; unnecessarily; undeservedly; unaccountably; startlingly; surprisingly; properly; deservedly; properly; politely; adroitly; in-

geniously; subtly; disconcertingly; promptly; urbanely; suavely; uncivilly; unceremoniously; sharply; definitely; officially; blandly.

REBUILD (v)
adverbs

patiently; vigorously; hopefully; courageously; repeatedly; gloriously; imitatively.
(See build, repair.)

REBUKE
adjectives

pertinent; merited; grave; whispered; sour; stinging; artless; delicate; savage; frightened; stern; uncompromising; paternal; dignified; proud; smart; standing; sulphurous; scornful; sad; promptest.

verbs

administer—; endure—; imply—; offset—; submit to—; suffer—; thrust—at; —abashes; —corrects; —disconcerts; —hurts; —maddens; —silences.
(See rebuff, reprimand, ridicule.)

REBUKE (v)
adverbs

indignantly; priggishly; sternly; pertinently; gravely; stingingly; paternally; sulphurously; scornfully; briskly; curtly; cuttingly; incisively.
(See admonish, censure, reprove.)

REBUKED
adverbs

sternly; harshly; unreasonably; unaccountably; undeservedly; constantly; recently; saucily; officially; seriously; gravely; ominously; publicly; openly; quietly; deservedly; properly; naturally; necessarily; woefully; rudely; ungraciously; unwarrantably; unjustly; cruelly; wantonly; subtly; loudly; furiously; brusquely; bluntly; rudely; unforgivably; unforgettably.

RECALCITRANT
adverbs

cantankerously; habitually; always; disagreeably; unpleasantly; offensively; politically; obnoxiously; detestably; despicably; unfailingly; obstinately; stubbornly; unreasonably; unaccountably; naturally; stupidly; boorishly; doggedly; singularly; peculiarly; presumptiously; bumptiously.

RECALL (v)
adverbs

vividly; affectionately; palpably; momentarily; distinctively; perpetually; bitterly; vaguely; greedily; idly; passionately.
(See annul, retract.)

RECEIVE (v)
adverbs

courteously; precisely; graciously; affably; reluctantly; hospitably; opportunely; glowingly; morosely; willingly; scornfully; consciously; mournfully; credulously; gratuitously; supinely; indiscriminately; haughtily; cordially; royally; ceremoniously; frostily.
(See accept, take.)

RECEIVERSHIP
verbs

accept—; anticipate—; avoid—; demand—; enter into—; fall into—; grant—; lapse into—; repel—; resist—; save from—; succor from—; verge on—; —embarrasses; —safeguards; —satisfies; —terminates.
(See bankruptcy.)

RECEPTACLE
adjectives

sacred; unsightly; unworthy; hideous; secret; hidden.

RECEPTION
adjectives

unfriendly; sumptuous; canine; flattering; popular; suitable; favorable; enthusiastic; affectionate; honorable; courteous; critical; problematical; ceremonious; unprejudiced; instant; general; cordial; wonderful; traditional; frosty; grand; stormy; official; magnificent; bloody; court; extraordinary; welcome; royal; friendly; sympathetic; hospitable; tame; sullen.

RECEPTIVE
adverbs

intelligently; astonishingly; brilliantly; attentively; eagerly; ardently; gratefully; thankfully; utterly; actively; pleasantly; helpfully; sharply; keenly; particularly.

RECESS
adjectives

fathomless; remotest; dark; dim; glowing; tangled; innermost; profound; various (pl); mystic; grassy; appalling; cool; capacious; intimate; little-known; soul-haunting; shy; shady.

verbs
deny—; enjoy—; grant—; lull in—; prescribe—; suggest—; welcome—; —affords; —allays; —disburdens; —dispels; —eases; —refreshes; —relaxes; —relieves; —revivifies; —vents.
(See rest, vacation, pause.)

RECESSION
adjectives
financial; business; widespread; nationwide; gripping.

RECIPE
verbs
adhere to—; attempt—; clip—; commend—; devise—; follow—; interpret—; necessitate —; refer to—; scan—; seek—; study—; — acquaints; —eases; —edifies; —enlightens; —guides; —informs; —prevents; —satisfies; —suggests.
(See formula, method.)

RECIPROCAL
adverbs
agreeably; pleasantly; accommodatingly; publicly; readily; systematically; contractually; interchangeably; helpfully; sympathetically; openly; reluctantly; eagerly; proportionally; satisfactorily; conveniently; advantageously; profitably.

RECITAL
adjectives
bolting; warm; light; summary; amusing; quaint; dejected; tedious; dispassionate; instructive.

verbs
narrate—; rehearse—; render—; sum up—; unfold—; —edifies; —enchants; —enlightens; —enthralls; —entrances; —inspires; — pictures; —portrays; —recounts; —relates; —unravels.
(See performance, concert, speech, poem.)

RECITATIVE
adverbs
crooningly; endlessly; effectively; monotonously; raucously; huskily; dully; unmelodiously; comically; hilariously; clownishly; curiously; dramatically; melodiously; rhythmically; qauintly; dramatically; incomparably; strangely; pleasantly.

RECITE (*v*)
adverbs
drolly; faithfully; feelingly; passionately; ardently; quaintly; instructively; repetitiously; monotonously; drearily.
(See relate, repeat.)

RECKLESS
adverbs
desperately; daringly; audaciously; blithely; merrily; hilariously; bitterly; cruelly; inconsiderately; thoughtlessly; heedlessly; deliberately; optimistically; wickedly; disconcertingly; improvidently; extravagantly; exceedingly; fantastically; outlandishly; outrageously; grotesquely; ostentatiously; spectacularly; dramatically; wildly; indiscreetly; financially; commercially; politically; personally; inexcusably; insensately; angrily; furiously; jealously; pitiably.

RECKLESSNESS
adjectives
wanton; stubborn; unfelt; lavish; uncalculating; staid; fastidious; daring; fatal; gallant.

verbs
admonish—; protest—; repent—; rue—; tempt—; tolerate—; warn against—; —destroys; —endangers; —exposes to; —ignores; —irritates; —provokes; —risks; — suffers; —ventures; —wrecks.
(See audacity, indiscretion.)

RECKONING
adjectives
annual; lunar; dreadful; final; false; dead; swift.

verbs
confuse—; demand—; discharge—; discount—; estimate—; ignore—; probe—; value—; weed out of—; —accounts for; —acquits; —balances; —clarifies; —dishonors; —fathoms; —nullifies; —repays.
(See account, computation, calculation, consideration.)

RECLINE (*v*)
adverbs
lazily; somnolently; cozily; comfortably; swinishly; calmly; artlessly; unambitiously.
(See rest, relax.)

RECLUSE

adjectives

literary; curious; poetical; sanctified; churlish; venerable; staid.

RECOGNITION

adjectives

abbreviated; instant; reverent; warmest; rigid; deserved; continuous; momentary; enforced; long-awaited; critical; unbroken; increasing; welcome; cold; unmistakable; faint; intelligent; courteous; legislative; mutual; dismayed; admiring; tacit; grateful; orderly; affectionate; public; sole; formal; emphatic; full; familiar; premature; clouded; flattering; hard-won.

verbs

accord—; alter beyond—; arouse—; concede—; confer—; demand—; evade—; escape—; extend—; gain—; lose—; merit—; permit—; prompt—; receive—; refuse—; struggle for—; suggest—; win—; —confirms; —corroborates; —recalls.

(See fame, greatness, position.)

RECOGNIZABLE

adverbs

easily; readily; distinctly; unfailingly; instantly; unmistakably; singularly; manifestly; memorably; unforgettably; peculiarly; particularly; positively; transparently; conspicuously; glaringly; unconcealably; strikingly; remarkably.

RECOGNIZE (*v*)

adverbs

distinctly; instinctively; definitely; universally; formally; frankly; deservedly; coldly; courteously; mutually; affectionately; tacitly; formally; publicly; prematurely.

(See distinguish, acknowledge.)

RECOIL

adjectives

vicious; impetuous; silent; tardy; nervous.

RECOIL (*v*)

adverbs

instinctively; involuntarily; modestly; impatiently; impetuously; nervously; abruptly; abnormally; tremblingly.

(See react, shrink.)

RECOLLECT (*v*)

adverbs

agreeably; humiliatingly; delightfully; hatefully; gratefully; remorsefully; vaguely; uneasily; romantically; painfully; affectionately.

(See remember, recall.)

RECOLLECTION

adjectives

nightmare; agreeable; humiliating; delightful; grateful; hateful; glorious; contemptuous; dark; stern; remorseful; vanished; importunate; dim; vague; sweet; eternal; uneasy; romantic; sudden; simultaneous; humbling; distinct; melancholy; painful; accurate; faithful; perfect; tangled; livelier; pleasant; dormant; vivid; hazy; blissful; ungracious; cloudy; affectionate.

verbs

attempt—; betray—; crowd—s; drown—; escape—; evade—; hallow—; hinder—; obliterate—; prompt—; seek—; shudder at —; sink into—; stimulate—; stir—; suggest —; urge—; verify—; —dawns; —dims; —fades; —refreshes.

(See memory, remembrance, reminiscence.)

RECOMMEND (*v*)

adverbs

conscientiously; respectfully; unreservedly; cordially; urgently; expressly; unanimously; confidently; unhesitatingly; vigorously; earnestly; aptly; eloquently; subtly; emphatically; consistently.

(See suggest, commend, praise.)

RECOMMENDATION

adjectives

definite; additional; nimble; sweet; subtle; novel; emphatic; hesitating; sound; impolitic; consistent.

verbs

carry out—; confer—; consult—; demand—; gain—; glean—s; incorporate—s; offer—; sketch—s; —advises; —advocates; —favors; —flatters; —glows; —impresses; — informs; —refers to; —reports; —suggests.

(See commendation, approval, approbation, reference.)

RECOMMENDED

adverbs

highly; enthusiastically; favorably; well; exceptionally; unconditionally; earnestly;

justly; readily; acceptably; thoughtfully; unreservedly; strongly; eminently; explicitly; expressly.

RECOMPENSE
adjectives
godlike; solid; immortal; earnest; noblest; friendly; generous; exciting; abundant; insufficient; scant.

RECONCILABLE
adverbs
easily; readily; scarcely; hardly; wholly; partially; entirely; logically; reasonably; sensibly; naturally; fortunately; pleasantly; amiably; generously; amicably; fortunately; consistently.

RECONCILE (*v*)
adverbs
peremptorily; briefly; conveniently; permanently; forgivingly; touchingly; dramatically; logically; philosophically.
(See adjust, settle.)

RECONCILIATION
adjectives
perfect; convenient; short-lived; sweet; lasting; generous; forgiving.

verbs
arrange—; declare—; draw—; effect—; exact—; gain—; refuse—; seek—; —allays; —appeases; —heals; —hushes; —pacifies; —placates; —renews; —restores; —settles; —smooths; —squares.
(See conciliation, peace, reunion.)

RECONDITION (*v*)
adverbs
efficiently; professionally; thoroughly; permanently; periodically.
(See renew, repair.)

RECONNOITRE (*v*)
adverbs
audaciously; slyly; dutifully; courageously; cautiously; brazenly.
(See examine, inspect.)

RECONSIDER (*v*)
adverbs
hastily; subsequently; consequentially; meditatively; contemplatively; reflectively; serenely.
(See review, contemplate.)

RECONSTRUCTION
adjectives
orderly; benign; inartistic; voluntary.

verbs
advise—; facilitate—; necessitate—; retard —; —converts; —corrects; —cures; —heals; —recoups; —rectifies; —redresses; —refreshes; —reinforces; —rights.
(See repairs, improvement, change.)

RECORD
adjectives
attainable; successful; enviable; reliable; long; indispensable; unsavory; scriptural; manifold (pl); authenticated; mystical; honorable; engrossed; splendid; imperfect; woeful; forlorn; formless; faithful; creditable; distinguished; chronological; continuous; vivid; subtlest; illustrious; unapproachable; earliest; historic; stenographic; boasted; bristling; erroneous; lingering; shameful; surprising; trivial; fond; illustrated; contemporary; parliamentary; voluminous; damning; priceless; definite; terse; cold; literal; comparable; accurate; individual; progressive; glorious; formal; lasting; tabulated; valuable; supernatural; available; confessed; trustworthy; indelible; notarial; pathetic; dumb; accumulated; aggregated; official; flawless; unpretending; artistic; clinical; imperishable; enthralling; factual; romantic; commendable; tragic; exemplary; phenomenal; heraldic.

verbs
achieve—; afford—; assemble—s; best—; blast—; bolster—; catalogue—s; compare —s; compile—s; delve into—s; divulge—; establish—; filch from—s; hang up—; illuminate—; inscribe—; live up to—; obliterate—; pound out—; pore over—s; probe —s; produce—; top—s; —s set forth; —s vary.
(See chronicle, archives, list, reputation.)

RECORD (*v*)
adverbs
faithfully; accurately; precisely; amusingly; regularly; minutely; authentically; industriously; impassively; uninterruptedly; scripturally; mystically; creditably; chronologically; vividly; subtly; historically; graphically; trivially; voluminously; literally; formally; flawlessly; clinically; factually; commendably; phenomenally.
(See note, reserve.)

RECORDED

adverbs

duly; accurately; carefully; meticulously; indelibly; graphically; intricately; officially; memorably; secretly; punctiliously; promptly; instantly; immediately; beautifully; realistically; photostatically; precisely; faithfully; legally; methodically; systematically; lovingly; vividly; completely.

RECOVER (v)

adverbs

mechanically; sufficiently; extraordinarily; miraculously; swiftly; speedily; tardily; moderately; fortunately; gradually; spectacularly; normally.

(See repair, restore.)

RECOVERY

adjectives

slow; gradual; rapid; ultimate; languid; spontaneous; happy; noble; spectacular; permanent; extraordinary; receding.

verbs

anticipate—; attribute—to; effect—; envisage—; expedite—; facilitate—; fumble with—; hasten—; hinder—; impede—; insure—; jeopardize—; promote—; retard—; speed—; stimulate—; —cheers; —ensues; —follows.

(See improvement, convalescence, restoration.)

RECREANT

adverbs

detestably; incredibly; shamefully; grossly; meanly; stubbornly; disgracefully; blasphemously; fearfully; infirmly; infamously; tortuously; insidiously; ignominiously; knavishly; unworthily; gracelessly; irreclaimably; unconscionably; basely.

RECREATION

adjectives

stimulating; intellectual; sweet; healthful; inexpensive; joyous; subsidiary; luxurious; innocent; solitary; wholesome; mutual; constructive.

verbs

arrange—; enjoy—; indulge in—; plan—; provide for—; seek—; —amuses; —beguiles; —bores; —cheers; —diverts; — drags; —enlivens; —entertains; —palls;

—relaxes; —revivifies; —tires; —wearies.

(See game, entertainment, jollity, diversion, amusement.)

RECRIMINATION

adjectives

mutual; bitter; incessant; cruel; repeated (pl).

RECRUDESCENT

adverbs

fortunately; surprisingly; advantageously; profitably; startlingly; strangely; luckily; opportunely; periodically; conveniently; fortuitously; resurgently; providentially; blessedly.

RECRUIT (v)

adverbs

intelligently; forcefully; faithfully; mainly; militaristically; martially; haphazardly.

(See furnish, raise.)

RECRUITS

adjectives

clownish; manifold; raw; unwilling; well-drilled; flustered; trustworthy; intelligent; unarmed; discouraged.

verbs

attract—; contribute—; furnish—; initiate —; lure—; tempt—; —advance; —assist; —attend; —brace; —cheer; —expedite; — fortify; —prop; —protect; —reenforce; — rescue; —steel; —sustain; —vivify.

(See volunteers, soldier.)

RECTITUDE

adjectives

extreme; utter; absolute; conscious; primeval; aesthetic; strict; self-styled.

RECTOR

adjectives

lisping; stern; devout; earnest; pious.

verbs

consult—; support—; unfrock—; —administers; —admonishes; —announces; —conducts; —crusades; —directs; —governs; —guides; —ministers; —orates; —preaches; —prepares; —prescribes; —presides; — supervises.

(See minister.)

RECTUM

verbs

abscess—; act on—; cleanse—; dilate—; distend—; flush—; inflame—; inject into—; irritate—; plug—; purge—; support—; terminate in—; trouble—; —extends.

(See bowels.)

RECUPERATE (v)

adverbs

expectedly; normally; beneficently; placidly; markedly; tardily; extendedly; passively; entirely.

(See rally, improve.)

RECUPERATIVE

adverbs

highly; strongly; vigorously; happily; fortunately; wholesomely; healthfully; sturdily; slowly; steadily; quietly; incredibly; luckily; carefully; successfully; patiently; resolutely; calmly; undeniably.

RECUR (v)

adverbs

successively; intermittently; constantly; insanely; sporadically; unexpectedly; infrequently; abruptly; irritatingly; explosively.

(See return, restore.)

RECURRENCE

adjectives

infrequent; delicate; sweet; constant; emphatic; intermittent; noisy; angry.

verbs

anticipate—; endure—; insure against—; prepare for—; suffer—; survive—; —bores; —drums; —redoubles; —refreshes; —renews; —resumes; —revolves; —rings; —shocks; —surprises; —wearies.

(See frequency, occurrence, repetition.)

RED

adjectives

deep; bloody; hectic; ruby; flamingo; latest; blazing; shimmering; livid; angry; tuneful; vivid; cochineal; unnatural; bright; orange; gleaming; rich; velvety; rosy; lifeless; brightish; monochromatic; fiery; gaudy; eye-closing; garish.

REDDEN (v)

adverbs

hotly; coyly; blushingly; shyly; modestly; timidly; enthusiastically; visibly; furiously; feverishly; indignantly.

(See flush, blush.)

REDEEM (v)

adverbs

ultimately; promptly; spiritually; subsequently; everlastingly; honorably; faithfully.

(See recover, rescue.)

REDEEMABLE

adverbs

currently; locally; immediately; fortunately; conveniently; profitably; undoubtedly; warrantably; fairly; easily; proportionally; lucratively; admissibly; unquestionably; legally; definitely; contractually; readily.

REDEMPTION

adjectives

ultimate; everlasting; foul; prompt; subsequent; spiritual; complete.

REDNESS

adjectives

shimmering; dewy; startling; rheumy.

REDOLENT

adverbs

pungently; spicily; sweetly; fragrantly; deliciously; delightfully; pleasantly; aromatically; refreshingly; suggestively; woodsily; surprisingly; lingeringly; strongly; highly; uncommonly.

REDRESS

adjectives

adequate; instant; warlike; immediate.

REDS

(communists)

verbs

support—; suppress—; —advocate; —agitate; —aggravate; —band; —forfeit; —idealize; —inflame; —instigate; —invade; —pillage; —plot; —promise; —resist; —revolt; —riot; —strike; —undermine.

(See communist, anarchist.)

REDUCE (v)

adverbs

materially; sharply; correspondingly; emphatically; deliberately; necessarily; rigorously; substantially; markedly; radically; drastically.

(See diminish, lower.)

adjectives

substantial; successive (pl); inexplicable; tremendous; marked; enormous; proper; radical; honest; ample; drastic; smashing; equitable; perpetual; scant.

REED

adjectives

jungle; pastoral; balmy; stiff; solacing; bruised; swampy; bending; unsustaining; plaited; vocal; whispering; silvery.

REEF

adjectives

submerged; hidden; sunken; encircling; subterranean; lisping; bluff; leering; scowling; frowning; darkling; dangerous; black-browed.

verbs

avoid—; cast upon—; drift to—; drive upon—; doom to—; founder on—; lash—; pound—; shatter on—s; thunder on—; —descends; —extends; —menaces; —ranges; —stretches; —threatens.

(See beach, rocks, shore.)

REEK (*v*)

adverbs

foully; alcoholically; vilely; powerfully; nauseatingly; disgustingly.

(See smoke, smell.)

REEL (*v*)

adverbs

visibly; weakly; drunkenly; dizzily; abruptly; sickeningly; swayingly.

(See stagger, sway.)

REFER (*v*)

adverbs

sarcastically; ironically; indelicately; pointedly; caustically; vaguely; satirically; unequivocally; sneeringly; sagaciously; affectionately; cursorily; contemptuously; pertinently; hilariously; obscurely; vaguely.

(See allude, hint, intimate.)

REFERENCE

adjectives

contemptuous; satisfying; constant; complimentary; barren; innumerable (pl); pathetic; pertinent; bibliographical; polite; solitary; never-ending; unmistakable; figurative; hilarious; documentary; mutual; offhand; obscure; touching; specific; sudden; sly; gratifying; vague; slighting.

verbs

avoid—to; demand—s; furnish—s; heed—; request—s; seek—s; vouchsafe—s; weigh—s; —compliments; —concerns; —counsels; —flatters; —instructs; —justifies; —mentions; —pertains to; —prescribes; —relates to; —satisfies; —suggests; —warns.

(See allusion, recommendation, mention, hint, record.)

REFINEMENT

adjectives

vital; technical; conscious; artistic; subtle; structural; utmost; high; intellectual; fresh; inventive; studied; nameless; classic; elaborate; sophistical; characteristic; delicate; accentuated; expert; exquisite; distilled; soft; false; incidental.

verbs

cultivate—; discern—; infuse—; profit by —; touch with—; weigh—; —ameliorates; —discriminates; —distinguishes; —enhances; —enriches; —graces; —improves; —mellows; —mitigates; —polishes; —promotes; —sifts.

(See elegance, civilization, refinement, culture.)

REFLECT (*v*)

adverbs

calmly; meditatively; sparklingly; contemplatively; cannily; piously; pensively; moodily; morbidly; somberly; grimly; opportunely; serenely; ingenuously; cynically; bitterly; miserably; delicately; philosophically; coherently; candidly; logically.

(See mirror, revert.)

REFLECTION

adjectives

delicate; vivid; surface; opposite; dreadful; somber; sagacious; gloomy; grave; unpleasant; sobering; impersonal; colorless; mature; injurious; sage; passionate; solemn; admirable; unbroken; wicked; judicious; interesting; cheering; dazzling; rusty; satirical; rich; best; philosophic; melancholy; bitter; careful; subtle; calm; unconscious; dim; perturbed; mortifying; unquiet; dancing; rosy; perplexing; drowsy; powerful; spectral; shortest; profound; brooding; distracting; nostalgic; silvery; recurring; homely; disagreeable; agitating; adequate; philosophical; coherent; assuring; heart-shaking; candid; prosaic; continuous; harrowing; disturbing; splendid; logical.

verbs
absorb in—; air—; bolster by—; bury in—; console with—; emerge from—; feign—; immerse in—; sustain by—; veil in—; wrap in—; —calms; —convinces; —flatters; —mirrors.
(See consideration, contemplation, image, study, meditation.)

REFLECTIVE
adverbs
philosophically; lazily; idly; pensively; wistfully; actively; alertly; keenly; gravely; seriously; earnestly; studiously; deeply; profoundly; aimlessly; restfully; quietly; calmly; serenely; gloomily; pessimistically; sadly; happily; pleasantly; peacefully; unwontedly; habitually.

REFORM
adjectives
obstinate; headlong; subsequent; constitutional; valuable; great; liberal; beneficent; mimetic; effectual; important; educational; ideological; dietary; phonetic; baronial; simultaneous; rigid; radical; feverish; temperance; energetic; imposed; rational.

verbs
adapt to—; adopt—; advocate—; approve —; deal with—; dramatize—; effect—; enforce—; facilitate—; formulate—; initiate —; institute—; labor for—; overemphasize —; proffer—; propose—; stalemate—; — overtakes; —slogs along; —surges over.
(See improvement, change, amendment.)

REFORM (v)
adverbs
speedily; constitutionally; beneficently; educationally; ideologically; radically; temperately; energetically; rationally.
(See convert, change.)

REFORMER
adjectives
hardy; prison; ardent; pugnacious; theoretical; phonetic; joy-killing; meretricious; disorderly; impetuous; respectable; temperance.

verbs
—advocates; —ameliorates; —betters; — corrects; —cultivates; —directs; —doctors; —eases; —foists upon; —fosters; —mends; —prates; —promotes; —purifies; —rants; —relieves; —remedies; —reorganizes; — repairs.
(See apostle, minister.)

REFRACTORY
adverbs
hopelessly; uncommonly; highly; remarkably; incredibly; incomparably; unmanageably; stubbornly; doggedly; mulishly; obstinately; obdurately; contumaciously; naturally; incorrigibly; desperately; uncontrollably; stiffly; perversely; disobediently; impertinently; mischievously; vexatiously; intolerably; inscrutably; inexplicably; unreasonably; embarrassingly; atrociously.

REFRAIN
adjectives
everlasting; drear; wild; unmeaning; recurring; plaintive; irreverent; sadder; wearisome; constant; weird.

verbs
chant—; chorus—; drum—; endure—; join in on—; paraphrase—; renew—; resume—; shout—; sing—; —bores; —refreshes; —revolves; —hinges; —rings; —shocks; —surprises; —survives; —tires; —wearies.
(See chorus, melody, verse, song.)

REFRAIN (v)
adverbs
prudently; deliberately; purposely; pointedly; sagely; resolutely; cautiously; wisely.
(See restrain, check, curb.)

REFRESH (v)
adverbs
deliciously; delectably; periodically; deliberately; potently; seasonally; hospitably.
(See renew, restore, revive.)

REFRESHED
adverbs
delightfully; wholly; unbelievably; completely; permanently; momentarily; temporarily; pleasantly; helpfully; heartily; incredibly; surprisingly; unexpectedly; visibly; noticeably; evidently; marvelously; miraculously; curiously; mysteriously; highly; amazingly; deeply; profoundly; unmistakably.

REFRESHING

adverbs

healthfully; wholesomely; thoughtfully; delightfully; pleasantly; interestingly; surprisingly; strikingly; gloriously; vigorously; restfully; peacefully; quietly; extremely; deliciously; coolly; comfortably; graciously; keenly; hospitably; invigoratingly; sharply; simply; wholly.

REFRESHMENTS

adjectives

delicate; potent; invigorating; apparent; elaborate; suitable; cool; nightcap; delicious; edible; smoky; surprising; delectable.

verbs

afford—; gorge on—; relish—; —appeal; —appease; —cheer; —comfort; —console; —delight; —invigorate; —quench; —repair; —restore; —revive; —sate; —stimulate.

(See food, luncheon.)

REFUGE

adjectives

hunted; walled; sheltered; flimsy; comforting; grateful; soothing; time-honored; secret; unavailing; temporary; modest; blessed; permanent.

verbs

abandon—; afford—; erect—; establish—; find—; grant—; hide in—; offer—; provide —; seek—; threaten—; uncover—; yield—; —assures; —comforts; —conceals; —defends; —preserves; —protects; —secures; —shelters; —shrouds.

(See shelter, protection, lodging, haven, nest, home.)

REFUGEE

adjectives

repatriating; testy; penniless; favorite; sick; unwelcome.

verbs

aid—; harbor—; overtake—; prosecute—; pursue—; search for—; shelter—; succor—; —s abandon; —absconds; —departs; —eludes; —endeavors; —escapes; —evades; —flees; —migrates; —s pour into; —s retreat; —trudges.

(See prisoner, criminal, fugitive.)

REFUSAL

adjectives

frightened; explicit; peremptory; persistent;

periodic; positive; obstinate; varied; resolute; decided; energetic; melodramatic; kind; courteous; flat; gracious; contemptuous.

verbs

confront with—; consider—; ignore—; incur —; issue—; rehearse—; —contravenes; —declines; —denies; —depresses; —irks; —nullifies; —oppresses; —rebuffs; —revokes; —saddens; —squelches; —stays; —suppresses.

(See denial, dissent, rebuff, repulse.)

REFUSE (v)

adverbs

curtly; tacitly; mutinously; courteously; obdurately; scornfully; sternly; doggedly; positively; arbitrarily; inexorably; austerely; snobbishly; flatly; emphatically; sullenly; steadfastly; scrupulously; peremptorily; indignantly; spitefully; prudently; persistently; contumaciously; vehemently; delicately; unequivocally; haughtily; honorably; characteristically; invariably; habitually; graciously.

(See deny, repulse.)

REFUTATION

adjectives

serious; violent; sincere; practical; labored; complete; adequate.

REFUTE (v)

adverbs

undeniably; indisputably; violently; completely; adequately; laboredly; spectacularly; rudely.

(See question.)

REGAL

adverbs

gloriously; grandly; majestically; brilliantly; gorgeously; splendidly; magnificently; sumptuously; ceremonially; ceremoniously; processionally; incredibly; pompously; proudly; superbly; appropriately; suitably; marvelously; incomparably; unsurpassably; uncommonly; resplendently; eminently; consummately; mightily; imposingly; impressively; richly.

REGALE (v)

adverbs

pleasingly; boisterously; affluently; convivially; ostentatiously; hospitably; sumptuously; joyously; fraternally.

(See entertain, feast, gratify.)

REGARD

adjectives

cordial; affectionate; cold; platonic; reverential; eloquent; glorious; general; rueful; intense; delicate; mutual; prudential; due; profound; deepening; repulsive; wearisome; scrupulous; conscientious; sagacious; unalterable; popular; infantine; undue; deep; heartiest; faint; austere; pure; candid; tender; habitual; indispensable; religious; charitable; critical; decorous; slightest; deliberate.

verbs

acquire—; bear—; command—; entertain—; feign—; gain—; inspire—; observe with—; recognize—; relax—; signalize—; solicit—; win—; —arises from; —distinguishes; —flatters; —glorifies; —honors; —outshadows; —shines.

(See favor, esteem, deference, attention.)

REGARD (v)

adverbs

contemptuously; patiently; affectionately; passionately; ruthlessly; lewdly; practically; fondly; narrowly; enviously; attentively; pensively; appraisingly; solemnly; severely; pugnaciously; skeptically; vindictively; curiously; hopelessly; maliciously; ruefully; cordially; platonically; reverentially; sagaciously; austerely; candidly; tenderly; religiously; decorously.

(See observe, consider, heed.)

REGARDFUL

adverbs

deferentially; carefully; considerately; graciously; ingratiatingly; respectfully; punctiliously; meticulously; diplomatically; cautiously; vigilantly; warily; shrewdly; keenly; watchfully; mindfully; attentively; highly; profoundly; alertly; courteously; unfailingly.

REGENERATION

adjectives

political; physical; successful; spiritual; remarkable.

REGIME

adjectives

fascist; competitive; acid-neutralizing; sanguinary; scandalous; despotic; complete; dominant; established; totalitarian; royalistic; democratic; memorable; tyrannical.

verbs

abolish—; control—; denounce—; discredit —; enjoy—; encroach on—; establish—; influence—; introduce—; labor under—; overthrow—; relax—; shape—; support—; sway —; tolerate—; —alters; —dictates; —exercises; —overawes; —usurps.

(See reign, rule, government, power.)

REGIMEN

adjectives

better; strict; unruly; careful; systematic.

REGIMENT

adjectives

ragged; red-coated; magnificent; opinionated; various (pl); redoubtable; crack; splendid.

verbs

distribute—; locate—; lodge—; quarter—; —advances; —assembles; —attacks; —concentrates; —disbands; —flocks; —focuses on; —gathers; —overspreads; —pitches; —retreats; —separates; —throngs .

(See brigade, infantry, militia, soldier.)

REGIMENTED

adverbs

overly; bureaucratically; dangerously; hopelessly; strictly; helplessly; terribly; ominously; unconsciously; frankly; unwillingly; insidiously; alarmingly; unsuspectingly; portentously; deliberately; significantly; disastrously; tyrannically; despotically; calamitously.

REGION

adjectives

devastated; tenuous; remote; spiritual; considerable; untraversed; indiscriminate; saturnine; shadowy; equatorial; ugly; raw; dreaded; airy; desolate; dreary; caudal; mountainous; fertile; wild; antique; inland; nobler; ionized; humid; lonely; unfooted; icy; enchanting; dense; inspiring; equinoctial; interesting; grazing; sequestered; burning; afflicted; constellated; empyreal; disputed; mystical; sterile; ravaged; subterranean; celestial; frontal; arid; unknown; reflecting; barbarous; purer; inferior; boundless; embryonic; hospitable; romantic; idyllic; prolific; unexplored; neighboring; condensed; immense; atmospheric; forest; extensive; infernal; crooked; habitable; healthy; industrial; untrod; low; lumbar; cardiac; gloomy; wooded; enchanted; picturesque; blooming; tropical; imperiled; agricultural; rarefied; adjacent; hypogastric; limited; uncultivated; fruitful; exhausted; semibarbarous; lacustrine; insulated; bleak; ill-defined; thrilling.

verbs

bound—; divide—; dominate—; dwell in —; endow—with; evacuate—; fortify—; infest—; inhabit—; invade—; locate in—; mark—; migrate to—; occupy—; rule—; settle in—; skirt—; visit—.

(See field, country, district, locality, valley, plain.)

REGRET

adjectives

pious; undersigned; relentful; idle; unspeakable; fond; tender; contrite; indignant; mingled (pl); continued; passionate; bitter; serious; unmeaning; dead; keenest; constant; deep; hopeless; meek; vain; frantic; proud; repentant; immeasurable; formal; torturing; sweet; sensible; vague; wistful; inextinguishable; immense; sincere; unfeigned; momentary; endless; unhappy; fierce; subsequent; inexpressible; restless; fundamental; maudlin; unequivocal; unavailing.

verbs

accept—s; betoken—; bewail in—; cherish —; convey—s; croak—s; express—; lament —s; offer—s; plague with—s; send—s; —s chafe; —s confuse; —s disappoint; —s disconcert; —s dishearten; —s humiliate; — oppresses; —saddens; —s vex.

(See sorrow, grief, misery.)

REGRET (v)

adverbs

audibly; pitifully; officially; deeply; bitterly; exceedingly; mournfully; piously; fondly; passionately; keenly; vainly; inexpressibly; vaguely; wistfully; maudlinly; unequivocally; unavailingly.

(See deprecate, deplore.)

REGULAR

adverbs

strictly; sternly; horribly; chastely; systematically; methodically; altogether; painfully; strangely; artificially; stiffly; formidably;

unnaturally; formally; legally; detestably; beautifully; curiously; perfectly; unnecessarily; conveniently; surprisingly; marvelously.

REGULARITY

adjectives

chronological; vulgar; mechanical; absolute; commonplace; surprising; comparative; rhythmic; accustomed; unfailing; faultless; bashful; monotonous; clock-like.

verbs

acquire—; adjust to—; chime in—; drum with—; fall in—; form with—; level to—; maintain—; perform with—; range in—; sustain—; —conforms to; —offsets; —wearies.

(See consistency, harmony, persistence.)

REGULATE (v)

adverbs

stringently; socially; solely; mechanically; scientifically; bureaucratically; autonomously; dictatorially; tyrannically; austerely.

(See direct, control.)

REGULATIONS

adjectives

existing; labeling; influential; arbitrary; stupid; special; conflicting; cast-iron; elaborate; stringent; complicated; administrative; admirable; sanitary; military; martial; hostile; celebrated; barbarous; inviolable; local; wide-spread; federal; civic.

verbs

adopt—; approve—; bar by—; block—; comply with—; conform to—; control by—; decry—; defy—; denounce—; enforce—; govern by—; legislate—; impose—upon; improve—; promulgate—; provide—; revise —; submit—; sustain—; violate—.

(See legislation, bill, arrangement, law, mandate, rule.)

REHABILITATE (v)

adverbs

completely; entirely; refreshingly; spectacularly; miraculously; superficially.

(See restore, renew, revive.)

REHEARSE (v)

adverbs

incessantly; harmoniously; perfunctorily; dutifully; painstakingly; faithfully.

(See practice, say.)

adjectives

transient; dismal; passionate; present; illustrious; imperial; unbreathing; subsequent; reasoning; secure; inexorable; abdicated; horrid; preceding; unsurpassed; liberal; unmolested; remotest; prosperous; gaudy; troublous; happy.

verbs

force—; limit—; overthrow—; submit to—; suffer under—; terminate—; undermine—; tolerate—; usurp—; —chafes; —contents; —dictates; —symbolizes; —trammels; —tramples on; —treads upon; —tyrannizes.

(See regime, government, dominion.)

REIGN (v)

adverbs

imperially; inexorably; liberally; prosperously; tyrannically; lustfully; beneficently; imperiously; supremely; austerely; contemporaneously; gloriously; royally.

(See govern, rule.)

REIMBURSE (v)

adverbs

appreciatively; satisfactorily; fully; generously; financially; liberally; unstintingly.

(See repay, avenge.)

REINDEER

verbs

bag—; domesticate—; exhibit—; mount—; preserve—; stalk—; team—; —draws; —herds; —inhabits; —migrates; —retreats; —scrapes; —sheds; —shies; —traverses.

(See animal, deer.)

REINFORCE (v)

adverbs

substantially; materially; firmly; enormously; strategically.

(See aid, assist.)

REINFORCED

adverbs

strongly; firmly; unbreakably; suddenly; necessarily; conveniently; advantageously; completely; appropriately; suitably; substantially; enormously; materially; providentially; immensely; opportunely; duly.

REINFORCEMENT

adjectives

enormous; seasonable; material; welcome; momentary; unexpected.

adjectives

commanding; jingling; loosened; leathern; dangling.

verbs

check with—; control—; discard—; dress—; grasp—; grease—; hand over—; jerk on—; knot—; loop—; master—; pluck at—; relax —; release—; respond to—; rustle—; saw with—; slap with—; spank—; take over—; tangle—; yank (colloq.)—; —check; —control; —dangle; —direct.

(See bit.)

REITERATE (v)

adverbs

incessantly; substantially; emphatically; characteristically; monotonously; maddeningly; intermittently.

(See repeat.)

REJECT (v)

adverbs

summarily; scornfully; disdainfully; scoffingly; unconditionally; overwhelmingly; airily; petulantly; incontinently; contemptuously; utterly; haughtily; stubbornly; indignantly; peremptorily; flatly; unanimously; sullenly; brusquely; bluntly; pointedly.

(See refuse, repulse.)

REJECTION

adjectives

sullen; intellectual; subsequent; pointed; blunt; brusque.

REJOICE (v)

adverbs

convivially; immoderately; festively; hilariously; exultantly; openly; gleefully; enthusiastically; spontaneously; impulsively; fraternally.

(See cheer, exult.)

REJOICED

adverbs

greatly; highly; uncommonly; radiantly; gloriously; proudly; triumphantly; splendidly; exultantly; elatedly; naturally; genuinely.

REJOICING

adjectives

endless; enthusiastic; excited; ravenous; spontaneous; surface; incessant; half-hearted.

adverbs

reverently; hilariously; uproariously; riotously; loudly; quietly; calmly; deeply; profoundly; thoughtfully; boisterously; triumphantly; gayly; merrily; happily; rapturously; wildly; enthusiastically; hysterically; excitedly; exuberantly; madly; tumultuously; heartily.

REJOIN (v)
adverbs

ultimately; laughingly; daringly; stingingly; passionately; flippantly; curtly; pointedly; tartly; quaintly; tardily; shrewdly; bitterly; sympathetically; reluctantly; icily; haughtily; calmly; musingly.

(See reply, answer.)

REJOINDER
adjectives

laughing; daring; stinging; passionate; flippant; curt; pointed; tart; clever; quaint; sad; usual; nasty; tardy.

REJUVENATION
verbs

buy—; draw—from; induce—; quaff—; retard—; seek—; —aids; —cures; —eludes; —rallies; —reanimates; —rectifies; —redresses; —repairs; —stimulates; —thrills.

(See youth, health, cure, remedy.)

RELAPSE
adjectives

subsequent; moral; fatal; momentary; swift; sure; unavoidable; inevitable.

verbs

anticipate—; deplore—; fall into—; incur —; lament—; preclude—; sink into—; slide into—; undergo—; verge on—; warn against—; —occurs; —recoils; —retrogrades; —reverts to.

(See recurrence.)

RELATE (v)
adverbs

mirthfully; speciously; variously; tediously; succulently; incredibly; intimately; gravely; confidently; graphically; sympathetically; monotonously.

(See tell, narrate.)

RELATED
adverbs

closely; remotely; intimately; personally; officially; scarcely; materially; inescapably;

obviously; naturally; circumstantially; conditionally; accidentally; casually; incomprehensibly; practically; obviously; manifestly; conveniently.

RELATIONS
adjectives

brotherly; hostile; uninterrupted; definite; long-dreaded; exacting; intimate; selfish; delicate; ecclesiastical; wretched; harmonious; pedagogic; causative; domestic; truthful; evident; sublimest; unbroken; genial; agreeable; confiding; pacific; veiled; peculiar; paternal; filial; diplomatic; untried; blessed; typical; mysterious; unobtrusive; sympathetic; conjugal; occult; amicable; prejudiced; nominal; friendly; necessary; supernatural; uncaressing; unsympathizing; dynamical; independent; complex; current; healthful; antagonistic; marital; coetaneous; incestuous; distinct; parallel; causal; scandalous; far-reaching; frank; simultaneous; cordial; piquant; amiable; perverse; confidential; innumerable; organic; mutual; fixed; uniform; established; determinate; passional; external; feudal; conflicting; unnatural; sex; altruistic; mathematical; antenuptial; consistent; symbolic; industrial; decorative; subsequent; clerical; strained.

verbs

achieve—; bear—with; break off—; cement —; cloud—; cripple—; deny—with; disturb —; entertain—with; establish—; facilitate —; govern—; harmonize—; ignore—; maintain—; mar—; preserve—; reestablish—; sever—; sharpen—; shun—; smooth—; strain—; suppress—; sustain—; —bind; —cool; —prevail; —tie.

(See relationship, affairs, connection.)

RELATIONSHIP
adjectives

intimate; unconventional; confidential; harmonious; hierarchical; personal; simple; monotonous; illicit; family; intelligible; intellectual; domestic; healthful; closer; sympathetic; marked; economic.

RELATIVES
(kin)
adjectives

distant; harmless; elderly; endangered; illustrious; erring; reluctant; interfering; interested; portly; unsympathetic; departing; circumspect; disagreeable; unpleasant.

verbs

characterize—; claim—; endure—; link—; plague with—; reconcile—; support—; —assemble; —bicker; —commemorate; —congregate; —convene; —criticize; —drift; —honor; —implore; —intrude; —pester; —quarrel; —recount; —report; —sanction; —trace.

(See friend, family.)

RELATIONSHIP

verbs

affect—; claim—; comprehend—; criticize —; discern—; draw from—; endure—; enter into—; expose—; form—; intrude on—; mar—; probe—; prove—; report—; sanction—; sever—; split—; terminate—; warp —; —associates; —binds; —comforts; —involves; —links.

(See alliance, connection, affiliation, relation.)

RELAX (v)

adverbs

momentarily; restfully; contentedly; totally; completely; beneficially; healthfully; blissfully; drowsily; refreshingly.

(See slacken, rest.)

RELAXATION

adjectives

acquiescent; complete; attendant; humanizing; universal; momentary; amused; necessary.

verbs

attain—; conduce toward—; loll in—; lounge in—; participate in—; practice—; seek—; —alleviates; —arouses; —calms; —composes; —modifies; —pacifies; —palliates; —quiets; —refreshes; —rests; —smoothes; —stills; —subdues; —tempers; —tranquilizes; —wastes.

(See diversion, jollity, recreation.)

RELAXED

adverbs

pleasantly; mentally; idly; momentarily; suddenly; wholly; delightfully; restfully; rarely; serenely; lazily; irresponsibly; unwontedly; surprisingly; comfortably; fortunately; beautifully; finally; drowsily; dreamily; satisfactorily; refreshingly; unbelievably; miraculously; curiously.

RELEASE

adjectives

impassioned; speedy; merciful; ultimate; eventual; anticipated; unaccountable; long-sought.

verbs

attempt—; beg for—; grant—; hinder—; permit—; procure—; sanction—; schedule for—; secure—; withhold—; —absolves; —acquits; —clears; —exonerates; —frees; —unbars; —unclogs; —unlooses.

(See bail, deliverance, discharge.)

RELEASE (v)

adverbs

unconditionally; instantaneously; blamelessly; consequently; subsequently; deftly; ultimately; unaccountably.

(See free, acquit.)

RELENT (v)

adverbs

graciously; grudgingly; tardily; beneficently; remorsefully; partially; smilingly.

(See yield, repent.)

RELIANCE

adjectives

affectionate; rugged; implicit; noble; sober; loving; just; calm; pretended; reciprocal; manly; centering; imbecilic; humble.

verbs

cherish—; consider—; doubt—; foster—; place—in; presume—; produce—; prove—; rest on—; shake—; trust—; —buoys; —encourages; —impresses; —inspires; —persuades; —satisfies.

(See hope, confidence, assurance, trust.)

RELIC

adjectives

antediluvian; hoary; visible; lacustrine; precious; melancholy; holy; fascinating; pathetic; prehistoric; sartorial; exquisite; venerable; sacred; unmistakable; quaint; supposed; amusing; incensing; celebrated; curious; archaeological; unseemly; tender; quivering; cherished; moldering.

RELIEF

verbs

administer—; afford—; derive—from; experience—; extend—; gain—; gasp with—;

grant—; hail—; heave a sigh of—; indulge
—; mark by—; seek—; speed—; voice—.
(See help, aid, assistance, consolation.)

RELIEF
(charity, dole.)
verbs
apply for—; infringe upon—; promote—;
slash—; —allays; —assuages; —cheers;
—comforts; —disburdens; —eases; —encourages; —insures; —mitigates; —remedies; —solves; —smooths; —sustains.
(See payment, dole, charity.)

RELIEF
(general)
adjectives
consequent; speedy; hysterical; parochial;
intense; joyous; beautiful; inevitable; delighted; complete; permanent; temporary;
marked; distinct; regular; pronounced; infinite; immediate; effective; actual; spiritual; pretended; considerable; delicious;
partial; decided; mean; instant; scant;
sheer; welcome; urgent; national; decorative; reliable.

RELIEVE (v)
adverbs
tactfully; effectually; painlessly; ultimately;
intensely; temporarily; spiritually; partially; economically; nationally.
(See alleviate, lessen.)

RELIGION
adjectives
scurvy; ritual; rudimentary; concentrated;
positive; fierce; absurd; austere; profane;
constructive; inaccessible; sanguinary;
powerful; fervent; blessed; unalterable;
irrevocable; distinct; revealed; peaceful;
maudlin; professed; easy-minded; blatant;
doctrinal; gripping; saving.

verbs
adopt—; attack—; cast aside—; cherish—;
corrupt—; defile—; define—; devote to—;
discredit—; embrace—; formulate—; inculcate—; interpret—; profess—; renounce
—; ridicule—; side-track—; stamp out—;
traduce—; venerate—; —comforts; —consoles; —elevates; —fetters; —influences;
—moulds; —nourishes; —paralyzes; —perishes; —prevails; —purges; —purifies; —
sanctifies; —sways; —unifies; —wanes.
(See devotion, faith, worship, Christianity,
modernism.)

RELINQUISH (v)
adverbs
silently; nobly; gallantly; magnanimously;
voluntarily; completely; reluctantly; philosophically; gloomily; unselfishly; logically.
(See surrender, waive, cede.)

RELISH
adjectives
savory; exciting; peculiar; anticipatory;
derisive; insatiable; unwonted; evident;
higher; callous; complacent; keen; savage;
added; natural; acquired.

RELISH (v)
adverbs
heartily; appreciatively; intellectually; spicily; pungently; enjoyably.
(See enjoy, taste.)

RELUCTANCE
adjectives
resentful; sullen; unfeigned; fierce; reverent; unaffected; infinite; pretty; lingering;
natural; insurmountable; shuddering; evident; double; general; untamed; curious;
studied.

verbs
assume—; complain of—; dispel—; employ
with—; feign—; harbor—; imply—; incite
—; incur—; invite—; overcome—; prompt
—; stifle—; —baits; —provokes; —resists;
—restrains; —sharpens; —tantalizes; —
whets.
(See distaste, aversion, unwillingness,
repugnance, dislike.)

RELUCTANT
adverbs
inexplicably; terribly; visibly; evidently;
sternly; inflexibly; unyieldingly; palpably;
manifestly; strangely; harshly; morosely;
undeniably; resentfully; unpleasantly; discourteously; impolitely; sullenly; uncivilly;
roughly; unaffectedly; naturally; curiously;
superstitiously; timidly; shyly; bashfully;
fearfully; timorously; senselessly; sensibly;
wisely; thoughtfully; profoundly; secretly;
oddly; peculiarly; significantly; particularly; uncommonly.

RELY (v)
adverbs
implicitly; exclusively; chiefly; trustfully;

faithfully; tacitly; affectionately; reciprocally; soberly; humbly; calmly.

(See depend, trust.)

REMAIN (v)

adverbs

constantly; hopefully; tensely; determinedly; indefinitely; courageously; voluntarily; impassively; motionlessly; tranquilly; inflexibly; wilfully; permanently; peacefully.

(See stay, linger.)

REMAINS

adjectives

mangled; undemolished; mutilated; honored; numerous; jagged; august; fossilized; dreary; lifeless; insensible; imperishable; charred; mortal; architectural; heterogeneous; comic; disinterred; dingy; scattered; petrified; colorless; archaeological.

verbs

cart away—; conceal—; consign—to; cremate—; disinter—; dispose of—; dissect—; embalm—; entomb—; exhume—; expose—; honor—; inter—; mummify—; rescue—; ship—; trace—.

(See ashes, debris, dust, corpse, remnants.)

REMARK

adjectives

laughing; bantering; automatic; delighted; editorial; pregnant; noncommittal; ill-bred; futile; felicitous; stinging; harsh; preliminary; taunting; fertile; disparaging; commonplace; inaccurate; terse; hasty; vicious; candid; malicious; concluding; immortal; cryptic; appreciative; unpremeditated; enigmatical; unexpected; profound; brittle; opprobrious; deprecatory; chance; sententious; derogatory; outspoken; complimentary; incidental; tomfool; satiric; material; boorish; insubordinate; sage; insolent; coarse; cheerful; desultory; treasonable; merry; philosophic; withering; sarcastic; drunken; significant; casual; illuminating; laconic; feeble; caustic; pat; obscure; verbal; simultaneous (pl); surly; skeptical; mischievous; philosophical; egotistical; independent; special; characteristic; graceful; frolicsome; priceless; careless; indiscreet; prelusory; slurring; ejaculatory; animated; scintillating; epithetical; facetious; deathless; calescent; disputed; trivial; acrimonious; disgusting; critical; allusive; appropriate; judicious.

verbs

ban—; bar—; comprehend—; couch—; deliver—; digest—; drop—; emit—; exchange —s; insert—; occasion—; open—s; poise—; preface—; propose—; punctuate—; repress —; —deprecates; —disparages; —embitters; —falls; —indicates; —issues from; —interrupts.

(See mention, comment, observation, statement.)

REMARK (v)

adverbs

gratuitously; banteringly; ambiguously; anxiously; dryly; wittily; significantly; dispassionately; disparingly; illogically; mendaciously; casually; emphatically; judicially; modestly; complacently; affably; ruefully; vigorously; inquisitively; confidently; whimsically; indifferently; exuberantly; pathetically; sympathetically; sententiously; contemptuously; cynically; deftly; laconically; demurely; pointedly; wistfully; tenatively; caustically; editorially; pregnantly; noncommittally; felicitously; disparagingly; viciously; candidly; appreciatively; boorishly; obscurely; acrimoniously; allusively; appropriately; judiciously; skeptically; egotistically.

(See comment, assert.)

REMEDIABLE

adverbs

easily; fortunately; luckily; quickly; immediately; supposedly; probably; expensively; distinctly; definitely; manifestly; now; altogether; undoubtedly.

REMEDY

adjectives

worthless; potent; favorite; time-tested; present; similar; valuable; misbranded; fraudulent; mythical; accepted; manifold (pl); rational; insidious; infallible; palliative; celebrated; universal; unavailing; irrational; precious; radical; ancient; drug; original; effective; fruitless; costly; extreme; innocent; heroic; futile; makeshift.

verbs

advocate—; apply—; concoct—; denounce —; employ—; furnish—; grope for—; hail —; persevere with—; prescribe—; propose —; provide—; recommend—; rely upon—;

seek—; —alleviates; —eases; —palliates; —purges; —relieves; —soothes.

(See cure, liniment, laxative, purgative, medicine.)

REMEDY (v)
adverbs
concurrently; similarly; rationally; fraudulently; traditionally; heroically; medically; beneficially; miraculously.

(See cure, heal.)

REMEMBER (v)
adverbs
vividly; mechanically; graphically; sorrowfully; remorsefully; irrelevantly; dimly; subconsciously; vaguely; passionately; generously; superstitiously; gratefully; fondly; affectionately; morbidly; eternally; mournfully; involuntarily.

(See recollect, recall.)

REMEMBRANCE
adjectives
pleasant; affectionate; clear; lasting; loving; proud; grateful; fond; dull; discourteous; intuitive; melancholy; morbid; gray; desolate; yielding; burning; fevered; ennobling; ineffaceable; lively; personal; deep; triumphant; tender; ancestral; undimmed; foul; mournful; eternal; faithful; ignominious; listening; evil; gracious; involuntary; stern; worthiest; slow; honorable; sufficient; unwelcome; fading; delighted; constant; kindly; grateful; vivid; lifelong.

verbs
con—; bear in—; honor—; incite—; indulge in—; prompt—; retain—; rivet in—; suggest—; —commemorates; —diverts; —fades; —flatters; —impresses; —renews; —stings; —wanes.

(See memory, compliment, recollection, reminiscence.)

REMIND (v)
adverbs
relentlessly; grimly; persistently; poignantly; irksomely; demurely; accusingly; irrationally; determinedly; vigorously; vividly; pleasantly; personally; tenderly; painfully; laughingly; spitefully.

(See recall.)

REMINDER
adjectives
grim; curious; visible; painful; neat; tangible; pitiful; laughing; continual.

REMINISCENCE
adjectives
agreeable; uncomfortable; indistinct; haunting; glorified; vulgarized; distinguishable; tender; historical; pleasing; vague; barren; commonplace; crisp; humorous; incoherent; divine; fascinating.

verbs
awaken—; delight in—; dispel—; embarrass by—; enjoy—; indulge in—; interpose —; prolong—; revel in—; review in—; steep in—; veil—; —cheers; —colors; —consoles; —delights; —s flood; —warms; interrupt—.

(See remembrance, recollection, memory.)

REMINISCENT
adverbs
delightfully; happily; tiresomely; unendingly; crisply; humorously; divinely; fascinatingly; vaguely; pleasingly; tenderly; gloriously; teasingly; incoherently; uproariously; convivially; genially; embarrassingly; surprisingly; foolishly; deliriously; garrulously; unsteadily; wistfully; feebly; constantly.

REMISS
adverbs
apologetically; confessedly; admittedly; terribly; unpardonably; gravely; seriously; heedlessly; nonchalantly; criminally; tragically; inexplicably; unaccountably; strangely; curiously; unconsciously; unintentionally; carelessly; hopelessly; sorely; unacceptably; frequently; negligently; indifferently; atrociously.

REMNANTS
adjectives
sufficing; laggard; straggling; placable; salvaged; shrunken; scorched; enduring; shattered; discarded; miserable; pathetic; quaint; wretched; fugitive; lingering; greater; saving.

verbs
bag—; cherish—; collect—; conceal—; consume—; gather—; heap—; leave—; market —; offer—; piece—; proffer—; salvage—;

scatter—; store—; utilize—; value; —disappear; —survive.

(See fragment, residue, piece, remains.)

REMONSTRANCE

adjectives

passionate; energetic; rash; urgent; mutinous; bitter; temperate; tender; lukewarm; childish; indignant; peaceful; final; earnest; useless; obvious; eloquent; angry; rational; resentful.

REMONSTRATE (v)

adverbs

waggishly; vainly; rudely; incessantly; earnestly; calmly; passionately; energetically; mutinously; bitterly; tenderly; childishly; eloquently; rationally; resentfully.

(See protest, expostulate.)

REMORSE

adjectives

useless; sisterly; gnawing; fictitious; bitter; unconfessed; light; violent; vile; abrupt; unceasing; dull; poignant.

verbs

burden with—; confess—; depress by—; experience—; incite—; overcome with—; overwhelm with—; palliate—; relieve—; shake with—; shroud in—; smite with—; sober by—; suffer—; tinge with—; wrap in—; —colors; —devours; —humbles; —maddens; —overwhelms; —racks; —shatters; —subdues; —stirs; —surges within; —undermines.

(See contrition, regret, qualm, repentance.)

REMORSEFUL

adverbs

naturally; admittedly; openly; manifestly; miserably; tardily; wretchedly; pitiably; pitifully; pathetically; tragically; immeasurably; terribly; sorely; significantly; sincerely; sobbingly; weakly; duly; penitently; contritely; deeply; profoundly.

REMOTE

adverbs

coldly; distantly; proudly; shyly; timidly; arrogantly; superciliously; intellectually; absent-mindedly; abstractedly; philosophically; naturally; dreamily; discourteously; deliberately; resolutely; gravely; unsocially; inscrutably; mysteriously; vexatiously; gruffly; gravely; judiciously; absurdly.

REMOTENESS

adjectives

romantic; apparent; comparative; patent.

REMOVAL

adjectives

successful; prompt; repeated; forcible; swift.

verbs

advocate—; allow—; balk at—; compel—; delay—; demand—; ease by—; entail—; hamper—; hinder—; impede—; instigate—; order—; recommend—; rejoice in—; resist —; upset by—; —alters; —annoys; —confuses; —disturbs.

(See dismissal, displacement, withdrawal, change.)

REMOVE (v)

adverbs

dexterously; clumsily; skillfully; cautiously; surreptitiously; slyly; permanently; temporarily; forcefully; promptly; swiftly.

(See transfer, withdraw.)

REMUNERATIVE

adverbs

providentially; extravagantly; sufficiently; fairly; justly; adequately; highly; satisfactorily; surprisingly; astoundingly; remarkably; gratifyingly; incredibly; opportunely; finally; profitably; scarcely; duly; advantageously; usefully; fantastically; richly; uncommonly.

RENAISSANCE

verbs

anticipate—; characterize—; contribute to —; create—; foster—; hail—; instigate—; pertain to—; promote—; prompt—; terminate—; voice—; —alters; —flourishes; —produces; —reforms; —renews; —restores; —reveals; —revivifies; —stimulates; —unfolds.

(See birth, revival, restoration.)

RENDER (v)

adverbs

passively; powerfully; exquisitely; peculiarly; necessarily; infallibly; barely; charmingly; admirably; poetically; realistically; artistically.

(See repay, restore.)

RENDERING

adjectives
realistic; photographic; elusive; exquisite; independent; artistic.

RENDEZVOUS

adjectives
picturesque; favorite; charming; famous; appointed; storied; legendary; modern.

RENEW (v)

adverbs
modernistically; periodically; auspiciously; mysteriously; generously; harmoniously; incessantly; wholly; reverently; seasonally.
(See repair, restore.)

RENOUNCE (v)

adverbs
dogmatically; courageously; boldly; rashly; lawfully; faithlessly; virtually; eternally; voluntarily; passionately; shamelessly; explicitly; frankly.
(See reject, disclaim.)

RENOVATED

adverbs
perfectly; pleasingly; usefully; delightfully; acceptably; inexpensively; skilfully; marvelously; astoundingly; amazingly; opportunely; duly; attractively; newly; recently; properly; appropriately; lately; cleverly; artistically; substantially; admirably; satisfactorily; beautifully.

RENOWN

adjectives
splendid; posthumous; unfulfilled; ancient; chaste; temporary; contemporary; godlike; provincial; unspeakable; wide-spread; notorious.

verbs
accept—; accredit—; achieve—; acquire—; cherish—; feign—; gain—; glean—; radiate—; reflect—; respect—; rise to—; sing —; win—; —glorifies; —overshadows; — overwhelms; —shines; —spoils.
(See glory, fame, limelight, distinction, notoriety.)

RENT

adjectives
great; ragged; artificial; ghastly; economic; reconciling; preposterous; numerous (pl); outrageous.

RENUNCIATION

adjectives
passionate; shameless; sublime; frank; perfect; explicit.

REORGANIZATION

adjectives
intensive; careful; economic; periodical; necessary.

REPAIR (v)

adverbs
temporarily; hastily; haphazardly; amply; ceaselessly; extensively; technically; judiciously; medically.
(See restore, mend.)

REPAIRED

adverbs
obviously; recently; badly; handsomely; adroitly; secretly; visibly; skilfully; beautifully; marvelously; completely; aptly; expensively; reasonably; extensively; shoddily; ably; expertly; ingeniously; wonderfully; unnoticeably; perfectly; patently; imperceptibly; exquisitely; awkwardly; clumsily; sufficiently; satisfactorily.

REPAIRS

adjectives
extensive; judicious; necessary; expensive; technical; obvious; happy.

verbs
effect—; resume—; undergo—; view—; — ameliorate; —bolster; —compensate; —convert; —enhance; —purge; —rectify—; redeem; —refresh; —relieve; —remedy; — restore; —strengthen.
(See reconstruction, improvement.)

REPARATIONS

verbs
cancel—; demand—; forego—; liquidate—; offer—; refuse—; repudiate—; review—; — acknowledge; —appease; —atone; —correct; —indemnify; —pacify; —recompense; —redeem; —redress; —requite; —restore; —reward; —satisfy.
(See insurance, atonement, restoration.)

REPARTEE

adjectives
insulting; clever; humorous; colloquial; icy; restless; victorious; spicy; sparkling; witty.

verbs

banter—; engage in—; excel in—; furnish —; prolong—; quicken—; school in—; stimulate—; suffer—; surpass in—; —amuses; —arouses; —beguiles; —cheers; —delights; —diverts; —entertains; —excels; —frisks; —romps; —scintillates; —sparkles; — wanes.

(See answer, banter, reply.)

REPAST

adjectives

unsavory; sumptuous; cannibal; nocturnal; precious; disgusting; substantial; satisfying; ridiculous; extravagant; delicious; tumultuous.

verbs

crave—; devour—; donate—; gorge—; invite to—; partake of—; prepare—; relish—; spread—; wash down—; yield to—; —allays; —appeases; —attracts; —nourishes; —quells; —sates.

(See eating, luncheon, feast, meal, food.)

REPAY (v)

adverbs

promptly; severely; cheerfully; lavishly; amply; faithfully; conscientiously; legally; graciously.

(See reimburse, avenge.)

REPEAL

verbs

abolish—; advocate—; agitate for—; authorize—; celebrate—; demand—; desire—; discard—; favor—; fight—; induce—; overrule—; permit—; promote—; recommend—; reverse—; sanction—; seek—; welcome—; —ameliorates; —cheers; —dissolves; — gladdens; —improves; —nullifies; —relieves.

(See dismissal, displacement.)

REPEAL (v)

adverbs

expressly; totally; legally; harshly; dogmatically; unanimously; promptly.

(See retract, recall.)

REPEAT (v)

adverbs

idiotically; tediously; foolishly; maliciously; vindictively; icily; incredulously; insistently; vaguely; fatuously; insultingly; emphatically; peevishly; multitudinously; stubbornly; mechanically; simultaneously; musingly; fluently; deprecatingly; monotonously; interrogatively; authoritatively; aimlessly; tenderly; musically.

(See reiterate.)

REPEATED

adverbs

endlessly; monotonously; emphatically; frequently; necessarily; tediously; whiningly; sullenly; unbearably; tiresomely; foolishly; maliciously; garrulously; senselessly; accurately; erroneously; imprudently; indiscreetly; secretly; confidentially; cruelly; derisively; unfortunately; unluckily; malevolently; scoffingly; deliberately; treacherously; surreptitiously; slyly; intelligibly; audibly; authoritatively; ominously; significantly.

REPEL (v)

adverbs

obstinately; stubbornly; vigorously; forcefully; courageously; staunchly; determinedly; gallantly.

(See oppose, repulse.)

REPENT (v)

adverbs

religiously; remorsefully; bitterly; genuinely; submissively; sincerely.

(See regret, grieve.)

REPENTANCE

adjectives

genuine; unavailing; bitter; submissive; generous; deep; sad; shamefaced; deathbed; sincere; sullen.

verbs

burden with—; confess—; experience—; feign—; incite—; overcome with—; wrap in—; —appeases; —condones; —humbles; —oppresses; —overwhelms; —pacifies; — palliates; —relieves; —shrouds; —sobers; —subdues; —tinges.

(See remorse, contrition, regret.)

REPERTOIRE

verbs

acclaim—; acquire—; announce—; applaud —; arrange—; balance—; choose—; enact —; enlarge—; exhaust—; expand—; include in—; increase—; list—; plan—; practice—; rehearse—; round out—; —covers; —delights; —embraces; —engages; —includes; —unfolds.

(See program, plan, list.)

adjectives

insane; mannered; verbal; constant; monotonous; wholesale; frequent; musical; maddening; fine; unmeaning; steady; endless; broken; emphatic; undulating; useless; decorative; injudicious; vague; tragic; idiotic; deadly; suasive; meaningless; diverting; explanatory; forceful.

verbs

clamor for—; demand—; endure—; influence—; justify—; permit—; request—; stifle —; suffer—; survive—; threaten—; — bores; —emphasizes; —impresses; —irritates; —prolongs; —recalls; —refreshes; — teaches; —tires; —wearies.
(See mention, recurrence.)

REPLACE (v)

adverbs

surreptitiously; effectively; effectually; faithfully; graciously; promptly; intelligently; skillfully.
(See repay, restore.)

REPLICA

verbs

commend—; compare—; criticize—; prepare —; produce—; —adheres to; —appears; — attracts; —condenses; —copies; —deceives; —duplicates; —follows; —recalls; —reproduces.
(See duplicate, copy.)

REPLY

adjectives

suitable; lackadaisical; unexpected; frank; modest; judicial; unembarrassed; shameless; monosyllabic; disrespectful; short; temperate; haughty; elaborate; silly; immediate; ungracious; good-humored; noncommittal; guarded; discouraging; cold; pettish; memorable; gracious; categorical; contemptuous; impatient; ready; biting; caustic; tart; scornful; unmoved; intelligent; inarticulate; incoherent; tactful; tremulous; humble; proper; audible; chaffing; austere; obvious; correct; negative; preoccupied; conclusive; stumbling; impromptu; sound; impertinent; garbled; distorted; satisfactory; politic; magnanimous; chilling; languid; impressive; idiotic; chary; pungent; consolatory; evasive; angry; emphatic; unanimous.

verbs

calculate—; contemplate—; demand—; deign—; elicit—; evoke—; mutter—; overhaul—; probe—; propose—; provoke—; rejoin—; —acknowledges; —affirms; —alleviates; —answers; —clarifies; —clears; — determines; —explains; —informs; —interrogates; —rebuts; —refutes; —satisfies; — solves.
(See answer, response, retort, repartee.)

REPLY (v)

adverbs

evasively; solemnly; tonelessly; affirmatively; crisply; bitingly; equivocally; impertinently; promptly; auspiciously; grimly; dolefully; defiantly; wistfully; mechanically; elusively; falteringly; gravely; archly; laboriously; hilariously; dubiously; incoherently; inexorably; tremulously; petulantly; casually; tensely; modestly; placidly; jocosely; listlessly; cautiously; musingly; dejectedly; reflectively; mordantly; haughtily; serenely; maliciously; decisively; acrimoniously; pensively; meekly; dryly; sententiously; laconically; pettishly; ambiguously; indulgently; monosyllabically; temperately; noncommittally; magnanimously; pungently; emphatically.
(See answer, respond.)

REPORT

adjectives

verbatim; exact; unbiased; unanimous; distant; illustrated; first-hand; stimulating; clear; understandable; supplementary; complete; unconfined; successive (pl); dependable; inflammatory; untruthful; precise; flattering; plausible; gratifying; preliminary; press; energetic; sly; insidious; formal; official; partial; detailed; inaccurate; dazzling; hearsay; critical; archeological; suppressed; statistical; disheartening; neat; reassuring; ardent; vague; alarming; typical; regular; aggregated; voluble; orderly; condensed; annual; authentic; snobbish; veracious; written; admirable; pestiferous; outspoken; hopeless; voluminous; sensational; elaborate; shocking; frightened; thundering; commercial; reverberating; varying; random; astounding; enthusiastic; exaggerated; published; confused; pretentious; stenographic; unwelcome; explicit.

verbs

allay—s; append to—; bungle—; challenge —; chronicle—s; circulate—; confirm—;

corroborate—; counteract—; deluge with —s; draw up—; echo—; evaluate—; fudge —; indorse—; pigeon-hole—; prepare—; qualify—; render—; scoff at—; shelve—; summarize—; transmit—; verify—; wind up —; —bears out; —bolsters; —discloses; — emanates from; —embodies; —persists; — recommends; —spreads.

(See fame, account, news, rumor, record.)

REPORT (v)
adverbs
faithfully; precisely; currently; alarmingly; capably; officially; adversely; duly; glumly; graciously; verbally; insidiously; formally; partially; critically; archeologically; statistically; reassuringly; vaguely; volubly; annually; authentically; veraciously; sensationally; reverberatingly; exaggeratedly; pretentiously; stenographically.

(See announce, describe.)

REPORTER
adjectives
rushing; mere; prying; realistic; inquisitive; disreputable; disgruntled; clever; skilled.

verbs
besiege by—s; hush up—s; loathe—s; muffle —s; stifle—s; —alludes to; —announces; —s beleaguer; —s descend upon; —disguises; —eavesdrops; —expresses; —fences; —hints; —imparts; —imposes; —interviews; —intimates; —libels; —mentions; — mobs; —prowls; —reserves; —reviews; — "scoops"; —slanders; —specifies; —tips off; —withholds.

(See journalist, detective, writer.)

REPORTING
adjectives
franker; alert; candid.

REPOSE
adjectives
soothing; calm; innocent; serene; undisturbed; sullen; delicious; charmed; noble; blissful; final; comforting; grave; irksome; profitless; chronic; supreme; mental; stolid; permanent; scornful; effeminate; statuesque; long-coveted; profound; peaceful; solemn; comparative; orbed; unreached; vile; languorous; dreamy; passionless; weak; healthful; everlasting; fathomless; equivocal; intellectual; infamous; exquisite; last; rheumatic; particular; spacious; exasperating;

deep; echoless; fitful; indolent; placid; dull; sweet; dignified; complete; stupid; prolonged; cultivated; studied; momentary; outward; grave-like; grim; stern; thoughtful; reason-wrought; voluptuous.

verbs
advocate—; disturb—; dwell in—; indulge in—; seek—; while away in—; —energizes; —frees; —lulls; —preserves; —refreshes; —relaxes; —relieves; —rests; —soothes; — stagnates; —stems; —vivifies.

(See composure, rest, sleep, quiet, peace.)

REPOSE (v)
adverbs
lazily; soothingly; calmly; serenely; sullenly; deliciously; effeminately; profoundly; passionlessly; rheumatically; placidly; momentarily; voluptuously.

(See rest, relax.)

REPOSEFUL
adverbs
pleasantly; sweetly; oddly; calmly; serenely; unusually; gratefully; duly; dully; prosaically; quietly; lazily; blissfully; deliciously; soothingly; somnolently; drowsily; dreamily; idly; languidly; listlessly; deliberately; heavily; silently; immovably; incredibly; unexpectedly; utterly; happily.

REPREHENSIBLE
adverbs
lamentably; undeniably; openly; flagrantly; particularly; unpardonably; admittedly; miserably; shamefully; wretchedly; curiously; unwarrantably; uncommonly; highly; utterly; exceptionally; gravely; indiscreetly; unconscionably; inordinately; terribly.

REPRESENT (v)
adverbs
copiously; faithfully; magnificently; initially; beneficently; allegorically; fantastically; diagrammatically; materially; adequately; speciously; personally; orally; substantially; symbolically; conventionally; fictitiously; ludicrously; realistically.

(See portray, depict.)

REPRESENTATION
adjectives
oral; adequate; easily-understood; hallucinatory; pasteboard; hearty; disproportionate; concrete; animated; distinct; substantial; graphic; definite; direct; diplomatic; count-

less (pl) ; urgent; decennial; striking; vigorous; symbolic; democratic; renewed; just; faithful; pictorial; mental; material; fraudulent; proportioned; august; mere; earnest; specious; tolerable; abstract; wild; conventional; mimic; dramatic; one-sided; untruthful; harmonious; factual; fictitious; softened; sensuous; ludicrous; natural; unfair; realistic; archaic.

verbs
carve—; comprehend—; deprive of—; dress up—; mold—; rehearse—; yield to—s; —alludes to; —betokens; —depicts; —describes; —designates; —enlightens; —illustrates; —indicates; —informs; —points out; —portrays; —signifies; —symbolizes; —typifies.
(See description, comedy, design, reproduction, art, portrayal, drama.)

REPRESENTATIVE
adjectives
dwarfed; local-minded; fitting; dazzling; mentionable; assembled (pl) ; accredited; prominent; cold; correct; tremulous; striking; exemplary; placement; shy; awkward; authorized; diplomatic; surviving; lineal; avowed; arrogant; cold-brained; brilliant; fraudulent; traveling.

verbs
accredit—; apportion—s; antagonize—; delegate—; interchange—s; obligate—; replace —; —bandies; —calls; —commutes; —introduces; —offers; —reciprocates; —redeems; —retaliates; —serves; —solicits; —supersedes; —supplants.
(See consul, delegate, agent, deputy.)

adverbs
typically; truly; fairly; justly; altogether; officially; authoritatively; adequately; satisfactorily; substantially; diplomatically; tolerably; unfairly; scarcely; hardly; entirely; accurately; concisely; legally; uncommonly; warrantably; specifically; appropriately; singularly; functionally; appointively.

REPRESS (v)
adverbs
sternly; tyrannically; stoically; impatiently; amiably; severely; dictatorially; dogmatically; rudely; ruthlessly; systematically.
(See restrain, suppress.)

REPRESSED
adverbs
cruelly; naturally; morbidly; sternly; severely; harshly; unduly; pitiably; successfully; immediately; barbarously; opportunely; promptly; effectively; pitiably.

REPRESSION
adjectives
prompt; impartial; intense; sublime; self; particular; sexual; severe; definite.

REPRIMAND
verbs
expose to—; inflict—; load with—s; protest —; resist—; submit to—; subject to—; taunt with—s; —accuses; —anathematizes; —annoys; —cavils; —condemns; —corrects; —deprecates; —disparages; —execrates; —lashes; —rebukes; —reproaches.
(See rebuke, blame, censure, reproach.)

REPRIMAND (v)
adverbs
rigorously; sternly; publicly; officially; severely; sharply; violently; paternally; judicially.
(See reproach, scold.)

REPRINT (v)
adverbs
popularly; widely; multitudinously; perpetually; extensively; accurately; legally; faithfully.
(See print, reproduce.)

REPRISAL
adjectives
prompt; legitimate; indiscriminate; fearful; legal; swift; deadly; unerring.

verbs
anticipate—; breast—; check—; deserve—; draw—; elicit—; face—; fear—; grapple with—; offer—; provoke—; return—; stifle —; suppress—; visit—upon; —caps; —climaxes; —confronts; —dismays; —exchanges; —strikes; —subdues.
(See retaliation, punishment, penalty.)

REPROACH
adjectives
sorrowful; violent; constant; continual; disgustful; subtle; unutterable; thick-tongued; serious; bitter; ingenuous; mute; passion-

ate; galling; unjust; mild; smiling; dumb; tacit; mystic; selfish; fierce; self; mingled; undeserved; angry; generous.

verbs
attach—to; cast—upon; disfavor—; expose to—; fling—at; imply—; justify—; overwhelm with—; resist—; support—; warrant —; —blots; —corrects; —cuts; —disgraces; —implicates; —reflects; —slurs; —sullies; —upsets.
(See blame, dishonor, disgrace, censure, disapproval.)

REPROACH (v)
adverbs
passionately; bitterly; abusively; violently; sorrowfully; subtly; mutely; gallingly; tacitly; fiercely; undeservedly; ungenerously; selfishly.
(See reprimand, scold.)

REPROACHFUL
adverbs
mildly; gently; softly; harshly; cruelly; moderately; sternly; severely; unforgivingly; hatefully; atrociously; intolerably; openly; publicly; secretly; abusively; immoderately; unnecessarily; needlessly; violently; vehemently; loudly; vociferously; vengefully; vituperously; unfairly; brutally; offensively; terribly; inflexibly; outrageously; arrantly; unwarrantably; pitilessly; viciously; gravely.

REPROBATE
adjectives
thorough; degenerate; notorious; malicious; energetic; self-styled.

REPRODUCE (v)
adverbs
superbly; scrupulously; perfectly; voluntarily; plastically; authentically; quaintly; historically; adequately; slavishly; mechanically; painstakingly; accurately; elaborately.
(See imitate, portray.)

REPRODUCTION
adjectives
plastic; authentic; quaint; historic; incessant; adequate; slavish; mechanical; subsequent; painstaking; accurate; elaborate.

REPROOF
adjectives
tacit; stinging; distinct; sour.

REPROVE (v)
adverbs
acridly; smartly; harshly; sternly; vigorously; bitterly; stingingly; tacitly; mutely; violently; verbally; expressly; explicitly; furiously; spiritedly.
(See reprimand, reproach.)

REPTILE
adjectives
venomous; hideous; characteristic; scaly; croaking; fishy; abhorrent; snakish; ugly; useful; groveling.

verbs
—coils; —consists; —contorts; —crushes; — encircles; —entwines; —glides; —lashes; —lies in wait; —meanders; —poisons; — slithers; —springs; —squeezes; —squirms; —strains; —strikes; —swirls; —swishes; — tightens; —twists; —undulates; —warns; — wounds; —writhes.
(See crocodile, alligator, lizard, snake.)

REPUBLIC
adjectives
model; visionary; peaceful; progressive; long-lived; rebellious; well-ordered; popular.

verbs
administer—; approve—; betray—; control —; disrupt—; dominate—; establish—; form—; govern—; organize—; override—; preserve—; preside over—; revolt against —; rule—; sway—; tolerate—; undermine —; wreck—; —relaxes; —triumphs.
(See country, democracy, government, state.)

REPUDIATE (v)
adverbs
instinctively; utterly; wholly; violently; faithlessly; unreservedly; flatly; ultimately.
(See reject, renounce.)

REPUGNANCE
adjectives
unforeseen; loathing; secret; invincible; sentimental; horrible; undefinable; strong; real; deep-seated.

verbs
allay—; arouse—; assuage—; avoid—; bear —; conceive—; dispel—; entertain—; excite —; feign—; incur—; mitigate—; mollify—;

overwhelm—; recoil from—; withdraw in
—; —estranges; —intrudes; —palls; —riles
(colloq.) ; —shocks.
(See disgust, dislike, opposition, antipathy,
inconsistency, aversion.)

REPULSE
adjectives
virtual; bloody; severe; brisk; complete.

verbs
encounter—; —abduces; —chases; —dashes;
—dispels; —hurtles; —impedes; —impinges; —jerks; —jogs; —prods; —pushes;
—resounds; —slaps; —spurs on.
(See defeat, refusal, rebuff, denial.)

REPULSE (v)
adverbs
briskly; stoutly; stalwartly; successfully;
sharply; readily; unceremoniously; severely;
violently.
(See repel, reject.)

REPULSION
adjectives
reciprocal; lively; utter; mutual; instinctive; deadly; bitter; indescribable; singular;
remarkable.

REPUTATION
adjectives
freshest; popular; rising; senseless; local;
unassailable; well-earned; murdered; magnificent; swollen; formidable; subverted;
enviable; commonplace; civic; evanescent;
posthumous; untarnished; immature; artistic; unblemished; literary; mushroom; exceptional; wounded; established; merited;
spotless; exaggerated; reverend; enduring;
undue; skittish; slender; bubble; unquestioned; professional; priceless; outstanding;
terrible; pious; vile; tender; savory; damaged; fabulous; poetic; lamentable.

verbs
achieve—; acquire—; belie—; blacken—;
build—; carve—; destroy—; enhance—; enjoy—; establish—; injure—; jeopardize—;
justify—; mar—; mature—; merit—; outlive—; prostitute—; protect—; rival—; sacrifice—; save—; stake—on; —blooms; —
languishes; —precedes; —precludes; —
spreads; —swells; —withers.
(See fame, name, character, distinction,
honor, notoriety, glory.)

REPUTE
adjectives
grave; ill; considerable; honorable; doubtful; prominent; local; scientific; charitable;
provincial; high.

REQUEST
adjectives
conflicting; unusual; continual; commonplace; inopportune; dying; special; urgent;
humble; whispered; emphatic; unreasonable; unconsidered; universal; pointed.

verbs
accede to—; acquiesce in—; assail with—s;
bombard with—s; comply with—; convey—;
dodge—; grant—; gratify—; heed—; justify—; meet—; pester with—s; repeat—;
swamp with—s; urge—.
(See desire, entreaty, application, appeal,
demand.)

REQUEST (v)
adverbs
urgently; haughtily; earnestly; fawningly;
emphatically; reluctantly; graciously; ultimately; insistently; particularly; reasonably; humbly; importunately.
(See ask, beg, entreat.)

REQUIRE (v)
adverbs
passionately; urgently; perpetually; vitally;
imperatively; strictly; reasonably; ethically;
personally; physically; medically; aesthetically.
(See exact, want, demand.)

REQUIRED
adverbs
legally; inescapably; naturally; technically;
inexorably; peremptorily; recently; authoritatively; officially; arbitrarily; tyrannically; dogmatically; reasonably; rigorously;
rigidly; absolutely; socially; conventionally;
prescriptively; lawfully; openly; duly; constitutionally; decently; traditionally.

REQUIREMENTS
adjectives
postnatal; eminent; classic; reasonable; relative; ethical; basic; collective; exacting;
hygienic; traditional; rigorous; technical;
strictest; human; personnel; specific; professional; complex; certain; maximum; minimum; residential; absolute; physical; rhythmic; aesthetic; sanitary; imperative.

verbs

check—; comply with—; condemn—; dispense with—; draw up—; fulfill—; furnish —; justify—; lack—; meet—; necessitate—; occasion—; offer—; overlook—; point out —; produce—; raise—; remove—; respect —; supply—; tabulate—; violate—; —apply to; —call for; —demand; —impede.

(See demand, injunction, necessity.)

REQUISITE

adjectives
regular; prime; definite; essential; indispensable.

REQUITAL

adjectives
humble; ungenerous; unworthy; poor; scant; fair; satisfactory.

RESCUE

verbs
aid in—; dash to—; deplore—; clog—; cumber—; expedite—; hamper—; hasten—; hinder—; impede—; interrupt—; obstruct—; perform—; pray for—; retard—; speed—; —delivers; —discommodes; —embarrasses; —preserves; —relieves; —saves.

(See deliverance, release.)

RESCUE (v)

adverbs
nobly; heroically; triumphantly; gallantly; stalwartly; rashly; boldly; courageously.

(See save, release.)

RESEARCH

adjectives
vigilant; philosophical; indefatigable; antiquarian; abstract; hydrological; subsequent; perpetual; relentless; celestial; original; brilliant; infinite; useless; enthusiastic; conscientious; scientific; extensive; microscopical; commercial; philological; bold; ingenious; effective; exhaustive; photographic; valuable; painstaking; patient; profound; deliberate; sociological; mysterious; laborious; masterly; comprehensive; stellar; ceaseless; critical; historical; malignant; archaeological; tireless; multitudinous (pl); psychoanalytic; obscure; profitable.

verbs
commence—; conduct—; direct—; engage in —; enter upon—; instigate—; launch—; maintain—; promote—; publish—; stimulate —; —analyzes; —awakens; —contributes;

—culminates in; —determines; —discloses; —enlightens; —enriches; —exposes; —explores; —fathoms; —ferrets out; —imparts; —peers; —reveals.

(See inquiry, investigation, inquisition, study.)

RESEMBLANCE

adjectives
intricate; mimetic; enchanted; successful; extraordinary; fancied; natural; striking; faraway; vague; distant; self-evident; divine; partial; mysterious; close; protective; inaccurate; defensive; aggressive; capital; inexplicable; recognizable; unexpected; startling.

verbs
accentuate—; approximate—; assimilate—; bear—; detect—; discern—; evoke—; kindle —; savor of—; sharpen—; —amazes; —astounds; —disturbs; —moves; —shocks; —smites; —stirs; —strikes.

(See similarity, identity.)

RESEMBLE (v)

adverbs
strikingly; curiously; precisely; particularly; spectacularly; adequately; protectively; recognizably; startlingly; mysteriously; markedly; superficially.

(See favor.)

RESENT (v)

adverbs
forcibly; morbidly; vehemently; bitterly; subconsciously; indignantly; sternly; passionately; humorously; secretly; mutely; violently; keenly; fiercely; murderously; disdainfully; sullenly.

(See disapprove, begrudge.)

RESENTFUL

adverbs
angrily; dangerously; bitterly; passionately; sullenly; bluntly; sadly; cruelly; venomously; maliciously; vengefully; acrimoniously; violently; vociferously; strangely; unaccountably; unreasonably; insatiably; stubbornly; implacably; unappeasably; openly; secretly; fantastically; obviously; manifestly; evidently; furiously; irascibly; truculently; uncommonly; ominously; disastrously; permanently.

RESENTMENT

adjectives

terrible; increasing; admiring; individual; implacable; obstinate; dull; furious; keen; angry; impulsive; blind; half-sore; animal; fierce; intense; murderous; incipient; vigorous; sturdy; hot; disdainful; momentary; jealous; brooding; bitter; impotent; sagged; hasty; spirited; sullen; hard; viperish; astonished; impatient; additional; passionate; protecting; personal; desperate; general; generous; just; fancied.

verbs

arouse—; call forth—; cherish—; display—; engender—; evoke—; excite—; exhibit—; fill with—; flood with—; kindle—; reflect with—; shake off—; smother—; stir up—; —flares; —is born; —melts; —mounts; — wells; —yields to.

(See grudge, ill-will, anger, grievance.)

RESERVATION

adjectives

mental; explicit; express; common-sense; forest; experimental; heedful; definite; specific.

RESERVE

adjectives

scholarly; cash; considerable; substantial; emotional; chaste; appreciable; haughty; preliminary; habitual; dignified; sullen; mistrustful; maidenly; stately; sorrowful; stern; cold; unsympathizing; timberland; stubborn; approaching; singular; natural; compulsory; lawful; precious; womanly; ungenerous; freezing; naive; analytical; mysterious; alkaline; impenetrable; defective; delicate; mutual; watchful; critical.

verbs

break down—; deplete—; discard—; emerge from—; ignore—; inspire—; intensify—; penetrate—; pierce—; prick—; retain—; — cloaks; —conceals; —covers; —masks; — melts; —mystifies; —piques; —protects; — secludes.

(See aloofness, modesty, reticence, restraint, shyness, diffidence, fund.)

RESERVE (v)

adverbs

expressly; shrewdly; delicately; covetously; exclusively; faithfully.

(See retain, restrain.)

RESERVED

adverbs

quietly; demurely; sedately; characteristically; habitually; naturally; inherently; discreetly; strategically; prudently; wisely; gravely; judicially; arrogantly; proudly; shyly; bashfully; unduly; unfortunately; extremely; strangely; curiously; oddly; placidly; serenely; coyly; timidly; mysteriously; extraordinarily; sensibly; vexatiously.

RESERVOIR

adjectives

tapering; immense; ducal; copious; sheltered; inexhaustible.

verbs

construct—; dam—; exhaust—; flow from —; form—; inspect—; replenish—; tax—; —accumulates; —collects; —preserves; — reserves; —stores; —yields.

(See supply, tank.)

RESIDENCE

adjectives

episcopal; commodious; costly; palatial; comfortable; handsome; peculiar; official; ungarnished; stately; enlarged; wretched; permanent; seasonal; picturesque; temporary; monastic; ambitious; baronial; paternal; suitable; prolonged; sumptuous; modest.

verbs

establish—; frequent—; guard—; lack—; maintain—; neglect—; occupy—; regulate —; secure—; take up—; view—; invite to—.

(See home, establishment, mansion, dwelling.)

RESIDENT

adjectives

influential; distinguished; valued; temporary; permanent.

RESIDENTIAL

adverbs

pleasantly; strictly; expensively; exclusively; desirably; aristocratically; swankily; modestly; primarily; wholly; assuredly; delightfully; scrupulously; unmistakably; quietly; peacefully; agreeably.

RESIDUE

adjectives

harmful; visible; sweetest; solid; miserable; final; greasy; gummy; soapy; mournful.

verbs

bag—; consume—; cherish—; conceal—; discard—; gather—; heap—; "junk"—; leave—; offer—; proffer—; retain—; salvage—; scatter—; scrap—; store—; utilize —; value—; —disperses; —survives.

(See ashes, excess, cinders, remnant.)

RESIGN (v)

adverbs

reluctantly; voluntarily; nominally; officially; cheerfully; piously; fatalistically; irrevocably; philosophically; wearily.

(See abdicate, withdraw.)

RESIGNATION

adjectives

fatalistic; grim; virtual; dreamy; melancholy; serene; unsurprised; meek; patient; irrevocable; perverted; conscious; apparent; unwilling; quiet; infinite; philosophical; appalling; angelical; unhappy; spiritless; youthful; sorrowful; perfect; pathetic; tacit; passive; somber; gentle; mournful; despondent; voluntary; wearied; gloomy.

verbs

announce—; anticipate—; bewail—; compel —; decline—; deplore—; grant—; lament —; offer—; order—; present—; regret—; tender—; weigh—; —alters; —confuses; — disappoints; —disconcerts; —humbles; — mortifies.

(See surrender, retirement.)

RESIGNED

adverbs

philosophically; passively; quietly; scarcely; hardly; apathetically; resolutely; grimly; meekly; apparently; perfectly; shamelessly; appallingly; incredibly; eventually; obviously; strangely; humbly; pathetically; obediently; submissively; pliantly; weakly; calmly; imperturbably; stolidly; stupidly.

RESILIENT

adverbs

satisfactorily; unusually; highly; extraordinarily; smoothly; appreciably; pleasantly; desirably; adequately; extremely; conveniently; surprisingly; suitably; buoyantly; advantageously; uncommonly.

RESIST (v)

adverbs

stubbornly; vigorously; skillfully; dexterously; passively; blusteringly; modestly; stern-

ly; heroically; effectively; violently; stoutly; physically; insurmountably; feebly; resolutely.

(See oppose, withstand.)

RESISTANCE

adjectives

rust; permanent; unexpected; forcible; popular; stern; unyielding; strenuous; heroic; prompt; amazing; pretended; successful; prolonged; stubborn; indignant; glorious; increased; warlike; crushed; desperate; enfeebled; stout; substantial; sad; perceiving; vague; militant; fierce; faint; humble; bold; incredulous; keener; tenacious; ineffectual; organized; gladiatorial; countervailing; rationalized; unlawful; unconscious; determined; patriotic; creditable; passive; severest; awed; earnest; coy; physical; meditating; stagnated; obstinate; rugged; hopeless; insurmountable; armed; feeble; resolute; vain; appreciable; angry.

verbs

acquire—; batter down—; break down—; build—; compensate for—; crush—; deplete —; determine—; encounter—; exercise—; harden for—; increase—; lower—; meet with—; prolong—; rationalize—; reduce—; stiffen—; weaken—; —collapses; —cracks; —lessens; —melts away.

(See antagonism, strength, opposition, hostility.)

RESOLUTE

adverbs

courageously; doggedly; stubbornly; intrepidly; gallantly; staunchly; persistently; immovably; steadily; unwaveringly; stoutly; dauntlessly; obstinately; cruelly; bitterly; determinedly; tragically; pluckily; tenaciously; indomitably; sadly; fanatically; dogmatically; ungenerously; inexorably; relentlessly; admirably; commendably; earnestly; zealously; enthusiastically; confidently; heroically; amazingly; remarkably; terribly.

RESOLUTION

adjectives

constitutional; settled; defiant; dogged; sensible; inflexible; virtuous; submissive; deliberate; jaunty; unanimous; daring; restless; generous; thoughtful; robust; gloomy; stern; tremendous; determined; austere; firm; immense; rash; obituary; indomitable; undaunted; desperate; philosophical; bold; early; stubborn; energetic; impulsive;

concurrent; invincible; passionate; dangerous; joint; vigorous; loyal; essential; satisfactory; freighted; fierce; unalterable; chivalrous; sacred; evanescent; memorable; momentous; gathering; congressional; pious; irrevocable; wise; courageous; godly; determined; heroic; imprudent; epic; unchangeable; queer; decisive.

verbs
abandon—; acclaim—; adhere to—; adopt —; applaud—; bolster—; convey—; crystalize into—; draft—; formulate—; fortify—; introduce—; prime with—s; shake—; stiffen —; uphold—; weaken—; —s pour in; —s strengthen.
(See decision, determination, bill, law.)

RESOLVE
adjectives
absolute; strained; secret; deliberate; fearless; rash; added; stern; desperate; virtuous; firm; deeper; mental; pertinacious; iron; concluding; excellent; courageous; calm; dominant; high; wise; terrible; unswerving; dauntless; mortified; inflexible; feeble-framed.

RESOLVE (v)
adverbs
ultimately; prudently; mentally; rationally; solemnly; privately; unanimously; stubbornly; inflexibly; deliberately; impulsively; fiercely; chivalrously; momentously; imprudently.
(See determine, dissolve.)

RESONANT
adverbs
pleasantly; deeply; unusually; harmoniously; surprisingly; marvellously; admirably; distinctly; hollowly; agreeably; strikingly; peculiarly; curiously; remarkably.

RESORT
adjectives
strict; brilliant; cold; lowest; fair; pleasure; attractive; little; embryonic; mountain; seasonal; favorite; fashionable; expanding; imposing; dissolute; habitual; desperate; summer; mundane; complete; seashore; family; self-contained; beach; delightful; best-loved; premier; world-famous; wonderful.

verbs
crowd—; fill—; frequent—; infest—; retire to—; repair to—; swamp—s; —advertises; —appeals; —attracts; —consoles; —delights; —eases; —offers; —refreshes; — strengthens.
(See hotel, refuge.)

RESOUND (v)
adverbs
thunderingly; discordantly; tremendously; dreadfully; awesomely; thunderously; reverberatingly.
(See peal, reverberate.)

RESOURCEFUL
adverbs
ingeniously; amazingly; skilfully; conveniently; fortunately; luckily; unusually; miraculously; incredibly; inventively; cleverly; adroitly; expediently; expertly; handily; adaptably; deftly; intelligently; felicitously; happily; particularly; manifestly; unfailingly; naturally; inimitably.

RESOURCES
adjectives
natural; decorative; perpetual; ever-present; fertile; meager; spiritual; financial; utmost; therapeutic; magnificent; manifold; productive; unfailing; mineral; artistic; boundless; reasonable; enormous; gigantic; technical; infallible; visual; limited; despairing; legitimate; exhausted; immense; physical; cyclopedic; immeasurable; temporal; material; healing; military; diplomatic; delightful; sole; insignificant; colossal; extensive; vast; tremendous; dramatic; strategic; privileged; unfailing; endless; slender; pecuniary; ready; adequate; scanty; prodigious.

verbs
assemble—; augment—; cast upon—; concentrate—; cultivate—; deplete—; develop —; employ—; encourage—; exhaust—; expend—; fortify—; impair—; liquidate—; mobilize—; paralyze—; squander—; strain —; tap—; tax—.
(See finances, assets, property, means.)

RESPECT
adjectives
exalted; regretful; greatest; idolatrous; reverential; utmost; impassive; continued; affectionate; proper; astonished; wholesome; compassionate; graceful; self; dignified; profound; temporal; haughty; deferential; pitying; punctilious; merited; apologetic;

indignant; unfeigned; listening; mutual; essential; delicate; tender; unqualified; grudging; devout; reluctant; important; high; lasting; credulous; weak; infinite; indescribable; extorted; extreme; considerate; habitual; corresponding; scant; diminished; genuine; remarkable; enormous; undefinable; unbounded; ambiguous; regretful; increased; expensive; constant; dutiful; particular; astonishing; popular; thoughtful; pusillanimous; diffident; marked.

verbs

broaden into—; command—; compel—; deepen—; deserve—; draw—; earn—; engender—; entitle to—; forfeit—; heighten —; impair—; inspire—; insure—; merit—; pay—s; preserve—; reflect—; retain—; train in—; violate—; win—.
(See esteem, deference, honor, homage, admiration, respectability.)

RESPECT (v)

adverbs

scrupulously; sympathetically; intuitively; universally; deferentially; punctiliously; unfeignedly; mutually; reluctantly; genuinely; unboundedly; dutifully; wholesomely; markedly; affectionately.
(See revere, esteem.)

RESPECTABILITY

adjectives

decent; indisputable; bourgeois; unshadowed; worldly; irreproachable; unimpeachable; unblemished; private; undeniable; obvious; dignified; spotless; triumphant; suburban; utilitarian.

verbs

acquire—; assume—; claim—; cleave to—; confer—; crown with—; don—; emulate—; feign—; gain—; preserve—; reflect—; renounce—; sacrifice—; shed—; wear—; —dignifies; —distinguishes; —elevates; —flourishes; —narrows; —restricts; —stifles.
(See respect.)

RESPECTABLE

adverbs

highly; eminently; decently; notably; unimpeachably; undeniably; obviously; admirably; extremely; admittedly; uncommonly; estimably; oppressively; painfully; ostentatiously; self-righteously; flauntingly; indisputably; scarcely; supposedly; pleasantly; harmlessly.

RESPECTFUL

adverbs

deferentially; ingratiatingly; servilely; slavishly; enthusiastically; affectionately; genuinely; sincerely; devotedly; devoutly; piously; reverently; graciously; gravely; flatteringly; amiably; courteously; politely; attentively; earnestly; ardently; nonchalantly; casually; significantly; solemnly; filially; dutifully; ardently; officiously; diplomatically; subserviently; gracefully; pleasantly; agreeably; hospitably; exceedingly; chivalrously; significantly; overwhelmingly; habitually.

RESPIRATION

adjectives

momentary; diminished; violent; labored; artificial.

verbs

clog—; disorder—; embarrass—; force—; govern—; heighten—; impede—; increase —; involve—; labor—; persevere with—; record—; stimulate—; sustain—.
(See breath, breathing.)

RESPITE

verbs

appeal for—; consume—; cut short—; demand—; enjoy—; grant—; seek—; spend —; —arrests; —delays; —elapses; —interrupts; —intervenes; —overjoys; —refreshes; —rescues; —stems; —tides over.
(See delay, rest, suspension, pause.)

RESPOND (v)

adverbs

royally; affably; felicitously; brilliantly; generously; curtly; brusquely; pertly; acridly; sarcastically; reluctantly; enigmatically; passionately; imperturbably; grimly; nervously; enthusiastically; patriotically; gallantly; genially; humorously; suitably; affectionately; ambiguously; felicitously; crabbedly; boisterously; sententiously; tardily.
(See reply, answer.)

RESPONSE

adjectives

unpalatable; affectionate; eager; astounding; loving; blessed; unfavorable; ready; gloomy; generous; cordial; patriotic; emotional; appropriate; feminine; immediate; popular; copious; instinctive; evident; oracular; verbal; ambiguous; sympathetic;

characteristic; hearty; felicitous; instantaneous; beauteous; tremendous; typical; accurate; crabbed; calm; quick; liquid; untimely; boisterous; remote; passive; enthusiastic; shallow; brutal; joint; sententious; rough.

verbs
avert—; awaken—; bark—; bolster—; call forth—; convey—; correlate—s; determine —; elicit—; evoke—; force—; gain—; guard—; hail—; invite—; level—at; mumble—; mutter—; provoke—; question—; quicken—; restrain—; welcome—; —dismays; —encourages; —gladdens; —heightens; —lessens.
(See answer, echo.)

RESPONSIBILITY
adjectives
executive; unending; fearful; pecuniary; colossal; immense; sacred; dubious; painful; divided; individual; incidental; administrative; gravest; moral; serious; dreadful; direct; frightful; tremendous; numerous (pl); weighty; corresponding.

verbs
absolve from—; awaken to—; assume—; bear—; cast off—; charge with—; confer—; deviate from—; delegate—; discard—; disregard—; dodge—; dread—; entail—; evade—; expand—; face—; impose—; incur—; inherit—; involve—; lighten—; meet—; obviate—; overburden with—; realize—; relieve of—; saddle with—; shield from—; shift—; shirk—; shoulder —; shrink from—; shy away from—; tackle—; undertake—; —devolves upon; —exacts; —presses; —reposes in; —rests on.
(See duty, charge.)

RESPONSIBLE
adverbs
admittedly; personally; individually; fearfully; unfortunately; entirely; directly; criminally; legally; accidently; voluntarily; peculiarly; indisputably; terribly; undoubtedly; officially; allegedly; indirectly; certainly; partially; reliably; sincerely; heavily; altogether; perfectly; safely; gravely; seriously; unhappily; completely; tragically; frightly; tremendously; naturally; incidentally; temporarily; permanently; momentarily; duly; morally; financially; deeply; carefully; wholly.

REST
adjectives
ecstatic; listless; ignoble; needful; saintly; unutterable; heavy-laden; comfortable; peaceful; common; prolonged; life-preserving; spacious; everlasting; fitting; unadulterated; grave; wholesome; predestined; eternal; tumultuous; sullen; gracious; mental; refreshing; frequent; happy; placid; noontide; recumbent; interminable; absolute; perpetual; balmy; breathless; comparative; saintly.

verbs
abstain from—; advocate—; afford—; deserve—; desist from—; enjoin—; enjoy—; fold in—; refrain from—; terminate—; —comforts; —delays; —eases; —invigorates; —refreshes; —rejuvenates; —relaxes; —relieves; —renews; —slackens; —soothes; —stagnates; —unburdens.
(See delay, pause, respite, sleep.)

REST (v)
adverbs
ultimately; unsoundly; implicitly; perpetually; philosophically; impassively; ostentatiously; placidly; serenely; firmly; securely; listlessly; eternally; interminably.
(See relax, stop, repose.)

RESTAURANT
adjectives
celebrated; exclusive; world-famous; exotic; modest; open-air; low-ceilinged; clattering; bustling; unpretentious; dingy; little; lighted; gay; bright; modern; excellent; glamorous; diverting; exciting; fine; distinctive; air-cooled; moderate; colorful; fashionable; renowned.

verbs
inspect—; license—; rig up—; —advertises; —appeals; —attracts; —caters to; —delights; —employs; —patronizes; —plans; —pleases; —prepares; —offers; —solicits; —specializes.
(See hotel, tavern, inn.)

RESTFUL
adverbs
quietly; pleasantly; agreeably; beautifully; unusually; lazily; moderately; comparatively; entirely; wholly; extremely; singularly; curiously; peculiarly; incomparably; unspeakably; gratefully; strangely; simply; irresponsibly; unutterably; refreshingly; in-

effably; inexpressibly; unbelievably; easily; invitingly; irresistibly; dreamily; drowsily; safely; miraculously; marvelously; soporiferously.

RESTITUTION
adjectives
quantitative; hopeless; spiritual; complete.

RESTIVE
adverbs
strangely; oddly; unmanageably; naturally; hopelessly; incurably; pathetically; obstinately; constantly; pitiably; understandably; helplessly; painfully; impatiently; nervously; feverishly; fractiously; reluctantly; openly; visibly; unconcealably; undisguisedly; unhappily; wretchedly; extraordinarily.

RESTLESS
adverbs
noticeably; visibly; hopelessly; actively; energetically; painfully; undisguisedly; ostentatiously; impolitely; inattentively; feverishly; nervously; heedlessly; strangely; curiously; significantly; oddly; unpleasantly; disagreeably; sullenly; unhappily; impatiently; physically; inordinately; extraordinarily; inexplicably; unaccountably; unreasonably; seriously; alarmingly; dangerously; irritably; vexatiously; anxiously; uncomfortably; disquietingly; distressingly; disturbingly.

RESTLESSNESS
adjectives
morbid; incessant; fevered; undulating; covert; pallid; inexplicable; repining; abrupt; unsteady; mercurial; infinite; ragged.

verbs
allay—; appease—; breed—; brook—; calm —; endure—; foment—; master—; overcome—; repress—; suffer—; toss in—; undergo—; yield to—; —chafes; —distresses; —fumes; —grips; —pains; —rages; —tears; —torments.
(See impatience, agitation, excitement, delirium, uneasiness, discontent.)

RESTORATION
adjectives
joyful; tranquil; refreshing; prompt; speedy; cleansing.

verbs
authorize—; direct—; discuss—; inspire—;

lament—; order—; plead for—; repel—; resist—; sanction—; —appeases; —converts; —corrects; —enhances; —humbles; —improves; —pacifies; —repairs.
(See revival, reconstruction.)

RESTORATIVE
adverbs
pleasantly; effectively; successfully; usually; safely; definitely; distinctly; notably; prescriptively; supposedly; agreeably; dependably; reliably; actively; powerfully; adequately; satisfactorily; remarkably; highly.

RESTORE (v)
adverbs
accurately; unquestionably; ultimately; genuinely; miraculously; subsequently; skillfully; dexterously; faithfully; medically; speedily; promptly.
(See repair, renew.)

RESTRAIN (v)
adverbs
vigorously; voluntarily; gently; firmly; forcibly; narrowly; unreasonably; judiciously; legally; lawfully; tyrannically; artificially; irksomely; rigidly; vexatiously; oppressively; benevolently; commercially.
(See repress, suppress.)

RESTRAINED
adverbs
cautiously; discreetly; prudently; warily; austerely; patiently; judicially; wisely; carefully; politely; courteously; absurdly; unduly; stiffly; cruelly; determinedly; deliberately; resolutely; significantly; unusually; habitually; ominously; portentously; extraordinarily; strangely; singularly; oddly; unaccountably.

RESTRAINT
adjectives
parental; irksome; conventional; apparent; moral; strange; needful; artistic; uncommon; dignified; perceptible; strict; noble; outrageous; necessary; comparative; intense; rigid; practiced; wearisome; dry; grim; compelled; severe; professional; heroic; determined; habitual.

verbs
burst—; compel—; deplore—; dispel—; enforce—; exercise—; forge—; impose—; insist upon—; loosen—; necessitate—; relax

—; require—; resist—; throw off—; —binds; —burdens; —checks; —controls; —curbs; —despairs; —gags; —intensifies; —melts.

(See constraint, embargo, denial, inhibition, limitation.)

RESTRICT (v)

adverbs

parentally; irksomely; grimly; rigidly; severely; selfishly; ascetically; maddeningly; pettishly.

(See restrain, limit.)

RESTRICTIONS

adjectives

commercial; narrow; arbitrary; quantitative; impassable; oppressive; benevolent; diet; unreasonable; sharp; judicious; enforced; vexatious; regulatory; rigid; irksome; artificial; tyrannical.

verbs

abolish—; advocate—; disregard—; establish—; impose—; lift—; maintain—; subject to—; surmount—; throw off—; tighten —; yield to—; —ban; —chafe; —check; —destroy; —doom; —embrace; —forbid; —hedge in; —inhibit; —limit; —prohibit; —restrain; —stifle.

(See limits, inhibition, restraint, limitations.)

RESULT

adjectives

historical; admirable; indecisive; promising; exquisite; barren; declared; discouraging; magnificent; half-starving; pernicious; tangible; observed; ripe; immediate; ultimate; substantial; gratifying; disastrous; outstanding; intractable; astounding; brilliant; amazing; dazzling; astonishing; consistent; momentous; pertinent; involuntary; deducible; decorative; splendid; detrimental; creditable; bewildering; positive; triumphant; natural; unfailing; pecuniary; moral; estimated; salubrious; winning; direct; beneficial; effective; calculated; appreciable; proportional; invariable; tangible; vociferated; hilarious; multitudinous (pl); casual; primary; encouraging; unobserved; crowning; fatal; necessary; naked; tardy; advantageous; lasting; honest; ambrosian; excellent; revealing; satisfactory; successful; inevitable; unanticipated; quantitative; accomplishing; speculative; unbelievable; pitiful; conclusive; startling; re-

markable; wonderful; abundant; extraordinary; profitable; therapeutic; agreeable; notable; satisfactory; desirable; intelligible; practical; confusing; fine; disappointing; outward; sifted; unquestionable; scientific; identical; valuable; accurate; infallible; marvelous; capital; auspicious; typical; startling; memorable; obvious; competent; educative; sweeping; surprising; rapid; partial; ethereal; expectable; living; prosperous; extreme; salutary; established; fruitful; equivocal; riotous; happy; comic; deferred; important; verified; feverish; exhausting; logical; gradual; factitious; disheartening; contradictory; traceable; ludicrous; demoralizing; delightful; damaging; chastening; beneficent; valid; sentimental; required; secondary; unreliable; compromising; unified; legitimate; stupendous; deplorable; fearful; net.

verbs

accept—; accomplish—; achieve—; anticipate—; assay—; attain—; cap—; challenge —; claim—; confirm—; decry—; discredit —; embody—; envisage—; evaluate—; falsify—; forecast—; garner—s; predict—; sum up—s; tally—s; trace—s; visualize—; yield—s; —s accrue; —s attend; —s justify.

(See consequence, effect, issue, outcome.)

RESULT (v)

adverbs

fatally; invariably; inevitably; appreciably; ludicrously; damagingly; demoralizingly; legitimately; deplorably; astonishingly; proportionally; infallibly.

(See terminate, end.)

RESUME (v)

adverbs

reluctantly; haughtily; diligently; placidly; traditionally; complacently; cheerily; voluntarily; uncomplainingly; blandly; customarily.

(See begin, start.)

RESURRECTION

adjectives

artificial; joyful; queer; summer; spiritual.

verbs

anticipate—; arrange for—; escape—; evade—; inspire—; mold—; plan—; prom-

ise—; seek—; shape—; stay—; suggest—;
support—; warn of—; —restores; —threatens.
(See renaissance, restoration, revival.)

RETAIN (v)
adverbs
invariably; indefinitely; selfishly; voluptuously; basely; gloriously; righteously.
(See hold, keep, reserve.)

RETAINER
adjectives
taciturn; gorgeous; confidential; faithful;
marshaled.

verbs
beckon—; chastise—; despatch—; discharge
—; flout—; order—; recommend—; reprove
—; suffer—; —accompanies; —aids; —arranges; —attends; —betrays; —confronts;
—eases; —endures; —refers; —serves.
(See following, servant, matron.)

RETALIATE (v)
adverbs
revengefully; viciously; vindictively; pitilessly; treacherously; poisonously; hatefully;
despicably; violently; insidiously; traitorously.
(See repay, avenge.)

RETALIATION
adjectives
pitiless; provoking; youthful; treacherous;
angry.

verbs
avert—; draw—; grapple with—; ignore
—; incur—; invite—; offer—; overlook—;
smother—; threaten with—; withstand—;
—avenges; —harms; —inflames; —kicks; —
pierces; —rankles; —repulses; —revenges;
—stems; —stings.
(See punishment, revenge, discipline, penalty.)

RETARD (v)
adverbs
mechanically; deliberately; inevitably; cautiously; expediently; automatically.
(See hinder, obstruct.)

RETENTION
adjectives
undue; stubborn; corresponding; enforced.

RETENTIVE
adverbs
highly; unusually; phenomenally; miraculously; extraordinarily; marvelously; astonishingly; amazingly; unbelievably; incredibly; conveniently; curiously; peculiarly;
singularly; particularly; incomparably.

RETICENCE
adjectives
noble; diplomatic; exaggerated; introspective; masterly; strict; womanly; haughty;
dignified; excessive; dogged; cautious; judicious.

verbs
couch in—; discard—; lapse into—; penetrate—; pierce—; shroud in—; sink into—;
—blinds; —cloaks; —conceals; —curtains;
—envelops; —masks; —mystifies; —perplexes; —puzzles; —screens; —veils; —withholds.
(See modesty, reserve, aloofness.)

RETICENT
adverbs
austerely; needlessly; absurdly; naturally;
habitually; unnecessarily; highly; curiously;
unreasonably; sensibly; singularly; oddly;
peculiarly; unduly; taciturnly; foolishly;
disagreeably; noticeably; unfortunately.

RETINUE
adjectives
glittering; brilliant; imperial; numerous
(pl); copious; radiant; perilous.

RETIRE (v)
adverbs
timidly; cautiously; snobbishly; unwillingly;
meekly; modestly; deferentially; shamefacedly; noiselessly; discreetly; decently;
voluntarily; precipitately.
(See retreat, withdraw.)

RETIREMENT
adjectives
voluntary; imminent; short; quiet; suspicious; comparative; peaceful; secular; close;
unobtrusive; romantic; precipitate; sweet;
monastic; ostentatious; beloved; temporary.

verbs
creep into—; draw into—; drive into—;
emerge from—; forego—; hasten—; hold in
—; loathe—; remain in—; resist—; shame

into—; shut into—; sink into—; slate for —; surrender to—; —abjures; —bores; —cuts off; —deprives; —stagnates.

(See isolation, resignation, retreat, seclusion.)

RETIRING

adverbs

unusually; shyly; timidly; studiously; habitually; naturally; diffidently; unsocially; inhospitably; reticently; taciturnly; forbiddingly.

RETORT

adjectives

gruff; famous; skillful; impulsive; scornful; spirited; readiest; instant; severest; stinging.

verbs

draw—; fire—; parry—; provoke—; —acknowledges; —appeases; —clinches; —confutes; —crushes; —defeats; —determines; —explains; —irks; —leaps to one's lips; —parries; —rebuts; —solves; —shatters; —silences; —verifies.

(See answer, reply, response, repartee.)

RETORT (*v*)

adverbs

sharply; curtly; absurdly; shrewdly; effectively; acrimoniously; comically; resentfully; spiritedly; caustically; facetiously; scurrilously; waspishly; petulantly; gruffly; stingingly.

(See respond, reply.)

RETRACT (*v*)

adverbs

pusillanimously; timidly; ultimately; cautiously; fearfully; ignominiously; hastily; dishonorably; despairingly.

(See recall, disavow.)

RETREAT

adjectives

tardy; ignominious; hasty; immediate; subterranean; verdant; hospitable; bloody; sacred; timely; final; hurried; sunless; precipitate; reckless; swift; panic-stricken; dignified; grateful; epic; flurried; chosen; beloved; circuitous; masterly; lonely; secluded; orderly; crippled; hasty; base; ultimate; snug; double-quick; disastrous; cavernous; rural; gracious; foul; ruinous; secure; serene; secret; favorite; despairing; soft; honorable; glorious.

verbs

advocate—; beat—; censure—; chase into —; drive into—; fall back in—; flee in—; force into—; hasten—; move in—; occasion —; order—; shrink in—; sound—; withdraw in—; —averts; —defeats; —saves.

(See retirement, isolation.)

RETREAT (*v*)

adverbs

cringingly; ignominiously; precipitately; irrationally; coquettishly; cravenly; disastrously; ruinously; serenely; honorably; despairingly; pusillanimously.

(See retire, withdraw.)

RETRENCH (*v*)

adverbs

financially; cautiously; conservatively; sensibly; enforcedly; periodically; disastrously; shrewdly.

(See lessen, limit.)

RETRIBUTION

adjectives

trenchant; severest; utmost; tardy; righteous; bloody; just; speedy.

verbs

anticipate—; award—; defy—; deserve—; fear—; ignore—; measure—; reap—; resist —; reveal—; sow—; —amends; —atones; —harries; —evens; —retaliates; —revenges; —upbraids.

(See justice, compensation, punishment, penalty.)

RETROACTIVE

adverbs

fortunately; disastrously; luckily; happily; opportunely; expediently; legally; wisely; unconditionally; unexpectedly; acceptably.

RETROSPECT

adjectives

widening; melancholy; drowsy; foregoing; deep; briefest; gratifying; entertaining.

RETROSPECTIVE

adverbs

lamentably; curiously; tiresomely; unprofitably; unfortunately; dismally; stagnantly; stubbornly; sorrowfully; obstinately; fearfully; incorrigibly; incurably; inveterately.

adjectives

ordinary; periodical; honorable; tedious; successive (pl); infallible; pecuniary; physical; exuberant; inevitable; speedy; visible; reassuring; adequate; alleged; impending; bountiful; unprofited; scant; monetary; diminishing; abundant; circling; material; peaceful; tangible; swift; beggarly; immediate; imperfect; fortuitous.

verbs

anticipate—; deter—; foresee—; forestall—; foretell—; hamper—; hinder—; narrate—; observe—s; predict—; presage—; recount —s; relate—; resume on—; —s echo; —overjoys; —pleases; —s pour in; —redoubles; —renews.

(See harvest, report, profit, reply.)

RETURN (*v*)

adverbs

periodically; seasonally; sardonically; traditionally; habitually; customarily; testily; dubiously; deliberately; unceremoniously; subsequently; expeditiously; reluctantly; incessantly; triumphantly; fortuitously; infallibly; tediously; honorably.

(See recur, repay.)

REUNION

adjectives

chaotic; select; plotting; prominent; formal; ultimate; happy.

verbs

arrange—; attend—; band in—; bring about—; clasp in—; delay—; effect—; embrace in—; entwine in—; gather in—; invite to—; participate in—; plan—; —embodies; —interests; —overjoys; —recalls; —renews; —unites.

(See meeting, gathering, union.)

REVEAL (*v*)

adverbs

penetratingly; candidly; vividly; graphically; immodestly; daringly; traitorously; partially; concisely; deplorably; spaciously; strikingly; unmistakably; fluently; injudiciously; dismally; painfully; courageously; supernaturally.

(See disclose, expose.)

adjectives

lurid; nightly; bestial; heavy-headed; profligate.

REVELATION

adjectives

astonishing; unexpected; lightning; sickening; fluent; divine; deathlike; injudicious; ultimate; startling; veritable; awful; curious; vivid; unsuspected; successive (pl); celestial; appalling; dismal; unforeseen; cool; judicial; painful; incessant; intimate; supernatural; guarded; frightful; amazing; courageous.

verbs

color—; deplore—; fear—; inspire—; interpret—; prod to—; resist—; —admits; —awes; —bares; —concedes; —corrects; —disburdens; —discloses; —divulges; —embarrasses; —enlightens; —exposes.

(See disclosure, exposure, discovery.)

REVELER

adjectives

joyous; lusty; bright; profane; unconventional.

REVELRY

adjectives

wild; gay; wanton; drunken; rustic; wildest; ardent.

REVENGE

adjectives

dire; luscious-toothed; unlearned; sworn; desperate; frightful; implacable; passionate; undisturbing; stinging; delicate; meaningless; bloody; fierce; prophesied; timid; meditated; swift; secret; spiteful; just; wild; refined; doubtful; sweet.

verbs

aggravate to—; avert—; contrive—; evoke —; incur—; itch for—; provoke to—; restrain—; suppress—; vow—; wreak—; —angers; —confuses; —enrages; —evens; —exasperates; —flares; —foams; —grinds; —infuriates; —stings.

(See retaliation, vengeance, hatred, hate.)

REVENGE (*v*)

adverbs

diabolically; ingeniously; logically; direly;

frightfully; implacably; passionately; swiftly; secretly; spitefully; deliberately.

(See avenge, retaliate.)

REVENUE

adjectives

confiscated; royal; overflowing; advertising; surplus; princely; accruing; requisite; gross; expected; present.

verbs

acquire—; apportion—; bear—; boost (colloq.)—; claim—; derive—; dissipate—; draw—; expend—; forfeit—; gain—; increase—; invest—; possess—; produce—; promise—; seek—; spend—; untie—; yield —; —accrues; —dribbles in.

(See income, money, profit, wages.)

REVERBERATE (v)

adverbs

raucously; thunderously; overwhelmingly; threateningly; portentously; musically; crashingly; clangingly; deafeningly.

(See resound, peal.)

REVERBERATING

adverbs

dimly; loudly; thunderously; resonantly; faintly; distantly; strangely; hollowly; sepulchrally; frightfully; fearfully; dully; rumblingly; mournfully; dolefully; madly; jubilantly; triumphantly; wildly.

REVERBERATION

adjectives

rocking; surly; crashing; clanging; thunderous; deafening.

REVERE (v)

adverbs

religiously; blindly; adoringly; idolatrously; spiritually; physically; fanatically.

(See honor, respect.)

REVERENCE

adjectives

professed; increasing; unquestioning; profound; easy; infinite; worshipful; mystical; devotional; meek; habitual; involuntary; superstitious; apprehensive; pious; subdued; peculiar; grateful; serious; high; honest; dutiful; awed; defensive; unaffected; instinctive; forward; personal; wanting; servile; special; religious; nominal; implicit; instant; better-proportioned; overgreat; inexpressible; filial.

verbs

arouse—; bear—; bestow—; cherish—; command—; dedicate in—; deserve—; entertain —; evince—; feign—; inculcate—; ingrain —; inspire—; kneel in—; observe with—; pay—; present—; produce—; question—; win—; —edifies; —elevates; —enshrines; —overawes.

(See awe, honor, adoration, respect, obeisance.)

REVERENCE (v)

adverbs

devoutly; unquestionably; profoundly; infinitely; mystically; superstitiously; piously; dutifully; religiously; servilely; filially; inexpressibly.

(See venerate, revere.)

REVERENT

adverbs

respectfully; devoutly; piously; quietly; silently; duly; becomingly; fittingly; sincerely; deeply; profoundly; noticeably; commendably; visibly; carefully; habitually; inherently; truly; unusually; worshipfully; unaffectedly; unobtrusively; implicitly.

REVERIE

adjectives

dreamful; embowered; abstracted; absorbed; voluptuous; pensive; sublime; scornful; perplexed; anxious; gloomy; celestial; silent; uneasy; brief; delicious; motionless; pleasant; indignant; indefinable; blissful; intoxicating; unconscious; fantastic; enamored.

verbs

absorb in—; awake from—; base on—; bask in—; compose—; crack—; drift into—; engage in—; envelop in—; fall into—; fashion—; float into—; imbibe in—; indulge in —; intoxicate with—; lapse into—; lose in —; pursue in—; recall in—; rouse from—; shroud in—; sink into—; start from—; steep in—; —attains; —dances; —exalts; —promises; —reflects; —revolves; —sustains.

(See dream, meditation.)

REVERSE

adjectives

occasional; ominous; appalling; disastrous; catastrophic.

allay—; bear—; compare—s; contend with
—s; encounter—s; lament—; mitigate—;
shoulder—; suffer—; teach—; —annuls; —
cancels; —damages; —deposes; —depresses; —dissolves; —overrides; —saddles.
(See misfortune, calamity, defeat, adversity.)

REVERSE (v)
adverbs
dramatically; automatically; mechanically;
strategically; desperately; strikingly; appreciably.
(See invert, overthrow.)

REVERSIBLE
adverbs
conveniently; adaptably; fittingly; appropriately; easily; readily; comfortably; advantageously; usefully; serviceably; quickly; instantly; smartly; handsomely.

REVERSION
adjectives
far-off; natural; certain; inevitable.

REVERT (v)
adverbs
normally; customarily; traditionally; historically; instinctively; naturally; inevitably.
(See return, recur.)

REVIEW
adjectives
balanced; impartial; crisp; accurate; honest; unbiased; news; up-to-the-minute; annual; embracing; enthusiastic; competent;
prejudiced; financial; artistic; dispassionate; critical; sweeping; elaborate; exhaustive; strict; dignified; prodigal; learned;
lumbering; involuntary; copious; philosophical; adulatory; brief; flippant.

verbs
march in—; pass in—; —blasts; —censures;
—commends; —criticizes; —discusses; —exposes; —fatigues; —honors; —lauds; —
scorches; —suggests; —surveys; —treats
of; —unfolds.
(See analysis, study, parade, survey, examination.)

REVIEW (v)
adverbs
appreciatively; courteously; briefly; cursorily; formally; perfunctorily; critically; im-

partially; accurately; unbiasedly; annually;
competently; dispassionately; elaborately;
exhaustively; philosophically; acrimoniously.
(See reconsider, contemplate.)

REVISED
adverbs
recently; cleverly; handsomely; advantageously; profitably; wisely; ably; considerably; skilfully; satisfactorily; appropriately; acceptably; broadly; somewhat; ingeniously; capably; completely; substantially;
carefully; admirably.

REVISION
adjectives
substantial; patient; endless; downward;
quarrelsome; slight; careful; desperate.

verbs
advise—; advocate—; balk at—; complete
—; consider—; guide—; meditate on—; note
—; pass—; prepare—; publish—; survive
—; —astonishes; —condenses; —corrects;
—improves; —seasons; —suppresses .
(See censorship, change, correction, alteration.)

REVIVAL
adjectives
neo-classic; poetic; impetuous; incidental; .
literary; religious; romantic; wide-spread.

verbs
assume—; attempt—; costume—; deserve—;
display—; hiss—; justify—; merit—; necessitate—; rejoice over—; retard—; wish for
—; —commences; —exhausts; —confuses;
—reawakens; —refreshes; —regains.
(See resurrection, renaissance.)

REVIVE (v)
adverbs
popularly; neo-classically; seasonally; poetically; religiously; spectacularly; dramatically; athletically; spiritually; physically.
(See restore, rally.)

REVOLT
adjectives
successful; meditated; wide-spread; minor;
projected; healthy; tentative; mental; incoherent; energetic; personal; inconsistent.

REVOLT (v)
adverbs
traitorously; viciously; vigorously; vindic-

tively; successfully; tentatively; abortively; unanimously; bloodlessly; violently; periodically; socially; ineffectively; inevitably.

(See rebel, shock.)

REVOLTING

adverbs

hideously; grossly; inordinately; extraordinarily; extremely; abominably; atrociously; nauseatingly; incredibly; unspeakably; detestably; unutterably; inexpressibly; particularly; strangely; painfully; appallingly; shockingly; grimly; unbearably.

REVOLUTION

adjectives

anomalistic; bloodless; veritable; successive (pl); interior; public; complete; impending; synodic; radical; dynastic; incarnate; social; industrial; sidereal; inevitable; ineffective; orbital; hideous; violent; solemn; proletarian; periodic; fickle; salutary.

verbs

betray—; consummate—; chronicle—; crush —; drive to—; engineer—; foment—; forestall—; hail—; hatch—; instigate—; justify —; launch—; map—; plunge into—; promote—; resist—; shatter—; sponsor—; spur —; stamp out—; stave off—; subdue—.

(See anarchy, insurrection, mutiny, outbreak, rebellion.)

REVOLUTIONARY

adverbs

ominously; completely; moderately; incredibly; genuinely; dangerously; alarmingly; fearfully; dreadfully; significantly; pointedly; appallingly; shockingly; grimly; restively; ungovernably; uncontrollably; riotously; mutinously; unsubmissively; insurgently; sullenly.

REVOLVE (v)

adverbs

incessantly; mechanically; automatically; perpetually; periodically; sidereally; synodically.

(See roll, spin.)

REVOLVER

verbs

conceal—; confiscate—; discharge—; display —; draw—; juggle—; oil—; pack—; pocket

—; prohibit—; snatch—; —barks; —frightens; —peppers; —protects; —reassures; — spatters; —spits fire.

(See machine-gun, gun, weapon, pistol.)

REVULSION

adjectives

bitter; rapid; extraordinary; violent; desperate.

verbs

develop—; direct—; encounter—; fall into —; incur—; meet with—; recover from—; shake off—; suffer—; —dizzies; —evolves; —overturns; —shocks; —spins; —uncoils; —whirls.

(See disgust, aversion, repugnance, dislike, sickness.)

REWARD

adjectives

comprehensive; particular; swift; dazzling; palpable; sufficient; material; slender; momentary; temporal; flat; ample; adequate; rich; destined; utmost; arbitrary; tangible; sure; due; coveted; political; just; crowning; pecuniary; monetary.

verbs

assign—; assure of—; confer—; contend for —; gather—; increase—; merit—; offer—; post—; promise—; reap—; scorn—; strive for—; woo—; —blesses; —decorates; —inspires; —recompenses.

(See merit, laurel, fee, dowry, medal, prize.)

REWARD (v)

adverbs

munificently; lavishly; graciously; handsomely; fitly; amply; abundantly; dazzlingly; monetarily; financially; tangibly; politically; pecuniarily.

(See offer, compensate.)

RHAPSODIZE (v)

adverbs

furiously; bombastically; vigorously; oratorically; maddeningly; eloquently; superfluously.

(See improvise, recite, play.)

RHAPSODY

adjectives

extravagant; romantic; incoherent; mystical.

1008

•

adjectives
subtle; empty; heavenly; florid; full-voiced; ambitious; glowing; exuberant; judicial.

verbs
adhere to—; condemn—; consider—; exhibit —; frame—; hammer—into; heed—; indulge in—; inspect—; unmask—; lecture in —; obey—; observe—; polish—; refurbish —; school in—; steep in—; —confuses; —convinces; —expresses; —impresses; —influences; —languishes; —persuades.
(See style, prose, art, eloquence, elegance, oratory.)

RHEUMATIC
adverbs
painfully; gallantly; laughingly; embarrassingly; helplessly; hopelessly; desperately; permanently; incurably; extremely; obviously; manifestly; irremediably; crookedly; unfortunately; terribly; slightly; somewhat; distressingly; undoubtedly; noticeably; woefully.

RHEUMATISM
verbs
afflict with—; endure—; inflict with—; mitigate—; salve—; suffer from—; —attacks; —confines; —irks; —irritates; —lames; —locates; —pains; —racks; —ravages.
(See disease, pain.)

RHINOCEROS
verbs
cage—; capture—; —batters; —charges; —defends; —drowses; —feeds; —gores; —inflicts; —inhabits; —preys on; —puffs; —rams; —roams; —snorts; —waters.
(See animal.)

RHYME
adjectives
pairing (pl); lofty; feverish; uncouth; ruder; golden; bootless; tender; efficacious; ringing; visionary; facile; feminine; careless; nondescript; ever-varying; nobler; meaningless; accepted; refluent; scornful; fettered; unbaptized; brawling; rollicking; emblazoned; unmoving; frozen; nursery; euphonious; mournful; initiative; silvery; innocent; dangerous.

RHYTHM
adjectives
blithe; tantalizing; tenderest; doggerel; accelerated; settled; trotting; vibrating; visual; seductive; intriguing; wailing; sensuous; fluctuating; mighty; rowdy; dull; monotonous; incisive; abrupt; regulated; insinuating; characteristic; maddening; graceful; perfect; rustic; vehement; whirring; exquisite; maudlin; tragic; jarring; primal; natural; pulsating; throbbing; harmonious.

verbs
abuse—; accelerate—; accent—; attune to —; break—; dash into—; depend on—; derive—; determine—; lose—; measure—; regulate—; sing in—; set to—; stress—; sway to—; "swing" to—; synchronize—; —charms; —descends; —flows; —harmonizes; —persists; —reigns.
(See swing, flow.)

RIBALD
adverbs
coarsely; comically; hilariously; disgustingly; grossly; indecently; uproariously; boisterously; shockingly; appallingly; crassly; brazenly; blatantly; flagrantly; openly; notoriously; infamously; inexcusably; unpardonably; villainously; deliberately; impudently; shamelessly; shamefully; daringly.

RIBALDRY
adjectives
public; raucous.

RIBS
adjectives
overweathered; internal; irregular; glistening.

verbs
adhere to—; cling to—; crack—; crush—; develop—; divide into—; grate—; injure—; knuckle—; poke—; rend—; smash—; stick to—; stuff—; —brace; —compose; —extend; —frame; —protect; —snap; —support.

RICH
adverbs
moderately; affluently; opulently; comfortably; unbelievably; incredibly; immeasurably; incalculably; magnificently; mysteriously; suddenly; unquestionably; extremely; secretly; unimaginably; surreptitiously; exceedingly; sumptuously; abundantly marvelously.

RICHES

adjectives

boundless; inherent; ineffectual; unsearchable; manifold; exceeding; intellectual; generous; singular; countless; heavy; unbelievable; .fabulous; inordinate; enormous; undreamed-of; superfluous.

verbs

accumulate—; acquire—; administer—; amass—; bestow—; command—; covet—; desire—; despise—; draw—; enjoy—; estimate—; gather—; overwhelm with—; pile up—; possess—; spurn—; store—; treasure —; trust—; worship—; wring—; —abound; —content; —corrupt; —endanger; —enslave; —flow; —govern; —hinder; —serve. (See affluence, wealth, money, income.)

RICHNESS

adjectives

inexhaustible; vivid; mellow; smooth; changing; vibrant; gilded; decorative; amazing; singular; exceeding; medieval.

RICKETY

adverbs

absurdly; comically; dangerously; fearfully; amusingly; extremely; hazardously; impossibly; alarmingly; curiously; noisily; perilously; laughably.

RID (v)

adverbs

effectually; permanently; ultimately; completely; logically; thoroughly; scientifically. (See dispose.)

RIDDLE

adjectives

fustian; psychological; diplomatic; puzzling; insoluble; unread; inscrutable; miserable; torturing.

verbs

compose—; construct—; contrive—; couch in—s; desire—; dissolve—; evolve—; guess —; interpret—; propose—; propound—; record—; resolve—; solve—; speak in—s; weave—; —amuses; —diverts; —perplexes; —puzzles; —torments; —vexes; —yields. (See enigma, puzzle, problem, mystery.)

RIDE

adjectives

dusty; daring; subsequent; starry; desperate; tedious; delightful; tireless; midnight; fabled.

verbs

accept—; enjoy—; extend—; gain—; hasten —; invite for—; promise—; solicit—; terminate—; "thumb"—; —bores; —delights; —refreshes; —thrills; —tires; —wearies; —diverts. (See trip, journey, tour.)

RIDE (v)

adverbs

thunderously; swiftly; triumphantly; furiously; victoriously; gallantly; blindly; leisurely; wildly; proudly; blithely; ruthlessly; roughly; desperately; dashingly; daringly; gracefully; decisively; superbly. (See move, travel.)

RIDER

adjectives

consummate; heavy; gallant; superb; unmovable; dashing; expert; audacious; warlike; daring; decisive; groomless; graceful.

verbs

bear—; carry—; equal—; obey—; throw—; train—; unnerve—; —charges; —dismounts; —drags; —drives; —joggles; —lashes; —mounts; —pats; —reigns; —soothes; —spurs; —tires; —travels; —vaults; —wearies; —whips. (See horseman.)

RIDGE

adjectives

cruciform; melancholy; woody; parallel; hummocky; hog-backed; wind-swept; barren; perpendicular; tremendous; mountain; formidable; lofty; precipitous; loosened; ice; craggy; gentle; encircling; shaggy; commanding; uncultivated; sunken; extended; crowned; hillocky.

verbs

climb to—; dance on—; discern—; dread—; drive to—; dwarf—; form—; fortify—; quit—; —beams; —caps; —chains; —crests; —elevates; —rises; —runs; —stretches; —tempts. (See bank, range, mountain, hill.)

RIDICULE

adjectives

stinging; comic; raucous; merciless; personal; angry; bitter; traditional; abusive; sarcastic; scathing; biting.

verbs
bear—; defy—; expose to—; fear—; heap —; indulge in—; move to—; overcome—; resort to—; share—; subject to—; sustain—; taste—; turn to—; —bites; —checks; — cuts; —disgraces; —embarrasses; —embitters; —enrages; —pains; —smothers; — storms; —strips.
(See banter, **jeer**, irony, mockery, derision.)

RIDICULE (v)
adverbs
ruthlessly; sarcastically; cruelly; tenderly; spitefully; stingingly; raucously; mercilessly; angrily; bitterly; abusively; bitingly; scathingly.
(See mock, jeer.)

RIDICULOUS
adverbs
foolishly; absurdly; unreasonably; laughably; palpably; crazily; extravagantly; irrationally; childishly; stupidly; grotesquely; blatantly; whimsically; gaily; airily; intentionally; injudiciously; recklessly; weakly; senselessly; nonsensically; grossly; manifestly; rashly; unwisely; pathetically.

RIFLE
adjectives
leather-cased; handled; speckless; omnipresent; unwieldy; pneumatic; handsome; new; grimy; deathdealing; express; crackling; dreaded.

verbs
arm with—; brandish—; bristle with—s; conceal—; discharge—; examine—; fear—; inspect—; point—; provide with—s; shoulder— ;—crackles; —frightens; —gleams; — mows down; —speaks.
(See gun, machine-gun, musket.)

RIFT
adjectives
horrid; savage; gusty; keen; little; widening; convenient.

verbs
fill—; lament—; span—; —appears; — breaches; —brews; —disjoins; —disunites;

—gapes; —heals; —overhangs; —rends; — rips; —ruptures; —separates; —splits; — widens.
(See breach, gap.)

RIGHT
adjectives
outward; authoritative; individual; inalienable; hereditary; unrestricted; colonial; prescriptive; litigious; indefeasible; peculiar; legal; belligerent; relative; legitimate; marital; sacred; inviolable; unquestionable; undisputed; natural; respective; concrete; undoubted; exclusive; purchased; immemorial; substantial; inestimable; municipal; injured; prime; invaded; inborn; constitutional; derivative; inherent; obedient; vanquished; common; riparian (pl); conceded; poetical; autonomic; conjugal; functional; vested; unquestioned; beautiful; proprietary; antique; terrible; illimitable; civil; perfected; manorial; executive; formal; sable-vested; shameful; feudal; covenanted; immutable; invulnerable; unalterable; abstract; ecclesiastical; unclaimed; statutable; possessory; proprietary; lucrative; impugned; questionable; absolute; vital; senescent; uncontested; divine; irrevocable; provincial; vindicated.

verbs
abolish—; accord—; acknowledge—; arrogate—; assert—; assume—; cherish—; clamor for—; concede—; confer—; confiscate—; curtail—; defend—; deprive of—; derive—; dispose of—; dispute—; disregard —; earn—; embody—; encroach on—; establish—; exercise—; forfeit—; grant—; impair—; infringe upon—; insure—; invade —; invest with—; prate of—s; preserve—; protest—; relinquish—; remand—; respect —; restore—; retain—; revoke—; safeguard—; surrender—; suspend—; suppress —; terminate—; transgress—; undermine —; uphold—; urge—; vindicate—; violate —; vouchsafe—; waive—; win—; wrest—; — resides with; —triumphs.
(See liberty, license, franchise, **justice**, privilege, **authority**, prerogative.)

RIGHTEOUS
adverbs
rigidly; sincerely; consciously; utterly; completely; uprightly; inherently; carefully; ostentatiously; austerely; undeviatingly; strictly; painfully; ostensibly; incredibly; apparently; overly; dutifully; duly; unduly;

pretentiously; manifestly; pharisaically; uncompromisingly; stiffly.

RIGHTEOUSNESS
adjectives
divine; inherent; ungodly; final; spotless; haughty; imputed.

verbs
forsake—; found on—; garb in—; hunger for—; judge in—; maintain—; observe with —; proclaim—; thirst for—; uphold—; — advances; —exalts; —falters; —flourishes; —rewards; —withstands; —yields; impute —.

(See justice, good, virtue, purity.)

RIGID
adverbs
stiffly; painfully; terribly; dreadfully; stonily; bleakly; uncompromisingly; intolerably; woefully; coldly; harshly; austerely; cruelly; bitterly; sternly; severely; brutally; ungenerously; narrow-mindedly; dogmatically; tyrannically; puritanically; doctrinally; intolerantly.

RIGOR
adjectives
utmost; merciless; logical; decisive; religious; protracted; grizzly; coveted; unsparing; remorseless; pedantic.

RIGORS
verbs
allay—; alleviate—; ease—; endure—; enforce—; fear—; feel—; ferment—; guard against—; preserve from—; relax—; resist —; shelter from—; smart under—; survive —; temper—; —affect; —distress; —harden; —reduce.

(See difficulty, trouble, obstacle, severity, harshness.)

RILL
adjectives
narrow; wandering; babbling; dancing; tinkling; solitary; winding; sylvan; clear; fuming; glancing; gushing; waking; frosted; limpid; rebounding; singing; summer; flowing; purling; classic.

RING
adjectives
metallic; ducal; marriage; granite; tinkling; jubilant; carved; babyish; magnificent; diamond; diurnal; dry; subtle; typic;

glittering; rhythmic; betrothal; determined; watery; wondrous; closing; luminous; superb; old; scaly; mournful; insistent; diverting; contorted; stifling; clustering; lubricous; tense; monumental; familiar; sinister; dancing; flat; oval; solid; great; massive; dingy; continuous; concentric (pl).

verbs
admire—; appraise—; bedeck with—s; finger—; mislay—; restore—to; return—; tinkle—s; value—; —adorns; —binds; — dazzles; —encircles; —espouses; —imitates; —gleams; —glimmers; —glitters; —recalls; —seals; —sparkles; —weds.

(See diamond, jewel, gem.)

RING (v)
adverbs
incessantly; musically; harshly; dolefully; drowsily; monotonously; feebly; impatiently; blithely; resonantly; piercingly; metalically; vigorously; jubilantly; tinklingly.

(See resound, chime.)

RIOT
adjectives
prodigal; noiseless; bloody; subsequent; prison; licentious; golden; wild; senseless; springtide; transient.

verbs
deplore—; describe—; expose to—; incite to—; instigate—; pitch into—; provoke—; quash—; quell—; subdue—; suppress—; —bursts forth; —disorders; —ensues; — jeopardizes; —protests; —strikes; —upsets; —violates.

(See commotion, revolution, strike, disturbance, turmoil, violence.)

RIOTERS
verbs
calm—; condemn—; disperse—; incite—; pardon—; punish—; quell—; restrain—; suppress—; —agitate; —aggravate; —attack; —clamor; —demand; —harry; —pillage; —plunder; —ravage; —storm; — transgress.

(See striker, anarchist, terrorist, communist, scab.)

RIOTOUS
adverbs
dangerously; alarmingly; boisterously; seditiously; mutinously; disgracefully; inordinately; extraordinarily; strangely; uncon-

trollably; ungovernably; murderously; insensately; wildly; violently; vociferously; grimly; daringly; defiantly; tumultuously; seditiously; uproariously; terribly; sullenly.

RIPE

adverbs
finally; quite; entirely; altogether; lusciously; deliciously; completely; satisfactorily; perfectly; unexpectedly; pleasantly; sufficiently; extremely; unduly; evidently.

RIPEN (v)

adverbs
seasonally; wholesomely; deliciously; normally; luxuriantly; goldenly; succulently.
(See develop, complete.)

RIPPLE (v)

adverbs
idly; sleekly; liquidly; bubblingly; luminously; gildedly.
(See wave, sway.)

RIPPLES

adjectives
glad; silvery; purled; innumerable; foamy; moon-lit; timid; minute; bubbling; passing; luminous; breeze-ridden; transparent; sungilt; liquid.

verbs
agitate—; blow—; flow in—; form—; mark by—; observe—; smooth—; —fascinate; —glisten; —ruffle; —shimmer; —subside; —undulate; —wash.
(See wave, billow, breaker.)

RIPPLING

adverbs
merrily; cheerfully; pleasantly; clearly; smoothly; pleasantly; sparklingly; flashily; plashily; happily; blithely; brightly; brilliantly; laughingly; quietly; audibly; noisily.

RISE

adjectives
meteoric; successful; sufficient; miraculous; unprecedented; phenomenal; important; thermometric; nocturnal; gradual; corresponding; extraordinary; unpredictable; speedy.

verbs
anticipate—; check—; deplore—; forestall —; gauge—; heighten—; mount—; predict —; produce—; stem—; stimulate—; tremble

on—; —advances; —ceases; —continues; —frightens; —indicates; —profits; —thrills.
(See beginning, advance, progress, increase.)

RISE (v)

adverbs
dizzily; abruptly; majestically; airily; militantly; reluctantly; unanimously; gradually; mysteriously; solemnly; impulsively; leisurely; ceremoniously; conspicuously; deliberately; involuntarily; lingeringly; reverently; obediently; perpendicularly; instinctively; amiably; meteorically; phenomenally; unpredictably.
(See arise, ascend.)

RISK

adjectives
imminent; tremendous; operative; alarming; infinite; serious; continual; unaccustomed; canine; known; desirable; considerable; unjustifiable; extraordinary.

verbs
accept—; assume—; avoid—; balk at—; court—; decry—; diminish—; entail—; exclude—; expose to—; free from—; guard against—; harbor—; increase—; incur—; involve—; justify—; lessen—; obviate—; preclude—; preserve from—; question—; undergo—; underwrite—.
(See danger, chance, hazard, speculation.)

RISK (v)

adverbs
alarmingly; unjustifiably; rashly; heroically; needlessly; considerably; superfluously.
(See endanger, imperil.)

RISKY

adverbs
dangerously; ominously; perilously; alarmingly; hazardously; definitely; peculiarly; particularly; immensely; incalculably; admittedly; unwarrantably; unfortunately; always; manifestly; extremely; uncommonly; commercially; altogether; notoriously; obviously; gravely; seriously; inescapably; unavoidably; undeniably; inordinately; unaccountably; immeasurably; incalculably; desperately; appallingly; hideously; pitiably; fearfully; tragically; adventurously; distinctly.

RITE

adjectives

superstitious; purifying; pleasing; funeral; sanguinary; sensual; true; sacramental; courtly; bloody; pagan; nuptial; connubial; ecclesiastical; abominable; sacred; gorgeous; dismal; mysterious; wanton; barbaric; religious; gloomy; hideous; ceremonial; blessed; ancient; obnoxious; various (pl); horrid; preparatory; repulsive; propitiatory; gentle; solemn.

verbs

adhere to—; celebrate—; follow—; ignore —; institute—; observe—; perform—; prolong—; refrain from—; relinquish—; retain—; stage—; value—; —consists of; — honors; —impresses; —symbolizes.

(See ceremony, function, ritual.)

RITUAL

adjectives

social; captivating; visible; complicated; artistic; elaborate; burdensome.

verbs

adhere to—; adopt—; attempt—; attend—; elaborate—; evolve—; instruct in—; mumble—; observe—; offend by—; perform—; prepare for—; recite—; supply—; suspend —; —animates; —beautifies; —celebrates; —colors; —dignifies; —sanctifies; —symbolizes.

(See form, formula, rite, ceremony, function.)

RITUALISTIC

adverbs

elaborately; ceremonially; reverently; extravagantly; unusually; highly; profoundly; peculiarly; particularly; exotically; mysteriously; strangely.

RIVAL

adjectives

insolent; mutinous; unworthy; formidable; ribald; potent; irresistable; disagreeable; intolerable; vexatious; insolent; celebrated; successful; gallant; richer; traditional; guiltless; powerful; fallen; testy; scheming; hostile; confiding; incredible; favorable; importunate; circumstanced; angry; covetous; dangerous; strenuous; worthy; patriotic; distinguished; hopeless; domestic; rising; hated.

verbs

appraise—; defy—; emulate—; encounter —; excel—; oust—; outlast—; restrain—; shoulder aside—; surpass—; tolerate—; trail—; —aspires; —bewails; —s clash; — competes; —contends; —disputes; —equals; —excels; —glares; —opposes; —pursues; —s scramble; —spars; —squares off; — strives; —vies.

(See enemy, competitor, contestant, antagonist, insurgent.)

RIVALRY

adjectives

female; impious; dawning; fierce; ruthless; malignant; generous; unwitting; amiable; professional; ambitious; jealous; passionate; keen; sectional; kindly; municipal; bloody; inherent; dangerous; eager; bitter.

verbs

confess—; create—; eliminate—; endure—; engage in—; forbid—; forsake—; intensify —; promote—; subordinate—; —confronts; —continues; —divides; —intervenes; —separates; —subsides; —wanes; —threatens.

(See competition, enmity, opposition, antagonism.)

RIVER

adjectives

channeled; raucous; solemn; foaming; noble; unfranked; chafing; brimming; crystal; narrowed; exulting; far-off; pelting; babbling; ringing; racing; saturnine; rapid; fruitful; leaping; clear; deep-banked; booming; limpid; swollen; abominable; rushing; rife; turbid; ruinous; slow; noiseless; flowing; remarkable; ironical; encroaching; torrential; murmuring; roaring; peculiar; majestic; spectral; winding; mighty; darkening; unfordable; full-grown; peaceful; sunlit; meandering; cheerful; pebble-paved; immense; wandering; turbulent; incorrigible; glassy; brattling; capricious; hurrying; sparkling; resplendent; sobbing; weariest; useless; failing; reflecting; royal; quiet; doubling; hesitating; white-robed; subterranean; trickling; golden; unbridged; whirling; solitary; speeding; sluggish; mystic; subsiding; salmon-thronged; soft-flowing; ever-deepening; imaginary; freshening; frozen; long; gray; swanlike; impassable; hissing; swift; silent; sweet-voiced; hard-working; historic; mocking.

verbs

breast—; bridge—; divert—; emerge from —; ford—; ply—; plunge into—; stock—; —abounds in; —babbles; —batters; —bawls; —chatters; —churns; —eddies; —flows; —foams; —frets; —glides; —glitters; —growls; —gurgles; —laps; —laughs; —leaps; —loiters; —meanders; —murmurs; —races; —rises; —roars; —sallies; —stirs; —subsides; —swells; —threads.

(See liquid, stream, brook.)

RIVET

verbs

beat—; bind with—; bucket—; force—; hammer—; heat—; insert—; join with—; loose—; secure with—; set—; strain—; —braces; —s clatter; —clinches; —fastens; —projects; —secures; —tightens; —unites; —welds.

(See nail, link, bond, fetter, band.)

RIVULET

adjectives

merry; shady; woodland; shrunken; clear; babbling; noisy; tinkling; cheerful; glittering; ever-joyous; melancholy; widely-wandering.

ROAD

adjectives

endless; beaten; unfrequented; homeward; arduous; gliding; country; grass-grown; monotonous; impassable; lifeless; miry; shady; sunny; winding; smiling; serpentine; misty; worthless; conventional; parched; dusty; corduroy; superb; dilapidated; wood; rutty; rugged; vicinal; circuitous; white; sand; sun-splashed; tortuous; steep; hilly; silver; swarming; mended; half-defined; romantic; turfy; unguarded; lakeside; starless; forsaken; military; thorny; fated; unknown; coral-bordered; red; rutted; surest; moon-lit; wrong; disused; miraculous; chocolate-colored; holy; intricate; dreary; elevated; bumpy; glaring; subtler; dubious; frozen; shaded; heavenly; indistinguishable; interminable; various (pl); treacherous; miserable; smoother; level; macadamized; translucent; narrow; sinuous; weary; unfamiliar; dappled; scenic; uneven; undulating; zigzagging; ready; unbroken.

verbs

bank—; bounce over—; clock—; clog—; deviate from—; diverge from—; infest—;

jog along—; jounce over—; level—; patrol —; plod along—; skim along—; slog over —; skirt—; surface—; trudge along—; —ambles; —s converge; —meanders; —s radiate from; —rambles; —swarms; —sweeps along; —wanders; —wearies; —winds.

(See avenue, highway, lane, drive.)

ROADSIDE

verbs

bank—; beautify—; border—; carpet—; defile—; dot—; fall to—; follow—; grace —; lie along—; lodge on—; plant—; sprawl over—; strew—; tramp—; tread—; view from—; —appeals; —borders; —charms.

(See countryside, field, land.)

ROADSTER

adjectives

asthmatic; resplendent; low-slung; sport; sleek; swift; streamlined; battered; shiny.

verbs

sport (colloq.)—; —bounces along; —careens; —chugs; —gleams; —glitters; —hurtles; —performs; —rattles; —rolls along; —slows up; —speeds; —sputters; —spurts; —thrills; —whirs; —whizzes.

(See car, automobile.)

ROAM (v)

adverbs

casually; freely; leisurely; carelessly; buoyantly; lightly; circuitously; extensively.

(See wander, stray.)

ROAR

adjectives

deep; incessant; snarling; perpetual; majestic; indistinguishable; ebbing; shutterlike; swelling; quavering; continuous; dreadful; cannon-like; living; sullen; endless; incredible; hoarse; subdued; solemn; baffled; hideous; unremitting; drumming; deepening; heavy; monotonous; gusty; painful; distressed; awful; massive; sealike; enormous; universal; stifled; muffled; deafening; dull; suppressed; confused; moaning; intermittent; tremendous; gesturing; wildest; mingled; simultaneous; prolonged; suggestive; vague; wavering; unceasing; full-throated; dry; wild; triumphant; angry; steady; tumultuous; high-keyed; crackling; appalling.

verbs
deafen by—; imitate—; muffle—; restrain
—; suppress—; swell into—; utter—; —
blasts; —deafens; —disembowels; —drowns
out; —echoes; —enrages; —excites; —
frightens; —horrifies; —interrupts; —pains;
—rends; —splits the air.
(See noise, sound, uproar, thunder, rumble.)

ROAR (v)

adverbs
thunderously; awesomely; terrifically;
brutally; imperiously; vigorously; unremittingly; incessantly; incredibly; hoarsely;
hideously; deafeningly; triumphantly; tumultuously; appallingly; full-throatedly.
(See bellow, boom.)

ROB (v)

adverbs
systematically; professionally; slyly; insidiously; successfully; nocturnally; brazenly;
boldly; impudently.
(See plunder, steal.)

ROBBER

adjectives
nocturnal; bloody; prowling; brutalized;
successful.

verbs
apprehend—; deliver from—; incarcerate
—; —s congregate; —s conspire; —depredates; —despoils; —divests; —dodges; —
evades; —filches; —guts; —s infest; —s
invade; —loots; —marauds; —pilfers —
pillages; —plucks; —plunders; —purloins;
—ranges; —ransacks; —rifles; —sacks; —
strips; —tricks.
(See burglar, bandit, hoodlum, intruder,
liar, offender.)

ROBBERY

verbs
addict to—; commit—; conceal—; contrive
—; discover—; escape—; fear—; implicate
in—; interrupt—; mourn—; perform—; perpetrate—; plot—; punish—; report—; reveal—; uncover—; —impoverishes; —occurs; —strips.
(See "holdup", plagiarism, theft, plunder.)

ROBE

adjectives
canonical; luxuriant; tattered; tinsel; foot-catching; flowing; flaunting; gossamer;
trailing; glistening; magnificent; operatic;
fantastic; painted; outspread; snowy; unconfined; sable; virgin; brocaded; spotless;
ceremonial; gorgeous; shimmering; conventional; somber; glittering; unreverent; sacerdotal; festive; priestly; woven; sweeping;
brilliant; dripping; cerulean; incomplete;
freckled; princely; transitory; ducal; officious; ruddy; royal; close-fitting; bloodstained; transparent; vestal; musty; ample;
saffron; mortal; festal; gold-trimmed;
shroudlike; delicate; bridal; pompous;
little.

verbs
array in—; bestow—upon; cast off—; clothe
in—; disguise in—; doff—; don—; embroider—; fold—; huddle in—; gather—; invest
—; line—; strip of—; —beautifies; —enfolds; —envelops; —flows; —glorifies; —
heightens; —streams; —trails.
(See frock, blanket, gown, clothing.)

ROBE (v)

adverbs
magnificently; luxuriantly; fantastically;
spectacularly; ceremonially; conventionally;
sacerdotally; ecclesiastically.
(See shroud, cloak.)

ROBIN

verbs
befriend—; welcome—; —announces
Spring; —booms; —braves; —busies; —
cheers; —chirrups; —cocks; —darts; —
defies; —digs; —flutters; —hops; —moults;
—pokes; —snaps up; —swoops; —soars.
(See bird.)

ROBUST

adverbs
sturdily; splendidly; stoutly; healthily; vigorously; wholesomely; magnificently; enviably; admirably; stockily; brawnily; physically; amazingly; heartily.

ROCK (v)

adverbs
paternally; maternally; desolately; disconsolately; dizzily; patiently; tenderly.
(See sway, vacillate.)

ROCKET

verbs
bombard with—s; discharge—; display—;
eject—; fire—; fuse—; ignite—; project—;
propel—; set off—; signal with—; spark—;

touch off—; —bursts; —darts; —endangers; —hurtles; —illumines; —s scatter; —showers; —sizzles; —terrifies; —vanishes; — zooms.

(See bullet, shot, projectile.)

ROCKS

adjectives

bare; torpid; porphyritic; hospitable; darker; native; volcanic; craggy; glistening; fantastic; dazzling; picturesque; chalky; friable; jagged; sheltering; single; naked; ragged; spiritual; adamant; shelving; ancient; steep; sun-heated; rough-hewn; lichen-covered; fissured; cloven; miraculous; calcareous; low-browed; irresistable; living; igneous; perilous; precipitous; enwombed; sharp; splintered; riven; gaunt; flinty; stubborn; dun-colored; wave-encircled; disintegrated; inhospitable; sheer; tempest-beaten; submissive; sublime; traitorous; shadowing; jutting; steadfast; tidal; silver-fretted; impregnable; vine-clad; imperishable; hanging; unmistakable; merchant-marring; tall; cruel; burly-shouldered; shapeless; mantel-like; sea-beaten; shivering; wave-lapped; noticeable; senseless; sacrificial; gloomy; ice-bound; grass-covered; fearful; storied; incumbent; shining; rooted; cavernous; gneissic; sedimentary; genial; humid; monumental; ashy; mossy; projecting; massive; sparkling; sliding; peaked; curved; hoary; smitten; vaulted; churning; multitudinous; rigid; cream-colored; conspicuous; onlooking; echoing; unhewn; frowning; sullen; high-ascending; field; galled; kelp-covered; storm-drenched; cliffy; rugged; overhanging; wrinkled; glaciated; highest; insensible; basaltic; raging; serrated; time-stained; underlying; dangerous; dreary; weed-hung.

verbs

avoid—; bivouac on—; blast—; carve from —; crack—; crush—; dash against—; direct—; dislodge—; fear—; heap—; hew—; hurl—; quarry—; run upon—; shatter on —; split—; strike—; surmount—; —batter; —bound; —crest; —disintegrate; —erode; —fortify; —girdle; —hurtle; —jut; —project; —stud; —tower.

(See crag, reef, stone, granite, cliff.)

ROCKY

adverbs

painfully; arduously; extremely; impassably; roughly; dangerously; exceedingly; incredibly; unexpectedly; surprizingly; amazingly; terribly; perilously.

ROD

adjectives

chastening; pastoral; bayonet; mystic; avenging; radiant; metallic; sharpest; transparent; sin-avenging; uplifted; gubernatorial; merciless.

ROGUE

adjectives

unconscionable; poor; drunken; damnable; false-hearted; cunning; dissentious; wenching; cowardly; fair-haired; little; consummate; unmitigated; tedious; pestilent; loitering; complete; overweening.

verbs

accuse—; apprehend—; deal with—s; denounce—; discomfit—; distrust—; punish —; quell—; rebuke—; reproach—; —baits; —beguiles; —deceives; —designs; —deviates; —devises; —entices; —fools; — "foxes"; —lures; —shirks; —swindles; — tricks.

(See robber, scoundrel, profligate.)

ROGUISH

adverbs

mischievously; comically; lovably; rascally; innocently; merrily; teasingly; tormentingly; actively; ingeniously; inveterately; incurably; incorrigibly; naturally; wantonly; secretly; trickily; craftily; knavishly; particularly; villainously; peculiarly; singularly; notoriously.

ROISTERING

adverbs

noisily; playfully; mirthfully; boisterously; capriciously; boldly; waggishly; wantonly; uproariously; sportively; prankishly; absurdly; inordinately; swaggeringly; boastfully; fantastically; outlandishly; blusteringly; tumultuously; turbulently; bombastically; merrily.

ROLE

adjectives

inquisitorial; crucial; subordinate; inglorious; dominating; important; restricted; decisive; benevolent; influential; essential; pessimistic; responsible; unsavory; villainous; significant; prominent; destined; tremendous; suitable; self-imposed.

verbs

acclaim—; adopt—; animate—; bolster—; color—; convey—; denounce—; enact—; ennoble—; exploit—; extol—; fill—; fire—; illuminate—; immortalize—; jade—; overact—; portray—; renounce—; romp through —; spice—.

(See part, character.)

ROLL

adjectives

luscious; harsh; delicate; lumbering; bloody; uncanny; condescending; mystic; mathematic; rhythmic.

ROLL (v)

adverbs

heavily; furiously; enchantingly; impetuously; luxuriously; dangerously; exultantly; fiercely; smoothly; sluggishly; lumberingly; rhythmically.

(See whirl, revolve.)

ROLLICKING

adverbs

blithely; gaily; happily; frivolously; hilariously; boisterously; laughingly; divertingly; entertainingly; loudly; comically; clownishly; cheerfully; buoyantly; recklessly; jauntily; vivaciously; noisily; gleefully; sportively; joyously; mirthfully; jubilantly.

ROMANCE

adjectives

picaresque; somber; fictitious; touching; rooted; veritable; synthetic; bottled; budding; unknown; boyish; chivalrous; brilliant; spirited; pure; ennobling; pastoral; degenerate; headlong; elegant; passionate; singular; stormy; tempestuous; tawdry; interminable; enthralling; nautical; mawkish; comic; tragic; prose; prodigal; charming; audacious; fiery; insipid; colorless; cosmopolitan; fantastic; habitual; metrical; blighted; discursive; wild; bloody; hazy; sentimental.

verbs

color with—; crave—; culminate in—; delve into—; denude of—; divest of—; dull—; embalm—; enact—; guard—; nurture—; permeate with—; repudiate—; taste—; tinge with—; wreck—; —blinds; —blooms; —blossoms; —conceives; —dissolves; —fades; —flourishes; —flowers; —glows; —illuminates; —soars; —transports; —uplifts.

(See love, passion.)

adverbs

incurably; naturally; venturously; adventurously; unusually; absurdly; incorrigibly; extravagantly; wildly; fantastically; sentimentally; imaginatively; picturesquely; incredibly; singularly; oddly; boldly; recklessly; whimsically; capriciously; magnificently; brilliantly; daringly; splendidly.

ROMP (v)

adverbs

sportively; boisterously; gaily; enthusiastically; irresistibly; intoxicatedly; pastorally; amorously; rustically.

(See play, frolic.)

ROOF

adjectives

matted; distant; pyramidal; multitudinous; (pl); consecrated; crumbling; picturesque; gabled; timbered; weather-toned; unpretentious; terraced; milky; huddling; leafy; sloping; brook-eaved; irregular; gambrel; fantastic; embowered; purple-peaked; projected; moonwashed; slanting; majestical; radiant; high-pitched; verdant; branching; fretted; permanent; blackening; wavy; crystal; graceful; arched; high-peaked; mansard; lowly; vaulted; flowery; sagging; ragged; thatched; dusky; mountainous; atrocious; long; movable; waving; collapsing; great; massive.

verbs

examine—; ornament—; paint—; patch—; pierce—; provide—; repair—; ruin—; shatter—; test—; thatch—; vault—; —affords; —crests; —extends; —leaks; —projects; —shades; —sheds; —shelters; —slants.

(See cover, ledge, dome.)

ROOK

verbs

—builds; —caws; —clamors; —flocks; —s jangle; —mounts; —plunders; —pours forth; —s quarrel; —s swarm; —torments; —s wrangle.

(See bird.)

ROOM

adjectives

vaulted; modest; furnished; peaceful; shadowy; secluded; bleak; spacious; well-swept; neighboring; immaculate; reading; sunny; abutting; luxurious; desolate; well-proportioned; charming; livable; warmed; fireproof; light; slashing; ink-smelling; paper-littered; commodious; crowded; midnight; frescoed; tobacco-scented; emergency; colorless; haunted; utmost; wide; spiritual; dismal; disordered; habitable; cheerless; sunlit; saddening; sundry (pl); comfortable; wretched; gracious; octagonal; beam-roofed; rectangular; barny; squalid; scanty; generous; pleasant; drafty; poverty-stricken; plaster-dropping; adjoining; shabby; large; clean; dim; sick; dingy; dreary; dimly-lit; fencing; tranquil; guest; tolerable; stiff; moon-lit; immense; solitary; low-ceilinged; dark; uncarpeted; low; smoke-filled; banqueting; unattractive; remote; awesome; foul; polluted; elegant; slant-roofed; earthly; dull; musty; handsome; sunny; raftered; airy; upper; quaint; mirror; projection; squalid; air-conditioned; uncomfortable; sordid; stuffy; charming; dormer-windowed; gloomy; darkening; lonely; eerie; cozy; smart; impressive; intimate; restful; remarkable; delightful; ultra-modern; homelike; perfect; unusual; beautiful; exquisite; appointed; outside; tasteful; attractive; livable; modern; sleeping; well-planned; inexpensive; appealing; excellent; faultless; amazing; fine; great; decorated; becoming; sound-proof; bright; oversize.

verbs

air—; bar—; barge into (colloq.)—; bundle out of—; bunk in—; burst into—; bustle out of—; confine to—; clutter—; darken—; direct to—; flank—; fresco—; furnish—; jam —; mass in—; pace—; pop into—; repair to—; saunter into—; scuttle from—; seclude in—; slip from—; stalk out of—; stump out of—; sweep from—; ventilate—; —buzzes; —invites.

(See classroom, lounge, lobby, cell, hall, chamber, apartment, bedroom, kitchen, office.)

ROOMY

adverbs

delightfully; charmingly; pleasantly; comfortably; satisfactorily; acceptably; unnecessarily; spaciously; magnificently; adequately; amply; pleasantly; luxuriously; agreeably; conveniently.

ROOSTER

verbs

behead—; exhibit—; fatten—; pen up—; wire in—; —flutters about; —gobbles up;

—invades the hennery; —molts; —pecks; —perches; —scratches; —squawks; —struts; —waxes indignant.

(See fowl, hen.)

ROOTS

adjectives

nocturnal; grasping; aerial; ulcerating; lurid; mucilaginous; insipid; antique; vigorous; nutritious; fibrous; giant; unsearchable; musty; inconsiderable; extraneous; spreading; wasting; parched; bulbous; sexless; powdered; moss-cushioned; orbed; goodly; gnarled; deep-lying; aromatic; venerable; cooling; fantastic; palatable; homeliest; vile; corrugated; babbling; wiry; old; uptorn; clasping; social; severed.

verbs

affix to—; choke—; dig to—; enrich—; feed —; fertilize—; ground—; grub among—; involve—; kill—; manure—; nourish—; stimulate—; uncover—; unearth—; —absorb; —bury in; —canker; —function; —go deep; —insinuate themselves into; —moor to; —project above; —supply; —thrust.

(See stem, cause, source, plant.)

ROPE

adjectives

graceful; greasy; hempen; rag; dangling; fatal; dragging; efficacious; innumerable (pl); rescuing; improvised; rain-bleached.

verbs

attach—; bind with—; braid—; cast—; haul on—; knife—; lay—; plait—; secure with—; snag—; strain—; tighten—; tug—; twist—; wind—; —binds; —chafes; —entwines; —fastens; —girdles; —secures.

(See cable, cord, string, chain.)

ROSE

adjectives

transient; fading; refreshing; quaint; distinctive; colorful; full-blown; fresh-blown; belated; wild; damask; dusty; shaken; panting; white-petaled; golden-centered; imperial; bubbled; winter; transcendent; amorous; fossil; glimmering; glowing; flowerless; newborn; burning; snowy; branching; delicate; blooming; embroidered; autumnal; countless (pl); fragrant; blushing; deeper; victorious; heavenly; living; immeasurable; wide-hearted; queenliest; virgin; magic; late.

verbs
bear—; crown with—s; gather—s; hawk —s; infect—s; pluck—; prize—; strew with —s; strip—; —adorns; —blooms; —blossoms; —blushes; —buds; —charms; — fades; —flames; —glows; —lingers; —perfumes; —perishes; —strews; —survives; — trembles; —withers; prune—.
(See flower, plant.)

ROSTRUM
verbs
adorn—; advance toward—; appeal from—; ascend—; assemble on—; erect—; exhort from—; glide into—; harangue from—; mount—; orate from—; pace—; speak from —; —quakes; —tremors.
(See pulpit, platform, stage.)

ROSY
adverbs
beautifully; charmingly; bewitchingly; blushingly; bloomingly; buxomly; happily; shyly; bashfully; modestly; hopefully; artlessly; naturally; sweetly; innocently; childishly; laughingly; healthfully; wholesomely; pleasantly; prettily.

ROTE
adjectives
rapt; aesthetic; rhythmal.

ROTTEN
adverbs
utterly; uselessly; ruinously; abominably; unfortunately; disgustingly; unserviceably; unusably; disastrously; disgustingly; dangerously; hopelessly; indescribably.

ROTUND
adverbs
amusingly; prosperously; becomingly; perfectly; healthily; laughably; ludicrously; slightly; somewhat.

ROUGH
adverbs
unpleasantly; extremely; uncommonly; disagreeably; unevenly; jaggedly; unusually; peculiarly; strangely; curiously; stiffly; harshly; rockily; unexpectedly; surprisingly; distressingly; uncomfortably; dreadfully; intolerably.

ROUND
adjectives
diurnal; dutiful; mazy; ambitious; tedious; unheroic; lucent; subsequent; monotonous; merciful; heathen; airy; weary; terrible; unfailing; luminous; solemn; frequent; periodical; ceaseless; dizzy; mortal; daily.

ROUSE (v)
adverbs
abruptly; violently; startlingly; dutifully; daily; faithfully; harshly; habitually; instinctively.
(See arouse, excite.)

ROUTE
adjectives
circuitous; rigorous; diversified; branching; baffled; river; caravan; slow; laborious; disused; shorter; sylvan; convenient; quaint; ignominious; extensive; unobstructed; unusual; principal; roundabout; dangerous; pilgrim; time-honored; rebellious; wanton; practicable; meandering; direct; devious; passable; regular; profitable; common; traditional; elusive; untried.

verbs
assure of—; chart—; choose—; clog—; conceive—; course—; cover—; deviate from—; direct to—; enter by—; follow—; invade —; memorize—; reconnoiter—; seek—; signify—; survey—; travel—; traverse—; — diverges; —entrances.
(See line, channel, road, course.)

ROUTE (v)
adverbs
completely; devastatingly; ignominiously; wholly; rebelliously; ruthlessly.
(See direct, plan.)

ROUTINE
adjectives
irksome; obscure; home; pleasure-seeking; foul; mechanized; ostentatious; systematic; hack; ordinary; laborious; slavish; dull; dreary; pleasant; wearisome; habituated; professional; indolent; systematized; monotonously; hated; soul-degrading; regular.

verbs
acquaint with—; adhere to—; adopt—; chafe under—; discharge—; eliminate—; endure—; establish—; fix—; identify with —; lift from—; mire in—; perform—; quit

—; reduce to—; relax—; settle into—; sink into—; —bores; —dulls; —encases; —rusts; —stagnates; —wears.

(See rule, conventionality, habit, custom.)

ROW

adjectives
parallel; endless; bowing; everlasting; courtesying; straggling; interminable; legioned; branchy; pale; tranquil; burnished; flaring; monotonous; serried; formal; answering; tenement; impenetrable; lusty; tremendous; dreadful; numberless (pl); venerable.

verbs
arrange in—s; break—; disrupt—; draw from—; emerge from—; file in—; fix—; mark in—; mow down—; rank in—; realign —; reinforce—; station in—; string in—s; verge from—; —dazzles; —impresses; interrupt—.

(See line, series.)

ROW (v)

adverbs
strenuously; energetically; industriously; heroically; monotonously; tirelessly; vigorously; victoriously.

(See paddle, propel.)

ROWDY

adverbs
uncommonly; indecorously; uncivilly; intolerably; disagreeably; coarsely; boorishly; outlandishly; disreputably; shamefully; opprobriously; arrantly; shockingly; appallingly; disturbingly; outrageously; scandalously; boisterously; audaciously; uncontrollably; inherently; deliberately; daringly; naturally; incorrigibly; insufferably; blusteringly; defiantly.

ROYAL

adverbs
magnificently; splendidly; brilliantly; gorgeously; gloriously; imperiously; dominantly; imperially; arrogantly; proudly; authoritatively; absolutely; superbly; grandly; augustly; magnanimously; justly; majestically; sumptuously; munificently; lavishly; extravagantly.

ROYALISTS

adjectives
triumphant; ardent; passionate; staunch; erratic; economic; loyal.

verbs
exterminate—; favor—; inspire—; oust—; overthrow—; repel—; resist—; restore—; —adhere; —advance; —deplore; —flee; —progress; —support; —yield.

(See nobility, aristocracy, peerage.)

ROYALTY (v)

verbs
ascribe to—; assume—; desert—; fear—; imitate—; inherit—; mingle with—; pretend —; profane—; regain—; regard—; relinquish—; support—; suspect—; treat as—; usurp—; worship—; —departs; —functions; —oppresses; —privileges.

(See royalists, monarch, aristocracy, peerage.)

RUB (v)

adverbs
briskly; frantically; industriously; vigorously; mechanically; incessantly; injuriously; maddeningly; furiously; skillfully.

(See polish, massage.)

RUBBISH

adjectives
worthless; dripping; fragmentary; inconceivable; unutterable; intelligent-sounding; hypocritical; delightful; sea-drifted; noxious; mental.

verbs
cart—; cast—; clutter with—; consign to—; dig in—; dispose of—; haul—; heap—; mingle with—; object to—; reject as—; relegate to—; remove—; sweep away—; trample on—; —offends; —reeks; —stains.

(See junk, dust, debris, filth, dirt.)

RUBY

verbs
adorn with—ies; appraise—; blemish—; crust with—ies; cut—; deck with—ies; distinguish—; imitate—; polish—; prize—; set —; tinge—; value—; —blazes; —flushes; —gleams; —glitters; —glows; —sparkles; —ies stud.

(See gem, jewel, ornament, stone.)

RUDDERLESS

adverbs
hopelessly; helplessly; flounderingly; pathetically; desolately; forlornly; woefully; unfortunately; aimlessly; sadly; powerlessly; unhappily.

adverbs

coarsely; ignorantly; bitterly; boorishly; naturally; characteristically; inexcusably; unnecessarily; vulgarly; unintentionally; indefensibly; awkwardly; particularly; contemptibly; inordinately; unwittingly; colossally; shockingly; drunkenly; churlishly; disrespectfully; impudently; mischievously; moodily; morosely; coolly; unpardonably; unpleasantly; disagreeably; deliberately; boisterously; offensively; unconsciously; artlessly; insufferably; innately; unceremoniously.

RUDENESS

adjectives

downright; ineffaceable; apparent; equal; barbarous.

verbs

betray into—; encounter—; forgive—; loathe—; palliate—; pardon—; soften—; subject to—; tolerate—; —appears; —irks; —offends; —provokes; —shames; —springs from; —unveils; —vexes.

(See barbarism, coarseness, disrespect.)

RUDIMENTS

verbs

acquire—; convey—; detect—; drill in—; embellish—; furnish—; inculcate—; ingrain —; instruct in—; master—; pick up—; nourish—; receive—; reduce to—; teach—; tutor in—.

(See knowledge, elements, idea, principles, essentials.)

RUEFUL

adverbs

forlornly; terribly; pathetically; sorrowfully; dismally; desolately; hopelessly; pitiably; drearily; darkly; helplessly; miserably; wretchedly; unspeakably; strangely; distressingly.

RUFFIAN

adjectives

burly; black-looking; solitary; sordid; staring; shy; young; true; malignant-looking; miserable; swaggering; madcap; cowardly; unprincipled.

adverbs

truculently; frivolously; jocosely; boisterously; placidly; violently; deliberately.

(See pucker, wrinkle.)

RUFFLES

adjectives

triple; full; frivolous; atheistic; shirred; hemmed; double-picot.

verbs

arrange in—; draw into—; gather—; iron out—; press into—; smooth—; —adorn; —decorate; —droop; —enhance; —frill; —ornament; —sag; —trim; —wilt.

(See wrinkle, braids, lace, fringe.)

RUG

adjectives

thick; sumptuous; brilliant; luxurious; shaggy; lustrous; reversible; valuable.

verbs

beat—; cushion—; dye—; fold—; pattern—; place—; roll—; shampoo—; tack—; trip over—; weave—; —covers; —protects; —shields.

(See carpet.)

RUIN

adjectives

rambling; picturesque; dustless; temporary; irremediable; financial; dismantled; mossy; calamitous; magnificent; silent; remarkable; undistinguished; smoldering; mental; glorious; partial; treasured; weed-covered; irretrievable; blood-stained; accumulated; wild; reeking; moldering; twisted; hungry; venerable; ivy-wreathed; hideous; final; complete; crumbling; barricaded; fragmentary; unsightly; blazing; dirty; scattered; undecipherable; frowning; majestic; pathetic; chaotic; promiscuous; deathless; piteous; impending; smoking; sudden; graceful; sprawling; private; melancholy; sandswept; stark; gloomy; mournful; hopeless; discreditable; black.

verbs

avert—; batter to—; behold—; brood over —; bury in—; drag to—; drift to—; escape —; expire in—; fall to—; foresee—; hide —; mourn—; prophesy—; reduce to—; reflect—; repair—; rescue from—; restore—;

secure from—; shield from—; speed—; verge on—; —impends; —threatens.
(See defeat, downfall, destruction.)

RUIN, (v)

adverbs

irreparably; miserably; utterly; ruthlessly; ingeniously; traitorously; vindictively; vengefully; irretrievably; irremediably; hideously; calamitously; financially; economically; politically.
(See overthrow, destroy.)

RULE

adjectives

artificial; bayonet; dynastic; brutal; declaratory; invariable; fixed; prescribed; odalisque; stipulated; mistaken; cut-and-dried; military; benign; uncivil; arbitrary; elaborate; melodic; beneficent; ethical; absurd; dictatorial; disciplinary; rigid; capricious; chivalrous; parliamentary; vexatious; drastic; paternal; classical; meticulous; strict; unavoidable; eligibility; violent; aristocratic; supposititious; abstemious; cardinal; orthodox; accepted; general; long; brutal; fundamental; special; redtape; stern; authentic; mob; maiden; enlightened; inflexible; convenient; infallible; profitable; respected; eventful; municipal; sceptral; awful; definite; adequate; unfailing; clogging; ancient; austere; common; operose; vigorous; iron-clad; equitable; inviolable; contradictory; inexorable; conventional.

verbs

abandon—; abide by—s; adhere to—; apply—; ascertain—; chafe under—; challenge —; cleave to—; conform to—; devise—; disregard—; enforce—; establish—; fix—; formulate—; ignore—; impose—; lay down —; liberalize—; memorize—; observe—; prescribe—s; reiterate—; revise—; subject to—; submit to—; sum up—; violate—; yield to—; —decrees; —fetters; —hampers; —prevails; —regulates; —stipulates.
(See ethics, routine, law, decree, formula, fundamental, method.)

RULE (v)

adverbs

imperiously; indomitably; despotically; munificently; cunningly; democratically; implicitly; arbitrarily; capriciously; brutally; conventionally; inexorably.
(See dominate, govern, influence.)

RULER

adjectives

predominant; ruthless; beneficient; incapable; effete; venerated; constitutional; influential; absolute; distant; despotic; discredited; ecclesiastical; sagacious; moneyed; dynastic; unscrupulous; successive (pl).

verbs

acclaim—; advise—; bless—; bow to—; crown—; dethrone—; dictate to—; exile—; ordain—; praise—; trust—; yield to—; — abdicates; —administers; —authorizes; — commands; —controls; —defends; —divines; —heads; —judges; —manages; — respects.
(See king, God, sovereign, dictator.)

RULING

verbs

abide by—; adhere to—; amend—; anticipate—; authorize—; comprehend—; correct —; decry—; ignore—; justify—; manufacture—; post—; presage—; question—; refer to—; sustain—; threaten—; uphold—; warrant—; —decrees; —forbids; —menaces; —prohibits.
(See regulation, announcement, decision, proclamation, amendment.)

RUMBLE

adjectives

confused; formidable; endless; throbbing; subterranean; dull; low; incessant; terrifying; mysterious.

verbs

dull—; emit—; muffle—; prolong—; scorn —; utter—; —arouses; —breaks; —bursts; —clashes; —cracks; —dins; —disturbs; — drowns out; —issues from; —rends; —resounds; —rolls; —travels.
(See growl, roar, echo, noise, thunder.)

RUMBLE (v)

adverbs

portentously; ominously; threateningly; resoundingly; reechoingly; formidably; mysteriously; terrifyingly; incessantly; intermittently.
(See reverberate, resound.)

RUMOR

adjectives

absurd; perennial; malicious; persistent; untimely; hideous; vague; traditionary; convincing; pitiful; faint; insane; wild;

universal; exciting; contradictory; apparent; wildest; dreadful; false; ghastly; painful; splintered; sinister; fake; baseless; scandalous.

verbs
brand as—; bruit about—; buzz with—; confirm—; deny—; discount—; disprove—; explode—; foster—; further—; give rise to—; lend color to—; manufacture—; overshadow—; promulgate—; ridicule—; scotch —; seethe with—; set afloat—; set to rest —; suppress—; track down—; —blossoms; —buds; —carries weight; —circulates; — flies; —gains ground; —grows; —hints at; —menaces; —persists; —seeps out; — spreads; —startles; —suggests.

(See libel, gossip, news, secret, report, lie.)

RUMOR (v)

adverbs
ridiculously; absurdly; perennially; maliciously; persistently; falsely; baselessly; slyly; scandalously; vindictively.

(See circulate, spread.)

RUMPUS
(colloq)

verbs
denounce—; design—; devise—; endure—; loathe—; muffle—; plan—; quell—; restrain —; stir up—; suffer—; suppress—; —disconcerts; —distracts; —diverts; —enrages; —horrifies; —terminates in; —vexes.

(See fight, brawl, quarrel, wrangle, disturbance, fracas.)

RUN (v)

adverbs
refractorily; blindly; obediently; efficiently; deliberately; capriciously; noiselessly; infallibly; smoothly; greedily; spontaneously; tortuously; frantically; riotously; violently.

(See hasten, scamper.)

RUPTURE

adjectives
final; violent; irreducible; sudden; inexplicable; public.

verbs
acquire—; avert—; brace—; complete—; cure—; develop—; excite—; hint at—; incur—; induce—; suffer—; —breaches; —

discloses; —ensues; —severs; —strangulates; —weakens.

(See fracture, discord, dissension, breach.)

RURAL

adverbs
delightfully; charmingly; pleasantly; refreshingly; expensively; invitingly; attractively; advantageously; desirably; gratifyingly; appropriately; conveniently; spaciously; invigoratingly; healthfully; wholesomely; admirably; commendably; enviably; enjoyably; dismally; drearily; inconveniently; undesirably; shabbily.

RUSE

adjectives
innocent; favorite; desperate; ready-witted; clever.

verbs
contrive—; detect—; design—; devise—; elude—; evade—; plan—; plant—; suggest —; —ambushes; —baits; —beguiles; —distracts; —diverts; —ensnares; —lures; — succeeds; —tempts; —traps; —tricks; — waylays.

(See trick, hoax, subterfuge, stratagem.)

RUSH

adjectives
headlong; swift; hectic; precipitate; despairing; violent; blowing; flying; impulsive; engulfing; shrieking; blossomy; trampling; sickening; steady; titanic; madder; furious; pounding; rioting; never-ending; nodding; tumultuous; veritable; memorable; impetuous; recurrent; mighty; soft; chilly; onward; slimy.

verbs
attempt—; avert—; check—; control—; curb—; discharge—; foresee—; halt—; predict—; prophesy—; stem—; —abates; — carries along; —drives; —forces; —impels; —overcomes; —overwhelms; —severs; — strains; —surges; —swells; —sweeps; — traps.

(See attack, charge.)

RUSH (v)

adverbs
tumultuously; deliberately; powerfully; incoherently; blindly; irrepressibly; unceremoniously; impetuously; violently; recklessly; madly; sickeningly; precipitately.

(See press, hurry.)

RUST

adjectives
devouring; killing; protective.

RUSTIC

adjectives
boorish; austere; impudent; honest; patient; egregious; simple.

adverbs
artlessly; shabbily; quaintly; boorishly; bluntly; rudely; clownishly; cheaply; remotely; inconveniently; uncomfortably; undesirably; intolerably; roughly; clumsily; outlandishly; unattractively.

RUSTLE

adjectives
silken; delicate; indefinable; slow; occasional; sad; uncertain; attractive.

verbs
emit—; muffle—; produce—; restrain—; suppress—; —arouses; —attracts; —bestirs; —discloses; —distracts; —disturbs; —falls; —issues; —perturbs; —reveals.

(See sound, hum, murmur, whisper.)

RUSTY

adverbs
ruinously; unserviceably; unusably; horribly; impossibly; dangerously; unfortunately; terribly; singularly; extremely; hopelessly; uselessly; worthlessly; disagreeably.

RUT

verbs
approach—; avoid—; bounce over—; cut—; deplore—; drift into—; erode—; excavate —; groove—; heed—; hollow out—; lumber along—s; pursue—; settle into—; sink into —; wear—; —deepens; —disgraces; —envelops.

(See groove, hole, channel, track, habit.)

RUTHLESS

adverbs
atrociously; viciously; maliciously; vengefully; bitterly; cruelly; barbarously; brutally; ferociously; malevolently; venomously; outrageously; unbelievably; unimaginably; nefariously; wickedly; unutterably; strangely; unaccountably; inherently; terribly; shockingly; appallingly; astonishingly; horribly.

S

adjectives
hilted; gilded; cruel; clashing; gleaming.

SABOTAGE

verbs
accomplish—; advocate—; charge with—; convict of—; disclose—; frustrate—; resort to—; thwart—; uncover—; unveil—; —cripples; —delays; —destroys; —disorganizes; —hinders; —impedes; —injures; —obstructs; —violates.

(See mutilation, destruction, delay.)

SAC

verbs
clog—; dilate—; distend—; impair—; incise —; irritate—; lodge in—; obliterate—; penetrate—; pierce—; rupture—; tap— ;—contracts; —discharges; —encloses.

SACK

verbs
bear—; convey in—; dip into—; emerge from—; forage with—; hoist—; mend—; plunge into—; transport in—; twill—; weave—; —yields.

(See basket, box, case.)

SACRAMENT

verbs
administer—; deny—; observe—; partake of—; receive—; take—; —baptizes; —betokens; —binds; —canonizes; —christens; —confirms; —consecrates; —dedicates; —imposes; —impresses; —obligates; —ordains; —pledges; —promises; —ritualizes; —sanctifies; —seals; —signifies; —symbolizes.

(See ceremony, rite, benediction, matrimony.)

SACRED

adverbs
unutterably; inviolably; personally; universally; traditionally; locally; racially; curiously; inexplicably; affectionately; solemnly; carefully; augustly; impressively; genuinely; nationally; peculiarly; inordinately; **unaccountably; inscrutably; mysteriously.**

verbs
attach—to; blaspheme—; blemish—; despoil —; encroach on—; enshrine in—; esteem—; infringe upon—; mar—; preserve—; revere —; sense—; taint—; tamper with—; venerate—; violate—; —consecrates; —hallows; —glorifies; —secludes; —sets apart.

(See holiness, religion, benevolence, justice, integrity, sanctity, piety.)

SACRIFICE

adjectives
useless; prodigious; vicarious; living; idle; bloodless; fatal; patriotic; willing; personal; ruinous; superstitious; supreme; approaching; fearful; easy; tremendous; enormous; severe; ghastly; dreadful; exposed; inevitable; virtuous; appropriate; unimaginable; necessary; saving; sweeping; deliberate; unprofitable; mock; undue; eucharistic; economic; gratifying; numberless (pl); heroic; searching.

verbs
bemoan—; decry—; dramatize—; entail—; impose—; involve—; modify—; occasion—; offer—; ritualize—; submit to—; suffer—; undergo—; —absolves; —atones for; —compensates; —deifies; —deprives; —exemplifies; —expiates; —hallows; —purges; —purifies; —sanctifies; —sheds; —shrives; —symbolizes.

(See atonement, loss.)

SACRIFICE (v)

adverbs
repentantly; deliberately; economically; heartlessly; wantonly; shamefully; bloodlessly; patriotically; superstitiously; heroically; personally; supremely; fatally.

(See surrender.)

SACRILEGE

verbs
brand with—; commit—; deplore—; —blasphemes; —curses; —defiles; —desecrates; —injures; —insults; —offends; —outrages; —profanes; —reviles; —scandalizes; —violates.

(See sin, crime, vice.)

adverbs

habitually; naturally; inherently; incurably; lonesomely; curiously; unaccountably; heedlessly; inconsolably; inexplicably; awfully; profoundly; anxiously; deplorably; grievously; piteously; pathetically; pensively; ostentatiously; plaintively; dreamily; uncommonly; ominously; strangely.

SADDLE

verbs

break to—; cling to—; cushion—; ease from —; grip—; hop into—; ornament—; pad—; perch on—; polish—; rub—; slip from—; stir in—; straddle—; stud—; sway in—; sweep from—; swing into—; tear from—; vault into—.

(See seat ,chair.)

SADNESS

adjectives

settled; deadly; unmannered; uncultivated; treasured; great; real; simple; lyrical; pensive; inexpressible; wintry; shady; mild; sober; pleasing; unfathomable; unrecumbent; sudden; unbidden; clinging; preposterous; penetrating; thrilling; primeval; tender; good; prophetic; breathed; silent; mortal; humorous; painful; moody; haunting; profound; grateful; quaintest; utter; galling; compassionate; exquisite.

verbs

afflict with—; bow in—; brood in—; dispel —; exude—; incline toward—; induce—; mope in—; occasion—; —dampens; —deepens; —dejects; —depresses; —disheartens; —downcasts; —envelops; —hangs over; — pains; —pervades; —prevails; —racks; — rends; —seizes; —sheathes; —shrouds; — sobers; —touches; —weighs upon; .—wrings.

(See grief, melancholy, homesickness, nostalgia, pathos.)

SAFARI

verbs

equip—; fit out—; gear—; guide—; organize—; outfit—; rig up—; —beats a path; —breaks camp; —explores; —fatigues; — films; —halts; —hunts; —records; —takes the trail; —thrills; —trails; —traverses; — treks; —uncovers.

(See expedition.)

adverbs

fortunately; luckily; happily; thankfully; comparatively; fairly; altogether; reasonably; supposedly; presumably; probably; forever; finally; ultimately; gratefully; relatively; permanently.

SAFEGUARD

verbs

adopt—; dispense with—; employ—; inspect —; offer—; prescribe—; preserve—; promote—; sweep away—; —affords; — bridles; —exempts; —flanks; —insures; — protects; —reassures; —screens; —shelters; —shields; —shrouds; —wards off.

(See guard, protection.)

SAFETY

adjectives

precious; maximum; greatest; inglorious; comparative.

verbs

advance with—; advocate—; afford—; campaign for—; contrive for—; dwell in—; endanger—; engender—; enhance—; foster—; further—; hazard—; heighten—; insure—; jeopardize—; menace—; preach—; promote—; reduce—; risk—; scurry to—; threaten—.

(See security, protection, stability.)

SAG (*v*)

adverbs

concavely; dilapidatedly; hideously; mournfully; partially; weakly; abruptly; markedly; weakly.

(See sink, yield.)

SAGA

verbs

compose—; edit—; narrate—; publish—; relate—; treasure—; unfold—; —depicts; —entertains; —fascinates; —glories in; — honors; —interweaves; —intrigues; —perishes; —portrays; —recites; —recounts; — sings of; —stirs; —grips.

(See adventure, book, story, narrative.)

SAGACIOUS

adverbs

shrewdly; drolly; drily; eminently; dependably; notably; reputably; maturely; unusually; unexpectedly; strangely; coolly; marvelously; admirably; surprisingly; sharply; astutely; keenly; uncommonly; unfailingly.

S
T

SAGACITY

adjectives
superior; strange; clear-sighted; undimmed; shrewd; political; commercial; cool; crafty; mortal; unerring; marvelous; equal; practical; consummate; characteristic.

SAGE

verbs
acclaim—; consult—; venerate—; —counsels; —decrees; —foresees; —foretells; —predicts; —prescribes; —proclaims; —pronounces; —prophesies; —visions.
(See philosopher, scientist, master, counselor.)

adverbs
perceptibly; discerningly; profoundly; shrewdly; reputedly; notably; remarkably; unusually; uncommonly; extraordinarily; estimably; learnedly.

SAGES

adjectives
literary; rapt; puissant; honored; ancient; pungent; blundering; venerable; martyred; dusty; august; life-taught; hoary; erudite; analytical; cautious.

SAIL

verbs
cross—s; distend—; draw—; expand—; hoist—; lash—; lower—; puff out—; reef —; reenforce—; rig—; shorten—; slack—; stain—; strain—; stretch—; strike—; unfurl—; whip—; —billows; —booms; —dips; —droops; —flaps; —flutters; —propels; —shudders.
(See canvas, cloth.)

SAIL (v)

adverbs
peacefully; pensively; majestically; adventurously; prosperously; invincibly; gracefully; longitudinally; deftly; serenely.
(See embark, navigate.)

SAIL-BOAT

verbs
(See ship.)

SAILING

adjectives
emotional; gossiping; deft; smooth; superior; skilled; adept; seaworthy; landlubberly; graceful; accomplished; notable; crowded; intermittent; regular; spasmodic; announced; final; expected.

SAILOR

adjectives
shanghaied; storm-driven; outlandish-looking; swarthy; stray; apparent; sufficient; roistering; unwary; gesticulating; skillful; slow; homesick; roving; practical; drenched; mahogany-faced; stalwart; practised; trained; experienced; dissolute; debauched.

verbs
drill—s; elevate—; maroon—; quarter—s; —charts; —departs; —embarks; —fares; —guides; —mutinies; —navigates; —provisions; —voyages; command—; court-martial—; decorate—.
(See midshipman, soldier.)

SAILS

adjectives
bellying; cunning; swelling; gliding; roaring; snowy; vapory; drifting; flashing; slanting; rising; whitening; winglike; tattered; dead-leaf; slippery; riddled; flapping; torn; noisy; useless; sere.

SAINT

adjectives
criticizing; mounting; imaged; elder; loveliest; sublimest; particular; honored; toiling; felicitous; heavenly; apostolic; propitious; invisible; canonized; shoddy; glorious; beatified; latest; espoused; guardian; mortal; pastoral; mild-eyed; earthly; sentimental; pagan; reviling; lost; martyred; impolluted.

verbs
acclaim—; address—s; canonize—; esteem —; exalt—; glorify—; hail as—; hallow—; honor—; importune—; invoke—s; martyr —; persecute—; placate—s; prostrate before—; reverence—; supplicate—s; venerate—; worship—.
(See God, hero, angel, idol.)

SAINTED

adverbs
recently; devoutly; ceremoniously; ritualistically; deservedly; happily; piously; solemnly; formally; ceremonially; publicly; magnificently; officially; ecclesiastically.

SAINTLY

adverbs

downright; incredibly; drolly; sincerely; punctiliously; piously; ostentatiously; absurdly; unnecessarily; incongruously; excessively; stiffly; genuinely; extraordinarily; comically.

SALACIOUS

adverbs

unnecessarily; disagreeably; unreadably; abominably; detestably; loosely; disgustingly; coarsely; grossly; indecently; dreadfully; inordinately; highly.

SALADS

adjectives

excellent; tempting; crisp; cold; floating; bitter; green.

SALARY

adjectives

picayune; admirable; weekly; meager; terrific; substantial; moderate; tiny; exceptional; scanty; stated; adequate; unearned.

verbs

attach—; deprive of—; draw—; fix—; invest—; reap—; restore—; shear—; slash —; withhold—; —compensates; —fluctuates; —recompenses; —redresses; —remunerates; —rewards.

(See income, livelihood, earnings, wages.)

SALES

adjectives

thrilling; spectacular; periodic; miscellaneous; insignificant; summer; sensational; sluggish; private; dynamic; previous; widespread; current.

verbs

advertise—; advise—; advocate—; balk at —; bolster—; climax—; close—; contrive—; disclose—; double—; facilitate—; force—; interfere with—; jeopardize—; kill—; prohibit—; promote—; push—; restrict—; stimulate—; unearth—; —accelerate; —decline; —diminish; —drop; —dwindle; — ebb; —jump; —rise; —soar; —spurt; — toboggan.

(See trade, traffic, purchase.)

SALESMAN

adjectives

traveling; live; direct; aggressive; real;

well-paid; slick; super-annuated; invaluable; able; unusual; persuasive; well-dressed; suave; sleek; pleasant.

verbs

commission—; drill—; employ—; engage—; organize—; stall—; teach—; train—; — arouses interest; —beguiles; —colors; — convinces; —creates; —demonstrates; — enables; —exhibits; —explains; —interviews; —lures; —markets; —paints; — points out; —pushes; —tempts.

(See employee, clerk, worker.)

SALIVA

verbs

absorb—; convey—; drivel—; drool—; emit—; excrete—; issue—; ooze—; pour out—; remove—; secrete—; slaver—; slobber—; swallow—; —aids; —defiles; — flows; —mixes; —moistens; —sterilizes.

SALLIES

adjectives

erratic; piquant; impotent; brilliant; massed; liveliest; occasional; sudden; futile; hot; outrageous; bitter.

SALONS

adjectives

glittering; philosophical; illegal; artistic; gaudy; gilded.

SALOON

adjectives

gorgeous; gilded; shadowy; luxurious; spacious; decorous; old-time; mirrored.

verbs

abolish—; assemble in—; crowd—; denounce—; frequent—; furnish—; hie to—; license—; line—; maintain—; permit—; renounce—; tax—; wreck—; —clamors; —reeks of; —resounds.

(See tavern, restaurant, inn, hotel.)

SALT

adjectives

insinuating; resultant; solid; valuable; mineral; specific; complex; relaxing; systematic; desolating; insoluble; deliquescent; shrill; atmospheric; iodized; celery.

verbs

add—; apply—; conserve—; dab in—; dash —; dissolve—; export—; imbue with—; immerse in—; impregnate with—; iodize—;

lack—; powder—; prepare—; preserve in
—; refine—; require—; season with—;
spice with—; sprinkle—; —destroys; —influences.

(See mustard, sugar, spice.)

SALTY

adverbs
impossibly; extremely; dangerously; satisfactorily; unnecessarily; bitterly; stingingly;
sharply; unexpectedly; unsavorily; brackishly; disagreeably; impossibly; unpleasantly; unpalatably; rankly; unappetizingly; inexcusably.

SALUBRIOUS

adverbs
invigoratingly; stimulatingly; measurably;
unquestionably; bracingly; usefully; definitely; obviously; manifestly; famously; notably; reputably; undeniably; advantageously.

SALUTATION

adjectives
rude; elaborate; original; friendly; courteous; cordial; mock; boisterous; impressive;
noisy; grateful; murmured; expressive;
pleasant; grim; crude; hearty.

verbs
acknowledge—; condense—; discharge—;
dispense with—; exchange—s; express—;
gain—; greet with—; ignore—; rehearse—;
return—; shout—; word—; —befits; —compliments; —favors; —honors.

(See greeting, kiss, embrace.)

SALUTE

adjectives
obedient; reverential; characteristic; rattling; roistering; royal; noisy; parting;
graceful; sketched; customary; silent; presidential.

verbs
acknowledge—; bestow—; bow to—; conceive—; fire—; give—; greet with—; master
—; perform—; present—; return—; —announces; —compliments; —expresses; —
favors; —honors; —troubles.

(See greeting, kiss.)

SALUTE (v)

adverbs
courteously; formally; cordially; thunderously; respectfully; civilly; vehemently;

gravely; obediently; fraternally; affectionately; obsequiously.

(See hail, greet.)

SALVATION

adjectives
lovely; eternal; certain; promised; rosy;
imaged.

verbs
achieve—; desire—; despair of—; exhort—;
find—; gain—; interfere with—; offer—;
plead—; preach—; prove—; relish—; secure—; seek—; suffer—; venture—; win—;
work out—; —depends on; —opens to.

(See atonement, deliverance.)

SALVE

verbs
apply—; anoint with—; concoct—; daub—;
mix—; smear—; spread—; —comforts; —
consoles; —cures; —eases; —heals; —mitigates; —palliates; —soothes.

(See lotion, balm, liniment, poultice, ointment.)

SAMENESS

adjectives
deadly; long; illusive; very; dull; boring;
repetitious.

SAMPLE

adjectives
original; fair; random; disheartening; odd;
pretty; splendid; generous.

verbs
apply for—; collect—s; examine—; furnish
—; judge by—; match—; obtain—; present
with—; secure—; show—; survey—s; view
—; witness—; —confirms; —illustrates; —
represents; —serves.

(See merchandise, goods, example, specimen.)

SANATIVE

adverbs
commendably; approvedly; acceptably; reputably; exceptionally; assuredly; securely;
conclusively; decisively; demonstrably; conspicuously; successfully; unusually; miraculously; marvelously; unexpectedly; unfailingly.

SANCTIFIED

adverbs

sincerely; piously; devoutly; strangely; suddenly; rapturously; contentedly; serenely; recently; naturally; ecclesiastically; ceremonially; actually; reverently; fervently; solemnly; radiantly; zealously.

SANCTIMONIOUS

adverbs

absurdly; ridiculously; affectedly; ostentatiously; laughably; insincerely; disagreeably; pretentiously; smoothly; blandly; suavely; unctuously; prudishly; pharasaically; hollowly; intolerably.

SANCTION

adjectives

philosophical; express; tacit; highest; pragmatic; legislative; rational; theologic; divine; unequivocal; venerable.

verbs

abolish—s; announce—; invoke—s; lend—; offer—; receive—; regard—; require—; seek—; —allows; —assures; —authorizes; —benefits; —confirms; —encourages; — establishes; —permits; —pleases; —supports.

(See approval, indorsement, confirmation, approbation.)

SANCTION (v)

adverbs

unequivocally; solemnly; expressly; philosophically; tacitly; ecclesiastically; legislatively; beneficently; paternally.

(See approve, conform.)

SANCTITY

adjectives

marital; purest; superior; profound; angelic; quiet; magical; supposed; humorless.

verbs

abrogate—; approach—; assume—; cloak in—; conceive in—; defile—; exhibit—; fame for—; hallow—; honor—; intrude upon—; possess—; question—; retain—; simulate—; tamper with—; translate—; vindicate—; violate—; —decays; —invades.

(See holiness, piety, sacredness.)

SANCTUARY

adjectives

startled; heavenly; ancient; tapering; desecrated; vast; veiled; lifelong.

verbs

admit to—; afford—; crowd—; dedicate—; defile—; dwell in—; embrace—; enshrine in—; expel from—; frequent—; gain—; hallow—; inhabit—; raze—; seek—; unveil —; —consoles; —invites; —protects; — shelters.

(See refuge, immunity, cathedral, church, temple, retreat.)

SAND

adjectives

ribbed; spangling; tinted; unending; milky; drooping; sea-deserted; shifting; pathless; torrid; angry; damp; quick; perpetual; swampy; conniving; silver; sounding; slippery; sun-bleached; restless; drifting; slushy; bituminous; dissolving; auriferous; wrinkled; ruby; dreary; worthless; clinging; treeless; sweltering; coralline; wan; volatile; shallower; parched; sinking; sighing; endless; penurious; tropic; stinging; swishing.

verbs

bury in—; crush into—; elevate—; finger—; heap—; intermix with—; lose in—; overlay with—; plod through—; plough through—; polish with—; precipitate—; shovel—; sift —; trace in—; tread—; wade through—; wrinkle—; —hems; —shifts; —smooths.

(See grit, powder, dust.)

SANDALS

adjectives

placid; ambrosial; winged; tropic; worn.

SANDPIPER

verbs

bog—; decoy—; gun for—; —arrays; — bobs; —booms; —bows; —darts; —defies; —flits; —flutes; —glides; —honks; —patters about; —probes; —sails; —settles down; — soars; —squats; —whirs; —zigzags.

(See bird.)

SANDWICH

verbs

broil—; consume—; devour—; fill—; garnish—; gobble—; lunch on—es; munch—; pack—es; relish—; savor—; serve—; spread —; sup on—es; toast—; —appeals; —refreshes.

(See food.)

adverbs

admirably; usefully; satisfactorily; advantageously; fortunately; grittily; disagreeably; unluckily; ordinarily; unpleasantly; unpalatably; terribly; dreadfully.

SANGUINE

adverbs

groundlessly; unreasonably; overly; cheerfully; absurdly; brightly; optimistically; buoyantly; happily; enthusiastically; unwarrantably; foolishly; confidently; ardently; warmly; earnestly; excitedly; characteristically; naturally; inherently.

SANITARY

adverbs

wholly; satisfactorily; surprisingly; completely; safely; meticulously; carefully; intelligently; adequately; extremely; sufficiently; uncommonly; highly; scrupulously.

SANITY

verbs

approach—; attest to—; derange—; display —; doubt—; enjoy—; forsake—; gain—; guard—; jeopardize—; question—; recover —; restore to—; retain—; return to—; test —; —flags; —languishes; —wanes.

(See reason, knowledge, sense.)

SAP

adjectives

torpid; impregnate; sciential; tasty.

SAPIENT

adverbs

acutely; cunningly; discerningly; perceptibly; sensibly; intelligently; profoundly; reasonably; subtly; pompously; proudly; garrulously; chattily; brightly; jocosely; astutely; slyly; cannily; cleverly; piercingly; sharply; shrewdly; soundly; nimbly; wittily.

SAPLINGS

adjectives

flimsy; round; silvered; spiny; sturdy; bent; twisted; hardy.

SARCASM

adjectives

coarse; chilling; taunting; evident; good-natured; needless; irritating; sweeping; quiet; elaborate; cutting; sneering; juster; mocking; withering; hurtling; keener; pre-

meditated; deadly; biting; mild; veiled; obvious; bludgeoning; savage; shivering; painful.

verbs

employ—; flout—; gird in—; indulge in—; pour forth—; vary—; vent—; temper—; — affronts; —bites; —cuts; —detracts; —embitters; —flays; —insults; —piques; —scars; squelches; —strikes; —taunts; —scathes; — smarts.

(See cynicism, **invective,** mockery, derision, irony.)

SASH

adjectives

tarnished; silken; flaunting; voluminous.

SATCHEL

verbs

check—; clasp—; cram—; dig into—; explore—; guard—; hug—; mislay—; probe —; replenish—; stuff—; tuck in—; — bulges; —contains; —discloses; —swings.

(See bag, baggage, grip, brief-case.)

SATIN

adjectives

lustrous; glossy; shimmering; creamy; gleaming; sheeny; wrinkled; warm.

SATIRE

adjectives

delicate; sharp-pointed; effective; harmless; humorous; scorching; coarse; sober; cosmic; irresistible; shy; genial; deadly; nobler; modest; mild; personal; implied; biting; social; unsparing; scathing; keen; critical; ribald; savage; political.

verbs

aim—at; direct—; employ—; fear—; flash —; interpret—; introduce—; partake in—; resent—; sharpen—; soften—; subject in—; wield—; —amuses; —cuts; —declaims; — denounces; —derides; —exaggerates; —exposes; —jeers; —lashes at; —reproves; — ridicules; —runs riot.

(See irony, jest, joke, mockery.)

SATIRICAL

adverbs

bitterly; cruelly; stingingly; curiously; cleverly; unexpectedly; unnecessarily; scathingly; savagely; derisively; ironically; caustically; contemptibly; boorishly; disagreeably; meanly; unpleasantly; gracelessly; grossly; keenly; brilliantly; effectively.

SATIRIZE (v)
adverbs
spitefully; pungently; ruthlessly; delicately; effectively; comically; bitterly; scorchingly; passionately; politically; socially; diabolically; astutely; acrimoniously.
(See ridicule, lash.)

SATISFACTION
adjectives
relaxing; inexpressible; tolerable; aesthetic; obtrusive; obscure; proud; mutual; partial; subjective; excessive; complete; unspeakable; unbounded; suitable; comfortable; outward; disguised; evident; anxious; fine; phonetic; nostalgic; mirthful; immense; mournful; peculiar; compensating; lasting; enduring; all-around; absolute; elegant; unctuous; sweet; unique; lively; ferocious; melancholy; subtle; smug; inward; grim; cold; unhappy; hearty; elevated; mental; mundane; unconcealed; pecuniary; hauling; unfeigned; rash; physical; wholesome; pleasurable; unmarried; meager; indwelling; paltry; complacent; sinister; deep; lasting; inner; fleeting; unnatural; universal; obvious; drunken; full; solemn; secret; ample; heartfelt; vicarious; internal; permanent; extreme; reasonable; ultimate; keenest; lofty; honest.

verbs
achieve—; afford—; beam in—; conceal—; consume with—; crave—; derive—; demand —; desire—; experience—; express—; feign —; gain—; heighten—; indulge in—; lessen —; offer—; procure—; scorn—; yield—; — results; —soothes; seek—.
(See delight, contentment, gratification, happiness, enjoyment.)

SATISFACTORY
adverbs
highly; charmingly; wholly; genuinely; providentially; luckily; gratifyingly; acceptably; reasonably; vastly; unexpectedly; profoundly; particularly; absolutely; unusually; socially; financially; universally; generally; officially; utterly; entirely; seldom; rarely; scarcely; happily.

SATISFIED
adverbs
completely; perfectly; adequately; sufficiently; utterly; wholly; pleasantly; happily; contentedly; luckily; altogether; comfortably; complacently; easily; serenely; cheerfully.

SATISFY (v)
adverbs
temporarily; amply; abundantly; aesthetically; uniquely; pecuniarily; vicariously; sexually; reasonably; ultimately; keenly; rationally; intellectually; philosophically; lustfully; lasciviously; sensually.
(See appease, gratify.)

SATYRIC
adverbs
horribly; leeringly; foully; evilly; frightfully; hideously; monstrously; repulsively; grinningly.

SAUCE
adjectives
luscious; delicate; unstudied; well-seasoned; inimitable; tasty; sizzling.

SAUCY
adverbs
impertinently; incredibly; incurably; impudently; boldly; prettily; insolently; pertly; grossly; unpleasantly; disrespectfully; oddly; singularly; inexplicably; brazenly; smartly; cheaply; audaciously; flippantly; presumptuously; unpardonably; inexcusably; brashly; discourteously; amazingly; singularly; dreadfully; foolishly; dangerously.

SAUNTER (v)
adverbs
lazily; leisurely; unconcernedly; carelessly; brazenly; boldly; nonchalantly.
(See loiter, linger.)

SAVAGE
adverbs
cruelly; bestially; unbelievably; inhumanly; brutally; ferociously; fiercely; furiously; barbarously; pitilessly; ruthlessly; unmercifully; grossly; relentlessly; wildly; singularly; lawlessly.

SAVAGERY
adjectives
asserted; untamed; absolute; idiotic; genial; degraded; outlying; eternal; methodized; abject.

adjectives

incurable; hostile; primitive; squalid; shiftless; sensitive; naked; brown; superstitious; unchristian; innocent; guileless; malicious; carnivorous; dreadful; livid; rudimentary; untutored; howling; sentimental; splendid; malignant.

verbs

appease—; civilize—; condemn—; encourage—; fear—; incite—; quell—; quiet—; soothe—; tame—; —attack; —beset; — charm; —distress; —guide; —inhabit; — murder; —overtake; —rage; —spare; — stampede; —worship.

(See monster, barbarian, Indian, ferocity, native.)

SAVE (*v*)

adverbs

prudently; judiciously; scrupulously; substantially; phenomenally; spectacularly; privately; unprecedentedly; miraculously; penuriously; rashly; courageously; heroically.

(See rescue, deliver.)

SAVING

adjectives

considerable; great; guaranteed; substantial; systematic; conventional; miraculous; phenomenal; bankable; epigrammatic; unbelievable; additional; important; exciting; tremendous; aggregate; definite; private; valuable; unprecedented; supreme; sensational; extraordinary; spectacular.

SAVINGS

verbs

acquire—; afford—; amass—; apply—to; bequeath—; deplete—; deposit—; effect—; entrust with—; exhaust—; heap—; hoard—; preserve—; put by—; rake together—; retire on—; store—; treasure up—; —accrue; —accumulate; —dwindle; —pension.

(See money, profits, income, earnings.)

SAVOR

adjectives

luscious; sharp; immortal; odious; putrid; lovely; appetizing.

verbs

blend—; destroy—; dispel—; lack—; lose —; perfect—; relinquish—; retain—; —al-

lures; —baits; —beguiles; —departs; — differs; —excites; —relishes; —tempts; — varies.

(See flavor, taste, fragrance, perfume, odor.)

SAY (*v*)

adverbs

plaintively; fiercely; cryptically; artlessly; graciously; tremulously; compassionately; complacently; impatiently; brokenly; casually; hoarsely; ruefully; reflectively; insistently; decisively; unsteadily; consolingly; acutely; deprecatingly; reflectively; roisterously; resignedly; emotionally; passionately; soothingly; involuntarily; wistfully; craftily; sententiously; reassuringly; searchingly; tentatively; doggedly; dogmatically; derisively; exultingly; sardonically; impetuously; musingly; coaxingly; wrathfully; authoritatively; emphatically; triumphantly; candidly; blandly; demurely; naively; impetuously; brusquely; magnanimously; philosophically; bluntly; dubiously; tremulously; sensitively; ostentatiously; insinuatingly; decisively.

(See speak, utter.)

SAYING

adjectives

humorous; skin-deep; magnanimous; faithful; blunt; apt; prudent; sententious; bold; quaint; pregnant; mirthful; well-known; pithy; indiscreet; needle-pointed; witty; dim; deft; true; wise.

verbs

accept—; advance—; amend—; attribute— to; compose—; contradict—; heed—; quote —; recall—; refer to—; —amplifies; — angers; —attests; —emphasizes; —epitomizes; —summarizes; —voices.

(See adage, epigram, quotation, motto.)

SCAB
(*industry*)

verbs

disband—s; lynch—; manhandle—; oust—; prohibit—s; protect—; threaten—; —s offend; —s organize; —rebels; —resists; — troubles; —s unite.

(See striker, rioter.)

SCALES

adjectives

grander; chromatic; glistening; diatonic; extensive; colossal; sordid; stupendous; generous; artistic; lavish; prodigal; elaborate; manifest; glittering; gigantic; diminutive; realistic; defective; adequate; ambitious; industrial; burnished; respectable; miniature.

verbs
collect—; detach—; form—; peel off—; penetrate—; separate—; shed—; strip of—; — armor; —cover; —defend; —enhance; — fall; —overlap; —overlay; —protect; — radiate.
(See flake, film.)

SCALP

adjectives
bare; fearful; transformed; clean; sickly; dry; itching; diseased; scaly.

verbs
adorn—; affect—; apply to—; cover—; crust —; cut—; distend—; heal—; imbed in—; irritate—; lacerate—; massage—; move—; pierce—; rip—; strip—; tear—; wound—; —erodes; —reddens; —tenses; —tingles.
(See head, skin.)

SCAMP

adjectives
slick; premature; pitiful; conscienceless; frolicsome; potential; worthless; wicked; unsocial.

SCAMPER (*v*)

adverbs
hurriedly; swiftly; playfully; boisterously; friskily; joyously; blithely.
(See run, hasten.)

SCAN (*v*)

adverbs
earnestly; anxiously; minutely; industriously; wearily; studiously; critically; eagerly; casually; superficially; desultorily; intently; pedantically.
(See look, distinguish.)

SCANDAL

adjectives
darker; latest; typical; inconspicuous; frightful; amazing; frequent (pl); fantastic; judicial; family; appalling; tea-table; foul; vulgar; flagrant; grave.

verbs
air—; bear—; blaze into—; breathe—; curb —; degenerate into—; despise—; dig up—;

diffuse—; disclose—; discredit—; dissect—; enjoy—; face—; free from—; garnish with —; involve in—; monger—; shroud in—; spread—; wipe away—; —allures; —arises; —damages; —defaces; —defames; —disgraces; —excommunicates; —harms; —injures; —offends; —persecutes; —shames; —shocks; —trickles in.
(See infamy, aspersion, slander, gossip.)

SCANDALOUS

adverbs
unfortunately; openly; uncommonly; arrantly; terribly; shamefully; undeniably; flagrantly; admittedly; highly; regrettably; sadly; deplorably; grossly; notably.

SCANT

adverbs
dangerously; alarmingly; indecently; pitiably; inexplicably; unmercifully; shamefully; curiously; significantly; fearfully.

SCAR

adjectives
honorable; raised; deep; mental; private; frightful; hideous; dreadful; unsightly; fratricidal.

verbs
bear—; expose—; inflict—; jest at—; plaster —; retain—; reveal—; seam with—s; — attests to; —blemishes; —disfigures; — mars; —marks; —proves; —remains; —results from; —sustains; —traces.
(See blemish, defect, flaw, sore.)

SCARCE

adverbs
alarmingly; seriously; critically; locally; universally; lamentably; fearfully; uncommonly; unusually; curiously; unaccountably; inexplicably; inconveniently; miserably; unexpectedly; evidently; deplorably; remarkably; singularly; suddenly.

SCARCITY

adjectives
restful; increasing; definite; chronic; noticeable; dangerous; fearful.

SCARE

adjectives
baseless; wild; sorry; hopeless.

verbs
exaggerate—; foment—; heed—; manufac-

ture—; occasion—; report—; strike with—; work—; —arouses; —fizzles out (colloq.); —overcomes; —seizes; —stimulates; —terrifies; —unnerves; —excites; —fades.

(See fright, terror, fear, dread, anxiety.)

SCARE (v)

adverbs

instinctively; baselessly; unavoidably; agitatingly; dreadfully; abominably; waggishly.

(See frighten, terrify.)

SCARED

adverbs

terribly; shockingly; awfully; irrecoverably; frightfully; unmercifully; cruelly; brutally; desperately; apparently; somewhat; wildly; foolishly; hideously; ignorantly; miserably; heartlessly; secretly; suddenly; mortally.

SCARF

adjectives

flaunting; downy; fluttering; traditional; square; fringed; flamboyant; daring; flashing.

SCATTER (v)

adverbs

profusely; liberally; generously; promiscuously; philanthropically; confusedly; haphazardly; carelessly.

(See separate, dispel.)

SCATTERED

adverbs

widely; pitifully; wastefully; erratically; lavishly; wantonly; fortunately; luckily; sparsely; extravagantly; thinly; thickly; singularly; intentionally; cleverly; diplomatically; profitably; intentionally.

SCENARIO

verbs

alter—; collaborate on—; complete—; compose—; condense—; detail—; draw up—; elaborate on—; fill in—; outline—; purchase —; reject—; rewrite—; sketch—; submit—; —calls for; —depicts; —dramatizes; —portrays; —thrills; —unfolds.

(See story, play.)

SCENE

adjectives

striking; moving; appropriate; painful; pastoral; mad; magnificent; solemn; shameless; sanguinary; sublime; grotesque; ted-

ious; frightful; idyllic; desolate; lively; licentious; dramatic; affecting; decorous; chaotic; animating; hopeful; delicious; brilliant; semi-tragic; violent; passionate; comical; pitiable; circling; martial; distant; enchanting; lofty; remote; novel; mythological; celestial; garish; foregoing; barren; fine; enveloping; cheerless; troubled; riotous; visionary; sylvan; wondrous; convivial; mountain; sunny; powerful; trial; tropical; odious; immediate; binding; classic; picturesque; exquisite; murky; shifting; droll; torturing; grateful; flattering; varied; melodramatic; death-bed; adventurous; squalid; fateful; historic; astonishing; mournful; pirate; pathetic; turbulent; previous; terse; wild; imposing; conspicuous; animated; human; dreadful; memorable; engrossing; realistic; night; impressive; imprisoned; mimic; shocking; pungent; horrible; distressing; harrowing; preliminary; soul-searching; ennobling; fearful; dismal; stirring; rollicking; vivid; agitating; perilous; heroic; touching; awful; renovated; sequestered; strange; trying; toiling; festive; tragic; quaint; singular; universal; monotonous; precarious; verdant; pacific; tranquil; beauteous.

verbs

alter—; applaud—; behold—; cloud—; conceive—; conjure up—; contemplate—; detail —; dispatch to—; dominate—; dramatize—; eavesdrop upon—; enact—; flee—; hover over—; indulge in—; overshadow—; portray—; reconstruct—; reproduce—; retire from—; smirk at—; storm across—; stumble upon—; visualize—; weigh—; —depicts; —drifts; —motivates; —shifts; —takes momentum.

(See aspect, spectacle, view, place, scenery.)

SCENERY

adjectives

picturesque; distant; rugged; salient; impressive; glorious; noble; savage; diversified; quieting; grandiose; monstrous; fascinating; superlative; mountainous; sumptuous; gaudy; animated; admirable.

verbs

admire—; behold—; contemplate—; design —; devour—; enjoy—; feed on—; light—; present—; view—; —affects; —attracts; —awes; —changes; —delights; —enhances;

—enraptures; —enthralls; —impresses; —
inspires; —magnetizes.
(See landscape, scene.)

SCENT

adjectives
foreign; pleasing; floral; alluring; spicy;
faint; delicious; keen; remarkable; patriarchal; chosen; dusty; dry; sweet; delicate;
exalted; lingering; hot; flower; pungent;
cunning; unmemoried; impromptu; dull;
peppery; balmy; pretty.

verbs
abhor—; breathe—; convey—; derive—
from; detect—; discern—; employ—; eschew
—; extract—; follow—; impregnate with—;
inhale—; load with—; lose—; pick out—;
pursue—; recognize—; recover—; seek—;
sniff up—; stimulate—; visualize—; —aids;
—disguises; —indicates; —overwhelms; —
perceives; —permeates; —pervades; —recalls; —rises; —survives; —wanes; —yields
to.
(See essence, fragrance, aroma, odor.)

SCENT (v)

adverbs
instinctively; fragrantly; deliciously; pungently; delicately; brazenly; boldly.
(See perfume.)

SCENTED

adverbs
permanently; odiously; disgustingly; fragrantly; sweetly; exotically; expensively; exquisitely; delicately; opulently; seductively;
alluringly; excitingly; pleasantly; nauseatingly; sickeningly; cheaply; mysteriously;
evanescently; delightfully; cleverly.

SCEPTRE

adjectives
social; pacific; golden; age-old; jeweled;
beauteous; royal; magic.

verbs
bear—; confer—on; entitle to—; govern
with—; invest with—; ornament—; rule
with—; shake—; sway—; swear by—; touch
with—; wield—; —awes; —dignifies; —
empowers; —signifies; —symbolizes.
(See baton, power, staff.)

SCHEDULE

adjectives
preconcerted; rigorous; diverse (pl); fixed;
timed; daily; temporary.

verbs
abolish—; adhere to—; alter—; arrange—;
consult—; discard—; establish—; expand—;
fall behind—; follow—; insert in—; maintain—; map out—; observe—; note—; present—; publish—; refer to—; slash—;
threaten—; throw off—; —regulates; —
sets forth; —specifies.
(See list, calendar, itinerary.)

SCHEME

adjectives
curious; artistic; nameless; recognized; comprehensive; suitable; subtile; beautiful; selling; ambitious; philanthropic; systematic;
ingenious; illusory; unphilosophical; mature; marvelous; impractical; dualistic;
seditious; educational; critical; far-reaching; imperial; iconographic; poaching; dubious; hostile; gigantic; cherished; social;
multiform (pl); elaborate; improvident; decorative; extensive; despotic; rascally; visionary; promising; constructive; wild; speculative; gardening; unbodied; prearranged;
entangled; abominable; interesting; tortuous; iniquitous; rational; ludicrous; extravagant; feasible; generous; well-weighed;
detailed; warm; cheery; perfidious; chimerical; digesting; eternal; desolate; providential; prodigal; cowardly; particular; flying; fantastic; vast; homely; harmonious;
artless; selfish; colossal; bold; notable; advantageous; flimsy; seductive; wonderful;
darling; complicated; shallow; monotonous.

verbs
abandon—; administer—; adopt—; back out
of—; blast—; broach—; commit to—; concoct—; contemplate—; dally with—; demonstrate—; devise—; discern—; foist—upon;
formulate—; fulfill—; further—; immerse
in—; launch—; mature—; mull over—s;
organize—; promote—; prosecute—; puzzle
out—; resurrect—; scrap—; scrutinize—;
seethe with—s; spin—; stymie—; undertake
—; view—; —concentrates on; —goes awry;
—hatches; —intrigues; —unfolds.
(See idea, project, plan.)

SCHEME (v)

adverbs
covetously; traitorously; diabolically; vic-

iously; abominably; extravagantly; chimerically; artlessly; advantageously; systematically; politically; seditiously; tortuously; perfidiously.

(See plan, plot.)

SCHEMING

adjectives

wily; political; amiable; nefarious; wicked; skillful.

adverbs

innocently; mischievously; childishly; pleasantly; mysteriously; secretly; openly; brazenly; maliciously; meanly; cleverly; politically; astutely; adroitly; madly; viciously; criminally; heartlessly; cattily; brutally; dangerously; lovingly; hatefully; successfully; artfully; ingeniously; cunningly; craftily; sharply; slyly; warily; unscrupulously; insidiously; disloyally; treacherously; thoughtfully; prudently.

SCHOLAR

adjectives

learned; elegant; tolerable; potential; distinguished; convent; renowned; eminent; quiet; reserved; brilliant; famous; studious; ivory-towered; absent-minded; profound; reputed; classical; astonished; feeble; famishing; desperate; crude; credulous; facile; austere; advanced; professional; rude; ripe; amiable; painstaking; imaginative; pedantic; competent; able; grammatical; true; refractory.

verbs

discipline—; enlighten—; guide—; honor—; instruct—; reward—; test—; tutor—; train —; —acknowledges; —acquaints with; — attains; —attends; —comprehends; — crams; —embraces; —follows; —inquires; —investigates; —merits; —professes; — searches.

(See reader, student, pupil, disciple, follower.)

SCHOLARLY

adverbs

extremely; amazingly; brilliantly; deeply; profoundly; singularly; eminently; particularly; reasonably; broadly; assiduously; industriously; forbiddingly; abstrusely; alarmingly; splendidly; consciously.

SCHOLARSHIP

adjectives

theological; eminent; profound; deficient; unusual.

SCHOOL

adjectives

vigorous; trivial; hostile; hungering; monastic; cursory; archaeological; law; creditable; fashionable; eclectic; spasmodic; collegiate; skill-contending; elaborate; up-to-date; hard-boiled; realistic; red-brick; immemorial; illustrious; foremost; decadent; haggard; magazine; formal; parochial; consummate; evolutionary; subordinate; toilful; celebrated.

verbs

approve—; attend—; bar from—; disband —; endow—; enroll in—; enter—; exclude from—; expel from—; father—; foster—; found—; graduate from—; impair—; join —; maintain—; rank—; rate—; revisit—; —attracts; —designates; —examines; — flourishes; —prepares; —suspends; — thrives.

(See college, institution, seminary, library, university.)

SCHOOL-BOY

verbs

chastise—; discipline—; enlighten—; examine—; harass—; impress—; oppress—; rebuke—; reprimand—; reproach—; tutor—; —attends; —cheers; —comprehends; —derides; —detects; —enjoys; —s gather; — pens; —romps; —sports; —taunts; —violates.

(See student, pupil, scholar.)

SCHOOLING

verbs

afford—; confine to—; continue—; ignore—; lack—; neglect—; overlook—; profit by—; refuse—; test—; utilize—; value—; —edifies; —enlightens; —grounds; —imbues; — infuses; —instills; —overcomes; —polishes; —prepares; —trains.

(See training, preparation, education.)

SCHOONER

adjectives

splendid; helpless; respectable; dilapidated; coasting; piratical; trading.

verbs
anchor—; becalm—; con—; convert—; convey by—; design—; fit out—; handle—; launch—; navigate—; rig—; steer—; —bears off; —clears; —cruises; —gleams; —graces; —heels; —plies; —ports; —rushes; —sheers; —shoves off; —signals; —skims; —sounds; —tacks; —tosses.
(See boat, launch, ship.)

SCIENCE

adjectives
substantial; principal; adequate; universal; physical; pseudo; mysterious; experimental; practical; laborious; economic; dominant; non-remunerative; biological; kindred (pl); contiguous; astronomical; industrial; spatial; liberal; specific; miracle; profane; systematic; political; grotesque; falsified; deepest; hypnotic; abstract; speculative; occult; intricate; daring; applied; imaginary; sister; pure; auxiliary; mechanical; visionary; various (pl); direct; bloodless; collateral.

verbs
acclaim—; applaud—; apply—; bolster by —; correlate—s; elucidate—; foster—; further—; grapple with—; live for—; pertain to—; suppress—; —contributes to; —contrives; —demonstrates; —dissects; —explores; —flourishes; —investigates; —proves; —pursues; —reveals; —scoffs at; —scorns —surpasses; —sustains; —teaches; —tests; —trains; —utilizes; —voices; —wages a fight.
(See economics, anatomy, psychology.)

SCIENTIFIC

adverbs
carefully; meticulously; accurately; highly; gravely; extremely; necessarily; scarcely; distinctly; profoundly; undeniably.

SCIENTIST

adjectives
heckling; over-impulsive; distinguished; attuned; pure; dissecting; rejuvenated; equipped; enraptured; objective; skilled; famous.

verbs
enrage—; honor—; perplex—s; puzzle—s; —concludes; —considers; —converts; —cultivates; —deduces; —delves; —devotes; —discerns; —discloses; —disputes; —dissects; —envisions; —examines; —fathoms; —

formulizes; —infers; —reasons; —researches; —seeks; —solves; —stresses; —studies; —verifies.
(See naturalist, philosopher.)

SCION

adjectives
dormant; remaining; fiery; illustrious; gentler; decadent; dissipated; royal.

SCISSORS

verbs
grind—; ply—; resharpen—; wield—; —clips; —crops; —dangles; —nicks; —pares; —pieces; —pierces; —removes; —shears; —smooths; —snips.
(See shears.)

SCOLD (v)

adverbs
harshly; pedantically; maddeningly; monotonously; irritatingly; exasperatingly; malignantly; shrewishly.
(See reprimand, lecture.)

SCOLDING

verbs
addict to—; incur—; inflict—; justify—; merit—; relent—; rue—; vent—; —abuses; —bites; —corrects; —curbs; —cuts; —descends upon; —disciplines; —disturbs; —mortifies; —rebukes; —reproaches; —shames.
(See lashing, rebuke, ridicule.)

SCOPE

adjectives
ample; determined; economic; confined; unlimited; gracious; intellectual; international; institutional; plentiful; utmost; unrestricted; free; comprehensive; unusual; unsuspected.

verbs
appreciate—; afford—; ascertain—; broaden —; comprehend—; confine—; desire—; dissipate—; dwarf—; enlarge—; exceed—; extend—; gain in—; limit—; measure—; muse over—; narrow—; question—; restrict—; survey—; widen—; —embraces; —extends; —ranges.
(See limit, range, extent.)

SCORCH (v)

adverbs
superficially; ruinously; hopelessly; carelessly; partially; markedly; obviously.
(See burn, shrivel.)

adjectives

mortal; creditable; voluminous; operatic; trifling; one-sided; brilliant; breath-taking.

verbs

collate—s; compose—; compress—; copy—; distribute—; familiarize with—; mark—; note—; play—; practice—; recall—; rehearse—; strike off—; tabulate—.

(See music, manuscript, account, reckoning.)

SCORE (v)

adverbs

deftly; precisely; accurately; brilliantly; repeatedly; victoriously; creditably; overwhelmingly.

(See record, enter.)

SCORN

adjectives

sullen; compassionate; rising; indignant; ineffable; casual; virtuous; supercilious; helpless; hopeless; merry; revengeful; unconcealed; quiet; tameless; haughty; curious; intolerable; unaffected; languid; tender; triumphant; indescribable; infidel; shameful; profound; defiant; hard; superficial; superior; writhing; bitter; frank; casual; withering; sensitive; mingled; magnanimous; spitting; fine; chivalric; idle; constant; contemptuous; amused; foul; old-fashioned; supreme; ribald; dazzling; womanly; unutterable; unsavory; incredulous; incalculable; contemptuous.

verbs

bristle in—; cloak in—; convey—; deride in —; expose to—; express—; feign—; heap—; imply—; point in—; quiver in—; regard with—; sneer in—; snort in—; submit to—; treat with—; wither with—; —deepens; — grows; —offends.

(See disdain, derision, contempt.)

SCORN (v)

adverbs

theoretically; unutterably; sullenly; indignantly; superciliously; haughtily; intolerably; triumphantly; indescribably; casually; contemptuously; hatefully.

(See reject, disregard.)

SCORNFUL

adverbs

arrogantly; pompously; insolently; unbearably; offensively; youthfully; blithely; ridiculously; ignorantly; significantly; pityingly; unpleasantly; defiantly; learnedly; utterly; thoughtlessly; laughingly; malignantly.

SCOUNDREL

adjectives

unscrupulous; upstanding; infamous; pompous; church-going; blatant; unprincipled; hypocritical; infernal; murderous; remorseless; dissolute; swindling; insolent.

verbs

associate with—; berate—; harbor—; master—; oust—; punish—; regiment—s; rebuke—; reprimand—; shelter—; —degrades; —eludes; —evades; —shocks; — sullies; —tricks.

(See profligate, villian, rogue, criminal.)

SCOURGE

adjectives

national; appointed; dreadful; appalling; inexorable; lifted; controversial; fatal; chastening; penitential; dreaded.

verbs

afflict with—; anticipate—; bemoan—; check—; curb—; cure of—; deplore—; halt —; incur—; lift—; overcome—; prevent—; stamp out—; succumb to—; —befalls; —besets; —destroys; —exterminates; —plagues; —ravishes; —routs; —settles on; —spreads; —wipes out.

(See curse, disease, plague.)

SCOUTING

verbs

discover—; encourage—; engage in—; enjoy—; foster—; found—; instruct in—; perform—; practice—; train in—; venture into —; —conduces to; —drills; —engenders; —offers; —prepares; —teaches; —toughens.

(See athletics, exercise, activity.)

SCOWL

adjectives

envious; unbecoming; slight; swarthy; anxious; sullen; suffering; malignant; fierce; terrific; lowering.

verbs

assume—; cast—; draw into—; exhibit—; gather into—; ignore—; incur—; perpetuate—; receive—; send forth—; —darkens;

—departs; —expresses; —fouls; —glowers; —relents; —sours; —threatens; —wilts; — withers.
(See frown, glare, look, sneer.)

SCOWL (v)
adverbs
morosely; vindictively; bitterly; savagely; threateningly; pugnaciously; belligerently; enviously; sullenly; malignantly; fiercely; rudely; uncouthly.
(See frown.)

SCRAMBLE
adjectives
ethical; wild; persistent; rough; unseemly; exhilarating; nerve-destroying; fearful; noisy.

verbs
decipher—; define—; degenerate into—; interpret—; protest—; regard—; survey—; —confuses; —disorders; —disperses; —displeases; —disturbs; —hampers; —impedes; —perplexes; —upsets; —wanes.
(See rush, struggle.)

SCRAPE
adjectives
unfortunate; typhoid; frequent (pl); tight.

SCRAPS
adjectives
sundry; reminiscent; abject; babbling; infected; disdained; discreditable.

SCRATCH (v)
adverbs
industriously; eagerly; perplexedly; harassedly; composedly; complacently; reflectively; meditatively; uncouthly.
(See scribble, scrawl.)

SCRATCHING
verbs
induce—; necessitate—; weary of—; — annoys; —chafes; —eases; —endangers; —gratifies; —infects; —inflames; —irks; —irritates; —mars; —relieves; —vexes.

SCRAWL
adjecives
unhallowed; blotted; rapid; tragic; anguished; hurried; illegible.

SCRAWL (v)
adverbs
illegibly; laboriously; feebly; crudely; rudely; clumsily; hurriedly; unconventionally.
(See scribble, scratch.)

SCRAWNY
adverbs
dingily; haggardly; pitiably; terribly; inexplicably; decrepitly; horridly; scurvily; sorrily; pitifully; feebly.

SCREAM
adjectives
half-stifled; ear-splitting; feminine; frantic; faint; long; mocking; unearthly; eloquent; inarticulate; defiant; hoarse; sharp; piercing; querulous; shrill; piteous; pretty; multitudinous (pl); pulsating; ecstatic; suppressed.

verbs
emit—; issue—; muffle—; pour forth—; resound with—s; restrain—; silence—; stifle —; suppress—; —alarms; —curdles; — freezes; —lances; —penetrates; —pierces; —rends; —rocks; —shakes; —shatters; — terrorizes.
(See cry, yell, noise, howl, roar.)

SCREAM (v)
adverbs
piercingly; shrilly; madly; frantically; triumphantly; agonizedly; harshly; mockingly; eloquently; ecstatically; piteously.
(See yell, shriek, screech.)

SCREECH (v)
adverbs
dissonantly; insanely; wildly; bestially; hideously; irrationally; shamefully; ribaldly.
(See scream, shriek.)

SCREEN
adjectives
featureless; leafy; costly; omnipresent; mendacious; little; hand; impenetrable; luminous; stubble; theoretical; shadowy; fluorescent.

verbs
contrive—; employ—; fold—; frame—; hinge—; insert—; necessitate—; observe through—; project on—; remove—; view on—; —encloses; —envelops; —guards; —

obscures; —prevents; —protects; —shelters; —shields; —shrouds; —wards off.

SCREEN (v)
adverbs
protectively; effectually; leafily; faithfully; modernistically; coveniently.
(See protect, conceal.)

SCRIBBLE (v)
adverbs
carelessly; unbeautifully; furiously; illegibly; unreadably; crabbedly; grotesquely; characteristically.
(See scrawl, scratch.)

SCRIBBLED
adverbs
weakly; dimly; faintly; coarsely; grossly; childishly; illegibly; crookedly; sprawlingly; finely; clearly; feebly; desperately; hurriedly; hastily; hopefully; eagerly; carelessly; untidily; secretly.

SCRIBE
adjectives
romantic; daily; deft; professional; poison-spirited; capable.

SCRIPT
adjectives
legible; spidery; unfinished; tiny; unreadable.

verbs
abolish—; clarify—; comprehend—; decipher—; decode—; direct from—; form—; imitate—; interpret—; practise—; recognize—; reproduce—; revise—; study—; translate—; —attracts; —awes; —confuses; —differs; —puzzles; —resembles.
(See handwriting, writing, manuscript.)

SCRIPTURAL
adverbs
genuinely; authentically; authoritatively; piously; incontrovertibly; convincingly; persuasively; undeniably; provokingly; unanswerably; formidably; comfortingly; prophetically; highly.

SCRIPTURES
verbs
accept—; attack—; bolster with—; cite—; con—; embody in—; embrace—; employ—; enjoy—; limit—; mark—; memorize—;

mouth—; recall—; refer to—; regard—; review—; study—; —enlighten; —guide; —illuminate; —reveal; —sanctify.
(See Bible, Gospel, writing.)

SCROLL
adjectives
scented; bible; brilliant; talismanic; unsullied; graven; awful; gentle; parchment.

SCRUB (v)
adverbs
scrupulously; diligently; spotlessly; industriously; methodically; ambitiously; tirelessly; vigorously; ceaselessly,
(See rub, polish.)

SCRUPLES
adjectives
weak; conscientious; ceremonious; utmost; immovable; commendable; spiritual; tiresome; religious; desperate; formal; wayward; ceremonial; confirmed.

verbs
avoid—; banish—; cling to—; disregard—; dull—; entertain—; express—; lack—; mold —; overcome—; override—; question—; raise—; shape—; sharpen—; shelve—; silence—; stand on—; tamper with—; —plague; —restrain; —trouble; —weigh upon.
(See qualm. doubt, skepticism, suspicion, hesitation.)

SCRUPULOUS
adverbs
habitually; carefully; dependably; unusually; remarkably; admirably; commendably; highly; vigilantly; laudably; reliably; painstakingly; genuinely; meticulously; honestly.

SCRUTINIZE (v)
adverbs
avidly; critically; intently; cannily; quizzically; keenly; minutely; circumspectly; cautiously; persistently; suspiciously; hostilely; irreverently; boldly; shrewdly.
(See examine, inspect.)

SCRUTINY
adjectives
persistent; prolonged; assiduous; suspicious; terrible; distant; calm; curious; intent; searching; accurate; hostile; critical; sullen;

deliberate; attentive; cool; irreverent; silent; keen; overclose; bold; telescopic; appalling; strictest; shrewd; ignorant; earnest; wondering.

verbs
avoid—; cringe under—; defy—; discard on—; invite—; lead to—; meet—; resent—; sharpen—; stretch—; subject to—; threaten with—; undergo—; —detects; —discloses; —disqualifies; —informs; —reveals; —rewards; endure—; expose to—.
(See look, examination, search, inquiry.)

SCUFFLE

adjectives
rough; momentary; noisy; veritable; violent.

verbs
encounter—; join in—; lament—; subdue in—; —bursts forth; —confuses; —cripples; —disturbs; —ensues; —irks; —irritates; —menaces; —rages; —results in; —roars; —threatens; —upsets; —vexes; —wearies.
(See fight, struggle.)

SCULPTOR

verbs
acclaim—; award to—; criticize—; model for—; pose for—; —adorns; —carves; —chisels; —conceives; —engraves; —executes; —expresses; —finishes; —forms; —hews; —immortalizes; —molds; —shapes.
(See artist, painter.)

SCULPTURE

adjectives
monumental; shapeless; classic; antique; symbolic; mortuary; shadowy; matchless; colossal.

SCULPTURE (*v*)

adverbs
curiously; quaintly; deftly; exquisitely; monumentally; modernistically; bizarrely; intricately.
(See carve, engrave.)

SCUM

adjectives
precocious; muddy; leprous; vulgar; common.

verbs
clear of—; collect—; form—; gather—; purge—; reject—; retain—; sift off—;

strain—; throw off—; work up—; —covers; —films; —floats; —rises; —settles; —thickens; —veils.
(See dross, dirt, debris, filth.)

SCURRILOUS

adverbs
illegally; unpardonably; meanly; maliciously; basely; vulgarly; damagingly; hideously; intentionally; unforgivably; unforgettably; foully; indecently; unnecessarily; vilely; audaciously; boldly; challengingly; tauntingly; opprobriously.

SCURVY

verbs
afflict with—; communicate—; cure of—; ease—; heal of—; remedy—; salve—; suffer from—; —blemishes; —blights; —mars; —scourges; —spreads; —visits; —wipes out.
(See disease.)

SCUTTLED

adverbs
shamefully; ignominiously; secretly; necessarily; finally; desperately; furtively; reluctantly; completely.

SEA

adjectives
fair; boisterous; bland; sterile; sepulchral; savage; motionless; circumfluous; billowy; depraved; turbulent; choppy; coral; shoreless; crystal; glistening; varied; multitudinous (pl); unknown; shimmering; full-toned; homeless; orient; whispering; foaming; rocking; walled; moon-lit; heartless; glassy; sullen; primeval; tideless; wrinkled; insatiate; dense; flowing; undreamed; rough; complaining; unsalted; spacious; calmest; discharged; laughing; tropic; rushing; unfirm; sharp; voracious; wild; abhorred; remorseless; tranquil; treacherous; chainless; illumined; choral; uncanny; dim; leaden; tempestuous; sleeping; raging; troubled; ancient; isolating; throbbing; islanded; arctic; silken; mossy; opaline; empty; whelming; soundless; heaving; slimy; polished; gradual; agitated; murderous; summer; sparkling; plangent; democratic; wondering; lucent; unfathomed; climbing; hoary; intervening; straitened; waveless; arching; corpse-encumbered; misty; unpastured; wan; interlunar; undulating; distant; tossing; molten; full; boiling; unreluctant; peaceful; sandy; terrestrial; neglected; slumbrous; lulled; surging; inward; ugly;

extended; stainless; inviolate; violent; tumbling; careening; hindering; rainy; elongated; moral; winter; spendthrift; changeless; shoaling; rolling; enchanted; azure; delicious; phosphoric; mighty; placid; brilliant; wasting; sunny; pleasant; shivering; windy; abysmal; immemorial; trackless; barren; milky; harmonious; ordinary; narrow; rippling; tinted; incessant; southern; swollen; unresting; stern; limpid; farthest; glad; dancing; haughty; familiar; unstable; invisible; triumphant; rosy; perfumed; incarnadined.

verbs
cast up by—; challenge—; chart—; embark on—; fan—; head out for—; launch on—; plow through—; streak—; traverse—; —allures; —beats against; —bristles; —chastises; —chops; —dashes; —foams; —hems in; —murmurs; —s pile up; —pounds; —pursues; —retreats; —ripples; —rustles; —sighs; —sleeps; —sweeps; —thrashes; —thunders; —whispers; —yields up.
(See lake, ocean, wave, river, surf.)

SEAL
adjectives
dangling; sulphur; violated; experimental; sweet; wax; official; broken.

SEAL (v)
adverbs
hermetically; effectively; mechanically; scientifically; officially; automatically; nominally; legally; bindingly.
(See confirm, attest.)

SEALED
adverbs
hermetically; tightly; completely; successfully; properly; finally; officially; securely; safely; confidently; expertly; sufficiently; satisfactorily; hopelessly; firmly; legally.

SEAMAN
adjectives
distant; broken; disbanded (pl); skillful; proficient; doughty; unimaginative; conscientious; obsequious; groaning.

SEAMED
adverbs
oddly; conspicuously; remarkably; extremely; senilely; frostily; merrily; terribly; deeply.

SEAMS
adjectives
fossiliferous; chintz-welted; innumerable; whitened.

SEAPORT
adjectives
old; drowsy; conspicuous; populous; busy; modern.

SEARCH
adjectives
diligent; preliminary; keen; futile; quiet; breathless; fruitless; unreasonable; evident; deliberate; repeated; systematic; reckless; exhaustive; resolute; protracted; obnoxious; blindfolded; vain; intensive; vague; patient; relentless; superstitious; terrestrial; proposed; personal; narrow; prolonged; studious; frantic; roaming; vigorous; weary; nationwide.

verbs
baffle in—; cease—; conduct—; commence —; devote to—; discontinue—; entail—; enter into—; entrust—to; escape—; instigate —; institute—; justify—; relinquish—; renew—; undertake—; venture on—; weary of—; —ascertains; —consumes; —extends to; —pains; —reveals; —results in; —uncovers; —unearths.
(See examination, exploration, scrutiny, inquiry.)

SEARCH (v)
adverbs
deliberately; diligently; frenziedly; blindly; frantically; intently; rigorously; fruitlessly; cautiously; tirelessly; systematically; recklessly; protractedly; vainly; relentlessly; vaguely; legally; indefatigably.
(See hunt, seek.)

SEARCHING
adjectives
patient; intelligent; laborious; restless.

adverbs
unusually; rigorously; thoroughly; profoundly; uncommonly; rigidly; unpleasantly; heartlessly; inescapably.

SEARCH-LIGHT
verbs
desire—; exhibit—; fit with—; supply—; suspend—; switch on—; —beams; —dazzles; —diffuses; —enables; —exposes; —

facilitates; —flickers; —gleams; —illumines; —pierces; —penetrates; —reflects; —reveals; —signals.
(See light.)

SEASON

adjectives
singing; sickly; glorious; buried; tempestuous; heated; due; ordinary; rainy; favored; sultry; propitious; modish; virtuous; unapparent; festive; winter; holiday; gala; due; faithful; adverse; gentle; true; ominous; pestilential; youthful; beneficent; suitable; advancing; autumnal; convenient; unchanged.

verbs
adapt to—; divide into—s; fill—; inaugurate—; launch—; measure—s; —s alternate; —advances; —clothes; —creeps along; —develops; —drifts by; —fades; —flowers; —lapses; —matures; —s merge; —proceeds; —progresses; —promises; —ripens; —rolls around; —s vary; —waxes.
(See autumn, spring, summer, winter.)

SEASON (v)

adverbs
pungently; deftly; professionally; skillfully; richly; deliciously.
(See flavor.)

SEASONABLE

adverbs
pleasantly; safely; congruously; stylishly; fashionably; reasonably; appropriately; carefully; fastidiously; conveniently; happily; luckily; agreeably; fairly; sensibly.

SEAT

adjectives
proffered; rustic; glorious; battered; pleasant; splayed; favorite; airy; chiefest; princely; storied; regal; supreme; cheap; blissful; dismal; shady; secure; venerable; rural; capacious; luxurious; exalted; imperial; ancestral.

verbs
arrange—s; discover—; emerge from—; fill—s; group—s; mark—; number—s; occupy—; offer—; order—; pad—; proffer—; range—s; relinquish—; reserve—; slump in —; vacate—; wedge into—; —accommodates; —collapses.
(See chair, saddle.)

SEAT (v)

adverbs
musingly; peacefully; airily; cozily; carelessly; abruptly; wearily; drowsily; idly; calmly; rustically; regally; blissfully; exaltedly; imperially; ostentatiously; modestly; demurely; unobtrusively.
(See usher, establish.)

SEATED

adverbs
firmly; gingerly; shakily; nervously; permanently; resolutely; immovably; shyly; timidly; determinedly; finally; primly; demurely; stiffly; gravely; pompously; carefully; respectfully; slouchily; disrespectfully; lazily.

SECESSION

adjectives
successful; timely; foolish; peaceable.

SECLUDED

adverbs
carefully; happily; distantly; completely; pleasantly; comfortably; desirably; terribly; desolately; palatially; unsociably; conveniently; agreeably; inhospitably; delightfully; inexplicably; singularly; curiously; significantly.

SECLUSION

adjectives
obliterating; wearisome; elegant; mummied; dignified; studied; comforting; deep; haughty; bleak; aristocratic; motionless; strict; sweet; utter; tropical; slothful; ascetic; comparative; sullen; torpid; flowery; virtual; sunshiny; blank.

verbs
advise—; advocate—; afford—; attempt—; contemplate in—; emerge from—; enjoy—; gain—; hide in—; interrupt—; meditate in —; offer—; prize—; raise in—; rouse from —; seek—; strive for—; subject to—; —bores; —consoles; —dulls, —stagnates; —disciplines.
(See isolation, loneliness, concealment, retirement, retreat.)

SECOND

adjectives
condemned; supercharged; frozen; significant; reckless; precise; fleeting; precious; recaptured; wasted; breathless.

adjectives

mysterious; enjoined; half-pretended; inviolate; romantic; strictest; indispensable; profound; infinite; tremendous; necessary; sworn.

verbs

delve into—; encroach upon—; intrude upon —; obscure with—; pervade—; pierce—; — fosters; —mystifies; —solaces; —veils.

(See seclusion, privacy, retirement, retreat, solitude.)

SECRET

adjectives

unnecessary; enrapturing; golden; tender; yearning; solemn; terrible; guilty; precious; close-locked; fatal; sublime; effective; minute; open; delicious; damaging; dreadful; mysterious; unrevealed; innocent; priceless; efficient; scientific; ultimate; subtle; treasured; serious; sterile; elfish; grim; divine; curious; shameful; conventual; vital; untold; elemental; unsavory.

verbs

betray—; disclose—; discover—; divulge—; entrust—; explore—; expose—; exult in—; ferret into—; ferret out—; glean—s; guard —; harbor—; hug—; impart—; laden with —s; penetrate—; probe—; pry into—; recount—; rediscover—; rejoice in—; relieve of—; relish—; reveal—; secure—; share—; spill—; take into—; unbosom—; unearth—; unfold—; unlock—; utter—; wheedle—; wrest—from; wring—from; yield—; — breaks; —leaks out; —mystifies.

(See confidence, mystery.)

adverbs

apparently; closely; carefully; profoundly; inviolably; necessarily; dangerously; darkly; pleasantly; mysteriously; deeply; furtively; vexatiously; foolishly; wisely; inscrutably; childishly.

SECRETARY

adjectives

indefatigable; confidential; delinquent; honorary; obsequious; legation; subservient; household; flippant; suave; diplomatic.

verbs

acquaint—; confide in—; depend on—; despatch—; dispense with—; entrust—; pro-

vide with—; —attends; —records; —transacts.

(See assistant, accessory.)

SECRETION

adjectives

nauseating; acrid; animal; pungent; endocrinous; curdy; life-giving.

verbs

deposit—; discharge—; emit—; extract—; furnish—; influence—; inject—; limit—; pour—; stimulate—; suppress—; throw off —; undergo—; —covers; —flows; —emanates; —exudes; —increases; —issues; — oozes.

(See liquid, saliva, bile.)

SECRETIVE

adverbs

curiously; furtively; mysteriously; unpleasantly; unnecessarily; oddly; importantly; absurdly; ridiculously; laughably; foolishly; craftily; extraordinarily; inordinately; unreasonably; senselessly; habitually; fantastically; crazily; morbidly; comically.

SECT

adjectives

persecuted; denominational; dissenting; unresting; reigning; separated; dogmatical.

verbs

attach to—; distinguish—; divide into—s; extirpate—; honor—; found—; originate—; persecute—; profess—; scatter—; test—; — adheres; —believes; —confounds; —deviates; —distracts; —endures; —observes; — banishes; —springs up; —worships.

(See party, religion.)

SECTION

adjectives

fresh; concluding; pointed; elongated; adjunctive; remote; identical; covered; rugged; rural; insurgent; progressive; benighted; geographical; colored; peaceful; pure; omitted; subsequent; luscious; internal.

verbs

break up into—s; combine—s; curtain off—; desert—; designate—; detach—; divide into —s; enlarge—; present—; rate—; split up into—s; unite—s; —constitutes; —s join.

(See division, compartment, department, segment.)

adverbs

entirely; remarkably; financially; reasonably; probably; unusually; extraordinarily; prosperously; fortunately; undeniably; palpably; dependably; reliably; confidently; authentically; happily.

SECURE (v)

adverbs

conditionally; expeditiously; triumphantly; blamelessly; questionably; privately; eventually; legitimately; promptly; fortunately; effectually; financially.

(See gain, obtain.)

SECURITY

adjectives

unfathomable; false; stable; specific; mundane; comparative; fancied; individual; absolute; carnal; imperfect; universal; symbolized; tolerable; proper; reasonable; effectual; foreign; financial; smiling; essential; contented.

verbs

attain—; build up—; dwell in—; enjoy—; evince—; guarantee—; imperil—; insure—; lull into—; maintain—; preserve—; receive —; ruffle—; threaten—; undermine—.

(See impregnability, independence, safety.)

SEDATE

adverbs

gravely; comically; habitually; naturally; pleasantly; priggishly; ridiculously; peculiarly; unusually; properly; modestly; serenely; thoughtfully; calmly; occasionally; forbiddingly; curiously.

SEDATIVE

adjectives

admirable; efficient; bitter; harmful.

verbs

act as—; addict to—s; administer—; employ—; prescribe—; —calms; —eases; — lulls; —mitigates; —palliates; —quells; — quiets; —relieves; —weakens; —soothes.

(See medicine, opiate.)

SEDENTARY

adverbs

disagreeably; unfortunately; monotonously; conveniently; comfortably; harmfully; injuriously; necessarily; providentially; tediously.

SEDGE

adjectives

waving; rustling; bonnet; thick.

SEDIMENT

adjectives

ignoble; dark; useless.

SEDITION

verbs

convict of—; direct—; protest against—; seethe with—; —agitates; —arouses; —disorders; —disparages; —distracts; —disturbs; —incites; —offends; —prejudices; — upsets.

(See treason, disturbance, agitation, commotion.)

SEDITIOUS

adverbs

viciously; desperately; meanly; secretly; vilely; dangerously; alarmingly; powerfully; churlishly; insidiously; furtively; loudly; resentfully; aggressively; actively; openly; audaciously; boldly; influentially.

SEDUCTION

adjectives

vulgar; didactic; deliberate; lulling; invisible.

SEDUCTIVE

adverbs

mysteriously; deliberately; utterly; delightfully; disturbingly; provokingly; intentionally; cleverly; designedly; diabolically; successfully; bewilderingly; amazingly; irresistibly; unquestionably; wondrously; marvelously; unexpectedly; remarkably; surprisingly; coolly; radiantly; joyously; quietly; consciously; tauntingly; tormentingly; overwhelmingly; provocatively; unconsciously.

SEE (v)

adverbs

vividly; graphically: objectively; subjectively; dimly; faintly; distinctly; picturesquely; nakedly; comprehensively; belatedly; previously.

(See view, observe, notice.)

SEED

adjectives

deathless; fruitful; heavenly; worthy; spurting; generous; untainted; true; blind; vigorous; healthy; sanguine; diversified; noxious; alated; degenerate; extensive; foreign; winged; spiritual; germinating; shriveled.

verbs
bear—; bruise—; carry—; implant—; propagate—; scatter—; sow—; —clings; —falls; —flowers; —fructifies; —germinates; —matures; —splits; —springs open; —springs up; —yields.
(See germ, grain.)

SEEDY
adverbs
disagreeably; unpleasantly; decrepitly; sorrily; shabbily; wearily; distressingly; pitiably; miserably; lamentably; deplorably; carelessly; raggedly; wretchedly; unhappily; unusually; unnecessarily; gracelesssly; desolately.

SEEK (*v*)
adverbs
frivolously; sensually; patiently; idly; sedulously; contemptuously; unavailingly; desperately; habitually; persistently; instinctively; contentiously; adventurously; diligently; vainly; aimlessly; scientifically; involuntarily; tirelessly; faithfully; impiously; perseveringly; industriously; obstinately.
(See search, hunt.)

SEEKER
adjectives
frivolous; sincere; tranquil; selfless; inactive; inexperienced; vivacious; sensation.

SEERS
adjectives
profound; pretentious; discomfited; infallible; vegetarian; solitary; statistical; worldly-wise; omniscent.

SEGMENTS
adjectives
decorated; manageable; separated; equal.

verbs
arrange—; compose—; compress—; designate—; divide—; join—; rivet—; unite—; —constitute; —form.
(See section, division, department, part.)

SEGREGATE (*v*)
adverbs
racially; designedly; dictatorially; vicious-

ly; invidiously; seasonally; virtually; diplomatically.
(See isolate, separate.)

SEGREGATED
adverbs
carefully; inhospitably; cruelly; unnecessarily; happily; preferably; mercilessly; significantly; thoughtfully; intolerantly; arrogantly; illegally; undemocratically; uncharitably; perniciously.

SEIZE (*v*)
adverbs
peremptorily; selfishly; impulsively; roughly; rapaciously; greedily; lustfully; diabolically; bestially; unceremoniously; summarily; rudely; uncouthly; desperately; arbitrarily; illegally.
(See snatch, grasp.)

SEIZURE
adjectives
prolonged; epileptic; impending; arbitrary; convulsive; permanent; abrupt; peremptory; illegal; unwarranted.

SELECT (*v*)
adverbs
intelligently; discreetly; painstakingly; arbitrarily; tastefully; variously; fastidiously; ostentatiously; judiciously; exquisitely; infallibly; methodically; legitimately.
(See choose, pick.)

SELECTION
adjectives
marvelous; smartest; extensive; huge; enormous; perverse; customary; dazzling; unusual; noteworthy; careful; judicious; vocational; grand; current; natural; exquisite; unlimited; intelligent; methodical; representative; widest; infallible; artificial; dire; euphuistic; copious; fine; vast; occasional; rapid; conscious; singular; eager; immediate; legitimate; confident; complete; varied.

SELF
adjectives
inmost; past-created; unchanged; progressive; insignificant; whimsical; full-formed; reverend; beautiful; profane; gushing; substantial; piquant; buoyant; perfect; pretended; fancied; malignant; dead; worthless; central; bold; customary; real; gracious; wittiest; sweet; maternal; irregular; tortured; double; forgotten.

SELF-APPRECIATION

verbs

bear—; dissipate—; flush with—; inflate—; inspire—; promote—; puff up with—; resort to—; —contents; —provokes; —rewards.

(See egotism, self-esteem.)

SELF-CONFIDENCE

adjectives

sturdy; brave; youthful; sublime; brash; bright; hard-won; serene.

SELF-CONSCIOUSNESS

adjectives

sharp; perpetual; absurd; puerile; exaggerated; embarrassed; obvious.

verbs

affect—; afflict with—; attain—; blush in—; conquer—; defeat—; dispel—; divert from —; free from—; ignite—; nettle by—; overcome—; plague with—; relinquish—; rout —; simper in—; sweep away—; triumph over—; —absorbs; —affects; —annoys; — hinders; —irks; —provokes; —sensitizes.

(See awkwardness, clumsiness, embarrassment.)

SELF-CONTROL

adjectives

persistent; rigid; systematic; supreme; long-practiced; resolute; wondrous.

SELF-ESTEEM

verbs

alter—; build—; center in—; enlarge—; favor—; flatter—; impair—; lower—; modify—; pique—; polish—; raise—; smite—; value—; —assures; —grounds on; —melts; —overrates; —profits.

(See egotism, conceit, pride, vanity.)

SELFISH

adverbs

incredibly; shamelessly; lazily; incurably; inherently; habitually; naturally; unbelievably; atrociously; thoughtlessly; abominably; cruelly; unforgivably; shamefully; blithely; heedlessly; undutifully; ungrateably; remarkably; arrantly; egregiously; grossly; stingily; arrogantly; sordidly; indolently; uncommonly; unhappily; miserably; grossly; greedily; avariciously; blatantly; openly; curiously; strangely .

SELFISHNESS

adjectives

inconsiderate; blind; intense; enlightened; rigid; obstinate; sordid; willful; cold; debasing; ghastly; overweening; shallow; individual; solitary; petty; sheer; querulous; intelligent.

verbs

censure—; coddle—; conquer—; decry—; foster—; inculcate—; indulge in—; nurse—; practice—; pursue—; overcome—; oppose —; restrain—; route—; screen—; transcend —; —angers; —centers; —concentrates; — covets; —curses; —embroils; —narrows; — pains; —pampers.

(See jealousy, ingratitude, materialism, egotism, cruelty.)

SELF-RELIANCE

verbs

admire—; appreciate—; beget—; breed—; demand—; destroy—; display—; encourage —; engender—; esteem—; evince—; foster —; generate—; implant—; inculcate—; infuse—; instil—; praise—; prize—; smother —; stifle—; urge—; value—; —fortifies; — sustains.

(See confidence, faith, assurance.)

SELF-RESPECT

verbs

betray—; brace—; breed—; debase—; degrade—; destroy—; foster—; heighten—; hoist—; humble—; inculcate—; lower—; maintain—; nurture—; promote—; sustain —; reduce—; value—; weaken—; wound—.

(See pride, vanity, egotism, respect.)

SELF-RESTRAINT

verbs

discard—; esteem—; exercise—; impose—; train in—; value—; —abstains; —binds; — coerces; —checks; —curbs; —declines; — desists; —disciplines; —fetters; —forbears; —governs; —impels; —inures; —moderates; —shackles; —restricts; —tempers.

(See discipline, training, restraint, control.)

SELL (*v*)

adverbs

systematically; professionally; constructively; rationally; profitably; legitimately; irregularly; intelligently.

(See exchange, transfer.)

SELVES

adjectives

gross; glorified; restored; corruptible; deserted; petty.

SEMBLANCE

adjectives

tragic; striking; equal; princely; simple; rare; ghostly; sham; grotesque; airy; figurative; bustling; outward.

verbs

admit—; afford—; ascertain—; assume—; bear—; communicate—; discern—; expose —; furnish—; impart—; maintain—; offer —; recognize—; regard—; reveal—; ridicule—; scrutinize—; sustain—; uncover—; wear—of; —approximates; —burlesques; —caricatures; —copies; —deceives; —mirrors; —parallels; —simulates; —smacks of.

(See appearance, aspect, look, similarity.)

SEMINARY

verbs

enroll in—; father—; found—; —breeds; —cherishes; —cultivates; —disciplines; —enlightens; —equips; —expands; —expels; —flourishes; —fosters; —inculcates; —informs; —infuses; —instructs; —nurtures; —polishes; —prepares; —propagates; —qualifies; —refines; —trains.

(See college, school, institution, university.)

SENATE

adjectives

venerable; complaisant; servile; reverend; venal; strong; popular.

SENATORS

adjectives

energetic; businesslike; influential; odious; easily-influenced; brilliant; lame-duck; independent.

verbs

convoke—; embroil—; impeach—; muster —; support—; —address; —adjourn; —admit; —assemble; —campaign; —confirm; —convene; —demand; —formulate; —legislate; —orate; —propose; —sit; —stampede; —filibuster.

(See legislator, congressman, judge, lawyer.)

SEND (v)

adverbs

swiftly; despairingly; providentially; equitably; expressly; anonymously; simultaneously; tirelessly; incessantly; vigorously; peremptorily; promptly; precipitately.

(See forward, dispatch.)

SENILE

adverbs

terribly; tragically; pathetically; dingily; ridiculously; desolately; rosily; drunkenly; lamentably; crabbedly; feebly; disgustingly; horribly; weakly; degenerately; gracelessly; depressingly; startlingly; woefully; hopelessly; prematurely; mournfully.

SENILITY

adjectives

sheer; sham; self-indulgent

SENSATION

adjectives

enlightening; disagreeable; wonderful; delicious; sinking; buoyant; literary; tingling; satisfying; pleasing; overpowering; formless; void; spry; variable; sparkling; luxurious; burning; queer; beneficent; strong; tremendous; strange; overnight; immense; peculiar; perverted; unique; smashing; prodigious; profound; tactual; creeping; enormous; bright; funny; crazed; broken; refined; horrible; aristocratic; restful; exuberant; stinging; abrupt; curtain; passive; reigning; advertising; inner; tactile; absorbing; outstanding; atrocious; heavy; nervous; wretched; darting; pricking; extraordinary.

verbs

convey—; create—; excite—; derive—; experience—; fan—; illustrate—; impart—; interpret—; inspire—; lower—; jade with —; overshadow—; parade—; perceive—; produce—; retain—; revive—; stir—; transmit—; —agitates; —animates; —arouses; —enkindles; —enraptures; —fascinates; —flushes; —flusters; —galvanizes; —impresses; —infects; —inflames; —infuriates; —intoxicates; —penetrates; —perishes; —perturbs; —petrifies; —pierces; —piques; —overwhelms; —ravishes; —renders; —ruffles; —rushes; —staggers; —startles; —strikes; —warms; —entrances; rekindle—; report—; reproduce—.

(See perception, consciousness, mood, emotion, feeling, sensationalism.)

SENSATIONAL

adverbs

definitely; curiously; intentionally; shockingly; offensively; singularly; undeniably; garishly; wickedly; extraordinarily; downright; cleverly; tremendously; profitably; deliberately; designedly; purposely; adroitly; ingeniously; attractively; dramatically; spectacularly; surprisingly.

SENSATIONALISM

verbs

abominate—; abhor—; addict to—; avoid —; bear—; condone—; detest—; deplore—; dispose toward—; dodge—; eschew—; frown upon—; incline toward—; recoil from—; refrain from—; reject—; shun—; shy from—; —blazons; —cheapens; —corrupts; —defiles; —disgusts; —publicizes; —sullies.

(See notoriety, publicity, sensation.)

SENSE

adjectives

real; miraculous; pleading; evil; indefatigable; cowering; abounding; moral; accommodated; final; soothing; confused; instinctive; crude; vulgar; intuitive; prophetic; exaggerated; dreary; supplementary; aesthetic; helpless; wakeful; superstitious; false; disparaging; practical; deepening; different; unscientific; distinct; inward; common; crushing; artistic; vigorous; corporeal; elementary; glimmering; intellectual; penetrating; cruel; mystical; colder; sterling; surly; strictest; baffled; extravagant; sickening; normal; suffocating; human; secret; dusty; serene; shrewd; automatic; unwitting; insidious; critical; curious; divers (pl); literal; momentary; accretive; mobile; external; exhilarating; genuine; superior; just; dull; seeming; modest; jubilant; cultivated; mysterious; innate; brute; scriptural; academic; imperturbable; half-conscious; delicate; lingering; practical; devout; sobering; pedagogical; magnetic; noisome; leaping; ethnological; renewed; morbid; anguished; realizing; universal; humble; dimmer; rhetorical; subtile; eminent; sardonic; impaired; hazy; pleasant; constant; tacit; painful; stable; jealous; complimentary; puzzled; narrow; uncanny; absorbed; dewy; rigorous; caviling; kennel; boiling; precocious; jaded; blunted; perceptive; untechnical; warring; palpitating; esoteric; dismal;

arithmetical; architectonic; half-dormant; degraded; irresistable; pseudo-pantheistic; nascent; sudden; immanent; plain; wretched; terrible; withering; odious; balancing; apparent; military; dim; symbolic; inborn; reputable; etymological; hypothetical; ineffaceable; eternal; sleepy; inarticulate; pedantic; acquired; implicit; benumbed; solemn; keener; reverted; exterior; lofty; magic; stored; languid; testifying; lively; finer; abstract; social; quibbling; amiable; earnest; material; mobile; offended; sound; exceeding; deficient; due; mechanical; seeing; pathological; receptive; grosser; slumbering; acute; gratified; oppressive.

SENSE (v)

adverbs

intuitively; instinctively; vaguely; uncannily; morbidly; nervously; miraculously; prophetically; secretly; automatically; mysteriously; jealously; precociously; keenly.

(See recognize, perceive.)

SENSE of HUMOR

verbs

cultivate—; derange—; develop—; display —; dull—; exhibit—; foster—; instil—; lack —; necessitate—; pervert—; prize—; require—; treasure—; value—; —eases; —lightens; —responds; —rewards.

(See wisdom, knowledge, ability.)

SENSES

verbs

annihilate—; assail—; awaken—; benumb —; bereave—; blunt—; cultivate—; conquer —; deaden—; deprave—; distort—; doubt —; dull—; educate—; enrapture—; govern —; gratify—; heighten—; inflame—; impair —; injure—; lose—; outrage—; overwhelm —; paralyze—; perceive by—; possess—; purify—; quicken—; refine—; regain—; stimulate—; stir—; titillate—; vex—; —convey; —deceive; —delude; —dictate; —disconcert; —endow; —estrange; —guide; —play; —respond; —stifle; —stray; —swim; —tingle; —conflict.

(See emotion, feeling, sensation, mood.)

SENSIBILITIES

verbs

awaken—; benumb—; blunt—; cloud—; cultivate—; deaden—; discern—; dull—; dwarf—; engender—; lose—; offend—;

paralyze—; perceive—; restore—; revive—; resuscitate—; sharpen—; stupefy—; surrender to—.

(See senses.)

SENSIBILITY
adjectives
quivering; refined; finer; glowing; elegant; profound; natural; tender; delicate; exquisite.

SENSIBLE
adverbs
undoubtedly; scarcely; financially; economically; practicably; solidly; profoundly; usually; stolidly; soundly; substantially; particularly; honestly; thoughtfully; wisely; instinctively; crudely; cruelly; serenely; shrewdly; curiously; dully; imperturbably; pleasantly; painfully; dismally; eminently; remarkably; sincerely; apparently; palpably; evidently; manifestly; highly; altogether; entirely; commendably; laudably; admirably; delightfully; refreshingly; inherently; naturally; innately; discreetly; sagely; gravely; stodgily; odiously; oppressively.

SENSITIVE
adverbs
morbidly; unusually; unreasonably; curiously; oddly; extravagantly; nervously; timidly; shyly; awkwardly; extremely; unfortunately; unnaturally; foolishly; ridiculously; absurdly; deplorably; distressingly; heartbreakingly; preposterously; terribly.

SENSITIVENESS
adjectives
astonishing; pardonable; quivering; morbid; abnormal; fantastic; artistic; overstrained; excessive; infinite; unnatural; emotional; perilous; womanly; feverish.

verbs
dull—; lack—; sharpen—; —pains; —pierces; —prompts; —shocks; —varies; —wrings.

(See feeling, emotion, pain.)

SENSUAL
adverbs
coarsely; basely; grossly; dissolutely; vilely; undeniably; unfortunately; scandalously; broadly; indecently; deplorably; flagrantly; outrageously; utterly.

SENSUOUS
adverbs
keenly; artistically; refreshingly; poetically; enthusiastically; eagerly; appreciatively; responsively; acutely; intensively; quickly; poignantly; avidly; deeply; profoundly; unusually; alertly.

SENSUOUSNESS
adjectives
inert; controlled; rarefied; captivating; rare.

SENTENCE
(*general*)
adjectives
dispossessed; suspended; extravagant; turgid; involved; hurried; merciful; animated; charming; epigrammatic; vigorous; memorable; concluding; incoherent; suggestive; characteristic; functionary; fragmentary; monotonous; lucid; obscure; final; irritable; drastic; angry; incoherent; weird; vibrant; telegraphic; haunting; jerky; dreadful; dumb; childish; swift; stimulating; discreet; scathing; mangled; whispered; favorite; frigid; oracular; appalling; too-lenient; pithy; hard; immediate; consecutive; fresh; slovenly; declarative.

SENTENCE
(*punishment*)
verbs
advocate—; annul—; commute—; deal out —; defer—; execute—; faint at—; impose —; justify—; mete out—; pass—; proclaim —; pronounce—; —binds; —expires.

(See judgment, punishment, justice.)

SENTENCES
(*words*)
verbs
balance—; build—; construct—; declaim—; disclaim—; detach—; embody—; hurl—; mutter—; paraphrase—; quote—; recast—; recollect—; reconstruct—; round—; sum up —; toss—; transcribe—; —pound; —roll; —swing.

(See thought, paragraph, idea, word.)

SENTIMENT
adjectives
affectionate; baseless; filthy; tender; favorable; contradictory; ennobling; growing; mawkish; elevated; incongruous; liberal; enduring; aristocratic; patriotic; frivolous; secret; universal; public; delicate; fresh;

fiery; emotional; poetical; mingled; vague; noble; kindly; recurring; adverse; collective; profane; grateful; delicious; natural; absorbing; vivid; congenial; generous; traditional; buried; maudlin; trivial; warm; creeping; virtuous; humanizing; chivalric; ominous; unaltered; national; pious; exotic; elusive; romantic; artistic; unexpressed; pompous; unexaggerated; altruistic; enduring; detached; silky; potent; heroic; similar; sympathetic; moral; confused; warm; affectionate; false; serious; decisive; contemptuous; fitting; noble; slighting; perpetual; lackadaisical; bombastic; opposite; wintry; endearing; uneasy; stubborn; grandiose; aroused; excessive; muddled; growing; outspoken; pretty; exalted; puerile; minority; masculine; morbid; paltry; reactionary; delectable.

verbs
arouse—; awaken—; check—; communicate—; control—; consummate—; convey—; corrupt—; crystallize—; discard—; echo—; encourage—; express—; gag—; induce—; inscribe—; moderate—; reflect—; sweep—; venerate—; voice—; —blossoms; —blurs; —chills; —defies; —expresses; —falls; —flits; —flowers; —grows; —hangs; —nurtures; —possesses; —reflects; —shifts; —shapes; —solidifies; —swings; —switches; —survives; —veers; —violates; —works.
(See feeling, emotion, tenderness, sentimentality.)

SENTIMENTAL
adverbs
pleasantly; extremely; absurdly; touchingly; incurably; secretly; openly; probably; romantically; feelingly; unusually; somewhat; deeply; profoundly; particularly; ostentatiously; mawkishly; sincerely; genuinely.

SENTIMENTALISM
adjectives
racial; unmanly; romantic; spurious; feigned; western.

SENTIMENTALIST
adjectives
gushing; slobbering; sincere.

SENTIMENTALITY
adjectives
sheer; foolish; posturing; stupid; queer; be-.aying; unnatural; silly; erotic; sallow.

verbs
affect—; appeal to—; avoid—; burlesque—; confess—; depreciate—; detect—; discard—; dismiss—; disparage—; display—; evince—; exclude—; exhibit—; express—; feign—; profess—; reject—; ridicule—; scoff at—; shun—; —complicates; —creeps; —exaggerates; —oozes; —riles (colloq.); —softens.
(See sentiment.)

SENTINELS
adjectives
watchful; dauntless; delinquent; vigilant; cheerful; motionless; faithful; sleeping.

SENTRIES
adjectives
successive; pacing; red-coated.

SENTRY
verbs
address—; appoint—; circumvent—; discharge—; elude—; escape—; evade—; ignore—; lure—; post—; replace—; salute—; shun—; stand—; —abandons; —accosts; —admits; —advances; —alarms; —arouses; —bars; —challenges; —dozes; —escorts; —guards; —hails; —intrenches; —paces; —patrols; —signals; —warns.
(See patrol, guard.)

SEPARATE (v)
adverbs
cruelly; symmetrically; partially; insuperably; formally; nominally; subsequently; legally; permanently; effectually; physically; fatally; inevitably; deplorably; eternally; conventionally; gradually; austerely.
(See sever, divide.)

SEPARATION
adjectives
physical; unavoidable; laborious; uncertain; prolonged; fatal; inevitable; deplorable; eternal; earthly; conventional; gradual; forcible; austere; subsequent; mysterious; compulsory.

verbs
cement—; effect—; endure—; hazard—; propose—; recommend—; —accomplishes; —bisects; —breaches; —disengages; —disjoins; —dismembers; —enforces; —isolates; —jeopardizes; —reconciles; —rends; —sad-

dens; —segregates; —severs; —splices; —sunders; —unleashes; —wrings.

(See exile, divorce, excommunication, departure, seclusion.)

SEPULCHER
adjectives
fair; uncovered; enormous; magnificent; dreamless; august; tenantless; immense.

SEPULCHRAL
adverbs
deeply; coldly; hollowly; darkly; gauntly; dreadfully; alarmingly; woefully; lugubriously; gloomily; miserably; incongruously; inexplicably; curiously; preposterously; absurdly; designedly; terrifyingly; inauspiciously; repulsively; needlessly; terribly; unwontedly; mournfully; bafflingly.

SEQUENCE
adjectives
logical; invariable; melancholy; historical; natural; dramatic; impressive; unusual; fragmentary; consecutive; chronological; true; interminable; rapid; intended; inflexible; honorable; chromatic; passionate; coherent; single; listless.

SERAPH
adjectives
burning; unseen; sinless.

SERENADE
verbs
applaud—; compose—; execute—; perform —; praise—; silence—; sing—; utter—; —arouses; —awakens; —charms; —enchants; —enraptures; —entertains; —expresses; —extols; —moves; —soothes; —stills; —stirs; —thrills; —unfolds.

(See music, song.)

SERENITY
adjectives
conceited; domestic; undisturbed; cloudless; calm; symmetrical; ineffable; celestial; wondrous; stern; sweet; unalterable; supreme; radiant.

verbs
bask in—; bathe in—; bear—; blast—; discompose—; disperse—; disturb—; menace —; recover—; repose in—; threaten—; —

breaks; —dominates; —charms; —composes; —enchants; —pacifies; —radiates; —reconciles; —reigns; —ruffles.

(See calm, complacency, composure.)

SERFDOM
verbs
abolish—; deliver from—; denounce—; emancipate from—; eradicate—; liberate from—; reduce to—; release from—; sink into—; —binds; —debases; —constrains; —enchains; —fetters; —harnesses; —oppresses; —represses; —shackles; —subjugates; —suppresses; —tethers; —tramples; —enslaves.

(See slavery, bondage, servitude.)

SERIES
adjectives
attractive; interesting; stately; well-known; periodical; distinct; regressive; definite; extensive; painstaking; rhythmic; continuous; ingenious; graduated; unbroken; deliberate.

verbs
alternate—; arrange in—; blend into—; break—; chain in—; compile—; construct —; continue—; deliver—; discontinue—; edit—; endure—; engage in—; enumerate —; extend—; file in—; follow in—; grade in—; interrupt—; issue—; join in—; partition—; pen—; prolong—; protract—; publish—; record—; regulate—; relate—; sponsor—; sum up—; tabulate in—; wind in—.

(See row, set, group.)

SERIOUS
adverbs
gravely; critically; extremely; unquestionably; apparently; evidently; manifestly; curiously; secretly; palpably; ominously; portentously; mysteriously; admittedly; oddly; resolutely; decidedly; emphatically; grimly; severely.

SERIOUSNESS
adjectives
conscientious; portentous; unpleasant; nervous; unnecessary; owl-like; touching; especial; melancholy; ironic; sudden; apparent; pitiful; mock; reverential; surpassing.

verbs
abate—; acknowledge—; aggravate—; alleviate—; assuage—; compensate for—; conjecture—; decry—; detect—; determine—;

diminish—; doubt—; estimate—; exaggerate—; heighten—; intensify—; ignore—;
judge—; magnify—; minimize—; mitigate
—; modify—; reflect upon—; recognize—;
—assures; —invades; —sobers.
(See gravity, earnestness, solemnity.)

SERMON

adjectives
extempore; controversial; funeral; soft;
assize; elaborate; erudite; incomparable;
splendid; stirring; sincere; brilliant.

verbs
acclaim—; borrow—; deliver—; design—;
extol—; feed on—s; misinterpret—; prepare—; polish up—; revise—; —bores; —
censures; —declaims; —discourses on; —
edifies; —elucidates; —enlightens; —eulogizes; —exhorts; —expatiates on; —expounds; —guides; —harangues; —inspires;
—moralizes; —rebukes; —reproves; —
thunders; —uplifts; —wearies.
(See oration, address, homily, speech.)

SERMONIZE (v)

adverbs
allegorically; monotonously; paternally;
morally; bombastically; mawkishly; conventionally; turgidly; irritably; animatedly;
epigrammatically; characteristically; religiously; fanatically.
(See compose, preach.)

SERPENT

adjectives
poisonous; fiery; gilt; immense; treacherous; cursed; troubled; traitorous; writhing;
lumbering; belligerent; venomous; monstrous; swollen.

verbs
exhibit—; slay—; —beguiles; —buzzes; —
churns; —coils; —entwines; —glides; —
hisses; —rustles; —sibilates; —spirals; —
stings; —strikes; —struggles; —uncoils; —
undulates; —writhes; —envenoms.
(See dragon, snake, reptile.)

SERUM

verbs
administer—; dilute—; derive—; devise—;
discover—; drain—; employ—; impregnate
with—; infuse—; inoculate—; inject—; introduce—; invent—; prepare—; rush—; —
assists; —checks; —combats; —controls; —
exempts; —generates; —immunizes; —in-

sures; —moderates; —neutralizes; —overcomes; —remedies; —stagnates; —stems.
(See medicine, fluid, remedy, tonic, anti-
toxin.)

SERVANT

adjectives
cloistered; shining; numerous (pl); diligent;
good natured; gracious; primitive; menial;
indentured; authorized; private; confidential; natural; trustworthy; domestic; voluntary; respectful; solitary; stolid; disinterested; faithful; zealous; vile; gentle; assigned;
laden; magnanimous; noiseless; unjust; inattentive; corrupt; public; flowered; natty;
obedient; docile; superannuated; sorrowful.

verbs
bond—; command—; commend—; curse—;
discharge—; dismiss—; employ—; extol—;
humble—; rebuke—; reimburse—; reproach
—; reprove—; retain—; reward—; sack—;
station—; —announces; —attends; —beguiles; —betrays; —devotes; —details; —
enlightens; —humbles; —identifies; —obeys;
—pilfers; —ushers in; reprimand—.
(See matron, slave, assistant.)

SERVE (v)

adverbs
deftly; graciously; whole-heartedly; elegantly; gratuitously; conspicuously; unwittingly;
valiantly; judiciously; indifferently; admirably; exclusively; eminently; generously;
simultaneously; gloriously; faithfully; apathetically; tenderly.
(See deal, distribute.)

SERVICE

adjectives
right; courteous; efficient; thoughtful; unmatched; celebrated; gracious; willing;
flawless; fine; unusual; alert; deft; helpful;
extra; fast; expert; gallant; lip; financial;
insurgent; domestic; unedifying; invidious;
trustworthy; distinguished; meritorious; inestimable; deferred; memorial; typographic;
professional; priestly; peaceful; suitable;
religious; imposing; costly; gratuitous; humblest; valuable; haulage; exalted; gruelling;
maximum; reluctant; economical; perfunctory; abiding; engineering; impressive; essential; thankless; desperate; dependable;
perpetual; honorable; promising; brisk; consecrated; immense; unionized; superior;
committal; disastrous; proffered; beneficial;
table; scant; eminent; civil; diplomatic;

scientific; gloomy; garrison; reasonable; unselfish; surgical; superlative; industrial; imperative; utility; erection; unique; satisfactory; management; continuous; lasting; hazardous; charitable; meticulous; unmenaced; silver; ceremonious; arduous; glorious; solitary; strenuous; specific; secretarial; mutual; hateful; particular; duteous; advisory; supervisory; auxiliary; filial; golden; dependable; prompt; consular; diffused; manifold (pl); musical; meager.

verbs
abandon—; arise in—; attend—; attribute —; bribe—; call for—; command—; conduct —; correlate—; crave—; culminate—; dedicate—; dislocate—; dispense with—; display—; dispose of—; distinguish—; draw into—; engage in—; enlist—; experience—; force from—; induce into—; introduce into —; lay down—; maintain—; modernize—; obligate to—; paralyze—; participate in—; prepare for—; press into—; provide—; regiment into—; render—; review—; reward—; slash—; sublimate—; supplant—; suspend—; terminate—; toil in—; unify—; volunteer—.

(See work, employment, practice.)

SERVICEABLE
adverbs
extremely; undeniably; valuably; helpfully; practically; infinitely; generously; unusually; highly; conveniently; extraordinarily; obediently.

SERVILE
adverbs
obsequiously; disgustingly; pitiably; cringingly; miserably; innately; sickeningly; pitifully; abjectly; unctuously; blandly; basely; humbly; meekly; ingratiatingly; fawningly; subserviently; remarkably; significantly; oddly; inexplicably; unaccountably; openly.

SERVITOR
adjectives
faithful; swarthy; favored.

SERVITUDE
adjectives
penal; involuntary; loving; political; gilded; marital; prisoned; martial.

verbs
abolish—; bear—; betray into—; debase by —; deliver from—; drag into—; free from

—; lead into—; liberate from—; reduce to —; resign to—; sentence to—; subject to—; —degrades; —chains; —enslaves; —expires; —fetters; —harnesses; —shackles; —weighs upon.

(See bondage, serfdom.)

SESSION
adjectives
executive; prolonged; nominal; secret; winter; all-night; plenary; extraordinary; lengthy; fruitless; extra; special.

verbs
adjourn—; attend—; complicate—; conclude —; convoke—; disband—; dismiss—; disperse—; emphasize—; extend—; open—; prolong—; protract—; resume—; wind up —; —administers; —achieves; —accomplishes; —appropriates; —assembles; —convenes; —deliberates; —effects; —formulates; —frames; —legislates; —recesses.

(See court, meeting, conference, assembly, council.)

SET
adjectives
unreasonable; artistic; brawling; unwelcome; gambling; hard-drinking; military; basic; uncut; prosaic; deplorable; intelligent; fair; poisonous; shiftless; social.

verbs
accumulate—; acquire—; associate in—s; arrange—s; classify in—s; collect—; compile—; complete—; compose—; compound —; conclude—; consort in—s; constitute—; create—; cut—; designate—; dispose of—; dissolve—; divide—; effect—; employ—; form—; fuse—; muster—; pair off in—s; procure—; sever—; sort into—s; supply—; weld—; —comprises; —includes.

(See series, group.)

SET (*v*)
adverbs
cunningly; perceptibly; resolutely; grimly; firmly; stubbornly; sternly; ingeniously; illogically; intuitively; primly; obstinately; deliberately; calmly; relentlessly; coquettishly; daintily; partially; courageously; awkwardly.

(See place, establish.)

SET-BACK
verbs
bear—; brood over—; endure—; fear—;

meet with—; suffer—; —abashes; —confuses; —crushes; —dejects; —discourages; —hinders; —humiliates; —impedes; —mortifies; —rebuffs; —relapses; —retards; —retrogrades; —reverses; —weakens.

(See disaster, calamity, mishap, misfortune.)

SETTING

adjectives

irrational; incongruous; atmospheric; half-comic; contemporary; tragic; insensitive; balanced; pastoral; superb; romantic; brilliant; gorgeous; drab; cumbrous; suggestive.

verbs

—assures; —calls for; —confuses; —depicts; —enhances; —extorts; —hinders; —impedes; —implies; —necessitates; —obstructs; —provides.

(See background, scene, environment.)

SETTLE (*v*)

adverbs

traditionally; cozily; sparsely; voluntarily; colonially; permanently; conclusively; mercilessly; satisfactorily; peacefully; amicably; contentedly; thinly; vaguely; prosperously; pecuniarily; arbitrarily; harmoniously.

(See adjust, fix.)

SETTLEMENT
(*colony*)

verbs

abandon—; attack—; attempt—; defend—; desert—; endanger—; establish—; forsake —; fortify—; garrison—; guide—; imperil —; oppress—; plant—; ravage—; reinforce —; rule—; tyrannize over—; —decays; —colonizes; —dwindles; —governs; —flourishes; —languishes; —perishes; —pioneers; —progresses; —prospers; —thrives.

(See colony.)

SETTLEMENT
(*decision*)

verbs

appeal for—; award—; arrange for—; arrive at—; balk at—; conclude—; confirm —; contract—; delay—; denounce—; dictate —; dispute—; effect—; favor—; gain—; hasten—; negotiate—; pledge—; postpone

—; procure—; question—; ratify—; —determines; —disposes of; —grants; —provides for; —stipulates.

(See litigation, compromise, decision, adjustment.)

SETTLEMENT
(*general*)

adjectives

amicable; prosperous; sparse; rapid; pecuniary; ultimate; defenseless; pretty; lasting; flourishing; equitable; arbitrary; scattered (pl); organized; peaceful; stable; separate; speedy; quiet; numerous (pl); sensible; penal; discordant; harmonious; ecclesiastical; parochial; upper; important.

SETTLER

adjectives

important; befuddled; outlying; early; staunch; brave; hardy; pious; first.

SEVER (*v*)

adverbs

permanently; completely; fatally; partially; hopelessly; voluntarily; legally; financially; economically; socially.

(See divide, separate.)

SEVERE

adverbs

harshly; gravely; puritanically; rigorously; rigidly; uncompromisingly; inflexibly; unsparingly; arbitrarily; domineeringly; imperiously; sternly; unmitigatedly; unrelentingly; relentlessly; odiously; atrociously; detestably; tyrannically; haughtily; brutally; needlessly; intolerably; abominably; barbarously; unwisely; senselessly; unreasonably; warrantably; properly.

SEVERITY

adjectives

unjust; uncompromising; stern; unsmiling; inexorable; unrelaxed; exemplary; unbending; extraordinary; mingled; brutal; presaging; intemperate; amused; burlesque; unnecessary; wholesome; hypocritical; righteous; relentless; formidable; calm; clear-cut; merciless; just; unusual; ill-directed.

verbs

abate—; abolish—; accentuate—; acknowledge—; aggravate—; allay—; ameliorate —; apologize for—; assuage—; determine —; ease—; extenuate—; heighten—; ignore —; impose—; increase—; intensify—; judge

with—; magnify—; mitigate—; modify—; palliate—; relax—; relieve—; scrutinize—; vary—; —exacts; —tires; —wears down.
(See cruelty, hardness, harshness.)

SEW (v)
adverbs
domestically; exquisitely; delicately; professionally; habitually; fastidiously; artistically.
(See stitch, fasten.)

SEWAGE
verbs
carry off—; convey—; discharge—; dispose of—; drain—; filter—; wallow in—; —breeds; —contaminates; —emanates from; —fouls; —hatches; —infects; —overflows; —pollutes; —precipitates; —reeks; spreads; —taints.
(See junk, garbage, filth, waste.)

SEX
adjectives
immured; gentle; fragile; inconstant; variable; bewitching; sterner; respective; dominant; grasping; enigmatical; weaker; dependent; deadlier.

verbs
arouse—; characterize—; cloak—; conceal —; debauch—; destroy—; determine—; distinguish—; equalize—s; eulogize—; honor —; pervert—; purify—; respect—; screen —; segregate—s; shroud—; unite—s; — boasts; —claims; —emphasizes; —mystifies.
(See males, women, distinction.)

SHACKLES
verbs
fuse—; liberate from—; rend—; sever—; sunder—; tear—; throw off—; unleash—; weld—; —bind; —burden; —encumber; —frustrate; —hamper; —link; —restrict; —restrain; —torture; —yoke.
(See chain, fetter.)

SHADE
adjectives
thick; cool; melancholy; symbolic; desolate; chequered; odorous; forlorn; deepest; awful; grim; heavenly; thorny; various (pl); numberless (pl); noonday; minutest; venerable; fleeting; solemn; unmoving; exact; consecrated; sullen; tender; tremulous; illustrious; brilliant; translucent; smoky; emphatic; summer; deepening; silent; bashful; evening; tangled; mottled; somber; sprouting; hideous; harmonious; complementary; finer; doleful; religious; grateful; waning; murky; fragrant; mellow; tufted; peaceful; leafy; veiled; vengeful; popular; floating; suburban; stunted; dewy; midnight; natural-looking; beautiful; quivering; reluctant; delicate; cerise; endless; partial; pulsating; pointed; blank; balmy; weltering; imperial; arching; pastel; blending; slender; new; pleasant; smart; wanted; solid; virile; lengthened; plain; popular; rich; exclusive; inviting; welcome; pendent; unexpected; endless; moonlight; implacable; steadfast; monastic; wandering; audacious; blessed; heterogeneous; powerful; disfiguring; lucid; wider; wavering.

verbs
abandon—; afford—; bury in—; gain—; illuminate—; recline in—; repose in—; retire to—; search for—; seek—; welcome—; —curtains; —deepens; —dims; —eclipses; —envelops; —obscures; —overcasts; —screens; —shelters; —shrouds; —veils.
(See darkness, gloom, shadow.)

SHADE (v)
adverbs
dismally; somberly; sullenly; invitingly; coolly; monastically; partially.
(See screen, cloud.)

SHADOW
adjectives
silvery; wandering; magnified; somber; impervious; stupendous; pale; brooding; luminous; gathering; swift; spectral; gentle; misty; lengthening; majestic; grotesque; thoughtful; sudden; protecting; eloquent; mellow; flocking; thin; transparent; tremulous; clear; portentous; monstrous; dappled; opaque; vague; lifelong; walking; gigantic; ghostly; heavy; deepest; magic-lantern; condemning; swimming; grim; gloomy; cool; noble; fantastic; horrible; mysterious; moonlight; twilight; dim; baleful; popular; softest; absurd; skulking; rustling; illuminated; distorted; flickering; haughty; intermittent; dense; violet; shapeless; evening; rosy; empty; translucent; sinister; weird; glimmering; defensive; fitful; ghastly; straight; unnatural; celestial; meager; ambrosial; apotheosized; vaporous; gusty; noisome; shining; slatted; illusive; impalpable; slanting; elongated; transparent; changing; whispering; misty; bold; dread;

veiled; solemn; encroaching; lifeless; thickening; bounding; trembling; houseless; liquid; citron; characteristic; lessening; disturbing; meaner; lank; chiseled; constitutional.

verbs
banish—; cast—; clutch at—; devise—; emerge from—; extend—; grope in—; haunt—; lurk in—; penetrate—; pierce—; repose in—; —blots; —casts; —creeps; —crouches; —dances; —dims; —disintegrates; —eclipses; —encircles; —engulfs; —falls; —flickers; —flits; —hangs; —haunts; —hovers; —hugs; —lengthens; —loiters; —looms; —melts; —plays; —radiates; —retreats; —shifts; —shrouds; —stretches; —trembles; —tosses.
(See shade, ghost, phantom, reflection.)

SHADY

adverbs
refreshingly; gratifyingly; pleasantly; excessively; beautifully; attractively; fortunately; questionably; suspiciously; darkly; invitingly; providentially.

SHAFT

adjectives
serene; granite; spotless; clustering; various (pl); rich; oblique; fluted.

verbs
ascend—; cleave—; descend—; erect—; grasp—; ground—; imbed—; loose—; mount—; sink—; shoulder—; splinter—; straddle—; suspend from—; —bears; —commemorates; —projects; —protrudes; —soars; —supports; —sustains; —towers.
(See column, post, tower, spear, arrow, lance, handle.)

SHAGGY

adverbs
roughly; softly; expensively; pleasantly; naturally; warmly; fashionably; extremely; slightly; beautifully; stylishly; untidily.

SHAKE

adjectives
impressive; impatient; melancholy; solemn; nervous; dubious; significant; respectful; weary.

SHAKE (v)

adverbs
convulsively; nervously; agitatedly; furiously; rudely; violently; negatively; skeptically; energetically; pitilessly; inwardly; pathetically; lustily; viciously; vigorously; sternly; ominously; vehemently; passionately.
(See jar, jolt.)

SHAKESPEARE

verbs
analyze—; commemorate—; criticize—; discuss—; disparage—; glorify—; honor—; idolize—; immortalize—; laud—; perform —; perpetuate—; portray—; revere—; venerate—; worship—; —depicts; —dramatizes; —eternizes; —excels; —lives.
(See literature, artist, poet, creator, dramatist.)

SHAKY

adverbs
tremulously; feebly; weakly; nervously; insecurely; helplessly; hopelessly; desperately; undeniably; obviously; hazardously; perilously; ominously; critically; precariously; forlornly; incurably; infirmly; decrepitly; embarrassingly.

SHALLOW

adverbs
extremely; pleasantly; safely; scandalously; impracticably; desperately; dangerously; obviously; particularly; sufficiently; fortunately; conveniently; unduly; disappointingly.

SHAM

verbs
cloak—; denounce—; discard—; disclose—; divulge—; expose—; fabricate—; uncover —; penetrate—; rebuke—; resort to—; reveal—; suppress—; unveil—; —deceives; —defrauds; —deludes; —disguises; —distorts; —feigns; —imposes upon; —mimics; —perverts; —pretends; —simulates.
(See fake, imitation, deception, counterfeit, hypocrisy.)

SHAME

adjectives
divulged; alluring; sweet; irreparable; maiden; perpetual; conscious; notable; eternal; stinging; sluggish; pure; innocent; passing; burning; penetrative; treble; bashful; sudden; blushing; wounding; virtuous; guilty; tender; murderous; notorious; sec-

ret; ingenious; infernal; deep; passionate; blighting; primal; engendered; earthly; naked; desolate; cherished; disgusting; defiant; tolerated; humble; utter; girlish; villainous; angry; lovely; crying; unvalued; lasting; natural.

verbs
accept—; avenge—; bequeath—; blush in—; bow in—; cloak—; condemn—; cover—; cower in—; cringe in—; deaden to—; disparage—; endure—; evoke—; expel in—; flush with—; hide in—; impute to—; put to —; rid of—; sink with—; slink away in—; suffer—; —blots; —burns; —debases; —defames; —defiles; —degrades; —dishonors; —humiliates; —mixes; —overcomes; —possesses; —scandalizes; —slurs; —stains; —stigmatizes; —sullies; —sweeps; —taints; —tarnishes; —villifies; —disgraces; bring to—.
(See humiliation, disgrace, dishonor, mortification.)

SHAME (v)
adverbs
consciously; viciously; ingeniously; jealously; disgustingly; traitorously; lustfully; vindictively.
(See humiliate, mock.)

SHAME-FACED
adverbs
embarrassingly; sheepishly; guiltily; foolishly; ridiculously; comically; absurdly; unnecessarily; instantly; curiously; significantly; amazingly; modestly; demurely; timidly; fearfully; childishly; awkwardly.

SHAPE
adjectives
vague; graceful; fundamental; sublime; stray; vampire; manifold (pl); imagined; lordly; phantom; ultimate; globular; nobler; streaming; slim; articulate; withered; invisible; various (pl); questionable; uniform; unaccustomed; goodly; delicate; monstrous; expanded; chimerical; clownish; archaic; convenient; cowled; gaudy; false; coarser; uncouth; transitory; prodigious; obscene; execrable; original; orthodox; delusive; lusty; checkered; perfect; glorious; exquisite; stalwart; airy; tangible; dim; minutest; distinctive; oblong; unimagined; quaint; imposing; stately; pillared; elliptic;

gross; human; unique; pigmy; symmetrical; castled; alien; swarthy; habitable; **nameless**; peculiar; frightful; loathly.

verbs
alter—; caricaturize—; define—; delineate —; depict—; determine—; dim—; discern —; disguise—; distort—; draft—; hack at —; hack into—; hew into—; knead—; lick into—; modify—; mold—; obscure—; outline—; pad—; perceive—; regard—; sketch —; twist into—; —assumes; —suggests.
(See figure, feature, form, outline.)

SHAPE (v)
adverbs
adroitly; divinely; deftly; skillfully; professionally; gracefully; delicately; conveniently; conventionally; exquisitely; distinctively; quaintly; elliptically; symmetrically.
(See form, fashion, mould.)

SHAPELESS
adverbs
lumpishly; cumbrously; heavily; grotesquely; carelessly; awkwardly; fantastically; coarsely; grossly; loutishly; gawkily; consciously; hopelessly; pitiably; miserably; wretchedly; curiously; utterly; pathetically.

SHAPELY
adverbs
beautifully; alluringly; perfectly; divinely; seductively; prettily; unusually; remarkably; strikingly; noticeably; conspicuously; attractively.

SHARE
adjectives
ample; proportionate; individual; sufficient; adequate; full; fertile; fair; due; horrid; considerable; major; requisite; insignificant; proper; scanty; eccentric; usual; corresponding.

verbs
accept—; acquire—; adjust—; allocate—; allot—; apportion—; assign—; assume—; bequeath—; claim—; command—; consume —; deprive of—; disclaim—; distribute—; divert—; draw—; forfeit—; issue—; net—; partake of—; procure—; reap—; refuse—; regulate—; retain—; scorn—; usurp—; waive—; —doubles; —drops; —entitles.
(See part, investment, portion, proportion.)

SHARE (v)

adverbs
vicariously; affectionately; profitably; unsparingly; philanthropically; richly; equitably; gratuitously; faithfully; proportionately; adequately.
(See apportion, divide.)

SHARK

verbs
elude—s; repel—s; —s abound; —attacks; —bolts; —devours; —s endanger; —overturns; —plunges; —preys upon; —pursues; —s ravage; —skims; —skulks; —thrashes; —s victimize.
(See whale, fish.)

SHARP

adverbs
maliciously; unnecessarily; deliberately; bitterly; viciously; purposely; hatefully; spitefully; resentfully; venomously; designedly; cunningly; insinuatingly; incisively; antagonistically; needlessly; unwisely; mercilessly; obnoxiously; churlishly; snarlingly; rancourously; unsparingly; bitingly; adroitly; strategically; unwontedly; naturally; subtly; sensibly; schemingly; extremely; alertly; shrewdly; mysteriously; indubitably; obviously; supremely; unexpectedly; infallibly; infinitely; broadly; precociously; sympathetically; astoundingly; sagaciously; politically; cleverly; profoundly; deeply.

SHATTER (v)

adverbs
utterly; devastatingly; ruinously; spiritually; morally; physically; economically; financially; fundamentally.
(See shiver, demolish.)

SHAVE (v)

adverbs
daily; industriously; fastidiously; neatly; cleanly; closely; meticulously; customarily; habitually.
(See cut, clip.)

SHEARS

adjectives
abhorred; sounding; large; sharp.

verbs
apply—; blunt—; edge—; employ—; clip with—; file—; grind—; manipulate—; sharpen—; whet—; —bristle; —curtail; —level; —lop off; —reduce; —shave.
(See scissors.)

SHEATH

verbs
deposit in—; discard—; divest of—; draw from—; enclose in—; ensconce in—; extract from—; penetrate—; pierce—; pluck from —; repose in—; rest in—; withdraw from —; —encases; —encompasses; —enfolds; —envelops; —girds; —houses; —preserves; —protects; perforate— .
(See envelope, case.)

SHEAVES

adjectives
scattered; nodding; ripened; rusted.

SHED

adjectives
battered; nightly; tumbling; rickety.

SHED (v)

adverbs
periodically; seasonally; annually; naturally; normally; wastefully; luminously.
(See discard, cast.)

SHEEN

adjectives
starlight; spangled; dissolving; changing; original; placid; glistening; glorious; wavy; weird; alternate; superb; tremulous; variegated; metallic; dazzling; lustrous; smoky.

SHEEP

verbs
auction—; breed—; clip—; confine—; cross —; domesticate—; fleece—; herd—; market —; shear—; shelter—; slaughter—; tend —; —bleat; —browse; —climb; —graze; — huddle; —pasture; —produce; —ramble; — roam; —secrete; —straggle; —stray; — taint; —flock.
(See lamb, livestock, animal.)

SHEEPISH

adverbs
somewhat; obviously; naturally; naively; blushingly; absurdly; comically; laughably; ludicrously; awkwardly; guiltily; modestly; bashfully; uncomfortably; adorably.

SHEETS
(*general*)

adjectives
cotton; stray; smooth; crisp; winding; bedraggled; tattered; torn; dampened; silver; unintermitting; delicious; loneliest; slumbrous; troublesome; standard; stinging; ghostlike; written.

SHEETS
(bed)

verbs

air—; befoul—; begrime—; bleach—; crease—; deodorize—; disinfect—;˙ dispose of—; flounce—; fumigate—; gather—; hem —; launder—; pin—; plait—; reverse—; roll—; ruck—; ruffle—; rumple—; stain—; smooth—; snuggle in—; sully—; tuck in—; wrinkle—.

(See pillow, cloth, fabric.)

SHELF

adjectives

crowded; empty; pendent; continental; hanging; china.

verbs

adhere to—; bolster—; brace—; deplete—; deposit on—; dislodge from—; disorder on —; elevate—; hoist to—; incline—; lodge on—; prop—; recline on—; replenish—; repose on—; suspend from—; —facilitates; —rocks; —slopes; —sustains; —totters; — supports.

(See ledge, board.)

SHELL
(cannon)

verbs

clinch—; crack—; deflect—; rain—s; —annihilates; —blots out; —bursts; —crashes; —cripples; —demolishes; —detonates; — devastates; —discharges; —dismembers; — effaces; —erases; —obliterates; —plasters; —puffs; —rends; —screams; —sighs; — shatters; —smoulders; —uproots; —whines; —whistles; —whizzes.

(See bomb, grenade, shot, projectile.)

SHELL
(general)

adjectives

curved; fantastic; skimmed; hissing; rifled; awe-inspiring; orchestra; blazing; almond-shaped; veined; withered; crumbling; bivalve; splitting; knife-edged; screeching; chorded; spherical; tainted; sputtering; outgrown; box-like; misgrown; clinging; microscopic; single; solid; glass; bursting; soundless; woody; reflecting; sea; castaway.

SHELTER

adjectives

offered; sacred; solacing; delightful; generous; despicable; treacherous; grateful; hospitable; insufficient; rude; continual; artificial; noontide; respectable; safe; honorable.

verbs

abandon—; afford—; avail oneself of—; deny—; escort to—; expose—; extend—; gain—; grant—; imperil—; jeopardize—; maintain—; obtain—; procure—; retreat to —; scurry for—; secure—; seek—; utilize —; withdraw from—; —nurtures; — screens; —wards off.

(See haven, sanctuary, security, defense.)

SHELTER (v)

adverbs

paternally; faithfully; gratefully; generously; hospitably; artificially; protectively; honorably.

(See defend, protest.)

SHELTERED

adverbs

carefully; extremely; tenderly; unduly; prudishly; protectively; safely; warmly; securely; satisfactorily; duly; grudgingly; hospitably; painfully; comfortably; adequately; affectionately; permanently; insecurely; temporarily; pleasantly; barely.

SHEPHERD

adjectives

faithful; erratic; wandering; boding; homeless.

SHERIFF

adjectives

varlet; burly; brooding; mean.

verbs

authorize—; baffle—; commission—; delegate—; dodge—; elude—; empower—; evade—; frustrate—; perplex—; thwart—; vest in—; —apprehends; —compels; —confines; —deputizes; —enforces; —escorts; — grapples; —implicates; —incriminates; — repossesses; —restrains; —sanctions; — serves; —snares.

(See police, officer, constable.)

SHIELD

adjectives

mirrored; brazen; gilded; caudal; serried; ponderous; bright; protecting; worthless; clanging; dusky; siliceous; heraldic.

verbs
adorn—; batter—; bear—; emblazon—; engrave—; forge—; polish—; split—; —burdens; —protects.
(See badge, emblem, armor, screen.)

SHIFT (*v*)
adverbs
nervously; obligingly; uneasily; restlessly; momentarily; visibly; impatiently; inoffensively; perceptibly.
(See turn, change.)

SHIFTLESS
adverbs
incurably; habitually; constitutionally; inherently; naturally; oddly; curiously; singularly; unpardonably; crazily; offensively; provokingly; audaciously; openly; negligently; foolishly; loutishly; lazily; indolently; untidily; nonchalantly; indifferently; shamefully; grossly; unwarrantably; improvidently; stupidly; senselessly; stolidly; ineptly.

SHIFTY
adverbs
untrustworthily; shamefully; terribly; inherently; naturally; disgracefully; obviously; manifestly; miserably; wickedly; extremely; cleverly; adroitly; notably; notoriously; insidiously; treacherously; dangerously; despicably; contemptibly; artfully; warily; infamously.

SHIMMER (*v*)
adverbs
sparklingly; gloriously; metallically; tremulously; gildedly; brightly.
(See shine, flicker.)

SHIN
verbs
abrade—; bandage—; bare—; bark—; batter—; brace—; bruise—; buffet—; expose —; fracture—; gash—; lacerate—; pad—; rend—; scrape—; shield—; skin—; splinter —.
(See leg.)

SHINE (*v*)
adverbs
serenely; auspiciously; brilliantly; glaringly; perpendicularly; lucidly; radiantly; hazily; luminously; gloriously; goldenly; dazzlingly; feverishly; fitfully; tremulously; majestically; intermittently; fiercely; capriciously.
(See gleam, glitter.)

SHINY
adverbs
attractively; conspicuously; brilliantly; garishly; brightly; gloriously; momentarily; gaudily; unbearably; unpleasantly; gorgeously; proudly; glitteringly; scintillatingly; luminously; phosphorescently; unfashionably; conspicuously; intolerably; admirably; commendably; amazingly; singularly; peculiarly.

SHIP
adjectives
opposing; stratosphere; rolling; advertising; hostile; full-rigged; fearful; turbine-driven; stranded; tempest-winged; ocean-going; expected; blowing; distressed; pursuing; isolated; laboring; embryo; stately; rickety; shapely; specter; cloud; disastrous; myriad (pl); gallant; dismantled; water-logged; butchered; deep-water; whaling; leather-armored; unfortunate.

verbs
abandon—; apportion—; board—; charter —; delay—; drive—; escort—; man—; moor—; navigate—; nose—; propel—; scuttle—; —anchors; —bears; —blows; —bounds; —churns; —crawls; —flounders; —grounds; —lurches; —plies; —plows; —rears; —runs; —sails; —scuds; —shears; —shudders; —sidles; —slithers; —steams; —swings; —tosses; —turns.
(See boat, motorboat, aeroplane, launch.)

SHIP (*v*)
adverbs
seasonally; internationally; expressly; disastrously; promptly; customarily; faithfully.
(See transport, dismiss, send.)

SHIPMENT
verbs
allow—; admit—; authorize—; bear—; charge with—; check—; consign—; convey —; curtail—; dispose of—; exclude—; guarantee—; imperil—; insure—; limit—; obtain —; pledge—; prohibit—; release—; safeguard—; slate—; tax—; transport—; underwrite—; verify—; —burdens; —includes.
(See goods, merchandise.)

SHIRK (*v*)
adverbs
timidly; faithlessly; pusillanimously; basely; meanly; cowardly; ingeniously; falsely.
(See neglect, avoid, evade.)

adjectives

fringed; clammy; foul; higher; homespun; woven; unwearable; ruffled; spotless; sleeveless; pleated; wrinkled; irreproachable; fringed; buckskin; hair; dress; work; shrunken.

verbs

attire in—; damage—; divest of—; doff—; don—; expose—; mend—; patch—; pierce —; rend—; shred—; slit—; starch—; strip off—; stuff—; tatter—; tuck—; vend—; — frays; —shields; —swathes.

(See clothing, dress, garment.)

SHIVER

adjectives

cold; electric; simultaneous; protesting; timid; live; nervous.

verbs

allay—s; calm—s; repress—; restrain—; tremble with—; —agitates; —betrays; — convulses; —disquiets; —perturbs; —quavers; —ripples; —runs; —stirs.

(See sob, sigh, thrill, shudder.)

SHIVER (*v*)

adverbs

involuntarily; coldly; abnormally; timorously; inwardly; ceaselessly; feverishly.

(See shake, tremble.)

SHOALS

adjectives

narrow; dangerous; sable; deadly; treacherous.

verbs

circumvent—; encounter—; escape—; espy —; evade—; extricate from—; discern—; flounder on—; ground on—; risk—; snag on —; sight—; shunt—; —abound; —endanger; —force; —imperil; —jeopardize; —menace; —restrain.

(See reefs, rocks, shore, coast, island.)

SHOCK

adjectives

suggestive; surgical; psychic; paralyzing; overpowering; foaming; immediate; terrific; thundering; surging; unlooked-for; stern; moral; galvanic; dreadful; irresistible; fearful; quivering; rude; feeble; deso-

lating; shivering; shattering; acknowledged; tremendous; harmonious; sudden; jangling; violent; visiting; stunned; physical; sublunar.

verbs

absorb—; attribute—; cushion—; displace —; outweigh—; receive—; subject to—; suffer—; survive—; withstand—; throw off —; —s ensue; —freezes; —galvanizes; — occurs; —persists; —reacts; —recurs.

(See collision, impact, agitation.)

SHOCK (*v*)

adverbs

morally; profoundly; astoundingly; unspeakably; physically; paralyzingly; terrifically; irresistibly; tremendously; violently; surgically.

(See terrify, astound.)

SHOCKED

adverbs

immeasurably; intensely; duly; indignantly; suddenly; terribly; awfully; incalculably; horribly; desperately; alarmingly; appallingly; fearfully; wildly; miserably; perilously; genuinely; manifestly; shamefully; cruelly; irrecoverably; obviously.

SHOCKING

adverbs

tragically; terribly; scandalously; outlandishly; unexpectedly; grossly; unquestionably; oddly; horribly; undeniably; miserably; wretchedly; shamefully; brutally; needlessly.

SHOD

adverbs

daintily; finely; extravagantly; expensively; stylishly; fashionably; incongruously; inharmoniously; crudely; heavily; warmly; insufficiently; coarsely; cloddishly; carelessly; comfortably; wretchedly; miserably; poorly; ridiculously; inadequately; meanly; raggedly; outlandishly; conspicuously; tastefully; well.

SHOES

adjectives

clumsy; capacious; preposterous; patched; silken; russet; worn; well-cut; abusive; sorry-looking; little; sun-baked; spiked; tin; tattered; irksome; nail-clad; battered; flimsy.

verbs

don—; bear—; fashion—; gloss—; hurl—; manufacture—; mend—; polish—; retrieve —; revamp (colloq.)—; sheathe in—; sole —; —compress; —crunch; —nip; —pinch; —support; —squeeze; —torture.

SHOOT (v)

adverbs

accurately; obliquely; involuntarily; professionally; skillfully; fatally; tragically; maniacally; blindly; wildly.

(See fire, discharge.)

SHOP

adjectives

endless; exclusive; garish; desolate; filth-strewn; multiple (pl); inviting; showy; decent; dull; dingy; discriminating; intrepid; out-of-the-way; glittering; fashionable; specialty; matrimonial; dirty.

verbs

clutter up—; enlarge—; equip—; line—; loot—; man—; patronize—; support—; — accommodates; —adjusts; —caters to; — dispenses; —disposes of; —expands; —furnishes; —offers; —prospers; —purveys; — flourishes; —pledges; —retails; —stocks; — thrives; —undersells; —vends.

(See factory, garage, store.)

SHOP (v)

adverbs

voraciously; meticulously; tirelessly; fashionably; daily; gregariously; industriously; enthusiastically; vigorously; insensately.

(See purchase, visit.)

SHORE

adjectives

fading; pebbled; happy; fertile; beaten; swampy; receding; desolate; concave; exalted; far-off; crescent; rocky; sundered; emerald; inhospitable; waveless; dreadful; solitary; sighing; grateful; gloomy; cliff-like; scanty; delicious; shining; smiling; sterile; verdant; lily-lined; melancholy; pastoral; slimy; celestial; treeless; craggy; hoary; lonely; tumbling; accessible; pleasant; crepuscular; laughing; wasting; rival; kindred; upbraiding; sunny; bold; beautiful; chill; distant; furrowed; pitiless; sordid; porous; proximate; cressy; crumbling; friendlier; cheerless; peopled; savage; darksome; teeming; unprotected; changeless; boundless; tranquil; ghostly; mist-

covered; peaceful; rugged; breezy; caressing; lonesome; radiant; spicy; stormless; bloody; imagined; weary; sandy; wintry; arid; perilous; alluvial; heterogeneous; echoic.

verbs

batter—; behold—; blockade—; buffet—; buttress—; coast to—; dash upon—; espy —; explore—; fortify—; frequent—; gain —; hail—; hasten to—; intrench on—; kiss —; maroon on—; pace—; patrol—; plant on—; ramble on—; repel from—; roam—; saunter on—; seek—; skirt—; strive for—; stroll along—; view from—; wash—; win —; —resounds; —tapers.

(See coast, island, beach, shoals, rocks.)

SHORT

adverbs

ridiculously; offensively; delightfully; agreeably; pitifully; disappointingly; relatively; tragically; scandalously; mercifully; wantonly; humanely; unreasonably; dramatically; disgustingly; smartly; inexcusably; characteristically; shamefully; curiously; extremely; remarkably; unconscionably; unpardonably; unexpectedly.

SHORTCOMING

adjectives

intellectual; obvious; spiritual; convenient; pleasant.

verbs

adjust—; atone for—; balance—; betray—; cloak—; compensate for—; condemn—; cope with—; correct—; counteract—; countervail —; denounce—; develop—; discern—; disclose—; divulge—; equalize—; expose—; indicate—; neutralize—; nullify—; overcome—; reconcile to—; redeem—; reproach —; reprove—; reveal—; perceive—.

(See defect, deficiency, failing, failure, imperfection.)

SHORT-HANDED

adverbs

obviously; manifestly; unfortunately; undeniably; lamentably; dreadfully; curiously; admittedly; helplessly; desperately; despairingly; distressingly; painfully; inconveniently; unprofitably; gloomily; sadly.

SHORT-SIGHTED

adverbs

deplorably; unintelligently; formidably; inauspiciously; unforgivably; politically; horribly; despicably; improvidently; foolishly; unhappily; disastrously; ruinously; calamitously; unpardonably; ineptly; hopelessly; irretrievably; lamentably; tragically; sorrily; selfishly; unwarrantably.

SHOT

adjectives
quick; succulent; tender; successive (pl); effectual; candid; chance; sprouting; calamitous; stray; deflected; pelting; native; hostile; scattering (pl); desultory; wondrous; hopeful; pendulous; argumentative; deadsure; steady.

verbs
fill with—; hurl—; pour—; pump—; — beats; —belches; —bombards; —cracks; — fusillades; —nicks; —rains; —reverberates; —ricochets; —spatters; —sprays; —sputters; —streams; —thunders; —wails; — whistles; —whizzes.
(See bullet, shell, gun-fire, projectile, missile.)

SHOULDER

verbs
brush—; huddle—; lower—; shrug—; strengthen—; —dislocates; —droops; — flinches; —humps; —hunches; —inclines; — rubs; —sags; —stoops; —twitches; — wriggles.

SHOULDER (v)

adverbs
courageously; staunchly; vigorously; gallantly; bravely; patiently; reluctantly; stalwartly; promptly.
(See assume, bear.)

SHOULDERS

adjectives
naked; drawn; lofty; weary; careless; bowed; patient; shabby; unworthy; averted; decisive; slim; competent; reluctant; indolent; stooped; drooping; slender; quaking; resolute; dislocated; glorious; glimmering; disproportionate; milk-white; misshapen; ponderous; stalwart; heavy; broad; collective; strapping; submissive; hunched; shining; unresponsive; massive; slouching; willing; artful; half-nude; lurching; glossy; immortal; bony; jutting.

SHOUT

adjectives
faint; confused; unrestrained; clamorous; answering; universal; exultant; joyous; defiant; reckless; unreal; melancholy; gratified; uproarious; tumultuous; derisive; enthusiastic; untimely; windy; lusty; painful; distant; muffled; tiny; incessant; rough; cordial; deferential; blithesome; sporadic; deafening; involuntary.

verbs
muffle—; mute—; raise—; restrain—; stifle —; still—; smother—; —alarms; —arises; —breaks; —deafens; —dims; —s drown out; —entreats; —penetrates; —pierces; — rends; —rings; —resounds; —rouses; — splits; —spurs; —stabs; —startles; —terrifies; —thunders; —weaves.
(See call, cry, yell, shriek.)

SHOUT (v)

adverbs
profanely; turbulently; obstreperously; vociferously; jovially; dramatically; hoarsely; ecstatically; derisively; furiously; impatiently; triumphantly; stentoriously; defiantly; clamorously; recklessly; enthusiastically; roughly; cordially; fraternally; deafeningly; blithesomely.
(See yell, call.)

SHOVE (v)

adverbs
rudely; uncouthly; vulgarly; boisterously; playfully; bullyingly; brutally; carelessly; vigorously.
(See crowd, push.)

SHOVEL

verbs
apply—; brandish—; discard—; employ—; muster—s; scoop in—; till with—; —burrows; —clatters; —cuts; —delves; —discloses; —excavates; —exposes; —gouges; —grates against; —lays bare; —unearths.

SHOW
(colloq)

verbs
acclaim—; applaud—; back—; censor—; conclude—; extol—; finance—; flock to—; hail—; offer—; produce—; render—; review—; revise—; stage—; —beguiles; — draws; —traduces.
(See circus, display, exhibition, play, performance.)

SHOW (v)

adverbs
distinctly; conclusively; vaguely; picturesquely; deftly; negatively; devoutly; conspicuously; adroitly; accurately; unequivocally; ingeniously; photographically; subsequently; reluctantly; ostentatiously; delusively; spectacularly; formidably; imperially.

(See display, exhibit.)

SHOWER

adjectives
genial; fiery; russet; intellectual; frizzling; passing; dewy; honeyed; arrowy; icy; myriad; soft; winking; sprinkling; sulphurous; frequent; gracious; fruitful; distilling; ambient; blinding; shimmering; pelting; rainbow-winged; sunlit; continual; whitening; accidental; dropping; scant; summer; spectacular; vernal; falling; heavy.

verbs
long for—; welcome—; —abates; —chills; —continues; —darkens; —deluges; —diminishes; —gushes; —inundates; —issues; —lets up; —plunges; —streams; —surges; —whirls.

(See rain.)

SHOWER (v)

adverbs
generously; genially; unstintedly; fruitfully; ceaselessly; intermittently; vernally.

(See rain, pour.)

SHOWMANSHIP

verbs
applaud—; proclaim—; —acclaims; —advertises; —attracts; —bandies; —dazzles; —embellishes; —emblazons; —features (colloq.); —flames; —flashes; —garnishes; —glitters; —heralds; —parades; —publicizes; —promulgates; —trumpets.

(See display, exhibition.)

SHOWS

adjectives
kingly; unrivaled; temporal; regional; grouped; ostentatious; brilliant; delightful; brave; giddy; miserable; triumphal; frightful; delusive; hideous; spectacular; venerable; outstanding; sorry; harmless; formidable; glittering; pitiful; master; extensive; tumultuous; idle; elaborate; detestable; farcical; mock; brilliant; shallow; rich; gaudy; gallant; brave; imperious; full; phantasmagoric; spangled; marionette.

SHOWY

adverbs
garishly; ornately; cheaply; miserably; unnecessarily; unduly; disgracefully; tawdrily; grossly; foolishly; stupidly; childishly; gracelessly; elaborately; deceptively; gorgeously; pompously; magnificently; inordinately; delusively; expensively; outlandishly; fantastically; excessively.

SHREDS

verbs
bind—; cement—; convert into—; lacerate into—; pare—; reduce to—; rend into—; sever—; snatch—; snip—; tatter into—; tear to—; wear to—.

(See fragment, pieces.)

SHREW

adjectives
chirping; aquatic; occasional; ferret; curst; humorous; noisy; blatant; clamant; raucous.

SHREWD

adverbs
suavely; infinitely; uncannily; adroitly; cleverly; subtly; urbanely; artfully; designingly; slyly; insidiously; dangerously; admirably; practically; commercially; alarmingly; extremely; astoundingly; singularly; thoughtfully; profoundly; precociously; obviously; amazingly; unexpectedly; socially; deliberately; politically; sagaciously; cautiously; wisely; invariably; habitually; customarily; astutely; deftly.

SHREWDNESS

adjectives
infinite; uncanny; apparent; cynical; suave.

verbs
acquire—; ascertain—; commend—; contrive with—; cultivate—; demand—; develop—; discern—; exercise—; gain—; inherit —; intensify—; lack—; mark—; parallel—; penetrate—; recognize—; respect—; reveal —; value—; —dazzles; —discriminates; —endows; —foresees; —impresses; —qualifies.

(See diplomacy, tact, skill, ingenuity.)

SHREWISH

adverbs
disagreeably; scurrilously; scandalously; unpleasantly; intolerably; unbearably; poignantly; sarcastically; unbelievably; notoriously; inexcusably; outlandishly; infamous-

ly; inordinately; despicably; contemptibly; abominably; trenchantly; particularly; brutally; scorchingly; cruelly; bitterly; mercilessly.

SHRIEK

adjectives
vehement; myriad; wailing; hilarious; faint; passionate; inquiring; shrill; piercing; loud; unrestrained; great; long; ghastly; sensational; frantic; delirious; discordant; piteous; demoniacal.

verbs
drown out—; emit—; muffle—; restrain—; stifle—; utter—; —alarms; —chills; —curdles; —echoes; —harrows; —penetrates; —petrifies; —pierces; —rends; —resounds; —rings; —rouses; —smothers; —splits; —startles; —unnerves.
(See cry, shout, call, yell.)

SHRIEK (v)

adverbs
agonizingly; heartrendingly; imperatively; stridently; shrewishly; vehemently; passionately; unrestrainedly; piteously; discordantly; demoniacally.
(See yell, scream.)

SHRILL

adverbs
piercingly; cuttingly; alarmingly; horribly; murderously; intolerably; fearfully; incredibly; horridly; raucously; suddenly; contemptibly; disagreeably; naturally; incurably; desperately; cruelly; undisguisedly; deliberately; designedly; purposely; meanly; penetratingly; sharply.

SHRINE

adjectives
popular; tourist; despoiled; innumerable (pl); unhallowed; mysterious; desecrated; veritable; haunted; exploited; cherished; celebrated; echoing; secret; competing; wayside; nameless; inmost; fragrant; happy; gloomy; unrivaled; miraculous.

verbs
abandon—; banish from—; bar from—; consecrate—; contaminate—; convert into —; dedicate—; deface—; defile—; desecrate —; dismantle—; enthrone in—; exalt—; hallow—; immortalize—; invade—; isolate —; mutilate—; penetrate—; pervert—;

prostitute—; sanctify—; seclude in—; sequester in—; transgress—; violate—; worship in—; —symbolizes.
(See altar, tomb, sanctuary, temple.)

SHRINK (v)

adverbs
perceptibly; timorously; modestly; instinctively; visibly; dumbly; involuntarily; shyly.
(See recoil, wince.)

SHRINKING

adverbs
shyly; painfully; coldly; terribly; desperately; visibly; instinctively; pitiably; guiltily; pathetically; timidly; submissively; servilely; slavishly; basely; tragically; inwardly; noticeably; childishly; perceptibly; pitiably; unaccountably; significantly.

SHRIVEL (v)

adverbs
abnormally; prematurely; markedly; partially; ruinously; sadly; tragically.
(See shrink, dwindle.)

SHRIVELED

adverbs
slightly; meagerly; cadaverously; gauntly; emaciatedly; haggardly; scrawnily; skinnily; dreadfully; curiously.

SHROUD

adjectives
vibrant; bloody; flecked; misty; sable; spotted; leafy; clinging; rattling; streamlined; putrid; thin.

verbs
clothe in—; discard—; divest of—; invest in —; —circumscribes; —cloaks; —darkens; —dims; —disguises; —eclipses; —enfolds; —envelops; —obscures; —overcasts; —screens; —shades; —veils.
(See raiment.)

SHROUD (v)

adverbs
effectually; permanently; modestly; closely; protectively; partially; darkly; somberly; gloomily.
(See screen, cloak.)

SHRUB

adjectives
blossoming; aromatic; crowding (pl); luxuriant; ornamental; skirting; tranquil; unpruned; widowed; warm-tinted; stunted.

verbs
blast—; blight—; choke—; cultivate—; debilitate—; eradicate—; extirpate—; fertilize—; impoverish—; starve—; strangle—; trim—; uproot—; —beautifies; —declines; —droops; —s enhance; —fades; —flourishes; —graces; —luxuriates; —languishes; —thrives; —trembles; —wanes.
(See bush, honeysuckle, bud, plant.)

SHRUGS

adjectives
expressive; dumb; impertinent; good-natured; impatient; indifferent; significant; contemptuous.

SHUDDER

adjectives
strong; involuntary; passing; ecstatic; visible; slight; repressed; pious; elaborate; intuitive; violent.

verbs
arrest—; elicit—; excite—; feign—; impel —; induce—; inspire—; occasion—; provoke —; repress—; restrain—; —agitates; —betrays; —convulses; —disconcerts; —electrifies; —paralyzes; —perturbs; —ripples through; —ruffles.
(See shiver, sob, sigh.)

SHUDDER (v)

adverbs
spasmodically; physically; instinctively; figuratively; apprehensively; involuntarily; violently; feverishly; abnormally; perceptibly.
(See tremble, shake, shiver.)

SHUFFLE (v)

adverbs
noiselessly; slyly; wearily; uncouthly; sluggishly; clumsily; imperturbably; drearily.
(See drag, walk.)

SHUN (v)

adverbs
timorously; fastidiously; aristocratically; intelligently; cautiously; scrupulously; systematically; studiously.
(See elude, shift, avoid.)

SHUT (v)

adverbs
clamorously; obligingly; stealthily; inexor-

ably; convulsively; sullenly; mysteriously; impatiently; drowsily; abruptly; cautiously.
(See close, exclude.)

SHUTTER

adjectives
awry; heavy-barred; supplementary; iron-cased; closed.

verbs
draw—; elevate—; unfold—; —bars; —blinds; —eclipses; —mantles; —masks; —obscures; —rattles; —restrains; —shades; —veils.
(See screen.)

SHUTTLE

verbs
propel—; swivel—; —alternates; —gyrates; —lurches; —oscillates; —pulsates; —quivers; —revolves; —rotates; —see-saws; —swerves; —swirls; —trembles; —trundles; —wabbles; —whirls; —vibrates.

SHY

adverbs
awkwardly; uneasily; childishly; self-consciously; timidly; uncomfortably; engagingly; embarrassingly; charmingly; painfully; peculiarly; strangely; unwontedly; becomingly; unnaturally; fearfully; clumsily; foolishly; ridiculously; pitiably; touchingly; adorably; comically; absurdly; exquisitely; habitually; deliciously; extremely; incredibly; oddly; curiously; unnecessarily.

SHYNESS

adjectives
delicious; provincial; confused; virgin; rural; exquisite; innate; wonted; girlish; unconquerable; maiden; blushing.

verbs
blush in—; falter in—; feign—; flinch in—; overcome with—; quail in—; —abashes; —afflicts; —arrests; —blenches; —bridles; —confuses; —constrains; —cows; —curbs; —daunts; —deters; —distorts; —distresses; —fetters; —humiliates; —leashes; —overawes; —overwhelms; —perturbs; —represses; —restrains; —smothers.
(See bashfulness, modesty.)

SIBILANT

adverbs
softly; affectedly; ridiculously; laughably; hissingly; toothlessly; lispingly; comically;

warningly; persistently; curiously; derisively; mockingly; disturbingly; pitiably; unpleasantly; strangely; disagreeably.

SICK

verbs
comfort—; heal—; palliate—; prescribe for —; rebuild—; reclaim—; regenerate—; rehabilitate—; relieve—; rescue—; restore—; revive—; soothe—.
(See patient, invalid.)

adverbs
chronically; continually; seriously; habitually; unfortunately; unusually; curiously; oddly; strangely; unaccountably; inexplicably; seriously; critically; recently; definitely; unfortunately; frequently; squeamishly; feverishly; mentally; dangerously; painfully; embarrassingly; inopportunely; inconveniently; awkwardly; desperately; slightly; unendurably.

SICKEN (v)

adverbs
visibly; swooningly; biliously; fatally; tragically; woefully; gradually; speechlessly; mutely; nauseatingly.
(See disgust, languish.)

SICKLY

adverbs
distressingly; unfortunately; bafflingly; always; strangely; inexplicably; wretchedly; unhappily; apparently; curiously.

SICKNESS

adjectives
speechless; desperate; prolonged; swooning; everlasting; pining; violent; bilious; deadly; lasting; soul.

verbs
allay—; alleviate—; banish—; check—; combat—; conquer—; convalesce from—; curse—; eradicate—; feign—; induce—; occasion—; subdue—; —abates; —afflicts; —aggravates; —besets; —cankers; —confines; —cripples; —desolates; —harasses; —heals; —incommodes; —indisposes; —induces; —invalids; —maims; —oppresses; —overcomes; —predisposes; —racks; —ravages; —sears; —seizes; —smites; —sours; —torments; —undermines; —vitiates; —wastes; —withers.
(See ailment, disease, illness, malady.)

SIDE

adjectives
ludicrous; balanced; unbaked; instrumental; paternal; humane; gruesome; seamy; rusty; perilous; luminous; unengaged; massive; verdant; windy; pierced; liberal; stretched-out; obverse; ample; sorrowful; practical; engaging; interminable; nobler; tangled; grassy; ridiculous; bank; valuable; translucent; hairy; wounded; gaping; deep; precipitous; semi-nomadic; perpendicular; distinctive; sloping; lighter; respective; intellectual; outward; emotional; shrinking; spiritual; extravagant; fathomless; pierced; showy; administrative; executive; psychological; spotted; gorgeous; brawny; craggy; neglected; aesthetic; diametrical; opposite; fanciful; starboard; maternal; ventral; exposed; protected; dreamy; winning; objective; superstitious; shuddering; woolly.

SIDE-SPLITTING

adverbs
absurdly; mirthfully; uproariously; boisterously; comically; ridiculously; laughably; farcically; drolly; tumultuously; prankishly; outlandishly; merrily; ludicrously.

SIDEWALK

adjectives
swarming; gravel; moving; unpaved; scented; innocent-looking; broken; wide; cobbled; brick; winding; slippery.

verbs
fence—; gad about—; jog along—; pace—; patrol—; promenade—; ramble along—; saunter along—; straggle along—; traverse —; trudge over—; —crumbles; —deviates; —glistens; —jams.
(See walk.)

SIEGE

adjectives
vigorous; lingering; wanton; severe; bitter; disastrous; moving; protracted; creditable; wreckful; amiable; fatal; famous; fearful; implacable; repeated; hateful; bloody.

verbs
brave—; breast—; endure—; engage in—; extend—; intrench against—; lay—; maintain—; parry—; prolong—; protract—; repel—; resist—; submit to—; survive—; yield to—; weather—; withstand—; —anni-

hilates; —beleaguers; —devastates; —grips; —impoverishes; —lags; —ravages; — starves; —undermines; —blockades.
(See attack, blockade.)

SIEVE

adjectives
meshed; trembling; captious.

verbs
—filters; —purges; —refines; —separates; —sifts; —sorts; —strains; —winnows.

SIFT (*v*)

adverbs
mechanically; academically; curiously; patiently; industriously; painstakingly; suspiciously; legally; automatically.
(See investigate, bolt.)

SIGH

adjectives
gasping; thriftless; gusty; impatient; aimless; fruitless; expiring; deep; burning; sharp; puzzled; plenteous (pl); perpetual; relieved; desponding; perfumed; vain; friendly; delicious; reproachful; sultry; monitorial; lingering; compassionate; mournful; sympathetic; piteous; profound; heavy; quick; slumberous; useless; contrite; false; wistful; feeble; thirsty; pensive; alien; restful; repentant; half-forlorn; audible; inauspicious; inharmonious; short; joyous; passing; impatient; interjectional; watery; philosophic; wasteful; sumptuous; sad; amorous; short; tantalizing; gasping; exasperated; mistaken; miserable; odorous; reckless; infallible; comprehensive; relaxing; desolate; feigned; inaudible; occasional; sorry; yearning; pleased; stifled; disgusted; loud; long; persuasive; gratified; moral; involuntary; relieved; thriftless; convulsive.

verbs
breathe—; burst into—; draw—; elicit—; evoke—; heave—; hush—; muffle—; murmur—; mute—; restrain—; smother—; stifle—; suppress—; utter—; whisper—; — betrays; —bursts from; —deprecates; — flutters; —laments; —racks; —rends; — stirs; —wrings.
(See groan, sob, moan, murmur.)

SIGH (*v*)

adverbs
dismally; profoundly; soulfully; romantically; audibly; pensively; retrospectively; sentimentally; plaintively; appealingly; woefully; tremulously; dejectedly; reminiscently; nostalgically; wistfully; involuntarily; eloquently; compassionately; contritely; forlornly; desolately; inaudibly.
(See grieve, lament.)

SIGHT

adjectives
inward; melting; wondrous; novel; weird; startling; wide; stirring; goodly; uncommon; piteous; enraptured; stimulating; irresistible; aching; holiest; impressive; dilated; refreshing; dismal; touching; remarkable; doleful; spiritual; richer; purer; fairer; heterogeneous; dubious; ravishing; amusing; cheery; instructive; wretched; portentous; clouded; exhilarating; imposing; horrifying; unusual; curtained; solemn; gorgeous; triumphant; precious; fearful; loveliest; continuous; infant; grand; thrilling; unaided; disturbing; curious; quickened; wished; ludicrous; marvelous; appalling; translatable; ghastliest; gallant; truest; bleared; distressing; horrible; swimming; majestic; fine; exceptional; welcome; powerful; sickening; glorious; purblind; joyful; inspiring; all-searching; steadfast; unacquainted; approved; gladdened; straining; extraordinary; splendid; worthless; loathsome; lucent; unveiled; absolute; deadening; glistening; bewildered; unaided; mortal; awful; sorry; genial; saltatory; nocturnal; priceless; secret; whimsical; prettiest; feebler; perfect.

verbs
abhor—; blur—; check—; cloud—; confuse —; conjure—; control—; dim—; distort—; distract—; dull—; focus—; impair—; intensify—; loathe—; lose—; obscure—; obstruct—; recover—; regain—; rely upon—; restore—; sharpen—; shun—; sink from—; stimulate—; tuck out of—; veil—; visualize —; —dazzles; —dissipates; —declines; — enriches; —fails; —invigorates; —outrages; —pollutes; —weakens.
(See vision, view, phenomenon, spectacle, mirage.)

SIGHTLY

adverbs
agreeably; pleasantly; splendidly; magnifi-

cently; unusually; delightfully; extraordinarily; unexpectedly; gloriously; gorgeously; beautifully; entrancingly; remarkably; exceptionally; impressively; thrillingly; dramatically; inexpressibly.

SIGN

adjectives

encouraging; mournful; conspicuous; deep-drawn; premonitory; ideographic; ghastly; indubitable; extreme; hopeful; mute; incomprehensible; regretful; fraternal; important; fluttering; perpetual; visible; ambitious; assured; supplementary; watery; subtle; undoubted; geometric; inauspicious; palpable; bursting; celestial; impressive; depressing; labial; creaking; ominous; frantic; peculiar; optimistic; fragrant; lying; visible; eloquent; translucent; manifold (pl); fearful; natural; symbolic; cabalistic; physical; doubtful; infallible; obscure; elaborate; mysterious; decreased; useless; evident; abject; imperial; characteristic; affecting; faintest; conclusive; sacred; discernible; lamentable; perceptible; talismanic.

verbs

betray—; discern—; drape—; evince—; experience—; interpret—; mistakes—s; question—; trace—s; visit—; watch for—; wipe out—; —appears; —characterizes; —glares; —warns.

(See emblem, indication, signal, notice, mark.)

SIGN (v)

adverbs

legally; formally; perfunctorily; nominally; bindingly; willingly; felicitously.

(See signify, indicate.)

SIGNAL

adjectives

emergency; customary; imperceptible; suggestive; descriptive; preconcerted; true; prompt; cautionary; warning; unheeded.

verbs

await—; beat—; blaze—; breathe—; dispatch—; disperse at—; drum—; exchange —s; flash—; flourish—s; flout—; heed—; gather at—; interpret—; issue—; predetermine—; prescribe—; respond to—; —cautions; —summons; —winks.

(See alarm, beacon, sign.)

SIGNATURE

adjectives

bold; scrawling; sundry; conscious; sprawling; scribbled; unreadable.

verbs

affix—; attest to—; counterfeit—; dash off —; duplicate—; embellish—; enter—; familiarize with—; identify—; pen—; produce —; scratch out—; scrawl—; scribble—; stereotype—; strike out—; submit—; trace —; transcribe—; verify—; vouch for—; witness—; —endorses; —flows; —ripples from; —seals; —s tally.

SIGNIFICANCE

adjectives

drear; mental; emotional; lofty; ghastly; particular; sufficient; supreme; intense; tremendous; spiritual; sad; unsuspected; historic; sound; functional; representative; special; popular; malign; symbolical; mystifying; double; profound; dramatic; ultimate; fine; enormous; vital; tragic; social; immense; contemptuous; intrinsic; lasting; artistic; cruel; prophetic; rude; poignant; gloomy; threatening; highest; arresting; larger; stinging; deep; permanent; transcendent; insolent; convincing; musical; ominous; prime; curious; minor; fatal; moral.

verbs

acquire—; assign—; assume—; attach—; attain—; awaken to—; broaden—; consider —; convey—; dwell upon—; eschew—; fathom—; feel—; forget—; grasp—; heighten—; measure—; narrow—; unfold—; —grows; —overshadows.

(See importance, consequence, import, meaning.)

SIGNIFICANT

adverbs

horribly; menacingly; portentously; pleasantly; happily; immensely; remarkably; distinctly; suddenly; curiously; ominously; deliberately; unmistakably; alarmingly; threateningly; openly; marvelously; tremendously; auspiciously; cruelly.

SIGNIFY (v)

adverbs

clearly; concretely; vividly; undeniably;

affirmatively; comprehensively; plainly; obviously; graphically.

(See show, indicate.)

SILENCE

adjectives

profound; obstinate; mysterious; complete; discomfited; infant; horrid; sullen; majestic; pale; sickening; indignant; melodious; deep; sarcastic; reverent; roaring; morose; heated; honorable; listening; chilling; awkward; demure; musing; stagnant; suitable; unaccountable; voluptuous; resentful; horrified; fearful; astonished; expectant; respectful; oppressive; dignified; deathly; distressful; chagrined; awed; luxurious; bashful; stern; total; snowy; religious; solemn; involuntary; warm; perfumed; defiant; apologetic; lazy; everlasting; moody; attentive; absolute; abstracted; heavy; motionless; stifling; tense; sympathetic; discreet; slumberous; limp; sunlit; momentary; industrious; embarrassed; somber; sulky; dogged; prevailing; hushed; depressing; blank; mute; fruitful; punctuated; painful; broken; ominous; mannerless; grateful; awful; funeral; universal; gathered; uninterrupted; silvery; infinite; tearless; appalling; fragile; eloquent; severe; sepulchral; thoughtful; dismal; empty; thick; sunken; mysterious; guilty; enforced; strange; magical; solvent; freezing; infuriated; bewildered; vibrant; imperative; curious; cold; complete; long; meditative; inhuman; gracious; intense; passive; spellbound; noisy; monumental; museful; brooding; perfect; breathless; lengthened; white; hostile; hideous; dignified; poetic; disciplined; sacred; smiling; forbidding; aggravating; tangible; flushing; unreproved; unsociable; stern; grim; comparative; arid; appealing; maiden; azure; deafening; rapturous; horrible; simple; welcome; bashful; mournful; enamored; despairing; pregnant; shaded; eternal.

verbs

acquiesce in—; appraise—; awaken—; bear—; break—; cajole into—; constrain—; covet—; drop into—; endure—; enjoin—; feel—; impose—; inculcate—; interpret—; lapse into—; lie in—; maintain—; penetrate —; plead for—; preserve—; press into—; put to—; quench—; reduce to—; reflect in —; relapse into—; retreat in—; rip—; sift —; sink into—; slump into—; survey in—; wrap in—; worship—; —cloaks; —descends; —enchants; —encompasses; —en-

sues; —explodes; —falls; —fills; —follows; —grows; —hammers; —hangs; —imposes; —pervades; —pounces; —prevails; —reigns; —rolls; —settles; —sinks; —supervenes; —swallows; —throbs; —troubles.

(See hush, quiet, stillness.)

SILENCE (v)

adverbs

effectually; completely; mysteriously; sarcastically; discreetly; awkwardly; sternly; apologetically; momentarily; grimly.

(See suppress, hush.)

SILENT

adverbs

absolutely; remarkably; unusually; pleasantly; practically; sufficiently; warrantably; reasonably; positively; significantly; usually; reticently; gravely; alarmingly; amusedly; impressively; dangerously; ominously; indulgently; haughtily; angrily; happily; magnanimously; charitably; bewilderingly; strangely; singularly; maddeningly; obstinately; stolidly; sadly; sullenly; mischievously; furtively; stealthily; warily; cautiously; carefully; naturally; guardedly; breathlessly; dreadfully; terrifyingly; gloomily.

SILHOUETTE

adjectives

dark; sliding; streamline; sleek; shadowy; grim; fitted; meager.

SILK

adjectives

watered; seeded; pompadour; domestic; heavy; fresh; delicate; faded; exquisite; glistening; pleated; scarlet; flimsy; newspun; delicate-filmed.

verbs

apparel in—; arrange—; array in—; attire in—; bale—; begrime—; braid—; cast off —; divest of—; drape—; dress in—; entwine—; export—; fabricate—; fringe with —; import—; impregnate—; invest in—; lace—; mat—; net—; plait—; shear—; shred—; skein—; spin—; tangle—; veil in —; warp—; weave—; —fades; —rustles; —tears.

(See handkerchief, cloth, gauze, lining, linen.)

SILLY

adverbs

miserably; incurably; senselessly; stupidly;

loutishly; clownishly; purposely; amusingly; entertainingly; feignedly; absurdly; laughably; imprudently; indiscreetly; hopelessly; disagreeably; intolerably; disgustingly; contemptibly; curiously; pitiably; lamentably; deplorably; wretchedly; disastrously; utterly; hopelessly.

SILVER

adjectives
sheeny; quivering; rippling; transparent; gleaming; wavering; glowing; burnished; shimmering; filigree; massive.

verbs
bedeck with—; burnish—; caparison in—; chase (emboss)—; devaluate—; fabricate—; fashion—; glorify with—; hoard—; mine—; refine—; work in—; —blazons; —coruscates; —enriches; —glints; —glitters; —glows; —tarnishes.
(See metal, steel, jewel.)

SIMILAR

adverbs
indistinguishably; bewilderingly; inconveniently; dangerously; curiously; strangely; naturally; laughably; somewhat; congenially; sufficiently; accidentally; intentionally; deliberately.

SIMILARITY

adjectives
assumed; singular; increasing; psychological.

verbs
attend with—; direct attention to—; discern —; indicate—; observe—; regard—; sense —; —bewilders; —bores; —ceases; —confuses; —echoes; —flusters; —reflects; — mirrors; —parallels; —perplexes; —reproduces; —strikes.
(See identity, resemblance.)

SIMILE

adjectives
absurd; chilling; amiable; expressive; good; swift; felicitous; sickly; oft-repeated; natural; arctic; happy; apt.

verbs
employ—; enlist—; garble—; resort to—; revel in—; —alludes; —colors; —contrasts; —conveys; —clarifies; —expresses; —implies; —paints; —parallels; —pictures; — strikes.
(See metaphor, comparison.)

SIMPER (v)

adverbs
affectedly; coyly; bashfully; embarrassedly; coquettishly; naively; childishly.
(See smile, smirk.)

SIMPERING

adverbs
coyly; demurely; deliberately; foolishly; provokingly; cleverly; designingly; senselessly; hopefully; flirtatiously; ridiculously; archly; cunningly; subtly; wittingly; girlishly; craftily; engagingly.

SIMPLE

adverbs
beautifully; expensively; unnecessarily; utterly; delightfully; artlessly; graciously; refreshingly; intelligibly; pleasantly; fortunately; needlessly; starkly; childishly; severely; chastely; elegantly; gracefully; tastefully; harmoniously; appropriately; ingenuously; naively; bluntly; foolishly; delicately; daintily; charmingly; idiotically; crazily; inanely; fatuously; mindlessly.

SIMPLICITY

adjectives
rich; extreme; precise; subtle; orthographic; sublime; gradual; impressive; chaste; touching; primitive; everlasting; striking; thoroughgoing; scanty; unostentatious; severe; studied; luminous; noble; childlike; solid; medieval; pathetic; laughable; courteous; classic; majestic; low; rude; idyllic; healthful; fundamental; patrician; stolid; limpid; naive; habitual; grave; unique; native; frank; austere; unconscious; sad; patriarchal; serious; absolute; affectionate; stunning; miraculous; antique; pastoral; poignant; inscrutable; rustic; cheerful; exquisite; polite; boyish; striking; vigorous; venerable.

verbs
abandon—; acclaim—; achieve—; advocate —; afford—; applaud—; aspire to—; commend—; desert—; feign—; forsake—; glory in—; inspire—; pretend—; relinquish—; seek—; simulate—; welcome—; —allures;

—attracts; —beguiles; —charms; —deceives; —delights; —disarms; —enchants; —entrances; —fascinates; —inveigles; — refreshes; —renounces.

(See innocence, sincerity, frankness, plainness.)

SIMPLIFY (v)

adverbs
extremely; amazingly; precisely; subtly; orthographically; impressively; fundamentally; uniquely.

(See arrange.)

SIMULATE (v)

adverbs
ingeniously; deftly; artfully; skillfully; professionally; traitorously; slyly; insidiously; venomously.

(See feign, pretend.)

SIMULATED

adverbs
carefully; cleverly; fraudulently; deceptively; adroitly; skillfully; wickedly; deliberately; viciously; artfully; secretly; successfully; mendaciously; smoothly; accurately; exactly; correctly; authentically; theatrically; dramatically; spectacularly; impressively; graphically; wonderfully.

SIN

adjectives
maddening; fundamental; unpardonable; original; dark; deadly; fleshly; grievous; cardinal; damning; regretted; heinous; familiar; unexpiated; shameful; untold; vilest; hidden; foul; mystic; implied; besetting; appalling; bygone; cunning; virtuous; intellectual; grave; venial; detested; imaginary; delightful; conscious; characteristic; precious; penitential; disorderly; superficial.

verbs
abandon—; absolve of—; abstain from—; acknowledge—; ameliorate—; atone for—; banish—; clean from—; commit—; compensate for—; conceive in—; deliver from—; do penance for—; divest of—; excoriate—s; expiate—; extenuate—; forsake—; grapple with—; inherit—; lapse into—; offer for —s; overcome—; pardon—; plunge into—; purge of—; relinquish—; repeat—; reproach—; reveal—; shrive of—; steep in—; stray into—; uncover—; unveil—; wash away—; wallow in—; whip for—; wrestle with—; —corrupts; —damns; —defiles; —

depraves; —flourishes; —hardens; —pollutes; —purges; —surges; —tortures; — traduces; —transgresses; —weighs upon.

(See iniquity, licentiousness, abomination, evil, crime, lust.)

SIN (v)

adverbs
fundamentally; incorrigibly; unwittingly; grievously; egregiously; carnally; intellectually; venially; knowingly; unsuspectingly; lustfully.

(See transgress, trespass.)

SINCERE

adverbs
unaffectedly; charmingly; graciously; affably; cordially; pleasantly; utterly; delightfully ; ardently; honestly; remarkably; plainly; genuinely; dependably; scrupulously; earnestly; fervently; enthusiastically; punctiliously; particularly; reliably.

SINCERITY

adjectives
evident; transparent; artistic; flaming; perfect; despairing; well-feigned; worshiping; obvious; impetuous; unaffected; noble; deep; forlorn; sterling; grave; violent; fierce; youthful; bashful; robust; abominable; sorrowful; patent; grim.

verbs
attest to—; cherish—; declare—; doubt—; express—; feign—; impeach—; impugn—; maintain—; pledge—; pretend—; question —; ring with—; smack of—; stir—; test—; value—; verify—; vow—; —beguiles; — burns; —deludes; —falters; —impresses; — pervades; —vacillates.

(See candor, simplicity, earnestness, honesty, innocence, integrity.)

SINFUL

adverbs
deliberately; wilfully; maliciously; blasphemously; coarsely; consciously; boldly; audaciously; defiantly; impiously; brazenly; openly; flagrantly; incredibly.

SING (v)

adverbs
fervently; quaveringly; nocturnally; effortlessly; audibly; angelically; lustily; bewitchingly; blithely; responsively; derisively; impetuously; exultingly; merrily; conscientiously; extemporaneously; vigorously;

raptly; melodiously; vibrantly; hilariously; magnificently; discordantly; vociferously; throatily; congregationally; professionally; lucretively.

(See hum, croon.)

SINGER

adjectives

notable; malignant; eloquent; inimitable; flattering; pensive; cunning; skillful; splendid; renowned; trained; unseen.

verbs

acclaim—; accompany—; applaud—; belittle—; extol—; prepare—; train—; —carols; —enraptures; —enthralls; —executes; —s harmonize; —impresses; —intones; —matures; —modulates; —pitches; —renders; —stirs; —syncopates; —thrills; —trills; —uplifts.

(See choir, chorus, singing, musician, artist.)

SINGING

adjectives

magical; merry; remote; clear; concerted; congregational; delectable; interlaced; comic; vociferous; fervent; hearty; throaty.

verbs

accompany—; arrange—; coach—; direct—; dominate—; harmonize—; modulate—; rejoice in—; syncopate—; —amuses; —diverts; —echoes; —penetrates; —pervades; —precipitates; —smites; —voices.

(See singer, music.)

SINGSONG

adverbs

intolerably; monotonously; dully; droningly; tediously; unbearably; lullingly; soothingly; drowsily; deliberately; dreamily; sleepily; prosaically; persistently; interminably; endlessly; maddeningly; outlandishly; disagreeably.

SINISTER

adverbs

horribly; ominously; portentously; alarmingly; terrifyingly; deliberately; oppressively; gloomily; unhappily; disturbingly; distressingly; significantly; unmistakably; darkly; hopelessly; fearfully; dismally; deplorably; insidiously; uncommonly; actually; unquestionably; seriously; undoubtedly.

SINK (v)

adverbs

exhaustedly; despondently; swiftly; fatally; gratefully; unfathomably; dejectedly; partially; relaxedly; markedly; continuously.

(See fall, descend.)

SINLESS

adverbs

impossibly; immaculately; chastely; incredibly; sacredly; divinely; beatifically; blessedly; angelically; immortally; eternally; seraphically; innocently.

SINNER

adjectives

tortured; corrigible; wretched; vile; rebellious; ever-living; obdurate; dainty; reckless; hardened.

SINUS

verbs

cauterize—; congest—; drain—; infect—; inflame—; irrigate—; obliterate—; obstruct —; suppurate—; tap—; —clogs; —discharges; —poisons; —secretes; —tortures; —undermines; —racks.

(See sore, cavity, opening.)

SIP (v)

adverbs

demurely; sparingly; fastidiously; aristocratically; delicately; sickeningly; disgustingly; noisily; vulgarly.

(See drink, absorb, suck.)

SIRE

adjectives

sweet; sapient; heathen; illustrious; loving.

SIREN

verbs

resist—; withstand—; yield to—; —allures; —attracts; —beckons; —bewitches; —cajoles; —captivates; —charms; —enamours; —entices; —fascinates; —impels; —inveigles; —intrigues; —lures; —magnetizes; —tempts; —screams; —seduces; —shrieks; —wheedles.

(See lover, woman.)

SISTER

adjectives

impressionable; droll; diverting; desolate; fair; erring; beauteous; barren; unchaste;

weird; hard-boiled; woodland; honored; religious; sterner; younger; incredulous; innocent.

verbs
adore—; caress—; cherish—; claim—; dote on—; embosom—; embrace—; endear to—; esteem—; favor—; glorify—; idolize—; prize—; revere—; worship—.
(See mother.)

SISTERLY
adverbs
warmly; sympathetically; comfortingly; tenderly; affectionately; assiduously; persistently; adroitly; patiently; indulgently; hopefully; insistently; consistently; cleverly; impulsively; noticeably; carefully; unfailingly; pleasantly; agreeably.

SIT (*v*)
adverbs
decorously; ignominiously; mutely; moodily; calmly; inscrutably; placidly; unobtrusively; picturesquely; impassively; dejectedly; disconsolately; despondently; voicelessly; spiritlessly; dispiritedly; quiescently; majestically.
(See rest, repose.)

SITE
adjectives
admirable; impregnable; noble; suitable; magnificent; restricted; appropriate; splendid.

SITUATE (*v*)
adverbs
conveniently; centrally; fortunately; geographically; romantically; favorably; picturesquely; alarmingly; dramatically; uniquely; remotely; depressingly; dismally; secludedly; ridiculously; precariously; perilously; anomalously.
(See place, establish.)

SITUATION
adjectives
sentimental; silly; messiest; equivocal; dramatic; ticklish; cheerful; recurrent; enviable; unpleasant; extreme; alarming; horrifying; tragic; embarrassing; peculiar; speech; tense; detrimental; momentous; dangerous; farcical; desolate; unique; slippery; economic; international; effective; social; urgent; charming; analogous; painful; dependent; aggravating; remote; ma-

terial; depressing; financial; defiant; unhappy; countless (pl); rational; humorous; precise; secluded; curious; relative; important; insular; hopeless; lonesome; incredible; immoral; dismal; strategical; favorable; arduous; defenseless; conspicuous; parlous; dispersed; pragmatic; dismaying; strained; unfortunate; picturesque; melancholy; appalling; commanding; accessible; ridiculous; subordinate; paradoxical; delicate; difficult; much-coveted; awkward; isolated; distressing; diplomatic; precarious; sequestered; desperate; exposed; forfeited; military; healthy; romantic; comfortable; fearful; perilous; ironic; anomalous.

verbs
alleviate—; alter—; analyze—; barge into (colloq.)—; contemplate—; control—; crash into—; define—; denounce—; dismiss—; dramatize—; clarify—; command—; conceive—; confess—; cope with—; create—; cripple—; deal with—; divulge—; evaluate —; exaggerate—; excogitate—s; gloss over —; grapple with—; grasp—; handle—; master—; plunge into—; ponder over—; relieve—; remedy—; resolve—; save—; sense —; size up—; soften—; sum up—; take stock of—; trace—; unscramble—; utilize—; view—; visualize—; —aggravates; —appeals; —s arise; —baffles; —calculates; — carries; —clears; —confronts; —demonstrates; —develops; —discloses; —disturbs; —dominates; —eases; —grows; —illuminates; —intensifies; —portrays; —recurs; — relaxes; —relinquishes; —revolves; — solves; —suffers; mull over—; neglect—; overdramatize—.
(See position, condition, predicament.)

SIZE
adjectives
enormous; remarkable; immense; cap; apparent; defined; prodigious; stunted; comparative; generous; respectable; stupendous; imposing; sensational; unusual; unwieldy; minute; inexpensive; substantial; convenient; formidable; monstrous; gargantuan; heroic; graduated; sample; small; serving; requisite; undue; tangible.

verbs
attenuate—; augment—; calibrate—s; compute—; diminish—; distend—; estimate—; exaggerate—; exceed—; expand—; fix—; gauge—; grade—s; graduate—s; inflate—; magnify—; modify—; plumb—; reduce—;

register—; restrict—; standardize—; surpass in—; swell—; tabulate—s; vary—; —dwindles; —s range from; —shrinks.

(See dimension, measurement, extent, magnitude.)

SKELETON
adjectives
decaying; sheeted; fleshless; homogeneous; rickety; moldering; colossal; human; metallic; uncouth; bleached; grinning; moldy.

verbs
build on—; cremate—; disinter—; embalm —; exhume—; expose—; inter—; preserve —; prop—; reduce to—; shrivel to—; uncover—; unearth—; —bears; —crumbles; —grins; —reveals; —supports; —sustains.

SKEPTIC
adjectives
obstinate; staunch; satisfied; complete; confirmed.

verbs
assure—; brook—; overawe—s; overwhelm —s; impress—; persuade—; quiet—; stagger—s; —cavils; —challenges; —demurs; —discredits; —disputes; —dissents; —distrusts; —entertains; —doubts; —hesitates; —queries; —vacillates; —wavers.

(See atheist, critic, heretic.)

SKEPTICAL
adverbs
openly; publicly; scoffingly; jeeringly; derisively; contemptuously; significantly; conspicuously; persistently; obstinately; stubbornly; stolidly; distrustfully; arrogantly; oddly; curiously; extremely; profoundly; secretly.

SKEPTICISM
adjectives
pretended; indulgent; cold; inveterate; painful; native; learned; extreme; happy; definite; flippant; worthwhile; safe; rationalistic.

verbs
assume—; attribute to—; betray—; break down—; collapse into—; confute—; criticize—; deny—; dispose to—; excuse—; fall into—; incline to—; incur—; involve—; justify—; lament—; minimize—; profess—; prompt—; rebuke—; regard—; taint by—;

—amuses; —asserts; —overthrows; —persuades; —prevails; —sweeps; —vanishes.

(See atheism, disbelief, doubt.)

SKETCH
adjectives
pastel; charming; unfinished; occasional; faint; historical; insufficient; vigorous; impressionistic; autobiographical; loose; effective; brief; colossal; concise; panoramic; biographical; hospital; vivid; vignette; critical; characteristic; orchestral; malignant; dramatic; imaginative; good-humored; accompanying; rambling; belated; spirited; despairing; ingenious; lifelike.

verbs
dash off—; design—; disclose—; draft—; execute—; reproduce—; scrutinize—; submit—; trace—; transcribe—; —charts; —delineates; —depicts; —details; —diagrams; —enlightens; —facilitates; —guides; —illustrates; —outlines; —portrays; —prescribes; —represents; —sets forth.

(See drawing, design, illustration, plan, outline.)

SKETCH (v)
adverbs
realistically; vaguely; imperfectly; roughly; artistically; vividly; graphically; covertly; ridiculously; satirically; impressionistically; autobiographically; panoramically; biographically; dramatically; imaginatively; ingeniously.

(See draw, portray.)

SKETCHY
adverbs
inadequately; unsatisfactorily; carelessly; unserviceably; hopelessly; disappointingly; singularly; curiously; ineffectively; provokingly; inexcusably; unpardonably.

SKI (v)
adverbs
boisterously; dexterously; artfully; professionally; sportively; amateurishly; daringly.
(See slide, skim.)

SKIFF
verbs
batter—; buffet—; convoy—; embark on—; man—; navigate—; punt—; ram—; scull —; swamp—; waft—; —bears; —conveys;

—drifts; —glides; —plies; —puts to sea; —sallies forth; —scuds; —sweeps; —weighs anchor.

(See boat.)

SKILL

adjectives

experimental; inordinate; persevering; diagnostic; dangerous; tactical; moderate; ancient; profound; manual; technical; artistic; trained; superior; exceptional; subtle; acquired; dramatic; linguistic; deft; infinite; descriptive; acknowledged; inventive; competent; matchless; tattered; martial; prodigious; strict; uncanny; untaught; professional; diplomatic; considerable; consummate; daredevil; executive; shallow; exquisite; simple; barren; quaint; detached; methodic; journalistic; masterly; practical; unavailing; athletic; unusual; creative; analytical; potent; monastic; unsurpassed; fearful; unfaltering; comparative; mechanical; rare; quick; sufficient.

verbs

absorb—; acquire—; applaud—; capitalize —; challenge—; confound—; contend with —; develop—; devise—; discern—; display —; evince—; execute with—; exhaust—; exhibit—; extol—; manifest—; overestimate —; surpass—; transfer—.

(See ability, faculty, ingenuity, capability.)

SKILLED

adverbs

moderately; exceptionally; professionally; profoundly; subtly; definitely; admittedly; infinitely; matchlessly; prodigiously; uncannily; diplomatically; consummately; exquisitely; quaintly; rarely; undeniably; incontrovertibly; unusually; creatively; powerfully; fearfully; comparatively; notably; strikingly; diabolically; marvelously; incredibly; dangerously; obviously; constitutionally; naturally; innately; inherently; instinctively; capably; competently; proficiently; deftly; discreetly; conveniently.

SKILLFUL

adverbs

amazingly; remarkably; particularly; miraculously; eminently; conspicuously; unusually; genuinely; admittedly; adequately; presumably; brilliantly; famously; inexpressibly; modestly.

SKIM (*v*)

adverbs

cursorily; perfunctorily; carelessly; hastily; rapidly; studiously; critically.

(See scan, read.)

SKIMP (*v*)

adverbs

penuriously; niggardly; meanly; parsimoniously; selfishly; fanatically.

(See save.)

SKIMPY

adverbs

ridiculously; fantastically; comically; absurdly; inexcusably; outrageously; miserably; inadequately; pitifully; pitiably; pathetically; grotesquely; ingenerously; stingily; carelessly; awkwardly; unbecomingly; unfashionably; uncomfortably; unfortunately.

SKIN

adjectives

clear; ruddy; tanned; mortal; dainty; tawny; parchment; tender; dry; scratchy; shaggy; accumulated; tough; defensive; roughened; ivory; olive; ardent; incarnate; wrinkled; transparent; sensitive; sleekest; edible; sunburned; lustrous; untanned; sallow; gay; dead; painted; scaling; waxy; bronzed; superfluous; crinkled; redundant; mottled; narrow.

verbs

affect—; aggravate—; bathe—; chafe—; dust—; enervate—; expose—; harden—; inflame—; ingrain—; injure—; irritate—; macerate—; paint—; pat—; peel—; prick —; pull off—; rejuvenate—; rinse—; rub —; ruffle—; safeguard—; save one's—; scratch—; shed—; smear—; soften—; soothe —; sponge—; ulcerate—; —adapts; — blanches; —erupts; —forms; —furrows; — glows; —jaundices; —parches; —quivers; —scars; —shrinks; —splits; —stains; — thickens; —warts; —wrinkles.

(See epidermis, surface.)

SKIRT

adjectives

sable; close-clinging; silken; short; awful; antiquated; tight; divided; ample; jaunty; flared; voluminous; fleecy; cloudy; smooth; draggled; vaporous; gaudy; wide; hoop; gloomy; umbrella; rustling; gathered; pleated; slit; form-fitting; wrinkled.

verbs

accoutre in—; attire in—; bare—; baste—; cling to—; divest of—; enfold in—; garb in —; gusset—; hem—; pleat—; rig in—; rumple—; ruffle—; soil—; strip off—; swaddle in—; tack—; tuck in—; —cloaks; —s flutter; —mantles; —swathes; —s swirl; —s swish.

(See dress.)

SKITTISH

adverbs

nervously; wildly; fearfully; spiritedly; alarmingly; dangerously; absurdly; ridiculously; laughably; outlandishly; awkwardly; simperingly; fatuously; wantonly; capriciously; captiously; unreliably; unsteadily; undependably; unsteadily; erratically; unpredictably; vexatiously; remarkably.

SKULKING

adverbs

furtively; warily; cautiously; soundlessly; fearfully; constantly; unhappily; miserably; wretchedly; guiltily; frightfully; watchfully; secretly; abjectly; pitiably.

SKULL

adjectives

brainless; eyeless; cast-iron; perfect; grinning; gleaming; empty.

verbs

abrade—; batter—; compress—; contuse—; crack—; crush—; drain—; fracture—; imbed in—; lacerate—; measure—; mummify —; penetrate—; perforate—; pierce—; scrape—; split—; tap—; trepan—; trephine —; —contracts; —deflects; —protects.

(See head, brain, mind.)

SKUNK

verbs

rear—; skin—; trap—; —burrows; —controls; —defiles; —depredates; —digs; — ejects; —exudes; —grunts; —hibernates; — inhabits; —plagues; —preys on; —robs; — secretes; —squirts; —stalks; —stinks.

(See animal.)

SKY

adjectives

flooded; crystal; far; distant; radiant; moon-lit; nether; insufficient; thickening; sweltering; fair; twinkling; viewless; ancient; fantastic; lurid; starry; cloudless; turbulent; glowing; wintry; unruffled; in-teresting; frightening; dappled; stormy; sullen; balmy; leaden; empty; kindred; utmost; mature; beneficent; natural; elusive; upper; smiling; wonted; sunset; pathless; flaming; glorious; broad; frowning; domestic; copper; velvety; violent; nocturnal; delicious; curdled; humid; bright; narrowing; arched; burning; grinning; showery; granite; haunted; overcast; bitter; palpitating; deep; luminous; roseate; unconscious; lulling; sounding; ethereal; blinding; shrinking; softest; western; boundless; sapphire; barren; serene; enchanting; fragrant; alien; frosty; embroiling; triumphant; lowering; changing; unbarred; tidy; middle; pitiless; flawless; palpitant; fated; envious; star-studded; living; rosy; stainless; candid; gorgeous; peacock; tropic; hueless; sultry; night; summer; windless; resplendent; adverse; spacious; turquoise; sombre; placid; menacing; universal; primrose; angry; wonted; steely; vaulted; winking; saffron; nimbus.

verbs

clothe—; fleck—; flutter from—; freak—; gaze at—; gild—; lighten—; rule—; scan —; streak—; weave across—; —blackens; —blazes; —broods; —casts; —clouds; — darkens; —entrances; —glows; —marbles; —obscures; —patterns; —rifts; —curdles.

(See heaven, cloud.)

SLABS

adjectives

mortuary; thick; steaming; monolithic; shattered; boneless; original; huge; sepulchral.

SLACK

adverbs

weakly; lazily; shiftlessly; indolently; incorrigibly; habitually; naturally; inherently; innately; curiously; dreadfully; unpardonably; inexcusably; intolerably; unprofitably; thriftlessly; negligently; improvidently; uncommonly; utterly; apathetically; dangerously; languidly; carelessly; heedlessly; thoughtlessly; inconsiderately; clumsily; indifferently.

SLACKEN (v)

adverbs

materially; markedly; appreciably; gradually; abruptly; experimentally; comparatively.

(See reduce, loosen.)

SLANDER

adjectives

cursing; malicious; honest; cruel; lame; covered; cunning; abominable; impossible; libelous.

verbs

acquit of—; babble—; decry—; disprove—; inveigh against—; refute—; spread—; vindicate of—; —bespatters; —blackens; —brands; —calumniates; —defames; —deprecates; —derogates; —detracts; —disparages; —incenses; —infuriates; —libels; —maligns; —stigmatizes; —traduces; —vilifies.

(See aspersion, calumny, libel, malediction.)

SLANDER (*v*)

adverbs

libelously; scurrilously; foully; viciously; hatefully; vindictively; criminally; illegally; spitefully; maliciously; cunningly; cruelly; covertly; abominably; libelously.

(See defame, traduce.)

SLANDEROUS

adverbs

shamefully; boldly; altogether; openly; actually; admittedly; unexpectedly; shockingly; disgracefully; utterly; infamously; notoriously; uncommonly.

SLANG

adjectives

picturesque; vulgar; descriptive; polyglot; current; sporting; two-fisted; bold; understandable; local; accepted.

verbs

adopt—; ban—; colloquialize—; debar—; evolve—; express in—; frown upon—; interpret—; invent—; popularize—; taboo—; translate—; —amuses; —assumes; —colors; —corrupts; —enlivens; —invigorates; —mutilates; —revises; —spreads; —tends; —vulgarizes.

(See jargon, language.)

SLANGY

adverbs

disagreeably; unpleasantly; trenchantly; catchily; cheaply; coarsely; unnecessarily; crudely; tawdrily; boorishly; loutishly; ignorantly; gruffly; churlishly; indelicately; remarkably; gracelessly.

SLAP (*v*)

adverbs

smartly; brutally; cruelly; viciously; impatiently; indignantly.

(See box, strike.)

SLAP-DASH

adverbs

carelessly; blithely; hastily; nonchalantly; excitedly; hurriedly; untidily; thoughtlessly; inconsiderately; boyishly; inexcusably; habitually; incorrigibly; hopelessly; unsatisfactorily; unpleasantly; unluckily.

SLASH (*v*)

adverbs

ruthlessly; economically; murderously; energetically; conclusively; furiously; vindictively; bestially.

(See cut, gash.)

SLATTERNLY

adverbs

wretchedly; miserably; untidily; intolerably; incorrigibly; unattractively; unpleasantly; unfortunately; actually; carelessly; unconventionally; nonchalantly; desperately; sadly; hopelessly; habitually; unwontedly; displeasingly; offensively.

SLAUGHTER

adjectives

needless; terrific; deep; deadly; dreadful; ignoble; red; fratricidal; ruthless; sheer; persistent; brutal; indiscriminate; terrible; hopeless; unheard-of; causeless; awful; unworthy; fearful; subsequent; treacherous; incidental; wholesale.

verbs

avenge—; check—; condone—; countenance —; curb—; denounce—; exonerate of—; justify—; implicate in—; prosecute for—; regret—; restrain—; subdue—; succumb in —; stem—; —debauches; —decimates; —defiles; —deletes; —depraves; —ravages; —shames.

(See bloodshed, massacre.)

SLAUGHTER (*v*)

adverbs

professionally; blindly; ruthlessly; carelessly; bellicosely; insensately; needlessly; ignobly; indiscriminately; causelessly; treacherously; fearfully.

(See butcher, kill.)

SLAVE

adjectives

perfidious; veriest; humble; submissive; observant; delegated; fugitive; mercenary; ferocious; cringing; sceptered; myriad (pl); devilish; absconding; tawdry; supernumerary; thin; swarming (pl); pernicious; hollow-chested; runaway; factious; transgressing; crouching; drunken; absolute; faithful; purchased; fingering; past-saving; unmannerly; meanest; refractory; groveling; classified; insulting; monastic; luxurious; sanguine; base; superfluous; liberated; gigantic; loathed.

verbs

awe—; chastise—; emancipate—s; castigate —; fetter—; lash—; leash—s; liberate—s; manacle—s; market—s; oversee—s; repress —; return—; shackle—s; spare—; subdue —; subjugate—s; trade in—s; tyrannize over —; yoke—s; —attends; —bows; —s colonize; —drudges; —ministers to; —reveres; —s revolt; —salaams.

(See servant, captive.)

SLAVERY

adjectives

virtual; social; voluntary; blissful; abject; merciful; mechanical.

verbs

abolish—; ban—; deliver from—; denounce —; drudge in—; efface—; enforce—; lead into—; liberate from—; outlaw—; perpetuate—; prohibit—; redeem from—; sell into —; subject to—; submit to—; suppress—; traffic in—; —binds; —crushes; —chains; —demoralizes; —fetters; —flourishes; —manacles; —restrains; —shackles; —subjugates.

(See bondage, enslavement, captivity.)

SLAVISH

adverbs

amazingly; unspeakably; meanly; servilely; pitiably; unbearably; totally; willingly; cheerfully; sullenly; temporarily; rebelliously; patently; mockingly; devotedly; ludicrously; ridiculously; apparently; pathetically; humbly; basely; manifestly; contentedly; contemptibly; openly; markedly; exaggeratedly.

SLAY (*v*)

adverbs

treacherously; traitorously; vindictively; re-

vengefully; soullessly; nefariously; heartlessly; ruthlessly.

(See kill, slaughter.)

SLEEK

adverbs

smoothly; glossily; extremely; inordinately; unpleasantly; blandly; smugly; consciously; remarkably; excessively; suavely; attractively; unbelievably.

SLEEP

adjectives

flattering; noble; comfortable; common noonday; night; profound; trembling; bankrupt; heavy; eternal; pink-tinged; magnetic; fatal; transient; smiling; bestial; tranquil; scanty; deep; secret; marble; breathing; quiet; restful; sound; unbroken; refreshing; wintry; dreamless; peaceful; fitful; beloved; mystic; metamorphic; downy; lethargic; unstirring; portioned; poppied; sudden; drunken; alcoholic; short; convulsed; uninterrupted; fevered; pleasing; enchanted; mysterious; stealthy; startling; forgetful; hypnotic; frozen; troubled; filmy-eyed; speechless; violated; watchful; solacing.

verbs

arouse from—; beguile in—; call in—; desire—; disturb—; feign—; incline to—; induce—; intensify—; lack—; lull to—; mutter in—; produce—; relieve—; repose in—; require—; rock to—; rouse from—; secure —; sink into—; trail into—; —curtains; —curtails; —engulfs; —insures; —overpowers; —reigns; —renews; —soothes; —steals; —transfers.

(See repose, rest, slumber.)

SLEEP (*v*)

adverbs

heavily; peacefully; stertorously; profoundly; habitually; fitfully; comfortably; transiently; tranquilly; dreamlessly; alcoholically; hypnotically.

(See doze, slumber.)

SLEEPLESS

adverbs

vigilantly; alertly; nervously; deliriously; feverishly; anxiously; distressingly; painfully; unfortunately; remarkably; puzzlingly; unaccountably; incurably; alarmingly; disturbingly; unhappily; excitedly; curiously; wakefully; restlessly; restively; apprehensively; uneasily; vexatiously; ironically; inconveniently; dangerously; confoundedly; strangely.

SLEEPY

adverbs

uncontrollably; irresistibly; inordinately; strangely; oddly; curiously; particularly; significantly; extremely; alarmingly; dangerously; specially; unusually; wretchedly; miserably; naturally; abnormally; surprisingly; unaccountably; inexplicably; mysteriously; conveniently; perilously; confoundedly; strangely.

SLEET

adjectives

slapping; driving; eddying; arrowy; stimulated; shiny; dangerous.

verbs

brave—; encounter—; melt—; precipitate —; —assails; —bites; —blasts; —blights; —devastates; —endangers; —glazes; —impairs; —imperils; —nips; —pelts; —penetrates; —pierces; —pinches; —rattles on; —ravages; —thaws.

(See ice, snow, hail.)

SLEETY

adverbs

miserably; fearfully; dangerously; suddenly; wretchedly; unmanageably; dreadfully; terribly; freezingly; disagreeably; unpleasantly; frightfully; chillingly; bitterly; perilously; hazardously.

SLEEVE

adjectives

puffed; long; short; flowing; pendent; capacious; tapered; luxurious; charming; slashed; lounging; molded; draw-string.

verbs

adorn—; alter—; append—; baste—; chuckle into—; cuff—; drape—; embellish —; extend—; flounce—; fray—; frill—; fringe—; hem—; knit up—; ruffle—; rumple—; shred—; starch—; tatter—; trim —; —girds.

SLENDER

adverbs

gracefully; unusually; remarkably; delightfully; pleasantly; attractively; exceptionally; marvelously; extremely; beautifully; exquisitely; youthfully; prettily.

verbs

employ—; engage—; tip off (colloq.)—; — analyzes; —apprehends; —beguiles; — cloaks—; cross-examines—; —deduces; — detects; —discloses; —disguises; —divulges; —dodges; —exposes; —fathoms; —ferrets out; —grills; —interrogates; —investigates; —mystifies; —outwits; —overhauls; — peers; —pries into; —probes; —prowls; — queries; —questions; —ransacks; —reveals; —scents; —scrutinizes; —shadows; — threshes out; —traces; —tracks down; — trails; —uncovers; —unearths; —unmasks; —veils.

(See detective.)

SLIDE (*v*)

adverbs

imperceptibly; appreciably; terrifyingly; greasily; languidly; violently; deftly; cautiously.

(See glide, slip.)

SLIM

adverbs

boyishly; girlishly; childishly; delightfully; gracefully; unusually; extremely; normally; abnormally; attractively; noticeably; youthfully; unwontedly; distressingly; admirably; pleasantly.

SLIME

adjectives

subsiding; blistering; brute; primeval; bestial.

SLIP

adjectives

artless; warped; native; costly; silken; shapely; sheeny; fitted; necessary.

SLIP (*v*)

adverbs

stealthily; elusively; artfully; treacherously; evanescently; surreptitiously; insidiously; silently.

(See slide, glide.)

SLIPPER

adjectives

mended; imaginary; high-heeled; fur-lined; flowered; sharp-pointed; comfortable; battered; pinching.

adverbs

unmanageably; always; alarmingly; perilously; dangerously; hazardously; terribly; desperately; wretchedly; miserably; disturbingly; evidently; dreadfully; frightfully; unusually; extremely.

SLOGAN

verbs

adopt—; assail—; chant—; chorus—; dramatize—; coin—; flaunt—; hail—; offer—; rally to—; reject—; shout—; shrill—; thunder—; —elaborates; —rings; —stirs; —symbolizes; —takes hold; —wafts.

(See motto, cry, phrase.)

SLOP (v)

adverbs

carelessly; disgustingly; violently; abruptly; clumsily.

(See soil, drink.)

SLOPE

adjectives

fruitful; inaccessible; dappled; parallel; inclined; haunted; sunny; springing; grassy; intervening; declivitous; luminous; gentler; slippery; verdant; scarred; swelling; reverse; trampled; precipitous; rapid; flattish; upland; glimmering; terraced; neglected; westering; desert; wooded; monotonous; savage.

verbs

afford—; avoid—; capsize on—; careen down—; grade—; level—; maintain—; scale—; scamper down—; skirt—; sustain —; —ascends; —banks; —distorts; —endangers; —inclines; —lurches; —recedes; —sags; —streams; —tilts.

(See bank, hill.)

SLOPE (v)

adverbs

gradually; markedly; steeply; gently; greenly; inaccessibly; grassily; swellingly; precipitously.

(See incline.)

SLOTH

adjectives

silken; dilatory; cowardly; cushioned; sensual; deliberate; drowsy.

adverbs

notoriously; habitually; naturally; incorrigibly; incurably; lazily; indolently; evidently; openly; admittedly; brazenly; laughingly; unaccountably; drowsily.

SLOUCH (v)

adverbs

heavily; carelessly; sullenly; obnoxiously; wearily; visibly; deliberately.

(See droop, hang.)

SLOUGH

adjectives

dreadful; pestiferous; humble; deadly; dreaded.

SLOVENLY

adverbs

inexcusably; unreasonably; shamefully; sadly; embarrassingly; unpardonably; lazily; shamelessly; unpleasantly; repulsively; curiously; negligently; thoughtlessly; insouciantly; casually; nonchalantly; laughingly; unbecomingly; discourteously; crassly; boorishly; outlandishly; outrageously; scandalously; unnecessarily; offensively.

SLUGGISH

adverbs

strangely; stupidly; loutishly; dully; torpidly; indolently; inertly; supinely; negligently; carelessly; indifferently; lethargically; strangely; unwontedly; unusually; exceptionally; intolerably; provokingly; vexatiously; hopelessly; wretchedly; unprofitably.

SLUMBER

adjectives

refreshed; pleasant; profound; heavy; dreamless; weary; unnatural; troubled; breathless; rigid; riveted; shady; careless; charmed; sufficient; famous; alert; eternal; fearful; soft; noontide; tickled; enervating; tranquil; healthful; colossal; unconscious; stagnant; prostrate; silent; lighter; dusty.

verbs

blast—; burst from—; consume in—; curtail —; doze into—; induce—; shatter—; toss in —; —enfolds; —envelops; —grips; —reanimates; —regenerates; —relaxes; —renews; —revitalizes; —revives; —seizes.

(See sleep.)

SLUMBER (v)

adverbs
refreshingly; sweetly; pleasantly; profoundly; dreamlessly; enervatingly; tranquilly; healthfully.
(See doze, sleep.)

SLUMP

verbs
allay—; alleviate—; balance—; check—; counteract—; curb—; descend into—; emerge from—; halt—; mitigate—; moderate —; stem—; suffer—; survive—; —abates; —depresses; —endangers; —fizzles out (colloq.); —jeopardizes; —reduces; —relaxes; —retards; —slackens; —troubles.
(See depression, fall, melancholy.)

SLUMS

verbs
abolish—; comb—; dismantle—; efface—; eradicate—; erase—; explore—; exterminate—; infest—; level—; prowl about—; lurk in—; raze—; rise from—; roam—; root out—; scour—; skulk in—; stamp out —; wallow in—; —breed; —congest; —deface; —defile; —pollute; —reek; —screen; —sully; —teem.
(See district.)

SLUSHY

adverbs
miserably; unhealthfully; disagreeably; wretchedly; messily; unpleasantly; unusually; deucedly.

SLY

adverbs
subtly; surreptitiously; furtively; actually; insidiously; abominably; dangerously; warily; undiscoverably; undoubtedly; extremely; successfully; miserably; hatefully; maliciously; cleverly; adroitly; astutely; politically; commercially; trickily; curiously; marvelously.

SMACK

adjectives
emphatic; hearty; clamorous; affectionate; loud; stunning.

SMALL

adverbs
gracefully; pleasantly; prettily; infinitesimally; minutely; extraordinarily; pitifully; pathetically; miserably; compactly; handily; conveniently; daintily; delicately; miraculously; unbelievably.

SMALLNESS

adjectives
compact; frivolous; suggestive; aristocratic; dainty; handy.

SMALLPOX

verbs
afflict with—; characterize—; contract—; convey—; diagnose as—; expose to—; exterminate—; extirpate—; immunize to—; infect with—; inoculate against—; isolate —; prevent—; quarantine—; succumb to—; transmit—; usher in—; —communicates; —confines; —disfigures; —incubates; —invalids; —marks; —pits; —prostrates; —ravages; —scars; —taints; —vitiates.
(See epidemic, measles, disease.)

SMART

adverbs
comically; facetiously; banteringly; foolishly; jestingly; cleverly; felicitously; uncommonly; brilliantly; unusually; thoroughly; ingeniously; amazingly; admirably; wonderfully; wittily; drolly; sparklingly; acutely, capably; cunningly; craftily; sensibly; reasonably; sagely; prudently; subtly; consciously; impressively; learnedly; notoriously; proverbially; assiduously; alertly; sedulously; earnestly; actively.

SMARTNESS

adjectives
figure; lasting; style; exceptional; distinguished; dramatic; stimulating; superficial; uncouth; fabulous; slovenly; alert; conservative; demure; forced; clumsy

SMASH (v)

adverbs
relentlessly; ruthlessly; vigorously; impulsively; violently; thunderously; terrifically; frightfully.
(See wreck, crush.)

SMELL

adjectives
offensive; pungent; rutting; rank; sharp; foul; conglomerate; musty; villainous; luscious; putrid; faint; concentrated; warning; sickish; sweet; dreadful; grateful; elegant; pervading; spicy; powerful; rebellious; hor-

rid; unholy; evil; heavy; acrid; fishy; damp; moldy; balsam; overpowering; breathless; heavenly; balmy; odious; cold; oppressive; dank.

verbs

abhor—; abominate—; banish—; deodorize —; inhale—; intensify—; loathe—; recognize—; relish—; retain—; waft—; —asphyxiates; —assails; —clings; —corrupts; —edges; —entices; —floats; —gags; —incenses; —irritates; —lures; —mingles; — nauseates; —offends; —permeates; —pervades; —ranks; —repels; —revolts; — sickens; —suggests; —taints; —tempts.

(See fragrance, stench, scent, odor.)

SMELL (v)

adverbs

repulsively; objectionably; heavenly; evilly; repugnantly; offensively; noisomely; pungently; abominably; provokingly; potently; sweetly; odiously; dankly; delectably.

(See scent, perfume.)

SMELLY

adverbs

hideously; odiously; horridly; sickeningly; nauseatingly; startlingly; definitely; disgustingly; unbearably; curiously; overpoweringly; suffocatingly.

SMILE

adjectives

rustic; uneasy; gracious; regretful; winning; surprised; radiant; broad; bitter; reminiscent; whimsical; wreathed; metallic; faint; apologetic; affectionate; sweet; amiable; solitary; pitying; ridiculous; quizzical; spicy; special; contagious; fawning; amused; icy; wistful; courteous; crafty; withering; beaming; ravished; enormous; uncontrolled; sickly; sly; maternal; eager; naked; frank; joyous; complacent; brilliant; answering; forced; angry; sympathetic; wanton; contemptuous; deadly; sad; simulated; audible; illumined; parting; approving; ironical; mocking; sudden; indulgent; welcoming; irradiating; agreeable; restrained; watery; rare; playful; superior; arch; perpetual; innocent; big; somber; polished; responding; irrepressible; religious; peculiar; convenient; everlasting; tolerant; vapid; priceless; vague; racked; complicated; smart; polite; murderous; disdainful; sunny; indomitable; sinister; diabolical;

complaisant; dim; patient; haughty; endless; rapid; passing; benign; lurid; crooked; placid; hot; grave; malicious; incredulous; timid; nervous; kind; involuntary; smothered; ardent; bland; provocative; peerless; vivacious; mellow; wan; new; quiet; calm; abrupt; loving; sagacious; buoyant; greasy; sardonic; conciliatory; sidelong; nasty; dawning; grim; ironical; false; meaning; sustaining; saucy; atoning; cynical; prodigal; charming; natural; indifferent; tolerant; wry; little; visible; mournful; weary; patronizing; languid; deprecating; fitful; humorous; seductive; sarcastic; mutual; idiotic; frigid; enrapt; doleful; hospitable; doubtful; ingratiating; counterfeit; curious; mischievous; childlike; exultant; saturnine; speculative; pensive; immutable; condescending; pert; impish; roguish; ghastly; rueful; hollow; unctuous; inane; joyless; wild; satirical; reassuring; slow; hideous; flattering; listless; parting; fleeting; engaging; severe; immortal; insipid; moonshine; fascinating; facile; beatific; restless; scornful; bosomed; wondering; moony; senile; ambrosial; covert; airy; incisive; faded; shy; social; angelic; envious; debonair; bashful; artificial; waking; antiseptic; paternal; dubious; hungry; pale; ready; clear; thoughtless; gentle; infectious; conscious; timorous; haughty; frequent; backward; enamored; obnoxious; pallid; derisive; beguiling; excited.

verbs

achieve—; answer with—; bestow—; cloud —; conceal—; crinkle into—; extinguish—; extract—; flash—; grant—; illuminate with —; induce—; loosen—; manage—; mock—; permit—; provoke—; quench—; repress—; rouse—; share—; shed—; suppress—; throw—; toss—; wear—; wreathe in—; wrinkle into—; —abashes; —basks; — confronts; —contorts; —creases; —crinkles; —deludes; —departs; —disconcerts; —disparages; —fades; —flashes; —flickers; — hides; —hovers; —lightens; —lingers; — mantles; —plays; —reassures; —renders; —reveals; —twitches.

(See grin, laughter, smirk.)

SMILE (v)

adverbs

delightedly; approvingly; shrewdly; affectionately; cherubically; reluctantly; ecstatically; whimsically; tolerantly; radiantly; indulgently; benevolently; tremulously;

grimly; sympathetically; blandly; beamingly; wanly; auspiciously; impudently; disarmingly; mischievously; magnanimously; unctuously; contemptuously; lewdly; winsomely; wryly; languidly; artificially; automatically; apathetically; benignly; contagiously; ingratiatingly; facetiously; superciliously; superficially; demurely; guilelessly; angelically; affably; ambiguously; coyly; cynically; cunningly; exultantly; exaggeratedly; cryptically; ruefully; benevolently.

(See grin, laugh.)

SMIRK

adjectives
conscious; genteel; empty; confidential; nasty.

verbs
affect—; check—; curb—; force—; raise—; repress—; restrain—; wipe away—; wither with—; —dampens; —depresses; —derides; —disdains; —droops; —flushes; —indicates; —reveals; —ridicules; —scorns; —sinks; —sours.

(See grin, smile.)

SMIRK (v)

adverbs
unpleasantly; slyly; treacherously; cynically; sarcastically; hideously; covertly; artificially; obnoxiously; satirically; saturninely.

(See sneer, simper.)

SMITE (v)

adverbs
ruthlessly; resoundingly; mercilessly; cruelly; bestially; heartlessly; shatteringly.

(See strike, hit.)

SMOKE

adjectives
after-dinner; favorite; stale; filthy; suffocating; thin; ribbon; pallid; curling; sulphur; helpless; inky; lurid; eddying; leaping; bituminous; faint; dense; resinous; blinding; sour; crooked; foul; columned; acrid; venomous.

verbs
enfold with—; spurt—; —asphyxiates; — belches; —billows; —blinds; —blackens; —blights; —carries; —chokes; —clouds; — conceals; —curls; —dissolves; —drifts; — eclipses; —emits; —envelops; —floats; — gags; —grimes; —hangs; —hovers; —

looms; —obscures; —overcomes; —penetrates; —pervades; —pours; —puffs; — reeks; —screens; —seeps in; —shrouds; —shuts out; —smothers; —smudges; — soars; —spirals; —stifles; —suffocates; — swirls; —uncurls; —veils; —vitiates; — whirls; —wraps; —wreathes.

(See fumes, haze, mist, soot, fog.)

SMOKE (v)

adverbs
complacently; jovially; fraternally; leisurely; somnolently; gravely; endlessly; atrociously; deliciously; philosophically; reflectively; meditatively; incessantly.

(See fume, reek.)

SMOKY

adverbs
densely; alarmingly; suffocatingly; terribly; dangerously; dingily; invisibly; perilously; unpleasantly; unbearably; disagreeably; odiously; acridly; blindingly; abominably; hazardously.

SMOOTH

adverbs
politely; mysteriously; significantly; amiably; civilly; genteely; courteously; craftily; obsequiously; good-temperedly; suavely; urbanely; suspiciously; sweetly; graciously; ingratiatingly; fashionably; alluringly; superficially; seductively; hypocritically.

SMOOTH (v)

adverbs
diplomatically; socially; mechanically; skillfully; artfully; benevolently.

(See stroke, calm.)

SMOOTHNESS

adjectives
polished; fashionable; exclusive; alluring; oily; excessive; matronly; surface.

SMOTHER (v)

adverbs
fatally; painfully; incontinently; politely; insidiously; socially; economically; politically; viciously.

(See repress, extinguish.)

SMOULDERING

adverbs
slowly; dangerously; luridly; fantastically; glowingly; alarmingly; actively; dully;

dimly; faintly; perilously; hazardously; hatefully; evidently; persistently; steadily; apparently.

SMUDGY
adverbs
unacceptably; carelessly; illegibly; dingily; grimily; grittily; darkly; unpleasantly; offensively; unattractively; amazingly; inexplicably; deliberately; intentionally; impossibly; contemptibly; disagreeably.

SMUG
adverbs
unbearably; disgustingly; disagreeably; irritatingly; unreasonably; ridiculously; pompously; chestily; overly; vexatiously; maddeningly; ostentatiously; complacently; pretentiously; laughably; contentedly; priggishly; imperturbably.

SMUGGLING
verbs
abandon—; abolish—; charge with—; cloak —; confess to—; convict of—; countenance —; cover—; deter—; disclose—; engage in —; expose—; frown upon—; justify—; practice—; screen—; suppress—; traffic in —; uncover—; —defrauds; —mulcts; — profits; —violates.
(See robbery, theft.)

SNAIL
verbs
cultivate—; prey on—; search for—; uncover—; —buries; —crawls; —emerges; — hides.
(See animal.)

SNAKE
adjectives
sinuous; sacred; venomous; gaping; dazzling; strong; quick; watching; hissing; gigantic; poisonous.

verbs
cage—; capture—; charm—; —coils; —constricts; —contorts; —crawls; —deposits eggs; —drapes around; —drops upon; — emerges; —encircles; —engulfs its prey; —entwines; —feigns; —frightens; —glides; —hibernates; —hisses; —lunges; —poisons; —recoils; —retreats; —scurries; —seizes; —slides; —slithers; —squirms; —stalks; —stings; —stirs; —strangles its prey; — strikes; —struggles; —suns itself; —surprises its prey; —swallows its prey; —

sways; —terrorizes; —thrashes about; — threatens; —twines; —twists; —undulates; —vibrates; —whips its tail; —worms its way; —wraps around; —wriggles; — writhes; —zigzags.
(See lizard, reptile.)

SNAKY
adverbs
circuitously; sinuously; insidiously; maliciously; artfully; craftily; subtly; slanderously; insinuatingly; surreptitiously; deceitfully; despicably; treacherously; wilily; subtly; archly; crookedly.

SNAP (*v*)
adverbs
explosively; exultantly; joyously; irritatingly; nervously; intermittently; repeatedly.
(See snarl, growl.)

SNAPPY
adverbs
disagreeably; bracingly; stimulatingly; coldly; unpleasantly; extremely; bitterly; cruelly; stingingly; harshly; exceedingly; terribly; dreadfully.

SNARE
adjectives
silken; wavering; female; alluring; sensual; treacherous; drowsing; harmless; opal; lying; elfish; marvelous; sentimental; cursed.

verbs
bait—; decoy into—; entangle in—; escape —; lure into—; mend—; plant—; —attracts; —deludes; —entices; —intrigues; —menaces; —tempts; —victimizes.
(See cobweb, net, trap.)

SNARL (*v*)
adverbs
tigerishly; fiendishly; formidably; fiercely; viciously; portentously; furiously; rapaciously; terrifyingly; bestially; diabolically.
(See growl, snap.)

SNARLS
adjectives
perfect; hoarse; angry; rasping; screaming.

SNATCH (*v*)
adverbs
instantaneously; swiftly; thievingly; insolently; hurriedly; selfishly; callously; gluttonously.
(See grasp, grab.)

SNEAKY

adverbs
notoriously; infamously; reputedly; disagreeably; detestably; abominably; atrociously; shamefully; wickedly; viciously; maliciously; incurably; fearfully; strangely; naturally; habitually; alarmingly; suspiciously; furtively; guiltily.

SNEER

adjectives
dull; veiled; significant; copious (pl); perceptible; subtle; drifting; powdery; haughty; frozen; bitter; infernal; chronic; sinister; twisted; mocking.

verbs
check—; curb—; curl into—; force—; indulge in—; parry—; repress—; restrain—; wither with—; —affronts; —castigates; —chides; —derides; —desecrates; —disparages; —gibes; —jeers; —mocks; —outrages; —rebukes; —scorns; —taunts.
(See jeer, ridicule, contempt.)

SNEER (v)

adverbs
derisively; contemptuously; aristocratically; scornfully; hatefully; superciliously; fastidiously; priggishly.
(See jeer, smirk.)

SNEEZE (v)

adverbs
violently; explosively; abruptly; repeatedly; significantly; obstreperously; exasperatingly.
(See cough.)

SNICKER

verbs
check—; curb—; disregard—; restrain—; voice—; —admonishes; —chides; —derides; —disparages; —insults; —issues; —mimics; —scoffs; —taunts; —withers; —twits.
(See giggle, laughter, smirk, grin.)

SNICKER (v)

adverbs
contemptuously; indecently; irreverently; ribaldly; ludicrously; exasperatingly; slyly; maliciously; irresistibly; insolently.
(See titter, smirk, simper.)

SNIFF

adjectives
tremendous; sarcastic; hearty; prodigious; premonitory.

SNIFF (v)

adverbs
greedily; haughtily; warily; instinctively; audibly; suspiciously; ostentatiously.
(See scent, smell.)

SNOB

verbs
crush—; deflate—; humble—; loathe—; pique—; sober—; —affects; —apes; —assumes; —condescends; —cringes; —cuts (colloq.); —disdains; —flushes; —humiliates; —inflates; —overbears; —overweens; —preens; —pretends; —puffs up; —regards; —scoffs at; —scorns; —swaggers; —swells; —worships.
(See hypocrite.)

SNOBBISH

adverbs
unwarrantably; groundlessly; absurdly; curiously; oddly; meanly; grossly; crudely; crazily; pompously; bombastically; cheaply; laughably; arrogantly; haughtily; ridiculously; ludicrously; particularly; uncommonly; unpardonably; unbearably; disagreeably; unpleasantly.

SNORE

adjectives
simultaneous; melodious; feminine; smothered; annoying; regular; buzzing.

SNORE (v)

adverbs
intoxicatedly; sonorously; peacefully; stertorously; irritatingly; exasperatingly; melodiously; incessantly; annoyingly; perpetually.
(See sleep, slumber, breathe.)

SNORT

adjectives
impatient; angry; loud; trumpeting; audible; roaring.

SNORT (v)

adverbs
impatiently; indignantly; audibly; trumpetingly; roaringly; terrifically; disgustingly; violently; vulgarly.
(See snarl, growl.)

SNOW

adjectives
wintry; flaky; feathery; melting; downy; driven; whirling; benumbing; trackless;

eternal; summer; innocent; chilling; caressing; consecrated; glittering; shrinking; powerful; winged; rugged; drifting; crunching; scattering; untrampled; dazzling; solidified; crisp; sharp; virgin; unfathomable; shrouded; pure; homogeneous; receding; perpetual; wondrous; strange; crusted; dissolving; frozen; sculptured; flying; unsunned; sparkling; untrodden; hard; heavy; wasting; powdery; whipped; crackling; dreaded.

verbs
crunch—; scan—; scrunch (colloq.)—; sculpture in—; stamp—; thaw—; —avalanches; —blankets; —caps; —crowns; —dazzles; —deadens; —diminishes; —drifts; —envelops; —falls; —flashes; —flurries; —glistens; —hides; —hushes; —lies; —mantles; —masks; —muffles; —pelts; —penetrates; —piles; —retreats; —ribs; —sails; —scuds; —sculptures; —settles; —shrouds; —sifts; —tinges; —tints; —veils; —wraps.
(See snowflakes.)

SNOW-BLIND
adverbs
completely; momentarily; temporarily; frantically; terrifyingly; suddenly; perilously; inopportunely; curiously; merely; unluckily; tormentingly.

SNOWFLAKES
verbs
drive—; —accumulate; —adorn; —bite; —blanch; —checker; —chill; —cling; —dazzle; —deluge; —fleck; —frost; —glitter; —nip; —obscure; —shudder; —silver.
(See snow, crystal, flake.)

SNOWY
adverbs
beautifully; exquisitely; fortunately; spectacularly; brilliantly; dazzlingly; dangerously; unbelievably; deeply; persistently; incredibly; unseasonably; unexpectedly; surprisingly; perilously; blindingly; hazardously; dreadfully; fearfully; frightfully; suddenly; windily.

SNUB
adjectives
deliberate; suggestive; cold; shrewd; nasty.

verbs
construe as—; expose to—; resent—; risk—;

rue—; —abashes; —bewilders; —discomposes; —disconcerts; —discredits; —humbles; —humiliates; —overwhelms; —petrifies; —reddens; —reproaches; —slurs; —staggers; —stuns; —takes down a peg.
(See insult, rebuff, rebuke.)

SNUB (v)
adverbs
deliberately; coldly; acrimoniously; invidiously; permanently; contemptuously; hatefully; conceitedly.
(See ignore, disregard.)

SNUG
adverbs
compactly; securely; safely; closely; comfortably; happily; fortunately; pleasantly; warmly; reasonably; agreeably; delightfully; luckily; sufficiently; satisfactorily; deliciously.

SOAP
verbs
adulterate—; enrich—; rinse off—; —agrees with; —deodorizes; —disinfects; —fortifies; —invigorates; —lathers; —launders; —laves; —protects; —purges; —refreshes; —restores; —saturates; —scours; —shampoos; —soothes; —stimulates; —tingles.
(See lather, lotion.)

SOAPY
adverbs
sufficiently; warmly; satisfactorily; pleasantly; reasonably; slightly; strongly; occasionally; unpleasantly; pungently; comfortably; comfortingly.

SOAR (v)
adverbs
magnificently; lazily; serenely; majestically; pretentiously; daringly; gracefully; incessantly; loftily; effortlessly; daringly; transcendingly.
(See fly, mount.)

SOB
adjectives
tearless; dying; convulsive; hysterical; heaving; tremulous; noiseless; desolate; innumerable (pl); loud; indignant; audible; hopeless; diminished; confused; gulping; choked; painful; feeble; commingled (pl); conventional; wild; stifled; gasping; panting; racking; renewed; stormy; deep.

verbs
burst into—s; check—; heave—; repress—;
restrain—; smother—; stifle—; strangle—;
suppress—; whimper—; —disarms; —engulfs; —gurgles; —lacerates; —laments;
—melts; —moves; —overwhelms; —racks;
—rends; —shakes; —softens; —touches; —
wells up; —wrings.
(See moan, murmur, sigh, shiver, shudder.)

SOB (*v*)
adverbs
piteously; audibly; miserably; bleakly; passionately; hysterically; violently; convulsively; bitterly; monotonously; tearlessly;
tremulously; rackingly; pantingly; gaspingly.
(See weep, cry.)

SOBBING
adjectives
gentle; frightened; unrestrained; monotonous.

adverbs
convulsively; heavily; desolately; lonesomely; heartbreakingly; repentantly; remorsefully; bitterly; cruelly; miserably; loudly;
quietly; silently; interminably; continually;
unreasonably; absurdly; ridiculously; deliberately; purposefully; profitably; suddenly; violently; unaccountably; hysterically;
grievously; angrily; happily; nervously.

SOBER
adverbs
unusually; gravely; unwontedly; uncommonly; extremely; unquestionably; occasionally;
usually; seldom; rarely; scarcely; reluctantly; habitually; substantially; moderately;
drearily; dismally; pensively; thoughtfully;
speculatively; wistfully; wishfully; reasonably; dispassionately; judicially; suddenly;
earnestly; judiciously; amazingly; strangely; studiously; alarmingly.

SOBRIETY
verbs
commend—; conduce to—; dispose toward
—; dwell in—; lack—; maintain—; moderate—; persist in—; preserve—; pursue—;
restore—; suspend—; —represses; —restrains; —spares; —tempers.
(See temperance, moderation, gravity.)

SOCIABLE
adverbs
delightfully; sincerely; charmingly; agreeably; habitually; extremely; usually; rarely;
scarcely; affably; genially; highly; cordially; familiarly; quietly; noisily; hilariously;
heartily; gracefully; chattily; unusually;
exceedingly; extraordinarily; clumsily;
suddenly; unexpectedly; excessively; designedly; chummily; warmly; truly; uncommonly; remarkably; significantly; ostentatiously.

SOCIAL
adverbs
pleasantly; agreeably; genially; jovially;
happily; festively; sportively; affably; usually; highly; companionably; remarkably;
openly.

SOCIALISM
verbs
advocate—; combat—; define—; frown upon—; oppose—; prate of—; promote—;
rant against—; reject—; —burrows into;
—cankers; —confiscates; —controls; —disposes of; —ebbs; —equals; —flourishes;
—frees; —humanizes; —levels; —liberates;
—manifests; —paralyzes; —regulates; —
relinquishes; —remedies; —shares; —shatters; —undermines; —wages; —wars a-
gainst.
(See communism, liberalism, modernism,
nationalism.)

SOCIALIST
verbs
silence—; —abolishes; —bands; —cements;
—clashes; —discards; —distributes; —expatiates on; —hails; —harangues; —heckles; —indoctrinates; —organizes; —prates;
—rants; —spreads; —theorizes; —undermines.
(See anarchist, communist.)

SOCIETY
adjectives
plutocratic; polished; vigorous; cultivated;
fashionable; cold; open; integrated; agreeable; desolate; exotic; honorable; competitive; provincial; artistic; civilized; charitable; cheerful; distinguished; human; frivolous; shattered; unevolved; distinct; formal; martyrized; decorous; polite; heartless; inorganic; intellectual; fastidious; insensitive; brilliant; literary; aristocratic;
primitive; high-toned; perpetual; congenial;

purified; benevolent; exclusive; peripatetic; reputable; sordid; monastic; immoral; notorious; respectable; wild; scientific; contemporary; industrial.

verbs
abandon—; admit to—; debar from—; denounce—; deprive—; destroy—; displease —; elevate—; expel from—; introduce into —; mingle with—; negate—; plunge—; purge—; redeem—; remodel—; shun—; step into—; usher into—; —animates; — arrays; —binds; —brands; —campaigns; —conciliates; —conforms; —controls; — copes; —disintegrates; —establishes; —expands; —expels; —frowns upon; —lauds; —obligates; —organizes; —outlaws; — plagues; —polishes; —recruits; —rends asunder; —revolutionizes; —sanctions; — serves; —shackles; —springs from; —uproots; —wars on; —withdraws.
(See brotherhood, community, companionship, state.)

SOCIETY
(*association*)
verbs
address—; conciliate—; convoke—; disband —; found—; harangue—; head—; league in—; link in—; mobilize—; muster—; preside over—; sever—; —adjourns; —assembles; —convenes; —defines; —disseminates; —elects; —flocks to; —pledges; — preys; —promulgates; —supports.
(See league, association, club, guild, lodge.)

SOD
adjectives
peace-giving; stubborn; velvet; verdant; spongy; lifeless; moldering.

SODA
verbs
bottle—s; cap—s; carbonate—; charge—; color—; dispense—; dissolve in—; down—; flavor—; manufacture—; mix—; prepare—; purvey—s; siphon—; sweeten—; —effervesces; —exhilarates; —refreshes.
(See beverage, drink, liquor.)

SODDEN
adverbs
dismally; gloomily; heavily; irretrievably; disagreeably; unpleasantly; strangely.

SOFA
adjectives
imposing; embroidered; matted; satin-damask; comfortable; battered.

verbs
bolster—; crouch behind—; curl in—; ensconce in—; loll on—; lounge on—; prop —; perch on—; recline on—; refurbish—; renovate—; repose on—; slump on—; straddle—; upholster—; —accommodates; — bears; —beckons; —graces; —sinks; —supports; —sustains.
(See couch.)

SOFT
adverbs
deliciously; adorably; pleasantly; delightfully; comfortably; admirably; conveniently; invitingly; warmly; comfortingly; curiously; particularly; commendably; pliably; delicately; tenderly; compassionately; sympathetically; gently; adaptably.

SOFT-HEARTED
adverbs
leniently; indulgently; judiciously; understandingly; occasionally; pliably; naturally; usually; unwontedly; graciously; hospitably; admirably; curiously; charitably; generously; magnanimously; notoriously; foolishly; usually.

SOFTNESS
adjectives
passionate; sapping; lovely; liquid; musical; purring; tremulous; feline; infinite; melting; bewitching; displeasing; velvet; shy; unbelievable; sudden; cat-like.

SOFT-SPOKEN
adverbs
blandly; usually; habitually; normally; pleasantly; agreeably; delightfully; deceivingly; indulgently; naturally; invariably; curiously; admirably; deliberately; purposely.

SOGGY
adverbs
unpleasantly; unserviceably; curiously; unwholesomely; heavily; irredeemably; unfortunately; unprofitably; admittedly; irremediably; unexpectedly; remarkably; dreadfully.

SOIL

adjectives

humid; volcanic; fenny; blood-stained; hallowed; luxuriant; teeming; sterile; sifted; repressed; alluvial; enchanted; thirsty; marshy; unbroken; unproductive; friendly; noxious; ill-smelling; fertile; wholesome; friable; sacred; desolate; accursed; fruitful; parched; arid; sandy; indistinguishable; ancient; smoking; niggardly; poor; rich; radiant; favored; fallow; cultivated; kind; surrounding; ungrateful; neglected; peaty; wretched; congenial; tillable; swampy; burning; mangled; barren; foreign; adjacent; drenched; crusty; virgin; exhausted; devastated; mortal; tropic; native; alien; nitrous; conquered; oozy; crumbling.

verbs

cleave—; conserve—; cultivate—; devitalize—; drain—; enrich—; fertilize—; furrow—; harrow—; irrigate—; impregnate—; preserve—; pry from—; renew—; renounce —; revitalize—; ridge up—; rob—; root in —; scratch—; set foot on—; smell—; sow—; starve—; till—; wring from—; —begrimes; —blesses; —erodes; —procreates; —satisfies; —smudges.

(See land, earth, ground, farm.)

SOIL (*v*)

adverbs

carelessly; obnoxiously; markedly; hopelessly; disgustingly; annoyingly; exasperatingly.

(See taint, spoil.)

SOJOURN

adjectives

dreary; aimless; endless; short; enforced; protracted; permanent; bloody; previous; brief; accursed; autumnal; obscure; pleasant.

SOLACE

adjectives

individual; airy; idle; melancholy; immeasurable; ecstatic; scant; repenting; little.

verbs

afford—; accord—; bestow—; decline—; derive—; extend—; grant—; offer—; proffer —; reject—; tender—; volunteer—; yield —; —allays; —appeases; —assuages; —beguiles; —cheers; —comforts; —draws; — diverts; —mitigates; —palliates; —salves; —smooths.

(See comfort, consolation.)

SOLDIERS

adjectives

fanatical; languid; wilted; faceless; gallant; brave; illiterate; true; trusty; rough; career; drunken; godless; volunteer; surviving; harassed; well-tried; distinguished; capable; maddened; struggling; brutal; sausage-legged; valiant; weary; rowdy; unrelenting; mercenary; butchered; disbanded; decorative; deluded; accomplished; improvident; straggling; disorderly; good; hardy; wandering; disaffected; lion-hearted; stout; demoralized; gaunt; intrepid; stern; fearless; hot-tempered; heroic; veteran; lice-ridden; sentimental; indomitable; obdurate; eager; doughty; steady; fortunate; condemned; besotted; chivalrous; vulgar; magnanimous; forlorn; staring; resolute; inebriated; weary; mutilated; sleepy; disillusioned.

verbs

arm—; command—; conciliate—; court-martial—; dispatch—; drill—; harry—; mobilize—; mow down—; quarter—; train—; — advance; —barricade; —beleaguer; —besiege; —brandish; —break step; —bristle; —bluster; —campaign; —charge; —coerce; —crusade; —desert; —enlist; —enroll; — engage; —flock; —garrison; —invade; — intrench; —jostle; —lay siege; —mutiny; — patrol; —parry; —plod—; rake; —repulse; —retaliate; —revive; —slog; —snipe; — squander; —storm; —surrender; —tramp; —trudge; —ward off; —wield.

(See besieger, infantry, army, invader, militia.)

SOLDIERY

adjectives

ruthless; insolent; ferocious; desperate; sanguine; brutal; well-clad; riotous; vagabond; grim-faced; licentious; architectural; fierce.

SOLEMN

adverbs

unduly; curiously; ceremoniously; sacredly; piously; religiously; devoutly; reverentially; fervently; ritualistically; judicially; sternly; austerely; ponderously; gravely; seriously; alarmingly; forbiddingly; unnecessarily; ominously; portentously; depressingly; impressively; magnificently; extraordinarily; gravely; grimly; ridiculously; absurdly; ludicrously; unreasonably; occasionally; unexpectedly; unusually; curiously; strangely; reverently; uncommonly.

adjectives

severe; majestic; religious; rare; mysterious; quaint; guarded; significant; pretentious; accustomed; symmetrical; grievous; unutterable; impressive; formal; professional; inaccessible; profound; dismal; preternatural; sweet; shallow; mournful; livid; royal.

verbs

alleviate—; dedicate in—; ease—; enthrone in—; impress—; maintain—; mar—; perform with—; preserve—; relax—; ruffle—; sustain—; temper—; —abashes; —awes; —chastens; —dampens; —dazzles; —depresses; —deters; —glooms; —inspires; —oppresses; —pervades; —sobers; —subdues.

(See ceremony, gravity, seriousness.)

SOLICIT (v)

adverbs

impudently; courteously; importunately; pertinaciously; timorously; underhandedly; earnestly; pressingly; urgently; insinuatingly.

(See request, ask, seek.)

SOLICITATION

adjectives

hinted; earnest; sickening; pressing; tearful; urgent; insinuating.

verbs

brush aside—s; dismiss—; elicit—; endure —; ignore—; pursue—s; yield to—; —s carry weight; —influences; —irks; —moves; —plagues; —provokes; —riles (colloq.); —ruffles; —sways; —touches; —vexes; —wrings.

(See request, invitation, entreaty.)

SOLICITORS

adjectives

best-moving; fair; government; prominent; insistent.

SOLICITOUS

adverbs

tenderly; anxiously; eagerly; frantically; curiously; strangely; pretentiously; ostentatiously; cursorily; lovingly; affectionately; protectively; absurdly; ridiculously; responsibly; forebodingly; terribly.

adjectives

constant; peculiar; passionate; quiet; liveliest; dismal; tenderest; loving; frozen; selfish; affectionate; profound; glorious; trembling; pitying; sincere; voluntary; paternal; friendly; deep.

verbs

allay—; assuage—; blench in—; cloak—; conceal—; deserve—; display—; distrust—; dwell in—; ease—; exhibit—; expose—; feign—; manifest—; relieve—; relish—; screen—; —besets; —deters; —harrows; —haunts; —obsesses; —perturbs; —preys on; —unnerves; —wracks; —wrings; inspire—.

(See anxiety, misgiving, care, concern, attention.)

SOLID

adverbs

unusually; satisfactorily; fortunately; securely; stably; remarkably; immovably; finally; desirably; sufficiently; safely; financially; structurally; commercially; warrantably; splendidly; undoubtedly; unbreakably.

SOLIDARITY

verbs

cement—; cleave—; compromise—; disrupt —; endanger—; fracture—; gnaw at—; hazard—; impair—; jeopardize—; link in —; maintain—; mar—; menace—; mould —; nurse—; preserve—; rend—; rupture—; sap—; shake—; split—; strain—; sustain —; threaten—; undermine—; weld—; —crumbles; —disintegrates; —prevails; —totters.

(See power, authority, leadership, union.)

SOLIDITY

adjectives

combined; moral; little; primitive; costly; imposing; mellow; false; stable.

SOLIDS

adjectives

atomic; precipitated; flaccid; geometrical; quiescent; elastic.

verbs

compress—; congeal into—; convert into—; dissolve—; excrete—; liquefy—; pierce—; precipitate—; pulverize—; vaporize—; —cohere; —contract; —disintegrate; —displace; —expand.

(See mass.)

SOLILOQUIZE (v)

adverbs

philosophically; morbidly; dejectedly; monotonously; ceaselessly; academically; sepulchrally.

(See utter, talk.)

SOLILOQUY

verbs

breathe—; deliver—; emit—; indulge in—; murmur—; mutter—; reflect in—; unfold —; utter—; voice—; —considers; —contemplates; —discourses; —expatiates on; —mediates; —moves; —ponders; —reasons; —reproaches; —reveals; —revolves; —touches.

(See speech, talk.)

SOLITARY

adverbs

restfully; delightfully; formidably; gloomily; forbiddingly; cheerlessly; pathetically; unhappily; remotely; alarmingly; disagreeably; desperately; desolately; impossibly; tragically; preferably; comfortably; selfishly; unexpectedly; undesirably; uncommonly; curiously; amazingly; insistently.

SOLITUDE

adjectives

mighty; unhallowed; dismal; heaving; tranquil; great; sylvan; proud; expectant; gladsome; splendid; social; musing; crowded; decent; dreary; sealed; oppressive; perfect; wildest; unbroken; mountain; vast; misty; populous; convenient; careless; morose; meditative; patient; arctic; fearful; rural; chilly; mystic; unweeping; delicious; utter; obscure; midnight; grave; dewy; gigantic; twilight; artificial; deep; majestic; moorland; solemn; inaccessible; sullen; serene; pastoral; restored.

verbs

abandon to—; abide in—; afford—; burden —; bear—; crave—; encompass—; endure —; evince—; incline to—; loathe—; long for—; mope in—; muse in—; ponder in—; recall in—; relegate to—; relish—; retire to—; sequester in—; shatter—; shun—; suffer—; welcome—; yearn for—; —cloaks; —deceives; —depresses; —detaches; —isolates; —penetrates; —stagnates.

(See isolation, loneliness, seclusion.)

SOLUBLE

adverbs

scarcely; highly; instantly; chemically; easily; obviously; manifestly; conveniently; handily; quickly; adaptably; commendably.

SOLUTION
(explanation)

verbs

approach—; arrive at—; clarify—; comprehend—; demonstrate—; disagree with—; facilitate—; formulate—; furnish—; gain—; offer—; reach—; seek—; trace—; —coincides; —implies; —points; —racks.

(See explanation, interpretation.)

SOLUTION
(general)

adjectives

dilute; saline; partial; attenuated; elusive; commonplace; classic; irritating; logical; colloidal; formless; transparent; decent; pacific; ultimate; dirt; deodorizing; obvious; antiseptic; adaptive; delightful; consequent; rational; supernatural; basic; successful; supersaturated; practical; satisfying; contemporary; sensible; equitable; ideal; peaceful; ordinary; lofty.

SOLUTION
(mixture)

verbs

dilute—; dip—; gargle—; inject—; saturate with—; sponge—; —mixes; —strengthens; seek—.

(See mixture, juice, liquid, medicine.)

SOLVE (v)

adverbs

definitely; accurately; promptly; swiftly; mechanically; scientifically; ultimately; constructively; ingeniously; practically; basically; partially.

(See clear, explain.)

SOLVENT

adverbs

responsibly; reputedly; reputably; admirably; safely; financially; manifestly; acceptably; satisfactorily; fortunately; absolutely.

SOMBERNESS

verbs

alleviate—; brighten—; brood in—; droop in—; reflect—; relax—; relieve of—; ruffle —; sink into—; sulk in—; sustain—; —abashes; —awes; —dampens; —darkens; —

deepens; —dejects; —depresses; —envelops; —glooms; —illuminates; —oppresses; —permeates; —pervades; —saddens; —shadows; —weights.

(See darkness, melancholy, gravity, gloom.)

SOMBRE

adverbs

lugubriously; gloomily; dismally; unaccountably; unnecessarily; unpleasantly; richly; sumptuously; harmoniously; fashionably; conventionally; disagreeably; overwhelmingly; mournfully; gravely; gruesomely; terribly; hauntingly; horribly.

SOMERSAULT

verbs

achieve—; avert—; avoid—; culminate in —; execute—; perfect—; perform—; practise—s; reverse—; —amazes; —astounds; —climaxes; —inverts; —surprises.

(See trick, leap.)

SOMETHING

adjectives

undefinable; coquettish; intangible; infinitesimal; misty; solemn; inestimable; unnatural; ghastly; unnamable; curious.

SOMNOLENT

adverbs

overwhelmingly; unaccountably; irresistibly; strangely; dully; overpoweringly; uncontrollably; inexplicably; abnormally; embarrassingly; alarmingly; inexpressibly.

SON

adjectives

giddy; mutilated; slow-minded; intended; scapegrace; accursed; hardy; illegitimate; reckless; instinctive; lawful; patriotic; enigmatic; murdered; hapless; prodigal; equivocal; misunderstood; degenerate; virtuous; astonished; blooming; surviving; indolent; observant; unkempt; gallant; ransomed; poor; illustrious; dutiful; purblind; filmloving; admirable; accursed; docile; stalwart; valiant; obedient; accomplished; wayward; humbled; tortured; first-born; enchanting; ungracious; goodly; brisk; eldest; handsome; patriotic; elegant; amiable; free-hearted; insignificant; mercenary; unappreciated; rude; energetic; exiled.

verbs

alienate—; bear—; beget—; castigate—;

chastise—; conceive—; crave—; discipline —; disinherit—; disown—; endear to—; expel—; guide—; hunger for—; inculcate in —; ingrain in—; instill in—; pamper—; renounce—; yearn for—; —assumes; —begets; —cherishes; —inherits; —relinquishes; —toddles.

(See child, offspring, daughter.)

SONG

adjectives

emotional; melodious; dramatic; characteristic; throbbing; shanty; voluntary; comic; faultless; boisterous; spiritual; mournful; scurrilous; pealing; solemn; humorous; ineffable; choral; monotonous; rapturous; tranquil; echoing; vapid; immortal; buoyant; deathless; cheerful; weird; antiquated; impassioned; speechless; perpetual; artful; amorous; affectionate; irksome; unconnected; everlasting; protracted; joyous; provoking; unmusical; indolent; savage; drawling; ringing; lifeless; ribald; generous; gusty; rich; blithe; unpremeditated; mystic; shrill; laborious; foolish; magnetic; quivering; syncopated; pastoral; dropping; wondrous; jubilant; plaintive; tragic; parting; chastening; saucy; desperate; ear-breaking; coarse; sunny; eddying; arduous; grandest; wailing; fatal; medicinal; worthless; doleful; visible; yearning; piquant; rollicking; fiery; stifling; hideous; twilight; adventurous; belligerent; noble; nuptial

verbs

accompany—; break out into—; breathe—; carol—; chant—; compose—; dash into —; diffuse—; echo—; execute—; exploit —; flood with—; hum—; improvise—; intone—; lilt—; perform—; pipe—; perpetuate—; render—; stifle—; strike up—; trill —; twitter—; warble—; whistle—; —breaks out; —descends upon; —dwindles; —expresses; —evolves; —laments; —merges; —moderates; —modulates; —pierces; —s pour; —quavers; —recaptures; —ripples; —shatters; —subsides; —swells; —uplifts; —vibrates.

(See melody, jazz, ditty, incantation, music, chant, refrain, carol, hymn.)

SONGSTER

adjectives

exquisite; plumed; lingering; feathered; lifeless; medieval; radio.

adjectives
commendatory; true; glowing; halting; wailful; memorable; soaring; conventional; stock; beauteous; insincere.

verbs
compose—; consecrate—; dash off—; dedicate—to; indite—; peruse—s; scan—; transcribe—; weave—; —amuses; —delights; —expresses; —glorifies; —immortalizes; —impresses; —reflects; —rhymes; —sentimentalizes; —treats of; —versifies.
(See poem.)

SONOROUS
adverbs
impressively; unctuously; chantingly; deeply; profoundly; resoundingly; challengingly; richly; magnificently; splendidly; remarkably; strangely; compellingly; majestically; regally; authoritatively.

SOOT
verbs
—begrimes; —besmears; —besmirches; —blackens; —blots; —blurs; —contaminates; —defiles; —eclipses; —flocculates; —jets; —obscures; —reeks; —screens; —settles; —smears; —smirches; —smudges; —soils; —sullies; —tarnishes; —veils.
(See carbon, powder, dust, smoke, fog.)

SOOTHE (v)
adverbs
maternally; infinitely; benevolently; compassionately; harmoniously; effectually; pleasingly.
(See pacify, calm.)

SOOTHING
adverbs
refreshingly; comfortingly; curatively; graciously; serenely; mildly; pleasantly; softly; gratefully; quietly; coolly; gently; blandly; especially; satisfyingly; remarkably; marvelously; tenderly; maternally; mercifully.

SOPHISTICATED
adverbs
consciously; impressively; proudly; vivaciously; absurdly; ridiculously; haughtily; pretentiously; extremely; unexpectedly; bitterly; stylishly; fashionably.

SOPHISTICATION
adjectives
subtle; sly; cool; quaint; hard-boiled; studied; brittle; surface; cruel.

verbs
acquire—; breed—; cultivate—; develop—; discard—; ingrain--; jar—; mould—; pierce—; stamp with—; shock—; —attracts; —beguiles; —bores; —enhances; —glosses; —impresses; —polishes; —reeks; —varnishes; —veneers.
(See manner, style.)

SOPHISTRY
adjectives
subtle; pompous; wild; delinquent; apparent.

SOPRANO
verbs
acclaim—; applaud—; present—; train—; —carols; —cracks; —cultivates; —enthralls; —entrances; —executes; —exercises; —expresses; —flutes; —lilts; —modulates; —moves; —performs; —renders; —strains; —tours; —trills; —twitters.
(See singer, choir, chorus.)

SORCERER
adjectives
miserable; hostile; unfortunate; accused; wicked.

SORDID
adverbs
disagreeably; undoubtedly; atrociously; curiously; basely; uncommonly; unreasonably; unbelievably; incredibly; unthinkably; outrageously; outlandishly; scandalously; terribly; fearfully; detestably; barbarously; unspeakably; stingily; grossly; miserably; churlishly; greedily; foully; unaccountably; unwarrantably; strangely; utterly; undeniably.

SORE
adjectives
swollen; embossed; inward; festering; everfretting; raw; horrid.

verbs
aggravate—; cauterize—; diagnose—; disinfect—; dress—; extirpate—; irritate—; lance—; lick—; salve—; treat—; —atrophies; —breaks out; —cankers; —chafes; —defaces; —discharges; —disfigures; —en-

venoms; —festers; —ferments; —infects; —inflames; —occurs; —persists; —rankles; —responds; —scabs; —suppurates; —taints; —throbs.

(See rash, inflammation, canker, abscess, blister, boil.)

adverbs
painfully; curiously; extremely; miserably; infectiously; dangerously; alarmingly; unaccountably; strangely; fearfully; feverishly; unfortunately; cruelly; exceedingly; naturally.

SORROW

adjectives
dreaming; querulous; sole; profound; despondent; inextinguishable; poignant; sacred; slow; imperious; human; stormy; transient; impetuous; faithless; helpless; unfeigned; sleepless; premature; stifled; domestic; dying; eternal; bitter; silent; deep; hearty; trampling; mortal; uncheered; sentimental; dark; dumb; passionate; crushing; unmitigated; sincere; romantic; imagined; fantastic; foolish; vehement; dried; accumulated; gnarling; noisy; desperate; oppressive; peculiar; grievous; dull; present; aesthetic; inarticulate; strange; concealed.

verbs
afflict with—; appease—; assail with—; assuage—; brim with—; cast—; cloak—; console—; contain—; couch in—; crush—; depict—; derive—; fade out of—; inflict—; intensify—; lament—; multiply—s; relieve—; remedy—; restrain—; share—; swallow—; unfold—; —befalls; —blights; —burdens; —chastens; —consumes; —darkens; —deepens; —embraces; —mars; —overburdens; —overwhelms; —purges.

(See commiseration, sadness, suffering, grief.)

SORRY

adverbs
pitifully; wretchedly; sincerely; genuinely; truly; pitiably; miserably; grievously; profoundly; deeply; abjectly; remorsefully; embarrassingly; humbly; bitterly; regretfully; penitently; admittedly; extremely; immeasurably; reasonably; somewhat.

SORT

adjectives
particular; unsatisfactory; enthusiastic; whimsical; barren; vulgar; prophetical; stimulating; grossest; truest; meanest; desultory; outspoken; odd.

SOUL

adjectives
repentant; harmonic; circling; stormy; witty; genial; learned; troubled; hopeful; flaming; lost; living; amiable; kindred; sinful; erring; frank; reviving; poisonous; ardent; aesthetic; pagan; raptured; maddened; pervading; poetic; wronged; cheated; stagnant; unblemished; zealous; sensitive; loving; neat; gentle; departed; passive; tortured; malignant; impassive; noblest; helpless; starved; susceptible; silly; ravished; withered; luckless; chastened; desolate; lofty; singular; eager; radiant; wondrous; vile; daring; suspended; genial; trusting; polluted; vigorous; willing; separate; fettered; visionary; human; righteous; heroic; grateful; ingenious; deathless; rapt; naked; lifted; ecstatic; flagging; heated; dear; dawning; deluded; vitriolic; artist; full; loyal; groveling; solitary; agitated; gross; fainting; secret; silent; resolute; defeated; common; maddening; divine; brooding; incarnate; harmonious; convivial; morbid; comprehensive; speaking; priceless; wounded; craven; inmost; smitten; offending; spheric; guilty; poisonous; tender; pervading; universal; delicious; haughty; debilitated; passionate; progressive; saturate; feeble; liberal; multitudinous (pl); plastic; unripened; unstained; antique; agitated; festered; regal; truthful; trembling; kingly; emaciated; torpid; nimble; embryonic; redeemed; manly; devastated; reptile; shuddering; unwasting; frivolous; exploring; blotched; dead; scintillating; ransomed; pious; enthralling; delicate; pessimistic; tardy; virile; active; dauntless; altered; crude; eccentric; wakeful; elevated; cavalier; cantankerous; bleeding; clearest; stubborn; yearning; truant; dying; prevailing; introspective; credulous; misguided; exalted; angelic; cautious; charitable; grieved; timid; ardent; merry; spotted; callous; watchful; jealous; departed; intercurrent; countless (pl); rational; hungry; abstracted; wiser; patient; inviolable; obstinate; sordid; guileless; preserved; rich; bewildered; mean; knightly; sober; hideous; distracted; practical; simple; immortal; torn; famished; straying.

verbs

beguile—; beleaguer—; benefit—; bruise—; clothe—; clutter—; commit—; consign—; crush—; deliver—; deplore—; drain—; drown—; empty—; ennoble—; enrapture—; explore—; feast—; feed—; fire—; fortify—; gratify—; harrow—; impel—; incarnate—; incrust—; inflame—; loose—; mask—; mold —; nourish—; perjure—; pour—; purge—; purify—; rack—; raise—; release—; rend —; reveal—; salve—; satisfy—; saturate—; scourge—; sear—; search—; sell—; shadow —; smite—; soothe—; stain—; steep—; stir —; surrender—; tear— touch— transplant —; unburden—; untrim—; unveil—; wrap —; weary—; wrench—; —awakens; — bows; —breathes; —cries; —dares; —exults; —flames; —grieves; —governs; — lives; —palsies; —pants; —perishes; — quails; —quickens; —rebels; —revolts; — sees; —shudders; —struggles; —thirsts for; —wakens; —wavers; —wells up.

(See spirit.)

SOUND

adjectives

incongruous; obdurate; joyful; financial; explosive; ecstatic; numerous (pl); roaring; hissing; peculiar; quavering; plaintive; sprinkled; similar; lamentable; languid; unauthorized; elementary; crisp; muffled; unearthly; affrighting; thundering; lulling; empty; winged; perfidious; tinkling; imposing; ear-splitting; flat; petulant; scratching; powerful; human; horrid; answering; pulsating; puffing; monotonous; cropping; discordant; ominous; multitudinous (pl); articulate; distinct; terrible; mysterious; harmonious; faint; moaning; jarring; agreeable; perfect; blithe; thwacking; sad; romantic; weird; furtive; immortal; obnoxious; maddening; unresting; hideous; menacing; onomatopoeic; agglomerative; endearing; tuneful; stormy; incessant; plain; strange; dentilingual; obstructed; hoarse; chuckling; caressing; murmuring; animated; understanding; munching; increasing; howling; hollow; sullen; meaningless; cruel; heterogeneous; droning; pinging; wandering; delicious; cracking; kindred; spiritual; convulsed; clattering; perpetual; humming; evil; flattering; various (pl); murderous; consecutive; rumbling; gurgling; sensuous; rattling; joyous; dubious; rushing; monosyllabic; muttering; celestial; sweet; stealthy; whizzing; soothing; slight; throaty; suggestive; melodious; eminent;

confused; melancholy; healing; whistling; vague; clashing; raving; siren; repining; soft; recurrent; lambent; portentous; carefree; grunting; mirthful; false; sighing; raspy; idle; vocal; conversational; hammering; chirping; shocking; rhythmic; blissful; scientific; droll; harsh; fundamental; continuous; appalling; ghostly.

verbs

absorb—; alter—; attune to—; carry—; communicate—; deaden—; detect—; dilute —; direct—; disguise—; echo—; elicit—; emit—; give forth—; induce—; lessen—; limit—; mellow—; muffle—; interpret—; sharpen—; smother—; transmit—; waft—; visualize—; smother—; —alarms; —babbles; —ceases; —comforts; —dins; —echoes; —emanates; —s emerge; —falls; —s gibber; —s gurgle; —lulls; —penetrates; — reawakens; —reechoes; —registers; —reverberates; —scatters; —s trouble; —vanishes.

(See noise.)

SOUND

adverbs

fortunately; wholesomely; securely; luckily; admirably; commendably; satisfactorily; unusually; magnificently; splendidly; impressively; gloriously; perfectly; remarkably; excellently; sufficiently; superbly; miraculously.

SOUND (v)

adverbs

peremptorily; exasperatingly; incessantly; harshly; audibly; incredibly; importunately; celestially; mournfully; incongruously; thunderously; monotonously; discordantly; ominously; mysteriously; jarringly; thwackingly; weirdly; obnoxiously; portentously; appallingly.

(See express, hear.)

SOUNDLESS

adverbs

breathlessly; curiously; strangely; eerily; mysteriously; oddly; extraordinarily; miraculously; admirably; pleasantly; fortunately; furtively; stealthily; carefully; cautiously; warily; perfectly; remarkably; incredibly.

SOUP

adjectives

thick; substantial; hearty; savory; scalding; canned.

verbs

administer—; bolt—; brew—; concoct—; dispatch—; gulp—; guzzle—; imbibe—; ladle—; prepare—; relish—; savor—; season—; sip—; spice—; strain—; swill—; —gelatinizes; —invigorates; —nourishes; —replenishes; —scalds; —tempts; —thickens; —tickles the palate.

(See broth, food, liquid.)

SOUR

adverbs

disagreeably; acridly; yeastily; pleasantly; horribly; startlingly; unexpectedly; oddly; mustily; offensively; inedibly; overly; extremely; curiously; unpalatably; unpleasantly; rancidly.

SOURCE

adjectives

copious (pl); reliable; various (pl); authentic; abundant (pl); external; outside; delightful; usual; proximate; inexhaustible; scanty; respectable; distorted; vital; real; occult; festering; fruitful; paternal; worthwhile; known; classical; valuable; bounteous; recurrent; vulgar; artificial; full-fed; radiant; prolific; frequent; unrelated; continued; grand; editorial; important; shallow; true; inactive; miscellaneous; invisible; authoritative.

verbs

attack—; borrow from—; determine—; dry up—; flow from—; emanate from—; exhaust —; poison—; replenish from—; search for —; spring from—; stamp out—; strike at —; tap—; trace to—; track down—; utilize —; —constitutes; —feeds; —supplies.

(See origin, beginning.)

SOUTH

adjectives

aromatic; fragrant; far; soft; fiery; quiet; feudal; warm.

SOVEREIGN

adjectives

neutral; successive (pl); ruthless; ambitious; legitimate; hapless; territorial; hereditary; joint; youthful; sceptered; vigilant; squatter; spiritual; unchallenged; inscrutable; tribal; feeble; diminished; glorious; gracious; individual.

SOVEREIGNTY

verbs

ascend to—; assume—; endanger—; exercise —; exert—; extend—; gain—; impair—; invest with—; jeopardize—; limit—; maintain—; relinquish—; respect—; retain—; usurp—; weaken—; yield—; —crumbles; —spreads; —sways; —totters; —wields.

(See crown, dominion, power.)

SOW (*v*)

adverbs

mechanically; scientifically; scatteredly; widely; sparsely; thickly; luxuriantly.

(See scatter, plant.)

SPACE

adjectives

shoreless; encumbered; furlong; ample; plenteous; eternal; coming; boundless; allotted; inconsiderable; porous; astonishing; globular; unnecessary; limitless; tumultuous; immense; adequate; stabling; intervening; trackless; vast; endless; editorial; unoccupied; wide; infinite; successive (pl); watery; projecting; sufficient; weary; choking; unbounded; awful; pervading; shaded; hoary; stellar; vaulted; neutral; storage; restricted; azure; generous; interminable; imaginary; dimensional; intermediate; ethereal; tenantless; breathing; grudging; surface; mightiest; betokened; available; soundless; angry.

verbs

acquire—; augment—; confine to—; cramp for—; dash—; define—; determine—; devote—; diminish—; encamp on—; estimate —; evacuate—; extend—; grant—; insert in —; lack—; limit—; lodge in—; narrow—; nestle in—; penetrate—; permeate—; pervade—; provide—; regulate—; stare in—; tenant—; transmit through—; withdraw from—; —accommodates; —dwindles; —expands; —ranges.

(See capacity, area.)

SPACIOUS

adverbs

adequately; satisfactorily; delightfully; wonderfully; amply; unexpectedly; amazingly; uncommonly; extremely; unnecessarily; admirably; commendably; extraordinarily; magnificently; splendidly; remarkably; conveniently; charmingly; reasonably; vastly.

verbs

disclose—; relax in—; reveal—; revel in—; survey—; —affords; —allows; —dazzles; —emancipates; —enables; —enthralls; —facilitates; —frees; —gives scope; —leaves; —liberates; —overawes; —overwhelms; —permits; —unfolds.

(See luxury, comfort, vastness.)

SPAN

adjectives

incredible; toil-stained; fleeting; artistic; infinitesimal; pitiful; allotted; sapphire; natural; life; useful.

verbs

abbreviate—; bridge—; elongate—; fuse—; interlink—; limit—; prolong—; protract—; reduce—; shorten—; stretch—; survive—; terminate—; unite—; —breaches; —elapses; —extends; —spreads; —stretches.

(See bridge, spread, extent.)

SPANK (v)

adverbs

resoundingly; heartlessly; cruelly; penally; repeatedly; viciously; explosively.

(See whip, paddle.)

SPARE (v)

adverbs

mercifully; generously; benevolently; willingly; voluntarily; magnanimously; nobly; benignantly.

(See save, refrain.)

SPARKLE

adjectives

fiery; exciting; phosphoric; odd; epigrammatic; conversational.

SPARKLE (v)

adverbs

splendidly; radiantly; frostily; keenly; luminously; phosphorically; gaily; spectacularly.

(See glitter, gleam.)

SPARKLING

adverbs

brightly; youthfully; ingenuously; happily; comically; brilliantly; wittily; facetiously; humorously; pleasantly; whimsically; nonsensically; fantastically; drolly; scintillatingly; delightfully; entrancingly; piquantly; thrillingly; stimulatingly.

adjectives

wandering; poor; glimmering; smoldering; enkindling; glowing; broad; bold; angry; starry; numbered; primitive; benignant; luminous; involuntary; immortal; feeble; hot; compensatory; latent; dubious; lively.

verbs

apply—; extinguish—; fan—; kindle—; quench—; smother—; snuff out—; —dazzle; —die; —dwell; —endanger; —enkindle; —flicker; —fly; —glow; —grow; —ignite; —illuminate; —inflame; —radiate; —shoot from; —smoulder; —strike; —tremble.

(See light, fire, flame, flash.)

SPARROW

verbs

—busies; —chases; —cheers; —chirps; —circles; —drifts; —flocks; —flutters; —s haunt; —perks up; —plagues; —robs; —soars; —steals; —thrives on; —tucks away; —twitters; —wanders; —warbles; —wheels; —whistles.

(See bird.)

SPARTAN

adverbs

resolutely; intrepidly; dauntlessly; determinedly; unflinchingly; marvelously; invincibly; fearlessly; heroically; valiantly; doughtily.

SPASM

adjectives

blind; unseemly; terrible; temporary; social; fierce; clonic; tonic; violent; sudden; painful.

verbs

afflict with—s; alleviate—; assuage—; burst into—; characterize by—s; check—; contract in—s; diagnose—; excite—; mitigate —; moderate—; pacify—; prevent—; prolong—; quell—; reduce—; relieve—; subdue —; —affects; —agonizes; —convulses; —denotes; —jerks; —lessens; —overcomes; —passes; —ruffles; —seizes; —strains; —s wrack.

(See convulsion, fit, contraction.)

SPASMODIC

adverbs

convulsively; curiously; strangely; inexplicably; regularly; oddly; terrifyingly; violently; bafflingly; perplexingly; heartbreakingly; unpredictably.

SPEAK (v)

adverbs

epigrammatically; euphemistically; characteristically; impressively; vaguely; pompously; grandiloquently; verbosely; melodiously; euphonically; pointedly; periodically; mournfully; rationally; derogatorily; disparagingly; judiciously; coaxingly; optimistically; respectfully; articulately; conservatively; tremulously; uncompromisingly; reassuringly; energetically; laconically; icily; mellifluously; glibly; contemptuously; indulgently; discursively; tensely; venomously; circuitously; edifyingly; directly; simply; impudently; figuratively; passionately; sublimely; scurrilously; precipitantly; solicitously; warily; emphatically; volubly; ironically; negatively; persuasively; exquisitely.
(See talk, say, express.)

SPEAKER

adjectives

distinguished; influential; conspicuous; adequate; fluent; brilliant; liberal; adroit; inspiring; dependable; impressive; boring; eloquent; timorous; scarred; hardy; flippant; principal; effective; polished; obstreperous; finished; handicapped; unintelligible; scintillating; deft.

verbs

applaud—; badger—; compliment—; confuse—; divert—; eulogize—; heckle—; introduce—; jibe—; laud—; silence—; —addresses; —admonishes; —articulates; —besmirches; —blares; —castigates; —chastises; —condemns; —conveys; —disclaims; —delivers; —digresses; —drawls; —drives home; —enunciates; —expatiates; —expostulates; —fulminates; —gesticulates; —gestures; —harangues; —insinuates; —inveighs against; —laments; —orates; —pounds; —prates; —proclaims; —rants; —raps; —rebuts; —refutes; —shocks; —slanders; —slings; —slurs; —snaps; —stammers; —stutters; —utters; —discourses.
(See debater, orator, politician, minister.)

SPEAR

adjectives

battled; glittering; enormous; broad; well-balanced; serried; splintering; stabbing; bloody; couched; barbed; beaming; shadowy; poisoned; brazen-headed.

verbs

arm with—; barb—; brandish—; cast—; edge—; extract—; fashion—; fling—; hurl —; impale on—; let fly—; level—; taper—; —s bristle; —fells; —flies; —gores; —penetrates; —perforates; —pricks; —punctures; —riddles; —spikes; —stabs; —staves in; —whirs; —whizzes.
(See dart, lance, missile.)

SPECIALIST

adjectives

celebrated; pretended; minute; cold-blooded; qualified; experienced; high-priced.

verbs

baffle—; consult—; employ—; engage—; recommend—; recruit—s; —advocates; —analyzes; —assures; —concludes; —s confer; —counsels; —diagnoses; —discerns; —exhorts; —prescribes; —relieves; —resurrects; —restores.
(See expert, physician, scholar.)

SPECIALTY

verbs

characterize—; designate—; determine—; devote to—; emphasize—; engage in—; excel in—; foster—; indicate—; master—; recognize—; restrict to—; stress—; warrant—.
(See work, science, art, knowledge.)

SPECIES

adjectives

particular; gigantic; important; superior; representative; prehistoric; foreign; tropical; new; dominant; extinct; distinct; collective; terrestrial; principal; mimetic; delightful; incipient; corresponding; subtle; unique; domesticated; nobler; nigh-perfected; rare.

verbs

breed—; classify—; corrupt—; cross—; discover—; elevate—; exalt—; exterminate—; group—; inbreed—; perpetuate—; preserve —; propagate—; refine—; reproduce—; revive—; segregate—; uplift—; vitiate—; —abounds; —congregates; —degenerates; —embraces; —evolves; —includes; —ornaments; —rehabilitates; —relates; —survives.
(See race, group, classification, variety, category.)

adverbs
highly; helpfully; particularly; accurately; singularly; intimately; markedly; appropriately; typically; usually; uncommonly; satisfactorily; duly; conveniently; pertinently; advantageously; especially; minutely; sufficiently; conclusively; opportunely.

SPECIFICATIONS
adjectives
factory; provisional; essential; exact; strict; broad; detailed; minute; manufacturing; stated; licensed; general; sweeping; all-inclusive.

verbs
abide by—; adhere to—; cleave to—; deviate from—; diverge from—; draw—; embody in—; follow—; require—; standardize —; —call for; —conform; —define; —demand; —describe; —designate; —detail; —determine; —embrace; —enumerate; —itemize; —particularize; —regulate.
(See regulations, definition, details, items.)

SPECIFY (*v*)
adverbs
definitely; distinctly; provisionally; essentially; strictly; broadly; minutely; generally.
(See designate, name.)

SPECIMEN
adjectives
stalwart; active; unique; marvelous; abundant (pl); splendid; favorable; knobby; sundry (pl); hard-looking; precious; complete; admirable; acknowledged; superb; handsome; genuine; huge; lingering; superior; excellent; sickly; occasional; ferocious; prolonged; pleasing; puny; given; enormous; good-looking; unfair.

verbs
attract—; bag—; collect—s; dissect—; exhibit—; guard—; hunt—; mount—; preserve—; prize—; pursue—; search for—; seek—; snare—; stalk—; stuff—; trap—; value—; —evades; —exemplifies; —illustrates.
(See animal, sample.)

SPECK
adjectives
frothy; nebulous; morbid; inconsequential; eccentric; tiniest; swimming; microscopic; isolated; brilliant; shadowy; furthest; pitted.

adverbs
unpleasantly; unfortunately; unluckily; prettily; beautifully; artificially; inconveniently; unsalably; unprofitably; completely; strangely; oddly; perplexingly; unaccountably; inexplicably.

SPECTACLE
(*general*)
adjectives
ghastly; pleasant; wild; impressive; weird; singular; garish; bewildering; placid; awful; imposing; depressing; appalling; revolting; remarkable; religious; owl-eyed; solemn; lordly; striking; stupendous; damp; theatrical; picturesque; hideous; finer; shameful; elaborate; fairy; odious; inspiring; unhallowed; impassioned; fearful; miserable; gorgeous; sly; beaming; savage; gala; silent; triumphant; pitiful; novel; benevolent; magnificent; direful; daring; wondrous; entrancing; ignoble; attractive; unwonted; unexpected; unique; grandmotherly; extraordinary; splendid; everlasting; mossy; monstrous; menacing; chorographic; unprecedented.

SPECTACLE
(*show*)
verbs
unfold—; view—; witness—; —affords; —appeals; —caricatures; —fascinates.
(See exhibition, show, display.)

SPECTACLED
adverbs
heavily; forbiddingly; formidably; grimly; primly; unwillingly; unattractively; unbecomingly; horribly; comically; carefully; helpfully; carefully; skilfully; finally; stylishly; protectively; fashionably; demurely; deceptively.

SPECTACLES
(*glasses*)
verbs
adjust—; blink through—; exhibit—; prescribe—; toy with—.

SPECTACULAR
adverbs
highly; impressively; magnificently; splendidly; brilliantly; regally; royally; colorfully; gorgeously; gloriously; imposingly; ma-

jestically; dazzlingly; processionally; dramatically; fantastically; unusually; sensationally; superbly.

SPECTATORS

adjectives
passing; broad; bold; angry; unpracticed; indifferent; festive; singular; curious; distinguished; impartial; patient; unlearned; passive; crowded; astonished; dignified; plebeian; bored; ambitious; attentive; callous.

verbs
accommodate—; affront—; amaze—; amuse —; astound—; attract—; awe—; beguile—; bore—; cheat—; dazzle—; dumbfound—; electrify—; enrage—; entrance—; impress —; petrify—; regale—; scan—; stun—; thrill—; —applaud; —behold; —clamor; —cram; —disperse; —fret; —gasp; — heckle; —irk; —jam; —lure; —marvel; —pour; —rivet; —witness.
(See hearer, crowd, bystander, audience.)

SPECTER

adjectives
ridiculous; gibbering; looming; dancing; ghastly; gloomy; ghostly; confused; grim; grisly; horrid.

verbs
cast—; fight off—; goggle at—; —dissolves; —dreads; —evaporates; —fades; —floats; —glares; —glowers; —haunts; —looms; — melts away; —penetrates; —permeates; — petrifies; —plagues; —terrifies; —vanishes.
(See apparition, phantom, ghost.)

SPECULATE (v)

adverbs
disastrously; rashly; divertingly; chimerically; philosophically; casually; adroitly; financially; contemplatively; ridiculously; abstractly; vaguely; theoretically; ingeniously; shrewdly.
(See meditate, guess.)

SPECULATION

adjectives
grandest; casual; discursive; sympathetic; delighted; daring; philosophic; adroit; colossal; presumptuous; abstruse; financial; humble; enthusiastic; humanitarian; idle; imaginative; contemplative; doubtful; loftier; fantastic; visionary; ridiculous; moody; gambling; delectable; awful; mercenary; disastrous; abstract; rational; improbable; favorite; empty; vague; sad; wild; unpremeditated; amused; adventurous; original; heedless; affectionate; erring; theoretical; ingenious; prejudicial; deep.

verbs
absorb in—; admonish—; arouse—; denounce—; deter from—; discourage—; dismiss—; dominate—; engage in—; hush—; indulge in—; license—; plunge into—; prohibit—; restrain—; resume—; risk in—; stake on—; torture—; —chances; —endangers; —fascinates; —gropes; —jeopardizes; —lures; —prohibits; —ventures.
(See gambling, meditation, transaction.)

SPECULATOR

adjectives
unscrupulous; dauntless; ingenious; grasping; keen; able; scientific; curbstone; shrewd; plunging; rich.

SPEECH

adjectives
thoughtless; voluble; angry; goodly; copious; long; stirring; maiden; gracious; heartless; chanting; epigrammatic; purest; wholesome; noblest; unrestrained; irrelevant; whispered; ambiguous; occasional; dual; sacred; moderate; impromptu; dedicatory; average; normal; saucy; meaningless; familiar; true; strict; after-luncheon; nebulous; laughing; decent; muchabused; impertinent; strong; vague; wellprepared; oracular; disrespectful; impressive; indignant; devoted; candid; elaborate; derogatory; characteristic; voiceless; extraordinary; eloquent; perfunctory; persuasive; masterly; articulate; demonstrative; rough; facetious; muddled; rasping; plaintive; powerful; whining; fraudulent; graceless; sibilant; complimentary; winged; taciturn; resistance; appropriate; sententious; consonantal; immemorial; intolerant; yearning; pedantic; supposititious; seditious; appreciative; villainous; patriotic; intelligible; expressive; champagne; stump; explosive; inflammatory; treasonable; high; momentous; pursuing; melted; deprecatory; flattering; lazy; composite; private; deliberating; flamboyant; explicit; flirtatious; fluent; luxuriant; royal; ghost-written; effective; reserved; rhetorical; voluble; fastidious; stifled; funeral; artistic; morning; inaudible; incharitable; wandering; dangerous; previous; strict; corrupted; free; manly;

broken; rattling; skillful; triumphant; graceful; higher; untimely; aimless; desolate; florid; fervid; common; impudent; nasal; uncensored; farewell; long-winded; memorized.

verbs
adjust—; ape—; augment—; book—; coach —; color—; compose—; confine—; cultivate —; deliver—; deprecate—; dismiss—; embellish—; endow—; extend—; flood—; incorporate in—; interlard—; intersperse—; polish—; pour forth—; prolong—; recite—; reel off—; respond to—; salt—; spout—; stumble through—; suppress—; time—; — appraises; —betrays; —declaims; —degenerates; —drones; —eulogizes; —flows; —glitters; —humors; —matures; —mingles; —thunders; —transcends; —wearies.
(See lecture, recital, declamation, discourse, oration, address.)

SPEECHLESS
adverbs
suddenly; strangely; utterly; curiously; embarrassingly; pathetically; bashfully; awkwardly; ineptly; shyly; clumsily; timidly; boorishly; loutishly; overwhelmingly; emotionally; miserably; wretchedly; unaccountably.

SPEED
adjectives
violent; dependable; superior; furious; imagined; convenient; breakneck; impressive; wonted; requisite; initial; amazing; thrilling; noiseless; specified; railway; evil; frightful; uninterrupted; incredible; utmost; high; accelerated; skyey; desired; fabulous; surprising; sufficient; diminished; careless; incredible; flashing; electric; lightning; moderate; reasonable; sustained; intoxicating; bidding.

verbs
accelerate—; arrest—; attain—; check—; curb—; diminish—; exceed—; gauge—; goad to—; maintain—; moderate—; propel at—; regale—; slacken—; spur to—; sustain —; throttle—; urge—; —alarms; —endangers; —exhilarates; —facilitates; —intoxicates; —jeopardizes; —menaces; —outstrips; —spurts.
(See momentum, velocity.)

SPEEDY
adverbs
incredibly; increasingly; effortlessly; mercifully; crazily; tragically; awkwardly; uncomfortably; distressingly; painfully; breathlessly; impetuously; perilously; unaccountably; surprisingly; astonishingly; moderately; dangerously; lightly; remarkably; precipitately; incalculably.

SPELL
adjectives
potent; unsolvable; heavenly; fascinating; mesmeric; drowsy; breathing; springtime; subtle; melancholy; hideous; maddened; baleful; appreciable; beguiling; cabalistical; funereal; wondrous; ineffable; savage; mighty; undying; wizard.

verbs
allay—; assuage—; cast—; conjure up—; exercise—; exert—; intensify—; overcome —; struggle under—; weave—; wield—; —bewitches; —charms; —enthralls; —fascinates; —hypnotizes; —lures; —magnetizes; —overwhelms; —permeates; —persists; —prevails; —ruffles; —entrances.
(See charm, enchantment, glamor, incantation.)

SPELL (*v*)
adverbs
accurately; promptly; involvedly; complicatedly; abbreviatedly; originally.
(See unravel, unfold.)

SPELLBOUND
adverbs
rapturously; raptly; earnestly; intently; magically; fascinatedly; eagerly; completely; utterly; curiously; strangely; marvelously; involuntarily; helplessly.

SPEND (*v*)
adverbs
tranquilly; recklessly; exclusively; lavishly; rashly; affluently; liberally; fabulously; idly; clandestinely; royally.
(See expend, squander.)

SPHERE
adjectives
glimmering; exalted; higher; bewildering; wheeling; murderous; mortal; youthful; native; diurnal; dusky; starriest; lucid; kingless; sublunary; luscious; ripe; great; mental; unthinking; crystal; softer; danc-

ing; stormy; pure; social; destined; heavenly; singing; unknown; calmer; mundane; alien; blazing; martial; political; far-off; willing; different; enchanted; celestial; humble; reachless; sensuous; untrodden; benighted; legitimate; whirling; poised; interstellar.

verbs
allot—; broaden—; confine to—; deepen—; dominate—; emerge from—; enlarge—; extend—; invade—; limit—; narrow—; penetrate—; permeate—; pierce—; preserve—; reject from—; restrict—; rule—; tread—; widen—; —s narrow; —s overlap; —ranges.
(See jurisdiction, region, position, province, globe.)

SPICE
adjectives
pungent; rich; strange; bartered; powerful; strong; odorous.

verbs
adulterate—; blend with—; impart—; infuse—; inject—; savor—; —bites; —embalms; —flavors; —nauseates; —pervades; —pickles; —preserves; —scents; —seasons.
(See mustard, flavoring.)

SPICY
adverbs
pleasantly; fragrantly; pungently; redolently; lingeringly; arrestingly; refreshingly; freshly; pleasingly; strongly; delicately; exquisitely; enchantingly; charmingly; delectably; intoxicatingly; richly; attractively; exotically.

SPIDER
adjectives
intrusive; bloated; putrid; weaving; hardy.

verbs
—attacks; —clambers up; —clings; —constructs; —dances; —dangles; —devours; —emerges; —entices; —envenoms; —s infest; —inhabits; —lies in wait; —loops; —paralyzes; —poisons; —s possess; —preys upon; —scrambles; —scurries; —snares; —spins; —stalks; —strikes; —suspends from; —traps; —weaves.
(See insect.)

SPIN (*v*)
adverbs
scientifically; assiduously; tirelessly; automatically; vigorously; industriously; dizzily; monotonously; sickeningly.
(See twirl, whirl.)

SPINE
verbs
brace—; compress—; curve—; damage—; dislocate—; expose—; fracture—; impair—; inflame—; inject into—; irritate—; lacerate —; protect—; puncture—; sheathe—; strengthen—; support—; tap—; x ray—; —bristles; —controls; —flashes; —quivers; —shudders; —transmits.
(See bone.)

SPINELESS
adverbs
utterly; despicably; contemptibly; cravenly; arrantly; palpably; obviously; notoriously; confessedly; openly; pitiably; shamefully; ingloriously; infamously; terribly; unconscionably; recreantly; distressingly; pitifully; disgustingly.

SPINSTER
adjectives
ardent; unpredictable; resigned; anemic; withered; hopeless; contented; man-shy; miserable.

SPIRE
adjectives
humble; ornate; tapering; slender; friendly; jagged; feathery; tranquil; flaming; graceful; gleaming; soaring; mountain; steadfast; diminishing; rocky; numberless (pl); octagonal; exquisite; far-off.

verbs
ascend—; clamber up—; descend—; discern —; erect—; impale on—; mount—; raze—; scale—; surmount—; suspend from—; —s bristle; —s cluster; —looms; —s shimmer; —soars; —tapers; —topples.
(See tower, stalk.)

SPIRIT
adjectives
abiding; absent; adventurous; aggravated; aggressive; airy; alleged; altruistic; animal; animating; apathetic; ardent; arrogant; artistic; aspiring; audacious; barren; beauteous; becoming; bellicose; belligerent; benevolent; bodiless; benignant; blessed;

boastful; bold; boundless; braced; braver; brazen; bubbling; buoyant; burgeoning; Byronic; burlesquing; calculating; cernuous; combative; charming; chaste; chastened; cherished; chimerical; churlish; commercial; common; compassionate; competitive; complacent; confident; congenial; contagious; contented; contrite; courageous; courtier; craving; creative; critical; damned; dangerous; darksome; dedicated; dejected; demonic; determined; devilish; disconsolate; disembodied; divine; drooping; earnest; ebbing; electric; embittered; emancipated; emulous; encumbered; enlightened; enlivened; enticing; ephemeral; equable; erect; erring; ever-soaring; ethereal; excellent; excited; evil; exclusive; exuberant; facinorous; faint; fallen; familiar; fantastic; fastidious; fervent; festive; feverish; fiery; fighting; flabby; flaming; flashy; flexible; fluttering; foreign; fractious; fraternal; free; fresh; gay; generous; genial; gentle; gloomy; glorious; goaded; grave; gray; grudging; guiding; hackneyed; happy; harassed; hardy; haughty; heedless; helpless; heroic; high; horrible; hospitable; hostile; huge; illustrious; imaged; immaterial; immortal; impatient; imperial; imperishable; impertinent; impetuous; inborn; incongruous; inconstant; indefatigable; independent; indignant; indomitable; inexorable; inexpiable; insurgent; internal; intrepid; introspective; intuitive; invincible; irascible; iron; joyous; judicial; kindly; kindred; kingly; laboring; laggard; lavish; leading; lewd; liberal; lonely; lovable; low; lustrous; magnanimous; majestic; malicious; malignant; managing; martial; masculine; meanest; mercenary; mercurial; migratory; militant; ministering; misguided; mixed; moderate; moving; mutinous; mysterious; nameless; neighboring; neutral; nimble; normal; noble; noxious; obdurate; paradoxical; parting; patronizing; perfect; persecuting; pert; perturbed; pervading; petulant; philanthropic; philosophical; poetic; practical; predominant; presumptuous; profane; prosaic; proscriptive; provincial; public; purest; purged; pythonic; quaint; queer; querulous; rabid; questioning; racial; radical; rallied; rampant; ransomed; rapacious; rare; rational; reasonable; rebellious; regenerate; released; repugnant; resolute; responsive; restless; romantic; roving; ruling; sacerdotal; sacred; scattered; scientific; searching; secret; secular; self-conscious; sensitive; serene; serious; silent; skipping; skittish; lewd; sleeping; slothful; slow; smoothed; smug; soaring; soldiering; solemn; somber; sound; sparkling; stanch; stern; stout; submissive; supercilious; sympathetic; tempered; tolerable; tolerant; tough; traditional; tragic; troubled; turbulent; tumultuous; unbridled; uncaged; undefiled; unfair; unfettered; unhaggling; unhappy; unmoved; unnatural; unquiet; unresting; valiant; valorous; valuable; vanguard; vanishing; vanquished; vital; vehement; venomous; vivid; volatile; wandering; wanton; warlike; weak; weary; weeping; wicked; wild; worthy; wounded; zealous.

verbs

allude to—; annihilate—; affront—; bolster —; bruise—; burn—; chafe—; commend—; commune with—; comprehend—; drink of —; drench—; exalt—; exorcise—; fetter—; flood—; hamper—; humble—; immortalize —; implant—; inflame—; inject—; oppose —; purge—; raise—; re-animate—; recapture—; reveal—; reverence—; stamp out—; submerge—; sustain—; symbolize—; teach—; typify—; violate—; war against—; wash—; worship—; yield to—; —abides; —actuates; —animates; —appeases; —arises; —awakens; —blights; —bolsters; —breathes; —broods; —buoys; —caters; —cheers; —climbs; —communes with; —communicates; —conjures; —connotes; —conquers; —conveys; —dampens; —daunts; —departs; —displays; —diverts; —embodies; —endows; —engages; —excites; —exhausts; —exhibits; —expands; —expresses; —extracts; —fatigues; —frets; —haunts; —imbibes; —imbues; —impoverishes; —inculcates; —indulges; —infuses; —lags; —lingers; —maintains; —molests; —narrows; —obscures; —overrules; —paralyzes; —partakes; —perceives; —permeates; —pervades; —pierces; —pours out; —preserves; —prevails; —rankles; —reflects; —reigns; —relates; —reveres; —revives; —sinks; —stalks; —stems; —stimulates; —stirs; —strengthens; —strives; —succumbs; —survives; —summons; —swells; —tempers; —tires; —touches; —unfolds; —uplifts; —wails; —wars; —washes. (See soul, life, specter.)

SPIRITED

adverbs

ardently; briskly; unusually; uncommonly; exceedingly; alertly; busily; friskily; vivaciously; unwontedly; delightfully; splendidly; actively; intelligently.

SPIRITUAL

adverbs
naturally; personally; subjectively; devoutly; faithfully; piously; religiously; reverently; instinctively; celestially; gloriously; intuitively; beautifully; immoderately; blessedly; humbly; solemnly; consciously; innately; simply; inherently.

SPIT

verbs
eject—; emit—; excrete—; exude—; moisten with—; regurgitate—; slaver—; slobber—; squirt—; —drivels; —drools; —nauseates; —showers; —slobbers.

(See saliva, liquid, sputum, expectoration.)

SPIT (v)

adverbs
venomously; vulgarly; carelessly; disgustingly; nauseatingly; incessantly; obstreperously; accurately; explosively.

(See sputter.)

SPITEFUL

adverbs
naturally; habitually; always; detestably; dangerously; maliciously; viciously; abominably; incorrigibly; incurably; atrociously; hatefully; enviously; unhappily; unfortunately; strangely; absurdly; deplorably; bitterly; cruelly.

SPLASH

adjectives
gaudy; tremendous; quickening; confounded; tiny; ignominious; audible; weltering; rhythmic.

verbs
avert—; raise—; —begrimes; —besmirches; —deluges; —douses; —drenches; —fouls; —inundates; —moistens; —ruffles; —rumples; —showers; —smears; —smudges; —souses; —spatters; —swashes.

(See wave, water, liquid.)

SPLEEN

adjectives
merry; scornful; weakest; testy; heaving.

verbs
affect—; enlarge—; excise—; excite—; provoke—; remove—; rile (colloq.)—; ruffle

—; vent—; vex—; —depresses; —enlarges; —execrates; —ferments; —functions; —governs; —secretes.

(See bile.)

SPLENDID

adverbs
gorgeously; luminously; brilliantly; vividly; dazzlingly; radiantly; richly; sumptuously; artistically; extraordinarily; amazingly; regally; unexpectedly; barbarically; fantastically; romantically; imposingly; impressively; majestically; imperially; royally; colorfully; imperishably; unforgettably; ornately; dramatically; ceremonially; ritualistically.

SPLENDOR

adjectives
oriental; reflected; intrinsic; glamorous; divine; temporal; lonely; dazzling; scarlet; superficial; infernal; reminiscent; dark; transitory; prodigious; immense; liquid; intellectual; hurrying; vermeil; profuse; passionless; clinging; celestial; sumptuous; lofty; spectral; barbaric; mild; queenly; magnificent; external; meaning; wasteful; crimson; faded; lurid; mellow; dewy; new; starry; chilled; sultry; ancient; modest; baleful; meridian; opulent; prismatic; radiant; scaly; level; unhealthy; monarchical; visionary; chromatic; delusive; arrogant; lustrous; vulgar.

verbs
belittle—; blur—; crown—; envy—; mar—; rejoice in—; —blazes; —blinds; —bursts forth; —crowns; —dazzles; —intoxicates.

(See brilliance, glory, grandeur.)

SPLINT

verbs
apply—; bear—; bind—; discard—; improvise—; pad—; wear—; —affords; —assures; —bolsters; —braces; —maintains; —necessitates; —props; —protects; —serves; —supports; —sustains; —trusses; —underpins.

(See brace, protection.)

SPLINTER

verbs
cleave into—s; draw—; eject—; extract—; impale on—; pluck—; remove—; rend into —s; sever into—; shiver into—s; transfix on

—; withdraw—; —barbs; —gashes; —gauges; —infects; —perforates; —pierces; —punctures.
(See fragment, piece.)

SPLIT

verbs
cement—; fuse—; intervene—; wedge in—; weld—; —bisects; —breaches; —disjoins; —disrupts; —extends; —fractures; —gapes; —halves; —leaves; —mars; —rives; —shatters; —shivers; —splinters; —widens.
(See breach, crack.)

SPLURGE
(*colloq.*)

verbs
create—; cut—; deplore—; indulge in—; lament—; reproach—; rue—; —beguiles; —celebrates; —dazzles; —deludes; —displays; —exhibits; —flaunts; —flourishes; —glitters; —swaggers; —shows off; —splashes.
(See extravagance, waste, demonstration.)

SPOIL (*v*)

adverbs
ultimately; hopelessly; sadly; disastrously; effectively; partially; sickeningly.
(See plunder, damage.)

SPOILS

adjectives
envied; frequent; glittering; private; recking; sluttish; consecrated; trophied.

verbs
appropriate—; cache—; capture—; confiscate—; covet—; display—; dispose of—; exhaust—; exhibit—; filch—; hunger for—; lust for—; pilfer—; pillage for—; pounce upon—; plunder for—; prize—; purloin—; reap—; retain—; sack—; scramble for—; seize—; swoop to—; value—; win—; wrench—; —accrue; —allure; —attract.
(See loot, graft.)

SPONGE

verbs
apply—; dampen—; fish for—s; hook—; infiltrate—; market—; moisten—; mop with —; rinse—; saturate—; scour with—; swab with—; —absorbs; —soaks up; —sucks up.

SPONGY

adverbs
usefully; naturally; profitably; convenient-

ly; adaptably; flexibly; yieldingly; absorbently; pleasantly; comfortably; hopelessly; porously; swampily; quaggily; dangerously; impassably.

SPONSER (*v*)

adverbs
enthusiastically; financially; annually; necessarily; faithfully.
(See indorse, finance.)

SPONSOR

verbs
acquire—; conciliate—s; gain—; inspire—s; obligate to—; redeem—; seek—; —assures; —contracts; —discharges; —encourages; —exhorts; —finances; —furthers; —guarantees; —indorses; —observes; —pioneers; —pledges; —vouches for.
(See contributor, owner, manager.)

SPONTANEOUS

adverbs
eagerly; obviously; enthusiastically; utterly; manifestly; remarkably; absolutely; palpably; unquestionably; warmly; fervently: heartily; undoubtedly; intensely; exceptionally; sympathetically; unusually.

SPOOKY

adverbs
designedly; deliberately; pleasantly; mischievously; unusually; mysteriously; disagreeably; creepily; dismally; desolately; alarmingly; weirdly; uncannily; eerily; fearfully; wretchedly; miserably; uncomfortably; startlingly; horribly; ominously.

SPORT

adjectives
false; rare; willing; noisy; spectator; cruel; merry; sanguinary; biologic; equestrian; rustic; glorious; healthy; solitary; competitive; childish; malicious; domestic.

verbs
coach—; engage in—; enthuse about (colloq.)—; excel in—s; follow—; forsake —; hurl into—; indulge in—; pursue—; revive—; take up—; —attracts; —beguiles; —diverts; —endangers; —enlivens; —fascinates; —invigorates; —strains; —takes hold; —wearies.
(See amusement, diversion, fishing, frolic, game, golf, baseball, etc.)

SPORT (v)

adverbs

ludicrously; boisterously; enthusiastically; animatedly; merrily; competitively; childishly; rustically; noisily; uncouthly.

(See frolic, play.)

SPOT

adjectives

secluded; sheltered; distinguishable; tuneful; convenient; hovering; dusky; delicious; threadbare; unpromising; chosen; hallowed; shady; retired; dreary; sunlit; selfsame; forsaken; elevated; sleek; wet; treacherous; sore; unknown; dry; beauty; mildewed; curious; desolate; seductive; devoted; perceptible; faulty; unsightly; formidable; sequestered; secure; moist; sacred; swampy; malarial; plague; trysting; vital; lovely; haunted; drearest; barren; memorable; remote; vicious; infinitesimal; secure; insidious; weak; doleful; consecrated; solitary; dreariest; neglected; limited; tender; designated; unfertile; isolated; vulnerable; silent; tranquil; burning; loathsome; ulcer; sanctified; attention-arresting; favorable; veritable; wave-walled.

verbs

bear—s; confine—; designate—; detect—; efface—; eradicate—; lurk near—; incrust —; obliterate—; patch—; scatter—s; scour —; —attracts; —s bespatter; —s besmirch; —betokens; —blemishes; —blurs; —blotches; —s checker; —connotates; —defiles; — mars; —represents; —smudges; —sullies; — transfixes.

(See freckles, mark, blemish.)

SPOTLIGHT

verbs

concentrate—; eclipse—; elude—; evade—; extinguish—; focus—; obscure—; retire from—; share—; shrink from—; shun—; shy from—; steal—; —dazzles; —diffuses; —disperses; —flickers; —glares; —glimmers; —guides; —illuminates; —penetrates; —pierces; —plays upon; —radiates; —scintillates; —shimmers.

(See light, limelight.)

SPOUSE

adjectives

indignant; tempestuous; expatriated; faithful; repulsive; pesty; skillful; plighted; exquisite; preternatural; waxen.

SPRAWL (v)

adverbs

grotesquely; drunkenly; violently; lazily; indolently; clumsily; uncouthly.

(See spread, lie.)

SPRAWLY

adverbs

inconveniently; awkwardly; inexpediently; unnecessarily; terribly; unhandily; unfortunately; undesirably; objectionably.

SPRAY

adjectives

belching; out-wafting; glistening; salt-sea; bloomy; brackish; heavy; vagrant; beechen; sleepless; bent; white-hot; trailing; radiant; dissolving; drooping; yeasty; blinding; delicate; saltless; birchen; seething; writhen; flying; lofty; tumbling; sheeted; misty; deadly.

verbs

diffuse—; distil—; expel—; —beclouds; — befogs; —disinfects; —evaporates; —fizzes; —foams; —fumigates; —gleams; —glitters; —hazes; —mists; —moistens; —obscures; —overcasts; —radiates; —saturates; — sparkles; —spatters; —spumes; —drenches.

(See fountain, mist, moïsture, steam, vapor.)

SPRAY (v)

adverbs

periodically; scientifically; automatically; annually; agriculturally.

(See scatter, sprinkle.)

SPREAD

adjectives

stunning; mortal; cloudless; dainty; solemn; delicious; immeasurable; tasty; delectable; eye-filling.

verbs

augment—; confine—; diminish—; enhance —; enlarge—; exaggerate—; expand—; extend—; extenuate—; heighten—; intensify —; limit—; magnify—; prevent—; reduce —; swell—; —embraces; —ranges.

(See cover, extent.)

SPREAD (v)

adverbs

insidiously; contagiously; swiftly; malicious-

ly; spaciously; industriously; generously; parsimoniously; invidiously; internationally.
(See expand, circulate.)

SPREE

adjectives
gigantic; conquering; periodic; prolonged; measured; violent; headlong.

SPRIGHTLY

adverbs
inordinately; exceedingly; unusually; extremely; pleasantly; nimbly; delightfully; gleefully; divertingly; merrily; briskly; vivaciously; alertly; blithely; vigorously; joyously; mercurially.

SPRING

adjectives
trickling; sparkling; hasty; delightful; elegant; plashy; convulsive; fruitless; smiling; wayside; copious; muscular; bubbling; sagging; clear; perpetual; tongue-tied; secret; crystal; bitter; inexhaustible; powerful; quivering; amorous-breathing; bursting; fern-wreathed; purling; covert; young; whispering; tardy; lasting; latent; limpid; filthy; lagging; balmy; exulting; budding; portentous; endless; sinuous; babbling; unfading; living; phantom; fathomless; unsealed; humbler; unusual.

verbs
apostrophize—; bid—to; greet—; hail—; prophesy—; reveal—; salute—; taste—; welcome—; —adorns; —arrives; —boasts; —breathes; —brings; —bursts; —calls forth; —comes; —cries; —departs; —flies; —flourishes; —forsakes; —greets; —laughs; —murmurs; —questions; —returns; —rushes; —says good-bye; —smiles; —spreads; —supplies; —takes leave; —takes wing; —unbosoms; —unlocks; —visits; —wakens; —whips away; —works.
(See autumn, summer, winter.)

SPRING
(well)

verbs
contaminate—; drain—; drill—; emanate from—; issue from—; pollute—; seep into —; tap—; trace—; vent—; —advances; —awakens; —babbles; —discharges; —dribbles; —gurgles; —gushes; —jets; —murmurs; —oozes; —opens; —originates in; —

pulsates; —refreshes; —reinforces; —rises; —swashes; —swells; —trickles.
(See fountain, geyser, well, brook.)

SPRING (v)

adverbs
agilely; impetuously; hazardously; independently; amazingly; spontaneously; impulsively; joyously; viciously; vindictively; dexterously.
(See leap, bound.)

SPRINKLE (v)

adverbs
freshly; thickly; uniformly; liberally; profusely; delicately; sporadically.
(See scatter, spray.)

SPRITE

adjectives
elfin; shadowy; bright-eyed; wretched; dusky; melancholy; airy; elusive; devilish; mischievous; impish.

SPRUCE

adverbs
jauntily; nattily; unusually; habitually; attractively; smugly; carefully; designedly; unwontedly; remarkably; consciously; admirably; proudly; curiously; noticeably; conspicuously.

SPRY

adverbs
ostentatiously; absurdly; foolishly; proudly; pretentiously; resolutely; conspicuously; fatuously; deceptively; jauntily; curiously; showily; remarkably; unusually; ridiculously; crookedly; actively; naturally; habitually; pleasantly; alertly.

SPUNKY

adverbs
delightfully; sufficiently; smartly; inherently; merrily; actually; independently; absurdly; comically; ridiculously; extremely; unreasonably; uncommonly.

SPUR

adjectives
pricking; sluggish; continental; continual; clanking; dizzy; knightly; goading.

SPURIOUS

adverbs
disgracefully; obviously; evidently; manifestly; shamefully; cleverly; deceptively; in-

geniously; unquestionably; transparently; admittedly; unexpectedly; daringly; outrageously; ostensibly; visibly; ridiculously; cheaply.

SPUTTER (v)
adverbs
irately; indignantly; furiously; vindictively; violently; obnoxiously; vulgarly.
(See spit.)

SPUTTERING
adverbs
constantly; fitfully; fretfully; unreasonably; tetchily; shrewishly; irritably; ill-temperedly; futilely; uselessly; vainly; loudly; sullenly; excitedly; eternally.

SPUTUM
verbs
charge—; cough up—; discharge—; emit—; examine—; expectorate—; sterilize—; test —; —accumulates; —characterizes; —congests; —contaminates; —conveys; —dries; —disseminates; —endangers.
(See spit.)

SPY
adjectives
true; prying; universal; omnipresent; unfortunate; jealous; traveling; clumsy; frail; involuntary.

SPY (v)
adverbs
pryingly; jealously; professionally; slyly; involuntarily; insidiously; unscrupulously; traitorously; treacherously; suspiciously; omnisciently; cautiously.
(See watch, search.)

SPYING
verbs
charge with—; cloak—; convict of—; detect—; deter—; disclose—; expose—; goad into—; harry—; mask—; penalize—; perpetrate—; reveal—; uncover—; —acquaints one with; —adorns; —betrays; —brands; —divulges; —enables; —informs; —intrigues; —jeopardizes; —menaces; —reveals; —stigmatizes; —unveils.
(See curiosity, examination, search, discovery, scrutiny.)

SQUABBLE
adjectives
personal; contemptible; musty; money; petty; grudge; lulling; vulgar; miserable.

verbs
obviate—; arbitrate—; avert—; avoid—; check—; conclude—; curtail—; intervene in —; join in—; judge—; pacify—; precipitate —; preclude—; stage—; subdue—; terminate—; —breaches; —disconcerts; —embroils; —estranges; —expires; —fractures; —ill-becomes; —mars; —rages; —ruptures; —threatens; —vexes.
(See fight, quarrel, dispute.)

SQUAD
adjectives
trained; investigation; motorized; formidable; awkward; mustering; firing; death; narcotic.

verbs
augment—; bar from—; bolster—; captain —; caution—; condition—; disband—; dispatch—; enlarge—; flank—; limit—; maintain—; mobilize—; muster—; quarter—; reanimate—; regiment—; reinforce—; reinstate—; rejuvenate—; revamp (colloq.)—; —assembles; —demolishes; —disperses; —embarks; —huddles; —intrenches; —mobilizes; —patrols; —sallies forth; —s troop.
(See gang, band, group.)

SQUADRON
adjectives
outflanking; feinting; reconnoitering; rushing; prancing; blockading; retreating; magnificent; kindred; lucid; thundering; watchful; well-built; woven-winged; murderous.

SQUALID
adverbs
miserably; wretchedly; incredibly; impossibly; inexpressibly; utterly; pitiably; deplorably; lamentably; shamefully; unnecessarily; needlessly; grossly; terribly; horribly; hopelessly.

SQUALOR
verbs
abolish—; endure—; eradicate—; fester in —; purge—; thrive amidst—; —begrimes; —blots; —contaminates; —corrupts; —de-

bases; —defaces; —defiles; —emphasizes; —offends; —pollutes; —rankles; —reeks; —smothers; —sullies; —tarnishes.
(See dirt, filth, abomination.)

SQUANDER (v)
adverbs
recklessly; rashly; improvidently; liberally; royally; prodigiously; fantastically; wantonly.
(See waste, spend, expend.)

SQUARE
adjectives
quaint; open; desolate; inverse; drawling; fountained; principal; hollow; dusty; silent; diagonal; budding; conspicuous; perfect.

SQUAT (v)
adverbs
vulgarly; cozily; somnolently; pugnaciously; characteristically; habitually; complacently; threateningly.
(See corner, crouch.)

SQUATTERS
verbs
allure—; attract—; dislodge—; encourage —; evict—; invite—; tax—; tempt—; — abound; —claim; —colonize; —deprive; — domesticate; —encamp; —lease; —settle on; —tenant; —usurp.
(See denizen.)

SQUAWK (v)
adverbs
cacophonously; raucously; indignantly; hideously; persistently; plaintively; endurably.
(See squeal, yell.)

SQUEAK
adjectives
shrill; impassioned; high-pitched; serene; tiny; persistent; elusive.

SQUEAKY
adverbs
shrilly; comically; curiously; oddly; unfortunately; annoyingly; embarrassingly; vexatiously; alarmingly; ominously; unfortunately; unluckily; treacherously; dangerously; provokingly.

SQUEAL (v)
adverbs
piteously; shrilly; agonizingly; piercingly; penetratingly; desolately; wrathfully; impassionedly.
(See cry, yell.)

SQUEAMISH
adverbs
unusually; delicately; extremely; terribly; prudishly; pretentiously; ostentatiously; presumably; notoriously; fastidiously; daintily; absurdly; comically; ridiculously; helplessly; disgustingly; overly; nervously.

SQUEEZE
adjectives
brotherly; mollifying; affectionate; hard; warm; tender.

SQUEEZE (v)
adverbs
imploringly; passionately; mollifyingly; affectionately; fraternally; warmly; tenderly; oppressively; impetuously.
(See compress, crowd.)

SQUINT (v)
adverbs
drolly; sinisterly; suspiciously; knowingly; penetratingly; affectedly; comically; threateningly.
(See wince, peer.)

SQUIRE
adjectives
stupid; rustic; ponderous; parliamentary; proper; blunt.

SQUIRREL
adjectives
flippant; tawny; watchful.

verbs
protect—s; tame—s; —barks; —burrows; —cracks; —curses; —darts; —digs; — dodges; —evades; —flirts its tail; —frolics; —gathers; —harvests; —hides; —jeers; — munches; —nibbles; —quivers; —scampers; —shies; —stores; —trembles; —whisks himself off.
(See animal, chipmunk.)

STAB
adjectives
adroit; bleeding; gashed; hateful; verbal.

verbs
deflect—; inflict—; —agonizes; —convulses; —despatches; —excruciates; —impales; —

inflames; —gushes; —gnaws; —lacerates;
—penetrates; —perforates; —pierces; —
punctures; —slays; —throbs; —twinges; —
twitches.
(See wound.)

STAB (v)

adverbs
adroitly; fatally; dangerously; hideously;
vindictively; passionately; treacherously.
(See pierce, thrust.)

STABILITY

adjectives
emotional; social; razor-keen; great; civic.

verbs
afford—; ascertain—; assure of—; attain—;
cherish—; commend—; confirm—; destroy
—; determine—; detract from—; endanger
—; forfeit—; insure—; investigate—; jeopardize—; maintain—; measure—; necessitate—; nurture—; offer—; question—; reinforce—; restore—; retain—; secure—; sustain—; value—; wreck—; —hinges on; —
insures; —ruffles; —totters; —wanes.
(See permanence, constancy, firmness,
strength, steadiness.)

STABILIZE (v)

adverbs
economically; effectively; politically; democratically; emotionally; governmentally;
legislatively; socially.
(See fix.)

STABLE

adverbs
reliably; dependably; fortunately; securely; safely; entirely; financially; emotionally;
creditably; eminently; commercially; indestructibly; delightfully; supposedly; presumably; reputably; uncommonly; solidly.

STAFF
(cane)

verbs
arm with—; bear—; brandish—; cudgel
with—; discard—; flourish—; flutter on—;
relinquish—; shatter—; shoulder—; splinter
—; surrender—; wield—; —bludgeons; —
braces; —deflects; —sags; —supports; —
sustains; —sways.
(See cane, baton, stick.)

STAFF
(general)

adjectives
knotted; managerial; faithful; official; efficient; consultant; inventive; research; energetic; intelligent; glittering.

STAFF
(personal)

verbs
appoint to—; augment—; clutter—; discharge—; employ—; evacuate—; inspect—;
resign from—; recruit—; suspend from—;
—surrenders.
(See personnel.)

STAFF (v)

adverbs
efficiently; faithfully; officially; scientifically; periodically; annually; seasonally.
(See support, provide.)

STAGE

adjectives
verdant; primitive; well-set; mental; com-
mencing; formative; inglorious; momentous;
incipient; successive (pl); veiled; obstructed; various (pl); miraculous; analytic;
realistic; developmental; trembling; uncertain; restorative; early; domestic; infantile;
tentative; rudimentary; middle; well-trod;
experimental; indifferent; tragic; legitimate; explosive; worthier; hypothetical;
pudding; condensed; baffling; intermediate;
infectious; important; imperceptible; dilapidated; milky; maturing; initial; diminutive;
perilous; naked; painful; buskined; regressive; embryonic; uncontrollable; usurped.

verbs
abandon—; advance—; cherish—; conceive
—; connect—s; dedicate to—s; define—;
desert—; destine for—; devote to—; elevate
—; exalt—; extol—; forsake—; frisk onto
—; glorify—; hoot off—; install—; perform
—; prostitute—; quit—; relinquish—; renounce—; retire from—; set—; strut upon
—; unsettle—; vindicate—; wed to—; —
allures; —attracts; —debases; —entices; —
fascinates; —immortalizes; —impassions;
—notorizes; —seduces; —succeeds; —s unfold.
(See board, footlights, platform, theatre.)

adverbs

stupendously; spectacularly; awesomely; grandiosely; handsomely; dramatically.
(See produce, effect.)

STAGE-FRIGHT

verbs

afflict with—; induce—; intensify—; manifest—; quell—; smite with—; subdue—; suffer—; surmount—; vanquish—; —abates; —barbs; —chills; —consumes; —curdles; —disconcerts; —distresses; —harasses; —hounds; —irks; —nauseates; —overawes; —overcomes; —overwhelms; —plagues; —racks; —ruffles; —sickens; —tenses; —terrifies.
(See fright, fear, terror, nervousness.)

STAGEY

adverbs

absurdly; pretentiously; undisguisedly; outlandishly; transparently; ridiculously; obviously; fantastically; outrageously; flimsily; cheaply; manifestly; disagreeably; unpleasantly; undeniably; bombastically; pompously; laughably; patently.

STAGGER (v)

adverbs

intoxicatedly; weakly; clumsily; stumblingly; helplessly; blindly; faintingly.
(See reel, sway.)

STAGNANT

adverbs

hopelessly; unfortunately; putridly; pestiferously; dangerously; inexplicably; palpably; uselessly; completely; dully; carelessly; indifferently; stolidly; contentedly; lazily.

STAIN

adjectives

primal; perspiration; tender; cloudy; hot; tyrant; haunting; powder; indelible; imputed; crimson; inborn; ineradicable.

STAIRCASE

adjectives

labored; pinched; twisted; steep; monumental; marble; secret; palatial; principal; quaint; little; lofty; filthy; winding; mossy; graceful.

STAIRS

adjectives

broken; skatish; lazar; mountain; wooden; singing; cramped; dingy; ill-kept; cold; cheerless; rocking; interminable; dark; winding; discolored; spacious; polished; dim; tackled; corkscrew.

verbs

ascend—; avoid—; bear up—; blockade—; bolt down—; bounce down—; bound from —; clamber up—; clatter down—; climb—; descend—; design—; grope on—; guide down—; labor up—; limp up—; mount—; pause on—; scale—; scramble up—; scurry up—; skip up—; survey from—; tear up—; thrust down—; thunder down—; topple from —; totter on—; tumble from—; vault—; —creak; —diverge; —spiral; —wind.
(See ladder, step.)

STAKE

adjectives

black; windward; sharp-pointed; metal.

verbs

affix to—; avoid—; drive—; extract—; hitch to—; impale on—; implant—; moor to—; plant—; sink—; shackle to—; suspend from—; transfix to—; withdraw—; —directs; —fences; —guides; —indicates; —marks; —penetrates; —signalizes.
(See post.)

STALACTITES

verbs

—bracket; —dazzle; —derive from; —fashion; —gleam; —glitter; —glimmer; —incrust; —line; —ornament; —radiate; —spur; —stud; —suspend; —taper.
(See icicle.)

STALE

adverbs

uselessly; terribly; obviously; unluckily; alarmingly; indubitably; mustily; unprofitably; tastelessly; inexcusably; unacceptably; disgustingly; wearily; injuriously; unhealthfully; unwholesomely; unwarrantably; objectionably; disagreeably; unpleasantly.

STALENESS

verbs

bar—; estimate—; incur—; loathe—; resent —; resist—; —alters; —flattens; —prevails; —provokes; —offsets; —shames.
(See odor, stench, smell.)

adjectives
green; juicy; martial; tall; withered.

verbs
attach to—; cast away—; crush—; dry—; gather—; pile—; shake—; sickle—; — bears; —connects; —curves; —s elevate; —juts; —protrudes; —rises; —springs; — supports; —sways; —s tangle; —tapers; — waves.
(See stem.)

STALK (*v*)

adverbs
dramatically; implacably; grimly; jauntily; nonchalantly; haughtily; stealthily; martially; vigorously; triumphantly; swaggeringly.
(See stride, strut.)

STALWART

adverbs
sturdily; remarkably; huskily; resolutely; valorously; intrepidly; trustworthily; amazingly; conspicuously; unusually; remarkably; marvelously; uncommonly; obviously; vigorously; doggedly; splendidly; dependably; uncommonly; naturally; reliably.

STAMENS

verbs
bear—; examine—; form—; support—; — burst; —cohere; —contain; —discharge; —shed; —split open.

STAMINA

verbs
break—; calculate—; deteriorate in—; develop—; evince—; lack—; exhaust—; increase—; lower—; possess—; preserve—; require—; restore—; supply—; test—; — ebbs; —endures; —lessens; —mounts; — resists; —succumbs; —wanes; —withstands.
(See strength, endurance.)

STAMMER (*v*)

adverbs
chokingly; inarticulately; laboriously; confusedly; hesitatingly; incoherently; timidly; embarrassedly.
(See stumble, falter.)

STAMP

adjectives
broken; legal; indelible; legislative; witching; occasional; intellectual; unmistakable; rubber.

verbs
affix—; attach—; bear—; collect—; design —; display—; hammer—; impress—; issue —; lick—; mark—; moisten—; pound—; provide—; sponge—; —adheres; —attests; —authorizes; —certifies; —s cover; —guarantees; —seals; —signifies; —sticks; —validates; —warrants.
(See label, mark, impression.)

STAMP (*v*)

adverbs
petulantly; angrily; indelibly; violently; vigorously; viciously; ruthlessly; impotently; unmistakably; permanently.
(See imprint, impress.)

STANCH

adverbs
loyally; fearlessly; unwaveringly; steadily; firmly; reliably; admirably; commendably; laudably; unusually; marvelously; courageously; gallantly; intrepidly; valiantly; valorously; unexpectedly; enthusiastically; eagerly; earnestly; immovably.

STAND

adjectives
drowsy; desperate; stubborn; unalterable; dimension; brutal; last; unflinching; lofty; unequivocal; final; roadside; definite.

verbs
advocate—; appreciate—; criticize—; depend on—; drive from—; hold—; maintain —; plan—; prepare for—; reiterate—; resist—; retain—; —annoys; —arrests; — checks; —recoups; —refreshes; —repels.
(See position, opinion.)

STAND (*v*)

adverbs
preeminently; militantly; stalwartly; indubitably; obediently; squarely; habitually; tremulously; haughtily; forlornly; conspicuously; precariously; courageously; picturesquely; valiantly; meekly; irresolutely; ostentatiously; sullenly; boldly; perilously; wistfully; unfalteringly; erectly.
(See endure, bear.)

STANDARD

adjectives
critical; ethical; altered; accepted; zoned; inherent; abstract; superior; dingy; infallible; artistic; accursed; unrivaled; barbarian; highest; hackneyed; crafty; persistent;

quantitative; capricious; moral; minimum; tentative; legal; well-defined; average; ordinary; tattered; acknowledged; shadowy; unconscious; secular; ponderous; proud; lofty; prospective; artificial; dietary; unhonored; exacting; rigorous; tangible; intellectual; inflexible; journalistic; accessible; rising; rigid; incontestable; single; recognized; unimpeachable; complaisant; conventional.

verbs

accept—; adopt—; advance—; apply—; attain—; conform—; desert—; deviate from —; elevate—; establish—; degrade—; formulate—; frame—; improve—; indoctrinate —; judge—; lift to—; lower—; maintain—; measure up to—; obtain—; prescribe—; preserve—; raise—; rally to—; reconcile—; record—; represent—; require—; serve—; set—; unfurl—; uplift—; violate—; —s collapse; —s conform; —s dictate; —s melt away; —prevails; —reflects.

(See flag, ideal.)

STANDARDIZATION
verbs

adopt—; advocate—; apply—; approve—; assume—; demand—; devise—; encourage —; examine—; formulate—; necessitate—; overcome—; perfect—; promise—; —insures; —progresses; —rears.

(See system.)

STANDING
adjectives

scholastic; better; scientific; legal; worldwide; logical; amateur; requisite; social.

verbs

aspire to—; better—; command—; confine —; create—; declare—; elevate—; esteem —; exceed in—; favor—; grade—; honor —; inquire as to—; judge—; reckon—; regain—; respect—; threaten—.

(See position, reputation, status.)

STANDPOINT
adjectives

elementary; artistic; favorable; psychoanalytic; outside; critical; prejudiced; academic; anagogic; decorative; practical; pagan; unbiased.

verbs

adopt—; alter—; assume—; compare—; contemplate—; criticize—; direct—; insure

—; interpret—; maintain—; measure—; move—; occupy—; regard—; sanction—; select—; shake—; view from—; —affords; —contents.

(See view, position, conception.)

STANZA
adjectives

elegiac; quaint; complicated; pious; long; staccato; unrhyming; experimental; sweeping.

STAR
(actor)

verbs

abuse—; admire—; advertise—; celebrate —; credit—; direct—; discover—; distinguish—; glimpse—; glorify—; groom—; hail—; highlight—; interview—; laud—; mob—; present—; publicize—; uncover—; —appears; —attracts; —delights; —interprets; —performs; —portrays; —thrills; —triumphs.

(See hero, actor, artist.)

STAR
(celestial)

verbs

discern—; —appears; —beams; —dims; —s flee; —gleams; —glitters; —guides; —hangs; —kindles; —lingers; —s perform; —plumes; —s reign; —s revolve; —s shed radiance; —spangles; —s unfold; —s wander; —s wane.

(See sun.)

STAR
(general)

adjectives

celestial; sanguine; mightiest; innumerable (pl); unsetting; evening; air-dissolved; bright; unchanging; ever-burning; polar; gold; glistening; innocent; scattered (pl); literal; happy; glory-beaming; sparkling; luckiest; tenderer; blinking; wide; pink; shy; waking; charitable; blazing; soaring; scintillating; dynastic; solemn; guiding; keen; fixed; remote; fiery; consenting; swart; panting; periodical; tremulous; folding; occulted; azure; guardian; teeming (pl); fragrant; ushering; brooding; meliorating; vagabond; mighty; deathless; wizard; wild; dying; friendly; summer; equidistant; secret; dumb; twinkling; unfinished; vanished; intense; steadfast; burning; patient; watery; pendulous; sentinel; rushing; solitary; dependent; baneful; wheeling; glancing; lurid; bright; downcast; tranquil; solid; winking; sliding; clear; intimate; obscure; gaudy; actual; moist; melancholy; declining; luminous; alien; beamless; prickly; pilot; budding; imperial; favorable; unanchored; cooperative; untroubled; lonely; elderly; newest; white; splendor-winged; utmost; journeying; attending; remorseless; truer; tyrant; palpitating; unstable; fortunate; sinking.

STARCH
verbs
apply—; convert—; dip into—; immerse in —; lose—; object to—; prepare—; remove —; store up—; —finishes; —galls; —hardens; —irritates; —stiffens.
(See food, constituent, carbohydrate.)

STARE
adjectives
studious; dull; stupid; algid; defiant; disfigured; glassy; fascinated; hostile; audible; vacant; grave; angry; meditative; absent-minded; sidelong; frigid; concentrated; appraising; unwinking; gloomy; fixed; dreamy; long; admiring; wondering; irreverent; stony; maniac; noncommittal; disgusted; spectral; superior; wild; bemused; questioning; hesitating; incredulous; hungry; sullen; limpid; owlish; insolent; unmitigated; oily; fascinated; solemn; wide-eyed.

verbs
blanket—; comprehend—; cast—; fix—; note —; prolong—; transfer—; —absorbs; —arouses; —astonishes; —excites; —irritates; —provokes; —startles.
(See look.)

STARE (v)
adverbs
impudently; fixedly; sullenly; persistently; solemnly; abstractedly; impassively; hypnotically; perplexedly; obtrusively; moodily; hostilely; arrogantly; apathetically; incredulously; fixedly; truculently; speculatively; insolently; fascinatedly; morbidly; rudely; vacantly.
(See look, gaze.)

STARLIGHT
adjectives
glittering; cool; boundless; glorious; pale; bright; shining; wondrous; magic; romantic.

verbs
be wrought by—; emerge from—; exhibit —; reveal—; shed—; view—; —appears; —awes; —cheers; —comforts; —creeps; —dimples; —embraces; —frames; —glitters; —guides; —scatters; —spangles; —splits; —unfolds; —works.
(See light, star.)

STARLING
verbs
introduce—; naturalize—; rid of—s; —s blot out; —s damage; —dives; —s feast on; —passes over; —quarters; —robs; —thrives.
(See bird.)

STARRY
adverbs
luminously; brilliantly; luckily; fortunately; unusually; brightly; helpfully; romantically; desirably; providentially; auspiciously; remarkably; amazingly.

START
adjectives
theatrical; undisguised; palpable; rheumatic; infinite; hopeful; reluctant; convulsive; guilty; running; involuntary; troubled; vigorous; tremulous; slight; longing; answering; painful; terrified; sudden; fitful.

START (v)
adverbs
violently; precipitately; perceptibly; distractedly; simultaneously; impetuously; reluctantly; jauntily; involuntarily; tremulously; fitfully.
(See embark, launch.)

STARTLE (v)
adverbs
inexpressibly; abruptly; playfully; ludicrously; stupidly; repeatedly.
(See scare, surprise.)

STARTLING
adverbs
unbelievably; unusually; utterly; alarmingly; extremely; unpleasantly; suddenly; strangely; curiously; disconcertingly; painfully; terribly; dreadfully; fearfully; tremendously; remarkably; singularly; oddly; appallingly; disturbingly; unexpectedly; disagreeably; peculiarly.

adjectives
absolute; oxygen; bitter; aesthetic; mental; cruel; slow.

verbs
alleviate—; avoid—; brave—; conceal—; endure—; face with—; hide—; influence—; perish by—; produce—; overcome—; reduce —; reveal—; stave off—; subject to—; — burdens; —devastates; —stalks; —threatens; —victimizes; —weakens.
(See hunger, suffering, need, death.)

STARVE (*v*)

adverbs
deliberately; cruelly; pennilessly; genteelly; parsimoniously; penuriously; niggardly; mentally; gradually; agonizingly; ceaselessly; miserably.
(See weaken.)

STATE
(*condition*)

verbs
aggravate—; allay—; alleviate—; arrest—; assuage—; attribute—; breed—; cloak—; comprehend—; conceal—; condemn—; ease —; establish—; excite—; expose—; induce —; intensify—; palliate—; prolong—; relieve—; restore—; resuscitate—; reveal—; revive—; screen—; shroud—.
(See condition, predicament, plight.)

STATE
(*general*)

adjectives
happy; unpropitious; deplorable; ordered; hopeful; kingly; humble; healthy; wandering; transitional; insipid; distended; totalitarian; bastard; sepulchral; disordered; throned; altered; lamentable; turbulent; dropsical; political; fossil; semi-conscious; feverish; frenzied; blissful; burdened; needful; pathetic; flourishing; honorable; excessive; deplorable; slovenly; anterior; cramped; crude; relaxed; supernal; deluded; spirited; ecstatic; variable (pl); dejected; inarticulate; primitive; impressible; autonomous; surrounding; morbid; feeble; former; dilapidated; democratic; semi-liquid; peaceful; enlightened; industrious; homogeneous; populated; tangled; emotional; authoritative; opulent; neurotic; compound; deliberate; existing; destitute; well-settled; semi-savage; impressible; comatose; depressed; corresponding; ordered; indissoluble; dread-

ful; bedraggled; retired; bulwarked; infant; transitional; social; primordial; slow; undetermined; scrambled; unsteadfast; neutral; passionless; dormant; exalted; perpetual; stronger; neutral; anomalous; unravaged; decapitated; unpleasant; knotted; unassailable; embryonic; conflicting; solitary; regal; stoic; vacillating; unique; frail; loose; electrical; quiescent; unwonted; melancholy; miserable; joyless; alarming; wretched; troubled; fair; outcast; forlorn; self-governing; distracted; dissolved; candid; enfeebled; pitiful; rebellious; palmy; coward; rapid; disadvantageous; natural; joyful; stable; budding; unwelcome; savage; apparent; enviable; desirable.

STATE
(*political*)

verbs
ally with—; annex—; bow to—; carve out —; dominate—; empower—; encroach upon —; enslave—; evacuate—; exalt—; forfeit to—; found—; industrialize—; infringe upon—; invade—; partition—; quell—; reduce—; subdue—; subjugate—; unite—; vanquish—; weld—; yield to—; —administers; —appropriates; —domiciles; —exercises; —s federate; —maintains; —persecutes; —racks with; —requisitions; — tramples; —tyrannizes; —wields.
(See empire, commonwealth, republic, country, nation.)

STATE (*v*)

adverbs
parenthetically; succinctly; tersely; concisely; impressively; broadly; specifically; metaphorically; authoritatively; emphatically; laconically; explicitly; solemnly; officially; substantially; tranquilly.
(See say, affirm, declare.)

STATELY

adverbs
becomingly; unusually; habitually; naturally; inherently; attractively; beautifully; proudly; regally; royally; majestically; magnificently; splendidly; appropriately; pompously; ceremoniously; gravely; properly; graciously; impressively.

STATEMENT

adjectives
misleading; big; hurtful; irrefutable; preceding; explicit; souring; terse; emphatic; fallacious; sententious; itemized; facetious;

contradictory; lucid; cardinal; unproved; colorless; written; definite; ineradicable; judicious; conflicting; defamatory; comparative; quaint; admirable; humorous; adroit; confident; intelligible; inaccurate; conservative; groundless; naked; specious; plausible; previous; remarkable; uncompromising; hazardous; ridiculous; penetrating; accompanying; publicized; distorted; oracular; attributive; precise; ingenuous; comprehensive; sensible; trifle-sounding; absurd; startling; hyperbolical; vague; foregoing; elucidated; derogatory; fervid; immortal; amazing; reiterated; graphic; detailed; articulate; erroneous; periphrastic; sweeping; dogmatic; positive; direct; superfluous; candid; authoritative; substantial.

verbs
allude to—; alter—; amplify—; base—on; bolster—; buttress—; certify to—; cite—; compile—; contradict—; controvert—; convey—; correlate—; dig up—; discredit—; draft—; edit—; elaborate—; elicit—; evade —; exaggerate—; extract—; fling out—; follow up—; heed—; impugn—; infer from —; issue—; label—; misquote—; modify—; qualify—; quote—; reiterate—; rest upon—; subsidize—; transmit—; unravel—; utter—; verify—; weigh—; —challenges; —depresses; —discloses; —implies; —jars; — justifies.
(See allegation, assertion, declaration, expression, remark.)

STATESMAN
adjectives
influential; sagacious; unhackneyed; darksome; bold; eminent; contending; practised; astute; senile; distinguished; wary; brash; far-seeing; liberal; haughty; dogmatic; brilliant; deft.

verbs
acclaim—; commemorate—; honor—; laud —; —arbitrates; —confers; —contracts; — counsels; —directs; —emancipates; —elevates; —executes; —exhorts; —formulates; —forges; —furthers; —governs; —guides; —helms; —manipulates; —negotiates; — steers; —struggles; —takes over; —transacts; —uplifts.
(See diplomat, legislator, ambassador, statesmanship.)

STATESMANSHIP
adjectives
businesslike; perjured; treacherous; inade-

quate; clear-sighted; far-seeing; conservative; pitiful.

verbs
acclaim—; cloak in—; demonstrate—; discern—; employ—; endow with—; exercise —; —alleviates; —averts; —dodges; — eases tension; —extricates; —flounders; — lightens; —machinates; —maneuvers; — pilots; —smooths; —steers; —unravels.
(See statesman, diplomacy, management.)

STATION
adjectives
enviable; desolate; supernatural; allotted; recruiting; way; unmoving; equivocal; biological; unshrinking; elevated; responsible; dust-driven; distributing; intermediate; fragile; conspicuous; meteorological; dingy; smoky; native; low; service; future; passenger; retreading; control; prostrate; dinky.

verbs
accumulate at—; confine to—; deposit at—; maintain—; remain at—; trundle to—; wait at—; —distributes; —quarters.
(See place, post, location.)

STATION (v)
adverbs
ingeniously; elevatedly; conspicuously; intermittently; frequently; advantageously.
(See post, place.)

STATIONARY
adverbs
mysteriously; alarmingly; bewilderingly; apparently; deliberately; helpfully; significantly; curiously; evidently.

STATISTICS
adjectives
complex; staple; stupendous; controversial; appalling; cold; official; available; accurate; scanty; untrustworthy; glowing; devastating; remarkable; pitiless; convincing; definite.

verbs
combine—; compile—; dig into—; eschew —; marshal—; plow through—; quote—; — arm; —bury under; —demonstrate; —dis-

close; —embrace; —hammer; —substantiate; —support; —terrify; —unleash; —verify.
(See list, information, book, knowledge.)

STATUE

adjectives

gigantic; plaster; impulsive; urgent; sepulchral; sylvan; portrait; earthen; colossal; symbolic; charming; strict; grotesque; memorial; emblematic; insignificant; mutilated; grave; multi-farious (pl); magic; marble; rigorous; dominating; painted.

verbs

carve—; cast—; chisel—; disrobe—; erect —; exhibit—; hew—; inscribe on—; model —; mould—; mount—; mutilate—; perch on—; prize—; prop—; shatter—; straddle —; topple—; unveil—; value—; —adorns; —commemorates; —depicts; —embellishes; —honors; —illustrates; —portrays; —symbolizes.
(See figure, masterpiece, monument, plaque.)

STATURE

adjectives

intellectual; veritable; simulated; commanding; mental; physical; moral; unusual; frail; gigantic; diminutive; stately; proud; dilating; slender; apparent; middle; financial; intellectual; political; herculean; unusual; exceptional; colossal; tall.

verbs

achieve—; alter—; attain—; augment—; check—; determine—; exalt—; extend—; heighten—; lack—; limit—; magnify—; measure—; stunt—; surpass in—; —bulks; —dwindles; —looms; —overawes; —towers.
(See height, growth, development.)

STATUS

adjectives

recognized; financial; front-rank; primitive; honorific; present; moral; usual; definite.

verbs

abandon—; acquire—; alter—; approve—; ascertain—; assume—; attack—; attain—; confuse—; corrupt—; defend—; define—; degrade—; designate—; detect—; determine —; dignify—; discredit—; elevate—; ennoble—; exalt—; forfeit—; glorify—; grant —; humble—; improve upon—; impugn—; insure—; investigate—; maintain—; merit

—; recover—; relinquish—; restore—; resurrect—; retain—; revolutionize—; suspend—; sustain—; taint—.
(See position, standing, state, condition.)

STATUTE

adjectives

penal; contravened; dead; oppressive; protective; unfair; age-old; unenforced; heartless; unjustifiable.

verbs

advocate—; abolish—; abrogate—; annul—; codify—; comply with—; countermand—; decry—; denounce—; discard—; doom—; enact—; enforce—; evade—; flout—; formulate—; frame—; ignore—; infringe—; invoke—; nullify—; observe—; ratify—; repeal—; retract—; transgress—; uphold—; veto—; violate—; void—; —annuls; —authorizes; —bans; —bars; —classifies; —decrees; —delegates; —enlightens; —empowers; —establishes; —exists; —legalizes; —limits; —prescribes; —prohibits; —provides.
(See law, legislation.)

STATUTORY

adverbs

impressively; inescapably; recently; unfortunately; luckily; inflexibly; vexatiously; curiously; wisely.

STAY

adjectives

fruitless; protracted; transient; pertinacious; subsequent; laggard; unprofitable; prolonged; tremulous; short; pleasant; amusing; lengthy.

verbs

abandon—; anticipate—; conclude—; discontinue—; enforce—; extend—; grant—; interrupt—; plead for—; press for—; prolong—; protract—; resume—; terminate—; welcome—; —defers; —elapses; —expires; —relaxes; —reprieves; —retards; —wanes.
(See stand, support.)

STAY (*v*)

adverbs

unobtrusively; adamantly; stubbornly; miraculously; traditionally; customarily; habitually; perpetually; temporarily; fruitlessly; protractedly; transiently; briefly; pertinaciously.
(See remain, lodge.)

STEADFAST

adverbs

loyally; dutifully; affectionately; properly; dependably; reliably; faithfully; eagerly; enthusiastically; zealously; filially; lovingly; fondly; piously; fervently; ardently; unwaveringly; curiously; remarkably; utterly.

STEAL (*v*)

adverbs

furtively; craftily; slyly; insidiously; basely; covertly; subtly; discreetly; mercilessly; noiselessly; jealously; suspiciously; ominously.

(See rob, plunder.)

STEALING

verbs

charge with—; convict of—; deplore—; disclose—; forsake—; indict for—; penalize—; practise—; rebuke for—; reduce to—; relinquish—; renounce—; reproach for—; resort to—; reveal—; scorn—; —defiles; —degrades; —deprives; —dishonors.

(See theft.)

STEALTHY

adverbs

guiltily; necessarily; warily; unusually; suspiciously; extraordinarily; remarkably; mischievously; furtively; carefully; naturally; uncommonly; craftily; cleverly; adroitly; mysteriously; cautiously; suspiciously; gingerly.

STEAM

adjectives

corrosive; scalding; fainting; sanguine; oppressive; exhaust; unsavory; poisonous; fragrant; spouting; hot; stinking; hissing; rich.

verbs

compress—; gauge—; generate—; harness —; inhale—; meter—; spew—; spout—; spray—; vent—; —befogs; —bursts; —clouds; —condenses; —drenches; —forces; —jets; —mists; —moistens; —obscures; —propels; —scalds; —wilts.

(See mist, spray, smoke.)

STEAMER

adjectives

charter; borrowed; prosaic; boarded; tramp; coastwise; filibustering; delinquent; lazy; dismantled; ocean; sumptuous; elegant; warping.

verbs

convoy—; launch—; —circumnavigates; —ferries; —glides; —hauls; —maneuvers; —plies; —rolls; —rots; —rusts; —speeds; —transports.

(See boat, launch, motor-boat, ship.)

STEAM-SHOVEL

verbs

—batters; —burrows; —s clank; —deepens; —devours; —discloses; —effaces; —erases; —excavates; —facilitates; —gorges; —gnaws at; —gulps; —hollows; —levels; —ravages; —swallows; —trenches; —unearths.

STEED

adjectives

bounding; angular; proud; fiery; flying; dashing; ribbed; unmanageable; mangy; fine-limbed; snowy; mercurial; heavenly; resistless; prancing; border; mottled; fire-breathing; well-proportioned; riderless; reinless; strong; livid; headstrong; frantic; smoking; noble; mighty; shadowy; aerial; stalwart; spirited; wild.

STEEL

adjectives

vengeful; ingot; thrusting; rushing; coarse; thin; nervous; well-tempered; field; jagged; massive; gleaming; shrewd; scorching; mirroring; unpolished; toughened; incomplete; brandished; lateral; carbonized; flashing; molten; crashing; fiery; roweled.

verbs

alloy—; analyze—; cast—; clash against—; compound—; convert into—; deoxidize—; desulphurize—; encase in—; forge—; frame with—; ladle—; lathe—; magnetize—; melt—; mold—; polish—; process—; purify —; roll—; smelt—; tap—; temper—; test—; weld—; —armors; —congeals; —corrodes; —decomposes; —deflects; —oxidizes; —reinforces; —resists; —transmits.

(See iron, lead, metal.)

STEEP

adverbs

precipitously; alarmingly; impossibly; startlingly; unexpectedly; perilously; hazardously; suddenly; starkly; abruptly; unreasonably; excessively; remarkably; incalculably;

inaccessibly; boldly; exorbitantly; extravagantly; unwarrantably; unreasonably; painfully; formidably; forbiddingly; curiously; particularly; immoderately.

STEEPNESS

verbs

bolt—; cap—; culminate—; elevate—; exaggerate—; mount—; surmount—; —declines; —exalts; —impresses; —inspires; —looms; —overwhelms; —soars; —towers.

(See height, altitude.)

STEER (*v*)

adverbs

erratically; unerringly; dexterously; deftly; skillfully; cautiously; accurately; conscientiously.

(See control, guide.)

STEM

adjectives

enchanted; deathless; gnarled; immovable; tapering; supple; tough; knotted; fibrous; apparent; sacred; insignificant; succulent; climbing; nourishing; straggling; fanedged; fruitless; slender; bending.

verbs

clasp—; crop—; ground—; heighten—; hinge on—; level—; pivot on—; pluck from —; snip—; spring from—; sway on—; —curves; —extends; —forks; —rises; —supports; —sustains.

(See stalk.)

STENCH

adjectives

noisome; fetid; obscene; horrible; nasty; intolerable; nauseating.

verbs

cast—; diffuse—; emit—; inhale—; —assails; —clings; —contaminates; —corrupts; —defiles; —galls; —lingers; —nauseates; —offends; —overcomes; —overwhelms; —penetrates; —pervades; —pollutes; —reeks; —sickens; —taints; —thickens; —turns.

(See odor, smell, staleness.)

STEP

adjectives

decisive; quickened; radical; important; imperious; weary; restless; tremulous; painful;

pilgrim; homeless; elastic; impudent; lascivious; desperate; fainting; toiling; firm; unfaltering; cautious; single; false; dragging; light; fleet; ungainly; rugged; swinging; uncertain; innumerable; listless; fearless; certain; tottering; rapid; mincing; echoless; zigzag; winding; incomprehensible; successive; witching; assured; gradual; vast; desirable; inadvertent; laggard; graceful; stately; devious; backward; conquering; unpracticed; uneven; timid; reeling; feeble; dictating; trembling; buoyant; practicable; pregnant; irrevocable; gigantic; grassy; drastic; vacillating; sagging; suspended; joyful; dignified; requisite; sedative; long; slow; concluding; still; instinctive; honest; resounding; slackened; furtive; ponderous; social; doubtful; disordered; inevitable; slippery; military; languid; reluctant; ample; rustic; rude; parting; shuffled; hospitable; crunching; boundless; measurable; precautionary; gentle; weak; flagging; rosy; stone; jerky; comely; confident; hasty; gradual; immense; unhurrying; beehived; springy; homeward; irreverent; hushed; decorous; constructive; haughty; threatening; stealthy; undeviating; indispensable; silken; wandering; logical; subsequent; dainty; hazardous; momentous; bold; panting; finite; erratic; deft; noiseless; palsied; tottering; impious; soldierly; intermediate; martial; disspirited; stiff.

verbs

acclaim—; advance—; advocate—; applaud —; appraise—; approve—; ascend—; avert —; comprehend—; contrive—; defend—; design—; devise—; frame—; graduate—; lay out—; loll on—; lumber up—; map out —s; mount—; ooze down—s; plan—; reconsider—; regard—; regret—; retrace—s; rue —; scale—s; slant down—; slip down—s; steal down—s; survey—; systematize—; toil up—; trip down—; urge—; weigh—; —commences; —intrudes; —retreats; —s retrograde.

(See ladder, stairs, footstep, advance.)

STEP (*v*)

adverbs

discreetly; mincingly; awkwardly; clumsily; boldly; gingerly; defiantly; noiselessly; deliberately; resolutely; reluctantly; majestically; fearlessly; shufflingly; stealthily.

(See stride, pace.)

adverbs
safely; securely; absolutely; warrantably; completely; assuredly; protectively; supposedly; presumably; carefully.

STERILITY

adjectives
general; panting; superficial; artistic; painful; shamed.

verbs
advocate—; bewail—; decry—; determine —; induce—; produce—; —annuls; —blasts; —blights; —dashes; —deprives; —devitalizes; —disconcerts; —emasculates; —frustrates; —nullifies; —thwarts.
(See weakness, fatigue.)

STERN

adverbs
gravely; puritanically; rigorously; uncompromisingly; inflexibly; unsparingly; arbitrarily; imperiously; severely; tyrannically; brutally; odiously; atrociously; needlessly; intolerably; senselessly; unreasonably; properly; necessarily.

STERNNESS

adjectives
strange; awful; considerable; unwonted; black; meaningful; frowning.

STEW

adjectives
hot; sickly; peppered; savory-looking; terrible.

verbs
bolt—; brew—; compound—; concoct—; dispatch—; fare on—; gulp—; prepare—; relish—; savor—; season—; sniff—; swill—; —blisters; —quells; —satiates; —seethes; —simmers; —slakes; —whets.
(See meat, food.)

STICK

adjectives
dead-brown; gnarled; knobbed; thick; knotted; sturdy; twisted; pointed.

verbs
arm with—; bear—; belabor with—; brandish—; deflect with—; fling—; flog with—; flourish—; goad with—; hurl—; prop on—; repulse with—; splinter—; thrash with—; thrust—; thwack with—; twirl—; wave—; whack with—; whittle—; —coerces; —intimidates; —supports; —sustains.
(See cane, baton, club.)

STICK (*v*)

adverbs
tenaciously; manfully; faithfully; firmly; adhesively; sturdily; jealously.
(See jab, stab.)

STICKY

adverbs
unaccountably; perniciously; inconveniently; unpleasantly; disagreeably; terribly; unexpectedly; hatefully; inexcusably; carelessly; messily; unfortunately; handily; usefully; serviceably; properly; suitably; adaptably; amazingly; dependably; insufficiently.

STIGMA

adjectives
infernal; irredeemable; lifelong; viscid; social; scandalous.

verbs
abolish—; bear—; destroy—; efface—; endure—; eradicate—; escape—; extricate—; incur—; inveigh against—; nullify—; purge of—; shun—; suffer—; tolerate—; vindicate of—; wipe out—; —aggravates; —brands; —clings; —defames; —detracts from; —humiliates; —marks; —ostracizes; —reflects upon; —sullies; —taints; —traduces; —defiles.
(See disgrace, dishonor.)

STILETTO

verbs
bury—; edge—; extract—; fling—; hilt—; hurl—; impale on—; plunge—; sheathe—; withdraw—; —s clash; —cleaves; —gashes; —lacerates; —penetrates; —perforates; —pierces; —pricks; —punctures; —rends; —severs; —slashes; —slits; —sunders.
(See knife.)

STILL

adverbs
alarmingly; desolately; lonesomely; absolutely; strangely; peculiarly; curiously; oddly; gruesomely; pleasantly; comfortably; serenely; calmly; refreshingly; appropriately; happily; contentedly; peacefully; suddenly; unaccountably; exceptionally; unusually; remarkably; amazingly; mysteriously; significantly; appallingly.

adjectives
comparative; monastic; prolonged; modest; gloomy; hideous; solemn; earnest; ominous; deathly; profound; appalling; majestic; deepest; utter; glittering; sepulchral; ghostly; unearthly; weird; succeeding; sullen; soft; rural; reverential; curtained; outdoor; sacred; abysmal; intense; fetid; prevailing; suffocating; sabbatical; willful; pensive; deep; black; obstinate; sunny; absolute; audible; dreaming; unwonted; midnight; hushed; awed.

verbs
break—; cherish—; endure—; murmur in—; penetrate—; permeate—; perpetuate—; pervade—; prolong—; rend—; resound in—; ruffle—; shatter—; shroud in—; —calms; —dejects; —depresses; —envelops; —grips; —haunts; —pervades; —reigns; —soothes; —stifles; —sulks; —unnerves.
(See calm, hush, silence.)

STILTED
adverbs
formally; uncomfortably; uneasily; stupidly; ineptly; unfortunately; curiously; crudely; awkwardly; terribly; nervously; gracelessly; pretentiously; absurdly; fantastically; outlandishly; bombastically; bashfully; inexpertly; grossly; unwontedly; unreasonably.

STIMULANT
adjectives
active; overpowering; mental; excellent; strange; intoxicating; favorite; necessary; helpful.

verbs
abstain from—; addict to—; administer—; avoid—; dilute—; impart—; indulge in—; infuse—; inject—; introduce—; prescribe—; require—; —agitates; —buoys; —compresses; —electrifies; —enkindles; —excites; —flushes; —galvanizes; —impassions; —inflames; —intoxicates; —provokes; —quickens; —reanimates; —rejuvenates; —rekindles; —revives; —shocks.
(See coffee, tonic, medicine, alcohol, whiskey.)

STIMULATE (v)
adverbs
lasciviously; artificially; alcoholically; electrically; simultaneously; instantaneously; erotically; refreshingly; injuriously; healthfully; beneficially; perniciously; agreeably; languidly; morbidly; sexually; psychologically.
(See incite, excite.)

STIMULATION
adjectives
sensory; self-satisfying; unnatural; psychological; sexual; useless; painful; gentle.

verbs
acquire—; afford—; convey—; derive—; furnish—; impart—; indulge in—; offer—; provide—; resist—; supply—; yield to—; —accelerates; —overexerts; —quickens; —subsides.
(See excitement, exhilaration.)

STIMULUS
adjectives
temporary; peculiar; reviving; new; sufficient; provocative; external; intellectual; immense; artificial; natural; native; unsound; keen; biting; sharp.

verbs
add—; afford—; apply—; balance—; furnish—; gain—; implant—; lessen—; react to—; reduce—; respond to—; want—; —allures; —assails; —baits; —declines; —diminishes; —incites; —induces; —produces; —recedes; —responds; —survives; —tempts; —wanes.
(See impetus, inducement, incentive.)

STING
adjectives
momentary; jealous; sudden; unworthy; painful; galling; rancorous; brutish; fiery; myriad; careless; venomous.

verbs
allay—; alleviate—; escape—; inflict—; mitigate—; palliate—; relieve—; salve—; treat—; wince at—; —envenoms; —incenses; —inflames; —irritates; —lancinates; —nettles; —perforates; —piques; —poisons; —pricks; —punctures; —rends; —tingles.
(See bite.)

STINK
verbs
(See stench.)

STINT (v)

adverbs

parsimoniously; fanatically; meanly; niggardly; selfishly; scandalously; unwontedly.

(See limit, restrain.)

STIPULATE (v)

adverbs

solemnly; financially; specifically; shrewdly; generally; minutely.

(See agree, state.)

STIR

adjectives

fluttering; quick; multitudinous; tremulous; nervous; gentle; tremendous; angry; noiseless; pleasant; enormous; ceaseless; restless; subdued; faint; considerable; unnoticed.

verbs

agitate—; brook—; create—; embroil in—; endure—; quash—; quell—; restrain—; subdue—; suppress—; tolerate—; —bustles; —convulses; —disconcerts; —disquiets; —distracts; —diverts; —ebbs; —excites; —intensifies; —persists; —perturbs; —sharpens; —subsides.

(See commotion, agitation, movement, activity.)

STIR (v)

adverbs

contentiously; frantically; emotionally; spiritually; imperceptibly; profoundly; incessantly; restively; caressingly; tremulously; ceaselessly; agitatedly.

(See move, arouse, rouse.)

STIRRUPS

verbs

adjust—; discard—; loll on—; maintain—; mount by—; polish—; post on—; reinforce —; rise in—; slip from—; stand up in—; strain—; suspend—; weaken—; —afford; —bear; —brace; —dangle; —enable; —gird; —hang; —receive; —relieve; —support; —sustain.

STITCH (v)

adverbs

patiently; diligently; dexterously; cleverly; ceaselessly; indefatigably; industriously; skillfully.

(See sew, fasten.)

STITCHES

verbs

alternate—; bias—; dissolve—; interlace—; interlink—; rend—; unravel—; —baste; —bind; —conjoin; —fuse; —hem; —insure; —knit; —reinforce; —restrain; —seal; —save; —tack; —unite.

STOCK
(finance)

verbs

bear—; bull—; burden with—; certify—; counterfeit—; dabble in—; devaluate—; dispose of—; dump—; inflate—; invest in—; issue—; juggle—; liquidate—; market—; recommend—; renew—; retain—; relinquish —; speculate with—; stabilize—; traffic in —; unload—; —ascends; —booms; —crashes; —dwindles; —fluctuates; —impoverishes; —oscillates; —skyrockets (colloq.); —soars; —toboggans; —vacillates.

(See business, investment, capital, thermometer, barometer, shares.)

STOCK
(general)

adjectives

chitinous; parent; diversified; rejuvenated; calcareous; gilt-edged; inferior; reputable; revolutionary; rolling; suspicious; peaceful; heterogeneous; degenerate; serious; enormous; linguistic; inclusive; parish; tremendous; replaceable; sapling; surplus; extensive; common; fine; venturesome; pioneer; deficient; pathetic; ranging; selected; wild.

STOCKING

adjectives

foul; prosaic; merino; silk; wool; rayon; cotton; webbed; coarse; rough; rubber; wrinkled; rolled.

STOCKY

adverbs

sturdily; huskily; stalwartly; thickly; exceptionally; remarkably; distinctly; peculiarly; unusually; noticeably; unforgettably; chubbily; brawnily.

STOICAL

adverbs

marvellously; naturally; philosophically; courageously; intrepidly; calmly; serenely; valiantly; inflexibly; patiently; coolly; imperturbably; immovably; resolutely; exceptionally.

adverbs

strangely; dully; apathetically; singularly; oddly; curiously; unaccountably; inscrutably; irritatingly; vexatiously; shockingly; callously; abysmally; hopelessly; inexplicably; incurably.

STOMACH

adjectives

tripartite; grateful; excellent; heroic; distended; empty; lean; outraged; unbounded; queasy; nervous; upset; hollow; bulging; protruding.

verbs

abuse—; alkalize—; constrict—; cramp —; derange—; dilate—; displace—; distend—; drain—; empty—; flood—; incise—; irritate—; knead—; lodge in—; offend—; overload—; pump from—; purge —; reduce—; remove from—; scald—; sour —; strangulate—; turn—; upset—; wash out —; —assimilates; —converts; —distresses; —excretes; —falls; —houses; —prolapses; —protests; —reduces; —regurgitates; —retains; —revolts; —shrinks; —turns.

STONE

adjectives

mossy; sacrificial; senseless; heavy; ragged; jagged; votive; pallid; timeworn; graven; veritable; ribbed; crumbling; moldering; ancient; crystal; shattered; stumbling; quarried; flying; wrought; misshapen; scarlet; flawless; contumelious; cold; miry; typical; sizzling; destructive; corresponding; hollow; coarse; lithographic; sun-heated; precious; dangerous; showering; blasted; unpolished; barren; silent; greasy; monumental; enameled; uneven; rifted; breathing; bruising; solemn; rigid; massive; splintered; nameless; smoldered; chiseled; perfect; priceless.

verbs

carve in—; cast in—; chisel in—; dislodge —; face—; fashion of—; heave—; hew from—; hurl—; inscribe on—; perpetuate in—; project—; quarry—; rib with—; unveil—; work in—; —bruises; —crushes; — erodes; —facets; —s rattle; —rumbles; — supports; —sustains; —wedges.

(See rock, gem, jewel.)

adverbs

roughly; unpleasantly; ruggedly; disagreeably; impassably; curiously; amazingly; indescribably; terribly; unmanageably; cruelly.

STOOP (*v*)

adverbs

cautiously; humbly; dejectedly; wearily; miserably; subserviently; abjectly; obsequiously.

(See bend, descend.)

STOP

adjectives

sudden; tender; multiple; occasional; traffic; express; surprising.

STOP (*v*)

adverbs

abruptly; suddenly; instantaneously; instinctively; imperiously; constantly; effectually; timorously; virtually.

(See halt, pause.)

STOPPER

verbs

employ—; fasten—; perforate—; ram in—; stave in—; tamp—; valve—; —checks; — chokes; —corks; —dams; —gags; —insures; —obstructs; —plugs; —restrains; —seals; —stems.

(See plug.)

STORE

adjectives

hideous; wholesome; commodious; hidden; heterogeneous; priceless; strange; corner; frugal; department; fragrant; truly-beautiful; tributary; increasing; plundered; rich; chain; vegetable; bounteous; sorrowful; shoe; overflowing; swanky; smart; glistening; plentiful; wondrous; inexhaustible; gorgeous; mystic; unprotected; ordnance; milky; humble; exclusive; abundant; reliable; provident; vast; cooperative; subsistence; gigantic; literary; undiminished; mustering; huge; immense; proud; untried; prodigious; lavish; winnowing; present; colorful; sparkling; absorbing; exciting; action; adventure; entertaining; amazing; amusing; picked; delightful; captivating; thrilling; true.

verbs

canvass—s; departmentalize—; draw from

—s; expand—; patronize—; —adjusts; —branches out; —caters to; —dispenses; —disposes of; —flourishes; —guarantees; —markets; —purveys; —renovates; —retails; —services; —thrives; —undersells; —unloads; —vends; —wholesales.
(See market, shop, source, supply, provision, food.)

STORE (v)
adverbs
providentially; consequently; secretly; bounteously; inexhaustibly; abundantly; immensely; lavishly; prodigiously; adequately.
(See save, hoard.)

STORK
adjectives
stilted; devouring; brisk; unwelcome; gawky; awkward.

verbs
alarm—; gun for—; stir up—; —claws; —fishes; —floats; —gyrates; —hovers; —rakes; —sails over; —skims; —soars; —strokes; —wades; —wheels.
(See bird.)

STORM
adjectives
teacup; lurid; freezing; irresistible; majestic; blinding; blustering; tumultuous; driving; maddened; harsh; adverse; murky; wintry; fearful; mocking; wrestling; gathering; factual; insatiate; devastating; cyclonic; purifying; conflicting; rising; surly; mingling; slanted; revolving; violent; forgotten; howling; bloody; persistent; rushing; clarifying; dissipated; psychologic; terrific; heavy; raging; confluent; coming; shipwrecking; vicious; beating; expiring; pelting; financial; cyclic; unkind; transitory; recurrent; coast; whistling; perfect; subsiding; blinding; appraising; commingling (pl); rollicking; savage; full-grown; slanting; driving; momentary; deluging; long-continued; tremendous; theologic; awakening; wreckful; drenching; political.

verbs
allay—; battle through—; encounter—; fly before—; foretell—; front—; ride—; scoff at—; shelter from—; stir up—; survive—; tarry in—; unleash—; weather—; —abates; —batters; —brawls; —breaks; —brews; —bursts; —calms; —develops; —flashes; —gathers; —grumbles; —lashes; —rages; —

roars; —seethes; —thunders; —wears out; —whips through; —whistles.
(See blizzard, hurricane, lightning, rain.)

STORM (v)
adverbs
overpoweringly; relentlessly; furiously; irresistibly; thunderously; passionately; devastatingly.
(See fume, rage.)

STORMY
adverbs
wildly; drearily; inordinately; terribly; perilously; tempestuously; thunderously; gustily; roughly; furiously; relentlessly; alarmingly; extraordinarily; violently; fiercely; intensely; unusually; disastrously; dreadfully; fearfully; unusually; extremely; uncommonly; cyclonically; icily.

STORY
adjectives
pathetic; candid; stirring; mouthed; chivalrous; complicated; wonderful; plausible; ludicrous; priceless; naive; moving; roaring; sublime; unexpurgated; eye-opening; authentic; detailed; graphic; specious; woeful; improbable; harrowing; idyllic; rambling; poignant; outrageous; self-told; true; ill-natured; gripping; unpublished; painful; legendary; rudimentary; mystery; absorbing; stupendous; incredible; cruel; mournful; inimitable; apocryphal; unembellished; shameful; threadbare; circumstantial; speaking; typical; thrilling; perishing; revealing; hackneyed; dubious; ribald; conflicting; calumniating; unfinished; veritable; dismal; squalid; wondrous; well-known; age-worn; amusing; time-honored; unbelievable; priceless; adventure; self-effacing; blood-curdling; delectable; inspiring; pungent; fictitious; witty; racy; rapid; complete; amorous; laborious; heroic; commonplace; smooth-flowing; sea; fruitful; innocent; eloquent; darling; appropriate; absurd; perpetual; horrid; abominable; unconnected; tragic; curious; edifying; lustful; copious; spicy; readable; ridiculous; realistic; uppermost; lame; finest; romantic; monotonous; facetious; sad; thought-provoking; sordid; slanderous; eventful; melodramatic; uninterrupted; homely; accredited; grim; tender; didactic; unbiased; tribal; mess-worn; disastrous; well-told; instructive; fascinating; upper; shallow; garbled; delicious; hall-marked;

unreticent; heinous; elaborate; sensational; exquisite; accepted; harrowing; alive; complete; distinguished; deep; entertaining; horror; full-blooded; intimate; inside; light; swift-moving; top-notch; veracious; well-written; well-paced.

verbs
accumulate—s; belittle—; bolster—; cast—; circulate—; climax—; conceive—; concoct —; construct—; dash off—; criticize—; devour—; discredit—; dominate—; dramatize —; dwarf—; embroider—; enact—; fabricate—; fashion—; forge—; hail—; interpret—; invent—; issue—; load—; manufacture—s; narrate—; overload—; paint—; peg away at—; pour out—; present—; peruse—; question—; recapitulate—; reel off —; reiterate—; relate—; release—; relish —; scoff at—; scotch—; spin—; thread—; transcend—; turn out—; verify—; wade thru—; weave—; worm out—; —centers; —confirms; —consoles; —corroborates; —degenerates; —denounces; —depends; —elicits; —emanates; —embellishes; —engrosses; —enhances; —etches; —fascinates; —flows; —hurtles; —implicates; —inspires; —lacks; —links; —marches; —moves; —originates; —pictures; —pieces; —plunges; —progresses; —recounts; —regales; —reigns; —revolves; —rounds off; —shapes; —skirts; —slanders; —slants; —survives; —throws; —tingles; —touches; —travels; —unfolds.
(See legend, fiction, prose, "movie," history, narrative, myth, narration, manuscript, anecdote, book, episode, novel.)

STOUT

adverbs
brawnily; vigorously; unexpectedly; incredibly; invincibly; dependably; unusually; reliably; intrepidly; unbelievably; fortunately; remarkably; surprisingly; uncommonly.

STOUT-HEARTED

adverbs
intrepidly; fearlessly; ridiculously; uncommonly; admirably; undauntedly; immovably; cheerfully; steadfastly; wonderfully; valiantly; boldly; unfailingly; gaily; heroically; pluckily; resolutely; confidently; indomitably; uncommonly; spunkily.

STOUTNESS

verbs
accentuate—; augment—; deplore—; de-

ride—; exaggerate—; magnify—; mitigate —; predispose to—; reduce—; ridicule—; scoff at—; snigger at—; tend toward—; —aggravates; —deforms; —discommodes; —distorts; —dwarfs; —embarrasses; —endangers; —hampers; —hinders; —inconveniences; —mars; —renders ugly; —restrains; —restricts; —stagnates; —threatens; —towers; —wanes.
(See obesity.)

STOVE

adjectives
solemn; nameless; diminutive; roaring; hot; ancient; fiery; sputtering.

verbs
bask by—; consign to—; dampen—; draft —; extinguish—; feed—; hover over—; kindle—; quench—; replenish—; tend—; —affords; —comforts; —diffuses; —dies; —fumes; —insures; —reeks; —roars; —smoulders; —thaws.
(See fire, flame.)

STRAIGHT

adverbs
invariably; perfectly; unwaveringly; commendably; undeniably; exactly; accurately; correctly; admirably; unquestionably; uncommonly; exceptionally; unerringly; authentically; officially; conveniently; comparatively.

STRAIGHTFORWARD

adverbs
commendably; admirably; eminently; unusually; manifestly; evidently; reliably; unquestionably; delightfully; helpfully; artlessly; candidly; unaffectedly; naturally; inherently; obviously; bluntly; ingenuously; childishly; remarkably; uncommonly; scrupulously.

STRAIN

adjectives
sunny; metaphysical; inspiring; harmonious; terrific; bastard; impure; celestial-ordered; subtle; indomitable; echoing; windy; wild; passionate; parting; true-breeding; jubilant; self-same; soft; andante; majestic; exalted; tidal; lofty; untaught; ceaseless; meditative; strenuous; thrilling; singular; unwonted; sublime; aesthetic; adoring; onward; seraphic; taut; minor; thrilling; virile; homiletic; heated; mystical; musical; haunting; audacious; furious;

melancholy; shrill; intellectual; magic; creeping; nameless; unending; delicious; solemn; ventriloquous; gloomy; exultant; epic; lamentable; humorous; immortal; nervous; ravishing; fluent; intense; melodious; dirgeful; noble; thrilling; severe; pompous; intolerable; arresting; serious; mournful; extraordinary; full-fraught; sententious; chaste; racial; emotional; semi-humorous; muscular; individual; violent; true; profitless; indigenous; tender; steady; existing; successive (pl); mystic; pathetic; half-forgotten; polemic; vicious; curious; iterant; somber; martial; tremendous; terrible; inspired; syncopated; subdued; evoked; local; humble; unpolished; sweet; fierce; divine; crushing; enchanting; inevitable.

verbs
avoid—; develop—; disturb—; endure—; entail—; impose—; lift—; mutate—; relieve of—; overtake—; remove—; risk—; slacken—; stand—; subject to—; withstand —; —swells.
(See tension, exertion, stress.)

STRAIN (*v*)
adverbs
incompatibly; prodigiously; inordinately; feebly; passionately; furiously; intellectually; lamentably; excessively.
(See force, stretch.)

STRAIT-LACED
adverbs
absurdly; extremely; priggishly; puritanically; ridiculously; immovably; austerely; arbitrarily; unreasonably; unfortunately; rigidly; unwisely; uncompromisingly; forbiddingly; peremptorily; inexorably; tyrannically; foolishly; prudishly.

STRAITS
adjectives
pecuniary; dire; interminable; imaginary; sounding; desperate; narrow; great; bitter.

STRAND
adjectives
braided; remotest; everlasting; rippling; deserted; great; deep; dark; tragic; mysterious; siren-footed; genial; intertwisted (pl); blistering; dreary; uneven; lonely.

STRANGER
adjectives
formidable; mysterious; unutterable; illustrious; witless; unfriended; well-bred; wandering; forlorn; curious; waiting; humble; unsuspecting; audacious; comparative; thorough; inferior; wayfaring; dreadful; distinguished; swarthy; total; casual; ungenial; sympathetic; neat; unsavory; strange; queer; fluttering; passing; houseless; adulated; unnaturalized; insignificant; unheralded; blooming; detested; shrewd; plain-spoken; earth-born; rough-looking; drunken; drawling-voiced.

verbs
acquaint—with; admit—; appraise—; apprehend—; beguile—; bilk—; confide in—; cultivate—; deceive—; defraud—; delude —; discuss—; distrust—; dupe—; enlighten—; entertain—; exclude—s; extend to—; greet—; guide—; hail—; harbor—; implicate—; inform—; interrogate—; investigate—; mislead—; question—; receive—; regard—; salute—; snarl at—; trail—; usher in—; victimize—; welcome—.
(See alien, immigrant, newcomers, foreigners.)

STRANGLE (*v*)
adverbs
cruelly; excruciatingly; demoniacally; fiendishly; deliberately; maniacally; lustfully; sordidly; horridly; sensationally; horribly; amorously.
(See choke, kill.)

STRAP
verbs
affix—; braid—; buckle—; clasp—; detach —; reinforce—; rend—; sever—; slacken —; tense—; —binds; —couples; —curbs; —fetters; —impedes; —leashes; —links; —restrains; —supports; —sustains.
(See leash, belt, band.)

STRATEGIC
adverbs
cleverly; opportunely; conveniently; expediently; diplomatically; profoundly; secretly; wisely; prudently; discreetly; brilliantly; cunningly; craftily; insidiously; cannily; successfully; splendidly; usefully; profitably; immeasurably; financially; politically; commercially.

adjectives
successful; deadlier; vicious; daring; clumsy; clever; brilliant; military.

verbs
conceive—; concoct—; devise—; employ—; frame—; hatch—; practice—; resort to—; —accomplishes; —baffles; —baits; —befools; —beguiles; —bluffs; —confounds; —decoys; —defrauds; —deludes; —distracts; —diverts; —entices; —frustrates; —hoodwinks; —lures; —rebuffs; —repulses; —routs; —snares; —succeeds; —thwarts.
(See fraud, strategy, deception.)

STRATEGY
adjectives
half-baked; adroit; military; triumphant; ancient; superlative; absurd; sound; naval; aggressive; offensive; thrill-packed.

verbs
achieve—; administer—; adopt—; advise—; approve—; beguile with—; condemn—; counsel—; direct—; effect—; employ—; execute—; fashion—; frame—; guide—; pilot —; plan—; prescribe—; proceed with—; resort to—; steer—; work out—; —defeats; —outwits; —stems from.
(See maneuver, method, stratagem.)

STRAW
adjectives
patient; plaiting; helpful; apparent; damp; frowzy; synthetic; oaten.

verbs
bale—; bed with—; bleach—; discard—; embed in—; glean—; macerate—; plait—; scatter—; shed—; stuff with—; thresh—; weave—; —insures; —litters; —pads; —protects; —thatches.
(See chaff, hair, hay.)

STRAY (v)
adverbs
ostensibly; widely; irrationally; idiotically; adventurously; lustfully; senselessly.
(See roam, wander.)

STREAK
adjectives
ruthless; momentary; rotary; blood-red; uncouth; dingy; shy; cruel; tenderer; glimmering; faithless; vivid; zigzag; dancing; evident; pale; amphibious; glittering; long.

adverbs
dingily; unfortunately; carelessly; sorrily; strangely; unaccountably; shabbily; dimly; luminously; curiously; disagreeably; faintly; shamefully; unattractively; unpleasantly.

STREAM
adjectives
swampy; bounding; echoing; whispering; turning; turbid; crystalline; rude; sharp; rippled; torrent; crystal; playful; straining; purling; shoreless; sluggish; eddying; immemorial; rushing; muddy; murmuring; trickling; rock-encumbered; translucent; fiery; feeding; dancing; summer; gliding; eternal; forbidden; steady; reedy; milky; sullen; solitary; gentle; sourceless; augmented; intervening; surcharged; trembling; fervid; plashing; cooling; glacial; salutary; lucid; sylvan; brown; quickening; livelier; fond; silly; wizard; tributary; voiceless; slender; flashing; lurid; cleansing; impetuous; yellow; constant; placid; fertilizing; simpering; bashful; unreluctant; fascinating; chiding; precipitous; intermittent; volcanic; ever-flowing; precious; fleeting; gushing; inert; navigable; pebbly; constant; enormous; comet-like; wayward; muddied; merry; visible; mighty; rapid; irrigating; whispering; living; delicate; substantial; boundless; celestial; Stygian; picturesque; bleeding; branching; feeble; blended; innumberable (pl); accepted; running; hairy; hurrying; hidden; formidable; indolent; reverent; sinister; pale; melancholy; doubled; storied; haunted; equable; formless; continuous; languid; cascading; copious; swollen; flowing; leaping; exuberant; bone-dry; imperial; golden; attractive; rippling; mountain; icy; undulating; petty; epigrammatic; diverging; inland; shallow; joyous; electric; gracious; singing; motionless; childhood; ignoble; lyrical; venomous; traffic; subterranean; returning; limpid; salt; mighty; numerous; brackish; foaming; verbose; dwindling; desolate; flattering; adventurous; brimming.

verbs
bridge—; ford—; head—; purify—; trace —; —boils; —bubbles; —clogs; —complains; —disappears; —drifts; —dwindles; —s harass; —s languish; —s meander; —narrows; —races; —ripples; —shimmers;

—s splash; —trickles; —tumbles; —washes; —s wind.

(See brook, creek, river.)

STREAM (v)

adverbs

tortuously; monotonously; unceasingly; perpetually; giddily; incessantly; boundingly; turbulently; turbidly; torrentially; eddyingly; translucently; copiously; exuberantly; undulatingly; subterraneanly; limpidly.

(See gush, pour, run.)

STREET

adjectives

dingy; medieval; winding; disreputable; squalid; crooked; blazing; quiet; sleepy; narrow; shaded; paved; silent; filthy; attractive; monotonous; littered; still; prominent; startled; unlovely; crowded; embowered; desolate; misty; impassable; moon-lit; forbidden; greasy; populous; unwatered; prominent; darksome; glaring; gutted; deep; darkling; sloppy; racy; straggling; arcaded; dusty; fearful; surging; charted; tortuous; peopled; intersecting; waking; dazzling; slippery; sunny; irregular; frozen; principal; wandering; obscure; deserted; adjacent; respectable; starry; twilight; glittering; little; clean-washed; ill-kept; palaced; corresponding; throngful; unpaved; spacious; rugged; murmuring; roaring; crooked; sultry; marching; residential; adroit; sunburnt; arid; gray; miry; melancholy; thronged.

verbs

amble about—; bedeck—; clutter—; deface —; front—; gain—; lay out—s; litter—; maintain—; patrol—; parade—; ramble thru—; roam—; strew—; stride thru—s; thread—s; throng in—; trudge along—; wander down—; —bakes; —flanks; — joins; —s shine; —swarms; —thunders.

(See sidewalk, lane, avenue, alley, thoroughfare.)

STRENGTH

adjectives

humble; fragile; clumsy; monstrous; raw; hairy; exhaustless; repellant; numerical; vigorous; passionate; sacred; augmented; national; united; central; shining; living; immortal; undivided; superhuman; effective; untiring; elastic; needless; superior; full; remarkable; herculean; barbaric; concentrated; masterful; magnificent; unwasting; natural; alcoholic; unyielding; unimaginative; rockbound; dogged; joyous; remaining; sudden; brute; double; ultimate; lusty; victorious; fear-crazed; desperate; thoughtful; enormous; awkward; voting; unconquerable; immense; immeasurable; silent; lavish; social; impregnable; sturdy; intellectual; unaided; determined; party; sinewy; tensile; massive; artistic; irresistible; renovated; intense; dominating; prodigious; financial; drowsy; superior; revived; aggressive; firm; lasting; muscular; evident; innate; banded; unbroken; conscious; reserved; lofty; excellent; steadfast; divine; ruthless; huge; comparative; placid; relative; pungent; unabated; manlier; solid; sufficient; concentrated; incredible; residing; surprising; unerring; matchless; authorized; spiritual; moral; gigantic; inseverable; skilled; sober; nervous; ambitious; passionless; lyric; honorable; unfolding; mysterious; welded; splendid; fiery; infinite.

verbs

accumulate—; augment—; betray—; confer —upon; conserve—; deny—; derive—; diffuse—; diminish—; drain—; endow with —; equal—; exhaust—; gain—; gather—; husband—; imbibe—; indicate—; maintain —; match—; measure—; muster—; pit—; possess—; pray for—; preserve—; prune—; recover—; regain—; reserve—; restore—; restrain—; sap—; scatter—; signify—; strain—; tax—; undermine—; unite—; — declines; —endures; —falters; —flows; — manifests itself; —spends itself.

(See energy, fortitude, force, power, health, impregnability.)

STRENUOUS

adverbs

disagreeably; dangerously; zealously; eagerly; laboriously; painfully; terribly; extremely; arduously; incredibly; dreadfully; impossibly; energetically; doggedly; vigorously; intensely; indefatigably; wearisomely; formidably; remarkably; unbelievably; unspeakably; unusually; exceptionally; particularly; singularly; peculiarly; unwholesomely.

STRESS

adjectives

unavailing; emotional; special; urgent; adamantine; particular; critical; unobtrusive; unnatural; artificial; plastic; tremendous; intestinal.

verbs

allay—; alleviate—; attach—to; avoid—;
demand—; ease—; emphasize—; entail—;
lay—upon; mitigate—; occasion—; palliate
—; pronounce—; redouble—; relax—; subject to—; —accentuates; —aggravates; —
declines; —taxes; —tenses; —wanes; —
weighs upon.

(See emphasis, accent, pressure, strain.)

STRESS (*v*)

adverbs

faintly; markedly; precisely; particularly;
exclusively; repeatedly; adamantinely; artificially; obtrusively; vigorously.

(See accent, emphasize.)

STRETCH (*v*)

adverbs

inordinately; gruesomely; indulgently; beauteously; dismayingly; generously; moderately; tightly; abnormally; piteously; consciously; symmetrically; interminably; indolently;
casually.

(See extend, spread.)

STRETCHES

adjectives

sun-scorched; haggard; symmetrical; lilac;
mighty; magnificent; interminable; treeless;
ample; fragrant; indolent; endless; barren;
mysterious; fertile; mossy; casual; wide.

STRICT

adverbs

unreasonably; particularly; singularily;
needlessly; narrowly; dogmatically; narrow-
mindedly; intolerantly; uncharitably; unnecessarily; foolishly; unwisely; cruelly;
bitterly; moderately; severely; oddly; illogically; inconsistently; brutally; piously; conventionally; viciously; habitually; dreadfully; wisely; sensibly; moderately; uncommonly; austerely; uncompromisingly; terribly; hideously.

STRICTNESS

verbs

adhere to—; ameliorate—; conform to—;
diminish—; ease—; enforce—; infringe—;
mitigate—; relax—; violate—; —crushes;
—demands; —disciplines; —domineers; —
exacts; —hampers; —impresses; —inures;
—oppresses; —overrides; —restricts; —revolts; —strains; —taxes; —tramples; —
tyrannizes; —yokes.

(See severity, rules, harshness.)

adjectives

heavy; tumultuous; nervous; proud; rhythmical; careless; consuming; self-assuring;
enormous; slouching; unprecedented; swinging; prodigious; immense; disordered; free;
athletic; short; lofty; majestic; irregular;
fearless; formidable; sinking; ravishing;
restless; martial; manly; rapid; sober.

verbs

accelerate—; break—; burlesque—; exaggerate—; halt—; hasten—; lengthen—;
mimic—; quicken—; regain—; regulate—;
relax—; ridicule—; secure—; smooth—;
spur to—; —covers; —devours; —outdis-
tances; —overhauls; —shuffles; —spurts;
—strains; —taxes.

(See step, walk, pace, gait.)

STRIDE (*v*)

adverbs

vigorously; austerely; grimly; furiously;
swiftly; dramatically; fearlessly; tirelessly;
sturdily; rhythmically; prodigiously; athletically; majestically; martially; rapidly;
soberly.

(See strut, stalk.)

STRIDENT

adverbs

unpleasantly; raucously; disagreeably;
loudly; harshly; quarrelsomely; inelegantly;
naturally; insistently; hatefully; offensively;
coarsely; cruelly; brutally; pugnaciously;
daringly; suddenly; broadly; repulsively;
shockingly; disgustingly; ridiculously.

STRIFE

adjectives

unprofitable; elemental; deadly; stern; sexual; frivolous; murderous; fragrant; patient; sacrificial; noble; ambiguous; harmonious; domestic; continued; fruitful;
party; barren; unceasing; eternal; vain;
inward; harmless; civil; victorious; bloody;
dying; absorbing; ignoble; midnight; surging; household; languid; sordid; political;
ineffectual; harsh; expiring; constant; idle;
inevitable; whirlwind; turbulent; industrial;
uncongenial; tortured; feverish; unselfish;
victorious; convulsive; theological; varied;
bitter; selfish; inhuman; classic; dawning;
spiritual; perpetual; unreposing; useless;
foolish.

verbs

avert—; maneuver—; perpetuate—; plague with—; renew—; stir up—; —afflicts; —breaks out; —breeds; —brings; —dissolves; —flares; —harasses; —locks; —prolongs; —racks; —seethes; —surges; —tears.

(See discord, dissension, fued, conflict, contention, competition.)

STRIKE

verbs

avert—; ban—; break—; condemn—; crush —; deal with—; direct—; engage in—; foment—; forbid—; forestall—; handle—; interfere in—; precipitate—; prolong—; resort to—; stage—; stave off—; submit without—; support—; terminate—; tolerate—; weigh—; —breaks out; —develops; —s drag on; —embroils; —grips; —intervenes; —paralyzes; —rages; —spreads; —threatens; —wanes; breed—.

(See strife, conflict, feud.)

STRIKE (v)

adverbs

firmly; sullenly; pronouncedly; simultaneously; forcibly; spontaneously; instinctively; energetically; significantly; thunderously; heavily; intermittently; aimlessly; accidently; swiftly; mysteriously.

(See hit, slap.)

STRIKERS

verbs

acquit—; bow to—; champion—; conciliate —; disperse—; exonerate—; harangue—; pacify—; placate—; unite—; —arbitrate; —arm; —bar; —charge; —cooperate; —deride; —evict; —heckle; —intimidate; —jeer; —organize; —picket; —pillage; —relent; —repudiate; —riot; —sit down; —taunt; —violate; —demand.

(See rioters, crowd.)

STRIKING

adverbs

conspicuously; impressively; significantly; unusually; ominously; brilliantly; gorgeously; blatantly; garishly; gaudily; unbecomingly; inelegantly; magnificently; gloriously; beautifully; satisfactorily; artistically; luminously; overwhelmingly; delicately; daringly; boldly.

adjectives

hampering; friendly; sleeping; trembling; sinless; dissonant; silken; melodious; speaking; clanging; stubborn; tinkling; twined; tremulous; consecrated; quivering; veritable; sturdy; dusty; gouty; tightening; dangling; wayward; vibrating; tuneful; slackened.

verbs

braid—; cleave—; draw—; plait—; secure with—; sever—; shred—; slash—; stretch —; sunder—; suspend from—; tense—; —couples; —girds; —sustains; —yokes.

(See cord, leash, chains.)

STRINGENT

adverbs

unwisely; disagreeably; unbearably; intolerably; unintelligently; necessarily; inescapably; terribly; irritatingly; vexatiously; dangerously; ominously; unreasonably; injudiciously; stupidly; inexpediently; ill-advisedly; absurdly.

STRINGY

adverbs

unpleasantly; inconveniently; disagreeably; necessarily; unavoidably; naturally; gummily; uselessly; sufficiently; satisfactorily.

STRIP

adjectives

tenacious; popular; marginal; shadowy; pestilential; tiny; strong.

STRIPES

adjectives

brisk; contrast; vivid; severe; oblique; polychromatic; longitudinal; bright; broad; service; tiny.

STRIVE (v)

adverbs

ineffectually; laboriously; ambitiously; earnestly; indomitably; energetically; incessantly; valiantly; patiently; bull-headedly; stubbornly; ineffectively; nobly; dutifully; filially; fiercely; seditiously; diligently; vainly.

(See try, struggle.)

STRIVING

adjectives

human; eternal; earnest; ineradicable; hopeful; wishful; useful; bitter; wistful; vain.

STROKE (v)

adverbs

reflectively; meditatively; caressingly; affectionately; tenderly; absently; moodily; gently.

(See calm, smooth, touch.)

STROKES
(boating)

verbs

accelerate—; coach—; develop—; employ—; execute—; invigorate—; pace—; perfect—; polish—; regulate—; scull with—; synchronize—; time—; —cut; —exhaust; —lash; —outdistance; —overhaul; —propel; —strain; —tax; —tell; —tire; —weary.

(See blow.)

STROKES
(general)

adjectives

fatal; parliamentary; overhand; crowning; silver; unkind; vulgar; paralytic; heavy; bloodless; careful; cautious; ignorant; vicious; prevailing; impulsive; vigorous; concussive; subtle; blessed; specious; fragrant; lusty; spasmodic; rapid; rhythmic; blind; mortal; apoplectic; disastrous; mortuary; oft-repeated; calumnious; forceful; stinted; fanciful; hostile; curious; brilliant; terrific; coarse; sturdy; despairing; measured; unprecedented.

STROLL

adjectives

aimless; meditative; memorable; undisturbed.

STROLL (v)

adverbs

leisurely; languidly; dejectedly; philosophically; reflectively; nonchalantly; idly; contemplatively; pleasantly; dreamily .

(See roam, ramble.)

STRONG

adverbs

brutally; remarkably; physically; powerfully; vigorously; vitally; incontestably; pitilessly; tenaciously; toughly; unquestionably; indubitably; remarkably; exceedingly; undeniably; manifestly; evidently; unexpectedly; determinedly; resolutely; cruelly; unyieldingly; incredibly; obviously; supremely; amazingly; incalculably.

STRONGHOLD

adjectives

impregnable; unconquerable; abandoned; gloomy; ruined.

verbs

abandon—; abdicate—; bar—; barricade—; bolt—; bombard—; escort to—; fortify—; garrison—; imperil—; intrench in—; invade —; jeopardize—; maintain—; menace—; padlock—; patrol—; repel from—; retire to —; retreat to—; screen—; subject—; —preserves; —shields.

(See fortifications, castle, citadel.)

STRUCTURE

adjectives

pyramidal; interesting; domineering; intricate; cosmical; rudimentary; ill-smelling; intended; fanciful; economic; serpentine; naked; mossy; asteriated; elaborate; circular; bonelike; metropolitan; solid; classical; dignified; ephemeral; ambitious; hideous; cellular; imposing; confused; rhythmical; chemical; vernacular; inner; stereotyped; cell; restless; inorganic; sensible; spiritual; streamlined; feathery; phantasmic; substantial; worldly; choral; patchwork; ecumenical; jointed; industrial; commodious; natural; unsightly; hair-growing; administrative; flexible; complicated; institutional; airy; continuous; underlying; ill-conceived; flimsy; internal; laminated; graceful; grave; supporting; artistic; various (pl); unwieldy; rambling; uniform; fragile; stately; urbane; sensible; unambitious; synthetic; magnificent; patriarchal; barn-like.

verbs

bind—; bore into—; complete—; elevate—; erect—; house in—; obliterate—; prop up —; rebuild—; tear down—; threaten—; underlie—.

(See building, edifice, frame, mansion.)

STRUGGLE

adjectives

tragic; intestinal; convulsive; protracted; brutal; obstinate; ineffectual; actual; intense; constant; inner; impending; arduous; continuous; painful; confused; perpetual; unending; imperialist; tremendous; fearful; dying; dire; terrific; heroic; vehement; strenuous; vain; gallant; victorious; stouthearted; prodigious; embittered; wild; unceasing; spiritual; thwarted; savage; sustained; eternal; ancient; deplorable; unequal; herculean; impotent; universal; unbrotherly; awful; bitter; foolish; lifelong; passionate; severe; inevitable; internecine; sanguine; subjective; desperate; slight; despairing; unaided; bloody; sharp; titanic; doubtful; bootless; parochial; fierce; unlettered; unremitting; brilliant; pioneer; apprehended; hidden; obscure; rough; melancholy; muscular; writhing; selfish; ardent; human; evident; moral; expressionable; creative; momentous.

verbs

desert—; engage in—; finance—; indulge in —; intercede in—; localize—; look upon—; participate in—; settle down to—; undergo —; wage—; yield in—; —culminates; —eliminates; —emaciates; —fills; —resolves; —harries; —summons; —swings in.

(See combat, contention, fight, effort, exertion, contest.)

STRUGGLE (v)

adverbs

flounderingly; terrifically; frantically; vainly; heroically; vigorously; savagely; weakly; feebly; manfully; ingeniously; obstinately; gallantly; turbulently; protractedly; vehemently; herculeanly; bootlessly; momentously.

(See labor, grapple.)

STRUT (v)

adverbs

stalwartly; vainly; proudly; conceitedly; arrogantly; pompously; complacently; jauntily; preposterously; magnificently; vulgarly; pugnaciously; valiantly.

(See swell, swagger.)

STUBBORN

adverbs

obstinately; astonishingly; surprisingly; naturally; incorrigibly; wonderfully; unexpectedly; infinitely; implacably; sternly; bull-headedly; doggedly; brutally; inveterately; desperately; inflexibly; habitually; obdurately; viciously; dreadfully.

STUBBORNNESS

adjectives

infinite; impious; implacable; stern; vainglorious; bull-headed.

verbs

allay—; conciliate—; decry—; denounce—; display—; evince—; exhibit—; moderate—;

rebuke—; relax—; reproach—; reprove—; revolt at—; submit to—; —goads; —irks; — resists; —riles (colloq.); —stiffens; —withstands; —yields to.

(See obstinacy, perversity.)

STUDENT

adjectives

diligent; research; discriminating; deep; promising; earnest; fastidious; formal; impartial; docile; special; facetious; ardent; aspiring; insatiable; careless; assiduous; indefatigable; veritable; irresponsible; tireless; thorough; languid; abstract; unprejudiced; historical; noble; able; sober-minded; learned; painstaking; talented; subsequent; tireless; candid; self-helping; laboratory; divinity; apathetic; enthusiastic; agile; negligent; inquisitive; critical; philosophical; scientific; thoughtful; impassioned.

verbs

assign—; bewilder—; baffle—; delude—; discipline—; dismiss—; edify—; enlighten —; enroll—; examine—; expound to—s; grade—; guide—; herd—s; honor—; inculcate in—; indoctrinate—s; ingrain—; initiate—; propound to—s; rear—; recruit—s; reprimand—; reproach—; tutor—; vex—s; —acquires; —advances; —attains; —attunes himself to; —s carouse; —concentrates; — cows; —crams; —cuts; —dips into; —drills; —familiarizes himself with; —flunks (colloq.); —gleams; —interprets; —peruses; —prepares; —qualifies; —translates; —wades through.

(See reader, pupil, graduate, apprentice, classmate.)

STUDIO

adjectives

shabby; wonderful; separate; silk-hung; aggressive; lofty; colossal; comfortable; broadcasting.

STUDIOUS

adverbs

earnestly; curiously; keenly; avidly; eagerly; energetically; tirelessly; actively; naturally; feverishly; gravely; seriously; resolutely; delightfully; overly; alarmingly; profoundly; deeply; uncommonly; happily; ambitiously; obviously; diligently; enthusiastically; oppressively; solemnly; erratically; spasmodically; occasionally.

adjectives
antiquarian; unsympathetic; superficial; graduate; modern; comparative; remarkable; illuminating; long-continued; scientific; painstaking; extraordinary; systematic; unfavorable; preparatory; revealing; proper; comprehensive; extensive; booklined; judicial; concise; forthright; up-to-the-minute; provocative; expert; full-length; fundamental; flippant; exhaustive; philosophical; continuous; assiduous; daring; delightful; watchful; careful; serious; old; desperate; concentrated; patient; theological; authoritative; morbid; analytical; technical; advanced; striking; instructive; candid; crude; suggestive; academic; intensive; satirical; vigorous; compulsory; fossil; obvious; diversified; profitless; linguistic; detailed; actual; thorough; curious; measured; topographical; ornamental; valuable; practical; searching; artistic; cartographic; tempting; clever; immediate; qualitative; perpetual; useless; passionate; lifetime; whimsical; sample; persistent; slight; consecutive; historic; constant; sociological; diligent; rational; economic; indispensable; illusory; rough-hewn; brilliant-hued; convincing; long-interrupted; solitary; utmost; exalted; laborious; statistical; contrapuntal; profound; daily; conscientious; energetic; sublime; penetrating; vivid; incessant; exciting; complicated; mathematical; desultory; previous; ethnographical; probing; intimate; monumental.

verbs
carry on—s; commence—; confine—; delve into—; devote time to—; direct—; distract from—; embrace—of; engage in—; engross in—; enlarge range of—; facilitate—; focus —on; further—; guide—s; impel—; incorporate—; neglect—; plunge into—; proclaim —of; pursue—; select—; simplify—; specialize in—; stabilize—; standardize—s; thirst for—; toy with—; undertake—; — compensates; —discloses; —edifies; —enlightens; —occupies; —reveals; —rewards; —sharpens; absorb in—; apply—; buckle down to—.
(See curriculum, research, learning, application, history, English, science, etc.)

STUDY (v)
adverbs
desultorily; diligently; extensively; minutely; assiduously; scrupulously; meticulously; persistently; exhaustively; historically; systematically; conscientiously; earnestly; fervently; obstinately; theoretically; monastically; unremittingly; indefatigably; abstractly; philosophically.
(See muse, concentrate.)

STUFF
adjectives
pleasing; fiery; masquing; dismal; immortal; rich; colored; mortifying; stern; garden; embroidered; vitriolic; proud; branded; stinging; warming; luminous.

STUFFY
adverbs
intolerably; overwhelmingly; absurdly; uncommonly; odorously; aristocratically; elegantly; pedantically; snuffily; uncomfortably; distressingly; oppressively; stupidly; unbearably; clamorously; noisily; swarmingly.

STUMBLE (v)
adverbs
blindly; stupidly; awkwardly; falteringly; inadvertently; drunkenly; soddenly; vacantly.
(See trip, fall.)

STUN (v)
adverbs
momentarily; physically; emotionally; staggeringly; spiritually; utterly; partially; terrifically.
(See overcome, bewilder.)

STUNTED
adverbs
cruelly; crookedly; distressingly; criminally; pitiably; oddly; wretchedly; miserably; dwarfishly; scrawnily; elfishly; queerly; unfortunately; incredibly; hopelessly; pudgily.

STUPEFIED
adverbs
oddly; suddenly; astonishingly; bewilderingly; grievously; queerly; curiously; dopily; soddenly; utterly; strangely; helplessly; hopelessly; maliciously; hypnotically; sleepily; mysteriously; unaccountably; dazedly.

STUPID
adverbs
abysmally; strangely; unutterably; vacuously; ridiculously; oddly; peculiarly; curiously; unaccountably; irritatingly; vexatious-

ly; shockingly; fatally; callously; carelessly; hopelessly; unpardonably; inexplicably; innately; soddenly; sullenly; grossly; direly; blankly.

STUPIDITY
adjectives
innate; sodden; impenetrable; ineffable; sullen; stultifying; blundering; pompous; designed; gross; useless; current; vacant; insuperable; dire.

verbs
bemoan—; betoken—; bewail—; contemplate —; decry—; deplore—; deride—; disclose —; display—; evince—; feign—; manifest —; marvel at—; observe—; overcome—; realize—; reveal—; ridicule—; shriek at—; stress—; —confounds; —flabbergasts colloq.); —overwhelms; —prejudices.
(See inefficiency, mediocrity, imbecility, inability, dullness, incompetence, ignorance.)

STUPOR
adjectives
dull; partial; obstructing; vacant; empty; silly; blank.

verbs
arouse from—; bring on—; collapse in—; induce—; shock into—; —benumbs; —binds; —blunts; —deadens; —dulls, —envelops; — ensues; —exhausts; —overtakes; —paralyzes; —petrifies; —prostrates; —shatters; —stuns; —suspends; —overcomes.
(See coma, lethargy, languor, unconsciousness.)

STURDY
adverbs
splendidly; admirably; remarkably; surprisingly; stoutly; healthily; vigorously; boyishly; magnificently; stockily; brawnily; enviably; physically.

STYLE
adjectives
slenderizing; tailored; frilly; florid; artificial; dashing; architectural; concise; effective; halting; figurative; extra-colloquial; episodical; anithetical; correct; pleasing; all-pervading; comprehensible; heathenish; slovenly; fantastic; grotesque; balanced; conservative; honorable; latinized; showy; literary; satirical; classic; unsurpassed; impeccable; authentic; complimentary; trim; genuine; sparkling; alert; distinctive; advance; permanent; commanding; behavioristic; friendly; clear; baronial; polished; brilliant; admirable; rushing; secular; barbaric; lucid; unacademic; dapper; legitimate; single; expensive; established; important; gigantic; swagger; magniloquent; pianoforte; loving; conventional; vigorous; monumental; captivating; pungent; simple; habitual; inherited; arrogant; offensive; flamboyant; browbeating; ceremonious; limited; piquant; epistolary; representative; soft; journalistic; swashbuckling; engaging; dramatic; unambiguous; elegant; ambitious; burial; peculiar; learned; elevated; cataloguing; quiet; incongruous; inoffensive; handsome; fitted; architectural; sleek-fitting; youthful; decent; becoming; pointed; pathetic; superior; interesting; cryptic; ostentatious; stilted; nervous; lucid; epigrammatic; forcible; inimitable; laminated; logical; bald; imperial; reprehensible; thrill-provoking; metrical; dissimilar; typical; sonorous; conceivable; didactic; historic; successive (pl); rebellious; prose; puny; damnatory; native; patriarchal; exclamatory; unequaled; poetic; fine; wrought; singular; dazzling; appropriate; favored.

verbs
acclaim—; adopt—; affect—; approve—; breed—; burlesque—; characterize—; cling to—; cloak—; coarsen—; conceive—; conform to—; couch—; cramp—; cultivate—; design—; develop—; distinguish—; distort —; elaborate—; fabricate—; fashion—; fix —; flag—; formulate—; introduce—; lack —; mar—; mature—; model—; modify—; mold—; polish—; popularize—; purify—; refine—; ridicule—; satirize—; set—; strain —; study—; —bears; —s decree; —discriminates; —embraces; —expresses; —glitters; —indicates; —lends charm; —palls; —takes your fancy; —varies.
(See form, manner, character, fashion.)

STYLE (v)
adverbs
smartly; individually; spectacularly; exquisitely; casually; correctly; euphemistically; universally.
(See fashion, create.)

STYLISH
adverbs
conventionally; extremely; elegantly; properly; unusually; curiously; engagingly; enchantingly; inordinately; consciously; not-

iceably; conspicuously; impressively; imposingly; aristocratically; undeniably; amazingly; astoundingly; skillfully; expensively; naturally; delightfully; charmingly; beautifully; agreeably.

SUAVE
adverbs
unctuously; blandly; resolutely; steadily; deliberately; ominously; politely; ceremoniously; chivalrously; conspicuously; gently; helpfully; craftily; adroitly; disarmingly; charmingly; engagingly; unwontedly; painstakingly; diplomatically; carefully; warily; cleverly.

SUBCONSCIOUSNESS
verbs
arouse from—; control—; fix in—; induce —; influence—; penetrate—; pervade—; reduce to—; —clings to; —dematerializes; —disembodies; —dwells; —ensues; —retains; —reigns; —roams; —spiritualizes; —strays; —wanders.
(See mind, intellect.)

SUBDUE (v)
adverbs
valiantly; unconditionally; absolutely; ignominiously; degradingly; compulsorily.
(See conquer, overpower.)

SUBJECT
adjectives
contemporary; congenial; cognate; bruited; unhappy; abstract; apt; truer; humble; elevated; practical; tragical; touching; imaginable; despairing; dutiful; recurring; distressed; rebellious; incongruous; turbulent; daring; controversial; unruly; absorbing; varied (pl); analogous; fruitful; painful; related; utilitarian; historical; well-determined; idealistic; copious (pl); immediate; hypnotic; impressionable; intoxicating; diversified; rich; miscellaneous (pl); delicate; responsive; base; scriptural; antiquated; facetious; non-technical; allegorical; extraneous; unpleasant; proposed; dominant; precipient; docile; kindred; thinking; suitable; abstruse; dehydrated; unwelcome; invaluable; horrified; corpulent; unwilling; traitorous; ephemeral; foolscap; stern; passive; coherent; striking; ethical; admissable; tributary; somber; decorative; obscure; vexed; isolated; leisure; least; unfortunate; tempted; philosophical; sentient; dehumanized; aggrieved; obtuse.

verbs
abuse—; allude to—; ally to—; approach—; assail—; bedevil—; branch off—; broach—; brood over—; brush upon—; circumvent—; comment on—; comprehend—; converse on —; debate on—; delve into—; depict—; dismiss—; draw upon—; edit—; evade—; exhaust—; exorcise—; expatiate on—; expound—; grasp—; hurry through—; introduce—; investigate—; master—; mention—; nourish—; obscure—; phrase—; ponder over—; pursue—; return to—; scorn—; shake—; summarize—; tackle—; wrap oneself up in—; —associates; —baffles; —s bruit; —deals; —engages; —exalts; —illuminates; —s interweave; —intrigues; —s range; —reacts; —recurs; —stimulates; —takes shape; —throws; —treats; —unfolds; —warms; harp on—.
(See matter, proposition, question, history, English, etc.)

SUBJECT (v)
adverbs
minutely; perpetually; humiliatingly; rigorously; civilly; morally; debasingly; tyrannically; dictatorially.
(See expose, uncover.)

SUBJECTION
adjectives
entire; debasing; discomfited; enforced; civil; total; absolute; moral; humble.

verbs
accomplish—; achieve—; assail—; batter to —; coerce into—; complete—; contrive—; culminate in—; curb—; exempt from—; gain—; halt—; reduce to—; repress—; resist—; restrain—; secure—; terminate—; undermine—; wrestle into—; —binds; —oppresses; control—.
(See discipline, enslavement, exposure, subjugation, subserviency.)

SUBJUGATION
verbs
endure—; escape—; lead into—; liberate from—; reduce to—; resist—; —bridles; —blights; —constrains; —curbs; —enslaves; —fetters; —leashes; —muzzles; —restricts; —shackles; —suppresses; —weighs upon; —yokes.
(See bondage, enslavement, subjection.)

SUBMARINE

verbs

batter—; charter—; command—; communicate with—; engulf—; ground—; navigate —; propel—; ram—; scuttle—; swamp—; —s blockade; —convoys; —descends; — dips; —dives; —ejects; —endangers; — escorts; —explores; —founders; —immerses; —s patrol; —plummets; —plunges; —probes; —scurries; —settles; —slides; — sounds; —squats; —submerges; —tips; — torpedoes.

SUBMERGE (v)

adverbs

forcibly; totally; completely; fatally; instinctively; involuntarily.

(See plunge, sink.)

SUBMISSION

adjectives

unconditional; absolute; calm; vile; dishonorable; willing; unexpected; hopeless; tame; humble; quiet; ignominious; coy; continued; supine; abject; prompt; slavish; degrading; piteous; gentle; formal; proud; patient; pretended; deprecating; compulsory; mute.

verbs

advise—; advocate—; bait into—; bend in —; bow in—; coerce into—; compel—; cuff into—; demand—; endure—; enforce—; enjoin—; exact—; force into—; reduce to—; resign to—; tame into—; tolerate—; yield to—; —chastens; —humbles; —humilitates; batter into—.

(See acquiescence, compliance, obedience.)

SUBMISSIVE

adverbs

obsequiously; compliantly; loyally; passively; obediently; modestly; meekly; humbly; philosophically; necessarily; quietly; apathetically; dully; grimly; apparently; perfectly; shamelessly; appallingly; incredibly; strangely; pathetically; pliantly; weakly; calmly; resolutely; imperturbably; stolidly; stupidly; curiously; mysteriously; evidently; tragically; presumably.

SUBMIT (v)

adverbs

graciously; willingly; passively; uxoriously; spinelessly; coyly; voluntarily; placidly; informally; tamely; ignominiously; uncondi-

tionally; docilely; apathetically; supinely; slavishly; mutely; deprecatingly.

(See surrender, yield.)

SUBORDINATE

adverbs

gracefully; cheerfully; respectfully; deferentially; carefully; cautiously; unfailingly; abjectly; slavishly; miserably; wretchedly; pleasantly; courteously; obediently; contentedly; admiringly; willingly; admittedly; apparently.

SUBPOENA

verbs

default—; dispatch—; evade—; issue—; request—; serve—; —apprehends; —arraigns; —bids; —calls upon; —commands; —compels; —constrains; —informs; —instructs; —orders; —requires; —specifies; —summons.

(See order, command.)

SUBSCRIBE (v)

adverbs

heartily; sincerely; earnestly; willingly; immediately; annually; cheerfully; voluntarily.

(See sign, agree.)

SUBSCRIPTION

adjectives

voluntary; annual; huge; cheerful; suggested.

verbs

advance—; afford—; bestow—; cancel—; conclude—; confer—; contribute—; donate —; entrust with—; favor with—; increase —; plead for—; pledge—; raise—; reduce —; renew—; swamp with—s; —aids; —assists; —s pour in; —reinforces; —relieves; —rescues; —succors.

(See contribution.)

SUBSERVIENCY

adverbs

assail—; bow in—; cower in—; cringe in—; decry—; emancipate from—; grovel in—; kneel in—; prostrate in—; reduce to—; stoop in—; submit to—; —abases; —defaces; —degrades; —discountenances; — humiliates; —oppresses; —yokes.

(See subjection.)

1140

adverbs

willingly; unfortunately; humbly; meekly; slavishly; wretchedly; abjectly; helplessly; sullenly; agreeably; deferentially; respectfully; voluntarily; eagerly; zealously; remarkably; amazingly; oddly; strangely; unaccountably; curiously; unwontedly.

SUBSIDE (v)

adverbs

abruptly; gradually; growlingly; brokenly; ultimately; spontaneously; markedly; intermittently.

(See sink, fall.)

SUBSIDY

verbs

advance—; appropriate—; disburse—; expend—; yield—; —abets; —assists; —bolsters; —enables; —encourages; —fosters; —furthers; —protests; —rejuvenates; —relieves; —rescues; —resuscitates; —succors; —supports; —sustains; —wrests.

(See aid, gift.)

SUBSIST (v)

adverbs

frugally; intellectually; meagerly; precariously; scantily; barely; penuriously.

(See maintain, exist.)

SUBSISTENCE

adjectives

meager; precarious; degraded; scanty; bare; mere.

verbs

animate—; destroy—; ennoble—; justify—; maintain—; preserve—; prolong—; protract —; rely on for—; revive—; support—; vitalize—; vivify—; invest—; wrest—; —furnishes; —wanes; —waxes.

(See livelihood, living, employment.)

SUBSTANCE

adjectives

natural; softening; unsightly; poisonous; combustible; essential; spiritual; tremendous; obstructing; tolerated; sterner; toxic; demulcent; emotional; intellectual; earthly; noble; insulating; viscid; gelatinous; perfumed; innocuous; permeable; authenticating; inert; injurious; scanty; metallic; waste; watery; abrasive; adulterate; pulpy; deleterious; luminous; delicate; innumerable (pl); gummy; artificial; material; life-

giving; synthetic; convertible; reorganized; vital; incorruptible; homogeneous; prepared; solid; bituminous; dilated; harsh; caustic; refulgent; rebellious; vitreous; glossy; tenacious; malleable; gaseous; porous; desiccated; durable; mollifying; slovenly; putrid; versatile.

verbs

absorb—; administer—; alter—; compound —; condense—; convert—; dehydrate—; desiccate—; disperse—; dissolve—; embody in—; employ—; express—; fritter away—; lack—; lose—; market—; oxidize—; pulverize—; reach—; reflect—; secrete—; value —; —activates; —congeals; —crumbles; — disintegrates; —endures; —ossifies; —petrifies; —produces; —resists; —yields; produce—.

(See chemical, essence, material, matter.)

SUBSTANTIAL

adverbs

admirably; unusually; remarkably; financially; structurally; commendably; luckily; acceptably; satisfactorily; unexpectedly; agreeably; amazingly; delightfully; providentially.

SUBSTITUTE

adjectives

improvised; sufficient; acceptable; comprehensive; facile; agreeable; ancient; temporary; satisfactory; reasonable; ingenious; occasional; wooden; bloodless; plausible; inadequate; appropriate; selective; human; solid.

verbs

accept—; accredit—; approve—; authorize —; commend—; commission—; concede to —; consent to—; consider—; create—; delegate—; deprecate—; discard—; employ—; frown upon—; grant—; hail—; indorse—; invest—with; offer—; regard—; reimburse —; reject—; sanction—; weigh—; yield to —; —conforms to; —constitutes; —replaces; —supersedes; —supplants; empower—.

(See delegate, agent, representative.)

SUBSTITUTE (v)

adverbs

successfully; definitely; deftly; slyly; insidiously; ingeniously; plausibly; adequately; appropriately; invidiously.

(See exchange.)

SUBTERFUGE

verbs

cloak in—; employ—; resort to—; screen—; veil in—; —beguiles; —conceals; —counterfeits; —deceives; —deludes; —dodges; —eludes; —evades; —falsifies; —feigns; —glosses over; —impostures; —juggles; —misleads; —misrepresents; —obscures.

(See evasion, artifice.)

SUBTLETY

adjectives

ceremonious; absurd; obvious; airy; delicate; hidden; natural; shadowy; time-woven.

verbs

bare—; comprehend—; discern—; enlighten—; interpret—; mask in—; pierce—; see through—; —beguiles; —cloaks; —curtails; —deludes; —disguises; —hints; —misleads; —obscures; —pervades; —prompts; —screens; —shrouds; —suggests; —veils.

(See cunning, deceit, distinction.)

SUBURB

adjectives

smiling; residential; initial; dingy; depressing; thriving; adjoining; flourishing; smug; convenient; fragrant; charming; obscure; foreign; immediate; picturesque; shabby; gardened; mysterious; remote.

SUBVERT (v)

adverbs

monstrously; utterly; viciously; completely; insidiously; secretly; debasingly; civilly; politically; governmentally.

(See overthrow, destroy.)

SUBWAY

verbs

construct—; dash into—; flow from—; jam —; —bears; —bores; —conveys; —courses; —extends to; —facilitates; —hums; —replaces; —roars; —screams; —traverses; —tunnels; —unloads; —unites.

(See train, railroad, tunnel.)

SUCCEED (v)

adverbs

patently; credibly; notably; inevitably; eminently; legitimately; admirably; scholastically; financially; triumphantly; precociously; superficially; materialistically; phenomenally; significantly; sensationally; ephemerally; commercially; economically.

(See attain, accomplish.)

SUCCESS

adjectives

scholastic; undoubted; international; popular; bad; social; pretentious; booming; enduring; grand; prodigious; mounting; continued; alternate; dawning; instantaneous; pecuniary; inferior; competitive; particular; tremendous; unexampled; imperial; unreached; triumphant; checkered; immense; precocious; transient; superficial; proper; political; indifferent; ill; clumsy; material; brilliant; emphatic; petty; overawed; ultimate; gratifying; enduring; lasting; unbroken; substantial; howling; phenomenal; significant; outstanding; fugitive; considerable; conspicuous; soaring; universal; overnight; amazing; sensational; artistic; perfect; superb; grandiose; ephemeral; commercial; financial; poor; youthful; extraordinary; definite; prompt; unqualified; dramatic; equal; dubious; established; signal; double; spontaneous; notable; permanent; marvelous; facile; astonishing; monetary; evanescent; sufficient; well-merited; temporary; economic; noticeable; growing; worldly; eventual; reigning.

verbs

achieve—; aspire to—; assure—; attain—; attend with—; beset—; claim—; correlate —; crown with—; earn—; enjoy—; fight to—; flush with—; glean—; hinder—; impede—; jeopardize—; predict—; reckon with—; score—; secure—; smash into—; taste—; train for—; —arises; —attests to; —blasts; —comes; —completes; —crowns; —embitters; —emboldens; —encourages; —hails; —hinges; —insures; —paves; —pays for; —pursues; —signalizes; —springs; —tempts; —wears.

(See fortune, victory, triumph, achievement, supremacy, wealth, fame.)

SUCCESSFUL

adverbs

happily; unusually; consistently; fortunately; triumphantly; extremely; unexpectedly; luckily; felicitously; buoyantly; hilariously; thrillingly; boisterously; excitedly; highly; incomparably; uncommonly; marvelously.

adjectives

uninterrupted; dreary; perpetual; observed; lashing; swift; delicious; destined; strange; rapid; continual; sweet; tragic; barbarous; fierce; hereditary; rigid; melodious; medieval; connected; fortuitous; constant.

SUCCOR

verbs

afford—; cherish—; extend—; find—; gain—; furnish—; lend—; plead for—; refuse—; reject—; render—; seek—; withdraw—; withhold—; yield—; —cheers; —nurtures; —relieves; —supports; —sustains.

(See aid, help, relief, assistance.)

SUCCULENT

adverbs

lusciously; deliciously; delightfully; palatably; nutritiously; strangely; unexpectedly; especially; unusually; incomparably; agreeably; pleasantly; delicately; commendably; healthfully.

SUCCUMB (v)

adverbs

fatally; feebly; unconditionally; weakly; gradually; partially; dangerously; ultimately; unresistingly; promptly

(See submit, sink, yield.)

SUCK (v)

adverbs

thirstily; vigorously; greedily; insatiably.

(See absorb, imbibe.)

SUDDEN

adverbs

rudely; unfortunately; startlingly; whimsically; intentionally; astonishingly; mercifully; shockingly; amusingly; disconcertingly; ridiculously; laughably; offensively; inexcusably; unforgivably; dangerously; unreasonably; lamentably; unintentionally; abruptly; breathlessly; unpardonably; precipitately; prematurely.

SUE (v)

adverbs

importunately; legally; litigiously; ruthlessly; vindictively; logically; irrationally.

(See prosecute, arrest.)

SUFFER (v)

adverbs

agonizingly; distressingly; severely; stoically; intensely; dismally; atrociously; grievously; acutely; keenly; proportionately; deservedly; heroically; mentally; extensively; mutely; monetarily; infinitely; miserably; chronically; wretchedly.

(See endure, bear.)

SUFFERER

adjectives

lifelong; innocent; glorious; distinguished; chronic; mighty; indignant; surviving; wretched; immediate.

verbs

agonize—; attend—; cheer—; comfort—; condole with—; console—; convulse—; crucify—; deliver—; depress—; disburden—; ease—; flog—; nurse—; soothe—; treat—; wrack—; wrap up—; wring—; —baffles; —endures; —groans; —laments; —moans; —rallies; —retaliates; —revives; —survives.

(See invalid, victim.)

SUFFERING

adjectives

prolong; imitative; indignant; passive; self-inflicted; awful; needless; subtle; intense; meek; angelic; vicarious; spiritual; supreme; cruel; ignominious; pecuniary; virtuous; fictitious; tempestuous; poignant; unnecessary; protracted; inevitable; patient; unmerited; terrible; acute; untold; petty; decisive; universal; mortal; everlasting.

verbs

antidote—; appease—; assuage—; augment—; avoid—; bear—; doom to—; endure—; exhibit—; experience—; fight—; impose—; indulge—; lessen—; minimize—; palliate—; perfect through—; persevere in—; probe—; prolong—; quench—; reassure—; remedy—; —aggravates; —alleviates; —burdens; —convinces; —defaces; —diminishes; —entails; —expiates; —mitigates; —obviates; —racks; protract—.

(See distress, pain.)

SUFFICIENT

adverbs

sufficient; luckily; gratifyingly; wonderfully; quite; satisfactorily; admirably; luxuriantly; abundantly; amply; copiously; inexhaustibly; amazingly; happily; fortunately.

SUFFOCATION

verbs

avert—; await—; doom to—; escape—; face with—; forestall—; hazard—; rescue from—; result in—; risk—; stave off—; verge on—; —cuts short; —ensues; —follows; —impends; —looms; —menaces; —occurs; —severs; —supervenes; —threatens; —wipes out.

(See drowning, failure.)

SUFFRAGE

adjectives

popular; unsolicited; unrestricted; universal; unappreciated.

verbs

authorize—; campaign for—; claim—; confer—on; curtail—; demand—; deny—; deprive of—; endow with—; enjoy—; entitle to—; extend—; gain—; merit—; relinquish —;restore—; restrict—; revoke—; sanction —; solicit—; throttle—; yield—; —voices.

(See right, vote.)

SUGAR

adjectives

swarthy; permissible; vital; energy-giving; tasty.

verbs

abstain from—; adulterate—; box—; consume—; convert—; crystallize—; cure with —; decompose—; dissolve—; excrete—; grade—; granulate—; market—; prepare —; pulverize—; purify—; refine—; transform into—; utilize—; —candies; —honeys; extract—.

(See nectar, sweetness.)

SUGGEST (*v*)

adverbs

promptly; slyly; insidiously; respectfully; tactfully; whimsically; sagaciously; facetiously; pacifically; deftly; mildly; casually; subtly; wistfully; significantly; poetically; gloomily; sardonically; rationally; contemptuously; craftily; irrelevantly; hypnotically; specifically.

(See intimate, hint, insinuate.)

SUGGESTION

adjectives

taunting; detailed; sinful; compelling; hypnotic; sound; sensible; inexhaustible; meritless; wild; plausible; pregnant; delicate; obvious; subtle; delusive; least; startling; perpetual; hopeful; fantastic; imaginative; timorous; sorrowful; rational; implied; ironical; pantomimic; illusory; remotest; reasonable; helpful; adverse; constructive; outside; ashamed; pained; casual; inspiring; terrifying; native; endless; mute; practical; specific; opulent; timely; cheerful; bare; solemn; hopeful.

verbs

acknowledge—; adopt—; afford—; combat —; conceive—; contribute—; convey—; dare —; enforce—; frame—; hazard—; launch —; offer—; propound—; put forth—; reject —; submit—; venture—; waive—; yield to —; —alludes to; —assumes; —counsels; —dies; —expedites; —facilitates; —hints; —misleads; —prescribes; —recommends; —speculates; —stimulates; —surmises; —theorizes.

(See intimation, hint, insinuation, implication, innuendo.)

SUICIDE

adjectives

involuntary; would-be; eventual; political; cold; brave; planned.

verbs

avert—; commit—; conceal—; contemplate —; feign—; flirt with—; goad to—; grieve over—; incite to—; resign to—; resort to—; reveal—; —allures; —betrays; —closes; —dramatizes; —exposes; —frees; —mystifies; —relinquishes.

(See death, murder.)

SUIT

adjectives

elaborate; exclusive; hopeless; washable; riding; luxury; classic; play; tardy; excellent; humble; strong; imported; new; striking; summer; choice; suave; durable; draped; wool; terraced; charming; sumptuous; business; fresh; smart; dressy; distinctive; smooth; conservative; sturdy; worsted; fine; rainy-day; losing; faded; pepper-and-salt; habitual; boldest; sober; customary; gorgeous; libel; honest; superb; neat; repeated; wrong; presumptuous.

verbs

adorn—; alter—; apparel in—; array in—; attire in—; divest of—; doff—; don—; fray —; garb in—; mend—; tatter—; vest in—;

1144

—disguises; —mantles; —protects; — shields.

(See uniform, coat, overcoat, garment.)

SUIT (v)

adverbs

specifically; exactly; definitely; admirably; logically; rationally; precisely; peculiarly; superbly.

(See fit, adapt.)

SUITABLE

adverbs

eminently; wholly; ineffably; conveniently; opportunely; seasonably; comfortably; stylishly; highly; delightfully; unquestionably; fortunately; appropriately; becomingly; providentially; beautifully.

SUITOR

adjectives

unnumbered (pl); bashful; anxious; importunate; eligible; princely; renowned; bold; probable; accepted; slighted; scrupulous; pernicious; woeful.

verbs

attract—s; bind—; cherish—; discourage—; encourage—; gain—; secure—; slight—; —adores; —affiances; —aspires to; —bids for; —bows; —s clamor for; —idolizes; —implores; —importunes; —kneels; —offers; —pleads; —plights; —presses; —professes; —reveres; —solicits; —s throng; —vows; —woos; —troths.

(See lover, sweetheart.)

SULK (v)

adverbs

obstinately; glumly; adamantly; persistently; mutely; unreasonably; miserably; hatefully; woefully.

(See pout, brood.)

SULKY

adverbs

disagreeably; actively; poutingly; glumly; noisily; grimly; dangerously; unpleasantly; vengefully; hatefully; smoulderingly; unaccountably; unreasonably; absurdly; ridiculously; oddly; comically; strangely; gloomily; intolerably.

SULLEN

adverbs

desperately; glumly; dourly; inveterately; habitually; usually; incorrigibly; defiantly; perversely; stolidly; silently; moodily; obstinately; ungraciously; uncivilly; resentfully; angrily; shamefully; disagreeably; unpleasantly; obviously; undisguisedly.

SULTRINESS

verbs

droop in—; swelter in—; —chokes; —dampens; —depresses; —disheartens; —dispirits; —envelops; —flushes; —frets; —glooms; —oppresses; —permeates; —prostrates; —reeks; —seethes; —simmers; —smothers; —sulks; —weighs upon.

(See heat, weather.)

SULTRY

adverbs

unpleasantly; disagreeably; ominously; significantly; distressingly; wretchedly; miserably; strangely; oppressively; smotheringly; curiously; steamily; inauspiciously; intolerably; uncomfortably; alarmingly; extremely; breathlessly.

SUM

adjectives

nominal; fabulous; moderate; untold; successive (pl); meager; pitiful; gross; vast; reasonable; stupendous; trifling; substantial; lawful; formidable; exorbitant; munificent; phonetic; staggering; utmost; unprecedented; round; appalling; pretty; small; enormous; paltry; objective; aggregate; satisfying; tabled; tidy; specified; high; modest.

verbs

accrue—; accumulate—; aggregate—; allot —; amass—; arrive at—; audit—; bestow —; calculate—; check—; compute—; disburse—; discount—; distribute—; embezzle —; entail—; expend—; file—; issue—; necessitate—; realize—; reckon—; register—; represent—; subscribe—; —diminishes; —dwindles; —soars; —staggers.

(See amount, list, number, overhead, profits.)

SUMMARIZE (v)

adverbs

roughly; casually; generally; completely; concisely; statistically; luminously; logically; vividly; convincingly; intelligibly.

(See add, combine.)

SUMMARY

adjectives

statistical; running; intimate; authoritative; apt; contradictory; luminous; logical; concise; slumberous; singular; striking; necessary; helpful.

SUMMER

adjectives

parting; bitter; relentless; broiling; costly; gorgeous; slow; humid; troubled; hot; promised; husky; trailing; northern; luxurious; strenuous; exciting; colorful; proud; economic; delicate; heavy; perished; perpetual; epitomized; immediate.

verbs

await—; bask in—; bear the stamp of—; long for—; prolong—; suspend for—; thrive in—; usher in—; welcome—; yearn for—; —begets; —blooms; —breeds; —burgeons; —colors; —conceives; —dresses; —enriches; —fades; —gilds; —kisses; —mellows; —parches; —renews; —unfolds; —vitalizes; —wanes; —waxes; —wilts; —yields.
(See autumn, spring, winter, season.)

SUMMIT

adjectives

peaked; serene; towering; jagged; snow-clad; feathery; ornamental; dreadful; topmost; snowy; wild; pathless; lone; seared; blasted; sacred; sloping; breathless; flowering; hoary; islanded; unique; subordinate; commanding; bleak; sunburned; roofless; unscaled; intangible; toppling.

verbs

achieve—; ascend to—; aspire to—; cap—; clamber to—; crown—; grope for—; link—; mount to—; plunge from—; precipitate from —; scale—; soar to—; strive for—; topple from—; view from—; —allures; —climaxes; —crests; —culminates; —erodes; —tempts.
(See crown, culmination, height, pinnacle.)

SUMMON (v)

adverbs

domineeringly; commandingly; dictatorially; dogmatically; harshly; sternly; peremptorily; courteously; unceremoniously; tersely; arrogantly; emphatically; petulantly; urgently; vociferously.
(See command, call.)

SUMMONS

adjectives

emphatic; collective; peremptory; gracious; petulant; authoritative; coincident; silent; final; hasty; urgent; dread; long-waited; vociferous; strange.

verbs

abrogate—; announce—; answer—; countermand—; dismiss—; dispatch—; enforce—; heed—; ignore—; nullify—; quash—; serve with—; —apprehends; —arraigns; —bids; —cites; —coerces; —commands; —demands; —directs; —informs; —notifies; —orders.
(See call, invitation, mandate, order, command.)

SUMPTUOUS

adverbs

comfortably; surprisingly; actually; luxuriously; delightfully; unexpectedly; miraculously; significantly; invitingly; unnecessarily; extravagantly; pleasantly; designedly; lavishly.

SUN

adjectives

noontide; withdrawing; scarlet; warm; pleasant; never-hurrying; soul-expanding; waning; devouring; traveling; extinguished; external; burning; keen; morning; night; meridian; invisible; declining; rising; dipping; lowering; centrifugal; dazzling; unconquered; pitiless; kindling; blazing; bronze; material; sinking; fierce; retiring; vanished; setting; cruel; earthly; ancient; climbing; ardent; glorious; outdoor; brazen; dying; cloudless; scorching; lurid; rounding; smoldering; tropic; vertical; slanting; circling; majestic; vernal; merciless; killing; radiant; mimic; autumn; descended; glaring; unveiled; temperate; retreating; warmer; conflagrant; sickly; wheeling; early; impassioned; surviving; unruly; gaudy; fair; utmost; worshipped; garish; hateful; insistent; fervent; uncurled; central; bleak; naked; universal; smiting; westering; liberal; vaporous; broiling; blushing; sleepy; fierce; ruddy; sudden; sovereign; treacherous; unshaded; alien; bloody; earth-invisible (pl).

verbs

bask in—; bathe in—; block off—; eclipse —; expose to—; obscure—; protect from—; revel in—; salute—; scorn—; shield from—;

1146

squint at—; worship—; —anneals; —ascends; —bakes; —beats down; —blinds; —blisters; —blushes; —breaks; —burnishes; —climbs; —clouds; —clothes; —creeps; —crowns; —dazzles; —declines; —dims; —dips; —dogs; —draws; —drenches; —eclipses; —fades; —filters; —flames; —flays; —floods; —gilds; —gyrates; —haunts; —heralds; —melts; —mirrors; —nourishes; —paints; —parches; —peeps out; —penetrates; —pours; —presses down; —radiates; —renews; —retreats; —salutes; —sears; —shadows; —shines; —sinks; —smiles upon; —smites; —stimulates; —strikes; —tinges; —vanishes; —veils; —wearies; —withdraws; —withers.
(See moon, heat, sunlight.)

SUNLIGHT

adjectives
morning; flowing; bright; thinned; reflected; hazy; marvelous; ardent; roseate; windy; sweet; slanting; choicer; naked; mellow; purging; stealing; unfallen; glancing; blinding; forenoon; laughing; dancing; imprisoned; watery; joyous; quivering; pitiless; mocking; parting; dappled; shaded; healthful; spring-eyed.

verbs
bask in—; emerge into—; flash in—; —arises; —dies; —exposes; —filters; —hallows; —lingers; —penetrates; —quivers; —slides through; —streams; —touches.
(See moonbeam, light, sun.)

SUNNY

adverbs
radiantly; pleasantly; happily; wholesomely; delightfully; cheerily; vivaciously; merrily; brightly; blithely; buoyantly; helpfully; winsomely; exultantly; optimistically; sparklingly; jauntily.

SUNSET

adjectives
forlorn; crimson; sunken; hollow; brilliant; sinking; fiery; dying; silent; pompous; lingering; glorious; peaceful; polychrome; fading; refulgent; wintry; bloody.

verbs
cloud—; loiter till—; linger to—; obscure —; view—; —beams; —colors; —dazzles; —declines; —diffuses; —eclipses; —enchants; —enthralls; —entrances; —gilds;

—gleams; —glimmers; —glows; —glowers; —radiates; —reflects; —scintillates; —shimmers.
(See twilight, daylight, dawn.)

SUNSHINE

adjectives
perpetual; brilliant; sudden; sparkling; searching; westering; tawny; cruel; eternal; clear; radiant; embodied; vital; glancing; dreaming; tingling; satin; sweet; mellow; vivid; open; harsh; broad; pitiless; illimitable; everlasting; imprisoned; peaceful; unclouded; beauteous; precious; continuous; genial; merciless.

verbs
drink in—; flood with—; luxuriate in—; —bleaches; —bursts forth; —caresses; —dances; —energizes; —enlivens; —filters through; —flatters; —gladdens; —glitters; —greets; —illumines; —melts; —parches; —permeates; —pervades; —renews; —shimmers; —showers.
(See light, moonbeam, sunlight, sun.)

SUNSHINY

adverbs
brilliantly; gorgeously; gloriously; delightfully; unusually; fortunately; luckily; wonderfully; marvelously; dazzlingly; faintly; scarcely; hotly; unbearably; intolerably; scorchingly; burningly; mercilessly; glaringly.

SUP (v)

adverbs
sumptuously; regally; bountifully; clandestinely; domestically; fraternally; formally; genially.
(See dine, eat.)

SUPERCILIOUS

adverbs
intolerably; uncivilly; deplorably; haughtily; stupidly; oddly; magnificently; laughably; arrogantly; proudly; offensively; ridiculously; incurably; unpardonably; smugly; irritatingly; insolently; presumptuously; coolly; insufferably; condescendingly; purposely; splendidly; brashly; brazenly; idiotically; ostentatiously; rudely; egotistically; conceitedly; pretentiously; unblushingly; impudently; saucily; swaggeringly; flippantly; shamelessly.

SUPERINTENDENT

adjectives
tutorial; strict; immediate; personal; careful; watchful.

verbs
closet with—; consult—; —admonishes; —arbitrates; —commends; —deliberates; —dickers with; —directs; —exhorts; —goads; —governs; —guides; —manages; —officiates; —pilots; —prescribes; —presides; —pulls strings; —regulates; —sacks; —steers.
(See manager, employer, boss.)

SUPERIOR

adjectives
race; intellectual; immediate.

•

SUPERIORITY

adjectives
feline; racial; cool; innate; muscular; spurious; numerical; overwhelming; intellectual; essential; absolute; economic; whimsical; scornful; astonishing; obvious; compassionate; ineffable; menaced; lofty; simpering; contemptuous; historical; infinite; fancied; dignified; inherent; masculine; base; adventitious; conscious; immense; extraordinary; assumed.

verbs
acclaim—; achieve—; assert—; assume—; attest to—; belittle—; challenge—; consider —; demonstrate—; disclose—; display—; enhance—; evince—; exaggerate—; exalt—; exhibit—; manifest—; proclaim—; prove—; regard—; reveal—; verify—; vie for—; weigh—; —eclipses; —outshines; establish —.
(See supremacy, eminence.)

SUPERSEDE (v)

adverbs
gradually; temporarily; invidiously; ultimately; logically; expectedly.
(See replace, supplant.)

SUPERSTITION

adjectives
barbarous; colorful; idle; monstrous; exploded; fantastic; capricious; brutal; religious; ethnic; silly; deepest; contemporary; narrow; vain; enormous; popular; conflicting; pure; childish; puerile; vulgar; imaginative; pestilent; singular; degrading; illustrious; bizarre; insatiate; grossest; primitive; unbelievable; fanciful; confused; ancient; haunting; pre-existing.

verbs
abolish—; efface—; encrust with—; eradicate—; explode—; free from—; ignore—; refute—; revive—; rid of—; swallow—; —beguiles; —blinds; —chains; —deludes; —dominates; —dupes; —enslaves; —fetters; —persists; —prejudices; —prevails; —shackles; —shrouds; —subjugates; —warps.
(See fanaticism, ignorance, prejudice, myth.)

SUPERSTITIOUS

adverbs
absurdly; sincerely; ridiculously; unreasonably; foolishly; terribly; fearfully; honestly; gullibly; nervously; incredibly; fanatically; piously; exceedingly; curiously; oddly; strangely; credulously; romantically; fearsomely; inveterately; incurably; anxiously.

SUPERVISE (v)

adverbs
personally; intelligently; successfully; strictly; cautiously; professionally.
(See manage, direct.)

SUPERVISION

adjectives
constant; censorial; direct; rigid; jealous; provincial; voluntary; human; chilling; controlling; governmental; strict; careful.

verbs
assume—; enforce—; maintain—; prescribe —; recommend—; relax—; retain—; subject to—; —administers; —chains; —curbs; —fetters; —guides; —irks; —leashes; —pilots; —restrains; —restricts; —wanes.
(See management, control.)

SUPPER

adjectives
champagne; bountiful; scanty; hearty; solemn; sumptuous; bare; rich.

verbs
bid to—; bolt—; climax—; conclude—; cram in—; deprive of—; devour—; gobble —; gorge—; grace—; gulp—; relish—; savor—; summon to—; —nauseates; —refreshes; —reinvigorates; —renews; —satiates; —tickles the palate.
(See meal, luncheon, breakfast, dinner.)

SUPPLANT (v)

adverbs

inevitably; permanently; ultimately; temporarily; unexpectedly; ruthlessly; dictatorially.

(See supersede, replace.)

SUPPLE

adverbs

youthfully; incredibly; naturally; slenderly; sturdily; amazingly; extremely; uncommonly; admirably; particularly; delightfully; unusually; remarkably; fortunately.

SUPPLEMENT (v)

adverbs

elaborately; fully; completely; authoritatively; definitely; adequately.

(See add, complete.)

SUPPLICATION

adjectives

formal; strong; affecting; frantic; fervent; piteous; reverent; honest.

SUPPLIES

adjectives

stable; continuous; inexhaustible; plentiful; abundant; precarious; visible; regulated; virgin; providential; needed; pecuniary; liberal; considerable; limited; constant; deficient; perennial; adequate; unbounded; scant; table; ample; warlike; extensive; dependable; bountiful; countless; permanent; miserable; muddy; vast; commercial.

SUPPLY

verbs

augment—; avail oneself of—; bolster—; check—; crave—; curb—; curtail—; deplete —; dispense—; entreat—; exceed—; exhaust—; facilitate—; guarantee—; insure —; procure—; replenish—; stabilize—; stock with—; warehouse—; —dwindles; —evaporates; —flows.

(See store, merchandise, stock, surplus, product.)

SUPPLY (v)

adverbs

bounteously; liberally; indifferently; exclusively; infallibly; amply; abundantly; plentifully; faithfully; scantily; continuously; pecuniarily; adequately; permanently; commercially; liberally.

(See furnish, yield.)

SUPPORT

adjectives

substantial; powerful; generous; overwhelming; intermediate; eloquent; wholesale; warm; earnest; mere; thoughtful; zealous; uniform; effective; firm; frail; elusive; principal; hearty; abated; stalwart; urgent; ephemeral; enthusiastic; scarce; vigorous; adequate; superficial.

verbs

angle for—; barter for—; bestow—upon; command—of; consolidate—; derive—; earn —; enlist—; foster—; lend—; lessen—; line up—; maintain—; muster—; pledge—; rally to—; repel—; repudiate—; seek—; share in—; whip up—; —comforts; —consoles; —dissolves; —fails.

(See living, help, livelihood, assistance.)

SUPPORT (v)

adverbs

adequately; steadfastly; appreciatively; respectfully; structurally; plausibly; conscientiously; adamantly; abundantly; substantially; theoretically; warmly; zealously; effectively; heartily; enthusiastically; vigorously.

(See defend, back.)

SUPPORTERS

adjectives

shadowy; ardent; persistent; staunchest; faithful; devoted; fanatical; unconditional; jubilant; regular.

verbs

alienate—; assure of—; estrange—; gather —; lure—; rally—; vex—; —advance; —authenticate; —back; —bear; —bolster; —cheer; —comfort; —expedite; —foster; —found; —further; —maintain; —promote; —sustain.

(See contributor, friend, advocate.)

SUPPOSE (v)

adverbs

rationally; erroneously; falsely; fallaciously; unsuspectingly; hopefully; optimistically.

(See assume, presume.)

SUPPOSITION

adjectives

false; analogous; indolent; staggering; contrary; probable; mitigating.

verbs

argue on—; concede—; confirm—; contra-

dict—; forsake—; grant—; hazard—; maintain—; overthrow—; refute—; speculate on
—; support—; unfold—; weigh—; work on
—; —alludes; —assumes; —carries weight;
—conjectures; —hints; —originates in; —
presumes; —presupposes; —surmises; —
theorizes; ridicule—.
(See assumption, guess, hypothesis, conjecture.)

SUPPRESS (v)
adverbs
silently; insidiously; traitorously; ruthlessly; undemocratically; viciously; vindictively; overtly; covertly; rigorously; generally;
summarily; studiously; tyrannically.
(See repress, restrain.)

SUPREMACY
adjectives
literal; feudal; authorized; universal; maritime; scholarly; secular; naval; ecclesiastical; political; restored; righteous; long-
sought; matrimonial; domestic.

verbs
achieve—; acknowledge—; admit—; assert
—; battle for—; bolster—; confirm—; demonstrate—; dispute—; insure—; maintain
—; preserve—; prove—; renounce—; reveal
—; seek—; struggle for—; surrender—; veil
—; —crumbles; —sways; —totters.
(See domination, success, achievement,
victory.)

SURE-FOOTED
adverbs
amazingly; sufficiently; particularly; unfailingly; fortunately; assuredly; comfortingly;
luckily; alertly; gracefully; faithfully; confidently; intrepidly; fearlessly; unquestionably; reliably; trustworthily.

SURF
adjectives
booming; roaring; boiling; raging; damaging; foamy; retreating; relentless; murderous; turmoiling.

verbs
—agitates; —babbles; —batters; —billows;
—boils; —booms; —breaks; —buffets; —
chops; —deluges; —drenches; —foams; —
froths; —hisses; —inundates; —licks; —
murmurs; —pounds; —ripples; —roars; —

seethes; —sluices; —sprays; —spumes; —
surges; —swashes; —swells; —washes.
(See billow, wave, breaker.)

SURFACE
adjectives
silky; simmering; inferior; temporary; highway; brushed; rough; sparkling; shaggy;
heaving; mirror-like; limiting; leaden; inelastic; refracting; troubled; raised; rugged; crawling; vibratory; undulating; reasonable; polished; sensitive; smooth; gleaming; faceted; rolling; agitated; glassy; intellectual; lumpy; metallic; unbroken; radiant; vitreous; sloping; broad; burnished;
sprayed; convex; prismatic; sluggish; slot-
ted; plaited; external; tourist; warmer; exposed; muddy; bright; stony; pliant; tenacious; general; plane; driving; suede-like.

verbs
abrade—; becalm—; burnish—; corrugate
—; dent—; detect upon—; dip below—;
duck below—; engrave on—; explore—;
face—; finish—; flash upon—; furrow—;
glaze—; inflame—; level—; mar—; penetrate—; plunge beneath—; polish—; probe
below—; ruffle—; rumple—; scan—; scour
—; scratch—; skim—; smite—; smooth—;
veneer—; venture upon—; warp—; weather
—; wrinkle—.

SURGE
adjectives
eternal; furious; relentless; toiling; fiery;
sulphurous; knelling; rolling; volcanic; boiling; whispering; roaring; restless; broken;
imperious.

SURGE (v)
adverbs
confusedly; wildly; thunderously; turbulently; violently; relentlessly; sulphurously; volcanically; boilingly; roaringly; imperiously.
(See swell, heave.)

SURGERY
adjectives
plastic; radical; painful; bold; bloody;
magic; life-saving.

verbs
advise—; baffle—; botch—; defy—; employ
—; hail—; perform—; practise—; rally
from—; resort to—; skill in—; survive—;
weather—; —adjusts; —binds; —converts;
—delivers; —endangers; —facilitates; —

reanimates; —reconstructs; —rectifies; — rehabilitates; —rejuvenates; —removes; — renovates; —repairs; —restores; —resuscitates; —staunches.

(See operation, remedy, medicine.)

SURLY

adverbs

bluntly; terrifyingly; cruelly; unnecessarily; heedlessly; inexcusably; discourteously; disrespectfully; unpardonably; unwarrantably; boorishly; angrily; roughly; intolerably; churlishly; unaccountably; strangely; curiously; alarmingly; darkly; ominously; unusually.

SURMISE

adjectives

false; intellectual; vague; anxious; wide; wild.

verbs

advance—; concede—; denounce—; form—; grant—; hazard—; offer—; refute—; resort to—; speculate on—; submit—; —alleges; —alludes to; —assumes; —coincides with; —conjectures; —hints; —postulates; —presumes; —presupposes; —suggests; —theorizes.

(See guess, conjecture.)

SURMISE (v)

adverbs

shrewdly; intuitively; rationally; slyly; astutely; vaguely; anxiously; pessimistically; jealously; enviously.

(See suppose, guess.)

SURMOUNT (v)

adverbs

exultantly; victoriously; boisterously; triumphantly; ambitiously; incredibly.

(See conquer, overcome.)

SURPASS (v)

adverbs

amazingly; exultantly; exceedingly; incredibly; astoundingly; spectacularly; sensationally.

(See excel, exceed.)

SURPLUS

adjectives

destructive; labor; unavoidable; re-invested; unsellable; huge; undistributed; profitable.

verbs

accrue—; accumulate—; afford—; amass—; avert—; discard—; disclose—; dispose of —; exaggerate—; invest—; market—; pile up—; reveal—; squander—; swallow—; — assures; —augments; —brims; —burdens; —congests; —deluges; —floods the market; —gorges; —gluts; —insures; —overflows; —strains; —supersaturates; —weighs upon.

(See excess, supply.)

SURPRISE

adjectives

unspeakable; dull; wistful; pleasant; perpetual; quaint; unfortunate; unfeigned; amiable; delightful; unaffected; infinite; contemptuous; calm; charming; effusive; admiring; geological; solemn; shameful; sordid; sweet; bewildered; acceptable; painful; strange; melancholy; glad; excessive; hollow; curt; pompous; horrified; agreeable; blank; puzzled; annoyed; dramatic; drab; swift; exquisite; cordial; inexcusable; continual; quick; speculative; tremendous; mingled; hurt; immense; comic.

verbs

affect—; anticipate—; conceal—; express—; feign—; gape in—; induce—; manifest—; occasion—; prepare—; reveal—; strike with —; —bewilders; —dazzles; —electrifies; — flabbergasts; —overwhelms; —petrifies; — ruffles; —rumples; —shocks; —staggers; — startles; —stuns; —throws one off guard.

(See amazement, miracle, astonishment.)

SURPRISE (v)

adverbs

curiously; agreeably; innocently; utterly; mildly; faintly; mutually; unspeakably; amiably; quaintly; unfeignedly; delightfully; infinitely; painfully; excessively; exquisitely; cordially; tremendously; comically.

(See astonish, amaze.)

SURRENDER

adjectives

easy; traitorous; joyous; pusillanimous; instant; unconditional; forced; forlorn; verbal; resigned; peaceable.

SURRENDER (v)

adverbs

utterly; impatiently; meekly; affectionately; peaceably; unconditionally; voluntarily;

graciously; traitorously; forlornly; pusillanimously.

(See yield, abandon.)

SURROUND (v)

adverbs
opulently; inextricably; enthusiastically; triumphantly; fraternally; apprehensively; artificially; uncongenially; felicitously; luxuriously; tranquilly; picturesquely; grotesquely; nobly; trivially; quaintly; rustically; pastorally; inspiringly.

(See entrench, inclose.)

SURROUNDINGS

adjectives
artificial; uncongenial; iron; appalling; felicitous; tropical; sociable; pleasant; superb; smart; cultural; refined; luxurious; tranquil; picturesque; dignified; affectionate; unique; harsh; primitive; grotesque; grander; indulgent; noble; trivial; quaint; frigid; charming; beautiful; dingy; rustic; pastoral; unwonted; inspiring; modern.

verbs
absorb in—; acclimate to—; acquaint with —; adapt to—; alter—; blind to—; condition by—; contemplate—; darken—; deduce from —; encompass—; engross in—; escape—; explore—; inspect—; orient to—; pervade —; recognize—; reconnoiter—; regard—; rise above—; scan—; scrutinize—; skirt—; survey—; transcend—; —breed; —depress; —enchant; —enthrall; —foster; —impress; —oppress; —suggest; —symbolize.

(See environment, circumstances, conditions.)

SURVEILLANT

adverbs
warily; vigilantly; suspiciously; significantly; carefully; alertly; inquisitively; constantly; watchfully; incessantly; generally; conscientiously; meticulously; punctiliously; dependably; reliably.

SURVEY

adjectives
mournful; calm; ordnance; cursory; interior; official; leisure; compiled; recent; hopeless; impassioned; casual; severe; quick; optimistic; independent; sweeping; chronological; decisive; unbiased; preliminary; perspective; impartial; exhaustive.

verbs
authenticate—; check—; cite—; condense—; conduct—; contemplate—; extend—; initiate —; regard—; scan—; —astounds; —calculates; —catalogues; —computes; —confirms; —demonstrates; —discloses; —discovers; — embraces; —enables; —enumerates; —estimates; —evaluates; —gauges; —indicates; —informs; —measures; —probes; —records; —reveals; —scales; —startles; —uncovers; —verifies.

(See study, investigation, examination.)

SURVEY (v)

adverbs
extensively; gloomily; tranquilly; critically; curiously; morbidly; maliciously; suspiciously; officially; leisurely; optimistically; unbiasedly; impartially.

(See view, examine.)

SURVIVAL

adjectives
unique; barbaric; unconscious; fortunate; race; evolutionary; bare.

SURVIVE (v)

adverbs
vigorously; miraculously; heroically; undauntedly; staunchly; courageously.

(See live, exist.)

SURVIVORS

adjectives
terrified; ill-fated; reimbursed; heroic; injured; struggling; belated.

SUSCEPTIBILITY

adjectives
morbid; exquisite; excessive; strong; foolish; obvious; observant; moral; vivid; extreme; patent.

verbs
affect—; allay—; augment—; cancel—; conceal—; compensate for—; counteract—; cultivate—; excite—; exempt from—; increase —; intensify—; neutralize—; promote—; raise—; repress—; sense—; sharpen—; stir —; —endangers; —exposes; —inclines; — jeopardizes; —predisposes; —tends toward.

(See propensity, inclination, tendency.)

SUSCEPTIBLE

adverbs
highly; unusually; easily; emotionally; extremely; quickly; alarmingly; romantically;

strangely; curiously; uncommonly; amazingly; inherently; naturally.

SUSPECT

verbs

absolve—; acquit—; bail—; challenge—; clear—; cross-examine—; defend—; detain —; discharge—; dismiss—; exculpate—; exempt—; exonerate—; free—; grill—; harbor—; hold—; jail—; liberate—; lynch—; question—; release—; retain—; round up —s; shake—; trap—; vindicate—; whitewash—; —denies; —defends; —escapes; — vindicates.

(See prisoner, criminal.)

SUSPECT (v)

adverbs

unjustifiably; shrewdly; secretly; previously; gravely; unfairly; generally; justly; insanely; jealously; personally; intrusively.

(See surmise, doubt.)

SUSPENSE

adjectives

absorbed; waiting; agonizing; irresolute; tremulous; sultry; lowering; painful; frighted; unrelaxed; dramatic; clever; intolerable; agitated; prolonged; awful; tedious; awakening.

verbs

allay—; alleviate—; bear—; cower in—; ease—; face—; flinch at—; heighten—; intensify—; lessen—; maintain—; mitigate—; moderate—; palliate—; preserve—; relinquish—; survive—; sustain—; swoon in—; withdraw—; —abates; —agonizes; —embarasses; —relaxes; —rends; —shatters; — strains; —subsides; —taxes; —tenses; — wanes; —weighs upon.

(See perplexity, excitement, tension, anxiety, uncertainty.)

SUSPENSION

adjectives

premature; simultaneous; mature; critical; permanent; definite.

SUSPICION

adjectives

mingled; habitual; mean; mutual; bitter; aggressive; horrible; overawing; harsh; common; inscrutable; special; deep; plentiful; lingering; unworthy; dull; aroused; lively; hard; terrible; prying; jealous; waked; chilly; furtive; infusing; perpetual;

groundless; merest; faint; horrid; diminished; tormented; additional; shrewd; excited; angry; unmanly; personal; general; intrusive; sharp; sly.

verbs

absolve of—; allay—; arouse—; brand with —; breed—; cherish—; confirm—; conquer —; consolidate—s; dispel—; entertain—; evade—; excite—; ground—; heighten—; inspire—; justify—; lull—; occasion—; regard with—; resent—; sweep aside—; veil —; voice—; —crosses the mind; —dawns upon; —deepens; —grows; —pervades; — prevails; —thickens.

(See distrust, jealousy, anxiety, doubt.)

SUSPICIOUS

adverbs

unreasonably; jealously; meanly; cruelly; foolishly; dangerously; terribly; ridiculously; warily; extravagantly; inordinately; curiously; significantly; fearfully; uncertainly; vaguely; definitely; oddly; absurdly; needlessly; wildly; strangely; disagreeably; unpleasantly; odiously; perplexingly; unworthily; craftily.

SUSTAIN (v)

adverbs

precisely; spiritually; materially; faithfully; casually; honorably; unanimously; magnificently; heroically; vigorously; faithfully; disastrously; courageously.

(See support, uphold.)

SUSTENANCE

verbs

afford—; arrest—; avail of—; begrudge—; deprive of—; dispatch—; dispense—; exhaust—; furnish—; grant—; grope for—; grovel for—; obtain—; offer—; plead for —; proffer—; provide—; refuse—; strive for—; struggle for—; suspend—; tender—; yield—; extract—.

(See living, livelihood.)

SWAB

verbs

begrime—; besmirch—; brush with—; contaminate—; dab with—; discard—; disinfect with—; dispose of—; foul—; introduce —; precipitate on—; rinse—; saturate—; scour with—; smudge—; taint—; —absorbs; —purges; —soaks up; —sponges.

(See sponge, mop.)

SWAGGER

adjectives

lordly; indolent; imposing; consequential; new; boxy; outstanding; shallow; jaunty; loose; brusque; impudent.

SWAGGER (v)

adverbs

theatrically; boisterously; obstreperously; pretentiously; shamelessly; impudently; dramatically; indolently; jauntily; nonchalantly.
(See swell, strut.)

SWAIN

adjectives

low-spirited; responsive; bashful; rustic; lusty; laboring; ephemeral; despairing; awkward; forlorn; ashy; country; reaping; wary; mistrustful.

verbs

deride—; ground—; impassion—; —attracts; —bewitches; —captivates; —caresses; —cherishes; —courts; —declares; —enamours of; —endears; —pleads; —prates of; —proclaims; —professes; —reveres; —serenades; —woos; —yearns.
(See lover, sweetheart, peasant.)

SWALLOW

adjectives

skimming; twittering; innumerable (pl); blithe; garrulous; chaffering; beauteous.

verbs

—arranges; —banks; —busies; —chirps; —circles; —s colonize; —dares; —s flock; —flutters; —journeys; —migrates; —swims low; —smooths; —snatches; —spreads wings; —sweeps; —twitters.
(See bird, martin.)

SWALLOW (v)

adverbs

avidly; vigorously; hastily; glumly; greedily; thickly; embarrassedly; spasmodically.
(See gulp, eat.)

SWAMP

adjectives

torrid; busy; moss-hung; impassable; fetid; pestilential; tamarack; tangled; unsightly; overtowering; adjacent; brackish; tropical; unhealthy; lonely; salty; inaccessible; social.

verbs

bog in—; brave—; drain—; foul in—; frequent—; hazard—; infest—; inhabit—; meander through—; mire in—; prowl in—; restore—; roam—; skirt—; slog through—; stray into—; traverse—; vanish into—; wallow through—; —breeds; —endangers; —enfolds; —engulfs; —jeopardizes; —mars.
(See marsh, mire, morass, mud.)

SWAMPY

adverbs

muddily; quaggishly; squashily; softly; unwholesomely; malarially; pestilentially; irremediably; hopelessly; unpleasantly; impracticably; disturbingly; distressingly; dangerously; deplorably; undesirably; unfortunately; unhealthfully; unluckily.

SWAN

adjectives

mysterious; drowsy; floating; solitary; ruthless; ruffling; graceful; dying.

verbs

—arches; —chants; —dips; —floats; —idles on water; —immerses; —lies; —mantles; —murmurs; —nibbles; —probes; —sails; —shies away, —steers; —strays; —swims; —trumpets; —wanders; —whoops; —flocks.
(See bird, duck, goose.)

SWANKY

adverbs

absurdly; luxuriously; pompously; arrogantly; superbly; aggressively; ostentatiously; extraordinarily; stylishly; sumptuously; elegantly; manifestly; flauntingly; gorgeously; conspicuously; consciously; quietly; genuinely.

SWARM

adjectives

unsuspected; solar; countless (pl); snowsoft; bony; prodigious; tremendous; ignoble; invading; droning; singing; meteoric; thieving; prolific.

verbs

capture—; disperse—; herd—; restrain—; rout—; smoke—; stir up—; —bristles; —buzzes; —clamors; —clusters; —converges on; —deluges; —emigrates; —filters from;

—focuses on; —hums; —multiplies; —over-whelms; —pours out; —presses; —**settles**; —surges; —teems; —throngs.
(See hive, horde, crowd.)

SWARM (v)

adverbs
noisomely; prodigiously; prolifically; thunderously; multitudinously; spectacularly; rushingly; engulfingly.
(See flock, cluster.)

SWAY

adjectives
illimitable; righteous; feeble; departed; un-questioned; long-time; potent; ancient; un-disputed; mightier; steadfast; insolent; kin-dred; arbitrary; gracious; territorial; vice-regal; double; singular; patriarchal; uncom-querable; antique; despotic; sovereign; frigid; intolerable; murmurous; usurped; omni-potent; mischievous.

verbs
administer—; augment—; cripple—; deaden —; diminish—; exercise—; exert—; extend —; invalidate—; paralyze—; scotch—; un-dermine—; strengthen—; wield—; —con-trols; —dominates; —dwindles.
(See dominion, influence, power.)

SWAY (v)

adverbs
dizzily; rhythmically; musically; gently; in-dolently; perilously; alluringly; entrancing-ly; violently; restlessly; emotionally; psycho-logically; tremendously; dreamily; religious-ly.
(See lurch, swing.)

SWEAR (v)

adverbs
vigorously; fiercely; ferociously; solemnly; lustily; audibly; roundly; abominably; trait-orously; earnestly.
(See curse, affirm, testify.)

SWEAT

adjectives
bitter; body; profuse; chilly; bloody; cold; tremendous; copious; continual; peasant; goblin.

verbs
check—; glisten with—; induce—; secrete —; —beads; —chills; —develops; —dif-fuses; —diminishes; —drenches; —drips;

—droops; —glistens; —pours off; —**rolls**; —stains; —starts; —wilts.
(See perspiration.)

SWEAT (v)

adverbs
copiously; prodigiously; profusely; tremen-dously; coldly; abnormally.
(See perspire, exude.)

SWEEP

adjectives
outward; wavering; everlasting; soft; long; heaving; exulting; comprehensive; windy; majestic; gentle; irresistible; pitiless; mag-nificent; wild; enormous; dramatic; dread; liberal; joyous; shining; semi-circular.

verbs
condense—; deflect—; determine—; direct —; enlarge—; extend—; limit—; magnify —; realign—; restrict—; shift—; switch—; —declines; —deviates; —diverges; —em-braces; —expands; —ranges; —swerves; —zigzags.
(See speed, range.)

SWEEP (v)

adverbs
capriciously; irresistibly; bitterly; majesti-cally; resistlessly; frightfully; terrifically; silently; mutely; hoarsely; gracefully; sur-reptitiously; vigorously; tumultuously; re-lentlessly; heartlessly; confusedly; magnifi-cently; dramatically.
(See carry, move, sway.)

SWEETHEART

verbs
adore—; betroth to—; caress—; cherish—; devote to—; dismiss—; estrange—; forsake —; gain—; idolize—; jilt—; libel—; reject —; revere—; treasure—; woo—; yearn for —; —bewitches; —captivates; —charms; —enchants; —endears; —enraptures; —in-fatuates.
(See lover, mistress, siren, swain.)

SWEETNESS

adjectives
liquid; mournful; seductive; subtle; woman-ly; voluptuous; brooding; wild; earnest; penetrating; venerable; palling; ineffable; tender; wanton; balmy; admirable; listless; enduring; deceptive; ravishing; continuous; infantile; exceeding; unbelievable; luscious; drowsy; patient; plaintive; withering;

strained; direful; earthly; penetrative; alarming; awful; saucy; summer; capricious; fragrant; cloying; singular; sacred; wayward; sunny; girlish; prattling; secret; twittering; benign; candied; profuse; simpering.

verbs
adulterate—; affect—; commend—; emit—; enjoy—; feign—; inhale—; inject—; relish —; savor—; —allures; —baits; —cloys; —deceives; —depresses; —nauseates; — permeates; —revolts; —sickens; —smothers; —tempts.
(See nectar, fragrance, sugar, candy.)

SWELL (v)
adverbs
abnormally; hideously; pretentiously; indignantly; gently; powerfully; perceptibly; proudly; enormously; voluptuously; bulbously; incredibly; spectacularly.
(See expand, dilate.)

SWELLING
adjectives
imperceptible; proudest; puffy; slight; harmless; stormy; unfathomed; alternate; hive-like; solemn; gentle; cockney; serious; enormous; voluptuous; bulbous; secret.

verbs
accentuate—; allay—; alleviate—; avert—; characterize by—; compress—; diagnose—; ease—; extend—; overcome—; reduce—; remedy—; restrain—; vent—; —abates; —dilates; —diminishes; —disfigures; —distends; —dwindles; —ebbs; —exaggerates; —indicates; —mars; —presses; —projects; —protrudes; —stiffens; —subsides; —tortures; —wanes.
(See inflammation.)

SWERVE (v)
adverbs
deviously; perilously; dangerously; fatally; erratically; drunkenly.
(See deviate, turn.)

SWIFTNESS
adjectives
incredible; electric; tireless; usual; feline; stunning; menacing; bounding; amazing; wave-like.

SWIM (v)
adverbs
desperately; heroically; vigorously; unflaggingly; lustily; courageously; boldly; staunchly; gallantly.
(See float, move.)

SWINDLE
adjectives
churlish; loving; squealing; enormous; obstinate; snorting; public; huge; monstrous; wide-spread.

verbs
disclose—; execute—; guard against—; participate in—; penalize—; perpetrate—; reveal—; uncover—; unearth—; —bilks; — deprives; —despoils; —diverts; —extorts; —fleeces; —impoverishes; —infuriates; — mulcts; —rooks; —shears; —strips.
(See fake, fraud.)

SWING
adjectives
sensuous; breathless; undulating; rhythmic; unrestricted; smooth; romantic; graceful; saber; glittering; unerring; sweet; fascinating; swaying; crazed.

SWING (v)
adverbs
gracefully; playfully; noiselessly; creakingly; recklessly; gratingly; peremptorily; grotesquely; adroitly; lazily.
(See sway, wave.)

SWIRL
adjectives
eddying; unmistakable; nasty.

SWIRL (v)
adverbs
turbulently; dizzily; incessantly; aimlessly; eddyingly; vertiginously.
(See whirl, twist.)

SWOON
adjectives
profound; interlunar; deathlike; summer; drunken; amorous; sweet; pretended; opportune.

SWORD
adjectives
deputed; drawn; shining; unsheathed; glittering; angry; bold; senseless; naked; virgin; pitiless; reeking; tapered; temporal;

victorious; handsome; self-pointed; ponderous; unsullied; theological; tyrannous; prompted; swift; leaden; two-edged; flaming; boisterous; trusty; noisy; grasping; rusty; knightly; ornamented; sated.

verbs
accoutre with—; affix—; arm with—; bear —; besmirch—; brandish—; draw—; edge —; equip with—; extract—; fall before—; fence with—; flaunt—; flourish—; govern by—; insert—; oppose with—; perish by—; plunge—; purge by—; send home—; sheathe —; slash with—; slay with—; smite with—; stain—; strike with—; swish—; temper—; thrust—; unsheathe—; wave—; wear—; wield—; win by—; woo with—; —clanks; —s clash; —s cut; —drips; —flames; —flashes down; —glitters; —hacks; —pierces; —s slash against; —stuns; —whirs; —wounds.
(See knife, rapier, lance, cutlass, stiletto.)

SYCOPHANCY
adjectives
prodigious; courtly; crude.

verbs
approve—; brand with—; detect—; favor —; forbid—; induce—; lament—; patronize —; ply—; practise—; pursue with—; reject —; resist—; ridicule—; —infests; —irks; —irritates; —nauseates; —pollutes; —wins.
(See flattery.)

SYLLABLES
adjectives
ponderous; liquid; redundant; hideous; hissing; stressed; difficult; long; staccato; unaccented.

SYLVAN
adverbs
delightfully; refreshingly; shadily; sweetly; songfully; pleasantly; charmingly; fragrantly; attractively; spaciously.

SYMBOL
adjectives
mystic; prefiguring; appropriated; rigid; graphic; repulsive; shining; magic; national; valiant; barren; companionable; impressive; universal; sacred; accidental; elaborate; mingled (pl); living; everlasting; hallowed; suggestive; dramatic; revolutionary; crude; archaic; sound.

verbs
compose—; comprehend—; conceive—; define—; engrave—; examine—; inquire into —; interpret—; regard—; renounce—; seek —; study—; substitute—; value—; —denotes; —overshadows; —proves; —represents; —signifies; —suggests; —typifies.
(See attribute, device, emblem, mark, sign.)

SYMBOLIC
adverbs
mystically; inscrutably; significantly; faintly; clearly; definitely; intentionally; artistically; mysteriously; curiously; abstrusely; cleverly; consistently; conspicuously; apparently.

SYMMETRY
adjectives
studied; adolescent; absolute; vertical; artificial; admirable; exquisite; broken; structural; rare; matchless; bilateral; sinewy; perfect.

SYMPATHETIC
adverbs
delightfully; warmly; lovingly; companionably; comfortingly; ardently; understandingly; intelligently; cooperatively; actively; zealously; energetically; feelingly; compassionately; indignantly; touchingly; harmoniously; pitifully; altogether; heartily; cordially; effusively; amiably; affectionately; helpfully; humanely; benevolently; generously.

SYMPATHIZE (*v*)
adverbs
gushingly; profoundly; effusively; complacently; keenly; warmly; earnestly; paternally; spontaneously; compassionately; frankly.
(See understand.)

SYMPATHY
adjectives
vivacious; fatherly; imperfect; awful; silent; active; understanding; filial; instinctive; unspoken; poetic; trivial; genuine; noble; mock; wholehearted; extensive; delighted; tender; vivid; rebel; secret; loving; intelligent; consoling; utter; spiritual; glorious; passionate; nameless; inexplicable; irrepressible; frightened; reverent; fervent; mysterious; intense; mystic; irresistible; inborn; jeering; natural; impotent; mental; infinite; effusive; unconscious; energetic;

fanciful; fervid; spasmodic; boundless; divided; middle; conditional; placid; ardent; morbid; painful; presumed; healing; patient; cordial; magnetic; imaginative; practical; flaunted; respective; apparent; generous; prudent; subtle; spontaneous; warm; instantaneous; tentative; majestic; sincere; emotional; elaborate; profound; fraternal; unwelcome; synthetic; affectionate; peculiar; sobbing; loving; indissoluble; young; sweet; deferential; intelligent; kindly; passionate; adaptable; demonstrative; impersonal; gentle; radical; frank; solemn; universal; fearful.

verbs
afford—; alienate—s; arouse—; attract—; bestow—; desire—; elicit—; engage—; enlist—; evince—; exercise—; extend—; exude —; feign—; flare up in—; gain—; lack—; limit—; pledge—; reject—; shut off from—; spare—; steel against—; stir—; suppress—; whip up—; win—; woo—; —binds; —consoles; —cools; —eases; —lashes together; —moves; —tempers; —touches; —twinges; —unites.
(See compassion, pity, tenderness, affection.)

SYMPHONIC
adverbs
triumphantly; gloriously; brilliantly; dazzlingly; hamoniously; blaringly; delicately; beautifully; tenderly; merrily; scarcely; thunderously; soothingly; pleasantly; ineffably; impressively; splendidly; magnificently.

SYMPHONY
adjectives
light; airy; pathetic; descriptive; majestic; massive; angelic; universal; seraphic; pert; marvelous; awe-inspiring.

verbs
attend—; compose—; constitute—; develop —; direct—; execute—; introduce—; interpret—; join in—; perform—; present—; produce—; score—; —bursts forth; — charms; —delights; —enchants; —entices; —floats; —provokes; —thrills; —uplifts.
(See music, composition, orchestra.)

SYMPTOMS
adjectives
alarming; positive; terrifying; terminal; prevailing; anomalous; marked; inward;

subsequent; dangerous; ominous; warning; dramatic; serious; peculiar; premonitory; unpleasant; distressing; hysterical; troublesome; insidious; bellicose; mitigated; feverish; characteristic; aggravated; decisive; individual; constant; threatening; recurring.

verbs
aggravate—; allay—; alleviate—; attend with—; complicate—; deprecate—; describe —; detail—; develop—; discern—; distrust —; eliminate—; enumerate—; evaluate—; evince—; exhibit—; give rise to—; heed—; ignore—; interpret—; mask—; observe—; regard—; relieve—; subdue—; —abate; — accompany; —advance; —appear; —confound; —continue; —decline; —distress; — indicate; —manifest; —mark; —subside; — vanish; —vary.
(See evidence, sign, indication.)

SYNCHRONIZE (v)
adverbs
delicately; nicely; scientifically; automatically; exactly.

SYNCOPE
verbs
endure—; expire from—; induce—; lapse into—; produce—; suffer—; —contracts; — endangers; —strains; —unnerves.

SYNDICATE
verbs
appoint to—; combine in—; empower—; form—; head—; —adjourns; —contracts for; —controls; —directs; —disposes of; — dupes; —forces; —introduces; —manages; —meets; —promotes; —purchases; — pushes; —raises; —schemes; —transacts; —undertakes.
(See committee, board, group, association, concern.)

SYNTHESIS
verbs
arise from—; comprehend—; construct by—; delve into—; devise—; disclose—; effect—; employ—; exhibit—; facilitate—; form—; hail—; observe—; produce by—; unite in—; —compounds; —restores; —results in; — yields.
(See combination, method.)

SYPHILIS
verbs
afflict with—; campaign against—; contract

—; control—; cure—; diagnose as—; eradicate—; expose—; fear—; indicate—; inflict with—; recognize—; relieve—; reveal—; stamp out—; suspect—; test for—; treat—; —attacks; —cripples; —destroys; —devastates; —menaces; —ravages; —strikes; — yields to.

(See disease.)

SYRINGE

verbs

compress—; employ—; exhaust—; fit—; force from—; inject with—; manipulate—; squeeze—; —cleanses; —discharges; — draws in; —ejects; —emits; —pours; — spouts; —sprinkles into; —squirts.

(See pump.)

SYSTEM
(general)

adjectives

pure; monetary; runaway; star; terrestrial; flexible; rational; corporate; constitutional; delicate; cumbrous; foul; elective; optical; pernicious; maudlin; digestive; mythic; rotting; intricate; dark; prefectorial; monarchical; nervous; overtaxed; routined; innovating; differing; bloc; reducing; judicial; enormous; expensive; utmost; proposed; gymnastic; defective; cumbersome; complicated; correlated; absolute; anatomical; preposterous; stellar; pedantic; beneficent; feudal; ecclesiastical; rigorous; harmonious; sequential; barbarous; infallible; elliptic; native; addled; metrical; prudent; tragic; voluntary; atrocious; equitable; selfish; medieval; debased; feasible; vicious; respected; effective; rapid; voluminous; defensive; conventual; diverse; elevated; closed; expiring; weak; inferior; scientific; harmful; equivalent; merit; subtle; formidable; existing; elastic; extraordinary; philosophic; sympathetic; competitive; imperial; reflective; disastrous; antiquated; subversive; respiratory; vascular; chronological; vigilant; unstable; impersonal; representative; profit; excellent; severe; fruit-

less; vain; infant; patronage; magnificent; distribution; experimental; ethical; full; compact; discordant; regulated; imperial; antiseptic; abstruse; drying.

SYSTEM
(plan, scheme, etc.)

verbs

accept—; adapt to—; adhere to—; adopt—; afford—; apply—; base on—; brace—; buck —; cling to—; consolidate—; contrive—; corrupt—; curb—; demonstrate—; devise—; discard—; disrupt—; dominate—; elucidate —; entrench—; establish—; evolve—; extend—; fashion—; father—; formulate—; forsake—; found—; inaugurate—; incorporate in—; install—; institute—; "knock"—; map out—; master—; modify—; mold—; outmode—; overthrow—; promulgate—; reduce to—; reform—; restore—; shake—; shatter—; subscribe to—; supervise—; vindicate—; wed to—; —bars; —decrees; — disintegrates; —functions; —governs; — hinges on; —insures; —rears; —totters.

(See plan, program, scheme, method, order.)

SYSTEM
(human body)

verbs

absorb into—; alkalize—; animate—; break down—; build up—; deplete—; derange—; drain—; emaciate—; fetter—; gear—; impoverish—; invade—; invigorate—; involve —; nourish—; poison—; purge—; recharge —; regulate—; relieve—; tone up—; traverse—.

(See body.)

SYSTEMATIC

adverbs

habitually; naturally; carefully; cautiously; painfully; pedantically; punctiliously; meticulously; incredibly; painstakingly; satisfactorily; commendably; admirably; tiresomely; needlessly; overly; unnecessarily; occasionally; emphatically.

T

TABERNACLE

adjectives

cloudy; mortal; earthly; quivering; fleshy; incarnate; spiritual.

verbs

abide in—; achieve—; conceive—; construct —; create—; disseminate through—; dwell in—; erect—; establish—; fill—; form—of; frequent—; inhabit—; lay foundation of—; occupy—; organize—; people—; permeate —; put together—; raise—; revere—; shun —; take up one's abode in—; —arises; — breeds; —brings forth; —fosters; —stands; —teems with.

(See church, temple, tent.)

TABLE

adjectives

shrouded; imperial; padded; tottering; wine-smeared; transparent; warped; tolerable; comely; bounteous; clean; zinc-topped; work; modest; rude; separate; abundant (pl); sphered; banqueting; polished; cluttered; immense; hospitable; gaming; sturdy; extension; reading; well-spread; cheerful; washing; rickety; weather-beaten.

verbs

adorn—with; burrow under—; carve—; compose—of; construct—; clutter—; drape —; drum upon—; emboss—; fashion—; furnish—; gild—; grace—; gorge at—; head —; inlay—; litter—; load—with; pile on—; prepare—; spread—; support—; —bears; —groans; —stands; —sustains.

(See desk, bench, furniture.)

TABLOID

verbs

decipher—; interpret—; launch—; —abuses; —adulterates; —clamors; —commits; — cries out; —defiles; —disseminates; —holds forth; —horrifies; —inculcates; —nurtures; —pictures; —prostitutes; —seduces; — teems with; —violates; —vulgarizes.

(See press, newspaper.)

TABOO

verbs

countenance—; denounce—; enforce—; ignore—; impose—; observe—; remove—; set up—; —bans; —bars; —debars; —excludes;

—forbids; —hampers; —hinders; —inhibits; —interdicts; —prohibits; —restrains; —restricts; —stands in the way.

(See ban, restriction.)

adverbs

racially; conventionally; inanely; snobbishly; socially; piously; ceremonially; strictly; traditionally; ecclesiastically; irrationally; inexplicably; utterly; politically; seriously; curiously; gravely.

TABULATE (*v*)

adverbs

tirelessly; accurately; industriously; statistically; neatly; mathematically.

(See record, arrange.)

TACIT

adverbs

implicitly; unobtrusively; inferentially; inarticulately; usually; timorously; validly; legally.

TACITURN

adverbs

provokingly; reticently; shyly; morosely; gloomily; observantly; amazingly; deliberately; habitually; naturally; unusually; incurably; usually; inexplicably; unaccountably; interestingly; curtly; laconically; notoriously; secretively; evasively; incredibly; strangely; usually; oddly; peculiarly; inveterately; consistently; extraordinarily.

TACT

adjectives

subtle; external; sympathetic; gracious; delicate; unerring; perfect; cheerful; diplomatic; exquisite; rare; pecuniary; admirable; female; genuine; discriminating; requisite; faultless; extraordinary; critical; consummate; customary; fine.

apply—; bring—into play; cast—to the winds; discard—; dispense with—; employ —; enlist—; evince—; make away with—; practice—; require—; shelve—; throw aside —; throw—overboard; utilize—; —brings to bear; —conduces; —serves; —subserves.

(See diplomacy, shrewdness, discretion.)

TACTFUL

adverbs

easily; graciously; pleasantly; affably; urbanely; agreeably; ingratiatingly; pleasingly; inoffensively; diplomatically; prudently; discreetly; unusually; notoriously; signally; significantly; gratefully; gracefully; helpfully; serviceably; unwontedly; carefully; cautiously; warily; sympathetically; unctuously; deliberately; wisely; tenderly; acutely; delicately; shrewdly; expertly; reasonably; profoundly; cleverly; thoughtfully; subtly; courteously; chivalrously; politely

TACTICS

adjectives

piscatory; able; skillful; terrorist; astute; medieval; imperfect; preliminary; wily; militant; tough; company; defensive; cautious; amazing; successful; driving; obstructive; ingenious; original; matrimonial; similar; turncoat.

verbs

adopt—; apply—; base—on; condone—; credit—; denounce—; develop—; devise—; dispute—; employ—; engage in—; influence —; introduce—; modify—; predict—; resort to—; revamp (colloq.)—; shift—; vary—; —aim; —assist; —cause; —demand; —effect; —enable; —evolve; —produce; —protect; —result in; —revolt; —shift.

(See maneuver, strategy, plan.)

TACTLESS

adverbs

unfortunately; unwittingly; thoughtlessly; ineptly; blunderingly; awkwardly; gracelessly; cruelly; embarrassingly; unluckily; clumsily; innocently; bluntly; ungraciously; carelessly; brutally; unfeelingly; unsympathetically; coldly; strangely; unexpectedly; lamentably; deplorably; unpardonably; insufferably; unpleasantly; disagreeably; unpredictably; blindly.

TADPOLE

verbs

convert—into; evolve from—; swarm with —s; view—; —adheres to the surface; — approaches; —s attach themselves; — breathes; —breeds; —changes to; —clings; —develops into; —emerges; —glides; — hatches; —is transformed into; —metamor- phoses; —nibbles; —regenerates; —rushes; —sallies; —undergoes transformation; — wiggles; —wriggles.

(See fish.)

TAIL

adjectives

real; curling; flickering; forked; prehensible; stumpy; monstrous; false; fantastic; lambent; lashing; deadly; stinging; scraggy.

verbs

agitate—; cover—; fasten—; flick—; flourish—; hitch—; infest—; swish—; toss—; wag—; whisk—; —balances; —collides with; —dangles; —dashes; —hangs; — jerks; —lashes; —quivers; —slaps; — smacks; —strikes; —sweeps; —swings; — taps; —twitches; —whacks; —whisks; — wiggles.

(See braid, hair, end, rear.)

TAILOR

adjectives

trained; efficient; master; custom; union; experienced; faultless; loquacious; careful; hand; fine; lusty; soft; skillful; artistic; elaborate; casual; provincial; meticulous.

verbs

—accoutres; —alters; —apparels; —arrays; —attires; —biases; —borders; —designs; — drapes; —fits out; —flounces; —frills; — fringes; —gears; —hems; —outfits; —refurbishes; —renovates; —rigs; —seams; — sheathes; —styles; —tacks.

TAILOR (v)

adverbs

expertly; superbly; smartly; properly; stylishly; luxuriously; expensively; handsomely; faultlessly; exquisitely; flawlessly; scientifically; meticulously; impeccably; artistically.

(See fit, clothe.)

TAINT (v)

adverbs

disgustingly; sickeningly; dangerously; poisonously; partially; subtly; odorously; vilely.

(See corrupt.)

TAINTED

adverbs

unfortunately; ineradicably; indelibly; undisguisedly; fatally; indubitably; vilely; slightly; terribly; lamentably; strangely; unexpectedly; immeasurably; infectiously; noxiously; disgracefully; dangerously; completely; curiously; thoroughly; undeniably; unpleasantly; disagreeably; inexplicably.

TAKE (v)

adverbs

selfishly; invariably; graciously; voluntarily; figuratively; consciously; voraciously; recklessly; unhesitatingly; reluctantly; forcibly; sparingly; literally; ostentatiously; affectionately; seriously; indiscriminately; ostensibly; ceremoniously; roughly.

(See seize, apprehend.)

TAKING

adverbs

marvellously; attractively; charmingly; remarkably; prettily; beautifully; unusually; especially; pleasantly; interestingly; arrestingly; irresistibly; curiously; extraordinarily; enchantingly.

TALE

adjectives

half-told; monotonous; scandalous; sentimental; apocryphal; unbelievable; ecclesiastical; ridiculous; gloomy; foam-like; specious; supernatural; wondrous; pathetic; dismal; legendary; instructive; untold; tedious; mournful; exquisite; beautiful; passionate; flattering; effective; grievous; enchanting; true; riotous; shameful; diverting; evil; extraordinary; soothing; idle; definite; harrowing; melancholy; heavy; romantic; childish; uneventful; successful; crowning; gruesome; desolating; horrible; blissful; sensible; tragic; blood-curdling; artless; ever-young; saddest; magical; incoherent; tempting; merry; wild; transmitted; improbable; family; baseless; unpainted; tavern; taking; piteous; unvarnished; facetious; incomprehensible; intoxicating; sinister; amorous; long-winded; thrilling; melodramatic; mystic; abbreviated; touching; boastful; analogous; trifling; debonair; mingled (pl); seafaring; graphic; metrical; idle; free.

verbs

bear—; beguile with —s; center—; close—; compose—; conceive—; concoct—; construct —; depict—; drink in—; embody in—; follow up—; pervade—; plunge into—; pour out—; relate—; revive—; spin—; testify to —; treat—; unfold—; vary—; weave—; —s abound; —s drift into mind; —enhances

in interest; —entertains; —lengthens; —portrays; —progresses.

(See legend, narrative, narration, novel, story, "yarn," poem.)

TALENT

adjectives

genuine; distinguished; peculiar; superficial; satirical; histrionic; stifled; dramatic; marked; copious; kindred; administrative; brilliant; hidden; intuitive; inherited; native; undisciplined; vivid; social; admirable; innate; conspicuous; rare; precocious; evinced; delicate; original; sturdy; eminent; inconsiderable; gastronomic; choice; undoubted; uncommon; musical; wild; inventive; practical; interior; inborn; extraordinary; rising; latent; constructive; outside; mediocre; undoubted; comic; adoring; culinary; military; exquisite; budding.

verbs

applaud—; bring to light—; call upon—; confine—; cultivate—; demonstrate—; detect—; develop—; discover—; display—; dissipate—; enlist—; esteem—; eulogize—; expand—; exploit—; extol—; glorify—; inherit—; laud—; magnify—; misuse—; nurture—; panegyrize—; pay tribute to—; pervert—; prostitute—; smother—; stifle—; trace—; transcend—; weigh—; worship—; —buds; —decays; —germinates; —issues from; —ministers; —nourishes; —sprouts; —sustains; —transcends.

(See ability, mentality, intelligence, capacity, genius, skill.)

TALENTED

adverbs

eminently; conspicuously; extraordinarily; genuinely; peculiarly; particularly; remarkably; admirably; uncommonly; ingeniously; amazingly; signally; dazzlingly; surprisingly; splendidly; magnificently.

TALK

adjectives

buoyant; hearty; revolutionary; comprehending; fanciful; heartening; ineffable; passionate; furtive; prodigious; vainglorious; blasphemous; sneering; obscene; scandalous; heated; vigorous; unpleasant; willful; casual; yelling; loud; arduous; tedious; fragmentary; elliptical; rambling; everlasting; brilliant; indeterminate; bawdy; unmeaning; customary; spontaneous; vile; unmannerly; imperious; assuming; endless;

racy; confounded; solemn; droning; abundant; convincing; delightful; straight; impersonal; unusual; wanton; desultory; masculine; common; sprightly; buzzing; provincial; vain; loose; boyish; stimulating; inflammatory; inane; frivolous; vague; enjoyable; wicked; malignant; stammering; pious; discursive; alluring; facile; empty; silly; heart-searching; interesting; poetic; half-whispered; tumultuous; eloquent; bantering; wearisome; spasmodic; confidential.

verbs
cease—; compose—; deliver—; distinguish —; hush—; muffle—; mute—; muzzle—; silence—; stifle—; still—; substantiate—; tone down—; —allures; —annoys; —baits; —charms; —convinces; —distracts; —disturbs; —diverts; —edifies; —elucidates; — enlightens; —induces; —interests; —rumors.
(See speech, conversation, discourse, lecture.)

TALK (v)
adverbs
ramblingly; briskly; indefinitely; garrulously; animatedly; fluently; tediously; volubly; amicably; articulately; indiscreetly; blithely; shrewdly; casually; incoherently; pathetically; vivaciously; informally; interminably; mysteriously; unceasingly; eloquently; affectedly.
(See converse, speak.)

TALKATIVE
adverbs
incorrigibly; fluently; garrulously; chattily; informatively; incessantly; pleasantly; graciously; sociably; inveterately; naturally; habitually; incurably; happily; foolishly; loosely; effusively; eloquently; gushingly; prolixly; glibly; flippantly; unwisely; indiscreetly; imprudently; endlessly; tiresomely; strangely; remarkably; marvelously; incredibly; wearisomely; repetitively.

TALL
adverbs
slenderly; extraordinarily; splendidly; handsomely; lankily; absurdly; magnificently; commandingly; cadaverously; gauntly; awkwardly; laughably; gawkily; consciously; proudly; admirably; wonderfully; amazingly; unfortunately; ungainly; immeasurably; unusually; incredibly; attractively; conveniently.

TALLOW
verbs
affect—; boil—; compress—; convert into—; dissolve—; harden—; ignite—; liquefy—; melt—; mold—; purify—; refine—; separate—; solidify—; yield—; —consolidates; —confuses; —lumps; —thaws; —thickens.
(See wax.)

TALONS
verbs
bag with—; bare—; clip—; clutch in—; grasp in—; hook—; lay hold with—; pare —; pinion with—; retain in—; seize in—; sharpen—; —claw; —clench; —clinch; —detain; —gash; —gripe; —lacerate; —rend; —scar; —slash; —tear; —throttle.
(See fang, claw.)

TAME
adverbs
strangely; unexpectedly; finally; curiously; affectionately; tractably; unusually; downright; harmlessly; vexatiously; uninterestingly; dully; insipidly; submissively; lamentably; deplorably; compliantly; dutifully; apparently; obediently; surprisingly; sycophantically; tediously; insufferably.

TAME (v)
adverbs
partially; domestically; thoroughly; sufficiently; subtly; assiduously; rationally.
(See discipline, conquer.)

TAMELESS
adverbs
ardently; vehemently; enthusiastically; irrepressibly; utterly; violently; wildly; absolutely; savagely; ferociously; impatiently; stormily; inordinately; boisterously; crazily; riotously; temperamentally.

TANGIBLE
adverbs
comfortably; solidly; comfortingly; incontrovertibly; actually; finally; scarcely; ultimately; eventually; unexpectedly.

TANGLE
adjectives
dense; hopeless; confused; shining; mossy; feudal; matted; mazy; hereditary; complicated; blossoming; unexpected.

verbs

decipher—; dissolve—; elucidate—; extricate from—; fathom—; key—; liquidate—; resolve—; unravel—; unriddle—; unsnarl —; —confounds; —convulses; —deranges; —disconcerts; —dishevels; —jumbles; —meshes; —muddles; —perplexes; —perturbs; —puzzles; —ruffles; —rumples; —shuffles; —weaves; —webs.

(See intricacy, entanglement, mystery, riddle.)

TANGLE (v)

adverbs

perplexingly; desperately; hopelessly; complicatedly; designedly; confusedly; haphazardly; diplomatically; economically.

(See involve, perplex.)

TANGLED

adverbs

hopelessly; terribly; unfortunately; financially; curiously; embarrassingly; inextricably; strangely; deplorably; lamentably; oddly; darkly; odiously; laughably; ineptly; awkwardly; uncommonly; ridiculously; ludicrously; unskilfully; perplexingly; bewilderingly; guiltily; innocently; unwittingly; gullibly; helplessly; pitifully.

TANK
(general)

adjectives

special; septic; large; spacious; clogged; rusty; useful.

TANK
(military)

verbs

armor—; bullet-proof—; construct—; convert into—; design—; evade—; man—; manoeuvre—; mount—; propel—; surrender —; turret—; —attacks; —bombards; —caterpillars; —climbs; —crushes; —disperses; —lumbers; —negotiates; —repels; —rolls; —rumbles; —wheels.

TANTALIZING

adverbs

idly; absurdly; tormentingly; playfully; unbearably; teasingly; incalculably; terribly; oddly; merrily; continually; comically; outlandishly; uncommonly.

TAP (v)

adverbs

nervously; impatiently; rudely; gracefully; lightly; significantly; intermittently; irritatingly; incessantly; periodically.

(See rap, knock.)

TAPE

verbs

rend—; shred—; —adheres; —agglutinates; —binds; —cements; —cleaves; —clings; —coheres; —conglutinates; —couples; —glues; —gums; —seals; —shackles; —unites.

(See ligature, band, bandage.)

TAPER

adjectives

glimmering; gleaming; beaming; midnight; waxen; burning; sickly; flickering; tall; graceful; slender.

verbs

glut with—s; obscure—; quench—; snuff out—; —beams; —diffuses; —flames; —flares; —flickers; —flutters; —gleams; —glimmers; —glows; —gutters; —illuminates; —radiates; —scintillates; —shadows; —twinkles.

(See candle, wick, light.)

TAPERING

adverbs

gracefully; symmetrically; slenderly; gradually; suddenly; eventually; unfortunately; beautifully; lamentably; unexpectedly.

TAPESTRY

adjectives

star-inwoven; fluttering; desolate; sun-colored; blossoming; luxuriant; low-toned; smirched; enameled.

verbs

embellish—; exhibit—; hang—; line—; mount—; mutilate—; prize—; rend—; shade —; suspend—; value—; weave—; —adorns; —beautifies; —decorates; —depicts; —landscapes; —portrays.

(See picture, painting.)

TARDY

adverbs

unfortunately; disastrously; unluckily; extremely; unaccountably; deleteriously; unreasonably; needlessly; infamously; unaccountably; indiscreetly; lamentably; deplorably; fatally; unconscionably; habitually; characteristically; exasperatingly; inexcusably; unpardonably; discourteously; impolitely; grossly; indecorously; surprisingly; disappointingly; irreparably.

TARGET

adjectives

uplifted; flaming; sensible; suitable; vulnerable; conspicuous; momentary; superb; helpless; receptive; rapid; moving; human; disappearing.

verbs

align with—; batter—; buffet—; collide with —; deflect from—; deflect—; deviate from —; direct toward—; diverge from—; fall short of—; flay—; level at—; rebound from —; riddle—; smite—; speed toward—; steer toward—; swerve from—; thwack—; — eludes.

(See mark, object.)

TARIFF

verbs

abolish—; absorb in—; adopt—; bandy—; bear—; bruit about—; exact—; legislate—; levy—; modify—; nullify—; parry—; rate —; reciprocate—; reduce—; regale with—; regulate—; revise—; scrap—; set—; silence —; slash—; steer—; yield—; —bamboozles (colloq.); —discourages; —distrains; — fades; —flows; —impedes; —limits; —prohibits; —protects; —ranges; —rates; —restrains; —restricts; —schedules; —subsides; —touches upon; —veers toward.

(See taxes, amount.)

TARNISHED

adverbs

slightly; remediably; temporarily; momentarily; wholly; unfortunately; curiously; ingloriously; morally; deeply; irrecoverably; pitiably; deplorably; unluckily; irretrievably; suddenly; hopelessly; sadly; manifestly.

TART

adverbs

sharply; pleasantly; interestingly; disagreeably; unnecessarily; keenly; discriminatingly; tastefully; laughably; cleverly; piquantly; poignantly; bewilderingly; ungraciously; deliberately; unpleasantly; gracelessly; tactlessly; extremely; suddenly; overly; inexcusably.

adjectives

barren; acrid; incongruous; diabolical; humble; pensive; considerable; self-imposed; toilsome; glorious; zealous; perilous; imaginative; present-day; uninspired; unpleasing; weary; appalling; tremendous; difficult; strenuous; bleak; ungracious; painful; willing; inevitable; hazardous; dormant; amusing; staggering; cheerless; mental; pedagogical; delightful; knotty; spiritual; irksome; arduous; dreaded; hopeless; delicate; simplified; futile; endless; unfulfilled; impossible; herculean; costly; thankless; onerous; graceful; alloted; anxious; abhorrent; rough; pleasing; laborious; unnatural; noble; primary; astounding; prosaic; formidable; musical; colossal; congenial; recurring; neglected; ungrateful; vulgar; heavy; exacting; suitable; disheartening; menial; priestlike; self-appointed; troublesome; tender; distasteful; useless; easy; discordant; venturesome; intellectual; sales; basic; discouraging; joyous; docile; fatiguing; appalling; dizzy; sublime.

verbs

absorb in—; accept—; achieve—; allot—; appoint—; approach—; assign—; assume —; attempt—; buckle down to—; charge with—; complicate—; confront—; consecrate to—; dedicate to—; develop—; devote to—; discharge—; dispose of—; ease—; engage in—; engross in—; enlist in—; entrust —; essay—; expend on—; facilitate—; fit for—; fulfill—; glorify—; impose—; intrust —; inure to—; lighten—; lump—s; perform —; plunge into—; prescribe—; present—; rally to—; render—; reward—; rob—; set to—; shirk—; shoulder—; shunt—; spur on to—; toil at—; undertake—; view—; whittle down—; —bores; —confronts; —consumes; —exhausts; —fatigues; —involves; —taxes; —wearies.

(See labor, chore, work, job.)

TASTE

adjectives

worst; impeccable; distinctive; congenial; artificial; pictureque; startling; acrid; artistic; luxurious; agreeable; aesthetic; considerable; fanciful; unpleasant; barbarous; educated; nauseous; bizarre; provincial; fastidious; incongruous; desultory; native; refreshing; controlling; exquisite; intellectual; superior; bookkeeping; cultivated; unusual; costly; execrable; elevated; vulgar;

classical; horrible; magic; varying; ludicrous; lustrous; cosmopolitan; barbaric; philanthropic; tangy; good; scientific; admirable; ancestral; erroneous; musical; precious; astringent; literary; uncertain; developed; popular; brazen; massive; instinctive; diminished; enlightened; ephemeral; pronounced; elegant; mortal; clean; honorable; gross; individual; delicious; aromatic; radical; savage; odious; characteristic; surprising; questionable; critical; unperverted; inimitable; plebeian; histrionic; taffy; bitter; schoolmastery; fashionable.

verbs

accumulate—; alter—; betray—; concoct—; criticize—; cultivate—; deprave—; disguise —; dispel—; elevate—; endure—; feign—; gratify—; impair—; indulge in—; manifest —; minister to—; modify—; outgrow—; overrate—; pander to—; pervert—; possess —; polish—; purify—; refine—; reflect—; relish—; simplify—; spice—; —appeals; — bites; —blossoms; —characterizes; —clings; —collapses; —crystallizes; —discriminates; —guides; —gormandizes; —intoxicates; — lingers; —nauseates; —rasps; —reflects; — sickens; —smacks of.

(See desire, craving, impulse, inclination, flavor, appreciation.)

TASTE (v)
adverbs
sparingly; tentatively; fastidiously; perniciously; poisonously; odiously; horribly.
(See relish, eat.)

TASTEFUL
adverbs
delicately; deftly; naturally; richly; chastely; instinctively; inherently; innately; unerringly; exquisitely; fastidiously; quaintly; ingeniously; intrinsically; discriminatingly; expertly; correctly; academically; admirably.

TASTY
adverbs
pleasantly; unusually; gracefully; beautifully; delicately; delightfully; unexpectedly; surprisingly; deliberately; laboriously; invitingly; luxuriously; artistically.

TATTLE (v)
adverbs
childishly; faithlessly; traitorously; pettishly; hatefully; peevishly; vindictively.
(See babble, gossip.)

TATTLING
adverbs
maliciously; garrulously; innocently; cheerily; cheerfully; deliberately; dangerously; purposely; intentionally; childishly; meanly; mischievously; idly; diffusely; endlessly; snidely; dangerously; viciously; vindictively; malignantly; venomously; inanely; mindlessly; senselessly; thoughtlessly; witlessly; contemptibly; despicably; basely.

TAUNT
adjectives
parting; bitter; stinging; unmerited; unfeeling; good; reproachful.

verbs
bristle at—s; disregard—; fling—; hurl—; ignore—; repay—; repress—; restrain—; stifle—; tolerate—; utter—s; —affronts; — brands; —cuts; —disparages; —irks; —irritates; —jeers; —lashes; —outrages; — pervades; —ridicules; —slurs; —stings; — twits.
(See jeer, insult, reproach.)

TAUT
adverbs
curiously; nervously; dangerously; solidly; securely; sufficiently; perilously; finally; completely; lamentably; deplorably; inconveniently; rigidly; strangely; unaccountably.

TAVERN
adjectives
dusky; uninviting; well-restored; popular.

verbs
beguile in—; frequent—; frolic at—; haunt —; patronize—; regale in—; relax in—; reside at—; revel in—; stagger from—; visit —; weary of—; —accommodates; —beckons; —dispenses; —diverts; —lodges; —lures; — resounds; —rings; —welcomes.
(See hotel, inn.)

TAWDRY
adverbs
cheaply; unacceptably; reprehensibly; inexcusably; definitely; positively; inconceivably; incredibly; emphatically; admittedly; inadmissibly; disagreeably; contemptibly; insubstantially; obtrusively; dreadfully; noticeably; conspicuously; undisguisedly; blatantly; inordinately; extremely; sordidly; meanly; cheaply; offensively.

adjectives
confiscatory; direct; excessive; equitable; ingenious; oppressive; unequal; stealthy; extortionate; merciless; enormous; staggering; arbitrary; unpitying; burdensome.

TAXES

adjectives
hidden; local; inspection; prohibitive; punitive; social; fantastic; exclusive; grievous; external; superfluous; onerous; arbitrary; oppressive; exceptionable; inequitable; personal; incredible; odious.

verbs
abscond with—; apply—; appraise for—; appropriate from—; assess—; authorize—; default—; denounce—; derive—; discount—; divert from—; dodge—; eliminate—; enact —; evade—; exempt from—; extort—; grumble about—; impose—; inveigh against —; legislate—; levy—; outlaw—; question —; rate—; reduce—; repeal—; squeeze—; —accrue; —burden; —constitute; —crush; —defray; —design; —enable; —extend; — impoverish; —mount; —prorate; —ruin; — stifle; —support; —total; —yield; expend—.
(See tariff.)

TAXI

verbs
avail oneself of—; commandeer—; employ —; flag—; hail—; hire—; license—; man—; mobilize—s; pursue in—; recruit—s; resort to—; scramble for—; whistle for—; —careens; —conveys; —s file by; —meanders; —pick its way; —rolls away; —rumbles; —scuds; —s scurry; —skids; —swerves; — threads thru traffic; —transports; —traverses; —whizzes.
(See automobile.)

TAXPAYERS

verbs
address—; besiege—; burden—; coerce—; delude—; harass—; impoverish—; irk—; overburden—; promise—; ruffle—; soothe —; stir—; swindle—; tyrannize over—; — array against; —band; —campaign for; — declaim; —decry; —elect; —groan; — clamor; —league; —moan; —petition; — protest; —repudiate; —rise; —unite; — voice.
(See citizen, public, people.)

adjectives
numberless (pl); well-creamed; smuggled; elemental; contraband; rare; licorice; softened; melodious; perfumed; fragrant; aphrodisiac.

verbs
abstain from—; addict to—; brew—; concoct—; dispatch—; dispense—; drain—; entertain at—; flavor—; gulp—; ice—; imbibe—; import—; quaff—; sip—; spice—; strain—; sweeten—; swill down—; —appeases; —moistens; —quenches; —revives; —simmers; —stimulates; —thickens.
(See coffee, drink, beverage.)

TEACH (v)

adverbs
professionally; explicitly; elaborately; exclusively; extensively; laboriously; effectually; systematically; dispassionately; ethically; scrupulously; conscientiously; competently; eminently; zealously; erroneously; inspirationally.
(See instruct.)

TEACHABLE

adverbs
easily; scarcely; hardly; eagerly; responsively; clearly; manifestly; readily; ordinarily; extraordinarily; unusually; alertly; quickly; intelligently; admirably; exceptionally; surprisingly.

TEACHER

adjectives
perspicacious; competent; well-trained; mute; pious; imaginative; established; enthusiastic; delightful; admirable; discontented; notable; eminent; fledged; brilliant; illustrious; foremost; understanding; zealous; distinguished; religious; discouraged; primary; incapable; stimulating.

verbs
commend—; disqualify—; extol—; honor—; prejudice—; revere—; —adjusts; —breeds; —coaches; —cultivates; —disciplines; —discourses; —drills; —edifies; —emancipates; —enlightens; —equips; —expounds; — fledges; —fosters; —guides; —harangues; —hews; —holds forth; —illumines; —impregnates; —inculcates; —indoctrinates; — infiltrates; —infuses; —interprets; —initiates; —inspires; —instils; —instructs; — liberates; —matures; —molds; —nurtures;

—poises; —prepares; —shapes; —sheds light; —sows; —rears; —tutors; —uplifts.
(See master, orator, scholar.)

TEACHING

adjectives

assiduous; blind; austere; orthodox; political; time-honored; positive; inspired; inner; basic; rational; erroneous; stern; polytheistic; ethical; false; lofty; skeptical.

verbs

accept—; acquaint with—; adhere to—; advance—; afford—; bias—; blind to—; certify for—; contradict—; convey—; demonstrate—; enlarge—; evolve—; follow—; glean from—; heed—; introduce—; labor at —; memorize—; practise—; prejudice—; propagandize—; reiterate—; reject—; standardize—; suppress—s; treasure—; — affords; —directs; —embraces; —enlightens; —guides; —inculcates; —infuses; — instils; —matures; —qualifies; —prepares; —unveils.
(See doctrine, gospel, precept, instruction, profession.)

TEA-CUP

adjectives

rattling; tiny; dainty; china; fragile.

TEAM

adjectives

well-matched; splendid; phlegmatic; ill-mated; willing; panting; serviceable.

verbs

acclaim—; assemble—; captain—; cleave—; coach—; condition—; discipline—; dominate —; drill—; forsake—; harangue—; harness —; heckle—; inspire—; instil in—; mobilize—; oppose—; rend—; reward—; sever —; subsidize—; transport—; —bows; —concedes; —conquers; —contends; —cooperates; —drubs; —files out; —flounders; — hampers; —manoeuvers; —proselytes; — surmounts; —trains; —triumphs; —upsets; —vanquishes.
(See crew, athlete, contestant.)

TEAR (v)

adverbs

distractedly; viciously; hideously; extensively; impatiently; ravenously; rudely; wolfishly; literally; wantonly; ceaselessly; ruthlessly; dreadfully.
(See divide, sever.)

TEARFUL

adverbs

touchingly; maddeningly; vexatiously; deliberately; purposely; profitably; pathetically; sympathetically; pitiably; unfortunately; readily; easily; ridiculously; comically; ludicrously; hysterically; nervously; timidly; shyly; bashfully; tragically; angrily; fearfully; overwhelmingly; embarrassingly; helplessly; anxiously; happily; boisterously; noisily; piteously.

TEARS

adjectives

superabundant; solemn; unshed; melodious; sorrowful; hysterical; timid; passionate; unavailing; heartbroken; fruitless; flowing; glowing; dying; passion-ridden; soul-brought; subduing; glorious; silent; weak; unreclaiming; stealing; idiot; sharp; sweet; bitter; dewy; struggling; treacherous; crystal; impending; grateful; honest; frozen; immortal; happy; salt; undropped; scalding; maudlin; untimely; eternal; joyful; repentant; unremembered; plenteous; tributary; emotional; ungovernable; immense; kindred; continual; gathering; contending; solemn; reminiscent; unavailing; sparkling; briny; unconscious; sympathetic; noiseless; sleepless; merry; crocodile; foolish; supplicating; patriotic; obsequious; excessive; imploring; intermittent; future; celestial; smarting; spiteful; involuntary; resistless; furious; parting; softening; mingled; submissive; saccharine; foreboding; purple; stanchless; contrite; peevish; quenched; humble; feigned; brimming; noble; penitential; dreadful; transparent; vanished; impotent; silver-shedding; mighty; fertile.

verbs

agitate to—; allay—; bathe in—; blind with —; brush away—; burst into—; check—; conceal—; consecrate with—; dab at—; dim with—; dissolve into—; dry—; emit —; feign—; flood with—; give vent to—; ignore—; inspire—; melt down—; move to —; provoke—; relieve—; secrete—; shed —; snivel in—; stem—; sting to—; summon —; swallow—; tinge with—; water with —; wink back—; wipe away—; wring—; —bedew; —blind; —choke; —dissolve; — dry up; —fall; —flow; —glisten; —glitter; —gush forth; —impassion; —melt; —move; —rack; —rain down; —scald; —soften; — start; —sting; —stream down; —sway; —

touch; —tremble; —trickle; —wash away; —well up; —wet; blink back—.
(See lamentation, dew, grief.)

TEASE (v)
adverbs
wilfully; provokingly; irritatingly; exasperatingly; bullyingly; boisterously; slyly; insidiously; viciously; vindictively; subtly; blithely.
(See torment, harass.)

TEASING
adverbs
blithely; playfully; persistently; comically; merrily; wildly; noisily; tormentingly; foolishly; inordinately; pestiferously; ludicrously; nonsensically; absurdly; merrily; airily; immoderately; hilariously.

TECHNICAL
adverbs
clearly; purely; merely; probably; narrowly; strictly; wholly.

TECHNICALITIES
verbs
acquire—; avoid—; bores one with—; botch —; bungle—; denote—; detail—; discard —; dispense with—; dissolve—; enlighten —; exhibit—; explain—; ignore—; insist upon—; master—; necessitate—; plague with —; simplify—; strip—; weigh—; —bewilder; —confuse; —particularize; —perplex.
(See detail, technique.)

TECHNICALITY
adjectives
theological; ecclesiastical; selling; trivial; tiny.

TECHNIQUE
adjectives
comprehensive; scarce; specified; perfected; grooming; inborn; natural; creative; operating; educational; photographic; administrative; first-rate; incredible; piano; impressionistic; remarkable; dramatic; masterly; sterile; histological; surgical; brushing; delicate; facile; amazing; complex.

verbs
acclaim—; achieve—; acquire—; attain—; change—; commend—; contrive—; crown —; dispatch with—; display—; develop—; devise—; employ—; endow with—; evolve —; excel in—; exhibit—; forge—; formulate—; improve—; introduce—; laud—; master—; perfect—; practise—; revolutionize—; stamp with—; suggest—; —aids; —enhances; —equips.
(See skill, method, manner.)

TEDIOUS
adverbs
intolerably; monotonously; profoundly; irksomely; tiresomely; uniformly; boringly; terribly; wearisomely; inordinately; feebly; exhaustingly; dully; mortally; prosily; disgustingly; unbearably; wearily; flatly; stupidly.

TEDIUM
verbs
allay—; chafe at—; decry—; disperse—; divert from—; ease—; relieve—; revolt at —; —assails; —beguiles; —bores; —burdens; —disintegrates; —exhausts; —fags; —fatigues; —harasses; —irks; —jades; —overwhelms; —prostrates; —sours; —stagnates; —strains; —taxes; —vexes; —wearies; —weighs upon.
(See monotony, weariness.)

TEETER (v)
adverbs
precariously; dizzily; dangerously; comically; drunkenly; weakly; painfully.
(See sway, balance.)

TEETH
adjectives
feeble; mottled; dazzling; tortuous; milky; ravenous; sharpened; jagged; clenched; hooked; pearly; tartarous; compressed; ferocious; flashing; foam-laced; blunted; glittering; chattering; convulsive; horrid; neglected; decayed; black; lacquered; wolfish; short; ivory; gnashing; snowy; close-shut; dagger-like; grinding.

verbs
abscess—; brace—; clamp—on; clench in—; cut—; dislodge—; drill—; engage with—; extract—; gnash—; grate—; grit—; groove —; imbed—in; lock—; polish—; retain—; —chatter; —crunch; —cut; —disintegrate; —emerge; —erupt; —flash; —gnaw; —lacerate; —pierce; —poison; —project; —reduce.
(See fang, bone.)

adjectives

congratulatory; visual; ocular; co-working; worrying; speedy.

verbs

acknowledge by—; convey—; decipher—; decode—; dispatch—; seal—; unfold—; — advises; —alarms; —announces; —authorizes; —s bombard; —confirms; —congratulates; —discloses; —divulges; —directs; — excites; —informs; —orders; —s pour in; — protests; —reveals.

(See letter, dispatch, news, message.)

TELEGRAPH (v)

adverbs

swiftly; instantly; faithfully; peremptorily; authoritatively; fraternally.

(See communicate, dispatch.)

TELEGRAPHIC

adverbs

mysteriously; swiftly; emotionally; marvellously; silently; confidentially; comically; fleetly; unmistakably; mercifully; sympathetically.

TELEPATHIC

adverbs

emotionally; sympathetically; instinctively; unmistakably; mysteriously; naturally; definitely; demonstrably; presumably; distinctly; possibly; imaginably; curiously; strangely; admissibly; credibly.

TELEPHONE

adjectives

limitless; effective; clattering; mute.

verbs

acquire—; communicate by—; confirm by—; disconnect—; drone into—; inform by—; install—; necessitate—; remove—; repair—; scurry to—; sever—; —assists; —awakens; —clamors; —distracts; —diverts; —eases; —enables; —facilitates; —jangles; —lightens; —persists; —shrills.

TELESCOPE

verbs

contemplate through—; design—; direct— at; discern through—; level—at; mount—; peek through—; rivet—on; scan with—; squint into—; study through—; survey with—; — aids; —clarifies; —discovers; —distinguish-

es; —enlarges; —enlightens; —facilitates; —magnifies; —ranges; —reveals; —sweeps the heavens.

(See microscope.)

TELESCOPIC

adverbs

amazingly; incredibly; marvellously; authentically; credibly; highly; evidently; conveniently; compactly; cleverly; handily; disconcertingly.

TELL (v)

adverbs

succinctly; impassively; hysterically; vehemently; conclusively; frankly; vigorously; jestingly; vividly; reluctantly; impressively; vaguely; musically; candidly; effectively; complacently; fluently; simply; circumstantially; reverently; artfully; reproachfully; accordingly; bluntly; genially; dispassionately; arrogantly; fervently; glibly; poignantly; gravely; inconsistently.

(See communicate, speak.)

TELLING

adverbs

vividly; trenchantly; brilliantly; eloquently; unusually; impressively; uniquely; significantly; graphically; dramatically; vigorously; authoritatively; positively; sensationally; remarkably; extremely; singularly; marvellously.

TELLTALE

adverbs

undisguisably; innocently; embarrassingly; indubitably; convincingly; ineradicably; inescapably; manifestly; ridiculously; undeniably; significantly; remarkably; conspicuously; noticeably; visibly; graphically.

TEMPER

adjectives

generous; reckless; subjective; suspended; creative; critical; gusty; querulous; peevish; suspicious; inflammable; gracious; charitable; terrible; ethereal; youthful; judicial; penurious; violent; dauntless; ruffled; indolent; collective (pl); frayed; bad; easy; convivial; uncertain; predominant; revengeful; skeptical; chivalrous; complacent; malignant; malleable; slumbering; imperious; independent; fixed; haughty; jarring; serene; buoyant; amiable; indifferent; chastened; earthly; ruthless; jovial; unspent; unsunned; fiery; lively; loquacious; self-willed; passionate; columned; delicate; noble; docile; imperturbable; characteristic; mirthful; sweet; queer; philosophic; irritable; lethargic; meek; placid; sunny; equable; changeable; curious; polemical; cold; irreligious; merry; conciliatory; unforgiving; fretful; invincible; pedantic; heroic; unaltered; keen; despondent; ungovernable; inquisitive; impatient; admirable; combative; childish; turbulent; choleric; gunpowder; aspiring; dignified; villainous; boisterous; resentful; coddled; schizoid; benevolent; calm; ferocious; submissive; confident; crusading; eddying; iron-like; tart; feeble.

verbs
allay—; assuage—; blunt—; calm—; chasten—; compose—; curb—; dulcify—; exhibit —; fire—; ignite—; lull—; manifest—; moderate—; mollify—; pacify—; palliate—; quell—; quench—; restrain—; rule—; smooth—; sober—; subdue—; sweeten—; —blazes; —erupts; —explodes; —flames; —flares; —foams; —foments; —fumes; — seethes; —simmers; —snaps.
(See ire, anger, disposition, temperament.)

TEMPERAMENT
adjectives
adventurous; uncertain; artistic; cheerful; nervous; bilious; romantic; brooding; poetical; fierce; ardent; sanguine; morbid; observing; restless; nerveless; classic; highbred; individual; aspiring; unchangeable; philanthropic; sprightly; apathetic; emotional; mercurial; equable; grave; warlike; peculiar; heroic; inborn; fervent; oratorical; impetuous; undisciplined; genial; melancholy; mournful; indolent; pugnacious; fitful; delicate; rare; sunny; passionate; peculiar; physical; overcharged.

verbs
attune—to; bend—; characterize—; curse with—; display—; dispose toward—; exhibit—; fire—; foment—; harmonize—s; imbue with—; incline toward—; inflame—; influence—; inherit—; modulate—; mollify —; mould—; warp—; wrestle with—; —s clash; —flares; —indicates; —piques; — seethes; —simmers.
(See character, disposition.)

TEMPERAMENTAL
adverbs
highly; inconveniently; tempestuously; pro-

vokingly; bewilderingly; naturally; proverbially; characteristically; insufferably; unpredictably; allegedly; unmanageably; uncontrollably; violently; interestingly; perplexingly.

TEMPERANCE
verbs
advocate—; campaign for—; commend—; exhort—; laud—; pledge—; promote—; — abstains; —allays; —alleviates; —chastens; —composes; —denies; —forbears; —mitigates; —moderates; —refrains; —sobers; — softens; —spares; —tranquillizes.
(See moderation, sobriety, restraint.)

TEMPERATE
adverbs
definitely; mildly; judiciously; moderately; calmly; pleasantly; safely; honestly; cautiously; discreetly; prudently; reasonably; certainly; occasionally; habitually; naturally; soberly; consistently; modestly; quietly; inveterately; surprisingly; meticulously; punctiliously; scrupulously; usually.

TEMPERATURE
adjectives
accurate; congenial; equable; unexpected; high; balmy; tepid; terrestrial; physical; low; critical; ruinous; debilitating; varying; aggregate; uniform; intolerable; mean; cheap; consistent; elevated.

verbs
ascertain—; determine—; expose to—of; indicate—; maintain—; measure—; record —; regulate—; swelter in—of; —chars; — chills; —chafes; —climbs; —congeals; — descends; —fluctuates; —flushes; —fuses; —ignites; —mounts; —nips; —parches; — petrifies; —pinches; —refreshes; —sinks; —skyrockets (colloq.); —soars; —thaws; —toboggans.
(See mercury, barometer, meter, weather.)

TEMPEST
adjectives
terrible; howling; winter; renewed; spirit-brewed; shadowy; embattled; hideous; giddy; aerial; social; weltering; thundering; laboring; furious; careening; commanding; ruinous; damaging.

verbs
calm—; still—; sway in—; —abates; —agitates; —batters; —bellows; —blusters; —

buffets; —churns; —clamors; —crackles; —
devastates; —drenches; —fumes; —howls;
—lashes; —rages; —roars; —seethes; —
shrieks; —subdues; —swells; —uproots; —
whisks; —whistles; —subsides.
(See gale, hurricane, storm.)

TEMPESTUOUS
adverbs
violently; uncontrollably; passionately;
stormily; dangerously; unmanageably; remarkably; unusually; insufferably; notoriously; sensationally; melodramatically;
feverishly.

TEMPLE
adjectives
druidical; blushing; foreign; mystical; unworthy; versatile; abolished; graceful;
wind-swept; throbbing; soniferous; burning; shattered; hairy; pagan; proud; pillared; wooden; gorgeous; projecting; ancient;
holy; arching; magnificent; veined; heated;
solemn; sumptuous; shattered; battered;
numerous (pl); anointed; airy; glass;
monumental.

verbs
attend—; banish from—; beseech in—; blas_
pheme—; bow in—; commune in—; convert
into—; dedicate—; defile—; degrade—;
desecrate—; design—; enshrine in—; erect
—; expel from—; found—; ordain—; profane—; purge—; quarter in—; refuge in—;
rend—; retire to—; sully—; swear by—;
taint—; visit—; whip from—; —rises; —
sanctifies.
(See church, tabernacle, cathedral.)

TEMPORAL
adverbs
evanescently; merely; transitorily; briefly;
fleetingly; fugitively; perishably; transiently; mutably; precariously; impermanently;
painfully; unhappily; frailly; ephemerally;
utterly; sadly; uncertainly; insecurely.

TEMPORARY
adverbs
fortunately; merely; definitely; presumably;
luckily; unfortunately; probably; presumably; definitely; supposedly; allegedly.

TEMPT (*v*)
adverbs
diabolically; fiendishly; insidiously; viciously; lewdly; appetizingly; intolerably; unwit-

tingly; irresistibly; unduly; incestuously;
mystically; maddeningly; goadingly.
(See induce, lead.)

TEMPTATION
adjectives
constant; incestuous; sore; stronger; fierce;
irresistible; external; various (pl); succulent; inviting; urban; insidious; testy; urgent; mystical; repeated; enticing; usurped.

verbs
accede to—; avoid—; conquer—; deliver
from—; fling aside—; grapple with—;
heighten—; intensify—; prevail against—;
resist—; shun—; steel to—; subdue—; succumb to—; surrender to—; vanquish—;
withstand—; wrestle with—; subdue—; —
allures; —attracts; —baits; —beckons; —
beguiles; —biases; —goads; —lures; —
overcomes; —overwhelms; —seduces; —
spurs; —sways; —tantalizes.
(See desire, passion, appetite.)

TEMPTING
adverbs
delectably; alluringly; subtly; viciously;
cleverly; slily; guilelessly; seductively; irresistibly; curiously; strangely; exotically;
perilously; boldly; wickedly; deliciously;
charmingly; pleasurably; insidiously.

TENABLE
adverbs
scarcely; soundly; rationally; reasonably;
logically; incontrovertibly; obviously; undeniably; easily; manifestly; validly; legally; satisfactorily; basically; effectively; inferentially; sensibly; fundamentally; essentially.

TENACIOUS
adverbs
stubbornly; obstinately; piously; dogmatically; doctrinally; doggedly; toughly; persistently; obdurately; resolutely; grimly;
uncompromisingly; indomitably; stiffly; fanatically; inexplicably; disagreeably; ungraciously; tactlessly; surprisingly; churlishly; grossly; vexatiously.

TENACITY
adjectives
unyielding; peculiar; pathetic; amazing;
bulldog; breathless; obstinate; desperate;

extraordinary; unmatched; dogged; agonized; marvelous.

verbs
buckle with—; cling with—; display—; exhibit—; inherit—; marvel at—; value—; —droops; —fails; —flags; —flinches; — impresses; —irks; —piques; —rankles; — resists; —riles (colloq.); —stiffens; — wavers; —yields to.
(See impregnability, stubbornness, persistence, strength.)

TENANT
adjectives
delinquent; peripatetic; impoverished; previous; worshipful; shuddering; defaulting; noisome; troublesome.

TEND (v)
adverbs
progressively; auspiciously; affectionately; subversively; obliquely; sedulously; faithfully; maternally; materially; religiously; fervently.
(See contribute, incline.)

TENDENCY
adjectives
pensive; sadistic; moralizing; abnormal; consequent; contrary; general; inevitable; exhibitionistic; decadent; abortive; immoral; dominant; latent; worldly; picturesque; belated; remote; revolutionary; marked; overruling; hereditary; evil; boyish; vicious; rationalistic; opposing; neurotic; abounding; pernicious; ambivalent; diverging; apprehensive; curtailed; philosophical; unconscious; speculative; primitive; morbid; life-abridging; transitory; herding; incestuous; rising; tubercular; undevout; natural; progressive; youthful; extravagant; erratic; notable; irreligious; conflicting; realistic; cancerous; centripetal; social; chronic; growing; powerful; stubborn; pseudo-classic; gravitating; materializing; obnoxious; dispositional; constitutional; pragmatic; aggravating; prevalent; remarkable; dangerous; healthy; observable; incorrigible; curious; devotional; pernicious; dispersive; culinary; commercial; monopolistic.

verbs
augment—; bolster—; check—; combat—; counteract—; counterbalance—; cultivate—; decry—; deplore—; deprecate—; dispose of

—; eliminate—; encourage—; exhibit—; foster—; inherit—; neutralize—; nurse—; nurture—; observe—; offset—; outgrow—; overcome—; perceive—; promote—; reflect —; resist—; restrain—; smother—; stifle—; temper—; warp—; —conduces toward; — endangers; —jeopardizes; —predisposes.
(See inclination, proclivity, disposition.)

TENDER
adverbs
affectionately; maternally; infinitely; mercifully; passionately; amorously; impulsively; impetuously; eagerly; amiably; gently; curiously; naturally; oddly; unexpectedly; lovingly; caressingly.

TENDERNESS
adjectives
respectful; wounded; tearful; solemn; passionate; renewed; marked; sexual; dawning; yearning; melting; latent; pardonable; quaint; compassionate; human; spontaneous; newborn; bountiful; boundless; exquisite; conjugal; maternal; growing; unutterable; secondary; paternal; natural; deep; laughing; patriarchal; credulous; brief; immense; profound; elephantine; saddened; masculine; ineffable; touching; increasing; pathetic; grateful; infinite; unaccustomed; majestic; flowery; rugged; zealous; connubial; wishful; infinite; malicious; grave; wild; ineffable; excessive; rough; unvarying; flavorsome; graceful; universal; etherealized; brooding; shy; surpassing; patronizing; ideal; searching; sufficient; eternal; heavenly; uneradicated; peculiar.

verbs
affect—; arouse—; cherish—; display—; evince—; excite—; exhibit—; infuse—; inspire—; move to—; propitiate in—; relent in—; sense—; temper with—; treasure—; —assuages; —captivates; —charms; —disarms; —engages; —floods; —melts; — mitigates; —mollifies; —pervades; — pierces; —stirs.
(See love, kindness, compassion, pity, mercy.)

TENDON
verbs
bind—; cleave—; dissect—; incise—; lacerate—; penetrate—; pull—; rend—; seg-

ment—; sever—; strain—; strip—; —couples; —jams; —knots; —pains; —supports; —unites.

(See muscle, ligament.)

TENEMENTS
adjectives
spacious; frail; tessellated; dreary; newly-painted; fire-trap; dilapidated; unsafe; nauseating; filthy; close-packed; unsightly; disgusting; squalid.

verbs
condemn—; decry—; dwell in—; eject from —; evict from—; inhabit—; inveigh against —; poke about—; raze—; reside in—; roost in—; scurry through—; —breed; —confine; —defile; —dot; —engender; —harden; —overspread; —reek; —sully.

(See building, structure, home, slums.)

TENOR
adjectives
constant; noiseless; general; loud; expressionless; diminutive; same; habitual; operatic; even.

TENSE
adverbs
nervously; utterly; anxiously; rigidly; stiffly; terribly; oddly; uneasily; apprehensively; dreadfully; curiously; visibly; noticeably; manifestly; fearfully; self-consciously; excitedly; eagerly; unusually; remarkably; feverishly; warily; watchfully; quietly.

TENSION
adjectives
diminished; surface; severe; tremendous; increased; relieved; ocular; wonted; nervous; mental; spasmodic; unendurable; vigorous; bitter; emotional; extreme; unnatural; ominous; elastic; awful; high; electric.

verbs
allay—; alleviate—; ameliorate—; blunt—; ease—; erase—; generate—; inure to—; reduce—; relax—; release—; relieve—; soothe—; stir up—; sustain—; —burdens; —exhausts; —flares; —heightens; —jades; —mounts; —prostrates; —snaps; —strains; —taxes; —unnerves; —wearies.

(See misapprehension, anxiety, fear, strain, intensity.)

TENT
adjectives
invading; striped; tall; mat-walled; little; swarthy; stationary; convenient; superfluous; abominable; gauze; solitary; prim; tight.

verbs
assemble in—; avail oneself of—; batter—; buffet—; dwell in—; encamp in—; pelt—; pitch—; stake—; whisk away—; —affords; —comforts; —conceals; —enshrouds; —envelops; —flaps; —flutters; —obscures; —preserves; —shelters.

(See canvas, home, house, pavilion.)

TENTACLES
adjectives
long; trailing; murderous; multitudinous; clutching.

verbs
clutch in—; deliver from—; disengage—; elude—; ensnare in—; escape—; evade—; expand—; extricate from—; hug in—; liberate from—; relax—; release from—; seize in—; sever—; unloose—; —cling to; —contract; —entwine; —grasp; —retain; —smother; —snatch; —suffocate.

(See grasp, grip, talons, claw, clutch.)

TENURE
adjectives
property; fixed; solitary; lifelong; permanent; indefinite.

TEPID
adverbs
sickeningly; nauseously; uninterestingly; pleasantly; harmlessly; agreeably; safely; disagreeably.

TERM
(*general*)
adjectives
stringent; mechanistic; concrete; triumphant; remunerative; inexorable; appreciative; uncompromising; precise; brilliant; purposed; mysterious; familiar; interchangeable; plain; warm; ambiguous; proffered; unexpired; dubious; unhallowed; disastrous; convincing; abusive; modest; sudden; limited; strong; vile; festival; subsequent; equivalent; respectable; growling; impending; vague; hyperbolical; personal; unqualified; successful; downright; specific; generous; explicit; glowing; wrathful; con-

ciliatory; budget; honorable; obscure; silent; rash; affectionate; convertible; installment; speedy; anagogic; emphatic; disapproving; attractive; original; indefinite; complied; gross; measured; absolute; uncalculating; following; misapplied; extravagant; equal; silken; liberal; uncouth; synonymous; flattering; satisfactory; hyperbolical; chameleon; advantageous; immense; tedious; convenient; endurable; psychoanalytic; unreasonable; generic; relative; intimate; eloquent; terrible; tender; fashionable; amicable; equivocal; favorable; complimentary; penitentiary; recollected; degrading; much-abused; express; comprehensive; antiquated; impressive; feeble; technical; essential; respectful; fundamental; abominable; unmistakable; graphic; energetic; monetary; figurative; opprobrious; unmistakable.

TERM
(words)
verbs
accentuate—; amplify—; analyze—; apply —; clarify—; cloak in—s; clothe in—s; coin—; condense—; confine—; corrupt—; couch in—; define—; derive—; employ—; illustrate—; interpret—; object to—; paraphrase—; stilt—; stress—; voice in—s; — bewilders; —colors; —confuses; —degenerates; —disgraces; —embraces; —emphasizes; —expresses; —implies; —insinuates; —veils.
(See phrase, expression, word.)

TERM (v)
adverbs
vulgarly; improperly; euphemistically; confidentially; appropriately; aptly; irrelevantly; sneeringly; jestingly; satirically; equivocally; degradingly; technically; graphically; figuratively; opprobriously; affectionately; modestly; wrathfully; ambiguously; hyperbolically.
(See call, name.)

TERMAGANT
adverbs
brazenly; uncontrollably; boisterously; savagely; rudely; incredibly; obviously; laughably; ridiculously; unreasoningly; habitually; oddly; crazily; biliously; excitably; pugnaciously; truculently; bewilderingly; cruelly; scurrilously; obscenely.

TERMINATE (v)
adverbs
abruptly; tediously; innocently; happily; disastrously; seedily; inevitably; effectually; fatally; legitimately; swiftly; successfully; amazingly.
(See end, conclude.)

TERMITES
verbs
control—; deter—; exterminate—; infest with—; resist—; seethe with—; shield from —; teem with—; trample—; —abound; — ally with; —attack; —blight; —bore through; —burrow; —colonize; —construct; —deface; —despoil; —destroy; —devastate; —devour; —excavate; —forage; —gnaw; —hollow out; —impair; —incubate; —injure; —invade; —menace; —moult; — mound; —mutilate; —nest; —overrun; — penetrate; —raid; —ravage; —raise; — sap foundations; —store; —swarm; — tunnel through; —undermine.
(See ant, insect.)

TERMS
(conditions)
verbs
accede to—; acknowledge—; acquiesce to —; adopt—; allude to—; approve—; assent to—; challenge—; comply with—; concede to—; confine to—; consent to—; consider —; contract on—; corroborate—; couch in —; dictate—; disclose—; divulge—; enforce—; haggle over—; impose—; indorse —; mince—; propound—; ratify—; regard —; restrict to—; shorten—; sign—; submit —; subscribe to—; translate into—; yield to—; —apply; —conciliate; —imply; —include; —pacify; —placate; —yoke.
(See condition, demand, proposition, provision, limitation.)

TERRACE
adjectives
successive (pl); sloping; spacious; narrow; zigzag; beautiful; rounded; landscaped.

TERRESTRIAL
adverbs
manifestly; disappointingly; materially; comfortably; obviously; ridiculously.

TERRIBLE
adverbs
utterly; consummately; unbearably; appall-

1175

ingly; fascinatingly; luridly; overwhelmingly; indescribably; astoundingly; portentously.

TERRIFIED
adverbs

utterly; basely; brutally; cruelly; mercilessly; irrationally; unusually; highly; dismally; hopelessly; desperately; distressingly; painfully; pathetically; secretly; dreadfully; inwardly; strangely; curiously; wildly; violently; hysterically.

TERRIFY (*v*)
adverbs

pusillanimously; psychically; unreasoningly; manifestly; irrationally; superstitiously; secretly; frantically; vicariously; immoderately; direly; blindly; overwhelmingly; supernaturally; abjectly.
(See frighten, scare.)

TERRITORY
adjectives

extensive; adjacent; contiguous; debatable; adjoining; valuable; disputed; immense; imperial; worthless; contracted; neutral; condemned; excellent; dangerous; virgin; ideal; productive; paltry; vast; annexed; choice; rich; unassigned; inexhaustible; restricted; best; protected.

verbs

abandon—; absorb—; administer—s; annex —; border—; cede—; claim—; commandeer —; covet—; devastate—; dispose of—; embrace—; endow with—; expropriate—; flank—; forfeit—; fortify—; gain—; impound—; invade—; lay waste—; lease—; mandate—; partition—; patrol—; ravage —; reconquer—; retain—; reward with—; rule—; seek—; skirt—; traverse—; value —; yield—; —confronts; —flourishes; — revolts; —seethes.
(See district, province, locality, jurisdiction, country.)

TERROR
adjectives

mute; avowed; blasphemous; striking; pusillanimous; loving; mutual; bodily; abject; abysmal; mysterious; coquettish; conventional; chastening; conquering; psychic; manifest; rattling; hasty; inconceivable; avenging; haunting; forest; imaginary; instinctive; vague; limitless; unreasoning; sheer; absurd; majestic; dissolving; wild;

grisly; superstitious; shuddering; bouncing; roaring; rigid; secret; breathless; dispelled; vigorous; frantic; natural; undefinable; solemn; rhythmic; deadly; fantastic; vicarious; tinkling; vengeful; faltering; prudential; dreadful; groundless; panicky; moderate; anticipative; veritable; pregnant; scattered; cold; paralyzing; dire; sickly; blind; constant; soul-chilling; overwhelming; unreasonable; supernatural; suppressed; simultaneous; efficient; increasing; unconvinced; ignoble.

verbs

allay—; attest to—; beleaguer by—; bend in—; blanch with—; cower in—; dispel—; entertain—; flinch in—; hesitate in—; incite—; inspire—; live in—; pale in—; palpitate in—; paralyze—; plunge into—; prostrate with—; quake in—; quiver in—; read—; retreat in—; sense—; shrink in—; shudder in—; squirm in—; tremble in—; —aggravates; —catches; —chills; —deters; —harrows; —haunts; —looms; —nauseates; —overwhelms; —petrifies; —racks; —recoils; —reigns; —seizes; —shapes itself; —springs; —stalks; —strikes; —stuns; — weighs upon.
(See dread, dismay, fear, alarm, fright, consternation.)

TERRORISM
verbs

assail—; castigate—; check—; curb—; inflict—; have recourse to—; revolt against —; subject to—; suppress—; tolerate—; —cankers; —coerces; —crushes; —dictates; —domineers; —oppresses; —overrides; — persecutes; —ravages; —reigns; —restrains; —rides roughshod; —snuffs out; —stings; —tyrannizes; —tramples; — wreaks; —yokes.
(See tyranny, intimidation.)

TERRORIST
verbs

quail before—; root out—s; —bridles; — coerces; —desecrates; —devastates; —domineers; —intimidates; —outrages; —pillages; —plunders; —ravages; —restrains; —retaliates; —sheds; —shocks; —suppresses; —tramples; —usurps.
(See anarchist, striker, revolutionist.)

TERROR-STRICKEN
adverbs

disastrously; nervously; awfully; unaccountably; unmercifully; tragically; utterly; hopelessly; curiously; helplessly; pitiably; irrecoverably; direly; sorely; unduly; grievously; naturally; inevitably; appallingly.

TERSE
adverbs
carefully; incisively; bitterly; cuttingly; sarcastically; insolently; indifferently; coldly; officially; wearily; cautiously; discreetly; formidably; rigidly; frigidly; curiously; perplexingly; unreasonably; unnecessarily; brusquely; bluntly; ominously; significantly; oddly.

TEST
adjectives
microscopic; summit; crucial; quick; fiery; acid; practical; universal; elaborate; exhaustive; innumerable (pl); conceiving; grueling; stringent; selective; triumphant; bacteriological; preliminary; careful; rigid; convincing; dangerous; supreme; experimental; actual; great; definite; discriminative; supplementary; instrumental; theological; temporal; complicated; infallible; provocative; prescribed; routine.

verbs
apply—; broaden—; cite—; concoct—; confront with—; conceive—; conduct—; —confirm—; devise—; employ—; essay—; exercise—; fail in—; flunk (colloq.)—; grapple with—; institute—; perform—; question—; rehearse—; repeat—; subject to—; submit to—; survive—; undergo—; utilize—; work out—; wrestle with—; —analyzes; —ascertains; —appraises; —authenticates; —confirms; —determines; —discloses; —dissects; —judges; —overwhelms; —reveals; —springs; —verifies; —vindicates; —weighs.
(See experiment, examination, criterion.)

TEST (v)
adverbs
scientifically; experimentally; practically; thoroughly; periodically; crucially; elaborately; exhaustively; rigidly; definitely; discriminatively; theologically; infallibly; provocatively.
(See quiz, question.)

TESTIFY (v)
adverbs
ethically; essentially; obstreperously; traitorously; flatteringly; falteringly; abundantly; mutely; unflinchingly; solemnly; unequivocally; corroboratively; irrelevantly; negatively; consequently; unanimously; unbiasedly; personally; unimpeachably; conflictingly; sincerely; incontrovertibly; emphatically.
(See assert, tell.)

TESTIMONIAL
adverbs
vividly; reminiscently; suggestively; intimately; pleasantly; flatteringly; deservedly; significantly; unforgettably; indelibly; permanently.

TESTIMONY
adjectives
solitary; jubilant; concurrent; equivocal; miraculous; honeyed; corroborative; irrelevant; remarkable; appreciative; negative; contemporary; inward; consequential; unsupported; indubitable; unanimous; abundant; silent; sufficient; unbiased; uniform; princely; magnificent; personal; willing; ample; unimpeachable; genuine; unique; conflicting; venerable; clear; professional; precious; enthusiastic; damaging; glorious; cheerful; sincere; explicit; oral; unbroken; incontrovertible; emphatic.

verbs
adduce—; analyze—; authenticate—; bear —; blast—; cite—; conform—; contradict—; corroborate—; deduce—; deliver as—; deny —; dispute—; expose—; express—; falsify —; file—; impair—; marshal—; perjure—; punctuate—; question—; record—; refute —; repudiate—; reverse—; review—; substantiate—; sustain—; uncover—; undermine—; uphold—; verify—; —authenticates; —bears; —carries weight; —conflicts; —convinces; —deludes; —differs; —discloses; —disturbs; —divulges; —floods; —reveals; —stuns; —vindicates; —warrants.
(See evidence, proof, declaration.)

TEXT
adjectives
trivial; pregnant; trite; faultless; miraculous; holy; sanguine; adopted; descriptive; infallible; authentic; expanded; obscene; widely-used; brilliant; edited.

verbs
acquaint with—; adhere to—; allude to—; analyze—; bear upon—; contemplate—; con-

tradict—; convey—; copyright—; digress from—; engross in—; explore—; express in —; follow—; heed—; peruse—; ponder—; pore over—; ransack—; regard—; reflect on—; review—; revise—; scan—; scrutinize—; supplement—; tamper with—; transform—; —depicts; —informs; —portrays.

(See matter, composition, book, story, subject, topic, theme.)

TEXTURE
adjectives
mysterious; basic; satiny; exquisite; grainy; permanent; delicate; misty; superb; soft; fine; springy; homely; unstylish; porous; rude; harmonic; historical; slippery; exclusive; crinkled; sheer; delicious; substantial; orthodox; even; fragile; smooth; shimmering; translucent; bubbled; surface; peach-like.

THANK (*v*)
adverbs
adequately; inarticulately; devoutly; cordially; heartily; formally; humbly; profusely; reverently; sincerely; appreciatively; fulsomely; haughtily; cursorily; dutifully; churlishly.
(See appreciate.)

THANKFUL
adverbs
utterly; delightedly; joyously; gratefully; unusually; particularly; singularly; exceptionally; enthusiastically; devoutly; reverently; deeply; profoundly; appreciatively; inordinately; obviously; earnestly; sincerely; truly; redundantly; unquestionably; remarkably; peculiarly.

THANKLESS
adverbs
dismally; sadly; ungraciously; grimly; heartbreakingly; utterly; bitterly; tragically; distressingly; drearily; cruelly; amazingly.

THANKS
adjectives
distracted; allegiant; humble; shy; fulsome; haughty; savage; impious; cordial; lively; dutiful; public; hearty; beggarly; silent; churlish; mumbled; half-hearted.

verbs
accept—; acknowledge—; declare—; derive —; express—; extend—; feign—; gush—;

inspire—; offer—; overflow with—; proclaim—; proffer—; render—; return—; reward with—; tender—; —beguile; —gratify.
(See gratitude, appreciation.)

THATCHED
adverbs
attractively; recently; picturesquely; admirably; quaintly; satisfactorily; inadequately; thickly; greenly; fragrantly; curiously; intricately; generously; sparsely; thinly; stingily.

THEATRE
adjectives
legitimate; elegant; stupendous; imaginary; sensational; outdoor; woody; vast; gigantic; sublime; air-cooled; immense; comfortable; pleasant; troublesome; costly.

verbs
acclaim—; convert—; flow from—; forsake —; frequent—; install in—; jam—; participate in—; reject—; renounce—; storm—; —affords; —allures; —beckons; —beguiles; —claims; —diverts; —emblazons; —fascinates; —glitters; —immortalizes; —inspires; —presents; —publicizes; —relaxes; —solaces; pack—.
(See opera, footlights, stage, drama.)

THEATRICAL
adverbs
absurdly; ridiculously; professionally; unexpectedly; skilfully; artistically; surprisingly; laughably; imposingly; impressively; pompously; bombastically; extravagantly; crassly; affectedly; crudely; showily; insincerely; gaudily; sensationally; consummately.

THEFT
verbs
accomplish—; acquire by—; apprehend for —; bewail—; charge with—; commit—; denounce—; disclose—; divulge—; forestall —; insure against—; penalize—; plan—; plot—; reveal—; uncover—; —baffles; —distresses; —impoverishes; —violates.
(See plagiarism, robbery.)

THEME
adjectives
lofty; abstract; everlasting; anti-social; pathetic; prolific; gracious; inspiring; majestic; unpleasant; paramount; inviting;

curious; earnest; amusing; unsympathetic; spiritual; characteristic; animating; exotic; weak; idle; imperial; debatable; supermundane; pastoral; poetic; varying; irksome; inexhaustible; realistic; extraneous; fruitful; favorite; rusty; dangerous; conversational; immediate; romantic; human; pregnant; copious (pl); prevailing.

verbs
allot—; alter—; clothe—; color—; comprehend—; criticize—; discard—; dramatize—; elucidate—; embellish—; embody—; evolve —; exhaust—; expatiate on—; expound—; found—; give rise to—; handle—; harp on —; interpret—; intertwine—; launch—; plunge into—; revert—; set forth—; tackle —; unfold—; variate—; vary—; ventilate —; voice—; weave—; —deals; —depicts; —dominates; —portrays; —stands upright; —symolizes.
(See text, subject, topic, idea, essay, composition.)

THEOLOGICAL
adverbs
strictly; narrowly; bigotedly; dogmatically; completely; soundly; devoutly; liberally; restrictively; obstinately; broadly; intolerantly.

THEOREM
verbs
admit—; analyze—; apply—; base on—; comprehend—; contrive—; expound—; fashion—; formulize—; ground on—; ponder —; refer to—; regard—; unfold—; —assumes; —derives from; —postulates; — proves; —solves.
(See problem, principle, law, formula.)

THEORETICAL
adverbs
obstinately; absurdly; impractically; unreasonably; infeasibly; stupidly; impracticably; impossibly; absolutely; merely; vaguely; presumably; fanatically; obscurely; entirely.

THEORIZE (v)
adverbs
philosophically; abstractly; optimistically; plausibly; psychoanalytically; experimentally; atomically; coherently; psychologically; nebulously; poetically; geometrically;

destructively; ingeniously; extravagantly; classically; absurdly; relatively; dynamically; morally; politically; economically; vaguely.
(See philosophize, talk.)

THEORY
adjectives
favorite; plausible; vibratory; psychoanalytic; experimental; undulatory; imaginative; unsound; universal; constructive; atomic; fanciful; antediluvian; coherent; unsatisfactory; elaborate; psychological; rounded; shaky; buttressed; nebulous; physical; artistic; vague; communistic; protectionist; elliptic; geometrical; evolutionary; color; straightforward; antiquated; ethical; mistaken; collision; philosophical; aesthetic; destructive; cherished; reprehensible; underlying; ingenious; deliberate; extravagant; chemical; classical; absurd; unsupported; oft-expressed; plausible; preconceived; tremendous; fantastic; secular; fossilized; coherential; radical; original; futile; abstract; relative; dynamic; irreconcilable; musical; impracticable; utopian; moral; religious; vague; suicide; economic.

verbs
abandon—; absorb in—; accept—; adopt—; advance—; antiquate—; apply—; arrive at —; authenticate—; base on—; blast—; check—; commit to—; comprehend—; conceive—; confirm—; contradict—; corroborate—; crush—; defend—; demolish—; devise—; discard—; discredit—; dismiss—; disprove—; dispute—; elaborate—; embrace —; entertain—; evolve—; exhaust—; explode—; explain—; hail—; hazard—; illustrate—; incline to—; incorporate in—; investigate—; maintain—; nurse—; outline—; propound—; refute—; reject—; relinquish —; scorn—; set forth—; speculate on—; submit—; subscribe to—; substantiate—; support—; test—; unveil—; upset—; verify —; visualize—; —s clash; —concludes; — deludes; —holds water; —opposes; —proposes; herald—.
(See idea, interpretation, hypothesis, logic.)

THERAPY
adjectives
vaccine; occupational; analytic; radio.

verbs
apply—; baffle—; devise—; expound—;

hail—; herald—; practise—; prolong—; protract—; recommend—; revolutionize—; —ameliorates; —mitigates; —palliates; —rectifies; —relieves; —restores; —resuscitates; —revives.

(See cure, treatment.)

THERMOMETER

verbs

consult—; disinfect—; grade—; immerse—in; insert—; impair—; obscure—; shake down—; shatter—; suspend—; —ascends; —deceives; —dives; —indicates; —measures; —ranges from; —records; —registers; —reveals; —rises; —skyrockets (colloq.); —soars; —testifies; —toboggans; —warns; —wavers.

(See meter, price, barometer, mercury.)

THESIS

adjectives

aesthetic; alternative; voluminous; graduate; requisite; dull; pedantic; plagiarized; useless; incompetent; startling; established; brilliant; heavily-footnoted; well-documented.

verbs

acclaim—; analyze—; applaud—; build—; compose—; criticize—; dash off—; elaborate on—; formulate—; illustrate—; peruse—; propound—; submit—; support—; sustain — ;—airs; —brings to light; —comments on; —compiles; —discusses; —dissertates; —embraces; —expatiates; —proposes; —recites; —theorizes; —treats of; —ventilates.

(See manuscript, book, composition, essay.)

THICK

adverbs

substantially; satisfactorily; acceptably; admirably; commendably; impenetrably; sufficiently; tremendously; unimaginably; distressingly; unmanageably; densely; suffocatingly; unreasonably; impassably; curiously; strangely; undesirably.

THICKET

adjectives

bowery; high; spicy; neighboring; branch; straggling; impenetrable; shady; grotesque; dripping; miniature; cool; darksome; fragrant; leafless; impervious; thorny; prickly.

verbs

conceal in—; frequent—; lop off—; nest in —; plunge into—; prune—; spring from—;

stir among—s; trim—; uproot—; —affords; —s choke; —s eclipses; —hinders; —impedes; —obscures; —restrains; —rustles; —shelters.

(See bush, jungle.)

THICK-SET

adverbs

solidly; substantially; sturdily; healthily; stoutly; remarkably; noticeably; staunchly; unusually; particularly; conspicuously; singularly; curiously; uncommonly.

THIEF

adjectives

arrant; filthy; door-waylaying; contented; self-satisfied; insect; child; low; vile; sacrilegious; adulterous; practised; slovenly; deformed; unimaginative; hard-headed; raw-boned; snaky-haired; dwarfish; injured; timorous; subtle; merciless; escaped; deft; honorable.

verbs

apprehend—; convict—; grapple with—; handcuff—; incarcerate—; interpret—; parole—; penalize—; pinion—; sentence—; —assaults; —bilks; —defrauds; —eludes; —evades; —extorts; —filches; —fleeces; —loots; —marauds; —mulcts; —palms; —pilfers; —plunders; —poaches; —purloins; —rifles; —rooks; —sacks; —strips.

(See highwayman, gangster, kidnapper, intruder, robber.)

THIEVISH

adverbs

impishly; naturally; habitually; watchfully; incorrigibly; viciously; incurably; wickedly; inveterately; loutishly; dangerously; remarkably; uncommonly; trickily; mischievously; smartly; furtively; stealthily; adroitly; dexterously; cunningly; artfully; ingeniously .

THIN

adverbs

astonishingly; extremely; excessively; tenuously; pathetically; insecurely; alarmingly; dangerously; palpably; flimsily; unsatisfactorily; terribly; sufficiently; extraordinarily; expensively; dreadfully; incredibly; conveniently.

THING

adjectives

goodly; extravagant; travailing; heterogeneous; existing; fantastic; disproportioned; blind; sharp; single; terrestrial; unutterable; fragile; brute-hooved; insatiable; living; delightful; horrible; atrocious; subtle; elusive; unstable; contemptible; inexplicable; faraway; sublunary; terrene; inanimate; glorious; good; ignoble; treacherous; dreadful; distressful; ill-used; quixotic; ridiculous; painful; groping; plaguy; exasperating; sacred; intangible; desirable; manifold; plaintive; pitiful; semi-accidental; demented; secondary; devastating; rustling; created; willful; grotesque; logical; miserable; haunting; hazardous; interesting; essential; peculiar; prudent; traditional; dark; irrelevant; manly; trivial; infinite; unusual; feathered; kingly; horrid; castaway; venomous; pesky; flimsy; improbable; external; roguish; weird; piquant; odious; powerless; hateful; indispensable; insulting; complete; sinister; heartbreaking; inferior; incongruous; squirming; unheeded; petty; mealy-mouthed; ticklish; accepted; unpardonable; incalculable; divine; blamed; mischievous; rightful; immaterial; serious; unprecedented; salutary; omnipotent; creaking; unchained; momentous; detestable; arduous; portentous; unintelligible; interminable; devilish; needful; senseless; hidden; spectral; rotten; native; fresh; priceless; fearful; extraordinary; bohemian; combustible; vast; stupid; terrible; creepy; uncommon; melancholy; valueless; gaudy; dear; vulgar; formed; precious; pinched; subordinate; ruthless; brittle; selfsame; unkind.

THINK (v)

adverbs

abstractly; sensually; despairingly; humorously; frenziedly; contemplatively; habitually; desolately; conscientiously; precisely; instinctively; vaguely; incessantly; idly; poetically; deliberately; remorsefully; constructively; grimly; anxiously; candidly; erratically; scoffingly; divergently; morosely; desultorily; contemptuously; connectedly; hysterically; rapturously; shrewdly; vehemently; dispassionately; diversely; independently; grievously; dismally; creatively; wishfully; incisively; psychoanalytically; subtly; cunningly.

(See meditate, muse.)

THINKING

adjectives

independent; ill; archaic; infantile; infer-

ior; sustained; honest; clear; differentiated; exact; thorough; inventive; original; grievous; dismal; untrammeled; conceptive; creative; wishful; accurate; incisive; psychoanalytic; spacious; subtle; cunning; symmetrical.

verbs

absorb in—; avoid—; bias—; betray—; clarify—; confuse—; discipline—; distract —; divert—; encourage—; engender—; engross in—; exercise—; foster—; give food for—; guide— ;indulge in—; influence—; lose in—; nurture—; occupy in—; pervert —; prejudice—; stimulate—; trust to—; — depresses; —digresses; —focuses on; — penetrates; —revolves about.

(See thought, contemplation, reflection, meditation.)

THIN-SKINNED

adverbs

unfortunately; delicately; inordinately; sensitively; terribly; evidently; acutely; abnormally; unusually; exceptionally; strangely; absurdly; unreasonably; noticeably; palpably; foolishly.

THIRST

adjectives

immortal; unqeunchable; insatiable; vulgar; sanctifying; hot; burning; eternal; baffled; fierce; aimless; inextinguishable; human; ardent; opulent; wholesome; reckless; inordinate; universal; pretended; exacting; unhallowed; incessant; savage; slakeless; feverish; parching; urgent; intolerable; perpetual; frantic; distressing; pallid; acquired; marked.

verbs

allay—; arouse—; assuage—; create—; experience—; extinguish—; gratify—; indulge in—; intensify—; kindle—; overcome by—; quell—; quench—; satiate—; satisfy—; sharpen—; slake—; stimulate—; subdue—; suffice—; whet—; —maddens; —plagues; —rages; —torments.

(See appetite, desire, craving, longing.)

THIRSTY

adverbs

continually; painfully; terribly; habitually; strangely; feverishly; inordinately; crazily; constitutionally; curiously; cravingly; desperately; alarmingly; inveterately; cruelly; conveniently; avidly; significantly; dreadfully; evidently; suddenly; distressingly.

THORN

adjectives
flowering; barren; fruitful; poisonous; pungent; prickly; mean; insipid; venomed; cruel; blazing; piercing; wind-warped.

verbs
bristle with—s; escape—s; impale on—; snag on—; —barbs; —s crucify; —s fence about; —s harass; —lacerates; —lancinates; —penetrates; —pierces; —plagues; —pricks; —punctures; —rends; —spikes; —s torture.
(See sting, needle, nail.)

THORNY

adverbs
painfully; extremely; dangerously; perilously; strangely; intolerably; undesirably; disagreeably; thickly; unpleasantly; unexpectedly; surprisingly; disadvantageously; inconveniently; slightly; terribly; exceptionally; unusually; unfortunately.

THOROUGHBRED

adverbs
unmistakably; conspicuously; unquestionably; warrantably; decidedly; authentically; highly; obviously; manifestly; palpably; patently; positively; absolutely; notably.

THOROUGHFARE

adjectives
dusty; celebrated; bewildering; glistening; busy; trodden; ambitious; murmurous; tumultuous.

verbs
amble down—; blockade—; clog—; clutter —; cut—; direct to—; enter—; evade—; extend—; file along—; forsake—; frequent —; intersect—; jam—; line—; litter—; obstruct—; pave—; proceed down—; promenade—; strike—; traverse—; —deviates; —swerves; —winds in and out.
(See highway, avenue, street.)

THOUGHT

adjectives
undecided; lingering; leading; angry; systematic; chiming; dream; naked; shining; horrible; flurried; importunate; lofty; numbing; forcible; effective; translucent; marvelous; golden; vagrant; fiery; poetic; habitual; self-torturing; abstract; impassioned; appalling; boundless; high; myriad; accidental; dissonant; unseasonable; restless; ripe; clever; heaven-born; speculative; divine; bitter; darting; darkling; complacent; carking; ill; longing; faithful; soft; unresisting; ennobled; metaphysical; contemplative; virtuous; inscrutable; sober; sinful; impetuous; distracting; knitted; narrow; exhilarating; trustful; teeming; pensive; empirical; moody; innermost; reproachful; contradictory; gentle; dying; odious; adventurous; holy; quiet; eclectic; invisible; wrecked; desponding; roving; hairy; engrossing; brutal; viper; dangerous; discontented; rebellious; selfsame; interesting; economic; studious; suggesting; unutterable; painful; sifted; transcending; endless; fond; thankful; satirical; sorrowful; awakened; disconnected; woundless; haunting; persistent; rash; irreverent; sorry; benighted; uncertain; wistful; morbid; anxious; oftspurned; lifting; frail; tumultuous; incestuous; constant; laborious; treasonable; grand; pleasant; heartwarming; paramount; insupportable; presumptuous; mere; mournful; monopolized; everpresent; halfformed; collateral; associated; winged; pedantic; serene; tangible; unwelcome; soaring; pacific; shattered; clamorous; gastronomic; ungovernable; lawless; rational; misanthropic; unfathomable; licentious; flattering; chaotic; slaughterous; freezing; somber; fleeting; concentrated; morbid; luminous; far-soaring; indistinct; philosophic; intimate; compelling; celebrated; vain; unquiet; intransigent; unschooled; unpractised; swift; passing; dismal; genial; hasty; likely; formless; hateful; thornless; manlike; matchless; aidless; unstained; loving; innocent; deliberate; dreamy; harsh; confused; exhaustive; **vigorous**; questioning; humiliating.

verbs
absorb in—; analyze—s; appraise—; arrest —; associate with—; awaken—; banish—; bias—s; blend—s; brood over—; center—s upon; check—; cherish—; clarify—s; collect—s; color—; comprehend—; compress—; confirm—; convey—; counterbalance—; cultivate—; dally with—; disclose—; disorder —s; distort—s; divert—s; divine—; dwell upon—; echo—s; efface—; electrify—; embody in—; endure—; engage in—; engross in—; enlarge upon—; enrich—s; entertain

—; erase—; etch—; evoke—; exclude—; execute—; expand—; expel from—s; expose—s; fashion—; formulate—s; furnish food for—; further—; fuse into—s; govern —s; grasp—; groove—s; hamper—; harbor—; immerse in—; impart—; implant—; impregnate with—; induce—; indulge in—; —; interpret—; interrupt—; isolate—; jot down—; kindle the pulse of—; lose in—; impede—; mould—; nurse—; obliterate—; occupy with—; open avenues of—; parallel —; paralyze—s; perpetuate—; preserve—; prompt—; purify—s; react upon—; read—s; recoil from—; reflect—s; reject—; restate —; reveal—; round out—s; saturate—s; scramble—s; scoff at—; shape—s; shrink from—; spit out—; stimulate—; tincture —s; toy with—; transcribe—s; tremble at —; unite—s; utter—; vent—s; vitiate—; voice—; weigh—; wrap in—; —appeals; — corrodes; —creeps into; —crosses the mind; —s crowd; —dominates; —enraptures; — enthralls; —escapes; —filters into; —flashes; —germinates; —haunts; —impresses; — intrudes; —leans toward; —leaps into; — matures; —numbs; —obsesses; —oppresses; —permeates; —perturbs; —petrifies; —possesses; —presents itself; —s ramble; —recalls; —recurs; —relapses into; —s revert to; —s revolve about; —shakes; —shifts to; —sobers; —springs from; —stings; — strikes; —suggests; —swirls up; —symbolizes; —terrifies; —torments; —uplifts; —s waver.
(See idea, concept, conception, consideration, imagination, opinion, meditation.)

THOUGHTFUL
adverbs
graciously; pleasantly; courteously; considerately; agreeably; unusually; quietly; busily; naively; unfailingly; remarkably; marvellously; practically; helpfully; prudently; providently; tactfully; sensibly; thoroughly; completely; charmingly; studiously; earnestly; gravely; seriously; judicially; deliberately; significantly; wonderfully; soberly; profoundly; deeply; dreamily; wistfully.

THOUGHTLESS
adverbs
carelessly; selfishly; dreamily; blindly; innocently; youthfully; boyishly; girlishly; blithely; unwittingly; unconsciously; cruelly; bitterly; meanly; inconsiderately; ungraciously; impolitely; discourteously; terribly; dangerously; significantly; desperately; hopelessly; unpardonably; inexcusably; remarkably; strangely; incredibly; gaily.

THRASH (v)
adverbs
brutally; soundly; wildly; cruelly; viciously; bestially; penally; fiercely; passionately.
(See beat, whip.)

THREAD
adjectives
imaginary; aimless; scarlet; dramatic; protecting; snagged; sacred; broken; crossed; delicate; ligeneous; gossamer; basting; swift-running; darkened; fluffy; wool-like; rhyming; knotted; allotted; frayed.

verbs
baste with—; cleave—; dangle by—; draw —; entwine in—; fray—; loop—; reinforce —; rend—; sever—; shear—; stitch with—; sunder—; suspend from—; tack—; weave —; wear to—.
(See cotton, fibre, string, cord.)

THREAD (v)
adverbs
skillfully; dexterously; delicately; complicatedly; involvedly; intricately; unerringly.
(See wind, weave.)

THREADBARE
adverbs
shabbily; shockingly; dreadfully; dingily; carelessly; pathetically; diaphanously; pitiably; miserably; curiously; inexplicably; mustily; desperately; cruelly; unutterably; sadly; grotesquely; fantastically; unnecessarily; parsimoniously; terribly; distressingly; painfully; humiliatingly; shamefully; nonchalantly; imperturbably.

THREAT
adjectives
invincible; silent; bawling; thundering; terrible; cloudy; stifled; obscure; serious; muttered; ruffian; dark; playful; mysterious; desperate; fearful; insolent; parting; fantastic; bitter; petty; absurd; contemporaneous; drunken; implied; private; tense; whispered; violent; sullen; tyrannous; sibylline.

verbs
aim—at; bandy—s; fling—at; fulminate—; hurl—; mutter—; retract—; resort to—s;

roar—; thunder—; thwart—; unleash—; veil—; yield to—s; —alarms; —bluffs; — browbeats; —coerces; —compromises; — cows; —daunts; —deters; —disconcerts; — distresses; —hangs over; —haunts; —indicts; —intimidates; —jeopardizes; —menaces; —obsesses; —perturbs; —preys upon; —stings; —unnerves; —weighs upon; — awes.

(See menace, oath, curse, imprecation.)

THREATEN (v)
adverbs
illimitably; direfully; darkly; terrifyingly; sinisterly; seriously; adroitly; mutteringly; sullenly; violently; tyrannically; bitterly.

(See menace, portend.)

THREATENING
adverbs
undeniably; plainly; odiously; hatefully; alarmingly; significantly; seriously; gravely; desperately; clearly; definitely; absolutely; positively; graphically; sensationally; dramatically; obviously; terribly; dreadfully; ominously; curiously; darkly; mysteriously; palpably; obscurely; vaguely; dimly; feebly; violently; truculently; absurdly; ridiculously; openly; apparently; frankly; furtively; stealthily.

THRESHOLD
adjectives
unhallowed; shadowed; sacred; glimmering; dread; lucky.

verbs
achieve—; arrive at—; attain—; bar from —; bestride—; block—; cloud—; dwell on —; enter—; file through—; flank—; gain —; huddle at—; reach—; reverence—; screen—; seek—; skirt—; strand at—; stumble over—; veil—.

(See entrance, gate, door.)

THRIFT
adjectives
prudent; extreme; constant; balanced; contented; pecuniary; incomprehensible; reasonable.

verbs
demand—; emphasize—; encourage—; enforce—; extol—; foster—; imbue with—;

implant—; inculcate—; ingrain—; necessitate—; practise—; preach—; stress—; — grudges; —infects; —redeems; —saves.

(See economy, frugality.)

THRIFTLESS
adverbs
inexcusably; habitually; naturally; inherently; strangely; picturesquely; presumably; possibly; odiously; hopelessly; incurably; incorrigibly; carelessly; thoughtlessly; improvidently; distressingly; shabbily; deplorably; lamentably; provokingly; intolerably; insufferably; vexatiously; terribly; blithely; gaily; insouciantly.

THRIFTY
adverbs
fortunately; carefully; providently; shrewdly; invariably; unfailingly; wisely; sagely; sensibly; happily; pleasantly; profitably; distinctly; moderately; judiciously; graspingly; overly; uncomfortably; ostentatiously; flourishingly; manifestly; enviably; admirably; commendably; laudably; unusually; habitually; naturally; intensely; inherently; innately; particularly; commercially; happily; luckily; thoughtfully.

THRILL
adjectives
double; distinguished; charmful; warming; renewed; shuddering; delicious; awed; amazed; intoxicating; continuous; restoring; silent; incredulous; horrible; tragic; metallic; original; sympathetic; supernal; biggest; involuntary; vicarious; nascent; poetic; gentle; unpleasant; amusing; exultant; compensating; electric; passionate; comforting; equestrian; eloquent.

verbs
cherish—; crave—; derive—from; excite—; experience—; furnish—; gain—; glow with —; inspire—; itch for—; respond to—; seek —; sense—; —enthuses (colloq.); —fires; —flushes; —impassions; —infects; — pierces; —prickles; —shoots through; — stabs; —tickles; —vibrates through; — warms; —warns; —tingles.

(See shiver, vibration, excitement, tremor.)

THRILL (v)
adverbs
blissfully; tenderly; involuntarily; vicariously; poetically; exultantly; passionately; eloquently.

(See excite, arouse.)

THRILLED

adverbs

enchantingly; interestingly; excitably; tremendously; emotionally; unutterably; remarkably; apparently; evidently; visibly; terribly; utterly; strangely; oddly; marvellously; inexpressibly; utterly; magnificently; splendidly; completely; unwontedly; apparently; immensely; thoroughly; indescribably; positively.

THRILLING

adverbs

utterly; indescribably; unusually; inexpressibly; marvellously; tremendously; superbly; magnificently; immensely; completely; unusually.

THRIVE (v)

adverbs

miraculously; bountifully; exceedingly; markedly; amazingly; prodigiously.

(See prosper, succeed.)

THRIVING

adverbs

steadily; gradually; remarkably; amazingly; indubitably; miraculously; incredibly; deservedly; unquestionably; suddenly; curiously; strangely; marvellously; splendidly; stupendously; salubriously; slowly; substantially; pleasantly; happily.

THROAT

adjectives

sinewy; blithest; dreadful; lucid; thundering; soft; impudent; thick; stretching; dazzling; unslaked; slender; infantile; sanded; sore; creamy; harsh; irritated; parched; shaggy; quivering; warbling; swan-like; exquisite; mellow; feminine; supple; scorched; swelling; brown; bursting; corded; careless; listless; myriad (pl); furry; incapable; snowy; slit; gushing; vulture; dividing; careless.

verbs

clear—; clutch—; congest—; disinfect—; dust—; ease—; emerge from—; clog—; infect—; inflame—; introduce into—; irritate —; lacerate—; lodge in—; massage—; medicate—; paint—; ram down—; ravage —; seize by—; sponge—; spray—; strain—; swab—; tickle—; ulcerate—; —contracts; —swells; —tightens.

THROB

adjectives

rhythmic; trembling; belated; harmonic; fondest; minutest; romantic; exulting; fleeing; steady; fluttering; heart; ecstatic; blissful.

THROB (v)

adverbs

palpitatingly; violently; rapidly; riotously; swiftly; visibly; fitfully; tumultuously; rhythmically; romantically; exultingly; ecstatically; blissfully.

(See pulsate, beat.)

THRONE

adjectives

angelic; heavenly; sanguine; everlasting; jeweled; conspicuous; tear-gemmed; ivory; maiden; towering; empyreal; usurped; sunlike; crystalline; venerable; unenvied; western; lofty; dynastic; sullen; sublime; tarnished; boundless; glorious; cambric; malignant; stately; universal; meridian; ancestral; rocky; peaceful; disputed; constellated; forsaken; tottering; sovereign; blissful; imperial; sapphire; moldy.

verbs

abandon—; abdicate—; accede to—; ascend aspire to—; attend—; bow before—; burnish—; covet—; defy—; depose from—; desert—; ensconce on—; establish on—; forsake—; gain—; lay claim to—; loll on—; occupy—; overthrow—; plant on—; relinquish—; renounce—; restore to—; retire from—; seek—; usurp—; vacate—; vest in —; win—; —authorizes; —empowers; —tyrannizes; seize—.

(See kingdom, kingship, power, sovereignty, seat, chair.)

THRONG

adjectives

trampling; demoniac; well-dressed; countless (pl); burdened; motley; shadowy; grateful; tumultuous; ragged; threadbare; accusing; ill-bred; billowy; worshipping; sinless; unreposing; innumerable (pl); riotous; fearful; eager; thoughtless; seething; lean; exultant; hungry; starving; ghostly; angelic; excited; expectant; blood-washed; terror-stricken; beauteous; bewinged; adoring; laughing; chattering; moveless; trembling; crushed-down; spectral; listening; sceptered; invisible; festal; armed; emotional; spending; foolish; shining; prostrate; immense; base; impish; multitudinous; bestial; pressing; teeming; shoeless; struggling; shaggy; ravenous; unhealthy; edifying; toiling; whirling; amorous; moiling.

verbs
disband—; disperse—; muster—; pacify—; plunge through—; provoke—; rejoin—; scatter—; silence—; slip through—; —assembles; —concentrates; —clamors; —converges on; —deluges; —eddies 'round; —flocks; —masses; —mills about; —mobs; —presses; —swarms; —focuses on.
(See mob, crowd, multitude.)

THRONG (v)
adverbs
tumultuously; ceaselessly; **demoniacally;** countlessly; innumerably; seethingly, hungrily; expectantly; multitudinously; incongruously; bestially; moilingly .
(See swarm, congregate.)

THROW (v)
adverbs
violently; recklessly; haughtily; deliberately; dejectedly; bodily; savagely; profligately; passionately; lavishly; systematically; significantly; defiantly; adroitly.
(See hurl, heave.)

THRUSH
verbs
—bodes; —cheers; —choruses; —gushes; —hymns; —moults; —pipes; —pours forth; —retires; —trills.
(See bird.)

THRUST
adjectives
vain; repeated (pl); vital; prompt; final; shrewd-planned; unlikely; sore; tireless; unlucky.

THRUST (v)
adverbs
impudently; impatiently; brutally; determinedly; agilely; obtrusively; conspicuously; methodically; resolutely; demurely; belligerently; rudely; wrathfully.
(See stab, stick.)

THUMB
adjectives
black; shuffling; peaked; vigorous; wadded; solitary; broken; waving; fatty.

verbs
bind—; brush with—; crush—; deform—; dislocate—; extend—; flex—; knead with —s; lacerate—; manipulate—; sever—; sprain—; twiddle—s; —gropes; —throbs.
(See finger.)

THUMP (v)
adverbs
furiously; emphatically; repetitiously; impatiently; indignantly; thunderously; powerfully; dramatically.
(See beat, hit.)

THUNDER
adjectives
howling; blasting; intermittent; interrupted; heavy; frightful; thrilling; melodious; mountain; angry; swarthy; sullen; editorial; muttering; branding; oracular; suspended; flameless; ominous; harmless; rumbling; direful; serious; muffled; wrathful; lounging; artillery; hateful; clothed; incessant; threatening; stage; earthly; sweet; rattling; brazen; volleying.

verbs
brave—; shoot forth—; —blusters; —booms; —claps; —crashes; —deafens; —detonates; —dins; —discords; —disturbs; —echoes; —fulminates; —menaces; —petrifies; —pierces; —rattles; —rends;; —reverberates; —roars; —rolls; —rumbles; —shatters; —shocks; —splits; —startles; —threatens; —volleys.
(See lightning, detonation, noise, discharge, report, explosion.)

THUNDER (v)
adverbs
appallingly; violently; ominously; tremendously; terrifically; frightfully; rumblingly; muffledly; wrathfully; threateningly; repeatedly; awesomely.
(See crash, resound.)

THUNDEROUS
adverbs
ominously; positively; portentously; triumphantly; enthusiastically; acclaimingly; mutinously; threateningly; significantly; swellingly; curiously; strangely; deafeningly; splendidly; loyally.

THWART (v)
adverbs
effectually; diligently; successfully; tempo-

rarily; discouragingly; righteously.
(See defeat, baffle.)

THWARTED
adverbs
dangerously; hopelessly; suddenly; painfully; distressingly; unfairly; meanly; odiously; hatefully; cruelly; desperately; curiously; strangely; inscrutably; adroitly; maliciously; cleverly; ingeniously; artfully; craftily; shrewdly; inexplicably; stealthily; quietly; successfully; helplessly; unaccountably; maliciously; dreadfully; discouragingly.

TICKER-TAPE
verbs
festoon with—; insert—; perforate—; read —; shower with—; stabilize—; steady—; —announces; —clutters; —communicates with; —fluctuates; —indicates; —informs; —lists; —litters; —notifies; —oscillates; — quotes; —records; —transmits; —unreels; —vacillates.

TICKET
verbs
arm with—; counterfeit—s; discard—; dispense—s; enumerate—s; grant—; hawk—s; purchase—; register—s; speculate on—s; stamp—s; tag with—s; —admits; —authorizes; —betokens; —checks; —enables; — evidences; —informs; —indicates; —labels; —permits; —testifies to; —vouchsafes.
(See ballot, coupon, label, permit, certificate.)

TICKLE (v)
adverbs
humorously; boisterously; playfully; teasingly; verbally; rudely; roughly; clownishly.
(See tease.)

TICKLED
adverbs
roguishly; mischievously; merrily; enormously; gleefully; ridiculously; obviously; visibly; prankishly; jubilantly; exceedingly; inordinately; wickedly; naughtily; amazingly.

TIDE
adjectives
undulating; brimming; ebbing; insurging; aerial; eventful; boundless (pl); multitudinous (pl); human; restless; falling; arrested; waveless; silent; terrible; mysterious; tossing; joyous; sidereal; ancient; surging; chafing; reactionary; capricious; passionate; forward-flowing; sultry; confused; overwhelming; subsiding; tumultuous; headlong; swollen; rippling; green-blue; conflicting; theologic; over-running; hastening; primal; refluent; glassy; brimful; rising; whelming; billowing; retiring; fickle; pellucid; foaming; interminable; incoming; trackless; latent; lulling; adverse; patriotic; sucking; angry; roving; golden; hurrying; flooding; perennial; contrary; westering; crystal; turbid; dusty-gray; misty; river; silvery; summer; deep-breathing; sliding; treacherous; rhythmic.

verbs
battle with—; breast—; drift with—; harness—; oppose—; stem—; swim with—; yield to—; —crawls out; —deluges; —ebbs; —fluctuates; —inundates; —invades; — moans; —overtakes; —recedes; —regresses; —retires; —retreats; —roars; —swamps; —swells; —throbs; —wanes; —washes; — withdraws.
(See flow, flood, current.)

TIDINGS
adjectives
dismal; bad; joyful; unpleasant; frightful; inarticulate; glad; blissful; unimpeded; evil; gracious; accurate; astonishing; startling; heart-stirring; swift; hopeless.

TIDY
adverbs
scrupulously; painfully; terribly; carefully; unwontedly; unusually; dreadfully; spotlessly; remarkably; unexpectedly; suddenly; attractively; invitingly; pleasantly; agreeably; sufficiently; cosily; alluringly; distressingly; starkly; oppressively; miraculously; incredibly.

TIE
adjectives
subtle; weakened; cunning; common; primary; senseless; sordid; lifelong; mysterious; tenderest; singular; indissoluble; deep; domestic; silken; conjugal; sacred; foppish; unsubstantial; frail.

TIE (v)
adverbs
securely; fantastically; heroically; intri-

cately; involvedly; complicatedly; firmly; cunningly; indissolubly.
(See fasten, bind.)

TIER
adjectives
ascending; graceful; proportioned; blazing.

TIES
verbs
acknowledge—; adhere to—; cement—; cherish—; dissolve—; forsake—; knit—; preserve—; rend—; renounce—; saddle with—; sever—; shatter—; strain—; sunder —; treasure—; —affiliate; —bind; — couple; —fetter; —link; —obligate; — pledge; —restrain; —restrict; —shackle; — weaken.
(See bond, band, obligation.)

TIFF
adjectives
domestic; daily; lifelong; hateful; unnerving.

TIGER
adjectives
tawny; brindled; enraged; pouncing; man-eating; mangled; shrinking; clawing; murderous; lightning-fast; muscled; vicious; cunning; lunging; circling; snapping; growling; leaping; skulking; furious; mighty; teeth-baring; ferocious; creeping; catapulting; royal; determined; striped; spotted; fractious; frenzied; deadly; Sumatra; sabre-toothed; swift; slinking; villainous; demoniac; coughing; treacherous; cantering.

verbs
cage—; exterminate—s; infuriate—; lash—; perform with—s; train—; —climb; — crouches; —depredates; —devours; — haunts; —s infest; —lashes out at; — maims; —marauds; —mauls; —mews; — paws; —preys; —purrs; —rages; —ravages; —rends; —roars; —romps; —seizes; —slithers along the path; —snarls; — springs; —tears.
(See animal, lion, leopard.)

TIGERISH
adverbs
vaguely; furtively; fawningly; warily; vigilantly; fearsomely; attractively; slinkingly; alluringly; seductively; alarmingly; dangerously; contemptibly; slinkily; fiercely; per- ceptibly; indubitably; unmistakably; fatally; indescribably; inexpressibly; inescapably; undeniably.

TIGHT
adverbs
uncomfortably; sufficiently; unfortunately; fatally; terribly; occasionally; dreadfully; happily; blithely; completely; painfully; odiously; distressingly; gloriously; blissfully; permanently; momentarily; disgracefully; shamefully; strangely; unusually; ridiculously; dangerously; injuriously; revealingly; satisfactorily.

TIGHTEN (v)
adverbs
gradually; partially; remorselessly; lovingly; passionately; abruptly; insidiously; subtly.
(See grip, squeeze.)

TIGHTS
verbs
accoutre in—; array in—; attire in—; bare —; cavort in—; divest of—; doff—; don—; equip with—; fray—; spangle—; strip of —; tatter—; vest in—; —display; —enable; —expose; —facilitate.
(See costume, uniform, garment.)

TILT (v)
adverbs
awkwardly; negligently; jauntily; nonchalantly; precariously.
(See teeter, sway.)

TIMBER
adjectives
shaky; massive; long-used; slashed; marketable; reverberating; rotten; superb; fringing; graceful; useful.

verbs
avail oneself of—; blast—; conserve—; debark—; fell—; knot—; level—; market—; preserve—; process—; provide—; raze—; reinforce—; strip of—; treat—; value—; —decays; —erodes; —jams; —rots.
(See log, beam, wood.)

TIMBERED
adverbs
heavily; profitably; densely; wisely; fortunately; well; luckily; thickly; amazingly; sparsely; thinly; neglibly; valuably; reputedly; allegedly; immensely.

adjectives
valuable; sufficient; troublous; inexpedient; curious; happy; righteous; irresponsible; unconscionable; precious; primitive; arduous; historic; auspicious; predestined; patristic; solemn; evil; official; tolerating; troubled; reasonable; unfit; glorious; fantastic; thoughtless; later; frivolous; rococo; dark; considerable; former; palmy; unsettled; priceless; injurious; appointed; bygone; substantial; fruitful; halcyon; impatient; fleeting; ample; boundless; descending; civilized; recorded; intervening; trying; woeful; sorry; appreciable; casting; measurable; degenerate; fittest; unseasonable; stormy; mutual; lessened; uneasy; turbulent; indefinite; despicable; unquiet; factious; immemorial; sacred; fated; apostolic; moral; periodic; unused; record-breaking; virtuous; distracted; tuning; affirmed; chaotic; opportune; fitting; abundant; corroding; pairing; exciting; unemployed; sultry; costly; millennium; propitious; rough-and-tumble; subversive; potential; scented; calamitous; gleaning; leisure; unborn; melodious; charitable; barbarous; anxious; flowering; ridiculous; blissful; squalid; dicing; administrative; invaluable; mournful; pleasant; specified; remote; pointed; abysmal; thin-faced; terrible; discouraging; feudal; stirring; naughty; restless; statutory; perilous; altered; conquering; shadowed; accustomed; unhallowed; limited; envious; significant; awful; intermediate; various (pl); classic; inconvenient; broadening; inevitable; breathing; regenerated; prehistoric; equinoctial; scriptural; scant; dusky; ill-devouring; portentous; assigned; limited; disorderly; revolutionary; unaccustomed; hasty; balmy; prosperous; guilty; growing; distant; profitable; subsequent; enormous; rippling; amphibious; short; swift-footed; regretted; spacious; cloudless; discouraging; stormy; unfavorable; fairy; future; due; consumed; emotional.

verbs
abide—; allot—; begrudge—; beguile—; bide for—; budget—; calculate—; conserve —; consume—; devote—to; devour—; endure—; engross—; exhaust—; fritter away —; indicate—; inform of—; lack—; lavish —on; limit—; mark—; measure—; prolong —; protract—; record—; reveal in—; spare —; squander—; "stall for"—; tarry for—;

terminate—; while away—; —advances; —approaches; —blots out; —discloses; —disintegrates; —dissolves; —dwindles; —elapses; —expires; —fades; —flies; —flits; —glides on; —heals; —marches on; —matures; —mellows; —nears; —outmodes; —presses; —races; —ripens; —recedes; —rolls around; —rolls back; —shadows; —tempers; —unfolds; —vanishes; —vindicates; —wanes; —withers.

(See interval, hour, leisure, month, instant, moment, day.)

TIMED

adverbs
opportunely; wisely; seasonably; wonderfully; fatally; precisely; meticulously; exactly; uncannily; viciously; brutally; heinously; tragically; carefully; scientifically; automatically; cautiously; cleverly; auspiciously; apparently; murderously; punctiliously; promptly; considerately; thoughtfully; graciously; obviously.

TIMELY

adverbs
pleasantly; fortunately; altogether; unusually; particularly; singularly; providentially; remarkably; miraculously; marvellously; curiously; felicitously; wonderfully.

TIMID

adverbs
modestly; constitutionally; shyly; bashfully; groundlessly; anxiously; deliciously; unreasonably; unwontedly; tremulously; childishly; nervously; foolishly; incredibly; naturally; vaguely; momentarily; secretly; excessively; strangely; distressingly; incomprehensibly; temperamentally; helplessly; hopelessly; unaccountably; uneasily; queerly; curiously; genuinely; unaffectedly; significantly.

TIMIDITY

adjectives
modest; early; scrupulous; constitutional; ill-grounded; shy; bashful; refined; anxious; delicious; skulking; irrational; sententious; unwonted; tremulous.

verbs
conceal—; conquer—; cower in—; despise —; feign—; flinch in—; induce—; inspire —; master—; mock—; overcome—; pretend —; prevail over—; quail in—; retire in—; reveal—; simulate—; smite with—; suffer

—; —abashes; —besets; —cows; —daunts; —deters; —dismays; —distresses; —haunts; —overwhelms; —petrifies.

(See cowardice, bashfulness, shyness, modesty, fear.)

TIMOROUS
adverbs
shyly; bashfully; self-consciously; modestly; guiltily; sheepishly; naturally; inherently; merely; habitually; usually; foolishly; sadly; pitiably; miserably; unfortunately; childishly; wretchedly; unreasonably; needlessly; strangely; oddly; curiously; inexplicably; unaccountably; ridiculously; positively; actually.

TINGE
adjectives
sunset; bright; silky-green; confidential; pantheistic; mauve; transient; sanguinary; abundant; slight.

TINGE (v)
adverbs
brilliantly; markedly; slightly; occasionally; deeply; transiently; luridly.
(See imbue, color.)

TINKER
adjectives
itinerant; mean; preaching; strong.

TINKLE
adjectives
inviting; pleasant; cheery; liquid; laughing; lilting.

TINNY
adverbs
unpleasantly; inexcusably; unacceptably; disagreeably; curiously; raucously; intolerably; strangely; unpalatably; tawdrily.

TINT
adjectives
vivid; dismal; acquainted; delicate; pearly; exquisite; unobtrusive; shifting; somber; prophetic; smoky; rainbowed; combative; bloody; delicate; gathering; changing; positive; beauteous; prismatic; prevailing; general; brilliant; mellow; harmonious; tender; original.

TINT (v)
adverbs
delicately; gracefully; richly; vividly; somberly; beauteously; prismatically; brilliantly; harmoniously; mellowly.
(See tinge, color.)

TINY
adverbs
unbelievably; incredibly; infinitesimally; microscopically; minutely; extremely; remarkably; actually; marvelously; positively; dwarfishly; insignificantly; elfishly; fantastically; unimaginably; grotesquely; terribly.

TIP
verbs
cap—; crown—; daub on—; gild—; impale on—; veneer—; whet—; —bristles; —penetrates; —pierces; —projects; —protrudes; —punctures; —stabs.
(See edge, point.)

TIPSY
adverbs
gloriously; shamefully; helplessly; comically; sadly; alarmingly; insecurely; happily; foolishly; comically; ridiculously; laughably; ludicrously; grossly; crassly; offensively; disagreeably; unpleasantly; hopelessly; inordinately; slightly; extremely; terribly; continually; occasionally; definitely; indubitably; suddenly; inexplicably; undeniably; hilariously; noisily; boisterously; uproariously; sullenly.

TIRADE
adjectives
jeering; tedious; patriotic; shrill; positive; cumulative; belated; bitter; lengthy.

verbs
declaim in—; deliver—; fulminate—; halt —; launch—; pour out—; prolong—; rant —; recite—; silence—; spout—; utter—; — anathematizes; —castigates; —censors; — chastises; —declaims; —defames; —denounces; —deprecates; —disparages; —excoriates; —execrates; —harangues; —inveighs against; —lampoons; —lashes; — reprimands; —reproaches; —reproves; — thunders.
(See diatribe, scolding, invective, speech.)

TIRE

adjectives

spare; pneumatic; first; strong; deflated; retreaded; worn; slippery; useless.

verbs

deflate—; depress—; dilate—; distend—; fray—; gauge—; imbed in—; inflate—; mount on—s; perforate—; pierce—; pump —; puncture—; retread—; scrape—; value —; vulcanize—; —erodes; —grazes; — pads; —preserves; —skids.

TIRE (v)

adverbs

acutely; rapidly; abnormally; sadly; noticably; patently.

(See exhaust, bore.)

TIRESOME

adverbs

pedantically; monotonously; gushingly; garrulously; dully; uninterestingly; prosaically; long-windedly; endlessly; preachily; tediously; irksomely; boresomely; intolerably; unpleasantly; harmlessly; disagreeably; undeniably; terribly; needlessly; dreadfully; unfortunately; abominably; disgustingly; desperately; droningly.

TIRING

adverbs

unexpectedly; unwittingly; uncommonly; extraordinarily; dangerously; extremely; unintentionally; terribly; dreadfully; unwontedly; sadly; unfortunately; strangely; curiously; oddly; unnecessarily; needlessly; distressingly; painfully; obviously; palpably; inconsiderately; unaccountably; terrifically; grievously; unwarrantably; pitifully; seriously; oppressively; profoundly; inordinately.

TISSUE

adjectives

superficial; rich; silver; muscular; dermatoid; vegetable; damaged; disposable; cellular; social; desensitized; adipose; glandular; fibrous; abundant; innermost; plaited; excess; transpicuous; siliceous.

verbs

abscess—; canker—; consume—; cramp—; crush—; curette away—; desiccate—; destroy—; distend—; excise—; graft—; harden—; incise—; infect—; inflame—; inject into—; invade—; involve—; knead—; massage—; mould—; nourish—; regenerate

—; support—; suture—; transplant—; —degenerates; —infiltrates; —languishes; —relaxes; —shrivels; —wastes; —withers.

TITANIC

adverbs

monstrously; tremendously; unbelievably; unimaginably; superbly; magnificently; gloriously; majestically; overwhelmingly; gorgeously; stupendously; inconceivably; cumbersomely; incomparably; unsurpassably.

TITLE

adjectives

honorary; precarious; elusive; religious; fabulous; trumped-up; bombastic; imposing; soul-stirring; vague; successive (pl); preliminary; forfeited; neglected; optimistic; seductive; pompous; impressive; shrill; legitimist; grotesque; attractive; hereditary; quaint; numerous (pl); clerical; imperial; distinguishing; illogical; vainglorious; appertinent; fantastic; ingenious; significant; ironic; prescriptive; smoothing; subscriptive; whimsical; homely; honorable; resounding; worse; dubious; newly-obtained; suggestive.

verbs

assume—; award—; bear—; claim—; covet —; decorate with—; defile—; degrade—; disparage—; dub with—; earn—; inherit—; invent—; renounce—; respect—; retain—; revere—; surrender—; underline—; usurp —; —awes; —connotes; —cows; —distinguishes; —epitomizes; —implies; —impresses; —misleads; —symbolizes; —signifies; —veils.

(See name, degree, nickname, rank.)

TITLED

adverbs

nobly; grandly; gloriously; proudly; royally; imperially; austerely; ecclesiastically; divinely; piously; devoutly; legitimately; officially; absurdly; bombastically; ridiculously; ironically; truly; self-; vainly; foolishly; unreasonably; realistically; popularly; ignominously; jeeringly; affectionately; lovingly; derisively; comically; shamefully.

TITTER

adjectives

slight; shamefaced; electric; damaging; explosive.

adverbs

affectedly; irrepressibly; involuntarily; girlishly; unsophisticatedly; explosively; naively; rudely; comically; hysterically; affectedly; coyly.

(See laugh, giggle.)

TOAD

adjectives

loathed; soft; sizable; well-fed; blinking;
ugly; venomous; bucolic.

verbs

infest with —s; —burrows; —s bury themselves; —creeps; —croaks; —emits a noise;
—hibernates; —hops; —jumps; —leaps; —
metamorphoses; —plagues; —secretes; —
springs; —squats; —vaults.

TOAST

adjectives

complimentary; appropriate; enthusiastic;
celebrated; tasty; scorching; crisp; burned;
crackling; crunching.

verbs

cheer—; drink—; hail—; join in—; propose
—; rejoice in—; suggest—; utter—; voice
—; acclaims—; —commemorates; —compliments; —eulogizes; —extols; —flatters; —
glorifies; —hallows; —honors; —pledges;
—solemnizes.

(See tribute, praise, sentiment, bread.)

TOAST (v)

adverbs

convivially; appropriately; crisply; crackl-
ingly; victoriously; fraternally; boisterously.

(See congratulate, celebrate.)

TOBACCO

adjectives

aromatic; heavy; suggestive; coarse.

verbs

abhor—; abstain from—; addict to—; age
—; auction—; blend —s; consume—; crave
—; cross —s; cultivate—; cure—; denicoti-
nize—; ferment—; filter—; grade—; hunger
for—; inhale—; market—; mellow—; mentholize—; moisten—; plug—; powder—;
purvey—; ripen—; roast—; scent—; store
—; toast—; yearn for—; —braces; —calms;
—clouds; —deteriorates; —discolors; —
dulls; —impairs; —irritates; —lifts; —ma-

tures; —ravages; —reeks; —repels; —
soothes; —steadies; —stunts; —tempts; —
tranquillizes; —undermines; —vitiates.

TOE

adjectives

jagged; elfin; pliant; superfluous; contemptuous; shuffling; blunt; nimble; outraged;
fantastic; dance-weary; festered; infected.

verbs

amputate—; bare—; brace—; bruise—;
cramp—; crush—; dance on—; deform—;
dislocate—; distort—; flex—; fracture—;
pad—; sever—; skip on —s; splint—; stub
—; teeter on—; web—; —pinches; —projects; —protrudes.

TOIL

adjectives

precarious; unhonored; manly; unrequited;
exhausting; terrible; profitable; wholesome;
philanthropic; unremitting; irksome; contented; hideous; pernicious; happy; filthy;
sporadic; wasting; eager; smiling; rugged;
blundering; griping; unceasing; earnest;
delicious; fragrant; loving; arduous; sickening; desperate; earthly; successful; anxious; double; brave; stormy; noble; honest;
meridian; ferocious; sultry; humble; squalid; elaborate; unrepaid; spasmodic; wasting; sullen; drudging; captive; patient;
unhallowed; benignant; productive; fatiguing; congenial; ingenious; unusual; incessant; pernicious; sportive.

verbs

abate—; achieve by—; amass by—; cease—;
consume in—; delight in—; ease—; hallow
—; mitigate—; necessitate—; obviate—;
plunge into—; relax—; reward—; shirk—;
slacken—; —exhausts; —fags; —fatigues;
—jades; —strains; —taxes; —wearies.

(See labor, drudgery, work, effort.)

TOIL (v)

adverbs

patiently; laboriously; ceaselessly; uncomplainingly; manfully; bodily; stealthily;
painfully; assiduously; conscientiously; vigorously; sickeningly; precariously; exhaustingly; philanthropically; irksomely; incessantly; arduously; fatiguingly; perniciously.

(See work, labor.)

adjectives
self-sufficient; patient; possessionless; laborious.

adjectives
elaborate; hasty; unfinished; hurried.

adverbs
terribly; dreadfully; undesirably; inescapably; unavoidably; brutally; cruelly; bitterly; exhaustingly; horribly; curiously; inordinately; extremely; unexpectedly; shockingly; miserably; wretchedly; shamefully; monotonously; tediously.

adverbs
terribly; pathetically; significantly; apparently; palpably; extremely; unusually; miserably; obviously; evidently; wretchedly; lamentably; unaccountably; unexpectedly; deplorably; pitiably; inexcusably; remarkably; unmistakably; utterly.

adjectives
unmistakable; especial; tiniest; expressive; personal; unanimous; crushing; unique; singular; mystic; sensible; glorious; visible; palpable; bounteous; beauteous; outward; tremendous; sunny; amorous; leaden; irritating; meaningful.

adverbs
scarcely; barely; fairly; apparently; easily; eventually; finally; gradually; evidently; hardly; actually.

adjectives
kindly; legal; habitual; courteous; lazy; contemptuous; scientific; moral; apathetic; easygoing; amused; mischievous; indolent; gentle.

verbs
acclaim—; achieve—; advocate—; bear with —; breed—; cherish—; commend—; exemplify—; exhort—; foster—; further—; lack—; nurture—; preach—; preserve—; regard with—; sustain—; temper with—; —ameliorates; —pervades.
(See charity, forbearance, kindness, benevolence.)

adverbs
sensibly; generously; broadly; wisely; discreetly; diplomatically; tactfully; overly; indulgently; reasonably; moderately; unusually; inordinately; unwisely; charitably; foolishly; rabidly; patiently; calmly; imperturbably; quietly; serenely; easily; mildly; sagely; marvellously; magnanimously; splendidly.

adverbs
eternally; consciously; patiently; magnanimously; generously; legally; courteously; lazily; contemptuously; morally; indolently; gently.
(See endure, permit.)

adjectives
universal; further; religious; generous; absolute; quiet; superficial; indifferent; continued.

adjectives
devilish; patient; terrible; enormous; death; preposterous.

verbs
assess—; augment—; bear—; charge—; deflate—; demand—; enforce—; exact—; fix —; levy—; quote—; rate—; set—; take—; subject to—; —burdens; —enables; —mounts; —taxes; —yields.
(See price, payment, tap.)

adverbs
solemnly; mournfully; dismally; repetitiously; funereally; fatally; heavily; vibrantly.
(See ring, clang.)

adjectives
rock-hewn; sumptuous; brazen; dateless; neglected; wandering; ancestral; vacant; gilded; traditional; crumbling; antenatal; interdicted; indefinable; fin-winged; flowering; melancholy; untimely; fiery; ponderous; lingering; wintry; vast; impregnable; ferocious; watery; murmurous; slender; unlamented; reverend; drear; somber; miry.

verbs
adorn—; bar—; consign to—; deface—; de-

file—; delve in—; desecrate—; disinter from —; erect—; explore—; guard—; haunt—; illuminate—; incarcerate in—; inter in—; mould in—; patrol—; register upon—; rest in—; seal—; shadow—; unearth—; wreath —; —depresses; —envelops; —muffles; — receives; —reeks; —shrouds; —yields up. (See shrine, grave, monument.)

TOMB-LIKE

adverbs

coldly; horribly; unbearably; supernaturally; terribly; fearfully; wretchedly; intolerably; frighteningly; appallingly; gruesomely; grimly; depressingly; dispiritingly; dismally; woefully; forbiddingly; curiously; grotesquely; fantastically.

TOME

verbs

compose—; concoct—; criticize—; dash off —; deliver—; immortalize—; inscribe—; pen—; polish—; pour forth—; publish—; wade through—; —commemorates; —eulogizes; —honors; —soliloquizes; —treats.

(See book, volume.)

TONE

adjectives

faltering; contemptuous; deprecating; soothing; passive; clear; angelic; deep-strung; provocative; milder; customary; diverse (pl); rueful; answering; solitary; frightened; braggart; ethereal; saddened; dearest; varying (pl); suggestive; victory; vindictive; low; lover-like; gentlest; confidential; sweet; gracious; joyous; regretful; rich; smothered; imperative; sanctimonious; moral; elastic; agitated; startled; careless; romantic; senatorial; breathless; pleading; pitiful; conciliatory; anguished; dictatorial; pastel; dominant; ringing; wailing; dark; bright; intermediate; marine; modified; colorful; didactic; inward; free; callous; hearty; beautiful; unceremonious; unconscious; boisterous; sullen; timid; flippant; blunt; nasal; moral; beseeching; shapeless; mean; menacing; soft; stentorian; confident; savage; faltering; preoccupied; child-like; earnest; imperious; dispassionate; conversational; scorching; intimate; sarcastic; threatening; soul-stirring; exulting; solemn; yearning; vibrating; impatient; luscious; tremulous; philosophic; supercilious; enamored; altered; crimson; distressful; amicable; honeyed; cathedral; ironical; displeasing; monotonous; ordinary; listless; ag-

gressive; ivory; melodious; melting; tranquil; caressing; intriguing; half-pensive; indescribable; transient; well-guarded; promiscuous; martial; subdued; authoritative; maniac; unctuous; contrasting; assured; measured; despairing; archaic; mournful; whining; composite; paternal; drawling; bellicose; officer-like; ruminative; piping; metallic; bantering; incongruous; well-remembered; fretful; exquisite; hollow; vigorous; vexed; animated; witching; clarion; constituent; agonized; eager; healthy; complimentary; brisk; audible; penetrating; subduing; dreamy; piqued; apologetic; fluttering; caustic; proper; courteous; argumentative; nauseated; good-humored; haunting; dulcet; wonted; general; imperious; abominable; doubtful; abrupt; terrified; wheedling; innocent; considerable; tranquil; scoffing; thin; emphatic; sepulchral; liquid; silvery; jocular; harmonious; insolent; condescending; wistful; suppressed; fundamental; reflective; blustering; reproachful; controversial; burnt; unworldly; respectful; precious; lachrymose; unemotional; hungry; revolutionary; convinced; indifferent; untrammeled; strong; expostulating; insinuating; stately; inadequate; feeble; ever-pealing; grown-up; reminiscent; determined; musing; thoughtful; unmusical; exotic; mimic; professional; lugubrious; mordant; suppressed; mollified; frosted.

verbs

accentuate—; adopt—; alter—; amplify—; chasten—; deepen—; elevate—; falsify—; govern—; impart—; inflect—; lack—; lend —; lower—; magnify—; mimic—; modulate—; muffle—; silence—; strengthen—; subdue—; utter—; —betrays; —chastises; — elevates; —expresses; —harmonizes; —indicates; —irritates; —manifests; —mocks; —nettles; —predominates; —reproaches; — reproves; —reveals; —reverberates; —vibrates.

(See note, sound.)

TONGUE

adjectives

serpent; tuneful; partial; piercing; hissing; envious; forked; golden; indignant; wagging; moistened; dead; prattling; cloven; wily; complaining; lambent; gluttonous; foamless; evil; caustic; raise; immortal; furred; feverish; quivering; rapid; dominant; slick; leaping; unbound; classic; calumnious; lolling; earnest; unintelligible; gossiping; faltering; shrewish; gentle; polished; carping; cautious; boyish; halting; biting; coated; hasty; scoffing; silent; slurring; fervent; perfidious; flattering; finedividing; ancient; glowing; base; boundless; romancing; casual; heedless; proper; multitudinous (pl); uncivilized; oily; bitter; unbridled; joyous; unwilling; iron; soul-subduing; persuasive; slanderous; malicious; double; nimble; national; candied; pleading; discreet; lamenting; droning; viperish; railing; forbidden; woe-wearied; facile; flexible; foul; censorious; unintelligible; ill; lying; pliant; learned; modern; pioneer; glib; railing; nerveless; boastful; unknowable; brazen; liquid; soothing; slippery; stammering; scorched; teasing; glowing; shallow; whispering; pleasing; immortal; cynical; masterful; captious; gentle; guileless; inestimable; woodland; mother; selfsame.

adjectives
blister—; bridle—; candy—; chafe—; clip cluck—; curb—; discipline—; envenom—; examine—; fur—; furrow—; hold—; hush —; hypnotize—; inflame—; insert—; irritate—; lap with—; loosen—; mute—; paralyze—; provoke—; roll off—; sever—; silence—; smack—; stifle—; still—; suppress —; swab—; tempt—; tickle—; tie—; train —; wag—; —charms; —cleaves to; — falters; —laps; —lashes; —licks; —moistens; —projects; —protrudes; —rasps; — relishes; —savors; —slanders; —slips; — traduces; —voices; —wounds.

TONGUE-TIED
adverbs
deplorably; congenitally; lamentably; unfortunately; pitiably; pathetically; wretchedly; miserably; clumsily; awkwardly; unluckily; embarrassingly; shockingly; uncomfortably; bashfully; shyly; timidly; self-consciously; guiltily; curiously; unwontedly; unusually; peculiarly; strangely; unaccountably; suddenly; apparently.

TONIC
adjectives
valuable; intellectual; antiseptic; exhilarating; bracing; useful; provocative; bitter; healthful; mental; excellent.

verbs
addict to—s; administer—; consume—; dose

with—; prescribe—; recommend—; —bolsters; —builds up; —enriches; —nauseates; —purges; —reanimates; —rejuvenates; — renews; —renovates; —restores; —resuscitates; —revivifies; —stimulates.
(See laxative, medicine, wine.)

TONIC
adverbs
refreshingly; wholesomely; definitely; effectively; really; dependably; reliably; assuredly; strongly; splendidly; invigoratingly; desirably; noticeably; evidently; positively; indubitably; admirably; wonderfully; commendably; marvellously; miraculously; incredibly; unexpectedly; delightfully; satisfactorily; remarkably; particularly .

TONSILS
verbs
apply to—; attack—; coat—; disease—; drain—; enlarge—; enucleate—; excite—; extract—; infect—; inflame—; invade—; swab—; swell—; —envenom; —filter; — indicate; —poison; —project; —suppurate; —ulcerate; paint—; scrutinize—; sever—; shrink—.

TOOL
adjectives
unconscious; passive; obedient; legitimate; vital; tempered; shaped; dexterous; edged; brittle; trenchant; unaccustomed; ready; obsolete; congenial; subservient; exquisite; keen.

verbs
apply—; devise—; employ—; enlist—; fashion—; guide—; hew with—; manipulate—; mechanize—; operate—; skill with—; stamp —; strain—; tax—; utilize—; wield—; — bevels; —bores; —eases; —facilitates; — lightens; —smooths.
(See instrument, apparatus, machine.)

TOOLING
adjectives
vigorous; firm; dazzling.

TOOTH
adjectives
rankling; determined; raging; rotten; cavity-eaten; filled; aching; film-covered; sparkling; false; broken; jagged.

verbs
(See teeth.)

TOOTHACHE

adjectives

serious; agonizing; unrelieved; comic; painful.

TOOTHLESS

adverbs

hideously; repulsively; pitifully; incoherently; unintelligibly; powerlessly; infirmly; utterly.

TOOTHSOME

adverbs

especially; particularly; agreeably; surprisingly; definitely; actually; unexpectedly; delectably; deliciously; lusciously; temptingly; extremely; undeniably; unusually; uncommonly; invitingly; pleasantly .

TOP

adjectives

slender; inviolate; grisly; hill; sterile; gloomy; sun-bleached; singed; massive; eminent; pryamided; lofty.

TOP-HEAVY

adverbs

dangerously; inartistically; unfortunately; peculiarly; unsatisfactorily; objectionably; oddly; strangely; unluckily; hazardously; clumsily; awkwardly; impractically; unreliably; riskily; obviously; manifestly; unreasonably; crazily; unacceptably; abnormally; precariously; insecurely; uncommonly.

TOPIC

adjectives

dangerous; recondite; related; aforementioned; conversational; wary; religious; hackneyed; various (pl); disagreeable; dreadful; current; absorbing; conservative; tempting; concrete; conceivable; numerous (pl); forbidden; doubtful; political; one-sided; allied; abandoned; important; tiresome; celestial; magazine; commonplace; complicated; wholesome.

verbs

absorb in—; air—; analyze—; argue—; condense—; converse on—; digress from—; disclose—; dismiss—; dissect—; dissertate on—; divert from—; do justice to—; exhaust—; expatiate on—; expound—; grapple with—; limit—; obscure—; probe—; propose—; pursue—; rant about—; resume—;

revive—; seize upon—; shrink from—; unfold—; ventilate—; —fascinates; —treats of.

(See subject, theme, question.)

TOPSY-TURVY

adverbs

unpleasantly; crazily; carelessly; inexcusably; disagreeably; negligently; objectionably; untidily; hastily; irremediably; terribly; oddly; fantastically; unexpectedly; gaily; perplexingly; inextricably; madly; mischievously; deliberately; inconsiderately; thoughtlessly; heedlessly; wildly; wantonly.

TORCH

adjectives

inverted; bridal; fiery; nuptial; smoldering; flaring; feeble; extemporized; broidered; incandescent; blazing; extemporary; processional.

verbs

apply—; bear—; eclipse—; employ—; extend—; extinguish—; flourish—; obscure—; quench—; screen—; smother—; snuff out—; ·thrust—; —beams; —chars; —dazzles; -- enkindles; —flares; —flashes; —flickers; — gleams; —glimmers; —ignites; —radiates; —scintillates; —scorches; —sheds; —shimmers; —singes; —smoulders.

(See lamp, flame, light.)

TORMENT

adjectives

happy; numberless (pl); invented; abiding; exhausted; human; eternal; haunting; protracted; dreadful; perpetual; exquisite; especial; endless; continual; studied.

verbs

allay—; alleviate—; bear—; dull—; ease—; endure—; experience—; induce—; inflict—; mitigate—; occasion—; suffer—; tolerate—; —agonizes; —crushes; —curses; —galls; — gnaws; —rends; —rings; —shatters; — sours; —wracks.

(See punishment, anguish, itching, torture.)

TORMENT (v)

adverbs

constantly; protractedly; exquisitely; endlessly; diabolically; cruelly; heartlessly; unrelentingly; barbarously; devilishly; fiendishly.

(See hurt, pain, torture.)

adverbs

vaguely; distinctly; mischievously; wantonly; offensively; vexatiously; intolerably; insufferably; unbearably; unwittingly; wilfully; deliberately; intentionally; constantly; unconsciously; purposely; viciously; maliciously; venomously; childishly; youthfully; blithely; continually; consistently; particularly; peculiarly; abominably; detestably; atrociously; facetiously; foolishly.

TORNADO

flounder in—; stagger in—; totter in—; —batters; —blasts; —bowls over; —cripples; —devastates; —ebbs; —effaces; —exterminates; —gyrates; —howls; —levels; — mangles; —plays havoc; —prostrates; — razes; —revolves; —rips over; —roars; — rotates; —scuttles; —smashes; —spends itself; —swamps; —swirls; —topples; — wheezes; —whistles.

(See storm, hurricane, wind.)

TORPID
adverbs

safely; securely; wanly; peculiarly; seasonally; naturally; stupidly; dully; merely; apathetically; terribly; unaccountably; unusually; alarmingly; helplessly; hopelessly; particularly; oddly; peculiarly; uncommonly; mercifully; inertly; contentedly; sluggishly; remarkably; inexplicably; habitually.

TORPOR
adjectives

momentary; guilty; heavy; vegetable; dead; frozen; intellectual; delicious; blank; dazed; death-like.

TORRENT
adjectives

wild; rushing; impetuous; irregular; tempestuous; streaming; furious; fiery; thundering; driving; angry; boiling; muddy; seething; dangerous; racing; living; windy; drenching; rapid; turbid; plunging; instantaneous; silver; deep; narrow; swirling; eddying; restless; tremendous; resistless; noisy; mad; fierce; hushed; flashing; swift; foaming; raging; radical; icy; mountain; descending; lava; turbulent; pent-up.

verbs

check—; dam—; immerse in—; pacify—; slacken—; staunch—; stem—; swell into—; tranquillize—; —batters; —buffets; —cas-

cades; —deluges; —devastates; —foams; —gushes; —inundates; —issues from; — roars; —rolls; —surges; —sweeps; — swirls; —washes; —waves.

(See maelstrom, storm, rain, flood, stream.)

TORRENTIAL
adverbs

unusually; unseasonably; unexpectedly; suddenly; alarmingly; destructively; calamitously; disastrously; violently; viciously; swirlingly; inescapably; windily; frigidly; lamentably; mercilessly; furiously; perilously; frightfully; terribly; indescribably; incomparably; tragically; ominously; positively; actually.

TORRID
adverbs

unpleasantly; unfortunately; mercilessly; cruelly; intolerably; unbearably; parchingly; distressingly; injuriously; disastrously; calamitously; unexpectedly; unseasonably; suddenly; terribly; curiously; oddly; particularly; usually; uncommonly; painfully; inescapably.

TORSO
adjectives

slender; youthful; well-proportioned; antique.

TORTUOUS
adverbs

circuitously; painfully; perplexingly; wonderfully; intricately; unusually; arduously; unnecessarily; craftily; sinuously; deceptively; bewilderingly; distressingly; bothersomely; deliberately; objectionably; unpleasantly; disagreeably; maddeningly; discouragingly; vexatiously; curiously; unreasonably; confusingly; needlessly; terribly; dreadfully; tiresomely.

TORTURE
adjectives

excruciating; bitter; mental; lingering; physical; everlasting; exquisite; measured; hideous; endless; unrepressed; horrible; innate; slow; consuming; supreme; secret; utmost; tightening; eternal; memorable; rational; intense; untold; subtle; curdling; cruel; abominable; righteous; fiendish; burning; showy; grating.

verbs
avert—; contrive—; devise—; endure—; enforce—; palliate—; release from—; submit to—; subject to—; —benumbs; —convulses; —crucifies; —harrows; —lingers; —racks.
(See ordeal, torment, punishment, pain.)

TORTURE (v)
adverbs
excruciatingly; bitterly; lingeringly; physically; hideously; horribly; secretly; irrationally; exquisitely; barbarically; grotesquely.
(See torment, hurt, pain.)

TOSS
adjectives
tremendous; pretty; merry; coquettish; disdainful; careless.

TOSS (v)
adverbs
angrily; carelessly; restlessly; arrogantly; indiscriminately; restively; fretfully; impatiently; pettishly; coyly; coquettishly; disdainfully.
(See hurl, heave.)

TOTAL
adjectives
impressive; alarming; tremendous; enormous; attainable; staggering; incorrect; huge; amazing; erroneous.

verbs
amass—; appraise—; ascertain—; assess—; augment—; balance—; calculate—; check—; compile—; compute—; determine—; dispute —; divulge—; estimate—; integrate—; plumb—; rate—; reckon—; reveal—; underestimate—; weigh—; whittle down—; — aggregates; —astounds; —embraces; — mounts; —soars; —staggers; —totters.
(See amount.)

TOTAL
adverbs
finally; undeniably; grossly; substantially; presumably; indivisably; tentatively; staggeringly; roughly; unconditionally.

TOTTERING
adverbs
tremulously; waveringly; uncertainly; odd-

ly; queerly; agedly; helplessly; pitiably; extremely; effetely; dejectedly.

TOUCH
adjectives
starry; soft; pleading; composing; distinctive; fairy; casual; impassioned; featherlike; caustic; felicitous; innumerable (pl); vivifying; continuous; magic; daughterly; hasty; corroding; subtile; exciting; nurselike; unwonted; polluting; passing; consoling; mortal; mysterious; sophisticated; chilling; dramatic; flexible; quivering; aristocratic; truthful; celestial; pardonable; luxurious; masterly; satiric; humorous; soothing; alien; simplifying; lively; mellow; sensitive; couturier; musical; demoralizing; clinging; crowning; icy; dreamy; uncivil; desperate; glowing; unfelt; ethereal; ironical; sweetest; inspiriting; fascinating; facile; convincing; tainting; finishing; summery; immaculate; all-pervading; immediate; caressing; arch; slight; incautious; simple; deathly; discriminative; abominable; skillful; beastly; plastic; innocent; vulgar; sparkling; superficial; faultless; final; classic; rare; grotesque; lyrical; inimitable; passionate; sophisticated; trial-fire.

verbs
avert—; avoid—; evade—; sense—; sensitize—; —benumbs; —brushes; —chills; — comforts; —contaminates; —defiles; —degrades; —electrifies; —excites; —grazes; —impassions; —petrifies; —pollutes; —reveals; —revolts; —tickles.
(See contact.)

TOUCH (v)
adverbs
delicately; affectionately; lingeringly; reverently; piquantly; inadequately; profoundly; confidingly; genuinely; inexpressibly; angelically; timidly; respectfully; fitfully; cautiously.
(See finger, feel.)

TOUCHDOWN
verbs
achieve—; aim at—; annul—; avert—; bid for—; block—; charge for—; clamor for—; culminate in—; pass to—; pile up—s; plunge for—; prevent—; recall—; score—; sneak over—; stem—; sweep for—; void—; yield—; —climaxes; —demoralizes; —determines.

TOUCHING

adverbs

infinitely; poignantly; extremely; unusually; positively; utterly; tenderly; hauntingly; curiously; pathetically; thrillingly; overwhelmingly; incomparably; unexpectedly; undeniably.

TOUCHY

adverbs

absurdly; unreasonably; vexatiously; significantly; arrogantly; indescribably; nervously; cholerically; churlishly; pugnaciously; curiously; strangely; inexplicably; unaccountably; inherently; naturally; unbecomingly; unpleasantly; disagreeably; atrociously; painfully; distressingly; ridiculously.

TOUGH

adverbs

disagreeably; unpleasantly; unpalatably; inedibly; unwarrantably; inadmissibly; curiously; unreasonably; unpardonably; outrageously; scandalously; shamefully; troublesomely; wantonly; dreadfully; inconceivably; uncommonly; extraordinarily; singularly; particularly; viciously; wickedly; ridiculously.

TOUGHNESS

verbs

acquire—; augment—; boast of—; deplore —; glory in—; mitigate—; preserve—; — affords; —breasts; —defies; —endures; — insures; —protects; —rebuffs; —repels; — resists; —supports; —sustains; —withstands; —yields.
(See strength, tenacity.)

TOUR

adjectives

prolonged; extended; creative; systematic; walking; triumphal; protracted; lecture; expensive; reconnoitering; memorable.

verbs

arrange—; cater for—; conclude—; conduct —; direct—; embark on—; extend—; guide —; map out—; organize—; plan—; project —; protract—; recruit for—; sponsor—; standardize—; —attracts; —broadens; — covers; —embraces; —includes; —provides; —skirts; —touches.
(See journey, trip, voyage, excursion.)

TOUR (v)

adverbs

enthusiastically; extendedly; listlessly; hurriedly; drearily; wearily; indefatigably; systematically.
(See travel, visit.)

TOURISTS

adjectives

guileless; romantic; rewarded; listless; hurried; dreary; clever; experienced; wary; weary.

verbs

accommodate—; accompany—; attract—; cater to—; convey—; divert—; entertain—; exploit—; guide—; lecture to—; lure—; shelter—; —consult; —embark; —flock; — marvel at; —mill; —motor; —purchase; — sail; —throng; —view.
(See traveler, passenger.)

TOURNAMENT

adjectives

mock; chivalric; independent; open; national; amateur.

verbs

advance in—; cheer—; color—; compete in —; conduct—; dominate—; emerge from—; engage in—; enter—; judge—; referee—; triumph in—; vie in—; witness—; —excites; —glorifies; —impassions; —publicizes; —rages.
(See contest, game.)

TOWEL

adjectives

ragged; hospitable; cordial; snowy; rough; rubbing; huge; crumpled; soggy.

verbs

begrime—; besmirch—; boil—; defile—; disinfect—; embroider—; employ—; filch—s; launder—; rack—; scour—; spatter—; sully —; swab with—; wrap in—; whip—; — absorbs; —envelops.
(See napkin, handkerchief, cloth.)

TOWER

adjectives

preserved; flying; immortal; quaint; opal; crumbling; meridian; warlike; weird; machicolated; tranquil; nodding; martial-like; impertinent; rent; gigantic; stalagmite; feudal; baroque; temporary; square; leaning; low; tottering; church; strong; topless; irregular; showy; flanking; worn; lurching; gleaming; stone; stunted; upper; shattered; slender; ivy-mantled; precipitous; stately; fortified; moldering; massive; overthrown; marshalled; external; shining; turret; skyey; rustic; ecclesiastical; barbaric; cylindrical; movable; tall; time-twin (pl).

verbs
ascend—; assail—; besiege—; clamber up —; convey to—; dismantle—; encompass—; erect—; flank—with; fortify—; hover over —; imprison in—; incarcerate in—; level—; mount—; raze—; repose in—; scale—; storm—; summon to—; surmount—; surround—; topple from—; view from—; — caps; —commemorates; —dominates; — flanks; —frowns; —honors; —looms; — rears; —soars; —symbolizes.
(See pinnacle, peak, mountain, spire.)

TOWER (v)
adverbs
magnificently; sublimely; martially; gigantically; precipitously; massively; awesomely; prodigiously; impressively.
(See rise.)

TOWN
adjectives
mute; quaint; storm-swept; tumultuous; queer; many-languaged; self-respecting; terror-stricken; combustible; seven-faced; drowsy; murmuring; imaginary; scenic; shapeless; provincial; breeding; sedate; everyday; defenseless; cheerful; industrial; bustling; rebel; high-perched; gray; placid; peaceful; beleaguered; adjacent; toiling; natal; inland; pretentious; ragged; haunted; dark; majestic; resurrecting; glittering; adverse; walled; retreating; famished; prosperous; hapless; picturesque; spiry; forest-girdled; benighted; populous; burning; lesser; native; festival; crude; ambitious; abominable; harbor; massive; cosmopolitan; fortified; insignificant; extraordinary; outlying; veritable; fated; colorful; straggling; wondrous; filthy; fascinating; respective; inexorable; thriving; corrupt; dirty; permanent; petty; snow-thatched; grass-grown; bleak.

verbs
abide in—; allude to—; assault—; besiege —; border—; distinguish—; evacuate—; extend—; father—; flank—; forsake—; found

—; govern—; guide—; inhabit—; invade—; loot—; make the rounds of—; parade—; people—; potter about—; reclaim—; reconnoiter—; scurry around—; set foot in—; skirt—; sojourn in—; throng—; settle in—; trek across—; trudge around—; wall—; — booms; —flourishes; —s snuggle; —springs up; —thrives; —throngs.
(See city, neighborhood, community, village.)

TOXIC
adverbs
indubitably; truly; dangerously; fatally; alarmingly; curiously; evidently; apparently; immediately; instantly; deeply; palpably; cruelly; usually; irremediably; disturbingly; terribly; incontrovertibly.

TOXIN
verbs
dilute—; dispel—; inject—; liberate—; neutralize—; purge of—; secrete—; succumb to —; —circulates; —envenoms; —s fatigue; —invades; —overruns; —poisons; —pollutes; —s propagate; —ravishes; —taints; —vitiates; —weakens.
(See poison, germ.)

TOY
adjectives
tremulous; rude; lamenting; saccharine; adorable; vulgar; battered; inconstant; amorous; expensive; attractive; fond; imaginative; fairy; trifling; garish.

verbs
absorb in—s; caress—; cherish—; deprive of—s; disburse—s; engross in—s; fondle—; model—; regard—; reward with—s; tempt with—s; tinker with—s; weary of—s; wheedle—s away; —amuses; —beguiles; — cheers; —caricatures; —delights; —distracts; —diverts; —excites; —fascinates; — solaces.
(See rattle, doll.)

TOY (v)
adverbs
valiantly; irresistibly; idly; amorously; vulgarly; triflingly; adoringly; quaintly.
(See play, sport.)

TRACE (v)
adverbs
skillfully; accurately; roughly; laboriously;

painfully; unconsciously; ethnologically; unmistakably; perceptibly.
  (See investigate, search.)

TRACEABLE
adverbs
easily; dimly; vaguely; distinctly; reasonably; calculably; obviously; discernibly;
hardly; actually; conclusively; manifestly;
clearly; allegedly; presumably; vestigially;
objectively; psychologically; physically.

TRACES
adjectives
ancient; historical; corroding; abundant;
generous; partial; servile; tangled; archaeological; anthropological; ethnological;
slight; marked; effacing; sensible; unmistakable; perceptible; undiscovered; phantom;
visible; surviving.

verbs
bear—; confirm—; convey—; detect—; dim
—; disclose—; discover—; eclipse—; efface
—; eradicate—; erase—; examine—; obscure—; obliterate—; outline—; recognize
—; record—; reveal—; scent—; scrutinize
—; stumble upon—; uncover—; unearth—;
veil—; verify—; —disappear; —vanish.
  (See evidence, impression, mark, sign,
multiply.)

TRACK
adjectives
steep; indelible; foamy; beaten; zigzag;
ant; well-chosen; sorrowless; myriad (pl);
luminous; resplendent; untraveled; vengeful; receding; shining; adjacent; unending;
thirsty; glistening; cloud-swept; solar; suitable; grooved.

verbs
blot out—; careen down—; clear—; deduce
from—; efface—; eradicate—; erase—; espy
—; expunge—; follow in—; jump—; obliterate—; steal across—; stumble upon—;
trace—; uncover—; —s afford; —s bear evidence; —s betoken; —s blaze; —s denote;
—enables; —ensnares; —s indicate; —s record; —s reveal.
  (See course, groove, trail, trace.)

TRACKLESS
adverbs
bewilderingly; terrifyingly; utterly; hopelessly; completely; incredibly; appallingly;
dismally; overwhelmingly; dishearteningly;
absolutely.

adjectives
inflammable; latent; controversial; much-
desired; distributing; uncultivated; wicked;
untrodden; considerable; inviting; stifling;
dry; missionary; irritable; theologic;
marshy; vast; diffusing; humane; alimentary; generous; tender; digestive; adjoining; singular; broad; large; partisan.

verbs
claim—; confine—; cultivate—; enlarge—;
entitle to—; expand—; explore—; fence in
—; grant—; harrow—; limit—; plow—;
reclaim—; sow—; stake out—; till—; work
—; —bears; —flourishes; —fructifies; —
ranges; —thrives.
  (See farm, area, district, field, land.)

TRACTABLE
adverbs
easily; pleasantly; agreeably; conveniently;
handily; deceptively; amazingly; unexpectedly; accommodatingly; docilely; surprisingly; dully; quietly; humbly; willingly;
happily; fortunately; suddenly; grudgingly;
momentarily; amenably; apparently; delightfully; silently; wearily; placidly; tearfully.

TRADE
adjectives
considerable; clandestine; immense; peaceable; savory; melancholy; depressed; dreadful; monstrous; profitable; flourishing; military; lucrative; constant; discordant; penitent; languishing; abominable; essential;
harsh; vilest; illicit; wholesale; hereditary;
doubtful; permanent; beastly; external; sedentary; diverted; stagnated; unlawful; intermediary; earthly; reciprocal; thriving;
frivolous; magnificent.

verbs
abandon—; alienate—; augment—; blockade—; bolster—; cement—; conciliate—;
cut into—; decrease—; discontinue—; disrupt—; dominate—; encourage—; endanger
—; engage in—; establish—; expand—; facilitate—; foster—; hamper—; impede—;
increase—; inspire—; make roads upon—;
monopolize—; nurture—; originate—; ply
—; promote—; pursue—; regiment—; relinquish—; restrain—; revive—; spur—;
stimulate—; strangle—; strengthen—; stymie—; swamp with—; swell—; tackle—;

teach—; threaten—; traffic in—; trample down—; —collapses; —dwindles; —freezes; —jumps up; —lures; —slumps.

(See employment, market, exchange, commerce, industry, calling, business.)

TRADEMARK

verbs

acquaint with—; appropriate—; glorify—; patent—; popularize—; recognize—; stamp —; —attests to; —betokens; —distinguishes; —emblazons; —guarantees; —heralds; —indicates; —insures; —labels; —represents; —symbolizes; —vouches.

(See label, copyright, patent.)

TRADESMEN

verbs

bargain with—; barter with—; dicker with —; cater to—; —deal in; —dispense; —dispose of; —engage in; —haggle; —hawk; —market; —peddle; —ply; —purvey; —retail; —trade; —traffic in; —transact; —vend; —vie.

(See hawker, merchant, salesman.)

TRADITION

adjectives

sacred; mysterious; precise; ancient; soberest; superstitious; venerable; cumulative; social; historic; culinary; inherited; patriotic; simple; saner; time-honored; sentimental; exquisite; ghostly; current; moldy; gentlemanly; ritualistic; intellectual; unscientific; sporting; hospitable; family; high; rare; sweet; dim; hoary; liberal; heroic; aesthetic; untrustworthy; living; remote; medieval; decorous; poetic; remarkable; pleasant; tribal; conventional; popular; established; cherished; imperial; renowned; fine; immutable.

verbs

absorb—; acquire—; adhere to—; annihilate —; authenticate—; "ballyhoo"—; bare—; batter—; better—; bound by—; break down —; cast aside—; carry on—; cherish—; conform to—; continue—; create—; cut loose from—; defend—; derive from—; destroy —; disclose—; discrepit—; disregard—; dissolve—; emancipate—; emasculate—; embody in—; endure—; enrich—; establish —; exist in—; express—; force—; fortify—; found—; glory in—; guard—; honor—; ignore—; illustrate—; imbue—; impair—; imperial—; infuse—; ingrain—; inherit—; "junk"—; limit—s; maintain—; mock—;

nourish—; nurture—; observe—; perpetuate —; preserve—; profit by—; rear in—; relate—; relinquish—; repudiate—; revive—; respect—; root in—; saturate with—; shake off—; shatter—; smash—; stand for—; steep in—; stick to—; strangle—; sweep away—; take over—; tinge with—; trace—; undermine—; unfold—; violate—; weld—; —accentuates; —ascribes; —binds; —blinds; —brands; —carries on; —colors; —describes; —determines; —dictates; —enriches; —fetters; —governs; —hands down; —immortalizes; —narrates; —preserves; —persists; —prescribes; —recounts; —regulates; —reports; —rules; —stands; —threatens; —s topple.

(See belief, attitude, culture, habit, custom, usage.)

TRADITIONAL

adverbs

devoutly; deeply; racially; innately; reverently; profoundly; curiously; manifestly; pleasantly; seriously; ineradicably; conventionally; delightfully; apparently; popularly; locally; indestructibly; inflexibly; vaguely; clearly.

TRADUCE (v)

adverbs

viciously; scandalously; libelously; hatefully; savagely; vindictively; revengefully.

(See slander, assail.)

TRAFFIC

adjectives

congested; rushing; metropolitan; aerial; dense; heavy; incessant; petty; abominable; ceaseless; roaring; terminate; din-producing; wearisome.

verbs

avert—; check—; choke—; congest—; control—; converge—; direct—; engage in—; escape—; evade—; facilitate—; guide—; hamper—; impede—; jam—; obstruct—; paralyze—; quell—; regulate—; retard—; shun—; speed—; support—; tangle—; —blares; —clogs; —confuses; —converges; —endangers; —flows; —jangles; —jeopardizes; —roars; —surges; —sweeps by; —thunders.

(See intercourse, exchange, commerce.)

TRAGEDY

adjectives

poetic; vast; shocking; unimaginable; de-

1202

rived; inexcusable; bourgeois; radical; unequalled; dark; bombastic; dream; philosophic; classical; bloody; supreme; fantastic; stark; nocturnal; ancient; national; countless (pl); tribal; dismal; terrible; impressive; domestic; timeless; climacteric; successful; terrestrial; world; unavoidable.

verbs
avert—; banish—; bear—; belittle—; bewail—; decry—; deplore—; develop into —; disclose—; facilitate—; heighten—; intensify—; lament—; mourn—; play—; plot—; plunge into—; precipitate—; sense —; shudder at—; skirt the edge of—; stay —; submerge—; suffer—; surmount—; verge on—; —afflicts; —appalls; —bereaves; —curdles; —curses; —deals a blow; —depresses; —descends; —distorts; —excites; —foredooms; —harrows; —haunts; —mows down; —oppresses; —overtakes; —purges; —racks; —rends; —sears; —shakes; —shocks; —sours; —spells; —unfolds; —weighs upon; —wrings.
(See melodrama, atrocity, outrage, calamity, drama, catastrophe.)

TRAGIC
adverbs
overwhelmingly; calamitously; bitterly; cruelly; incredibly; unexpectedly; dismally; appallingly; shockingly; devastatingly; unmitigatedly; hopelessly; unrelievedly; utterly; splendidly; superbly; highly; profoundly; consummately; incalculably; immeasurably.

TRAIL
adjectives
hurrying; downward; sidling; lonesome; traveled; resplendent; recent; dusty; endless; milky; unique; pungent; majestic; arduous; hour-old; winding; sinuous; wellworn; twisting; elusive; spiritual; ancestral.

verbs
blaze—; break—; clarify—; clutter—; construct—; deviate from—; diverge from—; efface—; erase—; explore—; forsake—; illuminate—; jog along—; lay out—; map—; mark—; obliterate—; obscure—; obstruct —; plunge along—; pursue—; scan—; shadow—; skirt—; stir up—; strike into—; veil—; —bewilders; —recedes; —threads its course; —twists; —veers; —winds.
(See track, road, lane.)

TRAIL (v)
adverbs
demurely; faithfully; humbly; tediously; arduously; sinuously; twistingly; elusively; incessantly.
(See follow, trace.)

TRAIN
adjectives
reaper; starry; unparalleled; funeral; illustrious; imperial; crawling; belated; night; retreating; prodigious; express; inferior; gigantic; suburban; shining; grisly; hurtling; fast-flying; virgin; complicated; pointed; harmless; crack; long-laid; additional; pensive; vagrant; incoming; unfeeling; unpainted; gloom-stricken; wooden; immediate; melancholy; haughty; celestial; pompous; sweeping; streamlined.

verbs
assign to—; board—; collide with—; consign to—; convey—; couple—; derail—; flag—; fuel—; hop aboard (colloq.)—; insert in—; launch—; section—; schedule—s; scurry for—; shunt—; signal—; switch—s; transport by—; —bears; —chugs (colloq.); —conveys; —departs; —facilitates; —glides; —plunges; —puffs; —pulls into; —rattles; —rocks; —rolls; —shunts; —shrieks; —steams; —sways; —sweeps away; —thunders; —wheels away; —whistles; —whizzes; —winds its way.
(See automobile, locomotive, trolley-car.)

TRAIN (v)
adverbs
exquisitely; sedulously; scientifically; specially; competently; intellectually; judiciously; technically; adequately; intensively; monastically; academically; arduously; systematically; subtly; theoretically.
(See discipline, teach.)

TRAINED
adverbs
successfully; highly; moderately; skilfully; adequately; recently; well-; badly; inadequately; consummately; carefully; scarcely; cleverly; marvelously; brilliantly; cruelly; mercilessly; patiently; persistently; consistently; effectively; sufficiently; specifically; constantly.

TRAINING
adjectives
continuous; intellectual; judicious; vicious;

elementary; technical; valuable; preparatory; rigid; persistent; watchful; ethical;
industrial; disciplinary; adequate; rural;
intensive; lifelong; monastic; requisite;
vocational; classical; scholarly; precedent;
supplementary; arduous; superficial; loving;
pious; admirable; secretarial; practical;
systematic; rigorous; amatory; leisurely;
stabilized; subtle; architectural; theoretical.

verbs

entrust to—; fit for—; imbibe—; persevere
with—; prescribe—; relax—; subject to—;
undergo—; —accustoms; —breeds; —disciplines; —equips; —forearms; —habituates;
—hardens; —impregnates; —inculcates; —
infuses; —instils; —inures; —matures; —
mellows; —polishes; —prepares; —qualifies; —sharpens; —smooths; —veneers.
(See preparation, education, discipline,
exercise.)

TRAIT

adjectives

redeeming; petty; striking; intellectual;
boyish; ridiculous; bestial; dominant; overbearing; predominating; advanced; distinguished; outstanding; conspicuous; royal;
feminine; multiplex (pl); noble; salient;
common; singular; outward; scrupulous;
generous; sectional; characteristic; humane;
national; essential; desirable; lasting; hereditary; notable; varied (pl); obnoxious;
introvert; quantitative; childish; valuable;
visible; physiological; ostensible.

verbs

assentuate—; acquire—; breed—s; commend
—; cultivate—; discover—s; emphasize—;
exhibit—; foster—; illuminate—s; intensify
—; manifest—; play a part in—; portray
—; relate—; stamp—; value—; —allures;
—appears; —attracts; —betokens; —characterizes; —distinguishes; —s etch deeper;
—fascinates; —indicates; —individualizes;
—s stamp out.
(See characteristic, habit, quality.)

TRAITOR

verbs

accuse—; banish—; denounce—; dub—;
exile—; expose—; hiss—; hoot—; ostracize
—; outlaw—; proclaim—; pursue—; redeem—; scorn—; sneer at—; spurn—; subdue—; —betrays; —debases; —demeans;

—falsifies; —loses caste; —repudiates; —
secedes.
(See betrayer, conspirators, plotters,
criminal.)

TRAITOROUS

adverbs

despicably; abominably; stealthily; furtively; unbelievably; unexpectedly; suddenly;
curiously; detestably; murderously; meretriciously; insidiously; atrociously; odiously; hatefully; venomously; vilely; grossly;
ungratefully; confessedly; traceably; evidently; incalculably; cleverly; invidiously;
utterly; presumably; allegedly.

TRAJECTION

adjectives

free; limited; swift; uncanny.

TRAMP

adjectives

collier; measured; penniless; steady; dusty;
derisible; plashy; echoing; impecunious;
dingy; clattering; sullen; beggarly.

TRAMP (v)

adverbs

ruthlessly; vigorously; sullenly; monotonously; dingily; indefatigably; remorselessly.
(See march, trudge.)

TRAMPLE (v)

adverbs

ruthlessly; heedlessly; speedily; cruelly;
viciously; contemptuously; heartlessly.
(See tramp, stamp.)

TRANCE

adjectives

spectral; rigid; magic; mystic; compassionate; blissful; icy; stupid; restless; ecstatic;
cataleptic; dizzy; spiritual; stilly; lethargic;
doleful; speechless; detested.

TRANQUIL

adverbs

sweetly; amazingly; restfully; contentedly;
incredibly; suddenly; surprisingly; refreshingly; delightfully; naturally; habitually;
always; seldom; enviably; admirably;
happily; contentedly; blissfully; extremely;
uncommonly.

TRANQUILITY

adjectives

wishless; misty; dignified; well-regulated;

mist-wrapped; divine; magnanimous; honey-sweet; sumptuous; profound; flustered; long-desired; monotonous; perfect; serene; dry; physical; innocent; boresome; empty; dull.

verbs
break—; disturb—; lull into—; recapture —; recollect in—; shatter—; tolerate—; — alleviates; —assuages; —becalms; —chastens; —composes; —deadens; —depresses; —dulcifies; —pacifies; —settles over; — smooths; —smothers; —stagnates; —subdues.
(See calm, apathy, quiet.)

TRANSACT (v)
adverbs
profitably; industriously; efficiently; ethically; momentously; monetarily; fraudulently; spiritually; nefariously; discreditably; philosophically; ephemerally.
(See conduct, negotiate.)

TRANSACTION
adjectives
momentous; mercantile; monetary; notorious; important; fraudulent; clouded; private; flowery; spiritual; extortionate; nefarious; discreditable; philosophical; ritualistic.

verbs
abandon—; bind to—; carry on—; conceal —; conduct—; consummate—; divulge—; draft—; engage in—; endanger—; execute —; facilitate—; insure—; negotiate—; nullify—; outline—; participate in—; plan—; press—; profit by—; promote—; reject—; release from—; rue—; underwrite—; withdraw from—; —obligates; —stipulates.
(See procedure, deal, bargain, intercourse.)

TRANSCEND (v)
adverbs
boundlessly; gloriously; infinitely; obviously; markedly; amazingly; spectacularly.
(See surpass, excel.)

TRANSCENDENTAL
adverbs
presumably; indubitably; impractically; satisfactorily; altogether; curiously; obviously; incalculably; loosely; strictly.

TRANSCRIBE (v)
adverbs
faithfully; diligently; laboriously; patiently; indefatigably; industriously; ambitiously; accurately.
(See copy, write.)

TRANSCRIBED
adverbs
carefully; accurately; usually; responsibly; legally; necessarily; scrupulously; immediately; intelligibly; perfectly; punctiliously; painstakingly; mechanically; scientifically; carelessly; imperfectly.

TRANSFER (v)
adverbs
temporarily; satisfactorily; forcibly; rapidly; professionally; individually.
(See shift, change.)

TRANSFIGURED
adverbs
radiantly; gloriously; celestially; divinely; brilliantly; glowingly; piously; devoutly; unimaginably; incredibly; beauteously; luminously; curiously; brightly; spiritually; idealistically; marvelously; miraculously; supernaturally; utterly; suddenly.

TRANSFORM (v)
adverbs
miraculously; magically; ingeniously; topographically; uniquely; supernaturally; amazingly; extensively; spectacularly.
(See change.)

TRANSFORMATION
adjectives
magical; striking; bucolic; epic; weird; successive (pl); solemn; tremendous; ingenious; unique; supernatural; topographical.

verbs
achieve—; analyze—; condone—; discern —; facilitate—; undergo—; —accentuates; —alters; —deviates; —innovates; —introduces; —modifies; —modulates; —revamps; —swerves from.
(See fermentation, change, alteration, transition.)

TRANSFORMED
adverbs
marvelously; miraculously; suddenly; gloriously; divinely; utterly; luminously;

strangely; peculiarly; oddly; unaccountably; inexplicably; radiantly; grotesquely; palpably; manifestly; unbelievably; undeniably; incredibly.

TRANSGRESS (v)
adverbs
outrageously; repetitiously; wantonly; venially; notoriously; incestuously; egregiously.
(See sin, violate.)

TRANSIENT
adverbs
painfully; lamentably; fortunately; fleetingly; merely; pathetically; sadly; tragically; ephemerally; bitterly; meteorically; brilliantly.

TRANSITION
adjectives
ethnological; soft; terrible; quick; hard; sudden; awful; perilous; stormy; violent; delicious; fine; necessary; painful; bitter; swift.

verbs
accomplish—; balk at—; bemoan—; complete—; decry—; denounce—; endure—; necessitate—; smooth—; trace—; undergo —; undertake—; —converts; —involves; —matures; —mellows; —revolutionizes; —ripens.
(See change, modification, transformation.)

TRANSITIONAL
adverbs
expediently; merely; conveniently; practically; feasibly; quickly; profitably; suitably; advantageously; briefly; serviceably; presumably; probably; adaptably; providentially; helpfully; admirably; aptly.

TRANSITORY
adverbs
briefly; ephemerally; impermanently; perishably; sadly; lamentably; unhappily; mortally; evanescently.

TRANSLATE (v)
adverbs
literally; fluently; extensively; faithfully; flawlessly; exquisitely; freely; exactly; copiously; skillfully; mentally.
(See interpret, construe.)

TRANSLUCENT
adverbs
mysteriously; strangely; incredibly; scientifically; unbelievably; uncommonly; admirably; commendably; sufficiently; surprisingly; pleasantly; attractively; conveniently; cleverly; agreeably; reasonably; surprisingly; unexpectedly; usefully; practically; satisfactorily.

TRANSPARENT
adverbs
entirely; inconveniently; uncomfortably; delightfully; attractively; unexpectedly; amazingly; conveniently; admirably; commendably; satisfactorily; oddly; comically; absurdly; shamefully; unnecessarily; remarkably; uncommonly; highly; exceptionally; perfectly.

TRANSPLANT (v)
adverbs
unceremoniously; agriculturally; patiently; skillfully; ingeniously; successfully; prudently.
(See shift, move, change.)

TRANSPLANTED
adverbs
carelessly; unskilfully; unsuccessfully; seldom; easily; safely; skilfully; carefully; successfully; often; usually; unwisely; clumsily; inexpertly; improperly; properly; experimentally.

TRANSPORT (v)
adverbs
swiftly; recklessly; laboriously; dramatically; periodically; annually; regularly; seasonally; continuously; deftly; uniquely.
(See move, ship.)

TRANSPORTATION
adjectives
water; ruined; laborious; swift; air; faultless; reckless.

verbs
accelerate—; afford—; assign—; assure of —; avail of—; block—; cripple—; direct —; disrupt—; expedite—; facilitate—; grant—; hamper—; impede—; manage—; rate—; retard—; slacken—; —cements; —communicates with; —enables; —links; —unites.
(See shipment, conveyance.)

1206

adjectives
unyielding; baited; palpable; dramatic; dreaded; ridiculous.

verbs
bait—; circumvent—; elude—; evade—; inveigle into—; lure into—; mask—; spring —; warn of—; —beguiles; —claws; —decoys; —deludes; —dupes; —ensnares; —grasps; —gulls; —hoaxes; —masks; —menaces.
(See pitfall, net, snare, ambush.)

TRAPPED

adverbs
hideously; helplessly; hopelessly; desperately; abominably; maliciously; grimly; unspeakably; utterly; inescapably; fatally; precariously; perilously; permanently; terribly; horribly; frightfuly; appallingly; shockingly; frantically; cleverly; cunningly; finally; ultimately; legally; subtly; adroitly; treacherously.

TRASHY

adverbs
utterly; abominably; terribly; cheaply; worthlessly; horribly; unspeakably; undisguisedly; irretrievably; irredeemably; grossly; crassly; irreclaimably; unacceptably; hopelessly; disagreeably; disgustingly; manifestly; undeniably; arrantly.

TRAVEL

adjectives
earthly; dreary; unknown; riotous; air; irrelevant; tiresome; horseback; prudent; extensive; transient; frequent; equatorial; continental; nomadic; fatiguing.

verbs
afford—; extend—s; facilitate—; forsake —; long for—; modernize—; recall—s; recite—s; recount—s; relinquish—s; widen—s; —acquaints one with; —broadens; —cultivates; —cultures; —edifies; —educates; —endangers; —enlightens; —polishes; —veneers.
(See tour, cruise, adventure, education.)

TRAVEL (*v*)

adverbs
extensively; circuitously; luxuriously; methodically; laboriously; perceptibly; sedately; expensively; advantageously; recklessly.
(See tour, journey.)

TRAVELED

adverbs
widely; highly; broadly; brilliantly; unusually; admirably; wonderfully; far; much; frequently; infrequently; seldom; little; marvelously; extensively.

TRAVELER

adjectives
ephemeral; zealous; wayworn; elegant; weary; cheerful; defenseless; mysterious; unprotected; unwary; desperate; expectant; unprofessional; dawdling; dispirited; shrewd; contemporary; present; thoughtful; economical; colonial; veteran; hoary; storm-tossed; late-arriving; rustic; gaping; sleepless; well-assorted (pl); discriminating; unwilling; fastidious; casual; reputable; disconcerting; arctic; wise; sophisticated; refined; seasoned; epicurean.

verbs
accommodate—; cater to—s; comfort—; enchant—s; enthrall—s; exhaust—; fatigue —; guide—; lecture to—; organize—; plunder—s; route—s; waylay—s; welcome —; —journeys; —lingers; —s mill about; —plans; —prolongs; —protracts; —repairs to; —resides at; —roams; —roves; —views; —wearies of; —wends; —witnesses.
(See marcher, tourists.)

TREACHEROUS

adverbs
abominably; dangerously; alarmingly; ominously; portentously; slyly; smoothly; insidiously; hypocritically; flatteringly; furtively; cleverly; disloyally; despicably; boldly; hideously; subtly; maliciously; grossly; deliberately; adroitly; vilely; astutely; inscrutably; undoubtedly; infinitely; deeply; darkly.

TREACHERY

adjectives
cruel; meditated; base; subtle; signal; bitter.

verbs
condemn—; court-martial for—; disclose—; denounce—; expose—; fear—; frame—; plot—; resort to—; screen—; shroud—; stoop to—; suspect—; uncover—; untangle —; veil—; —baits; —beguiles; —betrays; —debases; —deceives; —decoys; —deludes;

—dishonors; —disillusions; —engulfs; —lures; —lurks; —pollutes; —snares; —stains; —sullies.

(See insincerity, ingratitude, infidelity, betrayal.)

TREAD

adjectives

hasty; quick; elastic; viewless; swinging; limping; winter; victorious; slow; measured; firm; fairy; martial; sacred; monotonous; stately; imperious; stealthy; nervous; delicate; resilient; pointed; scandaled; thundering; persistent; springy; self-assured; conquering; undazzled; muffled; backward; unflinching; cat-like; clanging.

TREAD (v)

adverbs

sorrowfully; lightly; boldly; profanely; noiselessly; soundlessly; cautiously; rhythmically; painfully; consciously; gaily; unheedingly; tenderly.

(See walk, proceed.)

TREASON

adjectives

strong; household; detested; pretended; unpardonable; domestic; manifest; ugly; certain; passive; defiant; proud.

verbs

accuse of—; acquit of—; arraign for—; charge with—; cite—; combat—; commit—; condemn for—; confess—; convict of—; deny—; exile for—; indict for—; penalize for—; revenge—; unveil—; uncover—; —betrays; —breaches; —corrupts; —debases; —degrades; —demeans; —dishonors; —stigmatizes.

(See betrayal, crime, treachery.)

TREASONABLE

adverbs

indubitably; utterly; wickedly; admittedly; allegedly; subtly; frankly; assuredly; immeasurably; deliberately; indefeasibly; indefensibly; defiantly; arrantly; unutterably; daringly; boldly; peculiarly; palpably; highly; dangerously; darkly.

TREASURE

adjectives

valued; countless (pl); inexhaustible; sacred; royal; patrimonial; garnered; priceless; celestial; subsequent; vast; portable; precious; costly; heavenly; accursed; life-time; perishing; dear-bought; self-consuming; chaste; autumn; nobler; numbered (pl); eternal; drainless; sterling; superfluous; golden; accumulated; notable; earthly; ruffling; orphaned; long-lost; sleeping; cherished; unsuspected; dewy; longed-for; purloined; buried.

verbs

accumulate—; adorn—; amass—; appraise —; bury—; cache—; cherish—; disclose—; dispose of—; dive for—; exaggerate—; explore for—; extort—; garner—; harbor—; hoard—; impound—; lavish—upon; pilfer —; reclaim—; reveal—; salvage—; secrete —; seek—; stow away—; swallow—; uncover—; unearth—; —astounds; —dazzles; —enriches.

(See wealth, money.)

TREASURED

adverbs

highly; greatly; carefully; piously; affectionately; fondly; lovingly; tenderly; always; truly; especially; deeply; openly; strangely; oddly; unaccountably; sincerely; nationally; decorously; ceremoniously; insistently.

TREASURY

adjectives

exhaustless; infinite; provincial; veritable; depleted; enfeebled; anemic; national; vestpocket.

verbs

augment—; bankrupt—; deplete—; divert from—; drain—; embarrass—; embezzle from—; raid—; reinforce—; replenish—; replete—; repose in—; stabilize—; tap—; —accrues; —accumulates; —amasses; —appropriates; —authorizes; —declines; —inflates; —issues; —languishes; —lifts; —mounts; —recalls; —swells; —totters.

(See coffer, bank, reserve.)

TREAT

adjectives

popular; delightful; optical; splendid.

verbs

afford—; extend—; indulge in—; luxuriate in—; offer—; procure—; provide—; relish —; rejoice in—; revel in—; welcome—; yield—; —absorbs; —amuses; —delights; —enlivens; —fascinates; —gladdens; —regales; —solaces; —tickles.

(See dainty, entertainment, feast, repast.)

TREAT (v)

adverbs
rationally; barbarously; circumspectly; humanely; systematically; tenderly; adequately; harshly; elaborately; brutally; deferentially; compassionately; reverently; mercilessly; roughly; histrionically; elaborately; objectively; sympathetically; essentially; hospitably; conscientiously; jocosely; capriciously; contemptuously; surgically; medically; courteously.

(See behave, act.)

TREATISE

adjectives
extensive; erudite; laborious; scholarly; distinguished; lucid; philosophical; pedagogical; far-sighted; important; abstruse; pedantic; musical; celebrated; voluminous; masterly; hard-headed; distinct; elaborate; valuable.

verbs
absorb in—; acclaim—; commend—; comprehend—; condense—; consolidate—; denounce—; illustrate—; peruse—; present—; produce—; publish—; revise—; summarize —; write—; —airs; —boxes; —deals with; —digresses; —discourses; —dissertates; — does justice to; —elaborates on; —exhausts; —extends; —sets forth; —recites; —unfolds; —wearies.

(See dissertation, article, book.)

TREATMENT

adjectives
miraculous; infamous; prompt; acoustical; diabetic; proposed; triple-acting; drastic; abominable; scientific; superficial; dietary; persuasive; bold; thematic; heroic; jocose; intelligent; technical; contemptuous; harsh; pessimistic; realistic; cruel; proper; humane; psychoanalytic; symphonic; affectionate; unjust; preferential; successful; osteopathic; unfilial; inhuman; barbarous; severe; well-considered; judicious; summary; sufficient; axial; statistical; ceiling; appropriate; harmonic; architectural; voluntary; hospitable; routine; cathartic; attentive; torturing; ruthless; reliable; competent; delicate; insolent; surgical; standard; sportive; interior; scandalous; harmonious; remote; beautifying; preferential; perfidious; ungererous; respectful; conscientious; preventive; courteous; hypnotic; capricious; impolite; antiquated; immediate; mosaic; realistic; playful; disrespectful; frank; artistic; original.

verbs
acquaint with—; administer—; adopt—; advise—; advocate—; alter—; apply—; attribute—; carry on—; check—; commence—; conduct—; confer—on; constitute—; consult for—; co-ordinate—; counsel—; discard—; discontinue—; direct—; employ—; endure —; excel in—; expose—; extend—; facilitate —; indicate—; improve—; institute—; modernize—; modify—; neglect—; outline—; place—; prescribe—; prolong—; protract—; pursue—; question—; recommend—; regulate—; render—; repeat—; require—; respond to—; resume—; skill in—; standardize—; subject to—; tolerate—; undergo—; urge—; yield to—; —accomplishes; —allays; —ameliorates; —antidotes; —assuages; —falls; —incenses; —metes out; — misleads; —mitigates; —perseveres; —palliates; —relieves; —remedies; —represents; —varies.

(See * cure, method, act, performance, usage.)

TREATY

adjectives
far-sighted; separate; successive (pl); defensive; definitive; supplementary; ambiguous; secret; advantageous; pleasing; monstrous; equitable; obnoxious; outrageous; violated.

verbs
abrogate—; adopt—; comply with—; condition—; condemn—; confirm—; conform to —; contract—; create—; discharge—; disregard—; dissolve—; draft—; frame—; ignore—; infringe upon—; negotiate—; nullify—; observe—; press—; ratify—; repudiate—; rip—; sanction—; scrap—; sign—; trample—; transgress—; violate—; void—; —affords; —aims; —allies; —binds; —cements; —circumvents; —concludes; —embroils; —guarantees; —insures; —leagues; —pledges; —stipulates; —strengthens; — ties; —unites.

(See lease, covenant, agreement.)

TREE

adjectives
rich; ominous; whispering; brittle; cringing; wide-spreading; ragged; overgrown; tropical; trimmed; stately; fledged; inter-

posing; accursed; tangled; wind-swept; well-branched; kindred; assailed; dusty; feathery; tottering; cleft; stunted; hardy; well-cared-for; thread-like; gloomy; embowering; breathless; slender; white-starred; paradise; low; scrubby; dewy-tasseled; resinous; over-hanging; murdered; stretching; mute; shady; patriarchal; tufted; shining-leaved; enticing; notched; waking; unhewn; draped; rejoicing; water-loving; bare; genealogic; unwaving; darling; immortal; blasted; flowering; somber; unguarded; unlawful; lofty; senseless; yielding; parched; pleached; deserted; spectral; exotic; celestial; drooping; attractive; rifled; hoary; sheltering; forbidden; fantastic; stubby; dooryard; deciduous; prostrate; perfect; tempting; pomegranate; coveted; dripping; new-leafed; gnarled; denuded; sturdy; hollow; wayside; virtuous; twisted; interdicted; sprawling; friendly; lusty; gracious; listening; half-budded; slumberous; massive; blossoming; venerable; indigenous; faded; voluptuous; overarching; magnificent; broad-armed; sapient; naked; centennial; hereditary; tortured; undecaying; celestial; waving; fruit-laden; aromatic; bending; long-lived; eldest; full-branched; girdled; gaunt; unbrageous; glittering; gift-bearing; over-leaning; contorted; quivering; luxuriate; antique; trysting; intolerable; shivering; ornamental; pauper; spicy; shadowy; glistening; blessed; unaccustomed; short; majestic; lowering; misshapen; grafted.

verbs

blight—; clamber up—; conserve —s; cultivate —s; dot with —s; fell—; fertilize —s; graft—; hack at—; hew—; label—; level—; nest in—; prune—; raze—; suspend from—; tap—; thin out—; transplant—; uproot—; —affords; —bears; —bends; —blooms; — blossoms; —bows under; —buds; —s cluster; —creaks; —dips; —falls; —flanks; — flourishes; —flowers; —forms; —forsakes; —fructifies; —garlands; —hints; —lashes; —lifts; —loads; —obscures; —occupies; — overspreads; —plunges; —relinquishes; — rises; —rustles; —scourges; —screens; — shades; —sheds; —shelters; —shimmers; — shivers; —shrouds; —soars; —spreads; —s straggle; —sways; —swishes; —thrives; — throws; —thunders; —topples; —totters; — towers; —whips; —whispers; —writhes; — yields.

(See leaf, branch, oak, elm, etc.)

TREMBLE (v)

adverbs

fearsomely; fearfully; violently; inwardly; abominably; visibly; spasmodically; nervously; morbidly; abnormally; agitatedly.

(See shiver, move.)

TREMBLING

adverbs

helplessly; dreadfully; uncertainly; uncontrollably; awkwardly; perceptibly; pitiably; ineptly; paralytically; weakly; feebly.

TREMOR

adjectives

touching; nervous; sharp; immeasurable; emotional; eager; slight; awful; luminous; fierce; earthquake.

verbs

allay —s; excite to —s; inspire—; record—; respond to—; stir with —s; —agitates; — alarms; —convulses; —creeps; —dislodges; —indicates; —jars; —jolts; —jostles; — jounces; —pulsates; —ripples thru; — shocks; —swells; —terrifies; —trickles; — warms; —quivers.

(See agitation, earthquake, shiver, shudder.)

TRENCH

adjectives

slimy; abhorred; trial; current; political; bold; bloody; artificial; flanking; adjacent; defensive; muddy.

TRENCHANT

adverbs

effectively; unusually; famously; remarkably; wonderfully; cleverly; aptly; uncommonly; powerfully; tellingly; savagely; viciously; unmercifully; sarcastically; drolly; brutally; bluntly; sharply.

TRENCHES

verbs

beseige—; blast—; bolster—; bombard—; burrow—; confine to—; excavate—; fortify —; flow from—; lodge in—; maintain—; map—; patrol—; plan—; raid—; repulse from—; scoop out—; straggle to—; stream to—; swarm from—; tunnel—; —afford; — deface; —furrow; —shelter; —shield.

(See ditch, drain, fortification.)

TREND

adjectives

significant; important; radical; philosophic; noticeable; recent; future; mystical; practical; probable; impressive; unhealthy; gambling; significant.

verbs

affect—; approve—; detect—; discern—; divert—; emphasize—; encourage—; foster—; govern—; hail—; herald—; illustrate—; indicate—; influence—; obscure—; promote—; recognize—; regulate—; retard—; reverse—; scotch—; sense—; sway—; warp —; —departs from; —deviates; —inclines toward; —shifts; —signifies; —swerves.

(See mode, fashion, style, tendency.)

TRESPASS (*v*)

adverbs

nefariously; boldly; illegally; brazenly; lawlessly; flagrantly.

(See transgress, intrude.)

TRESPASSER

verbs

admonish—; banish—; bar—; caution—; dispel—; eject—; expel—; inveigh against —; oust—; penalize—; prosecute—; —encroaches on; —infringes on; —intrudes; —invades; , —obtrudes; —offends; —oversteps; —violates.

(See aggressor, intruder.)

TRESS

adjectives

raven; ebon; flaming; beauteous; unbound.

TRIAL

adjectives

repeated; fiery; ancient; memorable; ludicrous; harassing; speedy; hurried; religious; gracious; mutual; intensified; terrible; weary; still; bitter; countless (pl); impartial; unnecessary; supreme; petty; amicable; mock; grueling.

verbs

appeal—; arraign for—; arrange for—; bear—; behold—; bias—; challenge to—; conclude—; conduct—; determine—; docket —; judge—; prejudice—; preside over—; protract—; scorn—; summon for—; warrant—; —absolves; —acquits; —airs; —

clears; —commences; —discloses; —exculpates; —exonerates; —notorizes; —publicizes; —ventilates; —whitewashes.

(See effort, attempt, endeavor, tribunal, examination.)

TRIBAL

adverbs

ceremonially; strictly; narrowly; originally; characteristically; singularly; peculiarly; exclusively; oddly; actually; apparently; obviously; manifestly; conspicuously.

TRIBE

adjectives

beaten; finny; kindred; rebellious; malignant; predatory; cervine; hostile; crushed; pastoral; illustrious; sylvan; scattered (pl); swarming (pl); cognate; barbarian; unfriendly; neighboring; scaly; contemptible; perishing; indolent; wandering; protected; aboriginal; feline; feathered; unlearned; thriftless; primitive; unnumbered (pl); invisible; swarthy; powerful; fierce; native; carnivorous.

verbs

affiliate with—; ban from—; band in—; cement—; evolve from—; exterminate—; father—; found—; head—; inflame—; mobilize—; muster—; perpetuate—; scatter—; unite—; weld—s; —expands; —multiplies; —ostracizes; —prospers; —survives; —thrives; —vanishes; —wanes.

(See clan, family.)

TRIBULATIONS

verbs

afflict with—; allay—; assuage—; augment —; ease—; encounter—; endure—; experience—; lament—; mitigate—; mourn—; occasion—; palliate—; suffer—; —consume; —distress; —harass; —harrow; —rack; —subdue; —weigh upon.

(See affliction, trouble.)

TRIBUNAL

adjectives

legal; international; judicious; secret; tardy; independent; impartial; peaceful; revolutionary; bustling; arbitral; mock; revolting; supreme; military; just; righteous.

verbs

adjourn—; appeal to—; bias—; convoke—; hamper—; prejudice—; resort to—; —adjudicates; —arbitrates; —awards; —brings in a verdict; —confirms; —decides; —determines; —dooms; —evaluates; —judges; — passes an opinion; —proclaims; —reviews; —sentences; —sets aside; —settles.

(See court, jury.)

TRIBUTE

adjectives

tardy; august; odorous; extravagant; sincere; unconscious; significant; fitting; requisite; eloquent; noble; unwilling; touching; impressive; remarkable; manifold (pl); expressive; everlasting; elaborate; grim; extraordinary; floral; stipulated; joyous; sisterly; generous; anonymous; spontaneous; obtrusive; virgin; poetic; personal; russet; complacent; curious; honorable; intuitive; magnificent; whole-hearted.

verbs

accept—; acknowledge—; award—; bestow —; decline—; decry—; demand—; disdain —; extort—; grant—; indulge—; lavish—; levy—; merit—; offer—; owe—; pour—; scorn—; yield—; —acclaims; —compliments; —flatters; —glorifies; —indemnifies; —lauds; —recompenses; —remunerates; — rewards.

(See graft, tax, bribe.)

TRICK

adjectives

psychological; innocent; hideous; juggling; juvenile; perfidious; foremost; scurvy; forgotten; unwarrantable; commercial; ultramontane; pretty; strategic; singular; sardonic; harsh; perverse; ingenious; admiration; momentary; raw; artistic; speeding; ceremonious; unconsidered; shy; mad; fantastical; innate; nasty; extra; cowardly; abominable; ugly; amusing; political; unbecoming; barbarous; stage; trashy; unworthy; fascinating; mathematical; valorous; favorite; villainous; practical.

verbs

concoct—; contrive—; devise—; discern—; disclose—; hatch—; master—; perform—; perpetrate—; practise—; reveal—; spring —; study—; —ambushes; —baffles; —bewilders; —bores; —confounds; —deceives; —defrauds; —deludes; —mystifies; — amuses.

(See puzzle, manipulation, fraud, deceit, magic, mystery.)

TRICK (v)

adverbs

ridiculously; mystifyingly; deftly; unscrupulously; psychologically; perfidiously; singularly; sardonically; ingeniously; amusingly; mathematically; villainously; practically; politically.

(See deceive, fool.)

TRICKERY

adjectives

obvious; successful; low; transparent; base; foreign; shameless.

verbs

disclose—; employ—; fear—; foil—; hint at—; resort to—; scorn—; sense—; surmise —; suspect—; uncover—; unearth—; — baffles; —baits; —bilks; —deceives; —decoys; —defrauds; —deludes; —ensnares; —gulls; —infuriates; —swindles; —victimizes.

(See cunning, hyprocisy, deception, deceit, fraud.)

TRICKSY

adverbs

cleverly; playfully; whimsically; childishly; wildly; uncontrollably; nonsensically; clownishly; roguishly; mischievously; waggishly; comically; laughably; farcically; ludicrously.

TRICKY

adverbs

subtly; cunningly; insidiously; surreptitiously; artfully; slyly; craftily; deceitfully; delightfully; dangerously; cleverly; adroitly; alarmingly; mischievously; playfully; harmlessly; provokingly; disagreeably; plaguedly; foolishly; maneuveringly; underhandedly.

TRIFLE

adjectives

consequential; unspeakable; useless; glittering; laborious; insignificant; nameless; countless (pl); honest; musical; merest; satirical; inconsiderable; inconsequential; important; enchanted; silliest; logical; careless; petty; pedantic.

TRIFLE (v)

adverbs

leeringly; ridiculously; ludicrously; unspeakably; insignificantly; illogically; inconsequentially; pettishly; pedantically.

(See toy, play.)

TRIFLES
verbs

belittle—; chatter about—; discount—; disregard—; emphasize—; fret over—; ignore —; minimize—; omit—; scrutinize—; shelve —; skim over—; skip—; stress—; underestimate—; —irk; —irritate; —pique; —rile (colloq.); —plague.

(See insignificance, trivialities.)

TRIFLING
adverbs

absurdly; foolishly; facetiously; flippantly; languidly; senselessly; nonsensically; giddily; airily; ridiculously; farcically; clownishly; intolerably; vainly; uncommonly.

TRIGGER
verbs

caress—; cock—; draw—; ease—; finger—; flick—; fondle—; gear—; jam—; jerk—; jiggle—; oil—; lock—; lubricate—; release—; snap—; wedge—; —clicks; —controls; —discharges; —endangers; —menaces; —recedes; —threatens.

(See knob, lever.)

TRIM
adverbs

naturally; pleasantly; agreeably; usually; habitually; unwontedly; stiffly; jauntily; daintily; smoothly; delicately; neatly; unusually; particularly; noticeably; conspicuously; indescribably; painfully; marvelously; delightfully.

TRIM (*v*)
adverbs

cautiously; judiciously; exquisitely; gaudily; garrishly; tastefully; symbolically; neatly; fastidiously.

(See arrange, adjust.)

TRIP
adjectives

fairy; perilous; constant; phantasmagoric; periodic; bridal; shopping; foreign; innumerable (pl); mysterious; ghastly; infernal; stimulating; overland; sight-seeing; curious; delightful; strenuous; previous.

verbs

conclude—; contemplate—; depart on—; embark on—; entrain on—; extend—; journey on—; plan—; prolong—; protract—; sally forth on—; —acquaints one with; —embraces; —enchants; —enlightens; —fatigues; —intrigues; —proceeds; —progresses; —relaxes; —spans; —traverses.

(See flight, journey, excursion, quest, tour.)

TRIP (*v*)
adverbs

rhythmically; gaily; dexterously; lightly; noiselessly; blithely; strenuously; fantastically.

(See dance, move.)

TRIPPING
adverbs

lightly; gaily; merrily; jauntily; blithely; nimbly; tunefully; pleasantly; childishly; girlishly; joyously; happily; beautifully; quickly; buoyantly; ecstatically; melodiously.

TRITE
adverbs

monotonously; tiresomely; vapidly; disagreeably; invariably; trivially; facetiously; fatuously; intolerably; sententiously; uninterestingly; wearily; tediously; flatly; senselessly; vacuously; prosily.

TRIUMPH
adjectives

unworthy; pitiless; crowning; consummate; delusive; melancholy; fiendish; hideous; intoxicating; rare; dawning; gay; paltry; splendid; rhetorical; superficial; turbulent; forensic; ill-concealed; temporary; bitter; assured; absent; unsought; demiurgic; vindictive; final; social; unapproachable; intimate; inimitable; chuckling; strategic; recent; brilliant; nameless; unspeakable; perpetual; wearisome; secure; permanent; malicious; veritable; ultimate; dramatic; awful; debonair; personal; scornful; delirious; ultimate; unmistakable; conscious; passionate; unbroken; remorseless; diplomatic; ceremonial; marvelous; magnificent; peaceful; glorious; melodious; laboring; slight; shameful; contemptible; veritable; bacchanal; temporary.

verbs

acclaim—; attend with—; belittle—; blaze into—; boast—; commemorate—; concede —; congratulate one on—; dilute—; emerge in—; exult in—; foreshadow—; frustrate—; gain—; hail—; mar—; presage—; record —; rejoice in—; return in—; signalize—; sing of—; spur to—; thwart—; witness—; —elates; —emancipates; —flushes; —vanquishes.

(See conquest, ovation.)

TRIUMPH (v)

adverbs

markedly; notably; supremely; gloriously; pitilessly; consummately; intoxicatingly; rhetorically; forensically; politically; strategically; ultimately; diplomatically; veritably.

(See win, succeed.)

TRIUMPHANT

adverbs

proudly; elatedly; justly; naturally; exultingly; wholly; gloriously; splendidly; magnificently; happily; radiantly; delightedly; joyously; jubilantly; merrily; laughingly; heartily; mockingly; jeeringly; scoffingly.

TRIVIAL

adverbs

absurdly; foolishly; altogether; wholly; senselessly; nonsensically; ridiculously; intolerably; uncommonly; insignificantly; inconsequentially; particularly; vexatiously; bothersomely; cheaply; childishly.

TRIVIALITIES

verbs

amplify—; babble—; charge with—; clarify —; cloak in—; content with—; discard—; dismiss—; escape—; evade—; flounder on —; magnify—; prate about—; scoff at—; scorn—; shrink from—; —arise; —bore; —crop up; —harass.

(See trifles.)

TROLLEY-CAR

verbs

collide with—; derail—; jam—; man—; outstrip—; pilot—; schedule—s; stream from—; —accelerates; —clatters; —con-

verges on; —crawls along; —disburdens; —jangles by; —jars; —jolts; —lurches; — rumbles; —screeches; —tears.

(See train.)

TROOPING

adverbs

merrily; noisily; gaily; purposefully; sullenly; angrily; boisterously; truculently; pugnaciously; ominously; threateningly; menacingly; mischievously; derisively; happily; shyly; defiantly; resolutely; encouragingly; triumphantly; laughingly.

TROOPS

adjectives

dispirited; sleepy; ragged; shoeless; ill-equipped; mutinous; light-armed; furious; hated; vulgar; servile; available; predatory; parti-colored; raw; flexible; scattered; exhausted; obtained; infectious; radiant; mercenary; wearied; supplementary; fresh; disembarking; organized; disciplined.

verbs

accoutre—; amass—; arm—; assemble—; ban—; conceal—; concentrate—; dispatch —; disperse—; draft—; enhearten—; enlist —; enforce with—; equip—; garrison—; halt—; harry—; mass—; mobilize—; muster —; quarter—; transport—; yield to—; —advance; —beleaguer; —besiege; —bolster; —charge; —coerce; —disband; —drive; — invade; —mutiny; —occupy; —patrol; — pour into; —reconnoitre; —retaliate; — rout; —storm; —throng.

(See brigade, army, besieger, invader, militia.)

TROPHY

adjectives

glorious; grisly; evil-smelling; ghastly; bloody; shining; melancholy; ostentatious.

verbs

acquire—; annex—; attain—; award—; carry off—; cherish—; clinch—; collect—s; compete for—; contend for—; covet—; display—; engrave—; exhibit—; gain—; gather—s; merit—; procure—; recover—; regain—; relinquish—; retain—; retrieve—; treasure—; value—; —commemorates; — elates; —honors; —signifies; —symbolizes.

(See laurels, monument, memorial, medal.)

TROPICAL
adverbs
narrowly; essentially; fundamentally; peculiarly; definitely; scientifically; geographically; preferably; characteristically; distinctly; presumably; unpleasantly; agreeably; intolerably.

TROT (v)
adverbs
doggedly; obediently; faithfully; listlessly; monotonously; diligently; jubilantly.
(See gallop, run.)

TROUBLE
adjectives
wretched; associate; endless; unfortunate; personal; perpetual; disciplinary; monetary; annoying; powerful; inflammatory; joyful; intolerable; vague; obscure; major; nocturnal; infinite; lifelong; hesitant; poor; delicious; cruel; constant; garrulous; complex; distressing; pathetic; contagious; invincible; luxurious; measurable.

verbs
afflict with—; anticipate—; arrest—; attend with—; avert—; avoid—; bear—; bewail —; breed—; compensate for—; cure—; diagnose—; endure—; experience—; explore —; foment—; instigate—; lament—; localize—; minimize—; mourn—; pour out—s; probe—; remedy—; repay—; stir up—; undergo—; ward off—; —besets; —blasts; —blights; —crops up; —deranges; —harasses; —haunts; —irks; —irritates; —looms; —lurks; —manifests itself; —originates in; —piques; —preys upon; —rankles; —recurs; —ruffles; —rumples; —seethes; —simmers; —smites; —strikes; —waxes; —weighs upon; —wracks.
(See affliction, hardship, difficulty, adversity, obstacles, tribulation.)

TROUBLE (v)
adverbs
impudently; perpetually; vaguely; obscurely; nocturnally; infinitely; distressingly; profoundly.
(See disturb, irritate.)

TROUBLED
adverbs
nervously; frenziedly; unnaturally; laughably; ridiculously; pathetically; lamentably; curiously; abnormally; naturally; touchingly; supremely; unduly; deeply; indescribably; perceptibly; suspiciously; significantly; pitiably; miserably; terribly; tenderly.

TROUBLESOME
adverbs
persistently; increasingly; sometimes; slightly; devilishly; deucedly; perplexingly; mysteriously; conspicuously; palpably; visibly; manifestly; unusually; naturally; particularly; diplomatically; vexatiously; distressingly; painfully; consistently; remarkably; deliberately; despicably; grossly; boldly; defiantly; intentionally; always.

TROUSERS
adjectives
voluminous; baggy; fluttering; plaid; mustard-colored; creaseless; sport.

verbs
alter—; array in—; bare—; divest of—; doff—; don—; drape—; fray—; garb in —; hitch up—; peg—; pleat—; refurbish—; rend—; retrieve—; strip of—; sunder—; tatter—; vest in—; —clothe; —cover; —protect.
(See clothing.)

TRUANT
adverbs
vexatiously; intolerably; deliberately; heedlessly; carelessly; triflingly; negligently; indifferently; worthlessly; incorrigibly; derisively; brazenly; inexplicably; unaccountably; wantonly; unprofitably; unendurably; bafflingly.

TRUCE
adjectives
reasonable; temporary; faithless; broken; perpetual.

verbs
adopt—; agree to—; arrive at—; beseech —; clamor for—; consent to—; declare—; effect—; hail—; hamper—; impede—; invite—; petition for—; plead for—; press for—; proclaim—; project—; refuse—; reject—; rejoice in—; sign—; welcome—; —arrests; —checks; —curtails; —liberates; —lulls; —pacifies; —reprieves; —rescues; —suspends.
(See halt, peace, respite.)

1215

TRUCK

adjectives

rumbling; passing; clattering.

verbs

assign to—; consign to—; fuel—; guide—; license—; lubricate—; manoeuvre—; overhaul—; recondition—; shift—; —bears; —booms; —chugs (colloq.); —clatters; —conveys; —groans; —jars; —jolts; —pounds along; —roars; —rolls; —rumbles; —swerves; —transports.

(See cart, automobile, bus, vehicle.)

TRUCULENT

adverbs

unbearably; offensively; boldly; daringly; intolerably; boorishly; unmistakably; openly; brutally; challengingly; brazenly; grossly; ominously; inordinately; alarmingly; disagreeably; unreasonably; always; sullenly; singularly; curiously; uncommonly; viciously; vengefully; villainously.

TRUDGE (*v*)

adverbs

wearily; monotonously; heavily; tirelessly; lazily; solemnly; indefatigably; bravely; buoyantly; patiently; laboriously.

(See walk, proceed.)

TRUE

adverbs

apparently; positively; unquestionably; avowedly; confessedly; admittedly; professedly; palpably; essentially; obviously; evidently; manifestly; officially; reliably; solemnly; disagreeably; accidentally; fundamentally; profoundly; disgracefully; unpleasantly; horribly; intrinsically; gloriously; unanswerably; painfully; heavily; ironically; shockingly; sublimely; universally.

TRUMPET

adjectives

shattering; martial; hideous; silver; snarling; hostile; fierce; discordant; splitting; unblown.

verbs

flourish—s; hearken to—; sound—; toot—; —alarms; —awakens; —blares; —blasts; —blazes; —calls forth; —deafens; —hails; —

heralds; —mobilizes; —musters; —proclaims; —rends; —resounds; —reverberates; —screams; —shatters; —trills.

(See bugle, loudspeaker.)

TRUNK

adjectives

formless; nameless; forest; ungainly; uniform; overhanging; prostrate; silicified; comfortable; quivering; columnar; palpitating; charred; ghostlike; scraggy; knotty; fleshy; decaying; crackling; gnarled; split; ponderous; hoary; fibrous; barky; crashing; moss-grown.

TRUST

adjectives

gentle; boyish; investment; serene; guileless; humble; honorable; unfaltering; blind; changeless; fearless; devoted; stupendous; buoyant; false; unswerving; impious; important; instinctive; delusive; serious; theologic; complete; earnest; human; commercial; implicit; dreadful; sacred; unattainable; ample.

verbs

abuse—; afford—; bestow—; betray—; breach—; breed—; charge with—; cherish —; confide—in; encourage—; entertain—of; fix—; foster—; found—on; inspire—; misplace—; nurse—; nurture—; relinquish—; retain—; root—; rue—; shake—; shatter—; shock out of—; strengthen—; violate—; —crumbles; —falters; —flatters; —reposes in; —wanes; —wavers.

(See hope, assurance, faith, confidence, idealism.)

TRUST (*v*)

adverbs

implicitly; assuredly; fondly; indolently; tacitly; shrewdly; reverentially; credulously; explicitly; guilelessly; delusively; amply; unfalteringly.

(See rely, depend.)

TRUSTFUL

adverbs

innocently; gullibly; overly; wistfully; childishly; foolishly; unwisely; inordinately; singularly; particularly; incredibly; unbelievably; curiously; remarkably; peculiarly; uncommonly; idiotically; touchingly; unaffectedly; pitifully; confidently; terribly; ingenuously; naively.

adverbs

admirably; commendably; unusually; exceptionally; absolutely; utterly; uncommonly; singularly; obviously; apparently; undoubtedly; dependably; truly; supposedly; presumably.

TRUTH

adjectives

disagreeable; dual; unlovely; conceivable; accidental; fundamental; invincible; profound; pursuing; abstract; gloomy; clear; hackneyed; striking; delicious; innocent; disgraceful; unpleasant; intense; solemn; transparent; undoubted; distracted; distorted; outspoken; unconscious; searching; fragmentary; absolute; disguised; horrible; bare; consequent; hateful; perfect; sweet; unfaltering; gracious; useful; innate; unequivocal; practical; rigorous; intrinsic; perennial; granite; austere; unadulterated; glorious; crystal; rudimentary; unsophisticated; dramatic; perverting; palpable; historic; objective; unanswerable; demonstrated; religious; astounding; established; magnificent; slighted; moral; painful; remorseless; hideous; burning; lasting; indelible; priceless; unfathomable; domestic; injured; flattering; apparent; immutable; heavenly; benignant; heavy; consolatory; revered; crushing; valid; constant; barbed; naked; substantial; shocking; unornamented; golden; unvarnished; obvious; stretched; serviceable; scattered; droll; general; solid; unique; humbling; unrecognized; melancholy; informing; appalling; sober; relative; heartrending; comparative; dawning; naturalistic; formidable; imageless; irrefragable; physical; maiden; effectual; royal; sacred; essential; precious; unwelcome; bitter; underlying; stately; steadfast; necessary; good; symmetrical; sublime; indestructible; philosophical; extraordinary; approximate; divine; pure; indwelling; guileless; brilliant; strenuous; sensuous; inviolable; poignant; universal.

verbs

accept—; acknowledge—; adumbrate—; affirm—; annihilate—; apprehend—; approach—; arrive at—; ascertain—; attest to—; blurt out—; cherish—; cloud—; color—; commit to—; communicate—; compromise—; conceal—; consecrate to—; contradict—; convey—; counterfeit—; credit —; demand—; demonstrate—; deny—; determine—; discern—; disclose—; dispute—; distort—; divulge—; dodge—; dress up—; embroider—; emphasize—; establish—; evade—; expose—; face—; falsify—; flinch before—; forecast—; foster—; foreshadow—; garble—; gloss over—; grace with—; grasp—; herald—; imitate—; impart—; inspire—; intermingle with—; misrepresent—; modify—; obscure—; obstruct—; open—; persuade one of—; pervert—; preach —; probe for—; proclaim—; propagate—; question—; re-echo—; reflect on—; refuge in—; reject—; repudiate—; reveal—; seduce from—; seek—; shadow—; shrink at—; simulate—; sift—; skirt—; smother—; stretch—; stumble over—; support—; sustain—; upholster—; utter—; value—; varnish—; verify—; voice—; vouch for—; warp—; welcome—; —blazes; —burns; —dawns upon; —emerges from; —flatters; —looms; —pierces; —prevails; —shines; —triumphs; —vanquishes.

(See gospel, integrity, verity, veracity, sincerity, realism, reality.)

TRUTHFUL

adverbs

dependably; reliably; absolutely; always; altogether; painfully; brutally; fanatically; childishly; completely; dangerously; evidently; reputedly; allegedly; avowedly; inconveniently; usually; notably; fairly; scarcely; faithfully; precisely; literally; glumly; innocently; technically; volubly; statistically; sensationally; frankly; vividly; graphically; impressively; simply; artfully; bluntly; glibly; reluctantly; gravely.

TRY (v)

adverbs

exceedingly; sorely; insistently; surreptitiously; deliberately; variously; perfunctorily; conscientiously; piteously; energetically; manfully; sorely; convulsively; obstinately; blunderingly; elaborately; abominably; faithfully; vainly; nervously; falteringly; guiltily; strenuously.

(See attempt, endeavor.)

TRYST

adjectives

clandestine; childish; bloody; moonlight; amorous; fatal.

verbs

agree upon—; anticipate—; appoint—; cloak—; curtail—; fulfill—; hamper—; impede—; keep—; observe—; plan—; pledge to—; shroud—; suggest—; veil—; —allures; —beguiles; —transgresses; —violates.

(See appointment, place, meeting.)

TUB

adjectives

odious; fermenting; insignificant; daily; refreshing.

verbs

convey in—; dip into—; drain—; emerge from—; ground—; immerse in—; invert—; plug—; plunge into—; propel—; scour—; scuttle—; soak in—; submerge in—; swamp —; swish in—; tap—.

(See kettle, vat, barrel.)

TUBE

adjectives

pneumatic; elegant; ivory; tortuous; magic; hollow; perforated; delicate; slender; golden; railway; twisted.

verbs

coke—; clog—; convolute—; couple—s; dam —; deflate—; dilate—; distend—; drain—; inflate—; insert—; line—; narrow—; obstruct—; penetrate—; perforate—; pierce—; plug—; puncture—; riddle—; seal—; tap—; throttle—; value—; —bursts; —conveys; —expands; —transmits.

(See nozzle, pipe, conduit, tunnel.)

TUBERCULOSIS

verbs

allay—; check—; combat—; contract—; convey—; diagnose as—; predispose to—; succumb to—; tend toward—; wipe out—; —blasts; —blights; —decimates; —devours; —eats; —impairs; —infects; —moulders; —ravages; —saps; —scathes; —taints; —taxes; —undermines; —wastes.

(See consumption, disease.)

TUCK (v)

adverbs

cautiously; mentally; meticulously; picturesquely; snugly; cozily.

(See fold, press.)

TUFT

adjectives

feathery; obligatory; flowery; amber; inky.

TUG (v)

adverbs

hysterically; drowsily; repeatedly; nervously; agitatedly; repetitiously; exasperatingly.

(See pull, draw.)

TUGBOAT

adjectives

vulgar; little; innumerable (pl); straining; squat; sturdy; pug-nosed.

verbs

employ—; guide—; pilot—; ram—; recruit —; —batters; —bestirs; —chugs (colloq.); —draws; —exerts; —s flock about; —hauls; —plies; —puffs; —s retire; —scurries; —snorts; —steams; —strains; —struggles; —s surround; —tows.

(See boat, motor-boat, launch.)

TULIP

adjectives

red; gold; grandiose; lovely; beauteous.

TUMBLE (v)

adverbs

clownishly; comically; clumsily; drunkenly; wretchedly; abruptly; precipitately.

(See fall, heave.)

TUMOR

verbs

confine—; diagnose—; dissolve—; excise—; extirpate—; incise—; reduce—; relieve—; restrict—; treat—; —atrophies; —blocks; —cankers; —compresses; —distends; —enlarges; —expands; —hardens; —invades; —infiltrates; —obstructs; —protrudes; —subsides; —ulcerates.

(See cancer, abscess, growth.)

TUMULT

adjectives

murmuring; fast-gathering; tempestuous; growing; intestinal; formidable; sickening; ensuing; portentous; wild; rolling; surging; internal; inward; passionate; ceaseless; fiery; civic.

verbs
calm—; quell—; restrain—; —bewilders; —
breaks loose; —ceases; —dies; —disconcerts; —disorders; —embroils; —ensues; —
muddles; —rages; —reigns; —roars; —
ruffles; —subsides; —wanes; —waxes.
(See clamor, confusion, disturbance, commotion, noise, turmoil.)

TUMULTUOUS
adverbs
terribly; unmanageably; boisterously; truculently; inordinately; ungovernably; riotously; uproariously; dangerously; dreadfully; fearfully; alarmingly; ominously; significantly; threateningly; lawlessly; defiantly; boldly; grossly; portentously; desperately; derisively; angrily; triumphantly; madly; crazily; deafeningly; hilariously; drunkenly.

TUNE
adjectives
lingering; stirring; plaintive; warbling;
fat; fulsome; light; touching; melodious;
sentimental; half-remembered; loyal; saucy;
enthralling; trivial; tremulous; mysterious;
merry; pathetic; greedy; fandango; superfluous; tempting; ecstatic; facile; catchy;
pert; lilting; rollicking; romantic.

verbs
accompany—; arrange—; bleat—; carol—;
chant—; coax—from; compose—; fake
(colloq.)—; fiddle—; harmonize—; hum—;
march to—; modulate—; orchestrate—; recall—; render—; score—; strike up—; synchronize—; transpose—; trill—; twitter—;
vocalize—; warble—; yodel—; —amuses;
—delights; —lilts.
(See ditty, air, incantation, song, music.)

TUNE (*v*)
adverbs
automatically; professionally; skillfully; accurately; melodiously; delicately; deftly.
(See adjust.)

TUNEFUL
adverbs
pleasantly; merrily; happily; melodiously;
musically; rhythmically; childishly; naturally; delightfully; simply; sweetly; smoothly;
harmoniously; joyously; joyfully; boyishly.

TUNIC
adjectives
sleeveless; spotless; ungirlish; velvet;
adamantine; rich; gauzy; revealing.

TUNNEL
adjectives
deep-level; brilliant; unsupported; signaled;
clattering; hot; long; snowy; stuffy.

verbs
blast—; blockade—; bore—; burrow—;
drive—through; engineer—; gouge out—;
guide through—; patrol—; project—; seal
—; —couples; —facilitates; —gapes; —
links; —pierces; —penetrates; —unites; —
yawns.
(See tube, conduit, pipe.)

TURBID
adverbs
peculiarly; singularly; slightly; unfortunately; significantly; unpleasantly; momentarily; temporarily; definitely; particularly;
noticeably; obviously.

TURBULENCE
adjectives
licentious; bloody; infantile; bewildering;
riotous; frightening; raucous; nasty.

TURBULENT
adverbs
shamefully; riotously; raucously; ruthlessly;
desperately; tumultuously; mutinously; uproariously; unmanageably; ungovernably;
violently; recklessly; frightfully; implacably; unappeasably; vengefully; brazenly;
murderously; unreasoningly; wildly; furiously; madly; dangerously; ominously; significantly.

TURF
adjectives
trodden; moss-inwoven; firm; flowery;
frost-bit; close-cropped; wet; spongy; emerald; springing; fine; mountain; ragged;
crisp; compact; unscarred.

verbs
corrugate—; delve in—; furrow—; fertilize—; gambol on—; level—; mar—; plow
under—; replace—; smooth—; tamp—;
trim—; —beautifies; —blankets; —extends;
—greens; —mats; —pads; —mow.
(See meadow, grass, tract, ground.)

TURKEY

verbs

carve—; dine on—; domesticate—; gun for
—; market—s; pluck—; roast—; savor—;
spice—; —dances about; —displays feathers; —s flock; —flutters; —gobbles; —gyrates; —hovers; —preens; —rakes; —
ranges; —stirs up; —strokes; —struts; —
symbolizes; —wheels.

(See bird, fowl, rooster.)

TURMOIL

adjectives

fierce; urban; destructive; strenuous; stern;
bloody; hideous; historic; whizzing; noisy.

verbs

embroil in—; ferment—; foment—; provoke
—; quiet—; throw into—; tranquillize—;
—accompanies; —agitates; —confuses; —
convulses; —deranges; —dishevels; —disquiets; —distracts; —diverts; —follows; —
persists; —perturbs; —prevails; —ruffles;
—seethes; —tangles.

(See commotion, tumult, confusion.)

TURN

adjectives

romantic; radical; light; extravagant; ostentatious; countless (pl); sensational; administrative; thoughtful; comic; sudden;
good; fanciful; melodic; sentimental; epi-
grammatical; satirical; intimate; unquiet;
conversational; unexpected; cynical; artificial; marvelous.

TURN (v)

adverbs

snarlingly; tortuously; petulantly; sinuously; deviously; abruptly; reluctantly; gracefully; deliberately; solemnly; imploringly;
exultingly; doggedly; awkwardly; distractedly; insensibly; instinctively; wearily; amiably; insolently; involuntarily; perversely;
radiantly; wistfully; simultaneously; disdainfully; capriciously; resolutely; grudgingly; noiselessly; miraculously; indifferently; discreetly; energetically; listlessly;
treacherously.

(See spin, revolve.)

TURNING

adjectives

incessant; gentle; fateful; acute; accurate.

TURRET

adjectives

squat; glittering; highest; equal; sequestered; fåding; fort.

verbs

armor—; beseige—; command—; festoon—;
fortify—; hover over—; imprison in—;
level—; mount to—; perch on—; plate—;
raze—; surmount—; topple from—; train
—s; view from—; —looms; —revolves; —
rotates.

(See tower, spire, cannon.)

TURTLE

verbs

capture—; crush—; market—s; relish—;
stew—; —s abound; —attains; —breeds;
—burrows; —calls; —creeps; —deposits
eggs; —exudes; —hibernates; —hisses; —
paddles; —perseveres; —protrudes; —snaps
at; —snatches; —submerges; —swims; —
swishes; —withdraws.

(See reptile.)

TUSKS

adjectives

enormous; ingrown; valuable; sharp;
spiral; protective.

TUTOR

adjectives

threadbare; lively; shrewd; deft; skilled;
wise; experienced.

TWANG

adjectives

nasal; familiar; peevish; provincial; annoying.

TWANG (v)

adverbs

exasperatingly; nasally; sharply; tunelessly; harshly; hideously; annoyingly; peevishly.

(See sound.)

TWEEDS

adjectives

imported; sturdy; roughish; rugged; inevitable; exquisite; handsome; hand-loomed.

TWIG

adjectives

tired; overhanging; unsightly; fragile;
hardwood; insignificant; bleak; upreared;

nervous; gleaming; thorny; threatening; ice-coated; crackling.

verbs
bend—; brace—; burden—; clip—; deform —; gather—s; glean—s; ingraft—; prune —s; restrain—; snip off—; support—; thin out—s; —bears; —projects; —protrudes; —shoots out; —spreads.
(See branch, stem.)

TWILIGHT
adjectives
brightening; silvery; sad; deepening; dark; gruesome; obscure; intermediate; shadowy; cool; brilliant; dubious; rainy; darkling; dim; amber; perpetual; magical; unhurried; blank; uncomfortable; slow-dropping; white; disastrous; sulphurous; mystic; thickening; fading; wintry; gathering; winsome; mournful; ancient; departing; hollow; summer; hot; breathless; hesitant; lingering; hushed; mellow; stilly; dense; chilling; luminous; balmy; sympathetic; beautiful; closing.

verbs
approach—; bathe in—; flicker in—; melt into—; reflect—; twinkle in—; —bedims; —creeps upon; —curtails; —curtains; —declines; —deepens; —descends; —diffuses; —dims; —drapes; —fades; —gathers 'round; —glimmers; —hazes; —obscures; —screens; —shades; —shadows; —veils; — wanes; —wraps; —yields to.
(See night, dusk, evening, light, shadow.)

TWILIGHT
adverbs
faintly; delicately; rosily; dully; dimly; windily; fearsomely; beautifully; seductively; romantically; unforgettably; roseately; coldly; darksomely.

TWIN
adjectives
tributary; fraternal; identical.

adverbs
identically; attractively; apparently; interestingly; affectionately; perplexingly; inseparably.

TWINE (v)
adverbs
caressingly; nervously; tortuously; affection-

ately; complicatedly; intricately; involvedly; abundantly.
(See cling, fasten.)

TWINGE
adjectives
warning; smart; hereditary; conscience; painful.

TWINKLE
adjectives
humorous; rapid; peculiar; vicious; merry; mischievous; lewd.

TWINKLE (v)
adverbs
jovially; frostily; softly; luminously; merrily; humorously; peculiarly; mischievously.
(See shimmer, shine.)

TWINKLING
adverbs
brightly; keenly; sharply; affectionately; fondly; mischievously; laughingly; distinctly; irregularly; unmistakably; wittily; brilliantly; intermittently; regularly; indulgently; actually; significantly.

TWIRL (v)
adverbs
nonchalantly; languidly; fiercely; gallantly; sophisticatedly; idly; picturesquely.
(See whirl, revolve.)

TWIST
adjectives
infernal; dexterous; restless; worst; spiral; heroic; antique; unusual; brutal.

TWIST (v)
adverbs
deftly; drearily; slyly; dexterously; insidiously; craftily; tortuously; superciliously; infernally; ruthlessly; restlessly; brutally; viciously.
(See contort, coil.)

TWIT (v)
adverbs
facetiously; vindictively; maliciously; remorselessly; hatefully; spitefully; humorously; comically; blithely; impudently.
(See chide, reproach.)

TWITCH

adjectives

involuntary; vicious; innocent; agonized; virulent.

TWITCH (v)

adverbs

convulsively; weakly; spasmodically; abnormally; morbidly; pathologically; agitatedly; agonizingly.

(See snatch, jerk.)

TWITCHING

adjectives

uneasy; nervous; spasmodic; convulsive.

TWITTER (v)

adverbs

melodiously; sweetly; blithesomely; merrily; innumerably; irritatingly; maddeningly.

(See chirp, sing.)

TWO-FACED

adverbs

despicably; undoubtedly; contemptibly; deceptively; smoothly; smugly; suavely; grossly; subtly; unexpectedly; shamefully; treacherously; disloyally; naturally; craftily; adroitly; artfully; cunningly; slyly.

TYPE

adjectives

innocent; contemplative; existing; rugged; barren; conspicuous; temperamental; severe; shiftless; civilized; austere; myriad (pl); constitutional; conventional; coadequate; psychologic; dominant; nonpareil; sturdy; various (pl); individual; girlish; attentive; established; militant; conceivable; pompous; delicious; feline; ritualist; unchangeable; spirited; aristocratic; unscrupulous; dignified; tender; vulgar; manufactured; dominant; prevalent; fatalistic; chest-heaving; unrealized; faddist; charming; aesthetic; engrossing; delectable; bachelor; evanescent; heroic; spontaneous; gamin; characteristic; unfamiliar; representative; transcendent; malignant; florid; picturesque; myopic; marrying; original; objectionable; intellectual; innumerable (pl); indigenous; ethnic; conceivable; ingenue;

lax; crackling; beautiful; primitive; preferred; didactic; elaborate; primeval; favorable; man-hunting; superficial; hideous; perverted; uncanny; consummate; sunny; manifold (pl); lofty.

verbs

breed—; cast—; characterize—; classify—; conceive—; conform to—; denote—; depict —; designate—; determine—; distinguish—; efface—; enact—; exploit—; fall into—; hew—; idealize—; mold—; portray—; register—; reproduce—; revert to—; specify —; warp—; —embodies; —embraces; — includes; —mystifies; —perplexes.

(See symbol, style, class, model, print.)

TYPE (v)

adverbs

individually; swiftly; accurately; originally; consummately; characteristically.

(See represent.)

TYPEWRITER

verbs

bang—; instruct on—; lubricate—; manipulate—; master—; necessitate—; overhaul —; peck at—; pound on—; service—s; silence—; —clicks; —clatters; —disconcerts; —distracts; —disturbs; —eases; —enables; —facilitates; —lightens; —plagues; —rings; —shifts.

TYPHOON

verbs

—abates; —batters; —devastates; —endangers; —howls; —rages; —ravages; —revolves; —roars; —shrieks; —subsides; — sweeps; —topples; —trammels; —uproots; —whirls.

(See hurricane, blizzard, storm.)

TYPICAL

adverbs

absolutely; entirely; truly; accurately; dependably; reliably; substantially; realistically; symbolically; curiously; incidentally; satisfactorily; approximately; exactly; unerringly; distinctly; indicatively; graphically.

TYRANNICAL

adverbs

quietly; adroitly; unendurably; imperiously;

1222

confidently; socially; selfishly; hopelessly; sweetly; gracefully; wantonly; unscrupulously; insupportably; inexorably; cruelly; vindictively; remorselessly; ruthlessly; intolerably; unreasonably; dangerously; viciously; heartlessly; recklessly; outrageously.

TYRANNY

adjectives

municipal; barefaced; odious; clerical; decided; quiet; adroit; unendurable; imperious; worn-out; watchful; confident; social; selfish; hopeless; legal; grinding; sweet; graceful; wanton; petty; unscrupulous; exacting; insupportable.

verbs

exercise—; impose—upon; inflict with—; germinate—; overthrow—; resist—; revolt against—; savor of—; subject to—; — abuses; —crushes; —distresses; —enslaves; —fetters; —harasses; —oppresses; —re-

stricts; —shackles; —tramples; —treads on; —yokes.

(See despotism, domination, persecution.)

TYRANT

adjectives

unpersuaded; professed; inexorable; implacable; early; despotic; cunning; cruel; sportive; petty; vindictive; remorseless; domestic; power-mad; avaricious; guiltiest; benevolent; invaluable; feminine; pious; sanguinary; ambitious; maniacal; haughty; cloud-piercing; usurping.

verbs

oppose—; play—; prove—; rebel against—; repel—; resist—; serve—; submit to—; — administers; —arrogates; —assumes; —beguiles; —butchers; —coerces; —crushes; — dictates; —domineers; —enslaves; —oppresses; —overrides; —persecutes; —subjugates; —tramples; —usurps; —wields; — yokes.

(See dictator, oppressor; monarch; sovereign.)

U

UBIQUITOUS

adverbs

valuably; extraordinarily; comically; importantly; dominantly; aggressively; conspicuously; pompously; curiously; apparently; eagerly; officiously; ostentatiously; undeniably; proudly; quietly; assertively; enterprisingly; busily; actively; patronizingly.

UGLINESS

adjectives

racy; grotesque; ultimate; shapeless; unmitigated; bare; insipid; ferocious; grim; bestial.

verbs

abhor—; accentuate—; aggravate—; deplore—; dispel—; efface—; enhance—; heighten—; lament—; level—; mitigate—; portray—; revolt at—; —blemishes; —defaces; —deforms; —distorts; —embitters; —mars; —pervades; —robs; —sours; —weighs upon.

(See squalor, deformity.)

UGLY

adverbs

awkwardly; fantastically; grotesquely; amusingly; repulsively; pathetically; unbelievably; distressingly; angularly; terribly; horribly; oddly; touchingly; grievously; ludicrously; ridiculously; deplorably; lamentably; singularly; drolly; strangely; queerly; curiously; forbiddingly; frightfully; grossly; clumsily; hideously; grimly; shockingly.

ULCER

verbs

afflict with—s; cauterize—; detect—; expose —; poultice—; probe—; remedy—; salve—; suffer from—; —blemishes; —blights; —cankers; —cicatrizes; —deteriorates; —devours; —disfigures; —erodes; —festers; —infiltrates; —inflames; —rankles; —ravages; —scars; —scathes; —spreads; —taints.

(See abscess, canker, inflammation, blister, sore, cancer.)

ULCEROUS

adverbs

unfortunately; fatally; seriously; slightly; annoyingly; unpleasantly; disagreeably; presumably; obviously; gnawingly; dangerously; alarmingly; chronically; recently; acutely; painfully; disturbingly; distressingly; unaccountably; finally; extremely.

ULTIMATE

verbs

acclaim—; achieve—; afford—; anticipate —; apply—; attain—; dedicate to—; delay —; demand—; determine—; employ—; gain—; necessitate—; proclaim—; seek—; survive—; temporize—; undergo—; waive —; —endures.

(See extreme, goal, aim.)

adverbs

irrevocably; eventually; significantly; tragically; fatally; decisively; unchangeably; hopelessly.

ULTIMATUM

verbs

accede to—; acknowledge—; bow to—; comply with—; contemplate—; contest—; decree—; deliver—; draw up—; enforce—; execute—; file—; ignore—; issue—; reject —; resist—; retract—; slap down—; thunder—; —admonishes; —demands; —impends; —stipulates; —threatens; —warns.

(See warning, demand, challenge, proposition.)

UMBRAGEOUS

adverbs

refreshingly; pleasantly; gloomily; alarmingly; dismally; mysteriously; delightfully; coolly; gratefully; sensitively; curiously; uncommonly; exceptionally; highly; unexpectedly; surprisingly; suddenly; deeply.

UMBRELLA

adjectives

ubiquitous; formidable; protective; leaking.

verbs

arm with—; borrow—; brandish—; discard —; display—; employ—; flourish—; loll under—; mislay—; resort to—; —affords;

—eclipses; —hoods; —insures; —obscures; —obstructs; —screens; —shades; —shelters; —shrouds.

(See pavilion, cane, canopy.)

UMPIRE
verbs
appeal to—; bias—; boo—; bribe—; mob—; prejudice—; protest to—; "razz"—; —admonishes; —arbitrates; —awards; —bars; —confers with; —decides; —determines; —expels; —hands down a decision; —mediates; —penalizes; —referees.
(See judge.)

UNABASHED
adverbs
courageously; frankly; innocently; childishly; boldly; clearly; admirably; surprisingly; entirely; obviously; defiantly; positively; curiously; steadily; strangely; oddly; marvelously; remarkably; fearlessly; calmly; serenely; quietly; composedly; justly; brazenly.

UNACCEPTABLE
adverbs
obviously; cheaply; unfortunately; deplorably; utterly; curiously; vexatiously; embarrassingly; awkwardly; palpably; crudely; shamefully; outrageously; scandalously; seriously; hopelessly.

UNACCOMMODATING
adverbs
gruffly; ungraciously; embarrassingly; grimly; brusquely; crudely; vexatiously; churlishly; sternly; harshly; indifferently; coolly; curiously; strangely; nonchalantly; coldly; cruelly; crisply; bitterly; appraisingly; imperturbably; disturbingly; distressingly; hopelessly; perplexingly; bewilderingly; unconscionably; absurdly; insolently.

UNACCOMPANIED
adverbs
rarely; lonesomely; occasionally; forlornly; courageously; singularly; oddly; preferably; usually; noticeably; obviously; invitingly; manifestly; precariously; embarrassingly; boldly; daringly; challengingly; unfortunately; audaciously; brazenly; oddly; mysteriously; significantly; foolishly; inadvertently.

UNACCOUNTABLE
adverbs
strangely; outlandishly; utterly; perplexingly; bafflingly; apparently; curiously; challengingly.

UNACCUSTOMED
adverbs
apparently; obviously; manifestly; curiously; oddly; significantly; embarrassingly; awkwardly; clearly; appallingly; crudely.

UNADORNED
adverbs
chastely; severely; casually; deliberately; humbly; noticeably; indifferently; carelessly; distinctly; purposely; vexatiously; intentionally; significantly; curiously; remarkably; conspicuously.

UNAIDED
adverbs
surprisingly; obviously; remarkably; utterly; proudly; triumphantly; completely; curiously; manifestly; distinctly; supposedly; presumably; prescriptively; avowedly.

UNALTERABLE
adverbs
deplorably; inconveniently; officially; constitutionally; unfortunately; definitely; presumably; supposedly; luckily; tragically; wretchedly; obviously; regrettably.

UNANIMOUS
adverbs
whole-heartedly; enthusiastically; warmly; practically; absolutely; eagerly; ardently; vociferously; astonishingly; significantly; comfortingly; completely; cheerfully; sensibly; reassuringly; emphatically; impressively; promptly; gladly; miraculously; happily.

UNAPPETIZING
adverbs
dingily; insipidly; colorlessly; miserably; utterly; unfortunately; curiously; unhappily; suddenly; surprisingly; disappointingly; desperately; hopelessly; completely; dismally;

UNAPPROACHABLE
adverbs
sternly; unaccountably; reticently; gloomily;

U
V

harshly; cruelly; austerely; pompously; arrogantly; imperially; brutally; coldly; unfortunately; strangely; manifestly; forbiddingly; fearfully; frightfully; gravely; rigorously; unsmilingly; tragically; oddly.

UNASSAILABLE
adverbs
virtuously; pompously; officially; self-righteously; powerfully; imperially; royally; safely; securely; righteously; judicially; constitutionally; happily; arrogantly; presumably; haughtily; hatefully; oddly; monstrously; heartbreakingly; abominably.

UNASSUMING
adverbs
modestly; quietly; demurely; sweetly; shyly; unobtrusively; attractively; charmingly; unaffectedly; delightfully; pleasantly; habitually; naturally; agreeably; artlessly; naively; ingenuously; informally.

UNATTRACTIVE
adverbs
awkwardly; grotesquely; repulsively; unbelievably; pitiably; oddly; angularly; deplorably; strangely; fantastically; pathetically; distressingly; terribly; horridly; touchingly; ridiculously; lamentably; singularly; drolly; queerly: curiously; crudely; painfully.

UNAUTHORIZED
adverbs
blatantly; boldly; brazenly; daringly; unluckily; tragically; foolishly; rashly; recklessly; obviously; palpably; gravely; defiantly; carelessly.

UNAVOIDABLE
adverbs
regrettably; completely; vexatiously; unfortunately; unluckily; awkwardly; embarrassingly; humiliatingly; mortifyingly; incontrovertibly; frankly; fatally; allegedly; manifestly; evidently; obviously; curiously; undoubtedly; legally.

UNAWARE
adverbs
blissfully; innocently; happily; astonishingly; oddly; ironically; curiously; singularly; incredibly; strangely; incongruously; stupidly; carelessly; heedlessly; blithely; nonchalantly; blindly; absurdly.

UNBALANCED
adverbs
dangerously; obviously; palpably; outlandishly; grotesquely; crazily; manifestly; tragically; oddly; singularly; naturally; peculiarly; definitely; presumably; allegedly; unhappily; unfortunately; irresponsibly; curiously; overwhelmingly; incurably; irremediably; deplorably; wretchedly; dangerously; utterly; recently; temporarily.

UNBECOMING
adverbs
utterly; entirely; wholly; frightfully; indecorously; terribly; immodestly; uncommonly; palpably; frankly; awkwardly; exceptionally; discreditably; unworthily; extremely; shamefully; disgracefully.

UNBENDING
adverbs
cruelly; gravely; pompously; austerely; coldly; harshly; severely; bitterly; proudly; taciturnly; implacably; unappeasably; naturally; pridefully; horribly; preposterously; inconceivably; proudly.

UNBIASED
adverbs
delightfully; dependably; truly; actually; sincerely; commendably; admirably; laudably; warrantably; personally; broadly; allegedly; reputedly; avowedly; indisputably; palpably; absolutely; wholly; dispassionately; disinterestedly; fortunately; tolerantly; judiciously; luckily.

UNBURDEN (*v*)
adverbs
deliberately; remorsefully; articulately; freely; faithfully; tremulously; unconsciously.
(See relieve, empty.)

UNBUSINESSLIKE
adverbs
astonishingly; flippantly; astoundingly; disappointingly; surprisingly; curiously; absurdly; disagreeably; disconcertingly; perplexingly; disturbingly; foolishly; seriously; palpably; strangely; unaccountably; remarkably; amazingly; uncommonly; facet-

iously; annoyingly; impractically; suspiciously; evasively; equivocally; shiftily; indecisively; oddly; impossibly.

UNCANNY

adverbs

alarmingly; peculiarly; weirdly; curiously; strangely; inexplicably; unaccountably; harrowingly; oppressively; mysteriously; viciously; vaguely; unreasonably; hauntingly; gloomily; indefinably; obscurely; inescapably; absurdly; inscrutably; eerily.

UNCEREMONIOUS

adverbs

delightfully; independently; casually; pleasantly; brusquely; facetiously; gruffly; hastily; smilingly; nervously; agreeably; portentously; ominously; naturally; usually; remarkably; singularly; unexpectedly; oddly; peculiarly; characteristically; suddenly; marvellously.

UNCERTAIN

adverbs

timidly; clumsily; shyly; tremulously; blindly; feebly; pathetically; curiously; strangely; vexatiously; indecisively; oddly; miserably; wretchedly; terribly; peculiarly; singularly; significantly; awkwardly; nervously.

UNCERTAINTY

adjectives

unconscious; momentary; prevalent; full; horrible; anxious; tremulous; painful; intolerable; pleasing.

verbs

abolish—; consume—; destroy—; dispel—; efface—; erase—; exhibit—; extinguish—; falter in—; flounder in—; hesitate in—; sweep aside—; vacillate in—; wallow in—; waver in—; —clouds; —dogs; —muddles; —perplexes; —persists; —pervades; —plagues; —prevails; —shrouds; —unnerves; —veils.

(See misapprehension, ambiguity, hesitation, doubt.)

UNCHANGEABLE

adverbs

obstinately; stubbornly; obdurately; egotistically; manifestly; obviously; hopelessly; vexatiously; fatefully; dependably; officially; authoritatively; definitely; cruelly; legally; constitutionally; humanly.

UNCHARITABLE

adverbs

selfishly; narrowly; intolerantly; dogmatically; naturally; unfortunately; stubbornly; harshly; thoughtlessly; sternly; abominably; curiously; viciously; disagreeably; coldly; callously; grimly; heartlessly; terribly.

UNCHRISTIAN

adverbs

dreadfully; blatantly; defiantly; definitely; positively; abominably; appallingly; shockingly; boldly; openly; curiously; savagely; barbarously; cruelly; selfishly; flauntingly; gracelessly; indifferently; callously; horribly.

UNCIVIL

adverbs

deliberately; intentionally; significantly; challengingly; rudely; plainly; clearly; inexcusably; unpardonably; contemptibly; arrogantly; crudely; curtly; gruffly; boorishly; churlishly; dangerously; defiantly; boldly; audaciously; curiously; particularly; grossly.

UNCLEAN

adverbs

odiously; squalidly; grossly; obscenely; singularly; indescribably; detestably; abominably; despicably; offensively; disgustingly; impiously; carelessly; arrantly; grievously; scandalously; disastrously; shamefully; infamously; infectiously; horribly; noxiously; deleteriously.

UNCOMFORTABLE

adverbs

definitely; painfully; distressingly; unpleasantly; horribly; dangerously; utterly; coldly; dimly; obscurely; inexcusably; shamefully; uneasily; genuinely; needlessly; extremely; exceedingly; curiously; devilishly; confoundedly; thoroughly; strangely; physically; angrily; embarrassingly; outrageously.

UNCOMMUNICATIVE

adverbs

disagreeably; unsociably; resolutely; doggedly; awkwardly; taciturnly; secretively;

deliberately; stubbornly; loyally; silently; profoundly; determinedly; unpleasantly; desperately; hopelessly; reticently; obstinately; evasively; unflinchingly; exceptionally; immovably; extraordinarily; hopelessly.

UNCOMPLAINING
adverbs
submissively; humbly; curiously; docilely; wisely; fearfully; meekly; singularly; doggedly; resolutely; sullenly; cheerfully; timidly; astutely; craftily; suspiciously; helplessly; shrewdly; patiently; sagaciously; discreetly; cunningly; prudently; knowingly.

UNCOMPLIMENTARY
adverbs
obviously; openly; subtly; maliciously; enviously; terribly; suavely; derisively; cunningly; insidiously; meanly; jealously; smartly; venomously; scandalously; deleteriously; libellously; slightly; highly; unreasonably; curiously; singularly; particularly; smoothly; definitely; contemptibly; deliberately; dreadfully; appallingly; shockingly.

UNCOMPROMISING
adverbs
stiffly; rigidly; unappeasably; obstinately; stubbornly; doctrinally; piously; dogmatically; puritannically; impossibly; terribly; disagreeably; unpleasantly; austerely; severely; sternly; cruelly; brutally; frankly; boldly; truculently; turbulently; gruffly; callously; definitely; indomitably; inexorably; resolutely; fanatically; proudly; arrogantly.

UNCONCERNED
adverbs
indifferently; nonchalantly; blithely; happily; selfishly; thoughtlessly; blindly; ignorantly; pathetically; terribly; deliberately; inconsiderately; curiously; ominously; apparently; singularly; absurdly; strangely; unnaturally; abominably.

UNCONDITIONAL
adverbs
presumably; allegedly; entirely; happily; fortunately; liberally; definitely; constitutionally; practically; generously; broadly; flatly; gloriously; triumphantly; reliably.

UNCONGENIAL
adverbs
unhappily; obviously; bitterly; oddly; surprisingly; helplessly; terribly; dreadfully; intolerably; unfortunately; hopelessly; desperately; singularly; definitely; temperamentally; ominously; fearfully.

UNCONSCIOUS
adverbs
blindly; childishly; selfishly; pathetically; happily; blissfully; momentarily; temporarily; singularly; apparently; obviously; manifestly; presumably; undoubtedly.

UNCONSCIOUSNESS
verbs
approach—; arouse from—; avert—; diagnose—; dope into—; drug into—; fade into —; feign—; hover near—; lapse into—; pretend—; repose in—; shock into—; sink into—; stun into—; —deadens; —endures; —paralyzes; —persists; —seals; —terrifies. (See coma, lethargy.)

UNCONSTITUTIONAL
adverbs
odiously; presumably; flagrantly; supposedly; lamentably; dangerously; daringly; defiantly; trickily; craftily; definitely; manifestly; openly; incontrovertibly; postively; decidedly; flagitiously; unfortunately.

UNCONVENTIONAL
adverbs
absurdly; ridiculously; flauntingly; flagrantly; daringly; slightly; oddly; peculiarly; astonishingly; surprisingly; quaintly; sweetly; singularly; notionally; delightfully; outlandishly; shamefully; purposely; attractively; refreshingly; vexatiously; bewilderingly; unpleasantly; boorishly; crudely.

UNCOUTH
adverbs
rudely; boorishly; naturally; inexcusably; lamentably; awkwardly; fantastically; inordinately; contemptibly; colossally; shockingly; drunkenly; impudently; morosely; unpleasantly; disagreeably; deliberately; boisterously; blatantly; offensively; insufferably; innately; intolerably; unbearably.

adjectives
vain; awkward; embarrassing.

UNCOVER (v)
adverbs
mercilessly; ruthlessly; searchingly; diligently; fruitfully; formidably; slyly; grimly; cruelly; despotically; cunningly.
(See reveal, disclose.)

UNCTUOUS
adverbs
disgustingly; professionally; pedantically; smugly; blandly; intolerably; obsequiously; submissively; deceptively; ominously; maddeningly; solemnly; softly; persuasively; carefully; properly; ingratiatingly; suavely; adroitly.

UNDAUNTED
adverbs
resolutely; intrepidly; courageously; blithely; gaily; serenely; calmly; curiously; remarkably; gallantly; laughingly; grimly; absurdly; foolishly; daringly; recklessly; apparently; singularly; confidently; amazingly.

UNDECIPHERABLE
adverbs
sadly; strangely; unfortunately; childishly; dimly; curiously; singularly; vexatiously; awkwardly; disappointingly; heartbreakingly; inexcusably; unpardonably; unreasonably; significantly; deliberately; intentionally; craftily; purposely; cruelly.

UNDEMONSTRATIVE
adverbs
habitually; naturally; inherently; significantly; coolly; surprisingly; perplexingly; churlishly; ungratefully; meanly; disappointingly; shyly; bashfully; modestly; awkwardly; demurely; augustly; sternly; forbiddingly; painfully; curiously; oddly; calmly; chillingly; unluckily; unfortunately; temperamentally.

UNDERGO (v)
adverbs
heroically; gallantly; stoically; generously; willingly; staunchly; courageously; peacefully.
(See endure, experience.)

UNDERHANDED
adverbs
wickedly; curiously; significantly; nefariously; despicably; detestably; craftily; shrewdly; carefully; mysteriously; cunningly; abominably; adroitly; atrociously; cruelly; disgracefully; basely; viciously; grossly.

UNDERNOURISHED
adverbs
pathetically; cruelly; undeniably; positively; definitely; obviously; miserably; wretchedly; pitiably; dangerously; alarmingly; desperately; helplessly; hopelessly; unconsciously; generally; surprisingly; deplorably; unwisely; impecuniously; dreadfully; terribly; inexcusably; recently; emphatically; bitterly.

UNDERPAID
adverbs
contemptibly; inexcusably; cruelly; terribly; needlessly; obviously; absurdly; remarkably; preposterously; presumably; manifestly; definitely; wretchedly; miserably; unwarrantably; emphatically.

UNDERSCORE (v)
adverbs
heavily; blackly; redundantly; indelibly.
(See mark.)

UNDERSELL (v)
adverbs
astutely; ethically; secretively; legitimately; momentously; boldly; financially; desperately.
(See transact, win.)

UNDERSTAND (v)
adverbs
literally; distinctly; cleverly; dimly; sympathetically; expressly; properly; assuredly; intimately; vaguely; keenly; accurately; theoretically; adequately; subtly; exceptionally; shrewdly; sympathetically; tacitly.
(See comprehend, discern.)

UNDERSTANDING
adjectives
friendly; robust; keen; previous; courteous; prospective; analytical; theoretical; adequate; subtle; slow; unconscious; instinctive; definite; speedy; cynical; cordial; synthetic; useful; retrospective; close; general; comprehensive; masculine; profound; dis-

cursive; exceptional; enlarged; vague; chronic; secret; veiled; barren; shrewd; human; distinct; mutual; kind; sympathetic; furtive; mean; emotional; tacit; verbal; momentary; consummate; full-bodied.

verbs
achieve—; acquire—; arrive at—; attain—; awaken—; blossom into—; chill—; convey to —; demonstrate—; destroy—; display—; engrave on—; enlarge—; enlighten—; enrich —; enter into—; escape—; evince—; feign —; foster—; further—; gain—; grasp—; grope for—; illuminate—; impart—; impede—; inhibit—; lack—; lead to—; manifest—; obtain—; promote—; reflect—; require—; school—; seek—; swell—; temper with—; yield to—; —dawns; —discerns; —discriminates; —harmonizes; —pacifies; —tranquillizes; —triumphs.
(See insight, knowledge, commonsense, intellect, learning.)

adverbs
sympathetically; generously; pleasantly; unusually; remarkably; helpfully; patiently; profoundly; momentarily; marvellously; mercifully; completely.

UNDERTAKE (v)
adverbs
sporadically; rashly; reluctantly; successfully; boldly; ill-advisedly; illicitly; scientifically; desperately; hazardously; perilously; grimly; ridicuously; arduously; financially.
(See assume.)

UNDERTAKING
adjectives
scientific; tangible; desperate; unconnected; momentous; remarkable; bold; spurious; aimless; conciliatory; hazardous; chimerical; illicit; solemn; important; tremendous; munificent; unparalleled; perilous; grim; exciting; ridiculous; involved; arduous; herculean; stupendous; desperate; formidable; financial.

verbs
abandon—; analyze—; bind to—; commend —; conceive—; desert—; encourage—; endanger—; essay—; forego—; forestall—; forsake—; insure—; jeopardize—; laud—; outline—; plan—; relinquish—; promote—; renounce—; tackle—; venture on—; withdraw from—; —embraces; —endeavors; —

flourishes; —promises; —thrives.
(See enterprise, plan, deal, program.)

UNDISMAYED
adverbs
gallantly; confidently; optimistically; curiously; admirably; wondrously; apparently; evidently; fortunately; recklessly; pathetically; courageously; singularly; fanatically; zealously; blindly; imperturbably; astonishingly; surprisingly; remarkably; significantly; audaciously; absurdly; arrogantly; brashly.

UNDISTURBED
adverbs
serenely; blindly; stoically; pedantically; witlessly; irresponsibly; calmly; vexatiously; infuriatingly; strangely; amazingly; suspiciously; blandly; unaccountably; surprisingly; philosophically.

UNDULATE (v)
adverbs
restlessly; incessantly; sinuously; gently.
(See wave, curve.)

UNDULATING
adverbs
regularly; smoothly; endlessly; restlessly; dizzily; disturbingly; monotonously; ceaselessly; pleasantly; arably; advantageously; fortunately; crazily; fascinatingly; delightfully; curiously; vastly; extensively; mysteriously; iridescently; colorfully; singularly; marvellously; incessantly; continuously.

UNDUTIFUL
adverbs
curiously; desperately; disagreeably; cruelly; heartbreakingly; incorrigibly; blindly; bitterly; inexcusably; terribly; singularly; coldly; strangely; unquestionably; unbelievably; incredibly; preposterously; shamefully; miserably; unwarrantably; unconcernedly.

UNEASINESS
adjectives
longing; vague; transitory; abrupt; idle; restless; faint; unhappy; growing.

verbs
afflict with—; allay—; assuage—; burden with—; calm—; dispel—; experience—; inspire—; ridicule—; scoff at—; sense—; sweep away—; —accompanies; —distresses;

—dwells in; —envelopes; —gnaws at; —haunts; —oppresses; —persists; —pervades; —prevails; —shrouds; —stabs; —takes hold; —unnerves; —weighs upon; —yields. (See impatience, discomfort, discontent, anxiety.)

UNEASY

adverbs

naturally; timidly; shyly; unacountably; suddenly; justifiably; unusually; extremely; unnecessarily; needlessly; oddly; ominously; visibly; seriously; obviously; inexplicably; painfully; foolishly; distinctly; inordinately; apparently; profoundly.

UNEDUCATED

adverbs

frankly; unfortunately; academically; supposedly; paradoxically; blessedly; blatantly; strangely; apparently; coarsely; grossly; avowedly; allegedly; manifestly.

UNEMOTIONAL

adverbs

coldly; sternly; gravely; terrifyingly; brutally; harshly; austerely; stoically; unbelievably; unnaturally; abnormally; strangely; singularly; frightfully; ungenerously; stingily; selfishly; terribly; peculiarly; notoriously; reputedly; ostensibly; presumably; conspicuously.

UNEMPLOYED

adverbs

idly; lazily; indolently; unfortunately; miserably; helplessly; inadvertently; unhappily; temporarily; evidently; frequently; manifestly; involuntarily.

UNEMPLOYMENT

adjectives

technological; devastating; partial; continued; nation-wide; artificially-relieved; supposed; appalling; dreaded; frightening.

verbs

absorb—; analyze—; augment—; banish—; bewail—; cancel out—; cause—; check—; decrease—; decry—; deplore—; fear—; increase—; insure against—; legislate against —; lament—; outlaw—; predict—; reduce —; relieve—; remedy—; tackle—; —breeds; —depresses; —deprives; —diminishes; —dwindles; —endangers; —mitigates; —oppresses; —overwhelms; —rav-

ages; —satirizes; —scourges; —shelves; —sweeps; —victimizes.

UNEVEN

adverbs

curiously; perilously; raggedly; roughly; inconveniently; unpleasantly; unjustly; inequitably; unfairly; meanly; disagreeably; absurdly; sadly; crookedly.

UNEVENTFUL

adverbs

tiresomely; dully; flatly; uninterestingly; boresomely; monotonously; curiously; unexpectedly; unpardonably; undeniably; tediously; restfully; fortunately; blessedly; smoothly; conspicuously; placidly; utterly; happily.

UNEXPECTED

adverbs

provokingly; bewilderingly; curiously; utterly; unfeignedly; pitifully; sadly; completely; tragically; suddenly; stunningly; startlingly; terribly; obviously; manifestly; undoubtedly.

UNFAILING

adverbs

blessedly; presumably; generously; usually; reliably; notoriously; reputedly; supposedly; manifestly; miraculously; apparently; conspicuously; notably; dependably; reliably.

UNFAIR

adverbs

manifestly; terribly; openly; flagrantly; abominably; shamefully; cruelly; bitterly; egregiously; despicably; maliciously; unmistakably; daringly; deliberately; dishonorably; uncommonly; secretly; greedily; arrogantly; high-handedly; atrociously.

UNFAIRNESS

verbs

ameliorate—; avenge—; avert—; betray—; condone—; denounce—; deplore—; disclose —; divulge—; mitigate—; rebuke—; remedy—; reveal—; uncover—; —colors; —distorts; —embroiders; —garbles; —glosses over; —taints.

(See injustice, partiality, grievance, wrong.)

UNFAITHFUL

adverbs
notoriously; allegedly; conspicuously; flagrantly; openly; terribly; carelessly; cruelly; irresponsibly; treacherously; curiously; secretly; furtively; actually; presumably; recklessly; undependably; intolerably; abominably; wickedly; viciously; reprehensibly; provokingly; vexatiously; unbearably; unprofitably; deplorably; uselessly; surreptitiously; heinously; wretchedly; miserably; definitely; despicably; detestably; dreadfully; worthlessly; incorrigibly.

UNFAITHFULNESS

verbs
absolve of—; atone for—; avenge—; bear —; breed—; charge—; display—; evince —; expiate—; forgive—; foster—; frown upon—; punish—; regret—; repent—; rue —; —beckons; —disgraces; —dishonors; —tempts.

(See infidelity, insincerity, treachery.)

UNFAMILIAR

adverbs
sadly; embarrassingly; awkwardly; admittedly; evidently; obviously; unconcealably; tragically; helplessly; hopelessly; self-consciously; openly; shamelessly; unsophisticatedly; dreadfully; ineptly; oddly.

UNFASHIONABLE

adverbs
daringly; audaciously; carelessly; slouchily; untidily; dowdily; independently; boldly; recklessly; openly; definitely; admittedly; artistically; strikingly; smartly; ridiculously; bizarrely; ludicrously; intentionally; serenely; indifferently; consciously; naturally; curiously; magnificently; arrogantly; negligently; barbarically; casually; nonchalantly; happily; blithely; thoughtlessly; emphatically; positively; flippantly; notoriously; unashamedly; interestingly; vexatiously; laughingly; foolishly; unwisely.

UNFASTEN (*v*)

adverbs
readily; automatically; easily; tremblingly; carelessly; artfully; deftly; customarily; strategically.

(See release, relieve.)

UNFATHOMABLE

adverbs
obscurely; mysteriously; darkly; dimly; vaguely; impenetrably; nebulously; perplexingly; eternally; wondrously; abstrusely; muddily; mystically; occultly; inscrutably; puzzlingly; reconditely; unaccountably; unreasonably; irrationally; profoundly; abysmally; infinitely; perpetually; forever.

UNFAVORABLE

adverbs
definitely; unappeasably; uncompromisingly; defiantly; rebelliously; forbiddingly; discouragingly; resolutely; sternly; implacably; emphatically; downright; openly; secretly; surreptitiously; ominously; undeniably; influentially; indifferently; actively; mildly; positively; energetically; dangerously; frankly; expressly; harshly; powerfully; lamentably; fortuitously; stubbornly.

UNFEELING

adverbs
callously; cruelly; coldly; downright; evidently; curiously; strangely; obdurately; implacably; terribly; preposterously; extremely; inexplainably; utterly; harshly; stubbornly; wickedly; brutally; unbelievably; selfishly; incredibly; unimaginably; singularly; viciously; stonily; inhumanly; sternly; austerely; heartlessly.

UNFEIGNED

adverbs
clearly; unquestionably; perceptibly; ingenuously; apparently.

UNFILIAL

adverbs
unnaturally; strangely; horribly; appallingly; incredibly; unreasonably; utterly; unimaginably; astoundingly; justifiably; eventually; sadly; deplorably; wretchedly; miserably; curiously; strangely; remarkably; terribly; inexplicably; ungratefully; inconsiderately; heartbreakingly; surprisingly; stonily; openly.

UNFINISH (*v*)

adverbs
deservedly; carelessly; sadly; incomprehensibly; unwisely; improvidently.

(See cease, stop.)

UNFIT

adverbs

palpably; altogether; manifestly; allegedly; presumably; ostensibly; utterly; temperamentally; physically; morally; lamentably; deplorably; miserably; wretchedly; curiously; downright.

UNFLINCHING

adverbs

courageously; sturdily; staunchly; boldly; steadily; splendidly; chivalrously; admirably; surprisingly; quietly; imperturbably; firmly; gallantly; heroically; marvellously; magnificently.

UNFOLD (*v*)

adverbs

beauteously; swiftly; joyously; vividly; prominently; maturely.

(See reveal, uncover.)

UNFORGIVING

adverbs

uncompromisingly; sternly; austerely; seriously; gravely; censoriously; callously; unmercifully; coldly; obdurately; stubbornly; hopelessly; wretchedly; unfortunately; curiously; pharisaically; harshly.

UNFORTUNATE

adverbs

sadly; miserably; tragically; wretchedly; chronically; direly; unexpectedly; suddenly; shamefully; surprisingly; terribly; really; unusually; strangely; oddly; naturally; extremely.

UNFREQUENTED

adverbs

usually; perilously; dangerously; hazardously; notoriously; notably; conspicuously; riskily; unpleasantly; desolately; gloomily; eerily.

UNFRIENDLY

adverbs

cruelly; bitterly; terribly; unreasonably; meanly; hatefully; spitefully; strangely; unwontedly; suddenly; curiously; unwarrantably; disagreeably; snobbishly; inexcusably; churlishly; boorishly; narrow-mindedly; intolerantly; uncharitably; discouragingly; painfully; extremely; uncommonly.

UNFURL (*v*)

adverbs

automatically; gallantly; awesomely; impressively; picturesquely.

(See release, unfold.)

UNGAINLY

adverbs

miserably; unfortunately; comically; undeniably; terribly; dreadfully; unpleasantly; sadly; curiously; particularly; conspicuously; pathetically; oddly; clumsily; positively; laughably; regrettably; unsuitably; nonchalantly; carelessly; slouchily; indifferently; blandly.

UNGENEROUS

adverbs

surprisingly; suddenly; appallingly; unexpectedly; curiously; unluckily; shockingly; miserably; short-sightedly; foolishly; unwisely; intolerantly; uncharitably; bigotedly; narrowly; terribly; dreadfully; uncommonly.

UNGODLY

adverbs

shamefully; unconscionably; surprisingly; flagrantly; openly; flauntingly; shockingly; appallingly; atrociously; blasphemously; impiously; despicably; offensively; heartbreakingly; viciously; daringly; wickedly; conspicuously; dreadfully; strangely.

UNGOVERNABLE

adverbs

sadly; gracelessly; conspicuously; heinously; highly; inexplicably; atrociously; incomprehensibly; suddenly; sometimes; habitually; boldly; defiantly; mutinously; hopelessly; dreadfully; dangerously; violently; curiously; occasionally; eventually; admittedly; terribly.

UNGRACIOUS

adverbs

curtly; strangely; oddly; significantly; conspicuously; unaccountably; curiously; momentarily; deliberately; intentionally; pointedly; dreadfully; unwontedly; purposely; regrettably; sadly; unfortunately; inadvertently; clumsily; unintentionally; awkwardly; snobbishly.

adverbs

boorishly; ignorantly; selfishly; indifferently; thoughtlessly; callously; incredibly; unbelievably; oddly; terribly; crassly; grossly; significantly; dreadfully; coldly; stupidly; shamefully; remarkably; unpardonably; astoundingly; cruelly; arrogantly.

UNGUARDED

adverbs

carelessly; inadvertently; momentarily; indifferently; temporarily; insecurely; crassly; strangely; inexplicably; happily; unaccountably; blessedly; advantageously; fortuitously; trustfully; stupidly; incautiously; unexpectedly; seldom; rarely.

UNHANDY

adverbs

deucedly; vexatiously; terribly; foolishly; wastefully; frequently; dreadfully; downright; admittedly; curiously; short-sightedly; extravagantly.

UNHAPPINESS

verbs

bear—; curse with—; dispel—; endure—; evince—; exhibit—; languish in—; lessen—; mitigate—; mollify—; soothe—; suffer—; undergo—; —afflicts; —blasts; —blights; —burdens; —clouds; —crucifies; —dampens; —dejects; —depresses; —desolates; —pervades; —prostrates; —racks; —sprouts; —stabs; —torments; —weighs upon.

(See pathos, distress, misery, sadness.)

UNHAPPY

adverbs

cruelly; bitterly; sadly; desolately; gloomily; moodily; naturally; terribly; dreadfully; unaccountably; inexplicably; curiously; particularly; selfishly; childishly; painfully; admittedly; sullenly; particularly; helplessly; hopelessly; desperately; suddenly; eventually; openly; obviously; frankly; wretchedly; miserably.

UNHEALTHY

adverbs

definitely; terribly; curiously; naturally; apparently; malarially; obviously; manifestly; unfortunately; wickedly; oddly; positively; miserably; wretchedly; congenitally.

adverbs

frightfully; blasphemously; impiously; terribly; accursedly; profanely; sacrilegiously; wantonly; carelessly; recklessly; appallingly; flippantly; execrably; damnably; dreadfully; horribly.

UNIFORM

adjectives

brilliant; handsome; full; striking; undress; continuous; resplendent; finished; glittering; shabby; outstanding; greasy; practical; gorgeous; dress; gaudy.

verbs

array in—; besmirch—; bestow—s; defile—; discard—; dishonor—; divest of—; don—; espy—; frill—; invest in—; march in—; masquerade in—; recognize—; strip of—; tatter—; —attracts; —denotes; —flatters; —impresses; —symbolizes; —stamps one as; —betokens.

(See tights, clothing, dress.)

adverbs

monotonously; wearisomely; conveniently; adaptably; comfortably; assuredly; pleasantly; tiresomely; flatly; uninterestingly; beautifully; symmetrically; presumably; allegedly; obviously; conspicuously; economically; dependably; reliably; conventionally.

UNIFORM (*v*)

adverbs

gaudily; gaily; impressively; dramatically; vividly; patriotically; brilliantly; somberly; drably.

(See garb, dress.)

UNION

adjectives

splendid; contingent; mystic; eternal; solemn; incestuous; ultimate; conjugal; habitual; unjust; constant; indissoluble; potent; powerful; fertile; conscious; perpetual; existing; legislative; precipitate; unfathomable; moribund; hurried; illicit; fruitful; visible; labor; celestial; consummate; checkoff; complete; substantial; immemorial; perfect; fructifying; loathed; confederated; outstanding.

verbs

band into—; bind into—; consummate—; defend—; destroy—; disrupt—; encourage—; enter into—; foster—; further—; hallow—;

hinder—; impede—; lack—; partition—; preserve—; promote—; protect—; rend—; signify—; solemnize—; sunder—; —affords; —enables; —flourishes; —insures; —strengthens; —suffers.

(See marriage, connection, matrimony, attachment, coalition, combination.)

UNIONS

verbs

affiliate with—; alienate—; ally—; arbitrate—; betray—; cement—; centralize—; combat—; consolidate—; crush—; effect—; enlist in—; enroll in—; dispel—; foster—; head—; install—; league with—; mediate with—; operate—; pacify—; recruit for —; rend—; rule—; scorn—; sympathize with—; —achieve; —band; —call out; —challenge; —clash with; —demand; —embroil; —foment; —link; —merge with; —picket; —preserve; —protect; —strike; —support.

(See strikers, labor.)

UNIT

adjectives

regulatory; myriad (pl); topical; versatile; efficient; functioning; fire-fighting; unmanageable; single; sounding; inseparable; research; harmonious; primary; mechanical; similar; parallactic; potent; political; arbitrary; perfected.

verbs

affiliate with—; amass—; complete—; demolish—; design—; dissolve—; integrate—; isolate—; mould—; partition—; perform as —; rend—; replenish—; shatter—; strengthen—; sunder—; —expands; —swells.

(See cell, property, part.)

UNITE (*v*)

adverbs

stubbornly; strangely; fraternally; substantially; indissolubly; cordially; subsequently; promptly; unanimously; vigorously; ultimately; dramatically; politically; spiritually; harmoniously; enduringly; strategically; logically; morally; fundamentally; practically.

(See join, ally.)

UNITY

adjectives

distinct; unbroken; political; wielded; necessary; rigorous; dramatic; essential; artistic; pervading; territorial; moral; contin-

ental; spiritual; internal; harmonious; enduring; dim; compendious; lasting; brilliant; uncompounded; early; strategic; dramatic; imperial; logical; solid; fundamental; practical; mad.

verbs

accomplish—; achieve—; bind in—; blend in—; clamor for—; commend—; demand—; demolish—; endanger—; foster—; further —; impair—; jeopardize—; lack—; necessitate—; preserve—; promote—; rend—; sunder—; unfold—; verify—; want—; work for—; —enables; —insures; —perpetuates; —persists; —pervades; —prevails; —resists; —rules; —strengthens.

(See harmony, cooperation, agreement.)

UNIVERSAL

adverbs

fundamentally; woefully; universally; significantly; strikingly; curiously; ominously; surprisingly; astonishingly; terribly.

UNIVERSE

adjectives

moral; mad; vast; practical; lampless; useless; illimitable; well-conducted; visible; enduring; conceivable; spiritual; collective; boundless; insubstantial; harmonious; infinite; wise; myriad (pl); expanding; malign; aerial; material; incomprehensible; offensive; effectless; objective; foundering.

verbs

bound—; cloak—; cloud—; comprise—; contemplate—; "debunk"—; dim—; dwell in —; embrace—; encompass—; fathom—; glory in—; govern—; illumine—; impart to —; interpret—; limit—; map—; pervade—; re-create—; regard—; save—; scan—; shroud—; span—; sunder from—; survey—; —acclaims; —evolves from; —links; —mystifies; —mourns; —seethes; —teems; —whirls.

(See creation, life.)

UNIVERSITY

adjectives

studious; sedate; well-rounded; theological; splendid; great; significant; national; state.

verbs

affiliate with—; converge upon—; endow—; enroll in—; enter—; expel from—; found—; guide—; —advances; —breeds; —disciplines; —edifies; —enlightens; —equips; —

facilitates; —fosters; —functions; —furthers; —grounds one in; —honors; —imparts; —instructs; —mothers; —nurtures; —offers; —polishes; —prepares; —primes; —proselytes; —qualifies; —rears; —subsidizes; —verses one in.
(See college, institution, school.)

UNJUST
adverbs
cruelly; bitterly; keenly; unaccountably; unexpectedly; palpably; uncommonly; arrantly; wantonly; intolerably; illogically; vengefully; inexcusably; hatefully; hideously; miserably; wretchedly; incredibly; openly; crassly; stupidly; gravely; seriously; inadvertently; deliberately; intentionally; incredibly; inexplicably; remarkably; incomprehensibly.

UNKEMPT
adverbs
surprisingly; carelessly; deliberately; coolly; nonchalantly; comfortably; provokingly; shamefully; dowdily; embarrassingly; inexcusably; unfortunately; casually; notoriously; conspicuously; unconcealably; horribly; unluckily; deplorably; scandalously; merrily; blowzily; boldly; audaciously; flagrantly.

UNKNOWABLE
adverbs
obscurely; eternally; mysteriously; latently; darkly; dimly; vaguely; impenetratingly; incomprehensibly; perplexingly; wonderfully; mystically; occultly; inscrutably; puzzlingly; elusively; unaccountably; inexplicably; unreasonably; tormentingly; irrationally; profoundly; abysmally; infinitely; perpetually.

UNLAWFUL
adverbs
definitely; implicitly; riskily; perilously; strictly; positively; absurdly; specifically; explicitly; actually; allegedly; presumably; probably; certainly; avowedly; admittedly.

UNLIKELY
adverbs
naturally; utterly; legally; morally; particularly; emphatically; positively.

UNLOCK (v)
adverbs
automatically; readily; rustily; smoothly; easily; temporarily; dexterously.
(See unfasten, release.)

UNMANNERLY
adverbs
strangely; grossly; barbarously; naturally; incredibly; crassly; stupidly; boorishly; cruelly; rustically; provincially; unpleasantly; foolishly; apparently; manifestly; embarrassingly; shamefully; gracelessly; naively; ignorantly; unsophisticatedly; unluckily; wretchedly; unpardonably; oddly; conspicuously; remarkably; highly; uncommonly; unwontedly; disagreeably.

UNMERCIFUL
adverbs
cruelly; coldly; miserably; hatefully; inflexibly; stubbornly; boorishly; brutally; selfishly; unyieldingly; dreadfully; intractably; shamefully; scandalously; wickedly; immovably; sternly; inscrutably; mysteriously; strangely; significantly; remarkably; unwontedly; unaccountably; oddly; surprisingly.

UNMISTAKABLE
adverbs
clearly; explicitly; positively; manifestly; obviously; conspicuously; conveniently; safely; felicitously; fortunately; luckily; happily; definitely; purposely; singularly; designedly.

UNNERVED
adverbs
strangely; naturally; shakily; utterly; oddly; curiously; probably; completely; unreasonably; foolishly; shockingly; palpably; apparently; mysteriously; conspicuously; tremulously; helplessly.

UNOBJECTIONABLE
adverbs
personally; entirely; quite; naturally; pleasantly; harmlessly; manifestly; locally; politically; financially; generally; reasonably; frankly; wholly; fairly; presumably; singularly; altogether.

UNOSTENTATIOUS
adverbs
modestly; quietly; serenely; carefully; calmly; curiously; preferably; always; strangely; shyly; bashfully.

UNPALATABLE

adverbs
strangely; altogether; manifestly; curiously; noxiously; disagreeably; disgustingly; hopelessly; terribly; wretchedly; impossibly; embarrassingly; cruelly; bitterly; disappointingly; outlandishly; dreadfully.

UNPARLIAMENTARY

adverbs
openly; manifestly; wholly; foolishly; ignorantly; boldly; flauntingly; consciously; obstinately; absurdly; entirely; evidently; conspicuously; loosely; casually; carelessly.

UNPERTURBED

adverbs
quietly; strangely; confidently; optimistically; trustfully; curiously; particularly; noticeably; altogether; serenely; certainly; palpably; hopefully.

UNPOPULAR

adverbs
generally; strangely; noticeably; significantly; desperately; currently; terribly; definitely; conspicuously; apparently; manifestly; disturbingly; miserably; mysteriously; curiously; distinctly; emphatically; intensely; seriously; consciously.

UNPREJUDICED

adverbs
admirably; nobly; particularly; admittedly; distinctly; emphatically; curiously; palpably; commendably; dependably; hearteningly; judicially; gravely; honorably; honestly; entirely; wonderfully; happily.

UNPREPARED

adverbs
grossly; carelessly; unpardonably; miserably; palpably; inadvertently; wantonly; financially; socially; wretchedly; undisguisedly; openly; admittedly; unluckily; laughably; comically; tragically; ridiculously; nonchalantly; blithely; merrily.

UNPRESENTABLE

adverbs
horribly; laughably; ridiculously; embarrassingly; muddily; soggily; carelessly; altogether; shamefully; comically; ludicrously; utterly; messily; cruelly; bashfully; obviously; momentarily; always.

UNPROFITABLE

adverbs
disastrously; probably; sadly; extremely; terribly; naturally; seasonally; curiously; suddenly; desperately.

UNQUESTIONABLE

adverbs
utterly; admittedly; luckily; absolutely; momentarily; recognizably; palpably; socially; financially.

UNRAVEL (*v*)

adverbs
persistently; easily; intelligently; patiently; diligently; monotonously.
(See open, reveal.)

UNREAL

adverbs
darkly; abstrusely; obscurely; immaterially; indefinably; chimerically; phantasmally; vaguely; nebulously; evanescently; fantastically; strangely; fabulously; queerly; mystically; insubstantially; virtually; enigmatically; subtly; wildly; spectrally; dimly.

UNREASONABLE

adverbs
foolishly; blunderingly; ridiculously; absurdly; ludicrously; extravagantly; senselessly; egregiously; preposterously; comically; monstrously; fantastically; grotesquely; outlandishly; strangely; manifestly; patently; palpably; perversely; pathetically; grossly; incredibly.

UNREGENERATE

adverbs
obviously; manifestly; evidently; pitiably; stubbornly; obstinately; unfortunately; openly; flagrantly; blasphemously; flippantly; audaciously; impiously; terribly; dreadfully; impenitently.

UNRELENTING

adverbs
wilfully; indomitably; bitterly; sternly; obdurately; pitiably; lamentably; unpardonably; unreasonably; pitilessly; inexorably; obstinately; stubbornly; mulishly; doggedly; perversely; fanatically; pig-headedly; contumaciously; bigotedly; implacably; rancourously; vengefully; ruthlessly; maliciously; cruelly; unmercifully.

UNRELIABLE

adverbs

unfortunately; manifestly; entirely; unluckily; desperately; admittedly; obviously; terribly; actually; furtively; secretly; downright; notoriously; infamously; shamefully; wickedly; palpably; certainly.

UNREST

adjectives

wearisome; secret; political; sickening; unsettled; vain; essential; bitter; ghoulish; eager; sweet.

verbs

allay—; assuage—; calm—; cloak—; cope with—; dispel—; dwell in—; incite—; provoke—; quell—; silence—; still—; stave off—; subdue—; —disconcerts; —gnaws; —irks; —irritates; —racks; —rends; —smoulders; —spreads; —wanes; —weighs upon; —wrings.

(See restlessness, confusion, dissatisfaction, discontent.)

UNRESTRAINED

adverbs

excessively; rakishly; wildly; playfully; wickedly; hilariously; gleefully; joyously; crazily; airily; youthfully; ludicrously; brazenly; monstrously; outlandishly; delightfully; recklessly; wantonly; amazingly; audaciously; impetuously; ardently; heedlessly; indiscreetly.

UNRIGHTEOUS

adverbs

openly; unheedingly; deliberately; heinously; wickedly; impiously; blasphemously; deplorably; wretchedly; miserably; heathenishly.

UNRUFFLED

adverbs

admirably; surprisingly; restrainedly; wonderfully; utterly; calmly; actually; apparently; palpably; evidently; strangely; curiously; fortunately; securely; beautifully.

UNRULY

adverbs

ominously; dreadfully; unmanageably; obstinately; significantly; terribly; oddly; uproariously; boisterously; viciously; politically; truculently; dangerously; violently; unreasonably; ungovernably; obstreperously; jeeringly; designedly; maliciously; viciously; alarmingly; turbulently.

UNSAVORY

adverbs

notoriously; slightly; decidedly; extremely; admittedly; terribly; undisguisedly; dreadfully; manifestly; wickedly.

UNSCATHED

adverbs

mercifully; apparently; blessedly; surprisingly; gloriously; happily; luckily; unexpectedly; blissfully; evidently.

UNSCRUPULOUS

adverbs

notoriously; shamefully; cleverly; astutely; adroitly; infamously; reputedly; allegedly; curiously; terribly; extremely; shamelessly; triumphantly; arrogantly; openly; cruelly; bitterly; desperately; hard-heartedly; greedily; meanly; aggressively; boldly; daringly; criminally; selfishly; hatefully; atrociously.

UNSEASONABLE

adverbs

manifestly; surprisingly; unhealthfully; unprofitably; dangerously; desperately; hazardously; undeniably; highly; uncommonly; curiously; strangely; oddly; significantly; ominously; definitely.

UNSEEMLY

adverbs

desperately; shamefully; unpleasantly; disagreeably; surprisingly; unpardonably; absolutely; inexcusably; indefensibly; daringly; flauntingly; miserably; wantonly; frightfully; horridly; impertinently; blatantly.

UNSELFISH

adverbs

utterly; unnecessarily; ostentatiously; delightfully; remarkably; always; altogether; downright; absurdly; generously; altruistically; charitably; thoughtfully; considerately; graciously; courteously; unexpectedly; usually; naturally; habitually; tenderly; lovingly; extremely; uncommonly; singularly; unexpectedly; unwontedly; sweetly.

UNSETTLED

adverbs

curiously; indecisively; obviously; manifestly; unfortunately; evidently; pitiably; dangerously; temporarily; pathetically; miserably; secretly; confusedly; mentally; financially; sadly; temperamentally; habitually; naturally.

UNSIGHTLY

adverbs

hideously; loathesomely; disgustingly; shabbily; filthily; repulsively; horridly; shockingly; monstrously; gruesomely; dreadfully; positively; terribly; unbearably.

UNSKILFUL

adverbs

naturally; pitiably; awkwardly; clumsily; ineptly; inexpertly; ignorantly; carelessly; heedlessly; pathetically; unacceptably; grossly; undeniably; surprisingly; miserably; terribly; criminally; admittedly; undisguisedly; naively; shyly; self-consciously.

UNSOCIABLE

adverbs

painfully; shyly; disagreeably; terribly; awkwardly; naturally; naively; ungraciously; selfishly; inconsiderately; unwontedly; habitually; unpardonably; miserably; reticently; gravely; surprisingly; unfortunately; pitifully; inexcusably; strangely; offensively.

UNSOPHISTICATED

adverbs

naively; undisguisedly; apparently; palpably; manifestly; ludicrously; ridiculously; embarrassingly; shyly; consciously; painfully; childishly; innocently; awkwardly; clumsily; unhappily; unfortunately; laughably; pathetically.

UNSOUND

adverbs

unfortunately; curiously; inexcusably; untenably; ridiculously; absurdly; dreadfully; wickedly; admittedly; miserably; dangerously; significantly; manifestly; openly; daringly; utterly; unreliably.

UNSPARING

adverbs

sternly; harshly; gravely; unjustly; obstinately; inflexibly; fanatically; narrowly; bigotedly; ridiculously; bitterly; cruelly; unreasoningly; unreasonably; obdurately; gravely; solemnly; frightfully.

UNSTABLE

adverbs

lamentably; deplorably; miserably; ridiculously;_obviously; dangerously; alarmingly;

ominously; desperately; manifestly; perilously; unpardonably; carelessly; notoriously; flagrantly; unforgivably.

UNSUBSTANTIAL

adverbs

baselessly; fabulously; fantastically; fancifully; suppositiously; virtually; mockingly; illusively; mythically; notionally; romantically; visionarily; quixotically; whimsically; ethereally; tenuously; chimerically.

UNSUITABLE

adverbs

distinctly; positively; altogether; wholly; entirely; incongruously; socially; awkwardly; absurdly; foolishly; extravagantly; unbecomingly; comically; outlandishly; inappropriately; shockingly; crudely; horribly; laughably; singularly.

UNSYSTEMATIC

adverbs

carelessly; bewilderingly; confusingly; chaotically; terribly; unpardonably; inexcusably; criminally; provokingly; irritatingly; inconveniently; vexatiously; ruinously; ignorantly; foolishly; confoundedly; strangely; lazily; negligently; heedlessly; unwarrantably.

UNTENABLE

adverbs

fallibly; unreliably; inaccurately; insubstantially; absolutely; manifestly; carelessly; inconclusively; fallaciously; ultimately; obviously; absurdly; hopelessly; wholly; ridiculously; laughably.

UNTIMELY

adverbs

strangely; obviously; unfortunately; politically; financially; distressingly; terribly.

UNTOUCHED

adverbs

curiously; singularly; momentarily; mercifully; fortunately; blessedly; strangely; absolutely; carefully; providently; luckily; heedfully; apparently; absolutely.

UNTRAMMEL (*v*)

adverbs

entirely; nominally; legally; apparently; obviously.

(See release, free.)

UNTUTORED

adverbs

naively; unbelievably; miraculously; marvelously; curiously; childishly; utterly; obviously; manifestly; miserably; wretchedly; helplessly; distressingly; pathetically; pitiably; fortunately; palpably; blessedly; gloriously; apparently; brilliantly.

UNUSUAL

adverbs

extremely; fortunately; luckily; believably; apparently; obviously; manifestly; gloriously; mercifully; unfortunately; significantly; delightfully; altogether.

UNWARRANTABLE

adverbs

obviously; naturally; altogether; legally; socially; conventionally; decently; judicially; politically; terribly; admittedly; absurdly; ridiculously; ludicrously; wretchedly; miserably; indefensibly; dreadfully; altogether; downright; utterly.

UNWARY

adverbs

youthfully; flippantly; heedlessly; bravely; foolishly; naively; carelessly; ignorantly; wantonly; ridiculously; unbelievably; absurdly; blithely; inconceivably; rashly; witlessly.

UNWEARIED

adverbs

incredibly; fondly; affectionately; helpfully; patriotically; resolutely; intrepidly; unbelievably; miraculously; splendidly; incomprehensibly; lovingly; desperately; marvelously; strangely; oddly; fanatically; amazingly; remarkably.

UNWIELDY

adverbs

awkwardly; clumsily; terribly; unpleasantly; embarrassingly; disagreeably; massively; altogether; manifestly; inconveniently; lumberingly; vexatiously; plaguedly; confoundedly; singularly.

UNWILLINGNESS

adjectives

sheer; dull; deliberate; obstinate; studied.

verbs

acknowledge—; announce—; assert—; aver —; conquer—; contain—; deplore—; dis-

cern—; dispel—; display—; dissolve—; emphasize—; express—; indicate—; justify—; maintain—; overcome—; prevail against—; subdue—; surmount—; sweep away—; swerve from—; voice—; —irks; —persists; —piques; —riles (colloq.).
(See indisposition, reluctance.)

UNWISE

adverbs

incredibly; stubbornly; absurdly; habitually; naturally; obstinately; outrageously; palpably; obviously; cruelly; undeniably; flagrantly; fantastically; politically; terribly; utterly; absolutely; bitterly; disastrously; calamitously.

UNWOMANLY

adverbs

strangely; unbelievably; hoydenishly; terribly; lamentably; deplorably; surprisingly; utterly; dreadfully; ungraciously; curiously.

UNWORLDLY

adverbs

curiously; piously; peculiarly; wholly; indubitably; admirably; blessedly; happily; serenely; blandly; truly.

UNWORTHY

adverbs

entirely; deeply; utterly; undeniably; despicably; contemptibly; sadly; selfishly; lamentably; indisputably; peculiarly; particularly; censoriously; outrageously; bitterly.

UPBRAID (v)

adverbs

viciously; vindictively; brutally; obstreperously; laughingly; ferociously; unjustly; volubly; rigorously; paternally; hatefully; jealously.
(See chide, rebuke.)

UPHEAVAL

adjectives

volcanic; economic; religious; devastating; sensuous; business; fatal; passionate; violent; sudden; wild.

verbs

avert—; precipitate—; quash—; quell—; suppress—; —agitates; —arouses; — awakens; —characterizes; —convulses; — dashes; —demolishes; —discloses; —elevates; —jars; —jolts; —jounces; —levels; —prostrates; —razes; —reveals; —revolutionizes; —uncovers.

(See uprising, convulsion, revolution, strike.)

UPHOLD (v)

adverbs

staunchly; faithfully; patiently; patriotically; virtually; solemnly; fiercely; gallantly; extraordinarily; economically; politically; philosophically; metaphysically; nationally.

(See support, defend.)

UPRIGHT

adverbs

splendidly; reputably; admittedly; virtuously; admirably; sincerely; openly; unfailingly; conspicuously; estimably; honorably; boldly; undauntedly; firmly; stably.

UPRISING

adjectives

sudden; armed; courageous; seditious; concerted; marvelous; feared; wide-spread; national; growing .

verbs

annihilate—; blot out—; check—; defeat—; foment—; forestall—; incite—; inspire—; instigate—; provoke—; smash—; squelch —; stem—; subdue—; suppress—; swamp —; —breaks out; —peters out (colloq.); — seethes; —spreads; —violates.

(See upheaval, revolution, strike.)

UPROAR

adjectives

wild; everlasting; positive; stupendous; tremendous; furious; musical; ghastly; stultifying.

verbs

hush—; muffle—; mute—; quash—; quell—; silence—; stifle—; still—; subdue—; suppress—; —abates; —bewilders; —confuses; —deafens; —drowns out; —mounts; — pierces; —rends; —shatters; —splits; — startles; —subsides; —swells; —thunders.

(See clamor, disturbance, din, fracas, roar, rumble.)

UPROARIOUS

adverbs

boisterously; comically; foolishly; hilariously; clownishly; merrily; blithely; gaily; amusingly; divertingly; farcically; fantasti-

cally; inimitably; excitedly; hysterically; enthusiastically; jubilantly; exultantly; triumphantly; rampantly; irrepressibly; laughingly.

UPSET

adverbs

peculiarly; utterly; strangely; significantly; inconsolably; grievously; wearily; nervously; physically; mentally; cruelly; miserably; bitterly; oddly; curiously; amazingly; remarkably; mysteriously; unexpectedly; suddenly; inexplicably; unaccountably.

UPSET (v)

adverbs

ultimately; practically; physically; emotionally; incomprehensibly; cruelly; gravely.

(See otherthrow, overpower.)

URBAN

adverbs

smoothly; distinctly; self-consciously; insistantly; ridiculously; scarcely; absurdly; pseudo-; recently; ridiculously; earnestly.

URBANE

adverbs

pleasantly; courteously; unusually; markedly; conspicuously; agreeably; ingratiatingly; skilfully; smoothly; carefully; diplomatically; serenely; complaisantly; graciously; splendidly; elegantly; unfailingly; resolutely; imperturbably; quietly; tolerantly; indulgently.

URGE

adjectives

biological; evolutionary; irresistible; sudden; strong; deep-seated; universal; self-satisfying; demon-like; glandular; swarthy; creative.

verbs

awaken—; check—; choke back—; conquer —; counteract—; dull—; gratify—; quell—; resist—; restrain—; smother—; squelch—; stem—; stifle—; —impels; —overpowers; —overwhelms; —seizes; —swells; intensify —.

(See importunity, desire, impulse.)

URGE (v)

adverbs

diplomatically; passionately; secretly; blandly; disingenuously; plausibly; insolently; ineffectually; blatantly; eloquently; importunately; explicitly; enthusiastically; continually; persistently; ostentatiously; strenuously; powerfully; insidiously; traitorously; clamorously; mutely; irresistibly.

(See impel, incite.)

URGENT

adverbs

vitally; terribly; essentially; immediately; pressingly; personally; sorely; desperately; dreadfully; ominously; significantly; extremely; supremely; singularly; particularly; peculiarly; presumably; conspicuously; momentously; gravely; seriously.

URINE

verbs

acidify—; analyze—; cloud—; contaminate —; convey—; darken—; dilute—; discharge —; drain—; draw off—; egest—; eliminate —; emit—; evacuate—; excrete—; expel—; extract—; purge of—; retain—; saturate with—; secrete—; store—; tap—; vent—; void—; —accumulates; —colors; —concentrates; —emanates; —indicates; —passes; —pollutes; —reeks; —stinks.

(See liquid, odor, excretion.)

USAGE

adjectives

laudable; hereditary; abnormal; pedantic; traditional; general; effective; cruel; diplomatic; sinister; ill; grammatical; established; symphonic; immemorial; dietetic; rough; traditional; troglodytic; social; common.

verbs

accustom to—; approve—; condemn—; condone—; decry—; determine—; encourage—; foster—; govern—; marvel at—; practise—; prescribe—; promote—; rebuke—; recommend—; reproach—; reprove—; set forth —; subject to—; violate—; —infringes; — offends; —persists; —prevails; —sanctions; —violates.

(See procedure, use, custom, fashion, conventionality.)

USE

adjectives

refined; repeated; unsuspected; unspecified; excessive; experimental; inordinate; lavish; economical; amiable; creative; unsparing; assiduous; infrequent; habitual; vain; ignoble; senseless; consistent; occasional; far-reaching; unholy; grave; prolonged; long-

continued; brutal; outspoken; diligent; narrow; respective; increased; decorative; metaphorical; unwonted; temporary; transcendent; domestic; particular; remarkable; infinite; ample; imperfect; growing; barren; congenial; valuable; fruitful; effective; uncaged; exclusive; imaginative; specific; instinctive; unreasoning; judicious; singular; delicate; efficient; dexterous; brilliant; constant; immediate; charitable; plentiful; deliberate; recurrent; varied (pl); concealed; common; accepted; mandatory; precocious; subordinate; unauthorized; industrious; ultimate; indiscriminate; immoderate; unnatural; voluntary; homespun.

verbs

accede to—; addict to—; advance—; advocate—; approve—; assure of—; authorize —; begrudge—; bid for—; concede—; condemn—; confer upon—; confine—to; consider—; counsel—; crave—; cultivate—; curb—; curtail—; debar—; debase—; decline—; decry—; deprecate—; design for—; develop—; disclaim—; discontinue—; discourage—; encourage—; enforce—; enjoin from—; exhort—; facilitate—; foster—; frown upon—; grant—; guide—; impair—; impede—; induce—; inspire—; involve—; master—; obviate—; offer—; outlive—; petition for—; pledge—; ponder—; press to—; prolong—; prompt—; propose—; provoke—; protest—; recommend—; request—; resort to—; restrain—; restrict—; ridicule —; suppress—; tender—; —dishonors; — entails; —facilitates; —habituates; —hardens; —insures.

(See service, need, employment, application.)

USE (v)

adverbs

indiscriminately; similarly; mercifully; promiscuously; universally; exclusively; extensively; lavishly; chiefly; conspicuously; intermittently; ostentatiously; effectively; officially; simultaneously; artfully; deftly; tenderly; ethically; magnanimously; economically; creatively; assiduously; consistently; diligently; domestically; congenially; singularly; judiciously; dexterously; ultimately; voluntarily.

(See employ, utilize.)

USEFUL

adverbs

conveniently; constantly; wholly; unusually;

particularly; specially; peculiarly; amazingly; wonderfully; admirably; curiously; frequently; remarkably; unexpectedly; politically; suddenly; actually; extremely; marvellously; socially; adaptably; invariably; dependably; downright.

USEFULNESS
adjectives
sheer; varied; desultory; partial; increased; high; conspicuous; extraordinary; practical; lively; prodigious; preeminent.

verbs
acclaim—; acquire—; appreciate—; augment—; belittle—; commend—; consider—; contemplate—; discern—; disclose—; hamper—; heighten—; impair—; judge—; lack —; laud—; measure—; minimize—; outlive —; recognize—; regard—; reveal—; weigh —; —ceases; —ebbs; —impresses.
(See value, advantage, benefit.)

USELESS
adverbs
eventually; definitely; utterly; absolutely; probably; finally; ultimately; absurdly; certainly; fantastically; ridiculously; possibly; undoubtedly; completely; pathetically; admittedly; unaccountably; manifestly; obviously.

USELESSNESS
verbs
decry—; deplore—; disclose—; fall into—; inveigh against—; overcome—; rebuke—; scoff at—; set forth—; —burdens; —irks; —irritates; —oppresses; —riles (colloq.); —stigmatizes; —vexes; —weighs upon.
(See futility, waste.)

USHER (*v*)
adverbs
hospitably; gallantly; politely; formally; habitually; professionally.
(See escort, introduce.)

USUAL
adverbs
altogether; scarcely; quite; absolutely; too; rather; admittedly.

USURP (*v*)
adverbs
treacherously; violently; murderously; dictatorially; tyrannically; illegally; sternly; vigorously; politically; arbitrarily.
(See seize, take.)

UTENSIL
adjectives
washing; primitive; cooking; valuable; practical.

verbs
blacken—; cleanse—; discard—; edge—; employ—; encumber—; equip with—s; exhibit—; fashion—; grind—; pilfer—; plate —; polish—; renew—; rinse—; scour—; scrape—; sharpen—; soak—; —enables; —facilitates.
(See instrument, knife, fork, cup, kettle, tool.)

UTILITARIAN
adverbs
handsomely; truly; altogether; sordidly; plainly; entirely; possibly; conveniently; admittedly; warrantably; sensibly; obviously; distinctly.

UTILITY
(*general*)
adjectives
respectable; universal; industrial; misconceived; practical; social; ultimate; heartless; essential; vulgar; definite; wide; obvious.

UTILITY
(*public utility*)
verbs
cater to—; charge—with; dance attendance to—; enrich—; govern—; head—; inveigh against—; investigate—; legislate against —; regulate—; tax—; —s amass; —bribes; —s "crack"; —s crack up (colloq.); —s facilitate; —s function; —s grind; —s lobby; —s perform; —s profit; —s rule; —serves; —s subserve; —tyrannizes.
(See power, company.)

UTILIZE (*v*)
adverbs
economically; effectively; politically; strategically; heartlessly; obviously; essentially; prodigiously; potently.
(See use, employ.)

UTOPIA
adjectives
mechanistic; economic; incorrigible; long-awaited; planned.

verbs
abide in—; cherish—; contrive—; depict—;

desert—; desire—; dream of—; dwell in—; fancy—; forsake—; gain—; hail—; imagine—; inspire—; picture—; portray—; predict—; proclaim—; promise—; quit—; relinquish—; renounce—; reside in—; strive for—; struggle for—.

(See heaven, perfection, ideal.)

UTOPIAN

adverbs

brightly; cheerfully; desirably; airily; illusively; promisingly; elusively; roseately; romantically; fancifully; phantasmally; hopefully; optimistically; whimsically; seriously; boldly; fallaciously; fantastically; notionally; chimerically; ingeniously.

UTTER (v)

adverbs

drolly; involuntarily; tremulously; decisively; articulately; prophetically; disparagingly; foolishly; coaxingly; mechanically; inarticulately; impassionately; lyrically; incisively; exquisitely; indiscriminately; voluntarily; specifically; delicately; deliberately.

(See speak, say.)

UTTERANCE

adjectives

bare; mordant; effective; unblushing; rapid; impassioned; mere; audible; rhythmical; graphic; broken; ill-considered; discouraging; homogeneous; full; characteristic; rending; death-defying; articulate; private; prophetic; premature; lyrical; exquisite; lofty; historic; incisive; noble; perfect; calm; lively; spontaneous; loving; imperfect; unheard; monotonous; mastered; public; hearty; numberless (pl); recent; glowing; rapid; fiery; supreme; impressive; simulated; intimate; recorded; luminous; harmonized; caustic; practical; injudicious; brute; spasmodic; simple; indistinct; expansive; vivid; roseate; important; grave; reasonable; powerful; weighty; precise.

verbs

acclaim—; clarify—; clothe—; condense—; deprecate—; magnify—; muffle—; mumble —; mute—; mutter—; rue—; silence—; smother—; stifle—; still—; voice—; weigh —; —astounds; —electrifies; —irks; —perplexes; —rings out; —sears; —shocks; — startles; —stuns.

(See exclamation, drawl, expression, statement.)

UXORIOUS

adverbs

noticeably; absurdly; notoriously; openly; absurdly; ridiculously; conspicuously; foolishly; outlandishly; obviously; ludicrously.

V

VACANCY

adjectives

dull; prospective; stony; rectangular; soundless; blank; utter; absolute; astounding; complete.

VACANT

adverbs

apparently; recently; obviously; coldly; mysteriously; forbiddingly; dismally; unexpectedly; gloriously; opportunely; actually; presumably; allegedly; seldom; happily; fortunately; unfortunately; unprofitably; gloomily; blankly; seasonally; temporarily; frequently.

VACATION

adjectives

memorable; peaceful; unspoiled; thorough; complete; thrilling; never-to-be-forgotten; carefree; summer; inclusive; unique; pictorial; glorious; frequent (pl); restful; giddy; wild; joyous; longed-for; wonderful.

verbs

advise—; conclude—; counsel—; crave—; curtail—; depart on—; extend—; grant—; loll on—; lounge on—; merit—; necessitate —; prolong—; protract—; recommend—; reward with—; terminate—; warrant—; yearn for—; —distracts; —diverts; —reanimates; —refreshes; —relaxes; —renews; —restores; —unbends; —vivifies; —wanes.
(See recess, rest, respite.)

VACATION (v)

adverbs

luxuriously; jovially; sumptuously; fraternally; memorably; peacefully; thrillingly; uniquely; gloriously; giddily; joyously; exquisitely.
(See refresh, travel.)

VACCINATION

verbs

advise—; compel—; employ—; prescribe—; procure—; submit to—; undergo—; —assures; —benefits; —discommodes; —erases; —erupts; —immunizes; —inflames; —insures; —modifies; —safeguards; —scars; —stamps out.
(See operation, serum.)

VACCINE

verbs

assimilate—; diffuse—; dispense; —glycerinate—; inject—; inoculate with—; insert —; introduce—; prepare—; prescribe—; sensitize—; utilize—; —builds up; —exempts; —immunizes; —induces; —inflames; —insures; —irritates; —modifies; —protects; —resists; —safeguards; —stimulates.

VACILLATE (v)

adverbs

irresolutely; weakly; pusillanimously; irrationally; indecisively; desultorily; improvidently.
(See sway, waver.)

VACILLATING

adverbs

vexatiously; hopelessly; indecisively; wantonly; intolerably; foolishly; incorrigibly; habitually; strangely; absurdly; mindlessly; incurably; naturally; inherently; irresolutely; deplorably; unfortunately; sluggishly; helplessly; lamentably; feebly; witlessly; remarkably; inordinately; unreasonably; unbearably; disgustingly.

VACUOUS

adverbs

deplorably; wantonly; sluggishly; lamentably; irremediably; irrecoverably; helplessly; pitiably; strangely; mysteriously; unaccountably; suddenly; unintelligibly; irresponsibly; evidently; manifestly; curiously; grotesquely; miserably; wretchedly.

VACUUM

adjectives

luminous; sterile; dreary; absolute.

verbs

achieve—; create—; employ—; exhaust to —; fill—; induce—; obtain—; reduce to—; require—; seal—; utilize—; valve—; — fails; —retains; —preserves.

VAGABOND

adjectives

incorrigible; royal; nondescript; seedy; precious; wandering; romantic; clever-appearing; lazy; roaming; alluring.

delightfully; whimsically; foolishly; notionally; irresponsibly; crazily; elfishly; irrepressibly; merrily; blithely; wholesomely; gaily; happily; uncontrollably; wittily; affably; genially.

VAGARIES
adjectives
superstitious; metaphysical; strange; queer; unusual; wild.

VAGINA
verbs
abscess—; dilate—; distend—; drain—; examine—; explore—; incise—; infect—; inflame—; inseminate—; insert into—; invade—; irritate—; lacerate—; line—; obstruct—; occlude—; plug—; probe—; suppurate—; syringe—; —discharges; —emits.

VAGRANT
adjectives
scattered (pl); undeveloped; apprehended; arrested.

adverbs
blithely; gaily; jauntily; happily; carelessly; irresponsibly; suspiciously; joyously; alertly; profitably; enviably; inconveniently; selfishly; luxuriously; habitually; pleasantly; nervously; furtively; stealthily; merrily; nonchalantly; delightfully; wretchedly; uncertainly; miserably; lonesomely; preferably; hazardously; independently; innocently; harmlessly.

VAGUE
adverbs
intentionally; perplexingly; embarrassingly; obscurely; dimly; stupidly; precariously; ambiguously; unintelligibly; distressingly; mysteriously; unwisely; uncertainly; casually; airily; delusively; evasively; subtly; inconclusively; darkly; abstrusely; impenetrably; remotely; unwarrantably; foolishly; speciously; misleadingly; tenuously; terribly; nonsensically; senselessly; completely; perilously; fearfully; alarmingly; ominously; significantly; fantastically; needlessly; unreliably.

VAGUENESS
adjectives
mysterious; comprehensible; voluptuous; studied; calculated; intentional.

VAIN
adverbs
awkwardly; fantastically; inordinately; offensively; contemptibly; amusingly; artlessly; morbidly; prodigiously; complacently; colossally; tediously.

VAINGLORIOUS
adverbs
bombastically; egregiously; incredibly; disgustingly; curiously; unreasonably; absurdly; insanely; harmlessly; ridiculously; ludicrously; laughably; sadly; extremely; manifestly; blindly; pompously; fantastically; preposterously; singularly.

VALE
adjectives
hopeless; melancholy; pleasant; fast-filling; sequestered; horrid; well-watered; hollow; simmering; shadowy; sunny; dimpling; dimmer; grassy; tuneful; gloomy; lonely; wondrous; intervening; dewy; spicy; luxuriant; smooth; sinuous; dreary; long; lit; deep.

verbs
(See valley, dale.)

VALEDICTORY
adverbs
sadly; seriously; appraisingly; analytically; admonitory; complimentarily; apparently; manifestly; obviously; warningly; critically; bitterly; affectionately; fondly; touchingly; affectingly; conventionally; comprehensively.

VALET
adjectives
inestimable; obsequious; bowing; quiet; effective; artful; deft; efficient; silk-hosed.

VALIANT
adverbs
resolutely; steadily; unfalteringly; boldly; admirably; wonderfully; marvellously; particularly; amazingly; gloriously; notably; surpassingly; incomparably; immeasurably; indescribably; intrepidly; superhumanly; superbly; splendidly; magnificently; unforgettably; fearlessly; supremely.

VALID
adverbs
reasonably; undoubtedly; assuredly; legally; financially; manifestly; obviously; evi-

dently; reputably; presumably; probably; unquestionably; altogether; substantially; effectively; curiously; definitely.

VALIDITY

adjectives
incontestable; legal; objective; eternal; supreme; scientific; independent; demonstrated; definite.

verbs
analyze—; attack—; avow—; challenge—; defend—; destroy—; discuss—; dispute—; emphasize—; endanger—; exhibit—; honor —; imperil—; impugn—; interfere with—; jeopardize—; maintain—; preserve—; question—; respect—; stamp with—; sustain—; test—; view—; —signifies; —stands.
(See value, position.)

VALLEY

adjectives
fantastic; stretching; fertile; overshadowed; precipitous; placid; solitary; sun-baked; pleasant; delectable; tributary; lofty; rugged; canyon-like; seductive; miserable; heated; copse-clad; picturesque; fabled; serene; blooming; fog-obscured; profound; irregular; branching; beautiful; breathless; solitary; pastoral; fruitful; wooded; flowering; watered; lovely; nest-like; desolate; immense; widening; conspicuous; shallow; redolent; grassy; oblivious; receding; haystack-dotted; verdant; cozy; little; terrible; formless; tiny; untenable; hill-beholden; flat-bottomed; dizzy; lonely; mountain; dusky; southern; imperial; winding; viewless; pathless.

verbs
command—; dash to—; devastate—; discern —; dot—; dwell in—; fill—; haunt—; inhabit—; overrun—; overspread—; penetrate —; people—; permeate—; pervade—; revisit—; ring through—; settle in—; view—; —awakes; —bestirs; —blossoms; —bristles; —dozes; —endures; —glistens; —inspires; —sleeps; —snuggles; —thickens; —waxes; —winds.
(See plain, dale, dell.)

VALOR

adjectives
deliberated; heroic; exceeding; unquestioned; unaffected; loyal; naked; idealized; sheer; free; honorable; bloody; dormouse; personal; distinguished; approved; deliber-

ate; self-respecting; desperate; redoubled; unsurpassed; truculent; mock; reverend; true; frantic; indomitable; patient; pristine; individual; splendid.

verbs
awaken—; call forth—; confirm—; consecrate—; counterfeit—; dedicate to—; discard—; dispense with—; display—; endow with—; gape at—; herald—; impeach—; impugn—; marvel at—; practise—; proclaim—; report—; reward—; tax—; —beggars description; —bewilders; —confounds; —dazzles; —figures; —vanishes.
(See courage, heroism, morale.)

VALOROUS

adverbs
highly; wonderfully; intrepidly; amazingly; commendably; unusually; uncommonly; admirably; tremendously; brilliantly; resolutely; stubbornly; incredibly; invincibly; remarkably.

VALUABLE

adverbs
curiously; exceptionably; exceptionally; extremely; marvellously; seriously; magnificently; incredibly; incalculably; immeasurably; unbelievably; significantly; wonderfully; oddly; unexpectedly; rarely; immensely; enormously; suddenly; immediately; absurdly; fabulously; extraordinarily.

VALUATION

adjectives
false; mental; cordial; fair; common; altered; assessed; improper; reduced.

VALUE

adjectives
historical; rental; thrilling; artistic; independent; priceless; desirable; anticipatory; investment; inestimable; speculative; apologetic; determining; relative; unjust; intrinsic; unescapable; additional; material; positive; restorative; fictitious; sacred; tremendous; incalculable; opposite; symbolic; demonstrated; excellent; amazing; therapeutic; important; outstanding; fundamental; remarkable; heating; exchange; retail; sheer; energy-yielding; sound; uniform; decorative; grand; verified; memorable; prime; essential; food; big; extraordinary; aesthetic; compensating; monetary; unappreciable; local; caloric; asserted; intellectual; independent; prodigious; aggregate; annual;

potential; comparative; vitamin; immeasurable; psychological; paper; survival; practical; marvelous; rare; half-mystical; chief; extra; cultural; reasonable; literary; scientific; full; proper; sensational; nominal; numerical; psychopathic; ultimate; property; fallacious; thrifty; fancy; representative; mere; sentimental; emotional; educational; uncertain; needful; economic; nutritional; permanent; enormous; corresponding; distinct; immense; determinate; splendid; exciting; enduring; customary; specific; beneficial; affective; expressive; unprecedented; conducive; consequent; ethical; critical; diagnostic; refrigerating; social; sacred; unexpected; varying; unrivaled; cherished; additive; face; fluctuating; surprise; moral; extrinsic; compelling; unbelievable; irresistible; exceptional; unbeatable; good; true; unmatchable; surpassed; supreme; entire; lasting; questionable; documentary; exquisite; cash; insulation; top; conspicuous; negotiable; rachitic; fabulous; honest; eye; experimental; brighter; market; dollar; unusual; quality; heart-warming; transcendental; crowning; genuine; scarcity; specified; delusive; peculiar.

verbs
abuse—; advance—; advertise—; analyze —; appraise—; ascertain—; ascribe—to; assess—; attach—to; atribute—to; audit—; authenticate—; belittle—; bolster— —; boast —; broadcast—; calculate—; certify—; cite —; comprehend—; compute—; contribute—; debase—; declare—; deflate—; demonstrate —; depreciate—; depress—; determine—; detract from—; dilute—; discount—; dispute—; distort—; dwell upon—; emasculate —; enhance—; establish—; estimate—; exploit—; fathom—; grasp—; impair—; intensify—; judge—; maintain—; misjudge—; negate—; overestimate—; predetermine—; preserve—; proclaim—; rate—; readjust—; reckon—; recognize—; repudiate—; salvage —; sense—; share—; stress—; substantiate —; tender—; testify to—; verify—; vindicate—; weigh—; yield—; —dawns upon; —diminishes; —enriches; —fluctuates; — —hurtles; —inheres; —leaps; —melts away; —mounts; —shrivels; —soars.
(See esteem, usefulness, worth, significance, importance.)

VALUE (v)
adverbs
inordinately; adequately; artistically; historically; pricelessly; sacredly; symbolically; extraordinarily; aesthetically; locally; potentially; immeasurably; psychologically; scientifically; emotionally; economically; politically; ethically; critically; morally; transcendentally; genuinely.
(See estimate, prize.)

VANDAL
adjectives
arrogant; literary; lawless.

VANISH (v)
adverbs
ultimately; mysteriously; utterly; simultaneously; noiselessly; speedily; swiftly; wholly; magically; completely.
(See disappear.)

VANISHING
adverbs
mysteriously; inconsiderately; strangely; inconveniently; magically; outlandishly; deliberately; curiously; strangely; suddenly; unaccountably; mischievously; fantastically; impishly; selfishly.

VANITY
adjectives
flattering; awkward; fantastic; soothed; foolish; petty; violent; generous; roused; racial; inordinate; mundane; unpunctured; courageous; offensive; contemptible; amusing; ingenuous; artless; punctured; insatiable; reawakened; earthly; morbid; literary; innocent; wounded; motherly; restless; complacent; professed; chargeable; prodigious; colossal; selfish; sanguine; ingenious; offended; sheer; masculine; outworn; trampled; tedious; unconscious; ill-bred.

verbs
appease—; betray—; cater to—; conceal—; counteract—; down—; eradicate—; exhibit —; gratify—; humble—; indulge—; irritate —; loathe—; measure—; mollify—; pander to—; prick—; puncture—; ridicule—; ruffle —; satirize—; tickle—; yield to—; —angers; —cloys; —despoils; —diminishes; — functions; —nauseates; —operates; —repulses; —singes; —stirs.
(See egotism, conceit, pedantry, futility.)

VAPID
adverbs
disappointingly; disagreeably; hopelessly; unbelievably; utterly; strangely; unexpect-

edly; hopelessly; monotonously; uninterestingly; curiously; horribly.

VAPOR

adjectives
oracular; sulphurous; obscuring; aqueous; portentous; black; deathly; foul; gross; swimming; sealike; miasmatic; sunless; steaming; impalpable; misty; sympathetic; poisonous; smoke; soothing; relieving; oracular; radiant; noxious; agitated; rent; gaseous; invisible; stifling; gloomy; midnight; wintry; milky; hideous; imponderable; unctuous; quivering; dim; noontide; suffocating; temperate; corrosive; mercury; ghostly; pale; murky; noxious; alcoholic; quick; evil; diaphanous; motionless.

verbs
diffuse—; distill—; emit—; exhale—; free —; inhale—; liquefy—; —arises; —asphyxiates; —bedims; —befogs; —clouds; —condenses; —eddies; —explodes; —floats; — fumes; —hovers over; —infiltrates; —melts; —obscures; —offends; —permeates; — reeks; —rises; —shrouds; —smothers; — vanishes; —veils.
(See haze, fog, fume, mist, moisture.)

VAPOROUS

adverbs
curiously; strangely; terribly; confusingly; alarmingly; insecurely; mysteriously; intensely; foggily; mistily; steamily; bewilderingly; unhealthfully; dankly; hotly; suffocatingly; mustily.

VARIABLE

adverbs
vexatiously; mysteriously; irritatingly; unpredictably; strangely; unreasonably; mischievously; absurdly; inexplicably; unwarrantably; unstably; unreliably; provokingly; remarkably; unaccountably; intensely; inconveniently; uncomfortably; uselessly; unnecessarily.

VARIANCE

adjectives
internal; usual; perpetual; wide; noticeable.

VARIATION

adjectives
graceful; periodic; momentary; secular; diurnal; visible; sure; divers (pl); incessant; discreet; seasonal; occasional; skillful; fantastic; pyro-technical; erratic; verbal;

slight; injurious; pleasing; distracting; endless; beneficial; numerous (pl); dignified; appreciable; perpetual; transient; emotional.

verbs
account for—; afford—; ascertain—; augment—; calculate—; check—; condone—; correct—; countenance—; decry—; determine—; discern—; disclose—; discount—; dispel—; evolve—; record—; register—; result in—; welcome—; —arises; —deviates; —modifies; —modulates; —occurs.
(See difference, discrepancy, deviation, change, alteration, modification.)

VARIEGATED

adverbs
beautifully; iridescently; colorfully; opalescently; constantly; unpredictably; remarkably; amazingly; curiously; unusually; mysteriously; handsomely.

VARIETY

adjectives
extraordinary; unmotived; improved; dominant; endless; interesting; considerable; immense; amazing; enchanting; distinct; natural; delicious; continental; boundless; manifold (pl); impressive; multiform (pl); infinite; internal; cultivated; epileptic; sportive; splendid; tubular; crafty; graceful; multifarious (pl); bewildering; coarse; picturesque; aquatic; stout; rich; external; embarrassing; tumultuous; stubborn; inordinate; fresh; dull; conceivable; hideous; gorgeous; agreeable; clinging; remarkable; accurate; distinct; limited; wide; colorful.

verbs
achieve—; afford—; crave—; demand—; display—; distinguish by—; encourage—; foster—; indulge in—; infuse—; inspire—; lack—; offer—; procure—; value—; want —; yield—; —animates; —dazes; —diversifies; —diverts; —enlivens; —entertains; — seasons; —spices.
(See collection, change, violation.)

VARLET

adjectives
wicked; abominable; graceless; crimson; incontinent; naughty.

VARNISH (v)

adverbs
sickly; sleekly; luxuriously; thickly; lustrously; smoothly.
(See polish, shine.)

VARY (v)

adverbs

widely; radically; infinitely; indefinitely; heterogeneously; periodically; incessantly; bewilderingly; distinctly.

(See charge, modify.)

VASE

adjectives

exquisite; ponderous; cloisonne; priceless; broken; patched; inimitable.

VASSAL

adjectives

rebellious; gallant; skillful; tributary; belligerent; dreaded; duteous; humble; obsequious.

VASSALAGE

adjectives

commercial; hereditary; economic; complete; effectual.

VAST

adjectives

populous; current; fathomless; boundless; unimagined.

adverbs

enormously; mysteriously; stupendously; impossibly; overwhelmingly; strangely; colossally; prodigiously; astonishingly; marvellously; extraordinarily; miraculously.

VASTNESS

adjectives

tangled; mysterious; encircling; physical; unending.

verbs

bridge—; comprehend—; explore—; measure—; scale—; scan—; span—; survey—; —affords; —allows; —astounds; —awes; —bewilders; —bulks large; —cows; —embraces; —enraptures; —extends; —fascinates; —impresses; —inspires; —intrigues; —looms; —overawes; —overwhelms; —staggers; —stuns; —transcends.

(See spaciousness, magnitude, size.)

VAT

verbs

age in—; char—; contaminate—; deplete—; drain—; ferment in—; immerse in—; label

—; plunge into—; replenish—; store in—; submerge in—; tap—; —diffuses; —emits; —preserves; —reeks.

(See kettle, tub.)

VAULT

adjectives

choked-up; adjoining; gloomy; intersecting; unribbed; majestic; lurid; heavenly; deep; midnight; opaque; celestial; noxious; sinuous; fathomless; wintry; starry; measurable; lofty; inexhaustible; resounding; dungeon-like; imbowered; azure; ebon; dankish; flaming; funereal.

verbs

amass in—; consign to—; defile—; deposit in—; desecrate—; engrave on—; entomb in —; filch from—; haunt—; inscribe on—; inter in—; invade—; pillage—; plunder—; repose in—; seal—; store in—; stow in—; —depresses; —honors; —insures; —muffles; —receives; —reeks; —resounds; —safeguards.

(See cellar, tomb, box.)

VAULT (v)

adverbs

agilely; skillfully; precipitately; rashly; vigorously; lightly; thrillingly.

(See jump, spring.)

VAULTED

adverbs

ethereally; beautifully; immensely; magnificently; splendidly; brilliantly; safely; closely; tightly; securely.

VAUNT

adjectives

obligatory; vainglorious; ostentatious; nauseating.

VAUNT (v)

adverbs

arrogantly; unduly; obstreperously; vaingloriously; ostentatiously; belligerently; verbally.

(See boast, extol.)

VAUNTING

adjectives

compulsory; idle; boastful.

VEGETABLES

adjectives

frozen; thriving; indigenous; succulent; unpalatable; flabby; shade-living; out-of-season; fresh; raw; green.

verbs
bed out—; broil—; consume—; cultivate—; delve among—; fertilize—; hawk—; husband—; label—; market—; partake of—; pluck—; nurse—; prize—; purvey—; reap —; —relish—; savor—; sow—; sprout—; steam—; transplant—.
(See peanut, plant, fruit, food, peas, etc.)

VEGETATION
adjectives
spontaneous; riotous; luxuriant; decaying; exuberant; tropical; treacherous; aboreal; delicate; objectionable; reeking; thriving; velvet; noxious; spiteful; repulsive; slumbering; coarse; variegated; vigorous.

verbs
tame—; —bourgeons; —buds; —bursts forth; —chokes; —curtains; —eclipses; — flourishes; —flowers; —germinates; — mantles; —obscures; —overruns; —overspreads; —pullulates; —screens; —shades; —shadows; —shoots up; —smothers; — sprouts; —strangles; —thickens; —veils.
(See vegetables.)

VEHEMENCE
adjectives
noisy; unaccountable; petitionary; earnest; suppressed; essential; passionate; excessive; sudden; lively; hasty; wild; corresponding; equal.

VEHEMENT
adverbs
unnecessarily; absurdly; laughably; earnestly; foolishly; wildly; loudly; enthusiastically; zealously; ridiculously; gravely; seriously; passionately; forcibly; energetically; pleadingly; fanatically; oddly; singularly; dogmatically; unwisely; vexatiously.

VEHICLE
adjectives
muddled; passing; appropriate; gleaming; favored; poor; groaning; abused; motor; wind-driven; fluid; mechanical; propelled; nominal; crazy; festive; lumbering; sole; back-country; humble; mimic; commonplace; up-to-date; moldering.

verbs
accelerate—; brake—; draw—; fuel—; guide—; impair—; lubricate—; park—; pilot—; —bears; —conveys; —jars; —jolts; —jounces; —rattles; —roars by; —trundles; —whizzes by.
(See cart, conveyance, carriage, chariot, truck.)

VEIL
adjectives
emerald; snowy; inmost; pitchy; misty; dusky; leafy; gloomy; intervening; star-studded; lucid; ugly; solemnizing; gauzy; impenetrable; twilight; obligatory; tangled; mystic; turbid; close-spun; diaphanous; hieroglyphic; sinuous; overhanging; filmy; trembling; fluttering; raw; golden-tissued; borrowed; adamantine; amethystine; fleecy; fearful; maiden.

verbs
bare—; bedeck with—; cast off—; discard —; dispel—; divest of—; doff—; don—; drape—over; draw—; envelop in—; maintain—; penetrate—; rend—; suspend—over; withdraw—; —beguiles; —billows behind; —conceals; —curtains; —deceives; —deludes; —dims; —disguises; —eclipses; — mantles; —muffles; —obstructs; —obscures; —screens; —shades; —shadows.
(See mask, cloak, disguise, fabric, cloth.)

VEIL (v)
adverbs
curiously; unconsciously; impenetrably; skillfully; gloomily; mystically; diaphanously.
(See conceal, hide.)

VEILED
adverbs
beautifully; closely; msyteriously; heavily; luminously; colorfully; provocatively; secretly; furtively; remarkably; marvellously; splendidly; lightly; thinly; deeply; mystically; symbolically; resolutely; exotically.

VEINS
adjectives
hepatic; freezing; moralizing; throbbing; masterful; aging; scorching; rapid; sap-transmitting; sacred; flushed; sanguine; philosophical; prevalent; cloven; idealistic; empty; azure; agreeable; languid; strenuous; whimsical; merry; swollen; fluent; purple-pulsing; translucent; humorous; dra-

matic; varicose; heroic; melodic; equivocating; contaminated; superstitious; prominent; benignant; enamored; prolific; satirical; sluggish; indurated; furtive; rich; laboring; reminiscent; didactic.

verbs
abscess—; attack—; block—; calcify—; compress—; constrict—; dilate—; disperse through—; distend—; drain—; inflame—; inject into—; issue from—; ligature—; occlude—; puncture—; stir in—; tap—; traverse—; trickle through—; —anastomose; —atrophy; —branch off; —clot; —convey; —degenerate; —harden; —proliferate; —pulsate; —thicken; —ulcerate.
(See blood-vessel, artery.)

VELOCITY
adjectives
high; angular; extraneous; extravagant; accentuated; unrelaxed; inconceivable; ascertained; elliptic; linear; standard; undetermined.

verbs
accelerate—; ascertain—; attain—; check—; determine—; diminish—; gain—; heighten —; measure—; stablize—; —abates; —declines; —dwindles; —ebbs; —endangers; —fluctuates; —subsides; —vacillates; —wanes.
(See momentum, speed.)

VELVET
adjectives
prodigious; slashed; fawn-tinted; transparent; smooth; ruffled; regal; wrinkled; flattering.

verbs
array in—; attire in—; bask on—; crumple —; divest of—; garb in—; lounge in—; ruffle—; rumple—; swathe in—; upholster in—; —adds; —colors; —enhances; —enriches; —signifies; —symbolizes.
(See linen, silk.)

VENDIBLE
adverbs
readily; conveniently; easily; profitably; remarkably; extremely; universally; marvellously; incredibly.

VENERABLE
adverbs
ripely; reputably; extraordinarily; signally;

conspicuously; notoriously; estimably; distinctly; nobly; justly; illustriously; virtuously; splendidly; eminently.

VENERATE (v)
adverbs
highly; deeply; religiously; superstitiously; profoundly; obsequiously; humbly; abjectly.
(See respect, esteem.)

VENERATION
adjectives
superstitious; unsympathetic; striking; partial; profound; defective; high; special; deep; remarkable.

VENGEANCE
adjectives
savage; hoarded; gratified; eternal; heroic; bloody; dark; spiteful; cowardly; exemplary; political; vulgar; dastardly; brooding; ample; summary; popular; kindred; pleasing; fiery; worthy; wreakful; satisfied; instant; indiscriminate; gloomy; legal; ripened.

verbs
achieve—; bear—; claim—; clamor for—; conspire—; crave—; demand—; enact—; exact—; forego—; pledge—; press for—; promise—; pursue—; rain—on; seek—; swear—; vow—; wreak—; yield—; —overtakes.
(See revenge, retribution.)

VENGEFUL
adverbs
openly; notoriously; spitefully; murderously; naturally; temperamentally; remarkably; cruelly; bitterly; unrestrainedly; dangerously; secretly; alarmingly; fanatically; wickedly; unforgivingly; reprehensibly; curiously; outrageously; furtively; stealthily; savagely.

VENOM
adjectives
subtle; palsying; spider; lasting; rank.

verbs
anoint with—; antidote—; assimilate—; extract—; immunize to—; infuse—; inject—; neutralize—; resist—; steep in—; succumb to—; suck up—; weaken—; —courses through; —deadens; —overcomes; —paralyzes; —rankles; —seeps through; —stuns.
(See poison, toxin.)

adverbs

notoriously; incredibly; hatefully; unfortunately; incurably; fatally; mortally; naturally; terribly; manifestly; horribly; fearfully; conspicuously; outrageously; reprehensibly; uncommonly; highly; intensely.

VENTILATE (*v*)

adverbs

adequately; thoroughly; defectively; healthfully; beneficially; automatically.

VENTILATION

adjectives

controlled; defective; adequate; automatic; necessary; healthful.

verbs

accomplish—; adjust—; afford—; allow—; facilitate—; furnish—; impair—; lack—; offer—; prescribe—; prevent—; promote—; require—; stabilize—; starve for—; systematize—; want—; —reanimates; —refreshes; —restores; —revivifies.

(See breathing, respiration.)

VENTURE

adjectives

advantageous; revolutionary; maiden; disillusioning; successful; uncertain; amateur; scientific; short-lived; private; matrimonial; speculative; prodigious; fruitful; maritime; succeeding; money-making; biographical; profitable.

verbs

abandon—; acclaim—; back—; contemplate —; decry—; defeat—; denounce—; disclose —; embark on—; encourage—; endanger—; eye—; finance—; forsake—; further—; gamble on—; imperil—; insure—; menace —; promote—; pursue—; relinquish—; threaten—; undertake—; stake on—; withdraw from—; —crashes; —entails; —flourishes; —tempts; —thrives.

(See effort, enterprise, project, undertaking.)

VENTURE (*v*)

adverbs

buoyantly; soothingly; boldly; timidly; hazardously; trustfully; wistfully; occasionally; cautiously; oracularly; imperiously; openly; solemnly; daringly; rashly; madly; sullenly;

complacently; tactfully; timorously; fruitlessly; profitably.

(See dare, risk.)

VENTURESOME

adverbs

distressingly; boyishly; joyously; fantastically; disturbingly; unaccountably; alarmingly; colossally; terribly; dramatically; crazily; spectacularly; notoriously; strangely; singularly; amazingly; recklessly; incredibly; foolishly; boldly; bravely; audaciously; romantically; vicariously; courageously; unnecessarily; disconcertingly; ostentatiously; showily; daringly.

VERACIOUS

adverbs

naturally; habitually; dependably; utterly; absolutely; reliably; strictly; wholly; courageously; boldly; defiantly.

VERACITY

adjectives

scrupulous; attested; unalloyed; simple; inflexible; proved; innate.

verbs

affirm—; assure of—; authenticate—; confirm—; contravene—; demand—; discipline to—; dispute—; doubt—; gainsay—; impugn —; insure of—; maintain—; profess—; question—; reassert—; rebut—; refute—; regard—; repudiate—; swear to—; trust—; vow to—.

(See honesty, truth, frankness.)

VERANDA

adjectives

spreading; glass-enclosed; canvas-covered; sunken; shady; cool.

VERB

verbs

abuse—; accentuate—; adorn with—; avoid —; bandy—s; bristle with—; classify—; choose—; coin—; condense—; conjugate—; corrupt—; cull—s; decide on—; dedicate —; discard—; dispense with—; elect—; eliminate—; employ—; encounter—; eschew —; espouse—s; examine—s; exclude—s; explore—; fancy—; fix upon—; gasp at—; gather—; go in quest of—; grind out—s; identify—; indulge in—; inspire—; intone—; lavish—; manipulate—; marvel at—; misemploy—; modify—; overwork—; pluck—; prefer—; probe—; reel off—s; reject—; repudiate—s; sanction—; search for—; scrutinize—; seek—; select—; shun—; tabulate —s; thirst for—; —accomplishes; — achieves; —alludes to; —animates; —appeals; —asserts; —bites; —caps; —carries out; —colors; —compels; —complements; — completes; —connotes; —consummates; — controls; —conveys; —crowns; —crystallizes; —declares; —defines; —delineates; — depicts; —derives from; —denotes; —distorts; —drives home; —effects; —energizes; —enlivens; —enriches; —exaggerates; — expresses; —frolics; —fulfills; —gyrates; — impels; —implies; —imports; —improves; —indicates; —informs; —interprets; —invigorates; —kindles; —maintains; —moves; —overshadows; —penetrates; —perfects; — performs; —s plunge into; —portrays; — predicates; —provokes; —renders complete; —responds; —rounds out; —rouses; — seals; —s seethe with; —signifies; —s spring into; —states; —stimulates; —strengthens; —suggests; —supplies action; —swings into action; —urges; —wages, analyzes—; — purports.

VERBOSE
adverbs
incurably; tiresomely; inveterately; monotonously; wearisomely; awkwardly; unexpectedly; grossly; crassly; ineptly; clumsily; childishly; garrulously; fulsomely; terribly; extravagantly; unacceptably; unfortunately.

VERDANT
adverbs
delightfully; luxuriantly; invitingly; alluringly; lushly; properly; unexpectedly; gratifyingly; brilliantly; remarkably; unusually; beautifully.

VERDICT
adjectives
lawful; unanimous; manic-depressive; inevitable; consistent; emphatic; intelligent; differing; favorable; adverse; contrary; just; preposterous; fair; inexplicable.

verbs
affect—; appeal—; arrive at—; bias—; carry—; cast—; clarify—; confirm—; contest—; dally with—; deliver—; denounce—; determine—; disclose—; dispute—; elicit—; enter—; evolve—; influence—; justify—; maintain—; ponder—; prejudice—; present —; pronounce—; propound—; question—; render—; return—; reverse—; secure—; sustain—; venture—; verify—; voice—; warrant—; —awards; —dooms; —involves; —misjudges; —startles.
(See judgment, award, finding, decision.)

VERDURE
adjectives
lush; perpetual; profuse; deepening; rank; gloomy; restful; living; perennial; vigorous; tropical; virgin; black; complex; endless; vivid; close-cropped; unchanging.

verbs
clothe in—; prune—; reflect—; thin out—; trim—; —blankets; —cloaks; —colors; — curtains; —flourishes; —freshens; — mantles; —obscures; —overspreads; — screens; —shades; —smothers; —veils.
(See grass, vegetation.)

VERGE
adjectives
utmost; inclusive; uppermost; farthest; beetling; extreme; outward.

verbs
achieve—; ascend to—; approach—; attain —; skirt—; steer to—; tread on—; —borders; —bounds; —encloses.
(See boundary, edge.)

VERIFICATION
adjectives
official; decisive; experimental; attempted.

VERIFY (*v*)
adverbs
unaccountably; accurately; substantially; impartially; officially; experimentally; decisively; specifically.
(See confirm, prove.)

VERITY
adjectives
continual; intense; eternal; conditional; fundamental; bitter; faithful.

verbs
acclaim—; adulterate—; apprehend—; arm with—; demonstrate—; deny—; establish—; evidence—; garble—; ponder—; proclaim —; pronounce—; realize—; reveal—; substantiate—; sustain—; testify to—; unfold —; utter—; voice—.
(See veracity, reality.)

VERMIN

adjectives
creeping; invisible; filthy; parasitic; unpleasant.

verbs
abhor—; breed—; dispel—; eradicate—; exterminate—; swarm with—; —abound; —carry; —contaminate; —defile; —endanger; —infect; —infest; —nauseate; —offend; —overrun; —plague; —pollute; —thrive.
(See insects, cockroach, bug.)

VERMINOUS

adverbs
dangerously; filthily; disgustingly; deplorably; hopelessly; unhealthfully; unsanitarily; unfortunately; damnably; grossly; terribly; dreadfully; unspeakably; indescribably; irremediably; foully; revoltingly; awfully; incredibly.

VERSATILE

adverbs
delightfully; amazingly; charmingly; curiously; admirably; surprisingly; incredibly; marvellously; unbelievably; eminently; illustriously; uncommonly; distinctly; conspicuously; consummately; remarkably; highly.

VERSATILITY

adjectives
vivacious; enormous; characteristic; established; apparent.

verbs
acclaim—; acquire—; appreciate—; attain —; commend—; display—; evince—; exhibit —; marvel at—; value—; —affords; —amazes; —astounds; —embraces; —enables; —excels; —staggers.
(See skill, ability.)

VERSE

adjectives
unpremeditated; mature; evocative; ironic; abominable; flower-sweet; golden; deathless; luxurious; dramatic; magnificent; prosaic; little; magnanimous; well-cadenced; jolly; metaphysical; immortal; marvellous; graceful; introspective; devotional; macaronic; malicious; supererogatory; graceful; slumberous; polished; society; various (pl); measured; heroic; flattering; homely; blank; realistic; faultless; exquisite; sonorous; caustic; singable; sanguinary; halting; rustic; numerous (pl); neglected; faltering;

patriotic; poetic; fascinating; goodly; doggerel; trashy; matchless; piercing; common; undistinguished; musical; balanced; classical; mournful; distinctive; satiric; quill-writ; soothing; galloping; insulting; delicate; melodious; non-dramatic; sorrowful; alliterative; inspired; tolerable; ennobling; clever; octosyllabic; circulated; mechanical; commonplace; comic; unfinished; coarse; outstanding; ridiculous; assonanced; occasional.

verbs
bawl—; carol—; compose—; dash off—; declaim—; divide into—s; enumerate—s; inscribe—on; improvise—; measure—; memorize—; peruse—; polish—; quote—; render —; scan—; scrawl—; sing—; —delights; —effloresces; —eulogizes; —proclaims; —rhymes; —sings of.
(See poetry, poem.)

VERSED

adverbs
well; remarkably; consummately; learnedly; completely; unusually; extraordinarily; supremely; distinctly; effectively.

VERSIFIER

adjectives
ingenious; skillful; mere; melodious.

VERSIFY (v)

adverbs
wittily; cleverly; beautifully; exquisitely; scurrilously; ingeniously; melodiously; skillfully.
(See write, compose.)

VERSION

adjectives
corrected; discordant; condensed; spirited; difficult; vamped-up; coarse; dramatic; rhymed; brisk; virulent; defunct; trimmed-down; garbled; thrilling; pedantic; useful; varying (pl); different; radical; scurrilous; casual; faithful; authorized; modified; artistic; classic; exaggerated; improved; authentic; appealing.

verbs
afford—; authenticate—; color—; confirm —; dash off—; distort—; garble—; illustrate—; maintain—; modify—; offer—; pervert—; simplify—; sustain—; unearth—; varnish—; verify—; —s conflict; —contradicts; —differs; —falsifies; —glosses over;

—interprets; —misrepresents; —slanders.
(See comparison, description, meaning.)

VESICAL
verbs
compress—; contract—; dilate—; distend—; drain—; excise—; incise—; inflame—; irritate—; occlude—; pierce—; puncture—; strangulate—; tap—; —bursts; —dries up; —expands; —protrudes; —shrinks; —shrivels.
(See cell, cavity, sac.)

VESSEL
(boat)
verbs
abandon—; batter—; buffet—; captain—; embark on—; equip—; fit out—; fuel—; ground—; helm—; man—; moor—; navigate—; pilot—; punt—; rig out—; scull—; strand—; waft—; —conveys; —departs; —plies; —plows; —sallies forth; —scuds; —shoves off; —skims; —straggles in; —tosses; —weighs anchor.
(See launch, boat, motor-boat, ship.)

VESSEL
(general)
adjectives
primitive; anchored; ship-wrecked; surrendered; tossing; precious; perished; contaminated; rowing; excretory; convenient; rich-laden; populous; disabled; earthen; effective; weather-beaten; superb; foundering; communicating; fragile; overcrowded; capillary; half-empty; sacred; lymphatic; puny; puffing; staggering; seaworthy; gentle; endangered; straggling; suspicious; suitable.

VEST
adjectives
jeweled; warm; bedecked; plain; stylish.

VEST (v)
adverbs
exclusively; specifically; diplomatically; legislatively; religiously; temporarily.
(See invest.)

VESTIBULE
adjectives
crowded; well-designed; monumental.

VESTIGE
adjectives
last; remaining; enormous; lone.

verbs
bear—; discern—; disclose—; display—; exhibit—; mark—; recognize—; reveal—; stamp out—; uncover—; unearth—; —betokens; —evidences; —fades; —indicates; —remains; —survives; —tesifies to.
(See sign, mark, trace, remnant, remains.)

VESTIGIAL
adverbs
probably; undoubtedly; apparently; manifestly; unmistakably; possibly; credibly; curiously; interestingly; traceably; definitely.

VESTMENT
adjectives
gorgeous; coarse; tattered; purchasable; antique; glorious; somber.

VESTURE
adjectives
imperfect; muddy; pretty; mechanic; napless; choral; pompous; linen; fatal.

VETERAN
adjectives
shoeless; surviving; wary; old; experienced; seasoned; war-worn; gallant; right-minded; decrepit; battered; stalwart; invalided; grim-visaged; hardy; callous.

VETO
adjectives
suspensive; exasperating; equivocal; final; overruled.

verbs
anticipate—; clamp down—; exercise—; fear—; override—; sustain—; table—; —annuls; —checks; —curtails; —dashes the hopes; —debars; —declines; —excludes; —nullifies; —overrides; —overrules; —quashes; —quells; —rejects; —sets aside; —stems; —voids; —withholds.
(See vote, restriction, prohibition.)

VEX (v)
adverbs
intolerably; shrewdly; exceedingly; maddeningly; bitterly; ceaselessly; mutely; horridly; violently; mentally; fiercely; tryingly.
(See irritate, annoy.)

VEXATION
adjectives
silent; resentful; mutual; insupportable; horrid; extreme; evident; puzzled; fierce;

tearful; violent; mental; bitter; trying.

verbs
allay—; arouse—; bear—; conceal—; conciliate—; disclose—; display—; evince—; exhibit—; feign—; foment—; fret in—; incite—; induce—; occasion—; overcome—; palliate—; provoke—; restrain—; writhe in—; —cankers; —irks; —gnaws at; —riles (colloq.); —ruffles; —sours.
(See anger, annoyance, displeasure, irritation, ire, chagrin.)

VEXATIOUS
adverbs
especially; unusually; naturally; occasionally; recently; particularly; monotonously; pettily; terribly; inopportunely; plaguedly; deucedly; intolerably; unfortunately; unimaginably; horribly.

VEXED
adverbs
definitely; unreasonably; foolishly; senselessly; unfairly; deeply; unjustly; distinctly; quickly; easily; unhappily; miserably; wretchedly; ill-temperedly; annoyingly; bitterly; plaguedly; pathetically; sorely; grievously; frightfully; intolerably; distressingly; unbearably; furiously; mightily; hotly.

VIAL
adjectives
wrathful; blasting; tiny; bitter; poisonous.

verbs
analyze—; charge—; despatch—; drain—; eject—; filter—; imbibe from—; inhale from —; label—; quaff from—; seal—; snuff up from—; sterilize—; swill—; uncork—; —befuddles; —enlivens; —envenoms; —paralyzes.
(See medicine, glass bottle.)

VIANDS
adjectives
ruder; exotic; mortal; dainty; ready-baked; tasty; savory.

verbs
bolt—; despatch—; devour—; display—; do justice to—; fall to—; gobble—; gulp—; market—; nibble—; preserve—; purvey—; regale with—; relish—; savor—; tuck in—; —nourish; —revive; —tempt.
(See food, victuals, provisions, fare.)

VIBRATE (*v*)
adverbs
resonantly; discordantly; tunelessly; curiously; rhythmically; mournfully; audibly; sonorously; tremulously; mysteriously.
(See swing, vacillate.)

VIBRATING
adverbs
constantly; thunderously; regularly; tremulously; sympathetically; rapidly; curiously; magically; tunefully; mysteriously; noisily; silently; strangely; secretly; incomprehensibly; dependably; inexplicably; ominously; steadily.

VIBRATION
adjectives
stimulating; rhythmical; deep; touching; braced; nervous; constant; superimposed; mysterious; longitudinal; brave; mournful; audible; sonorous; heart-quaking; rapid; tremulous; ravishing; isochronous; uncomfortable; definite.

verbs
avert—; curb—; record—s; transmit—; —agitates; —ceases; —churns; —disconcerts; —disquiets; —jars; —jiggles; —joggles; —jolts; —jostles; —jounces; —oscillates; —perturbs; —pitches; —pulsates; —rocks; —throbs.
(See pulse, earthquake.)

VICARIOUS
adverbs
altogether; comfortably; perilously; wholly; strangely; generously; curiously; merely.

VICE
adjectives
solemn; enemy; ultimate; incurable; selfish; discordant; encroaching; virtuous; kindred; respective; disgusting; monstrous; gilded; beneficial; hereditary; distinguished; black; ineffable; distorted; plausible; infamous; searing; overshadowing; ruling; alluring; reckless; engendering; unmarred; trivial; heathen; distressing; deliberate; fashionable; supreme; depicting; abstract; notorious; hateful; gross; coarse; bold; reputed; solitary; ingrained; popular; essential; embodied; walking; redeeming; filthy.

verbs
abandon—; addict to—; campaign against check—; clothe in—; combat—; commercial-

ize—; condemn—; condone—; confess—; crusade against—; curb—; cure—; denounce —; expose—; fall into—; forsake—; foster —; indulge in—; renounce—; reveal—; smack of—; sow—; stem—; stray into—; succumb to—; uncover—; weed out—; — corrupts; —debauches; —demoralizes; — depraves; —desecrates; —flourishes; — fouls; —perverts; —stains; —sullies; — taints; lapse into—.

(See knavery, lawlessness, licentiousness, crime.)

VICINITY
adjectives
immediate; apogeal; perilous; proximate.

verbs
abandon—; acquaint one with—; adjoin—; approach—; betake oneself to—; border—; comb—; converge on—; denude—; devastate—; drift to—; encircle—; encompass—; expel from—; flank—; forsake—; frequent —; guard—; patrol—; picket—; prowl about—; ramble about—; roam—; rove—; screen—; shroud—; skirt—; stroll about—.

(See locality, neighborhood.)

VICIOUS
adverbs
notoriously; famously; incomparably; alarmingly; criminally; heinously; nefariously; brutally; incredibly; indescribably; incomparably; wholly; politically; obviously; deplorably; manifestly; terribly; basely; grossly; obscenely; morally; notably; indefensibly; dangerously; intolerably.

VICIOUSNESS
adjectives
inherent; senile; compounded; essential; natural; characteristic.

VICISSITUDES
adjectives
myriad; sublime; sweet; sudden; mortal; sad; strange.

verbs
acquaint one with—; avert—; control—; decry—; denounce—; deplore—; dwell upon —; forecast—; forestall—; foretell—; hazard—; meet—; prepare for—; prophesy—; risk—; suffer—; welcome—; —alter; —imperil; —jeopardize; —revolutionize; — threaten.

(See change, misfortune.)

VICTIM
adjectives
unsuspicious; noble; unfortunate; struggling; hapless; miserable; desirable; ulster-clad; prospective; unspotted; penitent; wretched; choking; immediate; bridal; potential; slaughtered; unresisting; deluded; hunted; illustrious; innumerable (pl); unthinking; contemptible; cowering; countless (pl); unshriven; unnamed; supposed; ingenuous; mutilated; livid; squalid; multifarious (pl).

verbs
avenge—; bait—; beguile—; bilk—; console—; decoy—; defraud—; dupe—; ease —; ensnare—; entice—; exonerate—; goad —; harass—; harrow—; lure—; maim—; martyrize—; sacrifice—; snare—; solicit—s; succor—s; trap—; wrack—; wring—; — bewails; —decries; —despairs; —endures; —grieves; —laments; —languishes; — mourns; —pines; —suffers; —testifies; — tolerates; —succumbs to.

(See prey, quarry, amateur.)

VICTOR
adjectives
laurel-crowned; joyless; loving; upborne; modest.

VICTORIOUS
adverbs
ultimately; finally; eventually; immediately; recently; grandly; brilliantly; magnificently; gloriously; splendidly; royally; modestly; triumphantly; quietly; logically; reasonably; suddenly; unexpectedly; deservedly; happily; luckily; blessedly; utterly.

VICTORY
adjectives
smashing; splendid; subsequent; glorious; brilliant; dialectic; decisive; barren; undeclining; approaching; partisan; ultimate; triumphant; sweeping; marvelous; inevitable; overwhelming; publicized; enormous; fresh; unvarying; superb; prospective; world-famous; ineffective; self-assured; bloody; wholesome; retributive; manifold (pl); signal; endless; speedy; secret; obligatory; gladsome; strategic; Pyrrhic.

verbs
acclaim—; achieve—; advance to—; anticipate—; assure of—; botch—; celebrate—; chalk up—; clinch—; commemorate—;

crown with—; emerge with—; eventuate in —; fall short of—; gain—; glorify—; goad to—; grace—; grind out—; guide to—; hail —; inspire—; insure—; magnify—; pledge to—; proclaim—; promise—; purchase—; radiate—; rob of—; romp to—; result in—; salute—; score—; seal—; sense—; signify —; snatch—; spur to—; sweep to—; temper —; wreathe in—; wrest—from; —demoralizes; —eludes; —evades; —overwhelms; —routs; —vanquishes.

(See conquest, advantage, triumph, success, supremacy.)

VICTUALS

verbs
bolt—; consume—; deluge with—; deplete —; despatch—; devour—; dispense—; furnish with—; gobble—; gorge—; gulp—; laud—; munch—; praise—; preserve—; prepare—; provide—; purvey—; refrigerate—; relish—; replenish—; savor—; stint on—; stock with—; —attract; —lure; —nourish; —refresh; —renew; —restore; —tempt.

(See food, viands.)

VIEW
(general)

adjectives
extensive; provincial; splendid; comprehensive; topographical; modern; regimentalist; historical; respective (pl); foregoing; definite; monarchical; wide; representative; personal; broad; solemn; reiterated; clashing; enlarged; spiritual; systematized; theological; religious; divergent; masculine; gloomy; prehistoric; realistic; bloody; rationalist; stereopticon; philosophic; dismayed; differing; pessimistic; magnificent; distinct; enchanting; optimistic; perspective; dubious; architectural; humanistic; infinite; dynamic; trustworthy; lucid; celebrated; exaggerated; prophetic; benighted; interesting; experimental; anti-democratic; vivid; complete; unmitigated; intensive; spectacular; elaborate; successive (pl); deliberate; panoramic; dissolving; sentimental; esthetic; superb; metaphysical; charitable; illuminated; individualistic; unbounded; intellectual; peculiar; unwashed; liberal; nihilistic; sudden; injurious; aberrant; unobstructed; continuous; partial; stable; mischievous; worldly; unfavorable; glorious; luminous; lofty; idealistic; impressive; practical; prevalent; ample; mechanical; cynic; human; similar; mystical; sharp; clear;

orthodox; believing; angelic; erroneous; nerve-trying; subjective; romantic; beautiful; shuddering; hopeless; dismal; sympathetic; primitive; cheerful; gorgeous; old-fashioned; superficial; many-sided; fascinating; mortal; rosy; undulating; startled; disparaging; dignified; prudent; calm; sanguine; deep; advanced; materialistic; despairing; evolutionary; irresponsible; investigating; charming; disheartened; constitutional; rational; especial; collateral; dissolving; limited; pecuniary; tenable; straining; benevolent; theoretic; matured; retrospective; unfair; uninterrupted; rigid; indescribable; dissolving; sightless; enlightened; melancholy; cross-section; partial; stately; conservative; top-lofty; settled; picturesque; disputed; world-famous; thrilling; splendid; skyline; river; exceptional; overpowering; orthodox.

VIEW
(intellectual)

verbs
advertise—; air—; alter—; analyze—; arrive at—; balance—; bias—; bolster—; broaden—; cancel—; cherish—; clarify—; color—; conceive—; conciliate—; confide—; confirm—; countenance—; credit—; demonstrate—; dispute—; distort—; embrace—; entertain—; establish—; evaluate—; exchange—s; expose—s; expound—; falsify—; fix—; formulate—; grasp—; illustrate—; inculcate—; indoctrinate—; indorse—; influence—; inspire—; integrate—s; interpret —; justify—; lack—; maintain—; narrow —; nurse—; object to—; oppose—; originate —; present—; proclaim—; profess—; reconsider—; repudiate—; retain—; reveal—; set forth—; shape—; share—; shift—; substantiate—; sum up—; support—; sustain—; thwart—; uphold—; voice—; warp—; warrant—; —prevails; —shocks.

(See belief, aim, mission, notion, aspect, perspective, perception, opinion.)

VIEW
(landscape, sight, etc.)

verbs
afford—; bare to—; beautify—; blemish—; cloud—; command—; contemplate—; deface —; distort—; dull—; emblazon—; enjoy—; exalt—; frame—; gaze at—; glimpse—; mar—; obliterate—; obscure—; obstruct—; photograph—; pop into—; portray—; preserve—; rivet upon—; screen—; shade—; sketch—; telescope—; vanish from—; —

blurs; —dazzles; —enchants; —enkindles; —enraptures; —enthralls; —impassions; —impresses; —inspires; —petrifies; —unfolds.
(See sight, scene, prospect, panorama, landscape.)

VIEW (v)
adverbs
regretfully; historically; cynically; sardonically; incessantly; dispassionately; faintly; fitfully; hastily; curiously; extensively; solemnly; philosophically; optimistically; charitably; idealistically; subjectively; sympathetically; objectively; theoretically; panoramically.
(See regard, see.)

VIEWPOINT
adjectives
hard-boiled; short-sighted; national; practical; impersonal; unbiased; fresh; optimistic; evolutionistic; customary; universal; sociological; pessimistic; prejudiced.

VIGIL
adjectives
tearless; lone; late; bitter; dangerous; heart-chilling; weary; solemn; unhallowed; anxious; tongueless.

verbs
allay—; arrest—; curtail—; dread—; ease —; eke out—; endure—; interrupt—; maintain—; necessitate—; prolong—; protract—; relax—; relinquish—; resume—; slacken—; survive—; suspend—; sustain—; terminate —; —fatigues; —tells; —weakens; —wearies; —weighs upon.
(See vigilance, interest, watch, scrutiny.)

VIGILANCE
adjectives
eternal; remarkable; utmost; constant; increasing; unceasing; determined; extraordinary; redoubled; jealous; habitual; stern.

verbs
admonish—; circumvent—; ease—; enforce —; escape—; exhort—; heighten—; intensify—; lighten—; maintain—; mitigate—; necessitate—; reduce—; relax—; sharpen —; slacken—; —declines; —discovers; —insures; —lapses; —safeguards; —subsides; —wanes; —wearies.
(See interest, vigil, caution.)

VIGILANT
adverbs
eternally; constantly; unrelentingly; carefully; intelligently; ordinarily; usually; uncommonly; especially; particularly; unremittingly; cruelly; lovingly; fondly; affectionately; gently; anxiously; fearfully; timidly; nervously; sternly; harshly; curiously; inquisitively; inexcusably; vexatiously; inescapably.

VIGNETTE
verbs
adorn with—s; dash off—; embellish with —s; enamel—; etch—; execute—; frame—; impress—; print—; sketch—; stipple—; varnish—; —delineates; —depicts; —describes; —illustrates; —ornaments; —pictures; —portrays.
(See portrait, picture, sketch.)

VIGOR
adjectives
mortal; ethereal; disciplined; hybrid; prime; uninterrupted; florid; excessive; tireless; sinewy; remarkable; accustomed; terse; quickened; coarse; wild; dramatic; muscular; athletic; wonted; intellectual; pristine; furious; rude; aggressive; manly; plastic; incisive; contrary; bodily; selfish; incredible; extraordinary; original; renewing; increased; peristaltic; conscious; customary; dynamic; remorseless; emulating; recuperative; glorious; determined; rustic; redoubled; lusty; classic; especial; elastic; hardy; graceful; masculine; mighty; purposeful; youthful; mental; terrible; unabated; astonishing; superabundant; full; sudden; original; unimpaired; native; offhand; renovated.

verbs
acquire—; demand—; deplete—; display—; endow with—; enhance—; exert—; exhibit —; infuse—; inject—; instill—; lessen—; maintain—; perform with—; preserve—; radiate—; renew—; retain—; restore—; sap up—; stimulate—; store up—; sustain —; —buttresses; —fades; —fortifies.
(See force, energy, "pep", strength.)

VIGOROUS
adverbs
splendidly; sufficiently; brawnily; healthily; warrantably; actually; fortunately; necessarily; apparently; mysteriously; manifestly; uncommonly; remarkably; luckily.

VILIFY (v)

adverbs
blackly; wrathfully; maliciously; malignantly; cruelly; viciously; jealously; furiously; terribly; coarsely; rudely; hatefully; grossly.
(See slander, traduce.)

VILLA

adjectives
glittering; enchanting; expensive; commodious; peaceful; dainty; restful; gaudy; handsome; spacious; suburban; voluptuous; sumptuous; medieval.

VILLAGE

adjectives
smiling; toy-like; poverty-stricken; cool; shady; damp; worn-out; patriarchal; incurious; straggling; dependent; adjacent; innumerable (pl); obscure; rustic; neighboring; ordinary; provincial; whitewashed; poor; dusky; ghost-like; pathetic; retired; pleasant; well-ordered; preoccupied; miserable; insensible; rural; native; deserted; squalid; insignificant; forsaken; producing; self-supporting; isolated; delightful; stupid-looking; little; stony; picturesque; manufacturing; sprawling; embowered; remote; shabby; lovely; sweet; smiling; red-roofed; helpless; pastoral; benighted.

verbs
abide in—; arouse—; border—; commute from—; desert—; devastate—; dot with—s; ensconce in—; flank—; forsake—; frequent —; inhabit—; lull—; nestle in—; quarter in—; raze—; repair to—; skirt—; storm—; —expands; —flourishes; —hums; —straggles; —thrives.
(See neighborhood, community, town, city.)

VILLAGER

verbs
alarm—; beseech—; bilk—; dominate—; educate—; enslave—; harangue—; plague —; rook—; rouse—; summon—; swindle —; tax—; —bands; —commutes; —cultivates; —descends upon; —flocks to; —markets; —prospers; —rises; —scatters; — thwarts.
(See citizen, individual, inhabitant, taxpayer, public.)

VILLAIN

adjectives
plain-dealing; replenished; ungrateful; dissembling; precise; white; sweet; monstrous; soulless; repulsive; murdering; rich; senseless; false; infernal; cursed; notorious; prodigious; wicked; skulking; accomplished; penurious; scheming; murderous; shaghaired; fine; hoary; inflexible; trusty; honorable; abandoned; atrocious; deliberate; cool.

verbs
apprehend—; banish—; band—; condemn —; curtail—; denounce—; expose—; ferret out—; incarcerate—; inveigh against—; jail—; portray—; prosecute—; reveal—; scourge—; seize—; sniff out—; —s band; —betrays; —confesses; —conspires; —defiles; —desecrates; —eludes; —evades; — plots; —seduces; —slanders; —transgresses.
(See profligate, actor, scoundrel, criminal, monster, character.)

VILLAINOUS

adverbs
unmistakably; utterly; despicably; unhappily; terribly; dreadfully; unspeakably; infamously; conspicuously; incredibly; unimaginably; remarkably; contemptibly; defiantly; openly; secretly; blandly; actually; manifestly.

VILLAINY

adjectives
cold-blooded; multiplying; deliberate; unusual; naked; superfluous; reeking; systematic; stupendous; vocal; sensual; deliberate; demoniacal; subtle.

verbs
accuse of—; charge with—; denounce—; deplore—; detect—; disclose—; expose—; forsake—; involve—; lapse into—; practise—; punish—; renounce—; resort to—; reveal —; rue—; sink into—; turn from—; uncover —; —defames; —degrades.
(See sin, wickedness, crime.)

VINDICATE (v)

adverbs
amply; sufficiently; triumphantly; gallantly; honorably; magnanimously; heroically; creditably; ingeniously; simply.
(See justify, correct.)

VINDICATION

adjectives
alleged; gloomy; culminating; prompt; attempted; triumphant; labored; simple; cred-

itable; vicarious; ingenious; mischievous; pampered.

VINDICTIVE

adverbs
utterly; openly; secretly; defiantly; violently; dangerously; furtively; alarmingly; portentously; ominously; oddly; peculiarly; smoothly; cruelly; bitterly; brutally.

VINDICTIVENESS

adjectives
satanic; detestable; vicious; spiteful; hateful.

verbs
appease—; assert—; assuage—; calm—; dispose toward—; ease—; express—; indulge in—; justify—; harbor—; quell—; relax—; relent—; reveal—; satisfy—; temper—; tranquillize—; warrant—; — grows; —subsides; —wanes; —wakes.
(See hatred, animosity, contempt.)

VINE

adjectives
withering; never-flowering; gadding; tangled; clinging; trellised; scented; delicate; springing; arching; thorny; sovereign; trailing; delicious; intricate; clustering; bordering; ambitious; well-pruned; perfume-breathing; flaming; riotous; luxuriant; creeping; strangling; ambrosial; cloistral; rose-flecked; immense; parasitic; sweet; breathed; interwoven; twisted; choice.

verbs
bunch on—; graft into—; husband—; load —; lop—; prune—; screen with—s; smother in—s; support—; transplant—; —bears; —bows with; —clambers; —clings; — creeps; —embowers; —enriches; —entwines; —flourishes; —overspreads; — scents; —thickens; —thrives; —trails; — yields.
(See honeysuckle, etc.)

VINEYARD

adjectives
sloping; blood-tinctured; terraced; luscious; productive.

VIOLATE (v)

adverbs
flagrantly; expressly; palpably; basely; grossly; flatly; wickedly; persistently; undisguisedly; expressly; criminally; spiritually.
(See transgress, trespass.)

VIOLATION

adjectives
gross; flat; denouncing; wide-spread; wicked; conscious; signal; persistent; undisguised; express.

verbs
condone—; constitute—; disapprove of—; disclose—; dismiss for—; frown on—; ignore—; justify—; penalize—; protest—; wink at—; —desecrates; —encroaches upon; —infringes; —nullifies; —ostracizes; —piques; —repudiates; —riles (colloq.); — tramples; —transgresses; —voids.
(See breach, infringement, infraction.)

VIOLATOR

adjectives
apparent; sacrilegious.

verbs
apprehend—; check—; denounce—; disclose —; exile—; fine—; jail—; "nab"—; pounce upon—; punish—; seize—; trail—; — abuses; —baffles; —breaks; —despoils; — disregards; —eludes; —encroaches; — evades; —infringes; —mulcts; —profanes; —ravishes.
(See criminal.)

VIOLENCE

adjectives
frightful; murderous; unlooked-for; sheer; spontaneous; physical; reckless; passionate; high-handed; unwonted; brutal; unjustifiable; glorious; unscrupulous; theatric; impetuous; irreconcilable; ghostly; gentle; midnight; unreasoning; swift; bloody; needful; uncommon; loud; extreme; odious; meditated; irregular; personal; momentary; aggressive; stunning; sacrilegious; devilish; cowardly; invisible; undiminished; occasional; tragic; threatening; restless; increasing; quiet.

verbs
advocate—; allay—; avert—; balk at—; bar—; burst into—; condone—; cow by—; curb—; denounce—; deplore—; deprecate —; discountenance—; employ—; foment—; frustrate—; incite—; indulge in—; inflame to—; instigate—; lull—; pacify—; precipi-

tate—; provoke—; quell—; resort to—; restrain—; subdue—; —erupts; —rages.

(See malice, impetuosity, indignation, intensify, fury, anger.)

VIOLENT
adverbs
ungovernably; dangerously; lawlessly; youthfully; heedlessly; lamentably; deplorably; openly; actively; defiantly; insurgently; restively; mutinously; rebelliously; tumultuously; treasonably; incorrigibly; persistently; obstinately.

VIOLET
adjectives
glowing; blue-veined; royal; nodding; shrinking; purple; dewy; first; blown; lucid.

VIOLIN
adjectives
alto; beautiful; masterful; priceless.

VIPER
adjectives
universal; jumping; startled.

VIRGIN
adjectives
wily; white-robed; young; budding; vestal; regarded; pale-eyed; poor; learned; powerful; ill-drawn; ultimate; charming; bashful; blushing.

verbs
befit—; bestow upon—; defile—; deflower —; despoil—; esteem—; play the—; respect —; revere—; seduce—; sully—; touch—; —binds; —brags; —captives; —exults; — flaunts; —flouts; —glories; —scolds; — stifles.

(See girl, woman, wife.)

VIRGINITY
adjectives
pretty; irrevocable; indestructible; antiquated; long-preserved.

verbs
acknowledge—; ascribe—; blemish—; dig-

nify—; preserve—; pride oneself on—; profess—; question—; stain—; taint—; take—; tarnish—; threaten—; violate—; worship —; —imparts.

(See chastity, purity, virtue.)

VIRTUE
adjectives
disinterested; hereditary; acquired; slender; manly; unselfish; self-abnegating; conscious; commonplace; attractive; negative; imputed; stellar; domestic; sounding; sterling; vestal; infinite; peculiar; rigid; heroic; admirable; rare; impregnable; barbaric; paltry; distinguished; new-built; abstract; consummate; sober; well-known; surface; unassailable; exemplary; external; unpretending; perfect; unquestionable; diuretic; delightful; dominant; fanciful; honorable; active; ennobling; illustrious; beaming; wondrous; proud; suffering; healing; probable; proverbial; outraged; distressed; aromatic; contradictory; magnetic; outstanding; prime; redeeming; humble; lofty; wearied; beatific; grateful; possible; personal; ever-flourishing; supposed; unique; political; simple; superstitious; thoughtful; godlike; chief; inimitable; boasted; excellent; artificial; manifold (pl); legitimate; proper; nameless; eminent; high; spirited; preserved; knightly; intrinsic; certain; sublime; eclipsed; natural; unbecoming; old-fashioned; healing; ruining; comely; sweet; rude; ruffled; right; strict; sober; solid; public; prosaic; pure; nectarous; disputable; injurious; liberal; politic; cardinal; low; succored; religious; infant; medicinal; flowering; severe; reawakening; moral; middle; untainted; fundamental; marvelous; tangible; loving; aristocratic; definite; traditionary; boasted; small; philanthropic; powerful; cheap; incessant; rural; befriending; feminine; bastard; sundry (pl); leading; private; uncertain; amiable; grand; special; soporific; prodigious; ignominious.

verbs
acclaim—s; blot out—; commend—; cultivate—s; defend—; delight in—; embody—s; emphasize—s; esteem—; exemplify—; extol —s; forsake—; foster—; hail—; impart— to; implant—; incarnate—s; inculcate—; instil—; magnify—s; nurture—; observe—s; preserve—; proclaim—s; question—; recognize—s; redeem—; relinquish—; reward—; scoff at—; scorn—; sing—s; stray from—;

sustain—; —distinguishes; —prevails; —
triumphs; —uplifts; embrace—.

(See chastity, integrity, morality, courage,
prudence, honesty, fortitude, temperance, justice.)

VIRTUOUS
adverbs

pretentiously; unctuously; pharasaically; ostentatiously; actually; notably; entirely; conspicuously; apparently; supposedly; utterly;
unquestionably; manifestly; palpably; definitely; remarkably; honestly; sincerely.

VIRULENT
adverbs

disastrously; unfortunately; cruelly; bitterly; admittedly; unusually; terribly; remarkably; insidiously; unbelievably; uncommonly; highly; dreadfully; dangerously.

VIRUS
verbs

allay—; antidote—; check—; combat—; confine—; counteract—; immunize to—; inacti-
vate—; infect with—; inject—; isolate—;
neutralize—; weaken—; —attacks; —consumes; —devastates; —inflames; —invades;
—paralyzes; —prostrates; —ravages.

(See germ, disease, poison, venom.)

VISAGE
adjectives

grotesque; tawny; shattered; unmutilated;
gory; grim; great; bloody; impassive;
wrinkled; puckered; swarthy; fierce; monstrous; storied; infernal; importing; bleared; silver; favored; borrowed; illuminated; horrent; ironical; sickly; grotesque;
hard-favored; glimmering; revolting; saintly; unrepentant; dark; passionless; weather-
beaten; leathery; pale; choleric; ancient;
coppery.

VISIBLE
adverbs

easily; undoubtedly; dimly; clearly; usually;
wholly; completely; faintly; brightly; obscurely; distinctly; conspicuously; embarrassingly; inadvertently; unavoidably; purposely; inconveniently; awkwardly.

VISION
(*eyesight, etc.*)
verbs

astigmatize—; augment—; blur—; cloud—;
conserve—; correct—; dazzle—; deprive of

—; dim—; distort—; dull—; eclipse—;
focus—upon; impair—; infract—; measure
—; obscure—; obstruct—; preserve—;
quicken—; ravage—; refract—; scathe—;
screen—; sharpen—; shield from—; value
—; veil—; warp—.

(See sight.)

VISION
(*general*)
adjectives

sudden; frightful; telescopic; sun-compell-
ing; moral; transitory; tender; ravishing;
foregone; delightful; alleged; vivid; specialized; remarkable; appointed; angelic;
sweet; light; radiant; rectified; fresh;
stunted; mental; early; concentrated; failing; gloomy; spiritual; horrible; calm; relentless; prophetic; useful; disturbing; embodied; unremembered; anxious; uncertain;
harassing; artless; dying; frightful; dreadful; singular; ecstatic; tranced; charmed;
skyey; world; unforgettable; transcendent;
myopic; subjective; halting; transient; dim;
fatal; chill; airy; baseless; blissful; nar-
rating; painful; unreal; troubled; mysterious; culminating; morning; earthly; infinite; subtle; alluring; enchanted; unsubstantial; heavenly; saintly; rapturous; entrancing; hawk-like; glorious; cosmic; aesthetic;
imaginary; extended; inspiring; subsequent;
importunate; cold; confused; delirious; par-
adisical; impaired; encompassed; tranquil;
ominous; pleasing; beautiful; long-promised; discriminating; beatific; downcast;
obscure; lucid; hallowed; intellectual; unaided; creative; crystal; cradled; mental;
clear; midday; pious; unclouded; overwhelming; singular; bored; sweet; rare;
yearning; everlasting; earth-dimmed; defective; philosophical; vague; sun; window; fruitless; far-seeing; apocalyptic.

VISION
(*imagination*)
verbs

blur—; cherish—; conjure up—; fire by—;
flirt with—; fulfill—; resolve—; reveal—;
shake off—; train on—; —appears; —
arises; —dances; —dawns upon; —dazes;
—departs; —fascinates; —flashes before; —
flees; —flits; —foretells; —haunts; —materializes; —prophesies.

(See imagination, phantom, dream, phan-
tasy, mirage, nightmare, image.)

1264

adverbs
fantastically; quixotically; chimerically; ephemerally; unsubstantially; imponderably; tenuously; mystically; mythically; fancifully; uncommonly; highly; inanely; vacuously; airily; blankly; dreamily; groundlessly.

VISIT

adjectives
delightful; dramatic; ultimate; surreptitious; unlooked-for; flying; proffered; cordial; doubtful; courteous; unceremonious; yearly; imperial; casual; frequent (pl); distinguished; intended; transient; extraordinary; dreaded; volunteered; ill-timed; agreeable; unavailing; momentous; intemperate; meditated; unwelcome; gentle; prolonged; approaching; parochial; wonted; flying; last-mentioned; hurried; occasional; untimely; perfunctory; domiciliary; impending; stated; cool; comfortable; quiet; happy; pleasant; well-rounded.

verbs
abbreviate—; alternate—; cancel—; close —; conclude—; curtail—; defer—; depart on—; draw out—; extend—; plan—; prolong—; protract—; reciprocate—; resume —; return—; season—; schedule—; terminate—; welcome—; —delights; —wearies.
(See vacation, interview.)

VISIT (v)

adverbs
habitually; customarily; traditionally; periodically; seasonally; surreptitiously; cordially; courteously; ceremoniously; annually; imperially; agreeably; momentously; intemperately.
(See call, journey.)

VISITANT

adjectives
ghostly; weird; undesirable; strange.

VISITATION

adjectives
wide-spread; loving; gentle; transient; providential; heavenly; supernatural; troublesome; undeserved; nightly; sudden.

VISITING

adjectives
compunctious; continual; yearly; routine.

adjectives
transient; assiduous; unseen; anonymous; favored; struggling; nightly; distraught; gaping; pedestrian; enthusiastic; transcendental; dwindling; prominent; casual; uninitiated; wondering; gentle; frequent; haggard; savage; constant; distinguished; celestial; wandering; pauper; ordinary; belated; time-stealing; transitory; accustomed; dreadful; unwelcome.

verbs
amuse—; anticipate—; ban—; bar—; beam at—; confront—; discourage—; elude—; embrace—; entertain—; exclude—; greet—; hail—; ignore—; limit—; receive—; regale —; salute—; shun—; welcome—; —bore; —distract; —divert; —interrupt; —stream in; —surge in; —throng; —weary.
(See guest, listener.)

VISTA

adjectives
economic; pillared; enticing; distant; boundless; backward; frequent; mental; stately; unexpected; spectral.

verbs
cloud—; gaze at—; glory in—; obscure—; pore over—; rivet upon—; scan—; screen —; stare at—; survey—; —dazzles; —enraptures; —enthralls; —extends; —glitters; —opens before; —yawns.
(See view, landscape.)

VITAL

adverbs
obviously; indisputably; clearly; admittedly; curiously; strangely; significantly; particularly; absolutely; fundamentally; palpably; manifestly; remarkably.

VITALITY

adjectives
undreamed-of; intellectual; sportive; hilarious; protracted; restless; aggressive; creative; genuine; lingering; sparkling; continued; departing; brisk; enfeebled; abounding; mental; characteristic; inherent; forgotten; enormous; subterranean; unfailing; immaculate; vigorous; dimensional; glorious; unrivaled; inexhaustible; persistent; overpowering; brutal; miserable; great; low.

verbs
absorb—; acquire—; brim with—; build—; charge with—; concentrate—; conserve—; deprive of—; destroy—; detract from—; dull—; endow with—; exhaust—; glow with —; impair—; instil—; invest with—; lack —; maintain—; preserve—; recruit—; reduce—; reinforce—; renew—; rob of—; retain—; sap—; spare—; sustain—; throb with—; undermine—; —ebbs; —endures; — wanes; —wavers.

(See strength, health.)

VITAMINS
adjectives
toxic; essential; prevailing; helpful; over-emphasized.

verbs
classify—; condense—; demand—; despatch —; enrich in—; instil—; lack—; measure —; necessitate—; prate of—; require—; rob of—; —build resistance; —deteriorate; — immunize; —nourish; —sustain.

(See nourishment, food.)

VITUPERATE (v)
adverbs
bitterly; cruelly; insidiously; vitriolically; personally; emotionally; exceedingly; viciously; craftily; savagely; sardonically; snarlingly; horribly; jubilantly; shrilly; stridently; vulgarly; unspeakably.

(See vilify, slander.)

VITUPERATION
adjectives
personal; emotional; nasty; vitriolic.

VITUPERATIVE
adverbs
profanely; obscenely; loudly; blatantly; boisterously; insanely; furiously; justly; unreasonably; terribly; unjustly; coarsely; openly; particularly; shamefully; blisteringly; brutally; unspeakably; incredibly; noisily; shamelessly; publicly; scathingly.

VIVACIOUS
adverbs
delightfully; pleasantly; merrily; nonsensically; comically; entertainingly; divertingly; extremely; uncommonly; highly; amusingly; excitably; enthusiastically; briskly; restlessly; alertly.

VIVACITY
adjectives
violent; nervous; ingenuous; high; unflagging; immense; unsurpassable; unabated; exuberant; sparkling; pert; artificial; unbelievable.

verbs
awaken—; cultivate—; destroy—; display —; lack—; preserve—; recapture—; value —; —animates; —bubbles; —cheers; —declines; —delights; —enlivens; —endears; — exhilarates; —gladdens; —infects; —inspirits; —refreshes; —tires; —vivifies; — wanes.

(See gayety, liveliness, animation.)

VIVID
adverbs
extremely; supernaturally; terribly; frightfully; beautifully; admirably; commendably; unusually; splendidly; wonderfully; miraculously; unbelievably; uncommonly; particularly; peculiarly; curiously; mysteriously; delightfully.

VIVIDNESS
adjectives
shocking; painful; tremendous; transparent; burning; bright; startling; journalistic.

VIXENISH
adverbs
impishly; comically; childishly; significantly; portentously; unbecomingly; ridiculously; unwarrantably; inexplicably; suddenly; hysterically; violently; surprisingly; unwontedly; alarmingly; dreadfully; momentarily.

VOCABULARY
adjectives
lurid; workable; adequate; copious; fundamental; enormous; scientific; picturesque; fashionable; full; varied; working; reading; reserve; valuable; speaking; built-up; stimulated; choice; wide; notable; well-balanced; normal; brilliant; scant; lively; rich; racy; saucy; unusual.

verbs
acquire—; add to—; adopt—; aggrandize —; amass—; analyze—; arrange—; augment—; better—; broaden—; build—; color —; compare—; compile—; contrast—; criticize—; cultivate—; culture—; derive—; develop—; display—; eliminate from—; employ—; enhance—; enlarge—; enrich—; ex-

amine—; exhaust—; familiarize oneself with
—; furnish with—; gather—; improve—;
increase—; limit—; make—active; mature
—; narrow—; ransack—; refine—; require
—; retain—; select—; simplify—; strength-
en—; swell—; vary—; vulgarize—; weaken
—; —accrrues; —aids; —amazes; —a-
stounds; —colors; —derives from; —embraces; —equips; —excels; —expresses; —
flowers; —fructifies; —grows; —includes;
—indicates; —insures; —invigorates; —
multiplies; —provides; —ranges; —reveals.

VOCAL CHORDS
verbs
discipline—; distend—; ease—; elongate—;
impair—; injure—; irritate—; rasp—;
soothe—; strain—; tax—; tighten—; train
—; trap—; weaken—; —change; —contract; —emit; —lengthen; —quiver; —utter; —vibrate.

VOCALIST
adjectives
eminent; prominent; wonderful; thrilling.

verbs
acclaim—; accompany—; applaud—; arrange for—; laud—; train—; —carols; —
enraptures; —enthralls; —entrances; —executes; —improvises; —intones; —lilts; —
quavers; —records; —renders; —scales; —
thrills; —trills; —twitters.
(See singer, soprano, choir.)

VOCALIZATION
adjectives
enormous; delicious; picturesque; proper.

VOCATION
adjectives
perilous; sane; sacred; legitimate; peaceful;
lifelong.

verbs
desert—; employ in—; enter—; fit for—;
forsake—; master—; overcrowd—; prepare
for—; pursue—; qualify for—; skill in—;
—allures; —attracts; —beckons; —demands; —exacts; —fascinates; —interests;
—necessitates; —requires; —treats of.
(See hobby, employment, industry, calling,
teaching, law, etc.)

VOCIFERATION
adjectives
harsh; ferocious; raging.

VOCIFEROUS
adverbs
unnecessarily; comically; naturally; earnestly; excitedly; hysterically; enthusiastically;
riotously; shrilly; clamorously; inexcusably;
disagreeably; unbecomingly; coarsely; surprisingly; grossly; foolishly; unfortunately.

VOGUE
adjectives
instigated; appreciable; tremendous; immense; decorative; fashionable.

verbs
adhere to—; alter—; create—; design—;
devise—; dictate—; dignify—; emulate—;
establish—; exalt—; fashion—; foster—;
glorify—; maintain—; outlive—; popularize
—; —dies; —diminishes; —fades; —glitters; —persists; —prevails; —wanes.
(See mode, fashion.)

VOICE
adjectives
able; abrupt; accusing; admirable; admonishing; affectionate; agonized; agitated;
airy; alarmed; alien; angelic; angry; antagonistic; anxious; apocalyptic; apologetic;
appropriate; arbitrary; assuring; audible;
authoritative; awe-struck; babbling; bari-
tone; barren; base; bass; beautiful; beguiling; bellowing; beloved; bemused; bewildered; bitter; blatant; bleating; bluff; blunt;
blurred; booming; breathless; brisk; buzzing; broken; calm; caressing; carrying; cavernous; celestial; charming; checked; cheerful; cheering; childish; choked; clamoring;
clarion; clashing; clear; clinging; cold; collective; commanding; compelling; complete;
concentrated; contentious; controlling; convinced; corrupted; courteous; cracked;
crashing; crisp; croaking; darkening; deceptive; decisive; decorous; deep; deferential;
deliberate; demoniac; desired; determined;
dictatorial; discordant; disembodied; dispassionate; dissentient; dissenting; distant;
distinct; divine; doleful; dominant; dragging; dreaded; droning; drunken; dry;
dull; eager; ear-deafening; earnest; easy;
effective; elegant; eloquent; embarrassed;
erect; exasperating; excited; exhilarating;
expressionless; exquisite; extinguished; extraordinary; exultant; faint; false; falsetto;

faltering; familiar; far-away; far-off; far-ringing; fascinating; fearful; fear-struck; feeble; feigned; feminine; fiendish; fine; firm; flexible; flowing; flute-like; fluttering; foghorn; frequent; fretful; fresh; frightened; full; functioning; gentle; ghostly; gibing; gleeful; glorious; godly; good; gorgeous; gracious; great; growling; gruff; guiding; guttural; habitual; half-hesitant; half-whispered; hard; harsh; harmonious; hearty; heathen; heavenly; heavy; helpless; high; high-pitched; hoarse; hollow; horrible; hurried; hushed; husky; icy; ignorant; imaginary; impassioned; impressive; improved; impelling; imperative; inarticulate; inaudible; incarnate; incessant; incisive; independent; indistinct; ineffectual; inexorable; infallible; inflexible; inner; insinuating; insolent; inward; iron; irritable; jerky; jubilant; labored; languid; languorous; laughing; lazy; leafy; level; lifeless; lifted; lingering; lisping; living; loathing; loud; loving; low; lowered; low-keyed; low-pitched; lusty; magnificent; magniloquent; majestic; manful; manly; masculine; matchless; maudlin; measured; meek; melancholy; mellifluous; mellow; melodious; melting; merciless; metallic; meteoric; mighty; mingled (pl); mirthful; modulated; monotonous; monstrous; mortal; motherly; mournful; multitudinous (pl); muffled; mumbling; murmuring; musical; mute; myriad (pl); mysterious; nagging; nasal; native; natural; odious; offended; oily; omniscient; ominous; painful; palpitant; parrot-like; passionate; patient; patriotic; peaceful; peevish; penetrating; perpetual; pertinent; pettish; petulant; phantom-like; piercing; piping; pitying; placating; plaining; plaintive; playful; pleading; pleasant; polite; powerful; prodigious; purring; puzzled; quarreling; quavering; querulous; questioning; quiet; quivering; rapid; raised; rasping; raucous; reckless; recognized; reedy; remarkable; reminiscent; reprehensible; reproachful; resonant; respectful; responsive; reverential; ringing; rough; rowdy; rusty; sacred; sad; salutary; sardonic; savage; secret; seductive; sepulchral; seraphic; serious; shaken; sharp; short-breathed; shrieking; shrill; silky; silvery; singsong; sleep-thick; slender; slow; slurring; smooth; smothered; snapping; snarling; snuffling; sobbing; soft; solemn; sonorous; soothing; sorrowful; soul-piercing; soul-subduing; sprightly; stammering; stately; stationary; steady; stentorian; stern; stifled; still; stir-

ring; strained; strange; strangled; stricken; strident; strong; stumbling; stupendous; subdued; subterranean; sudden; suitable; suppressed; surmounting; suspicious; sweet; swelled; synchronized; taunting; tearful; tender; tentative; tenuous; thick; thin; thundering; tiny; toneless; tottering; tragic; tranquil; transcendent; transformed; transported; trembling; tremulous; triumphant; troubled; trumpeting; tyrannical; uncertain; unctuous; uneducated; unearthly; unheeded; universal; unmistakable; unmodulated; unmoved; unrestrained; unruffled; unruly; unshaded; unshaken; unsteady; unsyllabic; uttered; vacuous; vague; velvet; venal; venomous; veritable; vigorous; virgin; vociferous; vulgar; wailing; warbled; warning; weary; welcoming; well-attuned; well-bred; well-known; well-modulated; well-tuned; wheedling; whining; whispering; wistful; wondering; woodland; wondrous; wretched; yawning; yearning; young; impatient; impersonal.

verbs

acclaim—; attune to—; blot out—; candy —; choke—; *control—; dampen—; discipline—; disguise—; drop—; drown out—; dull—; echo—; exercise—; guard—; harken to—; heed—; hush—; irritate—; laud —; lift—; mellow—; modulate—; muffle —; mute—; muzzle—; pitch—; place—; recognize—; silence—; still—; strain—; study —; sugar—; sweeten—; thrill to—; throttle —; tinge—; train—; —awakens; —bawls; —beguiles; —booms; —breaks; —carols; —carries; —censures; —changes; —charms; —chokes; —cracks; —cuts; —deepens; —drones on; —dwindles; —enraptures; —fascinates; —flags; —flames; —floats up; —lashes; —murmurs; —palpitates; —penetrates; —pierces; —quavers; —ranges; —rasps; —registers; —resounds; —rings out; —rises; —rolls; —sharpens; —slurs; —squeaks; —stirs; —swells; —thickens; —throbs; —thunders; —tightens; —trails off; —trembles; —twitters; —vibrates; —warms; —wavers; —wheedles; —whines; —whispers; —wracks; —wrings.

(See sound, utterance, tone.)

VOICE (v)

adverbs

tenderly; harmoniously; accusingly; antagonistically; anxiously; authoritatively; bluntly; exultantly; ominously; sternly; patriotically; lustily; audibly; **monotonously**; petu-

1268

lantly; raucously; reproachfully; sepulchrally; vulgarly; vigorously; vociferously; venomously.

(See express, say.)

VOID

adjectives

trackless; foggy; pale; bare; absolute; mysterious; boundless; populous; fathomless;
immeasurable; illimitable; blank.

adverbs

legally; unluckily; apparently; manifestly;
unfortunately; blessedly; fortunately; utterly; recently; temporarily; hopelessly; undeniably; definitely; curiously.

VOLCANO

adjectives

extinct; perilous; concealed; slumbering;
barren; drowned; spiritual; smoldering.

verbs

fling into—; gaze into—; pacify—; placate
—; toss into—; —activates; —awakens; —
belches; —buries; —chokes; —destroys; —
devastates; —discharges; —ejects; —embroils; —emits; —endangers; —erupts; —
flows; —foments; —fulminates; —fumes; —
lies dormant; —looms; —quiets; —rampages; —rises; —roars; —rumbles; —seethes; —simmers; —sleeps; —smoulders; —
spews forth; —strangles; —streams over;
—threatens; —vents.

(See eruption, crater.)

VOLITION

adjectives

distinct; special; true; passionate; conscious; particular.

VOLLEY

adjectives

severe; fine; bombastic; pyrotechnic; instantaneous; incessant; intermitting; useless;
deafening.

verbs

blast—; discharge—; flash—; fulminate—;
prolong—; renew—; —assaults; —bombards; —crashes; —decimates; —destroys;
—detonates; —devastates; —echoes; —
flares; —levels; —rattles; —razes; —rends;
—resounds; —rings out; —roars; —rolls;
—rumbles; —shatters; —splits; —thunders;
—wreaks.

(See gun-fire, shots, fussilade.)

VOLUBILITY

adjectives

startling; accustomed; infinite; fierce.

VOLUBLE

adverbs

usually; habitually; comically; chattily; torrentially; ridiculously; unnecessarily; peculiarly; characteristically; momentarily; unusually; hysterically; excitedly; officiously;
vexatiously; intolerably; amusingly.

VOLUME

adjectives

separate; immense; added; record; sympathetic; respective; published; comfortable;
ambitious; increasing; unprecedented; random; dusky; ragged; penultimate; inexhaustible; thumb-scarred; pale; magnificent;
enormous; arid; precious; attractive; ponderous; endless; unlimited; growing; rushing; valuable; library; thundering; remarkable; swelling; respectable; charming; solemn; supplementary; worthless; far-reaching; poetic; tasteful; long-coveted; subsequent; forthcoming; dog-eared; serried
(pl); tremendous; substantial; collected;
thrilling; proud; pathetic; posthumous; universal; fascinating; masterful; brilliant;
momentous; sturdy; vast; venerable; splendid; printed; blinding; mere; bulky; sulphurous; enormous; weighty; instructive;
stray; odd; scholarly; sumptuous; inspired;
comprehensive.

verbs

author—; autograph—; bind—; browse
through—; compile—; con—; confiscate—;
consult—; curtail—; delve into—; display
—; entitle—; fray—; illustrate—; immerse
in—; interpret—; peruse—; ponder—; prepare—; prize—; publish—; review—; revise—; scan—; skim over—; summarize—;
tackle—; value—; —airs; —circulates; —
condemns; —deals with; —discourses on; —
dissertates; —diverts; —exposes; —libels;
—narrates; —plagiarizes; —recites; —recounts; —relates; —slanders; —treats of;
—unfolds; —ventilates; devote—to.

(See book, manuscript, story, work, tome.)

VOLUMINOUS

adverbs

overwhelmingly; stupendously; inclusively;
pedantically; ambitiously; monumentally;
sufficiently; immensely; manifestly; absurdly; unnecessarily.

VOLUNTARY

adverbs

freely; generously; impetuously; eagerly; earnestly; energetically; emphatically; unmistakably; undoubtedly; unquestionably; usually; frankly; necessarily; amicably; delightfully; completely.

VOLUNTEERS

adjectives

raw; devoted; zealous; tireless; fanatic; susceptible; doughty; brave.

verbs

acclaim—; arm—; command—; compose of —; discipline—; equip—; furnish—; honor —; laud—; plead for—; quarter—; recruit —; rig out—; train—; transport—; —bid for; —brave; —comprise; —defend; —disband; —enlist; —offer; —proffer; —serve; —storm; —tackle; —tender.

(See soldier, recruit.)

VOLUPTUARY

adjectives

cautious; refined; hedonistic.

VOLUPTUOUS

adverbs

pleasantly; buxomly; luxuriously; delightedly; naturally; habitually; notoriously; conspicuously; openly; utterly; unmistakably.

VOLUPTUOUSNESS

adjectives

inebriating; supposed; gorgeous.

VOMIT (v)

adverbs

nauseatingly; sickeningly; disgustingly; recurringly; drunkenly.

VOMITING

verbs

allay—; ameliorate—; check—; curtail—; diagnose—; encourage—; force—; forestall—; induce—; produce—; stem—; stimulate to—; —cleanses; —dislodges; —eases; —ejects; —eliminates; —endangers; —expels; —indicates; —purges; —sheds; —unburdens; —vents; —weakens.

(See nausea.)

VORACIOUS

adverbs

overweeningly; rabidly; insatiately; incredibly; dreadfully; unspeakably; frightfully; unbelievably; wolfishly; bestially.

VORACITY

adjectives

impotent; insatiable; unscrupulous.

VORTEX

verbs

form—; sweep into—; tumble into—; —agitates; —billows; —boils; —churns; —circumvolutes; —convolutes; —eddies; —engulfs; —expands; —foams; —gyrates; —immerses; —pirouettes; —revolves; —ripples; —rotates; —submerges; —surges; —swells; —swirls; —trundles; —twirls; —whirls.

(See whirlpool, maelstrom.)

VOTARY

adjectives

boyish; dull; firm; mistaken.

VOTE

adjectives

majority; overhanging; overwhelming; disputed; injudicious; unanimous; purchasable; direct; negative; reluctant; decisive; ignorant; appalling; valid; dissenting; simple; plurality; deciding; heavy; loyal; crooked.

VOTE (v)

adverbs

unanimously; progressively; overwhelmingly; democratically; inconsistently; regularly; affirmatively; loyally; intelligently; legally; judiciously; ignorantly; decisively.

(See elect, declare.)

VOTERS

adjectives

independent-minded; submissive; patient; stupid; blinded; purchased; intelligent; thinking.

verbs

address—; appeal to—; assure—; beguile —; coerce—; dictate to—; divide—; harangue—; pledge to—; poll—; promise—; sway—; woo—; —acknowledge; —approve; —ballot; —choose; —determine; —elect; —endorse; —overwhelm; —reign; —rule; —select; —stream to; —subscribe to; —support; —sustain; —vacillate; —voice.

(See constituent, public, citizen.)

verbs

aggregate—; alienate—; amass—; angle for —; apportion—; assure of—; bag—; bias —; calculate—; campaign for—; compute —; conciliate—; corral—; gain—; gather —; guarantee—; hazard—; imperil—; influence—; insure—; jeopardize—; line up —; muster—; poll—; procure—; promise—; record—; recount—; register—; risk—; separate—; sew up—; split—; sway—; swing —; void—; win—; —determine; —pile up; —pour in.

(See election, nomination, plurality, ballot.)

VOTIVE

adverbs

sacredly; sacrificially; devoutly; undeniably; apparently; sincerely; truly; completely; contritely.

VOW

adjectives

earthly; capricious; rash; musical; unheedful; violated; truant; passionate; unbroken; moist; bridal; ardent; intermingled; sainted; hollow; frail; noble; slighted; monastic; limber; monkish; solemn; marital; sacred; dread; grateful; self-imposed; idle; generous; heavenly; serviceable.

verbs

annul—; breathe—; commit to—; comply with—; contract—; declare—; desecrate—; discharge from—; divorce from—; embody in—; enforce—; forfeit—; fulfill—; heed—; ignore—; infringe—; liberate from—; maintain—; observe—; pursue—; register—; relax—; respect—; sanctify—; slacken—; solemnize—; swear to—; undertake—; violate—; —binds; —burdens; —chains; — fetters; —pledges; —prohibits; —restrains; —restricts; —weighs upon.

(See pledge, oath, promise, contract.)

VOW (*v*)

adverbs

patiently; passionately; languidly; capriciously; rashly; ardently; nobly; magnanimously; monastically; sacredly; generously; maritally.

(See promise, swear.)

VOWEL

adjectives

open; various (pl); softening; euphonious;

nasalized; drawled; guttural; mispronounced; throaty.

verbs

ablaut—; accent—; accentuate—; articulate —; discard—; economize on—s; emphasize —; employ—; lengthen—; misuse—; pronounce—; silence—; shorten—; stress—; umlaut—; trip up on—s; —changes; — sharpens.

(See sound.)

VOYAGE

adjectives

prosperous; loving; projected; aimless; tedious; eventful; magnificent; determinate; stormy; tempestuous; ill-fated; frequent (pl); uncertain; romantic; perilous; mysterious; homeward.

verbs

brave—; chart—; conclude—; curtail—; delay—; deviate from—; embark on—; extend —; hazard—; plan—; prolong—; protract —; set forth on—; terminate—; venture upon—; —broadens; —embraces; —fascinates; —lures; —intrigues; —refreshes; — relaxes; —touches upon; —tranquillizes.

(See journey, trip.)

VOYAGER

adjectives

dusty-throated; battered; uninstructed; seasick.

VULGAR

adverbs

incredibly; strangely; habitually; unwontedly; grossly; boorishly; defiantly; crassly; strangely; purposely; arrantly; definitely; openly; conspicuously; shamefully; carelessly; unmistakably; singularly; surprisingly; intentionally; deliberately; flagrantly.

VULGARITY

adjectives

patent; hideous; rude; vigorous; impertinent; unutterable; innumerable (pl); purseproud; finished; pathetic; stupid; private; blatant; odious; intense; superlative; petty; universal; studied.

verbs

abhor—; blush at—; breed—; countenance —; deplore—; descend to—; exhibit—; flaunt—; frown upon—; recoil from—; —

coarsens; —debases; —degrades; —irks; —
mortifies; —ostracizes; —repels; —shocks;
—surrounds.

(See coarseness.)

VULNERABLE
adverbs

sadly; unfortunately; admittedly; wretchedly; miserably; probably; unluckily; terribly;
alarmingly; portentously; ominously; significantly; dangerously; perilously; carelessly; incautiously; criminally; dreadfully; unbelievably; unforgivably; negligently; unhappily.

VULTURE
adjectives

famished; gnawing; carrion; hovering;
greedy; swooping; ugly.

verbs

—circles; —clutches; —descends; —devours; —dives; —divests; —flutters; —
glides; —gorges; —hisses; —hovers over;
—picks clean; —plucks; —pounces upon; —
preys upon; —ravishes; —regurgitates; —
scales; —scavenges; —seizes; —soars; —
shrieks; —subsists; —swoops down; —
whirls.

(See bird, eagle, hawk.)

W

WADE (v)
adverbs
laboriously; conscientiously; cautiously; fastidiously; carefully.
(See swim.)

WAFT (v)
adverbs
delicately; pungently; insidiously; gently; capriciously.
(See carry, float.)

WAG (v)
adverbs
humorously; sardonically; slowly; feebly; mutely; wordlessly; sagely; cryptically.
(See nod, move.)

WAGE
adjectives
preposterous; satisfactory; aggregate; hard-earned; comparative; prevailing; monetary; actual; scanty; unsteady; uncertain; exorbitant; inflated; youthful; daily; living.

WAGER
verbs
accept—; agree upon—; cast—; chance—; claim—; contest—; decide—; determine—; force—; frame—; gamble on—; lay—; propose—; record—; release from—; speculate on—; stake—on; transact—; venture—; —challenges; —hazards; —pledges.
(See bet, gambling.)

WAGES
verbs
advance—; boost—; default—; determine—; distribute—; engage for—; expend—; fix—; forfeit—; grudge—; halve—; increase—; invest—; level—; lift—; proportion—; raise—; rate—; realize—; reap—; reduce —; regulate—; scale—; scorn—; serve for —; slash—; squander—; step up—; stimulate—; supplement—; tabulate—; withhold —; —compensate; —conform; —decline; —indemnify; —remunerate; —reward; —soar.
(See income, earnings, fee, pittance, living, livelihood.)

WAGGISH
adverbs
jocosely; facetiously; fatuously; banteringly; boastfully; drolly; clownishly; pleasantly; foolishly; playfully; intolerably; disagreeably; smartly; conceitedly; whimsically; fantastically; vexatiously; disgustingly; merrily; mischievously.

WAGON
adjectives
ancient; lumbering; serviceable; jolting; creaking; wobbling; emigrant; clanking; broken-down; hooded; ramshackle; vengeful.

verbs
brake—; cart on—; convoy—; dispatch—; draw—; harness to—; hitch—; journey by —; —conveys; —creeps along; —draws up; —jolts; —jounces; —rattles; —rolls; —transports.
(See caravan, automobile, cart, vehicle.)

WAIL
adjectives
piteous; faint; infantile; obstreperous; lusty; articulate; windy; inward; melodramatic; thin; fretful; dismal; doleful; dying; hideous; damned; confused; heartbroken; young; passionate; patriotic; pathetic; murmured; tender; moaning; wild; liquid; weird; far-off; mournful; amazed; angry; nightly; flute-like.

verbs
emit—; prolong—; set up—; shrill—; utter —; —complains of; —deplores; —deprecates; —grieves; —laments; —mourns; —pierces; —rends; —rings out; —rises; —wrings.
(See cry, howl, lamentation.)

WAIL (v)
adverbs
distressfully; mournfully; dismally; piteously; inarticulately; fretfully; dolefully; passionately; wildly; weirdly; mournfully; lustily; obstreperously.
(See moan, lament.)

W
X

WAILING

adverbs

mournfully; incessantly; continually; intermittently; hopefully; piously; confoundedly; petulantly; disagreeably; feebly; vociferously; loudly; wistfully; ostentatiously; pitifully; hungrily; sleepily; drowsily; insincerely; tiresomely; monotonously; desperately; vexatiously; pettishly.

WAIST

adjectives

snug; thickening; imperceptible; tapering; enormous; collective; trackless; slender; winsome; wasplike; well-fitting; capacious.

WAIT (v)

adverbs

breathlessly; passively; sadly; reverently; anxiously; exultantly; mutely; devotedly; placidly; instinctively; calmly; apprehensively; boldly; hungrily; morbidly; disastrously; indecisively; tensely.

(See pause, delay.)

WAITER

adjectives

smug; oblivious; rowdy; obsequious; swarthy; corpulent; stately; efficient.

verbs

beckon to—; bid—; bow—out; employ—; engage—; rebuke—; reproach—; ring for —; signal—; summon—; tip—; uniform—; —announces; —approaches; —attends; —directs to; —fumbles; —hovers near; —informs; —recommends; —serves; —suggests.

(See matron, nurse, servant.)

WAITING

adverbs

silently; doggedly; resolutely; hopelessly; helplessly; intolerably; restlessly; feverishly; optimistically; trustfully; happily; forlornly; eagerly; boisterously; cruelly; miserably; interminably; insistently.

WAIVE (v)

adverbs

magnanimously; willingly; voluntarily; deliberately; nobly; generously; affectionately; informally.

(See dispense, relinquish.)

WAKEFUL

adverbs

nervously; mysteriously; alertly; anxiously;

miserably; wretchedly; vigilantly; habitually; watchfully; unnaturally; peculiarly; strangely; significantly; fortunately; luckily; suddenly; feverishly; comfortably.

WALK
(general)

adjectives

solar; winding; strenuous; long; sunken; gravel; aimless; sanguine; flagged; exhilarating; cheerful; moderate; cloistered; lumbering; obscure; sunny; rough; windy; fatiguing; leisurely; lingering; tangling; cultured; mincing; haphazard; laurel; solitary; hedge-lined; contemplative; rampart; willowy; shady; slow; undulating; rhythmic; moonlight; enrapturing; roaming; royal; humble; swarming; tremendous; silent; visionary; smart; mind-clearing; dark; night; restless; glorious; opposite; spacious; sequestered; imposing; tangling; lazy; murmuring; substantial; oval; umbrageous.

WALK
(path)

verbs

beautify—; border—; block—; bound—; circle—; designate—; elevate—; enclose—; fence in—; flank—; intersect—; occupy—; parallel—; pave—; plank—; promenade—; repair—; run up—; seclude—; shade—; skirt—.

(See lane, alley, path.)

WALK (v)

adverbs

cavalierly; gingerly; sprightly; blindly; spirally; deliberately; defiantly; meekly; humbly; unsteadily; characteristically; mutely; monotonously; untiringly; tempestuously; stealthily; strenuously; musingly; restlessly; languidly; foppishly; aimlessly; wantonly; reflectively; defiantly; jauntily; calmly; briskly; warily; abstractedly; sedately; haphazardly; contemplatively; lazily.

(See trudge, stroll.)

WALLET

verbs

adorn—; appropriate—; cram—; emboss—; engrave—; examine—; filch—; guard—; lift—; mulct of—; palm—; pilfer—; prize —; protrude from—; rifle—; stuff—; swell —; thrust into—; —bulges; —wears.

(See bag, purse.)

adverbs
bestially; voluptuously; hoggishly; disgustingly; revoltingly; carnally; lewdly; insatiably; vulgarly.
(See flounder, grovel.)

WALLS

adjectives
naked; massive; rugged; crannied; crumbling; shattered; eloquent; high; espaliered; garden; bartizan; sapphire; gloomy; adamantine; tired; thick; crenelated; staring; tinted; forsaken; weltering; well-built; verdurous; unsurmounted; emblazoned; proscenium; continuous; impregnable; imperial; pretty; impassable; forested; outward; obliterated; impenetrable; celestial; beauteous; ruined; munimental; abdominal; dignified; flaming; expressionless; far-reaching; buttressed; decaying; wicked; dainty; trembling; moldering; ancient; ruinous; humid; courteous; chancel; battlemented; venerable; dungeon; illuminated; exterior; everlasting; dull; damp; fluttering; roofless; low; unplastered; paneled; high-jutting; pictured; dark; grimy; prison; frowning; fortress; tottering; inaccessible; protecting; sheer; remote; unbroken; leafy-bannered; conventual; vertical; steep; jointed; rocky; lengthy; living; soft; evenly-tinted; gleaming; mossy; shiny; sunny; yonder; wailing; rose-bannered; garden; wind-proofed; austered; cerulean; majestic; towering; girdling; unornamented; unfinished; moaning; mountain; lofty; protecting; silver-seamed; somber; melted; unpeopled; projecting; brazen; eternal; intervening; triple; leprous; lateral; beloved; multitudinous; blistered; fragmentary; rustling; weathered; ageless; scarped; confining; mirrored; moss-covered; dingy; distempered.

verbs
barricade behind—; batter down—; bedaub—; clamber over—; decorate—; deface—; drape—; drive to—; emboss—; erect—; flank—; fortify—; fresco—; harbor within—; mount—; paper—; pierce—; rib—; scale—; scan—; smite—; surmount—; vault—; —arise; —confine; —crumble; —defend; —enclose; —envelop; —gird; —impede; —partition; —obscure; —shelter; —shield; —shoulder; —surround.
(See fence, barricade, fortification.)

WALTZ

adjectives
lilting; wheeling; ingratiating; old-fashioned; whirling; graceful; appealing.

verbs
compose—; embrace in—; enjoy—; fling into—; introduce—; popularize—; portray—; sway to—; whirl in—; —calms; —enthralls; —entrances; —graces; —gyrates; —relaxes; —revolves; —rolls; —survives; —thrills.
(See dance, minuet.)

WALTZ (*v*)

adverbs
gracefully; harmoniously; deftly; energetically; charmingly; seductively; rhythmically; liltingly; ingratiatingly; appealingly.
(See dance, trip.)

WAN

adverbs
pitifully; unfortunately; alarmingly; miserably; feebly; unhealthily; wretchedly; dreadfully; unaccountably; unusually; naturally; strangely; curiously; unnaturally; ghastly.

WAND

adjectives
opiate; streaked; potent; scribbling; snake-encircled; certain; sable.

verbs
bear—; brandish—; cleave—; endow—; fashion—; flex—; flourish—; magnetize—; ply—; smite with—; splinter—; split—; strike with—; stroke—; tip—; whittle—; —charms; —chastises; —enchants; —guides; —mesmerizes; —mystifies; —symbolizes.
(See baton, cane, scepter, twig.)

WANDER (*v*)

adverbs
desolately; erratically; deviously; dilatorily; errantly; listlessly; aimlessly; disconsolately; blindly; ruefully; stupidly; hopelessly; promiscuously; rashly; wearily.
(See roam, ramble.)

WANDERER

adjectives
bodiless; fantastic; forlorn; night; weary; unwilling; immortal; archetypical; blithe; half-frozen; long-lost; undisciplined.

WANDERING

adjectives

eccentric; devious; difficult; weary; sleepless; restless; vague; unquiet; aimless; accidental; dream-led; enfranchised; much; occasional.

adverbs

inanely; fruitlessly; incessantly; doggedly; hopefully; idly; actually; mentally; confusedly; nervously; nonchalantly; irresponsibly.

WANDERINGS

verbs

cease—; chart—; color—; condemn to—; describe—; embark on—; experience in—; extend—; narrate—; prolong—; protract—; record—; relate—; retire from—; unfold—; weary of—; —aberrate; —age; —amuse; —embrace; —interest; —thrill.

(See travel, voyage.)

WANDERLUST

adjectives

unconquerable; reoccurring; uncontrollable.

verbs

extinguish—; nip—; obey—; quash—; quell —; quench—; resist—; stamp out—; subdue —; succumb to—; surrender to—; yield to —; suppress—; —fires; —grips; —impels; —overwhelms; —perishes; —prods; —pushes; —seizes; —urges.

(See desire, longing, impulse.)

WANT

adjectives

abject; burning; thirsty; fiery; gnawing; acute; actual; spontaneous; unreflected; needful; artificial; common; utter; frank; fearless; passionate; respective; material; immediate; total; unpardonable; unbounded; shameful; endless; wondrous; tender; squalid; divine; present; narrow; curious; presumptive; ripe; absolute; modest; lower; spiritual; conscious; returning; sufficient.

verbs

administer to—s; anticipate—s; come to—; consult—s; correct—; diminish—s; discharge —s; express—; gratify—; impoverish with —; intensify—; mark by—; occasion—; provide for—s; reduce to—; subject to—; suffer—; —blemishes; —goads on; —s multiply.

(See need, lack, necessity, destitution.)

WANT (v)

adverbs

desperately; distressingly; intensely; vaguely; immediately; manifestly; particularly; shamelessly; absolutely; immodestly; spiritually; wistfully; conspicuously; abjectly; passionately.

(See need, desire.)

WANTON

adverbs

recklessly; playfully; immorally; irrepressibly; loosely; unrestrainedly; wickedly; provocatively; delightedly; hilariously; drunkenly; airily; emotionally; insanely; crazily; childishly; ludicrously; pitiably; brazenly; audaciously; heedlessly; imprudently; incorrigibly; eccentrically; monstrously; lawlessly; outlandishly; unwontedly; bafflingly.

WAR

adjectives

suicidal; glorious; brooding; vigorous; impious; exhausting; guerrilla; diabolical; ruthless; expensive; aggressive; ferocious; defensive; internecine; offensive; desolating; mimic; mustering; bitter; grim; impending; universal; increasing; horrible; aboriginal; glorified; inevitable; imminent; classical; barbarous; undeclared; virtuous; fratricidal; open; manful; cormorant; victorious; fearful; intrepid; successive (pl); deadly; successful; tribal; unearthly; meritorious; righteous; unholy; interminable; raging; ensuing; disastrous; banded; brutal; pelting; unvanquished; unjust; incessant; rebellious; devastating; nonsparing; silvan; plangent; elemental; imperialist; contemplated; ghastly; mercenary; renewed; silent; sanguinary; strenuous; social; servile; innocent; irrepressible; intellectual; contumelious; beastly; mad-brained; realistic; fierce; courageous; petty; theologic; religious; witching; tremendous; passive.

verbs

abstain from—; aggravate—; anticipate—; avert—; banish—; cease—; control—; dedicate to—; determine—; dramatize—; dread —; drift into—; embrace—; entangle in—; enter—; envisage—; fend off—; flame into —; foment—; gird for—; halt—; launch—; localize—; muster for—; outlaw—; plunge into—; prolong—; promote—; provoke—; resort to—; romanticize—; stage—; stave off—; stem—; survive—; taboo—; throttle

—; vilify—; wage—; witness—; —arises; —bestializes; —blasts; —bristles; —drags on; —endangers; —entangles; —looms; — overclouds; —overshadows; —progresses; —rages; —ravages; —runs rampant; —sunders; —terminates; —vilifies.

(See fight, combat, battle, warfare.)

WARD

adjectives

unguarded; close; legitimate; hard; slow-turning; airy; intricate; mutinous; surgical; gracious.

WARDROBE

adjectives

sophisticated; natty; all-occasion; personalized; endless; summer; outdoor; holiday.

verbs

attain—; augment—; complete—; delete—; envy—; equip with—; expend on—; fit out with—; luxuriate in—; mend—; mutilate —; perfect—; provide—; purchase—; renew—; repair—; replenish—; restore—; — suffers; —suffices.

(See clothing, apparel.)

WARE

adjectives

varnished; universal; tawdry; gaudy.

WARES

verbs

auction—; bargain for—; bid for—; cheapen —; dispense—; display—; dispose of—; examine—; hawk—; inflate—; inspect—; liquidate—; loot—; market—; peddle—; pilfer—; proclaim—; purvey—; put—under the hammer; retail—; scatter—; test—; undersell—; vend—; —allure; —depreciate.

(See merchandise, product.)

WARFARE

adjectives

manful; curious; dulcet; cruel; chivalrous; incessant; nightly; friendless; deadly; desperate; foreign; unceasing; offensive; tremendous; unrelenting; eternal; aggressive; wanton; devastating; hopeless; internecine; sylvan; perpetual; unsuccessful; bloody; critical; protracted; vigorous; disjointed; impending; predatory; guerrilla; mimic; licentious; partisan; heartrending.

verbs

abolish—; arm for—; array for—; balk at —; carry on—; conclude—; decry—; engage in—; force into—; incite—; inflame to—; initiate into—; instigate—; kindle—; light the torch of—; mobilize for—; precipitate into—; resign to—; revolt at—; threaten—; train for—; —devastates; —exterminates; —menaces; —pillages; —plunders; — seethes; —takes toll: —undermines: — wreaks.

(See hostility, war, struggle, conflict.)

WARLIKE

adverbs

insatiably; recklessly; criminally; bestially; flagrantly; viciously; inherently; foully; systematically; abominably; inhumanly; atrociously; brutally; infamously; iniquitously; nefariously; scandalously; savagely; ferociously; vilely; wickedly; barbarously; incorrigibly; unfeelingly; sinfully; horribly; unspeakably; fiendishly; flagitiously; villainously; needlessly; indecently.

WARM

adverbs

unseasonably; uncomfortably; unreasonably; curiously; terribly; comfortably; securely; gratefully; surprisingly; slightly; dreadfully; suffocatingly; unnecessarily; extremely; sufficiently; pleasantly.

WARM (v)

adverbs

perceptibly; appreciably; uncomfortably; frightfully; dangerously; significantly.

(See heat, arouse.)

WARM-HEARTED

adverbs

delightfully; impulsively; lovingly; generously; philanthropically; naturally; dependably; especially; marvelously; pleasantly; wonderfully; altruistically; cordially; hospitably; unusually; uncommonly; sincerely; conspicuously; genuinely; really; truly; always; frankly; earnestly.

WARMTH

adjectives

genial; comfortable; thrilling; redolent; juvenile; life-giving; personal; soft; native; grateful; bright; added; balmy; considerable; unseemly; vivacious; trustworthy; deceitful; feeble; loathy; refreshing; virile; varying; peculiar; ethereal; brooding; passionate; heartfelt; tongueless; friendly; dissolving; tingling; true; human; added; eccentric; rugged; confiding; voluptuous; fostering; utmost.

verbs

accustom to—; afford—; bask in—; diffuse —; drowse in—; enjoy—; excite—; exude —; glow with—; impart—; inhale—; provide—; radiate—; regain—; retain—; sense —; swelter in—; temper with—; welcome—; —animates; —chafes; —comforts; —flushes; —fuses; —lingers; —pervades; —renews; —revives; —revivifies; —thaws.

(See glow, geniality, fervor, ardor, heat.)

WARN (v)

adverbs

providentially; solemnly; amply; sufficiently; grimly; prophetically; urgently; graciously; forcefully; subtly; soberly; earnestly; faithfully.

(See admonish.)

WARNING

adjectives

grim; prophetic; ecclesiastical; celestial; competent; sundry (pl); gracious; urgent; open; preliminary; startling; eternal; slender; forceful; important; hoarse; subtle; timely; anonymous; displeasing; terrible; anxious; secular; fair; pathetic; sober; earnest; paradoxical.

verbs

accept—; broadcast—; convey—; disregard —; distribute—s; explode—; furnish—; heed—; ignore—; issue—; protest—; regard —; rumble—; signal—; sound—; stress—; tender—; voice—; yield to—; —alarms; —impends; —terrifies.

(See counsel, portent, admonition.)

WARRANT

adjectives

external; lawful; bloody; sufficient; seeming; scriptural; doubtful; valid; avowed; infallible; further.

verbs

arm with—; draw up—; exercise—; flourish —; issue—; procure—; resort to—; retain on—; swear out—; wield—; —accredits; —apprehends; —authorizes; —commissions; —delegates; —deputizes; —empowers; —permits; —pledges; —proclaims; —protects.

(See authority, mandate, summons.)

WARRANTABLE

adverbs

thoroughly; entirely; soundly; altogether; wholly; justly; properly; safely; reasonably; sufficiently; probably; presumably; supposedly; definitely.

WARRIOR

adjectives

sullen; painful; intrepid; inferior; flaming; simple-minded; charging; care-stricken; delighted; naked; redoubtable; savage; struggling; indefatigable; stern-faced; discomfited; long-dead; gloomy-looking; veteran; fierce; illustrious; exhausted; devilish; magnificent; invincible; tiny; dauntless; fell-handed.

verbs

acclaim—; arm—; beribbon—; commemorate—; conciliate—; confer upon—; decorate—; dedicate to—; distinguish—; draft —; elevate—; emulate—; ennoble—; enshrine—; esteem—; exalt—; exhort—; glorify—; hail—; honor—; idealize—; immortalize—; knight—; laud—; lionize—; pacify —; pay homage to—; rank—; revere—; reward—; salute—; worship—; —combats; —engages; —intrenches; —s mobilize; —parries; —perishes; —repels; —sheathes; —wields.

(See soldier, fighter, hero.)

WARSHIP

verbs

anchor—; bomb—; command—; confine on —; engage—; evade—; dodge—; scale—; —blockades; —bombards; —conveys; —convoys; —founders; —hems in; —maneuvers; —s mass; —patrols; —plies; —raids; —rakes; —rams; —retaliates; —rolls; —rushes; —sallies; —shells; —threatens; —transports.

(See boat, ship, army.)

WART

verbs

apply to—; burn—; cauterize—; cut—; daub on—; detach—; dissect—; excise—s; grease—; incise—; patch—s; peel—; remove—; salve—; sever—; subject to—s; treat—; —appears; —blemishes; —bulges; —s develop; —disfigures; —erupts; —flattens; —maligns; —mars; —protrudes; —swells; —thickens; —vanishes.

(See sore, wound.)

adverbs

habitually; constantly; necessarily; alertly; uncommonly; significantly; extraordinarily; noticeably; nervously; wisely; ordinarily; curiously; tiresomely; conspicuously; timidly; sagaciously; deliberately; anxiously; admirably.

WASH (v)

adverbs

surreptitiously; scrupulously; listlessly; fastidiously; habitually; laboriously; deliberately.

(See clean, scrub.)

WASHING

verbs

obviate—; require—; subject to—; —ablutes; —cleanses; —deodorizes; —deterges; —disinfects; —elutriates; —expurgates; —eliminates; —laves; —lixiviates; —purges; —purifies; —refreshes; —renews; —vivifies.

(See bath, water.)

WASPS

adjectives

injurious; stinging; buzzing; rowdy.

verbs

avoid—; classify—; —barb; —burrow; —buzz; —dig; —excavate; —hum; —flit; —molest; —nest; —paralyze; —poison; —provision; —pursue; —snare; —sting; —store; —tunnel; —wing.

(See hornet, insect, bee.)

WASTE

adjectives

unbridled; trackless; wandering; sinful; deliberate; dismal; encompassing; watery; woeful; colorless; indeterminate; gloomy; senseless; vast; thriftless; solemn-sounding; stupendous; unnecessary; terrible; inexcusable; wintry; glimmering; unproductive; arctic; barren; widening; sprinkled; spiritual; lonely; putrid; melancholy; simple; premature; colossal; tragic; aching; positive; nitrogenous; inward; desolate; hurried; remote; snowy; frightful; hopeless; burning; pathless; muscular; weltering; garden; flowering; sanctuary; shoreless; lavish; unpardonable; fruitless; boundless; ruinous; digestive; uninhabited; woodland; full; sandy; merciless; monstrous; howling; arid; frozen; turbid; war-worn; useless; dreary; dangerous; sterile; insidious; desert; wanton; verdant; enormous; tedious; billowy; illimitable; untamed; profligate; dread; moldering.

verbs

abate—; bewail—; check—; countenance—; curb—; curtail—; decry—; detect—; diminish—; discharge—; eliminate—; excrete—; harvest—; imply—; incur—; manufacture —; rebuke for—; reproach for—; restore —; result in—; retrieve—; rid of—; upbraid for—; wipe out—; withdraw—; —abuses; —accumulates; —appals; —declines; —denudes; —desecrates; —diminishes; —dissipates; —endangers; —shrinks; —squanders; —threatens.

(See junk, mess, garbage, extravagance.)

WASTE (v)

adverbs

unprofitably; improvidently; rashly; carelessly; heedlessly; deliberately; woefully; senselessly; stupendously; unnecessarily; unproductively; spiritually; ruthlessly; fruitlessly; wantonly; profligately.

(See sqaunder, dissipate.)

WASTE-BASKET

verbs

cast into—; consign to—; cram into—; deluge—; empty—; find in—; mouse around —; relegate to—; stuff—; —provides; —serves; —overflows.

(See basket.)

WASTED
(emaciated)

adverbs

pitiably; remarkably; haggardly; gauntly; helplessly; lankly; feebly; desperately; wretchedly; extremely.

WASTEFUL

adverbs

criminally; wickedly; extremely; wantonly; thoughtlessly; inconsiderately; immoderately; terribly; carelessly; negligently; foolishly; enormously; indolently; improvidently; ignorantly; crazily; unconscionably; inordinately; egregiously; atrociously; incredibly; miserably; extremely; imprudently; wretchedly.

WATCH

adjectives

happy; railroad; neglected; solitary; clamorous; fierce; advised; adventuring; vigilant; tireless; celestial; sympathetic; expensive; airy; couchant; brotherly; breathless; unnatural; strict; unceasing; patient; furtive; incessant; faithful; thrilling.

verbs
adjust—; check—; consult—; embellish—; engrave—; fondle—; illuminate—; jewel—; lubricate—; observe—; overwind—; pawn —; refer to—; regulate—; rely upon—; repair—; set—; snatch—; value—; wind—; —fails; —informs; —reminds; —runs down.
(See dial, clock.)

WATCH (v)

adverbs
vigilantly; anxiously; surreptitiously; sullenly; furtively; narrowly; assiduously; disconsolately; absently; minutely; keenly; vaguely; listlessly; slyly; idly; breathlessly; wistfully; apprehensively; attentively; stealthily; greedily; incessantly; moodily; covertly; defiantly; somberly; pensively; lazily; faithfully.
(See observe, scrutinize.)

WATCHER

adjectives
indolent; wingless; unsuspected; lone; sleepless.

WATCHFUL

adverbs
carefully; cautiously; responsibly; properly; stingily; greedily; hungrily; coldly; slyly; alertly; wisely; justifiably; sagaciously; inquisitively; curiously; maliciously; fondly; devotedly; jealously; enviously; constantly; anxiously; timidly.

WATCHFULNESS

adjectives
incumbent; calm; heavy; stealthy; constant; suspicious; assiduous; sharp; alert; silent; strenuous.

WATER

adjectives
poisonous; murky; wrinkled; brackish; gentle; golden; pellucid; swishing; impounded; shining; marching; sunny; purplish; winding; honeyed; unshaken; precious; steaming; greasy; saline; putrid; bitter; gliding; hidden; rampant; sky-hued; limpid; rocking; darkening; stagnant; shadow-less; hurrying; clear; sparkling; hot; glittering; silvery; seaward; surplus; numberless (pl); glistening; emerald; thundering; sleepy; blessed; ready; burning; blue-bosomed; streaming; muddy; invisible; huddling; climbing; living; wind-swept; lonely; reflecting; cleansing; ornamental; brooding; yielding; insipid; weary; swollen; navigable; transparent; festering; reef-strewn; trackless; starlit; moving; virgin; shoal-impatient; swift; giddy; annihilating; quivering; seething; placid; rose-white; glaring; restless; heaving; meager; dropping; sluggish; bickering; reviving; ebbing; imprisoned; dreamy; land-locked; crystal; flowing; gloomy; turbid; broken; perilous; vivifying; healing; moon-clear; tepid; enchanted; cloistered; sunshiny; fetid; dreary; azure; fastflowing; moon-lit; angry; wasteful; perennial; pliant; unsuspected; hydrant; chanting; loathsome; abundant; fluvial; smooth; idle; silent; booming; still; wide; sweltering; distilled; darkling; inviolable; flashing; scalding; treacherous; devouring; circumfluous; glorious; mysterious; dimpled; surging; life-giving; purling; fleecy; sweet; trickling; blushing; journalistic; tree-fringed; bleak; deep; cold; tributary; bubbling; warm; slow-moving; filthy; odorous; spreading; stormy; nearing; glorious; unclean; distant; glassy; roaring; wild; troubled; retreating; glimmering; western; fleeting; imprisoned; mountainous; jumbled; brilliant; benevolent; green; unknown; unstirring; august; tangy; medicinal; forest; fretting; polished; fatal; sharked; slimy; resistant; rushing; lisping; peaceful; smitten; milky; calm; sliding; tormented; rippling; tideless; running; unruffled; teeming; inundating; mute; destined; faint; black; turbulent; adjacent; fragrant; phosphorescent; unflinching; invisible; frothy.

verbs
administer—; agitate—; cart—; cast upon —; chart—; contaminate—; dabble in—; dam up—; dilute with—; distil—; disturb —; draw—; excrete—; filter—; frisk in—; gaze upon—; harness—; immerse in—; infest—; ingest—; pacify—; partake of—; plod through—; plunge into—; ply with—; pollute—; resort to—; saturate with—; slither into—; slash—; smooth—; steep in—; submerge in—; suck up—; —babbles; — drenches; —dribbles; —drips; —engulfs; —evaporates; —glimmers; —gurgles; —

1280

gushes; —invigorates; —laps; —lashes; —murmurs; —oozes out; —penetrates; —precipitates; —quenches; —recedes; —ripples; —roars; —seeps in; —simmers; —snuffs out; —spurts; —stagnates; —subsides; —surges; —stains; —swells; —swirls; —trickles in.

(See moisture, bath, liquid, pond, juice, lava.)

WATER (v)
adverbs
diligently; literally; faithfully; daily; constantly; superfluously; patiently.

(See refresh, supply.)

WATERFALL
adjectives
ethereal; sheeted; distant; babbling; misty; overhanging; sudden; blazing; dashing; living; roaring; gamboling; rainbowed; graceful.

verbs
approach—; bridge—; erode into—; span —; view—; —cascades; —churns; —deluges; —descends; —endangers; —froths; —gurgles; —s lace; —leaps; —pitches; —roars; —rolls; —rumbles; —scuds over; —sprays; —threatens; —thunders; —tinkles.

(See cataract, spray, mist.)

WAVE
adjectives
sanguine; dark; voiceless; weltering; moon-whitened; tremendous; accompanying; playful; petulant; warring; transcendent; plunging; troubled; unnumbered (pl); sloping; foaming; sordid; successive (pl); tidal; glowing; bounteous; scornful; long; throbbing; turbid; surging; bright; translucent; dignified; furious; lava; fleecy; towering; gliding; rugged; all-powerful; rolling; never-tiring; feathery; lustrous; charming; fluctuating; delicate; glittering; eternal; greedy; burning; whirling; immeasurable; lapsing; flashing; drunken; dividual (pl); yeasty; sparkling; fierce; green; wintry; dull; monstrous; amber; petrified; vivid; haunted; oblivious; rippling; inveterate; hurrying; turbulent; startled; bellowing; rebellious; reckless; inflated; chilly; mounting; softening; impressive; weltering; painted; great; white-crested; pent; impetuous; flinging; whispering; hiding; fiery; yellow; breaking; indented; wobbly; uneven; glossy; frolicsome; audacious; gleaming; lasting; tempestuous; surf; glooming; dissolving; sheltering; dashing; sullen; conquered; starry; blackening; high-rolling; engulfing; melodious; wireless; caressing; calm; ruthless; careless; moon-lit; mirrored; full-flushed; late; rhythmical; curling; ever-deepening; undulating; tossing; wide-wallowing; blind; restless; migratory; lustrous; tractable; bounding; peaceful; dashing; refluent; shattered; wan; slumberous; sparkling; tepid; intermingled (pl); electric; brimming; peaked; mountainous; slimy; salt; wandering; pandemic; infinitesimal; frantic; breaking; foam-figured; whistling; slight; creative; lambent; thin-edged; unfathomable; lonely; mournful; eerie; uncharted; rival; enormous; conflicting; angry; burnished; grassy; conciliatory; crisp; dimpled; quivering; advancing; sable; sympathetic; spent; implacable; ruffled; alarming; loyal; urgent; wildered; jostling; rising; shallow; fretting; mighty; mimic; sonorous; receding; gurgling; siren-haunted; sun-kissed; charmed; frothy; inconstant; unsullied; raging; heaving; peristaltic; stormy; summer; western; blind.

WAVE (v)
adverbs
gaily; gracefully; magically; helplessly; frantically; amicably; cheerfully; energetically; desolately; tremulously; rhythmically; constantly; languidly; erratically; impudently; mournfully; eloquently; gently; contemptuously; surreptitiously.

(See flaunt, brandish.)

WAVER (v)
adverbs
indecisively; irresolutely; weakly; morbidly; vacillatingly; erratically; doubtfully.

(See vacillate.)

WAVERING
adverbs
feebly; decrepitly; indecisively; hesitantly; weakly; finally; seldom; vexatiously; foolishly; irresponsibly; weakly; shyly; timidly; terribly; anxiously; strangely.

WAVES
verbs
breast—; command—; launch upon—; ride —; stem—; walk upon—; —batter; —beat; —break; —buffet; —chant; —dance; —dash; —emanate; —fall; —fizzle; —foam; —lap; —lash; —lift their heads; —lull;

—pound; —rage; —recede; —ripple; —rise; —show their teeth; —sigh; —slap; —slop; —swamp; —toss their manes; —tremble; —tumble; —vibrate.

(See ocean, breaker, billow, maelstrom.)

WAX

adjectives
yielding; incorruptible; plastic; soft; dental.

verbs
accumulate—; bleach—; candle—; collect—; derive—; extract—; fuse—; impress on—; model in—; mould—; plug with—; scrape —; seal with—; secrete—; wick—; yield—; —adheres; —melts; —polishes; —seals; —smooths; —waterproofs.

(See candle, putty.)

WAX (v)

adverbs
mightily; indignantly; boisterously; prodigiously; abnormally; spectacularly.

(See grow, increase.)

WAY

adjectives
abnormal; absolute; admirable; abstract; accommodating; admonitory; adroit; advantageous; agitated; agreeable; aimless; airy; allegorical; ancient; ambitious; amorous; applauded; arched; appointed; artful; assured; astounding; avoidable; bachelor; busy; calculating; caressing; categorical; celestial; challenged; chance; characteristic; charming; cheap; cheerful; childish; comical; circuitous; cold; comfortable; compact; companionable; comparative; complete; composed; comradely; confidential; convenient; cordial; creative; critical; cynical; dank; dark; darkling; dauntless; defiant; deep; delicate; delicious; delightful; depreciating; desolate; desultory; devious; dignified; dim; direct; disagreeable; dishonest; disorderly; distant; distempered; divers (pl); divine; dogged; dolorous; doubtful; doubtless; dreamy; dull; dusty; easy; eccentric; effective; endearing; egoistic; elaborate; enigmatical; enlightened; erring; everlasting; existing; execrable; expeditious; expensive; explicable; expressive; false; fantastic; farthest; fathomable; fiery; flaming; flowered; foul; fumbling; genial; glib; gloomy; good-humored; gracious; gratifying; grave; grim; guileless; happy; half-frightened; hateful; hearty; heavenward;

heavy-hearted; heedful; heterogeneous; hilarious; honorable; humble; idiomatic; idle; illogical; immortal; imperious; impersonal; impetuous; impregnable; incomprehensible; inconsequent; indefinite; indifferent; indirect; inexplicable; infinite; inflexible; ingenious; inscrutable; insolent; insular; inspired; intimate; introverted; irregular; invisible; irresistible; irritating; jerky; jostling; kind; laborious; lampless; labyrinthine; languid; last; laudable; lawful; leafy; learned; legendary; leisure; listless; lofty; loitering; lonely; luxurious; magical; marvelous; melancholy; mild; military; mischievous; modern; monstrous; moon-lit; muddled; murderous; muffled; mysterious; mystical; narrow; nasty; negative; noiseless; objective; night-wandering; nudging; obscure; obedient; offensive; oily; old; organic; original; ostentatious; outmoded; over-darkened; particular; peaceable; passive; paved; pebbly; peculiar; penetrating; peremptory; perfunctory; perilous; perplexing; picturesque; pilgrim; plausible; practical; prefatory; preoccupied; priestly; primrose; privy; promiscuous; promising; prosperous; provincial; provoking; prudent; public; quaint; queer; quick; rakish; random; rational; ready; realistic; reasonable; reassuring; reckless; reflective; respected; restless; restrained; restricted; roundabout; rude; rugged; safe; satisfactory; scaly; scornful; scrupulous; secret; self-chosen; self-made; self-pleasing; servile; shameful; facile; sharp; sheepish; shy; silly; sinuous; slimy; slippery; sodden; soft; solitary; sophisticated; sound; spasmodic; special; spectacular; spiky; spirited; sporadic; spring; squalid; starry; steadfast; stiff-necked; stolid; strange; stylish; sublime; subterranean; successful; sunken; supernatural; suspicious; symmetrical; sympathetic; systematic; temporary; tainted; tentative; theological; thorny; toilsome; tortuous; trackless; tranquil; treacherous; tricky; tumultuous; unaccountable; unceremonious; unchristian; uncompromising; uncouth; undynamic; unemotional; unerring; unexpected; uneven; unfriendly; ungenerous; ungracious; unhandsome; unimpassioned; unique; unkindled; unknown; unmeaning; unmerciful; unmistakable; unmitigated; unobtrusive; unpremeditated; unskilled; unslackened; unsuspected; untrodden; untutored; unwithered; upland; varied; venturous; vigorous; vulgar; wandering; wanton; wary; weary; weedy; whimsical; wildering; willowy; winding; woodland; workable; conscientious; constrained; contrary; half-fascinated.

verbs
adapt to—s; bar—; betray—; block—; bluff —; clutter—; contemplate—; demonstrate —; designate—; devise—; discern—; disclose—; elbow—; emulate—s; err in—; explore—; forge—; forsake—s; grope—; guide—; hew—; illumine—; inaugurate—; initiate in—s; inspire—; interpret—; lurk along—; mark—; mend—s; muddle—; pave —; pick—; plod—; plow—; point out—; pursue—; renounce—s; retrace—; smash—; smooth—; stray from—; strew—; thread—; veer from—; wangle—; welter—; wend—; worm—; yield—.

(See fashion, highway, gate, alley, avenue, manner, course, habit, lane.)

WAYWARD
adverbs
reprehensibly; heartbreakingly; incredibly; miserably; wretchedly; pitiably; curiously; remarkably; unaccountably; unmanageably; incorrigibly; strangely; haplessly; peculiarly; unfortunately; uncommonly; singularly; hopelessly; desperately; childishly.

WAYWORN
adverbs
terribly; weakly; feebly; pitiably; pathetically; undoubtedly; naturally; credibly; extremely; completely; utterly; ominously; momentarily; dreadfully.

WEAK
adverbs
pathetically; terribly; unusually; naturally; extremely; inordinately; significantly; palpably; languidly; remarkably; strangely; curiously; unexpectedly; surprisingly; unaccountably; distressingly; disappointingly; fatally; mortally; alarmingly; unfortunately.

WEAKEN (*v*)
adverbs
painfully; constitutionally; unsuspectedly; alarmingly; tragically; treacherously; precipitately; materially; basically; ostensibly; insidiously.

(See impair, decline.)

WEAKNESS
adjectives
cold-pale; youthful; normal; mortal; an-

archical; potential; veriest; hereditary; childish; extraordinary; disordered; bodily; relative; physical; endearing; momentary; incurable; inherent; curious; unworthy; progressive; absolute; overmastering; confessed; extreme; deadly; amiable; earthly; intellectual; fatal; permanent; contemptible; prevalent; inborn; hollow.

verbs
arise from—; betray—; bewail—; blame—; confess to—; conquer—; deride—; dress up —; exploit—; increase—; indicate—; lament —; overcome—; pander to—; parade—; produce—; redeem—; reproach for—; speculate upon—; spurn—; —assails; —forfeits; —impairs; —prostrates; —thwarts; induce —.

(See infirmity, inability, disability, impotence, frailty, helplessness.)

WEAL
adjectives
common; public; universal; all-embracing.

WEALTH
adjectives
incipient; personal; incalculable; flowing; estimated; melodic; comparative; boundless; enormous; wanton; ill-gotten; unlimited; diminished; fabulous; proverbial; maiden; undeveloped; mineral; independent; movable; sole; hoarded; substantive; intellectual; growing; concentrated; complacent; monopolistic; lavished; priceless; crystal; progressive; natural; tremendous; material; conspicuous; squandering; magic; unwieldy; veritable; many-sided; lacteal; emotional; religious; disregarded; physical; inherited; immense; spiritual; available; gleaned; sparkling.

verbs
accumulate—; affect—; apportion—; attain —; confer—; confiscate—; consume—; destroy—; diffuse—; dissipate—; drain—; efface—; euphemize—; forfeit—; gather—; groan with—; hoard—; labor for—; lavish —; load with—; lust for—; obviate—; plunder—; redistribute—; reject—; roll in—; scatter—; scramble for—; squander—; tap —; tax—; toil for—; winnow—; —destines; —menaces; —multiplies; —surpasses.

(See fortune, affluence, legacy, capital, luxury, money, riches, plenty.)

WEALTHY

adverbs

gorgeously; enormously; comfortably; fortunately; pleasantly; agreeably; serenely; snugly; enviably; complacently; sufficiently; smugly; graciously; fabulously; independently; substantially; tremendously; conspicuously; immensely; crassly; excessively; fairly.

WEAPON

adjectives

slight; spiritual; enticing; ancipital; lethal; unsheathed; respectable; resistless; fierce; habitual; mimic; economic; inadequate; ceremonial; saintly; climatic; pitiless; prohibited; keen; formidable; devastating; ghastly; idle; defensive; fatal; blood-tipped; effective; primitive; death-dealing; trusty; lavish; dripping; heroic; dangerous; imperial; competent.

verbs

brandish—; conceal—; devise—; discredit —; display—; draw—; flourish—; forge—; furnish with—; resort to—; scorn—; sheathe —; stroke—; shield from—; temper—; wield—; wrest—; —s clang; —s clash; — cracks; —s crash; —flashes; —intimidates; —roars; —coerces.

(See arms, cannon, bow, cutlass, dagger, missile, gun, sword.)

WEAR

adjectives

abundant; minimum; worthy; immediate; superfluous; forcible; fashionable; prolonging; satisfactory.

WEAR (v)

adverbs

habitually; absurdly; customarily; religiously; gracefully; conventionally; invariably; jauntily; loosely; haughtily; superfluously; fashionably.

(See use, sport.)

WEARINESS

adjectives

elemental; humble; delicious; despairing; simple; utter; exasperated; satisfied; sheer; mortal; everlasting; blissful; silent; colossal; never-ending; eternal.

verbs

allay—; alleviate—; assuage—; augment—; complain of—; endure—; induce—; mitigate —; relieve—; result in—; succumb to—; — besets; —consumes; —creeps; —deters; — diminishes; —drags; —engulfs; —irks; — irritates; —oppresses; —overtakes; —overwhelms.

(See impotence, fatigue, languor, exhaustion, lassitude, lethargy, ennui.)

WEARISOME

adverbs

intolerably; tediously; monotonously; profoundly; irksomely; terribly; inordinately; exhaustingly; prosily; disgustingly; unbearably; stupidly; vexatiously; annoyingly; excessively; utterly; painfully; dreadfully.

WEARY

adverbs

naturally; inordinately; terribly; utterly; strangely; pitifully; forlornly; physically; nervously; unutterably; immeasurably; profoundly; extremely; mortally; inexpressibly; distressingly; pathetically; sadly.

WEASEL

verbs

—claws; —climbs; —constructs; —defends; —deposits; —inhabits; —pillages; —preys on; —plunders; —slays; —swims.

(See animal.)

WEATHER

adjectives

fair; green; heavy; high; windy; frosty; prized; harsh; inclement; bitter; portentous; overhung; unsullied; thick; warm; sunshiny; damp; foggy; sticky; summer; capricious; foul; whirling; militant; ripening; bright; hard; glad; wintry; unseasonable; darkening; somber; common; extreme; unfavorable; sultry; gypsy; mild; blue; rough; oppressive; humid; starless; unsettled; loud; delicious; glorious; golden; wilting; surface; tough; ripening; gusty; blusterous; unpropitious; cloudless; feverish; detestable; intemperate; singing.

verbs

anticipate—; bare to—; bear—; becloud—; chart—; conjecture on—; converse about—; endure—; expose to—; exult in—; forecast —; predict—; prophesy—; stomach—; unsettle—; —affects; —brightens; —clears; —damages; —dejects; —demoralizes; —depresses; —discourages; —disheartens; —en-

1284

livens; —frowns; —hovers; —invigorates; —limits; —modifies; —permits; —thickens.
(See climate, cold, heat.)

WEATHER-BEATEN
adverbs
curiously; hopelessly; sturdily; dingily; apparently; admittedly; probably; naturally; obviously; palpably; manifestly; laughingly; harmlessly; oddly; shabbily; dingily.

WEATHERED
adverbs
decrepitly; invincibly; sturdily; anciently; admirably; pitifully; languidly; outrageously; definitely; agedly; gauntly; desperately; hopelessly.

WEAVE (v)
adverbs
deceptively; coarsely; subtly; laboriously; ingeniously; inextricably; deftly; skillfully; dexterously; artfully.
(See braid, fabricate.)

WEB
adjectives
singularly-formed; mysterious; bandana; tangled; dark; illuminated; contrapuntal; atrocious; unfinished; intricate; thick-spun; frail; luminous; wondrous; graceful-looking; braided.

verbs
avoid—; elude—; escape—; evade—; spin —; weave—; wreathe—; —ambushes; — attracts; —baits; —beguiles; —convolutes; —curves; —decussates; —enmeshes; —entangles; —entwines; —intersects; —lures; —reticulates; —snares; —traps; —vibrates.
(See cobweb, trap, net.)

WED (v)
adverbs
auspiciously; admirably; happily; gaily; blissfully; genially; perfunctorily; passionately.
(See marry, unite.)

WEDDING
verbs
approve of—; attend—; bar from—; bless —; celebrate—; ceremonialize—; contemplate—; entertain at—; feast at—; officiate at—; perform—; ritualize—; witness—; — binds; —cements; —contracts; —joins; — pledges; —ties; —unites.
(See nuptials, matrimony, marriage.)

WEEDS
adjectives
hardy; pageant; luxuriant; offensive; sea; bladdery; troublesome; unwholesome; mourning; coarse; brittle; silver-budded; fancy; rank; dank; valueless; wretched-looking; little; scented; flowerless; loathed; huddling; clinging; convent; blossoming; amphibious; bending; noisome; fragrant; deleterious; undulating; ineradicable; wasting; encumbering; swaying; thin; choking; noxious; unsightly; berry-spotted.

verbs
clear of—; exterminate—; eradicate—; nip —; pluck—; sever—; suffocate by—; teem with—; —attain; —choke; —crowd; —cumber; —deprive; —destroy; —entwine; —fringe; —hamper; —hinder; —overgrow; —parch; —strangle.
(See grass, plant.)

WEEDY
adverbs
excessively; horribly; hopelessly; inordinately; extraordinarily; naturally; offensively; vexatiously; terribly; unnecessarily; inexcusably; carelessly; hideously; rankly; unwholesomely; disgustingly; discouragingly.

WEEK
adjectives
consecutive (pl); bewildering; tempestuous; momentous; previous; ensuing; successive (pl); eventful; disturbing; dreary; happy; intoxicating; long; tedious; weary.

verbs
abide—; beguile—; celebrate—; commemorate—; endure—; extend—; fix—; forecast —; fritter away—; gain—; outlast—; prolong—; reckon—s; remain—; survive—; terminate—; tolerate for—; while away—; —elapses; —expires; —inaugurates; — lapses; —marks; —s stretch.
(See month, day, hour, time.)

WEEP (v)
adverbs
pitifully; plaintively; piteously; bitterly; wildly; tumultuously; sentimentally; pathetically; intermittently; stormily; hysterically; abundantly; furiously; copiously; ludicrously; sympathetically.
(See lament, moan.)

adjectives

responsive; mysterious; incessant; hysterical; violent; passionate; continual; ludicrous; sore; chronic; wild; focused; untimely.

WEIGH (*v*)

adverbs

gravely; judiciously; reflectively; empirically; correctly; onerously; heavily; minutely; momentously; ponderously.

(See balance, estimate.)

WEIGHT

adjectives

nightmare; slumberous; undue; soft; dark; mass; excess; increasing; overwhelming; panting; superior; sweet; enormous; withering; unsolicited; panting; patent; caressing; portcullis; co-extensive; lesser; dead; comfortable; unaccustomed; hard; icy; noticeable; prodigal; definite; descending; weary; augmented; emotional; specific; idle; crushing; finite; momentous; ponderous; relative; surplus; massive; cruel; exceptional; light; sufficient; combined.

verbs

adjust—; ascertain—; attain—; bear—; carry—; cast off—; convey—; determine—; exert—; flounder under—; groan under—; manipulate—; match—; modify—; propel —; regulate—; shoulder—; support—; suspend—; unburden—; vary in—; —balances; —bruises; —burdens; —compresses; —constricts; —crumples; —crushes; —descends; —diminishes; —fatigues; —oppresses; — overwhelms; —submerges.

(See load, heaviness, burden.)

WEIRD

adverbs

strangely; gloomily; uncannily; terribly; dismally; fearfully; mysteriously; darkly; curiously; fantastically; grotesquely; incomprehensibly; unpleasantly; disagreeably; peculiarly; eerily.

WELCOME

adjectives

formal; courteous; healthful; comfortless; chill; familiar; tepid; hearty; smiling; preposterous; cordial; awkward; unclouded; pathetic; homely; triumphant; pure; majestic; friendly; noisy; kindred; heart-sped; royal; dismal; generous; intuitive; gracious; unquestioned; premeditated; scant; boisterous; kindly; languid; urbane; immemorial; unostentatious; frank; energetic; extraordinary; joyous; hospitable; genial; cheerful; reverend; warm; lavish; frolic.

verbs

assure—; bark—; bid—; bow—; embrace in—; extend—; greet with—; hail—; insure —; nod—; offer—; overstay—; rejoice in—; roar—; salute—; shout—; smile—; thunder —; win—; —cools; —flatters; —greets; — heartens; —rings.

(See greeting, friendship.)

adverbs

gratefully; refreshingly; cordially; sincerely; hospitably; warmly; truly; unexpectedly; supremely; encouragingly; frankly; acceptably; pleasantly; genially; graciously.

WELCOME (*v*)

adverbs

smilingly; spaciously; hospitably; enthusiastically; fondly; heartily; affectionately; ecstatically; gleefully; courteously; majestically; generously; languidly; urbanely; ostentatiously; frankly; energetically; joyously; genially; lavishly.

(See greet, hail.)

WELD (*v*)

adverbs

electrically; sturdily; staunchly; firmly.

WELDING

adjectives

intimate; sturdy; gradual; necessary.

WELFARE

adjectives

immediate; bodily; real; general; human; material; permanent; spiritual; financial; commercial; national; eternal.

verbs

administer—; advance—; aid—; concern—; consider—; consult—; contribute to—; determine—; devote to—; disregard—; encourage —; endanger—; forward—; foster—; further—; ignore—; impair—; improve—; jeopardize—; neglect—; overlook—; plan —; promote—; raise—; regard—; respect —; sacrifice—; safeguard—; seek—; serve —; study—; threaten—; —ascends; —flourishes; —thrives.

(See good, health, happiness, well-being.)

adjectives

deep; calm; handsome; stone; decorated; poisoned; projected; fathomable; crystal; transparent; mossy; extreme; babbling; connected; polluted; harmonious; bubbling.

verbs

bare—; case—; contaminate—; drain—; drill—; emanate from—; excavate—; issue from—; line—; pollute—; probe—; pump from—; sink—; sound—; submerge in—; tap—; test—; —affords; —bubbles; —facilitates; —offers; —overflows; —springs up; —yields.

(See spring, shaft, source, fountain, volcano.)

adverbs

gloriously; splendidly; magnificently; wholly; gaily; entirely; seldom; recently; finally; radiantly; miraculously; happily; fortunately; luckily; naturally; surprisingly; extremely; incomparably; sturdily; rosily.

WELL-BEING

verbs

administer to—; advance—; afford—; bask in—; contribute toward—; desire—; discern —; encourage—; envy—; indicate—; jeopardize—; promote—; sense—; serve—; threaten—; wrap up in—; —flourishes; —permeates; —pervades; —prospers; —thrives.

(See welfare.)

WELL-BRED

adverbs

extremely; satisfactorily; gratifyingly; acceptably; unusually; delightfully; extraordinarily; beautifully; marvelously; surprisingly; unexpectedly; obviously; manifestly; meticulously; charmingly; naturally.

WELL-INFORMED

adverbs

remarkably; eminently; illustriously; exceptionally; consummately; distinctly; particularly; marvelously; wonderfully; profoundly; incredibly; surprisingly; undeniably; intelligently; unusually; certainly; impressively.

WELL-MEANING

adverbs

possibly; probably; apparently; evidently; manifestly; painfully; obviously; hopefully; awkwardly; clumsily; sufficiently.

adjectives

sublimated; faded; bountiful; infinite; flameless; unfooted; shadowy; vagrant; rich; glowing; fiery; crimson; bloody.

verbs

determine—; drift to—; establish in—; filter into—; invade—; migrate to—; penetrate—; pioneer—; settle in—; —absorbs; —attracts; —beckons; —calls; —flourishes; —importunes; —invites; —lures; —offers; —retreats; —thrives.

(See territory, country, region, locality.)

WET

adverbs

terribly; obnoxiously; unwholesomely; soppily; hopelessly; unseasonably; swampily; quaggily; mysteriously; strangely; disgustingly; unpleasantly; unhealthfully; utterly.

WETNESS

adjectives

dripping; sticky; red; annoying; permanent.

WETTING

adjectives

hearty; customary; voluntary; necessary.

WHALE

adjectives

wanton; large-finned; awkward; belching; monstrous; trained.

verbs

conserve—; derive from—s; dissect—; encounter—; exterminate—; glimpse—; harpoon—; haul in—; land—; market—; pursue—; sight—; spot—; strand—; strip—; value—; —s frequent; —gives battle; —s haunt; —inhabits; —looms; —plunges; —preys upon; —spouts; —submerges; —tows; —yields.

(See shark, fish, animal.)

WHEAT

adjectives

fruitless; scythed; yellowing; tender; nodding; ripe; whole; cracked; ground; bleached.

verbs

attack—; consume—; convert—; cultivate—; enrich—; glean—; grind—; harvest—; import—; market—; mill—; pulverize—; sow —; thresh—; trade in—; winnow the chaff from—; —booms; —fails; —flourishes; — fluctuates; —germinates; —matures; — ripens; —ripples; —thrives.

(See crop, harvest, grain, cereal, grass, plant.)

WHEEDLING

adverbs

teasingly; coaxingly; flatteringly; fondly; carefully; foxily; tenderly; persistently; successfully; constantly.

WHEEL

adjectives

ardent; muffled; toothed; sentient; tardy; interior; flaming; buckled; whirling; fervid; humming; formidable; jarring; worm-eaten; gilded; living; westering; broad-tired; massive; shining; wobbling; rolling; restless; ponderous; creaking; glowing; retreating; worn-out; waggly; spinning; whirring; gambling.

verbs

derail—; grip—; lubricate—; maneuver—; pad—; réalign—s; shatter—; tread—; trundle—; twirl—; —clicks; —creaks; — deviates; —drones; —encompasses; —encircles; —girdles; —facilitates; —gyrates; —lurches; —jars; —jolts; —jounces; —pivots on; —recoils; —responds; —revolves; —rumbles; —spins; —swerves; —twirls; — whirls.

(See helm, cycle.)

WHEEL (v)

adverbs

automatically; serenely; sharply; swiftly; dizzily; drunkenly; mechanically; ceaselessly; whirringly; smoothly.

(See roll, move.)

WHEREABOUTS

verbs

allude to—; ascertain—; bare—; betray—; bring to light—; conceal—; confirm—; determine—; discern—; disclose—; discover —; divulge—; establish—; expose—; fix—; inform of—; report—; reveal—; screen—; solve—; trace—; unearth—; veil—; verify —; —baffles; —creeps out; —mystifies.

(See existence, position, place.)

WHIFF

adjectives

jealous; subtle; odorous; suggestive; gentle.

WHIM

adjectives

wild; eccentric; epicurean; delightful; illogical; abrupt; mere; ornamental; arbitrary; idle; anti-social; inconvenient; humorous; arrant; curious; mad; silly.

verbs

accede to—; conceive—; deny—; deplore—; discard—; dismiss as—; excite—; grant—; gratify—; humor—; indulge in—; outgrow —; play up to—; provoke—; satisfy—; smother—; yield to—; —intoxicates; —irritates; —piques; —riles (colloq.); —seizes.

(See humor, fad, fancy, caprice.)

WHIMPER (v)

adverbs

fretfully; distractedly; pusillanimously; reproachfully; feebly; pitifully; nervously; weakly; brokenly; hysterically; fruitlessly.

(See weep, cry.)

WHIMPERING

adjectives

nervous; secret; everlasting; continual; frightened; pitiful.

WHIMSICAL

adverbs

ludicrously; fancifully; fantastically; amusingly; pleasantly; cleverly; subtly; agreeably; fascinatingly; charmingly; grotesquely; outlandishly; delightfully; immensely; absurdly; unusually; oddly.

WHINE

adjectives

shrill; pusillanimous; friendly; cracked; peculiar; hungry; begging.

verbs

choke back—; discern—; elicit—; emit—; provoke—; restrain—; smother—; stifle—; subdue—; —distresses; —expresses; —irks; —irritates; —laments; —moves; —riles (colloq.); —s subside; —touches.

(See moan, sob, complaint.)

WHINE (v)

adverbs

piteously; wretchedly; churlishly; shrilly; pusillanimously; beggingly; mournfully; intolerably; hungrily.

(See whimper, cry.)

WHINNY

adjectives
colt-like; shrill; nervous; excited.

WHIP

adjectives
gigantic; remorseless; cutting; keen; deadly; brutal.

verbs
apply—; brandish—; crack—; cut with—; flick—; flog with—; lay on—; prod with—; utilize—; yield to—; —accelerates; —belabors; —bestirs; —coerces; —crackles; —cracks; —flays; —cuts; —impels; —induces; —lashes; —pricks; —reddens; —scourges; —spurs; —stimulates; —stings; —urges; —goads.

WHIP (v)

adverbs
unmercifully; deservedly; savagely; brutally; remorselessly; viciously.
(See beat, thrash.)

WHIPPOORWILL

verbs
—calls; —moans; —reiterates; —vociferates; —wails.
(See bird.)

WHIRL

adjectives
little; powdery; foamy; continuous; social; giddy.

WHIRL (v)

adverbs
crazily; dizzily; madly; gaily; joyously; incessantly; furiously; giddily; continuously.
(See revolve, swirl.)

WHIRLPOOL

adjectives
everlasting; continued; foamy; fatal; heartless.

verbs
avoid—; drift into—; escape—; ferment—; flounder in—; quiver in—; sweep into—; yield to—; —agitates; —batters; —boils; —buffets; —churns; —dashes; —eddies; —endangers; —foams; —froths; —gyrates; —imperils; —jostles; —jounces; —menaces;

—plays; —roars; —seethes; —spouts; —sucks; —swirls; —threatens; —whips.
(See maelstrom, vortex, waves.)

WHIRLWIND

adjectives
drear; cloudy; weltering; dark; awful; rending; eddying; good; undulating; toying; fatal; unexpected.

WHISK (v)

adverbs
deftly; cleverly; eagerly; abruptly; resolutely; noiselessly; cunningly.
(See sweep, whirl.)

WHISKERS

adjectives
solitary; grizzled; sere; miserable; half-starved; shaggy; educated; combed; closely-cropped; bushy; unruly; optimistic; huge; fuzzy; bountiful; unkempt; ingrown.

verbs
affect—; clip—; crop—; cultivate—; discard—; lop off—; pluck—; respect—; ruffle —; rumple—; shag—; shampoo—; shear—; smooth—; stroke—; thin out—; trim—; —adorn; —cloak; —disguise; —fringe; —gray; —quiver; —transform; —tuft.
(See moustache, mane, hair, beard.)

WHISKEY

adjectives
indispensable; hot; commissary; straight; blended; bonded; young; medicinal; cheap; smooth; fiery; burning; synthetic.

verbs
abstain from—; addict to—; age—; assimilate—; bond—; bootleg—; bottle—; consume—; dispatch—; distil—; drain—; inure to—; legalize—; prohibit—; quaff—; refine—; sip—; swill—; tax—; value—; —anaesthetizes; —befogs; —deadens; —dulls; —enlivens; —flows; —flings down; —inebriates; —enslaves; —intoxicates; —narcotizes; —perverts; —revives; swig—.
(See brandy, liquor, alcohol, gin, wine.)

WHISPER

adjectives
delightful; gentle; sullen; friendly; dainty; icy; sibilant; soothing; awe-stricken; stirring; naked; subdued; ragged; little; rapid; hysteric; broken; persuasive; insistent; stage; imperturbable; laughing; silken;

stealthy; confidential; frantic; resolute; ceaseless; indolent; answering; intense; solemn; unnatural; keen; wheezing; busy; blasphemous; significant; low; muttered; hoarse; failing; vibrating; swelling; precautionary; benignant; bearded; husky; multitudinous (pl); fierce; tragic; hollow; ghostly; hideous; bass; audible; hurried; frightened; serene; overt; eloquent; agonized; strained; occasional; caressing; complaining; fanatical; distressed.

verbs
amplify—; conspire in—s; converse in—s; convey in—; drown out—; emit—; harken to—; hush—; inform in—; muffle—; overhear—; raise above—; reduce to—; resort to—; revive—; stifle—; suppress—; — beckons; —buzzes; —dies; —distracts; — diverts; —hints; —prompts; —quavers; — rebukes; —sears; still—.
(See sound, tone, noise, hum.)

WHISPER (v)
adverbs
hoarsely; treasonably; brokenly; passionately; impressively; eagerly; tremulously; urgently; mysteriously; audibly; affectionately; discreetly; petulantly; breathlessly; fiercely; savagely; feebly; defiantly; appealingly; compassionately; insidiously; vehemently; feverishly; stealthily; overtly; eloquently; impressively.
(See gossip, speak.)

WHISTLE
adjectives
noiseless; plaintive; hoarse; careless; expressive; fierce; denouncing; shrill; incessant; congratulatory; occasional.

verbs
blow on—; toot—; —alarms; —announces; —awakens; —beckons; —deafens; —distracts; —drowns out; —pierces; —proclaims; —rends; —screams; —shrieks; — shrills; —signals; —sounds; —splits; — startles; —wails; —warns.
(See warning, flute, note, scream.)

WHISTLE (v)
adverbs
sharply; briskly; piercingly; incisively; warningly; desperately; weirdly; thinly; tunelessly; mockingly; gently; repetitiously; melodiously; plaintively.
(See sound, sing.)

WHITE
adjectives
pure; new; snow; artemisia; frosty; clinging; unendurable; moon-washed; brilliant; beach; billowy; delicate; silvery; translucent; uncanny; popular; smart; plain; wanted; smooth; dazzling; creamy; foaming; shining; whirling; argent; deadly; immaculate; bloodless; slashing; luminous.

adverbs
ghastly; utterly; suddenly; brilliantly; dingily; dustily; dully; nervously; sickly; frightfully; gleamingly; blazingly; chalkily; ghostly; surprisingly; inappropriately; startlingly.

WHITE-LIVERED
adverbs
disgustingly; foolishly; shamefully; terribly; despicably; contemptibly; obviously; manifestly; notoriously; infamously; unusually; spinelessly; abjectly; helplessly; undisguisedly; hideously; terribly.

WHITENESS
adjectives
dazzling; splendid; immaculate; gleaming; downy; pristine; spotless; ghastly; unbroken; chalky; silent; bony; evanescent; dead; odious.

WHITEWASHED
adverbs
neatly; gleamingly; recently; tidily; sanitarily; pleasantly; conveniently; hilariously; quickly; diplomatically; wisely; cheaply; delightfully; cheerfully; ingeniously; thoughtfully; carefully; deceptively; artistically.

WHOLE
adjectives
consistent; magnificent; stupendous; homogeneous; coherent; immeasurable; complete; great; weltering.

WHOLESOME
adverbs
pleasantly; delightfully; palatably; tastily; notably; admittedly; soundly; nutritiously; splendidly; happily; admirably; commendably; attractively; smilingly; rosily; sturdily.

WHOOP (v)
adverbs
hideously; madly; wildly; insanely; barbar-

ously; terrifyingly; viciously; insistently; hysterically.

(See cry, yell.)

WICK

adjectives

flaring; homemade; burned; cotton; low.

verbs

enkindle—; ignite—; immerse—; lower—; raise—; renew—; saturate—; smother—; snuff out—; soak—; —blazes; —diffuses; — flares; —flickers; —flutters; —glimmers; — glows; —illumines; —radiates; —scintillates; —sears; —singes; —sparkles.

(See candle.)

WICKED

adverbs

scarcely; slightly; interestingly; alluringly; terribly; brutally; heinously; undeniably; palpably; manifestly; nefariously; unspeakably; inexpressibly; dreadfully; obscenely; conspicuously; notoriously; infamously.

WICKEDNESS

adjectives

loathsome; idolatrous; flagrant; unforgivable; exceeding.

verbs

acquit of—; atone for—; breed—; condone —; convert from—; denounce—; deplore—; disclose—; do penance for—; expiate—; expose—; extirpate—; forsake—; impute- to; inveigh against—; paint—; purge of—; renounce—; repent—; reproach for—; reveal—; rue—; shrive of—; stamp out—; stew in—; work—; —corrupts; —prevails; —reigns; —taints.

(See lawlessness, abomination, iniquity, licentiousness, immorality, evil.)

WIDE

adverbs

amply; sufficiently; generously; unexpectedly; capaciously; voluminously; exceptionally; particularly; peculiarly; conveniently; commodiously; spaciously; advantageously; tremendously; immensely; adequately; suitably; properly; fortunately; outlandishly; unnecessarily.

WIDEN (v)

adverbs

perceptibly; appreciably; gradually; mark-

edly; proportionately; sufficiently; immeasurably; illimitably.

(See broaden, increase.)

WIDE-SPREAD

adverbs

unfortunately; manifestly; remarkably; amazingly; alarmingly; fearfully; luckily; dangerously; profitably; ineradicably; presumably; allegedly; fantastically; curiously.

WIDOW

adjectives

charming; agreeable; disconsolate; broken-hearted; wanton; childless; perverse; loving; pious; sentimental; virginal; lusty; unpensioned; polygamous; intrepid; austere; superabundant (pl).

WIELD (v)

adverbs

magically; potently; honorably; viciously; dictatorially; tyrannically; cunningly; dangerously; slyly; hatefully; deceitfully; craftily; subtly; ambitiously; ambiguously; virtuously; vigorously; powerfully; ruthlessly.

(See employ, use.)

WIFE

adjectives

shrewish; meek-eyed; worthy; tearful; disrespectful; legitimate; stainless; delicate; profligate; faithless; high-corseted; prideful; sprightly; bejeweled; coquettish; devoted; high-spirited; splendid; querulous; flattered; unsustained; exemplary; playful; dutiful; burdensome; slovenly; frantic; respective (pl); conquering; affectionate; trustful; sainted; temporary; spotless; forward; churchly; begotten; bullied; gracious; beaten; affianced; patient; sweet; virtuous; pale-faced; murdered; undivorced; unalienable; whimpering; smooth-haired; celebrated; amiable; strong-willed; tyrannical; diminutive; mercenary; constant; lewd-tongued; chaste; lawful; attractive; innocent; young; execrable; shameless; nervous; simple; common-law; slippery; perjured; aristocratic; pale-cheeked; tender; prudent; pining.

verbs

adore—; alienate—; caress—; choose—; cohabit with—; court—; desert—; embrace—; escort—; estrange from—; extol—; forsake —; intimidate—; seduce—; seek—; slander

—; strike—; take—; win—; —begets; —betrays; —comforts; —conceives; —haggles; —inspires; —mothers; —nags; —presides over; —rails; —shares.

(See mate, husband, mistress.)

WIG

adjectives

glossy; curly; formidable; elastic; frizzled; obvious; tangled; little; flaxen; towering; comical-looking.

WILD

adjectives

vast; impenetrable; sequestered; hidden; unapprehensive; dawning; fretted; luscious; untrodden; dreary.

adverbs

apparently; terribly; unmanageably; rankly; rampantly; fantastically; outrageously; outlandishly; savagely; ungovernably; naturally; inexpressibly; inordinately; boisterously; crazily; frantically; unconscionably; inveterately; hopelessly; manifestly; extraordinarily; pestiferously.

WILDCAT

adjectives

docile; cunning; vicious; sly; dangerous.

verbs

encounter—; skin—; trap—; —carries away; —claws; —depredates; —devours; —glares; —growls; —preys on; —roams; —slinks; —springs; —stalks.

(See animal.)

WILDERNESS

adjectives

vast; sub-arctic; intricate; unwithered; howling; watery; uneasy; rough; trackless; ancient; woody; indiscriminate; equal; untamed; obscure; pristine; remote; reluctant; barren; virgin; leafy; boundless; tangled; lonely; glowing; native; world-wide; unsettled; death-fraught; untrodden; broad; wild; shadowed; frozen; tangled; snowy; intricate; fertile; wasteful; uninhabited; untraveled; savage; measureless; constellated; adoring; interminable; pathless; untamable; marshy; inquiring; parched; arid.

verbs

brave—; circumvent—; clear—; dare—; explore—; fertilize—; flee into—; forsake—; frequent—; infest—; inhabit—; issue from

—; level—; penetrate into—; pioneer into —; plunge into—; range—; retire to—; roam—; skirt—; subdue—; tame—; tangle in—; traverse—; venture into—; —beckons; —broods; —cloaks; —extends; —fascinates; —lures; —screens; —shrouds; invade—.

(See jungle, forest, desert.)

WILDNESS

adjectives

dreaming; wailing; graceful.

WILES

adjectives

intrinsic; instinctive; wanton; insidious; manifold; feminine; endearing; imaginary; winning; subtle; deceitful; crafty.

verbs

discern—; disguise—; fall victim to—; pierce—; resist—; resort to—; succumb to —; yield to—; —allure; —attract; —bait; —deceive; —defraud; —delude; —dupe; —ensnare; —entangle; —gull; —hook; —inveigle; —lure; —seduce; —succeed; —trap.

(See trick, deception, ruse, cunning.)

WILFUL

adverbs

naturally; inveterately; uncontrollably; notoriously; wickedly; stubbornly; foolishly; unreasonably; unmanageably; erratically; fanatically; impudently; inconsiderately; ungraciously; rudely; grossly; brutally; selfishly.

WILL
(*document*)

verbs

abide by—; attest to—; comply with—; contest—; direct in—; discharge—; dispute—; evidence—; execute—; file—; invalidate—; negate—; nullify—; observe—; probate—; seal—; set aside—; stipulate in—; witness —; wrangle over—; —assigns; —bequeaths; —bestows upon; —confers on; —consigns; —contributes to; —declares; —decrees; —discloses; —dispenses; —disposes of; —doles out; —endows; —enriches; —entrusts with; —estranges; —grants; —invests; —metes out; —restores; —settles; —subsidizes; —transfers.

(See contract, legacy, document.)

adjectives

passionless; individual; vulgar; overmastering; ambitious; cheerful; irresistible; unstable; grumbling; ill; intense; fiery; gracious; incorporated; inexorable; virtuous; devilish; firm-set; indomitable; unconquerable; holy; rational; never-daunted; vigorous; strenuous; inscrutable; powerful; regenerate; hindering; sturdy; unreined; invincible; tyrant; fallible; tormenting; idiotic; uncontrolled; dauntless; overruling; nerveless; natural; arbitrary; potent; genuine; good; lordly; sublime; basic; universal; arch-imperial; opposing; mutual; imperious; cruel; incorruptible; sensory; sovereign; sanguine; self-determined; undivided; sacred; honest; expressive; tremendous; lawless; clearly-expressed; tempered; despotic; tyrannic; benumbed; entangled; tendril-like; royal; imperative; imminent; unrelaxing; gracious.

verbs

accede to—; annihilate—; assert—; bend to —; blind—; blunt—; control—; curb—; effect—; energize—; enforce—; exercise—; express—; flout—; harden—; impose—; ignore—; liberate—; mold to—; obey—; oppose—; perform—; restore—; subject to—; subjugate—; subordinate—; weaken—; work—; yield to—; —s clash; —moves; — prevails; indulge—.

(See preference, desire, determination, willpower.)

WILLFULNESS

verbs

brook—; curb—; decry—; denounce—; deplore—; dispel—; dispose toward—; dissolve—; endure—; govern by—; incline toward—; put up with—; relax—; relent—; repent—; rue—; tolerate—; —irks; —irritates; —piques; —riles (colloq.); —succumbs to; —yields to.

(See perversity, obstinacy, stubbornness.)

WILLING

adverbs

usually; graciously; politely; considerately; indulgently; generously; agreeably; pleasantly; helpfully; indifferently; enthusiastically; surprisingly; suspiciously; curiously; generously; unexpectedly.

adjectives

gruff; repeated; obvious; ready; surface.

WILLOW

adjectives

idling; silken; sprouting; shivery; weeping; slender.

WILLPOWER

verbs

breed—; cultivate—; discern—; display—; evince—; exhibit—; foster—; inherit—; lack —; lower—; necessitate—; rejuvenate—; require—; stimulate—; test—; want—; weaken—; —banishes; —curbs; —determines; —directs; —dominates; —droops; — flags; —flinches; —perseveres; —rebels; — rejects; —relaxes; —resists; —swerves; — wavers.

(See will, strength, desire, power.)

WIN (*v*)

adverbs

strategically; decisively; effectually; spectacularly; phenomenally; competitively; gallantly; substantially; intrepidly; treacherously.

(See triumph, achieve.)

WINCE (*v*)

adverbs

visibly; perceptibly; markedly; painfully; abruptly; revealingly; guiltily.

(See recoil, shrink.)

WINCING

adverbs

fearfully; constantly; suddenly; significantly; tremulously; painfully; haggardly; arrantly; senselessly; timidly; abjectly; indescribably; secretly; inwardly; openly; miserably; wretchedly; timorously; dreadfully; pathetically; curiously.

WIND

adjectives

crannying; worldly; southerly; good; swift; ill; cruel; biting; wandering; whispering; boisterous; hurtling; rolling; rough; poisonous; shrill; mad; curdling; dew-impearled; wild; chilling; whimsical; ocean; continuous; noiseless; streaming; sharp; rising; wailing; wanton; rude; nimble; special; spleenless; contrary; passing; foul; bleak; whitening; viewless; red-hot; roaring; crackling; fierce; gentle; dirty; sunny; bitter; keen; merry; favoring; shifting; restless; sleepy; sudden; sleety; gusty; cutting; whistling; murderous; dirgeful; pensive; uplifting; soughing; dying; wrinkling; wooing; weighty; unwilling; intricate; doleful; dead; hollow; moaning; mysterious; lulled; light; baffling; fabulous; azure; listening; inanimate; wintry; desert; woven; ferocious; delicate; fresh; panting; ravishing; hurricane; amorous; luscious; weak; tearing; felon; sportive; driving; boisterous; impetuous; mournful; adverse; piercing; tempestuous; contending; baleful; perverse; thirsty; ill-dispersing; tossing; monotonous; soothing; bracing; rustling; throwing; contrary; supple; wrecking; careless; bone-piercing; prevailing; serviceable; sighing; beating; impotent; fitful; quickening; petulant; winged; clinging; weary; lowered; treacherous; awakening; billowy; warring; fickle; life-breathing; unseen; frolic; screaming; dull; illuminated; sole; buffeting; eddying; gathering; marsh-bred; evil; murmuring; swift-winged; merciful; idle; sounding; sweeping; false; rainless; hot; stormy; furious; powerful; withering; warbling; frosty; surly; wave-building; parching; burdened; ungovernable; suffocating; burning; shrieking; repining; stray; drying; unwholesome; inconstant; soothed; mighty; worn-out; unfettered; prophetic; rushing; unbreathed; vagrant; lazy; summer; icy; unleashed; pious; relentless; hungry; odorous; cold; riotous; mounting; intermitting; lapsing; insulting; invisible; laughing; morning; voiceless; howling; translucent; stifling; lifting; visiting; speaking; wicked; tainted; chainless; forgetting; nimble; noble; envious; endless; blustering; mindless; melodious; life-breathing.

verbs

bear on— breast—; expose to—; harness—; ride—; ripple in—; sniff—; soar on—; still —; —abates; —assails; —bites; —blasts; —blusters; —breathes; —buffets; —caresses; —chants; —chills; —s conflict; —cuts; —dallies; —diminishes; —disturbs; —enfolds; —etches; —extinguishes; —grieves; —howls; —hums; —knifes; —lashes; — moans; —mourns; —murmurs; —rages; — rakes; —ranges; —rattles; —roars; — ruffles; —rustles; —scatters; —scourges; — shrieks; —sighs; —sings; —slaps; —slashes; —smites; —snaps; —soughs; —stings; —strips; —sweeps; —swells; —swirls; — threatens; —tugs; —twists; —uproots; —

veers; —wafts; —wails; —wanders; — whines; —whips; —whispers; —whistles; —winnows; shelter from—.

(See gale, blizzard, air, breeze.)

WIND (v)

adverbs

tortuously; sinuously; picturesquely; intricately; monotonously; incessantly.

(See coil, curve.)

WINDMILL

verbs

agitate—; becalm—; drive—; employ—; outmode—; —churns; —circumvolves; — clatters; —s dot; —flaps; —gyrates; — quivers; —revolves; —rotates; —spins; — swirls; —twirls; —whirls.

(See propeller.)

WINDOW

adjectives

embayed; downy; hallowed; eye-like; stained-glass; pictured; foul; shattered; gaping; modern; prominent; bay; oriel; goggle-eyed; mullioned; iron-barred; steamy; irregular; lofty; filmy; diamond-paned; jeweled; dusky; glittering; dark; eastern; grimy; shuttered; thick; curtained; heat-clouded; latticed; emblazoned; delicate; panoramic; countrified; translucent; unglazed; scullery; fading; outjutting; shop; showy; fitted; rusty; iron-grilled; arched; tight; shut; barred; dingy; transparent; panting; regular; memorial; well-glazed; viewless; moon-lit.

verbs

beat on—; besiege—s; besmirch—; besmudge—; confront—; curtain—; drum on —; frame—; glower through—; jimmy—; peep out—; peer through—; pelt—; pour through—; putty—; rap on—; scour—; screen—; scrutinize through—; seal—; shade—; shatter—; spatter—; view from —; weatherstrip—; yank up (colloq.)—; — admits; —affords; —discloses; —glitters; — rattles; —vents; —ventilates.

(See glass, opening.)

WINDOW-PANE

adjectives

shining; grimy; well-fitted; dirt-streaked.

WINDY

adverbs

gustily; terribly; fatally; alarmingly; ominously; frigidly; freezingly; hotly; bitterly;

scorchingly; dreadfully; curiously; increasingly; cruelly; bitterly; bitingly; cuttingly; deucedly; plaguedly; infernally.

WINE

adjectives

diluted; sepulchral; generous; home-brewed; scuppernong; fierce; costly; agitated; raging; nectareous; new; copious; opulent; thick-purpled; straining; windy; heady; wholesome; fermented; medicated; mirthful; remembering; resplendent; inspiring; split; murmuring; heart-warming; splashing; foaming; frothing; forbearing; glimmering; palmy; enchanted; unmingled; fiery.

verbs

age—; brew—; chill—; cure in—; derive —from; distil—; ferment into—; gulp—; guzzle—; heat with—; imbibe—; ply with —; quaff—; reek of—; regale with—; savor —; sip—; sour—; swill—; value—; —animates; —dulls; —enlivens; —exhilarates; —flows; —flushes; —heats; —inflames; — inspires; —inspirits; —putrefies; —relaxes; —revives; —stimulates; —tempts; —warms; —intoxicates.

(See beverage, alcohol, liquor, champagne, beer.)

WING (*v*)

adverbs

gaily; sublimely; tirelessly; gracefully; joyously; unflaggingly; angelically; serenely; powerfully.

(See fly, float.)

WINGS
(*general*)

adjectives

leathern; curbed; trustless; joyous; fiery; hovering; glad; crumpled; snowy; divine; speckled; untiring; budding; light; steady; spacious; gleaming; huge; shadowy; flagging; redoubled; errant; overhanging; vibrating; folded; fateful; peaceful; rushing; silken; scare-crow; glowing; restless; futile; celestial; peerless; feeble; odoriferous; linen; fluttering; expanded; wide-open; invisible; noiseless; slow; laboring; winnowing; swift-rushing; feathered; untried; reverberate; mighty; motionless; fearless; aggressive; plume-plucked; sumptuous; wandering; wavering; dusky; sheltering; grisly; joyful; dawn-white; intended; outspread; rich; ruffled; viewless; hurrying;

trembling; filmy; ebon; languid; nimble; dewy; aerial; twinkling; fanning; aurora; oaring; angelic; cherubic; parental; luminous; airy; unhallowed; immortal; overshadowing; gelid; moving; murmurous; gorgeous; quivering; outstretched; healing; unsustaining; enchanted; gauzy; jealous; unconquerable; multicolored; daedal; drooping; serene; expanded; inconstant; sunny; shower-struck; thunderous; rugged; sounding; unfledged; mealy; gaudy; velvet; fairy; shadowing; glassy; parted; tremulous; glossy; imprisoned; downy; sportive; swift; wheeling; laden; clanking; dyedusty; unconfined; quickening; mutable; radiant; shrouding; rustling; bruised; agile; dipping; merciful; melancholy; blessed; shivering; glancing; quivering.

verbs

clip—; disable—; flap—; flit on—; fracture —; gather beneath—; hover on—; lend—; pluck—; preen—; prune—; singe—; soar on—; sprout—; strengthen—; take to—; try —; tuck under—; waft on—; —beat; — droop; —enable; —enfold; —flag; —flutter; —liberate; —quiver; —rustle; —wither.

WINGS
(*parts of a building*)

verbs

add—; explore—; extend into—; face—; flank—; gain access to—; haunt—; install —; level—; partition—; raze—; renovate —; restore—; seal—; shout from—; skirt —; skulk in—; view from—; —adjoin; — annex; —append; —project; —supplement.

(See passage, addition.)

WINK

adjectives

single; significant; unfatherly; lasting; cunning; impudent; sly; furtive; suggestive; pitying.

verbs

burlesque—; discern—; exaggerate—; exchange—s; swap—s (colloq.); tip—to; — allures; —amuses; —beckons; —beguiles; — betokens; —conveys; —denotes; —discloses; —distorts; —distracts; —entices; —expresses; —flirts; —indicates; —lures; —passes between; —prompts; —warns.

(See look, grin.)

adverbs

coyly; triumphantly; significantly; wickedly; broadly; saucily; cunningly; impudently: furtively; suggestively.

(See blink, overlook.)

WINNER

adjectives

outstanding; capable; bread; practical; consistent.

verbs

acclaim—; announce—; applaud—; award to—; crown—; declare—; dispute—; emerge —; entertain—; fete—; glorify—; hail—; herald—; honor—; judge—; proclaim—; publicize—; reward—; —annexes; —profits; —reaps; —surmounts.

(See champion, hero, conqueror.)

WINSOME

adverbs

bonnily; sweetly; consciously; happily; merrily; rosily; graciously; innocently; childishly; youthfully; quietly; laughingly; irresistibly; wholly; alluringly; incomparably; daintily; airily; blithely; wholesomely; truly.

WINTER

adjectives

withered; rough; tedious; semi-arctic; dreadful; belated; rude; terrible; dreary; oblivious; laggard; bitter; brown; collapsing; stern; grand; dumb; dogged; brilliant; fatal; weeping; immortalizing; veritable; polar; trembling; monstrous; cheerless; unearthly; oppressive.

verbs

approach—; evade—; survive—; usher in —; —benumbs; —bites; —blankets; — blasts; —blights; —cloaks; —continues; — declines; —exterminates; —frosts; —glistens; —grips; —impoverishes; —nips; — persists; —presses; —relaxes; —roars; — wanes; —whips across.

(See cold, blizzard, storm, fall.)

WINTRY

adverbs

bracingly; bitterly; invigoratingly; snappily; nippingly; frigidly; delightfully; pleasantly; gloriously; picturesquely; delightfully; freezingly; unpleasantly; bleakly; barely.

WIPE (v)

adverbs

gently; timidly; sedately; quietly; hastily; mechanically; cautiously; medicinally.

(See whisk, obliterate.)

WIRE

adjectives

vertical; braided; flaxen; silver; tattered; telephone; leased; old-fashioned; singing; magnetic; envious; flexible; gilded; cunning.

verbs

base—; coat—; encase—; entwine—; fish with—; insulate—; tape—; —binds; — braces; —communicates with; —conveys; —electrifies; —furnishes; —hums; —reinforces; —transmits; —vibrates.

(See cable.)

WIRY

adverbs

inexhaustibly; sturdily; huskily; indefatigably; untiringly; dependably; wonderfully; amazingly; unbelievably; marvellously.

WISDOM

adjectives

divine; slow; memorable; infinite; wasted; practical; united; quaint; astute; stupendous; assimilable; incomparable; weighty; unseasonable; smiling; ancient; surpassing; calculating; revered; peculiar; limitless; protecting; profound; powerless; worldly; polished; political; moral; heavenly; determined; rich; presumptuous; ripe; deep; aphoristic; sufficient; Magian; supreme; collective; gnomic; honest; dark; musical; parabolical; selfsame; cunning; divine; mature; inner; magisterial; earthly; passion-starved; sifted; ruthless; superhuman; eternal; detestable; conceited; whimsy; sinister; crooked; undefiled; incomprehensible; pointed; prophetic; modest; housewifey; vulgar; fair; just.

verbs

accumulate—; belittle—; bow to—; challenge—; cloak—; conceal—; disclose—; distil—from; doubt—; enthrone in—; garner—; impugn—; inspire with—; invoke—; judge—; lack—; manifest—; partake of—; require—; school in—; seek—; simulate—; steep in—; temper with—; unfold—; yield

to—; —decrees; —guides; —ripens; —
rules; —warns.

(See information, philosophy, erudition,
learning, intelligence, enlightenment, knowledge.)

WISE
adverbs

infinitely; unassailably; astutely; incomparably; surpassingly; particularly; ripely; expertly; sufficiently; supremely; honestly;
darkly; cunningly; cleverly; divinely; magisterially; genially; ruthlessly; eternally; detestably; whimsically; significantly; pointedly; prophetically; affectionately; modestly;
indubitably; scarcely; financially; discreetly; practically; profoundly; politically; usually; selfishly; surprisingly; undeniably;
instinctively; intuitively; sensibly; judicially; capably; sagaciously; acutely; intelligently; sagely; cannily; coolly; equitably;
solidly; discerningly.

WISE-CRACKING
adverbs

ridiculously; entertainingly; divertingly;
amusingly; cleverly; nonsensically; comically; continually; crazily; smartly; clownishly; drolly; ludicrously; facetiously; waggishly; ridiculously.

WISH
adjectives

ardent; pious; gnawing; lifelong; reasonable; earnest; idle; faint; conscious; homicidal; audible; changing; vague; unrealized; cruel; forbidden; utmost; eager; doleful; docile; distinct; avaricious; fondest;
irreconcilable; unaccomplished; slight; irrational; lawless; humble; incestuous; willful; repressed; poor; petty; inordinate; dignified; urgent; ambitious; sensual; venturous; fervent; careless; vehement; added; repressed; ardent; fleeting; anxious; dying;
granted; dominant; feeble; foolish; dubious; helpless; passing; pious.

verbs

abandon—; accede to—; achieve—; acquiesce to—; anticipate—; assent to—; betray—; cater to—s; comply with—; conceive—; convey—; defy—s; disclose—; entertain—; express—; favor—; fulfill—;
govern—; grant—; gratify—; harbor—;
honor—; indicate—; indulge—; inform of
—; manifest—; mask—; override—; real-

ize—; repress—; satisfy—; submit to—;
subordinate—; uphold—; voice—; yield to
—; —consumes; —materializes; —prevails.

(See desire, want, need.)

WISH (v)
adverbs

heartily; devoutly; earnestly; ardently; solemnly; fervently; craftily; seriously; deliberately; viciously; conscientiously; piously;
fondly; irrationally; vehemently; foolishly;
vainly.

(See desire, want.)

WISP
adjectives

stringy; dewy; lazy.

WISTFULNESS
adjectives

pathetic; queer; tearful.

WIT
adjectives

licentious; shallow; out-of-fashion; undergraduate; blunted; scholarly; fresh; mellow; simple; bitter; obscene; mighty; sarcastic; keen; sprightly; mobile; caustic;
courteous; admirable; perplexed; mixed;
sparkling; comic; foolish; open; fastidious;
paradoxical; sparkling; prodigal; unstrain-
ed; inexhaustible; insidious; conversational;
vigorous; shrewd; homely; quick; trenchant; various (pl); inimitable; threadbare;
human; metaphysic; crack-brained; unseasonable; native; loyal; microscopic; shattered; merciless; strayed; rude; aimless;
sharpened; diabolic; assured; fouled; fog-
ged; worthless; acidulous; sluggish; sudden; acute; dextrous; light; confounded;
spontaneous; verbal; alert; subtle; delicate;
unpremeditated; ebullient; satirical; airy;
incomparable; exhilarating; eminent; unmatched; vulgar; ready.

verbs

clothe in—; dampen—; display—; draw—;
dull—; exhibit—; grasp—; infuse—; inject
—; kindle—; match—; pervert—; refine—;
scatter—; sharpen—; tinge with—; —
amuses; —beguiles; —bores; —cuts; —delights; —flashes; —flourishes; —flowers; —
flows; —penetrates; —rebounds; —scathes;
—scintillates; —shines; —sparkles; —totters; —victimizes.

(See understanding, humor, banter, repartee, witticism.)

WITCH

adjectives

soul-killing; potent; wrinkled; foul; reputed.

WITCHCRAFT

verbs

charge with—; condemn—; delve into—; embrace—; employ—; exercise—; explode —; hang for—; practise—; resort to—; suspect of—; —bewitches; —charms; — conjures up; —enchants; —flourishes; — intrigues; —mesmerizes; —presages; employ—; exercise—.

(See enchantment, magic, mysticism.)

WITCHERY

adjectives

dear; languorous; traditional; strange; romantic.

WITHDRAW (v)

adverbs

honorably; modestly; steadily; definitely; hostilely; apologetically; involuntarily; mysteriously; courteously; formally; gracefully; shamefacedly; noiselessly; precipitately; unmolestedly; pusillanimously.

(See retreat, retract.)

WITHDRAWAL

adjectives

timely; unmolested; contemporaneous; early.

verbs

advise—; advocate—; announce—; attend —; begrudge—; contemplate—; consider—; curtail—; promote—; recommend—; regard —; shrink from—; subject to—; —closes; — devoids; —disturbs; —ebbs; —evacuates; —strains; —taxes.

(See removal, departure, evacuation.)

WITHERED

adverbs

pitiably; helplessly; remarkably; surprisingly; gauntly; desperately; paralytically; perceptibly.

WITHHOLD (v)

adverbs

deliberately; purposely; mystically; insidiously; venomously; hatefully; relentlessly; tenaciously; perfidiously.

(See deny, refuse.)

WITHSTAND (v)

adverbs

manfully; gallantly; vigorously; staunchly; stalwartly; admirably; perpetually; economically; boldly.

(See resist, oppose.)

WITLESS

adverbs

provokingly; utterly; absolutely; helplessly; crazily; pitiably; pathetically; miserably; wretchedly; piteously; allegedly; vexatiously.

WITNESS

adjectives

mute; trustworthy; laughing; material; missing; singular; actual; striking; eloquent; perjured; divers (pl); long-lost; perpetual; impartial; terror-stricken; awful; creditable; reluctant; silent; surviving; alljudging; eternal; too-willing; followed; crushing; credible; thorough; steadfast; relentless; petrified; sympathizing.

verbs

bear—; bias—; bribe—; cite—; coach—; confront with—; contradict—; cross-examine —; intimidate—; introduce—; prejudice—; present—; produce—; rake up—s; suborn —; subpoena—; summon—; —acknowledges; —alleges; —attests to; —authenticates; —avers; —bears on; —beholds; — certifies; —confesses; —confirms; —contends; —contradicts; —corroborates; — damns; —endorses; —evidences; —falsifies; —impugns; —perjures; —pictures; — pleads; —records; —reports; —reveals; — seals; —signs; —substantiates; —supports; —testifies; —upholds; —verifies; —views; —vouches for; —vows.

(See observer, bystander, evidence.)

WITTICISM

adjectives

characteristic; pert; neat; coarse; constrained; obscene; painful; withering.

verbs

banter—s; evoke—; exchange—s; flash—; indulge in—s; roar at—; trade—s; —bites; —glitters; —retorts; —salts; —scintillates; —sparkles; —spices; —stings.

(See wit, joke, jest, humor.)

WITTY

adverbs

profoundly; divertingly; amusingly; delightfully; uncommonly; extremely; mischievously; comically; roguishly; mischievously; scintillatingly; brilliantly; splendidly; unusually; broadly; drolly; facetiously; fatuously; pleasantly; smartly; whimsically; waggishly; cruelly; merrily; fantastically; sparklingly.

WIZARD

adjectives

reputed; doting; egregious; glancing; baffled; bounteous; aged.

WOE

adjectives

silent; unavailing; gloomy; unwieldy; unutterable; comic; lesser; intolerable; outward; imaginative; holy; speechless; bitter; endless; tedious; unreposing; human; immedicable; life-consuming; harboring; guilty; pious; tedious; immortal; irredeemable; wearied; earthly; conscious; unprevailing; nameless; imaginary; discordant; impending; eternal; black; worthless; outward; everlasting; mortal; incommunicable; ending; thankless; stagnant; perplexing; lofty; great; rank; inexpressible; constant; wanton; insuperable.

verbs

afflict with—; allay—; alleviate—; babble —; bewail—; bow in—; burden with—; ease—; exclaim—; hide—; induce—; nurse —; occasion—; overcome with—; palliate —; predict—; recompense for—; remedy—; sink into—; spin out—; suffer—; triumph over—; whimper of—; —curses; —lacerates; —overwhelms; —rends; —saddens; —sours; —wracks; —wrings.

(See grief, sadness, sorrow.)

WOEFUL

adverbs

sadly; dolefully; habitually; utterly; wretchedly; helplessly; terribly; naturally; pathetically; pitiably.

WOLF

verbs

pay a bounty on—s; —s assemble; —s chase; —s devastate; —s infest; —s overpower; — preys on; —prowls; —pursues; —ranges; —runs down; —skulks; —slinks; —snarls; —stalks; —s terrorize; —s troop; —s visit. (See animal.)

WOLVES

adjectives

famished; snapping; snarling; mangled; bloodless; shrewd; rabid; human; ravenous; fearful; genteel; universal.

WOMAN

adjectives

abject; accomplished; admirable; affected; affectionate; aggressive; ambitious; amiable; appealing; aproned; artful; ashy-hued; attractive; beautiful; awe-stricken; baby-faced; bedraggled; bedridden; bent; bewitching; brawny; bread-winning; brilliant; broken-hearted; bustling; careworn; celebrated; charming; chaste; childless; clear-eyed; clear-headed; clever; clinging; comely; compassionate; composed; consonant; corpulent; courageous; crabby; crisp; cruel; curious; cynical; decent; decrepit; defenseless; delicate; desireful; determined; devout; discontented; distinguished; dutiful; dowdyish; dressed; earthly; economical; ecstatic; elaborate; elegant; embroidering; emerging; enduring; energetic; equable; erring; estimable; excellent; exemplary; fair-faced; fanatic; fantastic; fascinating; fashionable; fervent; feverish; flashy; flat; foolish; forsaken; fragile; frantic; frightened; fruitful; frigid; frowsy; full-blossomed; garrulous; gaunt; ghastly; glamorous; glittering; gray; grim; grizzled; handsome; happy; hard-faced; hard-worked; headstrong; haughty; heartless; helpless; heroic; hesitating; high-minded; home-keeping; home-loving; hypersensitive; hysterical; idealistic; illiterate; imperious; impish; implacable; importunate; impressible; incorrigible; indefatigable; independent; indigent; industrious; infidel; informal; insipid; intelligent; intrepid; jealous; jocose; large-souled; lewd; limping; listless; lithe; little; lonely; loitering; long; loose; loquacious; lovely; lumpish; lustful; managing; marble-limbed; mean; middle-aged; mincing; miserable; miserly; modern; modest; morbid; mortal; motherly; much-loved; mulatto; mystic; new; nice; noble; observant; odious; old; over-virtuous; over-worked; over-wrought; pale; perfidious; perjured; pernicious; pinched; pitiless; plain-featured; plainly-dressed; plump; poor; preeminent; presumptuous; pretty; promiscuous; prosaic;

prosperous; proud; prudent; querulous; radiant; rapacious; remarkable; repentant; resolute; respected; reticent; rheumatic; romantic; sad-eyed; scrawny; seductive; self-loving; sensible; sensitive; serene-eyed; serious; shabby; shadowy; shallow; showy; shrewd; shriveled; silken-tressed; silly; slatternly; slender; slim; smooth-limbed; sorrowful; sour-faced; sporting; spotless; square-browed; stalwart; stout; striking; sumptuous; super-annuated; superior; sweet; sweet-voiced; tactful; tattling; tawdry; tenacious; tender; terrified; timid; timorous; tremendous; tremulous; unconstant; uncultivated; uncultured; unenlightened; unescorted; unkempt; unprotected; unworldly; vain; versatile; virtuous; vivacious; warm-hearted; wayside; wayward; weak-willed; wearied; wearisome; weeping; weird; well-dressed; well-favored; white-faced; wilted; witchlike; withered; witty; wooden; worldly; wretched; wrinkled; young.

WOMANLY
adverbs
truly; sweetly; graciously; delightfully; comfortingly; quietly; gracefully; compassionately; serenely; gently; hospitably; pleasantly; naturally; unusually; particularly; remarkably; surprisingly; unexpectedly; attractively; extremely.

WOMB
adjectives
solemn; hollow; tortured; unfathomed; shuddering; fruitful.

verbs
abscess—; develop in—; displace—; empty —; enter—; infect—; incise—; lacerate—; manipulate—; retain in—; support—; ulcerate—; —atrophies; —bends; —contracts; — discharges; —dilates; —dislodges; —distends; —encloses; —engenders; —enlarges; —expels; —falls; —involutes; —manipulates; —pulsates; —quickens; —relaxes; — sags; —yields.

WOMEN
verbs
appeal to—; ban—; bar—; cater to—; charm—; consort with—; defame—; defile —; degrade—; disparage—; emancipate—; enchant—; enfranchise—; enlighten—; liberate—; persecute—; rally—; rape—;

ravish—; spurn—; sway—; typify—; uplift —; —bear; —beget; —beguile; —charm; —conceive; —flock about; —inflame; — labor; —mature; —provide; —nag; —scold.
(See damsel, girl, daughter.)

WONDER
adjectives
natural; varied (pl); small; breathing; envious; utmost; ignorant; lying; listening; breathless; midnight; despairing; sickened; perplexed; sullen; admiring; prodigious; curling; universal; elderly; loving; ornithological; vague; admiring; scornful; peerless; unreasoning; troubled; stupid; reverent; unimaginative; dramatic; lustrous; incredulous; estimable; unearthed; perpetual; isolated; speculative; special; snaky; late; scientific; supernatural; overwhelming; comedy; half-reproachful; silent; effusive.

verbs
acclaim—; bare—s; delve into—s; disclose —s; excite—; explore—s; gain—; gape at —; hail—; inspire—; marvel at—; occasion —; overcome with—; reveal—; stare with —; strike with—; —allures; —amazes; — astounds; —awes; —baffles; —bewilders; —dazzles; —dumbfounds; —mystifies; — petrifies; —startles.
(See curiosity, astonishment, incredulity, admiration, miracle, marvel.)

WONDER (v)
adverbs
confusedly; desperately; wistfully; anxiously; idly; uneasily; vaguely; irrelevantly; distractedly; detachedly; abjectly; capriciously; gloomily; blindly; ironically; uncomfortably; dazedly; sneeringly; miserably; enviously.
(See marvel, amaze.)

WONDERFUL
adverbs
utterly; amazingly; spectacularly; mysteriously; magically; unsurpassably; incredibly; fantastically.

WOO (v)
adverbs
roughly; affectionately; tenderly; timorously; ardently; vigorously; genially; subtly; lackadaisically; abortively; eloquently; earnestly; amusingly.
(See court, love.)

verbs

comb—; encamp in—; flank—; forsake—; frequent—; infest—; inhabit—; nest in—; prowl—; roam—; rove—; scour—; shelter in—; skirt—; thread through—; —blooms; —extends; —flowers; —obscures; —ranges; —screens; —shades; —shadows; —veils.

(See jungle, forest.)

WOOD
(*general*)

adjectives

sheltering; bushy; stormy; untrodden: boundless; split; green; tangled; sportive; intricate; wild; solemn; extensive; rippling; swampy; sonorous; violet; echoing; odorous; interminable; scented; ancient; plundered; darkling; dense; vernal; thorny; glowing; gloomy; snow-choked; mistrustful; rooky; soft-textured; crimson; sleeping; unfrequented; pathless; stilly; tuneful; dusky; rare; volumned; native; visionless; roundbosomed; primitive; fragrant; budding; naked; shaded; resinous; haughty; high; beechen; desolate; shining; wet; widestretching; sun-bedappled; trackless; dimseen; distant; unshorn; ragged; aromatic; branching; rank; intervening; thick; ruined; gray-colored; delightsome; changing; hanging; whispering; shaggy; surrounding; dewy; variegated; chestnut; prehistoric; waving; precious; mazy; legendary; oracular; musical; autumnal; pheasant; inaccessible; ruthless; vast; competing; dreadful; deaf; dull; virgin; fatal; magnificent; wild; primeval.

WOOD
(*material*)

verbs

bevel—; carve in—; char—; chisel—; compress—; debark—; enkindle—; hack—; hew —; gather—; glean—; level—; model in—; plan—; sand—; sear—; shatter—; shave—; splinter—; whittle—; —blazes; —braces; —erodes; —hardens; —petrifies; —rots; —supports.

(See forest, carpenter, board, log, timber.)

WOODCHUCK

verbs

—hole; —burrows; —claws; —damages; —defends; —digs; —holes up; —pops into its hole; —preys on; —pursues; —rips; —tears; —slays; —snatches; —waddles away.

(See animal.)

WOODCOCK

verbs

bag—; decoy—; gun for—; —booms;—defies; —flits; —flocks; —glides; —honks; —inflates; —nips; —probes; —squats; —whirs; —zigzags.

(See bird.)

WOODED

adverbs

densely; thickly; valuably; wonderfully; profitably; beautifully; venerably; gently; sparsely; thinly; carefully; scientifically; intelligently; selectively; variously; impenetrably; gratefully; pleasantly.

WOODPECKER

verbs

—axes; —bores; —chisels; —clings; —digs; —hammers; —laps; —pecks; —prevents; —protects; —taps.

(See bird.)

WOOL

adjectives

soft; unbleached; mineral; ticklish; prickly.

verbs

bear—; brush—; card—; comb—; line with —; market—; oil—; rumple—; shear—; sort—; value—; weave of—; yield—; —affords; —comforts; —frays; —insures; —shelters; —shields.

(See cloth, leather, cotton.)

WORD

adjectives

abhorred; abounding; abrupt; abused: action; agonizing; altered; amazing; ambiguous; amusing; angry; appropriate; archaic; ardent; articulate; astonishing; audible; balanced; barbarous; barbed; bare; barren; bawled; biographical; biting; bitter; blameful; bland; blasphemous; blazing; blessed; bludgeoning; blundering; blunt; boastful; brave; bracketed; brawling; brotherly; brief; broken; burning; cabalistic; careless; caressing; casual; celebrated; certain; ceremonial; chanted; cheering; cherished; choice; choleric; coarse; coaxing; coined; comfortable; comforted; common-sense; comprehensive; conciliatory; conquering; considerate; consoling; constructive; contumelious; conventional; cordial; courteous; cruel; cunning; cutting; dainty; dangerous; daring; deadly; deathful; deathless; debasing; defensive; deliberate; delicate; deprecatory; derisive; descriptive; devastating; devout; dismal; disputatious; distinct; distracted; divided; doubtful; dread; dreadful; dying; eager; earnest; eloquent; elusive; emotional; emphatic; empty; encouraging; endearing; enriched; equivocal; eternal; explanatory; excusing; exotic; evangelical; explicit; extended; exultant; faithful; faltering; famed; fancy; farewell; fatal; favorite; feeble; fervent; fiery; fitting; flaming; flat; flattering; flowery; flying; foul; frequent; frivolous; futile; general; generous; gentle; genial; gigantic; glorious; glowing; golden; good; Gordian; graceful; gracious; grand; grateful; grave; great; half-extinguished; happy; hard; harsh; hasty; healing; heart-easing; heartrending; hesitant; hideous; high; high-born; homely; honest; honeyed; honorable; honored; hopeful; horrible; hot; household; hyphenated; identical (pl); idle; ill; imbedded; impious; imposing; impressive; inappropriate; inarticulate; incarnate; incautious; incoherent; incongruous; indignant; inexcusable; insane; inspiring; insulated; insulting; interchangeable; interrogative; iron; irrevocable; irritable; isolated; jeering; joking; just; keenly-felt; light; lilting; liquid; living; loved; loving; low-pitched; low-spoken; low-toned; luminous; lying; magic; magnanimous; majestic; matchless; meandering; meaningful; measured; meditated; mellifluous; mellow; melting; memorable; merciful; mere; metaphorical; meticulous; mighty; modified; momentary; momentous; monosyllabic; monotonous; moral; mortal; motherly; moving; much-abused; musical; muttered; mystic; naive; naughty; nauseous; nice; necromantic; noble; noisy; noted; obscure; obsolete; odd; odious; offending; oft-repeated; ominous; oppressive; orthodox; overpowering; passing; passionate; pathetic; peerless; perennial; persuasive; petulant; pithy; pitiful; plain; plausible; pleading; plighted; plump; plundered; poetic; poignant; polysyllable; pompous; portentous; potent; precious; precise; pregnant; provocative; quaint; qualified; queer; quenchless; quick; quickening; quiet; rabble-rousing; racy; radical; ragged; rallying; rapturous; rare; rash; ravishing; ready; reasoning; reconciling; recreative; reread; reproachful; repulsive; resonant; restless; revengeful; ringing;

rough; rude; sacred; scientific; scornful; scurrilous; seafaring; sea-going; senseless; serious; serviceable; shy; shameful; sharp; significant; simple; simple-seeming; single; smooth; sneering; sober; soft; soggy; solemn; soothing; soulful; spoken; standardized; stemmed; stifled; stinging; stirring; stormy; strange; strong; stumbling; submissive; successful; sugared; sulphurous; sumptuous; superfluous; sweet; swelling; sympathetic; talismanic; tender; thick; thin; thoughtful; thought-up; threatening; torrential; touching; transparent; tremulous; trite; trenchant; tricky; tumbled; twanging; ugly; unalterable; unchosen; uncomprehended; uncompromising; undecided; understandable; unfamiliar; unfeeling; unflattering; unforgettable; ungrateful; unhappy; unheeded; universal; unkind; unlucky; unmistakable; unmodest; unmodulated; unmoving; unpleasant; unspeakable; unusual; unmuttered; unwinged; unwonted; useless; uttered; vague; veritable; vilified; vituperative; vivid; vulgar; wandering; warning; weak; weird; whirling; whispering; wild; wily; wise; witty; woeful; wondrous; woolly; worthless; woven; written; yearning; superlative; suppliant; suspicious.

WORD (v)

adverbs

courteously; succinctly; cautiously; ingeniously; deftly; insidiously; theoretically; meticulously; religiously; musically; quaintly; modestly; vaguely; vividly; sulphurously.

(See express, speak.)

WORDS

verbs

accept—; amend—; blink at—; boggle over —; breathe—; burble (colloq.)—; clip—; coax—; comprehend—; confirm—; conjure up —; contradict—; convey—; coo—; coin —; cram—; crowd—; cull—; debase—; decipher—; define—; derive—; detect—; digest—; discharge—; dissect—; distort—; dog—; drawl—; drink—; emphasize—; employ—; encounter—; enunciate—; epitomize—; exchange—; exemplify—; fear—; flounder for—; fondle—; forge—; fumble with—; grasp—; grope for—; hang on—; hum—; hurl—; interpose—; interpret—; interrupt—; loose—; measure—; meditate upon—; mince—; misuse—; modify—; mould—; mouth—; muffle—; mumble—; play on—; ponder—; prune down—; quote

—; recall—; record—; reject—; relay—; retract—; rob of—; scrutinize—; search for —; seek—; set forth—; shun—; shy at—; snap at—; snarl—; span—; speak—; spread —; stem—; strain—; string—; stumble through—; swallow—; sweep—; tangle—; tap—; trade—; toss—; toy with—; transcribe—; utter—; verify—; voice—; weave —; weigh—; wrench—; —add; —arrest; —awaken; —boom; —burst; —cluster; —come forth; —crash; —designate; —drift; —drone; —echo; —elude; —embed; —embody; —escape; —expound; —express; —fail; —filter; —flash; —fling; —float; —flow; —gull; —haunt; —imply; —imprison; —inspire; —leak out; —make sense; —overwhelm; —play; —pour; —rebound; —resuscitate; —ring; —rise; —salve; —set forth; —signify; —shower; —slur; —stab; —stare; —sting; —storm; —strangle; —suggest; —surge; —sweep; —symbolize; —toll; —trail; —trickle out; —vibrate; —waft; —wing; —drip.

(See idiom, metaphor, derivative, expression, thought.)

WORDY

adverbs

endlessly; tiresomely; inexpertly; grossly; intolerably; disappointingly; incomprehensibly; monotonously; wearisomely; impossibly; tediously; repetitiously; vilely; confoundedly; unsatisfactorily; crudely.

WORK

adjectives

able; abortive; absurd; accessible; accomplished; admired; aesthetic; aggressive; airy; alleged; ambitious; analogous; anatomical; architectural; arduous; artistic; authentic; authoritative; barbarous; beneficent; biographical; blessed; blundering; brain-directed; celebrated; bread-winning; calamitous; caretaking; catalogue; chamber; changeless; characteristic; charming; cherished; choicest; clean; clerical; colossal; commemorative; compassionate; comprehensive; conscienceless; conscientous; conspicuous; constructive; contemporary; continued; creative; creditable; critical; damp; defective; dental; desolate; destructive; desultory; development; dignified; diplomatic; diversified; domestic; dramatic; dreary; drudgery; durable; easy; ecclesiastical; editorial; egocentric; elaborate; elegant; embroidered; entertaining; epoch-making; exact; executive; exhaustive; experimental; explicable; expressive; exquisite; extemporaneous; extension; exterior; extravagant; fanciful; fascinating; fatiguing; fiendish; finicky; flourishing; free-lance; frenzied; ghastly; gigantic; graceful; grim; hand; harassing; hard; harmonious; hasty; hazardous; heartbreaking; helpless; home; hospital; humblest; humorous; idealistic; immediate; immoral; immortal; impassioned; imperishable; important; imposing; impressive; incomparable; indifferent; individual; ingenious; inimitable; inner; intellectual; intensive; interesting; irregular; irreligious; irreproachable; journalistic; laboratory; laborious; lacework; lax; licentious; literary; lofty; long-baffled; luminous; lyrical; majestic; makeshift; manifold (pl); masterful; masterly; mature; mechanical; memorable; menial; meretricious; meritorious; merry; monumental; multitudinous (pl); mystical; mythological; nefarious; new; noble; noted; noteworthy; objective; operative; orchestral; ornamental; outer; painful; patriotic; peaceful; permanent; perpendicular; persistent; philanthropic; philosophic; photographic; pianoforte; pioneer; piquant; pleasant; ponderous; popular; practical; profitable; prose; radiant; redeeming; regretful; remarkable; remunerate; reposing; representative; reproductive; risky; rhapsodical; routine; rudimentary; ruinous; rural; scandalous; sensational; sensitive; serious; sham; shielding; short; shriving; significant; sinful; sinless; solid; solitary; spontaneous; startling; statistical; steady; stellar; stern; subsequent; straightforward; stupendous; substantial; subtle; superficial; supplementary; suspended; symbolic; symphonic; systematic; tasteful; tawdry; technical; tedious; theological; theoretical; ticklish; tiring; titanic; toilsome; tolerable; unaccountable; tragic; unfruitful; unhallowed; uniting; unnecessary; unremitting; unsatisfactory; unstinted; unworthy; uplifting; urgent; valorous; variegated; valuable; vigorous; vital; vocal; voluntary; wearisome; well-composed; wholesome; winter; wondrous; worldly; master.

verbs

abandon—; acclaim—; accomplish—; buckle down to—; carry on—; christen—; comprehend—; conceive—; conclude—; delegate—; deprive of—; detail—; differentiate—; digest—; discredit—; distinguish—; dive into—; drug with—; efface—; embark upon

—; enlarge—; execute—; flinch at—; force
—; foster—; fulfill—; hamper—; hinder—;
immerse in—; impair—; improve—; investigate—; issue—; knock off—; mar—; master
—; merge—; minimize—; nurture—; outdo
—; perfect—; perform—; pigeonhole—;
prosecute—; provide—; reconstruct—; recount—; regulate—; remunerate for—;
retard—; shirk—; simplify—; submit—;
supplement—; suspend from—; swamp with
—; terminate—; thrive on—; undo—; wind
up with—; wrestle with—; —blunts; —
ceases; —commences; —confirms; —confounds; —constitutes; —devolves; —eases;
—encumbers; —engrosses; —ennobles; —
entails; —exacts; —extolls; —galls; —
glorifies; —honors; —imbeds; —involves;
—inspires; —overwhelms; —rectifies; —
suspends.

(See drudgery, duty, enterprise, job, labor,
occupation, business, grind.)

WORK (v)
adverbs
diligently; feverishly; passionately; energetically; zealously; automatically; faithfully;
diurnally; persistently; furiously; simultaneously; concertedly; strenuously; indefatigably; minutely; assiduously; prodigiously;
unremittingly; sedulously; spasmodically;
continuously; effectually; exquisitely; harmoniously; independently; conscientiously;
competently; listlessly.

(See labor, toil.)

WORKABLE
adverbs
splendidly; altogether; happily; practically;
conveniently; opportunely; entirely; absolutely; easily; satisfactorily; adequately; actually; readily; luckily.

WORKERS
adjectives
energetic; subservient; mechanical; brisk;
overburdened; copious; deceased; eligible;
subtle; indefatigable; zealous; offending;
routine; faithful; prodigious; bunchy; conservative; inert; chosen; ardent; methodical; swarming; migratory; rotund; rosy;
noble; able-bodied; relief.

verbs
address—; battle—; bind—; discharge—;
engage—; entitle—; exhaust—; exploit—;
fag—; fatigue—; ferret out—; goad—; harangue—; house—; incite—; inveigle—; lock

out—; master—; oust—; oversee—; prod
—; refresh—; regiment—; reimburse—; reinstate—; reward—; ride—; speed—; spur
—; superintend—; —accomplish; —arbitrate; —contribute; —lag; —parade; —pile
into; —plunge into; —relax; —strain; —
strike; —toil; —unionize; —weary.

(See labor, employee, striker.)

WORKMANSHIP
adjectives
exquisite; impeccable; intricate; meticulous;
domestic; experienced; sterling; intrinsic;
reliable; perfect; exacting; gossamer-like;
cumbrous; competent; masterly; expert; cunning; delicate; fine; highest; elaborate; artistic; crude.

WORLD
adjectives
giddy; operatic; expectant; epicurean; outside; drowsy; immense; custom-laden; organic; humming; polite; gloomy; tolerant;
good-tempered; well-breeding; impure; industrial; pagan; demolished; shadowy; unspotted; mighty; unsympathizing; noisy; unending; suffering; romantic; naughty; dim-
eyed; injurious; contemporary; insulted; innumerable (pl); interminable; mundane;
fantastic; unconscious; dissolving; pitiful;
countless (pl); frozen; bustling; spiritual;
intellectual; candid; uncounted (pl); disordered; supernatural; financial; dense; degenerate; commonplace; everyday; sensual;
untraveled; breathing; diagrammed; wondering; invisible; hollow-hearted; crashing;
assembled; unimaginable; fictitious; globular; convex; boisterous; workaday; clamorous; grieved; shaggy; material; flaming;
unseen; busy; turbulent; alien; dingy; congregated; sorrowful; exclusive; neglected;
seething; limited; conscious; benighted; listening; intelligible; contradictory; pulseless;
writhing; famous; teeming; spacious; thinking; unusual; busy; witty; recreant; pendant; frantic; recorded; lazy; working;
manifold; extraordinary; falling; unfamiliar; new-born; atheistic; chilling; arduous;
contemptible; snowy; approving; archetypal; war-convulsed; desert; heaving; unbelieving; quivering; false; monstrous; selfish; despicable; contumelious; fashionable;
angry; inexpressive; rain-wet; fast; moving; distasteful; decomposed; ever-advanc-
ing; godless; hero-worshipping; fighting;
monotonous; corrupted; sin-bound; sympa-

thizing; unremembered; celestial; hoary; altered; heartless; obscure; splendor-winged; divided; fascinating; undiscriminating; literary; careless; censorious; enduring; undisparaged; undespoiled; amphibious; merciless; unfriendly; insipid; infinite; watery; artistic; insecure; imaginative; unfathomable; sphered; warring; carping; commercial; merry; interdependent; well-loved; beautiful; beggared; distraught; sacrilegious; insurgent; shabby; golden; unsteady; dim; mazed; beseiged; offended; ancient; waiting; rough; eugenic; supernatural; external; mechanized; enlightened; white; voiceless; antique; vegetable; unappreciative; practical; ranking; inaccessible; united; boundless; imperfect; mechanistic; resplendent; civilized; panicky; indifferent; simple; violent; unstable; perfumed; ghostly; somber; dream; cautious; feminized; surrounding; spacious; groaning; resplendent; primeval; renovated; too-busy; sublime; thankless; faithless; wide; lampless; apostate; unroofed; war-pliant; hostile; fallen; imperfect; ungoverned.

verbs
bedevil—; befuddle—; benefit—; bestride —; blight—; confront—; consolidate—; contemplate—; convulse—; disease—; dislocate—; doom—; dwarf—; encompass—; enrich—; entangle—; flood—; grace—; heal —; hide from—; ignore—; isolate from—; people—; present to—; proclaim to—; redeem—; reform—; renounce—; revolutionize—; roam—; rock—; shape—; stir—; storm—; struggle with—; survey—; trample on—; transfigure—; triumph over—; withdraw from—; —acclaims; —acknowledges; —collapses; —crumbles; —rejects; —revolves; —slumbers; —teems with; —turns.
(See mankind, humanity, individual, globe, earth, creation, universe.)

WORLDLINESS
verbs
abhor—; achieve—; attain—; declaim—; decry—; denounce—; deplore—; envelop in —; exhibit—; feign—; forsake—; gain—; pretend—; purge of—; quit—; reject—; renounce—; supplant—; wrap in—; —callouses; —centers; —cloaks; —doubts; — hardens; —polishes; —questions; —veneers.
(See erudition, ambition, cynicism, experience.)

WORLDLY
adverbs
godlessly; selfishly; egotistically; covetously; immensely; pitiably; extraordinarily; lazily; contemptibly; deplorably; monstrously; heartlessly; gracelessly; stubbornly; callously; mercenarily; inexplicably; unreasonably; irritatingly; insensately; irreligiously; sacrilegiously; atheistically; irreverently; irrevocably; apostately; horribly; impiously; perversely; fanatically; recklessly; avowedly; blasphemously; profanely; heartbreakingly; grievously; obstinately; obdurately; unhappily; irrationally; unreasonably; openly.

WORM
adjectives
destitute; surfeited; unwholesome; obscene; invisible; lowly; humble; pollution-nourished; sluggish; nameless; voracious; resuscitated; venomous; reluctant; fiery; trodden; dead; crawling; lucky; worthless; velvet; vile.

verbs
angle with—; attract—s; bait with—; crush —; dig for—; excavate for—; hook—; impale—; —s annihilate; —attacks; —bores; —burrows; —creeps; —gnaws; —infects; —pupates; —screws; —slithers; —spirals; —symbolizes; —wriggles.
(See bait, animal.)

WORN
adverbs
shabbily; uselessly; irrecoverably; terribly; naturally; utterly; dingily; undesirably; utterly; pitifully; miserably; dreadfully.

WORRIED
adverbs
unnaturally; nervously; excitedly; terribly; miserably; frantically; pitiably; keenly; significantly; perceptibly; indescribably; deeply; unduly; touchingly; abnormally; naturally; curiously; lamentably; pathetically; ridiculously; ludicrously.

WORRY
adjectives
manifold (pl); mental; faint; territorial; eternal; death-dealing.

verbs
afflict with—; allay—; bear—; beset with —; betray—; dispel—; drown—; experience

—; immerse in—; induce—; occasion—; plunge into—; relieve of—; submerge in—; imburden—; —harasses; —harrows; —haunts; —hounds; —lashes; —oppresses; —plagues; —preys upon; —racks; —rends; —retards; —rings; —shatters; —weighs upon.

(See anxiety, misgivings, liability, care.)

WORRY (v)
adverbs
morbidly; miserably; neurotically; perpetually; abnormally; needlessly; desperately.
(See fret, vex.)

WORSHIP
adjectives
pagan; outward; astral; mystical; inhuman; spiritual; reverent; sane; idealistic; silent; cynical; imploring; coterie; divine; passionate; reverential; ardent; worthy; unhesitating; continual; interrupted; lifelong.

verbs
bow in—; chant—; congregate for—; defile —; desecrate—; dogmatize—; exalt—; intone—; join in—; kneel in—; lead—; perform—; persecute—; rejoice in—; renounce —; ridicule—; ritualize—; scorn—; sing—; —deifies; —exalts; —glorifies; —idolizes; —invokes; —lauds; —supplicates; —survives.

(See cult, devotion, adoration, love, prayer, mass.)

WORSHIP (v)
adverbs
blindly; inconsistently; religiously; solemnly; idolatrously; mystically; reverently; silently; passionately; ardently; continually.
(See adore, reverence.)

WORSHIPERS
adjectives
insensate; false; frenzied; vulgar; idol; heathen; devout.

verbs
address—; awe—; convoke—; electrify—; elevate—; hallow—; inspire—; preach to —; —adore; —beseech; —bow; —deify; —enshrine; —give thanks; —glorify; —invoke; —kneel; —pay homage; —pay tribute; —petition; —prostrate; —revere; —sacrifice; —supplicate; —vow.
(See church-goers, priest, minister.)

WORSHIPFUL
adverbs
fatuously; foolishly; obviously; conspicuously; devotedly; devoutly; faithfully; fanatically; sincerely; gloriously; admirably; ostentatiously; unctuously; smugly; blandly; truly; laudably; pharasaically; humbly; abjectly; adoringly; meekly.

WORTH
adjectives
transcendent; priceless; individual; passing; inestimable; artistic; imaginary; venerable; intrinsic; known; matchless; martial; nameless; sterling; high; unspeakable; additional; spiritual; reverend; divine; ultimate; genuine.

verbs
appraise—; appreciate—; ascertain—; assert—; assess—; attest to—; challenge—; degrade—; derive—from; determine—; disclose—; display—; endow with—; establish —; estimate—; exhibit—; gauge—; judge —; measure—; probe—; prove—; question —; reflect upon—; signify—; stamp—; weigh—; —ascends; —depreciates; —mounts; —skyrockets.
(See value, merit, ability.)

WORTHLESS
adverbs
terribly; undeniably; altogether; absolutely; hopelessly; scandalously; abominably; curiously; peculiarly; outlandishly; trashily; shabbily; miserably; wretchedly; atrociously; completely; contemptibly.

WORTHLESSNESS
verbs
acknowledge—; admit—; balance—; bare —; bemoan—; betray—; bewail—; concede —; consider—; contemplate—; decry—; denounce—; deplore—; divulge—; evidence—; expose—; inveigh against—; lapse into—; mask—; regard—; reveal—; ridicule—; scoff at—; scorn—; stray into—; unveil—.
(See futility, inferiority, inefficiency, mediocrity, stupidity.)

WORTHY
adverbs
completely; utterly; laudably; meritoriously; notably; conspicuously; sincerely; truly; incomparably; surpassingly; extraordinarily; amazingly; obviously; recognizably; manifestly; singularly.

adjectives

sharp; starched; gaping; unprobed; obstinate; desperate; lifelong; unhealed; sterile; sharp; unadvised; stiffening; self-inflicted; dark; bleeding; ancient; external; immedicable; ghastly; fatal; infected; punctured; lacerated; mortal; grievous; suppurating; cruel; serious; aching; frightful; reeking; recurring; raw; numerous (pl); surface; immediate; hideous; disastrous; severe.

verbs

allay—; alleviate—; assuage—; balm—; caress—; cauterize—; cleanse—; disinfect —; drain—; dress—; inflict—; irrigate—; pack—; probe—; soothe—; staunch—; suck —; swab—; weather—; —bleeds; —punctures; —scars.

(See cut, laceration, injury.)

adverbs

indirectly; mortally; spiritually; dangerously; frightfully; cruelly; seriously; severely; critically; sorely; fatally; internally; grievously; hideously; disastrously.

(See hurt, injure.)

adjectives

meek; likely; unusual.

adjectives

bloody; vestry; conjugal; political; brutal.

verbs

arbitrate—; avert—; curb—; curtail—; engage in—; incite—; instigate—; quell—; subdue—; —annoys; —arises; —bickers; —breaches; —clashes; —disputes; —distracts; —diverts; —ebbs; —embroils; —estranges; —jars; —jolts; —shocks; —wanes.

(See brawl, dispute, argument, quarrel.)

adverbs

stridently; vociferously; indignantly; furiously; conjugally; politically; brutally; viciously; vindictively; heatedly; incessantly; jealously; pettishly; argumentatively.

(See quarrel, argue.)

adverbs

snugly; clumsily; punctiliously; impeccably; festively; meticulously; competently; artistically; crudely.

(See cover, conceal.)

adjectives

protective; formless; holiday.

verbs

bind—; cast off—; divest of—; enclose in —; husk—; invest in—; package in—s; penetrate—; pierce—; seal—; shed—; strip off—; superimpose—; —affords; —armors; —envelops; —girds; —insures; —preserves; — protects; —safeguards; —shelters; — shields; —swathes.

(See envelope, lining, cover.)

adjectives

tiger-like; indignant; dead; volcanic; infinite; jealous; immoderate; swollen; righteous; unconscious; intolerable; glutinous; treacherous; mingled; passionate; desolating; whimsical; vindictive; drunken; popular; fiercest; uncaged; chastening; scornful; patient; ill-suppressed; silent; bitter; naked; envious; stormy; celestial; crazy; awakened; relentless; intense; mysterious; helpless; deathless; senile; destructive; parental; eternal; reproachful; unholy; headlong; foolish; revengeful; celebrated; threatening; righteous.

verbs

appease—; brave—; bring to—; burst into —; dampen—; draw—; encounter—; endure—; escape—; explode in—; fire with —; incur—; mollify—; move to—; pacify —; placate—; provoke—; repent—; rouse —; slake—; uncork—; vent—; —abates; — abuses; —bites; —blazes —clouds; —descends upon; —melts; —oppresses; — smoulders.

(See ire, anger, indignation, rage.)

adverbs

desperately; dangerously; inordinately; brutally; ominously; portentously; alarmingly; terribly; frightfully; unusually; unmitigably; unreasoningly; insensately; senselessly.

adjectives

wanton; flavored; branching; rosy; light; variegated; flimsy; summer; noble; festal; odorous; bridal.

WRECK

adjectives

isolated; passive; sunken; pensile; irredeemable; silent; human; stunted; profitable; dilapidated; emotional; colossal; leafless; pulverized; shattered; crimson; moral; mangled; horrid; centennial; complicated; dreaded; ghastly; pitiable.

verbs

avert—; avoid—; escape—; explore—; glean from—; investigate—; perish in—; probe—; rummage through—; salvage—; survive—; —annihilates; —blights; —defaces; —demolishes; —devastates; —disheartens; —encumbers; —impairs; —impedes; —mars; —obstructs; —scars; —scathes; —strews.

(See ruins, debris, remains, accident.)

WRECK (v)

adverbs

deliberately; wantonly; revengefully; vindictively; desperately; hideously; disastrously; spiritually; destructively; insanely; treacherously.

(See destroy, ruin.)

WREN

verbs

—bubbles along; —busies; —chatters; —cheers; —cuddles; —dances; —hops; —peeps; —runs; —skips; —warms.

(See bird.)

WRENCH (v)

adverbs

violently; abruptly; distressfully; simultaneously; drastically; fiercely; disastrously; diabolically; rudely.

(See seize, grasp.)

WRESTLE (v)

adverbs

persuasively; religiously; prodigiously; arduously; ignominiously; industrially; economically; politically; wrathfully; fanatically; fiercely.

(See contend, fight.)

WRESTLER

verbs

coach—; manage—; train—; —batters; —buffets; —contends; —crouches; —dives; —engages; —fends; —flattens; —flings; —feints; —grapples; —groans; —grunts; —hugs; —hurls; —locks; —pancakes; —pinions; —rams; —scrambles; —spread-eagles; —strains; —strips; —tackles; —trains; —tussles; —vies for; —wards off.

WRETCH

adjectives

wondrous; mutinous; timorous; base; despairing; stupid; extreme; trembling; pretty; utter; short-sighted; imperturbable; tame; hollow-eyed; miserable; pitied; profligate; loathed; restless; fanatical; scandalous; enormous; self-nurtured; abandoned; nameless; barbarous; famishing; hunted; ephemeral; execrable; caitiff; shattered; delicate; disobedient; cruel; disabled; cowering; intense; fond; tortured; rude; miserable; famished; dishonest; drunken; jealous; deceptive; violent; sodden; smoky; inhuman; stupid; dew-bedabbled; conscious-stricken; odious; needy; houseless; irreparable; filthy.

WRETCHED

adverbs

miserably; pitiably; wordlessly; silently; utterly; inexpressibly; unspeakably; helplessly; feebly; hopelessly; cruelly; bitterly; singularly; inconsolably; disconsolately.

WRIGGLE (v)

adverbs

ecstatically; uncomfortably; uneasily; nervously; oppressively; distressfully; impatiently; impulsively; slickly; deftly; slyly.

(See move, writhe.)

WRING (v)

adverbs

fiercely; hysterically; vehemently; imperiously; convulsively; wildly; demoniacally; jubilantly; barbarically; sickeningly; fiendishly; iniquitously.

(See clutch, grasp.)

WRINKLE (v)

adverbs

carelessly; furiously; curiously; impatiently; prematurely; superciliously; fastidiously; scornfully.

(See pucker, crease.)

adverbs

oddly; deeply; remarkably; excessively; terribly; merrily; agedly; uncommonly; curiously; noticeably; surprisingly; perceptibly.

adjectives

upright; facial; weeping; frown-caused.

verbs

acquire—; avoid—; decry—; deplore—; knead—; smooth—; —appear; —blemish; —corrugate; —crease; —deepen; —disfigure; —distress; —furrow; —line; —mar; —ruffle.

adjectives

fettered; limp; blue-veined; gallant; compact; slim; strong.

verbs

adorn—; band—; bare—; benumb—; bind —; brace—; bruise—; dislocate—; distort —; encircle—; extend—; flex—; fracture —; grasp—; handcuff—; lacerate—; manipulate—; misshape—; paralyze—; prick —; seize by—; sprain—.

(See arm, hand, joint.)

adjectives

ingenious; hallowed; apostolic; moving; deathless; legal.

verbs

apply for—; draw up—; file—; grant—; honor—; refuse—; respect—; —absolves; —accords; —allows; —authorizes; —confirms; —decrees; —disposes; —empowers; —evicts; —exempts; —exonerates; —immunizes; —informs; —legalizes; —pardons; —privileges; —releases; —sanctions; —summons; —verifies.

(See decree, award, decision, edict, order.)

adverbs

diplomatically; ·admirably; bombastically; trenchantly; graphically; crudely; barbarously; devastatingly; convincingly; pornographically; scintillatingly; profusely; magnanimously; scientifically; laboriously; ironically; irresolutely; irresistibly; pretentiously; tremulously; elegantly; desultorily; anonymously; satirically; hypothetically; harshly; affectionately; expressly; faultlessly; industriously; legibly; prosaically; salaciously; erotically; sensuously; contemporaneously; authoritatively; genially; avidly; solemnly; incoherently; vigorously; urgently; dogmatically; didactically; eclectically; voluminously; inscrutably; realistically; cynically.

(See compose, inscribe.)

adjectives

outstanding; foremost; verbose; nature; world-famous; fatigued; controversial; credible; ancient; profane; neo-romantic; prolific; theoretic; travel; authoritative; ecclesiastical; illustrious; distinguished; public; opera; miscellaneous; quaint; sociological; sensational; inspiring; discouraged; unscientific; impressionistic; well-known; promising; juvenile; wretched; designing; seduced; eminent; vivacious; historical; roguish; original; anonymous; polemical; tragic; imaginative; convincing; passionate; discriminating; splendid; creative; influential; monkish; native; fertile; talented; thoughtful; philosophical; early; copious; ghost; practised; vigorous; estimable; nondescript; classic; revolutionary; charming; meritorious; previous; prose; diestical; voluminous; reputed; embryo; entertaining.

verbs

acclaim—; honor—; immortalize—; inspire —; laud—; —climaxes; —clothes in; —colors; —composes; —concocts; —couches in; —dashes off; —decries; —depicts; —elucidates; —eulogizes; —fabricates; —fascinates; —infers; —interprets; —libels; —molds; —narrates; —pens; —plagiarizes; —portrays; —recounts; —relates; —reports; —slanders; —soliloquizes; —styles; —unfolds; —vitalizes; —voices; —weaves.

(See dramatist, novelist, journalist, author, poet.)

adverbs

spiritually; convulsively; sickeningly; agonizingly; pitiably.

(See wriggle, struggle.)

adjectives

mental; gnarled; imaginative; splendid; ignominious.

WRITINGS

WRITINGS

adjectives

superb; first-class; breezy; contrapuntal; philosophical; epistolary; biographical; voluminous; humorous; undecipherable; wedge-shaped; hieroglyphic; tropical; free-lance; controversial; metaphorical; foremost; impressive; contemporary; descriptive; elaborate; clear; ghost; imaginative; copious; tragic; historical; propagandist; theoretical; inter-twisted; classic; commercial; prophetical; pernicious; dimmed; superb; representative; figurative; straightforward; unfinished; undistinguished; phonetic; miscellaneous; clerkly; distinct; admirable; sacred; cryptic; dramatic; poignant; unacademic; unpublished; excellent; lucid; scholarly; stylistic.

verbs

abridge—; acclaim—; analyze—; ban—; comprehend—; dissect—; disseminate—; engross in—; ferret out—; herald—; immortalize—; interpret—; laud—; permeate—; peruse—; pervade—; pervert—; probe—; prostitute—; publish—; rival—; —air; —dissertate; —embody; —embrace; —enthrall; —impassion; —inspire; —live; —particularize; —treat of; —ventilate.

(See editorial, epistle, epigram, handwriting, literature, prose, poetry.)

WRONG

adjectives

avenged; uncomplaining; revenging; cruel; deadly; great; bitter; ruthless; grievous; deep; hideous; fancied; intrinsic; culminating; enforced; irrevocable; willful; private; petty; perfidious; inevitable; early; fierce; trifling; illegal; foul; heinous; hoarded; irreparable; unredeemed; diabolic; mutual; deplored; inexpiable; accumulated; brazen; abstract; secret; drastic.

verbs

amend—; avenge—; challenge—; combat—; defeat—; denounce—; discern—; efface—; expose—; extenuate—; heal—; implant—; intend—; perpetuate—; redress—; reform —; remedy—; repent—; reproach—; reveal—; sustain—; —blemishes; —blots; —corrupts; —harasses; —injures; —mars; —offends; —oppresses; —weighs upon.

(See guilt, evil, injustice, grievance, crime.)

adverbs

utterly; absolutely; altogether; singularly; curiously; completely; wickedly; mischievously; deliberately; blunderingly; knowingly; outrageously; scandalously; brutally; cruelly; fatally.

WRONG (v)

adverbs

grievously; irreparably; deeply; grossly; iniquitously; ignominiously; insidiously; dishonestly; treacherously; egregiously; ruthlessly; diabolically; secretly.

(See deceive, trick.)

WRONG-DOING

verbs

ameliorate—; atone for—; avert—; campaign against—; check—; condone—; countenance—; decry—; deplore—; expiate—; inveigh against—; penalize—; quell—; reprove—; —despoils; —embitters; —invalidates; —saps; —undermines.

(See wrong, crime, sin.)

WRY

adverbs

fantastically; comically; decrepitly; curiously; cynically; pathetically; congenitally; pitiably; miserably; tragically; hopelessly; irremediably; permanently.

X

verbs

blur—; diagnose by—; dim—; examine under—; employ—; introduce—; observe—; resort to—; scrutinize—; study—; —delineates; —depicts; —discloses; —outlines; —photographs; —reveals; —shadows; —traces.

(See picture, microscope, photograph.)

Y

YACHT

adjectives
graceful; magnificent; furtive; converted.

verbs
batter—; board—; buffet—; captain—; christen—; collide with—; dock—; ground —; guide—; lash—; launch—; luxuriate on —; navigate—; pilot—; provision—; quarter on—; ram—; refurbish—; salvage—; scuttle—; swamp—; waft—; —flounders; —reels; —signals.
(See launch, boat, motor-boat, ship.)

YAMMERING

adverbs
hungrily; excitedly; pathetically; pitifully; pitiably; miserably; touchingly; affectingly; heartbreakingly; agonizedly; painfully; distressingly; pleadingly; wretchedly; hopefully; clamorously; feebly; despairingly; madly; dolefully; exhaustedly.

YAPPING

adverbs
spitefully; derisively; threateningly; disagreeably; noisily; clamorously; unpleasantly; grossly; coarsely; excitedly; viciously; eagerly; uncontrollably; unmanageably; alarmingly; snappishly; menacingly; fearfully.

YARD

adjectives
bustling; spacious; industrial; back; snowy; discreet; embowered; obscure; diminutive.

verbs
border—; bound—; circumscribe—; clutter —; confine to—; embrace—; encamp in—; enclose—; fence—; festoon—; flank—; garland—; litter—; provision—; restock—; romp in—; skirt—; span—; survey—; — affords; —extends.
(See area, garden, park.)

YARN
(colloq.)
(tale)

verbs
blast—; climax—; color—; debunk—; digress from—; embroider—; exaggerate—; explode—; fabricate—; magnify—; narrate —; recite—; recount—; relate—; retail—; spin—; stretch—; swap—s; terminate—; unfold—; varnish—; weave—; —delights; — distracts; —enthralls; —thrills.
(See story, tale.)

YARN
(general)

adjectives
mingled; rollicking; mystical; interminable; periodic; unlikely.

YARN
(thread)

verbs
arrange—; baste—; chain with—; entwine in—; fabricate—; interlace—; knit with—; pad with—; rend—; spin—; tack with—; twist—; unravel—; unsnarl—; unwind—; weave—; web—.
(See knitting, thread.)

YAWN

adjectives
smothered; suppressed; slight; prodigious; prolonged; imitative.

verbs
camouflage—; choke back—; conceal—; gag —; interpret—; muzzle—; restrain—; smother—; stifle—; suppress—; veil—; — betrays; —implies; —indicates; —insults; —masks; —silences; —widens.

YAWN (v)

adverbs
ferociously; prodigiously; drowsily; audibly; lazily; dreamily; surreptitiously; furtively; secretly; imitatively.

YAWNING

adverbs
embarrassingly; uncontrollably; significantly; undisguisedly; openly; unaccountably; impolitely; discourteously; deliberately; suggestively; unconscionably; wearily; drowsily; sleepily; oddly; continually; prodigiously; nonchalantly; indifferently; audibly; monstrously; loudly; ridiculously; cavernously; frankly; purposely; unconsciously; inadvertently.

adjectives

virgin; elder; young; declining; golden; eternal; blighted; fineless (pl); desolate; vanished; studious; early; tender; childish; dying; successful; important; dangerous; unripe; formative; mature; short; undawned; magnificent; allotted; varied; revolving; troublous; mellowed; plenteous; good; healing; quiet; ominous; countless (pl); reluctant; exasperating; imperial; creeping; cruel; revealing; experimental; enormous; unfulfilling; previous; mighty; mournful; blessed; blooming; arduous; impatient; unique; gilded; rolling (pl); adolescent; ensuing; silent; rare; beauteous; endless; far; distant; synodical; sidereal; peaceful; sanguine; weary; infinite; rapid; dreary; advancing; active; green; inverted; vernal; hopeless; innocent; tempestuous; sleeping; gracious; darkling; hallowed; ravaged; subsequent; trembling; iron-footed; fleeting; flying; rolling; slanting; lengthened; lapsing; strong; bitter; impending; heavy-footed; paltry; dreaded; long-vanished; grueling; extinguished; unreluctant; soon-ended; envenomed; recent (pl); peaceful; precious; disastrous; lying; moldering; turbulent; successive (pl); achieving; consecutive (pl); troubled; illimitable; pregnant; alternate (pl); merry; blissful; absent; industrious; memorable; probationary; unreckoned; columned; bountiful; swelling; long-buried; departed; eventful; canceled; straitened; ill-starred; terrible; innumerable (pl); ragged; blurred; laborious; fabulous; ripened; hoarded; changing; wasted; withering; fiscal; plenteous; execrated.

YEARN (v)

adverbs

vaguely; tenderly; passionately; pensively; compassionately; ineffably; deeply; honestly; restlessly; mutely; inchoately.

(See desire, wish.)

YEARNING

adjectives

rhythmical; passionate; affectionate; anguished; nebulous; poignant; strange; heavenly; pitiful; keen; mortal; tender; intense; silent; precious; innermost; moral; equal; double; inchoate; naive; ineffable; restless; awful; natural; deep; honest; earnest.

verbs

allay—; cherish—; crush—; disclose—; dull—; ease—; gratify—; intensify—; mitigate—; palliate—; quell—; quench—; reveal—; satiate—; satisfy—; slake—; smother—; stifle—; suppress—; —intoxicates; —overwhelms; —seizes.

(See craving, longing.)

adverbs

anxiously; affectionately; fondly; lovingly; amorously; solicitously; hungrily; wearily; eagerly; manifestly; ambitiously; politically; conspicuously; obviously.

YEARS

verbs

advance in—; blank out—; curtail—; devote—to; dream away—; ease—; enliven—; enumerate—; extend—; forsee—; order—; prolong—; record—; rob of—; romp through—; shorten—; span—; survive—; —accumulate; —age; —creep by; —dim; —expire; —file by; —fly; —gnarl; —intervene; —lapse; —mature; —mellow; —parch; —race by; —ripen; —sear; —shrivel; —steal by; —twist.

(See months, time.)

YELL

adjectives

mingled (pl); incessant; long-drawn; simultaneous; fiendish; exultant; doleful; demoniac; jubilant; sickening; frantic; mocking; responsive; excited; deafening; barbaric; fierce; clamorous; triumphant; taunting; distressful; shrill; blood-curdling.

verbs

emit—; muffle—; mute—; muzzle—; restrain—; smother—; stifle—; suppress—; —agonizes; —alarms; —betrays; —discloses; —echoes; —penetrates; —pierces; —rends; —rings out; —shatters; —shrills; —startles.

(See shout, shriek, cry.)

YELL (v)

adverbs

stridently; enthusiastically; violently; furiously; barbarically; viciously; mockingly; demoniacally; fiercely; clamorously; triumphantly; tauntingly; fiendishly; jubilantly; exultantly.

(See cry, bellow.)

Y
Z

adjectives

dazzling; brass; gay; soft; durable; **rich**; canary; cheerful; bright; eye-taking.

adverbs

dreadfully; deeply; uncommonly; perceptibly; agedly; significantly; ominously; sadly; sorrily; **darkly**; biliously; mopishly; desperately.

adjectives

throaty; deep; **hot**; **unmistakable**; hostile.

adjectives

pyramidal; **gigantic.**

adjectives

excellent; abundant; desired; glorious; astounding; bloodless; remarkable; reassuring; prosperous; fabulous.

verbs

conserve—; consume—; curtail—; augment —; deplete—; disperse—; enhance—; estimate—; exhaust—; forecast—; garner—; market—; multiply—; squander—; treasure —; value—; —accrues; —ascends; —descends; —exceeds; —floods; —gluts; —mounts; —replenishes; —soars; —swells.

(See harvest, crop.)

adverbs

unequivocally; copiously; ostensibly; dejectedly; reluctantly; submissively; unwillingly; gracefully; blindly; prudently; begrudgingly; heroically; gallantly; abundantly; pusillanimously; gloriously.

(See submit, surrender.)

adverbs

suddenly; warmly; reluctantly; ardently; eagerly; agreeably; politely; courteously; finally; grudgingly; inconsistently; unwillingly; voluntarily; eventually; harmoniously; helpfully; pleasantly; suavely; urbanly.

adjectives

unsought; galling; oppressive; detested; equal; brazen; chafing; heavy; bloody; tyrannical; cruel; **servile**; **insufferable**; harnessed.

verbs

bow to—; **cast off**—; deliver from—; ease —; emancipate from—; endure—; escape—; evade—; harness to—; liberate from—; rend—; sever—; subject to—; **throw off**—; tolerate—; unburden—; —couples; —curbs; —detains; —enslaves; —fetters; —irritates; —limits; —manacles; —restrains; —restricts; —shackles; —subjugates; —tethers.

(See manacle, chain, authority, band, tyranny.)

verbs

beget—; befriend—; cherish—; **conceive**—; defend—; devour—; fledge—; guard—; harass—; mother—; nest—; nurse—; prey upon—; protect—; raise—; restrain—; shield—; succor—; suckle—; teach—; **wean** —; —mature; —take wings; —test.

(See offspring, child.)

adverbs

adorably; sweetly; refreshingly; ridiculously; ecstatically; rapturously; delightfully; unsuitably; unfortunately; charmingly; appealingly; shyly; absurdly; hopelessly; extremely; wretchedly; terribly; childishly; blithely; happily; joyously; hilariously; infinitely; immortally; unbelievably; excitably; ardently; ingenuously; vividly; gloriously; splendidly; exuberantly; radiantly; blessedly.

adjectives

abashed; sturdy; thoughtless; inquisitive; impatient; irresponsible; vigorous; inexperienced; admiring; sensitive; adolescent; nondescript; impertinent.

verbs

adopt—; amuse—; chasten—; discipline—; divert—; entertain—; guide—; nurse—; scold—; sober—; subdue—; —clambers; —clamors; —naps; —plagues; —questions; —romps; —scampers; —scurries; —wearies.

(See child.)

adjectives

courteous; ardent; home-keeping; poetic; ingenuous; **unarmed**; dashing; immortal;

glorious; vigorous; ambitious; extreme; un-thinking; affected; studious; guarded; sanctimonious; illiterate; splendid; self-enamored; affluent; dazzling; uncouth; philosophical; smiling; malignant; ill-fed; hopeless; facile; mortal; sensitive; foolhardy; venturous; gracious; fragrant; exuberant; fertile; inexperienced; tenacious; timid; sinless; academic; sportive; heroic; everlasting; pensive; busy; handsome; perpetual; romantic; straying; overconfident; thankful; reverend; scorbutic; martial; willful; sweet; disdainful; radiant; burning; early; raucous; unhardened; restless; blessed; mischievous; moonish; unhappy; deflowered; fine; gallant; pretty; saintly; virtuous; bereaved; eager; personable; fresh; ill-kept; afflicted; tranquil; reckless; wasted; self-willed; haughty; extreme; lonely; expanding; refined; obstreperous; thoughtful; consecrated; protracted; shaggy-headed; rustic; lusty; high-spirited; inexplicable; venturesome; bruised; unregenerate; shrinking; soothing; callow; unsociable; unspent; dire; complaining; hapless; scant; loquacious; insensible; impetuous; fair-haired; illustrious; weather-beaten; departed; emulous; lumbering; corrupt; upright; trembling; joyous; tattered; haggard; fadeless; dumb; wooden; dissolute; unfriended; misguided; wretched; passionate; absurd; fantastic; inflammable; ill-boding; dark; irrepressible; yearning; visioning; smirking; emaciated; personable; curly-headed; fervent; handy; flaming; swart; shambling; dapper; post-war; close-lipped; alert.

verbs
attain—; burden—; cherish—; clutch—; commune with—; conscript—; corrupt—; counsel—; curtail—; depict—; discipline—; distress—; exalt—; extend—; exult in—; govern—; guide—; infuse—; inject—; instil —; lecture to—; maintain—; mar—; personify—; prate of—; prepare—; prolong—; quell—; recall—; recapture—; reflect on—; regain—; reminisce of—; reproach—; revel in—; revert to—; ripen into—; rob of—; sacrifice—; stride toward—; struggle to—; survive—; swamp—; symbolize—; —blooms; —emulates; —fades; —fires; —ignites; —impassions; —inspires; —inspirits; —invigorates; —matures; —mellows; —pervades; —reveres; —strays; —surmounts; —sweeps aside; —vaults; —wanes.

(See girl, childhood, maturity.)

YOUTHFUL
adverbs
delightfully; refreshingly; touchingly; wondrously; manifestly; charmingly; surprisingly; unbelievably; ingenuously; alluringly; adorably; artlessly; innocently; joyously; radiantly; blithely; cheerily; rapturously; gloriously; splendidly; adventurously; sweetly; restlessly; mischievously; blessedly; eagerly.

YOUTHFULNESS
adjectives
abounding; joyous; perpetual; mercurial; sparkling.

Z

adverbs

amusingly; divertingly; ridiculously; absurdly; nonsensically; utterly; laughably; farcically; clownishly; mischievously; roguishly; playfully; cleverly; ingeniously.

ZEAL

adjectives

untiring; equal; puritan; inconsiderate; unflagging; lofty; cruel; wise; undaunted; peaceful; reformatory; misguided; overtaxed; artistic; benevolent; ancestral; unflinching; high-bred; unselfish; neverwearying; fervent; divine; wavering; accustomed; missionary; indiscreet; plastic; flaming; indomitable; flagging; incredible; hot; ardent; characteristic; solemn; noble; petulant; insensate; unwearied; humble; furious; commendable; religious; pious; upright; immoderate; diminishing.

verbs

attend with—; burn with—; check—; constrain—; cool—; counterfeit—; devote with —; display—; express—; extinguish—; feign—; fire with—; flush with—; heighten —; imbue with—; infuse—; inject—; inspire —; instil—; intensify—; lack—; match—; misguide—; promote—; quench—; regain—; share—; sharpen—; slake—; stimulate—; want—; —blazes; —burns; —consumes; — declines; —ebbs; —goads; —impassions; — melts; —quickens; —spurs; —subsides; — surges; —wanes; —waxes.

(See "pep", ardor, enthusiasm, intensity, fervor, eagerness, energy.)

ZEALOTS

adjectives

religious; wild; fiery; graceless; poetic; crazy-brained; patriotic.

ZEALOUS

adverbs

earnestly; actively; ardently; passionately; energetically; impetuously; eagerly; nervously; excitedly; absurdly; irresistibly; helpfully; extraordinarily; serviceably; delightfully; ridiculously; seriously; devoutly; piously; remarkably; distinctly; efficiently; boldly; willingly; generously.

verbs

alarm—; cage—; captivate—; cross with—; domesticate—; exterminate—; fetter—; snare—; team with—; thrash—; —abounds in; —balks; —bolts; —bounds; —frequents; —grazes; —herds; —leaps; —pulls; — scurries; —sniffs; —springs.

(See animal, horse.)

ZENITH

verbs

achieve—; ascend to—; attain—; culminate in—, elevate to—; skyrocket to (colloq.)—; toboggan from—; topple from—; whirl to—; —climaxes.

(See height, pinnacle, fame, summit, peak.)

ZEPHYR

adjectives

reckless; delicious; sweet; playful; gracious.

ZERO
(rating)

verbs

achieve—; bestow—; concede—; degrade to —; dole out—; fling—; impose—; incur—; merit—; rate—; scorn—; solicit—; tender —; threaten—; withdraw—; —confounds; —contradicts; —destroys; —disorders; — strikes.

(See punishment, reward, grade.)

ZEST

adjectives

special; sporting; prodigious; insatiable; inherent; hearty; adventurous; savage; scalping; rollicking; invidious; soldierly; smiling; inextinguishable; exquisite; glorious; hungry; infinite; keen; unflagging; eager; special; cynical; monotonous.

verbs

afford—; arouse—; augment—; curb—; derive—; devour with—; enhance—; excite—; harness—; impart—; inspire—; repress—; savor with—; stimulate—; subdue—; whet —; —animates; —burns; —charms; —ebbs;

—enlivens; —fortifies; —heartens; —invigorates; —pervades; —promotes; —reassures; —refreshes; —restrains; —suffuses; —sustains; —wanes.

(See zeal, ardor, fervor, flavor.)

ZESTFUL

adverbs

eagerly; alertly; happily; earnestly; avidly; energetically; enthusiastically; unusually; marvelously; unexpectedly; remarkably; inordinately; curiously; miraculously; incalculably; splendidly; superbly; joyously; helpfully; ardently; delightfully; boyishly; youthfully; noticeably; unwontedly.

ZIGZAG

adverbs

interestingly; purposely; profitably; curiously; conveniently; oddly; artistically; peculiarly; miserably; clumsily; adroitly; cleverly; intentionally; characteristically; quaintly; disagreeably; attractively; unexpectedly; deliberately.

ZONE

adjectives

temperate; frozen; arctic; inner; verdant; fringed; bodiced; interminable; fortunate; arable; wide-spread.

verbs

amplify—; apportion—; belt—; bisect—; carve out—; chop up—; circumscribe—; detach—; encircle—; encompass—; enlarge—; flank—; incise—; intersect—; invade—; label—; measure—; outline—; overreach—; pare—; patrol—; penetrate—; permeate—; prescribe—; restrict to—; skirt—; slice up —; subdivide—; swerve from—; widen—; —insulates; —isolates; —partitions; —secludes; —segregates.

(See section, neighborhood, area, locality, whereabouts.)